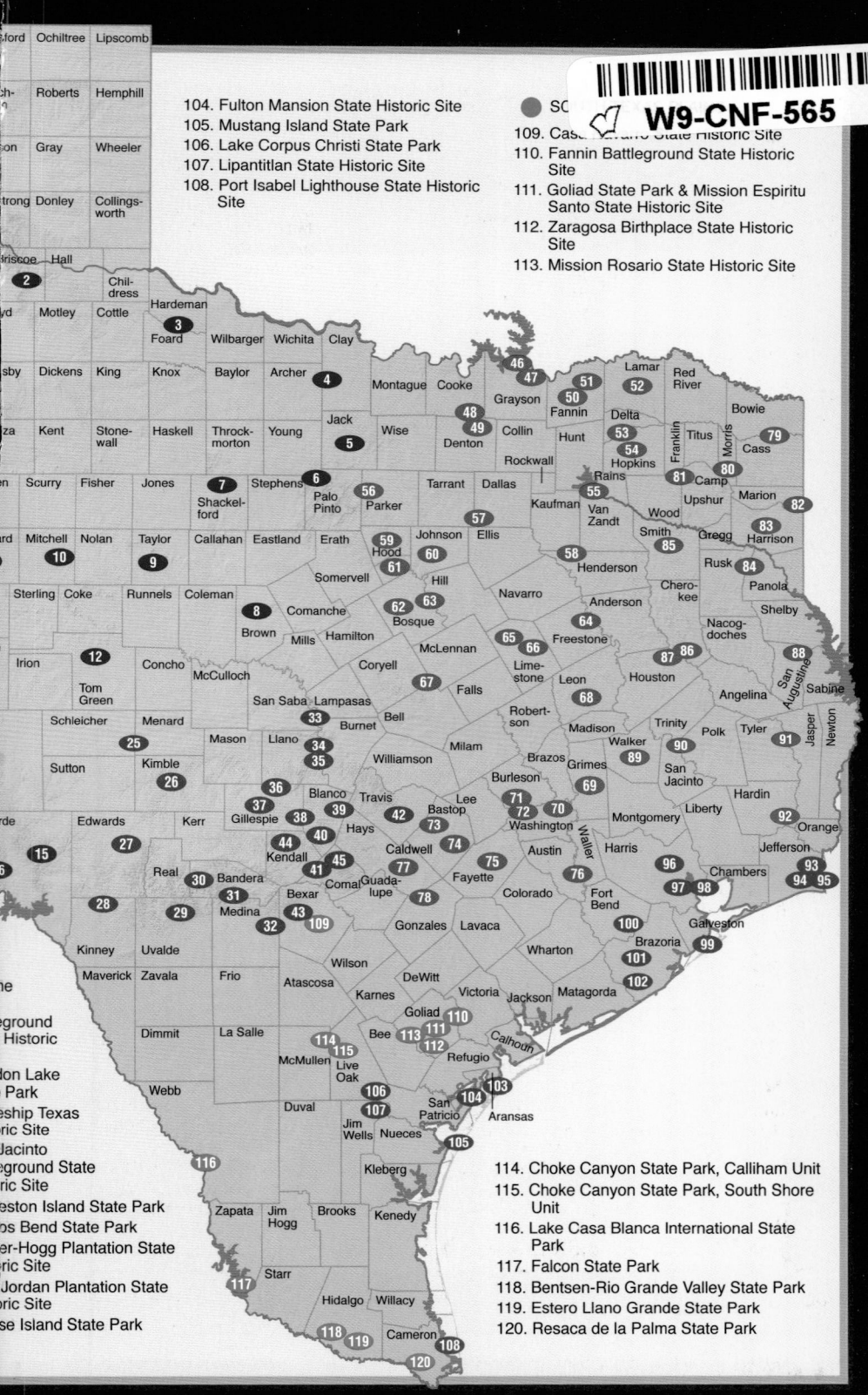

104. Fulton Mansion State Historic Site
105. Mustang Island State Park
106. Lake Corpus Christi State Park
107. Lipantitlan State Historic Site
108. Port Isabel Lighthouse State Historic Site

● SO...

109. Cas... ...o State Historic Site
110. Fannin Battleground State Historic Site
111. Goliad State Park & Mission Espiritu Santo State Historic Site
112. Zaragosa Birthplace State Historic Site
113. Mission Rosario State Historic Site

114. Choke Canyon State Park, Calliham Unit
115. Choke Canyon State Park, South Shore Unit
116. Lake Casa Blanca International State Park
117. Falcon State Park
118. Bentsen-Rio Grande Valley State Park
119. Estero Llano Grande State Park
120. Resaca de la Palma State Park

W9-CNF-565

1-20
STC
$40.00

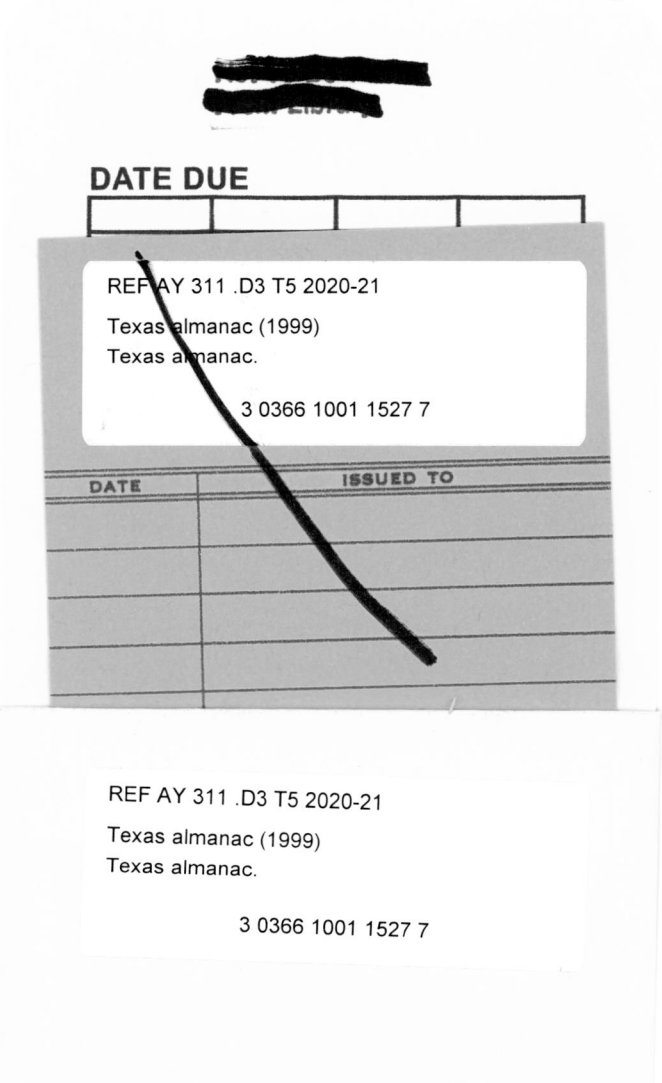

DATE DUE

REF AY 311 .D3 T5 2020-21

Texas almanac (1999)

Texas almanac.

3 0366 1001 1527 7

DATE	ISSUED TO

REF AY 311 .D3 T5 2020-21

Texas almanac (1999)

Texas almanac.

3 0366 1001 1527 7

DEMCO

TEXAS ALMANAC

2020-2021

70th Edition

Texas State Historical Association

LUSHER COLLECTIONS

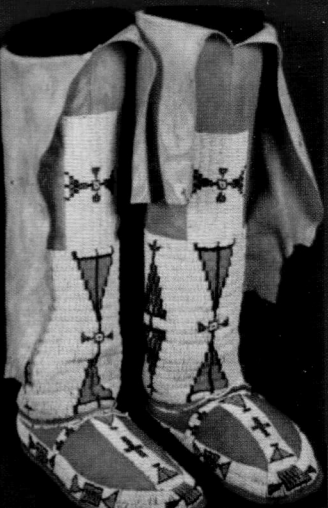

JEWELRY, FINE ART, AND INDIAN ARTIFACTS OF THE SOUTHWEST
WWW.LUSHERCOLLECTIONS.COM
AUSTIN – SANTA FE

Educational offerings
for all Texans!

Each of TSHA's educational programs and resources for students are designed to enhance the education of Texas youth while deepening their appreciation of the state's history; such as Junior Historians (4th-12th grade), Texas History Day (6th-12th grade), and Webb Society (College/University). TSHA provides educators with resources including workshops, professional development opportunities, and classroom curriculum via our educational department and TeachingTexas.org. Beyond the classroom, we seek to engage the public in Texas history through Texas Talks, the TSHA Annual Meeting, the San Jacinto Symposium, and various publications.

Texas State Historical Association
An Independent Nonprofit Since 1897

For more, visit **TSHAonline.org/Education**

Advertisement 3

YOUR GO-TO STORE FOR TEXAS HISTORY

All Proceeds Benefit the Texas History
Publications and Programs of TSHA

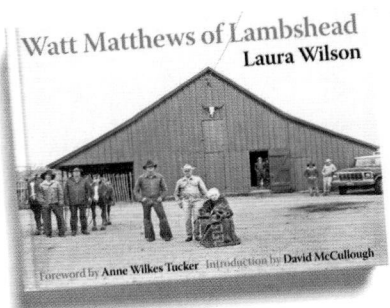

SHOP OUR ONLINE STORE TODAY
Visit www.LegacyofTexas.com

TEXAS ALMANAC

2020-2021

MANAGING EDITOR
Rosie Hatch

ASSOCIATE EDITOR
Robert Plocheck

ASSISTANT EDITORS
Nathaniel Muñiz and John Willis

COVER DESIGN
Joel Phillips and Michéle R. Newton

ISBN (hardcover) 978-1-62511-054-1
ISBN (flexbound) 978-1-62511-055-8
ISBN (ebook) 978-1-62511-056-5

Library of Congress ISSN: 2378-2188 (Print)
Library of Congress ISSN: 2378-2234 (Digital)

Copyright © 2020

All rights reserved.

TEXAS STATE HISTORICAL ASSOCIATION

The University of Texas at Austin
3001 Lake Austin Blvd., Ste. 3.116, Austin, TX 78703; (512) 471-2600

TSHAonline.org and LegacyofTexas.com

Printed in Dallas by Taylor Specialty Books
Bound in San Antonio by Universal Bookbindery
For permission requests, contact **Rosie.Hatch@TSHAonline.org**.

Distributed by Texas A&M University Press and the Texas Book Consortium
4354 TAMU, College Station, TX 77843-4354

Order hardcover or flexbound editions at **(800) 826-8911**
or online at www.tamupress.com

TexasAlmanac.com

PREFACE

*T*he *Texas Almanac 2020–2021* is the 70th of its kind in print, and my first alone in the driver's seat. Working on a book with so much history behind it is a great honor, and extremely daunting. But with the help of my team and the rest of the TSHA, I think we've delivered a new edition fit to continue the grand legacy.

As you may already know, the first *Texas Almanac* was published in 1857 in Galveston as a means of informing residents about the state and attracting new immigrants. I doubt anyone can tell for sure if it was successful in bringing people to the state, but here are some figures for you: The first five editions (1857, 1858, 1859, 1860, and 1861) sold as many as 100,000 copies. According to the U.S. Census, 605,987 people moved to Texas between 1850 and 1870, swelling the population by 285 percent. Something was bringing people to Texas – who's to say it wasn't the *Texas Almanac*?

I found those census figures in this year's first feature article, "Texas Population: Still Growing and Becoming Increasingly Diverse," written by Steve Murdock and Michael Cline. The year 2020 is a census year, and there has been speculation about how the demographics in Texas have been changing. In the article, Murdock and Cline take a deep dive into the numbers to show us where the state is today, and a few possibilities for where we may be in 2050. The full article starts on page 373.

The second feature article is "Asian Indians in Texas" by Ayshea Khan. This growing minority has made important contributions to our state's economy and culture, yet Asian Indian immigrants were not allowed to become citizens until 1946, and many were barred from coming here at all until 1965. Check out the full story, starting on page 532. Previous Almanacs have profiled other immigrant groups in Texas, including Irish, German, and Czech. You can find those articles and many more on our website: TexasAlmanac.com.

Whatever it was that brought you to Texas, I'm glad that it also brought you to the *Texas Almanac*, and I hope you enjoy reading it as much as I enjoyed working on it. Thank you for your support, and a special thanks to Robert, Nathaniel, John, and Marian for the hard work and care they put in to making each chapter as accurate and up-to-date as possible.

Rosie Hatch
Managing Editor, *Texas Almanac*

THE KENEDY RANCH MUSEUM
of SOUTH TEXAS

LARRY D. MOORE CC BY-SA 3.0

See the fascinating history of South Texas come alive in vibrant murals and learn about the area's cultural, economic and religious development. View "Vaquero", a video describing cowboy life in the Wild Horse Desert.

Open Tues. – Sat. 10 a.m. to 4 p.m. – Sunday 12 noon to 4 p.m.

Admission:
$3.00 Adults • $2.00 Seniors and Teens 13-18
Children 12 and under and organized school groups are free.

280 La Parra Ave • Sarita, Texas 78385
361-294-5751

www.kenedyranchmuseum.org

Emilio Zamora

On behalf of the Texas State Historical Association (TSHA), I welcome you to the most comprehensive resource on Texas history and culture that we offer biennially. Our Association's Board of Directors, Executive Committee, staff and its thousands of members throughout the state are gratified to bring you the long-running *Texas Almanac*, dating back to 1857.

Over the years, our Association has built a reputation for its outstanding contributions to Texas history and culture, including the *Southwestern Historical Quarterly*, an annual scholarly conference, the online Handbook of Texas, History Day, additional book-length publications, and other programs and events. The *Texas Almanac* stands proudly among them. It is the most reliable single source for data and information on Texas counties, weather, and much more. The current issue of the Almanac highlights Texas' changing demography.

We are especially grateful to the readers and members of the TSHA for sustaining the Texas Almanac over the years, and to the University of Texas at Austin for hosting us.

Visit us in Austin or online at www.tshaonline.org so that you can see all that we do. Thank you for your interest and enjoy the *Texas Almanac*!

Emilio Zamora
President, Texas State Historical Association

"Other music history books read like Wikipedia entries by comparison."
—*Austin Chronicle*

ALL OVER THE MAP:
TRUE HEROES OF TEXAS MUSIC

AVAILABLE FROM UNIVERSITY OF NORTH TEXAS PRESS
Orders: 1-800-826-8911 • UNTPress.unt.edu

Discover the
history of revolution
and independence at

THE
STORIED
SITES OF
TEXAS

FANNIN BATTLEGROUND

SAN FELIPE de AUSTIN

BARRINGTON PLANTATION

SAN JACINTO BATTLEGROUND

WASHINGTON-ON-THE-BRAZOS

Our 31 sites preserve and chronicle
the epic story of the Lone Star State.
Find one near you today.

TEXAS
HISTORICAL
COMMISSION
REAL PLACES TELLING REAL STORIES

storiedsites.com

Texas State Historical Association

An Independent Nonprofit Since 1897

Organized in Austin on March 2, 1897, the Texas State Historical Association is the oldest learned society in the state. Its mission is to "foster the appreciation, understanding, and teaching of the rich and unique history of Texas and, by example and through programs and activities, encourage and promote research, preservation, and publication of historical material affecting the state of Texas." The association's publications include the *Southwestern Historical Quarterly*, more than 150 scholarly books, the *Texas Almanac*, and the well-known *Handbook of Texas Online*. The online Handbook, the nation's preeminent state history encyclopedia, attracts 400,000 visitors per month from more than 200 countries and territories around the world. Through its varied education programs, the Association directly serves more than 50,000 elementary through college-aged students each year, while indirectly reaching an additional 86,000 through its teacher training opportunities.

TSHA Board of Directors, 2019-2020

Officers

Emilio Zamora
Austin . . . . President

Mary Margaret McAllen
San Antonio . . . . .First Vice President

Patrick Cox
Wimberley . . . . Second Vice President

Sarita Hixon
Houston . . . . .Past President (2018)

Paula Mitchell Marks
Austin . . . . .Past President (2017)

Thomas R. Phillips
Austin . . . . (2017-2020) Secretary

R. Lance Lolley
Austin. . . . . (2019-2022) Treasurer

Board Members

Jessica Brannon-Wranosky
McKinney . . . . (2018-2021)
Second Term

H. Scott Caven Jr.
Houston . . . . (2019-2022)
Second Term

Stephanie Cole
Arlington . . . . (2018-2021)

Sean Cunningham
Lubbock . . . . (2017-2020)

Carlos R. Hamilton, Jr.
Houston . . . . (2018-2021)

Kent Hance
Austin . . . . (2019-2022)

Nancy Baker Jones
Austin . . . . (2019-2022)

Larry Ketchersid
Austin . . . . (2018-2021)

Ted Lusher
Austin . . . . (2017-2020)

Nancy Painter Paup
Fort Worth . . . . (2017-2020)
Second Term

Trevor Rees-Jones
Dallas . . . . (2018-2021)

Andrew J. Torget
Denton . . . . (2019-2022)

Alan Tully
Austin . . . . (2019-2022)
Second Term

Heather Wooten
Houston . . . . (2019-2022)

Homero S. Vera
Premont and Sarita . . . . (2018-2021)
Second Term

Frank de La Teja
Austin . . . . .Chief Executive Officer, Ex-Officio

Walter L. Buenger
Bryan . . . . .Chief Historian, Honorary Life Board Member

J. P. Bryan
Houston . . . . Honorary Life Board Member

John W. Crain
Dallas . . . . Honorary Life Board Member

*G*reetings,

As Governor of Texas, it is my pleasure to welcome you to the pages of the *Texas Almanac*, published by the Texas State Historical Association.

With its long and storied history, wide range of geographical features, diverse populations and robust economy, Texas is worthy of intensive study. Fortunately, inside this go-to guide for all things Texas are all the facts, information, and figures you could ever want to discover about our beloved Lone Star State.

GREG ABBOTT
Governor of Texas

Our great state is renowned for its rich heritage and culture. Part of what makes Texas "Texas" is that across her more than 268,500 square miles, everyone can experience a vibrant array of customs which are a reflection of the people from near and far who have settled here to pursue their dreams.

Our communities, music, and culinary scenes have been inspired by many cultures from around the country and around the world. There is truly no place like the Lone Star State.

Texans are defined by their fiery can-do spirit. We believe that anyone can achieve anything in Texas so long as they are willing to put in the work. That is how we have become widely recognized as having the strongest economy in the nation. Just take a look at the facts: Texas has been the nation's top exporter for more than a decade, we are a national leader in job creation, a global leader in oil and natural gas production, and we remain a top relocation destination for businesses and families. The Lone Star State boasts a thriving business climate that promotes fairness, job growth, and economic prosperity.

As you turn the pages of the 70th edition of the *Texas Almanac*, I hope you come to see what I know to be true: Texas is an amazing and extraordinary place, made even more special by the citizens who call it home.

First Lady Cecilia Abbott joins me in thanking the Texas State Historical Association for its hard work in promoting our state's rich history.

Greg Abbott

Greg Abbott
Governor of Texas

*P*eople from all over the world look to the wonders of Texas.

Our economy is the tenth largest in the world, our natural landscapes have inspired artists for decades, and our history is legendary.

Our state story is a story of liberty, hard won through revolution and sanctified by the blood of patriots and heroes. It is a story of generations of settlers, immigrants, native people, freedmen, and even carpetbaggers and outlaws, all of whom have deep roots here and have made their own contribution to our shared history.

DAN PATRICK
Lt. Governor of Texas

Our beautiful state is united by our commitment to personal freedom and innovative government with the goal of allowing everyone the opportunity to prosper.

This Almanac provides a wonderful resource to learn about the extraordinary culture and history that make Texas a beacon for the world. I hope you join me in honoring it as you learn about the greatest state that God ever made: Texas.

Dan Patrick
Lt. Governor of Texas

February 27-29th, 2020
AT&T Hotel and Conference Center in Austin

The largest gathering of its kind for the Texas history community. Join us for three days of sessions on the latest research in the field. Enjoy networking, events, and professional development that will expand your knowledge, energize you, and help you to deepen your connections with the state's extraordinary past.

For more information on all annual meetings: TSHAonline.org/Annual-Meeting

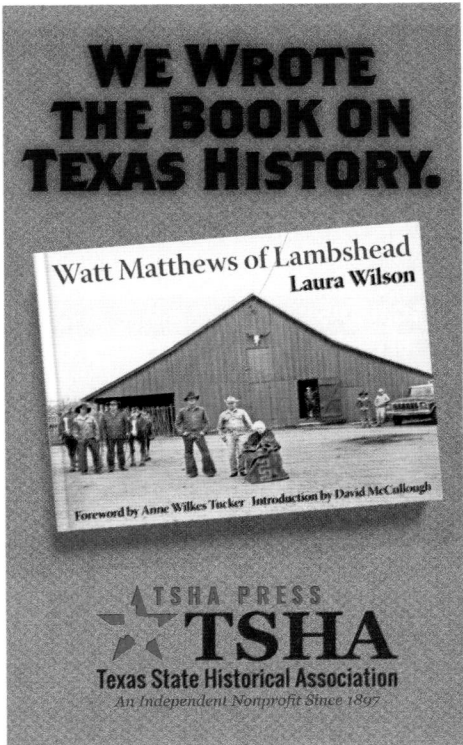

TABLE OF CONTENTS

Contents

INDEX OF TABLES

INDEX OF MAPS

This section offers a demographic and geographic profile of the second-largest, second-most-populous state in the United States. Check the **Table of Contents** and the **Index** for more-detailed information about each subject.

GOVERNMENT

Capital: Austin
Government: Bicameral Legislature
28th State to enter the Union: Dec. 29, 1845
Present Constitution adopted: 1876
State motto: Friendship (1930)
State symbols:

Flower:	Bluebonnet	(1901)
Bird:	Mockingbird	(1927)
Tree:	Pecan	(1919)
Song:	"Texas, Our Texas"	(1929)

Origin of name: Texas, or Tejas, was the Spanish pronunciation of a Caddo Indian word meaning "friends" or "allies."
Nickname: Texas is called the **Lone Star State** because of the design of the state flag: a broad vertical blue stripe at left centered by a single white star, and at right, horizontal bars of white (top) and red.

TEN LARGEST CITIES

Houston (Harris Co.)	2,331,354
San Antonio (Bexar Co.)	1,462,766
Dallas (Dallas Co.)	1,298,196
Austin (Travis Co.)	.921,781
Fort Worth (Tarrant Co.)	832,030
El Paso (El Paso Co.)	678,253
Arlington (Tarrant Co.)	.387,148
Corpus Christi (Nueces Co.)	325,080
Plano (Collin Co.)	296,641
Laredo (Webb Co.)	260,799

Number of counties	.254
Largest by pop: Harris Co.	4,660,474
Smallest by pop: Loving Co.	81

Number of incorporated cities	.1,216
Number of cities of 100,000 pop. or more . . .	38
Number of cities of 50,000 pop. or more	70
Number of cities of 10,000 pop. or more	.254

(Texas Demographic Center estimates for Jan. 1, 2018.)

PEOPLE

Population, 2018*	**28,525,596**
Population, 2010 U.S. Census.	**25,145,561**
Population increase, 2010–2018	**13.4%**
Population, 2000 U.S. Census. . . .	**20,851,820**
Population increase, 2000–2018	**37.8%**

Ethnicity, 2018

Group	Percent
White, NH.	.41.5%
Hispanic	.39.5%
Black	.12.8%
Asian	. 5.2%
Other	. 1%

Veterans, 2013–2017. . . . . **1,482,871**

* Jan. 1, 2018, U.S. Census Bureau estimate.
(Sources: U.S. Census Bureau, Texas Demographic Center)

BUSINESS

Per Capita Personal Income (2018)	.$49,161
Per Capita Consumption (2017)	$37,486

Top spending categories:

Housing and utilities	$6,264
Health care	$6,025

Non-Farm Employment (2018) 13,314,203
Employment by industry:

Industry Group	Percent
Education and health services	23.4%
Trade, transportation, utilities	21.0%
Professional and business services	14.3%
Leisure and hospitality	11.0%
Manufacturing	7.2%
Construction	6.3%
All others	16.8%

(Per capita income/consumption: U.S. Bureau of Economic Analysis. Employment: Texas Workforce Commission.)

NATURAL ENVIRONMENT

Area (total) . . . . 268,596 sq. miles
. . . . (171,901,440 acres)

Land Area . . . . 261,232 sq. miles
. . . . (167,188,480 acres)

Water Area . . . . .7,365 sq. miles
. . . .(4,713,600 acres)

Geographic Center:
About 15 miles northeast of Brady in northern
McCulloch County.

Highest Point:
Guadalupe Peak (8,749 ft.) in Culberson County
in far West Texas.

Lowest Point:
Gulf of Mexico (sea level).

Normal Average Annual Precipitation Range:
From 60.57 inches at Jasper County in far East
Texas to 9.43 inches at El Paso, in far West Texas.

Record Highest Temperature:
Seymour, Baylor Co., ... Aug. 12, 1936, 120°F
Monahans, Ward Co., ... June 28, 1994, 120°F

Record Lowest Temperature:
Tulia, Swisher Co., ... Feb. 12, 1899, –23°F
Seminole, Gaines Co., ... Feb. 8, 1933, –23°F

PRINCIPAL PRODUCTS

Manufacturing: Chemicals and allied products,
petroleum and coal products, food and kindred
products, transportation equipment.

Farm Products: Cattle, cotton, vegetables, fruits,
nursery and greenhouse, dairy products.

Minerals: Petroleum, natural gas, and natural gas
liquids.

Finance (as of 12/31/2018):
Number of banks 409
Total deposits. $328,907,699,000
Number of savings & loan associations 5
Total deposits. $73,570,292,000
Number of savings banks 24
Total deposits. $17,635,204,000
*(Banks: Federal Reserve Bank of Dallas; savings and loans
and savings banks: Texas Dept. of Savings and Mortgage
Lending.)*

Agriculture:
Total cash receipts, 2017 . . . . . . $26.47 billion
Animals & products, 2017. . . . . . $14.59 billion
Crops, 2017 . . . . $7.62 billion
Total exports . . . . $6.06 billion
Land in farms in acres, 2017 . . . . .129.6 million
*(U.S. Department of Agriculture, National Agricultural
Statistics Service Farm Numbers.)*

Sunrise over the Margaret Hunt Hill Bridge in Dallas. Photo by TheGabeC (CC).

Texas' Rank Among the States

Sources for these tables are: the Bureau of Economic Analysis, Centers for Disease Control and Prevention, U.S. Census Bureau, U.S. Dept. of Agriculture, and the U.S. Energy Information Administration.

GDP by State, FYE 2018

	State	In Millions
1.	California	$2,968,079.0
2.	**Texas**	**$1,775,796.5**
3.	New York	$1,676,350.2
4.	Florida	$1,036,323.2
5.	Illinois	$864,587.3
6.	Pennsylvania	$788,537.8
7.	Ohio	$676,192.5
8.	New Jersey	$624,851.9
9.	Georgia	$588,171.7
10.	Massachusetts	$567,254.8
	United States: $20,494,079.0	

Number of Births, 2017

	State	Total
1.	California	471,658
2.	**Texas**	**382,050**
3.	New York	229,737
4.	Florida	223,630
5.	Illinois	149,390
6.	Pennsylvania	137,745
7.	Ohio	136,832
8.	Georgia	129,243
9.	North Carolina	120,125
10.	Michigan	111,426
	United States: 3,855,500	

Net Farm Income, 2017

	State	Income
1.	California	$17,858,524
2.	**Texas**	**$4,407,992**
3.	Iowa	$3,403,253
4.	North Carolina	$3,193,369
5.	Washington	$3,163,742
6.	Nebraska	$2,672,742
7.	Georgia	$2,672,552
8.	Florida	$2,636,155
9.	Illinois	$2,061,179
10.	Minnesota	$1,841,099

Domestic Migration, 2010–2018

	State	Net Migration
1.	Florida	+1,160,387
2.	**Texas**	**1,019,434**
3.	North Carolina	402,389
4.	Arizona	362,015
5.	Colorado	321,782
6.	South Carolina	314,775
7.	Washington	295,480
8.	Tennessee	219,385
9.	Oregon	206,712
10.	Georgia	205,405

Crude Oil Production, 2017

	State	1,000's of Barrels
1.	**Texas**	**1,282,692**
2.	North Dakota	392,127
3.	Alaska	180,467
4.	California	174,107
5.	New Mexico	171,440
6.	Oklahoma	161,678
7.	Colorado	130,732
8.	Wyoming	75,669
9.	Louisiana	52,024
10.	Kansas	35,822
	United States: 3,413,338	

Percent of Population Lacking Health Insurance, 2017

	State	Percent
1.	**Texas**	**17.3%**
2.	Oklahoma	14.2%
3.	Alaska	13.7%
4.	Georgia	13.4%
5.	Florida	12.9%
6.	Wyoming	12.3%
7.	Mississippi	12.0%
8.	Nevada	11.2%
9.	South Carolina	11.0%
10.	North Carolina	10.7%
	United States: 8.7%	

VC LIBRARY

Flags of Texas

United States
1845-Present

Spain
1519-1821

France
1685-1690

Republic
Republic: 1836-1845; State: 1845-Present

Mexico
1821-1836

Confederate States of America
1861-1865

Texas is called the **Lone Star State** because of its state flag with a single star. The state flag was also the **flag of the Republic of Texas**.

The following information about historic Texas flags, the current flag, and other Texas symbols is from the **Texas State Library & Archives** in Austin. More information is at:

www.tsl.state.tx.us/ref/abouttx/index.html#flags
and
https://texasalmanac.com/topics/flags-symbols/flags-other-symbols

Six Flags of Texas

Six different flags have flown over Texas during eight changes of sovereignty. The accepted sequence of these flags follows:

Spanish: 1519–1821
French: 1685–1690
Mexican: 1821–1836
Republic of Texas: 1836–1845
Confederate States of America: 1861–1865
United States: 1845 to the present.

Evolution of the Lone Star Flag

The Convention at Washington-on-the-Brazos in March 1836 allegedly adopted a flag for the Republic that was designed by **Lorenzo de Zavala.** The design of de Zavala's flag is unknown, but the convention journals state that a "Rainbow and star of five points above the western horizon; and a star of six points sinking below" was added to de Zavala's flag.

There was a suggestion the letters "T E X A S" be placed around the star in the flag, but there is no evidence that the Convention ever approved a final flag design. Probably because of the hasty dispersion of the Convention and the loss of part of the Convention notes, nothing further was done with the Convention's proposals for a national flag.

A **so-called "Zavala flag"** is sometimes flown in Texas today that consists of a blue field with a white five-pointed star in the center and the letters "T E X A S" between the star points, but there is no historical evidence to support this flag's design.

The **first official flag of the Republic,** known as the **National Standard of Texas** or **David G. Burnet's**

flag, was adopted by the Texas Congress and approved by President Sam Houston on Dec. 10, 1836. The design **"shall be an azure ground with a large golden star central."**

The Lone Star Flag

On Jan. 25, 1839, President Mirabeau B. Lamar approved the adoption by Congress of a new national flag. This flag consisted of "a blue perpendicular stripe of the width of one third of the whole length of the flag, with a white star of five points in the centre thereof, and two horizontal stripes of equal breadth, the upper stripe white, the lower red, of the length of two thirds of the length of the whole flag." This is the **Lone Star Flag,** which later became the state flag.

Although Senator William H. Wharton proposed the adoption of the Lone Star Flag in 1838, no one knows who actually designed the flag. The legislature in 1879 inadvertently repealed the law establishing the state flag, but the legislature adopted a new law in 1933 that legally re-established the flag's design.

The red, white, and blue of the state flag stand, respectively, for bravery, purity, and loyalty. The proper **finial** for use with the state flag is either **a star or a spearhead.** Texas is one of only two states that has a flag that formerly served as the flag of an independent nation. The other is Hawaii.

Displaying the State Flag

The Texas Flag Code was first adopted in 1933 and completely revised in 1993. Laws governing display of the state flag are found in sections 3100.002 through 3100.152 of the Texas Government Code: **www.tsl.state.tx.us/ref/abouttx/flagcode.html.** Here is a summary of those rules:

★ The Texas flag should be **displayed on state and national holidays** and on special occasions of historical significance, and it should be displayed at every school on regular school days. **When flown out of doors,** the Texas flag should not be flown earlier than sunrise nor later than sunset unless properly illuminated. It should not be left out in inclement weather unless a weather-proof flag is used. It should be flown with the white stripe uppermost **except in case of distress.**

★ **No flag other than the United States flag should be placed above or,** if on the same level, to the state flag's right (observer's left). The state flag should be underneath the national flag when the two are flown from the same halyard. **When flown from adjacent flagpoles,** the national flag and the state flag should be of approximately the same size and on flagpoles of equal height; the national flag should be on the flag's own right (observer's left).

★ If the state flag is displayed **with the flag of another U.S. state, a nation other than the United States, or an international organization,** the state flag should be, from an observer's perspective, to the left of the other flag on a separate flagpole or flagstaff, and the state flag should not be above the other flag on the same flagpole or flagstaff or on a taller flagpole or flagstaff. If the state flag and the U.S. flag are **displayed from crossed flagstaffs,** the state flag should be, from an observer's perspective, to the right of the U.S. flag and the state flag's flagstaff should be behind the U.S. flag's flagstaff.

★ **When the flag is displayed horizontally,** the white stripe should be above the red stripe and, from an observer's perspective, to the right of the blue stripe. **When the flag is displayed vertically,** the blue stripe should be uppermost and the white stripe should be to the state flag's right (observer's left).

★ If the state and national flags are both **carried in a procession,** the national flag should be on the marching right and state flag should be on the national flag's left (observer's right).

★ **On Memorial Day,** the state flag should be displayed at half-staff until noon and then completely raised. **On Peace Officers Memorial Day** (May 15), the state flag should be displayed at half-staff all day, unless that day is also Armed Forces Day.

★ The state flag should not touch anything beneath it or be dipped to any person or thing except the U.S. flag. Advertising should not be fastened to a flagpole, flagstaff, or halyard on which the state flag is displayed.

★ If a state flag is no longer used or useful as an emblem for display, it should be destroyed, preferably by burning. A **flag retirement ceremony** is set out in the Texas Government Code mentioned earlier.

Pledge to the Texas Flag

> *Honor the Texas flag;*
> *I pledge allegiance*
> *to thee, Texas,*
> *one state under God,*
> *one and indivisible.*

A pledge to the Texas flag was adopted in 1933 by the 43rd Legislature. It contained a phrase, "Flag of 1836," which inadvertently referred to the **David G. Burnet flag** instead of the Lone Star Flag adopted in 1839. In 2007, the 80th Legislature changed the pledge to its current form:

A person reciting the pledge to the state flag should face the flag, place the right hand over the heart, and remove any easily removable hat.

The pledge to the Texas flag may be recited at all public and private meetings at which the Pledge of Allegiance to the national flag is recited and at state historical events and celebrations.

The pledge to the Texas flag should be recited after the pledge of allegiance to the United States flag, if both are recited. ☆

Texas State Symbols

State Song

The state song of Texas is "Texas, Our Texas." The music was written by the late William J. Marsh (who died Feb. 1, 1971, in Fort Worth at age 90), and the words by Marsh and Gladys Yoakum Wright, also of Fort Worth. It was the winner of a state song contest sponsored by the 41st Legislature and was adopted in 1929. The wording has been changed once: Shortly after Alaska became a state in January 1959, the word "Largest" in the third line was changed by Mr. Marsh to "Boldest." The text follows:

TEXAS, OUR TEXAS

Texas, our Texas! All hail the mighty State!

Texas, our Texas! So wonderful, so great!

Boldest and grandest, Withstanding ev'ry test;

O Empire wide and glorious, You stand supremely blest.

CHORUS

God bless you Texas!

And keep you brave and strong,

That you may grow in power and worth,

Thro'out the ages long.

REFRAIN

Texas, O Texas! Your freeborn single star,

Sends out its radiance to nations near and far.

Emblem of freedom! It sets our hearts aglow,

With thoughts of San Jacinto and glorious Alamo.

Texas, dear Texas! From tyrant grip now free,

Shines forth in splendor your star of destiny!

Mother of heroes! We come your children true,

Proclaiming our allegiance, our faith, our love for you.

State Motto

The state motto is "Friendship." The word Texas, or Tejas, was the Spanish pronunciation of a Caddo Indian word meaning "friends" or "allies." It was designated by the 41st Legislature in 1930.

State Citizenship Designation

The people of Texas usually call themselves Texans. However, Texian was generally used in the early period of the state's history.

State Seal

The design of the obverse (front) of the State Seal consists of "a star of five points encircled by olive and live oak branches, and the words, 'The State of Texas.' " (State Constitution, Art. IV, Sec. 19.) This design is a slight modification of the Great Seal of the Republic of Texas, adopted by the Congress of the Republic, Dec. 10, 1836, and readopted with modifications in 1839.

Front of Seal

An official design for the reverse (back) of the seal was adopted by the 57th Legislature in 1961, but there were discrepancies between the written description and the artistic rendering that was adopted at the same time. To resolve the problems, the 72nd Legislature in 1991 adopted an official design.

The 73rd Legislature in 1993 finally adopted the reverse by law. The current description is in the Texas

Back of Seal

Government Code, section 3101.001:

"(b) The reverse side of the state seal contains a shield displaying a depiction of:

(1) the Alamo; (2) the cannon of the Battle of Gonzales; and (3) Vince's Bridge.

(c) The shield on the reverse side of the state seal is encircled by:

(1) live oak and olive branches; and (2) the unfurled flags of: (A) the Kingdom of France; (B) the Kingdom of Spain; (C) the United Mexican States; (D) the Republic of Texas; (E) the Confederate States of America; and (F) the United States of America.

(d) Above the shield is emblazoned the motto, 'REMEMBER THE ALAMO,' and beneath are the words, 'TEXAS ONE AND INDIVISIBLE.'

(e) A white five-pointed star hangs over the shield, centered between the flags."

Texas State Symbols

State Bird: The mockingbird (Mimus polyglottos) is the state bird of Texas, adopted by the 40th Legislature of 1927 at the request of the Texas Federation of Women's Clubs.

State Flower: The state flower of Texas is the bluebonnet, also called buffalo clover, wolf flower, and el conejo (the rabbit). The bluebonnet was adopted as the state flower, at the request of the Society of Colonial Dames in Texas, by the 27th Legislature in 1901. The original resolution made Lupinus subcarnosus the state flower, but a resolution by the 62nd Legislature in 1971 provided legal status as the state flower of Texas for "Lupinus Texensis and any other variety of bluebonnet."

State Tree: The pecan tree (Carya illinoinensis) was adopted as the state tree of Texas by the 36th Legislature in 1919. The sentiment that led to its adoption probably grew out of the request of Gov. James Stephen Hogg that a pecan tree be planted at his grave.

Other State Symbols

(In 2001, the Texas Legislature placed restrictions on the adoption of future symbols by requiring that a joint resolution to designate a symbol must specify the item's historical or cultural significance to the state.)

State Air Force: The Commemorative Air Force (formerly known as the Confederate Air Force), based in Midland at Midland International Airport, was proclaimed the state air force of Texas by the 71st Legislature in 1989.

State Amphibian: The Texas toad was named the state amphibian by the 81st Legislature in 2009.

State Aquarium: The Texas State Aquarium in Corpus Christi was designated the state aquarium of Texas by the 69th Legislature in 1985.

State Bison Herd: The bison herd at Caprock Canyons State Park was named the official Texas State Bison Herd by the 82nd Legislature in 2011.

State Bluebonnet City: The city of Ennis in Ellis County was designated the state bluebonnet city by the 75th Legislature in 1997.

State Bluebonnet Festival: The Chappell Hill Bluebonnet Festival, held in April, was named state bluebonnet festival by the 75th Legislature in 1997.

State Bluebonnet Trail: The city of Ennis was proclaimed the official state bluebonnet trail by the 75th Legislature in 1997.

State Bread: Pan de campo, translated "camp bread" and often called cowboy bread, was named the state bread by the 79th Legislature in 2005. It is a simple baking-powder bread that was a staple of early Texans and often baked in a Dutch oven.

State Cobbler: Peach cobbler was named the state cobbler of Texas by the 83rd Legislature in 2013.

State Cooking Implement: The cast iron Dutch oven was named the cooking implement of Texas by the 79th Legislature in 2005.

State Crustacean: Texas Gulf Shrimp was designated the state crustacean by the 84th Legislature in 2015.

State Dinosaur: Paluxysaurus jonesi was proclaimed the state dinosaur by the 81st Legislature in 2009, after it was discovered that the previous state dinosaur, the Brachiosaur Sauropod, Pleurocoelus, (75th Legislature in 1997) had been a misidentification.

State Dish: Chili was proclaimed the Texas state dish by the 65th Legislature in 1977.

State Dog Breed: The Blue Lacy was designated the state dog breed by the 79th Legislature in 2005. The Blue Lacy is a herding and hunting breed descended from greyhound, scent-hound, and coyote stock and developed by the Lacy brothers, who left Kentucky and settled near Marble Falls in 1858.

State Domino Game: 42 was named the state domino game by the 82nd Legislature in 2011.

State Epic Poem: "The Legend of Old Stone Ranch," written by John Worth Cloud, was named the epic poem of Texas by the 61st Legislature in 1969. The work is a 400-page history of the Albany–Fort Griffin area written in verse form.

State Fiber and Fabric: Cotton was designated the state fiber and fabric of Texas by the 75th Legislature in 1997.

State Fish: The Guadalupe bass, a member of the genus Micropterus within the sunfish family, was named the state fish of Texas by the 71st Legislature in 1989. It is one of a group of fish collectively known as black bass.

State Flower Song: "Bluebonnets," written by Julia D. Booth and Lora C. Crockett, was named the state flower song by the 43rd Legislature in 1933.

State Folk Dance: The square dance was designated the state folk dance by the 72nd Legislature in 1991.

State Footwear: The cowboy boot was named the state footwear by the 80th Legislature in 2007.

State Fruit: Texas red grapefruit was designated the state fruit by the 73rd Legislature in 1993.

Our state bird: the mockingbird.

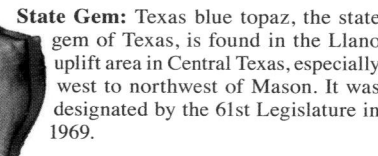

State Gem: Texas blue topaz, the state gem of Texas, is found in the Llano uplift area in Central Texas, especially west to northwest of Mason. It was designated by the 61st Legislature in 1969.

State Gemstone Cut: The Lone Star Cut was named the state gemstone cut by the 65th Legislature in 1977.

State Grass: Sideoats grama (Bouteloua curtipendula), a native grass found on many different Texas soils, was designated the state grass of Texas by the 62nd Legislature in 1971.

State Hashtags: #Texas (state), #TexasToDo (tourism), and #txlege (legislature) were all proclaimed state hashtags by the 84th Legislature in 2015.

State Hat: The cowboy hat was named the state hat of Texas by the 84th Legislature in 2015.

State Health Nut: The pecan was designated the state health nut by the 77th Legislature in 2001.

> **Psst! The images on these two pages can be matched to the state symbol descriptions in red. Can you match them all? (Answers on the next page.)**

State Horse: The American Quarter Horse was named state horse by the 81st Legislature in 2009.

State Insect: The Monarch butterfly (Danaus plexippus) was designated the state insect by the 74th Legislature in 1995.

State Longhorn Herd: The longhorn herd at Fort Griffin State Historic Site was named the state longhorn herd by the 61st Legislature in 1969.

State Mammals: The state mammals were all designated by the 74th Legislature in 1995:

- **Flying:** Mexican free-tailed bat (Tadarida brasiliensis);
- **Large:** Longhorn (Bos Texanus);
- **Small:** Armadillo (Dasypus novemcinctus).

State Maritime Museum: The Texas Maritime Museum in Rockport was named the state maritime museum by the 70th Legislature in 1987.

State Music: Western swing was named the state's official music by the 82nd Legislature in 2011.

State Musical Instrument: The guitar was designated the state musical instrument by the 75th Legislature in 1997.

State Native Pepper: The chiltepin (Capsicum annuum var. glabriusculum) was named the native pepper of Texas by the 75th Legislature in 1997.

State Native Shrub: Texas purple sage (Leucophyllum frutescens) was designated the state native shrub by the 79th Legislature in 2005.

State Nickname: "The Lone Star State" was designated the state nickname of Texas by the 84th Legislature in 2015.

State Pastries: Both the sopaipilla and strudel were named the state pastries of Texas by the 78th Legislature in 2003.

State Pepper: The jalapeño pepper (Capsicum annuum) was designated the state pepper by the 74th Legislature in 1995.

State Pie: Pecan pie was named the state pie by the 83rd Legislature in 2013.

State Plant: The prickly pear cactus (Genus Opuntia) was named the state plant by the 74th Legislature in 1995.

State Plays: There are four official state plays that were designated by the 66th Legislature in 1979:

1. **The Lone Star**
2. **Texas**
3. **Beyond the Sundown**
4. **Fandangle**

State Pollinator: The Western Honey Bee (Apis mellifera) was designated the official pollinator of Texas by the 84th Legislature in 2015.

State Precious Metal: Silver was named the official precious metal by the 80th Legislature in 2007.

State Railroad: The Texas State Railroad was designated the state railroad by the 78th Legislature in 2003. It is a steam-powered tourist excursion train that runs between the towns of Rusk and Palestine.

State Reptile: The Texas horned lizard (Phrynosoma cornutum) was named the state reptile by the 73rd Legislature in 1993.

State Rodeo Drill Team: Ghostriders were named the official rodeo drill team of Texas by the 80th Legislature in 2007.

State Saltwater Fish: Red Drum (Sciaenops ocellatus) was named the state's saltwater fish by the 82nd Legislature in 2011.

State Sea Turtle: Kemp's Ridley Sea Turtle was named the state sea turtle of Texas by the 83rd Legislature in 2013.

State Seashell: The lightning whelk (Busycon perversum pulleyi) was named the state seashell by the 70th Legislature in 1987. One of the few shells that open on the left side, the lightning whelk is named for its colored stripes and is found only on the Gulf Coast.

State Ship: The battleship USS Texas was designated the state ship by the 74th Legislature in 1995. The USS Texas was launched on May 18, 1912, from Newport News, Virginia, and commissioned on March 12, 1914. In 1919, it became the first U.S. battleship to launch an aircraft, and in 1939, it received the first commercial radar in the U.S. Navy. In 1940, the Texas was designated flagship of the U.S. Atlantic Fleet and was the last of the battleships to participate in both World Wars I and II. It was decommissioned on April 21, 1948, and is a National Historic Landmark and a National Mechanical Engineering Landmark. It is docked along the Houston Ship Channel.

State Shrub: The crape myrtle (Lagerstroemia indica) was designated the official state shrub by the 75th Legislature in 1997.

State Snack: Tortilla chips and salsa was named the state snack by the 78th Legislature in 2003.

State Sport: Rodeo was named the state sport of Texas by the 75th Legislature in 1997.

State Squash: Pumpkin was designated the state squash of Texas by the 83rd Legislature in 2013.

State Stone: Petrified palmwood, found in Texas principally near the Gulf Coast, was designated the state stone by the 61st Legislature in 1969.

State Tall Ship: The Elissa was named the state tall ship by the 79th Legislature in 2005. The 1877 ship makes its home at the Texas Seaport Museum at the port of Galveston.

State Tartan: The Texas Bluebonnet Tartan was named the official state tartan by the 71st Texas Legislature in 1989.

State 10K: The Texas Roundup 10K was named the official state 10K by the 79th Legislature in 2005 to encourage Texans to exercise and incorporate physical activity into their daily lives.

State Tie: The bolo tie was designated the state tie by the 80th Legislature in 2007.

State Vegetable: The Texas sweet onion was designated the state vegetable by the 75th Legislature in 1997.

State Vehicle: The chuck wagon was named the state vehicle by the 79th Legislature in 2005. Texas rancher Charles Goodnight is credited with inventing the chuck wagon to carry food and supplies for the cowboys on trail drives.

State Waterlily: The Nymphaea "Texas Dawn" was named the state waterlily by the 82nd Legislature in 2011. ☆

★ ★ ★ ★ ★
State symbol images, clockwise from top left:
Lightning whelk (seashell), photo by James St. John, CC
Jalapeno (pepper)
Chiltepin (native pepper)
Crape myrtle (shrub)
Blue Topaz (gem), photo by Michelle Jo, CC
Monarch butterfly (insect)
Chuck wagon (vehicle)
Texas Maritime Museum (maritime museum), Photo courtesy of the Texas Maritime Museum

Left: Chuck wagon racing in Alberta, Canada. Photo by Becks (CC)

Explore Texas History 🔍 Texas State Historical Association
HANDBOOK OF TEXAS

The *Texas Almanac* has long published feature articles about various aspects of Texas history, all of which are still available on our website, **TexasAlmanac.com**. In recent years, many of those articles were edited and combined to create a single article, "A Brief Sketch of Texas History," which was featured in several editions of the book. That article served its purpose, but a brief look has obvious limitations. After all, the history of Texas is anything but brief.

For this edition we are calling upon our colleagues at the *Handbook of Texas* to present an introductory selection of entries you can read online to learn about the history of Texas. Every entry offers a piece of the fabric of Texas past and present, and just as originally envisioned, the goal of those who write, revise, and edit entries remains ensuring that the *Handbook* is accurate, inclusive, accessible, and reflective of current scholarly standards.

Consider this list a starting point in your further study of Texas history, and explore our chronological overview entries and a few examples of our entries on cities and regions, specific topics, and biographies of deceased individuals. Dig in to these interesting samples of Texas history, and then go on to discover more at the *Handbook of Texas Online,* **tshaonline.org/handbook**.

Chronological Overview

Prehistory
https://tshaonline.org/handbook/online/articles/bfp02

Spanish Texas
https://tshaonline.org/handbook/online/articles/nps01

Texas in the Age of Mexican Independence
https://tshaonline.org/handbook/online/articles/nptsd

Mexican Texas
https://tshaonline.org/handbook/online/articles/npm01

Texas Revolution
https://tshaonline.org/handbook/online/articles/qdt01

Republic of Texas
https://tshaonline.org/handbook/online/articles/mzr02

Antebellum Texas
https://tshaonline.org/handbook/online/articles/npa01

Civil War
https://tshaonline.org/handbook/online/articles/qdc02

Reconstruction
https://tshaonline.org/handbook/online/articles/mzr01

Late-Nineteenth Century Texas
https://tshaonline.org/handbook/online/articles/npl01

Progressive Era
https://tshaonline.org/handbook/online/articles/npp01

Texas in the 1920s
https://tshaonline.org/handbook/online/articles/npt01

Great Depression
https://tshaonline.org/handbook/online/articles/npg01

World War II
https://tshaonline.org/handbook/online/articles/npwnj

Texas Post World War II
https://tshaonline.org/handbook/online/articles/npt02

Texas in the 21st Century
https://tshaonline.org/handbook/online/articles/npt21

Biographical

Athanase de Mézières
https://tshaonline.org/handbook/online/articles/fme69

Sam Houston
https://tshaonline.org/handbook/online/articles/fho73

Stephen F. Austin
https://tshaonline.org/handbook/online/articles/fau14

Mary Eleanor Brackenridge
https://tshaonline.org/handbook/online/articles/fbr04

Lyndon B. Johnson
https://tshaonline.org/handbook/online/articles/fjo19

Minnie Fisher Cunningham
https://tshaonline.org/handbook/online/articles/fcu24

Jesse H. Jones
https://tshaonline.org/handbook/online/articles/fjo53

Ernie Banks
https://tshaonline.org/handbook/online/articles/fbank

George H. W. Bush
https://tshaonline.org/handbook/online/articles/fbuhw

José Francisco Ruiz
https://tshaonline.org/handbook/online/articles/fru11

Barbara Jordan
https://tshaonline.org/handbook/online/articles/fjoas

George T. Ruby
https://tshaonline.org/handbook/online/articles/fru02

Jovita Idar
https://tshaonline.org/handbook/online/articles/fid03

Lady Bird Johnson
https://tshaonline.org/handbook/online/articles/fjocd

Henry B. González
https://tshaonline.org/handbook/online/articles/fgo76

Katherine Stinson
https://tshaonline.org/handbook/online/articles/fst97

Babe Didrikson Zaharias
https://tshaonline.org/handbook/online/articles/fza01

Barbara Pierce Bush
https://tshaonline.org/handbook/online/articles/fbubr

Topical

Spanish Missions https://tshaonline.org/handbook/online/articles/its02	**Comanche** https://tshaonline.org/handbook/online/articles/bmc72
Slavery https://tshaonline.org/handbook/online/articles/yps01	**People's Party** https://tshaonline.org/handbook/online/articles/wap01
Battle of the Alamo https://tshaonline.org/handbook/online/articles/qea02	**Houston Astros** https://tshaonline.org/handbook/online/articles/xoh01
Civil Rights in Texas https://tshaonline.org/handbook/online/articles/pkcfl	**San Antonio Spurs** https://tshaonline.org/handbook/online/articles/xos01
Music https://tshaonline.org/handbook/online/articles/xmm01	**Witte Museum** https://tshaonline.org/handbook/online/articles/lbw03
Woman Suffrage https://tshaonline.org/handbook/online/articles/viw01	**Railroads** https://tshaonline.org/handbook/online/articles/eqr01
Germans https://tshaonline.org/handbook/online/articles/png02	**Vietnamese** https://tshaonline.org/handbook/online/articles/pjv01
African Americans https://tshaonline.org/handbook/online/articles/pkaan	**Mexican Americans** https://tshaonline.org/handbook/online/articles/pqmue
Anglo American Colonization https://tshaonline.org/handbook/online/articles/uma01	**Segregation** https://tshaonline.org/handbook/online/articles/pks01
LULAC https://tshaonline.org/handbook/online/articles/wel01	**Porvenir Massacre** https://tshaonline.org/handbook/online/articles/jcp02
Kerrville Folk Festival https://tshaonline.org/handbook/online/articles/xfk01	**Armadillo** https://tshaonline.org/handbook/online/articles/tca02
Surface Water https://tshaonline.org/handbook/online/articles/grs01	**Visual Arts** https://tshaonline.org/handbook/online/articles/kjvtz

Cities and Regions

Dallas https://tshaonline.org/handbook/online/articles/hdd01	**El Paso** https://tshaonline.org/handbook/online/articles/hde01
Fort Worth https://tshaonline.org/handbook/online/articles/hdf01	**Austin** https://tshaonline.org/handbook/online/articles/hda03
Houston https://tshaonline.org/handbook/online/articles/hdh03	**San Antonio** https://tshaonline.org/handbook/online/articles/hds02
Panhandle https://tshaonline.org/handbook/online/articles/ryp01	**Rio Grande Valley** https://tshaonline.org/handbook/online/articles/ryr01
Trans-Pecos https://tshaonline.org/handbook/online/articles/ryt02	**East Texas** https://tshaonline.org/handbook/online/articles/rye01
Hill Country https://tshaonline.org/handbook/online/articles/ryh02	**Permian Basin** https://tshaonline.org/handbook/online/articles/ryp02

The *Handbook of Texas* is a collaborative scholarly project of the Texas State Historical Association (TSHA) that began in 1939 under the direction of Professor Walter Prescott Webb at the University of Texas at Austin to create, "the most useful book that has ever been published in Texas."

- **FREE** and Accessible on computers, phones, and tablets
- Nearly 27,000 entries by 6,000+ authors
- 10 million page views annually
- 4.5 million users annually

Immigrants just arrived in Galveston, 1890s. Photo courtesy of the Texas State Archives

ENVIRONMENT

Hikers at Big Bend National Park
Photo by Jonathan Cutrer (jcutrer.com).

PHYSICAL REGIONS

GEOLOGY AND SOILS

AQUIFERS, RIVERS, LAKES, ESTUARIES

PLANT LIFE, FORESTS, GRASSLANDS

WILDLIFE

The Physical State of Texas

The Area of Texas

Texas occupies about 7 percent of the total water and land area of the United States. Second in size among the states, Texas has a land and water area of 268,596 square miles, as compared with Alaska's 665,384 square miles, according to the United States Bureau of the Census. California, the third-largest state, has 163,695 square miles. Texas is as large as all of New England, New York, Delaware, Pennsylvania, Ohio, and Virginia combined.

The state's total area consists of 261,232 square miles of land and 7,365 square miles of water.

Length and Breadth

The longest straight-line distance in a general north-south direction is 801 miles from the northwest corner of the Panhandle to the extreme southern tip of Texas on the Rio Grande southeast of Brownsville. The greatest east-west distance is 773 miles from the extreme eastward bend in the Sabine River in Newton County to the extreme western bulge of the Rio Grande just northwest of El Paso.

Texas' Boundary Lines

The boundary of Texas by segments, including only larger river bends and only the great arc of the coastline, is as follows:

Boundary	Miles
Rio Grande	889.0
Coastline	367.0
Sabine River, Lake, and Pass	180.0
Sabine River to Red River	106.5
Red River	480.0
East Panhandle line	133.6
North Panhandle line	167.0
West Panhandle line	310.2
Along 32nd parallel	209.0
TOTAL	**2,842.3**

Following the smaller meanderings of the rivers and the tidewater coastline, the following are the boundary measurements:

Boundary	Miles
Rio Grande	1,254.0
Coastline (tidewater)	624.0
Sabine River, Lake, and Pass	292.0
Sabine River to Red River	106.5
Red River	726.0
East Panhandle line	133.6
North Panhandle line	167.0
West Panhandle line	310.2
Along 32nd parallel	209.0
TOTAL	**3,822.3**

Latitude and Longitude

The extremes of latitude and longitude in Texas are as follows:

★ From 25° 50' North latitude at the extreme southern turn of the Rio Grande on the south line of Cameron County to 36° 30' North latitude along the north line of the Panhandle, and

★ From 93° 31' West longitude at the extreme eastern point of the Sabine River on the east line of Newton County to 106° 38' West longitude at the extreme westward point of the Rio Grande on the western edge of El Paso.

Named Mountain Peaks in Texas Above 8,000 Feet

The highest point in the state is Guadalupe Peak at 8,749 feet above sea level. Its twin, El Capitan, stands at 8,085 feet and also is located in Culberson County near the New Mexico state line. Both are in Guadalupe Mountains National Park, which includes the scenic McKittrick Canyon.

The elevations used on this page are from various sources, including the U.S. Geological Survey, the National Park Service, and the Texas Department of Transportation. The named peaks above 8,000 feet and the counties in which they are located are listed below.

Name	County	Height (Ft.)
Guadalupe Peak	Culberson	8,749
Bush Mountain	Culberson	8,631
Shumard Peak	Culberson	8,615
Bartlett Peak	Culberson	8,508
Mount Livermore (Baldy Peak)	Jeff Davis	8,378
Hunter Peak (Pine Top Mtn.)	Culberson	8,368
El Capitan	Culberson	8,085

Elevation Highs and Lows

Highest Town: Fort Davis in Jeff Davis County is the highest town of any size in Texas at 5,050 feet above sea level, and the county has the highest average elevation.

Highest Highway: The highest state highway point also is in Jeff Davis County at McDonald Observatory on Mount Locke, where the road reaches 6,781 feet above sea level, as determined by the Texas Department of Transportation.

Highest Railway: The highest railway point is Paisano Pass, 14 miles east of Marfa in Presidio County, which is 5,074 above sea level.

Lowest Point: Sea level is the lowest elevation determined in Texas, and it can be found in all the coastal counties. No point in the state has been found by the geological survey to be below sea level. ☆

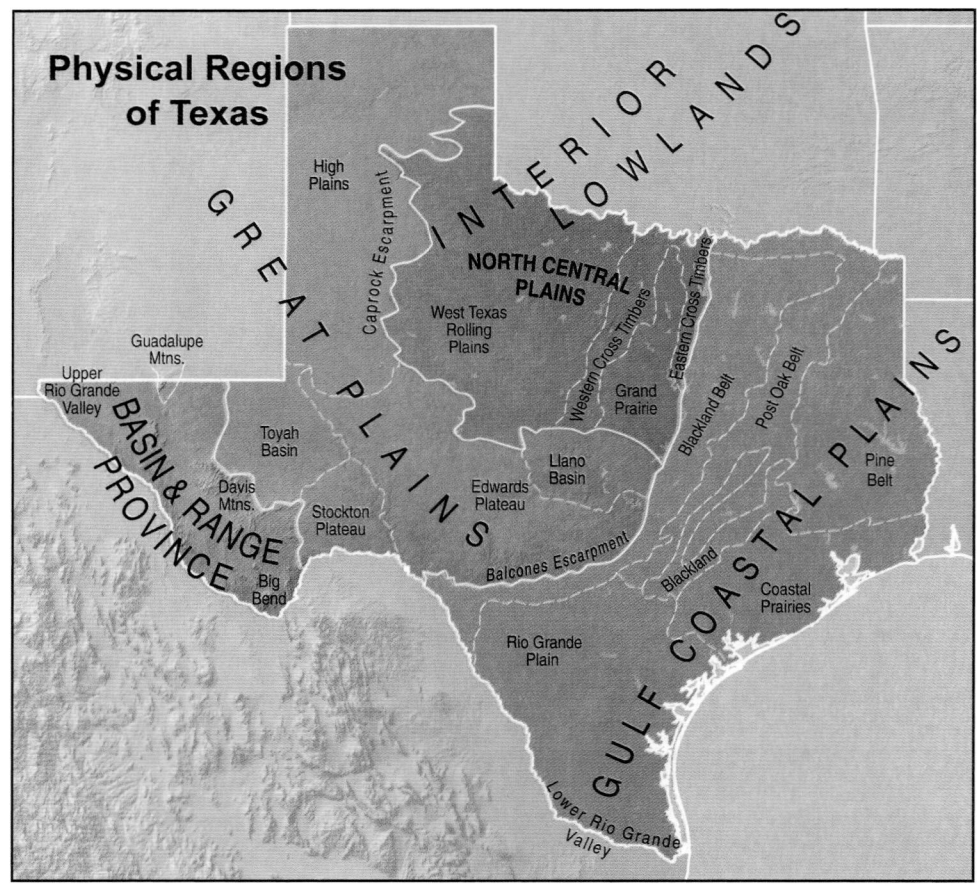

Physical Regions of Texas

Physical Regions

This section was reviewed by Dr. David R. Butler, Texas State University System Regents' Professor of Geography

The principal physical regions of Texas are usually listed as follows:

I. Gulf Coastal Plains

Texas' Gulf Coastal Plains are the western extension of the coastal plain extending from the Atlantic Ocean to beyond the Rio Grande. Its characteristic rolling to hilly surface covered with a heavy growth of pine and hardwoods extends into East Texas. In the increasingly arid west, however, its forests become secondary in nature, consisting largely of post oaks and, farther west, prairies and brushlands.

The interior limit of the Gulf Coastal Plains in Texas is the line of the Balcones Fault and Escarpment. This geologic fault or shearing of underground strata extends eastward from a point on the Rio Grande near Del Rio. It extends to the northwestern part of Bexar County, where it turns northeastward and extends through Comal, Hays, and Travis counties, intersecting the Colorado River immediately north of Austin. The fault line is a single, definite geologic feature,

accompanied by a line of southward- and eastward-facing hills.

The resemblance of the hills to balconies when viewed from the plain below accounts for the Spanish name for this area: balcones.

North of Waco, features of the fault zone are sufficiently inconspicuous that the interior boundary of the Coastal Plain follows the traditional geologic contact between upper and lower Cretaceous rocks. This contact is along the eastern edge of the Eastern Cross Timbers.

This fault line is usually accepted as the boundary between lowland and upland Texas. Below the fault line, the surface is characteristically coastal plains. Above the Balcones Fault, the surface is characteristically interior rolling plains.

A. Pine Belt or "Piney Woods"

The Pine Belt, called the "Piney Woods," extends 75 to 125 miles into Texas from the east. From north to south, it extends from the Red River to within about 25 miles of the Gulf Coast. Interspersed among the pines are hardwood timbers, usually in valleys of rivers and creeks. This area is the source of practically all of Texas' commercial timber production (see Texas Forest Resources, page 115). It was settled early in Texas' history and is one of the oldest farming areas in the state.

This area's soils and climate are adaptable to the production of a variety of fruit and vegetable crops. Cattle raising is widespread, along with the development of pastures planted to improved grasses. Lumber production is the principal industry. There is a large iron-and-steel industry near Daingerfield in Morris County based on nearby iron deposits. Iron deposits are also worked in Rusk and one or two other counties.

A great oil field discovered in Gregg, Rusk, and Smith counties in 1931 has done more than anything else to contribute to the economic growth of the area. This area has a variety of clays, lignite, and other minerals as potentials for development.

B. Post Oak Belt

The main Post Oak Belt of Texas is wedged between the Pine Belt on the east, Blacklands on the west, and the Coastal Prairies on the south, covering a considerable area in East-Central Texas. The principal industry is diversified farming and livestock raising.

It is spotty in character, with some insular areas of blackland soil and some that closely resemble those of the Pine Belt. There is a small, isolated area of loblolly pines in Bastrop, Caldwell, Fayette, and Lee counties known as the "Lost Pines," the westernmost southern pines in the United States. The Post Oak Belt has lignite, commercial clays, and some other minerals.

C. Blackland Belt

The Blackland Belt stretches from the Rio Grande to the Red River, lying just below the line of the Balcones Fault and varying in width from 15 to 70 miles. It is narrowest below the segment of the Balcones Fault from the Rio Grande to Bexar County and gradually widens as it runs northeast to the Red River.

Its rolling prairie, easily turned by the plow, developed rapidly as a farming area until the 1930s and was the principal cotton-producing area of Texas. Now, however, other Texas areas that are irrigated and mechanized lead in farming.

Because of the early growth, the Blackland Belt is still the most thickly populated area in the state and contains within it and along its border more of the state's large and middle-sized cities than any other area. Primarily because of this concentration of population, this belt has the most diversified manufacturing industry of the state.

D. Coastal Prairies

The Texas Coastal Prairies extend westward along the coast from the Sabine River, reaching inland 30 to 60 miles. Between the Sabine and Galveston Bay, the line of demarcation between the prairies and the Pine Belt forests to the north is very distinct. The Coastal Prairies extend along the Gulf of Mexico from the Sabine to the Lower Rio Grande Valley.

The eastern half is covered with a heavy growth of grass; the western half, which is more arid, is covered

with short grass and, in some places, with small timber and brush. The soil is heavy clay. Grass supports the densest cattle population in Texas, and cattle ranching is the principal agricultural industry. Rice is a major crop, grown under irrigation from wells and rivers. Cotton, grain sorghum, and truck crops also are grown.

Coastal Prairie areas have seen the greatest industrial development in Texas history since World War II. Chief concentration has been from Orange and Beaumont to Houston, and much of the development has been in petrochemicals and the aerospace industry.

Corpus Christi, in the Coastal Bend, and Brownsville, in the Lower Rio Grande Valley, have seaports and agricultural and industrial sections. Cotton, grain, vegetables, and citrus fruits are the principal crops. Cattle production is significant, with the famed King Ranch and other large ranches located here.

E. Lower Rio Grande Valley

The deep alluvial soils and distinctive economy cause the Lower Rio Grande Valley to be classified as a subregion of the Gulf Coastal Plains. "The Valley," as it is called locally, is Texas' greatest citrus and winter vegetable growing region because of the normal absence of freezing weather and the rich delta soils of the Rio Grande. Despite occasional damaging freezes, the Lower Valley ranks high among the nation's fruit and truck-farming regions. Much of the acreage is irrigated, although dry-land farming also is practiced.

F. Rio Grande Plain

This area may be roughly defined as lying south of San Antonio between the Rio Grande and the Gulf Coast. The Rio Grande Plain shows characteristics of both the Gulf Coastal Plains and the North Mexico Plains because there is similarity of topography, climate, and plant life all the way from the Balcones Escarpment in Texas to the Sierra Madre Oriental in Mexico, which runs past Monterrey about 160 miles south of Laredo.

The Rio Grande Plain is partly prairie, but much of it is covered with a dense growth of prickly pear, mesquite, dwarf oak, catclaw, guajillo, huisache, blackbrush, cenizo, and other cactus and wild shrubs. It is devoted primarily to raising cattle, sheep, and goats. The Texas Angora goat and mohair industry centers in this area and on the Edwards Plateau, which borders it on the north. San Antonio and Laredo are its chief commercial centers, with San Antonio dominating trade.

There is some farming, and the Winter Garden, centering in Dimmit and Zavala counties north of Laredo, is irrigated from wells and streams to produce vegetables in late winter and early spring. Primarily, however, the central and western part of the Rio Grande Plain is devoted to livestock raising.

The rainfall is less than 25 inches annually, and the hot summers cause heavy evaporation, so that cultivation without irrigation is limited.

Over a large area in the central and western parts of the Rio Grande Plain, the growth of small oaks, mesquite, prickly pear (Opuntia) cactus, and a variety of wild shrubs is very dense, and it is often called the

Brush Country. It is also referred to as the chaparral and the monte, from a Spanish word that can mean dense brush.)

II. Interior Lowlands

North Central Plains

The North Central Plains of Texas are a southwestern extension into Texas of the interior, or central, lowlands that extend northward to the Canadian border, paralleling the Great Plains to the West. The North Central Plains of Texas extend from the Blackland Belt on the east to the Caprock Escarpment on the west. From north to south, they extend from the Red River to the Colorado River.

A. West Texas Rolling Plains

The West Texas Rolling Plains, approximately the western two-thirds of the North Central Plains in Texas, rise from east to west in altitude from about 750 feet to 2,000 feet at the base of the Caprock Escarpment. Annual rainfall ranges from about 30 inches on the east to 20 inches on the west. In general, as one progresses westward in Texas, the precipitation not only declines but also becomes more variable from year to year. Temperature varies rather widely between summer's heat and winter's cold.

This area still has a large cattle-raising industry with many of the state's largest ranches. However, there is much level, cultivable land.

B. Grand Prairie

Near the eastern edge of the North Central Plains is the Grand Prairie, extending south from the Red River in an irregular band through Cooke, Montague, Wise, Denton, Tarrant, Parker, Hood, Johnson, Bosque, Coryell, and some adjacent counties.

It is a limestone-based area, usually treeless except along the numerous streams, and adapted primarily to raising livestock and growing staple crops. Sometimes called the Fort Worth Prairie, it has an agricultural economy and largely rural population, with no large cities, except Fort Worth on its eastern boundary.

C. Eastern and Western Cross Timbers

Hanging over the top of the Grand Prairie and dropping down on each side are the Eastern and Western Cross Timbers. The two southward-extending bands are connected by a narrow strip along the Red River.

The Eastern Cross Timbers extend southward from the Red River through eastern Denton County and along the boundary between Dallas and Tarrant counties. It then stretches through Johnson County to the Brazos River and into Hill County.

The much larger Western Cross Timbers extend from the Red River south through Clay, Montague, Jack, Wise, Parker, Palo Pinto, Hood, Erath, Eastland, Comanche, Brown, and Mills counties to the Colorado River, where they meet the Llano Basin.

Their soils are adapted to fruit and vegetable crops, which reach considerable commercial production in some areas in Parker, Erath, Eastland, and Comanche counties.

III. Great Plains

A. High Plains

The Great Plains, which lie to the east of the base of the Rocky Mountains, extend into northwestern Texas. This area, commonly known as the High Plains, is a vast, flat, high plain covered with thick layers of alluvial material. It is also known as the Staked Plains or Llano Estacado.

Historians differ as to the origin of this name. Some say it came from the fact that the explorer Coronado's expedition used stakes to mark its route across the trackless sea of grass so that it would be guided on its return trip. Others think that the estacado refers to the palisaded appearance of the Caprock in many places, especially the west-facing escarpment in New Mexico.

The Caprock Escarpment is the dividing line between the High Plains and the lower West Texas Rolling Plains. Like the Balcones Escarpment, the Caprock Escarpment is a striking physical feature, rising abruptly 200 feet, 500 feet, and in some places almost 1,000 feet above the plains. Unlike the Balcones Escarpment, the Caprock was caused by surface erosion.

Where rivers issue from the eastern face of the Caprock, there frequently are notable canyons, such as Palo Duro Canyon on the Prairie Dog Town Fork of the Red River, Blanco Canyon on the White River, as well as the breaks along the Canadian River as it crosses the Panhandle north of Amarillo.

Along the eastern edge of the Panhandle, there is a gradual descent of the land's surface from high to low plains; but at the Red River, the Caprock Escarpment becomes a striking surface feature.

It continues as an east-facing wall south through Briscoe, Floyd, Motley, Dickens, Crosby, Garza, and Borden counties, gradually decreasing in elevation. South of Borden County, the escarpment is less obvious, and the boundary between the High Plains and the Edwards Plateau occurs where the alluvial cover of the High Plains disappears.

Stretching over the largest level plain of its kind in the United States, the High Plains rise gradually from about 2,700 feet on the east to more than 4,000 in spots along the New Mexico border.

Chiefly because of climate and the resultant agriculture, subdivisions are called the North Plains and South Plains. The North Plains, from Hale County north, has primarily wheat and grain sorghum farming, but with significant ranching and petroleum developments. Amarillo is the largest city, with Plainview on the south and Borger on the north as important commercial centers.

The South Plains, also a leading grain sorghum region, leads Texas in cotton production. Lubbock is the principal city, and Lubbock County is one of the state's largest cotton producers. Irrigation from underground reservoirs, centered around Lubbock and Plainview, waters much of the crop acreage.

B. Edwards Plateau

Geographers usually consider that the Great Plains at the foot of the Rocky Mountains actually continue

Galveston Island State Park is part of the Coastal Prairies region. Photo by Yinan Chen (CC).

southward from the High Plains of Texas to the Rio Grande and the Balcones Escarpment. This southern and lower extension of the Great Plains in Texas is known as the Edwards Plateau.

It lies between the Rio Grande and the Colorado River. Its southeastern border is the Balcones Escarpment from the Rio Grande at Del Rio eastward to San Antonio and thence to Austin on the Colorado River. Its upper boundary is the Pecos River, though the Stockton Plateau is geologically and topographically classed with the Edwards Plateau.

The Edwards Plateau varies from about 750 feet high at its southern and eastern borders to about 2,700 feet in places. Almost the entire surface is a thin, limestone-based soil covered with a medium to thick growth of cedar, small oak, and mesquite and a varying growth of prickly pear. Grass for cattle, weeds for sheep, and tree foliage for the browsing goats support three industries — cattle, goat, and sheep raising — upon which the area's economy depends. It is the nation's leading Angora goat and mohair producing region and one of the nation's leading sheep and wool areas. A few crops are grown.

Hill Country

The Hill Country is a popular name for the eastern portion of the Edwards Plateau south of the Llano Basin. Its notable large springs include Barton Springs at Austin, San Marcos Springs at San Marcos, Comal Springs at New Braunfels, several springs at San Antonio, and a number of others.

The Hill Country is characterized by rugged hills with relatively steep slopes and thin soils overlying limestone bedrock. High gradient streams combine with these steep hillslopes and occasionally heavy precipitation to produce an area with a significant flash-flood hazard.

C. Toyah Basin

To the northwest of the Edwards and Stockton plateaus is the Toyah Basin, a broad, flat remnant of an old sea floor that occupied the region as recently as Quaternary time.

Located in the Pecos River Valley, this region, in relatively recent time, has become important for many agricultural products as a result of irrigation. Additional economic activity is afforded by local oil fields.

D. Llano Basin

The Llano Basin lies at the junction of the Colorado and Llano rivers in Burnet and Llano counties. Earlier, this was known as the "Central Mineral Region" because of evidence there of a large number of minerals.

On the Colorado River in this area, a succession of dams impounds two large and five small reservoirs. Uppermost is Lake Buchanan, one of the large reservoirs, between Burnet and Llano counties. Below it in the western part of Travis County is Lake Travis.

Between these two large reservoirs are three smaller ones, Inks, Lyndon B. Johnson (formerly Granite Shoals), and Marble Falls reservoirs, used primarily to produce electric power from the overflow from Lake Buchanan. Lake Austin is along the western part of the city of Austin. Still another small lake, Lady Bird Lake (formerly Town Lake), is formed by a low-water dam in Austin.

The recreational area around these lakes has been called the Highland Lakes Country. This is an interesting area with Precambrian and Paleozoic rocks found on the surface. Granitic domes, exemplified by Enchanted Rock north of Fredericksburg, form the core of this area of ancient rocks.

IV. Basin and Range Province

The Basin and Range Province, with its center in Nevada, surrounds the Colorado Plateau on the west and south and enters far West Texas from southern New Mexico on the east. It consists of broad interior drainage basins interspersed with scattered fault-block mountain ranges.

Although this is the only part of Texas regarded as mountainous, these should not be confused with the Rocky Mountains. Of all the independent ranges in West Texas, only the Davis Mountains resemble the Rockies, and there is much debate about this.

Texas west of the Edwards Plateau, bounded on the north by New Mexico and on the south by the Rio Grande, is distinctive in its physical and economic conditions. Traversed from north to south by fault-block mountains, it contains all of Texas' true mountains and also is very interesting geologically.

A. Guadalupe Mountains

Highest of the Trans-Pecos Mountains is the Guadalupe Range, which enters Texas from New Mexico. It abruptly ends about 20 miles south of the boundary line, where Guadalupe Peak, (8,749 feet, highest in Texas) and El Capitan (8,085 feet) are situated. El Capitan, because of perspective, appears to the observer on the plain below to be higher than Guadalupe.

Lying just west of the Guadalupe Range and extending to the Hueco Mountains a short distance east of El Paso is the Diablo Plateau or basin. It has no drainage outlet to the sea. The runoff from the scant rain that falls on its surface drains into a series of salt lakes that lie just west of the Guadalupe Mountains. These lakes are dry during periods of low rainfall, exposing bottoms of solid salt; for years they were a source of commercial salt. West of the Hueco Mountains are the Franklin Mountains in El Paso, with the Hueco Bolson (a down-dropped area approximately 4,000 feet above sea level) separating the two fault-block ranges.

B. Davis Mountains

The Davis Mountains are principally in Jeff Davis County. The highest peak, Mount Livermore (8,378 feet), is one of the highest in Texas; there are several others more than 7,000 feet high. These mountains intercept the moisture-bearing winds and receive more precipitation than elsewhere in the Trans-Pecos, so they have more vegetation than the other Trans-Pecos mountains. Noteworthy are the San Solomon Springs at the northern base of these mountains.

C. Big Bend

South of the Davis Mountains lies the Big Bend country, so called because it is encompassed on three sides by a great southward swing of the Rio Grande. It is a mountainous country of scant rainfall and sparse population. Its principal mountains, the Chisos, rise to 7,825 feet in Mount Emory.

Along the Rio Grande are the Santa Elena, Mariscal, and Boquillas canyons with rim elevations of 3,500 to 3,775 feet. They are among the noteworthy canyons of the North American continent.

Because of its remarkable topography and plant and animal life, the southern part of this region along the Rio Grande is home to Big Bend National Park, with headquarters in the Chisos Basin, a deep valley in the Chisos Mountains. It is a favorite recreation area.

D. Upper Rio Grande Valley

The Upper Rio Grande Valley, or El Paso Valley, is a narrow strip of irrigated land running down the river from El Paso for a distance of 75 miles or more.

In this area are the historic towns and missions of Ysleta, Socorro, and San Elizario, some of the oldest in Texas. Cotton is the chief product of this valley, much of it the long-staple variety. This limited area has a dense urban and rural population, in marked contrast to the territory surrounding it. ☆

Palo Duro Canyon is in the High Plains of Texas, near Amarillo. Photo by Joe Diaz (CC).

Geology of Texas

Source: Bureau of Economic Geology, The University of Texas at Austin; www.beg.utexas.edu

Mountains, seas, coastal plains, rocky plateaus, high plains, forests — all of this physiographic variety in Texas is controlled by the varied rocks and structures that underlie and crop out across the state. The fascinating geologic history of Texas is recorded in the rocks — both those exposed at the surface and those penetrated by holes drilled in search of oil and natural gas.

The rocks reveal a dynamic, ever-changing earth: ancient mountains, seas, volcanoes, earthquake belts, rivers, hurricanes, and winds. Today, the volcanoes and great earthquake belts are no longer active, but rivers and streams, wind and rain, and the slow, inexorable alterations of rocks at or near the surface continue to change the face of Texas.

The geologic history of Texas, as documented by the rocks, began more than a billion years ago. Its legacy is the mineral wealth and varied land forms of modern Texas.

Geologic Time Travel

The story preserved in rocks requires an understanding of the origin of strata and how they have been deformed. **Stratigraphy is the study of the composition, sequence, and origin of rocks**: what rocks are made of, how they were formed, and the order in which the layers were formed.

Structural geology reveals the architecture of rocks: the locations of the mountains, volcanoes, sedimentary basins, and earthquake belts.

The map on page 36 shows where rocks of various geologic ages are visible on the surface of Texas today. History concerns events through time, but geologic time is such a grandiose concept, most find it difficult to comprehend. So geologists have **named the various chapters of earth history.**

Precambrian Eon

Precambrian rocks, more than 600 million years old, are exposed at the surface in the Llano Uplift of Central Texas and in scattered outcrops in West Texas, around and north of Van Horn and near El Paso.

These rocks, some more than a billion years old, include complexly deformed rocks that were originally formed by cooling from a liquid state, as well as rocks that were altered from pre-existing rocks.

Precambrian rocks, often called the "basement complex," are thought to form the foundation of continental masses. They underlie all of Texas. The outcrop in Central Texas is only the exposed part of the Texas Craton, which is primarily buried by younger rocks. (A craton is a stable, almost immovable portion of the earth's crust that forms the nuclear mass of a continent.)

Paleozoic Era

During the early part of the Paleozoic Era (approximately 600 million to 350 million years ago), **broad, relatively shallow seas repeatedly inundated the Texas Craton and much of North and West Texas.** The evidence for these events is found exposed around the Llano Uplift and in far West Texas near Van Horn and El Paso, and also in the subsurface throughout most of West and North Texas.

The evidence includes early Paleozoic rocks, sandstones, shales, and limestones, similar to sediments that form in seas today, and the fossils of animals, similar to modern crustaceans: the brachiopods, clams, snails, and related organisms that live in modern marine environments.

By late Paleozoic (approximately 350 million to 240 million years ago), the Texas Craton was bordered on the east and south by a long, deep marine basin called the Ouachita Trough. Sediments slowly accumulated in this trough until late in the Paleozoic Era.

Plate-tectonic theory postulates that the collision of the North American Plate (upon which the Texas Craton is located) with the European and African–South American plates uplifted the thick sediments that had accumulated in the trough **to form the Ouachita Mountains**.

At that time, the Ouachitas extended across Texas. Today, the Texas portion of the old mountain range is mostly buried by younger rocks. Ancient remnants can be seen in the Marathon Basin of West Texas due to uplift and erosion of younger sediments.

The public can see the remains of this once-majestic Ouachita Mountain range at Post Park, just south of Marathon in Brewster County. Other remnants at the surface are exposed in southeastern Oklahoma and southwestern Arkansas.

During the **Pennsylvanian** Period, however, the Ouachita Mountains bordered the eastern margin of shallow inland seas that covered most of West Texas. Rivers flowed westward from the mountains to the seas bringing sediment to form deltas along an ever-changing coastline.

The sediments were then reworked by the waves and currents of the inland sea. Today, these fluvial, delta, and shallow marine deposits compose the late Paleozoic rocks that crop out and underlie the surface of North-Central Texas.

Broad marine shelves divided the West Texas seas into several sub-basins, or deeper areas, that received more sediments than accumulated on the limestone shelves. Limestone reefs rimmed the deeper basins. **Today, these limestone reefs are important oil reservoirs in West Texas.**

These seas gradually withdrew from Texas, and by the late **Permian** Period, all that was left in West Texas were shallow basins and wide tidal flats in which salt, gypsum, and red muds accumulated in a hot, arid land. Strata deposited during the Permian Period are exposed today along the edge of the Panhandle, as far east as Wichita Falls and south to Concho County, and in the Trans-Pecos.

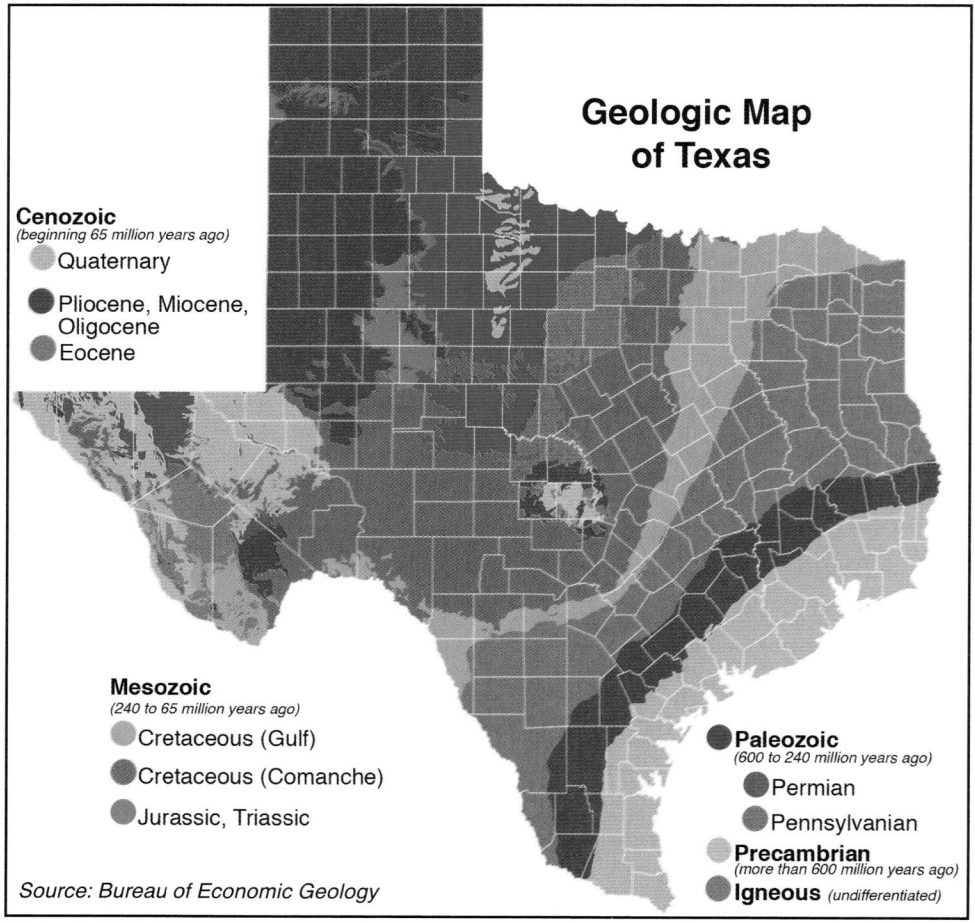

Geologic Map of Texas

Cenozoic
(beginning 65 million years ago)
- Quaternary
- Pliocene, Miocene, Oligocene
- Eocene

Mesozoic
(240 to 65 million years ago)
- Cretaceous (Gulf)
- Cretaceous (Comanche)
- Jurassic, Triassic

Paleozoic
(600 to 240 million years ago)
- Permian
- Pennsylvanian

Precambrian
(more than 600 million years ago)
- Igneous *(undifferentiated)*

Source: Bureau of Economic Geology

Mesozoic Era

Approximately 240 million years ago, the major geologic events in Texas shifted from West Texas to East and Southeast Texas. The European and African–South American plates, which had collided with the North American plate to form the Ouachita Mountains, began to separate from North America.

A series of faulted basins, or rifts, extending from Mexico to Nova Scotia were formed. These rifted basins received sediments from adjacent uplifts. As Europe and the southern continents continued to drift away from North America, **the Texas basins were eventually buried beneath thick deposits of marine salt within the newly formed East Texas and Gulf Coast basins.**

Jurassic and Cretaceous rocks in East and Southeast Texas document a sequence of broad limestone shelves at the edge of the developing Gulf of Mexico. From time to time, the shelves were buried beneath deltaic sandstones and shales, which built the northwestern margin of the widening Gulf of Mexico to the south and southeast.

As the underlying salt was buried more deeply by dense sediments, the salt became unstable and moved toward areas of least pressure. As the salt moved, it arched or pierced overlying sediments forming, in some cases, columns known as "salt domes." In some cases, these salt domes moved to the surface; others remain beneath a sedimentary overburden. This mobile salt formed numerous structures that would later serve to trap oil and natural gas.

By the early **Cretaceous** (approximately 140 million years ago), the shallow Mesozoic seas covered a large part of Texas, eventually extending west to the Trans-Pecos area and north almost to present-day state boundaries.

Today, the **limestone deposited in those seas is exposed in the walls of the magnificent canyons of the Rio Grande in the Big Bend National Park area** and in the canyons and headwaters of streams that drain the Edwards Plateau, as well as in Central Texas from San Antonio to Dallas.

Animals of many types lived in the shallow Mesozoic seas, tidal pools, and coastal swamps. Today, these lower Cretaceous rocks are some of the most fossiliferous in the state. **Tracks of dinosaurs occur in several places**, and remains of terrestrial, aquatic, and flying reptiles have been collected from Cretaceous rocks in many areas.

During most of the late Cretaceous, much of Texas lay beneath marine waters that were deeper than those of the early Cretaceous seas, except where rivers, deltas, and shallow marine shelves existed.

River delta and strandline sandstones are the reservoir rocks for the most prolific oil field in Texas. When discovered in 1930, this East Texas oil field contained recoverable reserves estimated at 5.6 billion barrels.

The chalky rock that we now call the "Austin Chalk" was deposited when the Texas seas became deeper. Today, the chalk and other Upper Cretaceous rocks crop out in a wide band that extends from near Eagle Pass on the Rio Grande, east to San Antonio, north to Dallas, and east to the Texarkana area. The Austin Chalk and other upper Cretaceous rocks dip southeastward beneath the East Texas and Gulf Coast basins.

The late Cretaceous was the time of the last major seaway across Texas, because mountains were forming in the western United States that influenced areas as far away as Texas.

A chain of volcanoes formed beneath the late Cretaceous seas in an area roughly parallel to and south and east of the old, buried Ouachita Mountains. The eruptions of these volcanoes were primarily on the sea floor and great clouds of steam and ash likely accompanied them.

Between eruptions, invertebrate marine animals built reefs on the shallow volcanic cones. Pilot Knob, located southeast of Austin, is one of these old volcanoes that is now exposed at the surface.

Cenozoic Era

At the dawn of the Cenozoic Era, approximately 65 million years ago, deltas fed by rivers were in the northern and northwestern margins of the East Texas Basin. These streams flowed eastward, draining areas to the north and west. Although there were minor incursions of the seas, the Cenozoic rocks principally document extensive seaward building by broad deltas, marshy lagoons, sandy barrier islands, and embayments.

Thick vegetation covered the levees and areas between the streams. Coastal plains were taking shape under the same processes still at work today.

The Mesozoic marine salt became buried by thick sediments in the coastal plain area. The salt began to form ridges and domes in the Houston and Rio Grande areas. The heavy load of sand, silt, and mud deposited by the deltas eventually caused some areas of the coast to subside and form large fault systems, essentially parallel to the coast.

Many of these coastal faults moved slowly and probably generated little earthquake activity. However, movement along the Balcones and Luling-Mexia-Talco zones, a complex system of faults along the western and northern edge of the basins, likely generated large earthquakes millions of years ago.

Predecessors of modern animals roamed the Texas Cenozoic coastal plains and woodlands. Bones and teeth of horses, camels, sloths, giant armadillos,

mammoths, mastodons, bats, rats, large cats, and other modern or extinct mammals have been excavated from coastal plain deposits.

Vegetation in the area included varieties of plants and trees both similar and dissimilar to modern ones. Fossil palmwood, the Texas "state stone," is found in sediments of early Cenozoic age.

The Cenozoic Era in Trans-Pecos Texas was entirely different. There, extensive volcanic eruptions formed great calderas and produced copious lava flows. These eruptions ejected great clouds of volcanic ash and rock particles into the air — many times the amount of material ejected by the 1980 eruption of Mount St. Helens.

Ash from the eruptions drifted eastward and is found in many of the sand-and-siltstones of the Gulf Coastal Plains. Lava flowed over older Paleozoic and Mesozoic rocks, and igneous intrusions melted their way upward into crustal rocks. These volcanic and intrusive igneous rocks are well exposed in arid areas of the Trans-Pecos today.

In the Texas Panhandle, streams originating in the recently elevated southern Rocky Mountains brought floods of gravel and sand into Texas. As the braided streams crisscrossed the area, they formed great alluvial fans.

These fans, which were deposited on the older Paleozoic and Mesozoic rocks, occur from northwestern Texas into Nebraska. Between 1 million and 2 million years ago, the streams of the Panhandle were isolated from their Rocky Mountain source, and the eastern edge of this sheet of alluvial material began to retreat westward, forming the Caprock of the modern High Plains.

Late in the Cenozoic Era, a great Ice Age descended on the northern North American continent. For more than 2 million years, there were successive advances and retreats of the thick sheets of glacial ice. Four periods of extensive glaciation were separated by warmer interglacial periods. Although the glaciers never reached as far south as Texas, the state's climate and sea level underwent major changes with each period of glacial advance and retreat.

Sea level during times of glacial advance was 300 to 450 feet lower than during the warmer interglacial periods because so much sea water was captured in the ice sheets. The climate was both more humid and cooler than today, and the major Texas rivers carried more water and more sand and gravel to the sea. These deposits underlie the outer 50 miles or more of the Gulf Coastal Plain.

Approximately 3,000 years ago, sea level reached its modern position. The rivers, deltas, lagoons, beaches, and barrier islands that we know as coastal Texas today have formed since that time. ☆

Soils of Texas

Source: Natural Resources Conservation Service, U.S. Department of Agriculture, www.tx.nrcs.usda.gov

One of Texas' most important natural resources is its soil. Texas soils are complex because of the wide diversity of climate, vegetation, geology, and landscape. More than 1,300 different kinds of soil are recognized in Texas. Each has a specific set of properties that affect its use.

Soils information that was once available only through paper maps or books is now easily accessed online through the Web Soil Survey, found here: **http://websoilsurvey.nrcs.usda.gov.**

As the state's population continues to move from rural to urban areas, the Web Soil Survey is a tool landowners can use to make land-use and management decisions. This free tool allows landowners to analyze soil data and maps. It is used by farmers and ranchers to find information about soil properties and qualities to optimize agricultural production.

The soil survey is also used by homeowners and commercial builders looking for information on the suitability or the limitations of a building site.

For more information, contact the Natural Resources Conservation Service at 101 S. Main, Temple 76501-7602; (254) 742-9800; or visit www.tx.nrcs.usda.gov; find the "Topic" menu and choose the "Soils" option.

Major Soil Areas

Texas can be divided into **21 Major Land Resource Areas** that have similar or related soils, vegetation, topography, climate, and land uses. Following are brief descriptions of these 21 areas:

Trans-Pecos Soils

The 18.7 million acres of the Trans-Pecos, mostly west of the Pecos River, are diverse plains and valleys intermixed with mountains. Surface drainage is slow to rapid. This arid region is used mainly as rangeland. A small amount of irrigated cropland lies on the more fertile soils along the Rio Grande and the Pecos River. Vineyards are a more recent use of these soils, as is the disposal of large volumes of municipal wastes.

Upland soils are mostly well-drained, light reddish-brown to brown clay loams, clays, and sands. Some have a large amount of gypsum or other salts. Many areas have shallow soils and rock outcrops, and sizable areas have deep sands.

Bottomland soils are deep, well-drained, dark grayish-brown to reddish-brown silt loams, loams, clay loams, and clays. The lack of soil moisture and wind erosion are the major soil-management problems. Only irrigated crops can be grown on these soils, and most areas lack an adequate source of good water.

Upper Pecos, Canadian Valleys and Plains Soils

The Upper Pecos, Canadian Valleys, and Plains area occupies a little over a half-million acres and is in the northwest part of Texas near the Texas–New Mexico border. It is characterized by broad rolling plains and tablelands broken by drainageways and tributaries of the Canadian River. It includes the Canadian Breaks, which are rough, steep lands below the adjacent High Plains. The average annual precipitation is about 15 inches, but it fluctuates widely from year to year. Surface drainage is slow to rapid.

The soils are well drained and alkaline. The mostly reddish-brown clay loams and sandy loams were formed mostly in material weathered from sandstone and shale. Depths range from shallow to very deep.

The area is used mainly as rangeland and wildlife habitat. Native vegetation is mid- to short-grass prairie species, such as hairy grama, sideoats grama, little bluestem, alkali sacaton, vine-mesquite, and galleta in the plains and tablelands. Juniper and mesquite grow on the relatively higher breaks. Soil management problems include low soil moisture and brush control.

High Plains Soils

The High Plains area comprises a vast high plateau of more than 19.4 million acres in northwestern Texas. It lies in the southern part of the Great Plains province that includes large, similar areas in Oklahoma and New Mexico. The flat, nearly level treeless plain has few streams to cause local relief. However, several major rivers originate in the High Plains or cross the area. The largest is the Canadian River, which has cut a deep valley across the Panhandle section.

Playas, small intermittent lakes scattered through the area, lie up to 20 feet below the surrounding plains. A 1965 survey counted more than 19,000 playas in 44 counties occupying some 340,000 acres. Most runoff from rainfall is collected in the playas, but only 10 to 40 percent of this water percolates back to the Ogallala Aquifer. The aquifer is virtually the exclusive water source in this area.

Upland soils are mostly well-drained, deep, neutral to alkaline clay loams and sandy loams in shades of brown or red. Sandy soils are in the southern part. Many soils have large amounts of lime at various depths and some are shallow over caliche. Soils of bottomlands are minor in extent.

The area is used mostly for cropland, but significant areas of rangeland are in the southwestern and extreme northern parts. Millions of cattle populate the many large feedlots in the area. The soils are moderately productive, and the flat surface encourages irrigation and mechanization. Limited soil moisture, constant danger of wind erosion, and irrigation water management are the major soil-management problems, but the region is Texas' leading producer of three important crops: cotton, grain sorghums, and wheat.

Rolling Plains Soils

The Rolling Plains include 21.7 million acres east of the High Plains in northwestern Texas. The area lies west of the North Central Prairies and extends from the edge of the Edwards Plateau in Tom Green County northward into Oklahoma. The landscape is nearly level to strongly rolling, and surface drainage is moderate to rapid. Outcrops of red beds, geologic materials, and associated reddish soils have led some scientists to use the name "Red Plains." Limestone underlies the soils in the southeastern part. The eastern part contains large areas of badlands (dry terrain with extensive erosion).

Upland soils are mostly deep, pale-brown through reddish-brown to dark grayish-brown, neutral to alkaline sandy loams, clay loams, and clays; some are deep sands.

Many soils have a large amount of lime in the lower part, and a few others are saline; some are shallow and stony. Bottomland soils are mostly reddish-brown and sandy to clayey; some are saline.

This area is used mostly for rangeland, but cotton, grain sorghums, and wheat are important crops. The major soil-management problems are brush control, wind erosion, low fertility, and lack of soil moisture. Salt spots are a concern in some areas.

North Central Prairie Soils

The North Central Prairie occupies about 7 million acres in North Central Texas. Adjacent to this area on the north is the rather small area (less than 1 million acres) called Rolling Red Prairies, which extends into Oklahoma and is included here because the soils and land use are similar.

This area lies between the Western Cross Timbers and the Rolling Plains. It is predominantly grassland intermixed with small wooded areas. The landscape is undulating with slow to rapid surface drainage.

Upland soils are mostly deep, well-drained, brown or reddish-brown, slightly acid loams over neutral to alkaline, clayey subsoils. Some soils are shallow or moderately deep to shale. Bottomland soils are mostly well-drained, dark-brown or gray loams and clays.

This area is used mostly as rangeland, but wheat, grain sorghums, and other crops are grown on the better soils. Brush control, wind and water erosion, and limited soil moisture are the major management concerns.

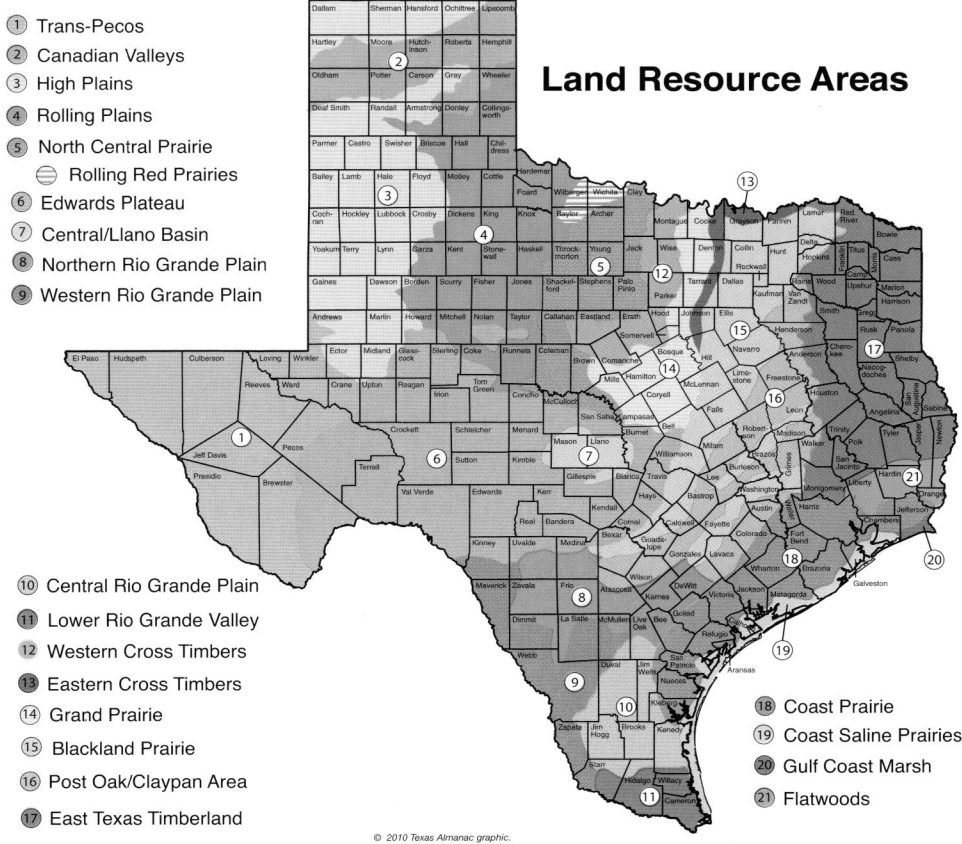

1. Trans-Pecos
2. Canadian Valleys
3. High Plains
4. Rolling Plains
5. North Central Prairie
   ⊜ Rolling Red Prairies
6. Edwards Plateau
7. Central/Llano Basin
8. Northern Rio Grande Plain
9. Western Rio Grande Plain

10. Central Rio Grande Plain
11. Lower Rio Grande Valley
12. Western Cross Timbers
13. Eastern Cross Timbers
14. Grand Prairie
15. Blackland Prairie
16. Post Oak/Claypan Area
17. East Texas Timberland

18. Coast Prairie
19. Coast Saline Prairies
20. Gulf Coast Marsh
21. Flatwoods

Land Resource Areas

© 2010 Texas Almanac graphic.
Source: Natural Resources Conservation Service of the U.S. Department of Agriculture.

The map above shows the land resource areas of Texas, as defined by the Natural Resources Conservation Service at the U.S. Department of Agriculture. A land resource area is defined as "a geographic area, usually several thousand acres in extent, that is characterized by a particular pattern of soils, climate, water resources, land uses, and type of farming."

Edwards Plateau Soils

The 22.7 million acres of the Edwards Plateau are in South Central Texas east of the Trans-Pecos and west of the Blackland Prairie. Uplands are nearly level to undulating except near large stream valleys, where the landscape is hilly with deep canyons and steep slopes. There are many cedar brakes in this area. Surface drainage is rapid.

Upland soils are mostly shallow, stony, or gravelly, dark alkaline clays and clay loams underlain by limestone. Lighter-colored soils are on steep sideslopes and deep, less-stony soils are in the valleys. Bottomland soils are mostly deep, dark-gray or brown, alkaline loams and clays.

Raising beef cattle is the main enterprise in this region, but it is also the center of Texas' and the nation's mohair and wool production. The area is a major deer habitat, and hunting leases produce income. Cropland is mostly in the valleys on the deeper soils and is used mainly for growing forage crops and hay. The major soil-management concerns are brush control, large stones, low fertility, excess lime, and limited soil moisture.

Central or Llano Basin Soils

The Central Basin, also known as the Llano Basin, occupies a relatively small area in Central Texas. It includes parts or all of Llano, Mason, Gillespie, and adjoining counties. The total area is about 1.6 million acres of undulating to hilly landscape.

Upland soils are mostly shallow, reddish-brown to brown, mostly gravelly and stony, neutral to slightly acid sandy loams over granite, limestone, gneiss, and schist bedrock. Large boulders are on the soil surface in some areas. Deeper, less stony sandy-loam soils are in the valleys. Bottomland soils are minor areas of deep, dark-gray or brown loams and clays.

Ranching is the main enterprise, with some farms producing peaches, grain sorghum, and wheat. The area provides excellent deer habitat, and hunting leases are a major source of income. Brush control, large stones, and limited soil moisture are soil-management concerns.

Northern Rio Grande Plain Soils

The Northern Rio Grande Plain comprises about 6.3 million acres in South Texas extending from Uvalde to Beeville. The landscape is nearly level to rolling, mostly brush-covered plains with slow to rapid surface drainage.

The major upland soils are deep, reddish-brown or dark grayish-brown, neutral to alkaline loams and clays. Bottomland soils are mostly dark-colored loams.

The area is mostly rangeland with significant areas of cropland. Grain sorghums, cotton, corn, and small grains are the major crops. Crops are irrigated in the western part, especially in the Winter Garden area, where vegetables such as spinach, carrots, and cabbage are grown. Much of the area is good deer and dove habitat; hunting leases are a major source of income. Brush control, soil fertility, and irrigation-water management are the major soil-management concerns.

Western Rio Grande Plain Soils

The Western Rio Grande Plain comprises about 5.3 million acres in an area of southwestern Texas from Del Rio to Rio Grande City. The landscape is nearly level to undulating except near the Rio Grande where it is hilly. Surface drainage is slow to rapid.

The major soils are mostly deep, brown or gray alkaline clays and loams. Some are saline.

Most of the soils are used for rangeland. Irrigated grain sorghums and vegetables are grown along the Rio Grande. Hunting leases are a major source of income. Brush control and limited soil moisture are the major soil-management problems.

Central Rio Grande Plain Soils

The Central Rio Grande Plain comprises about 5.9 million acres in an area of South Texas from Live Oak County to Hidalgo County. It includes the South Texas Sand Sheet, an area of deep, sandy soils and active sand dunes. The landscape is nearly level to gently undulating. Surface drainage is slow to rapid. Upland soils are mostly deep, light-colored, neutral to alkaline sands and loams. Many are saline or sodic. Bottomland soils are of minor extent.

Most of the area is used for raising beef cattle. A few areas, mostly in the northeast part, are used for growing grain sorghums, cotton, and small grains. Hunting leases are a major source of income. Brush control is the major soil-management problem on rangeland; wind erosion and limited soil moisture are major concerns on cropland.

Lower Rio Grande Valley Soils

The Lower Rio Grande Valley comprises about 2.1 million acres in extreme southern Texas. The landscape is level to gently sloping with slow surface drainage.

Upland soils are mostly deep, grayish-brown, neutral to alkaline loams; coastal areas are mostly gray, silty clay loam and silty clay; some are saline. Bottomland soils are minor in extent.

Most of the soils are used for growing irrigated vegetables and citrus, along with cotton, grain sorghums, and sugar cane. Some areas are used for growing beef cattle. Irrigation water management and wind erosion are the major soil-management problems on cropland; brush control is the major problem on rangeland.

Western Cross Timbers Soils

The Western Cross Timbers area comprises about 2.6 million acres. It includes the wooded section west of the Grand Prairie and extends from the Red River southward to the north edge of Brown County. The landscape is undulating and is dissected by many drainageways including the Brazos and Red rivers. Surface drainage is rapid.

Upland soils are mostly deep, grayish-brown, slightly acid sandy loams with loamy and clayey subsoils. Bottomland soils along the major rivers are deep, reddish-brown, neutral to alkaline silt loams and clays.

The area is used mostly for grazing beef and dairy cattle on native range and improved pastures. Crops are peanuts, grain sorghums, small grains, peaches, pecans, and vegetables. The major soil-management problem on grazing lands is brush control. Waste management on dairy farms is a more recent concern. Wind and water erosion are the major problems on cropland.

Eastern Cross Timbers Soils

The Eastern Cross Timbers area comprises about 1 million acres in a long narrow strip of wooded land that separates the northern parts of the Blackland Prairie and Grand Prairie and extends from the Red River southward to Hill County. The landscape is gently undulating to rolling and is dissected by many streams, including the Red and Trinity rivers. Sandstone-capped hills are prominent in some areas. Surface runoff is moderate to rapid.

The upland soils are mostly deep, light-colored, slightly acid sandy loams and loamy sands with reddish loamy or clayey subsoils. Bottomland soils are reddish-brown to dark gray, slightly acid to alkaline loams or gray clays.

Grassland consisting of native range and improved pastures is the major land use. Peanuts, grain sorghums, small grains, peaches, pecans, and vegetables are grown in some areas. Brush control, water erosion, and low fertility are the major soil concerns in management.

Grand Prairie Soils

The Grand Prairie comprises about 6.3 million acres in North Central Texas. It extends from the Red River to about the Colorado River. It lies between the Eastern and Western Cross Timbers in the northern part and just west of the Blackland Prairie in the southern part. The landscape is undulating to hilly and is dissected by many streams including the Red, Trinity, and Brazos rivers. Surface drainage is rapid.

Upland soils are mostly dark-gray, alkaline clays; some are shallow over limestone and some are stony. Some areas have light-colored loamy soils over chalky limestone. Bottomland soils along the Red and Brazos rivers are reddish silt loams and clays. Other bottomlands have dark-gray loams and clays.

Land use is a mixture of rangeland, pastureland, and cropland. The area is mainly used for growing beef cattle. Some small grain, grain sorghums, corn, and hay are grown. Brush control and water erosion are the major management concerns.

Blackland Prairie Soils

The Blackland Prairies consist of about 12.6 million acres of east-central Texas extending southwesterly from the Red River to Bexar County. There are smaller areas to the southeast. The landscape is undulating with few scattered wooded areas that are mostly in the bottomlands. Surface drainage is moderate to rapid.

Both upland and bottomland soils are deep, dark-gray to black alkaline clays. Some soils in the western part are shallow to moderately deep over chalk. Some soils on the eastern edge are neutral to slightly acid, grayish clays and loams over mottled clay subsoils (sometimes called graylands).

Houston Black Soil

The Professional Soil Scientists of Texas consider Houston Black **the state soil of Texas,** and they're working to make it official.

From the USDA: "Houston Black soils are important agricultural soils used extensively for growing grain sorghum, cotton, corn, small grains, and forage grasses. They are also important soils in many urban areas. They occur throughout the Blackland Prairie region of Central Texas from Bonham to San Antonio. Houston Black soils are not found in any other state."

Houston black soil. Photo by John A. Kelley, USDA Natural Resources Conservation Service.

Blackland soils are known as "cracking clays" because of the large, deep cracks that form in dry weather. This high shrink-swell property can cause serious damage to foundations, highways, and other structures and is a safety hazard in pits and trenches.

Land use is divided about equally between cropland and grassland. Cotton, grain sorghums, corn, wheat, oats, and hay are grown. Grassland is mostly improved pastures, with native range on the shallower and steeper soils. Water erosion, cotton root rot, soil tilth, and brush control are the major management problems.

Claypan Area Soils

The Claypan Area consists of about 6.1 million acres in east-central Texas just east of the Blackland Prairie. The landscape is a gently undulating to rolling, moderately dissected woodland also known as the Post Oak Belt or Post Oak Savannah. Surface drainage is moderate.

Upland soils commonly have a thin, light-colored, acid sandy loam surface layer over dense, mottled red, yellow, and gray claypan subsoils. Some deep, sandy soils with less clayey subsoils exist. Bottomlands are deep, highly fertile, reddish-brown to dark-gray loamy to clayey soils.

Land use is mainly rangeland. Some areas are in improved pastures. Most cropland is in bottomlands that are protected from flooding. Major crops are cotton, grain sorghums, corn, hay, and forage crops, most of which are irrigated. Brush control on rangeland and irrigation water management on cropland are the major soil-management problems. Water erosion is a serious problem on the highly erosive claypan soils, especially where they are overgrazed.

East Texas Timberland Soils

The East Texas Timberlands area comprises about 16.1 million acres of the forested eastern part of the state. The land is gently undulating to hilly and well dissected by many streams. Surface drainage is moderate to rapid.

This area has many kinds of upland soils but most are deep, light-colored, acid sands and loams over loamy and clayey subsoils. Deep sands are in scattered areas, and red clays are in areas of "redlands." Bottomland soils are mostly brown to dark-gray, acid loams and some clays.

The land is used mostly for growing commercial pine timber and for woodland grazing. Improved pastures are scattered throughout and are used for grazing beef and dairy cattle and for hay production. Some commercial hardwoods are in the bottomlands. Woodland management problems include seedling survival, invasion of hardwoods in pine stands, effects of logging on water quality, and control of the southern pine beetle. Lime and fertilizers are necessary for productive cropland and pastures.

Coast Prairie Soils

The Coast Prairie includes about 8.7 million acres near the Gulf Coast. It ranges from 30 miles to 80 miles in width and parallels the coast from the Sabine River in Orange County in Southeast Texas to Baffin Bay in Kleberg County in South Texas. The landscape is level to gently undulating with slow surface drainage.

Upland soils are mostly deep, dark-gray, neutral to slightly acid clay loams and clays. Lighter-colored and more-sandy soils are in a strip on the northwestern edge. Some soils in the southern part are alkaline; some are saline and sodic. Bottomland soils are mostly deep, dark-colored clays and loams along small streams but are greatly varied along the rivers.

Land use is mainly grazing lands and cropland. Some hardwood timber is in the bottomlands. Many areas are also managed for wetland wildlife habitat. The nearly level topography and productive soils encourage farming. Rice, grain sorghums, cotton, corn, and hay are the main crops. Brush management on grasslands and removal of excess water on cropland are the major management concerns.

Coast Saline Prairies Soils

The Coast Saline Prairies area includes about 3.2 million acres along a narrow strip of wet lowlands adjacent to the coast; it includes the barrier islands that extend from Mexico to Louisiana. The surface is at or only a few feet above sea level with many areas of salt-water marsh. Surface drainage is very slow.

The soils are mostly deep, dark-colored clays and loams; many are saline and sodic. Light-colored sandy soils are on the barrier islands. The water table is at or near the surface of most soils.

Cattle grazing is the chief economic use of the various salt-tolerant cordgrasses and sedges. Many areas are managed for wetland wildlife. Recreation is popular on the barrier islands. Providing fresh water and access to grazing areas are the major management concerns.

Gulf Coast Marsh Soils

This 150,000-acre area lies in the extreme southeastern corner of Texas. The area can be subdivided into four parts: freshwater, intermediate, brackish, and saline (saltwater) marsh. The degree of salinity of this system grades landward from saltwater marshes along the coast to freshwater marshes inland. Surface drainage is very slow.

This area contains many lakes, bayous, tidal channels, and man-made canals. About one-half of the marsh is fresh; one-half is salty. Most of it is susceptible to flooding either by fresh water drained from lands adjacent to the marsh or by saltwater from the Gulf of Mexico.

Most of the soils are poorly drained, continuously saturated, soft, and can carry little weight. In general, the organic soils have a thick layer of dark gray, relatively undecomposed organic material over a gray, clayey subsoil. The mineral soils have a surface of dark gray, highly decomposed organic material over a gray, clayey subsoil.

Most of the almost treeless and uninhabited area is in marsh vegetation, such as grasses, sedges, and rushes. It is used mainly for wildlife habitat. Part of the fertile and productive estuarine complex supports marine life of the Gulf of Mexico. It also provides wintering ground for waterfowl and habitat for many fur-bearing animals and alligators. A significant acreage is firm enough to support livestock and is used for winter grazing of cattle. The major management problems are providing fresh water and access to grazing areas.

Flatwoods Soils

The Flatwoods area includes about 2.5 million acres of woodland in humid Southeast Texas just north of the Coast Prairie and extending into Louisiana. The landscape is level to gently undulating. Surface drainage is slow.

Upland soils are mostly deep, light-colored, acid loams with gray, loamy, or clayey subsoils. Bottomland soils are deep, dark-colored, acid clays and loams. The water table is near the surface at least part of the year.

The land is mainly used for forest, although cattle are grazed in some areas. Woodland management problems include seedling survival, invasion of hardwoods in pine stands, effects of logging on water quality, and control of the southern pine beetle. ☆

The waterfall at Hamilton Pool Reserve. Photo by Jonathan Cutrer (jcutrer.com).

Texas Water Resources

Water shortage is the **most serious** natural resource issue facing Texas today.

Here, as elsewhere in the world, the struggle over the uses to which water should be put — and who has the right to decide on those uses — is **intense and escalating**, particularly as the cyclical occurrence of severe flooding and drought increase. The bottom line is that Texas' population is going to double in the next fifty years (for more about this, see our feature article on page 373) and if all the water rights we have issued in our major rivers since Texas was a colony of Spain were fully exercised, many of them would be dry today. Thus, **many of our most iconic rivers**, which are vital to both our economy and the environment, **are at risk**.

Due in part to increasing stress on our rivers and lakes in Texas, we are also increasingly dependent on groundwater from the State's diverse major and minor aquifers. Unfortunately, **we do not recognize in law or policy the hydrologic linkage of our groundwater resources to surface water** — this failure will complicate sound water management of both in the future.

Texas' sensational system of bays and estuaries are arguably the finest such system of any state in the union. These coastal systems provide billions of dollars of economic benefit to the State and constitute some of the most prolific marine ecosystems in the world. What is less understood is that this spectacular natural resource is entirely dependent on continued supplies of freshwater flowing down our rivers and streams to mix with saltwater to **create the unique conditions vital to the existence of so many species of fish and wildlife**. Despite the enormous economic and environmental benefits we receive from these freshwater inflows, we have done a very inadequate job of insuring their continuation.

Historically, we have been reluctant to make difficult choices and decisions relating to water but when faced with crisis we have reacted. Following the drought of the 1950's, which we formally consider the worst on record, we built over 200 major reservoirs for flood control, water supply, and hydropower and they have served us well. However, since the 1970's there has been a dramatic decline in reservoir construction, due to a number of reasons.

More and more communities are creating underground reservoirs in a process called aquifer storage and retrieval, which captures water in times of high flows and stores it to avoid evaporation. We also have millions of acre feet of **brackish groundwater** in Texas **which has been largely untapped** and is less saline than water from the Gulf and closer to the consumer, making it less costly to produce and deliver.

But will that be enough to ensure our future? Despite much progress in water conservation, particularly in cities like San Antonio and El Paso, we still waste far too much water. **It is likely that the key to having a healthy water supply in the future will be increased efficiency.**

Our rivers and streams, our bays, estuaries, and our aquifers not only help define us as a state but are essential components of the one resource that no plant and animal can live without: water. We must do everything we can to make sure it is there for our economy, our environment, and our children. ☆

Contributed by Dr. Andrew Sansom, leading conservationist and executive director of the Meadows Center for Water and the Environment.

Major Aquifers of Texas

Sources: Texas Water Development Board, www.twdb.texas.gov; U.S. Geological Survey, https://www.usgs.gov/centers/tx-water

Aquifers are water-bearing rock formations beneath the earth's surface. Texas has a wealth of fresh to slightly saline groundwater in **nine major and 22 minor aquifers** that underlie more than 81 percent of the state.

Each year, groundwater provides approximately 60 percent of the water used in the state. Annual water use ranged from 14.23 million acre-feet in 2016 to 18.18 million acre-feet in 2011. The median annual water use between the years 2007 and 2016 was 14.6 million acre-feet.

Groundwater is an important resource to every industry in Texas, from farming, ranching, and manufacturing to energy exploration and refining.

Groundwater also provides water for municipal and environmental needs. Approximately 55 percent of the groundwater produced in 2016 was used for agriculture (mostly for irrigation). About half of this amount is used in the Panhandle region of the state. In 2016, groundwater supplied approximately 31 percent of the state's municipal water needs.

For more information about the aquifers of Texas and groundwater management, watch these videos created by the Texas Water Development Board:

www.twdb.texas.gov/groundwater/video/index.asp

Ogallala

The Ogallala Aquifer underlies most of the Texas Panhandle. It is the southernmost extension of the largest aquifer (High Plains Aquifer) in North America. The Ogallala Formation of late Miocene to early Pliocene age consists of heterogeneous sequences of coarse-grained sand and gravel in the lower part, grading upward into clay, silt, and fine sand.

The formation reaches a maximum thickness of 800 feet, and its freshwater saturated thickness averages 95 feet. In Texas, the Panhandle is the most extensive region irrigated with groundwater. About 95 percent of the water pumped from the Ogallala Aquifer is used for irrigation.

Extensive pumping that exceeds the amount of recharge has resulted in consistently declining water levels throughout much of the aquifer. Water conservation measures promoted by agricultural and municipal users have slowed the rate of decline, and water levels have risen in a few areas. Several agencies are investigating playa recharge and agricultural reuse projects in the aquifer area.

Gulf Coast

The Gulf Coast Aquifer system forms a broad belt parallel to the Texas coastline, extending through 54 counties from the Rio Grande northeastward to the Louisiana border. The aquifer system is composed of Quaternary- and Tertiary-age layers including the Catahoula, Oakville, Fleming, Goliad, Willis, Lissie, Bentley, Montgomery, and Beaumont formations.

The Gulf Coast Aquifer system has been divided into three major water-producing components referred to as the Chicot, Evangeline, and Jasper aquifers. These aquifers are composed of discontinuous layers of sand, silt, clay, and gravel.

The maximum total sand thickness of the Gulf Coast Aquifer system ranges from 700 feet in the south to 1,300 feet in the north. Freshwater saturated thickness averages 1,000 feet. The Gulf Coast Aquifer system is used primarily for municipal, industrial, and agricultural purposes.

Water quality is generally good in the central and northeastern parts of the aquifer but deteriorates to the southwest. Years of heavy pumping have caused significant water-level declines in portions of the aquifer. Some of these declines have resulted in land subsidence, particularly in the Houston-Galveston area.

Edwards Balcones Fault Zone

The Edwards Balcones Fault Zone (BFZ) Aquifer forms a narrow belt extending through the south-central part of the state from a groundwater divide in Kinney County through the San Antonio area northeastward to the Leon River in Bell County. A groundwater divide in Hays County hydrologically separates the aquifer into the San Antonio and Austin regions.

The aquifer is highly permeable, with water occurring in fractures, honeycomb-like zones (or intergranular pores), and solution channels that characterize the Edwards and associated limestone formations of Cretaceous age. Because the aquifer is highly permeable, water levels and spring flows respond quickly to rainfall, drought, and pumping. Aquifer thickness ranges from 200 to 600 feet, and freshwater saturated thickness averages 560 feet in the southern part of the aquifer.

Water from the Edwards BFZ is used primarily for municipal, irrigation, and recreational purposes. The City of San Antonio meets the majority of its water needs with Edwards BFZ water. The aquifer also feeds several well-known recreational springs and underlies some of Texas's most environmentally sensitive areas.

In 1993, the Texas Legislature created the Edwards Aquifer Authority (EAA) to regulate pumping from the aquifer to benefit all users within EAA's jurisdiction. The Barton Springs/Edwards Aquifer Conservation District and the Kinney County Groundwater Conservation District also provide aquifer management in the areas of the aquifer that are not within the EAA boundaries.

The EAA has an active outreach program used to educate the public on water conservation. It also operates several active groundwater recharge sites. The San Antonio River Authority also has a number of flood-control structures that effectively recharge the aquifer.

Carrizo-Wilcox

The Carrizo-Wilcox Aquifer extends from south of the Rio Grande in Mexico through Texas northeastward into Arkansas and Louisiana in a wide band parallel to and northwest of the Gulf Coast Aquifer.

The aquifer consists of the Tertiary-age Wilcox Group and overlying Carrizo Sand Formation of the Claiborne Group. The aquifer is composed of a hydrologically connected system of sand locally interbedded with clay, silt, lignite, and gravel. Although the Carrizo-Wilcox Aquifer reaches 3,000 feet in thickness, the freshwater saturated thickness of the sands averages 670 feet.

Throughout most of its extent in Texas, the aquifer yields fresh to slightly saline water. A little more than half of the water pumped from the aquifer is used for irrigation; the remaining amount pumped is used for municipal, industrial, domestic, and livestock purposes.

Recently, the Carrizo-Wilcox Aquifer has been considered as an alternative water supply for growing central Texas communities that have traditionally used the Edwards BFZ Aquifer to meet municipal needs.

Trinity

The Trinity Aquifer consists of Cretaceous-age Trinity Group formations that extend from the Red River in North Texas southward to the Hill Country of Central Texas. It is composed of several smaller aquifers contained within the Trinity Group. Depending on where they occur in the state, they are referred to as the Antlers, Glen Rose, Paluxy, Twin Mountains, Travis Peak, Hensell, and Hosston aquifers.

These aquifers consist of limestones, sands, clays, gravels, and conglomerates. Their combined freshwater saturated thickness averages about 600 feet in North Texas, and about 1,900 feet in Central Texas. The aquifer discharges to many small springs, with most flowing less than 10 cubic feet per second.

The Trinity Aquifer is primarily used to meet municipal water demands, but also provides water for irrigation, livestock, and other domestic purposes. Extensive development of the Trinity Aquifer in the Dallas–Fort Worth and Waco areas has resulted in water-level declines of 350 feet to more than 1,000 feet, though these declines have slowed with more reliance on surface water and reductions in groundwater pumping.

Edwards-Trinity Plateau

The Edwards-Trinity Plateau Aquifer extends from the Hill Country of Central Texas westward and southwestward to the Trans-Pecos region, covering much of the southwestern part of the state. The aquifer consists of early Cretaceous limestone and dolomites of the Edwards Group and sands of the Trinity Group. Although the maximum saturated thickness of the

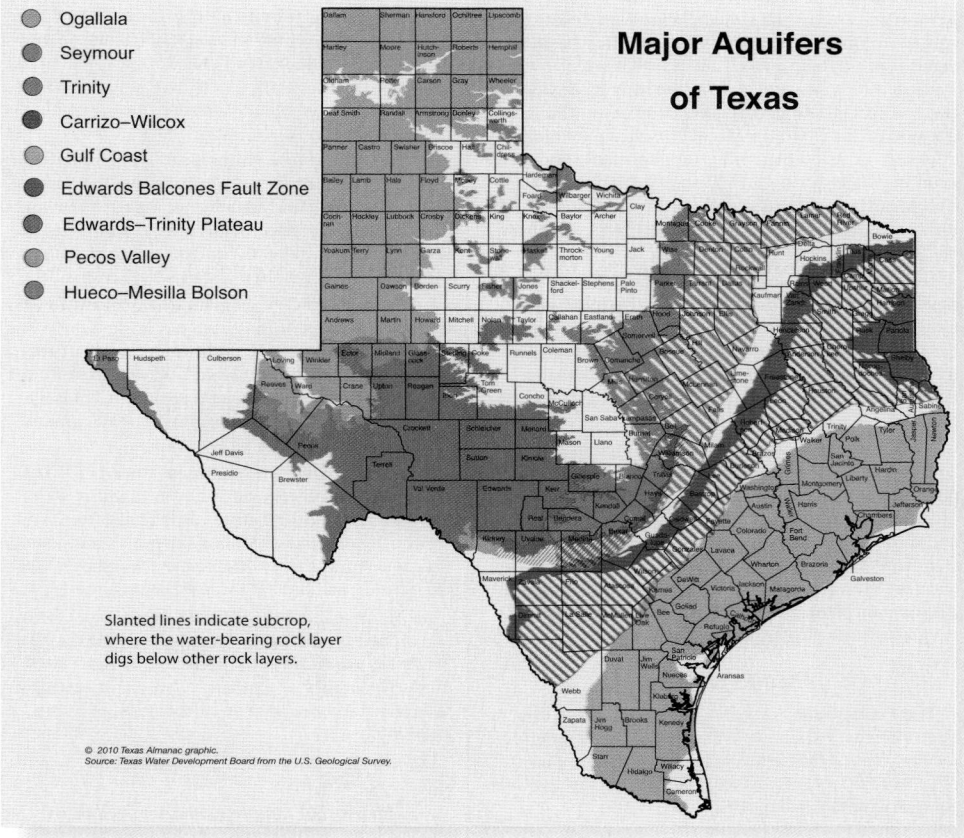

Ogallala
Seymour
Trinity
Carrizo–Wilcox
Gulf Coast
Edwards Balcones Fault Zone
Edwards–Trinity Plateau
Pecos Valley
Hueco–Mesilla Bolson

Major Aquifers of Texas

Slanted lines indicate subcrop, where the water-bearing rock layer digs below other rock layers.

© 2010 Texas Almanac graphic.
Source: Texas Water Development Board from the U.S. Geological Survey.

aquifer is greater than 800 feet, freshwater saturated thickness averages 433 feet.

The aquifer lies beneath the Edwards Plateau. Near the plateau's edge, along the northern, eastern, and southern margins of the aquifer, groundwater flows towards streams, where water discharges from springs. Irrigation, mainly in the northwestern portion of the region, accounts for more than two-thirds of aquifer use.

Seymour

The Seymour Aquifer extends across north-central Texas. It consists of Quaternary-age, alluvial sediments unconformably overlying Permian-age rocks. Water is contained within isolated patches of discontinuous beds of poorly sorted gravel, conglomerate, sand, and silty clay. These deposits may reach 360 feet in thickness, but most of the Seymour is less than 100 feet thick.

About 90 percent of the water pumped from the Seymour is used for irrigation. Water quality generally ranges from fresh to slightly saline; however, some areas have moderately to very saline water quality. Nitrate concentrations occur above primary drinking water standards throughout much of the aquifer.

Hueco-Mesilla Bolsons

The Hueco-Mesilla Bolsons Aquifer is located in El Paso and Hudspeth counties in far West Texas. The aquifer consists of Tertiary and Quaternary basin-fill deposits of silt, sand, gravel, and clay that extend northward into New Mexico and westward into Mexico in two basins. The Hueco Bolson, located on the eastern side of the Franklin Mountains, has a maximum thickness of 9,000 feet and is an important source of drinking water for both El Paso and Juárez, Mexico. The Mesilla Bolson, located on the western side of the Franklin Mountains, has a maximum thickness of 2,000 feet.

Historical large-scale groundwater withdrawals, especially for the municipal uses of El Paso and Juárez, have caused major water-level declines. This pumping has also caused a deterioration of the chemical quality of the groundwater in the aquifer, according to El Paso Water Utilities and the United States Geological Survey.

Nearly 90 percent of the water pumped from the aquifer in the Texas extent of the bolsons is used for public supply. The City of El Paso has reduced its use of groundwater from the Hueco Bolson since 1989, and observation wells indicate that water levels have stabilized from a previously declining trend. El Paso and Fort Bliss also have built the world's largest inland desalination plant in El Paso County, which uses brackish groundwater from the Hueco Bolson.

Pecos Valley

The Pecos Valley Aquifer is located in the upper Pecos River Valley of West Texas. This aquifer, formerly called the Cenozoic Pecos Alluvium, consists of up to 1,500 feet of Tertiary and Quaternary alluvial fill and windblown deposits.

The aquifer occupies two hydrologically separate basins: the Pecos Trough in the west and the Monument Draw Trough in the east. The alluvial fill reaches 1,500 feet thick, and freshwater saturated thickness averages about 250 feet. Naturally occurring arsenic and radionuclides occur in excess of primary drinking water standards.

More than 80 percent of groundwater pumped from the aquifer is used for irrigation, and the remainder is withdrawn for industrial, power supply, and municipal uses. Water-level declines in excess of 200 feet have occurred in Reeves and Pecos counties but have slowed since the mid-1970s as irrigation pumping has decreased. Declines continue in Ward County due to increased municipal and industrial pumping. ☆

Water Regulation in Texas

In Texas, water law historically has been different for surface water and groundwater. Surface water belongs to the state and, except for limited amounts of water for household and on-farm livestock use, requires a permit for use.

The **Texas Commission on Environmental Quality (TCEQ)** is responsible for permitting and adjudicating surface water rights. The TCEQ is the primary regulator of surface water and polices contamination and pollution of both surface and groundwater.

In general, groundwater is considered the private property of the surface landowner by "rule of capture," meaning the landowner may pump as much water as he wishes from beneath his land for any beneficial use and that does not harm neighboring property.

This right may be limited only by groundwater conservation districts, which are the state's preferred method of groundwater management and provide for the conservation, preservation, protection, recharging, and prevention of waste of groundwater resources within their jurisdictions.

As of August 2019, 98 **groundwater conservation districts** exist in Texas, covering nearly 70 percent of the state. In addition, two subsidence districts cover Harris, Galveston, and Fort Bend counties. Subsidence districts regulate groundwater production to prevent land subsidence: the gradual caving in or sinking of an area of land.

The **Texas Water Development Board (TWDB)** collects data on water quality and availability within the state, plans for future supply and use, and administers the state's funds for grants and loans to finance future water development and supply. See the current members of the TWDB on page 477.

In January 2017, the TWDB released the latest comprehensive statewide water plan, which the 75th Texas Legislature (1997) required of the TWDB every five years. It outlines water conservation strategies for meeting projected water supply needs in 2070.

You can see an interactive version of the current state water plan here:

https://2017.texasstatewaterplan.org/statewide

Children playing water games on the Guadalupe River at Guadalupe River State Park. Photo courtesy of TrekTexas (www.TrekTexas.com).

Major Rivers of Texas

Sources: Texas Water Development Board, www.twdb.texas.gov; U.S. Geological Survey, https://www.usgs.gov/centers/tx-water

There are 11,247 named Texas streams identified in the U.S. Geological Survey Geographic Names Information System. Their combined length is about 80,000 miles, and they drain 263,513 square miles within Texas. Fourteen major rivers are described in this section, starting with the southernmost and moving northward.

Rio Grande

The Pueblo Indians called this river P'osoge, which means the "river of great water." In 1582, Antonio de Espejo of Nueva Vizcaya, Mexico, followed the course of the Río Conchos to its confluence with a great river, which he named Río del Norte (River of the North). The name Rio Grande was first used, apparently by the explorer Juan de Oñate, who arrived on its banks near present-day El Paso in 1598.

Thereafter the names were often consolidated as Río Grande del Norte. It was shown also on early Spanish maps as Río San Buenaventura and Río Ganapetuán. In its lower course, it early acquired the name Río Bravo, which is its name on most Mexican maps. At times it has also been known as Río Turbio, probably because of its muddy appearance during its frequent rises. Some people erroneously call this watercourse the Rio Grande River.

This river forms the boundary of Texas and the international U.S.-Mexican border for 889 or 1,254 river miles, depending upon method of measurement. (See Texas Boundary Lines, page 29.)

Average Annual Flow		
	River	Acre-Feet*
1.	Brazos	6,074,000
2.	Sabine	5,864,000
3.	Trinity	5,727,000
4.	Neches	4,323,000
5.	Red	3,464,000
6.	Colorado	1,904,000

* One acre-foot equals 325,851 gallons of water.
Source: Texas Water Development Board, 2017 State Water Plan.

Lengths Of Major Rivers		
	River	Length-Miles
1.	Rio Grande	1,900
2.	Red	1,290
3.	Brazos	1,280
4.	Pecos	926
5.	Canadian	906
6.	Colorado	865

Source: U.S. Geological Survey, 2008.

The U.S. Geological Survey figure for the total length from its headwaters to its mouth on the Gulf of Mexico is 1,900 miles.

According to the USGS, the Rio Grande is tied with the St. Lawrence River (also 1,900 miles) as the fourth-longest North American river, exceeded only by the Missouri-Mississippi, McKenzie-Peace, and Yukon rivers. Since all of these except the Missouri-Mississippi are partly in Canada, the Rio Grande is the second-longest river entirely within or bordering the United States. It is Texas' longest river.

The snow-fed flow of the Rio Grande is used for irrigation in Colorado below the San Juan Mountains, where the river rises at the Continental Divide. Turning south, it flows through a canyon in northern New Mexico and again irrigates a broad valley of central New Mexico. Southern New Mexico impounds Rio Grande waters in Elephant Butte Reservoir for irrigation of the valley above and below El Paso.

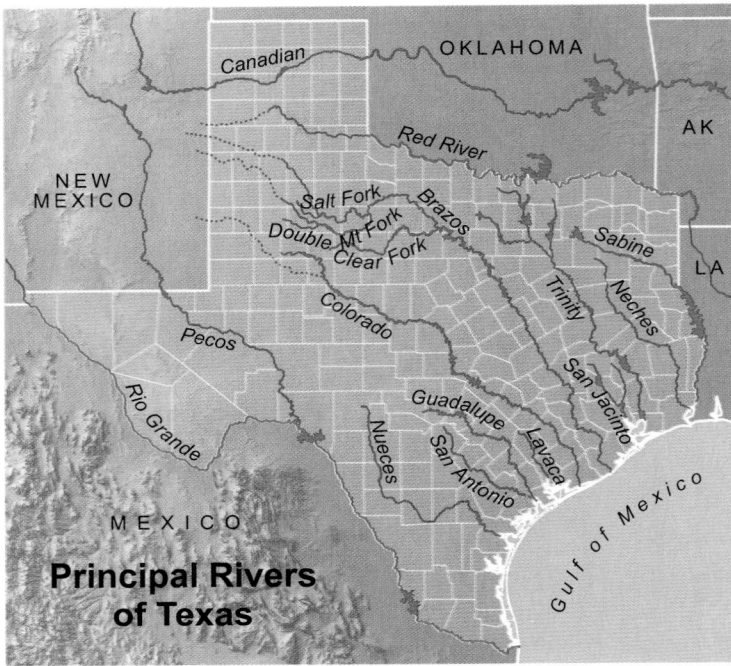

Principal Rivers of Texas

The valley near El Paso is thought to be the oldest irrigated area in Texas because Indians were irrigating crops here when Spanish explorers arrived in the early 1500s.

From source to mouth, the Rio Grande drops 12,000 feet to sea level as a mountain torrent, desert stream, and meandering coastal river. Along its banks and in its valley, Europeans established some of their first North American settlements. Here are situated three of the oldest towns in Texas: Ysleta, Socorro, and San Elizario.

Because of the extensive irrigation, the Rio Grande virtually ends at the lower end of the El Paso valley, except in seasons of above-normal flow.

The river starts again as a perennially flowing stream where the Río Conchos of Mexico flows into it at Presidio-Ojinaga. Through the Big Bend, the Rio Grande flows through three successive canyons, the Santa Elena, the Mariscal, and the Boquillas. The Santa Elena has a river bed elevation of 2,145 feet and a canyon-rim elevation of 3,661. Corresponding figures for Mariscal are 1,925 and 3,625, and for Boquillas, 1,850 and 3,490. The river here flows for about 100 miles around the base of the Chisos Mountains as the southern boundary of Big Bend National Park.

Below the Big Bend, the Rio Grande gradually emerges from mountains onto the Coastal Plains. A 191.2-mile strip on the U.S. side from Big Bend

National Park downstream to the Terrell–Val Verde county line has federal designation as the Rio Grande Wild and Scenic River.

At the confluence of the Rio Grande and Devils River, the United States and Mexico have built Amistad Dam, to impound 3,275,532 acre-feet of water, of which Texas' share is 56.2 percent. Falcon Reservoir, also an international project in Zapata and Starr counties, impounds 2,646,813 acre-feet of water, of which Texas' share in Zapata and Starr counties is 58.6 percent.

The Rio Grande, where it joins the Gulf of Mexico, has created a fertile delta called the Lower Rio Grande Valley, a major vegetable- and fruit-growing area. The river drains 49,387 square miles of Texas and has an average annual flow of 1,064,613 acre-feet.

Principal tributaries flowing from the Texas side are the Pecos and Devils rivers. On the Mexican side are Río Conchos, Río Salado, and Río San Juan. About three-fourths of the water running into the Rio Grande below El Paso comes from the Mexican side.

Pecos River

The Pecos, one of the major tributaries of the Rio Grande, rises on the western slope of the Santa Fe Mountains in the Sangre de Cristo Range of northern New Mexico. It enters Texas as the boundary between Loving and Reeves counties and flows 350 miles southeast as the boundary for several other counties, entering Val Verde County at its northwestern corner and angles across that county to its mouth on the Rio Grande, northwest of Del Rio.

According to the Handbook of Texas, the origins of the river's several names began with Antonio de Espejo, who called the river the Río de las Vacas ("river of the cows") because of the number of buffalo in the vicinity. Gaspar Castaño de Sosa, who followed the Pecos northward, called it the Río Salado because of its salty taste, which caused it to be shunned by men and animals alike.

It is believed that the name "Pecos" first appears in Juan de Oñate's reports concerning the Indian pueblo of Cicuye, now known as the Pecos Pueblo in New Mexico, and is of unknown origin.

Through most of its 926-mile-long course from its headwaters, the Pecos River parallels the Rio Grande. The total drainage area of the Pecos in New Mexico and Texas is about 44,000 square miles. Most of its tributaries flow from the west; these include the Delaware River and Toyah Creek.

The topography of the river valley in Texas ranges from semi-arid irrigated farmlands, desert with sparse vegetation, and, in the lowermost reaches of the river, deep canyons.

Nueces River

The Nueces River rises in two forks in Edwards and Real counties and flows 315 miles to Nueces Bay on the Gulf near Corpus Christi. Draining 16,700 square miles, it is a beautiful, spring-fed stream flowing through canyons until it issues from the Balcones Escarpment onto the Coastal Plains in northern Uvalde County.

Alonso de León, in 1689, gave it its name. Nueces, plural of nuez, means nuts in Spanish. (More than a century earlier, Cabeza de Vaca had referred to a Río de las Nueces in this region, but that is now thought to have been the Guadalupe.)

The original Indian name for this river seems to have been Chotilapacquen. Crossing Texas in 1691, Terán de los Ríos named the river San Diego.

The Nueces was the boundary line between the Spanish provinces of Texas and Nuevo Santander. After the Texas Revolution of 1836, both Texas and Mexico claimed the territory between the Nueces and the Rio Grande, a dispute that was settled in 1848 by the Treaty of Guadalupe Hidalgo, which fixed the international boundary at the Rio Grande.

Average runoff of the Nueces is about 539,700 acre-feet a year. Principal water supply projects are Lake Corpus Christi and Choke Canyon Reservoir. Principal tributaries of the Nueces are the Frio and the Atascosa rivers. The river terminates in Nueces and Corpus Christi bays along the Coastal Bend.

San Antonio River

The San Antonio River has at its source large springs within and near the city limits of San Antonio. It flows 180 miles across the Coastal Plains to a junction with the Guadalupe River to enter San Antonio Bay along the Gulf Coast. Its channel through San Antonio has been developed into a parkway known as the River Walk.

Its principal tributaries are the Medina River and Cibolo Creek, both spring-fed streams, and this, with its own spring origin, gives it remarkably clear water and makes it one of the steadiest of Texas rivers. Including the Medina River headwaters, it is 238 miles in length.

The river was first named the León by Alonso de León in 1689; the name was not for himself, but he

A view of the Colorado River with the Austin skyline. Photo by Tony Webster (CC).

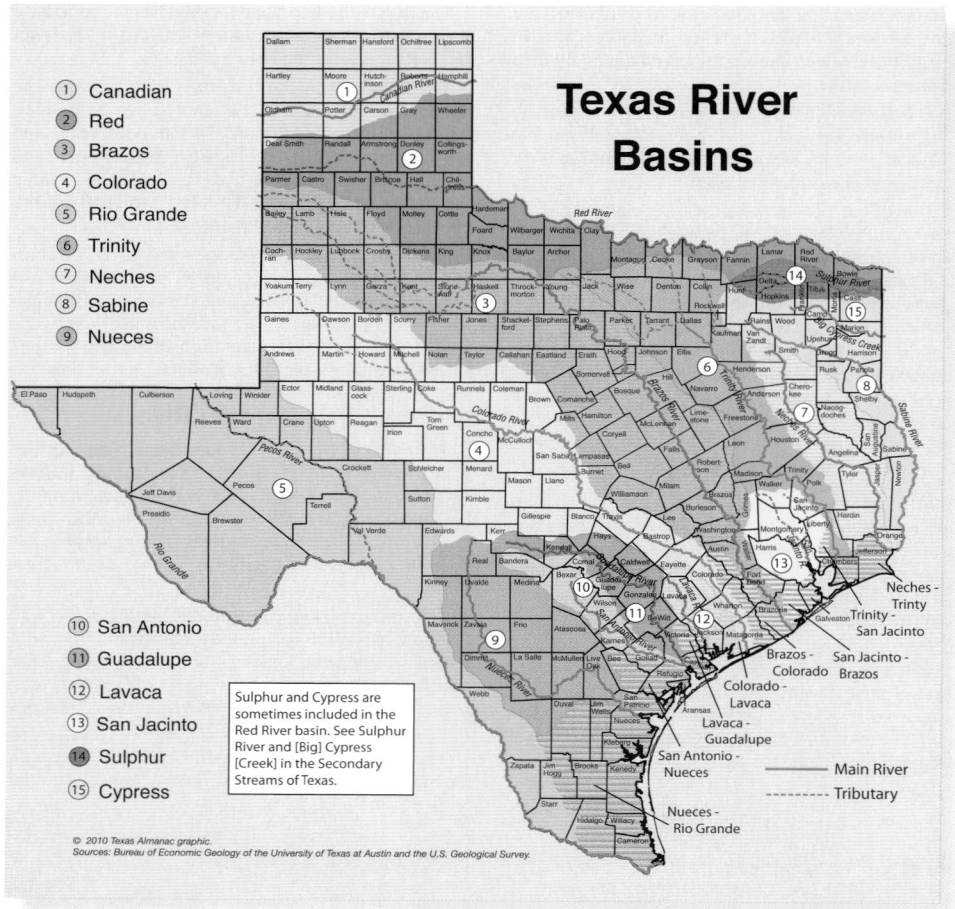

Texas River Basins

1. Canadian
2. Red
3. Brazos
4. Colorado
5. Rio Grande
6. Trinity
7. Neches
8. Sabine
9. Nueces
10. San Antonio
11. Guadalupe
12. Lavaca
13. San Jacinto
14. Sulphur
15. Cypress

Sulphur and Cypress are sometimes included in the Red River basin. See Sulphur River and [Big] Cypress [Creek] in the Secondary Streams of Texas.

Neches - Trinty
Trinity - San Jacinto
San Jacinto - Brazos
Brazos - Colorado
Colorado - Lavaca
Lavaca - Guadalupe
San Antonio - Nueces
Nueces - Rio Grande

—— Main River
------ Tributary

© 2010 Texas Almanac graphic.
Sources: Bureau of Economic Geology of the University of Texas at Austin and the U.S. Geological Survey.

called it "lion" because its channel was filled with a rampaging flood.

Because of its limited and arid drainage area (4,180 square miles) the average runoff of the San Antonio River is relatively small, about 562,700 acre-feet annually.

Guadalupe River

The Guadalupe rises in its North and South forks in western Kerr County. A spring-fed stream, it flows eastward through the Hill Country until it issues from the Balcones Escarpment near New Braunfels. It then crosses the Coastal Plains to San Antonio Bay. Its total length is 409 miles, and its drainage area is 5,953 square miles. Its principal tributaries are the Comal, which joins it at New Braunfels; the San Marcos, another spring-fed stream, which joins it in Gonzales County; and the San Antonio, which joins it just above its mouth on San Antonio Bay.

There has been power development on the Guadalupe near Gonzales and Cuero for many years, and there is also power generation at Canyon Lake. Because of its springs and its considerable drainage

area, the Guadalupe has an average annual runoff of more than 1.42 million acre-feet.

The name Guadalupe is derived from Nuestra Señora de Guadalupe, the name given the stream by Alonso de León.

Lavaca River

The Lavaca rises in extreme southwestern Fayette County and flows 117 miles to terminate in Lavaca Bay. Without a spring-fed water source and with only a small watershed, including that of its principal tributary, the Navidad, its flow is intermittent. Runoff averages about 277,000 acre-feet yearly.

The Spanish called it the Lavaca (the cow) because of the numerous bison found near it. It is the principal stream flowing to the Texas Coast between the Guadalupe and the Colorado, and drains 2,309 square miles. The principal lake on the Navidad is Lake Texana.

Colorado River

The Colorado River rises in east-central Dawson County and flows 600 miles to Matagorda Bay. Its drainage area, which extends into New Mexico, is 42,318 square miles. The U.S. Geological Survey puts is total length from source at 865 miles.

Its average annual runoff reaches a volume of 1.9 million acre-feet near the coast. Its name is a Spanish word meaning "reddish." There is evidence that Spanish explorers originally named the muddy Brazos "Colorado," but Spanish mapmakers later transposed the two names.

The river flows through a rolling, mostly prairie terrain to the vicinity of San Saba County, where it enters the rugged Hill Country and Llano Basin. It passes through a picturesque series of canyons until it issues from the Balcones Escarpment at Austin and flows across the Coastal Plains.

In the Hill Country, a remarkable series of reservoirs has been built to provide hydoelectric power, flood control, and water supply. The largest of these are Lake Buchanan in Burnet and Llano counties and Lake Travis in Travis County. Between the two in Burnet County are three smaller reservoirs: Inks, Lyndon B. Johnson (formerly Granite Shoals), and Marble Falls. Below Lake Travis is the older Lake Austin, largely filled with silt, whose dam is used to produce power from waters flowing down from the lakes above. Lady Bird Lake (formerly Town Lake) is in the city of Austin. This entire area is known as the Highland Lakes Country.

As early as the 1820s, Anglo-Americans settled on the banks of the lower Colorado, and in 1839, the Capital Commission of the Republic of Texas chose the picturesque area where the river flows from the Balcones Escarpment as the site of a new capital of the Republic — now Austin, capital of the state.

The early colonists encouraged navigation along the lower channel with some success. However, a natural log raft that formed 10 miles from the Gulf blocked river traffic after 1839, although shallow-draught vessels occasionally ventured as far upstream as Austin.

Conservation and utilization of the waters of the Colorado are under the jurisdiction of two agencies created by the Legislature — the Lower and Upper Colorado River authorities.

The principal tributaries of the Colorado River are the several prongs of the Concho River on its upper course, Pecan Bayou (farthest west "bayou" in the United States), and the Llano, San Saba, and Pedernales rivers. All except Pecan Bayou flow into the Colorado from the Edwards Plateau and are spring-fed, perennially flowing rivers. In the numerous mussels found along these streams, pearls occasionally have been found. On early Spanish maps, the Middle Concho was called Río de las Perlas.

Brazos River

The Brazos River proper is considered to begin where the Double Mountain and Salt Forks flow together in northeastern Stonewall County; it then flows 840 miles across Texas. The U.S. Geological Survey puts the total length from the New Mexico source of its longest upper prong at 1,280 miles.

With a drainage area of about 42,865 square miles, it is the second-largest river basin in Texas, after the Rio Grande. It flows directly into the Gulf southwest of Freeport in Brazoria County. Its average annual flow approaches 6.1 million acre-feet, the largest volume of any river in the state.

The Brazos' third upper fork is the Clear Fork, which joins the main stream in Young County, just above Possum Kingdom Lake. The Brazos crosses most of the main physiographic regions of Texas: High Plains, West Texas Rolling Plains, Western Cross Timbers, Grand Prairie, and Gulf Coastal Plains.

The original name of this river was Brazos de Dios, meaning "Arms of God." There are several legends as to why. One story is that the Coronado expedition, wandering on the trackless Llano Estacado, exhausted its water and was threatened with death from thirst. Arriving at the bank of the river, they gave it the name "Brazos de Dios" in thankfulness. Another legend is that a ship exhausted its water supply, and its crew was saved when they found the mouth of the Brazos. Still another story is that miners on the San Saba were forced by drought to seek water near present-day Waco and in gratitude called it Brazos de Dios.

Much early Anglo-American colonization of Texas took place in the Brazos Valley. Along its channel were San Felipe de Austin, capital of Austin's colony; Washington-on-the-Brazos, where Texans declared independence from Mexico; and other historic settlements. There was some navigation of the lower channel of the Brazos in this period. Near its mouth, it intersects the Gulf Intracoastal Waterway, which provides connection with commerce throughout Texas and the Gulf Coast.

Most of the Brazos Valley lies within the boundaries of the Brazos River Authority, which conducts a multi-purpose program for development. A large reservoir on the main channel of the Brazos is Lake Whitney (554,203 acre-feet capacity), where it is the boundary line between Hill and Bosque counties. Lake Waco on the Bosque and Belton Lake on the Leon are among the principal reservoirs on its tributaries. In addition to its three upper forks, other chief tributaries are the Paluxy, Little, and Navasota rivers.

San Jacinto River

The San Jacinto is a short river with a drainage basin of 3,936 square miles and an average annual runoff of about 1.36 million acre-feet. It is formed by the junction of its East and West forks in northeastern Harris County and runs to the Gulf through Galveston Bay. Its total length, including the East Fork, is about 85 miles.

Lake Conroe is on the West Fork, and Lake Houston is at the junction of the West Fork and the East Fork. The Houston Ship Channel runs through the lower course of the San Jacinto and its tributary, Buffalo Bayou, connecting the Port of Houston to the Gulf.

There are two stories concerning the origin of its name. One is that when early explorers discovered it, its channel was choked with hyacinth ("jacinto" is the Spanish word for hyacinth). The other is that it was discovered on Aug. 17, St. Hyacinth's Day.

The Brazos River flows under this bridge on TX 16. Photo by Larry D. Moore (CC).

The Battle of San Jacinto was fought on the bank of this river on April 21, 1836, when Texas won its independence from Mexico. San Jacinto Battleground State Historic Site and monument commemorate the battle.

Trinity River

The Trinity rises in its East Fork, Elm Fork, West Fork, and Clear Fork in Grayson, Montague, Archer, and Parker counties, respectively. The main stream begins with the junction of the Elm and West forks at Dallas. Its length is 550 miles, and its drainage area is 17,913 square miles. Because of moderate to heavy rainfall over its drainage area, it has an average annual flow of 5.7 million acre-feet near its mouth on Trinity Bay in the Galveston Bay system.

The Trinity derives its name from the Spanish "Trinidad." Alonso de León named it La Santísima Trinidad (the Most Holy Trinity).

Navigation was developed along its lower course with several riverport towns, such as Sebastopol in Trinity County. For many years, there has been a basin-wide movement for navigation, conservation, and utilization of its water. The Trinity River Authority is a state agency and the Trinity Improvement Association is a publicly supported nonprofit organization that has advocated its development.

The Trinity has in its valley more large cities, greater population, and more industrial development than any other river basin in Texas. On the Coastal Plains, there is large use of its waters for rice irrigation. Large reservoirs on the Elm Fork are Lewisville Lake and Ray Roberts Lake. There are four reservoirs above Fort Worth: Lake Worth, Eagle Mountain Lake, and Lake Bridgeport on the West Fork and Benbrook Lake on the Clear Fork.

Lake Lavon in southeast Collin County and Lake Ray Hubbard in Collin, Dallas, Kaufman,

and Rockwall counties are on the East Fork. Lake Livingston is in Polk, San Jacinto, Trinity, and Walker counties. Two other reservoirs in the Trinity basin below the Dallas–Fort Worth area are Cedar Creek Reservoir and Richland-Chambers Reservoir.

Neches River

The Neches rises in Van Zandt County in East Texas and flows 416 miles to Sabine Lake near Port Arthur. It has a drainage area of 9,937 square miles. Abundant rainfall over its entire basin gives it an average annual flow near the Gulf of about 4.3 million acre-feet a year. The river takes its name from the Neches Indians, who the early Spanish explorers found living along its banks. Principal tributary of the Neches, and comparable with the Neches in length and flow above their confluence, is the Angelina River, so named for Angelina (Little Angel), a Hainai Indian girl who converted to Christianity and played an important role in the early development of this region.

Both the Neches and the Angelina run most of their courses in the Piney Woods, and there was much settlement along them as early as the 1820s.

Sam Rayburn Reservoir, near Jasper on the Angelina River, was completed and dedicated in 1965. With a storage capacity of 2.88 million acre-feet, it is the fourth-largest reservoir in Texas. Reservoirs located on the Neches River include Lake Palestine in the upper basin and B. A. Steinhagen Lake located at the junction of the Neches and the Angelina rivers.

Sabine River

The Sabine River is formed by three forks rising in Collin and Hunt counties. From its sources to its mouth on Sabine Lake, it flows approximately 360 miles and drains 7,570 square miles.

Sabine comes from the Spanish word for cypress, as does the name of the Sabinal River, which flows into the Frio River in Southwest Texas. The Sabine has an average annual flow volume of 5.8 million acre-feet.

Throughout most of Texas history, the lower Sabine has been the eastern Texas boundary line, although for a while there was doubt as to whether the Sabine or the Arroyo Hondo, east of the Sabine in Louisiana, was the boundary. For a number of years, the outlaw-infested neutral ground lay between them. There was also a boundary dispute in which it was alleged that the Neches River was really the Sabine and, therefore, the boundary.

Travelers over the part of the Camino Real known as the Old San Antonio Road crossed the Sabine at the Gaines Ferry in Sabine County, and there were crossings for the Atascosito Road and other travel and trade routes of that day.

Toledo Bend Reservoir is the largest lake lying wholly or partly in Texas. The reservoir impounds 4.47 million acre-feet of water on the Sabine River in Newton, Panola, Sabine, and Shelby counties. It is the 16th-largest reservoir (in capacity by volume) in the United States. This is a joint project of Texas and Louisiana, through the Sabine River Authority.

Red River

The Red River, with a length of 1,290 miles from its headwaters, is exceeded in length only by the Rio Grande among rivers associated with Texas. Its original source is water in Curry County, New Mexico, near the Texas boundary, forming a definite channel as it crosses Deaf Smith County, Texas, in tributaries that flow into the Prairie Dog Town Fork of the Red River. These waters carve the spectacular Palo Duro Canyon of the High Plains before the Red River leaves the Caprock Escarpment, flowing eastward.

Where the Red River crosses the 100th meridian at the bottom of the Panhandle, the river becomes the Texas-Oklahoma boundary and is soon joined by Buck Creek to form the main channel, according to the U.S. Geological Survey. Its length in Texas is 695 miles, before it flows into Arkansas, where it swings south to flow through Louisiana.

The Red River, which drains 24,297 square miles in Texas, is a part of the Mississippi drainage basin, and at one time emptied all of its water into the Mississippi. In recent years, however, part of its water, especially at flood stage, has flowed to the Gulf via the Atchafalaya River in Louisiana.

The Red River takes its name from the red color of the water. This caused every explorer who came to its banks to call it "red" regardless of the language he spoke — Río Rojo or Río Roxo in Spanish, Rivière Rouge in French. At an early date, the river became the axis for French advance from Louisiana northwestward as far as present-day Montague County. There was consistent early navigation of the river from its mouth on the Mississippi to Shreveport, above which navigation was blocked by a natural log raft.

A number of important gateways into Texas from the north were established along the stream, such as Pecan Point and Jonesborough in Red River County,

Colbert's Ferry and Preston in Grayson County, and later, Doan's Store Crossing in Wilbarger County. The river was a menace to the early traveler because of both its variable current and its quicksands, which brought disaster to many a trail-herd cow, as well as ox team and covered wagon.

The largest water conservation project on the Red River is Lake Texoma, with a conservation storage capacity of 2.5 million acre-feet.

The Red River's high content of salt and other minerals limits the usefulness of its water along its upper reaches. Ten salt springs and tributaries in Texas and Oklahoma contribute most of these minerals.

The uppermost tributaries of the Red River in Texas are Tierra Blanca Creek, which rises in Curry County, N.M., and flows easterly across Deaf Smith and Randall counties to meet Palo Duro Creek and form the Prairie Dog Town Fork a few miles east of Canyon.

Other principal tributaries in Texas are the Pease and the Wichita in North Central Texas and the Sulphur in Northeast Texas, which flows through Wright Patman Lake, then into the Red River after it has crossed the boundary line into Arkansas.

The last major tributary in Northeast Texas is the Cypress Creek system, which flows into Louisiana before joining with the Red River. Major reservoirs in this basin are Lake O' The Pines and Caddo Lake.

From Oklahoma, the principal tributary is the Washita, which has its headwaters in Roberts County, Texas. The Ouachita, a river with the same pronunciation though spelled differently, is the principal tributary to the Red River's lower course in Arkansas.

The Red River boundary dispute, a long-standing feud between Oklahoma and Texas, was finally settled in 2000 when the boundary was set at the vegetation line on the south bank, except for Lake Texoma, where the boundary was set within the channel of the lake.

Canadian River

The Canadian River heads near Raton Pass in northern New Mexico near the Colorado boundary line and flows into Texas on the west line of Oldham County. It crosses the Texas Panhandle into Oklahoma and there flows into the Arkansas River, a total distance of 906 miles. It drains 12,865 square miles in Texas, and much of its 213-mile course across the Panhandle is in a deep gorge.

A tributary, the North Canadian River, dips briefly into the Texas Panhandle in Sherman County before it joins the main channel in Oklahoma.

One of several theories as to how the Canadian got its name is that some early explorers thought it flowed into Canada. Lake Meredith, formed by Sanford Dam, provides water for several Panhandle cities.

Because of the deep gorge and the quicksand that occurs in many places, the Canadian River has been a particularly difficult stream to bridge. It is known, especially in its lower course in Oklahoma, as outstanding among the streams of the country for the great amount of quicksand in its channel. ☆

The Llano River flooding in 2018. Photo by Jonathan Cutrer (jcutrer.com).

Secondary Streams of Texas

In addition to the principal rivers, Texas has many other streams of various size. The following list gives a few of these streams as designated by the U.S. Geological Survey, with additional information from the new Handbook of Texas and previous Texas Almanacs.

ALAMITO CREEK: Formed by confluence of North, South forks 3 mi. N Marfa in Presidio County. Flows SE 82 mi. to Rio Grande 5 mi. S Presidio.

ANGELINA RIVER: Rises in central Rusk County; flows SE 120 mi. through Cherokee, Nacogdoches, Angelina, San Augustine counties into Sam Rayburn Reservoir, then into Jasper County to the Neches River 12 mi. west of Jasper. A meandering stream through forested country.

ARANSAS RIVER: Formed 2 mi. N Skidmore in SC Bee County by union of Poesta and Aransas creeks; flows SE 40 mi. forming boundary between San Patricio and Refugio counties; then briefly into Aransas County where it empties into Copano Bay.

ATASCOSA RIVER: Formed NW Atascosa County by confluence of North, West prongs, flows SE 92 mi. through Atascosa and Live Oak counties into Frio River 2 mi. NW Three Rivers.

ATTOYAC BAYOU: Rises 2.8 mi. NE Mount Enterprise in SE Rusk County; flows SE 67 mi. through Shelby, San Augustine and Nacogdoches counties into Angelina River at Sam Rayburn Reservoir.

BARTON CREEK: Rises NE of Henly in NW Hays County; flows E 40 mi. through Travis County to Colorado River at Lady Bird Lake in Austin.

BEALS CREEK: Formed by confluence of Sulphur Springs and Mustang draws 4 mi. W Big Spring SW Howard County; flows E 55 mi. into Mitchell County to mouth on Colorado River.

BIG CYPRESS CREEK: Forms in SE Hopkins County E of Pickton; flows SE 60 mi. to mouth on Big Cypress Bayou 3 mi. E Jefferson in Marion County and just before the bayou flows into Caddo Lake. The creek forms the boundary lines between Camp and Titus, Camp and Morris, and Morris and Upshur counties. It passes through Lake Cypress Springs, Lake Bob Sandlin, and Lake O' The Pines, and is part of the Red River drainage basin.

BLACKWATER DRAW: Rises in Curry County, N.M.; flows into Texas in extreme NW Bailey County; flows SE through Lamb, Hale, and Lubbock counties to junction with Yellow House Draw to form North Fork of the Double Mountain Fork Brazos River. Length, 100 mi.

BLANCO CREEK: Rises near the intersection of Bee, Goliad and Karnes county lines in extreme S Karnes County; flows SE 45 mi. forming boundary of Bee and Goliad counties. Joins Medio Creek in Refugio County to form Mission River.

BLANCO CREEK: Rises E of Concan in Uvalde County; flows S 44 mi. to Frio River.

BLANCO RIVER: Rises W Lindendale in NE Kendall County; flows SE 64 mi. through Blanco and Hays counties; joins San Marcos River, a tributary of the Guadalupe; fed by many springs.

BOSQUE RIVER: Flows from Lake Waco in McLennan County 5 mi. into Brazos River.

BOSQUE RIVER, NORTH: Formed at Stephenville by the union of North, South forks in Erath County; flows generally SE 96 mi. through Hamilton, Bosque and McLennan counties into Lake Waco.

BOSQUE RIVER, SOUTH: Rises near Coryell-McLennan county line; flows NE 24 mi. into Lake Waco.

BRADY CREEK: Rises 14 mi. SW Eden in SW Concho County; flows 90 mi. through McCulloch and San Saba counties into San Saba River 10 mi. SW of Richland Springs.

BRAZOS RIVER, CLEAR FORK: Rises 8 mi. E Snyder in Scurry County; flows NE 180 mi. through Fisher, Jones, Haskell, Throckmorton, Shackelford and Stephens counties into Brazos River in S Young County; drainage area 5,728 sq. mi.

BRAZOS RIVER, DOUBLE MOUNTAIN FORK: Rises 12 mi. SE Tahoka, Lynn County; flows E 175 mi. through Garza, Kent, Fisher and Haskell counties to confluence with Salt Fork of the Brazos, north of Old Glory in Stonewall County.

BRAZOS RIVER, NORTH FORK: DOUBLE MOUNTAIN FORK: Formed by union of Yellow House and Blackwater draws in Lubbock; flows SE 75 miles through Crosby, Garza and Kent counties to junction with Double Mountain Fork Brazos River.

BRAZOS RIVER, SALT FORK: Rises in SE Crosby County; flows 150 mi. through Garza and Kent counties to confluence with Double Mountain Fork in NE Stonewall County to form the main stream of Brazos River.

BUCK CREEK: Also called Spiller Creek. Rises SE Donley County; flows SE 49 mi. through Collingsworth and Childress counties to Texas-Oklahoma boundary; then 3 mi. through Oklahoma to junction with Prairie Dog Town Fork of Red River NW Hardeman County to form main stream of the Red River.

BUFFALO BAYOU: Rises in extreme N Fort Bend County; flows E 46 mi. through Houston into San Jacinto River in Harris County. Part of Houston Ship Channel.

CALIFORNIA CREEK: Rises 10 mi. NE Roby in Fisher County; flows NE 70 mi. through Jones County into Paint Creek in E Haskell County.

CANEY CREEK: Rises near Wharton in Wharton County; flows 75 mi. through Matagorda County into east end of Matagorda Bay. Centuries ago, the current Caney Creek channel was the channel for the Colorado River.

CAPOTE/WILDHORSE DRAW: Rises N of Van Horn in Culberson County; runs 86 mi. S through Jeff Davis County to SW of Marfa in Presidio County. One of a number of streams in this area with no outlet to the sea.

CEDAR BAYOU: Rises 11 mi. NW Liberty in Liberty County; flows 46 mi. S as boundary between Harris County and Liberty and Chambers counties, and into Trinity Bay.

CHAMBERS CREEK: Formed SW Waxahachie in Ellis County by union North, South forks; flows SE 45 mi. through Navarro County into Richland Creek at Richland-Chambers Reservoir.

CIBOLO CREEK: Rises 7 mi. W Boerne in Kendall County; flows SE through Bexar, Comal, Guadalupe and Wilson counties into San Antonio River in Karnes County; 96 mi. in length. Spring-fed, perennially flowing stream.

COLETO CREEK: Formed SW of Mission Valley in NW Victoria County by union of Twelve Mile and Fifteen Mile creeks forming boundary between Victoria and Goliad counties. From Coleto Creek Reservoir flows to Guadalupe River in Victoria County.

COMAL RIVER: Rises in Comal Springs in City of New Braunfels and flows SE about 2.5 miles to Guadalupe River. Shortest river in Texas by name.

CONCHO RIVER: Formed at San Angelo by conjunction North, South Concho rivers; flows E 24 mi. through Tom Green County, then 29 mi. through Concho County into Colorado River 12 m. NE Paint Rock. Drainage basin, including North and South Concho, 6,613 sq. mi. A spring-fed stream.

CONCHO RIVER, MIDDLE: Rises SW Sterling County; flows S, then E 66 mi. through Tom Green panhandle, Irion and Reagan counties into South Concho River at Lake Nasworthy near Tankersley in Tom Green County.

CONCHO RIVER, NORTH: Rises in S Howard County; flows 137 mi. through Glasscock, Sterling and Coke counties to confluence with South Concho to form Concho River in Tom Green County. Drainage basin, 1,510 sq. mi.

CONCHO RIVER, SOUTH: Rises in C Schleicher County; flows N through Lake Nasworthy to confluence with North Concho River in Tom Green County; length, 41 mi.; drainage basin area 3, 866 sq. mi. Perennial flow from springs.

COWLEECH FORK SABINE RIVER: Rises 2 mi. NW Celeste NW Hunt County; flows SE 40 mi. to Lake Tawakoni.

DEEP CREEK: Rises SE Baird, Callahan County; flows N 55 mi. into Hubbard Creek in Shackelford County near McCatherine Mountain.

DEEP CREEK: Rises 4 mi. N Fluvanna NW Scurry County; flows SSE 70 mi. to mouth on Colorado River in extreme N Mitchell County.

DELAWARE RIVER: Rises eastern slope Delaware Mountains in N Culberson County; flows in NE course; crosses Texas-New Mexico state line and enters Pecos River; length, 50 mi.

DEVILS RIVER: Formed SW Sutton County by union Dry Devils River and Granger Draw; flows SE 95 mi. through Val Verde County into Rio Grande at Amistad Reservoir. Spring-fed, perennially flowing stream throughout most of its course.

ELM CREEK: Rises 3 mi. SE Nolan in Nolan County; flows NE 60 mi., passes through Lake

Abilene, Buffalo Gap and Abilene in Taylor County and through Lake Fort Phantom Hill into Clear Fork Brazos River near Nugent, SE Jones County.

FRIO RIVER: Formed at Leakey in Real County by union of West and East Frio rivers; flows S 190 mi. through Uvalde, Medina, Frio, La Salle, McMullen counties (Choke Canyon Reservoir); joins Nueces River S of Three Rivers in Live Oak County. Drainage area, 7,310 sq. mi. Fed by springs in northern part, where it flows through picturesque canyon.

GREENS BAYOU: Rises 9 mi. W Aldine, C Harris County; flows ESE into Houston Ship Channel; 42 mi. long.

HONDO CREEK: Rises 7.5 mi. NW Tarpley C Bandera County; flows SSE 67 mi. through Medina and Frio counties to Frio River 5 mi. NW Pearsall.

HOWARD DRAW: Rises at Crockett-Reagan county line; flows SSW 45 mi. through Val Verde County to Pecos River near Pandale.

HUBBARD CREEK: Rises 3 mi. NW Baird N Callahan County; flows NE 62 mi. through Shackelford County; then into Stephens County (Hubbard Creek Reservoir) and joins Clear Fork of the Brazos River 10 mi. NW Breckenridge.

JAMES RIVER: Rises SE Kimble County; flows NE 37 mi. to join Llano River in Mason County.

JIM NED CREEK: Rises 10 mi. NW Tuscola SC Taylor County; flows SE 71 mi. through Callahan and Coleman counties to Brown County to join Pecan Bayou, a tributary of Colorado River.

JOHNSON DRAW: Rises NE Crockett County; runs SSE 66 miles to mouth on Devils River in Val Verde County.

LAMPASAS RIVER: Rises NW Mills County; flows SE 100 miles through Hamilton, Lampasas, Burnet and Bell counties (Stillhouse Hollow Lake); unites with Leon River to form Little River.

LEON RIVER: Formed by confluence North, Middle and South Forks in NC Eastland County; flows SE 185 mi. through Comanche, Hamilton and Coryell counties to junction with Lampasas River to form Little River in Bell County.

LEONA RIVER: Rises N Uvalde in central Uvalde County; flows SE 83 mi. through Zavala County into Frio River in Frio County.

LIMPIA CREEK: Heads in the Davis Mountains on the NE slope of Mount Livermore in Jeff Davis County and flows 52 mi. E, NE and E through Limpia Canyon to disappear at the head of Barrilla Draw in Pecos County. Part of course through Limpia Canyon noted for its scenic beauty.

LITTLE BRAZOS RIVER: Rises 5 mi. SW Thornton, SW Limestone County; flows 72 mi. SE through Falls and Robertson counties into Brazos River in Brazos County.

LITTLE RIVER: Formed central Bell County by union Leon, Lampasas rivers; flows 75 mi. SE through Milam County into Brazos River.

LLANO RIVER: Formed C Kimble County by union North, South Llano rivers; flows E 100 mi. through Mason, Llano counties to Colorado River. Drainage area, including North, South Llano rivers, 4,460 sq. mi. A spring-fed stream of the Edwards Plateau, known for scenic beauty.

LLANO RIVER, NORTH: Rises C Sutton County; flows E 40 mi. to union with South Llano River at Junction in Kimble County.

LLANO RIVER, SOUTH: Rises in NC Edwards County; flows 55 mi. NE to confluence with North Llano River at Junction in Kimble County.

LOS OLMOS CREEK: Rises central Duval County; flows SE 71 mi. through Jim Wells and Brooks counties; forms boundary between Kenedy and Kleberg counties; into Baffin Bay.

MADERA CANYON: Rises N slope Mount Livermore, Jeff Davis County, at altitude of 7,500 ft.; flows 40 mi. NE to join Aguja Creek at Reeves County line to form Toyah Creek, tributary through Pecos River to Rio Grande. Intermittent stream. Noteworthy for its beauty.

MEDINA RIVER: Rises in North, West prongs in W Bandera County; flows SE 116 mi. through Medina and Bexar counties to San Antonio River. A spring-fed stream. Scenically beautiful along upper course.

MEDIO CREEK: Rises S Karnes County; flows SE 2 mi. through Karnes County, then 7 mi. along boundary Karnes and Bee counties, then SE 37 mi. through Bee County, SE 7 mi. through Refugio County to junction with Blanco Creek to form Mission River.

MISSION RIVER: Formed by confluence of Blanco and Medio creeks in C Refugio County; flows SE 24 mi. to mouth on Mission Bay, an inlet of Copano Bay.

MULBERRY CREEK: Rises NW Armstrong County at Fairview; flows SE 58 mi. through Donley and Briscoe counties into Prairie Dog Town Fork Red River in NW Hall County.

NAVASOTA RIVER: Rises SE Hill County; flows SE 125 mi. through Limestone County and along boundary Leon, Madison, Robertson, Brazos and Grimes counties to Brazos River near Navasota.

NAVIDAD RIVER: Forms at juncture of East and West Navidad rivers in NE Lavaca County; flows 74 mi. through Lavaca and Jackson counties into Lake Texana near Ganado; then joins Lavaca River.

NOLAN RIVER: Rises in NW Johnson County; flows S 30 mi. through Lake Pat Cleburne and into Hill County, where it empties into Brazos River at Lake Whitney.

ONION CREEK: Rises 1 mi. W of Hays-Blanco county line SE Blanco County; flows SE 37 mi.

Exploring Texas this year? Submit your photos to our Flickr group:
https://www.flickr.com/groups/texasalmanac/
Your photo might be chosen to be on our website, or even in our next book!

through N Hays County; then 22 mi. through S Travis County into Colorado River near Garfield.

PAINT CREEK: Rises in extreme NW Jones County near Tuxedo; flows NE, then SE 53 mi. through SE corner of Stonewall County; then across S Haskell County (Lake Stamford) and into W Throckmorton County to mouth on Clear Fork Brazos River.

PALO BLANCO CREEK: Rises SE Hebbronville in N Jim Hogg County; flows SE 59 mi. through Duval and Brooks, where it passes through Laguna Salada; then into NW Kenedy County.

PALO DURO CREEK: Rises in W Deaf Smith County; flows E 45 mi. into C Randall County to junction with Tierra Blanca Creek near Canyon to form the Prairie Dog Town Fork of the Red River. Lends its name to the notable canyon.

PALUXY RIVER: Formed in E Erath County by convergence of North and South branches at Bluff Dale; flows SE 29 mi. through Hood and Somervell counties to mouth on Brazos River. Dinosaur Valley State Park at a large bend of the river in Somervell County is site of 100-million-year-old dinosaur tracks.

PEASE RIVER: Formed by union of North and Middle Pease rivers in NE Cottle County; flows E 100 mi. through Hardeman, Foard and Wilbarger counties into Red River 8 mi. NE of Vernon.

PEASE RIVER, MIDDLE: Rises 8 mi. NW Matador in WC Motley County; flows E 63 miles into North Pease River to form the Pease River in NE Cottle County.

PEASE RIVER, NORTH: Rises 9 mi. SE Cedar Hill in E Floyd County; flows E 60 mi. through Motley, Hall and Cottle counties. Joins Middle Pease to form Pease River.

PEASE RIVER, SOUTH: Also called Tongue River. Rises 11 mi. SW Roaring Springs in SW Motley County; flows ENE 40 mi. to mouth on Middle Pease River in W Cottle County.

PECAN BAYOU: Formed by union of South, North prongs in SC Callahan County; flows SE 90 mi. through Coleman, Brown (Lake Brownwood) and Mills counties into Colorado River SW Goldthwaite. Westernmost bayou.

PEDERNALES RIVER: Rises NE corner of Kerr County; flows E 106 mi. through Kimble, Gillespie, Blanco, Hays and Travis counties into Colorado River at Lake Travis. Spring-fed; a beautiful stream.

PINE ISLAND BAYOU: Rises near Rye, NE Liberty County; flows 76 mi. SE through Hardin and Jefferson counties into Neches River.

RED RIVER, PRAIRIE DOG TOWN FORK: Formed by union of Palo Duro and Tierra Blanca creeks in Randall County; flows E 160 mi. through Armstrong, Briscoe, Hall, and Childress counties to junction with Buck Creek to form Red River in NW corner of Hardeman County. Palo Duro Canyon is along course of this stream as it descends from Great Plains.

RED RIVER, NORTH FORK: Rises W Gray County; flows SE 180 mi. through Wheeler County

into Oklahoma to junction with the Red River NE Vernon in Wilbarger County.

RED RIVER, SALT FORK: Rises N Armstrong County; flows SE 155 mi. through Donley and Collingsworth counties and into Oklahoma. It joins the Red River opposite the northernmost point of Wilbarger County.

RICHLAND CREEK: Rises 3.5 mi. E Itasca N Hill County; flows E 50 mi. through Ellis and Navarro counties, through Navarro Mills Lake and Richland-Chambers Reservoir; then into the Trinity River in Freestone County.

RUNNING WATER DRAW: Rises 24 mi. WNW Clovis, N.M.; flows ESE into Texas in C Parmer County; then through Castro, Lamb, Hale and Floyd counties to join Callahan Draw 8 mi. W Floydada at head of White River, a tributary of the Brazos River.

SABANA RIVER: Rises at Callahan-Eastland county line; flows SE 50 mi. through Comanche County into Leon River at Proctor Lake.

SABINAL RIVER: Rises 7 mi. N Vanderpool in NW Bandera County; flows S 60 mi. to junction with Frio River in SE Uvalde County. The West Sabinal River, which rises in Real County, joins the main stream at the Bandera-Uvalde county line.

SAN BERNARD RIVER: Rises 1 mi. S New Ulm in W Austin County; flows SE, forming boundary Austin and Colorado counties, 31 mi.; Austin and Wharton counties, 8 mi.; Wharton and Fort Bend counties, 28 mi.; approaches Gulf of Mexico in Brazoria County. Total length, 120 mi. (For more than 100 years locals have reported hearing the wail of a violin from the river. The mystery has never been solved, although some say the musical sounds are caused by escaping gas. The phenomenon has caused the stream to be called the Singing River: Handbook of Texas.)

SAN GABRIEL RIVER: Formed at Georgetown in C Williamson County by union of North and South forks; flows NE 50 mi. into Milam County to join Little River. Originally called San Xavier River.

SAN JACINTO RIVER, EAST: Rises E Walker County; flows SE and S 69 mi. through San Jacinto, Liberty, Montgomery and Harris counties into Lake Houston and San Jacinto River.

SAN JACINTO RIVER, WEST: Rises E Grimes County NE Shiro; flows SE 90 mi. through Walker County; into Lake Conroe in Montgomery County; then through Montgomery County to Lake Houston in Harris County.

SAN MARCOS RIVER: Formed near N limits City of San Marcos, Hays County, by several large springs, although watershed extends about 10 mi. NE of springs; Blanco River joins the San Marcos River 4 mi. downstream; flows SE 59 mi. as boundary between Guadalupe and Caldwell counties; then through Gonzales County to join Guadalupe River 2 mi. W Gonzales.

SANDY CREEK: Rises SW Colorado County; flows SSE 42 mi. through Lavaca, Wharton and Jackson counties into Lake Texana.

SAN SABA RIVER: Formed W Fort McKavett at Schleicher-Menard county line by union of North Valley and Middle Valley prongs; flows NE 140 mi. through Menard, Mason, McCulloch and San Saba counties into Colorado River 8 mi. NE San Saba. One of the picturesque streams of the Edwards Plateau.

SPRING CREEK: Rises NE Waller County near Fields Store; flows E 64 mi. forming boundary between Waller and Harris counties, and Montgomery and Harris counties to junction with West Fork San Jacinto River and Lake Houston.

SULPHUR RIVER: Formed E Delta County by junction North, South branches; flows E 183 miles forming boundary between Franklin and Red River counties; Titus and Red River counties; Morris and Red River and Bowie counties; then between Bowie and Cass counties, where it flows into Wright Patman Lake; continues on into Red River in S Miller County, Ark.

SULPHUR RIVER, NORTH: Rises 1 mi. SW Gober S Fannin County; flows SE, E 54 mi. as boundary between Delta and Lamar counties and to union with South Sulphur River to form Sulphur River.

SULPHUR RIVER, SOUTH: Rises N Leonard S Fannin County; flows ESE 50 mi. through Hunt County; then as boundary between Hopkins and Delta counties (through Cooper Lake) to union with North Sulphur to form Sulphur River.

SULPHUR SPRINGS DRAW: Rises in E Lea County, N.M.; enters Texas W Yoakum County at Bronco; flows SE 100 mi. through Terry, Gaines, Dawson, Martin, and Howard counties to confluence with Mustang Creek to form Beals Creek, a tributary of Colorado River.

SWEETWATER CREEK: Rises 2 mi. W Maryneal, C Nolan County; flows NE 45 mi. through Fisher and Jones counties into Clear Fork Brazos River.

TERLINGUA CREEK: Rises WC Brewster County; flows S 83 mi. into Rio Grande just E Santa Elena Canyon.

TIERRA BLANCA CREEK: Rises N Curry County, N.M.; flows E across Texas state line in SW Deaf Smith County and 75 mi. through Deaf Smith, Parmer and Randall counties to junction with Palo Duro Creek where it forms Prairie Dog Town Fork Red River.

TOYAH CREEK: Forms near boundary Jeff Davis-Reeves counties; flows NE 50 mi. into Pecos River NC Reeves County.

TRINITY RIVER, CLEAR FORK: Rises NW Poolville in NW Parker County; flows SE 56 mi. through Tarrant County into West Fork Trinity River at Fort Worth.

TRINITY RIVER, EAST FORK: Rises 1.5 mi. NW Dorchester in SC Grayson County; flows S 85 mi. through Collin County (Lake Lavon and Lake Ray Hubbard); then Rockwall and Dallas counties into Trinity River in SE Kaufman County.

TRINITY RIVER, ELM FORK: Rises 1 mi. NW Saint Jo in E Montague County; flows 85 mi. SE through Cooke, Denton counties (Ray Roberts Lake and Lewisville Lake) to junction with West Fork to form Trinity River proper at Irving in WC Dallas County.

TRINITY RIVER, WEST FORK: Rises in SC Archer County; flows SE 145 mi. through Jack, Wise (Lake Bridgeport) and Tarrant (Eagle Mountain Lake and Lake Worth) counties to conjunction with Elm Fork to form Trinity River proper in WC Dallas County.

TULE CREEK: Formed in Swisher County by union of North, Middle and South Tule draws; flows E 40 mi. through Mackenzie Reservoir and Briscoe County into Prairie Dog Town Fork Red River. Remarkably beautiful Tule Canyon along lower course.

TURKEY CREEK: Rises near Turkey Mountain EC Kinney County; flows SE 54 mi. through Uvalde, Zavala, Dimmit counties to Nueces River.

WASHITA RIVER: Rises SE Roberts County; flows E 35 mi. through Hemphill County to Oklahoma state line, then SE to Red River at Lake Texoma. Total length, 295 mi.

WEST CANEY CREEK: Rises 1 mi. SW Normangee in SW Leon County; flows SW 11 mi. through NW Madison County to junction with Navasota River on Brazos county line. The historic Old San Antonio Road, a thoroughfare for early Spanish and French explorers, crossed the headwaters of the stream.

WHITE RIVER: Formed 8 mi. W Floydada in WC Floyd County by union of Running Water and Callahan draws; flows SE 62 mi. through Blanco Canyon and White River Lake in Crosby County; then through Garza and Kent counties into Salt Fork Brazos River; principal tributary to Salt Fork.

WICHITA RIVER: Formed NE Knox County by union North, South Wichita rivers; flows NE 90 mi. through Baylor (Lake Kemp and Lake Diversion), Archer, Wichita and Clay counties to Red River N Byers.

WICHITA RIVER, LITTLE: Formed in C Archer County by union of its North, Middle and South forks; flows NE 62 mi. through Clay County (Lake Arrowhead) into Red River.

WICHITA RIVER, NORTH: Rises 6 mi. E East Afton in NE Dickens County; flows E through King, Cottle, Foard counties; then as boundary for Foard and Knox counties; then briefly into Baylor County to junction with South Wichita River to form Wichita River proper NE Vera in Knox County. Length, 100 mi.

WICHITA RIVER, SOUTH: Rises 10 mi. E Dickens in EC Dickens County; flows E 85 mi. through King and Knox counties to junction with North Wichita to form Wichita River.

YELLOW HOUSE DRAW: Rises in SE Bailey County; flows SE 80 mi. through Cochran, Hockley and Lubbock counties to confluence with Blackwater Draw at Lubbock to form the North Fork of Double Mountain Fork Brazos River. ☆

Possum Kingdom Lake and Morris Sheppard Dam. Photo by Nicolas Henderson (CC).

Artificial Lakes and Reservoirs

Sources: U.S. Geological Survey; Texas Water Development Board; New Handbook of Texas; Texas Parks & Wildlife; U.S. Army Corps of Engineers; various river basin authorities; reservoir websites.

The large increase in the number of reservoirs in Texas during the past half-century has greatly improved water conservation and supplies.

As late as 1917, Texas had only four major reservoirs with a total storage capacity of 288,340 acre-feet. (*One acre-foot is the amount of water necessary to cover an acre of surface area with water one foot deep, about 325,851 gallons of water.*) Most of this capacity was in Medina Lake in southwest Texas, with 254,000 acre-feet capacity, created by a dam completed in May 1913.

By January 2012, Texas had 188 major water supply reservoirs (those with a normal capacity of 5,000 acre-feet or larger) and 21 major non-water supply reservoirs (those that do not have a water supply function). The 188 water supply reservoirs have a total conservation surface area of 1.67 million acres and an original conservation storage capacity of 35 million acre-feet (only Texas' share is counted in border reservoirs). The 21 non-water supply reservoirs have a total normal surface area of 62,079 acres and an original normal storage capacity of 760,000 acre-feet.

According to the U.S. Statistical Abstract of 2018, Texas has 5,612 square miles of inland water, ranking it first in the 48 contiguous states, followed by Florida, with 5,023 sq. mi. The only state with more inland water is Alaska, with 19,346 sq. mi.

There are 6,976 reservoirs in Texas with a normal storage capacity of 10 acre-feet or larger.

Natural Lakes in Texas

There are many natural lakes in Texas, though none is of great size. The largest designated natural lake touching the border of Texas is **Sabine Lake**, into which the Sabine and Neches rivers discharge. It is more properly called the **Sabine-Neches Estuary** of the Gulf of Mexico. (Find more information about this estuary on page 66.)

Also near the coast, in Calhoun County, is **Green Lake**, which has about 10,000 acre-feet of storage capacity. It is one of the state's largest natural freshwater lakes.

Caddo Lake, on the Texas-Louisiana border, was a natural lake originally, but its present capacity and surface area are largely due to dams built to raise the surface of the original body of water.

Natural Dam Lake, in Howard County, has a similar history to Caddo Lake.

In East Texas, there are many small natural lakes formed by "horse-shoe" bends that have been eliminated from the main channel of a river. There are also a number of these "horse-shoe" lakes along the Rio Grande in the Lower Valley, where they are called resacas.

On the South Plains and west of San Angelo there are lakes, such as **Big Lake** in Reagan County, that are usually dry.

List of Lakes and Reservoirs

The table below lists lakes and reservoirs in Texas having **more than 5,000 acre-feet of storage capacity**. Some industrial cooling reservoirs are not included in this table.

The surface area listed in the table is the **area at conservation elevation** as calculated by the Texas Water Development Board (TWDB). Because sediment deposition constantly changes reservoir volumes over time, storage capacity figures are from the most recent surveys available.

Various methods of computing capacity area are used, and detailed information may be obtained from the TWDB, from the U.S. Army Corps of Engineers, or from local sources. Boundary reservoir capacities include water designated for Texas and non-Texas water. Texas' share will be included in the description.

Information is in the following order: (1) Name of lake or reservoir; (2) year of first impounding of water; (3) county or counties in which it is located; (4) river or creek on which it is located; (5) location with respect to some city or town; (6) purpose of reservoir; (7) owner of reservoir.

Some of these items, when not listed, are not available. For the larger lakes and reservoirs, the dam impounding water to form the lake bears the same name, unless otherwise indicated. The years in the table refer to first impounding of water. Double years refer to later, larger dams.

Lakes and Reservoirs, Date of Origin	Surface Area (acres)	Storage Capacity (acre-ft.)
ABILENE, L.: (1919) Taylor Co.; Elm Cr.; 6 mi. NW Tuscola; (M-In.-R); City of Abilene	588	7,900
ADDICKS RESERVOIR: (1948) Harris Co.; South Mayde Cr.; 1 mi. E of Addicks; (FC only); USAE; Addicks only has water during times of flood and is dry most of the year	16,780	202,128
ALAN HENRY, L.: (1993) Garza Co.; Double Mountain Fork Brazos River; 10 mi. E Justiceburg; (M-In.-Ir.); City of Lubbock	2,395	96,207
ALCOA L.: (1952) Milam Co.; Sandy Cr.; 7 mi. SW Rockdale; (In.-R); Alcoa Aluminum (also called Sandow L.)	914	15,650
AMISTAD RESERVOIR, INTERNATIONAL: (1969) Val Verde Co.; Rio Grande; an international project of the U.S. and Mexico; 12 mi. NW Del Rio; (C-R-Ir.-P-FC); International Boundary and Water Commission (Texas' share of conservation capacity is 56.2 percent.) (Formerly Diablo Reservoir)	65,597	3,275,532
AMON G. CARTER, L.: (1961) Montague Co.; Big Sandy Cr.; 6 mi. S Bowie; (M-In.); City of Bowie	1,524	19,266
ANAHUAC, L.: (1936, 1954) Chambers Co.; Turtle Bayou; near Anahuac; (Ir.-In.-Mi.); Chambers-Liberty Counties Navigation District. (also called Turtle Bayou Reservoir)	5,035	33,348
ANZALDUAS CHANNEL DAM: Hidalgo Co.; Rio Grande; 11 mi. upstream from Hidalgo; (Ir.-FC); United States and Mexico	1,472	13,910
AQUILLA L.: (1983) Hill Co.; Aquilla Cr.; 10.2 mi. W of Hillsboro; (FC-M-Ir.-In.-R); USAE–Brazos R. Auth.	3,119	43,243
ARLINGTON, L.: (1957) Tarrant Co.; Village Cr.; 7 mi. W Arlington; (M-In.); City of Arlington	1,908	40,188
ARROWHEAD, L.: (1966) Clay-Archer counties.; Little Wichita R.; 13 mi. SE Wichita Falls; (M); City of Wichita Falls	14,372	230,359
ATHENS, L.: (1962) Henderson Co.; 8 mi. E Athens; (M-FC-R); Athens Municipal Water Authority (formerly Flat Creek Reservoir)	1,799	29,503
AUSTIN, L.: (1893, 1915, 1939) Travis Co.; Colorado R.; W Austin city limits; (M-In.-P); City of Austin, leased to LCRA (Imp. by Tom Miller Dam) (In 1893, the first dam was completed. It broke in 1900. In 1915, a second dam was partially built but not completed. In 1939, the present Tom Miller Dam was completed.)	1,589	23,972
BALLINGER L.: (1947) Runnels Co.; Valley Creek; 5 mi. W Ballinger; (M); City of Ballinger (also known as Lake Moonen)	500	8,215
BALMORHEA L.: (1917) Reeves Co.; Sandia Cr.; 3 mi. SE Balmorhea; (Ir.-R); Reeves Co. WID No. 1	573	6,350
BARDWELL L.: (1965) Ellis Co.; Waxahachie Cr.; 3 mi. SE Bardwell; (FC-C-R); USAE	3,138	46,122
BARKER RESERVOIR: (1945) Harris Co.; above Buffalo Bayou; (FC only); USAE; Barker only has water during times of flood and is dry most of the year	17,225	206,860
B. A. STEINHAGEN L.: (1951) Tyler-Jasper counties; Neches R.; 1/2 mi. N Town Bluff; (FC-R-C); USAE; (also called Town Bluff Reservoir and Dam B. Reservoir); (Imp. by Town Bluff Dam)	10,421	66,961
BASTROP, L.: (1964) Bastrop Co.; Spicer Cr.; 3 mi. NE Bastrop; (In.-R); LCRA	906	16,590
BAYLOR L.: (1950) Childress Co.; 10 mi. NW Childress; (M-R); City of Childress (also called Baylor Creek Reservoir)	610	9,220
BELTON L.: (1954) Bell-Coryell counties; Leon R.; 3 mi. N. Belton; (M-FC-R); USAE–Brazos R. Auth.	12,135	435,225
BENBROOK L.: (1952) Tarrant Co.; Clear Fk. Trinity R.; 10 mi. SW Fort Worth; (FC-R); USAE	3,635	85,648
BIVINS L.: (1927) Randall Co.; Palo Duro Cr.; 8 mi. NW Canyon; (M); Amarillo; City of Amarillo (also called Amarillo City Lake)	379	5,122
BOB SANDLIN, L.: (1977) Titus-Wood-Camp-Franklin counties; Big Cypress Cr.; 5 mi. SW Mount Pleasant; (In.-M-R); Titus Co. FWSD No. 1 (Imp. by Fort Sherman Dam)	8,888	203,148
BONHAM, L.: (1969) Fannin Co.; Timber Cr.; 5 mi. NE Bonham; (M); Bonham Municipal Water Auth.	1,056	11,027
BRADY CREEK RESERVOIR: (1963) McCulloch Co.; Brady Cr.; 3 mi. W Brady; (M-In.-R); City of Brady	2,020	30,430

Abbreviations used in this table: L., lake; R., river; Co., county; Cr., creek; (C) conservation; (FC) flood control; (R) recreation; (P) power; (M) municipal; (D) domestic; (Ir.) irrigation; (In.) industry; (Mi.) mining, including oil production; (FH) fish hatchery; USAE, United States Army Corps of Engineers; WC&ID, Water Control and Improvement District; WID, Water Improvement District; USBR, United States Bureau of Reclamation; Auth., Authority; LCRA, Lower Colorado River Authority; TPWD, Texas Parks & Wildlife Dept.; USDA, United States Department of Agriculture; Imp., impounded.

Lakes and Reservoirs, Date of Origin	Surface Area (acres)	Storage Capacity (acre-ft.)
BRANDY BRANCH RESERVOIR: (1983) Harrison Co.; Brandy Br.; 10 mi. SW Marshall; (In.); AEP-Southwestern Electric Power Co.	1,242	29,513
BRAZORIA RESERVOIR: (1954) Brazoria Co.; off-channel reservoir; 1 mi. NE Brazoria; (In.); Dow Chemical Co.	1,865	21,970
BRIDGEPORT, L.: (1932) Wise-Jack counties; W. Fk. of Trinity R.; 4 mi. W Bridgeport; (M-FC-R); Tarrant Regional Water District	11,712	366,236
BROWNWOOD, L.: (1933) Brown Co.; Pecan Bayou; 8 mi. N Brownwood; (M-R); Brown Co. WID No. 1	6,460	128,839
BRYAN UTILITIES L.: (1977) Brazos Co.; unnamed stream; 6 mi. NW Bryan; (In.); City of Bryan (also called Lake Bryan)	818	14,163
BUCHANAN, L.: (1937) Burnet-Llano-San Saba counties; Colorado R.; 13 mi. W Burnet; (M-FC-R-P); LCRA	21,618	860,607
BUFFALO L.: (1938) Randall Co.; Tierra Blanca Cr.; 2 mi. S. Umbarger; (C-FC); U.S. Fish and Wildlife Service; Imp. by Umbarger Dam; See Buffalo Lake entry in Wildlife Refuge section for more info. Buffalo Lake is dry most of the year.	1,900	18,150
CADDO L.: (1873, 1914, 1971) Harrison-Marion counties, Texas, and Caddo Parish, La.; Cypress Bayou; 29 mi. NE Marshall; (C-R-M); Northeast Texas Municipal Water District; An original natural lake, whose surface and capacity were increased by construction of dams.	26,138	129,000
CALAVERAS L.: (1969) Bexar Co.; Calaveras Cr.; 15 mi. SE San Antonio; (In.-R); CPS Energy of San Antonio	3,624	63,200
CAMP CREEK L.: (1949) Robertson Co.; 13 mi. E Franklin; (R); Camp Creek Water Co.	750	8,550
CANYON L.: (1964) Comal Co.; Guadalupe R.; 12 mi. NW New Braunfels; (M-R-P-FC); Guadalupe-Blanco R. Authority & USAE	8,308	378,781
CASA BLANCA, L.: (1951) Webb Co.; Chacon Cr.; 3 mi. NE Laredo; (R); Webb Co.; (Imp. by Country Club Dam)	1,680	20,000
CEDAR CREEK RESERVOIR: (1965) Henderson-Kaufman counties; Cedar Cr.; 3 mi. NE Trinidad; (M-R);Tarrant Regional Water District; (also called Lake Joe B. Hogsett)	32,796	644,686
CHAMPION CREEK RESERVOIR: (1959) Mitchell Co.; 7 mi. S. Colorado City; (M-In.); City of Colorado City	1,196	41,580
CHEROKEE, L.: (1948) Gregg-Rusk counties; Cherokee Bayou; 12 mi. SE Longview; (M-In.-R); Cherokee Water Co.	3,889	40,094
CHOKE CANYON RESERVOIR: (1982) Live Oak-McMullen counties; Frio R.; 4 mi. W Three Rivers; (M-In.-R-FC); City of Corpus Christi-USBR	17,660	662,820
CISCO, L.: (1923) Eastland Co.; Sandy Cr.; 4 mi. N. Cisco; (M); City of Cisco (Imp. by Williamson Dam)	985	29,003
CLYDE, L.: (1970) Callahan Co.; N. Prong Pecan Bayou; 6 mi. S. Clyde; (M-R); City of Clyde and USDA Soil Conservation Service	449	5,748
COFFEE MILL L.: (1939, 1967) Fannin Co.; Coffee Mill Cr.; 12 mi. NW Honey Grove; (R); U.S. Forest Service	650	8,000
COLEMAN L.: (1966) Coleman Co.; Jim Ned Cr.; 14 mi. N. Coleman; (M-In.); City of Coleman	1,811	38,094
COLETO CREEK RESERVOIR: (1980) Goliad–Victoria counties; Coleto Cr.; 12 mi. SW Victoria; (In); Guadalupe-Blanco River Auth.	3,100	31,040
COLORADO CITY, L.: (1949) Mitchell Co.; Morgan Cr.; 4 mi. SW Colorado City; (M-In.-P); TXU	1,612	30,758
CONROE, L.: (1973) Montgomery-Walker counties; W. Fork San Jacinto R.; 7 mi. NW Conroe; (M-In.); San Jacinto River Authority, City of Houston and Texas Water Development Board	19,590	410,988
COOPER, L./OLNEY: (1935) Archer Co.; Mesquite Crk; 8 mi. E Megargel; (M-R); City of Olney; (see L. Olney)	446	6,650
COOPER L.: (1991) Delta-Hopkins counties; Sulphur R.; 3 mi.SE Cooper; (FC-M-R); USAE; (also called Jim Chapman Lake)	17,958	260,332
CORPUS CHRISTI, L.: (1930) Live Oak-San Patricio-Jim Wells counties; Nueces R.; 4 mi. SW Mathis; (M-R); City of Corpus Christi (Imp. by Wesley E. Seale Dam)	18,700	256,062
COX CREEK RESERVOIR: Calhoun Co.; Cox Creek; 2 mi. E Point Comfort; (In); Alcoa Aluminum; (Also called Raw Water Lake and Recycle Lake)	541	5,034
CROOK, L.: (1923) Lamar Co.; Pine Cr.; 5 Mi. N. Paris; (M); City of Paris	1,051	9,195
CYPRESS SPRINGS, L.: (1970) Franklin Co.; Big Cypress Cr.; 8 mi. SE Mount Vernon; (In-M); Franklin Co. Water Development and Texas Water Development Board (formerly Franklin Co. L.); (Imp. by Franklin Co. Dam)	3,252	66,756
DANIEL, L.: (1948) Stephens Co.; Gunsolus Cr.; 7 mi. S Breckenridge; (M-In.); City of Breckenridge; (Imp. by Gunsolus Creek Dam)	924	9,515
DAVIS, L.: Knox Co.; Double Dutchman Cr.; 5 mi. SE Benjamin; (Ir); League Ranch	585	5,454
DELTA LAKE RES. UNITS 1 AND 2: (1939) Hidalgo Co.; Rio Grande (off channel); 4 mi. N. Monte Alto; (Ir.); Hidalgo-Willacy counties WC&ID No. 1 (formerly Monte Alto Reservoir)	2,371	14,000
DIVERSION, L.: (1924) Archer-Baylor counties; Wichita R.; 14 mi. W Holliday; (M-In.); City of Wichita Falls and Wichita Co. WID No. 2	3,397	35,324
DUNLAP, L.: (1928) Guadalupe Co.; Guadalupe R.; 9 mi. NW Seguin; (P); Guadalupe-Blanco R. Auth.; (Imp. by TP-1 Dam)	410	5,900
EAGLE L.: (1900) Colorado Co.; Colorado R. (off channel); in Eagle Lake; (Ir.); Lakeside Irrigation Co.	1,200	9,600
EAGLE MOUNTAIN L.: (1934) Tarrant-Wise counties; West Fork Trinity R.; 14 mi. NW Fort Worth; (M-In.-Ir.); Tarrant Regional Water District	8,666	179,880
EAGLE NEST L.: (1951) Brazoria Co.; off-channel Brazos R.; 12 mi. WNW Angleton; (Ir.); T.M. Smith, et al. (also called Manor Lake)	N/A	18,000
EASTMAN LAKES: 8 lakes; Harrison Co.; Sabine R. basin; NW of Longview; Texas Eastman Co.	N/A	8,135

Abbreviations used in this table: L., lake; R., river; Co., county; Cr., creek; (C) conservation; (FC) flood control; (R) recreation; (P) power; (M) municipal; (D) domestic; (Ir.) irrigation; (In.) industry; (Mi.) mining, including oil production; (FH) fish hatchery; USAE, United States Army Corps of Engineers; WC&ID, Water Control and Improvement District; WID, Water Improvement District; USBR, United States Bureau of Reclamation; Auth., Authority; LCRA, Lower Colorado River Authority; TPWD, Texas Parks & Wildlife Dept.; USDA, United States Department of Agriculture; Imp., impounded.

Lakes and Reservoirs, Date of Origin	Surface Area (acres)	Storage Capacity (acre-ft.)
ELECTRA, L.: (1950) Wilbarger Co.; Camp Cr. and Beaver Cr.; 7 mi. SW Electra; (In.-M); City of Electra	731	5,626
ELLISON CREEK RESERVOIR: (1943) Morris Co.; Ellison Cr.; 8 mi. S. Daingerfield; (P-In.); Lone Star Steel	1,516	24,700
E. V. SPENCE RESERVOIR: (1969) Coke Co.; Colorado R.; 2 mi. W. Robert Lee; (M-In.-Mi); Colorado R. Municipal Water District; (Imp. by Robert Lee Dam)	6,372	517,272
FAIRFIELD L.: (1970) Freestone Co.; Big Brown Cr.; 11 mi. NE Fairfield; (In.); TXU; (formerly Big Brown Creek Reservoir)	2,159	44,169
FALCON INTERNATIONAL RESERVOIR: (1954) Starr-Zapata counties; Rio Grande; (International U.S.-Mexico); 3 mi. W Falcon Heights; (M-In.-Ir.-FC-P-R); International Boundary and Water Commission; (Texas' share of total conservation capacity is 58.6 percent)	85,195	2,646,765
FAYETTE COUNTY RESERVOIR: (1978) Fayette Co.; Cedar Cr.; 8.5 mi. E. La Grange; (P-R); LCRA (also called Cedar Creek Reservoir)	2,400	71,400
FOREST GROVE RESERVOIR: (1982) Henderson Co.; Caney Cr.; 7 mi. NW Athens; (In.); TXU, Agent	1,502	20,038
FORT PHANTOM HILL, L.: (1938) Jones Co.; Elm Cr.; 5 mi. S. Nugent; (M-R); City of Abilene	4,213	70,030
GEORGETOWN, L.: (1980) Williamson Co.; N. Fk. San Gabriel R.; 3.5 mi. W Georgetown; (FC-M-In.); USAE	1,287	36,823
GIBBONS CREEK RESERVOIR: (1981) Grimes Co.; Gibbons Cr.; 9.5 mi NW Anderson; (In.); Texas Municipal Power Agency	2,576	27,603
GILMER RESERVOIR: (2001) Upshur Co.; Kelsey Creek; 15 mi. N of Longview; 4 mi. W of Gilmer; (M); City of Gilmer	895	12,720
GLADEWATER, L.: (1952) Upshur Co.; Glade Cr.; in Gladewater; (M-R); City of Gladewater	481	4,637
GONZALES, L.: (1931) Gonzales Co.; Guadalupe R.; 4.5 mi. SE Belmont; (P); Guadalupe-Blanco R. Auth.(also called H-4 Reservoir)	696	6,500
GRAHAM, L.: (1929) Young Co.; Flint and Salt creeks; 2 mi. NW Graham; (M-In.); City of Graham	2,436	45,288
GRANBURY, L.: (1969) Hood Co.; Brazos R.; 8 mi. SE Granbury; (M-In.-Ir.-P); Brazos River Authority (Imp. by DeCordova Bend Dam)	8,139	132,949
GRANGER L.: (1980) Williamson Co.; San Gabriel R.; 10 mi. NE Taylor; (FC-M-In.); USAE (formerly Laneport L.)	4,159	51,822
GRAPEVINE L.: (1952) Tarrant-Denton counties; Denton Cr.; 2 mi. NE Grapevine; (M-FC-In.-R.); USAE	6,978	164,703
GREENBELT L.: (1967) Donley Co.; Salt Fork of Red R.; 5 mi. N Clarendon; (M-In.); Greenbelt Municipal and Industrial Water Auth.	668	59,968
GREENVILLE CITY LAKES: 6 lakes; Hunt Co.; Cowleech Fork, Sabine R.; 2 mi. Greenville; (M-Other); City of Greenville	N/A	6,864
HALBERT, L.: (1921) Navarro Co.; Elm Cr.; 4 mi. SE Corsicana; (M-In-R); City of Corsicana	549	6,033
HAWKINS, L.: (1962) Wood Co.; Little Sandy Cr.; 3 mi. NW Hawkins; (FC-R); Wood County; (Imp. by Wood Co. Dam No. 3)	776	11,690
HOLBROOK, L.: (1962) Wood Co.; Keys Cr.; 4 mi. NW Mineola; (FC-R); Wood County; (Imp. by Wood Co. Dam No. 2)	653	7,790
HORDS CREEK L.: (1948) Coleman Co.; Hords Cr.; 5 mi. NW Valera; (M-FC); City of Coleman and USAE	364	8,443
HOUSTON, L.: (1954) Harris Co.; San Jacinto R.; 4 mi. N Sheldon; (M-In.-Ir.-Mi.-R); City of Houston	10,023	120,686
HOUSTON COUNTY L.: (1966) Houston Co.; Little Elkhart Cr.; 10 mi. NW Crockett; (M-In.); Houston Co. WC&ID No. 1	1,330	17,113
HUBBARD CREEK RESERVOIR: (1962) Stephens Co.; 6 mi. NW Breckenridge; (M-In.-Mi.); West Central Texas Municipal Water Authority	15,687	313,174
HUBERT H. MOSS L.: (1960) Cooke Co.; Fish Cr.; 10 mi. NW Gainesville; (M-In.); City of Gainesville	1,121	24,058
IMPERIAL RESERVOIR: (1912) Reeves-Pecos counties; Pecos R.; 35 mi. N Fort Stockton; (Ir.); Pecos County WC&ID No. 2	1,530	6,000
INKS L.: (1938) Burnet-Llano counties; Colorado R.; 12 mi. W Burnet; (M-Ir.-Mi.-P); LCRA	757	13,962
JACKSONVILLE, L.: (1959) Cherokee Co.; Gum Cr.; 5 mi. SW Jacksonville; (M-R); City of Jacksonville; (Imp. by Buckner Dam)	1,164	25,670
J. B. THOMAS, L.: (1952) Scurry-Borden counties; Colorado R.; 16 mi. SW Snyder; (M- In.-R); Colorado River Municipal Water District; (Imp. by Colorado R. Dam)	4,060	199,931
J. D. MURPHREE WILDLIFE MANAGEMENT AREA IMPOUNDMENTS: Jefferson Co.; off-channel reservoirs between Big Hill and Taylor bayous; at Port Acres; (FH-R); TPWD (formerly Big Hill Reservoir)	6,881	32,000
JOE POOL L.: (1986) Dallas-Tarrant-Ellis counties; Mountain Cr.; 14 mi. SW Dallas; (FC-M-R); USAE–Trinity River Auth. (formerly Lakeview Lake)	7,470	175,358
JOHNSON CREEK RESERVOIR: (1961) Marion Co.; 13 mi. NW Jefferson; (In.); AEP-Southwestern Electric Power Co.	650	10,100
KEMP, L.: (1923) Baylor Co.; Wichita R.; 6 mi. N Mabelle; (M-P-Ir.); City of Wichita Falls; Wichita Co. WID 2	15,357	245,307
KICKAPOO, L.: (1945) Archer Co.; N. Fk. Little Wichita R.; 10 mi. NW Archer City; (M); City of Wichita Falls	5,861	86,345
KIOWA, L.: (1967) Cooke Co.; Indian Cr.; 8 mi. SE Gainesville; (R); Lake Kiowa, Inc.	560	7,000
KIRBY, L.: (1928) Taylor Co.; Cedar Cr.; 5 mi. S. Abilene; (M); City of Abilene	740	7,620
KURTH, L.: (1950) Angelina Co.; off-channel reservoir; 8 mi. N Lufkin; (In.); Abitibi Consolidated Industries	726	14,769

Abbreviations used in this table: L., lake; R., river; Co., county; Cr., creek; (C) conservation; (FC) flood control; (R) recreation; (P) power; (M) municipal; (D) domestic; (Ir.) irrigation; (In.) industry; (Mi.) mining, including oil production; (FH) fish hatchery; USAE, United States Army Corps of Engineers; WC&ID, Water Control and Improvement District; WID, Water Improvement District; USBR, United States Bureau of Reclamation; Auth., Authority; LCRA, Lower Colorado River Authority; TPWD, Texas Parks & Wildlife Dept.; USDA, United States Department of Agriculture; Imp., impounded.

Sailboats on White Rock Lake in Dallas. Photo by John McStravick (CC).

Lakes and Reservoirs, Date of Origin	Surface Area (acres)	Storage Capacity (acre-ft.)
LADY BIRD L.: (1960) Travis Co.; Colorado R.; within Austin city limits; (R); City of Austin (formerly Town Lake)	468	6,409
LAKE CREEK L.: (1952) McLennan Co.; Manos Cr.; 4 mi. SW Riesel; (In.); TXU	550	8,400
LAKE FORK RESERVOIR: (1980) Wood-Rains counties; Lake Fork Cr.; 5 mi. W Quitman; (M-In.); Sabine River Authority	26,889	605,061
LAKE O' THE PINES: (1959) Marion-Upshur-Morris counties; Cypress Cr.; 9 mi. W Jefferson; (FC-C-R-In.-M); USAE; (Imp. by Ferrell's Bridge Dam)	17,638	241,363
LAVON, L.: (1953) Collin Co.; East Fk. Trinity R.; 2 mi. W Lavon; (M-FC-In.); USAE	20,650	406,388
LEON, LAKE: (1954) Eastland Co.; Leon R.; 7 mi. S Ranger; (M-In.); Eastland Co. Water Supply District	1,738	27,762
LEWIS CREEK RESERVOIR: (1969) Montgomery Co.; Lewis Cr.; 10 mi. NW Conroe; (In.); Entergy	1,010	16,400
LEWISVILLE L.: (1929, 1954) Denton Co.; Elm Fork of Trinity R.; 2 mi. NE Lewisville; (M-FC-In.-R); USAE; (also called Lake Dallas and Garza-Little Elm)	27,175	563,228
LIMESTONE, L.: (1978) Leon-Limestone-Robertson counties; Navasota R.; 7 mi. NW Marquez; (M-In.-Ir.); Brazos River Authority	12,486	203,780
LIVINGSTON, L.: (1969) Polk-San Jacinto-Trinity-Walker counties; Trinity R.; 6 mi. SW Livingston; (M-In.-Ir.); City of Houston and Trinity River Authority	83,730	1,785,348
LOMA ALTA LAKE: (1963) Cameron Co.; off-channel Rio Grande; 8 mi. NE Brownsville; (M-In.); Brownsville Navigation District	2,490	26,500
LOST CREEK RESERVOIR: (1990) Jack Co.; Lost Cr.; 4 mi. NE Jacksboro; (M); City of Jacksboro	413	11,950
LYNDON B. JOHNSON, L.: (1951) Burnet-Llano counties; Colorado R.; 5 mi. SW Marble Falls; (P); LCRA; (Imp. by Alvin Wirtz Dam); (formerly Granite Shoals L.)	6,110	115,249
MACKENZIE RESERVOIR: (1974) Briscoe Co.; Tule Cr.; 9 mi. NW Silverton; (M); Mackenzie Mun. Water Auth.	253	46,450
MARBLE FALLS, L.: (1951) Burnet Co.; Colorado R.; 1.25 mi. SE Marble Falls; (P); LCRA; (Imp. by Max Starcke Dam)	347	6,901
MARTIN CREEK L.: (1974) Rusk-Panola counties; Martin Cr.; 17 mi. NE Henderson; (P); TXU.	4,954	75,726
MEDINA L.: (1913) Medina-Bandera counties; Medina R.; 8 mi. W Rio Medina; (Ir.); Bexar-Medina-Atascosa Co. WID No. 1	6,059	254,823
MEREDITH, L.: (1965) Moore-Potter-Hutchinson counties; Canadian R.; 10 mi. NW Borger; (M-In.-FC-R); cooperative project for municipal water supply by Amarillo, Lubbock and other High Plains cities. Canadian R. Municipal Water Authority–USBR; (Imp. by Sanford Dam); Governed by the Canadian R. Compact (1950), Lake Meredith can only hold 500,000 acre-ft. before it must release water to flow to Oklahoma.	7,097	500,000
MILLERS CREEK RESERVOIR: (1990) Baylor-Throckmorton counties.; Millers Cr.; 9 mi. SE Goree; (M); North Central Texas Municipal Water Auth. and Texas Water Development Board	2,212	26,768
MINERAL WELLS, L.: (1920) Parker Co.; Rock Cr.; 4 mi. E Mineral Wells; (M); Palo Pinto Co. Municipal Water District No. 1	473	5,273
MITCHELL COUNTY RESERVOIR: (1993) Mitchell Co.; branch of Beals Creek; (Mi.-In.); Colorado River Municipal Water District	1,463	27,266
Abbreviations used in this table: L., lake; R., river; Co., county; Cr., creek; (C) conservation; (FC) flood control; (R) recreation; (P) power; (M) municipal; (D) domestic; (Ir.) irrigation; (In.) industry; (Mi.) mining, including oil production; (FH) fish hatchery; USAE, United States Army Corps of Engineers; WC&ID, Water Control and Improvement District; WID, Water Improvement District; USBR, United States Bureau of Reclamation; Auth., Authority; LCRA, Lower Colorado River Authority; TPWD, Texas Parks & Wildlife Dept.; USDA, United States Department of Agriculture; Imp., impounded.		

Lakes and Reservoirs, Date of Origin	Surface Area (acres)	Storage Capacity (acre-ft.)
MONTICELLO RESERVOIR: (1972) Titus Co.; Blundell Cr.; 2.5 mi. E. Monticello; (In.); TXU	1,795	34,740
MOUNTAIN CREEK L.: (1937) Dallas Co.; Mountain Cr.; 4 mi. SE Grand Prairie; (In.); TXU.	2,710	22,840
MURVAUL, L.: (1958) Panola Co.; Murvaul Bayou; 10 mi. W Carthage; (M-In.-R) Panola Co. Fresh Water Supply District No. 1	3,507	38,285
MUSTANG LAKE EAST/WEST: Brazoria Co.; Mustang Bayou; 6 mi. S Alvin; (Ir.-In.-R); Chocolate Bayou Land & Water Co.	N/A	6,451
NACOGDOCHES, L.: (1976) Nacogdoches Co.; Bayou Loco Cr.; 10 mi. W Nacogdoches; (M); City of Nacogdoches	2,180	39,522
NACONICHE, L.: (2009) Nacogdoches Co.; Naconishe Cr. and Telesco Cr.; 14 mi. NE Nacogdoches; (R); Nacogdoches Co.	692	15,031
NASWORTHY, L.: (1930) Tom Green Co.; S Concho R.; 6 mi. SW San Angelo; (M-In.-Ir); City of San Angelo	1,249	9,615
NATURAL DAM L.: (1957, 1989) Howard Co.; Sulphur Springs Draw; 8 mi. W Big Spring; An original natural lake, whose surface and capacity were increased by construction of dams; (FC); Wilkinson Ranch & Colorado River Municipal Water District. Natural Dam Lake only has water during times of flood and is dry most of the year	2,272	54,560
NAVARRO MILLS L.: (1963) Navarro-Hill counties; Richland Cr.; 16 mi. SW Corsicana; (M-FC); USAE	4,736	49,827
NOCONA, L.: (1960) Montague Co.; 8 mi. NE Nocona; (M-In.-Mi.); North Montague County Water Supply District (also known as Farmers Creek Reservoir)	1,362	21,444
NORTH FORK BUFFALO CREEK RESERVOIR: (1964) Wichita Co.; 5 mi. NW Iowa Park; (M); Wichita Co. WC&ID No.3	1,489	15,400
NORTH L.: (1957) Dallas Co.; S. Fork Grapevine Cr.; 2 mi. SE Coppell; (In.); TXU	800	9,400
OAK CREEK RESERVOIR: (1952) Coke Co.; 5 mi. SE Blackwell; (M-In.); City of Sweetwater	2,389	39,210
O. C. FISHER L.: (1952) Tom Green Co.; N Concho R.; 3 mi. NW San Angelo; (M-FC-C- Ir.-R-In.-Mi.); USAE; Upper Colorado River Auth. (formerly San Angelo L.)	1,265	119,445
O. H. IVIE RESERVOIR: (1990) Coleman-Concho-Runnels counties; 24 mi. SE Ballinger; (M-In.), Colorado R. Municipal Water District (formerly Stacy Reservoir)	19,149	554,340
OLNEY, L./COOPER: (1935) Archer Co.; Mesquite Crk; 8 mi. E Megargel; (M-R); City of Olney; (see L. Cooper)	432	4,546
PALESTINE, L.: (1962) Anderson-Cherokee-Henderson-Smith counties; Neches R.; 4 mi. E Frankston; (M-In.-R); Upper Neches R. Municipal Water Auth.; (Imp. by Blackburn Crossing Dam)	23,112	367,303
PALO DURO RESERVOIR: (1991) Hansford Co.; Palo Duro Cr.; 12 mi. N Spearman; (M-R); Palo Duro River Auth.	2,407	61,066
PALO PINTO, L.: (1964) Palo Pinto Co.; 15 mi. SW Mineral Wells; (M-In.); Palo Pinto Co. Municipal Water District 1	2,173	26,766
PAT CLEBURNE, L.: (1964) Johnson Co.; Nolan R.; 4 mi. S. Cleburne; (M-FC-In.-Ir.); City of Cleburne	1,568	26,008
PAT MAYSE L.: (1967) Lamar Co.; Sanders Cr.; 2 mi. SW Arthur City; (M-In.-FC); USAE	5,638	113,683
PINKSTON RESERVOIR: (1976) Shelby Co.; Sandy Cr.; 12.5 mi. SW Center; (M); City of Center; (formerly Sandy Creek Reservoir)	523	7,380
POSSUM KINGDOM L.: (1941) Palo Pinto-Young-Stephens-Jack counties; Brazos R.; 11 mi. SW Graford; (M-In.-Ir.-Mi.-P-R); Brazos R. Auth.; (Imp. by Morris Sheppard Dam)	17,970	538,139
PROCTOR L.: (1963) Comanche Co.; Leon R.; 9 mi. NE Comanche; (M-In.-Ir.-FC); USAE–Brazos River Auth.	4,715	54,762
QUITMAN, L.: (1962) Wood Co.; Dry Cr.; 4 mi. N Quitman; (FC-R); Wood County; (Imp. by Wood Co. Dam No.1)	814	7,440
RANDELL L.: (1909) Grayson Co.; Shawnee Cr.; 4 mi. NW Denison; (M); City of Denison	311	5,900
RAY HUBBARD, L.: (1968) Collin-Dallas-Kaufman-Rockwall counties; (formerly Forney Reservoir); E. Fork of Trinity R.; 15 mi. E Dallas; (M); City of Dallas	20,739	439,559
RAY ROBERTS, L.: (1987) Denton-Cooke-Grayson counties; Elm Fk. Trinity R.; 11 mi. NE Denton; (FC-M-D); City of Denton, Dallas, USAE; (also known as Aubrey Reservoir)	28,612	788,167
RED BLUFF RESERVOIR: (1937) Loving-Reeves counties, Texas; and Eddy Co.; N.M.; Pecos R.; 5 mi. N Orla; (Ir.-P); Red Bluff Water Power Control District	7,495	151,110
RED DRAW RESERVOIR: (1985) Howard Co.; Red Draw; 5 mi. E Bi Spring; (Mi.-In.); Colorado River Municipal Water District	374	8,538
RICHLAND-CHAMBERS RESERVOIR: (1987) Freestone-Navarro counties; Richland Cr.; 20 mi. SE Corsicana; (M); Tarrant Regional Water District.	43,384	1,087,839
RITA BLANCA, L.: (1940) Hartley Co.; Rita Blanca Cr.; 2 mi. S Dalhart; (R) City of Dalhart	524	12,050
RIVER CREST L.: (1953) Red River Co.; off-channel reservoir; 7 mi. SE Bogata; (In.); TXU	555	7,000
SAM RAYBURN RESERVOIR: (1965) Jasper-Angelina-Sabine-Nacogdoches-San Augustine counties; Angelina R.; (FC-P-M-In.-Ir.-R); USAE; (formerly McGee Bend Reservoir)	112,590	2,857,077
SAN BERNARD RESERVOIRS #1, #2, #3: Brazoria Co.; Off-Channel San Bernard R.; 3 mi. N Sweeney; (In.); ConocoPhillips	N/A	8,610
SANTA ROSA L.: (1929) Wilbarger Co.; Beaver Cr.; 15 mi. S Vernon; (Mi.); W. T. Waggoner Estate	1,500	11,570
SHELDON RESERVOIR: (1943) Harris Co.; Carpenters Bayou; 2 mi. SW Sheldon; (R-FH); TPWD	1,244	4,224
SMITHERS L.: (1957) Fort Bend Co.; Dry Creek; 10 mi. SE Richmond; (In.); Texas Genco	2,480	18,700
SOMERVILLE L.: (1967) Burleson-Washington-Lee counties; Yegua Cr.; 2 mi. S Somerville; (M-In.-Ir.-FC); USAE–Brazos River Authority	10,928	147,104

Abbreviations used in this table: L., lake; R., river; Co., county; Cr., creek; (C) conservation; (FC) flood control; (R) recreation; (P) power; (M) municipal; (D) domestic; (Ir.) irrigation; (In.) industry; (Mi.) mining, including oil production; (FH) fish hatchery; USAE, United States Army Corps of Engineers; WC&ID, Water Control and Improvement District; WID, Water Improvement District; USBR, United States Bureau of Reclamation; Auth., Authority; LCRA, Lower Colorado River Authority; TPWD, Texas Parks & Wildlife Dept.; USDA, United States Department of Agriculture; Imp., impounded.

Lakes and Reservoirs, Date of Origin	Surface Area (acres)	Storage Capacity (acre-ft.)
SOUTH TEXAS PROJECT RESERVOIR: (1983) Matagorda Co.; off-channel Colorado R.; 16 mi. S Bay City; (In.); STP Nuclear Operating Co.	7,000	202,600
SQUAW CREEK RESERVOIR: (1983) Somervell-Hood counties; Squaw Cr.; 4.5 mi. N Glen Rose; (In.); TXU	3,163	151,250
STAMFORD, L.: (1953) Haskell Co.; Paint Cr.; 10 mi. SE Haskell; (M-In.); City of Stamford	5,316	51,570
STILLHOUSE HOLLOW L.: (1968) Bell Co.; Lampasas R.; 5 mi. SW Belton; (M-In.-Ir.-FC); USAE– Brazos River Authority; (also called Lampasas Reservoir)	6,484	227,825
STRIKER CREEK RESERVOIR: (1957) Rusk-Cherokee counties; Striker Cr.; 18 mi. SW Henderson; (M-In.); Angelina-Nacogdoches WC&ID No. 1	1,920	16,934
SULPHUR SPRINGS, L.: (1950) Hopkins Co.; White Oak Cr.; 2 mi. N Sulphur Springs; (M) Sulphur Springs Water District; (formerly called White Oak Creek Reservoir)	1,340	17,747
SULPHUR SPRINGS DRAW RESERVOIR: (1992) Martin Co.; Sulphur Springs Draw; 12 mi. NE Stanton; (FC); Colorado River Municipal Water District	970	7,997
SWEETWATER, L.: (1930) Nolan Co.; Bitter Creek; 6 mi. SE Sweetwater (M-R); City of Sweetwater	652	12,267
TAWAKONI, L.: (1960) Rains-Van Zandt-Hunt counties; Sabine R.; 9 mi. NE Wills Point; (M-In.-Ir-R); Sabine River Authority; (Imp. by Iron Bridge Dam)	37,325	871,695
TERRELL CITY L.: (1955) Kaufman Co.; Muddy Cedar Cr.; 6 mi. E Terrell; (M-R); City of Terrell	849	8,594
TEXANA, L.: (1980) Jackson Co.; Navidad R. and Sandy Cr.; 6.8 mi. SE Edna; (M-Ir); USBR, Lavaca-Navidad R. Auth., Texas Water Dev. Bd.; (formerly Palmetto Bend Reservoir)	9,154	159,566
TEXOMA, L.: (1943) Grayson-Cooke counties, Texas; Bryan-Marshall-Love counties, Okla.; (Imp. by Denison Dam) on Red R. below confluence of Red and Washita rivers; (P-FC-C-R); USAE; Texas and Oklahoma each have the right to 50 percent of capacity	71,975	2,516,226
TOLEDO BEND RESERVOIR: (1967) Newton-Panola-Sabine-Shelby counties; Sabine R.; 14 mi. NE Burkeville; (M-In.-Ir.-PR); Sabine River Authority; Texas and Louisiana each have rights to 50 percent capacity	178,553	4,472,900
TRADINGHOUSE CREEK RESERVOIR: (1968) McLennan Co.; Tradinghouse Cr.; 9 mi. E Waco; (In.); TXU	2,010	35,124
TRAVIS, L.: (1942) Travis-Burnet counties; Colorado R.; 13 mi. NW Austin; (M-In.-Ir.- Mi.-P-FC-R); LCRA; (Imp. by Mansfield Dam)	19,533	1,113,348
TRINIDAD L.: (1923) Henderson Co.; off-channel reservoir Trinity R.; 2 mi. S. Trinidad; (P); TXU	690	6,200
TRUSCOTT BRINE L.: (1987) Knox Co.; Bluff Cr.; 26 mi. NNW Knox City; (Chlorine Control); Red River Auth.	3,146	111,147
TWIN BUTTES RESERVOIR: (1963) Tom Green Co.; Concho R.; 8 mi. SW San Angelo; (M-In. -FC-Ir.-R.); City of San Angelo, USBR, Tom Green Co. WC&ID No. 1	6,320	182,454
TWIN OAKS RESERVOIR: (1982) Robertson Co.; Duck Cr.; 12 mi. N. Franklin; (In) TXU	2,330	30,319
TYLER, L. /LAKE TYLER EAST: (1949/1967) Smith Co.; Prairie and Mud creeks.; 12 mi. SE Tyler; (M-In); City of Tyler; (Imp. by Whitehouse and Mud Creek dams)	4,714	72,073
UPPER NUECES L.: (1926, 1948) Zavala Co.; Nueces R.; 6 mi. N Crystal City; (Ir.); Zavala-Dimmit Co. WID No. 1	316	5,200
VALLEY ACRES RESERVOIR: (1956) Hidalgo Co.; off-channel Rio Grande; 7 mi. N Mercedes; (Ir-M-FC); Valley Acres Water District.	325	1,950
VALLEY L.: (1961) Fannin-Grayson counties; 2.5 mi. N Savoy; (P); TXU; (formerly Brushy Creek Reservoir)	1,080	16,400
VICTOR BRAUNIG LAKE: (1962) Bexar Co.; Arroyo Seco; 15 mi. SE San Antonio; (In.-R); CPS Energy of San Antonio	1,350	26,500
WACO, L.: (1929) McLennan Co.; Bosque R.; 2 mi. W Waco; (M-FC-C-R); City of Waco, USAE, Brazos River Authority	8,161	189,418
WALTER E. LONG, L.: (1967) Travis Co.; Decker Cr.; 9 mi. E Austin; (M-In.-R); City of Austin; (formerly Decker Lake)	1,269	33,940
WAXAHACHIE, L.: (1956) Ellis Co.; S Prong Waxahachie Cr.; 4 mi. SE Waxahachie; (M-In) Ellis County WC&ID No. 1; (Imp. by S. Prong Dam)	656	10,780
WEATHERFORD, L.: (1956) Parker Co.; Clear Fork Trinity River; 7 mi. E Weatherford; (M-In.); City of Weatherford	1,083	17,812
WELSH RESERVOIR: (1976) Titus Co.; Swauano Cr.; 11 mi. SE Mount Pleasant; (R-In.); AEP-Southwestern Electric Power Co.; (formerly Swauano Creek Reservoir)	1,269	18,431
WHITE RIVER L.: (1963) Crosby Co.; 16 mi. SE Crosbyton; (M-In.-Mi.); White River Municipal Water District	653	29,880
WHITE ROCK L.: (1911) Dallas Co.; White Rock Cr.; within NE Dallas city limits; (R); City of Dallas	1,088	9,004
WHITNEY, L.: (1951) Hill-Bosque-Johnson counties; Brazos R.; 5.5 mi. SW Whitney; (FC-P); USAE	21,442	553,344
WICHITA, L.: (1901) Wichita Co.; Holliday Cr.; 6 mi. SW Wichita Falls; (M-P-R); City of Wichita Falls	2,200	14,000
WILLIAM HARRIS RESERVOIR: (1947) Brazoria Co.; off-channel between Brazos R. and Oyster Cr.; 8 mi. NW Angleton; (In.); Dow Chemical Co.	1,663	9,200
WINNSBORO, L.: (1962) Wood Co.; Big Sandy Cr.; 6 mi. SW Winnsboro; (FC-R); Wood County; (Imp. by Wood Co. Dam No. 4)	806	8,100
WINTERS, L.: (1983) Runnels Co.; Elm Cr.; 4.5 mi. E Winters; (M); City of Winters (also known as Elm Creek Lake and New Lake Winters)	638	7,779
WORTH, L.: (1914) Tarrant Co.; West Fork of Trinity R.; in NW Fort Worth; (M); City of Fort Worth	3,377	33,495
WRIGHT PATMAN L.: (1957) Bowie-Cass-Morris-Titus-Red River counties; Sulphur R.; 8 mi. SW Texarkana; (FC-M); USAE; (formerly Lake Texarkana)	18,247	97,927
Abbreviations used in this table: L., lake; R., river; Co., county; Cr., creek; (C) conservation; (FC) flood control; (R) recreation; (P) power; (M) municipal; (D) domestic; (Ir.) irrigation; (In.) industry; (Mi.) mining, including oil production; (FH) fish hatchery; USAE, United States Army Corps of Engineers; WC&ID, Water Control and Improvement District; WID, Water Improvement District; USBR, United States Bureau of Reclamation; Auth., Authority; LCRA, Lower Colorado River Authority; TPWD, Texas Parks & Wildlife Dept.; USDA, United States Department of Agriculture; Imp., impounded.		

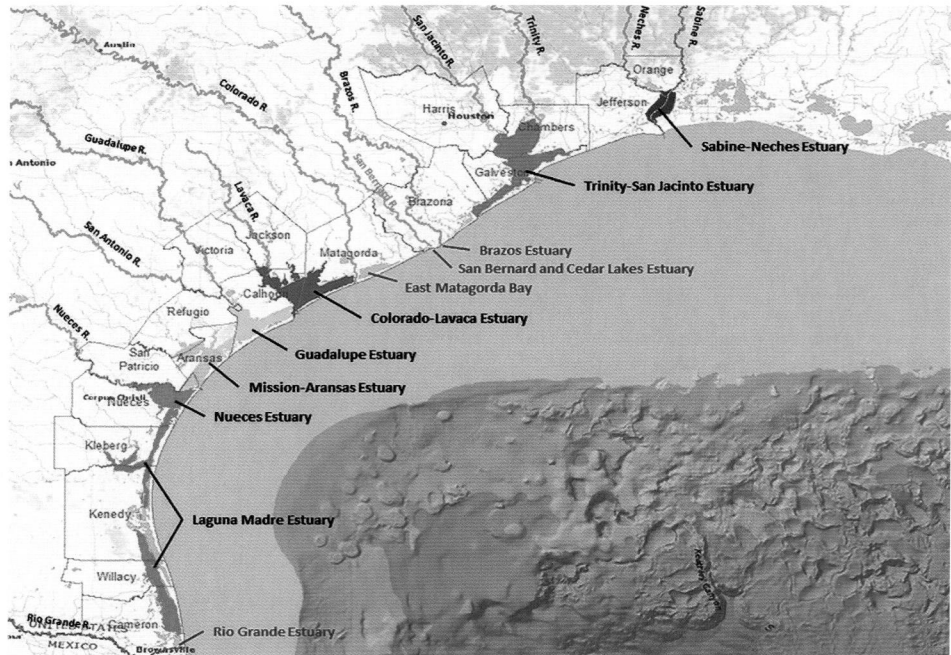

Map courtesy of the Texas Water Development Board.

Estuaries and Bays on the Texas Coast

Source: Texas Water Development Board; www.twdb.texas.gov

Texas has 367 miles of coastline along which 11 major river basins and eight coastal basins terminate, bringing fresh water from rivers, streams, and surface runoff to the coast to mix with the Gulf of Mexico seawater. These unique zones, known as estuaries, are a significant feature of the Texas coast.

Texas has seven major estuaries, which are formed by a complex of individual bays separated from the Gulf by barrier islands, and five minor, riverine estuaries, which occur near the mouths of major rivers that flow directly into the Gulf.

Texas estuaries range from the nearly fresh-water Sabine-Neches, which borders Louisiana, to the frequently hypersaline Laguna Madre along the southern coast.

Most Texas bays are shallow, ranging in average depth from two feet to ten feet.

Although each estuary differs in size and hydrological and ecological characteristics, together they support a diverse array of species that serve as the raw materials for a variety of economic activities associated with commercial and recreational fishing, hunting, and birding.

In addition, estuaries provide many other ecological services, such as:

• Water filtration and nutrient regulation through nutrient cycling

• Storm surge protection

• Shoreline stabilization through trapping sediments that support the growth of wetlands

The major estuaries, in order from east to west, include:

Sabine-Neches Estuary (Sabine Lake)

The Sabine-Neches Estuary, commonly known as Sabine Lake, is located along the Texas-Louisiana border and is the smallest of Texas' seven major estuaries with an area of 45,320 acres.

This estuary receives around 14 million acre-feet of fresh water inflow per year from the Sabine and Neches rivers and surrounding coastal watersheds, making it the freshest estuary along the Texas coast. Average bay salinity is eight parts per thousand.

The Sabine-Neches Waterway and Gulf Intracoastal Waterway are important shipping channels in this system.

The estuary is connected to the Gulf by Sabine Pass and lies within Orange and Jefferson counties on the Texas side.

Trinity-San Jacinto Estuary (Galveston Bay)

The Trinity-San Jacinto Estuary, also known as Galveston Bay, is located on the upper Texas coast. It is the largest estuary in Texas, with an area of 345,280 acres, and is the seventh largest in the United States.

Key features include Trinity Bay, Galveston Bay, East Bay, West Bay, and connections with the Gulf at Bolivar Roads, San Luis Pass, and Rollover Pass.

The Houston Ship Channel and the Gulf Intracoastal Waterway are notable man-made features of the system.

This estuary receives on average 11 million acre-feet of fresh water inflow annually from the Trinity and San Jacinto rivers and surrounding coastal watersheds. It is bounded by Bolivar Peninsula and Galveston Island and lies within Chambers, Harris, Galveston, and Brazoria counties.

Colorado-Lavaca Estuary (Matagorda Bay System)

The Colorado-Lavaca Estuary, or Matagorda Bay system, is located along the mid-Texas coast and covers an area of 244,490 acres. The estuary is bounded by Matagorda Island and consists of Matagorda Bay, Lavaca Bay, and several smaller bays, including Carancahua Bay, Tres Palacios Bay, Keller Bay, Cox Bay, and Turtle Bay.

Other key features include Pass Cavallo, the Matagorda Ship Channel, and the Gulf Intracoastal Waterway.

The estuary averages 3.5 million acre-feet of fresh water inflow annually from the Colorado, Lavaca, and Tres Palacios rivers and surrounding coastal watersheds. It is bordered by Matagorda, Jackson, Victoria, and Calhoun counties.

Guadalupe Estuary

The Guadalupe Estuary is located on the mid-Texas coast and covers 148,703 acres. The estuary includes San Antonio Bay, Mission Lake, Hynes Bay, Espiritu Santo Bay, and Mesquite Bay.

This estuary is largely protected from the Gulf by Matagorda Island and typically does not have a direct connection to the Gulf except through Cedar Bayou.

The other closest connection with the Gulf is through Pass Cavallo to the northeast in the Colorado-Lavaca Estuary.

The Guadalupe Estuary typically receives an average of 2.5 million acre-feet of fresh water inflow per year from the Guadalupe and San Antonio rivers and from surrounding coastal watersheds. The estuary lies adjacent to Calhoun, Aransas, and Refugio counties.

Mission-Aransas Estuary

The Mission-Aransas Estuary, located in the Coastal Bend, covers 111,780 acres and consists of Aransas Bay, Copano Bay, and several smaller bays, including Saint Charles Bay, Mission Bay, and Redfish Bay.

The estuary has a direct connection to the Gulf through Aransas Pass but is largely protected by a barrier island, San Jose Island.

Typically, the estuary receives 490,000 acre-feet of freshwater inflow per year from the Aransas and Mission rivers and surrounding coastal basins. The estuary is bordered by Aransas, Refugio, and San Patricio counties.

Nueces Estuary

The Nueces Estuary, located in the Coastal Bend, consists of Nueces Bay, Corpus Christi Bay, and Oso Bay. It spans 106,990 acres and is separated from the Gulf by Mustang Island, except for a direct connection through Aransas Pass.

The Corpus Christi Ship Channel and the Gulf Intracoastal Waterway are notable man-made features of the system.

This estuary typically receives 587,000 acre-feet of fresh water inflow per year from the Nueces River, Oso Creek, and surrounding coastal watersheds. The estuary is bordered by San Patricio and Nueces counties.

Laguna Madre Estuary

The Laguna Madre Estuary is the southernmost major estuary in Texas and extends almost to the Texas-Mexico border.

The Laguna Madre is a unique hypersaline lagoon with an average salinity between 32 and 38 parts per thousand. It is the only hypersaline estuary in the nation and one of only a handful that exist worldwide.

The estuary spans 280,910 acres but is divided by a coastal land mass known as Saltillo Flats, though more commonly referred to as the Landcut, and separated from the Gulf by Padre Island.

The Upper Laguna Madre has one major bay, Baffin Bay, and is hydrologically connected to the Nueces Estuary on its northern end and to the Gulf via the Packery Channel.

San Fernando Creek is the principal source of freshwater inflow to this arid estuary, where freshwater inflows typically are 326,000 acre-feet per year.

The Lower Laguna Madre has one major bay, South Bay, and is connected to the Gulf via the Port Mansfield Channel and Brazos-Santiago Pass.

The Arroyo Colorado and surrounding coastal watersheds are principal sources of freshwater inflow to the Lower Laguna Madre, providing on average 425,000 acre-feet of inflows per year.

The estuary is bordered by Nueces, Kleberg, Kenedy, Willacy, and Cameron counties.

Minor Estuaries and Bays

Christmas Bay

Southwest of Galveston Bay, this system includes both Bastrop Bay and Drum Bay, and it is protected from the Gulf of Mexico by Follet's Island. It has two connections to the gulf, through Cold Pass and San Luis Pass.

It receives fresh water from runoff and through Bastrop Bayou.

Brazos River Estuary

The Brazos River Estuary, located on the upper Texas coast, is a riverine estuary that flows directly into the Gulf rather than into a system of bays. The estuarine portion of the river occurs near the mouth where tidal water from the Gulf mixes with river water.

A gray day on Burnet Bay, part of the Trinity-San Jacinto Estuary. Photo by Robert Plocheck.

Typically, this estuary receives 6.3 million acre-feet of fresh water inflow per year. It is located in Brazoria county.

San Bernard Estuary

The San Bernard Estuary is a minor estuary located along the mid-Texas coast, covering an area of 3,760 acres.

While the San Bernard River flows directly into the Gulf, creating a riverine estuary, neighboring Cowtrap Lake and Cedar Lake are small bays that connect with the Gulf through small tidal inlets.

On average, this estuary receives 683,753 acre-feet of fresh water inflow per year from the San Bernard River and surrounding coastal watersheds. It is located in Brazoria and Matagorda counties.

East Matagorda Bay

East Matagorda Bay is a small bay covering an area of 37,810 acres and is separated from the larger estuary by the Colorado River delta. There are no direct sources of river inflow into this bay, which receives an average of 536,165 acre-feet of fresh water per year from runoff of surrounding coastal watersheds.

Rio Grande Estuary

The Rio Grande Estuary forms a natural border between the United States and Mexico and is a riverine estuary, which flows directly into the Gulf with no associated bay system.

The estuarine portion of the river occurs where tides from the Gulf mix with fresh water from the river. Annual average inflow from the Rio Grande is 370,722 acre-feet per year. The estuary is bordered by Cameron County on the north, and Mexico on the south. ☆

Water Conservation Tips

- Check all faucets, pipes, and toilets for leaks.
- Install water-saving showerheads and ultra-low-flush toilets.
- Take shorter showers.
- Never use the toilet as a wastebasket.
- Turn off the water while brushing teeth or shaving.
- Wash full loads of clothes.
- Fully load the dishwasher.
- Rinse dishes and vegetables in a full sink or pot of water and not under running water.
- Defrost frozen food in the refrigerator and not under running water.
- Do not over-water landscaping.
- Water the lawn or garden early in the morning or late in evening.
- Adjust sprinklers so they do not water the sidewalk or street.
- Do not water on cool, rainy, or windy days.
- Equip all hoses with shut-off nozzles.
- Use drip irrigation systems.
- Plant drought-tolerant or low-water-use plants and grasses.
- Place mulch around plants to reduce evaporation and discourage weeds.
- Set mower blades one notch higher, because longer grass means less evaporation.
- Use a bucket instead of a hose to wash vehicles, boats, and trailers.
- Use a broom rather than a hose to clean sidewalks, driveways, loading docks, and parking lots.

Texas Plant Life

Source: This article was updated for the Texas Almanac by Stephan L. Hatch, Director, S.M. Tracy Herbarium and professor, Department of Ecosystem Science and Management, Texas A&M University

The types of plants found in Texas vary widely from one region to the next. This is due to the amount and frequency of rainfall, diversity of soils, and the number of frost-free days. From the forests of East Texas to the deserts of West Texas, from the grassy plains of North Texas to the semi-arid brushlands of South Texas, plant species change continuously.

More than 100 million acres of Texas are devoted to grazing, both for domestic and wild animals. This is the largest single use of land in the state. More than 80 percent of the acreage is devoted to range in the Edwards Plateau, Cross Timbers and Prairies, South Texas Plains, and Trans-Pecos Mountains and Basins.

Sideoats grama, which occurs on more different soils in Texas than any other native grass, was officially designated as the state grass of Texas by the Texas Legislature in 1971.

The 10 principal plant life areas of Texas, starting in the east, are:

1. Piney Woods

Most of this area of some 16 million acres ranges from about 50 to 700 feet above sea level and receives 40 to 56 inches of rain yearly. Many rivers, creeks, and bayous drain the region. Nearly all of Texas' commercial timber comes from this area. There are three native species of pine, the principal timber: longleaf, shortleaf, and loblolly. An introduced species, the slash pine, also is widely grown. Hardwoods include oaks, elm, hickory, magnolia, sweet and black gum, tupelo, and others.

The area is interspersed with native and improved grasslands. Cattle are the primary grazing animals. Deer and quail are abundant in properly managed habitats. Primary forage plants, under proper grazing management, include species of bluestems, rosettegrass, panicums, paspalums, blackseed needlegrass, Canada and Virginia wildryes, purpletop, broadleaf and spike woodoats, switchcane, lovegrasses, indiangrass, and numerous legume species.

Highly disturbed areas have understory and overstory of undesirable woody plants that suppress growth of pine and desirable grasses. The primary forage grasses have been reduced, and the grasslands have been invaded by threeawns, annual grasses, weeds, broomsedge bluestem, red lovegrass, and shrubby woody species.

2. Gulf Prairies and Marshes

The Gulf Prairies and Marshes cover approximately 10 million acres. There are two subunits: (a) the marsh and salt grasses immediately at tidewater, and (b) a little farther inland, a strip of bluestems and tall grasses, with some gramas in the western part. Many of these grasses make excellent grazing.

Oaks, elm, and other hardwoods grow to some extent, especially along streams, and the area has some post oak and brushy extensions along its borders.

Much of the Gulf Prairies is fertile farmland, and the area is well suited for cattle.

Principal grasses of the Gulf Prairies are tall bunchgrasses, including big bluestem, little bluestem, seacoast bluestem, indiangrass, eastern gamagrass, Texas wintergrass, switchgrass, and gulf cordgrass. Saltgrass occurs on moist saline sites.

Heavy grazing has changed the native vegetation in many cases so the predominant grasses are the less desirable broomsedge bluestem, smutgrass, threeawns, tumblegrass, and many other less desirable grasses. Other plants that have invaded the productive grasslands include oak underbrush, Macartney rose, huisache, mesquite, prickly pear, ragweed, bitter sneezeweed, broomweed, and others.

Vegetation of the Gulf Marshes consists primarily of sedges, bullrush, flat-sedges, beakrush and other rushes, smooth cordgrass, marshhay cordgrass, marshmillet, and maidencane. The marshes are grazed best during winter.

3. Post Oak Savannah

This secondary forest area, also called the Post Oak Belt, covers some 7 million acres. It is immediately west of the primary forest region, with less annual rainfall and a little higher elevation. Principal trees are post oak, blackjack oak, and elm. Pecans, walnuts, and other kinds of water-demanding trees grow along streams. The southwestern extension of this belt is often poorly defined, with large areas of prairie.

The upland soils are sandy and sandy loam, while the bottomlands are sandy loams and clays.

The original vegetation consisted mainly of little bluestem, big bluestem, indiangrass, switchgrass, purpletop, silver bluestem, Texas wintergrass, woodoats, narrowleaf, post oak, and blackjack oak. The area is still largely native or improved grasslands, with small farms located throughout. Intensive grazing has contributed to dense stands of a woody understory of yaupon, greenbriar, and oak brush.

Mesquite has become a serious problem. Good forage plants have been replaced by such plants as split-beard bluestem, red lovegrass, broomsedge bluestem, broomweed, bullnettle, and western ragweed.

4. Blackland Prairies

This area of about 12 million acres, while called a "prairie," has much timber along the streams, including a variety of oaks, pecan, elm, bois d'arc, and mesquite. In its native state, it was largely a grassy plain — the first native grassland in the westward extension of the Southern Forest Region.

Most of this fertile area has been cultivated, and only small acreages of grassland remain in original vegetation. In heavily grazed pastures, the tall bunchgrass has been replaced by buffalograss, Texas grama, and other less productive grasses. Mesquite, lotebush, and other woody plants have invaded the grasslands.

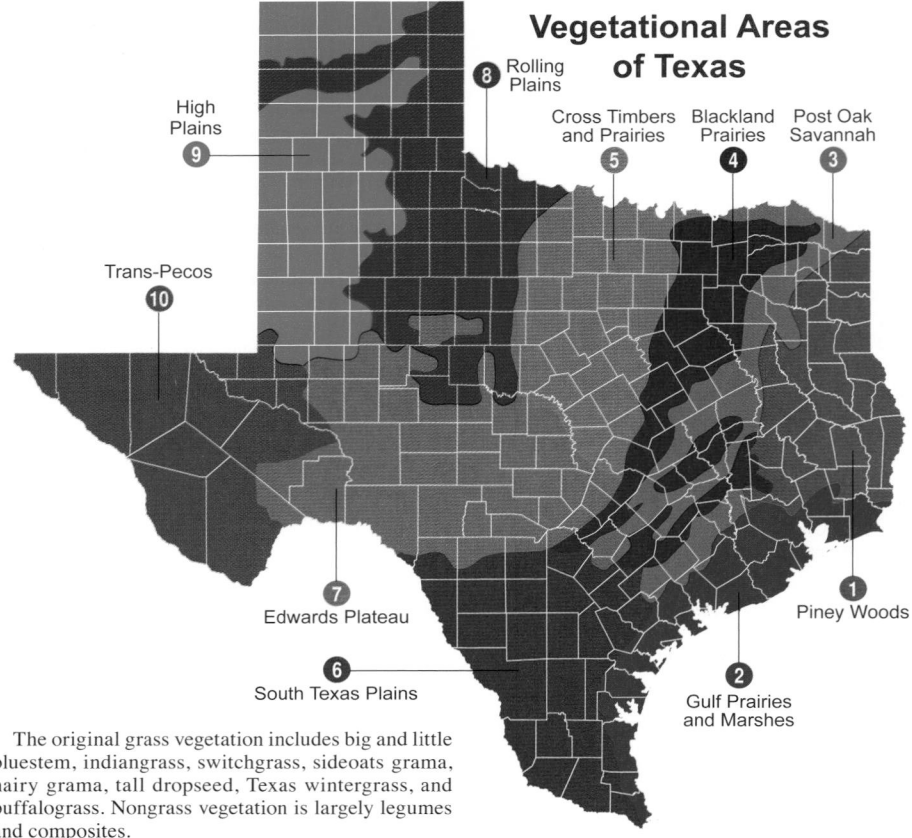

Vegetational Areas of Texas

- **8** Rolling Plains
- High Plains **9**
- Cross Timbers and Prairies **5**
- Blackland Prairies **4**
- Post Oak Savannah **3**
- Trans-Pecos **10**
- Edwards Plateau **7**
- **6** South Texas Plains
- **1** Piney Woods
- **2** Gulf Prairies and Marshes

The original grass vegetation includes big and little bluestem, indiangrass, switchgrass, sideoats grama, hairy grama, tall dropseed, Texas wintergrass, and buffalograss. Nongrass vegetation is largely legumes and composites.

5. Cross Timbers and Prairies

Approximately 15 million acres of alternating woodlands and prairies, often called the Western Cross Timbers, constitute this region. Sharp changes in the vegetational cover are associated with different soils and topography, but the grass composition is rather uniform.

The prairie grasses are big bluestem, little bluestem, indiangrass, switchgrass, Canada wildrye, sideoats grama, hairy grama, tall grama, tall dropseed, Texas wintergrass, blue grama, and buffalograss.

On Cross Timbers soils, the vegetation is composed of big bluestem, little bluestem, hooded windmillgrass, sand lovegrass, indiangrass, switchgrass, and many species of legumes. The woody vegetation includes shinnery, blackjack, post, and live oaks.

The entire area has been invaded heavily by woody brush plants of oaks, mesquite, juniper, and other unpalatable plants that furnish little forage for livestock.

6. South Texas Plains

South of San Antonio, between the coast and the Rio Grande, are some 21 million acres of subtropical dryland vegetation, consisting of small trees, shrubs, cactus, weeds, and grasses. The area is noteworthy for extensive brushlands and is known as the Brush Country, or the Spanish equivalents of chaparral or monte. Principal plants are mesquite, small live oak, post oak, prickly pear (Opuntia) cactus, catclaw, blackbrush, whitebrush, guajillo, huisache, cenizo, and others that often grow very densely.

The original vegetation was mainly perennial warm-season bunchgrasses in savannahs of post oak, live oak, and mesquite. Other brush species form dense thickets on the ridges and along streams. Long-continued grazing has contributed to the dense cover of brush. Most of the desirable grasses have only persisted under the protection of brush and cacti.

There are distinct differences in the original plant communities on various soils. Dominant grasses on the sandy loam soils are seacoast bluestem, bristle-grass, paspalum, windmillgrass, silver bluestem, big sandbur, and tanglehead. Dominant grasses on the clay and clay loams are silver bluestem, Arizona cottontop, buffalograss, common curly mesquite, bristlegrass, pappusgrass, gramas, plains lovegrass, Texas cupgrass, vine mesquite, other panicums, and Texas wintergrass.

Low saline areas are characterized by gulf cord-grass, saltgrass, alkali sacaton, and switchgrass. In

US 190 cuts through the hills of Crockett County. Photo by Robert Plocheck.

the post oak and live oak savannahs, the grasses are mainly seacoast bluestem, indiangrass, switchgrass, crinkleawn, paspalums, and panicums. Today much of the area has been reseeded to buffelgrass.

7. Edwards Plateau

These 25 million acres are rolling to mountainous, with woodlands in the eastern part and grassy prairies in the west. There is a good deal of brushy growth in the central and eastern areas. The combination of grasses, weeds, and small trees is ideal for cattle, sheep, goats, deer, and wild turkey.

This limestone-based area is characterized by the large number of springfed, perennially flowing streams that originate in its interior and flow across the Balcones Escarpment, which bounds it on the south and east. The soils are shallow, ranging from sands to clays, and are calcareous in reaction. This area is predominantly rangeland, with cultivation confined to the deeper soils.

In the east-central portion is the well-marked Central or Llano Basin, centering in Mason, Llano, and Burnet counties, with a mixture of granitic and sandy soils. The western portion of the area comprises the semi-arid Stockton Plateau.

Noteworthy is the growth of cypress along the perennially flowing streams. Separated by many miles from the cypress growth of the moist Southern Forest Belt, they constitute one of Texas' several "islands" of vegetation. These trees, which grow to stately proportions, were commercialized in the past.

The principal grasses of the clay soils are cane bluestem, silver bluestem, little bluestem, sideoats grama, hairy grama, indiangrass, curly mesquite, buffalograss, fall witchgrass, plains lovegrass, wildryes, and Texas wintergrass.

The rocky areas support tall or mid-grasses with an overstory of live oak, shinnery oak, juniper, and mesquite. The heavy clay soils have a mixture of tobosagrass, buffalograss, sideoats grama, and mesquite.

Throughout the Edwards Plateau, live oak, shinnery oak, mesquite, and juniper dominate the woody vegetation. Woody plants have invaded to the degree that they must be controlled before range forage plants can re-establish.

8. Rolling Plains

This is a region of approximately 24 million acres of alternating woodlands and prairies. The area is half mesquite woodland and half prairie. Mesquite trees have steadily invaded and increased in the grasslands for many years, despite constant control efforts.

Soils range from coarse sands along outwash terraces adjacent to streams to tight or compact clays on redbed clays and shales. Rough broken lands on steep slopes are found in the western portion. About two-thirds of the area is rangeland, but cultivation is important in certain localities.

Taking a road trip around the state? Submit your photos to our Flickr group: https://www.flickr.com/groups/texasalmanac/
Your photo might be chosen to be on our website, or even in our next book!

The original vegetation includes big, little, sand and silver bluestems, Texas wintergrass, indiangrass, switchgrass, sideoats and blue gramas, wildryes, tobosagrass, and buffalograss on the clay soils.

The sandy soils support tall bunchgrasses, mainly sand bluestem. Sand shinnery oak, sand sagebrush, and mesquite are the dominant woody plants.

Continued heavy grazing contributes to the increase in woody plants, low-value grasses such as red grama, red lovegrass, tumblegrass, gummy lovegrass, Texas grama, sand dropseed, and sandbur, with western ragweed, croton, and many other weedy forbs. Yucca is a problem plant on certain rangelands.

9. High Plains

The High Plains, some 19 million treeless acres, are an extension of the Great Plains to the north. Its level nature and porous soils prevent drainage over wide areas.

The relatively light rainfall flows into the numerous shallow playa lakes or sinks into the ground to feed the great underground aquifer that is the source of water for the countless wells that irrigate the surface of the plains. A large part of this area is under irrigated farming, but native grassland remains in about one-half of the High Plains.

Blue grama and buffalograss comprise the principal vegetation on the clay and clay loam "hardland" soils. Important grasses on the sandy loam "sandy land" soils are little bluestem, western wheatgrass, indiangrass, switchgrass, and sand reedgrass. Sand shinnery oak, sand sagebrush, mesquite, and yucca are conspicuous invading brushy plants.

10. Trans-Pecos Mountains and Basins

With as little as eight inches of annual rainfall, long hot summers, and usually cloudless skies to encourage evaporation, this 18-million-acre area produces only drought-resistant vegetation without irrigation. Grass is usually short and sparse.

The principal vegetation consists of lechuguilla, ocotillo, yucca, cenizo, prickly pear, and other arid land plants. In the more arid areas, gypsum and chino grama, and tobosagrass prevail. There is some mesquite. The vegetation includes creosote-tarbush, desert shrub, grama grassland, yucca and juniper savannahs, pine oak forest, and saline flats.

The mountains are 3,000 to 8,749 feet in elevation and support piñon pine, juniper, and some ponderosa pine and other forest vegetation on a few of the higher slopes. The grass vegetation, especially on the higher mountain slopes, includes many southwestern and Rocky Mountain species not present elsewhere in Texas. On the desert flats, black grama, burrograss, and fluffgrass are frequent.

More productive sites have numerous species of grama, muhly, Arizona cottontop, dropseed, and perennial threeawn grasses. At the higher elevations, plains bristlegrass, little bluestem, Texas bluestem, sideoats grama, chino grama, blue grama, piñon ricegrass, wolftail, and several species of needlegrass are frequent.

The common invaders on all depleted ranges are woody plants, burrograss, fluffgrass, hairy erioneuron, ear muhly, sand muhly, red grama, broom snakeweed, croton, cacti, and several poisonous plants. ☆

Rangeland in Gray County in the Panhandle. Gray County contains land in both the Rolling Plains and the High Plains. Photo by USDA NCRS Texas.

Public Forests and Grasslands in Texas

Sources: U.S. Forest Service, www.fs.usda.gov/texas/ and the Texas A&M Forest Service, tfsweb.tamu.edu

There are **four national forests and five national grasslands in Texas**. These federally owned lands are administered by the U.S. Department of Agriculture Forest Service and by district rangers. The **five state forests** in Texas are **I.D. Fairchild State Forest, W. Goodrich Jones State Forest, John Henry Kirby Memorial State Forest, Paul N. Masterson Memorial Forest,** and **E.O. Siecke State Forest.**

The national forests are managed to achieve sustainable conditions and provide wildlife habitat, outdoor recreation, water, wood, minerals, and forage for public use while retaining the aesthetic, historic, and spiritual qualities of the land.

In 1960, the Multiple Use–Sustained Yield Act put into law what had been practiced in Texas for almost 30 years: that resources on public lands will be managed so that they are used in ways that best meet the needs of the people, that the benefits obtained will exist indefinitely, and that each natural resource will be managed in balance with other resources.

However, even the most carefully planned system of management cannot foresee factors that can cause drastic changes in a forest. Fire, storms, insects, and disease, for example, can prompt managers to deviate from land management plans and can alter the way a forest is managed.

1. Timber Production

About 486,000 acres of the national forests in Texas are suitable for timber production. Sales of sawtimber, pulpwood, and other forest products are initiated to implement forest plans and objectives. The estimated net growth is more than 200 million board feet per year and is valued at $40 million. A portion of this growth is normally removed by cutting.

2. Cattle Grazing

Permits to graze cattle on national grasslands are granted to the public for an annual fee. About 600 head of cattle are grazed on the Caddo–Lyndon B. Johnson National Grasslands annually. On the Rita Blanca National Grasslands, 5,425 head of cattle are grazed each year, most of them in Texas.

3. Hunting and Fishing

State hunting and fishing laws and regulations apply to all national forest land. Game law enforcement is carried out by the Texas Parks and Wildlife Department.

A wide variety of fishing opportunities are available on the Angelina, Sabine, Neches, and San Jacinto rivers; the Sam Rayburn and Toledo Bend reservoirs; Lake Conroe; and many small streams. Hunting is not permitted on the McClellan Creek National Grassland nor at the Lake Marvin Unit of the Black Kettle National Grassland.

4. Recreational Facilities

An estimated 3 million people visit the recreational areas in the national forests and grasslands in Texas each year, primarily for picnicking, swimming, fishing, camping, boating, and nature enjoyment.

The Sabine and Angelina national forests are on the shores of Toledo Bend and Sam Rayburn reservoirs, two large East Texas lakes featuring fishing and other water sports. Lake Conroe and Lake Livingston offer water-related outdoor recreation opportunities on and near the Sam Houston National Forest.

(See page 151 for additional recreation information.)

National Forests

National forests in Texas were established by invitation of the Texas Legislature by an Act of 1933, authorizing the purchase of lands in Texas for the establishment of national forests. President Franklin D. Roosevelt proclaimed these purchases on Oct. 15, 1936.

The national forests cover 639,959 acres in parts of 12 Texas counties.

The four East Texas forests and two North Texas grasslands are under the supervision of the National Forests and Grasslands office in Lufkin. The three West Texas grasslands (Black Kettle, McClellan Creek, and Rita Blanca) are administered by the Forest Supervisor in Albuquerque, N.M., as units of the Cibola National Forest.

Each of Texas' national forests contains wilderness areas, made possible by the Texas Wilderness Act of 1984, introduced by Representative John W. Bryant of Texas' 5th Congressional district and signed into law by President Ronald Regan. These areas are allowed to return to a completely natural state with limited intervention, and visitors must follow strict guidelines while within those areas.

Angelina National Forest (154,474 acres) is spread across five East Texas counties: San Augustine (64,906 acres), Angelina (57,471), Jasper (21,867), Nacogdoches (10,222), and Tyler (8). The southern portion of the forest is predominantly covered by the longleaf pine. Loblolly and shortleaf pine cover much of the rest of the forest. Angelina NF is home to two wilderness areas: Upland Island (13,331 acres), found south of the Sam Rayburn Reservoir, and Turkey Hill (5,473), north of the reservoir.

Davy Crockett National Forest (161,141 acres) is found in Houston and Trinity counties (93,746 acres and 67,395 acres, respectively). This is a diverse forest, with both hardwoods (including white oak, red oak, hickory, chestnut oak, cherrybark oak, sweetgum, nuttall oak, and willow) and pines (loblolly and shortleaf). In the northern part of Davy Crockett NF, you'll find the Big Slough Wilderness Area (3,639 acres). The forest also contains the Alabama Creek Wildlife Management Area, 14,500 acres.

Sabine National Forest (161,087 acres) is another wide-ranging forest that touches five different counties, Sabine (95,195 acres), Shelby (59,897),

San Augustine (4,184), Newton (1,754), and Jasper (57), and even forms part of the border between Texas and Louisiana. The forest contains both hardwoods (American beech, southern red oak) and pines (loblolly, shortleaf, and longleaf). The Toledo Bend Reservoir runs along the eastern edge of much of the forest, including the Indian Mounds Wilderness Area (12,369 acres) near the middle.

Sam Houston National Forest (163,257 acres) is about 50 miles north of Houston, with parts found in San Jacinto (60,970 acres), Walker (55,115), and Montgomery (47,172) counties. It contains a variety of pines and hardwoods, and features redbuds and dogwoods, which are said to create a spectacular show of flowers in mid-February (redbud) and March (dogwood). Part of the forest stretches around the northern end of Lake Conroe, including the Little Lake Creek Wilderness (3,855 acres). Big Creek Scenic Area is near the easternmost part of the forest.

National Grasslands

The national grasslands were originally submarginal Dust Bowl project lands, purchased by the federal government primarily under the Bankhead-Jones Farm Tenant Act (1937). Today they are well covered with grasses and native shrubs.

The national grasslands cover 117,077 acres in six Texas counties. Two of these grasslands extend into Oklahoma, as well.

Lyndon B. Johnson National Grassland (20,102 acres) and Caddo National Grassland (17,630 acres) are located northeast and northwest of DFW, with a district ranger office at Decatur. These grasslands provide grazing land for cattle, but also habitat for native wildlife, including white-tailed deer, bobcats, red foxes, and several game birds. Lyndon B. Johnson NG is found mostly in Wise County (20,042 acres). The remaining 60 acres are in Montague County. Caddo NG is only in Fannin County. The Bois d'Arc unit of Caddo contains Lake Fannin, Coffee Mill Lake, and Lake Crockett, which are popular for fishing.

Black Kettle National Grassland (31,264 acres) and McClellan Creek National Grassland (1,402 acres) are both administered by the Cibola National Forest & National Grasslands in Albuquerque, N.M. Black Kettle NG lies mostly in Oklahoma, with a mere 577 acres in Texas' Hemphill County; McClellan Creek NG is found near Pampa in Gray County and includes the Lake McClellan Recreation area. Both grasslands have active oil and gas wells and lie within the Anadarko Basin.

Rita Blanca National Grassland (117,077 acres) is also managed by Cibola National Forest & National Grasslands, in Albuquerque. These grasslands also stretch across the Texas border, from Dallam County (77,366 acres) into Oklahoma (15,653).

State Forests

Texas has **five state forests**, all of which are used primarily for demonstration and research. They are

Forests and Grasslands in Texas

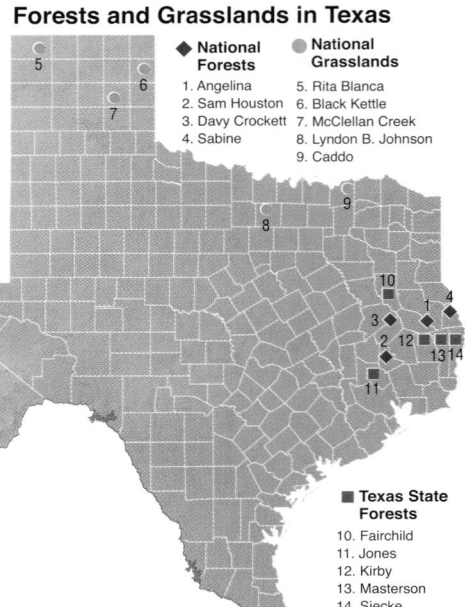

◆ National Forests   ● National Grasslands

1. Angelina
2. Sam Houston
3. Davy Crockett
4. Sabine
5. Rita Blanca
6. Black Kettle
7. McClellan Creek
8. Lyndon B. Johnson
9. Caddo

■ Texas State Forests
10. Fairchild
11. Jones
12. Kirby
13. Masterson
14. Siecke

all game sanctuaries with no firearms or hunting allowed.

Recreational opportunities, such as horseback riding, hiking, bird watching, and picnicking, are available in all but the Masterson Forest.

I.D. Fairchild State Forest: Texas' largest forest is located west of Rusk in Cherokee County. This forest was transferred from the state prison system in 1925. Additional land was obtained in 1963 from the Texas State Hospitals and Special Schools for a total acreage of 2,740.

W. Goodrich Jones State Forest: Located south of Conroe in Montgomery County, it comprises 1,733 acres. It was purchased in 1926 and named for the founder of the Texas Forestry Association.

John Henry Kirby Memorial State Forest: This 600-acre forest in Tyler County was donated by lumberman John Henry Kirby in 1929, as well as later donors. Revenue from this forest is given to the Association of Former Students of Texas A&M University for student-loan purposes.

Paul N. Masterson Memorial Forest: Mrs. Leonora O'Neal Masterson of Beaumont donated these 519 acres in Jasper County in 1984 in honor of her husband, who was a tree farmer and an active member of the Texas Forestry Association.

E.O. Siecke State Forest: The first state forest, it was purchased by the state in 1924. It contains 1,722 acres of pine land in Newton County. An additional 100 acres was obtained by a 99-year lease in 1946.

Texas Forest Resources

Source: Texas A&M Forest Service, Texas A&M University System; http://tfsweb.tamu.edu.

Forest resources in Texas are abundant and diverse. Forest land covers roughly 38 percent of the state's land area. According to 2017 figures from the Forest Inventory and Analysis (FIA), there are over 63 million acres of forests and woodlands in Texas.

The principal forest region in Texas is called the **East Texas Piney Woods**, due to the abundance of pine-hardwood in the region. The 43-county region forms the western edge of the southern pine region, extending from Bowie and Red River counties in northeast Texas to Jefferson, Harris, and Waller counties in southeast Texas. The counties contain 12.1 million acres of forestland of which 11.9 million acres are classified as productive timberland and produce nearly all of the state's commercial timber.

Following is a summary of the findings of the Forest Inventory of East Texas, completed in 2017 by the Texas A&M Forest Service (TFS) in cooperation with the USDA Forest Service Southern Research Station.

Timberland Acreage and Ownership

Nearly all (11.9 million of 12.1 million acres) of the East Texas forest is classified as "timberland," which is suitable for production of timber products and not reserved as parks or wilderness areas. Texas timberland acreage had a decrease of 22.4 thousand acres between 2016 and 2017.

Ninety-two percent of East Texas timberland is owned by approximately 210,000 private individuals, families, partnerships, corporations, forest-products companies, and timber investment groups. The remaining 8 percent is owned by federal, state, and local governments.

East Texas has undergone major shifts in private ownership during the past decade, primarily a transfer of land from forest industry owners to non-industrial private owners. Information from several sources, such as the FIA, National Woodland Owner Survey, and timberland transaction records, suggests that the forest industry now accounts for no more than 50 thousand acres. Nonindustrial private corporations, which include timber investment corporations, account for 3.5 million to 4.2 million acres, and family forest landowners account for 5.5 million to 5.8 million acres.

Timberland by Ownership	
Ownership Class	**Area (acres)**
Private	10,920,800
Public:	
National Forest	577,300
Misc. Federal	186,900
State & Local	236,900
Total	**11,921,900**

Forest Types

Six major forest types are found in the East Texas Piney Woods. Two pine-forest types are most common. The loblolly-shortleaf and longleaf-slash forest types are dominated by the four species of southern yellow pine. In these forests, the various pine trees make up at least 50 percent of the trees.

Oak-hickory is the next most common forest type. These are upland hardwood forests in which oaks or hickories make up at least 50 percent of the trees, and pine species are less than 25 percent. Oak-pine is a mixed-forest type in which more than 50 percent of the trees are hardwoods, but pines make up 25–49 percent of the trees.

Two forest types, oak-gum-cypress and elm-ash-cottonwood, are bottomland types that are commonly found along creeks, river bottoms, swamps, and other wet areas. The oak-gum-cypress forests are typically made up of many species including blackgum, sweetgum, oaks, and southern cypress. The elm-ash-cottonwood bottomland forests are dominated by those trees but also contain many other species, such as willow, sycamore, and maple.

Other forest types found in East Texas include small acreages of mesquite, exotic hardwoods, red cedar, and unproductive lands that are considered forested but do not meet stocking requirements. The following table shows the **breakdown in acreage by forest type**:

Forest Types in Texas	
Forest Type Group	**Area (acres)**
Southern Pine:	
Loblolly-shortleaf	108,600
Longleaf-slash	5,375,000
Oak-hickory	2,746,200
Oak-pine	1,378,900
Bottomland Hardwood:	
Oak-gum-cypress	1,331,200
Elm-ash-cottonwood	560,000
Other	422,100
Total	**11,922,000**

Southern pine plantations, established by tree planting and usually managed intensively to maximize timber production, are an important source of wood fiber. Texas forests include 3.2 million acres of pine plantations, 63 percent of which are on industrially managed land, 34 percent on nonindustrial private land, and 3 percent on public land. Genetically superior tree seedlings are usually planted to improve survival and growth.

Timber Volume and Number of Trees

Based on 2017 Forest Inventory & Analysis Data, Texas timberland contains about 15 billion cubic feet of timber "growing-stock" volume. One billion cubic feet of growing stock produces roughly enough lumber to build a 2,000-square-foot home for one out of every three Texans. Between 2016 and 2017, the inventory of softwood increased from 9.8 billion cubic feet to 10.3 billion cubic feet, while the hardwood inventory decreased from 5 billion cubic feet to 4.7 billion cubic feet.

Beyond the Piney Woods: Texas' Other Tree Regions

In addition to the 12 million acres of timberland in East Texas, there are an additional 51.1 million acres of land in the remainder of Texas that are considered forestland. These forests consist of mesquite woodlands, oak-hickory forests, juniper woodlands, and other western forest types. These forests do not have the commercial timber value of the East Texas Piney Woods but are environmentally important with benefits of wildlife habitat, improved water quality, recreation, and aesthetics.

- **Post Oak Belt**: The Post Oak Belt forms a band of wooded savanna mixed with pasture and cropland immediately west of the Piney Woods. It extends from Lamar and Red River counties southwest as far as Bee and Atascosa counties. Predominant species include post oak, blackjack oak, and elm. An interesting area called the "Lost Pines" forms an isolated island of southern-pine forest in Bastrop, Caldwell, Fayette, and Lee counties just a few miles southeast of Austin.

- **Eastern and Western Cross Timbers:** The Eastern and Western Cross Timbers cover an area of about 3 million acres in North-Central Texas. The term "cross timbers" originated with the early settlers who, in their travels from east to west, crossed alternating patches of oak forest and prairies and so affixed the name "cross timbers" to these forests.

- **Cedar Brakes:** Farther south in the Edwards Plateau region are the cedar brakes, which extend over 3.7 million acres. Cedar, live oak, and mesquite dominate these steep slopes and rolling hills. Mesquite is harvested for cooking wood, knickknacks, and woodworking. Live oak in this region is declining because of the oak wilt disease.

- **Mountain Forests:** The mountain forests of the Trans-Pecos region, including Jeff Davis County and the Big Bend, are rugged and picturesque. Several western tree species, including piñon pine, ponderosa pine, southwestern white pine, and even Douglas fir are found there, along with aspen and several species of oak.

- **Coastal Forests:** The coastal forests of the southern Gulf Coast are characterized by a mix of brush and short, scrubby trees. Common species include mesquite, live oak, and acacia. Some of these scrub forests are particularly important as migratory bird habitat.

There are an estimated 7.2 billion live trees in East Texas, according to the 2017 survey. This includes 2.2 billion softwoods and 5.0 billion hardwoods. The predominant species are loblolly and shortleaf pine; 1.9 billion pine trees are found in East Texas.

Timber Growth and Removals

An annual average of 574.3 million cubic feet of growing-stock timber was removed from the inventory, either through harvest or land-use changes. Meanwhile, 639.8 million cubic feet of growing stock were added to the inventory through growth each year.

For pine, an average of 450.3 million cubic feet was removed during those years, while 568.7 million cubic feet were added by growth. For hardwoods, 124 million cubic feet were removed, while 71.1 million cubic feet were added by growth.

The 2017 Timber Harvest

Total Removals

Total removals of growing stock in East Texas in 2017, including both pine and hardwood, decreased 8.7 percent from 2016. The total volume of growing stock that was removed from the 43-county timber region was 481.5 million cubic feet in 2017, compared to 527.3 million cubic feet in 2016. Included in the total growing-stock removals are timber harvested for industrial use and an estimate of logging residue.

Industrial roundwood harvest in Texas in 2017, the portion of the total removal that was subsequently utilized in the manufacture of wood products, totaled 415.1 million cubic feet for pine and 66.4 million cubic feet for hardwood. The pine industrial roundwood harvest was down 7.5 percent from 2016, and the hardwood roundwood harvest was down 16.2 percent. The combined harvest decreased 8.7 percent in 2017 to 498.8 million cubic feet. Top producing counties included Polk, Newton, Jasper, Harrison, and Angelina.

Total Harvest Value

Stumpage value of the East Texas timber harvest in 2017 was $244.8 million, an 18.3-percent decrease from 2016. The delivered value of timber was down 13.5 percent to $597.6 million. Pine timber accounted for 86 percent of the total stumpage value and 85.8 percent of the total delivered value.

Compared with 2016, the harvest of sawlogs for production of lumber decreased 7.4 percent in 2017 to 1.1 billion board feet. The pine sawlog cut totaled 1 billion board feet, down 6 percent from 2016, and the hardwood sawlog harvest decreased 23 percent to 73.1 million board feet. Newton, Polk, Angelina, Cherokee, and Jasper counties were the top producers of sawlogs.

Timber cut for the production of structural panels, including both plywood and OSB (oriented strand board) and hardwood veneer, totaled 130.8 million cubic feet, a 0.2 percent decrease from 2016. Harrison, Polk, Angelina, Nacogdoches, and Panola counties were the top producers of veneer and panel roundwood.

Pine trees in Huntsville State Park. Photo by Roy Luck (CC).

Harvest of timber for manufacture of pulp and paper products decreased 15.1 percent from 2016 to 2017 to 2.3 million cords. Cass, Polk, Cherokee, Tyler, and Rusk counties were the top producers of pulpwood.

Other roundwood harvest, including posts, poles, and pilings, totaled 3.9 million cubic feet in 2017.

Import-Export Trends

Texas was a net importer of timber products in 2017. Total import from other states was 90.7 million cubic feet, while the total export was 60.9 million cubic feet. Texas mills utilized 87.8 percent of the timber harvested in the state in 2017. The remainder was processed mainly by mills in Arkansas, Louisiana, and Oklahoma.

Production of Forest Products

Lumber: Texas sawmills produced 1.5 billion board feet of lumber in 2017, an increase of 2.3 percent over 2016. Production of pine lumber increased 3.1 percent to 1.4 billion board feet in 2017, and hardwood lumber production decreased 10.1 percent to 79.1 million board feet in 2017.

Structural Panel Products: Production of structural panels, including plywood and OSB, increased 10.5 percent to 2.4 billion square feet in 2017.

Paper Products: Production of pulp and paperboard products (includes fiberboard, paperboard, market pulp, and miscellaneous products) totaled 2.4 million tons in 2017, up 2.9 percent from a year earlier. There has not been any major paper production in Texas since 2003.

Treated Wood: There was a 4.5 percent decrease in the volume of wood processed by Texas wood treaters in 2017 from 2016. The total volume treated in 2017 was 40.3 million cubic feet. Among major treated products, lumber accounted for 61.1 percent of the total volume; railroad crossties accounted for 14 percent; utility poles accounted for 9.2 percent.

Primary Mill Residue: Total mill residue, including chips, sawdust, shavings, and bark in primary mills, such as sawmills, panel mills, and chip mills, was 5.5 million tons in 2017. Eighty-nine percent of the residue was from pine species and 11 percent was from hardwood species. Chips accounted for 48.9 percent of mill residue, followed by bark (31.7 percent), sawdust (13.3 percent), and shavings (6.1 percent).

Reforestation

A total of 94,655 acres were planted during the winter 2016 and spring 2017 planting season. Industrial landowners, including acres planted by Timber Investment Management Organizations and timberland Real Estate Investment Trusts, planted 64,551 acres, up 1.7 percent from the previous season.

Participants in the Family Forest Program planted 29,575 acres in 2016–2017, and public landowners planted 530 acres. Family forest owners received $1.8 million in cost-share assistance for reforestation through federal cost-share programs.

Fire Protection

Texas has a tiered approach to emergencies, such as wildland fires, with response coming from local, district, state, and federal levels. When a fire

Pine tree thinning in Nacogdoches County. Photo by USDA-NCRS Texas.

surpasses the capabilities of local fire departments, the TFS steps in to help. On average, TFS personnel respond to 15 percent of the wildland fires that burn across the state; however, those fires burn 70 percent of total acres lost to wildland fires each year.

More information on state wildfire response, wildfire risk assessments, fire department assistance programs, and how homeowners and communities can reduce their wildfire risk is online at: **http://tfsweb.tamu.edu** and **http://ticc.tamu.edu.**

Forest Pests

The southern pine beetle is the most destructive insect pest in the 12 million acres of commercial forests in East Texas. Typically, this bark beetle kills more timber annually than forest fires.

This destructive insect is currently at very low levels in East Texas. When outbreaks do occur, the TFS coordinates all direct control activity on state and private forestlands, including detecting infestations from the air, checking infestations on the ground to evaluate the need for control, notifying landowners, and providing technical assistance.

Recent efforts have focused on rating the susceptibility of pine stands to future southern pine beetle outbreaks, as well as prevention of infestations. Since 2003, the TFS has offered federal cost shares to private-forest landowners in East Texas as an incentive to thin the young pine stands that are most susceptible to bark beetles. Thinning dense forests to promote vigorous tree growth is the preferred long-run method to reduce tree losses caused by bark beetles.

Extensive mortality of live oaks in Central Texas is caused by a vascular wilt disease called oak wilt. A suppression project,

Texas Forest Products Production 2005–2017

Year	Lumber* (thousand board feet) Pine	Lumber* (thousand board feet) Hardwood	Paper Products (short tons) Paperboard	Structural Panel (thousand square feet*) Pine
2005	1,733,314	230,090	2,512,262	3,249,558
2006	1,676,461	240,214	2,781,865	2,935,637
2007	1,550,716	180,713	2,788,308	2,503,941
2008	1,406,103	213,191	2,329,347	2,204,544
2009	1,237,801	171,514	2,007,054	1,958,794
2010	1,188,294	139,389	2,089,521	1,881,763
2011	1,308,427	154,593	2,029,405	1,915,605
2012	1,291,578	118,823	2,081,521	2,049,084
2013	1,385,043	140,427	2,168,403	2,017,406
2014	1,444,203	104,089	2,213,026	2,348,023
2015	1,410,472	107,029	2,106,412	2,444,464
2016	1,357,409	88,001	2,317,537	2,729,569
2017	1,399,502	79,090	2,384,711	2,443,043
* Includes tie volumes.				* 3/8-inch basis
Sources: Annual Harvest Trends reports by Texas A&M Forest Service.				

administered by TFS Forest Health personnel, assists affected landowners.

Invasive (non-native) insects, diseases, and plants are an increasing problem for Texas' forest landowners. The soapberry borer, a wood-boring beetle introduced from Mexico, has killed western soapberry trees in some 50 counties in Central Texas. Invasive plants, such as Japanese climbing fern, Chinese tallow, and non-native privets, have also spread rapidly.

In 2012, TFS, Texas A&M AgriLife Extension Service, Sam Houston State University, and other collaborators conducted a widespread detection survey for the emerald ash borer, a major pest of ash trees introduced from Asia. There have been no confirmed cases of ash trees infested with the borers to date.

Urban Forests

An estimated 86 percent of Texans live in urban areas, making urban trees and forests important. Trees reduce urban heat island effect with shade and evaporative cooling. They purify the air by absorbing pollutants, slowing chemical reactions that produce harmful ozone, and filter dust. They reduce storm water runoff and soil erosion; buffer against noise, glare, and strong winds; and provide habitat for urban wildlife. ☆

Total Timber Production and Value by County in Texas, 2017

County	Pine	Hardwood	Total	Stumpage Value	Delivered Value
	(cubic feet)			(thousand dollars)	
Anderson	6,580,699	952,137	7,532,836	$3,844	$9,187
Angelina	25,168,511	2,164,874	27,333,385	$15,358	$34,554
Bowie	16,778,852	4,036,595	20,815,447	$11,379	$26,339
Camp	3,290,217	285,724	3,575,941	$1,922	$4,458
Cass	19,546,669	6,301,672	25,848,341	$12,258	$30,744
Chambers	15,997	0	15,997	$12	$23
Cherokee	18,508,081	2,607,540	21,115,621	$12,633	$27,824
Franklin	17,424	47,990	65,414	$67	$121
Gregg	1,636,273	707,712	2,343,985	$1,217	$2,917
Grimes	797,697	0	797,697	$561	$1,135
Hardin	20,842,153	1,322,089	22,164,242	$8,775	$24,106
Harris	1,458,189	9,785	1,467,974	$1,184	$2,256
Harrison	23,160,805	4,448,801	27,609,606	$13,800	$33,442
Henderson	394,304	256,480	650,784	$257	$723
Houston	9,251,192	674,102	9,925,294	$5,210	$12,220
Jasper	29,616,777	727,314	30,344,091	$12,215	$33,140
Jefferson	484,694	0	484,694	$248	$587
Leon	296,680	1,487,600	1,784,280	$669	$2,000
Liberty	10,137,986	2,863,572	13,001,558	$6,913	$16,255
Madison	18,357	560	18,917	$13	$26
Marion	6,356,975	2,046,534	8,403,509	$3,520	$9,479
Montgomery	3,873,234	84,231	3,957,465	$2,003	$4,781
Morris	324,962	584,411	909,373	$454	$1,134
Nacogdoches	20,962,401	3,587,858	24,550,259	$12,489	$29,944
Newton	30,619,922	403,284	31,023,206	$15,015	$36,630
Orange	1,664,997	85,120	1,750,117	$631	$1,837
Panola	18,408,681	2,778,619	21,187,300	$9,928	$24,886
Polk	32,917,848	1,398,012	34,315,860	$17,535	$41,574
Red River	7,689,356	2,561,886	10,251,242	$4,188	$11,470
Rusk	17,200,228	2,788,424	19,988,652	$11,237	$25,558
Sabine	13,321,843	1,115,360	14,437,203	$6,808	$16,927
San Augustine	15,055,046	4,299,495	19,354,541	$9,003	$22,770
San Jacinto	4,547,032	235,117	4,782,149	$2,490	$5,857
Shelby	17,219,308	3,546,321	20,765,629	$9,305	$23,970
Smith	4,138,187	1,604,591	5,742,778	$2,774	$6,897
Titus	435,802	328,019	763,821	$537	$1,113
Trinity	12,095,995	2,246,270	14,342,265	$7,288	$17,455
Tyler	24,490,827	1,184,079	25,674,906	$11,206	$29,045
Upshur	5,850,593	2,226,138	8,076,731	$3,536	$9,309
Van Zandt	159,895	104,560	264,455	$108	$298
Walker	2,229,219	108,960	2,338,179	$1,292	$2,941
Waller	686,032	0	686,032	$515	$1,012
Wood	2,551,990	1,848,928	4,400,918	$2,040	$5,236
Other counties	1,472,453	2,447,143	3,919,596	$2,396	$5,393
Totals	**432,274,383**	**66,507,907**	**498,782,290**	**$244,833**	**$597,573**

Source: Harvest Trends 2017, Texas A&M Forest Service.

A roseate spoonbill flying over a swamp near High Island. Photo by Ivan Kuzmin/Shutterstock.

Texas Wildlife

Source: Texas Parks and Wildlife Department; The Mammals of Texas Online Edition (Texas Tech University)

The wide variation of soils, climate, topography, and vegetation in Texas has resulted in an unusually rich diversity of animal life. The Texas environment supports **141 species of native terrestrial mammals**, a number exceeded in the United States only by California and New Mexico. In addition to native species, there are also 12 exotics or non-native species that have been introduced by man either accidentally (house mouse, roof rat, Norway rat) or intentionally (nutria, red fox, feral pig, axis deer, fallow deer, sika deer, nilgai, barbary sheep, and blackbuck) and have become established in the environment.

A few of the leading land mammals of Texas are described here. Those marked by an asterisk (*) are non-native species. Information was provided by the **Nongame and Urban Program**, Texas Parks and Wildlife Department, and updated using the online version of *The Mammals of Texas* by David J. Schmidly and the late William B. Davis: **www.nsrl. ttu.edu/tmot1/**. The print version was first published in 1947 and updated in 1994 by Texas Parks and Wildlife Press, Austin. The online version is maintained by Texas Tech University. For additional wildlife information on the web: **www.tpwd.state.tx.us/ huntwild/wild/species/**.

Mammals

Armadillo: The **nine-banded armadillo** *(Dasypus novemcinctus)* is one of Texas' most iconic mammals. It is found in most of the state except the western Trans-Pecos. It is now common as far north and east as Kansas and Mississippi.

Badger: The **badger** *(Taxidea taxus)* is most common in parts of West and South Texas, and is occasionally spotted in the eastern part of the state. It is a fierce fighter and is valuable in helping control the rodent population.

Bat: Thirty-two species of these winged mammals have been found in Texas, more than in any other state in the United States. Of these, 27 species are known residents, though they are seldom seen by the casual observer. The **Mexican**, or **Brazilian**, **free-tailed bat** *(Tadarida brasiliensis)* and the **cave myotis** *(Myotis velifer)* constitute most of the cave-dwelling bats of Central and West Texas.

They have some economic value for their deposits of nitrogen-rich **guano**. Some commercial guano has been produced from **James River Bat Cave**, Mason County; **Beaver Creek Cavern**, Burnet County; and from large deposits in other caves including **Devil's Sinkhole**, Edwards County; **Blowout Cave**, Blanco County; and **Bandera Bat Cave**, Bandera County. The largest concentration of bats in the world is found at **Bracken Cave** in Comal County, which is thought to hold between 20 million and 40 million bats. The **big brown bat** *(Eptesicus fuscus)*, the **red bat** *(Lasiurus borealis)*, and the **evening bat** *(Nycticeius humeralis)* are found in East and Southeast

Texas. The evening and big brown bats are forest and woodland dwelling mammals.

The rarer species of Texas bats have been found along the Rio Grande and in the Trans-Pecos. Bats can be observed at dusk near a water source, and many species may also be found foraging on insects attracted to street lights. Everywhere bats occur, they are the main predators of night-flying insects, including mosquitoes and many crop pests. On the web: **www.batcon.org/**

Bear: The **black bear** *(Ursus americanus)*, formerly common throughout most of the state, is now surviving in remnant populations in mountainous areas of the Trans-Pecos. Some are fleeing the drought and wildfires in Mexico and moving into the Big Bend area.

Beaver: The **American beaver** *(Castor canadensis)* is found over most of the state except for the Llano Estacado and parts of the Trans-Pecos.

Bighorn: (See **Sheep**.)

Bison: The largest of native terrestrial wild mammals of North America, the **American bison** *(Bos bison)*, commonly called **buffalo**, was formerly found in the western two-thirds of the state. Today, it is extirpated or confined on ranches. Deliberate slaughter of this majestic animal for hides and to eliminate the Plains Indians' main food source reached a peak about 1877–78, and the bison was almost eradicated by 1885. Estimates of the number of buffalo killed vary, but as many as 200,000 hides were sold in Fort Worth at a single two-day sale. Except for the interest of the late **Col. Charles Goodnight** and a few other foresighted men, the bison might be extinct.

Cat: The **jaguar** *(Felis onca)* is probably now extinct in Texas and, along with the **ocelot, jaguarundi,** and **margay**, is listed as endangered or threatened by both federal and state wildlife agencies. The **mountain lion** *(Felis concolor)*, also known as **cougar** and **puma**, was once found statewide. It is now found in the mountainous areas of the Trans-Pecos and the dense Rio Grande Plain brushland. The **ocelot** *(Felis pardalis)*, also known as the **leopard cat**, is found usually along the border. The **red-and-gray cat,** or **jaguarundi** *(Felis yagouaroundi Geoffroy)* is found, rarely, in extreme South Texas. The **margay** *(Felis wiedii)* was reported in the 1850s near Eagle Pass. The **bobcat** *(Lynx rufus)* is found throughout the state in large numbers.

Chipmunk: The **gray-footed chipmunk** *(Tamias canipes)* is found at high altitudes in the Guadalupe and Sierra Diablo ranges of the Trans-Pecos. (*See also* **Ground Squirrel**, with which the chipmunk is often confused in public reference.)

Coati: The **white-nosed coati** *(Nasua narica)*, a relative of the raccoon, is occasionally found in southern Texas from Brownsville to the Big Bend. It inhabits woodland areas and feeds both on the ground and in trees. The coati, which is on the list of threatened species, is also found occasionally in Big Bend National Park.

Coyote: The **coyote** *(Canis latrans)* exists in great numbers in Texas. It is the most destructive predator of Texas livestock. On the other hand, it is probably the most valuable predator in the balance of nature. It is a protection to crops and range lands by its control of rodents and rabbits. It is found throughout the state but is most numerous in the brush country of Southwest Texas. It is the second-most important fur-bearing animal in the state.

Deer: The **white-tailed deer** *(Odocoileus virginianus)*, found throughout the state in brushy or wooded areas, is the most important Texas game animal. Its numbers in Texas are estimated at more than 3 million. The **mule deer** *(Odocoileus heminous)* is found principally in the Trans-Pecos and Panhandle areas. It has increased in number in recent years. The little **Del Carmen deer**

(white-tailed subspecies) is found in limited numbers in the high valleys of the Chisos Mountains in the Big Bend. The only native **elk** in Texas *(Cervus merriami)*, found in the southern Guadalupe Mountains, became extinct about the turn of the 20th century. The **wapiti** or **elk** *(Cervus elaphus)* was introduced into the same area about 1928. There are currently several herds totaling several hundred individuals.

A number of exotic deer species have been introduced, mostly for hunting purposes. The **axis deer*** *(Cervus axis)* is the most numerous of the exotics. Native to India, it is found mostly in Central and South Texas, both free-ranging and confined on ranches. **Blackbuck*** *(Antilope cervicapra)*, also native to India, is the second-most numerous exotic deer in the state and is found on ranches in 86 counties. **Fallow deer*** *(Cervus dama)*, native to the Mediterranean, has been introduced to 93 counties, while the **nilgai*** *(Boselaphus tragocamelus)*, native of India and Pakistan, is found mostly on ranches in Kenedy and Willacy counties. The **sika deer*** *(Cervus nippon)*, native of southern Siberia, Japan, and China, has been introduced in 77 counties in Central and South Texas.

Dolphin: The **Atlantic spotted dolphin** *(Stenella frontalis)* is rather small, long-snouted, and spotted; it is purplish gray, appearing blackish at a distance, usually with numerous small white or gray spots on its sides and back. In the Gulf of Mexico, this dolphin is second in abundance only to the bottlenose dolphin. The bottlenose *(Tursiops truncatus)* is stout and short-beaked with sloping forehead, projecting lower jaw, and high dorsal fin. Other species, such as the Clymene, Common, Pantropical Spotted, Risso's, Rough-toothed, Spinner, and Striped are unusual and known in Texas only through strandings along Gulf beaches.

Ferret: The **black-footed ferret** *(Mustela nigripes)* was formerly found widely ranging through the West Texas country of the prairie dog on which it preyed. It is now considered extinct in Texas. It is of the same genus as the weasel and the mink.

Fox: The **common gray fox** *(Urocyon cinereoargenteus)* is found throughout most of the state, primarily in the woods of East Texas, in broken parts of the Edwards Plateau, and in the rough country at the foot of the High Plains. The **kit** or **swift fox** *(Vulpes velox)* is found in the western third of the state. A second species of **kit fox** *(Vulpes macrotis)* is found in the Trans-Pecos and is fairly numerous in some localities. The **red fox*** *(Vulpes vulpes)*, which ranges across Central Texas, was introduced for sport.

Gopher: Nine species of pocket gopher occur in Texas. The **Botta's pocket gopher** *(Thomomys bottae)* is found from the Trans-Pecos eastward across the Edwards Plateau. The **plains pocket gopher** *(Geomys bursarius)* is found from Midland and Tom Green counties east and north to McLennan, Dallas, and Grayson counties. The **desert pocket gopher** *(Geomys arenarius)* is found only in the Trans-Pecos, while the **yellow-faced pocket gopher** *(Cratogeomys castanops)* is found in the western third of the state, with occasional sightings along the Rio Grande in Maverick and Cameron counties. The **Texas pocket gopher** *(Geomys personatus)* is found in South Texas from San Patricio County to Val Verde County. **Attwater's pocket gopher** *(Geomys attwateri)* and **Baird's pocket gopher** *(Geomys breviceps)* are both found generally in South-Central and Coastal Texas from the Brazos River to the San Antonio River and south to Matagorda and San Patricio counties. **Jones' pocket gopher** *(Geomys knoxjonesi)* is found only in far West Texas, while the **Llano pocket gopher** *(Geomys texensis)* is found only in two isolated areas of the Hill Country.

Ground Squirrel: Five or more species of ground squirrel live in Texas, mostly in the western part of the state.

The **rock squirrel** *(Spermophilus variegatus)* is found throughout the Edwards Plateau and Trans-Pecos. The Mexican ground squirrel *(Spermophilus mexicanus)* occurs throughout much of South Texas, the Trans-Pecos, and almost to the Red River just east of the Panhandle. The **spotted ground squirrel** *(Spermophilus spilosoma)* is found generally in the western half of the state. The **thirteen-lined ground squirrel** *(Spermophilus tridecemlineatus)* is found in a narrow strip from Dallas and Tarrant counties to the Gulf. The **Texas antelope squirrel** *(Ammospermophilus interpres)* is found along the Rio Grande from El Paso to Val Verde County.

Hog, Feral: (See Pig, Feral.)

Javelina: The **javelina** or **collared peccary** *(Tayassu tajacu)* is found in brushy semidesert areas where prickly pear, a favorite food, is found. The javelina was hunted commercially for its hide until 1939. They are harmless to livestock and to people, though they can defend themselves ferociously when attacked by hunting dogs.

Mink: The **mink** *(Mustela vison)* is found in the eastern half of the state, always near streams, lakes, or other water sources. Although it is an economically important fur-bearing animal in the eastern United States, it ranked only 13th in numbers and 9th in economic value to trappers in Texas in 1988–89, according to a Texas Parks and Wildlife Department survey.

Mole: The **eastern mole** *(Scalopus aquaticus)* is found in the eastern two-thirds of Texas. Moles cannot see and spend most of their life in underground burrows they excavate for themselves or usurp from other mammals, such as pocket gophers. The burrowing of moles can damage lawns, row crops, and the greens of golf courses. Benefits, however, are aerating soil and eating larval insects that destroy roots of grass and crops.

Muskrat: The **common muskrat** *(Ondatra zibethica)* occurs in aquatic habitats in the northern, southeastern, and southwestern parts of the state. Although the muskrat was once economically valuable for its fur, its numbers have declined, mostly because of the loss of habitat.

Nutria*: This introduced species *(Myocastor coypus)*, native to South America, is found in the eastern two-thirds of the state. The fur is not highly valued and, because nutrias are in competition with muskrats, their spread is discouraged. They have been used widely in Texas as a cure-all for ponds choked with vegetation, with spotty results.

Opossum: A **marsupial**, the **Virginia opossum** *(Didelphis virginiana)* is found in nearly all parts of the state. The opossum has economic value for its pelt, and its meat is considered a delicacy by some.

Otter: A few **river otters** *(Lutra canadensis)* are found in the eastern quarter of the state. It has probably been extirpated from the Panhandle, North-Central, and South Texas.

Pig, Feral*: Feral pigs are found throughout Texas but especially in areas of the Rio Grande and Coastal Plains, as well as in the woods of East Texas. They are descendants of escaped domestic hogs or of European wild hogs that were imported for sport. Their rooting habits can extensively destroy vegetation and soil.

Porcupine: The **yellow-haired porcupine** *(Erethizon dorsatum)* is found from the western half of the state east to Bosque County. It is adapted to a variety of habitats and, in recent years, has expanded into South Texas. Porcupines are expert at climbing trees but are as much at home in rocks as on the ground or in trees. They have a relatively long lifespan; one marked female lived more than 10 years under natural conditions.

Prairie Dog: Until recent years, probably no sight was so universal in West Texas as the **black-tailed prairie dog** *(Cynomys ludovicianus)*. Naturalists estimated its population in the hundreds of millions, and prairie-dog towns often covered many acres with thickly spaced burrows. Its destruction of range grasses and cultivated crops has caused farmers and ranchers to destroy many of them, and it is extirpated from much of its former range. It is being propagated in several public zoos, notably in the **prairie dog town in Mackenzie Park** at Lubbock. It has been honored in Texas by the naming of the **Prairie Dog Town Fork** of the Red River, in one segment of which is located the beautiful **Palo Duro Canyon**.

Pronghorn: The **pronghorn** *(Antilocapra americana)* formerly was found in the western two-thirds of the state. It is currently found only in limited areas from the Panhandle to the Trans-Pecos. Despite management efforts, its numbers have been decreasing in recent years.

Rabbit: The **black-tailed jackrabbit** *(Lepus californicus)* is found throughout Texas except the Big Thicket area of East Texas. It breeds rapidly, and its long hind legs make it one of the world's faster-running animals. The **Eastern cottontail** *(Sylvilagus floridanus)* is found mostly in the eastern three-quarters of the state. The **desert cottontail** *(Sylvilagus auduboni)* is found in the western half of the state, usually on the open range. The **swamp rabbit** *(Sylvilagus aquaticus)* is found in East Texas and the coastal area.

Raccoon: The **raccoon** *(Procyon lotor)* is found throughout Texas, especially in woodlands and near water. It is strictly nocturnal. A raccoon makes its den in a large hollow tree or hollow log, in which its spends the daylight hours sleeping and in which it also rears its young. In western areas, dens usually are in crevices of rocky bluffs.

Rats, Mice, and Voles: There are 40 to 50 species of rats, mice, and voles in Texas of varying characteristics, habitats, and economic destructiveness. The **Norway rat*** *(Rattus norvegicus)* and the **roof rat*** *(Rattus rattus)*, both non-native species, are probably the most common and most destructive. They also are instrumental in the transmission of several dread diseases, including bubonic plague and typhus. The **common house mouse*** *(Mus musculis)* is estimated in the hundreds of millions annually. The **Mexican vole** *(Microtus mexicanus guadalupensis)*, also called the **Guadalupe Mountain vole**, is found only in the higher elevations of Guadalupe Mountains National Park and just over the border into New Mexico.

Ringtail: The **ringtail** *(Bassariscus astutus)* is a cat-sized carnivore resembling a small fox with a long raccoon-like tail. It found statewide but is rare in the Lower Valley and the Coastal Plains. Ringtails are nocturnal and live in a variety of habitats, preferring rocky areas, such as rock piles, stone fences, and canyon walls.

Sheep: The **mountain sheep** *(Ovis canadensis)*, or **desert bighorn**, formerly was found in isolated areas of the mountainous Trans-Pecos, but the last native sheep were seen in 1959. Recently, they have been introduced into the same areas with success. The **barbary sheep*** *(Ammotragus lervia)*, or **aoudad**, first introduced to the Palo Duro Canyon area in 1957–1958, has become firmly established. A multipartner wildlife restoration project has brought the bighorn sheep into the Edwards Plateau, Trans-Pecos, South Texas, Rolling Plains, and Post Oak Savannah regions, including Big Bend Ranch State Park.

Shrew: The shrew is one of the smallest mammals. Four species are found in Texas: the **southern short-tailed shrew** *(Blarina Carolinensis)*, found in the eastern fourth of the state; the **least shrew** *(Cryptotis parva)*, in eastern and central areas; **Elliot's short-tailed shrew** *(Blarina hylophaga)*, known to live in Aransas, Montague, and Bastrop counties; and the **desert shrew** *(Notiosorex crawfordi)*, found in the western two-thirds of the state.

Barbary sheep in Big Bend National Park. Photo by Diane Isabel/Shutterstock.

Skunk: There are six species of skunk in Texas. The **Eastern spotted skunk** *(Spilogale putorius)* is found in the eastern half of the state, the Gulf area, and across North-Central Texas to the Panhandle. A small skunk, it is often erroneously called civet cat. The **Western spotted skunk** *(Spilogale gracilis)* is found in the southwestern part of the state north to Garza and Howard counties and east to Bexar and Duval counties. The **striped skunk** *(Mephitis mephitis)* is found statewide, mostly in brush or wooded areas. The **hooded skunk** *(Mephitis macroura)* is found in limited numbers in the Big Bend and adjacent parts of the Trans-Pecos. The **eastern hog-nosed skunk** *(Conepatus leuconotus)*, found in the Gulf Coastal Plains, ranges southward into Mexico. The **common hog-nosed skunk** *(Conepatus mesoleucus)* is found in southwestern, central, and southern Texas, north to Collin and Lubbock counties.

Squirrel: The **eastern fox squirrel** *(Sciurus niger)* is found in the eastern two-thirds of the state. The **eastern gray squirrel** *(Sciurus carolinensis)* is found generally in the eastern third of the state. The **flying squirrel** *(Glaucomys volans)* is found in wooded areas of East Texas. The fox and gray squirrels are important small-game animals. See also **Ground Squirrel**.

Weasel: The **long-tailed weasel** *(Mustela frenata)*, akin to the mink, is found statewide but is scarce in West Texas and the far north Panhandle. In general, their destruction of mice, ground squirrels, and pocket gophers benefits agriculture. Also known to enter poultry houses and kill chickens.

Whale: Some species that are found in the Gulf of Mexico include: **dwarf sperm whale** *(Kogia simus)*; **pygmy sperm whale** *(Kogia breviceps)*, found near the Texas coast where strandings occur relatively frequently; **short-finned pilot whale** *(Globicephala macrorhynchus)*, common in the Gulf, where there are numerous strandings and sightings; **sperm whale** *(Physeter macrocephalus)*, an endangered species and the most numerous of the great whales in the Gulf, where sightings are relatively common. Other species are known in Texas only through strandings on Gulf beaches.

Wolf: The **red wolf** *(Canis rufus)* was once found throughout the eastern half of the state. It has now been extirpated from the wild, with the only known remnants of the population now in captive propagation. The **gray wolf** *(Canis lupus)* once had a wide range over the western two-thirds of the state. It is now considered extinct in Texas. The **red wolf** and **gray wolf** are on the federal and state endangered species lists.

Reptiles and Arachnids

Reptiles and arachnids are found throughout the state. Commonly found reptiles include the **American alligator** *(Alligator mississippiensis)*, **Eastern box turtle** *(Terrapene carolina)*, and the **Texas horned lizard** or "horny toad" *(Phrynosoma cornutum)*.

There are more than 100 species and subspecies of snakes found in Texas of which only 16 are venomous. Venomous snakes include three species of **copperheads** (southern, broad-banded, and Trans-Pecos); one kind of **cottonmouth** (western); 11 kinds of **rattlesnakes** (canebrake, western massasauga, desert massasauga, western pigmy, western diamondback, timber, banded rock, mottled rock, northern blacktailed, Mojave, and prairie); and the **Texas coral snake**.

The most common arachnids in the state include scorpions, centipedes, and spiders. Of the nearly 900 species of spider in Texas, the ones you are most likely to see include the **American grass spider** *(Agelenopsis)*, **Carolina wolf spider** *(Hogna carolinensis)*, and the **long-bodied cellar spider** or "daddy long-legs" *(Pholcus phalangioides)*. Only two groups of venomous spiders in Texas are considered dangerous to humans: the **brown recluse** *(Loxosceles reclusa)* and the **black widow** *(Latrodectus mactans)*. ☆

National Wildlife Refuges in Texas

Source: U.S. Fish and Wildlife Service, U.S. Department of the Interior.

Texas has more than 470,000 acres in 18 national wildlife refuges. Their descriptions, with date of acquisition in parentheses, follow.

Included in this acreage are two conservation easement refuges, which may be visited at different times of the year for bird watching and wildlife viewing, as well as hunting and fishing. Write or call before visiting to check on facilities and days and hours of operation. On the web: **www.fws.gov/southwest/**.

Anahuac (1963): The more than 37,000 acres of this refuge are located along the upper Gulf Coast in Chambers County. Fresh and saltwater marshes and miles of beautiful, sweeping coastal prairie provide wintering habitat for large flocks of waterfowl, including geese, 27 species of ducks, and six species of rails. Roseate spoonbills, great and snowy egrets, and white-faced ibis are among the other birds frequenting the refuge. Other species include alligator, muskrat, and bobcat. Fishing, bird watching, auto tours, and hunting are available. Office: Box 278, Anahuac 77514; (409) 267-3337.

Aransas (1937): This refuge complex comprises 115,000 acres including Blackjack Peninsula, Matagorda Island, and three satellite units in Aransas and Refugio counties. Besides providing wintering grounds for the largest wild flock of endangered whooping cranes, the refuge is home to more than 390 species of waterfowl and other migratory birds. Refuge Tour Loop is open daily, sunrise to sunset. Claude F. Lard Visitor Center is open daily, 6:45 am to 7:30 pm. Other facilities include a 40-foot observation tower and walking trails. Office: Box 100, Austwell 77950; (361) 349-1181.

Attwater Prairie Chicken (1972): Established in Colorado County to preserve habitat for the endangered Attwater's prairie chicken (a ground-dwelling grouse), the refuge comprises 10,528 acres of native tallgrass prairie, sandy knolls, and wooded areas. A 5-mile auto tour loop is available year-round. There are two hiking trails — the Sycamore and the Pipit trails — that traverse the prairie potholes and riparian areas. The auto tour loop can also serve as a hiking trail. Refuge open sunrise to sunset. Office: Box 519, Eagle Lake 77434; (979) 234-3021.

Balcones Canyonlands (1992): This 25,000-acre refuge is located in Burnet, Travis, and Williamson counties northwest of Austin. It was established to protect the nesting habitat of two endangered birds: black-capped vireo and golden-cheeked warbler. The Shin Oak Observation Deck is open almost year round (excluding a few weekends in the fall). Hunting available. Open Monday–Friday, 8:00 am–4:30 pm. Office: 24518 FM-1431, Marble Falls 78654; (512) 339-9432.

Big Boggy (1983): This refuge occupies 5,000 acres of coastal prairie and salt marsh along East Matagorda Bay for the benefit of wintering waterfowl. The refuge is only open to waterfowl hunting in season. Office: 6801 County Road 306, Brazoria 77422; (979) 964-4011.

Brazoria (1966): The 43,388 acres of this refuge, located along the Gulf Coast in Brazoria County, serve as haven for wintering waterfowl and a wide variety of other migratory birds. The refuge also supports many marsh and water birds, from roseate spoonbills and great blue herons to white-faced ibis and sandhill cranes. Brazoria Refuge is within the Freeport Christmas Bird Count circle, which frequently achieves the highest number of species seen in a 24-hour period. Open daily sunrise to sunset. Hunting and fishing also available. Office: 24907 FM 2004, Angleton 77515; (979) 922-1037.

Buffalo Lake (1958): Comprising 7,664 acres in the Central Flyway in Randall County in the Panhandle, this refuge contains some of the best remaining shortgrass prairie in the United States. Buffalo Lake is now dry; a marsh area is artificially maintained for the numerous birds, reptiles, and mammals. Available activities include picnicking, auto tour, birding, photography, and hiking. Office: Box 179, Umbarger 79091; (806) 499-3382.

Caddo Lake (2000): Established on portions of the 8,500-acre Longhorn Army Ammunition Plant in Harrison County, this refuge contains a mature flooded bald cypress forest, with some trees nearly 400 years old. The wetlands support a diverse plant community. The bottomland hardwood forest ecosystem provides essential habitat for migratory and resident wildlife. The wetlands of Caddo Lake are important to migratory birds within the Central Flyway. The area supports one of the highest breeding populations of wood ducks and prothonotary warblers. Bird watching, hunting, equestrian use, auto tour, hiking, and biking are available. Office: 15600 Hwy. 134, Karnack 75661; (903) 679-9144.

Hagerman (1946): Hagerman National Wildlife Refuge lies on the Big Mineral arm of Lake Texoma in Grayson County. The 4,500 acres of marsh and water and 6,900 acres of upland and farmland provide a feeding and resting place for migrating waterfowl. Bird watching, fishing, and hunting are available. Office: 6465 Refuge Road, Sherman 75092-5817; (903) 786-2826.

Laguna Atascosa (1946): This refuge is the southernmost waterfowl refuge in the Central Flyway and contains more than 45,000 acres fronting on the Laguna Madre in the Lower Rio Grande Valley in Cameron and Willacy counties. Open lagoons, coastal prairies, salt flats, and brushlands support a wide diversity of wildlife. The United States' largest concentration of redhead ducks winters here, along with many other species of waterfowl and shorebirds. White-tailed deer, javelina, and armadillo can be found, along with endangered ocelot. Bird watching and nature study are popular; auto-tour roads and nature trails are available. Camping and fishing are permitted within Adolph Thomae Jr. County Park. Hunting also available. Office: 22817 Ocelot Road, Los Fresnos 78566; (956) 748-3607.

Lower Rio Grande Valley (1979): Part of the 180,000-acre South Texas Refuge Complex, this refuge lies within Cameron, Hidalgo, Starr, and Willacy counties. It comprises more than 100 separate tracts of land, some fallow farm fields connecting healthy habitat that can become travel corridors for wildlife. The refuge includes 11 different habitat types, including sabal palm forest, tidal flats, coastal brushland, mid-delta thorn forest, woodland potholes and basins, upland thorn scrub, flood forest, barretal, riparian woodland, and Chihuahuan thorn forest. Nearly 500 species of birds and over 300 butterfly species have been found there, as well as four of the five cats that occur within the United States: jaguarundi, ocelot, bobcat, and mountain lion. Seasonal hunting and canoe tours are available. Office: 3325 Green Jay Road, Alamo 78516; (956) 784-7500.

McFaddin (1980): This refuge's 55,000 acres in Jefferson and Chambers counties are of great importance to wintering populations of migratory waterfowl. One of the densest populations of alligators in Texas is found here. Activities on the refuge include wildlife observation, hunting, fishing, and crabbing. Seven boat ramps provide access to inland lakes and waterways; limited roadways. Open daily from sunrise until sunset. Office: Box 358, Sabine Pass 77655; (409) 971-2909.

Muleshoe (1935): Oldest of the national refuges in Texas, Muleshoe provides winter habitat for waterfowl and the continent's largest wintering population of sandhill cranes. Comprising 5,809 acres in the High Plains of Bailey County, the refuge contains playa lakes, marsh areas, caliche outcroppings, and native grasslands. A nature trail, campground, and picnic area are available. Office: Box 549, Muleshoe 79347; (806) 946-3341.

Neches River (2013): Anderson and Cherokee counties. It was established to protect wintering and nesting habitat for migratory birds of the Central Flyway and the bottomland hardwoods for their diverse biological value. Office: 262 West Highway 79, Jacksonville 75766; (956) 245-9426.

San Bernard (1968): Located in Brazoria and Matagorda counties on the Gulf Coast near Freeport, this refuge's 27,414 acres attract migrating waterfowl, including white-fronted and Canada geese and several species of duck, which spend the winter on the refuge. Habitats, consisting of coastal prairies, salt-mud flats, and saltwater and fresh-water ponds and potholes, also attract yellow rails, roseate spoonbills, reddish egrets, and American bitterns. Visitors enjoy auto and hiking trails, photography, bird watching, fishing, and waterfowl hunting in season. Office: 6801 County Road 306, Brazoria 77422; (979) 964-4011.

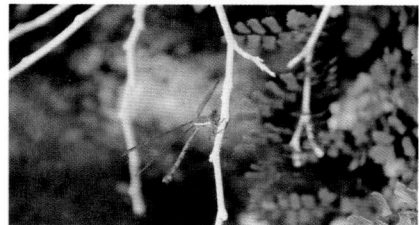

Santa Ana (1943): Santa Ana is located on the north bank of the Rio Grande in Hidalgo County. Santa Ana's 2,088 acres of subtropical forest and native brushland are at an ecological crossroads of subtropical, Gulf Coast, Great Plains, and Chihuahuan desert habitats. Santa Ana attracts birders from across the United States who can view many species of Mexican birds as they reach the northern edge of their ranges in South Texas. Also found at Santa Ana are ocelot and jaguarundi, endangered members of the cat family. Visitors enjoy a tram or auto drive, bicycling and hiking trails, and a tower overlook. Office: 3325 Green Jay Road, Alamo 78516; (956) 784-7500.

Texas Point (1980): Texas Point's 8,900 acres are located in Jefferson County on the upper Gulf Coast, 12 miles east of McFaddin NWR, where they serve a large wintering popu-lation of waterfowl and migratory birds. The endangered southern bald eagle and peregrine falcon may occasionally be seen during peak fall and spring migrations. Alligators are commonly observed during the spring, summer, and fall months. Activities include wildlife observation, hunt-ing, fishing, and crabbing. Access to the refuge is by boat and on foot only. Open daily from sunrise until sunset. Office: Box 358, Sabine Pass 77655; (409) 971-2909.

Trinity River (1994): Established to protect remnant bottomland hardwood forests and associated wetlands, this refuge, located in northern Liberty County off State Highway 787 about 15 miles east of Cleveland, provides habitat for wintering, migrating, and breeding waterfowl and a variety of other wetland-dependent wildlife. A tract south of Liberty includes Champion Lake. Office: Box 10015, Liberty 77575; (936) 336-9786. ☆

The photographs on this page were all taken at the Balcones Canyonlands National Wildlife Refuge. Top to bottom: Black-capped Vireo, photo by Isaac Sanchez (CC); Dragonfly, photo by Vince Smith (CC); Lesser Goldfinch, photo by Vince Smith (CC); Flower of the Toxicoscordion nuttallii (common name: Nuttall's Death Camas), photo by Danielle Bridgida (CC); and native trees under a beautiful sky, photo by Mark Bonica (CC).

Texas Wildlife Management Areas

Source: Texas Parks and Wildlife Department; http://tpwd.texas.gov/huntwild/hunt/wma/

Texas Parks and Wildlife Department is responsible for managing 47 wildlife management areas (WMAs) in the state totaling more than 710,000 acres. Every vegetational area in the state has at least one WMA, with the exception of the Cross Timbers and Prairies area in north central Texas. (See page 69 for more information about the Vegetational Areas of Texas.)

Wildlife management areas are used principally for hunting, but many are also used for research, fishing, wildlife viewing, hiking, camping, bicycling, and horseback riding, when those activities are compatible with the primary goals for which the WMA was established. See the table below for activities available in Texas' WMAs.

Access to WMAs at times designated for public use is provided through various permits, depending on the activity.

A Limited Public Use Permit ($12) allows access for such activities as birdwatching, hiking, camping, or picnicking.

On most WMAs, restrooms and drinking water are not provided; check with the TPWD about facilities before visiting a WMA.

For further information, contact the Texas Parks and Wildlife Department, 4200 Smith School Rd., Austin 78744. ☆

Texas Wildlife Management Areas Name (Acreage)	County	Hunting	Fishing	Camping	Wildlife Viewing	Hiking	Driving	Bicycling	Equestrian	Comments
Alabama Creek (14,561)	Trinity	★	★	★	★	★	★	★	★	In Davy Crockett NF
Alazan Bayou (2,063)	Nacogdoches	★	★	★	★				★	
Angelina-Neches/Dam B (12,636)	Jasper/Tyler	★	★	★	★	★		★		
Atkinson Island (150)	Harris		★		★					Boat access only
Bannister (25,695)	San Augustine	★	★	★	★	★		★	★	In Angelina NF
Big Lake Bottom (3,894)	Anderson	★	★		★					
Black Gap (103,000)	Brewster	★	★	★	★	★	★	★	★	NW of Big Bend NP
Caddo Lake (8,124)	Marion/Harrison	★	★	★	★				★	
Caddo National Grasslands (16,140)	Fannin	★	★	★	★	★		★	★	Separated into two units
Candy Cain Abshier (207)	Chambers				★					Excellent birding spring and fall
Cedar Creek Islands (160)	Henderson		★		★					Wildlife viewing from boat or bank of reservoir only
Chaparral (15,200)	La Salle/Dimmit	★	★	★	★	★	★	★	★	
Cooper (14,480)	Delta/Hopkins	★	★		★	★		★		Camping: Cooper Lake SP
D.R. Wintermann (246)	Wharton				★					Restricted access; bird refuge
East Texas Conservation Center (223)	Jasper				★		★	★		Register at office upon arrival
Elephant Mountain (23,147)	Brewster	★		★	★	★	★			
Gene Howe (5,886)	Hemphill	★	★	★	★	★		★	★	Riding March–August only
Gene Howe: W.A. "Pat" Murphy (889)	Lipscomb	★	★		★	★				
Guadalupe Delta (7,411)	Calhoun/Refugio	★	★		★	★		★		Freshwater marsh
Gus Engling (10,958)	Anderson	★	★	★	★	★	★	★	★	
J.D. Murphree (24,498)	Jefferson	★	★		★					Access by boat only
James E. Daughtrey (34,000)	Live Oak/McMullen	★			★					Primitive camping requires special permit
Justin Hurst (15,612)	Brazoria	★	★		★	★		★		On Texas Coastal Birding Trail
Keechi Creek (1,500)	Leon	★								
Kerr (6,493)	Kerr	★	★		★		★	★		On Guadalupe River
Las Palomas: Anacua (222)	Cameron	★			★					
Las Palomas: Lower Rio Grande Valley (3,311)	Cameron/Hidalgo	★			★	★				Also Starr and Willacy counties
Lower Neches (7,998)	Orange	★	★		★	★				Coastal marsh
M.O. Neasloney (100)	Gonzales				★	★				Primarily for school groups
Mad Island (7,200)	Matagorda	★			★					Reservations needed for wildlife tours
Mason Mountain (5,300)	Mason	★								Restricted access
Matador (28,183)	Cottle	★	★	★	★	★	★		★	Primitive camping; tours
Matagorda Island (56,688)	Calhoun	★	★	★	★	★		★		
Moore Plantation (26,772)	Sabine/Jasper	★	★	★	★	★		★	★	In Sabine National Forest
Muse (1,972)	Brown	★			★					
Nannie M. Stringfellow (3,666)	Brazoria	★			★					Open for special hunts only
Nature Center (82)	Smith				★	★				Primarily for school groups

Hardwood trees in a swampy area of Sam Houston National Forest. Parts of the forest are designated Wildlife Management Areas. Photo by Chris M. (CC).

Texas Wildlife Management Areas Name (Acreage)	County	Hunting	Fishing	Camping	Wildlife Viewing	Hiking	Driving	Bicycling	Equestrian	Comments
North Toledo Bend (3,650)	Shelby	★	★	★	★	★			★	
Old Sabine Bottom (5,158)	Smith	★	★	★	★	★		★	★	
Pat Mayse (8,925)	Lamar	★	★	★	★	★			★	
Playa Lakes: Armstrong (160)	Castro				★					Registration req., must stay on the roads
Playa Lakes: Dimmitt (422)	Castro	★								Limited access
Playa Lakes: Taylor Lakes (530)	Donley	★			★	★				
Redhead Pond (37)	Nueces				★					Freshwater wetland; part of Great Texas Birding Trail
Richland Creek (13,783)	Freestone/Navarro	★	★	★	★	★		★	★	
Sam Houston National Forest (161,508)	San Jacinto/Walker	★	★	★	★	★	★	★	★	Also Montgomery County
Sierra Diablo (11,624)	Hudspeth/Culberson	★								Restricted access
Tawakoni (2,335)	Hunt/Van Zandt	★	★	★	★	★			★	Primitive camping
Tony Houseman (3,985)	Orange	★	★	★	★	★				Canoeing
Welder Flats (1,480)	Calhoun		★		★					Boat access only
White Oak Creek (25,777)	Bowie/Cass/Morris/Titus	★	★		★	★			★	Camp in Atlanta and Daingerfield SPs
Yoakum Dunes (14,037)	Cochran/Terry/Yoakum	In development, not yet open to the public. Commissioned and authorized in 2014, this site will preserve the breeding and nesting habitats of the lesser prairie chicken, as well as many other native wildlife, including quail, mule deer, and Texas horned lizards.								

The tiny Tobusch fishhook cactus, a golden-cheeked warbler, and a Houston toad. All are endangered. Photos by U.S. Fish and Wildlife Service photographers Chris Best (cactus), Steve Maslowski (warbler), and Paige Najvar (toad).

Texas' Threatened and Endangered Species

Source: Texas Parks and Wildlife Department

Endangered species are those the TPWD has named as being at risk of statewide extinction. Threatened species are likely to become endangered in the future. The following lists include species that are either endangered or threatened as of February 2018 (the most recent list available) and vary slightly from the federal list. Learn more, and see the TPWD Conservation Action Plan at: **https://tpwd.texas.gov/ huntwild/wild/wildlife_diversity/nongame/**

Endangered Species

MAMMALS: Bats: Mexican long-nosed bat. **Marine Mammals**: West Indian manatee; finback and humpback whales. **Carnivores**: jaguar; jaguarundi; ocelot; gray and red wolves.

BIRDS: Waterbirds: whooping crane. **Raptors**: northern aplomado falcon. **Upland Birds**: Attwater's greater prairie chicken. **Shorebirds**: Eskimo curlew; interior least tern. **Woodpeckers**: red-cockaded woodpecker. **Songbirds**: southwestern willow flycatcher; black-capped vireo; golden-cheeked warbler.

REPTILES: Hawksbill, Kemp's Ridley, and leatherback sea turtles.

AMPHIBIANS: Salamanders: Austin blind, Barton Springs, and Texas blind salamanders. **Frogs & Toads**: Houston toad.

FISHES: Minnows: Rio Grande silvery minnow. **Killifish**: Comanche Springs and Leon Springs pupfish. **Livebearers**: Big Bend, Pecos, and San Marcos gambusias. **Perches**: fountain darter. **Coastal Fishes**: smalltooth sawfish. **Catfish**: Mexican blindcat.

INVERTEBRATES: Crustaceans: Peck's cave, Pecos, and diminuitive amphipods. **Mollusks & Snails**: Pecos assiminea, Diamond Y Spring, Phantom Cave, Phantom Spring, and Gonzales Spring snails. **Beetles**: Comal Springs dryopid and riffle beetles.

PLANTS: Cacti: Black lace, Nellie's Cory, Sneed's pincushion, star, and Tobusch fishhook cacti; Davis' green pitaya. **Trees, Shrubs, Sub-shrubs**: Texas ayenia; Walker's manioc; Texas snowbell. **Wildflowers**: South Texas ambrosia; Zapata and white bladderpod; Terlingua Creek cat's-eye; ashy dogweed; Texas trailing phlox; Texas poppy-mallow; Texas prairie dawn; slender rushpea; large-fruited sand-verbena; Texas golden gladecress. **Orchids**: Navasota ladies'-tresses. **Grasses**: little aguja pondweed; Texas wild-rice.

Threatened Species

MAMMALS: Bats: Rafinesque's big-eared, southern yellow, and spotted bats. **Carnivores**: black and Louisiana black bears; white-nosed coati. **Marine Mammals**: Atlantic spotted and rough-toothed dolphins; dwarf sperm, false killer, Gervais' beaked, goose-beaked, killer, pygmy killer, pygmy sperm, and short-finned pilot whales. **Rodents**: Palo Duro mouse; Coues' rice rat and Texas kangaroo rat.

BIRDS: Waterbirds: reddish egret; white-faced ibis; wood stork. **Raptors**: bald eagle; peregrine falcon; common black, gray, white-tailed, and zone-tailed hawks; swallow-tailed kite; Mexican spotted owl; cactus ferruginous pygmy-owl. **Shorebirds**: piping plover; sooty tern. **Songbirds**: rose-throated becard; tropical parula; Bachman's, Texas Botteri's, and Arizona Botteri's sparrows; northern beardless tyrannulet.

REPTILES: Turtles: loggerhead and green sea turtles; Texas tortoise; alligator snapping, Cagle's map, and Chihuahuan mud turtles. **Lizards**: reticulated gecko; mountain short-horned, reticulate collared, and Texas horned lizards. **Snakes**: speckled racer; black-striped, Brazos water, Chihuahuan desert lyre, Louisiana pine, northern cat-eyed, smooth green, northern scarlet, Texas scarlet, Texas indigo, and Trans-Pecos black-headed snakes; timber (canebrake) rattlesnake.

AMPHIBIANS: Salamanders: black-spotted newt; Blanco blind, Cascade Caverns, Comal blind, and San Marcos salamanders; South Texas siren (large form). **Frogs & Toads**: sheep and white-lipped frogs; Mexican treefrog; Mexican burrowing toad.

FISHES: Large River Fish: paddlefish and shovelnose sturgeon. **Minnows**: Rio Grande chub; Devils River minnow; Arkansas River, bluehead, bluntnose, Chihuahua, and proserpine shiners; Mexican stoneroller. **Killifish**: Conchos and Pecos pupfish. **Livebearers**: blotched and San Felipe gambusias. **Suckers**: blue sucker and creek chubsucker. **Perches**: blackside and Rio Grande darters. **Coastal Fishes**: opossum pipefish; river and Mexican gobies. **Catfish**: toothless blindcat and widemouth blindcat.

INVERTEBRATES: Mollusks & Snails: Texas fatmucket; Mexican and Texas fawnsfoot; Texas heelsplitter; Southern hickorynut; Texas hornshell; salina mucket; golden orb; Louisiana, Texas, and triangle pigtoe; smooth and Texas pimpleback; sandbank pocketbook; false spike.

PLANTS: Cacti: Bunched cory, Chisos Mountains hedgehog, Lloyd's mariposa cacti. **Trees, Shrubs, Sub-shrubs**: Hinckley's oak. **Wildflowers**: Pecos sunflower; earth fruit; Neches River rose mallow. ☆

WEATHER

A storm supercell near Seymour in Baylor County.
Photo by Daniel Rodriguez (CC).

HIGHLIGHTS & SUMMARIES, 2017 & 2018

TEMPERATURES, PRECIPITATION

TORNADOS, DROUGHTS

DESTRUCTIVE WEATHER 1766-2018

RECORDS BY COUNTY

Weather

Source: Unless otherwise noted, this information is provided by Texas State Climatologist John W. Nielsen-Gammon and graduate research assistants Brooke Barker and Jeramy Dedrick, Texas A&M University.

Weather Highlights 2017

January 14–15, 2017: A strong winter weather system made its way through the northern portions of the Panhandle bringing frigid temperatures and freezing precipitation. Some 58,000 electric customers were impacted at the storm's peak. This ice storm was the one of the costliest experienced in nearly 17 years with damages totaling more than $14 million. In Southwest Texas a passing line of storms dumped hail up to 3 inches in diameter and provided wind gusts up to 90 mph. A storm survey by the National Weather Service (NWS) determined that an EF-2 tornado passed through a rural area near Brady.

February 14, 2017: Early morning thunderstorms in Southeast Texas caught many residents by surprise as conditions quickly turned severe. Windows, roofs, and other property sustained extensive damage from winds measured to be in excess of 50 mph, causing an overall $2.9 million in damages. A rain-wrapped tornado, later classified as an EF-2 (peak winds at 115 mph), passed through Fort Bend Co. injuring six people.

April 14–17, 2017: Several days of pronounced severe weather in northern Texas and the Panhandle led to torrential downpours, hail, and tornadoes. Excessive rain over the four days of storms caused major flooding in the region, with areas observing 4–6 inches throughout the storm days. Hail measuring 1–3 inches in diameter fell nearly every day leading to extensive property and crop damages. An EF-3 tornado tore through Castro Co. in the southern Panhandle. Damages from these days of storms totaled nearly $2 million.

Climatic Data Regions of Texas

April 29, 2017: A devastating tornado outbreak in East Texas took the lives of four people and injured more than 50. Rains, Hopkins, Henderson, and Van Zandt counties were affected by 7 tornadoes in the late afternoon and evening hours; the most intense of these tornadoes, in Van Zandt Co., was given an EF-4 rating. Farmers suffered a $507,000 loss, while overall property damage exceeded $2 million.

	Average Temperatures 2017										Precipitation in Inches 2017									
	High Plains	Low Plains	North Central	East Texas	Trans-Pecos	Edwards Plateau	South Central	Upper Coast	South Texas	Lower Valley	High Plains	Low Plains	North Central	East Texas	Trans-Pecos	Edwards Plateau	South Central	Upper Coast	South Texas	Lower Valley
Jan.	40.7	44.7	49.2	54.0	48.9	51.2	58.3	59.9	61.0	64.8	1.83	1.72	2.86	5.11	0.72	1.64	2.74	4.48	0.53	0.91
Feb.	49.5	53.7	57.8	60.4	55.9	58.8	65.2	66.0	68.3	72.2	0.60	1.62	2.48	2.72	0.23	2.04	2.73	2.85	1.25	1.11
Mar.	56.3	60.6	62.7	63.6	63.5	64.4	68.5	68.5	71.1	74.1	1.38	1.66	1.55	3.02	0.11	1.02	3.23	4.73	3.00	2.99
April	60.1	64.0	66.4	68.0	66.9	67.6	71.4	71.4	74.6	77.0	2.29	1.97	4.12	5.34	0.84	2.38	2.51	3.57	1.80	0.98
May	66.0	70.0	71.6	71.2	72.0	72.5	75.6	75.4	78.9	81.1	1.16	1.83	2.59	6.19	0.88	2.45	2.48	3.61	2.64	1.80
June	78.0	80.2	79.4	78.9	81.5	80.7	82.7	81.4	85.0	85.8	2.20	2.24	5.30	4.69	1.40	2.19	3.46	6.89	1.52	1.45
July	80.7	84.0	84.4	83.2	80.9	83.9	86.3	84.7	87.3	86.4	2.61	2.65	3.10	4.04	2.66	1.98	0.81	2.96	0.43	0.83
Aug.	75.1	79.2	81.6	81.0	78.7	81.3	84.3	83.4	86.5	87.8	4.88	4.01	5.32	14.20	2.84	3.32	12.19	29.13	2.33	1.95
Sep.	71.2	74.9	77.0	76.7	75.6	76.6	79.1	79.6	82.1	83.9	3.18	3.86	2.14	0.86	2.11	2.80	2.49	1.81	4.76	2.00
Oct.	60.4	64.2	66.5	67.3	65.6	66.1	70.4	71.6	72.5	75.4	1.64	0.90	1.60	2.06	0.41	0.60	1.27	1.97	0.96	3.34
Nov.	53.1	55.9	59.6	61.5	58.8	60.2	66.4	66.9	68.2	72.1	0.13	0.41	1.09	1.93	0.16	0.55	0.61	1.37	0.71	2.00
Dec.	40.3	43.7	47.0	48.6	47.4	48.2	53.4	54.2	55.3	59.7	0.10	0.30	2.45	4.60	0.89	1.70	3.47	3.77	2.28	1.34
Ann.	61.0	64.6	66.9	67.9	66.3	67.6	71.8	71.9	74.2	76.7	22.00	23.17	34.60	54.76	13.25	22.67	37.99	67.14	22.21	20.70

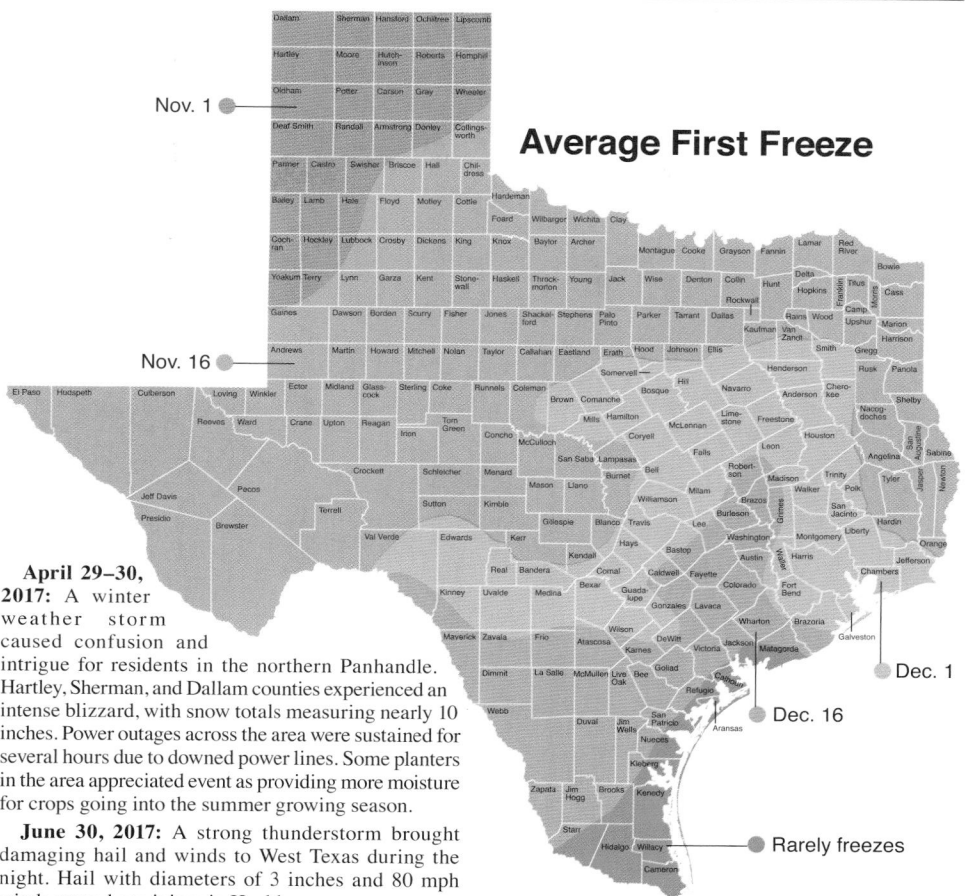

Average First Freeze

Nov. 1

Nov. 16

Dec. 1

Dec. 16

Rarely freezes

April 29–30, 2017: A winter weather storm caused confusion and intrigue for residents in the northern Panhandle. Hartley, Sherman, and Dallam counties experienced an intense blizzard, with snow totals measuring nearly 10 inches. Power outages across the area were sustained for several hours due to downed power lines. Some planters in the area appreciated event as providing more moisture for crops going into the summer growing season.

June 30, 2017: A strong thunderstorm brought damaging hail and winds to West Texas during the night. Hail with diameters of 3 inches and 80 mph winds caused one injury in Hockley Co. Residents and ranchers saw property and crop damage estimated above $20 million and $30 million, respectively.

August 25–29, 2017: Hurricane Harvey made landfall in southeast Texas and impacted the coastal region of the state, joining the list of the costliest weather events in U.S. history. Rain totals in excess of 50 inches were observed in some areas, with a maximum of 60 inches as the storm stalled in the southeastern Texas interior. The storm was responsible for 68 deaths and $125 billion in damages in Texas.

December 7–8, 2017: A mix of wintry precipitation across Central and South Texas during the evening and early night hours of December 7. As temperatures continued to drop into the night, precipitation developed into snow for most regions. Some areas observed 4–6 inches of snow accumulation, with a maximum of 7 inches near Corpus Christi. Freezing fog and heavy snow rates led to traffic accidents and power outages in numerous areas, causing $85,000 in property damages.

2017 WEATHER EXTREMES

Lowest Temp.: Lipscomb, Lipscomb Co., January 16 . . . . .–10°
Highest Temp.: Rio Grande Village, Brewster Co., July 15 . . 114°
24-hour Precip.: Port Arthur, Jefferson Co., August 29 . . 26.03"
Monthly Precip.: Port Arthur, Jefferson Co., August . . . 54.74"
Least Annual Precip.: El Paso, El Paso Co. . . . . 5.68"
Greatest Annual Precip.: Port Arthur, Jefferson Co. . . . 104.30"

Monthly Summaries 2017

January was an abnormally warm month for the majority of the state. The eastern and southern portions of Texas observed the warmest conditions, with record-breaking high temperatures in Brownsville, Corpus Christi, and Galveston, while the Panhandle and portions of West Texas saw average and cooler-than-average temperatures. The northern sector of the Panhandle saw precipitation totals that were 300 percent to 600 percent above normal. South Texas was significantly drier, observing only 5 percent to 25 percent of normal precipitation.

It was an unseasonably warm month in **February**. With the exception of the Trans-Pecos region,

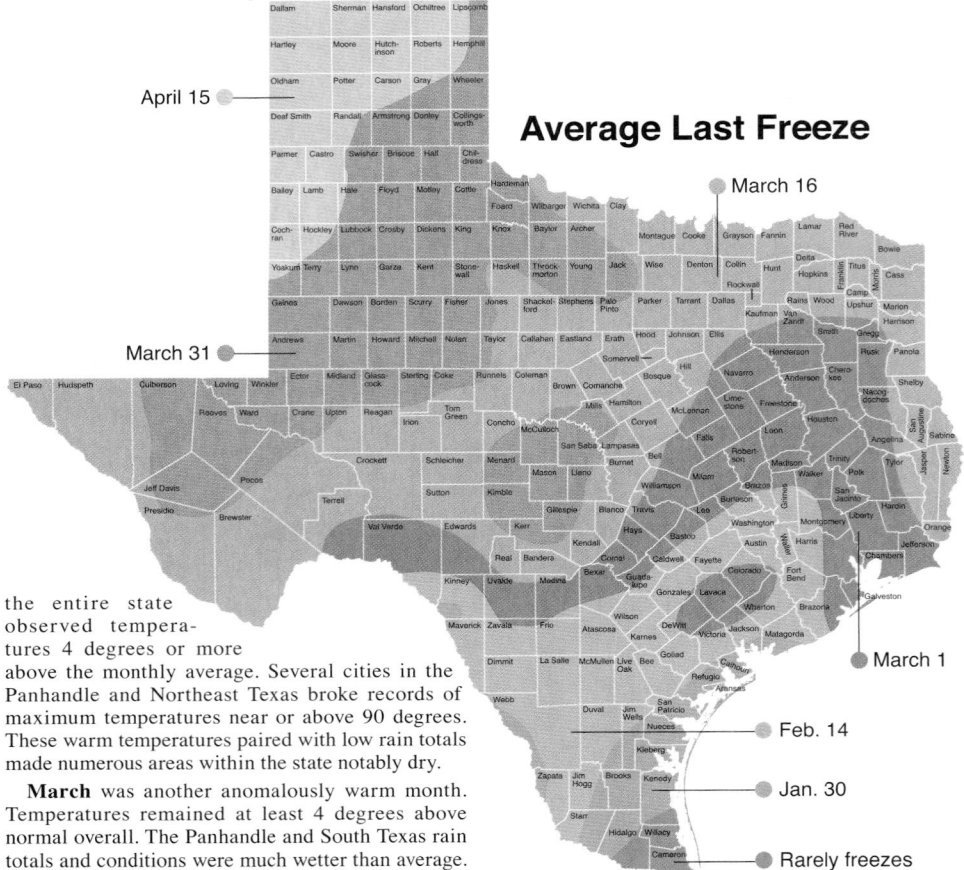

Average Last Freeze

April 15

March 31

March 16

March 1

Feb. 14

Jan. 30

Rarely freezes

the entire state observed temperatures 4 degrees or more above the monthly average. Several cities in the Panhandle and Northeast Texas broke records of maximum temperatures near or above 90 degrees. These warm temperatures paired with low rain totals made numerous areas within the state notably dry.

March was another anomalously warm month. Temperatures remained at least 4 degrees above normal overall. The Panhandle and South Texas rain totals and conditions were much wetter than average. South Texas and the Lower Valley were the wettest regions during the month, with precipitation exceeding 200 percent. The interior regions saw much lower-than-average precipitation. Northeastern and Central Texas were the most heavily impacted by the dryness.

As with the preceding months, **April** temperatures were warmer than the monthly average. Most regions remained within 2 percent to 3 percent of the monthly average. North Central Texas and a portion of the Upper Coast were the warmest, with temperatures of 3 degrees to 4 degrees above normal, while the Low Rolling Plains remained at or just below average. It was also a wet month for a large portion of the state; however, the Lower Valley saw a relative dry spell.

May was on the cooler side with observed temperatures 1 degree to 3 degrees below normal in the majority of the state. No regions were significantly wet other than a few areas in East Texas. Notable dryness prevailed in nearly every other region, especially the Trans-Pecos and southern High Plains. By the end of May, abnormal dryness increased to 30 percent from 7 percent across the state.

For most Texans, **June** was average in terms of temperature. The High Plains observed temperatures at 2 degrees to 3 degrees above normal, while the Central and Coastal regions had normal and 1 degree to 2 degrees below normal temperatures. The DFW

Metroplex had the wettest conditions at nearly 200 percent above the norm. Most other regions experienced atypical dryness.

With summer in full swing, temperatures crept back up to above average for several regions in **July.** The South Central, Edwards Plateau, and northern High Plains regions felt the heat the most, with temperatures pushing 2 degrees to 4 degrees above normal. Though rainfall across the majority of the state remained at normal for July, extensive dryness in the southern portions of the state allowed for issuance of Burn Bans in several counties.

August brought relief from significant heat and dryness. Temperatures on average were cooler by at least 1 degree and up to 4 degrees for every region, excluding the South. The High Plains was the coolest region as average temperatures were 3 degrees or more below normal. Hurricane Harvey hit the Gulf Coast and Southeast, dropping precipitation up to 600 percent above normal on some areas. The western portion of the state observed normal and just below normal precipitation during the month.

Above normal temperatures returned to many areas in **September**. North Central Texas, the western Edwards Plateau, and the Trans-Pecos regions saw

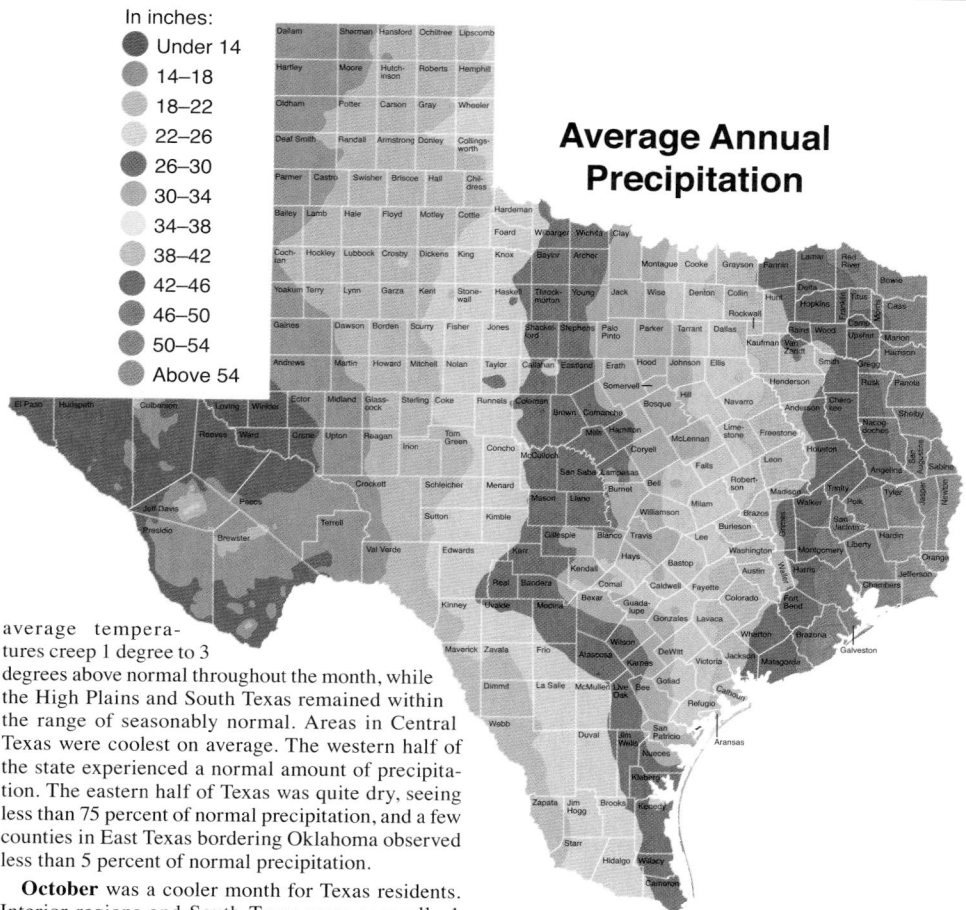

In inches:
- Under 14
- 14–18
- 18–22
- 22–26
- 26–30
- 30–34
- 34–38
- 38–42
- 42–46
- 46–50
- 50–54
- Above 54

Average Annual Precipitation

average temperatures creep 1 degree to 3 degrees above normal throughout the month, while the High Plains and South Texas remained within the range of seasonably normal. Areas in Central Texas were coolest on average. The western half of the state experienced a normal amount of precipitation. The eastern half of Texas was quite dry, seeing less than 75 percent of normal precipitation, and a few counties in East Texas bordering Oklahoma observed less than 5 percent of normal precipitation.

October was a cooler month for Texas residents. Interior regions and South Texas were generally 1 degree to 2 degrees cooler than normal. The High Plains and North Central Texas remained at average, while Northeastern Texas and the Trans-Pecos were again just above average. It was also a notably dry month for the state. The central regions were the driest, with less than 10 percent of normal precipitation.

It was a notably warm and dry **November** for all Texas residents. Temperatures 4 degrees or more above normal dominated the High Plains, Trans Pecos, and Central regions. This, along with significantly below normal precipitation, broadened drought conditions throughout the state. A large area within Northeastern Texas was classified as Severe Drought by the end of the month, along with expanding Moderate Drought in Central Texas, where percent of normal precipitation was less than 10.

December brought varying weather patterns to Texas. The South and Southeast Texas saw a cooler and wetter-than-average month, with temperatures that were 3 degrees below normal and precipitation of more than 100 percent of normal. In contrast, West Texas, the Low Rolling Plains, and High Plains had a warmer and drier month, and many counties in the Panhandle did not see any measurable rainfall.

Drought and abnormally dry conditions were mostly erased in the South and improved in Central and East Texas, while degradation occurred in the Panhandle. This month marked the first classification of extreme drought since early February.

Weather Highlights 2018

January–October 2018: Particularly dry conditions aided by a moderate La Niña led to significant drought coverage in the state. Severe and extreme drought were designated in the Panhandle and continued to degrade. A trend of low rainfall during the Spring in the Panhandle led to **exceptional drought**, the first designation of this severity anywhere in the state since October 2015.

January 21, 2018: The interaction of cold and warm airmasses in the Southern High Plains ignited severe weather in north Central and Northeast Texas. Moderately-sized hail and strong winds impacted many counties within the region. A tornado in Bowie Co. reached maximum intensity as an EF-2 in De Kalb.

March 10–11, 2018: A system of severe storms moved through the Ark-La-Tex region in the late night to early morning hours, bringing hazardous conditions to East Texas. Strong winds in excess of 70 mph were observed in Marion and Upshur counties causing

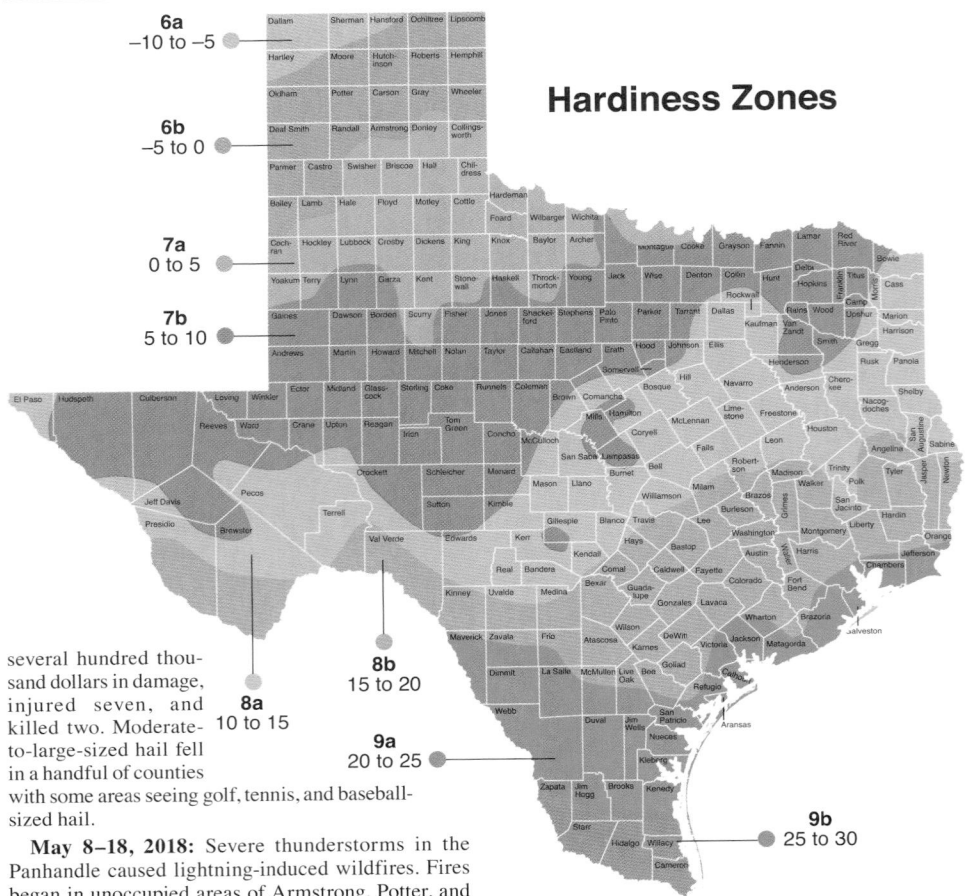

Hardiness Zones

6a
−10 to −5

6b
−5 to 0

7a
0 to 5

7b
5 to 10

8a
10 to 15

8b
15 to 20

9a
20 to 25

9b
25 to 30

several hundred thousand dollars in damage, injured seven, and killed two. Moderate-to-large-sized hail fell in a handful of counties with some areas seeing golf, tennis, and baseball-sized hail.

May 8–18, 2018: Severe thunderstorms in the Panhandle caused lightning-induced wildfires. Fires began in unoccupied areas of Armstrong, Potter, and Randall counties. Two of the wildfires, Summer Field and Mallard, merged and burned approximately 75,530 acres. No property damage was reported.

June 1, 2018: A storm with rapid intensification hit towns in Crosby, Dickens, Kent, and Stonewall counties causing over $4.5 million in damage. The storm also caused a downburst in Ralls with sustained winds of 50–70 mph and gusts as high as 90 mph.

June 6–10, 2018: Intense storms caused dangerous conditions across Texas. During the evening and night hours of the five-day period, atmospheric disturbances produced storms with hurricane-force winds, large hail, and torrential downpours. Winds in Scurry and Mitchell counties were estimated to be 110–120 mph and caused one injury. Dallas and Denton counties reported baseball-sized hail.

September 19–22, 2018: North and Central Texas experienced several days of showers and thunderstorms that caused flash flooding throughout the area and led to nearly $300,000 in property damage. Fast-moving high water caused one death.

2018 WEATHER EXTREMES

Lowest Temp.: Lipscomb, Lipscomb Co., January 17 . . . . . −7°
Highest Temp.: Rio Grande Village, Brewster Co., June 25 . . 116°
24-hour Precip.: Weslaco ARC, Hidalgo Co., June 21 . . . . 11.98"
Monthly Precip.: Galveston, Galveston Co., September . 34.03"
Least Annual Precip.: Tornillo, El Paso Co. . . . . 6.32"
Greatest Annual Precip.: Colmesneil, Tyler Co. . . . . . . 97.92"

October 8, 2018: A strong weather disturbance created heavy rains in Central Texas. Rainfall totalled between 8 inches and 12 inches and flooded nearby rivers and creeks, including South Llano River and Cedar Creek. Flash flooding forced the evacuation of residents at an RV resort; however, four people died and three were injured.

November 11–12, 2018: Winter came early for residents in the Panhandle, as a low-pressure system from New Mexico brought frozen precipitation and strong winds into the region. The winter storm dumped about 6 inches of snow on average in the western Panhandle, with isolated areas observing up to 9 inches of snow.

December 7–8, 2018: Western Texas was blanketed with snow after a slow-moving, unstable northern air mass passed eastward through the region. Most snow accumulation observations were on the range of 3–5 inches, with the largest totals near 10 inches observed in Lubbock.

Monthly Summaries 2018

Almost the entire state was colder than normal in **January.** Parts of South, Southeast, and East Texas saw the greatest temperature anomalies at more than 4 degrees below normal. In terms of precipitation, most of Texas was below normal. The Panhandle and parts of North Central and West Texas observed less than 5 percent of normal precipitation. However, Southeast Texas received between 125 percent and 150 percent of normal precipitation.

February temperatures were normal to slightly below normal in upper North Central Texas. The rest of the state experienced above-normal temperatures. The upper Panhandle received less than 5 percent of normal precipitation. Parts of Northeast Texas received between 300 percent and 400 percent of normal precipitation, and most of East Texas saw between 200 percent and 300 percent of normal rainfall. A large part of the Trans-Pecos saw less than 25 percent of normal rainfall, but far West Texas saw up to 200 percent of normal rainfall.

March saw very warm temperatures across Texas. Most regions saw temperatures more than 4 degrees above normal. The upper Panhandle also saw low precipitation, and the northwest corner recorded no rain. Most of West Texas and Edwards Plateau saw between 25 percent and 50 percent of normal precipitation, but the lower Trans-Pecos recorded less than 25 percent of normal precipitation. Parts of East and Central Texas had between 150 percent and 200 percent of normal precipitation.

April was cool and dry for most of the state. Temperatures ranged from more than 4 degrees below normal in North Central Texas, between 3 degrees and 4 degrees below normal in East Texas and the Low Rolling Plains, and up to 2 degrees below normal in South Texas. West Texas saw above-normal

temperatures. Parts of West Texas and the Panhandle had less than 5 percent of normal rainfall. Most of North Central Texas measured rainfall between 25 percent and 50 percent of normal. East Texas was the only region to see above-normal rainfall.

Generally warmer spring temperatures were seen in **May,** with most of the state at least 2 degrees to 4 degrees above normal. Areas of West Texas and the Panhandle were particularly warm, averaging greater than 6 degrees above normal. Small parts of the High Plains, Edwards Plateau, South Central, and South Texas had more than average precipitation, while the majority of other regions saw less than 75 percent of the May normal.

June provided a warm start to the summer with temperatures above average statewide. As in May, Southern and Eastern regions remained within 2 degrees of normal. Central, Northern, and Western regions experienced up to 8 degrees above normal. June provided another variety of statewide precipitation conditions, with the Southern and Northern regions receiving more than average precipitation while the interior regions of the state were notably dry.

The warm Texas summer continued in **July** when above-average temperatures dominated nearly all of the state. The largest anomalies, averaging about 3 degrees above normal, were in the North Central and Edwards Plateau regions. Precipitation was generally low in July with a number of areas experiencing much drier than normal conditions. Some counties in West Texas and an appreciable part of Southeast Texas managed wetter than normal conditions (100 percent to 200 percent) this month.

For large portions of the state, temperatures were at normal to just above normal for the month of **August.** The Trans-Pecos had notably the warmest departure with temperatures generally 1 degree to 4 degrees above the monthly normal. It was a relatively dry August for many areas. Portions of the Trans-Pecos and counties extending from the northeast to deep South Texas were the driest, with precipitation of 75 percent or less than the monthly normal.

	Average Temperatures 2018										Precipitation in Inches 2018									
	High Plains	Low Plains	North Central	East Texas	Trans-Pecos	Edwards Plateau	South Central	Upper Coast	South Texas	Lower Valley	High Plains	Low Plains	North Central	East Texas	Trans-Pecos	Edwards Plateau	South Central	Upper Coast	South Texas	Lower Valley
Jan.	38.2	40.8	42.1	43.0	44.4	44.6	48.6	48.5	51.2	55.3	0.01	0.06	0.42	2.43	0.03	0.13	0.67	3.11	0.45	0.91
Feb.	42.9	46.0	48.4	54.0	53.4	53.7	58.5	62.1	63.4	68.3	0.16	0.82	4.89	8.25	0.10	1.34	1.87	3.96	0.62	0.65
Mar.	54.1	58.4	60.5	62.3	60.4	62.8	67.4	67.1	71.0	73.9	0.38	0.98	2.94	5.87	0.16	0.85	3.23	2.94	1.43	0.45
April	56.5	59.9	60.2	61.3	65.8	64.8	67.0	66.4	71.4	73.6	0.51	0.48	1.15	3.43	0.11	0.35	1.28	2.29	0.58	1.23
May	75.1	78.7	77.3	76.9	78.4	78.3	79.8	79.1	81.9	81.9	1.54	3.09	2.93	1.84	0.71	2.68	1.96	2.31	2.12	0.92
June	80.5	84.1	84.6	83.1	84.0	84.7	85.2	83.9	86.8	85.9	2.07	2.34	1.37	2.75	1.53	0.98	3.75	6.89	3.21	9.36
July	80.9	85.4	87.0	84.6	82.0	85.2	85.4	84.3	86.6	86.7	2.14	1.48	1.48	3.42	1.68	1.78	2.66	4.64	1.78	1.05
Aug.	78.9	83.2	84.2	83.5	81.2	82.8	85.8	84.8	86.8	87.6	2.64	2.07	3.10	2.25	1.18	2.67	1.26	2.78	1.28	0.42
Sep.	71.2	74.2	77.0	78.8	73.4	75.3	80.2	80.1	81.3	83.9	2.74	5.58	7.68	8.37	2.56	7.55	9.27	11.37	10.72	10.27
Oct.	58.3	62.1	65.3	67.3	63.2	65.5	70.3	72.3	71.8	75.2	4.64	8.09	10.51	8.89	3.46	9.41	6.32	6.12	3.60	2.97
Nov.	44.5	48.9	51.2	52.5	50.8	52.6	57.3	58.5	60.1	63.9	0.28	0.79	1.97	6.02	0.24	0.60	2.80	4.55	0.81	0.94
Dec.	39.9	43.7	47.3	50.0	47.0	48.5	54.9	56.4	57.7	62.9	0.92	1.82	4.61	9.17	0.75	2.70	4.16	6.65	1.37	0.63
Ann.	60.1	63.8	65.4	66.4	65.3	66.6	70.0	70.3	72.5	74.9	18.66	27.60	43.05	62.69	12.51	31.04	39.23	57.61	27.97	29.80

September saw mixed average-temperature conditions throughout the state. Most regions within the eastern half of the state observed temperatures up to 3 degrees above normal, while much of the western half of the state was as much as 2 degrees cooler than normal. The start of a period of exceptionally moist conditions began in September. Record-breaking rainfall was observed in many regions, most notably in North Central, Upper Coast, and South, which saw a large range of 5 inches to 20 inches above normal conditions. The substantial rainfall in September 2018 made it the third wettest in Texas history.

Average temperatures for the month of **October** were generally 0 degrees to 4 degrees below normal, from the High Plains to the Lower Valley. It was a second consecutive month of exceptional rainfall. In the heart of the state, San Saba, Mills, and Lampasas counties set their all-time October rainfall records at over 13 inches each, compared to long-term monthly averages below 3 inches. October 2018 was the second wettest month in Texas history, and September and October were the wettest consecutive months ever. The Lower Valley was an area of notable dryness,

with about half the stations receiving less than 50 percent of normal rainfall.

Intermittent cold spells during **November** reduced regional average temperatures across the state. Almost all of the state was in the range of normal to 5 degrees below normal, with only El Paso recording above-normal temperatures for the month. Precipitation accumulation in the state's western sectors were generally well below normal, averaging about 50 percent of normal precipitation. Parts of East Texas and the Upper Coast exceeded 200 percent of normal precipitation.

December was a month of generally higher-than-average temperatures in the state of Texas. Most of the state averaged 0 degrees to 2 degrees above the monthly normal. Most of the state saw a normal to above-normal month of precipitation. The Edwards Plateau, North Central, and East Texas regions were wettest, each receiving about twice the normal precipitation for the month. The northern High Plains, western Trans-Pecos, and Lower Valley regions had total accumulations less than 75 percent of normal. ☆

Meteorological Data

Source: National Climatic Data Center. Additional data for these locations are listed by county in the table of Texas Climatological Normals for 1981–2010 and Extreme Weather Records by County, beginning on page 110.

City	Temperature — No. Days Max. 90° and Above	Temperature — No. Days Min. 32° and Below	Precipitation — Maximum in 24 Hours	Precipitation — Month & Year	Precipitation — Snowfall (Mean Annual)	Precipitation — Max. Snowfall in 24 Hours	Precipitation — Month & Year	Relative Humidity — 6:00 a.m., CT	Relative Humidity — Noon, CT	Wind — Speed, MPH (Mean Annual)	Wind — Highest MPH	Wind — Month & Year	Sun — Percent Possible Sunshine
Abilene	90	45	6.70	9/1961	5.2	9.3	4/1996	75	50	10.9	55	4/1998	70
Amarillo	61	107	7.25	7/2010	17.8	20.6	3/1934	75	46	12.8	68	6/2008	74
Austin	111	12	15.00	9/1931	1.0	9.7	11/1937	84	57	7.0	52	5/1997	60
Brownsville	123	1	12.19	9/1967	0.0	**	3/1993	90	61	10.4	51	7/2008	59
Corpus Christi	106	4	11.52	6/2006	0.2	2.3	12/2004	90	62	11.7	56	5/1999	60
Dallas-Fort Worth	95	29	5.91	10/1959	1.2	12.1	1/1964	82	56	10.5	73	8/1959	61
Del Rio	131	15	17.03	8/1998	0.9	8.6	1/1985	73	65	8.8	60	8/1970	84
El Paso	99	44	6.50	7/1881	6.9	16.8	12/1987	58	35	8.1	64	1/1996	84
Galveston	30	5	13.91	10/1901	0.2	15.4	2/1895	91	64	11.0	*100	9/1900	62
Houston †	102	10	11.02	6/2001	0.1	2.0	1/1973	90	60	7.5	51	8/1983	59
Lubbock	78	84	7.80	9/2008	8.2	16.3	1/1983	75	46	12.0	70	3/1952	72
Midland-Odessa	101	58	5.99	7/1961	5.1	10.6	1/2012	74	43	10.9	67	2/1960	74
Port Arthur-Beaumont	80	9	17.16	9/1980	0.0	4.4	2/1960	91	64	8.6	105	8/2005	58
San Angelo	102	46	6.25	9/1980	2.4	7.4	1/1978	80	49	9.7	75	4/1969	70
San Antonio	111	15	13.35	10/1998	0.7	13.2	1/1985	84	56	8.2	51	6/2010	60
Victoria	107	11	9.87	4/1991	0.1	2.1	1/1985	91	60	9.5	99	7/1963	49
Waco	104	31	7.98	12/1997	1.2	7.0	1/1949	86	57	10.1	69	6/1961	59
Wichita Falls	98	59	6.22	9/1980	4.2	9.7	3/1989	82	52	11.2	69	6/2002	60
Shreveport, LA §	88	32	10.76	5/2008	1.0	5.6	1/1982	89	59	7.3	63	5/2000	64

*100 mph recorded at 6:15 p.m., Sept. 8, 1900, just before the anemometer blew away. Maximum velocity was estimated to be 120 mph from the northeast between 7:30 p.m. and 8:30 p.m.
†The official Houston station was moved from near downtown to Intercontinental Airport, 12 miles north of the old station.

§Shreveport is included because it is near the boundary line and its data can be considered representative of Texas' east border.
**Trace is an amount too small to measure.

Texas Is Tornado Capital

Source: The Office of the State Climatologist.

An average of 130 tornadoes touch Texas soil each year. The annual total varies considerably, and certain areas are struck more often than others. Tornadoes occur with **greatest frequency in the Red River Valley**.

Tornadoes may occur in any month and at any hour of the day, but they occur with greatest frequency during the late spring and early summer months, and between the hours of 4:00 p.m. and 8:00 p.m. In the period 1951–2016, 63.4 percent of all Texas tornadoes occurred within the three-month period of April, May, and June, with almost one-third of the total tornadoes occurring in May.

More tornadoes have been recorded in Texas than in any other state, which is partly due to the state's size. Between 1951–2018, 8,599 funnel clouds are known to have reached the ground, thus becoming tornadoes. Texas ranks 11th among the 50 states in the density of tornadoes, experiencing an annual average of 5.8 tornadoes per 10,000 square miles.

The greatest outbreak of tornadoes on record in Texas was associated with Hurricane Beulah in September 1967. **Within a five-day period (Sept. 19-23), 115 known tornadoes,** all in Texas, were spawned by this great hurricane. **Sixty-seven occurred on Sept. 20**, a Texas record for a single day.

In May 2015, there were 130 tornadoes, which is a Texas record for a single month. The greatest number of tornadoes in Texas in a single year was 248, which was also in 2015. The second-highest number in a single year was in 1967, when 232 tornadoes occurred in Texas.

On average, May has the highest number of tornadoes with 40.05. January has the lowest average number of tornadoes with 2.48.

The accompanying table, compiled by the National Climatic Data Center, Environmental Data Service, and the National Oceanic and Atmospheric Administration, lists tornado occurrences in Texas, by months, for the period 1980–2018. ☆

Tornadoes by Year and Month

Year	Jan.	Feb.	March	April	May	June	July	Aug.	Sept.	Oct.	Nov.	Dec.	TOTAL
1951-53	0	1	2	3	4	3	1	2	0	1	0	2	20
1954-56	0	2	4	14	27	17	4	3	3	5	1	0	79
1957	0	1	21	69	33	5	0	3	2	6	5	0	145
1958-60	6	0	5	8	25	14	8	5	2	5	5	0	77
1961-63	0	2	12	11	23	37	10	7	8	2	5	0	116
1964-66	0	3	3	17	27	17	5	8	3	2	1	1	87
1967	0	2	11	17	34	22	10	5	124	2	0	5	232
1968-70	0	2	3	17	45	15	5	12	7	12	4	6	128
1971	0	20	10	24	27	33	7	20	7	16	4	23	191
1972	1	0	19	13	43	12	19	13	8	9	7	0	144
1973	14	1	29	25	21	24	4	8	5	3	9	4	147
1974	2	1	8	19	18	26	3	9	6	22	2	0	116
1975	5	2	9	12	50	18	10	3	3	3	1	1	117
1976	1	1	8	53	63	11	16	6	13	4	0	0	176
1977	0	0	3	34	50	4	5	5	12	0	6	4	123
1978	0	0	0	34	65	10	13	6	6	1	2	0	137
1979	1	2	24	33	39	14	12	10	4	15	3	0	157
1980	0	2	7	26	44	21	2	34	10	5	0	2	153
1981	0	7	7	9	71	26	5	20	5	23	3	0	176
1982	0	0	6	27	123	36	4	0	3	0	3	1	203
1983	5	7	24	1	62	35	4	22	5	0	7	14	186
1984	0	13	9	18	19	19	0	4	1	5	2	5	95
1985	0	0	5	41	28	5	3	1	1	3	1	2	90
1986	0	12	4	21	50	24	3	5	4	7	1	0	131
1987	1	1	7	0	54	19	11	3	8	0	16	4	124
1988	0	0	0	11	7	7	6	2	42	4	10	0	89
1989	3	0	5	3	70	63	0	6	3	6	1	0	160
1990	3	3	4	56	62	20	5	2	3	0	0	0	158
1991	20	5	2	39	72	36	1	2	3	8	4	0	192
1992	0	5	13	22	43	66	4	4	4	7	21	0	189
1993	1	4	5	17	39	4	4	0	12	23	8	0	117
1994	0	1	1	48	88	2	1	4	3	9	8	0	165
1995	6	0	13	36	66	75	11	3	2	1	0	10	223
1996	7	1	2	21	33	9	3	8	33	8	4	1	130
1997	0	6	7	31	59	50	2	2	1	16	3	0	177
1998	24	15	4	9	11	6	3	5	3	28	1	0	109
1999	22	0	22	23	70	26	3	8	0	0	0	4	178
2000	0	7	49	33	23	8	3	0	0	10	20	1	154
2001	0	0	4	12	36	12	0	7	15	24	27	5	142
2002	0	0	44	25	61	5	1	4	13	8	0	22	183
2003	0	0	4	31	50	29	6	1	4	12	29	0	166
2004	1	1	27	25	29	34	1	5	0	4	55	2	184
2005	0	0	6	7	27	46	15	4	2	0	0	2	109
2006	0	1	4	20	43	7	3	3	0	9	0	27	117
2007	2	1	56	61	43	21	8	4	14	2	1	3	216
2008	0	3	15	48	33	9	5	1	2	3	1	3	123
2009	0	5	4	48	18	32	2	4	1	4	1	12	131
2010	10	0	0	19	34	23	3	1	12	10	0	0	112
2011	1	1	3	57	20	6	1	4	1	2	8	0	104
2012	22	3	9	36	31	3	0	1	2	3	0	5	115
2013	1	16	0	8	41	3	0	6	0	6	0	3	84
2014	0	0	0	6	15	15	5	0	0	2	0	3	46
2015	0	0	0	48	130	3	0	0	2	20	23	22	248
2016	0	1	14	33	43	4	1	1	5	0	0	0	102
2017	22	17	36	29	43	3	3	25	1	1	0	3	183
2018	5	0	9	4	6	3	3	2	1	22	1	2	58
Total	180	174	570	1318	2301	1058	253	320	427	386	303	203	7493
Avg.	3	3	11	25	44	20	5	6	8	7	6	4	144
Max	24	20	56	61	130	75	19	34	124	28	55	27	248

Texas Droughts

Source: Texas State Climatologist and the New Mexico Drought Planning Team.

Drought is difficult to define, and there is no universally accepted definition. The most commonly used drought definitions are based on meteorological, agricultural, hydrological, and socioeconomic effects.

Meteorological drought is often defined as a period when precipitation is diminished in duration and/or intensity. The commonly used definition of meteorological drought is an interval of time, generally on the order of months or years, during which the moisture supply at a given place consistently falls below the climatically appropriate amount.

Agricultural drought occurs when there is inadequate soil moisture to meet the needs of a particular crop at a particular time. Agricultural drought usually occurs after or during meteorological drought but before hydrological drought and can also affect livestock and other dry-land agricultural operations.

Hydrological drought refers to deficiencies in surface and subsurface water supplies. It is measured as streamflow and as lake, reservoir, and groundwater levels. There is usually a delay between lack of rain and less measurable water in streams, lakes, and reservoirs. Therefore, hydrological measurements tend to lag other drought indicators.

Socioeconomic drought occurs when physical water shortages start to affect the health, well-being, and quality of life of the population, or when the drought starts to affect the supply and demand of an economic product.

The table on this page uses the **Palmer drought severity index (PDSI)**, the index preferred by the Texas State Climatologist's Office, the National Weather Service, and NOAA. It was developed by meteorologist Wayne Palmer, who first published this method in 1965.

The PDSI is based on a **supply-and-demand model of soil moisture** that factors in temperature, the amount of moisture in the soil, evapotranspiration, and recharge rates. It is most effective in determining long-term drought. Years were included in the table if at least one climate division had a PDSI of -4 or below, and the past 10 years, even when no periods of drought occurred. ☆

PDSI Table Indicators

Moderate drought, PDSI between -2 and -4

Severe drought, PDSI between -4 and -6

Extreme drought, PDSI below -6

Palmer Drought Severity Index

	High Plains	Low Rolling Plains	North Central	East Texas	Trans–Pecos	Edwards Plateau	South Central	Upper Coast	South Texas	Lower Valley
Frequency	27	28	27	25	28	28	26	26	25	25
1901	-2.01	-2.55	-4.58	-2.39	-2.28	-3.14	-3.84	-2.78	-3.21	-5.05
1902	-2.54	-3.73	-5.64	-3.23	-3.23	-4.05	-4.99	-3.45	-4.97	-5.70
1910	-3.47	-3.89	-5.04	-3.99	-4.21	-4.48	-3.63	-2.51	-3.26	-3.43
1911	-3.69	-4.10	-5.97	-5.02	-4.02	-4.03	-4.21	-4.31	-4.39	-3.03
1916	-2.60	-2.79	-2.49	-3.23	-3.53	-2.37	-4.19	-3.26	-4.71	-4.51
1917	-3.90	-4.66	-4.53	-4.90	-4.58	-4.88	-6.00	-6.03	-4.56	-3.91
1918	-3.88	-5.97	-6.11	-6.42	-3.75	-5.61	-6.13	-7.00	-4.50	-4.09
1925	-2.96	-3.26	-6.41	-6.20	-3.09	-3.95	-6.09	-5.20	-3.79	-2.51
1934	-4.66	-4.42	-4.84	-3.55	-4.88	-4.51	-2.82	-2.27	-1.54	-1.33
1935	-4.57	-3.83	-0.58	0.19	-4.68	-3.99	0.66	-0.39	0.10	-1.76
1951	-1.65	-3.36	-4.26	-3.84	-4.15	-4.66	-4.64	-4.37	-3.91	-4.10
1952	-4.23	-5.38	-5.53	-3.72	-4.28	-5.10	-4.53	-4.47	-4.45	-3.71
1953	-5.33	-5.41	-3.12	-1.27	-5.67	-4.64	-2.58	-2.21	-5.26	-4.45
1954	-4.46	-4.24	-4.29	-4.27	-4.59	-5.09	-4.87	-3.89	-3.59	-3.38
1955	-4.13	-3.76	-3.81	-3.18	-3.35	-4.78	-4.95	-3.75	-4.59	-3.60
1956	-5.62	-6.25	-6.82	-5.09	-5.47	-6.16	-6.68	-5.72	-4.77	-3.81
1957	-4.94	-5.02	-5.08	-4.92	-4.85	-5.10	-5.82	-5.64	-4.29	-4.12
1963	-2.38	-2.91	-3.95	-3.77	-2.07	-4.29	-4.80	-4.15	-3.71	-3.57
1967	-3.31	-3.42	-4.61	-3.34	-2.55	-4.12	-4.73	-2.99	-3.62	-2.44
1971	-3.33	-4.18	-4.41	-3.11	-2.80	-3.46	-5.01	-3.28	-3.68	-2.70
1974	-4.43	-4.20	-2.44	1.60	-3.44	-3.09	1.26	1.95	-1.29	-1.97
1996	-3.83	-3.57	-4.28	-3.63	-3.76	-3.88	-4.51	-2.59	-3.64	-3.04
2000	-3.88	-3.97	-3.76	-4.34	-4.93	-4.78	-4.39	-5.17	-4.12	-3.73
2006	-4.58	-4.80	-4.93	-4.16	-3.72	-4.14	-5.23	-4.32	-4.73	-4.77
2009	-2.24	-2.97	-3.88	-2.43	-2.35	-3.82	-6.36	-4.23	-5.19	-4.09
2010	-1.13	-1.20	-1.27	-3.67	-2.08	-2.02	-1.49	-1.19	-1.59	-1.68
2011	-6.98	-6.99	-5.99	-6.86	-6.52	-6.39	-6.21	-5.70	-5.45	-4.87
2012	-5.12	-4.75	-3.70	-4.36	-4.93	-3.75	-4.37	-4.72	-4.17	-4.69
2013	-4.16	-4.26	-3.43	-2.94	-3.02	-3.40	-4.47	-3.47	-4.33	-4.94
2014	-3.45	-3.29	-2.56	-1.34	-2.85	-2.93	-3.29	-2.49	-2.72	-1.23
2015	0.69	0.39	0.38	0.84	1.74	0.33	0.41	-0.59	-1.14	-0.56
2016	1.30	2.57	2.85	-2.04	-1.15	1.98	-0.47	-1.63	-1.50	-2.86
2017	-1.15	-1.43	-1.31	-2.40	-1.82	-1.47	-1.72	0.59	-1.97	-3.72
2018	-3.84	-4.35	-3.30	-2.16	-3.18	-3.67	-2.31	0.79	-2.72	-4.09

Normal Annual Rainfall in Inches by Texas Climatic Region

Listed below is the normal annual rainfall in inches for three 30-year periods in each geographical region (See map, p. 93).

Region	HP	LRP	NC	ET	TP	EP	SC	UC	ST	LV
1961–1990	18.88	23.77	33.99	45.67	13.01	24.00	34.49	47.63	23.47	25.31
1971–2000	19.64	24.51	35.23	48.08	13.19	24.73	36.21	50.31	24.08	25.43
1981–2010	20.02	24.85	36.17	48.21	13.16	24.86	35.54	51.14	24.17	24.67

A supercell near Wichita Falls. Photo by Daniel Rodriguez (CC).

Extreme Weather Records in Texas

Sources: Office of the State Climatologist and the National Weather Service, Dallas–Fort Worth.

TEMPERATURE			
Lowest	-23°F	Tulia	Feb. 12, 1899
	-23°F	Seminole	Feb. 8, 1933
Highest	120°F	Seymour	Aug. 12, 1936
	120°F	Monahans	June 28, 1994
Coldest Winter	41.3°F average		1898–1899
Hottest Summer	86.8°F average		2011

WIND VELOCITY		
Highest sustained wind		
145 mph SE	Matagorda	Sept. 11, 1961
145 mph NE	Port Lavaca	Sept. 11, 1961
Highest peak gust		
180 mph SW	Aransas Pass	Aug. 3, 1970
180 mph WSW	Robstown	Aug. 3, 1970

These winds occurred during Hurricane Carla in 1961 and Hurricane Celia in 1970.

TORNADOES		
Since 1950, there have been six tornadoes of the F-5 category, that is, with winds between 261–318 mph.		
Waco	McLennan County	May 11, 1953
Wichita Falls	Wichita County	April 3, 1964
Lubbock	Lubbock County	May 11, 1970
Valley Mills	McLennan County	May 6, 1973
Brownwood	Brown County	April 19, 1976
Jarrell	Williamson County	May 27, 1997

RAINFALL			
Wettest year statewide		2015	41.23 in.
Driest year statewide		1917	14.06 in.
Most annual	Clarksville	1874	109.38 in.
Least annual	Presidio	1956	1.64 in.
Most in 24 hours†	Alvin	July 25–26 1979	43.00 in.
Most in 18 hours	Thrall	Sept. 9, 1921	36.40 in.

†Unofficial estimate of rainfall during Tropical Storm Claudette.
Greatest 24-hour rainfall at an official site occurred at Albany, Shackelford County, on Aug. 4, 1978: 29.05 inches.

HAIL		
(Hailstones six inches or greater, since 1950)		
8.00 in.	Winkler County	May 31, 1960
7.50 in.	Young County	April 14, 1965
6.00 in.	Ward County	May 10, 1991
7.05 in.	Burleson County	Dec. 17, 1995

SNOWFALL			
65.0 in.	Season	Romero*	1923–1924
61.0 in.	Month	Vega	Feb. 1956
61.0 in.	Single storm	Vega	Feb. 1–8, 1956
26.0 in.	24 hours	Cleburne	Dec. 21–22, 1929
24.2 in	Annual avg.	Vega, Oldham County	
Romero was in southwestern Hartley County.			

Significant and Destructive Weather

This list of significant weather events in Texas since 1766 was compiled from ESSA–Weather Bureau information, previous Texas Almanacs, the Handbook of Texas, The Dallas Morning News, and the Office of the State Climatologist.

Sept. 4, 1766: Hurricane. Galveston Bay. Spanish Mission Nuestra Señora de la Luz destroyed.

Sept. 12, 1818: Hurricane. Galveston Island. Salt water flowed four feet deep. Only six buildings remained habitable. Of the six vessels and two barges in the harbor, even the two not seriously damaged were reduced to dismasted hulks. Pirate Jean Lafitte moved to one hulk so his Red House might serve as a hospital.

Aug. 6, 1844: Hurricane. Mouth of Rio Grande. All houses destroyed at the mouth of the river and at Brazos Santiago, eight miles north; 70 lives lost.

Sept. 19, 1854: Hurricane. Struck near Matagorda and moved inland, northwestward over Columbus. Main impact felt in Matagorda and Lavaca bays. Four lives were lost in town; more lives were lost on the peninsula. Almost all buildings in Matagorda were destroyed.

Oct. 3, 1867: Hurricane. Moved inland south of Galveston but raked the entire Texas coast from the Rio Grande to the Sabine. Bagdad and Clarksville, towns at the mouth of the Rio Grande, were destroyed. Much of Galveston was flooded; property damage there was estimated at $1 million.

Sept. 16, 1875: Hurricane. Struck Indianola, Calhoun County. Three-fourths of town swept away; 176 lives lost. Flooding from the bay caused nearly all destruction.

Aug. 13, 1880: Hurricane. Center struck Matamoros, Mexico; lower Texas coast affected.

Oct. 12–13, 1880: Hurricane. Brownsville. City nearly destroyed, many lives lost.

Dec. 29, 1880: Snow. Brownsville. A rare snowstorm in the Lower Rio Grande Valley.

Aug. 23–24, 1882: Torrential rains caused flooding on the North and South Concho and Bosque rivers (South Concho reported 45 feet above normal level), destroying Benficklen, then county seat of Tom Green County, leaving only the courthouse and jail. More than 50 persons drowned in Tom Green and Erath counties, with property damage at $200,000 and 10,000 to 15,000 head of livestock lost.

Aug. 19–21, 1886: Hurricane. Indianola. Every house destroyed or damaged. Indianola was never rebuilt.

Oct. 12, 1886: Hurricane. Sabine, Jefferson County. Hurricane passed over Sabine. The inundation extended 20 miles inland; 150 persons drowned and nearly every house in the vicinity was moved from its foundation.

April 28, 1893: Tornado. Cisco, Eastland County. 23 killed, 93 injured; damage, $400,000.

Feb. 1895: Freeze-Snow. Coastal Texas. Probably the greatest heavy-snow anomaly in the climatic history of the U.S. resulted from a snowstorm along the Texas coast on the 14th–15th. Houston; Orange; Stafford, Fort Bend County; and Columbus, Colorado County, each reported a snowfall of 20 inches. Galveston had a snowfall of 15.4 inches. Snow fell as far south as the Lower Rio Grande Valley, where Brownsville received 5 inches. Lower Valley had lows of 22 degrees the 14th–17th, destroying vegetable crops.

May 15, 1896: Tornadoes. Sherman, Grayson County; Justin and Gribble Springs, Denton County. 76 killed; damage, $225,000.

Sept. 12, 1897: Hurricane. Port Arthur. Many houses were demolished; 13 killed; damage, $150,000.

May 1, 1898: Tornado. Mobeetie, Wheeler County. Four killed; several injured; damage, $35,000.

Feb. 11–13, 1899: Freeze. Disastrous cold wave that newspapers described as the worst freeze ever known in the state. Brownsville's temperature reach 16 degrees on the 12th and remained below freezing through the 13th. Much destruction of vegetable crops.

June 27–July 1, 1899: Rainstorm. A storm, centered over the Brazos River watershed, dropped an average of 17 inches over 7,000 square miles. At Hearne, the gauge overflowed at 24 inches and was estimated at 30 inches. At Turnersville, Coryell County, 33 inches were recorded in three days. The rain caused the worst Brazos River flood on record; 30 and 35 lives lost; property damage, $9 million.

April 5–8, 1900: Rainstorm. This storm began in two centers, over Val Verde County on the Rio Grande and over Swisher County on the High Plains, and converged in the vicinity of Travis County, causing disastrous floods in the Colorado, Brazos, and Guadalupe rivers. McDonald Dam on the Colorado River at Austin crumbled suddenly. A wall of water swept through the city taking at least 23 lives. Damage was estimated at $1.3 million.

Sept. 8–9, 1900: Hurricane. Galveston. The Great Galveston Storm was the worst natural disaster in U.S. history in terms of human life. Loss of life at Galveston has been estimated at 6,000 to 8,000, but the exact number has never been determined. The island was completely inundated; not a single structure escaped damage. Most loss of life was due to drowning when storm tides that reached 15 feet or more. The anemometer blew away when the wind reached 100 mph at 6:15 p.m. on the 8th. Wind reached an estimated maximum velocity of 120 mph between 7:30 and 8:30 p.m. Property damage was estimated at $30 million to $40 million.

May 18, 1902: Tornado. Goliad. The tornado cut a 250-yard-wide path through town, turning 150 buildings into rubble. Several churches were destroyed, one of which was holding services; all 40 worshippers were either killed or injured. Total deaths, 114; injured, 230; damage, $200,000.

April 26, 1906: Tornado. Bellevue, Clay County. Bellevue was demolished. Considerable damage done at Stoneburg, seven miles east in Montague County. In all, 17 killed; 20 injured; damage, $300,000.

May 6, 1907: Tornado. North of Sulphur Springs, Hopkins County. Five killed, 19 injured.

May 13, 1908: Tornado. Linden, Cass County. Four killed; seven injured; damage, $75,000.

May 22–25, 1908: Rainstorm. Unique because it originated on the Pacific Coast. It moved first into North Texas and southern Oklahoma and then to Central Texas, precipitating as much as 10 inches. Heaviest floods were in the upper Trinity basin but extended south to the Nueces. Eleven killed near Dallas; property damage, more than $5 million.

March 23, 1909: Tornado. Slidell, Wise County; 11 killed, 10 injured; damage, $30,000.

May 30, 1909: Tornado. Zephyr, Brown County; 28 killed, many injured; damage, $90,000.

July 21, 1909: Hurricane. Velasco, Brazoria County. Half of town destroyed; 41 lives lost; damage, $2 million.

Dec. 1–5, 1913: Rainstorm. Caused the second major Brazos River flood and more deaths than the 1899 storm. Formed over Central Texas; spread southwest and northeast, dumping 15 inches of rain at San Marcos and 11 inches at Kaufman. Floods killed 177; damage, $8.5 million.

April 20–26, 1915: Rainstorm. Developed over Central Texas; spread into North and East Texas. Up to 17 inches of rain caused floods in Trinity, Brazos, Colorado and Guadalupe rivers. More than 40 killed; damage, $2.3 million.

Aug. 16–19, 1915: Hurricane. Galveston. Peak wind gusts of 120 miles recorded at Galveston; tide ranged 9.5 to 14.3 feet above mean sea level in the city, and up to 16.1 feet near the causeway. Business section flooded with 5–6 feet of water. At least 275 lives lost; damage, $56 million. A new seawall prevented a repetition of the 1900 disaster.

Aug. 18, 1916: Hurricane. Corpus Christi. Maximum wind speed, 100 mph; 20 lives lost; damage, $1.6 million.

Jan. 10–12, 1918: Blizzard. The most severe since February 1899, it was accompanied by zero-degree temperatures in North Texas and temperatures from 7–12 degrees below freezing along the lower coast.

April 9, 1919: Tornado. Leonard, Ector, and Ravenna, Fannin County; 20 killed; 45 injured; damage, $125,000.

April 9, 1919: Tornado. Henderson, Van Zandt, Wood, Camp, and Red River counties; 42 killed; 150 injured; damage, $450,000.

May 7, 1919: Windstorms. Starr, Hidalgo, Willacy, and Cameron counties. Violent thunderstorms with high winds, hail, and rain occurred between Rio Grande City and the coast, killing 10 persons. Damage to property and crops was $500,000. Seven were killed at Mission.

Sept. 14, 1919: Hurricane. Near Corpus Christi. Center moved inland south of Corpus Christi; tides were 16 feet above normal in that area and 8.8 feet above normal at Galveston. Extreme wind at Corpus Christi measured at 110 mph; 284 lives lost; damage, $20.3 million.

April 13, 1921: Tornado. Melissa, Collin County, and Petty, Lamar County. Melissa was practically destroyed; 12 killed; 80 injured; damage, $500,000.

April 15, 1921: Tornado. Wood, Cass, and Bowie counties; 10 killed; 50 injured; damage, $85,000.

Sept. 8–10, 1921: Rainstorm. Probably the greatest rainstorm in Texas history, it entered Mexico as a hurricane from the Gulf. Torrential rains fell as the storm moved northeasterly across Texas. Record floods occurred in Bexar, Travis, Williamson, Bell, and Milam counties, killing 215 persons, with property losses over $19 million. Five to nine feet of water stood in downtown San Antonio. A total of 24 inches was measured at the U.S. Weather Bureau station at Taylor during a period of 35 hours, with a 24-hour maximum of 23.1 inches on Sept. 9–10. The greatest rainfall recorded in U.S. history during 18 consecutive hours (measured at an unofficial weather-monitoring site) fell at Thrall, Williamson County: 36.4 inches fell on Sept. 9.

April 8, 1922: Tornado. Rowena, Runnels County. Seven killed; 52 injured; damage, $55,000.

April 8, 1922: Tornado. Oplin, Callahan County. Five killed; 30 injured; damage, $15,000.

April 23–28, 1922: Rainstorm. An exceptional storm entered Texas from the west and moved from the Panhandle to North Central and East Texas. Rains up to 12.6 inches over Parker, Tarrant, and Dallas counties caused severe floods in the Upper Trinity at Fort Worth; 11 lives were lost; damage was estimated at $1 million.

May 4, 1922: Tornado. Austin, Travis County; 12 killed; 50 injured; damage, $500,000.

May 14, 1923: Tornado. Howard and Mitchell counties; 23 killed; 100 injured; damage, $50,000.

April 12, 1927: Tornado. Edwards, Real, and Uvalde counties; 74 killed; 205 injured; damage, $1.2 million. Most damage was in Rocksprings, where 72 deaths occurred and the town was practically destroyed.

May 9, 1927: Tornado. Garland; 11 killed; damage, $100,000.

May 9, 1927: Tornado. Nevada, Collin County; Wolfe City, Hunt County; and Tigertown, Lamar County; 28 killed; more than 200 injured; damage, $900,000.

Jan. 4, 1929: Tornado. Near Bay City, Matagorda County. Five killed, 14 injured.

April 24, 1929: Tornado. Slocum, Anderson County; seven killed; 20 injured; damage, $200,000.

May 24–31, 1929: Rainstorm. Beginning over Caldwell County, the storm spread over much of Central and Coastal Texas with maximum rainfall of 12.9 inches, causing floods

in Colorado, Guadalupe, Brazos, Trinity, Neches, and Sabine rivers. Much damage at Houston from overflow of bayous. Damage estimated at $6 million.

May 6, 1930: Tornado. Bynum, Irene, and Mertens in Hill County; Ennis, Ellis County; and Frost, Navarro County; 41 killed; damage, $2.1 million.

May 6, 1930: Tornado. Kenedy and Runge in Karnes County; Nordheim, DeWitt County; 36 killed; 34 injured; damage, $127,000.

June 30–July 2, 1932: Rainstorm. Torrential rains fell over the upper watersheds of the Nueces and Guadalupe rivers, causing destructive floods. Seven persons drowned; property losses exceeded $500,000.

Aug. 13, 1932: Hurricane. Near Freeport, Brazoria County. Wind speed at East Columbia estimated at 100 mph; 40 lives lost; 200 injured; damage, $7.5 million.

March 1, 1933: Tornado. Angelina, Nacogdoches, and San Augustine counties; 10 killed; 56 injured; damage, $200,000.

April 26, 1933: Tornado. Bowie County near Texarkana. Five killed, 38 injured; damage, $14,000.

April 29, 1933: Dust storm. Panhandle, South Plains. The dust storm extended from Sweetwater north to Central Kansas and from Albuquerque, N.M., to Oklahoma. Newspaper accounts described it as the worst sandstorm in years; "as dark as any night" in Perryton. Thousands of acres of small grain crops were blown from the soil.

July 22–25, 1933: Tropical Storm. One of the greatest U.S. storms in area and general rainfall. The storm reached the vicinity of Freeport late on the 22nd and moved slowly overland across eastern Texas through the 25th. Its center moved into northern Louisiana on the 25th. Rainfall averaged 12.5 inches over an area of about 25,000 square miles. Twenty inches or more fell in a small area of eastern Texas and western Louisiana surrounding Logansport, La. The four-day total at Logansport was 22.3 inches. Property damage was estimated at $1.1 million.

July 30, 1933: Tornado. Oak Cliff section of Dallas. Five killed; 30 injured; damage, $500,000.

Sept. 4–5, 1933: Hurricane. Near Brownsville. Center passed inland a short distance north of Brownsville, where an extreme wind of 106 mph was measured before the anemometer blew away. Peak wind gusts were estimated at 120–125 mph; 40 known dead; 500 injured; damage, $16.9 million. About 90 percent of the citrus crop in the Lower Rio Grande Valley was destroyed.

July 25, 1934: Hurricane. Near Seadrift, Calhoun County; 19 lives lost; many minor injuries; damage, $4.5 million. About 85 percent of damage was to crops.

Jan.–March 1935: Dust storms. Amarillo. Seven times, the visibility in Amarillo declined to zero from dust storms. One of these complete blackouts lasted 11 hours. One of the storms raged for 3 ½ days.

Sept. 15–18, 1936: Rainstorm. Excessive rains over the North Concho and Middle Concho rivers caused a sharp rise in the Concho River, which overflowed San Angelo. Much of the business district and 500 homes were flooded. Four persons drowned and property losses were estimated at $5 million. Four-day storm rainfall at San Angelo measured 25.2 inches; 11.8 inches fell on the 15th.

June 10, 1938: Tornado. Clyde, Callahan County; 14 killed; 9 injured; damage, $85,000.

Sept. 23, 1941: Hurricane. Center moved inland near Matagorda and passed over Houston about midnight. Extremely high tides along coast in the Matagorda to Galveston area. Heaviest property and crop losses were in counties from Matagorda County to the Sabine River. Four lives lost. Damage was $6.5 million.

April 28, 1942: Tornado. Crowell, Foard County; 11 killed; 250 injured; damage, $1.5 million.

Aug. 30, 1942: Hurricane. Matagorda Bay. Highest wind estimated at 115 mph at Seadrift. Tide at Matagorda was 14.7

feet. Storm moved west-north westward and finally diminished over the Edwards Plateau; eight lives lost; property damage, $11.5 million; crop damage, $15 million.

May 10, 1943: Tornado. Laird Hill, Rusk County, and Kilgore, Gregg County; four killed; 25 injured; damage, $1 million.

July 27, 1943: Hurricane. Near Galveston. Center moved inland across Bolivar Peninsula and Trinity Bay. A wind gust of 104 mph was recorded at Texas City; 19 lives lost; damage estimated at $16.6 million.

Aug. 26–27, 1945: Hurricane. Aransas–San Antonio Bay area. At Port O'Connor, the wind reached 105 mph when the cups were torn from the anemometer. Peak gusts of 135 mph were estimated at Seadrift, Port O'Connor, and Port Lavaca; three killed; 25 injured; damage, $20.1 million.

Jan. 4, 1946: Tornado. Near Lufkin, Angelina County, and Nacogdoches, Nacogdoches County; 13 killed; 250 injured; damage, $2.1 million.

Jan. 4, 1946: Tornado. Near Palestine, Anderson County; 15 killed; 60 injured; damage, $500,000.

May 18, 1946: Tornado. Clay, Montague, and Denton counties. Four killed; damage, $112,000.

April 9, 1947: Tornado. White Deer, Carson County; Glazier, Hemphill County; and Higgins, Lipscomb County; 68 killed; 201 injured; damage, $1.6 million. Glazier was destroyed. One of the largest tornadoes on record. Width of path, 1 mile at Higgins; length of path, 221 miles across portions of Texas, Oklahoma, and Kansas. This tornado also struck Woodward, Okla.

May 3, 1948: Tornado. McKinney, Collin County. Three killed; 43 injured; damage, $2 million.

May 15, 1949: Tornado. Amarillo and vicinity; six killed; 83 injured. Total damage from tornado, wind, and hail, $5.3 million. Total destruction over one-block by three-block area in southern part of city; airport and 45 airplanes damaged; 28 railroad boxcars blown off track.

Jan.–Feb. 1951: Freeze. On Jan. 31.–Feb. 3 and again on Feb. 13–17, cold waves swept over the entire state, bringing snow and sleet. Heavy damage was done in the Lower Rio Grande Valley to truck and citrus crops, notably in the earlier of these northers. During the norther of Jan. 31–Feb. 3, the temperature went to minus 19 degrees in Dalhart.

Sept. 8–10, 1952: Rainstorm. Heavy rains over the Colorado and Guadalupe river watersheds in southwestern Texas caused major flooding. From 23–26 inches fell between Kerrville, Blanco, and Boerne. Highest stages ever known occurred in the Pedernales River; five lives lost; three injured; 17 homes destroyed, 454 damaged. Property loss, several million dollars.

March 13, 1953: Tornado. Jud and O'Brien, Haskell County; and Knox City, Knox County; 17 killed; 25 injured; damage, $600,000.

May 11, 1953: Tornado. Near San Angelo, Tom Green County. Eleven killed; 159 injured; damage, $3.2 million.

May 11, 1953: Tornado. Waco, McLennan County; 114 killed; 597 injured; damage, $41.2 million. One of two most disastrous tornadoes; 150 homes destroyed, 900 damaged; 185 other buildings destroyed, 500 damaged.

Feb. 1–5, 1956: Blizzard. Northwestern Texas. A major blizzard moved into the Panhandle and South Plains on the 1st. Snow and high winds continued through the 5th. Snowfall was the heaviest on record in Texas; 20 killed.

April 2, 1957: Tornado. Dallas. Ten killed; 200 injured; damage, $4 million. Moving through Oak Cliff and West Dallas, it damaged 574 buildings, largely homes.

April–May, 1957: Torrential Rains. Excessive flooding occurred in the area east of the Pecos River to the Sabine River during the last 10 days of April; 17 lives were lost; several hundred homes were destroyed. During May, more than 4,000 persons were evacuated from unprotected lowlands on the West Fork of the Trinity north of Fort

Worth and along creeks in Fort Worth. Twenty-nine houses at Christoval were damaged or destroyed; 83 houses at San Angelo were damaged. Five persons drowned in South Central Texas.

May 15, 1957: Tornado. Silverton, Briscoe County; 21 killed; 80 injured; damage, $500,000.

June 27, 1957: Hurricane Audrey. Center crossed the Gulf Coast near the Texas-Louisiana line. Orange was in the western portion of the eye between 9 a.m.–10 a.m. In Texas, nine lives were lost; 450 persons injured; property damage was $8 million. Damage was extensive in Jefferson and Orange counties, with less in Chambers and Galveston counties. Maximum wind reported in Texas, 85 mph. at Sabine Pass, with gusts to 100 mph.

Oct. 28, 1960: Rainstorm. Rains of 7–10 inches fell in South Central Texas; 11 died from drowning in flash floods. In Austin, about 300 families were driven from their homes. Damage in Austin was estimated at $2.5 million.

Sept. 8–14, 1961: Hurricane Carla. Port O'Connor. Maximum wind gust at Port Lavaca estimated at 175 mph. Highest tide was 18.5 feet at Port Lavaca. Most damage was to coastal counties between Corpus Christi and Port Arthur, and inland, in Jackson, Harris, and Wharton counties. In Texas, 34 persons died, seven in a tornado that swept across Galveston Island; 465 persons were injured. Property and crop damage conservatively estimated at $300 million. Evacuation of an estimated 250,000 persons kept loss of life low. Hurricane Carla was the largest hurricane of record.

Jan. 9–12, 1962: Freeze. A disastrous cold wave comparable to those of 1899 and 1951. Low temperatures ranged from minus 15 degrees in the Panhandle to 10 degrees at Rio Grande City. Agricultural loss estimate, $50 million.

Sept. 7, 1962: Rainstorm. Fort Worth. Rains fell over the Big Fossil Creek and Denton Creek watersheds, ranging up to 11 inches in three hours. Extensive damage from flash flooding occurred in Richland Hills and Haltom City.

Sept. 16–20, 1963: Hurricane Cindy. Rains of 15 to 23.5 inches fell in portions of Jefferson, Newton, and Orange counties when Hurricane Cindy became stationary west of Port Arthur. Flooding resulted in property damage of $11.6 million and agricultural losses of $500,000.

April 3, 1964: Tornado. Wichita Falls; 7 killed, 111 injured; damage, $15 million; 225 homes destroyed, 50 with major damage and 200 with minor damage. Sixteen other buildings received major damage.

Sept. 21–23, 1964: Rainstorm. Collin, Dallas, and Tarrant counties. More than 12 inches of rain fell during the first eight hours on the 21st. Flash flooding of tributaries of the Trinity River and smaller creeks and streams resulted in two drownings and an estimated $3 million in property damage. Flooding of homes occurred in all sections of McKinney. In Fort Worth, there was considerable damage to residences along Big Fossil and White Rock creeks.

Jan. 25, 1965: Dust Storm. West Texas. The worst dust storm since February 1956 developed on the southern High Plains. Winds, gusting up to 75 mph at Lubbock, sent dust billowing to 31,000 feet in the area from the Texas–New Mexico border eastward to a line from Tulia to Abilene. Ground visibility was reduced to about 100 yards in many areas. The worst hit was the Muleshoe, Seminole, Plains, Morton area on the South Plains. The rain gauge at Reese Air Force Base, Lubbock, contained 3 inches of fine sand.

June 2, 1965: Tornado. Hale Center, Hale County. Four killed, 76 injured; damage, $8 million.

June 11, 1965: Rainstorm. Sanderson, Terrell County. Torrential rains of up to eight inches in two hours near Sanderson caused a major flash flood that swept through the town; 26 persons drowned; property losses, $2.7 million.

April 22–29, 1966: Flooding. Northeast Texas. Twenty to 26 inches of rain fell in portions of Wood, Smith, Morris, Upshur, Gregg, Marion, and Harrison counties; 19 persons drowned in the rampaging rivers and creeks that swept away bridges, roads, and dams; damage, $12 million.

April 28, 1966: Flash flooding. Dallas County. Flash flooding from torrential rains in Dallas County resulted in 14 persons drowned and property losses of $15 million.

Sept. 18–23, 1967: Hurricane Beulah. Near Brownsville. The third largest hurricane of record, Hurricane Beulah moved inland near the mouth of the Rio Grande on the 20th. Wind gusts of 136 mph were reported during Beulah's passage. Rains 10–20 inches over much of the area south of San Antonio resulted in record-breaking floods. An unofficial gauging station at Falfurrias registered the highest accumulated rainfall, 36 inches. Stream overflow and surface runoff inundated 1.4 million acres. Beulah spawned 115 tornadoes, all in Texas, the greatest number of tornadoes on record for any hurricane. There were 13 deaths and 37 injuries (5 deaths and 34 injuries attributed to tornadoes); property losses, $100 million; crop losses, $50 million.

April 18, 1970: Tornado. Near Clarendon, Donley County; 17 killed; 42 injured; damage, $2.1 million. Fourteen persons were killed at a resort community at Green Belt Reservoir, 7 miles north of Clarendon.

May 11, 1970: Tornado. Lubbock, Lubbock County; 26 killed; 500 injured; damage, $135 million. Fifteen square miles, almost 1/4 of the city of Lubbock, suffered damage.

Aug. 3–5, 1970: Hurricane Celia. Corpus Christi. Hurricane Celia was a unique but severe storm. Measured in dollars, it was the costliest in the state's history to that time. Sustained wind speeds reached 130 mph, but it was great bursts of kinetic energy of short duration that appeared to cause the severe damage. Wind gusts of 161 mph were measured at the Corpus Christi National Weather Service Office. At Aransas Pass, peak wind gusts were estimated as high as 180 mph after the wind equipment blew away. In Texas, Celia caused 11 deaths, at least 466 injuries, and total property and crop damage of $453.8 million. Hurricane Celia crossed the Texas coastline midway between Corpus Christi and Aransas Pass about 3:30 p.m. CST on Aug. 3. Hardest hit was the metropolitan area of Corpus Christi, including Robstown, Aransas Pass, Port Aransas, and small towns on the north side of Corpus Christi Bay.

Feb. 20–22, 1971: Blizzard. Panhandle. Paralyzing blizzard, the worst since March 22–25, 1957, transformed the Panhandle into one vast snowfield as 6–26 inches of snow were whipped by 40–60 mph winds into drifts up to 12 feet high. At Follett, 3-day snowfall was 26 inches. Three persons killed; property and livestock losses were $3.1 million.

Sept. 9–13, 1971: Hurricane Fern. Coastal Bend. Rain of 10–26 inches resulted in some of the worst flooding since Hurricane Beulah in 1967; 2 killed; damage, $30.2 million.

May 11–12, 1972: Rainstorm. South Central Texas. Seventeen drowned at New Braunfels, one at McQueeney. New Braunfels and Seguin hardest hit. Property damage, $17.5 million.

June 12–13, 1973: Rainstorm. Southeastern Texas. From 10–15 inches of rain recorded; 10 drowned; property and crop damage, more than $50 million.

Nov. 23–24, 1974: Flash Flooding. Central Texas. Thirteen killed, 10 in Travis County; damage, $1 million.

Jan. 31–Feb. 1, 1975: Flooding. Nacogdoches County. Widespread heavy rain caused flash flooding, resulting in three deaths; damage, more than $5.5 million.

May 23, 1975: Rainstorm. Austin area. Heavy rains, high winds, and hail caused 4 deaths from drowning; 40 injuries; and damage of more than $5 million.

April 19, 1976: Tornado. Brownwood. An F-5 tornado destroyed a few homes and airplanes; 9 people injured.

June 15, 1976: Rainstorm. Harris County. Rains in excess of 13 inches caused eight deaths, including three drownings; damage was nearly $25 million.

Aug. 1–4, 1978: Heavy Rains, Flooding. Edwards Plateau, Low Rolling Plains. Remnants of Tropical Storm Amelia caused some of the worst flooding of the century. As much as 30 inches of rain fell near Albany in Shackelford County, where six drownings were reported. In Bandera, Kerr, Kendall, and Gillespie counties, 27 people drowned; damage was at least $50 million.

Dec. 30–31, 1978: Ice Storm. North Central Texas. Possibly the worst ice storm in 30 years hit Dallas County particularly hard; six deaths; damage, $14 million.

April 10, 1979: Tornado. Wichita Falls. The worst single tornado in Texas' history hit Wichita Falls. Earlier on the same day, several tornadoes hit farther west. The destruction in Wichita Falls resulted in 42 dead, 1,740 injured, more than 3,000 homes destroyed, and damage of approximately $400 million. An estimated 20,000 persons were left homeless. In all, the tornadoes on April 10 killed 53 people, injured 1,812, and caused over $500 million in damages.

May 3, 1979: Thunderstorms. Dallas County. The county was hit by a wave of the most destructive thunderstorms in many years; 37 injuries; damages, $5 million.

July 25–26, 1979: Tropical Storm Claudette. This storm caused more than $750 million in property and crop damage, but fortunately only few injuries. Near Alvin, an estimated 43 inches of rain fell, a new state record for 24 hours.

Aug. 24, 1979: Hailstorms. West Texas. One of the worst hailstorms in the past 100 years; $200 million in crops, mostly cotton, were destroyed.

Sept. 18–20, 1979: Flooding. Aransas Pass. Coastal flooding from heavy rain: 18 inches in 24 hours at Aransas Pass, and 13 inches at Rockport.

Aug. 9–11, 1980: Hurricane Allen. South Texas. Three persons killed; property and crop damage, $650 million to $750 million; more than 250,000 coastal residents evacuated. The worst damage was along Padre Island and in Corpus Christi; 20 inches of rain fell on extreme South Texas; 29 tornadoes, one of the worst hurricane-related outbreaks.

Summer 1980: Heat. One of the hottest summers in the history of the Lone Star State.

Sept. 5–8, 1980: Hurricane Danielle. The storm brought rain and flooding to Southeast and Central Texas; 17 inches of rain fell at Port Arthur; 25 inches near Junction.

May 24–25, 1981: Severe Flooding. Austin. Thirteen killed; 100 injured; damage, $40 million. Up to 5.5 inches of rain fell in one hour west of the city.

Oct. 11–14, 1981: Rain. North Central Texas. Record rain caused by the remains of Pacific Hurricane Norma reached more than 20 inches in some locations.

April 2, 1982: Tornadoes. Northeast Texas. A tornado outbreak with the most severe striking Paris; 10 people killed; 170 injured; 1,000 left homeless; damage, $50 million. In all, seven tornadoes that day left 11 dead and 174 injured.

May 1982: Tornadoes. Texas recorded 123 tornadoes, the most ever in May and one less than the most recorded in any single month in the state; 1 death; 23 injuries.

Dec. 1982: Heavy Snow. El Paso. Snowfall recorded at 18.2 inches was the most to fall there in any month.

Aug. 15–21, 1983: Hurricane Alicia. This was the first hurricane to make landfall in the continental U.S. in three years (Aug. 18) and one of the costliest in Texas history ($3 billion). Alicia caused widespread damage to a large section of Southeast Texas, including coastal areas near Galveston and the entire Houston area. Alicia spawned 22 tornadoes; highest winds were estimated near 130 mph. In all, 18 people were killed and 1,800 injured.

Jan. 12–13, 1985: Snowstorm. West and South Central Texas. A record-breaking snowstorm struck with up to 15 inches falling at many locations between San Antonio and the Rio Grande. San Antonio recorded 13.2 inches of snow on Jan. 12 (the greatest in a day) and 13.5 inches for the two-day total. Eagle Pass reported 14.5 inches of snow.

June 26, 1986: Hurricane Bonnie. The storm made landfall between High Island and Sabine Pass around 3:45 a.m. Highest wind measured in the area was a 97-mph gust, recorded at Sea Rim State Park. As much as 13 inches of rain fell in Ace, southern Polk County. There were several reports of funnel clouds, but no confirmed tornadoes. While the storm caused no major structural damage, there was widespread minor damage and numerous injuries.

May 22, 1987: Tornado. Saragosa. A strong, multiple-vortex tornado struck the town of Saragosa, Reeves County. Of the town's 183 inhabitants, 30 were killed and 121 were injured. Eight-five percent of the town's structures were destroyed; total damage topped $1.3 million.

Oct. 15–19, 1994: Rain. Southeast Texas. Extreme amounts of rainfall, up to 28.9 inches over a 4-day period, fell throughout southeastern Texas; 17 killed, mostly in flash flooding. Many rivers reached record flood levels. Houston was cut off as numerous roads, including Interstate 10, were under water. Damage was estimated at $700 million; 26 counties were declared disaster areas.

May 5, 1995: Thunderstorm and Hail. Dallas–Fort Worth. A thunderstorm moved across the area with 70 mph wind gusts and rainfall rates of almost 3 inches in 30 minutes (5 inches in one hour); 20 people killed; 109 injured by large hail, many at Fort Worth's outdoor Mayfest near the Trinity River. With more than $2 billion in damage, NOAA dubbed it the "costliest thunderstorm event in history."

May 28, 1995: Supercell Thunderstorm. San Angelo. The storm produced extreme winds and giant hail, injuring at least 80 people and causing about $120 million in damage. Sixty-one homes were destroyed; more than 9,000 were slightly damaged. In some areas, hail was 6 inches deep, with drifts to 2 feet.

Feb. 21, 1996: Heat. Anomalously high temperatures were reported over the entire state, breaking records in nearly every region. Temperatures near 100 degrees shattered previous records by as many as 10 degrees, and Texans experienced heat more characteristic of mid-summer than winter.

May 10, 1996: Hail. Howard County. Hail up to 5 inches in diameter fell; 48 injuries; property damage, $30 million.

May 27, 1997: Tornado. Jarrell. A half-mile-wide F-5 tornado struck Jarrell, Williamson County, leveling the Double Creek subdivision, claiming 27 lives, injuring 12 others, and causing more than $40 million in damage.

March–May 1998: Drought. According to the Climate Prediction Center, this three-month period ranks as the seventh driest for a region, including Texas, Oklahoma, Arkansas, Louisiana, and Mississippi. May 1998 has been ranked as both the warmest and the driest May in this region.

Aug. 22–25, 1998: Tropical Storm Charley. Hill Country. The storm dumped torrential rains in the area that caused flash floods; 13 killed; more than 200 were injured.

Oct. 17–19, 1998: Rainstorm. Hill Country. A massive, devastating flood set all-time records for rainfall and river levels; 25 killed; more than 2,000 injured; damage, more than $500 million from the Hill Country to counties south and east of San Antonio.

Jan. 22, 1999: Hail. Brazos County. Golf ball- and softball-sized hail fell in the Bryan–College Station area; damage, $10 million to cars, homes, and offices.

May 1999: Storms. Tornadoes. East, Central, West Texas. Numerous severe-weather outbreaks caused damaging winds, large hail, dangerous lightning, and numerous tornadoes. An F-3 tornado moved through downtown area and high school of De Kalb, Bowie County, on the 4th, injuring 22 people and causing $125 million in damage to the community. On the same day, two F-2 tornadoes roared through Kilgore

simultaneously. On the 11th, an F-4 tornado moved through parts of Loyal Valley, Mason County, and Castell, Llano County, killing one and injuring six. The 25th saw storms produce 2.5-inch hail in Levelland and Amarillo. Total damages, more than $157 million.

August 1999: Heat. Dallas–Fort Worth. Excessive heat throughout the month resulted in 16 fatalities. The airport reported 26 consecutive days of 100 degrees or greater.

January–October 2000: Drought. A severe drought plagued most of Texas. Some regions experienced little to no rain for several months during the summer. Abilene saw no rain for 72 consecutive days, while Dallas had no rain for 84 consecutive days during the summer. During July, aquifers hit all-time lows, and lakes and streams fell to critical levels. Most regions had to cut back or stop agricultural activities, which resulted in $515 million in agricultural loss, according to USDA figures.

March 28, 2000: Tornado. Fort Worth. A supercell over Fort Worth produced an F-3 tornado, which injured 80 people and caused significant damage. Flooding killed two people.

May 20, 2000: Rainstorm. Southeast Texas. A flash flood in the Liberty and Dayton area was caused by 18.3 inches of rain falling in five hours. Up to 80 people were rescued from flood waters; property damage, $10 million.

July 2000: Heat. Dallas–Fort Worth. Excessive heat resulted from a high-pressure ridge, particularly from the 12th–21st. DFW Airport reported a 10-day average of 103.3 degrees. College Station had 12 consecutive days of 100 degrees or greater. The heat caused 34 deaths in North and Southeast Texas, primarily among the elderly.

Aug. 2, 2000: Storm. Houston. Lightning struck a tree at Astroworld in Houston injuring 17 teens.

Sept. 5, 2000: Heat. Excessive heat resulted in at least eight all-time high temperature records around the state, one of which was Possum Kingdom Lake, which reached 114 degrees. This day is regarded as the hottest day ever in Texas, considering the state as a whole.

Dec. 13 and 24–25, 2000: Ice and Snow. Northeast Texas. Two major winter storms blanketed the area with up to 6 inches of ice from each storm. Eight inches of snow fell in the Panhandle, while areas in North Texas received 12 inches. Thousands of motorists were stranded on Interstate 20 and had to be rescued by the National Guard; 235,000 people lost electric service from the first storm alone. Roads were treacherous, driving was halted in several counties; total cost of damages from both storms, more than $156 million.

Jan. 1–31, 2001: Drought. South Texas. The USDA's Farm Service Agency received a Presidential Disaster Declaration in December 2000 because of persistent drought conditions in South Texas; $125 million in damage was reported in the region.

May 2001: Storms. San Antonio, High Plains. Numerous storms caused excessive damage. Four-inch hail caused nearly $150 million in damage in San Antonio on the 6th. On the 30th, supercell thunderstorms in the High Plains produced winds over 100 mph, and golf-ball-sized hail caused more than $186 million in damage; 36 injured; property and agriculture damage, $358 million.

June–December 2001: Drought. Significant drought-like conditions occurred in Texas from early summer through December. After the yearly drought report was filed, it was determined that total crop damage across the South Plains was about $420 million. Losses occurred to crops such as cotton, wheat, grain sorghum, and corn.

June 5–10, 2001: Tropical Storm Allison. Houston area. The storm dumped large amounts of rain on the city and made landfall on the western end of Galveston Island.

Have you seen crazy weather in your area? Submit your photos to our Flickr group at:
www.flickr.com/groups/texasalmanac/
Your photo might be chosen to be on our website, or even in our next book!

Over the next five days, it produced record rainfall, which led to devastating flooding across southeastern Texas. Some weather stations in the Houston area reported more than 40 inches of rain total and more than 18 inches in a 24-hour period. Twenty-two deaths; damage, $5.2 billion.

July–August 2001: Heat. Excessive heat plagued Texas, resulting in 17 deaths in the Houston area.

Oct. 12, 2001: Tornado. Hondo. An F-2 tornado caused $20 million in damage. The tornado injured 25 people and damaged the National Guard Armory, a large hangar at the Hondo Airport, and nearly two dozen aircraft. Also damaged were some 150 homes in Hondo, 50 on its outskirts, and nearly 100 mobile homes.

Nov. 15, 2001: Rainstorms. Central Texas. Storms caused flash flooding and weak tornadoes in the Edwards Plateau, South-Central, and southern portions of North-Central Texas. Flash flooding caused 8 deaths and 198 injuries.

March 2002: Storms. Central Texas. Several violent storms occurred, which produced hail, tornadoes, and strong winds. Hail 1-3/4 inches in diameter caused $16 million in damage to San Angelo on the 19th, while 30 people where injured on the same day by an F-2 tornado in Somerset, Bexar County, that caused $2 million in damage. For the month: 3 fatalities; 64 injuries; damage, $37.5 million.

June 30–July 7, 2002: Rainstorm. Central Texas. Excessive rainfall occurred in the South Central and Edwards Plateau regions, with some areas reporting more than 30 inches of rain. Damage in the South Central region alone was nearly $250 million. In Central Texas, 29 counties were devastated by flooding and declared federal disaster areas by President George W. Bush. Total event damage, $2 billion.

Sept. 5–7, 2002: Tropical Storm Fay. Coastal Plains. The storm made landfall along the coast on the 6th. This system produced extremely heavy rainfall, strong damaging wind gusts, and tornadoes. Ten to 20 inches of rain fell in eastern Wharton County. Brazoria County was hit the hardest with about 1,500 homes flooded. The storm produced five tornadoes, flooded many areas, and caused significant wind damage; total damage, $4.5 million.

Oct. 24, 2002: Raintorms. South Texas. Severe thunderstorms in South Texas produced heavy rain, causing flooding and two tornadoes in Corpus Christi. The most extensive damage occurred across Del Mar College. The storm caused one death and 26 injuries; total damages, more than $85 million.

Feb. 24–26, 2003: Snow and Ice. North Central Texas. A severe cold front brought freezing rain, sleet, and snow to the region. Snow accumulations were as high as 5 inches, resulting in $15 million in damages. Most schools and businesses were closed for this period.

April 8, 2003: Rainstorm. Brownsville. A severe thunderstorm caused one of the most destructive hail events in the history of Brownsville. Hail exceeded 2.75 inches in diameter and caused $50 million in damage to the city. At least 5 injuries were reported.

July 14–16, 2003: Hurricane Claudette. Port O'Connor. The hurricane made landfall near Port O'Connor in the late morning hours of the 14th. At landfall, wind speeds were more than 90 mph. The system then moved westward toward Big Bend and northern Mexico; 1 death; 2 injuries; damage, more than $100 million.

September 2003: Floods. Upper Coast, South Texas. Persistent flooding caused more than $2 million in damage. The remnants of Tropical Storm Grace caused flash flooding along the Upper Coast region near Galveston early in September, with rainfall estimates in Matagorda County ranging from 6–12 inches. During the second half of the month, South Texas was hit with a deluge of rain caused by a tropical wave combined with cold fronts. Monthly rainfall totals ranged from 7–15 inches in the deep south.

June 1–9, 2004: Floods. North Central Texas. Flash flooding due to an upper air disturbance and a cold front caused damage to more than 1,000 homes. This was the first of many days in which heavy rains fell throughout the state. Estimated damage was more than $7.5 million.

June 21, 2004: Tornadoes. Panhandle. Severe weather kicked up just ahead of a frontal boundary causing damage to Amarillo and the surrounding area. Eight tornadoes were reported around the Panhandle, and there were many reports of hail, topping out at 4.3 inches in diameter in Potter County. Thousands of homes were damaged, and the total damage was estimated at more than $150 million.

July 28–29, 2004: Rainstorm. North Central Texas. A stationary front led to torrential rainfall in Dallas and Waco. Hundreds of homes were damaged by flash flooding, as 24-hour rainfall totals for the two cities approached 5 inches. Outlying areas of the cities reported as much as 7 inches of rain in a 12-hour period on the 29th. Damage estimates topped $20 million.

Sept. 14, 2004: Storm. Grapeland. A lightning strike during football practice at Grapeland High School, Houston County, caused one death and injuries to 40 players and coaches.

Dec. 24–26, 2004: Snow. Coastal Texas. Large portions of Southeast and South Texas saw their first white Christmas in recorded history. A cold front passed over the state a few days prior to Christmas Eve dropping temperatures below freezing. Another cold front brought snow, which accumulated Christmas Eve night and into Christmas Day. Galveston and Houston recorded 4 inches of snow, while areas further south, such as Victoria, had 12 inches. Brownsville recorded 1.5 inches of snow.

March 25, 2005: Hail. Austin. In the evening, the most destructive hailstorm in 10 years struck the greater Austin area. The storm knocked out power to 5,000 homes in northwest Austin. Hail 2 inches in diameter was reported near the Travis County Exposition Center. Total damage was estimated at $100 million.

May 2005–December 2006: Drought. North Central Texas. In May, portions of the area were upgraded from moderate to severe drought. By month's end, the drought had made significant agricultural and hydrological impacts on the region. In November, many Central Texas counties were added to the drought. The Texas Cooperative Extension estimated statewide drought losses at $4.1 billion, $1.9 billion in North Texas alone.

June 9, 2005: Tornado. Petersburg. An F-3 tornado affected an area from Petersburg in southeast Hale County to portions of southwest and south-central Floyd County. Total damage was estimated at $70 million.

Sept. 23, 2005: Hurricane Rita. Southeast Texas. The eye of Hurricane Rita moved ashore in extreme southwest Louisiana between Sabine Pass and Johnson's Bayou in Cameron Parish with maximum sustained winds of 120 mph, category-3 strength. On the 22nd, Rita had strengthened to a peak intensity of 175 mph winds. In Southeast Texas, Rita caused 3 fatalities, 3 injuries, and $159.5 million in property and crop damage. Total property damage, $2.1 billion.

Dec. 27, 2005: Wildfire. Cross Plains, Callahan County. The fire started just west of Cross Plains and, fanned by winds gusting near 40 mph, quickly moved east into town. Two elderly people were unable to escape the flames; 16 firefighters were also injured; property damage, $11 million.

Jan. 1, 2006: Wildfires. North Texas. Several wildfires exploded across North Texas due to low humidity, strong winds, and the ongoing drought. Fires were reported in Montague, Eastland, and Palo Pinto counties. Five injuries were reported, as well as $10.8 million in property damage.

March 12–18, 2006: Wildfires. Borger. A wildfire now known as the Borger wildfire started four miles southwest of Borger, Hutchinson County. It killed seven people and burned 479,500 acres and 28 structures; total property damage, $49.9 million; crop damage, $45.4 million. A second wildfire known as the Interstate 40 wildfire burned 427,696 acres. The Texas Forest Service named the two wildfires the East Amarillo Complex. In all, 12 people were killed; total property damage, $49.9 million; crop damage, $45.4 million.

March 19, 2006: Tornado. Uvalde. An F-2 tornado moved through the Uvalde area causing $1.5 million in property damage. It was the strongest tornado in South Central Texas since Oct. 12, 2001.

April 11–13, 2006: Wildfire. Canadian. A wildfire 10 miles north of Canadian, Hemphill County, injured two; burned 18,000 acres; and destroyed $90 million of crops.

April 18, 2006: Hail. Gillespie County. Hailstones as large as 2.5 inches in diameter destroyed windows in homes and car windshields between Harper and Doss in Gillespie County. The hail also damaged 70 percent of the area's peach crop, an estimated loss of $5 million.

April 20, 2006: Hail. San Marcos. Hailstones as large as 4.3 inches in diameter (grapefruit-size) were reported south of San Marcos, damaging 10,000 vehicles on the road and another 7,000 vehicles at homes; total damage was estimated at $100 million.

May 4, 2006: Hail. Snyder. Lime-to-baseball-size hail fell across Snyder in Scurry County for at least 15 minutes. The hail was blown sideways at times by 60-to-70-mph winds. Total damage was estimated at $15 million.

May 5, 2006: Tornado. Waco. A tornado with peak intensity estimated at low F-2 caused damage of $3 million.

May 9, 2006: Tornado. Childress. An F-2 tornado caused significant damage along a 1-½-mile path through the north side of Childress in the evening. An instrument at Childress High School measured a wind gust of 109 mph. Property damage was estimated at $5.7 million.

Aug. 1, 2006: Thunderstorms. El Paso. Storms in a saturated atmosphere repeatedly developed and moved over the northwest third of El Paso County, concentrating near the Franklin Mountains. Rainfall reports varied from 4–6 inches within 15 hours, with an isolated report of about 8 inches on the western slope of the mountain range. Four days of heavy rains, combined with the mountains' terrain, led to excessive runoff and flooding not seen on such a large scale in the El Paso area in more than 100 years. Property damage was estimated at $180 million.

March 29, 2007: Floods. Corsicana. Flash flooding along Interstate 45 submerged two cars in Navarro County, north of Corsicana, and 2 feet of water was reported on I-45 and Texas 31, east of town; damage to businesses, roads, and bridges, $19 million.

April 13, 2007: Hail. Colleyville. Teacup-size hail was reported as strong storms developed in Tarrant County. Hail damage to 5,500 cars and 3,500 homes and businesses was estimated at $10 million.

April 24, 2007: Tornado. Eagle Pass. A large tornado crossed the Rio Grande from Mexico around 6 p.m., striking Rosita Valley, near Eagle Pass. Ten deaths were reported, including a family of five in a mobile home. Golf-ball-sized hail and the tornado struck Rosita Valley Elementary School, leaving only the interior walls standing. Damage indicated wind speeds near 140 mph and an F-3 level, with a path ¼ mile wide and 4 miles long. The tornado also destroyed 59 manufactured homes and 57 houses. Total damage was estimated at $80 million.

June 17–18, 2007: Floods. North Texas. Torrential rain fell as an upper-level low lingered for several days. In Tarrant County, one person drowned after her rescue boat capsized. Hundreds of people were rescued from high water. In Grayson County, a woman died in floodwaters as she drove under an overpass, and another death occurred in a flooded truck. Three people in Cooke County died when a mobile home was carried away by floodwaters. Damage was estimated at $30 million in Tarrant County, $20 million in Grayson County, and $28 million in Cooke County.

June 27, 2007: Floods. Marble Falls. Two lines of thunderstorms produced 10–19 inches of rain in southern Burnet County. Hardest hit was Marble Falls, where two young men died in the early morning when their jeep was swept into high water east of town. Damage to more than 315 homes and businesses was $130 million.

Sept. 13, 2007: Hurricane Humberto. Jefferson County. The hurricane made landfall around 1 a.m. in rural southwestern Jefferson County near McFaddin National Wildlife Refuge. Minimum pressure was around 985 millibars, with maximum winds at 90 mph. Flash flooding occurred in urban areas between Beaumont and Orange, as 11 inches of rain fell. Coastal storm tides were 3–5 feet, with the highest storm surge occurring at Texas Point. Humberto caused one death, 12 injuries, and $25 million in damage.

March 31, 2008: Hail. Northeast Texas. Severe thunderstorms developed across the Red River valley, many producing large hail that damaged car windows, skylights, and roofs in Texarkana and elsewhere in Bowie County. Damage was estimated at $120 million.

April 10, 2008: Tornadoes. Johnson County. A lone supercell thunderstorm evolved in the afternoon of the 9th, producing tornadoes and large hail. A tornado touched down near Happy Hill and traveled northeast 3 miles to Pleasant Point, where it dissipated. The F-1 tornado, with maximum wind speeds of 90–95 mph, destroyed three homes and damaged more than 30 homes and other buildings. Damage was $25 million.

May 14, 2008: Hail. Austin. A severe thunderstorm southwest of Austin moved northeast across downtown, causing extensive damage from winds and large hail. Large trees and branches were knocked down, and baseball-sized hail and 70–80 mph winds blew out windows in apartments and office buildings, including the State Capitol. Total damage was estimated at $50 million.

August 18, 2008: Floods. Wichita Falls. An unseasonably strong upper-level storm system moved over North Texas, and several waves of heavy thunderstorms caused heavy rain and widespread flooding in the Iowa Park, Burkburnett, and Wichita Falls areas. In Wichita Falls, at least 118 homes were flooded, 19 of which were destroyed, and residents were evacuated by boat. Burkburnett and Iowa Park were isolated for a few hours because of street flooding. Damage was estimated at $25 million, and Gov. Rick Perry declared Wichita County a disaster area.

Sept. 12, 2008: Hurricane Ike. Galveston. The eye of the hurricane moved ashore near Galveston with central pressure of 951.6 millibars and maximum sustained winds around 110 mph, which made Hurricane Ike a strong category-2 storm. There were 12 deaths directly related to Ike (11 occurring in Galveston County from drowning due to storm surge) and at least another 25 fatalities either due to carbon monoxide poisoning from generators, accidents while clearing debris, or house fires from candles. Storm tide and storm surge caused the majority of property damage at the coast. Damage in Harris, Chambers, Galveston, Liberty, Polk, Matagorda, Brazoria, Fort Bend, San Jacinto, and Montgomery counties totaled $14 billion.

Jan. 19, 2009: Wildfire. Hidalgo County. Aided by strong gusts, low humidity, lack of rain, and warm temperatures, a wildfire spread across 2,560 acres in Hidalgo County and consumed four buildings at Moore Air Force Base. Damage at the base was $10 million.

March 30, 2009: Hail. Northeast Tarrant County. A strong line of severe storms dumped ping-pong- to baseball-sized hail on numerous cities in northeast Tarrant County. Much of the damage was to automobiles; overall damage was $95 million.

April 11, 2009: Hail. Midland. Up to golf-ball-sized hail caused tremendous damage to homes and vehicles during a severe storm, with an estimated $160 million in roof damage. A woman was pelted in the stomach by a hailstone that broke through the window in her dining room.

May 2, 2009: Thunderstorm Wind. Irving. The National Weather Service determined that a microburst caused the Dallas Cowboys' bubble practice facility to collapse from winds estimated at 70 mph. Twelve people were injured, including one coach who was paralyzed from the waist down. The damage was estimated at $5 million.

June 11, 2009: Thunderstorm Wind. Burnet. A peak wind of 67 mph was measured at the Burnet Airport and numerous planes were flipped or blown across the tarmac. Damage in the city was $5 million.

Sept. 16, 2009: Hail. El Paso. A series of supercell storms produced golf-ball- to tennis-ball-sized hail and the most costly hailstorm in recorded history for the El Paso area. Estimated damage was $150 million.

Dec. 23, 2009: Tornado. Lufkin. An EF-3 tornado touched down in Lufkin, damaging structures, homes, and vehicles. The twister and heavy rains caused damage estimated at $10 million.

June 9, 2010: Flash Flood. New Braunfels. Storms produced rains in excess of 11 inches, which caused the Guadalupe River to rise over 20 feet in just two hours. Campers, vehicles, boats, homes, and businesses suffered extensive damages along the riverbanks. The flash flood resulted in one death; damage, more than $10 million.

July 2, 2010: Tornado. Hebbronville. An EF-1 tornado that developed following Hurricane Alex caused considerable damage in Hebbronville. Over half of the town's population lost power, and the tornado was reported to be as wide as a football field. Estimated damage, $1.5 million.

July 4, 2010: Flood. Terry, Lubbock, Garza, and Lynn Counties. A series of thunderstorms erupted in the early morning of the Fourth of July over the west South Texas Plains. Local flooding caused roadway closures and damage to more than 100 vehicles. More than 300 homes and businesses were affected; economic losses were around $16.5 million.

July 8, 2010: Flood. Starr County. Another storm that formed in the aftermath of Hurricane Alex dumped an estimated 50 inches or more of rain on the lower Rio Grande Valley over 10 days leading up to the 8th. Falcon Reservoir rose during days of rain and finally spilled over on the 8th. The Rio Grande was nearly 2 miles wide at some points. Estimated damage was around $37 million.

Oct. 24, 2010: Tornado. Rice, Navarro County. An intense EF-2 tornado struck with maximum winds of 135 mph. Vehicles were overturned on Interstate 45 and 11 train cars were derailed when the tornado hit the tracks. The football, baseball, and softball fields of the local high school were damaged; the intermediate school lost the gymnasium roof and suffered a caved-in wall; damage was $1 million.

Jan. 8, 2011: Heavy Snow. Sherman. Between 3–7 inches of snow fell across Northeast Texas, causing hundreds of vehicle accidents, including more than 40 in Sherman and one fatality. Total damage, $1 million.

Feb. 27, 2011: Wildfire. West Texas. High winds and temperatures produced a series of wildfire complexes. The costliest was in Tanglewood, burning 1,659 acres and destroying 26 homes at a cost of $25 million. The biggest was in Willow Creek, burning 24,310 acres and 29 homes at a cost of $10 million. A combination of fires near Lubbock, Matador, Post, and Levelland burned 60,500 acres and several urban dwellings, costing $3.5 million.

March 11, 2011: Wildfire. Jack, Wise counties. High heat, dry air, and high winds produced several fires in North Central Texas. More than 10,000 acres burned, including fields of hay bales worth $4 million. Three injuries were reported; other property losses were around $1 million.

April 6, 2011: Wildfire. Swenson, Stonewall County. A wildfire near Swenson was spawned during critical fire conditions due to a cutting torch. The fire burned for 15 days, burning 122,500 acres of grass and ranchland; damage, $2.5 million.

April 9–13, 2011: Wildfire. Possum Kingdom Lake. Drought and high winds helped spark a massive fire complex that burned for 16 days, destroying 167 homes, 126 other buildings, and 90 percent of Possum Kingdom State Park — about 126,734 acres total. Damage was $120 million, not including the estimated $11 million needed to combat the fire, nor the loss of cattle.

April 9, 2011: Wildfire. West Texas. Dry conditions near the Pecos River spawned two fires near Midland and Marfa. The former burned 16,500 acres and 34 homes, causing 500 evacuations; the latter was caused by an electrical problem and burned 314,444 acres, 41 homes, and hundreds of cattle and utility poles. Total property damage was estimated at $7.7 million.

April 15, 2011: Wildfire. Cisco. Dry conditions caused several wildfires in North Texas. The largest was near Cisco, burning around 2,000 acres and destroying five homes. The fires burned 18,000 acres, costing $1 million.

April 17, 2011: Wildfire. Oak Hill. Dry conditions and human negligence combined to cause a wildfire in Travis County. Although it covered only 100 acres, it destroyed 11 homes and damage estimates reached $2 million.

April 19, 2011: Hail. North Texas. A series of supercells brought widespread hail ranging from 0.8 inches to 3.5 inches over the course of the 5-hour storm. Damage was around $1 million.

April 25–26, 2011: Supercells. East Texas. An upper-level trough brought severe storms to East Texas for two days. On the 25th, 3 tornadoes touched down in Cherokee and Angelina counties, including two EF-1s; moderate hail was seen and downburst winds of 90-plus mph were reported. The next day, 10 tornadoes were reported, two of which were EF-1s near Ben Wheeler and Groesbeck, causing injuries. Total damage, $2.7 million.

May 1, 2011: Thunderstorm Wind. Clyde. Isolated thunderstorms popped up in the Big Country, bringing hail and strong winds. In Clyde, straight-line winds were reported in excess of 100 mph; damage, $2 million.

May 11, 2011: Thunderstorm Wind. Scattered thunderstorms from Killeen to Burns in Bowie County caused strong winds, hail, flash flooding, and an EF-0 tornado near Lake Kiowa; damage, $1 million.

June 18, 2011: Thunderstorm Wind. Muenster. Thunderstorms followed by a strong microburst in the early evening and straight-line winds greater than 80 mph caused widespread damage in excess of $1.36 million.

June 20–21, 2011: Thunderstorm Wind. East Texas. Severe thunderstorms culminated in strong downburst winds, hail, and an EF-0 tornado. Winds greater than 80 mph occurred in Nacogdoches and San Augustine, a tornado in Shelby County, and moderate hail; damage, $1 million.

June 28, 2011: Thunderstorm Wind. Titus County. Thunderstorms with 65 mph winds caused widespread damage at a cost of $1.6 million.

Aug. 11, 2011: Flash Flood. Lubbock. Scattered thunderstorms brought heavy rain, wind, and hail to the Lubbock area. Some areas received 1–4 inches of rain in an hour, causing high-water damage to homes and vehicles. Farm and weather equipment in Dimmit was damaged by 90 mph winds. Total damage, $1.2 million.

September–October 2011: Wildfires. Bastrop County. Three separate fires that began Sept. 4 merged into a single blaze east of the city of Bastrop and became known as the Bastrop County Complex fire. The fire destroyed 1,691 homes, and much of Bastrop State Park was burned. Declared the most destructive wildfire in Texas history, it was finally extinguished on Oct. 29.

Oct. 9, 2011: Tornado. San Antonio. An EF-1 tornado with winds up to 90–100 mph tore apart roofs, utility poles, and vehicles; damage, $1 million.

Jan. 9, 2012: Supercells. South Texas. Squall-line thunderstorms, hail, and an EF-1 tornado hit southeast of Alice

International Airport and parts of Robstown, causing an estimated $5 million in damage. Other straight-line winds and hail caused total damage of $8.7 million.

March 29, 2012: Hail. McAllen. Strong thunderstorms, with wind gusts over 70 mph at Edinburg Airport, and severe hail up to 2.8 inches caused $50 million in property damage to homes and $1 million to crops. Rainfall between 4–6 inches fell in less than two hours, causing $5 million in flood damage.

April 16, 2012: Tornadoes and Flash Floods. Gregory. Thunderstorms along the Coastal Bend caused four tornadoes, including an EF-1 in Portland, two EF-0 tornadoes in Gregory, and another in Kleberg County. The Portland tornado caused $2 million in damage to homes and property. Around 80 percent of all homes in Gregory were flooded when storms dumped 2–6 inches of rain; some locations received up to 15 inches over several hours. Total damages topped $8.3 million.

April 29, 2012: Hail. Lubbock County. Several severe storms blew up in West Texas near Lubbock with damaging hail and winds. Hailstones up to 4.5 inches fell in Whitharral, and winds gusts up to 95 mph near Wolfforth tore apart homes and cars. Damage estimates were $20 million from hail in Lubbock and more than $5 million from wind.

Nov. 22, 2012: Fog. Winnie, Chambers County. Dense fog early Thanksgiving morning caused a massive 150-car pileup on both sides of Interstate 10, causing two deaths and 80 injuries, 12 serious. Vehicular damage was $6 million.

Dec. 19, 2012: Dust Storm. Lubbock. A strong Pacific front kicked up winds up to 70 mph, reducing visibility below ½ mile for more than 5 hours, the longest such event since 1977; property damage, $1 million.

Dec. 25, 2012: Heavy Snow. Plano. A moderate cold front and minor storms in North Texas produced wrap-around snow between 3–6 inches that caused 89 traffic accidents and costing $1.2 million.

May 15, 2013: Tornado Outbreak. North Texas. A deadly tornado outbreak in North Texas claimed the lives of six people and injured more than 100 others. $250 million in damages were a result of an EF-4 tornado in Mambrino and an EF-3 tornado in Cleburne.

May 28, 2013: Hailstorm. Amarillo. A massive hailstorm moving through the Amarillo area dropped hail as big as baseballs and caused $200 million in damages. An estimated 35,000 vehicles and thousands of homes in Amarillo were damaged.

June 5, 2013: Hailstorm. Lubbock. Baseball-sized hail along with winds in excess of 90 mph caused more than $400 million in property damage in Lubbock. There were numerous reports of damage to homes and vehicles, as well as downed trees and power lines.

Oct. 30–31, 2013: Flash Flooding. Travis County. Six to ten inches of rain fell in Travis County and more than a foot of rain fell near Wimberley and Driftwood. Near Oak Hill, four people died and the flooding caused $100 million in property damage.

April 3, 2014: Hailstorm. Denton. A severe thunderstorm moving through the Denton area dropped hail as big as softballs, which caused more than $500 million in damages to homes, businesses, and vehicles.

May 11, 2014: Wildfire. Hutchinson County. A wildfire in Hutchinson County destroyed about 100 homes and caused the evacuation of more than 700 residents. The fire burned more than 1,000 acres and caused at least $10 million in damages.

June 12, 2014: Hailstorm. Abilene. A severe hailstorm moving through Abilene dropped hail up to 4.5 inches in diameter across the city. There were 12 injuries and $400 million in property damage.

May 4, 2015: Flood. Lubbock. Dozens of motorists from Lubbock to Tahoka needed to be rescued from their vehicles after driving into deep floodwaters. Combined damage

to vehicles, homes, and thousands of acres of wheat crops exceeded $300 million.

May 8, 2015: Hail. Lubbock. Widespread hail damage to homes, businesses, vehicles, and wheat crops. Nearly $500 million of combined property damage and $100 million in crop damage.

May 23–30, 2015: Flash Flood. Central Texas. More than 25 deaths from flash floods and tornadoes from North Central to South Central Texas. Flood waters inundated at least 2,585 homes and 73 commercial buildings. Property damage exceeded $1 billion.

Oct. 23–24, 2015: Flash Flood. North Central Texas. Heavy rain led to flash flooding across portions of North Central Texas. Rainfall totals in flood-damaged areas ranged from 5 inches to 21-plus inches within a 36-hour period. Property damage estimated at $1 billion.

Dec. 26–27, 2015: Tornado. North Texas. A potent storm system brought blizzard conditions to Lubbock and 12 deadly tornadoes to North Texas, followed by significant flooding across parts of North and Central Texas. In total, 15 people died, more than 600 were injured, and tens of thousands of dairy cows in West Texas were killed.

March 9–10, 2016: Flood. East Texas. Multiple days of heavy rain fell across the Sabine River Valley causing massive flooding in the basin. More than 1,500 homes received flood damage, and damage in Texas and Louisiana was estimated at $2.4 billion.

March 17, 2016: Hail. North Central Texas. Intense, warm advection led to thunderstorm development over the western counties of North Texas. Damage from hail as large as tennis balls was estimated at $600 million.

March 23, 2016: Hail. North Central Texas. Severe thunderstorms developed along a dry line as it surged east to the Interstate 35 corridor. Damaging winds, hail, and one tornado caused $2.3 billion in damage.

April 11–12, 2016: Hail. South Central Texas. Severe thunderstorms produced 4.3-inch hail that damaged an estimated 136,000 vehicles and 125,000 homes. Combined damage of $3.5 billion made this the costliest hail storm ever in Texas.

April 17, 2016: Flood. Southeast Texas. Ten to 15 inches of rain in less than 12 hours produced devastating flooding in west Houston in an event called the "Tax Day Flood." There were eight deaths and $2.7 billion in property damage.

May 21–26, 2016: Widespread Severe Weather. Five-inch hail and tornadoes were reported in the Panhandle. Rainfall totals of 6 to 10 inches occurred there and in Southeast Texas. The storms caused four deaths and a combined $1.2 billion in damage.

Jan. 14–15, 2017: Ice Storm. High Plains. A strong winter storm made its way from the western U.S. into the Texas Panhandle in the second weekend of January bringing frigid temperatures, strong winds, ice, and snow. Ice and snow accumulations were measured to be 1-3 inches across the region. Many residents lost power during this event, along with damages to some infrastructure and economic losses to businesses. Total damages were estimated to be nearly $50 million for both the Texas and Oklahoma panhandles.

Jan. 21, 2017: Tornadoes. East Texas. An advancing cold front from the Southern High Plains made its way into East Texas, where it interacted with unstable and unseasonably warm air developing into strong thunderstorms and supercells. Twelve tornadoes touched down across the Ark-La-Tex region, with two destructive EF-2s pushing through East Texas. The severe storms were responsible for over $4 million in damages to vehicles, local infrastructure, and resident homes.

March 7, 2017: Fire Weather. High Plains. Hot, dry, and windy conditions led to the ignition of a wildfire in the Texas Panhandle along with other fires within the Great Plains. The Gray County fire took the lives of three who were attempting to save livestock. After more than 521,000 acres of land burned, damages and losses of land, livestock, and infrastructure were estimated to be over $25.1 million.

April 14, 2017: Tornado. High Plains. Strong thunderstorms firing in the Texas Panhandle produced a significant tornadic supercell in the southern High Plains. A post-storm survey conducted by the National Weather Service (NWS) determined that the tornado that tore through Castro County during the early evening hours was an EF-3 with a massive diameter of 1.1 miles. Reports by the NWS affirmed no deaths or injuries, though damages were estimated to be nearly $2 million.

April 29, 2017: Tornadoes. East Texas. Four deaths and over 50 injuries were the result of a devastating tornado outbreak in East Texas. There was a total of Seven confirmed tornadoes passing through Henderson, Hopkins, Rains, and Van Zandt counties. Post-storm surveys confirmed the strongest storm was an EF-4 that had estimated wind speeds near 180 mph in Van Zandt County.

June 4, 2017: Hail. West Texas. The development of a strong line of thunderstorms produced strong winds and large hail in Odessa. Five-inch hail and 100 mph winds were recorded when the storm was at its peak. These conditions significantly damaged vehicles and infrastructure, uprooted trees, and caused power outages across the area. Damages of $208 million were sustained from these storms.

August 25–29, 2017: Hurricane. Southeast Texas. Hurricane Harvey made landfall in Southeast Texas, the first Category 4 landfall in the state since 1961. Strong winds and torrential downpours were the most destructive impacts to the region; maximum wind speeds reached 130 mph, and the largest observed rainfall total was 60 inches. There were 68 deaths directly related to the storm and an estimate of $125 billion in damage.

Jan. 16–17, 2018: Winter Weather. North Central Texas. North Texas citizens experienced a frigid Martin Luther King Jr. Day as a strong Arctic cold front pushed through the region. The air mass brought freezing temperatures, snow, sleet, and freezing rain. Two homeless citizens in Dallas lost their lives from the extreme cold conditions.

Jan. 21, 2018: Tornado. East Texas. Unstable atmospheric conditions produced supercell thunderstorms in the Ark-La-Tex midwinter season. Moderate-sized hail and strong winds were products of the intense storms. An EF-2 tornado on the ground for 7 miles in Bowie County reached an estimated maximum wind speed of 125 mph. Many homes were damaged, as well as injuries sustained by local residents and farm animals, with an estimated loss of $2.5 million.

April 3, 2018: Strong Winds. Upper Coast. Strong storms along the Texas coast produced damaging winds and gusts in Harris County. The most damaging winds were short-lived in a phenomenon known as a "microburst," a powerful downward rush of air from a thunderstorm. Sustained winds from this event reached an estimated maximum of 80 mph, causing $2 million in damages to a hangar at Houston Hobby Airport.

May 19–20, 2018: Hail. High Plains. Slow-moving supercell thunderstorms caused a great deal of damage to residents of West Texas during the evening hours and into the night. The storms produced heavy rainfall that led to flash flooding and large-size hail. The magnitude of hail produced had the greatest toll on residents. Several observations of tennis- to baseball-sized hail were reported during the event, which caused an estimated $30 million in damages to property.

June 7, 2018: Severe Weather. High Plains and Low Rolling Plains. A late-spring storm produced heavy rains and destructive winds in West Texas. Estimated winds during this event reached hurricane force, peaking near 115 mph. One family in Scurry County reported an overturned manufactured home that resulted in one injury. Total damages by flash flooding and strong winds were estimated at over $600,000.

June 19–22, 2018: Flooding/Tropical Weather. Lower Valley and South Texas. A low-pressure system originating from the Caribbean made landfall in South Texas in the early days of summer. The system interacted with other atmospheric features to create strong, heavy-rain producing storms. For nearly four days, the region was drenched with continual precipitation that caused widespread flooding. Locally flooded areas saw water depths of 2 to 4 feet. Disaster responders in the region reported more than 2,000 rescues during the event. With at least 20,000 residents and businesses considered affected by the storms, a preliminary estimate of $115 million in property damage was reported.

Oct. 16–17, 2018: Flooding. Central Texas. Strong thunderstorms slowly rolled through Central Texas during the early morning hours bringing torrential downpours to the region. Flash flooding was extensive in the western areas of the region, where rainfall totals between 6 to 9 inches caused overfilling of the Llano River, Lake LBJ, Lake Marble Falls, and Lake Travis. One loss of life was reported in Llano County. The combined property damage in Llano, Burnet, and Travis counties exceeded $100 million. ☆

Hurricane Harvey Recovery So Far

The Legislative Budget Board report *Fiscal Impact of Hurricane Harvey on State Agencies* (April 2019) states: "The early aftermath of Hurricane Harvey left more than 18 inches of standing floodwater in nearly 80,000 homes, with more than five feet of floodwater in almost 30 percent of those homes. Eighty percent of households affected by Hurricane Harvey did not have flood insurance. Initial estimates projected that approximately 32,500 households would need direct housing assistance."

In the years since, most of those affected by the storm have completed repairs to their homes and businesses, but there are many who have yet to recover.

FEMA reports show that as of January 4, 2019, there were 17,145 Harvey survivors still in "temporary housing and innovative repair programs" in Texas. The following list includes the counties identified by HUD as most affected by the storm, the amount that has already been spent on housing and other disaster-related expenses within the county, and the number of people in FEMA housing as of January 4, 2019:

- **Aransas** ($29.8 million; 229 in housing)
- **Brazoria** ($74.3 million; 188 in housing)
- **Chambers** ($25.6 million; 65 in housing)
- **Ford Bend** ($96.9 million; 46 in housing)
- **Galveston** ($108.2 million; 151 in housing)
- **Hardin** ($35.5 million; 254 in housing)
- **Harris** ($771.7 million; 388 in housing)
- **Jefferson** ($177.4 million; 697 in housing)
- **Liberty** ($29.5 million; 44 in housing)
- **Montgomery** ($38.7 million; 75 in housing)
- **Nueces** ($18.4 million; 12 in housing)
- **Orange** ($124.8 million; 588 in housing)
- **San Jacinto** ($8.0 million; 24 in housing)
- **San Patricio** ($17.0 million; 18 in housing)
- **Victoria** ($13.0 million; 9 in housing)
- **Wharton** ($15.2 million; 63 in housing)

Texas Climatological Normals for 1981–2010 and Extreme Weather Records by County through 2018

Explanations and Sources

Data in this table are provided by the Office of the Texas State Climatologist, Texas A&M University, College Station, Texas.

The Climatological Normals include Mean Maximum July Temperature, Mean Minimum January Temperature, Average Freeze Dates, Growing Season, and Mean Precipitation. They are calculated every 10 years and are based on the previous 30-year period, which is 1981–2010. Data in italics are from the period 1971–2000.

Data for counties where a weather station has not been maintained long enough to establish a reliable mean are interpolated from isoline charts prepared from mean values from stations with long-established records.

Mean Maximum for July is computed from the sum of the daily maxima. Mean Minimum for January is computed from the sum of the daily minima.

Extreme Weather Records include Record High Temperature, Record Low Temperature, and Record Rainfall; they are compiled yearly and are current through 2018.

The far left column lists Texas' 254 counties and identifies the town or landmark nearest to the National Weather Service station used to calculate Climatological Normals. If that weather station is outside the county, the town or landmark is in italics.

Extreme Weather Records may have occurred at any weather station in that county and are identified only for Record Rainfall.

An asterisk (*) preceding an Extreme Weather Record means it also occurred on a previous date.

COUNTY, TOWN OR LANDMARK CLOSEST TO STATION FOR NORMALS	TEMPERATURE								AVERAGE FREEZE DATES			
	Mean Max. July	No. At or Above 100°F	Mean Min. January	No. At or Below 32°F	Record Highest	Record High Date	Record Lowest	Record Low Date	Last in Spring		First in Fall	
	F.	Days	F.	Days	F.	M-D-Y	F.	M-D-Y	Mo.	Day	Mo.	Day
Anderson, Palestine	92.3	4	34.5	44	114	7-26-1954	−6	2-12-1899	Mar.	24	Nov.	12
Andrews, Andrews	94.8	15	30.7	59	113	6-27-1994	−1	2-2-1985	Mar.	31	Nov.	10
Angelina, County Airport	93.3	5	38.3	27	*110	8-19-1909	−2	2-2-1951	Mar.	10	Nov.	20
Aransas, Rockport	91.6	0	46.0	5	107	9-5-2000	9	12-23-1989	Feb.	6	Dec.	20
Archer, Archer City	96.5	22	29.0	63	114	6-28-1980	*−10	12-23-1989	Mar.	27	Nov.	8
Armstrong, Claude	90.6	3	22.4	114	*108	6-28-1980	−16	2-13-1905	Apr.	16	Oct.	24
Atascosa, Pleasanton	95.4	15	39.3	18	*113	8-22-1917	−1	1-31-1949	Feb.	27	Nov.	29
Austin, Sealy	93.7	7	41.0	13	*111	9-4-2000	0	12-23-1989	Feb.	22	Dec.	5
Bailey, Muleshoe NWR	92.6	9	22.0	117	*112	6-28-1994	−21	2-8-1933	Apr.	20	Oct.	23
Bandera, Medina	93.0	4	34.5	45	*110	7-9-1939	*−5	2-2-1951	Mar.	24	Nov.	13
Bastrop, Elgin	95.3	13	39.3	21	*111	9-5-2000	−3	12-23-1989	Mar.	5	Nov.	28
Baylor, Seymour	96.5	24	28.1	70	120	8-12-1936	−14	1-4-1947	Mar.	28	Nov.	7
Bee, Beeville	93.9	7	43.7	9	114	6-22-1990	5	2-12-1899	Feb.	18	Dec.	10
Bell, Stillhouse Hollow Dam	95.4	13	35.9	27	*112	8-11-1947	−5	12-23-1989	Mar.	10	Nov.	27
Bexar, San Antonio Intl. Airport	94.6	8	40.7	16	*113	8-28-2011	*0	1-31-1949	Mar.	1	Dec.	1
Blanco, Blanco	92.8	5	34.8	42	110	9-6-2000	*−6	1-31-1949	Mar.	22	Nov.	13
Borden, Gail	94.8	15	33.1	46	116	6-27-1994	−1	12-23-1989	Mar.	24	Nov.	12
Bosque, Lake Whitney Dam	96.4	20	34.8	37	113	9-5-2000	*−3	12-23-1989	Mar.	13	Nov.	18
Bowie, Texarkana	92.9	7	33.1	45	*112	8-5-2011	−9	2-12-1899	Mar.	16	Nov.	19
Brazoria, Angleton	90.3	0	45.6	6	109	9-4-2000	6	2-12-1899	Feb.	6	Dec.	17
Brazos, College Station	94.8	12	41.2	14	112	9-4-2000	−3	1-31-1949	Feb.	26	Dec.	2
Brewster, Alpine	88.5	2	30.3	66	*117	6-17-1992	*−6	1-12-1962	Apr.	4	Nov.	2
Briscoe, Silverton	90.9	4	23.2	109	111	6-27-2011	−10	12-25-2004	Apr.	13	Oct.	27
Brooks, Falfurrias	97.0	28	42.5	13	116	7-13-2016	9	1-12-1962	Feb.	23	Dec.	5
Brown, Brownwood	95.7	18	30.1	60	113	7-19-1925	−6	12-23-1989	Mar.	29	Nov.	7
Burleson, Somerville Dam	95.2	13	36.8	29	114	9-5-2000	3	12-23-1989	Mar.	8	Nov.	24
Burnet, Burnet Muni. Airport	94.0	6	37.6	26	*114	7-11-1917	*−4	12-23-1989	Mar.	6	Nov.	24
Caldwell, Luling	94.8	13	37.8	28	111	8-28-2011	−3	1-31-1949	Mar.	9	Nov.	23
Calhoun, Port O'Connor	89.0	1	46.5	4	*109	8-29-2011	9	12-23-1989	Jan.	29	Dec.	22
Callahan, Putnam	94.8	15	31.4	55	*110	5-28-2011	−8	12-23-1989	Mar.	31	Nov.	8
Cameron, Brownsville	93.6	1	51.6	1	108	8-18-1915	12	2-13-1899	Dec.	25	Jan.	24
Camp, *Daingerfield*	94.1	9	35.1	34	111	8-3-2011	*10	12-9-2005	Mar.	8	Nov.	23
Carson, Panhandle	92.2	7	20.3	127	112	6-27-2011	*−10	1-12-1963	Apr.	22	Oct.	19

Table Highlights

Record Highs in 2011

Thirty-five new record highs were set in 2011 from the Gulf Coast to West Texas and the Panhandle. The highest records were 118 degrees set in Knox County on June 20 and in Cottle County on June 27. That year began a severe drought that lasted through part of 2015. This period is now considered a "drought of record" by some water suppliers.

The years 1951–1957, however, are still considered the drought of record for other officials and agencies. On a statewide basis, the most intense drought, as measured by the Palmer Drought Severity Index, was in 2011, but the most severe drought, as measured by combined intensity and duration, was 1951–1957.

Rain Records in 2015

Eleven rainfall records were set in 2015, including six records during Oct. 24–25. Most records were set in Central and East Texas and ranged from 9.5 inches in Mineola in Wood County to 18.95 inches in Corsicana in Navarro County.

Rain Records in 2017

Twenty-one rainfall records were set in 2017, 17 of which occurred between August 26 and August 30, during Hurricane Harvey. Six counties recorded more than 20 inches of rain: Galveston, Harris, Jefferson, Lavaca, Liberty, and Orange. The highest rainfall total, 26.03 inches, fell on Port Arthur in Jefferson County.

Rain Records in 2018

Eight rain records were set in 2018. Six of those occurred in the months of September (the third wettest month in Texas history) and October (the second wettest month in Texas history). Combined, September–October 2018 are the wettest consecutive months ever. ☆

GROWING SEASON	MEAN PRECIPITATION													RECORD RAINFALL HIGHEST DAILY TOTAL		
	January	February	March	April	May	June	July	August	September	October	November	December	Annual			
Days	In.	In.	In.	In.	In.	In.	In.	In.	In.	In.	In.	In.	In.	Location	In.	M-D-Y
232	3.66	3.90	3.89	3.29	4.21	4.97	2.65	3.31	3.21	5.07	4.24	4.20	46.60	Palestine	9.10	8-14-1991
224	0.56	0.69	0.86	0.66	1.63	2.03	1.83	1.65	1.85	1.58	0.71	0.69	14.74	Andrews	7.60	7-2-1914
252	4.18	3.87	3.78	3.05	4.64	4.68	3.05	3.34	4.08	4.83	5.01	4.44	48.95	Lufkin	10.65	10-17-1994
316	2.42	2.20	2.40	1.76	3.10	3.17	3.46	2.57	5.08	4.22	3.02	1.78	35.18	Aransas NWR	14.25	11-1-1974
227	1.36	2.07	2.24	2.53	4.09	3.81	1.92	2.61	2.62	3.81	1.82	1.84	30.72	Olney	8.45	5-15-1989
190	0.59	0.64	1.33	1.70	2.44	3.64	2.81	3.00	2.33	2.17	0.86	0.74	22.25	Claude	6.42	5-16-1951
277	1.94	1.95	2.19	2.06	4.05	4.19	2.78	2.36	3.22	3.03	2.43	1.87	32.07	Rossville	9.09	9-15-1919
288	3.25	2.72	2.84	3.56	4.57	3.62	2.65	3.56	3.91	4.84	4.51	2.89	42.92	San Felipe	12.25	4-18-2016
185	0.54	0.48	0.86	0.81	2.32	2.50	2.18	2.88	2.50	1.73	0.71	0.73	18.24	Muleshoe	5.25	5-16-1951
233	2.00	1.92	3.28	2.37	4.74	4.17	3.96	2.14	3.58	4.36	2.61	2.24	37.37	Vanderpool	11.53	8-1-1978
266	2.41	2.30	2.81	2.13	4.29	4.03	2.00	2.05	2.74	4.07	3.13	2.47	34.43	Smithville	16.05	6-30-1940
225	1.21	1.89	1.94	1.95	4.11	4.00	2.38	2.76	2.91	2.71	1.66	1.43	28.95	Lake Kemp	6.25	9-1-1986
297	1.96	1.74	2.28	2.55	2.88	3.86	3.39	2.30	3.74	3.45	2.14	1.68	31.97	Chase Field	11.55	7-16-1990
261	2.13	2.59	3.19	2.59	4.51	4.23	1.93	2.25	3.70	3.97	2.94	2.75	36.78	Killeen	11.43	9-8-2010
274	1.76	1.79	2.31	2.10	4.01	4.14	2.74	2.09	3.03	4.11	2.28	1.91	32.27	San Antonio	14.33	10-18-1998
236	2.11	2.04	2.92	2.29	4.16	4.23	2.41	1.90	3.33	4.26	2.88	2.34	34.87	Hye	20.70	9-11-1952
234	0.66	0.77	1.06	1.44	2.68	2.62	1.73	2.30	2.32	1.78	0.97	0.73	19.06	Gail	10.79	9-20-2014
248	2.16	2.42	3.50	2.81	4.16	4.58	1.76	2.04	3.28	3.98	2.75	2.75	36.19	Kopperl	11.87	6-23-2014
246	3.90	4.32	4.65	4.16	5.13	4.79	3.78	2.17	3.59	5.25	4.99	5.23	51.96	New Boston	8.15	5-10-2009
313	4.65	3.30	3.59	3.42	4.32	6.19	5.17	4.23	7.03	5.41	4.65	4.51	56.47	Alvin	25.75	7-26-1979
280	3.24	2.85	3.17	2.66	4.33	4.45	2.14	2.68	3.18	4.91	3.22	3.23	40.06	College Station	13.39	10-16-1994
211	0.54	0.57	0.46	0.60	1.48	2.62	2.74	2.93	2.60	1.40	0.47	0.59	17.00	O2 Ranch	7.80	8-6-1920
195	0.72	0.82	1.32	1.60	2.86	4.15	2.34	2.78	2.18	1.87	0.92	0.85	22.41	Quitaque	8.58	6-1-1957
290	1.13	1.53	1.14	1.46	3.10	2.85	3.08	2.49	4.07	3.23	1.12	1.27	26.47	Falfurrias	10.00	9-20-1967
223	1.35	2.38	2.68	2.31	3.75	4.49	2.01	2.24	2.93	3.07	1.68	1.54	30.43	Winchell	8.20	9-23-1955
259	2.98	2.91	3.05	2.73	3.96	4.35	1.89	2.50	3.19	4.47	3.53	3.11	38.67	Somerville Dam	15.25	10-17-1994
261	1.84	2.03	2.98	2.15	4.03	4.25	2.04	1.82	3.10	3.40	2.76	2.01	32.41	Marble Falls	11.00	9-10-1921
257	2.30	2.30	2.56	2.66	4.30	4.28	2.04	2.14	3.34	4.56	2.89	2.56	35.93	Lockhart	13.38	10-18-1998
332	3.90	1.88	2.09	1.39	2.94	3.87	5.32	1.84	3.47	3.13	2.52	3.58	35.93	Point Comfort	14.65	6-26-1960
223	1.10	1.78	2.35	1.77	3.32	4.01	2.12	2.05	2.58	3.06	1.93	1.35	27.42	Baird	10.29	8-3-1978
365	1.27	1.08	1.23	1.54	2.64	2.57	2.04	2.44	5.92	3.74	1.82	1.15	27.44	San Benito	12.67	9-5-1933
258	3.24	3.85	4.55	3.56	4.75	4.16	3.29	2.72	3.22	4.58	4.45	4.42	46.79	Pittsburg	8.11	4-27-1958
178	0.61	0.61	1.35	1.68	2.74	3.53	2.57	2.94	2.19	1.87	0.93	0.76	21.78	Panhandle	8.05	5-16-1951

COUNTY, TOWN OR LANDMARK CLOSEST TO STATION FOR NORMALS	TEMPERATURE								AVERAGE FREEZE DATES			
	Mean Max. July	No. At or Above 100°F	Mean Min. January	No. At or Below 32°F	Record Highest	Record High Date	Record Lowest	Record Low Date	Last in Spring		First in Fall	
	F.	Days	F.	Days	F.	M-D-Y	F.	M-D-Y	Mo.	Day	Mo.	Day
Cass, Wright Patman Dam	92.1	4	34.6	35	*111	8-5-2011	−1	12-23-1989	Mar.	5	Nov.	21
Castro, Dimmitt	91.0	4	21.3	131	111	7-4-1983	−11	12-25-2004	Apr.	23	Oct.	20
Chambers, Anahuac	90.6	1	42.2	10	106	7-9-1939	8	12-23-1989	Feb.	15	Dec.	7
Cherokee, Rusk	91.2	3	36.3	29	*111	8-20-1925	*−5	2-13-1899	Mar.	11	Nov.	24
Childress, Childress	95.7	20	26.8	79	*117	6-26-2011	−13	1-17-1930	Apr.	1	Nov.	7
Clay, Henrietta	96.6	23	28.7	66	*116	8-7-1951	*−8	12-24-1989	Mar.	27	Nov.	9
Cochran, Morton	91.5	6	24.4	101	111	6-26-2011	−12	1-13-1963	Apr.	8	Oct.	31
Coke, Robert Lee	96.7	27	28.4	71	114	5-25-2000	−2	12-24-1989	Mar.	31	Nov.	6
Coleman, Coleman	95.7	20	33.7	40	114	8-3-1943	−9	12-23-1989	Mar.	19	Nov.	17
Collin, McKinney	91.5	3	30.1	60	115	8-4-2001	−11	12-23-1989	Mar.	28	Nov.	7
Collingsworth, Wellington	97.6	30	27.4	74	117	6-26-2011	−6	12-23-1989	Apr.	1	Nov.	5
Colorado, Columbus	94.3	15	40.8	17	116	9-4-2000	*4	12-24-1989	Feb.	25	Dec.	2
Comal, Canyon Dam	92.1	4	38.9	18	*112	8-4-2011	*2	12-23-1989	Mar.	1	Dec.	3
Comanche, Proctor Reservoir	95.7	19	31.4	51	113	8-3-2000	−8	12-23-1989	Mar.	20	Nov.	14
Concho, Paint Rock	95.2	17	29.5	65	*111	5-29-2011	−8	2-2-1985	Apr.	1	Nov.	5
Cooke, Gainesville	93.4	14	31.3	49	114	8-10-1936	−12	2-12-1899	Mar.	20	Nov.	17
Coryell, Gatesville	94.2	8	31.9	55	*112	9-5-2000	−6	1-31-1949	Mar.	29	Nov.	6
Cottle, Paducah	97.2	31	27.9	68	*118	6-27-2011	*−7	12-24-1989	Mar.	27	Nov.	8
Crane, Crane	93.3	7	31.9	52	115	6-27-1994	−6	2-2-1985	Mar.	24	Nov.	11
Crockett, Ozona	93.4	8	30.2	63	113	8-3-2015	−8	2-2-1951	Mar.	29	Nov.	7
Crosby, Crosbyton	92.3	8	25.9	88	113	6-28-1994	−14	2-12-1899	Apr.	4	Nov.	3
Culberson, Van Horn	92.3	8	28.3	70	112	6-25-1969	−14	2-3-2011	Mar.	31	Nov.	7
Dallam, Dalhart (6 mi. SW)	90.0	2	17.2	153	110	6-26-2011	−21	1-4-1959	Apr.	28	Oct.	12
Dallas, Dallas Love Field	96.0	17	37.3	23	115	8-18-1909	−10	2-12-1899	Mar.	4	Nov.	30
Dawson, Lamesa	93.1	10	26.0	90	114	6-28-1994	−12	2-8-1933	Apr.	3	Nov.	5
Deaf Smith, Hereford	91.4	4	22.5	116	111	6-8-1910	−17	2-1-1951	Apr.	14	Oct.	26
Delta, Cooper Dam	94.0		30.0		110		−1		Mar.	25	Nov.	13
Denton, Denton	95.3	15	33.0	42	*113	7-25-1954	−3	1-31-1949	Mar.	19	Nov.	17
DeWitt, Cuero	96.5	20	39.1	27	114	8-29-2011	2	1-31-1949	Mar.	13	Nov.	18
Dickens, Spur	94.7	17	26.6	86	117	6-28-1994	*−17	2-8-1933	Apr.	4	Nov.	4
Dimmit, Carrizo Springs	97.8	40	40.5	17	*114	6-11-1942	8	12-24-1989	Feb.	22	Dec.	3
Donley, Clarendon	94.7	17	23.8	102	117	8-12-1936	*−13	1-19-1984	Apr.	10	Oct.	26
Duval, Freer	97.0	32	43.1	11	116	6-15-1998	*12	1-24-1963	Feb.	13	Dec.	8
Eastland, Eastland	94.6	13	28.8	68	*115	8-11-1936	−8	12-24-1989	Mar.	31	Nov.	5
Ector, Penwell	95.3	20	28.7	67	116	6-28-1994	−12	2-2-1985	Mar.	31	Nov.	7
Edwards, Rocksprings	90.4	1	36.6	30	110	6-9-1988	0	12-22-1929	Mar.	16	Nov.	22
Ellis, Waxahachie	93.9	7	33.8	41	115	8-18-1909	−9	2-12-1899	Mar.	19	Nov.	17
El Paso, El Paso Intl. Airport	94.7	14	32.5	44	*115	8-18-2002	*−13	2-5-2011	Mar.	17	Nov.	14
Erath, Stephenville	94.2	11	31.0	55	114	8-11-1936	−9	2-12-1899	Mar.	27	Nov.	11
Falls, Marlin	94.2	8	35.4	37	*112	8-11-1969	*−7	1-31-1949	Mar.	16	Nov.	15
Fannin, Bonham	92.3	6	30.9	56	115	8-10-1936	−5	1-19-1930	Mar.	26	Nov.	8
Fayette, La Grange	95.5	15	39.2	24	111	8-23-1917	3	12-23-1989	Mar.	8	Nov.	23
Fisher, Rotan	94.6	13	30.5	59	116	6-27-1994	−12	2-12-1899	Mar.	30	Nov.	8
Floyd, Floydada	92.4	7	25.1	94	111	6-28-1994	−9	1-13-1963	Apr.	5	Nov.	3
Foard, Truscott	96.8	29	28.0	70	114		−7		Mar.	28	Nov.	9
Fort Bend, Sugar Land	94.9	7	44.1	6	*108	8-27-2011	8	12-23-1989	Feb.	6	Dec.	16
Franklin, Mount Vernon	92.0	6	31.9	50	112	8-3-2011	*−5	12-23-1989	Mar.	24	Nov.	12
Freestone, Fairfield	93.5	9	35.3	40	*110	9-4-2000	−2	12-23-1989	Mar.	19	Nov.	17
Frio, Dilley	96.7	27	41.7	9	113	9-6-2000	7	12-23-1989	Feb.	18	Dec.	6
Gaines, Seminole	93.4	11	27.7	79	114	6-28-1994	*−23	2-8-1933	Mar.	31	Nov.	7
Galveston, Galveston	89.2	0	45.1	5	106	9-4-2000	7	2-12-1899	Feb.	3	Dec.	28
Garza, Lake Alan Henry	93.4	9	29.2	65	116	6-28-1994	−1	12-22-1989	Mar.	26	Nov.	11
Gillespie, Fredericksburg	92.7	4	34.3	47	*109	9-5-2000	−5	1-31-1949	Mar.	26	Nov.	9
Glasscock, Garden City	92.6	6	28.3	71	114	6-27-1994	*−3	12-22-1989	Mar.	31	Nov.	5
Goliad, Goliad	93.8	7	42.5	16	*112	6-14-1998	7	1-12-1962	Mar.	2	Nov.	26

MEAN PRECIPITATION

GROWING SEASON	January	February	March	April	May	June	July	August	September	October	November	December	Annual	Location	RECORD RAINFALL HIGHEST DAILY TOTAL In.	M-D-Y
Days	In.	In.	In.	In.	In.	In.	In.	In.	In.	In.	In.	In.	In.		In.	
258	3.75	4.04	4.52	3.79	4.74	4.58	3.29	2.53	3.14	4.92	4.87	5.00	49.17	Linden	8.45	3-28-1989
179	0.62	0.56	1.04	1.05	2.83	3.72	2.21	3.21	2.59	1.86	0.75	0.78	21.22	Hart	5.17	6-11-1965
297	4.47	3.21	3.40	3.59	5.20	6.50	5.45	5.09	6.39	5.06	4.21	4.54	57.11	Anahuac	15.87	8-28-1945
258	4.08	4.35	4.44	3.34	4.36	4.73	3.25	3.07	3.55	5.27	4.57	4.53	49.54	Jacksonville	11.00	11-22-1940
220	0.85	1.16	1.74	2.28	3.95	4.33	2.23	2.50	3.21	2.04	1.18	0.96	26.43	Childress Airport	5.32	10-20-1983
226	1.56	2.17	2.70	2.74	4.57	4.28	1.89	2.59	2.73	3.31	2.01	2.13	32.68	Henrietta	6.07	6-23-1959
204	0.64	0.67	1.11	0.89	2.09	2.50	2.55	2.57	2.35	1.78	0.92	0.86	18.93	Morton	4.69	7-7-1960
221	0.88	1.35	1.41	1.55	2.94	3.11	1.51	2.52	2.55	2.76	1.21	0.96	22.75	Robert Lee	8.40	10-13-1957
242	1.11	2.07	2.45	1.92	3.62	4.43	1.99	2.38	2.57	3.00	1.85	1.35	28.74	Burkett	9.47	7-5-2002
224	2.63	3.17	4.06	3.69	5.72	4.48	2.43	1.90	3.03	4.31	3.85	3.05	42.32	Gunter	11.03	5-13-1982
218	0.79	0.73	1.44	1.86	3.02	3.45	2.25	1.86	2.32	2.45	1.18	0.91	22.26	Wellington	9.50	10-3-1986
282	3.57	2.88	3.18	3.12	4.77	4.98	3.24	2.87	3.06	4.68	4.42	3.16	43.93	New Ulm	12.13	4-18-2016
276	2.24	2.10	2.91	2.48	4.20	5.14	2.93	2.24	3.39	4.30	3.22	2.29	37.44	New Braunfels	18.35	10-18-1998
237	1.38	2.23	2.70	2.42	4.36	4.90	1.89	2.46	3.02	3.27	2.13	1.62	32.38	Comanche	8.86	8-19-2004
219	1.00	1.64	1.92	1.33	3.26	3.92	1.98	2.13	2.31	2.68	1.60	1.19	24.96	Paint Rock	8.25	9-9-1980
242	1.96	2.70	3.63	3.87	5.34	5.69	2.58	2.39	4.02	4.64	2.98	2.90	42.70	Gainesville	10.07	7-2-1903
222	1.65	2.35	2.57	2.90	4.38	3.66	2.36	2.53	2.87	3.30	2.51	2.35	33.43	Gatesville	8.67	9-8-2010
227	0.88	1.09	1.58	2.17	3.47	4.05	1.96	2.05	2.73	2.38	1.47	1.11	24.94	Paducah	7.00	6-2-1991
232	0.77	0.69	0.59	0.87	1.47	1.79	1.60	2.17	2.11	1.89	0.81	0.84	15.60	Crane	5.55	8-11-1986
222	0.93	1.04	1.63	1.74	2.20	2.04	1.39	1.97	2.00	2.36	0.90	0.66	18.86	Ozona (22 mi. SE)	8.02	8-18-2007
214	0.82	0.99	1.41	2.05	2.75	3.17	2.36	2.52	2.99	2.22	1.10	0.96	23.34	Crosbyton	5.78	6-30-1913
223	0.45	0.49	0.20	0.32	0.53	1.22	2.37	2.15	1.50	1.31	0.49	0.55	11.58	Pine Springs	9.42	9-12-2014
166	0.59	0.45	1.37	1.01	2.32	2.27	2.31	2.70	1.40	1.51	0.73	0.70	17.36	Bunker Hill	5.25	7-11-1959
269	2.06	2.59	3.49	3.07	4.92	4.11	2.21	1.87	2.84	4.79	2.88	2.74	37.57	Joe Pool Lake	12.05	7-29-2004
216	0.58	0.86	1.11	0.90	2.30	2.96	1.83	1.73	3.19	1.93	0.93	0.82	19.14	Lamesa	6.24	10-10-1985
194	0.72	0.56	1.27	1.01	2.03	3.53	2.17	3.43	2.07	1.68	0.74	0.84	20.05	Hereford	*5.30	8-3-1976
233	3.00	3.61	4.37	3.41	5.11	4.11	3.29	2.46	2.92	4.06	4.35	4.11	44.80	Cooper	8.46	5-13-1982
243	2.06	2.81	3.23	3.25	5.11	3.59	2.39	2.14	3.09	4.96	2.90	2.56	38.09	Isle Du Bois SP	13.00	5-13-1982
248	2.23	1.88	2.64	3.05	4.02	4.58	2.93	2.41	3.33	3.60	2.80	2.20	35.67	Cuero	12.40	6-30-1940
213	0.78	0.95	1.26	1.87	2.95	3.40	2.11	2.52	2.26	2.50	1.15	1.00	22.75	Pitchfork Ranch	7.60	9-18-1996
284	1.10	1.12	1.16	1.59	2.82	2.06	1.96	1.53	2.42	2.12	1.12	0.77	19.77	Carrizo Springs	11.48	10-14-2013
198	0.76	0.81	1.48	2.27	3.31	3.53	2.13	3.02	2.54	2.20	1.02	0.95	24.02	Clarendon	9.25	5-4-2001
297	1.43	1.56	2.26	2.08	3.16	3.68	2.24	2.11	2.49	2.47	1.47	1.04	25.99	Benavides	9.60	9-12-1971
218	1.17	2.05	2.57	1.98	3.45	4.21	1.77	2.43	2.56	3.44	1.74	1.65	29.02	Eastland	7.00	10-13-1957
222	0.53	0.75	0.65	0.62	2.25	1.38	1.17	1.61	1.92	1.34	0.73	0.58	13.53	Pleasant Farms	4.57	8-01-2017
250	0.99	1.16	1.80	1.97	3.37	3.22	2.07	2.74	2.83	3.62	1.58	1.21	26.56	Carta Valley	10.75	8-24-1998
241	2.27	2.93	3.84	3.34	3.99	4.12	2.66	2.34	3.05	4.45	3.03	3.10	39.12	Waxahachie	10.80	9-19-1958
242	0.40	0.46	0.26	0.23	0.47	0.94	1.55	2.01	1.51	0.61	0.49	0.78	9.71	El Paso	6.50	7-9-1881
228	1.45	2.25	2.86	2.52	4.39	4.01	1.56	2.38	3.02	3.11	2.09	1.90	31.54	Huckabay	10.21	4-26-1990
243	2.63	2.78	3.52	2.72	4.76	3.91	2.07	2.57	2.77	4.25	3.15	3.33	38.46	Marlin	11.90	7-31-1903
227	2.69	3.60	4.37	3.87	5.57	5.30	3.15	2.17	3.41	5.06	3.37	3.57	46.13	Bonham	13.30	7-3-1903
260	3.07	3.08	2.99	2.58	4.25	4.16	2.48	2.57	3.61	4.91	3.55	3.21	40.46	La Grange	14.69	8-27-2017
225	0.89	1.59	1.70	1.96	3.68	2.93	2.22	2.44	2.71	2.19	1.33	1.12	24.76	Rotan	6.85	8-13-1972
210	0.61	0.75	1.28	1.65	2.82	3.96	2.11	2.23	2.82	1.73	0.82	0.82	21.60	Floydada	7.75	9-12-2008
226	1.12	1.52	1.78	2.19	4.33	3.63	2.08	2.15	2.85	2.85	1.63	1.10	27.23	Crowell	8.25	9-19-1965
314	3.55	3.07	3.43	3.36	4.30	5.65	3.97	4.43	5.10	5.28	4.84	3.37	50.35	Katy	16.43	8-28-2017
232	2.77	3.62	4.47	3.34	5.13	4.61	3.68	2.43	3.25	5.22	4.57	4.33	47.42	Winfield	10.44	9-15-1913
242	2.96	3.64	3.84	3.12	5.14	4.29	2.08	2.58	3.02	4.37	4.30	3.78	43.12	Fairfield	7.90	1-29-1999
293	1.36	1.33	1.85	1.86	2.85	2.92	2.71	2.01	2.46	3.00	1.46	1.13	24.94	Derby	12.80	5-16-1980
220	0.71	0.84	0.98	0.96	2.46	2.37	2.51	1.85	2.47	1.48	0.91	0.82	18.36	Loop	6.35	10-19-1983
327	3.69	2.99	2.85	2.19	3.01	4.83	3.85	3.35	5.36	4.15	3.42	3.36	43.05	Bacliff	21.62	8-27-2017
230	0.72	1.15	1.34	1.57	2.29	3.00	2.40	2.30	2.16	2.12	1.07	0.77	20.89	Polar	9.00	9-25-1955
228	1.60	2.01	2.45	2.34	3.90	3.80	2.40	2.20	2.91	3.71	2.20	2.01	31.53	Gold	13.80	9-10-1952
219	0.87	0.92	1.18	1.17	2.31	1.82	1.53	1.97	2.48	1.68	0.94	0.70	17.57	Garden City	8.75	7-7-1945
267	2.41	1.98	2.44	2.52	4.06	4.14	3.71	2.94	4.26	3.85	2.56	1.91	36.78	Goliad	12.15	7-16-1990

COUNTY, TOWN OR LANDMARK CLOSEST TO STATION FOR NORMALS	TEMPERATURE								AVERAGE FREEZE DATES			
	Mean Max. July	No. At or Above 100°F	Mean Min. January	No. At or Below 32°F	Record Highest	Record High Date	Record Lowest	Record Low Date	Last in Spring		First in Fall	
	F.	Days	F.	Days	F.	M-D-Y	F.	M-D-Y	Mo.	Day	Mo.	Day
Gonzales, Gonzales	94.2	10	39.9	18	*114	8-10-1962	1	1-31-1949	Feb.	28	Dec.	1
Gray, Pampa	91.4	5	23.3	107	113	6-27-2011	−12	1-11-1962	Apr.	14	Oct.	27
Grayson, Sherman	92.1	5	33.1	42	113	8-10-1936	−3	12-23-1989	Mar.	17	Nov.	19
Gregg, Longview	93.8	6	34.2	43	113	8-10-1936	−7	2-12-1899	Mar.	17	Nov.	18
Grimes, Washington St. Park	95.1	17	36.3	33	108	8-11-1969	14	1-7-1970	Mar.	14	Nov.	19
Guadalupe, New Braunfels	93.3	3	38.1	26	112	9-5-2000	0	1-30-1949	Mar.	9	Nov.	25
Hale, Plainview	91.0	4	25.8	90	112	6-27-2011	−8	2-8-1933	Apr.	5	Nov.	1
Hall, Memphis	95.7	21	26.0	84	*117	8-3-1944	−11	1-18-1930	Apr.	1	Nov.	4
Hamilton, Hico	94.0	9	30.8	61	113	8-11-1936	−11	1-31-1949	Mar.	31	Nov.	6
Hansford, Spearman	95.6	19	24.8	97	111	8-13-1936	−22	1-4-1959	Apr.	11	Oct.	28
Hardeman, Quanah	95.7	20	26.2	83	*119	6-27-1994	−15	12-23-1989	Apr.	3	Nov.	1
Hardin, Evadale	93.0		37.0		110	9-1-2000	15	12-22-2000	Mar.	31	Nov.	14
Harris, Houston Hobby Airport	92.1	1	45.1	5	111	9-4-2000	5	1-18-1930	Feb.	3	Dec.	20
Harrison, Marshall	92.3	5	35.3	34	*112	8-18-1909	*−9	2-12-1899	Mar.	11	Nov.	22
Hartley, Channing	91.6	5	21.4	122	110	9-7-1907	*−20	2-8-1933	Apr.	17	Oct.	24
Haskell, Haskell	94.9	15	29.1	63	115	6-27-1994	*−6	12-23-1989	Mar.	28	Nov.	9
Hays, Dripping Springs	93.0	6	38.1	29	111	9-5-2000	−2	1-31-1949	Mar.	19	Nov.	17
Hemphill, Canadian	93.2	10	21.2	117	*112	6-26-1994	−14	1-5-1942	Apr.	16	Oct.	20
Henderson, Athens	92.6	5	34.5	41	*109	9-5-2000	−6	2-2-1985	Mar.	19	Nov.	14
Hidalgo, McAllen Intl. Airport	97.1	26	50.7	1	113	6-16-1998	10	1-12-1962	Jan.	13	Dec.	31
Hill, Hillsboro	95.0	10	34.8	40	113	7-10-1917	−6	12-23-1989	Mar.	23	Nov.	13
Hockley, Levelland	91.6	7	26.1	91	115	6-28-1994	−16	1-13-1963	Apr.	4	Nov.	3
Hood, Cresson	97.0		33.0		*111	8-10-1947	−6	1-31-1949	Mar.	26	Nov.	13
Hopkins, Sulphur Springs	91.5	5	32.9	45	*115	8-10-1969	−10	2-12-1899	Mar.	21	Nov.	13
Houston, Crockett	93.4	9	36.8	30	114	8-18-1909	0	2-1-1951	Mar.	9	Nov.	24
Howard, Big Spring	94.6	14	31.3	52	114	6-28-1994	−7	1-11-1962	Mar.	22	Nov.	16
Hudspeth, Sierra Blanca	92.5	7	25.7	96	115	6-28-1994	−10	2-2-1985	Apr.	12	Oct.	29
Hunt, Greenville	96.4	23	32.7	45	116	8-10-1936	*−4	1-18-1930	Mar.	19	Nov.	18
Hutchinson, Borger	93.8	12	25.2	95	*113	6-26-2011	−19	1-8-1912	Apr.	13	Oct.	27
Irion, Cope Ranch	94.5	15	27.1	84	*108	6-9-1985	4	2-1-1985	Apr.	8	Oct.	31
Jack, Jacksboro	94.4	13	29.7	57	*113	8-29-2011	−8	12-22-1989	Mar.	25	Nov.	9
Jackson, Point Comfort	90.7	0	45.1	6	107	7-27-1954	8	1-31-1949	Feb.	8	Dec.	16
Jasper, Sam Rayburn Dam	91.4	2	38.7	23	109	9-5-2000	*2	2-2-1951	Mar.	6	Nov.	27
Jeff Davis, Fort Davis	87.0	1	28.9	73	*108	6-27-1994	*−10	1-11-1962	Apr.	8	Oct.	30
Jefferson, Port Arthur / Airport	91.7	1	43.2	9	*108	8-31-2000	4	2-12-1899	Feb.	16	Dec.	8
Jim Hogg, Hebbronville	96.7	25	44.8	7	118	7-9-2009	12	12-23-1989	Feb.	14	Dec.	12
Jim Wells, Alice	96.0	18	45.0	5	*114	7-6-1997	11	12-25-1989	Feb.	5	Dec.	17
Johnson, Cleburne	95.7	15	32.6	48	114	9-2-1939	−6	12-23-1989	Mar.	24	Nov.	11
Jones, Anson	96.2	23	31.1	55	118	6-28-1994	*−12	12-23-1989	Mar.	27	Nov.	11
Karnes, Karnes City	95.1	14	41.8	13	112	7-27-1954	6	2-12-1899	Feb.	24	Dec.	5
Kaufman, Kaufman	94.3	11	33.1	43	113	8-10-1936	−3	12-23-1989	Mar.	20	Nov.	16
Kendall, Boerne	92.5	4	35.4	41	112	8-23-1925	−4	1-31-1949	Mar.	20	Nov.	14
Kenedy, Port Mansfield	89.8	0	50.2	3	110	6-16-1963	14	1-13-1975	Jan.	22	Dec.	30
Kent, Jayton	94.6	16	27.2	79	116	6-28-1994	−6	2-3-1985	Apr.	1	Nov.	6
Kerr, Kerrville	92.2	5	33.8	46	110	7-27-1954	−7	1-31-1949	Mar.	29	Nov.	8
Kimble, Junction / Co. Airport	94.6	12	33.1	52	112	8-2-2011	−11	12-22-1929	Mar.	25	Nov.	7
King, Guthrie	95.9	23	27.0	80	119	6-28-1994	−10	12-23-1989	Apr.	2	Nov.	4
Kinney, Brackettville	94.8	17	36.9	28	111	6-10-1988	4	1-12-1962	Mar.	6	Nov.	27
Kleberg, Kingsville Air Station	95.1	8	45.8	6	115	6-15-1998	10	12-24-1989	Feb.	5	Dec.	13
Knox, Munday	96.3	21	29.1	64	*118	6-20-2011	−11	1-4-1947	Mar.	27	Nov.	9
Lamar, Paris	95.8	20	31.8	46	115	8-10-1936	−13	2-12-1899	Mar.	18	Nov.	17
Lamb, Littlefield	92.0	6	24.5	101	112	6-28-1994	*−14	1-13-1963	Apr.	8	Oct.	31
Lampasas, Lampasas	95.6	17	33.4	47	*112	7-11-1917	−12	1-31-1949	Mar.	22	Nov.	15
La Salle, Fowlerton	96.9	33	38.9	24	*116	9-8-1893	9	1-12-1962	Mar.	3	Nov.	26
Lavaca, Hallettsville	93.4	4	41.3	15	112	8-29-2011	5	12-23-1989	Mar.	2	Nov.	30

GROWING SEASON Days	January In.	February In.	March In.	April In.	May In.	June In.	July In.	August In.	September In.	October In.	November In.	December In.	Annual In.	Location	In.	M-D-Y
278	2.39	2.15	2.44	2.51	4.23	4.17	2.23	2.27	3.07	3.92	2.99	2.54	34.91	Gonzales	16.31	8-31-1981
195	0.70	0.69	1.64	2.04	2.98	3.65	2.71	2.77	2.12	1.95	1.06	0.88	23.19	McLean	7.60	4-3-1997
247	2.47	2.94	3.92	3.55	5.32	5.00	2.62	2.06	3.59	5.29	3.70	3.14	43.60	Van Alstyne	9.30	9-22-2018
246	3.69	4.26	4.28	3.73	4.79	4.44	2.95	2.87	3.46	4.46	4.47	4.69	48.09	Longview	12.03	3-9-2016
249	3.54	2.83	3.52	2.80	3.90	4.76	2.37	2.79	3.36	4.63	3.80	3.38	41.68	Richards	11.98	10-16-1994
260	1.95	1.98	2.58	2.03	3.95	4.78	2.93	2.11	3.04	3.80	2.46	2.36	33.97	Kingsbury	9.25	10-9-2002
210	0.72	0.63	1.16	1.64	2.80	3.20	2.42	2.25	2.17	1.74	0.92	0.80	20.45	Plainview	7.00	7-8-1960
218	0.69	0.94	1.47	2.05	3.07	3.32	2.05	2.56	2.49	1.89	1.12	0.94	22.59	Memphis	8.80	6-7-1960
221	2.00	2.58	3.16	2.63	4.91	4.86	1.97	2.48	3.02	3.44	2.20	2.03	35.28	Hamilton	8.20	10-4-1959
198	0.47	0.63	1.62	1.68	2.50	3.89	2.69	2.62	1.97	1.55	0.83	0.74	21.19	Gruver	9.72	6-13-2010
211	1.00	1.19	1.90	2.13	3.29	3.95	2.42	2.79	2.83	2.56	1.64	1.15	26.85	Quanah	8.03	8-2-1995
246	4.73	4.31	3.56	3.01	5.14	5.65	4.20	4.38	4.60	4.75	4.82	5.60	54.75	Kountze	15.50	8-30-2017
320	3.87	3.21	3.20	3.25	4.75	7.10	4.66	5.06	5.21	5.99	4.32	4.03	54.65	Houston-South	20.84	8-27-2017
253	3.72	4.33	4.49	3.64	4.85	5.18	3.49	2.61	3.32	4.93	4.58	5.04	50.18	Harleton	10.50	3-29-1989
188	2.70	0.61	1.58	0.80	1.91	2.02	2.64	3.85	1.68	1.52	0.79	0.92	21.02	Romero	8.27	5-17-1914
228	1.04	1.75	1.80	2.20	3.43	3.95	1.92	2.20	2.63	2.54	1.48	1.46	26.40	Haskell	14.29	8-4-1978
243	2.36	2.24	3.00	2.20	4.13	5.02	2.09	1.76	3.08	4.08	3.17	2.61	35.74	San Marcos	15.78	10-17-1998
186	0.53	0.66	1.81	1.69	3.30	3.62	2.37	2.20	2.17	1.93	0.71	0.78	21.77	Canadian	7.00	6-8-2008
238	2.98	3.87	4.04	3.21	4.77	4.35	2.11	2.37	2.56	4.96	3.74	3.98	42.94	Payne Springs	11.28	10-25-2015
360	1.05	1.11	1.03	1.34	2.25	2.58	2.00	2.21	4.47	2.08	0.89	1.19	22.20	Weslaco	15.00	9-5-1933
235	2.39	2.92	3.78	2.95	4.37	4.34	1.59	2.10	3.03	4.53	2.84	3.09	37.93	Aquilla	11.49	10-24-2015
211	0.72	0.68	1.02	1.02	2.48	2.84	2.17	2.63	2.74	1.68	0.99	0.87	19.84	Ropesville	5.06	9-12-2008
232	1.79	2.56	3.42	2.71	4.57	4.44	1.63	2.25	2.94	3.87	2.77	2.13	35.08	Cresson	11.08	6-4-2000
236	3.07	3.66	4.41	3.83	4.79	4.36	3.38	2.44	2.99	5.39	4.54	4.32	47.18	Cumby	8.64	4-11-2017
258	3.77	3.62	3.66	3.16	4.41	4.64	3.02	3.03	3.02	4.76	4.09	4.00	45.18	Crockett	9.11	6-8-2001
239	0.71	0.90	1.02	1.36	2.41	2.69	1.64	2.55	2.65	1.88	1.09	0.60	19.50	Ackerly	6.40	6-9-1993
200	0.40	0.65	0.30	0.33	0.52	1.13	2.13	2.15	1.45	1.15	0.41	0.62	11.24	Dell City	7.10	9-12-2013
243	2.75	3.44	4.22	3.48	5.52	4.18	3.16	1.88	3.34	5.09	4.01	3.58	44.65	Commerce	12.00	8-13-2017
196	0.71	0.69	1.54	1.79	2.68	3.28	2.68	3.56	2.09	1.94	1.03	0.86	22.85	Borger	6.27	9-22-2004
204	0.79	1.04	1.08	1.14	2.19	2.78	1.76	2.22	2.58	2.06	0.90	0.95	19.49	Mertzon	8.35	8-12-1971
228	1.31	2.19	2.82	2.67	4.80	4.19	1.91	1.54	3.36	3.86	2.29	1.98	32.92	Antelope	11.18	5-16-1989
311	3.06	2.46	3.10	2.30	4.27	4.72	4.06	2.66	4.42	4.78	3.93	2.63	42.39	Maurbro	14.80	6-26-1960
264	5.27	4.70	4.95	3.94	4.50	6.18	3.89	4.01	4.29	5.54	6.33	6.15	59.75	Evadale	14.52	9-18-1963
203	0.48	0.51	0.46	0.67	1.50	2.46	3.26	3.28	2.23	1.45	0.52	0.65	17.47	Jasper	8.05	3-29-2018
298	5.26	3.58	3.53	3.21	5.23	7.09	5.95	5.38	5.97	5.58	4.40	5.29	60.47	Port Arthur Reg AP	26.03	8-29-2017
304	1.25	1.45	1.19	1.46	3.10	2.57	2.67	1.69	3.30	2.36	1.35	1.40	23.79	Kaffie Ranch	21.02	9-12-1971
315	1.21	1.51	1.34	1.65	3.16	3.41	1.76	2.70	4.52	3.55	1.50	1.21	27.52	Alice Intl. Airport	13.21	9-13-1951
232	2.24	2.59	3.64	2.91	4.85	4.27	2.10	2.59	3.15	3.89	2.80	2.58	37.61	Lillian	9.30	5-17-1989
229	1.12	1.55	1.69	2.10	3.32	3.66	2.32	2.42	2.35	2.66	1.51	1.36	26.06	Stamford	8.22	8-4-1978
287	1.63	1.68	2.20	2.20	3.03	3.47	2.97	2.35	3.06	3.33	2.30	1.92	30.14	Cibolo Creek	13.75	9-21-1967
239	2.85	3.03	3.89	2.68	4.50	3.51	2.20	2.50	2.83	5.07	3.56	3.30	39.92	Crandall	10.22	4-19-1976
237	2.08	2.39	2.95	2.26	4.64	4.63	3.27	2.73	3.41	4.38	3.12	2.24	38.10	Kendalia	12.32	5-24-2015
351	1.32	1.68	1.34	1.39	2.45	2.19	2.43	1.43	5.33	3.30	1.73	1.32	25.91	Sarita	9.30	10-12-1973
219	0.96	1.22	1.42	1.83	3.39	3.46	2.40	2.21	2.25	2.36	1.17	0.84	23.51	Jayton	*6.50	7-29-2004
224	1.58	1.81	2.48	2.10	4.00	3.97	2.82	1.69	3.65	3.66	2.43	1.86	32.05	Lynxhaven Ranch	15.20	8-2-1978
227	0.86	1.57	2.41	2.12	3.29	3.61	1.95	2.34	2.76	2.96	1.89	1.22	26.98	Junction	8.56	10-08-2018
215	1.03	1.42	1.53	2.06	3.42	3.66	2.27	2.69	2.58	2.50	1.30	1.07	25.53	Guthrie	8.85	7-4-1986
266	0.73	0.92	1.61	1.56	3.16	2.81	1.92	2.52	3.15	2.88	1.29	1.01	23.56	Fort Clark	18.00	6-15-1899
312	1.55	1.79	1.45	1.64	3.59	3.49	2.46	2.67	5.15	3.39	1.75	1.45	30.38	Ricardo	11.30	6-21-1924
227	1.12	1.67	2.08	2.11	3.49	4.16	1.83	2.24	2.48	2.72	1.33	1.20	26.43	Munday	8.00	6-14-1930
244	2.70	3.28	4.44	3.41	5.56	4.17	3.68	2.22	3.84	5.10	4.68	3.99	47.07	Arthur City	10.50	5-12-1920
204	0.65	0.63	1.08	1.10	2.05	3.08	2.30	2.53	2.20	1.55	0.86	0.84	18.87	Olton	6.30	6-4-1985
236	1.88	2.23	2.79	2.25	4.20	3.96	2.05	2.28	2.62	3.49	2.31	2.17	32.23	Lometa	9.50	10-4-1959
265	1.15	1.16	1.85	1.96	2.95	2.75	2.61	1.83	2.96	2.76	1.44	1.28	24.70	Fowlerton	12.80	9-9-2002
270	3.01	2.50	2.72	3.14	4.66	4.73	2.81	2.80	3.87	4.44	3.74	2.64	41.06	Halletsville	20.60	8-27-2017

COUNTY, TOWN OR LANDMARK CLOSEST TO STATION FOR NORMALS	TEMPERATURE								AVERAGE FREEZE DATES			
	Mean Max. July	No. At or Above 100°F	Mean Min. January	No. At or Below 32°F	Record Highest	Record High Date	Record Lowest	Record Low Date	Last in Spring		First in Fall	
	F.	Days	F.	Days	F.	M-D-Y	F.	M-D-Y	Mo.	Day	Mo.	Day
Lee, Lexington	94.1	7	37.2	27	111	9-6-2000	*2	12-23-1989	Mar.	7	Nov.	24
Leon, Centerville	93.7	7	34.9	42	113	8-18-1909	0	2-1-1951	Mar.	21	Nov.	16
Liberty, Liberty	92.1	1	41.2	14	112	8-9-1962	5	12-24-1989	Feb.	24	Dec.	4
Limestone, Mexia	94.1	10	35.2	30	112	8-18-1909	−5	12-23-1989	Mar.	10	Nov.	24
Lipscomb, Lipscomb	94.0	16	18.1	134	*114	6-27-2011	−19	1-19-1984	Apr.	23	Oct.	14
Live Oak, Choke Canyon Dam	95.5	20	42.4	11	112	9-6-2000	11	12-26-1983	Feb.	17	Dec.	9
Llano, Llano	97.7	34	32.2	52	115	7-14-1933	−7	12-22-1929	Mar.	24	Nov.	10
Loving, *Red Bluff Dam*	99.3	52	29.7	61	*112	7-30-1944	0	1-5-1947	Mar.	29	Nov.	9
Lubbock, Lubbock	92.8	7	26.4	84	114	6-27-1994	−17	2-8-1933	Apr.	4	Nov.	2
Lynn, Tahoka	91.9	6	28.0	75	111	6-28-1994	−15	2-8-1933	Apr.	1	Nov.	8
Madison, Madisonville	94.4	9	36.9	35	112	9-5-2000	*−2	1-31-1949	Mar.	17	Nov.	14
Marion, Jefferson	92.6	6	32.7	50	*112	8-5-2011	*−5	12-23-1989	Mar.	21	Nov.	10
Martin, Lenorah	*94.0*		*30.0*		*109*		*−8*		*Apr.*	*5*	*Nov.*	*6*
Mason, Mason	92.3	4	32.1	53	*109	8-12-1962	*3	2-2-1985	Mar.	27	Nov.	10
Matagorda, Bay City	91.5	1	45.4	6	109	9-4-2000	7	12-23-1989	Feb.	10	Dec.	18
Maverick, Eagle Pass	98.1	42	41.5	10	*115	7-25-1944	7	2-12-1899	Feb.	14	Dec.	8
McCulloch, Brady	94.2	11	32.2	51	110	6-29-1980	*−2	1-18-1930	Mar.	26	Nov.	11
McLennan, Waco Reg. Airport	96.3	17	36.1	31	*114	7-23-2018	*−7	1-31-1949	Mar.	13	Nov.	21
McMullen, Tilden	96.4	26	42.6	9	119	7-2-1910	5	12-22-1989	Feb.	16	Dec.	6
Medina, Hondo Muni. Airport	94.6	12	39.0	23	*112	9-5-2000	4	2-1-1949	Mar.	6	Nov.	24
Menard, Menard	93.1	6	29.3	72	114	5-29-1927	−6	1-9-1879	Apr.	9	Oct.	30
Midland, Midland	94.6	15	30.3	58	*116	6-27-1994	*−12	1-11-1962	Mar.	29	Nov.	10
Milam, Cameron	88.7	0	33.8	47	114	7-10-1917	−7	1-17-1930	Mar.	25	Nov.	10
Mills, Goldthwaite	91.5	2	33.0	42	110	8-6-1964	−7	12-23-1989	Mar.	21	Nov.	13
Mitchell, Lake Colorado City	94.7	12	30.1	56	115	6-30-1907	*−7	1-4-1947	Mar.	25	Nov.	15
Montague, Bowie	93.3	9	29.2	65	115	6-28-1980	−12	2-12-1899	Mar.	30	Nov.	9
Montgomery, Conroe	93.5	5	40.4	18	113	9-4-2000	2	2-12-1899	Feb.	28	Dec.	1
Moore, Dumas	91.6	5	22.1	118	*109	6-28-1980	−18	1-5-1959	Apr.	17	Oct.	24
Morris, Daingerfield	94.1	9	35.1	34	112	8-4-1998	4	1-10-1962	Mar.	8	Nov.	23
Motley, Matador	94.2	13	29.6	66	116	6-28-1994	*−5	12-23-1989	Apr.	1	Nov.	7
Nacogdoches, Nacogdoches	93.2	7	35.8	40	*113	9-3-2000	−4	1-18-1930	Mar.	19	Nov.	16
Navarro, Corsicana	94.1	10	34.7	36	*113	7-26-1954	−7	2-12-1899	Mar.	13	Nov.	21
Newton, Toledo Bend Dam	93.1	4	36.5	35	110	6-5-2011	4	1-19-1930	Mar.	14	Nov.	20
Nolan, Roscoe	93.9	11	29.0	67	113	6-27-1994	−11	1-5-1947	Apr.	2	Nov.	6
Nueces, Corpus Christi	93.1	2	47.2	4	113	8-31-1983	*7	2-12-1899	Feb.	2	Dec.	19
Ochiltree, Perryton	92.4	9	19.0	135	*113	6-10-1981	−17	1-7-1988	Apr.	25	Oct.	18
Oldham, Vega	90.6	3	19.8	132	110	7-27-1982	*−17	2-1-1951	Apr.	22	Oct.	19
Orange, Orange	91.2	1	39.6	22	107	9-1-2000	10	12-25-1989	Feb.	28	Nov.	26
Palo Pinto, Mineral Wells	95.5	16	32.2	48	115	8-14-1999	−8	12-23-1989	Mar.	23	Nov.	11
Panola, Carthage	93.0	5	35.2	39	109	9-5-2000	1	12-24-1989	Mar.	14	Nov.	19
Parker, Weatherford	93.2	8	30.1	63	119	6-26-1980	*−11	2-12-1899	Mar.	31	Nov.	5
Parmer, Friona	89.8	3	22.5	120	109	6-19-2017	−15	1-13-1963	Apr.	20	Oct.	23
Pecos, Fort Stockton	94.3	15	33.2	42	117	6-29-1994	−7	1-3-1911	Mar.	17	Nov.	18
Polk, Livingston	93.7	5	39.6	24	116	8-3-2016	*3	12-24-1989	Mar.	4	Nov.	26
Potter, Amarillo	91.4	5	23.4	107	111	6-26-2011	−16	2-12-1899	Apr.	15	Oct.	24
Presidio, Presidio	100.4	73	34.5	30	*117	6-18-1960	−2	1-5-1972	Feb.	27	Nov.	28
Rains, Emory	91.4	4	31.4	56	112	9-5-2000	−5	12-25-1989	Mar.	25	Nov.	10
Randall, Canyon	91.7	4	21.5	116	*109	6-27-2011	−14	2-1-1951	Apr.	16	Oct.	22
Reagan, Big Lake	93.5	9	30.8	57	115	6-28-1994	−9	2-2-1985	Mar.	27	Nov.	10
Real, Camp Wood	93.0	5	33.6	47	*109	9-6-2000	0	11-29-1976	Mar.	22	Nov.	12
Red River, *DeKalb*	93.4	7	31.5	54	115	8-10-1936	*−7	1-18-1930	Mar.	27	Nov.	7
Reeves, Balmorhea	94.4	15	30.3	65	118	6-29-1968	−14	1-11-1962	Mar.	29	Nov.	10
Refugio, Refugio	92.0	2	44.3	11	112	9-5-2000	8	1-12-1962	Feb.	24	Dec.	5
Roberts, Miami	92.1	7	22.1	113	114	6-11-1917	−15	1-5-1942	Apr.	16	Oct.	21
Robertson, Franklin	94.9	12	38.8	23	112	9-4-2000	−1	12-23-1989	Mar.	8	Nov.	22
Rockwall, *Lavon Dam*	94.3	10	34.2	33	*109	7-25-1954	4	2-2-1951	Mar.	10	Nov.	24

GROWING SEASON Days	January In.	February In.	March In.	April In.	May In.	June In.	July In.	August In.	September In.	October In.	November In.	December In.	Annual In.	Location	In.	M-D-Y
259	2.58	2.43	2.84	2.05	4.20	3.74	2.11	2.17	2.98	5.04	3.52	2.95	36.61	Fedor	13.00	10-17-1994
239	3.16	3.45	3.82	2.73	4.61	4.18	2.49	2.65	2.79	4.96	3.80	3.65	42.29	Buffalo	9.19	10-14-1957
286	4.42	4.18	3.90	3.88	5.58	7.35	5.20	4.24	5.49	6.51	5.25	5.25	61.25	Dayton	25.00	8-27-2017
259	2.46	3.34	3.82	2.91	4.39	3.92	1.93	2.35	3.46	4.35	3.64	3.77	40.34	Mexia	8.63	2-4-1986
173	0.56	0.74	1.79	1.76	2.91	3.92	2.35	2.68	1.84	1.77	1.02	0.91	22.25	Booker	7.76	6-9-1997
298	1.45	1.47	1.88	2.16	2.62	3.16	3.38	1.53	3.07	2.45	1.70	1.49	26.36	Whitsett	15.69	9-22-1967
232	1.43	1.83	2.51	1.92	3.64	3.57	2.00	1.55	2.21	2.97	2.22	1.85	27.70	Moss Ranch	13.53	9-11-1952
226	0.63	0.34	0.23	0.72	0.94	2.09	2.37	1.41	1.54	1.15	0.45	0.70	12.57	Mentone	3.79	9-24-1955
211	0.65	0.75	1.10	1.41	2.30	3.04	1.91	1.91	2.51	1.93	0.85	0.76	19.12	Lubbock	7.81	9-12-2008
221	0.76	0.85	1.07	1.44	2.82	3.16	2.63	2.25	2.28	2.07	1.00	0.88	21.21	Tahoka	9.10	5-5-2015
242	3.86	3.28	3.26	2.82	4.49	4.10	3.84	2.91	3.42	4.84	4.38	3.92	45.12	Madisonville	8.89	10-16-2018
234	3.96	4.45	4.48	3.50	4.61	5.17	2.88	2.25	3.43	5.01	4.51	4.71	48.96	Jefferson	9.10	4-26-1921
215	0.66	0.88	0.86	1.30	2.13	2.42	1.58	1.62	2.54	1.93	0.96	0.68	17.56	Tarzan	6.54	9-20-2014
227	1.13	1.97	2.30	2.16	3.58	4.31	2.47	1.95	2.73	3.12	2.08	1.39	29.19	Mason	7.80	10-16-2018
313	3.86	2.69	3.07	2.98	4.45	5.30	4.78	3.75	5.11	5.06	4.25	3.59	48.89	Matagorda	12.20	5-7-1951
299	0.90	0.96	1.01	1.88	2.55	2.73	2.08	1.46	3.11	2.07	0.95	0.71	20.41	Eagle Pass	15.60	6-29-1936
230	1.18	1.81	2.24	1.94	3.61	3.40	2.23	2.21	2.83	2.75	1.84	1.56	27.60	Brady	9.13	7-8-2015
250	2.12	2.63	3.15	2.69	4.30	3.43	1.79	2.05	3.06	3.90	2.82	2.75	34.69	McGregor	13.08	6-16-1964
294	1.11	1.30	1.64	2.05	3.15	3.24	1.74	1.95	3.16	2.11	1.24	1.30	23.99	Calliham	12.00	4-17-2010
262	1.38	1.49	2.13	1.98	3.38	3.49	2.09	1.67	2.60	3.31	1.58	1.14	26.24	Natalia	11.47	9-27-1973
202	1.17	1.52	2.01	1.47	2.97	3.17	1.86	1.90	2.10	2.43	1.56	1.16	23.32	Callan	7.67	10-10-1961
227	0.56	0.71	0.60	0.65	1.74	1.80	1.82	1.84	1.86	1.73	0.69	0.60	14.60	Midland	7.20	5-9-1968
230	2.29	2.66	2.74	2.53	4.94	3.69	2.17	2.15	3.44	4.14	3.33	2.89	36.97	Cameron	12.45	9-10-1921
236	1.43	2.34	2.57	2.15	3.87	4.79	1.89	2.16	2.60	3.15	2.05	1.61	30.61	Goldthwaite	7.20	10-5-1969
236	0.44	0.89	1.07	1.33	2.49	2.84	1.23	2.29	3.09	2.22	0.90	0.64	19.43	Colorado City	8.65	4-6-1900
224	1.45	2.44	3.08	2.99	5.00	4.34	1.98	2.07	3.41	4.02	2.21	2.07	35.06	Bonita	12.47	4-30-2009
276	3.85	3.47	3.25	2.91	4.94	5.26	3.07	3.61	3.75	5.73	5.09	3.84	48.77	Montgomery	14.72	8-27-2017
188	0.62	0.52	1.26	1.28	2.17	2.41	2.43	2.89	1.87	1.37	0.73	0.82	18.37	Sunray	4.49	10-16-1968
258	3.24	3.85	4.55	3.56	4.75	4.16	3.29	2.72	3.22	4.58	4.45	4.42	46.79	Daingerfield	7.50	7-28-2009
220	0.80	0.90	1.49	1.92	2.91	3.67	2.19	2.44	2.90	2.15	1.14	0.92	23.43	Flomot	7.08	7-9-1994
240	4.13	4.42	4.20	3.73	4.38	4.42	3.01	3.25	3.64	4.70	4.56	4.84	49.28	Nacogdoches	14.22	6-28-1902
252	2.64	3.39	3.91	3.02	4.70	3.52	2.25	2.14	2.96	4.50	3.30	3.45	39.78	Corsicana	18.95	10-24-2015
248	4.74	4.94	4.47	3.57	4.62	5.50	4.00	3.11	3.38	5.07	5.53	5.99	54.92	Deweyville	20.60	9-18-1963
217	0.98	1.21	1.23	1.62	2.86	3.38	2.17	2.16	2.38	2.45	0.93	1.05	22.42	Roscoe	8.28	9-9-1980
321	1.54	1.93	1.89	1.84	3.07	3.36	2.79	2.92	4.98	3.64	1.97	1.83	31.76	Port Aransas	13.89	8-22-1999
175	0.47	0.62	1.75	1.82	2.96	3.32	3.12	2.63	1.86	1.83	0.88	0.84	22.10	Perryton	7.11	5-17-1989
178	0.62	0.51	1.22	1.12	2.28	3.07	2.69	3.51	2.08	1.68	0.76	0.78	20.32	Vega	6.07	5-16-1951
271	5.40	4.63	3.67	3.50	5.45	7.32	5.77	5.69	6.23	6.04	4.99	5.52	64.21	Bridge City	23.82	8-30-2017
232	1.45	2.14	3.19	2.38	3.95	4.16	1.99	2.24	2.82	3.73	2.16	1.84	32.05	Gordon	8.20	5-8-1997
248	4.38	4.46	4.22	3.78	4.53	4.73	3.31	2.92	3.64	5.15	4.94	5.37	51.43	Carthage	9.25	4-14-1991
219	1.57	2.82	3.27	2.54	4.59	4.56	2.14	2.07	3.10	4.00	2.95	2.16	35.77	Weatherford	8.57	8-20-2016
185	0.72	0.63	1.20	1.03	2.20	2.65	2.48	3.33	2.40	1.81	0.83	0.86	20.14	Bovina	4.73	7-21-1918
244	0.61	0.59	0.53	0.84	1.40	2.23	1.75	2.29	2.08	1.76	0.53	0.54	15.15	Bakersfield	7.10	4-30-2007
265	4.24	3.92	3.87	3.26	4.88	5.70	3.56	3.34	4.06	4.85	5.15	4.70	51.53	Corrigan	14.69	10-17-1994
192	0.72	0.56	1.39	1.40	2.29	3.16	2.84	2.91	1.92	1.66	0.80	0.71	20.36	Amarillo	5.89	10-08-2018
272	0.51	0.47	0.22	0.28	0.65	1.27	1.66	1.73	1.20	0.94	0.34	0.39	9.66	Bunton Rch	5.50	8-23-1944
230	2.87	3.82	4.60	3.30	4.91	4.20	2.99	2.22	2.97	4.87	3.95	3.77	44.47	Lake Tawakoni	10.05	10-25-2015
188	0.60	0.48	1.12	1.10	2.55	3.33	2.24	3.43	2.13	1.81	0.76	0.60	20.15	Canyon	7.87	8-29-1968
228	0.95	1.11	1.29	1.48	2.19	2.14	2.77	1.96	2.00	1.69	0.91	0.80	19.29	Big Lake	5.87	8-15-2005
235	1.21	1.30	1.96	1.99	2.91	3.40	2.35	2.41	3.22	3.14	2.14	1.35	27.38	Leakey	11.95	9-26-2016
226	3.54	4.19	5.19	4.17	5.67	4.35	4.10	2.70	3.60	6.01	5.33	5.26	54.11	Avery	9.29	12-28-2015
225	0.58	0.73	0.29	0.79	1.22	1.27	1.73	2.23	2.29	1.24	0.50	0.67	13.54	Red Bluff Dam	7.24	6-19-1984
287	2.15	2.39	3.01	2.27	3.17	3.52	3.64	3.15	4.39	4.31	2.82	2.07	36.89	Austwell	15.96	8-26-2017
187	0.91	0.76	2.04	1.97	3.42	3.36	2.33	2.65	2.30	2.30	1.02	1.02	24.08	Miami	5.58	10-10-1985
258	2.92	2.99	3.22	2.58	4.54	3.52	1.84	2.90	3.08	4.71	3.57	3.63	39.50	Bremond	8.49	8-19-2008
259	2.45	2.97	3.67	3.44	5.17	4.47	2.02	1.85	3.17	4.55	3.55	3.22	40.53	Rockwall	7.08	9-22-2018

COUNTY, TOWN OR LANDMARK CLOSEST TO STATION FOR NORMALS	Mean Max. July	No. At or Above 100°F	Mean Min. January	No. At or Below 32°F	Record Highest	Record High Date	Record Lowest	Record Low Date	Last in Spring		First in Fall	
	F.	Days	F.	Days	F.	M-D-Y	F.	M-D-Y	Mo.	Day	Mo.	Day
Runnels, Ballinger	94.4	11	31.2	54	116	6-30-1907	−6	1-31-1949	Mar.	25	Nov.	10
Rusk, Henderson	92.7	6	34.9	40	*111	9-2-2000	*−1	12-23-1989	Mar.	19	Nov.	18
Sabine, Toledo Bend Dam	93.1	4	36.5	35	114	8-9-1947	6	2-2-1951	Mar.	14	Nov.	20
San Augustine, Broaddus	93.0		35.0		112	8-18-1909	7	1-17-2018	Mar.	19	Nov.	12
San Jacinto, Coldspring	92.4	6	38.2	28	110	8-2-1998	3	12-24-1989	Mar.	8	Nov.	27
San Patricio, Sinton	93.4	4	44.2	8	111	9-6-2000	10	12-23-1989	Feb.	9	Dec.	13
San Saba, San Saba	95.7	16	34.6	37	112	7-17-1978	−1	12-23-1989	Mar.	13	Nov.	18
Schleicher, Fort McKavett	93.6	8	31.6	58	*107	6-26-1972	−7	2-2-1985	Mar.	29	Nov.	6
Scurry, Snyder	93.9	10	28.2	71	115	8-12-1936	−11	2-2-1985	Mar.	30	Nov.	10
Shackelford, Albany	94.4	16	30.2	62	115	6-27-1972	−8	1-4-1947	Apr.	1	Nov.	6
Shelby, Center	94.4	10	35.1	42	112	9-2-2000	0	2-2-1951	Mar.	16	Nov.	16
Sherman, Stratford	91.5	4	19.5	138	108	6-24-1953	−20	2-9-1933	Apr.	25	Oct.	17
Smith, Tyler	92.7	4	36.4	32	*110	8-3-2011	−8	2-12-1899	Mar.	14	Nov.	19
Somervell, Glen Rose	97.0	24	27.4	76	115	8-19-1984	−15	12-23-1989	Apr.	8	Oct.	22
Starr, Rio Grande City	98.4	44	45.9	5	*116	6-14-1998	7	2-13-1899	Jan.	30	Dec.	19
Stephens, Breckenridge	95.8	19	30.3	62	114	8-12-1936	−7	12-22-1989	Mar.	29	Nov.	9
Sterling, Sterling City	93.6	8	28.2	74	112	6-27-1994	−13	2-2-1985	Apr.	4	Nov.	2
Stonewall, Aspermont	97.0	29	28.5	71	117	6-28-1994	−10	12-23-1989	Mar.	30	Nov.	8
Sutton, Sonora	94.4	10	29.2	69	109	6-28-1980	−8	2-2-1951	Apr.	4	Nov.	3
Swisher, Tulia	91.9	6	22.0	121	111	6-27-2011	*−23	2-12-1899	Apr.	16	Oct.	23
Tarrant, Benbrook Dam	95.5	16	32.4	42	115	8-18-1909	*−12	2-12-1899	Mar.	16	Nov.	18
Taylor, Abilene Reg. Airport	94.2	10	33.0	45	*111	8-3-1943	−9	1-4-1947	Mar.	24	Nov.	12
Terrell, Sanderson	92.2	7	31.5	50	120	6-14-2008	1	12-22-1989	Mar.	18	Nov.	11
Terry, Brownfield	92.4	7	26.9	82	111	6-28-1994	−8	1-14-1963	Apr.	1	Nov.	6
Throckmorton, Throckmorton	95.8	22	29.6	62	119	8-30-1947	−11	12-23-1989	Mar.	31	Nov.	7
Titus, Mount Pleasant	92.9	6	31.1	60	109	8-5-2011	−12	2-2-1951	Mar.	28	Nov.	7
Tom Green, San Angelo	95.1	15	33.3	46	113	6-30-1907	−6	1-18-1930	Mar.	26	Nov.	11
Travis, Austin-Camp Mabry	95.6	16	41.5	12	112	9-5-2000	*−5	1-31-1949	Feb.	19	Dec.	6
Trinity, Groveton	92.9	5	35.1	38	111	9-4-2000	1	12-23-1989	Mar.	19	Nov.	14
Tyler, Town Bluff Dam	91.8	2	37.5	27	*111	9-4-2000	*2	1-31-1949	Mar.	9	Nov.	24
Upshur, Gilmer	93.1	7	31.9	59	114	8-10-1936	*−4	12-24-1989	Mar.	31	Nov.	7
Upton, McCamey	95.3	18	31.9	48	*113	6-27-1994	*−2	1-11-1962	Mar.	20	Nov.	14
Uvalde, Uvalde	96.1	23	38.6	20	114	6-9-1910	*6	2-3-1951	Mar.	1	Nov.	28
Val Verde, Del Rio Intl. Airport	96.6	25	40.6	11	*114	7-30-1995	*2	2-3-1985	Feb.	19	Dec.	4
Van Zandt, Wills Point	93.7	10	33.7	41	115	8-18-1909	−2	12-24-1989	Mar.	16	Nov.	21
Victoria, Victoria Reg. Airport	93.8	4	43.1	11	*111	9-5-2000	*9	1-18-1930	Feb.	22	Dec.	6
Walker, Huntsville	93.3	4	39.7	17	110	9-4-2000	*−2	2-12-1899	Feb.	28	Dec.	3
Waller, Sealy	93.7	7	41.0	13	107	8-12-1969	13	1-30-1966	Feb.	22	Dec.	5
Ward, Monahans	97.2	33	28.2	72	120	6-28-1994	−9	1-11-1962	Mar.	31	Nov.	7
Washington, Brenham	94.2	8	39.0	21	113	9-5-2000	−2	1-19-1930	Mar.	2	Dec.	1
Webb, Laredo	99.3	54	46.1	6	116	6-17-1998	5	2-12-1899	Feb.	3	Dec.	14
Wharton, Pierce	92.2	2	43.0	10	112	9-5-2000	3	2-12-1899	Feb.	21	Dec.	8
Wheeler, Shamrock	93.3	11	24.0	98	117	7-12-2011	*−13	1-19-1984	Apr.	6	Oct.	29
Wichita, Wichita Falls Airport	96.9	25	29.8	59	117	6-28-1980	−15	1-4-1947	Mar.	28	Nov.	10
Wilbarger, Lake Kemp	97.0	26	29.5	56	119	8-3-1943	−9	12-23-1989	Mar.	21	Nov.	14
Willacy, Raymondville	96.7	18	47.6	4	109	6-6-1916	14	1-13-1962	Jan.	31	Dec.	22
Williamson, Taylor	94.9	9	36.5	29	113	7-11-1917	*−5	1-31-1949	Mar.	7	Nov.	24
Wilson, Floresville	95.5	15	37.2	30	*114	7-6-1984	5	1-21-1985	Mar.	12	Nov.	22
Winkler, County Airport	96.9	32	28.9	69	117	6-27-1994	*−14	1-11-1962	Mar.	31	Nov.	5
Wise, Bridgeport	94.2	13	29.7	65	*115	6-29-1980	*−8	12-23-1989	Apr.	2	Nov.	5
Wood, Mineola	93.0	8	32.0	57	114	6-18-1996	1	12-30-1983	Mar.	29	Nov.	8
Yoakum, Plains	91.7	7	25.7	90	113	6-27-1994	−12	2-1-1951	Apr.	6	Nov.	2
Young, Olney	95.7	22	29.3	65	*120	6-3-1998	−8	12-23-1989	Apr.	1	Nov.	6
Zapata, Zapata	97.8	39	46.3	4	116	6-16-1998	13	1-4-1911	Jan.	27	Dec.	23
Zavala, Crystal City	97.2	29	43.6	8	115	9-5-2000	6	1-12-1962	Feb.	13	Dec.	7

GROWING SEASON	MEAN PRECIPITATION													RECORD RAINFALL HIGHEST DAILY TOTAL		
	January	February	March	April	May	June	July	August	September	October	November	December	Annual	Location	In.	M-D-Y
Days	In.	In.	In.	In.	In.	In.	In.	In.	In.	In.	In.	In.	In.	Location	In.	M-D-Y
230	0.99	1.59	1.92	1.41	3.33	3.40	1.60	2.37	2.36	2.52	1.44	1.11	24.04	Wingate	7.68	6-19-1982
242	3.68	4.22	4.40	3.65	4.70	5.22	3.06	2.86	3.48	4.84	4.78	4.47	49.36	Henderson	11.05	3-29-1989
248	4.74	4.94	4.47	3.57	4.62	5.50	4.00	3.11	3.38	5.07	5.53	5.99	54.92	Hemphill	11.70	3-10-2018
238	4.46	4.58	4.12	3.55	4.16	5.12	3.07	3.44	4.02	4.96	4.89	5.52	51.89	San Augustine	10.60	8-18-1915
262	4.14	3.82	3.53	3.33	4.87	6.07	3.05	3.15	3.64	5.11	5.35	4.62	50.68	Oakhurst	16.50	8-28-2017
307	1.75	2.15	2.25	1.85	3.26	3.28	3.52	2.36	5.29	4.75	2.27	1.55	34.28	Welder Wildlife	14.40	9-13-1974
246	1.35	2.00	2.42	1.99	3.86	4.05	1.96	2.02	2.55	2.79	1.98	1.53	28.50	San Saba	11.20	10-5-1969
223	0.93	1.30	2.13	2.17	2.95	3.76	1.76	2.82	2.44	2.43	1.80	0.60	25.09	D. Wilson Ranch	9.51	7-16-1990
225	0.82	1.14	1.55	1.74	2.96	3.37	2.22	2.28	2.28	2.22	1.06	1.04	22.68	Knapp	5.93	5-15-1980
219	1.12	1.92	2.35	2.47	3.64	4.07	2.11	2.01	2.40	3.00	1.70	1.57	28.36	Albany	29.05	8-4-1978
244	4.45	4.95	4.60	4.16	4.47	5.30	3.31	3.52	3.65	5.32	5.04	5.43	54.20	Neuville	10.20	10-30-1941
173	0.54	0.45	1.27	1.26	2.41	2.37	2.25	2.75	1.74	1.35	0.70	0.68	17.77	Stratford	5.60	8-17-1992
250	3.42	4.12	4.19	3.10	4.41	5.15	2.75	2.66	3.05	4.91	4.38	4.49	46.63	Eads	8.24	6-7-1943
194	1.91	2.64	3.48	2.78	5.20	4.74	2.24	2.45	3.00	3.81	2.44	2.18	36.87	Glen Rose	10.73	6-22-2014
325	1.00	1.25	0.89	1.14	2.22	3.07	2.26	1.89	4.46	2.48	1.14	0.85	22.65	Rio Grande City	12.51	9-22-1967
225	1.44	1.89	2.58	2.12	4.01	4.09	2.23	2.36	2.65	3.48	1.56	1.57	29.98	Breckenridge	15.70	10-13-1981
211	0.89	1.12	1.21	1.33	2.59	2.37	1.72	2.57	2.48	2.20	0.98	1.00	20.46	Case Ranch	6.79	9-21-1972
223	1.00	1.36	1.64	1.88	3.22	3.56	1.86	2.75	2.10	2.16	1.14	1.10	23.77	Aspermont	6.92	4-28-1930
213	0.97	1.31	1.57	1.71	2.60	2.59	1.92	2.62	2.96	2.54	1.30	0.94	23.03	Humble Pump Stn	8.60	7-11-1988
189	0.77	0.75	1.38	1.54	2.79	3.32	2.26	2.91	2.13	1.95	0.95	0.82	21.57	Tulia	6.01	10-21-1918
246	1.90	2.42	3.33	2.86	4.69	3.98	1.91	2.16	3.26	3.98	2.66	2.35	35.50	Arlington	9.70	5-17-1949
234	1.02	1.36	1.74	1.64	3.18	3.56	1.87	2.59	2.24	2.98	1.41	1.23	24.82	Lawn	9.19	8-4-1978
238	0.55	0.65	0.65	0.73	1.68	2.25	2.04	1.60	1.70	1.74	0.63	0.50	14.72	Dryden	6.30	9-23-1990
220	0.68	0.75	1.03	1.18	2.75	3.01	2.41	1.95	2.38	1.77	0.90	0.77	19.58	Brownfield	7.85	9-21-1936
221	1.16	1.74	1.96	2.49	3.64	4.21	2.00	2.53	2.21	2.72	1.51	1.50	27.67	Throckmorton	6.53	8-4-1978
224	3.17	4.12	4.30	3.49	5.54	4.63	3.51	2.21	3.03	5.09	4.19	4.42	47.70	Mount Pleasant	8.06	11-5-1994
231	0.93	1.35	1.50	1.42	2.82	2.59	1.20	2.26	2.46	2.73	1.14	0.85	21.25	Mathis Field	11.75	9-15-1936
291	2.22	2.02	2.76	2.09	4.44	4.33	1.88	2.35	2.99	3.88	2.96	2.40	34.32	Hill's Ranch	16.02	9-10-1921
238	3.90	3.71	3.96	2.82	4.81	5.23	3.16	3.20	3.81	5.57	4.90	4.24	49.31	Groveton	12.10	10-17-1994
258	4.57	4.58	4.12	3.89	4.94	5.97	3.85	3.90	4.66	4.85	5.29	5.56	56.18	Spurger	11.50	8-30-2017
222	3.46	4.16	4.37	3.38	4.55	3.90	3.08	2.79	3.40	4.98	4.31	4.46	46.84	Gilmer	7.88	4-23-1966
239	0.68	0.64	0.48	1.02	1.31	2.11	1.32	2.14	1.85	2.23	0.70	0.66	15.14	McCamey	9.13	10-4-1986
272	1.18	1.25	1.76	1.71	3.03	2.97	2.79	1.81	2.59	2.88	1.54	1.09	24.60	Montell	20.05	6-29-1913
289	0.72	0.88	1.14	1.65	2.81	2.35	1.78	2.18	2.20	2.23	0.93	0.65	19.52	Del Rio Intl. AP	17.03	8-23-1998
250	3.18	3.58	4.30	3.01	4.73	4.47	2.19	2.25	3.23	4.96	4.41	3.84	44.15	South County Line	11.55	10-24-2015
290	2.52	2.08	2.77	2.82	5.19	4.46	4.18	2.85	4.16	4.64	3.24	2.31	41.22	Inez	10.45	8-26-2017
279	4.25	3.33	3.70	3.26	4.45	5.45	2.80	3.67	4.16	4.68	5.19	4.14	49.08	Huntsville	14.75	8-28-2017
288	3.25	2.72	2.84	3.56	4.57	3.62	2.65	3.56	3.91	4.84	4.51	2.89	42.92	Brookshire	16.75	8-28-2017
221	0.58	0.70	0.59	0.64	1.44	1.37	1.94	1.68	2.16	1.66	0.60	0.79	14.15	Grandfalls	5.87	9-4-1986
272	3.46	3.09	3.42	2.89	4.66	4.88	2.56	2.93	4.46	5.09	4.28	3.42	45.14	Brenham	21.46	5-27-2016
316	0.90	0.94	1.12	1.42	2.49	2.23	2.01	1.88	2.93	2.21	1.19	0.88	20.20	Laredo	9.70	5-10-1972
291	3.37	3.08	3.06	3.28	5.03	3.83	4.03	3.18	5.17	5.55	4.53	3.36	47.47	New Gulf	14.00	6-26-1960
205	0.76	0.88	1.96	2.13	3.56	3.99	2.25	2.45	2.59	2.27	1.35	0.97	25.16	Shamrock	8.24	6-4-1995
227	1.14	1.75	2.20	2.61	3.79	4.15	1.59	2.50	2.81	3.11	1.65	1.62	28.92	Wichita V. Farm	8.00	8-15-1971
238	1.06	1.66	1.91	1.79	3.48	3.98	1.70	1.93	2.76	2.60	1.55	1.22	25.64	Vernon	14.82	8-2-1995
331	1.14	1.55	1.24	1.46	3.03	2.31	2.27	2.31	5.51	3.12	0.99	1.15	26.08	Raymondville	9.90	9-1-1975
260	2.26	2.28	3.07	2.32	4.82	4.20	1.89	2.12	3.10	3.96	3.07	2.64	35.73	Taylor	16.11	9-10-1921
253	1.59	1.76	2.01	2.14	3.39	3.05	2.48	2.11	3.08	3.36	2.20	1.90	29.07	Falls City	8.83	9-15-1968
220	0.43	0.56	0.75	0.59	1.62	1.60	1.99	1.49	1.35	1.56	0.59	0.56	13.09	NE of Kermit	3.80	9-20-2014
217	1.55	2.38	3.09	2.88	5.23	4.22	2.04	1.98	3.06	4.01	2.20	2.07	34.71	Boyd	9.15	10-31-1981
224	3.09	3.76	4.13	3.66	4.63	4.23	3.15	2.41	2.99	5.41	4.31	4.43	46.20	Mineola	9.50	10-24-2015
209	0.46	0.70	0.90	0.82	1.89	2.78	2.58	2.32	2.63	1.35	0.84	0.93	18.20	Plains	6.11	7-5-1960
219	1.40	1.86	2.56	2.70	5.00	4.03	2.41	1.98	2.43	3.56	1.89	1.64	31.46	Olney	8.74	7-28-2004
334	0.95	0.99	0.80	1.33	2.50	2.11	2.71	1.50	3.53	1.38	1.22	0.75	19.77	Zapata	6.10	4-14-1966
299	1.06	1.06	1.43	1.52	2.15	2.54	2.25	1.54	2.08	2.08	1.11	0.76	19.58	Crystal City	13.88	10-14-2013

CALENDAR

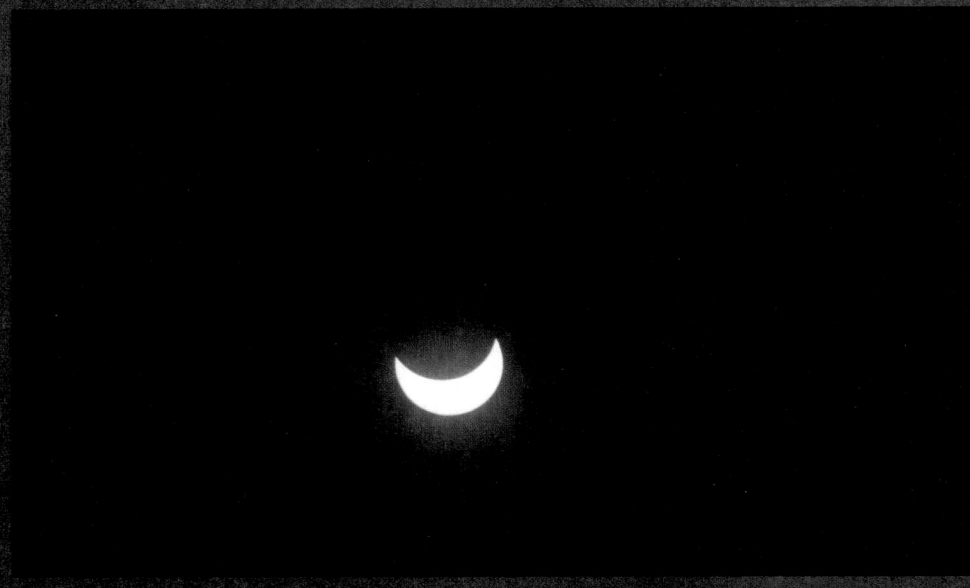

The 2017 solar eclipse as viewed in Bruceville.
Photo by Jason Kaechler (CC).

MORNING AND EVENING STARS

SEASONS, ECLIPSES, METEOR SHOWERS

CHRONOLOGICAL ERAS AND CYCLES

CALENDARS FOR 2020 AND 2021

Eras and Events for 2020 & 2021

Sources: McDonald Observatory; U.S. Naval Observatory's website (https://aa.usno.navy.mil/index.php) and publications, Astronomical Phenomena For The Year 2020 *and* Astronomical Phenomena For The Year 2021; *In-The-Sky.org*

The Year 2020

The year 2020 CE comprises the latter part of the 244th and the beginning of the 245th year of the independence of the United States of America. All dates in this book are given in terms of the Gregorian calendar.

The Seasons

Spring begins on Thursday, March 19, at 10:13 pm (CDT);
Summer begins on Saturday, June 20, at 4:07 pm (CDT);
Autumn begins on Tuesday, Sept. 22, at 7:54 am (CDT);
Winter begins on Monday, Dec. 21, at 3:25 am (CST).

Chronological Eras, 2020		
Era	**Year**	**Begins**
Julian	6733	Jan. 14
Byzantine	7529	Sept. 14
Jewish (A.M.)*	5781	Sept. 18
Chinese (gēng zǐ)	—	Jan. 25
Roman (A.U.C.)	2773	Jan. 14
Nabonassar	2769	April 18
Japanese	2680	Jan. 1
Seleucidæ (Grecian)	2332	Sept. 14 or Oct. 14
Saka (Indian)	1942	March 21
Diocletian (Coptic)	1737	Sept. 11
Islamic (Hegira)	1442	Aug. 19
Year begins at sunset.		

Chronological Cycles, 2020				
Dominical Letter	ED	Golden Number	VII	
Epact	5	(Lunar Cycle)		
Roman Indiction	13	Solar Cycle	13	

Morning & Evening Stars, 2020	
Morning Stars	
Venus ♀	June 11–Dec. 31
Mars ♂	Jan. 1–Oct. 13
Jupiter ♃	Jan. 10–July 14
Saturn ♄	Jan. 31–July 20
Evening Stars	
Venus ♀	Jan. 1–May 28
Mars ♂	Oct. 13–Dec. 31
Jupiter ♃	July 14–Dec. 31
Saturn ♄	July 20–Dec. 31

Eclipses 2020

January 10: Lunar, partial. Visible in N.W. North America, W. Pacific Ocean, most of Australaisa, Asia, Europe, Africa, E. South America, N.E. North America.

June 5: Lunar, partial. Visible in W. Pacific Ocean, Australasia, Asia (except parts of Russia), Antarctica, most of Europe, Africa, E. and S. South America.

June 21: Solar, partial. Visible in most of Africa, S.E. Europe, Middle East, Asia (except parts of Russia), Indonesia, Micronesia.

July 5: Lunar, partial. Visible in North America except for Alaska and westernmost parts of Canada, most of Africa, S. and W. Europe, Antarctica, most of Polynesia, New Zealand.

November 30: Lunar, partial. Visible in N.W. Europe, North and South America Oceania, Australasia, most of Asia.

December 14: Solar, total. Visible in Southern Pacific Ocean, Galapogos Islands, most of South America, part of Antarctica, parts of S.W. Africa.

The Year 2021

The year 2021 CE comprises the latter part of the 245th and the beginning of the 246th year of the independence of the United States of America.

The Seasons

Spring begins on Saturday, March 20, at 4:00 am (CDT);
Summer begins on Sunday, June 20, at 9:55 pm (CDT);
Autumn begins on Wednesday, Sept. 22, at 1:44 pm (CDT);
Winter begins on Tuesday, Dec. 21, at 9:22 am (CST).

Chronological Eras, 2021		
Era	**Year**	**Begins**
Julian	6734	Jan. 14
Byzantine	7530	Sept. 14
Jewish (A.M.)*	5782	Sept. 6
Chinese (xin chou)	—	Feb 12
Roman (A.U.C.)	2774	Jan. 14
Nabonassar	2770	April 18
Japanese	2681	Jan. 1
Seleucidæ (Grecian)	2333	Sept. 14 or Oct. 14
Saka (Indian)	1943	March 22
Diocletian (Coptic)	1738	Sept. 11
Islamic (Hegira)*	1443	Aug. 9
Year begins at sunset.		

Chronological Cycles, 2021				
Dominical Letter	C	Golden Number	VIII	
Epact	16	(Lunar Cycle)		
Roman Indiction	14	Solar Cycle	14	

Morning & Evening Stars, 2021	
Morning Stars	
Venus ♀	Jan. 1–Feb. 14
Mars ♂	Nov. 23–Dec. 31
Jupiter ♃	Feb. 11–Aug. 20
Saturn ♄	Feb. 10–Aug. 2
Evening Stars	
Venus ♀	May 5–Dec. 31
Mars ♂	Jan. 1–Aug. 23
Jupiter ♃	Jan. 1–Jan. 16, Aug. 20–Dec. 31
Saturn ♄	Jan. 1–Jan. 7, Aug. 2–Dec. 31

Eclipses 2021

May 26: Lunar, total. Visible to W. South America, W. North America, Pacific Ocean, Australasia, E. Asia.

June 10: Solar, partial. Visible to N. and N.E. North America, Greenland, most of Europe, most of Russia, N. and W. China.

November 19: Lunar, partial. Visible to N.W. Europe, the Americas, Oceania, Australasia, most of Asia.

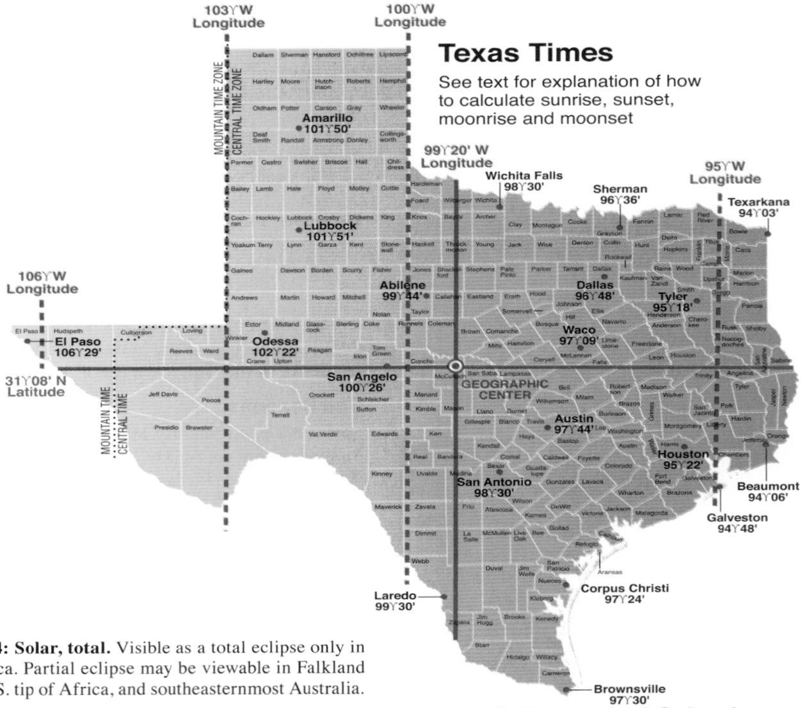

Texas Times

See text for explanation of how to calculate sunrise, sunset, moonrise and moonset

December 4: Solar, total. Visible as a total eclipse only in Antarctica. Partial eclipse may be viewable in Falkland Islands, S. tip of Africa, and southeasternmost Australia.

An Explanation of Texas Time

Times listed here are **Central Standard Time**, except for the period from 2:00 a.m. on the second Sunday in March until 2:00 a.m. on the first Sunday in November, when **Daylight Saving Time**, which is one hour later than Central Standard Time, is in effect.

All of Texas is in the Central Time Zone, except El Paso and Hudspeth counties and the northwest corner of Culberson County, which observe **Mountain Time**. Mountain Time is one hour earlier than Central Time.

All times are calculated for the intersection of 99° 20' west longitude and 31° 08' north latitude, which is **closest to the town of Mercury and** about 15 miles northeast of Brady, McCulloch County. This point is the **approximate geographical center of the state.**

How to Adjust Rise & Set Times

To adjust the time of sunrise or sunset, moonrise or moonset for any point in Texas, apply the following rules:

- For each degree of longitude that the place lies **west** of the 99th meridian, **add four minutes** to the times given in the calendar.
- For each degree of longitude the place lies **east** of the 99th meridian, **subtract four minutes**.

At times there will be considerable variation for distances north and south of the line of 31° 08' north latitude, but this formula will give sufficiently close results.

The map above shows the intersection for which all times given in this chapter are calculated, with some major cities and longitudes to aid in calculating times.

Astronomical Calendars

The calendars on the following pages feature phenomena and planetary configurations of the heavens for 2020 and 2021 in the center columns. The table to the right is a key to those symbols. You'll find find additional keys below the calendars.

Symbol	Meaning
☉	The Sun
☿	Mercury
♀	Venus
●	The Earth
☾	The Moon
♂	Mars
♃	Jupiter
♄	Saturn
⛢	Uranus
♆	Neptune
☌	conjunction
☍	opposition

Aspects: Conjunction & Opposition

☌ This symbol, appearing between symbols for heavenly bodies, means they are "in conjunction," that is, having the same longitude in the sky and appearing near each other. For example, ♀ ☌ ☾ means Venus is north or south of the moon by a few degrees. Conjunctions listed in this calendar are separated by 10 degrees or less. Inferior and superior conjuctions mean an inner plant, Venus or Mercury, is in line with the Sun, either between the Earth and the Sun (inferior) or on the opposite side of the Sun (superior).

☍ This symbol means that the heavenly body listed is in "opposition" to the Sun, or that they differ by 180 degrees of longitude.

Common Astronomical Terms

Aphelion: Point at which a planet's orbit is farthest from the sun.

Perihelion: Point at which a planet's orbit is nearest the sun.

Apogee: Point of the moon's orbit farthest from the earth.

Perigee: Point of the moon's orbit nearest the earth.

2020

Times are **Central Standard Time**, except from **March 8 to Nov. 1**, during which **Daylight Saving Time** is observed. **Boldface times for moonrise and moonset indicate p.m.** Times are figured for the point **31° 08' N 99° 20' W**, the approximate geographical center of the state. **See page 122 for explanation of how to get the approximate time at any other Texas point.**

1st Month — January 2020 — 31 Days

Moon Phases — *First Qtr.*, Jan. 2, 10:08 pm.; *Full*, Jan. 10, 12:44 pm; *Last Qtr.*, Jan. 17, 6:21 pm; *New*, Jan. 24, 3:05 pm

Day of Year	Day of Month	Day of Week	Planetary Configurations and Phenomena	Sunrise	Sunset	Moon-rise	Moon-set
1	1	We.	☾ at apogee (8 pm)	7:36	5:46	**12:01**	**11:53**
2	2	Th.	First qtr. ☾	7:36	5:47	**12:30**	
3	3	Fr.		7:36	5:47	**12:59**	12:45
4	4	Sa.	♅ ☌ ☾ (12 pm)	7:36	5:48	**1:29**	1:38
5	5	Su.	● perihelion (2 am)	7:37	5:49	**2:01**	2:33
6	6	Mo.		7:37	5:50	**2:37**	3:30
7	7	Tu.		7:37	5:50	**3:17**	4:29
8	8	We.		7:37	5:51	**4:04**	5:29
9	9	Th.		7:37	5:52	**4:58**	6:31
10	10	Fr.	Full ☾; ☿ in superior ☌	7:37	5:53	**5:58**	7:31
11	11	Sa.	♅ stationary (1 am)	7:37	5:54	**7:04**	8:26
12	12	Su.		7:37	5:55	**8:12**	9:17
13	13	Mo.	☾ at perigee (2 pm)	7:37	5:55	**9:20**	10:02
14	14	Tu.		7:36	5:56	**10:27**	10:43
15	15	We.		7:36	5:57	**11:32**	11:21
16	16	Th.		7:36	5:58		11:57
17	17	Fr.	Last qtr. ☾	7:36	5:59	12:37	**12:32**
18	18	Sa.		7:36	6:00	1:41	**1:09**
19	19	Su.		7:35	6:01	2:44	**1:48**
20	20	Mo.	♂ ☌ ☾ (1 pm)	7:35	6:02	3:47	**2:31**
21	21	Tu.		7:35	6:03	4:49	**3:19**
22	22	We.	♃ ☌ ☾ (9 pm)	7:35	6:03	5:48	**4:10**
23	23	Th.		7:34	6:04	6:43	**5:05**
24	24	Fr.	New ☾	7:34	6:05	7:32	**6:02**
25	25	Sa.		7:33	6:06	8:16	**6:59**
26	26	Su.		7:33	6:07	8:54	**7:55**
27	27	Mo.		7:32	6:08	9:29	**8:50**
28	28	Tu.	♀ ☌ ☾ (12 am)	7:32	6:09	10:01	**9:44**
29	29	We.	☾ at apogee (3 pm)	7:31	6:10	10:30	**10:36**
30	30	Th.		7:31	6:11	10:59	**11:29**
31	31	Fr.	♅ ☌ ☾ (9 pm)	7:30	6:12	11:28	

2nd Month — February 2020 — 29 Days

Moon Phases — *First Qtr.*, Feb. 1, 7:05 pm; *Full*, Feb. 9, 12:56 am; *Last Qtr.*, Feb. 15, 3:40 pm; *New Qtr.*, Feb. 23, 8:55 am

Day of Year	Day of Month	Day of Week	Planetary Configurations and Phenomena	Sunrise	Sunset	Moon-rise	Moon-set
32	1	Sa.	First qtr. ☾	7:30	6:12	11:59	12:22
33	2	Su.	Vesta ☌ ☾ (3 am)	7:29	6:13	**12:32**	1:17
34	3	Mo.		7:28	6:14	**1:09**	2:14
35	4	Tu.		7:28	6:15	**1:52**	3:12
36	5	We.		7:27	6:16	**2:41**	4:12
37	6	Th.		7:26	6:17	**3:38**	5:12
38	7	Fr.		7:26	6:18	**4:42**	6:10
39	8	Sa.		7:25	6:19	**5:50**	7:04
40	9	Su.	Full ☾	7:24	6:19	**7:00**	7:53
41	10	Mo.	☾ at perigee (2 pm)	7:23	6:20	**8:10**	8:37
42	11	Tu.		7:22	6:21	**9:19**	9:17
43	12	We.		7:21	6:22	**10:26**	9:55
44	13	Th.	Juno ☌ ☾ (4 am)	7:21	6:23	**11:32**	10:32
45	14	Fr.		7:20	6:24		11:09
46	15	Sa.	Last qtr. ☾	7:19	6:24	12:37	11:48
47	16	Su.	☿ stationary (4 am)	7:18	6:25	1:41	**12:30**
48	17	Mo.		7:17	6:26	2:44	**1:16**
49	18	Tu.	♂ ☌ ☾ (7 am)	7:16	6:27	3:43	**2:06**
50	19	We.	♃ ☌ ☾ (2 pm)	7:15	6:28	4:39	**2:59**
51	20	Th.	♄ ☌ ☾ (8 am)	7:14	6:29	5:29	**3:55**
52	21	Fr.		7:13	6:29	6:14	**4:51**
53	22	Sa.		7:12	6:30	6:54	**5:47**
54	23	Su.	New ☾	7:11	6:31	7:29	**6:43**
55	24	Mo.		7:10	6:32	8:01	**7:37**
56	25	Tu.	☿ in inferior ☌ (8 pm)	7:09	6:32	8:31	**8:30**
57	26	We.	☾ at apogee (6 am)	7:08	6:33	9:00	**9:22**
58	27	Th.	♀ ☌ ☾ (6 am)	7:07	6:34	9:29	**10:15**
59	28	Fr.	♅ ☌ ☾ (6 am)	7:06	6:35	9:59	**11:09**
60	29	Sa.		7:04	6:35	10:30	

3rd Month — March 2020 — 31 Days

Moon Phases — *First Qtr.*, March 2, 1:20 pm; *Full*, March 9, 12:11 pm; *Last Qtr.*, March 16, 3:57 am; *New*, March 24, 3:51 am

Day of Year	Day of Month	Day of Week	Planetary Configurations and Phenomena	Sunrise	Sunset	Moon-rise	Moon-set
61	1	Su.	Vesta ☌ ☾ (12 am)	7:03	6:36	11:05	12:04
62	2	Mo.	First qtr. ☾	7:02	6:37	11:44	1:00
63	3	Tu.		7:01	6:38	**12:29**	1:58
64	4	We.		7:00	6:38	**1:21**	2:57
65	5	Th.		6:59	6:39	**2:20**	3:54
66	6	Fr.		6:58	6:40	**3:25**	4:49
67	7	Sa.		6:56	6:40	**4:34**	5:39
68	8	Su.	**DST begins** (2 am)	7:55	7:41	**6:45**	7:25
69	9	Mo.	Full ☾; ☿ (3 am)	7:54	7:42	**7:55**	8:08
70	10	Tu.	☾ at perigee (1 am)	7:53	7:43	**9:05**	8:47
71	11	We.		7:52	7:43	**10:15**	9:26
72	12	Th.		7:50	7:44	**11:23**	10:04
73	13	Fr.		7:49	7:45		10:44
74	14	Sa.		7:48	7:45	12:30	11:26
75	15	Su.		7:47	7:46	1:36	**12:12**
76	16	Mo.	Last qtr. ☾	7:45	7:47	2:38	**1:02**
77	17	Tu.		7:44	7:47	3:35	**1:55**
78	18	We.	♂ ♃ ♄ ☌ ☾ (3 am)	7:43	7:48	4:27	**2:50**
79	19	Th.	Equinox (10:13 pm)	7:42	7:49	5:14	**3:46**
80	20	Fr.		7:40	7:49	5:55	**4:42**
81	21	Sa.	☿ ☌ ☾ (1 pm)	7:39	7:50	6:31	**5:37**
82	22	Su.		7:38	7:51	7:04	**6:32**
83	23	Mo.	☿ gr. elongation W. (9 pm)	7:37	7:51	7:34	**7:25**
84	24	Tu.	New ☾ at apogee (10 am)	7:35	7:52	8:03	**8:18**
85	25	We.		7:34	7:53	8:32	**9:10**
86	26	Th.	♅ ☌ ☾ (4 pm)	7:33	7:53	9:01	**10:04**
87	27	Fr.		7:32	7:54	9:31	**10:58**
88	28	Sa.	♀ ☌ ☾ (6 am)	7:30	7:54	10:05	**11:54**
89	29	Su.	Vesta ☌ ☾ (2 am)	7:29	7:55	10:42	
90	30	Mo.		7:28	7:56	11:24	12:51
91	31	Tu.	♂ ☌ ♄ (6 am)	7:27	7:56	**12:12**	1:48

Astronomical Calendar for 2020

4th Month — April 2020 — 30 Days

Moon Phases — *First Qtr.*, April 1, 4:44 am; *Full*, April 7, 10:58 pm; *Last Qtr.*, April 14, 5:19 pm; *New*, April 22, 8:49 pm; *First Qtr.*, April 30, 3:01 pm

Day of Year	Day of Month	Day of Week	Planetary Configurations and Phenomena	Sunrise	Sunset	Moonrise	Moonset
92	1	We.	First qtr. ☾	7:25	7:57	**1:06**	2:45
93	2	Th.		7:24	7:58	**2:07**	3:39
94	3	Fr.		7:23	7:58	**3:12**	4:29
95	4	Sa.		7:22	7:59	4:20	5:15
96	5	Su.		7:21	8:00	5:29	5:58
97	6	Mo.		7:19	8:00	6:39	6:38
98	7	Tu.	Full ☾ at perigee (1 pm)	7:18	8:01	7:49	**7:16**
99	8	We.		7:17	8:02	9:00	**7:55**
100	9	Th.		7:16	8:02	10:10	**8:34**
101	10	Fr.		7:15	8:03	11:19	**9:17**
102	11	Sa.		7:13	8:03		**10:03**
103	12	Su.		7:12	8:04	12:25	**10:52**
104	13	Mo.		7:11	8:05	1:27	**11:46**
105	14	Tu.	♃ ☌ ☾ (6 pm)	7:10	8:05	2:23	**12:42**
106	15	We.	♄ ☌ ☾ (4 am)	7:09	8:06	3:12	**1:39**
107	16	Th.	♂ ☌ ☾ (12 am)	7:08	8:07	3:55	**2:36**
108	17	Fr.		7:07	8:07	4:33	**3:32**
109	18	Sa.		7:05	8:08	5:07	**4:27**
110	19	Su.	♆ ☌ ☾ (2 am)	7:04	8:09	5:37	5:20
111	20	Mo.	☾ at apogee (2 pm)	7:03	8:09	6:07	6:13
112	21	Tu.		7:02	8:10	6:35	7:06
113	22	We.	New ☾	7:01	8:11	**7:04**	7:59
114	23	Th.		7:00	8:11	**7:34**	8:54
115	24	Fr.		6:59	8:12	**8:06**	9:49
116	25	Sa.		6:58	8:13	**8:42**	10:46
117	26	Su.	♀ ☌ ☾ (10 am)	6:57	8:13	**9:22**	11:44
118	27	Mo.	♀ gr. illumination (8 pm)	6:56	8:14	**10:08**	
119	28	Tu.		6:55	8:15	**11:00**	12:40
120	29	We.		6:54	8:16	**11:57**	1:34
121	30	Th.	First qtr. ☾	6:53	8:16	**12:59**	2:25

5th Month — May 2020 — 31 Days

Moon Phases — *Full*, May 7, 5:08 am; *Last Qtr.*, May 14, 8:26 am; *New*, May 22, 12:02 pm; *First Qtr.*, May 29, 9:53 pm

Day of Year	Day of Month	Day of Week	Planetary Configurations and Phenomena	Sunrise	Sunset	Moonrise	Moonset
122	1	Fr.		6:52	8:17	**2:04**	3:11
123	2	Sa.		6:51	8:18	**3:10**	3:53
124	3	Su.		6:50	8:18	**4:18**	4:33
125	4	Mo.	☿ in superior ☌ (5 pm)	6:50	8:19	**5:26**	5:10
126	5	Tu.	☾ at perigee (10 pm)	6:49	8:20	**6:35**	5:47
127	6	We.		6:48	8:20	**7:45**	6:25
128	7	Th.	Full ☾	6:47	8:21	**8:55**	7:06
129	8	Fr.		6:46	8:22	**10:04**	7:50
130	9	Sa.		6:46	8:22	**11:10**	8:39
131	10	Su.		6:45	8:23		9:32
132	11	Mo.	♄ stationary (4 am)	6:44	8:24	12:11	10:29
133	12	Tu.	♃ ♄ ☌ ☾ (5 am)	6:43	8:24	1:05	11:28
134	13	We.	♀ stationary (5 am)	6:43	8:25	1:52	**12:26**
135	14	Th.	♃ stationary (1 pm)	6:42	8:26	2:33	**1:24**
136	15	Fr.		6:41	8:26	3:08	**2:20**
137	16	Sa.	♆ ☌ ☾ (10 am)	6:41	8:27	3:40	**3:14**
138	17	Su.		6:40	8:28	4:10	**4:07**
139	18	Mo.	☾ at apogee (3 am)	6:40	8:28	4:38	**5:00**
140	19	Tu.		6:39	8:29	5:06	**5:53**
141	20	We.	⛢ ☌ ☾ (11 am)	6:39	8:30	5:36	**6:47**
142	21	Th.		6:38	8:30	6:07	**7:43**
143	22	Fr.	New ☾; ☿ ☌ ♀ (3 am)	6:38	8:31	6:42	**8:40**
144	23	Sa.	♀ ☌ ☾ (10 pm)	6:37	8:32	7:21	**9:38**
145	24	Su.	☿ ☌ ☾ (6 am)	6:37	8:32	8:05	**10:36**
146	25	Mo.		6:36	8:33	8:56	**11:31**
147	26	Tu.		6:36	8:33	9:52	
148	27	We.		6:35	8:34	10:52	12:23
149	28	Th.		6:35	8:35	11:56	1:10
150	29	Fr.	First qtr. ☾	6:35	8:35	1:00	1:53
151	30	Sa.		6:35	8:36	2:06	2:32
152	31	Su.		6:34	8:36	3:11	3:09

6th Month — June 2020 — 30 Days

Moon Phases — *Full*, June 5, 1:35 pm; *Last Qtr.*, June 13, 12:47 am; *New*, July 21, 1:04 am; *First Qtr.*, July 28, 2:39 am

Day of Year	Day of Month	Day of Week	Planetary Configurations and Phenomena	Sunrise	Sunset	Moonrise	Moonset
153	1	Mo.		6:34	8:37	**4:17**	3:45
154	2	Tu.	☾ at perigee (11 pm)	6:34	8:37	**5:24**	4:21
155	3	We.	♀ in inferior ☌ (1 pm)	6:34	8:38	**6:33**	4:58
156	4	Th.	☿ gr. elongation E (8 am)	6:33	8:38	**7:42**	5:40
157	5	Fr.	Full ☾	6:33	8:39	**8:50**	6:25
158	6	Sa.		6:33	8:39	**9:54**	7:17
159	7	Su.		6:33	8:40	**10:53**	8:13
160	8	Mo.	♃ ♄ ☌ ☾ (12 pm)	6:33	8:40	**11:44**	9:12
161	9	Tu.		6:33	8:41		10:12
162	10	We.		6:33	8:41	12:28	11:12
163	11	Th.		6:33	8:41	1:07	**12:09**
164	12	Fr.	♆ ♂ ☌ ☾ (6 pm)	6:33	8:42	1:40	**1:05**
165	13	Sa.	Last qtr. ☾	6:33	8:42	2:11	**2:59**
166	14	Su.	☾ at apogee (8 pm)	6:33	8:43	2:40	**2:52**
167	15	Mo.		6:33	8:43	3:08	**3:45**
168	16	Tu.	⛢ ☌ ☾ (9 pm)	6:33	8:43	3:37	**4:38**
169	17	We.	☿ stationary (3 pm)	6:33	8:43	4:07	**5:33**
170	18	Th.		6:34	8:44	4:40	**6:30**
171	19	Fr.	♀ ☌ ☾ (4 am)	6:34	8:44	5:18	**7:29**
172	20	Sa.	Solstice (4:07 pm)	6:34	8:44	6:00	**8:27**
173	21	Su.	New ☾	6:34	8:44	6:49	**9:25**
174	22	Mo.		6:34	8:45	7:45	**10:19**
175	23	Tu.	♆ stationary (1 pm)	6:35	8:45	8:45	**11:09**
176	24	We.	♀ stationary (1 pm)	6:35	8:45	9:49	**11:53**
177	25	Th.		6:35	8:45	10:54	
178	26	Fr.		6:36	8:45	11:59	12:34
179	27	Sa.		6:36	8:45	**1:03**	1:11
180	28	Su.	First qtr. ☾	6:36	8:45	**2:08**	1:46
181	29	Mo.	☾ at perigee (9 pm)	6:37	8:45	**3:13**	2:21
182	30	Tu.	☿ in inferior ☌ (10 pm)	6:37	8:45	**4:19**	2:57

☉ The Sun ● The Earth ☾ The Moon ☿ Mercury ♀ Venus ♂ Mars ♃ Jupiter ♄ Saturn ♆ Neptune ⛢ Uranus ☌ = in conjunction ☍ = opposition to the ☉

Astronomical Calendar for 2020

7th Month — July 2020 — 31 Days

Moon Phases — *Full*, July 4, 11:07 pm; *Last Qtr.*, July 12 5:52 pm; *New*, July 20, 11:56 am; *First Qtr.*, July 27, 6:56 am

Day of			Planetary Configurations and Phenomena	Hour of			
Year	Month	Week		Sunrise	Sunset	Moon-rise	Moon-set
183	1	We.		6:37	8:45	**5:26**	3:35
184	2	Th.		6:38	8:45	**6:33**	4:18
185	3	Fr.		6:38	8:45	**7:38**	5:06
186	4	Sa.	● aphelion (7 am)	6:39	8:45	**8:39**	5:59
187	5	Su.	♃ ☌ ☾ (5 pm)	6:39	8:45	**9:33**	6:56
188	6	Mo.	♄ ☌ ☾ (4 am)	6:40	8:45	**10:21**	7:57
189	7	Tu.		6:40	8:45	**11:02**	8:57
190	8	We.		6:41	8:44	**11:38**	9:56
191	9	Th.		6:41	8:44		10:54
192	10	Fr.	♀ gr. illumination (3 am)	6:42	8:44	12:10	11:49
193	11	Sa.	♂ ☌ ☾ (3 pm)	6:42	8:44	12:40	**12:42**
194	12	Su.	☾ at apogee (2 pm)	6:43	8:43	1:09	**1:35**
195	13	Mo.		6:43	8:43	1:37	**2:28**
196	14	Tu.	♃ ☍ (3 am); ⛢ ☌ ☾ (7 am)	6:44	8:43	2:06	**3:23**
197	15	We.		6:44	8:42	2:38	**4:18**
198	16	Th.		6:45	8:42	3:13	**5:16**
199	17	Fr.	♀ ☌ ☾ (2 am)	6:45	8:41	3:54	**6:15**
200	18	Sa.	☿ ☌ ☾ (11 pm)	6:46	8:41	4:40	**7:13**
201	19	Su.		6:47	8:40	5:33	**8:10**
202	20	Mo.	New ☾; ♄ ☍ (5 pm)	6:47	8:40	6:32	**9:02**
203	21	Tu.		6:48	8:39	7:36	**9:50**
204	22	We.	☿ gr. elongation W (10 am)	6:48	8:39	8:43	**10:32**
205	23	Th.		6:49	8:38	9:50	**11:11**
206	24	Fr.		6:50	8:38	10:56	**11:48**
207	25	Sa.	☾ at perigee (12 am)	6:50	8:37	**12:01**	
208	26	Su.		6:51	8:36	**1:06**	12:23
209	27	Mo.	First qtr. ☾	6:52	8:36	**2:12**	12:58
210	28	Tu.		6:52	8:35	**3:17**	1:35
211	29	We.		6:53	8:34	**4:23**	2:16
212	30	Th.		6:53	8:34	**5:27**	3:01
213	31	Fr.		6:54	8:33	**6:28**	3:51

8th Month — August 2020 — 31 Days

Moon Phases — *Full*, Aug. 3, 10:22 am; *Last Qtr.*, Aug. 11, 11:08 am; *New*, Aug. 18, 9:05 pm; *First Qtr.*, Aug. 25, 12:21 pm

Day of			Planetary Configurations and Phenomena	Hour of			
Year	Month	Week		Sunrise	Sunset	Moon-rise	Moon-set
214	1	Sa.	♃ ☌ ☾ (7 pm)	6:55	8:32	**7:24**	4:46
215	2	Su.	♄ ☌ ☾ (8 am)	6:55	8:31	**8:14**	5:44
216	3	Mo.	Full ☾	6:56	8:31	**8:58**	6:44
217	4	Tu.		6:57	8:30	**9:36**	7:44
218	5	We.		6:57	8:29	**10:09**	8:42
219	6	Th.	♆ ☌ ☾ (10 am)	6:58	8:28	**10:40**	9:38
220	7	Fr.		6:59	8:27	**11:09**	10:33
221	8	Sa.		6:59	8:26	**11:37**	11:26
222	9	Su.	☾ at apogee (9 am)	7:00	8:25		**12:19**
223	10	Mo.	⛢ ☌ ☾ (4 pm)	7:00	8:24	12:06	**1:13**
224	11	Tu.	Last qtr. ☾	7:01	8:23	12:36	**2:07**
225	12	We.	♀ gr. elongation W (7 pm)	7:02	8:22	1:10	**3:03**
226	13	Th.		7:02	8:21	1:47	**4:01**
227	14	Fr.		7:03	8:20	2:30	**4:59**
228	15	Sa.	⛢ stationary (12 pm)	7:04	8:19	3:19	**5:56**
229	16	Su.		7:04	8:18	4:16	**6:50**
230	17	Mo.	☿ in superior ☌ (3 pm)	7:05	8:17	5:18	**7:40**
231	18	Tu.	New ☾	7:05	8:16	6:25	**8:26**
232	19	We.		7:06	8:15	7:33	**9:07**
233	20	Th.		7:07	8:14	8:41	**9:46**
234	21	Fr.	☾ at perigee (6 am)	7:07	8:13	9:49	**10:22**
235	22	Sa.		7:08	8:12	10:56	**10:58**
236	23	Su.		7:08	8:11	**12:03**	**11:35**
237	24	Mo.		7:09	8:09	**1:10**	
238	25	Tu.	First qtr. ☾	7:10	8:08	**2:16**	12:15
239	26	We.		7:10	8:07	**3:21**	12:59
240	27	Th.		7:11	8:06	**4:23**	1:47
241	28	Fr.	♃ ☌ ☾ (9 pm)	7:11	8:05	**5:20**	2:40
242	29	Sa.	♄ ☌ ☾ (2 pm)	7:12	8:04	**6:11**	3:37
243	30	Su.		7:13	8:02	**6:55**	4:36
244	31	Mo.		7:13	8:01	**7:35**	5:35

9th Month — September 2020 — 30 Days

Moon Phases — *Full*, Sept. 1, 11:45 pm; *Last Qtr.*, Sept. 10, 3:49 am; *New*, Sept. 17 5:23 am; *First Qtr.*, Sept. 23, 8:18 pm

Day of			Planetary Configurations and Phenomena	Hour of			
Year	Month	Week		Sunrise	Sunset	Moon-rise	Moon-set
245	1	Tu.	Full ☾	7:14	8:00	8:09	**6:33**
246	2	We.	♆ ☌ ☾ (4 pm)	7:14	7:59	8:41	**7:30**
247	3	Th.		7:15	7:57	9:10	**8:25**
248	4	Fr.		7:16	7:56	9:38	**9:19**
249	5	Sa.		7:16	7:55	10:07	**10:12**
250	6	Su.	☾ at apogee (1 am)	7:17	7:54	10:36	**11:05**
251	7	Mo.		7:17	7:52	11:08	**11:59**
252	8	Tu.		7:18	7:51	11:43	**12:54**
253	9	We.	♂ stationary (1 pm)	7:18	7:50		**1:50**
254	10	Th.	Last qtr. ☾	7:19	7:49	12:23	**2:47**
255	11	Fr.	♆ ☍ (3 pm)	7:20	7:47	1:08	**3:43**
256	12	Sa.	♃ stationary (7 pm)	7:20	7:46	2:00	**4:38**
257	13	Su.		7:21	7:45	2:59	**5:29**
258	14	Mo.	♀ ☌ ☾ (12 am)	7:21	7:43	**4:03**	**6:16**
259	15	Tu.		7:22	7:42	**5:10**	6:59
260	16	We.		7:22	7:41	**6:19**	7:39
261	17	Th.	New ☾	7:23	7:40	**7:29**	8:16
262	18	Fr.	☾ at perigee (9 am)	7:24	7:38	**8:38**	8:53
263	19	Sa.		7:24	7:37	**9:47**	9:31
264	20	Su.		7:25	7:36	**10:57**	10:11
265	21	Mo.		7:25	7:34	**12:06**	10:55
266	22	Tu.	Equinox (7:54 am)	7:26	7:33	**1:13**	11:43
267	23	We.	First qtr. ☾	7:27	7:32	**2:18**	
268	24	Th.		7:27	7:31	**3:17**	12:35
269	25	Fr.	♃ ♄ ☌ ☾ (2 am)	7:28	7:29	**4:09**	1:31
270	26	Sa.		7:28	7:28	**4:56**	2:30
271	27	Su.		7:29	7:27	**5:36**	3:29
272	28	Mo.	♄ stationary (10 pm)	7:30	7:25	**6:11**	4:27
273	29	Tu.	♆ ☌ ☾ (9 pm)	7:30	7:24	**6:43**	5:24
274	30	We.		7:31	7:23	**7:13**	**6:19**

Bright stars: Aldebaran, Antares, Spica, Pollux, Regulus. **Minor planets or asteroids:** Pluto, Ceres, Pallas, Juno, Vesta. ☌ = in conjunction by 10° or < ☍ = opposition to the ☉

Astronomical Calendar for 2020

10th Month — October 2020 — 31 Days

Moon Phases — *Full*, Oct. 1, 3:28 pm; *Last Qtr.*, Oct. 9, 7:03 pm; *New*, Oct. 16, 1:54 pm; *First Qtr.*, Oct. 23, 7:46 am; *Full*, Oct. 31, 9:12 am

Day of Year	Day of Month	Day of Week	Planetary Configurations and Phenomena	Sunrise	Sunset	Moonrise	Moonset
275	1	Th.	Full ☾; ☿ gr. elongation E	7:31	7:22	**7:41**	7:13
276	2	Fr.	♂ ☌ ☾ (10 pm)	7:32	7:20	**8:09**	8:06
277	3	Sa.	☾ at apogee (12 pm)	7:33	7:19	**8:38**	8:59
278	4	Su.	♅ ☌ ☾ (4 am)	7:33	7:18	**9:08**	9:53
279	5	Mo.		7:34	7:17	**9:42**	10:48
280	6	Tu.		7:34	7:15	**10:19**	11:43
281	7	We.		7:35	7:14	**11:02**	**12:39**
282	8	Th.		7:36	7:13	**11:51**	**1:35**
283	9	Fr.	Last qtr. ☾	7:36	7:12		**2:29**
284	10	Sa.		7:37	7:11	12:45	**3:20**
285	11	Su.		7:38	7:10	1:45	**4:07**
286	12	Mo.		7:38	7:08	2:49	**4:51**
287	13	Tu.	♂ ☍ (6 pm)	7:39	7:07	3:56	**5:31**
288	14	We.		7:40	7:06	5:04	**6:09**
289	15	Th.		7:40	7:05	6:13	**6:46**
290	16	Fr.	New ☾ at perigee (7 pm)	7:41	7:04	7:23	**7:23**
291	17	Sa.	☿ ☌ ☾ (2 pm)	7:42	7:03	8:34	**8:02**
292	18	Su.		7:43	7:02	9:45	**8:45**
293	19	Mo.		7:43	7:01	10:56	**9:33**
294	20	Tu.		7:44	7:00	**12:05**	**10:25**
295	21	We.		7:45	6:58	**1:09**	**11:22**
296	22	Th.	♃ ♄ ☌ ☾ (12 pm)	7:46	6:57	**2:06**	
297	23	Fr.	First qtr. ☾	7:46	6:56	**2:55**	12:22
298	24	Sa.		7:47	6:55	**3:37**	1:22
299	25	Su.	☿ in inferior ☌ (1 pm)	7:48	6:54	**4:14**	2:21
300	26	Mo.		7:49	6:54	**4:47**	3:19
301	27	Tu.	♆ ☌ ☾ (1 am)	7:49	6:53	**5:16**	4:14
302	28	We.		7:50	6:52	**5:44**	5:08
303	29	Th.	♂ ☌ ☾ (11 am)	7:51	6:51	**6:12**	6:01
304	30	Fr.	☾ at apogee (2 pm)	7:52	6:50	**6:40**	6:54
305	31	Sa.	Full ☾; ♅ ☍ (11 am)	7:52	6:49	**7:10**	7:48

11th Month — November 2020 — 30 Days

Moon Phases — *Last Qtr.*, Nov. 8, 7:09 am; *New*, Nov. 14, 10:30 pm; *First Qtr.*, Nov. 21, 10:08 pm; *Full*, Nov. 30, 2:53 am

Day of Year	Day of Month	Day of Week	Planetary Configurations and Phenomena	Sunrise	Sunset	Moonrise	Moonset
306	1	Su.	**DST ends** (2 am)	6:53	5:48	**6:43**	7:42
307	2	Mo.		6:54	5:47	**7:19**	8:38
308	3	Tu.	☿ stationary (2 am)	6:55	5:47	**8:00**	9:34
309	4	We.		6:56	5:46	**8:46**	10:30
310	5	Th.		6:56	5:45	**9:38**	11:24
311	6	Fr.		6:57	5:44	**10:35**	**12:16**
312	7	Sa.		6:58	5:44	**11:36**	**1:03**
313	8	Su.	Last qtr. ☾	6:59	5:43		**1:47**
314	9	Mo.		7:00	5:42	12:39	**2:26**
315	10	Tu.	☿ gr. elongation W (11 am)	7:01	5:42	1:44	**3:03**
316	11	We.		7:01	5:41	2:50	**3:39**
317	12	Th.	♀ ☌ ☾ (3 pm)	7:02	5:40	3:58	**4:15**
318	13	Fr.	☿ ☌ ☾ (3 pm)	7:03	5:40	5:07	**4:52**
319	14	Sa.	New ☾ at perigee (6 am)	7:04	5:39	6:18	**5:33**
320	15	Su.	♂ stationary (1 pm)	7:05	5:39	7:30	**6:19**
321	16	Mo.		7:06	5:38	8:42	**7:10**
322	17	Tu.		7:07	5:38	9:51	**8:07**
323	18	We.		7:08	5:38	10:54	**9:07**
324	19	Th.	♃ ♄ ☌ ☾ (3 am)	7:08	5:37	11:48	**10:10**
325	20	Fr.		7:09	5:37	**12:35**	**11:11**
326	21	Sa.	First qtr. ☾	7:10	5:36	**1:14**	
327	22	Su.		7:11	5:36	**1:49**	12:11
328	23	Mo.	♆ ☌ ☾ (6 am)	7:12	5:36	**2:19**	1:08
329	24	Tu.		7:13	5:36	**2:48**	2:02
330	25	We.	♂ ☌ ☾ (2 pm)	7:13	5:35	**3:16**	2:56
331	26	Th.	☾ at apogee (6 pm)	7:14	5:35	**3:43**	3:49
332	27	Fr.	♅ ☌ ☾ (11 am)	7:15	5:35	**4:12**	4:42
333	28	Sa.		7:16	5:35	**4:44**	5:36
334	29	Su.	♆ stationary (3 am)	7:17	5:35	**5:19**	6:32
335	30	Mo.	Full ☾	7:18	5:35	**5:58**	7:28

12th Month — December 2020 — 31 Days

Moon Phases — *Last Qtr.*, Dec. 7, 6:00 pm; *New*, Dec. 14, 9:40 am; *First Qtr.*, Dec. 21, 5:04 pm; *Full*, Dec. 29, 8:51 pm

Day of Year	Day of Month	Day of Week	Planetary Configurations and Phenomena	Sunrise	Sunset	Moonrise	Moonset
336	1	Tu.		7:18	5:35	**6:43**	8:25
337	2	We.		7:19	5:35	**7:34**	9:21
338	3	Th.		7:20	5:35	**8:29**	10:13
339	4	Fr.		7:21	5:35	**9:29**	11:02
340	5	Sa.		7:22	5:35	**10:31**	11:46
341	6	Su.		7:22	5:35	**11:34**	**12:26**
342	7	Mo.	Last qtr. ☾	7:23	5:35		**1:03**
343	8	Tu.		7:24	5:35	12:38	**1:38**
344	9	We.		7:25	5:35	1:42	**2:12**
345	10	Th.		7:25	5:35	2:47	**2:47**
346	11	Fr.		7:26	5:36	3:55	**3:24**
347	12	Sa.	☾ at perigee (3 pm)	7:27	5:36	5:04	**4:06**
348	13	Su.		7:27	5:36	6:16	**4:53**
349	14	Mo.	New ☾	7:28	5:37	7:26	**5:47**
350	15	Tu.		7:29	5:37	8:33	**6:47**
351	16	We.	♃ ♄ ☌ ☾ (10 pm)	7:29	5:37	9:33	**7:50**
352	17	Th.		7:30	5:38	10:25	**8:54**
353	18	Fr.		7:30	5:38	11:09	**9:57**
354	19	Sa.	☿ in superior ☌ (9 pm)	7:31	5:39	11:47	**10:56**
355	20	Su.	♆ ☌ ☾ (2 pm)	7:31	5:39	12:20	**11:53**
356	21	Mo.	Solstice (3:25 am);	7:32	5:40	**12:50**	
357	22	Tu.		7:32	5:40	**1:18**	12:48
358	23	We.	♂ ☌ ☾ (1 pm)	7:33	5:41	**1:45**	1:41
359	24	Th.	☾ at apogee (11 am)	7:33	5:41	**2:14**	2:34
360	25	Fr.		7:34	5:42	**2:44**	3:28
361	26	Sa.		7:34	5:42	**3:17**	4:23
362	27	Su.		7:35	5:43	**3:55**	5:19
363	28	Mo.		7:35	5:44	**4:38**	6:16
364	29	Tu.	Full ☾	7:35	5:44	**5:28**	7:13
365	30	We.		7:35	5:45	**6:22**	8:08
366	31	Th.		7:36	5:46	**7:22**	8:59

☉ The Sun ● The Earth ☾ The Moon ☿ Mercury ♀ Venus ♂ Mars ♃ Jupiter ♄ Saturn ♆ Neptune ♅ Uranus ☌ = in conjunction ☍ = opposition to the ☉

2021

Times are **Central Standard Time,** except from **March 14 to Nov. 7,** during which **Daylight Saving Time** is observed. **Boldface times for moonrise and moonset indicate p.m.** Times are figured for the point **99° 20' West and 31° 08' North,** the approximate geographical center of the state. **See page 122 for explanation of how to get the approximate time at any other Texas point.**

1st Month — January 2021 — 31 Days

Moon Phases — *Last Qtr.*, Jan. 6, 3:00 am; *New*, Jan. 12, 10:23 pm; *First Qtr.*, Jan. 20, 2:25 pm; *Full*, Jan. 28, 12:39 pm

Day of Year	Day of Month	Day of Week	Planetary Configurations and Phenomena	Sunrise	Sunset	Moon-rise	Moon-set
1	1	Fr.		7:36	5:46	**7:47**	9:08
2	2	Sa.	● perihelion (8 am)	7:36	5:47	**8:50**	9:50
3	3	Su.		7:36	5:48	**9:53**	10:28
4	4	Mo.		7:36	5:49	**10:57**	11:03
5	5	Tu.		7:37	5:49		11:36
6	6	We.	Last qtr. ☾	7:37	5:50	12:00	**12:10**
7	7	Th.		7:37	5:51	1:05	**12:45**
8	8	Fr.		7:37	5:52	2:11	**1:23**
9	9	Sa.	☾ at perigee (10 am)	7:37	5:53	3:19	**2:06**
10	10	Su.		7:37	5:54	4:28	**2:55**
11	11	Mo.	♀ ☌ ☾ (2 pm)	7:37	5:54	5:36	**3:51**
12	12	Tu.	New ☾	7:37	5:55	6:39	**4:53**
13	13	We.	♃ ☌ ☾ (7 pm)	7:37	5:56	7:35	**5:57**
14	14	Th.	☿ ☌ ☾ (2 am)	7:36	5:57	8:23	**7:01**
15	15	Fr.		7:36	5:58	9:04	**8:03**
16	16	Sa.		7:36	5:59	9:40	**9:02**
17	17	Su.	♆ ☌ ☾ (12 am)	7:36	6:00	10:12	**9:59**
18	18	Mo.		7:36	6:01	10:41	**10:54**
19	19	Tu.		7:35	6:01	11:09	**11:47**
20	20	We.	First qtr. ☾	7:35	6:02	11:37	
21	21	Th.	☾ at apogee (7 am)	7:35	6:03	**12:06**	12:41
22	22	Fr.		7:34	6:04	**12:38**	1:35
23	23	Sa.	☿ gr. elongation E (8 pm)	7:34	6:05	**1:14**	2:31
24	24	Su.		7:33	6:06	**1:54**	3:27
25	25	Mo.		7:33	6:07	**2:41**	4:24
26	26	Tu.		7:33	6:08	**3:34**	5:20
27	27	We.		7:32	6:09	**4:32**	6:13
28	28	Th.	Full ☾; ♃ ☌ (8 pm)	7:32	6:09	**5:35**	7:02
29	29	Fr.	☿ stationary (8 pm)	7:31	6:10	**6:39**	7:47
30	30	Sa.		7:30	6:11	**7:44**	8:27
31	31	Su.		7:30	6:12	**8:49**	9:03

2nd Month — February 2021 — 28 Days

Moon Phases — *Last Qtr.*, Feb. 4, 11:00 am; *New*, Feb. 11, 12:29 pm; *First Qtr.*, Feb. 19, 12:10 pm; *Full*, Feb. 27, 1:40 pm

Day of Year	Day of Month	Day of Week	Planetary Configurations and Phenomena	Sunrise	Sunset	Moon-rise	Moon-set
32	1	Mo.		7:29	6:13	**9:54**	9:38
33	2	Tu.		7:29	6:14	**10:58**	10:12
34	3	We.	☾ at perigee (1 pm)	7:28	6:15		10:46
35	4	Th.	Last qtr. ☾	7:27	6:16	12:04	11:23
36	5	Fr.		7:26	6:17	1:10	**12:03**
37	6	Sa.		7:26	6:17	2:18	**12:49**
38	7	Su.		7:25	6:18	3:24	**1:41**
39	8	Mo.	☿ in inferior ☌ (8 am)	7:24	6:19	4:27	**2:39**
40	9	Tu.		7:23	6:20	5:24	**3:41**
41	10	We.	♀ ♄ ☌ ☾ (5 am)	7:23	6:21	6:15	**4:45**
42	11	Th.	New ☾; ♀ ☌ ♃ (6 am)	7:22	6:22	6:58	**5:47**
43	12	Fr.		7:21	6:23	7:36	**6:48**
44	13	Sa.	♆ ☌ ☾ (11 am)	7:20	6:23	8:09	**7:46**
45	14	Su.		7:19	6:24	8:40	**8:42**
46	15	Mo.		7:18	6:25	9:08	**9:37**
47	16	Tu.		7:17	6:26	9:36	**10:31**
48	17	We.	♅ ☌ ☾ (10 am)	7:16	6:27	10:05	**11:25**
49	18	Th.	☾ at apogee (4 am)	7:15	6:28	10:36	
50	19	Fr.	First qtr. ☾	7:14	6:28	11:09	12:20
51	20	Sa.	☿ stationary (7 am)	7:13	6:29	11:47	1:15
52	21	Su.		7:12	6:30	**12:31**	2:12
53	22	Mo.		7:11	6:31	**1:20**	3:08
54	23	Tu.		7:10	6:31	**2:16**	4:02
55	24	We.		7:09	6:32	**3:17**	4:52
56	25	Th.		7:08	6:33	**4:21**	5:39
57	26	Fr.		7:07	6:34	**5:27**	6:21
58	27	Sa.	Full ☾	7:06	6:34	**6:34**	7:00
59	28	Su.		7:05	6:35	**7:41**	7:36

3rd Month — March 2021 — 31 Days

Moon Phases — *Last Qtr.*, March 5, 6:53 pm; *New*, March 13, 12:29 pm; *First Qtr.*, March 21, 9:03 am; *Full*, March 28, 1:11 pm;

Day of Year	Day of Month	Day of Week	Planetary Configurations and Phenomena	Sunrise	Sunset	Moon-rise	Moon-set
60	1	Mo.	☾ at perigee (11 pm)	7:04	6:36	**8:47**	8:11
61	2	Tu.		7:02	6:37	**9:55**	8:46
62	3	We.		7:01	6:37	**11:03**	9:22
63	4	Th.	Vesta ☍ (12 pm)	7:00	6:38		10:02
64	5	Fr.	☿ ☌ ♃ (1 am)	6:59	6:39	12:11	10:47
65	6	Sa.	☿ gr. elongation W	6:58	6:40	1:18	11:37
66	7	Su.		6:57	6:40	2:21	**12:33**
67	8	Mo.		6:55	6:41	3:20	**1:33**
68	9	Tu.	♄ ☌ ☾ (5 pm)	6:54	6:42	4:11	**2:35**
69	10	We.	☿ ♃ ☌ ☾ (10 am)	6:53	6:42	4:56	**3:37**
70	11	Th.		6:52	6:43	5:35	**4:37**
71	12	Fr.		6:51	6:44	6:09	**5:36**
72	13	Sa.	New ☾	6:49	6:44	6:40	**6:32**
73	14	Su.	**DST begins** (2 am)	7:48	7:45	8:09	**8:27**
74	15	Mo.		7:47	7:46	8:37	**9:22**
75	16	Tu.	♅ ☌ ☾ (9 pm)	7:46	7:46	9:05	**10:16**
76	17	We.		7:44	7:47	9:35	**11:11**
77	18	Th.	☾ at apogee (12 am)	7:43	7:48	10:07	
78	19	Fr.	♂ ☌ ☾ (1 pm)	7:42	7:48	10:43	12:06
79	20	Sa.	Equinox (4:00 am)	7:41	7:49	11:23	1:02
80	21	Su.	First qtr. ☾	7:39	7:50	**12:09**	1:57
81	22	Mo.	♂ ☌ Aldebaran (7 pm)	7:38	7:50	**1:01**	2:51
82	23	Tu.		7:37	7:51	**1:59**	3:42
83	24	We.		7:36	7:52	**3:01**	4:30
84	25	Th.		7:34	7:52	**4:06**	5:13
85	26	Fr.	♀ in superior ☌ (2 am)	7:33	7:53	**5:12**	5:53
86	27	Sa.		7:32	7:54	**6:19**	6:30
87	28	Su.	Full ☾	7:31	7:54	**7:27**	7:05
88	29	Mo.		7:29	7:55	**8:37**	7:41
89	30	Tu.	☾ at perigee (1 am)	7:28	7:56	**9:47**	8:17
90	31	We.		7:27	7:56	**10:58**	8:57

Astronomical Calendar for 2021

4th Month — April 2021 — 30 Days

Moon Phases — *Last Qtr.*, April 4, 4:25 am; *New*, April 11, 8:54 pm; First Qtr. April 20, 1:22 am; *Full*, April 26, 9:55 pm

Day of Year	Day of Month	Day of Week	Planetary Configurations and Phenomena	Sunrise	Sunset	Moon-rise	Moon-set
91	1	Th.		7:26	7:57		9:41
92	2	Fr.		7:24	7:57	12:08	10:31
93	3	Sa.		7:23	7:58	1:15	11:26
94	4	Su.	Last qtr. ☾	7:22	7:59	2:16	**12:26**
95	5	Mo.		7:21	7:59	3:10	**1:28**
96	6	Tu.	♄ ☌ ☾ (3 am)	7:20	8:00	3:57	**2:30**
97	7	We.	♃ ☌ ☾ (2 am)	7:18	8:01	4:36	**3:31**
98	8	Th.		7:17	8:01	5:11	**4:29**
99	9	Fr.	♆ ☌ ☾ (6 am)	7:16	8:02	5:42	**5:26**
100	10	Sa.		7:15	8:03	6:11	**6:21**
101	11	Su.	New ☾	7:14	8:03	6:39	**7:15**
102	12	Mo.		7:12	8:04	7:07	**8:09**
103	13	Tu.	⛢ ☌ ☾ (7 am)	7:11	8:05	7:36	**9:04**
104	14	We.	☾ at apogee (1 pm)	7:10	8:05	8:07	**9:59**
105	15	Th.		7:09	8:06	8:41	**10:55**
106	16	Fr.		7:08	8:07	9:20	**11:50**
107	17	Sa.	♂ ☌ ☾ (7 am)	7:07	8:07	10:03	
108	18	Su.	☿ in superior ☌ (9 pm)	7:06	8:08	10:52	12:44
109	19	Mo.		7:05	8:09	11:47	1:36
110	20	Tu.	First qtr. ☾	7:03	8:09	**12:46**	2:23
111	21	We.		7:02	8:10	**1:47**	3:07
112	22	Th.		7:01	8:11	**2:51**	3:47
113	23	Fr.		7:00	8:11	**3:57**	4:24
114	24	Sa.		6:59	8:12	**5:03**	4:59
115	25	Su.		6:58	8:13	**6:12**	5:34
116	26	Mo.	Full ☾	6:57	8:13	**7:22**	6:10
117	27	Tu.	☾ at perigee (10 am)	6:56	8:14	**8:34**	6:48
118	28	We.		6:55	8:15	**9:48**	7:31
119	29	Th.		6:54	8:15	**10:59**	8:20
120	30	Fr.	⛢ in ☌ (3 pm)	6:53	8:16		9:15

5th Month — May 2021 — 31 Days

Moon Phases — *Last Qtr.*, May 3, 2:13 pm; *New*, May 11, 1:23 pm; *First Qtr.*, May 19, 1:36 pm; *Full*, May 26, 5:37 am

Day of Year	Day of Month	Day of Week	Planetary Configurations and Phenomena	Sunrise	Sunset	Moon-rise	Moon-set
121	1	Sa.		6:52	8:17	12:06	10:15
122	2	Su.		6:52	8:17	1:05	11:19
123	3	Mo.	Last qtr. ☾	6:51	8:18	1:55	**12:23**
124	4	Tu.	♃ ☌ ☾ (4 pm)	6:50	8:19	2:38	**1:25**
125	5	We.		6:49	8:19	3:14	**2:24**
126	6	Th.	♆ ☌ ☾ (1 pm)	6:48	8:20	3:46	**3:21**
127	7	Fr.		6:47	8:21	4:15	**4:16**
128	8	Sa.		6:47	8:21	4:43	**5:10**
129	9	Su.		6:46	8:22	5:11	**6:04**
130	10	Mo.	☿ ☌ Aldebaran (10 pm)	6:45	8:23	5:39	**6:58**
131	11	Tu.	New ☾ at apogee (5 pm)	6:44	8:24	6:09	**7:53**
132	12	We.	♀ ☌ ☾ (5 pm)	6:44	8:24	6:42	**8:49**
133	13	Th.	☿ ☌ ☾ (1 pm)	6:43	8:25	7:19	**9:45**
134	14	Fr.		6:42	8:26	8:01	**10:39**
135	15	Sa.		6:42	8:26	8:48	**11:32**
136	16	Su.	♂ ☌ ☾ (12 am)	6:41	8:27	9:40	
137	17	Mo.	☿ gr. elongation E	6:40	8:28	10:37	12:20
138	18	Tu.		6:40	8:28	11:36	1:05
139	19	We.	First qtr. ☾	6:39	8:29	**12:38**	1:45
140	20	Th.		6:39	8:30	**1:40**	2:22
141	21	Fr.		6:38	8:30	**2:44**	2:56
142	22	Sa.		6:38	8:31	**3:50**	3:29
143	23	Su.	♄ stationary (3 pm)	6:37	8:31	**4:57**	4:03
144	24	Mo.		6:37	8:32	**6:07**	4:39
145	25	Tu.	☾ at perigee (9 pm)	6:36	8:33	**7:21**	5:19
146	26	We.	Full ☾	6:36	8:33	**8:34**	6:05
147	27	Th.		6:36	8:34	**9:46**	6:57
148	28	Fr.		6:35	8:34	**10:51**	7:57
149	29	Sa.	☿ stationary (9 pm)	6:35	8:35	**11:47**	9:02
150	30	Su.	♄ ☌ ☾ (8 pm)	6:35	8:36		10:08
151	31	Mo.		6:34	8:36	12:34	11:13

6th Month — June 2021 — 30 Days

Moon Phases — *Last Qtr.*, June 2, 1:47 am; *New*, June 10, 5:16 am; *First Qtr.*, June 17, 10:17 pm; *Full*, June 24, 1:03 pm

Day of Year	Day of Month	Day of Week	Planetary Configurations and Phenomena	Sunrise	Sunset	Moon-rise	Moon-set
152	1	Tu.	♃ ☌ ☾ (4 am)	6:34	8:37	1:14	**12:15**
153	2	We.	Last qtr. ☾	6:34	8:37	1:48	**1:14**
154	3	Th.		6:34	8:38	2:19	**2:11**
155	4	Fr.		6:33	8:38	2:47	**3:05**
156	5	Sa.		6:33	8:39	3:14	**3:59**
157	6	Su.		6:33	8:39	3:42	**4:53**
158	7	Mo.	☾ at apogee (9 pm)	6:33	8:40	4:11	**5:48**
159	8	Tu.		6:33	8:40	4:43	**6:43**
160	9	We.		6:33	8:41	5:19	**7:39**
161	10	Th.	New ☾; ☿ in inferior ☌	6:33	8:41	5:59	**8:35**
162	11	Fr.		6:33	8:41	6:45	**9:28**
163	12	Sa.	♀ ☌ ☾ (2 am)	6:33	8:42	7:36	**10:18**
164	13	Su.	☿ ☌ ☾ (3 pm)	6:33	8:42	8:31	**11:04**
165	14	Mo.		6:33	8:43	9:30	**11:45**
166	15	Tu.		6:33	8:43	10:31	
167	16	We.		6:33	8:43	11:32	12:22
168	17	Th.	First qtr. ☾	6:33	8:43	**12:33**	12:57
169	18	Fr.		6:34	8:44	**1:36**	1:29
170	19	Sa.		6:34	8:44	**2:40**	2:02
171	20	Su.	Solstice (9:55 pm)	6:34	8:44	**3:47**	2:35
172	21	Mo.	♃ stationary (12 am)	6:34	8:44	**4:56**	3:12
173	22	Tu.	☿ stationary (6 pm)	6:34	8:45	**6:09**	3:53
174	23	We.	☾ at perigee (5 am)	6:35	8:45	**7:21**	4:41
175	24	Th.	Full ☾	6:35	8:45	**8:30**	5:37
176	25	Fr.		6:35	8:45	**9:32**	6:40
177	26	Sa.	♆ stationary (5 am)	6:35	8:45	**10:24**	7:47
178	27	Su.	♄ ☌ ☾ (4 am)	6:36	8:45	**11:09**	8:55
179	28	Mo.	♃ ☌ ☾ (2 pm)	6:36	8:45	**11:46**	10:01
180	29	Tu.		6:36	8:45		11:03
181	30	We.	♆ ☌ ☾ (4 am)	6:37	8:45	12:19	12:01

⊙ The Sun ● The Earth ☾ The Moon ☿ Mercury ♀ Venus ♂ Mars ♃ Jupiter ♄ Saturn ♆ Neptune ⛢ Uranus ☌ = in conjunction ☍ = opposition to the ⊙

Astronomical Calendar for 2021

7th Month — July 2021 — 31 Days

Moon Phases — *Last Qtr.*, July 1, 3:34 pm; *New*, July 9, 7:40 pm; *First Qtr.*, July 17, 4:34 am; *Full*, July 23, 9:00 pm; *Last Qtr.*, July 31, 7:39 am

Day of: Year	Month	Week	Planetary Configurations and Phenomena	Hour of: Sunrise	Sunset	Moon-rise	Moon-set
182	1	Th.	Last qtr. ☾	6:37	8:45	12:49	**12:58**
183	2	Fr.		6:38	8:45	1:17	**1:52**
184	3	Sa.		6:38	8:45	1:44	**2:46**
185	4	Su.	☿ gr. elongation W	6:39	8:45	2:13	**3:41**
186	5	Mo.	● aphelion (5 pm)	6:39	8:45	2:44	**4:36**
187	6	Tu.		6:39	8:45	3:18	**5:32**
188	7	We.		6:40	8:45	3:57	**6:28**
189	8	Th.	☿ ☌ ☾ (12 am)	6:40	8:44	4:41	**7:23**
190	9	Fr.	New ☾	6:41	8:44	5:31	**8:14**
191	10	Sa.	♀ gr. illumination (3 am)	6:41	8:44	6:25	**9:02**
192	11	Su.		6:42	8:44	7:24	**9:45**
193	12	Mo.	♀ ♂ ☌ ☾ (4 am)	6:43	8:43	8:25	**10:24**
194	13	Tu.	♀ ☌ ♂ (2 am)	6:43	8:43	9:26	**10:59**
195	14	We.		6:44	8:43	10:28	**11:32**
196	15	Th.		6:44	8:42	11:29	
197	16	Fr.		6:45	8:42	**12:31**	12:03
198	17	Sa.	First qtr. ☾	6:45	8:41	**1:35**	12:36
199	18	Su.		6:46	8:41	**2:42**	1:10
200	19	Mo.		6:47	8:41	**3:51**	1:48
201	20	Tu.		6:47	8:40	**5:01**	2:31
202	21	We.	☾ at perigee (5 am)	6:48	8:40	**6:10**	3:22
203	22	Th.		6:48	8:39	**7:14**	4:21
204	23	Fr.	Full ☾	6:49	8:38	**8:11**	5:26
205	24	Sa.	♄ ☌ ☾ (12 pm)	6:50	8:38	**9:00**	6:34
206	25	Su.	♃ ☌ ☾ (8 pm)	6:50	8:37	**9:41**	7:41
207	26	Mo.		6:51	8:37	**10:16**	8:46
208	27	Tu.	♆ ☌ ☾ (1 pm)	6:51	8:36	**10:47**	9:48
209	28	We.		6:52	8:35	**11:17**	10:46
210	29	Th.	♂ ☌ Regulus (11 am)	6:53	8:35	**11:45**	11:42
211	30	Fr.		6:53	8:34		**12:37**
212	31	Sa.	Last qtr. ☾	6:54	8:33	12:13	**1:32**

8th Month — August 2021 — 31 Days

Moon Phases — *New*, Aug. 8, 8:13 am; *First Qtr.*, Aug. 15, 9:43 am; *Full*, Aug. 22, 6:25 am; *Last Qtr.*, Aug. 30, 1:36 am

Day of: Year	Month	Week	Planetary Configurations and Phenomena	Hour of: Sunrise	Sunset	Moon-rise	Moon-set
213	1	Su.	☿ in superior ☌ (9 am)	6:55	8:32	12:44	**2:28**
214	2	Mo.	☾ at apogee (3 am); ♄ ☍	6:55	8:32	1:17	**3:23**
215	3	Tu.		6:56	8:31	1:53	**4:19**
216	4	We.		6:56	8:30	2:35	**5:15**
217	5	Th.		6:57	8:29	3:23	**6:08**
218	6	Fr.		6:58	8:28	4:16	**6:57**
219	7	Sa.		6:58	8:27	5:14	**7:42**
220	8	Su.	New ☾	6:59	8:26	6:15	**8:23**
221	9	Mo.	♂ ☌ ☾ (8 pm)	7:00	8:25	7:17	**8:59**
222	10	Tu.		7:00	8:25	8:20	**9:33**
223	11	We.	♀ ☌ ☾ (2 am)	7:01	8:24	9:23	**10:06**
224	12	Th.		7:02	8:23	10:25	**10:38**
225	13	Fr.		7:02	8:22	11:29	**11:11**
226	14	Sa.		7:03	8:21	**12:34**	**11:47**
227	15	Su.	First qtr. ☾	7:03	8:20	**1:41**	
228	16	Mo.		7:04	8:19	**2:50**	12:28
229	17	Tu.	☾ at perigee (4 am)	7:05	8:17	**3:58**	1:15
230	18	We.	☿ ☌ ♂ (11 pm)	7:05	8:16	**5:02**	2:09
231	19	Th.	♃ ☍ (7 pm); ⛢ stationary	7:06	8:15	**6:01**	3:10
232	20	Fr.	♄ ☌ ☾ (5 pm)	7:06	8:14	**6:51**	4:16
233	21	Sa.		7:07	8:13	**7:35**	5:23
234	22	Su.	Full ☾	7:08	8:12	**8:12**	6:29
235	23	Mo.	♆ ☌ ☾ (9 pm)	7:08	8:11	**8:45**	7:32
236	24	Tu.		7:09	8:10	**9:15**	8:32
237	25	We.		7:09	8:09	**9:44**	9:30
238	26	Th.		7:10	8:07	**10:13**	10:26
239	27	Fr.		7:11	8:06	**10:42**	11:22
240	28	Sa.	⛢ ☌ ☾ (4 am)	7:11	8:05	**11:14**	**12:17**
241	29	Su.	☾ at apogee (9 pm)	7:12	8:04	**11:49**	**1:13**
242	30	Mo.	Last qtr. ☾	7:12	8:03		**2:09**
243	31	Tu.		7:13	8:01	12:29	**3:05**

9th Month — September 2021 — 30 Days

Moon Phases — *New*, Sept. 6, 7:15 pm; *First Qtr.*, Sept. 13, 3:02 pm; *Full*, Sept. 20, 6:18 pm; *Last Qtr.*, Sept. 28, 8:20 pm

Day of: Year	Month	Week	Planetary Configurations and Phenomena	Hour of: Sunrise	Sunset	Moon-rise	Moon-set
244	1	We.		7:14	8:00	1:14	**3:59**
245	2	Th.		7:14	7:59	2:05	**4:49**
246	3	Fr.		7:15	7:58	3:01	**5:36**
247	4	Sa.		7:15	7:57	4:01	**6:18**
248	5	Su.	♀ ☌ Spica (1 am)	7:16	7:55	5:03	**6:57**
249	6	Mo.	New ☾	7:17	7:54	6:07	**7:32**
250	7	Tu.		7:17	7:53	7:11	**8:05**
251	8	We.	☿ ☌ ☾ (3 pm)	7:18	7:51	8:15	**8:38**
252	9	Th.	♀ ☌ ☾ (9 pm)	7:18	7:50	9:20	**9:12**
253	10	Fr.		7:19	7:49	10:26	**9:47**
254	11	Sa.	☾ at perigee (5 am)	7:19	7:48	11:34	**10:27**
255	12	Su.		7:20	7:46	**12:43**	**11:12**
256	13	Mo.	First qtr. ☾	7:21	7:45	**1:51**	
257	14	Tu.	♆ in ☍ (4 am)	7:21	7:44	**2:56**	12:04
258	15	We.		7:22	7:43	**3:55**	1:02
259	16	Th.	♄ ☌ ☾ (9 pm)	7:22	7:41	**4:47**	2:05
260	17	Fr.		7:23	7:40	**5:32**	3:11
261	18	Sa.	♃ ☌ ☾ (2 am)	7:23	7:39	**6:10**	4:16
262	19	Su.		7:24	7:37	**6:44**	5:19
263	20	Mo.	Full ☾	7:25	7:36	**7:15**	6:20
264	21	Tu.		7:25	7:35	**7:44**	7:18
265	22	We.	Equinox (1:44 pm)	7:26	7:33	**8:12**	8:15
266	23	Th.	☿ ☌ Spica (7 am)	7:26	7:32	**8:41**	9:11
267	24	Fr.	⛢ ☌ ☾ (11 am)	7:27	7:31	**9:12**	10:07
268	25	Sa.		7:28	7:30	**9:46**	11:03
269	26	Su.	☾ at apogee (5 pm)	7:28	7:28	**10:24**	**12:00**
270	27	Mo.		7:29	7:27	**11:06**	**12:55**
271	28	Tu.	Last qtr. ☾	7:29	7:26	**11:54**	**1:50**
272	29	We.		7:30	7:24		**2:41**
273	30	Th.	☿ ☌ Spica (10 am)	7:31	7:23	12:48	**3:29**

Bright stars: Aldebaran, Antares, Spica, Pollux, Regulus. **Minor planets or asteroids:** Pluto, Ceres, Pallas, Juno, Vesta ☌ = in conjunction by 10° or < ☍ = opposition to the ☉

Astronomical Calendar for 2021

10th Month — October 2021 — 31 Days

Moon Phases — *New*, Oct. 6, 5:28 am; *First Qtr.*, Oct. 12, 9:48 pm; *Full*, Oct. 20, 9:20 am; *Last Qtr.*, Oct. 28, 2:28 pm

Day of Year	Day of Month	Day of Week	Planetary Configurations and Phenomena	Sunrise	Sunset	Moon-rise	Moon-set
274	1	Fr.		7:31	7:22	1:45	**4:12**
275	2	Sa.		7:32	7:21	2:46	**4:52**
276	3	Su.		7:32	7:19	3:49	**5:28**
277	4	Mo.		7:33	7:18	4:52	**6:02**
278	5	Tu.		7:34	7:17	5:57	**6:35**
279	6	We.	New ☾	7:34	7:16	7:03	**7:09**
280	7	Th.	♂ in ☌ (11 pm)	7:35	7:15	8:10	**7:44**
281	8	Fr.	☾ at perigee (12 pm)	7:36	7:13	9:20	**8:23**
282	9	Sa.	♀ ☌ ☾ (2 pm)	7:36	7:12	10:31	**9:07**
283	10	Su.	♄ stationary (9 pm)	7:37	7:11	11:42	**9:58**
284	11	Mo.		7:38	7:10	**12:50**	**10:56**
285	12	Tu.	First qtr. ☾	7:38	7:09	**1:52**	**11:58**
286	13	We.		7:39	7:07	**2:46**	
287	14	Th.	♄ ☌ ☾ (2 am)	7:40	7:06	**3:32**	1:03
288	15	Fr.	♃ ☌ ☾ (5 am)	7:40	7:05	**4:12**	2:08
289	16	Sa.	♀ ☌ Antares (9 am)	7:41	7:04	**4:46**	3:11
290	17	Su.	☿ stationary (8 pm)	7:42	7:03	**5:17**	4:11
291	18	Mo.	♃ stationary (6 am)	7:42	7:02	**5:46**	5:10
292	19	Tu.		7:43	7:01	**6:14**	6:06
293	20	We.	Full ☾	7:44	7:00	**6:42**	7:02
294	21	Th.	⛢ ☌ ☾ (5 pm)	7:45	6:59	**7:12**	7:58
295	22	Fr.		7:45	6:58	**7:45**	8:54
296	23	Sa.		7:46	6:57	**8:21**	9:51
297	24	Su.	☾ at apogee (10 am)	7:47	6:56	**9:01**	10:47
298	25	Mo.	☿ gr. elongation W (1 am)	7:48	6:55	**9:47**	11:42
299	26	Tu.		7:48	6:54	**10:38**	**12:34**
300	27	We.		7:49	6:53	**11:33**	**1:23**
301	28	Th.	Last qtr. ☾	7:50	6:52		**2:07**
302	29	Fr.	♀ gr. elongation E (4 pm)	7:51	6:51	12:31	**2:47**
303	30	Sa.		7:51	6:50	1:31	**3:24**
304	31	Su.	☿ ☌ Spica (9 pm)	7:52	6:49	2:33	**3:58**

11th Month — November 2021 — 30 Days

Moon Phases — *New*, Nov. 4, 3:28 pm; *First Qtr.*, Nov. 11, 6:09 am; *Full*, Nov. 19, 2:20 am; *Last Qtr.*, Nov. 27, 5:51 am

Day of Year	Day of Month	Day of Week	Planetary Configurations and Phenomena	Sunrise	Sunset	Moon-rise	Moon-set
305	1	Mo.		7:53	6:48	3:36	**4:30**
306	2	Tu.		7:54	6:48	4:40	**5:03**
307	3	We.	☿ ☌ ☾ (2 pm)	7:55	6:47	5:47	**5:37**
308	4	Th.	New ☾; ⛢ in ☍ (7 pm)	7:55	6:46	6:56	**6:15**
309	5	Fr.	☾ at perigee (5 pm)	7:56	6:45	8:08	**6:58**
310	6	Sa.		7:57	6:44	9:22	**7:47**
311	7	Su.	**DST ends** (2 am)	6:58	5:44	9:35	**7:44**
312	8	Mo.		6:59	5:43	10:42	**8:47**
313	9	Tu.		7:00	5:42	11:41	**9:54**
314	10	We.	♄ ☌ ☾ (8 am)	7:00	5:42	**12:31**	**11:00**
315	11	Th.	First qtr. ☾	7:01	5:41	**1:13**	
316	12	Fr.		7:02	5:41	**1:49**	12:05
317	13	Sa.	♆ ☌ ☾ (1 pm)	7:03	5:40	**2:21**	1:06
318	14	Su.		7:04	5:39	**2:50**	2:04
319	15	Mo.		7:05	5:39	**3:17**	3:01
320	16	Tu.		7:06	5:38	**3:45**	3:56
321	17	We.	⛢ ☌ ☾ (8 pm)	7:06	5:38	**4:14**	4:52
322	18	Th.		7:07	5:38	**4:45**	5:47
323	19	Fr.	Full ☾	7:08	5:37	**5:20**	6:44
324	20	Sa.	☾ at apogee (8 pm)	7:09	5:37	**5:59**	7:40
325	21	Su.		7:10	5:36	**6:43**	8:36
326	22	Mo.		7:11	5:36	**7:32**	9:29
327	23	Tu.		7:12	5:36	**8:25**	10:19
328	24	We.		7:12	5:36	**9:21**	11:04
329	25	Th.		7:13	5:35	**10:20**	11:45
330	26	Fr.		7:14	5:35	**11:20**	**12:22**
331	27	Sa.	Last qtr. ☾	7:15	5:35		**12:56**
332	28	Su.	☿ in superior ☌ (11 pm)	7:16	5:35	12:20	**1:27**
333	29	Mo.		7:17	5:35	1:21	**1:59**
334	30	Tu.		7:17	5:35	2:25	**2:31**

12th Month — December 2021 — 31 Days

Moon Phases — *New*, Dec. 4, 1:06 am; *First Qtr.*, Dec. 10, 6:59 pm; *Full*, Dec. 18, 9:58 pm; *Last Qtr.*, Dec. 26, 7:47 pm

Day of Year	Day of Month	Day of Week	Planetary Configurations and Phenomena	Sunrise	Sunset	Moon-rise	Moon-set
335	1	We.	♆ stationary (4 pm)	7:18	5:35	3:31	**3:06**
336	2	Th.	♂ ☌ ☾ (6 pm)	7:19	5:35	4:40	**3:45**
337	3	Fr.		7:20	5:35	5:53	**4:31**
338	4	Sa.	New ☾ at perigee (4 am)	7:21	5:35	7:08	**5:25**
339	5	Su.		7:21	5:35	8:21	**6:27**
340	6	Mo.	♀ ☌ ☾ (7 pm)	7:22	5:35	9:26	**7:35**
341	7	Tu.	♄ ☌ ☾ (8 pm)	7:23	5:35	10:23	**8:45**
342	8	We.		7:24	5:35	11:10	**9:53**
343	9	Th.	♃ ☌ ☾ (12 am)	7:24	5:35	11:49	**10:57**
344	10	Fr.	First qtr. ☾	7:25	5:35	**12:23**	**11:58**
345	11	Sa.		7:26	5:36	**12:53**	
346	12	Su.		7:27	5:36	**1:21**	12:56
347	13	Mo.		7:27	5:36	**1:49**	1:51
348	14	Tu.		7:28	5:36	**2:17**	2:47
349	15	We.	⛢ ☌ ☾ (12 am)	7:28	5:37	**2:47**	3:42
350	16	Th.		7:29	5:37	**3:20**	4:38
351	17	Fr.	☾ at apogee (8 pm)	7:30	5:38	**3:58**	5:34
352	18	Sa.	Full ☾; ♀ stationary	7:30	5:38	**4:40**	6:30
353	19	Su.		7:31	5:38	**5:28**	7:24
354	20	Mo.		7:31	5:39	**6:20**	8:16
355	21	Tu.	Solstice (9:22 am)	7:32	5:39	**7:16**	9:03
356	22	We.		7:32	5:40	**8:14**	9:45
357	23	Th.	☿ gr. elongation E	7:33	5:40	**9:12**	10:23
358	24	Fr.		7:33	5:41	**10:11**	10:57
359	25	Sa.		7:34	5:42	**11:11**	11:28
360	26	Su.	Last qtr. ☾	7:34	5:42		11:59
361	27	Mo.		7:34	5:43	12:11	**12:29**
362	28	Tu.	☿ ☌ ♀ (7 pm)	7:35	5:43	1:13	**1:01**
363	29	We.		7:35	5:44	2:18	**1:36**
364	30	Th.		7:35	5:45	3:27	**2:17**
365	31	Fr.	♂ ☌ ☾ (2 pm)	7:36	5:46	4:39	**3:06**

☉ The Sun ● The Earth ☾ The Moon ☿ Mercury ♀ Venus ♂ Mars ♃ Jupiter ♄ Saturn ♆ Neptune ⛢ Uranus ☌ = in conjunction ☍ = opposition to the ☉

We are more than iconic blue signs by the highway.

WE ARE TIME TRAVELERS, ADVENTURERS & STORYTELLERS...

TEXASBRAZOSTRAIL.COM

TEXAS BRAZOS TRAIL

TEXASFORESTTRAIL.COM

TEXAS FOREST TRAIL

TEXASFORTSTRAIL.COM

TEXAS FORTS TRAIL

TXHILLCOUNTRYTRAIL.COM

TEXAS HILL COUNTRY TRAIL

TEXASINDEPENDENCETRAIL.COM

TEXAS INDEPENDENCE TRAIL

TEXASLAKESTRAIL.COM

TEXAS LAKES TRAIL

TEXASMOUNTAINTRAIL.COM

TEXAS MOUNTAIN TRAIL

TEXASPECOSTRAIL.COM

TEXAS PECOS TRAIL

TEXASPLAINSTRAIL.COM

TEXAS PLAINS TRAIL

TEXASTROPICALTRAIL.COM

TEXAS TROPICAL TRAIL

WE ARE THE TEXAS HERITAGE TRAILS

Advocates for the Preservation of Texas Heritage & Leaders in Texas Tourism.
We represent the sites, stops, and stories throughout Texas' 254 counties.

TEXAS HERITAGE TRAILS PROGRAM - TEXASTIMETRAVEL.COM - TEXAS HISTORICAL COMMISSION

RECREATION

A boat heading out for the bay from Laguna Madre.
Photo by Jonathan Cutrer (jcutrer.com).

TEXAS STATE PARKS AND HISTORIC SITES

TEXAS STATE FORESTS

NATIONAL PARKS AND LANDMARKS

BIRDING

FAIRS & FESTIVALS

HUNTING AND FISHING

Texas State Parks and Historic Sites

Sources: Texas Parks and Wildlife, https://tpwd.texas.gov; and the Texas Historical Commission, www.thc.texas.gov

Texas' diverse system of state parks and historic sites offers contrasting attractions: mountains and canyons, arid deserts and lush forests, spring-fed streams, sandy dunes, saltwater surf, and fascinating historic sites.

The Texas Parks and Wildlife's (TPW) **Central Reservation Center** can take reservations for almost all state parks. Exceptions are the facilities not operated by the TPW. Call the center during usual business hours at 512-389-8900. The TDD line is 512-389-8915.

The following information is a brief glimpse of what each park has to offer. Refer to the chart on pages 136–137 for a more complete list of available activities and facilities. Entrance fees to state parks range from $1 to $5 per person. There are also fees for tours and some activities. For up-to-date information, call the information number listed above before you go.

Road abbreviations used in this list are:
- IH: interstate highway
- US: U.S. highway
- TX: state highway
- FM: farm-to-market road
- PR: park road

List of State Parks and Historic Sites

ABILENE STATE PARK, 16 miles southwest of Abilene on FM 89 and PR 32 in Taylor County, consists of 529.4 acres that were deeded by the City of Abilene in 1933. A part of the official Texas longhorn herd and bison are located in the park. Large groves of pecan trees that once shaded bands of Comanches now shade visitors at picnic tables. Activities include camping, hiking, picnicking, nature study, biking, and swimming and fishing on Lake Abilene. Nearby is Buffalo Gap, the original Taylor County seat (1878) and one of the early frontier settlements. Buffalo Gap was on the Western, or Goodnight-Loving, Trail, over which pioneer Texas cattlemen drove herds to railheads in Kansas.

ACTON STATE HISTORIC SITE is a 0.006-acre cemetery plot in Hood County where Davy Crockett's second wife, Elizabeth, was buried in 1860. It is 4.5 miles east of Granbury on US 377 to FM 167 south, then 2.4 miles south to Acton. Nearby attractions include Cleburne, Dinosaur Valley and Lake Whitney state parks.

ATLANTA STATE PARK is 1,475 acres located 11 miles northwest of Atlanta on FM 1154 in Cass County; adjacent to Wright Patman Dam and Reservoir. Land acquired from the U.S. Army in 1954 by license to 2004 with option to renew to 2054. Camping, biking and hiking in pine forests, as well as water activities, such as boating, fishing, and lake swimming. Nearby are the historic town of Jefferson and the Caddo Lake and Daingerfield state parks.

BALMORHEA STATE PARK is 45.9 acres four miles southwest of Balmorhea on TX 17 between Balmorhea and Toyahvale in Reeves County. Deeded in 1934-35 by private owners and Reeves Co. Water Imp. Dist. No. 1 and built by the Civilian Conservation Corps (CCC). Swimming pool (1¾ acres) fed by artesian San Solomon Springs; also provides water to aquatic refuge in park. Activities include swimming, picnicking,

---

Ready to Plan Your Trip?

The **Texas Department of Transportation** publishes the **Texas State Travel Guide**, a full-color publication with information about attractions, activities, history and historic sites, and the official **Texas state highway map**. You can get both sent to you for free by calling the toll-free number, **1-800-888-8TEX,** or download a free digital version at the site:

www.traveltex.com

The TPWD sells discount passes for youth groups, qualifying seniors, veterans and disabled persons, and families. For further information, call the TPW at 512-389-8900 or visit:

**https://tpwd.texas.gov/state-parks/
park-information/passes/park-passes**

---

camping, scuba and skin diving. Motel rooms available at San Solomon Springs Courts. Nearby are city of Pecos, Fort Davis National Historic Site, Davis Mountains State Park, and McDonald Observatory.

BARTON WARNOCK ENVIRONMENTAL EDUCATION CENTER consists of 99.9 acres in Brewster County on FM 170, one mile east of Lajitas. Originally built by the Lajitas Foundation in 1982 as the Lajitas Museum Desert Gardens, the TPW purchased it in 1990 and renamed it for Texas botanist Dr. Barton Warnock. The center is also the eastern entrance station to Big Bend Ranch State Park. Self-guiding museum and botanical tours in the Trans-Pecos Vegetation Area.

BASTROP STATE PARK is 6,600 acres, found one mile east of Bastrop on TX 21 or from TX 71. The park was acquired by deeds from the City of Bastrop and private owners in 1933-35. Site of famous "Lost Pines," an isolated region of loblolly pines and hardwoods. Swimming pool, cabins, and lodge are among facilities. The park offers fishing at Lake Bastrop, geocaching, picnicking, canoeing, bicycling, and hiking. A golf course lies adjacent to the park. The state capitol at Austin is 32 miles away; a 13-mile drive through forest leads to Buescher State Park.

BENTSEN-RIO GRANDE VALLEY STATE PARK, a scenic park, is along the Rio Grande five miles southwest of Mission off FM 2062 in Hidalgo County. Originally acquired from private owners in 1944, the park's subtropical resaca woodlands and brushlands have grown to 797 acres. Hiking trails provide chance to study unique plants and animals of park. Many birds unique to southern United States found here, including pauraque, groove-billed ani, green kingfisher, rose-throated becard, and tropical parula. Birdwatching tours guided by park naturalists offered daily December–March. The park is one of last natural refuges in Texas for ocelot and jaguarundi. Trees include cedar elm, anaqua, ebony, and Mexican ash. Camping, hiking, picnicking, boating, fishing also available. Nearby are Santa Ana National Wildlife Refuge, Falcon State Park, and Sabal Palm Sanctuary.

BIG BEND RANCH STATE PARK, more than 300,000 acres of Chihuahuan Desert wilderness in Brewster and Presidio counties along the Rio Grande, was purchased from private owners in 1988. The

A hiking trail in Cedar Hills State Park. Photo by Robert Plocheck.

purchase more than doubled the size of the state park system, which comprised at that time 220,000 acres. Eastern entrance at Barton Warnock Environmental Education Center one mile east of Lajitas on FM 170; western entrance is at Fort Leaton State Historic Site four miles east of Presidio on FM 170. The area includes extinct volcanoes, several waterfalls, two mountain ranges, at least 11 rare species of plants and animals, and 90 major archaeological sites. There is little development. Vehicular access limited; wilderness backpacking, hiking, scenic drive, picnicking, fishing, and swimming. There are longhorns in the park, although they are not part of the official state longhorn herd.

BIG SPRING STATE PARK is 382 acres located on FM 700 within the city limits of Big Spring in Howard County. Both city and park were named for a natural spring that was replaced by an artificial one. The park was deeded by the City of Big Spring in 1934 and 1935. Drive to top of Scenic Mountain provides panoramic view of surrounding country and look at prairie dog colony. The "big spring," nearby in a city park, provided watering place for herds of bison, antelope, and wild horses. Used extensively also as campsite for early Indians, explorers, and settlers.

BLANCO STATE PARK is 104.6 acres along the Blanco River four blocks south of Blanco's town square in Blanco County. The land was deeded by private owners in 1933. Park area was used as campsite by early explorers and settlers. The park offers fishing, camping, swimming, picnicking, and boating. LBJ Ranch and LBJ State Historic Site, Pedernales Falls and Guadalupe River state parks are nearby.

BONHAM STATE PARK is a 261-acre park located two miles southeast of Bonham on TX 78, then two miles southeast on FM 271 in Fannin County. It includes a 65-acre lake, rolling prairies, and woodlands. The land was acquired in 1933 from the City of Bonham. Swimming, camping, mountain-bike trail, lighted fishing pier, boating. Sam Rayburn Memorial Library in Bonham. Sam Rayburn Home and Valley Lake nearby.

BRAZOS BEND STATE PARK in Fort Bend County, eight miles east of Damon off FM 1462 on FM 762, approximately 28 miles southwest of Houston. The 4,897-acre park was purchased from private owners in 1976–77. George Observatory in park. Observation platform for spotting and photographing the 270 species of birds, 23 species of mammals, and 21 species of reptiles and amphibians, including American alligator, that frequent the park. Interpretive and educational programs every weekend. Backpacking, camping, hiking, biking, fishing. Creekfield Lake Nature Trail.

BUESCHER STATE PARK, a scenic area, is 1,016 acres, found two miles northwest of Smithville off TX 71 to FM 153 in Bastrop County. Acquired between 1933 and 1936, about one-third deeded by private owner; heirs donated a third; balance from City of Smithville. El Camino Real once ran near park, connecting San Antonio de Béxar with Spanish missions in East Texas. Park land was part of Stephen F. Austin's colonial grant. Some 250 species of birds can be seen. Camping, fishing, hiking, boating. Scenic park road connects with Bastrop State Park through Lost Pines area.

CADDO LAKE STATE PARK, north of Karnack one mile off TX 43 to FM 2198 in Harrison County, consists of 483.9 acres along Cypress Bayou, which runs into Caddo Lake. A scenic area, it was acquired from private owners in 1933. Nearby Karnack is childhood home of Lady Bird Johnson. Close by is old city of Jefferson, famous as commercial center of Northeast Texas during last half of 19th century. Caddo Indian legend attributes formation of Caddo Lake to a huge flood. Cypress trees, American lotus and lily pads, as well as 71 species of fish, predominate in lake. Nutria, beaver, mink, squirrel, armadillo, alligator, and turtle abound. Activities include camping, hiking, swimming, fishing, canoeing. Screened shelters, cabins.

CADDO MOUNDS STATE HISTORIC SITE in Cherokee County six miles southwest of Alto on TX 21. Total of 93.8 acres acquired in 1975. Open for day visits only, park offers exhibits and interpretive trails through reconstructed Caddo dwellings and ceremonial areas, including two temple mounds, a burial mound, and a village area typical of people who lived in region for 500 years beginning about A.D. 800. Open Tuesday–Sunday. Nearby are Jim Hogg and Mission Tejas State historic sites and Texas State Railroad.

CAPROCK CANYONS STATE PARK AND TRAILWAY, 100 miles southeast of Amarillo and 3.5 miles north of Quitaque off FM 1065 and TX 86 in Briscoe, Floyd, and Hall counties, has 15,313 acres. Purchased in 1975. Scenic escarpment's canyons provided camping areas for Indians of Folsom culture more than 10,000 years ago. Mesquite and cacti in the badlands give way to tall grasses, cottonwood, and plum thickets in the bottomlands. Wildlife includes aoudad sheep, coyote, bobcat, porcupine, and fox. Activities include scenic drive, camping, hiking, mountain-bike riding, horse riding, and horse camping. A 64.3-mile trailway (hike, bike, and equestrian trail) extends from South Plains to Estelline.

CASA NAVARRO STATE HISTORIC SITE, on 0.7 acres at corner of S. Laredo and W. Nueva streets in downtown San Antonio, was acquired by donation from San Antonio Conservation Society Foundation in 1975. The furnished Navarro House three-building complex, built about 1848, was home of statesman, rancher, and Texas patriot José Antonio Navarro. Guided tours; exhibits. Open Wednesday through Sunday.

CEDAR HILL STATE PARK, an urban park on 1,826 acres ten miles southwest of Dallas via US 67 and FM 1382 on Joe Pool Lake, was acquired by long-term lease from the Army Corp of Engineers in 1982. Camping mostly in wooded areas. Fishing from two lighted jetties and a perch pond for children. Swimming, boating, bicycling, birdwatching, and picnicking. Vegetation includes several sections of tall-grass prairie. Penn Farm Agricultural History Center includes reconstructed buildings of the 19th-century Penn Farm and exhibits; self-guided tours.

CHOKE CANYON STATE PARK consists of two units, South Shore and Calliham, located on 26,000-acre Choke Canyon Reservoir. Park acquired in 1981 in a 50-year agreement among Bureau of Reclamation, City of Corpus Christi, and Nueces River Authority. Thickets of mesquite and blackbrush acacia predominate, supporting populations of javelina, coyote, skunk, and alligator, as well as the crested caracara. The 385-acre South Shore Unit is located 3.5 miles west of Three Rivers on TX 72 in Live Oak County; the 1,100-acre Calliham Unit is located 12 miles west of Three Rivers, on TX 72, in McMullen County. Both units offer camping, picnicking, boating, fishing, lake swimming, and baseball and volleyball areas. The Calliham Unit also has a hiking trail, wildlife educational center, screened shelters, rentable gym and kitchen. Sports complex includes swimming pool and tennis, volleyball, shuffleboard, and basketball courts. Across dam from South Shore is North Shore Equestrian and Camping Area; 18 miles of horseback riding trails.

CLEBURNE STATE PARK is a 528-acre park located 10 miles southwest of Cleburne via US 67 and PR 21 in Johnson County with 116-acre spring-fed lake; acquired from the City of Cleburne and private owners in 1935 and 1936. Oak, elm, mesquite, cedar, and redbud cover white rocky hills. Bluebonnets in spring. Activities include camping, picnicking, hiking, bicycling, canoeing, swimming, boating, fishing. Nearby are Fossil Rim Wildlife Center and dinosaur tracks in Paluxy River at Dinosaur Valley State Park.

COLORADO BEND STATE PARK, a 5,328-acre facility, is 28 miles west of Lampasas in Lampasas and San Saba counties. Access is from Lampasas to Bend on FM 580 west, then follow signs (access road subject to flooding). Park was purchased partly in 1984, with balance acquired in 1987. Primitive camping, fishing, swimming, hiking, biking, and picnicking; guided tours to Gorman Falls; crawling cave tours require reservations. Rare and endangered species here include golden-cheeked warbler, black-capped vireo, and bald eagle.

CONFEDERATE REUNION GROUNDS STATE HISTORIC SITE, located in Limestone County on the Navasota River, is 77.1 acres in size. Acquired 1983 by deed from Joseph E. Johnston Camp No. 94 CSA. Entrance is 6 miles south of Mexia on TX 14, then 2.5 miles west on FM 2705. Historic buildings, two scenic footbridges span creek; hiking trail. Nearby are Fort Parker State Park and Old Fort Parker.

COOPER LAKE STATE PARK comprises 3,026 acres three miles southeast of Cooper in Delta and Hopkins counties. The park was acquired in 1991 by 25-year lease from Army Corps of Engineers. Two units, Doctors Creek and South Sulphur, adjoin 19,300-surface-acre Cooper Lake. Fishing, boating, camping, picnicking, and swimming are some activities available at the park. South Sulphur offers equestrian camping and horseback riding trails. Access to Doctors Creek Unit is via TX 24 east from Commerce to Cooper, then east on TX 154 to FM 1529 to park.

Parks text continues on page 138

Texas State Parks & State Historic Sites

Park †Type of Park (Special Features)	NEAREST TOWN	Day Use Only	Historic Site/	Museum Exhibit/Interpretive Center	Restrooms	Showers	Trailer Dump Stn.	Camping ††	Screened Shelters	Cabins	Group Facilities	Nature Trail	Hiking Trail	Picnicking	Boat Ramp	Fishing	Swimming	Canoe Rentals	Activities/Amenities
Abilene SP	BUFFALO GAP				★	★	★	15	★	★	BG	★		★		☆	★		C
Acton SHS ▲ (Grave of Davy Crockett's Wife)	GRANBURY	★	★																
Atlanta SP	ATLANTA				★	★	★	15			DG	★	★	★	★	★	☆	★	
Balmorhea SP (San Solomon Springs Courts)	BALMORHEA			★	★	★	★	14		★	DG			★			★		L
Barton Warnock Environmental Ed. Center	LAJITAS	★		★	★							★							
Bastrop SP	BASTROP				★	★	★	8		★	BG	★	★		★	★	★	★	G
Bentsen–Rio Grande Valley SP	MISSION			★	★	★		6			BG	★	★						H
Big Bend Ranch SP	LAJITAS			★	★	★		1			NG	★	★	★		☆	☆		B1, C, E
Big Spring SP	BIG SPRING					★					DG	★	★	★					B1, H
Blanco SP	BLANCO			★	★	★	16	★		DG	★	★		★	★	★			
Bonham SP	BONHAM			★	★	★	15		★	BG	★	★	★	★	★	☆	★	B1	
Brazos Bend SP (George Observatory)	RICHMOND			★	★	★	★	14	★	★	BG	★	★	★		★			B1/2,E,H
Buescher SP	SMITHVILLE			★	★	★	★	14	★	★	BG	★		★		★	☆	★	B2
Caddo Lake SP	KARNACK			★	★	★	★	15	★	★	BG	★	★	★	★	★		★	
Caddo Mounds SHS ▲	ALTO	★	★	★	★							★							
Caprock Canyons SP & TW	QUITAQUE			★	★	★	★	8			BG	★	★	★	★	☆	☆		B1, E
Casa Navarro SHS ▲	SAN ANTONIO	★	★	★	★														
Cedar Hill SP	CEDAR HILL			★	★	★	17			DG	★	★	★	★	★	☆		B1, H	
Choke Canyon SP, Calliham Unit	THREE RIVERS			★	★	★	13		★	BG	★	★	★	★	★	☆	☆		
South Shore Unit	THREE RIVERS	★		★						DG		★	★	★	★			B1	
Cleburne SP	CLEBURNE			★	★	★	16	★	★	BG	★	★	★	★	★	★		H	
Colorado Bend SP (Cave Tours)	BEND			★	★			6			NG	★	★	★	★	★	☆	★	B1
Confederate Reunion Grounds SHS ▲	MEXIA	★	★	★	★							★	★						
Cooper Lake SP, Doctors Creek Unit	COOPER			★	★	★	★	4	★		DG	★	★	★	★	★	★		
South Sulphur Unit	SULPHUR SPRINGS			★	★	★	13	★	★	DG	★	★	★	★	★	★	★	B1, E	
Copper Breaks SP	QUANAH			★	★	★	★	8			BG	★	★	★	★	★	☆		B1, E, C
Daingerfield SP	DAINGERFIELD			★	★	★	15	★	★	BG	★	★	★	★	★	☆	★		
Davis Mountains SP (Indian Lodge)	FORT DAVIS			★	★	★	★	11			DG	★	★						B1, L, E
Devils River SNA (Reservations Required)	DEL RIO						6			BG					☆	★		B1	
Devil's Sinkhole SNA	ROCKSPRINGS	No access to cavern. Tours of SNA by special request only.																
Dinosaur Valley SP (Dinosaur Footprints)	GLEN ROSE			★	★	★	★	7			DG	★	★	★			☆	☆	B1, E, C
Eisenhower SP (Marina)	DENISON			★	★	★	15	★	★	BG	★	★	★	★	★	☆		B1, R	
Eisenhower Birthplace SHS ▲	DENISON	★	★	★							DG								
Enchanted Rock SNA	FREDERICKSBURG			★	★		★	8			DG	★	★	★					R
Estero Llano Grande SP	WESLACO										BG	★							
Fairfield Lake SP	FAIRFIELD			★	★	★	13			DG	★	★	★	★	★	☆	★	B1, E	
Falcon SP (Airstrip)	ZAPATA			★	★	★	11	★	★	DG	★	★	★	★	★	☆			
Fannin Battleground SHS ▲	GOLIAD	★	★	★	★						DG		★						
Fanthorp Inn SHS	ANDERSON	★	★	★	★							★							
Fort Boggy SP	CENTERVILLE	★		★	★			6		★	DG	★	★	★	★	★	☆		B1
Fort Griffin SHS ▲	ALBANY		★	★	★	★	★	11			BG	★	★		☆				C, E
Fort Lancaster SHS ▲	OZONA	★	★	★	★							☆							
Fort Leaton SHS	PRESIDIO	★	★	★	★						★	★							
Fort McKavett SHS, ▲	FORT McKAVETT	★	★	★	★						★	★							
Fort Parker SP	MEXIA			★	★	★	14	★	★	BG	★	★	★	★	★	☆	★	B1	
Fort Richardson SP, HS & Lost Creek Res. TW	JACKSBORO	★	★	★	★	★	10		★	DG	★	★		★	★			B1, E
Franklin Mountains SP (Wyler Aerial Tramway)	EL PASO	★						6			BG	★	★						B1, R
French Legation SHS	AUSTIN	Undergoing restoration; not open to the public at this time.																
Fulton Mansion SHS ▲	FULTON	★	★	★															
Galveston Island SP (Summer Theater)	GALVESTON			★	★	★	★	4			NG	★	★		☆	☆		B1	
Garner SP	CONCAN			★	★	★	14	★	★	BG	★	★		☆	☆	★		B1	
Goliad SP & Mission Espíritu Santo HS	GOLIAD	★	★	★	★	★	★	15	★		DG	★	★		☆	★			
Goose Island SP	ROCKPORT			★	★	★	13			BG	★	★	★	★					
Government Canyon SNA	SAN ANTONIO			★				9			DG	★	★						B1
Guadalupe River SP & Honey Creek SNA	BOERNE			★	★	★	★	13			DG	★	★		☆	☆	★		B1, E
Hill Country SNA	BANDERA			★				6			NG	★	★		☆	☆		B1, E	
Hueco Tanks SP & HS (Indian Pictographs)	EL PASO	★	★	★	★	★	14			DG	★	★	★					R	
Huntsville SP	HUNTSVILLE			★	★	★	★	15	★	★	DG	★	★	★	★	★	☆	★	G
Inks Lake SP	BURNET			★	★	★	10		★	DG	★	★	★	★	★	★	★		
Kickapoo Cavern SP (Reservations Required)	BRACKETTVILLE			★	★	★	15				★	★	★					B1	
Lake Arrowhead SP	WICHITA FALLS			★	★	★	10			DG	★	★	★	★	★	★	☆	E	

† TYPES OF PARKS

SP	State Park	HS	Historic Site
SHS	State Historic Site	TW	Trailway
SNA	State Natural Area		
▲	Facilities not operated by Parks & Wildlife Department		

†† TYPES OF CAMPING

1	Primitive/Backpacking	2	Walk-in Tent	3	Tent
4	Water & Electric	5	Water, Electric & Sewer		
6	1 & 2	7	1, 2 & 4	8	1, 2, 3 & 4
9	1 & 3	10	1, 3 & 4	11	1, 3, 4 & 5
12	1 & 4	13	2, 3 & 4	14	3 & 4
15	3, 4 & 5	16	4 & 5	17	1, 3 & 5

Texas State Parks & State Historic Sites

Park †Type of Park (Special Features)	NEAREST TOWN	Day Use Only	Historic Site/Museum	Exhibit/Interpretive Center	Restrooms	Showers	Trailer Dump Stn.	Camping ††	Screened Shelters	Cabins	Group Facilities	Nature Trail	Hiking Trail	Picnicking	Boat Ramp	Fishing	Swimming	Canoe Rentals	Activities/Amenities
Lake Bob Sandlin SP	MOUNT PLEASANT				★	★	★	10	★	★	DG	★	★	★	★	☆			B1
Lake Brownwood SP	BROWNWOOD				★	★	★	15	★	★	BG	★	★	★	★	★	☆		
Lake Casa Blanca International SP	LAREDO				★	★	★	14			DG		★	★	☆	☆			B1
Lake Colorado City SP	COLORADO CITY				★	★	★	14	★		DG	★	★	★	★	☆			
Lake Corpus Christi SP	MATHIS				★	★	★	15	★		DG	★	★	★	☆	☆	★		
Lake Livingston SP	LIVINGSTON			★	★	★	★	15	★		DG	★	★	★	★	★	☆		B1, B2, E
Lake Mineral Wells SP & TW	MINERAL WELLS				★	★	★	10	★		DG	★	★	★	★	★	☆		B1, E, R
Lake Somerville SP & TW, Birch Creek Unit	SOMERVILLE			★	★	★	★	10			BG	★	★	★	★	★	☆	★	B1, E
Nails Creek Unit	LEDBETTER			★	★	★	★	10			DG	★	★	★	★	★	☆	★	B1, E
Lake Tawakoni SP	WILLS POINT				★	★	★	4			BG	★	★	★	★	☆			
Lake Whitney SP (Airstrip)	WHITNEY				★	★	★	15	★		BG	★	★	★	☆	☆			B1
Landmark Inn SHS ▲ (Hotel Rooms)	CASTROVILLE	★	★	★							DG	★		★		☆			L
Levi Jordan Plantation SHS	BRAZORIA	*Under development; not open to the public at this time.*																	
Lipantitlan SHS	SAN PATRICIO	★											★						
Lockhart SP	LOCKHART				★	★	★	16			DG		★		★	★			G
Longhorn Cavern SP ▲ (Cavern Tours)	BURNET	★	★	★								★	★	★					
Lost Maples SNA	VANDERPOOL			★	★	★	★	12				★	★	★			☆	☆	
Lyndon B. Johnson SP & HS	STONEWALL	★	★	★	★							DG	★		★			★		C
Magoffin Home SHS ▲	EL PASO	★	★	★	★														
Martin Creek Lake SP	TATUM				★	★	★	12	★	★	DG	★	★	★	★	☆			B1
Martin Dies Jr. SP	JASPER			★	★	★	★	14	★	★	BG	★	★	★	★	★	☆	★	B1
McKinney Falls SP	AUSTIN		★	★	★	★	★	13		★	BG	★	★	★			☆		B1, B2
Meridian SP	MERIDIAN				★	★	★	13	★		BG	★		★	★	☆	☆	★	
Mission Dolores SHS ▲ (El Camino Real Trail)	SAN AUGUSTINE	★	★	★	★			5			DG	★	★						
Mission Rosario SHS	GOLIAD	★	★	★	★		★	15	★		DG	★		★	★				
Mission Tejas SP	WECHES	★			★	★	★	14			BG	★	★		☆				
Monahans Sandhills SP	MONAHANS			★	★	★	★	14			DG	★		★					E
Monument Hill & Kreische Brewery SHS	LA GRANGE	★	★	★	★						DG	★		★					
Mother Neff SP	MOODY				★	★		17			BG	★	★		☆				
Mustang Island SP	PORT ARANSAS				★	★	★	12						★		☆	☆		
National Museum of the Pacific War ▲	FREDERICKSBURG	★	★	★	★							★							
Old Tunnel SP (Bat viewing, May – Oct.)	FREDERICKSBURG	★										★							
Palmetto SP	LULING				★	★	★	15		★	BC	★	★	★		★	★		
Palo Duro Canyon SP (Summer Drama: "Texas")	CANYON			★	★	★	★	8	★			★	★	★					B1, E, C
Pedernales Falls SP	JOHNSON CITY				★	★	★	13			NG	★	★	★		☆	☆		B1, E
Port Isabel Lighthouse SHS ▲	PORT ISABEL	★	★										★						
Possum Kingdom SP	CADDO				★	★	★	10	★			★	★	★	★	★	☆	★	
Purtis Creek SP	EUSTACE				★	★	★	10			DG	★	★	★	★	★	☆	★	
Ray Roberts Lake SP, Isle du Bois Unit	PILOT POINT			★	★	★	★	13			DG	★	★	★	★	★	☆	★	B1, B2, E
Johnson Branch Unit	VALLEY VIEW				★	★	★	7			DG	★	★	★	★	★	☆	★	B1, B2
Jordan Unit (Lantana Resort)	PILOT POINT																		L
Resaca de la Palma SP	BROWNSVILLE				★						DG								
Sabine Pass Battleground SHS ▲	SABINE PASS	★	★	★			★	12				★	★	☆					
Sam Bell Maxey House SHS ▲	PARIS	★	★	★	★														
Sam Rayburn House SHS ▲	BONHAM	★	★	★	★														
San Angelo SP	SAN ANGELO				★	★	★	8		★	BG	★	★	★	★	★			B1, E, C
San Felipe de Austin SHS ▲	SAN FELIPE																		
San Jacinto Battleground SHS (Battleship Texas)	HOUSTON	★	★	★	★						DG	★		★		☆			
Sea Rim SP	PORT ARTHUR				★	★	★	10				★	★	★	★	★	★	★	B1
Sebastopol House HS ▲	SEGUIN	★	★	★									★						
Seminole Canyon SP & HS (Indian Pictographs)	LANGTRY		★	★	★	★	★	10				★	★	★					B1
Sheldon Lake SP (Environmental Learning Center)	HOUSTON	★		★	★	★						★	☆	★	★				
South Llano River SP	JUNCTION		★		★	★	★	10				★	★	★		☆	☆		B1
Starr Family Home SHS ▲	MARSHALL	★	★	★															
Stephen F. Austin SP	SAN FELIPE			★	★	★	★	15	★		BG	★	★	★		☆			G
Tyler SP	TYLER				★	★	★	15	★		BG	★	★	★	★	★	☆	★	B1
Varner-Hogg Plantation SHS ▲	WEST COLUMBIA	★	★	★	★							★		★		☆			
Village Creek SP	LUMBERTON				★	★	★	13			BG	★	★	★		☆		★	B1
Walter Umphrey SP ▲	PORT ARTHUR	*(Managed by Jefferson County)*																	
Washington-on-the-Brazos SHS / Barrington Living History Farm (Anson Jones Home)	WASHINGTON	★	★	★	★						DG	★		★					
Zaragoza Birthplace SHS	GOLIAD	★	★	★															

FACILITIES CODES

★ Facilities or services available for activity

☆ Permitted, but facilities not provided

ACTIVITIES/AMENITIES CODES

B1	Mountain biking	E	Equestrian facilities and/or trails
B2	Surfaced bike trail	G	Golf
DG	Day-use group facilities	L	Hotel-type facilities
NG	Overnight group facilities	C	Texas Longhorn herd
BG	Both day and night group facilities	R	Rock climbing
H	Some handicap accessible facilities		

One of the dinosaurs on display in Dinosaur Valley State Park. Photo by Dill Tom (CC).

To South Sulpher Unit, take IH 30 to Exit 122 west to Sulphur Spings to TX 19, then TX 71, then FM 3505.

COPPER BREAKS STATE PARK, 12 miles south of Quanah on TX 6 in Hardeman County, was acquired by purchase from private owner in 1970. Park features rugged scenic beauty on 1,899 acres, two lakes, grass-covered mesas, and juniper breaks. Nearby medicine mounds were important ceremonial sites of Comanche Indians. Nearby Pease River was site of 1860 battle in which Cynthia Ann Parker was recovered from Comanches. Part of state longhorn herd lives at park. Abundant wildlife. Nature, hiking, and eques-trian trails; natural and historical exhibits; summer programs; horseback riding; camping, equestrian camping.

DAINGERFIELD STATE PARK, off TX 49 and PR 17 southeast of Daingerfield in Morris County, is a 550.9-acre recreational area that includes an 80-surface-acre lake; deeded in 1935 by private owners. This area is center of iron industry in Texas; nearby is Lone Star Steel Co. In spring, dogwood, redbuds, and wisteria bloom; in fall, brilliant foliage of sweetgum, oaks, and maples contrast with dark green pines. Campsites, lodge, and cabins.

DAVIS MOUNTAINS STATE PARK is 2,709 acres in Jeff Davis County, four miles northwest of Fort Davis via TX 118 and PR 3. The scenic area was deeded in 1933-1937 by private owners. First European, Antonio de Espejo, came to area in 1583. Extremes of altitude produce both plains grasslands and piñon-juniper-oak woodlands. Montezuma quail, rare in Texas, visit park. Scenic drives, camping, and hiking. Indian Lodge, built by the Civilian Conservation Corps during the early 1930s, has 39 rooms, restaurant, and swim-ming pool (reservations: 432-426-3254). Four-mile hiking trail leads to Fort Davis National Historic Site. Other nearby points of interest include McDonald Observatory and 74-mile scenic loop through Davis

Mountains. Nearby are scenic Limpia, Madera, Musquiz, and Keesey canyons; Camino del Rio; ghost town of Shafter; Big Bend National Park; Big Bend Ranch State Park; Fort Davis National Historic Site; and Fort Leaton State Historic Site.

DEVILS RIVER STATE NATURAL AREA comprises 37,000 acres in Val Verde County, 22 miles off US 277, about 65 miles north of Del Rio on graded road. It is an ecological and archaeological crossroads. Ecologically, it is in a transitional area between the Edwards Plateau, the Trans-Pecos desert, and the South Texas brush country. Archaeological studies suggest occupation and use by cultures from both east and west. Camping, hiking, and mountain biking. All camping, facility stays, canyon, and pictograph-site tours are by reservation only. Dolan Falls is nearby and is accessible only through The Nature Conservancy of Texas.

DEVIL'S SINKHOLE STATE NATURAL AREA, comprising 1,860 acres about six miles northeast of Rocksprings on US 377 in Edwards County, is a verti-cal cavern. The sinkhole, discovered by Anglo settlers in 1867, is a registered National Natural Landmark; it was purchased in 1985 from private owners. The cavern opening is about 40 by 60 feet, with a verti-cal drop of about 140 feet. Access by prearranged tour with Devil's Sinkhole Society (830-683-BATS). Bats can be viewed in summer leaving cave at dusk; no access to cave itself. Contact Kickapoo Cavern State Park to arrange a tour.

DINOSAUR VALLEY STATE PARK, located off US 67 four miles west of Glen Rose in Somervell County, is a 1,525-acre scenic park. Land was acquired from private owners in 1968. Features dinosaur tracks in bed of Paluxy River and two full-scale dinosaur models, originally created for New York World's Fair in 1964–65, on display. Part of state longhorn herd is in park. Camping, picnicking, hiking, mountain biking, swimming, fishing. The riverbed featuring the dinosaur tracks was designated a national landmark in 1968.

EISENHOWER BIRTHPLACE STATE HISTORIC SITE is six acres off US 75 at 609 S. Lamar, Denison, Grayson County. The property was acquired in 1958 from the Eisenhower Birthplace Foundation. Restoration of home of President Dwight Eisenhower includes furnishings of period and some personal effects of Gen. Eisenhower. Guided tour; call for schedule. Park open daily, except Christmas Day and New Year's Day; call for hours. Town of Denison established on Butterfield Overland Mail Route in 1858.

EISENHOWER STATE PARK, 423.1 acres five miles northwest of Denison via US 75 to TX 91 N to FM 1310 on the shores of Lake Texoma in Grayson County, was acquired by an Army lease in 1954. Named for the 34th U.S. president, Dwight D. Eisenhower. First Anglo settlers came to area in 1835; Fort Johnson was established in area in 1840; Colbert's Ferry established on Red River in 1853 and operated until 1931. Areas of tall-grass prairie exist. Hiking, camping, picnicking, fishing, swimming.

ENCHANTED ROCK STATE NATURAL AREA is 1,644 acres on Big Sandy Creek 18 miles north of Fredericksburg on FM 965 on the line between Gillespie and Llano counties. Acquired in 1978 by The Nature Conservancy of Texas; state acquired from TNCT in 1984. Enchanted Rock is huge pink granite boulder rising 425 feet above ground and covering 640 acres. It is second-largest batholith (underground rock formation uncovered by erosion) in the United States. Indians believed ghost fires flickered at top and were awed by weird creaking and groaning, which geologists say resulted from rock's heating and expanding by day, cooling and contracting at night. Enchanted Rock is a National Natural Landmark and is on the National Register of Historic Places. Activities include hiking, geological study, camping, rock climbing, and stargazing.

ESTERO LLANO GRANDE STATE PARK, part of the World Birding Center network, is a 176-acre wetlands refuge in HIdlago County 3.2 miles southeast of Weslaco off FM 1015. Birds seen here include waders, shorebirds, and migrating waterfowl, as well as coastal species such as roseate spoonbill and ibis. Rare spottings include red-crowned parrots and green parakeets. Opened daily. Guided tours offered.

FAIRFIELD LAKE STATE PARK is 1,460 acres adjacent to Fairfield Lake, six miles northeast of the city of Fairfield off FM 2570 and FM 3285 in Freestone County. It was leased from Texas Utilities in 1971-72. Surrounding woods offer sanctuary for many species of birds and wildlife. Camping, hiking, backpacking, nature study, water-related activities available. Extensive schedule of tours, seminars, and other activities.

FALCON STATE PARK is 572.6 acres located 15 miles north of Roma off US 83 and FM 2098 at southern end of Falcon Reservoir in Starr and Zapata counties. Park leased from International Boundary and Water Commission in 1949. Gently rolling hills covered with mesquite, huisache, wild olive, ebony, cactus. Excellent birding and fishing. Camping and water activities also. Nearby are Mexico, Fort Ringgold in Rio Grande City,

and historic city of Roma. Bentsen-Rio Grande Valley State Park is 65 miles away.

FANNIN BATTLEGROUND STATE HISTORIC SITE, nine miles east of Goliad in Goliad County off US 59 to PR 27. The 13.6-acre park site was acquired by the state in 1914; transferred to TPW by legislative enactment in 1965. At this site on March 20, 1836, Col. James Fannin surrendered to Mexican Gen. José Urrea after Battle of Coleto; 342 massacred and 28 escaped near what is now Goliad SP.

FANTHORP INN STATE HISTORIC SITE includes a historic double-pen cedar-log dogtrot house and 1.4 acres in Anderson, county seat of Grimes County, south of TX 90. Acquired by purchase in 1977 from a Fanthorp descendant and opened to the public in 1987. Inn records report visits from many prominent civic and military leaders, including Sam Houston, Anson Jones, and generals Ulysses S. Grant, Robert E. Lee and Stonewall Jackson. Originally built in 1834, it has been restored to its 1850 use as a family home and travelers' hotel. Tours available Friday, Saturday, Sunday. Call TPW for stagecoach-ride schedule. No dining or overnight facilities.

FORT BOGGY STATE PARK is 1,847 acres of wooded, rolling hills in Leon County near Boggy Creek, about four miles south of Centerville on TX 75. Land donated to TPWD in 1985 by Eileen Crain Sullivan. Area once home to Keechi and Kickapoo tribes. Log fort was built by settlers in 1840s; first settlement north of the Old San Antonio Road and between the Navasota and Trinity rivers. Swimming beach, fishing, picnicking, nature trails for hiking and mountain biking. Fifteen-acre lake open to small craft. Open-air group pavilion overlooking lake can be reserved ($50 per day). Nearby attractions include Rusk/Palestine, Fort Parker State Park, and Texas State Railroad. Open Wed.–Sun. for day use only; entrance fee. For reservations, call 512-389-8900.

FORT GRIFFIN STATE HISTORIC SITE is 506.2 acres 15 miles north of Albany off US 283 in Shackelford County. The state was deeded the land by the county in 1935. Portion of state longhorn herd resides in park. On bluff overlooking townsite of Fort Griffin and Clear Fork of Brazos River valley are partially restored ruins of Old Fort Griffin, restored bakery, replicas of enlisted men's huts. Fort constructed in 1867, deactivated 1881. Camping, equestrian camping, hiking. Nearby are Albany with restored courthouse square, Abilene, and Possum Kingdom state parks. Albany annually holds "Fandangle" musical show in commemoration of frontier times.

FORT LANCASTER STATE HISTORIC SITE, 81.6-acres located about eight miles east of Sheffield on TX 290 in Crockett County. Acquired in 1968 by deed from Crockett County; Henry Meadows donated 41 acres in 1975. Fort Lancaster established Aug. 20, 1855, to guard San Antonio-El Paso Road and protect movement of supplies and immigrants from Indian hostilities. Site of part of Camel Corps experiment. Fort abandoned March 19, 1861, after Texas seceded from Union. Exhibits on history, natural history, and archaeology; nature trail, picnicking. Open daily; day use only.

FORT LEATON STATE HISTORIC SITE, four miles southeast of Presidio in Presidio County on FM 170, was acquired in 1967 from private owners. Consists of 23.4 acres, five of which are on site of trading post. In 1848, Ben Leaton built fortified adobe trading post known as Fort Leaton near present Presidio. Ben Leaton died in 1851. Guided tours; exhibits trace history, natural history, and archaeological history of area. Serves as western entrance to Big Bend Ranch State Park. Day use only.

FORT MCKAVETT STATE HISTORIC SITE, 79.5 acres acquired from 1967 through the mid-1970s from Fort McKavett Restoration, Inc., Menard County, and private individuals, is located 23 miles west of Menard off US 190 and FM 864. Originally called Camp San Saba, the fort was built by War Department in 1852 to protect frontier settlers and travelers on Upper El Paso Road from Indians. Camp later renamed for Capt. Henry McKavett, killed at Battle of Monterrey, Sept. 21, 1846. Fort abandoned March 1859; reoccupied April 1868. A Buffalo Soldier post. Abandoned again June 30, 1883. Once called by Gen. Wm. T. Sherman, "the prettiest post in Texas." More than 25 restored buildings, ruins of many others. Interpretive exhibits. Day use only.

FORT PARKER STATE PARK includes 1,459 acres, including 758.8 land acres and 700-acre lake between Mexia and Groesbeck off TX 14 in Limestone County. Named for the former private fort built near present park in 1836, the site was acquired from private owners and the City of Mexia 1935-1937. Camping, fishing, swimming, canoeing, picnicking. Nearby is Old Fort Parker Historic Site, which is operated by the City of Groesbeck.

FORT RICHARDSON STATE PARK, Historic Site, and Lost Creek Reservoir Trailway, located one-half mile south of Jacksboro off US 281 in Jack County, contains 454 acres. Acquired in 1968 from City of Jacksboro. Fort founded in 1867, northernmost of line of federal forts established after Civil War for protection from Indians; originally named Fort Jacksboro. In April 1867, fort was moved to its present location from 20 miles farther south; on Nov. 19, 1867, made permanent post at Jacksboro and named for Israel Richardson, who was fatally wounded at Battle of Antietam. Expeditions sent from Fort Richardson arrested Indians responsible for Warren Wagon Train Massacre in 1871 and fought Comanches in Palo Duro Canyon. Fort abandoned in May 1878. Park contains seven restored buildings and two replicas. Interpretive center, picnicking, camping, fishing; ten-mile trailway.

FRANKLIN MOUNTAINS STATE PARK, created by an act of the legislature in 1979 to protect the mountain range as a wilderness preserve and acquired by TPW in 1981, comprises 24,248 acres, all within El Paso city limits. Largest urban park in the nation. It includes virtually an entire Chihuahuan Desert mountain range, with an elevation of 7,192 feet at the summit. The park is habitat for many Chihuahuan Desert plants including sotol, lechuguilla, ocotillo, cholla, and barrel cactus, and such animals as mule deer, fox, and an occasional cougar. Camping, mountain biking, nature study, hiking, picnicking, rock-climbing. Wyler Aerial Tramway, an aerial cable-car tramway on 195 acres of rugged mountain on east side of Franklin Mountains. Purchase tickets at tramway station on McKinley Ave. Check with park for fees and hours; 915-566-6622. Other area attractions include Hueco Tanks State Historic Site and Magoffin Home State Historic Site.

FRENCH LEGATION STATE HISTORIC SITE was built in 1841 as a private home in Austin for Alphonse Dubois, French chargé d'affaires to the Republic of Texas. In 1848 it was purchased by Dr. Joseph W. Robertson, who lived there with his large family and nine enslaved workers. Daughter Lillie Robertson lived in the house her entire life. The state acquired the house after her death and appointed the Daughters of the Republic as custodian. In 2017, HB 3810 transferred the French Legation to the THC. The site is currently closed for restoration.

FULTON MANSION STATE HISTORIC SITE in Fulton is 3.5 miles north of Rockport off TX Business 35 on South Fulton Beach Rd. in Aransas County. The 2.3-acre property was acquired by purchase from private owner in 1976. Three-story wooden structure, built in 1874-1877, was home of George W. Fulton, prominent in South Texas for economic and commercial influence; mansion derives significance from its innovative construction and Victorian design. Call ahead for days and hours of guided tours; open Wednesday–Sunday; 800-792-1112.

GALVESTON ISLAND STATE PARK, on the west end of Galveston Island on FM 3005, is a 2,013-acre site acquired in 1969 from private owners. Camping, birding, nature study, swimming, bicycling, and fishing amid **sand dunes and grassland**. Musical productions in amphitheater during summer.

GARNER STATE PARK is 1,420 acres of recreational facilities on US 83 on the Frio River in Uvalde County 9 miles south of Leakey. Named for John Nance Garner, U.S. Vice President, 1933-1941, the park was deeded in 1934-36 by private owners. Camping, hiking, picnicking, river recreation, miniature golf, biking, boat rentals. Cabins available. Nearby is John Nance "Cactus Jack" Garner Museum in Uvalde. Nearby also are ruins of historic Mission Nuestra Señora de la Candelaria del Cañon, founded in 1749; Camp Sabinal (a U.S. Cavalry post and later Texas Ranger camp) established 1856; Fort Inge, established 1849.

GOLIAD STATE PARK AND MISSION ESPÍRITU SANTO HISTORIC SITE are 188.3 acres one-fourth mile south of Goliad on US 183 and 77A, along the San Antonio River in Goliad County. The land was deeded to the state in 1931 by the City and County of Goliad; transferred to TPW 1949. Nearby are the sites of several battles in the Texas fight for independence from Mexico. The park includes a replica of Mission Nuestra Señora del Espíritu Santo de Zúñiga, originally established 1722 and settled at its present site in 1749. At Goliad State Park are camping, picnicking, historical exhibits, nature trail. (See also Fannin Battleground State Historic Site.)

GOOSE ISLAND STATE PARK, 321.4 acres 10 miles northeast of Rockport on TX 35 and PR 13 on St. Charles and Aransas bays in Aransas County, was deeded by private owners in 1931-1935 plus an additional seven acres donated in the early 1990s by Sun Oil Co. Located here is "Big Tree" estimated to be a 1,000-year-old live oak. Fishing, picnicking, and camping, plus excellent birding; no swimming. Rare and endangered whooping cranes can be viewed during winter just across St. Charles Bay in Aransas National Wildlife Refuge.

GOVERNMENT CANYON STATE NATURAL AREA is an 8,622-acre area in Bexar County, northwest of San Antonio, 3.5 miles northwest of Loop 1604 and FM 471, then 1.6 miles north on Galm Road. Day

Students enrolled in the Field Studies Program at NCO Leadership Center of Excellence explore Hueco Tanks State Park. Photo by Spc. James Seals.

use only. No camping. Open Friday–Monday. Trees such as mountain laurel, Ashe juniper, Mexican buckeye, and Escarpment black cherry.

GUADALUPE RIVER STATE PARK comprises 1,939 acres on cypress-shaded Guadalupe River in Kendall and Comal counties, 13 miles east of Boerne on TX 46. Acquired by deed from private owners in 1974. Park has four miles of river frontage with several whitewater rapids and is located in a stretch of Guadalupe River noted for canoeing, tubing. Picnicking, camping, hiking, nature study. Trees include sycamore, elm, basswood, pecan, walnut, persimmon, willow and hackberry (also, Honey Creek State Natural Area).

HILL COUNTRY STATE NATURAL AREA in Bandera and Medina counties, 9 miles southwest of Bandera on FM 1077. The 5,370-acre site acquired by gift from Merrick Bar-O-Ranch and purchased in 1976. Park is located in typical Texas Hill Country on West Verde Creek and contains several spring-fed streams. Primitive and equestrian camping, hiking, horseback riding, mountain biking, fishing. Group lodge.

HUECO TANKS STATE PARK AND HISTORIC SITE, located 32 miles northeast of El Paso in El Paso County on FM 2775 just north of US 62-180, was obtained from the county in 1969, with additional 121 acres purchased in 1970. Featured in this 860.3-acre park are large natural rock basins that provided water for archaic hunters, Plains Indians, Butterfield Overland Mail coach horses and passengers, and other travelers in this arid region. In park are Indian pictographs, old ranch house, and relocated ruins of stage station. Rock climbing, picnicking, camping, hiking. Wildlife includes gray fox, bobcat, prairie falcons,

golden eagles. Visitation is limited. Pictograph tours are by advanced request.

HUNTSVILLE STATE PARK is 2,083-acre recreational area off IH 45 and PR 40 six miles south of Huntsville in Walker County, acquired by deeds from private owners in 1937. Heavily wooded park adjoins Sam Houston National Forest and encloses Lake Raven. Hiking, camping, fishing, biking, paddle boats, canoeing. At nearby Huntsville are Sam Houston's old homestead (Steamboat House), containing some of his personal effects and his grave. Approximately 50 miles away is Alabama-Coushatta Indian Reservation in Polk County.

INKS LAKE STATE PARK is 1,201 acres of recreational facilities along Inks Lake, 9 miles west of Burnet on the Colorado River off TX 29 on PR 4 in Burnet County. Acquired by deeds from the Lower Colorado River Authority and private owners in 1940. Camping, hiking, fishing, swimming, boating, golf. Deer, turkey, and other wildlife abundant. Nearby are Longhorn Cavern State Park, LBJ Ranch, LBJ State Historic Site, Pedernales Falls State Park and Enchanted Rock State Natural Area. Granite Mountain quarry at nearby Marble Falls furnished red granite for Texas state capitol. Buchanan Dam, considered the largest multi-arch dam in the nation, located 4 miles from park.

KICKAPOO CAVERN STATE PARK is located about 22 miles north of Brackettville on RM 674 on the Kinney/Edwards county line in the southern Edwards Plateau. The park (6,368 acres) contains 20 known caves, two of which are large enough to be significant: Kickapoo Cavern, about ¼ mile in length, has impressive formations, and Stuart Bat

The Landmark Inn State Historic Site in Castroville, Medina County. Photo by Robert Plocheck.

Cave (formally Green Cave), slightly shorter, supports a nursery colony of Mexican freetail bats in summer. Public observations of bat flights are available with an entrance permit. Birds include rare species such as black-capped vireo, varied bunting, and Montezuma quail. Reptiles and amphibians include barking frog, mottled rock rattlesnake, and Texas alligator lizard. Open Friday–Monday. Cavern tours on Saturday by reservation. Group lodge; primitive camping; hiking and mountain-biking trails.

LAKE ARROWHEAD STATE PARK consists of 524 acres in Clay County, about 14 miles southeast of Wichita Falls on US 281 to FM 1954, then 8 miles to park. Acquired in 1970 from the City of Wichita Falls. Lake Arrowhead is a reservoir on the Little Wichita River with 106 miles of shoreline. The land surrounding the lake is generally semiarid, gently rolling prairie, much of which has been invaded by mesquite in recent decades. Fishing, camping, lake swimming, picnicking, horseback-riding area.

LAKE BOB SANDLIN STATE PARK, on the wooded shoreline of 9,400-acre Lake Bob Sandlin, is located 12 miles southwest of Mount Pleasant off FM 21 in Titus County. Activities in the 639.8-acre park include picnicking, camping, mountain biking, hiking, swimming, fishing, and boating. Oak, hickory, dogwood, redbud, maple, and pine produce spectacular fall color. Eagles can sometimes be spotted in winter months.

LAKE BROWNWOOD STATE PARK in Brown County is 537.5 acres acquired from Brown County Water Improvement District No. 1 in 1934. Park reached from TX 279 to PR 15, 16 miles northwest of Brownwood on Lake Brownwood near geographical center of Texas. Water sports, hiking, camping. Cabins available.

LAKE CASA BLANCA INTERNATIONAL STATE PARK, located one mile east of Laredo off US 59 on Loop 20, was formerly operated by the City of Laredo and Webb County and was acquired by TPW in 1990. Park includes 371 acres on Lake Casa Blanca. Recreation hall can be reserved. Camping, picnicking, fishing, ball fields, playgrounds, amphitheater, and tennis courts. County-operated golf course nearby.

LAKE COLORADO CITY STATE PARK, 500 acres leased for 99 years from a utility company. It is located in Mitchell County 11 miles southwest of Colorado City off 1H 20 on FM 2836. Water sports, picnicking, camping, hiking. Part of state longhorn herd can be seen in park.

LAKE CORPUS CHRISTI STATE PARK, a 14,112-acre park in San Patricio, Jim Wells and Live Oak counties. Located 35 miles northwest of Corpus Christi and four miles southwest of Mathis off TX 359 and Park Road 25. Was leased from City of Corpus Christi in 1934. Camping, picnicking, birding, water sports. Nearby are Padre Island National Seashore; Mustang Island, Choke Canyon, Goliad and Goose Island state parks; Aransas National Wildlife Refuge; and Fulton Mansion State Historic Site.

LAKE LIVINGSTON STATE PARK, in Polk County, about one mile southwest of Livingston on FM 3126 and PR 65, contains 635.5 acres along Lake Livingston. Acquired by deed from private landowners in 1971. Near ghost town of Swartwout, steamboat landing on Trinity River in 1830s and 1850s. Camping, picnicking, swimming pool, fishing, mountain biking, and stables.

LAKE MINERAL WELLS STATE PARK AND TRAILWAY, located four miles east of Mineral Wells on US 180 in Parker County, consists of 3,283 acres encompassing Lake Mineral Wells. In 1975, the

City of Mineral Wells donated 1,095 land acres and the lake to TPW; the federal government transferred additional land from Fort Wolters army post. Popular for rock-climbing/rappelling. Swimming, fishing, boating, camping; the 20-mile Lake Mineral Wells State Trailway available for hiking, bicycling, equestrian use.

LAKE SOMERVILLE STATE PARK, northwest of Brenham in Lee and Burleson counties, was leased from the federal government in 1969. Birch Creek Unit (2,365 acres reached from TX 60 and PR 57) and Nails Creek Unit (3,155 acres reached from US 290 and FM 180) are connected by a 13-mile trailway system, with equestrian and primitive camp sites, rest benches, shelters, and drinking water. Also camping, birding, picnicking, volleyball, and water sports. Somerville Wildlife Management Area, 3,180 acres, is nearby.

LAKE TAWAKONI STATE PARK is a 376.3-acre park in Hunt County along the shore of its namesake reservoir. It was acquired in 1984 through a 50-year lease agreement with the Sabine River Authority and opened in 2001. Includes a swimming beach, half-mile trail, picnic sites, boat ramp, and campsites. A 40-acre tallgrass prairie managed in the post-oak woodlands. The park is reached from IH 20 on TX 47 north to FM 2475 about 20 miles past Wills Point.

LAKE WHITNEY STATE PARK is 1,281 acres along the east shore of Lake Whitney west of Hillsboro via TX 22 and FM 1244 in Hill County. Acquired in 1954 by a Department of the Army lease. Located near ruins of Towash, early Texas settlement inundated by the lake. Towash Village named for chief of Hainai Indians. Park noted for bluebonnets in spring. Camping, hiking, birding, picnicking, water activities.

LANDMARK INN STATE HISTORIC SITE, 4.7 acres in Castroville, Medina County, about 15 miles west of San Antonio, was acquired through donation by Miss Ruth Lawler in 1974. Castroville, settled in the 1840s by Alsatian farmers, is called Little Alsace of Texas. Landmark Inn built about 1844 as residence and store for Cesar Monod, mayor of Castroville 1851-1864. Special workshops, tours, and events held at inn; grounds may be rented for receptions, family reunions, and weddings. Overnight lodging; all rooms air-conditioned and nonsmoking.

LEVI JORDAN PLANTATION STATE HISTORIC SITE was a sugar and cotton plantation, established in the 1850s. The site, in Sweeny, is currently under development and is not open to the public.

LIPANTITLAN STATE HISTORIC SITE is five acres, found nine miles east of Orange Grove in Nueces County off Texas 359, FM 624 and FM 70. The property was deeded by private owners in 1937. Fort constructed here in 1833 by Mexican government fell to Texas forces in 1835. Only facilities are picnic tables. Lake Corpus Christi State Park is nearby.

LOCKHART STATE PARK is 263.7 acres, found four miles south of Lockhart via US 183, FM 20 and PR 10 in Caldwell County. The land was deeded by private owners between 1934 and 1937. Camping, picnicking, hiking, fishing, 9-hole golf course. After Comanche raid at Linnville, the Battle of Plum Creek (1840) was fought in area.

LONGHORN CAVERN STATE PARK, off US 281 and PR 4 about six miles west and six miles south of Burnet in Burnet County, is 645.6 acres dedicated as

a natural landmark in 1971. It was acquired in 1932-1937 from private owners. The cave has been used as a shelter since prehistoric times. Among legends about the cave is that the outlaw Sam Bass hid stolen money there. Confederates made gunpowder in the cave during the Civil War. Nature trail; guided tours of cave; picnicking, hiking. Cavern operated by concession agreement. Inks Lake State Park and Lyndon B. Johnson Ranch located nearby.

LOST MAPLES STATE NATURAL AREA consists of 2,174 scenic acres on the Sabinal River in Bandera and Real counties, five miles north of Vanderpool on FM 187. Acquired by purchase from private owners in 1973-1974. Outstanding example of Edwards Plateau flora and fauna, features isolated stand of uncommon Uvalde bigtooth maple. Rare golden-cheeked warbler, black-capped vireo, and green kingfisher nest and feed in park. Fall foliage can be spectacular (late Oct. through early Nov.). Hiking trails, camping, fishing, picnicking, birding.

LYNDON B. JOHNSON STATE PARK & HISTORIC SITE, off US 290 in Gillespie County 14 miles west of Johnson City near Stonewall, contains 717.9 acres. Acquired in 1965 with private donations. Home of Lyndon B. Johnson located north bank of Pedernales River across Ranch Road 1 from park; portion of official Texas longhorn herd maintained at park. Wildlife exhibit includes turkey, deer, and bison. Living-history demonstrations at restored Sauer-Beckmann house. Reconstruction of Johnson birthplace is open to public. Historic structures, swimming pool, tennis courts, baseball field, picnicking. Day use only. Nearby is family cemetery where former president and relatives are buried. In Johnson City is boyhood home of President Johnson. (See National Parks.)

MAGOFFIN HOME STATE HISTORIC SITE, in El Paso, is a 19-room territorial-style adobe on a 1.5-acre site. Purchased by the state and City of El Paso in 1976, it is operated by TPW. Home was built in 1875 by El Pasoan Joseph Magoffin. Furnished with original family artifacts. Guided tours; call for schedule. Day use only.

MARTIN CREEK LAKE STATE PARK, 286.9 acres, is located four miles southwest of Tatum off TX 43 and CR 2183 in Rusk County. It was deeded to the TPW by Texas Utilities in 1976. Water activities; also cabins, camping, picnicking. Roadbed of Trammel's Trace, old Indian trail that became major route for settlers moving to Texas from Arkansas, can be seen. Hardwood and pine forest shelters abundant wildlife including swamp rabbits, gophers, nutria, and numerous species of land birds and waterfowl. Annual perch fishing contest for children ages 4–12 the first Saturday in September.

MARTIN DIES JR. STATE PARK is 705 acres in Jasper and Tyler counties on B. A. Steinhagen Lake between Woodville and Jasper via US 190. Land leased for 50 years from Corps of Engineers in 1964. Located at edge of Big Thicket. Plant and animal life varied and abundant. Winter bald eagle census conducted at nearby Sam Rayburn Reservoir. Camping, hiking, mountain biking, water activities. Wildscape herb garden. Park is about 30 miles from Alabama and Coushatta Indian Reservation.

MCKINNEY FALLS STATE PARK is 744.4 acres, located about 13 miles southeast of the state capitol in Austin, off US 183. Acquired in 1970 by gift from private owners. Named for Thomas F. McKinney, one of Stephen F. Austin's first 300 colonists, who built his home here in the mid-1800s on Onion Creek. Ruins of his homestead can be viewed. Swimming, hiking, biking, camping, picnicking, fishing, guided tours.

MERIDIAN STATE PARK in Bosque County is a 505.4-acre park. The heavily wooded land, on TX 22 three miles southwest of Meridian, was acquired from private owners in 1933-1935. Texas-Santa Fe expedition of 1841 passed through Bosque County near present site of park on Bee Creek. Endangered golden-cheeked warbler nests here. Camping, picnicking, hiking, fishing, lake swimming, birding, bicycling.

MISSION DOLORES STATE HISTORIC SITE was once a Spanish mission built in 1721 just 20 miles west of the Texas-Louisiana border, in San Augustine. There are no longer any above-ground remains of the mission. Visitors can camp, view the museum, and explore its rich history.,

MISSION ROSARIO STATE HISTORIC SITE is located four miles west of Goliad on US 59. It contains the ruins of Nuestra Señora del Rosario mission, established 1754.

MISSION TEJAS STATE PARK is a 363.5-acre park in Houston County. Situated 12 miles southwest of Alto via TX 21 and PR 44, the park was acquired from the Texas Forest Service in 1957. In the park is a representation of Mission San Francisco de los Tejas, the first mission in East Texas (1690). It was abandoned, then re-established 1716; abandoned again 1719; re-established again 1721; abandoned for last time in 1730 when the mission was moved to San Antonio. Also in park is restored Rice Family Log Home, built about 1828. Camping, hiking, fishing, picnicking.

MONAHANS SANDHILLS STATE PARK consists of 3,840 acres of sand dunes, some up to 70 feet high, in Ward and Winkler counties 5 miles northeast of Monahans on IH 20 to PR 41. Land leased by state from private foundation until 2056. Dunes used as meeting place by raiding Indians. Camping, hiking, picnicking, sand-surfing. Scheduled tours. Odessa meteor crater is nearby, as is Balmorhea State Park.

MONUMENT HILL STATE HISTORIC SITE AND KREISCHE BREWERY STATE HISTORIC SITE are operated as one park unit. Monument Hill consists of 40.4 acres one mile south of La Grange on US 77 to Spur Road 92 in Fayette County. Monument and tomb area acquired by state in 1907; additional acreage acquired from the Archdiocese of San Antonio in 1956. Brewery and home purchased from private owners in 1977. Monument is dedicated to Capt. Nicholas Dawson and his men, who fought at Salado Creek in 1842, in Mexican Gen. Adrián Woll's invasion of Texas, and to the men of the "black bean lottery" (1843) of the Mier Expedition. Remains were brought to Monument Hill for reburial in 1848. Kreische Complex, on 36 acres, is linked to Monument Hill through interpretive trail. Kreische Brewery State Historic Site includes the brewery and stone-and-wood house built between 1850–1855 on Colorado River. One of first commercial breweries in state, it closed in 1884. Smokehouse and barn also in complex. Guided tours of brewery and house; call for schedule. Also picnicking, nature study.

MOTHER NEFF STATE PARK was the first official state park in Texas. It originated with six acres donated by Mrs. I. E. Neff, mother of Pat M. Neff, governor of Texas from 1921 to 1925. Gov. Neff and Frank Smith

donated remainder in 1934. The park, located eight miles west of Moody on FM 107 and TX 236, now contains 259 acres along the Leon River in Coryell County. Heavily wooded. Camping, picnicking, fishing, hiking.

MUSTANG ISLAND STATE PARK, 3,954 acres on Gulf of Mexico in Nueces County, 14 miles south of Port Aransas on TX 361, was acquired from private owners in 1972. Mustang Island is a barrier island with a complicated ecosystem, dependent upon the sand dune. The foundation plants of the dunes are sea oats, beach panic grass, and soilbind morning glory. Beach camping, picnicking; sun, sand, and water activities. Excellent birding. Padre Island National Seashore 14 miles south.

NATIONAL MUSEUM OF THE PACIFIC WAR AND ADMIRAL NIMITZ STATE HISTORIC SITE is on seven acres in downtown Fredericksburg. First established as a state agency in 1969 by Texas Legislature; transferred to TPW in 1981. George Bush Gallery opened in 1999. Named for Adm. Chester W. Nimitz of World War II fame, it includes the Pacific War Museum in the Nimitz Steamboat Hotel; the Japanese Garden of Peace, donated by the people of Japan; the History Walk of the Pacific War, featuring planes, boats, and other equipment from World War II; and other special exhibits. Nearby is Kerrville-Schreiner Park.

OLD TUNNEL STATE PARK sits on 16.1 acres of land, making it the smallest state park in Texas. Located at 10619 Old San Antonio Road, 13.6 miles south of Fredericksburg in Kendall County, the park is great for wildlife-viewing opportunites. The abandoned railroad tunnel provides a home to over 3 million Mexican free-tailed bats and 3,000 cave myotis from May to October, and the park provides nightly bat viewing access. An upper viewing area, open seven days a week, is limited to 250 visitors. Thursday through Sunday, a secondary viewing area opens. Call (866) 978-2287 for viewing time information. The park also has a half-mile trail open year-round for bird-watching or for a short hike.

PALMETTO STATE PARK, a scenic park of 270.3 acres, is eight miles southeast of Luling on US 183 and PR 11 along the San Marcos River in Gonzales County. Land deeded in 1934-1936 by private owners and City of Gonzales. Named for tropical dwarf palmetto found there. Diverse plant and animal life; excellent birding. Also picnicking, fishing, hiking, pedal boats, swimming. Nearby Gonzales and Ottine important in early Texas history. Gonzales settled 1825 as center of Green DeWitt's colonies.

PALO DURO CANYON STATE PARK consists of 16,402 acres found 12 miles east of Canyon on TX 217 in Armstrong and Randall counties. The land was deeded by private owners in 1933 and is the scene of the annual summer production of the musical drama "Texas." Spectacular one-million-year-old scenic canyon exposes rocks spanning about 200 million years of geological time. Coronado may have visited canyon in 1541. Canyon officially discovered by Capt. R. B. Marcy in 1852. Scene of decisive battle in 1874 between Comanche and Kiowa Indians and U.S. Army troops under Gen. Ranald Mackenzie. Also scene of ranching enterprise started by Charles Goodnight in 1876. Part of state longhorn herd is kept here.

Camping, mountain biking, scenic drives, horseback and hiking trails, horse rentals.

PEDERNALES FALLS STATE PARK, 5,212 acres in Blanco County about nine miles east of Johnson City on FM 2766 along Pedernales River, was acquired from private owners in 1970. Typical Edwards Plateau terrain, with live oaks, deer, turkey, and stone hills. Camping, picnicking, hiking, swimming, tubing. Falls main scenic attraction.

PORT ISABEL LIGHTHOUSE STATE HISTORIC SITE consists of 0.9 acres in Port Isabel, Cameron County. Acquired by purchase from private owners in 1950, site includes lighthouse constructed in 1852; visitors can climb to top. Park is near sites of Civil War battle of Palmito Ranch (1865) and Mexican War battles of Palo Alto and Resaca de la Palma (1846). Operated by City of Port Isabel.

POSSUM KINGDOM STATE PARK, west of Mineral Wells via US 180 and PR 33 in Palo Pinto County, is 1,529 acres adjacent to Possum Kingdom Lake, in Palo Pinto Mountains and Brazos River Valley. Rugged canyons home to deer, other wildlife. Acquired from the Brazos River Authority in 1940. Camping, picnicking, swimming, fishing, boating. Cabins available.

PURTIS CREEK STATE PARK is 1,582 acres in Henderson and Van Zandt counties 3.5 miles north of Eustace on FM 316. Acquired in 1977 from private owners. Fishing, camping, hiking, picnicking, paddle boats and canoes.

RAY ROBERTS LAKE STATE PARK, with Isle du Bois Unit consisting of 2,263 acres on the south side of Ray Roberts Lake on FM 455 in Denton County. Johnson Branch Unit contains 1,514 acres on north side of the lake in Denton and Cooke counties, seven miles east of IH 35 on FM 3002. There are also six satellite parks. Land acquired in 1984 by lease from Department of the Army. Abundant and varied plant and animal life. Fishing, camping, picnicking, swimming, hiking, biking; tours of 19-century farm buildings at Johnson Branch. Includes Lantana Ridge Lodge on the east side of the lake. It is a full-service lodging facility with restaurant.

RESACA DE LA PALMA STATE PARK, part of the World Birding Center network, is 1,700 semi-tropical acres off US 281, four miles west of Brownsville in Cameron County. Park grounds are open seven days a week year-round from sunrise to sunset. Birding and natural history tours offered. Colorful neotropical and neartic migrant birds have been seen.

SABINE PASS BATTLEGROUND STATE HISTORIC SITE in Jefferson County 1.5 miles south of Sabine Pass on Dick Dowling Road, contains 57.6 acres acquired from Kountze and Couch Trust in 1972. Lt. Richard W. Dowling, with small Confederate force, repelled an attempted 1863 invasion of Texas by Union gunboats. Monument, World War II ammunition bunkers. Fishing, picnicking, camping.

SAM BELL MAXEY HOUSE STATE HISTORIC SITE, at the corner of South Church and Washington streets in Paris, Lamar County, was donated by City of Paris in 1976. Consists of 0.4 acres with 1868 Victorian Italianate-style frame house, plus outbuildings. Most of furnishings accumulated by Maxey family. Maxey served in Mexican and Civil wars and was two-term U.S. Senator. House is on the National Register of Historic Places. Open for tours Friday through Sunday.

SAM RAYBURN HOUSE STATE HISTORIC SITE, in Bonham, preserves personal belongings, original furniture, and photos just as they were when Sam Rayburn lived here. Visitors can explore the home and grounds to the once powerful and influential Texas politician.

SAN ANGELO STATE PARK, on O.C. Fisher Reservoir adjacent to the city of San Angelo in Tom Green County, contains 7,677 acres of land, most of which will remain undeveloped. Leased from U.S. Corps of Engineers in 1995. Access is from US 87 or US 67, then FM 2288. Highly diversified plant and animal life. Activities include boating, water activities, hiking, mountain biking, horseback riding, camping, picnicking. Part of state longhorn herd in park. Nearby is Fort Concho.

SAN FELIPE DE AUSTIN STATE HISTORIC SITE, in Austin County east of Sealy, was once the

A fisherman launching his boat at Possum Kingdom Lake. Photo by Robert Plocheck.

location of Stephen F. Austin's headquarters for his colony in Mexican Texas. Visitors are able to walk the grounds of the former political and economic center of American immigration to Texas before its fall in the War of Texas Independence.

SAN JACINTO BATTLEGROUND STATE HISTORIC SITE AND BATTLESHIP TEXAS STATE HISTORIC SITE are located 20 miles east of downtown Houston off TX 225 east to TX 134 to PR 1836 in east Harris County. The park is 1,200 acres with a 570-foot-tall monument erected in 1936-1939 in honor of Texans who defeated Mexican Gen. Antonio López de Santa Anna on April 21, 1836, to win Texas' independence from Mexico. The park is original site of Texans' camp acquired in 1883. Subsequent acquisitions made in 1897, 1899, and 1985. Park transferred to TPW in 1965. Park registered as National Historic Landmark. Elevator ride to observation tower near top of monument; museum. Monument known as tallest free-standing concrete structure in the world at the time it was erected. Interpretive trail around battleground. Adjacent to park is the U.S.S. *Texas*, commissioned in 1914. The battleship, the only survivor of the dreadnought class and the only surviving veteran of two world wars, was donated to the people of Texas by U.S. Navy. Ship was moored in the Houston Ship Channel at the San Jacinto Battleground on San Jacinto Day, 1948. Extensive repairs were done 1988-1990. Some renovation is ongoing, but ship is open for tours. Ship closed Christmas Eve and Christmas Day.

SEA RIM STATE PARK IN JEFFERSON COUNTY, 20 miles south of Port Arthur, off TX 87, contains 4,141 acres of marshland and 5.2 miles of Gulf beach shoreline, acquired from private owners in 1972. It is prime wintering area for waterfowl. Wetlands also shelter such wildlife as river otter, nutria, alligator, mink, muskrat. Camping, fishing, swimming; wildlife observation; nature trail; boating. Airboat tours of marsh. Near McFaddin National Wildlife Refuge.

SEBASTOPOL HOUSE HISTORIC SITE at 704 Zorn Street in Seguin, Guadalupe County, was acquired by purchase in 1976 from Seguin Conservation Society; approximately 2.2 acres. Built about 1856 by Col. Joshua W. Young of limecrete, concrete made from local gravel and lime, the Greek Revival-style house, which was restored to its 1880 appearance by the TPW, is on National Register of Historic Places. Tours available Friday and Sunday. Also of interest in the area is historic Seguin, founded 1838.

SEMINOLE CANYON STATE PARK & HISTORIC SITE in Val Verde County, nine miles west of Comstock off US 90, contains 2,172 acres; acquired by purchase from private owners 1973-1977. Fate Bell Shelter in canyon contains several important prehistoric Indian pictographs. Historic interpretive center. Tours of rock-art sites Wednesday-Sunday; also hiking, mountain biking, camping.

SHELDON LAKE STATE PARK AND ENVIRON-MENTAL LEARNING CENTER, 2,800 acres in Harris County on Garrett Road two miles east of Beltway 8. Acquired by purchase in 1952 from the City of Houston. Freshwater marsh habitat. Activities include nature study, birding, fishing. Wildscape gardens of native plants.

SOUTH LLANO RIVER STATE PARK, five miles south of Junction in Kimble County off US 377, is a 524-acre site donated to the TPW by a private owner

in 1977. Wooded bottomland along the winding South Llano River is the largest and oldest winter roosting site for the Rio Grande turkey in Central Texas. Roosting area closed to visitors October-March. Other animals include wood ducks, javelina, fox, beaver, bobcat, and armadillo. Camping, picnicking, tubing, swimming and fishing, hiking, mountain biking.

STARR FAMILY HOME STATE HISTORIC SITE, 3.1 acres at 407 W. Travis in Marshall, Harrison County. Greek Revival-style mansion, Maplecroft, built 1870-1871, was home to four generations of Starr family, powerful and economically influential Texans. Two other family homes also in park. Acquired by gift in 1976; additional land donated in 1982. Maplecroft is on National Register of Historic Places. Tours Friday–Sunday or by appointment. Special events during year.

STEPHEN F. AUSTIN STATE PARK is 663.3 acres along the Brazos River in San Felipe, Austin County, named for the "Father of Texas." The area was deeded by the San Felipe de Austin Corporation and the San Felipe Park Association in 1940. Site of township of San Felipe was seat of government where conventions of 1832 and 1833 and Consultation of 1835 held. These led to Texas Declaration of Independence. San Felipe was home of Stephen F. Austin and other famous early Texans; home of Texas' first Anglo newspaper (the *Texas Gazette*) founded in 1829; postal system of Texas originated here. Area called "Cradle of Texas Liberty." Museum. Camping, picnicking, golf, fishing, hiking.

TYLER STATE PARK is 985.5 acres found two miles north of IH 20 on FM 14 north of Tyler in Smith County. Includes 64-acre lake. The land was deeded by private owners in 1934–1935. Heavily wooded. Camping, hiking, fishing, boating, lake swimming. Nearby Tyler called Rose Capital of Nation, with Tyler Rose Garden and annual Tyler Rose Festival. Also in Tyler are Caldwell Children's Zoo and Goodman Museum.

VARNER-HOGG PLANTATION STATE HISTORIC SITE is 66 acres in Brazoria County, two miles north of West Columbia on FM 2852. Land originally owned by Martin Varner, a member of Stephen F. Austin's "Old Three Hundred" colony; later was home of Texas governor James Stephen Hogg. Property was deeded to the state in 1957 by Miss Ima Hogg, Gov. Hogg's daughter. First rum distillery in Texas established in 1829 by Varner. Mansion tours Tuesday through Saturday. Also picnicking, fishing.

VILLAGE CREEK STATE PARK, comprising 1,004 heavily forested acres, is located in Lumberton, Hardin County, ten miles north of Beaumont off US 69 and FM 3513. Purchased in 1979 from private owner, the park contains abundant flora and fauna typical of the Big Thicket area. The 200 species of birds found here include wood ducks, egrets, and herons. Activities include fishing, camping, canoeing, swimming, hiking, and picnicking. Nearby is the Big Thicket National Preserve.

WALTER UMPHREY STATE PARK is operated by Jefferson County on the south end of Pleasure Island off TX 82. For RV site reservations, contact SGS Causeway Bait & Tackle, 409-985-4811.

WASHINGTON-ON-THE-BRAZOS STATE HISTORIC SITE consists of 293.1 acres found seven miles southwest of Navasota in Washington County on TX 105 and FM 1155. Land acquired by deed from private owners in 1916, 1976, and 1996. Park includes the site of the signing on March 2, 1836, of the Texas Declaration of Independence from Mexico, as well as the site of the later signing of the Constitution of the Republic of Texas. In 1842 and 1845, the land included the capitol of the Republic. Star of the Republic Museum. Activities include picnicking and birding. Barrington Living History Farm is the home of Anson Jones, the last president of the Republic of Texas. Activities are guided by entries that Jones made in his daybook while living there. For more information: call 916-878-2214 or email office@wheretexas-becametexas.org.

ZARAGOZA BIRTHPLACE STATE HISTORIC SITE is located across the river from Goliad SP. Gen. Ignacio Zaragoza was the Mexican national hero who led troops in the fight for Mexican independence against the French at historic Battle of Puebla on May 5, 1862. The nearby Zaragoza statue was donated by the people of Puebla, Mexico. Also found nearby is Presidio la Bahía, which was originally constructed in 1721 near Matagorda Bay and moved to the present site in 1749. Adjacent is a memorial monument, marking the common burial site of Col. Fannin and his men, victims of Goliad massacre (1836).

Recreation in State Forests

All Texas State Forests are game sanctuaries with no firearms or hunting allowed. For general information about the Texas State Forests, see page 74 in the Environment chapter.

I.D. Fairchild State Forest

Located in Cherokee County, recreation includes hiking, horseback riding, picnicking, wildlife viewing, and biking. Special attractions are a historical fire tower site with plaque, Red Cockaded Woodpecker Management Area, and a pond with picnic area. Forest management demonstration sites throughout the forest. There are no restroom facilities in this forest.

Open year-round during daylight hours. Obtain information and maps at the Jacksonville District Office, 1015 SE Loop 456 or call (903) 586-7545 weekdays.

W. Goodrich Jones State Forest

Recreational opportunities in this forest, located in Montgomery County, include bird watching, hiking, horseback riding, picnicking, wildlife viewing, and biking.

Special attractions include Sweetleaf Nature Trail with State Champion Sweetleaf Tree, Red Cockaded Woodpecker Management Area, two small lakes with limited fishing, and picnicking. Forest management demonstration sites throughout the forest.

Open year-round during daylight hours. Information, maps, permits, and restrooms available at the Conroe District Office on FM 1488, 1.5 miles west of I-45. Call (936) 273-2261 for information.

John Henry Kirby Memorial State Forest

Located in Tyler County, forest resource educational opportunities at this forest include demonstrations and nature study. Group education tours available by appointment. Recreational opportunities include hiking, picnicking, bird and wildlife watching. Special attractions are forest management demonstration sites, small picnic area, and John Henry Kirby Monument.

Open year-round to foot traffic during daylight hours. Contact the district office prior to entry. Special arrangements are needed for vehicle access. Information and maps can be obtained at the Olive District Office on Hwy. 69 north of Kountze or by calling (409) 246-2484 weekdays. No restroom facilities are available in this forest.

Masterson State Forest

All use of this forest in Jasper County is by reservation only. Group resource education tours are available by appointment. No public facilities are available. Information and maps can be obtained at the Kirbyville District Office, FM 82, 4.5 miles southeast of Kirbyville; call weekdays at (409) 423-2890.

E.O. Siecke State Forest

Recreational opportunities in this Newton County forest include hiking, bird watching, nature study, horseback riding, picnicking, and wildlife viewing.

Special attractions are a historic fire tower, the oldest slash pine stand in Texas, and a trout creek. Forest management demonstration sites throughout.

Open year-round during daylight hours. Limited access by vehicle. Information, maps, and restrooms are available at the Kirbyville District Office, located at the state forest on FM 82, 4.5 miles southeast of Kirbyville. Call (409) 423-2890 weekdays for information. ☆

Recreational Facilities, Corps of Engineers Lakes, 2019

Reservoir	Swim Beaches	Boat Ramps	Picnic Sites	Camp Sites	Group Camping	Rental Cabins
Aquilla		★				
Bardwell	★	★	★	★	★	
Belton	★	★	★	★	★	★
Benbrook	★	★	★	★	★	★
Buffalo Bayou	★		★	★		★
Canyon	★	★	★	★	★	
Cooper	★	★	★	★	★	★
Georgetown	★	★	★	★	★	
Granger	★	★	★	★	★	
Grapevine	★	★	★	★	★	★
Hords Creek	★	★	★	★	★	
Joe Pool	★	★	★			★
Lake O' the Pines	★	★	★	★	★	
Lavon	★	★	★	★	★	
Lewisville	★	★	★	★		★
Navarro Mills	★	★	★	★		
O.C. Fisher		★	★	★		
Pat Mayse		★	★	★		★
Proctor	★	★	★	★	★	
Ray Roberts	★	★	★	★	★	
Sam Rayburn	★	★	★	★	★	★
Somerville	★	★	★	★	★	★
Stillhouse Hollow	★	★	★	★		
Texoma	★	★	★	★	★	★
Town Bluff	★	★	★	★		
Waco	★	★	★	★	★	★
Wallisville		★	★			
Whitney	★	★	★	★	★	★
Wright Patman	★	★	★	★	★	

Source: U.S. Army Corps of Engineers

Murals at the Chamizal National Memorial in El Paso. Photo by Ken Lund (CC).

National Parks, Historic Sites, Recreation Areas

Source: U.S. Dept of Interior, https://www.nps.gov/state/tx/index.htm

Below is a list of facilities and activities that can be enjoyed at Texas' two national parks, a national seashore, a biological preserve, a marine sanctuary, and several historic sites, memorials, and recreation areas in Texas. Most are under supervision of the **U.S. Department of Interior**. Recreational opportunities in the state and national forests and national grasslands in Texas are under the jurisdiction of the **U.S. Department of Agriculture**.

ALIBATES FLINT QUARRIES NATIONAL MONUMENT consists of 1,371 acres in Potter County. For more than 10,000 years, pre-Columbian Indians dug agatized limestone from the quarries to make projectile points, knives, scrapers, and other tools. The area is presently undeveloped. You may visit the flint quarries on guided walking tours with a park ranger. Tours are at 10:00 a.m. and 2:00 p.m. from Memorial Day to Labor Day. Off-season tours can be arranged by writing to Lake Meredith National Recreation Area, Box 1460, Fritch 79036, or by calling 806-857-3151.

AMISTAD NATIONAL RECREATION AREA is located on the U.S. side of Amistad Reservoir, an international reservoir on the Texas-Mexico border. The 57,292-acre park's attractions include boating, water skiing, swimming, fishing, camping, and archaeological sites. If lake level is normal, visitors can see 4,000-year-old prehistoric pictographs in Panther and Parida caves, which are accessible only by boat. Check with park before visiting. The area is one of the densest concentrations of Archaic rock art in North America — more than 300 sites. Commercial campgrounds, motels, and restaurants nearby. Marinas located at Diablo East and Rough Canyon. Open year round. NPS Administration, 4121 Hwy. 90 W, Del Rio 78840; 830-775-7491.

BIG BEND NATIONAL PARK, established in 1944, has spectacular mountain and desert scenery and a variety of unusual geological structures. It is the nation's largest protected area of Chihuahuan Desert. Located in the great bend of the Rio Grande, the 801,000-acre park, which is part of the international boundary between the United States and Mexico, was designated a U.S. Biosphere Reserve in 1976. Hiking, birding, and float trips are popular. Numerous campsites are located in park, and the Chisos Mountain Lodge has accommodations for approximately 345 guests. Write for reservations to National Park Concessions, Inc., Big Bend National Park, Texas 79834; 915-477-2291; www.chisosmountainslodge.com. Park open year-round; facilities most crowded during spring break. PO Box 129, Big Bend National Park 79834; 915-477-2251.

BIG THICKET NATIONAL PRESERVE, established in 1974, consists of 15 separate units totaling 97,000 acres of diverse flora and fauna, often nicknamed the "biological crossroads of North America." The preserve, which includes parts of seven East Texas counties, has been designated an "International Biosphere Reserve" by the United Nations Educational, Scientific and Cultural Organization (UNESCO). The preserve includes four different ecological systems: Southeastern swamps, Eastern forests, Central Plains, and Southwestern deserts. The visitor information station is located on FM 420, seven miles north of Kountze; phone 409-951-6725. Open daily from 9 a.m. to 5 p.m. Naturalist activities are available by reservation only; reservations are made through the station.

Eight trails, ranging in length from one-half mile to 18 miles, visit a variety of forest communities. The two shortest trails are handicapped-accessible. Trails are open year-round, but flooding may occur after heavy rains. Horses permitted on the Big Sandy Horse Trail only. Boating and canoeing are popular on preserve corridor units. Park headquarters are at 3785 Milam, Beaumont 77701; 409-246-2337.

CHAMIZAL NATIONAL MEMORIAL, established in 1963 and opened to the public in 1973, stands as a monument to Mexican-American friendship and goodwill. The memorial, on 52 acres in El Paso, commemorates the peaceful settlement on Aug. 29, 1963, of a 99-year-old boundary dispute between the United States and Mexico. Chamizal uses the visual and performing arts as a medium of interchange, helping people better understand not only other cultures but their own, as well. It hosts a variety of programs throughout the year, including: the fall Chamizal Festival musical event; the Siglo de Oro drama festival (early March); the Oñate Historical Festival celebrating the First Thanksgiving (April); and Music Under the Stars (Sundays, June-August). The park has a 1.8-mile walking trail and picnic areas. Phone: 915-532-7273.

EL CAMINO REAL DE LOS TEJAS was designated a National Historic Trail in 2004. It traces the "royal road" from Mexico to the Red River Valley, established when the area was under Spanish rule. The full route stretched over 2,500 miles, down to Mexico City, and connected to Spanish missions and posts along the way to Los Adaes, the first capital of the Texas province. Today's trail travels many roads, the longest straight route being TX 21 to Hwy 6 in Louisiana, connecting parks, historic sites, and museums along the way. The website, **https://www.nps.gov/elte/index.htm**, has tools to help you plan your trip, and photos and videos to learn more about travelers in the past.

EL CAMINO REAL DE TIERRA ADENTRO became a National Historic Trail in 2000. This royal road brought travelers from Mexico City through what is now El Paso and north into New Mexico, ending near Santa Fe, which was one of the capitals of New Mexico under Spanish rule. This path takes travelers to historic sites and museums along Interstate 25. Learn more and plan your trip at **https://www.nps.gov/elca/index.htm**.

FLOWER GARDEN BANKS NATIONAL MARINE SANCTUARY was named after the brightly colored sponges, plants, and other marine life found in the area. The reefs were discovered by snapper and grouper fishermen in the early 1900s. Situated 70–115 miles offshore, the sanctuary is only accessible by boat, so divers interested in visiting can book dive charters that depart from numerous Texas ports, including: Galveston, Freeport, Sabine Pass, and Surfside. The sanctuary protects three separate areas: East Flower Garden Bank and West Flower Garden Bank were designed as a sanctuary under the National Marine Sanctuary Act in 1992, and the algal-sponge communities of Stetson Bank were added to the sanctuary in 1996. Exceptional underwater visibility allows divers to experience spectacular sights, such as giant coral heads, schools of fish, eagle and manta rays, and even majestic whale sharks during summer visits to the area. The banks of the sanctuary include more than a dozen moored dive sites, with typical dive profiles of 70–130 feet. Several ports that offer dive trips are also home to commercial fishing charters for anglers wanting to fish the Flower Garden and Stetson Banks. Snappers, jacks, barracuda, and wahoo are just a few of the fish commonly caught by sportfishing enthusiasts. On the web: flowergarden.noaa.gov.

FORT DAVIS NATIONAL HISTORIC SITE in Jeff Davis County was a key post in the West Texas defense system, guarding immigrants and tradesmen on the San Antonio-El Paso road from 1854 to 1891. At one time, Fort Davis was manned by black troops, called "Buffalo Soldiers" (because of their curly hair), who fought with great distinction in the Indian Wars. Henry O. Flipper, the first black graduate of West Point, served at Fort Davis in the early 1880s. The 474-acre historic site is located on the north edge of the town of Fort Davis in the Davis Mountains, the second-highest mountain range in the state. The site includes a museum, an auditorium with daily audio-visual programs, restored and refurnished buildings, picnic area, and hiking trails. Open year-round except Christmas Day. PO Box 1379, Fort Davis 79734; 915-426-3224.

GUADALUPE MOUNTAINS NATIONAL PARK, established in 1972, includes 86,416 acres in Hudspeth and Culberson counties. The park contains one of the most extensive fossil reefs on record. Deep canyons cut through this reef and provide a rare opportunity for geological study. Special points of interest are McKittrick Canyon, a fragile riparian environment, and Guadalupe Peak, the highest in Texas. Camping, hiking on 80 miles of trails, Frijole Ranch Museum, summer amphitheater programs. Orientation, free information, and natural history exhibits available at Visitor Center. Open year-round. Lodging at Van Horn, Texas, and White's City or Carlsbad, NM. HC 60, Box 400, Salt Flat 79847; 915-828-3251.

LAKE MEREDITH NATIONAL RECREATION AREA, 30 miles northeast of Amarillo, centers on a reservoir on the Canadian River, in Moore, Hutchinson, and Potter counties. The 50,000-acre recreational area is popular for water-based activities. Boat ramps, picnic areas, unimproved campsites. Commercial lodging and trailer hookups available in nearby towns. Open year-round. PO Box 1460, Fritch 79036; 806-857-3151.

LYNDON B. JOHNSON NATIONAL HISTORICAL PARK includes two separate districts 14 miles apart. The Johnson City District comprises the boyhood home of the 36th president of United States and the Johnson Settlement, where his grandparents resided during the late 1800s. The LBJ Ranch District can be visited only by taking the National Park Service bus tour starting at the LBJ State Historic Site. The tour includes the reconstructed LBJ Birthplace, old school, family cemetery, show barn, and a view of the Texas White House. Site in Blanco and Gillespie counties was established in 1969 and contains 1,570 acres, 674 of which are federal. Open year-round except Thanksgiving, Christmas Day, and New Year's Day. No camping on site; commercial campgrounds, motels in area. PO Box 329, Johnson City 78636; 830-868-7128.

PADRE ISLAND NATIONAL SEASHORE consists of a 67.5-mile stretch of a barrier island along the Gulf Coast; noted for white-sand beaches, excellent fishing, and abundant bird and marine life. Contains 133,000 acres in Kleberg, Willacy, and Kenedy counties. Open year-round. One paved campground (fee charged)

The parade ground at Fort Davis National Historic Site in Jeff Davis County. Photo by Robert Plocheck.

located north of Malaquite Beach; unpaved (primitive) campground area south on beach. Five miles of beach are accessible by regular vehicles; 55 miles are accessible only by 4x4 vehicles. Off-road vehicles prohibited. Camping permitted in two designated areas. Commercial lodging available on the island outside the National Seashore boundaries. PO Box 181300, Corpus Christi 78480; 361-949-8068.

PALO ALTO BATTLEFIELD NATIONAL HISTORICAL PARK preserves the site of the first major battle in the Mexican-American War. Fought on May 8, 1846, near Brownsville, it is recognized for the innovative use of light or "flying" artillery. Participating in the battle were three future presidents: General Zachary Taylor and Ulysses S. Grant on the U.S. side, and Gen. Mariano Arista on the Mexican. Historical markers are located at the junction of Farm-to-Market roads 1847 and 511. Access to the 3,400-acre site is currently limited. Exhibits at the visitors center interpret the battle as well as the causes and consequences of the war. Phone 956-541-2785.

RIO GRANDE WILD AND SCENIC RIVER is a 196-mile strip on the U.S. shore of the Rio Grande in the Chihuahuan Desert, beginning in Big Bend National Park and continuing downstream to the Terrell-Val Verde county line. There are federal facilities in Big Bend National Park only. Contact Big Bend National Park for more information.

SAN ANTONIO MISSIONS NATIONAL HISTORICAL PARK preserves four Spanish Colonial Missions — Concepción, San José, San Juan, and Espada — as well as the Espada dam and aqueduct, which are two of the best-preserved remains in the United States of the Spanish Colonial irrigation system, and Rancho de las Cabras, the colonial ranch of Mission Espada. All were crucial elements to Spanish settlement on the Texas frontier. When Franciscan attempts to establish a chain of missions in East Texas in the late 1600s failed, the Spanish Crown ordered three missions transferred to the San Antonio River valley in 1731. The missions are located within the city limits of San Antonio, while Rancho de las Cabras is located 25 miles south in Wilson County near Floresville. The four missions, which are still in use as active parishes, are open to the public from 9 a.m. to 5 p.m. daily except Thanksgiving, Christmas, and New Year's. Public roadways connect the sites; a hike-bike trail is being developed. The visitor center for the mission complex is at San José. For more information, write to 2202 Roosevelt Ave., San Antonio 78210; 210-932-1001.

WACO MAMMOTH NATIONAL MONUMENT

was designated in 2015 and is the newest Texas unit of the National Park System. This paleontological site represents the nation's only recorded discovery of a nursery herd of Columbian mammoths. Visitors can view "in situ" fossils including female mammoths, a bull mammoth, and a camel that lived approximately 67,000 years ago. The park is managed in partnership by the National Park Service, the City of Waco, and Baylor University. Welcome Center located at 6220 Steinbeck Bend Road. It is open Tuesday through Saturday, except Thanksgiving, Christmas Day, and New Year's Day. ☆

National Forests

For general information about the National Forests and National Grasslands, see page 73 in the Environment chapter.

An estimated 3 million people visit the National Forests in Texas for recreation annually. These visitors use established recreation areas primarily for hiking, picnicking, swimming, fishing, camping, boating, and nature enjoyment. In the following list of some of these areas, Forest Service Road is abbreviated FSR:

Angelina National Forest

Boykin Springs, 14 miles southeast of Zavalla, has a 6-acre lake and facilities for hiking, swimming, picnicking, fishing, and camping. Bouton Lake, 14 miles southeast of Zavalla off Texas 63 and FSR 303, has a 9-acre natural lake with primitive facilities for camping, picnicking, and fishing.

Caney Creek on Sam Rayburn Reservoir, ten miles southeast of Zavalla off FM 2743, offers fishing, boating, and camping. Sandy Creek, 15.5 miles east of Zavalla on Sam Rayburn, offers fishing, boating, and camping.

The Sawmill Hiking Trail is 2.5 miles long and winds from Aldridge Sawmill trailhead to Boykin Springs Recreation Area.

Davy Crockett National Forest

Ratcliff Lake, 25 miles west of Lufkin on TX 7, is a 45-acre lake with facilities for picnicking, hiking, swimming, boating, fishing, and camping. There is also an amphitheater.

The 20-mile-long 4C National Recreation Trail connects Ratcliff Recreation Area to the Neches Bluff overlook. The Piney Creek Horse Trail is 54 miles long and can be entered approximately 5.5 miles south of Kennard off County Road 4625. There are two horse camps along this trail system.

Sabine National Forest

Indian Mounds Recreation Area, located 12 miles southeast of Hemphill off FM 83, has camping facilities and a boat ramp. Lakeview, on Toledo Bend Reservoir, 21 miles from Pineland, offers camping, hiking, and fishing and can be reached via Texas 87, FM 2928, and FSR 120.

Ragtown, 26 miles southeast of Center and accessible by Texas 87 and Texas 139, County Road 3184, and FSR 132, is also on Toledo Bend and has facilities for hiking, camping, and boating. Red Hill Lake, three miles north of Milam on Texas 87, has facilities for fishing, swimming,

camping, and picnicking. Willow Oak Recreation Area on Toledo Bend, 13 miles south of Hemphill off Texas 87, offers fishing, picnicking, camping, and boating. Trail Between the Lakes is 28 miles long from Lakeview Recreation Area on Toledo Bend to U.S. 96 near Sam Rayburn Reservoir.

Sam Houston National Forest

Cagle Recreation Area is located on the shores of Lake Conroe, 50 miles north of Houston and five miles west of I-45 at FM 1375. Cagle offers camping, fishing, hiking, birding, and other recreational opportunities in a forested lakeside setting.

Double Lake, three miles south of Coldspring on FM 2025, has facilities for picnicking, hiking, camping, swimming, and fishing.

Stubblefield Lake, 15 miles west-northwest of New Waverly off Texas 1375 on the shores of Lake Conroe, has facilities for camping, hiking, picnicking, and fishing.

The Lone Star Hiking Trail, approximately 128 miles long, is located in Sam Houston National Forest in Montgomery, Walker, and San Jacinto counties.

National Grasslands

North Texas

Lake Davy Crockett Recreation Area (**Caddo National Grassland**), 12 miles north of Honey Grove (Fannin County) on FM 409, just off FM 100, has a boat-launch ramp and camping sites on a 450-acre lake.

Coffee Mill Lake Recreation Area has camping and picnicking facilities on a 650-acre lake. This area is four miles west of Lake Davy Crockett Recreation Area.

The Caddo Multi-Use Trail system, also four miles west of Lake Crockett, offers camping, hiking, and horseback riding on 35 miles of trails.

Black Creek Lake Recreation Area (**Lyndon B. Johnson National Grassland**) is eight miles north of Decatur (Wise County) and has camping, picnic facilities, and a boat-launch ramp on a 35-acre lake.

Cottonwood Lake, 13 miles north of Decatur, is around 40 acres and offers hiking, boating, and fishing.

The Cottonwood-Black Creek Hiking Trail is four miles long and connects the two lakes. It is rated moderately difficult. There are nearly 75 miles of multipurpose trails that run in the Cottonwood Lake vicinity.

TADRA Horse Trail, ten miles north of Decatur, has camping and 75 miles of horse trails. Restrooms and parking facilities are available.

West Texas

Lake McClellan (**McClellan Creek National Grassland**) in Gray County and Lake Marvin, which is part of the **Black Kettle National Grassland** in Hemphill County, receive more than 28,000 recreational visitors annually.

These areas provide camping, picnicking, fishing, birdwatching, and boating facilities. Concessionaires operate facilities at Lake McClellan, and a nominal fee is charged for use of the areas.

At the **Rita Blanca National Grassland** (Dallam County), about 4,500 visitors a year enjoy picnicking and hunting. Thompson Grove Picnic Area is 14 miles northeast of Texline. ☆

Visiting the sites in Texas this year? Submit your photos to our Flickr group:
https://www.flickr.com/groups/texasalmanac/

Your photo might be chosen to be on our website, or even in our next book!

National Natural Landmarks in Texas

Source: National Natural Landmarks Directory, https://www.nps.gov/subjects/nnlandmarks/nation.htm

Formations in the Cave Without a Name. Photo courtesy The Lyda Hill Texas Collection of Photographs, Library of Congress.

Twenty Texas natural areas have been listed on the **National Registry of Natural Landmarks**.

The registry was established by the Secretary of the Interior in 1962 to identify and encourage the preservation of geological and ecological features that represent nationally significant examples of the nation's natural heritage.

The registry currently lists a total of 599 national natural landmarks. Below is the list of those landmarks found in Texas, as of August 2019, and their characteristics (year of listing in parentheses).

ATTWATER PRAIRIE CHICKEN PRESERVE: Colorado County, 55 miles west of Houston in the national wildlife refuge, is rejuvenated Gulf Coastal Prairie, which is habitat for Attwater's prairie chickens. (1968)

BAYSIDE RESACA AREA: Cameron County, Laguna Atascosa National Wildlife Refuge, 28 miles north of Brownsville. Excellent example of a resaca, supporting coastal salt-marsh vegetation and rare birds. (1980)

CATFISH CREEK: Anderson County, 20 miles northwest of Palestine, is undisturbed riparian habitat. (1983)

CAVE WITHOUT A NAME: Kendall County, 12 miles northeast of Boerne, is a cave of several rooms that are filled with spectacular formations. (2009)

CAVERNS OF SONORA: Sutton County, 16 miles southwest of Sonora, has unusual geological formations. (1965)

DEVIL'S SINK HOLE: Edwards County, 9 miles northeast of Rocksprings, is a deep, bell-shaped, collapsed limestone sink with cave passages extending below the regional water table. (1972)

DINOSAUR VALLEY: Somervell County, in Dinosaur Valley State Park, four miles west of Glen Rose, contains fossil footprints exposed in bed of Paluxy River. (1968)

ENCHANTED ROCK: Gillespie and Llano counties, 12 miles southwest of Oxford, is a classic batholith, composed of coarse-grained pink granite. (1971)

EZELL'S CAVE: Hays County, within the city limits of San Marcos, houses at least 36 species of cave creatures. (1971)

FORT WORTH NATURE CENTER AND REFUGE: Tarrant County, within the Fort Worth city limits. Contains remnants of the Grand Prairie and a portion of the Cross Timbers, with limestone ledges and marshes. Refuge for migratory birds and other wildlife, and home to 11 buffalo raised by the center's staff. Educational programs offered for youth and adults. Self-guided hiking. (1980)

GREENWOOD CANYON: Montague County, along a tributary of Braden Branch, is a rich source of Cretaceous fossils. (1975)

HIGH PLAINS NATURAL AREA: Randall County, Buffalo Lake National Wildlife Refuge, 26 miles southwest of Amarillo, is a grama-buffalo shortgrass area. (1980)

LITTLE BLANCO RIVER BLUFF: Blanco County, comprises an Edwards Plateau limestone-bluff plant community. (1982)

LONGHORN CAVERN, BURNET COUNTY: 11 miles southwest of Burnet. Formed at least 450 million years ago, cave contains several unusual geologic features. (1971)

LOST MAPLES STATE NATURAL AREA: Bandera and Real counties, 61 miles northwest of San Antonio, contains Edwards Plateau fauna and flora, including unusual bigtooth maple. Largest known nesting population of golden-cheeked warbler. (1980)

MULESHOE NATIONAL WILDLIFE REFUGE: Bailey County, 59 miles northwest of Lubbock, contains playa lakes and typical High Plains shortgrass grama grasslands. (1980)

NATURAL BRIDGE CAVERNS: Comal County, 16 miles west of New Braunfels, is a multilevel cavern system, with beautiful and unusual geological formations. (1971)

ODESSA METEOR CRATER: Ector County, 10 miles southwest of Odessa, is one of only two known meteor sites in the country. (1965)

PALO DURO CANYON STATE PARK: Armstrong and Randall counties, 22 miles south-southeast of Amarillo. Cut by waters of the Red River, it contains cross-sectional views of sedimentary rocks representing four geological periods. (1976)

SANTA ANA NATIONAL WILDLIFE REFUGE: Hidalgo County, 7 miles south of Alamo, is a lowland forested area with jungle-like vegetation. It is habitat for more than 300 species of birds and some rare mammals. (1966) ☆

Sea Center Texas

Source: Texas Parks and Wildlife Department, http://tpwd.texas.gov/spdest/visitorcenters/seacenter/

The Texas Parks and Wildlife Department operates Sea Center Texas: a marine aquarium, fish hatchery, and nature center that educates and entertains visitors. It is located in Lake Jackson, 50 miles south of Houston, off of Texas 288.

The visitor center opened in 1996 and has interpretive displays, a "touch tank," and native Texas habitat exhibits depicting a salt marsh, bay, jetty, reef, and open Gulf waters. The Gulf aquarium features "Cooper," a 50-pound grouper; a green moray eel; a nurse shark; and other offshore species.

Sea Center is said to be the world's largest redfish hatchery and is one of three marine hatcheries on the Texas coast that produce juvenile red drum and spotted seatrout for enhancing natural populations in Texas bays. The hatchery can produce 15 million juvenile fish yearly and is a testing ground for production of other marine species, such as flounder. Hatchery tours and educational programs are available by reservation.

A half-acre youth fishing pond introduces youngsters to saltwater fishing through scheduled activities. The pond is handicap accessible and stocked with a variety of marine fish.

The center's wetland area is part of the Great Texas Coastal Birding Trail, where more than 150 species of birds have been identified. They include one acre of salt marsh and three acres of freshwater marsh. Damselflies, dragonflies, butterflies, turtles, and frogs can be sighted off the boardwalk, and an outdoor pavilion is adjacent to butterfly and hummingbird gardens.

Sea Center Texas is operated in partnership with The Dow Chemical Company and the Coastal Conservation Association. Admission and parking are free. Hours are 9 a.m. to 4 p.m. Tuesday through Saturday, and 1 p.m. to 4 p.m. Sunday, except some holidays. Reservations are required for group tours, nature tours, and hatchery tours. For more information: 979-292-0100, or email Seacenter@tpwd.texas.gov. ☆

Texas State Aquarium

Sources: New Handbook of Texas Online; Texas State Aquarium, https://www.texasstateaquarium.org/

The Texas State Aquarium, 7.3 acres on the southernmost tip of Corpus Christi Beach in Corpus Christi, is operated by the Texas State Aquarium Association, a nonprofit, self-supporting organization established in 1978. Efforts to fund a public aquarium in South Texas began in 1952, and several nonprofit organizations founded over the years eventually grew into the Texas State Aquarium Association.

Since 1978, the association has raised more than $28 million in private and public funding to build and operate the aquarium. The City of Corpus Christi provided $14.5 million, including $4 million from a bond issue.

In 1985, the 69th Texas Legislature declared the project the "Official Aquarium of the State of Texas."

The Jesse H. and Mary Gibbs Jones Gulf of Mexico Exhibit Building was completed in July 1990. In 2003, Dolphin Bay opened for Atlantic bottlenose dolphins and the Environmental Discovery Center opened, featuring a library, a Family Learning Center, and the Flint Hills Resources Distance Learning Studio.

The aquarium's exhibits and research focus on the plants and animals of the Gulf of Mexico and the Caribbean. It is the first U.S. facility to do so.

The aquarium is open daily 9 a.m. to 5 p.m., Labor Day through March 1, and until 6 p.m. March 1 through Labor Day. There are admission and parking fees.

For more information, call 1-800-477-GULF. ☆

Children enjoying the sights at the Texas State Aquarium. Photo by The McGee (CC).

Col. Christopher Sallese, U.S. Army Corps of Engineers Galveston District commander, welcomes birders to the Corps Woods on the first day of FeatherFest. Photo by U.S. Army Corps of Engineers.

Birding in Texas

World Birding Center

The World Birding Center comprises nine birding education centers and observation sites in the Lower Rio Grande Valley designed to protect wildlife habitat and offer visitors a view of more than 500 species of birds. The center has partnered with the Texas Parks and Wildlife Department, the U.S. Fish and Wildlife Service ,and nine communities to turn 10,000 acres back into natural areas for birds, butterflies and other wildlife.

This area in Cameron, Hidalgo, and Starr counties is a natural migratory path for millions of birds that move between the Americas. The nine WBC sites listed here are situated along the border with Mexico. Learn more at **http://www.theworldbirdingcenter.com/**.

Bentsen–Rio Grande Valley State Park

This is the World Birding Center Headquarters and comprises the 760-acre Bentsen-RGV State Park and 1,700 acres of adjoining federal refuge land near Mission.

The site offers: daily tram service; four nature trails ranging in length from one-quarter mile to two miles; 2-story-high Hawk Observation Tower with a 210-foot-long handicapped access ramp; two observation decks; two accessible bird blinds; primitive camping sites (by reservation); rest areas; picnic sites with tables; exhibit hall; park store; coffee bar; meeting room (available for rental); catering kitchen; bike rentals (1- and 2-seat bikes). Access within the park is by foot, bike, and tram only; (956) 585-1107.

Hours: 6 a.m. to 10 p.m., seven days a week.

Edinburg Scenic Wetlands

This 40-acre wetlands in Edinburg is an oasis for water-loving birds, butterflies, and other wildlife. The site is currently offering: walking trails, nature tours, and classes; (956) 381-9922.

Hours: 8 a.m.–5 p.m., Monday through Wednesday; 8 a.m.–6 p.m., Thursday through Saturday. Closed Sunday.

Estero Llano Grande State Park

This 176-acre refuge in Weslaco attracts a wide array of South Texas wildlife with its varied landscape of shallow lake, woodlands, and thorn forest; (956) 565-3919.

Hours: 8 a.m.–5 p.m., Monday through Friday; 8 a.m.–7:30 p.m., Saturday and Sunday.

Harlingen Arroyo Colorado

This site in Harlingen is connected by an arroyo waterway, as well as hike-and-bike trails meandering through the city, Hugh Ramsey Nature Park to the east and the Harlingen Thicket to the west; (956) 427-8873.

Hours: Office, 8 a.m.–5:00 p.m., Monday through Friday. Nature trails are open seven days a week, sunrise to sunset.

Old Hidalgo Pumphouse

Visitors to this museum in Hidalgo on the Rio Grande can learn about the steam-driven irrigation pumps that transformed Hidalgo County into a year-round farming area. The museum's grounds feature hummingbird gardens, walking trails, and historic tours; (956) 843-8686.

Hours: 10 a.m.–5 p.m., Monday through Friday; 1 p.m.–5 p.m., Sunday. Closed Saturday.

Quinta Mazatlan

This 1930s country estate in McAllen is a historic Spanish Revival adobe hacienda surrounded by lush tropical landscaping and native woodland. It is also an urban oasis, where quiet trails wind through more than 15 acres of birding habitat; (956) 688-3370.

Hours: 8 a.m.–5 p.m., Tuesday through Saturday. Open until sunset on Thursdays. Closed Mondays and holidays.

Resaca de la Palma State Park

More than 1,700 acres of newly opened wilderness near Brownsville, this site comprises the largest tract of native habitat in the World Birding Center network. The park offers birding tours and natural history tours. Admission is by appointment and reservation only; (956) 565-3919.

Roma Bluffs

History and nature meet on scenic bluffs above the Rio Grande, where the World Birding Center in Roma is located on the old plaza of a once-thriving steamboat port. Part of a national historic district, the WBC Roma Bluffs includes a riverside nature area of three acres in Starr County. The site offers: walking trails, canoe trips, birding tours, natural history tours, and classes; (956) 849-4930.

Hours: 8 a.m.–4 p.m., Tuesday through Saturday, although trails are open seven days a week and are free to the public.

South Padre Island Birding and Nature Center

At the southern tip of the world's longest barrier island, South Padre Island Birding and Nature Center is a slender thread of land between the shallow Laguna Madre and the Gulf of Mexico. This site offers: a nature trail, boardwalk, and birding tours; 1-800-SOPADRE.

Hours: 9 a.m.–5 p.m., seven days a week.

Great Texas Coastal Birding Trail

This trail winds its way through 43 Texas counties along the entire Texas coastal region. The trail was

A pyrrhuloxia, commonly known as the desert cardinal, in Falcon State Park. Photo by Tom Bunker (CC).

completed in April 2000 and is divided into upper, central, and lower coastal regions. It includes 308 wildlife-viewing sites and such amenities as boardwalks, parking pullouts, kiosks, observation platforms, and landscaping to attract native wildlife.

Color-coded maps are available, and signs mark each site. Trail maps contain information about the birds and habitats likely to be found at each site, the best season to visit, and food and lodging.

For information, contact: Nature Tourism Coordinator, Texas Parks and Wildlife Department, 4200 Smith School Road, Austin, TX 78744; (512) 389-4396.

On the web: **http://tpwd.texas.gov/huntwild/wildlife/ wildlife-trails/coastal.**

I-20 Wildlife Preserve and Jenna Welch Nature Study Center

The I-20 Wildlife Preserve is an 87-acre urban playa lake in its natural state in southwest Midland that opened in 2013. It was maintained for many years by the Midland Naturalists and other volunteers, including Jenna Welch, a birding enthusiast and a member of the group. It comprises 3.4 miles of hiking trails, including 1.45 miles of ADA-accessible trails, seven bird observation blinds, four teaching platforms, the 24-foot tall Hawk Observation Platform, and the Merritt Pavilion.

Jenna Welch Nature Study Center operates an educational outreach program to local schools and area colleges and universities. Land was acquired to build a facility to house the nature study center.

The preserve, at 2201 S. Midland Dr., Midland, 79701, is open to the public daily from dawn until dusk. For more information, call (432) 853-9453. On the web: **www.i20wildlifepreserve.org**. ☆

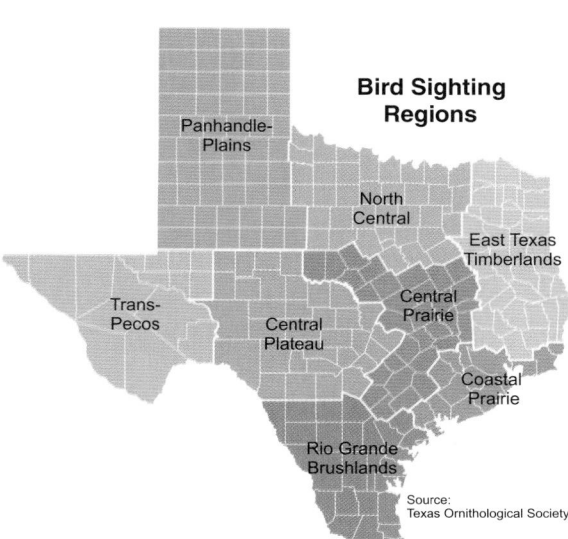

Bird Sighting Regions

Panhandle-Plains

North Central

East Texas Timberlands

Trans-Pecos

Central Plateau

Central Prairie

Coastal Prairie

Rio Grande Brushlands

Source: Texas Ornithological Society

Fairs, Festivals, and Special Events

Fairs, festivals, and other special events provide year-round recreation in Texas. Some are of national interest, while many attract visitors from across the state. Each county profile in the Counties section also lists events in the Recreation paragraph and following town names. Information here was furnished by event coordinators.

To have your town's event included here, submit your information in the form at:

www.TexasAlmanac.com/ListOurEvent

Abilene: West Texas Fair & Rodeo; September; 1700 Hwy. 36, 79602; www.taylorcountyexpocenter.com. Since 1897. rjohnson@expoctc.com. (325) 677-4376.

Albany: Fort Griffin Fandangle; June; PO Box 155, 76430; www.fortgriffinfandangle.org. Since 1938. info@fandangle.org. (325) 762-3838.

Alvarado: Johnson County Pioneers & Old Settlers Reunion; August; PO Box 217, 76009. Since 1893.

Amarillo: Tri-State Fair; September; 3301 SE 10th Ave., 79104; www.tristatefair.com. (806) 376-7767.

Anderson: Grimes County Fair; June; PO Box 435, 77830; www.grimescountyfair.com. (936)825-5995.

Angleton: Brazoria County Fair; October; PO Box 818, 77516; www.bcfa.org. Since 1939. (979) 849-6416.

Aransas Pass: Shrimporee; June, 130 W. Goodnight, 78336; www.aransaspass.org. Since 1949.

Athens: Texas Fiddlers' Asso. Reunion; May; Since 1932.

Austin: Rodeo Austin; March; 9100 Decker Lake Rd. 78724; www.rodeoaustin.com. Since 1937. Info@ rodeoaustin.com. (512) 919-3000.

Austin: Art City Austin; April; PO Box 5705, 78763; www.artcityaustin.org. info@artcityaustin.org. (512) 609.8587.

Bay City: Matagorda County Fair & Livestock Show; February; PO Box 1803, 77404; www.matagordacountyfair.com. Since 1945. mcfa@matagordacountyfair.com. (979) 245-2454.

Bay City: Bay City Rice Festival; September; PO Box 867; 77404; www.baycitylions.org. info@baycitylions.com.

Beaumont: South Texas State Fair; October; 7250 Wespark Cr., 77705; www.ymbl.org. Since 1943. info@ymbl.org. (409) 832-9991.

Bellville: Austin County Fair; October; PO Box 141, 77418; www.austincountyfair.com. ACFair@austincountyfair.com. (979) 865-5995.

Belton: 4th of July Celebration & PRCA Rodeo; July; PO Box 659, 76513; www.rodeobelton.com. (254) 939.3551.

Belton: Central Texas State Fair; Aug.-Sept.; PO Box 206, 76513; www.centraltexasstatefair.com. (254) 933-5353.

Big Spring: Howard County Fair; September; PO Box 2356, 79721; www.hcfair.org. Since 1973. howardcountyfairtx@gmail.com.

Boerne: Boerne Berges Fest; June; PO Box 748, 78006; www.bergesfest.com.

Boerne: Kendall County Fair; September (Labor Day Wknd.); PO Box 954, 78006; www.kcfa.org. Since 1906. info@kfca.org. (830) 249-2839.

Brenham: Washington County Fair; September; 1305 E. Blue Bell Rd., 77833; www.washingtoncofair.com. Since 1870. washingtoncofair@sbcglobal.net. (979) 836.4112.

Brownsville: Charro Days Fiesta; February; PO Box 3247, 78523; www.charrodaysfiesta.com. Since 1938. charrodaysfiesta@sbcglobal.net. (956) 542-4245.

Burnet: Burnet Bluebonnet Festival; April; 101 N. Pierce St., 78611; bluebonnetfestival.org. Since 1986. (512) 756-4297.

Burton: Cotton Gin Festival; April (3rd wknd.); PO Box 98; 77835; www.cottonginmuseum.org. Since 1990. texascottongin@gmail.com. (979) 289-3378.

Caldwell: Kolache Festival; September; 301 N. Main Street; www.burlesoncountytx.com. 77836; (979) 567-0000.

Caldwell: Burleson County Fair; September; PO Box 634, 77836; www.burlesoncountytx.com. (979) 567-3938.

Canyon: TEXAS! Outdoor Musical; June–August; 1514 5th Ave., 79015; www.texas-show.com. Since 1966. info@texas-show.com. (806) 655-2181.

Chappell Hill: Bluebonnet Festival; April; PO Box 547, 77426; chappellhillhistoricalsociety.com. chappellhill-festivals@gmail.com. (979) 203-1242.

Clifton: Norse Smorgasbord; November; 152 County Rd. 4145, 76634; www.oursaviorsnorse.org. oslcnorse1869@gmail.com. (254) 675-3962.

Clute: Great Texas Mosquito Festival; July; 100 Parkview Dr., 77531; www.mosquitofestival.com. Since 1981. (979) 265-8392.

Columbus: Colorado County Fair; September; PO Box 506, 78933; www.coloradocountyfair.org. info@coloradocountyfair.org. (979) 732-9266.

Conroe: Montgomery County Fair; March; PO Box 869, 77305; www.mcfa.org. Since 1957. (936) 760-3631.

Corpus Christi: Buc Days; April–May; PO Box 30404, 78463; www.bucdays.com. info@bucdays.com. (361) 882.3242.

Corsicana: Derrick Days; April; 301 S. Beaton St., 75110; www.derrickdays.com. Since 1976. (903) 654-4850.

Dalhart: XIT Rodeo & Reunion; August (1st full wknd.); www.xitrodeoreunion.com. Since 1937.

Dallas: State Fair of Texas; September–October; PO Box 150009, 75315; www.bigtex.com. Since 1886. info@bigtex.com. (214) 565-9931.

Decatur: Wise County Old Settlers Reunion; July (last full week).

De Leon: De Leon Peach & Melon Festival; August; PO Box 44, 76444; peachandmelonfestival.net. Since 1917. pmdeleon@cctc.net.

Denton: North Texas State Fair & Rodeo; August; 2217 N. Carroll Blvd., 76201; www.ntfair.com. Since 1929. info@ntfair.com. (940) 391-3452.

Edna: Jackson County Youth Fair; October; 284 Brackenridge Parkway, 77957; www.jcyf.org. Since 1949.

Ennis: National Polka Festival; May; PO Box 1177, 75120-1237; www.nationalpolkafestival.com. ennis4u@swbell.net.

Fairfield: Freestone County Fair; June; www.freestonecountyfairandrodeo.com.

Flatonia: Czhilispiel; October (4th full wknd.); PO Box 610, 78941; www.flatoniachamber.com. Since 1973. flatoniacofc@sbcglobal.net. (361) 865-3920.

Fort Worth: Pioneer Days; September; 131 E. Exchange Ave., Ste 100B, 76106; www.fortworthstockyards.org.

A roping event at the San Angelo Stock Show & Rodeo. Photo by Jonathan Cutrer (jcutrer.com).

Fort Worth: Southwestern Exposition & Livestock Show; January-February; PO Box 150, 76101; www.fwssr. com. Since 1896. contact@fwssr.com. (817) 877-2400.

Fredericksburg: Food and Wine Fest; October (4th Sat.); 703 N. Llano St., 78624; www.fbgfoodandwinefest. com. Since 1990. creativemarketing1975@gmail.com. (830) 997-8515.

Fredericksburg: Night in Old Fredericksburg; July; 302 E. Austin, 78624; www.gillespiefair.net. Since 1963. info@gillespiefair.com. (830) 997-2359.

Fredericksburg: Oktoberfest; October (1st wknd.); PO Box 222, 78624; www.oktoberfestinfbg.com. Since 1980. creativemarketing1975@gmail.com. (830) 997-4810.

Freer: Freer Rattlesnake Roundup; May; PO Box 717, 78357; www.therattlesnakeroundup.com. Since 1966. freercofc@yahoo.com. (361) 394-6891.

Galveston: Dickens on The Strand; December; 502 20th St., 77550; www.dickensonthestrand.org. Since 1973.

Galveston: Galveston Historic Homes Tour; May; 502 20th St., 77550-2014; www.galvestonhistory.org. Since 1974.

Gilmer: East Texas Yamboree; October; PO Box 854, 75644; www.yamboree.com. Since 1937. gilmerareachamber@gmail.com. (903) 843-2413.

Glen Flora: Wharton County Youth Fair; April; PO Box 167, 77443; www.whartoncountyyouthfair.org. Since 1976. wcyf@whartoncountyyouthfair.org. (979) 677-3350.

Graham: Art Splash on the Square; May.

Graham: Red, White & You Parade & Festivities; July; 608 Elm St.; 76450; www.visitgrahamtexas.com. (940) 549-0401.

Granbury: Annual July 4th Celebration; July; 116 W. Bridge St., 76048; www.granburychamber.com.

Granbury: Harvest Moon Festival; October; PO Box 2011 201 E. Pearl St., 76048; www.granburysquare.

com. Since 1977. granburyhgma@gmail.com. (682) 936-4550.

Grand Prairie: National Championship Pow-Wow; September; 2602 Mayfield Rd, 75052; www.tradersvillage.com. Since 1963. dfwinfo@tradersvillage.com. (972) 647-2331.

Grapevine: GrapeFest; September; 636 S. Main St., 76051; www.grapevinetexasusa.com. Since 1986. (800) 457-6338.

Greenville: Hunt County Fair; June; PO Box 1403, 75403; www.huntcountyfair.com. Since 1970. info@huntcountyfair.net. (903) 454-1503.

Groesbeck: Limestone County Fair; March–April; PO Box 965, 76642. limestonefair.org.

Hallettsville: Hallettsville Kolache Fest; September; PO Box 313, 77964; www.hallettsville.com. Since 1995.

Helotes: Helotes Cornyval; May (1st wknd.); PO Box 376, 78023; www.cornyval.com. Since 1967. cornyval@sbcglobal.net. (210) 695-2103.

Hempstead: Waller County Fair; September–October; PO Box 911, 77445. www.wallercountyfair.com. Since 1946. (979) 826-2825.

Hico: Hico Old Settler-Reunion; July; PO Box 93, 76457; www.hico-tx.com. Since 1887.

Hidalgo: BorderFest; March; PO Box 722; 78557; www.hidalgoborderfest.com.

Hondo: Medina County Fair; September (3rd wknd.); PO Box 4, 78861; www.medinacountyfair.net. Since 1980. havefun@medinacountyfair.net. (830) 426-5406.

Houston: Houston Livestock Show and Rodeo; March; PO Box 20070, 77225; www.rodeohouston.com. questions@rodeohouston.com. (832) 667-1134.

Hughes Springs: Wildflower Trails of Texas; April; PO Box 805, 75656; www.hughesspringstxusa.com. Since 1970. (903) 639-7519.

Huntsville: Walker County Fair & Rodeo; March–April; PO Box 1817, 77342; www.walkercountyfair.

com. Since 1979. wcfa@walkercountyfair.com. (936) 291-8763.

Ingram: The Official Texas State Arts & Crafts Fair; September; PO Box 489, 78025; txartsandcraftsfair.com. wgcash@hcaf.com. (830) 367-5121.

Jefferson: Historical Pilgrimage and Spring Festival; May (1st wknd.); PO Box 301, 75657-0301; www.jefferson-pilgrimage.com. Since 1947.

Johnson City: Blanco County Fair; August; PO Box 1257, 78636; www.bcfra.org. info@bcfra.org.

Kenedy: Bluebonnet Days; April; 205 S. 2nd St., 78119. kenedychamber.org. (830) 583-3223.

Kerrville: Kerr County Fair; October; PO Box 290842, 78029; www.kerrcountyfair.com. Since 1980. kcfa@kerrcountyfair.com. (830) 257-6833.

Kerrville: Kerrville Folk Festival; May–June; PO Box 291466, 78029; www.kerrvillefolkfestival.com. Since 1972. info@kerrville-music.com. (830) 257-3600.

Killeen: Take 190 WestArts Festival; 3601 S. WS Young Dr., 76542; www.take190west.com. info@take190west.com. (254) 501-3888.

La Grange: Fayette County Fair; September; PO Box 544, 78945; www.fayettecountyfairnet. Since 1926. info@fayettecountyfair.org. (979) 968-3911.

Laredo: Border Olympics; January–March; PO Box 450037, 78044; borderolympics.net. Since 1947.

Laredo: Laredo International Fair & Expo; March; PO Box 1770, 78043; www.laredofair.com. Since 1963. laredofair@att.net. (956) 722-9948.

Laredo: Washington's Birthday Celebration; January–February; 1819 E. Hillside Rd., 78041; www.wbcalaredo.com. Since 1898. wbca@wbcalaredo.org. (956) 722-0589.

Longview: Gregg County Fair & Exposition; September; 1511 Judson Rd., Ste. F, 75601; www.greggcountyfair.com. Since 1951. ayohe3184@gmail.com. (903) 753-4478.

Lubbock: 4th on Broadway Festival; July; PO Box 1643, 79408; www.broadwayfestivals.com. Since 1991. (806) 749.2929.

Lubbock: Lights on Broadway Celebration; December; PO Box 1643, 79408; www.broadwayfestivals.com.

Lubbock: Panhandle-South Plains Fair; September; PO Box 208, 79408; www.southplainsfair.com. Since 1914. info@southplainsfair.com. (806) 763-2833.

Lufkin: Texas Forest Festival; September; 1200 Ellen Trout Dr., 75904; www.texasforestfestival.com. (936) 634.6644.

Luling: Luling Watermelon Thump; June (last full wknd); PO Box 710, 78648; www.watermelonthump.com. Since 1953.

McKinney: Texas Scottish Festival & Highland Games; May; 1705 W. University Dr., Suite 108 - 110, 75069; www.texasscots.com.com. Since 1986. postmaster@texasscottishfestival.com. (469) 424.1930

Marshall: Fire Ant Festival; October; PO Box 520, 75671; www.marshalltexas.com. Since 1984.

Marshall: Stagecoach Days Festival; May; PO Box 520, 75671; www.marshalltexas.com. Since 1973.

Marshall: Wonderland of Lights; November–December; PO Box 520, 75671; www.marshalltxchamber.com.

Mercedes: Rio Grande Valley Livestock Show; March; 1000 N. Texas; www.rgvls.com. Since 1940. info@rgvls.com. (956) 565-2456.

Mesquite: Mesquite Championship Rodeo; June-August (each Fri. & Sat.); 1818 Rodeo Dr, 75149-3800; www.mesquiterodeo.com. Since 1957. info@ mesquiterodeo.com. (972) 285-8777.

Monahans: Butterfield-Overland Stage Coach and Wagon Festival; July; 401 S. Dwight Ave., 79756; www.monahans.org. Since 1994. chamber@monahans.org.

Mount Pleasant: Titus County Fair; September; PO Box 1232, 75456; www.tituscountyfair.com. Since 1975. info@tituscountyfair.com.

Fairies greet a visitor at the Texas Renaissance Festival near Todd Mission. Photo courtesy Texas Renaissance Festival.

Nacogdoches: Piney Woods Fair; October; 3805 NW Stallings Dr., 75964; www.nacexpo.net. Since 1978. nacexpo@co.nacogdoches.tx.us. (936) 564-0849.

Nederland: Nederland Heritage Festival; March; PO Box 1176, 77627; www.nederlandhf.org. Since 1973. (409) 724-2269.

New Braunfels: Comal County Fair; September; PO Box 310223, 78131; www.comalcountyfair.org. Since 1894. ccfa.nbtx@sbcglobal.net. (830) 625.1505.

New Braunfels: Wurstfest; October–November; PO Box 310309, 78131; www.wurstfest.com. info@ wurstfest.com. (830) 625-9167.

Odessa: Permian Basin Fair & Expo; September; 218 W. 46th St., 79764; www.pbfair.com.

Palestine: Dogwood Trails Festival; March–April; PO Box 2828, 75802-2828; www.visitpalestine.com.

Paris: Red River Valley Fair; August–September; 570 E. Center St., 75460; www.paristx-rrvfair.com. Since 1911. rrvfair@suddenlinkmail.com. (903) 785-7971.

Pasadena: Pasadena Livestock Show & Rodeo; September–October; 7601 Red Bluff Rd., 77507-1035; www.pasadenarodeo.com. contactus@ pasadenarodeo.com. (281) 487-0240.

Port Aransas: Whooping Crane Festival; February (last weekend); 403 W. Cotter, 78373; www.whoopingcranefestival.org. Since 1996. (361) 749-5919.

Port Arthur: cavOILcade; October; PO Box 2336, 77643; www.cavoilcade.portarthur.com. Since 1953. cavoilcade@portarthur.com. (409) 983-1009.

Port Lavaca: Calhoun County Fair; October (3rd wknd.); PO Box 42, 77979; http://www.calcofair.com. Since 1963. calcofair77979@gmail.com. (361) 250-0930.

Poteet: Poteet Strawberry Festival; April; PO Box 227, 78065; www.strawberryfestival.com. Since 1948. info@strawberryfestival.com. (830) 742-8144.

Refugio: Refugio County Fair & Rodeo & Livestock Show; March; PO Box 88, 78377. Since 1961.

Rio Grande City: Starr County Fair; March (1st full wknd.); PO Box 841, 78582; www.starrcountyfair.com. Since 1961. starrcountyfair@aol.com. (956) 488-0122.

Rosenberg: Fort Bend County Fair; September–October; PO Box 428, 77471; www.fortbendcountyfair.com. Since 1937. info@fbcfa.org. (281) 342-6171.

Salado: Salado Scottish Games and Competitions; November (2nd wknd.); 423 S. Main St.; www.saladomuseum.org. office@saladomuseum.org. (254) 947-5232.

San Angelo: San Angelo Stock Show & Rodeo; February; 200 W. 43rd St., 76903; www.sanangelorodeo.com. Since 1932. (325)653-7785.

San Antonio: Fiesta San Antonio; April; 2611 Broadway St.; 78215; www.fiesta-sa.org. Since 1891. info@fiesta-sa.org. (210) 227-5191.

San Antonio: Texas Folklife Festival; June; 801 E. Cesar E. Chavez Blvd., 78205; www.texasfolklifefestival.org. Since 1972. itcweb@utsa.edu. (210) 458-2300.

Sanderson: Cinco de Mayo Celebration; May; PO Box 598, 79848; www.sandersonchamber.com. sandersonchamber@yahoo.com. (432) 345-3331.

Sanderson: 4th of July Celebration; July; PO Box 598, 79848; www.sandersonchamber.com. Since 1908. sandersonchamber@yahoo.com. (432) 345-3331.

Sanderson: Pachanga!; November; PO Box 598, 79848; www.sandersonchamber.com. Since 2001. sandersonchamber@yahoo.com. (432) 345-3331.

Santa Fe: Galveston County Fair & Rodeo; April; PO Box 889, 77510; www.galvestoncountyfair.com. (409) 986-6010.

Schulenburg: Schulenburg Festival; August (1st full wknd.); PO Box 115; 78956; www.schulenburgfestival.com. Since 1976.

Shamrock: St. Patrick's Day Celebration; March; 207 N. Main St., 79079. www.shamrocktexas.net. Since 1947. shamrockedc@gmail.com. (806) 256-2516.

Stamford: Texas Cowboy Reunion; July; PO Box 928, 79553; www.texascowboyreunion.com. Since 1933. tcrrodeo@gmail.com.

Sulphur Springs: Hopkins County Fall Festival; September; 125 S. Davis St., 75482. www.sulphurspringstx.org. hopkinscountyfallfestival@gmail.com. (903) 243-1925.

Sweetwater: Rattlesnake Roundup; March; PO Box 416, 79556; www.rattlesnakeroundup.net. Since 1958.

Terlingua: Terlingua International Chili Championship; November; PO Box 39, 79852; www.casichili.net. Since 1947.

Texarkana: Four States Fair; September; 3700 E. 50th St., Texarkana AR, 75504; www.fourstatesfair.com. (870) 773-2941.

Todd Mission: Texas Renaissance Festival; October–November (8 weekends); 21778 FM 1774, 77363; www.texrenfest.com. Since 1975. info@texasrenfest.com. (800) 458-3435.

Tyler: East Texas State Fair; September; 2112 W. Front St., 75702; www.etstatefair.com. Since 1914. info@etstatefair.com. (903) 597-2501.

Tyler: Texas Rose Festival; Ocober (3rd wknd.); PO Box 8224, 75711; www.texasrosefestival.com. Since 1933. (903) 597-3130.

Waco: Heart O' Texas Fair & Rodeo; October; 4601 Bosque Blvd.; 76710; www.hotfair.com. Since 1954. (254) 776-1660.

Waxahachie: Gingerbread Trail Tour of Homes; June (1st full wknd.); PO Box 706, 75168; www.-rootsweb.com/~txecm/ginger. Since 1969.

Waxahachie: Scarborough Renaissance Festival; April–May; PO Box 538, 75168; www.srfestival.com. Since 1980. (972) 938-3247.

Weatherford: Parker County Peach Festival; July (2nd Sat.); PO Box 310, 76086; www.parkercountypeachfestival.org. Since 1985. info@weatherford-chamber.com. (817) 596-3801.

Weatherford: Christmas on the Square; December; PO Box 310, 76086; www.weatherford-chamber.com. Since 1988.

West: Westfest; September (Labor Day wknd.); PO Box 65, 76691; www.westfest.com. Since 1976. (254) 826-5058.

Winnsboro: Autumn Trails Festival; October (every wknd.); PO Box 464, 75494; www.winnsboroautumntrails.com. winnsboroautumntrails@gmail.com. (903) 342-1958.

Woodville: Tyler County Dogwood Festival; March–April; PO Box 2151, 75979-2151; www.tylercountydogwoodfestival.org. Since 1944. dogwood_festival@yahoo.com. (409) 283-2632.

Yorktown: Yorktown's Annual Western Days Celebration; October (3rd full wknd.); PO Box 488, 78164; www.yorktowntx.com. Since 1959. westerndays@yorktowntx.com. (361)564.2611. ☆

A foggy day on a pier in Galveston. Photo by IsleShire (CC).

Hunting and Fishing

Source: Texas Parks and Wildlife Department; http://tpwd.texas.gov

The popularity of hunting and fishing in Texas cannot be denied. Just ask the Texas Parks and Wildlife Department — which should probably be the place you start, because that's where you can find all of the current hunting and fishing regulations for the state.

According to the 2018 State of Texas Annual Cash Report, public hunting, fishing, and other participation fees (including sales of hunting and fishing licenses) brought in revenues of $106,511,841.49 in 2017 and $103,447,864.28 in 2018.

Hunting Licenses

A **hunting license** is required of Texas residents and non-residents who hunt any legal bird or animal. Hunting licenses and endorsements are valid during the period Sept. 1 through the following Aug. 31 of each year, except licenses issued for a specific number of days or time periods.

A hunting license (except the non-resident special hunting license and non-resident 5-day special hunting license) is valid for taking all legal species of wildlife in Texas including deer, turkey, javelina, antelope, aoudad (sheep), alligator, and all small game and migratory game birds. Endorsement and tag requirements apply.

A trapper's license is required for all persons to hunt, shoot, or take for sale those species classified as fur-bearing animals or their pelts.

In addition to a valid hunting license:

- An **Archery Endorsement** is required to hunt deer or turkey during Archery-Only open season.

Hunting and Fishing Licenses Sold	
2017	**Volume**
Hunting Licenses	524,111
Fishing Licenses	1,350,081
Combined Licenses	636,389
TOTALS	**2,510,581**
2018*	**Volume**
Hunting Licenses	501,116
Fishing Licenses	1,250,519
Combined Licenses	617,016
TOTALS	**2,368,651**

* Volumes for 2018 are estimated.
Source: 2020-21 Legislative Appropriation Request, TPWD

- An **Upland Game Bird Endorsement** is required to hunt turkey, pheasant, quail, or chachalaca. Non-residents who purchase the non-resident spring turkey license are exempt from this endorsement requirement.
- A **Migratory Game Bird Endorsement** and **HIP (Harvest Information Program) Certification** is required to hunt any migratory game birds, including waterfowl, coot, rail, gallinule, snipe, dove, sandhill crane, and woodcock.
- A valid **Federal Duck Stamp** is required of waterfowl hunters age 16 or older.

On the web, information from TPWD on hunting can be found at: **tpwd.texas.gov/huntwild/hunt/**

Game Harvest Estimates

The TPWD conducts random surveys of hunters every year to create estimates of hunter and harvest trends in two categories: small game (23 species total, birds and small mammals) and big game (white-tailed deer, mule deer, and javelina). It collects data not just on what animals were hunted, but also where and how. You can learn about the methodology and see the full results of these surveys on the web at: **https://tpwd.texas.gov/publications/huntwild/hunt.**

Wildlife Game Harvest		
Game	2017–2018 Estimates	2016–2017 Estimates
Dove, combined*	7,024,472	10,331,555
Duck	1,385,557	1,497,667
Gallinule	N/A	2,075
Goose	111,702	161,667
Pheasant	48,470	28,378
Quail, combined**	698,469	1,874,544
Rabbit	294,387	538,959
Rail	N/A	N/A
Snipe	2,559	7,024
Squirrel	427,699	474,314
Teal	200,085	253,879
Turkey (fall and spring)	42,471	50,235
Woodcock	303	7,515
White-tailed Deer	918,009	953,615
Mule Deer	17,620	18,062
Javalina	37,626	41,354

*Dove, combined includes the following species: Eurasian, mourning, white-tipped, and white-winged.
**Quail, combined includes the following species: bobwhite and scaled.

Source: TPWD Game Harvest Surveys

Fishing Licenses

All fishing licenses and endorsements are valid only from Sept. 1 through the following Aug. 31, except licenses issued for a specific number of days or time periods. If you own any valid freshwater-fishing package, you will be able to purchase a saltwater stamp and also fish saltwater.

If you own any valid saltwater-fishing package, you will be able to purchase a freshwater stamp and also fish freshwater. An all-water fishing package is available that enables anglers to fish both fresh- and saltwater.

Detailed information concerning licenses, endorsements, seasons, and regulations can be obtained from Texas Parks and Wildlife Department, 4200 Smith School Road, Austin 78744, (800) 792-1112 or (512) 389-4820; or on the web at: **tpwd.texas.gov/business/licenses.**

Freshwater Fishing

Freshwater fishing in Texas is an activity enjoyed by an estimated 1.2 million recreational anglers. In 2015, these anglers contributed an economic output of approximately $96 million to the Texas economy.

Among the 268 species of freshwater fish in Texas, the most popular fish for recreational fishing are: **largemouth bass, catfish, crappie, and striped, white, and hybrid striped bass.**

Texas anglers can fish in approximately 1,100 public reservoirs and about 191,000 miles of rivers and streams, together totaling 1.7 million acres.

The Texas Parks and Wildlife Department operates field stations, fish hatcheries, and research facilities to support the conservation and management of fishery resources. The hatcheries operated by TPWD raise largemouth and smallmouth bass, as well as catfish, striped and hybrid striped bass, and sunfish.

TPWD has continued its programs of stocking fish in public waters to increase angling opportunities. Many conservation-minded anglers who desire continued quality fishing practice catch-and-release fishing.

Texas Freshwater Fisheries Center

The Texas Freshwater Fisheries Center in Athens, about 75 miles southeast of Dallas, is an $18 million hatchery and educational center, where visitors can learn about underwater life.

The interactive Visitors Center includes aquarium displays of fish in their natural environment. Visitors get an "eye-to-eye" view of three authentically designed Texas freshwater habitats: a Hill Country stream, an East Texas pond, and a reservoir. A marsh exhibit features live American alligators.

A casting pond stocked with rainbow trout in the winter and catfish year-around provides a place for visitors to learn how to bait a hook, cast a line, and land a fish. The center has conference facilities and hosts groups by appointment.

The Texas Freshwater Fisheries Center is open Tuesday through Saturday, 9 a.m. to 4 p.m., and Sunday, 1 p.m. to 4 p.m. It is closed on Monday. Admission is charged. The center is located 4.5 miles east of Athens on FM 2495 at Lake Athens. Address: 5550 FM 2495, Athens 75752, or call (903) 676-2277. Download the free Texas Freshwater Fisheries Center smartphone app from the Apple app store or Google Play. For more information, visit: **http://tpwd.texas.gov/tffc/.**

Saltwater Fishing

According to the most recent report available, Texas has about 672,000 saltwater anglers (16 years old and older) who spend an estimated $1.1 billion annually on fishing-related expenditures. In 2013, anglers harvested 1.7 million fish from both Texas bays and the Gulf of Mexico off Texas.

The most popular saltwater sport fish in Texas bays are **spotted seatrout, sand seatrout, Atlantic croaker, red drum, southern flounder, black drum, sheepshead, and gafftopsail catfish.**

Offshore, some of the fish that anglers target are **red snapper, king mackerel, Spanish mackerel, dolphin-fish, cobia, tarpon, and yellowfin tuna.** ☆

For information about commercial fishing, see page 606 in the Business chapter.

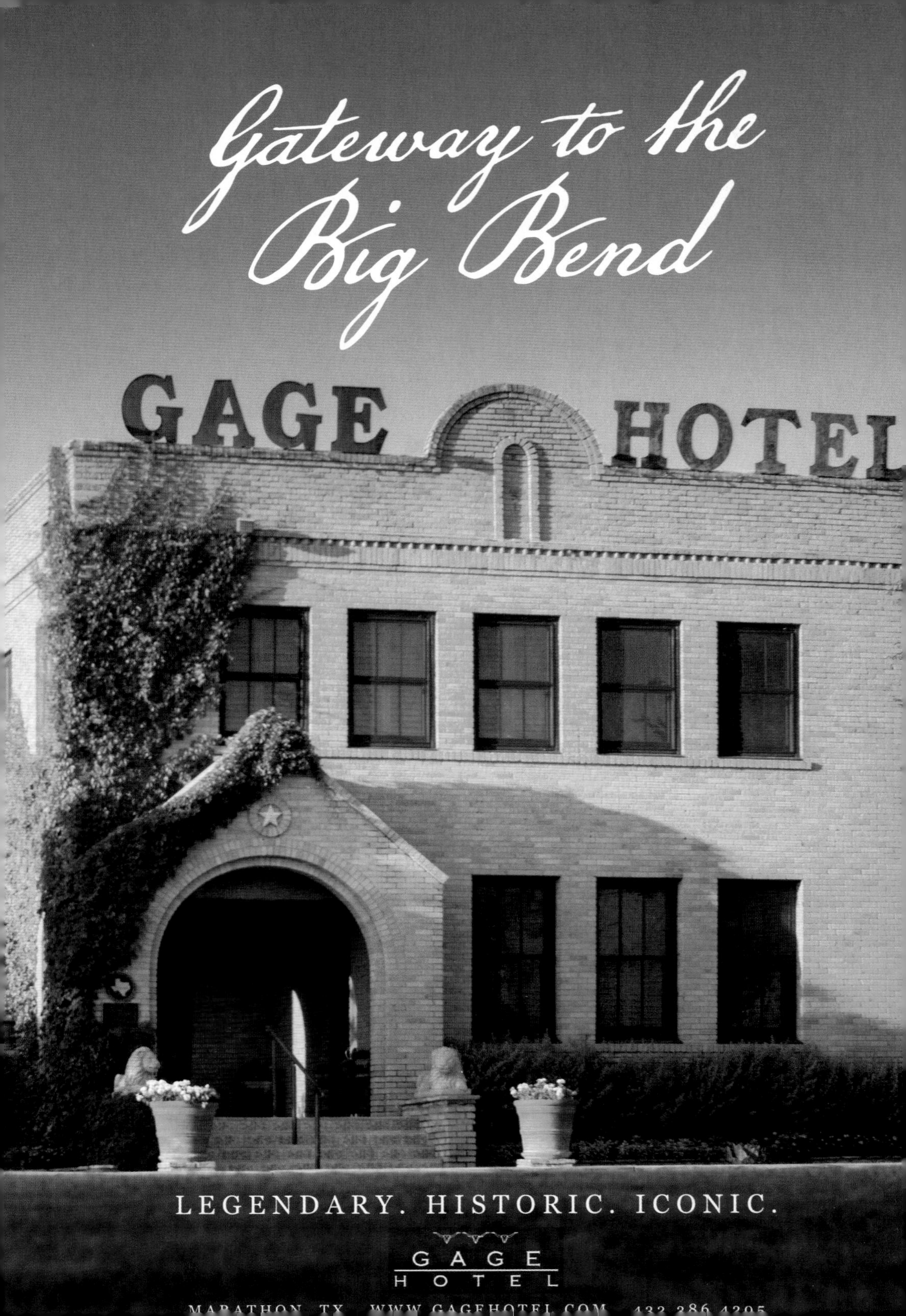

Gateway to the Big Bend

GAGE HOTEL

LEGENDARY. HISTORIC. ICONIC.

GAGE
HOTEL

MARATHON, TX WWW.GAGEHOTEL.COM 432.386.4205

SPORTS

Dallas Wings guard Alisha Gray in 2018. The team moved to Dallas from Tulsa in 2015.
Photo by Keeton Gale/Shutterstock.

HIGH SCHOOL CHAMPIONS

COLLEGE CHAMPIONS

PROFESSIONAL SPORTS TEAMS

HALL OF FAME, OLYMPIC MEDALISTS

STATE: High School Championships

UIL: The University Interscholastic League, which governs literary and athletic competition among public schools in Texas, was organized in 1910 as a division of the University of Texas extension service. Initially, it sponsored forensic competition. By 1920, the UIL organized the structure of the high school football game in response to the growing popularity of the sport in Texas.

TAPPS: The Texas Association of Private and Parochial Schools is the largest group of private schools in the state with more than 225 member institutions.

The interscholastic competition began in 1978 and was significantly expanded when the Texas Christian Interscholastic League ceased to exist in 2000 and many of those schools moved into TAPPS.

Listed are state champions and the game scores or series wins-loses.

Sources: The University Interscholastic League at www.uil.utexas.edu; the Texas Association of Private and Parochial Schools.

Football

Year	Division	Champion	Runner Up
UIL 2018	1A Division I	McLean 100	Milford 70
	1A Division II	Strawn 48	Follett 0
	2A Division I	Mason 44	New Deal 6
	2A Division II	Mart 76	Gruver 33
	3A Division I	Grandview 35	Malakoff 21
	3A Division II	Newton 21	Canadian 16
	4A Division I	La Vega (Waco) 35	Liberty Hill 21
	4A Division II	Cuero 40	Pleasant Grove (Texarkana) 28
	5A Division I	Highland Park (Dallas) 27	Alvin Shadow Creek 17
	5A Division II	Aledo 55	Fort Bend Marshall 19
	6A Division I	North Shore (Houston) 41	Duncanville 36
	6A Division II	Longview 35	Beaumont West Brook 34
TAPPS 2018	Division V	Katy St. John XXIII 38	San Antonio St. Mary's Hall 27
	Division IV	Shiner St. Paul 29	Fort Worth Lake Country 21
	Division III	Willow Park Trinity Christian 15	Boerne Geneva 14
	Division II	Cedar Hill Trinity 49	Austin Regents 24
	Division I	Dallas Bishop Dunne 13	Dallas Bishop Lynch 9

Year	Division	Champion	Runner Up
UIL 2017	1A Division I	Borden County 60	Jonesboro 22
	1A Division II	Strawn 78	Balmorhea 42
	2A Division I	Mart 34	Refugio 21
	2A Division II	Muenster 27	Tenaha 20
	3A Division I	Rockdale 45	Brock 29
	3A Division II	Newton 40	Gunter 16
	4A Division I	Carthage 49	Kennedale 21
	4A Division II	Pleasant Grove 41	West Orange-Stark 21
	5A Division I	Highland Park (Dallas) 53	Manvel 49
	5A Division II	College Station 20	Aledo 19
	6A Division I	Allen 35	Lake Travis (Austin) 33
	6A Division II	Cypress-Fairbanks 51	Midway (Waco) 35
TAPPS 2017	Division V	El Paso Cathedral 31	Houston Village School 28
	Division IV	Colleyville Covenant 14	The Woodlands Legacy Prep 0
	Division III	Houston Cypress Christian 68	McKinney Christian 34
	Division II	Cedar Hill Trinity 62	Austin Regents 30
	Division I	Plano Prestonwood Christian 42	Houston St. Pius 41

Muenster celebrates victory in the 2017 2A-Division II game at AT&T Stadium in Arlington. Photo by1stphototexas.

Volleyball

Year	Division	Champion	Runner Up
UIL 2018	1A	Neches 3	Water Valley 0
	2A	Beckville 3	Lindsay 2
	3A	Callisburg 3	Boyd 1
	4A	Decatur 3	Needville 1
	5A	Humble Kingwood 3	Lucas Lovejoy 0
	6A	Flower Mound 3	Fort Bend Ridge Point 1
TAPPS 2018	1A	Wichita Falls Christian Academy 3	Bellville Faith 1
	2A	Red Oak-Ovilla Christian 3	Austin Wladorf 2
	3A	Midland Classical 3	New Braunfels Christian 2
	4A	Arlington Grace Prep 3	Houston Northland 0
	5A	Victoria St. Joseph 3	Austin St. Michael's 1
	6A	Plano Prestonwood Baptist 3	Tomball Concordia 2
UIL 2017	1A	Bronte 3	Blum 1
	2A	Crawford 3	Iola 0
	3A	Goliad 3	Callisburg 1
	4A	Needville 3	Argyle 0
	5A	Prosper 3	Leander Rouse 2
	6A	Lewisville Hebron 3	League City Clear Creek 0
TAPPS 2017	1A	Granbury North Central 3	Bulverde Bracken 0
	2A	Lubbock All Saints 3	Waco Live Oak Classical 1
	3A	Round Rock Christian 3	Willow Park Trinity Christian 1
	4A	Lubbock Trinity Christian 3	The Woodlands Christian 0
	5A	Fort Worth All Saints 3	San Antonio Holy Cross 2
	6A	San Antonio Antonian 3	Plano Prestonwood Baptist 0

Girls Basketball

Year	Division	Champion	Runner Up
UIL 2019	1A	Nazareth 54	Dodd City 33
	2A	Martins Mill 60	Grapeland 56
	3A	Chapel Hill (Tyler) 55	Woodville 46
	4A	Argyle 49	Hardin-Jefferson 41
	5A	Amarillo 47	Frisco Liberty 42
	6A	Converse Judson 49	DeSoto 46
TAPPS 2019	1A	San Antonio Legacy Christian 50	Wichita Falls Notre Dame 39
	2A	Lubbock Southcrest Christian 41	Shiner St. Paul 34
	3A	Midland Classical 72	Beaumont Legacy Christian 47
	4A	Lubbock Trinity Christian 72	Houston Lutheran North 34
	5A	Cedar Hill Trinity Christian 76	San Antonio Christian 33
	6A	Dallas Bishop Lynch 81	Houston Village 62
UIL 2018	1A	Nazareth 56	Dodd City 43
	2A	Martins Mill 58	La Poynor 51
	3A	Mount Vernon 51	Marlin 47
	4A	Argyle 60	San Antonio Veterans Memorial 43
	5A	Amarillo 59	Mansfield Timberview 54
	6A	Plano 62	Converse Judson 58
TAPPS 2018	1A	DeSoto Canterbury Episcopal 53	San Antonio Legacy Christian 49
	2A	Lubbock Southcrest Christian 45	Shiner St. Paul 39
	3A	Midland Classical 59	Beaumont Legacy Christian 53 (2OT)
	4A	Fort Worth Lake Country 44	Austin Brentwood 19
	5A	Tyler Grace Community 37	Corpus Christi Incarnate Word 31
	6A	Dallas Parish Episcopal 61	Dallas Bishop Lynch 56

An Amarillo player flanked by Mansfield Timberview players in the 2018 5A final. Photo by1stphototexas.

Baseball

Year	Division	Champion	Runner Up
UIL 2019	1A	D'Hanis 4	New Home 0
	2A	Dallardsville Big Sandy 7	Linden-Kildare 1
	3A	Wall 2	Blanco 1
	4A	Argyle 6	Sweeny 3
	5A	Colleyville Heritage 14	Georgetown 2 (6 innings)
	6A	Southlake Carroll 17	Ft. Bend Ridge Point 0 (5 innings)
TAPPS 2019	Division V	Weatherford Chrisitan 7	Brazosport Chrisitan 6
	Division IV	Amarillo San Jacinto Christian 5	New Branfels Chrisitan 3
	Division III	Houston Northland Christian 3	Willow Park Tringity Christian 2
	Division II	Houston Lutheran South 11	Fort Worth Christian 1
	Division I	Argyle Liberty Christian 3	Fort Worth All Saints Episcopal 5
UIL 2018	1A	Slocum 6	Fayetteville 3
	2A	Dallardsville Big Sandy 13	Muenster 3
	3A	Beckville 5	Clifton 4
	4A	Argyle 5	Sweeny 0
	5A	FW Northwest Eaton 4	Forney 1
	6A	Southlake Carroll 7	San Antonio Reagan 2
TAPPS 2018	Division V	New Braunfels Christian 7	Muenster Sacred Heart 2
	Division IV	El Paso Faith Christian 11	Pasadena First Baptist 0
	Division III	Houston Cypress Christian 11	Lubbock Christian 0
	Division II	Houston Lutheran South 7	Bullard Brook Hill 3
	Division I	Liberty Christian 6	Beaumont Kelly 4
UIL 2017	1A	Abbott 11	Fayetteville 3
	2A	Muenster 6	Dallardsville Big Sandy 2
	3A	Nacogdoches Central Heights 10	Wall 0
	4A	Wylie (Abilene) 6	Robinson 5
	5A	Port Neches-Groves 4	Grapevine 2
	6A	Deer Park 7	San Antonio Reagan 2
TAPPS 2017	Division V	Longview Christian 3	Brazosport Christian 2
	Division IV	Tomball Rosehill 11	Dallas Lutheran 0
	Division III	Lubbock Christian 11	The Woodlands Christian 4
	Division II	Houston Emery 6	Fort Worth Christian 4
	Division I	Houston St. Thomas 15	Beaumont Kelly 1
UIL 2016	2A	Flatonia 7	Beckville 1
	3A	West 8	Van Alstyne 1
	4A	Wylie (Abilene) 3	Salado 2
	5A	Grapevine 9	Alamo Heights (San Antonio) 2
	6A	Dallas Jesuit 6	San Antonio Johnson 2
TAPPS 2016	1A and 2A	Tomball Rosehill 9	Conroe Covenant 2
	3A	Lubbock Christian 11	League City Bay Area 1
	4A	Houston Second Baptist 7	Midland Christian 2
	5A	Plano Prestonwood Baptist 7	Beaumont Kelly 1

For track, tennis, and other high school sports champions, see pages 574 in the Education section.

Boys Soccer

Year	Division	Champion	Runner Up
UIL 2019	4A	San Elizario 1	Midlothian Heritage 0 (OT)
	5A	El Paso Bel Air 2	Frisco Wakeland 1
	6A	Flower Mound 1	San Antonio Lee 0 (SO 4-1)
TAPPS 2019	Fall 2018	Nacogdoches Regents 2	Pflugerville Concordia 1
	Division III	Dallas Covenant 2	Houston St. Thomas Episcopal 1
	Division II	San Antonio TMI Episcopal 3	Carrollton Prince of Peace 2
	Division I	San Antonio Central Catholic 4	Dallas Bishop Lynch 0
UIL 2018	4A	San Elizario 1	Palestine 0
	5A	Frisco Wakeland 3	Aledo 1
	6A	Alief Elsik 1	San Antonio Reagan 0
TAPPS 2018	Fall 2017	Dallas International 3	Kingsville Pan American 1
	Division III	Dallas Covenant 2	Houston British School 1
	Division II	Houston Lutheran South 1	Garland Brighter Horizon 0 (SO)
	Division I	San Antonio Central Catholic 1	Houston St. Thomas 0
UIL 2017	4A	Kilgore 3	Bridgeport 2 (SO)
	5A	Frisco Wakeland 2	Waller 0
	6A	Dallas Jesuit 2	Arlington Houston 1
TAPPS 2017	Fall 2016	Dallas International 3	Kingsville Pan American 2
	Division III	Dallas British School 5	Dallas Covenant 2
	Division II	San Antonio TMI Episcopal 3	Grapevine Faith 1
	Division I	San Antonio Central Catholic 6	Houston St. Pius 1
UIL 2016	4A	Palestine 1	Progreso 0 (SO)
	5A	Brownsville Porter 3	Frisco Wakeland 2 (SO)
	6A	Coppell 6	Lake Travis 1
TAPPS 2016	Fall 2015	Sherman Texoma Christian 5	McAllen South Texas 2
	Division III	Houston St. Thomas Episcopal 2	Austin Hill Country 1 (SO)
	Division II	Houston Village School 2	Dallas Christian 0
	Division I	Addison Trinity Christian 2	Plano John Paul 1

Frisco Wakeland vs. Grapevine in the 5A final in 2018. Photo by 1stphototexas.

Year	Division	Champion	Runner Up
BOYS SOCCER continued			
UIL 2015	4A	San Elizario 4	Liberty Hill 2
	5A	Lufkin 3	Georgetown East View 1
	6A	Brownsville Rivera 2	Katy Cinco Ranch 0
TAPPS 2015	Fall 2014	Longview Christian Heritage 6	Austin Brentwood 4
	Division III	Pharr Oratory 2	Austin Hill Country Christian 0
	Division II	Houston Village School 3	Bullard Brook Hill 2
	Division I	El Paso Cathedral 3	Houston Awty 1
UIL 2014	4A	San Antonio Northwest Nelson 2	Pharr Valley View 1
	5A	Fort Bend Clements 3	Coppell 0
TAPPS 2014	Fall 2013	Houston British School 8	Sherman Texoma Christian 1
	Division III	Colleyville Covenant Christian 2	Houston Cypress 1
	Division II	Grapvince Faith Christian 2	Houston Awtry International 1
	Division I	San Antonio Central Catholic 2	Addison Trinity Christian 1 (SO)

Girls Soccer

Year	Division	Champion	Runner Up
UIL 2019	4A	Stephenville 2	Liberty Hill 0
	5A	Highland Park (Dallas) 2	Mansfield Legacy 0
	6A	Southlake Carroll 5	Katy Tompkins 0
TAPPS 2019	Division III	Houston St. Thomas Episcopal 6	Austin Veritas 0
	Division II	Grapevine Faith 7	Houston Second Baptist 0
	Division I	Dallas Bishop Lynch 1	Houston St. Agnes 0
UIL 2018	4A	Midlothian Heritage 2	Jasper 1 (OT)
	5A	Frisco Wakeland 4	Grapevine 3 (5-4 SO)
	6A	Houston Spring Branch Memorial 3	Flower Mound Marcus 0
TAPPS 2018	Division III	Kerrville Our Lady of the Hills 5	McKinney Christian 0
	Division II	Tyler Grace Community 4	San Antonio Christian 1
	Division I	Dallas Ursuline 2	Plano John Paul 0
UIL 2017	4A	Stephenville 2	Boerne 1
	5A	Highland Park (Dallas) 5	Aledo 3
	6A	Pflugerville Hendrickson 2	Katy Hopkins 0
TAPPS 2017	Division III	Austin Veritas 8	Colleyville Covenant 0
	Division II	Grapevine Faith 4	Corpus Christi Incarnate Word 0
	Division I	Dallas Ursuline 2	Houston St. Agnes 0
UIL 2016	4A	Kennedale 6	Jasper 0
	5A	Frisco Centennial 3	Grapevine 2 (SO)
	6A	Flower Mound 3	Highland Park (Dallas) 2 (SO)
TAPPS 2016	Division III	Austin Veritas 5	Kerrville Our Lady of the Hills 0
	Division II	Tyler Grace Community 4	San Antonio Christian 3
	Division I	Dallas Ursuline 1	Dallas Bishop Lynch 0
UIL 2015	4A	Kennedale 4	Princeton 3
	5A	Wylie East 1	Austin Vandgrift 0
	6A	Coppell 3	Highland Park (Dallas) 0
TAPPS 2015	Division III	Austin Veritas 7	Dallas Covenant 1
	Division II	San Antonio Christian 2	Colleyville Covenant 0
	Division I	Dallas Bishop Lynch 2	Dallas Ursuline 1

Port Arthur Memorial vs. Justin Northwest in the 5A final in 2018. Photo by 1stphototexas.

Boys Basketball

Year	Division	Champion	Runner Up
UIL 2019	1A	Slidell 49	Jayton 36
	2A	Shelbyville 67	Gruver 48
	3A	Dallas Madison 49	Brock 48
	4A	Oak Cliff Faith Family Academy 53	Liberty Hill 51
	5A	Mansfield Timberview 77	San Antonio Wagner 64
	6A	Duncanville 73	Klein Forest 69
TAPPS 2019	1A	Baytown Christian 63	Dallas Tyler Street 39
	2A	Bryan Allen Academy 68	Abilene Christian 47
	3A	Kerrville Our Lady of the Hills 50	Midland Classical 47
	4A	Arlington Grace Prep 58	The Woodlands Chrisitan 54
	5A	Frisco Legacy Christian 66	Houston Lutheran South 51
	6A	San Antonio Antonian 70	Plano Prestonwood Chrisitan 67
UIL 2018	1A	Lipan 49	Nazareth 42
	2A	Stinnett West Texas 61	Thorndale 55
	3A	Bowie 32	Mount Vernon 28
	4A	Silsbee 104	Dallas Carter 101
	5A	Port Arthur Memorial 75	Justin Northwest 69
	6A	Allen 49	Katy Tompkins 47 OT
TAPPS 2018	1A	Granbury North Central Texas 67	San Antonio Legacy Christian 50
	2A	Lubbock All Saints Episcopal 62	Conroe Covenant 41
	3A	El Paso Faith Christian 69	Kerrville Our Lady of the Hills 50
	4A	The Woodlands Christian 79	Arlington Grace Prep 76
	5A	Houston Second Baptist 60	Cedar Hill Trinity Christian 57
	6A	Tomball Concordia Lutheran 70	Houston St. Pius 48

Softball

Year	Division	Champion	Runner Up
UIL 2019	1A	D'Hanis 9	Chireno 7
	2A	Crawford 8	Thorndale 7 (8 innings)
	3A	Rains 6	Hallettsville 2
	4A	Huffamn Hargrave 12	Anna 0 (6 innings)
	5A	Angleton 8	Calallen 1
	6A	Katy 8	Klein Collins 2
TAPPS 2019	Division IV	Shiner St. Paul 15	Round Rock Concordia 0
	Division III	Waco Reicher 10	The Woodlands Christian 2
	Division II	Houston Lutheran South 6	Bullard Brook Hill 2
	Division I	Houston St. Agnes 3	Dallas Bishop Lynch 2
UIL 2018	1A	Slocum 3	Ector 0
	2A	Bells 9	Normangee 5
	3A	Santa Gertrudis Academy 8	Hughes Springs 3
	4A	Liberty 3	Vernon 1
	5A	Forney 4	Richmond Foster 1
	6A	Humble Atascocita 5	New Braunfels Canyon 3
TAPPS 2018	Division IV	Bellville Faith Academy 16	Sherman Texoma Christian 0
	Division III	Schertz John Paul 5	Waco Reicher 3
	Division II	Sugar Land Fort Bend Christian 10	Fort Worth Christian 0
	Division I	San Antonio Incarnate Word 3	Katy St. John 1
UIL 2017	1A	Slocum 10	Hermleigh 0
	2A	Bells 7	Shiner 6
	3A	Little River-Academy 5	Santa Gertrudis Academy 3
	4A	Krum 4	Liberty Hill 3
	5A	Lewisville The Colony 5	Willis 2
	6A	Keller 5	Austin Bowie 1
TAPPS 2017	Division IV	Bellville Faith Academy 13	Temple Central Texas Christian 0
	Division III	Waco Reicher 3	Schertz John Paul II 2
	Division II	Sugar Land Fort Bend Christian 6	Dallas Christian 2
	Division I	San Antonio Incarnate Word 21	San Antonio Antonian Prep 6
UIL 2016	2A	Shiner 13	Windthorst 0
	3A	West 11	Colorado City 0
	4A	La Grange 8	North Lamar (Paris) 1
	5A	North Richland Hills Birdville 8	Gregory-Portland 7
	6A	Keller 5	Pearland 0
TAPPS 2016	1A and 2A	Shiner St. Paul 9	Brazosport Christian 6
	3A	Schertz John Paul II 6	Lubbock Christian 3
	4A	Sugar Land Fort Bend Christian 6	Dallas Christian 1
	5A	San Antonio Incarnate Word 9	Houston St. Agnes 1
UIL 2015	2A	Shiner 3	Harelton 0
	3A	East Bernard 8	Hallettsville 1
	4A	Huffman Hargrave 6	Needville 4
	5A	Aledo 3	Cedar Park Vista Ridge 2
	6A	Katy 3	Lewisville 2

Texas College Sports — Division I

Big 12 Champions

In 2019, the Texas schools in the **Big 12** were:
University of Texas at Austin
Texas Tech University
Texas Christian University

Baylor University
Other schools in the Big 12 are the University of Kansas, Kansas State University, the University of Oklahoma, Oklahoma State University, Iowa State University, and West Virginia University.

2018–2019	Season	Tournament	National Playoffs
Football	Oklahoma		Lost semifinal to Alabama 45-34
Men's Basketball	K.State, TTech	Iowas State	TTech lost national title to Virginia 85-77 OT
Women's Basketball	Baylor	Baylor	**National champs**, over Notre Dame 82-81
Baseball	Texas Tech	Ok. State	TTech lost national semifinal to Michigan
Softball	Oklahoma	cancelled	Lost CWS to UCLA 2-0

2017–2018	Season	Tournament	National Playoffs
Football	Oklahoma		Lost semifinal to Georgia 54-48 (2OT)
Men's Basketball	Kansas	Kansas	Lost in Final 4 to Villanova 95-79
Women's Basketball	Baylor	Baylor	Lost in regionals to Oregon State 72-67
Baseball	Texas	Baylor	Texas lost first round; TTech lost second
Softball	Oklahoma	Oklahoma	Lost semifinal to Washington 3-0

2016–2017	Season	Tournament	National Playoffs
Football	Oklahoma		
Men's Basketball	Kansas	Iowa State	Kansas lost in Elite 8 to Oregon 74-60
Women's Basketball	Baylor	W. Virginia	West Virginia lost in second round
Baseball	TCU	OK State	TCU eliminated by Florida in CWS semifinals
Softball	Oklahoma	Oklahoma	**National champs**, beating Florida 7-5

2015–2016	Season	Tournament	National Playoffs
Football	Oklahoma		Lost in playoffs to Clemson 37-17
Men's Basketball	Kansas	Kansas	Kansas, OU lost Elite 8 games
Women's Basketball	Baylor	Baylor	Lost quarterfinals to Oregon State 60-57
Baseball	Texas Tech	TCU	TCU, TTech, OK State lost in World Series
Softball	Oklahoma	–	**National champs**, beating Auburn 2-1

2014–2015	Season	Tournament	National Playoffs
Football	Baylor, TCU (tie)		TCU won Peach Bowl, Baylor lost Cotton
Men's Basketball	Kansas	Iowa State	Kansas lost regional to Wichita State 78-65
Women's Basketball	Baylor	Baylor	Lost in Elite 8 to Notre Dame 77-68
Baseball	TCU	Texas	TCU lost in semifinals to Vanderbilt
Softball	Oklahoma	–	Lost super regional to Alabama

2013–2014	Season	Tournament	National Playoffs
Football	Baylor		Lost Fiesta Bowl to UCF 52-42
Men's Basketball	Kansas	Iowa State	Iowa State lost in regional to UConn 81-76
Women's Basketball	Baylor	Baylor	Lost regional to Notre Dame 88-69
Baseball	Oklahoma St.	TCU	Texas lost in semifinals to Vanderbilt
Softball	Oklahoma	–	Baylor lost in semifinals to Florida

Southeastern Conference Champions

Texas A&M University joined the **Southeastern Conference** in 2012 and competes in the West Division against Louisiana State University, the University of Arkansas, the University of Mississippi, Mississippi State University, the University of Alabama, and the University of Auburn.

Schools in the East Division are the Univerity of Missouri, the University of Kentucky, Vanderbilt University, the University of Tennessee, the University of Georgia, the University of South Carolina, and the University of Florida.

2018–2019	Season	Tournament	National Playoffs
Football	Alabama		Lost championship to Clemson 44-16
Men's Basketball	LSU	Auburn	Auburn lost in Final Four to Virginia 63-62
Women's Basketball	Miss. State	Miss. State	Lost regional final to Oregon 88-84
Baseball	Vanderbilt	Vanderbilt	Won College World Series over Michigan 2-1
Softball	Alabama	Florida	Alabama lost semi-final to Oklahoma

2017–2018	Season	Tournament	National Playoffs
Football	Georgia		Lost championship to Alabama 26-23 (OT)
Men's Basketball	Auburn/Tenn.	Kentucky	A&M, Alabama, Florida, Kentucky lost regionals
Women's Basketball	Miss. State	S. Carolina	Miss. State lost final to Notre Dame 61-58
Baseball	Florida	Ole Miss	Arkansas lost final series to Oregon State 2-1
Softball	Florida	Florida	Lost in second round to Oregon 6-5

2016–2017	Season	Tournament	National Playoffs
Football	Alabama		Lost championship to Clemson 35-31
Men's Basketball	Kentucky	Kentucky	Lost in Elite 8 to North Carolina 75-73
Women's Basketball	South Carolina	S. Carolina	**National champ**, beat Florida State 71-64
Baseball	Florida/LSU	LSU	A&M lost 1st of CWS; **Natl. champs,** Florida
Softball	Florida	Ole Miss	Florida lost final to Oklahoma 7-5

2015–2016	Season	Tournament	National Playoffs
Football	Alabama		**National champ**, beating Clemson 45-40
Men's Basketball	UK, A&M	Kentucky	A&M lost Sweet Sixteen to Okalhoma 77-63
Women's Basketball	South Carolina	S. Carolina	Lost third round to Syracuse 80-72
Baseball	Mississippi State	Texas A&M	**Both lost Super Regional games**
Softball	Florida	Auburn	Auburn lost final to Oklahoma 2-1

2014–2015	Season	Tournament	National Playoffs
Football	Alabama		Lost Sugar Bowl to Ohio State 42-35
Men's Basketball	Kentucky	Kentucky	Lost in Final Four to Wisconsin 71-64
Women's Basketball	South Carolina	S. Carolina	Lost in Final Four to Notre Dame 66-65
Baseball	LSU	Florida	Florida lost semifinals to Virginia
Softball	Florida	Auburn	**National champ** Florida over Michigan

2013–2014	Season	Tournament	National Playoffs
Football	Auburn		Lost BCS to Florida State 34-31
Men's Basketball	Florida	Florida	In Final Four, lost to UConn 63-53
Women's Basketball	South Carolina	Tennessee	S. Carolina lost regional semifinal
Baseball	Florida	LSU	Vanderbilt **national champs**
Softball	Alabama	Georgia	**National champ** Florida over Alabama

American Athletic Conference Champions

The 2013-14 season was the first for the AAC after the breakup of the Big East Conference. **Southern Methodist University** and the **University of Hous-** ton are in the Amercian Athletic Conference. Other schools in the conference are the University of Memphis, University of Cincinnati, University of Central Florida, East Carolina University, Temple University, University of South Florida, Tulane University, University of Tulsa, the University of Connecticut, and Wichita State University.

2018–2019	Season	Tournament	National Playoffs
Football	Central Florida		Lost Fiesta Bowl to LSU 40-32
Men's Basketball	U. of Houston	Cincinnati	Houston lost in regionals to Kentucky 62-58
Women's Basketball	UConn	UConn	Lost in Final Four to Notre Dame 81-76
Baseball	E. Carolina	Cincinnati	E. Carolina lost super regional to Louisville
Softball	South Florida	cancelled	Lost to Florida State in regional

2017–2018	Season	Tournament	National Playoffs
Football	Central Florida		Won Peach Bowl over Auburn 34-27
Men's Basketball	Cincinnati	Cincinnati	Lost in regional to Nevada 75-73
Women's Basketball	UConn	UConn	Lost semifinal to Notre Dame 91-89 (OT)
Baseball	U. of Houston	E.Carolina	U.of H, UConn lost regionals finals
Softball	S.Florida	Tulsa	Wichita State lost regional final

2016–2017	Season	Tournament	National Playoffs
Football	Temple		Lost Military Bowl to Wake Forest 34-26
Men's Basketball	SMU	SMU	Lost in first round to USC
Women's Basketball	UConn	UConn	Lost semifinal to Mississippi State
Baseball	UCF	U. of H.	U.of H. eliminated by A&M in regional final
Softball	Tulsa	Tulsa	Lost to Oklahoma in regional final

2015–2016	Season	Tournament	National Playoffs
Football	U. of Houston		Won Peach Bowl over Florida State 38-24
Men's Basketball	Temple	UConn	**Temple lost first, UConn second round**
Women's Basketball	UConn	UConn	**NCAA champions over Syracuse 82-51**
Baseball	Tulane	UConn	
Softball	South Florida	Tulsa	

2014–2015	Season	Tournament	National Playoffs
Football	UCF, Cincinnati, Memphis		Cincinnati lost Military, UCF lost St. Pete
Men's Basketball	SMU	SMU	
Women's Basketball	UConn	UConn	**NCAA champions** over Notre Dame 63-53
Baseball	U. of Houston	E. Carolina	
Softball	UCF	UCF	

2013–2014	Season	Tournament	National Playoffs
Football	U. of Central Florida		Won Fiesta Bowl over Baylor, 52-42
Men's Basketball	Louisville, Cin.	Louisville*	UConn went on to **National Champions**
Women's Basketball	UConn	UConn	**NCAA Champions**
Baseball	Louisville	U.of Houston	
Softball	UCF	Louisville	

Louisville left the AAC after the season for the Atlantic Coast Conference.

C-USA Champions

Texas schools in **Conference USA** in 2019 were:

Rice University
University of Texas at San Antonio
Univeristy of Texas at El Paso
University of North Texas

Rice and **UTEP** joined in 2005.
In 2013, the **University of North Texas** and the **University of Texas at San Antonio** joined the conference.

The University of Houston joined in 1996 and left in 2013.

Other teams in Conference USA are University of Alabama-Birmingham, Florida Atlantic University, Florida International University, Louisiana Tech University, and Marshall University.

Also, Middle Tennessee State University, University of North Carolina at Charlotte, Old Dominion University (in Virginia), University of Southern Mississippi, and Western Kentucky University.

2018–2019	Champion	Runner-up	National Playoffs
Football	UAB	Mid. Tenn.	UAB won Boca Raton over N. Illinois
Men's Basketball	Old Dominion	Old Dominion	Lost regional first round to Purdue 61-48
Women's Basketball	Rice	Rice	Lost in regional to Marquette 58-54 OT
Baseball	Fla. Atlantic	So. Miss.	So. Miss lost regional final to LSU
Softball	LA Tech	Marshall	LA Tech lost to TTech in regional

2017–2018	Champion	Runner-up	National Playoffs
Football	Fla. Atlantic	UNT	
Men's Basketball	Marshall	W. Kentucky	Marshall lost in regionals
Women's Basketball	W Kentucky	UAB	W Kentucky lost in regionals
Baseball	So. Miss.		Lost in regionals to Arkansas 10-2
Softball	Mid. Tenn.	Fla. Atlantic	Middle Tennessee lost in regionals

2016–2017	Champion	Runner-up	National Playoffs
Football	W Kentucky	LA Tech	Both teams won bowl games
Men's Basketball	Mid. Tenn.	LA Tech	Mid. Tenn lost second round to Butler
Women's Basketball	W Kentucky	So. Miss.	W Kentucky lost first round to Ohio State
Baseball	So. Miss.	Rice	
Softball	LA Tech	FIU	Both lost in 2nd round

2015–2016	Champion	Runner-up	National Playoffs
Football	W. Kentucky	So. Miss.	W. Kentucky, So. Miss. won bowl games
Men's Basketball	Mid. Tenn.	Old Dominion	Mid. Tenn. lost second round to Syracuse
Women's Basketball	Mid. Tenn.	Old Dominion	
Baseball	So. Miss.	Rice	Rice lost regionals to LSU
Softball	Florida Atlantic	UAB	

2014–2015	Champion	Runner-up	National Playoffs
Football	Marshall	LA Tech	Marshall won Boca Rotan, LT won Dallas
Men's Basketball	UAB	Mid. Tenn.	UAB lost in regional to UCLA 92-75
Women's Basketball	W Kentucky	So. Miss.	
Baseball	Florida Int.	UAB	
Softball	W Kentucky	FAU	

2013–2014	Champion	Runner-up	National Playoffs
Football	Rice	Marshall	Rice lost Liberty Bowl to Miss. State 44-7
Men's Basketball tie	LA Tech, Tulsa, M.Tenn., So. Miss.		Tulsa lost Round of 64 to UCLA 76-59
Women's Basketball	Tulsa	UCF	
Baseball	Rice	UTSA	Rice lost second round regional to Texas
Softball	Tulsa	Marshall	Tulsa lost regional final to Baylor

SWAC Champions

Texas schools in **Southwestern Athletic Conference** in 2019 were:

Prairie View A&M University
Texas Southern University

The Prairie View A&M Panthers have been in the conference since its founding in 1920 and the Texas Southern Tigers joined the conference in 1954.

Other teams in the SWAC Western Division are Grambling State University, Southern University (both in Louisiana), and University of Arkansas at Pine Bluff.

Schools in the Eastern Division are Jackson State University (in Mississippi), Mississippi Valley State University, Alcorn State University (in Mississippi), Alabama State University, and Alabama A&M University.

2018–2019	Season	Tournament	National Playoffs
Football	Alcorn State		Lost Celebration Bowl to NC A&T
Men's Basketball	Prairie View A&M	Prairie View A&M	Lost First Four to Fairleigh Dickinson
Women's Basketball	Southern	Southern	Lost in regionals to Miss. State 103-46
Baseball	Southern		Lost in regional first round
Softball	Alabama State		Lost in regionals to Lipscomb

2017–2018	Season	Tournament	National Playoffs
Football	Grambling		
Men's Basketball	Grambling	Texas Southern	Texas Southern lost in regionals
Women's Basketball	Southern	Grambling	Grambling lost in regionals
Baseball	Texas Southern		Lost in regionals
Softball	Prairie View A&M		Lost in regionals

2016–2017	Season	Tournament	National Playoffs
Football	Grambling		
Men's Basketball	Texas Southern	Texas Southern	Lost first round to North Carolina
Women's Basketball	Alabama State	Alabama State	
Baseball	Texas Southern		Lost first round to Rice
Softball	Texas Southern		Lost in first round to Texas A&M

2015–2016	Season	Tournament	National Playoffs
Football	Alcorn State		
Men's Basketball	Texas Southern	Southern	Southern lost first game to Holy Cross
Women's Basketball	3-way tie	Alabama State	AL St. lost first round to Texas 86-42
Baseball	Alabama State		Eliminated in regional by Florida State
Softball	Alabama State		Eliminated in regional by Florida

2014–2015	Season	Tournament	National Playoffs
Football	Alcorn Sate		
Men's Basketball	Texas Southern	Texas Southern	Lost second round to Arizona 93-72
Women's Basketball	Texas Southern	Alabama State	AL St. lost to Florida State 91-49
Baseball	Texas Southern		
Softball	Texas Southern		

2013–2014	Season	Tournament	National Playoffs
Football	Southern		
Men's Basketball	Southern	Texas Southern	
Women's Basketball	Southern	Prairie View	
Baseball	Jackson State		Lost regional 2nd round to Miss. State
Softball	Texas Southern		Lost regional 1st round to LA-Lafayette

Sun Belt Champions

In 2013, **Texas State University** and the **University of Texas at Arlington** joined the Sun Belt Conference.

Other schools in the conference are the University of Louisiana-Monroe, the University of Louisiana-La-fayette, the University of Arkansas-Little Rock, Arkansas State University, Coastal Carolina University, Troy University, the University of South Alabama, Middle Tennessee State University, Appalachian State University (N. Carolina), Georgia Southern University, and Georgia State University.

2018–2019	Season	Tournament	National Playoffs
Football	Appalachian State		
Men's Basketball	Georgia State	Georgia State	Lost regional first round to Houston 84-55
Women's Basketball	UT-Arlington	UA-Little Rock	Little Rock lost in regionals to Gonzaga 68-51
Baseball	TX St./GA St.	Co. Carolina	Co. Carolina lost regional second round
Softball	LA-Lafayette	LA-Lafayette	Lost regional final to Ole Miss

2017–2018	Season	Tournament	National Playoffs
Football	Appalachian State & Troy		
Men's Basketball	LA-Lafayette	Georgia State	GA State lost regional to Cincinnati 68-53
Women's Basketball	UA-Little Rock	UA-Little Rock	Lost regional to Florida State 91-49
Baseball	Co.Carolina / LA	Coastal Carolina	Lost regional to Washington 11-6
Softball	Texas State	Texas State	Lost regional Round 2 to UCLA 14-1

2016–2017	Season	Tournament	National Playoffs
Football	Appalachian St., Ark. St. (tie)		
Men's Basketball	UT-Arlington	Troy	Troy lost first round to Duke
Women's Basketball	UA-Little Rock	Troy	Troy lost first round to Mississippi State
Baseball	So. Alabama	So. Alabama	Lost in regional second round
Softball	LA-Lafayette	LA-Lafayette	Lost regional final to LSU

2015–2016	Season	Tournament	National Playoffs
Football	Arkansas State		Lost New Orleans Bowl to LA Tech 47-28
Men's Basketball	UA-Little Rock	UA-Little Rock	Lost second round to Iowa State 78-61
Women's Basketball	Arkansas State	Troy	Troy lost first round to Oregon State 73-31
Baseball	LA-Lafayette	LA-Lafayette	Lost regionals to Arizona
Softball	LA-Lafayette	LA-Lafayette	Lost super regionals to Oklahoma

2014–2015	Season	Tournament	National Playoffs
Football	Georgia Southern		
Men's Basketball	GA State	GA State	Lost regional to Xavier 75-67
Women's Basketball	UA-Little Rock	UA-Little Rock	Lost in regional to Arizona State 57-54
Baseball	So. Alabama	LA-Lafayette	LA-Lafayette lost super regional to LSU
Softball	LA-Lafayette	So. Alabama	LA-Lafayette lost super regional to Auburn

2013–2014	Season	Tournament	National Playoffs
Football	Arkansas State		Won GoDaddy over Ball State 23-20
Men's Basketball	GA State	LA-Lafayette	
Women's Basketball	Arkansas State	W. Kentucky	
Baseball	LA-Lafayette	LA-Lafayette	Lost regional final to Ole Miss
Softball	LA-Lafayette	LA-Lafayette	Lost in first round to Oklahoma

Southland Champions

Texas schools in the **Southland Conference** in 2019:

Abilene Christian Universtiy
Houston Baptist University
Texas A&M University–Corpus Christi
Stephen F. Austin State University

Sam Houston State University
Lamar University
Univserity of the Incarnate Word

Other schools are Central Arkansas University, McNeese State University, the University of New Orleans, Nicholls State University (LA), Northwestern State University (LA), and Southeastern Louisiana University.

2018–2019	Season	Tournament	National Playoffs
Football	Nicholls State		
Men's Basketball	Sam Houston	Abilene Christian	ACU lost regional to Kentucky 79-44
Women's Basketball	Lamar	Abilene Christian	ACU lost in regional to Baylor 95-38
Baseball	Sam Houston	McNeese	Dallas Baptist lost regional final
Softball	Sam Houston	Sam Houston	Lost in regionals to U. of Houston

2017–2018	Champion	Runner-up	National Playoffs
Football	Central Arkansas		Sam Houston lost semifinal
Men's Basketball	Stephen F. Austin	SE Louisiana	SFA lost regional to TTech
Women's Basketball	Nicholls State	Stephen F. Austin	Nicholls lost regional to Miss. State
Baseball	Northwestern	New Orleans	NW State lost regional to LSU
Softball	McNeese	Nicholls	McNeese lost regional to TX A&M

2017–2017	Champion	Runner-up	National Playoffs
Football	Sam Houston State		Lost quarterfinals to James Madison
Men's Basketball	New Orleans	A&M-Corpus	
Women's Basketball	Central Arkansas		
Baseball	Sam Houston	Central Arkansas	Sam Houston lost in super regional
Softball	McNeese	Abilene Chris.	McNeese lost in 2nd round to LSU

2015–2016	Champion	Runner-up	National Playoffs
Football	McNeese	Sam Houston	Sam Houston advanced to semifinals
Men's Basketball	Stephen F. Austin	A&M-Corpus	SFA eliminated in second round 76-75
Women's Basketball	Central Arkansas	Sam Houston	
Baseball	Sam Houston St.	SE Louisiana	
Softball	McNeese	Lamar	

2014–2015	Champion	Runner-up	National Playoffs
Football	Sam Houston State		Won quarterfinal over Villianova
Men's Basketball	Stephen F. Austin	Sam Houston	SFA lost second round to Utah 57-50
Women's Basketball	NW State	Houston Baptist	NW State lost to Baylor 77-36
Baseball	Houston Baptist	Sam Houston	
Softball	Central Arkansas	NW State	

2013–2014	Champion	Runner-up	National Playoffs
Football	Southeastern Louisiana		
Men's Basketball	Stephen F. Austin	Sam Houston St.	
Women's Basketball	NW State	Stephen F. Austin	NW State lost regional first round
Baseball	SE Louisiana	Central Arkansas	SE Louisiana lost regional second round
Softball	NW State	McNeese	NW State lost regional first round

Texas College Sports — Division II

Lone Star Champions

The **Lone Star Conference**, founded in 1931, has long been the athletic conference for Texas schools in the NCAA second tier of schools, Division II.

Texas schools in the conference in 2018 were:
Angelo State University
Midwestern State University
Tarleton State University
Texas A&M University—Commerce
Texas A&M University—Kingsville
Texas Woman's University
West Texas A&M University
University of Texas of the Permian Basin
Other teams in conference are Cameron University (Okla.), Western New Mexico University, and Eastern New Mexico State University.

In July 2019 the Heartland Conference schools (minus Newman) joined the Lone Star Conference.

The Universtiy of Texas at Tyler will become a member in the 2019-2020 academic year.

2018–2019	Season	Tournament	National Playoffs
Football	Tarleton State		
Men's Basketball	West Texas A&M	West Texas A&M	Lost quarterfinal to S Indiana
Women's Basketball	West Texas A&M	West Texas A&M	Angelo State lost regional final
Baseball	Angelo State	West Texas A&M	Angelo State lost in super regional
Softball	Kingsville	Kingsville	Lost national final to Augustana 2-1

2017–2018	Season	Tournament	National Playoffs
Football	Midwestern		A&M-Commerce **national champs**
Men's Basketball	West Texas A&M	West Texas A&M	
Women's Basketball	Angelo/WTX A&M	West Texas A&M	
Baseball	West Texas A&M	Tarleton	
Softball	Angelo State	Angelo State	

2016–2017	Season	Tournament	National Playoffs
Football	A&M-Commerce	Midwestern	A&M-Commerce lost second round
Men's Basketball	UT-Permian	UT-Permian	West Texas A&M lost regional final
Women's Basketball	Angelo State	Tarleton	West Texas A&M lost in Elite 8
Baseball	Angelo State	West Texas A&M	Both lost in regionals
Softball	Angelo State	West Texas A&M	Angelo lost final to MSU-Mankato

2015–2016	Season	Tournament	National Playoffs
Football	A&M–Commerce	Midwestern	A&M-Commerce lost first round
Men's Basketball	Tarleton	A&M–Commerce	Tarleton lost quarterfinal
Women's Basketball	West Texas A&M	West Texas A&M	Lost third round to Lubbock Chr.
Baseball	Angelo State	Angelo State	Angelo eliminated in second round
Softball	West Texas A&M	West Texas A&M	Lost 3rd round to Southern Ark.

2014–2015	Season	Tournament	National Playoffs
Football	A&M–Commerce	Angelo State	Angelo State lost in second round
Men's Basketball	Tarleton, Midwestern	Tarleton	Lost Final Four to Mt. Olive 77-59
Women's Basketball	West Texas A&M	West Texas A&M	Lost in Elite 8 to Emporia State
Baseball	WTX A&M, Kingsville (tie)	Angelo State	
Softball	West Texas A&M	West Texas A&M	

2013–2014	Season	Tournament	National Playoffs
Football	Eastern New Mexico and Tarleton		
Men's Basketball	Tarleton, Midwestern	Tarleton	Tarleton lost in round 2
Women's Basketball	West Texas A&M	West Texas A&M	Lost in final to Bentley 73-65
Baseball	Kingsville	Tarleton	
Softball	West Texas A&M	Angelo State	W Texas A&M **national champions**

Heartland Champions

The **Heartland Conference** was formed in 1999. Texas schools in the conference in 2018 were:

Texas A&M International University
St. Mary's University
St. Edward's University
Dallas Baptist University
Lubbock Christian University.

Other members were: University of Arkansas-Fort Smith, Oklahoma Christian University, Newman University (Kansas), and Rogers State University (Oklahoma). The conference does not have football competition.

In July 2019, all schools but Newman became members of the Lone Star Conference.

2018–2019	Season	Tournament	National Playoffs
Men's Basketball	St. Edward's	St. Edward's	Lost regional final to W Texas A&M
Women's Basketball	Lubbock Christian	Lubbock Christian	**National champs**, over SW Oklahoma
Baseball	Lubbock Christian	Rogers State	Lubbock Ch. lost in regional
Softball	OK Christian	OK Christian	

2017–2018	Season	Tournament	National Playoffs
Men's Basketball	Dallas Baptist	Dallas Baptist	Lost in regional to Regis 87-82
Women's Basketball	Lubbock Christian	Lubbock Christian	Lost in quarterfinals to Central Mo.
Baseball	St. Mary's	St. Edward's	St. Edward's lost in regional
Softball	St. Mary's	Rogers State	

2016–2017	Season	Tournament	National Playoffs
Men's Basketball	Dallas Baptist	UA-Fort Smith	
Women's Basketball	St. Edward's	St. Edward's	
Baseball	Lubbock Chris.	St. Edward's	Lubbock Chris. lost in regionals
Softball	St. Mary's	Lubbock Chris.	

2015–2016	Season	Tournament	National Playoffs
Men's Basketball	Rogers State	Dallas Baptist	Lubbock Chr. lost second round
Women's Basketball	Lubbock Christian		**National champs** over Alaska-Anch.
Baseball	St. Edward's	St. Edward's	Lost regional final to Angelo State
Softball	St. Mary's	Lubbock Christian	St. Mary's lost in super regional

2014–2015	Season	Tournament	National Playoffs
Men's Basketball	St. Mary's	St. Mary's	Lost first round to Tarleton 71-52
Women's Basketball	LCU, UA-Ft. Smith	UA-Fort Smith	Lost round 2 to W Texas A&M 70-57
Baseball	St. Ed, St Mary's	St. Mary's	
Softball	LCU, St. Mary's	St. Mary's	St. Mary's lost first round to Shorter

2013–2014	Season	Tournament	National Playoffs
Men's Basketball	UA-Fort Smith	A&M International	A&M Inter., St.Mary's lost 1st round
Women's Basketball	A&M International	St. Edward's	A&M Inter., St. Mary's lost 1st round
Baseball	St. Edward's	St. Edward's	Lost in regionals
Softball	St. Mary's	St. Mary's	Lost to W Texas A&M in regionals

Football Bowl Games 2018–2019

Following are the college football bowl games involving Texas schools, as well as bowl games held in the state and the national championship game.

Bowl	Winner	Opponent	Date, Place
Frisco Bowl	Ohio U. 27	San Diego State 0	Dec. 19, Frisco, Toyota Stadium
New Mexico Bowl	Utah State 52	North Texas 13	Dec. 15, Albuquerque, U. Stadium
Cheez-It Bowl	TCU 10 (OT)	California 7	Dec. 26, Phoenix, Chase Field
Alamo Bowl	Wash. State 28	Iowa State 26	Dec. 28, San Antonio, Alamodome
Texas Bowl	Baylor 45	Vanderbilt 38	Dec. 27, Houston, NRG Stadium
Cotton Bowl	Clemson 30	Notre Dame 3	Dec. 29, Arlington, AT&T Stadium
First Responder Bowl	Boston C./Boise St.	(canceled, weather)	Dec. 26, Dallas, Cotton Bowl
Sun Bowl	Stanford 14	Pittsburgh 13	Dec. 31, El Paso, Sun Bowl
Armed Forces Bowl	Army 70	U. of Houston 14	Dec. 22, Fort Worth, Amon Carter
Gator Bowl	Texas A&M 52	NC State 13	Dec. 30, Jacksonville, TIAA Field
Sugar Bowl	Texas 28	Georgia 21	Jan. 1, New Orleans, Superdome
Nat. Championship	Clemson 44	Alabama 16	Jan. 7, Santa Clara, Levi's Stadium

Football Bowl Games 2017–2018

Bowl	Winner	Opponent	Date, Place
Belk Bowl	Wake Forest 55	Texas A&M 52	Dec. 29, Charlotte, B. of Am. Stadium
Alamo Bowl	TCU 39	Stanford 37	Dec. 28, San Antonio, Alamodome
Texas Bowl	Texas 33	Missouri 16	Dec. 27, Houston, NRG Stadium
Heart of Dallas Bowl	Utah 30	West Virginia 14	Dec. 26, Dallas, Cotton Bowl
Cotton Bowl	Ohio State 24	USC 7	Dec. 29, Arlington, AT&T Stadium
Sun Bowl	N. Carolina St. 52	Arizona State 31	Dec. 30, El Paso, Sun Bowl
Armed Forces Bowl	Army 42	San Diego State 35	Dec. 23, Fort Worth, Amon Carter
New Orleans Bowl	Troy 50	North Texas 30	Dec. 16, New Orleans, Superdome
Frisco Bowl	Louisiana Tech 51	SMU 10	Dec. 20, Frisco, Toyota Stadium
Birmingham Bowl	South Florida 38	Texas Tech 34	Dec. 23, Birmingham, Legion Field
Hawaii Bowl	Fresno State 33	Houston 27	Dec. 24, Honolulu, Aloha Stadium
Nat. Championship	Alabama 26 (OT)	Georgia 23	Jan. 8, Atlanta, Mercedes-Benz Sta.

Football Bowl Games 2016–2017

Bowl	Winner	Opponent	Date, Place
Cactus Bowl	Baylor 31	Boise St. 12	Dec. 27, Phoenix, Chase Field
New Mexico Bowl	New Mexico 23	UTSA 20	Dec. 17, Albuquerque, U. Stadium
Las Vegas Bowl	San Diego St. 34	Houston 10	Dec. 17, Las Vegas, Boyd Stadium
Alamo Bowl	Oklahoma St. 38	Colorado 8	Dec. 29, San Antonio, Alamodome
Texas Bowl	Kansas St. 33	Texas A&M 28	Dec. 28, Houston, NRG Stadium
Heart of Dallas Bowl	Army 38 (OT)	North Texas 31	Dec. 27, Dallas, Cotton Bowl
Cotton Bowl	Wisconsin 24	W. Michigan 16	Jan. 2, Arlington, AT&T Stadium
Sun Bowl	Stanford 25	North Carolina 23	Dec. 30, El Paso, Sun Bowl
Armed Forces Bowl	Louisiana Tech 48	Navy 45	Dec. 23, Fort Worth, Amon Carter
Liberty Bowl	Georgia 31	TCU 23	Dec. 30, Memphis, Liberty Bowl
Nat. Championship	Clemson 35	Alabama 31	Jan. 9, Tampa, R. James Stadium

Major Professional Sports

Jose Altuve slides home in a 2017 game against Baltimore. Photo by Keith Allison, info@keithallisonphoto.com (CC).

World Series Champions 2017

For the second time in franchise history the Houston Astros went to the World Series, but this time won the major-league championship.

The Astros defeated the Los Angeles Dodgers four games to three in the first World Series since 1970 in which both teams had 100 wins in the regular season.

In 2005, Houston won the National League pennant but was swept in the World Series by the Chicago White Sox. The Astros, established in 1962 as the Colt .45s, moved to the American League West Division in 2013.

In 2017, the Astros beat the New York Yankees four games to three to win the American League pennant. The AL champs then faced the National League champion Dodgers, with Los Angeles having the home-field advantage for the finals.

Houston's outfielder George Springer was named the Most Valuable Player after hitting five home runs in the series' seven games.

The 101 Astros wins in the 2017 regular season was the result of a rebuilding that began after losing more than 100 games in three consecutive seasons.

In 2018, when they again went to the playoffs, they won 103 games but lost the American League title to the Boston Red Sox, who went on to win the 2018 World Series.

Texas' other major-league baseball team, the Texas Rangers, won the American League pennant back-to-back in 2010 and 2011. They lost the 2010 World Series to the San Francisco Giants four games to one, and the 2011 series to the St. Louis Cardinals four games to three.

Alliance of American Football (AAF)

San Antonio Commanders (Western Conference)

In February 2019, the first season of a new professional football league began and did not last the whole season. The Alliance of American Football included the San Antonio Commanders and seven other teams.

In the Western Conference with San Antonio were teams in Arizona, Salt Lake City, and San Diego.

In the Eastern Conference were teams in Atlanta, Birmingham, Memphis, and Orlando.

The Commanders, coached by former San Diego Chargers head coach Mike Riley, played their games in the 64,000-seat Alamodome.

The scheduled 10-week season ended after only eight weeks in April 2019 with the announcement that the league was suspending operatons. It filed for bankruptcy the same month.

Year	Win	Loss	Finish
2019	5	3	Tied with the Arizona Hotshots for the Western Conference lead

Major League Baseball
Houston Astros (National League Central / American League West)

Year	Win	Loss	%	Finish
2011	56	106	.346	6th in Central Divison, National League
2012	55	107	.340	6th in Central Division
			Realignment to American League, West Division	
2013	51	111	.315	5th in division
2014	70	92	.432	4th in division
2015	86	76	.531	2nd in division; lost division series to Kansas City Royals 3-2
2016	84	78	.519	3rd in division
2017	101	61	.623	**World Series champions**; defeated LA Dodgers 4-3
2018	103	59	.636	1st in division; lost ALCS to Boston Red Sox 4-1

Texas Rangers (American League West)

Year	Win	Loss	%	Finish
2011	96	66	.593	1st in division; lost **World Series** to St. Louis Cardinals 4-3
2012	93	69	.574	2nd in division; lost wild card to Baltimore Orioles 5-1
2013	91	72	.562	2nd in division
2014	67	95	.414	5th in division
2015	88	74	.543	1st in division; lost division series to Toronto Blue Jays 3-2
2016	95	67	.586	1st in division; lost division series to Toronto Blue Jays 3-0
2017	78	84	.481	Tied for 3rd in division
2018	67	95	.414	5th in division

National Football League (NFL)
Houston Texans (AFC South)

Year	Win	Loss	Finish
2011	10	6	1st AFC South; lost division playoff to Baltimore Ravens 20-13
2012	12	4	1st AFC South; lost division playoff to New England Patriots 41-28
2013	2	14	
2014	9	7	
2015	9	7	
2016	9	7	1st AFC South; lost division playoff to New England Patriots 34-16
2017	4	12	
2018	11	5	1st AFC South; lost wild-card playoff to Indianapolis Colts 21-7

Dallas Cowboys (NFC East)

Year	Win	Loss	Finish
2011	8	8	
2012	8	8	
2013	8	8	
2014	12	4	1st NFC East; lost divisional playoff to Green Bay Packers 26-21
2015	4	12	
2016	13	3	1st NFC East; lost divisional playoff to Green Bay Packers 34-31
2017	9	7	
2018	10	6	2nd NFC East; lost divisional playoff to Los Angeles Rams 30-22

National Basketball Association (NBA)

San Antonio Spurs (Southwest)

Year	Win	Loss	%	Finish
2011–12	50	16	.758	Lost Western conference finals to Oklahoma City Thunder 4-2
2012–13	58	24	.707	Western conference champions; lost finals to Miami Heat 4-3
2013–14	62	20	.756	Won **NBA championship** over Miami Heat 4–1
2014–15	55	27	.671	Lost first round to Los Angeles Clippers 4–3
2015–16	67	15	.817	Lost conference semifinals to Oklahoma City Thunder 4-2
2016–17	61	21	.744	Lost conference finals to Golden State Warriors 4–0
2017–18	47	35	.573	Lost first round to Golden State Warriors 4–1
2018–19	48	34	.582	Lost first round to Denver Nuggets 4-3

Houston Rockets (Southwest)

Year	Win	Loss	%	Finish
2011–12	34	32	.515	
2012–13	45	27	.549	Lost first round to Oklahoma City Thunder 4-2
2013–14	54	28	.659	Lost first round to Portland Trail Blazers 4-2
2014–15	56	26	.683	Lost conference finals to Golden State Warriors 4–1
2015–16	41	41	.500	Lost first round to Golden State Warriors 4-1
2016–17	55	27	.671	Lost conference semifinals to San Antonio Spurs 4–2
2017–18	65	17	.793	Lost Western conference finals to Golden State Warriors 4–3
2018–19	53	29	.646	Lost conference semifinals to Golden State Warriors 4-2

Dallas Mavericks (Southwest)

Year	Win	Loss	%	Finish
2011–12	36	30	.541	Lost first round to Oklahoma City Thunder 4-0
2012–13	41	41	.500	
2013–14	49	33	.598	Lost first round to San Antonio Spurs 4-3
2014–15	50	32	.610	Lost first round to Houston Rockets 4–1
2015–16	42	40	.512	Lost first round to Oklahoma City Thunder 4-1
2016–17	33	49	.402	
2017–18	24	58	.293	
2018–19	33	49	.402	

Womens National Basketball Association (WNBA)

Dallas Wings (Western Conference)

The franchise moved to Dallas-Fort Worth in 2015 from Tulsa. It was founded in 1998 as the Detroit Shock, where it played until 2010.

The Wings play in College Park Center at the University of Texas at Arlington.

The majority owner is Bill Cameron, who is an Oklahoma City businessman. He also owns part of the Oklahoma City Thunder in the NBA.

The WNBA has 12 teams, and its season is played from May to September.

The other WNBA team in Texas was the Houston Comets, who were an original franchise when the league was formed in 1997. The team folded in 2008 when no new owners could be found.

Year	Win	Loss	%	Finish
2016	11	23	.324	
2017	16	18	.470	Lost first-round game to Washington Mystics 86-76
2018	15	19	.441	Lost first-round game to Phoenix Mercury 101-83

National Hockey League (NHL)
Dallas Stars

Year	Win	Loss	Overtime loss	Finish
(Pacific Division)				
2011–12	42	35	5	
2012–13	22	22	4	(Lockout forced abbreviated season)
(Central Division)				
2013–14	40	30	11	Lost conference quarterfinals to Anaheim 4-2
2014–15	41	31	10	
2015–16	50	23	9	Lost second round to St. Louis Blues 4–3
2016–17	34	37	11	
2017–18	42	32	8	
2018–19	43	32	7	Lost second round to St. Louis Blues 4–3

Major League Soccer (MLS)
Houston Dynamo

Year	Win	Loss	Draw	Finish
EASTERN CONFERENCE				
2011	12	9	13	2nd in conference; lost final to Los Angeles Galaxy 1-0
2012	16	9	9	5th in conference; lost final to Los Angeles Galaxy 3-1
2013	14	11	9	4th in conference; lost final to Kansas City 2-1
2014	11	17	6	8th in conference
WESTERN CONFERENCE				
2015	11	14	9	8th in conference
2016	7	14	13	8th in conference
2017	13	10	11	4th in conference
2018	10	16	8	9th in conference

FC Dallas

Year	Win	Loss	Draw	Finish
WESTERN CONFERENCE				
2011	15	12	7	4th in conference; lost wild card game to New York Red Bulls 2-0
2012	9	13	12	6th in conference
2013	11	12	11	8th in conference
2014	16	12	6	4th in conference; lost semifinals to Seattle Sounders
2015	18	10	6	1st in conference; lost finals to Portland Timbers 5-3
2016	17	8	9	1st in conference; lost semifinals to Seattle Sounders 4-2
2017	11	10	13	7th in conference
2018	16	9	9	4th in conference; lost knockout round to Portland Timbers 2-1

National Womens Soccer League (NWSL)
Houston Dash

Year	Win	Loss	Draw	Finish
2014	5	16	3	9th
2015	6	8	6	5th
2016	6	10	4	8th
2017	7	14	3	8th
2018	9	10	5	6th

University of Texas quarterback Vince Young on the way to a touchdown against the Colorado Buffaloes in the 2005 Big 12 championship game at Reliant Stadium in Houston. The Texas Longhorns went on to win the game 70–3. Vince Young was inducted into the hall of fame in 2018. Photo by Johntex (CC).

Texas Sports Hall of Fame

The Texas Sports Hall of Fame was organized in 1951 by the Texas Sports Writers Association. Each year the honorees are inducted into the Hall of Fame at a gala dinner.

(The second such fete in 1952 was headlined by, "That filmland athlete, Ronald Reagan, and his actress wife, Nancy Davis," *The Dallas Morning News*, June 9, 1952.)

The hall was originally in Grand Prairie in the Dallas-Fort Worth area. The Hall of Fame was closed in 1986 for financial reasons, but in 1991 it was re-opened in Waco. In addition to memorabilia, the new location also houses archives.

Under the current selection process, dues-paying members of the Texas Sports Hall of Fame can nominate any number of individuals. (Anyone can become a member.)

The selection committee, chaired by Dave Campbell, founder of *Texas Football Magazine,* reviews all nominees and creates the "Official Voting Membership" ballot.

Ballots are then mailed to the voting membership, former Texas Sports Hall of Fame inductees, and the media selection committee.

The results of the balloting are announced in the autumn with the induction banquet following in the winter.

The hall of fame website is at **tshof.org**.

Year	Inductee	Sport	Texas connection, career
*Designation changed in 2013 from year the inductees were selected to the year the award was presented.			
Sources: Texas Sports Hall of Fame, The Handbook of Texas, The Dallas Morning News and other sources.			
2019	Maureen Connolly-Brinker	Tennis	Dallas, 9 Grand Slam singles titles 1950s
	Tony Franklin	Football	Big Spring, FW Arlington Heights, A&M, NFL kicker 1979–88
	Andre Johnson	Football	Wide receiver 14 years mostly with Houston Texans
	Nancy Liebermann	Basketball	First woman coach of men's professionals, for Texas Legends
	Loyd Phillips	Football	Longview, 1967–69 Chicago Bears, Outland Trophy
	Greg Swindell	Baseball	Houston Sharpstown High, UT, MLB pitcher 1986–2002
	Jason Witten	Football	All-Pro tight end, Dallas Cowboys 2003–17

Go to https://texasalmanac.com/topics/sports/texas-sports-hall-fame for a complete list of inductees beginning with 1951.

Year	Inductee	Sport	Texas connection, career
2018	Johnny Bailey	Football	Running back, Houston Yates, Texas A&I, NFL 1990-95
	Nell Fortner	Basketball	New Braunfels, UT, Olympics 2000, coach 1983-2012
	Pete Fredenburg	Football	Player SWT 1966-70, coach Mary Hardin-Baylor 1998–present
	Gary Kubiak	Football	QB Houston St. Pius, A&M 1983, coach Texans, Broncos
	Cathy Self-Morgan	Basketball	Jourdanton, coach Duncanville, 8 girls state champs 2003–19
	Gerald Myers	Basketball	Borger, player, coach, AD, Houston Baptist, Texas Tech – 2011
	Michael Young	Baseball	All-star infielder, Texas Rangers 2000-12
	Vince Young	Football	Houston Madison, QB UT national champs 2005, NFL
	Jill Sterkel	Swimming	UT 1980–83, Olympic medalist 1976, 1980, 1984
2017	Rita Buck-Crockett	Volleyball	San Antonio, U of H All-American 1977, Olympics 1980, 1984
	Dave Elmendorf	Football/Baseball	Houston, All-American at A&M 1970, LA Rams
	Pat Henry	Track	Blinn 1988–2004, A&M coach 2007–11, 35 team national titles
	Flo Hyman	Volleyball	U of H All-American 1970s, Olympics 1984
	Nastia Liukin	Gymnastics	Parker, 5 medals at Olympics 2008
	Eric Metcalf	Football/Track	UT 1980s All-American, NFL
	Wade Phillips	Football	Orange, U of H, coach Cowboys, Houston Oilers, Texans
	Darren Woodson	Football	Cowboys tackle 1992–2004
2016	Fred Akers	Football	Coach, Edinburg, Lubbock 1960s, UT 1977–86
	Larry Allen	Football	Dallas Cowboys All-Pro lineman 1994–2005
	Trevor Brazile	Rodeo	Amarillo, 13-time cowboy world champion 2006–15
	T.J. Ford	Basketball	Houston Willowridge, UT All-American, NBA 2003–12
	Ken Gray	Football	San Saba, Howard Payne, Cardinals, Oilers lineman 1958–70
	Jacob Green	Football	Pasadena, A&M, Seattle, 49ers lineman 1980–92
	Andy Pettitte	Baseball	Deer Park, Yankees, Astros pitcher 1995–2013
	"Smokey" Joe Williams	Baseball	Seguin, San Antonio, Negro Leagues pitcher 1907–32
2015	Zelmo Beaty	Basketball	Hillister, Woodville, Prairie View A&M, NBA-ABA 1962–75
	Gil Brandt	Football	Dallas Cowboys personnel executive 1960–88
	Ty Detmer	Football	Laredo, SA Southwest quarterback, 1990 Heisman at BYU
	Cliff Harris	Football	Dallas Cowboys safety 1970–79
	Richard Quick	Swimming	Highland Park, SMU, UT coach, Olympics coach 1984–2004
	Nolan Richardson	Basketball	El Paso, Texas Western 1961–64, Western Texas coach
	Everson Walls	Football	Richardson Berkner, Cowboys defensive back 1981–89
	Jeremy Wariner	Track	Arlington Lamar, Baylor, Olympic medalist 2004–08
2014*	Doug English	Football	Dallas Adams, UT tackle, Detroit Lions 1975–85
	Larry Johnson	Basketball	Dallas Skyline, Odessa College, UNLV, NBA 1991–2001
	Charlie Krueger	Football	Caldwell, A&M All-American under Bear Bryant, 49ers 1959–73
	Dat Nguyen	Football	Rockport-Fulton, A&M linebacker 1995-98, Dallas 1999–2005
	Pudge Rodriguez	Baseball	Texas Ranger starting in 1991, All-Star catcher 14 times
	Thurman Thomas	Football	Houston, Oklahoma State, NFL running back 1988–2000
	Sanya Richards-Ross	Track	Austin, UT track, Olympic medalist 2004, 2008, 2012
	Don Trull	Football	All-American quarterback Baylor 1960s, AFL-NFL 1963–74
2012*	Drew Brees	Football	Austin Westlake quarterback 1993–96, New Orleans Saints
	Walt Garrison	Football	Lewisville, fullback Dallas Cowboys 1966–74
	Eddie Mathews	Baseball	Texarkana, Boston/Milwaukee/Atlanta Braves 1952–66
	Bobby Moegle	Baseball	Winningest high school coach, Lubbock Monterey 1960–99
	Shaquille O'Neal	Basketball	San Antonio Cole, 19 years NBA, Lakers, Heat
	Cat Osterman	Softball	Houston, Cypress Springs, UT pitcher, Olympics
	Ricky Williams	Football	UT running back 1995–98, Heisman, NFL 1999–2011

Texas Olympic Medalists

This is a list of athletes with Texas connections who have won medals in the Olympics including the 2016 games in Rio de Janiero. This list includes those born here or have lived in Texas, as well as U.S. team members who spent their collegiate careers at Texas universities.

Information included is: the athlete's name, the sport and the year, as well as the types of medals (G-Gold, S-Silver, B-Bronze).

If the athlete won more than one of the same kind of medal in any one year, the number is noted before the letter code; i.e., 2G indicates that the athlete won two gold medals in the games that year.

The symbol (†) following the medal code indicates that the athlete participated in preliminary contests only; the medal was awarded because of membership on a winning team. Years in which the athlete participated but did not win a medal are not included.

Track indicates all track and field events except those noted separately.

Source: United States Olympic Committee.

Olympian	Sport	Year	Medal
Abdallah, Nia Nicole	Taekwondo	2004	S
Adams, Rachel	Volleyball	2016	B
Allen, Chad	Baseball	1996	B
Armstrong, Lance	*Cycling*	*2000*	*B**
Arnette, Jay Hoyland	Basketball	1960	G
Austin, Charles	Track	1996	G
Baker, Walter Thane	Track	1956	G,S,B
		1952	S
Baptiste, Kirk	Track	1984	S
Barr, Beth	Swimming	1988	S
Bassham, Lanny Robert	Shooting	1976	G
		1972	S
Bates, Michael D.	Track	1992	B
Beck, Robert Lee	Pentathlon	1960	2B
Beckie, Janine	Soccer	2016	B
Bedforth, B.J.	Swimming	2000	G
Berens, Ricky	Swimming	2012	G, S
		2008	G
Berube, Ryan Thomas	Swimming	1996	G
Biles, Simone	Gymnastics	2016	4G, B
Boudia, David	Diving	2016	S, B
		2012	G, B
Brew, Derrick K.	Track	2004	G, B
Brown, Earlene Dennis	Track	1960	B
Browning, David (Skippy)	Diving	1952	G
Buckner, William Quinn	Basketball	1976	G
Buford-Bailey, Tonja	Track	1996	B
Burrell, Leroy Russel	Track	1992	G
Butler, Jimmy	Basketball	2016	G
Carey, Rick	Swimming	1984	3G
Carlisle, Daniel T.	Shooting	1984	B
Carter, Michael D.	Shotput	1984	S
Carter, Michelle	Shotput	2016	G
Catchings, Tamika	Basketball	2016	G
		2012	G
Clay, Bryan E.	Decathlon	2008	G
		2004	S

• In January 2013, the International Olympic Committee disqualified Lance Armstrong from the 2000 events he competed in after he was found to have used drugs to enhance his performance.

Olympian	Sport	Year	Medal
Clement, Kerron	Track	2016	G
Cline, Nancy Lieberman	Basketball	1976	S
Cohen, Tiffany	Swimming	1984	G
Conger, Jack	Swimming	2016	G
Corbelli, Laurie Flachmeier	Volleyball	1984	S
Cotton, John	Baseball	2000	G
Crocker, Ian	Swimming	2008	G
		2004	G,S,B
		2000	G
Cross-Battle, Tara	Volleyball	1992	B
Crouser, Ryan	Shotput	2016	G
Davis, Clarissa G.	Basketball	1992	B
Davis, Jack Wells	Track	1956	S
		1952	S
Davis, Josh C.	Swimming	2000	2S
		1996	3G
Davis, W.F. (Buddy)	High Jump	1952	G
DeLoach, Joseph N. Jr.	Track	1988	G
Dersch, Hans	Swimming	1992	G
Didrikson, Mildred (Babe)	Track	1932	2G, S
Donie, Scott R.	Diving	1992	S
Drexler, Clyde	Basketball	1992	G
Dumais, Troy	Diving	2012	B
Durant, Kevin	Basketball	2016	G
		2012	G
Dusing, Nate	Swimming	2004	B
		2000	S
Eller, Glenn	Shooting	2008	G
Ethridge, Mary (Kamie)	Basketball	1988	G
Farmer-Patrick, Sandra	Track	1992	S
Feigen, Jimmy	Swimming	2016	G
		2012	S†
Fields, Connor	Cycling	2016	G
Finn-Burrell, Michelle Bonae	Track	1992	G
Forbes, James Ricardo	Basketball	1972	S
Ford, Gilbert (Gib)	Basketball	1956	G
Foreman, George	Boxing	1968	G
Fortenberry, Joe Cephis	Basketball	1936	G

Olympian	Sport	Year	Medal
Francis, Phyllis	Track	2016	G
Galloway, Jackie	Taekwondo	2016	B
Garrison, Zina	Tennis	1988	G, B
George, Chris	Baseball	2000	G
Gjertson, Doug	Swimming	1992	G, B
		1988	G
Glenesk, Dean William	Pentathlon	1984	S
Goldblatt, Scott	Swimming	2004	G
		2000	B
Gonzáles, Paul G. Jr.	Boxing	1984	G
Gordon, Chris-Ann	Track	2016	S
Griner, Brittney	Basketball	2016	G
Guidry, Carlette D.	Track	1996	G†
		1992	G
Haas, Townley	Swimming	2016	G
Hall, Gary Jr.	Swimming	2004	G, B
		2000	2G,S,B
		1996	2G, 2S
Hamm, Mia	Soccer	2004	G
		2000	S
		1996	G
Hannan, Tommy	Swimming	2000	G
Hansen, Brendan	Swimming	2012	G, B
		2008	G
		2004	G,S,B
Hansen, Fred Morgan	Track	1964	G
Hardee, Trey	Track	2012	S
Harkrider, Kiplan P.	Baseball	1996	B
Hartwell, Erin Wesley	Cycling	1996	S
		1992	B
Hays, Todd	Bobsled	2002	S
Heath, Michael Steward	Swimming	1984	2G, S
Hedgepeth, Whitney L.	Swimming	1996	G, 2S
Hedrick, Chad	Speed Skating	2010	S,B
		2006	G,S,B
Heidenreich, Jerry	Swimming	1972	2G,S,B
Henry, James Edward	Diving	1968	B
Hill, Denean E.	Track	1992	S
		1988	S
		1984	G
Hill, Grant Henry	Basketball	1996	G
Homfeld, Conrad E.	Equestrian	1984	G, S
Hooker, Destinee	Volleyball	2012	S
Hooper, Darrow	Shotput	1952	S
Horton, Jonathan	Gymnastics	2008	S
Howard, Sherri Francis	Track	1988	S
		1984	G
Jackson, Lucious Brown	Basketball	1964	G
Jacobs, Chris	Swimming	1988	2G, S
Johnson, Michael	Track	2000	2G
		1996	2G
		1992	G
Johnson, Rafer L.	Decathlon	1960	G
		1956	S

Olympian	Sport	Year	Medal
Jones, John Wesley (Lam)	Track	1976	G
Jordan, DeAndre	Basketball	2016	G
Jordan, Shaun	Swimming	1992	G
		1988	G
Juarez, Ricardo Rocky	Boxing	2000	S
Julich, Robert William	Cycling	2004	B
Keeler, Kathryn Elliott	Rowing	1984	G
Kern, Douglas James	Sailing	1992	S
Kiefer, Adolph	Swimming	1936	G
Kimmons, Trell	Track	2012	S
King, Judith Brown	Track	1984	S
Kleine, Megan	Swimming	1992	G†
Knight, Bianca	Track	2012	G
Kocian, Madison	Gymnastics	2016	G, S
Kolius, John Waldrip	Sailing	1976	S
Lane, Colleen	Swimming	2004	S
Langkop, Dorothy Franey	Speed Skating	1932	B
Leetch, Brian Joseph	Ice Hockey	2002	S
Lewis, F. (Carl) Carlton	Track	1996	G
		1992	2G
		1988	2G, S
		1984	4G
Lienhard, William Barner	Basketball	1952	G
Lipinski, Tara K.	Figure Skating	1998	G
Liukin, Nastia	Gymnastics	2008	G,3S,B
Lloyd, Andrea	Basketball	1988	G
Losey, Robert G. (Greg)	Pentathlon	1984	S
Lopez, Diana	Taekwondo	2008	B
Lopez, Mark	Taekwondo	2008	S
Lopez, Steven	Taekwondo	2008	B
		2004	G
		2000	G
Lowe, Sara Elizabeth	Swimming	2004	B
Magers, Rose Mary	Volleyball	1984	S
Malone, Jordan	Speed Skating	2014	S
		2010	B
Manuel, Simone	Swimming	2016	2G, 2S
Manzano, Leo	Track	2012	S
Marsh, Michael L.	Track	1996	S
		1992	2G
Marshall, Christine	Swimming	2008	B
Matson, James Randel (Randy)	Shotput	1968	G
		1964	G
Matson, Ollie G.	Track	1952	S, B
McFalls, Jennifer Yvonne	Softball	2000	G
McFarlane, Tracey	Swimming	1988	S
McKenzie, Kim	Track	1984	B
McNeir, Forest	Shooting	1920	G
Meadows, Earle	Track	1936	G
Meili, Katie	Swimming	2016	G, B
Mills, Ronald P.	Swimming	1968	B
Mitchell, Betsy	Swimming	1988	S
		1984	G, S

Olympian	Sport	Year	Medal
Moceanu, Dominique H.	Gymnastics	1996	G
Montgomery, James P.	Swimming	1976	3G, B
Moore, James Warren	Pentathlon	1964	S
Morrow, Bobby Joe	Track	1956	3G
Munoz, Felipe	Swimming	1968	G
Neilson-Bell, Sandy	Swimming	1972	3G
Nelson, Lianne Bennion	Rowing	2004	S
Newhouse, Frederick V.	Track	1976	G, S
Nott/Cunningham, Tara Lee	Weightlifting	2004	G
Okafor, Emeka	Basketball	2004	B
Okolo, Courtney	Track	2016	G
Olajuwon, Hakeem	Basketball	1996	G
Olsen, Justin	Bobsled	2010	G
Osterman, Catherine (Cat)	Softball	2008	S
		2004	G
Paddock, Charles W.	Track	1924	S
		1920	2G, S
Patterson, Carly	Gymnastics	2004	G, 2S
Patton, Darvis	Track	2004	S
Peirsol, Aaron	Swimming	2008	2G, S
		2004	3G
		2000	S
Perry, Nanceen L.	Track	2000	B
Pesthy, Paul Karoly	Fencing	1964	S
Phenix, Erin	Swimming	2000	G
Pinder, Demetrius	Track	2016	B
		2012	G
Postma, Joan Spillane	Swimming	1960	G
Potter, Cynthia Ann	Diving	1976	B
Rambo, John Barnett	Track	1964	B
Rauch, Jamie	Swimming	2000	S
Retton, Mary Lou	Gymnastics	1984	G, 2S, 2B
Richards, Robert E.	Track	1956	G
		1952	G
		1948	B
Richards-Ross, Sanya	Track	2012	2G
		2008	G, B
		2004	G
Ritter, Louise	Track	1988	G
Roberts, Gil	Track	2016	G
Robertson, Alvin Cyrrale	Basketball	1984	G
Robinson, David M.	Basketball	1996	G
		1992	G
		1988	B
Robinson, Moushaumi	Track	2004	G
Robinson, Robert J.	Basketball	1948	G
Robinzine, Kevin B.	Track	1988	G
Robles, Sarah	Weightlifting	2016	B
Roe, Frederick	Polo	1924	S
Russell, Douglas Albert	Swimming	1968	2G
Russell, John William	Equestrian	1952	B
Schneider, Marcus B.	Rowing	1996	B
Schooling, Joseph	Swimming	2016	G
Slay, Brandon Douglas	Wrestling	2000	G

Olympian	Sport	Year	Medal
Smith, Clark	Swimming	2016	G
Smith, Dean	Track	1952	G
Smith, Lamont	Track	1996	G
Smith, Owen Guinn	Track	1948	G
Smith, Tommie C.	Track	1968	G
Southern, S. Edward	Track	1956	S
Spencer, Ashley	Track	2016	B
Steinseifer, Carrie	Swimming	1984	2G
		1988	2B
Sterkle, Jill Ann	Swimming	1984	G
		1976	G
Stevenson, Toby	Pole Vault	2004	S
Stulce, Michael S.	Shotput	1992	G
Swoopes, Sheryl Denise	Basketball	2004	G
		2000	G
		1996	G
Sykora, Stacy	Volleyball	2008	S
Tarmoh, Jeneba	Track	2012	G
Taylor, Robert	Track	1972	G, S
Teagarden, Taylor	Baseball	2008	B
Tinsley, Michael	Track	2012	S
Tisdale, Wayman L.	Basketball	1984	G
Valdez, Jesse	Boxing	1972	B
Van, Allen	Ice Hockey	1952	S
Vollmer, Dana	Swimming	2016	G, S, B
		2012	3G
		2004	G
Walker, Laura Anne	Swimming	1988	B
Walker, Neil	Swimming	2004	G, B
		2000	G, S
Walters, Dave	Swimming	2008	G
Wariner, Jeremy	Track	2008	G, S
		2004	2G
Weatherspoon, Teresa G.	Basketball	1992	B
		1988	G
Weber-Gale, Garrett	Swimming	2008	2G
Wells, Rhoshii S.	Boxing	1996	B
Wells, Wayne A.	Wrestling	1972	G
Whitfield, Malvin G.	Track	1952	G, S
		1948	G, S
Wilkinson, Laura A.	Diving	2000	G
Williams, Christa L.	Softball	2000	G
		1996	G
Williamson, Darold	Track	2004	G
Wilson, Craig Martin	Water Polo	1988	S
		1984	S
Wolfe, Rowland (Flip)	Gymnastics	1932	G
Wrightson, Bernard C.	Diving	1968	G
Wylie, Paul Stanton	Figure Skating	1992	S
Young, Earl Verdelle	Track	1960	2G
Zmeskal, Kim	Gymnastics	1992	B

COUNTIES

The current Collin County Courthouse opened in 2008.
Photo by Larry D Moore (CC).

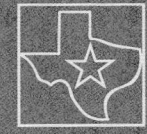

Counties of Texas

These pages describe Texas' 254 counties and hundreds of towns. Descriptions are based on reports from chambers of commerce, the Texas AgriLife Extension agents, federal and state agencies, the *Handbook of Texas,* and other sources. Consult the index for other county information.

County maps are based on those of the Texas Department of Transportation and are copyrighted, 2019, as are the entire contents.

Physical Features: Descriptions are from U.S. Geological Survey and local sources.

Economy: From information provided by local chambers of commerce and county extension agents.

History: From Texas statutes, *Fulmore's History and Geography of Texas as Told in County Names,* WPA Historical Records Survey, Texas Centennial Commission Report, and the *Handbook of Texas.*

Race/Ethnicity: Percentage estimates from the 2017 American Community Survey conducted by the U.S. Bureau of the Census. "Anglo" refers to non-Hispanic whites; "Asian" refers to persons having origins in the Far East, Southeast Asia, or the Indian subcontinent. "Other" includes those of American Indian origin, Pacific Islanders, and those who identify with two or more races. People may choose to report more than one race to indicate their racial mixture, such as "American Indian" and "White." People who identify their origin as Hispanic may be of any race. Thus, the totals may add up to more than 100 percent.

Vital Statistics: From the Texas Department of State Health Services Annual Report 2015 for births and deaths, 2014 for marriages and divorces.

Recreation: From information provided by local chambers of commerce and county extension agents. Attempts were made to note activities unique to the area or that point to ethnic or cultural heritage.

Minerals: From county extension agents.

Agriculture: Condensed from information provided to the *Texas Almanac* by county extension agents in 2019. Market value (total cash receipts) of agricultural products sold is from the **Census of Agriculture** of the U.S. Department of Agriculture that was conducted in 2012.

Cities: Towns listed include the county seat, incorporated cities, and towns with post offices, as well as certain census designated places (CDP). Population figures for incorporated towns and CDPs are estimates for Jan. 1, 2017, from the Texas Demographic Center. Population estimates for other towns are from local officials received through a Texas Almanac survey. When figures for small portions of major cities are given, they are in brackets, such as **part [46,885] of Dallas** in Collin County.

Sources of DATA LISTS

Population (of county): The county population estimate of July 1, 2018, U.S. Census Bureau. The line following gives the percentage of increase or decrease from the 2010 U.S. census count.

Area: Total area in square miles, including water surfaces, as determined in the 2010 U.S. census.

Land Area: The land area in square miles as determined by the U.S. Census Bureau in 2010.

Altitude (ft.): Principally from U.S. Geological Survey topographic maps, including revisions available in 2008. Not all of the surface of Texas has been precisely surveyed for elevation; in some cases data are from the Texas Railroad Commission or the Texas Department of Transportation.

Climate: Provided by the National Oceanic and Atmospheric Administration state climatologist, College Station. Data are revised at 10-year intervals to cover the previous three decades. Listed are the latest compilations, as of Feb. 1, 2013, and pertain to a particular site within the county

(usually the county seat). The data include: **Rainfall** (annual mean in inches); **Temperature** (in degrees Fahrenheit); January mean minimum and July mean maximum.

Workforce/Wages: Prepared by the Texas Workforce Commission, Austin, in cooperation with the Bureau of Labor Statistics of the U.S. Department of Labor. The data are computed from reports by all establishments subject to the Texas Unemployment Compensation Act.

(Agricultural employers are subject to the act if they employ as many as three workers for 20 weeks or pay cash wages of $6,250 in a quarter. Employers who pay $1,000 in wages in a quarter for domestic services are subject also. Still not mandatorily covered are self-employed, unpaid family workers, and those employed by churches and some small nonprofit organizations.)

The work/wage data include (state total, lowest county and highest county included here):

Civilian labor force as of Jan. 1, 2019. Texas, 13,976,348; Loving County, 99; Harris County, 22,356,016.

Unemployed: The unemployment rate (percentage of workforce) as of Jan. 1, 2019. Texas, 3.6; Hartley and McMullen counties, 1.8; Starr County, 9.4.

Total Wages paid in the second quarter of 2018. Texas, $169,512,543,606; King County, $1,257,282; Harris County, $37,997,626,697.

Per Capita Income is for 2017, as reported by the U.S. Bureau of Economic Analysis. Texas, $47,362; Kendall County, $83,808; Starr County, $24,981.

Property Values: Appraised gross market value of real and personal property in each county appraisal district in 2017 as reported to the State Property Tax Board.

Retail Sales: Figures for 2017 as reported to the state Comptroller of Public Accounts.

Anderson County

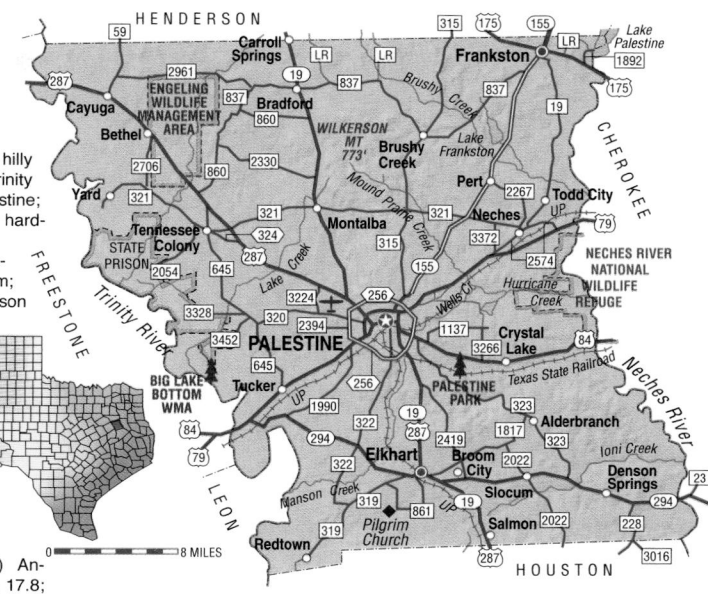

Physical Features: Forested, hilly East Texas county, slopes to Trinity and Neches rivers; Lake Palestine; sandy, clay, black soils; pines, hardwoods.

Economy: Manufacturing, distribution, agribusiness, tourism; hunting and fishing leases; prison units.

History: Comanche, Waco, other tribes. Anglo-American settlers arrived in the 1830s. Antebellum slaveholding area. County created and organized from Houston County in 1846; named for K.L. Anderson, last vice president of the Republic of Texas.

Race/Ethnicity: (In percent) Anglo, 59.1; Black, 21.5; Hispanic, 17.8; Asian, 0.9; Other, 0.8; Two or more races, 1.7.

Vital Statistics, annual: Births, 636; deaths, 655; marriages, 407; divorces, 121.

Recreation: Fishing and hunting, streams, lakes; dogwood trails; national wildlife refuge; historic sites; Texas State Railroad depot, park; museums.

Minerals: Oil and gas.

Agriculture: Beef cattle, hay, truck vegetables, melons, pecans, peaches. Market value $44.6 million. Timber sold.

PALESTINE (19,271), county seat; medical services, education, transportation; clothing, metal, wood products; scientific balloon station; historic bakery; library; vocational-technical facilities; hospital; UT-Tyler extension, community college; Museum of East Texas Culture; hot pepper festival in October.

Other towns include: **Cayuga** (137); **Elkhart** (1,284); **Frankston** (1,218), tourism, packaging industry, oil and gas, commuters to Tyler; depot museum, Square Fair in October; **Montalba** (110); **Neches** (175); and **Tennessee Colony** (300) site of state prisons.

Population	**58,057**
Change fm 2010	– 0.7
Area (sq. mi.)	1,078.0
Land Area (sq. mi.)	1,062.6
Altitude (ft.)	174-773
Rainfall (in.)	46.60
Jan. mean min.	34.5
July mean max.	92.3
Civ. Labor	23,718
Unemployed	3.1
Wages	$224,010,059
Per Capita Income	$33,362
Prop. Value	$3,944,849,392
Retail Sales	$497,346,744

Railroad Abbreviations

AAT	Austin Area Terminal Railroad
AGC	Alamo Gulf Coast Railway
ATK	AMTRAK
ANR	Angelina & Neches River Railroad
ATCX	Austin & Texas Central Railroad
BLR	Blacklands Railroad
BNSF	BNSF Railroad
BOP	Border Pacific Railroad
BRG	Brownsville & Rio Grande Int'l Railroad
CMC	CMC Railroad
DART	Dallas Area Rapid Transit
DGNO	Dallas, Garland & Northeastern Railroad
FWWR	Fort Worth & Western Railroad/Tarantula
GCSR	Gulf, Colorado & San Saba RailwayCorp.
GRR	Georgetown Railroad
GVSR	Galveston Railroad
KCS	Kansas City Southern Railway
KRR	Kiamichi Railroad Company
MCSA	Moscow, Camden & San Augustine RR
PCN	Point Comfort & Northern Railway
PNR	Panhandle Northern Railroad Company
PTRA	Port Terminal Railroad Association
PVS	Pecos Valley Southern Railway
RC	Rusk County Rural Rail Transportation District
RSS	Rockdale, Sandow & Southern Railroad
RVSC	Rio Valley Switching
SAW	South Plains Switching LTD
SRN	Sabine River & Northern Railroad Company
SSC	Southern Switching (Lone Star Railroad)
SW	Southwestern Shortline Railroad
TCT	Texas City Terminal Railway
TIBR	Timber Rock Railroad
TM	The Texas Mexican Railway Company
TN	Texas & Northern Railway
TNER	Texas Northeastern Railroad
TNMR	Texas & New Mexico Railroad
TNW	Texas North Western Railway
TP	Texas Pacifico Transportation
TSE	Texas South-Eastern Railroad Company
TXGN	Texas, Gonzales & Northern Railway
TXR	Texas Rock Crusher Railway
TSSR	Texas State Railroad
UP	Union Pacific Railroad Company
WTJR	Wichita, Tillman & Jackson Railway
WTLR	West Texas & Lubbock Railroad

Andrews County

Physical Features: South Plains, drain to playas; grass, mesquite, shin oak; red clay, sandy soils.

Economy: Natural resources/mining; manufacturing; construction; government/services; agribusiness.

History: Apache, Comanche area until U.S. Army campaigns of 1875. Ranching developed around 1900. Oil boom in 1940s. County created 1876 from Bexar Territory; organized 1910; named for Texas Revolutionary soldier Richard Andrews.

Race/Ethnicity: (In percent) Anglo, 40.2; Black, 1.9; Hispanic, 56.2; Asian, 0.8; Other, 1.5; Two or more races, 1.6.

Vital Statistics, annual: Births, 323; deaths, 137; marriages, 137; divorces, 55.

Recreation: Prairie dog town, wetlands, bird viewing; museum; camper facilities; Fall Fiesta in September.

Minerals: Oil and gas.

Agriculture: Beef, cotton, sorghums, grains, corn, hay; significant irrigation. Market value $12.6 million.

ANDREWS (13,520) county seat; trade center, amphitheatre, hospital.

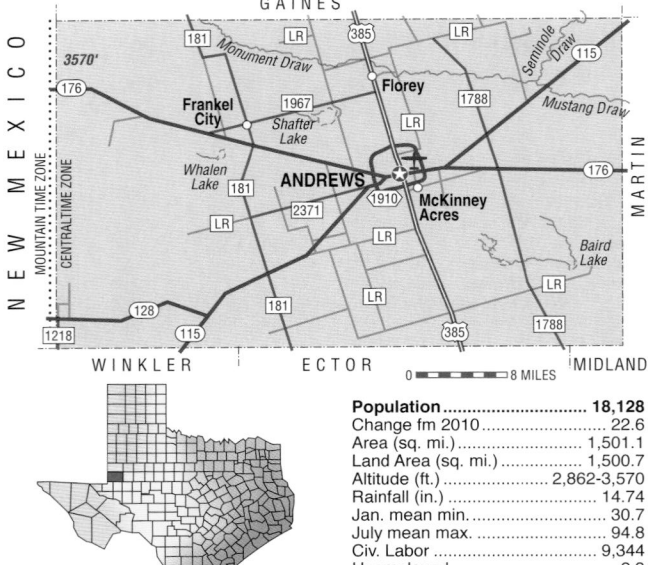

Other towns include, **McKinney Acres** (988).

Population	**18,128**
Change fm 2010	22.6
Area (sq. mi.)	1,501.1
Land Area (sq. mi.)	1,500.7
Altitude (ft.)	2,862-3,570
Rainfall (in.)	14.74
Jan. mean min.	30.7
July mean max.	94.8
Civ. Labor	9,344
Unemployed	2.3
Wages	$125,731,787
Per Capita Income	$43,105
Prop. Value	$4,724,857,970
Retail Sales	$257,621,576

Angelina County

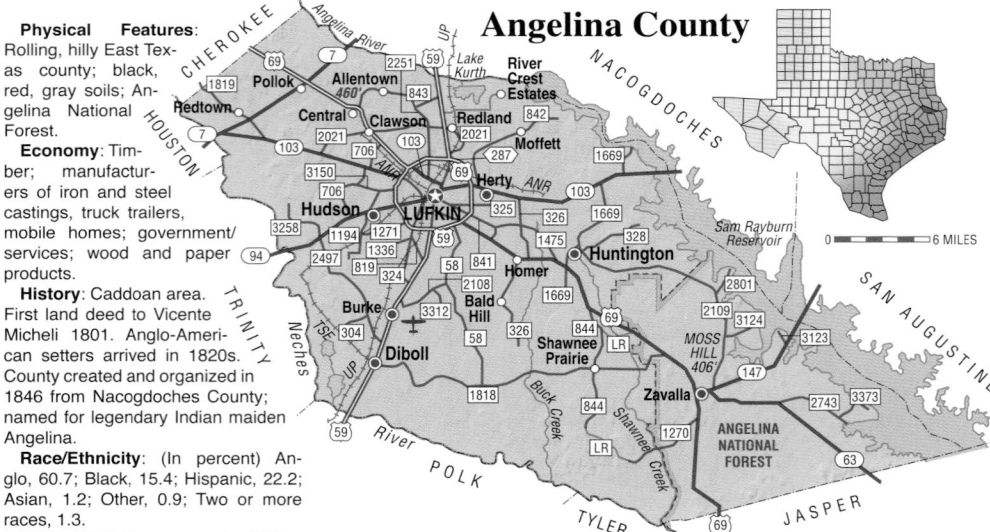

Physical Features: Rolling, hilly East Texas county; black, red, gray soils; Angelina National Forest.

Economy: Timber; manufacturers of iron and steel castings, truck trailers, mobile homes; government/services; wood and paper products.

History: Caddoan area. First land deed to Vicente Micheli 1801. Anglo-American setters arrived in 1820s. County created and organized in 1846 from Nacogdoches County; named for legendary Indian maiden Angelina.

Race/Ethnicity: (In percent) Anglo, 60.7; Black, 15.4; Hispanic, 22.2; Asian, 1.2; Other, 0.9; Two or more races, 1.3.

Vital Statistics, annual: Births, 1,215; deaths, 871; marriages, 662; divorces, 374.

Recreation: Sam Rayburn Reservoir; national, state forests, parks; locomotive exhibit; Forest Festival, bike ride in fall.

Minerals: Limited output of natural gas and oil.

Agriculture: Poultry, beef, horticulture, limited fruits and vegetables. Market value $46.4 million. A leading timber-producing county.

LUFKIN (37,204) county seat; manufacturing; Angelina College; hospitals; U.S., Texas Forest centers; zoo; Expo Center and Texas Forestry Museum.

Other towns include: **Burke** (741); **Diboll** (5,499); **Hudson** (4,820); **Huntington** (2,159); **Pollok** (400); **Redland** (1,108); **Zavalla** (731).

For explanation of sources, symbols and abbreviations, see p. 192, and foldout map.

Population	**87,092**
Change from 2010	0.4
Area (sq. mi.)	864.7
Land Area (sq. mi.)	797.8
Altitude (ft.)	102-460
Rainfall (in.)	48.95
Jan. mean min.	38.3
July mean max.	93.3
Civ. Labor	35,959
Unemployed	4.3
Wages	$352,621,482
Per Capita Income	$37,555
Prop. Value	$5,276,009,585
Retail Sales	$1,195,253,661

Aransas County

Physical Features: Coastal plains; sandy loam, coastal clays; bays, inlets; mesquites, oaks.

Economy: Tourism, recreational fishing, commercial shrimping, hunting.

History: Karankawa, Coahuiltecan area. Settlement by Irish and Mexicans began in 1829. County created and organized in 1871 from Refugio County; named for Rio Nuestra Señora de Aranzazu, derived from a Spanish palace.

Race/Ethnicity: (In percent) Anglo, 67.2; Black, 1.8; Hispanic, 27.7; Asian, 1.9; Other, 1.3; Two or more races, 1.9.

Vital Statistics, annual: Births, 276; deaths, 360; marriages, 242; divorces, 121.

Recreation: Sport fishing, waterfowl hunting; Fulton Mansion; state marine lab; Goose Island State Park; Texas Maritime Museum; bird sanctuaries (a nationally known birding hotspot); Rockport art center; Hummer Bird festival in September.

Minerals: Oil and gas, also oystershell and sand.

Agriculture: Cotton, hay, cow-calf operations. Market value $1.1 million. Fishing, hunting; redfish hatchery.

ROCKPORT (10,658) county seat; tourism, retail trade, health care, construction/real estate; Festival of Wines Memorial Day weekend.

Fulton (1,588) tourism, retail trade, oyster and shrimp harvesting, museums, Oysterfest in March; **Holiday Beach** (538); and **Lamar** (694).

Also, part [724] of **Aransas Pass**.

Population	**23,792**
Change fm 2010	2.7
Area (sq. mi.)	528.0
Land Area (sq. mi.)	252.1
Altitude (ft.)	sea level–55
Rainfall (in.)	34.59
Jan. mean min.	47.9
July mean max.	91.5
Civ. Labor	10,288
Unemployed	4.6
Wages	$49,821,346
Per Capita Income	$44,820
Prop. Value	$3,486,448,827
Retail Sales	$307,149,840

An oyster boat at Rockport-Fulton. Photo by Robert Plocheck.

Archer County

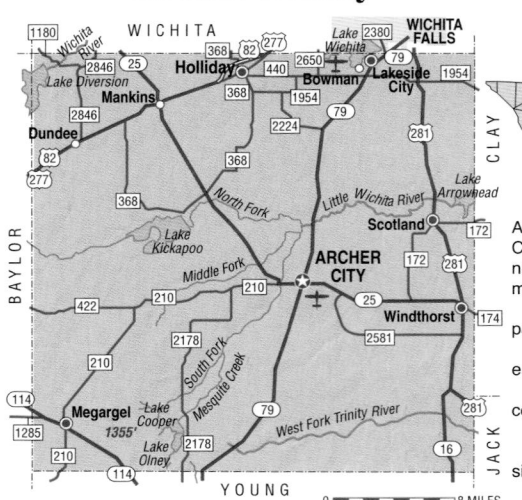

Physical Features: Northwestern county, rolling to hilly, drained by Wichita, Trinity River forks; Lake Kickapoo, Lake Diversion, Lake Wichita, Lake Arrowhead, Lake Cooper and Lake Olney; black, red loams, sandy soils; mesquites, post oaks.

Economy: Cattle, milk production, oil, hunting leases. Part of Wichita Falls metropolitan area.

History: Caddo, Comanche, Kiowas and other tribes in the area until 1875; Anglo-American settlement developed soon afterward. County created from Fannin Land District in 1858; organized in 1880. Named for Dr. B.T. Archer, Republic commissioner to United States.

Race/Ethnicity: (In percent) Anglo, 88.0; Black, 1.0; Hispanic, 8.7; Asian, 0.4; Other, 1.4; Two or more races, 1.5.

Vital Statistics, annual: Births, 78; deaths, 91; marriages, 32; divorces, 21.

Recreation: Hunting of deer, turkey, dove, feral hog, coyote; fishing in area lakes, rodeo in June.

Minerals: Oil and natural gas.

Agriculture: Cow/calf, stocker cattle, dairy, wheat, hay, silage and horses. Market value $76.8 million.

ARCHER CITY (1,826) county seat; cattle, oil field service center; museum; book center; Royal Theatre productions; some manufacturing.

Other towns include: **Holliday** (1,743) Mayfest in spring; **Lakeside City** (1,029); **Megargel** (196); **Scotland** (494); **Windthorst** (400), biannual German sausage festival (also in Scotland).

Population	8,786
Change fm 2010	–3.0
Area (sq. mi.)	925.4
Land Area (sq. mi.)	903,1
Altitude (ft.)	900-1,355
Rainfall (in.)	30.72
Jan. mean min.	29.0
July mean max.	96.5
Civ. Labor	4,110
Unemployed	3.0
Wages	$18,050,717
Per Capita Income	$47,110
Prop. Value	$1,892,220,681
Retail Sales	$33,789,036

For explanation of sources, symbols and abbreviations, see p. 192, and foldout map.

Armstrong County

Physical Features: Partly on High Plains, broken by Palo Duro Canyon. Chocolate loam, gray soils.

Economy: Agribusiness, tourism, commuting to Amarillo.

History: Apache tribal area, then Comanche territory until U.S. Army campaigns of 1874-75. Anglo-Americans began ranching soon afterward. County created from Bexar District, 1876; organized in 1890; name honors pioneer Texas family.

Race/Ethnicity: (In percent) Anglo, 89.6; Black, 1.1; Hispanic, 7.5; Asian, 0.1; Other, 1.5; Two or more races, 0.9.

Vital Statistics, annual: Births, 21; deaths, 38; marriages, 5; divorces, 13.

Recreation: Palo Duro Canyon State Park; Goodnight Ranch Home.

Minerals: Sand, gravel.

Agriculture: Stocker cattle, cow-calf operations; wheat, sorghum, cotton and hay; some irrigation. Market value $19.2 million.

CLAUDE (1,187) county seat; farm, ranch supplies; glass company; medical center; Caprock Roundup in July.

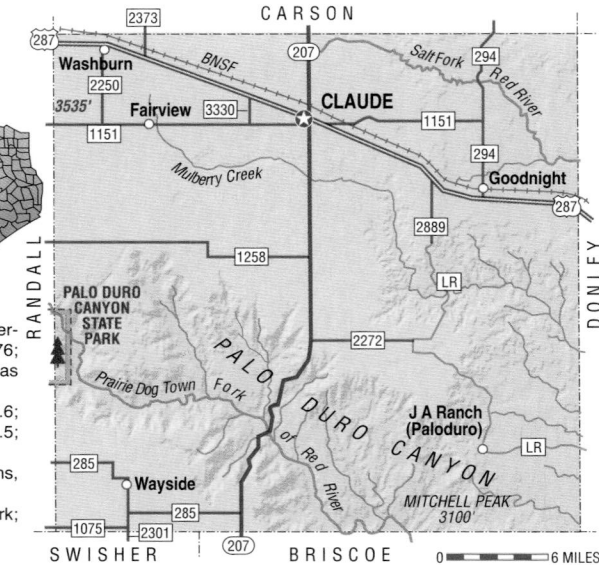

Population	1,892
Change fm 2010	–0.5
Area (sq. mi.)	913.8
Land Area (sq. mi.)	909.1
Altitude (ft.)	2,300–3,535
Rainfall (in.)	22.25
Jan. mean min.	22.4
July mean max.	90.6
Civ. Labor	928
Unemployed	2.5
Wages	$3,733,219
Per Capita Income	$45,262
Prop. Value	$816,595,680
Retail Sales	$11,363,867

Atascosa County

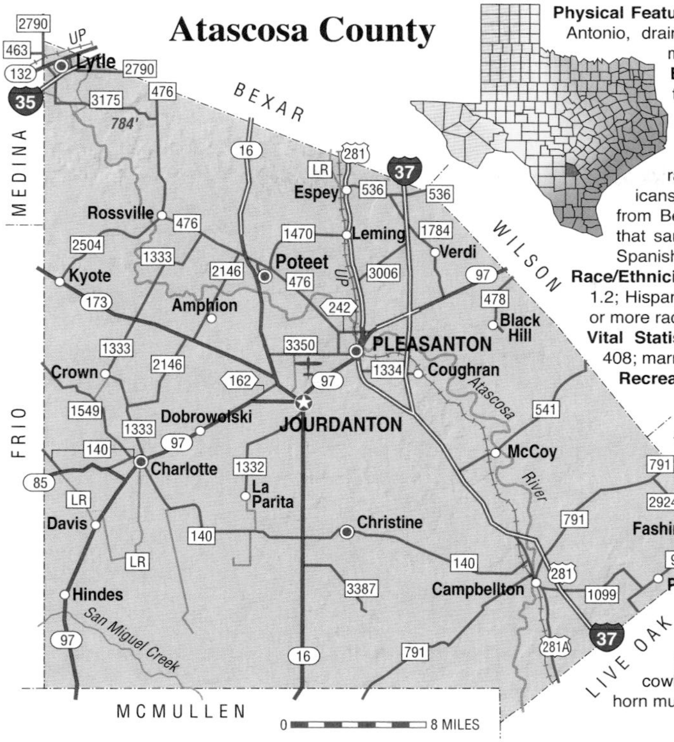

Physical Features: On grassy prairie south of San Antonio, drained by Atascosa River, tributaries; mesquites, other brush.

Economy: Coal plant, oil, commuters to San Antonio.

History: Coahuiltecan tribal area; later Apaches and Comanches. Families from Mexico established ranches in mid-1700s. Anglo-Americans arrived in 1840s. County created from Bexar District in 1856 and organized that same year. Atascosa means boggy in Spanish.

Race/Ethnicity: (In percent) Anglo, 33.4; Black, 1.2; Hispanic, 64.5; Asian, 0.6; Other, 1.3; Two or more races, 1.2.

Vital Statistics, annual: Births, 689; deaths, 408; marriages, 271; divorces, 61.

Recreation: Quail, deer hunting; museums; river park; theater group.

Minerals: Lignite, oil, gas.

Agriculture: Beef cattle, peanuts, vegetable farming. Some 25,000 acres irrigated. Market value $85 million.

JOURDANTON (4,276) county seat; coal mining; hospital; park, walking trail; chili cookoff in May, Czech Day in July.

PLEASANTON (10,657) farming, oil-field drilling, health services; cowboy homecoming in August, Longhorn museum; hospital.

Other towns include: **Campbellton** (350); **Charlotte** (1,812); **Christine** (413); **Leming** (1,085); **Lytle** (2,893) greenhouse, peanuts processed; **Peggy** (22); **Poteet** (3,520) government/services, library, strawberry festival in April.

Population	50,310
Change frm 2010	12.0
Area (sq. mi.)	1,221.5
Land Area (sq. mi.)	1,219,5
Altitude (ft.)	180–784
Rainfall (in.)	32.07
Jan. mean min.	39.3
July mean max.	95.4
Civ. Labor	21,445
Unemployed	3.7
Wages	$172,694,697
Per Capita Income	$34,372
Prop. Value	$4,814,880,380
Retail Sales	$611,675,322

The red soils of Palo Duro Canyon, Armstrong-Randall counties. Photo by Robert Plocheck.

Austin County

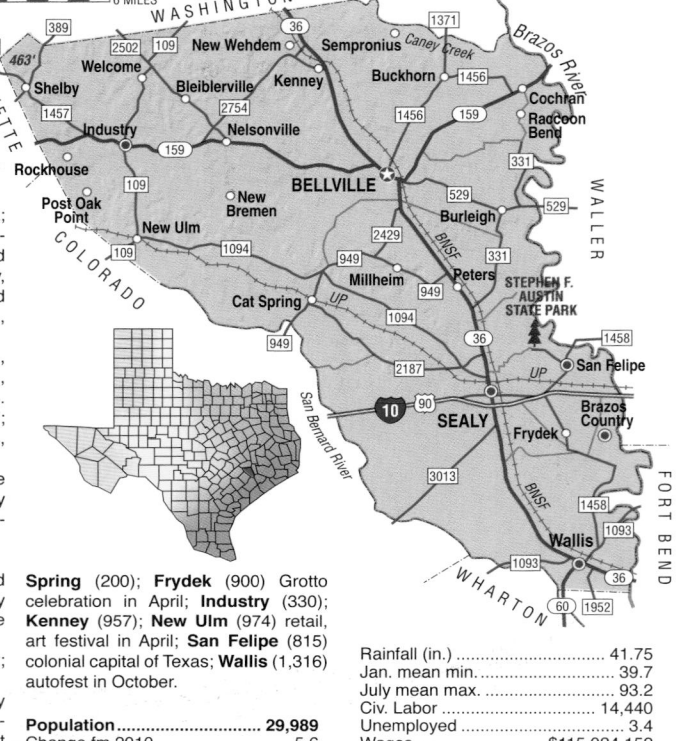

Physical Features: Level to hilly, drained by San Bernard, Brazos rivers; black prairie to sandy upland soils.

Economy: Agribusiness; tourism, government/services; metal, other manufacturing; commuting to Houston.

History: Tonkawa Indian tribal area; reduced by diseases. Birthplace of Anglo-American colonization, 1821, and German mother colony at Industry, 1831. County created and organized in 1837; named for Stephen F. Austin, father of Texas.

Race/Ethnicity: (In percent) Anglo, 62.0; Black, 9.5; Hispanic, 27.1; Asian, 0.7; Other, 0.8; Two or more races, 1.4.

Vital Statistics, annual: Births, 347; deaths, 272; marriages, 173; divorces, 107.

Recreation: Fishing, hunting; state park, Pioneer Trail; Bellville Country Livin' festival in April; Lone Star Raceway Park.

Minerals: Oil and natural gas.

Agriculture: Beef production and hay. Also rice, corn, sorghum, nursery crops, grapes, pecans. Market value $43.5 million.

BELLVILLE (4,375) county seat; varied manufacturing; hospital; oil.

SEALY (6,722) oil-field and military vehicle manufacturing, varied industries; Blinn College branch; polka fest in March.

Other towns include: **Bleiblerville** (125); **Brazos Country** (501); **Cat**

Spring (200); **Frydek** (900) Grotto celebration in April; **Industry** (330); **Kenney** (957); **New Ulm** (974) retail, art festival in April; **San Felipe** (815) colonial capital of Texas; **Wallis** (1,316) autofest in October.

Population	29,989
Change fm 2010	5.6
Area (sq. mi.)	656.4
Land Area (sq. mi.)	646.5
Altitude (ft.)	70–463

Rainfall (in.)	41.75
Jan. mean min.	39.7
July mean max.	93.2
Civ. Labor	14,440
Unemployed	3.4
Wages	$115,024,152
Per Capita Income	$49,262
Prop. Value	$5,825,189,375
Retail Sales	$304,311,905

Bailey County

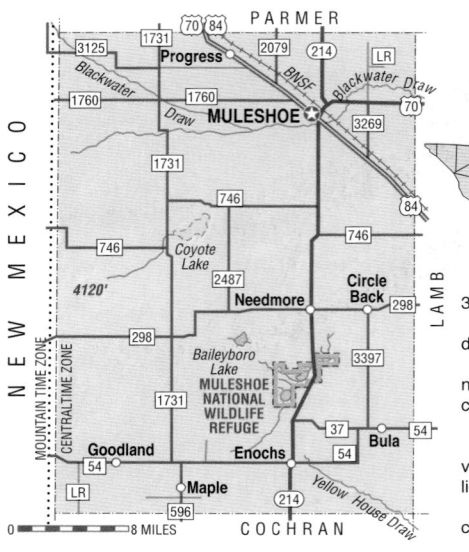

Physical Features: High Plains county, sandy loam soils; mesquite brush; drains to draws forming upper watershed of Brazos River, playas.

Economy: Farm supply manufacturing; electric generating plant; food-processing plants.

History: Settlement began after 1900. County created from Bexar District 1876, organized 1917. Named for Alamo hero Peter J. Bailey.

Race/Ethnicity: (In percent) Anglo, 32.9; Black, 1.9; Hispanic, 64.3; Asian, 0.8; Other, 3.5; Two or more races, 1.3.

Vital Statistics, annual: Births, 137; deaths, 50; marriages, 53; divorces, 9.

Recreation: Muleshoe National Wildlife Refuge; "Old Pete," the national mule memorial; historical building park; museum; motorcycle rally; mule deer, sandhill crane, pheasant hunting.

Minerals: Insignificant.

Agriculture: Feedlot, dairy cattle; cotton, wheat, sorghum, corn, vegetables; some 50,000 acres irrigated. Market value $292 million.

MULESHOE (5,134) county seat; agribusiness center; feedcorn milling; hospital; livestock show.

Other towns include: **Enochs** (80); **Maple** (40)

Population	7,027
Change fm 2010	– 1.9
Area (sq. mi.)	827.5
Land Area (sq. mi.)	826.8
Altitude (ft.)	3,660–4,120

Rainfall (in.)	18.38
Jan. mean min.	19.4
July mean max.	92.0
Civ. Labor	2,493
Unemployed	3.8

Wages	$25,600,753
Per Capita Income	$44,659
Prop. Value	$473,906,386
Retail Sales	$47,017,674

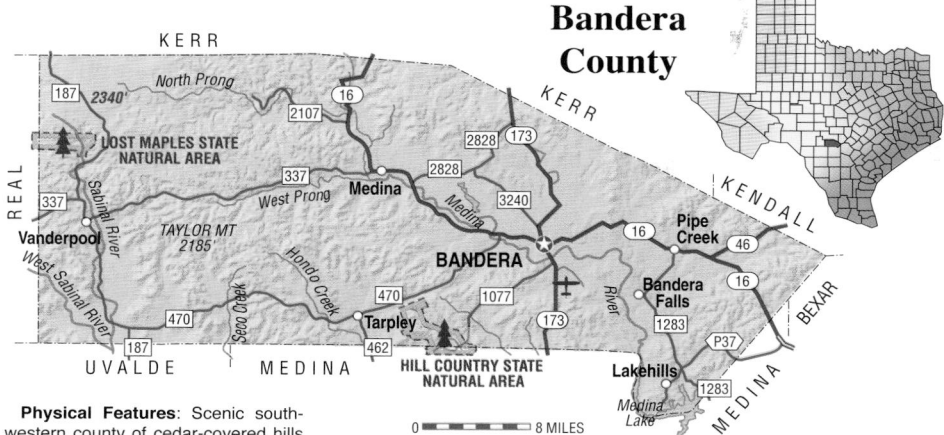

Bandera County

Physical Features: Scenic southwestern county of cedar-covered hills on the Edwards Plateau; Medina, Sabinal Rivers; limestone, sandy soils; species of oaks, walnuts, native cherry and Uvalde maple.

Economy: Tourism, hunting, fishing, ranching supplies, forest products.

History: Apache tribal area, then Comanche territory. White settlement began in the early 1850s, including Mormons and Poles. County, created, organized, from Bexar, Uvalde counties in 1856; named for Bandera (flag) Mountains.

Race/Ethnicity: (In percent) Anglo, 77.8; Black, 1.0; Hispanic, 18.8; Asian, 0.6; Other, 1.3; Two or more races, 1.6.

Vital Statistics, annual: Births, 154; deaths, 221; marriages, 149; divorces, 65.

Recreation: RV parks, resort ranches; Lost Maples and Hill Country State Natural Areas; rodeo, parade on Memorial Day weekend; Medina Lake.

Minerals: Not significant.

Agriculture: Beef cattle, sheep, goats, horses, deer (first in numbers in captivity), apples. Market value $11.2 million. Hunting and nature tourism important.

BANDERA (903) county seat; tourism, ranching, service industries; historic sites, Frontier Times Museum.

Other towns include: **Medina** (850) apple growing; **Pipe Creek** (130); **Tarpley** (30); **Vanderpool** (20). Also, the community of **Lakehills** (5,640) on Medina Lake, Cajun Fest in September, and **Lake Medina Shores** (1,277)

Population	**22,824**
Change fm 2010	11.4
Area (sq. mi.)	797.6
Land Area (sq. mi.)	791.0
Altitude (ft.)	1,064–2,340
Rainfall (in.)	37.37
Jan. mean min.	34.5
July mean max.	93.0
Civ. Labor	9,806
Unemployed	3.4
Wages	$29,743,080
Per Capita Income	$42,330
Prop. Value	$3,935,176,093
Retail Sales	$86,417,872

For explanation of sources, symbols and abbreviations, see p. 192, and foldout map.

Visitors at Lost Maples State Natural Area. Texas Parks & Wildlife photo.

Bastrop County

Physical Features: Rolling; alluvial, sandy, loam soils; varied timber, Lost Pines; bisected by Colorado River; Lake Bastrop.

Economy: Government/services; tourism; agribusiness; bio-technology research; computer-related industries; commuters to Austin.

History: Tonkawa Indian area; Comanches also present. Spanish fort established in 1804. County created in 1836, organized in 1837; named for Baron de Bastrop, who aided Moses and Stephen F. Austin in establishing the colony in the 1820s.

Race/Ethnicity: (In percent) Anglo, 52.6; Black, 7.6; Hispanic, 37.8; Asian, 0.9; Other, 2.2; Two or more races, 2.1.

Vital Statistics, annual: Births, 1,048; deaths, 660; marriages, 401; divorces, 225.

Recreation: Fishing; hunting; state parks; Lake Bastrop; historic sites; museum; railroad park; natural science center; nature trails.

Minerals: Lignite and clay.

Agriculture: Beef cattle, hay, pecans, turfgrass. Market value $35.3 million. Pine for lumber, oak for firewood.

BASTROP (8,712) county seat; government/services, tourism, hospitals, University of Texas cancer research center, federal prison; riverwalk; Yesterfest in April.

ELGIN (9,652) bricks, sausage manufacturing; horse, cattle breeding; medical research; depot museum; Western Days in June, Hogeye festival in October.

Smithville (4,188) government/services, hospital, railroad; parks, hike & bike trails, museums; jamboree on weekend after Easter, Reel Film Expo in May.

Other towns: **Cedar Creek** (145); **Circle D-KC Estates** (2,740); **McDade** (794) watermelon festival in July; **Paige** (275); **Red Rock** (40); **Rosanky** (210)

automotive museum; **Wyldwood** (2,746). Also, **Camp Swift** (7,414).

Population	86,976
Change fm 2010	17.2
Area (sq. mi.)	895.6
Land Area (sq. mi.)	888.2
Altitude (ft.)	300–729
Rainfall (in.)	37.62

Jan. mean min.	37.6
July mean max.	95.4
Civ. Labor	41,908
Unemployed	3.1
Wages	$179,336,259
Per Capita Income	$34,969
Prop. Value	$8,576,264,941
Retail Sales	$1,208,444,822

Bastrop State Park. Photo by Ron Billings, Texas A&M Forest Service.

Baylor County

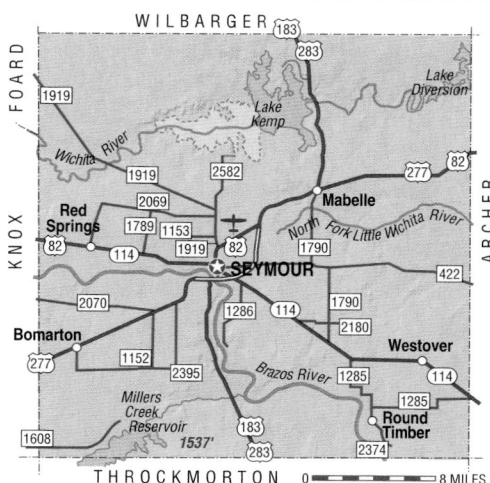

Physical Features: Northwest county; level to hilly; drains to Brazos, Wichita rivers; Lake Kemp, Lake Diversion, Millers Creek Reservoir; sandy, loam, red soils; grassy, mesquites, cedars.

Economy: Agribusiness; retail/service; health services.

History: Comanches, with Wichitas and other tribes also in the area; U.S. Army removed tribes in 1874-75. Anglo-Americans settled in the 1870s. County created from Fannin County in 1858; organized in 1879. Named for H.W. Baylor, Texas Ranger surgeon.

Race/Ethnicity: (In percent) Anglo, 82.0; Black, 3.0; Hispanic, 13.2; Asian, 0.4; Other, 0.8; Two or more races, 2.0.

Vital Statistics, annual: Births, 41; deaths, 61; marriages, 24; divorces, 3.

Recreation: Lakes; hunting; settlers reunion, rodeo, go-cart races in July.

Minerals: Oil, gas produced.

Population	3,582
Change fm 2010	-3.9
Area (sq. mi.)	901.1
Land Area (sq. mi.)	867.5
Altitude (ft.)	1,053–1,537
Rainfall (in.)	28.95
Jan. mean min.	28.1
July mean max.	96.5
Civ. Labor	1,550
Unemployed	2.9
Wages	$9,661,135
Per Capita Income	$39,650
Prop. Value	$1,013,541,400
Retail Sales	$29,113,662

Agriculture: Wheat, cattle, cow-calf operations, grain sorghum, cotton, hay. Market value $44.7 million.

SEYMOUR (2,880) county seat; agribusiness; hospital; dove hunters' breakfast in September.

Bee County

Physical Features: South Coastal Plain, level to rolling; black clay, sandy, loam soils; brushy.

Economy: Agriculture, government/services; hunting leases; oil and gas business.

History: Karankawa, Apache, Pawnee territory. First Spanish land grant, 1789. Irish settlers arrived 1826-29. County created from Karnes, Live Oak, Goliad, Refugio, San Patricio, 1857; organized 1858; named for Barnard Bee Sr., secretary of state and diplomat for the Republic.

Race/Ethnicity: (In percent) Anglo, 31.2; Black, 8.9; Hispanic, 59.1; Asian, 0.6; Other, 0.9; Two or more races, 1.2.

Vital Statistics, annual: Births, 412; deaths, 271; marriages, 166; divorces, 41.

Recreation: Hunting, birding, camping; historical sites, antiques; rodeo/roping events.

Minerals: Oil, gas produced.

Agriculture: Beef cattle, corn, cotton and grain sorghum. Market value $26 million. Hunting leases.

BEEVILLE (13,224) county seat; aircraft maintenance, waste-bind manufacturing; retail center; Costal Bend College; hospital; art museum; Diez y Seis festival in September.

Other towns and places include: **Blueberry Hill** (871); **Mineral** (65); **Normanna** (117); **Pawnee** (156); **Pettus** (554); **Skidmore** (912); **Tuleta** (295); **Tynan** (286).

For explanation of sources, symbols and abbreviations, see p. 192, and foldout map.

Population	32,587
Change fm 2010	2.3
Area (sq. mi.)	880.3
Land Area (sq. mi.)	880.2
Altitude (ft.)	39–540
Rainfall (in.)	31.95
Jan. mean min.	43.7
July mean max.	93.9
Civ. Labor	9,826
Unemployed	4.7
Wages	$80,064,742
Per Capita Income	$27,078
Prop. Value	$2,759,075,200
Retail Sales	$312,314,503

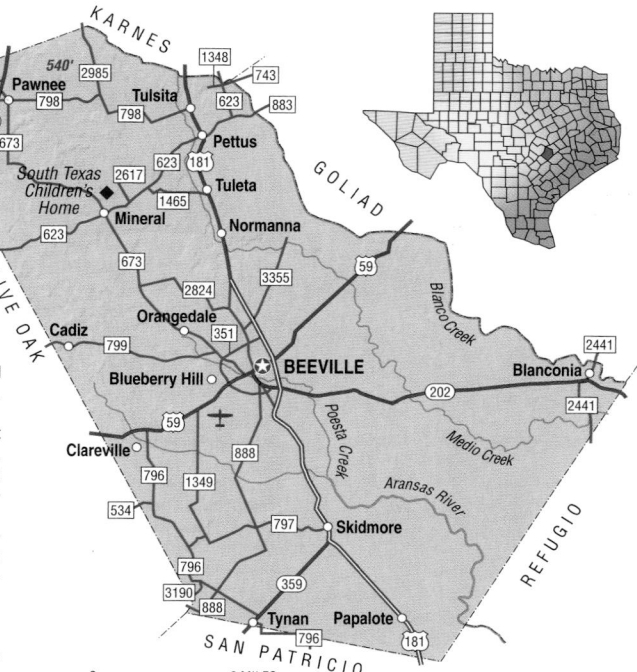

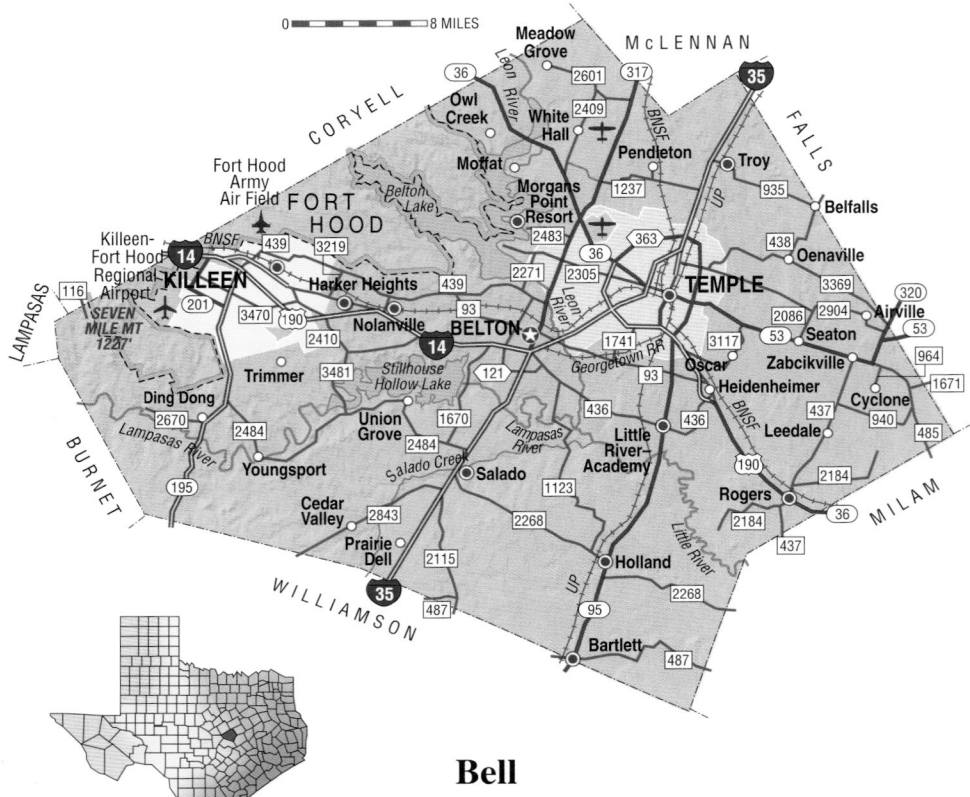

Bell County

Population **355,642**
Change fm 2010 .... 14.7
Area (sq. mi.) 1,087.8
Land Area (sq. mi.) 1,051.0
Altitude (ft.) 390–1,227
Rainfall (in.) 36.11
Jan. mean min. 35.6
July mean max. 94.6
Civ. Labor 145,439
Unemployed 3.9
Wages $1,386,437,960
Per Capita Income................ $42,024
Prop. Value $20,669,416,819
Retail Sales $4,540,180,554

Physical Features: Central Texas Blackland, level to hilly; black to light soils in west; mixed timber; Belton Lake, Stillhouse Hollow Lake.

Economy: Fort Hood; manufacturing includes computers, plastic goods, furniture, clothing; agribusiness; distribution center; tourism.

History: Tonkawas, Lipan Apaches; reduced by disease and advancing frontier by 1840s. Comanches raided into 1870s.

Settled in 1830s as part of Robertson's colony. A few slaveholders in 1850s. County created from Milam County in 1850; named for Gov. P.H. Bell.

Race/Ethnicity: (In percent) Anglo, 45.6; Black, 24.0; Hispanic, 24.8; Asian, 3.3; Other, 2.0; Two or more races, 4.6.

Vital Statistics, annual: Births, 6,496; deaths, 2,274; marriages, 3,688; divorces, 2,121.

Recreation: Fishing, hunting; lakes; historic sites; exposition center; Salado gathering of Scottish clans in November.

Minerals: Gravel.

Agriculture: Beef, corn, sorghum, wheat, cotton. Market value $84.9 million.

BELTON (21,157) county seat; University of Mary Hardin-Baylor; government/services; manufacturing; museum, nature center.

KILLEEN (143,334) Fort Hood; Texas A&M University–Central Texas and Central Texas College; regional airport; retail center, varied manufacturing; hospital; museums, planetarium; Four Winds Powwow in September.

TEMPLE (74,488) Major medical center with two hospitals and VA hospital; diversified industries; rail and wholesale distribution center; retail center; Temple College, Texas A&M College of Medicine; Azalee Marshall Cultural Activities Center; Czech museum; early-day tractor, engine show in October.

Other towns include: **Harker Heights** (30,328) Founder's Day in October; **Heidenheimer** (224); **Holland** (1,139) corn festival in June; **Little River-Academy** (2,000).

Also, **Morgan's Point Resort** (4,313); **Nolanville** (5,005); **Pendleton** (369); **Rogers** (1,250); **Salado** (2,062) tourism, civic center, amphitheathre, art fair in August; **Troy** (1,090).

Also, part [690] of **Bartlett**.

Fort Hood has a population of 30,959.

For explanation of sources, symbols and abbreviations, see p. 192, and foldout map.

Bexar County

Physical Features: On edge of Balcones Escarpment, Coastal Plain; heavy black to thin limestone soils; spring-fed streams; underground water; mesquite, other brush; Braunig Lake, Calaveras Lake.

Economy: Medical/biomedical research and services; government center with large federal payroll, military bases; tourism; education center.

History: Coahuiltecan Indian area; also Lipan Apache and Tonkawa tribes present. Mission San Antonio de Valero (Alamo) founded in 1718. Canary Islanders arrived in 1731. Anglo-American settlers began arriving in the late 1820s. County created and organized in 1836 from Spanish municipality named to honor the duke of Bexar; a colonial capital of Texas.

Race/Ethnicity: (In percent) Anglo, 27.7; Black, 8.5; Hispanic, 60.3; Asian, 3.1; Other, 1.4; Two or more races, 2.3.

Vital Statistics, annual: Births, 28,172; deaths, 12,982; marriages, 12,357; divorces, 3,318.

Recreation: Historic sites include the Alamo, other missions, Casa Navarro, La Villita; River Walk, El Mercado (market), Tower of the Americas, Brackenridge Park, zoo, SeaWorld, HemisFair Park, Institute of Texan Cultures; museums, symphony orchestra; hunting, fishing; NBA Spurs; Fiesta in April, Folklife Festival in June.

Minerals: Gravel, sand, limestone.

Agriculture: Nursery crops, beef cattle, grain sorghum, hay, corn. Market value $72.4 million.

Education: Fourteen colleges including Our Lady of the Lake, St. Mary's University, Texas A&M University–San Antonio, Trinity University, the University of Texas at San Antonio.

SAN ANTONIO (1,500,747) county seat; Texas' second largest city; healthcare/biosciences, government/services, manufacturing, tourism, information technology, aerospace, education, energy; Alamodome. Leon Springs is now part of San Antonio.

Other towns include: **Alamo Heights** (8,088); **Balcones Heights** (3,215); **Castle Hills** (4,502); **China Grove** (1,280); **Converse** (21,735); **Elmendorf** (1,883); **Fair Oaks Ranch** (9,003); **Grey Forest** (553); **Helotes** (8,889) government/services, retail trade, Cornyval Festival in May, Highland games in April, John T. Floore Country Store, Gugger Homestead; **Hill Country Village** (1,041); **Hollywood Park** (3,392).

Also, **Kirby** (8,492); **Leon Valley** (11,259); **Live Oak** (15,849); **Macdona** (633); **Olmos Park** (2,376); **St. Hedwig** (2,364); **Selma** (9,596, parts in Guadalupe and Comal counties); **Shavano Park** (3,722); **Somerset** (1,809); **Terrell Hills** (5,262); **Universal City** (20,961); **Von Ormy** (1,190); **Windcrest** (5,902).

Part [1,157] of **Schertz** (38,084).

Lackland Air Force Base (11,185); **Randolph Air Force Base** (1,340).

Population	**1,986,049**
Change fm 2010	15.8
Area (sq. mi.)	1,256.1
Land Area (sq. mi.)	1,239.8
Altitude (ft.)	400–1,896
Rainfall (in.)	32.27
Jan. mean min.	40.7
July mean max.	94.6
Civ. Labor	942,652
Unemployed	3.2
Wages	$10,592,802,212
Per Capita Income	$43,798
Prop. Value	$165,252,672,291
Retail Sales	$29,513,633,551

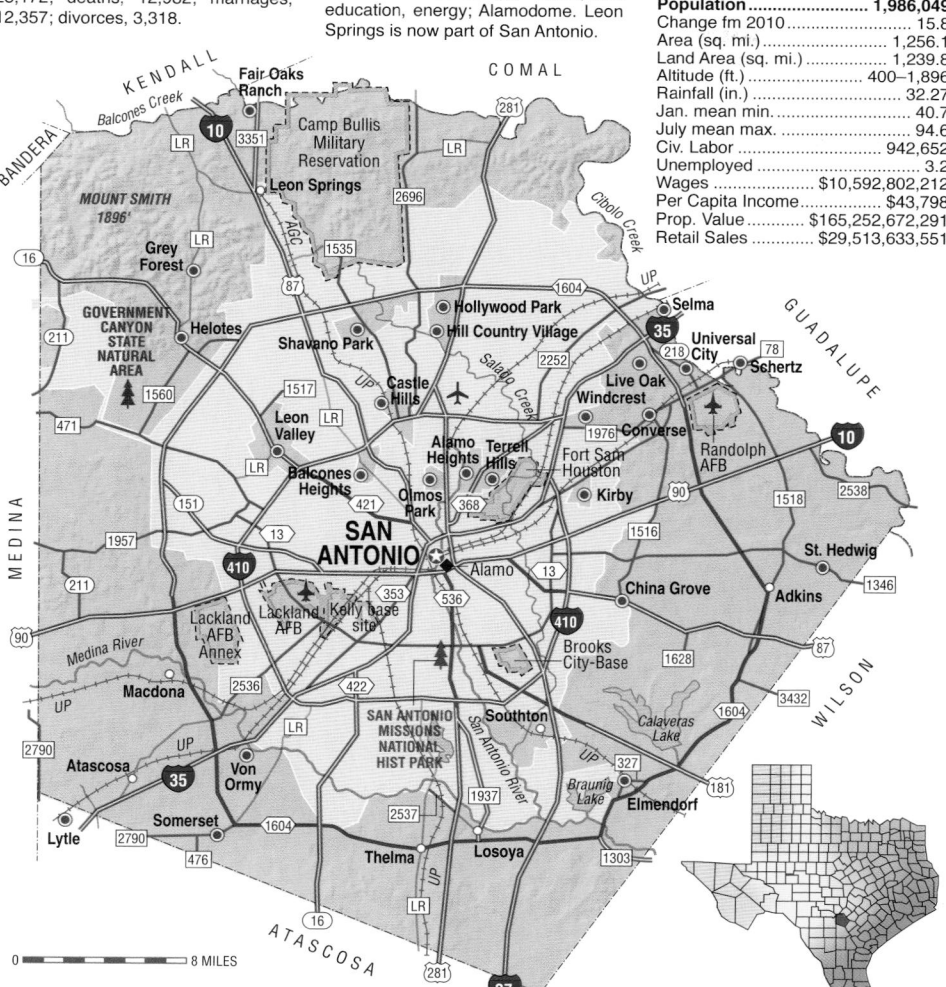

Blanco County

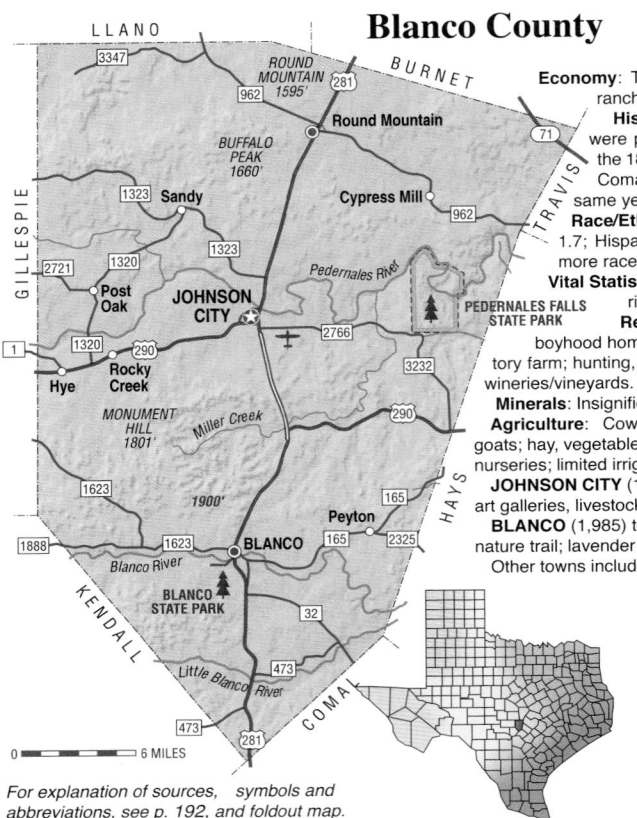

Physical Features: Hill Country county; Blanco, Pedernales rivers; cedars, pecans, live oaks, other trees.

Economy: Tourism, agribusiness/wholesale nursery, ranch supplies, hunting/fishing.

History: Lipan Apache area. Comanches were present when Anglo-Americans settled in the 1850s. County created in 1858 from Burnet, Comal, Gillespie, Hays counties, organized the same year; named for the Blanco (white) River.

Race/Ethnicity: (In percent), Anglo, 76.7; Black, 1.7; Hispanic, 19.7; Asian, 0.9; Other, 1.3; Two or more races, 1.5

Vital Statistics, annual: Births, 96; deaths, 122; marriages, 77; divorces, 25.

Recreation: President Lyndon B. Johnson's boyhood home, state parks, Saur-Beckmann history farm; hunting, fishing; bike ride in March; scenic drives, wineries/vineyards.

Minerals: Insignificant.

Agriculture: Cow-calf operation, stocker cattle; sheep, goats; hay, vegetables, peaches, grapes, pecans, greenhouse nurseries; limited irrigation. Market value $19.1 million.

JOHNSON CITY (1,880) county seat; tourism, electric co-op; art galleries, livestock center.

BLANCO (1,985) tourism, old courthouse, Pioneer museum, nature trail; lavender festival in June.

Other towns include: **Hye** (72) and **Round Mountain** (178).

Population	11,702
Change fm 2010	11.5
Area (sq. mi.)	713.4
Land Area (sq. mi.)	709.3
Altitude (ft.)	741–1,900
Rainfall (in.)	34.87
Jan. mean min.	34.8
July mean max.	92.8
Civ. Labor	6,211
Unemployed	2.6
Wages	$37,186,732
Per Capita Income	$48,978
Prop. Value	$5,068,963,794
Retail Sales	$70,220,693

For explanation of sources, symbols and abbreviations, see p. 192, and foldout map.

Borden County

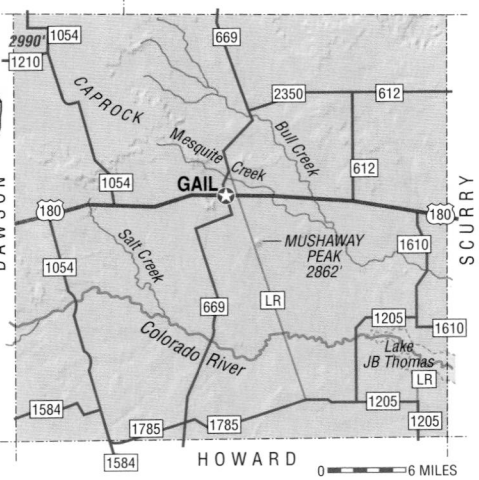

Physical Features: Rolling surface, broken by Caprock Escarpment; drains to Colorado River; sandy loam, clay soils.

Economy: Agriculture and hunting leases; oil; wind turbines.

History: Comanche area. Anglo-Americans settled in the 1870s. County created in 1876 from Bexar District, organized in 1891; named for Gail Borden, patriot, inventor, editor.

Race/Ethnicity: (In percent) Anglo, 77.3; Black, 1.5; Hispanic, 19.5; Asian, 0.1; Other, 0.7; Two or more races, 2.5.

Vital Statistics, annual: Births, 0; deaths, 10; marriages, 1; divorces, 2.

Recreation: Fishing; quail and deer hunting; Lake J.B. Thomas; museum; Coyote Opry in September; junior livestock show in January, ranch horse competition in September.

Minerals: Oil, gas, caliche, sand, gravel.

Agriculture: Beef cattle, cotton, wheat, hay, pecans, oats; some irrigation. Market value $9.4 million.

GAIL (262) county seat; museum; antique shop, ambulance service; "star" construction atop Gail Mountain.

Population	648
Change fm 2010	1.1
Area (sq. mi.)	906.1
Land Area (sq. mi.)	897.4
Altitude (ft.)	2,258–2,990
Rainfall (in.)	19.06
Jan. mean min.	33.1
July mean max.	94.8
Civ. Labor	301
Unemployed	3.3
Wages	$1,815,484
Per Capita Income	$51,776
Prop. Value	$876,249,120
Retail Sales	$17,803

Bosque County

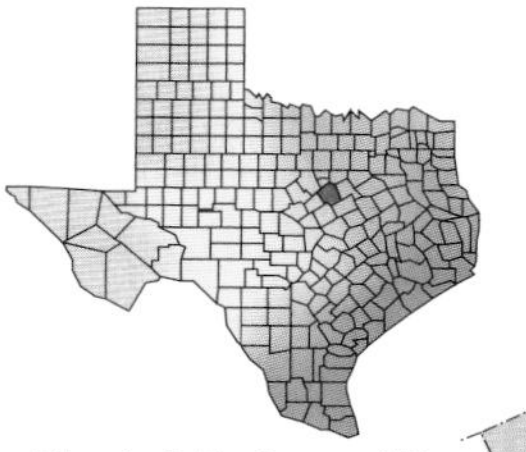

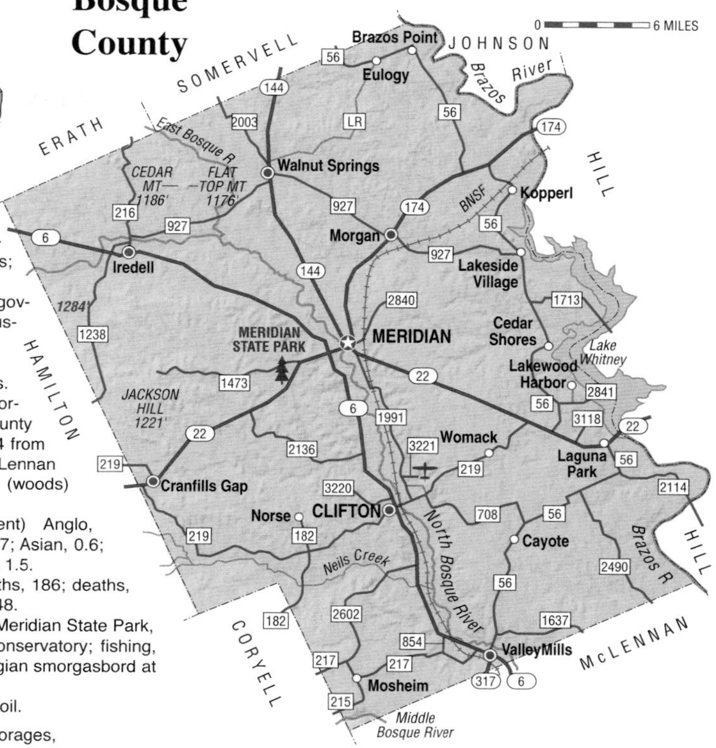

0 ▬▬▬▬ 6 MILES

Physical Features: Hilly, broken by Brazos, Bosque rivers; limestone to alluvial soils; cedars, oaks, mesquites.

Economy: Agribusiness, government/services, small industries, tourism.

History: Tonkawa, Waco, and Tawakoni Indian tribes. Settlers from England and Norway arrived in the 1850s. County created and organized in 1854 from the Milam District and McLennan County; named for Bosque (woods) River.

Race/Ethnicity: (In percent) Anglo, 77.6; Black, 2.1; Hispanic, 18.7; Asian, 0.6; Other, 1.0; Two or more races, 1.5.

Vital Statistics, annual: Births, 186; deaths, 224; marriages, 69; divorces, 48.

Recreation: Lake Whitney, Meridian State Park, museum at Clifton, fine art conservatory; fishing, hunting; scenic routes, Norwegian smorgasbord at Norse in November.

Minerals: Limestone, gas & oil.

Agriculture: Beef cattle, forages, small grains, turkeys. Market value $78.3 million. Hunting leases.

MERIDIAN (1,490) county seat; food processing, government/services, tourism; retirement home, community college; national championship barbecue cookoff in October.

CLIFTON (3,533) retirement/health care; hospital, nursing school; library; Norwegian historic district; Norwegian Country Christmas.

Other towns include: **Cranfills Gap** (275) Lutefisk dinner in December, Old Rock Church; **Iredell** (334); **Kopperl** (225); **Laguna Park** (1,250); **Morgan** (492); **Valley Mills** (1,220); **Walnut Springs** (872).

Population............................. 18,691
Change fm 2010........................... 2.6
Area (sq. mi.)......................... 1,002.5

Land Area (sq. mi.) 983.0
Altitude (ft.) 410–1,284
Rainfall (in.) 36.04
Jan. mean min. 34.8
July mean max. 96.4
Civ. Labor 8,216
Unemployed 3.5
Wages $35,893,283
Per Capita Income................ $40,704
Prop. Value $2,962,221,445
Retail Sales $84,379,499

A horse prances through spring flowers in Blanco County. Photo by Carol M. Highsmith, Library of Congress.

Bowie County

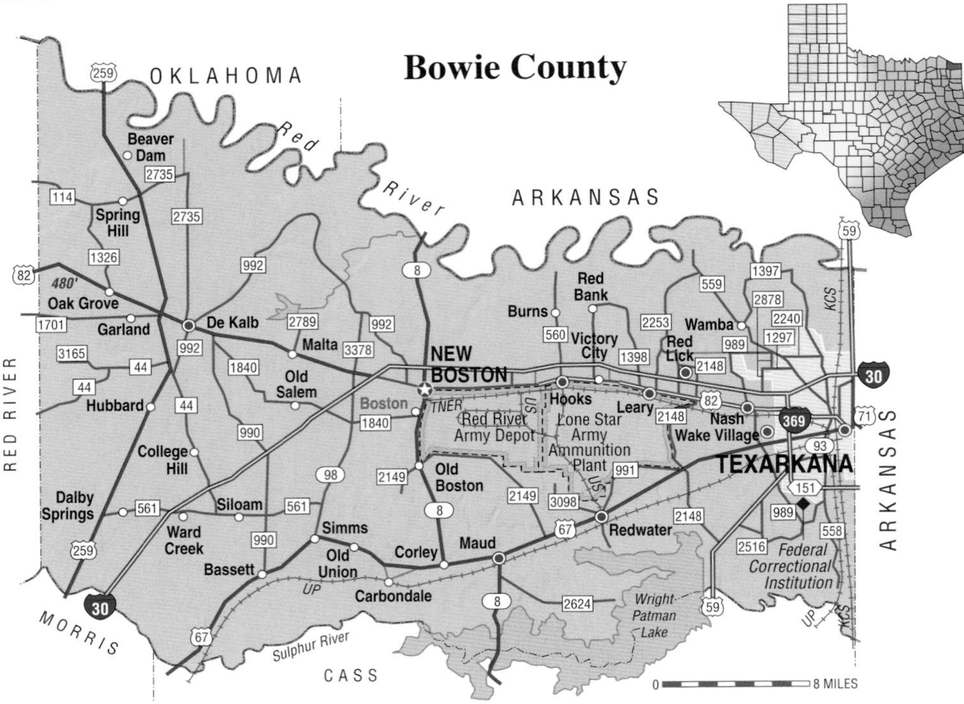

OKLAHOMA

ARKANSAS

Red River

Beaver Dam

Spring Hill

Oak Grove

Garland

De Kalb

Hubbard

College Hill

Dalby Springs

Ward Creek

Bassett

Siloam

Old Union

Simms

Carbondale

Malta

Old Salem

Boston

Old Boston

Corley

Maud

NEW BOSTON

Red River Army Depot

Lone Star Army Ammunition Plant

Red Bank

Burns

Victory City

Wamba

Red Lick

Hooks

Leary

Nash

Wake Village

TEXARKANA

Redwater

Federal Correctional Institution

Wright-Patman Lake

Sulphur River

RED RIVER

MORRIS

CASS

ARKANSAS

0 — 8 MILES

Physical Features: Forested hills at northeast corner of the state; clay, sandy, alluvial soils; drained by Red and Sulphur rivers; Wright Patman Lake.

Economy: Government/services, lumber, manufacturing, agribusiness.

History: Caddo tribal area, abandoned in the 1790s after trouble with the Osage tribe. Anglo-Americans began arriving 1815-20. County created and organized in 1840 from Red River County; named for the Alamo hero James Bowie.

Race/Ethnicity: (In percent) Anglo, 63.7; Black, 25.0; Hispanic, 7.8; Asian, 1.3; Other, 1.1; Two or more races, 2.3.

Vital Statistics, annual: Births, 1,259; deaths, 1,076; marriages, 558; divorces, 392.

Recreation: Lake activities, Crystal Springs beach; hunting, fishing; historic sites; Four-States Fair in September, Oktoberfest.

Minerals: Oil, gas, sand, gravel.

Agriculture: Beef cattle, pecans, hay, corn, poultry, soybeans, dairy, nurseries, wheat, rice, horses, milo. Market value $66 million. Pine timber, hardwoods, pulpwood harvested.

NEW BOSTON (4,860) site of county courthouse; army depot, lumber mill, steel manufacture, agribusiness, state prison; Pioneer Days in August. The area of Boston, officially designated as the county seat, has been annexed by New Boston.

TEXARKANA (38,012 in Texas, 30,259 in Arkansas) rubber company, paper manufacturing, distribution; hospitals; tourism; colleges; federal prison; Perot Theatre; Quadrangle Festival in September.

Other towns include: **De Kalb** (1,731) agriculture, government/services, commuting to Texarkana, Oktoberfest; **Hooks** (2,778); **Leary** (488); **Maud** (1,136); **Nash** (3,370); **Red Lick** (1,034); **Redwater** (1,122); **Simms** (300); **Wake Village** (5,644).

Population	**94,324**
Change fm 2010	1.9
Area (sq. mi.)	923.0
Land Area (sq. mi.)	885.0
Altitude (ft.)	200–480
Rainfall (in.)	51.96
Jan. mean min.	33.1
July mean max.	92.9
Civ. Labor	40,098
Unemployed	4.9
Wages	$414,293,482
Per Capita Income	$38,807
Prop. Value	$6,413,440,110
Retail Sales	$1,635,602,198

A flooded field at San Bernard National Wildlife Refuge, Brazoria County. U.S. Fish & Wildlife Service photo.

Physical Features: Flat Coastal Plain, coastal soils, drained by Brazos and San Bernard rivers; Brazoria Reservoir, Eagle Nest Lake, Harris Reservoir, Mustang Lake East/West, San Bernard Reservoirs.

Economy: Petroleum and chemical industry, fishing, tourism, agribusiness. Part of Houston metropolitan area.

History: Karankawa area. Part of Austin's "Old Three Hundred" colony of families arriving in early 1820s. County created 1836 from Municipality of Brazoria, organized in 1837; name derived from Brazos River.

Race/Ethnicity: (In percent) Anglo, 47.3; Black, 14.2; Hispanic, 30.6; Asian, 6.8; Other, 0.9; Two or more races, 2.0.

Vital Statistics, annual: Births, 4,939; deaths, 2,155; marriages, 2,043; divorces, 1,261.

Recreation: Beaches, water sports; fishing, hunting; wildlife refuges, historic sites, plantations; state and county parks; replica of the first capitol of the Republic of Texas at West Columbia.

Minerals: Oil, gas, sand, gravel.

Population	370,200
Change fm 2010	18.2
Area (sq. mi.)	1,608.6
Land Area (sq. mi.)	1,357.7
Altitude (ft.)	sea level–146
Rainfall (in.)	56.47
Jan. mean min.	45.6
July mean max.	90.3
Civ. Labor	178,219
Unemployed	4.2
Wages	$1,600,264,586
Per Capita Income	$45,925
Prop. Value	$41,000,984,653
Retail Sales	$4,577,533,924

Brazoria County

Agriculture: Cattle, hay, rice, soybeans, sorghum, nurseries, corn, cotton, aquaculture, bees. Some 20,000 acres of rice irrigated. Market value $118.2 million.

ANGLETON (20,310) county seat; banking and distribution center for oil, chemical, agricultural area; fish-processing plant; hospital.

BRAZOSPORT (60,138) is a community of eight cities; chemical complex, deepwater seaport, commercial fishing, tourism; college; hospital; Brazosport cities include: **Clute** (11,642) mosquito festival in July, **Freeport** (12,273) museum, Riverfest in late April, **Jones Creek** (2,039), **Lake Jackson** (28,392) research & development, museum, sea center, Gulf Coast Bird Observatory, **Oyster Creek** (1,126), **Quintana** (114); Neotropical Bird Sanctuary, **Richwood** (3,970), **Surfside Beach** (582) tourism, St. Patrick's Day parade.

PEARLAND (114,204, parts in Harris, Fort Bend counties) trucking, metal fabrication, oilfield, chemical production; commuting to Houston, NASA; community college; Hindu temple; Winter Fest in January.

Other towns include: **Alvin** (27,241) petrochemical processing, agribusiness, rail, trucking; junior college; hospital; Crawfest and Shrimp Boil in April. **Bailey's Prairie** (755); **Bonney** (330); **Brazoria** (3,397) government/services, retail, manufacturing; library; No-Name Festival in June, Santa Anna Ball in July; **Brookside Village** (1,624).

Also, **Damon** (593); **Danbury** (1,851); **Danciger** (90); **Hillcrest Village** (740); **Holiday Lakes** (1,202); **Iowa Colony** (1,365); **Liverpool** (572); **Manvel** (9,023); **Old Ocean** (150); **Rosharon** (1,295); **Sandy Point** (232); **Sweeny** (3,930) petrochemicals, government/services, hospital, library, Pride Day in May, Levi Jordan Plantation; **West Columbia** (3,978) chemical industry, retail, cattle, rice farming, museum, historic sites, plantation, San Jacinto Festival in April, Stephen F. Austin funeral procession re-enactment in October.

For explanation of sources, symbols and abbreviations, see p. 192, and foldout map.

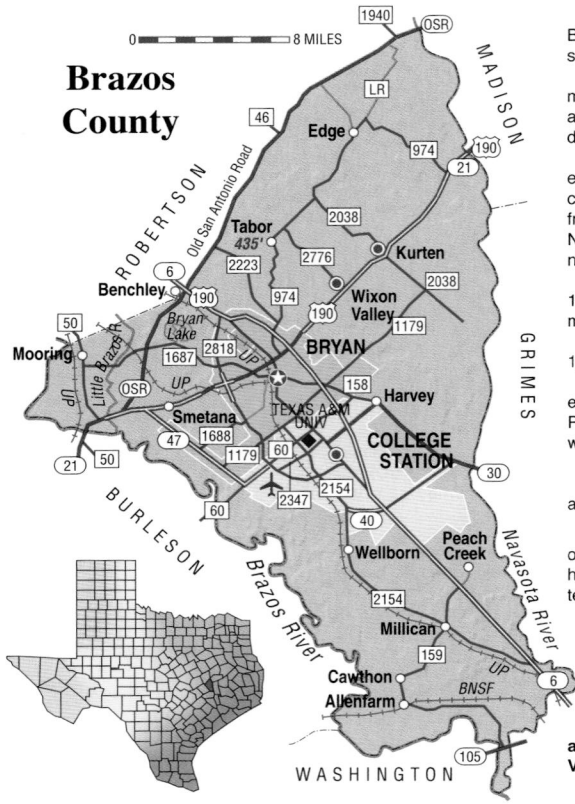

Brazos County

0 ◼◼◼◼ 8 MILES

Physical Features: South central county between Brazos, Navasota rivers; Bryan Lake; rich bottom soils, sandy, clays on rolling uplands; oak trees.

Economy: Texas A&M University; market and medical center; agribusiness; computers, research and development; government/services; winery; industrial parks; tourism.

History: Bidais and Tonkawas; Comanches hunted in the area. Part of Stephen F. Austin's second colony of the late 1820s. County created in 1841 from Robertson, Washington counties and named Navasota; renamed for Brazos River in 1842, organized in 1843.

Race/Ethnicity: (In percent) Anglo, 55.9; Black, 11.0; Hispanic, 25.8; Asian, 6.3; Other, 0.8; Two or more races, 2.0.

Vital Statistics, annual: Births, 2,903; deaths, 1,064; marriages, 1,394; divorces, 326.

Recreation: Fishing, hunting; raceway; many events related to Texas A&M activities; George Bush Presidential Library and Museum; winery harvest weekends in August.

Minerals: Sand and gravel, lignite, gas, oil.

Agriculture: Cattle, poultry, cotton, hay, horses and horticulture. Market value $95 million.

BRYAN (83,950) county seat; defense electronics, other varied manufacturing, agribusiness center; hospitals, psychiatric facilities; Blinn College extension; Brazos Valley African American Museum; steak & grape festival in June, Fiestas Patrias in September.

COLLEGE STATION (111,818) home of Texas A&M University, varied high-tech manufacturing, research; hospital.

Other towns include: **Kurten** (401); **Lake Bryan** (1,967); **Millican** (232); **Wellborn** (400); **Wixon Valley** (256).

Population 226,758	Rainfall (in.) 40.06	Wages $1,072,336,861
Change fm 2010 ....16.4	Jan. mean min. 41.2	Per Capita Income...................$37,352
Area (sq. mi.) 591.2	July mean max. 94.8	Prop. Value $19,951,923,410
Land Area (sq. mi.) 585.5	Civ. Labor 118,677	Retail Sales $3,297,031,352
Altitude (ft.) 157–435	Unemployed 2.7	

The Rio Grande near Boquillas Canyon, Brewster County. Photo by Robert Plocheck.

Brewster County

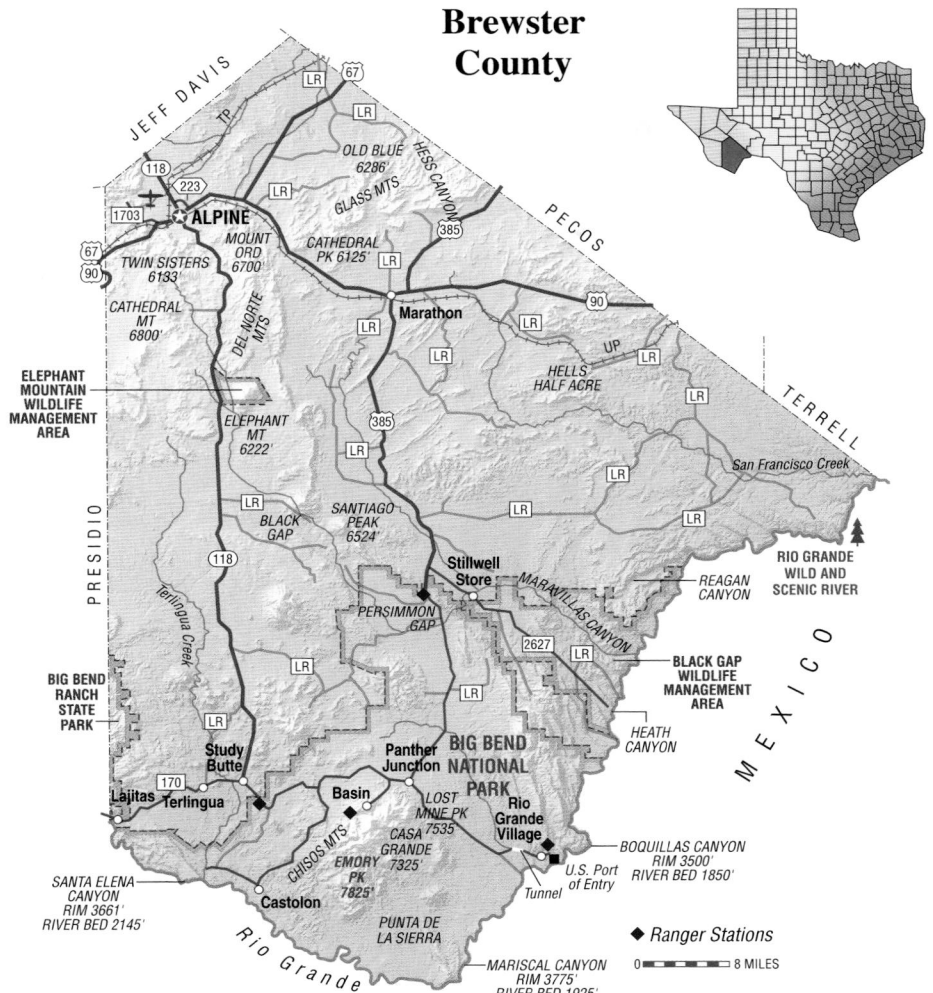

◆ *Ranger Stations*

0 ▬▬▬▬ 8 MILES

Physical Features: Largest county, with area slightly less than that of Connecticut plus Rhode Island; mountains, canyons, distinctive geology, plant life, animals.

Economy: Agriculture, tourism, government/services, Sul Ross State University, mining.

History: Pueblo culture had begun when Spanish explored in the 1500s. Mescalero Apaches in Chisos Mountains; Comanches raided in area.

Ranching developed in northern part in the 1880s, with Mexican agricultural communities along river. County created, organized, 1887 from Presidio County; named for Henry P. Brewster, Republic secretary of war.

Race/Ethnicity: (In percent) Anglo, 50.3; Black, 1.5; Hispanic, 45.4; Asian,

For explanation of sources, symbols and abbreviations, see p. 192, and foldout map.

1.2; Other, 1.9; Two or more races, 2.3.

Vital Statistics, annual: Births, 96; deaths, 81; marriages, 63; divorces, 0.

Recreation: Big Bend National Park, Big Bend Ranch State Park, Rio Grande Wild and Scenic River; ghost towns, scenic drives; hunting; museum; rockhound areas; cavalry post.

Also, Barton Warnock Environmental Education Center at Lajitas; cowboy poetry and Western art show in Feburary; Terlingua chili cookoff in November.

Minerals: Bentonite.

Agriculture: Beef cattle, meat goats, horses. Market value $9.9 million. Hunting leases important.

ALPINE (6,009) county seat; ranch trade center, tourism, varied manufacturing; Sul Ross State University; hospital.

Marathon (407) tourism, ranching center, Gage Hotel, Marathon Basin quilt show in October.

Also, **Basin** (30); **Study Butte** (254), and **Terlingua** (49).

Population	**9,267**
Change fm 2010	0.4
Area (sq. mi.)	6,192.3
Land Area (sq. mi.)	6,183.7
Altitude (ft.)	1,400–7,825
Rainfall (in.) Alpine	17.00
Rainfall (in.) Big Bend	19.17
Jan. mean min. Alpine	30.3
Jan. mean min. Big Bend	36.1
July mean max. Alpine	88.5
July mean max. Big Bend	84.2
Civ. Labor	4,045
Unemployed	3.1
Wages	$38,399,236
Per Capita Income	$44,418
Prop. Value	$1,191,402,216
Retail Sales	$86,363,189

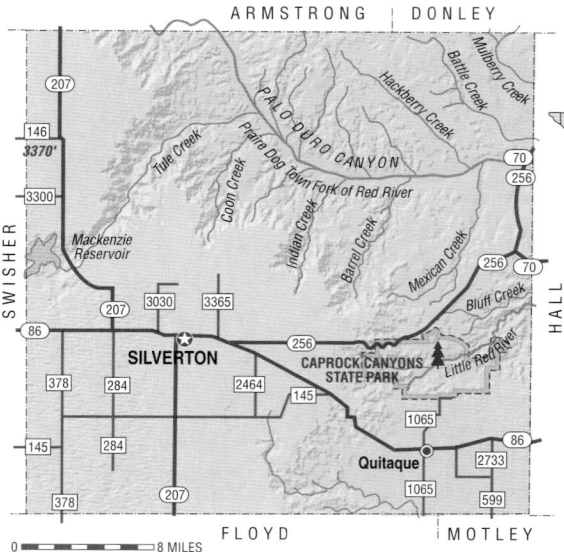

Briscoe County

Physical Features: Partly on High Plains, broken by Caprock Escarpment, fork of Red River; sandy, loam soils.

Economy: Agriculture, government/services.

History: Apaches in area, displaced by Comanches around 1700. Ranchers settled in the 1880s. County created from the Bexar District in 1876 and organized in 1892; named for Andrew Briscoe, Republic of Texas soldier.

Race/Ethnicity: (In percent) Anglo, 69.0; Black, 3.2; Hispanic, 25.4; Asian, 0.3; Other, 0.7; Two or more races, 2.3.

Vital Statistics, annual: Births, 13; deaths, 20; marriages, 12; divorces, 6.

Recreation: Hunting, fishing; scenic drives; museum at Quitaque; Caprock Canyons State Park, trailway, bison herd, Clarity tunnel with bats, Mackenzie Reservoir; Briscoe County Celebration in August, Bison Music Festival in September.

Minerals: Insignificant.

Agriculture: Cotton, beef, grain sorghum, wheat, hay. Some 23,000 acres irrigated. Market value $20.4 million.

SILVERTON (607) county seat; agribusiness center, irrigation supplies manufactured; clinics.

Quitaque (335) agribusiness, nature tourism, government/services.

Population	1,516	
Change fm 2010	− 7.4	
Area (sq. mi.)	901.6	
Land Area (sq. mi.)	900.0	
Altitude (ft.)	2,064–3,370	
Rainfall (in.)	22.41	
Jan. mean min.	23.2	
July mean max.	90.9	
Civ. Labor	542	
Unemployed	3.7	
Wages	$2,237,639	
Per Capita Income	$34,165	
Prop. Value	$611,452,520	
Retail Sales	$7,889,521	

Brooks County

Physical Features: On Rio Grande plain; level to rolling; brushy; light to dark sandy loam soils.

Economy: Oil, gas, hunting leases, cattle, watermelons and hay.

History: Coahuiltecan Indians. Spanish land grants date to around 1800. County created from Hidalgo, Starr, Zapata counties, 1911; organized in 1912. Named for J.A. Brooks, Texas Ranger and legislator.

Race/Ethnicity: (In percent) Anglo, 7.0; Black, 1.0; Hispanic, 89.8; Asian, 2.5; Other, 0.6; Two or more races, 0.4.

Vital Statistics, annual: Births, 117; deaths, 90; marriages, 38; divorces, 13.

Recreation: Hunting, fishing; Heritage Museum, Don Pedrito shrine; Fiesta del Campo in October.

Minerals: Oil, gas production; uranium.

Agriculture: Beef cow-calf operations, stocker; crops include hay, squash, watermelons, habanero peppers. Market value $50.8 million.

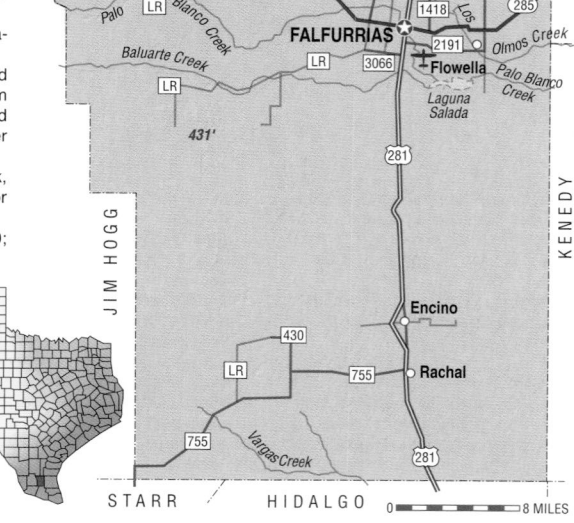

FALFURRIAS (4,931) county seat; oil and gas, agricultural, government/services.

Other towns include: **Encino** (137).

For explanation of sources, symbols and abbreviations, see p. 192, and foldout map.

Population	7,114	
Change fm 2010	− 1.5	
Area (sq. mi.)	943.7	
Land Area (sq. mi.)	943.4	
Altitude (ft.)	46–431	
Rainfall (in.)	26.47	
Jan. mean min.	42.5	
July mean max.	97.0	
Civ. Labor	2,385	
Unemployed	5.6	
Wages	$25,766,278	
Per Capita Income	$33,466	
Prop. Value	$1,317,586,381	
Retail Sales	$60,077,482	

Brown County

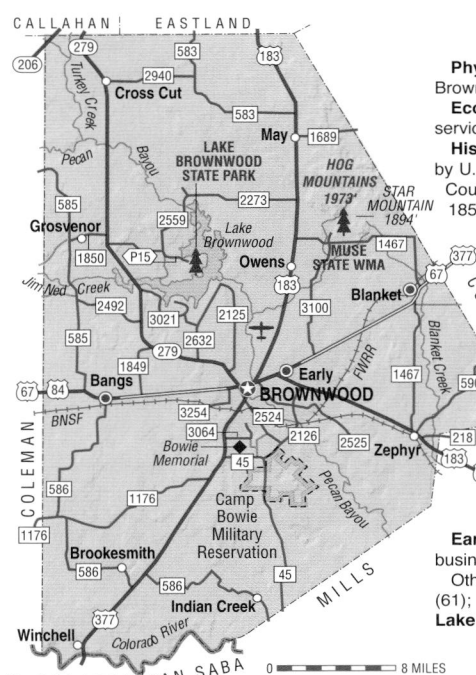

Physical Features: Rolling, hilly; drains to Colorado River; Lake Brownwood; varied soils, timber.

Economy: Manufacturing plants, distribution centers, government/services, agribusiness, medical, education.

History: Apaches; displaced by Comanches who were removed by U.S. Army in 1874-75. Anglo-Americans first settled in mid-1850s. County created 1856 from Comanche, Travis counties, organized in 1857. Named for frontiersman Henry S. Brown.

Race/Ethnicity: (In percent) Anglo, 71.6; Black, 3.9; Hispanic, 22.4; Asian; 0.8; Other, 0.9; Two or more races, 1.7.

Vital Statistics, annual: Births, 410; deaths, 515; marriages, 273; divorces, 65.

Recreation: State park; museums; fishing, hunting; wildflowers, walking trails.

Minerals: Oil, gas, paving materials, gravel, clays.

Agriculture: Cattle, hay, peanuts, pecans, meat goats, wheat, hogs. Market value $40.7 million.

BROWNWOOD (19,805) county seat; manufacturing, retail trade, distribution center; Howard Payne University, MacArthur Academy of Freedom; state substance abuse treatment center; state 4-H Club center; hospital; train museum, aquatic park; Reunion Celebration in September.

Early (3,024) retail, light manufacturing, government/services, agribusiness; motorcycle rally in October.

Other towns include: **Bangs** (1,601); **Blanket** (391); **Brookesmith** (61); **May** (270); **Zephyr** (201).

Lake Brownwood area (1,585).

Population	37,924
Change fm 2010	– 0.5
Area (sq. mi.)	957.0
Land Area (sq. mi.)	944.4
Altitude (ft.)	1,230–1,973
Rainfall (in.)	30.43
Jan. mean min.	30.1

July mean max.	95.7
Civ. Labor	16,212
Unemployed	3.4
Wages	$149,155,616
Per Capita Income	$37,041
Prop. Value	$3,867,229,566
Retail Sales	$467,022,462

A gas field on FM 755 in Brooks County. Photo by Robert Plocheck.

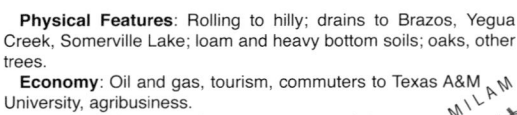

Burleson County

Physical Features: Rolling to hilly; drains to Brazos, Yegua Creek, Somerville Lake; loam and heavy bottom soils; oaks, other trees.

Economy: Oil and gas, tourism, commuters to Texas A&M University, agribusiness.

History: Tonkawa and Caddo tribes roamed the area. Mexicans and Anglo-Americans settled around Fort Tenoxtitlan in 1830. Black freedmen migration increased until 1910. Germans, Czechs, Italians migrated in the 1870s-80s. County created and organized in 1846 from Milam, Washington counties; named for Edward Burleson, a hero of the Texas Revolution.

Race/Ethnicity: (In percent) Anglo, 65.0; Black, 12.8; Hispanic, 20.6; Asian, 0.4; Other, 1.1; Two or more races, 1.7.

Vital Statistics, annual: Births, 215; deaths, 214; marriages, 106; divorces, 25.

Recreation: Fishing, hunting; lake recreation; historic sites; Czech heritage museum.

Minerals: Oil, gas, sand, gravel.

Agriculture: Cattle, cotton, corn, hay, sorghum, broiler production, soybeans; some irrigation. Market value $90.1 million.

CALDWELL (4,362) county seat; agribusiness, oil and gas, manufacturing, distribution center, tourism; hospital; civic center, museum; Kolache Festival in September.

Somerville (1,449) tourism, railroad center, some manufacturing; museum; Country Cajun festival in March.

Other towns include: **Chriesman** (30); **Deanville** (130); **Lyons** (360); **Snook** (531) Snookfest in June.

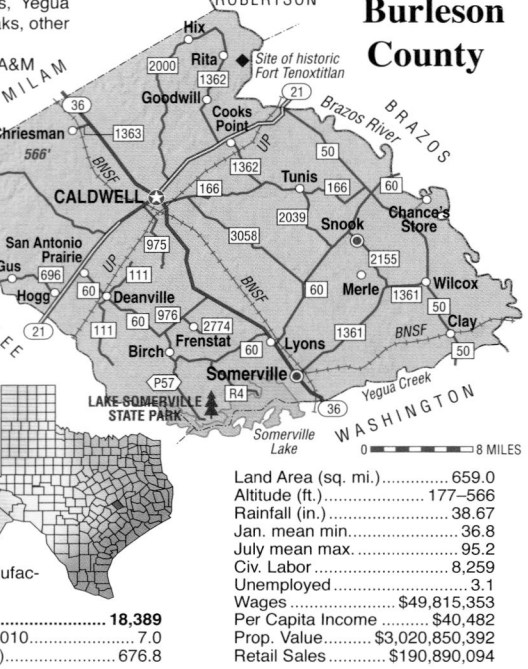

Population	18,389
Change fm 2010	7.0
Area (sq. mi.)	676.8
Land Area (sq. mi.)	659.0
Altitude (ft.)	177–566
Rainfall (in.)	38.67
Jan. mean min.	36.8
July mean max.	95.2
Civ. Labor	8,259
Unemployed	3.1
Wages	$49,815,353
Per Capita Income	$40,482
Prop. Value	$3,020,850,392
Retail Sales	$190,890,094

Burnet County

Physical Features: Scenic Hill Country county with Lake Buchanan, Inks Lake, Lake Lyndon B. Johnson, Lake Travis, Lake Marble Falls; caves; sandy, red, black waxy soils; cedars, other trees.

Economy: Tourism, stone processing, hunting leases.

History: Tonkawas, Lipan Apaches. Comanches raided in area. Frontier settlers arrived in the late 1840s. County created from Bell, Travis, Williamson counties, 1852; organized 1854; named for David G. Burnet, provisional president of the Republic.

Race/Ethnicity: (In percent) Anglo, 73.4; Black, 2.0; Hispanic, 22.5; Asian, 0.7; Other, 1.3; Two or more races, 1.4.

Vital Statistics, annual: Births, 526; deaths, 528; marriages, 258; divorces, 186.

Recreation: Water sports on lakes; sites of historic forts; hunting; state parks, wildlife refuge; wildflowers; birding; scenic train ride.

Minerals: Granite, limestone.

Agriculture: Cattle, goats, grapes, hay. Market value $14.7 million. Deer, wild hog, and turkey hunting leases.

BURNET (6,429) county seat; tourism, government/services, varied industries, ranching; hospital; museums; vineyards; bluebonnet festival in April.

MARBLE FALLS (6,717) tourism, retail, manufacturing; granite, limestone quarries; August drag boat race.

Other towns include: **Bertram** (1,430) Oatmeal festival on Labor Day; **Briggs** (172); **Cottonwood Shores** (1,245); **Granite Shoals** (5,057); **Highland Haven** (480); **Meadowlakes** (1,834); **Spicewood** (4,000). Also, part of **Horseshoe Bay** (3,758).

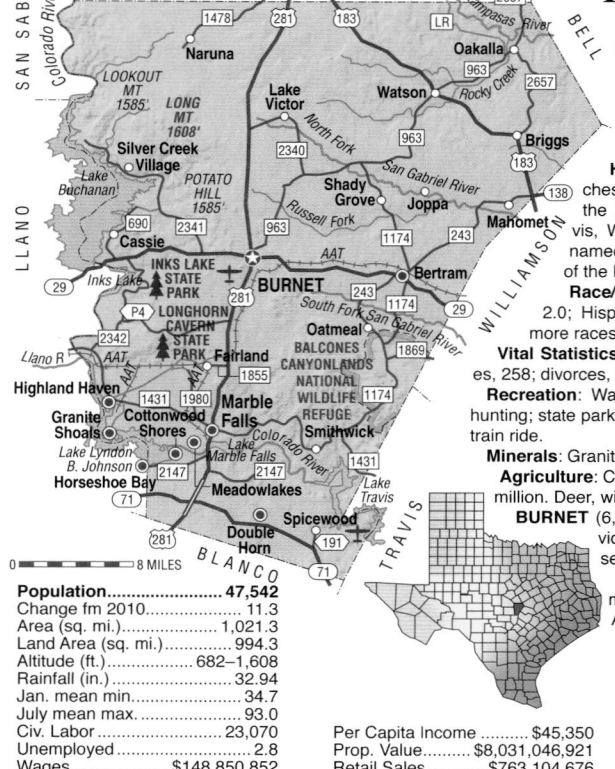

Population	47,542
Change fm 2010	11.3
Area (sq. mi.)	1,021.3
Land Area (sq. mi.)	994.3
Altitude (ft.)	682–1,608
Rainfall (in.)	32.94
Jan. mean min.	34.7
July mean max.	93.0
Civ. Labor	23,070
Unemployed	2.8
Wages	$148,850,852
Per Capita Income	$45,350
Prop. Value	$8,031,046,921
Retail Sales	$763,104,676

Caldwell County

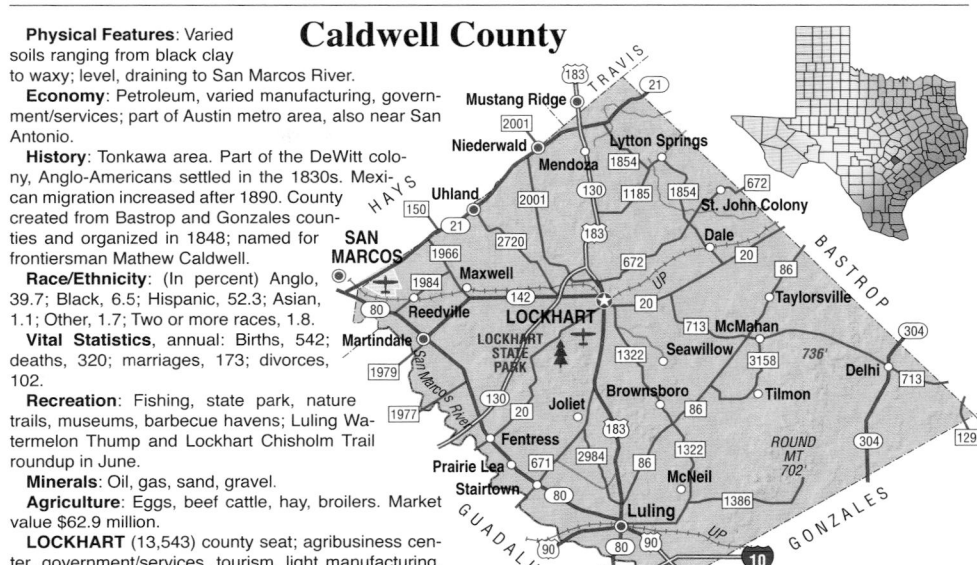

Physical Features: Varied soils ranging from black clay to waxy; level, draining to San Marcos River.

Economy: Petroleum, varied manufacturing, government/services; part of Austin metro area, also near San Antonio.

History: Tonkawa area. Part of the DeWitt colony, Anglo-Americans settled in the 1830s. Mexican migration increased after 1890. County created from Bastrop and Gonzales counties and organized in 1848; named for frontiersman Mathew Caldwell.

Race/Ethnicity: (In percent) Anglo, 39.7; Black, 6.5; Hispanic, 52.3; Asian, 1.1; Other, 1.7; Two or more races, 1.8.

Vital Statistics, annual: Births, 542; deaths, 320; marriages, 173; divorces, 102.

Recreation: Fishing, state park, nature trails, museums, barbecue havens; Luling Watermelon Thump and Lockhart Chisholm Trail roundup in June.

Minerals: Oil, gas, sand, gravel.

Agriculture: Eggs, beef cattle, hay, broilers. Market value $62.9 million.

LOCKHART (13,543) county seat; agribusiness center, government/services, tourism, light manufacturing, prison; renowned barbecue at Kreuz, Smitty's, Black's.

Luling (5,823) oil, tourism, agriculture; oil museum; hospital, barbecue cook-off in April.

Other towns include: **Dale** (300); **Fentress** (380); **Martindale** (1,247); **Maxwell** (500); part of **Mustang Ridge** (941, mostly in Travis County), and **Prairie Lea** (320).

Also, part of **Niederwald** (625), part of **Uhland** (1,331), and a small part of **San Marcos** (61,480), all mostly in Hays County.

Population	**43,247**
Change fm 2010	13.6
Area (sq. mi.)	547.2
Land Area (sq. mi.)	545.3
Altitude (ft.)	315–736
Rainfall (in.)	35.93
Jan. mean min.	37.8
July mean max.	94.8
Civ. Labor	19,228
Unemployed	3.4
Wages	$85,257,684
Per Capita Income	$32,889
Prop. Value	$3,257,897,671
Retail Sales	$363,884,079

For explanation of sources, symbols and abbreviations, see p. 192, and foldout map.

Balcones Canyonlands National Wildlife Refuge, Burnet/Travis counties. Photo by Matthew Rutledge (CC).

Calhoun County

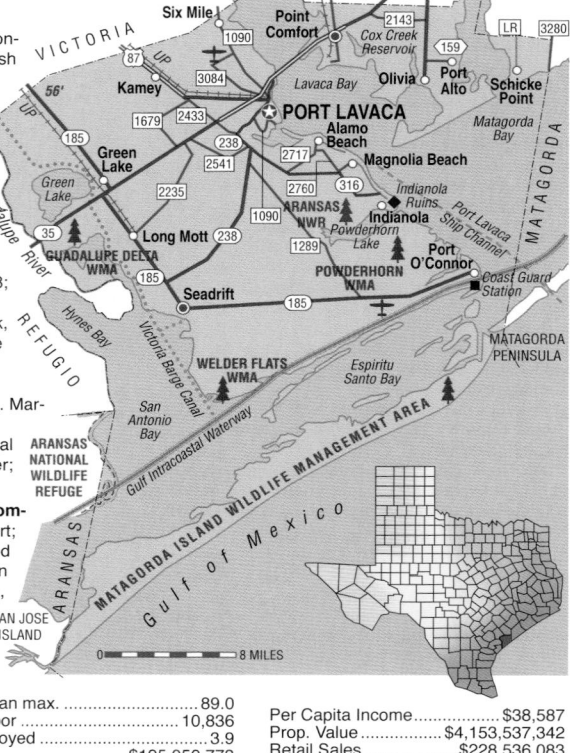

Physical Features: Sandy, broken by bays; Green Lake, Powderhorn Lake, Cox Creek Reservoir; partly on Matagorda Island.

Economy: Aluminum, plastics plants; marine construction; agribusinesses; petroleum; tourism; fish processing.

History: Karankawa tribal area. Empresario Martín De León brought 41 families in 1825. County created from Jackson, Matagorda, and Victoria counties in 1846; organized the same year. Named for John C. Calhoun, U.S. statesman.

Race/Ethnicity: (In percent) Anglo, 42.4; Black, 3.1; Hispanic, 48.8; Asian, 5.2; Other, 1.0; Two or more races, 1.3.

Vital Statistics, annual: Births, 319; deaths, 198; marriages, 141; divorces, 36.

Recreation: Beaches, fishing, water sports, duck, goose hunting; historic sites, county park; La Salle Days in April.

Minerals: Oil, gas.

Agriculture: Cotton, cattle, corn, grain sorghum. Market value $42.1 million. Commercial fishing.

PORT LAVACA (12,346) county seat; commercial seafood operations, offshore drilling, tourist center; some manufacturing; convention center; hospital.

Other towns include: **Long Mott** (76); **Point Comfort** (700) aluminum, plastic plants, deepwater port; **Port O'Connor** (1,254) tourist center, seafood processing, manufacturing, lighted boat parade in December; **Seadrift** (1,511) commercial fishing, processing plants, Bayfront Park, Shrimpfest in June.

Population	21,561
Change fm 2010	0.8
Area (sq. mi.)	1,032.7
Land Area (sq. mi.)	506.8
Altitude (ft.)	sea level–56
Rainfall (in.)	35.93
Jan. mean min.	46.5

July mean max.	89.0
Civ. Labor	10,836
Unemployed	3.9
Wages	$195,050,773

Per Capita Income	$38,587
Prop. Value	$4,153,537,342
Retail Sales	$228,536,083

Callahan County

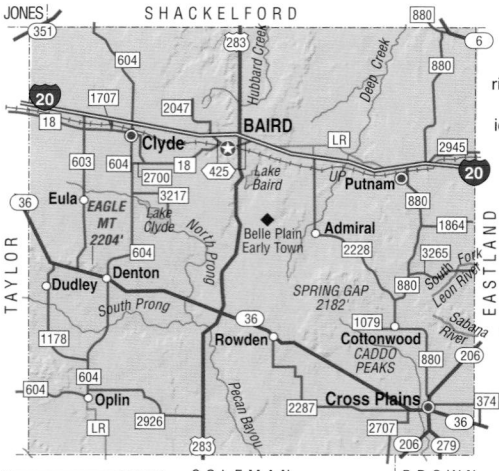

Physical Features: On divide between Brazos, Colorado rivers; Lake Clyde, Lake Baird; level to rolling.

Economy: Ranching; feed and fertilizer business; many residents commute to Abilene; 200,000 acres in hunting leases.

History: Comanche territory until the 1870s. Anglo-American settlement began around 1860. County created in 1858 from Bexar, Bosque, and Travis counties; organized in 1877. Named for Texas Ranger J.H. Callahan.

Race/Ethnicity: (In percent) Anglo, 85.9; Black, 1.7; Hispanic, 9.8; Asian, 0.6; Other, 0.9; Two or more races, 1.9.

Vital Statistics, annual: Births, 147; deaths, 179; marriages, 68; divorces, 42.

Recreation: Hunting, lakes; museums; Cross Plains Hunters' Feed at deer season.

Minerals: Oil and gas.

Agriculture: Cattle, wheat, sorghum, oats. Market value $29.9 million. Hunting leases important.

BAIRD (1,552) county seat; ranching/agricultural trade center, some manufacturing; shipping; historic sites; Railhead Day in May, depot museum.

Clyde (3,917) steel water systems manufacturing, government/services; library; Pecan Festival in October.

Other towns include: **Cross Plains** (996) oil and gas, agriculture, government/services, home of creator of Conan the Barbarian, museum, Barbarian Festival in June; **Putnam** (99).

Population	13,994
Change fm 2010	3.3
Area (sq. mi.)	901.3
Land Area (sq. mi.)	899.4
Altitude (ft.)	1,350–2,204
Rainfall (in.)	27.42
Jan. mean min.	31.4
July mean max.	94.8
Civ. Labor	6,003
Unemployed	3.4

Wages	$26,858,438
Per Capita Income	$38,029
Prop. Value	$1,789,882,822
Retail Sales	$154,431,262

Cameron County

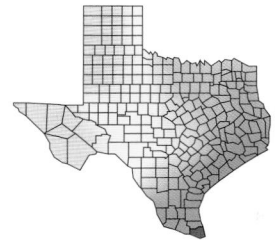

Physical Features: Southernmost county in rich Rio Grande Valley soils; flat landscape; semitropical climate; Loma Alta Lake.

Economy: Agribusiness, tourism, seafood processing, shipping, manufacturing, government/services.

History: Coahuiltecan tribal area. Spanish land grants date to 1781. County created from Nueces County, 1848; named for Capt. Ewen Cameron of Mier Expedition.

Race/Ethnicity: (In percent) Anglo, 8.9; Black, 0.8; Hispanic, 89.7; Asian, 0.8; Other, 0.8; Two or more races, 0.5.

Vital Statistics, annual: Births, 7,238; deaths, 2,684; marriages, 2,201; divorces, 872.

Recreation: South Padre Island: year-round resort; fishing, hunting, water sports; historical sites, Palo Alto visitors center; gateway to Mexico, state parks; wildlife refuge; recreational vehicle center.

Minerals: Natural gas, oil.

Agriculture: Cotton, grain sorghums, vegetables, corn, citrus. Ranked second in sugar cane acreage. Wholesale nursery plants raised. Small feedlot and cow-calf operations. Some 112,000 acres irrigated, mostly cotton and grain sorghums. Market value $160.4 million. Ranked third in value of aquaculture.

BROWNSVILLE (183,686) county seat; international trade, varied industries, shipping, tourism; college, hospitals, crippled children health center; Gladys Porter Zoo, historic Fort Brown; University of Texas–Rio Grande Valley, Texas Southmost College.

Harlingen (65,409) health care, government/services, tourism; hospitals; college extension campuses; nature center; birding festival in November.

San Benito (24,468) retail center, tourism, agriculture; hospital; museums, arts center, historic buildings; recreation facilities, including walking/jogging trail; ResacaFest on July 4.

South Padre Island (2,787) beaches, tourism/convention center, real estate and construction; birding/nature center, Sandcastle Days in October, Spring Break in March.

Other towns include: **Bayview** (405); **Bluetown** (351); **Cameron Park** (7,533); **Combes** (3,146); **Encantada-Ranchito El Calaboz** (2,222); **Indian Lake** (691); **La Feria** (7,791); **Laguna Heights** (4,102); **Laguna Vista** (3,364); **Laureles** (3,756); **Los Fresnos** (6,812) Little Graceland Museum, Butterfly Farm, library; **Los Indios** (1,064); **Olmito** (1,225); **Palm Valley** (1,259).

Also, **Port Isabel** (5,056) tourist center, fishing, museums, old lighthouse, Shrimp Cook-Off in November; **Primera** (4,760); **Rancho Viejo** (2,530); **Rangerville** (332); **Rio Hondo** (2,742); **Santa Maria** (731); **Santa Rosa** (2,932).

Population	**423,908**
Change fm 2010	4.4
Area (sq. mi.)	1,276.5
Land Area (sq. mi.)	890.9
Altitude (ft.)	sea level–67
Rainfall (in.)	27.44
Jan. mean min.	51.6
July mean max.	93.6
Civ. Labor	167,357
Unemployed	5.8
Wages	$1,154,773,068
Per Capita Income	$27,741
Prop. Value	$19,305,871,195
Retail Sales	$4,143,769,730

For explanation of sources, symbols and abbreviations, see p. 192, and foldout map.

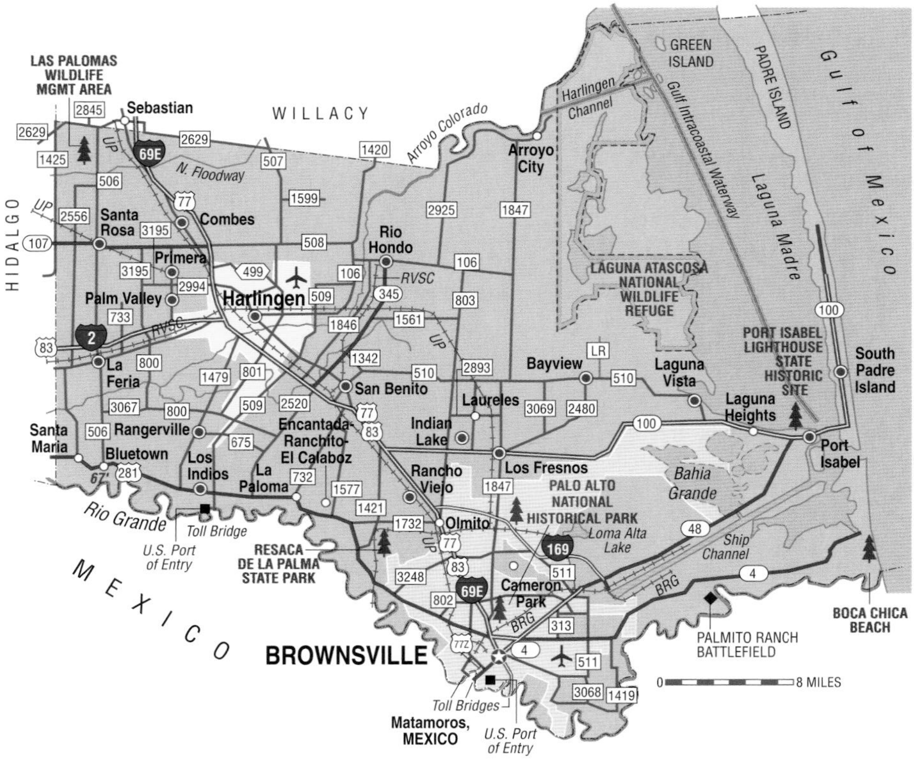

Population 13,033
Change fm 2010 .... 5.1
Area (sq. mi.) 203.2
Land Area (sq. mi.) 195.8
Altitude (ft.) 236–538
Rainfall (in.) 45.10
Jan. mean min. 33.1
July mean max. 95.2
Civ. Labor 4,970
Unemployed 4.7
Wages $36,321,746
Per Capita Income $38,491
Prop. Value $1,073,853,363
Retail Sales $125,293,558

Camp County

Physical Features: East Texas county with forested hills; drains to Big Cypress Creek on the north; Lake Bob Sandlin; third smallest county in Texas.

Economy: Agribusiness, chicken processing, timber industries, light manufacturing, retirement center.

History: Caddo area. Anglo-American settlers arrived in late 1830s. Antebellum slaveholding area. County created, organized, from Upshur County 1874; named for jurist J.L. Camp.

Race/Ethnicity: (In percent) Anglo, 55.8; Black, 16.6; Hispanic, 25.1; Asian, 0.9; Other, 1.2; Two or more races, 2.5.

Vital Statistics, annual: Births, 172; deaths, 132; marriages, 76; divorces, 11.

Recreation: Water sports, fishing on lakes; farmstead and airship museum; Pittsburg hot links; Chickfest in September.

Minerals: Oil, gas, clays, coal.

Agriculture: Poultry and products important; beef, dairy cattle, horses; peaches, hay, blueberries, vegetables. Market value $137.7 million. Forestry.

PITTSBURG (4,665) county seat; agribusiness, timber, tourism, food processing, light manufacturing, commuting to Longview, Tyler; hospital; community college; Prayer Tower.

Other towns include: **Leesburg** (128) and **Rocky Mound** (68).

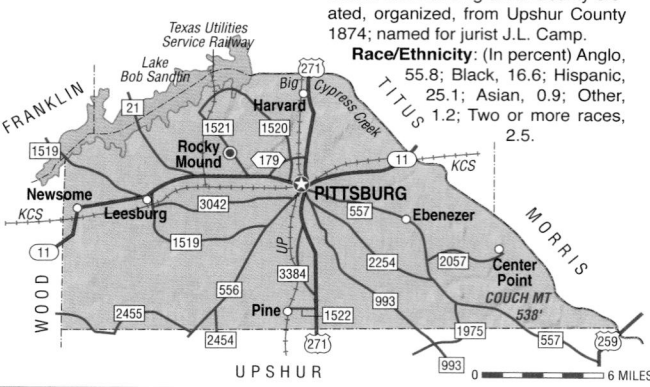

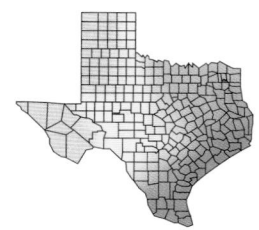

Physical Features: In center of Panhandle on level, some broken land; loam soils.

Economy: Pantex nuclear weapons assembly/disassembly facility (U.S. Department of Energy), commuting to Amarillo, petrochemical plants, agribusiness.

History: Apaches, displaced by Comanches. Anglo-American ranchers settled in the 1880s. German, Polish farmers arrived around 1910. County created from Bexar District, 1876; organized 1888. Named for Republic

Carson County

secretary of state S.P. Carson.

Race/Ethnicity: (In percent) Anglo, 85.5; Black, 0.8; Hispanic, 10.2; Asian, 0.4; Other, 1.6; Two or more races, 2.0.

Vital Statistics, annual: Births, 55; deaths, 58; marriages, 35; divorces, 14.

Recreation: Museum, The Cross at Groom; Square House Barbecue in fall.

Minerals: Oil, gas production.

Agriculture: Cattle, cotton, wheat, sorghum, corn, hay, soybeans. Market value $83 million.

PANHANDLE (2,409) county seat; government/services, agribusiness, petroleum center, commuters to Amarillo; Veterans Day celebration, car show in June.

Other towns include: **Groom** (566) farming center, government/services, Groom Day festival in August; **Skellytown** (471); **White Deer** (1,009) Polish sausage festival in November.

Population 6,005
Change fm 2010 .... – 2.9
Area (sq. mi.) 924.1
Land Area (sq. mi.) 920.2
Altitude (ft.) 2,926–3,595
Rainfall (in.) 21.78
Jan. mean min. 20.3
July mean max. 92.2
Civ. Labor 3,067
Unemployed 2.4
Wages $89,523,483
Per Capita Income $44,364
Prop. Value $2,148,574,950
Retail Sales $110,217,488

For explanation of sources, symbols and abbreviations, see p. 192, and foldout map.

Cass County

Physical Features: Forested Northeast county rolling to hilly; drained by Cypress Bayou, Sulphur River; Wright Patman Lake.

Economy: Timber and paper industries, government/services.

History: Caddoes, who were displaced by other tribes in the 1790s. Anglo-Americans arrived in the 1830s. Antebellum slaveholding area. County created and organized in 1846 from Bowie County; named for U.S. Sen. Lewis Cass.

Race/Ethnicity: (In percent) Anglo, 76.5; Black, 16.8; Hispanic, 4.5; Asian, 0.5; Other, 0.7; Two or more races, 1.6.

Vital Statistics, annual: Births, 386; deaths, 414; marriages, 165; divorces, 117.

Recreation: Fishing, hunting, water sports; state park, county park; lake, wildflower trails.

Minerals: Oil, iron ore.

Agriculture: Cattle, poultry. Market value $67.6 million. Timber important.

LINDEN (2,034) county seat, timber, agribusiness, tourism; oldest courthouse still in use as courthouse, hospital; Rock and Roll Hall of Fame.

ATLANTA (5,679) Paper and timber industries, government/services, varied manufacturing, hospital, library; Forest Festival in August.

Other towns include: **Avinger** (443) timber, paper industry, steel plant, ear-

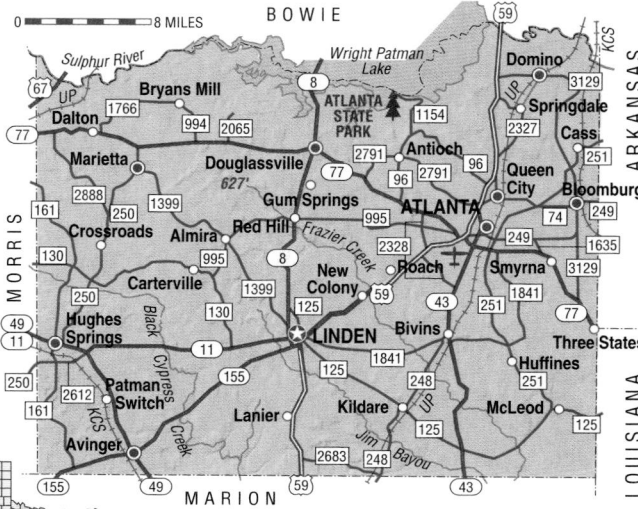

ly cemetery, Glory Days celebration in October; **Bivins** (215); **Bloomburg** (409); **Domino** (91); **Douglassville** (232); **Hughes Springs** (1,788) varied manufacturing, warehousing, trucking school, Pumpkin Glow in October; **Kildare** (104); **Marietta** (134); **McLeod** (600); **Queen City** (1,486) paper industry, commuters to Texarkana, government/services, historic sites.

Population	**30,119**
Change fm 2010	– 1.1
Area (sq. mi.)	960.3
Land Area (sq. mi.)	937.0
Altitude (ft.)	167–627
Rainfall (in.)	49.17
Jan. mean min.	34.6
July mean max.	92.1
Civ. Labor	12,228
Unemployed	4.8
Wages	$69,799,482
Per Capita Income	$35,996
Prop. Value	$2,815,488,358
Retail Sales	$254,704,714

Fishermen at dawn on South Padre Island, Cameron County. Photo by Robert Plocheck.

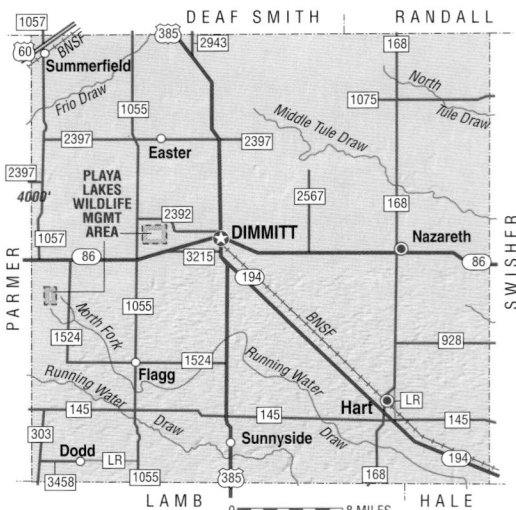

Castro County

Physical Features: Flat Panhandle county, drains to creeks, draws and playas; underground water.

Economy: Agribusiness.

History: Apaches, displaced by Comanches in the 1720s. Anglo-American ranchers began settling in the 1880s. Germans settled after 1900. Mexican migration increased after 1950. County created, 1876 from Bexar District, organized 1891. Named for Henri Castro, Texas colonizer.

Race/Ethnicity: (In percent) Anglo, 31.1; Black, 2.6; Hispanic, 65.4; Asian, 0.6; Other, 1.8; Two or more races, 1.0.

Vital Statistics, annual: Births, 125; deaths, 65; marriages, 39; divorces, 23.

Recreation: Pheasant hunting; Italian POW camp site; Dimmitt Harvest Days celebrated in August.

Minerals: Insignificant.

Agriculture: Beef cattle, dairies (first in number of milk cows), corn, cotton, wheat, sheep. Market value $1.31 billion; third in state.

Population	7,665
Change fm 2010	– 4.9
Area (sq. mi.)	899.3
Land Area (sq. mi.)	894.4
Altitude (ft.)	3,565–4,000
Rainfall (in.)	21.22
Jan. mean min.	21.3
July mean max.	91.0
Civ. Labor	3,373
Unemployed	3.0
Wages	$23,922,032
Per Capita Income	$50,209
Prop. Value	$1,826,771,510
Retail Sales	$54,501,601

DIMMITT (4,137) county seat; agribusiness center; library, hospital; quilt festival in April.

Other towns include: **Hart** (1,021) and **Nazareth** (290) German festival/ Suds & Sounds in July.

Chambers County

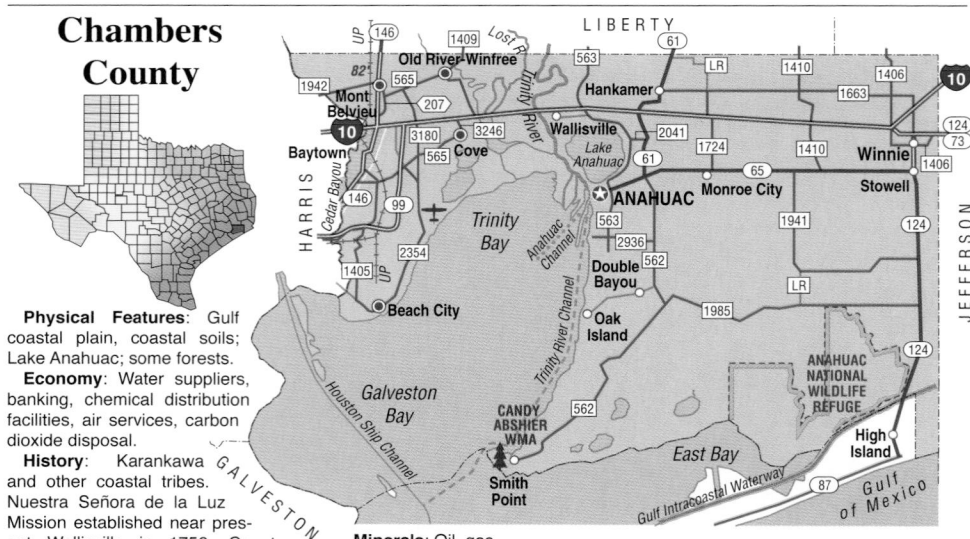

Physical Features: Gulf coastal plain, coastal soils; Lake Anahuac; some forests.

Economy: Water suppliers, banking, chemical distribution facilities, air services, carbon dioxide disposal.

History: Karankawa and other coastal tribes. Nuestra Señora de la Luz Mission established near present Wallisville in 1756. County created and organized in 1858 from Liberty, Jefferson counties. Named for Gen. T. J. Chambers, surveyor.

Race/Ethnicity: (In percent) Anglo, 67.0; Black, 8.4; Hispanic, 22.3; Asian, 1.4; Other, 1.1; Two or more races, 1.6.

Vital Statistics, annual: Births, 512; deaths, 290; marriages, 227; divorces, 160.

Recreation: Fishing, hunting; water sports; camping; county parks; wildlife refuge; historic sites; Wallisville Heritage Museum; Texas Gatorfest at Anahuac in September.

Minerals: Oil, gas.

Agriculture: Beef cattle, rice, hay, aquaculture; significant irrigation. Market value $25.6 million. Hunting, fishing important.

ANAHUAC (2,413) county seat; canal connects with Houston Ship Channel; agribusiness; hospital, library.

WINNIE (3,498) ecotourism; commuting to Beaumont, Houston; rice farming; antiques market; hospital; library, museum; Texas Rice Festival in early October.

Other towns include: **Beach City** (2,648), **Cove** (562), **Hankamer** (226), **Mont Belvieu** (5,658), **Old River-Winfree** (1,352), **Stowell** (1,967), and **Wallisville** (300).

Part [4,116] of **Baytown**.

Population	42,454
Change fm 2010	21.0
Area (sq. mi.)	871.2
Land Area (sq. mi.)	597.1
Altitude (ft.)	sea level–82
Rainfall (in.)	57.11
Jan. mean min.	42.2
July mean max.	90.6
Civ. Labor	19,103
Unemployed	4.9
Wages	$229,816,970
Per Capita Income	$51,832
Prop. Value	$14,646,874,482
Retail Sales	$386,888,874

Cherokee County

Physical Features: East Texas county; hilly, partly forested; drains to Angelina, Neches rivers; many streams; Lake Palestine, Lake Striker, Lake Jacksonville; sandy, clay soils.

Economy: Government/services, varied manufacturing, agribusiness.

History: Caddo tribes attracted Spanish missionaries around 1720. Cherokees began settling area around 1820, and soon afterward Anglo-Americans began to arrive. Cherokees forced to Indian Territory 1839. Named for Indian tribe; created 1846 from Nacogdoches County.

Race/Ethnicity: (In percent) Anglo, 60.5; Black, 14.5; Hispanic, 23.3; Asian, 0.6; Other, 1.7; Two or more races, 2.0.

Vital Statistics, annual: Births, 827; deaths, 557; marriages, 296; divorces, 160.

Recreation: Water sports; fishing, hunting; historic sites and parks, national wildlife refuge; Texas State Railroad; nature trails through forests; lakes.

Minerals: Gas, oil.

Agriculture: Nurseries (second in the state in value of sales), hay, beef cattle, dairies, poultry. Market value $134 million. Timber, hunting income significant.

RUSK (5,569) county seat; agribusiness, tourism, state mental hospital, prison unit; historic footbridge, heritage festival in October.

JACKSONVILLE (14,972) varied manufacturing, plastics, agribusiness, tourism, retail center; hospitals, junior colleges; Love's Lookout; Tomato Fest in June.

Other towns include: **Alto** (1,238) farming, timber, light manufacturing, pecan festival in November; **Cuney** (137); **Gallatin** (437); **Maydelle** (250); **New Summerfield** (1,165); **Reklaw** (390, partly in Rusk County); **Wells** (819). Part [47] of **Bullard** and part [61] of **Troup**.

Population	52,592
Change fm 2010	3.5
Area (sq. mi.)	1,062.2
Land Area (sq. mi.)	1,052.9
Altitude (ft.)	187–775
Rainfall (in.)	49.54
Jan. mean min.	36.3
uly mean max.	91.2
Civ. Labor	20,888

Unemployed	4.0
Wages	$129,575,126
Per Capita Income	$34,257
Prop. Value	$3,642,706,167
Retail Sales	$416,254,983

For explanation of sources, symbols and abbreviations, see p. 192, and foldout map.

Grain elevators at Dimmitt, Castro County. Photo by Robert Plocheck.

Childress County

COLLINGSWORTH

HALL

OKLAHOMA

HARDEMAN

COTTLE

Physical Features: Rolling prairie, at corner of Panhandle, draining to fork of Red River; Baylor Creek Lake, Lake Childress; mixed soils.

Economy: Government/services, retail trade, tourism, agriculture.

History: Apache tribal area, displaced by Comanches. Ranchers arrived around 1880. County created in 1876 from Bexar, Young districts; organized in 1887; named for writer of Texas Declaration of Independence, George C. Childress.

Race/Ethnicity: (In percent) Anglo, 57.0; Black, 10.2; Hispanic, 30.9; Asian, 0.7; Other, 0.9; Two or more races, 1.5.

Vital Statistics, annual: Births, 62; deaths, 75; marriages, 27; divorces, 11.

Recreation: Recreation on lakes and creeks, fishing; hunting of deer, turkey, wild hog, quail, dove; parks; county museum.

Minerals: Insignificant.

Agriculture: Cotton, beef cattle, wheat, hay, sorghum, peanuts; some 9,000 acres irrigated. Market value $19.9 million. Hunting leases.

CHILDRESS (5,994) county seat; agribusiness, hospital, prison unit; settlers reunion and rodeo in July.

Other towns include: **Tell** (20).

Population		7,291
Change fm 2010		3.6
Area (sq. mi.)		713.7
Land Area (sq. mi.)		696.4
Altitude (ft.)		1,560–2,060
Rainfall (in.)		26.43
Jan. mean min.		26.8
July mean max.		95.7
Civ. Labor		2,870
Unemployed		2.4
Wages		$24,334,765
Per Capita Income		$29,965
Prop. Value		$772,574,181
Retail Sales		$109,052,230

Clay County

Physical Features: Hilly, rolling; Northwest county drains to Red, Trinity rivers; Lake Arrowhead; sandy loam, chocolate soils; mesquites, post oaks.

Economy: Oil, agribusiness, commuting.

History: Wichitas arrived from north-central plains in mid-1700s, followed by Apaches and Comanches. Ranching attempts began in 1850s. County created from Cooke County, 1857; Indians forced disorganization, 1862; reorganized, 1873; named for Henry Clay, U.S. statesman.

Race/Ethnicity: (In percent) Anglo, 89.8; Black, 0.8; Hispanic, 6.1; Asian, 0.4; Other, 1.4; Two or more races, 2.3.

Vital Statistics, annual: Births, 84; deaths, 131; marriages, 70; divorces, 27.

Recreation: Fishing, hunting, horses, water sports; state park; pioneer reunion in September.

Minerals: Oil and gas, stone.

Agriculture: Beef cattle, wheat, pecans, peaches, dairy cattle. Market value $79.8 million. Oaks, cedar, elms sold to nurseries, mesquite cut for firewood.

HENRIETTA (3,011) county seat; agribusiness, government/services, manufacturing; hospital; museum; Turkey Fest in April.

Other towns include: **Bellevue** (350), **Bluegrove** (135), **Byers** (495), **Dean** (469), **Jolly** (175), **Petrolia** (661).

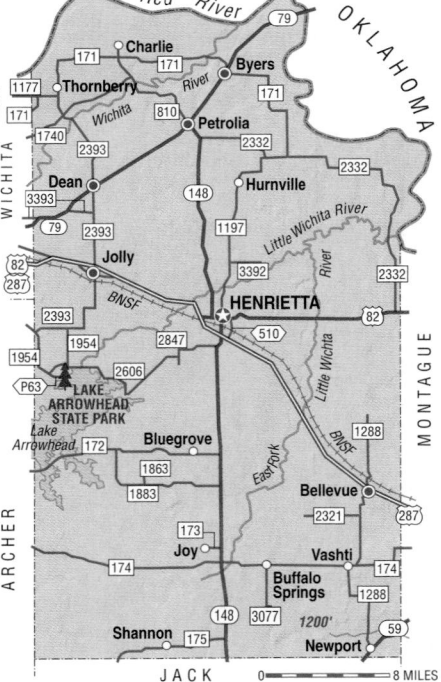

WICHITA

ARCHER

MONTAGUE

JACK

OKLAHOMA

Population		10,456
Change fm 2010		– 2.8
Area (sq. mi.)		1,116.8
Land Area (sq. mi.)		1,088.7
Altitude (ft.)		791–1,200
Rainfall (in.)		32.68
Jan. mean min.		28.7
July mean max.		96.6
Civ. Labor		4,800
Unemployed		3.2
Wages		$13,407,258
Per Capita Income		$42,522
Prop. Value		$2,206,868,350
Retail Sales		$63,055,833

For explanation of sources, symbols and abbreviations, see p. 192, and foldout map.

Cochran County

Physical Features: South Plains bordering New Mexico with small lakes (playas); underground water; loam, sandy loam soils.

Economy: Farming, government/services, retail.

History: Hunting area for various Indian tribes. Ranches operated in the 1880s but population in 1900 was still only 25. Farming began in the 1920s. County created from Bexar and Young districts in 1876; organized in 1924; named for Robert Cochran, who died at the Alamo.

Race/Ethnicity: (In percent) Anglo, 36.6; Black, 4.4; Hispanic, 58.1; Asian, 0.4; Other, 3.0; Two or more races, 1.0.

Vital Statistics, annual: Births, 39; deaths, 31; marriages, 21; divorces, 6.

Recreation: Museum; Last Frontier Trail Drive and Buffalo Soldier Day in June.

Minerals: Insignificant.

Agriculture: Cotton, peanuts, sorghum, peas, sunflowers, wheat. Crops 60 percent irrigated. Market value $100.8 million.

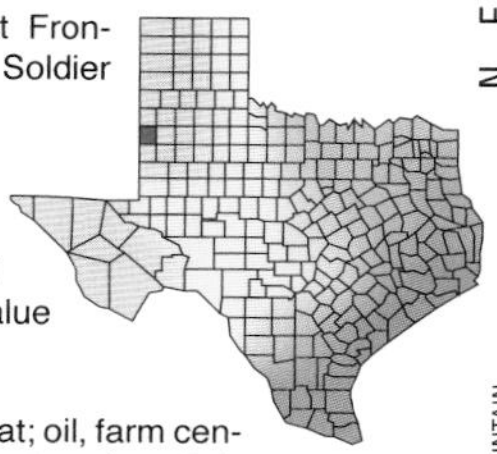

MORTON (1,903) county seat; oil, farm center, meat packing, light manufacture; hospital.

Other towns include: **Bledsoe** (126), **Whiteface** (424).

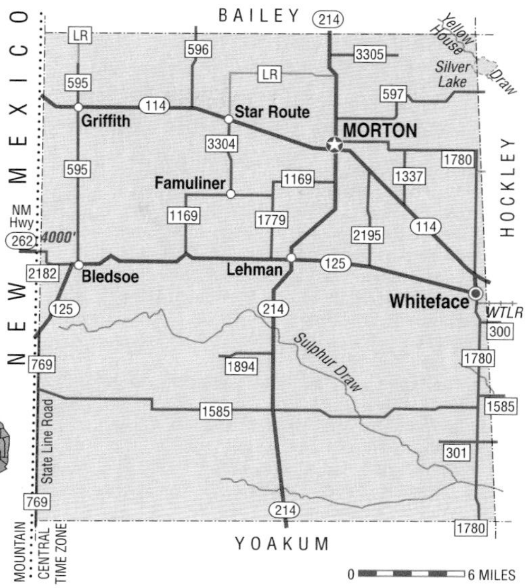

Population		**2,836**
Change fm 2010		– 9.3
Area (sq. mi.)		775.2
Land Area (sq. mi.)		775.2
Altitude (ft.)		3,565–4,000
Rainfall (in.)		18.93
Jan. temp. min.		24.4
July temp. max.		91.5
Civ. Labor		1,034
Unemployed		3.5
Wages		$6,102,844
Per Capita Income		$40,614
Prop. Value		$455,927,948
Retail Sales		$7,318,554

Fall foliage in Clay County near Charlie. Photo by Robert Plocheck.

Coke County

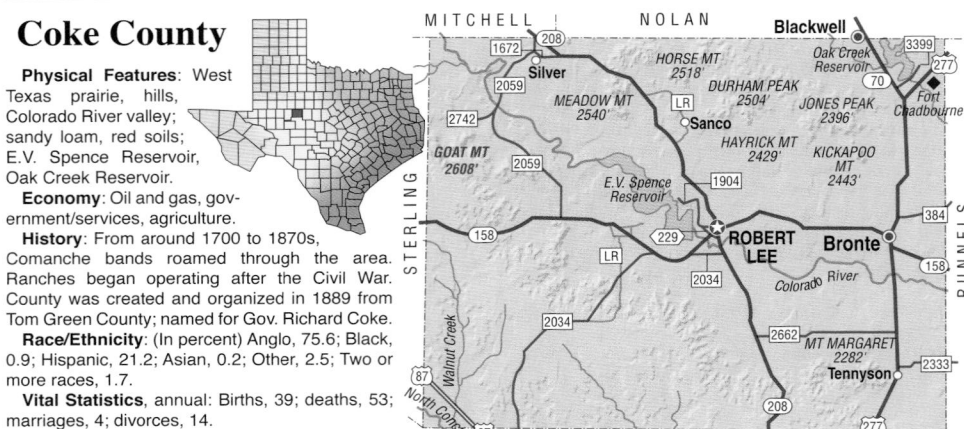

Physical Features: West Texas prairie, hills, Colorado River valley; sandy loam, red soils; E.V. Spence Reservoir, Oak Creek Reservoir.

Economy: Oil and gas, government/services, agriculture.

History: From around 1700 to 1870s, Comanche bands roamed through the area. Ranches began operating after the Civil War. County was created and organized in 1889 from Tom Green County; named for Gov. Richard Coke.

Race/Ethnicity: (In percent) Anglo, 75.6; Black, 0.9; Hispanic, 21.2; Asian, 0.2; Other, 2.5; Two or more races, 1.7.

Vital Statistics, annual: Births, 39; deaths, 53; marriages, 4; divorces, 14.

Recreation: Hunting, fishing, Caliche Loop birdwatching trail; lakes; Sumac hiking trail; historic sites, Fort Chadbourne, county museum, Fort Chadbourne Days in May; amphitheater.

Minerals: Oil, gas.

Agriculture: Beef cattle, small grains, sheep and goats, hay. Market value $7 million.

ROBERT LEE (1,029) county seat; oil and gas, wind farms, ranching, government/services; old jail museum.

Bronte (983) ranching, oil.

Other towns include: **Silver** (34) and **Tennyson** (46). Also, a small part of **Blackwell** (303).

Population	**3,370**
Change fm 2010	1.6
Area (sq. mi.)	928.0
Land Area (sq. mi.)	911.5
Altitude (ft.)	1,700–2,608
Rainfall (in.)	22.75
Jan. mean min.	28.4
July mean max.	96.7
Civ. Labor	1,437
Unemployed	3.0
Wages	$7,061,435
Per Capita Income	$38,586
Prop. Value	$955,014,500
Retail Sales	$20,629,141

Coleman County

Physical Features: Hilly, rolling; drains to Colorado River, Pecan Bayou; O.H. Ivie Reservoir Hords Creek Lake, Lake Coleman; mesquite, oaks.

Economy: Agribusiness, petroleum, ecotourism, varied manufacturing.

History: Presence of Apaches and Comanches brought military outpost, Camp Colorado, before the Civil War. Settlers arrived after organization. County created in 1858 from Brown, Travis counties; organized in 1864; named for Houston's aide, R.M. Coleman.

Race/Ethnicity: (In percent), Anglo, 76.5; Black, 3.2; Hispanic, 17.8; Asian, 1.0; Other, 1.4; Two or more races, 1.9.

Vital Statistics, annual: Births, 72; deaths, 131; marriages, 59; divorces, 44.

Recreation: Fishing, hunting; water sports; city park, historic sites; lakes; Santa Anna Peak; Santa Anna bison cook-off in May.

Minerals: Oil, gas, stone, clays.

Agriculture: Cattle, wheat, sheep, hay, grain sorghum, goats, oats, cotton. Market value $28.4 million. Mesquite for firewood and furniture.

COLEMAN (4,590) county seat; varied manufacturing; hospital, library, museums: Fiesta de la Paloma in October.

Santa Anna (1,084) agribusiness, oil, tourism; museum; Funtier days in May.

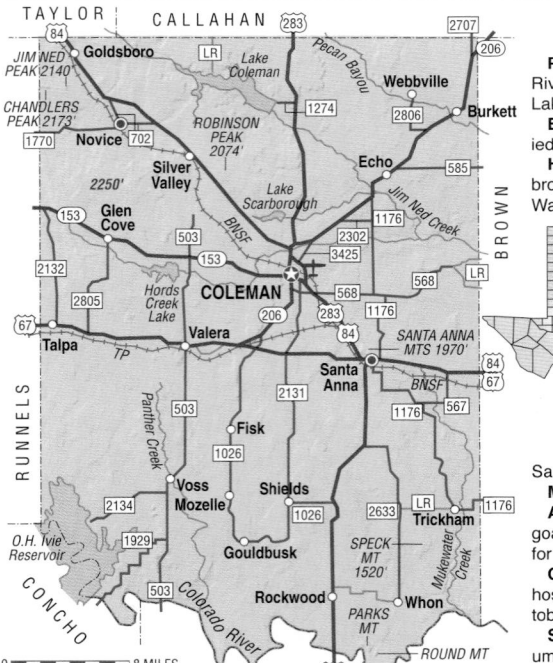

Other towns include: **Burkett** (90), **Goldsboro** (15), **Gouldbusk** (70), **Novice** (136), **Rockwood** (53), **Talpa** (127), and **Valera** (80).

For explanation of sources, symbols and abbreviations, see p. 192, and foldout map.

Population	**8,397**
Change fm 2000	– 5.6
Area (sq. mi.)	1,281.4
Land Area (sq. mi.)	1,262.0
Altitude (ft.)	1,289–2,250
Rainfall (in.)	28.74
Jan. mean min.	33.7
July mean max.	95.7
Civ. Labor	2,967
Unemployed	4.0
Wages	$14,937,077
Per Capita Income	$38,788
Prop. Value	$1,757,256,496
Retail Sales	$67,415,536

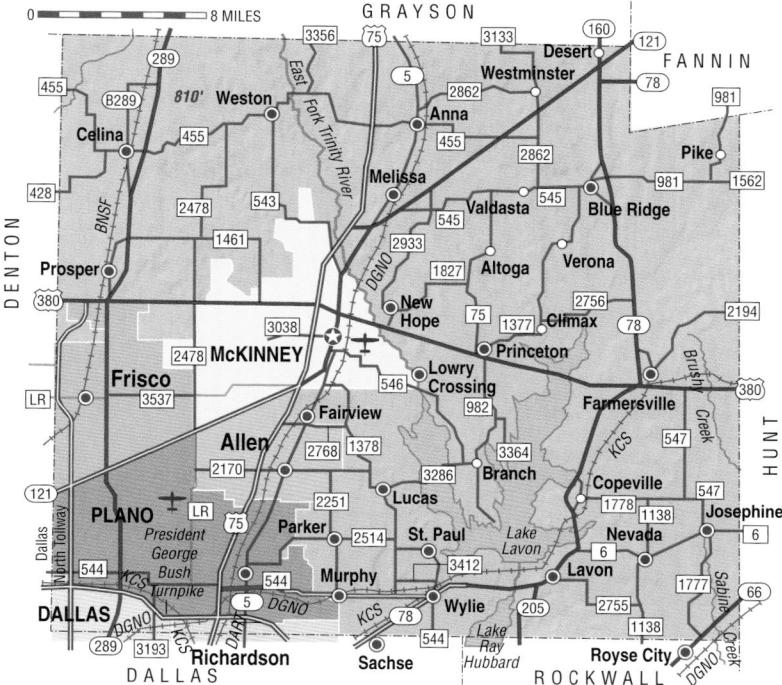

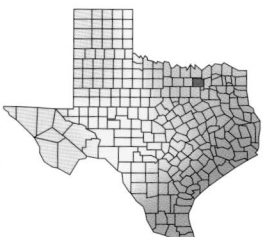

Physical Features: Heavy, black clay soil; level to rolling; drains to Trinity; Lake Lavon, Lake Ray Hubbard.

Economy: Government/services, manufacturing plants, retail and wholesale center, many residents work in Dallas.

History: Caddo tribal area until 1850s. Settlers of Peters colony arrived in the early 1840s. County created, organized, from Fannin County in 1846. Named for pioneer settler Collin McKinney.

Race/Ethnicity: (In percent) Anglo, 57.3; Black, 10.2; Hispanic, 15.3; Asian, 15.0; Other, 0.8; Two or more races, 2.7.

Vital Statistics, annual: Births, 10,921; deaths, 4,005; marriages, 5,225; divorces, 2,644.

Recreation: Fishing, water sports; historic sites; old homes restoration, tours; natural science museum.

Minerals: Insignificant.

Agriculture: Landscape nurseries, corn, wheat, cattle, hay, grain sorghum. Market value $77.8 million.

McKINNEY (175,129) county seat; agribusiness, trade center, varied industry; hospital, community college; museums.

PLANO (299,858) professional services, banking, finance, insurance, health care/hospitals; community college, university extensions; museums, fine arts organizations, nature pre-

Collin County

serves, hiking trails; balloon festival in September, AsiaFest in April.

FRISCO (171,982) technical, aerospace industry, hospital, community college.

Other towns include: **Allen** (100,003)

Population	1,005,146
Change fm 2010	28.5
Area (sq. mi.)	886.1
Land Area (sq. mi.)	841.2
Altitude (ft.)	434–810
Rainfall (in.)	42.32
Jan. mean min.	30.1
July mean max.	91.5
Civ. Labor	522,108
Unemployed	3.1
Wages	$6,678,384,694
Per Capita Income	$64,025
Prop. Value	$140,596,120,455
Retail Sales	$18,264,555,332

retail, manufacturing, wholesale trade, hospital, community college, nature conservatory, natatorium, historic stone dam, Stampede rodeo in October; **Anna** (11,904); **Blue Ridge** (920); **Celina** (8,147) museum, historic town square, Fun Day in September.

Also, **Copeville** (243); **Fairview** (9,278) government/services, retail center, commuters, museum, old mill site, wildlife sanctuary, veterans celebration in November; **Farmersville** (3,879) agriculture, light industries, Audie Murphy Day in June.

Also, **Josephine** (1,252); **Lavon** (3,260); **Lowry Crossing** (2,047); **Lucas** (7,238); **Melissa** (9,117) industrial plants, library, old town; **Murphy** (21,067); **Nevada** (1,069); **New Hope** (652); **Parker** (4,647); **Princeton** (9,669) manufacturing, commuters, Spring Onion festival in April.

Also, **Prosper** (19,659); **St. Paul** (1,388); **Westminster** (1,118); **Weston** (586); **Wylie** (50,658) manufacturing, retail, hospital, historic sites, big cat sanctuary, July Jubilee.

Also, part [46,885] of **Dallas**, part [28,569] of **Richardson** and part [6,301] of **Sachse**.

For explanation of sources, symbols and abbreviations, see p. 192, and foldout map.

Collingsworth County

Physical Features: Panhandle county of rolling, broken terrain, draining to Red River forks; sandy and loam soils.

Economy: Agribusiness.

History: Apaches, displaced by Comanches. Ranchers from England arrived in the late 1870s. County created in 1876, from Bexar and Young districts, organized in 1890. Named for Republic of Texas' first chief justice, James Collinsworth (name misspelled in law).

Race/Ethnicity: (In percent) Anglo, 57.6; Black, 6.2; Hispanic, 34.1; Asian, 0.5; Other, 3.0; Two or more races, 1.8.

Vital Statistics, annual: Births, 26; deaths, 39; marriages, 21; divorces, 5.

Recreation: Deer, quail hunting; children's camp, county museum, pioneer park; county fair/parade in September.

Minerals: Gas, oil production.

Agriculture: Cotton, peanuts, cow-calf operations, wheat, stocker cattle; 22,000 acres irrigated. Market value $43.1 million.

WELLINGTON (2,062) county seat; peanut-processing plants, varied manufacturing; agriculture; hospital; library; restored Ritz Theatre.

Other towns include: **Dodson** (106), **Quail** (15), **Samnorwood** (58).

Population	2,962
Change fm 2010	– 3.1
Area (sq. mi.)	919.3
Land Area (sq. mi.)	918.4
Altitude (ft.)	1,750–2,840
Rainfall (in.)	22.59
Jan. mean min.	27.4
July mean max.	97.6
Civ. Labor	1,146
Unemployed	3.4
Wages	$8,107,250
Per Capita Income	$38,186
Prop. Value	$706,698,760
Retail Sales	$15,340,421

Colorado County

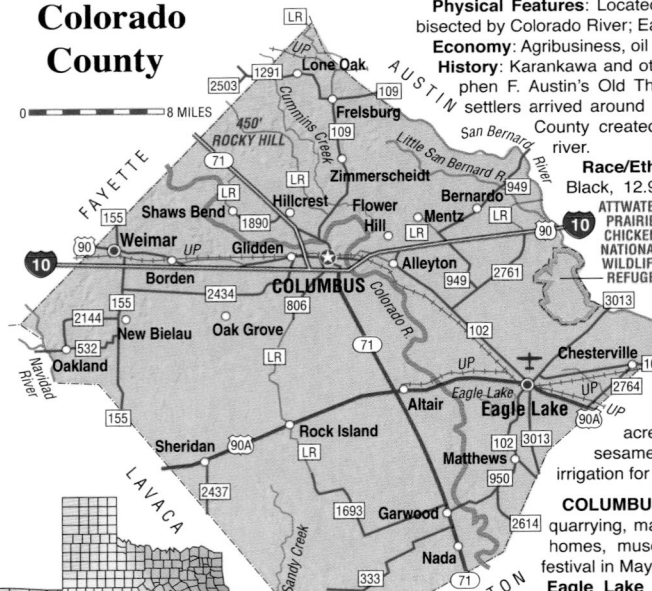

Physical Features: Located in three soil areas; level to rolling; bisected by Colorado River; Eagle Lake; oaks.

Economy: Agribusiness, oil and gas services, gravel mining.

History: Karankawa and other tribes. Anglo settlers among Stephen F. Austin's Old Three Hundred families. First German settlers arrived around 1840. Antebellum slaveholding area. County created 1836, organized 1837; named for river.

Race/Ethnicity: (In percent) Anglo, 56.3; Black, 12.9; Hispanic, 29.9; Asian, 0.8; Other, 1.2; Two or more races, 1.4.

Vital Statistics, annual: Births, 265; deaths, 256; marriages, 117; divorces, 45.

Recreation: Hunting of duck, geese, deer, exotics; canoeing, bicycling; historic sites; prairie chicken refuge; opera house in Columbus, water park in Sheridan.

Minerals: Gas, oil, gravel.

Agriculture: Rice (third in state in acres), cattle, corn, cotton, soybeans, sesame, hay, pecans, nurseries; significant irrigation for rice. Market value $68 million.

COLUMBUS (3,804) county seat; agriculture, quarrying, manufacturing; hospital; historical sites, homes, museums, walking tour; Magnolia Days festival in May.

Eagle Lake (3,809) rice drying center; hospital; goose hunting; Prairie Edge museum.

Weimar (2,317) agriculture, light industry, meat processing; retail; hospital, library; "Gedenke" (remember) celebration on Mother's Day weekend.

Other towns include: **Altair** (30), **Garwood** (600), **Glidden** (730), **Nada** (165), **Oakland** (80), **Rock Island** (160), **Sheridan** (300).

Population	21,217
Change fm 2010	1.7
Area (sq. mi.)	973.7
Land Area (sq. mi.)	960.3
Altitude (ft.)	125–450
Rainfall (in.)	43.93
Jan. mean min.	40.8
July mean max.	94.3
Civ. Labor	9,695
Unemployed	3.1
Wages	$71,406,015
Per Capita Income	$44,836
Prop. Value	$5,100,087,216
Retail Sales	$292,418,012

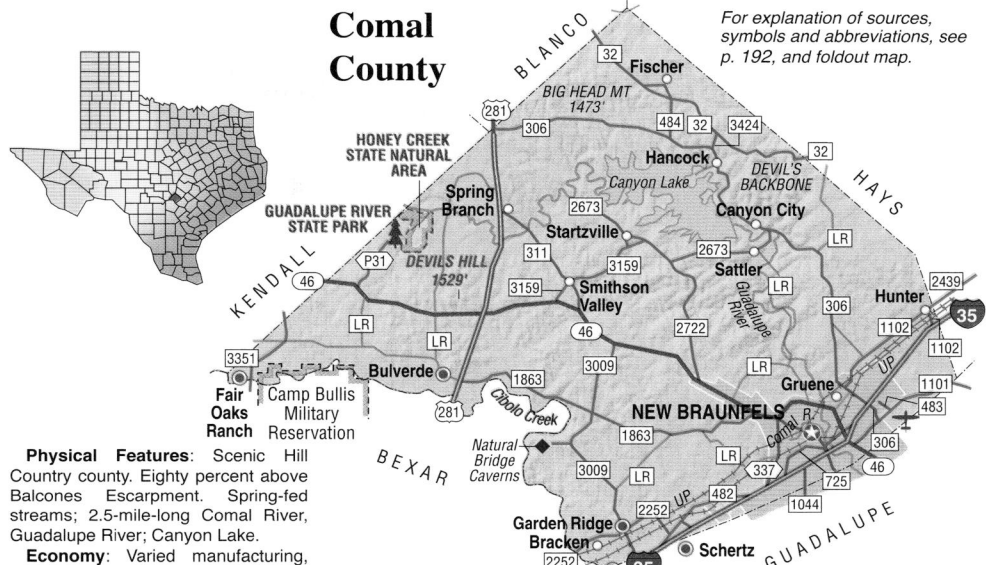

Comal County

For explanation of sources, symbols and abbreviations, see p. 192, and foldout map.

Physical Features: Scenic Hill Country county. Eighty percent above Balcones Escarpment. Spring-fed streams; 2.5-mile-long Comal River, Guadalupe River; Canyon Lake.

Economy: Varied manufacturing, tourism, government/services, agriculture; county in San Antonio metropolitan area.

History: Tonkawa, Waco Indians. A pioneer German settlement 1845. Mexican migration peaked during Mexican Revolution. County created from Bexar, Gonzales, Travis counties and organized in 1846; named for river, a name for Spanish earthenware or metal pan used for cooking tortillas.

Race/Ethnicity: (In percent) Anglo, 67.7; Black, 2.4; Hispanic, 27.5; Asian, 1.2; Other, 0.9; Two or more races, 1.8.

Vital Statistics, annual: Births, 1,632; deaths, 1,108; marriages, 1,112; divorces, 268.

Recreation: Fishing, hunting; historic sites; scenic drives, Devil's Backbone; lake facilities; Prince Solms Park, other county parks; Landa Park with 76 species of trees; Gruene

historic area; caverns; river resorts; river tubing; Schlitterbahn water park; Wurstfest in November, Wasselfest in December.

Minerals: Stone, lime, sand and gravel.

Agriculture: Cattle, goats, sheep, hogs, horses; nursery, hay, corn, sorghum, wheat.

NEW BRAUNFELS (74,930) county seat; manufacturing, retail, distribution center; picturesque city, making it a tourist center; Conservation Plaza; rose garden; hospital; library; mental health and retardation center. Gruene is now part of New Braunfels.

Canyon Lake (25,516), which includes **Startzville**, **Sattler**, **Smithson Valley**, **Canyon City**, **Fischer**, **Hancock**, and **Spring Branch**, retirement and recreation area, tourism, barbe-

cue cook-off in April.

Other towns include: **Bulverde** (5,410) retail center; **Garden Ridge** (3,966);

Also in the county, parts of **Fair Oaks Ranch** (9,003), **Selma** (9,596), and **Schertz** (38,084).

Population	**148,373**
Change fm 2010	36.8
Area (sq. mi.)	574.9
Land Area (sq. mi.)	559.5
Altitude (ft.)	560–1,529
Rainfall (in.)	33.97
Jan. mean min.	38.1
July mean max.	93.3
Civ. Labor	68,246
Unemployed	3.1
Wages	$593,106,670
Per Capita Income	$55,965
Prop. Value	$21,205,870,986
Retail Sales	$2,077,646,893

Fly fishing in the Guadalupe River. Photo by Chase Fountain, Texas Parks & Wildlife.

Comanche County

Physical Features: Rolling, hilly terrain; sandy, loam, waxy soils; drains to Leon River, Proctor Lake; pecans, oaks, mesquites, cedars.

Economy: Dairies, peanut-, pecan-shelling plants, manufacturing.

History: Comanche area. Anglo-American settlers arrived in 1854 on land granted earlier to Stephen F. Austin and Samuel May Williams. County created and organized in 1856 from Bosque and Coryell counties; named for the Indian tribe.

Race/Ethnicity: (In percent) Anglo, 69.5; Black, 1.1; Hispanic, 28.0; Asian, 0.5; Other, 1.4; Two or more races, 1.3.

Vital Statistics, annual: Births, 174; deaths, 188; marriages, 121; divorces, 18.

Recreation: Hunting, fishing, water sports, nature tourism; parks, community center, museums; Comanche Pow-Wow in September, rodeo in July.

Minerals: Limited gas, oil, stone, clay.

Agriculture: Dairies, beef cattle, pecans (first in state in acreage), hay, wildlife, melons. Market value $158.1 million.

COMANCHE (4,336) county seat; plants process feed, food; varied manufacturing; winery; hospital; Ranger College branch; library; state's oldest courthouse, "Old Cora," on display on town square.

De Leon (2,233) pecans, light manufacturing; hospital; car museum, Peach and Melon Festival in August.

Other towns include: **Energy** (70), **Gustine** (484), **Proctor** (228), and **Sidney** (148).

Population 13,534	July mean max. 95.7
Change fm 2010 .... – 3.1	Civ. Labor 5,290
Area (sq. mi.) 947.7	Unemployed 3.6
Land Area (sq. mi.) 937.8	Wages $31,331,825
Altitude (ft.) 1,020–1,847	Per Capita Income $39,842
Rainfall (in.) 32.38	Prop. Value $2,477,428,402
Jan. mean min. 31.4	Retail Sales $157,853,564

Concho County

Physical Features: On Edwards Plateau; rough, broken to south; level in north; sandy, loam and dark soils; drains to creeks and Colorado and Concho rivers.

Economy: Agribusiness, manufacturing.

History: Athabascan-speaking Plains Indians, then Jumanos in the 1600s, absorbed by Lipan Apaches in the 1700s. Comanches raided after 1800. Anglo-Americans began ranching around 1850; farming began after the Civil War. Mexican-Americans employed on sheep ranches in 1920s-30s. County created from Bexar District in 1858, organized in 1879; named for river.

Race/Ethnicity: (In percent) Anglo, 59.8; Black, 1.8; Hispanic, 36.6; Asian, 1.3; Other, 0.9; Two or more races, 1.0.

Vital Statistics, annual: Births, 33; deaths, 33; marriages, 10; divorces, 6.

Recreation: Famed for 1,500 Indian pictographs; O.H. Ivie Reservoir.

Minerals: Oil, gas, stone.

Agriculture: Sheep, cattle, goats; wheat, feed grains; 2,000 acres irrigated for cotton. Market value $22.8 million.

PAINT ROCK (275) county seat; named for Indian pictographs nearby; farming, ranching center.

EDEN (1,297) steel fabrication; hospital; fall fest.

Other towns include: **Eola** (215), **Lowake** (40), and **Millersview** (80).

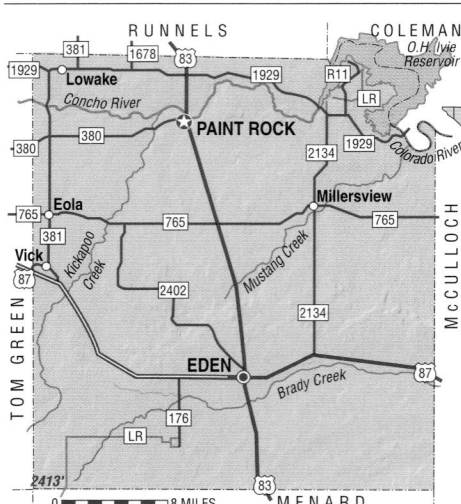

Population 4,276	Wages $5,296,112
Change fm 2010 .... 4.6	Per Capita Income $32,328
Area (sq. mi.) 993.7	Prop. Value $981,148,713
Land Area (sq. mi.) 983.8	Retail Sales $15,627,565
Altitude (ft.) 1,421–2,413	
Rainfall (in.) 24.96	*For explanation of sources,*
Jan. mean min. 29.5	*symbols and abbreviations, see*
July mean max. 95.2	*p. 192, and foldout map.*
Civ. Labor 1,044	
Unemployed 3.4	

Cooke County

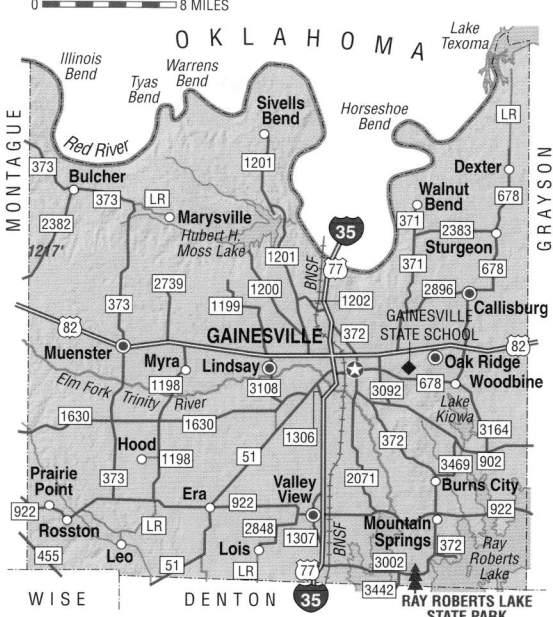

Physical Features: North Texas county; drains to Red, Trinity rivers; Ray Roberts Lake, Lake Texoma, Lake Kiowa, Hubert H. Moss Lake; sandy, red, loam soils.

Economy: Oil and gas, varied manufacturing, commuting to Dallas and Fort Worth.

History: Frontier between Caddoes and Comanches. Anglo-Americans arrived in the late 1840s. Germans settled western part around 1890. County created and organized in 1848 from Fannin County; named for Capt. W.G. Cooke of the Texas Revolution.

Race/Ethnicity: (In percent) Anglo, 75.3; Black, 3.4; Hispanic, 18.2; Asian, 1.1; Other, 1.6; Two or more races, 1.8.

Vital Statistics, annual: Births, 545; deaths, 413; marriages, 447; divorces, 143.

Recreation: Water sports; hunting, fishing; zoo; museum; park, Gainesville Depot Day/car show in October.

Minerals: Oil, natural gas, sand, gravel.

Agriculture: Beef cattle, horses, forages, wheat. Market value $63.3 million. Hunting leases important.

GAINESVILLE (16,373) county seat; aerospace, plastics, energy; Victorian homes, walking tours; hospital; community college, juvenile correction unit; Camp Sweeney for diabetic children; World War II Camp Howze site.

Muenster (1,603) varied manufacturing, food processing, water utilties; hospital, museum, Germanfest late April, Oktoberfest.

Other towns include: **Callisburg** (365), **Era** (150), **Lindsay** (1,081) 1919 Romanesque-style church, **Myra** (150), **Oak Ridge** (190), **Rosston** (75), **Valley View** (785), and the residential community around **Lake Kiowa** (1,970).

For explanation of sources, symbols and abbreviations, see p. 192, and foldout map.

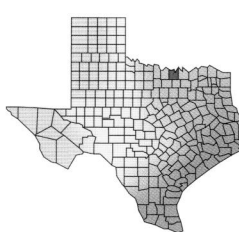

Population	40,574
Change fm 2010	5.6
Area (sq. mi.)	898.4
Land Area (sq. mi.)	874.8
Altitude (ft.)	617–1,217
Rainfall (in.)	42.70
Jan. mean min.	31.3
July mean max.	93.4
Civ. Labor	18,752
Unemployed	2.9
Wages	$163,677,032
Per Capita Income	$47,339
Prop. Value	$5,660,850,812
Retail Sales	$693,197,635

A cotton farm near Eola, Concho County. Photo by Robert Plocheck..

Physical Features: Leon Valley in center, remainder rolling, hilly; Belton Lake.

Economy: Fort Hood, prisons, agribusiness, manufacturing.

History: Tonkawa area, later various other tribes. Anglo-Americans settled around Fort Gates in late 1840s. Permanent establishment of Fort Hood in 1950 changed cultural geography. County created from Bell County, organized, 1854; named for local pioneer James Coryell.

Race/Ethnicity: (In percent) Anglo, 58.5; Black, 17.5; Hispanic, 18.3; Asian, 2.1; Other, 2.0; Two or more races, 4.6.

Vital Statistics, annual: Births, 1,045; deaths, 526; marriages, 474; divorces, 305.

Recreation: State park; deer hunting; fishing; lake, Leon River; bluebonnet area; historic homes; log jail; Shivaree in June.

Minerals: Oil and gas.

Agriculture: Beef, forages, oats, wildlife, row crops. Market value $68.8 million. Hunting leases, timber.

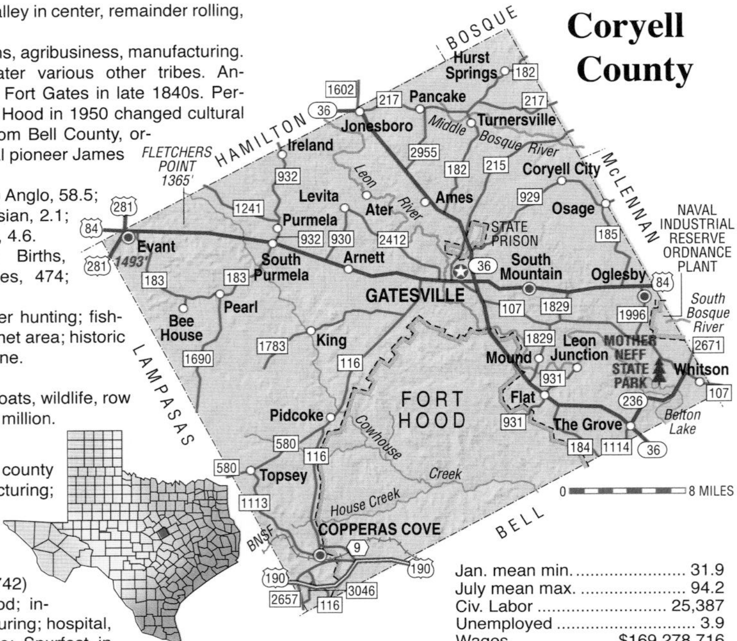

GATESVILLE (14,122) county seat; prisons, varied manufacturing; hospital; refurbished courthouse; museum; branch Central Texas College.

COPPERAS COVE (32,742) business center for Fort Hood; industrial filters, other manufacturing; hospital; library; Central Texas College; Spurfest in September.

Other towns include: **Evant** (388, partly in Hamilton County), **Flat** (210), **Jonesboro** (125), **Mound** (125), **Oglesby** (466), **Purmela** (50), **South Mountain** (367). Part [14,415] of **Fort Hood**.

Coryell County

Population	74,808
Change fm 2010	− 0.9
Area (sq. mi.)	1,056.8
Land Area (sq. mi.)	1,052.1
Altitude (ft.)	600–1,493
Rainfall (in.)	33.66

Jan. mean min.	31.9
July mean max.	94.2
Civ. Labor	25,387
Unemployed	3.9
Wages	$169,278,716
Per Capita Income	$32,904
Prop. Value	$4,113,738,342
Retail Sales	$516,956,484

For explanation of sources, symbols and abbreviations, see p. 192, and foldout map.

Plum Creek on FM 932, Coryell County. Photo by Robert Plocheck.

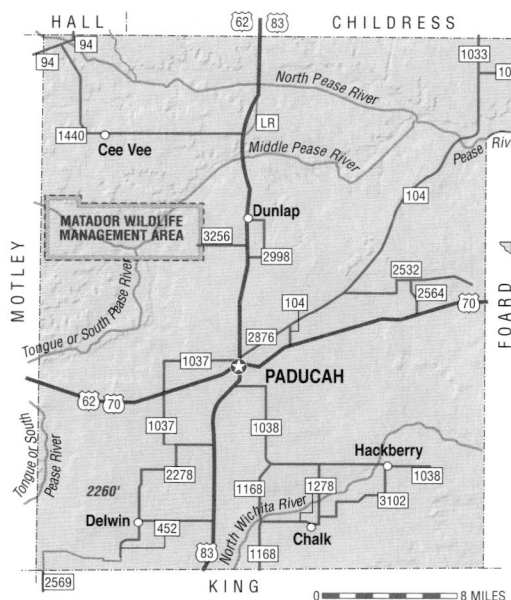

Cottle County

Physical Features: Northwest county below Caprock, rough in west, level in east; gray, black, sandy and loam soils; drains to Pease River.

Economy: Agribusiness, government/services.

History: Around 1700, Apaches were displaced by Comanches, who in turn were driven out by the U.S. Army the 1870s. Anglo-American settlers arrived in the 1880s. County created in 1876 from Fannin County; organized in 1892; named for George W. Cottle, Alamo hero.

Race/Ethnicity: (In percent) Anglo, 65.0; Black, 9.7; Hispanic, 24.4; Asian, 0.1; Other, 0.8; Two or more races, 2.0.

Vital Statistics, annual: Births, 0; deaths, 31; marriages, 0; divorces, 0.

Recreation: Hunting of quail, dove, wild hogs, deer; wildlife management area; museum, Fiestas Patrias in September, horse and colt show in April.

Minerals: Oil, natural gas.

Agriculture: Beef cattle, cotton, peanuts, wheat. 3,000 acres irrigated. Market value $15.9 million.

PADUCAH (1,133) county seat; government/services, library.

Other towns include: **Cee Vee** (45).

Population	1,389
Change fm 2010	− 7.8
Area (sq. mi.)	901.6
Land Area (sq. mi.)	900.6
Altitude (ft.)	1,470–2,260
Rainfall (in.)	24.94
Jan. mean min.	27.9
July mean max.	97.2
Civ. Labor	501
Unemployed	4.4
Wages	$3,591,341
Per Capita Income	$60,247
Prop. Value	$534,747,660
Retail Sales	$9,732,324

For explanation of sources, symbols and abbreviations, see p. 192, and foldout map.

Crane County

Physical Features: Rolling prairie, Pecos Valley, some hills; sandy, loam soils; Juan Cordona Lake (intermittent).

Economy: Oil and gas; agriculture; government/services.

History: Lipan Apache area. Ranching developed in the 1890s. Oil discovered in 1926. County created from Tom Green County in 1887, organized in 1927; named for Baylor University president W. C. Crane.

Race/Ethnicity: (In percent) Anglo, 32.0; Black, 3.8; Hispanic, 63.3; Asian, 0.9; Other, 1.8; Two or more races, 1.5.

Vital Statistics, annual: Births, 79; deaths, 36; marriages, 35; divorces, 10.

Recreation: Museum of the Desert Southwest; sites of pioneer trails and historic Horsehead Crossing on Pecos River; hunting of mule deer, quail; camping park; rodeo in May.

Minerals: Oil, gas production.

Agriculture: Beef cattle, goats. Market value $1.4 million.

CRANE (3,749) county seat; oil-well servicing and production, foundry, steel, surfboard manufacturing; hospital.

Population	4,794
Change fm 2010	9.6
Area (sq. mi.)	785.7
Land Area (sq. mi.)	785.1
Altitude (ft.)	2,290–2,945
Rainfall (in.)	15.60
Jan. mean min.	31.9
July mean max.	93.3
Civ. Labor	1,562
Unemployed	3.8
Wages	$23,889,013
Per Capita Income	$39,596
Prop. Value	$1,002,256,620
Retail Sales	$29,799,750

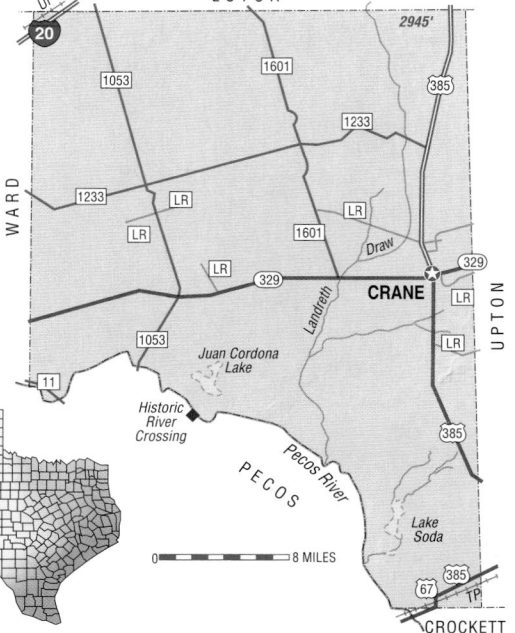

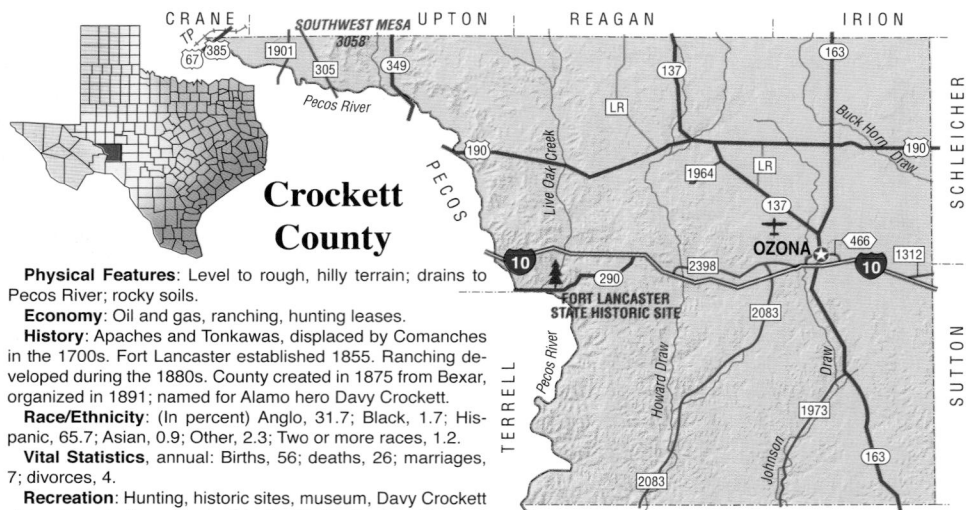

Crockett County

Physical Features: Level to rough, hilly terrain; drains to Pecos River; rocky soils.

Economy: Oil and gas, ranching, hunting leases.

History: Apaches and Tonkawas, displaced by Comanches in the 1700s. Fort Lancaster established 1855. Ranching developed during the 1880s. County created in 1875 from Bexar, organized in 1891; named for Alamo hero Davy Crockett.

Race/Ethnicity: (In percent) Anglo, 31.7; Black, 1.7; Hispanic, 65.7; Asian, 0.9; Other, 2.3; Two or more races, 1.2.

Vital Statistics, annual: Births, 56; deaths, 26; marriages, 7; divorces, 4.

Recreation: Hunting, historic sites, museum, Davy Crockett statue in park; Davy Crockett festival in September, Deerfest in December.

Minerals: Oil, gas production.

Agriculture: Sheep (first in numbers), goats; beef cattle. Market value $13.9 million.

OZONA (3,144) county seat; ranching, oil & gas, hunting, tourism; health care clinics.

Population		3,499
Change fm 2010		– 5.9
Area (sq. mi.)		2,807.4
Land Area (sq. mi.)		2,807.3
Altitude (ft.)		1,720–3,058
Rainfall (in.)		18.86
Jan. mean min.		30.2
July mean max.		93.4
Civ. Labor		1,610
Unemployed		2.8
Wages		$15,044,141
Per Capita Income		$36,757
Prop. Value		$1,589,828,660
Retail Sales		$30,516,503

Crosby County

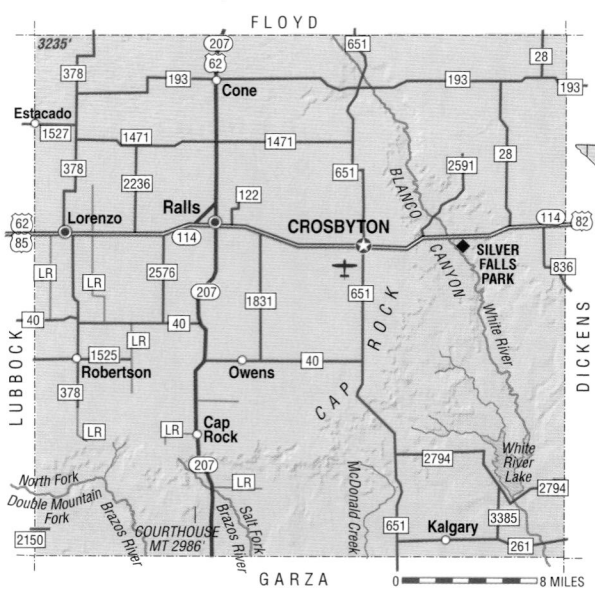

Physical Features: Flat, rich soil above Caprock, broken below; drains into Brazos River forks and playas.

Economy: Agribusiness, tourism, commuters to Lubbock.

History: Comanches, driven out by U.S. Army in 1870s; ranching developed soon afterward. Quaker colony founded in 1879. County created from Bexar District 1876, organized 1886; named for Texas Land Commissioner Stephen Crosby.

Race/Ethnicity: (In percent) Anglo, 39.5; Black, 3.9; Hispanic, 56.3; Asian, 0.2; Other, 1.2; Two or more races, 1.7.

Vital Statistics, annual: Births, 90; deaths, 77; marriages, 29; divorces, 14.

Recreation: White River Lake; Silver Falls Park; hunting.

Minerals: Sand, gravel, oil, gas.

Agriculture: Cotton, beef cattle, sorghum; about 112,000 acres irrigated. Market value $71.6 million.

CROSBYTON (1,644) county seat; agribusiness center; hospital, Pioneer Museum, Prairie Ladies Multi-Cultural Center, library; Cowboy Gathering in October.

Other towns include: **Lorenzo** (1,195); **Ralls** (1,857) government/services, agribusiness, museums, Cotton Boll Fest in September.

Population		5,779
Change fm 2010		– 4.6
Area (sq. mi.)		901.7
Land Area (sq. mi.)		900.2
Altitude (ft.)		2,250–3,235
Rainfall (in.)		23.34
Jan. mean min.		25.9
July mean max.		92.3
Civ. Labor		2,579
Unemployed		4.1
Wages		$11,531,198
Per Capita Income		$34,530
Prop. Value		$927,897,176
Retail Sales		$36,159,997

For explanation of sources, symbols and abbreviations, see p. 192, and foldout map.

Yucca plants with the Guadalupe Mountains in the background. Photo by Robert Plocheck.

Culberson County

Physical Features: Contains Texas' highest mountain; slopes toward Pecos Valley on east, Diablo Bolson on west; salt lakes; unique vegetation in canyons.

Economy: Tourism, government/services, talc mining and processing, agribusiness, sulfur mining.

History: Apaches arrived about 600 years ago. U.S. military frontier after Civil War. Ranching developed after 1880. Mexican migration increased after 1920. County created from El Paso County 1911, organized 1912; named for D.B. Culberson, Texas congressman.

Race/Ethnicity: (In percent) Anglo, 21.9; Black, 1.1; Hispanic, 73.1; Asian, 2.1; Other, 2.6; Two or more races, 3.0.

Vital Statistics, annual: Births, 36; deaths, 14; marriages, 5; divorces, 2.

Recreation: National park; Guadalupe and El Capitan, twin peaks; scenic canyons and mountains; classic car museum, antique saloon bar; frontier days in June, big buck tournament.

Minerals: Sulfur, talc, marble, oil.

Agriculture: Beef cattle; crops include cotton, vegetables, melons, pecans; 6,000 acres in irrigation. Market value $13.7 million.

VAN HORN (1,895) county seat; agribusiness, tourism, rock crushing, government/services; hospital.

Other towns: **Kent** (30).

Population	**2,204**
Change fm 2010	– 8.1
Area (sq. mi.)	3,813.0
Land Area (sq. mi.)	3,812.8
Altitude (ft.)	2,900–8,749
Rainfall (in.)	11.58
Jan. mean min.	28.3
July mean max.	92.3
Civ. Labor	858
Unemployed	4.1
Wages	$13,922,403
Per Capita Income	$47,127
Prop. Value	$1,563,448,800
Retail Sales	$95,322,005

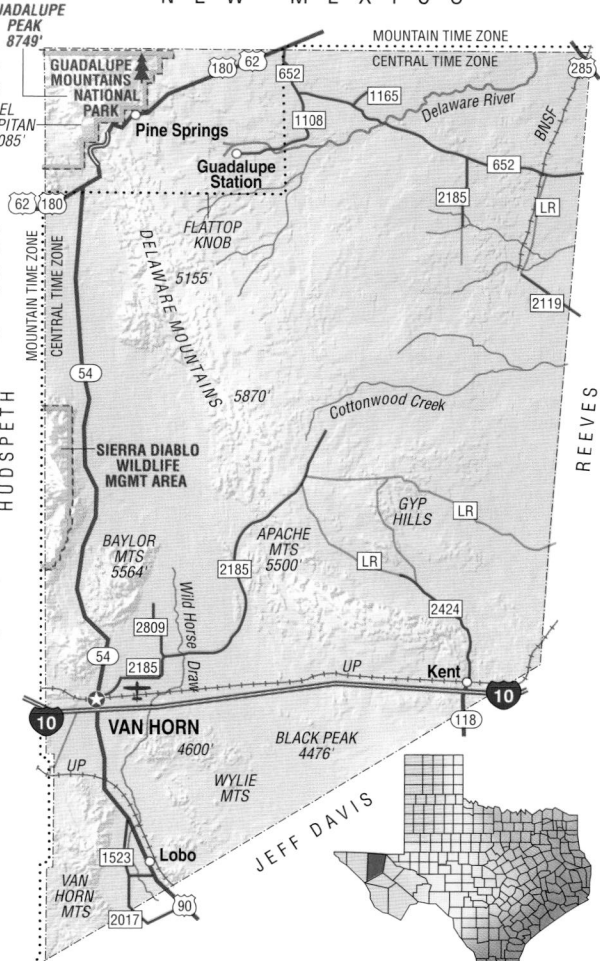

Dallam County

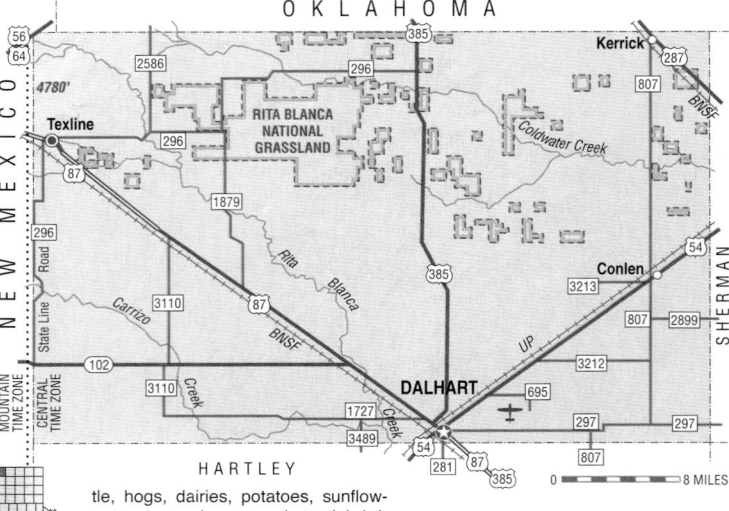

Physical Features: Prairie, broken by creeks; playas; sandy, loam soils; Rita Blanca National Grassland.

Economy: Agribusiness, dairies, cheese manufacturing, tourism.

History: Earliest Plains Apaches; displaced by Comanches and Kiowas. Ranching developed in late 19th century. Farming began after 1900. County created from Bexar District, 1876, organized 1891. Named for lawyer-editor James W. Dallam.

Race/Ethnicity: (In percent) Anglo, 49.1; Black, 2.2; Hispanic, 46.6; Asian, 1.1; Other, 2.4; Two or more races, 1.6.

Vital Statistics, annual: Births, 157; deaths, 38; marriages, 223; divorces, 32.

Recreation: XIT museum, XIT rodeo in August, pheasant hunting, wildlife, grasslands.

Minerals: Petroleum.

Agriculture: A leader in production of grain (corn, wheat, sorghum). Cattle, hogs, dairies, potatoes, sunflowers, beans; substantial irrigation. Market value $651.7 million.

DALHART (8,507, partly in Hartley County) county seat; government/services; agribusiness center for parts of Texas, New Mexico, Oklahoma; railroad; cheese plant; grain operations; junior college branch; hospital; prison.

Other towns include: **Kerrick** (35) and **Texline** (548).

Population	7,200
Change fm 2010	7.5
Area (sq. mi.)	1,505.3
Land Area (sq. mi.)	1,503.3
Altitude (ft.)	3,655–4,780
Rainfall (in.)	17.59
Jan. mean min.	18.3
July mean max.	91.1
Civ. Labor	4,001
Unemployed	2.1
Wages	$48,727,162
Per Capita Income	$54,562
Prop. Value	$1,651,671,636
Retail Sales	$135,167,986

Dallas County

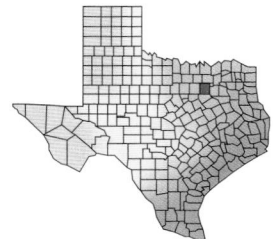

Physical Features: Mostly flat, heavy blackland soils, sandy clays in west; drains to Trinity River; Joe Pool Lake, White Rock Lake, Mountain Creek Lake, Lake Ray Hubbard, North Lake.

Economy: A national center for telecommunications, transportation, electronics manufacturing, data processing, conventions and trade shows; foreign-trade zone located at D/FW International Airport, U.S. Customs port of entry; government/services.

History: Caddoan area. Anglo-Americans began arriving in 1840. Antebellum slaveholding area. County created and organized in 1846 from Nacogdoches, Robertson counties; named for U.S. Vice President George Mifflin Dallas.

Race/Ethnicity: (In percent) Anglo, 29.2; Black, 23.4; Hispanic, 40.2; Asian, 6.5; Other, 1.2; Two or more races, 1.9.

Vital Statistics, annual: Births, 40,112; deaths, 15,727; marriages, 15,204; divorces, 7,391.

Recreation: One of the state's top tourist destinations and one of the nation's most popular convention centers; State Fair, museums, zoo, West End shopping and tourist district, historical sites, including Sixth Floor museum in the old Texas School Book Depository, site of the assassination of President Kennedy. Also, the Morton H. Meyerson Symphony Center; performing arts; professional sports; Texas broadcast museum; lakes, state park, Audubon center; theme and amusement parks.

Minerals: Sand, gravel, oil and gas.

Agriculture: Horticultural crops, wheat, hay, corn, soybeans, horses. Market value $44.5 million.

Education: Southern Methodist University, University of Dallas, Dallas Baptist University, University of Texas at Dallas, University of North Texas at Dallas, University of Texas Southwestern Medical Center and many other education centers.

DALLAS (1,345,452) county seat; center of state's largest consolidated metropolitan area and third-largest city in Texas; D/FW International Airport is one of the world's busiest; headquarters for the U.S. Army and Air Force Exchange Service; Federal Reserve Bank; a leader in fashions and in computer operations; hospitals; many hotels in downtown area offer adequate accommodations for most conventions.

Population	2,637,772
Change fm 2010	11.5
Area (sq. mi.)	908.6
Land Area (sq. mi.)	871.3
Altitude (ft.)	350–870
Rainfall (in.)	37.57
Jan. mean min.	37.3
July mean max.	96.0
Civ. Labor	1,396,085
Unemployed	3.4
Wages	$27,572,554,379
Per Capita Income	$55,859
Prop. Value	$266,283,725,220
Retail Sales	$45,684,905,996

Garland (238,534) varied manufacturing, community college branch, hospitals, performing arts center.

Irving (240,769) finance, technology, tourism, distribution center; Boy Scout headquarters and museum; North Lake College; hospitals; parks; Dragon Boat Festival in May.

Other cities include: **Addison** (15,475) general aviation airport, theater center; **Balch Springs** (24,997); part [49,392] of **Carrollton** (136,815) residential community, distribution center, hospital; **Cedar Hill** (50,320) residential, light manufacturing, retail, distribution center, Northwood University, community college, state park, Penn Farm, Country Day on the Hill in October; **Cockrell Hill** (4,501); **Coppell** (42,167) distribution, varied manufacturing, office center, hike and

For explanation of sources, symbols and abbreviations, see p. 192, and foldout map.

bike trails; **DeSoto** (51,886) residential community, light industry and distribution, hospitals; Toad Holler Creekfest in June.

Also, **Duncanville** (41,291) construction, health care, manufacturing; library, museums; Juneteenth celebration; **Farmers Branch** (34,500) distribution center, varied manufacturing, Brookhaven College, hospital; **Glenn Heights** (13,084, partly in Ellis County); most [123,487] of **Grand Prairie** (192,500) wholesale trade, aerospace, entertainment, hospital, library, Joe Pool Reservoir, Indian pow-wow in September, Lone Star horse-racing track; **Highland Park** (9,162); **Hutchins** (6,029) varied manufacturing; **Lancaster** (38,534) residential, industrial, distribution center, Cedar Valley College, Commemorative Air Force museum, Cold War air museum, Bear Creek nature preserve, depot, historic town square, Oktoberfest.

Also, **Mesquite** (142,823) shipping, rail port hub, retail, hospitals, arts center, championship rodeo July – September, rodeo parade in spring, Summer Sizzle festival in June, community college, historical parks; most [70,654] of **Richardson** (120,072) telecommunications, software development, financial services, hospital, library, Wildflower Music Festival in May; **Rowlett** (63,113) residential, manufacturing, government/services, hospital, library, park, hike and bike trails; **Sachse** (25,506, partly in Collin County) commuting to Dallas, government/services, Fallfest in October; **Seagoville** (16,204) rural/suburban setting, federal prison, Seagofest in October; **Sunnyvale** (6,337) tile manufacturing, hospital, Samuell Farm, Sunnyfest on July 4; **University Park** (24,401); **Wilmer** (4,056).

Part of **Combine** (2,132) and part of **Ovilla** (4,035).

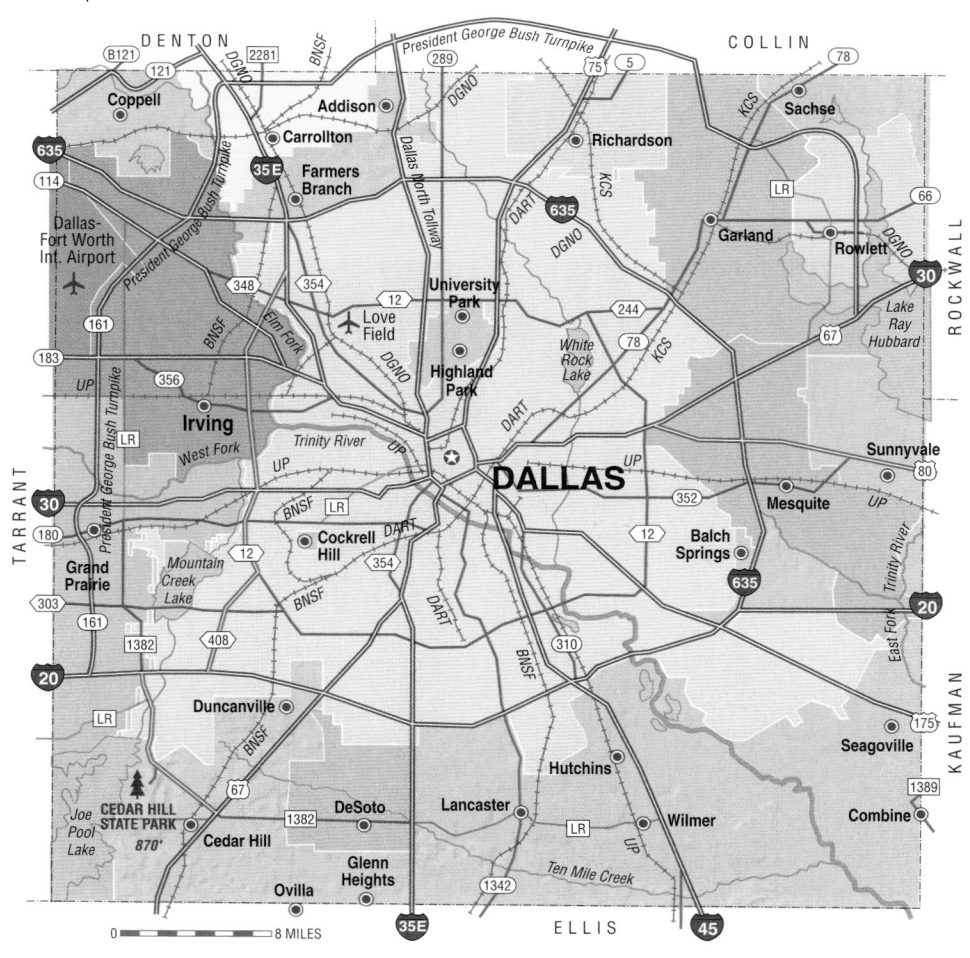

Dawson County

Physical Features: South Plains county, broken on the east; loam and sandy soils.

Economy: Agriculture, farm and gin equipment manufacturing, peanut plant, government/services.

History: Comanche, Kiowa area. Ranching developed in 1880s. Farming began after 1900. Hispanic population increased after 1940. County created from Bexar District, 1876, organized 1905; named for Nicholas M. Dawson, San Jacinto veteran.

Race/Ethnicity: (In percent) Anglo, 35.3; Black, 6.2; Hispanic, 57.4; Asian, 1.1; Other, 1.3; Two or more races, 1.5.

Vital Statistics, annual: Births, 205; deaths, 129; marriages, 77; divorces, 38.

Recreation: Parks, museum, campground, part of Quanah Parker Trail; Lamesa poetry and music fest in May.

Minerals: Oil, natural gas.

Agriculture: Cotton, peanuts, sorghums, watermelons, alfalfa, grapes. 60,000 acres irrigated. Market value $73.1 million.

LAMESA (9,505) county seat; agribusiness, food processing, oil-field services, some manufacturing, computerized cotton-classing office; hospital, library; Howard College branch; prison unit; chicken-fried steak festival last weekend in April.

Other towns include: **Ackerly** (237, partly in Martin County), **Los Ybanez** (18) and **Welch** (246).

Also, **O'Donnell** (817, mostly in Lynn County) bust of Dan Blocker.

For explanation of sources, symbols and abbreviations, see p. 192, and foldout map.

Population	**12,619**
Change fm 2010	− 8.8
Area (sq. mi.)	902.1
Land Area (sq. mi.)	900.3
Altitude (ft.)	2,580–3,220
Rainfall (in.)	19.14
Jan. mean min.	26.0
July mean max.	93.1
Civ. Labor	4,514
Unemployed	4.1
Wages	$41,806,781
Per Capita Income	$36,857
Prop. Value	$1,273,657,800
Retail Sales	$169,401,812

An irrigation system at a cotton field near Lamesa, Dawson County. Photo by Robert Plocheck.

Deaf Smith County

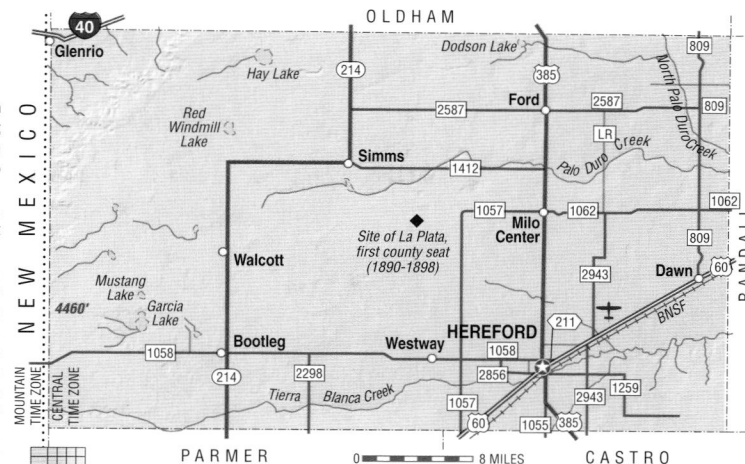

Physical Features: High Plains county, partly broken; chocolate and sandy loam soils; drains to Palo Duro and Tierra Blanca creeks.

Economy: Agriculture, varied industries, meat packing, offset printing.

History: Apache Indians, were displaced by Comanches and Kiowas. Ranching developed after the U.S. Army drove out the Indian tribes 1874-1875. Farming began after 1900. Hispanic settlement increased after 1950. County created in 1876 from the Bexar District; organized in 1890. Named for famed scout in Texas Revolution, Erastus "Deaf" Smith.

Race/Ethnicity: (In percent) Anglo, 24.7; Black, 1.8; Hispanic, 73.1; Asian, 0.6; Other, 1.8; Two or more races, 1.1.

Vital Statistics, annual: Births, 348; deaths, 143; marriages, 154; divorces, 37.

Recreation: Museum, tours, POW camp chapel; Cinco de Mayo, Pioneer Days in May.

Minerals: Insignificant.

Agriculture: Leading agricultural county, dairies (second in number of milk cows), feedlot operations, cotton, wheat, sorghum, corn; 50 percent irrigated. Market value $1.38 billion, first in state.

HEREFORD (15,554) county seat; cattle feeding, agriculture, trucking; hospital; Amarillo College branch; aquatic center.

Other towns include: **Dawn** (52).

Population	**18,760**
Change fm 2010	– 3.2
Area (sq. mi.)	1,498.4
Land Area (sq. mi.)	1,496.9
Altitude (ft.)	3,650–4,460
Rainfall (in.)	20.05
Jan. mean min.	22.5
July mean max.	91.4
Civ. Labor	8,228
Unemployed	2.8
Wages	$76,815,153
Per Capita Income	$41,634
Prop. Value	$2,300,095,075
Retail Sales	$362,288,372

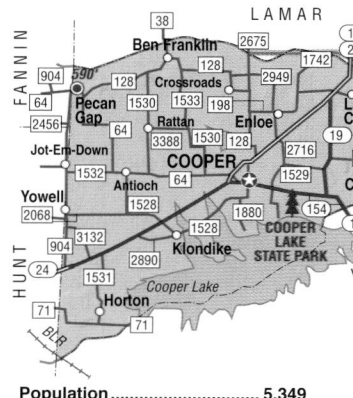

Population	**5,349**
Change fm 2010	2.3
Area (sq. mi.)	277.9
Land Area (sq. mi.)	256.8
Altitude (ft.)	322–590
Rainfall (in.)	44.80
Jan. mean min.	30.0
July mean max.	94.0
Civ. Labor	2,412
Unemployed	3.4
Wages	$6,587,862
Per Capita Income	$34,737
Prop. Value	$512,536,437
Retail Sales	$10,833,528

For explanation of sources, symbols and abbreviations, see p. 192, and foldout map.

Delta County

Physical Features: Northeastern county between two forks of Sulphur River; Cooper Lake (also designated Jim Chapman Lake); black, sandy loam soils.

Economy: Agriculture, government/services, retirement income.

History: Caddo area, but disease, other tribes caused displacement around 1790. Anglo-Americans arrived in 1820s. County created from Lamar, Hopkins counties 1870. Greek letter delta origin of name, because of shape of the county.

Race/Ethnicity: (In percent) Anglo, 81.0; Black, 6.5; Hispanic, 7.6; Asian, 0.7; Other, 2.5; Two or more races, 3.0.

Vital Statistics, annual: Births, 60;

deaths, 73; marriages, 41; divorces, 16.

Recreation: Fishing, hunting; lake, state park; Cooper Chiggerfest in October.

Minerals: Insignificant.

Agriculture: Beef, hay, soybeans, wheat, corn, sorghum, cotton. Market value $29.3 million.

COOPER (1,933) county seat; commuters, industrial park, some manufacturing, agribusiness; museum, library; post office mural.

Other towns include: **Ben Franklin** (60), **Enloe** (90), **Klondike** (175), **Lake Creek** (55), and **Pecan Gap** (185).

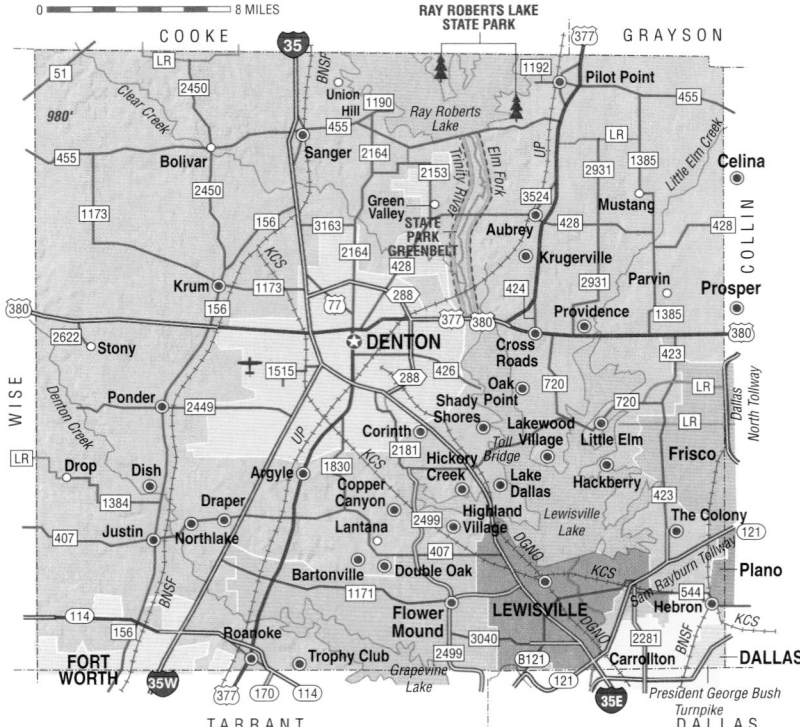

0 ■■■■■■■■ 8 MILES

RAY ROBERTS LAKE
STATE PARK

COOKE 35 GRAYSON

Denton County

Physical Features: North Texas county; partly hilly, draining to Elm Fork of Trinity River, Lewisville Lake, Ray Roberts Lake, Grapevine Lake; Blackland and Grand Prairie soils and terrain.

Economy: Varied industries, colleges, horse industry, tourism, government/services; part of Dallas-Fort Worth metropolitan area.

History: Land grant from Texas Congress 1841 for Peters colony. County created, organized, out of Fannin County in 1846; named for John B. Denton, pioneer Methodist minister.

Race/Ethnicity: (In percent) Anglo, 59.3; Black, 10.3; Hispanic, 19.4; Asian, 9.0; Other, 1.0; Two or more races, 2.6.

Vital Statistics, annual: Births, 10,040; deaths, 3,374; marriages, 4,404; divorces, 2,548.

Recreation: Lake activities, parks; universities' cultural, athletic activities, including "Texas Women; A Celebration of History"; "First Ladies of Texas" collection of memorabilia; Little Chapel in the Woods; Texas Motor Speedway; Denton Jazz Festival in April.

Minerals: Natural gas.

Education: University of North Texas, Texas Woman's University, and North Central Texas College.

Agriculture: Second in number of horses. Eggs, nurseries, turf, cattle; also, hay, sorghum, wheat, peanuts grown. Market value $137 million.

DENTON (141,923) county seat; universities; manufacturers of trucks (Peterbilt), medical, aviation; hospitals; historic courthouse square; storytelling festival in March.

LEWISVILLE (108,159) commuting to Dallas-Fort Worth, retail center, electronics and varied industries; hospital, library; Celtic Feis & Scottish Highland Games in March.

Flower Mound (74,318) residential community, library, mound of native grasses, bike classic in spring.

Carrollton (136,815, also in Dallas County), hospital.

Other towns include: **Argyle** (4,080) horse farms/training, bluegrass festival in March; **Aubrey** (3,405) horse farms/training, cabinet construction, museum, peanut festival early October; **Bartonville** (1,715); **Copper Canyon** (1,485); **Corinth** (22,429); **Cross Roads** (1,891); **Draper** (33); **Dish** (457); **Double Oak** (3,204); **Hackberry** (1,125); **Hebron** (426); **Hickory Creek** (4,425); **Highland Village** (17,037); **Justin** (3,837); **Krugerville** (1,917); **Krum** (5,191) commuters, old grain mill, heritage museum, North Pole Days in December; **Lake Dallas** (8,264) light manufacturing, marina, historic downtown, Mardi Gras.

Also, **Lakewood Village** (675); **Lantana** (7,965); **Little Elm** (42,771) real estate, retail, lake activities/beach area, summer concert series; **Northlake** (2,461); **Oak Point** (3,646); **Pilot Point** (4,465) light manufacturing, horse ranches, Fireman's Fest in April; **Ponder** (1,618); **Providence** (6,323); **Roanoke** (8,066); **Sanger** (8,831) distribution center, commuters, government/services, lakes, Sellabration in September; **Shady Shores** (3,038); **The Colony** (44,188) retail, business offices, industrial firms; parks, nature trails, salute to veterans on Veterans Day; and **Trophy Club** (12,923) commuters, retail.

Part [26,579] of **Dallas**, part [7,813] **Fort Worth**, part [44,500] **Frisco**, part [5,316] **Plano**, and small parts of **Coppell**, **Celina**, **Prosper**, **Southlake**, **Westlake**.

Population	859,064
Change fm 2010	29.7
Area (sq. mi.)	953.0
Land Area (sq. mi.)	878.4
Altitude (ft.)	433–980
Rainfall (in.)	38.09
Jan. mean min.	33.0
July mean max.	95.3
Civ. Labor	486,151
Unemployed	2.9
Wages	$3,044,692,915
Per Capita Income	$53,948
Prop. Value	$98,759,686,224
Retail Sales	$10,666,922,311

DeWitt County

Physical Features: Gulf Coastal Plain county drained by Guadalupe and tributaries; rolling to level; waxy, loam, sandy soils.

Economy: Oil, tourism.

History: Coahuiltecan area, then Karankawas and other tribes, finally the Comanches. Mexican and Anglo-American settlers arrived in the 1820s. County created, organized, in 1846 from Gonzales, Goliad, and Victoria counties; named for Green DeWitt, colonizer.

Race/Ethnicity: (In percent) Anglo, 54.7; Black, 9.6; Hispanic, 35.3; Asian, 0.4; Other, 0.9; Two or more races, 1.2.

Vital Statistics, annual: Births, 270; deaths, 253; marriages, 128; divorces, 85.

Recreation: Hunting, fishing, historic homes, museums, wildflowers, German dance halls.

Minerals: Oil and natural gas, gravel.

Agriculture: Cattle, pecans, row crops. Market value $61.4 million.

CUERO (7,605) county seat; medical/hospital, government/services, retail, ranching, oil and gas; Turkeyfest in October.

Yorktown (2,161) oil and gas, agriculture; library, museum, park, hike/bike trail; Western Days in October.

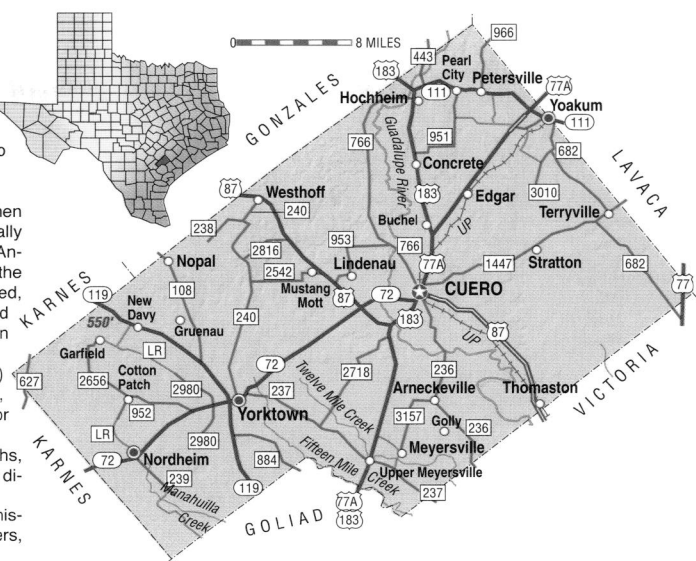

Other towns include: **Hochheim** (70), **Meyersville** (110), **Nordheim** (320), **Thomaston** (45), **Westhoff** (410).

Part [2,138] of **Yoakum** (6,017 total) cattle, leather, meat processing, hospital, museum, Tom Tom festival in June.

For explanation of sources, symbols and abbreviations, see p. 192, and foldout map.

Population	**20,187**
Change fm 2010	0.4
Area (sq. mi.)	910.5
Land Area (sq. mi.)	909.0
Altitude (ft.)	100–550
Rainfall (in.)	35.67
Jan. mean min.	39.1
July mean max.	96.5
Civ. Labor	9,626
Unemployed	3.0
Wages	$84,427,886
Per Capita Income	$51,896
Prop. Value	$5,873,149,670
Retail Sales	$212,462,411

Beaver Pond Creek Paddling Trail, Denton County. Photo by Earl Nottingham, Texas Parks & Wildlife.

Dickens County

Physical Features: West Texas county; broken land, Caprock in northwest; sandy, chocolate, red soils; drains to Croton, Duck creeks.

Economy: Agriculture, government services/prison unit, hunting leases, wind farms.

History: Comanches driven out by U.S. Army 1874-75. Ranching and some farming began in late 1880s. County created 1876, from Bexar District; organized 1891; named for Alamo hero who is variously listed as James R. Demkins or Dimpkins and J. Dickens.

Race/Ethnicity: (In percent) Anglo, 62.8; Black, 5.7; Hispanic, 29.6; Asian, 1.3; Other, 2.4; Two or more races, 1.8.

Vital Statistics, annual: Births, 25; deaths, 26; marriages, 10; divorces, 6.

Recreation: Hunting, fishing; Soldiers Mound site, Dickens Springs; downtown Spur.

Minerals: Oil, gas.

Agriculture: Cattle, horses, cotton, hay, small grains. Some irrigation. Market value $18.5 million. Hunting leases important.

DICKENS (230) county seat, market for ranching country.

SPUR (1,146) farming, ranching, hunting, government/services; museum; homecoming in October.

Other towns include: **Afton** (15) and **McAdoo** (75).

Population	2,249
Change fm 2010	– 7.9
Area (sq. mi.)	905.2
Land Area (sq. mi.)	901.7
Altitude (ft.)	1,800–3,037
Rainfall (in.)	22.75
Jan. mean min.	26.6
July mean max.	94.7
Civ. Labor	653
Unemployed	4.1
Wages	$3,612,876
Per Capita Income	$32,006
Prop. Value	$702,252,300
Retail Sales	$12,944,755

Dimmit County

Physical Features: Southwest county; level to rolling; much brush; sandy, loam, red soils; drained by Nueces River.

Economy: Government/services, agribusiness, petroleum products, tourism.

History: Coahuiltecan area, later Comanches. John Townsend, a black man from Nacogdoches, led the first attempt at settlement before the Civil War. Texas Rangers forced out the Comanches in 1877. Mexican migration increased after 1910. County created 1858 from Bexar, Maverick, Uval-de, Webb counties; organized 1880. Named for Philip Dimmitt of the Texas Revolution; law misspelled name.

Race/Ethnicity: (In percent) Anglo, 10.5; Black, 1.6; Hispanic, 87.5; Asian, 0.7; Other, 0.7; Two or more races, 0.8.

Vital Statistics, annual: Births, 173; deaths, 109; marriages, 61; divorces, 3.

Recreation: Hunting, fishing, camp-sites, wildlife area; winter haven for tourists; old jailhouse museum.

Minerals: Oil, natural gas.

Agriculture: Onions, pecans, cantaloupes, olives, tomatoes, tangerines, cattle, goats, horses, hay. Market value $35.2 million.

CARRIZO SPRINGS (5,590) county seat; agribusiness center, feedlot, food processing, oil, gas processing, hunting center; hospital; historic Baptist church; Mt. Hope cemetery with 17 Texas Rangers buried; bull riding event in April.

Other towns include: **Asherton** (1,065), **Big Wells** (742) Cinco de Mayo, and **Catarina** (107) Camino Real festival in April.

Population	10,308
Change fm 2010	3.1
Area (sq. mi.)	1,334.5
Land Area (sq. mi.)	1,328.9
Altitude (ft.)	410–871
Rainfall (in.)	19.77
Jan. mean min.	40.5
July mean max.	97.8
Civ. Labor	7,901
Unemployed	2.5
Wages	$87,709,032
Per Capita Income	$32,067
Prop. Value	$6,416,205,391
Retail Sales	$144,789,144

For explanation of sources, symbols and abbreviations, see p. 192, and foldout map.

Donley County

Physical Features: Panhandle county bisected by Red River Salt Fork; Greenbelt Lake, Lelia Lake; rolling to level; clay, loam, sandy soils.

Economy: Agribusiness, government/services, tourism.

History: Apaches displaced by Kiowas and Comanches, who were driven out in 1874-75 by U.S. Army. Methodist colony from New York settled in 1878. County created in 1876, organized 1882, out of Bexar District; named for Texas Supreme Court Justice S.P. Donley.

Race/Ethnicity: (In percent) Anglo, 80.9; Black, 5.1; Hispanic, 11.2; Asian, 0.6; Other, 0.9; Two or more races, 1.7.

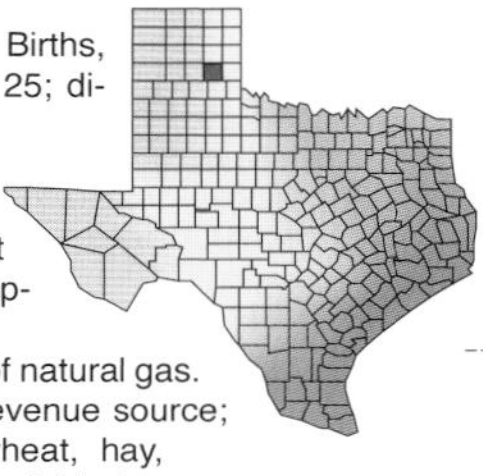

Vital Statistics, annual: Births, 32; deaths, 51; marriages, 25; divorces, 11.

Recreation: Lake, hunting, fishing, camping, water sports; Col. Goodnight Chuckwagon cook-off in September.

Minerals: Small amount of natural gas.

Agriculture: Cattle top revenue source; cotton, peanuts, alfalfa, wheat, hay, melons; 15,000 acres irrigated. Market value $95.1 million.

CLARENDON (1,878) county seat; higher education, agribusiness, tourism, medical center clinic; Saints Roost museum, library, junior college; restored historic buildings.

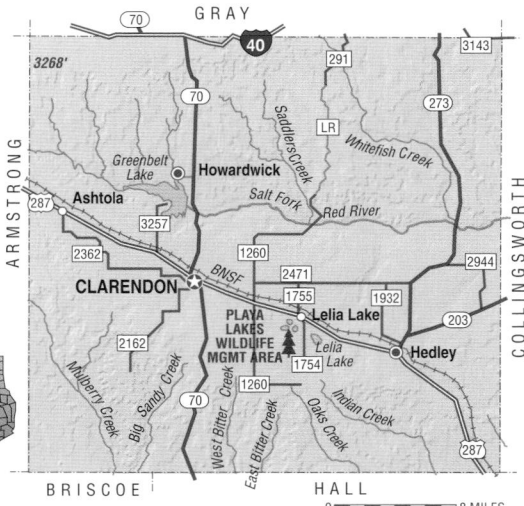

Other towns include: **Hedley** (317) cotton festival in October, **Howardwick** (384), and **Lelia Lake** (70).

Population	**3,319**
Change fm 2010	– 10.9
Area (sq. mi.)	933.1
Land Area (sq. mi.)	929.9

Altitude (ft.)	2,080–3,268
Rainfall (in.)	24.02
Jan. mean min.	23.8
July mean max.	94.7
Civ. Labor	1,467
Unemployed	3.6
Wages	$9,497,725
Per Capita Income	$44,176
Prop. Value	$843,346,027
Retail Sales	$33,939,560

The Donley County Courthouse in Clarendon. Photo by Robert Plocheck.

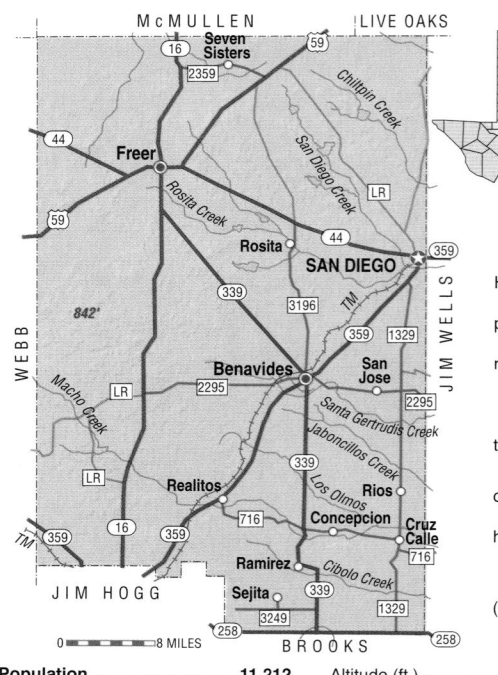

Duval County

Physical Features: South Texas county; level to hilly, brushy in most areas; varied soils.

Economy: Ranching, petroleum, tourism, government/services.

History: Coahuiltecans, displaced by Comanche bands. Mexican settlement began in 1812. County created from Live Oak, Nueces, and Starr counties in 1858, organized in 1876; named for Burr H. Duval, a victim of Goliad massacre.

Race/Ethnicity: (In percent) Anglo, 8.7; Black, 1.4; Hispanic, 89.6; Asian, 0.4; Other, 0.9; Two or more races, 0.6.

Vital Statistics, annual: Births, 181; deaths, 149; marriages, 71; divorces, 14.

Recreation: Hunting, tourist crossroads.

Minerals: Oil, gas, salt, sand, gravel, uranium.

Agriculture: Most income from beef cattle; grains, cotton, vegetables, hay, dairy. Market value $14.8 million.

SAN DIEGO (4,254, part [900] in Jim Wells County) county seat; ranching, oil field, tourist center; hospital.

Freer (2,608) oil and gas, construction, ranching and hunting; rattlesnake roundup in May.

Benavides (1,285) serves truck-farming area.

Other towns include: **Concepcion** (56) and **Realitos** (163).

Population	11,212
Change fm 2010	– 4.9
Area (sq. mi.)	1,795.6
Land Area (sq. mi.)	1,793.5
Altitude (ft.)	180–842
Rainfall (in.)	25.99
Jan. mean min.	43.1
July mean max.	97.0
Civ. Labor	4,870
Unemployed	4.9
Wages	$33,078,663
Per Capita Income	$34,579
Prop. Value	$2,543,969,034
Retail Sales	$49,556,271

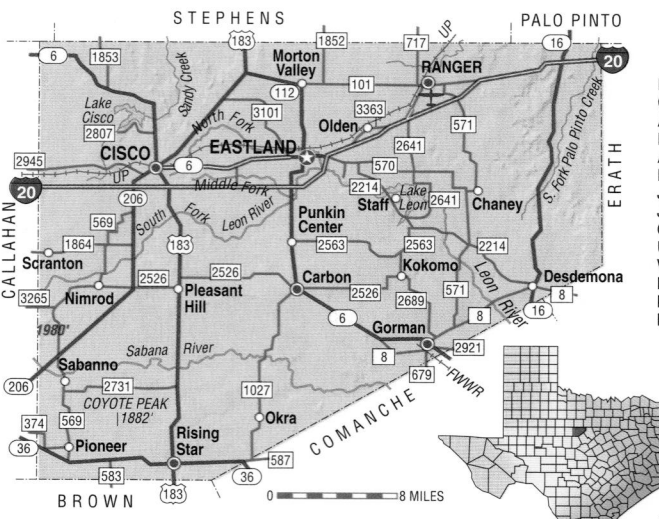

Eastland County

Population	18,322
Change fm 2010	– 1.4
Area (sq. mi.)	931.9
Land Area (sq. mi.)	926.5
Altitude (ft.)	960–1,980
Rainfall (in.)	29.02
Jan. mean min.	28.8
July mean max.	94.6
Civ. Labor	8,556
Unemployed	3.2
Wages	$115,575,541
Per Capita Income	$56,294
Prop. Value	$2,619,775,540
Retail Sales	$291,674,725

EASTLAND (3,967) county seat; tourism, government/services, petroleum industries, varied manufacturing; hospital, library; Old Ripfest in September.

CISCO (3,858) manufacturing, distribution, oilfield services; Conrad Hilton's first hotel restored, museums; community college; folklife festival in April.

RANGER (2,491) oil center, varied manufacturing, junior college.

Other towns include: **Carbon** (279) livestock equipment manufacturing; **Desdemona** (180); **Gorman** (1,037) peanut processing, agribusiness, hospital; **Olden** (113), and **Rising Star** (848) cap manufacturing, plant nursery; Octoberfest.

Physical Features: Hilly, rolling; sandy, loam soils; drains to Leon River forks; Lake Cisco, Lake Leon.

Economy: Agribusiness, education, petroleum industries.

History: Plains Indian area. Frank Sánchez among first settlers in 1850s. County created from Bosque, Coryell, Travis counties, 1858, organized 1873; named for W.M. Eastland, Mier Expedition casualty.

Race/Ethnicity: (In percent) Anglo, 79.1; Black, 2.1; Hispanic, 16.6; Asian, 0.6; Other, 1.3; Two or more races, 1.4.

Vital Statistics, annual: Births, 200; deaths, 265; marriages, 135; divorces, 57.

Recreation: Hunting, water sports; museums; historic sites and displays.

Minerals: Oil, natural gas.

Agriculture: Beef cattle, hay, cotton. Some 9,000 acres irrigated. Market value $27.9 million.

Ector County

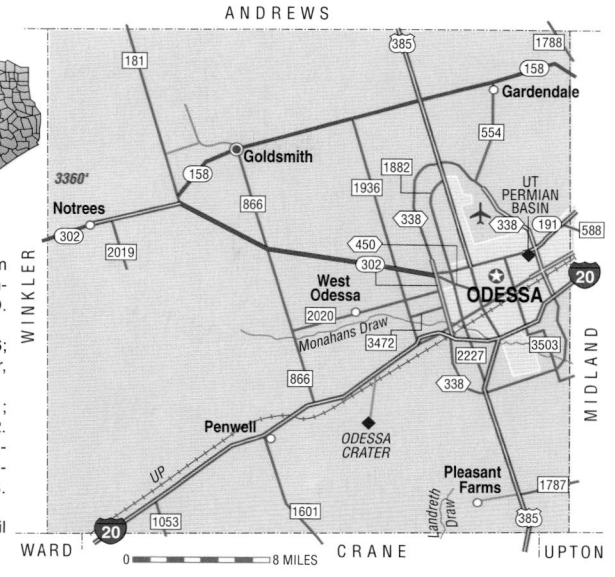

ANDREWS

Physical Features: West Texas county; level to rolling, some sand dunes; meteor crater; desert vegetation.

Economy: Center for Permian Basin oil field operations, plastics, electric generation plants.

History: First settlers in late 1880s. Oil boom in 1926. County created from Tom Green County, 1887; organized 1891; named for jurist M.D. Ector.

Race/Ethnicity: (In percent) Anglo, 32.6; Black, 5.1; Hispanic, 60.6; Asian, 1.2; Other, 1.6; Two or more races, 1.5.

Vital Statistics, annual: Births, 2,991; deaths, 1,196; marriages, 1,420; divorces, 422.

Recreation: Globe Theatre replica; presidential museum and Bush childhood home; ranching museum, art institute; second-largest U.S. meteor crater, museum; Stonehenge replica.

Minerals: More than 3 billion barrels of oil produced since 1926; gas, cement, stone.

Agriculture: Beef cattle, horses are chief producers; pecans, hay, poultry; minor irrigation. Market value $2.2 million.

Education: University of Texas of Permian Basin, Texas Tech University Health Sciences Center, Odessa (junior) College.

ODESSA (113,677, part [1,670] in Midland County) county seat; oil and gas, manufacturing, ranching; hospitals; cultural center; Permian Basin Fair and Expo in September.

Other towns include: **Gardendale** (1,902), **Goldsmith** (265), **Notrees** (20), **Penwell** (41), and **West Odessa** (27,725).

Population	162,124
Change fm 2010	18.2
Area (sq. mi.)	901.8
Land Area (sq. mi.)	897.7
Altitude (ft.)	2,780–3,360
Rainfall (in.)	13.45
Jan. mean min.	31.8
July mean max.	94.8
Civ. Labor	80,908
Unemployed	2.6
Wages	$1,164,880,469
Per Capita Income	$40,851
Prop. Value	$14,620,998,996
Retail Sales	$3,545,828,404

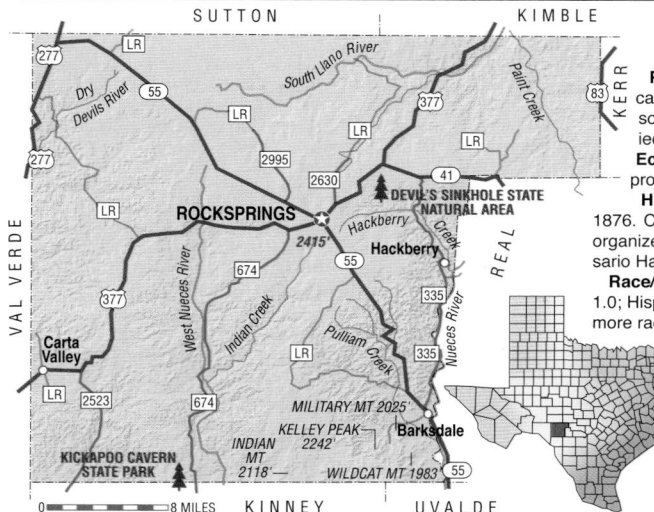

Edwards County

Physical Features: Rolling, hilly, with caves and spring-fed streams; rocky, thin soils; drained by Llano, Nueces rivers; varied timber.

Economy: Hunting leases, tourism, oil, gas production, ranching.

History: Apache area. First land sold in 1876. County created from Bexar District, 1858; organized 1883; named for Nacogdoches empresario Hayden Edwards.

Race/Ethnicity: (In percent) Anglo, 43.1; Black, 1.0; Hispanic, 55.1; Asian, 0.8; Other, 2.2; Two or more races, 0.7.

Vital Statistics, annual: Births, 22; deaths, 33; marriages, 10; divorces, 1.

Recreation: Hunting, fishing; scenic drives; Devil's Sinkhole, Kickapoo Cavern state parks.

Minerals: Gas.

Agriculture: Second in number of goats. Mohair-wool production, Angora goats (first in numbers), sheep, cattle, some pecans. Market value $8.2 million. Cedar for oil.

ROCKSPRINGS (1,115) county seat; government/services, hunting, ranching, oil and gas, hunters' barbecue in November.

Other towns include: **Barksdale** (100).

Population	1,928
Change fm 2010	– 3.7
Area (sq. mi.)	2,119.9
Land Area (sq. mi.)	2,117.9
Altitude (ft.)	1,480–2,415
Rainfall (in.)	26.56
Jan. mean min.	36.6
July mean max.	90.4
Civ. Labor	892
Unemployed	2.9
Wages	$3,212,234
Per Capita Income	$34,266
Prop. Value	$1,729,880,262
Retail Sales	$19,005,598

For explanation of sources, symbols and abbreviations, see p. 192, and foldout map.

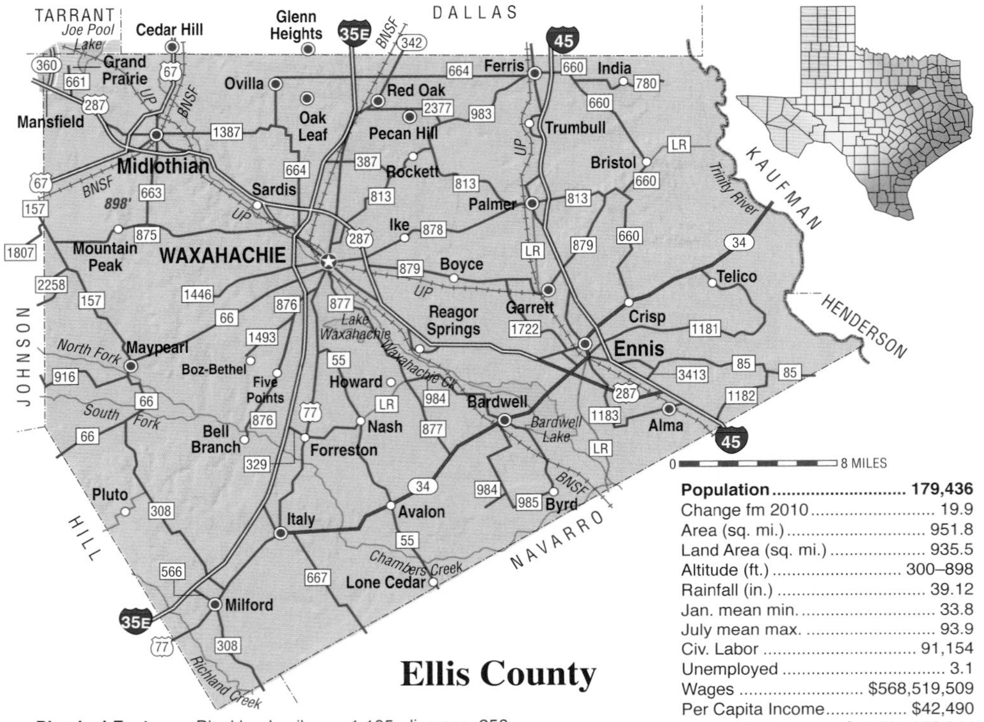

Ellis County

Map labels

TARRANT
Joe Pool Lake
Cedar Hill
Glenn Heights
DALLAS
360
Grand Prairie
67
Ovilla
35E
BNSF
342
45
664
Ferris
660
India
780
661
Mansfield
287
1387
Oak Leaf
Red Oak
2377
983
660
Trumbull
LR
UP
Pecan Hill
Midlothian
664
Sardis
387
Bockett
813
Bristol
660
67
BNSF
663
813
Palmer
813
KAUFMAN
Trinity River
157
898'
UP
Ike
878
879
660
34
1807
875
Mountain Peak
WAXAHACHIE
287
Boyce
LR
Telico
HENDERSON
2258
157
1446
876
877
Lake Waxahachie
Reagor Springs
Garrett
1722
Crisp
1181
JOHNSON
66
1493
55
Ennis
North Fork
Maypearl
Boz-Bethel
Five Points
Howard
984
Bardwell
287
3413
85
85
916
66
77
LR
1182
South Fork
876
Nash
877
Bardwell Lake
1183
Alma
66
Bell Branch
329
Forreston
LR
45
0 8 MILES
Pluto
308
Italy
34
984
Byrd
985
BNSF
NAVARRO
HILL
566
Chambers Creek
667
Lone Cedar
55
35E
Milford
77
308
Richland Creek

Statistics

Population	179,436
Change fm 2010	19.9
Area (sq. mi.)	951.8
Land Area (sq. mi.)	935.5
Altitude (ft.)	300–898
Rainfall (in.)	39.12
Jan. mean min.	33.8
July mean max.	93.9
Civ. Labor	91,154
Unemployed	3.1
Wages	$568,519,509
Per Capita Income	$42,490
Prop. Value	$16,291,962,344
Retail Sales	$2,028,884,802

Physical Features: Blackland soils; level to rolling; Chambers Creek, Trinity River; Bardwell Lake, Lake Waxahachie.

Economy: Cement, steel production, warehousing and distribution, government/services; many residents work in Dallas.

History: Tonkawa area. Part of Peters colony settled in 1843. County created 1849, organized 1850, from Navarro County. Named for Richard Ellis, president of convention that declared Texas' independence.

Race/Ethnicity: (In percent) Anglo, 60.8; Black, 10.8; Hispanic, 26.3; Asian, 0.8; Other, 1.0; Two or more races, 1.9.

Vital Statistics, annual: Births, 2,126; deaths, 1,209; marriages, 1,105; divorces, 256.

Recreation: Lakes, fishing, hunting; bluebonnet trails, historic homes, courthouse; Medieval-theme Scarborough Faire in spring.

Minerals: Cement, gas, sand, gravel.

Agriculture: Cattle, cotton, corn, hay, nurseries. Market value $91.4 million.

WAXAHACHIE (35,002) county seat; manufacturing, steel, aluminum, tourism; hospital; colleges, museums; hike/bike trail; Crape Myrtle festival in July.

Ennis (20,775) manufacturing, distribution, agribusiness, tourism; Czech museum and library; hospital; bluebonnet trails, National Polka Festival in May.

Midlothian (23,014) cement plants, steel plant, distribution center, manufacturing; heritage park, cabin; spring fling in April.

Other towns include: **Alma** (377); **Avalon** (400); **Bardwell** (707); **Bristol** (713); **Ferris** (2,559); **Forreston** (400); **Garrett** (862); **Howard** (60); **Italy** (1,962); **Maypearl** (1,309); **Milford** (782); **Oak Leaf** (1,422); **Ovilla** (4,035); **Palmer** (2,126); **Pecan Hill** (655); and **Red Oak** (12,784) manufacturing, Founders Day in September.

Also, **Glenn Heights** (12,603, mostly in Dallas County). Part of **Grand Prairie** and **Mansfield**.

The cemetery of the Socorro mission church, El Paso County. Photo by Robert Plocheck.

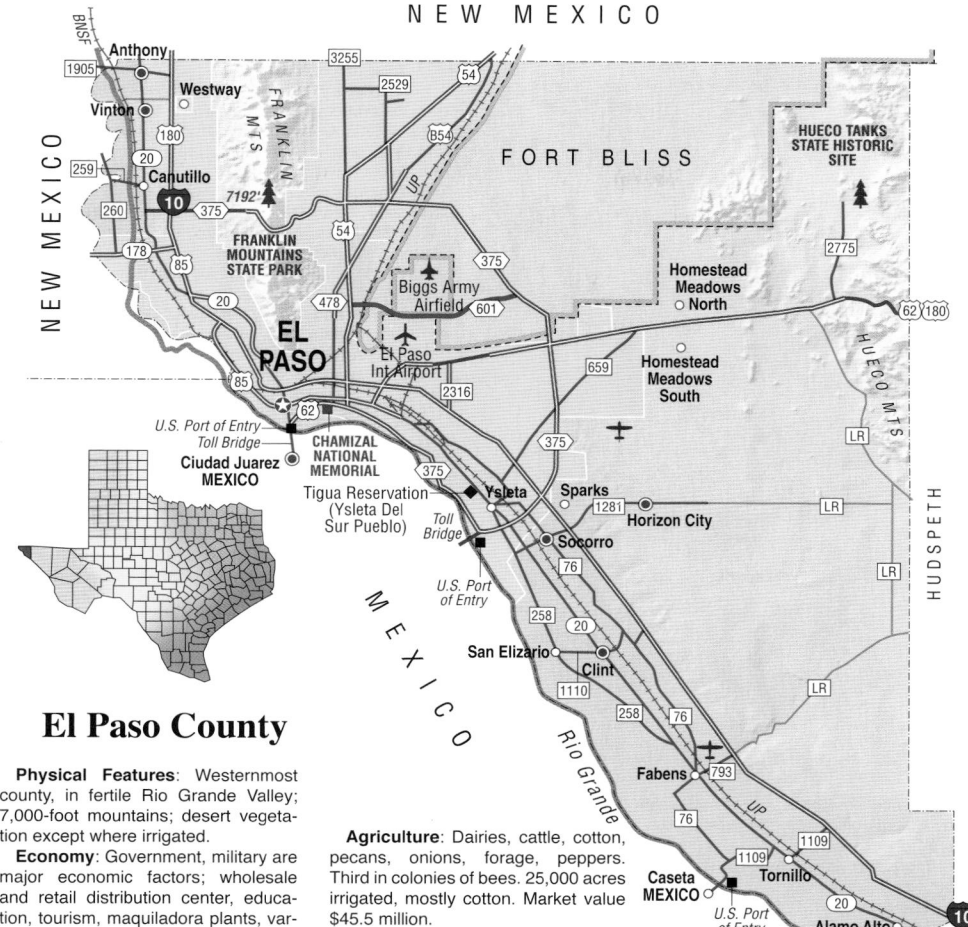

El Paso County

Physical Features: Westernmost county, in fertile Rio Grande Valley; 7,000-foot mountains; desert vegetation except where irrigated.

Economy: Government, military are major economic factors; wholesale and retail distribution center, education, tourism, maquiladora plants, varied manufacturing, oil refining, cotton, food processing.

History: Various Indian tribes inhabited the valley before Spanish civilization arrived in the late 1650s. Agriculture in area dates to at least 100 A.D. Spanish along with Tigua and Piro tribes fleeing Santa Fe uprising of 1680 sought refuge in the area. County created from the Bexar District in 1849; organized in 1850; named for historic pass (Paso del Norte), lowest all-weather pass through the southern Rocky Mountains.

Race/Ethnicity: (In percent) Anglo, 11.8; Black, 3.9; Hispanic, 82.8; Asian, 1.3; Other, 1.2; Two or more races, 1.5.

Vital Statistics, annual: Births, 13,521; deaths, 5,296; marriages, 6,819; divorces, 162.

Recreation: Gateway to Mexico; Chamizal Museum; major tourist center; December Sun Carnival with football game; state parks, mountain tramway, missions and other historic sites.

Minerals: Production of cement, stone, sand and gravel.

Agriculture: Dairies, cattle, cotton, pecans, onions, forage, peppers. Third in colonies of bees. 25,000 acres irrigated, mostly cotton. Market value $45.5 million.

Education: University of Texas at El Paso, UT School of Nursing at El Paso, Texas Tech University Health Sciences Center, El Paso Community College.

EL PASO (682,888) county seat; Texas' sixth-largest city and metro area, largest U.S. city on Mexican border.

A center for government operations. Federal installations include Fort Bliss, home of the U.S. Army 1st Armored Division, William Beaumont General Hospital, and La Tuna federal prison.

Manufactured products include clothing, electronics, auto equipment, plastics; trade and distribution; refining; processing oil, food, cotton, and other farm products.

Hospitals; museums; convention center; theater; symphony orchestra.

Other towns include: **Anthony** (5,600 in Texas, 9,360 in New Mexico); **Canutillo** (6,864); **Clint** (1,190);

For explanation of sources, symbols and abbreviations, see p. 192, and foldout map.

Fabens (8,415); **Homestead Meadows North** (5,470); **Homestead Meadows South** (7,595); **Horizon City** (18,592); **Prado Verde** (257); **San Elizario** (14,535), red & green chile war festival in September; **Socorro** (33,186) settled in 1680; **Sparks** (5,299); **Tornillo** (1,539); **Vinton** (2,007); **Westway** (4,275), and **Ysleta** (now within El Paso) settled in 1680, called the oldest town in Texas.

And, **Fort Bliss** (9,776).

Population	840,758
Change fm 2010	5.0
Area (sq. mi.)	1,015.0
Land Area (sq. mi.)	1,012.7
Altitude (ft.)	3,520–7,192
Rainfall (in.)	9.71
Jan. mean min.	32.5
July mean max.	94.7
Civ. Labor	362,089
Unemployed	4.0
Wages	$2,904,957,466
Per Capita Income	$34,582
Prop. Value	$44,956,797,581
Retail Sales	$9,808,594,473

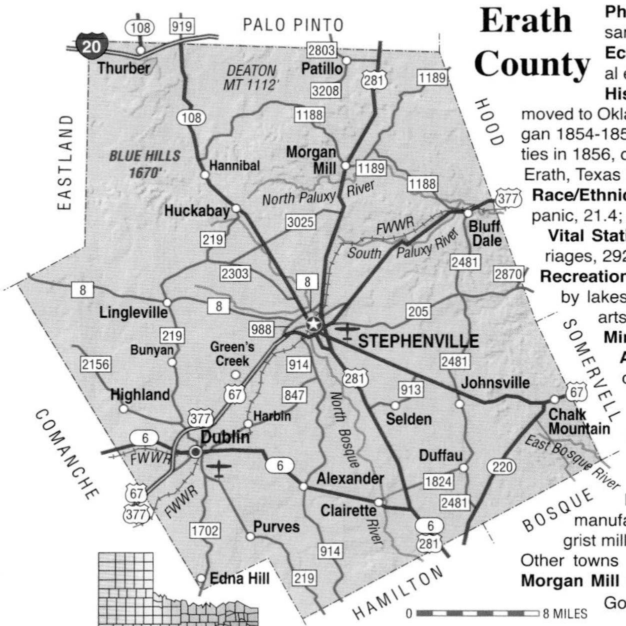

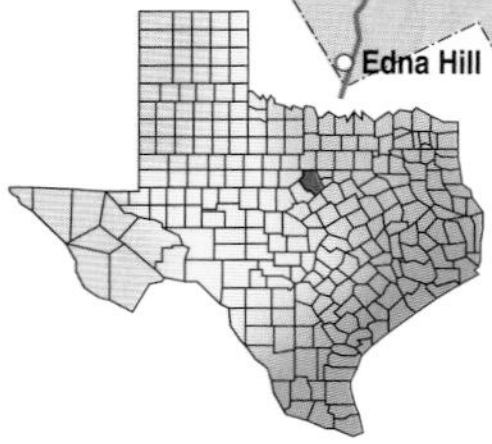

Erath County

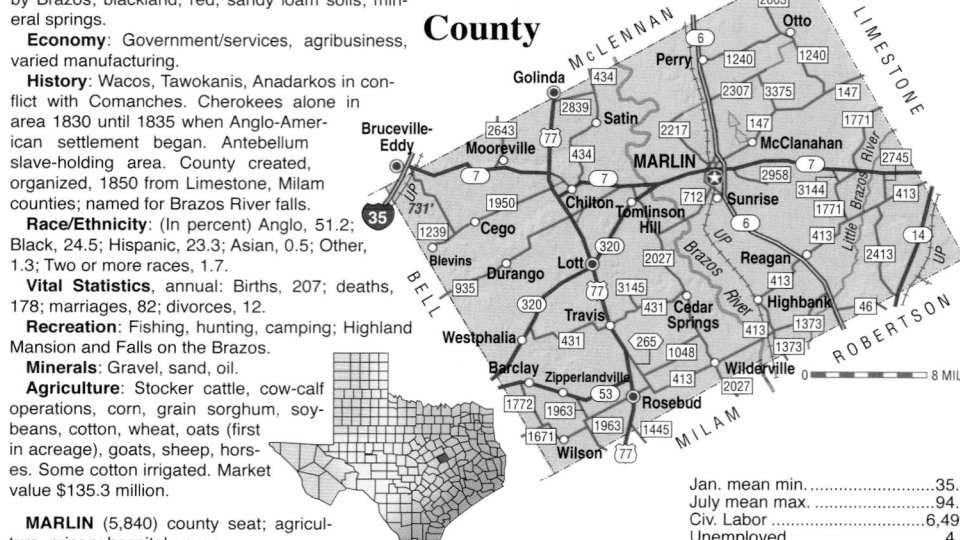

Physical Features: On Rolling Plains; clay loam, sandy soils; drains to Bosque, Paluxy rivers.

Economy: Agricultural, industrial, and educational enterprises.

History: Caddo and Anadarko Indians were moved to Oklahoma in 1860. Anglo-American settlement began 1854-1855. County created from Bosque, Coryell counties in 1856, organized the same year; named for George B. Erath, Texas Revolution figure.

Race/Ethnicity: (In percent) Anglo, 74.6; Black, 1.9; Hispanic, 21.4; Asian, 0.8; Other, 1.4; Two or more races, 1.5.

Vital Statistics, annual: Births, 448; deaths, 323; marriages, 292; divorces, 130.

Recreation: Old courthouse, log cabins, museums; nearby lakes, hunting, Bosque River Park; university fine arts center; Dairy Fest in June.

Minerals: Gas, oil.

Agriculture: Dairies (first in number of milk cows). Beef cattle, horticulture industry, horses raised. Market value $256.4 million.

STEPHENVILLE (20,150) county seat; Tarleton State University, varied manufacturing; hospital, mental health center; Texas A&M research and extension center.

Dublin (3,638) dairies, food processing, varied manufacturing, tourism; library; old Dr Pepper plant; grist mill; St. Patrick's Day celebration.

Other towns include: **Bluff Dale** (400); **Lingleville** (100); **Morgan Mill** (206); **Thurber** (48) former coal-mining town; Gordon Center for Industrial History of Texas.

Population	42,446
Change fm 2010	12.0
Area (sq. mi.)	1,089.8
Land Area (sq. mi.)	1,083.1
Altitude (ft.)	820–1,670
Rainfall (in.)	31.54
Jan. mean min.	31.0

July mean max.	94.2
Civ. Labor	20,968
Unemployed	3.0
Wages	$151,850,963
Per Capita Income	$37,624
Prop. Value	$5,131,521,950
Retail Sales	$580,967,665

Falls County

Physical Features: On rolling prairie; bisected by Brazos; blackland, red, sandy loam soils; mineral springs.

Economy: Government/services, agribusiness, varied manufacturing.

History: Wacos, Tawokanis, Anadarkos in conflict with Comanches. Cherokees alone in area 1830 until 1835 when Anglo-American settlement began. Antebellum slave-holding area. County created, organized, 1850 from Limestone, Milam counties; named for Brazos River falls.

Race/Ethnicity: (In percent) Anglo, 51.2; Black, 24.5; Hispanic, 23.3; Asian, 0.5; Other, 1.3; Two or more races, 1.7.

Vital Statistics, annual: Births, 207; deaths, 178; marriages, 82; divorces, 12.

Recreation: Fishing, hunting, camping; Highland Mansion and Falls on the Brazos.

Minerals: Gravel, sand, oil.

Agriculture: Stocker cattle, cow-calf operations, corn, grain sorghum, soybeans, cotton, wheat, oats (first in acreage), goats, sheep, horses. Some cotton irrigated. Market value $135.3 million.

MARLIN (5,840) county seat; agriculture, prison; hospital; museum.

Other towns include: **Chilton** (930); **Golinda** (600); **Lott** (772); **Reagan** (300); **Rosebud** (1,400) feed, fertilizer processing, clothing manufactured; **Satin** (86). Part of **Bruceville-Eddy** (1,873).

Population	17,335
Change fm 2010	– 3.0
Area (sq. mi.)	773.9
Land Area (sq. mi.)	765.5
Altitude (ft.)	282-731
Rainfall (in.)	38.46

Jan. mean min.	35.4
July mean max.	94.2
Civ. Labor	6,499
Unemployed	4.3
Wages	$27,825,884
Per Capita Income	$31,999
Prop. Value	$1,252,780,789
Retail Sales	$95,145,096

For explanation of sources, symbols and abbreviations, see p. 192, and foldout map.

Fannin County

Physical Features: North Texas county of rolling prairie, drained by Red River, Bois d'Arc Creek; Coffee Mill Lake, Lake Bonham, Valley Lake; mostly blackland soils; national grasslands.

Economy: Commuting to DFW metroplex, agribusiness.

History: Caddoes who later joined with Cherokees. Anglo-American settlement began in 1836. County created from Red River County in 1837 and organized in 1838; named for James W. Fannin, a victim of the Goliad massacre.

Race/Ethnicity: (In percent) Anglo, 79.0; Black, 6.8; Hispanic, 11.0; Asian, 0.7; Other, 1.4; Two or more races, 2.1.

Vital Statistics, annual: Births, 353; deaths, 458; marriages, 210; divorces, 153.

Recreation: Water activities on lakes; hunting; state park, fossil beds; winery; Sam Rayburn home, library; Bois D'Arc festival in May.

Minerals: Sand.

Agriculture: Beef cattle, wheat, corn. Market value $71.1 million. Hunting leases important.

BONHAM (10,628) county seat; varied manufacturing, veterans hospital/private hospital, state jail; Sam Rayburn birthday celebration in January.

Other towns include: **Bailey** (303); **Dodd City** (388); **Ector** (733); **Gober** (146); **Honey Grove** (1,762) agribusiness center, varied manufacturing, tourism, historic buildings, library, Davy Crockett Festival in October; **Ivanhoe** (110).

Also, **Ladonia** (651) restored historical downtown, tourism, varied manufacturing, commuters, rodeo; **Leonard** (2,074) government/services, power plant, retail, light industry, museums, community picnic in July; **Randolph** (600); **Ravenna** (222); **Savoy** (876); **Telephone** (210); **Trenton** (652); **Windom** (203).

Also, part of **Pecan Gap** (185) and part of **Whitewright** (1,618).

Population	35,286
Change fm 2010	4.1
Area (sq. mi.)	898.9
Land Area (sq. mi.)	890.8
Altitude (ft.)	450-800
Rainfall (in.)	46.13
Jan. mean min.	30.9
July mean max.	92.3
Civ. Labor	15,770
Unemployed	3.8
Wages	$72,838,955
Per Capita Income	$35,449
Prop. Value	$2,731,182,995
Retail Sales	$323,467,588

A lake at Bonham State Park, Fannin County. Photo by Robert Plocheck.

Fayette County

Physical Features: South central county bisected by Colorado River; Fayette County Reservoir; rolling to level; sandy loam, black waxy soils.

Economy: Agribusiness, production of electricity, mineral production, government/services, small manufacturing, tourism.

History: Lipan Apaches and Tonkawas. Austin's colonists arrived in 1822. Germans and Czechs began arriving in 1840s. County created from Bastrop, Colorado counties in 1837; organized in 1838; named for hero of American Revolution, Marquis de Lafayette.

Race/Ethnicity: (In percent) Anglo, 71.0; Black, 6.5; Hispanic, 21.3; Asian, 0.4; Other, 1.3; Two or more races, 1.2.

Vital Statistics, annual: Births, 282; deaths, 326; marriages, 117; divorces, 67.

Recreation: Monument Hill, Kreische brewery, Faison Home Museum, other historic sites including "Painted Churches"; hunting, fishing, lake; German and Czech ethnic foods; Prazska Pout in August, Octoberfests.

Minerals: Oil, gas, sand, gravel, bentonite clay.

Agriculture: Beef cattle, corn, hay, sorghum, pecans, dairies. Market value $66.4 million. Firewood sold.

LA GRANGE (4,726) county seat; electricity generation, manufacturing, food processing, retail trade, tourism; hospital, library, quilt museum, polka museum, archives; Czech heritage center; Best Little Cowboy Gathering in March.

Schulenburg (2,988) varied manufacturing, food processing; Blinn College extension; aircraft, polka music museums; sausagefest in April.

Round Top (93) music center, tourism; old Lutheran church, heritage museum; antiques shows, April/October; International Festival Institute, July-August; Shakespeare festival in April, Schuetzenfest in September, and **Winedale** (67), historic restorations including Winedale Inn.

Other towns include: **Carmine** (266); **Ellinger** (386) Tomato Festival in May; **Fayetteville** (261) tourism, antiques, old precinct courthouse, Lickskillet festival in October; **Flatonia** (1,413) food production, manufacturing, government/services; rail history museum, parks, Czhilispiel in October; **Ledbetter** (83); **Muldoon** (95); **Plum** (145); **Warda** (121); **Warrenton** (186) antique Cadillac museum; **West Point** (213), and **Winchester** (232).

Population	25,349
Change fm 2010	3.2
Area (sq. mi.)	959.8
Land Area (sq. mi.)	950.0
Altitude (ft.)	200-590
Rainfall (in.)	40.46
Jan. mean min.	39.2
July mean max.	95.5
Civ. Labor	12,277
Unemployed	3.8
Wages	$87,486,299
Per Capita Income	$51,176
Prop. Value	$5,643,034,869
Retail Sales	$363,889,637

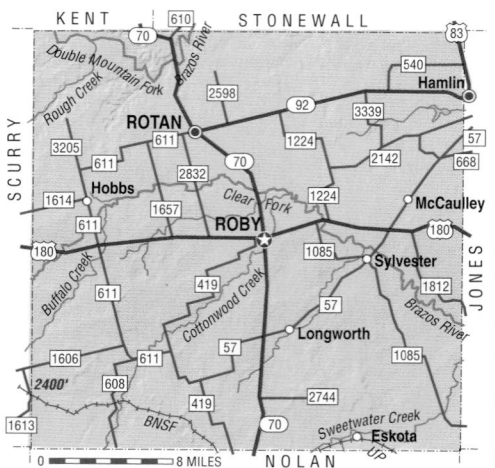

Fisher County

Physical Features: On rolling prairie; mesquite; red, sandy loam soils; drains to forks of Brazos River.

Economy: Agribusiness, hunting, gypsum.

History: Lipan Apaches, disrupted by Comanches and other tribes around 1700. Ranching began in 1876. County created from the Bexar District in 1876 and organized in 1886; named for S.R. Fisher, Republic of Texas secretary of navy.

Race/Ethnicity: (In percent) Anglo, 66.2; Black, 4.1; Hispanic, 28.4; Asian, 0.5; Other, 1.3; Two or more races, 2.2.

Vital Statistics, annual: Births, 50; deaths, 52; marriages, 25; divorces, 8.

Recreation: Quail, dove, turkey hunting; wildlife viewing; county fair, rodeo in August in Roby.

Minerals: Gypsum, oil.

Agriculture: Cattle, cotton, hay, wheat, sorghum, horses, sheep, goats. Irrigation for cotton and alfalfa. Market value $31.1 million.

ROBY (625) county seat; agribusiness, cotton gin; hospital between Roby and Rotan.

ROTAN (1,445) gypsum plant, oil mill, agribusiness.

Other towns include: **McCaulley** (96) and **Sylvester** (79). Part of **Hamlin** (2,119).

Population	3,839
Change fm 2010	– 3.5
Area (sq. mi.)	901.8
Land Area (sq. mi.)	898.9
Altitude (ft.)	1,720-2,405
Rainfall (in.)	24.76
Jan. mean min.	30.5
July mean max.	94.6
Civ. Labor	1,724
Unemployed	4.1
Wages	$8,881,581
Per Capita Income	$49,777
Prop. Value	$987,929,130
Retail Sales	$15,248,596

Floyd County

Physical Features: Flat High Plains, broken by Caprock on east, by White River on south; many playas; red, black loam soils.

Economy: Cotton, wind farm, varied manufacturing, government/services.

History: Plains Apaches in area, and later Comanches. First white settlers arrived in 1884. County created from the Bexar District in 1876 and organized in 1890. Named for Dolphin Ward Floyd, who died at the Alamo.

Race/Ethnicity: (In percent) Anglo, 36.2; Black, 4.0; Hispanic, 59.0; Asian, 0.5; Other, 1.4; Two or more races, 2.1.

Vital Statistics, annual: Births, 75; deaths, 67; marriages, 22; divorces, 9.

Recreation: Hunting of pheasant, deer, quail; fishing; Blanco Canyon; Floydada Punkin Day in October; museum.

Minerals: Not significant.

Agriculture: Cotton, wheat, sorghum, corn; pumpkins. Some 260,000 acres irrigated. Market value $282.7 million.

FLOYDADA (2,745) county seat; trucking, agriculture, retail, medical clinic, museum.

Lockney (1,688) agriculture center; manufacturing; hospital.

Other towns include: **Aiken** (52), **Dougherty** (91), and **South Plains** (67).

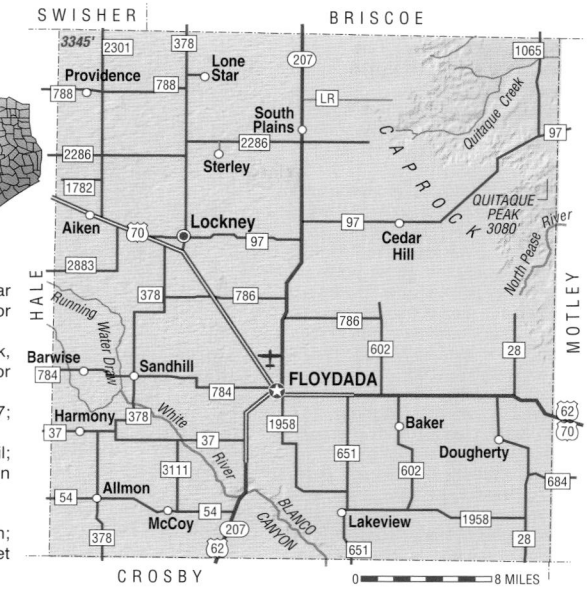

Population	5,837
Change fm 2010	– 9.4
Area (sq. mi.)	992.5
Land Area (sq. mi.)	992.1
Altitude (ft.)	2,440-3,345
Rainfall (in.)	21.60
Jan. mean min.	25.1
July mean max.	92.4
Civ. Labor	2,609
Unemployed	5.3
Wages	$13,969,445
Per Capita Income	$45,346
Prop. Value	$621,290,600
Retail Sales	$47,169,450

Foard County

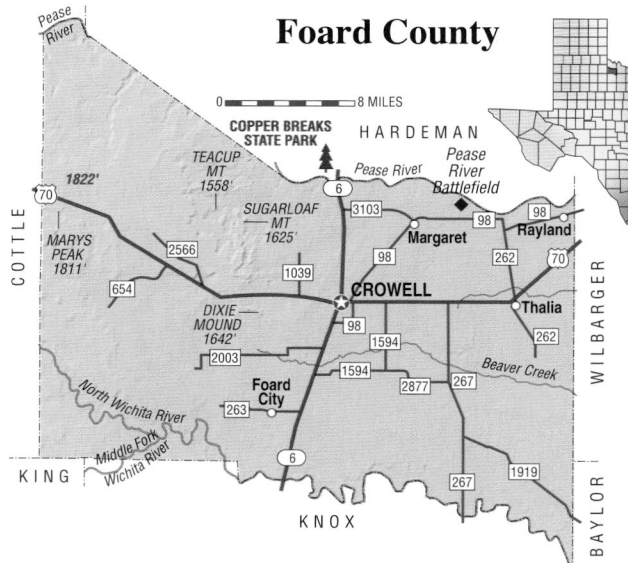

Physical Features: Northwest county drains to North Wichita, Pease rivers; sandy, loam soils, rolling surface.

Economy: Agribusiness, clothes manufacturing, government/service.

History: Comanches and Kiowas ranged the area until driven away in the 1870s. Ranching began in 1880. County created out of Cottle, Hardeman, King, and Knox counties in 1891, organized the same year; named for Maj. Robert L. Foard of the Confederate army.

Race/Ethnicity: (In percent) Anglo, 75.4; Black, 4.7; Hispanic, 17.8; Asian, 1.1; Other, 0.7; Two or more races, 1.3.

Vital Statistics, annual: Births, 10; deaths, 16; marriages, 0; divorces, 2.

Recreation: Three museums; hunting; astronomy and ecotourism foundation; wild hog cook-off in November.

Minerals: Natural gas, some oil.

Agriculture: Wheat, cattle, alfalfa, cotton, sorghum, dairies. Market value $13.8 million. Hunting leases important.

CROWELL (839) county seat; retail center, clothing manufacturing; library, Fire Hall museum.

Population	1,200
Change fm 2010	– 10.2
Area (sq. mi.)	707.7
Land Area (sq. mi.)	704.4
Altitude (ft.)	1,210–1,822
Rainfall (in.)	27.34
Jan. mean min.	26.0
July mean max.	98.0
Civ. Labor	591
Unemployed	2.7
Wages	$2,680,635
Per Capita Income	$37,809
Prop. Value	$602,614,480
Retail Sales	$5,026,804

For explanation of sources, symbols and abbreviations, see p. 192, and foldout map.

Fort Bend County

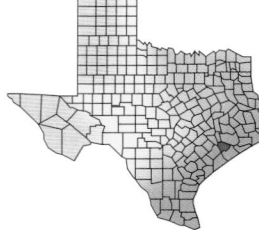

Physical Features: On Gulf Coastal Plain; drained by Brazos, San Bernard rivers; Smithers Lake; level to rolling; rich alluvial soils.

Economy: Agribusiness, petrochemicals, technology, government/services; many residents work in Houston.

History: Karankawa groups in area, who retreated to Mexico by the 1850s. Named for river bend where some of Austin's colonists settled in 1824 and built a blockhouse for protection against the Indians. Antebellum plantations made it one of six Texas counties with black majority in 1850. County created in 1837 from Austin County and organized in 1838.

Race/Ethnicity: (In percent) Anglo, 33.2; Black, 21.1; Hispanic, 24.5; Asian, 20.4; Other, 0.7; Two or more races, 2.2.

Vital Statistics, annual: Births, 9,887; deaths, 2,984; marriages, 3,145; divorces, 1,670.

Recreation: Many historic sites, museums, memorials, parks; George Ranch historical park; Brazos Bend State Park with George Observatory; fishing, waterfowl hunting.

Minerals: Oil, gas, sulfur, salt, clays, sand and gravel.

Agriculture: Nursery crops, cotton, sorghum, corn, hay, cattle, horses; irrigation for rice. Market value $103.8 million.

RICHMOND (13,401) county seat; foundry; University of Houston branch, Wharton County Junior College branch; Richmond State supported-living center, hospital.

SUGAR LAND (127,441) government/services, prisons, commuting to Houston; hospitals; University of Houston branch; Museum of Southern History. New Territory and Greatwood are now part of Sugar Land.

MISSOURI CITY (77,101, part [5,603] in Harris County) hospital.

ROSENBERG (40,484) varied industry, railroad museum.

Other towns include: **Arcola** (2,285); **Beasley** (759); **Cinco Ranch** (24,176); **Fairchilds** (1,012); **Fresno** (23,411); **Fulshear** (8,983); **Guy** (239); **Katy** (17,184, mostly in Harris County) hospital; **Kendleton** (408); **Meadows Place** (5,143); **Mission Bend** (41,119).

Also, **Needville** (3,357) agriculture, commuting, historic Schendel house, historic cemetery, Czech soup supper in January; **Orchard** (376); **Pecan Grove** (17,519); **Pleak** (1,439); **Simonton** (963); **Stafford** (19,007, partly in Harris County); **Thompsons** (308); **Weston Lakes** (2,807).

Also, part [38,124] of **Houston**.

Population	787,858
Change fm 2010	34.7
Area (sq. mi.)	885.3
Land Area (sq. mi.)	861.5
Altitude (ft.)	46–158
Rainfall (in.)	50.35
Jan. mean min.	44.1
July mean max.	94.9
Civ. Labor	384,031
Unemployment	3.6
Wages	$2,343,575,877
Per Capita Income	$54,510
Prop. Value	$81,585,882,575
Retail Sales	$8,215,753,882

For explanation of sources, symbols and abbreviations, see p. 192, and foldout map.

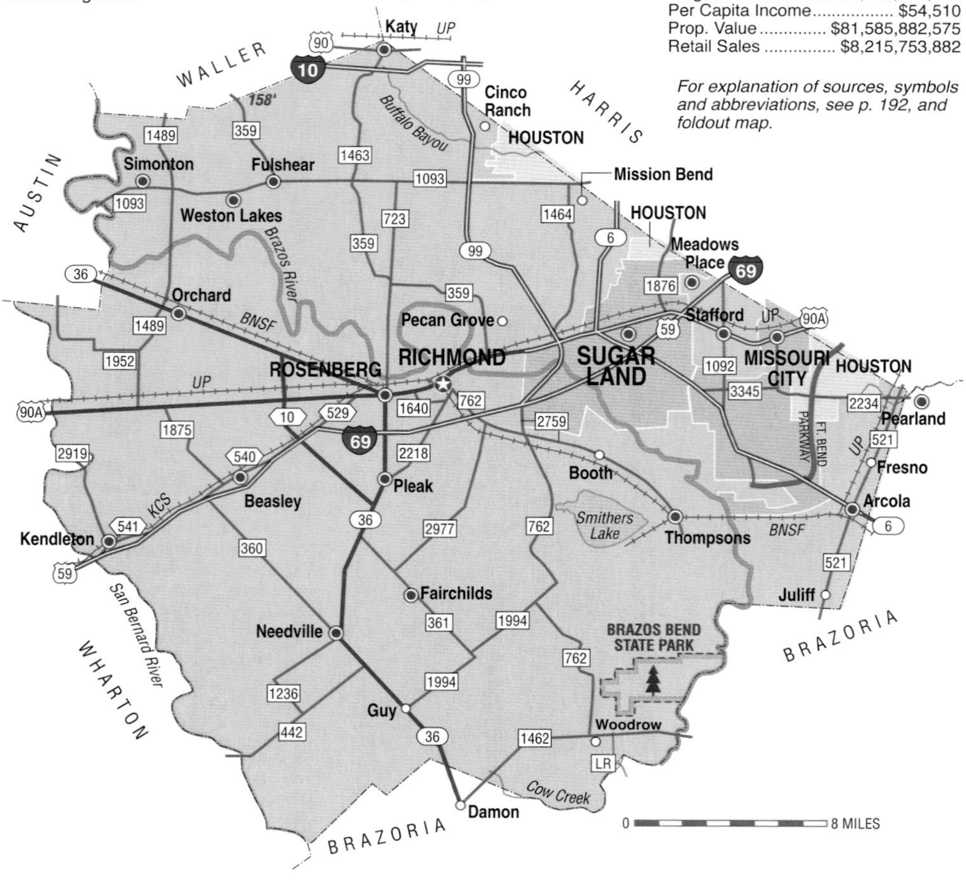

Franklin County

Physical Features: Small Northeast county with many wooded hills; drained by numerous streams; alluvial to sandy clay soils; Lake Bob Sandlin, Lake Cypress Springs.

Economy: Agribusiness, government/services, retirement area, distribution.

History: Caddoes abandoned the area in the 1790s because of disease and other tribes. First white settlers arrived around 1818. County created in 1875 from Titus County, organized the same year; named for jurist B.C. Franklin.

Race/Ethnicity: (In percent) Anglo, 78.9; Black, 3.9; Hispanic, 14.5; Asian, 0.9; Other, 1.1; Two or more races, 1.8.

Population	10,766
Change fm 2010	1.5
Area (sq. mi.)	294.8
Land Area (sq. mi.)	284.4
Altitude (ft.)	300–600
Rainfall (in.)	47.42
Jan. mean min.	31.9
July mean max.	92.0
Civ. Labor	4,474
Unemployed	3.9
Wages	$34,577,191
Per Capita Income	$38,351
Prop. Value	$1,537,760,200
Retail Sales	$98,877,721

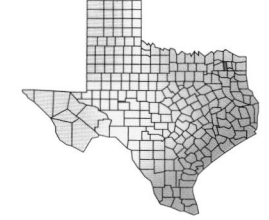

Vital Statistics, annual: Births, 123; deaths, 122; marriages, 51; divorces, 38.

Recreation: Fishing, water sports; historic homes; wild hog hunting, horse stables; stew cook-off in October.

Minerals: Lignite coal, oil and gas.

Agriculture: Beef cattle, milk production, poultry, hay. Market value $86 million. Timber marketed.

MOUNT VERNON (2,758) county seat; distribution center, manufacturing, tourism, antiques; hospital; nature preserves, museum with Don Meredith exhibit; wine festivals in May and October.

Other towns include: **Scroggins** (150), and **Winnsboro** (3,402, mostly in Wood County) commercial center, Autumn Trails.

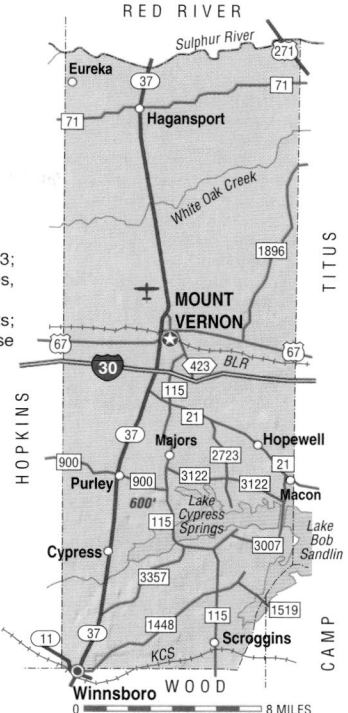

Freestone County

Physical Features: East central county bounded by the Trinity River; Richland-Chambers Reservoir, Fairfield Lake; rolling Blackland, sandy, loam soils.

Economy: Natural gas, agriculture.

History: Caddo and Tawakoni area. David G. Burnet received land grant in 1825. Seven Mexican citizens received grants in 1833. In 1860, more than half the population was black. County created in 1850 from Limestone County; organized in 1851. Named for the indigenous stone.

Race/Ethnicity: (In percent) Anglo, 67.0; Black, 16.2; Hispanic, 15.4; Asian, 0.7; Other, 1.3; Two or more races, 1.8.

Vital Statistics, annual: Births, 215; deaths, 202; marriages, 136; divorces, 60.

Recreation: Fishing, hunting; lakes; historic sites; state park; Teague amateur rodeo in July.

Minerals: Natural gas, oil.

Agriculture: Beef cattle, peaches (second in acreage), hay, blueberries, horticulture. Market value $44.1 million. Hunting leases.

FAIRFIELD (2,959) county seat; government/services, trade center; hospital, museum; wild game supper in July.

TEAGUE (3,558) railroad terminal, oil and gas, government/services, agriculture; library, museum; Parkfest in October.

Other towns include: **Donie** (250), **Kirvin** (131), **Streetman** (250), **Wortham** (1,056) agribusiness, blues festivals in September, Blind Lemon Jefferson gravesite.

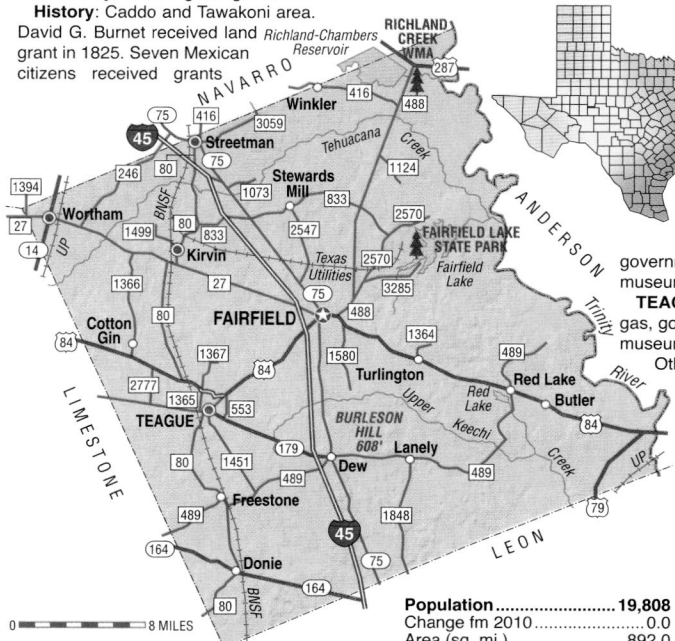

Population	19,808
Change fm 2010	0.0
Area (sq. mi.)	892.0
Land Area (sq. mi.)	877.7
Altitude (ft.)	200–608
Rainfall (in.)	43.12
Jan. mean min.	35.3
July mean max.	93.5
Civ. Labor	6,452
Unemployed	5.1
Wages	$48,813,424
Per Capita Income	$35,681
Prop. Value	$3,608,448,041
Retail Sales	$141,523,005

Frio County

Physical Features: South Texas county of rolling terrain with much brush; bisected by Frio River; sandy, red sandy loam soils.

Economy: Agribusiness, oil-field services, hunting leases.

History: Coahuiltecans; many taken into San Antonio missions. Comanches kept settlers out until after Civil War. Mexican citizens recruited for labor after 1900. County created in 1858 from Atascosa, Bexar, Uvalde counties, organized in 1871; named for the Frio (cold) River.

Race/Ethnicity: (In percent) Anglo, 14.8; Black, 3.9; Hispanic, 79.2; Asian, 2.5; Other, 1.0; Two or more races, 1.0.

Vital Statistics, annual: Births, 242; deaths, 155; marriages, 99; divorces, 12.

Recreation: Hunting, Big Foot Wallace Museum, Winter Garden area, splash pad/skate parks.

Minerals: Oil, natural gas, stone.

Agriculture: Peanuts, potatoes, sorghum, cotton, corn, spinach, cucumbers, watermelons, bees (second in number of colonies). Second in vegetables harvested. Market value $183.7 million. Hunting leases.

PEARSALL (10,057) county seat; agriculture center, oil and gas, food processing, shipping, government/services; old jail museum; hospital, junior college extension; Cinco de Mayo celebration.

Dilley (4,211) shipping center for melons and peanuts; hospital.

Other towns include: **Bigfoot** (522), **Hilltop** (285); **Moore** (501), and **North Pearsall** (653).

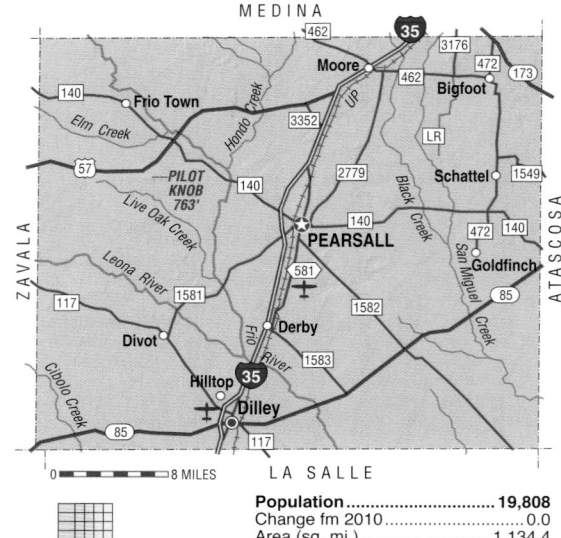

Population	19,808
Change fm 2010	0.0
Area (sq. mi.)	1,134.4
Land Area (sq. mi.)	1,133.5
Altitude (ft.)	400–763
Rainfall (in.)	24.73
Jan. mean min.	35.0
July mean max.	97.4
Civ. Labor	9,709
Unemployed	2.7
Wages	$98,882,029
Per Capita Income	$26,421
Prop. Value	$2,945,326,140
Retail Sales	$184,568,806

Gaines County

Population	20,901
Change fm 2010	19.3
Area (sq. mi.)	1,502.9
Land Area (sq. mi.)	1,502.4
Altitude (ft.)	2,935–3,695
Rainfall (in.)	18.36
Jan. mean min.	27.7
July mean max.	93.4
Civ. Labor	9,376
Unemployed	2.5
Wages	$77,110,526
Per Capita Income	$36,750
Prop. Value	$3,757,045,875
Retail Sales	$235,255,418

Physical Features: On South Plains, drains to draws; playas; underground water.

Economy: Oil, gas, cotton, peanuts.

History: Comanche country until the U.S. Army campaigns of 1875. Ranchers arrived in the 1880s; farming began around 1900. County created from Bexar District in 1876; organized in 1905; named for James Gaines, signer of the Texas Declaration of Independence.

Race/Ethnicity: (In percent) Anglo, 55.0; Black, 2.2; Hispanic, 41.9; Asian, 0.4; Other, 1.2; Two or more races, 1.3.

Vital Statistics, annual: Births, 460; deaths, 128; marriages, 179; divorces, 27.

Recreation: Cedar Lake one of largest alkali lakes on Texas plains.

Minerals: Oil, gas.

Agriculture: Cotton (first in bales produced), peanuts (first in acreage), small grains, pecans, paprika, rosemary; cattle, sheep, hogs; substantial irrigation. Market value $180.5 million.

SEMINOLE (7,335) county seat; manufacturing, oil and gas, agriculture; hospital, library, museum; Ag & Oil Day celebration in September.

Seagraves (2,733) market for three-county area; cotton, peanut farming; library, museum; Celebrate Seagraves in July.

Other towns include: **Loop** (228). Also, part of **Denver City** (5,062).

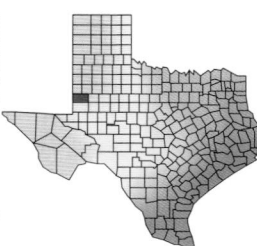

Physical Features: Partly island, partly coastal; flat, artificial drainage; sandy, loam, clay soils; broken by bays.

Economy: Port activities dominate economy; insurance and finance center, petrochemical plants, varied manufacturing, tourism, medical education, oceanographic research, ship building, commercial fishing.

History: Karankawa and other tribes roamed the area until 1850. French, Spanish, and American settlement began in 1815 and reached 1,000 by 1817.

County created from Brazoria County in 1838; organized in 1839; named for the Spanish governor of Louisiana Count Bernardo de Gálvez.

Race/Ethnicity: (In percent) Anglo, 57.3; Black, 13.4; Hispanic, 24.6; Asian, 3.5; Other, 0.9; Two or more races, 2.1.

Vital Statistics, annual: Births, 4,219; deaths, 2,675; marriages, 1,876; divorces, 1,026.

Recreation: One of Texas' most historic cities; popular tourist and convention center; fishing, surfing, boating, sailing and other water sports; state park; historic homes tour in spring, Moody Gardens.

Also, Mardi Gras celebration; Rosenberg Library; museums; restored sailing ship, "Elissa," railroad museum; Dickens on the Strand in early December.

Minerals: Oil, gas, clays, sand and gravel.

Agriculture: Cattle, aquaculture,

Galveston County

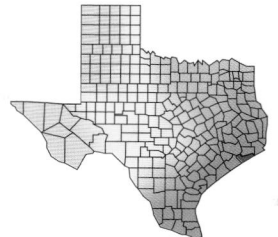

nursery crops, rice, hay, horses, soybeans, grain sorghum.

GALVESTON (49,979) county seat; tourist center, shipyard, other industries, insurance, port container facility; University of Texas Medical Branch; National Maritime Research Center; Texas A&M University at Galveston; Galveston College; hospitals.

League City (102,745, part [1,562] in Harris County) residential community, commuters to Houston, hospital.

Texas City (49,711) refining, petrochemical plants, port, rail shipping; College of the Mainland; hospital, library; dike; Cinco de Mayo, Shrimp Boil in August.

Bolivar Peninsula (2,743) includes: **Port Bolivar** (700) lighthouse, free ferry; **Crystal Beach** (800) seafood industry, sport fishing, tourism, Fort

Travis Seashore Park, shorebird sanctuary, Crab Festival in May; **Gilchrist** (400), and **High Island** (300).

Other towns include: **Bacliff** (10,025); **Bayou Vista** (1,552); **Clear Lake Shores** (1,195).

Also, **Dickinson** (20,217) manufacturing, commuters, strawberry festival in May; Friendswood (39,219, part [10,295] in Harris County); **Hitchcock** (7,884) residential community, tourism, fishing and shrimping, Good Ole Days in August, WWII blimp base, museum.

Also, **Jamaica Beach** (1,081); **Kemah** (1,984) tourism, boating, commuters, museum, Blessing of Fleet in August; **La Marque** (16,806) refining, greyhound racing, farming, hospital, library, Gulf Coast Grill-off in October; **San Leon** (5,488); **Santa Fe** (13,203); **Tiki Island** (1,053).

Population	**337,890**
Change fm 2010	16.0
Area (sq. mi.)	873.8
Land Area (sq. mi.)	378.4
Altitude (ft.)	sea level–40
Rainfall (in.)	50.76
Jan. mean min.	48.6
July mean max.	89.6
Civ. Labor	167,978
Unemployed	4.3
Wages	$1,288,345,428
Per Capita Income	$49,007
Prop. Value	$34,247,890,766
Retail Sales	$4,131,320,216

For explanation of sources, symbols and abbreviations, see p. 192, and foldout map.

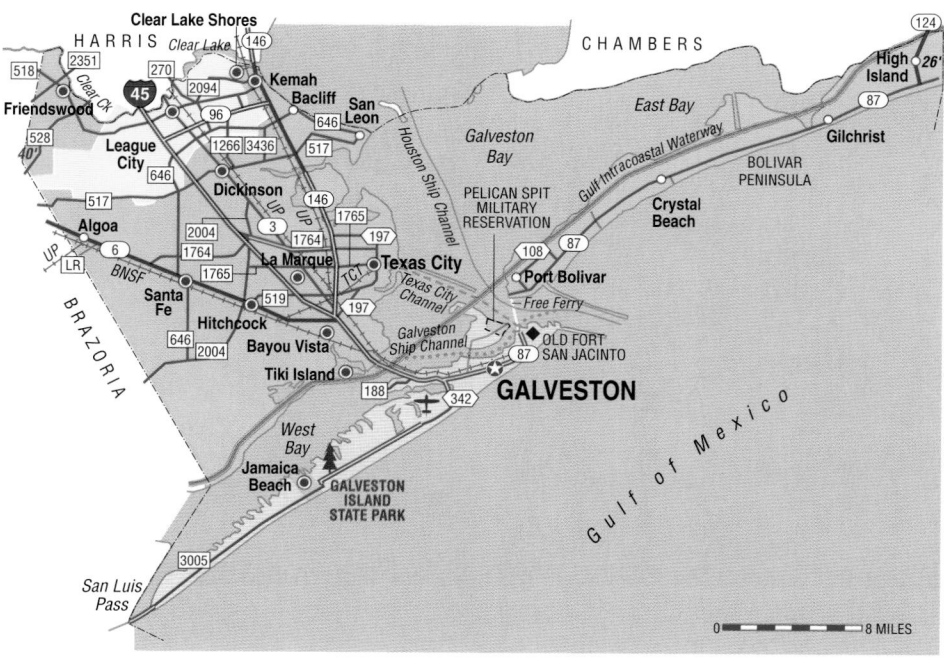

Garza County

Physical Features: On edge of Caprock; rough, broken land, with playas, gullies, canyons, Brazos River forks, Lake Alan Henry; sandy, loam, clay soils.

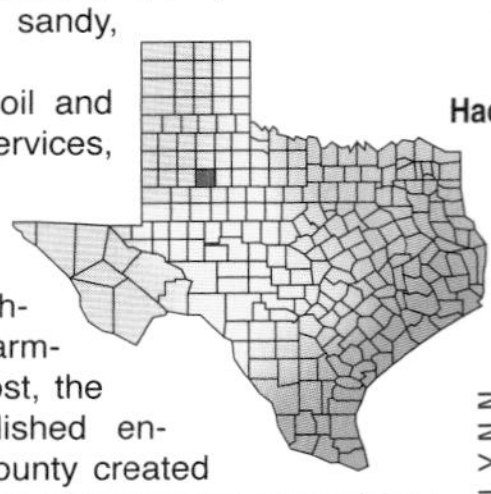

Economy: Agriculture, oil and gas, trade, government/services, hunting leases.

History: Kiowas and Comanches yielded to U.S. Army in 1875. Ranching began in the 1870s, farming in the 1890s. C.W. Post, the cereal millionaire, established enterprises here in 1906. County created from Bexar District 1876; organized 1907; named for a pioneer Bexar County family.

Race/Ethnicity: (In percent) Anglo, 40.1; Black, 7.5; Hispanic, 52.0; Asian, 0.5; Other, 1.0; Two or more races, 1.2.

Vital Statistics, annual: Births, 71; deaths, 56; marriages, 41; divorces, 7.

Recreation: Scenic areas, lake activities, Post-Garza Museum, trade days monthly.

Minerals: Oil, gas, sand, gravel.

Agriculture: Cotton, beef cattle, hay. Some 8,000 acres irrigated. Market value $12.4 million. Hunting leases.

POST (5,272) county seat; founded by C.W. Post; agriculture, tourism, government/services, prisons; museums, theater.

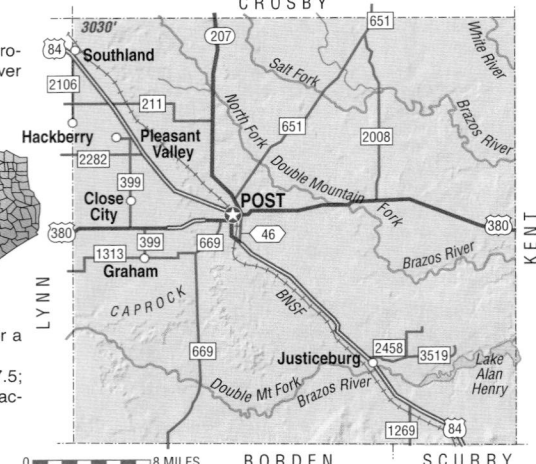

Population	**6,578**
Change fm 2010	1.8
Area (sq. mi.)	896.2
Land Area (sq. mi.)	893.4
Altitude (ft.)	2,140–3,030
Rainfall (in.)	21.99
Jan. mean min.	29.0
July mean max.	94.4
Civ. Labor	2,138
Unemployed	2.7
Wages	$17,837,632
Per Capita Income	$26,482
Prop. Value	$860,792,942
Retail Sales	$27,740,402

For explanation of sources, symbols and abbreviations, see p. 192, and foldout map.

Downtown Post, Garza County. Photo by Robert Plocheck.

Gillespie County

Physical Features: Picturesque Edwards Plateau area with hills, broken by spring-fed streams.

Economy: Tourism, government/services, agriculture, wine and specialty foods, hunting leases.

History: German settlement founded in 1846 in heart of Comanche country. County created in 1848 from Bexar and Travis counties, organized the same year; named for Texas Ranger Capt. R.A. Gillespie.

The birthplace of President Lyndon B. Johnson and Fleet Admiral Chester W. Nimitz.

Race/Ethnicity: (In percent) Anglo, 74.6; Black, 0.7; Hispanic, 23.5; Asian, 0.4; Other, 1.2; Two or more races, 1.0.

Vital Statistics, annual: Births, 254; deaths, 318; marriages, 193; divorces, 68.

Recreation: Among leading deer-hunting areas; numerous historic sites and tourist attractions include LBJ Ranch, Nimitz Hotel and Pacific war museum; Pioneer Museum Complex, Enchanted Rock, wineries, produce stands.

Minerals: Sand, gravel.

Agriculture: Beef cattle, wine,

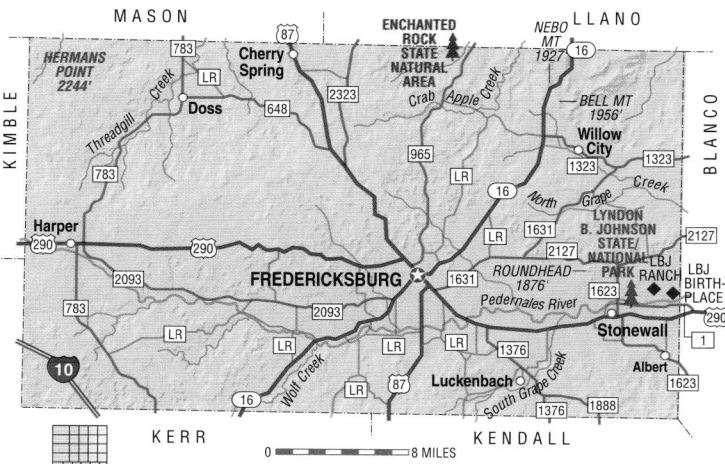

hay, peaches (first in acreage). Market value $46.1 million. Hunting leases important.

FREDERICKSBURG (11,542) county seat; agribusiness, tourism, wineries, food processing; museum; tourist attractions; hospital; Easter Fires, Oktoberfest.

Other towns include: **Doss** (100); **Harper** (1,326) ranching, deer hunting, Dachshund Hounds Downs race and Trades Day in October; **Luckenbach** (25) saloon, general store

and dance hall; **Stonewall** (524) agribusiness, wineries, tourism, hunting, Peach Jamboree in June, and **Willow City** (22) scenic drive.

Population	**26,804**
Change fm 2010	7.9
Area (sq. mi.)	1,061.7
Land Area (sq. mi.)	1,058.2
Altitude (ft.)	1,040–2,244
Rainfall (in.)	31.53
Jan. mean min.	34.3
July mean max.	92.7
Civ. Labor	13,587
Unemployed	2.6
Wages	$104,010,762
Per Capita Income	$57,382
Prop. Value	$8,246,251,790
Retail Sales	$520,146,658

Glasscock County

Physical Features: Western county on rolling plains, broken by small streams; sandy, loam soils.

Economy: Farming, ranching, hunting leases, oil and gas.

History: Hunting area for Kickapoos and Lipan Apaches. Anglo-American sheep ranchers and Mexican-American shepherds or pastores moved into the area in the 1880s. County created in 1887 from Tom Green County; organized in 1893; named for Texas pioneer George W. Glasscock.

Race/Ethnicity: (In percent) Anglo, 60.5; Black, 1.6; Hispanic, 37.2; Asian, 0.1; Other, 0.5; Two or more races, 0.7.

Vital Statistics, annual: Births, 16; deaths, 3; marriages, 4; divorces, 1.

Recreation: Hunting of deer, quail, turkey, fox, bobcat, coyote; St. Lawrence Fall Festival in October.

Minerals: Oil, gas, stone/rock.

Agriculture: Cotton, watermelons, wheat, sorghum, hay; 25,000 acres irrigated. Cattle, goats, sheep, hogs raised. Market value $25.9 million.

GARDEN CITY (371), county seat; serves sparsely settled ranching, oil area.

Also, **St. Lawrence** (90), farming.

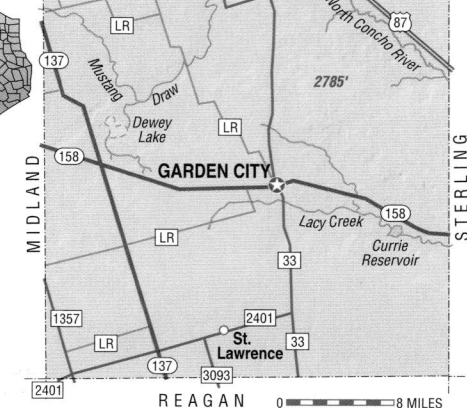

Population	**1,388**
Change fm 2010	13.2
Area (sq. mi.)	901.1
Land Area (sq. mi.)	900.2
Altitude (ft.)	2,470–2,785
Rainfall (in.)	17.57
Jan. mean min.	28.3
July mean max.	92.6
Civ. Labor	727
Unemployed	2.3
Wages	$7,549,619
Per Capita Income	$78,012
Prop. Value	$2,963,836,504
Retail Sales	$13,492,351

Physical Features: Coastal Plain county; rolling, brushy; bisected by San Antonio River; Coleto Creek Reservoir; sandy, loam, alluvial soils.

Economy: Government/services, oil/gas, agriculture, electricity-generating plant, tourism.

History: Karankawas, Comanches, other tribes in area in historic period. La Bahía presidio/mission established, 1749. County created, 1836, from Spanish municipality; organized, 1837; name is anagram of (H)idalgo. Birthplace of Gen. Ignacio Zaragoza, hero of Battle of Puebla.

Race/Ethnicity: (In percent) Anglo, 57.8; Black, 5.1; Hispanic, 36.4; Asian, 0.5; Other, 1.0; Two or more races, 1.3.

Vital Statistics, annual: Births, 78; deaths, 87; marriages, 47; divorces, 7.

Recreation: Missions, restored Presidio La Bahía, Fannin Battleground; Old Market House museum; lake, fishing, hunting (deer, quail, dove, hogs), camping, canoeing, birding.

Minerals: Production of oil, gas.

Agriculture: Beef cattle, stocker operations and fed cattle are top revenue producers; corn, grain sorghum, cotton, hay; minor irrigation for pasture. Market value $19.4 million. Hunting leases.

Goliad County

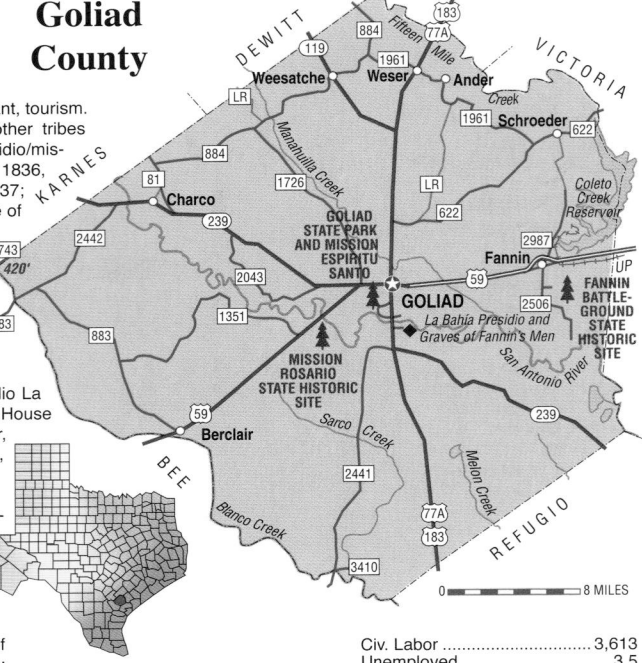

GOLIAD (2,022) county seat; one of state's oldest towns; power plant; tourism; library; Zaragoza Birthplace State Historic Site, statue; Goliad Massacre re-enactment in March, Diez y Seis celebration in September.

Other towns include: **Berclair** (253), **Fannin** (359), and **Weesatche** (411).

Population	**7,584**
Change fm 2010	5.2
Area (sq. mi.)	859.4
Land Area (sq. mi.)	852.0
Altitude (ft.)	50–420
Rainfall (in.)	36.78
Jan. mean min.	42.5
July mean max.	93.8

Civ. Labor	3,613
Unemployed	3.5
Wages	$11,036,301
Per Capita Income	$40,890
Prop. Value	$2,723,956,908
Retail Sales	36,728,673

For explanation of sources, symbols and abbreviations, see p. 192, and foldout map.

Ranch land in Gray County. Photo by Robert Plocheck.

Gonzales County

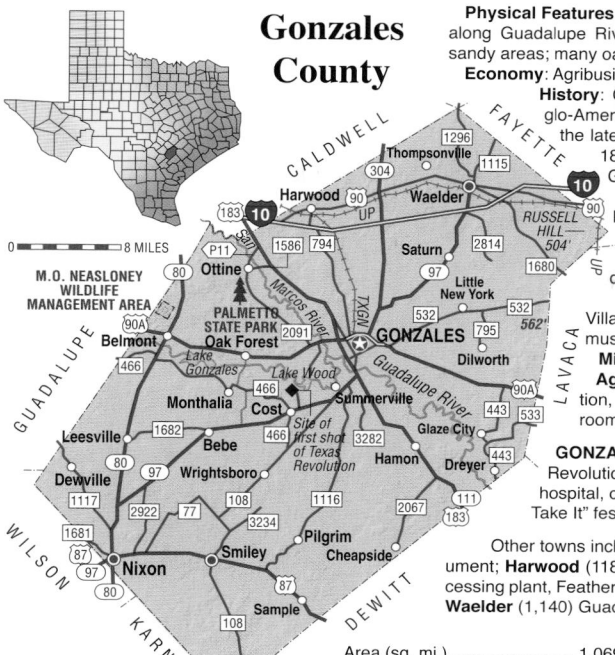

Physical Features: South central county; rolling, rich bottom soils along Guadalupe River and its tributaries; Lake Gonzales; some sandy areas; many oaks, pecans.

Economy: Agribusiness, hunting leases.

History: Coahuiltecan tribal area. Among the first Anglo-American settlements was the DeWitt colony in the late 1820s. County created in 1836; organized in 1837; named for Coahuila y Texas Gov. Rafael Gonzales.

Race/Ethnicity: (In percent) Anglo, 41.4; Black, 7.4; Hispanic, 51.0; Asian, 0.5; Other, 1.9; Two or more races, 1.2.

Vital Statistics, annual: Births, 342; deaths, 187; marriages, 103; divorces, 63.

Recreation: Historic sites, homes, Pioneer Village Living History Center, Palmetto State Park, museums, Independence Park.

Minerals: Gas, oil, clay, gravel.

Agriculture: Second in poultry and egg production, cattle; hay, corn, sorghum, pecans, mushrooms. Market value $517.8 million.

GONZALES (7,530) county seat; first shot in Texas Revolution fired here; cattle ranching, chicken farming; hospital, college extensions; pioneer village; "Come and Take It" festival in October.

Other towns include: **Belmont** (55); **Cost** (84) First Shot monument; **Harwood** (118); **Leesville** (152); **Nixon** (2,505) poultry-processing plant, Feather Fest in September; **Ottine** (80); **Smiley** (569); **Waelder** (1,140) Guacamole Fest in September; **Wrightsboro** (10).

Area (sq. mi.) 1,069.9	Civ. Labor 9,192
Land Area (sq. mi.) 1,066.7	Unemployed 2.9
Altitude (ft.) 200–562	Wages $74,711,500
Rainfall (in.) 34.91	Per Capita Income $41,154
Jan. mean min. 39.9	Prop. Value $5,666,819,180
July mean max. 94.2	Retail Sales $243,277,533
Population 20,826	
Change fm 2010 .... 5.1	

Gray County

Physical Features: High Plains, broken by Red River forks, tributaries; sandy loam, waxy soils.

Economy: Petroleum, agriculture, government/services.

History: Apaches, displaced by Comanches and Kiowas. Ranching began in the late 1870s. Farmers arrived around 1900. Oil discovered in 1926. County created in 1876 from Bexar District; organized in 1902; named for Peter W. Gray, member of first Legislature.

Race/Ethnicity: (In percent) Anglo, 63.2; Black, 5.3; Hispanic, 28.9; Asian, 0.7; Other, 1.6; Two or more races, 2.2.

Vital Statistics, annual: Births, 338; deaths, 267; marriages, 199; divorces, 97.

Recreation: Water sports, Lake McClellan and grassland; White Deer Land Museum, barbed-wire museum; Top of Texas livestock show in January.

Minerals: Natural gas, oil.

Agriculture: Cattle, hogs, wheat, cotton, corn, sorghum, hay, milk. Market value $207.7 million.

PAMPA (17,653) county seat; petroleum, agriculture; hospital; college; prison; Woody Guthrie museum; Mud Bog car show in June.

Other towns include: **Alanreed** (48); **Lefors** (492); **McLean** (770) commercial center for southern part of county.

Population 21,895	Civ. Labor 7,734
Change fm 2010 .... – 2.8	Unemployed 3.9
Area (sq. mi.) 929.3	Wages $91,524,237
Land Area (sq. mi.) 926.0	Per Capita Income $41,781
Altitude (ft.) 2,450–3,320	Prop. Value $2,296,376,180
Rainfall (in.) 23.19	Retail Sales $307,007,220
Jan. mean min. 23.3	
July mean max. 91.4	

For explanation of sources, symbols and abbreviations, see p. 192, and foldout map.

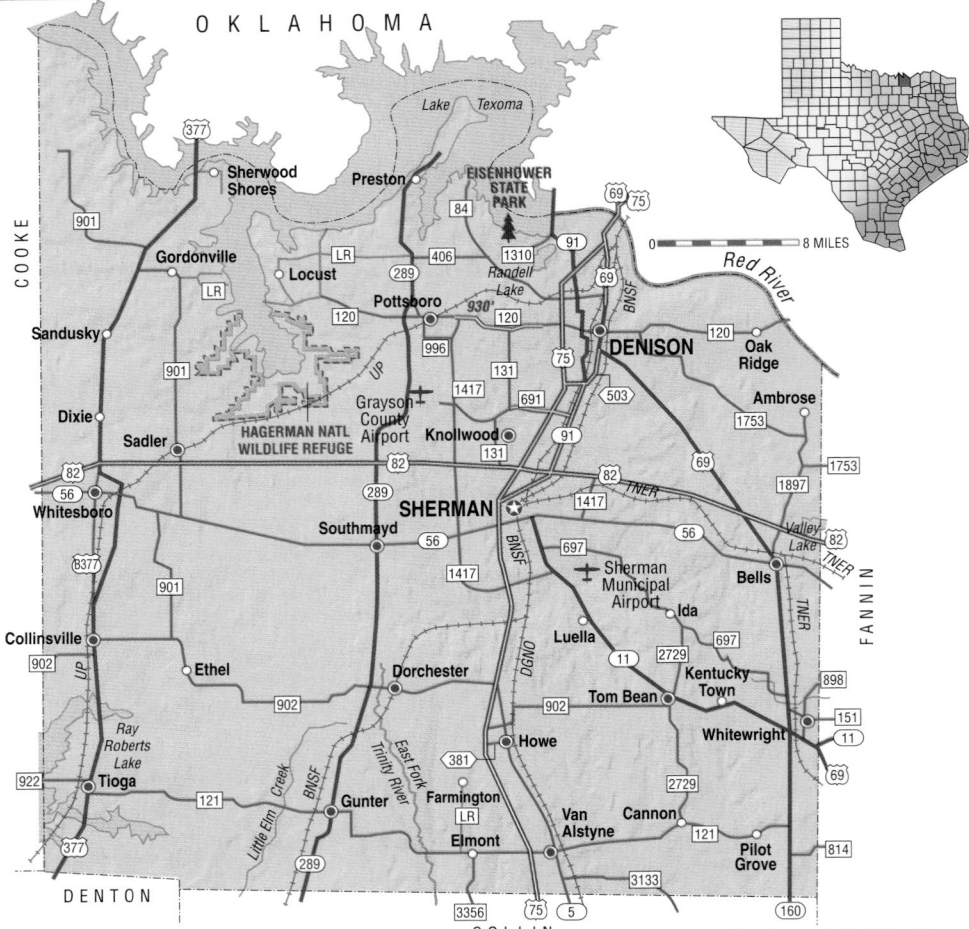

Physical Features: North Texas county; level, some low hills; sandy loam, blackland soils; drains to Red River and tributaries of Trinity River; Lake Texoma, Ray Roberts Lake, Valley Lake, Randell Lake.

Economy: A manufacturing, distribution and trade center for northern Texas and southern Oklahoma; nature tourism, mineral production.

History: Caddo and Tonkawa area. Preston Bend trading post established 1836-1837. Peters colony settlers arrived in the 1840s. County created in 1846 from Fannin County, organized the same year; named for Republic Attorney General Peter W. Grayson.

Race/Ethnicity: (In percent) Anglo, 76.2; Black, 6.2; Hispanic, 13.4; Asian, 1.4; Other, 1.9; Two or more races, 2.7.

Vital Statistics, annual: Births, 1,579; deaths, 1,461; marriages, 907; divorces, 251.

Recreation: Lakes, fishing, hunting, water sports, state park, cultural activities, Hagerman National Wildlife Refuge, Pioneer Village, railroad museum.

Grayson County

Minerals: Oil, gas, gravel, sand.

Agriculture: Wheat, corn, hay, beef cattle, horses. Market value $92 million.

Education: Austin College in Sherman and Grayson County College located between Sherman and Denison.

SHERMAN (41,556) county seat; varied manufacturing, processors and distributors for major companies; Austin College; hospital.

DENISON (23,695) health care, manufacturing, retail center; hospital; Eisenhower birthplace, air force base museum; Main Street Fall festival in October.

Other towns include: **Bells** (1,452); **Collinsville** (1,732); **Dorchester** (161); **Gordonville** (165); **Gunter** (1,460); **Howe** (2,772) manufacturing, agriculture, trucking services, library, Founders' Day in May; **Knollwood** (478); **Pottsboro** (2,308) lake activities, marinas, education, Frontier Days in September; **Sadler** (341).

Also, **Southmayd** (1,037); **Tioga** (840) Gene Autry museum, festival in September; **Tom Bean** (1,065); **Van Alstyne** (3,658) retail center, manufacturing, government/services, museum, Grayson County College-South Campus, Fall Der All in October; **Whitesboro** (3,928) agribusiness, tourism, manufacturing, library, Peanut Festival in October; **Whitewright** (1,618) government/services, retail, manufacturing, museum, truck & tractor pull in June.

Population	**133,991**
Change fm 2010	10.9
Area (sq. mi.)	979.2
Land Area (sq. mi.)	932.8
Altitude (ft.)	500–930
Rainfall (in.)	43.60
Jan. mean min.	33.1
July mean max.	92.1
Civ. Labor	64,158
Unemployed	3.0
Wages	$496,177,983
Per Capita Income	$41,250
Prop. Value	$12,726,482,052
Retail Sales	$1,940,504,715

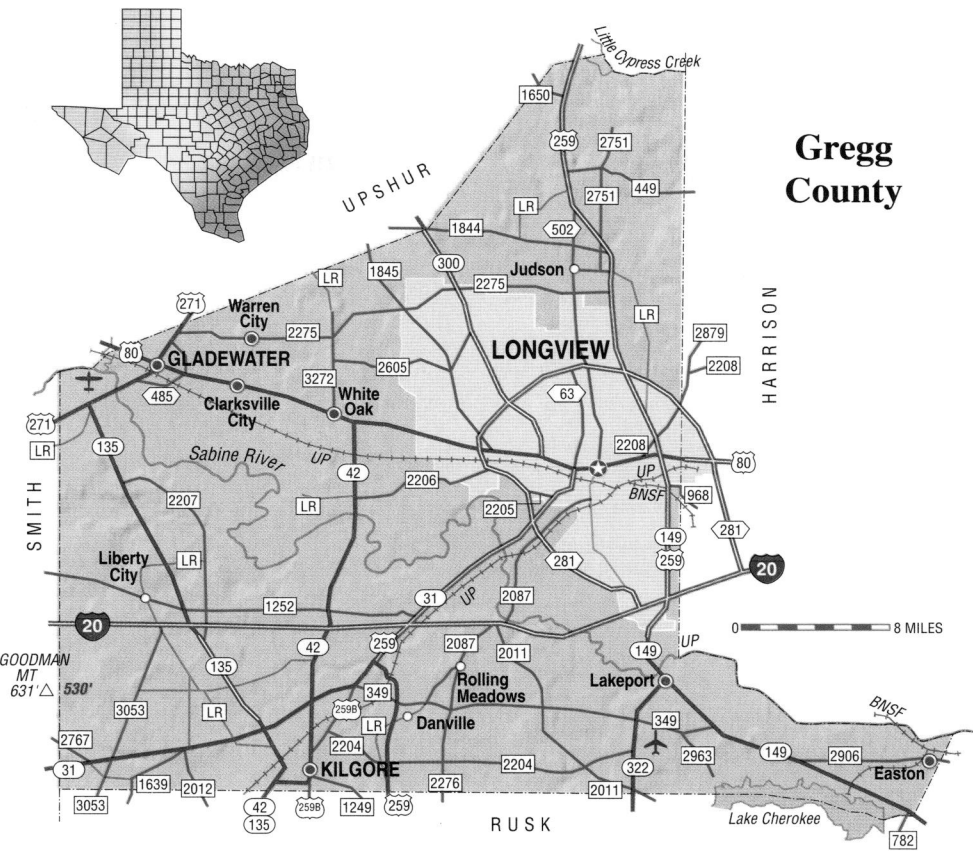

Gregg County

Physical Features: A populous, leading petroleum county, heart of the famed East Texas oil field; bisected by the Sabine River; hilly, timbered; with sandy, clay, alluvial soils.

Economy: Oil but with significant other manufacturing; tourism, conventions, agribusiness, and lignite coal production.

History: Caddoes; later Cherokees, who were driven out in 1838 by President Lamar. First land grants issued in 1835 by Republic of Mexico. County created and organized in 1873 from Rusk, Upshur counties; named for Confederate Gen. John Gregg. In U.S. censuses 1880-1910, blacks were more numerous than whites. Oil discovered in 1931.

Race/Ethnicity: (In percent) Anglo, 57.4; Black, 20.9; Hispanic, 19.0; Asian, 1.4; Other, 1.1; Two or more races, 2.0.

Vital Statistics, annual: Births, 1,858; deaths, 1,274; marriages, 1,192; divorces, 350.

Recreation: Water activities on Lake Cherokee, hunting, varied cultural events, East Texas Oil Museum in Kilgore.

Minerals: Leading oil-producing county with more than 3 billion barrels produced since 1931; also, sand, gravel and natural gas.

Agriculture: Cattle, horses, hay, nursery crops. Market value $3.6 million. Timber sales.

LONGVIEW (82,471, small part [1,870] in Harrison County) county seat; chemical manufacturing, oil industry, distribution and retail center; hospitals; LeTourneau University, University of Texas-Tyler Longview center; convention center; balloon race in July.

Kilgore (14,068, part [3,013] in Rusk County), oil, distribution center; Kilgore College, Rangerette museum; Shakespeare festival in summer.

Gladewater (6,794, part [2,447] in Upshur County) oil, manufacturing, tourism, antiques; library, airport, skydiving; Gusher Days in April; daffodils in February-March.

Other towns include: **Clarksville City** (910); **Easton** (636, partly in Rusk County); **Judson** (1,057); **Lakeport** (1,039); **Liberty City** (2,461) oil, tourism, government/services, Honor America Night in November.

Also, **Warren City** (357); **White Oak** (6,329) oil and gas, commuting to Longview, Tyler; park, Roughneck Days in spring every three years.

Population	123,707
Change fm 2010	1.6
Area (sq. mi.)	275.8
Land Area (sq. mi.)	273.3
Altitude (ft.)	240-530
Rainfall (in.)	48.09
Jan. mean min.	34.2
July mean max.	93.8
Civ. Labor	68,317
Unemployed	4.8
Wages	$844,803,032
Per Capita Income	$47,934
Prop. Value	$9,761,380,773
Retail Sales	$4,884,559,996

For explanation of sources, symbols and abbreviations, see p. 192, and foldout map.

Grimes County

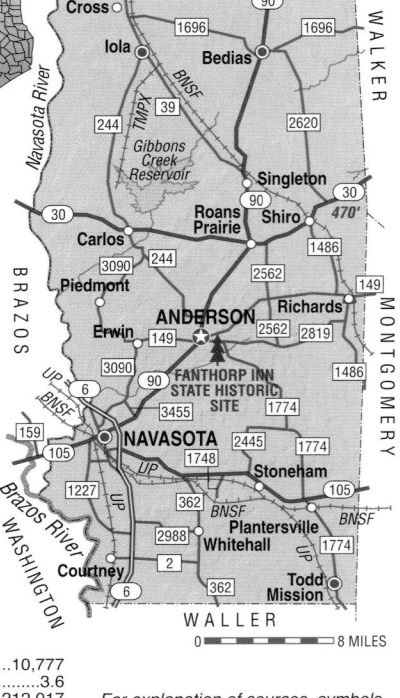

Physical Features: Rich bottom soils along Brazos, Navasota rivers; remainder hilly, partly forested; Gibbons Creek Reservoir.

Economy: Varied manufacturing, agribusiness, tourism.

History: Bidais (customs similar to the Caddoes) lived peacefully with Anglo-American settlers who arrived in 1820s, but tribe was removed to Indian Territory. Planter agriculture reflected in 1860 census, which listed 77 persons owning 20 or more slaves. County created from Montgomery County in 1846, organized the same year; named for Jesse Grimes, who signed Texas Declaration of Independence.

Race/Ethnicity: (In percent) Anglo, 58.3; Black, 15.8; Hispanic, 24.4; Asian, 0.4; Other, 1.1; Two or more races, 1.8.

Vital Statistics, annual: Births, 328; deaths, 279; marriages, 143; divorces, 52.

Recreation: Hunting, fishing; Gibbons Creek Reservoir; historic sites; fall Renaissance Festival at Plantersville.

Minerals: Lignite coal, natural gas.

Agriculture: Cattle, forage, horses, poultry; berries, pecans, honey sales significant. Market value $48.1 million. Some timber sold, Christmas tree farms.

ANDERSON (227) county seat; rural center; Fanthorp Inn historic site; Go-Texan weekend in February.

NAVASOTA (7,506) agribusiness center for parts of three counties; varied manufacturing; food, wood processing; hospital; prisons; La Salle statue; Blues Fest in August.

Other towns include: **Bedias** (445); **Iola** (417); **Plantersville** (260); **Richards** (300); **Roans Prairie** (64); **Shiro** (210); **Todd Mission** (111).

Population	**28,360**
Change fm 2010	6.7
Area (sq. mi.)	801.6
Land Area (sq. mi.)	787.5
Altitude (ft.)	150–470
Rainfall (in.)	43.51
Jan. mean min.	40.0
July mean max.	96.0

Civ. Labor	10,777
Unemployed	3.6
Wages	$87,212,017
Per Capita Income	$33,771
Prop. Value	$5,197,443,304
Retail Sales	$197,738,037

For explanation of sources, symbols and abbreviations, see p. 192, and foldout map.

Grain elevators along the railroad in Plainview, Hale County. Photo by Robert Plocheck.

Guadalupe County

Physical Features: South central county bisected by Guadalupe River, Lake Dunlap, Lake McQueeney; level to rolling surface; sandy, loam, blackland soils.

Economy: Varied manufacturing, commuting to San Antonio, agribusiness.

History: Karankawas, Comanches, and other tribes until the 1850s. The first Spanish land grant was in 1806 to José de la Baume. DeWitt colonists arrived in 1827. County created, organized, in 1846 from Bexar, Gonzales counties; named for the river.

Race/Ethnicity: (In percent) Anglo, 50.4; Black, 8.5; Hispanic, 38.0; Asian, 1.9; Other, 1.2; Two or more races, 2.7.

Vital Statistics, annual: Births, 1,838; deaths, 1,043; marriages, 582; divorces, 476.

Recreation: Fishing, hunting, river floating; Sebastopol House, other historic sites; river drive; Fiestas Juan Seguin in June, Diez y Seis in September in Seguin.

Minerals: Oil, gas, gravel, clays.

Agriculture: Cattle, corn, milo, wheat, cotton, hay, nursery crops, pecans. Market value $61.6 million.

SEGUIN (28,330) county seat; varied manufacturing/logistics, health care, government/services; hospital, museums, heritage village; Texas Lutheran University; Pecan Fest in late October.

Other towns include: **Cibolo** (28,207), **Geronimo** (1,140), **Kingsbury** (867), **Marion** (1,107), **McQueeney** (2,664), **New Berlin** (580), **Redwood** (4,902), **Santa C l a r a** (720), **Schertz** (38,084, parts in Bexar and Comal counties), **Staples** (278).

Also, part [10,154] of **New Braunfels**, part [1,377] of **Selma**, and a small part of **San Marcos**.

Population 163,694
Change fm 2010 .... 24.4
Area (sq. mi.) 714.8

Land Area (sq. mi.) 711.3
Altitude (ft.) 350–952
Rainfall (in.) 34.62
Jan. mean min. 40.5
July mean max. 95.2
Civ. Labor 78,961
Unemployed 3.1
Wages $457,705,467
Per Capita Income $43,019
Prop. Value $16,251,492,425
Retail Sales $1,679,030,184

Hale County

Physical Features: High Plains; fertile sandy, loam soils; playas; large underground water supply.

Economy: Agribusiness, food processing/ distribution, manufacturing, government/services.

History: Comanche hunters driven out by U.S. Army in 1875. Ranching began in 1880s. First motor-driven irrigation well drilled in 1911. County created from Bexar District in 1876; organized in 1888; named for Lt. J.C. Hale, who died at San Jacinto.

Race/Ethnicity: (In percent), Anglo, 33.9; Black, 5.7; Hispanic, 59.4; Asian, 0.6; Other, 1.8; Two or more races, 1.4.

Vital Statistics, annual: Births, 483; deaths, 322; marriages, 240; divorces, 53.

Recreation: Llano Estacado Museum; art gallery, antiques stores; pheasant hunting; Cowboy Days in September at Plainview.

Minerals: Some oil.

Agriculture: Cotton, fed beef, sorghum, dairies, corn, vegetables, wheat. Market value $409.9 million. Irrigation of 200,000 acres.

PLAINVIEW (21,276) county seat; agriculture, distribution, corn milling; Wayland Baptist University, South Plains College branch; hospital, library, mental health center; prisons.

Hale Center (2,112) trade center; farm museum, library, parks, murals, cacti gardens.

Abernathy (2,779, part [697] in Lubbock County) government/services, farm supplies, textile plant, gins.

Other towns include: **Cotton Center** (300), **Edmonson** (109), **Petersburg** (1,137), **Seth Ward** (1,965).

Population 33,830
Change fm 2010 .... – 6.6
Area (sq. mi.) 1,004.8
Land Area (sq. mi.) 1,004.7

Altitude (ft.) 3,180–3,620
Rainfall (in.) 20.45
Jan. mean min. 25.8
July mean max. 91.0
Civ. Labor 12,541
Unemployed 4.4
Wages $109,210,535
Per Capita Income $31,778
Prop. Value $2,802,576,208
Retail Sales $345,654,740

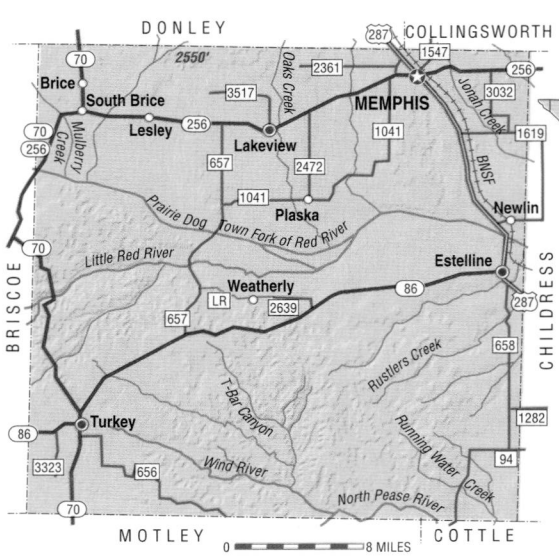

Hall County

Physical Features: Rolling to hilly, broken by Red River forks, tributaries; red and black sandy loam.

Economy: Agriculture, farm/ranch supplies.

History: Apaches displaced by Comanches, who were removed to Indian Territory in 1875. Ranching began in the 1880s. Farming expanded after 1910. County created in 1876 from Bexar, Young districts; organized in 1890; named for Republic of Texas secretary of war W.D.C. Hall.

Race/Ethnicity: (In percent) Anglo, 56.2; Black, 9.1; Hispanic, 34.1; Asian, 0.4; Other, 1.6; Two or more races, 1.6.

Vital Statistics, annual: Births, 22; deaths, 57; marriages, 0; divorces, 8.

Recreation: Hunting of deer, wild hog, dove; Rails to Trails system; Bob Wills museum; Memphis Picnic festival in September.

Minerals: None.

Agriculture: Cotton (lint and seed), beef cattle, hay, alfalfa, peanuts. Market value $24.8 million. Hunting leases important.

MEMPHIS (2,148) county seat; agriculture, foundry, trucking; historic buildings including Presbyterian church (1911); amphitheater built by WPA.

Other towns include: **Estelline** (138), motorcycle rally/chili cookoff in August, **Lakeview** (100), **Turkey** (383) Bob Wills Day in April.

Population **3,028**	July mean max. 95.7
Change fm 2010 .... – 9.7	Civ. Labor 1,063
Area (sq. mi.) 904.1	Unemployed 4.2
Land Area (sq. mi.) 883,5	Wages $5,586,227
Altitude (ft.) 1,750–2,550	Per Capita Income........ $30,033
Rainfall (in.) 22.59	Prop. Value $682,560,190
Jan. mean min. 26.0	Retail Sales $34,624,251

Hamilton County

Physical Features: Hilly north central county broken by scenic valleys; loam soils.

Economy: Varied manufacturing, agribusiness, hunting leases, tourism.

History: Waco and Tawakoni Indian area. Anglo-American settlers arrived in the mid-1850s. County created and organized in 1858, from Bosque, Comanche, Lampasas counties; named for South Carolina Gov. James Hamilton, who aided the Texas Revolution and Republic.

Race/Ethnicity: (In percent) Anglo, 84.6; Black, 1.0; Hispanic, 12.5; Asian, 0.8; Other, 1.9; Two or more races, 1.2.

Vital Statistics, annual: Births, 92; deaths, 154; marriages, 37; divorces, 40.

Recreation: Deer, quail, dove hunting; Linear Pecan Creek park in Hamilton; old Bulman (bowstring) bridge over Leon River; Hamilton dove festival in October.

Minerals: Natural gas.

Agriculture: Beef, milk, hay. Market value $55.8 million. Hunting leases important.

HAMILTON (3,182) county seat; manufacturing, agribusiness; hospital and medical clinics; museum, historical homes.

Hico (1,419) tourism, agriculture, varied manufacturing; antiques shops, Billy the Kid museum; steak cookoff in May.

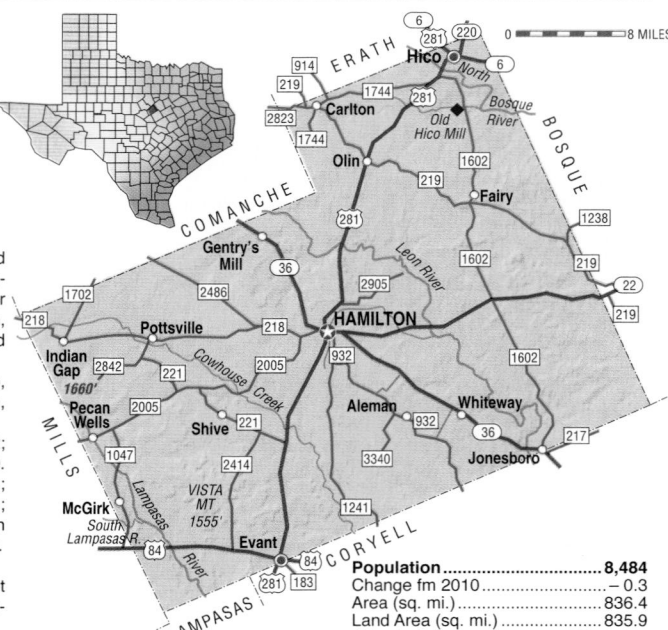

Other towns include: **Carlton** (75), **Evant** (388, partly in Coryell County), **Jonesboro** (125, partly in Coryell County); **Pottsville** (105).

For explanation of sources, symbols and abbreviations, see p. 192, and foldout map.

Population **8,484**	
Change fm 2010 .... – 0.3	
Area (sq. mi.) 836.4	
Land Area (sq. mi.) 835.9	
Altitude (ft.) 860–1,660	
Rainfall (in.) 35.28	
Jan. mean min. 30.8	
July mean max. 94.0	
Civ. Labor 3,530	
Unemployed 3.1	
Wages $22,654,439	
Per Capita Income................. $56,845	
Prop. Value $1,794,716,929	
Retail Sales $71,372,674	

Hansford County

Physical Features: High Plains, many playas, creeks, draws; sandy, loam, black soils; underground water; Palo Duro Reservoir.

Economy: Agribusinesses; oil, gas operations; wind energy.

History: Apaches in area, later pushed out by Comanches around 1700. The U.S. Army removed the Comanches to the Indian Territory in 1874-1875, and ranching began soon afterward. Farmers, including Norwegians, moved in around 1900. County created in 1876, from the Bexar, Young districts and organized in 1889; named for jurist J.M. Hansford.

Race/Ethnicity: (In percent) Anglo, 50.7; Black, 1.0; Hispanic, 47.4; Asian, 0.4; Other, 1.6; Two or more races, 1.1.

Vital Statistics, annual: Births, 75; deaths, 53; marriages, 36; divorces, 4.

Recreation: Stationmasters House Museum, hunting, lake activities, ecotourism, Lindbergh landing site.

Minerals: Production of gas, oil.

Agriculture: Large cattle-feeding operations; corn, wheat (first in acreage), sorghum; hogs. Substantial irrigation. Market value $783.2 million.

SPEARMAN (3,366) county seat; farming, cattle production, oil and gas, wind energy, biofuels; hospital, library, windmill collection; Heritage Days in May with rib cookoff.

Other towns include: **Gruver** (1,163) farm-ranch market, natural gas production, Fourth of July barbecue; **Morse** (133).

Population	**5,463**
Change fm 2010	– 2.7
Area (sq. mi.)	920.4
Land Area (sq. mi.)	919.8
Altitude (ft.)	2,750–3,378

Rainfall (in.)	21.19
Jan. mean min.	24.8
July mean max.	95.6
Civ. Labor	2,833
Unemployed	2.4
Wages	$27,054,863
Per Capita Income	$60,759
Prop. Value	$1,088,667,790
Retail Sales	$46,211,528

For explanation of sources, symbols and abbreviations, see p. 192, and foldout map.

Hall County Courthouse in Memphis. Photo by Robert Plocheck.

An old retail building now a museum at Medicine Mound, Hardeman County. Photo by Robert Plocheck.

Hardeman County

Physical Features: Rolling, broken area on divide between the Pease and Red rivers; Lake Pauline; sandy, loam soils.

Economy: Agriculture, gypsum production, oil and natural gas.

History: Apaches, later the semi-sedentary Wichitas and Comanche hunters. Ranching began in the late 1870s. Farming expanded after 1900. County created in 1858 from Fannin County; re-created in 1876, organized in 1884; named for pioneer brothers Bailey and T.J. Hardeman.

Race/Ethnicity: (In percent) Anglo, 68.8; Black, 5.7; Hispanic, 23.3; Asian, 0.6; Other, 1.2; Two or more races, 2.3.

Vital Statistics, annual: Births, 52; deaths, 49; marriages, 71; divorces, 11.

Recreation: State park; lake activities; Medicine Mound aborigine gathering site; Quanah Parker monument; hunting of deer, quail, wild hogs.

Minerals: Oil, natural gas, gypsum.

Agriculture: Wheat, cattle, cotton. Market value $25.4 million. Hunting leases.

QUANAH (2,482) county seat; manufacturing, farming, ranching, oil and gas; state hospital, general hospital; historical sites; Fall Festival in September.

Other towns include: **Chillicothe** (664) farm market center, hospital.

Population	3,922
Change fm 2010	– 5.2
Area (sq. mi.)	696.9
Land Area (sq. mi.)	695.1
Altitude (ft.)	1,250–1,850
Rainfall (in.)	26.85
Jan. mean min.	26.2
July mean max.	95.7
Civ. Labor	1,610

Unemployed	3.4
Wages	$10,645,072
Per Capita Income	$38,151
Prop. Value	$760,196,090
Retail Sales	$51,171,622

For explanation of sources, symbols and abbreviations, see p. 192, and foldout map.

Hardin County

Physical Features: Southeast county; timbered; many streams; sandy, loam soils; Big Thicket covers much of area.

Economy: Paper manufacturing, wood processing, minerals, food processing, oil and gas; county in Beaumont-Port Arthur-Orange metropolitan area.

History: Lorenzo de Zavala received first land grant in 1829. Anglo-American settlers arrived in 1830. County created and organized in 1858 from Jefferson, Liberty counties. Named for Texas Revolutionary leader William Hardin.

Race/Ethnicity: (In percent) Anglo, 86.6; Black, 5.6; Hispanic, 5.7; Asian, 0.7; Other, 0.6; Two or more races, 1.4.

Vital Statistics, annual: Births, 696; deaths, 536; marriages, 397; divorces, 236.

Recreation: Big Thicket with rare plant, animal life; national preserve; Red Cloud Water Park in Silsbee; hunting, fishing; state park; Cajun Country Music Festival in October in Kountze.

Minerals: Oil, gas, sand, gravel.

Agriculture: Beef cattle, hay, blueberries, bees and rice. Timber provides most income; more than 85 percent of county forested. Hunting leases.

KOUNTZE (2,197) county seat; government/services, retail center, commuting to Beaumont; library, museum.

SILSBEE (6,951) forest products, rail center, oil, gas; library, Ice House museum; Dulcimer Festival in fall.

LUMBERTON (12,836) construction, government/services, tourism; library; Village Creek Festival in October.

Other towns and places include: **Batson** (140); Pinewood Estates (1,704); **Rose Hill Acres** (434); **Saratoga** (1,000) Big Thicket Museum; **Sour Lake** (1,854) oil, lumbering; Old Timer's Day in September; **Thicket** (306); **Village Mills** (200); **Votaw** (160), and **Wildwood** (1,278).

Population	57,207
Change fm 2010	4.7
Area (sq. mi.)	897.6
Land Area (sq. mi.)	890.6
Altitude (ft.)	7–170
Rainfall (in.)	61.06
Jan. mean min.	37.5
July mean max.	93.6
Civ. Labor	24,666
Unemployed	5.0
Wages	$135,899,346
Per Capita Income	$44,456
Prop. Value	$3,974,558,601
Retail Sales	$854,728,217

The Big Thicket National Preserve. Photo by Larry Rana, U.S. Department of Agriculture.

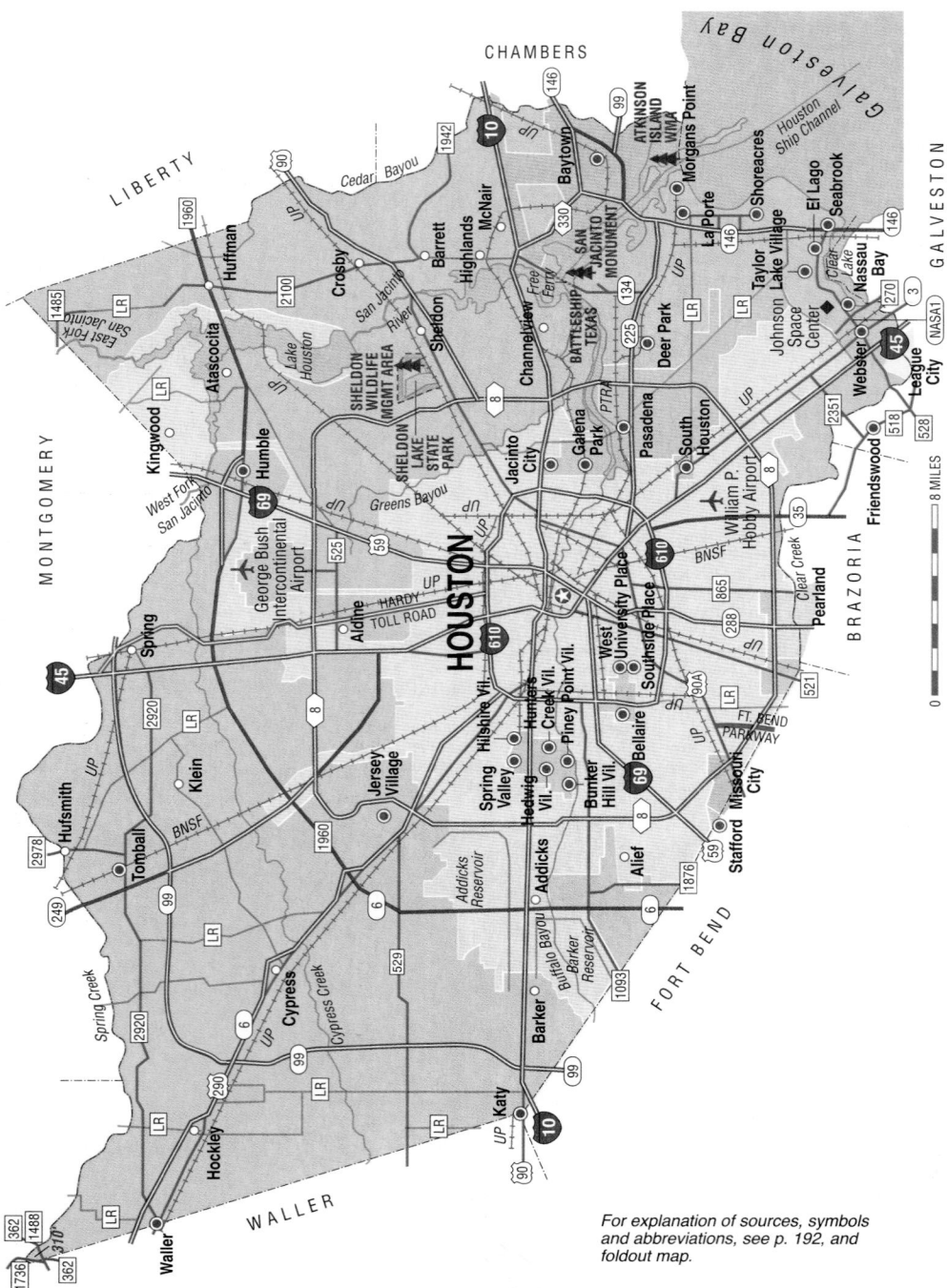

For explanation of sources, symbols
and abbreviations, see p. 192, and
foldout map.

Physical Features: Largest county in eastern half of state; level; typically coastal surface and soils; many bayous, canals for artificial drainage; Lake Houston, Sheldon Reservoir; partly forested.

Economy: Highly industrialized county with largest population; more than 92 foreign governments maintain offices in Houston; corporate management center; nation's largest concentration of petrochemical plants; largest U.S wheat-exporting port, among top U.S. ports in the value of foreign trade and total tonnage.

Petroleum refining, chemicals, food, fabricated metal products, non-electrical machinery, primary metals, scientific instruments; paper and allied products; printing and publishing; center for energy, space and medical research; center of international business.

History: Orcoquiza villages were visited by Spanish authorities in 1746. Pioneer settlers arrived by boat from Louisiana in 1822. Antebellum planters brought black slaves. Mexican migration increased after the Mexican Revolution. County created in 1836 and organized in 1837; named for John R. Harris, founder of Harrisburg (now part of Houston).

Race/Ethnicity: (In percent) Anglo, 29.7; Black, 19.7; Hispanic, 43.0; Asian, 7.3; Other, 1.2; Two or more races, 1.9.

Vital Statistics, annual: Births, 73,427; deaths, 25,342; marriages, 27,755; divorces, 11,902.

Recreation: Professional baseball, basketball, football, soccer; rodeo and livestock show; Jones Hall for the Performing Arts; Nina Vance Alley Theatre; Convention Center; Toyota Center, a 19,000-seat sports and entertainment center; Reliant Stadium and downtown ballpark.

Sam Houston Park, with restored early Houston homes, church, stores; Museum of Fine Arts, Contemporary Arts Museum, Rice Museum; Wortham Theater; Hobby Center for Performing Arts; museum of natural science, planetarium, zoo in Hermann Park.

San Jacinto Battleground, Battleship Texas; Johnson Space Center.

Fishing, boating, other freshwater and saltwater activities.

Minerals: Among leading oil, gas, petrochemical areas; production of petroleum, cement, natural gas, salt, lime, sulfur, sand and gravel, clays, stone.

Agriculture: Nursery crops, grass (third in acreage of sod), cattle, hay, horses, vegetables, Christmas trees (first in acreage), goats, rice, corn. Market value $65.2 million. Substantial income from forest products.

Education: Houston is a major center of higher education, with more than 300,000 students enrolled in 28

Harris County

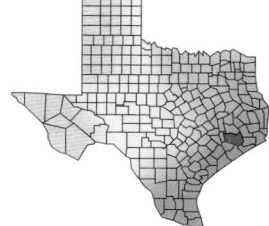

colleges and universities in the county. Among these are Rice University, the University of Houston, Texas Southern University, University of St. Thomas, Houston Baptist University.

Medical schools include Houston Baptist University School of Nursing, University of Texas Health Science Center, Baylor College of Medicine, Institute of Religion and Human Development, Texas Chiropractic College, Texas Woman's University-Houston Center.

HOUSTON (2,265,464, small parts in Fort Bend and Montgomery counties) county seat; largest Texas city; fourth-largest in nation.

A leading center for manufacture of petroleum equipment, agricultural chemicals, fertilizers, pesticides, oil and gas pipeline transmission; a leading scientific center; manufacture of machinery, fabricated metals; a major distribution, shipping center; engineering and research center; food processing; 85 hospitals.

Plants make apparel, lumber and wood products; furniture, paper, chemical, petroleum and coal products; publishing center; one of the nation's largest public school systems; prominent corporate center; Go Texan Days (rodeo) in February/March, international festival in March/April.

Pasadena (153,000) residential city with large industrial area manufacturing petrochemicals and other petroleum-related products; civic center; San Jacinto College, Texas Chiropractic College; hospitals; historical museum; Strawberry Festival in May.

Baytown (78,913, part [4,116] in Chambers County) refining, petrochemical center; commuters to Houston; Lee College; hospital, museum, library; historical homes; Chili When It's Chilly cookoff and the Great Bull Run in January.

The **Clear Lake Area** — which includes **El Lago** (2,583); **Nassau Bay**

(4,018); **Seabrook** (13,437); **Taylor Lake Village** (3,633); Webster (11,385) — tourism, Johnson Space Center, University of Houston-Clear Lake, commuting to Houston; Bayport Industrial Complex includes Port of Bayport; 12 major marinas; hospitals; Christmas lighted boat parade.

Other towns include: **Aldine** (17,177); **Atascocita** (75,566); **Barrett** (3,383); **Bellaire** (18,211) residential city with several major office buildings; **Bunker Hill Village** (3,796); **Channelview** (43,925) hospital; **Crosby** (2,753) government/services, chemical plant, Czech Fest in October; **Cypress** (120,000) ship-channel industries, Totally Texas celebration in April; **Galena Park** (11,092); **Hedwig Village** (2,731); **Highlands** (7,743) commuters, heritage museum, Jamboree in October; **Hilshire Village** (806); **Hockley** (400); **Huffman** (15,000); **Humble** (15,725) oil-field equipment manufactured, retail center, hospital; **Hunters Creek Village** (4,757); **Jacinto City** (10,634); **Jersey Village** (7,835).

Also, **Katy** (17,184, partly in Fort Bend and Waller counties) corporate headquarters, distribution center, hospitals; museums, park; Rice Harvest festival in October; **Klein** (45,000); **La Porte** (35,320) petrochemical industry; depot museum; Sylvan Beach Festival in April; Galveston Bay; **Morgan's Point** (362); **Piney Point Village** (3,386); **Sheldon** (2,076); **Shoreacres** (1,536); **South Houston** (17,656).

Also, **Southside Place** (1,800); **Spring** (60,802); **Spring Valley** (4,138); **Tomball** (11,470) health care, oil and gas, retail, hospital, museum, junior college, parks and nature preserve, German festival in March; **West University Place** (15,485).

Parts of **Friendswood, League City, Missouri City, Pearland, Stafford**, and **Waller**.

Addicks, Alief, and **Kingwood** are now within the city limits of Houston.

Population	4,698,619
Change fm 2010	14.8
Area (sq. mi.)	1,777.5
Land Area (sq. mi.)	1,703.5
Altitude (ft.)	sea level–310
Rainfall (in.)	56.81
Jan. mean min.	43.4
July mean max.	90.7
Civ. Labor	2,356,016
Unemployed	4.0
Wages	$37,997,626,697
Per Capita Income	$53,188
Prop. Value	$519,113,202,704
Retail Sales	$93,402,675,769

Harrison County

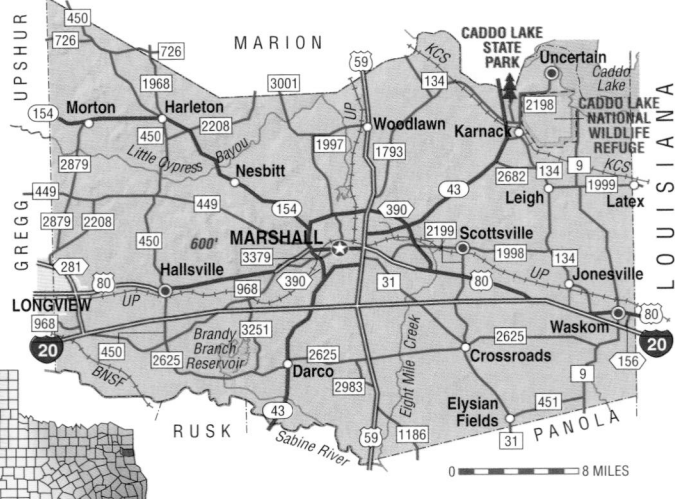

Physical Features: East Texas county; hilly, rolling; over half forested; Sabine River; Caddo Lake, Brandy Branch Reservoir.

Economy: Oil, gas processing, lumbering, pottery, other varied manufacturing.

History: Area was populated by agriculturist Caddo Indians whose numbers were reduced by disease. Anglo-Americans arrived in the 1830s. In 1850, the county had more slaves than any other in the state. County created in 1839 from Shelby County; organized in 1842. Named for eloquent advocate of the Texas Revolution, Jonas Harrison.

Race/Ethnicity: (In percent) Anglo, 63.3; Black, 21.2; Hispanic, 13.5; Asian, 0.8; Other, 1.3; Two or more races, 1.7.

Vital Statistics, annual: Births, 826; deaths, 677; marriages, 468; divorces, 115.

Recreation: Fishing, other water activities on Caddo and other lakes; hunting; plantation homes, historic sites; Stagecoach Days in May; Old Courthouse Museum; Old World Store; state park, performing arts; Fire Ant festival in October.

Minerals: Oil, gas, lignite coal, clays, sand and gravel.

Agriculture: Cattle, hay. Also, poultry, nursery plants, horses, vegetables, watermelons. Market value $19 million. Hunting leases important. Substantial timber industry.

MARSHALL (24,777) county seat; petroleum and lumber processing, varied manufacturing; civic center; historic sites, including Starr Family State Historic Site; hospital; Wiley College, East Texas Baptist University; Wonderland of Lights in December.

Other towns include: **Elysian Fields** (500); **Hallsville** (4,203) government/services, utilities, Western Days in October, museum; **Harleton** (390); **Jonesville** (70); **Karnack** (350); **Nesbitt** (270); **Scottsville** (393); **Uncertain** (105) tourism, fishing, hunting, Mayhaw Festival in May; **Waskom** (2,205) oil, gas, ranching, Armadillo Daze in April; **Woodlawn** (550).

Also, part [1,870] of **Longview**.

Population	66,726
Change fm 2010	1.6
Area (sq. mi.)	915.8
Land Area (sq. mi.)	900.0
Altitude (ft.)	168–600
Rainfall (in.)	50.18
Jan. mean min.	35.3
July mean max.	92.3
Civ. Labor	29,521
Unemployed	4.2
Wages	$286,605,202
Per Capita Income	$40,068
Prop. Value	$7,551,871,192
Retail Sales	$616,972,777

For explanation of sources, symbols and abbreviations, see p. 192, and foldout map.

Channing Methodist Church, Hartley County. Photo by Robert Plocheck.

Hartley County

Physical Features: Panhandle High Plains; drains to Canadian River tributaries, playas; sandy, loam, chocolate soils; lake.

Economy: Agriculture, dairies, gas production.

History: Apaches in area, pushed out by Comanches around 1700. The U.S. Army removed the Indians in 1875. Pastores (sheepmen) were in area until the 1880s when cattle ranching began. Farming expanded after 1900. County created in 1876 from the Bexar, Young districts; organized in 1891; named for Texas pioneers O.C. and R.K. Hartley.

Race/Ethnicity: (In percent) Anglo, 64.7; Black, 7.0; Hispanic, 26.8; Asian, 0.7; Other, 0.7; Two or more races, 1.1.

Vital Statistics, annual: Births, 54; deaths, 51; marriages, 1; divorces, 7.

Recreation: Lake Rita Blanca activities; ranch museum; XIT Rodeo and Reunion at Dalhart in August.

Minerals: Sand, gravel, natural gas.

Agriculture: Cattle, corn (second in acreage), wheat, hay, dairy cows, vegetables. 155,000 acres irrigated. Market value $1.18 billion. Hunting leases.

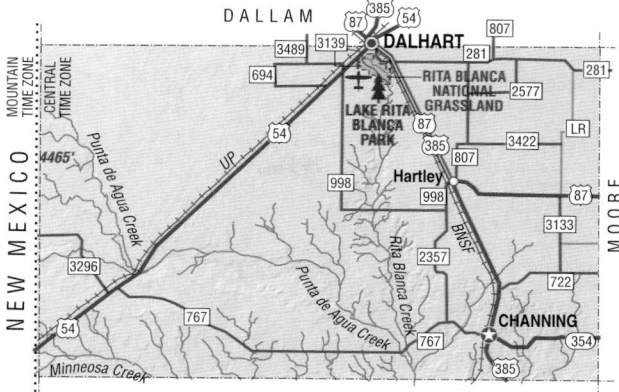

CHANNING (379) county seat; old XIT Ranch headquarters; Roundup in July.

DALHART (8,507, mostly in Dallam County), government/services; agribusiness center for parts of Texas, New Mexico, Oklahoma; railroad; cheese plant; grain operations; junior college branch; hospital; prison.

Also, **Hartley** (707).

Population	5,619
Change fm 2010	– 7.3
Area (sq. mi.)	1,463.2
Land Area (sq. mi.)	1,462.0
Altitude (ft.)	3,340–4,465
Rainfall (in.)	21.02
Jan. mean min.	21.4
July mean max.	91.6
Civ. Labor	2,870
Unemployed	1.8
Wages	$25,318,068
Per Capita Income	$62,274
Prop. Value	$1,318,177,531
Retail Sales	$53.753,443

Haskell County

Physical Features: Northwest county; rolling; broken areas; drained by Brazos tributaries; lake; sandy loam, gray, black soils.

Economy: Agribusiness, oil-field operations.

History: Apaches until 1700, then a Comanche area. Ranching began in the late 1870s after the Indians were removed. Farming expanded after 1900. County created in 1858, from Milam and Fannin counties; re-created in 1876 and organized in 1885; named for Goliad victim C.R. Haskell.

Race/Ethnicity: (In percent) Anglo, 64.1; Black, 4.5; Hispanic, 29.2; Asian, 0.9; Other, 1.1; Two or more races, 2.3.

Vital Statistics, annual: Births, 57; deaths, 62; marriages, 31; divorces, 21.

Recreation: Lake Stamford activities, bass tournament in August; Haskell arts & crafts show in November; hunting of deer, geese, wild hog.

Minerals: Oil and gas.

Agriculture: Wheat, cotton, peanuts; 28,000 acres irrigated. Beef cattle raised. Market value $38.7 million.

Population	5,813
Change fm 2010	– 1.5
Area (sq. mi.)	910.3
Land Area (sq. mi.)	903.1
Altitude (ft.)	1,340–1,795
Rainfall (in.)	26.40
Jan. mean min.	29.1
July mean max.	94.9
Civ. Labor	2,272
Unemployed	3.3
Wages	$13,971,731
Per Capita Income	$34,682
Prop. Value	$1,272,304,630
Retail Sales	$115,733,078

For explanation of sources, symbols and abbreviations, see p. 192, and foldout map.

HASKELL (3,217) county seat; farming center; hospital; city park; Wild Horse Prairie Days in June.

Other towns include: **O'Brien** (104), **Rochester** (314), **Rule** (618) farming, cotton gins/warehouses, oil, mural, park, Trunk or Treat in October, **Weinert** (167).

Hays County

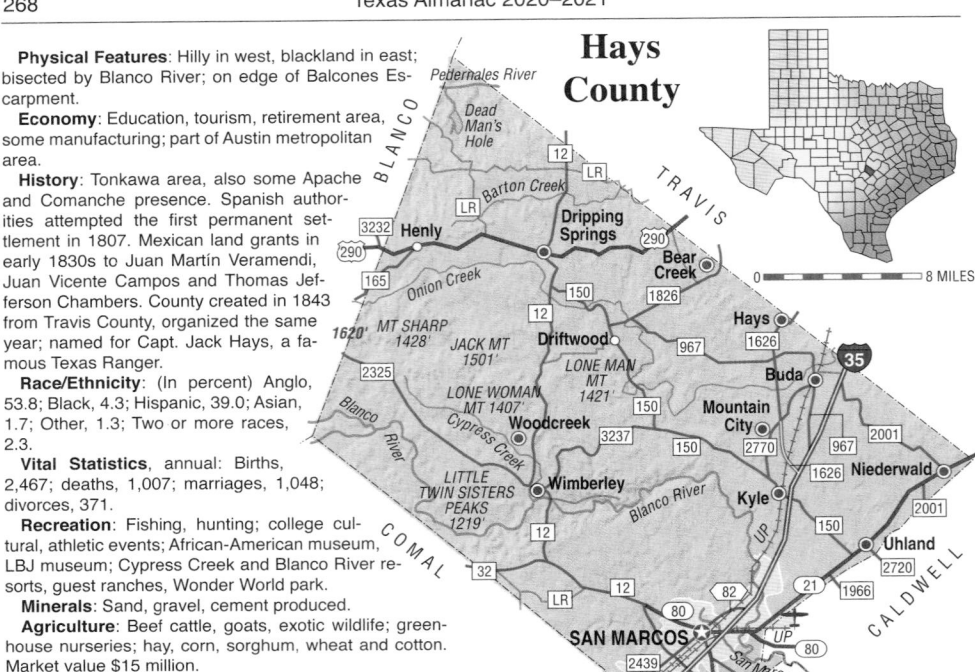

Physical Features: Hilly in west, blackland in east; bisected by Blanco River; on edge of Balcones Escarpment.

Economy: Education, tourism, retirement area, some manufacturing; part of Austin metropolitan area.

History: Tonkawa area, also some Apache and Comanche presence. Spanish authorities attempted the first permanent settlement in 1807. Mexican land grants in early 1830s to Juan Martín Veramendi, Juan Vicente Campos and Thomas Jefferson Chambers. County created in 1843 from Travis County, organized the same year; named for Capt. Jack Hays, a famous Texas Ranger.

Race/Ethnicity: (In percent) Anglo, 53.8; Black, 4.3; Hispanic, 39.0; Asian, 1.7; Other, 1.3; Two or more races, 2.3.

Vital Statistics, annual: Births, 2,467; deaths, 1,007; marriages, 1,048; divorces, 371.

Recreation: Fishing, hunting; college cultural, athletic events; African-American museum, LBJ museum; Cypress Creek and Blanco River resorts, guest ranches, Wonder World park.

Minerals: Sand, gravel, cement produced.

Agriculture: Beef cattle, goats, exotic wildlife; greenhouse nurseries; hay, corn, sorghum, wheat and cotton. Market value $15 million.

SAN MARCOS (61,480) county seat; Texas State University, outlet center, tourism, distribution center, commuting; hospital; San Marcos, Blanco rivers; jazz festival in February, Mermaid Fest in September.

Kyle (39,264) medical, education, retail center, Claiborne Kyle Log House, Katherine Anne Porter House, 5k Kyle-O-Meter in October.

Other towns include: **Bear Creek** (456); **Buda** (15,732) construction, manufacturing, retail, government/services, Stagecoach park, Weiner Dog races in April; **Driftwood** (168); **Dripping Springs** (3,348); **Hays** (251); **Mountain City** (752); **Niederwald** (625, partly in Caldwell County); **Uhland** (1,331, partly in Caldwell County); **Wimberley** (2,675) tourism, retirement community, artists, historic homes, museum, Blue Hole park/swimming, Jacob's Well spring/natural area, art festival in April; **Woodcreek** (1,688).

Population	222,631
Change fm 2010	41.7
Area (sq. mi.)	679.9
Land Area (sq. mi.)	678.0

For explanation of sources, symbols and abbreviations, see p. 192, and foldout map.

Altitude (ft.)	550–1,620
Rainfall (in.)	35.73
Jan. mean min.	38.7
July mean max.	94.3
Civ. Labor	113,249
Unemployed	2.9
Wages	$704,569,247
Av. Weekly Wage	$41,902
Prop. Value	$22,709,487,761
Retail Sales	$3,496,479,705

Tree-lined FM 2266 in the Canadian River Valley, Hemphill County. Photo by Robert Plocheck.

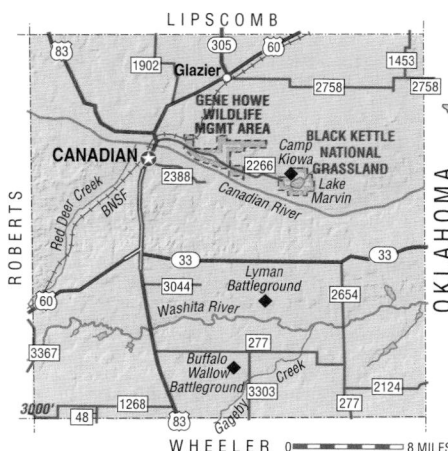

LIPSCOMB

83 · 1902 Glazier · 305 · 60 · 1453

2758 · 2758

GENE HOWE WILDLIFE MGMT AREA
Camp Kiowa · BLACK KETTLE NATIONAL GRASSLAND
CANADIAN · 2266 · Lake Marvin
2388 · Canadian River

Red Deer Creek · BNSF

ROBERTS

33 · Lyman Battleground · 33
3044 · 2654
60 · Washita River
3367
277
Buffalo Wallow Battleground · 3303 · Creek · 2124
3000' · 1268 · 83 · 277 · Gageby
48

WHEELER 0 ▬▬▬ 8 MILES

OKLAHOMA

Hemphill County

Physical Features: Sloping surface, broken by Canadian, Washita rivers; sandy, red, dark soils.

Economy: Oil, gas, agriculture, tourism, hunting, government/services.

History: Apaches who were in the area were later pushed out by Comanches and Kiowas. The tribes were removed to the Indian Territory in 1875. Ranching began in the late 1870s. Farmers began to arrive after 1900. County created from the Bexar and Young districts in 1876 and organized in 1887; named for Republic of Texas Justice John Hemphill.

Race/Ethnicity: (in percent) Anglo, 63.8; Black, 0.7; Hispanic, 33.2; Asian, 1.1; Other, 1.7; Two or more races, 1.2.

Vital Statistics, annual: Births, 76; deaths, 34; marriages, 43; divorces, 19.

Recreation: Lake Marvin; fall foliage tour; hunting, fishing; Indian Battleground, wildlife management area; museum; 4th of July rodeo; prairie chicken viewing in April.

Population	3,825
Change fm 2010	0.5
Area (sq. mi.)	912.2
Land Area (sq. mi.)	906.3
Altitude (ft.)	2,170–3,000
Rainfall (in.)	21.77
Jan. mean min.	21.2
July mean max.	93.2
Civ. Labor	2,359
Unemployed	1.9
Wages	$31,120,587
Per Capita Income	$52,632
Prop. Value	$1,836,805,740
Retail Sales	$31,122,669

Minerals: Oil, natural gas, caliche.

Agriculture: Cattle, wheat, horses, hay, alfalfa; some irrigation. Market value $110.6 million. Hunting, nature tourism.

CANADIAN (2,816) county seat; oil, gas production; hospital; art foundation.

KAUFMAN
Gun Barrel City · Seven Points · Mabank · PURTIS CREEK STATE PARK · VAN ZANDT
274 · 2613 · 316 · 1861 · 1861 · 19 · 773 · 2339 · 279
ELLIS · 85 · Aley · 85 · 334 · Eustace · 314 · 2010 · 315
274 · Cedar Creek Reservoir · 198 · 316 · 2709 · 1803 · Brownsboro · Chandler · 31
Tool · 2329 · Forest Grove Reservoir · 773 · UP · 3207
3225 · Payne Springs · 2752 · Murchison · 3079 · 315
Enchanted Oaks · 3054 · 1616 · 31 · 317 · 1803 · 607 · 317
Caney City · Log Cabin · 7 · 2495 · Lake Athens · Flat Creek · 314 · Lake Palestine
Star Harbor · 198 · 2892 · 804 · Moore Station · 155
ATHENS · TATER HILL · MT · 763'
Malakoff · 31 · 3062 · 2494 · 753 · New York · 607 · 315
Trinidad · 764 · 1667 · 753 · Shady Oaks · 60 · Larue · LR · Coffee City · 2215
3441 · 59 · 2970 · 1615 · 2588 · Poynor · 1305 · Berryville
Cross Roads · Coon Creek Lake · Carroll Springs · LR · 315 · 175 · 155
59 · 3273

Neches River
SMITH
CHEROKEE

ANDERSON 0 ▬▬▬ 8 MILES

Henderson County

Physical Features: East Texas county bounded by Neches and Trinity rivers; hilly, rolling; one-third forested; sandy, loam, clay soils; timber; Cedar Creek Reservoir, Lake Palestine, Lake Athens, Forest Grove Reservoir; Trinidad Lake.

NAVARRO
Trinity River
FREESTONE

Economy: Agribusiness, retail trade, varied manufacturing, minerals, recreation, tourism.

History: Caddo tribal area. Cherokees and other tribes migrated into the area in 1819-1820 ahead of white settlement. Cherokees were forced into Indian Territory in 1839. Anglo-American settlers arrived in the 1840s. County created in 1846 from Nacogdoches and Houston counties; organized the same year. County named for Gov. J. Pinckney Henderson.

Race/Ethnicity: (In percent) Anglo, 78.1; Black, 6.5; Hispanic, 12.9; Asian, 0.7; Other, 1.0; Two or more races, 1.9.

Vital Statistics, annual: Births, 897; deaths, 1,084; marriages, 457; divorces, 53.

Recreation: Cedar Creek Reservoir, Lake Palestine, other lakes; Purtis Creek State Park; hunting, fishing, bird-watching; aerial ropeslide at New York; East Texas Arboretum.

Minerals: Oil, gas, clays, lignite, sulfur, sand and gravel.

Agriculture: Beef cattle, forages, nurseries/horticulture, rodeo stock. Market value $49.5 million. Hunting leases and fishing. Timber important.

ATHENS (13,332) county seat; agribusiness center, varied manufacturing, tourism, state fish hatchery and museum, hospital, mental health center; Trinity Valley Community College; Texas Fiddlers' Contest in May.

Gun Barrel City (6,052) recreation, retirement, retail center.

Malakoff (2,361) brick factory, varied industry, tourism, library, Cornbread Festival in April.

Other towns include: **Berryville** (1,021); **Brownsboro** (1,089); **Caney City** (220); **Chandler** (3,083) commuting to Tyler, retail trade, tourism, Pow Wow Festival in October; **Coffee City** (1,492); **Enchanted Oaks** (332); **Eustace** (969); **Larue** (250); **Log Cabin** (690); **Moore Station** (194); **Murchison** (580); **Payne Springs** (785); **Poynor** (297); **Seven Points** (1,457) agribusiness, retail trade, recreation, Monte Carlo celebration in November; **Star Harbor** (458); **Tool** (2,309), and **Trinidad** (858).

Also, **Mabank** (3,423, mostly in Kaufman County).

Population	82,299
Change fm 2010	4.8
Area (sq. mi.)	949.3
Land Area (sq. mi.)	873.8
Altitude (ft.)	256–763
Rainfall (in.)	42.94
Jan. mean min.	34.5
July mean max.	92.6
Civ. Labor	36,731
Unemployed	3.6
Wages	$159,438,979
Per Capita Income	$38,216
Prop. Value	$7,299,795,172
Retail Sales	$799,444,730

Physical Features: Rich alluvial soils along Rio Grande; sandy, loam soils in north; semitropical vegetation; Anzalduas Channel Dam, Delta Lake, Valley Acres Reservoir.

Economy: Food processing and shipping, other agribusinesses, tourism, mineral operations; Texas' fifth-largest metro area.

History: Coahuiltecan and Karankawa area. Comanches forced Apaches southward into valley in the 1700s; Comanches arrived in valley in the 1800s. Spanish settlement occurred 1750-1800. County created in 1852 from Cameron and Starr counties, organized the same year; named for leader of Mexico's independence movement of 1810, Father Miguel Hidalgo y Costillo.

Race/Ethnicity: (In percent) Anglo, 6.2; Black, 0.8; Hispanic, 92.2; Asian, 1.1; Other, 0.5; Two or more races, 0.5.

Vital Statistics, annual: Births, 16,325; deaths, 4,179; marriages, 4,605; divorces, 0.

Recreation: Winter resort, retirement area; fishing, hunting; gateway to Mexico; historical sites; Bentsen-Rio Grande Valley State Park; museums; All-Valley Winter Vegetable Show at Pharr.

Minerals: Oil, gas, stone, sand and gravel.

Agriculture: Ninety percent of farm cash receipts from crops (ranked first in state), principally from sugar cane (first in acreage), grain sorghum (first in acreage), vegetables (first in acreage), citrus, cotton; livestock includes cattle; 184,000 acres irrigated. Market value $452.8 million.

EDINBURG (90,062) county seat; vegetable processing and packing, petroleum operations, tourism, clothing; planetarium; the University of Texas-Rio Grande Valley;

For explanation of sources, symbols and abbreviations, see p. 192, and foldout map.

Hidalgo County

Population **865,939**
Change fm 2010 .... 11.8
Area (sq. mi.) 1,582.9
Land Area (sq. mi.) 1,570.9
Altitude (ft.) 28–376
Rainfall (in.) 22.20
Jan. mean min. 49.3
July mean max. 96.2
Civ. Labor 351,108
Unemployed 6.7
Wages $2,193,068,492
Per Capita Income $25,617
Prop. Value $39,872,298,134
Retail Sales $9,606,080,935

hospitals; behavioral, health center; museum; Texas Cook'em High Steaks July 4 weekend, Fiesta Edinburg in February.

McALLEN (144,464) retail center, medical care/hospitals, government/services; community college; birding center, Mxlan arts/music celebration of Mexican culture in late July.

Mission (84,065) citrus groves, agricultural processing/distribution; hospital; community college; international butterfly park; Citrus Fiesta in January.

Pharr (78,815) agriculture, trading center; trucking; tourism; old clock, juke box museums; folklife festival in February.

Other towns include: **Abram** (2,337); **Alamo** (19,997) live steam museum; **Alton** (15,878); **Doffing** (5,730); **Donna** (17,427) citrus center, varied manufacturing; **Edcouch** (3,358); **Elsa** (6,871); **Granjeno** (298); **Hargill** (913); **Hidalgo** (13,334) trade zone, shipping, winter resort, agribusiness, historical sites, library, Borderfest in March; **La Blanca** (2,597); **La Homa** (11,801); **La Joya** (4,321); **La Villa** (2,425); **Los Ebanos** (362).

Also, **Mercedes** (16,130) "boot capital," citrus, and vegetable center, food processing, tourism, recreation vehicle show in January, Hispanic Fest July 4; **Mila Doce** (7,032); **Monte Alto** (2,121); **North Alamo** (3,847); **Nurillo** (8,874); **Palmhurst** (2,740); **Palmview** (6,845); **Palmview South** (5,999); **Peñitas** (4,946); **Perezville** (5,961); **Progreso** (6,177); **Progreso Lakes** (229); **San Carlos** (3,457); **San Juan** (37,042) retirement area, trucking, Shrine of Our Lady of San Juan, Spring Fiesta in February; **San Manuel-Linn** (787); **South Alamo** (3,879); **Sullivan City** (4,194); **Weslaco** (40,225) agriculture, nature tourism, South Texas College, hospital, Dragonfly Days in May.

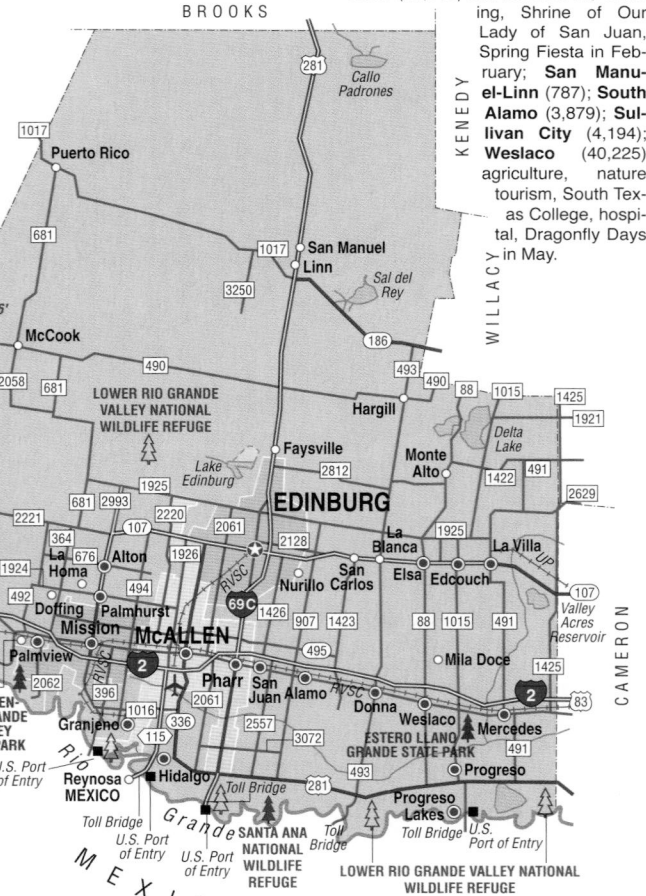

Hill County

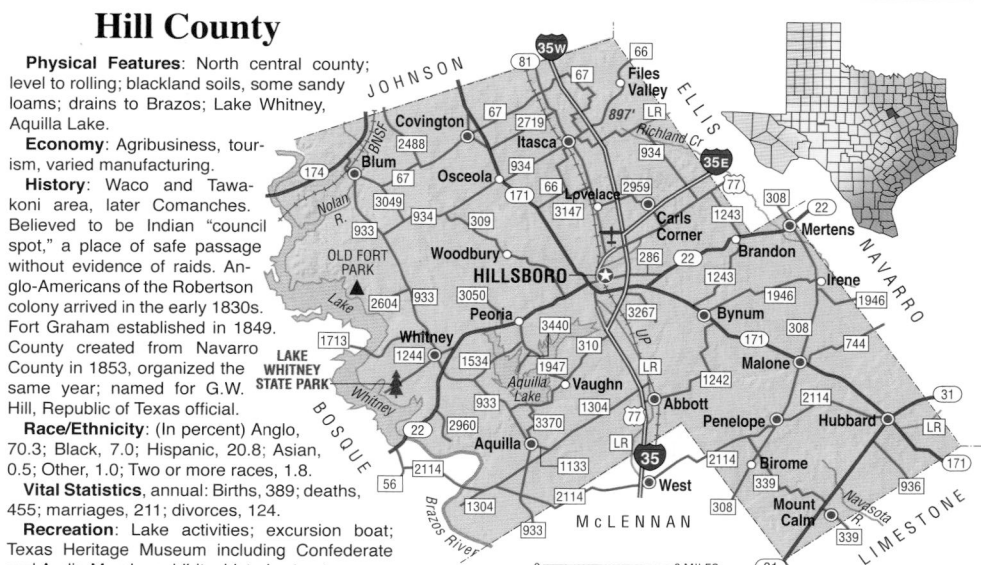

Physical Features: North central county; level to rolling; blackland soils, some sandy loams; drains to Brazos; Lake Whitney, Aquilla Lake.

Economy: Agribusiness, tourism, varied manufacturing.

History: Waco and Tawakoni area, later Comanches. Believed to be Indian "council spot," a place of safe passage without evidence of raids. Anglo-Americans of the Robertson colony arrived in the early 1830s. Fort Graham established in 1849. County created from Navarro County in 1853, organized the same year; named for G.W. Hill, Republic of Texas official.

Race/Ethnicity: (In percent) Anglo, 70.3; Black, 7.0; Hispanic, 20.8; Asian, 0.5; Other, 1.0; Two or more races, 1.8.

Vital Statistics, annual: Births, 389; deaths, 455; marriages, 211; divorces, 124.

Recreation: Lake activities; excursion boat; Texas Heritage Museum including Confederate and Audie Murphy exhibits, historic structures, rebuilt frontier fort barracks; motorcycle track.

Minerals: Gas, limestone.

Agriculture: Corn, cattle, sorghum, wheat, cotton, dairies, turkeys. Market value $119.9 million. Some firewood marketed.

HILLSBORO (8,456) county seat; agribusiness, varied manufacturing, retail, outlet center, tourism, antiques malls; Hill College; hospital; Cell Block museum, restored courthouse; Cotton Pickin Fair in September.

Whitney (2,162) manufacturing, stone works, government/services;

hospital; museum; Pioneer Days in October.

Other towns include: **Abbott** (366); **Aquilla** (106); **Blum** (452); Brandon (75); **Bynum** (200); **Carl's Corner** (171); **Covington** (276); **Hubbard** (1,404) agriculture, machine shop, antiques, museum, library, Magnolias & Mistletoe Victorian Christmas celebration; **Irene** (170); **Itasca** (1,689); **Malone** (274); **Mertens** (131); **Mount Calm** (317); **Penelope** (201).

Population	**36,354**
Change fm 2010	3.6
Area (sq. mi.)	985.7
Land Area (sq. mi.)	958.9
Altitude (ft.)	417–897
Rainfall (in.)	37.93
Jan. mean min.	34.8
July mean max.	95.0
Civ. Labor	16,435
Unemployed	3.4
Wages	$99,333,013
Per Capita Income	$37,502
Prop. Value	$3,718,379,468
Retail Sales	$412,148,124

Plant nursery at Bentsen-Rio Grande Valley State Park. Photo by Robert Plocheck.

Hockley County

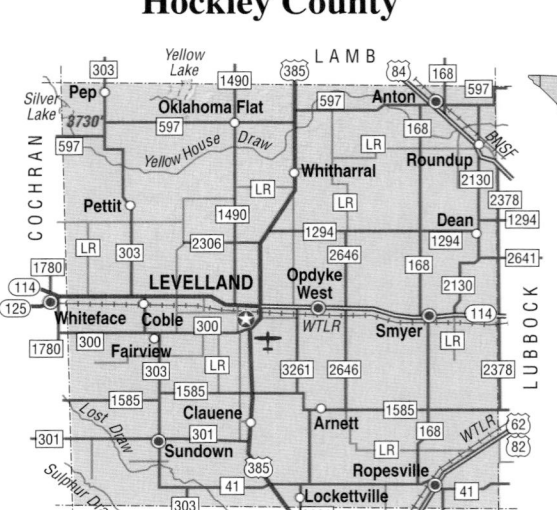

Physical Features: South Plains, numerous playas, drains to Yellow House Draw; loam, sandy loam soils.

Economy: Extensive oil, gas production and services; manufacturing; varied agribusiness.

History: Comanches displaced Apaches in the early 1700s. Large ranches of 1880s brought few residents. Homesteaders arrived after 1900. County created in 1876 from Bexar, Young districts; organized in 1921. Named for the Republic of Texas secretary of war Gen. G.W. Hockley.

Race/Ethnicity (in percent): Anglo, 46.6; Black, 4.1; Hispanic, 48.1; Asian, 0.6; Other, 1.4; Two or more races, 1.4.

Vital Statistics, annual: Births, 335; deaths, 224; marriages, 154; divorces, 70.

Recreation: Early Settlers' Day in July; Marigolds Arts, Crafts Festival in November.

Minerals: Oil, gas, stone; one of leading oil counties with more than 1 billion barrels produced.

Agriculture: Cotton, grain sorghum; cattle, hogs raised; substantial irrigation. Market value $78.7 million.

Population	22,980
Change fm 2010	0.2
Area (sq. mi.)	908.6
Land Area (sq. mi.)	908.4
Altitude (ft.)	3,300–3,730
Rainfall (in.)	19.84
Jan. mean min.	26.1
July mean max.	91.6
Civ. Labor	11,705
Unemployed	2.9
Wages	$128,705,908
Per Capita Income	$37,199
Prop. Value	$2,747,559,659
Retail Sales	$207,560,661

LEVELLAND (13,957) county seat; oil, cotton, cattle center; government/services; hospital; South Plains College; Hot Burrito & Bluegrass Music Festival in July.

Other towns include: **Anton** (1,127); **Opdyke West** (177); **Pep** (30); **Ropesville** (436); **Smyer** (483); **Sundown** (1,395); **Whitharral** (158).

Hood County

Physical Features: Hilly; broken by Paluxy, Brazos rivers; sandy loam soils; Lake Granbury, Squaw Creek Reservoir.

Economy: Tourism, commuting to Fort Worth and Dallas, nuclear power plant, agriculture.

History: Lipan Apache and Comanche area. Anglo-American settlers arrived in the late 1840s. County created in 1866 from Johnson and Erath counties, organized the same year; named for Confederate Gen. John B. Hood.

Race/Ethnicity: (In percent) Anglo, 83.9; Black, 0.9; Hispanic, 12.7; Asian, 0.9; Other, 1.1; Two or more races, 1.4.

Vital Statistics, annual: Births, 676; deaths, 751; marriages, 416; divorces, 184.

Recreation: Lakes, fishing, scenic areas; summer theater; Gen. Granbury's Bean & Rib cookoff in March; Acton historic site; hike & bike trail.

Minerals: Oil, gas, stone.

Agriculture: Hay, turfgrass, beef cattle, nursery crops, pecans, peaches; some irrigation. Market value $18.7 million.

GRANBURY (9,679) county seat; retail, tourism, medical services; historic downtown area, opera house,

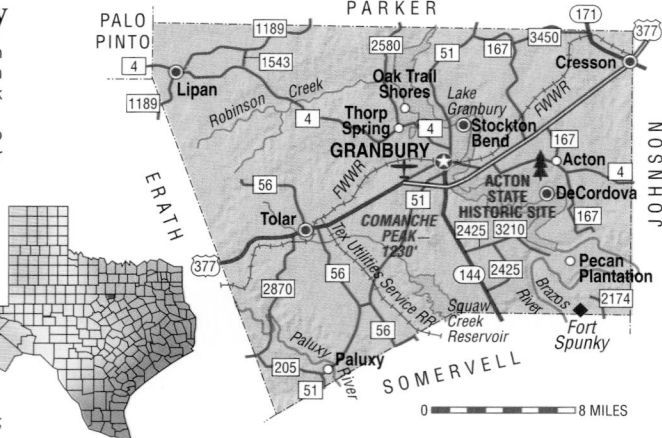

museums; hospital, library, college extensions; Harvest Moon festival in October.

Other towns include: **Acton** (1,129) grave of Elizabeth Crockett, wife of Davy; **Cresson** (789); **DeCordova** (3,130); **Lipan** (461); **Oak Trail Shores** (3,167); **Pecan Plantation** (5,465); **Stockton Bend** (330); **Tolar** (842).

Population	60,537
Change fm 2010	18.3
Area (sq. mi.)	436.8
Land Area (sq. mi.)	420.6
Altitude (ft.)	600–1,230
Rainfall (in.)	35.08
Jan. mean min.	30.1
July mean max.	95.1
Civ. Labor	26,529
Unemployed	3.4
Wages	$173,934,760
Per Capita Income	$47,368
Prop. Value	$7,486,351,730
Retail Sales	$924,736,604

For explanation of sources, symbols and abbreviations, see p. 192, and foldout map.

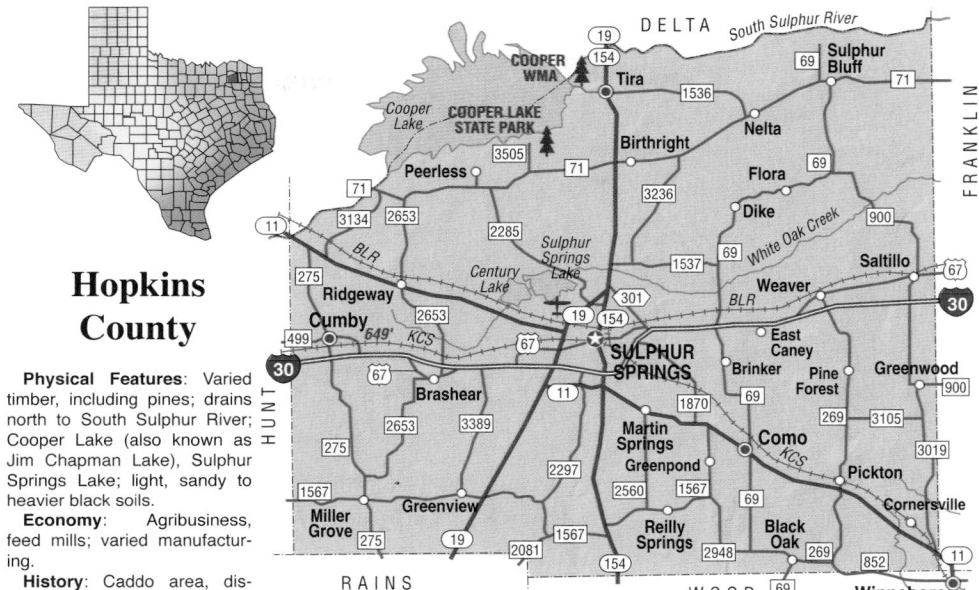

Hopkins County

Physical Features: Varied timber, including pines; drains north to South Sulphur River; Cooper Lake (also known as Jim Chapman Lake), Sulphur Springs Lake; light, sandy to heavier black soils.

Economy: Agribusiness, feed mills; varied manufacturing.

History: Caddo area, displaced by Cherokees, who in turn were forced out by President Lamar in 1839. First Anglo-American settlement in 1837. County created in 1846 from Lamar and Nacogdoches counties, organized the same year; named for pioneer Hopkins family.

Race/Ethnicity: (In percent) Anglo, 73.3; Black, 7.4; Hispanic, 16.9; Asian, 0.7; Other, 1.0; Two or more races, 2.1.

Vital Statistics, annual: Births, 444; deaths, 398; marriages, 264; divorces, 163.

Recreation: Fishing, hunting; state park, lake activities; dairy museum; dairy festival in June; stew contest in September.

Minerals: Lignite coal.

Agriculture: Dairies, beef cattle, hay (first in acreage). Market value $205.9 million. Firewood and hardwood lumber marketed.

SULPHUR SPRINGS (16,208) county seat; dairy farming, equine center, food processing and distribution, varied manufacturing, tourism; hospital; library, heritage park, music box gallery, civic center.

Other towns include: **Brashear** (280), **Como** (736), **Cumby** (796), **Dike** (170), **Pickton** (300), **Saltillo** (200), **Sulphur Bluff** (280), **Tira** (299).

Population	36,810
Change fm 2010	4.7
Area (sq. mi.)	792.8
Land Area (sq. mi.)	767.2
Altitude (ft.)	340–649
Rainfall (in.)	47.18
Jan. mean min.	32.9
July mean max.	93,1
Civ. Labor	17,123
Unemployed	3.2
Wages	$122,102,007
Per Capita Income	$37,868
Prop. Value	$2,939,315,363
Retail Sales	$587,146,040

For explanation of sources, symbols and abbreviations, see p. 192, and foldout map.

A pier at Cooper Lake State Park. Photo by Robert Plocheck.

Houston County

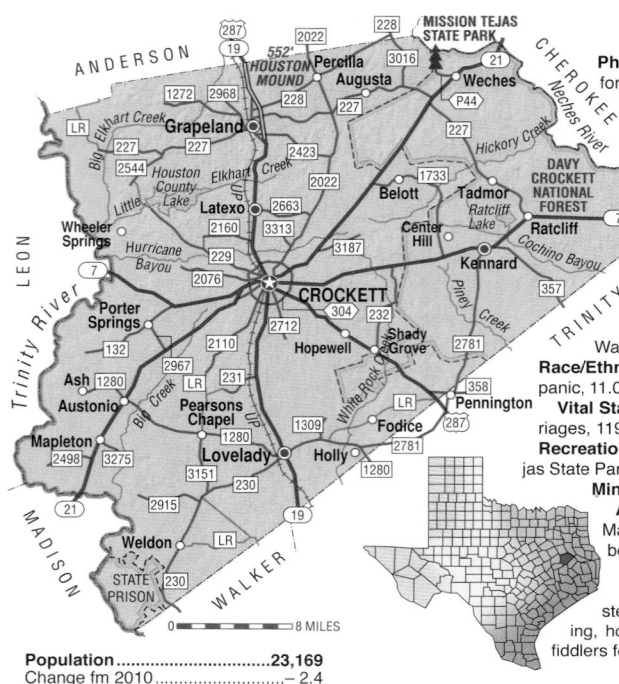

Physical Features: East Texas county over half forested; rolling terrain, draining to Neches, Trinity rivers; timber production.

Economy: Livestock, timber, government/services, manufacturing, tourism.

History: Caddo group attracted mission San Francisco de los Tejas in 1690. Spanish town of Bucareli established in 1774. Both lasted only a few years. Anglo-American settlers arrived in the 1820s. County created in 1837 from Nacogdoches County by Republic, organized the same year; named for Sam Houston. Cotton plantations before the Civil War had many slaves.

Race/Ethnicity: (In percent) Anglo, 61.8; Black, 25.7; Hispanic, 11.0; Asian, 0.7; Other, 0.7; Two or more races, 1.3.

Vital Statistics, annual: Births, 231; deaths, 268; marriages, 119; divorces, 57.

Recreation: Fishing, hunting; national forest; Mission Tejas State Park; 75 historical markers; Houston County Lake.

Minerals: Oil, gas, gravel.

Agriculture: Cattle, hay, watermelons, cotton. Market value $49.6 million. Hunting leases. Timber principal income source.

CROCKETT (6,789), county seat; timber, steel and plastic products, clothing manufacturing, hospital; historic sites; Black Expo in February; fiddlers festival in June.

Population	23,169
Change fm 2010	– 2.4
Area (sq. mi.)	1,236.6
Land Area (sq. mi.)	1,230.9
Altitude (ft.)	150–552
Rainfall (in.)	45.18
Jan. mean min.	36.8
July mean max.	93.4

Civ. Labor	10,377
Unemployed	3.2
Wages	$80,174,092
Per Capita Income	$36,552
Prop. Value	$2,893,197,240
Retail Sales	$171,969,579

Other towns include: **Grapeland** (1,490) steel, agribusiness, oil and gas, Peanut Festival in October; **Kennard** (327); **Latexo** (319); **Lovelady** (640) Lovefest in February; **Ratcliff** (106).

Howard County

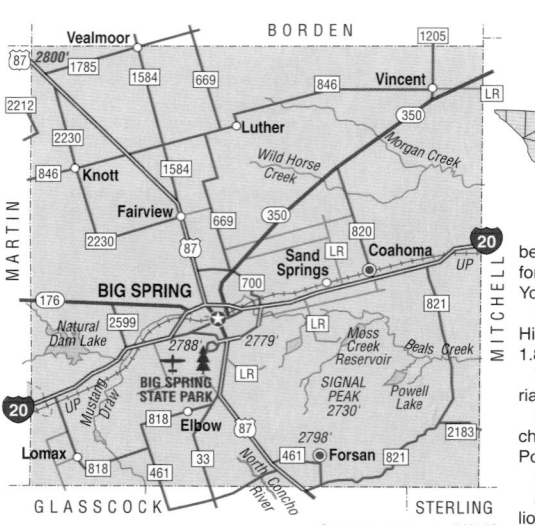

Physical Features: On edge of Llano Estacado; sandy loam soils; Natural Dam Lake.

Economy: Agriculture, petrochemicals, government/services.

History: Pawnee and Comanche area. Anglo-American settlement began in 1870. Oil boom in the mid-1920s. County named for V.E. Howard, legislator; created in 1876 from Bexar, Young districts; organized in 1882.

Race/Ethnicity: (In percent) Anglo, 48.6; Black, 7.3; Hispanic, 42.4; Asian, 1.2; Other, 1.8; Two or more races, 1.8.

Vital Statistics, annual: Births, 484; deaths, 416; marriages, 234; divorces, 18.

Recreation: Lakes, state park; campground in Comanche Trail Park, Native Plant Trail, museum, historical sites, Pow Wow in April, Pops in the Park in July.

Minerals: Oil, gas, sand, gravel, and stone.

Agriculture: Cotton, beef, hay. Market value $13.9 million.

BIG SPRING (28,057) county seat; agriculture, petrochemicals, varied manufacturing; hospitals including a state institution and Veterans Administration hospital; federal prison; Howard College; railroad plaza.

Population	36,459
Change fm 2010	4.1
Area (sq. mi.)	904.2
Land Area (sq. mi.)	900.8
Altitude (ft.)	2,180–2,800
Rainfall (in.)	19.50
Jan. mean min.	31.3
July mean max.	94.6
Civ. Labor	13,412

Unemployed	3.0
Wages	$161,884,399
Per Capita Income	$36,367
Prop. Value	$3,640,115,349
Retail Sales	$580,229,177

Other towns include: **Coahoma** (838), **Forsan** (207), **Knott** (200), and **Sand Springs** (836).

The Salt Basin and the Guadalupe Mountains. Photo by Robert Plocheck.

Hudspeth County

Physical Features: Plateau, basin terrain, draining to salt lakes; Rio Grande; mostly rocky, alkaline, clay soils and sandy loam soils, except alluvial along Rio Grande; desert, mountain vegetation. Fertile agricultural valley.

Economy: Agribusiness, mining, tourism, hunting leases.

History: Mescalero Apache area. Fort Quitman established in 1858 to protect routes to west. Railroad in 1881 brought Anglo-American settlers. Political turmoil in Mexico (1912–1929) brought more settlers from Mexico. County named for Texas political leader Claude B. Hudspeth; created in 1917 from El Paso County, organized the same year.

Race/Ethnicity: (In percent) Anglo, 17.6; Black, 2.8; Hispanic, 77.8; Asian, 1.6; Other, 2.1; Two or more races, 1.9.

Vital Statistics, annual: Births, 45; deaths, 12; marriages, 0; divorces, 0.

Recreation: Scenic drives; fort sites; hot springs; salt basin; white sands; hunting; birding; part of Guadalupe Mountains National Park, containing unique plant life, canyons.

Minerals: Talc, stone, gypsum.

Agriculture: Most income from cotton, vegetables, hay, alfalfa; beef cattle raised; 18,000 acres irrigated. Market value $34.5 million.

SIERRA BLANCA (570) county seat; ranching center, tourist stop on interstate highway; adobe courthouse; 4th of July fair, livestock show in January.

Other towns include: **Dell City** (468) agriculture, government/services, telephone co-op; some of largest water wells in state, Dell Valley Hudspeth fair in September, and **Fort Hancock** (1,853).

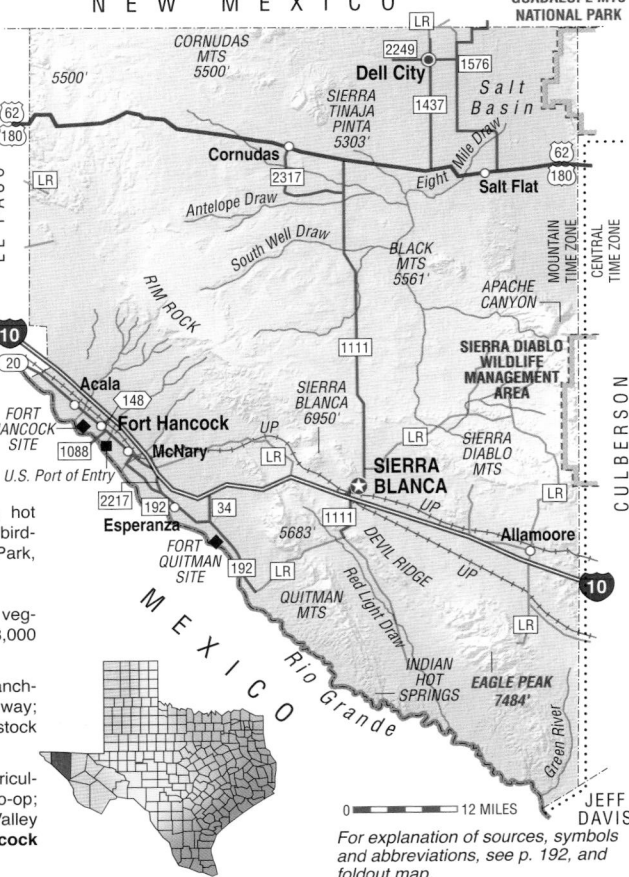

For explanation of sources, symbols and abbreviations, see p. 192, and foldout map.

Population		4,795
Change fm 2010		37.9
Area (sq. mi.)		4,571.8
Land Area (sq. mi.)		4,571.0
Altitude (ft.)		3,117–7,484

Rainfall (in.)		11.24
Jan. mean min.		25.7
July mean max.		92.5
Civ. Labor		1,509
Unemployed		4.5

Wages		$18,547,194
Per Capita Income		$33,241
Prop. Value		$806,013,886
Retail Sales		$8,607,337

Hunt County

Physical Features: Level to rolling surface; Sabine, Sulphur rivers; Lake Tawakoni, Greenville City Lakes; mostly heavy Blackland soil, some loam, sandy loams.

Economy: Education, varied manufacturing, agribusiness; several Fortune 500 companies in county; many residents employed in Dallas area.

History: Caddo Indians gone by 1790s. Kiowa bands in the area when Anglo-American settlers arrived in 1839. County named for Memucan Hunt, Republic secretary of navy; created in 1846 from Fannin, Nacogdoches counties, organized the same year.

Race/Ethnicity: (In percent) Anglo, 71.7; Black, 8.3; Hispanic, 16.4; Asian, 1.5; Other, 1.4; Two or more races, 2.1.

Vital Statistics, annual: Births, 1,097; deaths, 958; marriages, 531; divorces, 296.

Recreation: Lake Tawakoni sports, catfish tournament in August; Texas A&M University–Commerce events.

Minerals: Sand and white rock, gas, oil.

Agriculture: Cattle, forage, greenhouse crops, top revenue sources; horses, wheat, oats, cotton, grain sorghum. Market value $69.3 million. Some firewood sold.

GREENVILLE (27,492) county seat; varied manufacturing, retail trade, health and government services, commuters to Dallas; hospital; branch of Paris Junior College; cotton museum, Audie Murphy exhibit; fiddle festival in October.

Commerce (8,899) Texas A&M University–Commerce, government/services, varied manufacturing; emergency medical center; planetarium, children's museum; Bois d'Arc Bash in September.

Population	96493
Change fm 2010	12.0
Area (sq. mi.)	882.0
Land Area (sq. mi.)	840.3
Altitude (ft.)	437–730
Rainfall (in.)	44.65
Jan. mean min.	32.7
July mean max.	96.4
Civ. Labor	43,362
Unemployed	3.6
Wages	$370,580,259
Per Capita Income	$36,725
Prop. Value	$7,016,367,083
Retail Sales	$1,409,521,097

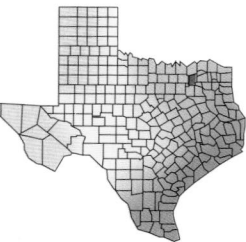

Other towns include: **Caddo Mills** (1,499); **Campbell** (772); **Celeste** (824); **Hawk Cove** (525); **Lone Oak** (632); **Merit** (225); **Neylandville** (103); **Quinlan** (1,463); **Union Valley** (351); **West Tawakoni** (1,689) tourist center, light industry, Lakefest in October; **Wolfe City** (1,454) manufacturing, antiques shops, commuters to Dallas, museum, library, car and truck show in October.

For explanation of sources, symbols and abbreviations, see p. 192, and foldout map.

The Canadian River valley near Adobe Walls, Hutchinson County. Photo by Robert Plocheck.

Hutchinson County

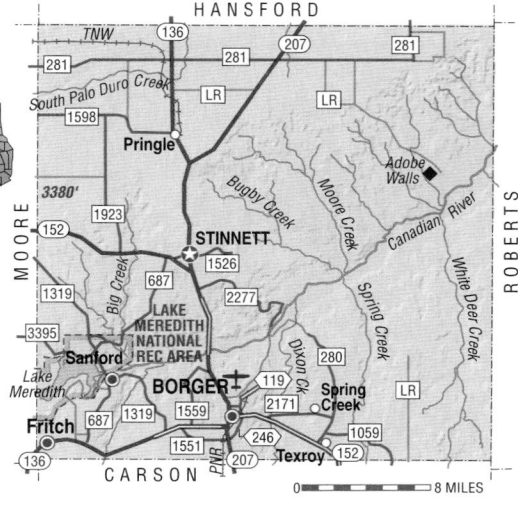

Physical Features: High Plains, broken by Canadian River and tributaries, Lake Meredith; fertile valleys along streams.

Economy: Oil and gas, petrochemicals, carbon black plants. **History**: Antelope Creek Indian area. Later, Comanches were driven out in U.S. cavalry campaigns of 1874-75. Adobe Walls site of two Indian attacks, in 1864 and 1874. Ranching began in the late 1870s. Oil boom in the early 1920s. County created in 1876 from Bexar Territory; organized in 1901; named for pioneer jurist Anderson Hutchinson.

Race/Ethnicity: (In percent) Anglo, 70.2; Black, 3.0; Hispanic, 23.4; Asian, 0.7; Other, 2.3; Two or more races, 2.4.

Vital Statistics, annual: Births, 287; deaths, 239; marriages, 189; divorces, 85.

Recreation: Meredith Lake activities, fishing, camping; Adobe Walls, historic Indian battle site; Alibates Flint Quarries.

Minerals: Oil and gas.

Agriculture: Beef cattle, corn, wheat; about 35,000 acres irrigated. Market value $55.9 million. Hunting important.

STINNETT (1,842) county seat; petroleum refining, farm center.

BORGER (12,873) petroleum refining, petrochemicals, nitrogen plant, carbon-black production, oil-field servicing, retail center; Frank Phillips College; museum; hospital; Downtown Merchants Beach Bash in June.

Other cities include: **Fritch** (2,067), **Sanford** (161).

Population	21,198
Change fm 2010	– 4.7
Area (sq. mi.)	895.0
Land Area (sq. mi.)	887.4
Altitude (ft.)	2,600–3,380
Rainfall (in.)	21.72
Jan. mean min.	25.2
July mean max.	93.8
Civ. Labor	8,565
Unemployed	4.8
Wages	$123,937,490
Per Capita Income	$42,053
Prop. Value	$3,057,351,030
Retail Sales	$223,498,427

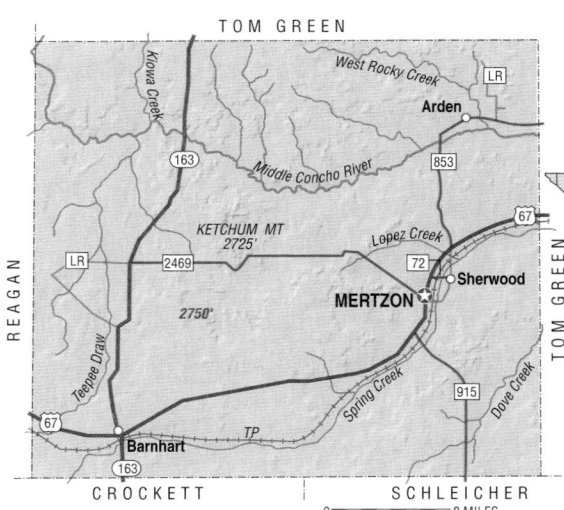

Irion County

Physical Features: West Texas county with hilly surface, broken by Middle Concho River, tributaries; clay, sandy soils.

Economy: Ranching, oil, gas production, wildlife recreation.

History: Tonkawa Indian area. Anglo-American settlement began in the late 1870s. County named for Republic leader R.A. Irion; created in 1889 from Tom Green County, organized the same year.

Race/Ethnicity: (In percent) Anglo, 70.4; Black, 1.3; Hispanic, 26.3; Asian, 0.3; Other, 1.2; Two or more races, 1.6.

Vital Statistics, annual: Births 12; deaths, 20; marriages, 6; divorces, 4.

Recreation: Hunting; historic sites, including Dove Creek battlefield and stagecoach stops, old Sherwood courthouse built 1900; hunters appreciation dinner in November.

Minerals: Oil, gas.

Agriculture: Beef cattle, sheep, goats; hay, wheat. Market value $7.5 million.

MERTZON (791) county seat; farm center, wool warehousing.

Other towns include: **Barnhart** (110).

Population	1,522
Change fm 2010	– 4.7
Area (sq. mi.)	1,051.6
Land Area (sq. mi.)	1,051.6
Altitude (ft.)	2,000–2,750
Rainfall (in.)	20.15
Jan. mean min.	32.0
July mean max.	95.0
Civ. Labor	782
Unemployed	2.9
Wages	$13,817,064
Per Capita Income	$55,231
Prop. Value	$1,670,007,770
Retail Sales	$5,710,207

For explanation of sources, symbols and abbreviations, see p. 192, and foldout map.

Jack County

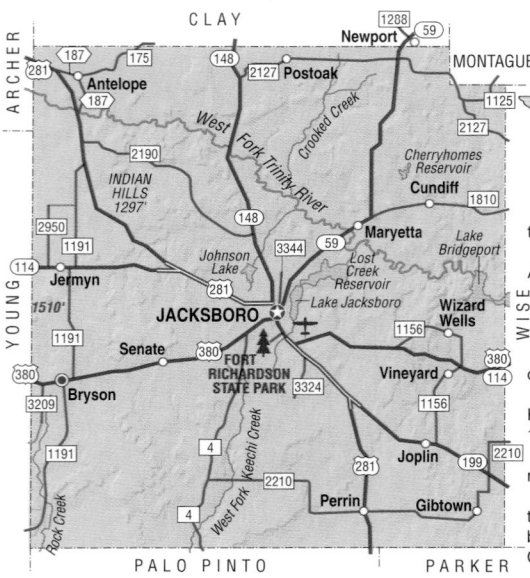

Physical Features: Rolling Cross Timbers, broken by West Fork of the Trinity, other streams; sandy, dark brown, loam soils; Lake Bridgeport, Lake Jacksboro, Lost Creek Reservoir.

Economy: Petroleum production, oil-field services, livestock, manufacturing, tourism.

History: A Caddo and Comanche borderland. The first Anglo-American settlers arrived in 1855 as part of the Peters Colony. County named for brothers P.C. and W.H. Jack, who were leaders in Texas' independence effort; created in 1856 from Cooke County; organized in 1857 with Mesquiteville (original name of Jacksboro) as the county seat.

Race/Ethnicity: (In percent) Anglo, 77.0; Black, 4.1; Hispanic, 16.9; Asian, 0.6; Other, 1.2; Two or more races, 1.2.

Vital Statistics, annual: Births, 104; deaths, 96; marriages, 74; divorces, 33.

Recreation: Hunting, wildlife leases; fishing; lake activities; Fort Richardson, Texas 4-H Museum (county is birthplace of 4-H clubs in Texas), other historic sites; Lost Creek Reservoir State Trailway.

Minerals: Oil, gas.

Agriculture: Cattle, hay, wheat, goats, sheep. Market value $22.5 million. Firewood sold.

JACKSBORO (4,556) county seat; agribusiness, petroleum production and services, tourism; hospital; library; Fort Richardson Living History Days in April.

Other towns include: **Bryson** (545), **Jermyn** (75), **Perrin** (427).

Population	8,843
Change fm 2010	– 2.2
Area (sq. mi.)	920.1
Land Area (sq. mi.)	910.7
Altitude (ft.)	836–1,510
Rainfall (in.)	32.92
Jan. mean min.	29.7
July mean max.	94.4
Civ. Labor	3,995
Unemployed	2.5
Wages	$59,448,802
Per Capita Income	$39,070
Prop. Value	$2,517,425,980
Retail Sales	$51,922,624

Jackson County

Physical Features: South coastal county of prairie and motts of trees; loam, clay, black soils; drains to creeks, rivers, bays.

Economy: Plastics manufacturing, agribusinesses.

History: Karankawa area. Lipan Apaches and Tonkawas arrived later. Six of Austin's Old Three Hundred families settled in the 1820s. Mexican municipality, created in 1835, became an original county the following year; named for U.S. President Andrew Jackson. Oil discovered in 1934.

Race/Ethnicity: (In percent) Anglo, 58.2; Black, 6.6; Hispanic, 33.4; Asian, 1.2; Other, 0.9; Two or more races 1.8.

Vital Statistics, annual: Births, 211; deaths, 146; marriages, 81; divorces, 37.

Recreation: Hunting, fishing, birding (southern bald eagle in area); historic sites; Texana Museum; Lake Texana, Brackenridge Plantation campground, state park; Chili Spill in November at Lake Texana, county fair, rodeo in April.

Minerals: Oil and natural gas.

Agriculture: Cotton, cattle, corn, rice; 13,000 acres of rice irrigated. Market value $101.8 million.

EDNA (5,692) county seat; oil and gas, chemical plants, agriculture; hospital, library, museums.

Other towns include: **Francitas** (125); **Ganado** (2,090) oil and gas, agriculture, historic movie theater, Crawfish Festival in May; **LaSalle** (110); **La Ward** (223); **Lolita** (580); **Vanderbilt** (417).

Population	14,874
Change fm 2010	5.7
Area (sq. mi.)	856.9
Land Area (sq. mi.)	829.4
Altitude (ft.)	sea level–155
Rainfall (in.)	43.25
Jan. mean min.	42.0
July mean max.	94.0
Civ. Labor	7,334
Unemployed	3.1
Wages	$64,043,936
Per Capita Income	$39,981
Prop. Value	$3,000,232,602
Retail Sales	$164,972,036

Jasper County

Physical Features: East Texas county; hilly to level; national forest; Sam Rayburn Reservoir, B.A. Steinhagen Lake; Neches River.

Economy: Timber industries; nature tourism, government/services.

History: Caddo and Atakapa Indian area. Land grants to John R. Bevil and Lorenzo de Zavala in 1829. County created in 1836, organized in 1837, from Mexican municipality; named for Sgt. William Jasper of American Revolution.

Race/Ethnicity: (In percent) Anglo, 74.8; Black, 16.3; Hispanic, 6.7; Asian, 0.5; Other, 0.8; Two or more races, 1.6.

Vital Statistics, annual: Births, 472; deaths, 458; marriages, 250; divorces, 119.

Recreation: Lake activities; hunting, fishing; state park, Big Thicket; Butterfly Festival in October at Jasper.

Minerals: Oil, gas produced.

Agriculture: Cattle, plant nurseries, fruits, vegetables. Market value $10.1 million. Timber is major income producer. Hunting leases and fishing tournaments are major income producers.

JASPER (7,649) county seat; tourism, government/services, timber; hospital; Angelina College extension; museum; Azalea Festival in March.

Other towns include: **Browndell** (187); **Buna** (2,124) timber, oil, polka dot house, redbud festival in March; **Evadale** (1,540); **Kirbyville** (2,180) electric co-op, government/services, retail, commuters, Caboose museum, library, Magnolia Festival in April; **Sam Rayburn** (1,159).

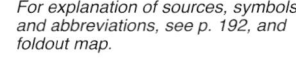

Population	35,872
Change fm 2010	0.5
Area (sq. mi.)	969.7
Land Area (sq. mi.)	938.9
Altitude (ft.)	10–580
Rainfall (in.)	59.75
Jan. mean min.	38.7
July mean max.	91.4

Civ. Labor	13,229
Unemployed	6.5
Wages	$101,643,661
Per Capita Income	$39,105
Prop. Value	$3,419,552,003
Retail Sales	$381,641,528

For explanation of sources, symbols and abbreviations, see p. 192, and foldout map.

Downtown Jacksboro, Jack County. Photo by Robert Plocheck.

Dawn in Limpia valley with McDonald Observatory on mountain tops. Photo by Robert Plocheck.

Jeff Davis County

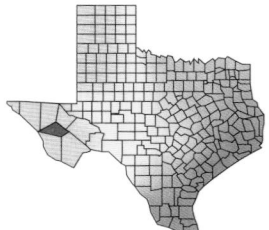

Physical Features: Highest average elevation in Texas; peaks (Mt. Livermore, 8,378 ft.), canyons, plateaus; intermountain wash, clay, loam soils; cedars, oaks in highlands.

Economy: Tourism, agriculture, McDonald Observatory.

History: Mescalero Apaches in area when Antonio de Espejo explored in 1583. U.S. Army established Fort Davis in 1854 to protect routes to west. Civilian settlers followed, including

Population	**2,252**
Change fm 2010	– 3.8
Area (sq. mi.)	2,264.6
Land Area (sq. mi.)	2,264.6
Altitude (ft.)	3,162–8,378
Rainfall (in.) Fort Davis	17.47
Rainfall (in.) Mt. Locke	20.37
Jan. mean min. Fort Davis	28.9
Jan. mean min. Mt. Locke	32.4
July mean max. Fort Davis	88.7
July mean max. Mt. Locke	84.5
Civ. Labor	1,012
Unemployed	2.9
Wages	$7,357,741
Per Capita Income	$39,627
Prop. Value	$599,508,350
Retail Sales	$8,973,498

Manuel Músquiz, a political refugee from Mexico. County named for Jefferson Davis, U.S. Secretary of War, Confederate president; created 1887 from Presidio County, organized the same year.

Race/Ethnicity: (In percent) Anglo, 61.7; Black, 1.6; Hispanic, 34.1; Asian, 1.0; Other, 1.4; Two or more races, 1.9.

Vital Statistics, annual: Births, 12; deaths, 16; marriages, 13; divorces, 1.

Recreation: Scenic drives including loop along Limpia Creek, Mt. Livermore, Blue Mountain; hunting; Fort Davis National Historic Site; state park; McDonald Observatory on Mt. Locke; Davis Mountain Preserve; Chihuahuan Desert Research Institute; hummingbird celebration in August.

Minerals: Not significant.

Agriculture: Greenhouse tomatoes, beef cattle, horses, meat goats. Hunting leases important.

FORT DAVIS (1,202), county seat; tourism, government/services, retail; library, Overland and Old Spanish trail museums; "Coolest July 4th in Texas" celebration.

Other town: **Valentine** (121).

For explanation of sources, symbols and abbreviations, see p. 192, and foldout map.

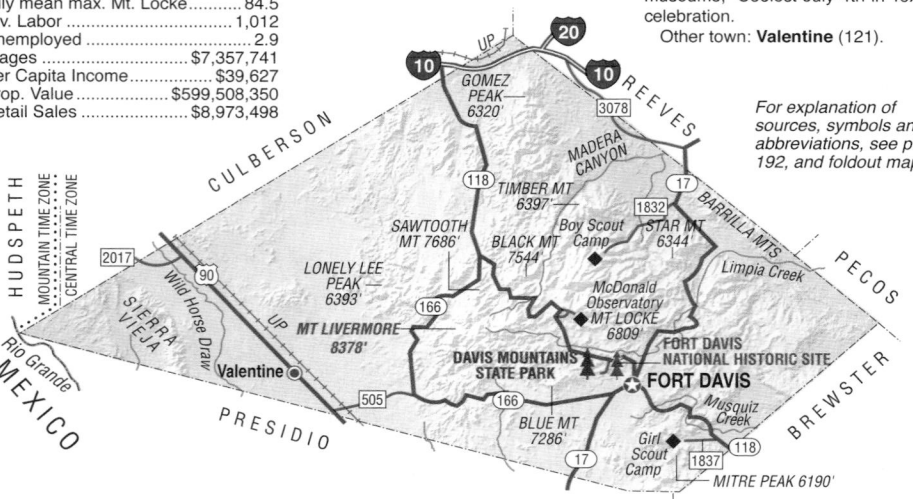

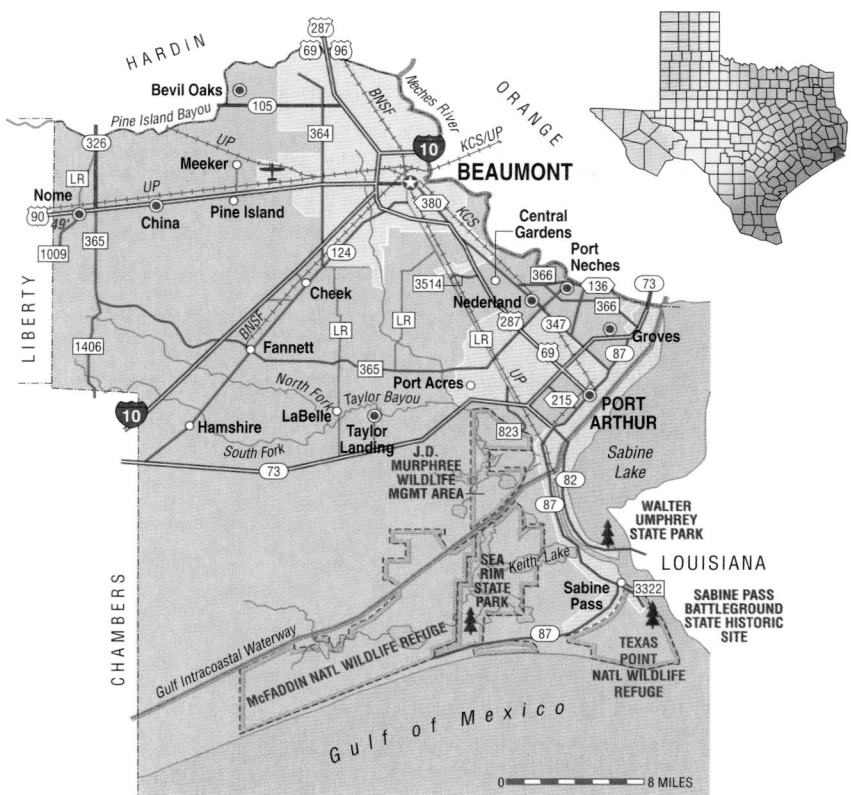

Physical Features: Gulf Coast grassy plain, with timber in northwest; beach sands, sandy loams, black clay soils; drains to Neches River, Gulf of Mexico.

Economy: Government/services, petrochemical and other chemical plants, shipbuilding, steel mill, port activity, oil-field supplies.

History: Atakapas and Orcoquizas, whose numbers were reduced by epidemics or migration before Anglo-American settlers arrived in the 1820s. Cajuns arrived in the 1840s; Europeans in the 1850s. Antebellum slaveholding area. County created in 1836 from Mexican municipality; organized in 1837; named for U.S. President Thomas Jefferson.

Race/Ethnicity: (In percent) Anglo, 40.4; Black, 34.3; Hispanic, 20.8; Asian, 4.0; Other, 1.1; Two or more races, 1.7.

Vital Statistics, annual: Births, 3,782; deaths, 2,514; marriages, 1,699; divorces, 616.

Recreation: Beaches, fresh and saltwater fishing; duck, goose hunting; water activities; Dick Dowling Monument and Park; Spindletop site, energy, fire museums; saltwater lake; J.D. Murphree WMA, McFaddin wildlife refuge, Texas Point wildlife refuge; Lamar

Jefferson County

University events; historic sites; South Texas Fair in March-April.

Minerals: Large producer of oil, gas, sulfur, salt, sand and gravel.

Agriculture: Rice, hay, beef cattle, crawfish; considerable rice irrigated. Market value $38 million. Timber sales significant.

BEAUMONT (117,245) county seat; oil and gas production, government/ services, engineering and industrial services, port; Lamar University, Institute of Technology; hospitals; entertainment district; Neches River Festival in April.

PORT ARTHUR (53,706) oil, chemical activities, shrimping and crawfishing, shipping, offshore marine, tourism; hospitals; museum; prison; Asian New Year Tet, Janis Joplin Birthday Bash in January. Sabine Pass and Port Acres are now within the city limits of Port Arthur.

Other towns include: **Bevil Oaks** (1,227); **Central Gardens** (4,241);

For explanation of sources, symbols and abbreviations, see p. 192, and foldout map.

China (1,186); **Fannett** (2,236); **Groves** (15,698) retail center, some manufacturing, government/services, tourism; hospital; pecan festival in September; **Hamshire** (759).

Also, **Nederland** (17,305) petrochemical refining, retail center, education; Windmill and French/Acadian museums; extended-care hospital; Tex Ritter memorial and park; heritage festival in March (city founded by Dutch immigrants in 1898).

Also, **Nome** (590); **Port Neches** (12,680) chemical and synthetic rubber industry, manufacturing, library, riverfront park with La Maison Beausoleil, RiverFest in May; **Taylor Landing** (209).

Population	**255,001**
Change fm 2010	1.1
Area (sq. mi.)	1,112.7
Land Area (sq. mi.)	876.3
Altitude (ft.)	sea level–49
Rainfall (in.)	60.42
Jan. mean min.	41.7
July mean max.	92.0
Civ. Labor	105,715
Unemployed	6.2
Wages	$1,706,192,068
Per Capita Income	$42,338
Prop. Value	$30,000,687,244
Retail Sales	$4,181,070,047

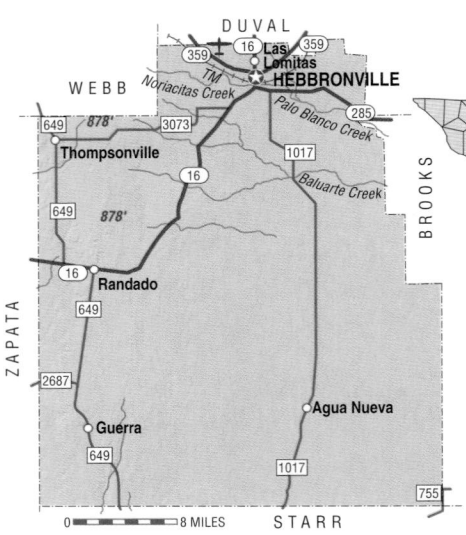

Jim Hogg County

Physical Features: South Texas county on rolling plain, with heavy brush cover; white blow sand and sandy loam; hilly, broken.

Economy: Oil, cattle operations.

History: Coahuiltecan area, then Lipan Apache. Spanish land grant in 1805 to Xavier Vela. County named for Gov. James Stephen Hogg; created and organized in 1913 from Brooks and Duval counties.

Race/Ethnicity: (In percent) Anglo, 5.6; Black, 0.8; Hispanic, 92.8; Asian, 0.5; Other, 0.5; Two or more races, 0.7.

Vital Statistics, annual: Births, 90; deaths, 50; marriages, 30; divorces, 2.

Recreation: White-tailed deer and bobwhite hunting.

Minerals: Oil and gas.

Agriculture: Cattle, hay, milk goats; some irrigation. Market value $11.1 million.

HEBBRONVILLE (4,485) county seat; ranching, oil-field center.

Other towns include: **Guerra** (5), **Las Lomitas** (216), **South Fork Estates** (77), and **Thompsonville** (48).

Population	5,248	Altitude (ft.)	230–878
Change fm 2010	– 1.0	Rainfall (in.)	23.79
Area (sq. mi.)	1,136.2	Jan. mean min.	44.8
Land Area (sq. mi.)	1,136.1	July mean max.	96.7

Civ. Labor	1,844
Unemployed	5.5
Wages	$15,294,818
Per Capita Income	$30,088
Prop. Value	$688,739,700
Retail Sales	$31,594,691

Jim Wells County

Physical Features: South Coastal Plains; level to rolling; sandy to dark soils; grassy with mesquite brush; Lake Corpus Christi.

Economy: Oil and gas production, agriculture, nature tourism.

History: Coahuiltecans, driven out by Lipan Apaches in 1775. Tomás Sánchez established settlement in 1754. Anglo-American settlement began in 1878. County created 1911 from Nueces County; organized 1912; named for developer J.B. Wells Jr.

Race/Ethnicity: (In percent) Anglo, 17.8; Black, 0.8; Hispanic, 80.6; Asian, 0.5; Other, 1.2; Two or more races, 0.9.

Vital Statistics, annual: Births, 639; deaths, 424; marriages, 222; divorces, 111.

Recreation: Hunting; fiestas; Tejano Roots hall of fame; South Texas museum.

Minerals: Oil, gas, caliche.

Agriculture: Cattle, sorghum, corn, cotton, dairies, goats, wheat, watermelons, sunflowers, peas, hay. Market value $82.9 million.

ALICE (18,499) county seat; oil-field service center, agribusiness, government/services; hospital; Bee County College extension; Fiesta Bandana (from original name of city) in May.

Other towns include: **Alfred** (85); **Ben Bolt** (1,600); **Orange Grove** (1,255); **Pernitas Point** (274, partly in Live Oak County); **Premont** (2,571) wildflower tour in spring; **Rancho Alegre** (1,646); **Sandia** (366).

Population	40,822
Change fm 2010	0.0
Area (sq. mi.)	868.3
Land Area (sq. mi.)	865.0
Altitude (ft.)	50–450
Rainfall (in.)	28.43
Jan. mean min.	44.9
July mean max.	97.2
Civ. Labor	16,881
Unemployed	4.9
Wages	$188,813,991
Per Capita Income	$37,906
Prop. Value	$2,356,670,761
Retail Sales	$440,324,185

Also, part [900] of San Diego (4,254).

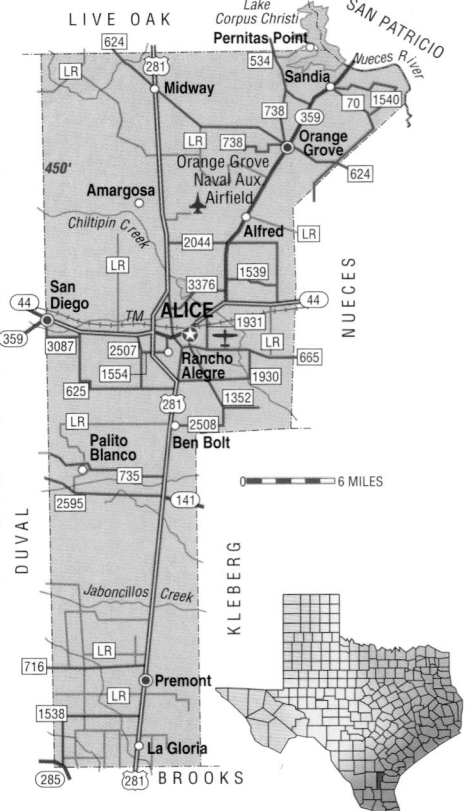

For explanation of sources, symbols and abbreviations, see p. 192, and foldout map.

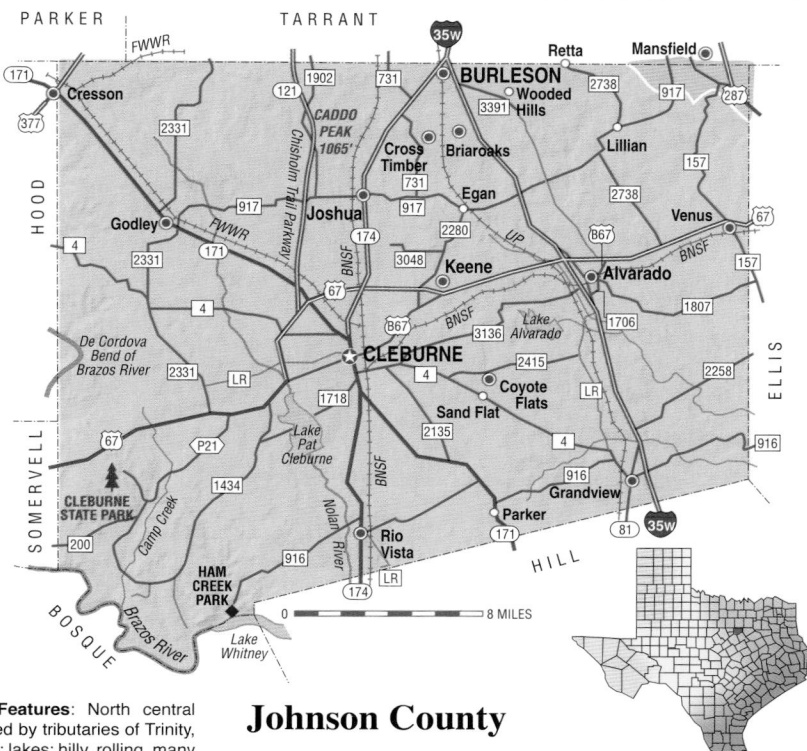

Johnson County

Physical Features: North central county drained by tributaries of Trinity, Brazos rivers; lakes; hilly, rolling, many soil types.

Economy: Agribusiness, railroad shops; manufacturing, distribution, lake activities, many residents employed in Fort Worth and Dallas; part of Fort Worth-Arlington metropolitan area.

History: No permanent Indian villages existed in the area. Anglo-American settlers arrived in the 1840s. County named for Col. M.T. Johnson of the Mexican War and Confederacy; created and organized in 1854. Formed from McLennan, Hill, and Navarro counties.

Race/Ethnicity: (In percent) Anglo, 72.2; Black, 3.6; Hispanic, 21.3; Asian, 0.9; Other, 1.5; Two or more races, 1.9.

Vital Statistics, annual: Births, 2,092; deaths, 1,340; marriages, 1,173; divorces, 576.

Recreation: Bird, deer hunting; water activities on Lake Pat Cleburne, Lake Whitney; state park; sports complex; museum; Chisholm Trail; Goatneck bike ride in July.

Minerals: Limestone, sand and gravel.

Agriculture: Cattle, hay, horses, dairies, cotton, sorghum, wheat, oats, hogs. Market value $78.9 million.

CLEBURNE (31,762) county seat; manufacturing, oil and gas; hospital, library, museum; Hill College campus; Whistle Stop Christmas.

BURLESON (44,161, part in Tarrant County) agriculture, retail center; hospital.

Other towns include: **Alvarado** (4,085) County Pioneer Days; **Briaroaks** (519); **Coyote Flats** (316); **Cross Timber** (291); Godley (1,139); **Grandview** (1,673); **Joshua** (7,156) many residents work in Fort Worth; **Keene** (6,700) Southwestern Adventist University; **Lillian** (1,160); **Rio Vista** (974), and **Venus** (3,520).

Also, part of **Cresson** (789), and part [1,652] of **Mansfield** (65,233, mostly in Tarrant County).

Population	**171,361**
Change fm 2010	13.5
Area (sq. mi.)	734.5
Land Area (sq. mi.)	724.7
Altitude (ft.)	500–1,065
Rainfall (in.)	37.61
Jan. mean min.	32.6
July mean max.	95.7
Civ. Labor	80,260
Unemployed	3.3
Wages	$527,917,978
Per Capita Income	$39,941
Prop. Value	$13,553,234,173
Retail Sales	$1,795,646,561

For explanation of sources, symbols and abbreviations, see p. 192, and foldout map.

Lake Pat Cleburne. Photo by Earl Nottingham/Texas Parks & Wildlife.

Jones County

Physical Features: West Texas Rolling Plains; drained by Brazos River fork, tributaries; Lake Fort Phantom Hill.

Economy: Agribusiness; government/services; varied manufacturing.

History: Comanches and other tribes hunted in the area. U.S. military presence began in 1851. Ranching established in the 1870s. County named for the last president of the Republic, Anson Jones; created in 1858 from Bexar and Bosque counties; re-created in 1876; organized in 1881.

Race/Ethnicity: (In percent) Anglo, 58.3; Black, 13.2; Hispanic, 27.9; Asian, 0.7; Other, 1.5; Two or more races, 1.6.

Vital Statistics, annual: Births, 147; deaths, 214; marriages, 82; divorces, 43.

Recreation: Lake activities, hunting, Fort Phantom Hill, Cowboy Reunion July 4 in Stamford.

Minerals: Oil, gas, sand and gravel, stone.

Agriculture: Cotton, wheat, sesame and peanuts; cattle. Some 3,500 acres irrigated for peanuts and hay. Market value $43.3 million.

ANSON (2,410) county seat; farming center, government/services; hospital; old courthouse, opera house, museums; Cowboys Christmas Ball in December.

STAMFORD (2,975) trade center for three counties, hospital, historic homes, cowboy museum.

HAMLIN (2,119) farm and ranching, oil and gas, electricity/steam plant using mesquite trees, hunting; hospital; museums; Runnin' the Buff 5K in December.

Other towns include: **Hawley** (638), **Lueders** (347) limestone quarries.

Part [5,145] of **Abilene**.

Population 19,817
Change fm 2010 .... – 1.9

Area (sq. mi.)	937.1
Land Area (sq. mi.)	928.6
Altitude (ft.)	1,480–1,970
Rainfall (in.)	26.06
Jan. mean min.	31.1
July mean max.	96.2
Civ. Labor	5,687
Unemployed	4.6
Wages	$27,763,980
Per Capita Income	$29,969
Prop. Value	$1,261,447,240
Retail Sales	$209,558,114

Karnes County

Physical Features: Sandy loam, dark clay, alluvial soils in rolling terrain; traversed by San Antonio River; mesquite, oak trees.

Economy: Oil and gas, agribusiness.

History: Coahuiltecan area. Spanish ranching began around 1750. Anglo-Americans arrived in 1840s; Polish in the 1850s. County created in 1854 from Bexar, Goliad, and San Patricio counties, organized the same year; named for Texas Revolutionary figure Henry W. Karnes.

Race/Ethnicity: (In percent) Anglo, 36.4; Black, 9.4; Hispanic, 54.0; Asian, 0.4; Other, 1.0; Two or more races, 0.8.

Vital Statistics, annual: Births, 180; deaths, 131; marriages, 16; divorces, 31.

Recreation: Panna Maria, nation's oldest Polish settlement, founded 1854; Old Helena restored courthouse, museum; hunting, nature tourism, guest ranches.

Minerals: Oil, gas, uranium.

Agriculture: Beef cattle, grain, cotton, hay. Market value $27.6 million.

KARNES CITY (3,315) county seat; oil and gas, agribusiness, tourism, processing center, oil-field servicing, manufacturing; library; Lonesome Dove Fest in September.

KENEDY (3,705) farm and oil center, library, dove/quail hunting, prison, hospital; Bluebonnet Days in April.

Other towns include: **Falls City** (681) ranching, sausage making, library, city park on river; **Gillett** (120); **Hobson** (135); **Panna Maria** (45); **Runge** (1,097) oil and gas services, farming, museum, library; cowboy breakfast in December.

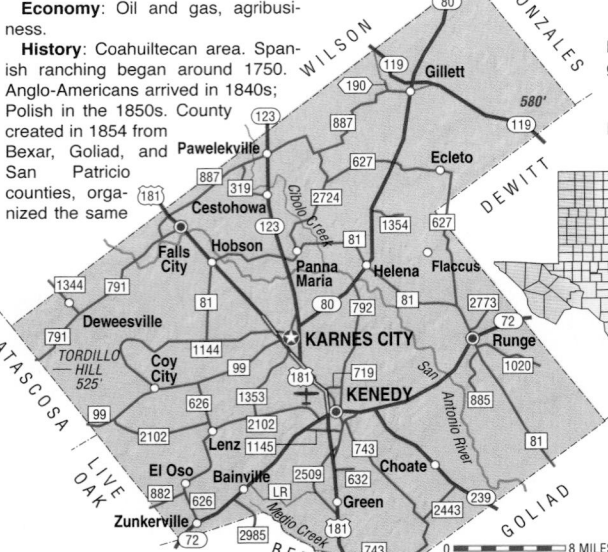

Population 15,650
Change fm 2010 .... 5.5
Area (sq. mi.) 753.6
Land Area (sq. mi.) 747.6
Altitude (ft.) 180–580
Rainfall (in.) 30.14

Jan. mean min.	41.8
July mean max.	95.1
Civ. Labor	6,555
Unemployed	2.8
Wages	$82,381,886
Per Capita Income	$44,986
Prop. Value	$7,089,126,533
Retail Sales	$165,225,121

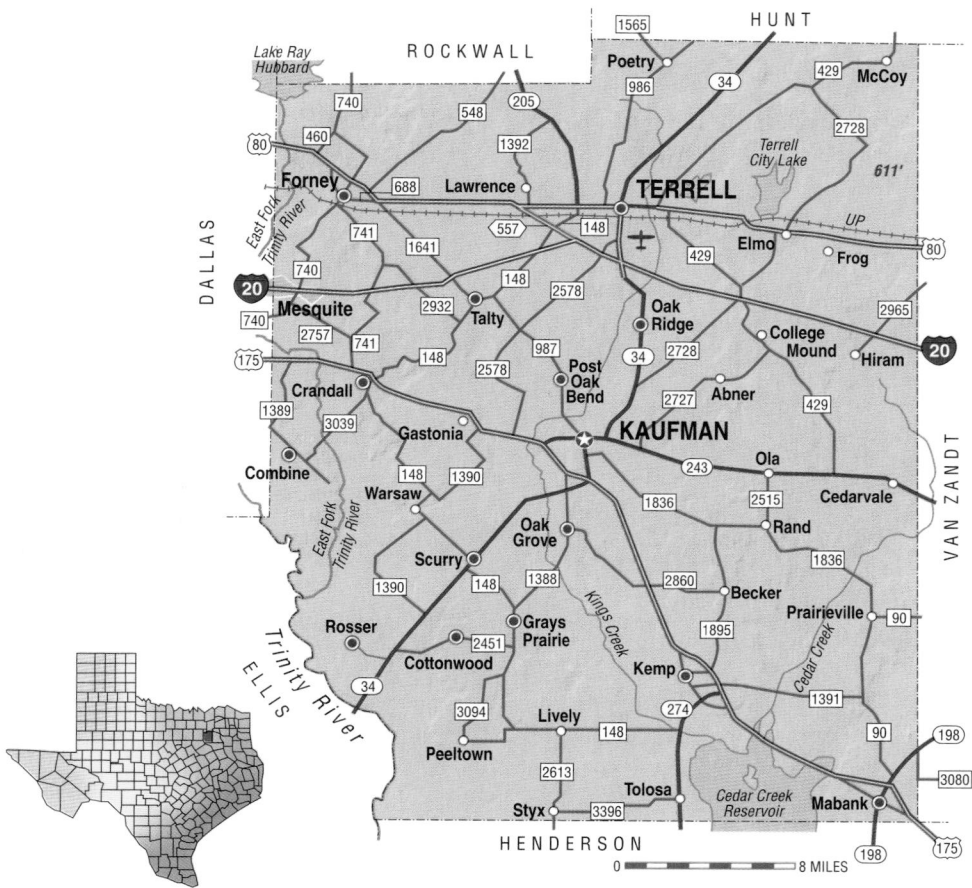

Kaufman County

Physical Features: North Black-land prairie, draining to Trinity River; Cedar Creek Reservoir, Lake Ray Hubbard and Terrell City Lake.

Economy: Agriculture, commuting to Dallas, government/services.

History: Caddo and later Cherokee Indians in the area; removed by 1840 when Anglo-American settlement began. County created from Henderson County and organized in 1848; named for member of Texas and U.S. congresses D.S. Kaufman.

Race/Ethnicity: (In percent) Anglo, 64.1; Black, 11.6; Hispanic, 21.4; Asian, 1.3; Other, 1.1; Two or more races, 2.1.

Vital Statistics, annual: Births, 1,539; deaths, 897; marriages, 669; divorces, 358.

Recreation: Lake activities; Porter Farm near Terrell is site of origin of U.S.-Texas Agricultural Extension program; antique centers near Forney; historic homes at Terrell.

Minerals: Gravel, sand, oil, gas.

Agriculture: Beef cattle, horticulture, hay/forage, row crops, horses. Market value $59 million.

KAUFMAN (7,089) county seat; government/services, manufacturing and distribution, commuters to Dallas; hospital; Octoberfest.

TERRELL (17,566) agribusiness, varied manufacturing, large outlet center; private hospital, state hospital; community college, Southwestern Christian College; British flying school museum, Heritage Jubilee in April.

FORNEY (19,481) important antiques center, light industrial, commuters to Dallas, historic homes, barbecue cook-off in June.

Other towns include: **Combine** (2,132, partly in Dallas County); **Cottonwood** (210); **Crandall** (3,231)

Cotton Festival in September; **Elmo** (899); **Grays Prairie** (364); **Kemp** (1,300); **Lawrence** (259); **Mabank** (3,423, partly in Henderson County) varied manufacturing, tourism, retail trade, Western Week in June; **Oak Grove** (708); **Oak Ridge** (604); **Post Oak Bend** (694); **Rosser** (361); **Scurry** (733); **Talty** (2,238).

Population	128,622
Change fm 2010	24.4
Area (sq. mi.)	807.7
Land Area (sq. mi.)	780.7
Altitude (ft.)	300–611
Rainfall (in.)	39.92
Jan. mean min.	33.1
July mean max.	94.3
Civ. Labor	62,279
Unemployed	3.2
Wages	$318,369,339
Per Capita Income	$41,140
Prop. Value	$10,233,250,926
Retail Sales	$1,427,416,700

For explanation of sources, symbols and abbreviations, see p. 192, and foldout map.

Kendall County

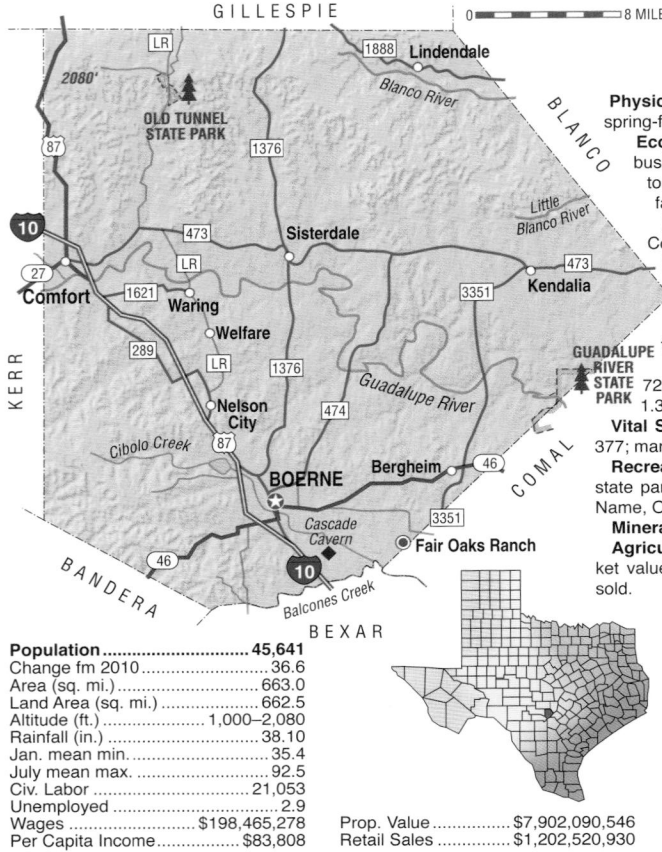

GILLESPIE

LR
2080'
OLD TUNNEL STATE PARK
87
1376
1888 Lindendale
Blanco River
Little Blanco River
473
Sisterdale
LR
27
Comfort
1621 Waring
Welfare
289
LR 1376
Guadalupe River
Nelson City
474
Cibolo Creek
87
Bergheim
BOERNE
Cascade Cavern
46
Balcones Creek
BANDERA
BEXAR
3351
473 Kendalia
GUADALUPE RIVER STATE PARK
COMAL
3351
Fair Oaks Ranch
10

0 ▬▬▬▬▬ 8 MILES

Physical Features: Hill Country, plateau, with spring-fed streams; caves; scenic drives.

Economy: Government/services, agri-business, commuters to San Antonio, tourism, retirement area, some manufacturing.

History: Lipan Apaches, Kiowas and Comanches in area when German settlers arrived in 1840s. County created, organized, from Blanco, Kerr counties 1862; named for pioneer journalist-sheepman and early contributor to Texas Almanac, George W. Kendall.

Race/Ethnicity: (In percent) Anglo, 72.0; Black, 1.3; Hispanic, 24.1; Asian, 1.3; Other, 0.8; Two or more races, 1.8.

Vital Statistics, annual: Births, 377; deaths, 377; marriages, 488; divorces, 104.

Recreation: Hunting, fishing, exotic wildlife, state parks; Cascade Cavern, Cave Without a Name, Old Tunnel; historic sites.

Minerals: Limestone rock, caliche.

Agriculture: Cattle, goats, sheep, hay. Market value $12.5 million. Cedar posts, firewood sold.

BOERNE (14,816) county seat; tourism, antiques, some manufacturing, ranching, commuting to San Antonio; library; Christmas in Comfort on Saturday after Thanksgiving.

Other towns include: **Comfort** (2,783) tourism, farming and ranching, manufacturing, Civil War monument honoring Unionists, library, museum, mountain bike trail; **Kendalia** (149); **Sisterdale** (110); **Waring** (73). Part of **Fair Oaks Ranch** (9,003).

Population	45,641
Change fm 2010	36.6
Area (sq. mi.)	663.0
Land Area (sq. mi.)	662.5
Altitude (ft.)	1,000–2,080
Rainfall (in.)	38.10
Jan. mean min.	35.4
July mean max.	92.5
Civ. Labor	21,053
Unemployed	2.9
Wages	$198,465,278
Per Capita Income	$83,808
Prop. Value	$7,902,090,546
Retail Sales	$1,202,520,930

A farmhouse near the Kendall-Gillespie county line. Photo by Robert Plocheck.

Kenedy County

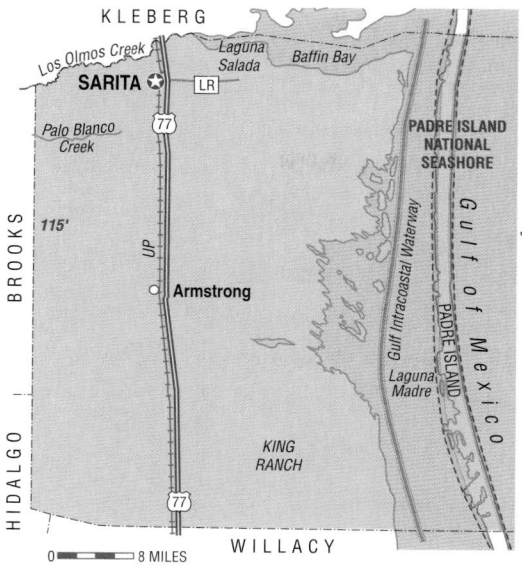

Physical Features: Gulf coastal county; flat, sandy terrain, some loam soils; motts of live oaks.

Economy: Oil, ranching, nature tourism, hunting leases, wind farm.

History: Coahuiltecan Indians who assimilated or were driven out by the Lipan Apaches. Spanish ranching began in the 1790s. Anglo-Americans arrived after the Mexican War. Among last counties created, organized, 1921 from Cameron, Hidalgo, and Willacy counties; named for pioneer steamboat operator and cattleman, Capt. Mifflin Kenedy.

Race/Ethnicity: (In percent) Anglo, 20.9; Black, 4.1; Hispanic, 74.3; Asian, 0.7; Other, 1.75; Two or more races, 0.5.

Vital Statistics, annual: Births, 0; deaths, 3; marriages, 4; divorces, 0.

Recreation: Hunting, fishing, nature tourism.

Minerals: Oil, gas.

Agriculture: Beef cattle, horses. Market value $23.7 million. Hunting leases, nature tourism important.

SARITA (244) county seat; cattle-shipping point, ranch headquarters, gas processing; one of state's least populous counties.

Also, **Armstrong** (4).

Population	442
Change fm 2010	7.0
Area (sq. mi.)	1,945.8
Land Area (sq. mi.)	1,458.3
Altitude (ft.)	sea level–115
Rainfall (in.)	29.17
Jan. mean min.	44.4
July mean max.	94.6
Civ. Labor	253
Unemployed	4.0
Wages	$9,275,210
Per Capita Income	$41,297
Prop. Value	$1,826,686,933
Retail Sales	NA

Kent County

Physical Features: Rolling, broken terrain; lake; drains to Salt and Double Mountain forks of Brazos River; sandy, loam soils.

Economy: Agribusiness, oil and gas operations, government/services, hunting leases.

History: Comanches driven out by the U.S. Army in the 1870s. Ranching developed in the 1880s. County created in 1876 from Bexar and Young territories; organized in 1892. Name honors Andrew Kent, one of 32 volunteers from Gonzales who died at the Alamo.

Race/Ethnicity: (In percent) Anglo, 75.6; Black, 1.6; Hispanic, 19.9; Asian, 0.0; Other, 1.7; Two or more races, 3.1.

Vital Statistics, annual: Births, 0; deaths, 9; marriages, 2; divorces, 1.

Recreation: Hunting, fishing; scenic croton breaks and salt flat; Winterfest in December.

Minerals: Oil, gas.

Agriculture: Cattle, cotton, wheat, sorghum.

JAYTON (534) county seat; oil-field services, farming center; Summerfest in August.

Other towns include: **Girard** (46).

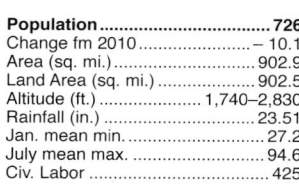

Population	726
Change fm 2010	– 10.1
Area (sq. mi.)	902.9
Land Area (sq. mi.)	902.5
Altitude (ft.)	1,740–2,830
Rainfall (in.)	23.51
Jan. mean min.	27.2
July mean max.	94.6
Civ. Labor	425
Unemployed	2.4
Wages	$2,539,087
Per Capita Income	$48,558
Prop. Value	$808,448,740
Retail Sales	$7,358,786

For explanation of sources, symbols and abbreviations, see p. 192, and foldout map.

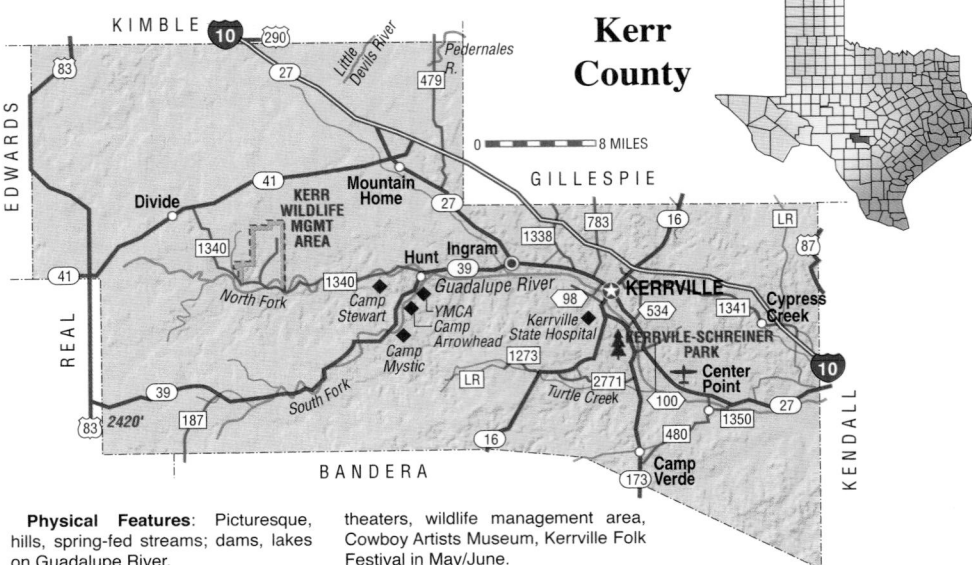

Kerr County

Physical Features: Picturesque, hills, spring-fed streams; dams, lakes on Guadalupe River.

Economy: Tourism, medical services, agribusiness, hunting leases.

History: Lipan Apaches, Kiowas and Comanches in area. Anglo-American settlers arrived in the late 1840s. County created in 1856 from Bexar County; organized the same year; named for a member of Austin's Colony, James Kerr.

Race/Ethnicity: (In percent) Anglo, 69.1; Black, 1.9; Hispanic, 26.8; Asian, 1.0; Other, 1.3; Two or more races, 1.8.

Vital Statistics, annual: Births, 540; deaths, 774; marriages, 311; divorces, 194.

Recreation: Youth camps, dude ranches, park, Cailloux and Point

theaters, wildlife management area, Cowboy Artists Museum, Kerrville Folk Festival in May/June.

Minerals: none.

Agriculture: Cattle, hay, goats and horses; deer (second in numbers as livestock). Market value $10.8 million. Hunting leases important.

KERRVILLE (23,559) county seat; tourist center, youth camps, agribusiness, aircraft and parts, varied manufacturing; Schreiner University; state hospital, veterans hospital, private hospital; retirement center; retail trade; state arts, crafts show in May.

Other towns include: **Camp Verde** (41); **Center Point** (800); **Hunt** (708) youth camps, hospital; **Ingram** (1,903) camps, cabins; **Mountain Home** (96).

Population 52,405
Change fm 2010 ....5.6
Area (sq. mi.) 1,107.3
Land Area (sq. mi.) 1,103.3
Altitude (ft.) 1,400–2,420
Rainfall (in.) 32.05
Jan. mean min. 33.8
July mean max. 92.2
Civ. Labor 21,680
Unemployed 3.0
Wages $192,457,420
Per Capita Income.............$47,288
Prop. Value $6,967,355,971
Retail Sales $904,598,603

For explanation of sources, symbols and abbreviations, see p. 192, and foldout map.

The King County courthouses, old and new, in Guthrie. Photo by Robert Plocheck.

Kimble County

Population **4,362**
Change fm 2010 .... − 5.3
Area (sq. mi.) 1,251.2
Land Area (sq. mi.) 1,251.0
Altitude (ft.) 1,476–2,460
Rainfall (in.) 26.98
Jan. mean min. 27.8
July mean max. 94.3
Civ. Labor 1,879
Unemployed 3.1
Wages $9,764,873
Per Capita Income $41,007
Prop. Value $2,366,576,335
Retail Sales $99,356,823

Physical Features: Picturesque Edwards Plateau; rugged, broken by numerous streams; drains to Llano River; sandy, gray, chocolate loam soils.

Economy: Livestock production and market, tourism, cedar oil and wood products, metal building materials.

History: Apache, Kiowa and Comanche area until the 1870s. U.S. military outposts protected the first Anglo-American settlers in the 1850s. County created from Bexar County in 1858 and organized in 1876. Named for George C. Kimble, a Gonzales volunteer who died at the Alamo.

Race/Ethnicity: (In percent) Anglo, 73.0; Black, 0.6; Hispanic, 24.6; Asian, 0.8; Other, 1.4; Two or more races, 0.6.

Vital Statistics, annual: Births, 39; deaths, 45; marriages, 34; divorces, 21.

Recreation: Hunting, fishing in spring-fed streams, nature tourism; among leading deer counties; state park; Kimble Kounty Kow Kick on Labor Day, Wild Game dinner on Thanksgiving Saturday.

Minerals: gravel.

Agriculture: Cattle, meat goats, sheep, Angora goats, pecans. Hunting leases important. Firewood, cedar sold.

JUNCTION (2,544) county seat; tourism, varied manufacturing; livestock production; two museums; Texas Tech University center; hospital; library; airport.

Other towns include: **London** (180); **Roosevelt** (14).

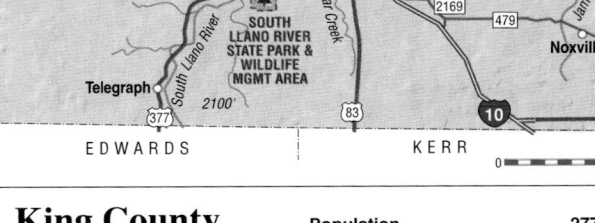

King County

Physical Features: Hilly, broken by Wichita, Brazos tributaries; extensive grassland; dark loam to red soils.

Economy: Oil and gas, ranching, government/services, horse sales, hunting leases.

History: Apache area until Comanches moved in about 1700. Comanches were removed by U.S. Army in 1874-75 after which ranching began. County created in 1876 from Bexar District; organized in 1891; named for William P. King, a volunteer from Gonzales who died at the Alamo.

Race/Ethnicity: (In percent) Anglo, 79.1; Black, 0.0; Hispanic, 18.2; Asian, 0.0; Other, 1.4; Two or more races, 2.0.

Vital Statistics, annual: Births, 0; deaths, 0; marriages, 2; divorces, 0.

Recreation: 6666 Ranch visits, hunting, roping and ranch horse competitions.

Minerals: Oil, gas.

Agriculture: Cattle, horses, wheat, hay, cotton. Market value $6.6 million. Hunting leases important.

GUTHRIE (183) county seat; ranch-supply center, government/services; community center complex, library; Thanksgiving community supper.

Population **277**
Change fm 2010 .... − 2.8
Area (sq. mi.) 913.3
Land Area (sq. mi.) 910.9
Altitude (ft.) 1,450–2,250
Rainfall (in.) 25.53
Jan. mean min. 27.0
July mean max. 95.9
Civ. Labor 154
Unemployed 3.5
Wages $1,257,282
Per Capita Income $37,689
Prop. Value $591,844,880
Retail Sales .... NA

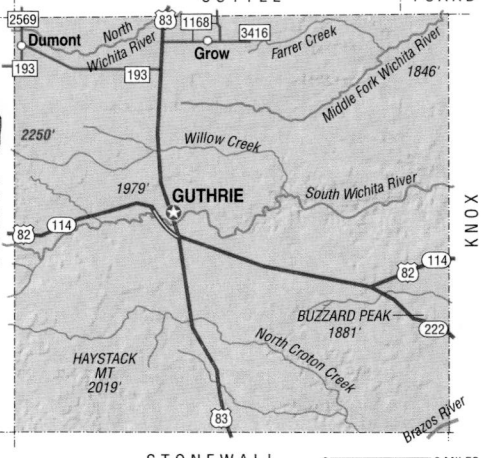

Kinney County

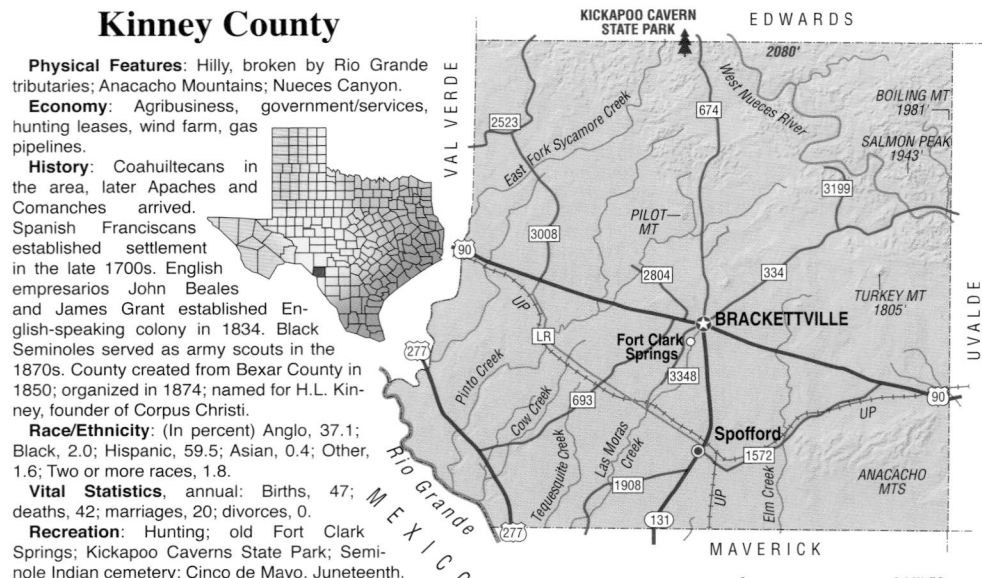

Physical Features: Hilly, broken by Rio Grande tributaries; Anacacho Mountains; Nueces Canyon.

Economy: Agribusiness, government/services, hunting leases, wind farm, gas pipelines.

History: Coahuiltecans in the area, later Apaches and Comanches arrived. Spanish Franciscans established settlement in the late 1700s. English empresarios John Beales and James Grant established English-speaking colony in 1834. Black Seminoles served as army scouts in the 1870s. County created from Bexar County in 1850; organized in 1874; named for H.L. Kinney, founder of Corpus Christi.

Race/Ethnicity: (In percent) Anglo, 37.1; Black, 2.0; Hispanic, 59.5; Asian, 0.4; Other, 1.6; Two or more races, 1.8.

Vital Statistics, annual: Births, 47; deaths, 42; marriages, 20; divorces, 0.

Recreation: Hunting; old Fort Clark Springs; Kickapoo Caverns State Park; Seminole Indian cemetery; Cinco de Mayo, Juneteenth.

Minerals: Not significant.

Agriculture: Cattle, sheep, goats, hay, sorghum, cotton, corn oats, wheat, pecans. Market value $4.7 million. Hunting important.

BRACKETTVILLE (1,766) county seat; agriculture, tourism; museum, Fort Clark Days in March.

Other towns include: **Fort Clark Springs** (1,249); **Spofford** (109).

Population	**3,767**
Change fm 2010	4.7
Area (sq. mi.)	1,365.1
Land Area (sq. mi.)	1,363.1
Altitude (ft.)	790–2,080
Rainfall (in.)	23.56
Jan. mean min.	38.8
July mean max.	93.9
Civ. Labor	1,166
Unemployed	4.3
Wages	$11,177,535
Per Capita Income	$28,964
Prop. Value	$1,582,180,493
Retail Sales	$8,497,000

Kleberg County

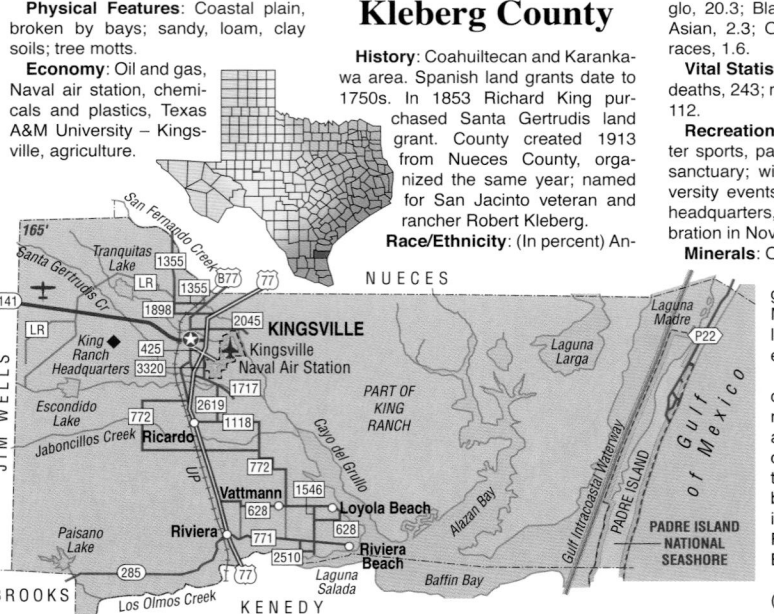

Physical Features: Coastal plain, broken by bays; sandy, loam, clay soils; tree motts.

Economy: Oil and gas, Naval air station, chemicals and plastics, Texas A&M University – Kingsville, agriculture.

History: Coahuiltecan and Karankawa area. Spanish land grants date to 1750s. In 1853 Richard King purchased Santa Gertrudis land grant. County created 1913 from Nueces County, organized the same year; named for San Jacinto veteran and rancher Robert Kleberg.

Race/Ethnicity: (In percent) Anglo, 20.3; Black, 4.4; Hispanic, 72.9; Asian, 2.3; Other, 1.1; Two or more races, 1.6.

Vital Statistics, annual: Births, 435; deaths, 243; marriages, 225; divorces, 112.

Recreation: Fishing, hunting, water sports, park at Baffin Bay; wildlife sanctuary; winter bird watching; university events, museum; King Ranch headquarters, tours; La Posada celebration in November.

Minerals: Oil, gas.

Agriculture: Cattle, grain sorghum, cotton. Market value $61.8 million. Hunting leases and ecotourism important.

KINGSVILLE (25,595) county seat; government/services, oil, gas, agribusiness, tourism, chemical plant, university, Coastal Bend College branch; hospital; ranching heritage festival in February, King Ranch Breakfast in November.

Other towns: **Ricardo** (1,044), **Riviera** (686).

Population	**31,129**
Change fm 2010	– 2.9
Area (sq. mi.)	1,090.2
Land Area (sq. mi.)	881.3
Altitude (ft.)	sea level–165
Rainfall (in.)	30.38
Jan. mean min.	45.8
July mean max.	95.1
Civ. Labor	13,312
Unemployed	4.7
Wages	$108,642,164
Per Capita Income	$37,123
Prop. Value	$2,240,000,702
Retail Sales	$419,256,957

Knox County

Physical Features: Eroded breaks on West Texas Rolling Plains; Brazos, Wichita rivers; sandy, loam soils; Lake Davis, Lake Catherine, and Truscott Brine Lake.

Economy: Oil, agriculture, government/services.

History: Indian conscripts were used as labor during the Spanish period to mine copper deposits along the Brazos River. Ranching and farming developed in the 1880s. German colony settled in 1895. County created from the Bexar, Young territories in 1858; re-created in 1876; organized in 1886; named for U.S. Secretary of War Henry Knox.

Race/Ethnicity: (In percent) Anglo, 58.1; Black, 5.9; Hispanic, 34.6; Asian, 0.3; Other, 1.3; Two or more races, 2.3.

Vital Statistics, annual: Births, 45; deaths, 61; marriages, 15; divorces, 9.

Recreation: Lake activities, fishing, hunting; Knox City seedless watermelon festival in July.

Minerals: Oil, gas.

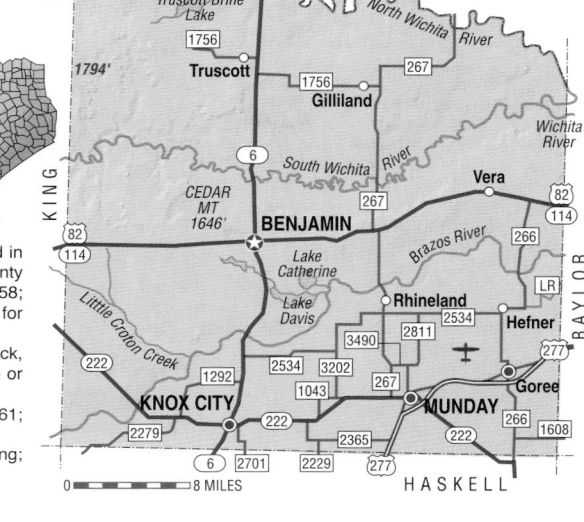

Agriculture: Wheat, cattle, cotton. Some cotton irrigated. Market value $59 million.

BENJAMIN (260) county seat; ranching, farm center; veterans memorial.

MUNDAY (1,187) portable buildings, other manufacturing; A&M vegetable research station.

KNOX CITY (1,085) agribusiness, petroleum center; USDA plant materials research center; hospital.

Other towns include: **Goree** (176); **Rhineland** (120) old church established by German immigrants.

Population 3,653
Change fm 2010 .... − 1.8
Area (sq. mi.) 855.5
Land Area (sq. mi.) 850.6
Altitude (ft.) 1,200–1,794
Rainfall (in.) 26.43

Jan. mean min. 29.1
July mean max. 96.3
Civ. Labor 1,428
Unemployed 3.2
Wages $10,511,604
Per Capita Income $36,564
Prop. Value $981,672,433
Retail Sales $33,078,203

For explanation of sources, symbols and abbreviations, see p. 192, and foldout map.

The Truscott Brine Lake, Knox County. Photo by Robert Plocheck.

Lamar County

Physical Features: North Texas county on divide between Red, Sulphur rivers; soils chiefly blackland, except along Red; pines, hardwoods; Pat Mayse Lake and Lake Crook.

Economy: Varied manufacturing, agribusiness, medical, government/services.

History: Caddo Indian area. First Anglo-American settlers arrived about 1815. County created in 1840 from Red River County; organized in 1841; named for second president of Republic, Mirabeau B. Lamar.

Race/Ethnicity: (In percent) Anglo, 74.4; Black, 13.2; Hispanic, 7.9; Asian, 0.8; Other, 1.8; Two or more races, 2.9.

Vital Statistics, annual: Births, 680; deaths, 641; marriages, 388; divorces, 268.

Recreation: Lake activities; Gambill goose refuge; hunting, fishing; state park; Trail de Paris rail-to-trail; Sam Bell Maxey Home; State Sen. A.M. Aikin Archives, other museums.

Minerals: Negligible.

Agriculture: Beef, hay, dairy, soybeans (first in acreage), wheat, corn, sorghum, cotton. Market value $84.9 million.

PARIS (25,207) county seat; varied manufacturing, food processing, government/services; hospitals; junior college; museums; Tour de Paris bicycle rally in July; archery pro-am tournament in March.

Other towns include: **Arthur City** (180), **Blossom** (1,561), **Brookston** (130), **Chicota** (150), **Cunningham** (110), **Deport** (560, partly in Red River County), **Pattonville** (180), **Petty** (130), **Powderly** (1,166), **Reno** (3,318), **Roxton** (652), **Sumner** (95), **Sun Valley** (75), **Toco** (74).

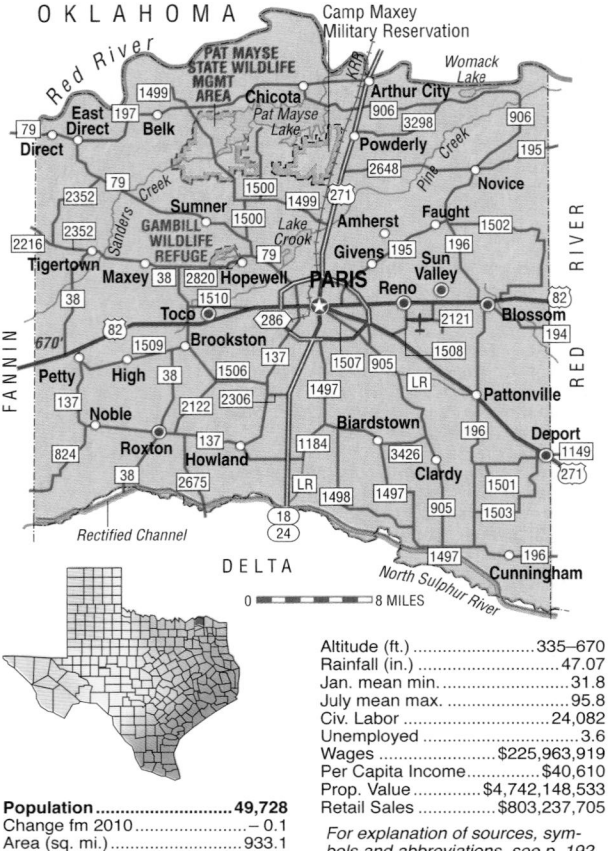

Population	49,728
Change fm 2010	– 0.1
Area (sq. mi.)	933.1
Land Area (sq. mi.)	907.2

Altitude (ft.)	335–670
Rainfall (in.)	47.07
Jan. mean min.	31.8
July mean max.	95.8
Civ. Labor	24,082
Unemployed	3.6
Wages	$225,963,919
Per Capita Income	$40,610
Prop. Value	$4,742,148,533
Retail Sales	$803,237,705

For explanation of sources, symbols and abbreviations, see p. 192, and foldout map.

The Red River valley along FM 906, Lamar County. Photo by Robert Plocheck.

Lamb County

Physical Features: Rich, red, brown soils on the High Plains; some hills; drains to upper Brazos River tributaries; numerous playas.

Economy: Agribusiness; distribution center; denim textiles.

History: Apache tribes, who were displaced by Comanches around 1700. The U.S. Army pushed the Comanches into the Indian Territory in 1875. Ranching began in the 1880s; farming started after 1900. County created in 1876 from the Bexar District and organized in 1908; named for Lt. G.A. Lamb, who died in battle of San Jacinto.

Race/Ethnicity: (In percent) Anglo, 38.8; Black, 4.8; Hispanic, 56.0; Asian, 0.4; Other, 1.9; Two or more races, 1.6.

Vital Statistics, annual: Births, 187; deaths, 147; marriages, 74; divorces, 32.

Recreation: Waylon Jennings Birthday Bash in June at Littlefield, museums, Earth Day in April.

Minerals: Oil, stone, gas.

Agriculture: Fed cattle; cotton, corn, wheat, grain sorghum, vegetables, soybeans, hay; sheep. 179,500 acres irrigated. Market value $575.3 million.

LITTLEFIELD (5,992) county seat; milk processing, agribusiness, manufacturing; hospital, prison, museum.

Olton (2,088) agribusiness, retail center; Sandcrawl museum; pheasant hunt in winter; Sandhills Celebration in August.

Other towns include: **Amherst** (670); **Earth** (975) farming center, dairies, feed lot; **Fieldton** (20); **Spade** (64); **Springlake** (98); **Sudan** (891) farming center, government/services, Homecoming Day in fall.

Population	13,158
Change fm 2010	– 5.9
Area (sq. mi.)	1,017.7
Land Area (sq. mi.)	1,016.2
Altitude (ft.)	3,390–3,870
Rainfall (in.)	18.87
Jan. mean min.	24.5
July mean max.	92.0
Civ. Labor	5,196
Unemployed	4.2
Wages	$39,767,417
Per Capita Income	$38,465
Prop. Value	$1,225,091,497
Retail Sales	$127,323,899

Lampasas County

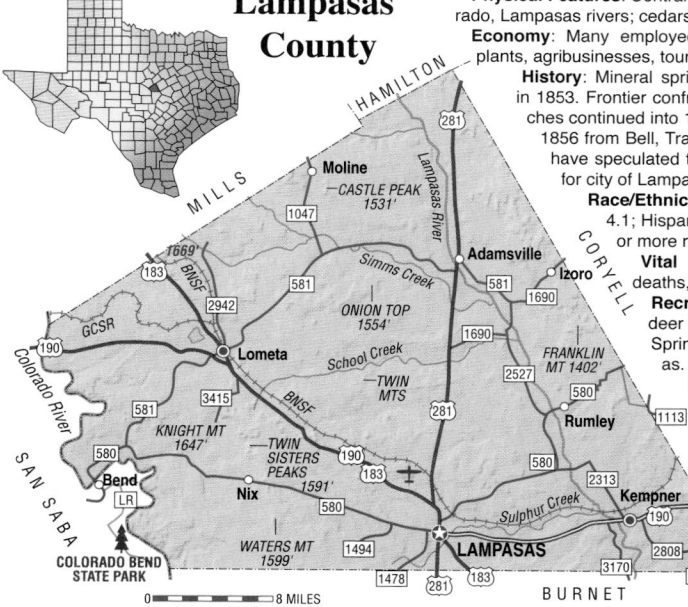

Physical Features: Central Texas on edge of Hill Country; Colorado, Lampasas rivers; cedars, oaks, pecans.

Economy: Many employed at Fort Hood, several industrial plants, agribusinesses, tourism.

History: Mineral springs attracted first Anglo-Americans in 1853. Frontier confrontations between settlers, Comanches continued into 1870s. County created, organized, in 1856 from Bell, Travis counties. Named for river. Some have speculated that an early expedition named river for city of Lampazos in Mexico.

Race/Ethnicity: (In percent) Anglo, 72.0; Black, 4.1; Hispanic, 20.0; Asian, 1.4; Other, 1.5; Two or more races, 2.9.

Vital Statistics, annual: Births, 219; deaths, 197; marriages, 118; divorces, 78.

Recreation: Scenic drives; state park; deer hunting, fishing in streams; Hancock Springs free-flow swim area at Lampasas.

Minerals: Sand and gravel, building stone.

Agriculture: Beef cattle, hay, goats, exotic animals. Market value $16.1 million. Hunting leases, ecotourism.

LAMPASAS (7,889) county seat; manufacturing, health care, retail; historic downtown; hospital, college extensions; museum; Spring Ho in July.

Other towns include: **Bend** (115, partly in San Saba County); **Izoro** (17); **Kempner** (1,066); **Lometa** (852) market and shipping point; Diamondback Jubilee in March.

Population	21,229
Change fm 2010	7.9
Area (sq. mi.)	713.9
Land Area (sq. mi.)	712.8
Altitude (ft.)	800–1,669
Rainfall (in.)	32.23
Jan. mean min.	33.4
July mean max.	95.6
Civ. Labor	9,488
Unemployed	3.5
Wages	$39,258,170
Per Capita Income	$48,098
Prop. Value	$2,689,357,060
Retail Sales	$221,915,927

La Salle County

Physical Features: Brushy plain, broken by Nueces, Frio rivers and their tributaries; chocolate, dark gray, sandy loam soils.

Economy: Agribusiness, hunting leases, tourism, government services.

History: Coahuiltecans, squeezed out by migrating Apaches. U.S. military outpost in the 1850s, settlers of Mexican descent established nearby village. Anglo-American ranching developed in the 1870s. County created from Bexar District in 1858; organized in 1880; named for Robert Cavelier Sieur de La Salle, French explorer who died in Texas.

Race/Ethnicity: (In percent) Anglo, 12.0; Black, 1.3; Hispanic, 86.4; Asian, 0.4; Other, 0.8; Two or more races, 0.6.

Vital Statistics, annual: Births, 104; deaths, 61; marriages, 31; divorces, 20.

Recreation: Nature trails; school where Lyndon B. Johnson taught; wildlife management area; deer, bird, javelina hunting, fishing; wild hog cookoff in March.

Minerals: Oil, gas.

Agriculture: Beef cattle, peanuts, watermelons, grain sorghum. Market value $18.7 million.

COTULLA (4,157) county seat; oil and lodging, state prison; hunting center; Brush Country museum.

Other towns include: **Encinal** (576), **Fowlerton** (49).

Population	7,531
Change fm 2010	9.4
Area (sq. mi.)	1,494.2
Land Area (sq. mi.)	1,486.7
Altitude (ft.)	255–650
Rainfall (in.)	24.70
Jan. mean min.	38.9
July mean max.	96.9
Civ. Labor	4,578
Unemployed	2.1
Wages	$54,060,425
Per Capita Income	$34,696
Prop. Value	$5,439,424,680
Retail Sales	$156,225,113

Lavaca County

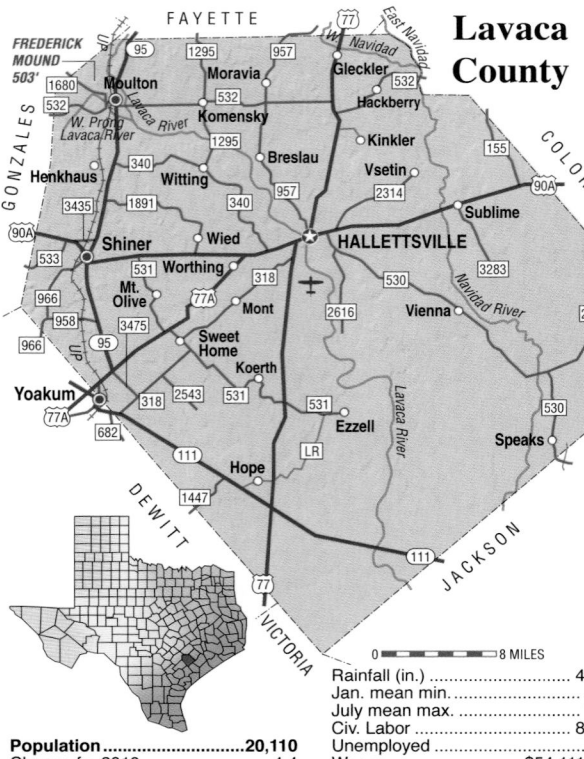

Physical Features: Coastal Plains county; north rolling; sandy loam, black waxy soils; drains to Lavaca, Navidad rivers.

Economy: Varied manufacturing, oil and gas production, agribusinesses, tourism.

History: Coahuiltecan area; later a Comanche area until 1850s. Anglo-Americans first settled in 1831. Germans and Czechs arrived 1880–1900. County created, organized, in 1846 from Colorado, Jackson, Gonzales, Victoria counties. Name is Spanish for cow, la vaca, from name of river.

Race/Ethnicity: (In percent) Anglo, 73.5; Black, 6.8; Hispanic, 18.8; Asian, 0.5; Other, 0.7; Two or more races, 1.4.

Vital Statistics, annual: Births, 231; deaths, 269; marriages, 109; divorces, 28.

Recreation: Deer, other hunting, fishing; wildflower trails, historic sites, churches; Fiddlers Frolics in Hallettsville in April.

Minerals: Some oil, gas.

Agriculture: Cattle, forage, poultry, rice, corn, sorghum. Market value $61.9 million. Hunting leases.

HALLETTSVILLE (2,629) county seat; retail center; varied manufacturing; agribusiness; museum, library, hospital; domino, "42" tournaments; Kolache Fest in September.

Yoakum (6,017, partly in DeWitt County); cattle, leather, meat processing; hospital; museum; Tom Tom festival in June.

Shiner (2,121) Spoetzl brewery, varied manufacturing; museum; clinic; Half Moon Holidays in July.

Other towns include: **Moulton** (912) agribusiness, Town & Country Jamboree in July; **Sublime** (75); **Sweet Home** (360).

Population	20,110
Change fm 2010	4.4
Area (sq. mi.)	970.4
Land Area (sq. mi.)	969.7
Altitude (ft.)	85–503
Rainfall (in.)	41.06
Jan. mean min.	41.3
July mean max.	93.4
Civ. Labor	8,658
Unemployed	2.9
Wages	$54,111,690
Per Capita Income	$47,880
Prop. Value	$4,419,219,229
Retail Sales	$229,012,128

Lee County

Physical Features: Rolling terrain, broken by Yegua and its tributaries; red to black soils, sandy to heavy loams; Somerville Lake.

Economy: Varied manufacturing, agribusiness, lignite coal operations, government/services.

History: Tonkawas; removed in 1855 to the Brazos Reservation. Most Anglo-American settlement occurred after the Texas Revolution. Slaveholding area. Germans, Wends, and other Europeans began arriving in the 1850s. County created from Bastrop, Burleson, Fayette, Washington counties in 1874 and organized the same year; named for Gen. Robert E. Lee.

Race/Ethnicity: (In percent) Anglo, 63.4; Black, 11.2; Hispanic, 23.4; Asian, 0.6; Other, 1.3; Two or more races, 1.8.

Vital Statistics, annual: Births, 208; deaths, 183; marriages, 85; divorces, 34.

Recreation: Fishing, hunting; lake activities, state park; pioneer village; historic sites.

Minerals: Lignite coal, iron ore, gravel.

Agriculture: Beef cattle, hay, nurseries, poultry, peanuts, goats, horses, aquaculture, corn; some irrigation. Market value $38.6 million. Firewood.

GIDDINGS (5,106) county seat; oil/gas, manufacturing, agriculture; museum, old Presbyterian church (1886); rodeo in May.

Other towns include: **Dime Box** (381); **Lexington** (1,208) utility plant, livestock-marketing center, small businesses, log cabins heritage center, homecoming rodeo and barbecue cookoff in May; **Lincoln** (336); **Serbin** (109) Wendish museum.

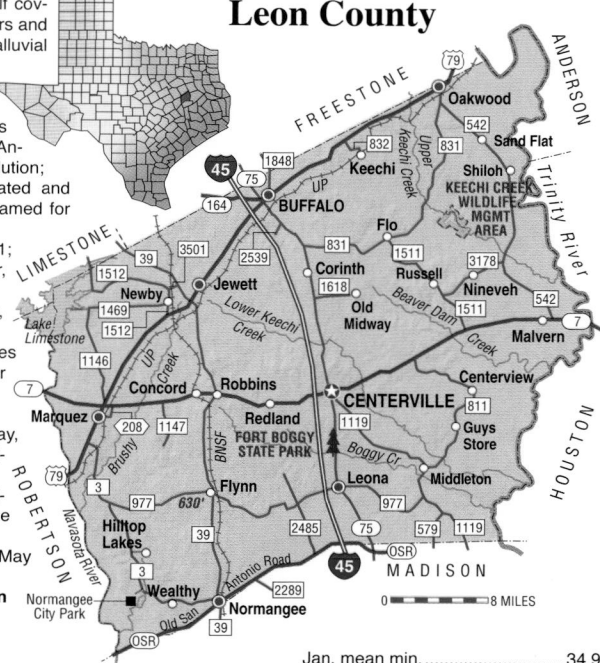

For explanation of sources, symbols and abbreviations, see p. 192, and foldout map.

Population	17,144
Change fm 2010	3.2
Area (sq. mi.)	634.1
Land Area (sq. mi.)	629.0
Altitude (ft.)	238-762
Rainfall (in.)	36.61
Jan. mean min.	37.2
July mean max.	94.1
Civ. Labor	9,272
Unemployed	3.8
Wages	$83,367,495
Per Capita Income	$45,849
Prop. Value	$2,798,199,735
Retail Sales	$548,690,521

Leon County

Physical Features: Hilly, rolling, almost half covered by timber; drains to Navasota, Trinity rivers and tributaries; Lake Limestone; sandy, dark, alluvial soils.

Economy: Poultry farming, cattle ranching, hay.

History: Bidais, absorbed into the Kickapoos and other groups. Permanent settlement by Anglo-Americans occurred after the Texas Revolution; Germans arrived in the 1870s. County created and organized in 1846 from Robertson County; named for founder of Victoria, Martín de León.

Race/Ethnicity: (In percent) Anglo, 76.1; Black, 7.3; Hispanic, 14.6; Asian, 0.7; Other, 0.9; Two or more races, 1.5.

Vital Statistics, annual: Births, 213; deaths, 223; marriages, 115; divorces, 61.

Recreation: Hilltop Lakes resort area; sites of Camino Real, Fort Boggy State Park; deer hunting.

Minerals: Oil, natural gas.

Agriculture: Poultry, cow-calf production, hay, small grains. Market value $148.7 million. Hardwoods, pine marketed.

CENTERVILLE (928) county seat; agriculture, government/services; Christmas on the Square in December.

BUFFALO (1,924) oil and gas; library; May Spring Fest with fiddlers' contest.

Other towns include: **Concord** (28); **Flynn** (81); **Hilltop Lakes** (1,025) resort and retirement center; **Jewett** (1,237) steel mill, civic center, museum, library, Classic Coon Hunt in January; **Leona** (177) candle factory; **Marquez** (282); **Normangee** (681, partly in Madison County) farming and tourism; library, museum, city park; **Oakwood** (518).

Population	17,270
Change fm 2010	2.8
Area (sq. mi.)	1,080.6
Land Area (sq. mi.)	1,073.2
Altitude (ft.)	150–630
Rainfall (in.)	42.29
Jan. mean min.	34.9
July mean max.	93.7
Civ. Labor	8,259
Unemployed	4.4
Wages	$66,588,044
Per Capita Income	$37,988
Prop. Value	$3,566,639,860
Retail Sales	$192,014,487

Liberty County

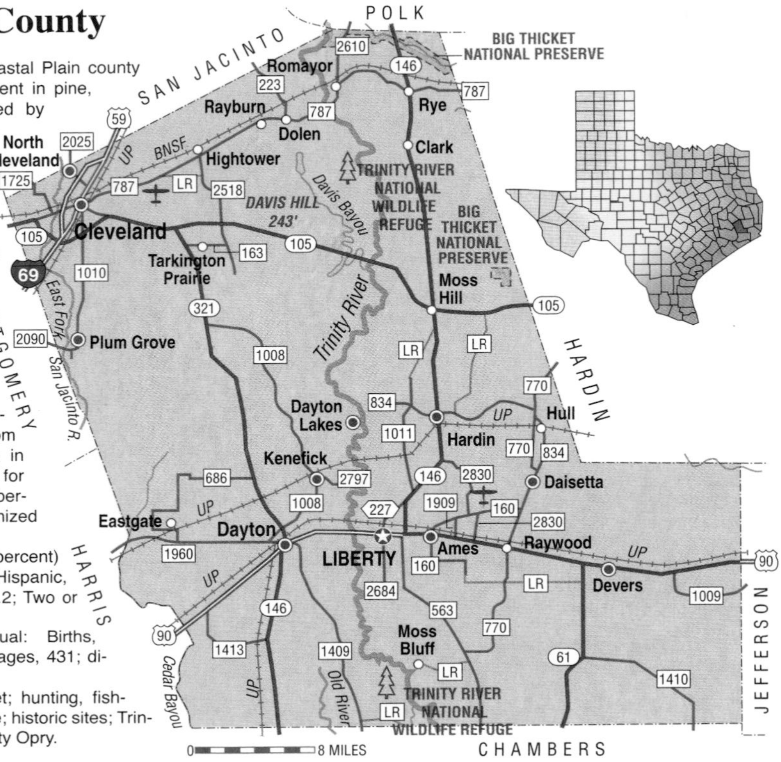

Physical Features: Coastal Plain county east of Houston; 60 percent in pine, hardwood timber; bisected by Trinity River; sandy, loam, black soils; Big Thicket.

Economy: Agribusiness; chemical plants; varied manufacturing; tourism; forest industries; prisons; many residents work in Houston; part of Houston metropolitan area.

History: Karankawa tribal area until the 1740s. Spanish established Atascosito settlement in 1756. Settlers from Louisiana began arriving in the 1810s. County named for Spanish municipality, Libertad; created in 1836, organized in 1837.

Race/Ethnicity: (In percent) Anglo, 63.3; Black, 10.2; Hispanic, 24.8; Asian, 0.6; Other, 1.2; Two or more races, 1.6.

Vital Statistics, annual: Births, 1,133; deaths, 765; marriages, 431; divorces, 243.

Recreation: Big Thicket; hunting, fishing; national wildlife refuge; historic sites; Trinity Valley exposition; Liberty Opry.

Minerals: Oil, gas.

Agriculture: Beef cattle; rice is principal crop. Also nursery crops, corn, hay, sorghum, bees (first in number of colonies). Market value $34.9 million. Some lumbering.

LIBERTY (9,327) county seat; petroleum-related industry, agribusiness; library, museum, regional historical resource depository; Liberty Bell, Price Daniel House; hospital; Jubilee in March.

Cleveland (8,131) forest products processed, shipped; tourism; library; museum; hospital.

Dayton (7,995) rice, oil center.

Other towns include: **Ames** (1,092); **Daisetta** (1,086); **Dayton Lakes** (98); **Devers** (513); **Hardin** (883); **Hull** (711); **Kenefick** (631); **North Cleveland** (258); **Plum Grove** (648); **Raywood** (231); **Romayor** (135); **Rye** (150).

For explanation of sources, symbols and abbreviations, see p. 192, and foldout map.

Population	86,323
Change fm 2010	14.1
Area (sq. mi.)	1,176.3
Land Area (sq. mi.)	1,158.4
Altitude (ft.)	3–243
Rainfall (in.)	61.25
Jan. mean min.	41.2
July mean max.	92.1
Civ. Labor	32,559
Unemployed	5.3
Wages	$202,927,132
Per Capita Income	$35,840
Prop. Value	$7,104,501,367
Retail Sales	$882,825,001

Sand hills of the Gene Howe Wildlife Management Area, Lipscomb County. Texas Parks & Wildlife photo.

Limestone County

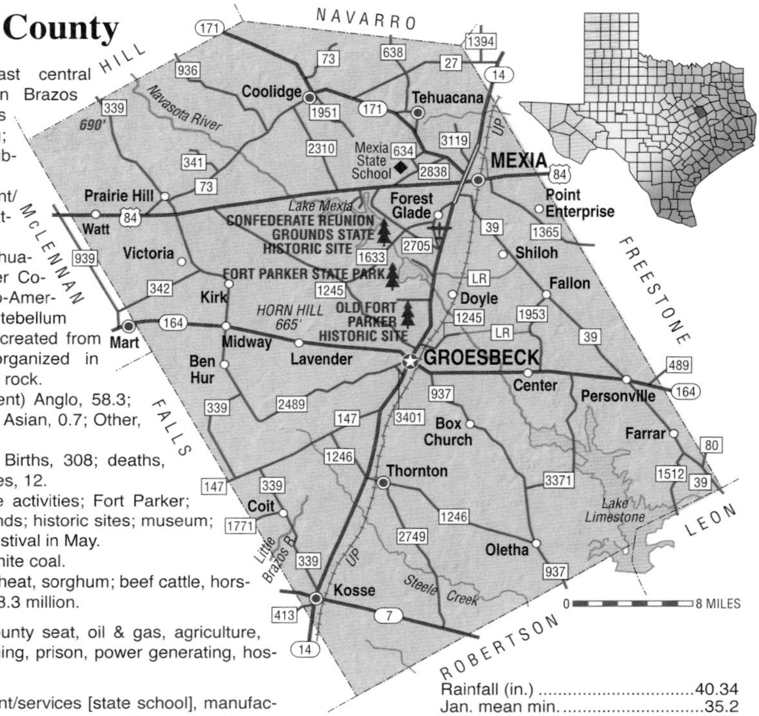

Physical Features: East central county on divide between Brazos and Trinity rivers; borders Blacklands, level to rolling; drained by Navasota and tributaries; Lake Limestone.

Economy: Government/services, electricity-generating plant.

History: Tawakoni (Tehuacana) and Waco area, later Comanche raiders. First Anglo-Americans arrived in 1833. Antebellum slaveholding area. County created from Robertson County and organized in 1846; named for indigenous rock.

Race/Ethnicity: (In percent) Anglo, 58.3; Black, 17.7; Hispanic, 22.4; Asian, 0.7; Other, 1.3; Two or more races, 1.8.

Vital Statistics, annual: Births, 308; deaths, 290; marriages, 129; divorces, 12.

Recreation: Fishing, lake activities; Fort Parker; Confederate Reunion Grounds; historic sites; museum; hunting; Groesbeck fiddle festival in May.

Minerals: Natural gas, lignite coal.

Agriculture: Hay, corn, wheat, sorghum; beef cattle, horses, poultry. Market value $48.3 million.

GROESBECK (4,320) county seat, oil & gas, agriculture, manufacturing, hunting, mining, prison, power generating, hospital, museum.

MEXIA (7,711) government/services [state school], manufacturing; hospital, college extension campus; Boomtown History Day in April.

Other towns include: **Coolidge** (984), **Kosse** (481), **Prairie Hill** (150), **Tehuacana** (288), **Thornton** (547).

Population	**23,519**
Change fm 2010	0.6
Area (sq. mi.)	933.2
Land Area (sq. mi.)	905.3
Altitude (ft.)	363–690
Rainfall (in.)	40.34
Jan. mean min.	35.2
July mean max.	94.1
Civ. Labor	8,190
Unemployed	5.3
Wages	$83,492,840
Per Capita Income	$33,945
Prop. Value	$3,057,554,118
Retail Sales	$244,238,794

Lipscomb County

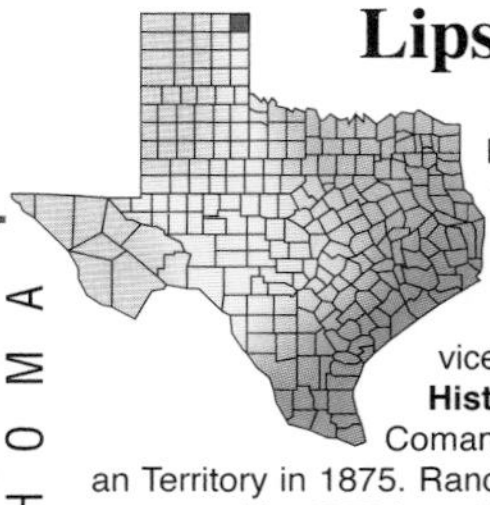

Physical Features: High Plains, broken in east; drains to tributaries of Canadian, Wolf Creek; sandy loam, black soils.

Economy: Oil and gas, agribusinesses, government/services.

History: Apaches, later Kiowas and Comanches who were driven into Indian Territory in 1875. Ranching began in late 1870s. County created in 1876 from Bexar District; organized in 1887; named for A.S. Lipscomb, Republic of Texas leader.

Race/Ethnicity: (In percent) Anglo, 62.0; Black, 1.8; Hispanic, 33.6; Asian, 0.7; Other, 2.3; Two or more races, 2.8.

Vital Statistics, annual: Births, 48; deaths, 21; marriages, 27; divorces, 11.

Recreation: Hunting; Wolf Creek museum, prairie chicken booming grounds.

Minerals: Oil, natural gas.

Agriculture: Cattle, corn, wheat, grain sorghum, hay, sunflowers. Some 23,000 acres irrigated. Market value $52.7 million.

LIPSCOMB (27), county seat; livestock center.

BOOKER (1,558, partly in Ochiltree County) trade center, library.

Other towns include: **Darrouzett** (367) Deutsches Fest in July; **Follett** (469); **Higgins** (413) library, Will Rogers Day in August.

Population	**3,355**
Change fm 2010	1.6
Area (sq. mi.)	932.3
Land Area (sq. mi.)	932.2
Altitude (ft.)	2,220–2,892
Rainfall (in.)	22.25
Jan. mean min.	18.1
July mean max.	94.0
Civ. Labor	1,642
Unemployed	2.8
Wages	$14,154,594
Per Capita Income	$54,838
Prop. Value	$792,679,978
Retail Sales	$23,718,628

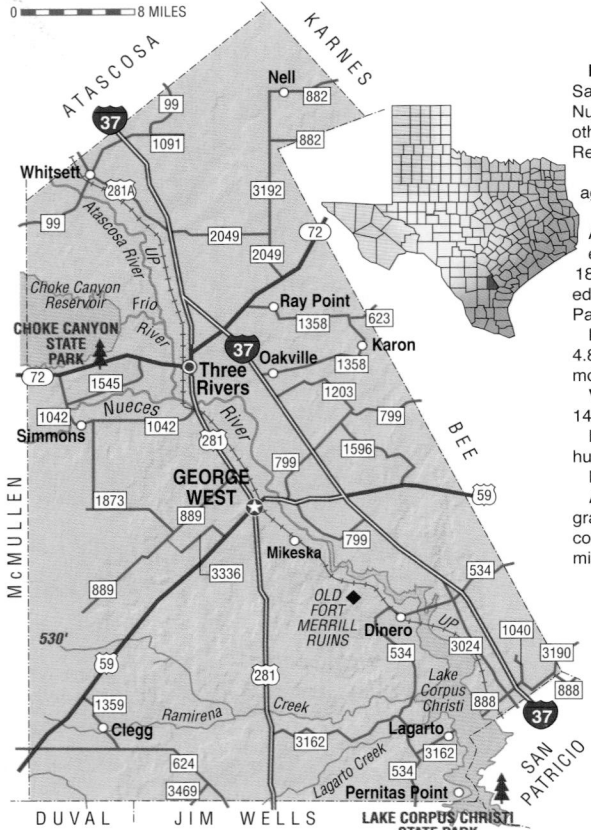

0 ━━━━ 8 MILES

Live Oak County

Physical Features: Brushy plains between San Antonio and Corpus Christi, partly broken by Nueces and tributaries; black waxy, gray sandy, other soils; Lake Corpus Christi, Choke Canyon Reservoir.

Economy: Oil, government/services, tourism, agribusinesses.

History: Coahuiltecans squeezed out by Lipan Apaches and Spanish. Spanish ranching started in the 1810s. Settlers from Ireland arrived in 1835. County named for predominant tree; created and organized in 1856 from Nueces and San Patricio counties.

Race/Ethnicity: (In percent) Anglo, 53.8; Black, 4.8; Hispanic, 40.0; Asian, 0.6; Other, 1.3; Two or more races, 1.0.

Vital Statistics, annual: Births, 133; deaths, 143; marriages, 65; divorces, 36.

Recreation: Lakes; water activities; state park; hunting; historic sites including Fort Merrill (1850s).

Minerals: Oil, gas, sand, gravel.

Agriculture: Cow-calf operations; hogs; corn, grain sorghum, cotton; some irrigation for hay, coastal Bermuda pastures. Market value $17.9 million.

GEORGE WEST (2,537) county seat, ranching, oil and gas operations, museums, library, Storyfest in November.

Three Rivers (1,925) oil and gas, hunting and fishing, agriculture, federal prison, salsa festival in April.

Other towns include: **Dinero** (344); **Lagarto** (735), **Pernitas Point** (274, partly in Jim Wells County), **Whitsett** (200).

Population 12,166		Unemployed 3.1
Change fm 2010 ....5.5	Rainfall (in.) 26.36	Wages $48,253,056
Area (sq. mi.) 1,078.9	Jan. mean min. 42.4	Per Capita Income $32,196
Land Area (sq. mi.) 1,039.7	July mean max. 95.5	Prop. Value $4,478,212,223
Altitude (ft.) 94–530	Civ. Labor 5,449	Retail Sales $189,032,383

The drive into Mentone, Loving County. Photo by Robert Plocheck.

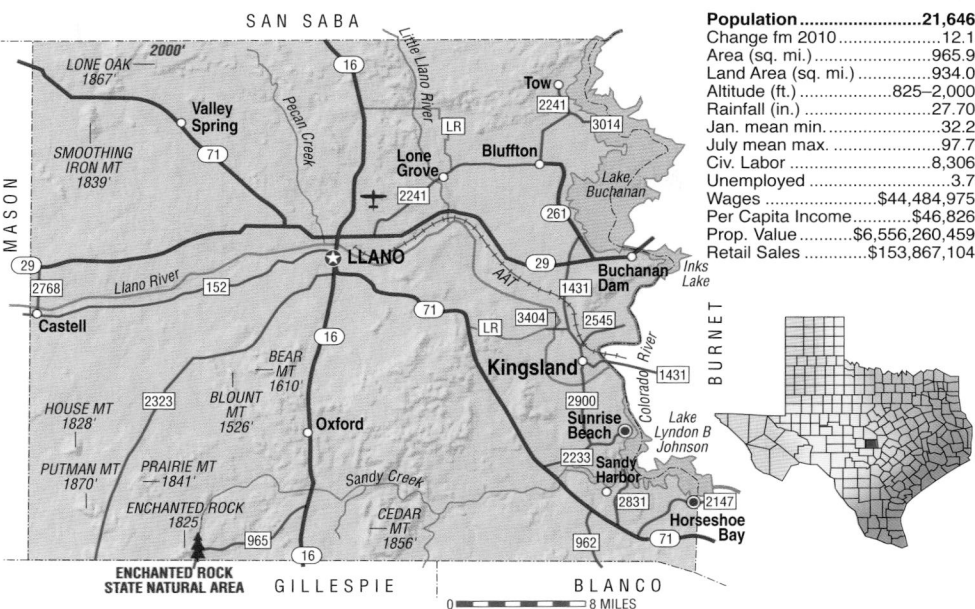

Population	**21,646**
Change fm 2010	12.1
Area (sq. mi.)	965.9
Land Area (sq. mi.)	934.0
Altitude (ft.)	825–2,000
Rainfall (in.)	27.70
Jan. mean min.	32.2
July mean max.	97.7
Civ. Labor	8,306
Unemployed	3.7
Wages	$44,484,975
Per Capita Income	$46,826
Prop. Value	$6,556,260,459
Retail Sales	$153,867,104

Llano County

Physical Features: Central county drains to Colorado, Llano rivers; rolling to hilly; Lake Buchanan, Inks Lake, Lake Lyndon B. Johnson.

Economy: Tourism, retirement, ranch trading center, vineyards.

History: Tonkawas, later Comanches. Anglo-American and German settlers arrived in the 1840s. County name is Spanish for plains; created and organized in 1856 from Bexar District and Gillespie County.

Race/Ethnicity: (In percent) Anglo, 86.1; Black, 1.2; Hispanic, 10.7; Asian, 0.6; Other, 1.0; Two or more races, 1.3.

Vital Statistics, annual: Births, 178; deaths, 311; marriages, 104; divorces, 64.

Recreation: Leading deer-hunting county; fishing, lake activities, major tourist area, Enchanted Rock, eagles' nest on Highway 29, bluebonnet festival, Hill Country Wine Trail in spring.

Minerals: Granite, vermiculite, llanite.

Agriculture: Beef cattle, sheep, goats. Market value $13.8 million. Deer-hunting, wildlife leases.

LLANO (3,301) county seat; agriculture, hunting, tourism; hospital; historic district; museum; Texas gold panning championship in September.

Kingsland (6,638) tourism, retirement community, recreation, vineyards; library; archaeological center; AquaBoom on July 4.

Other towns include: **Bluffton** (75); **Buchanan Dam** (1,523) hydroelectric industry, tourism, fishing, water sports; **Castell** (72); **Horseshoe Bay** (3,758, partly in Burnet County); **Sunrise Beach** (732); **Tow** (305); **Valley Spring** (50).

For explanation of sources, symbols and abbreviations, see p. 192, and foldout map.

Loving County

Physical Features: Flat desert terrain with a few low-rolling hills; slopes to Pecos River; Red Bluff Reservoir; sandy, loam, clay soils.

Economy: Oil and gas operations; cattle.

History: Land developers began operations in late 19th century. Oil discovered 1925. County created 1887 from Tom Green County; organized 1893, deorganized 1897, again organized 1931, the last organized. Named for Oliver Loving, trail driver. County is state's least populous.

Race/Ethnicity: (In percent) Anglo, 76.1; Black, 5.2; Hispanic, 19.4; Asian, 0.0; Other, 0.7; Two or more races, 0.0.

Vital Statistics, annual: Births, 0; deaths, 0; marriages, 2; divorces, 0.

Recreation: Pecos River, Red Bluff Lake.

Minerals: Oil, gas.

Agriculture: Cattle ranching. Market value $912,000.

MENTONE (25) county seat, oil-field supply center; the only town.

Population	152
Change fm 2010	85.4
Area (sq. mi.)	676.7
Land Area (sq. mi.)	668.9
Altitude (ft.)	2,660–3,374
Rainfall (in.)	12.57
Jan. mean min.	29.7
July mean max.	99.3
Civ. Labor	99
Unemployed	4.0
Wages	$1,309,659
Per Capita Income	$45,858
Prop. Value	$2,009,064,890
Retail Sales	4,582,556

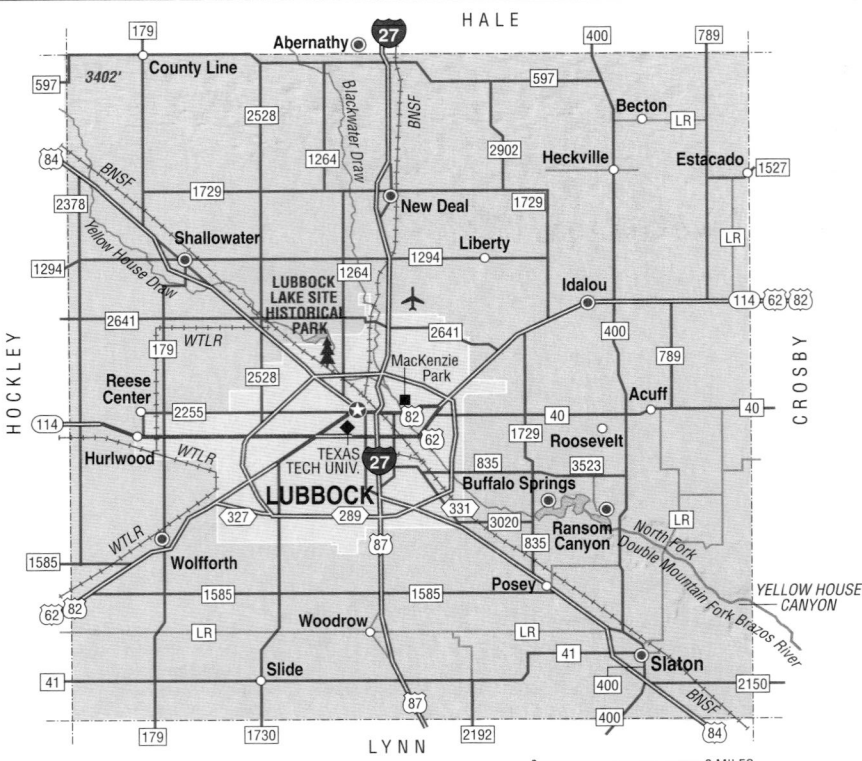

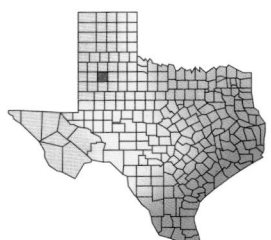

Lubbock County

Physical Features: South Plains, broken by 1,500 playas, upper Brazos River tributaries; rich soils with underground water.

Economy: Among world's largest cottonseed processing centers, a leading agribusiness center, cattle feedlots, varied manufacturing, higher education center, medical center, government/services.

History: Evidence of human habitation for 12,000 years. In historic period, Apache Indians, followed by Comanche hunters. Sheep raisers from Midwest arrived in the late 1870s. Cotton farms brought in Mexican laborers in the 1940s-1960s. County named for Col. Tom S. Lubbock, an organizer of the Confederate Terry's Rangers; county created in 1876 from Bexar District; organized in 1891.

Race/Ethnicity: (In percent) Anglo, 53.5; Black, 7.8; Hispanic, 35.5; Asian, 2.4; Other, 1.2; Two or more races, 1.8.

Vital Statistics, annual: Births, 4,112; deaths, 2,441; marriages, 2,009; divorces, 990.

Recreation: Lubbock Lake archaeological site; Texas Tech events; civic center; Buddy Holly statue, Walk of

For explanation of sources, symbols and abbreviations, see p. 192, and foldout map.

Fame, Lubbock Music Fest in fall; planetarium; Ranching Heritage Center; Panhandle-South Plains Fair, National Cowboy symposium in September; wine festivals; Buffalo Springs Lake.

Minerals: Oil, gas, stone, sand and gravel.

Agriculture: Second in bales of cotton produced. Fed beef, cow-calf operations; poultry, eggs; hogs. Other crops, nursery, grain sorghum, wheat, sunflowers, soybeans, hay, vegetables; more than 155,000 acres irrigated, mostly cotton. Market value $174.8 million.

Education: Texas Tech University with law and medical schools; Lubbock Christian University; South Plains Col-

lege branch; Wayland Baptist University off-campus center.

LUBBOCK (252,947) county seat; center for large agricultural area; manufacturing includes electronics, earth-moving equipment, food containers, fire-protection equipment, clothing, other products; distribution center for South Plains; feedlots; museum; government/services; hospitals, psychiatric hospital; wind power center.

Other towns include: **Buffalo Springs** (477); **Idalou** (2,350); **New Deal** (806); **Ransom Canyon** (1,094); **Shallowater** (2,557); **Slaton** (6,145) agriculture, government/services, Harvey House hotel, museums, sausagefest in October; **Wolfforth** (4,365) retail, government/services.

Also, part of **Abernathy** (2,779).

Population	307,412
Change fm 2010	10.2
Area (sq. mi.)	900.7
Land Area (sq. mi.)	895.6
Altitude (ft.)	2,821–3,402
Rainfall (in.)	19.12
Jan. mean min.	26.4
July mean max.	92.8
Civ. Labor	160,575
Unemployed	2.8
Wages	$1,530,050,078
Per Capita Income	$41,433
Prop. Value	$21,535,627,761
Retail Sales	$5,764,395,871

Lynn County

Physical Features: South Plains, broken by Caprock Escarpment, playas, draws; sandy loam, black, gray soils.

Economy: Agribusiness.

History: Apaches, ousted by Comanches who were removed to Indian Territory in 1875. Ranching began in 1880s. Farming developed after 1900. County created in 1876 from Bexar District; organized in 1903; named for Alamo victim W. Lynn.

Race/Ethnicity: (In percent) Anglo, 49.3; Black, 2.4; Hispanic, 47.4; Asian, 0.5; Other, 1.8; Two or more races, 1.7.

Vital Statistics, annual: Births, 70; deaths, 51; marriages, 31; divorces, 16.

Recreation: Pioneer museum in Tahoka; Dan Blocker museum in O'Donnell; sandhill crane migration in winter.

Minerals: Oil, natural gas.

Agriculture: Cotton produces largest income (first in acreage); 72,000 acres irrigated. Also, ranching, grain sorghum. Market value $67.6 million.

TAHOKA (2,681) county seat; agricultural center, electric/telephone cooperatives; hospital; museum; Harvest Festival in the fall.

O'Donnell (817, partly in Dawson County) commercial center.

Other towns include: **New Home** (350); **Wilson** (492).

Population **5,877**	July mean max. 91.9
Change fm 2010 .... – 0.6	Civ. Labor 2,693
Area (sq. mi.) 893.5	Unemployed 2.9
Land Area (sq. mi.) 891.9	Wages $18,780,815
Altitude (ft.) 2,660–3,300	Per Capita Income............$34,704
Rainfall (in.) 21.21	Prop. Value $969,673,630
Jan. mean min. 28.0	Retail Sales $18,192,190

Madison County

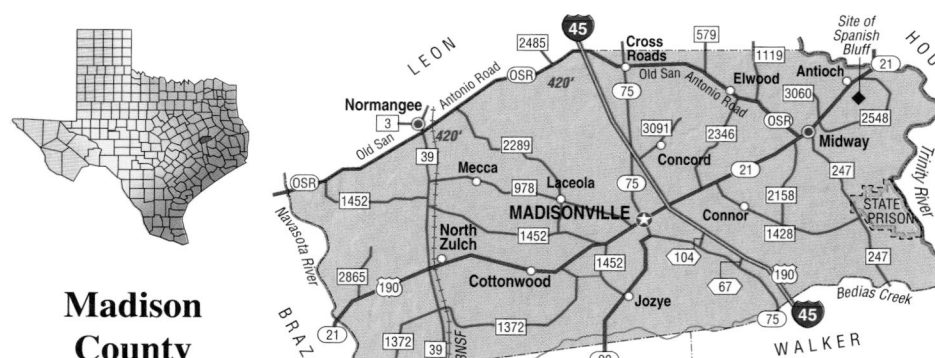

Physical Features: Hilly, draining to Trinity, Navasota rivers, Bedias Creek; one-fifth of area timbered; alluvial, loam, sandy soils.

Economy: Prison, government/services, varied manufacturing, agribusiness, oil production.

History: Caddo, Bidai Indian area; Kickapoos migrated from the east. Spanish settlements established in 1774 and 1805. Anglo-Americans arrived in 1829.

Census of 1860 showed 30 percent of population was black. County named for U.S. President James Madison; created from Grimes, Leon, and Walker counties 1853; organized 1854.

Race/Ethnicity: (In percent) Anglo, 54.9; Black, 20.6; Hispanic, 23.0; Asian, 0.7; Other, 1.4; Two or more races, 1.8.

Vital Statistics, annual: Births, 145; deaths, 126; marriages, 133; divorces, 50.

Recreation: Fishing, hunting; Spanish Bluff where survivors of the Gutierrez-Magee expedition were executed in 1813; other historic sites.

Minerals: sand, oil.

Agriculture: Nursery crops, cattle, horses, poultry raised; forage for livestock. Market value $82.9 million.

MADISONVILLE (4,695) county seat; farm-trade center, varied manu-

facturing; hospital, library; Spring Fling in April.

Other towns, **Midway** (232); **Normangee** (681, mostly in Leon County); **North Zulch** (600).

Population **14,422**	
Change fm 2010 ....5.5	
Area (sq. mi.) 472.4	
Land Area (sq. mi.) 466.1	
Altitude (ft.) 131–420	
Rainfall (in.) 45.12	
Jan. mean min. 36.9	
July mean max. 94.4	
Civ. Labor 4,491	
Unemployed 4.1	
Wages $42,736,637	
Per Capita Income.............$29,957	
Prop. Value $1,881,895,041	
Retail Sales $259,852,621	

Marion County

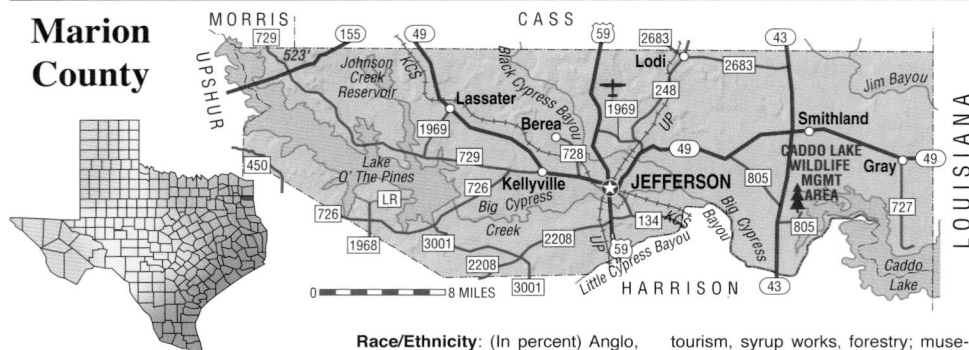

Physical Features: Northeastern county; hilly, three-quarters forested with pines, hardwoods; drains to Caddo Lake, Lake O' the Pines, Big Cypress Bayou; Johnson Creek Reservoir.

Economy: Agriculture, tourism, forestry, food processing.

History: Caddoes forced out in 1790s. Kickapoo in area when settlers arrived from Deep South around 1840. Antebellum slaveholding area. County created 1860 from Cass County, organized the same year; named for Gen. Francis Marion of American Revolution.

Race/Ethnicity: (In percent) Anglo, 71.1; Black, 21.3; Hispanic, 4.0; Asian, 0.8; Other, 1.2; Two or more races, 2.3.

Vital Statistics, annual: Births, 104; deaths, 167; marriages, 60; divorces, 37.

Recreation: Lake activities, hunting, Excelsior Hotel, 84 medallions on historic sites including Jay Gould railroad car, museum, historical homes tour in May, Spring Festival.

Minerals: Iron ore, natural gas, oil.

Agriculture: Beef cattle, hay. Market value $3.4 million. Forestry is most important industry.

JEFFERSON (2,060) county seat; tourism, syrup works, forestry; museum, library; historical sites.

Other towns include: **Lodi** (175).

Population	9,928
Change fm 2010	– 5.8
Area (sq. mi.)	420.3
Land Area (sq. mi.)	380.9
Altitude (ft.)	168–523
Rainfall (in.)	48.23
Jan. mean min.	32.7
July mean max.	92.6
Civ. Labor	4,446
Unemployed	4.4
Wages	$16,086,864
Per Capita Income	$36,419
Prop. Value	$1,084,281,810
Retail Sales	$61,592,975

Martin County

Physical Features: South Plains; sandy, loam soils, broken by playas, creeks; Sulphur Springs Draw Reservoir.

Economy: Oil and gas production, agribusiness.

History: Apaches, ousted by Comanches who in turn were forced out by the U.S. Army in 1875. Farming began in 1881. County created from Bexar District in 1876; organized in 1884; named for Wylie Martin, senator of Republic of Texas.

Race/Ethnicity: (In percent) Anglo, 49.6; Black, 2.9; Hispanic, 47.1; Asian, 0.5; Other, 1.5; Two or more races, 1.1.

Vital Statistics, annual: Births, 93; deaths, 52; marriages, 23; divorces, 16.

Recreation: Museum, settlers reunion in July at Stanton.

Minerals: Oil, gas.

Agriculture: Cotton, beef cattle, milo, wheat, horses, meat goats. Market value $20.3 million.

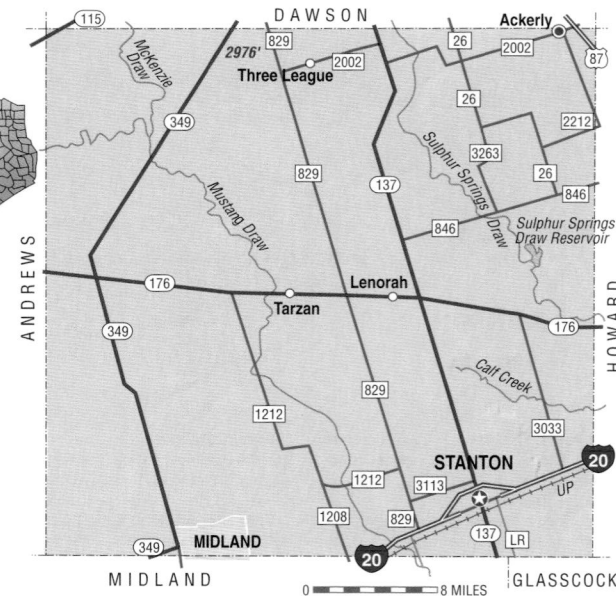

STANTON (2,937) county seat; oil and gas production, agribusiness; commuting to Midland, Big Spring; hospital; museum, historic monastery, other historic buildings; Old Sorehead trade days April, June, October.

Other towns include: **Ackerly** (237, partly in Dawson County); **Lenorah** (83); **Tarzan** (30). A small part of **Midland**.

Population	5,753
Change fm 2010	19.9
Area (sq. mi.)	915.7
Land Area (sq. mi.)	914.9
Altitude (ft.)	2,470–2,976
Rainfall (in.)	17.56
Jan. mean min.	30.0
July mean max.	94.0
Civ. Labor	2,750
Unemployed	2.7
Wages	$31,750,196
Per Capita Income	$46,781
Prop. Value	$4,705,459,400
Retail Sales	$101,786,413

For explanation of sources, symbols and abbreviations, see p. 192, and foldout map.

Mason County

Physical Features: Central county; hilly, draining to Llano and San Saba rivers and their tributaries; limestone, red soils; varied timber.

Economy: Sand plants, agriculture, tourism, hunting.

History: Lipan Apaches in area, driven south by Comanches around 1790. German settlers arrived in the mid-1840s, followed by Anglo-Americans. Mexican immigration increased after 1930. County created from Bexar and Gillespie counties in 1858, organized the same year; named for Mexican War victim U.S. Army Lt. G.T. Mason.

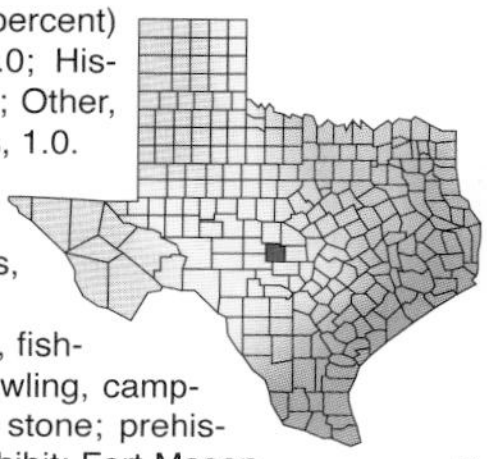

Race/Ethnicity: (In percent) Anglo, 72.7; Black, 1.0; Hispanic, 25.4; Asian, 0.3; Other, 1.1; Two or more races, 1.0.

Vital Statistics, annual: Births, 51; deaths, 44; marriages, 26; divorces, 18.

Recreation: Hunting, fishing; kayaking, rock crawling, camping; historic homes of stone; prehistoric Indian artifacts exhibit; Fort Mason, where Robert E. Lee served; bat cave; wildflower drives in spring, Roundup rodeo in July.

Minerals: Sand, topaz, granite.

Agriculture: Beef cattle, hay, meat goats. Market value $51.4 million. Hunting leases important.

MASON (2,172) county seat; agriculture, hunting, nature tourism; museums, historical district, homes, rock

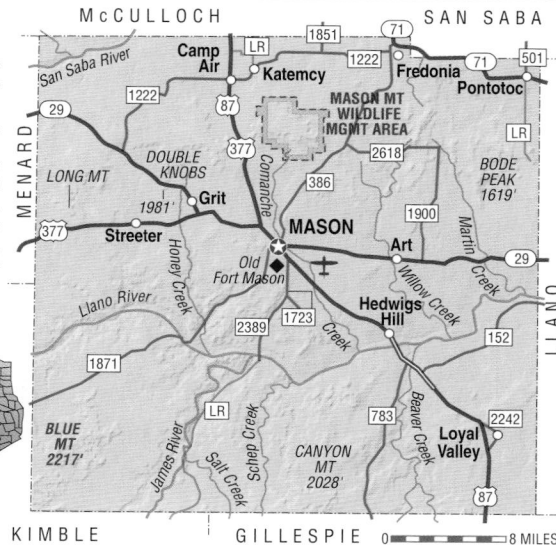

fences built by German settlers; wild game dinner in November.

Other towns include: **Art** (14), **Fredonia** (55), **Pontotoc** (125).

Population	**4,280**
Change fm 2010	6.7
Area (sq. mi.)	932.2
Land Area (sq. mi.)	928.8

Altitude (ft.)	1,180–2,217
Rainfall (in.)	29.19
Jan. mean min.	32.1
July mean max.	92.3
Civ. Labor	1,722
Unemployed	3.3
Wages	$8,806,859
Per Capita Income	$42,113
Prop. Value	$2,210,544,630
Retail Sales	$21,523,726

Texas 176 through Tarzan, Martin County. Photo by Robert Plocheck.

Matagorda County

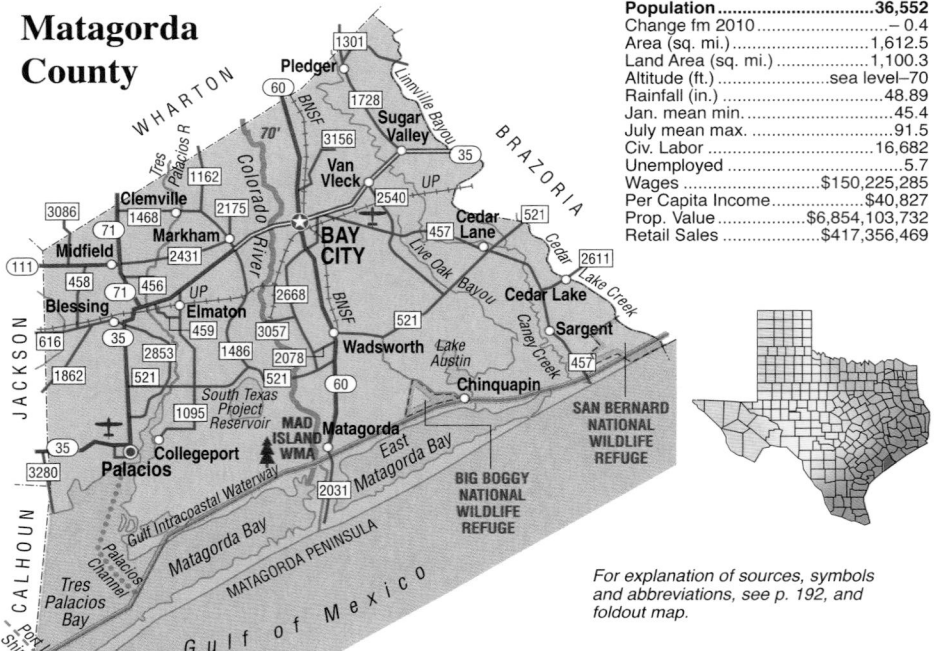

For explanation of sources, symbols and abbreviations, see p. 192, and foldout map.

Population	**36,552**
Change fm 2010	– 0.4
Area (sq. mi.)	1,612.5
Land Area (sq. mi.)	1,100.3
Altitude (ft.)	sea level–70
Rainfall (in.)	48.89
Jan. mean min.	45.4
July mean max.	91.5
Civ. Labor	16,682
Unemployed	5.7
Wages	$150,225,285
Per Capita Income	$40,827
Prop. Value	$6,854,103,732
Retail Sales	$417,356,469

Physical Features: Gulf Coastal Plain; flat, broken by bays; many different soils; drains to Colorado River, creeks, coast; South Texas Project Reservoir.

Economy: Agribusiness, oil and gas fields, refinery.

History: Karankawa tribal area, Tonkawas in the area later. Anglo-Americans arrived in 1822. Mexican immigration increased after 1920. An original county, created in 1836 from a Spanish municipality, named for canebrake; organized in 1837; settled by Austin colonists.

Race/Ethnicity: (In percent) Anglo, 43.8; Black, 11.2; Hispanic, 42.7; Asian, 2.0; Other, 1.4; Two or more races, 1.7.

Vital Statistics, annual: Births, 533; deaths, 407; marriages, 266; divorces, 114.

Recreation: Wildlife hunting and viewing, fishing (fresh and salt water), beaches, sailing, historic sites, museums; Bay City rice festival in October.

Minerals: Oil and gas.

Agriculture: Cotton, rice, soybeans, corn, grain sorgrum; some 33,000 acres of crops irrigated; cattle, turf, aquaculture (first in value). Market value $129.7 million.

BAY CITY (17,531) county seat;

government/services, education, nuclear power plant; petrochemicals; agribusiness; hospital; junior college branch.

Palacios (4,619) tourism, seafood industry; hospital; Marine Education Center; public fishing piers; Bay Festival on Labor Day.

Other towns include: **Blessing** (965) historic sites; **Cedar Lane** (300); **Collegeport** (80); **Elmaton** (160); **Markham** (1,048); **Matagorda** (528); **Midfield** (305); **Pledger** (265); **Sargent** (900) retirement community, fishing, birding, commercial fishing, barbecue cookoff in April; **Van Vleck** (1,979); **Wadsworth** (160).

Madagorda Harbor. Photo by Robert Plocheck.

Maverick County

Physical Features: Southwestern county on the Rio Grande; broken, rolling surface, with dense brush; clay, sandy, alluvial soils.

Economy: Oil, government/services, agribusiness, tourism.

History: Coahuiltecan area; later Comanches arrived. Spanish ranching began in the 1760s. Anglo-Americans arrived in 1834. County named for Sam A. Maverick, whose name is now a synonym for unbranded cattle; created in 1856 from Kinney County; organized in 1871.

Race/Ethnicity: (In percent) Anglo, 2.8; Black, 0.6; Hispanic, 95.1; Asian, 0.7; Other, 1.7; Two or more races, 0.5.

Vital Statistics, annual: Births, 1,150; deaths, 398; marriages, 594; divorces, 120.

Recreation: Tourist gateway to Mexico; white-tailed deer, bird hunting; fishing; historic sites, Fort Duncan museum.

Minerals: Oil, gas, sand, gravel.

Agriculture: Cattle feedlots; pecans, vegetables, sorghum, wheat; goats, sheep. Some irrigation from Rio Grande. Market value $32.6 million.

EAGLE PASS (28,202) county seat; government/services, retail center, tourism; hospital; junior college, Sul Ross college branch; entry point to Piedras Negras, Mex., Nacho Festival in Piedras Negras in October.

Other communities include: **Chula Vista** (3,888), **Eidson Road** (9,135), **El Indio** (172), **Las Quintas Fronterizas** (3,517), and **Rosita** (2,730), all immediately south of Eagle Pass. Also, **Elm Creek** (2,730) and **Quemado** (221).

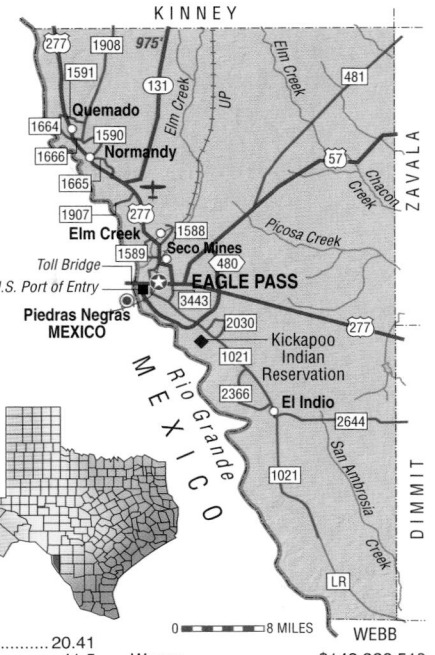

Population	58,485
Change fm 2010	7.8
Area (sq. mi.)	1,291.8
Land Area (sq. mi.)	1,279.3
Altitude (ft.)	550–975
Rainfall (in.)	20.41
Jan. mean min.	41.5
July mean max.	98.1
Civ. Labor	23,784
Unemployed	7.6
Wages	$148,326,519
Per Capita Income	$28,636
Prop. Value	$3,946,477,770
Retail Sales	$661,423,240

Population	7,987
Change fm 2010	– 3.6
Area (sq. mi.)	1,073.4
Land Area (sq. mi.)	1,065.6
Altitude (ft.)	1,280–2,021
Rainfall (in.)	27.60
Jan. mean min.	32.2
July mean max.	94.2
Civ. Labor	3,697
Unemployed	3.5
Wages	$30,311,285
Per Capita Income	$37,492
Prop. Value	$1,647,124,620
Retail Sales	$97,275,358

McCulloch County

Physical Features: Hilly and rolling; drains to Colorado River, Brady Creek and Brady Creek Reservoir, San Saba River; black loams to sandy soils.

Economy: Agribusiness, industrial sand production, hunting leases.

History: Apache area. First Anglo-American settlers arrived in the late 1850s, but Comanche raids delayed further settlement until the 1870s. County created from Bexar District in 1856; organized in 1876; named for San Jacinto veteran Gen. Ben McCulloch.

Race/Ethnicity: (In percent) Anglo, 63.5; Black, 2.8; Hispanic, 32.4; Asian, 0.8; Other, 1.2; Two or more races, 1.9.

Vital Statistics, annual: Births, 87; deaths, 117; marriages, 59; divorces, 33.

Recreation: Hunting, lake activities, museums, goat cookoff on Labor Day, Hogtoberfest in October, golf tournaments.

Minerals: Sand, oil, and gas.

Agriculture: Beef cattle and sheep; also small grains, goats, hay, cotton. Market value $22.6 million. Hunting leases.

BRADY (5,472) county seat; silica sand, oil-field equipment, ranching, tourism, other manufacturing; hospital; Heart of Texas car show in April, Cinco de Mayo.

Other towns: **Doole** (74), **Lohn** (149), **Melvin** (180), **Mercury** (166), **Rochelle** (163), and **Voca** (56).

McLennan County

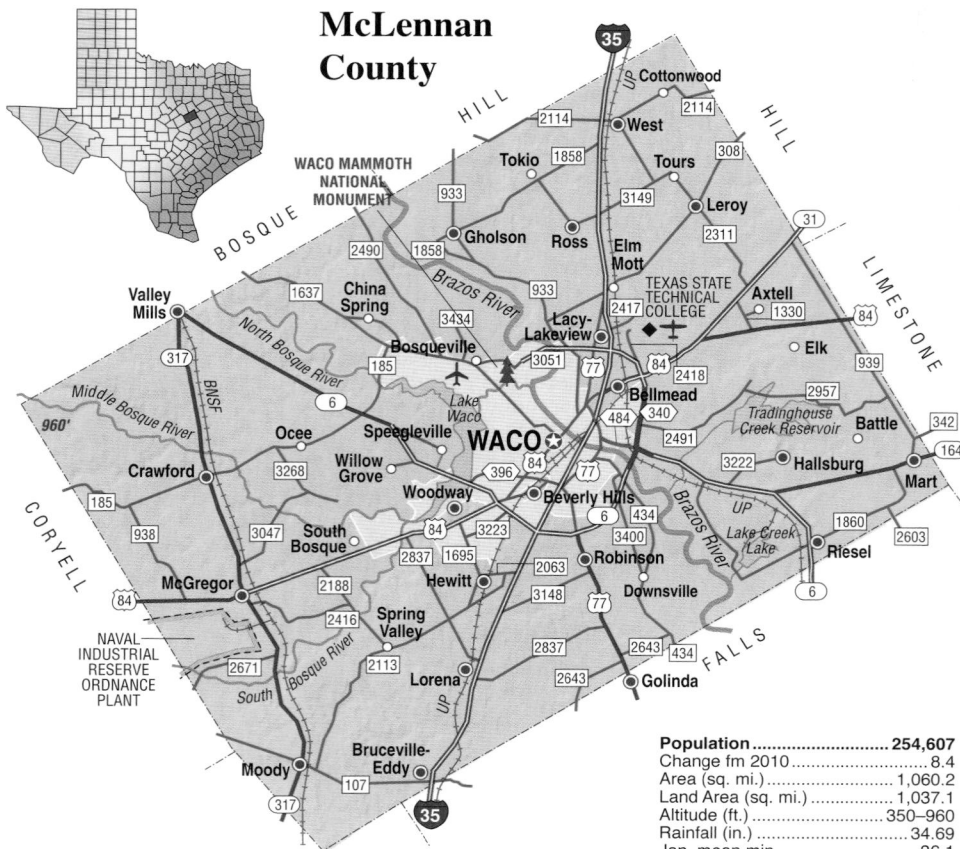

Population 254,607
Change fm 2010 .... 8.4
Area (sq. mi.) 1,060.2
Land Area (sq. mi.) 1,037.1
Altitude (ft.) 350–960
Rainfall (in.) 34.69
Jan. mean min. 36.1
July mean max. 96.3
Civ. Labor 119,271
Unemployed 3.3
Wages $1,299,492,120
Per Capita Income................. $39,740
Prop. Value $20,064,830,468
Retail Sales $3,772,799,470

Physical Features: Central Texas county of mostly Blackland prairie, but rolling hills in west; drains to Bosque, Brazos rivers and Lake Waco, Tradinghouse Creek Reservoir, Lake Creek Lake; heavy, loam, sandy soils.

Economy: Agribusiness, education, health services.

History: Tonkawas, Wichitas and Wacos in area. Anglo-American settlers arrived in the 1840s. Indians removed to Brazos reservations in 1854. County created from Milam County in 1850, organized the same year; named for settler, Neil McLennan Sr.

Race/Ethnicity: (In percent) Anglo, 56.0; Black, 15.0; Hispanic, 26.4; Asian, 1.7; Other, 1.2; Two or more races, 2.0.

Vital Statistics, annual: Births, 3,528; deaths, 2,123; marriages, 1,576; divorces, 886.

Recreation: Texas Ranger Hall of Fame, museum; Texas Sports Hall of Fame; Dr Pepper Museum; Cameron Park; drag boat races April and May; zoo; historic sites, homes; museums; libraries, art center; symphony; civic theater; Baylor University events; Heart o' Texas Fair in October.

Minerals: Sand, gravel, limestone.

Agriculture: Corn, silage, wheat, beef cattle, dairies. Market value $183 million.

Education: Baylor University; community college; Texas State Technical College; university extensions.

WACO (136,706) county seat; manufacturing, higher education, medical services/hospital, government/services, finance; riverside park, historic suspension bridge, zoo; Magnolia Silos market; Waco Mammoth National Monument; wine festivals in April and October.

Hewitt (14,217) medical services/hospital, construction, retail; car show and concert in April.

West (2,940) known for Czech foods; varied manufacturing; Westfest Labor Day weekend.

Other towns include: **Axtell** (300); **Bellmead** (10,655); **Beverly Hills** (2,025); **Bruceville-Eddy** (1,873, partly in Falls County); **China Spring** (1,378); **Crawford** (745); **Elm Mott** (300); **Gholson** (1,088); **Hallsburg** (504); **Lacy-Lakeview** (6,671); **Leroy** (336); **Lorena** (1,766); **Mart** (1,907) agricultural center, some manufacturing, museum, juvenile correction facility.

Also, **McGregor** (5,155) agriculture, manufacturing, distribution; private telephone museum; Frontier Founders Day in September; **Moody** (1,393) agriculture, commuting to Waco, Temple; library; Cotton Harvest fest in September; **Riesel** (1,027); **Robinson** (11,617); **Ross** (300); **Woodway** (8,955).

Part of **Golinda** (600, mostly in Falls County) and part of **Valley Mills** (1,220, mostly in Bosque County).

For explanation of sources, symbols and abbreviations, see p. 192, and foldout map.

McMullen County

Physical Features: Southern county of brushy plain, sloping to Frio, Nueces rivers and tributaries, Choke Canyon Reservoir; saline clay soils.

Economy: Government/services, retail, agriculture, oil and gas services.

History: Coahuiltecans, squeezed out by Lipan Apaches and other tribes. Anglo-American settlers arrived in 1858. Sheep ranching of 1870s attracted Mexican laborers. County created from Atascosa, Bexar, Live Oak counties 1858; organized 1862, reorganized 1877; named for Nueces River pioneer-empresario John McMullen.

Race/Ethnicity: (In percent) Anglo, 53.5; Black, 2.8; Hispanic, 42.4; Asian, 0.5; Other, 1.0; Two or more races, 2.4.

Vital Statistics, annual: Births, 0; deaths, 7; marriages, 9; divorces, 3.

Recreation: Hunting, wildlife viewing; lake activities, state park, wildlife management area; Labor Day rodeo.

Minerals: Gas, oil, lignite coal, caliche, kaolinite.

Agriculture: Beef cattle. Market value $8.3 million. Wildlife enterprises important.

TILDEN (338), county seat; oil, gas, lignite mining, ranch center, government/services.

Other towns include: **Calliham** (100).

Population	749
Change fm 2010	5.9
Area (sq. mi.)	1,156.8
Land Area (sq. mi.)	1,139.4
Altitude (ft.)	150–642
Rainfall (in.)	23.99
Jan. mean min.	42.6
July mean max.	96.4
Civ. Labor	715
Unemployed	1.8
Wages	$6,246,290
Per Capita Income	$58,513
Prop. Value	$3,195,671,226
Retail Sales	$28,103,144

Medina County

Physical Features: Southwestern county with scenic hills in north; south has fertile valleys, rolling surface; Medina River, Medina Lake.

Economy: Agribusiness, tourism, commuters to San Antonio.

History: Lipan Apaches and Comanches in area. Settled by Alsatians led by Henri Castro in 1844. Mexican immigration increased after 1900. County created and organized in 1848 from Bexar; named for river, probably for Spanish engineer Pedro Medina.

Race/Ethnicity: (In percent) Anglo, 43.8; Black, 2.9; Hispanic, 51.9; Asian, 0.8; Other, 1.3; Two or more races, 1.4.

Vital Statistics, annual: Births, 585; deaths, 428; marriages, 310; divorces, 112.

Recreation: A leading deer area; scenic drives, camping, fishing, historic buildings, museum, market trail days most months.

Minerals: Oil and natural gas.

Agriculture: Cattle, corn, grains, cotton, hay, vegetables, aquaculture; 50,000 acres irrigated. Market value $115.5 million.

HONDO (9,313) county seat; flight training center, aerospace industry, agribusiness, varied manufacturing, hunting leases; hospital; prisons; wild game festival in January.

Castroville (3,016) farming; tourism; commuting to San Antonio; Landmark Inn, museum; St. Louis Day celebration in August.

Devine (4,851) commuters, shipping for truck crop-livestock; fall festival in October.

Other towns: **D'Hanis** (859), **La Coste** (1,213), **Natalia** (1,545), **Riomedina** (60), **Yancey** (209). Also, **Lytle** (2,893, mostly in Atascosa County).

Population	50,921
Change fm 2010	10.7
Area (sq. mi.)	1,334.4
Land Area (sq. mi.)	1,325.4
Altitude (ft.)	570–1,995
Rainfall (in.)	30.32
Jan. mean min.	39.1
July mean max.	94.9
Civ. Labor	21,495
Unemployed	3.3
Wages	$92,404,690
Per Capita Income	$38,189
Prop. Value	$5,720,709,063
Retail Sales	$575,692,910

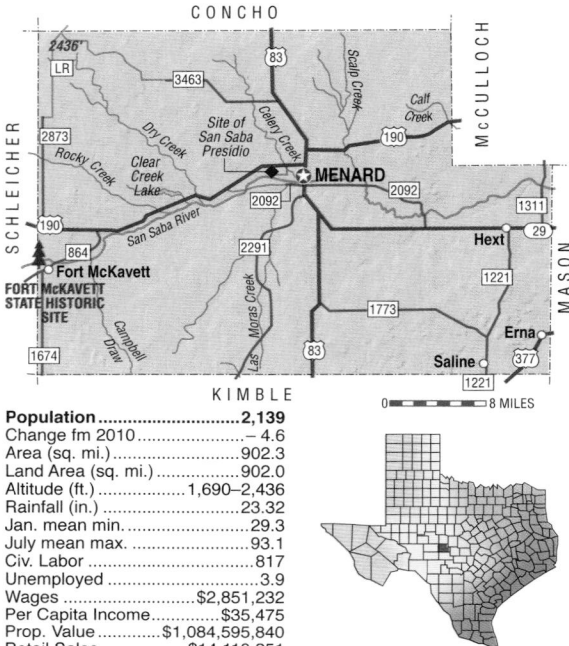

Menard County

Physical Features: West central county of rolling topography, draining to San Saba River and tributaries; limestone soils.

Economy: Agriculture, tourism, oil, gas production. **History**: Apaches, followed by Comanches in 18th century. Mission Santa Cruz de San Sabá established in 1757. A few Anglo-American and German settlers arrived in 1840s. County created from Bexar County 1858, organized 1871; named for Galveston's founder, Michel B. Menard.

Race/Ethnicity: (In percent) Anglo, 61.6; Black, 1.6; Hispanic, 36.1; Asian, 0.2; Other, 1.5; Two or more races, 0.8.

Vital Statistics, annual: Births, 15; deaths, 33; marriages, 9; divorces, 9.

Recreation: Hunting, fishing; historic sites, including Spanish presidio, mission, irrigation ditches; U.S. fort; railroad museum; Jim Bowie barbecue cook-off in May.

Minerals: Oil, gas.

Agriculture: Cattle, sheep, goats, pecans, hay. Market value $9.6 million. Hunting leases, ecotourism important.

MENARD (1,442) county seat; agribusiness, government/services; hunters blowout ball in early November.

Other towns include: **Fort McKavett** (50); **Hext** (75).

Population	**2,139**
Change fm 2010	– 4.6
Area (sq. mi.)	902.3
Land Area (sq. mi.)	902.0
Altitude (ft.)	1,690–2,436
Rainfall (in.)	23.32
Jan. mean min.	29.3
July mean max.	93.1
Civ. Labor	817
Unemployed	3.9
Wages	$2,851,232
Per Capita Income	$35,475
Prop. Value	$1,084,595,840
Retail Sales	$14,110,251

Midland County

Physical Features: Flat western county, broken by draws; sandy, loam soils with native grasses.

Economy: Among leading petroleum-producing counties; distribution, administrative center for oil industry; varied manufacturing; government/services.

History: Comanches in area in 19th century. Sheep ranching developed in the 1880s. Permian Basin oil boom began in the 1920s. County created from Tom Green County in 1885 and organized the same year; name came from midway location on the railroad between El Paso and Fort Worth. The Chihuahua Trail and Emigrant Road were pioneer trails that crossed the county.

Race/Ethnicity: (In percent) Anglo, 45.5; Black, 6.8; Hispanic, 45.0; Asian, 2.1; Other, 1.3; Two or more races, 1.6.

Vital Statistics, annual: Births, 3,032; deaths, 1,098; marriages, 1,394; divorces, 618.

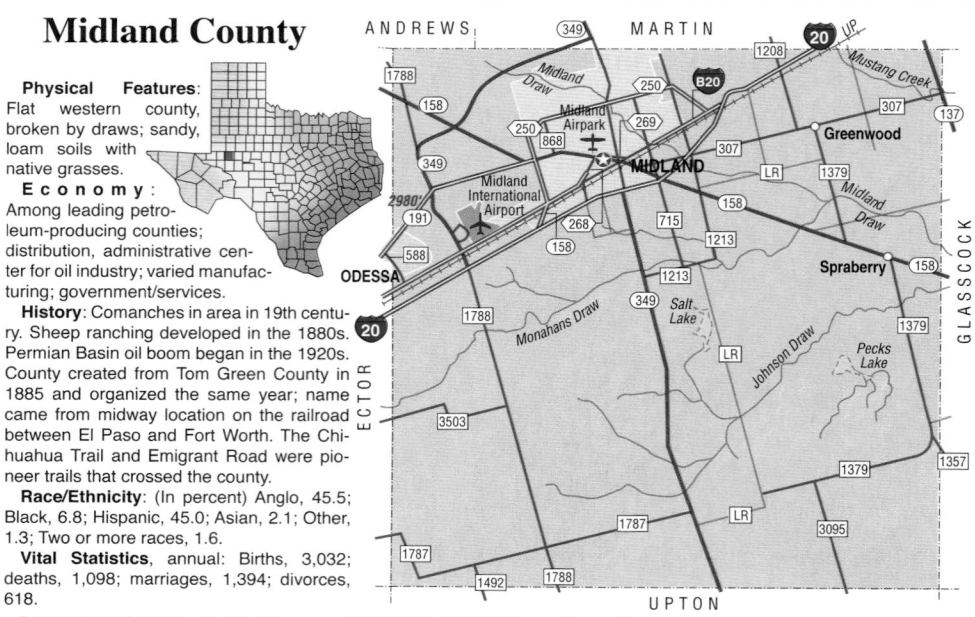

Recreation: Permian Basin Petroleum Museum, Library, Hall of Fame; Museum of Southwest; Commemorative Air Force and Museum; community theater; metropolitan events; homes of Presidents Bush.

Minerals: Oil, natural gas.

Agriculture: Beef cattle, horses, sheep and goats; cotton, hay, pecans; some 11,000 acres irrigated. Market value $17.2 million.

MIDLAND (134,372) county seat; petroleum, petrochemical center; varied manufacturing; livestock sale center; hospitals; cultural activities; community college; polo club, Texas League baseball; Celebration of the Arts in May.

Part [1,670] of **Odessa**.

Population	**172,578**
Change fm 2010	26.1
Area (sq. mi.)	902.1
Land Area (sq. mi.)	900.3
Altitude (ft.)	2,550–2,980
Rainfall (in.)	14.80
Jan. mean min.	31.5
July mean max.	96.2
Civ. Labor	98,007
Unemployed	2.1
Wages	$1,839,960,878
Per Capita Income	$75,002
Prop. Value	$25,484,388,774
Retail Sales	$3,806,294,064

Milam County

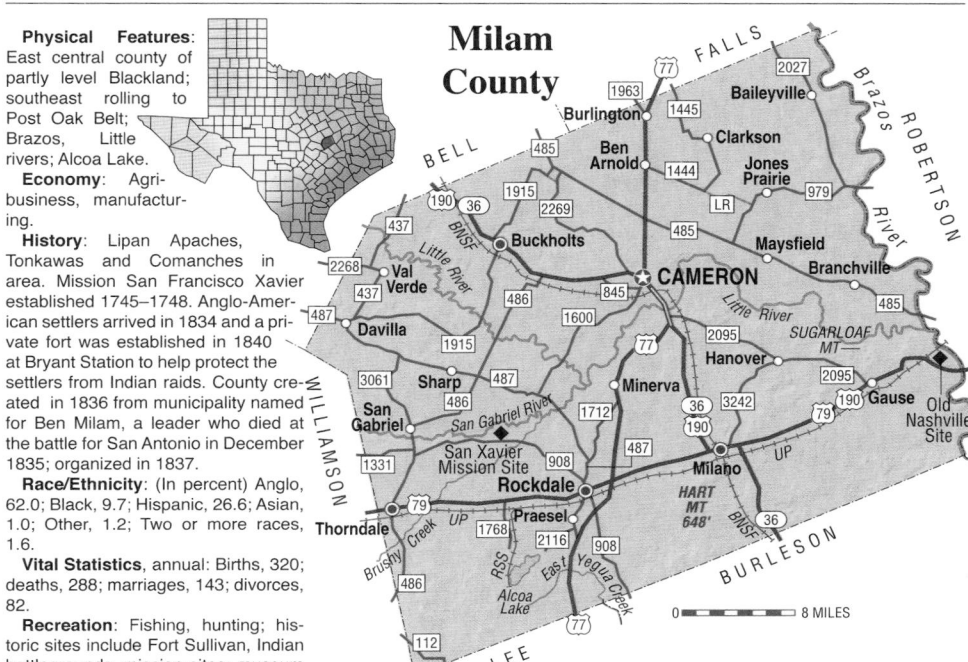

Physical Features: East central county of partly level Blackland; southeast rolling to Post Oak Belt; Brazos, Little rivers; Alcoa Lake.

Economy: Agribusiness, manufacturing.

History: Lipan Apaches, Tonkawas and Comanches in area. Mission San Francisco Xavier established 1745–1748. Anglo-American settlers arrived in 1834 and a private fort was established in 1840 at Bryant Station to help protect the settlers from Indian raids. County created in 1836 from municipality named for Ben Milam, a leader who died at the battle for San Antonio in December 1835; organized in 1837.

Race/Ethnicity: (In percent) Anglo, 62.0; Black, 9.7; Hispanic, 26.6; Asian, 1.0; Other, 1.2; Two or more races, 1.6.

Vital Statistics, annual: Births, 320; deaths, 288; marriages, 143; divorces, 82.

Recreation: Fishing, hunting; historic sites include Fort Sullivan, Indian battlegrounds, mission sites; museum in old jail at Cameron, El Camino Real.

Minerals: Barite, limited oil and gas production.

Agriculture: Cattle, poultry (first in number of turkeys), corn. Market value $144.7 million.

CAMERON (5,486) county seat; government/services, manufacturing; hospital, library; dewberry festival in April.

ROCKDALE (5,643) government/

services; hospital, juvenile detention center.

Other towns include: **Buckholts** (530); **Burlington** (100); **Davilla** (191); **Gause** (425); **Milano** (419); **Thorndale** (1,328) agribusiness, farming, ranching, antiques, barbecue cook-off in June.

For explanation of sources, symbols and abbreviations, see p. 192, and foldout map.

Population	25,131
Change fm 2010	1.5
Area (sq. mi.)	1,021.8
Land Area (sq. mi.)	1,016.9
Altitude (ft.)	250–648
Rainfall (in.)	36.97
Jan. mean min.	33.8
July mean max.	88.7
Civ. Labor	9,791
Unemployed	5.0
Wages	$52,495,334
Per Capita Income	$36,781
Prop. Value	$3,593,973,159
Retail Sales	$183,149,412

Downtown Menard, Menard County. Photo by Robert Plocheck.

Mills County

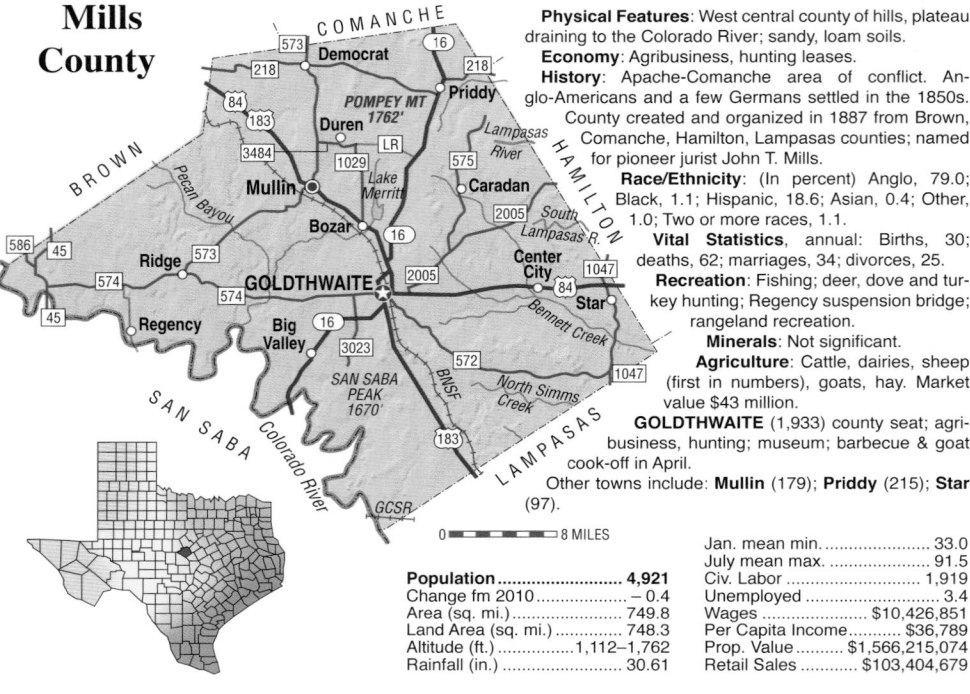

Physical Features: West central county of hills, plateau draining to the Colorado River; sandy, loam soils.

Economy: Agribusiness, hunting leases.

History: Apache-Comanche area of conflict. Anglo-Americans and a few Germans settled in the 1850s. County created and organized in 1887 from Brown, Comanche, Hamilton, Lampasas counties; named for pioneer jurist John T. Mills.

Race/Ethnicity: (In percent) Anglo, 79.0; Black, 1.1; Hispanic, 18.6; Asian, 0.4; Other, 1.0; Two or more races, 1.1.

Vital Statistics, annual: Births, 30; deaths, 62; marriages, 34; divorces, 25.

Recreation: Fishing; deer, dove and turkey hunting; Regency suspension bridge; rangeland recreation.

Minerals: Not significant.

Agriculture: Cattle, dairies, sheep (first in numbers), goats, hay. Market value $43 million.

GOLDTHWAITE (1,933) county seat; agribusiness, hunting; museum; barbecue & goat cook-off in April.

Other towns include: **Mullin** (179); **Priddy** (215); **Star** (97).

Population	4,921
Change fm 2010	– 0.4
Area (sq. mi.)	749.8
Land Area (sq. mi.)	748.3
Altitude (ft.)	1,112–1,762
Rainfall (in.)	30.61

Jan. mean min.	33.0
July mean max.	91.5
Civ. Labor	1,919
Unemployed	3.4
Wages	$10,426,851
Per Capita Income	$36,789
Prop. Value	$1,566,215,074
Retail Sales	$103,404,679

Mitchell County

Physical Features: Rolling, draining to Colorado and tributaries; sandy, red, dark soils; Lake Colorado City, Mitchell County Reservoir, and Champion Creek Reservoir.

Economy: Government/services, agribusiness, oil, some manufacturing.

History: Jumano Indians in area; Comanches arrived about 1780. Anglo-American settlers arrived in the late 1870s after Comanches were forced into Indian Territory. County created in 1876 from Bexar District and organized in 1881; named for pioneer brothers Asa and Eli Mitchell.

Race/Ethnicity: (In percent) Anglo, 48.5; Black, 11.2; Hispanic, 39.5; Asian, 0.7; Other, 1.8; Two or more races, 2.3.

Vital Statistics, annual: Births, 88; deaths, 109; marriages, 60; divorces, 33.

Recreation: Lake activities, state park, museums, hunting, Colorado City playhouse.

Minerals: Oil.

Agriculture: Cotton principal crop, grains also produced. Cattle, sheep, goats, hogs raised. Market value $21.2 million.

COLORADO CITY (3,815) county seat; cotton, cattle, oil; hospital/medical services; opera house; poppy-mallow blooms at sports complex; goat cook-off in October.

Other towns include: **Loraine** (573) and **Westbrook** (251), trade centers.

The community around **Lake Colorado City** (619).

Population	8,256
Change fm 2010	– 13.4
Area (sq. mi.)	915.9
Land Area (sq. mi.)	911.1
Altitude (ft.)	1,930–2,574
Rainfall (in.)	20.42

Jan. mean min.	28.3
July mean max.	95.0
Civ. Labor	2,216
Unemployed	4.2
Wages	$19,965,947
Per Capita Income	$30,037
Prop. Value	$1,347,069,923
Retail Sales	$38,058,647

For explanation of sources, symbols and abbreviations, see p. 192, and foldout map.

Montague County

Physical Features: Rolling, draining to tributaries of Trinity, Red rivers; sandy loams, red, black soils; Lake Nocona, Lake Amon G. Carter.

Economy: Agribusiness, oil, varied manufacturing, government/services.

History: Kiowas and Wichitas who allied with Comanches. Anglo-American settlements developed in the 1850s. County created from Cooke County in 1857, organized in 1858; named for pioneer Daniel Montague.

Race/Ethnicity: (In percent) Anglo, 85.7; Black, 0.7; Hispanic, 11.3; Asian, 0.4; Other, 1.4; Two or more races, 1.6.

Vital Statistics, annual: Births, 237; deaths, 263; marriages, 132; divorces, 66.

Recreation: Lake activities; quail, turkey, deer hunting; scenic drives; museums; historical sites, motorcycle dirt track.

Minerals: Oil, gas, rock.

Agriculture: Beef, hay, pecans, melons, peaches. Market value $44.9 million.

MONTAGUE (303) county seat.

BOWIE (5,119) varied manufacturing, oil and gas operations; hospital, library; Jim Bowie Days in June.

NOCONA (3,020) athletic goods, boot manufacturing; hospital; art galleries, museums; Wheels & Grills barbecue cook-off and car show in September.

Other towns include: **Forestburg** (50); **Ringgold** (100); **Saint Jo** (1,040) wineries, retail center, art galleries, museums, rodeo in August; **Sunset** (517).

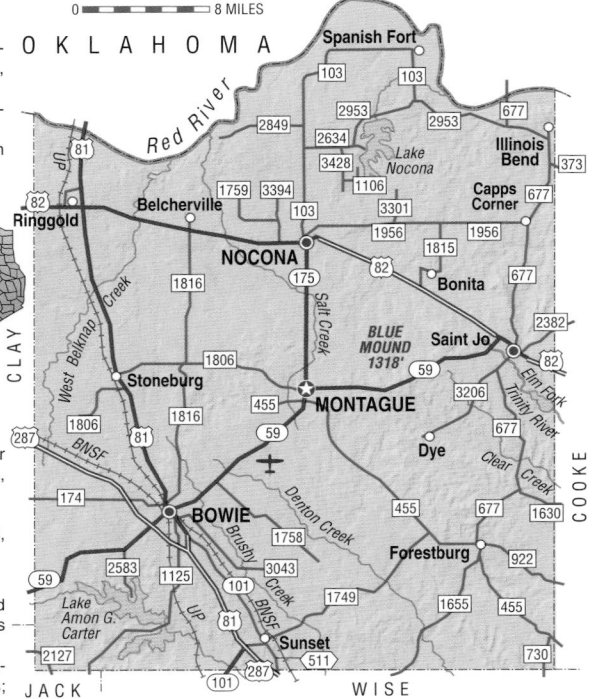

Population	**19,596**
Change fm 2010	– 0.6
Area (sq. mi.)	938.3
Land Area (sq. mi.)	930.9
Altitude (ft.)	715–1,318
Rainfall (in.)	35.06
Jan. mean min.	29.2
July mean max.	93.3
Civ. Labor	9,121
Unemployed	2.9
Wages	$48,127,916
Per Capita Income	$39,085
Prop. Value	$3,389,993,360
Retail Sales	$187,423,139

Cattle on the rolling landscape of Montague County near Spanish Fort. Photo by Robert Plocheck.

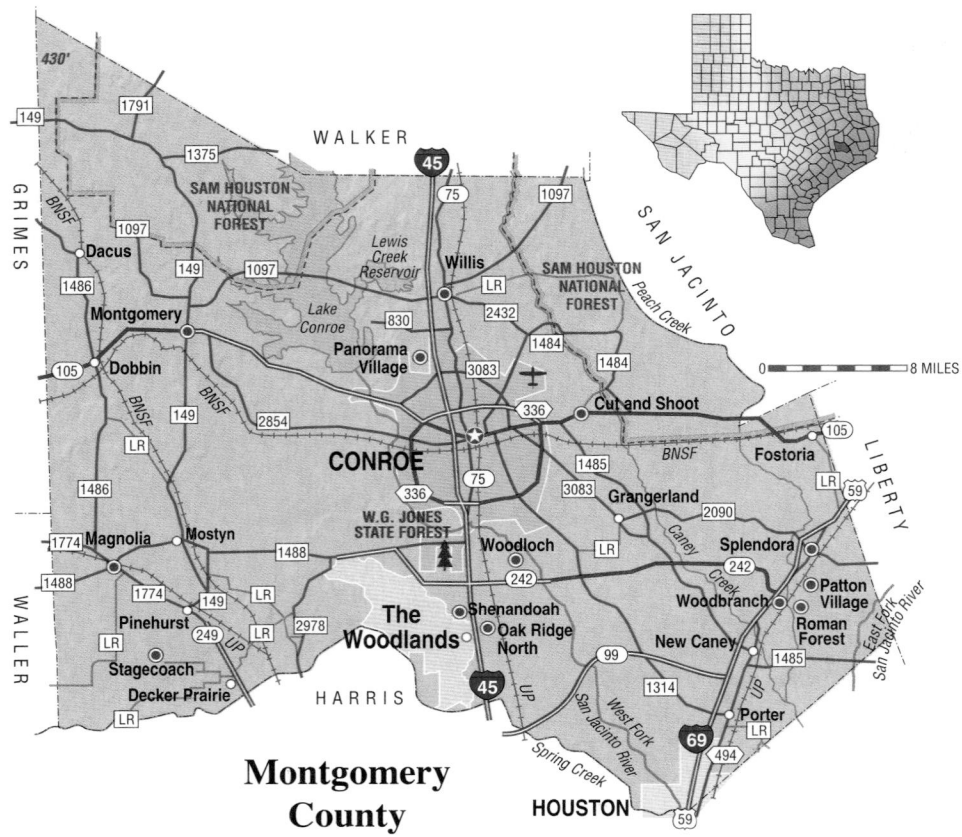

Montgomery County

Physical Features: Rolling, half timbered; Sam Houston National Forest; loam, sandy, alluvial soils; Lake Conroe and Lewis Creek Reservoir.

Economy: Varied manufacturing, oil production, medical research, government/services, many residents work in Houston.

History: Orcoquisac and Bidais tribes, removed from the area by the 1850s. Anglo-Americans arrived in the 1820s as part of Austin's colony. County created and organized in 1837 from Washington County; named for Richard Montgomery, American Revolution general.

Race/Ethnicity: (In percent) Anglo, 66.2; Black, 5.3; Hispanic, 24.1; Asian, 3.1; Other, 1.1; Two or more races, 1.9.

Vital Statistics, annual: Births, 7,336; deaths, 3,623; marriages, 3,350; divorces, 1,791.

Recreation: Hunting, fishing; Lake Conroe activities; national and state forests; hiking, boating, horseback riding; historic sites.

Minerals: Natural gas.

Agriculture: Greenhouse crops, hay, beef cattle, horses. Market value $23.8 million. Timber important.

CONROE (85,685) county seat; government/services, hospital/medical services, commuters to Houston; new Sam Houston State University medical school; community college, museum; Cajun catfish festival in October.

The Woodlands (116,958) commuters to Houston, energy, tourism; college branches, hospitals, museums, parks, concerts, festivals at Mitchell Pavilion.

Other towns include: **Cut and Shoot** (1,294); **Dobbin** (310); **Grangerland** (300); **Magnolia** (2,028) government/services, drilling technology, construction, depot museum, Love Bug Fest in June; **Montgomery** (963) commuters to Houston and Conroe, antiques stores, pioneer museum, historic homes tour in April; **New Caney** (6,800); **Oak Ridge North** (3,221);

Panorama Village (2,295); **Patton Village** (1,902).

Also, **Pinehurst** (5,166); **Porter** (4,200); **Porter Heights** (1,858); **Roman Forest** (1,905); **Shenandoah** (2,938); **Splendora** (2,034); **Stagecoach** (613); **Willis** (6,791) commuters to Conroe and Houston; **Woodbranch** (1,460); **Woodloch** (212).

Also, part [4,047] of **Houston** [**Kingwood**], hospital.

Population	590,925
Change fm 2010	29.7
Area (sq. mi.)	1,076.9
Land Area (sq. mi.)	1,041.9
Altitude (ft.)	50–430
Rainfall (in.)	48.77
Jan. mean min.	40.4
July mean max.	93.5
Civ. Labor	577,947
Unemployed	3.4
Wages	$2,538,416,772
Per Capita Income	$57,585
Prop. Value	$62,200,097,295
Retail Sales	$7,875,635,927

For explanation of sources, symbols and abbreviations, see p. 192, and foldout map.

Moore County

Physical Features: Flat to rolling, broken by creeks; sandy loams; Lake Meredith.

Economy: Varied agribusiness, petroleum, natural gas.

History: Comanches, removed to Indian Territory in 1874–1875; ranching began soon afterward. Farming developed after 1910. Oil boom in the 1920s. County created in 1876 from Bexar District; organized in 1892; named for Republic of Texas navy commander E.W. Moore.

Race/Ethnicity: (In percent) Anglo, 32.2; Black, 3.9; Hispanic, 55.3; Asian, 7.7; Other, 1.8; Two or more races, 1.4.

Vital Statistics, annual: Births, 438; deaths, 164; marriages, 142; divorces, 70.

Recreation: Lake Meredith activities; pheasant, deer, quail hunting; historical museum; arts center; free overnight RV park; Dogie Days in June.

Minerals: Oil and gas.

Agriculture: Fed beef, corn, wheat, stocker cattle, sorghum, cotton, soybeans, sunflowers. Market value $605 million. Irrigation of 122,000 acres.

DUMAS (15,246) county seat; tourism, retail trade, varied agribusiness; hospital, hospice, retirement complex.

Other towns include: **Cactus** (3,339), **Sunray** (1,949). Small part of **Fritch**.

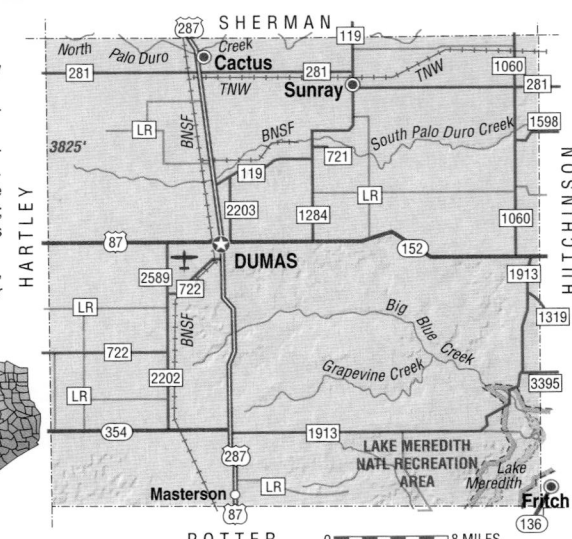

Population	21,485
Change fm 2010	– 1.9
Area (sq. mi.)	909.6
Land Area (sq. mi.)	899.7
Altitude (ft.)	2,915–3,825
Rainfall (in.)	18.37
Jan. mean min.	22.1
July mean max.	91.6
Civ. Labor	10,648
Unemployed	2.6
Wages	$122,526,196
Per Capita Income	$40,454
Prop. Value	$2,627,926,435
Retail Sales	$405,126,079

Morris County

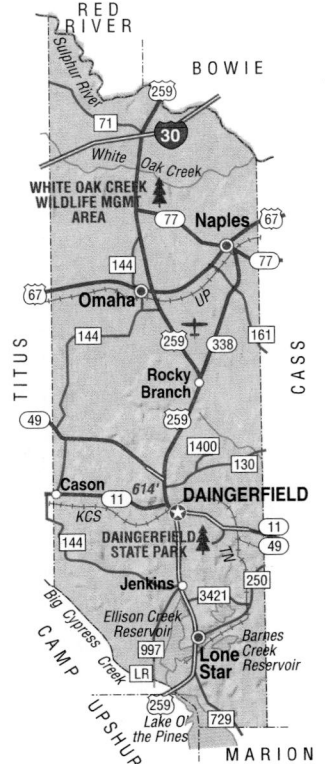

Physical Features: East Texas county of forested hills; drains to streams, Lake O' the Pines, Ellison Creek Reservoir, Barnes Creek Reservoir.

Economy: Steel manufacturing, agriculture, timber, government/services.

History: Caddo Indians until the 1790s. Kickapoo and other tribes in area 1820s-30s. Anglo-American settlement began in mid-1830s. Antebellum slaveholding area. County named for legislator-jurist W.W. Morris; created from Titus County and organized in 1875.

Race/Ethnicity: (In percent) Anglo, 63.8; Black, 23.0; Hispanic, 10.0; Asian, 0.6; Other, 1.4; Two or more races, 2.6.

Vital Statistics, annual: Births, 161; deaths, 179; marriages, 84; divorces, 23.

Recreation: Activities on Lake O' the Pines, small lakes; fishing, hunting; state park.

Minerals: Iron ore.

Agriculture: Beef cattle, broiler production, hay. Market value $46.9 million. Timber industry significant.

DAINGERFIELD (2,568) county seat; varied manufacturing, government/services; library, museum, city park, historic theater; Daingerfield Days in October.

Other towns include: **Cason** (173); **Lone Star** (1,585) oil-field equipment manufactured, catfish farming, Starfest in September; **Naples** (1,376) trailer manufacturing, livestock, watermelon festival in July; **Omaha** (1,038), retail center, government/services, commuters.

Population	12,339
Change fm 2010	– 4.6
Area (sq. mi.)	258.7
Land Area (sq. mi.)	252.0
Altitude (ft.)	228–614
Rainfall (in.)	46.79
Jan. mean min.	35.1
July mean max.	94.1
Civ. Labor	4,497
Unemployed	6.4
Wages	$47,739,260
Per Capita Income	$42,249
Prop. Value	$968,418,440
Retail Sales	$78,533,848

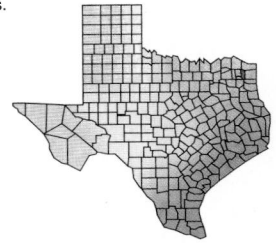

For explanation of sources, symbols and abbreviations, see p. 192, and foldout map.

Motley County

Physical Features: Western county just below Caprock; rough terrain, broken by Pease tributaries; sandy to red clay soils.

Economy: Agriculture, government/services, light manufacturing.

History: Comanche tribes in the area, removed to the Indian Territory by the U.S. Army in 1874–1875. Cattle ranching began in the late 1870s. County was created out of the Bexar District in 1876 and organized in 1891; named for Dr. J.W. Mottley, a signer of Texas Declaration of Independence (however name was misspelled in legislative statute).

Race/Ethnicity: (In percent) Anglo, 79.3; Black, 2.9; Hispanic, 16.8; Asian, 0.2; Other, 2.2; Two or more races, 0.5.

Vital Statistics, annual: Births, 0; deaths, 17; marriages, 24; divorces, 3.

Recreation: Quail, dove, turkey, deer, feral hog hunting; Matador Ranch headquarters; spring-fed pool at Roaring Springs; Motley-Dickens settlers reunion in August at Roaring Springs.

Minerals: Minimal.

Agriculture: Beef cattle, cotton, peanuts, hay, wheat. Some irrigation. Market value $12.8 million. Hunting leases important.

MATADOR (547) county seat; ranching, farming, government/services; museum, historic oil-derrick gas station; motorcycles race in April.

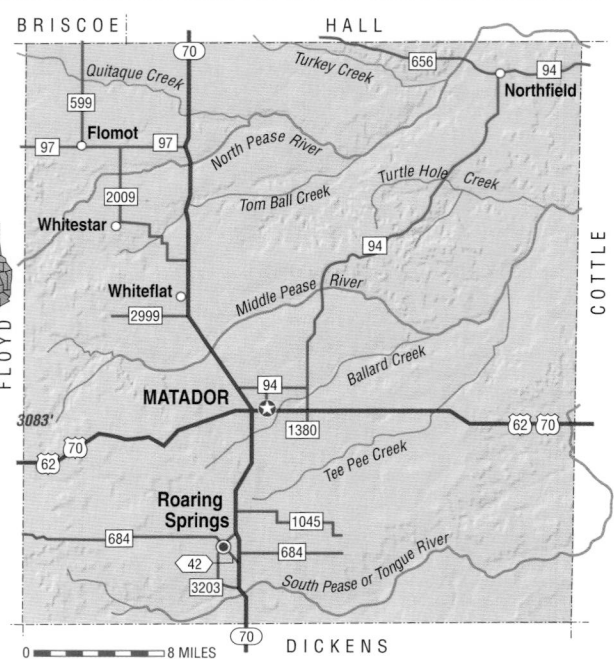

Other towns include: **Flomot** (181) bluegrass festival in May, and **Roaring Springs** (227).

Population	1,234
Change fm 2010	2.4
Area (sq. mi.)	989.8
Land Area (sq. mi.)	989.6
Altitude (ft.)	1,800–3,083

Rainfall (in.)	23.43
Jan. mean min.	29.6
July mean max.	94.2
Civ. Labor	443
Unemployed	3.6
Wages	$2,167,635
Per Capita Income	$28,447
Prop. Value	$350,324,040
Retail Sales	$6,702,956

A cattle pen and the hilly terrain along FM 95, Nacogdoches County. Photo by Robert Plocheck.

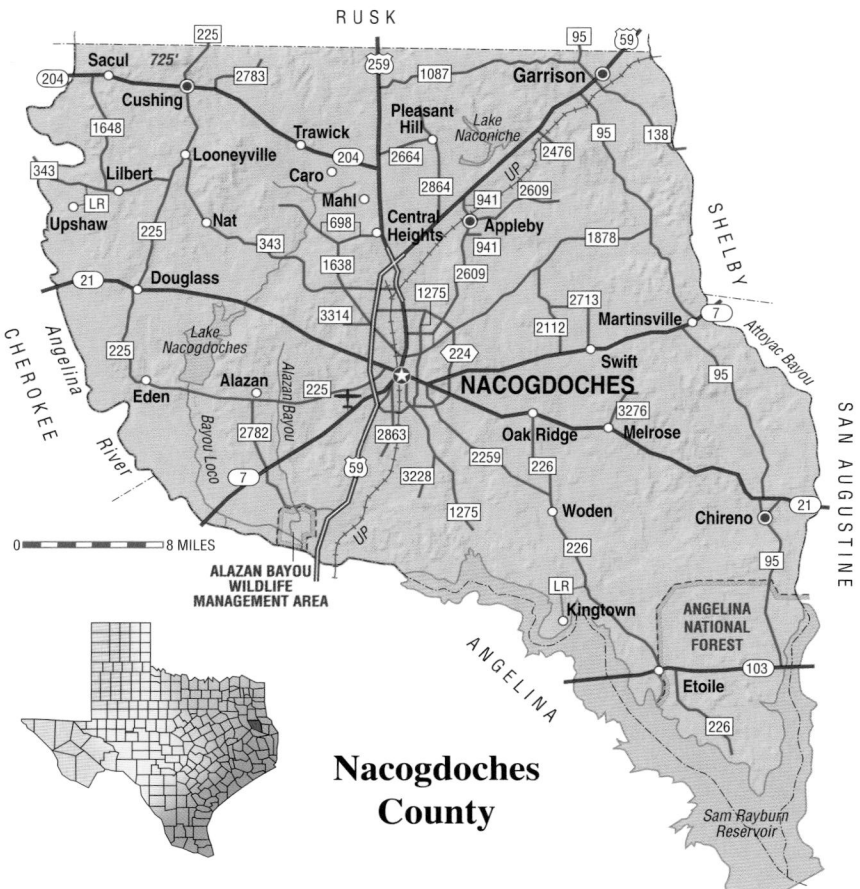

RUSK

Sacul *725'*
Cushing
Trawick
Pleasant Hill
Garrison
Looneyville
Caro
Lilbert
Mahl
Upshaw
Nat
Central Heights
Appleby
Douglass
Martinsville
Lake Nacogdoches
Swift
Alazan
Eden
NACOGDOCHES
Oak Ridge
Melrose
Woden
Chireno
ALAZAN BAYOU
WILDLIFE
MANAGEMENT AREA
Kingtown
ANGELINA
NATIONAL
FOREST
Etoile

0 ━━━━ 8 MILES

Lake Naconiche

SHELBY

SAN AUGUSTINE

CHEROKEE

Angelina River

Alazan Bayou

Bayou Loco

ANGELINA

Attoyac Bayou

Sam Rayburn Reservoir

Nacogdoches County

Physical Features: East Texas county on divide between the Angelina River and Attoyac Bayou; hilly; two-thirds is forested; red, gray, sandy soils; Sam Rayburn Reservoir, Lake Nacogdoches, Lake Naconiche.

Economy: Agribusiness, timber, manufacturing, education, tourism.

History: Caddo tribes, joined by displaced Cherokees in the 1820s. Indian tribes moved west of the Brazos River by 1840. Spanish missions established in 1716. Spanish settlers arrived in the mid-1700s.

Anglo-Americans arrived in the 1820s. An original county of the Republic in 1836, organized in 1837. Name comes from Caddo tribe in the area.

Race/Ethnicity: (In percent) Anglo, 59.4; Black, 18.5; Hispanic,

For explanation of sources, symbols and abbreviations, see p. 192, and foldout map.

19.5; Asian, 1.5; Other, 1.0; Two or more races, 1.8.

Vital Statistics, annual: Births, 864; deaths, 605; marriages, 463; divorces, 81.

Recreation: Lake and river activities; Stephen F. Austin State University events; Angelina National Forest; historic site.

Tourist attractions include the Old Stone Fort, pioneer homes, museums, Millard's Crossing Historic Village, Piney Woods Native Plant Center; Azalea Trail in March, Blueberry Festival in June.

Minerals: First Texas oil discovered here, 1866; gas, oil, clay, and stone.

Agriculture: A leading poultry-producing county (third in number of broilers); beef cattle raised. Market value $322.3 million. Substantial timber sold.

NACOGDOCHES (34,120) county seat; varied manufacturing, lumber

mills, wood products, trade center; hospitals; Stephen F. Austin State University; Nine Flags Festival in November/December.

Other towns include: **Appleby** (480), **Chireno** (382), **Cushing** (598), **Douglass** (380), **Etoile** (700), **Garrison** (886), **Martinsville** (350), **Sacul** (150), **Woden** (400).

Population	65,711
Change fm 2010	1.8
Area (sq. mi.)	981.2
Land Area (sq. mi.)	946.5
Altitude (ft.)	164–725
Rainfall (in.)	49.28
Jan. mean min.	35.8
July mean max.	93.2
Civ. Labor	28,751
Unemployed	3.8
Wages	$207,518,716
Per Capita Income	$36,398
Prop. Value	$5,288,277,800
Retail Sales	$845,563,830

Navarro County

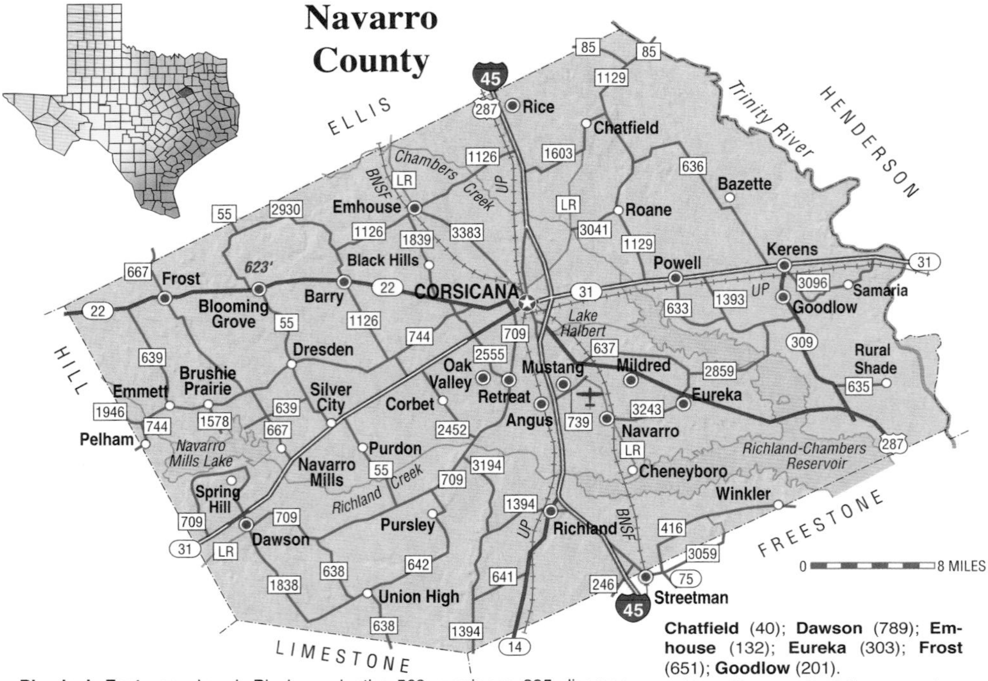

ELLIS

HENDERSON

Trinity River

85 85

1129

45

287 Rice

Chatfield

1126 1603

636

Bazette

Chambers Creek

BNSF LR

55 2930

Emhouse

LR

Roane

Powell

Kerens

31

1126 1839 3383

3041

1129

Black Hills

UP

3096 Samaria

667 Frost

623'

Barry 22 CORSICANA

31

633 1393 UP Goodlow

22 Blooming Grove 55 1126

Lake Halbert

Dresden 744 709

637

309

Rural Shade

HILL 639

2555

Brushie Prairie Emmett

Oak Valley Mustang Mildred

2859

635

1946 744 1578 Silver City 639 Corbet

Retreat

Eureka

667 2452

Angus 739

3243

Pelham Navarro Mills Lake

Purdon

Navarro

Navarro LR

Richland-Chambers Reservoir 287

Spring Hill 709 Navarro Mills 55 709

Richland Creek

3194

Cheneyboro

Winkler

709 1394

FREESTONE

31 LR Dawson

Pursley

BNSF Richland 416

3059

0 ▬▬▬ 8 MILES

1838 638 642 641 246 75 Streetman

Union High 45

638 1394 14

LIMESTONE

Physical Features
Level Blackland, some rolling; drains to creeks, Trinity River; Navarro Mills Lake, Richland-Chambers Reservoir, Lake Halbert.

Economy
Diversified manufacturing, agribusinesses, oil-field operations, distribution.

History
Kickapoo and Comanche area. Anglo-Americans settled in the late 1830s. Antebellum slaveholding area. County created in 1846 from Robertson County, organized the same year; named for Republic of Texas leader José Antonio Navarro.

Race/Ethnicity
(In percent) Anglo, 56.2; Black, 13.5; Hispanic, 27.3; Asian, 0.8; Other, 2.3; Two or more races, 1.9.

Vital Statistics, annual: Births, 664; deaths, 568; marriages, 335; divorces, 213.

Recreation
Lake activities; Pioneer Village; historic buildings; youth exposition, Derrick Days in April.

Minerals
Longest continuous Texas oil flow; more than 200 million barrels produced since 1895; natural gas, sand and gravel also produced.

Agriculture
Beef cattle, cotton, sorghum, corn, wheat, sunflowers, herbs, horses, dairies. Market value $66.4 million.

CORSICANA (24,304) county seat; major distribution center, pecans, candy, fruitcakes; varied manufacturing; agribusiness; hospital; Navarro College; Texas Youth Commission facility.

Other towns include: **Angus** (439); **Barry** (254); **Blooming Grove** (840); **Chatfield** (40); **Dawson** (789); **Emhouse** (132); **Eureka** (303); **Frost** (651); **Goodlow** (201).

Also, **Kerens** (1,581) commuting, nature tourism, Cotton Harvest Festival in October; **Mildred** (371); **Mustang** (19); **Navarro** (210); **Oak Valley** (383); **Powell** (148); **Purdon** (133); **Retreat** (395); **Rice** (985); **Richland** (254).

Population	49,565
Change fm 2010	3.6
Area (sq. mi.)	1,085.9
Land Area (sq. mi.)	1,009.6
Altitude (ft.)	250–623
Rainfall (in.)	39.78
Jan. mean min.	34.7
July mean max.	94.1
Civ. Labor	23,335
Unemployed	3.5
Wages	$159,699,507
Per Capita Income	$36,960
Prop. Value	$4,642,477,202
Retail Sales	$602,185,168

Wind turbines along FM 126, Nolan County. Photo by Robert Plocheck.

Newton County

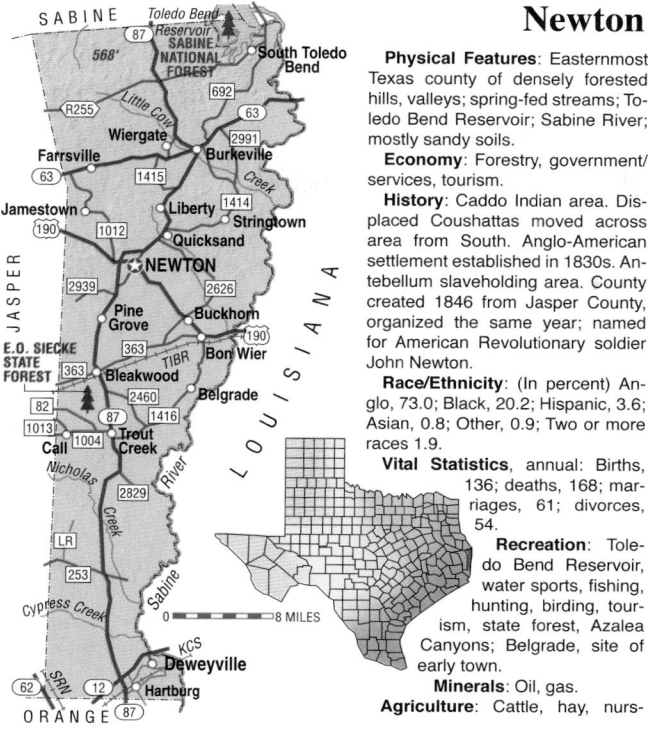

Physical Features: Easternmost Texas county of densely forested hills, valleys; spring-fed streams; Toledo Bend Reservoir; Sabine River; mostly sandy soils.

Economy: Forestry, government/services, tourism.

History: Caddo Indian area. Displaced Coushattas moved across area from South. Anglo-American settlement established in 1830s. Antebellum slaveholding area. County created 1846 from Jasper County, organized the same year; named for American Revolutionary soldier John Newton.

Race/Ethnicity: (In percent) Anglo, 73.0; Black, 20.2; Hispanic, 3.6; Asian, 0.8; Other, 0.9; Two or more races 1.9.

Vital Statistics, annual: Births, 136; deaths, 168; marriages, 61; divorces, 54.

Recreation: Toledo Bend Reservoir, water sports, fishing, hunting, birding, tourism, state forest, Azalea Canyons; Belgrade, site of early town.

Minerals: Oil, gas.

Agriculture: Cattle, hay, nursery crops, vegetables, goats, hogs. Market value $2.9 million. Hunting leases. Major forestry area.

NEWTON (2,400) county seat; lumber manufacturing, plywood mill, private prison unit, tourist center; genealogical library, museum; Wild Azalea festival in March.

Deweyville (960) power plant, commercial center for forestry, farming area.

Other towns include: **Bon Wier** (375); **Burkeville** (603); **Call** (493); **South Toledo Bend** (474); **Wiergate** (350).

Population	**13,746**
Change fm 2010	– 4.8
Area (sq. mi.)	939.7
Land Area (sq. mi.)	933.7
Altitude (ft.)	10–568
Rainfall (in.)	54.92
Jan. mean min.	36.5
July mean max.	93.1
Civ. Labor	5,215
Unemployed	6.8
Wages	$11,332,405
Per Capita Income	$31,306
Prop. Value	$2,195,907,805
Retail Sales	$39,869,797

For explanation of sources, symbols and abbreviations, see p. 192, and foldout map.

Nolan County

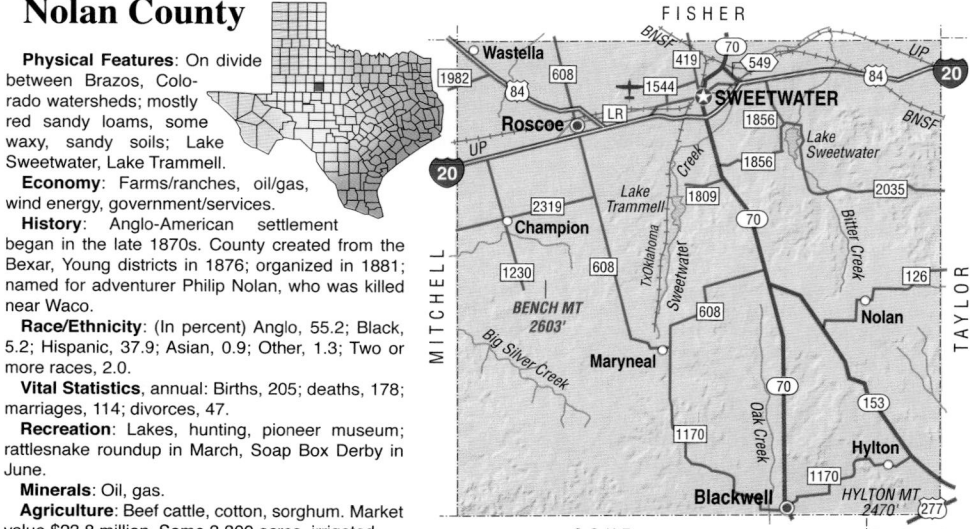

Physical Features: On divide between Brazos, Colorado watersheds; mostly red sandy loams, some waxy, sandy soils; Lake Sweetwater, Lake Trammell.

Economy: Farms/ranches, oil/gas, wind energy, government/services.

History: Anglo-American settlement began in the late 1870s. County created from the Bexar, Young districts in 1876; organized in 1881; named for adventurer Philip Nolan, who was killed near Waco.

Race/Ethnicity: (In percent) Anglo, 55.2; Black, 5.2; Hispanic, 37.9; Asian, 0.9; Other, 1.3; Two or more races, 2.0.

Vital Statistics, annual: Births, 205; deaths, 178; marriages, 114; divorces, 47.

Recreation: Lakes, hunting, pioneer museum; rattlesnake roundup in March, Soap Box Derby in June.

Minerals: Oil, gas.

Agriculture: Beef cattle, cotton, sorghum. Market value $23.8 million. Some 3,300 acres irrigated.

SWEETWATER (10,459) county seat; wind energy, varied manufacturing, gypsum; hospital; Texas State Technical College; WWII museum.

Other towns include: **Blackwell** (303, partly in Coke County), Oak Creek Reservoir to south; **Maryneal** (50); **Nolan** (60); **Roscoe** (1,246).

Population	14,751	July mean max.	93.9
Change fm 2010	– 3.0	Civ. Labor	6,627
Area (sq. mi.)	914.0	Unemployed	3.2
Land Area (sq. mi.)	912.0	Wages	$63,277,071
Altitude (ft.)	1,896–2,603	Per Capita Income	$40,256
Rainfall (in.)	22.42	Prop. Value	$2,838,738,510
Jan. mean min.	29.0	Retail Sales	$259,905,775

Nueces County

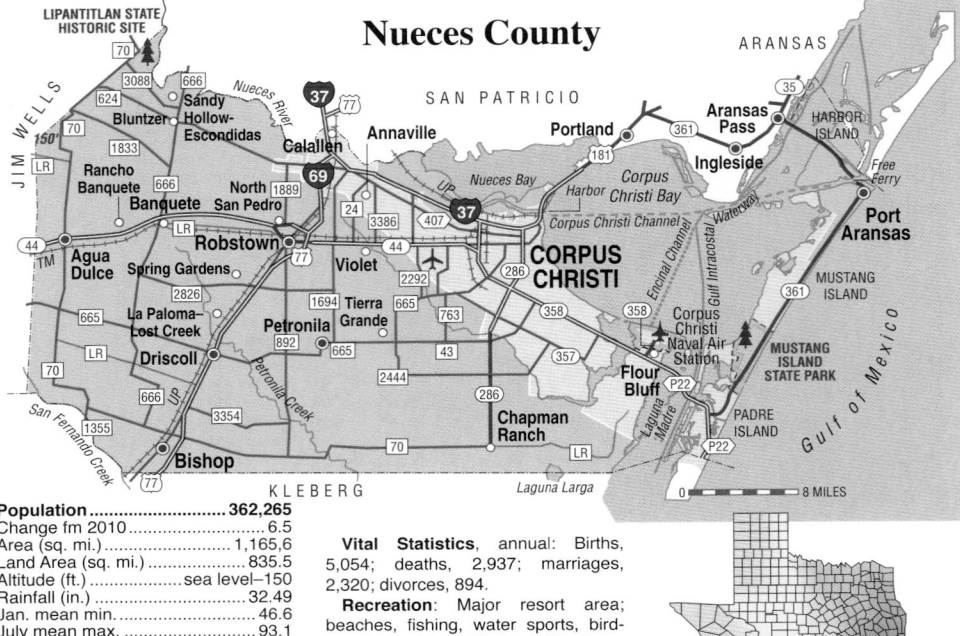

Population 362,265
Change fm 2010 .... 6.5
Area (sq. mi.) 1,165,6
Land Area (sq. mi.) 835.5
Altitude (ft.) .... sea level–150
Rainfall (in.) 32.49
Jan. mean min. 46.6
July mean max. 93.1
Civ. Labor 168,517
Unemployed 4.3
Wages $1,908,654,080
Per Capita Income................. $41,873
Prop. Value $34,654,546,470
Retail Sales $5,382,447,813

Physical Features: Southern Gulf Coast county; flat, rich soils, broken by bays, Nueces River, Petronila Creek; includes Mustang Island, north tip of Padre Island.

Economy: Petroleum processing, deepwater port facility, agriculture, tourism.

History: Coahuiltecan, Karankawa and other tribes who succumbed to disease or fled by 1840s. Spanish settlers arrived in the 1760s. Settlers from Ireland arrived around 1830. County name is Spanish for nuts; county named for river; created and organized in 1846 out of San Patricio County.

Race/Ethnicity: (In percent) Anglo, 29.4; Black, 4.3; Hispanic, 63.9; Asian, 2.2; Other, 0.9; Two or more races, 1.5.

Vital Statistics, annual: Births, 5,054; deaths, 2,937; marriages, 2,320; divorces, 894.

Recreation: Major resort area; beaches, fishing, water sports, birding; Padre Island National Seashore, Mustang Island State Park, Lipantitlan State Historic Site; Art Museum of South Texas, Corpus Christi Museum of Science and History; Texas State Aquarium; Museum of Asian Cultures; professional baseball, hockey; greyhound race track.

Minerals: Oil, gas, sand, gravel.

Agriculture: Grain sorghum (second in acreage), cotton, cattle, wheat, hay, nurseries/turfgrass. Market value $84.9 million.

CORPUS CHRISTI (326,071) county seat; seaport, naval bases, varied manufacturing, petroleum processing, tourism; hospitals; museums; Army depot; Texas A&M University-Corpus Christi, Del Mar College; USS Lexington museum, Harbor Lights; Buccaneer Days in late April.

Port Aransas (4,206) deepwater port, tourism, marine research, Coast Guard base, fishing industry; University of Texas Marine Science Institute; museum, beach; Celebration of

Whooping Cranes in February; Texas Sand Fest in April.

Robstown (11,392) agriculture, transportation, tourism, petroleum processing; regional fairgrounds; Cottonfest in October, Fiesta Mexicana in March.

Other towns include: **Agua Dulce** (830); **Banquete** (774); **Bishop** (3,222) petrochemicals, agriculture, pharmaceuticals, plastics, nature trail, Old Tyme Faire in April; **Chapman Ranch** (200); **Driscoll** (738); **La Paloma-Lost Creek** (500); **North San Pedro** (889); **Petronila** (115); **Rancho Banquete** (431); **Sandy Hollow-Escondidas** (261); **Spring Gardens** (618); **Tierra Grande** (434), and **Tierra Verde** (308).

Annaville, **Calallen**, and **Flour Bluff** are now part of Corpus Christi.

The marina at Corpus Christi. Photo by Rosie Hatch.

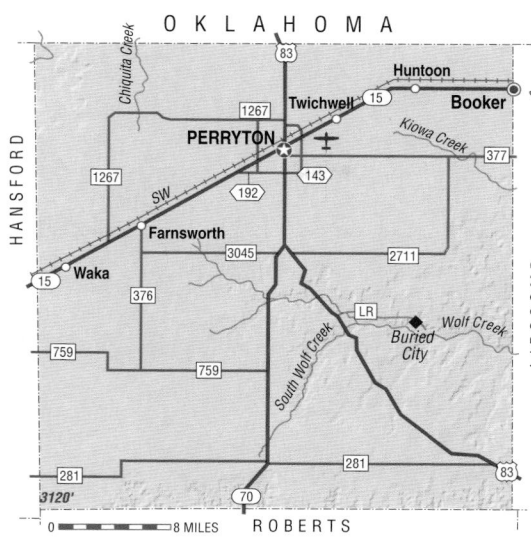

Ochiltree County

Physical Features: Panhandle county bordering Oklahoma; level, broken by creeks; deep loam, clay soils.

Economy: Agribusiness, oil/gas, government/services.

History: Apache groups, who were pushed out by Comanches in late 1700s. The Comanches were removed to the Indian Territory in 1874–1875 by U.S. Army. Ranching developed in 1880s; farming began after 1900. Created from the Bexar District in 1876, organized in 1889; named for Republic of Texas leader W.B. Ochiltree.

Race/Ethnicity: (In percent) Anglo, 42.8; Black, 1.1; Hispanic, 54.5; Asian, 0.6; Other, 1.8; Two or more races, 1.6.

Vital Statistics, annual: Births, 184; deaths, 83; marriages, 96; divorces, 37.

Recreation: Wolf Creek park; Museum of the Plains; Prehistoric settlement site of "Buried City"; pheasant hunting, also deer and dove; Wheatheart of the Nation celebration in August.

Minerals: Oil, natural gas, caliche.

Agriculture: Cattle, swine, corn, cotton, wheat (second in acreage), sorghum, hay and forages; some 50,000 acres irrigated. Market value $424.6 million.

PERRYTON (9,216) county seat; oil/gas, cattle feeding, grain center; hospital; college.

Other towns include: **Farnsworth** (130); **Waka** (65). Also, **Booker** (1,558, mostly in Lipscomb County).

Population	9,947
Change fm 2010	– 2.7
Area (sq. mi.)	918.1
Land Area (sq. mi.)	917.6
Altitude (ft.)	2,550–3,120
Rainfall (in.)	22.10
Jan. mean min.	19.0
July mean max.	92.4
Civ. Labor	4,462
Unemployed	2.7
Wages	$53,035,463
Per Capita Income	$50,251
Prop. Value	$1,974,136,789
Retail Sales	$93,580,778

For explanation of sources, symbols and abbreviations, see p. 192, and foldout map.

Oldham County

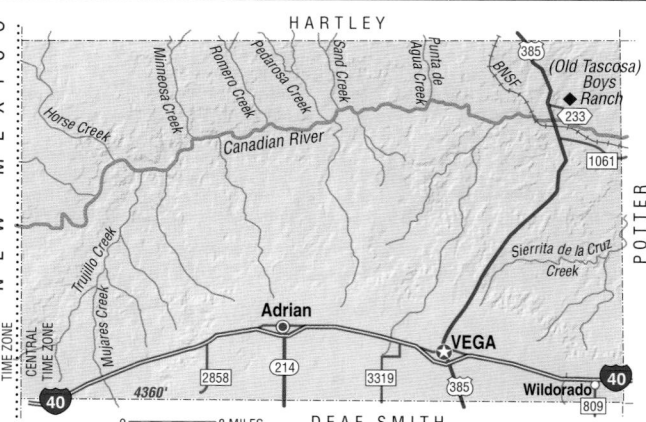

Physical Features: Northwestern Panhandle county; level, broken by Canadian River and tributaries.

Economy: Agriculture, wind energy, sand and gravel.

History: Apaches; followed later by Comanches, Kiowas. U.S. Army removed the Indians in 1875. Anglo ranchers and Spanish pastores (sheepmen) from New Mexico were in the area in the 1870s. County created in 1876 from Bexar District; organized in 1880; named for editor-Confederate senator W.S. Oldham.

Race/Ethnicity: (In percent) Anglo, 77.8; Black, 3.6; Hispanic, 15.6; Asian, 1.5; Other, 0.9; Two or more races, 1.9.

Vital Statistics, annual: Births, 23; deaths, 17; marriages, 14; divorces, 3.

Recreation: Old Tascosa, Cal Farley's Boys Ranch, Boot Hill Cemetery, museums; midway point on old Route 66; County Roundup in August, Boys Ranch rodeo Labor Day weekend.

Minerals: Sand and gravel, oil, natural gas, stone.

Agriculture: Beef cattle; crops include wheat, grain sorghum. Market value $113 million.

VEGA (867) county seat; farm and ranch trade center; transportation; museums.

Other towns: **Adrian** (164); **Wildorado** (210). Also, Cal Farley's **Boys Ranch** (297).

Population	2,131
Change fm 2010	3.8
Area (sq. mi.)	1,501.4
Land Area (sq. mi.)	1,500.5
Altitude (ft.)	3,140–4,360
Rainfall (in.)	19.16
Jan. mean min.	20.7
July mean max.	92.3
Civ. Labor	893
Unemployed	2.6
Wages	$9,882,662
Per Capita Income	$48,409
Prop. Value	$1,131,346,575
Retail Sales	$41,986,008

Orange County

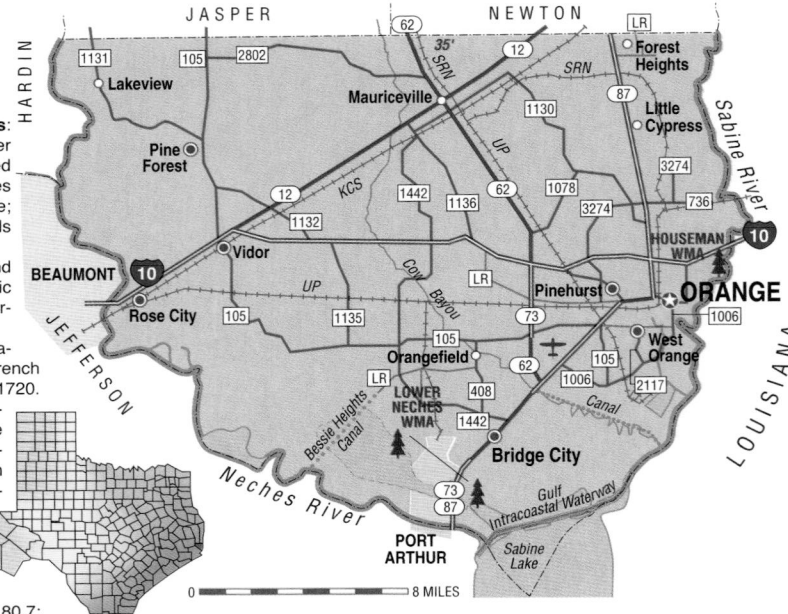

Physical Features: In southeastern corner of the state; bounded by Sabine, Neches rivers, Sabine Lake; coastal soils; two-thirds timbered.

Economy: Oil and gas production, electric power plants, commercial fishing.

History: Atakapan Indian area. French traders in area by 1720. Anglo-American settlement began in the 1820s. County created from Jefferson County in 1852, organized the same year; named for early orange grove.

Race/Ethnicity: (In percent) Anglo, 80.7; Black, 8.8; Hispanic, 7.7; Asian, 1.1; Other, 0.8; Two or more races, 1.6.

Vital Statistics, annual: Births, 1,218; deaths, 947; marriages, 630; divorces, 203.

Recreation: Fishing, hunting, water sports, birding, county park, museums; historical homes, crawfish and crab festivals in spring.

Minerals: Oil and gas.

Agriculture: Beef cattle, forages, citrus, bees. Market value $4.3 million. Hunting leases. Timber important.

ORANGE (19,416) county seat; seaport, petrochemical plants, varied manufacturing, food and timber pro-

cessing shipping; hospital, theater, museums; Lamar State College-Orange; Mardi Gras/gumbo festival in February.

Bridge City (8,092) varied manufacturing, ship repair yard, steel fabrication, fish farming, government/services; library; tall bridge and newer suspension bridge over Neches; stop for Monarch butterfly in fall during its migration to Mexico.

Vidor (10,937) steel processing, railroad-car refinishing; library; barbecue festival in April.

Other towns include: **Mauriceville** (3,526); **Orangefield** (725); **Pine Forest** (506); **Pinehurst** (2,138); **Rose City** (529); **West Orange** (3,549).

Population	**83,572**
Change fm 2010	2.1
Area (sq. mi.)	379.5
Land Area (sq. mi.)	333.7
Altitude (ft.)	sea level–35
Rainfall (in.)	64.21
Jan. mean min.	39.6
July mean max.	91.2
Civ. Labor	36.632
Unemployed	5.5
Wages	$288,458,160
Per Capita Income	$43,412
Prop. Value	$7,077,747,719
Retail Sales	$954,225,809

For explanation of sources, symbols and abbreviations, see p. 192, and foldout map.

Boaters and picnickers at Possum Kingdom Lake, Palo Pinto County. Photo by Robert Plocheck.

Mileage between Texas Cities

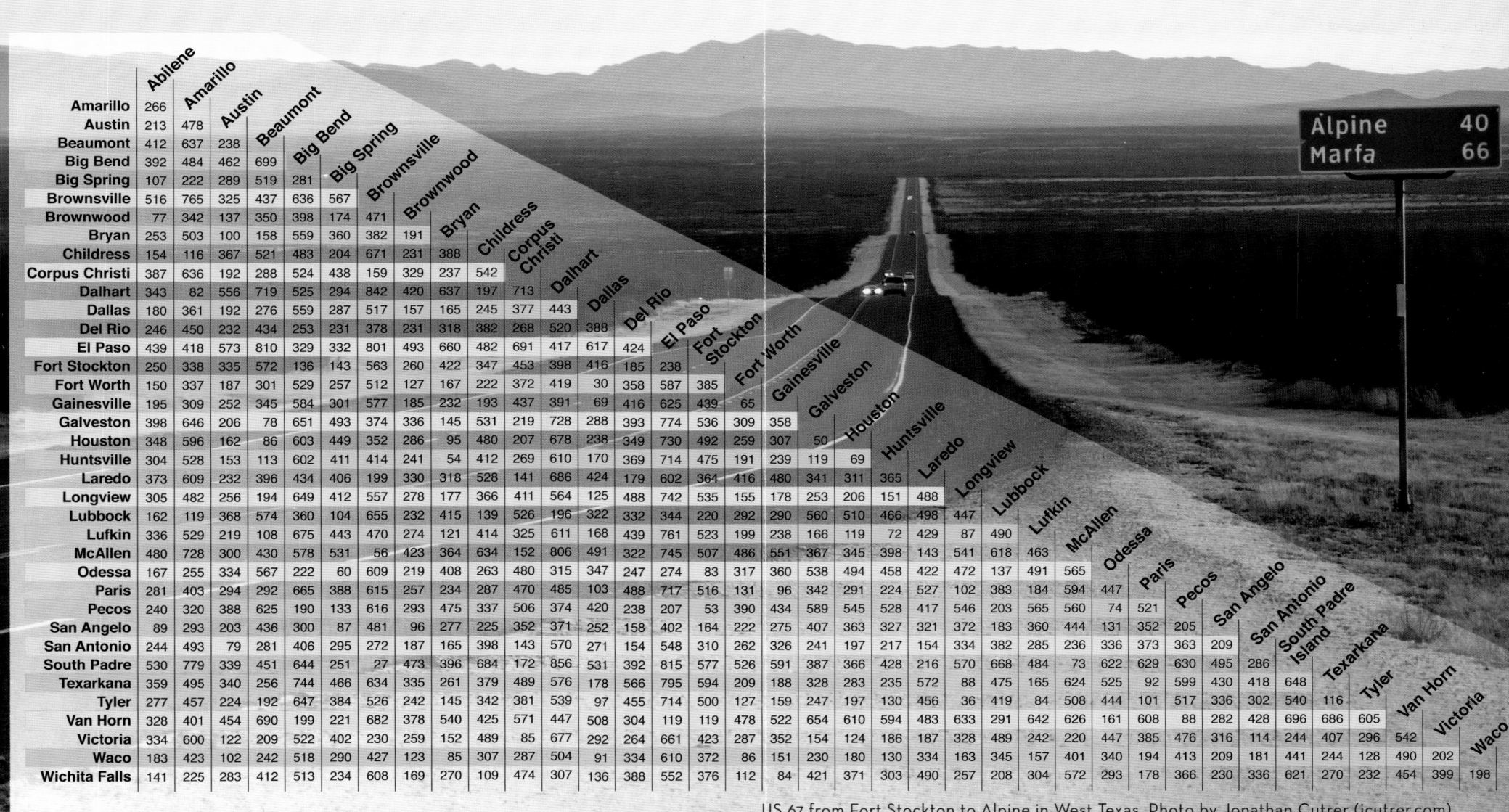

	Abilene	Amarillo	Austin	Beaumont	Big Bend	Big Spring	Brownsville	Brownwood	Bryan	Childress	Corpus Christi	Dalhart	Dallas	Del Rio	El Paso	Fort Stockton	Fort Worth	Gainesville	Galveston	Houston	Huntsville	Laredo	Longview	Lubbock	Lufkin	McAllen	Odessa	Paris	Pecos	San Angelo	San Antonio	South Padre Island	Texarkana	Tyler	Van Horn	Victoria	Waco
Amarillo	266																																				
Austin	213	478																																			
Beaumont	412	637	238																																		
Big Bend	392	484	462	699																																	
Big Spring	107	222	289	519	281																																
Brownsville	516	765	325	437	636	567																															
Brownwood	77	342	137	350	398	174	471																														
Bryan	253	503	100	158	559	360	382	191																													
Childress	154	116	367	521	483	204	671	231	388																												
Corpus Christi	387	636	192	288	524	438	159	329	237	542																											
Dalhart	343	82	556	719	525	294	842	420	637	197	713																										
Dallas	180	361	192	276	559	287	517	157	165	245	377	443																									
Del Rio	246	450	232	434	253	231	378	231	318	382	268	520	388																								
El Paso	439	418	573	810	329	332	801	493	660	482	691	417	617	424																							
Fort Stockton	250	338	335	572	136	143	563	260	422	347	453	398	416	185	238																						
Fort Worth	150	337	187	301	529	257	512	127	167	222	372	419	30	358	587	385																					
Gainesville	195	309	252	345	584	301	577	185	232	193	437	391	69	416	625	439	65																				
Galveston	398	646	206	78	651	493	374	336	145	531	219	728	288	393	774	536	309	358																			
Houston	348	596	162	86	603	449	352	286	95	480	207	678	238	349	730	492	259	307	50																		
Huntsville	304	528	153	113	602	411	414	241	54	412	269	610	170	369	714	475	191	239	119	69																	
Laredo	373	609	232	396	434	406	199	330	318	528	141	686	424	179	602	364	416	480	341	311	365																
Longview	305	482	256	194	649	412	557	278	177	366	411	564	125	488	742	535	155	178	253	206	151	488															
Lubbock	162	119	368	574	360	104	655	232	415	139	526	196	322	332	344	220	292	290	560	510	466	498	447														
Lufkin	336	529	219	108	675	443	470	274	121	414	325	611	168	439	761	523	199	238	166	119	72	429	87	490													
McAllen	480	728	300	430	578	531	56	423	364	634	152	806	491	322	745	507	486	551	367	345	398	143	541	618	463												
Odessa	167	255	334	567	222	60	609	219	408	263	480	315	347	247	274	83	317	360	538	494	458	422	472	137	491	565											
Paris	281	403	294	292	665	388	615	257	234	287	470	485	103	488	717	516	131	96	342	291	224	527	102	383	184	594	447										
Pecos	240	320	388	625	190	133	616	293	475	337	506	374	420	238	207	53	390	434	589	545	528	417	546	203	565	560	74	521									
San Angelo	89	293	203	436	300	87	481	96	277	225	352	371	158	402	164	222	275	407	363	327	321	372	183	360	444	131	352	205									
San Antonio	244	493	79	281	406	295	272	187	165	398	143	570	271	154	548	310	262	326	241	197	217	154	334	382	285	236	336	373	363	209							
South Padre	530	779	339	451	644	251	27	473	396	684	172	856	531	392	815	577	526	591	387	366	428	216	570	668	484	73	622	629	630	495	286						
Texarkana	359	495	340	256	744	466	634	335	261	379	489	576	178	566	795	594	209	188	328	283	235	572	88	475	165	624	525	92	599	430	418	648					
Tyler	277	457	224	192	647	384	526	242	145	342	381	539	97	455	714	500	127	159	247	197	130	456	36	419	84	508	444	101	517	336	302	540	116				
Van Horn	328	401	454	690	199	221	682	378	540	425	571	447	508	304	119	119	478	522	654	610	594	483	633	291	642	626	161	608	88	282	428	696	686	605			
Victoria	334	600	122	209	522	402	230	259	152	489	85	677	292	264	661	423	287	352	154	124	186	187	328	489	242	220	447	385	476	316	114	244	407	296	542		
Waco	183	423	102	242	518	290	427	123	85	307	287	504	91	334	610	372	86	151	230	180	130	334	163	345	157	401	340	194	413	209	181	441	244	128	490	202	
Wichita Falls	141	225	283	412	513	234	608	169	270	109	474	307	136	388	552	376	112	84	421	371	303	490	257	208	304	572	293	178	366	230	336	621	270	232	454	399	198

US 67 from Fort Stockton to Alpine in West Texas. Photo by Jonathan Cutrer (jcutrer.com)

Alpine 40
Marfa 66

Counties
of Texas

A detailed county map
accompanies each
of 254 county articles
on pages 191–369.

Below is the legend to the
symbols used on those maps:

Legend to counties

———	Principal road
———	Secondary road
———	Local road
═══	Divided highway
🛡10	Interstate highway
377	U.S. highway
81	State highway
308	Farm-to-market road
LR	Local roads
28	Loop
+++++	Railway
BNSF	Railway name
⌇	River or creek
⬭	Lake
⬯	Intermittent water source
━━	Intracoastal Waterway
✪	County seat
◉	Incorporated town
○	Unincorporated town
	County boundary
PECOS	Name of neighboring county
400'	Elevation
880'	Highest point in county
✈	Major airport with scheduled jet service
✛	Municipal airport
✦	Military airport
🌲	National park or wildlife management area
▭	Federal land
🌲	State park or wildlife management area
▭	State land
◆	Ranger station
········	Time zone line
▭	Boundary of prison or military installation

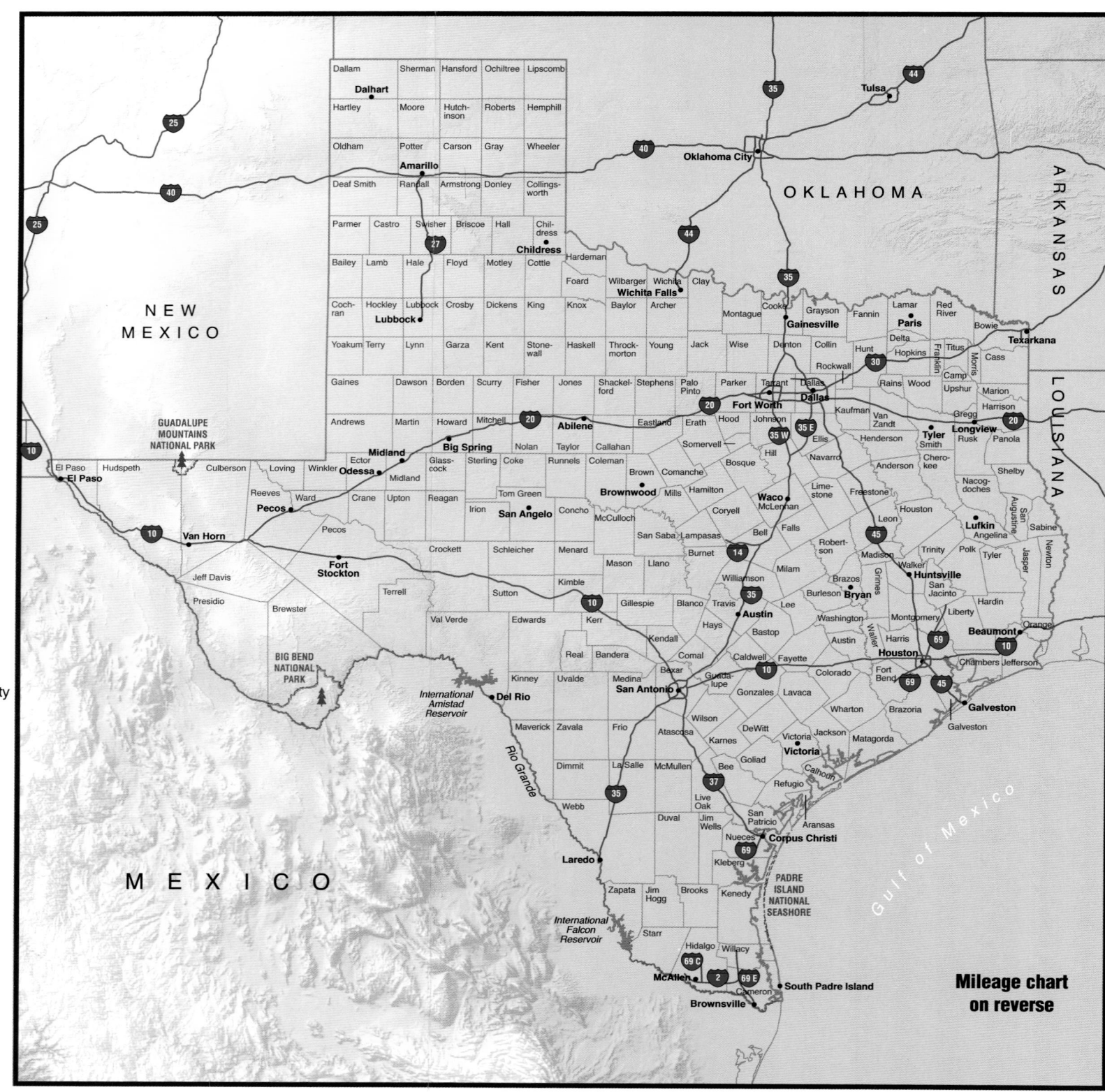

**Mileage chart
on reverse**

Palo Pinto County

Physical Features: North central county; broken, hilly, wooded in parts; Possum Kingdom Lake, Lake Palo Pinto; sandy, gray, black soils.

Economy: Varied manufacturing, tourism, petroleum, agribusiness.

History: Anglo-American ranchers arrived in the 1850s. Conflicts between settlers and numerous Indian tribes who had sought refuge on the Brazos River resulted in Texas Rangers removing the Indians in 1856. County created in 1856 from Bosque and Navarro counties; organized in 1857; named for creek (in Spanish name means painted stick).

Race/Ethnicity: (In percent) Anglo, 75.2; Black, 2.5; Hispanic, 19.9; Asian, 0.8; Other, 1.2; Two or more races, 1.6.

Vital Statistics, annual: Births, 353; deaths, 348; marriages, 167; divorces, 112.

Recreation: Lake activities, hunting, fishing, state parks, Rails to Trails hiking, biking, fossil park.

Minerals: Oil, gas, clays.

Agriculture: Cattle, dairy products, nursery crops, hay, wheat. Market value $53.8 million. Cedar posts marketed.

PALO PINTO (339) county seat; government center.

MINERAL WELLS (16,613, part [2,144] in Parker County) oil and gas, manufacturing, tourism; hospital, Weatherford College branch; art center; state park east of city in Parker County; Crazy Water Festival in October.

Other towns include: **Gordon** (472); **Graford** (590) retirement/recreation area, Possum Fest in October; **Mingus** (248); **Santo** (445), and **Strawn** (655).

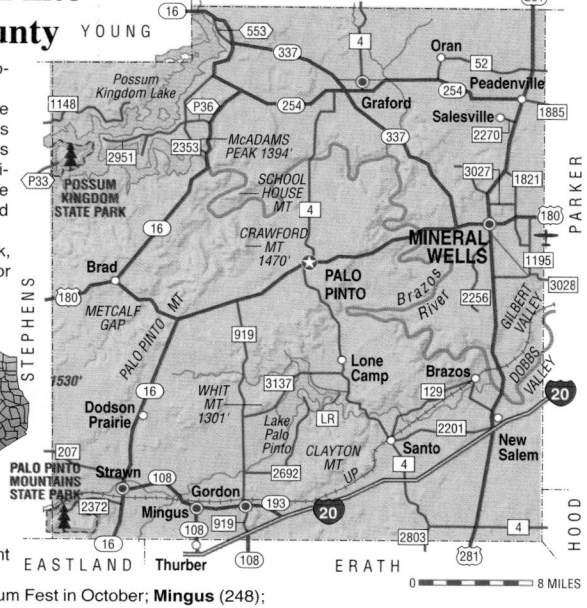

Population	28,875
Change fm 2010	2.7
Area (sq. mi.)	985.5
Land Area (sq. mi.)	951.8
Altitude (ft.)	782–1,530
Rainfall (in.)	32.05
Jan. mean min.	32.2
July mean max.	95.5
Civ. Labor	13,465
Unemployed	3.2
Wages	$93,825,267
Per Capita Income	$36,987
Prop. Value	$4,317,112,469
Retail Sales	$329,144,837

Panola County

Physical Features: East Texas county; sixty percent forested, rolling plain; broken by Sabine, Murvaul Creek; Toledo Bend Reservoir, Lake Murvaul, Martin Creek Lake.

Economy: Gas, oil-field operations, food processing, agribusiness.

History: A Caddo tribal area. Anglo-American settlement established in 1833. Antebellum slaveholding area. County name is Indian word for cotton; created from Harrison, Shelby counties in 1846; organized the same year.

Race/Ethnicity: (In percent) Anglo, 73.2; Black, 15.8; Hispanic, 8.8; Asian, 0.8; Other, 0.8; Two or more races, 2.0.

Vital Statistics, annual: Births, 287; deaths, 266; marriages, 164; divorces, 93.

Recreation: Fishing, water activities, hunting; Jim Reeves memorial, Tex Ritter museum and Texas Country Music Hall of Fame.

Minerals: Oil, gas, coal.

Agriculture: Broilers, cattle, forages. Market value $93.3 million. Timber sales significant.

CARTHAGE (6,934) county seat; petroleum processing, poultry, sawmills; hospital, junior college; Oil & Gas Blast in October.

Other towns include: **Beckville** (838), **Clayton** (125), **DeBerry** (301), **Gary** (301), **Long Branch** (150), **Panola** (305). Also, **Tatum** (1,416, mostly in Rusk County).

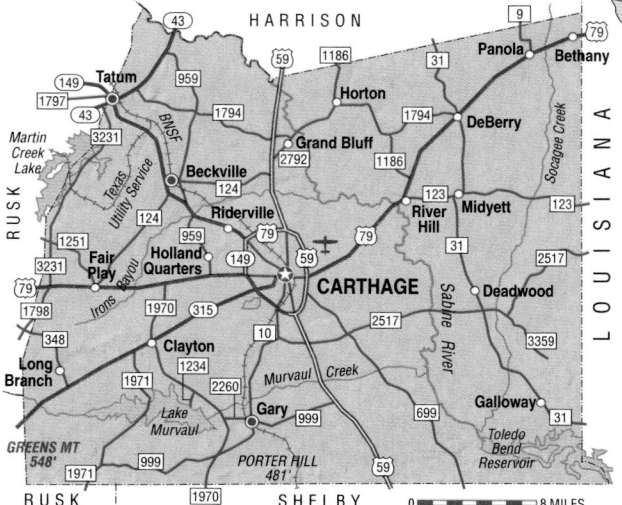

Population	23,148
Change fm 2010	– 2.7
Area (sq. mi.)	821.3
Land Area (sq. mi.)	801.8
Altitude (ft.)	172–548
Rainfall (in.)	51.43
Jan. mean min.	35.2
July mean max.	93.0
Civ. Labor	10,501
Unemployed	3.8
Wages	$100,563,001
Per Capita Income	$40,411
Prop. Value	$4,283,103,130
Retail Sales	$241,835,043

Parker County

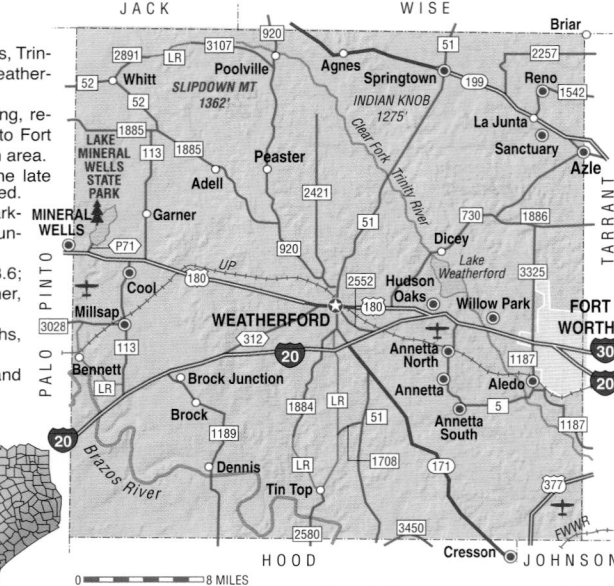

Physical Features: Hilly, broken by Brazos, Trinity tributaries, Lake Mineral Wells, Lake Weatherford; varied soils.

Economy: Agriculture, varied manufacturing, retail sales, government/services, commuting to Fort Worth; part of Dallas-Fort Worth metropolitan area.

History: Comanche and Kiowa area in the late 1840s when Anglo-American settlers arrived. County named for pioneer legislator Isaac Parker; created in 1855 from Bosque, Navarro counties, organized the same year.

Race/Ethnicity: (In percent) Anglo, 83.6; Black, 1.5; Hispanic, 12.2; Asian, 0.7; Other, 1.0; Two or more races, 1.7.

Vital Statistics, annual: Births, 1,484; deaths, 1,066; marriages, 761; divorces, 414.

Recreation: Water sports; state park and trailway; nature trails; hunting; Peach Festival in July and rodeo days in June; first Monday trade days monthly.

Minerals: Natural gas, oil, stone, sand and gravel, clays.

Agriculture: Beef cattle, greenhouses, hay, horses (first in number), peaches, sheep and goats, vegetables, pecans, aquaculture. Market value $74.3 million.

WEATHERFORD (30,351) county seat; retail center, manufacturing, warehousing, tourism, commuting to Fort Worth, government/services, equine industry; hospital, Weatherford College; museums, public gardens, historic buildings.

Other towns include: **Aledo** (3,426); **Annetta** (1,689), **Annetta North** (580) and **Annetta South** (589); **Cool** (174); **Dennis** (300); **Hudson Oaks** (2,248); **Millsap** (459); **Peaster** (1,000); **Poolville** (520); **Reno** (2,802); **Sanctuary** (338); **Springtown** (3,064) commuters, government/services, Wild West Festival in September; **Whitt** (38); **Willow Park** (5,400).

Also, parts of **Azle** (12,161); **Briar** (6,116), and **Cresson** (789); part [2,144] of **Mineral Wells**. Also, a small part of **Fort Worth**.

Population	138,371
Change fm 2010	18.3
Area (sq. mi.)	910.1
Land Area (sq. mi.)	903.5
Altitude (ft.)	700–1,362
Rainfall (in.)	35.77
Jan. mean min.	30.1
July mean max.	93.2
Civ. Labor	64,545
Unemployed	3.0
Wages	$369,767,843
Per Capita Income	$51,930
Prop. Value	$15,685,049,397
Retail Sales	$2,591,236,610

Parmer County

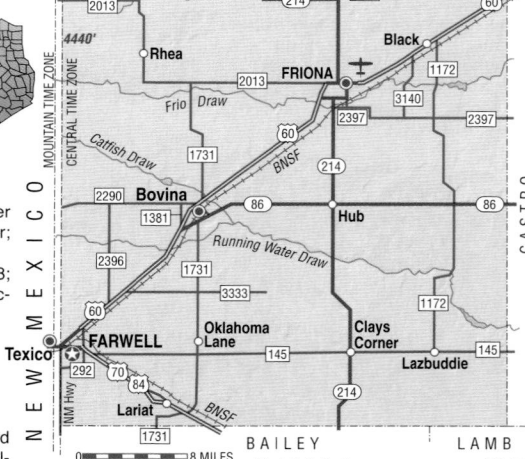

Physical Features: High Plains, broken by draws, playas; sandy, clay, loam soils.

Economy: Cattle feeding, grain elevators, meatpacking plant, other agribusiness.

History: Apaches, pushed out in late 1700s by Comanches and Kiowas. U.S. Army removed Indians in 1874–1875. Anglo-Americans arrived in 1880s. Mexican migration increased after 1950. County named for Republic figure Martin Parmer; created from Bexar District in 1876, organized in 1907.

Race/Ethnicity: (In percent) Anglo, 34.2; Black, 1.8; Hispanic, 63.5; Asian, 0.7; Other, 1.9; Two or more races, 1.3.

Vital Statistics, annual: Births, 159; deaths, 75; marriages, 35; divorces, 22.

Recreation: Hunting, playa lake, Border Town Days in July at Farwell.

Minerals: Not significant.

Agriculture: Cattle (second in numbers), dairies (third in number of cows); wheat, corn, cotton, sorghum, alfalfa; apples, potatoes. 163,000 acres irrigated. Market value $1.33 billion, second in state.

FARWELL (1,335) county seat; agribusiness, grain storage, farm equipment plants.

FRIONA (3,995) farming, feed lots, feed mill; hospital; museum; Cheeseburger Festival in July.

Other towns: **Bovina** (1,809) farm trade center; **Lazbuddie** (248).

Population	9,864
Change fm 2010	– 3.9
Area (sq. mi.)	885.2
Land Area (sq. mi.)	880.8
Altitude (ft.)	3,785–4,440
Rainfall (in.)	20.14
Jan. mean min.	22.5
July mean max.	89.8
Civ. Labor	4,759
Unemployed	2.3
Wages	$61,230,628
Per Capita Income	$47,274
Prop. Value	$1,674,223,104
Retail Sales	$73,040,139

Pecos County

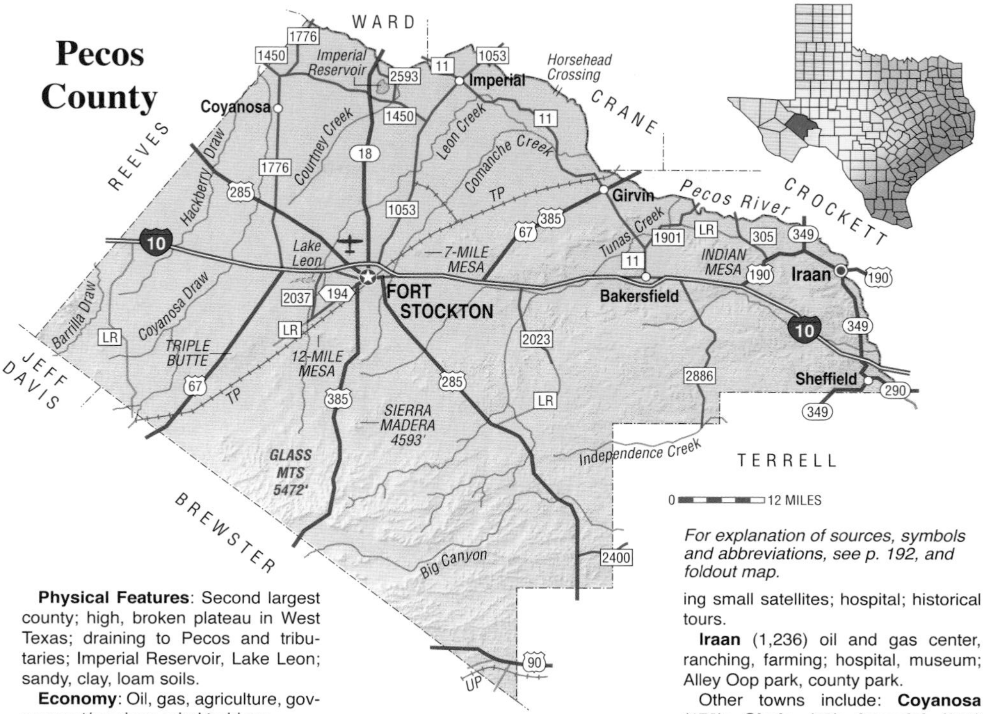

Physical Features: Second largest county; high, broken plateau in West Texas; draining to Pecos and tributaries; Imperial Reservoir, Lake Leon; sandy, clay, loam soils.

Economy: Oil, gas, agriculture, government/services, wind turbines.

History: Comanches in area when military outpost established in 1859. Settlement began after the Civil War. Created from Presidio County in 1871; organized in 1872; named for Pecos River, name origin uncertain.

Race/Ethnicity: (In percent) Anglo, 25.6; Black, 4.3; Hispanic, 68.8; Asian, 1.0; Other, 1.4; Two or more races, 1.2.

Vital Statistics, annual: Births, 203; deaths, 114; marriages, 81; divorces, 12.

Recreation: Old Fort Stockton, Annie Riggs Museum, stagecoach stop, scenic drives, Dinosaur Track Road-side Park, cattle-trail sites, archaeological museum with oil and ranch-heritage collections; Comanche Springs Water Carnival in summer.

Minerals: Natural gas, oil, gravel, caliche.

Agriculture: Cattle, alfalfa, pecans, sheep, goats, onions, peppers, melons. Market value $47.5 million. Aquaculture firm producing shrimp. Hunting leases.

FORT STOCKTON (8,558) county seat, distribution center for petroleum industry, government/services, agriculture, tourism, varied manufacturing, winery, prison units, spaceport launch-ing small satellites; hospital; historical tours.

Iraan (1,236) oil and gas center, ranching, farming; hospital; museum; Alley Oop park, county park.

Other towns include: **Coyanosa** (178); **Girvin** (20); **Imperial** (246) center for irrigated farming; **Sheffield** (322) oil, gas center.

Population	**15,673**
Change fm 2010	1.1
Area (sq. mi.)	4,764.8
Land Area (sq. mi.)	4,763.9
Altitude (ft.)	2,040–5,472
Rainfall (in.)	15.15
Jan. mean min.	33.2
July mean max.	94.3
Civ. Labor	6,452
Unemployed	3.5
Wages	$65,976,755
Per Capita Income	$33,461
Prop. Value	$3,748,132,940
Retail Sales	$549,074,256

For explanation of sources, symbols and abbreviations, see p. 192, and foldout map.

The Pecos River valley at Fort Lancaster near Sheffield, Crockett-Pecos counties. Photo by Robert Plocheck.

Polk County

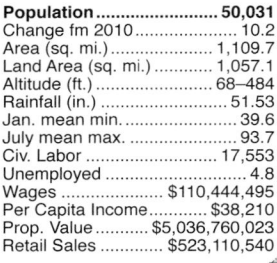
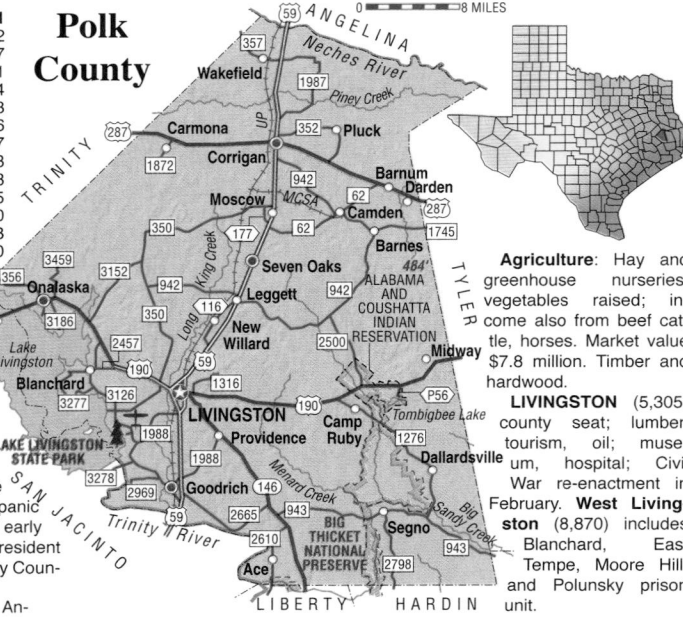

Population	50,031
Change fm 2010	10.2
Area (sq. mi.)	1,109.7
Land Area (sq. mi.)	1,057.1
Altitude (ft.)	68–484
Rainfall (in.)	51.53
Jan. mean min.	39.6
July mean max.	93.7
Civ. Labor	17,553
Unemployed	4.8
Wages	$110,444,495
Per Capita Income	$38,210
Prop. Value	$5,036,760,023
Retail Sales	$523,110,540

Physical Features: Rolling; densely forested, with Big Thicket, unique plant, animal life; Neches, Trinity rivers, tributaries; lake.

Economy: Timber, lumber production, tourism, manufacturing.

History: Caddo area; Alabama and Coushatta Indians arrived from Louisiana in the late 1700s. Anglo-American and Hispanic families received land grants in the early 1830s. County named for U.S. President James K. Polk; created from Liberty County and organized 1846.

Race/Ethnicity: (In percent) Anglo, 70.9; Black, 10.4; Hispanic, 15.3; Asian, 0.8; Other, 2.4; Two or more races, 1.6.

Vital Statistics, annual: Births, 562; deaths, 673; marriages, 325; divorces, 163.

Recreation: Lake and state park, water activities, fishing, hunting, Alabama-Coushatta Reservation, museum, Big Thicket, woodland trails, champion trees, historic homes.

Minerals: Oil, gas, sand, gravel.

Agriculture: Hay and greenhouse nurseries; vegetables raised; income also from beef cattle, horses. Market value $7.8 million. Timber and hardwood.

LIVINGSTON (5,305) county seat; lumber, tourism, oil; museum, hospital; Civil War re-enactment in February. **West Livingston** (8,870) includes Blanchard, East Tempe, Moore Hill, and Polunsky prison unit.

Other towns include: **Ace** (40); **Camden** (1,200); **Corrigan** (1,604) plywood plant; **Dallardsville** (350); **Goodrich** (294); **Leggett** (500); **Moscow** (170) historic sites; **Onalaska** (2,755); **Seven Oaks** (114).

Potter County

Physical Features: Mostly level, part rolling; broken by Canadian River and tributaries; sandy, sandy loam, chocolate loam, clay soils; Lake Meredith.

Economy: Transportation and distribution hub for large area, manufacturing, agribusiness, tourism, government/services, petrochemicals, gas processing.

History: Apaches, pushed out by Comanches in the 1700s. Comanches removed to Indian Territory in 1874–1875. Ranching began in the late 1870s. Oil boom in the 1920s. County named for Robert Potter, Republic leader; created in 1876 from Bexar District; organized in 1887.

Race/Ethnicity: (In percent) Anglo, 44.1; Black, 10.8; Hispanic, 38.3; Asian, 5.9; Other, 1.4; Two or more races, 2.1.

Vital Statistics, annual: Births, 1,944; deaths, 1,231; marriages, 1,383; divorces, 458.

Recreation: Lake activities, Alabates Flint Quarries National Monument, hunting, fishing, Wildcat Bluff nature center, Cadillac Ranch car sculpture, professional sports events, Tri-State Fair in September.

Minerals: Natural gas, oil, helium.

Agriculture: Beef cattle production and processing; wheat, sorghum, cotton. Market value $21 million.

AMARILLO (204,367 total, part [85,209] in Randall County) county seat; hub for northern Panhandle oil and ranching, distribution and marketing center, tourism, manufacturing, food processing, prison; hospitals; Amarillo College, Texas Tech University medical, engineering, pharmacy schools; Quarter Horse Hall of Fame, museum.

Other towns include: **Bishop Hills** (178) and **Bushland** (1,485).

Population	119,648
Change fm 2010	– 1.2
Area (sq. mi.)	922.0
Land Area (sq. mi.)	908.4
Altitude (ft.)	2,915–3,910
Rainfall (in.)	20.36
Jan. mean min.	23.4
July mean max.	91.4
Civ. Labor	57,293
Unemployed	2.7
Wages	$869,335,774
Per Capita Income	$40,456
Prop. Value	$8,464,316,930
Retail Sales	$2,488,660,459

The approach to the Rio Grande border at Presidio. Photo by Robert Plocheck.

Presidio County

Physical Features: Rugged, some of Texas' tallest mountains; clays, loams, sandy loams on uplands; intermountain wash; timber sparse; Capote Falls, state's highest.

Economy: Government/services, ranching, hunting leases, tourism.

History: Presidio area has been cultivated farmland since at least 1200 A.D. Spanish explorers of the 1500s encountered permanent villages along Rio Grande. Jumanos, Apaches, and Comanches in the area when Spanish missions began in 1680s. Anglo-Americans arrived in the 1840s. County created in 1850 from Bexar District; organized in 1875; named for Spanish Presidio del Norte (fort of the north).

Race/Ethnicity: (In percent) Anglo, 11.8; Black, 1.5; Hispanic, 83.6; Asian, 2.8; Other, 1.4; Two or more races, 1.2.

Vital Statistics, annual: Births, 108; deaths, 36; marriages, 55; divorces, 0.

Recreation: Hunting; scenic drives along Rio Grande, in mountains; ghost towns, mysterious Marfa Lights; Fort D.A. Russell; Big Bend Ranch State Park; hot springs; Cibolo Creek Ranch Resort; Chinati Foundation art festival in fall. (Chinati Mountains State Natural Area not yet open to public.)

Minerals: Sand, gravel, silver, zeolite.

Agriculture: Cattle, tomatoes, hay, onions, melons. Some irrigation near Rio Grande.

MARFA (1,840) county seat; ranching supply, Border Patrol headquarters, tourism, art center, gateway to mountainous area; Paisano Hotel, headquarters for movie *Giant*; Old Timers Roping on Memorial Day weekend.

PRESIDIO (4,352) international bridge to Ojinaga, Mex., gateway to Mexico's West Coast by rail; Fort Leaton historic site; asado cook-off in February.

Other towns include: **Redford** (80); **Shafter** (57) old mining town.

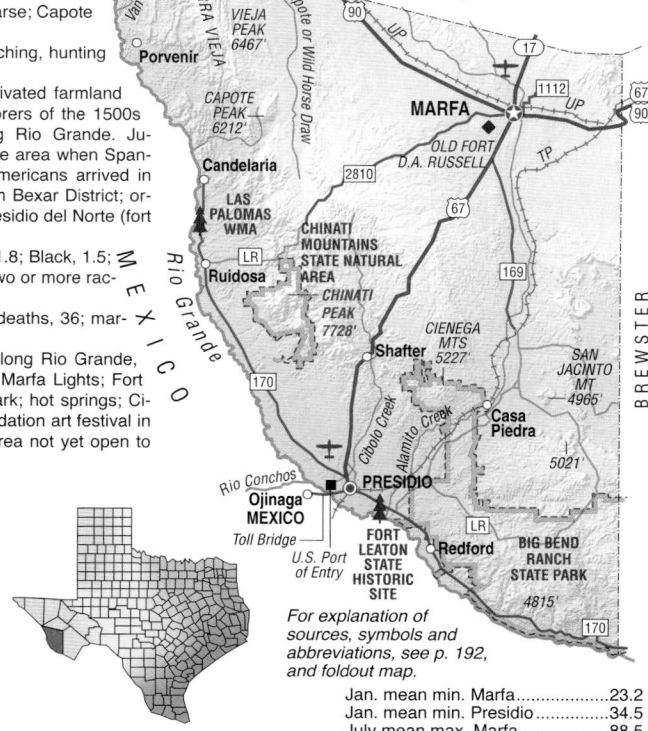

For explanation of sources, symbols and abbreviations, see p. 192, and foldout map.

Population	**6,948**
Change fm 2010	– 11.1
Area (sq. mi.)	3,855.9
Land Area (sq. mi.)	3,855.2
Altitude (ft.)	2,400–7,728
Rainfall (in.) Marfa	15.38
Rainfall (in.) Presidio	10.76

Jan. mean min. Marfa	23.2
Jan. mean min. Presidio	34.5
July mean max. Marfa	88.5
July mean max. Presidio	100.8
Civ. Labor	2,869
Unemployed	6.3
Wages	$20,369,075
Av. Weekly Wage	$39,183
Prop. Value	$1,253,850,538
Retail Sales	$56,104,221

Rains County

Physical Features: Northeastern county; rolling; partly Blackland, sandy loams, sandy soils; Sabine River, Lake Tawakoni, Lake Fork Reservoir.

Economy: Agribusiness, some manufacturing.

History: Caddo area. In the 1700s, Tawakoni Indians entered the area. Anglo-Americans arrived in the 1840s. County, county seat named for Emory Rains, Republic leader; created in 1870 from Hopkins, Hunt, and Wood counties, organized the same year; birthplace of National Farmers Union, 1902.

Race/Ethnicity: (In percent) Anglo, 85.5; Black, 2.6; Hispanic, 9.1; Asian, 1.0; Other, 1.1; Two or more races, 1.5.

Vital Statistics, annual: Births, 102; deaths, 150; marriages, 69; divorces, 53.

Recreation: Lake Tawakoni and Lake Fork Reservoir activities; birding, Eagle Fest in February.

Minerals: Gas, oil.

Agriculture: Beef, forages, dairies, vegetables (second in sweet potato acreage), fruits, nurseries. Market value $15.3 million.

EMORY (1,270) county seat; local trade, tourism, government/services, commuting to Greenville and Dallas; African-American museum.

Other towns include: **East Tawakoni** (927) and **Point** (857), manufacturing, tourism, tamale fest on July 4. Part of **Alba** (545), mostly in Wood County.

Population 12,159
Change fm 2010 .... 11.4

Area (sq. mi.) 258.8
Land Area (sq. mi.) 229.5

Altitude (ft.) 340–570
Rainfall (in.) 44.47
Jan. mean min. 31.4
July mean max. 91.4
Civ. Labor 5,984
Unemployed 3.2
Wages $15,754,481
Per Capita Income $32,379
Prop. Value $1,110,789,831
Retail Sales $106,087,967

Randall County

Population 136,271
Change fm 2010 .... 12.9
Area (sq. mi.) 922.4
Land Area (sq. mi.) 911.5
Altitude (ft.) 2,700–3,890
Rainfall (in.) 20.15
Jan. mean min. 21.5
July mean max. 91.7
Civ. Labor 71,866
Unemployed 2.5
Wages $333,283,547
Per Capita Income $46,718
Prop. Value $10,883,101,170
Retail Sales $1,785,378,341

Physical Features: Panhandle county; level, but broken by scenic Palo Duro Canyon, Buffalo Lake; Bivins Lake; silty clay, loam soils.

Economy: Agribusiness, education, tourism, part of Amarillo metropolitan area.

History: Comanche Indians removed in the mid-1870s; ranching began soon afterward. County created in 1876 from the Bexar District; organized in 1889; named for Confederate Gen. Horace Randal (name misspelled in statute).

Race/Ethnicity: (In percent) Anglo, 71.6; Black, 3.4; Hispanic, 21.8; Asian, 1.7; Other, 1.0; Two or more races, 2.0.

Vital Statistics, annual: Births, 1,667; deaths, 1,050; marriages, 465; divorces, 441.

Recreation: State park, with Texas outdoor musical drama each summer; Panhandle-Plains Historical Museum; West Texas A&M University events; aoudad sheep, migratory waterfowl hunting in season; Buffalo Lake National Wildlife Refuge; cowboy breakfasts at ranches.

Minerals: Not significant.

Agriculture: Grain sorghum, beef cattle, wheat, silage, cotton, dairies, hay. Market value $540.3 million.

CANYON (15,026) county seat; West Texas A&M University, tourism, commuting to Amarillo, ranching, farm center, light manufacturing, gateway to state park.

AMARILLO (204,367 total, part [105,486] in Potter County) hub for northern Panhandle oil and ranching, distribution and marketing center, manufacturing; hospitals.

Other towns include: **Lake Tanglewood** (934); **Palisades** (362); **Timbercreek Canyon** (456); **Umbarger** (327) German sausage festival in November.

Part of **Happy** (651, mostly in Swisher County).

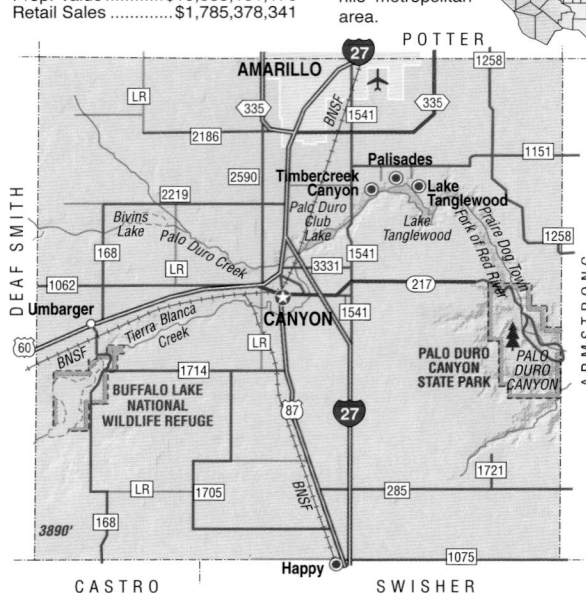

Reagan County

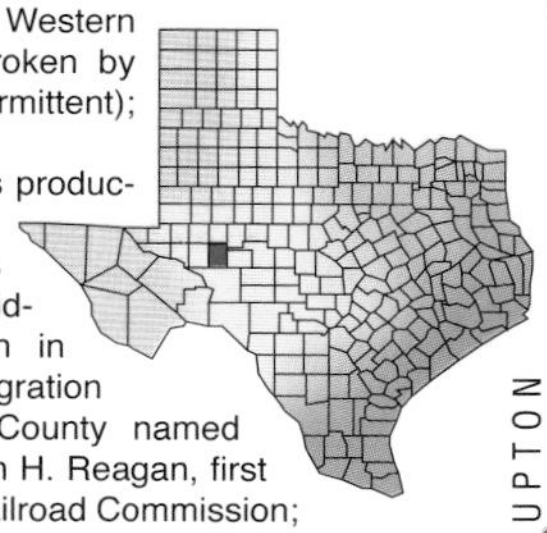

Physical Features: Western county; level to hilly, broken by draws, Big Lake (intermittent); sandy, loam, clay soils.

Economy: Oil and gas production, hunting, ranching.

History: Comanches in the area until the mid-1870s. Ranching began in the 1880s. Hispanic migration increased after 1950. County named for Texas' U.S. Sen. John H. Reagan, first chairman of the Texas Railroad Commission; county created and organized in 1903 from Tom Green County.

Race/Ethnicity: (In percent) Anglo, 27.1; Black, 3.1; Hispanic, 68.5; Asian, 0.6; Other, 1.2; Two or more races, 2.3.

Vital Statistics, annual: Births, 70; deaths, 29; marriages, 21; divorces, 20.

Recreation: Site of 1923 discovery well Santa Rita No. 1 on University of Texas land, Texon reunion in June.

Minerals: Gas, oil.

Agriculture: Cotton, cattle, sheep, goats. Market value $11.1 million. Hunting leases important.

BIG LAKE (3,448) county seat; center for oil activities, agriculture, government/services; hospital; Spring bluegrass festival, St. Rita festival in August.

For explanation of sources, symbols and abbreviations, see p. 192, and foldout map.

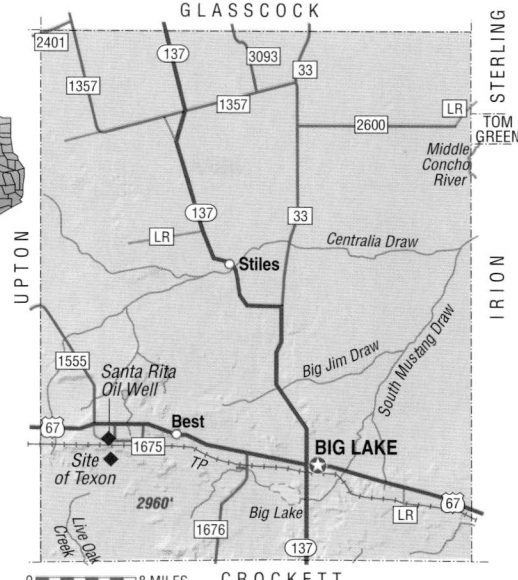

Population	3,741	July mean max.	93.5
Change fm 2010	11.1	Civ. Labor	1,813
Area (sq. mi.)	1,176.0	Unemployed	2.2
Land Area (sq. mi.)	1,175.3	Wages	$29,444,360
Altitude (ft.)	2,370–2,960	Per Capita Income	$40,496
Rainfall (in.)	19.29	Prop. Value	$2,757,444,187
Jan. mean min.	30.8	Retail Sales	$58,553,459

The Randall County Courthouse in Canyon. Photo by Robert Plocheck.

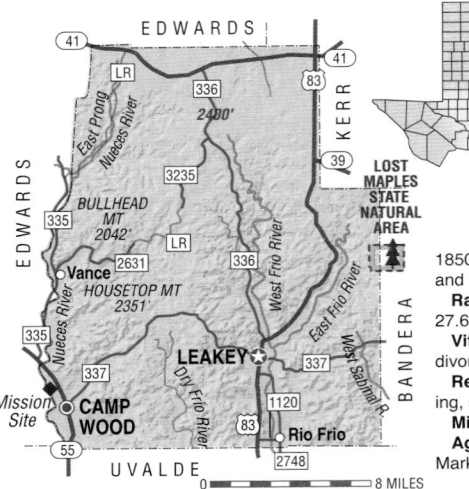

Real County

Physical Features: Hill Country, spring-fed streams, scenic canyons; Frio, Nueces rivers; cedars, pecans, walnuts, many live oaks.

Economy: Ranching, tourism, government/services, cedar cutting.

History: Tonkawa area; Lipan Apaches arrived in early 1700s; later, Comanche hunters arrived in the area. Spanish mission established in 1762. Anglo-Americans arrived in 1850s. County created, organized in 1913 from Bandera, Edwards, and Kerr counties; named for legislator-ranchman Julius Real.

Race/Ethnicity: (In percent) Anglo, 68.9; Black, 0.8; Hispanic, 27.6; Asian, 0.3; Other, 2.0; Two or more races, 1.9.

Vital Statistics, annual: Births, 41; deaths, 38; marriages, 17; divorces, 6.

Recreation: Tourist and hunting center, birding, fishing, camping, scenic drives, state natural area.

Minerals: Not significant.

Agriculture: Goats, sheep, beef cattle produce most income. Market value $1.6 million. Cedar posts processed.

LEAKEY (449) county seat; tourism, ranching; museums; July Jubilee.

CAMP WOOD (731) tourism, hunting, ranching; medical clinic; San Lorenzo de la Santa Cruz mission site; museum; Lindbergh Park, settlers reunion in August.

Other towns include: **Rio Frio** (50).

Population	3,478
Change fm 2010	5.1
Area (sq. mi.)	700.1
Land Area (sq. mi.)	699.2
Altitude (ft.)	1,400–2,400
Rainfall (in.)	27.38
Jan. mean min.	33.6
July mean max.	93.0
Civ. Labor	1,018
Unemployed	4.5
Wages	$4,909,232
Per Capita Income	$34,198
Prop. Value	$1,157,021,512
Retail Sales	$23,209,216

Red River County

Physical Features: On Red-Sulphur rivers' divide; 39 different soil types; half timbered; River Crest Reservoir.

Economy: Manufacturing, government/services, agriculture.

History: Caddo Indians abandoned the area in the 1790s. One of the oldest counties; settlers were moving in from the United States in the 1810s. Kickapoo and other tribes arrived in the 1820s. Antebellum slaveholding area. County created in 1836 as original county of the Republic; organized in 1837; named for Red River, its northern boundary.

Race/Ethnicity: (In percent) Anglo, 73.0; Black, 16.8; Hispanic, 7.6; Asian, 0.4; Other, 1.7; Two or more races, 1.9.

Vital Statistics, annual: Births, 115; deaths, 180; marriages, 67; divorces, 60.

Recreation: Historical sites include pioneer homes, birthplace of John Nance Garner; fall foliage; water activities; hunting of deer, turkey, duck, small game.

Minerals: Small oil flow.

Agriculture: Beef cattle, corn, soybeans, wheat, sorghum, hay. Market value $53.5 million. Timber sales substantial.

CLARKSVILLE (3,029) county seat; varied manufacturing; hospital, library; Historical Society bazaar in October.

Other towns include: **Annona** (289); **Avery** (444); **Bagwell** (150); **Bogata** (1,063); **Detroit** (670) commercial center in west. Part of **Deport** (560).

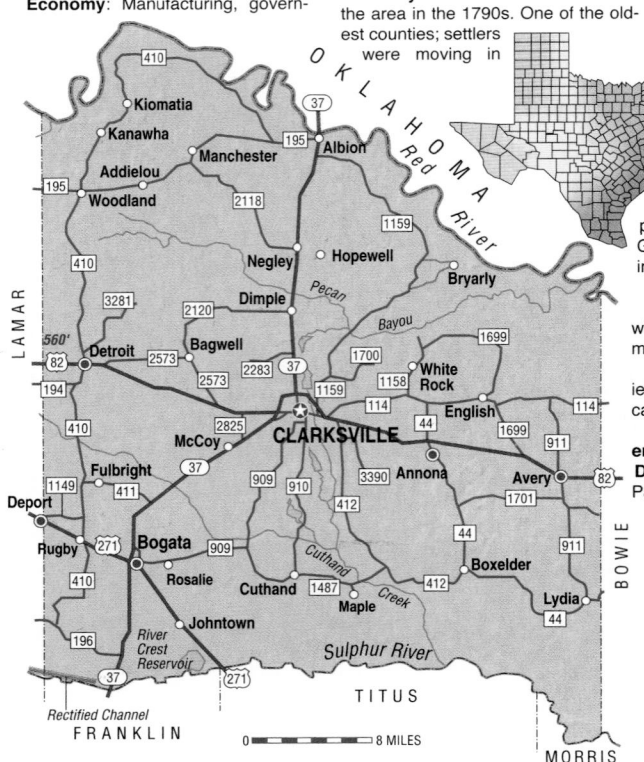

Population	12,175
Change fm 2010	– 5.4
Area (sq. mi.)	1,056.7
Land Area (sq. mi.)	1,036.6
Altitude (ft.)	260–560
Rainfall (in.)	48.77
Jan. mean min.	30.8
July mean max.	91.9
Civ. Labor	5,173
Unemployed	4.9
Wages	$22,074,780
Per Capita Income	$39,414
Prop. Value	$1,748,468,404
Retail Sales	$46,132,357

Reeves County

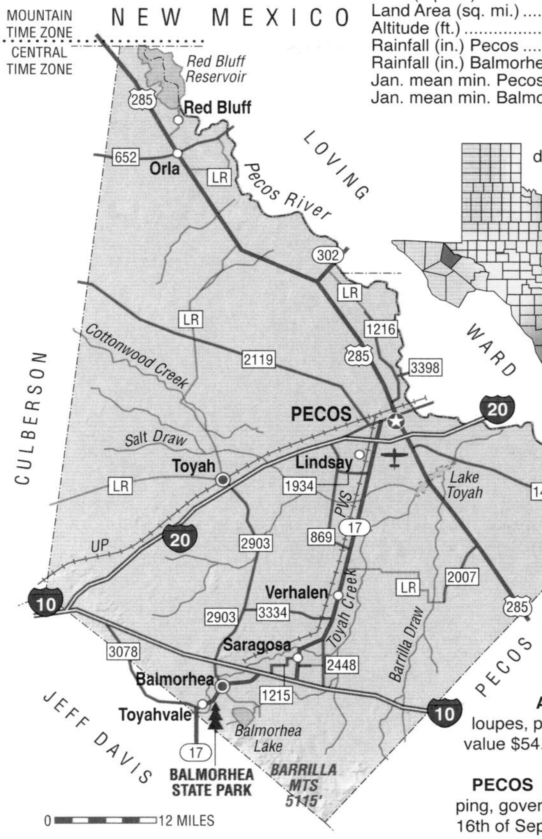

Population	**15,695**
Change fm 2010	13.9
Area (sq. mi.)	2,642.1
Land Area (sq. mi.)	2,635.4
Altitude (ft.)	2,460–5,115
Rainfall (in.) Pecos	11.61
Rainfall (in.) Balmorhea	13.54
Jan. mean min. Pecos	28.1
Jan. mean min. Balmorhea	30.3

July mean max. Pecos	98.5
July mean max. Balmorhea	94.4
Civ. Labor	8,197
Unemployed	2.0
Wages	$108,300,629
Per Capita Income	$32,859
Prop. Value	$4,626,538,330
Retail Sales	$322,961,386

Physical Features: Rolling plains, broken by many draws, Pecos River, Balmorhea Lake, Lake Toyah, Red Bluff Reservoir; Barrilla Mountains on the south; chocolate loam, clay, sandy, mountain wash soils.

Economy: Oil and gas, agriculture, tourism, food processing, government/services, gravel.

History: Jumanos were irrigating crops from springs (Balmorhea) when Spanish explored in 1583. Mexican farmers supplied nearby Fort Davis in the mid-19th century. Anglo-Americans arrived in the 1870s. County created in 1883 from Pecos County; organized in 1884; named for Confederate Col. George R. Reeves.

Race/Ethnicity: (In percent) Anglo, 17.9; Black, 5.3; Hispanic, 75.3; Asian, 1.4; Other, 1.0; Two or more races, 1.0.

Vital Statistics, annual: Births, 206; deaths, 114; marriages, 84; divorces, 24.

Recreation: Replica of Judge Roy Bean store, West of Pecos museum; park with javelina, prairie dogs; scenic drives; water activities; Balmorhea State Park with San Solomon Springs pool; Night in Old Pecos, cantaloupe festival in July.

Minerals: Oil, gas, gravel.

Agriculture: Ranching, dairies, hay, cotton, cantaloupes, pecans, pistachios. Some 11,000 acres irrigated. Market value $54.2 million.

PECOS (10,026) county seat; food processing, produce shipping, government/services, prison, tourism, agribusiness; hospital; 16th of September fiesta.

Other towns include: **Balmorhea** (551), **Lindsay** (267), **Orla** (80), **Saragosa** (185), **Toyah** (93), **Toyahvale** (60).

For explanation of sources, symbols and abbreviations, see p. 192, and foldout map.

Autumn in northern Red River County. Photo by Robert Plocheck.

Refugio County

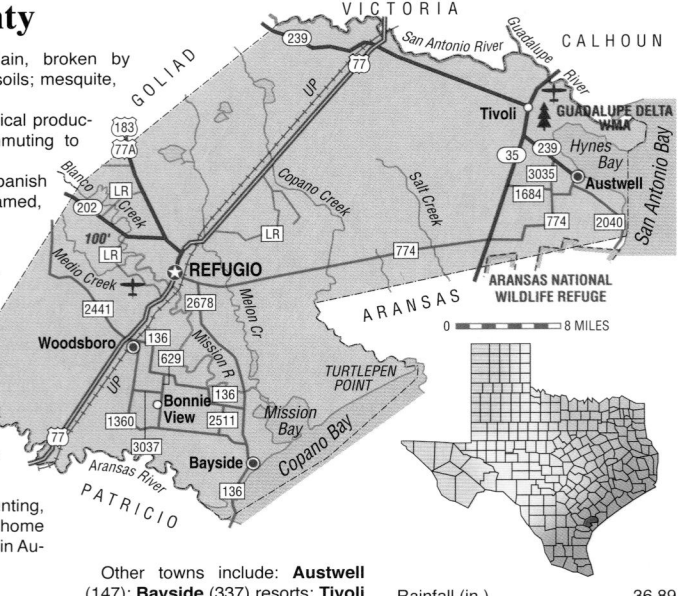

Physical Features: Coastal plain, broken by streams, bays; sandy, loam, black soils; mesquite, oak, huisache motts.

Economy: Petroleum, petrochemical production, agribusinesses, tourism, commuting to Corpus Christi, Victoria.

History: Karankawa area. Spanish mission, for which the county is named, Our Lady of Refuge, established in 1793. Colonists from Ireland and the United States arrived in the 1830s. Original county of the Republic created in 1836, organized in 1837.

Race/Ethnicity: (In percent) Anglo, 41.9; Black, 6.7; Hispanic, 50.0; Asian, 0.9; Other, 1.0; Two or more races, 1.9.

Vital Statistics, annual: Births, 99; deaths, 108; marriages, 47; divorces, 20.

Recreation: Water activities, hunting, fishing, historic sites, wildlife refuge, home of the whooping crane; chili cook-off in August, Festival of Flags in October.

Minerals: Oil, natural gas.

Agriculture: Cotton, beef cattle, sorghum, corn, soybeans, horses. Market value $43 million. Hunting leases.

REFUGIO (2,846) county seat; petroleum, agribusiness center; hospital; museum, historic homes.

Other towns include: **Austwell** (147); **Bayside** (337) resorts; **Tivoli** (503); **Woodsboro** (1,481) commercial center.

Population	**7,032**
Change fm 2010	– 4.8
Area (sq. mi.)	818.2
Land Area (sq. mi.)	770.4
Altitude (ft.)	sea level–100
Rainfall (in.)	36.89
Jan. mean min.	44.3
July mean max.	92.0
Civ. Labor	3,068
Unemployed	4.1
Wages	$22,271,020
Per Capita Income	$41,496
Prop. Value	$1,581,661,210
Retail Sales	$76,265,519

Roberts County

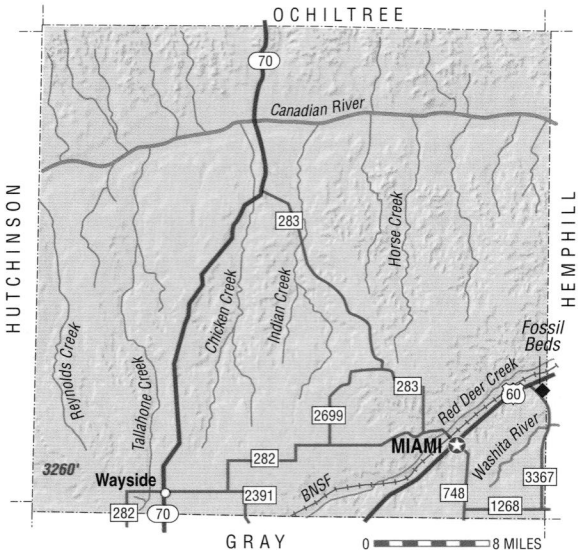

Physical Features: Rolling, broken by Canadian River and tributaries; Red Deer Creek; black, sandy loam, alluvial soils.

Economy: Oil-field operations, agribusiness.

History: Apaches; pushed out by Comanches who were removed in 1874–1875 by the U.S. Army. Ranching began in the late 1870s. County created in 1876 from Bexar District; organized in 1889; named for Texas leaders John S. Roberts and Gov. O.M. Roberts.

Race/Ethnicity: (In percent) Anglo, 85.8; Black, 0.1; Hispanic, 11.3; Asian, 0.3; Other, 0.7; Two or more races, 2.7.

Vital Statistics, annual: Births, 0; deaths, 6; marriages, 9; divorces, 1.

Recreation: Scenic drives, hunting, museum; national cow-calling contest in June.

Minerals: Production of gas, oil.

Agriculture: Beef cattle; wheat, sorghum, corn, soybeans, hay; 6,300 acres irrigated. Market value $16.4 million.

MIAMI (600) county seat; ranching, oil center, some manufacturing.

Population	**903**
Change fm 2010	– 2.8
Area (sq. mi.)	924.2
Land Area (sq. mi.)	924.1
Altitude (ft.)	2,380–3,260
Rainfall (in.)	24.08
Jan. mean min.	22.1
July mean max.	92.1
Civ. Labor	432
Unemployed	3.0
Wages	$2,649,130
Per Capita Income	$39,397
Prop. Value	$736,145,196
Retail Sales	$2,482,238

For explanation of sources, symbols and abbreviations, see p. 192, and foldout map.

Physical Features: Rolling in north and east, draining to bottoms along Brazos, Navasota rivers; sandy soils, heavy in bottoms; Lake Limestone, Twin Oaks Reservoir, Camp Creek Reservoir.

Economy: Agribusiness, government/services, oil and gas.

History: Tawakoni, Waco, Comanche, and other tribes. Anglo-Americans arrived in the 1820s. Antebellum slaveholding area. County created in 1837, organized in 1838, subdivided into many others later; named for pioneer Sterling Clack Robertson.

Race/Ethnicity: (In percent) Anglo, 57.5; Black, 20.5; Hispanic, 20.9; Asian, 0.7; Other, 1.1; Two or more races, 1.5.

Vital Statistics, annual: Births, 211; deaths, 173; marriages, 98; divorces, 25.

Recreation: Hunting, fishing; historic sites; dogwood trails, wildlife preserves.

Minerals: Gas, oil, lignite coal.

Agriculture: Poultry, beef cattle, cotton, hay, corn; 20,000 acres of cropland irrigated. Market value $136.4 million.

FRANKLIN (1,685) county seat; oil and gas, power plants, agriculture; Carnegie library.

HEARNE (4,648) railroad center; depot museum, historic homes, World War II POW camp; October Sticks & Stones golf and dominoes (Texas 42) tournament.

Other towns include: **Bremond** (958) mining, agriculture, power utilities, library, museum, Polish Days in late June; **Calvert** (1,151) agriculture, tourism, antiques, Maypole festival, tour of homes; **Mumford** (170); **New Baden** (150); **Wheelock** (225).

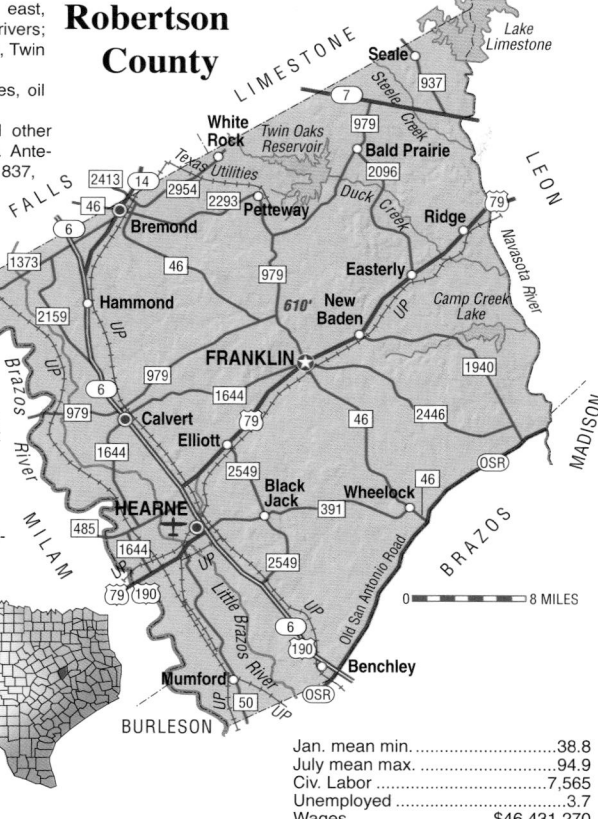

Robertson County

Population	17,284
Change fm 2010	4.0
Area (sq. mi.)	865.4
Land Area (sq. mi.)	855.7
Altitude (ft.)	230–610
Rainfall (in.)	39.50
Jan. mean min.	38.8
July mean max.	94.9
Civ. Labor	7,565
Unemployed	3.7
Wages	$46,431,270
Per Capita Income	$39,350
Prop. Value	$4,396,302,289
Retail Sales	$120,266,448

Copano Bay near Bayside, Refugio County. Photo by Rosie Hatch.

Rockwall County

Physical Features: Rolling prairie, mostly Blackland soil; Lake Ray Hubbard. Texas' smallest county.

Economy: Industrial employment in local plants and in Dallas; in Dallas metropolitan area; residential development around Lake Ray Hubbard.

History: Caddo area. Cherokees arrived in the 1820s. Anglo-American settlers arrived in the 1840s. County created in 1873 from Kaufman, organized the same year; named for wall-like rock formation.

Race/Ethnicity: (In percent) Anglo, 71.2; Black, 6.5; Hispanic, 17.7; Asian, 2.8; Other, 0.9; Two or more races, 2.0.

Vital Statistics, annual: Births, 1,034; deaths, 545; marriages, 1,389; divorces, 321.

Recreation: Lake activities; proximity to Dallas; unusual rock outcrop.

Minerals: Not significant.

Agriculture: Small grains, cattle, horticulture, horses. Market value $4.1 million.

ROCKWALL (45,435) county seat; commuters, varied manufacturing, government/services; hospital; harbor retail and entertainment district; Founders Day in April.

Other towns include: **Fate** (10,243); **Heath** (8,231); **McLendon-Chisholm** (2,438) chili cookoff in October; **Mobile City** (190); **Royse City** (12,476) government/services, varied manufacturing, agribusiness, museum, library, Funfest in October.

Part [7,011] of **Rowlett**, hospital, and a small part [1,055] of **Wylie**.

Population 100,657
Change fm 2010 .... 28.5
Area (sq. mi.) 148.7

Land Area (sq. mi.) 127.0
Altitude (ft.) 430–624
Rainfall (in.) 38,58
Jan. mean min. 33.0
July mean max. 96.0
Civ. Labor 50,949
Unemployed 3.1
Wages $321,824,114
Per Capita Income $58,717
Prop. Value $11,664,401,945
Retail Sales $1,986,935,133

Runnels County

Physical Features: Level to rolling; bisected by Colorado and tributaries; sandy loam, black waxy soils; O.H. Ivie Reservoir, Lake Ballinger.

Economy: Agribusiness, oil, government/services, manufacturing.

History: Spanish explorers found Jumanos in area in the 1650s; later, Apaches and Comanches driven out in the 1870s by U.S. military. First Anglo-Americans arrived in the 1850s; Germans, Czechs around 1900. County named for planter-legislator H.G. Runnels; created in 1858 from Bexar and Travis counties; organized in 1880.

Race/Ethnicity: (In percent) Anglo, 61.6; Black, 2.6; Hispanic, 34.3; Asian, 1.0; Other, 1.6; Two or more races, 1.2.

Vital Statistics, annual: Births, 112; deaths, 140; marriages, 56; divorces, 19.

Recreation: Deer, dove and turkey hunting; lakes; fishing; antique car museum; historical markers in county.

Minerals: Oil, gas, sand.

Agriculture: Cattle, cotton, wheat, sorghum, dairies, sheep and goats. Market value $47.4 million.

BALLINGER (3,700) county seat; varied manufacturing, meat processing; Carnegie Library, hospital, Western Texas College extension; the Cross, 100-ft. tall atop hill; city park; Festival of Ethnic Cultures in April.

Other towns include: **Miles** (862); **Norton** (50); **Rowena** (349); **Wingate** (100); **Winters** (2,525) manufacturing, museum, hospital.

Population 10,234
Change fm 2010 .... – 2.6
Area (sq. mi.) 1,057.1
Land Area (sq. mi.) 1,050.9
Altitude (ft.) 1,915–2,301
Rainfall (in.) 24.04
Jan. mean min. 31.2
July mean max. 94.4
Civ. Labor 4,509
Unemployed 3.0
Wages $24,159,566
Per Capita Income $39,215
Prop. Value $1,396,751,210
Retail Sales $87,077,520

For explanation of sources, symbols and abbreviations, see p. 192, and foldout map.

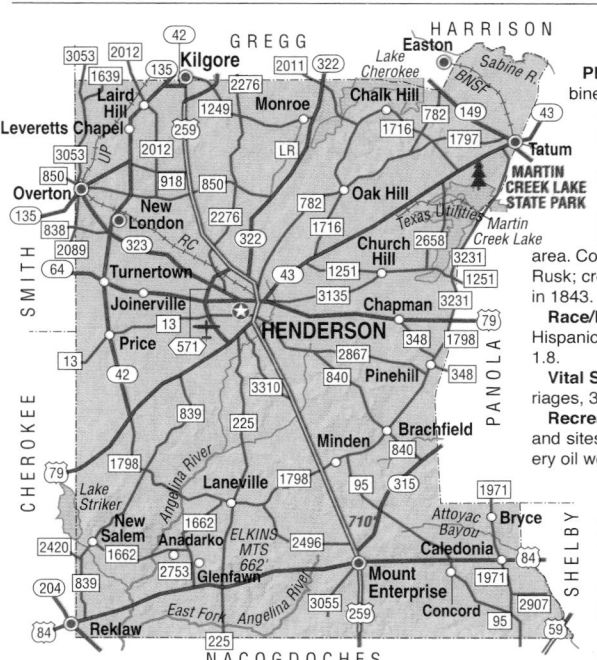

Rusk County

Physical Features: East Texas county on Sabine-Angelina divide; varied deep, sandy soils; over half in pines, hardwoods; Martin Creek Lake, Lake Cherokee, Lake Striker.

Economy: Oil and gas, lignite mining, electricity generation, agriculture.

History: Caddo area. Cherokees settled in the 1820s; removed in 1839. First Anglo-Americans arrived in 1829. Antebellum slaveholding area. County named for Republic, state leader Thomas J. Rusk; created and organized from Nacogdoches County in 1843.

Race/Ethnicity: (In percent) Anglo, 64.1; Black, 17.1; Hispanic, 16.9; Asian, 0.5; Other, 1.1; Two or more races, 1.8.

Vital Statistics, annual: Births, 645; deaths, 544; marriages, 335; divorces, 216.

Recreation: Water sports, state park, historic homes and sites, scenic drives, site of East Texas Field discovery oil well; Henderson syrup festival in November.

Minerals: Oil, natural gas, lignite.

Agriculture: Beef cattle, forage, poultry, nursery plants. Market value $75.3 million. Timber income substantial.

HENDERSON (13,708) county seat; power plant, mining, lumber, state jails; hospital, museum.

Other towns include: **Joinerville** (140); **Laird Hill** (300); **Laneville** (169); **Minden** (150); **Mount Enterprise** (448); **New London** (999) site of 1937 school explosion that killed 293 students and faculty; **Overton** (2,500, partly in Smith County) oil, lumbering center, petroleum processing, prison, A&M research center, blue-grass music festival in July; **Price** (275); **Tatum** (1,416, partly in Panola County); **Turnertown-Selman City** (271).

Also, part of **Easton** (636, mostly in Gregg County), part of **Reklaw** (390, mostly in Cherokee County), and part [3,013] of **Kilgore** (14,068 total).

Population	54,450
Change fm 2010	2.1
Area (sq. mi.)	938.4
Land Area (sq. mi.)	924.0
Altitude (ft.)	250–710
Rainfall (in.)	49.36
Jan. mean min.	34.9
July mean max.	92.7
Civ. Labor	22,242
Unemployed	3.9
Wages	$140,745,104
Per Capita Income	$35,508
Prop. Value	$5,113,499,630
Retail Sales	$359,592,702

0 ▆▆▆▆▆ 8 MILES

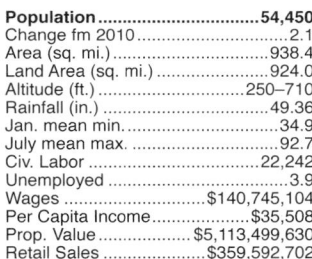

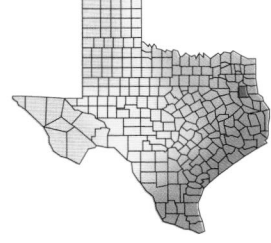

Cotton fields near Rowena, Runnels County. Photo by Robert Plocheck.

Sabine County

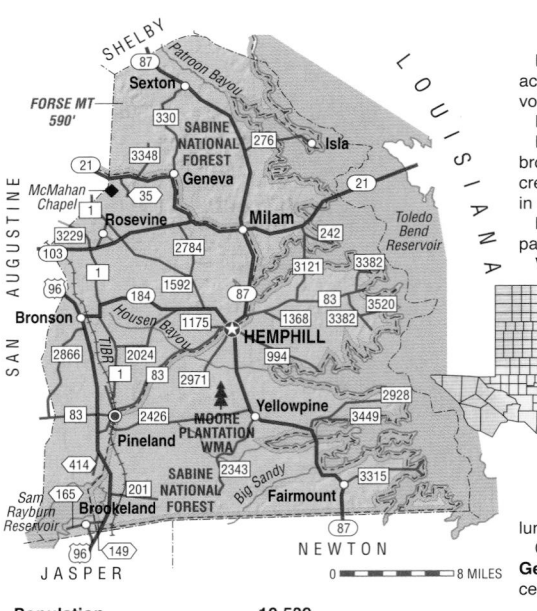

Physical Features: Eighty percent forested; 114,498 acres in national forest; Sabine River, Toledo Bend Reservoir on east; Sam Rayburn Reservoir on southwest.

Economy: Timber, government/services, tourism.

History: Caddo area. Spanish land grants in the 1790s brought first Spanish and Anglo settlers. An original county, created in 1836; organized in 1837. Name means cypress in Spanish.

Race/Ethnicity: (In percent) Anglo, 86.1; Black, 7.1; Hispanic, 4.5; Asian, 0.4; Other, 0.9; Two or more races, 1.7.

Vital Statistics, annual: Births, 111; deaths, 168; marriages, 83; divorces, 14.

Recreation: Lake activities, hunting, campsites, hiking trails, marinas, historic homes; McMahan's Chapel, pioneer Protestant church; Sabine National Forest; Lobanillo Swales historic trail.

Minerals: Glauconite, oil.

Agriculture: Beef cattle; forage, fruit raised. Market value $14.7 million. Significant timber industry.

HEMPHILL (1,229) county seat; timber, lake activities, tourism; hospital; NASA Columbia museum, library; Boo Bash at Halloween.

Other towns include: **Bronson** (377); **Brookeland** (300); **Geneva** (200); **Milam** (1,498); **Pineland** (793) timber processing.

Population	10,589	Rainfall (in.)	54.60
Change fm 2010	– 2.3	Jan. mean min.	36.5
Area (sq. mi.)	576.7	July mean max.	93.1
Land Area (sq. mi.)	491.4	Civ. Labor	3,673
Altitude (ft.)	164–590		

Unemployed	8.1
Wages	$20,832,322
Per Capita Income	$35,371
Prop. Value	$1,059,981,659
Retail Sales	$67,756,061

San Augustine County

Physical Features: Hilly East Texas county, 80 percent forested with 66,799 acres in Angelina National Forest, 4,317 in Sabine National Forest; Sam Rayburn Reservoir; varied soils, sandy to black alluvial.

Economy: Timber, poultry, tourism.

History: Presence of Ais Indians attracted Spanish mission in 1717. First Anglos and Indians from U.S. southern states arrived around 1800. Antebellum slaveholding area. County created and named for Mexican municipality in 1836; an original county; organized in 1837.

Race/Ethnicity: (In percent) Anglo, 69.1; Black, 22.0; Hispanic, 7.1; Asian, 0.4; Other, 0.8; Two or more races, 1.8.

Vital Statistics, annual: Births, 79; deaths, 128; marriages, 62; divorces, 8.

Recreation: Lake activities, historic homes, tourist facilities in national forests; sassafras festival in October.

Minerals: Small amount of oil.

Agriculture: Poultry, cattle, horses; watermelons, peas, corn, truck crops. Market value $63.2 million. Timber sales significant.

SAN AUGUSTINE (1,971) county seat; logging, poultry farms, tourism; hospital; Mission Dolores museum.

Other towns include: **Broaddus** (197).

Population	8,232
Change fm 2010	– 7.1
Area (sq. mi.)	592.3
Land Area (sq. mi.)	530.7
Altitude (ft.)	164–590
Rainfall (in.)	51.89
Jan. mean min.	35.6
July mean max.	92.7
Civ. Labor	3,020
Unemployed	6.3
Wages	$15,845,241
Per Capita Income	$38,277
Prop. Value	$1,052,031,660
Retail Sales	$54,477,836

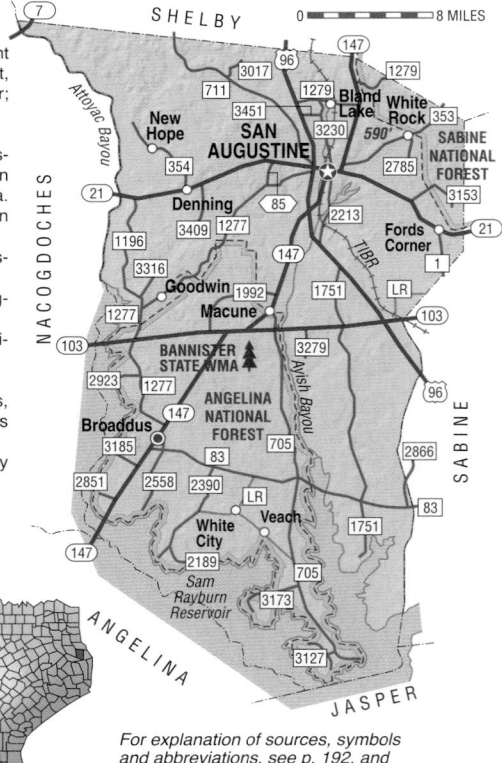

For explanation of sources, symbols and abbreviations, see p. 192, and foldout map.

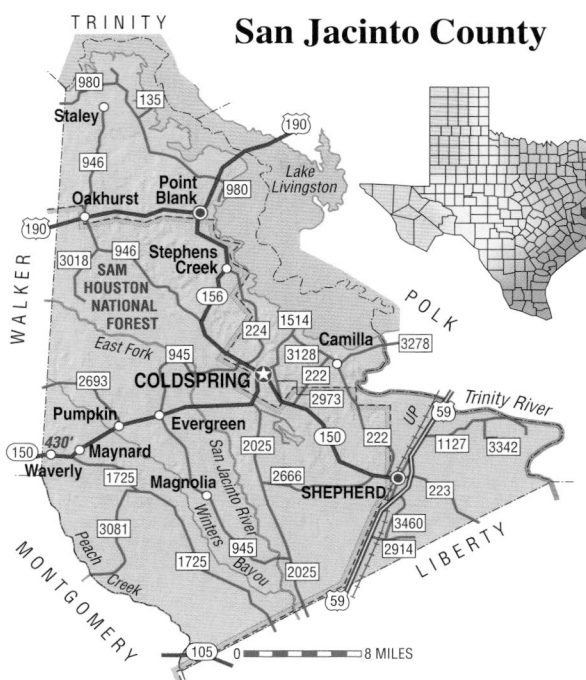

San Jacinto County

Physical Features: East Texas county north of Houston; rolling hills; eighty percent of area is forested; Sam Houston National Forest; Trinity and East Fork of San Jacinto rivers; Lake Livingston.

Economy: Timber and oil.

History: Atakapa Indian area. Anglo-Americans arrived in the 1820s. Land grants issued to Mexican families in the early 1830s. County created from Liberty, Montgomery, Polk, and Walker counties in 1869; organized in 1870; named for the battle.

Race/Ethnicity: (In percent) Anglo, 74.8; Black, 9.8; Hispanic, 13.1; Asian, 0.5; Other, 1.1; Two or more races, 2.1.

Vital Statistics, annual: Births, 283; deaths, 313; marriages, 113; divorces, 91.

Recreation: Lake activities, hunting, old courthouse and jail; Wolf Creek car show in Coldspring in October. Approximately 60 percent of county in national forest.

Minerals: Oil, rock, gravel and iron ore.

Agriculture: Beef cattle and forages. Market value $8.5 million. Timber is a principal product.

COLDSPRING (914) county seat; lumbering, oil, farming center, tourism; historic sites.

SHEPHERD (2,436) lumbering, tourism, ranching.

Other towns include: **Oakhurst** (242); **Point Blank** (716) logging, agribusiness, construction.

Population 28,719	Jan. mean min. 38.2	Prop. Value $2,564,340,382
Change fm 2010 .... 8.9	July mean max. 92.4	Retail Sales $57,449,594
Area (sq. mi.) 627.9	Civ. Labor 11,612	
Land Area (sq. mi.) 569.2	Unemployed 4.8	*For explanation of sources, symbols*
Altitude (ft.) 62–430	Wages $17,828,109	*and abbreviations, see p. 192, and*
Rainfall (in.) 50.68	Per Capita Income................ $33,712	*foldout map.*

Toledo Bend Reservoir, Sabine-Newton counties. Photo by Robert Plocheck.

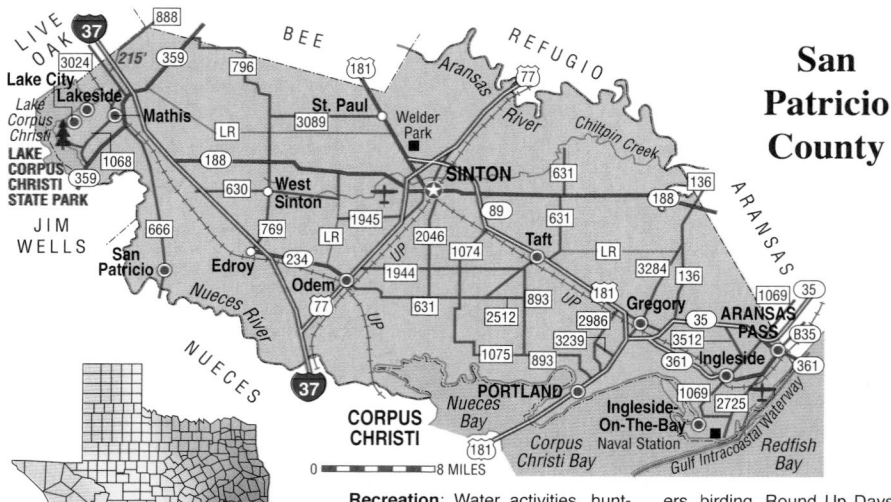

San Patricio County

Physical Features: Grassy, coastal prairie draining to Aransas, Nueces rivers and to bays; sandy loam, clay, black loam soils; Lake Corpus Christi.

Economy: Oil, petrochemicals, agribusiness, manufacturing, tourism, in Corpus Christi metropolitan area.

History: Karankawa area. Mexican sheep herders in the area before colonization. Settled by Irish families in 1830 (name is Spanish for St. Patrick). Created, named for municipality in 1836; organized in 1837, reorganized in 1847.

Race/Ethnicity: (In percent) Anglo, 38.3; Black, 2.0; Hispanic, 57.9; Asian, 1.1; Other, 1.1; Two or more races, 1.5.

Vital Statistics, annual: Births, 1,021; deaths, 642; marriages, 251; divorces, 207.

Recreation: Water activities, hunting, Corpus Christi Bay, state park, Welder Wildlife Foundation and Park, birdwatching.

Minerals: Oil, gas, gravel, caliche.

Agriculture: Cotton, grain sorghum, beef cattle, corn. Market value $86.2 million. Fisheries income significant.

SINTON (5,666) county seat; oil, agribusiness, tourism; Go Texan Days in October.

ARANSAS PASS (8,952, part [724] in Aransas County) deepwater port, shrimping, tourism, offshore oil-well servicing, aluminum and chemical plants; hospital; Shrimporee in May.

PORTLAND (15,841) retail center, petrochemicals, commuters to Corpus Christi; Indian Point pier; Windfest in April.

Other towns include: **Edroy** (312); **Gregory** (1,967); **Ingleside** (9,748) offshore well servicing, chemical and manufacturing plants, commut-

ers, birding, Round Up Days in April; **Ingleside-on-the-Bay** (622); **Lake City** (515); **Lakeside** (306); **Mathis** (4,821); **Odem** (2,423); **St. Paul** (593); **San Patricio** (412); **Taft** (2,999) agriculture, drug rehabilitation center, commuters, wind farm, blackland museum, barbecue, tamale and hot sauce cook-off in December; **Taft Southwest** (1,454).

Population	66,893
Change fm 2010	3.2
Area (sq. mi.)	707.8
Land Area (sq. mi.)	693.5
Altitude (ft.)	sea level–215
Rainfall (in.)	35.28
Jan. mean min.	44.2
July mean max.	93.4
Civ. Labor	30,382
Unemployed	5.6
Wages	$218,299,514
Per Capita Income	$42,852
Prop. Value	$10,782,261,587
Retail Sales	$894,646,531

For explanation of sources, symbols and abbreviations, see p. 192, and foldout map.

Oil pumping jack and wind turbines along FM 3284, San Patricio County. Photo by Rosie Hatch.

San Saba County

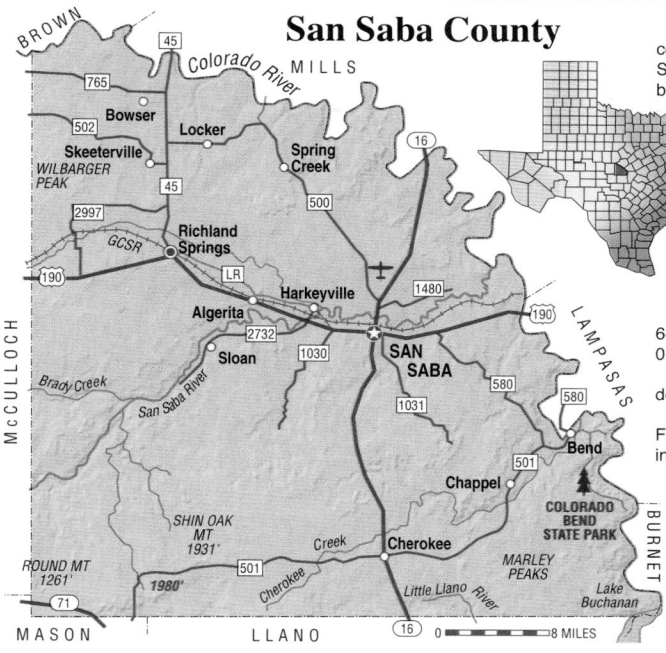

Physical Features: West central county; hilly, rolling; bisected by San Saba River; Colorado River on east; black, gray sandy loam, alluvial soils; northern tip of Lake Buchanan.

Economy: Pecan processing plants, tourism, hunting leases.

History: Apaches and Co-manches in the area when Spanish explored. Anglo-American settlers arrived in 1850s. County created from Bexar District in 1856, organized the same year; named for river.

Race/Ethnicity: (In percent) Anglo, 64.4; Black, 3.6; Hispanic, 30.3; Asian, 0.5; Other, 1.4; Two or more races, 1.9.

Vital Statistics, annual: Births, 73; deaths, 54; marriages, 40; divorces, 9.

Recreation: State park with Gorman Falls; deer hunting; historic sites; fishing; scenic drives; wildflower trail.

Minerals: Rock quarry, limestone and sand stone.

Agriculture: Cattle, pecans (second in acreage), wheat, hay, some sheep/goats. Market value $30 million. Hunting, wildlife leases.

SAN SABA (3,182) county seat; claims title "Pecan Capital of the World"; stone processing, varied manufacturing, prison; Cow Camp cookoff in May.

Other towns include: **Bend** (115, partly in Lampasas County); **Cherokee** (175); **Richland Springs** (340).

Population	6,054
Change fm 2010	– 1.2
Area (sq. mi.)	1,138.4
Land Area (sq. mi.)	1,135.3
Altitude (ft.)	1,020–1,980
Rainfall (in.)	28.50
Jan. mean min.	34.6
July mean max.	95.7
Civ. Labor	2,493
Unemployed	2.9
Wages	$17,623,048
Per Capita Income	$36,596
Prop. Value	$1,556,114,830
Retail Sales	$34,880,850

Schleicher County

Physical Features: West central county on edge of Edwards Plateau, broken by Devils, Concho, San Saba tributaries; part hilly; black soils.

Economy: Oil, ranching, hunting.

History: Jumanos in the area in the 1630s. Later, Apaches and Comanches; removed in the 1870s. Ranching began in the 1870s. Census of 1890 showed third of population from Mexico. County named for Gustav Schleicher, founder of German colony; county created from Crockett County in 1887, organized in 1901.

Race/Ethnicity: (In percent) Anglo, 44.6; Black, 1.7; Hispanic, 53.1; Asian, 0.3; Other, 0.9; Two or more races, 1.6.

Vital Statistics, annual: Births, 23; deaths, 23; marriages, 15; divorces, 5.

Recreation: Hunting, livestock show

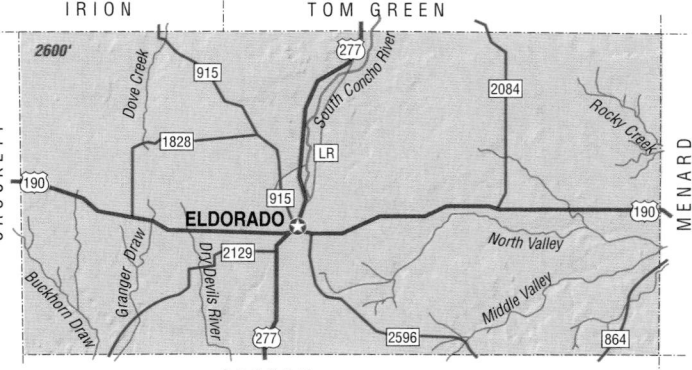

in January, youth and open rodeos, mountain bike events.

Minerals: Oil, natural gas.

Agriculture: Beef cattle, sheep, goats, and cotton, hay. Market value $13.6 million. Hunting leases important.

ELDORADO (1,720) county seat; oil activities, center for livestock, mohair marketing, woolen mill, government/services; hospital.

For explanation of sources, symbols and abbreviations, see p. 192, and foldout map.

Population	2,895
Change fm 2010	– 16.4
Area (sq. mi.)	1,310.7
Land Area (sq. mi.)	1,310.6
Altitude (ft.)	2,070–2,600
Rainfall (in.)	23.21
Jan. mean min.	31.1
July mean max.	92.1
Civ. Labor	1,274
Unemployed	2.9
Wages	$8,669,927
Per Capita Income	$35,836
Prop. Value	$952,469,472
Retail Sales	$10,620,448

Scurry County

Physical Features: Plains county below Caprock, some hills; drained by Colorado, Brazos tributaries; Lake J.B. Thomas; sandy, loam soils.

Economy: Oil, government/services, agribusiness, manufacturing.

History: Apaches; displaced later by Comanches who were relocated to Indian Territory in 1875. Ranching began in the late 1870s. County created from Bexar District in 1876; organized in 1884; named for Confederate Gen. W.R. Scurry.

Race/Ethnicity: (In percent) Anglo, 52.8; Black, 5.2; Hispanic, 40.6; Asian, 0.9; Other, 1.4; Two or more races, 1.8.

Vital Statistics, annual: Births, 230; deaths, 179; marriages, 132; divorces, 58.

Recreation: Lake J.B. Thomas water recreation; Towle Memorial Park; museums, community theater, White Buffalo Days and Bikefest in October.

Minerals: Oil, gas.

Agriculture: Cotton, wheat, cattle, hay. Market value $29 million.

SNYDER (11,582) county seat; oil, wind energy, agriculture; Western Texas College, hospital, museum; Western Swing days in June.

Other towns include: **Dunn** (75); **Fluvanna** (180); **Hermleigh** (315); **Ira** (250).

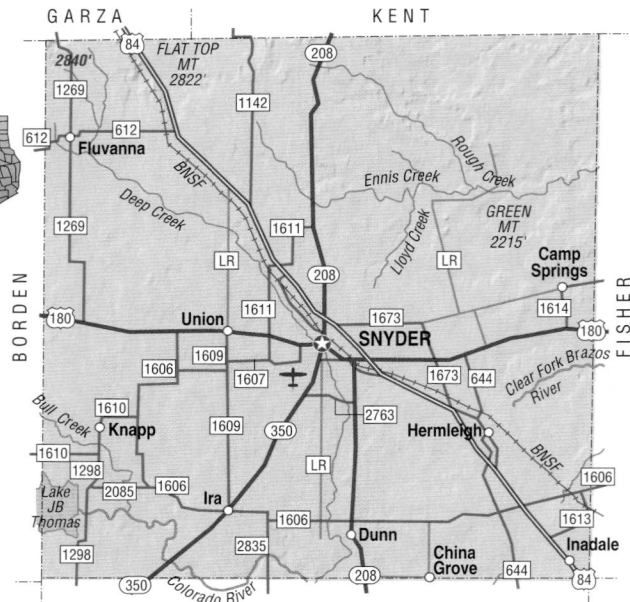

Population	16,866	July mean max.	93.9
Change fm 2010	– 0.3	Civ. Labor	6,767
Area (sq. mi.)	907.5	Unemployed	3.2
Land Area (sq. mi.)	905.4	Wages	$98,459,180
Altitude (ft.)	1,800–2,840	Per Capita Income	$37,542
Rainfall (in.)	22.68	Prop. Value	$3,196,880,481
Jan. mean min.	28.2	Retail Sales	$229,256,880

Shackelford County

Physical Features: Rolling, hilly, drained by tributaries of Brazos; sandy and chocolate loam soils; lake.

Economy: Oil and ranching, some manufacturing, hunting leases.

History: Apaches; driven out by Comanches. First Anglo-American settlers arrived soon after establishment of military outpost in the 1850s. County created from Bosque County in 1858; organized in 1874; named for Dr. Jack Shackelford (sometimes referred to as John), Texas Revolution hero.

Race/Ethnicity: (In percent) Anglo, 85.5; Black, 1.7; Hispanic, 11.6; Asian, 0.4; Other, 0.7; Two or more races, 1.4.

Vital Statistics, annual: Births, 43; deaths, 27; marriages, 29; divorces, 14.

Recreation: Fort Griffin historic site, courthouse historical district, hunting, lake, outdoor activities, June Fandangle musical about area history.

Minerals: Oil, natural gas.

Agriculture: Beef cattle, wheat, hay, cotton. Market value $22.3 million. Hunting leases.

ALBANY (2,018) county seat; oil, ranching, hunting; medical clinics; historical district, Old Jail art center, car museum.

Other town: **Moran** (302).

Population	3,253	July mean max.	94.4
Change fm 2010	– 3.8	Civ. Labor	1,949
Area (sq. mi.)	915.6	Unemployed	2.3
Land Area (sq. mi.)	914.3	Wages	$20,247,251
Altitude (ft.)	1,150–2,000	Per Capita Income	$77,918
Rainfall (in.)	28.36	Prop. Value	$1,323,616,752
Jan. mean min.	30.2	Retail Sales	$17,457,247

Shelby County

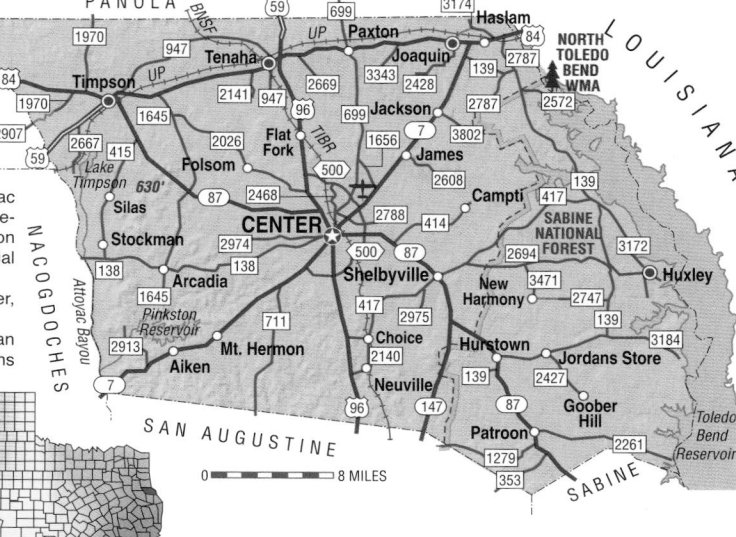

Physical Features: East Texas county; partly hills, much bottomland; well-timbered, 67,762 acres in national forest; Attoyac Bayou, other streams; Toledo Bend Reservoir, Pinkston Reservoir; sandy, clay, alluvial soils.

Economy: Poultry, timber, cattle, tourism.

History: Caddo Indian area. First Anglo-Americans settled in the 1810s. Antebellum slave-holding area. Original county of the Republic, created in 1836; organized in 1837; named for Isaac Shelby of the American Revolution.

Race/Ethnicity: (In percent) Anglo, 61.1; Black, 18.3; Hispanic, 18.5; Asian, 1.3; Other, 1.1; Two or more races, 1.4.

Vital Statistics, annual: Births, 390; deaths, 300; marriages, 178; divorces, 65.

Recreation: Toledo Bend Reservoir activities; Sabine National Forest; hunting, fishing, camping; historic sites, restored 1885 courthouse.

Minerals: Natural gas, oil.

Agriculture: First in poultry and egg production. Beef cattle and hay.

Market value $473.2 million. Timber sales significant.

CENTER (5,393) county seat; poultry, timber, oil and gas, tourism; hospital, Panola College extension, museum; What-A-Melon festival in July, poultry festival in October.

Other towns: **Huxley** (388); **Joaquin** (830); **Shelbyville** (600); **Tenaha** (1,164); **Timpson** (1,191) livestock, timber, farming, commuters, genealogy library, Frontier Days in July.

Population	25,418
Change fm 2010	– 0.1
Area (sq. mi.)	834.6
Land Area (sq. mi.)	795.6
Altitude (ft.)	174–630
Rainfall (in.)	54.20
Jan. mean min.	35.1
July mean max.	94.4
Civ. Labor	10,804
Unemployed	4.4
Wages	$75,926,763
Per Capita Income	$38,554
Prop. Value	$2,239,720,128
Retail Sales	$280,117,943

For explanation of sources, symbols and abbreviations, see p. 192, and foldout map.

The Shackelford County Courthouse in Albany. Photo by Robert Plocheck.

Sherman County

OKLAHOMA

North Canadian River

Texhoma

3805'

2677

UP

BNSF

287

Frisco Creek

119

1290

2349

STRATFORD

15

15

54

2232

Coldwater Creek

LR

2014

LR

1573

2899

DALLAM

1573

1573

520

LR

119

1060

297

BNSF

287

MOORE

North Palo Duro Creek

HANSFORD

0 ⬛⬛⬛ 8 MILES

Physical Features: A northern Panhandle county; level, broken by creeks, playas; sandy to dark loam soils; underground water.

Economy: Agribusiness, tourism.

History: Apaches; pushed out by Comanches in the 1700s. Comanches removed to Indian Territory in 1875. Ranching began around 1880; farming after 1900. County named for Republic of Texas Gen. Sidney Sherman; created from Bexar District in 1876; organized in 1889.

Race/Ethnicity: (In percent) Anglo, 53.3; Black, 1.7; Hispanic, 44.2; Asian, 0.8; Other, 1.2; Two or more races, 1.3.

Vital Statistics, annual: Births, 39; deaths, 34; marriages, 21; divorces, 9.

Recreation: Depot museum; pheasant, pronghorn hunting, jamboree and rodeo in July, carriage driving event in September.

Minerals: Natural gas, oil.

Agriculture: Beef and stocker cattle, wheat, corn, milo, cotton; 127,000 acres irrigated. Market value $590.4 million.

STRATFORD (2,177) county seat; agribusiness, petroleum, tourism, birdseed packaging; VA clinic; science and art museum.

Texhoma (1,285 [with 339 in Texas]) other principal town.

For explanation of sources, symbols and abbreviations, see p. 192, and foldout map.

Population	3,079
Change fm 2010	1.5
Area (sq. mi.)	923.2
Land Area (sq. mi.)	923.0
Altitude (ft.)	3,200–3,805
Rainfall (in.)	17.77
Jan. mean min.	19.5
July mean max.	91.5
Civ. Labor	1,216
Unemployed	3.0

Wages	$9,760,862
Per Capita Income	$64,897
Prop. Value	$1,042,885,100
Retail Sales	$44,791,459

Texhoma skyline, Sherman County, with utility line along Oklahoma boundary. Photo by Robert Plocheck.

Smith County

W O O D

UPSHUR

V A N   Z A N D T

G R E G G

H E N D E R S O N

R U S K

C H E R O K E E

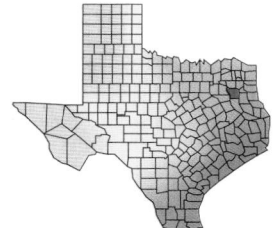

Physical Features: Populous East Texas county of rolling hills, many timbered; Sabine, Neches rivers, other streams; Lake Palestine, Lake Tyler, Lake Tyler East; alluvial, gray, sandy loam, clay soils.

Economy: Medical facilities, education, government/services, agribusiness, petroleum production, manufacturing, distribution center, tourism.

History: Caddoes of area reduced by disease and other tribes in the 1790s. Cherokees settled in the 1820s; removed in 1839. In the late 1820s, first Anglo-American settlers arrived. Antebellum slaveholding area. County named for Texas Revolution Gen. James Smith; county created and organized in 1846 from Nacogdoches County.

Race/Ethnicity: (In percent) Anglo, 59.6; Black, 17.8; Hispanic, 19.6; Asian, 1.7; Other, 0.9; Two or more races, 1.8.

Vital Statistics, annual: Births, 3,109; deaths, 2,111; marriages, 1,781; divorces, 563.

Recreation: Activities on Palestine, Tyler lakes; Rose Garden; state park; Goodman Museum; Caldwell Zoo; collegiate events; Juneteenth celebration,

Rose Festival in October, Azalea Trail, East Texas Fair in September/October.

Minerals: Oil, gas.

Agriculture: Horticultural crops and nurseries, beef cattle, forages, fruits and vegetables, horses, Christmas trees. Market value $76.8 million. Timber sales substantial.

TYLER (105,486) county seat; health services, education, retail center, varied manufacturing; University of Texas at Tyler, Tyler Junior College, Texas College, University of Texas Health Science Center; hospitals, nursing school; museums, Camp Ford historic park; styles itself, "City of Roses".

Other towns include: **Arp** (1,022) Strawberry Festival in April; **Bullard** (2,872, part in Cherokee County); **Flint** (2,500); **Hideaway** (2,986); **Lindale** (5,818) distribution center, foundry, varied manufacturing, Country Fest in October; **New Chapel Hill** (619); **Noonday** (777) Sweet Onion festival in June; **Troup** (1,980, part in Cherokee County) plastic manufacturing, motorcycle customization, Crawfish Boil in May; **Whitehouse** (8,371) commuters to Tyler, government/services, Yesteryear festival in June; and **Winona** (605).

Part of **Overton** (2,500, mostly in Rusk County).

Population	**230,221**
Change fm 2010	9.8
Area (sq. mi.)	949.7
Land Area (sq. mi.)	921.5
Altitude (ft.)	275–671
Rainfall (in.)	46.63
Jan. mean min.	36.4
July mean max.	92.7
Civ. Labor	110,590
Unemployed	3.5
Wages	$1,152,030,612
Per Capita Income	$47,200
Prop. Value	$19,067,014,343
Retail Sales	$4,015,694,610

Somervell County

Physical Features: Hilly terrain southwest of Fort Worth; Brazos, Paluxy rivers; Squaw Creek Reservoir; gray, dark, alluvial soils; second-smallest county.

Economy: Nuclear power plant, tourism.

History: Wichita, Tonkawa area; Comanches arrived later. Anglo-Americans arrived in the 1850s. County created in 1875 as Somerville County from Hood County, organized the same year. Spelling was changed in 1876; named for Republic of Texas Gen. Alexander Somervell.

Race/Ethnicity: (In percent) Anglo, 77.2; Black, 1.3; Hispanic, 18.7; Asian, 1.1; Other, 1.4; Two or more races, 2.3.

Vital Statistics, annual: Births, 77; deaths, 98; marriages, 74; divorces, 36.

Recreation: Fishing, hunting; unique geological formations; dinosaur tracks in state park; Glen Rose Big Rocks Park; Fossil Rim Wildlife Center; nature trails, museums; exposition center; Paluxy Pedal bicycle ride in October.

Minerals: Sand, gravel, silica, natural gas.

Agriculture: Cattle, hay. Market value $4.3 million. Hunting leases important.

GLEN ROSE (2,678) county seat; nuclear power plant, tourism, farm trade center; hospital; Hill College branch.

Other towns include: **Nemo** (56); **Rainbow** (121).

Population	**9,016**
Change fm 2010	6.2
Area (sq. mi.)	192,0
Land Area (sq. mi.)	186.5
Altitude (ft.)	550–1,310
Rainfall (in.)	36.87
Jan. mean min.	27.4
July mean max.	97.0
Civ. Labor	4,348
Unemployed	3.4
Wages	$52,640,499
Per Capita Income	$44,871
Prop. Value	$2,827,256,333
Retail Sales	$47,587,031

Starr County

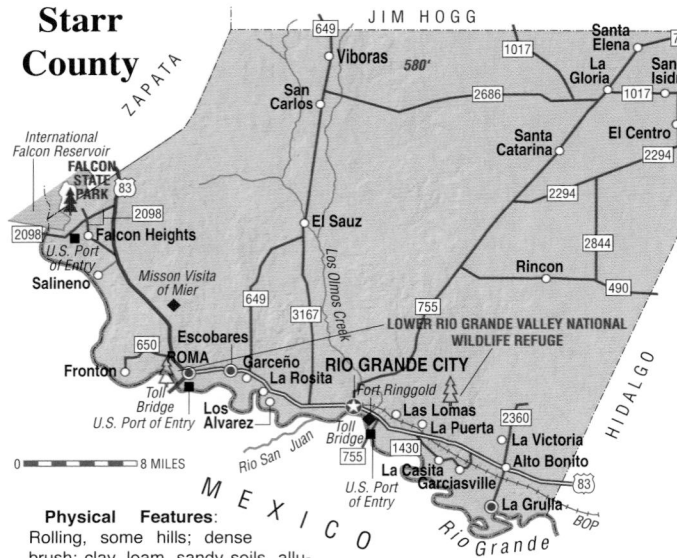

Physical Features: Rolling, some hills; dense brush; clay, loam, sandy soils, alluvial on Rio Grande; Falcon Reservoir.

Economy: Vegetable packing, other agribusiness, oil processing, tourism, government/services.

History: Coahuiltecan Indian area. Settlers from Spanish villages that were established in 1749 on south bank began to move across river soon afterward. Fort Ringgold established in 1848. County named for Dr. J.H. Starr, secretary of treasury of the Republic; county created from Nueces County and organized in 1848.

Race/Ethnicity: (In percent) Anglo, 3.3; Black, 0.4; Hispanic, 96.3; Asian, 0.2; Other, 0.4; Two or more races, 0.2.

Vital Statistics, annual: Births, 1,283; deaths, 397; marriages, 434; divorces, 0.

Recreation: Falcon Reservoir activities; deer, white-wing dove hunting; access to Mexico; historic houses, Lee House at Fort Ringgold; grotto at Rio Grande City; Roma Fest in November.

Minerals: Oil, gas, sand, gravel.

Agriculture: Beef and fed cattle; vegetables, cotton, sorghum; 8,500 acres irrigated for vegetables. Market value $108.5 million.

Population	**64,525**
Change fm 2010	5.8
Area (sq. mi.)	1,229.1
Land Area (sq. mi.)	1,223.2
Altitude (ft.)	125–580
Rainfall (in.)	22.65
Jan. mean min.	45.9
July mean max.	98.4
Civ. Labor	25,387
Unemployed	9.4
Wages	$111,166,299
Per Capita Income	$24,981
Prop. Value	$3,876,732,400
Retail Sales	$470,670,318

RIO GRANDE CITY (15,143) county seat; government/services, tourism, agriculture; hospital, college branches; trolley tours; Vaquero Days in February.

ROMA-Los Saenz (11,168) agriculture center; La Purísima Concepción Visita.

Other towns include: **Delmita** (225); **Escobares** (2,853); **Falcon Heights** (50); **Fronton** (172); **Garceño** (414); **Garciasville** (49); **La Casita** (122); **La Grulla** (1,698); **La Puerta** (620); **La Rosita** (75); **Las Lomas** (3,302); **La Victoria** (162); **Los Alvarez** (295); **North Escobares** (117); **Salineño** (182); **San Isidro** (240); **Santa Elena** (35).

Stephens County

Physical Features: West central county; broken, hilly; Hubbard Creek Reservoir, Possum Kingdom Lake, Lake Daniel; Brazos River; loam, sandy soils.

Economy: Oil, agribusiness, manufacturing, recreation.

History: Comanches, Tonkawas in the area when Anglo-American settlement began in the 1850s. County created as Buchanan in 1858 from Bosque County; renamed in 1861 for Confederate Vice President Alexander H. Stephens; organized in 1876.

Race/Ethnicity: (In percent) Anglo, 71.4; Black, 2.8; Hispanic, 24.0; Asian, 0.6; Other, 1.3; Two or more races, 1.3.

Vital Statistics, annual: Births, 119; deaths, 107; marriages, 63; divorces, 33.

Recreation: Lakes activities, state park, hunting, campsites, historical points, Swenson Museum, Sandefer Oil Museum, aviation museum, festival and car show in fall.

Minerals: Oil, natural gas, stone.

Agriculture: Beef cattle, hogs, goats, sheep; wheat, oats, hay, peanuts, grain sorghum, cotton, pecans. Market value $9.2 million.

BRECKENRIDGE (5,568) county seat; oil, agriculture, oil-field equipment, aircraft parts; hospital, prison, Texas State Technical College branch, library.

Other towns include: **Caddo** (70) gateway to Possum Kingdom State Park.

For explanation of sources, symbols and abbreviations, see p. 192, and foldout map.

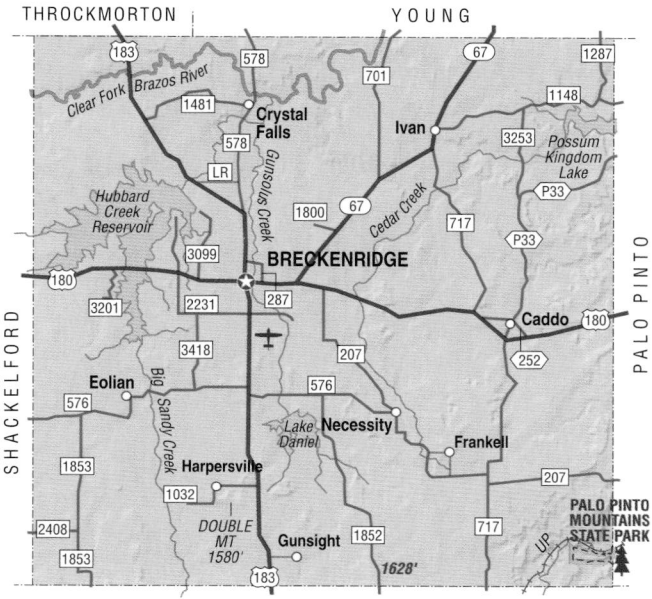

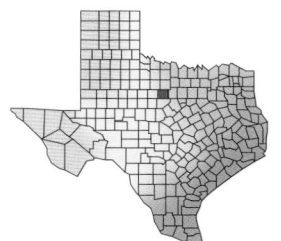

Population	**9,433**
Change fm 2010	− 2.0
Area (sq. mi.)	921.5
Land Area (sq. mi.)	896.7
Altitude (ft.)	995–1,628
Rainfall (in.)	29.98
Jan. mean min.	30.3
July mean max.	95.8
Civ. Labor	3,945
Unemployed	3.4
Wages	$30,820,831
Per Capita Inc.	$37,189
Prop. Value	$1,534,298,381
Retail Sales	$83,909,578

The Rio Grande at Roma, Starr County. Photo by Robert Plocheck.

Sterling County

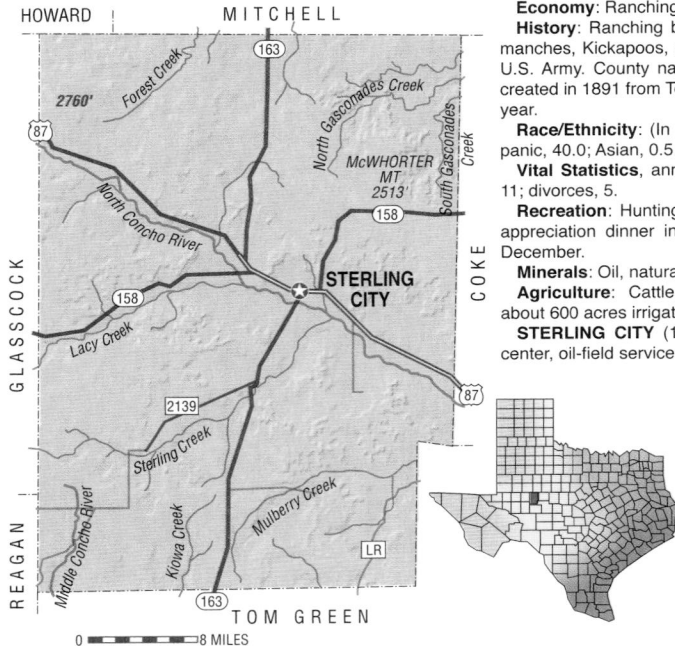

HOWARD

MITCHELL

2760'

Forest Creek

163

North Gasconades Creek

South Gasconades Creek

McWHORTER MT 2513'

158

87

North Concho River

GLASSCOCK

158

Lacy Creek

★ STERLING CITY

COKE

87

2139

Sterling Creek

Mulberry Creek

Kiowa Creek

LR

REAGAN

Middle Concho River

163

TOM GREEN

0 ⬛⬛⬛⬛ 8 MILES

Physical Features: Central prairie, surrounded by hills, broken by Concho River and tributaries; sandy to black soils.

Economy: Ranching, oil and gas, government/services.

History: Ranching began in the late 1870s after the Comanches, Kickapoos, and other tribes were removed by the U.S. Army. County named for buffalo hunter W.S. Sterling; created in 1891 from Tom Green County, organized the same year.

Race/Ethnicity: (In percent) Anglo, 55.3; Black, 2.0; Hispanic, 40.0; Asian, 0.5; Other, 2.2; Two or more races, 1.7.

Vital Statistics, annual: Births, 16; deaths, 9; marriages, 11; divorces, 5.

Recreation: Hunting of deer, quail, turkey, dove; hunters appreciation dinner in November; junior livestock show in December.

Minerals: Oil, natural gas.

Agriculture: Cattle, sheep/goats, horses, wheat, hay; about 600 acres irrigated. Hunting leases important.

STERLING CITY (1,059) county seat; farm, ranch trade center, oil-field services.

Population	1,311
Change fm 2010	14.7
Area (sq. mi.)	923.5
Land Area (sq. mi.)	923.5
Altitude (ft.)	2,000–2,760
Rainfall (in.)	20.46
Jan. mean min.	28.2
July mean max.	93.6
Civ. Labor	542
Unemployed	3.7
Wages	$5,484,119
Per Capita Income	$52,080
Prop. Value	$892,138,740
Retail Sales	$13,968,652

Stonewall County

Physical Features: Western county on Rolling Plains below Caprock, bisected by Brazos forks; sandy loam, sandy, other soils; some hills.

Economy: Agribusiness, light fabrication, government/services.

History: Anglo-American ranchers arrived in the 1870s after Comanches and other tribes were removed by U.S. Army. German farmers settled after 1900. County named for Confederate Gen. T.J. (Stonewall) Jackson; created from Bexar District in 1876, organized in 1888.

Race/Ethnicity: (In percent) Anglo, 75.0; Black, 3.8; Hispanic, 18.4; Asian, 1.6; Other, 1.7; Two or more races, 1.5.

Vital Statistics, annual: Births, 20; deaths, 29; marriages, 10; divorces, 3.

Recreation: Deer, quail, feral hog, turkey hunting; rodeos in June, September.

Minerals: Gypsum, gravel, oil.

Agriculture: Beef cattle, wheat, cotton, peanuts, hay. Also, grain sorghum, meat goats and swine. Market value $47.4 million.

ASPERMONT (912) county seat; oil field and ranching center, light fabrication; hospital; livestock show in February, Springfest.

Other towns include: **Old Glory** (100) farming center.

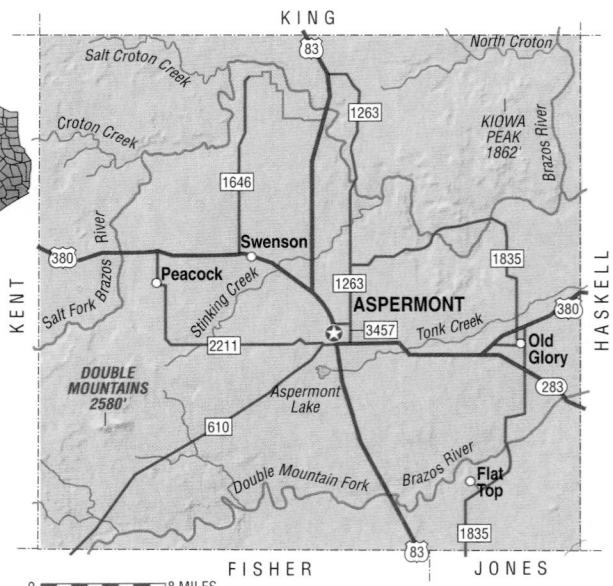

KING

Salt Croton Creek

83

North Croton

1263

KIOWA PEAK 1862'

Brazos River

Croton Creek

1646

KENT

Salt Fork Brazos River

380

Stinking Creek

Peacock

Swenson

1263

2211

DOUBLE MOUNTAINS 2580'

610

ASPERMONT ★

3457

Tonk Creek

Aspermont Lake

1835

Old Glory

283

HASKELL

380

Double Mountain Fork

Brazos River

Flat Top

1835

83

FISHER

JONES

0 ⬛⬛⬛⬛ 8 MILES

Population	1,362
Change fm 2010	– 8.6
Area (sq. mi.)	920.2
Land Area (sq. mi.)	916.3
Altitude (ft.)	1,450–2,580
Rainfall (in.)	23.77
Jan. mean min.	28.5
July mean max.	97.0
Civ. Labor	575
Unemployed	3.3
Wages	$4,435,839
Per Capita Income	$45,778
Prop. Value	$729,096,630
Retail Sales	$16,363,056

Sutton County

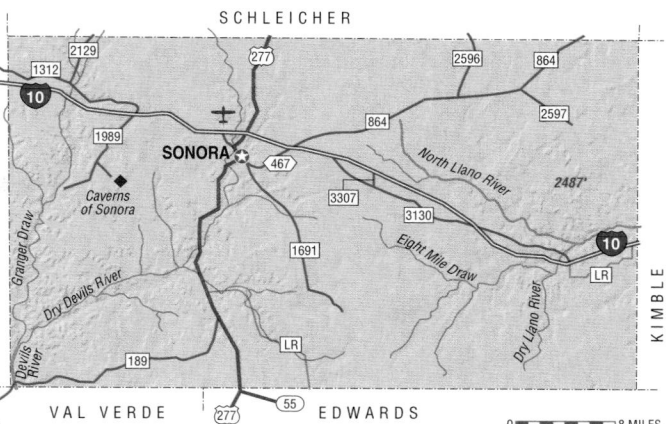

Physical Features: Southwestern county; level in west, rugged terrain in east, broken by tributaries of Devils, Llano rivers; black, red loam soils.

Economy: Natural gas, ranching, hunting.

History: Lipan Apaches drove out Tonkawas in 1600s. Comanches, military outpost, and disease forced Apaches south. Anglo-Americans settled in 1870s. Mexican immigration increased after 1890. County created from Crockett in 1887; organized in 1890; named for Confederate Col. John S. Sutton.

Race/Ethnicity: (In percent) Anglo, 36.2; Black, 1.2; Hispanic, 62.6; Asian, 0.6; Other, 1.2; Two or more races, 0.9.

Vital Statistics, annual: Births, 50; deaths, 30; marriages, 32; divorces, 12.

Recreation: Hunting, Miers Museum, ranch museum, Caverns of Sonora, wildlife sanctuary, Cinco de Mayo.

Minerals: Oil, natural gas.

Agriculture: Meat goats (first in numbers), sheep, cattle, Angora goats (second in numbers). Exotic wildlife. Wheat and oats raised for grazing, hay; minor irrigation. Market value $10.9 million. Hunting leases important.

SONORA (2,836) county seat; natural gas production, ranching, tourism; Dry Devils River Music Flood in October.

Population	3,758
Change fm 2010	– 9.0
Area (sq. mi.)	1,454.4
Land Area (sq. mi.)	1,453.9
Altitude (ft.)	1,840–2,487
Rainfall (in.)	23.03
Jan. mean min.	29.2
July mean max.	94.4
Civ. Labor	1,452
Unemployed	3.6
Wages	$30,009,815
Per Capita Income	$58,599
Prop. Value	$1,604,753,645
Retail Sales	$28,379,233

Swisher County

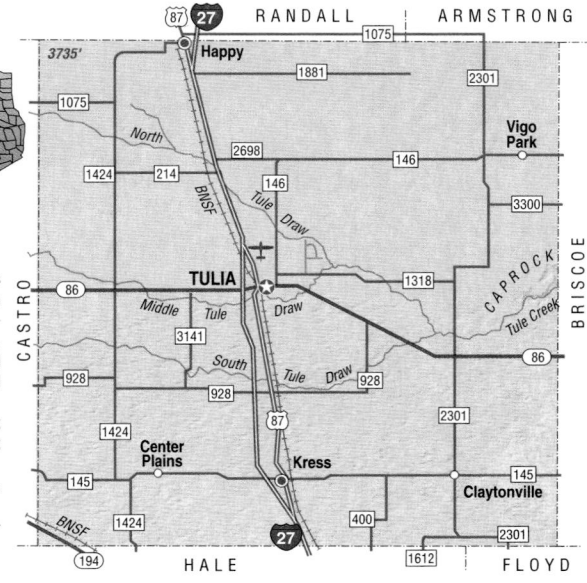

Physical Features: High Plains; level, broken by Tule Canyon and Creek; playas; large underground water supply; rich soils.

Economy: Cotton processing, manufacturing.

History: Apaches; displaced by Comanches around 1700. U.S. Army removed Comanches in 1874. Ranching began in the late 1870s. Farming developed after 1900. County named for J.G. Swisher of Texas Revolution; county created from Bexar, Young territories in 1876; organized in 1890.

Race/Ethnicity: (In percent) Anglo, 46.5; Black, 8.3; Hispanic, 44.1; Asian, 0.6; Other, 1.7; Two or more races, 1.7.

Vital Statistics, annual: Births, 111; deaths, 81; marriages, 40; divorces, 13.

Recreation: Mackenzie battle site, Picnic celebration in July at Tulia.

Minerals: Not significant.

Agriculture: Cotton, cattle, wheat, corn, sorghum, cucumbers. Some 65,000 acres irrigated. Market value $586.8 million.

TULIA (4,682) county seat; agriculture, government/services, manufacturing; hospital, library, museum.

Other towns include: **Happy** (651, partly in Randall County); **Kress** (678); **Vigo Park** (36).

Population	7,462
Change fm 2010	– 5.1
Area (sq. mi.)	900.7
Land Area (sq. mi.)	890.2
Altitude (ft.)	3,160–3,735
Rainfall (in.)	21.57
Jan. mean min.	22.0
July mean max.	91.9
Civ. Labor	2,657
Unemployed	4.0
Wages	$16,588,054
Per Capita Income	$44,632
Prop. Value	$729,431,033
Retail Sales	$51,757,785

For explanation of sources, symbols and abbreviations, see p. 192, and foldout map.

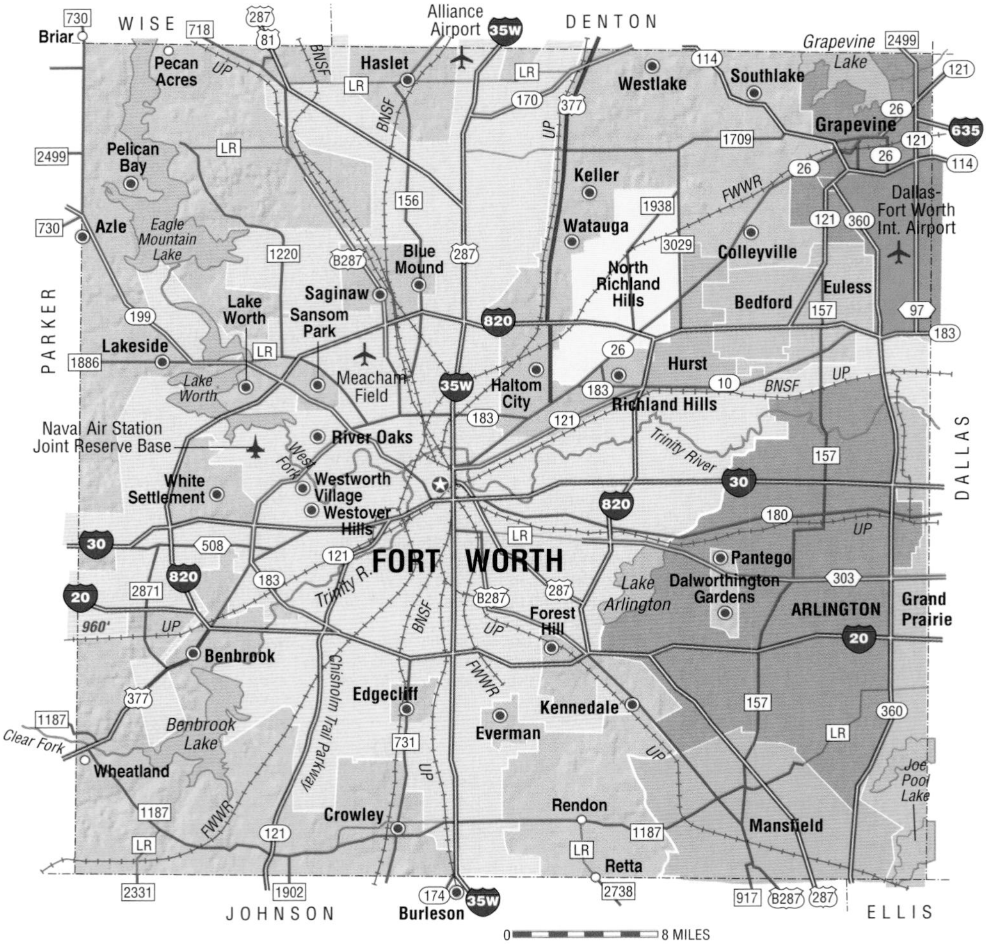

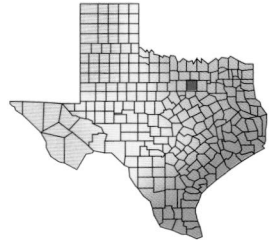

Tarrant County

Physical Features: Part Blackland, level to rolling; drains to Trinity; Lake Worth, Grapevine Lake, Eagle Mountain Lake, Benbrook Lake, Joe Pool Lake, Lake Arlington.

Economy: Tourism, planes, helicopters, foods, mobile homes, electronic equipment, chemicals, plastics among products of more than 1,000 factories, large federal expenditure, D/FW International Airport, economy closely associated with Dallas urban area.

History: Caddoes in area. Comanches, other tribes arrived about 1700. Anglo-Americans settled in the 1840s. Named for Republic of Texas Gen. Edward H. Tarrant, who helped drive Indian tribes from area. County created in 1849 from Navarro County; organized in 1850.

Race/Ethnicity: (In percent) Anglo, 46.8; Black, 17.1; Hispanic, 28.9; Asian, 5.7; Other, 1.1; Two or more races, 2.5.

Vital Statistics, annual: Births, 28,364; deaths, 12,277; marriages, 13,264; divorces, 7,133.

Recreation: Scott Theatre; Amon G. Carter Museum; Kimbell Art Museum; Modern Art Museum; Museum of Science and History; Casa Mañana; Botanic Gardens; Fort Worth Zoo; Log Cabin Village, all in Fort Worth.

Also, Six Flags Over Texas at Arlington; Southwestern Exposition, Stock Show; Convention Center; Stockyards Historical District; Texas Rangers and Dallas Cowboys at Arlington, other athletic events.

Minerals: Production of cement, sand, gravel, stone, gas.

Agriculture: Hay, beef cattle, wheat, horses, horticulture. Market value $34.6 million. Firewood marketed.

Education: Texas Christian University, University of Texas at Arlington, Texas Wesleyan University, Texas A&M University School of Law, University of North Texas Health Science Center, Southwestern Baptist Theological Seminary, Tarleton State University branch, and several other academic centers including a junior college system with five campuses and various centers.

FORT WORTH (851,655, small parts in Denton, Parker and Wise counties) county seat; a major mercantile, commercial and financial center; airplane, helicopter and other manufacturing plants; hospitals/health care; distribution center; oil and gas; stock show and rodeo January/February.

A cultural center with renowned art museums, Bass Performance Hall;

many conventions held in downtown center; agribusiness center for wide area with grain-storage and feed-mill operations; adjacent to D/FW International Airport.

ARLINGTON (389,386) University of Texas-Arlington, General Motors plant, tourism, the Texas Rangers baseball team, AT&T Stadium, retail, hospitals, bowling museum, art museum; Scottish festival in June.

Other towns include: **Hurst** (39,458); **Euless** (54,178); **Bedford** (49,500) helicopter plant, hospital, Celtic festival in fall (these three contiguous cities are sometimes referred to as H.E.B.).

Azle (12,161, partly in Parker County) government/services, retail, medical care/hospital, commuters to Fort Worth, museum, Sting Fling festival in September; **Benbrook** (23,788) varied manufacturing, hospitals; **Blue Mound** (2,484); **Briar** (6,166, parts in Wise and Parker counties).

Also, **Colleyville** (26,081) medical services, commuters, government/services, barbecue cookoff in April; **Crowley** (14,783) varied manufacturing, government/services, hospital; **Dalworthington Gardens** (2,372); **Edgecliff** (3,019); **Everman** (6,523); **Forest Hill** (12,699).

Also, **Grapevine** (51,700) tourist center, distribution, near the D/FW International Airport, hospitals, museums, art galleries, Grapefest in September; **Haltom City** (43,540) light manufacturing, food processing,

Largest U.S. Media Markets

Rank	TV Homes
1. New York	7.10 million
2. Los Angeles	5.28 million
3. Chicago	3.25 million
4. Philadelphia	2.82 million
5. Dallas/Fort Worth	2.62 million
6. Washington, D.C.	2.48 million
7. Houston	2.42 million
8. San Francisco	2.41 million
9. Boston	2.36 million
10. Atlanta	2.34 million

Source: Nielsen Media Research, 2019.

medical center; library; **Haslet** (1,868) commuters, government/services, chili fest and rodeo in May; **Keller** (44,749) Bear Creek Park, Wild West Fest.

Also, **Kennedale** (7,524) commuters, printing, manufacturing, library, drag strip, custom car show in May; **Lakeside** (1,665); **Lake Worth** (4,759) retail, tourism, museum, nature center; **Mansfield** (65,233, partly in Johnson, Ellis counties) varied manufacturing, retail, government/services, commuters, hospital, community college, library, museum, parks, Pecan festival in September; **North Richland Hills** (69,626) hospital; **Pantego** (2,798); **Pelican Bay** (1,657); **Rendon** (13,837); **Richland Hills** (7,857).

Also, **River Oaks** (7,990); **Saginaw**

(21,921) manufacturing, distribution/trucking, food processing/flour mill, Train & Grain festival in October; **Sansom Park** (4,881); **Southlake** (29,311) technology, financial, retail center, hospital, parks, Oktoberfest; **Watauga** (24,617); **Westlake** (1,324); **Westover Hills** (768); **Westworth Village** (2,742).

Also, **White Settlement** (17,288) aircraft manufacturing, drilling equipment, technological services, museums including Civil War museum, parks, historic sites; industrial park; settlers day festival in fall.

Also, part [7,579] of **Burleson** (44,161); part [51,864] of **Grand Prairie** (192,500), and part of **Pecan Acres** (4,480).

Population 2,084,931
Change fm 2010 .... 15.1
Area (sq. mi.) 902.3
Land Area (sq. mi.) 863.6
Altitude (ft.) 420–960
Rainfall (in.) 35.50
Jan. mean min. 32.4
July mean max. 95.5
Civ. Labor 1,074,048
Unemployed 3.2
Wages $12,092,353,375
Per Capita Income................. $47,525
Prop. Value $194,299,409,043
Retail Sales $34,951,513,855

For explanation of sources, symbols and abbreviations, see p. 192, and foldout map.

The Fort Worth skyline at night. Photo by Redshirt (CC).

Taylor County

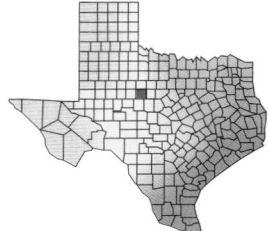

Physical Features: Prairies, with Callahan Divide, draining to Colorado River tributaries, Brazos River forks; Lake Abilene, Lake Kirby; mostly loam soils.

Economy: Agribusiness, oil and gas production, education, Dyess Air Force Base.

History: Comanches in the area about 1700. Anglo-American settlers arrived in the 1870s. Named for Alamo heroes Edward, James, and George Taylor, brothers; county created from Bexar, Travis counties in 1858 and organized in 1878.

Race/Ethnicity: (In percent) Anglo, 63.5; Black, 8.2; Hispanic, 24.5; Asian, 2.3; Other, 1.1; Two or more races, 2.8.

Vital Statistics, annual: Births, 2,097; deaths, 1,378; marriages, 1,206; divorces, 540.

Recreation: Abilene State Park, lake activities, Nelson Park Zoo, college events, Buffalo Gap historical tour and arts festival in April, Western Heritage ranch rodeo in May, as well as the West Texas Fair in September at Abilene.

Minerals: Oil, natural gas.

Agriculture: Beef cattle, small grains, cotton, milo. Market value $37.6 million.

Education: Abilene Christian University, Hardin-Simmons University, McMurry University, Texas Tech University pharmacy school, nursing school, and branch campus, and Cisco Junior College branch.

ABILENE (122,608, a small part in Jones County) county seat; retail center, oil and gas, military, colleges; hospitals, Abilene State School; Fort Phantom Hill (in Jones County). **Wylie** is now part of Abilene.

Other communities include: **Buffalo Gap** (468) historic sites; **Impact** (33); **Lawn** (330); **Merkel** (2,622) oil and wind energy, ranching, hunting, commuting, museum, health clinic, part of Bankhead Highway (early 1900s transcontinental route); classic car show in March; **Ovalo** (225); **Potosi** (3,221); **Trent** (329); **Tuscola** (746); **Tye** (1,270).

Population	137,640
Change fm 2010	4.7
Area (sq. mi.)	919.3
Land Area (sq. mi.)	915.6
Altitude (ft.)	1,640–2,490
Rainfall (in.)	24.82
Jan. mean min.	30.2
July mean max.	94.2
Civ. Labor	65,687
Unemployed	3.0
Wages	$655,928,980
Per Capita Income	$43,329
Prop. Value	$9,444,691,379
Retail Sales	$2,224,037,340

For explanation of sources, symbols and abbreviations, see p. 192, and foldout map.

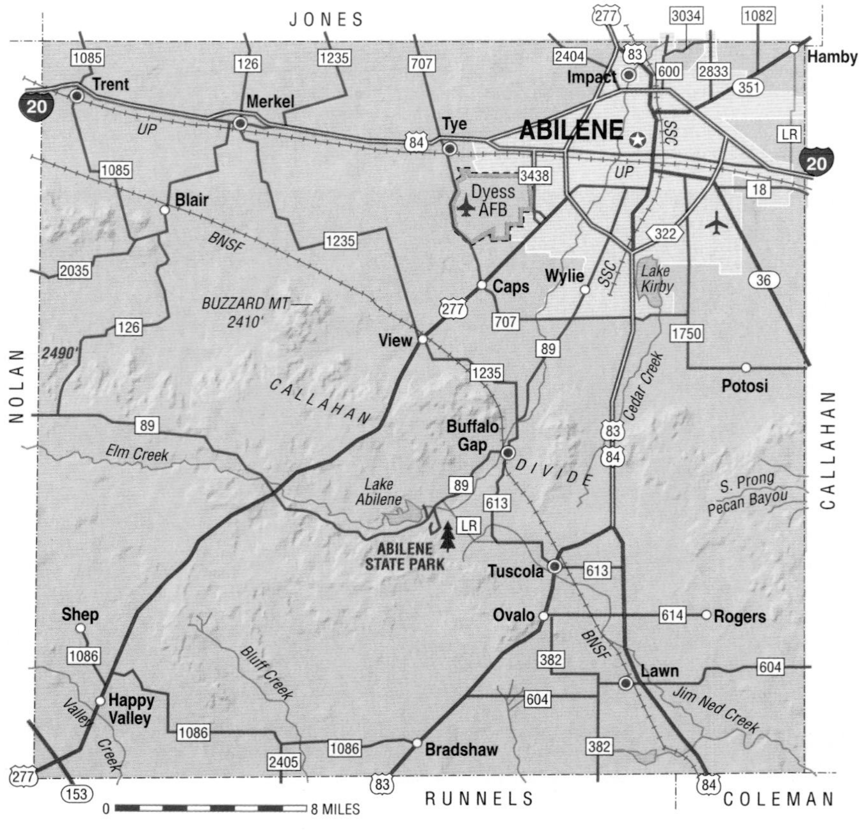

JONES

Trent · Merkel · Tye · ABILENE · Impact · Hamby

UP · 20 · 126 · 1235 · 707 · 2404 · 83 · 600 · 2833 · 351 · 1085 · LR · 20

84 · 3438 · UP · 18

Blair · Dyess AFB

BNSF · 1235 · 322 · 36

2035 · Caps · Wylie · Lake Kirby

BUZZARD MT — 2410' · 277 · 707

126 · View · 89 · 1750

NOLAN · 2490' · 1235 · Potosi

CALLAHAN

89 · Buffalo Gap · 83

Elm Creek · 84 · DIVIDE · S. Prong Pecan Bayou · CALLAHAN

Lake Abilene · 89 · 613 · LR

ABILENE STATE PARK · Tuscola · 613

Shep · Ovalo · 614 · Rogers

1086 · 382 · BNSF · 604

Happy Valley · 1086 · 604 · Lawn · Jim Ned Creek

Bluff Creek · Valley Creek · 1086 · 2405 · 1086 · Bradshaw · 382

277 · 153 · 83 · RUNNELS · 84 · COLEMAN

0 ▭▭▭▭ 8 MILES

Terrell County

Physical Features: Trans-Pecos southwestern county; semi-mountainous, many canyons; rocky, limestone soils.

Economy: Ranching, hunting leases, oil/gas exploration, tourism.

History: Coahuiltecans, Jumanos, and other tribes left many pictographs in area caves. Sheep ranching began in the 1880s. Named for Confederate Gen. A.W. Terrell; county created in 1905 from Pecos County, organized the same year.

Race/Ethnicity: (In percent) Anglo, 42.7; Black, 1.6; Hispanic, 52.7; Asian, 0.5; Other, 3.6; Two or more races, 2.2.

Vital Statistics, annual: Births, 0; deaths, 17; marriages, 6; divorces, 1.

Recreation: Nature tourism, hunting, especially white-tailed and mule deer, Rio Grande Wild and Scenic River, varied wildlife, hiking trail; Snake Days in June, Cactus Pachanga in October.

Minerals: Gas, oil, limestone.

Agriculture: Goats (meat, Angora); sheep (meat, wool); some beef cattle. Market value $3.1 million. Wildlife leases important.

SANDERSON (717) county seat; ranching, hunting, tourism, government/services; museum.

Other town: **Dryden** (13).

Population	823
Change fm 2010	– 16.4
Area (sq. mi.)	2,358.1
Land Area (sq. mi.)	2,358.0
Altitude (ft.)	1,180–3,765

Rainfall (in.)	14.72
Jan. mean min.	31.5
July mean max.	92.2
Civ. Labor	364
Unemployed	3.6

Wages	$2,737,467
Per Capita Income	$48,058
Prop. Value	$638,915,974
Retail Sales	$2,463,577

Terry County

Physical Features: South Plains, broken by draws, playas; sandy, sandy loam, loam soils.

Economy: Oil-field services, agribusiness, peanut processing.

History: Comanches removed in the 1870s by U.S. Army. Ranching developed in the 1890s; farming after 1900. Oil discovered in 1940. County named for Confederate Col. B.F. Terry, head of the Eighth Texas Cavalry (Terry's Texas Rangers). Created from the Bexar District in 1876; organized in 1904.

Race/Ethnicity: (In percent) Anglo, 39.3; Black, 5.1; Hispanic, 55.1; Asian, 0.7; Other, 1.3; Two or more races, 1.4.

Vital Statistics, annual: Births, 189; deaths, 139; marriages, 62; divorces, 32.

Recreation: Museum, aquatic center, vineyard festival in August, harvest festival in October.

Minerals: Oil, gas, salt mining.

Agriculture: Cotton is principal crop; peanuts (third in acreage), grain sorghum, guar, wheat, melons, cattle, grapes. 98,000 acres irrigated. Market value $125.8 million.

BROWNFIELD (9,808) county seat; oil-field services, government/services, vineyards, peanut processing; hospital; quilt trail displays in April.

Other towns include: **Meadow** (593); **Tokio** (6); **Wellman** (212).

Population	12,287
Change fm 2010	– 2.9
Area (sq. mi.)	890.9
Land Area (sq. mi.)	888.8
Altitude (ft.)	3,080–3,600
Rainfall (in.)	19.58
Jan. mean min.	26.9

July mean max.	92.4
Civ. Labor	5,084
Unemployed	3.9
Wages	$42,986,141
Per Capita Income	$32,649
Prop. Value	$1,166,827,625
Retail Sales	$117,189,305

Throckmorton County

Physical Features: Northwest county southwest of Wichita Falls; rolling, between Brazos forks; red to black soils.

Economy: Oil, agribusiness, hunting.

History: Site of Comanche Indian Reservation 1854-59. Ranching developed after Civil War. County named for Dr. W.E. Throckmorton, father of Gov. J.W. Throckmorton; county created from Fannin in 1858; organized in 1879.

Race/Ethnicity: (In percent) Anglo, 82.4; Black, 1.3; Hispanic, 14.4; Asian, 0.5; Other, 1.2; Two or more races, 1.0.

Vital Statistics, annual: Births, 10; deaths, 30; marriages, 9; divorces, 2.

Recreation: Hunting, fishing; historic sites include Camp Cooper, site of former Comanche reservation, restored ranch home; Millers Creek Reservoir; wild game dinner in January.

Minerals: Natural gas, oil.

Agriculture: Beef cattle, horses, wheat, hay. Market value $24.8 million. Mesquite firewood sold. Hunting leases important.

THROCKMORTON (744) county seat; varied manufacturing, oil-field services; hospital; Old Jail museum.

Other towns include: **Elbert** (24), **Woodson** (240).

Population	1,515
Change fm 2010	– 7.7
Area (sq. mi.)	915.5
Land Area (sq. mi.)	912.6
Altitude (ft.)	1,100–1,730
Rainfall (in.)	29.78
Jan. mean min.	29.6
July mean max.	95.8
Civ. Labor	640
Unemployed	3.4
Wages	$3,193,653
Per Capita Income	$33,732
Prop. Value	$797,883,950
Retail Sales	$6,559,090

Titus County

Physical Features: Northeast Texas county; hilly, timbered; drains to Big Cypress Creek, Sulphur River; Lake Bob Sandlin, Welsh Reservoir, Monticello Reservoir.

Economy: Agribusiness, varied manufacturing, electric power generation.

History: Caddo area. Cherokees and other tribes settled in the 1820s. Anglo-American settlers arrived in the 1840s. Named for pioneer settler A.J. Titus; county created from Bowie and Red River counties in 1846, organized the same year.

Race/Ethnicity: (In percent) Anglo, 45.1; Black, 10.1; Hispanic, 43.3; Asian, 1.2; Other, 2.6; Two or more races, 1.3.

Vital Statistics, annual: Births, 500; deaths, 311; marriages, 211; divorces, 64.

Recreation: Fishing, hunting, lake activities, state park, rodeo, railroad museum, flower gardens.

Minerals: Lignite coal, oil, gas.

Agriculture: Poultry, beef cattle, hay, horticulture, horses. Market value $81.2 million. Timber sales significant.

MOUNT PLEASANT (17,083) county seat; tourism, varied manufacturing, food-processing plants; hospital; Northeast Texas Community College; jubilee and outhouse races in May.

Other towns include: **Cookville** (105), **Millers Cove** (150), **Talco** (490), **Winfield** (526).

For explanation of sources, symbols and abbreviations, see p. 192, and foldout map.

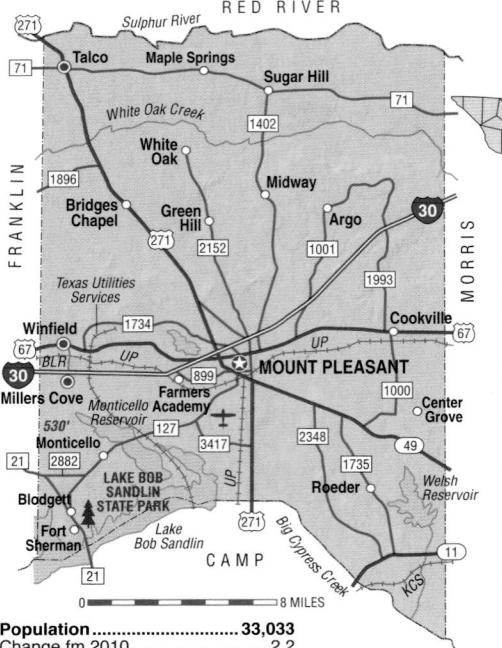

Population	33,033
Change fm 2010	2.2
Area (sq. mi.)	425.6
Land Area (sq. mi.)	406.1
Altitude (ft.)	250–530
Rainfall (in.)	47.70
Jan. mean min.	31.1
July mean max.	92.9
Civ. Labor	12,969
Unemployed	4.5
Wages	$143,711,287
Per Capita Income	$33,406
Prop. Value	$3,128,548,317
Retail Sales	$764,150,683

Tom Green County

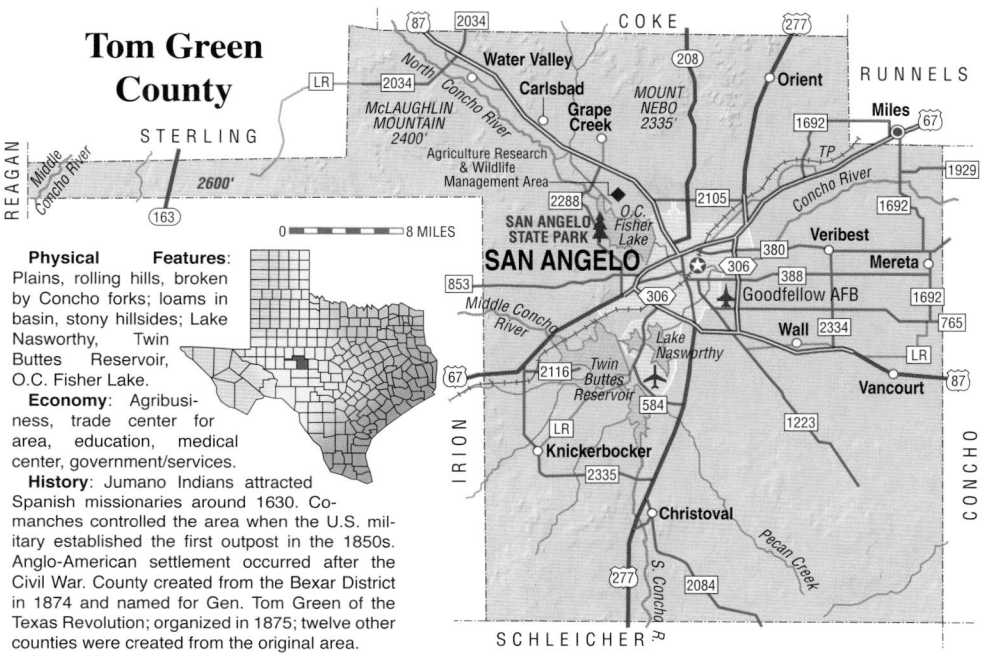

STERLING

REAGAN

Middle Concho River

2600'

(163)

0 ⊢━━━━┥ 8 MILES

COKE

(87) [2034]

Water Valley

[2034] Carlsbad
McLAUGHLIN
MOUNTAIN
2400'

Grape
Creek

MOUNT
NEBO
2335'

Agriculture Research
& Wildlife
Management Area

[2288]

[853]

Middle Concho River

SAN ANGELO
STATE PARK

O.C.
Fisher
Lake

SAN ANGELO

(306)

[2105]

(306)

(208)

Orient   RUNNELS

Miles (67)
[1692]

TP

Concho River   [1929]

[1692]

[380]   Veribest

[388]   Mereta

Goodfellow AFB   [1692]

Wall [2334]   [765]

LR

(67)   [2116]

Twin
Buttes
Reservoir

Lake
Nasworthy

[584]

[1223]

Vancourt (87)

IRION

LR

Knickerbocker

[2335]

Christoval

Pecan Creek

(277)   [2084]

S. Concho R.

SCHLEICHER

CONCHO

Physical Features:
Plains, rolling hills, broken by Concho forks; loams in basin, stony hillsides; Lake Nasworthy, Twin Buttes Reservoir, O.C. Fisher Lake.

Economy: Agribusiness, trade center for area, education, medical center, government/services.

History: Jumano Indians attracted Spanish missionaries around 1630. Comanches controlled the area when the U.S. military established the first outpost in the 1850s. Anglo-American settlement occurred after the Civil War. County created from the Bexar District in 1874 and named for Gen. Tom Green of the Texas Revolution; organized in 1875; twelve other counties were created from the original area.

Race/Ethnicity: (In percent) Anglo, 53.2; Black, 4.4; Hispanic, 40.0; Asian, 1.4; Other, 1.3; Two or more races, 2.1.

Vital Statistics, annual: Births, 1,721; deaths, 973; marriages, 1,060; divorces, 321.

Recreation: Water sports, hunting, Fort Concho museum, symphony, Christmas at Old Fort Concho, February rodeo.

Minerals: Oil, natural gas.

Agriculture: Cotton, beef cattle, goats, sheep (third in number), small grains, milo. About 30,000 acres irrigated. Market value $131.4 million.

SAN ANGELO (99,954) county seat; government/services, retail, transportation, education; hospitals; Angelo State University, Howard Junior College branch; riverwalk; Museum of Fine Arts, drag boat races in June.

Other towns include: **Carlsbad** (756); **Christoval** (558); **Grape Creek** (3,23,27059); **Knickerbocker** (94); **Mereta** (131); **Vancourt** (131); **Veribest** (115); **Wall** (329); **Water Valley** (203).

For explanation of sources, symbols and abbreviations, see p. 192, and foldout map.

Population	**118,189**
Change fm 2010	7.2
Area (sq. mi.)	1,540.6
Land Area (sq. mi.)	1,522.0
Altitude (ft.)	1,675–2,600
Rainfall (in.)	23.03
Jan. mean min.	29.6
July mean max.	94.5
Civ. Labor	55,187
Unemployed	3.1
Wages	$506,973,906
Per Capita Income	$42,688
Prop. Value	$9,118,468,148
Retail Sales	$1,852,459,954

The Capitol in Austin, Travis County. Photo by Robert Plocheck.

Travis County

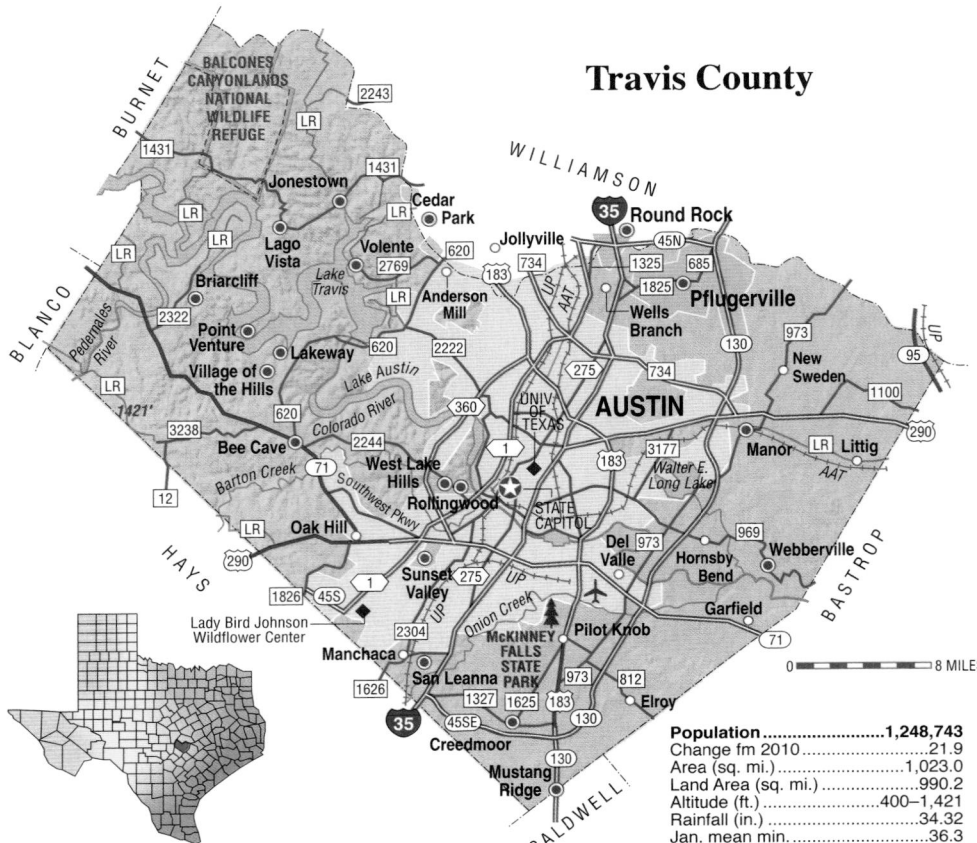

Population	1,248,743
Change fm 2010	21.9
Area (sq. mi.)	1,023.0
Land Area (sq. mi.)	990.2
Altitude (ft.)	400–1,421
Rainfall (in.)	34.32
Jan. mean min.	36.3
July mean max.	95.2
Civ. Labor	732,428
Unemployed	2.6
Wages	$11,895,367,147
Per Capita Income	$62,205
Prop. Value	$202,124,826,302
Retail Sales	$19,788,868,053

Physical Features: Central county of scenic hills, broken by Colorado River; Lake Travis, Lake Austin, Lady Bird Lake, Walter E. Long Lake; cedars, pecans, other trees; diverse soils, mineral deposits.

Economy: Government/services, education, technology, research, and industry.

History: Tonkawa and Lipan Apache area; Comanches, Kiowas arrived about 1700. Spanish missions from East Texas temporarily relocated near Barton Springs in 1730 before removing to San Antonio. Anglo-Americans arrived in the early 1830s. County created in 1840, when Austin became Republic's capital, from Bastrop County; organized in 1843; named for Alamo commander Col. William B. Travis; many other counties created from its original area.

Race/Ethnicity: (In percent) Anglo, 49.0; Black, 8.9; Hispanic, 33.9; Asian, 7.1; Other, 1.3; Two or more races, 2.6.

Vital Statistics, annual: Births, 16,297; deaths, 5,380; marriages, 8,618; divorces, 2,792.

Recreation: Colorado River lakes, hunting, fishing; McKinney Falls State Park; LBJ Presidential Library, Lady Bird Johnson Wildflower Center; collegiate, metropolitan, governmental events; official buildings and historic sites; museums, including Bullock state history museum; Sixth St. restoration area; scenic drives; many city parks; South by Southwest film, music festival in March.

Minerals: Production of lime, stone, sand, gravel, oil and gas.

Agriculture: Cattle, nursery crops, hogs; sorghum, corn, cotton, small grains, pecans. Market value $41.7 million.

Education: University of Texas, St. Edward's University, Concordia Lutheran University, Huston-Tillotson College, Austin Community College, Episcopal and Presbyterian seminaries.

AUSTIN (949,460, part [35,697] in Williamson County) county seat and state capital; state and federal payrolls, IRS center, high-tech industries, healthcare/hospitals, including state institutions for blind, deaf, mental illnesses; popular retirement area. **Anderson Mill**, **Del Valle**, and **Oak Hill** are now part of Austin.

Other towns include: **Bee Cave** (6,357) retail, tourism, SpringFest in April; **Briarcliff** (1,688); **Creedmoor** (217); **Garfield** (1,793); **Jonestown** (2,001) tourism, retail, commuters, Chili Pod chili cook-off in April; **Lago Vista** (6,965); **Lakeway** (15,100) residential real estate, retail, tourism, lake activities; **Manchaca** (1,309); **Manor** (7,524); **Mustang Ridge** (941, partly in Caldwell County).

Also, **Pflugerville** (61,271) high-tech industries, agriculture, government/services, Deutchenfest in May; **Point Venture** (922); **Rollingwood** (1,551); **San Leanna** (556); **Sunset Valley** (753); **The Hills** (2,687) residential community; **Volente** (504); **Webberville** (432); **Wells Branch** (12,836); **West Lake Hills** (3,209).

Also, part [489] of **Cedar Park**, part [882] of **Jollyville**, and part [1,362] of **Round Rock**, all mostly in Williamson County.

For explanation of sources, symbols and abbreviations, see p. 192, and foldout map.

Trinity County

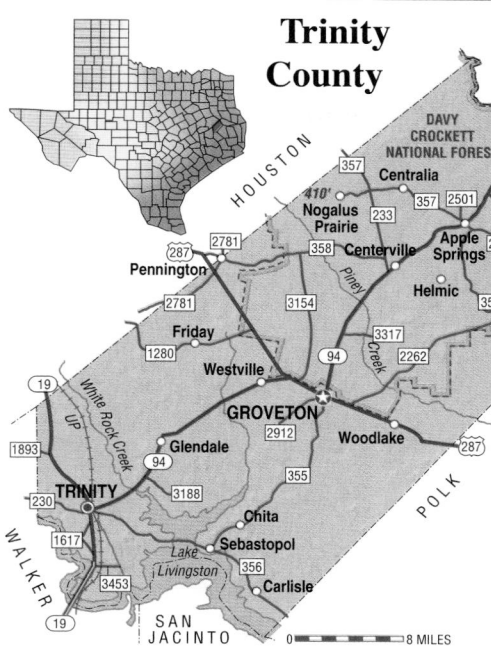

Physical Features: Heavily forested East Texas county of hills, between Neches and Trinity (Lake Livingston) rivers; rich alluvial soils, sandy upland; 67,910 acres in national forest.

Economy: Forestry, cattle, tourism, government/services.

History: Caddoes, reduced by disease in the late 1700s. Kickapoo, Alabama, and Coushatta in area when Anglo-Americans settled in the 1840s. Named for river; county created in 1850 out of Houston County, organized the same year.

Race/Ethnicity: (In percent) Anglo, 78.5; Black, 9.5; Hispanic, 9.7; Asian, 0.4; Other, 0.8; Two or more races, 1.8.

Vital Statistics, annual: Births, 151; deaths, 225; marriages, 64; divorces, 35.

Recreation: Lake activities, fishing, hiking, hunting, national forest, historic site.

Minerals: Limited oil, gas, sand and gravel.

Agriculture: Beef cattle. Market value $7.1 million. Timber sales significant. Hunting leases, fishing.

GROVETON (1,011) county seat; logging, government/services, recreation; museum, library; Bear Chase marathon in April.

TRINITY (2,793) government/services, steel fabrication, forest-industries center, commuters; hospital.

Other towns include: **Apple Springs** (350); **Centralia** (190); **Pennington** (67); **Sebastopol** (300) historic town; **Woodlake** (180).

Population..............................**14,740**	Altitude (ft.) 131–410	Unemployed 5.2
Change fm 2010............................0.4	Rainfall (in.) 49.31	Wages $18,940,994
Area (sq. mi.).............................714.0	Jan. mean min...............................35.1	Per Capita Income.................$33,383
Land Area (sq. mi.) 693.6	July mean max. 92.9	Prop. Value $1,878,108,442
	Civ. Labor 5,166	Retail Sales $66,580,232

Tyler County

Physical Features: Hilly East Texas county; densely timbered; drains to Neches River; B.A. Steinhagen Lake; Big Thicket is unique plant and animal area.

Economy: Lumbering, government/services, some manufacturing, tourism, hunting leases.

History: Caddoan area. Cherokees, Alabama, and Coushatta pushed into area from U.S. South in the 1820s. Anglo-Americans settled in the 1830s. Named for U.S. President John Tyler; county created in 1846 from Liberty County, organized the same year.

Race/Ethnicity: (In percent) Anglo, 79.1; Black, 11.2; Hispanic, 7.7; Asian, 0.6; Other, 0.9; Two or more races, 1.4.

Vital Statistics, annual: Births, 213; deaths, 274; marriages, 136; divorces, 97.

Recreation: Big Thicket National Preserve; Heritage Village; lake activities; Allan Shivers Museum; state forest; historic sites; dogwood festival in spring; rodeo, frontier frolics in September; gospel music fest in June.

Minerals: Oil, natural gas.

Agriculture: Cattle, hay, nursery crops, blueberries, horses. Market value $19.1 million. Timber sales significant.

WOODVILLE (2,711) county seat; lumber, cattle market, varied manufacturing, tourism; hospital; prison.

Other towns include: **Chester** (308) **Colmesneil** (579), **Doucette** (160), **Fred** (300), **Hillister** (250), **Ivanhoe** (1,489), **Spurger** (590), **Warren** (812).

Population..............................**21,696**	July mean max. 91.8
Change fm 2010..........................– 0.3	Civ. Labor 6,641
Area (sq. mi.).............................935.6	Unemployed 6.5
Land Area (sq. mi.) 924.5	Wages $32,254,870
Altitude (ft.) 50–461	Per Capita Income.................$33,551
Rainfall (in.) 56.18	Prop. Value $2,284,263,996
Jan. mean min...............................37.5	Retail Sales $127,013,423

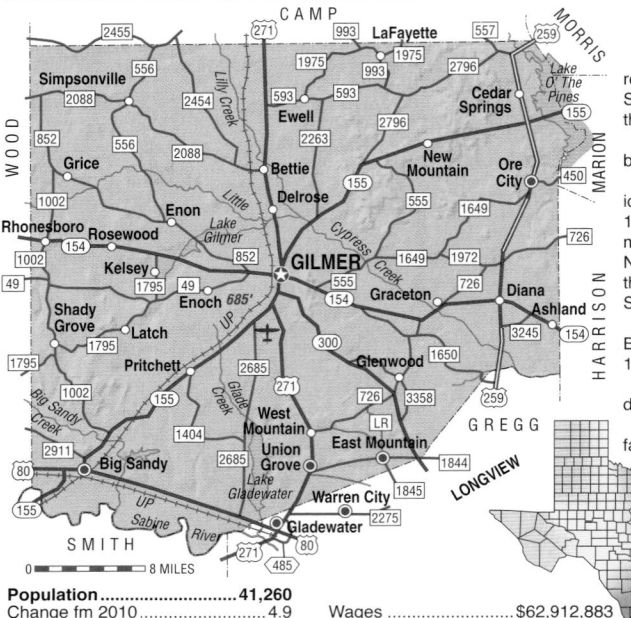

Upshur County

Physical Features: East Texas county; rolling to hilly, over half forested; drains to Sabine River, Little Cypress Creek, Lake O' the Pines, Lake Gilmer, Lake Gladewater.

Economy: Manufacturing, oil, gas, agri-business, timber.

History: Caddoes; reduced by epidemics in the 1700s. Cherokees in area in the 1820s. Anglo-American settlement in the mid-1830s. County created from Harrison, Nacogdoches counties in 1846, organized the same year; named for U.S. Secretary of State A.P. Upshur.

Race/Ethnicity: (In percent) Anglo, 80.3; Black, 8.3; Hispanic, 8.7; Asian, 0.5; Other, 1.2; Two or more races, 2.1.

Vital Statistics, annual: Births, 449; deaths, 471; marriages, 215; divorces, 193.

Recreation: Scenic trails, hunting, fishing, fall foliage, Yamboree in October at Gilmer.

Minerals: Oil, gas, sand, gravel.

Agriculture: Dairies, cattle, hay, vegetable crops, poultry. Market value $60.6 million. Timber a major product.

GILMER (5,252) county seat; agriculture, communications, electric power; museum; trails, parks; site of Cherokee village.

Other towns include: **Big Sandy** (1,379); **Diana** (585); **East Mountain** (839); **Ore City** (1,227); **Union Grove** (366). Part [2,447] of **Gladewater** (6,794).

Population	41,260
Change fm 2010	4.9
Area (sq. mi.)	592.6
Land Area (sq. mi.)	583.0
Altitude (ft.)	228–685
Rainfall (in.)	47.08
Jan. mean min.	31.4
July mean max.	93.4
Civ. Labor	17,710
Unemployed	4.0

Wages	$62,912,883
Per Capita Income	$34,783
Prop. Value	$3,016,045,746
Retail Sales	$277,280,792

For explanation of sources, symbols and abbreviations, see p. 192, and foldout map.

Upton County

Physical Features: Western county; north flat, south rolling, hilly; limestone, sandy loam soils, drains to creeks.

Economy: Oil, wind turbines, farming, ranching.

History: Apache and Comanche area until the tribes were removed by the U.S. Army in the 1870s. Sheep and cattle ranching developed in the 1880s. Oil discovered in 1925. County created in 1887 from Tom Green County; organized in 1910; the name honors brothers John and William Upton, Confederate colonels.

Race/Ethnicity: (In percent) Anglo, 42.3; Black, 3.0; Hispanic, 53.5; Asian, 0.7; Other, 2.7; Two or more races, 1.7.

Vital Statistics, annual: Births, 61; deaths, 36; marriages, 44; divorces, 19.

Recreation: Historic sites, Mendoza Trail museum, scenic areas, dinosaur tracks west of McCamey.

Minerals: Oil, natural gas.

Agriculture: Cotton, sheep, goats, cattle, watermelons, pecans. Extensive irrigation. Market value $12.7 million.

RANKIN (838) county seat, oil, ranching, farming; hospital; Barbados cookoff in May, All Kid rodeo in June.

McCAMEY (2,069) government/services, wind and solar power, oil; hospital; Wind Energy cookoff and festival in September.

Other town: **Midkiff** (182).

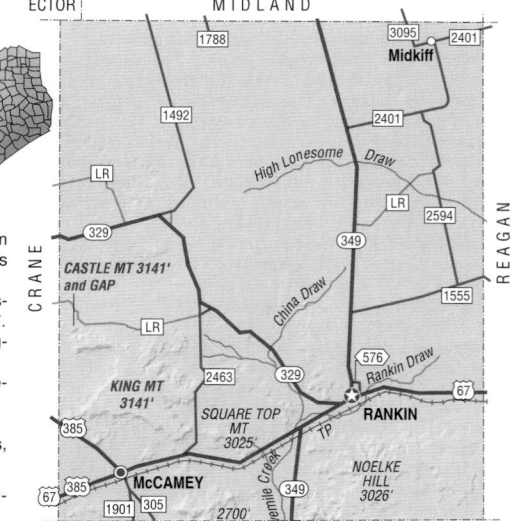

Population	3,671
Change fm 2010	9.6
Area (sq. mi.)	1,241.5
Land Area (sq. mi.)	1,241.3
Altitude (ft.)	2,310–3,141
Rainfall (in.)	15.14
Jan. mean min.	31.9
July mean max.	95.3
Civ. Labor	1,575
Unemployed	3.8
Wages	$24,901,574
Per Capita Income	$39,222
Prop. Value	$3,584,862,395
Retail Sales	$38,116,386

Uvalde County

Physical Features: Edwards Plateau, rolling hills below escarpment; spring-fed Sabinal, Frio, Leona, Nueces rivers; cypress, cedar, other trees, including maple groves.

Economy: Agribusinesses, hunting leases, light manufacturing, tourism.

History: Mission Nuestra Señora de la Candelaria founded in 1762 for Lipan Apaches near present-day Montell; Comanches harassed mission. U.S. military outpost established in 1849. County created from Bexar in 1850; re-created and organized in 1856; named for 1778 governor of Coahuila, Juan de Ugalde, with name Anglicized.

Race/Ethnicity: (In percent) Anglo, 26.5; Black, 1.3; Hispanic, 71.4; Asian, 0.9; Other, 1.3; Two or more races, 1.0.

Vital Statistics, annual: Births, 429; deaths, 233; marriages, 152; divorces, 21.

Recreation: Deer, turkey hunting; Garner State Park; water activities on rivers; John Nance Garner museum; Uvalde Memorial Park; scenic trails, historic sites.

Minerals: Asphalt, stone, sand, gravel.

Agriculture: Cattle, vegetables, corn, cotton, sorghum, sheep, goats, hay, wheat. Substantial irrigation. Market value $112.5 million.

UVALDE (16,609) county seat; vegetable, wool, mohair processing, tourism; opera house; junior college, A&M research center; hospital; Fort Inge Day in April.

Sabinal (1,687) farm, ranch center, tourism, retirement area.

Other towns include: **Concan** (500); **Knippa** (648); **Utopia** (222) resort; **Uvalde Estates** (2,309).

Population	26,846
Change fm 2010	1.7
Area (sq. mi.)	1,558.6
Land Area (sq. mi.)	1,552.0
Altitude (ft.)	650–2,200
Rainfall (in.)	24,60
Jan. mean min.	38.6
July mean max.	96.1
Civ. Labor	11,373
Unemployed	4.2
Wages	$81,746,782
Per Capita Income	$36,797
Prop. Value	$4,058,060,885
Retail Sales	$353,170,112

Val Verde County

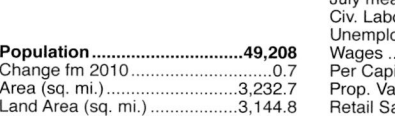

Physical Features: Southwestern county bordering Mexico, rolling, hilly; brushy; Devils, Pecos rivers, Rio Grande and Amistad Reservoir; limestone, alluvial soils.

Economy: Agribusiness, tourism, trade center, military, Border Patrol, hunting leases, fishing.

History: Apaches, Coahuiltecans, Jumanos present when Spanish came through in the late 1500s. Comanches arrived later. U.S. military outpost established in 1850s to protect settlers. Only county named for Civil War battle; Val Verde means green valley. Created in 1885 from Crockett, Kinney, Pecos counties, organized the same year.

Race/Ethnicity: (In percent) Anglo, 14.9; Black, 2.0; Hispanic, 82.3; Asian, 0.9; Other, 1.2; Two or more races, 1.1.

Vital Statistics, annual: Births, 904; deaths, 353; marriages, 458; divorces, 158.

Recreation: Gateway to Mexico; deer hunting, fishing; Amistad lake activities; two state parks; Langtry restoration of Judge Roy Bean's saloon; ancient pictographs; San Felipe Springs; winery.

Minerals: Production sand and gravel, gas, oil.

Agriculture: Sheep, Angora goats, meat goats (second in numbers); cattle; minor irrigation. Market value $10.7 million.

DEL RIO (34,790) county seat; government/services including federal agencies/military, agribusiness, tourism; hospital; extension colleges; Fiesta de Amistad in October.

Laughlin Air Force Base (1,583).

Other towns and places include: **Cienegas Terrace** (3,403); **Comstock** (344); **Langtry** (30); **Val Verde Park** (2,415).

Population	49,208
Change fm 2010	0.7
Area (sq. mi.)	3,232.7
Land Area (sq. mi.)	3,144.8
Altitude (ft.)	845-2,343
Rainfall (in.)	20.19
Jan. mean min.	38.7
July mean max.	96.4
Civ. Labor	19,880
Unemployed	6.2
Wages	$159,354,902
Per Capita Income	$34,100
Prop. Value	$3,245,192,433
Retail Sales	$547,960,343

Van Zandt County

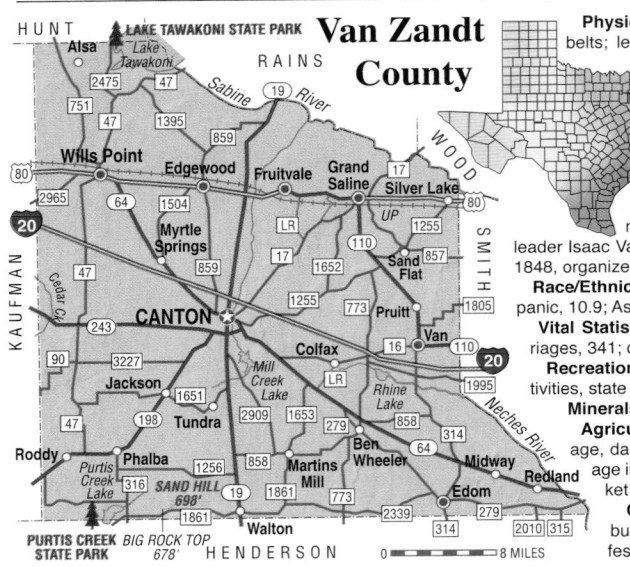

Physical Features: Eastern county in three soil belts; level to rolling; Sabine, Neches rivers; Lake Tawakoni; partly forested.

Economy: Agriculture, government/services, commuters to Dallas/Tyler.

History: Caddo tribes, reduced by epidemics before settlers arrived. Cherokees settled in the 1820s; removed in 1839 under policies of Republic President Lamar; Anglo-American settlement followed. County named for Republic leader Isaac Van Zandt; created from Henderson County in 1848, organized the same year.

Race/Ethnicity: (In percent) Anglo, 83.7; Black, 2.9; Hispanic, 10.9; Asian, 0.5; Other, 1.2; Two or more races, 1.7.

Vital Statistics, annual: Births, 608; deaths, 621; marriages, 341; divorces, 175.

Recreation: Canton First Monday trade days, lake activities, state parks, historic sites.

Minerals: Oil, gas.

Agriculture: Nurseries, beef cattle, hay and foliage, dairies, vegetables. First in nursery stock acreage in the open and in sweet potato acreage. Market value $94.3 million.

CANTON (3,864) county seat; tourism, agribusiness, commuters; museums, bluegrass festival in June.

Wills Point (3,590) government/services, retail, tourism, commuters to Dallas and Tyler; depot museum, bluebird festival in April.

Other towns include: **Ben Wheeler** (504); **Edgewood** (1,482) commuters, heritage park, antiques; **Edom** (390) arts and crafts; **Fruitvale** (419); **Grand Saline** (3,201) salt plant, agriculture, medical services/hospital, Salt Palace museum, salt prairie marsh, birding, Salt Festival in June; **Van** (2,680) oil center, hay, cattle, oil festival in October.

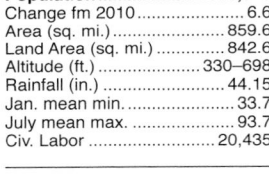

Population	56,019
Change fm 2010	6.6
Area (sq. mi.)	859.6
Land Area (sq. mi.)	842.6
Altitude (ft.)	330–698
Rainfall (in.)	44.15
Jan. mean min.	33.7
July mean max.	93.7
Civ. Labor	20,435

Unemployed	4.0
Wages	$163,957,596
Per Capita Income	$34,732
Prop. Value	$3,398,023,958
Retail Sales	$576,863,478

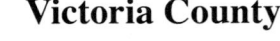

Victoria County

Physical Features: Rolling prairies, intersected by many streams; sandy loams, clays, alluvial soils.

Economy: Petrochemical plants, government/services, oil, manufacturing, agribusiness, tourism.

History: Karankawas and other tribes in the area when Spanish explored in 1528. Comanches, Tawakonis arrived later. La Salle's camp on Garcitas Creek 1685–1687. Spanish ranching developed in the 1750s. Anglo-Americans arrived after 1836. An original county, created in 1836 from Mexican municipality named for President Guadalupe Victoria of Mexico.

Race/Ethnicity: (In percent) Anglo, 44.6; Black, 6.7; Hispanic, 47.0; Asian, 1.4; Other, 1.0; Two or more races, 1.5.

Vital Statistics, annual: Births, 1,363; deaths, 847; marriages, 615; divorces, 381.

Recreation: Fishing, hunting; saltwater activities, historic homes, sites, riverside park, Coleto Creek Reservoir and park, zoo, Czech festival in September at Victoria.

Minerals: Oil, gas, sand, gravel.

Agriculture: Corn, beef cattle, grain sorghums, cotton, rice, soybeans. Market value $47.6 million.

VICTORIA (67,117) county seat; petrochemicals, government/services, hospitals/healthcare, retail, oil, manufacturing, agribusiness, tourism; Victoria College, University of Houston at Victoria; community theater, symphony, museums; Bootfeast in October.

Other towns include: **Bloomington** (2,590), **Inez** (2,430), **McFaddin** (50), **Nursery** (600), **Placedo** (758), **Telferner** (700).

Population	92,035
Change fm 2010	6.0
Area (sq. mi.)	888.8
Land Area (sq. mi.)	882.1
Altitude (ft.)	sea level–230
Rainfall (in.)	41.08

Jan. mean min.	40.7
July mean max.	94.1
Civ. Labor	42,120
Unemployed	3.7
Wages	$442,707,548
Per Capita Income	$42,484

Prop. Value	$8,727,869,705
Retail Sales	$1,798,882,695

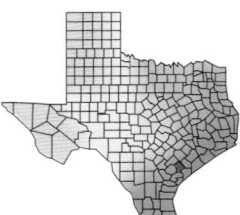

Walker County

Physical Features: South central county north of Houston of rolling hills; more than 70 percent forested; national forest; San Jacinto, Trinity rivers; Lake Livingston, Lake Conroe.

Economy: State employment in prison system, education.

History: Coahuiltecans, Bidais in area when Spanish explored around 1690. Later, area became trading ground for many Indian tribes. Anglo-Americans settled in the 1830s. Antebellum slaveholding area. County created in 1846 from Montgomery County and organized the same year; first named for U.S. Secretary of the Treasury R.J. Walker; renamed 1863 for Texas Ranger Capt. S.H. Walker.

Race/Ethnicity: (In percent) Anglo, 56.3; Black, 23.4; Hispanic, 18.1; Asian, 1.2; Other, 0.9; Two or more races, 1.6.

Vital Statistics, annual: Births, 667; deaths, 513; marriages, 418; divorces, 190.

Recreation: Fishing, hunting, lake activities; Sam Houston museum, homes, grave; prison museum; other historic sites, state park, Sam Houston National Forest; Sam Houston folk festival in spring.

Minerals: Clays, natural gas, oil, sand and gravel, stone.

Agriculture: Cattle, nursery plants, poultry, cotton, hay. Market value $34.5 million. Timber sales substantial.

HUNTSVILLE (41,511) county seat; state prison system, Sam Houston State University, forest products, varied manufacturing; hospital; museums, arts center.

Other towns include: **Dodge** (150), **New Waverly** (1,107), **Riverside** (555).

Population	72,480
Change fm 2010	6.8
Area (sq. mi.)	801.5
Land Area (sq. mi.)	784.2
Altitude (ft.)	131–500
Rainfall (in.)	49.08
Jan. mean min.	39.7
July mean max.	93.3
Civ. Labor	23,642
Unemployed	3.9
Wages	$250,356,897
Per Capita Income	$27,302
Prop. Value	$4,946,249,184
Retail Sales	$768,142,501

For explanation of sources, symbols and abbreviations, see p. 192, and foldout map.

A creek in Walker County. Photo by Ron Billings, Texas A&M Forest Service.

Waller County

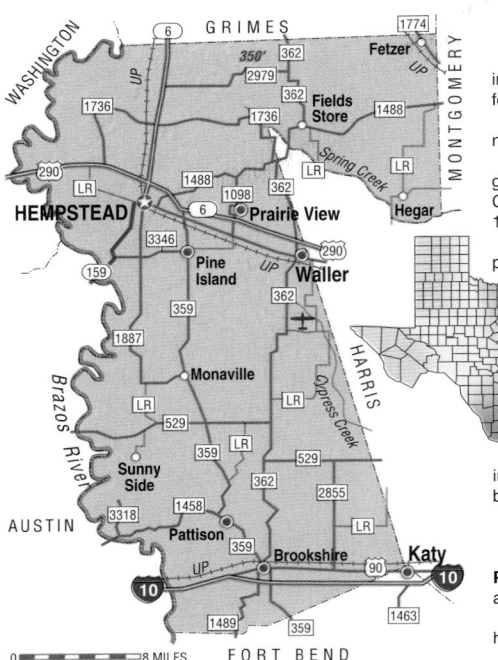

Physical Features: South central county Houston on rolling prairie; drains to Brazos; alluvial soils; about 20 percent forested.

Economy: Agribusiness, education, equine-related businesses, part of Houston metropolitan area.

History: Bidais Indians reduced to about 100 when Anglo-Americans settled in 1820s. Antebellum slaveholding area. County named for Edwin Waller, Republic leader; created in 1873 from Austin, Grimes counties, organized the same year.

Race/Ethnicity: (In percent), Anglo, 42.9; Black, 25.4; Hispanic, 30.1; Asian, 1.1; Other, 1.5; Two or more races, 1.5.

Vital Statistics, annual: Births, 592; deaths, 305; marriages, 345; divorces, 142.

Recreation: Fishing, hunting; historic sites; museum.

Minerals: Oil, gas.

Agriculture: Cattle, hay, rice, greenhouse nurseries, turf grass. 10,000 acres irrigated. Market value $91.7 million. Some timber marketed.

HEMPSTEAD (7,011) county seat; varied manufacturing, commuting to Houston, agribusiness center, large vegetable market; watermelon fest in July.

Prairie View (6,440) home of Prairie View A&M University.

Other towns include: **Brookshire** (5,283), **Pattison** (577), **Pine Island** (1,107), **Waller** (2,856, partly in Harris County) agriculture, education, construction.

Also, part [1,156] of **Katy** (17,184, mostly in Harris County) hospitals.

Population.............................53,126	Altitude (ft.)..........................100–350	Unemployed....................................3.8
Change fm 2010..........................22.8	Rainfall (in.)..............................45.53	Wages..........................$193,165,014
Area (sq. mi.)............................517.8	Jan. mean min..............................38.0	Per Capita Income.................$37,508
Land Area (sq. mi.).....................513.4	July mean max. 95.0	Prop. Value $7,711,391,370
	Civ. Labor 22,923	Retail Sales $583,692,187

Ward County

Physical Features: Western county on Pecos River; plain covered by grass, brush; sandy, loam soils.

Economy: Oil, gas, government/services.

History: Jumano Indians in area when Spanish explored in the 1580s. Comanches arrived later. Railroad stations established in the 1880s. Oil discovered in the 1920s. County named for Republic leader Thomas W. Ward; county created from Tom Green County in 1887; organized in 1892.

Race/Ethnicity: (In percent) Anglo, 39.9; Black, 5.2; Hispanic, 53.6; Asian, 0.6; Other, 1.6; Two or more races, 2.1.

Vital Statistics, annual: Births, 198; deaths, 134; marriages, 95; divorces, 31.

Recreation: Sandhills state park, camel treks, Million Barrel museum in Monahans, county park, Butterfield stagecoach festival in July.

Minerals: Oil, gas, caliche, sand, gravel.

Agriculture: Beef cattle, greenhouse crops, alfalfa, horses. Market value $1.8 million. Hunting leases important.

MONAHANS (7,312) county seat; oil and gas, tourism, ranching; hospital, Odessa College extension.

Other towns: **Barstow** (364); **Grandfalls** (377); **Pyote** (121) Rattlesnake bomber base museum; **Thorntonville** (497); **Wickett** (523).

For explanation of sources, symbols and abbreviations, see p. 192, and foldout map.

Population..............................11,720	
Change fm 2010..........................10.0	
Area (sq. mi.).............................835.8	
Land Area (sq. mi.)....................835.6	
Altitude (ft.)........................2,400–2,880	
Rainfall (in.)..............................13.87	
Jan. mean min...........................30.9	
July mean max. 94.9	
Civ. Labor 5,941	
Unemployed....................................2.8	
Wages...........................$84,591,476	
Per Capita Income.................$41,579	
Prop. Value $2,777,330,760	
Retail Sales $163,070,112	

Washington County

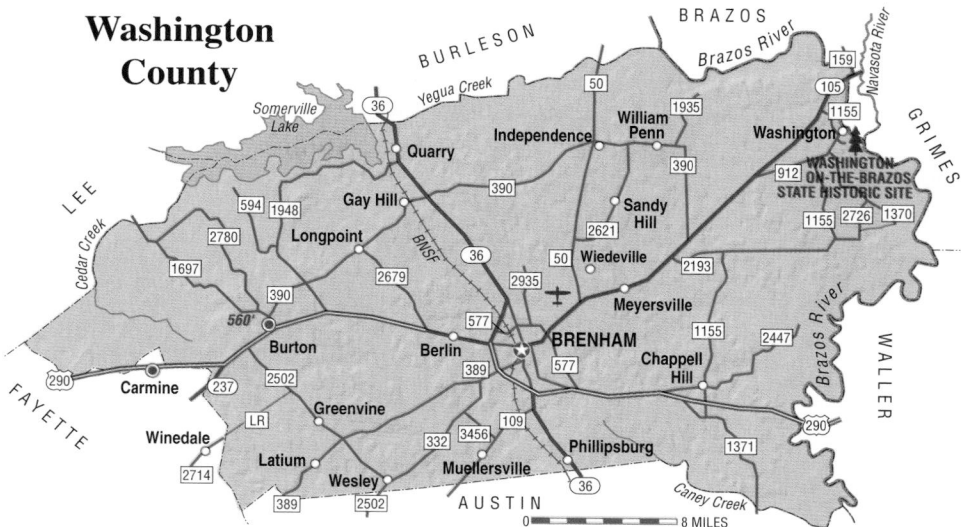

Physical Features: South central county in Brazos valley; rolling prairie of sandy loam, alluvial soils.

Economy: Agribusiness, oil, tourism, manufacturing, government/services.

History: Coahuiltecan tribes and Tonkawas in area when Anglo-American settlers arrived in 1821. Antebellum slaveholding area. Germans arrived around 1870. County named for George Washington; an original county, created in 1836, organized in 1837.

Race/Ethnicity: (In percent), Anglo, 63.7; Black, 17.5; Hispanic, 16.3; Asian, 1.9; Other, 0.5; Two or more races, 1.3.

Vital Statistics, annual: Births, 402; deaths, 389; marriages, 214; divorces, 100.

Recreation: Many historic sites, including Washington-on-the-Brazos, Texas Baptist Historical Museum,

Star of Republic Museum; wildflowers, Somerville Lake, fishing, hunting, birding; antique rose nursery; Bluebonnet festival in April.

Minerals: Oil, gas and stone.

Agriculture: Cattle, poultry, dairy products, hogs, horses; hay, corn, sorghum, cotton, small grains, nursery crops. Market value $45.7 million.

BRENHAM (17,262) county seat;

Blue Bell creamery, retail, tourism; hospital; Blinn College; Maifest.

Other towns include: **Burton** (298) agriculture, tourism, national landmark cotton gin, festival in April; **Chappell Hill** (750) agriculture, industrial, tourism, museum, historic homes, Scarecrow festival in October; **Washington** (100) site of signing of Texas Declaration of Independence.

Population	**35,108**
Change fm 2010	4.2
Area (sq. mi.)	621.8
Land Area (sq. mi.)	604.0
Altitude (ft.)	150–560
Rainfall (in.)	45.14
Jan. mean min.	39.0
July mean max.	94.2
Civ. Labor	14,631
Unemployed	3.6
Wages	$144,915,398
Per Capita Income	$47,741
Prop. Value	$6,333,191,802
Retail Sales	$513,242,587

Independence Hall at Washington-on-the-Brazos. Photo by Robert Plocheck.

Webb County

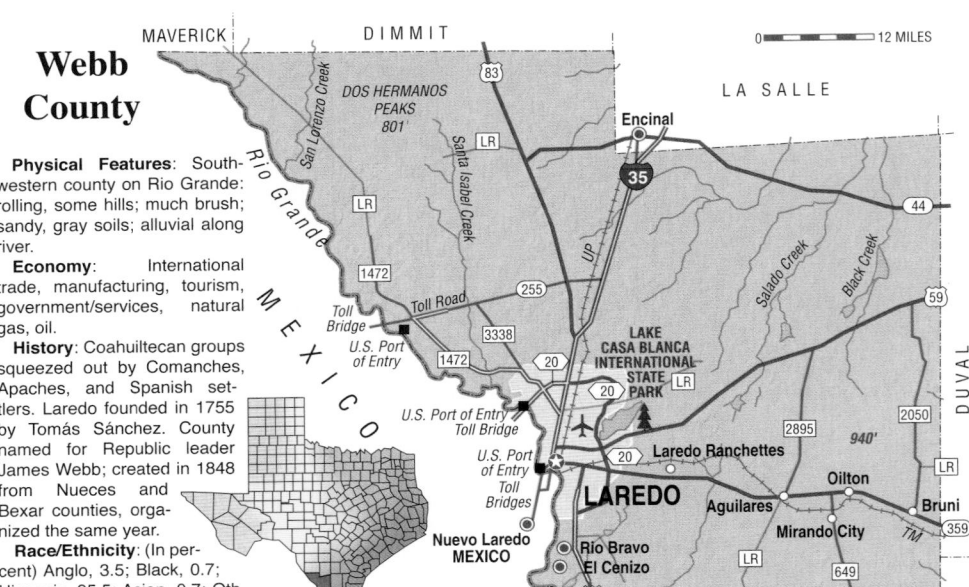

Physical Features: Southwestern county on Rio Grande: rolling, some hills; much brush; sandy, gray soils; alluvial along river.

Economy: International trade, manufacturing, tourism, government/services, natural gas, oil.

History: Coahuiltecan groups squeezed out by Comanches, Apaches, and Spanish settlers. Laredo founded in 1755 by Tomás Sánchez. County named for Republic leader James Webb; created in 1848 from Nueces and Bexar counties, organized the same year.

Race/Ethnicity: (In percent) Anglo, 3.5; Black, 0.7; Hispanic, 95.5; Asian, 0.7; Other, 0.7; Two or more races, 0.4.

Vital Statistics, annual: Births, 5,357; deaths, 1,356; marriages, 1,836; divorces, 171.

Recreation: Tourist gateway to Mexico; hunting, fishing; Lake Casa Blanca park, water recreation; historic sites; Museum of Republic of the Rio Grande; Fort McIntosh; minor league baseball, hockey; Washington's Birthday celebration.

Minerals: Natural gas, oil, coal.

Agriculture: Onions, melons, nursery crops, cattle, horses, goats. About 2,500 acres irrigated. Market value $30.3 million. Mesquite sold. Hunting leases important.

LAREDO (261,397) county seat; international trade, retail center, government/services; rail, highway gateway to Mexico; junior college, Texas A&M International University, community college; hospitals; entertainment/sports arena; "El Grito" on Sept. 15; Jalapeño festival in February.

Other towns and places include: **Bruni** (386); **El Cenizo** (3,132); **Mirando City** (341); **Oilton** (381); **Rio Bravo** (4,814).

Population	275,910
Change fm 2010	10.2
Area (sq. mi.)	3,375.6
Land Area (sq. mi.)	3,361.5
Altitude (ft.)	310–940
Rainfall (in.)	20.20
Jan. mean min.	46.1
July mean max.	99.3
Civ. Labor	116,571
Unemployed	3.8
Wages	$901,740,981
Per Capita Income	$30,008
Prop. Value	$22,539,565,878
Retail Sales	$3,406,322,437

The Texas Travel Information Center on I–35 near Laredo, Webb County. Photo by Robert Plocheck.

Wharton County

Physical Features: Gulf prairie; bisected by the Colorado River; alluvial, black, sandy loam soils.

Economy: Oil, agribusiness, hunting, manufacturing, government/services.

History: Karankawas in area until the 1840s. Anglo-American colonists settled in 1823. Czechs, Germans arrived in 1880s. Mexican migration increased after 1950. County named for John A. and William H. Wharton, brothers active in Texas Revolution; created in 1846 from Jackson, Matagorda, Colorado counties, organized the same year.

Race/Ethnicity: (In percent) Anglo, 44.3; Black, 14.0; Hispanic, 41.4; Asian, 0.5; Other, 0.8; Two or more races, 1.0.

Vital Statistics, annual: Births, 595; deaths, 417; marriages, 242; divorces, 97.

Recreation: Waterfowl hunting, fishing, big-game, birding; museums; river-front park at Wharton; historic sites; old Plaza Theater at Wharton.

Minerals: Oil, gas.

Agriculture: Rice (first in acreage); cotton, milo, corn, sorghum, soybeans; 72,000 acres irrigated. Also, eggs, nurseries/turf grass (first in value of sales), cattle, aquaculture. Market value $373.6 million.

WHARTON (8,690) county seat; health care, plastics, government/services; hospitals, junior college; Juneteenth, wine/arts festival in October.

EL CAMPO (11,727) agribusiness, hunting, varied manufacturing, oilfield services, rice processing; hospital; Polka Expo in November.

Other towns include: **Boling** (1,117); **Danevang** (61); **East Bernard** (2,320) commuters, agribusiness, retail, klobase-kolache festival in June; **Egypt** (26); **Glen Flora** (210); **Hungerford** (306); **Lane City** (111); **Lissie** (72); **Louise** (1,001); **Pierce** (51).

Population **41,619**
Change fm 2010 .... 0.8
Area (sq. mi.) 1,094.4
Land Area (sq. mi.) 1,086.2
Altitude (ft.) 50–165
Rainfall (in.) 47.47
Jan. mean min. 43.0
July mean max. 92.2
Civ. Labor 21,178
Unemployed 3.5
Wages $152,360,390
Per Capita Income $40,535
Prop. Value $5,692,922,100
Retail Sales $801,522,361

Wheeler County

Physical Features: Panhandle county adjoining Oklahoma. Plain, on edge of Caprock; Red River, Sweetwater Creek; some canyons; red sandy loam, black clay soils.

Economy: Oil, gas, agribusiness, tourism.

History: Apaches, displaced by Kiowas and Comanches around 1700. Fort Elliott established in 1875 after Indians forced into Oklahoma. Ranching began in the late 1870s. Oil boom in the 1920s. County named for pioneer jurist R.T. Wheeler; county created from Bexar, Young districts in 1876; organized in 1879.

Race/Ethnicity: (In percent) Anglo, 68.8; Black, 3.2; Hispanic, 25.6; Asian, 0.9; Other, 1.8; Two or more races, 1.9.

Vital Statistics, annual: Births, 81; deaths, 72; marriages, 87; divorces, 4.

Recreation: Pioneer West museum at Shamrock; historic sites; Old Mobeetie jail, trading post, Fort Elliott.

Minerals: Oil, natural gas.

Agriculture: Fed beef, cow-calf and stocker cattle, swine, horses; wheat, rye, grain sorghum, cotton. Market value $111.2 million.

WHEELER (1,590) county seat; oil & gas, agriculture, government/services; hospital, medical clinics, museum, library, aquatics center.

SHAMROCK (1,913) tourism, agribusiness antiques shops; hospital, library, old Route 66 sites; St. Patrick's Day event.

Other towns include: **Allison** (135); **Briscoe** (135); **Mobeetie** (102).

Population **5,191**
Change fm 2010 .... – 4.0
Area (sq. mi.) 915.5
Land Area (sq. mi.) 914.5
Altitude (ft.) 2,005–3,000
Rainfall (in.) 25.16
Jan. mean min. 24.0
July mean max. 93.3
Civ. Labor 2,515
Unemployed 2.8
Wages $20,699,294
Per Capita Income $38,978
Prop. Value $2,554,677,810
Retail Sales $71,340,033

For explanation of sources, symbols and abbreviations, see p. 192, and foldout map.

Wichita County

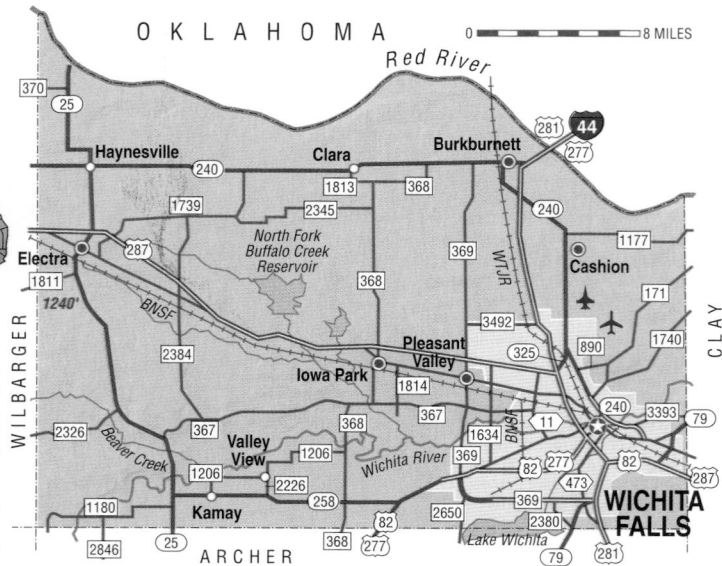

Physical Features: Northwest county in prairie bordering Oklahoma; drained by Red, Wichita rivers; North Fork Buffalo Creek Reservoir, Lake Wichita; sandy, loam soils.

Economy: Manufacturing, retail trade center, air base, government/services, agriculture.

History: Wichitas and other Caddoan tribes in the area in the 1700s; later, Comanches, Apaches also present until the 1850s. Anglo-American settlement increased after 1870. County named for tribe; created from Young Territory in 1858; organized in 1882.

Race/Ethnicity: (In percent) Anglo, 65.3; Black, 11.1; Hispanic, 19.2; Asian, 2.1; Other, 1.5; Two or more races, 2.8.

Vital Statistics, annual: Births, 1,740; deaths, 1,304; marriages, 1,120; divorces, 556.

Recreation: Museums; historic sites; Texas-Oklahoma High School Oil Bowl football game; collegiate activities; water sports; Fiestas Patrias parade, Ranch Round-up in August.

Minerals: Oil.

Agriculture: Beef cattle, horticulture, wheat, hay. Seventy-five percent of hay irrigated; 10 percent of wheat/cotton. Market value $37.9 million.

WICHITA FALLS (105,592) county seat; distribution center for large area of Texas and Oklahoma, government/services, varied manufacturing, oilfield services; hospitals, including North Texas state hospital; Midwestern State University, vocational-technical training center; hiking trails; Hotter'n Hell bicycle race in August; Sheppard Air Force Base.

Other cities include: **Burkburnett** (11,311) some manufacturing, Trails and Tales of Boomtown USA display and tours; **Cashion** (357); **Electra**

(2,738) oil, agriculture, manufacturing, commuters to Wichita Falls; hospital; goat barbecue in May; **Iowa Park** (6,450) manufacturing, prison, Parkfest in May; **Kamay** (640); **Pleasant Valley** (341).

Population	**132,064**
Change fm 2010	0.3
Area (sq. mi.)	633.1
Land Area (sq. mi.)	627.8
Altitude (ft.)	912–1,240
Rainfall (in.)	28.92
Jan. mean min.	29.8
July mean max.	96.9
Civ. Labor	56,795
Unemployed	3.3
Wages	$527,890,278
Per Capita Income	$40,034
Prop. Value	$7,389,170,982
Retail Sales	$1,721,300,970

A boat heads out from Port Mansfield, Willacy County. Photo by Robert Plocheck.

Wilbarger County

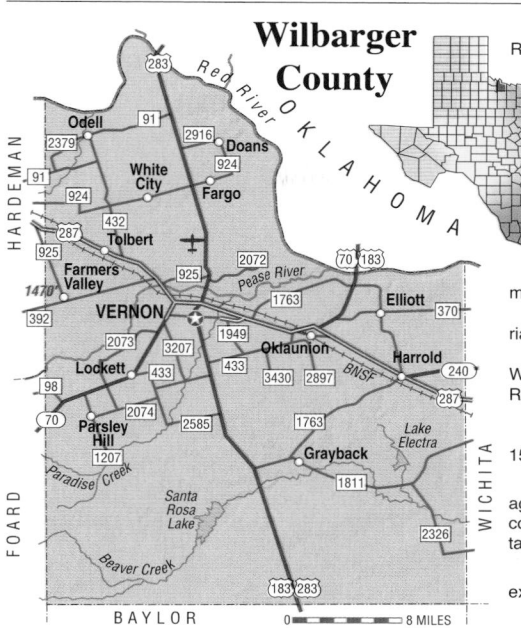

Physical Features: Gently rolling prairie draining to Red, Pease rivers, tributaries; sandy, loam, waxy soils; Santa Rosa Lake, Lake Electra.

Economy: Agribusiness, electricity generating plant, government/services.

History: Anglo-American settlement developed after removal of the Comanches into the Indian Territory in 1875. County named for pioneers Josiah and Mathias Wilbarger; created from the Bexar District in 1858 and organized in 1881.

Race/Ethnicity: (In percent) Anglo, 58.1; Black, 8.3; Hispanic, 29.3; Asian, 2.5; Other, 1.8; Two or more races, 2.2.

Vital Statistics, annual: Births, 177; deaths, 163; marriages, 138; divorces, 27.

Recreation: Doan's Crossing, on route of cattle drives; Waggoner Ranch, other historic sites; hunting, fishing; Red River Valley Museum; Santa Rosa roundup in May.

Minerals: Oil.

Agriculture: Wheat, cattle, cotton, alfalfa, peanuts; 15,000 acres irrigated. Market value $47.2 million.

VERNON (10,267) county seat; government/services, agribusiness, manufacturing, electricity-generating plant; college; state hospital/mental health center, private hospital, prison; museums; vintage car show in August.

Other towns include: **Harrold** (200); **Lockett** (150) A&M extension center; **Odell** (100); **Oklaunion** (138).

Population	12,820
Change fm 2010	– 5.3
Area (sq. mi.)	977.9
Land Area (sq. mi.)	970.8
Altitude (ft.)	1,030–1,470
Rainfall (in.)	27.94
Jan. mean min.	27.7
July mean max.	96.6
Civ. Labor	4,818
Unemployed	4.1
Wages	$53,773,950
Per Capita Income	$39,542
Prop. Value	$2,092,668,910
Retail Sales	$275,027,119

Willacy County

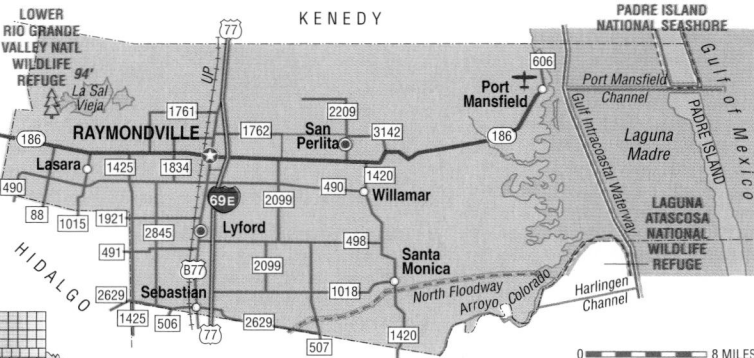

Physical Features: Flat coastal prairie sloping toward Gulf; alluvial, sandy, marshy soils; Padre Island; La Sal Vieja, salt lake; wildlife refuge.

Economy: Agribusiness, oil, government/services.

History: Coahuiltecan area when Spanish explored in the 1500s. Spanish ranching began in the 1790s. County named for legislator John G. Willacy; created in 1911 from Cameron, Hidalgo counties, organized in 1912; reorganized in 1921 after most of its territory was given over to the newly created Kenedy County.

Race/Ethnicity: (In percent) Anglo, 8.9; Black, 2.6; Hispanic, 88.3; Asian, 0.9; Other, 0.7; Two or more races, 0.5.

Vital Statistics, annual: Births, 291; deaths, 151; marriages, 81; divorces, 25.

Recreation: Fresh and saltwater fishing, hunting of deer, turkey, dove; mild climate attracts many winter tourists.

Minerals: Oil, natural gas.

Agriculture: Cotton, sorghum, corn, vegetables, sugar cane; 20 percent of cropland irrigated. Livestock includes cattle, horses, goats, hogs. Market value $82.6 million.

RAYMONDVILLE (11,373) county seat; agribusiness, oil, food processing, tourism, enterprise zone, prison; museum; Boot Fest in October.

Other towns include: **Lasara** (1,008); **Lyford** (2,630); **Port Mansfield** (190) charter fishing, bait and tackle, ecotourism/birding, nature trail, fishing tournament in July; **San Perlita** (577); **Sebastian** (1,841).

Population	21,515
Change fm 2010	– 2.8
Area (sq. mi.)	784.3
Land Area (sq. mi.)	590.6
Altitude (ft.)	sea level–94
Rainfall (in.)	26.08
Jan. mean min.	47.6
July mean max.	96.7
Civ. Labor	6,189
Unemployed	8.6
Wages	$30,370,386
Per Capita Income	$30,047
Prop. Value	$1,734,081,044
Retail Sales	$81,975,658

For explanation of sources, symbols and abbreviations, see p. 192, and foldout map.

Williamson County

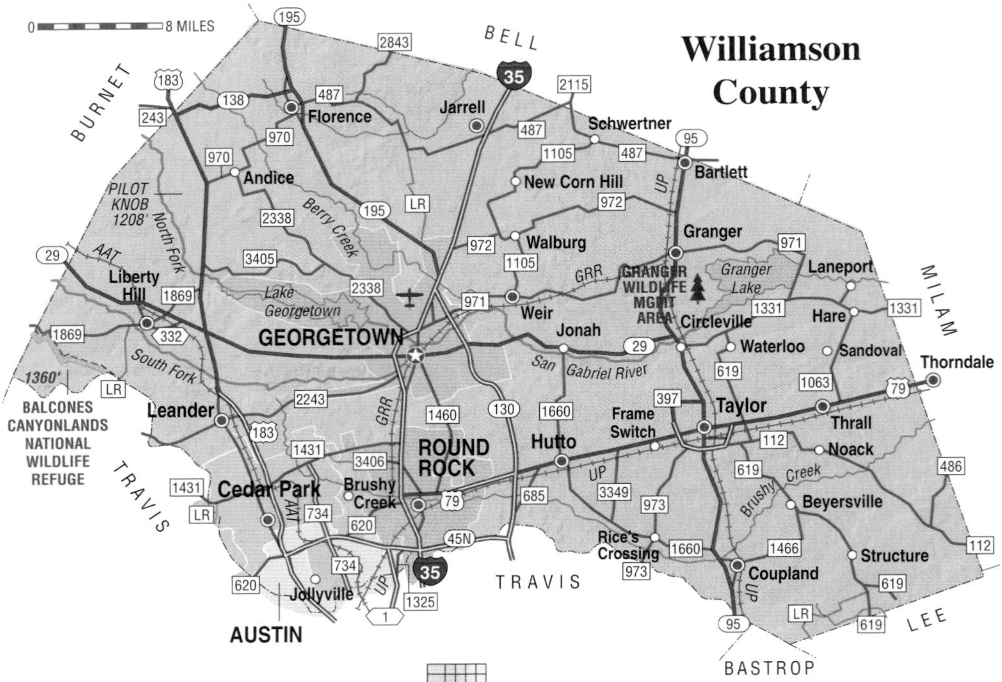

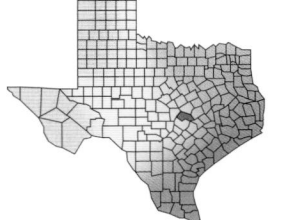

Physical Features: Central county near Austin. Level to rolling; mostly Blackland soil, some loam, sand; drained by San Gabriel River and tributaries; Granger Lake, Lake Georgetown.

Economy: Agribusinesses, varied manufacturing, education center, government/services; the county is part of Austin metropolitan area.

History: Tonkawa area; later, other tribes moved in. Comanches raided until the 1860s. Anglo-American settlement began in the late 1830s. County named for Robert M. Williamson, pioneer leader; created from Milam County and organized in 1848.

Race/Ethnicity: (In percent) Anglo, 59.6; Black, 7.1; Hispanic, 24.5; Asian, 7.2; Other, 1.1; Two or more races, 2.8.

Vital Statistics, annual: Births, 6,428; deaths, 2,625; marriages, 2,682; divorces, 872.

Recreation: Lake recreation; Inner Space Cavern; historic sites; deer hunting, fishing; Gov. Dan Moody Museum at Taylor; San Gabriel Park; old settlers park; walking tours, rattlesnake sacking, barbecue cookoff, frontier days in summer; Round Rock minor league baseball; Cedar Park Center, home of Austin Spurs NBA developmental basketball team and the Texas Stars AHL hockey team.

Minerals: Building stone, sand and gravel.

Agriculture: Corn, cattle, sorghum, cotton, wheat, hay, nursery crops. Market value $129.6 million.

GEORGETOWN (66,904) county seat; education, health, government/services, manufacturing, retail; hospital; Southwestern University; Red Poppy festival in April.

ROUND ROCK (124,455, part [1,362] in Travis County) semiconductor, varied manufacturing, tourism and distribution center; hospital; Texas Baptist Children's Home.

Cedar Park (70,375, part [489] in Travis County) energy equipment manufacturing, millwork, concrete production, commuting to Austin; hospital, community college extension; steam-engine train; Cedar Fest in the spring.

Taylor (17,451) varied manufacturing, wholesale, transportation, government/services; hospital, col-

For explanation of sources, symbols and abbreviations, see p. 192, and foldout map.

lege extension campuses, museum, parks; Blackland Prairie Day in May.

Other towns include: **Andice** (300); **Bartlett** (2,725, partly in Bell County) cotton, corn production, commuters, prison, first rural electrification in nation in 1933, clinic, library, Friendship Fest in September; **Brushy Creek** (24,749); **Coupland** (309); **Florence** (1,259).

Also, **Granger** (1,508); **Hutto** (23,443) agriculture, manufacturing, government/services, commuters to Austin, museum, Olde Tyme Days in October; **Jarrell** (1,209); **Jollyville** (15,877, partly in Travis County); **Leander** (39,202) varied manufacturing, government/services, community college campus, Old Town street festival in May, Leanderthal Lady prehistoric site; **Liberty Hill** (1,585) artisans center; **Schwertner** (175); **Thrall** (943); **Walburg** (277); **Weir** (479).

Also, part [35,697] of **Austin**.

Population	566,719
Change fm 2010	34.1
Area (sq. mi.)	1,134.4
Land Area (sq. mi.)	1,118.3
Altitude (ft.)	400–1,360
Rainfall (in.)	35.73
Jan. mean min.	36.5
July mean max.	94.9
Civ. Labor	301,123
Unemployed	2.9
Wages	$2,277,417,894
Per Capita Income	$48,091
Prop. Value	$66,034,178,034
Retail Sales	$9,659,868,162

Wilson County

0 ■■■■■■■ 8 MILES

Physical Features: Upper Coastal Plains; mostly sandy soils, some heavier; San Antonio River, Cibolo Creek.

Economy: Agribusiness, oil and gas, commuters to San Antonio; part of San Antonio metropolitan area.

History: Coahuiltecan Indians in area when Spanish began ranching around 1750. Anglo-American settlers arrived in the 1840s. Germans, Polish settled in the 1850s. County created from Bexar, Karnes counties and organized in 1860; named for James C. Wilson, a member of the Mier Expedition.

Race/Ethnicity: (In percent) Anglo, 57.2; Black, 1.7; Hispanic, 39.8; Asian, 0.5; Other, 1.1; Two or more races, 1.4.

Vital Statistics, annual: Births, 562; deaths, 410; marriages, 244; divorces, 118.

Recreation: Rancho de las Cabras mission ranch ruins, historic homes; the Stockdale watermelon jubilee in June; Floresville peanut festival in October.

Minerals: Oil, gas, clays.

Agriculture: Cattle, corn, sorghum, hay, cotton. Market value $102.1 million.

FLORESVILLE (7,653) county seat; government/services, distribution, retail trade; hospital; parks.

Other towns include: **La Vernia** (1,374); **Pandora** (110); **Poth** (2,223) agriculture, commuting to San Antonio; bicycle ride in September; **Stockdale** (1,656) agriculture, commuting

to San Antonio, museum, nature center, watermelon jubilee in June; **Sutherland Springs** (420).

Part of **Nixon** (2,505, mostly in Gonzales County).

For explanation of sources, symbols and abbreviations, see p. 192, and foldout map.

Population	**50,224**
Change fm 2010	17.0
Area (sq. mi.)	808.4
Land Area (sq. mi.)	803.7
Altitude (ft.)	300–804
Rainfall (in.)	29.07
Jan. mean min.	37.2
July mean max.	95.5
Civ. Labor	24,514
Unemployed	2.9
Wages	$82,658,646
Per Capita Income	$42,219
Prop. Value	$4,484,550,107
Retail Sales	$498,079,768

Winkler County

Physical Features: Western county adjoining New Mexico on plains, partly sandy hills.

Economy: Oil and natural gas, ranching, prison, some farming.

History: Apache area until arrival of Comanches in the 1700s. Anglo-Americans began ranching in the 1880s. Oil discovered in 1926. Mexican migration increased after 1960. County named for Confederate Col. C.M. Winkler; created from Tom Green County in 1887; organized in 1910.

Race/Ethnicity: (In percent) Anglo, 35.2; Black, 3.2; Hispanic, 60.8; Asian, 0.7; Other, 1.9; Two or more races, 1.2.

Vital Statistics, annual: Births, 136; deaths, 70; marriages, 32; divorces, 21.

Recreation: Part of Monahans Sandhills State Park; museum; Roy Orbison festival in June at Wink; Wink Sink, large sinkhole.

Minerals: Oil, gas.

Agriculture: Beef cattle. Market value $3.4 million.

KERMIT (6,366) county seat; oil, gas, ranching, some farming; hospital; Celebration Days in August.

Wink (1,056) oil, gas, ranching.

Population	**7,720**
Change fm 2010	8.6
Area (sq. mi.)	841.3
Land Area (sq. mi.)	841.1
Altitude (ft.)	2,665–3,400
Rainfall (in.)	13.09
Jan. mean min.	28.9
July mean max.	96.9
Civ. Labor	3,975
Unemployed	2.9
Wages	$55,351,674
Per Capita Income	$42,940
Prop. Value	$1,373,334,109
Retail Sales	$69,463,506

Wise County

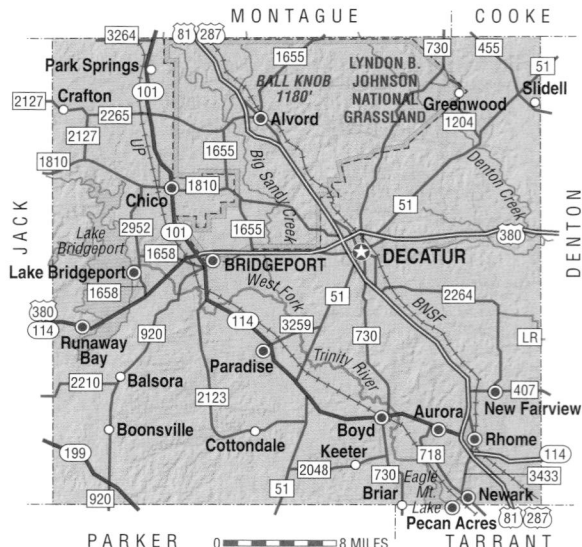

Physical Features: Northwest county of rolling prairie, some oaks; clay, loam, sandy soils; Lake Bridgeport, Eagle Mountain Lake.

Economy: Petroleum, sand and gravel, agribusiness, many residents work in Fort Worth.

History: Caddo Indian groups. Delaware tribe present when Anglo-Americans arrived in the 1850s. County created in 1856 from Cooke County, organized the same year; named for Virginian, U.S. Sen. Henry A. Wise, who favored annexation of Texas.

Race/Ethnicity: (In percent) Anglo, 76.5; Black, 1.7; Hispanic, 19.5; Asian, 0.6; Other, 1.2; Two or more races, 1.7.

Vital Statistics, annual: Births, 837; deaths, 554; marriages, 466; divorces, 327.

Recreation: Lake activities, hunting, exotic deer preserve, historical sites, Lyndon B. Johnson National Grassland, heritage museum; Decatur Chisholm trail days in June, Bridgeport Butterfield stage days in July.

Minerals: Gas, oil, sand, gravel.

Agriculture: Beef cattle, hay, dairies, horses, wheat, goats. Market value $49.9 million.

DECATUR (6,824) county seat; petroleum center, dairying, cattle marketing, some manufacturing; hospital.

BRIDGEPORT (6,533) trade center for lake resort, oil and gas production, manufacturing, prison release facility; time-share housing, art community.

Other towns include: **Alvord** (1,471); **Aurora** (1,383) sand and gravel, manufacturing, equestrian center, "alien crash" site; **Boyd** (1,395) chili cookoff in May; **Briar** (6,116, mostly in Tarrant County); **Chico** (1,105); **Greenwood** (76); **Lake Bridgeport** (366); **Newark** (1,126); **New Fairview** (1,408); **Paradise** (498); **Pecan Acres** (4,480, partly in Tarrant County); **Rhome** (1,712); **Runaway Bay** (1,519) tourism, fishing, boating, golf club, Firecracker Scramble in July; **Slidell** (175).

Population	**68,305**
Change fm 2010	15.6
Area (sq. mi.)	922.6
Land Area (sq. mi.)	904.4
Altitude (ft.)	649–1,180
Rainfall (in.)	34.71
Jan. mean min.	29.7
July mean max.	94.2
Civ. Labor	30,758
Unemployed	3.2
Wages	$244,681,519
Per Capita Income	$41,321
Prop. Value	$9,210,358,366
Retail Sales	$703,954,333

For explanation of sources, symbols and abbreviations, see p. 192, and foldout map.

Lake Bridgeport at Runaway Bay, Wise County. Photo by Robert Plocheck.

Wood County

Physical Features: Hilly northeastern county almost half forested; sandy to alluvial soils; drained by Sabine and tributaries; Lake Fork Reservoir, Lake Quitman, Lake Winnsboro, Lake Hawkins, Holbrook Lake.

Economy: Agribusiness, oil, gas, tourism.

History: Caddo Indians, reduced by disease. Anglo-American settlement developed in the 1840s. County created from Van Zandt County in 1850, organized the same year; named for Gov. George T. Wood.

Race/Ethnicity: (In percent) Anglo, 82.4; Black, 5.4; Hispanic, 10.1; Asian, 0.6; Other, 1.2; Two or more races, 1.4.

Vital Statistics, annual: Births, 417; deaths, 613; marriages, 243; divorces, 131.

Recreation: Autumn trails; lake activities; hunting, fishing, birding; Gov. Hogg shrine and museum; historic sites; scenic drives; Mineola depot.

Minerals: Gas, oil, sand, gravel.

Agriculture: Cattle, dairies, poultry, forages, vegetables, nurseries. Market value $105.9 million. Timber production significant.

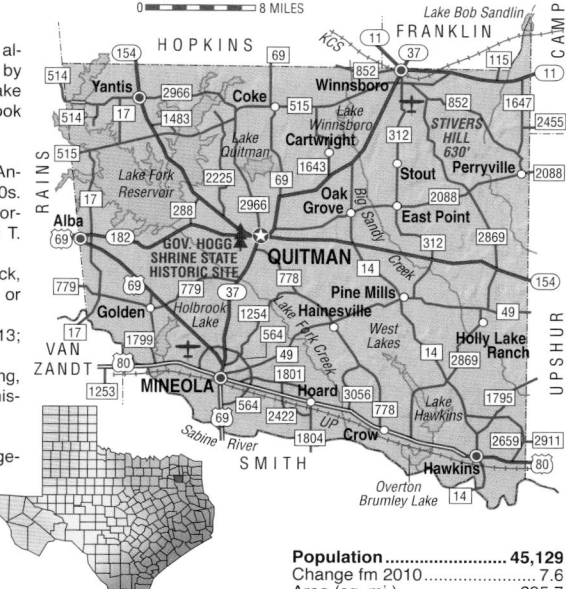

QUITMAN (1,806) county seat; tourism, food processing, some manufacturing; hospital; botanical gardens; Dogwood Fiesta.

MINEOLA (4,795) agriculture, railroad center (Amtrak), oil and gas, heritage and nature tourism; museum, library; nature preserve; Ironhorse Festival in November.

Winnsboro (3,402, partly in Franklin County) poultry production, dairies, distribution, prison; hospital.

Other towns include: **Alba** (545, partly in Rains County); **Golden** (398) Sweet Potato festival in October; **Hawkins** (1,343) petroleum, water bottling, Jarvis Christian College; oil festival in October; **Holly Lake Ranch** (2,762); **Yantis** (402).

Population	**45,129**
Change fm 2010	7.6
Area (sq. mi.)	695.7
Land Area (sq. mi.)	645.2
Altitude (ft.)	270–630
Rainfall (in.)	43.02
Jan. mean min.	32.5
July mean max.	94.4
Civ. Labor	17,456
Unemployed	4.1
Wages	$93,782,719
Per Capita Income	$37,426
Prop. Value	$3,933,834,141
Retail Sales	$448,601,817

Yoakum County

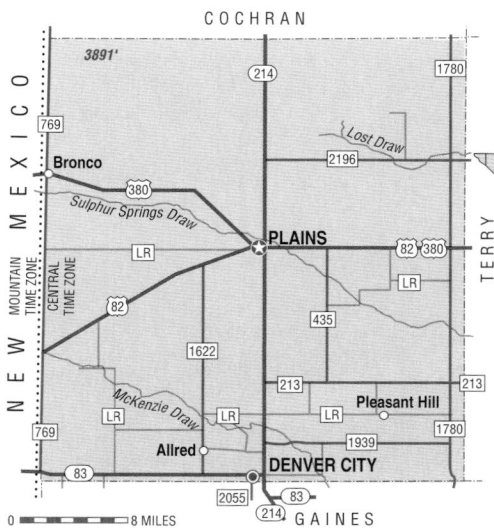

Physical Features: Western county is level to rolling; playas, draws; sandy, loam, chocolate soils.

Economy: Oil and gas, agriculture.

History: Comanche hunting area. Anglo-Americans began ranching in the 1890s. Oil discovered in 1936. Mexican migration increased in the 1950s. County named for Henderson Yoakum, pioneer historian; created from Bexar District in 1876; organized in 1907.

Race/Ethnicity: (In percent) Anglo, 30.9; Black, 1.4; Hispanic, 66.6; Asian, 0.6; Other, 1.8; Two or more races, 1.2.

Vital Statistics, annual: Births, 162; deaths, 63; marriages, 48; divorces, 15.

Recreation: Tsa Mo Ga museum at Plains; Plains watermelon roundup on Labor Day weekend.

Minerals: Oil, natural gas.

Agriculture: Cotton, peanuts (third in acreage), sorghum, wheat, watermelons, cattle. Some 90,000 acres irrigated. Market value $80 million.

PLAINS (1,628) county seat; oil, agribusiness center.

DENVER CITY (5,062) center for oil, agriculture activities in two counties; hospital/medical services, library, museum; Annie Armstrong dugout shelter.

Population	8,591
Change fm 2010	9.0
Area (sq. mi.)	799.7
Land Area (sq. mi.)	799.7
Altitude (ft.)	3,400–3,891
Rainfall (in.)	18.20
Jan. mean min.	25.7
July mean max.	91.7
Civ. Labor	3,577
Unemployed	2.8
Wages	$51,286,379
Per Capita Income	$39,807
Prop. Value	$2,320,334,162
Retail Sales	$79,026,565

Young County

Physical Features: Hilly, broken; drained by Brazos and tributaries; Possum Kingdom Lake, Lake Graham.

Economy: Oil, agribusiness, tourism, hunting leases.

History: U.S. military outpost established in 1851. Site of Brazos Indian Reservation from 1854–1859 with Caddoes, Wacos, and other tribes. Anglo-American settlers arrived in the 1850s. County named for early Texan, Col. W.C. Young; created from Bosque and Fannin counties, and organized in 1856; reorganized in 1874.

Race/Ethnicity: (In percent) Anglo, 77.8; Black, 1.5; Hispanic, 18.9; Asian, 0.6; Other, 1.3; Two or more races, 1.4.

Vital Statistics, annual: Births, 215; deaths, 239; marriages, 133; divorces, 42.

Recreation: Lake activities; hunting; Fort Belknap; marker at oak tree in Graham where ranchers formed forerunner of Texas and Southwestern Cattle Raisers Association.

Minerals: Oil, gas, sand, and gravel.

Agriculture: Beef cattle; wheat is the chief crop, also hay, cotton, pecans, nursery plants. Market value $23.7 million.

GRAHAM (9,054) county seat; oil and gas production, agriculture, tourism, government/services; hospital; old post office museum and art center; Western heritage days in September.

Other towns include: **Loving** (300);

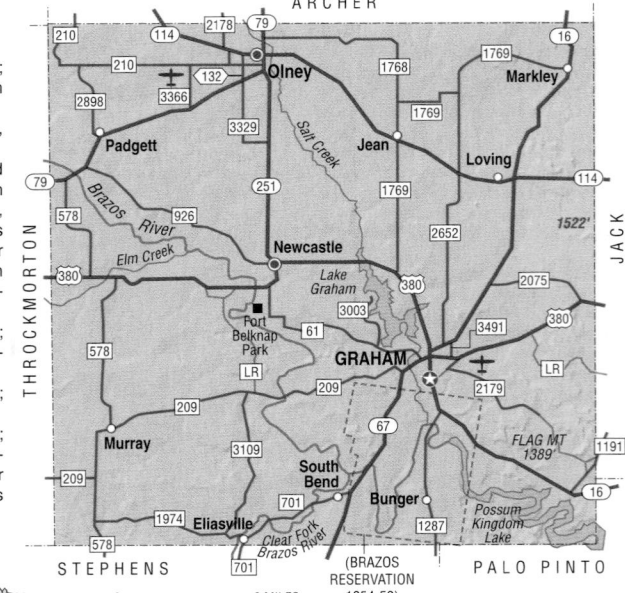

Newcastle (568) old coal-mining town; **Olney** (3,296) aluminum, varied manufacturing, hospital; One-Arm Dove Hunt in September; **South Bend** (100).

For explanation of sources, symbols and abbreviations, see p. 192, and foldout map.

Population	**18,045**
Change fm 2010	– 2.7
Area (sq. mi.)	930.9
Land Area (sq. mi.)	914.5
Altitude (ft.)	995–1,522
Rainfall (in.)	31.51
Jan. mean min.	28.3
July mean max.	96.2
Civ. Labor	8,049
Unemployed	3.1
Wages	$72,357,433
Per Capita Income	$45,405
Prop. Value	$2,000,046,316
Retail Sales	$263,566,000

The Rio Grande with Mexico on the right, Zapata County on the left. Photo by Robert Plocheck.

Zapata County

Physical Features: South Texas county of rolling, brushy topography; broken by tributaries of Rio Grande; Falcon Reservoir.

Economy: Natural gas and oil production and services, banking, tourism/Falcon Reservoir activities.

History: Coahuiltecan Indians in area when the ranch settlement of Nuestra Señora de los Dolores was established in 1750. Anglo-American migration increased after 1980. County named for Col. Antonio Zapata, pioneer rancher; created and organized in 1858 from Starr, Webb counties.

Race/Ethnicity: (In percent) Anglo, 4.9; Black, 0.4; Hispanic, 94.4; Asian, 0.3; Other, 0.5; Two or more races, 0.3.

Vital Statistics, annual: Births, 270; deaths, 85; marriages, 0; divorces, 2.

Recreation: Lake, state park, hunting, fishing, bird watching, golfing, Dolores Hacienda site, rock hunting.

Minerals: Natural gas, caliche.

Agriculture: Beef cattle, sorghum, meat goats. Market value $11.8 million. Hunting/wildlife leases important.

ZAPATA (4,977) county seat; tourism, agribusiness, oil, retirement center; clinic; fajita cook-off in November.

Other towns include: **Falcon** (186); **Lopeño** (184); **Medina** (4,308), and **San Ygnacio** (637) historic buildings, museum.

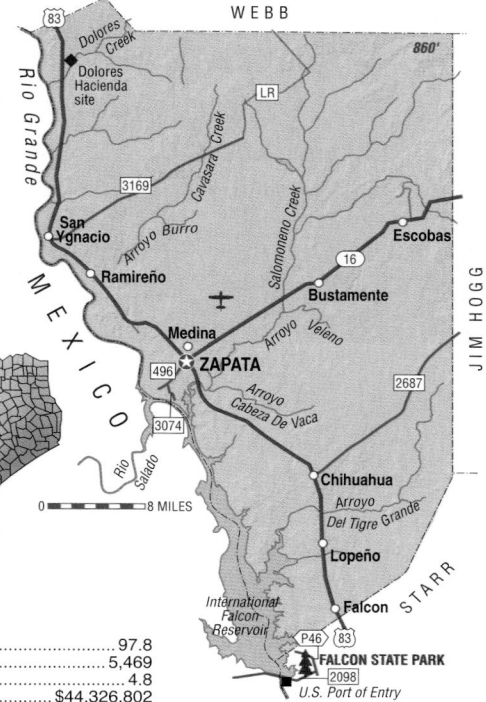

For explanation of sources, symbols and abbreviations, see p. 192, and foldout map.

Population	14,190
Change fm 2010	1.2
Area (sq. mi.)	1,058.0
Land Area (sq. mi.)	998.4
Altitude (ft.)	301–860
Rainfall (in.)	19.77
Jan. mean min.	46.3
July mean max.	97.8
Civ. Labor	5,469
Unemployed	4.8
Wages	$44,326,802
Per Capita INcome	$27,325
Prop. Value	$1,782,019,062
Retail Sales	$61,642,883

Zavala County

Physical Features: Southwestern county near Mexican border; rolling plains broken by much brush; Nueces, Leona, other streams; Upper Nueces Reservoir.

Economy: Agribusiness, food packaging, leading county in Winter Garden truck-farming area, government/services.

History: Coahuiltecan area; Apaches, Comanches arrived later. Ranching developed in the late 1860s. County created from Maverick and Uvalde counties in 1858; organized in 1884; named for Texas Revolutionary leader Lorenzo de Zavala.

Race/Ethnicity: (In percent) Anglo, 5.1; Black, 1.2; Hispanic, 93.9; Asian, 0.2; Other, 1.2; Two or more races, 0.7.

Vital Statistics, annual: Births, 195; deaths, 111; marriages, 40; divorces, 4.

Recreation: Hunting, fishing; spinach festival in November.

Minerals: Oil, natural gas.

Agriculture: Cattle, grains, vegetables, cotton, pecans. About 30,000 acres irrigated. Market value $72.7 million. Hunting leases important.

CRYSTAL CITY (7,261) county seat; agribusiness, food processing, oil-field services; site of World War II detention center. Home of Popeye statue.

Other towns include: **Batesville** (1,039) and **La Pryor** (1,710).

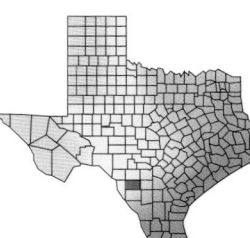

Population	11,983
Change fm 2010	2.6
Area (sq. mi.)	1,301.7
Land Area (sq. mi.)	1,297.4
Altitude (ft.)	540–956
Rainfall (in.)	19.58
Jan. mean min.	43.6
July mean max.	97.2
Civ. Labor	3,604
Unemployed	8.9
Wages	$22,127,655
Per Capita Income	$27,695
Prop. Value	$2,407,489,446
Retail Sales	$52,805,271

The Great Texas Land Rush

Stake your claim!

It seems unbelievable, but the **Great Texas Land Rush** has been active since 2011, and today it is stronger than ever! Funds raised through the Land Rush program are used to support the creation of each new edition of the Texas Almanac and improve our web presence at TexasAlmanac.com.

We'd like to extend a big ***Thank You!*** to our current adopters, listed below.

Ackerly, adopted by Merle Dickerson

Agua Dulce, adopted by AromaCP Fairie Mad Hatter

Alexander, adopted by Neil Green & Family

Anahuac, adopted by Kenneth Wayne Jones

Annie, adopted by Peter Leonard

Aransas Pass, adopted by Marie Halff

Argyle, adopted by Kay Teer

Arlington, adopted by Floreen Henry & Family

Austin, adopted by Austin Faith LaPorte

Bacon, adopted by Edward & Cherie Perez

Bartlett, adopted by John Poe, Jr.

Bastrop, adopted by Barbara Cederholm Stooksberry

Beeville, adopted by B&L Water Well Drilling

Belcherville, adopted by DeeDee & Harvey

Big Spring, adopted by Buddy Barnes

Birdville, adopted by Pam Musgrove-Burnett (Fort Worthy History)

Borger, adopted by Robert and Laura Garrett

Brad, adopted by Krista Fowles

Brileytown, adopted by Jena L. Briley

Brownsville, adopted by Thomas M Harris son of Joseph Foraker Harris

Buda, adopted by Thomas and Sandra Hughes

Byers, adopted by TFRBronzes

Castolon, adopted by Jason, Zach, Katie and Jaden

Castroville, adopted by Mary C. Mechler

Clardy, adopted by Kathy Ehmann-Clardy

Clay County, adopted by TFR Bronzes

College Station, adopted by Brents Family

Colton, adopted by Colton Kincaid

Cool, adopted by Katie Moore

Corpus Christi, adopted by Brian Miller

Corsicana, adopted by Shauna

Creedmoor, adopted by Jeani Smith

Cuero, adopted by Edward & Cherie Perez

Dale, adopted by Emilie Jones Siarkiewicz

Dan, adopted by Dan Tellman

Dayton, adopted by Caroline Wadzeck

Derby, adopted by William Lee Bennett

East River, adopted by Adele Dodd

Eastland, adopted by Rusty Williams, Author,

Emille, adopted by CALLIE Young

Erwin, adopted by Krista Fowles

Fairview, adopted by Mart and Minnie Crownover Descendents

Fedor, adopted by Photography by Jeremy Clifton

Fischer, adopted by Bryan H. Weidner

Fort Davis, adopted by Randy P. Parker

Fort Hood, adopted by Lane Abner Johnston

Fort Houston, adopted by Kim Ferrel Keehn

Fort Oldham, adopted by J's Wills and Testaments

Fort Worth, adopted by Floreen Henry & Family

Fredericksburg, adopted by Liebeskind, A Children's Boutique

Gainesville, adopted by Krista Fowles

Gillespie County, adopted by Friends of Gillespie County Country Schools, Inc. (https://historicschools.org)

Gladewater, adopted by The Gladewater Mirror Newspaper

Grapevine, adopted by M.E. and Barbara Musgrove

Grayrock, adopted by Mickey M. Sparkman

Greenville, adopted by Walt Hinton

Grigsby's Bluff, adopted by Glenda G

Hardin, adopted by The Hardin & Rangel Bunch

Harrold, adopted by Mindee Thweatt

Hatchton, adopted by Michael Carter

Helotes, adopted by Edna Marnock Smith

Hermleigh, adopted by Claire Cambell Stout

Hidalgo County, adopted by Misti Palacios

Hilbigville, adopted by Bill Hilbig

Houston, adopted by The Hughes Family

Houston Heights, adopted by Harley Grace LaPorte

Hughlett, adopted by Mart and Minnie Crownover Descendents

Ibex, adopted by Melinda Musselman

Indian Gap, adopted by Suzanne Culp

Irving, adopted by Linda Harper-Brown

Jim Town, adopted by Jim Werley

Jot-Em-Down, adopted by Black Ranches

Kamey, adopted by McKamey Bros

Kay, adopted by Kay Day

Keller, adopted by Robert Frank Keller

Kelley, adopted by Kelley Miller

Kemp, adopted by Annie Payne Epley

Killeen, adopted by Marvin Olier

Kleberg, adopted by Krista Fowles

Kyle, adopted by Kathleen Bergeron

La Porte, adopted by Georgia Malone

Lampasas, adopted by Carolyn Carter Malcolm Schiewe

Levelland, adopted by Troy Curl

Lindale, adopted by Lindale News & Times/Jim & Suzanne Bardwell

Lone Oak, adopted by Walt Hinton

Longview, adopted by Jim and Suzanne Bardwell

Luckenbach, adopted by Kathleen Bergeron

Marshall, adopted by Leigh Anne Rives Crowell

Matagorda, adopted by Georganna Triplett

Matthews, adopted by Linda Hulsey

Mcgregor, adopted by The Leslie Family

Melvin, adopted by Susan & Greg Reno

Minera, adopted by Judge Oscar Liendo

Morris County, adopted by Krista Fowles

Mound, adopted by Jim Mosier & Laura Clayton Mosier

Mountain Peak, adopted by Marilyn and Larry Jones

Neola, adopted by Karan Callaway

New Braunfels, adopted by Gina Perryman

New London, adopted by KLLS

North Waco, adopted by Michael Bauer

North Zulch, adopted by Lena Denman

Odessa, adopted by Jane, Eileen & Joe Suggs, Jr.

Oenaville, adopted by Richard and Cathy Dexter

Oxien, adopted by Diane McBurney Ferguson

Pampa, adopted by Tony Lyle

Parks Camp, adopted by Jan Hart

Patricia, adopted by Peter Leonard

Pendleton, adopted by A Pinky Promise

Perryman's Crossing, adopted by Gina Perryman

Pickton, adopted by Rose Brown Bryant

Pittsburg, adopted by John R. Pitts, Jr.

Poetry, adopted by Blake Balsley

Port Neches, adopted by Glenda G

Porvenir, adopted by Amanda Shields

Postoak, adopted by Xan Alexander

Reilly Springs, adopted by J. David Bowie

Rockdale, adopted by Joy Kornegay

Rosenfeld, adopted by Michael Rosenfeld

Salome, adopted by Eddie and Penelope Hernandez

San Antonio, adopted by His Eminence Archbishop Ray Gonia, ECLJ

San Felipe Del Rio, adopted by Andy Porras

San Gabriel, adopted by Darrell and Karen Burris

San Leon, adopted by FNG Images

San Ygnacio, adopted by GeorgiAnne Uribe Brochstein

Sandy Elm, adopted by Teddy and Gay Lynn Olsovsky

Schertz, adopted by Sandy McBride & Tina Schimonsky

Seagoville, adopted by Krista Fowles

Shallowater, adopted by Ruth Livingston

Star, adopted by John Poe, Jr.

Tennessee Valley, adopted by Emily Shaw

Trinity County, adopted by Frances B. Vick

Turkey, adopted by Ruth Livingston

Uncertain, adopted by Katy Waddell

Vinegarroon, adopted by Vinegaroon Table Hot Sauce

Waller, adopted by The McCaig Family

Waring, adopted by Lacey O‚Äôdelle

Washburn, adopted by Jan Hart

Webster, adopted by Sue Craddock Hamm

Whitewright, adopted by Molly Malinda M. Reed

Winfield, adopted by Mickey M. Sparkman

Wolfforth, adopted by Ruth Livingston

Woodal, adopted by Taylor Kanipe

Yorktown, adopted by Russell I. Alley 2nd (Cpt. John York)

Youngsport, adopted by Bill R. Shelton

Never heard of the Great Texas Land Rush?

Head over to **GreatTexasLandRush.com**, where you can adopt the Texas town or county of your choice. Adopters recieve an official adoption certificate and their names appear on their town's (or county's) page on TexasAlmanac.com.

We have thousands of towns and more than 200 counties still available for adoption. **Stake your claim today!**

POPULATION

Music fans crowding 6th Street in Austin during SXSW.
Photo by MACH Photos/Shutterstock.

**TEXAS POPULATION: STILL GROWING & BECOMING
INCREASINGLY DIVERSE**

U.S. CENSUS OF TOWNS

CENTER OF POPULATION BY DECADES

Texas Population: Still Growing and Becoming Increasingly Diverse

By Steve Murdock and Mike Cline

The population of Texas

has increased during every decade since Texas became a state, with recent population growth exceeding that of all other states in the nation (**Table 1**). In 1950 the Texas population was the sixth largest in the United States, but by the last decennial census count on April 1, 2010, at 25.1 million people, Texas's population was the second largest in the nation behind California (**Figure 1**).

Table 1: Total Population Change in Texas and the U.S., 1850–2010

Year	Total Population		Percent Change	
	Texas	U.S.	Texas	U.S.
1850	212,592	23,191,876	—	—
1860	604,215	31,443,321	184.2%	35.6%
1870	818,579	39,818,449	35.5%	26.6%
1880	1,591,749	50,155,783	94.5%	26.0%
1890	2,235,527	62,947,714	40.4%	25.5%
1900	3,048,710	75,994,575	36.4%	20.7%
1910	3,896,542	91,972,266	27.8%	21.0%
1920	4,663,228	105,710,620	19.7%	14.9%
1930	5,824,715	122,775,046	24.9%	16.1%
1940	6,414,824	131,669,275	10.1%	7.2%
1950	7,711,194	150,697,361	20.2%	14.5%
1960	9,579,677	179,323,175	24.2%	19.0%
1970	11,196,730	203,302,031	16.9%	13.4%
1980	14,229,191	226,545,805	27.1%	11.4%
1990	16,986,510	248,709,873	19.4%	9.8%
2000	20,851,820	281,421,906	22.8%	13.2%
2010	25,145,561	308,745,538	20.6%	9.7%

Source: Derived from the U.S. Census Bureau decennial census April 1 of reported year.

Figure 1: Five Largest States in the U.S. in 2018

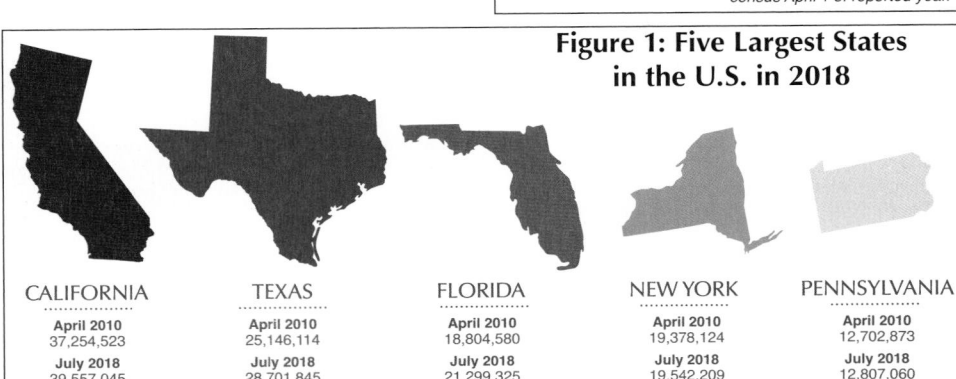

CALIFORNIA	TEXAS	FLORIDA	NEW YORK	PENNSYLVANIA
April 2010 37,254,523	**April 2010** 25,146,114	**April 2010** 18,804,580	**April 2010** 19,378,124	**April 2010** 12,702,873
July 2018 39,557,045	**July 2018** 28,701,845	**July 2018** 21,299,325	**July 2018** 19,542,209	**July 2018** 12,807,060
Change 6.2%	**Change** 14.1%	**Change** 13.3%	**Change** 0.8%	**Change** 0.8%

Note: April 1, 2010 estimate base includes adjustments.

Source: U.S. Census Bureau, Population Estimates, Vintage 2018.

Two Decades of Dominant Growth in Texas

Between 2000 and 2010, Texas' population increase of nearly 4.3 million was larger than that in all other states (**Table 2**) and its percentage growth of 20.6 percent exceeded that in all but four other states with much smaller populations:

- Nevada, which increased by 35.1 percent to 2.7 million in 2010;
- Arizona, which increased by 24.6 percent to 6.4 million in 2010;
- Utah, which increased by 23.8 percent to 2.8 million in 2010; and
- Idaho, which increased by 21.1 percent to 1.6 million in 2010.

According to the 2018 population estimates provided by the U.S. Census Bureau, Texas has, once again, added more people than all other states (an increase of 3.6 million people), and its percentage growth of 14.1 percent was surpassed by only Utah (which grew by 14.4 percent to an estimated 3.2 million by 2018). By July 1, 2018, there were an estimated 28.7 million people living in Texas.

Table 2: Ten States in the U.S. with the Largest Percentage Increase 2000–2010			Change, 2000–2010	
Geographical Area	April 1, 2000 Population	April 1, 2010 Population	Number	%
United States	281,421,906	308,745,538	27,323,632	9.7%
Nevada	1,998,257	2,700,551	702,294	35.1%
Arizona	5,130,632	6,392,017	1,261,385	24.6%
Utah	2,233,169	2,763,885	530,716	23.8%
Idaho	1,293,953	1,567,582	273,629	21.1%
Texas	20,851,820	25,145,561	4,293,741	20.6%
North Carolina	8,049,313	9,535,483	1,486,170	18.5%
Georgia	8,186,453	9,687,653	1,501,200	18.3%
Florida	15,982,378	18,801,310	2,818,932	17.6%
Colorado	4,301,261	5,029,196	727,935	16.9%
South Carolina	4,012,012	4,625,364	613,352	15.3%

Source: U.S. Census Bureau.

Growth in the Texas Triangle and Permian Basin

While the state has experienced substantial growth over the last few decades, that growth has not been equally distributed throughout the state. Over the course of the 20th century and into the 21st, population growth has occurred primarily in the largest cities and their surrounding counties – particularly in an area commonly called the Texas Triangle (the areas along the I-45, I-35 and I-10 corridors between Houston, Dallas-Ft. Worth, and San Antonio).

As you can see in **Table 3**, Texas' most populated county, Harris County, increased by an estimated 605,431 people from 2010 to 2018, followed by Tarrant County (with a population increase of 274,276 people), Bexar County (with an increase of 271,277 people), Dallas County (growth of 271,089 people), and Travis County (an increase of 224,281). In addition, in the most recent period, counties in the Permian Basin and parts of South Texas experienced resurgent population growth as a result of oil and gas development (**Figure 2**).

But not all county populations are growing. Between 2010 and 2018, 94 counties in Texas lost population, more than the 79 counties that lost population between 2000 and 2010. Many of these counties are located in the Rolling Plains and Panhandle regions of Texas – traditional farming and ranching areas distant from larger urban conglomerations. The population in Texas has become increasingly urban.

Largest Rural Population in the Country – But Most Texans Live in Metro Areas

At 3.8 million people in 2010, there were more people living in rural areas in Texas than in any other state in the nation. Fifty-eight counties, or 22.8 percent of Texas' 254 counties, had all of their population living in rural areas — on farms and ranches or in communities of fewer than 2,500 people. Another 78 counties (or 30.7 percent) had at least 50 percent of their population living in rural areas in 2010, while for the remaining 118 counties (or 46.5 percent) the majority of the population was living in urban areas.

Although Texas has a large rural population, the majority of Texans live in urban areas (or metropolitan statistical areas). In 2010, 84.7 percent of the Texas population lived in urban areas, and 75.4 percent lived in urban areas with 50,000 or more people.

Texas includes six of the 25 largest cities in the country including Houston (ranked fourth at 2.3 million people), San Antonio (ranked seventh at 1.5 million people), and Dallas (ranked ninth at 1.3 million people). Austin's population is just below 1 million people (at 964,000). At current rates of growth, Austin is expected to have more than 1 million people living within the city by 2020.

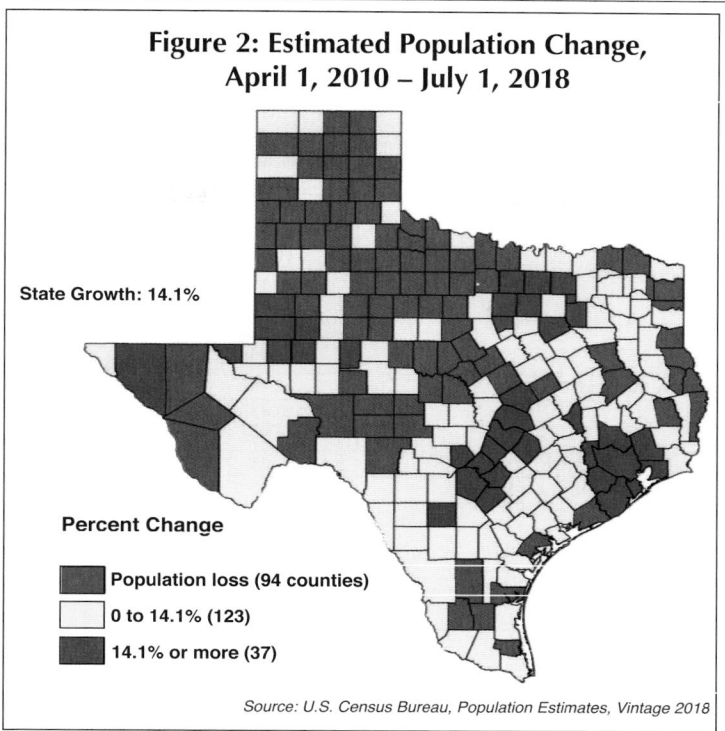

Figure 2: Estimated Population Change, April 1, 2010 – July 1, 2018

State Growth: 14.1%

Percent Change

■ Population loss (94 counties)

□ 0 to 14.1% (123)

■ 14.1% or more (37)

Source: U.S. Census Bureau, Population Estimates, Vintage 2018

Table 3: Population and Population Change for the Twenty Largest Counties in Texas in 2018

County	Population Estimates			Change 2000–2010		Change 2010–2018	
	2000	2010	2018	Number	Percent	Number	Percent
State of Texas	20,851,028	25,146,114	28,701,845	4,295,086	20.6%	3,555,731	14.1%
Harris	3,401,139	4,093,188	4,698,619	692,049	20.3%	605,431	14.8%
Dallas	2,216,808	2,366,683	2,637,772	149,875	6.8%	271,089	11.5%
Tarrant	1,449,290	1,810,655	2,084,931	361,365	24.9%	274,276	15.1%
Bexar	1,393,035	1,714,772	1,986,049	321,737	23.1%	271,277	15.8%
Travis	811,776	1,024,462	1,248,743	212,686	26.2%	224,281	21.9%
Collin	491,272	782,220	1,005,146	290,948	59.2%	222,926	28.5%
Hidalgo	569,099	774,768	865,939	205,669	36.1%	91,171	11.8%
Denton	433,065	662,554	859,064	229,489	53.0%	196,510	29.7%
El Paso	679,568	800,653	840,758	121,085	17.8%	40,105	5.0%
Fort Bend	354,286	584,690	787,858	230,404	65.0%	203,168	34.7%
Montgomery	293,779	455,750	590,925	161,971	55.1%	135,175	29.7%
Williamson	250,466	422,501	566,719	172,035	68.7%	144,218	34.1%
Cameron	334,884	406,215	423,908	71,331	21.3%	17,693	4.4%
Brazoria	241,805	313,123	370,200	71,318	29.5%	57,077	18.2%
Nueces	313,512	340,223	362,265	26,711	8.5%	22,042	6.5%
Bell	238,000	310,159	355,642	72,159	30.3%	45,483	14.7%
Galveston	250,178	291,307	337,890	41,129	16.4%	46,583	16.0%
Lubbock	242,644	278,918	307,412	36,274	14.9%	28,494	10.2%
Webb	193,124	250,304	275,910	57,180	29.6%	25,606	10.2%
Jefferson	251,968	252,277	255,001	309	0.1%	2,724	1.1%

Note: Population estimates are from April 1, 2000, April 1, 2010, and July 1, 2018. Time elapsed between April 1, 2010 to July 1, 2018 is 99 months. April 1, 2010 estimate base includes adjustments.

Source: U.S. Census Bureau, Population Estimates, Vintage 2018 and 2000-2010 Intercensal Estimates.
Prepared by the Hobby Center for the Study of Texas at Rice University.

Table 4: Twenty Metropolitan Areas with the Largest Percentage Population Change, 2010–2018

Metropolitan Statistical Area	Population 2010	Population 2018	Change, 2010–2018 Number	Change, 2010–2018 Percent
The Villages, FL	93,420	128,754	35,334	37.8%
Myrtle Beach-Conway-North Myrtle Beach, SC-NC	376,555	480,891	104,336	27.7%
Austin-Round Rock,TX	1,716,321	2,168,316	451,995	26.3%
Midland, TX	141,671	178,331	36,660	25.9%
St. George, UT	138,115	171,700	33,585	24.3%
Greeley, CO	252,847	314,305	61,458	24.3%
Cape Coral-Fort Myers, FL	618,754	754,610	135,856	22.0%
Bend-Redmond, OR	157,730	191,996	34,266	21.7%
Orlando-Kissimmee-Sanford, FL	2,134,402	2,572,962	438,560	20.5%
Raleigh, NC	1,130,488	1,362,540	232,052	20.5%
Provo-Orem, UT	526,885	633,768	106,883	20.3%
Daphne-Fairhope-Foley, AL	182,264	218,022	35,758	19.6%
Fayetteville-Springdale-Rogers, AR-MO	463,202	549,128	85,926	18.6%
Charleston-North Charleston, SC	664,639	787,643	123,004	18.5%
Boise, ID	616,566	730,426	113,860	18.5%
Odessa, TX	137,136	162,124	24,988	18.2%
Houston-The Woodlands-Sugar Land, TX	5,920,487	6,997,384	1,076,897	18.2%
Crestview-Fort Walton Beach-Destin, FL	235,868	278,644	42,776	18.1%
Naples-Immokalee-Marco Island, FL	321,521	378,488	56,967	17.7%
Lakeland-Winter Haven, FL	602,098	708,009	105,911	17.6%

Note: Time elapsed between April 1, 2010 to July 1, 2018 is 99 months.

Source: U.S. Census Bureau, Population Estimates, Vintage 2018.

Table 5: Twenty Metropolitan Areas with the Largest Numeric Population Change, 2010–2018

Metropolitan Statistical Area	Population 2010	Population 2018	Change 2010–2018 Number	Change 2010–2018 Percent
Dallas-Fort Worth-Arlington,TX	6,426,222	7,539,711	1,113,489	17.3%
Houston-The Woodlands-Sugar Land, TX	5,920,487	6,997,384	1,076,897	18.2%
Phoenix-Mesa-Scottsdale, AZ	4,193,127	4,857,962	664,835	15.9%
Atlanta-Sandy Springs-Roswell, GA	5,286,750	5,949,951	663,201	12.5%
Miami-Fort Lauderdale-West Palm Beach, FL	5,566,294	6,198,782	632,488	11.4%
Washington-Arlington-Alexandria, DC-VA-MD-WV	5,636,363	6,249,950	613,587	10.9%
Seattle-Tacoma-Bellevue, WA	3,439,805	3,939,363	499,558	14.5%
Los Angeles-Long Beach-Anaheim, CA	12,828,946	13,291,486	462,540	3.6%
Austin-Round Rock, TX	1,716,321	2,168,316	451,995	26.3%
Orlando-Kissimmee-Sanford, FL	2,134,402	2,572,962	438,560	20.5%
New York-Newark-Jersey City, NY-NJ-PA	19,566,527	19,979,477	412,950	2.1%
Riverside-San Bernardino-Ontario,CA	4,224,966	4,622,361	397,395	9.4%
San Francisco-Oakland-Hayward, CA	4,335,587	4,729,484	393,897	9.1%
Denver-Aurora-Lakewood, CO	2,543,602	2,932,415	388,813	15.3%
San Antonio-New Braunfels, TX	2,142,521	2,518,036	375,515	17.5%
Tampa-St. Petersburg-Clearwater, FL	2,783,462	3,142,663	359,201	12.9%
Charlotte-Concord-Gastonia, NC-SC	2,216,997	2,569,213	352,216	15.9%
Boston-Cambridge-Newton, MA-NH	4,552,598	4,875,390	322,792	7.1%
Las Vegas-Henderson-Paradise, NV	1,951,271	2,231,647	280,376	14.4%
Minneapolis-St. Paul-Bloomington, MN-WI	3,348,862	3,629,190	280,328	8.4%

Note: Time elapsed between April 1, 2010 to July 1, 2018 is 99 months.

Source: U.S. Census Bureau, Population Estimates, Vintage 2018.

Texas Metropolitan Areas Growing Faster Than Others in the Nation

The Dallas-Ft. Worth-Arlington Metropolitan Statistical Area (MSA) and the Houston-The Woodlands-Sugar Land MSA, ranked the fourth and fifth largest MSAs in the country, each added more than 1 million people between 2010 and 2018 — more than were added in the three largest MSAs in the nation combined.

But growth has not just occurred in Texas' largest urban conglomerations. An examination of MSAs relative to their numerical and percentage change in population from 2010 to 2018 in **Table 4** and **Table 5** indicates that the growth in Texas metropolitan areas is extraordinary.

Four Texas metropolitan areas were ranked among the nation's fastest-growing areas in percentage terms between 2010 and 2018, including Austin-Round Rock, Midland, Odessa, and Houston-The Woodlands-Sugar Land. The Austin-Round Rock MSA, with growth of 451,995 or 26.3 percent from 2010 to 2018, had the third-largest percentage increase in population (behind metropolitan areas less than a quarter its size). The two MSAs located within the Permian Basin, Midland (at 25.9 percent growth) and Odessa (at 18.2 percent growth), were ranked the fourth- and sixteenth-fastest-growing MSAs in percentage terms, respectively. Houston-The Woodlands-Sugar Land was ranked seventeenth-fastest-growing during this period — which is phenomenal given its large size (7.0 million people in 2018).

Texas' two largest metropolitan areas were the only metropolitan areas in the nation to have added more than 1 million people since 2010. The Dallas-Fort Worth-Arlington MSA added 1,113,489 from 2010 to 2018 while the Houston-The Woodlands-Sugar Land metropolitan area increased by 1,076,897. The Austin-Round Rock MSA was ranked ninth in numeric growth with an increase of 451,995 people while the San Antonio-New Braunfels MSA had the fifteenth-largest increase (it added 375,515 people).

According to the U.S. Census Bureau estimates, all other Texas metropolitan areas except Wichita Falls increased in population size during this period (**Table 6**).

Table 6: Population Change in Texas Metropolitan Areas, 2010–2018

Metropolitan Statistical Area	Population 2010	Population 2018	Change, 2010–2018 Number	Change, 2010–2018 Percent
Abilene	165,246	171,451	6,205	3.8%
Amarillo	251,937	265,947	14,010	5.6%
Austin-Round Rock	1,716,321	2,168,316	451,995	26.3%
Beaumont-Port Arthur	403,194	409,526	6,332	1.6%
Brownsville-Harlingen	406,215	423,908	17,693	4.4%
College Station-Bryan	228,668	262,431	33,763	14.8%
Corpus Christi	428,183	452,950	24,767	5.8%
Dallas-Fort Worth-Arlington	6,426,222	7,539,711	1,113,489	17.3%
El Paso	804,129	845,553	41,424	5.2%
Houston-The Woodlands-Sugar Land	5,920,487	6,997,384	1,076,897	18.2%
Killeen-Temple	405,313	451,679	46,366	11.4%
Laredo	250,304	275,910	25,606	10.2%
Longview	214,367	219,417	5,050	2.4%
Lubbock	290,889	319,068	28,179	9.7%
McAllen-Edinburg-Mission	774,768	865,939	91,171	11.8%
Midland	141,671	178,331	36,660	25.9%
Odessa	137,136	162,124	24,988	18.2%
San Angelo	111,825	119,711	7,886	7.1%
San Antonio-New Braunfels	2,142,521	2,518,036	375,515	17.5%
Sherman-Denison	120,875	133,991	13,116	10.9%
Texarkana, TX-AR	149,194	150,242	1,048	0.7%
Tyler	209,725	230,221	20,496	9.8%
Victoria	94,003	99,619	5,616	6.0%
Waco	252,766	271,942	19,176	7.6%
Wichita Falls	151,474	151,306	−168	-0.1%

Note: Time elapsed between April 1, 2010 to July 1, 2018 is 99 months.

Source: U.S. Census Bureau, Population Estimates, Vintage 2018.

Future Population Growth and Diversification in Texas

Texas' population growth has been substantial, and, assuming this growth continues into the future, Texas will see increasing demands on public resources. At the same time, this growth bodes well for continued economic development within the state as an increasing population creates more opportunities for businesses and a growing labor force to meet that demand. But change in the characteristics of the population itself can also bring about change in the demand for public resources and business services. Relative to other states, Texas' population is young, but as the baby boom generation enters retirement, a larger aged population will bring about increased demand for medical and other services to meet the changing needs of that aging population.

Demographers prepare population projections in order to assist governments, businesses, and nonprofits in planning for the future. Population grows as a result of natural increase (the excess of births over deaths) or positive net migration (more people moving into an area than moving out).

The Texas Demographic Center's latest population projection, which assumes that recent trends in fertility, mortality, and net migration continue, indicates that Texas' population is likely to grow substantially. In addition to this extraordinary population growth, Texas will continue to experience extensive racial/ethnic diversification and an overall aging of the population.

Under this projection scenario, the Texas population would almost double from 25.1 million people in 2010 to 47.3 million people in 2050 (**Table 7**). In addition, all race/ethnic populations will increase in size. The Non-Hispanic White population is projected to increase by 2.1 million people over the 40 years from 2010 to 2050. Over the same period, the Black population would increase by more than 3.1 million, the

Hispanic population by more than 10.7 million, and the Non-Hispanic Asian population by about 4.8 million.

The analysis shown in Table 7 reveals the impact of diverse patterns of racial/ethnic change. Thus, under this projection, the percentage of the population that is Non-Hispanic White could decrease to 28.6 percent of the total Texas population (from 45.3 percent in 2010), the percentage African-American could increase to 12.7 percent, the percentage Hispanic could increase to 42.7 percent, the percentage Non-Hispanic Asian could increase to 12.2 percent (from 3.8 percent in 2010), and all other groups could account for 3.8 percent of the population by 2050. Under this projection, the Hispanic population will be the largest population in Texas by 2025.

As shown in **Table 8**, Hispanics not only become the largest population group in numerical terms but, because of the extensive growth of the Hispanic population, although it has a younger population structure overall, it would come to account for the largest percentage in every age group but the oldest by 2050. How these changing demographic patterns will interact with other factors is not clear, but it is evident that all age groups will become more racially and ethnically diverse.

The elderly would become increasingly diverse, with Hispanics forming an increasing part of this population. The percentage of the elderly who are Hispanic would double from 2010 to 2050 (from 20.5 to 37.5 percent of the population 65 and older). Only Non-Hispanic Whites will see their representation in this age group decline.

Texas population is aging as well. In 2010, 10.3 percent of the population was age 65 or older, but by 2050 that percentage is projected to increase to 17.6 percent. In 46 counties in 2010, at least one of every five people were age 65 or older. By 2050, under the projections here, in 138 counties (more than half of

Table 7: Population in Texas by Race/Ethnicity in 2010 and Projected Population in Texas by Race/Ethnicity from 2020 to 2050
Assuming Race/Ethnicity-Specific Net Migration Equal to 2000–2015 for the State of Texas

Year	NH[1] White	NH Black	Hispanic	NH Asian	NH Other[2]	Total
Population						
2010	11,397,345	2,886,825	9,460,921	948,426	452,044	25,145,561
2020	12,138,523	3,557,892	11,804,659	1,525,629	651,069	29,677,772
2030	12,774,056	4,322,983	14,452,949	2,414,732	929,709	34,894,429
2040	13,203,514	5,141,963	17,260,820	3,772,125	1,308,068	40,686,490
2050	13,523,839	6,030,795	20,191,750	5,782,908	1,813,125	47,342,417
Percent						
2010	45.3%	11.5%	37.6%	3.8%	1.8%	100.0%
2020	40.9%	12.0%	39.8%	5.1%	2.2%	100.0%
2030	36.6%	12.4%	41.4%	6.9%	2.7%	100.0%
2040	32.5%	12.6%	42.4%	9.3%	3.2%	100.0%
2050	28.6%	12.7%	42.7%	12.2%	3.8%	100.0%

[1]NH refers to Non-Hispanic; values shown are only for the non-Hispanic persons in each race category. Hispanic includes Hispanics of all races.
[2]NH Other category includes non-Hispanic persons who identify themselves as belonging to two or more race groups.
Source: Texas Demographic Center at University of Texas at San Antonio, 2018 Population Projections.

Texas counties) the elderly will become 20 percent or more of the population.

If recent patterns in population growth and diversification continue, Texas will continue to be a leading state in the development of economic opportunities. At the same time, these demographic changes will likely continue to challenge the state in many different ways (such as developing and maintaining transportation infrastructure, developing additional water resources, ensuring that there is enough affordable housing, etc.). In addition, the state will be challenged to provide an array of educational opportunities to ensure that economic growth continues and is shared among all Texans. Its challenges are, at the same time, opportunities that should allow Texas to continue to be a place where opportunities may be developed and fulfilled for members of its relatively young and diverse population.

Table 8: Percent of the Population by Age Group and Race/Ethnicity in 2010 and Projected by Age Group and Race/Ethnicity in 2020 and 2050
Assuming Age and Race/Ethnicity-Specific Net Migration Equal to 2000–2015 for the State of Texas

Age	NH[1] White	NH Black	Hispanic	NH Asian	NH Other[2]	Total
2010						
<18	33.8%	11.8%	48.3%	3.4%	2.7%	100.0%
18–24	38.7%	12.6%	43.2%	3.6%	1.9%	100.0%
25–44	41.5%	11.9%	40.2%	4.8%	1.6%	100.0%
45–64	56.1%	11.5%	27.4%	3.6%	1.4%	100.0%
65–74	66.8%	8.5%	21.0%	2.7%	1.0%	100.0%
85+	73.9%	7.6%	16.4%	1.3%	0.8%	100.0%
2020						
<18	30.8%	11.8%	49.4%	4.6%	3.4%	100.0%
18–24	33.8%	12.7%	45.6%	5.1%	2.8%	100.0%
25–44	37.8%	13.0%	41.1%	6.1%	2.0%	100.0%
45–64	46.9%	12.1%	34.3%	5.3%	1.4%	100.0%
65–74	61.1%	9.7%	24.0%	3.9%	1.3%	100.0%
85+	66.1%	8.1%	22.1%	2.8%	0.9%	100.0%
2050						
<18	22.3%	12.0%	49.3%	10.9%	5.5%	100.0%
18–24	23.9%	12.6%	46.6%	12.0%	4.9%	100.0%
25–44	26.2%	13.3%	42.0%	14.4%	4.1%	100.0%
45–64	31.2%	13.8%	39.5%	12.5%	3.0%	100.0%
65–74	37.2%	11.7%	38.7%	10.5%	1.9%	100.0%
85+	48.4%	10.9%	30.2%	9.0%	1.5%	100.0%

[1] NH refers to Non-Hispanic; values shown are only for the non-Hispanic persons in each race category. Hispanic includes Hispanics of all races.
[2] NH Other category includes non-Hispanic persons who identify themselves as belonging to two or more race groups.
Source: Texas Demographic Center at University of Texas at San Antonio, 2018 Population Projections.

About the Authors

Steve Murdock, Ph.D., is the founding Director of the Hobby Center for the Study of Texas and the Allyn and Gladys Cline Chair in Sociology at Rice University. He is the former Director of the U.S. Census Bureau, the State Demographer of Texas, holder of a Regents Chair at Texas A&M University, the Lutcher Brown Distinguished Chair in Demography and Organization Studies at the University of Texas at San Antonio, and a noted scholar with 14 books and more than 150 articles and analytical reports. He has extensive experience in research on a wide variety of issues impacting Texas and the nation, and is widely known as a national expert in the areas of Demography, Rural Sociology, and Socioeconomic Impact Assessment.

Michael (Mike) Cline, Ph.D, a native of Snyder, currently serves as the State Demographer for the State of North Carolina. Dr. Cline previously served as the Associate Director at the Hobby Center for the Study of Texas, and most of his professional career has involved demographic research to support business planning, nonprofit and government decision making, and academic research in Texas. Dr. Cline has authored or co-authored several books, book chapters, and articles, including: *Population Change in the United States: Socioeconomic Challenges and Opportunities in the Twenty-First Century* and *Changing Texas: Implications of Addressing or Ignoring the Texas Challenge.*

Population 2010 and 2017

Population: Numbers in parentheses are from the 2010 U.S. census. The Census Bureau counts only incorporated cities and a few unincorporated towns called Census Designated Places.

Population figures at the far right for incorporated cities and CDPs are the Texas Demographic Center estimates for Jan. 1, 2017. Names of the incorporated cities are in capital letters, e.g., "ABBOTT".

The population figure given for other towns is an estimate received from local officials through a Texas Almanac survey.

When no 2010 census was conducted for a newly incorporated city, these places show "(nc)" for "not counted" in place of a 2010 population figure.

Location: The county in which the town is located follows the name of the town. If more than one county is listed, the town is principally in the first-named county, e.g., "ABERNATHY, Hale-Lubbock".

Businesses: For incorporated cities, the number following the county name indicates the number of business in the city as of January 2018 as reported by the state comptroller. For unincorporated towns, it is the number of businesses within the postal zip code as reported by the U.S. Bureau of the Census for 2016.

For example, "ABBOTT, Hill, 22" means Abbott in Hill County had 22 businesses.

Post Offices: Places with post offices, as of Nov. 2010, are marked with an asterisk (*), e.g., "*Afton".

Town, County ....Pop. 2017	Town, County ....Pop. 2017	Town, County ....Pop. 2017
*ABBOTT, Hill, 22, (356)..............366	*ALAMO, Hidalgo, 560,	Alto Bonito Heights, Starr, (342)...367
*ABERNATHY, Hale-Lubbock, 95,	(18,353)...........................19,977	Altoga, Collin 137
(2,805)..................................2,779	Alamo Alto, El Paso......................19	*ALTON, Hidalgo, 269,
*ABILENE, Taylor-Jones, 4,121,	Alamo Beach, Calhoun.................100	(12,341)..............................15,878
(117,063)........................122,608	ALAMO HEIGHTS, Bexar, 333,	Alum Creek, Bastrop 70
Ables Springs, Kaufman.................20	(7,031)................................8,088	*ALVARADO, Johnson, 224,
Abner, Kaufman.............................75	*Alanreed, Gray, 1 48	(3,785)..................................4,085
Abram, Hidalgo, (2,067)..........2,337	Alazan, Nacogdoches....................100	*ALVIN, Brazoria, 998,
*ACADEMY [Little River-], Bell, 36,	*ALBA, Wood-Rains, 70, (504).....545	(24,236)..............................27,241
(1,961)..................................2,000	*ALBANY, Shackelford, 123,	*ALVORD, Wise, 58, (1,334).....1,471
Acala, Hudspeth 25	(2,034)..................................2,018	Amada Acres, Starr, (92)...............87
*Ace, Polk, 1 40	Albert, Gillespie, ...25	Amargosa, Jim Wells, (291).........325
*ACKERLY, Dawson-Martin, 16,	Albion, Red River...........................52	*AMARILLO, Potter-Randall,
(220).......................................237	Alderbranch, Anderson....................3	6,780, (190,695)............204,367
Acme, Hardeman..............................7	Aldine, Harris, (15,869)...........17,177	Amaya, Zavala, (93) 88
Acton, Hood...............................1,129	*ALEDO, Parker, 278,	Ambia, Lamar 16
Acuff, Lubbock.............................152	(2,716)................................3,426	Ambrose, Grayson..........................90
Acworth, Red River........................50	Aleman, Hamilton 50	Ames, Coryell 10
Adams Gardens, Cameron...........350	Alexander, Erath 40	AMES, Liberty, 10, (1,003)........1,092
Adams Store, Panola.....................12	Aley, Henderson 45	Amherst, Lamar 125
Adamsville, Lampasas...................75	Alfred, Jim Wells, (91) 85	*AMHERST, Lamb, 14, (721).......670
Addicks, Harris .... [part of Houston]	Algerita, San Saba........................10	Amistad, Val Verde, (53)................46
Addielou, Red River.......................31	Algoa, Galveston 135	Ammannsville, Fayette.................137
*ADDISON, Dallas, 1,841,	*ALICE, Jim Wells, 687,	Amphion, Atascosa........................26
(13,056)..............................15,475	(19,104).............................18,499	Amsterdam, Brazoria....................193
Adell, Parker...............................100	Alice Acres, Jim Wells, (490).......486	Anacua, Starr, (12) 13
*Adkins, Bexar, 36 400	*Alief, Harris............. [part of Houston]	Anadarko, Rusk.............................30
Admiral, Callahan 18	Allamoore, Hudspeth....................10	*ANAHUAC, Chambers, 89,
Adobes, Presidio 5	*ALLEN, Collin, 2,916,	(2,243)..................................2,413
*ADRIAN, Oldham, 6, (166)..........159	(84,246)...........................100,003	Anchor, Brazoria...........................150
Advance, Parker..........................100	Allenfarm, Brazos 35	*ANDERSON, Grimes, 48,
*Afton, Dickens, 4..........................15	Allenhurst, Matagorda 72	(222).......................................227
Agnes, Parker 60	Allen's Chapel, Fannin..................30	Anderson Mill, Williamson-Travis
*AGUA DULCE, Nueces, 20,	Allen's Point, Fannin......................40	............................[part of Austin]
(812)..830	Allentown, Angelina 800	Ander-Weser-Kilgore, Goliad........322
Agua Dulce, El Paso, (3,014)....3,357	Alleyton, Colorado, 14 165	Andice, Williamson.......................300
Agua Nueva, Jim Hogg...................5	*Allison, Wheeler, 6 135	*ANDREWS, Andrews, 518,
Aguilares, Webb, (21)....................23	Allmon, Floyd................................24	(11,088)..............................13,520
*Aiken, Floyd, 1 52	Allred, Yoakum..............................90	*ANGLETON, Brazoria, 583,
Aiken, Shelby...............................150	ALMA, Ellis, 14, (331)..................377	(18,862)..............................20,310
Aikin Grove, Red River..................15	Almira, Cass..................................30	ANGUS, Navarro, 24, (414)..........439
Airport Heights, Starr, (161)..........176	*ALPINE, Brewster, 336,	*ANNA, Collin, 276, (8,249).....11,904
Airport Road Addition, Brooks,	(5,905)................................6,009	Annaville, Nueces
(93)...88	Alsa, Van Zandt 30	...............[part of Corpus Christi]
Airville, Bell...................................65	*Altair, Colorado, 6.......................30	ANNETTA, Parker, 70,
Alabama-Coushatta, Polk, (572) ..572	*ALTO, Cherokee, 57, (1,225)...1,238	(1,288)..................................1,689

For a complete list of more than 17,000 Texas communities, past and present, go to www.texasalmanac.com

CITIES & TOWNS

Town, County ....Pop. 2017	Town, County ....Pop. 2017	Town, County ....Pop. 2017

ANNETTA NORTH, Parker, 11,
  (518) 580
ANNETTA SOUTH, Parker, 10,
  (526) 589
*ANNONA, Red River, 5,
  (315) 289
*ANSON, Jones, 102,
  (2,430) 2,410
Antelope, Jack 65
*ANTHONY, El Paso, 133,
  (5,011) 5,600
Antioch, Cass 45
Antioch, Delta 10
Antioch, Madison 15
Antioch Colony, Hay 25
*ANTON, Hockley, 16,
  (1,126) 1,127
APPLEBY, Nacogdoches,
  (474) 480
*Apple Springs, Trinity, 10 350
*AQUILLA, Hill, 9, (109) 106
*ARANSAS PASS, San Patricio-
  Aransas, 341, (8,204) 8,952
Arbala, Hopkins 41
Arcadia, Shelby 35
*ARCHER CITY, Archer, 66,
  (1,834) 1,826
ARCOLA, Fort Bend, 67,
  (1,642) 2,285
Arden, Irion 7
Argo, Titus 90
*ARGYLE, Denton, 271,
  (3,282) 4,080
*ARLINGTON, Tarrant, 10,904,
  (365,438) 389,386
Armstrong, Bell 25
*Armstrong, Kenedy, 3 4
Arneckeville, DeWitt 50
Arnett, Coryell 15
Arnett, Hockley 5
*ARP, Smith, 70, (970) 1,022
Arroyo City, Cameron 600
Arroyo Colorado Estates,
  Cameron, (997) 1,086
Arroyo Gardens, Cameron,
  (456) 506
*Art, Mason 14
Artesia Wells, La Salle, 2 35
*Arthur City, Lamar, 6 180
Arvana, Dawson 8
Asa, McLennan 46
Ash, Houston 19
Ashby, Matagorda 60
*ASHERTON, Dimmit, 15,
  (1,084) 1,065
Ashland, Upshur 45
Ashtola, Donley 20
Ashwood, Matagorda 132
Asia, Polk 83
*ASPERMONT, Stonewall, 56,
  (919) 912
Atascocita, Harris, (65,844) 75,566
*Atascosa, Bexar, 46 600
Ater, Coryell 12
*ATHENS, Henderson, 595,
  (12,710) 13,332
*ATLANTA, Cass, 273, (5,675) .. 5,679
Atlas, Lamar 28
Atoy, Cherokee 50
*AUBREY, Denton, 208,
  (2,595) 3,405

Augusta, Houston 40
AURORA, Wise, 28, (1,220) 1,383
*AUSTIN, Travis-Williamson,
  37,458, (790,390) 949,460
Austonio, Houston 37
*AUSTWELL, Refugio, 9, (147) 147
Authon, Parker 15
*Avalon, Ellis, 3 400
*AVERY, Red River, 21, (482) 444
*AVINGER, Cass, 29, (444) 443
*Avoca, Jones, 2 121
*Axtell, McLennan, 21 300
*AZLE, Tarrant-Parker, 577,
  (10,947) 12,161

B

Back, Gray 6
*Bacliff, Galveston, 90,
  (8,619) 10,025
*Bagwell, Red River, 1 150
*BAILEY, Fannin, 10, (289) 303
BAILEY'S PRAIRIE, Brazoria, 16,
  (727) 755
Baileyville, Milam 32
Bainer, Lamb 10
Bainville, Karnes 8
*BAIRD, Callahan, 78, (1,496) ... 1,552

Baker, Floyd 28
Bakersfield, Pecos 9
*BALCH SPRINGS, Dallas, 615,
  (23,728) 24,997
BALCONES HEIGHTS, Bexar,
  175, (2,941) 3,215
Bald Hill, Angelina 100
Bald Prairie, Robertson 40
*BALLINGER, Runnels, 202,
  (3,767) 3,700
*BALMORHEA, Reeves, 18,
  (479) 551
Balsora, Wise 50
B and E, Starr, (518) 573
*BANDERA, Bandera, 286,
  (857) 903
Bandera Falls, Bandera 90
*BANGS, Brown, 48, (1,603) 1,601
*Banquete, Nueces, 9, (726) 774
Barbarosa, Guadalupe 46
Barclay, Falls 58
*BARDWELL, Ellis, 4, (649) 707
*Barker, Harris, 11 2,500
*Barksdale, Edwards, 2 100
Barnes, Polk 75
*Barnhart, Irion, 11 110
Barnum, Polk 50

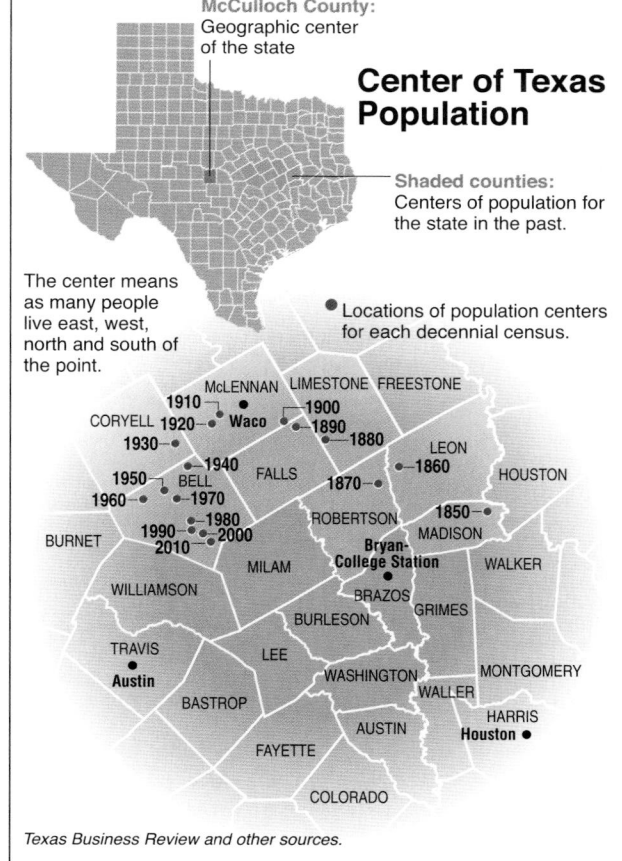

McCulloch County:
Geographic center
of the state

Center of Texas Population

Shaded counties:
Centers of population for
the state in the past.

The center means
as many people
live east, west,
north and south of
the point.

● Locations of population centers
for each decennial census.

McLENNAN LIMESTONE FREESTONE
1910
CORYELL 1920 Waco 1900
1930 1890
1880
LEON
1940
1950 FALLS 1860
1960 BELL 1870 HOUSTON
1970
1980 ROBERTSON 1850
1990 2000 MADISON
BURNET 2010 Bryan-
MILAM College Station WALKER
WILLIAMSON BRAZOS
BURLESON GRIMES
TRAVIS LEE
Austin WASHINGTON MONTGOMERY
BASTROP WALLER
AUSTIN HARRIS
Houston ●
FAYETTE

COLORADO

Texas Business Review and other sources.

CITIES & TOWNS

CITIES & TOWNS

Town, County ....Pop. 2017

Barrera, Starr, (108)..................... 131
*BARRETT, Harris, 21, (3,199) 3,383
*BARRY, Navarro, (242) 254
*BARSTOW, Ward, 3, (349) 364
*BARTLETT, Williamson-Bell, 61,
   (2,684) 2,725
Barton Corners, Lipscomb............... 4
Barton Creek, Travis, (3,077) 3,438
BARTONVILLE, Denton, 116,
   (1,469) 1,715
Barwise, Floyd 16
*Basin, Brewster, 3 30
Bassett, Bowie............................... 100
*BASTROP, Bastrop, 764,
   (7,218) 8,712
Bateman, Bastrop.......................... 12
Batesville, Red River 14
*Batesville, Zavala, 10,
   (1,068) 1,039
*Batson, Hardin, 14 140
Battle, McLennan........................... 100
Baxter, Henderson.......................... 150
*BAY CITY, Matagorda, 547,
   (17,614) 17,531
Baylor Lake, Childress................... 50
BAYOU VISTA, Galveston, 34,
   (1,537) 1,552
*BAYSIDE, Refugio, 13,
   (325) 337
*BAYTOWN, Harris-Chambers,
   1,940, (71,802) 78,913
BAYVIEW, Cameron, 12, (383) 405
Bazette, Navarro.......................... 30
BEACH CITY, Chambers,
   (2,198) 2,648
BEAR CREEK, Hays, (382).......... 456
*BEASLEY, Fort Bend, 22,
   (641) 759
Beattie, Comanche 48
*BEAUMONT, Jefferson, 3,768,
   (118,296) 117,245
Beaver Dam, Bowie........................ 10
Bebe, Gonzales 42
Becker, Kaufman 300
*BECKVILLE, Panola, 21, (847)... 838
Becton, Lubbock............................ 62
*BEDFORD, Tarrant, 1,409,
   (46,979) 49,500
*BEDIAS, Grimes, 31, (443)......... 445
BEE CAVE, Travis, 493,
   (3,925) 6,357
Bee House, Coryell......................... 15
*BEEVILLE, Bee, 470,
   (12,863) 13,224
Belcherville, Montague 25
Belfalls, Bell.................................... 30
Belgrade, Newton 20
Belk, Lamar 58
*BELLAIRE, Harris, 709,
   (16,855) 18,211
Bell Branch, Ellis............................ 125
*BELLEVUE, Clay, 18, (362) 350
*BELLMEAD, McLennan, 251,
   (9,901) 10,655
*BELLS, Grayson, 43,
   (1,392) 1,452
*BELLVILLE, Austin, 290,
   (4,097) 4,375
Belmena, Milam.............................. 15
*Belmont, Gonzales, 6.................... 55
Belott, Houston 101

Town, County ....Pop. 2017

*BELTON, Bell, 838,
   (18,216) 21,157
Ben Arnold, Milam 100
*BENAVIDES, Duval, 21,
   (1,362) 1,285
*Ben Bolt, Jim Wells, 4 1,600
*BENBROOK, Tarrant, 682,
   (21,234) 23,788
Benchley, Robertson-Brazos 110
*Bend, San Saba-Lampasas, 1 115
*Ben Franklin, Delta, 1.................... 60
Ben Hur, Limestone 42
*BENJAMIN, Knox, 14, (258) 260
Benjamin Perez, Starr, (34) 35
Bennett, Parker.............................. 120
Benoit, Runnels 10
Bentonville, Jim Wells.................... 15
*Ben Wheeler, Van Zandt, 70 504
*Berclair, Goliad, 3........................ 253
Berea, Houston.............................. 41
Berea, Marion 200
Bergheim, Kendall, 17 1,213
Berlin, Washington 40
Bernardo, Colorado 155
BERRYVILLE, Henderson, 8,
   (975) 1,021
*BERTRAM, Burnet, 86,
   (1,353) 1,430
Bessmay, Jasper 400
Best, Reagan 2
Bethany, Panola 50
Bethel, Anderson 75
Bethel, Henderson......................... 125
Bethel, Runnels 20
Bethlehem, Upshur......................... 75
Bettie, Upshur 110
Beulah, Limestone.......................... 12
BEVERLY HILLS, McLennan, 99,
   (1,995) 2,025
BEVIL OAKS, Jefferson, 29,
   (1,274) 1,227
Bevilport, Jasper............................ 12
Beyersville, Williamson.................. 80
Biardstown, Lamar......................... 75
*Bigfoot, Frio, 10, (450) 522
Big Hill, Limestone.......................... 9
*BIG LAKE, Reagan, 146,
   (2,936) 3,448
*BIG SANDY, Upshur, 87,
   (1,343) 1,379

Town, County ....Pop. 2017

*BIG SPRING, Howard, 669,
   (27,282) 28,057
Big Thicket Estates, Liberty-Polk,
   (742) 849
Big Valley, Mills............................. 35
*BIG WELLS, Dimmit, 8,
   (697) 742
Biloxi, Newton................................ 75
Birch, Burleson 200
Birome, Hill 30
Birthright, Hopkins 100
Biry, Medina................................... 24
*BISHOP, Nueces, 62,
   (3,134) 3,222
BISHOP HILLS, Potter, (193) 178
*Bivins, Cass, 6 215
Bixby, Cameron, (504).................. 579
Black, Parmer 100
Blackfoot, Anderson....................... 50
Black Hill, Atascosa........................ 60
Black Hills, Navarro........................ 80
Black Jack, Cherokee..................... 47
Black Jack, Robertson.................... 45
Black Oak, Hopkins 150
*BLACKWELL, Nolan-Coke, 16,
   (311) 303
Blair, Taylor 25
Blanchard, Polk 500
*BLANCO, Blanco, 248,
   (1,739) 1,985
Blanconia, Bee 100
Bland Lake, San Augustine 80
*BLANKET, Brown, 19, (390)........ 391
Blanton, Hill 5
Bleakwood, Newton........................ 450
*Bledsoe, Cochran, 1..................... 126
*Bleiblerville, Austin, 4 125
*Blessing, Matagorda, 22,
   (927) 965
Blevins, Falls 36
Blewett, Uvalde.............................. 7
Blodgett, Titus 60
*BLOOMBURG, Cass, 9,
   (404) 409
*BLOOMING GROVE, Navarro,
   19, (821) 840
*Bloomington, Victoria, 10,
   (2,459) 2,590
*BLOSSOM, Lamar, 59,
   (1,494) 1,561

Ten Largest U.S. Metro Areas		
Rank	**Metro Area**	**2017 Estimates**
1.	New York	20,320,876
2.	Los Angeles	13,353,907
3.	Chicago	9.533,040
4.	**Dallas-Fort Worth**	**7,399,622**
5.	**Houston**	**6,892,427**
6.	Washington, D.C.	6,216,589
7.	Miami	6,158,824
8.	Philadelphia	6,096,120
9.	Atlanta	5,884,736
10.	Boston	4,836,531
		Source: U.S. Census.

Town, County ....Pop. 2017	Town, County ....Pop. 2017	Town, County ....Pop. 2017
Blue, Lee 75	*BRADY, McCulloch, 243,	Brundage, Dimmit, (27) 26
Blueberry Hill, Bee, (866) 871	(5,528) 5,472	*Bruni, Webb, 6, (379) 386
*Bluegrove, Clay............................ 135	Branch, Collin 530	Brushie Prairie, Navarro 35
BLUE MOUND, Tarrant, 49,	Branchville, Milam 127	Brushy Creek, Anderson.............. 125
(2,394) 2,484	*Brandon, Hill, 3............................ 75	Brushy Creek, Williamson,
*BLUE RIDGE, Collin, 50,	*Brashear, Hopkins, 15................ 280	(21,764) 24,749
(822) 920	*BRAZORIA, Brazoria, 214,	*BRYAN, Brazos, 2,485,
Bluetown, Cameron, (356)............ 351	(3,019) 3,397	(76,201)............................. 83,950
*Bluff Dale, Erath, 24 400	Brazos, Palo Pinto 97	Bryans Mill, Cass......................... 150
*Bluffton, Llano, 5 75	BRAZOS COUNTRY, Austin, 16,	Bryarly, Red River.......................... 3
*BLUM, Hill, 16, (444).................... 452	(469) 501	Bryce, Rusk 15
Bluntzer, Nueces 150	Brazos Point, Bosque 20	*BRYSON, Jack, 12, (539) 545
Boca Chica Village, Cameron........ 34	Brazosport, Brazoria,	*Buchanan Dam, Llano, 41,
*BOERNE, Kendall, 1,419,	(57,288) 60,138	(1,519) 1,523
(10,471) 14,816	*BRECKENRIDGE, Stephens,	Buchanan Lake Village, Llano,
*BOGATA, Red River, 52,	277, (5,780) 5,568	(692) 732
(1,153) 1,063	*BREMOND, Robertson, 41,	Buchel, DeWitt............................... 45
Bois d'Arc, Anderson 25	(929) 958	Buckeye, Matagorda....................... 16
Bois d'Arc, Rains 6	*BRENHAM, Washington, 977,	*BUCKHOLTS, Milam, 14,
Bold Springs, Polk 100	(15,716) 17,262	(515) 530
Boles Home, Hunt 100	Breslau, Lavaca............................ 65	Buckhorn, Austin............................ 50
*Boling, Wharton, 32, (1,122) 1,117	Briar, Tarrant-Wise-Parker,	Buckhorn, Newton 80
Bolivar, Denton 140	(5,665) 6,116	Buckner, Parker 10
Bolivar Peninsula, Galveston,	BRIARCLIFF, Travis, 53,	*BUDA, Hays, 719,
(2,417) 2,743	(1,438) 1,688	(7,295) 15,732
Bomarton, Baylor............................ 15	BRIAROAKS, Johnson, 8,	Buena Vista, Shelby 20
Bonami, Jasper................................ 12	(495) 519	Buena Vista, Starr, (102) 115
Bonanza, Hopkins 26	Brice, Hall-Briscoe 20	*BUFFALO, Leon, 154,
Bonanza Hills, Webb, (37)............. 44	*BRIDGE CITY, Orange, 227,	(1,856) 1,924
*BONHAM, Fannin, 353,	(7,840) 8,092	*BUFFALO GAP, Taylor, 44,
(10,127) 10,628	*BRIDGEPORT, Wise, 302,	(464) 468
Bonita, Montague 25	(5,976) 6,533	Buffalo Mop, Limestone................. 21
BONNEY, Brazoria, (310) 330	Bridges Chapel, Titus 60	Buffalo Springs, Clay 45
Bonnie View, Refugio 97	*Briggs, Burnet, 9 172	BUFFALO SPRINGS, Lubbock,
Bonus, Wharton.............................. 44	Bright Star, Rains 25	(453) 477
*Bon Wier, Newton, 6 375	Brinker, Hopkins 100	Buford, Mitchell.............................. 30
*BOOKER, Lipscomb-Ochiltree,	*Briscoe, Wheeler, 2 135	Bugscuffle, Rusk 12
54, (1,516) 1,558	Bristol, Ellis, (668)........................ 713	Bula, Bailey,.................................... 35
Boonsville, Wise 52	*BROADDUS, San Augustine, 26,	Bulcher, Cooke 3
Booth, Fort Bend 50	(207) 197	*BULLARD, Smith-Cherokee,
Bootleg, Deaf Smith........................ 10	Broadway, Lamar 25	200, (2,463) 2,872
Borden, Colorado 20	Brock, Parker 2,000	Bull Run, Newton............................ 90
*BORGER, Hutchinson, 414,	Brock Junction, Parker 100	*BULVERDE, Comal, 428,
(13,251) 12,873	Bronco, Yoakum 30	(4,630) 5,410
Bosqueville, McLennan 200	*Bronson, Sabine, 7...................... 377	*Buna, Jasper, 87, (2,142)........ 2,124
Boston, Bowie.... [part of New Boston]	*BRONTE, Coke, 43, (999) 983	Buncombe, Panola 95
Botines, Webb, (117) 116	*Brookeland, Sabine, 29.............. 300	Bunger, Young 24
*BOVINA, Parmer, 42,	*Brookesmith, Brown, 1 61	BUNKER HILL VILLAGE, Harris,
(1,868) 1,809	Brooks, Panola 40	69, (3,633) 3,796
Bowers City, Gray.......................... 10	Brookshier, Runnels 15	Bunyan, Erath 20
*BOWIE, Montague, 357,	*BROOKSHIRE, Waller, 194,	*BURKBURNETT, Wichita, 228,
(5,218) 5,119	(4,702) 5,283	(10,811) 11,311
Bowman, Archer 300	BROOKSIDE VILLAGE, Brazoria,	BURKE, Angelina, (737).............. 741
Bowser, San Saba 20	39, (1,523) 1,624	*Burkett, Coleman 90
Box Canyon, Val Verde, (34) 22	*Brookston, Lamar, 14................ 130	*Burkeville, Newton, 25 603
Box Church, Limestone 45	Broom City, Anderson................... 20	Burleigh, Austin............................. 150
Boxelder, Red River....................... 100	BROWNDELL, Jasper, (197)........ 187	*BURLESON, Johnson-Tarrant,
Boxwood, Upshur 20	*BROWNFIELD, Terry, 245,	1,452, (36,690) 44,161
Boyce, Ellis 125	(9,657) 9,808	*Burlington, Milam, 3 100
Boyd, Fannin 105	Browning, Smith 25	*BURNET, Burnet, 432,
*BOYD, Wise, 132, (1,207)........ 1,395	Brownsboro, Caldwell.................... 50	(5,987) 6,429
*Boys Ranch, Oldham, 3, (282)... 305	*BROWNSBORO, Henderson, 70,	Burns, Bowie 400
Boz-Bethel, Ellis 100	(1,039) 1,089	Burns City, Cooke 45
Bozar, Mills 9	*BROWNSVILLE, Cameron, 4,930,	Burrantown, Houston...................... 70
Brachfield, Rusk 40	(175,023) 183,686	*BURTON, Washington, 81,
Bracken, Comal 95	*BROWNWOOD, Brown, 639,	(300) 298
*BRACKETTVILLE, Kinney, 65,	(19,288) 19,805	Bushland, Potter, 17.................. 1,485
(1,688) 1,766	Broyles Chapel, Anderson............. 60	Bustamante, Zapata 10
Brad, Palo Pinto 16	*BRUCEVILLE-EDDY, McLen-	Busterville, Hockley 6
Bradford, Anderson......................... 60	nan-Falls, 27, (1,475) 1,873	Butler, Bastrop 40
Bradshaw, Taylor 61	Brumley, Upshur 75	Butler, Freestone 67

Town, County .... Pop. 2017	Town, County .... Pop. 2017	Town, County .... Pop. 2017
Butterfield, El Paso, (114)............. 130	Cap Rock, Crosby 6	CELINA, Collin-Denton, 307,
*BYERS, Clay, 14, (496)............... 495	Caps, Taylor.................................. 300	(6,028) 8,147
*BYNUM, Hill, 9, (199).................. 200	Caradan, Mills.................................. 20	Center, Limestone 76
Byrd, Ellis.. 30	Carancahua, Jackson.................. 375	CENTER, Shelby, 349,
Byrdtown, Lamar 22	CARBON, Eastland, 10, (272)...... 279	(5,193)............................... 5,393
	Carbondale, Bowie 10	Center City, Mills............................ 27
C	Carey, Childress 25	Center Grove, Houston.................. 39
CACTUS, Moore, 35, (3,179) 3,339	Carlisle, Trinity 110	Center Grove, Titus 35
Caddo, Stephens, 4........................ 70	Carlos, Grimes................................ 60	Center Hill, Houston 105
CADDO MILLS, Hunt, 133,	Carlsbad, Tom Green, 10, (719)... 756	Center Plains, Swisher 20
(1,338) 1,499	CARL'S CORNER, Hill, 3,	Center Point, Camp 41
Cade Chapel, Navarro-Freestone .. 25	(173)................................... 171	Center Point, Kerr, 39.................. 800
Cadiz, Bee 15	Carlson, Travis................................ 20	Center Point, Upshur..................... 50
Calallen, Nueces	Carlton, Hamilton, 2........................ 75	Centerview, Leon 20
.... [part of Corpus Christi]	CARMINE, Fayette, 51, (250)...... 266	CENTERVILLE, Leon, 83,
Calaveras, Wilson 100	Carmona, Polk................................ 50	(892)................................... 928
CALDWELL, Burleson, 290,	Caro, Nacogdoches......................... 70	Centerville, Trinity 60
(4,104) 4,362	Carrizo Hill, Dimmit, (582) 606	Central, Angelina 1,400
Caledonia, Rusk 75	CARRIZO SPRINGS, Dimmit,	Central Gardens, Jefferson,
Calf Creek, McCulloch.................... 23	153, (5,368) 5,590	(4,347) 4,241
Calina, Limestone.......................... 10	Carroll, Smith.................................. 60	Central Heights, Nacogdoches..... 300
Call, Newton, 5 493	Carroll Springs, Anderson-	Central High, Cherokee 30
Callender Lake, Van Zandt,	Henderson......................... 20	Centralia, Trinity 190
(1,039) 1,301	CARROLLTON, Dallas-Denton,	Cesar Chavez, Hidalgo,
Calliham, McMullen, 4 100	5,038, (119,907) 136,815	(1,929) 2,195
CALLISBURG, Cooke, (353)........ 365	Carson, Fannin................................ 22	Cestohowa, Karnes 110
Call Junction, Jasper 50	Carta Valley, Edwards 12	Chalk, Cottle.................................. 17
CALVERT, Robertson, 50,	Carterville, Cass 39	Chalk Hill, Rusk 200
(1,192)............................... 1,151	CARTHAGE, Panola, 365,	Chalk Mountain, Erath-Somervell... 25
Camargito, Starr, (388)................. 420	(6,779) 6,934	Chambliss, Collin 29
Camden, Polk, 6 1,200	Cartwright, Wood.......................... 144	Champion, Nolan............................ 10
CAMERON, Milam, 203,	Casa Blanca, Starr, (54) 67	Champions, Harris 21,250
(5,552) 5,486	Casa Piedra, Presidio...................... 8	Chances Store, Burleson............... 15
Cameron Park, Cameron,	Casas, Starr, (39) 43	CHANDLER, Henderson, 157,
(6,963) 7,533	Cash, Hunt...................................... 56	(2,734) 3,083
Camilla, San Jacinto..................... 200	CASHION, Wichita, (348) 357	Chaney, Eastland 35
Camp Air, Mason 12	Cason, Morris, 1 173	Channelview, Harris, 398,
CAMPBELL, Hunt, 45, (638) 772	Cass, Cass 100	(38,289) 43,925
Campbellton, Atascosa, 5............. 350	Cassie, Burnet.............................. 496	CHANNING, Hartley, 5,
Camp Creek Lake, Robertson 350	Cassin, Bexar 200	(363) 379
Campo Verde, Starr, (132)............ 144	Castell, Llano, 2.............................. 72	Chaparrito, Starr, (114) 114
Camp Ruby, Polk............................ 35	CASTLE HILLS, Bexar, 302,	Chapeno, Starr, (47)...................... 52
Camp San Saba, McCulloch 36	(4,116) 4,502	Chapman, Rusk.............................. 20
Camp Seale, Polk........................... 53	Castolon, Brewster 8	Chapman Ranch, Nueces 200
Camp Springs, Scurry 10	CASTROVILLE, Medina, 194,	Chappel, San Saba 25
Camp Swift, Bastrop, (6,383) ... 7,414	(2,680) 3,016	Chappell Hill, Washington, 50 750
Camp Switch, Gregg 70	Catarina, Dimmit, 13, (118).......... 107	Charco, Goliad............................... 96
Campti, Shelby 25	Cat Spring, Austin, 24.................. 200	Charleston, Delta.......................... 150
Camp Verde, Kerr........................... 41	Caviness, Lamar.............................. 90	Charlie, Clay 70
CAMP WOOD, Real, 37, (706)..... 731	Cawthon, Brazos 75	CHARLOTTE, Atascosa, 40,
Canada Verde, Wilson 40	Cayote, Bosque 75	(1,715) 1,812
CANADIAN, Hemphill, 146,	Cayuga, Anderson, 2..................... 137	Chatfield, Navarro, 3...................... 40
(2,649) 2,816	Cedar Bayou, Harris.................. 1,555	Cheapside, Gonzales 5
Candelaria, Presidio 55	Cedar Creek, Bastrop 145	Cheek, Jefferson...................... 1,096
CANEY CITY, Henderson, 12,	CEDAR HILL, Dallas-Ellis, 1,228,	Cheneyboro, Navarro 100
(217) 220	(45,028) 50,320	Cherokee, San Saba, 10 175
Cannon, Grayson 50	Cedar Hill, Floyd 24	Cherry Spring, Gillespie................. 75
CANTON, Van Zandt, 812,	Cedar Lake, Matagorda................ 160	CHESTER, Tyler, 13, (312) 311
(3,581) 3,864	Cedar Lane, Matagorda, 3............ 300	Chesterville, Colorado 30
Cantu Addition, Brooks, (188)....... 194	CEDAR PARK, Williamson-Travis,	CHICO, Wise, 66, (1,002).......... 1,105
Canutillo, El Paso, 197,	2,495, (48,937) 70,375	Chicota, Lamar 150
(6,321) 6,864	Cedar Point, Polk, (630) 690	Chihuahua, Zapata, (84)................ 77
CANYON, Randall, 447,	Cedar Shores, Bosque 270	CHILDRESS, Childress, 177,
(13,303) 15,026	Cedar Springs, Falls....................... 90	(6,105) 5,994
Canyon City, Comal..................... 800	Cedar Springs, Upshur................. 100	CHILLICOTHE, Hardeman, 16,
Canyon Creek, Hood, (916)...... 1,002	Cedarvale, Kaufman........................ 50	(707) 664
Canyon Lake, Comal, 288,	Cedar Valley, Bell 14	Chilton, Falls, 10, (911)................ 930
(21,262) 25,516	Cee Vee, Cottle 45	CHINA, Jefferson, 30,
Cape Royale, San Jacinto,	Cego, Falls 42	(1,160) 1,186
(670) 614	Cele, Travis..................................... 20	CHINA GROVE, Bexar, 59,
Caplen, Galveston.......................... 60	CELESTE, Hunt, 34, (814) 824	(1,179) 1,280
Capps Corner, Montague 30		

Town, County .... Pop. 2017	Town, County .... Pop. 2017	Town, County .... Pop. 2017
China Grove, Scurry 15	CLEVELAND, Liberty, 492,	Concrete, DeWitt 46
China Spring, McLennan, 63,	(7,675) 8,131	Cone, Crosby 50
(1,281) 1,378	Cliffside, Potter 206	Conlen, Dallam 14
Chinati, Presidio 8	CLIFTON, Bosque, 223,	Connor, Madison 20
Chinquapin, Matagorda 6	(3,442) 3,533	CONROE, Montgomery, 3,454,
CHIRENO, Nacogdoches, 17,	Climax, Collin 82	(56,207) 85,685
(386) 382	Cline, Uvalde 15	Content, Bell 25
CHISHOLM [McLendon-], Rockwall,	CLINT, El Paso, 63, (926) 1,190	CONVERSE, Bexar, 528,
3, (1,373) 2,438	Clinton, Hunt 150	(18,198) 21,735
Chita, Trinity 81	Close City, Garza 65	Conway, Carson 20
Choate, Karnes 30	Cloverleaf, Harris, (22,942) 23,982	Cooks Point, Burleson 60
Chocolate Bayou, Brazoria 60	CLUTE, Brazoria, 355,	Cookville, Titus, 10 105
Choice, Shelby 35	(11,211) 11,642	COOL, Parker, 6, (157) 174
Chriesman, Burleson, 1 30	CLYDE, Callahan, 174,	COOLIDGE, Limestone, 13,
CHRISTINE, Atascosa,	(3,713) 3,917	(955) 984
(390) 413	COAHOMA, Howard, 27, (817) 838	COOPER, Delta, 72, (1,969) 1,933
Christoval, Tom Green, 26,	Coble, Hockley 11	Cooper, Houston 27
(504) 558	Cochran, Austin 200	Copano Village, Aransas 210
Chula Vista, Zavala, (450) 461	COCKRELL HILL, Dallas, 92,	Copeville, Collin, 4 243
Chula Vista, Cameron, (288) 287	(4,193) 4,501	COPPELL, Dallas-Denton, 1,376,
Chula Vista, Maverick,	COFFEE CITY, Henderson, 13,	(38,659) 42,167
(3,818) 3,888	(278) 1,492	COPPERAS COVE, Coryell, 658,
Church Hill, Rusk 20	Coffeeville, Upshur 50	(32,032) 32,742
Churchill, Brazoria 90	Cofferville, Lamb 4	COPPER CANYON, Denton, 37,
CIBOLO, Guadalupe, 474,	Coit, Limestone 25	(1,334) 1,485
(15,349) 28,207	Coke, Wood 53	Corbet, Navarro 80
Cienegas Terrace, Val Verde,	COLDSPRING, San Jacinto, 92,	Cordele, Jackson 51
(3,424) 3,403	(853) 914	CORINTH, Denton, 490,
Cinco Ranch, Fort Bend-Harris,	COLEMAN, Coleman, 207,	(19,935) 22,429
(18,274) 24,176	(4,709) 4,590	Corinth, Jones 10
Cipres, Hidalgo 20	Colfax, Van Zandt 94	Corinth, Leon 50
Circle, Lamb 6	Colita, Polk, Trinity 50	Corley, Bowie 35
Circle Back, Bailey 8	College Hill, Bowie 40	Cornersville, Hopkins 200
Circle D-KC Estates, Bastrop,	College Mound, Kaufman 500	Cornett, Cass 30
(2,393) 2,740	Collegeport, Matagorda 80	Cornudas, Hudspeth 5
Circleville, Williamson 50	COLLEGE STATION, Brazos,	CORPUS CHRISTI, Nueces,
CISCO, Eastland, 159,	2,576, (93,857) 111,818	9,140, (305,215) 326,071
(3,899) 3,858	COLLEYVILLE, Tarrant, 1,145,	CORRIGAN, Polk, 66,
Cistern, Fayette 137	(22,807) 26,081	(1,595) 1,604
Citrus City, Hidalgo, (2,321) 2,785	COLLINSVILLE, Grayson, 51,	CORSICANA, Navarro, 903,
Citrus Grove, Matagorda 30	(1,624) 1,732	(23,770) 24,304
Clairemont, Kent 12	COLMESNEIL, Tyler, 34,	Coryell City, Coryell 70
Clairette, Erath 55	(596) 583	Cost, Gonzales, 7 84
Clara, Wichita 100	Colony, Rains 35	Cotton Center, Fannin 33
Clardy, Lamar 160	Colorado Acres, Webb, (296) 325	Cotton Center, Hale, 4 300
CLARENDON, Donley, 94,	COLORADO CITY, Mitchell, 175,	Cottondale, Wise 300
(2,026) 1,878	(4,146) 3,815	Cotton Gin, Freestone 28
Clareville, Bee 25	Coltharp, Houston 40	Cotton Patch, DeWitt 11
Clark, Liberty 75	Colton, Travis 50	COTTONWOOD, Kaufman,
Clarkson, Milam 10	COLUMBUS, Colorado, 271,	(185) 210
CLARKSVILLE, Red River, 123,	(3,655) 3,804	Cottonwood, Madison 40
(3,285) 3,029	COMANCHE, Comanche, 218,	Cottonwood, McLennan 150
CLARKSVILLE CITY, Gregg-Upshur,	(4,335) 4,336	Cottonwood, Somervell 24
23, (865) 910	COMBES, Cameron, 45,	COTTONWOOD SHORES, Burnet,
CLAUDE, Armstrong, 60,	(2,895) 3,146	51, (1,123) 1,245
(1,196) 1,183	COMBINE, Kaufman-Dallas, 52,	COTULLA, La Salle, 144,
Clauene, Hockley 10	(1,942) 2,132	(3,603) 4,157
Clawson, Angelina 1,500	Cometa, Zavala 10	Couch, Karnes 10
Clay, Burleson 61	Comfort, Kendall, 140,	Coughran, Atascosa 20
Clays Corner, Parmer 15	(2,363) 2,783	Country Acres, San Patricio,
Clayton, Panola, 2 125	COMMERCE, Hunt, 237,	(185) 184
Claytonville, Swisher 85	(8,078) 8,899	County Line, Lubbock 59
Clear Creek, Burnet 78	COMO, Hopkins, 30, (702) 736	County Line, Rains 40
CLEAR LAKE SHORES, Galveston,	Comstock, Val Verde 344	COUPLAND, Williamson, 19 309
85, (1,063) 1,195	Comyn, Comanche 30	Courtney, Grimes 60
CLEBURNE, Johnson, 1,126,	Concan, Uvalde, 36 500	COVE, Chambers, 22, (510) 562
(29,337) 31,762	Concepcion, Duval, (62) 56	Cove Springs, Cherokee 49
Clegg, Live Oak 125	Concord, Cherokee 50	COVINGTON, Hill, 19, (269) 276
Clemville, Matagorda 25	Concord, Leon, 1 28	Cox, Upshur 30
Cleo, Kimble 3	Concord, Madison 50	Coyanosa, Pecos, 13, (163) 178
Cleveland, Austin 125	Concord, Rusk 23	Coy City, Karnes 30

CITIES & TOWNS

Town, County .... Pop. 2017	Town, County .... Pop. 2017	Town, County .... Pop. 2017

Coyote Acres, Jim Wells, (508) 541
COYOTE FLATS, Johnson,
(312) 316
Crabbs Prairie, Walker 240
Craft, Cherokee 21
Crafton, Wise 100
CRANDALL, Kaufman, 108,
(2,858) 3,231
CRANE, Crane, 101,
(3,353) 3,749
CRANFILLS GAP, Bosque, 16,
(281) 275
CRAWFORD, McLennan, 40,
(717) 745
Creath, Houston 20
Crecy, Trinity 15
CREEDMOOR, Travis, 35,
(202) 217
Crescent Heights, Henderson 180
CRESSON, Hood-Johnson-Parker,
87, (741) 789
Crews, Runnels 30
Crisp, Ellis 115
CROCKETT, Houston, 278,
(6,950) 6,789
Crosby, Harris, 388, (2,299) 2,753
CROSBYTON, Crosby, 51,
(1,741) 1,644
Cross, Grimes 53
Cross, McMullen 25
Cross Cut, Brown 22
Cross Mountain, Bexar,
(3,124) 3,589
CROSS PLAINS, Callahan, 57,
(982) 996
Crossroads, Cass 60
Crossroads, Delta 20
CROSS ROADS, Denton, 106,
(1,563) 1,891
Crossroads, Harrison 100
Cross Roads, Henderson 160
Crossroads, Hopkins 50
Cross Roads, Madison 75
Cross Roads, Milam 35
CROSS TIMBER, Johnson,
(268) 291
Croton, Dickens 7
Crow, Wood 178
CROWELL, Foard, 34,
(948) 839
CROWLEY, Tarrant, 352,
(12,838) 14,783
Crown, Atascosa 10
Cruz Calle, Duval 12
Cryer Creek, Navarro 15
Crystal Beach, Galveston 800
CRYSTAL CITY, Zavala, 101,
(7,136) 7,261
Crystal Falls, Stephens 10
Crystal Lake, Anderson 12
Cuadrilla, El Paso 67
CUERO, DeWitt, 320,
(6,841) 7,605
Cuevitas, Hidalgo, (40) 51
CUMBY, Hopkins, 42, (777) 796
Cumings, Fort Bend, (981) 1,330
Cundiff, Jack 45
CUNEY, Cherokee, 2, (140) 137
Cunningham, Lamar, 2 110
Currie, Navarro 25
Curtis, Jasper 150

CUSHING, Nacogdoches, 44,
(612) 598
Cusseta, Cass 30
CUT AND SHOOT, Montgomery,
62, (1,070) 1,294
Cuthand, Red River 116
Cyclone, Bell 47
Cypress, Franklin 20
Cypress Creek, Kerr 200
Cypress [-Fairbanks] , Harris,
2,552 120,000
Cypress Mill, Blanco 200

D

Dacosta, Victoria 89
Dacus, Montgomery 190
Daffan, Travis 500
*DAINGERFIELD, Morris, 90,
(2,560) 2,568
*DAISETTA, Liberty, 20, (966)... 1,086
Dalby Springs, Bowie 75
*Dale, Caldwell, 35 300
*DALHART, Dallam-Hartley, 323,
(7,930) 8,507
*Dallardsville, Polk, 1 350
*DALLAS, Dallas-Collin-Denton,
41,922, (1,197,816) 1,345,452
Dalton, Cass 50
DALWORTHINGTON GARDENS,
Tarrant, 153, (2,259) 2,372
*Damon, Brazoria, 25, (552) 593
*DANBURY, Brazoria, 48,
(1,715) 1,851
*Danciger, Brazoria, 1 90
*Danevang, Wharton, 5 61
Daniels, Panola 75
Danville, Gregg 200
Darby Hill, San Jacinto 25
Darco, Harrison 10
Darden, Polk 320
*DARROUZETT, Lipscomb, 16,
(350) 367
Datura, Limestone 2
*Davilla, Milam 191
Davis, Atascosa 8
Davis Prairie, Limestone 17
*Dawn, Deaf Smith 52
*DAWSON, Navarro, 23, (807) 789
*DAYTON, Liberty, 397,
(7,242) 7,995
DAYTON LAKES, Liberty, (93) 98
Deadwood, Panola 106
DEAN, Clay, 9, (493) 469
Dean, Hockley 20
*Deanville, Burleson, 4 130
*DeBerry, Panola, 23 200
*DECATUR, Wise, 495,
(6,042) 6,824
Decker Prairie, Montgomery 2,000
DeCORDOVA, Hood, (2,683) ... 3,130
*DEER PARK, Harris, 959,
(32,010) 34,217
*DE KALB, Bowie, 66,
(1,699) 1,731
*DE LEON, Comanche, 115,
(2,246) 2,233
Delhi, Caldwell 150
Delia, Limestone 20
*DELL CITY, Hudspeth, 17,
(365) 468
Del Mar Heights, Cameron, (113)... 98

*Delmita, Starr, 4, (216) 225
Delray, Panola 45
*DEL RIO, Val Verde, 882,
(35,591) 34,790
Delrose, Upshur 35
Del Sol, San Patricio, (239) 240
*Del Valle, Travis, 118
.... [part of Austin]
Delwin, Cottle 12
Demi-John, Brazoria 300
Democrat, Mills 8
Denhawken, Wilson 52
*DENISON, Grayson, 843,
(22,682) 23,695
Denning, San Augustine 100
*Dennis, Parker, 2 300
Denson Springs, Anderson 60
Denton, Callahan 6
*DENTON, Denton, 3,635,
(113,383) 141,923
*DENVER CITY, Yoakum, 159,
(4,479) 5,062
*DEPORT, Lamar-Red River, 15,
(578) 560
Derby, Frio 50
*Desdemona, Eastland 180
Desert, Collin 35
*DeSOTO, Dallas, 1,079,
(49,047) 51,886
*DETROIT, Red River, 36,
(732) 670
*DEVERS, Liberty, 20, (447) 513
*DEVINE, Medina, 233,
(4,350) 4,851
Dew, Freestone 150
DeWees, Wilson 60
Deweesville, Karnes 12
*Deweyville, Newton, 11,
(1,023) 960
Dewville, Gonzales 30
Dexter, Cooke 12
*D'Hanis, Medina, 21, (847) 859
Dial, Fannin 76
Dialville, Cherokee 200
*Diana, Upshur, 39 585
*DIBOLL, Angelina, 113,
(5,359) 5,499
Dicey, Parker 40
*DICKENS, Dickens, 12,
(286) 230
*DICKINSON, Galveston, 541,
(18,680) 20,217
*Dike, Hopkins, 6 170
*DILLEY, Frio, 86, (3,894) 4,211
Dilworth, Gonzales 18
Dilworth, Red River 25
*Dime Box, Lee, 15 381
*DIMMITT, Castro, 117,
(4,393) 4,137
Dimple, Red River 60
*Dinero, Live Oak, 1 344
Ding Dong, Bell 301
Direct, Lamar 85
Dirgin, Rusk 50
DISH, Denton, (201) 457
Divide, Kerr 50
Divot, Frio 30
Dixie, Grayson 17
Dixon, Hunt 31
Dixon-Hopewell, Houston 10
Doak Springs, Lee 50

CITIES & TOWNS

Town, County .... Pop. 2017	Town, County .... Pop. 2017	Town, County .... Pop. 2017

Doans, Wilbarger............................ 20
*Dobbin, Montgomery, 1 310
Dobrowolski, Atascosa 10
Dodd, Castro 12
*DODD CITY, Fannin, 17,
   (369) 388
*Dodge, Walker, 5........................ 150
*DODSON, Collingsworth, (109) .. 106
Dodson Prairie, Palo Pinto 18
Doffing, Hidalgo, (5,091)............ 5,730
Dog Ridge, Bell............................. 215
Dogwood City, Smith 800
Dolen, Liberty 75
DOMINO, Cass, 8, (93) 91
*Donie, Freestone, 7.................... 250
*DONNA, Hidalgo, 536,
   (15,798) 17,427
*Doole, McCulloch 74
Doolittle, Hidalgo, (2,769) 2,975
DORCHESTER, Grayson,
   (148) 161
Dorras, Stonewall 20
Doss, Cass 15
*Doss, Gillespie, 7 100
Dot, Falls 17
Dotson, Panola 35
Double Bayou, Chambers 200
DOUBLE HORN, Burnet (NC)...... 180
DOUBLE OAK, Denton, 100,
   (2,867) 3,204
*Doucette, Tyler, 3 160
*Dougherty, Floyd, 2 91
Dougherty, Rains 40
*Douglass, Nacogdoches, 20 ... 380
*DOUGLASSVILLE, Cass, 8,
   (229) 232
Downing, Comanche 30
Downsville, McLennan.................. 150
Downtown Texas, Milam 34
Doyle, Limestone........................... 50
Doyle, San Patricio, (254)............ 247
Dozier, Collingsworth........................ 4
Drane, Navarro 16
DRAPER, Denton, (27)................... 33
Drasco, Runnels 15
Draw, Lynn..................................... 18
Dreka, Shelby................................. 30
Dresden, Navarro 25
Dreyer, Gonzales........................... 20
*Driftwood, Hays, 89, (144) 168
*DRIPPING SPRINGS, Hays,
   622, (1,788) 3,348
*DRISCOLL, Nueces, 12, (739).... 738
Drop, Denton 90
*Dryden, Terrell, 1 13
Dubina, Fayette 272
*DUBLIN, Erath, 156, (3,654).... 3,638
Dudley, Callahan 25
Duffau, Erath 76
*DUMAS, Moore, 378,
   (14,691) 15,246
Dumont, King.................................. 19
Dunbar, Rains................................. 40
*DUNCANVILLE, Dallas, 1,139,
   (38,524) 41,291
Dundee, Archer............................... 12
Dunlap, Cottle................................. 10
Dunlap, Travis................................. 80
Dunlay, Medina 145
*Dunn, Scurry 75
Duplex, Fannin 25

Durango, Falls 54
Duren, Mills.................................... 15
Duster, Comanche.......................... 25
Dye, Montague 30

E

Eagle, Chambers............................ 30
*EAGLE LAKE, Colorado, 106,
   (3,639) 3,809
*EAGLE PASS, Maverick, 902,
   (26,248) 28,202
*EARLY, Brown, 183,
   (2,762) 3,024
*EARTH, Lamb, 23, (1,065).......... 975
East Afton, Dickens 13
East Alto Bonito, Starr, (824) 929
*EAST BERNARD, Wharton, 113,
   (2,272) 2,320
East Caney, Hopkins 100
East Columbia, Brazoria................ 95
East Delta, Delta............................ 60
East Direct, Lamar 48
Easter, Castro................................ 26
Easterly, Robertson 61
Eastgate, Liberty.......................... 200
East Hamilton, Shelby 25
*EASTLAND, Eastland, 211,
   (3,960) 3,967
East Lopez, Starr, (166)................ 183
EAST MOUNTAIN, Upshur, 20,
   (797) 839
*EASTON, Gregg-Rusk, 5,
   (510) 636
East Point, Wood............................ 40
East Sweden, McCulloch................ 40
EAST TAWAKONI, Rains, 24,
   (883) 927
Ebenezer, Camp............................. 55
Ebenezer, Jasper........................... 50
Echo, Coleman 6
Ecleto, Karnes 22
*ECTOR, Fannin, 12, (695) 733
*EDCOUCH, Hidalgo, 46,
   (3,161) 3,358
*EDDY [Bruceville-], McLennan-Falls,
   27, (1,475) 1,873
*EDEN, Concho, 54, (2,766) 1,297
Eden, Nacogdoches 100
Edgar, DeWitt 8
Edge, Brazos 10
EDGECLIFF, Tarrant, (2,776) 3,019
Edgewater Estates, San Patricio,
   (72) 76
*EDGEWOOD, Van Zandt, 97,
   (1,441) 1,482
Edgeworth, Bell 15
Edhube, Fannin 40
*EDINBURG, Hidalgo, 1,921,
   (74,588) 90,062
*EDMONSON, Hale, 5, (111)........ 109
*EDNA, Jackson, 257,
   (5,499) 5,692
Edna Hill, Erath.............................. 32
EDOM, Van Zandt, 16, (375) 390
*Edroy, San Patricio, 1, (331) 312
Egan, Johnson.............................. 133
*Egypt, Wharton, 3 26
Eidson Road, Maverick,
   (8,960) 9,135
Elam Springs, Upshur.................... 50
Elbert, Throckmorton, (30)............. 24

Elbow, Howard................................ 10
El Brazil, Starr, (47) 50
El Camino Angosto, Cameron,
   (253) 268
*EL CAMPO, Wharton, 609,
   (11,602) 11,727
El Castillo, Starr, (188).................. 214
EL CENIZO, Webb, 25,
   (3,273) 3,132
El Cenizo, Starr, (249) 279
El Centro, Starr................................ 50
El Chaparral, Starr, (464).............. 504
*ELDORADO, Schleicher, 67,
   (1,951) 1,720
Eldorado Center, Navarro.............. 20
Eldridge, Colorado.......................... 10
*ELECTRA, Wichita, 72,
   (2,791) 2,738
Elevation, Milam 12
*ELGIN, Bastrop, 419,
   (8,135) 9,652
Elias-Fela Solis, Starr, (30)............ 36
Eliasville, Young........................... 100
*El Indio, Maverick, 1, (190) 172
Elk, McLennan.............................. 150
*ELKHART, Anderson, 60,
   (1,371) 1,284
EL LAGO, Harris, 67,
   (2,706) 2,583
*Ellinger, Fayette, 9 386
Elliott, Robertson 55
Elliott, Wilbarger........................... 50
*Elmaton, Matagorda, 3.............. 160
Elm Creek, Maverick, (2,469) 2,730
*ELMENDORF, Bexar, 71,
   (1,488) 1,883
El Mesquite, Starr, (38).................. 45
Elm Grove, Cherokee..................... 50
Elm Grove, San Saba..................... 15
Elm Grove, Wharton....................... 76
Elm Grove Camp, Guadalupe 88
*Elm Mott, McLennan, 70 300
*Elmo, Kaufman, 1, (768) 899
Elmont, Grayson............................. 15
Elm Ridge, Milam 25
Elmwood, Anderson........................ 15
Eloise, Falls 19
El Oso, Karnes 35
*EL PASO, El Paso, 16,474,
   (649,121) 682,888
El Quiote, Starr, (208).................. 221
El Rancho Vela, Starr, (274)......... 299
El Refugio, Starr, (331)................. 384
Elroy, Travis 125
*ELSA, Hidalgo, 158, (5,660) 6,871
El Sauz, Starr 50
El Socio, Starr, (130) 133
Elton, Dickens.................................. 4
El Toro, Jackson........................... 136
Elwood, Fannin............................... 31
Elwood, Madison............................ 50
*Elysian Fields, Harrison, 7 500
Emberson, Lamar........................... 80
Emerald Bay, Smith, (1,047)...... 1,072
EMHOUSE, Navarro, 2,
   (133) 132
Emmett, Navarro 100
*EMORY, Rains, 179,
   (1,239) 1,270
Encantada-Ranchito El Calaboz,
   Cameron, (2,255) 2,222

Town, County .... Pop. 2017	Town, County .... Pop. 2017	Town, County .... Pop. 2017
ENCHANTED OAKS, Henderson, (326) 332	EUREKA, Navarro, 9, (307) 303	Falcon, Zapata, (191) 186
*ENCINAL, La Salle, 28, (559) 576	*EUSTACE, Henderson, 57, (991) 969	Falconaire, Starr, (132) 132
*Encino, Brooks, 6, (143) 137	*Evadale, Jasper, 16, (1,483) 1,540	*Falcon Heights, Starr, 1, (53) 50
*Energy, Comanche, 2................... 70	*EVANT, Coryell-Hamilton, 37, (426) 388	Falcon Lake Estates, Zapata, (1,036) 1,082
Engle, Fayette 141	Evergreen, San Jacinto 100	Falcon Mesa, Zapata, (405) 359
English, Red River...................... 100	Evergreen, Starr, (73) 83	Falcon Village, Starr, (47) 54
*Enloe, Delta, 1.............................. 90	EVERMAN, Tarrant, 117, (6,108) 6,523	*FALFURRIAS, Brooks, 133, (4,981) 4,931
*ENNIS, Ellis, 685, (18,513) 20,775	Ewell, Upshur 20	Fallon, Limestone 100
Enoch, Upshur................................ 25	Ezzell, Lavaca 55	*FALLS CITY, Karnes, 32, (611) ... 681
*Enochs, Bailey 80		Falman, San Patricio, (76).............. 76
Enon, Upshur............................... 204	**F**	Famuliner, Cochran 5
*Eola, Concho, 4........................... 215	*Fabens, El Paso, 67, (8,257) ... 8,415	Fannett, Jefferson, (2,252) 2,236
Eolian, Stephens 9	Fabrica, Maverick, (923).............. 956	*Fannin, Goliad, 6......................... 359
*Era, Cooke, 5 150	FAIRCHILDS, Fort Bend, (763) 1,012	Fargo, Wilbarger........................... 169
Ericksdahl, Jones 35	*FAIRFIELD, Freestone, 223, (2,951) 2,959	Farmers Academy, Titus 75
Erin, Jasper 70	Fairland, Burnet............................ 340	*FARMERS BRANCH, Dallas, 1,975, (28,616) 34,500
Erna, Menard.................................. 27	Fairlie, Hunt 80	Farmers Valley, Wilbarger 30
Erwin, Grimes................................. 52	Fairmount, Sabine 1,500	*FARMERSVILLE, Collin, 201, (3,301) 3,879
Escobares, Starr, 44, (1,188)..... 2,853	Fair Oaks, Limestone 15	Farmington, Grayson...................... 40
Escobar I, Starr, (324) 351	*FAIR OAKS RANCH, Bexar-Comal-Kendall, 154, (5,986) 9,003	*Farnsworth, Ochiltree, 6.............. 130
Escobas, Zapata............................. 2		Farrar, Limestone 51
Escondidas [Sandy Hollow-], Nueces, (296)........................ 261	Fair Play, Panola 80	Farrsville, Newton 152
Eskota, Fisher................................. 32	Fairview, Armstrong....................... 10	*FARWELL, Parmer, 47, (1,363) 1,335
Esperanza, Hudspeth 75	Fairview, Cass 20	Fashing, Atascosa 35
Espey, Atascosa 55	FAIRVIEW, Collin, 289, (7,248) 9,278	*FATE, Rockwall, 261, (6,357) 10,243
Estacado, Lubbock-Crosby 32	Fairview, Gaines 160	Faught, Lamar 25
*ESTELLINE, Hall, 3, (145) 138	Fairview, Hockley........................... 20	Faulkner, Lamar............................. 10
Estes, Aransas............................. 300	Fairview, Hood............................... 30	Fawil, Newton 183
Ethel, Grayson............................... 40	Fairview, Howard 5	*FAYETTEVILLE, Fayette, 69, (258) 261
*Etoile, Nacogdoches, 12 700	Fairview, Wilson............................. 95	Faysville, Hidalgo, (439) 475
Eugenio Saenz, Starr, (159) 173	Fairy, Hamilton............................... 40	Fedor, Lee 92
Eula, Callahan 125		*Fentress, Caldwell, 8.................. 380
*EULESS, Tarrant, 1,423, (51,277) 54,178		
Eulogy, Bosque............................. 10		
Eureka, Franklin 18		

Downtown Gonzales. Photo by Rosie Hatch.

Town, County ....Pop. 2017	Town, County ....Pop. 2017	Town, County ....Pop. 2017
Fernando Salinas, Starr, (15) 14	*Fort Hancock, Hudspeth, 8,	*FULSHEAR, Fort Bend, 318,
*FERRIS, Ellis, 101, (2,436)...... 2,559	(1,750) 1,853	(1,134).............................. 8,983
Fetzer, Waller 150	Fort Hood, Bell-Coryell,	*FULTON, Aransas, 98,
Fields Store, Waller 500	(29,589)........................... 30,959	(1,358).............................. 1,588
*Fieldton, Lamb, 1 20	*Fort McKavett, Menard................ 50	Funston, Jones............................. 26
Fife, McCulloch............................ 32	Fort Parker, Limestone 2	Furrh, Panola............................... 40
Fifth Street, Fort Bend,	Fort Parker State Park, Limestone . 30	
(2,486) 3,163	Fort Sherman, Titus.................... 200	**G**
Files Valley, Hill............................ 60	Fort Spunky, Hood......................... 15	Gadston, Lamar............................ 35
Fincastle, Henderson.................... 75	*FORT STOCKTON, Pecos, 314,	*Gail, Borden, 5, (231)............... 262
Finney, Hale.................................. 18	(8,283) 8,558	*GAINESVILLE, Cooke, 773,
*Fischer, Comal, 17 400	*FORT WORTH, Tarrant-Denton-	(16,002) 16,373
Fisk, Coleman............................... 40	Parker-Wise, 20,779,	Galena, Smith............................... 50
Five Points, Ellis 25	(741,206) 851,655	*GALENA PARK, Harris, 160,
Flaccus, Karnes............................ 15	Foster, Terry.................................... 6	(10,887) 11,092
Flagg, Castro 26	Fostoria, Montgomery.................. 586	Galilee, Smith.............................. 150
*Flat, Coryell, 2 210	Fouke, Wood 30	*GALLATIN, Cherokee, (419) 437
Flat Fork, Shelby 10	Four Corners, Brazoria 60	Galloway, Panola........................... 71
*FLATONIA, Fayette, 102,	Four Corners, Chambers............... 18	*GALVESTON, Galveston, 1,887,
(1,383) 1,413	Four Corners, Fort Bend,	(47,743) 49,979
Flat Prairie, Trinity......................... 33	(12,382) 15,153	*GANADO, Jackson, 112,
Flats, Rains.................................. 40	Four Corners, Montgomery 500	(2,003) 2,090
Flat Top, Stonewall 5	Four Points, Webb, (18) 16	Garceño, Starr, (420).................. 414
*Flint, Smith, 193 2,500	*Fowlerton, La Salle, 4, (55).......... 49	*Garciasville, Starr, 2, (46)........... 49
Flo, Leon...................................... 12	Frame Switch, Williamson 25	*Garden City, Glasscock, 31,
*Flomot, Motley............................ 181	*Francitas, Jackson, 2 125	(334) 371
Flora, Hopkins 20	Frankel City, Andrews...................... 2	*Gardendale, Ector, 45,
Flor del Rio, Starr, (122) 135	Frankell, Stephens........................... 8	(1,574) 1,902
*FLORENCE, Williamson, 103,	*FRANKLIN, Robertson, 83,	Gardendale, La Salle..................... 80
(1,136) 1,259	(1,564) 1,685	GARDEN RIDGE, Comal, 116,
*FLORESVILLE, Wilson, 355,	*FRANKSTON, Anderson, 89,	(3,259) 3,966
(6,448) 7,653	(1,229) 1,218	Garden Valley, Smith 150
Florey, Andrews 25	*Fred, Tyler, 6 300	Garfield, DeWitt 16
Flour Bluff, Nueces	*FREDERICKSBURG, Gillespie,	Garfield, Travis, (1,698)............. 1,793
.... [part of Corpus Christi]	1,193, (10,530) 11,542	Garland, Bowie 45
Flowella, Brooks, (118) 115	*Fredonia, Mason, 2 55	*GARLAND, Dallas, 5,949,
Flower Hill, Colorado 20	Freedom, Rains 32	(226,876) 238,534
*FLOWER MOUND, Denton,	*FREEPORT, Brazoria, 309,	Garner, Parker............................. 196
2,290, (64,669) 74,318	(12,049) 12,273	Garner State Park, Uvalde 50
Floyd, Hunt................................... 90	*FREER, Duval, 91, (2,818) 2,608	GARRETT, Ellis, 9, (806)............. 862
*FLOYDADA, Floyd, 115,	Freestone, Freestone 100	Garretts Bluff, Lamar 25
(3,038) 2,745	Frelsburg, Colorado........................ 75	*GARRISON, Nacogdoches, 43,
*Fluvanna, Scurry, 8 180	Frenstat, Burleson 50	(895)................................. 886
*Flynn, Leon, 4 81	Fresno, Collingsworth 10	*Garwood, Colorado, 21 600
Foard City, Foard........................... 10	*Fresno, Fort Bend, 113,	*GARY, Panola, (311) 301
Fodice, Houston 49	(19,069) 23,411	Garza-Salinas II, Starr, (719)........ 783
*FOLLETT, Lipscomb, 25,	Freyburg, Fayette 148	Gastonia, Kaufman...................... 100
(459)................................. 469	Friday, Trinity................................. 70	*GATESVILLE, Coryell, 372,
Folsom, Shelby.............................. 30	Friendship, Dawson........................ 40	(15,751) 14,122
Ford, Deaf Smith 25	Friendship, Smith......................... 200	*Gause, Milam, 6 425
Fords Corner, San Augustine 30	Friendship, Upshur 25	Gay Hill, Washington 40
Fordtran, Victoria 18	Friendship Village, Bowie 200	Geneva, Sabine........................... 200
Forest, Cherokee........................... 85	*FRIENDSWOOD, Galveston-Harris,	Geneview, Stonewall 3
*Forestburg, Montague, 14............. 50	1,179, (35,805) 39,219	Gentry's Mill, Hamilton 20
Forest Chapel, Lamar 105	Frio Town, Frio 9	George's Creek, Somervell 43
Forest Glade, Limestone 340	*FRIONA, Parmer, 86,	*GEORGETOWN, Williamson,
Forest Grove, Milam 60	(4,123) 3,995	2,136, (47,400) 66,904
Forest Heights, Orange 250	*FRISCO, Collin-Denton, 5,120,	*GEORGE WEST, Live Oak, 157,
Forest Hill, Lamar 50	(116,989) 171,982	(2,445).............................. 2,537
FOREST HILL, Tarrant, 328,	*FRITCH, Hutchinson-Moore, 66,	Georgia, Lamar............................. 55
(12,355) 12,699	(2,117) 2,067	Germany, Houston......................... 23
Forest Hill, Wood 30	Frog, Kaufman 90	*Geronimo, Guadalupe, 5,
*FORNEY, Kaufman, 761,	Fronton, Starr, (180) 172	(1,032) 1,140
(14,611) 19,481	Fronton Ranchettes, Starr,	GHOLSON, McLennan, 21,
*Forreston, Ellis, 2 400	(113) 121	(1,061) 1,088
*FORSAN, Howard, 9, (210) 207	*FROST, Navarro, 21, (643) 651	Gibtown, Jack 20
Fort Bliss, El Paso, (8,591)........ 9,776	Fruitland, Montague........................ 20	*GIDDINGS, Lee, 326,
Fort Clark Springs, Kinney,	*FRUITVALE, Van Zandt, 11,	(4,881) 5,106
(1,228).............................. 1,249	(408)................................. 419	*Gilchrist, Galveston, 1 300
*Fort Davis, Jeff Davis, 59,	Frydek, Austin.............................. 900	*Gillett, Karnes, 12..................... 120
(1,201) 1,202	Fulbright, Red River...................... 150	Gilliland, Knox............................... 20

Town, County .... Pop. 2017	Town, County .... Pop. 2017	Town, County .... Pop. 2017

CITIES & TOWNS

*GILMER, Upshur, 392,
   (4,905) 5,252
Gilpin, Dickens.................................. 2
Ginger, Rains................................... 70
*Girard, Kent, (50) 46
*Girvin, Pecos.................................. 20
Gist, Jasper 20
Givens, Lamar 135
*GLADEWATER, Gregg-Upshur,
   332, (6,441) 6,794
Glaze City, Gonzales 10
Glazier, Hemphill 48
Gleckler, Lavaca 78
Glen Cove, Coleman 40
Glendale, Trinity............................ 175
Glenfawn, Rusk 100
*Glen Flora, Wharton, 3 210
Glenn, Dickens 4
GLENN HEIGHTS, Dallas-Ellis,
   160, (11,278) 12,603
Glenrio, Deaf Smith 10
*GLEN ROSE, Somervell, 235,
   (2,444) 2,678
Glenwood, Upshur........................ 150
Glidden, Colorado, 1, (661) 730
Globe, Lamar 60
Glory, Lamar 30
*Gober, Fannin, 1 146
*GODLEY, Johnson, 65,
   (1,009) 1,139
*Golden, Wood, 6 398
Goldfinch, Frio 35
*Goldsboro, Coleman, 1 15
*GOLDSMITH, Ector, 18,
   (257) 265
*GOLDTHWAITE, Mills, 82,
   (1,878) 1,933
*GOLIAD, Goliad, 138,
   (1,908) 2,022
GOLINDA, Falls-McLennan, 18,
   (559) 600
Golly, DeWitt................................... 41
Gomez, Terry 6
*GONZALES, Gonzales, 360,
   (7,237) 7,530
Goober Hill, Shelby......................... 30
Goodland, Bailey 10
Goodlett, Hardeman 80
GOODLOW, Navarro, 4,
   (200) 201
Good Neighbor, Hopkins 40
Goodnight, Armstrong..................... 20
*GOODRICH, Polk, 32, (271) 294
Goodsprings, Rusk 40
Goodwill, Burleson.......................... 12
Goodwin, San Augustine 70
*GORDON, Palo Pinto, 30,
   (478) 472
*Gordonville, Grayson, 21 165
*GOREE, Knox, 8, (203)............... 176
*GORMAN, Eastland, 43,
   (1,083) 1,037
Goshen, Walker............................ 250
Gould, Cherokee 20
*Gouldbusk, Coleman, 3............... 70
Graceton, Upshur.......................... 100
*GRAFORD, Palo Pinto, 30,
   (584) 590
Graham, Garza 60
*GRAHAM, Young, 515,
   (8,903) 9,054

*GRANBURY, Hood, 1,249,
   (7,978) 9,679
Grand Acres, Cameron, (49) 47
Grand Bluff, Panola 115
*GRANDFALLS, Ward, 10,
   (360) 377
*GRAND PRAIRIE, Dallas-Tarrant-
   Ellis, 4,737,
   (175,396) 192,500
*GRAND SALINE, Van Zandt, 119,
   (3,136) 3,201
Grandview, Dawson......................... 8
Grandview, Gray............................. 13
*GRANDVIEW, Johnson, 109,
   (1,561) 1,673
*GRANGER, Williamson, 54,
   (1,419) 1,508
Grangerland, Montgomery........... 300
*GRANITE SHOALS, Burnet, 90,
   (4,910) 5,057
GRANJENO, Hidalgo, 2,
   (293) 298
Grape Creek, Tom Green,
   (3,154) 3,270
*GRAPELAND, Houston, 87,
   (1,489) 1,490
*GRAPEVINE, Tarrant, 2,825,
   (46,334) 51,700
Grassland, Lynn 40
Gray, Marion 12
Grayback, Wilbarger 10
GRAYS PRAIRIE, Kaufman, 6,
   (337) 364
Graytown, Wilson 85
Green, Karnes 50
Green Hill, Titus 80
Green Lake, Calhoun 51
Greenpond, Hopkins..................... 150
Green's Creek, Erath 75
Green Valley, Denton 100
Green Valley Farms, Cameron,
   (1,272) 1,492
Greenview, Hopkins........................ 25
*GREENVILLE, Hunt, 979,
   (25,557) 27,492
Greenvine, Washington 35
Greenwood, Hopkins 100
Greenwood, Midland 2,000
Greenwood, Red River 20
*Greenwood, Wise, 3..................... 76
*GREGORY, San Patricio, 38,
   (1,907) 1,967
Gresham, Smith......................... 1,000
GREY FOREST, Bexar, 16,
   (483) 553
Gribble Springs, Denton 55
Grice, Upshur 20
Griffith, Cochran 12
Grigsby, Shelby 15
Grit, Mason 15
*GROESBECK, Limestone, 131,
   (4,328) 4,320
*GROOM, Carson, 32,
   (574) 566
Grosvenor, Brown........................... 24
*GROVES, Jefferson, 316,
   (16,144) 15,698
*GROVETON, Trinity, 46,
   (1,057) 1,011
Grow, King... 9
Gruenau, DeWitt............................. 18

Gruene, Comal ....
   .... [part of New Braunfels]
*GRUVER, Hansford, 41,
   (1,194) 1,163
Guadalupe, Victoria 70
Guadalupe-Guerra, Starr, (37)........ 44
Guadalupe Station, Culberson 10
*Guerra, Jim Hogg, (6) 5
Gum Springs, Cass 59
*GUN BARREL CITY, Henderson,
   322, (5,672) 6,052
Gunsight, Stephens 6
*GUNTER, Grayson, 74,
   (1,498) 1,460
Gus, Burleson 50
*GUSTINE, Comanche, 10,
   (476) 484
*Guthrie, King, 1, (160)................. 183
Gutierrez, Starr, (79)....................... 83
*Guy, Fort Bend, 9 239
Guys Store, Leon............................ 20

H

Haciendito, Presidio........................ 10
Hackberry, Cottle 30
HACKBERRY, Denton, 53,
   (968) 1,125
Hackberry, Edwards 3
Hackberry, Garza 5
Hackberry, Lavaca.......................... 40
Hagansport, Franklin 40
Hagerville, Houston 70
Hail, Fannin 30
Hainesville, Wood 95
*HALE CENTER, Hale, 40,
   (2,252) 2,112
Halfway, Hale 165
Hall, San Saba 25
*HALLETTSVILLE, Lavaca, 213,
   (2,550) 2,629
Halls Bluff, Houston 67
HALLSBURG, McLennan, 12,
   (507) 504
*HALLSVILLE, Harrison, 123,
   (3,577) 4,203
*HALTOM CITY, Tarrant, 1,331,
   (42,409) 43,540
Hamby, Taylor 100
*HAMILTON, Hamilton, 181,
   (3,095) 3,182
*HAMLIN, Jones-Fisher, 70,
   (2,124) 2,119
Hammond, Robertson 44
Hamon, Gonzales 20
*Hamshire, Jefferson, 18 759
Hancock, Comal 1,000
Hancock, Dawson........................... 20
*Hankamer, Chambers, 12 226
Hannibal, Erath............................... 25
Hanover, Milam............................... 25
*HAPPY, Swisher-Randall, 34,
   (678) 651
Happy Union, Hale 25
Happy Valley, Taylor 12
Harbin, Erath 21
*HARDIN, Liberty, 11, (819).......... 894
Hare, Williamson 60
*Hargill, Hidalgo, 3, (877) 913
*HARKER HEIGHTS, Bell, 662,
   (26,700) 30,328
Harkeyville, San Saba 12

Town, County ....Pop. 2017	Town, County ....Pop. 2017	Town, County ....Pop. 2017
*Harleton, Harrison, 22.................390	*HEREFORD, Deaf Smith, 395,	HOLIDAY LAKES, Brazoria, 5,
*HARLINGEN, Cameron, 2,167,	(15,370)...........................15,554	(1,107)...............................1,202
(64,849)............................65,409	Hermits Cove, Rains.....................40	*HOLLAND, Bell, 49,
Harmon, Lamar.............................12	*Hermleigh, Scurry, 16, (345).......315	(1,121)...............................1,139
Harmony, Floyd.............................42	Hester, Navarro............................35	Holland Quarters, Panola..............40
Harmony, Grimes...........................12	*HEWITT, McLennan, 398,	*HOLLIDAY, Archer, 75,
Harmony, Kent...............................10	(13,549).............................14,217	(1,758)...............................1,743
Harmony, Nacogdoches.................50	*Hext, Menard, 1............................75	Holly, Houston...............................95
*Harper, Gillespie, 31,	HICKORY CREEK, Denton, 126,	Holly Grove, Polk...........................20
(1,192)...............................1,326	(3,247)................................4,425	Holly Lake Ranch, Wood,
Harpersville, Stephens....................5	Hickory Creek, Houston.................31	(2,774)...............................2,762
Harrison, McLennan.....................100	Hickory Creek, Hunt......................40	Holly Springs, Jasper.....................50
*Harrold, Wilbarger, 3..................200	*HICO, Hamilton, 143,	HOLLYWOOD PARK, Bexar, 121,
*HART, Castro, 23, (1,114)........1,021	(1,379)...............................1,419	(3,062)...............................3,392
Hartburg, Newton.........................893	*HIDALGO, Hidalgo, 481,	Holman, Fayette...........................101
Hart Camp, Lamb............................4	(11,198).............................13,334	Homer, Angelina..........................475
*Hartley, Hartley, 19, (540)...........707	Hidden Acres [Lakeshore Gardens-],	Homestead Meadows North, El Paso,
Harvard, Camp...............................48	San Patricio, (504).................471	(5,247)...............................5,470
Harvey, Brazos..........................1,000	HIDEAWAY, Smith, (3,083).......2,986	Homestead Meadows South, El Paso,
Harwell Point, Burnet...................138	Higginbotham, Gaines...................21	(7,247)...............................7,595
*Harwood, Gonzales, 12...............118	*HIGGINS, Lipscomb, 15,	*HONDO, Medina, 276,
*HASKELL, Haskell, 96,	(397).................................413	(8,803)...............................9,313
(3,322)...............................3,217	High, Lamar...................................14	*HONEY GROVE, Fannin, 63,
Haslam, Shelby............................100	Highbank, Falls..............................20	(1,668)...............................1,762
*HASLET, Tarrant, 249,	High Hill, Fayette.........................176	Honey Island, Hardin...................200
(1,517)...............................1,868	*High Island, Galveston, 5...........300	Hood, Cooke..................................13
Hasse, Comanche..........................50	Highland, Erath..............................60	Hooker Ridge, Rains....................250
Hatchel, Runnels.............................6	HIGHLAND HAVEN, Burnet,	*HOOKS, Bowie, 50, (2,769)....2,778
Hatchettville, Hopkins....................20	(431).................................480	Hoover, Gray...................................5
Havana, Hidalgo,(407)..................394	HIGHLAND PARK, Dallas, 457,	Hoover, Lamar................................20
HAWK COVE, Hunt, 3, (483)........525	(8,564)...............................9,162	Hope, Lavaca.................................45
*HAWKINS, Wood, 86,	*Highlands, Harris, 120,	Hopewell, Franklin.........................50
(1,278)...............................1,343	(7,522)...............................7,743	Hopewell, Houston.........................22
*HAWLEY, Jones, 55,	HIGHLAND VILLAGE, Denton, 511,	Hopewell, Lamar.............................90
(634).................................638	(15,056).............................17,037	Hopewell, Red River.....................152
Hawthorne, Walker......................100	Hightower, Liberty........................225	Hopewell, Smith.............................45
Haynesville, Wichita......................65	HILL COUNTRY VILLAGE, Bexar,	Hopewell [Dixon-], Houston...........10
HAYS, Hays, 2, (217)...................251	98, (985).........................1,041	HORIZON CITY, El Paso, 268,
Hazeldell, Comanche.....................12	Hillcrest, Colorado.........................25	(16,735)............................18,592
H. Cuellar Estates, Starr, (20).........19	HILLCREST VILLAGE, Brazoria,	Hornsby Bend, Travis,
*HEARNE, Robertson, 160,	(730).................................740	(6,791)...............................7,762
(4,459)...............................4,648	*Hillister, Tyler, 11........................250	HORSESHOE BAY, Llano-Burnet,
HEATH, Rockwall, 264,	Hillje, Wharton...............................51	168, (3,418).....................3,758
(6,921)...............................8,231	Hills, Lee.......................................20	Horseshoe Bend, Parker,
*Hebbronville, Jim Hogg, 84,	*HILLSBORO, Hill, 385,	(789).................................883
(4,558)...............................4,485	(8,456)...............................8,456	Hortense, Polk...............................20
HEBRON, Denton, 43, (415)........426	Hillside Acres, Webb, (30).............39	Horton, Delta.................................40
Heckville, Lubbock.........................91	Hilltop, Frio, (287).......................285	Horton, Panola.............................200
*HEDLEY, Donley, 7, (329)...........317	Hilltop, Starr, (77)..........................86	*HOUSTON, Harris-Fort Bend-
Hedwigs Hill, Mason......................12	*Hilltop Lakes, Leon,	Montgomery, 87,046,
HEDWIG VILLAGE, Harris, 253,	(1,101)...............................1,025	(2,100,263).................2,265,464
(2,557)...............................2,731	HILSHIRE VILLAGE, Harris, 18,	Howard, Ellis..................................60
Hefner, Knox...................................3	(746).................................806	HOWARDWICK, Donley, 9,
Hegar, Waller...............................100	Hinckley, Lamar.............................40	(402).................................384
Heidelberg, Hidalgo, (1,725)......1,885	Hindes, Atascosa...........................14	*HOWE, Grayson, 63,
*Heidenheimer, Bell, 6.................224	Hinkles Ferry, Brazoria.................100	(2,600)...............................2,772
Helena, Karnes..............................35	Hiram, Kaufman.............................75	Howland, Lamar.............................65
Helmic, Trinity...............................86	*HITCHCOCK, Galveston, 175,	Hoxie, Williamson..........................60
*HELOTES, Bexar, 515,	(6,961)...............................7,884	Hoyte, Milam..................................20
(7,341)...............................8,889	Hitchland, Hansford.......................15	Hub, Parmer...................................25
*HEMPHILL, Sabine, 136,	Hix, Burleson.................................35	Hubbard, Bowie............................350
(1,198)...............................1,229	Hoard, Wood..................................45	*HUBBARD, Hill, 64, (1,423).....1,404
*HEMPSTEAD, Waller, 241,	Hobbs, Fisher................................32	Huber, Shelby.................................15
(5,770)...............................7,011	*Hobson, Karnes, 11....................135	Huckabay, Erath...........................150
*HENDERSON, Rusk, 606,	*Hochheim, DeWitt........................70	HUDSON, Angelina, 81,
(13,712).............................13,708	*Hockley, Harris, 147...................400	(4,731)...............................4,820
Henkhaus, Lavaca..........................88	Hodges, Jones.............................150	Hudson Bend, Travis,
Henly, Hays.................................140	Hogansville, Rains.......................300	(2,981)...............................3,694
*HENRIETTA, Clay, 123,	Hogg, Burleson..............................20	HUDSON OAKS, Parker, 153,
(3,141)...............................3,011	Holiday Beach, Aransas,	(1,662)...............................2,248
Henry's Chapel, Cherokee.............75	(514).................................538	Huffines, Cass..............................140

Town, County .... Pop. 2017	Town, County .... Pop. 2017	Town, County .... Pop. 2017

*Huffman, Harris, 155 15,000
Hufsmith, Harris............................. 500
*HUGHES SPRINGS, Cass, 66,
   (1,760) 1,788
*Hull, Liberty, 15, (669) 711
*HUMBLE, Harris, 1,834,
   (15,133) 15,725
*Hungerford, Wharton, 16,
   (347)...................................... 306
*Hunt, Kerr, 38.............................. 708
Hunter, Comal................................. 40
HUNTERS CREEK VILLAGE, Harris,
   103, (4,367) 4,757
*HUNTINGTON, Angelina, 107,
   (2,118) 2,159
Huntoon, Ochiltree........................... 22
*HUNTSVILLE, Walker, 1,135,
   (38,548) 41,511
Hurley, Wood.................................. 30
Hurlwood, Lubbock........................ 152
Hurnville, Clay 10
*HURST, Tarrant, 1,601,
   (37,337) 39,458
Hurstown, Shelby 20
Hurst Springs, Coryell..................... 10
*HUTCHINS, Dallas, 134,
   (5,338) 6,029
*HUTTO, Williamson, 551,
   (14,698) 23,443
HUXLEY, Shelby, 5, (385) 388
*Hye, Blanco, 11 72
Hylton, Nolan 6

I

Iago, Wharton, (161)..................... 154
Ida, Grayson 30
*IDALOU, Lubbock, 88,
   (2,250) 2,350
Iglesia Antigua, Cameron, (413) ... 447
Ike, Ellis 50
Illinois Bend, Montague 40
IMPACT, Taylor, 1, (35) 33
*Imperial, Pecos, 6, (278) 246
Inadale, Scurry 12
Independence, Washington........... 140
India, Ellis 30
Indian Creek, Brown 28
Indian Creek, Smith 300
Indian Gap, Hamilton 35
Indian Hill, Newton........................... 7
Indian Hills, Hidalgo,
   (2,591) 2,952
INDIAN LAKE, Cameron,
   (640) 691
Indianola, Calhoun........................ 200
Indian Rock, Upshur 45
Indian Springs, Polk, (785) 791
Indio, Presidio.................................. 5
Indio, Starr, (50)............................. 60
*INDUSTRY, Austin, 44,
   (304) 330
*Inez, Victoria, 51, (2,098) 2,430
*INGLESIDE, San Patricio, 215,
   (9,387) 9,748
INGLESIDE-ON-THE-BAY,
   San Patricio, 13, (615).......... 622
*INGRAM, Kerr, 174,
   (1,804) 1,903
*IOLA, Grimes, 11, (401) 417
IOWA COLONY, Brazoria, 26,
   (1,170) 1,365

*IOWA PARK, Wichita, 173,
   (6,355) 6,450
*Ira, Scurry, 12.............................. 250
*IRAAN, Pecos, 58, (1,229)....... 1,236
*IREDELL, Bosque, 19,
   (339) 334
Ireland, Coryell 60
Irene, Hill 170
Ironton, Cherokee......................... 110
*IRVING, Dallas, 6,682,
   (216,290) 240,769
Isla, Sabine.................................. 350
Israel, Polk..................................... 25
*ITALY, Ellis, 59, (1,863) 1,962
*ITASCA, Hill, 55,
   (1,644) 1,689
Ivan, Stephens............................... 15
*Ivanhoe, Fannin, 8 110
IVANHOE, Tyler, (1,425)............. 2,264
Izoro, Lampasas.............................. 17

J

*JACINTO CITY, Harris, 206,
   (10,553) 10,634
*JACKSBORO, Jack, 188,
   (4,511) 4,556
Jackson, Shelby.............................. 50
Jackson, Van Zandt 25
*JACKSONVILLE, Cherokee, 708,
   (14,544) 14,972
Jacobia, Hunt................................. 60
Jakes Colony, Guadalupe............... 95
JAMAICA BEACH, Galveston, 43,
   (983) 1,081
James, Shelby 75
Jamestown, Newton 196
Jamestown, Smith 75
Jardin de San Julian, Starr, (22)..... 23
*JARRELL, Williamson, 138,
   (984) 1,209
*JASPER, Jasper, 409,
   (7,590) 7,649
*JAYTON, Kent, 21, (534) 534
Jean, Young 110
*JEFFERSON, Marion, 216,
   (2,106) 2,060
Jenkins, Morris 350
Jennings, Lamar 85
*Jermyn, Jack, 3 75
JERSEY VILLAGE, Harris, 262,
   (7,620) 7,835
*JEWETT, Leon, 67,
   (1,167) 1,237
JF Villarreal, Starr, (104)...............111
Jiba, Kaufman................................ 50
*JOAQUIN, Shelby, 40, (824) 830
Joe Lee, Bell.................................... 8
*JOHNSON CITY, Blanco, 146,
   (1,656) 1,880
Johnsville, Erath 45
Johntown, Red River 175
*Joinerville, Rusk 140
Joliet, Caldwell............................... 70
JOLLY, Clay, 5, (172) 175
Jollyville, Williamson-Travis
   (16,151) 15,877
Jonah, Williamson 60
*Jonesboro, Coryell-Hamilton, 8 ... 125
JONES CREEK, Brazoria, 26,
   (2,020) 2,039
Jones Prairie, Milam 20

JONESTOWN, Travis, 89,
   (1,834) 2,001
*Jonesville, Harrison, 2................... 70
Joplin, Jack.................................... 15
Joppa, Burnet................................. 84
Jordans Store, Shelby 20
*JOSEPHINE, Collin, 27,
   (812) 1,252
*JOSHUA, Johnson, 267,
   (5,910) 7,156
Josserand, Trinity 29
Jot-Em-Down, Delta 8
*JOURDANTON, Atascosa, 152,
   (3,871) 4,276
Joy, Clay 110
Jozye, Madison............................... 36
Juarez, Cameron, (1,017)........... 1,153
Jud, Haskell................................... 60
*Judson, Gregg, 9........................ 1,057
Juliff, Fort Bend 100
Jumbo, Panola............................... 60
*JUNCTION, Kimble, 182,
   (2,574) 2,544
Justiceburg, Garza, 3 45
*JUSTIN, Denton, 193,
   (3,246) 3,837

K

Kalgary, Crosby 2
*Kamay, Wichita, 5 640
Kamey, Calhoun 25
Kanawha, Red River........................ 90
*Karnack, Harrison, 22 350
*KARNES CITY, Karnes, 103,
   (3,042) 3,315
Karon, Live Oak.............................. 25
Katemcy, Mason 80
*KATY, Harris-Waller-Fort Bend,
   2,528, (14,102) 17,184
*KAUFMAN, Kaufman, 366,
   (6,703) 7,089
K-Bar Ranch, Jim Wells, (358) 328
Keechi, Leon................................. 15
*KEENE, Johnson, 103,
   (6,106) 6,700
Keeter, Wise 250
Keith, Grimes................................. 50
*KELLER, Tarrant, 1,437,
   (39,627) 44,749
Kellerville, Wheeler......................... 15
Kellogg, Hunt................................. 20
Kellyville, Marion............................ 75
Kelsey, Upshur 50
Kelton, Wheeler.............................. 34
*KEMAH, Galveston, 339,
   (1,773) 1,984
*KEMP, Kaufman, 103,
   (1,154) 1,300
Kemper City, Victoria 16
*KEMPNER, Lampasas, 82,
   (1,089) 1,066
*Kendalia, Kendall, 12 149
*KENDLETON, Fort Bend, 3,
   (380) 408
*KENEDY, Karnes, 142,
   (3,296) 3,705
KENEFICK, Liberty, 13, (563)....... 631
*KENNARD, Houston, 13,
   (337) 327
*KENNEDALE, Tarrant, 313,
   (6,763) 7,524

Town, County ....Pop. 2017	Town, County ....Pop. 2017	Town, County ....Pop. 2017
La Paloma Ranchettes, Starr, (239) 265	Laughlin Air Force Base, Val Verde, (1,569) 1,583	*Lenorah, Martin, 6 83
La Parita, Atascosa.........................48	Laurel, Newton 357	Lenz, Karnes 50
*LA PORTE, Harris, 948, (33,800) 35,320	Laureles, Cameron, (3,692).......3,756	Leo, Cooke 20
La Presa, Webb, (319) 297	Lavender, Limestone 30	Leo, Lee...10
*La Pryor, Zavala, 11, (1,643) 1,710	*LA VERNIA, Wilson, 217, (1,034) 1,374	*LEONA, Leon, 8, (175)...............177
La Puerta, Starr, (632) 620	La Victoria, Starr, (171)................162	*LEONARD, Fannin, 102, (1,990) 2,074
*LAREDO, Webb, 6,909, (236,091) 261,397	*LA VILLA, Hidalgo, 17, (1,957) 2,425	Leon Junction, Coryell 50
Laredo Ranchettes, Webb, (22) 20	*LAVON, Collin, 120, (2,219) 3,260	Leon Springs, Bexar........................... ....[part of San Antonio]
La Reforma, Starr..........................20	*LA WARD, Jackson, 5, (213) 223	*LEON VALLEY, Bexar, 475, (10,151) 11,259
Lariat, Parmer..............................100	*LAWN, Taylor, 10, (314) 330	*LEROY, McLennan, 10, (337) 336
La Rosita, Starr, (85) 75	Lawrence, Kaufman.....................259	Lesley, Hall 25
*Larue, Henderson, 23 250	*Lazbuddie, Parmer, 5 248	*LEVELLAND, Hockley, 424, (13,542) 13,957
*LaSalle, Jackson.........................110	*LEAGUE CITY, Galveston-Harris, 2,813, (83,560) 102,745	Leverett's Chapel, Rusk 400
Lasana, Cameron, (84)...................73	Leagueville, Henderson.................50	Levi, McLennan 50
*Lasara, Willacy, 1, (1,039)........1,008	*LEAKEY, Real, 66, (425)..............449	Levita, Coryell................................70
Las Escobas, Starr 5	*LEANDER, Williamson, 1,135, (26,521) 39,202	*LEWISVILLE, Denton, 3,655, (95,290) 108,159
Las Haciendas, Webb, (7)................8	LEARY, Bowie, 13, (495) 488	*LEXINGTON, Lee, 74, (1,177) 1,208
Las Lomas, Starr, (3,147)...........3,302	*Ledbetter, Fayette, 13 83	*LIBERTY, Liberty, 448, (8,397) 9,327
Las Lomitas, Jim Hogg, (244).......216	Leedale, Bell..................................24	Liberty, Lubbock 228
Las Palmas, Zapata, (67) 65	*Leesburg, Camp, 11...................128	Liberty, Milam 40
Las Palmas II, Cameron, (1,605) 1,869	*Leesville, Gonzales, 2 152	Liberty, Newton 128
Las Pilas, Webb, (28) 29	*LEFORS, Gray, 9, (497)..............492	Liberty City, Gregg, (2,351) 2,461
Las Quintas Fronterizas, Maverick, (3,290) 3,517	*Leggett, Polk, 5 500	Liberty Hill, Houston 73
Lassater, Marion 60	Lehman, Cochran 6	Liberty Hill, Milam 25
Las Yescas, Cameron...................221	Leigh, Harrison 60	*LIBERTY HILL, Williamson, 363, (967) 1,585
Latch, Upshur 50	Lela, Wheeler 135	Lilbert, Nacogdoches....................100
Latex, Harrison 75	*Lelia Lake, Donley, 1 70	*Lillian, Johnson, 9 1,160
*LATEXO, Houston, 9, (322) 319	*Leming, Atascosa, 6, (946) 1,085	
La Tina Ranch, Cameron, (618) ... 677		
Latium, Washington.......................30		

The water tower over Luling. Photo by Rosie Hatch.

Town, County .... Pop. 2017	Town, County .... Pop. 2017	Town, County .... Pop. 2017
*Lincoln, Lee, 11 336	Lone Cedar, Ellis 18	Loyal Valley, Mason 52
*LINDALE, Smith, 409,	Lone Grove, Llano 50	Loyola Beach, Kleberg 185
(4,818) 5,818	Lone Oak, Colorado 50	*Lozano, Cameron, (404) 442
*LINDEN, Cass, 77,	*LONE OAK, Hunt, 49, (598) 632	*LUBBOCK, Lubbock, 7,871,
(1,988) 2,034	Lone Pine, Houston 81	(229,573) 252,947
Lindenau, DeWitt 50	Lone Star, Cherokee 20	LUCAS, Collin, 209,
Lindendale, Kendall 70	Lone Star, Floyd 42	(5,166) 7,238
*LINDSAY, Cooke, 38,	Lone Star, Lamar 35	Luckenbach, Gillespie 25
(1,018) 1,081	*LONE STAR, Morris, 42,	*LUEDERS, Jones, 10, (346) 347
Lindsay, Reeves, (271) 267	(1,581) 1,585	Luella, Grayson 639
*Lingleville, Erath 100	*Long Branch, Panola, 4 150	*LUFKIN, Angelina, 1,810,
Linn Flat, Nacogdoches 60	Long Lake, Anderson 30	(35,067) 37,204
*Linn [San Manuel-], Hidalgo, 4,	Long Mott, Calhoun 76	*LULING, Caldwell, 248,
(801) 787	Longoria, Starr, (92) 100	(5,411) 5,823
Linwood, Cherokee 40	Longpoint, Washington 30	*LUMBERTON, Hardin, 449,
*LIPAN, Hood, 44, (430) 461	*LONGVIEW, Gregg-Harrison,	(11,943) 12,836
*Lipscomb, Lipscomb, (37) 27	3,509, (80,455) 82,471	Lums Chapel, Lamb 6
*Lissie, Wharton, 5 72	Longworth, Fisher 47	Luther, Howard 3
Littig, Travis 35	Looneyville, Nacogdoches 50	Lutie, Collingsworth 10
Little Cypress, Orange 900	*Loop, Gaines, 6, (225) 228	Lydia, Red River 109
*LITTLE ELM, Denton, 800,	*Lopeño, Zapata, (174) 184	*LYFORD, Willacy, 44,
(25,898) 42,771	Lopezville, Hidalgo, (4,333) 4,526	(2,611) 2,630
*LITTLEFIELD, Lamb, 147,	*LORAINE, Mitchell, 15,	Lynn Grove, Grimes 25
(6,372) 5,992	(602) 573	*Lyons, Burleson, 3 360
Little Hope, Wood 25	*LORENA, McLennan, 150,	*LYTLE, Atascosa-Medina-Bexar,
Little Midland, Burnet 82	(1,691) 1,766	190, (2,492) 2,893
Little New York, Gonzales 15	*LORENZO, Crosby, 30,	Lytton Springs, Caldwell 300
*LITTLE RIVER-ACADEMY, Bell,	(1,147) 1,195	
36, (1,961) 2,000	Los Altos, Webb, (140) 150	**M**
Lively, Kaufman 50	Los Alvarez, Starr, (303) 295	*MABANK, Kaufman-Henderson,
LIVE OAK, Bexar, 406,	Los Angeles, La Salle 15	222, (3,035) 3,423
(13,131) 15,849	Los Angeles Subdivision, Willacy,	Mabelle, Baylor 9
*LIVERPOOL, Brazoria, 21,	(121) 142	Mabry, Red River 60
(482) 572	Los Arcos, Webb, (127) 137	*Macdona, Bexar, 4, (559) 633
*LIVINGSTON, Polk, 588,	Los Arrieros, Starr, (91) 97	Macon, Franklin 21
(5,335) 5,305	Los Barreras, Starr, (288) 303	Macune, San Augustine 50
*LLANO, Llano, 240,	Los Centenarios, Webb, (87) 96	*MADISONVILLE, Madison, 205,
(3,232) 3,301	Los Corralitos, Webb, (35) 41	(4,396) 4,695
Llano Grande, Hidalgo,	*Los Ebanos, Hidalgo, 1,	Madras, Red River 61
(3,008) 3,254	(335) 362	Magnet, Wharton 42
Locker, San Saba 16	Los Ebanos, Starr, (280) 301	*MAGNOLIA, Montgomery, 954,
Lockett, Wilbarger 150	Los Escondidos, Burnet 80	(1,393) 2,028
Lockettville, Hockley 20	*LOS FRESNOS, Cameron, 219,	Magnolia, San Jacinto 150
*LOCKHART, Caldwell, 471,	(5,542) 6,812	Magnolia Beach, Calhoun 250
(12,698) 13,543	Los Fresnos, Webb, (67) 76	Magnolia Springs, Jasper 20
*LOCKNEY, Floyd, 46,	Los Huisaches, Webb, (17) 16	Maha, Travis 200
(1,842) 1,688	*LOS INDIOS, Cameron, 21,	Mahl, Nacogdoches 150
Locust, Grayson 118	(1,083) 1,064	Mahomet, Burnet 97
*Lodi, Marion, 1 175	Los Lobos, Zapata, (9) 7	Majors, Franklin 13
Loebau, Lee 35	Los Minerales, Webb, (20) 20	*MALAKOFF, Henderson, 113,
Logan, Panola 40	Los Nopalitos, Webb, (62) 65	(2,324) 2,361
LOG CABIN, Henderson, 6,	Losoya, Bexar 500	Mallard, Montague 12
(714) 690	LOS SAENZ [Roma-], Starr,	*MALONE, Hill, 13, (269) 274
*Lohn, McCulloch, 1 149	218, (9,765) 11,168	Malta, Bowie 350
Loire, Wilson 50	Lost Creek, Travis, (4,509) 4,523	Malvern, Leon 12
Lois, Cooke 10	Lost Creek [La Paloma-], Nueces,	Mambrino, Hood 74
*Lolita, Jackson, 19, (555) 580	(408) 500	*Manchaca, Travis, 106,
Loma Alta, McMullen 25	Lost Prairie, Limestone 2	(1,133) 1,309
Loma Alta, Val Verde 30	Los Veteranos I, Webb, (24) 26	Manchester, Red River 185
Loma Grande, Zavala, (107) 100	Los Veteranos II, Webb, (24) 26	Mangum, Eastland 15
Loma Linda, San Patricio, (122) ... 122	LOS YBANEZ, Dawson, 1, (19)..... 18	Manheim, Lee 50
Loma Linda East, Jim Wells,	*LOTT, Falls, 49, (759) 772	Mankin, Henderson 30
(254) 259	*Louise, Wharton, 37,	Mankins, Archer 10
Loma Linda East, Starr, (44) 43	(995) 1,001	*MANOR, Travis, 276,
Loma Linda West, Starr, (114) 129	Lovelace, Hill 30	(5,037) 7,524
Loma Vista, Starr, (160) 169	*LOVELADY, Houston, 33,	*MANSFIELD, Tarrant-Johnson-Ellis,
Lomax, Howard 25	(649) 640	2,003, (56,368) 65,233
*LOMETA, Lampasas, 38,	*Loving, Young, 4 300	Manuel Garcia, Starr, (203) 209
(856) 852	*Lowake, Concho, 1 40	Manuel Garcia II, Starr, (77) 74
*London, Kimble, 5 180	LOWRY CROSSING, Collin, 57,	*MANVEL, Brazoria, 342,
Lone Camp, Palo Pinto 110	(1,711) 2,047	(5,179) 9,023

CITIES & TOWNS

*Maple, Bailey.................................. 40
Maple, Red River........................... 30
Maple Springs, Titus...................... 25
Mapleton, Houston 32
*Marathon, Brewster, 18,
   (430) 407
*MARBLE FALLS, Burnet, 706,
   (6,077) 6,717
*MARFA, Presidio, 148,
   (1,981) 1,840
Margaret, Foard............................. 50
Marie, Runnels 10
*MARIETTA, Cass, (134).............. 134
*MARION, Guadalupe, 106,
   (1,066) 1,107
*Markham, Matagorda, 13,
   (1,082) 1,048
Markley, Young 25
*MARLIN, Falls, 154,
   (5,967) 5,840
Marlow, Milam 45
*MARQUEZ, Leon, 31, (263)........ 282
Mars, Van Zandt 20
*MARSHALL, Harrison, 853,
   (23,523) 24,777
Marston, Polk................................. 25
*MART, McLennan, 64,
   (1,897) 1,907
*MARTINDALE, Caldwell, 49,
   (1,116) 1,247
Martinez, Starr, (69)....................... 75
Martins Mill, Van Zandt 158
Martin Springs, Hopkins 200
*Martinsville, Nacogdoches, 2 350
Marvin, Lamar................................ 48
Maryetta, Jack................................. 7
*Maryneal, Nolan, 5....................... 50
Marysville, Cooke 12
*MASON, Mason, 216,
   (2,114) 2,172
Massey Lake, Anderson 30
Masterson, Moore, 2........................ 2
*MATADOR, Motley, 39, (607)...... 547
*Matagorda, Matagorda, 27,
   (503) 528
*MATHIS, San Patricio, 141,
   (4,942) 4,821
Matthews, Colorado....................... 20
*MAUD, Bowie, 37,
   (1,056) 1,136
*Mauriceville, Orange, 14,
   (3,252) 3,526
Maverick, Runnels 35
Maxdale, Bell 25
Maxey, Lamar................................. 70
*Maxwell, Caldwell, 26................. 500
*May, Brown, 13 270
*Maydelle, Cherokee, 1 250
Mayfield, Hale................................ 26
Mayfield, Hill 25
Mayflower, Newton 50
Maynard, San Jacinto 90
*MAYPEARL, Ellis, 47,
   (934) 1,309
Maysfield, Milam 140
*McAdoo, Dickens, 2 75
*McALLEN, Hidalgo, 5,480,
   (129,877) 144,464
McBeth, Brazoria............................ 20
*McCAMEY, Upton, 69,
   (1,887) 2,069

*McCaulley, Fisher.......................... 96
McClanahan, Falls.......................... 30
McCook, Hidalgo............................ 50
McCoy, Atascosa............................ 30
McCoy, Floyd.................................. 20
McCoy, Kaufman............................ 20
McCoy, Panola............................... 30
McCoy, Red River......................... 175
*McDade, Bastrop, 17, (685)........ 794
*McFaddin, Victoria 50
McGirk, Hamilton 18
*McGREGOR, McLennan, 197,
   (4,987) 5,155
*McKINNEY, Collin, 4,631,
   (131,117) 175,129
McKinney Acres, Andrews,
   (815) 988
*McLEAN, Gray, 24, (778) 770
McLENDON-CHISHOLM, Rockwall,
   5, (1,373) 2,438
*McLeod, Cass, 3 600
McMahan, Caldwell 90
McMillin, San Saba 15
McNair, Harris............................ 2,039
McNary, Hudspeth 100
McNeil, Caldwell 50
*McQueeney, Guadalupe, 41,
   (2,545) 2,664
*MEADOW, Terry, 16, (593)......... 593
Meadow Grove, Bell 22
MEADOWLAKES, Burnet, 41,
   (1,777) 1,834
MEADOWS PLACE, Fort Bend,
   111, (4,660)......................... 5,143
Mecca, Madison 48
Medicine Mound, Hardeman 25
Medill, Lamar................................. 50
*Medina, Bandera, 31.................. 850
Medina, Zapata, (3,935) 4,308
Meeker, Jefferson...................... 2,280
Meeks, Bell 6
*MEGARGEL, Archer, 11,
   (203) 196
*MELISSA, Collin, 206,
   (4,695) 9,117
Melrose, Nacogdoches................ 400
*MELVIN, McCulloch, 4,
   (178) 180
*MEMPHIS, Hall, 74, (2,290)..... 2,148
*MENARD, Menard, 59,
   (1,471) 1,442
Mendoza, Caldwell 100
Menlow, Hill 12
*Mentone, Loving, 5, (19) 25
Mentz, Colorado 100
*MERCEDES, Hidalgo, 502,
   (15,570)............................. 16,130
Mercury, McCulloch 166
*Mereta, Tom Green, 2 131
*MERIDIAN, Bosque, 78,
   (1,493) 1,490
*Merit, Hunt, 1............................. 225
*MERKEL, Taylor, 92,
   (2,590) 2,622
Merle, Burleson 10
Merriman, Eastland 14
*MERTENS, Hill, 6, (125) 131
*MERTZON, Irion, 52,
   (781) 791
*MESQUITE, Dallas-Kaufman,
   3,193, (139,824) 142,823

Mesquite, Starr, (505)................. 550
Metcalf Gap, Palo Pinto.................. 6
*MEXIA, Limestone, 260,
   (7,459) 7,711
*Meyersville, DeWitt, 6 110
Meyersville, Washington............... 15
*MIAMI, Roberts, 22, (597).......... 600
Mico, Medina 107
Midcity, Lamar 50
Middleton, Leon 26
*Midfield, Matagorda, 4............... 305
*Midkiff, Upton, 14 182
*MIDLAND, Midland-Martin,
   5,000, (111,147)............... 134,372
*MIDLOTHIAN, Ellis, 964,
   (18,037) 23,014
Midway, Dawson 12
Midway, Fannin.............................. 51
Midway, Jim Wells 24
Midway, Limestone 9
*MIDWAY, Madison, 20,
   (228) 232
Midway, Red River......................... 40
Midway, Titus 110
Midway, Upshur 20
Midway, Van Zandt 31
Midway, Polk................................ 525
Midway North, Hidalgo,
   (4,752) 5,163
Midway South, Hidalgo,
   (2,239) 2,497
Midyett, Panola 150
Miguel Barrera, Starr, (128).......... 139
Mikes, Starr, (910) 1,009
Mikeska, Live Oak 10
Mila Doce, Hidalgo, (6,222)...... 7,032
*Milam, Sabine, 11, (1,480) 1,498
*MILANO, Milam, 20, (428) 419
Milburn, McCulloch 8
MILDRED, Navarro, 6,
   (368) 371
*MILES, Runnels, 50, (829)......... 862
*MILFORD, Ellis, 16, (728).......... 782
Mill Creek, Washington.................. 40
Miller Grove, Hopkins 115
MILLERS COVE, Titus, 3,
   (149) 150
*Millersview, Concho, 5 80
Millett, La Salle.............................. 60
Millheim, Austin........................... 170
*Millican, Brazos, 3, (240)........... 232
*MILLSAP, Parker, 54, (403)........ 459
Milo Center, Deaf Smith.................. 5
Milton, Lamar................................. 50
Mims, Brazoria............................. 160
*Minden, Rusk, 4 150
*MINEOLA, Wood, 370,
   (4,515) 4,795
Mineral, Bee 65
*MINERAL WELLS, Palo Pinto-
   Parker, 591, (16,788)........ 16,613
Minerva, Milam 100
Mings Chapel, Upshur.................... 50
*MINGUS, Palo Pinto, 17,
   (235) 248
Minter, Lamar................................. 78
Mi Ranchito Estate, Starr,
   (281) 269
*Mirando City, Webb, 13, (375) 341
*MISSION, Hidalgo, 1,827,
   (77,058) 84,065

Town, County ....Pop. 2017	Town, County ....Pop. 2017	Town, County ....Pop. 2017

Mission Bend, Fort Bend-Harris,
(36,501) 41,119
Mission Valley, Victoria 225
*MISSOURI CITY, Fort Bend-Harris,
1,911, (67,358) 77,101
Mixon, Cherokee 50
*MOBEETIE, Wheeler, 10,
(101) 102
MOBILE CITY, Rockwall, 3,
(188) 190
Moffat, Bell 1,406
Moffett, Angelina 100
Moline, Lampasas 32
*MONAHANS, Ward, 280,
(6,953) 7,312
Monaville, Waller 180
Monkstown, Fannin 35
Monroe, Rusk 96
Monroe City, Chambers 5
Mont, Lavaca 30
*Montague, Montague, 18,
(304) 303
*Montalba, Anderson, 10 110
*MONT BELVIEU, Chambers,
193, (3,835) 5,658
Monte Alto, Hidalgo, (1,924) 2,121
Monte Grande, Cameron 97
Montell, Uvalde 20
*MONTGOMERY, Montgomery,
582, (621) 963
Monthalia, Gonzales 32
Monticello, Titus 20
*MOODY, McLennan, 74,
(1,371) 1,393
*Moore, Frio, 13, (475) 501
Moore's Crossing, Travis 25
MOORE STATION, Henderson,
(201) 194
Mooreville, Falls 96
Mooring, Brazos 80
Moraida, Starr, (212) 240
Morales, Jackson 72
*MORAN, Shackelford, 9,
(270) 302
Moravia, Lavaca 165
*MORGAN, Bosque, 15,
(490) 492
Morgan Creek, Burnet 126
Morgan Farm Area, San Patricio,
(463) 463
*Morgan Mill, Erath, 3 206
MORGAN'S POINT, Harris, 21,
(339) 362
MORGAN'S POINT RESORT, Bell,
70, (4,170) 4,313
Morning Glory, El Paso, (651) 641
*Morse, Hansford, 7, (147) 133
*MORTON, Cochran, 41,
(2,006) 1,903
Morton, Harrison 75
Morton Valley, Eastland 46
*Moscow, Polk, 12 170
Mosheim, Bosque 75
Moss Bluff, Liberty 65
Moss Hill, Liberty 180
Mostyn, Montgomery 90
*MOULTON, Lavaca, 62, (886) 912
*Mound, Coryell, 2 125
Mound City, Anderson-Houston 25
MOUNTAIN CITY, Hays, 13,
(648) 752

*Mountain Home, Kerr, 20 96
Mountain Peak, Ellis 300
Mountain Springs, Cooke 600
Mount Bethel, Panola 65
*MOUNT CALM, Hill, 21,
(320) 317
*MOUNT ENTERPRISE, Rusk,
45, (447) 448
Mount Haven, Cherokee 30
Mount Hermon, Shelby 80
Mount Olive, Lavaca 50
*MOUNT PLEASANT, Titus,
720, (15,564) 17,083
Mount Rose, Falls 15
Mount Selman, Cherokee 325
Mount Sylvan, Smith 181
*MOUNT VERNON, Franklin,
150, (2,662) 2,758
Mount Vernon, Houston 43
Mozelle, Coleman 15
Muellersville, Washington 20
*MUENSTER, Cooke, 137,
(1,544) 1,603
Mulberry, Fannin 141
*Muldoon, Fayette, 9 95
*MULESHOE, Bailey, 173,
(5,158) 5,134
*MULLIN, Mills, 10, (179) 179
Mullins Prairie, Fayette 107
*Mumford, Robertson, 3 170
*MUNDAY, Knox, 40,
(1,300) 1,187
Munger, Limestone 5
Mungerville, Dawson 20
Muniz, Hidalgo, (1,370) 1,543
*MURCHISON, Henderson, 44,
(594) 580
MURPHY, Collin, 506,
(17,708) 21,067
Murray, Young 29
Murvaul, Panola 150
Mustang, Denton 25
MUSTANG, Navarro, 1, (21) 19
Mustang Mott, DeWitt 20
MUSTANG RIDGE, Travis-Caldwell,
36, (861) 941
*Myra, Cooke, 3 150
Myrtle Springs, Van Zandt,
(828) 896

N

*NACOGDOCHES, Nacogdoches,
1,348, (32,996) 34,120
*Nada, Colorado, 12 165
*NAPLES, Morris, 46,
(1,378) 1,376
Narciso Pena, Starr, (30) 34
Naruna, Burnet 95
*NASH, Bowie, 122, (2,960) 3,370
Nash, Ellis 40
NASSAU BAY, Harris, 183,
(4,002) 4,018
Nat, Nacogdoches 50
*NATALIA, Medina, 64,
(1,431) 1,545
NAVARRO, Navarro, (210) 210
Navarro Mills, Navarro 90
*NAVASOTA, Grimes, 351,
(7,049) 7,506
Navidad, Jackson 227
*NAZARETH, Castro, 17, (311) 290

Necessity, Stephens 10
Nechanitz, Fayette 57
*Neches, Anderson, 4 175
*NEDERLAND, Jefferson, 642,
(17,547) 17,305
Needmore, Bailey 20
Needmore, Terry 7
*NEEDVILLE, Fort Bend, 137,
(2,823) 3,357
Negley, Red River 136
Neinda, Jones 21
Nell, Live Oak 60
Nelson City, Kendall 50
Nelsonville, Austin 200
Nelta, Hopkins 36
*Nemo, Somervell, 17 56
Nesbitt, Harrison, (281) 270
Netos, Starr (31) 38
Neuville, Shelby 65
*NEVADA, Collin, 55, (822) 1,069
*NEWARK, Wise, 56,
(1,005) 1,126
*New Baden, Robertson, 3 150
NEW BERLIN, Guadalupe, 11,
(511) 580
New Bielau, Colorado 30
*NEW BOSTON, Bowie, 171,
(4,550) 4,860
*NEW BRAUNFELS, Comal-
Guadalupe, 3,376,
(57,740) 74,930
New Bremen, Austin 125
Newburg, Comanche 32
Newby, Leon 40
*New Caney, Montgomery,
236 6,800
*NEWCASTLE, Young, 20,
(585) 568
NEW CHAPEL HILL, Smith, 8,
(594) 619
New Colony, Bell 12
New Colony, Cass 65
New Corn Hill, Williamson 475
New Davy, DeWitt 20
*NEW DEAL, Lubbock, 27,
(794) 806
NEW FAIRVIEW, Wise, 27,
(1,258) 1,408
Newgulf, Wharton 10
New Harmony, Shelby 40
New Harmony, Smith 350
*NEW HOME, Lynn, (334) 350
New Hope, Cherokee 50
NEW HOPE, Collin, 18, (614) 652
New Hope, Jones 9
New Hope, San Augustine 75
New Hope, Smith 75
New Hope, Wood 15
Newlin, Hall 27
*NEW LONDON, Rusk, 12,
(998) 999
New Lynn, Lynn 4
New Moore, Lynn 10
New Mountain, Upshur 20
Newport, Clay, Jack 75
New Salem, Palo Pinto 89
New Salem, Rusk 55
Newsome, Camp 113
*NEW SUMMERFIELD, Cherokee,
22, (1,111) 1,165
New Sweden, Travis 60

CITIES & TOWNS

CITIES & TOWNS

Town, County ....Pop. 2017	Town, County ....Pop. 2017	Town, County ....Pop. 2017
New Taiton, Wharton 10	Oak Grove, Bowie 90	Olivia Lopez de Gutierrez, Starr,
*NEWTON, Newton, 57,	Oak Grove, Colorado..................... 40	(93) 86
(2,478) 2,400	OAK GROVE, Kaufman, (603) 708	Ollie, Polk 5
*New Ulm, Austin, 41 974	Oak Grove, Wood 140	*Olmito, Cameron, 65,
*NEW WAVERLY, Walker, 93,	Oak Hill, Rusk................................ 200	(1,210) 1,225
(1,032) 1,107	Oak Hill, Travis .... [part of Austin]	Olmito and Olmito, Starr,
New Wehdem, Austin 414	*Oakhurst, San Jacinto, 6,	(271) 301
New Willard, Polk 160	(233) 242	Olmos, Guadalupe......................... 65
New York, Henderson.................... 60	Oak Island, Chambers, (363) 386	OLMOS PARK, Bexar, 108,
NEYLANDVILLE, Hunt, 1, (97)..... 103	Oakland, Cherokee......................... 50	(2,237).................................. 2,376
NIEDERWALD, Hays-Caldwell,	*Oakland, Colorado, Lavaca, 1....... 80	*OLNEY, Young, 123,
22, (565)................................. 625	Oakland, Van Zandt....................... 26	(3,285).................................. 3,296
Nigton, Trinity................................ 87	OAK LEAF, Ellis, 35,	*OLTON, Lamb, 64,
Nimrod, Eastland 45	(1,298).................................. 1,422	(2,215).................................. 2,088
Nina, Starr, (141) 152	OAK POINT, Denton, 106,	*OMAHA, Morris, 30,
Nineveh, Leon 50	(2,786)..................................3,646	(1,021).................................. 1,038
Nix, Lampasas.............................. 14	OAK RIDGE, Cooke, (141)........... 190	Omen, Smith................................ 150
*NIXON, Gonzales-Wilson, 66,	Oak Ridge, Grayson 161	*ONALASKA, Polk, 127,
(2,385) 2,505	OAK RIDGE, Kaufman, 14,	(1,764).................................. 2,755
Noack, Williamson......................... 70	(495) 604	Opdyke, Hockley 50
Nobility, Fannin 100	Oak Ridge, Nacogdoches............. 225	OPDYKE WEST, Hockley, 2,
Noble, Lamar 14	OAK RIDGE NORTH, Montgomery,	(174) 177
Nockernut, Wilson 20	229, (3,049) 3,221	Oplin, Callahan 75
*NOCONA, Montague, 133,	Oak Trail Shores, Hood,	O'Quinn, Fayette 191
(3,033)................................. 3,020	(2,755)................................. 3,167	Oran, Palo Pinto 61
Nocona Hills, Montague (675)...... 670	OAK VALLEY, Navarro, 2,	*ORANGE, Orange, 611,
Nogalus Prairie, Trinity 109	(368) 383	(18,595)............................... 19,416
*Nolan, Nolan, 1 60	Oakville, Live Oak, 4..................... 260	Orangedale, Bee 40
*NOLANVILLE, Bell, 63,	*OAKWOOD, Leon, 26, (510)....... 518	*Orangefield, Orange, 6................. 725
(4,259) 5,005	Oatmeal, Burnet 74	*ORANGE GROVE, Jim Wells,
*NOME, Jefferson, 25,	*O'BRIEN, Haskell, 2, (106) 104	109, (1,318) 1,255
(588) 590	Ocee, McLennan 84	Orangeville, Fannin 60
Noodle, Jones............................... 40	Odds, Limestone 24	Orason, Cameron, (129)............... 128
NOONDAY, Smith, 62, (777) 777	Odell, Wilbarger........................... 100	*ORCHARD, Fort Bend, 15,
Nopal, DeWitt 25	*ODEM, San Patricio, 65,	(352) 376
*NORDHEIM, DeWitt, 19, (307) ... 320	(2,389).................................. 2,423	*ORE CITY, Upshur, 52,
Norman, Williamson 40	*ODESSA, Ector-Midland, 4,021,	(1,144) 1,227
Normandy, Maverick..................... 114	(99,940) 113,677	Orient, Tom Green 57
*NORMANGEE, Leon-Madison,	*O'DONNELL, Lynn-Dawson, 22,	*Orla, Reeves, 14 80
70, (685)................................. 681	(831) 817	Osage, Colorado 10
*Normanna, Bee, 2, (113)............. 117	Oenaville, Bell.............................. 108	Osage, Coryell.............................. 30
Norse, Bosque............................. 110	O'Farrell, Cass............................. 20	Oscar, Bell 58
North Alamo, Hidalgo, (3,235) ... 3,847	Ogburn, Wood 10	Osceola, Hill 95
NORTH CLEVELAND, Liberty, 5,	*OGLESBY, Coryell, 19,	Otey, Brazoria 31
(247).. 258	(484) 466	Ottine, Gonzales 80
North Escobares, Starr, (118) 117	*Oilton, Webb, 1, (353) 381	Otto, Falls 48
Northfield, Motley........................... 15	Oklahoma, Montgomery 800	*Ovalo, Taylor, 3 225
NORTHLAKE, Denton, 56,	Oklahoma Flat, Hockley 4	*OVERTON, Rusk-Smith, 87,
(1,724) 2,461	Oklahoma Lane, Parmer 25	(2,554) 2,500
North Pearsall, Frio, (614) 653	*Oklaunion, Wilbarger, 4.............. 138	*OVILLA, Ellis-Dallas, 132,
*NORTH RICHLAND HILLS, Tarrant,	Okra, Eastland.............................. 20	(3,492).................................. 4,035
1,948, (63,343)..................... 69,626	Ola, Kaufman 65	Owens, Brown 16
Northridge, Starr, (78)................... 86	Old Boston, Bowie 100	Owens, Crosby 4
Northrup, Lee................................ 86	Old Center, Panola 83	Owentown, Smith 100
North San Pedro, Nueces, (895) .. 889	Old Dime Box, Lee 225	Owl Creek, Bell 130
North Star, Archer 10	*Olden, Eastland, 3...................... 113	Owl Ranch, Jim Wells,
*North Zulch, Madison, 13............ 600	Oldenburg, Fayette 92	(225) 195
Norton, Runnels............................ 50	Old Escobares, Starr, (97) 104	Oxford, Llano 18
*Notrees, Ector, 1 20	*Old Glory, Stonewall, 2............... 100	OYSTER CREEK, Brazoria, 34,
*NOVICE, Coleman, (139)............ 136	Old Midway, Leon 12	(1,111).................................. 1,126
Novice, Lamar 35	*Old Ocean, Brazoria, 14.............. 150	*Ozona, Crockett, 125,
Noxville, Kimble 3	OLD RIVER-WINFREE, Chambers,	(3,225).................................. 3,144
Nugent, Jones 50	17, (1,245)............................. 1,352	
Nunelee, Fannin 90	Old Salem, Bowie 50	**P**
Nurillo, Hidalgo, (7,344)............. 8,874	Old Union, Bowie 100	Pablo Pena, Starr, (63) 66
*Nursery, Victoria, 4 600	Old Union, Limestone 25	Pacio, Delta 35
	Oletha, Limestone 53	Padgett, Young 18
O	Olfen, Runnels.............................. 35	*PADUCAH, Cottle, 48,
	Olin, Hamilton 15	(1,186).................................. 1,133
Oakalla, Burnet............................. 99	Olivarez, Hidalgo, (3,827)........... 4,615	*Paige, Bastrop, 34..................... 275
Oakdale, Polk 25	Olivia, Calhoun 215	Paint Creek, Haskell..................... 150
Oak Forest, Gonzales.................... 24		

Town, County .... Pop. 2017	Town, County .... Pop. 2017	Town, County .... Pop. 2017
*PAINT ROCK, Concho, 12, (273) 275	PAYNE SPRINGS, Henderson, 26, (767) 785	*PHARR, Hidalgo, 1,751, (70,400) 80,054
Paisano Park, San Patricio (130) 125	Peach Creek, Brazos................... 150	Phelps, Walker 98
*PALACIOS, Matagorda, 113, (4,718) 4,619	Peacock, Stonewall 100	Phillipsburg, Washington 75
*PALESTINE, Anderson, 776, (18,712) 19,271	Peadenville, Palo Pinto................. 15	Pickens, Henderson 20
	Pearl, Coryell............................... 50	Pickett, Navarro 30
PALISADES, Randall, (325) 362	*PEARLAND, Brazoria-Harris-Fort Bend, 3,428, (91,252) 114,204	*Pickton, Hopkins, 11.................... 300
Palito Blanco, Jim Wells 750		Pidcoke, Coryell........................... 50
*PALMER, Ellis, 76, (2,000) 2,126	Pearl City, DeWitt 4	Piedmont, Grimes......................... 50
	*PEARSALL, Frio, 234, (9,146) 10,057	Piedmont, Upshur......................... 20
PALMHURST, Hidalgo, 109, (2,607) 2,740	Pearson, Medina 24	*Pierce, Wharton, 2 51
	Pearsons Chapel, Houston............. 95	Pike, Collin................................... 47
PALM VALLEY, Cameron, 18, (1,304) 1,259	Pear Valley, McCulloch 37	Pilgrim, Gonzales 22
	*Peaster, Parker, 2.................... 1,000	Pilgrim Rest, Rains 72
PALMVIEW, Hidalgo, 383, (5,460) 6,845	Pecan Acres, Tarrant-Wise, (4,099) 4,480	Pilot Grove, Grayson 48
		Pilot Knob, Travis......................... 500
Palmview South, Hidalgo (5,575) 5,999	*PECAN GAP, Delta-Fannin, 7, (203) 185	*PILOT POINT, Denton, 190, (3,856) 4,465
Palo Blanco, Starr (204) 227	Pecan Grove, Fort Bend (15,963) 17,519	Pine, Camp.................................. 78
Paloduro, Armstrong...................... 10		Pine Branch, Red River 40
Paloma Creek, Denton, (2,501) 2,972	PECAN HILL, Ellis, 12, (626)........ 655	Pine Forest, Hopkins 100
	Pecan Plantation, Hood, (5,294) 5,465	PINE FOREST, Orange, 15, (487) 506
Paloma Creek South, Denton (2,753) 3,276	Pecan Wells, Hamilton 6	Pine Grove, Cherokee 30
*Palo Pinto, Palo Pinto, 8, (333) 339	*PECOS, Reeves, 345, (8,780) 10,026	Pine Grove, Newton 180
		Pine Harbor, Marion, (810) 806
Paluxy, Hood 36	Peeltown, Kaufman 75	Pinehill, Rusk............................... 70
*PAMPA, Gray, 553, (17,994) 17,653	Peerless, Hopkins......................... 90	*Pinehurst, Montgomery, 108, (4,624) 5,166
	*Peggy, Atascosa.......................... 22	
Pancake, Coryell........................... 11	Pelham, Navarro........................... 75	PINEHURST, Orange, 210, (2,097) 2,138
Pandale, Val Verde 25	PELICAN BAY, Tarrant, 12, (1,547) 1,657	Pine Island, Jefferson 350
*Pandora, Wilson, 1 110		PINE ISLAND, Waller, (988) 1,107
*PANHANDLE, Carson, 80, (2,452) 2,409	Pena, Starr, (118) 129	
	*Pendleton, Bell, 1 369	*PINELAND, Sabine, 29, (850) 793
*Panna Maria, Karnes, 6 45	*PENELOPE, Hill, 4, (198) 201	Pine Mills, Wood 75
*Panola, Panola, 1.......................... 305	*PEÑITAS, Hidalgo, 98, (4,403) 4,946	Pine Prairie, Walker..................... 450
PANORAMA VILLAGE, Montgomery, 31, (2,170) 2,295		Pine Springs, Culberson............... 20
	*Pennington, Trinity-Houston, 7...... 67	Pine Springs, Smith 150
*PANTEGO, Tarrant, 393, (2,394) 2,798	*Penwell, Ector, 6 41	Pineview, Wood 10
	Peoria, Hill 105	Pinewood Estates, Hardin, (1,678) 1,704
Panther Junction, Brewster 130	*Pep, Hockley................................ 30	
Papalote, Bee................................ 75	Percilla, Houston 95	Piney, Austin 60
*PARADISE, Wise, 81, (441)........ 498	Perezville, Hidalgo, (5,376) 5,961	PINEY POINT VILLAGE, Harris, 59, (3,125) 3,386
*PARIS, Lamar, 1,127, (25,171) 25,207	Pernitas Point, Live Oak-Jim Wells. 274	
		Pin Hook, Lamar 48
Park, Fayette 25	*Perrin, Jack, 14, (398)................ 427	Pioneer, Eastland 20
PARKER, Collin, 124, (3,811) 4,647	Perry, Falls 76	*Pipe Creek, Bandera, 116 130
	*PERRYTON, Ochiltree, 404, (8,802) 9,216	Pitner Junction, Rusk.................... 20
Parker, Johnson............................ 93		*PITTSBURG, Camp, 231, (4,497) 4,665
Park Springs, Wise 90	Perryville, Wood 35	
Parsley Hill, Wilbarger 25	Personville, Limestone 50	*Placedo, Victoria, 4, (692).......... 758
Parvin, Denton 44	Pert, Anderson 20	Placid, McCulloch 32
*PASADENA, Harris, 3,246, (149,043) 153,000	Peters, Austin 150	Plain, Houston 30
	*PETERSBURG, Hale, 23, (1,202) 1,137	*PLAINS, Yoakum, 52, (1,481) 1,628
Patillo, Erath 10	Peter's Prairie, Red River.............. 40	
Patman Switch, Cass 40	Petersville, DeWitt 38	*PLAINVIEW, Hale, 718, (22,194) 21,276
Patonia, Polk 15	*PETROLIA, Clay, 12, (686) 661	
Patricia, Dawson............................ 50	PETRONILA, Nueces, 2, (113)..... 115	*PLANO, Collin-Denton, 10,742, (259,841) 299,858
Patroon, Shelby 25	Petteway, Robertson 25	
*PATTISON, Waller, 32, (472) 577	Pettibone, Milam 25	*Plantersville, Grimes, 56 260
	Pettit, Hockley.............................. 30	Plaska, Hall.................................. 20
PATTON VILLAGE, Montgomery, 17, (1,557) 1,902	*Pettus, Bee, 10, (558) 554	PLEAK, Fort Bend, 28, (1,044) 1,439
	*Petty, Lamar, 5 130	
*Pattonville, Lamar, 9.................... 180	Petty, Lynn..................................... 8	Pleasant Farms, Ector................. 800
Pattonfield, Upshur 20	Peyton, Blanco 30	Pleasant Grove, Falls 35
Pawelekville, Karnes 110	*PFLUGERVILLE, Travis, 1,666, (46,936) 61,271	Pleasant Grove, Limestone 20
*Pawnee, Bee, 6, (166) 156		Pleasant Grove, Upshur 35
Paxton, Shelby 50	Phalba, Van Zandt 73	Pleasant Grove, Wood 30
Paynes Corner, Gaines 18		Pleasant Hill, Eastland................... 15

Town, County ....Pop. 2017	Town, County ....Pop. 2017	Town, County ....Pop. 2017
Pleasant Hill, Nacogdoches...........250	*POTTSBORO, Grayson, 133,	Quarry, Washington........................60
Pleasant Hill, Yoakum.....................30	(2,160).................................2,308	Quarterway, Hale............................24
Pleasant Hill, Polk (522) 548	Pottsville, Hamilton.......................105	*QUEEN CITY, Cass, 74,
*PLEASANTON, Atascosa, 461,	*Powderly, Lamar, 40,	(1,476).................................1,486
(8,934)...............................10,657	(1,178).................................1,174	*Quemado, Maverick, 9,
Pleasant Valley, Garza 5	*POWELL, Navarro, 9,	(230)..221
PLEASANT VALLEY, Wichita,	(136)..148	Quesada, Starr, (25)........................32
(336)...341	*POYNOR, Henderson, 11,	Quicksand, Newton 50
Pledger, Matagorda 265	(305)..297	Quihi, Medina 125
Pluck, Polk.....................................53	Prado Verde, El Paso, (246).........257	*QUINLAN, Hunt, 203,
*Plum, Fayette, 2..........................145	Praesel, Milam..............................115	(1,394).................................1,463
PLUM GROVE, Liberty, 6,	Praha, Fayette................................90	QUINTANA, Brazoria, 3, (56) 114
(600)..648	Prairie Chapel, McLennan..............35	*QUITAQUE, Briscoe, 14,
Pluto, Ellis.....................................30	Prairie Dell, Bell.............................34	(411)..335
Poetry, Kaufman 90	*Prairie Hill, Limestone, 4 150	*QUITMAN, Wood, 191,
*POINT, Rains, 41, (820)..............857	Prairie Hill, Washington 20	(1,809).................................1,806
*POINT BLANK, San Jacinto, 17,	*Prairie Lea, Caldwell, 6 320	
(688)..716	Prairie Point, Cooke........................22	**R**
*POINT COMFORT, Calhoun, 30,	*PRAIRIE VIEW, Waller, 44,	Rabbs Prairie, Fayette....................79
(737)..700	(5,576)................................6,440	Raccoon Bend, Austin 775
Point Enterprise, Limestone 200	Prairieville, Kaufman.......................75	Rachal, Brooks 36
POINT VENTURE, Travis, 19,	*PREMONT, Jim Wells, 57,	Radar Base, Maverick, (762)........825
(800)..922	(2,653)................................2,571	Radium, Jones 10
Polar, Kent.....................................15	*PRESIDIO, Presidio, 93,	Rafael Pena, Starr, (17)..................16
*Pollok, Angelina, 34.....................400	(4,426)................................4,352	Ragtown, Lamar 30
PONDER, Denton, 68,	Preston, Grayson, (2,096) 1,844	*Rainbow, Somervell, 15 121
(1,395)................................1,618	*Price, Rusk, 4..............................275	Raisin, Victoria...............................85
Ponta, Cherokee.............................50	*Priddy, Mills, 8............................215	Raleigh, Navarro.............................40
*Pontotoc, Mason, 1......................125	PRIMERA, Cameron, 33,	*RALLS, Crosby, 50, (1,944) 1,857
Poole, Rains 20	(4,070)................................4,760	Ramireno, Zapata, (35) 31
*Poolville, Parker, 28 520	Primrose, Van Zandt.......................26	Ramirez, Duval 42
Port Acres, Jefferson	*PRINCETON, Collin, 263,	Ramirez-Perez, Starr, (78)..............76
......................[part of Port Arthur]	(6,807)................................9,669	Ramos, Starr, (116) 123
Port Alto, Calhoun...........................45	Pringle, Hutchinson 20	Ranchette Estates, Willacy,
*PORT ARANSAS, Nueces,	Pritchett, Upshur...........................125	(152)..147
418, (3,480).......................4,206	*Proctor, Comanche, 5 228	Ranchito El Calaboz [Encantada-],
*PORT ARTHUR, Jefferson,	*PROGRESO, Hidalgo, 55,	Cameron, (2,284) 2,222
1,082, (53,818)...............53,706	(5,507)................................6,177	Ranchitos Del Norte, Starr,
*Port Bolivar, Galveston, 60..........700	PROGRESO LAKES, Hidalgo, 9,	(112)..107
*Porter, Montgomery, 376..........4,200	(240)..229	Ranchitos East, Webb, (212)........233
Porter Heights, Montgomery,	Progress, Bailey 49	Ranchitos Las Lomas, Webb,
(1,653)................................1,858	Prospect, Rains 40	(266)..303
Porter Springs, Houston 50	*PROSPER, Collin-Denton, 650,	Rancho Alegre, Jim Wells,
*PORT ISABEL, Cameron, 269,	(9,423)..............................19,659	(1,704)................................1,646
(5,006).................................5,056	Providence, Floyd............................78	Rancho Banquete, Nueces,
*PORTLAND, San Patricio, 487,	Providence, Polk............................350	(424)..431
(15,099)............................15,841	PROVIDENCE, Denton,	Rancho Chico, San Patricio,
*PORT LAVACA, Calhoun, 437,	(4,786)................................6,323	(396)..445
(12,248)............................12,346	Pruitt, Cass....................................25	Ranchos Penitas West, Webb,
*Port Mansfield, Willacy, 11,	Pruitt, Van Zandt.............................45	(573)..597
(226)..190	Pueblo Nuevo, Webb, (521) 556	RANCHO VIEJO, Cameron, 43,
*PORT NECHES, Jefferson,	Puerto Rico, Hidalgo.......................50	(2,437)................................2,530
315, (13,040)...................12,680	Pullman, Potter...............................31	Rancho Viejo, Starr, (228) 253
*Port O'Connor , Calhoun, 46,	Pumphrey, Runnels 15	Rand, Kaufman...............................70
(1,253)................................1,254	Pumpkin, San Jacinto....................100	Randado, Jim Hogg..........................6
Port Sullivan, Milam........................15	Pumpville, Val Verde.......................25	*Randolph, Fannin, 2.....................600
Porvenir, Presidio 3	Punkin Center, Dawson....................8	Randolph Air Force Base, Bexar,
Posey, Hopkins 12	Punkin Center, Eastland.................12	(1,241)................................1,340
Posey, Lubbock 225	*Purdon, Navarro, 8......................133	*RANGER, Eastland, 83,
*POST, Garza, 173, (5,376).......5,272	Purley, Franklin.............................100	(2,468)................................2,491
Post Oak, Blanco 10	*Purmela, Coryell, 1........................50	RANGERVILLE, Cameron,
Postoak, Jack 20	Pursley, Navarro 40	(289)..332
Postoak, Lamar 65	Purves, Erath..................................50	Rankin, Ellis....................................10
Post Oak, Lee................................100	*PUTNAM, Callahan, 2, (94) 99	*RANKIN, Upton, 42, (778)...........838
POST OAK BEND, Kaufman, 9,	*PYOTE, Ward, 7, (114) 121	RANSOM CANYON, Lubbock,
(595)..694		42, (1,096).........................1,094
Post Oak Point, Austin....................60	**Q**	Ratamosa, Cameron, (254 260
*POTEET, Atascosa, 124,	*Quail, Collingsworth, 1, (19)..........15	*Ratcliff, Houston, 2......................106
(3,260).................................3,520	Quail Creek, Victoria, (1,628) 1,775	Ratibor, Bell....................................22
*POTH, Wilson, 48, (1,908).......2,223	*QUANAH, Hardeman, 100,	Rattan, Delta...................................10
Potosi, Taylor, (2,991) 3,221	(2,641).................................2,482	*RAVENNA, Fannin, 5, (209).......222

CITIES & TOWNS

Town, County ....Pop. 2017	Town, County ....Pop. 2017	Town, County ....Pop. 2017
Rayburn, Liberty 60	*REKLAW, Cherokee-Rusk, 8,	*RIO HONDO, Cameron, 58,
Rayland, Foard 30	(379) 390	(2,356) 2,742
*RAYMONDVILLE, Willacy, 181,	Relampago, Hidalgo, (132).......... 154	*Riomedina, Medina, 9 60
(11,284) 11,373	Rendon, Tarrant, (12,552) 13,837	Rios, Duval 75
Ray Point, Live Oak..................... 200	*RENO, Lamar, 104,	*RIO VISTA, Johnson, 38,
*Raywood, Liberty, 12.................. 231	(3,166) 3,318	(873) 974
Razor, Lamar................................. 20	RENO, Parker, Tarrant, 34,	*RISING STAR, Eastland, 41,
*Reagan, Falls, 2 300	(2,494) 2,802	(835) 848
Reagan Wells, Uvalde 30	Retreat, Grimes 25	Rita, Burleson 50
Reagor Springs, Ellis................... 250	RETREAT, Navarro, (377) 395	Rivera, Starr, (162) 181
*Realitos, Duval, 4, (184).............. 163	Reynard, Houston.......................... 75	Riverby, Fannin................................ 8
Red Bank, Bowie 125	Rhea, Parmer 98	River Crest Estates, Angelina....... 150
Red Bluff, Jackson......................... 45	Rhineland, Knox 120	Rivereno, Starr, (61) 88
Red Bluff, Reeves.......................... 40	*RHOME, Wise, 106, (1,522) 1,712	River Hill, Panola 125
Redfield, Nacogdoches, (441)...... 428	Rhonesboro, Upshur 40	RIVER OAKS, Tarrant, 151,
Redford, Presidio, (90) 80	Ricardo, Kleberg, (1,048) 1,044	(7,427) 7,990
Red Hill, Cass 28	*RICE, Navarro, 57,	Rivers End, Brazoria....................... 90
Red Hill, Limestone 20	(923) 985	*RIVERSIDE, Walker, 27,
Red Lake, Freestone 50	Rice's Crossing, Williamson 130	(510) 555
Redland, Angelina, (1,047)........ 1,108	*Richards, Grimes, 19 300	*Riviera, Kleberg, 27, (689) 686
Redland, Leon 35	*RICHARDSON, Dallas-Collin,	Riviera Beach, Kleberg................. 155
Redland, Van Zandt........................ 45	4,767, (99,223) 120,072	Roach, Cass 50
RED LICK, Bowie, (1,008)......... 1,034	*RICHLAND, Navarro, 6,	Roane, Navarro 120
*RED OAK, Ellis, 495,	(264) 254	*ROANOKE, Denton, 457,
(10,769) 12,784	Richland, Rains 50	(5,962) 8,066
Red Ranger, Bell 30	*RICHLAND HILLS, Tarrant, 376,	*Roans Prairie, Grimes, 4.............. 64
*Red Rock, Bastrop, 26................. 40	(7,801) 7,857	*ROARING SPRINGS, Motley, 8,
Red Springs, Baylor....................... 42	*RICHLAND SPRINGS, San Saba,	(234) 227
Red Springs, Smith....................... 350	8, (338) 340	Robbins, Leon 20
Redtown, Anderson 30	*RICHMOND, Fort Bend, 997,	*ROBERT LEE, Coke, 49,
Redtown, Angelina....................... 500	(11,679) 13,401	(1,049) 1,029
*REDWATER, Bowie, 18,	RICHWOOD, Brazoria, 79,	Robertson, Crosby.......................... 10
(1,057) 1,122	(3,510) 3,970	ROBINSON, McLennan, 350,
Redwood, Guadalupe,	Riderville, Panola........................... 50	(10,509) 11,617
(4,338) 4,902	Ridge, Mills 25	*ROBSTOWN, Nueces, 339,
Reeds Settlement, Red River........ 50	Ridge, Robertson........................... 67	(11,487) 11,392
Reedville, Caldwell 520	Ridgeway, Hopkins 54	*ROBY, Fisher, 28,
Reese, Cherokee........................... 75	Ridings, Fannin............................ 200	(643) 625
Refuge, Houston............................ 20	*RIESEL, McLennan, 61,	*Rochelle, McCulloch, 4 163
*REFUGIO, Refugio, 128,	(1,007) 1,027	*ROCHESTER, Haskell, 12,
(2,890) 2,846	Rincon, Starr.................................... 5	(324) 314
Regency, Mills 25	*Ringgold, Montague, 4 100	Rock Bluff, Burnet........................... 90
Regino Ramirez, Starr, (85)............ 97	RIO BRAVO, Webb, 60,	Rock Creek, Somervell.................... 70
Rehburg, Washington..................... 20	(4,794) 4,814	*ROCKDALE, Milam, 249,
Reid Hope King, Cameron,	*Rio Frio, Real, 4 50	(5,595) 5,643
(786) 866	*RIO GRANDE CITY, Starr,	Rockett, Ellis 300
Reilly Springs, Hopkins.................. 75	507, (13,834) 15,143	Rockford, Lamar 30
Rek Hill, Fayette 168	Rio Grande Village, Brewster 12	Rockhouse, Austin....................... 100

The main street in Roaring Springs. Photo by Robert Plocheck.

CITIES & TOWNS

CITIES & TOWNS

Town, County ....Pop. 2017	Town, County ....Pop. 2017	Town, County ....Pop. 2017
*Rock Island, Colorado, 3............. 160	Rowden, Callahan 15	*SAN ANTONIO, Bexar, 39,746,
Rockland, Tyler............................... 98	*Rowena, Runnels, 10.................. 349	(1,327,407)............ 1,500,747
Rockne, Bastrop........................... 190	*ROWLETT, Dallas-Rockwall,	San Antonio Prairie, Burleson......... 20
*ROCKPORT, Aransas, 685,	1,558, (56,199)................. 63,113	*SAN AUGUSTINE, San Augustine,
(8,766)............................... 10,635	*ROXTON, Lamar, 21, (650)........ 652	127, (2,108)................... 1,971
*ROCKSPRINGS, Edwards, 59,	Royalty, Ward 27	*SAN BENITO, Cameron, 581,
(1,182)............................... 1,115	*ROYSE CITY, Rockwall-Collin,	(24,250)........................... 24,468
*ROCKWALL, Rockwall, 1,952,	449, (9,349)...................... 12,476	San Carlos, Hidalgo,
(37,490)........................... 45,435	Rucker, Comanche......................... 28	(3,130).............................. 3,457
*Rockwood, Coleman, 3................. 53	Rugby, Red River 24	San Carlos, Starr 10
Rocky Branch, Morris 135	Ruidosa, Presidio 18	San Carlos I, Webb, (316)............ 337
Rocky Creek, Blanco 20	*RULE, Haskell, 15, (636) 618	San Carlos II, Webb, (261)........... 284
ROCKY MOUND, Camp, 2, (75) 68	Rumley, Lampasas 30	Sanco, Coke 15
Rocky Point, Burnet...................... 152	RUNAWAY BAY, Wise, 32,	SANCTUARY, Parker, 29,
Roddy, Van Zandt........................... 29	(1,286)............................... 1,519	(329)................................... 338
Rodney, Navarro............................. 15	*RUNGE, Karnes, 27,	Sand Branch, Dallas.................... 400
Roeder, Titus 75	(1,031)............................... 1,097	*Sanderson, Terrell, 13, (837)...... 717
Roganville, Jasper........................... 70	Rural Shade, Navarro.................... 30	Sand Flat, Johnson...................... 133
*ROGERS, Bell, 41, (1,218) 1,250	*RUSK, Cherokee, 163,	Sand Flat, Rains 45
Rogers, Taylor 151	(5,551).............................. 5,569	Sand Flat, Smith 100
Rolling Hills, Potter 1,000	Russell, Leon 27	Sand Flat, Van Zandt 25
Rolling Meadows, Gregg 362	Rutersville, Fayette...................... 137	Sand Flat, Leon 32
ROLLINGWOOD, Travis, 124,	Ruth Springs, Henderson 120	Sandhill, Floyd 33
(1,412).............................. 1,551	*Rye, Liberty, 4 150	Sand Hill, Upshur.......................... 75
Roma Creek, Starr, (350) 368		*Sandia, Jim Wells, 39, (379) 366
*ROMA-Los Saenz, Starr, 200,	**S**	*SAN DIEGO, Duval-Jim Wells,
(9,765).............................. 11,168	Sabanno, Eastland 12	99, (4,488).......................... 4,254
ROMAN FOREST, Montgomery,	*SABINAL, Uvalde, 52,	Sandlin, Stonewall 3
(1,538).............................. 1,905	(1,695).............................. 1,687	Sandoval, Williamson 60
*Romayor, Liberty, 2 135	*Sabine Pass, Jefferson, 13	Sandoval, Starr, (32).................... 37
*Roosevelt, Kimble, 1 14	....................[part of Port Arthur]	Sand Springs, Howard, (835) 836
Roosevelt, Lubbock....................... 362	*SACHSE, Dallas-Collin, 655,	Sandusky, Grayson 15
*ROPESVILLE, Hockley, 20,	(20,229)........................... 25,506	Sandy, Blanco............................... 150
(434)................................... 436	*Sacul, Nacogdoches 150	Sandy, Limestone 5
Rosalie, Red River....................... 100	*SADLER, Grayson, 16,	Sandy Harbor, Llano 85
*Rosanky, Bastrop, 18 210	(343)................................... 341	Sandy Hill, Washington 50
*ROSCOE, Nolan, 52,	Sagerton, Haskell 171	Sandy Hollow-Escondidas, Nueces,
(1,322).............................. 1,246	*SAGINAW, Tarrant, 527,	(296)................................... 261
*ROSEBUD, Falls, 49,	(19,806)........................... 21,921	SANDY POINT, Brazoria, (250).... 232
(1,412).............................. 1,400	St. Francis, Potter........................... 30	*SAN ELIZARIO, El Paso, 56,
ROSE CITY, Orange, 34,	*ST. HEDWIG, Bexar, 88,	(13,603)........................... 14,535
(502)................................... 529	(2,094).............................. 2,364	*SAN FELIPE, Austin, 33,
Rose Hill, Harris.......................... 3,500	*SAINT JO, Montague, 40,	(747)................................... 815
Rose Hill, San Jacinto 30	(1,043).............................. 1,040	San Fernando, Starr, (68).............. 75
ROSE HILL ACRES, Hardin,	St. John Colony, Caldwell............. 150	*SANFORD, Hutchinson, 5,
(441)................................... 434	St. Lawrence, Glasscock 90	(164)................................... 161
*ROSENBERG, Fort Bend, 1,139,	St. Mary's Colony, Bastrop 50	San Gabriel, Milam 70
(30,618)........................... 40,484	ST. PAUL, Collin, 38, (1,066).... 1,388	*SANGER, Denton, 311,
Rosevine, Sabine 50	St. Paul, San Patricio, (584) 593	(6,916)............................... 8,831
Rosewood, Upshur....................... 100	*SALADO, Bell, 309,	*San Isidro, Starr, 10, (240)......... 240
*Rosharon, Brazoria, 169,	(2,126).............................. 2,062	San Jose, Duval 15
(1,152).............................. 1,295	Salem, Cherokee........................... 20	*SAN JUAN, Hidalgo, 587,
Rosita, Duval 25	Salem, Grimes............................... 54	(33,856)........................... 37,042
Rosita, Maverick, (2,704).......... 2,730	Salem, Newton 218	San Juan, Starr, (129) 141
*ROSS, McLennan, 8, (283)........ 300	Salesville, Palo Pinto 88	SAN LEANNA, Travis, (497)......... 556
*ROSSER, Kaufman, 6,	Saline, Menard 70	San Leon, Galveston,
(332)................................... 361	*Salineño, Starr, (201) 187	(4,970).............................. 5,488
*Rosston, Cooke, 2......................... 75	Salineño North, Starr, (115) 130	*San Manuel-Linn, Hidalgo, 4,
Rossville, Atascosa....................... 200	Salmon, Anderson 20	(801)................................... 787
*ROTAN, Fisher, 53,	Salt Flat, Hudspeth 8	*SAN MARCOS, Hays-Caldwell-
(1,508).............................. 1,445	Salt Gap, McCulloch...................... 25	Guadalupe, 1,953,
Rough Creek, San Saba.................. 8	*Saltillo, Hopkins, 5...................... 200	(44,894)........................... 61,480
Round House, Navarro.................. 40	Samaria, Navarro 90	SAN PATRICIO, San Patricio,
*ROUND MOUNTAIN, Blanco, 14,	Sammy Martinez, Starr, (110)....... 116	(395)................................... 412
(181)................................... 178	*Samnorwood, Collingsworth,	San Pedro, Cameron, (530) 533
Round Mountain, Travis................. 59	(51)..................................... 58	*SAN PERLITA, Willacy,
Round Prairie, Navarro.................. 40	Sample, Gonzales 16	(573)................................... 566
*ROUND ROCK, Williamson-Travis,	Sam Rayburn, Jasper,	San Roman, Starr............................ 5
4,166, (99,887).............. 124,455	(1,181).............................. 1,159	*SAN SABA, San Saba, 157,
Round Timber, Baylor....................... 2	*SAN ANGELO, Tom Green,	(3,099).............................. 3,182
*ROUND TOP, Fayette, 75, (90)... 93	3,481, (93,200)............... 99,954	SANSOM PARK, Tarrant, 102,
Roundup, Hockley 20		(4,686).............................. 4,881

Town, County ....Pop. 2017	Town, County ....Pop. 2017	Town, County ....Pop. 2017

*SANTA ANNA, Coleman, 57,
(1,099) 1,084
Santa Anna, Starr, (13) 19
Santa Catarina, Starr 15
SANTA CLARA, Guadalupe, 22,
(725) 720
Santa Cruz, Starr, (54) 53
*Santa Elena, Starr, 2 35
*SANTA FE, Galveston, 419,
(12,222) 13,203
*Santa Maria, Cameron, 2,
(733) 731
Santa Monica, Willacy, (83) 92
*SANTA ROSA, Cameron, 39,
(2,873) 2,932
Santa Rosa, Starr, (241) 244
Santel, Starr, (44) 46
*Santo, Palo Pinto, 25 445
*San Ygnacio, Zapata, 4,
(667) 637
*Saragosa, Reeves, 3 185
*Saratoga, Hardin, 11 1,000
Sardis, Ellis 60
*Sarita, Kenedy, 18, (238) 244
Saron, Trinity 6
Saspamco, Wilson 300
*Satin, Falls, 2 86
Sattler, Comal 2,500
Saturn, Gonzales 15
Savannah, Denton, (3,318) 3,913
*SAVOY, Fannin, 29,
(831) 876
Scenic Oaks, Bexar, (4,957) 5,520
Schattel, Frio 30
*SCHERTZ, Guadalupe-Comal-Bexar,
1,107, (31,465) 38,084
Schicke Point, Calhoun 70
Schroeder, Goliad 347
*SCHULENBURG, Fayette, 330,
(2,852) 2,988
Schumansville, Guadalupe 678
Schwab City, Polk 120
*Schwertner, Williamson, 1 175
Scissors, Hidalgo, (3,186) 3,425
*SCOTLAND, Archer, 19,
(501) 494
*SCOTTSVILLE, Harrison, 20,
(376) 393
Scranton, Eastland 40
Scrappin Valley, Newton 25
*Scroggins, Franklin, 17 150
*SCURRY, Kaufman, 64, (681) 733
*SEABROOK, Harris, 479,
(11,952) 13,437
*SEADRIFT, Calhoun, 52,
(1,364) 1,511
*SEAGOVILLE, Dallas, 486,
(14,835) 16,204
*SEAGRAVES, Gaines, 47,
(2,417) 2,733
Seale, Robertson 60
*SEALY, Austin, 366,
(6,019) 6,722
Seaton, Bell 60
Seawillow, Caldwell 75
*Sebastian, Willacy, 10,
(1,917) 1,841
Sebastopol, Trinity 300
Seco Mines, Maverick, (560) 580
Security, Montgomery 200

Sedalia, Collin 24
Segno, Polk 80
Segovia, Kimble 12
*SEGUIN, Guadalupe, 1,223,
(25,175) 28,330
Sejita, Duval 24
Selden, Erath 55
Selfs, Fannin 30
SELMA, Bexar-Guadalupe-Comal,
325, (5,540) 9,596
*Selman City [Turnertown-], Rusk,
.... 3,271
*SEMINOLE, Gaines, 376,
(6,430) 7,335
Sempronius, Austin 25
Senate, Jack 20
Serbin, Lee 109
Serenada, Williamson,
(1,641) 1,648
Seth Ward, Hale, (2,025) 1,965
SEVEN OAKS, Polk, 4, (111) 114
Seven Pines, Gregg-Upshur 50
*SEVEN POINTS, Henderson,
101, (1,455) 1,457
Seven Sisters, Duval 25
Sexton, Sabine 29
*SEYMOUR, Baylor, 120,
(2,740) 2,880
Shadybrook, Cherokee,
(1,967) 2,009
Shady Grove, Burnet 114
Shady Grove, Cherokee 30
Shady Grove, Houston 83
Shady Grove, Panola 45
Shady Grove, Smith 250
Shady Grove, Upshur 40
Shady Hollow, Travis, (5,004) 5,068
Shady Oaks, Henderson 300
SHADY SHORES, Denton, 71,
(2,612) 3,038
Shafter, Presidio 57
*SHALLOWATER, Lubbock, 136,
(2,484) 2,557
*SHAMROCK, Wheeler, 103,
(1,910) 1,913
Shangri La, Burnet 108
Shankleville, Newton 35
Shannon, Clay 20
Sharp, Milam 52
SHAVANO PARK, Bexar, 100,
(3,035) 3,722
Shawnee Prairie, Angelina 20
Shaws Bend, Colorado 100
*Sheffield, Pecos, 11 322
Shelby, Austin 300
*Shelbyville, Shelby, 27 600
Sheldon, Harris, (1,990) 2,076
SHENANDOAH, Montgomery,
330, (2,134) 2,938
Shep, Taylor 25
*SHEPHERD, San Jacinto, 72,
(2,319) 2,436
*Sheridan, Colorado, 14 300
*SHERMAN, Grayson, 1,517,
(38,521) 41,556
Sherry, Red River 15
Sherwood, Irion 170
Sherwood Shores, Bell 774
Sherwood Shores, Burnet 920
Sherwood Shores, Grayson 950
Shields, Coleman 8

Shiloh, Leon 30
Shiloh, Limestone 250
*SHINER, Lavaca, 146,
(2,069) 2,121
Shirley, Hopkins 20
*Shiro, Grimes, 3 210
Shive, Hamilton 60
SHOREACRES, Harris, 21,
(1,493) 1,536
Short, Shelby 15
Shovel Mountain, Burnet 148
*Sidney, Comanche, 3 148
Sienna Plantation, Fort Bend,
(13,721) 16,868
*Sierra Blanca, Hudspeth, 12,
(553) 570
Siesta Acres, Maverick,
(1,885) 1,956
Siesta Shores, Zapata,
(1,382) 1,489
Silas, Shelby 75
Siloam, Bowie 50
*SILSBEE, Hardin, 307,
(6,611) 6,951
*Silver, Coke, 1 34
Silver City, Milam 25
Silver City, Navarro 100
Silver City, Red River 25
Silver Creek Village, Burnet 300
Silver Lake, Van Zandt 42
*SILVERTON, Briscoe, 35,
(731) 607
Silver Valley, Coleman 15
Simmons, Live Oak 65
*Simms, Bowie, 8 300
Simms, Deaf Smith 6
*SIMONTON, Fort Bend, 49,
(814) 963
Simpsonville, Matagorda 6
Simpsonville, Upshur 100
Sinclair City, Smith 50
Singleton, Grimes 45
*SINTON, San Patricio, 183,
(5,665) 5,666
Sipe Springs, Comanche 70
Sisterdale, Kendall 110
Sivells Bend, Cooke 36
Six Mile, Calhoun 300
Skeeterville, San Saba 10
*SKELLYTOWN, Carson, 12,
(473) 471
*Skidmore, Bee, 17, (925) 912
Slate Shoals, Lamar 10
*SLATON, Lubbock, 158,
(6,121) 6,145
Slayden, Gonzales 10
Slide, Lubbock 245
*Slidell, Wise, 2 175
Sloan, San Saba 30
Slocum, Anderson 150
Smetana, Brazos 80
*SMILEY, Gonzales, 8, (549) 569
Smithland, Marion 179
Smith Point, Chambers 180
Smithson Valley, Comal 1,000
*SMITHVILLE, Bastrop, 254,
(3,817) 4,188
Smithwick, Burnet 102
*SMYER, Hockley, 7, (474) 483
Smyrna, Cass 215
Smyrna, Rains 25

Town, County .... Pop. 2017	Town, County .... Pop. 2017	Town, County .... Pop. 2017

CITIES & TOWNS

*SNOOK, Burleson, 21, (511) 531
Snow Hill, Collin 23
Snow Hill, Upshur 75
*SNYDER, Scurry, 520,
  (11,202) 11,582
*SOCORRO, El Paso, 590,
  (32,013) 33,186
Soldier Mound, Dickens 10
Solis, Cameron, (512) 543
*SOMERSET, Bexar, 73,
  (1,631) 1,809
*SOMERVILLE, Burleson, 77,
  (1,376) 1,449
Sommer's Mill, Bell 27
*SONORA, Sutton, 133,
  (3,027) 2,836
*SOUR LAKE, Hardin, 103,
  (1,813) 1,864
South Alamo, Hidalgo, (3,361)... 3,879
*South Bend, Young, 2 100
South Bosque, McLennan 1,523
South Brice, Hall 19
South Fork Estates, Jim Hogg,
  (70) 77
*SOUTH HOUSTON, Harris,
  629, (16,983) 17,656
*SOUTHLAKE, Tarrant-Denton,
  1,743, (26,575) 29,311
Southland, Garza 157
South La Paloma, Jim Wells,
  (345) 325
*SOUTHMAYD, Grayson, 19,
  (992) 1,037
SOUTH MOUNTAIN, Coryell,
  (384) 367
*SOUTH PADRE ISLAND, Cameron,
  357, (2,816) 2,787
*South Plains, Floyd 67
South Point, Cameron, (1,376) .. 1,442
South Purmela, Coryell 10
South Shore, Bell 60
SOUTHSIDE PLACE, Harris, 61,
  (1,715) 1,800
South Sulphur, Hunt 60
South Toledo Bend, Newton,
  (524) 474
Southton, Bexar 113
*Spade, Lamb, 2, (73) 64
Spanish Fort, Montague 50
Sparenberg, Dawson 40
Sparks, Bell 40
Sparks, El Paso, (4,529) 5,299
Speaks, Lavaca 60
*SPEARMAN, Hansford, 111,
  (3,368) 3,366
Speegleville, McLennan 1,655
*Spicewood, Burnet, 279 4,000
Spider Mountain, Burnet 92
*SPLENDORA, Montgomery, 169,
  (1,615) 2,034
SPOFFORD, Kinney, (95) 109
Spraberry, Midland 46
*Spring, Harris, 2,188,
  (54,298) 60,802
*Spring Branch, Comal, 380 4,000
Spring Creek, Hutchinson 20
Spring Creek, San Saba 20
Springdale, Cass 55
Springfield, Anderson 30
Spring Gardens, Nueces, (563) 618
Spring Hill, Bowie 100

Spring Hill, Navarro 60
Spring Hill, San Jacinto 38
*SPRINGLAKE, Lamb, 9,
  (108) 98
*SPRINGTOWN, Parker, 306,
  (2,658) 3,064
SPRING VALLEY, Harris, 142,
  (3,715) 4,138
Spring Valley, McLennan 400
*SPUR, Dickens, 49,
  (1,318) 1,146
*Spurger, Tyler, 15 590
Stacy, McCulloch 20
Staff, Eastland 65
*STAFFORD, Fort Bend-Harris,
  1,410, (17,693) 19,007
Stag Creek, Comanche 45
STAGECOACH, Montgomery, 11,
  (538) 613
Stairtown, Caldwell 35
Staley, San Jacinto 30
*STAMFORD, Jones-Haskell,
  133, (3,124) 2,975
Stampede, Bell 6
Stamps, Upshur 45
*STANTON, Martin, 105,
  (2,492) 2,937
*Staples, Guadalupe, 5, (267) 278
*Star, Mills, 1 97
STAR HARBOR, Henderson, 13,
  (444) 458
Star Route, Cochran 15
Starrville, Smith 75
Startzville, Comal 7,000
Steele Hill, Dickens 4
Stephens Creek, San Jacinto 385
*STEPHENVILLE, Erath, 908,
  (17,123) 20,150
Sterley, Floyd 31
*STERLING CITY, Sterling, 46,
  (888) 1,059
Stewards Mill, Freestone 22
Stewart, Rusk 15
Stiles, Reagan 4
Stillwell Store, Brewster 2
*STINNETT, Hutchinson, 50,
  (1,881) 1,842
Stith, Jones 50
*STOCKDALE, Wilson, 80,
  (1,442) 1,656
Stockman, Shelby 55
STOCKTON BEND, Hood,
  (305) 330
Stoneburg, Montague 51
Stoneham, Grimes 15
*Stonewall, Gillespie, 25,
  (505) 524
Stony, Denton 25
Stout, Wood 302
*Stowell, Chambers, 9,
  (1,756) 1,967
Stranger, Falls 12
*STRATFORD, Sherman, 65,
  (2,017) 2,177
Stratton, DeWitt 25
*STRAWN, Palo Pinto, 34,
  (653) 655
Streeter, Mason 85
*STREETMAN, Freestone, 26,
  (247) 250
String Prairie, Bastrop 40

Stringtown, Newton 20
Structure, Williamson 50
Stubblefield, Houston 15
Stubbs, Kaufman 50
*Study Butte, Brewster, 29,
  (233) 254
Sturgeon, Cooke 10
Styx, Kaufman 50
*Sublime, Lavaca 75
*SUDAN, Lamb, 23, (958) 891
Sugar Hill, Titus 90
*SUGAR LAND, Fort Bend,
  4,317, (78,817) 127,441
Sugar Valley, Matagorda 45
*SULLIVAN CITY, Hidalgo, 67,
  (4,002) 4,194
*Sulphur Bluff, Hopkins, 4 280
*SULPHUR SPRINGS, Hopkins,
  794, (15,449) 16,208
Summerfield, Castro 48
Summerville, Gonzales 45
*Sumner, Lamar, 31 95
*SUNDOWN, Hockley, 41,
  (1,397) 1,395
Sunnyside, Castro 64
Sunny Side, Waller 250
Sunnyside, Wilson 100
SUNNYVALE, Dallas, 256,
  (5,130) 6,337
*SUNRAY, Moore, 45,
  (1,926) 1,949
Sunrise, Falls 200
*SUNRISE BEACH, Llano, 36,
  (713) 732
*Sunset, Montague, 15, (497) 517
Sunset, Starr, (47) 54
Sunset Acres, Webb, (23) 20
Sunset Oaks, Burnet 198
SUNSET VALLEY, Travis, 142,
  (648) 753
SUN VALLEY, Lamar, 32, (69) 75
SURFSIDE BEACH, Brazoria,
  34, (482) 582
*Sutherland Springs, Wilson, 6 420
Swamp City, Gregg 8
Swan, Smith 150
*SWEENY, Brazoria, 103,
  (3,684) 3,930
Sweet Home, Guadalupe 294
*Sweet Home, Lavaca, 5 360
Sweet Home, Lee 30
Sweet Union, Cherokee 40
*SWEETWATER, Nolan, 373,
  (10,906) 10,459
Swenson, Stonewall 80
Swift, Nacogdoches 210
Swiss Alp, Fayette 17
Sylvan, Lamar 68
*Sylvester, Fisher, 1 79

T

Tabor, Brazos 150
Tadmor, Houston 67
*TAFT, San Patricio, 61,
  (3,048) 2,999
Taft Southwest, San Patricio,
  (1,460) 1,454
*TAHOKA, Lynn, 70,
  (2,673) 2,681
*TALCO, Titus, 16, (516) 490
*Talpa, Coleman, 8 127

Town, County .... Pop. 2017	Town, County .... Pop. 2017	Town, County .... Pop. 2017

TALTY, Kaufman, 30,
 (1,535) 2,238
Tamina, Montgomery 900
Tanglewood, Lee 60
Tanquecitos South Acres, Webb,
 (233) 244
Tanquecitos South Acres II, Webb,
 (50) 53
Tarkington Prairie, Liberty 300
*Tarpley, Bandera, 6 30
*Tarzan, Martin, 7 30
Tascosa Hills, Potter 90
*TATUM, Rusk, Panola, 68,
 (1,385) 1,416
*TAYLOR, Williamson, 549,
 (15,191) 17,451
TAYLOR LAKE VILLAGE, Harris,
 66, (3,544) 3,633
TAYLOR LANDING, Jefferson,
 (228) 209
Taylorsville, Caldwell 35
Taylor Town, Lamar 40
Tazewell, Hopkins 20
*TEAGUE, Freestone, 115,
 (3,560) 3,558
Teaselville, Smith 150
*TEHUACANA, Limestone, 3,
 (283) 288
Telegraph, Kimble 3
*Telephone, Fannin, 7 210
*Telferner, Victoria, 5 700
Telico, Ellis, Navarro 115
*Tell, Childress 20
*TEMPLE, Bell, 2,199,
 (66,102) 74,488
*TENAHA, Shelby, 32,
 (1,150) 1,164
Tenmile, Dawson 30
*Tennessee Colony, Anderson,
 13 300
*Tennyson, Coke, 1 46
*Terlingua, Brewster, 2, (58) 49
*TERRELL, Kaufman, 836,
 (15,816) 17,566
TERRELL HILLS, Bexar, 113,
 (4,878) 5,262
Terry Chapel, Falls 30
Terryville, DeWitt 40
*TEXARKANA, Bowie, (Miller, Ark.)
 3,467, (66,035) 68,271
*TEXAS CITY, Galveston, 1,018,
 (45,099) 49,711
TEXHOMA, Sherman, (Texas Co.,
 Okla.) 27, (1,295) 1,285
*TEXLINE, Dallam, 26,
 (507) 548
Texroy, Hutchinson 50
Thalia, Foard 50
*THE COLONY, Denton, 929,
 (36,328) 44,188
Thedford, Smith 65
The Grove, Coryell 100
THE HILLS, Travis, (2,472) 2,687
Thelma, Bexar 150
Thelma, Limestone 20
Theon, Williamson 30
Thermo, Hopkins 56
*The Woodlands, Montgomery,
 766, (93,847) 116,958
*Thicket, Hardin, 2 306
*Thomaston, DeWitt 45

*THOMPSONS, Fort Bend, 6,
 (246) 308
Thompsonville, Gonzales 30
Thompsonville, Jim Hogg, (46) 48
Thornberry, Clay 75
*THORNDALE, Milam, 75,
 (1,336) 1,328
*THORNTON, Limestone, 16,
 (526) 547
THORNTONVILLE, Ward, 11,
 (476) 497
Thorp Spring, Hood 222
*THRALL, Williamson, 32,
 (839) 943
Three League, Martin 20
Three Oaks, Wilson 150
*THREE RIVERS, Live Oak, 101,
 (1,848) 1,925
Three States, Cass 45
*THROCKMORTON, Throckmorton,
 49, (828) 744
Thunderbird Bay, Brown, (663) 634
Thurber, Erath 48
Tidwell, Hunt 50
Tierra Bonita, Cameron, (141) 131
Tierra Dorada, Starr, (28) 35
Tierra Grande, Nueces, (403) 434
Tierra Verde, Nueces, (277) 308
Tigertown, Lamar 400
TIKI ISLAND, Galveston, 31,
 (968) 1,053
*Tilden, McMullen, 42,
 (261) 338
Tilmon, Caldwell 60
TIMBERCREEK CANYON, Randall,
 (418) 456
Timberwood, Bexar, (13,447) .. 16,020
*TIMPSON, Shelby, 68,
 (1,155) 1,191
Tin Top, Parker 500
*TIOGA, Grayson, 44,
 (803) 840
TIRA, Hopkins, (297) 299
*Tivoli, Refugio, 5, (479) 503
TOCO, Lamar, 3, (75) 74
Todd City, Anderson 10
TODD MISSION, Grimes, 93,
 (107) 111
Tokio, McLennan 250
Tokio, Terry 6
*TOLAR, Hood, 48, (681) 842
Tolbert, Wilbarger 15
Tolette, Lamar 40
Tolosa, Kaufman 65
*TOMBALL, Harris, 1,459,
 (10,753) 11,470
*TOM BEAN, Grayson, 27,
 (1,045) 1,065
Tomlinson Hill, Falls 64
TOOL, Henderson, 53,
 (2,240) 2,309
Topsey, Coryell 35
*Tornillo, El Paso, 12,
 (1,568) 1,539
Tours, McLennan 130
*Tow, Llano, 6 305
Town Bluff, Tyler 429
*TOYAH, Reeves, 3, (90) 93
*Toyahvale, Reeves, 1 60
Tradewinds, San Patricio, (180) ... 182
Travis, Falls 48

Travis Ranch, Kaufman,
 (2,556) 2,963
Trawick, Nacogdoches 375
Treasure Island, Guadalupe 172
Treasure Island, Brazoria 152
*TRENT, Taylor, 3, (337) 329
*TRENTON, Fannin, 58,
 (635) 652
Trickham, Coleman 29
Trimmer, Bell 390
*TRINIDAD, Henderson, 28,
 (886) 858
*TRINITY, Trinity, 138,
 (2,697) 2,793
TROPHY CLUB, Denton, 290,
 (8,024) 12,923
*TROUP, Smith-Cherokee, 102,
 (1,869) 1,980
Trout Creek, Newton 70
*TROY, Bell, 103, (1,645) 1,909
Truby, Jones 26
Trumbull, Ellis 100
Truscott, Knox 50
Tucker, Anderson 175
*Tuleta, Bee, 12, (288) 295
*TULIA, Swisher, 128,
 (4,967) 4,682
Tulip, Fannin 10
Tulsita, Bee, (14) 2
Tundra, Van Zandt 34
Tunis, Burleson 150
*TURKEY, Hall, 20,
 (421) 383
Turlington, Freestone 27
Turnersville, Coryell 125
Turnersville, Travis 90
*Turnertown-Selman City, Rusk,
 3 271
Turtle Bayou, Chambers 55
*TUSCOLA, Taylor, 73,
 (742) 746
Tuxedo, Jones 42
Twichell, Ochiltree 22
Twitty, Wheeler 12
*TYE, Taylor, 57, (1,242) 1,270
*TYLER, Smith, 4,648,
 (96,900) 105,486
*Tynan, Bee, 6, (278) 286
Type, Williamson-Bastrop 40

U
UHLAND, Hays-Caldwell, 22,
 (1,014) 1,331
*Umbarger, Randall, 2 327
UNCERTAIN, Harrison, 3,
 (94) 105
Union, Scurry 20
Union, Terry 8
Union, Wilson 52
Union Grove, Bell 12
UNION GROVE, Upshur, 2,
 (357) 366
Union High, Navarro 30
Union Hill, Denton 25
UNION VALLEY, Hunt,
 (307) 351
Unity, Lamar 60
*UNIVERSAL CITY, Bexar, 579,
 (18,530) 20,961
UNIVERSITY PARK, Dallas, 861,
 (23,068) 24,401

CITIES & TOWNS

CITIES & TOWNS

Town, County .... Pop. 2017	Town, County .... Pop. 2017	Town, County .... Pop. 2017

*WESTON, Collin, 14, (563) 586
WESTON LAKES, Fort Bend,
  (2,482) 2,807
WEST ORANGE, Orange, 107,
  (3,443) 3,549
Westover, Baylor 18
WESTOVER HILLS, Tarrant,
  (682) 768
Westphalia, Falls 186
*West Point, Fayette, 11 213
West Sharyland, Hidalgo,
  (2,309) 2,375
West Sinton, San Patricio 150
WEST TAWAKONI, Hunt, 41,
  (1,576) 1,689
WEST UNIVERSITY PLACE, Harris,
  280, (14,787) 15,485
Westville, Trinity 46
Westway, Deaf Smith 15
Westway, El Paso, (4,188) 4,275
Westwood Shores, Trinity,
  (1,162) 1,180
WESTWORTH VILLAGE, Tarrant,
  67, (2,472) 2,742
*WHARTON, Wharton, 335,
  (8,832) 8,690
Wheatland, Tarrant 175
*WHEELER, Wheeler, 61,
  (1,592) 1,590
Wheeler Springs, Houston 89
*Wheelock, Robertson, 4 225
White City, San Augustine 20
White City, Wilbarger 40
*WHITE DEER, Carson, 42,
  (1,000) 1,009
*WHITEFACE, Cochran, 15,
  (449) 424
Whiteflat, Motley 4
White Hall, Bell 262
Whitehall, Grimes 30
*WHITEHOUSE, Smith, 315,
  (7,660) 8,371
*WHITE OAK, Gregg, 249,
  (6,489) 6,329
White Oak, Titus 60
White River Lake, Crosby 83
White Rock, Hunt 60
White Rock, Red River 90
White Rock, Robertson 80
White Rock, San Augustine 60
*WHITESBORO, Grayson, 202,
  (3,793) 3,928
*WHITE SETTLEMENT, Tarrant,
  341, (16,116) 17,228
White Star, Motley 6
Whiteway, Hamilton 8
*WHITEWRIGHT, Grayson-Fannin,
  84, (1,604) 1,618
*Whitharral, Hockley 158
Whitman, Washington 25
*WHITNEY, Hill, 184,
  (2,087) 2,162
*Whitsett, Live Oak, 9 200
Whitson, Coryell 50
*Whitt, Parker 38
Whon, Coleman 35
*WICHITA FALLS, Wichita,
  3,030, (104,553) 105,592
*WICKETT, Ward, 34,
  (498) 523
Wied, Lavaca 65

Wiedeville, Washington 35
*Wiergate, Newton, 1 350
Wigginsville, Montgomery 100
Wilcox, Burleson 39
Wilderville, Falls 45
*Wildorado, Oldham, 10 210
Wild Peach, Brazoria,
  (2,452) 2,661
Wildwood, Hardin,
  (1,235) 1,278
Wilkins, Upshur 75
*Willamar, Willacy, (15) 10
William Penn, Washington 40
*WILLIS, Montgomery, 459,
  (5,662) 6,791
*Willow City, Gillespie, 3 22
Willow Grove, McLennan 100
WILLOW PARK, Parker, 173,
  (3,982) 5,400
Willow Springs, Fayette 74
Willow Springs, Rains 25
*WILLS POINT, Van Zandt, 211,
  (3,524) 3,590
*WILMER, Dallas, 66,
  (3,682) 4,056
Wilmeth, Runnels 15
Wilson, Falls 42
*WILSON, Lynn, 15, (489) 492
*WIMBERLEY, Hays, 669,
  (2,626) 2,675
Winchell, Brown 20
Winchester, Fayette 232
WINDCREST, Bexar, 237,
  (5,364) 5,902
Windemere, Travis, (1,037) 1,066
*WINDOM, Fannin, 14,
  (199) 203
*WINDTHORST, Archer, 45,
  (409) 400
Winedale, Fayette 67
*WINFIELD, Titus, 17, (524) 526
WINFREE [Old River-], Chambers,
  17, (1,245) 1,352
*Wingate, Runnels, 3 100
*WINK, Winkler, 33, (940) 1,056
Winkler, Navarro-Freestone 26
*Winnie, Chambers, 149,
  (3,254) 3,498
*WINNSBORO, Wood-Franklin,
  281, (3,252) 3,402
*WINONA, Smith, 42,
  (576) 605
Winter Haven, Dimmit 123
*WINTERS, Runnels, 81,
  (2,562) 2,525
Witting, Lavaca 90
WIXON VALLEY, Brazos, 18,
  (254) 256
Wizard Wells, Jack 69
*Woden, Nacogdoches, 3 400
*WOLFE CITY, Hunt, 53,
  (1,412) 1,454
*WOLFFORTH, Lubbock, 188,
  (3,670) 4,365
Womack, Bosque 25
Woodbine, Cooke 250
WOODBRANCH, Montgomery,
  (1,282) 1,460
Woodbury, Hill 45
WOODCREEK, Hays, 37,
  (1,457) 1,688

Wooded Hills, Johnson 580
Wood Hi, Victoria 35
*Woodlake, Trinity, 1 180
Woodland, Red River 128
*Woodlawn, Harrison, 5 550
WOODLOCH, Montgomery,
  (207) 212
Woodrow, Fort Bend 190
Woodrow, Lubbock 2,034
Woods, Panola 65
*WOODSBORO, Refugio, 58,
  (1,512) 1,481
*WOODSON, Throckmorton, 13,
  (264) 240
Wood Springs, Smith 200
Woodville, Cherokee 20
*WOODVILLE, Tyler, 177,
  (2,586) 2,670
Woodward, La Salle 6
WOODWAY, McLennan, 352,
  (8,452) 8,955
Woosley, Rains 47
*WORTHAM, Freestone, 30,
  (1,073) 1,056
Worthing, Lavaca 55
Wright City, Smith 172
Wrightsboro, Gonzales 10
Wyldwood, Bastrop, (2,505) 2,746
*WYLIE, Collin-Rockwall-Dallas,
  1,222, (41,427) 50,658
Wylie, Taylor .... [part of Abilene]

Y

*Yancey, Medina, 14 209
*YANTIS, Wood, 64, (388) 402
Yard, Anderson 50
Yarrellton, Milam 35
Yellowpine, Sabine 97
*YOAKUM, Lavaca-DeWitt, 224,
  (5,815) 6,017
*YORKTOWN, DeWitt, 130,
  (2,092) 2,161
Youngsport, Bell 49
Yowell, Delta, Hunt 30
Ysleta del Sur Pueblo, El Paso,
  (350) 350
Yznaga, Cameron, (91) 91

Z

Zabcikville, Bell 76
*Zapata, Zapata, 143,
  (5,089) 4,977
Zapata Ranch, Willacy,
  (108) 113
Zarate, Starr, (59) 62
*ZAVALLA, Angelina, 40,
  (713) 731
*Zephyr, Brown, 12 201
Zimmerscheidt, Colorado 50
Zion Hill, Guadalupe 595
Zipperlandville, Falls 22
Zorn, Guadalupe 287
Zuehl, Guadalupe, (376) 394
Zunkerville, Karnes 15

ELECTIONS

Campaign yard signs near a polling place in Irving on March 2, 2018.
Photo by Trong Nguyen/Shutterstock.

Red Texas Fades a Little: Close Race for U.S. Senate

By Carolyn Barta

Republicans in long reliably red Texas got a wake-up call in the 2018 mid-term elections – but continued to dominate.

Beto O'Rourke, a little-known El Paso congressman, held Republican U.S. Sen. Ted Cruz to less than 51 percent in the best statewide showing for a Democrat in decades – 2.6 points short of victory.

It propelled O'Rourke, a dynamic campaigner and successful fundraiser, into an unlikely run for the Democratic presidential nomination. It also propelled other Texas Democrats.

Democrats haven't won a statewide race since 1994. That didn't change. Gov. Greg Abbott coasted to re-election, with other state officials following. Republicans maintained a state house majority, electing 83 of 150 members and keeping state senate control with 19 of 31.

But Democrats were pumped when they picked up two seats in Congress, flipped 12 seats in the Texas House, two in the Texas Senate, reduced GOP tallies in some state races, and won eight seats on the 14-member Fifth District Court of Appeals.

Moving to just nine votes short of a House majority gave Democrats more leverage in the 2019 legislative session and bolstered their hopes for 2020 elections.

Two uber-conservative state senators, Don Huffines and Konni Burton, lost in Dallas and Tarrant County, as the electorate leaned more moderate, suggesting a decline in tea-party influence.

Congressional delegation dominance shifted

Democrat Beto O'Rourke campaigning in Austin in 2018. Photo by crockodile, Flickr (CC).

Republican Senator Ted Cruz speaking to the Conservative Political Action Conference in 2017. Photo by George Skidmore (CC).

Congressional Districts

© Texas Almanac

from 25 Rs and 11 Ds to 23-13. Dallas-area congressman Pete Sessions, a member since 1997, was defeated in District 32 by Colin Allred. Houston's District 7, a Republican seat since the 1960s once held by George H.W. Bush, also fell, to Democrat Lizzie Fletcher.

Turnout topped 8.3 million, a huge jump from the 4.7 million who voted in the 2014 off-year election, as voters sought to weigh in on the Trump presidency as well as the Senate race.

Hispanic influence continued to grow. Texas sent its first Latinas to the U.S. House with Sylvia Garcia of Houston (District 29) and Veronica Escobar of El Paso (District 16).

In 2020, more than one-third of the electorate in Texas is predicted to be nonwhite.

Carolyn Barta is a former political writer for the Dallas Morning News *and retired Journalism professor at Southern Methodist University.*

2018 Election for Senator, Governor by County

Below are the results by county in the races for governor and U.S senator. The Democratic Party candidate for senator was U.S. Rep. Beto O'Rourke of El Paso. The Republican Party candidate was incumbent Senator Ted Cruz.

The Republican Party candidate for governor was the incumbent Gov. Greg Abbott. The Democratic Party candidate was Lupe Valdez of Dallas.

The voting age population in November 2018 was estimated at 19,900,980.

The statewide turnout in the previous gubernatorial and senatorial elections in 2014 was 33.7 percent of the registered voters. *Source: Texas Secretary of State.*

SENATOR				COUNTY	Registered Voters	Turn-out %	GOVERNOR			
Cruz	%	O'Rourke	%				Abbott	%	Valdez	%
4,260,553	50.89	4,045,632	48.33	**Statewide**	**15,793,257**	**53.01**	4,656,196	55.81	3,546,615	42.51
11,335	76.92	3,307	22.44	Anderson	28,487	51.78	11,732	79.53	2,868	19.44
3,338	80.80	776	18.78	Andrews	9,574	43.15	3,400	82.42	687	16.65
19,166	72.46	7,130	26.96	Angelina	51,751	51.11	19,701	74.76	6,406	24.31
6,677	74.35	2,247	25.02	Aransas	17,308	51.88	7,075	78.79	1,797	20.01
3,208	89.06	376	10.44	Archer	6,317	57.15	3,259	90.28	323	8.95
819	91.10	74	8.23	Armstrong	1,428	62.96	822	91.84	59	6.59
7,753	63.53	4,332	35.50	Atascosa	27,338	44.64	8,361	68.68	3,655	30.02
8,722	78.95	2,241	20.29	Austin	19,406	56.93	9,009	81.68	1,897	17.20
1,204	74.50	405	25.06	Bailey	3,727	43.36	1,241	77.27	348	21.67
7,643	79.75	1,865	19.46	Bandera	15,869	60.42	7,866	82.04	1,602	16.71
15,067	54.87	12,082	44.00	Bastrop	47,438	57.89	16,351	59.68	10,407	37.98
1,070	86.64	156	12.63	Baylor	2,365	52.22	1,090	88.33	129	10.45
4,342	60.16	2,811	38.95	Bee	15,883	45.44	4,827	67.25	2,261	31.50
47,437	54.79	38,417	44.37	Bell	195,760	44.23	51,157	59.21	33,803	39.12
217,600	39.59	326,946	59.49	Bexar	1,098,257	50.04	251,043	45.95	285,502	52.25
4,181	71.99	1,570	27.03	Blanco	8,504	68.30	4,329	74.70	1,351	23.31
320	93.29	22	6.41	Borden	488	70.29	321	94.69	17	5.01
5,718	79.92	1,374	19.20	Bosque	12,209	58.63	5,948	83.10	1,104	15.42
20,157	71.17	7,982	28.18	Bowie	59,618	47.50	20,651	73.00	7,357	26.01
65,693	58.78	45,228	40.47	Brazoria	207,446	53.87	70,373	63.09	39,536	35.44
35,971	55.78	27,876	43.23	Brazos	114,377	56.38	39,424	61.44	23,361	36.41
1,879	45.99	2,147	52.55	Brewster	7,292	56.03	2,033	50.05	1,933	47.59
553	88.62	69	11.06	Briscoe	1,084	57.56	556	89.25	58	9.31
543	28.24	1,376	71.55	Brooks	5,843	32.91	658	35.22	1,198	64.13
10,391	85.65	1,670	13.77	Brown	23,368	51.92	10,640	86.93	1,458	11.91
5,079	77.53	1,427	21.78	Burleson	11,782	56.01	5,254	79.62	1,277	19.35
13,859	74.95	4,444	24.03	Burnet	31,072	59.70	14,497	78.16	3,712	20.01
6,147	53.54	5,227	45.53	Caldwell	23,777	48.29	6,723	58.68	4,509	39.36
4,198	68.61	1,874	30.63	Calhoun	12,835	47.67	4,409	72.07	1,627	26.59
4,373	87.06	610	12.14	Callahan	9,337	53.80	4,475	89.23	486	9.69
28,574	36.67	48,770	62.60	Cameron	206,966	37.64	34,407	44.39	41,991	54.17
2,749	70.63	1,119	28.75	Camp	7,648	50.89	2,816	72.48	1,028	26.46
2,192	89.14	245	9.96	Carson	4,263	57.68	2,209	90.05	208	8.48
8,148	79.75	2,024	19.81	Cass	20,119	51.14	8,323	80.89	1,890	18.37
1,219	75.11	394	24.28	Castro	3,842	42.24	1,226	75.91	371	22.97
12,146	80.01	2,926	19.27	Chambers	28,063	54.10	12,505	82.44	2,460	16.22
11,631	77.85	3,207	21.46	Cherokee	27,949	53.79	11,943	79.43	2,938	19.54
1,526	86.21	236	13.33	Childress	3,559	49.73	1,546	87.59	206	11.67
3,710	86.52	547	12.76	Clay	7,655	56.02	3,807	88.82	449	10.48
541	78.86	140	20.41	Cochran	1,729	39.68	550	81.00	122	17.97
1,150	88.67	137	10.56	Coke	2,285	57.77	1,187	89.92	118	8.94
2,759	88.26	351	11.23	Coleman	5,912	52.94	2,774	88.63	328	10.48
187,425	52.65	165,614	46.53	Collin	579,893	61.38	208,075	58.83	139,175	39.35
810	87.28	113	12.18	Collingsworth	1,906	49.27	827	88.07	101	10.76
5,779	75.67	1,825	23.90	Colorado	13,938	54.79	5,992	78.71	1,558	20.46
44,079	71.68	16,830	27.37	Comal	100,867	61.26	46,635	75.47	14,145	22.89
3,799	82.41	781	16.94	Comanche	9,197	50.16	3,906	84.67	657	14.24
803	81.94	163	16.63	Concho	1,677	58.62	825	83.93	145	14.75
11,879	81.70	2,550	17.54	Cooke	25,747	56.47	12,294	84.72	2,054	14.15
10,626	66.99	5,067	31.94	Coryell	38,635	41.23	11,281	70.81	4,392	27.57

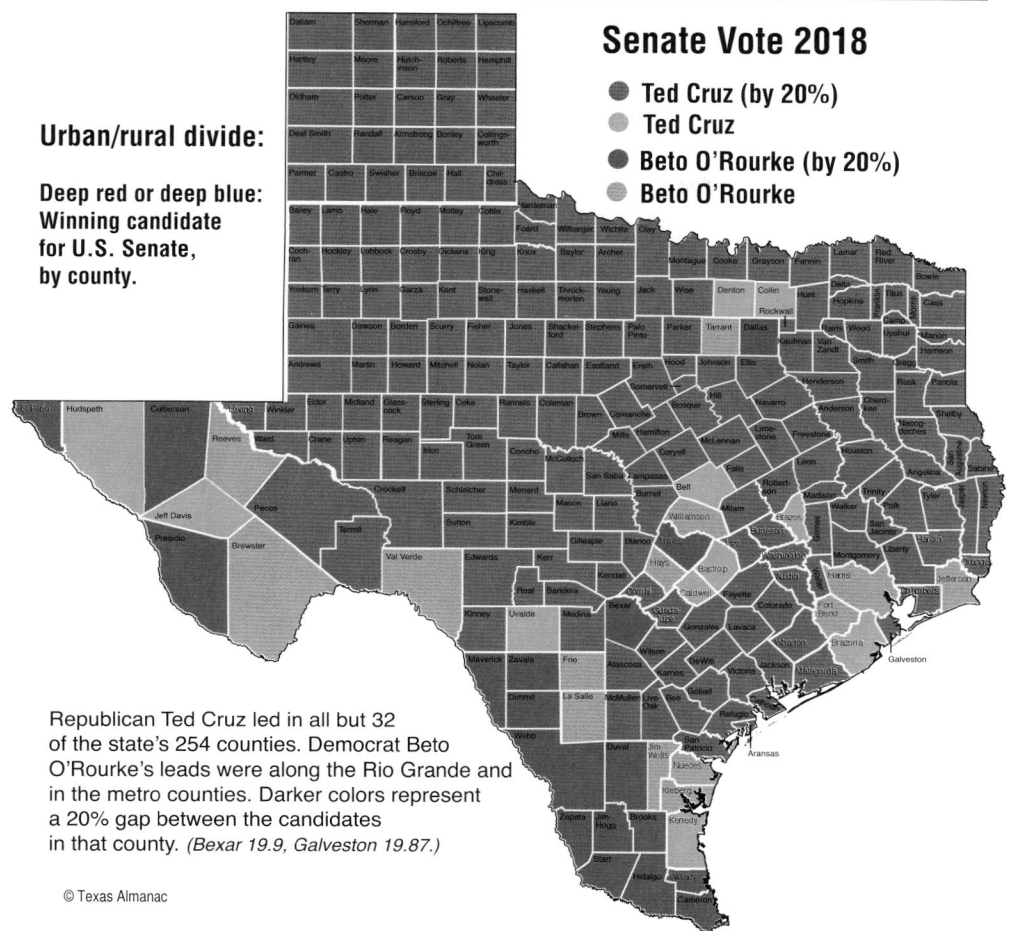

Senate Vote 2018

● Ted Cruz (by 20%)
◐ Ted Cruz
● Beto O'Rourke (by 20%)
◐ Beto O'Rourke

Urban/rural divide:

Deep red or deep blue:
Winning candidate
for U.S. Senate,
by county.

Republican Ted Cruz led in all but 32
of the state's 254 counties. Democrat Beto
O'Rourke's leads were along the Rio Grande and
in the metro counties. Darker colors represent
a 20% gap between the candidates
in that county. *(Bexar 19.9, Galveston 19.87.)*

© Texas Almanac

SENATOR				COUNTY	Registered	Turn-	GOVERNOR			
Cruz	%	O'Rourke	%		Voters	out %	Abbott	%	Valdez	%
458	82.23	97	17.41	Cottle	1,063	52.59	468	83.72	88	15.74
836	79.24	213	20.19	Crane	2,666	39.57	842	80.42	197	18.82
928	72.73	340	26.65	Crockett	2,497	51.10	921	72.75	333	26.30
978	68.78	437	30.73	Crosby	3,540	40.17	1,005	70.92	392	27.66
297	35.91	521	63.00	Culberson	1,722	48.03	324	42.80	422	55.75
970	87.00	139	12.47	Dallam	3,039	36.92	985	87.79	129	11.50
241,126	33.13	481,395	66.14	Dallas	1,335,313	54.51	283,659	39.18	425,208	58.74
2,192	72.70	811	26.90	Dawson	7,202	41.86	2,240	74.44	739	24.56
2,680	70.99	1,067	28.26	Deaf Smith	8,855	42.63	2,788	73.89	957	25.36
1,562	80.85	354	18.32	Delta	3,896	49.69	1,606	82.95	301	15.55
158,744	53.67	134,649	45.52	Denton	497,490	59.46	174,472	59.25	113,808	38.65
4,974	81.13	1,128	18.40	DeWitt	11,744	52.21	5,115	83.59	942	15.39
635	84.22	113	14.99	Dickens	1,288	58.85	656	86.54	96	12.66
840	29.03	2,042	70.56	Dimmit	7,378	39.22	1,042	36.55	1,787	62.68
1,110	86.79	161	12.59	Donley	2,237	57.40	1,130	88.01	134	10.44
1,330	32.34	2,765	67.23	Duval	8,377	49.10	1,479	37.37	2,457	62.08
5,377	86.66	800	12.89	Eastland	11,775	52.70	5,434	87.66	708	11.42
20,996	68.90	9,230	30.29	Ector	76,536	39.93	21,934	71.78	8,211	26.87
604	79.79	145	19.15	Edwards	1,449	52.24	635	85.58	100	13.48
41,022	67.71	19,106	31.53	Ellis	108,349	55.92	43,647	72.14	15,879	26.25
50,943	25.02	151,482	74.40	El Paso	455,992	44.65	62,749	31.28	134,181	66.88

SENATOR				COUNTY	Registered Voters	Turn-out %	GOVERNOR			
Cruz	%	O'Rourke	%				Abbott	%	Valdez	%
10,055	79.64	2,486	19.69	Erath	22,492	56.13	10,356	82.22	2,073	16.46
3,215	68.70	1,445	30.88	Falls	10,399	45.00	3,344	71.62	1,286	27.54
8,569	79.71	2,107	19.60	Fannin	20,756	51.81	8,856	82.35	1,767	16.43
8,228	78.52	2,198	20.98	Fayette	16,626	63.03	8,576	81.98	1,777	16.99
1,139	76.24	340	22.76	Fisher	2,682	55.70	1,161	78.02	310	20.83
1,394	74.19	476	25.33	Floyd	3,965	47.39	1,448	77.14	412	21.95
321	73.79	113	25.98	Foard	913	47.75	331	75.92	101	23.17
111,423	43.62	142,399	55.75	Fort Bend	431,832	59.15	125,867	49.39	125,374	49.19
3,300	83.04	639	16.08	Franklin	6,807	58.38	3,359	84.93	537	13.58
5,243	79.90	1,279	19.49	Freestone	11,978	54.78	5,336	81.60	1,143	17.48
1,636	44.46	2,016	54.78	Frio	8,606	42.76	1,844	50.74	1,739	47.85
3,317	86.18	513	13.33	Gaines	8,921	43.15	3,305	86.22	475	12.39
67,641	59.53	45,065	39.66	Galveston	212,630	53.44	72,104	63.56	39,314	34.66
1,068	82.98	203	15.77	Garza	2,712	47.46	1,078	84.42	186	14.57
9,890	78.85	2,572	20.51	Gillespie	19,294	65.02	10,351	82.51	2,030	16.18
513	92.60	37	6.68	Glasscock	782	70.84	515	93.13	36	6.51
2,326	75.72	717	23.34	Goliad	5,597	54.89	2,397	78.28	617	20.15
4,173	74.19	1,421	25.26	Gonzales	12,210	46.07	4,393	78.24	1,170	20.84
5,246	88.90	615	10.42	Gray	12,493	47.61	5,330	89.61	551	9.26
31,655	73.37	11,157	25.86	Grayson	80,863	53.35	32,562	75.68	9,857	22.91
24,469	68.37	11,133	30.98	Gregg	69,893	51.48	25,558	71.03	10,015	27.83
6,499	75.51	2,037	23.67	Grimes	16,176	53.44	6,684	77.33	1,858	21.49
33,938	62.19	20,079	36.79	Guadalupe	100,552	54.27	36,284	66.69	17,265	31.74
5,360	72.51	1,970	26.65	Hale	19,170	38.56	5,532	75.03	1,727	23.42
807	83.11	161	16.58	Hall	1,987	48.87	815	84.54	142	14.73
2,795	83.93	507	15.23	Hamilton	5,611	59.49	2,903	86.97	405	12.13
1,552	90.76	138	8.07	Hansford	3,034	56.36	1,548	91.54	118	6.98
973	83.73	185	15.92	Hardeman	2,459	47.25	997	86.17	154	13.31
17,391	86.53	2,636	13.12	Hardin	38,259	52.53	17,528	87.60	2,327	11.63
498,902	41.31	700,200	57.98	Harris	2,338,460	51.65	559,819	46.39	628,804	52.11
16,226	71.82	6,245	27.64	Harrison	44,462	50.81	16,747	74.21	5,562	24.65
1,467	90.33	153	9.42	Hartley	2,875	56.49	1,491	91.87	125	7.70
1,362	81.36	302	18.04	Haskell	3,331	50.26	1,387	83.15	267	16.01
33,308	41.77	45,584	57.16	Hays	134,403	59.33	37,895	47.65	39,486	49.65
1,209	87.93	157	11.42	Hemphill	2,289	60.07	1,199	87.84	152	11.14
20,891	78.80	5,415	20.43	Henderson	51,770	51.58	21,775	81.55	4,622	17.31
46,505	30.64	104,416	68.81	Hidalgo	361,562	41.97	55,421	36.70	93,935	62.20
8,927	78.08	2,443	21.37	Hill	22,743	50.27	9,262	81.03	2,052	17.95
4,844	79.49	1,211	19.87	Hockley	13,582	44.87	4,947	81.47	1,030	16.96
20,090	80.34	4,720	18.88	Hood	40,835	61.23	20,865	83.66	3,765	15.10
9,306	78.07	2,545	21.35	Hopkins	22,706	52.50	9,533	80.24	2,218	18.67
5,552	75.43	1,772	24.08	Houston	13,090	56.23	5,659	76.99	1,641	22.33
5,651	76.32	1,693	22.87	Howard	16,968	43.64	5,737	77.83	1,542	20.92
509	54.56	407	43.62	Hudspeth	1,922	48.54	538	60.72	335	37.81
21,115	74.12	7,151	25.10	Hunt	55,193	51.62	22,078	77.70	5,946	20.93
5,854	88.14	753	11.34	Hutchinson	13,547	49.03	5,874	88.46	687	10.35
636	86.18	96	13.01	Irion	1,314	56.16	641	86.97	87	11.80
2,498	88.80	296	10.52	Jack	5,082	56.09	2,539	90.32	246	8.75
3,991	82.46	832	17.19	Jackson	9,195	52.64	4,016	84.41	715	15.03
9,504	80.32	2,282	19.29	Jasper	22,848	51.79	9,732	82.42	1,990	16.85
683	58.03	466	39.59	Jeff Davis	1,719	68.57	719	61.72	407	34.94
36,731	49.48	37,128	50.01	Jefferson	148,344	50.06	38,999	52.51	34,516	46.48
410	27.74	1,060	71.72	Jim Hogg	3,833	38.56	509	34.98	938	64.47
4,520	45.66	5,331	53.85	Jim Wells	26,438	37.45	5,088	52.02	4,616	47.19
39,571	75.47	12,411	23.67	Johnson	97,157	53.97	41,485	79.22	10,105	19.30
4,115	82.56	832	16.69	Jones	10,024	49.72	4,167	83.66	757	15.20
2,900	70.12	1,203	29.09	Karnes	8,071	51.25	3,023	73.32	1,054	25.56
26,118	67.07	12,002	31.28	Kaufman	72,579	52.87	27,491	71.70	10,294	26.85
15,292	77.25	4,340	21.92	Kendall	30,774	64.33	16,076	81.42	3,382	17.13
100	55.56	77	42.78	Kenedy	309	58.25	111	64.91	57	33.33
288	85.46	44	13.06	Kent	588	57.31	299	88.72	34	10.09

Cruz	%	O'Rourke	%	COUNTY	Registered Voters	Turn-out %	Abbott	%	Valdez	%
							SENATOR spans Cruz..% ; GOVERNOR spans Abbott..%			

SENATOR				COUNTY	Registered Voters	Turn-out %	GOVERNOR			
Cruz	%	O'Rourke	%				Abbott	%	Valdez	%
16,822	75.76	5,198	23.41	Kerr	35,854	61.93	17,566	79.37	4,268	19.28
1,495	87.73	195	11.44	Kimble	2,908	58.91	1,529	89.26	161	9.40
124	94.66	6	4.58	King	184	71.20	120	94.49	6	4.72
827	68.97	358	29.86	Kinney	2,255	53.17	890	74.73	290	24.35
4,081	47.48	4,456	51.84	Kleberg	18,186	47.27	4,831	56.44	3,629	42.40
855	78.23	229	20.95	Knox	2,434	44.95	866	79.16	217	19.84
12,711	76.72	3,731	22.52	Lamar	31,591	52.45	13,103	79.25	3,231	19.54
2,741	79.29	699	20.22	Lamb	8,096	42.70	2,785	80.75	629	18.24
5,836	78.13	1,569	21.00	Lampasas	14,099	53.32	6,073	80.79	1,343	17.87
673	45.20	813	54.60	La Salle	4,300	34.63	728	49.86	725	49.66
6,688	86.44	1,019	13.17	Lavaca	13,234	58.46	6,856	88.68	830	10.74
4,487	76.74	1,322	22.61	Lee	10,453	55.94	4,650	79.68	1,129	19.35
5,711	86.67	855	12.98	Leon	11,163	59.03	5,781	87.82	751	11.41
16,041	77.96	4,421	21.49	Liberty	43,981	46.78	16,527	80.44	3,816	18.57
5,211	75.35	1,672	24.18	Limestone	13,621	50.78	5,330	77.06	1,535	22.19
942	88.28	116	10.87	Lipscomb	1,988	53.67	947	89.00	109	10.24
3,029	82.96	601	16.46	Live Oak	7,240	50.43	3,114	85.39	504	13.82
7,954	78.33	2,124	20.92	Llano	15,758	64.58	8,287	81.44	1,751	17.21
47	87.04	6	11.11	Loving	121	46.28	47	83.93	9	16.07
58,780	64.19	32,068	35.02	Lubbock	175,881	52.07	61,775	67.76	27,266	29.91
1,369	80.67	323	19.03	Lynn	3,945	43.02	1,380	81.37	302	17.81
3,033	79.17	780	20.36	Madison	7,428	51.59	3,081	80.40	722	18.84
2,448	70.00	1,018	29.11	Marion	7,368	47.84	2,553	72.43	939	26.64
1,297	83.46	243	15.64	Martin	3,252	47.79	1,303	84.28	229	14.81
1,560	79.31	402	20.44	Mason	2,956	66.54	1,605	81.93	333	17.00
7,330	70.10	3,049	29.16	Matagorda	21,654	48.42	7,705	73.49	2,673	25.50
2,951	27.38	7,727	71.71	Maverick	31,453	34.26	3,495	33.09	6,940	65.71
2,245	84.05	400	14.98	McCulloch	5,243	51.04	2,275	85.01	368	13.75
45,855	61.24	28,452	38.00	McLennan	139,699	53.69	49,195	65.59	24,734	32.98
387	90.00	41	9.53	McMullen	704	61.08	395	92.07	33	7.69
11,444	70.73	4,621	28.56	Medina	31,354	51.63	12,057	74.49	3,964	24.49
632	80.72	145	18.52	Menard	1,443	54.26	646	82.82	130	16.67
32,867	76.51	9,723	22.64	Midland	84,393	50.90	34,049	79.48	8,101	18.91
5,922	74.15	1,997	25.00	Milam	15,038	53.13	6,080	76.10	1,795	22.47
1,764	88.02	229	11.43	Mills	3,426	58.79	1,790	88.88	206	10.23
1,585	82.85	323	16.88	Mitchell	4,562	41.93	1,595	83.64	298	15.63
6,424	86.57	941	12.68	Montague	13,588	54.61	6,563	88.59	765	10.33
137,395	72.28	51,268	26.97	Montgomery	333,488	57.07	144,664	76.01	43,044	22.62
3,248	80.00	787	19.38	Moore	9,764	41.58	3,268	80.53	750	18.48
2,953	69.74	1,260	29.76	Morris	8,302	51.00	3,018	71.50	1,159	27.46
483	91.65	40	7.59	Motley	847	62.22	458	92.15	35	7.04
13,775	63.68	7,732	35.74	Nacogdoches	36,993	58.48	14,411	66.97	6,843	31.80
10,391	72.08	3,918	27.18	Navarro	28,641	50.33	10,818	75.08	3,411	23.67
3,660	78.27	993	21.24	Newton	9,293	50.32	3,771	80.75	870	18.63
3,120	76.58	928	22.78	Nolan	8,778	46.41	3,200	78.86	807	19.89
45,956	48.85	47,392	50.38	Nueces	205,176	45.85	52,918	56.33	39,720	42.28
2,160	89.44	230	9.52	Ochiltree	5,216	46.30	2,169	90.11	212	8.81
732	89.71	82	10.05	Oldham	1,417	57.59	742	91.72	62	7.66
21,164	80.37	5,050	19.18	Orange	53,392	49.32	21,724	82.64	4,348	16.54
7,547	80.03	1,837	19.48	Palo Pinto	17,984	52.44	7,811	82.83	1,529	16.21
7,120	81.38	1,598	18.26	Panola	16,392	53.37	7,182	82.20	1,494	17.10
44,071	80.87	9,956	18.27	Parker	91,858	59.68	45,981	83.87	8,099	14.77
1,675	81.43	372	18.08	Parmer	4,428	46.45	1,680	82.11	352	17.20
2,161	61.39	1,339	38.04	Pecos	8,223	42.81	2,299	65.63	1,167	33.31
12,794	76.38	3,850	22.99	Polk	38,018	44.06	13,130	78.49	3,378	20.19
16,689	68.33	7,521	30.79	Potter	55,580	43.94	17,299	71.01	6,674	27.40
436	26.15	1,221	73.25	Presidio	4,884	34.13	465	28.15	1,157	70.04
3,702	84.02	681	15.46	Rains	7,668	57.47	3,810	86.45	566	12.84
38,479	79.41	9,613	19.84	Randall	87,827	55.17	39,586	81.84	8,065	16.67
692	82.97	136	16.31	Reagan	1,845	45.31	697	83.37	127	15.19
1,311	83.82	245	15.66	Real	2,590	60.46	1,341	85.63	213	13.60

Cruz	%	O'Rourke	%	COUNTY	Registered Voters	Turn-out %	Abbott	%	Valdez	%
	SENATOR							GOVERNOR		
3,427	77.57	973	22.02	Red River	8,268	53.43	3,476	78.89	904	20.52
1,128	47.04	1,255	52.34	Reeves	7,089	33.83	1,210	51.34	1,123	47.65
1,636	65.65	847	33.99	Refugio	4,949	50.43	1,726	69.15	751	30.09
441	95.87	19	4.13	Roberts	707	66.34	448	95.52	16	3.41
4,295	68.52	1,942	30.98	Robertson	11,654	53.78	4,448	71.13	1,753	28.03
26,615	68.77	11,754	30.37	Rockwall	62,933	61.49	28,582	73.98	9,432	24.41
2,842	87.88	385	11.90	Runnels	6,692	48.68	2,885	88.55	345	10.59
12,597	77.37	3,609	22.17	Rusk	31,242	52.12	12,864	79.19	3,233	19.90
3,456	87.12	496	12.50	Sabine	7,802	50.85	3,477	87.85	458	11.57
2,266	75.13	734	24.34	San Augustine	5,989	50.36	2,296	76.53	684	22.80
7,499	80.30	1,785	19.11	San Jacinto	17,976	51.95	7,722	82.72	1,529	16.38
11,335	62.22	6,777	37.20	San Patricio	41,762	43.63	12,173	66.83	5,842	32.07
1,811	87.53	247	11.94	San Saba	3,737	55.37	1,835	89.12	211	10.24
735	77.21	209	21.95	Schleicher	1,789	53.49	758	79.21	187	19.54
3,705	84.92	642	14.71	Scurry	9,393	46.50	3,750	85.85	577	13.21
1,174	91.65	103	8.04	Shackelford	2,320	55.39	1,190	92.61	87	6.77
6,008	79.46	1,521	20.12	Shelby	15,294	49.31	6,132	81.30	1,366	18.11
692	84.18	87	10.58	Sherman	1,535	53.22	701	85.80	74	9.06
53,760	69.46	23,182	29.95	Smith	134,712	57.33	55,708	72.13	20,623	26.70
3,033	82.17	633	17.15	Somervell	6,287	58.71	3,143	85.31	499	13.55
2,443	22.65	8,273	76.72	Starr	33,110	32.57	3,217	31.29	6,968	67.78
2,631	88.65	324	10.92	Stephens	5,573	53.26	2,653	89.39	291	9.80
442	90.95	44	9.05	Sterling	880	55.45	445	91.19	39	7.99
497	80.94	112	18.24	Stonewall	957	64.16	503	82.46	96	15.74
934	77.45	265	21.97	Sutton	2,478	48.67	939	78.32	248	20.68
1,461	77.10	420	22.16	Swisher	3,968	47.70	1,491	79.10	368	19.52
309,189	49.24	313,497	49.93	Tarrant	1,122,597	55.93	340,404	54.39	273,814	43.75
29,811	73.32	10,489	25.80	Taylor	80,168	50.77	31,152	76.53	8,880	21.82
323	69.16	139	29.76	Terrell	694	67.29	316	69.45	136	29.87
2,169	77.11	629	22.36	Terry	6,633	42.41	2,221	79.26	552	19.70
617	87.77	77	10.95	Throckmorton	1,219	57.67	625	89.67	63	9.04
5,685	71.02	2,265	28.29	Titus	17,020	47.03	5,861	73.48	2,017	25.29
24,648	71.18	9,690	27.98	Tom Green	66,826	51.86	25,792	74.43	8,373	24.16
119,278	24.63	359,772	74.30	Travis	775,950	62.40	145,910	30.41	320,550	66.81
4,146	80.12	998	19.29	Trinity	11,455	45.18	4,293	83.05	835	16.15
5,919	82.91	1,185	16.60	Tyler	13,725	52.01	6,079	85.39	973	13.67
11,529	82.44	2,364	16.91	Upshur	27,708	50.56	11,638	83.08	2,177	15.54
854	82.83	169	16.39	Upton	2,116	48.72	860	84.65	148	14.57
4,348	54.80	3,528	44.46	Uvalde	17,118	46.35	4,755	60.15	3,070	38.84
5,345	46.87	5,955	52.21	Val Verde	27,972	40.77	5,993	52.73	5,241	46.12
15,182	84.66	2,634	14.69	Van Zandt	36,982	48.53	15,609	86.96	2,150	11.98
19,005	69.85	8,046	29.57	Victoria	55,473	49.05	19,599	72.20	7,245	26.69
11,535	64.61	6,186	34.65	Walker	33,422	53.42	12,199	68.55	5,331	29.96
10,167	61.24	6,335	38.16	Waller	32,584	50.95	10,639	64.09	5,791	34.89
2,096	71.78	800	27.40	Ward	6,522	44.86	2,201	75.22	690	23.58
10,134	75.11	3,263	24.18	Washington	23,253	58.02	10,532	78.19	2,730	20.27
13,814	27.97	35,159	71.20	Webb	130,784	37.76	16,287	33.30	32,055	65.54
9,094	70.27	3,793	29.31	Wharton	25,132	51.50	9,472	73.36	3,332	25.81
1,679	92.76	125	6.91	Wheeler	3,415	53.32	1,682	92.37	126	6.92
23,648	69.72	9,971	29.40	Wichita	81,419	41.66	24,817	73.16	8,614	25.40
2,639	76.74	776	22.56	Wilbarger	8,134	42.50	2,722	78.74	685	19.81
1,527	35.31	2,773	64.12	Willacy	12,405	34.86	1,931	45.69	2,257	53.41
99,857	47.96	105,850	50.84	Williamson	331,985	62.72	112,214	54.08	90,002	43.37
13,025	73.51	4,567	25.77	Wilson	32,537	54.46	13,704	77.41	3,800	21.47
1,123	77.18	321	22.06	Winkler	3,870	37.60	1,150	79.15	284	19.55
19,023	82.29	3,915	16.94	Wise	41,749	55.38	19,633	84.92	3,184	13.77
13,987	83.55	2,635	15.74	Wood	30,065	56.15	14,406	85.34	2,324	13.77
1,558	81.87	335	17.60	Yoakum	4,264	44.63	1,558	82.30	303	16.01
5,543	86.54	821	12.82	Young	11,854	54.03	5,579	87.28	726	11.36
821	36.93	1,392	62.62	Zapata	7,587	29.30	861	39.71	1,292	59.59
589	20.19	2,313	79.29	Zavala	8,157	35.76	748	26.25	2,082	73.05

General Election, 2018

Below are the voting results for the general election held November 6, 2018, for all statewide races and for contested congressional, state senate, courts of appeals, and state board of education races. These are official returns as canvassed by the State Canvassing Board. Abbreviations used are (Dem.) Democrat, (Rep.) Republican, (Lib.) Libertarian, (Ind.) Independent, and (W-I) Write-in.

U.S. Senator
Ted Cruz (Rep.)	4,260,553	50.89%
Beto O'Rourke (Dem.)	4,045,632	48.33%
Neal Dikeman (Lib.)	65,470	0.78%
Total Vote	8,371,655	

Governor
Greg Abbott (Rep.)	4,656,196	55.81%
Lupe Valdez (Dem.)	3,546,615	42.51%
Mark Jay Tippetts (Lib.)	140,632	1.69%
Total vote	8,343,443	

Lieutenant Governor
Dan Patrick (Rep.)	4,260,990	51.30%
Mike Collier (Dem.)	3,860,865	46.49%
Kerry Douglas McKennon (Lib.)	183,516	2.21%
Total vote	8,305,371	

Attorney General
Ken Paxton (Rep.)	4,193,207	50.57%
Justin Nelson (Dem.)	3,898,098	47.01%
Michael Ray Harris (Lib.)	201,310	2.43%
Total vote	8,292,615	

Comptroller of Public Accouts
Glenn Hegar (Rep.)	4,376,828	53.19%
Joi Chevalier (Dem.)	3,570,693	43.39%
Ben Sanders (Lib.)	281,081	3.42%
Total vote	8,228,602	

Commissioner of General Land Office
George P. Bush (Rep.)	4,435,202	53.68%
Miguel Suazo (Dem.)	3,567,927	43.19%
Matt Pina (Lib.)	258,482	3.13%
Total vote	8,261,611	

Commissioner of Agriculture
Sid Miller (Rep.)	4,221,527	51.26%
Kim Olson (Dem.)	3,822,137	46.41%
Richard Carpenter (Lib.)	191,639	2.33%
Total vote	8,235,303	

Railroad Commissioner
Christi Craddick (Rep.)	4,376,729	53.20%
Roman McAllen (Dem.)	3,612,130	43.91%
Mike Wright (Lib.)	237.984	2.89%
Total vote	8,226,843	

U.S. HOUSE OF REPRESENTATIVES
(See map of districts on p. 409.)

District 1
Louie Gohmert (Rep.)	168,165	72.26%
Shirley J. McKellar (Dem.)	61,263	26.32%
Jeff Callaway (Lib.)	3,292	1.41%
Total Vote	232,720	

District 2
Daniel Crenshaw (Rep.)	139,188	52.84%
Todd Litton (Dem.)	119,992	45.56%
Patrick Gunnels (Lib.)	2,373	0.90%
Scott Cubbler (Ind.)	1,839	0.70%
Total Vote	263,392	

District 3
Van Taylor (Rep.)	169,520	54.24%
Lorie Burch (Dem.)	138,234	44.23%
Christopher J. Claytor (Lib.)	4,604	1.47%
Jeff Simmons (W-I)	153	0.05%
Total Vote	312,511	

District 4
John Ratcliffe (Rep.)	188,667	75.70%
Catherine Krantz (Dem.)	57,400	23.03%
Ken Ashby (Lib.)	3,178	1.28%
Total Vote	249,245	

District 5
Lance Gooden (Rep.)	130,617	62.34%
Dan Wood (Dem.)	78,666	37.55%
Phil Gray (W-I)	224	0.11%
Total Vote	209,507	

District 6
Ron Wright (Rep.)	135,961	53.10%
Jana Lynne Sanchez (Dem.)	116,350	45.44%
Jason Allen Harber (Lib.)	3,731	1.46%
Total Vote	256,042	

District 7
Lizzie Pannill Fletcher (Dem.)	127,959	52.53%
John Culberson (Rep.)	115,642	47.47%
Total Vote	243,601	

District 8
Kevin Brady (Rep.)	200,619	73.44%
Steven David (Dem.)	67,930	24.87%
Chris Duncan (Lib.)	4,621	1.69%
Total Vote	273,170	

District 9
Al Green (Dem.)	136,256	89.06%
Phil Kurtz (Lib.)	5,940	3.88%
Benjamin Hernandez (Ind.)	5,774	3.77%
Kesha Rogers (Ind.)	5,031	3.29%
Total Vote	153,001	

District 10
Michael T. McCaul (Rep.)	157,166	51.06%
Mike Siegel (Dem.)	144,034	46.79%
Mike Ryan (Lib.)	6,627	2.15%
Total Vote	307,827	

District 11
Mike Conaway (Rep.)	176,603	80.14%
Jennie Lou Leeder (Dem.)	40,631	18.44%
Rhett Rosenquest Smith (Lib.)	3,143	1.43%
Total Vote	220,377	

District 12
Kay Granger (Rep.)	172,557	64.27%
Vanessa Adia (Dem.)	90,994	33.89%
Jacob Leddy (Lib.)	4,940	1.84%
Total Vote	268,491	

District 13
Mac Thornberry (Rep.)	169,027	81.54%
Greg Sagan (Dem.)	35,083	16.93%
Calvin DeWesse (Lib.)	3,175	1.53%
Total Vote	207,285	

District 14
Randy Weber (Rep.)	138,942	59.24%
Adrienne Bell (Dem.)	92,212	39.32%
Don E. Conley III (Lib.)	3,374	1.44%
Total Vote	234,528	

District 15
Vicente Gonzalez (Dem.)	98,333	59.67%
Tim Westley (Rep.)	63,862	38.75%
Anthony Cristo (Lib.)	2,607	1.58%
Total Vote	164,802	

District 16
Veronica Escobar (Dem.) .... 124,437 ...... 68.46%
Rick Seeberger (Rep.) .... 49,127 ...... 27.03%
Ben Mendoza (Ind.) .... 8,147 .... 4.48%
Samuel Williams (W-I) .... 43 .... 0.02%
    Total Vote 181,754

District 17
Bill Flores (Rep.) .... 134,841 ...... 56.81%
Rick Kennedy (Dem.) .... 98,070 ...... 41.32%
Peter Churchman (Lib.) .... 4,440 .... 1.87%
    Total Vote 237,351

District 18
Sheila Jackson Lee (Dem.) .... 138,704 ...... 75.25%
Ava Reynero Pate (Rep.) .... 38,368 ...... 20.81%
Luke Spencer (Lib.) .... 4,067 .... 2.21%
Vince Duncan (Ind.) .... 3,193 .... 1.73%
    Total Vote 184,332

District 19
Jodey Arrington (Rep.) .... 151,946 ...... 75.23%
Miguel Levario (Dem.) .... 50,039 ...... 24.77%
    Total Vote 201,985

District 20
Joaquin Castro (Dem.) .... 139,038 ...... 80.85%
Jeffrey Blunt (Lib.) .... 32,925 ...... 19.15%
    Total Vote 171,963

District 21
Chip Roy (Rep.) .... 177,654 ...... 50.24%
Joseph Kopser (Dem.) .... 168,421 ...... 47.63%
Lee Santos (Lib.) .... 7,542 .... 2.13%
    Total Vote 353,617

District 22
Pete Olson (Rep.) .... 152,750 ...... 51.36%
Sri Preston Kulkarni (Dem.) .... 138,153 ...... 46.45%
John B. McElligott (Lib.) .... 3,261 .... 1.10%
Kellen Sweny (Ind.) .... 3,241 .... 1.09%
    Total Vote 297,405

District 23
Will Hurd (Rep.) .... 103,285 ...... 49.17%
Gina Ortiz Jones (Dem.) .... 102,359 ...... 48.73%
Ruben Corvalan (Lib.) .... 4,425 .... 2.11%
    Total Vote 210,069

District 24
Kenny E. Marchant (Rep.) .... 133,317 ...... 50.61%
Jan McDowell (Dem.) .... 125,231 ...... 47.54%
Mike Kolls (Lib.) .... 4,870 .... 1.85%
    Total Vote 263,418

District 25
Roger Williams (Rep.) .... 163,023 ...... 53.53%
Julie Oliver (Dem.) .... 136,385 ...... 44.78%
Desarae Lindsey (Lib.) .... 5,145 .... 1.69%
    Total Vote 304,553

District 26
Michael Burgess (Rep.) .... 185,551 ...... 59.38%
Linsey Fagan (Dem.) .... 121,938 ...... 39.02%
Mark Boler (Lib.) .... 5,016 .... 1.61%
    Total Vote 312,505

District 27
Michael Cloud (Rep.) .... 125,118 ...... 60.32%
Eric Holguin (Dem.) .... 75,929 ...... 36.61%
Daniel Tinus (Lib.) .... 2,100 .... 1.01%
James Duerr (Ind.) .... 4,274 .... 2.06%
    Total Vote 207,421

District 28
Henry Cuellar (Dem.) .... 117,494 ...... 84.39%
Arthur Thomas IV (Lib.) .... 21,732 ...... 15.61%
    Total Vote 139,226

District 29
Sylvia Garcia (Dem.) .... 88,188 ...... 75.06%
Phillip Aronoff (Rep.) .... 28,098 ...... 23.91%
Cullen Burns (Lib.) .... 1,199 .... 1.02%
Johnathan Garza (W-I) .... 9 .... 0.01%
    Total Vote 117,494

District 30
Eddie Bernice Johnson (Dem.) .... 166,784 ...... 91.05%
Shawn Jones (Lib.) .... 16,390 .... 8.95%
    Total Vote 183,174

District 31
John Carter (Rep.) .... 144,680 ...... 50.59%
Mary Jennings "MJ" Hegar (Dem.) ...... 136,362 ...... 47.68%
Jason Hope (Lib.) .... 4,965 .... 1.74%
    Total Vote 286,007

District 32
Colin Allred (Dem.) .... 144,067 ...... 52.27%
Pete Sessions (Rep.) .... 126,101 ...... 45.75%
Melina Baker (Lib.) .... 5,452 .... 1.98%
    Total Vote 275,620

District 33
Marc Veasey (Dem.) .... 90,805 ...... 76.16%
Willie Billups (Rep.) .... 26,120 ...... 21.91%
Jason Reeves (Lib.) .... 2,299 .... 1.93%
    Total Vote 119,224

District 34
Filemon B. Vela (Dem.) .... 85,825 ...... 59.99%
Rey Gonzalez (Rep.) .... 57,243 ...... 40.01%
    Total Vote 143,068

District 35
Lloyd Doggett (Dem.) .... 138,278 ...... 71.25%
David Smalling (Rep.) .... 50,553 ...... 26.05%
Clark Patterson (Lib.) .... 5,236 .... 2.70%
    Total Vote 194,067

District 36
Brian Babin (Rep.) .... 161,048 ...... 72.56%
Dayna Steele (Dem.) .... 60,908 ...... 27.44%
    Total Vote 221,956

OTHER STATE RACES

Justice, Supreme Court, Place 2
Jimmy Blacklock (Rep.) .... 4,358,756 ...... 53.17%
Steven Kirkland (Dem.) .... 3,838,411 ...... 46.83%
    Total Vote 8,197,167

Justice, Supreme Court, Place 4
John Devine (Rep.) .... 4,399,890 ...... 53.71%
R.K. Sandill (Dem.) .... 3,792,144 ...... 46.29%
    Total Vote 8,192,034

Justice, Supreme Court, Place 6
Jeff Brown (Rep.) .... 4,404,602 ...... 53.71%
Kathy Cheng (Dem.) .... 3,796,001 ...... 46.29%
    Total Vote 8,200,603

Presiding Judge, Court of Criminal Appeals
Sharon Keller (Rep.) .... 4,288,913 ...... 52.24%
Maria T. "Terri" Jackson (Dem.) .... 3,734,179 ...... 45.48%
William Bryan Strange III (Lib.) .... 187,384 .... 2.28%
    Total Vote 8,210,476

Judge, Court of Criminal Appeals, Place 7
Barbara Parker Hervey (Rep.) .... 4,429,113 ...... 54.15%
Ramona Franklin (Dem.) .... 3,750,114 ...... 45.85%
    Total Vote 8,179,227

Judge, Court of Criminal Appeals, Place 8
Michelle Slaughter (Rep.) .... 4,760,576 ...... 74.68%
Mark Ash (Lib.) .... 1,614,119 ...... 25.32%
    Total Vote 6,374,695

STATE BOARD OF EDUCATION

District 2
Ruben Cortez Jr. (Dem.)......................206,689 ...... 53.60%
Charles "Tad" Hasse (Rep.)................ 178,928 .... 46.40%
Total Vote 385,612

District 7
Matt Robinson (Rep.) .... 369,752 ...... 59.45%
Elizabeth "Eliz" Markowitz (Dem.) ...... 252,158 .... 40.55%
Total Vote 621,910

District 11
Patricia "Pat" Hardy (Rep.) .... 366,245 ...... 57.16%
Carla Morton (Dem.).......................... 259,276 ...... 40.46%
Aaron Gutknecht (Lib.) .... 15,241 .... 2.38%
Total Vote 640,762

District 12
Pam Little (Rep.).............................. 334,584 ...... 49.43%
Suzanne Smith (Dem.) .... 324,307 .... 47.91%
Rachel Wester (Lib.).......................... 18,002 .... 2.66%
Total Vote 676,893

District 13
Aicha Davis (Dem.)........................... 309,926 ...... 76.32%
A. Denise Russell (Rep.) .... 96,136 .... 23.68%
Total Vote 406,062

STATE SENATE

District 2
Bob Hall (Rep.) .... 153,151 .... 59.35%
Kendall Scudder (Dem.) .... 104,897 .... 40.65%
Total Vote 258,048

District 3
Robert Nichols (Rep.) .... 215,058 .... 78.27%
Shirley Layton (Dem.) .... 56,398 .... 20.53%
Bruce Quarles (Lib.) .... 3,301 .... 1.20%
Total Vote 274,757

District 5
Charles Schwertner (Rep.) .... 182,550 .... 55.34%
Meg Walsh (Dem.)............................. 136,792 ...... 41.47%
Amy Lyons (Lib.) .... 10,500 .... 3.18%
Total Vote 329,842

District 7
Paul Bettencourt (Rep.) .... 177,864 .... 57.75%
David Romero (Dem.).......................... 124,232 ...... 40.34%
Tom Glass (Lib.) .... 5,878 .... 1.91%
Total Vote 307,974

District 8
Angela Paxton (Rep.) .... 169,995 .... 51.18%
Mark Pharriss (Dem.).......................... 162,157 ...... 48.82%
Total Vote 332,152

District 9
Kelly Hancock (Rep..) .... 132,256 .... 54.03%
Gween Burud (Dem.)........................... 112,537 .... 45.97%
Total Vote 244,793

District 10
Beverly Powell (Dem..) .... 148,959 .... 51.73%
Konni Burton (Rep.) .... 138,968 ...... 48.27%
Total Vote 287,927

District 14
Kirk Watson (Dem.) .... 276,052 ...... 71.93%
George W. Hindman (Rep.) .... 96,834 .... 25.23%
Micah M. Verlander (Lib.) .... 10,889 .... 2.84%
Total Vote 383,775

District 15
John Whitmire (Dem.)......................... 153,016 .... 65.18%
Randy Orr (Rep.)................................ 75,518 .... 32.17%
Gilberto "Gil" Velasquez Jr. (Lib.)............ 6,229 .... 2.65%
Total Vote 234,763

District 16
Nathan Johnson (Dem.) .... 159,228 .... 54.13%
Don Huffines (Rep.)........................... 134,933 .... 45.87%
Total Vote 294,161

District 17
Joan Huffman (Rep.) .... 158,263 .... 51.44%
Rita Lucido (Dem.)............................ 143,978 .... 46.80%
Lauren LaCount (Lib.)........................... 5,396 .... 1.75%
Total Vote 307,637

District 25
Donna Campbell (Rep.) .... 263,753 .... 57.68%
Steven Kling (Dem.) .... 173,698 ...... 42.32%
Total Vote 410,451

District 30
Pat Fallon (Rep.) .... 234,374 .... 73.92%
Kevin Lopez (Dem.)........................... 82,669 ...... 26.08%
Total Vote 317,043

District 31
Kel Seliger (Rep.) .... 174,367 ...... 87.52%
Jack B. Westbrook (Lib.) .... 24,869 ...... 12.48%
Total Vote 199,236

COURTS OF APPEALS

FIRST DISTRICT
Justice, Place 2
Gordon Goodman (Dem.)....................881,091 ...... 50.93%
Jane Bland (Rep.).............................. 849,077 ...... 49.07%
Total Vote 1,730,168

Justice, Place 6
Sarah Beth Landau (Dem.)..................895,562 ...... 51.78%
Harvey Brown (Rep.) .... 834,062 ...... 48.22%
Total Vote 1,729,624

Justice, Place 7
Julie Countiss (Dem.) .... 906,180 ...... 52.40%
Terry Yates (Rep.) .... 823,106 ...... 47.60%
Total Vote 1,729,286

Justice, Place 8
Richard Hightower (Dem.)..................909,756 ...... 52.63%
Michael Massengale (Rep.).................818,931 ...... 47.37%
Total Vote 1,728,687

Justice, Place 9
Peter Kelly (Dem.) .... 894,209 ...... 51.76%
Jennifer Caughey (Rep.) .... 833,319 .... 48.24%
Total Vote 1,727,528

SECOND DISTRICT
Justice, Place 5
Dabney Bassel (Rep.) ....622,466 ...... 58.33%
Delonia A. Watson (Dem.) ....444,612 ...... 41.67%
Total Vote 1,067,078

THIRD DISTRICT
Justice, Place 2
Edward Smith (Dem.) ....552,167 ...... 53.02%
Cindy Olson Bourland (Rep.)...............489,191 ...... 46.98%
Total Vote 1,041,358

Justice, Place 3
Chari Kelly (Dem.) ....566,246 ...... 54.38%
Scott Field (Rep.).............................. 475,074 ...... 45.62%
Total Vote 1,041,320

Justice, Place 5
Thomas J. Baker (Dem.) ....560,790 ...... 53.91%
David Puryear (Rep.).......................... 479,517 ...... 46.09%
Total Vote 1,040,307

Justice, Place 6
Gisela Triana (Dem.) ....566,064 ...... 54.40%
Michael Toth (Rep.) ....472,806 ...... 45.44%
Kerry O'Brien (W-I) ....1,694 .... 0.16%
Total Vote 1,040,564

FOURTH DISTRICT
Justice, Place 2

Beth Watkins (Dem.) ....429,521 ...... 52.00%
Marialyn Barnard (Rep.) ....396,458 ...... 48.00%
    Total Vote 825,979

Justice, Place 3

Patricia O'Connell Alvarez (Dem.).......438,709 ...... 53.07%
Jason Pulliam (Rep.) ....388,009 ...... 46.93%
    Total Vote 826,718

Justice, Place 4

Luz Elena Chapa (Dem.) ....445,672 ...... 53.89%
Patrick Ballantyne (Rep.)....................381,319 ...... 46.11%
    Total Vote 826,991

Justice, Place 5

Liza Rodriguez (Dem.).........................433,796 ...... 52.45%
Rebecca Simmons (Rep.) ....393,321 ...... 47.55%
    Total Vote 827,117

Justice, Place 7

Rebeca Martinez (Dem.) ....446,260 ...... 53.95%
Shane Stolarczyk (Rep.) ....380,905 ...... 46.05%
    Total Vote 827,165

FIFTH DISTRICT
Chief Justice

Robert Burns (Dem.) ....631,219 ...... 52.83%
Douglas S. Lang (Rep.) ....563,589 ......47.17%
    Total Vote 1,194,808

Justice, Place 2

Robbie Partida-Kipness (Dem.)...........622,131 ...... 52.13%
David Evans (Rep.) ....571,269 ...... 47.87%
    Total Vote 1,193,400

Justice, Place 5

Erin Nowell (Dem.) ....632,443 ...... 52.99%
Craig Stoddart (Rep.) ....561,120 ...... 47.01%
    Total Vote 1,193,563

Justice, Place 9

Bill Pedersen (Dem.) ....629,684 ...... 52.80%
Jason Boatright (Rep.).........................562,999 ...... 47.20%
    Total Vote 1,192,683

Justice, Place 10

Amanda Reichek (Dem.) ....627,548 ...... 52.63%
Molly Francis (Rep.) ....564,776 ...... 47.37%
    Total Vote 1,192,324

Justice, Place 11

Cory Carlyle (Dem.).............................627,198 ...... 52.66%
John Browning (Rep.)..........................563,864 ...... 47.34%
    Total Vote 1,191,062

Justice, Place 12

Ken Molberg (Dem.) ....637,698 ...... 53.51%
Jim Pikl (Rep.) ....554,098 ......46.49%
    Total Vote 1,191,796

Justice, Place 13

Leslie Lester Osborne (Dem.) ....625,147 ...... 52.45%
Elizabeth Lang Miers (Rep.)...............566,673 ......47.55%
    Total Vote 1,191,820

THIRTEENTH DISTRICT
Chief Justice

Dori Contreras (Dem.) ....241,673 ...... 53.56%
Ernie Aliseda (Rep.)............................209,556 ......46.44%
    Total Vote 451,229

Justice, Place 2

Nora Longoria (Dem.)..........................242,267 ...... 53.56%
Greg Perkes (Rep.) ....210,029 ......46.44%
    Total Vote 452,296

Justice, Place 4

Rudy Delgado (Dem.)..........................226,042 ...... 50.36%
Jaime Tijerina (Rep.) ....222,794 ....49.64%
    Total Vote 448,836

Justice, Place 5

Gina Benavides (Dem.) ....238,682 ...... 53.04%
Clarissa Silva (Rep.)............................211,308 ....46.96%
    Total Vote 449,990

FOURTEENTH DISTRICT
Justice, Place 3

Jerry Zimmerer (Dem.) ....884,260 ...... 51.21%
Brett Busby (Rep.)...............................842,634 ...... 48.79%
    Total Vote 1,726,894

Justice, Place 4

Charles Spain (Dem.) ....882,099 ...... 51.10%
Marc Brown (Rep.) ....844,280 ...... 48.90%
    Total Vote 1,726,379

Justice, Place 5

Frances Bourliot (Dem.) ....879,966 ...... 50.97%
Martha Hill Jamison (Rep.)..................846,487 ...... 49.03%
    Total Vote 1,726,453

Justice, Place 6

Meagan Hassan (Dem.) ....892,635 ...... 51.70%
Bill Boyce (Rep.)..................................833,950 ...... 48.30%
    Total Vote 1,726,585

Justice, Place 8

Margaret "Meg" Poissant (Dem.).........892,775 ...... 51.72%
John Donovan (Rep.) ....833,445 ...... 48.28%
    Total Vote 1,726,220

Special Elections
State Senate
District 19
Runoff held Sept. 18, 2018

Peter P. "Pete" Flores (Rep.) ....25,330 ...... 56.67%
Pete Gallego (Dem.)..............................19,367 ...... 43.33%
    Total Vote 44,697

District 19
Held July 31, 2018

Peter P. "Pete" Flores (Rep.) ....9,003 ...... 34.35%
Pete Gallego (Dem.)................................7,580 ...... 28.92%
Roland Gutierrez (Dem.) ....6,389 ...... 24.38%
Charlie Urbina Jones (Dem.) ....789 ...... 3.01%
Thomas Uresti (Dem.) ....799 ...... 3.05%
Carlos Antonio Raymond (Rep.)..................920 ...... 3.51%
Jesse "Jay" Alaniz (Rep.) ....461 ...... 1.76%
Tony Valdivia (Lib.) ....266 ...... 1.01%
    Total Vote 26,207

U.S. House of Representatives
District 27
Held June 30, 2018

Michael Cloud (Rep.)..............................19,872 ...... 54.76%
Eric Holguin (Dem.) ....11,599 ...... 31.96%
Raul "Roy" Barrera (Dem.) ....1,748 ...... 4.82%
Bech Bruun (Rep.).....................................1,571 ...... 4.33%
Judith Cutright (Ind.) ....172 ...... 0.47%
Marty Perez (Rep.) ....276 ...... 0.76%
Christopher Suprun (Ind.)..............................51 ...... 0.14%
Daniel Tinus (Lib.)..144 .... 0.44%
Michael Westergren (Dem.)..........................858 .... 2.36%
    Total Vote 36,291

Republican Primary Election, 2018

Following are the official results for the contested races in the Republican Party primary held March 6, 2018. Included are statewide races and selected district races. Runoffs were held on May 22, 2018.

U.S. Senator
Ted Cruz .... 1,322,724 .... 85.36%
Mary Miller .... 94,715 .... 6.11%
Bruce Jacobson Jr. .... 64,791 .... 4.18%
Stefano de Stefano .... 44,456 .... 2.87%
Geraldine Sam .... 22,887 .... 1.48%
    Total Vote 1,549,573

Governor
Greg Abbott .... 1,400,647 .... 90.42%
Barbara Kilgore .... 127,858 .... 8.25%
Secede Kilgore .... 20,501 .... 1.32%
    Total Vote 1,549,006

Lieutenant Governor
Dan Patrick .... 1,172,830 .... 76.07%
Scott Milder .... 368,995 .... 23.93%
    Total Vote 1,541,825

Commissioner of the General Land Office
George P. Bush .... 862,512 ...... 58.22%
Jerry Patterson .... 439,602 ...... 29.67%
Davey Edwards .... 101,359 .... 6.84%
Rick Range .... 78,124 .... 5.27%
    Total Vote 1,481,597

Agriculture Commissioner
Sid Miller .... 755,498 ...... 55.65%
Jim Hogan .... 310,431 ...... 22.87%
Trey Blocker .... 291,583 ...... 21.48%
    Total Vote 1,357,512

Railroad Commissioner
Christi Craddick .... 1,042,633 ...... 75.83%
Weston Martinez .... 332,374 .... 24.17%
    Total Vote 1,375,007

U.S. HOUSE OF REPRESENTATIVES
District 1
Louie Gohmert .... 64,241 .... 88.33%
Anthony Culler .... 6,526 .... 8.97%
Roshin Rowjee .... 1,962 .... 2.70%
    Total Vote 72,729

District 2
Kevin Roberts .... 15,273 .... 33.03%
Dan Crenshaw .... 12,679 .... 27.42%
Kathleen Wall .... 12,524 .... 27.08%
David Balat .... 348 .... 0.75%
Jonny Havens .... 936 .... 2.02%
Justin L. Lurie .... 425 .... 0.92%
Jon Spiers .... 418 .... 0.90%
Rick Walker .... 3,320 .... 7.18%
Malcolm Whittaker .... 322 .... 0.70%
    Total Vote 46,245

District 3
Van Taylor .... 45,650 .... 84.68%
David Niederkorn .... 5,065 .... 9.39%
Alex Donkervoet .... 3,197 .... 5.93%
    Total Vote 53,912

District 4
John Ratcliffe .... 63,275 .... 85.50%
John Cooper .... 10,735 .... 14.50%
    Total Vote 74,010

District 5
Lance Gooden .... 17,551 .... 29.97%
Bunni Pounds .... 12,851 .... 21.95%
Sam Deen .... 10,051 .... 17.16%
Danny Campbell .... 1,770 .... 3.02%
Charles Lingerfelt .... 1,022 .... 1.75%

Kenneth Sheets .... 7,024 .... 11.99%
David Williams .... 1,601 .... 2.73%
Jason Wright .... 6,690 .... 11.42%
    Total Vote 58,560

District 6
Ron Wright .... 20,750 .... 45.15%
J.K. "Jake" Ellzey .... 9,999 .... 21.76%
Ken Cope .... 3,540 .... 7.70%
Shawn Dandridge .... 518 .... 1.13%
Thomas Dillingham .... 544 .... 1.18%
Shannon Dubberly .... 2,884 .... 6.28%
Deborah Gagliardi .... 1,676 .... 3.65%
Kevin Harrison .... 1,771 .... 3.85%
Mel Hassell .... 268 .... 0.58%
Mark Mitchell .... 2,152 .... 4.68%
Troy Ratterree .... 1,858 .... 4.04%
    Total Vote 45,960

District 7
John Culberson .... 29,052 .... 76.11%
Edward Ziegler .... 9,117 .... 23.89%
    Total Vote 38,169

District 10
Michael T. McCaul .... 42,088 .... 80.10%
John W. Cook .... 10,458 .... 19.90%
    Total Vote 52,546

District 11
Mike Conaway .... 63,526 .... 82.96%
Paul Myers .... 13,049 .... 17.04%
    Total Vote 76,575

District 14
Randy Weber .... 33,720 .... 75.29%
Bill "Sarge" Sargent .... 8,770 .... 19.58%
Keith Casey .... 2,298 .... 5.13%
    Total Vote 44,788

District 16
Rick Seeberger .... 7,278 .... 69.35%
Alia Garcia-Ureste .... 3,238 .... 30.65%
    Total Vote 10,566

District 21
Chip Roy .... 19,428 .... 27.06%
Matt McCall .... 12,152 .... 16.93%
William Negley .... 11,163 .... 15.55%
Jason Isaac .... 7,208 .... 10.04%
Ivan A. Andarza .... 96 .... 0.13%
Eric Burkhart .... 723 .... 1.01%
Francsico "Quico" Canseco .... 2,489 .... 3.47%
Mauro Garza .... 663 .... 0.92%
Foster Hagen .... 394 .... 0.55%
Ryan Krause .... 2,300 .... 3.20%
Susan Narvaiz .... 2,720 .... 3.79%
Al M. Poteet .... 1,300 .... 1.81%
Autry J. Pruitt .... 455 .... 0.63%
Jenifer Sarver .... 4,027 .... 5.61%
Robert Stovall .... 3,414 .... 4.76%
Samuel Temple .... 1,020 .... 1.42%
Peggy Wardlaw .... 1,285 .... 1.79%
Anthonyt J. White .... 952 .... 1.33%
    Total Vote 71,789

District 22
Pete Olson .... 35,918 .... 78.41%
Danny Nguyen .... 6,181 .... 13.49%
James Green .... 2,531 .... 5.53%
Eric Zmrhal .... 1,177 .... 2.57%
    Total Vote 45,807

District 23
Will Hurd .... 25,001 .... 80.27%
Alma Arredondo-Lynch .... 6,144 .... 19.73%
    Total Vote 31,145

District 24
Kenny E. Marchant .... 30,310 .... 74.41%
Johnathan Kyle Davidson .... 10,425 .... 25.59%
    Total Vote 40,735

District 26
Michael Burgess .... 42,556 .... 76.99%
Veronica Birkenstock .... 12,720 .... 23.01%
    Total Vote 55,276

District 27
Bech Bruun .... 15,919 .... 36.09%
Michael Cloud .... 14,920 .... 33.83%
Christopher K. Mapp .... 5,356 .... 12.14%
Eddie Gassman .... 1,237 .... 2.80%
John Grunwald .... 3,027 .... 6.86%
Jerry Hall .... 3,649 .... 8.27%
    Total Vote 44,108

District 29
Phillip Aronoff .... 2,406 .... 38.60%
Carmen Maria Montiel .... 1,470 .... 23.58%
Jaimy Z. Blanco .... 1,314 .... 21.08%
Robert Schafranek .... 1,043 .... 16.73%
    Total Vote 6,233

District 31
John Carter .... 34,623 .... 65.50%
Mike Sweeney .... 18,236 .... 34.50%
    Total Vote 52,859

District 32
Pete Sessions .... 32,929 .... 79.29%
Paul Brown .... 8,599 .... 20.71%
    Total Vote 41,528

District 35
David Smalling .... 7,148 .... 53.30%
Sherrill Kenneth "SK" Alexander .... 6,264 .... 46.70%
    Total Vote 13,412

STATE COURTS
Presiding Judge, Court of Criminal Appeals
Sharon Keller .... 674,889 .... 52.16%
David Bridges .... 618,982 .... 47.84%
    Total Vote 1,293,871

Judge, Court of Criminal Appeals, Place 8
Michelle Slaughter .... 669,949 .... 52.84%
Jay Brandon .... 389,753 .... 30.74%
Dib Waldrip .... 208,179 .... 16.42%
    Total Vote 1,267,881

STATE SENATE
District 2
Bob Hall .... 35,530 .... 53.23%
Cindy Burkett .... 31,216 .... 46.77%
    Total Vote 66,746

District 5
Charles Schwertner .... 50,254 .... 75.12%
Harold Ramm .... 16,648 .... 24.88%
    Total Vote 66,902

District 8
Angela Paxton .... 32,756 .... 54.32%
Phillip Huffines .... 27,545 .... 45.68%
    Total Vote 60,301

District 17
Joan Huffman .... 36,830 .... 72.67%
Kristin Tassin .... 13,849 .... 27.33%
    Total Vote 50,679

District 25
Donna Campbell .... 59,143 .... 73.75%
Shannon K. McClendon .... 21,055 .... 26.25%
    Total Vote 80,198

District 30
Pat Fallon .... 53,881 .... 62.01%
Craig Estes .... 19,641 .... 22.60%
Craig Carter .... 13,371 .... 15.39%
    Total Vote 86,893

District 31
Kel Seliger .... 40,664 .... 50.41%
Mike Canon .... 25,335 .... 31.41%
Victor Leal .... 14,671 .... 18.19%
    Total Vote 80,670

STATE BOARD OF EDUCATION
District 2
Charles "Tad" Hasse .... 31,768 .... 67.13%
Eric Garza .... 15,558 .... 32.87%
    Total Vote 47,326

District 11
Patricia "Pat" Hardy .... 58,998 .... 55.78%
Feyi Obamehinti .... 25,656 .... 24.26%
Cheryl Surber .... 21,116 .... 19.96%
    Total Vote 105,770

PROPOSITIONS
Prop. 1 – Replace property tax with consumption tax
In Favor .... 958,379 .... 65.59%
Against .... 502,748 .... 32.41%
    Total Vote 1,461,127

Prop. 2 – Require voter approval for toll roads
In Favor .... 1,377,530 .... 89.91%
Against .... 154,599 .... 10.09%
    Total Vote 1,532,129

Prop. 3 – Elect House speaker by party caucus
In Favor .... 1,282,385 .... 85.11%
Against .... 224,432 .... 14.89%
    Total Vote 1,506,817

Prop. 4 – Screen hiring for legal status
In Favor .... 1,377,946 .... 90.28%
Against .... 148,426 .... 9.72%
    Total Vote 1,526,372

Prop. 5 – Tax credits/exemptions for school choice
In Favor .... 1,206,597 .... 78.67%
Against .... 327,159 .... 21.33%
    Total Vote 1,533,776

Prop. 6 – Privacy protection for bathrooms
In Favor .... 1,391,732 .... 90.25%
Against .... 150,331 .... 9.75%
    Total Vote 1,542,063

Prop. 7 – Abolish abortion
In Favor .... 1,030,986 .... 68.19%
Against .... 481,002 .... 31.81%
    Total Vote 1,511,988

Prop. 8 – Make voter fraud a felony
In Favor .... 1,465,652 .... 94.82%
Against .... 80,073 .... 5.18%
    Total Vote 1,545,725

Prop. 9 – Repeal Obamacare
In Favor .... 1,331,855 .... 86.97%
Against .... 199,474 .... 13.03%
    Total Vote 1,531,329

Prop. 10 – Cap property tax increases
In Favor .... 1,423,528 .... 93.89%
Against .... 92,600 .... 6.11%
    Total Vote 1,516,128

Prop. 11 – No tax dollars for pro sports stadiums
In Favor .... 1,330,473 ....86.71%
Against.. 203,967 .... 13.29%
    Total Vote................................. 1,534,440

COURTS OF APPEALS
Justice, First District, Place 7
Terry Yates................................... 120,476 .... 53.92%
Katy Boatman................................. 102,942 .... 46.08%
    Total Vote................................... 223,418

Justice, Third District, Place 6
Michael "Mike" Toth .... 53,382 ....39.15%
Donna Davidson .... 43,325 ....31.78%
Jennifer S. Freel .... 27,564 .... 20.22%
Kristofer Monson .... 12,077 .... 8.86%
    Total Vote................................... 136,348

Justice, Fifth District, Place 11
John Browning................................... 84,175 .... 57.06%
Tom Nowak....................................... 41,976 .... 28.45%
Dan Wyde... 21,368 .... 14.48%
    Total Vote................................... 147,519

Justice, Fifth District, Place 12
Jim Pikl. .... 61,083 .... 41.44%
William "Randy" Johnson..................... 58,216 .... 39.50%
Perry Cockerell.................................. 28,087 .... 19.06%
    Total Vote................................... 147,386

REPUBLICAN RUNOFF
U.S. HOUSE OF REPRESENTATIVES
District 2
Dan Crenshaw.................................... 20,392 .... 69.84%
Kevin Roberts...................................... 8,808 .... 30.16%
    Total Vote..................................... 29,200

District 5
Lance Gooden..................................... 18,364 .... 54.01%
Bunni Pounds..................................... 15,634 .... 45.99%
    Total Vote................................... 33,998

District 6
Ron Wright.. 12,775 .... 52.17%
J.K. "Jake" Ellzey................................11,711 .... 47.83%
    Total Vote................................... 24,486

District 21
Chip Roy.. 18,088 .... 52.69%
Matt McCall.. 16,243 .... 47.31%
    Total Vote................................... 34,331

District 27
Michael Cloud..................................... 15,249 .... 61.02%
Bech Bruun... 9,741 .... 38.98%
    Total Vote................................... 24,990

District 29
Phillip Aronoff...................................... 1,153 .... 51.82%
Carmen Maria Montiel .... 1,072 .... 48.18%
    Total Vote................................... 2,225

COURTS OF APPEALS
Justice, Third District, Place 6
Michael "Mike" Toth .... 28,836 .... 52.83%
Donna Davidson .... 25,743 .... 47.17%
    Total Vote................................... 54,579

Justice, Fifth District, Place 12
Jim Pikl. .... 26,325 .... 57.61%
William "Randy" Johnson..................... 19,374 .... 42.39%
    Total Vote................................... 45,699

Texas Election Turnout by Voting Age Population

Year	2016	2012	2008	2004	2000	1996	1992	1988	1984	1980	1976	1972
Major Candidates	Trump / Clinton	Obama / Romney	Obama / McCain	Bush / Kerry	Bush / Gore	Clinton / Dole	Clinton/Bush/Perot	Bush / Dukakis	Reagan / Mondale	Reagan / Carter	Carter / Ford	Nixon / McGovern
Percent of VAP that voted	46.5	43.7	45.6	46.1	44.3	41.0	47.6	44.3	47.6	45.6	46.1	44.9
Percent of registered voters that voted	59.4	58.6	59.5	56.6	51.8	53.2	72.9	66.2	68.3	68.4	64.8	66.6

The **voting age population (VAP)** refers to the total number of persons of voting age regardless of citizenship, military status, felony conviction, or mental state. The Bureau of the Census is the source for the VAP estimates.

Since the National Voter Registration Act of 1993, nonvoters cannot be removed from registration rolls of a county until two federal elections have been held. So, for instance, if a person moved in December 2012 from one county to another, that person could be counted as a nonvoter in the previous county of residence through the general election of November 2016.

These are called "suspense voters" on county rolls and have affected the statistical reports of the percentage of registered voters participating in elections.

In the early 1970s, various election reforms were enacted by the Legislature, including eliminating the requirement for an annual registration and allowing for a continuing voter registration system.

The presidential elections have a larger voter turnout than off-year and state elections. — RP

Sources: Federal Election Commission and the Texas Secretary of State office.

Democratic Primary Election, 2018

Following are the official results for the contested races in the Democratic Party primary held March 6, 2018. Included are statewide races and selected district races.

U.S. Senator
Beto O'Rourke .... 644,632 .... 61.81%
Sema Hernandez .... 247,424 .... 23.72%
Edward Kimbrough .... 150,858 .... 14.47%
Total Vote 1,042,914

Governor
Lupe Valdez .... 438,820 .... 42.91%
Andrew White .... 280,200 .... 27.40%
James Jolly Clark .... 21,994 .... 2.15%
Cedric Davis Sr. .... 84,215 .... 8.24%
Joe Mumback .... 13,950 .... 1.36%
Adrian Ocegueda .... 45,020 .... 4.40%
Jeffrey Payne .... 48,590 .... 4.75%
Tom Wakely .... 34,834 .... 3.41%
Grady Yarbrough .... 54,935 .... 5.37%
Total vote 1,022,558

Lieutenant Governor
Mike Collier .... 504,220 .... 52.38%
Michael Cooper .... 458,404 .... 47.62%
Total Vote 962,624

Comptroller of Public Accounts
Joi Chevalier .... 486,702 .... 51.87%
Tim Mahoney .... 451,687 .... 48.13%
Total Vote 938,389

Commissioner of General Land Office
Miguel Suazo .... 665,344 .... 70.15%
Tex Morgan .... 283,096 .... 29.85%
Total Vote 948,440

Railroad Commissioner
Roman McAllen .... 539,785 .... 58.51%
Chris Spellmon .... 382,795 .... 41.49%
Total Vote 922,580

U.S. HOUSE OF REPRESENTATIVES

District 1
Shirley J. McKellar .... 9,234 .... 61.04%
Brent Beal .... 5,895 .... 38.96%
Total Vote 15,129

District 2
Todd Litton .... 15,152 .... 52.81%
J. Darnell Jones .... 6,336 .... 22.08%
Ali A. Khorasani .... 2,152 .... 7.50%
Silky Malik .... 2,783 .... 9.70%
H.P. Parvizian .... 2,269 .... 7.91%
Total Vote 28,692

District 3
Lorie Burch .... 15,519 .... 49.61%
Sam Johnson .... 8,971 .... 28.68%
Adam P. Bell .... 5,617 .... 17.96%
Medrick Yhap .... 1,175 .... 3.76%
Total Vote 31,282

District 4
Catherine Krantz .... 9,040 .... 68.62%
Lander Bethel .... 4,134 .... 31.38%
Total Vote 13,174

District 6
Ruby Faye Woolridge .... 10,895 .... 36.95%
Jana Lynne Sanchez .... 10,880 .... 36.90%
John W. Duncan .... 3,987 .... 13.52%
Levii R. Shocklee .... 1,704 .... 5.78%
Justin Snider .... 2,021 .... 6.85%
Total Vote 29,487

District 7
Lizzie Pannill Fletcher .... 9,768 .... 29.36%
Laura Moser .... 8,099 .... 24.34%
Joshua A. Butler .... 1,253 .... 3.77%
James Cargas .... 651 .... 1.96%
Ivan Sanchez .... 1,895 .... 5.69%
Alex Triantaphyllis .... 5,234 .... 15.73%
Jason Westin .... 6,375 .... 19.16%
Total Vote 33,275

District 10
Mike Siegel .... 15,511 .... 40.00%
Tawana Walter-Cadien .... 6,963 .... 17.96%
Richie DeGrow .... 302 .... 0.78%
Madeline K. Eden .... 5,532 .... 14.27%
Matt Harris .... 2,838 .... 7.32%
Kevin Nelson .... 1,597 .... 4.13%
Tami Walker .... 6,033 .... 15.56%
Total Vote 38,776

District 11
Jennie Lou Leeder .... 7,273 .... 82.91%
Eric Pfalzgraf .... 1,499 .... 17.09%
Total Vote 8,772

District 14
Adrienne Bell .... 19,600 .... 79.83%
Levy Q. Barnes Jr. .... 4,951 .... 20.17%
Total Vote 24,551

District 16
Veronica Escobar .... 31,009 .... 61.53%
Dori Fenenbock .... 11,071 .... 21.97%
John Carrillo .... 780 .... 1.55%
Norma Chavez .... 3,357 .... 6.66%
Enrique Garcia .... 2,684 .... 5.33%
Jerome Tilghman .... 1,495 .... 2.97%
Total Vote 50,396

District 17
Rick Kennedy .... 14,424 .... 63.40%
Dale Mantey .... 8,326 .... 36.60%
Total Vote 22,750

District 18
Sheila Jackson Lee .... 32,625 .... 85.30%
Richard Johnson .... 5,622 .... 14.70%
Total Vote 38,247

District 21
Mary Street Wilson .... 15,736 .... 30.90%
Joseph Kopser .... 14,787 .... 29.03%
Derrick Crowe .... 11,742 .... 23.05%
Elliot McFadden .... 8,667 .... 17.02%
Total Vote 50,932

District 22
Sri Preston Kulkarni .... 9,515 .... 31.85%
Letitia Plummer .... 7,258 .... 24.29%
Steve Brown .... 6,269 .... 20.98%
Mark Gibson .... 3,060 .... 10.24%
Margarita Ruiz Johnson .... 3,776 .... 12.64%
Total Vote 29,878

District 23
Gina Ortiz Jones .... 18,443 .... 41.56%
Rick Trevino .... 7,710 .... 17.38%
Judy Canales .... 7,538 .... 16.99%
Jay Hulings .... 6,649 .... 14.98%
Angela "Angie" Villescaz .... 4,032 .... 9.09%
Total Vote 44,372

District 24

Jan McDowell	14,626	52.47%
John Biggan	5,998	21.52%
Edward "Todd" Allen	5,574	20.00%
Josh Imhoff	1,678	6.02%
Total Vote	27,876	

District 25

Chris Perri	13,984	32.79%
Julie Oliver	11,274	26.44%
West Hansen	4,508	10.57%
Chetan Panda	3,853	9.04%
Kathi Thomas	9,024	21.16%
Total Vote	42,643	

District 26

Linsey Fagan	13,895	52.66%
Will Fisher	12,489	47.34%
Total Vote	26,384	

District 27

Raul "Roy" Barrera	8,766	41.23%
Eric Holguin	4,953	23.30%
Vanessa Edwards Foster	4,057	19.08%
Ronnie McDonald	3,484	16.39%
Total Vote	21,260	

District 29

Sylvia R. Garcia	11,727	63.26%
Tahir Javed	3,851	20.67%
Dominique Michelle Garcia	478	2.58%
Roel Garcia	1,221	6.59%
Hector Morales	563	3.04%
Augustine H. Reyes	525	2.83%
Pedro Valencia	193	1.04%
Total Vote	18,538	

District 30

Eddie Bernice Johnson	32,669	63.60%
Barbara Mallory Caraway	11,723	22.82%
Eric Williams	6,971	13.57%
Total Vote	51,363	

District 31

Mary Jennings "MJ" Hegar	13,900	44.93%
Christine Eady Mann	10,368	33.51%
Mike Clark	3,475	11.23%
Kent Lester	3,193	10.32%
Total Vote	30,936	

District 32

Colin Allred	15,498	38.43%
Lillian Salerno	7,400	18.35%
Ron Marshall	1,306	3.24%
Todd Maternowski	952	2.36%
Ed Meier	5,525	13.70%
George Rodriguez	3,062	7.59%
Brett Shipp	6,589	16.34%
Total Vote	40,332	

District 33

Marc Veasey	15,175	70.32%
Carlos Quintanilla	6,405	29.68%
Total Vote	21,580	

District 36

Dayna Steele	9,891	72.00%
Jon Powell	3,847	28.00%
Total Vote	13,738	

STATE SENATE
District 5

Meg Walsh	22,605	71.13%
Brian E. Cronin	5,383	16.94%
Glenn "Grumpy" Williams	3,791	11.93%
Total Vote	31,779	

District 8

Mark Phariss	16,748	50.91%
Brian Chaput	16,148	49.09%
Total Vote	32,896	

District 10

Beverly Powell	23,148	61.60%
Allison Campolo	14,432	38.40%
Total Vote	37,580	

District 15

John Whitmire	27,307	74.92%
Damien LaCroix	6,520	17.89%
Hank Segelke	2,619	7.19%
Total Vote	36,446	

District 16

Nathan Johnson	25,437	69.57%
Joe Bogen	11,125	30.43%
Total Vote	36,562	

District 17

Rita Lucido	17,669	48.96%
Fran Watson	12,663	35.09%
Ahmad R. Hassan	5,757	15.95%
Total Vote	36,089	

District 25

Steven Kling	23,017	51.06%
Jack Guerra	22,064	48.94%
Total Vote	45,081	

STATE BOARD OF EDUCATION
District 2

Ruben Cortez Jr.	31,329	52.32%
Michelle Arévalo Dávila	28,553	47.68%
Total Vote	59,882	

District 3

Marisa B. Perez	60,275	75.94%
Dan Arellano	19,097	24.06%
Total Vote	79,372	

District 4

Lawrence Allen Jr.	45,335	66.91%
Steven A. Chambers	22,416	33.09%
Total Vote	67,751	

District 11

Carla Morton	33,392	57.98%
Celeste Light	24,205	42.02%
Total Vote	57,597	

District 12

Suzanne Smith	35,646	48.12%
Laura Malone-Miller	19,490	26.31%
Tina Green	18,948	25.58%
Total Vote	74,084	

PROPOSITIONS
Prop. 1 – Right to School & Training

In Favor	1,021,693	96.02%
Against	42,368	3.98%
Total Vote	1,064,061	

Prop. 2 – Refinance Student Loan Debt

In Favor	990,991	93.46%
Against	69,389	6.54%
Total Vote	1,060,380	

Prop. 3 – Right to Universal Health Care

In Favor	1,009,219	94.46%
Against	59,244	5.54%
Total Vote	1,068,463	

Prop. 4 – Right to Economic Security

In Favor	1,013,665	95.77%
Against	44,785	4.23%
Total Vote	1,058,450	

Prop. 5 – Promote National Jobs Program

In Favor	970,870	93.06%
Against	72,436	6.94%
Total Vote	1,043,306	

Prop. 6 – Right to Clean Environment
In Favor .... 1,046,094 .... 98.55%
Against .... 15,441 .... 1.45%
Total Vote 1,061,535

Prop. 7 – Right to Dignity & Respect
In Favor .... 1,024,562 .... 97.01%
Against .... 31,617 .... 2.99%
Total Vote 1,056,179

Prop. 8 – Right to Housing & Utilities
In Favor .... 961,493 .... 91.83%
Against .... 85,579 .... 8.17%
Total Vote 1,047,072

Prop. 9 – Right to Vote
In Favor .... 996,322 .... 94.58%
Against .... 57,144 .... 5.42%
Total Vote 1,053,466

Prop. 10 – Right to Fair Justice System
In Favor .... 1,018,366 .... 96.77%
Against .... 33,956 .... 3.23%
Total Vote 1,052,322

Prop. 11 – Immigrant Rights Reform
In Favor .... 996,632 .... 94.46%
Against .... 58,497 .... 5.54%
Total Vote 1,055,129

Prop. 12 – Fair State Taxation
In Favor .... 1,014,909 .... 96.59%
Against .... 35,782 .... 3.41%
Total Vote 1,050,691

COURTS OF APPEALS
Chief Justice, Thirteenth District
Dori Contreras .... 51,495 .... 63.87%
Ray Thomas. .... 29,125 .... 36.13%
Total Vote 80,620

Justice, Fourteenth District, Place 3
Jerry Zimmerer .... 96,818 .... 51.20%
Joseph R. Willie II .... 92,291 .... 48.80%
Total Vote 189,109

Justice, Fourteenth District, Place 8
Margaret "Meg" Poissant .... 110,682 .... 58.60%
Michele Barber Chimene. .... 78,206 .... 41.40%
Total Vote 188,888

DEMOCRATIC RUNOFF
Governor
Lupe Valdez .... 232,020 .... 53.35%
Andrew White .... 202,869 .... 46.65%
Total Vote 434,889

U.S. HOUSE OF REPRESENTATIVES
District 3
Lorie Burch .... 9,377 .... 75.02%
Sam Johnson .... 3,123 .... 24.98%
Total Vote 12,500

District 6
Jana Lynne Sanchez .... 6,117 .... 53.12%
Ruby Faye Woolridge .... 5,398 .... 46.88%
Total Vote 11,515

District 7
Lizzie Pannill Fletcher .... 11,506 .... 67.12%
Laura Moser .... 5,637 .... 32.88%
Total Vote 17,143

District 10
Mike Siegel .... 12,333 .... 69.82%
Tawana Walter-Cadien .... 5,330 .... 30.18%
Total Vote 17,663

District 21
Joseph Kopser .... 14,765 .... 57.93%
Mary Street Wilson .... 10,722 .... 42.07%
Total Vote 25,487

District 22
Sri Preston Kulkarni .... 9,517 .... 62.11%
Letitia Plummer .... 5,805 .... 37.89%
Total Vote 15,322

District 23
Gina Ortiz Jones .... 17,570 .... 67.93%
Rick Trevino .... 8,296 .... 32.07%
Total Vote 25,866

District 25
Julie Oliver .... 12,052 .... 52.18%
Chris Perri .... 11,043 .... 47.82%
Total Vote 23,095

District 27
Eric Holguin .... 6,448 .... 61.93%
Raul "Roy" Barrera .... 3,964 .... 38.07%
Total Vote 10,412

District 31
Mary Jennings "MJ" Hegar .... 8,879 .... 62.27%
Christine Eady Mann .... 5,380 .... 37.73%
Total Vote 14,259

District 32
Colin Allred .... 15,823 .... 69.35%
Lillian Salerno .... 6,992 .... 30.65%
Total Vote 22,815

STATE SENATE
District 17
Rita Lucido .... 10,533 .... 57.79%
Fran Watson .... 7,694 .... 42.21%
Total Vote 18.227

STATE BOARD OF EDUCATION
District 12
Suzanne Smith .... 0 .... 0%
Laura Malone-Miller* .... 0 .... 0%
withdrew prior to runoff

Political Party Organizations

DEMOCRATIC State Executive Committee
www.txdemocrats.org
Chairman, Gilberto Hinojosa, PO Box 116, Austin 78767.

REPUBLICAN State Executive Committee
www.texasgop.org
Chairman, James Dickey, P.O. Box 2206, Austin 78768.

LIBERTARIAN State Executive Committee
www.lptexas.org
Chair, John Wilford, 111 Congress Ave. Ste. 400, Austin 78701.

GREEN State Executive Committee
txgreens.org
Co-Chairs, Wesson Gaige and Janis Richards, P.O. Box 271080, Houston 77277-1080.

GOVERNMENT

The Intergovernmental Relations Committee at the desk of chair Senator
Eddie Lucio of Brownsville during the 86th Legislative Session.
Texas Senate photo.

HISTORICAL DOCUMENTS

CONSTITUTIONAL AMENDMENTS

CHIEF OFFICIALS, 1691–2019

STATE, LOCAL, FEDERAL GOVERNMENT

Legislative sessions in May sometimes extend late into the evening, and later. Texas Senate photo.

86th Legislature Increases School Funding, Sets Limits on Local Property Tax Raises

By Carolyn Barta

Texas legislators grappled successfully, and at last, with two major issues that have hounded state government for years — school finance reform and property tax relief — in the 86th legislative session that ran from Jan. 8 to May 27, 2019.

Following a tight-fisted and rancorous session in 2017, lawmakers unanimously agreed during a more collaborative gathering to a historically high $250.7 billion two-year budget, enabled by revenue expectations from record oil production and economic growth.

The two big goals, to provide more money for schools and tamp down local tax escalation, were achieved with an $11.6 billion package that allocated $6.5 billion in new state money for public education, mandated a teacher pay raise, funded full day pre-kindergarten, and offered $5.1 billion to buy down local property taxes.

The plan began to wean the state from the long criticized and oft-legally challenged "Robin Hood" system of recapturing funds from property-rich to poorer districts. After years of neglect, Lawmakers increased the state's share of educating students from 35 to 45 percent, vaulting the per-student allotment from $5,180 to $6,160.

Thirty percent of new money must go to teacher/staff salary increases. Lt. Gov. Dan Patrick's proposal to grant teachers an across-the-board $5,000 fizzled, leaving districts with their desired flexibility to dole out the raises.

But local officials lost their fight to keep the Legislature from putting a lid on how the extent to which local governments and school districts can raise property taxes. Legislators imposed a 3.5 percent cap on annual increases in city and county tax bills and limited school tax hikes to 2.5 percent per year. A local election would be required to exceed the caps.

Leaders in Austin called the plan "transformative," but some lawmakers questioned its affordability long term as limiting local tax revenue could force greater state reimbursements. The $11.6 billion initial cost was projected to grow by $2 billion in two years. A one-cent sales tax increase proposed by state leaders for new revenue faced fierce pushback.

The mostly drama-free session reflected a different tone from 2017 when public flare-ups, threats, and hard feelings resulted over controversial issues including an approved sanctuary cities measure and "bathroom bill" that would have affected transgender people.

Chalk up the more harmonious session to 2018 election consequences and solidarity of the top three Republican leaders: Gov. Greg Abbott, Lt. Gov. Dan Patrick and House Speaker Dennis Bonnen. The "Big Three" announced a unified focus on schools and tax reform at the session's beginning.

In contrast, the 85th Legislature was marked by conflicts between a more conservative Senate, presided over by Patrick, and a more moderate House, led by 5-term Speaker Joe Straus. Bonnen, a 22-year veteran of the House, provided new leadership after Straus retired, and Abbott was more involved in the process. Patrick credited the productive session to "teamwork."

But Republicans also were looking over their shoulders at the 2018 election, when Democrats flipped 12 House seats, two Senate seats, and Democrat Beto O'Rourke gave U.S. Sen. Ted Cruz a frightening close election.

Republicans continued to hold all statewide offices, plus the majority in both houses, but sought to halt further Democrat inroads by creating a platform of success on pocketbook issues. Democrats, who had gained leverage, hoped to continue momentum to win nine more seats in 2020 to gain House control.

Conservative activists made less headway on social issues than previously. They delivered a blow to Planned Parenthood by banning cities and counties from entering into contracts with any abortion provider for any service, even those unrelated to abortion. And a "Born Alive" bill was passed to impose fines and potential imprisonment on doctors who fail to provide medical treatment to babies born alive after failed abortion attempts.

Citing the need to protect religious liberty, lawmakers passed the "Save Chick-fil-A bill," preventing local governments from adverse action against companies based on charitable contributions. The bill followed Chick-fil-A being denied a San Antonio airport location after donations to certain Christian organizations. The newly formed LGBTQ caucus contended the bill would lessen gay and transgender rights.

A much-watched bill to reduce criminal penalties for possession of small amounts of marijuana failed. It passed the House but failed to make it to the Senate floor after the lieutenant governor announced opposition.

However, lawmakers did approve a bill to legalize low-THC cannabidiol, or CBC oil, expanding the prescription of medical marijuana by specialty doctors from epilepsy to a wider range of health conditions such as terminal cancer, multiple sclerosis, Parkinson's disease and autism.

In other action, the 86th Legislature:
- Banned red light cameras, but allowed impacted cities to keep them until contracts with vendors expire.
- Raised the minimum age to buy cigarettes and e-cigs to 21, except for active duty members of the U.S. military.

- Authorized citizens to carry guns, open or concealed, without a permit for a week following a declared state or natural disaster.
- Let places of religious worship decide whether to allow handguns on their premises.
- Approved the sale of craft beer for take-home customers but declined to allow beer and wine sales to start at 10 a.m. on Sunday instead of noon.
- Created a special flood infrastructure fund to help communities hurt by natural disasters like Hurricane Harvey.
- Approved a plan to reduce the backlog of 15,000 untested rape kits in police evidence rooms and imposed a 90-day deadline for testing new rape kits to prevent future backlogs.
- Shored up the teacher pension fund by increasing state contributions.

Measures that failed included:
- A plan that would have negated the need to change clocks twice a year by letting Texas voters pick either Daylight Savings Time or standard time year-round.
- A last-minute proposal emanating from the governor's office to spend $100 million for federal "surge operations" to secure the U.S. Mexico border. Members objected to the Rainy Day Fund draw-down when they were already spending $800 million for border law enforcement and saw no need to jeopardize the session's accord with a late fight over border security.

On the lighter side, lawmakers voted to make child-run lemonaid stands legal in Texas! ☆

Carolyn Barta is a former political writer for The Dallas Morning News and retired journalism professor at Southern Methodist University. Much of the research for this article came from the Texas Tribune and The Dallas Morning News.

Senator Lois Kolkhorst of Brenham chaired the Health and Human Services Committee during the 86th Legislature. Texas Senate photo.

Declaration of Independence of the Republic of Texas

The Declaration of Independence of the Republic of Texas was adopted in general convention at Washington-on-the-Brazos, March 2, 1836.

Richard Ellis, president of the convention, appointed a committee of five to write the declaration for submission to the convention. However, there is much evidence that George C. Childress, one of the members, wrote the document with little or no help from the other members. Childress is therefore generally accepted as the author.

The text of the declaration is followed by the names of the signers of the document. The names are presented here as the signers actually signed the document.

Our thanks to the staff of the Texas State Archives for furnishing a photocopy of the signatures.

UNANIMOUS

Declaration of Independence,

BY THE
DELEGATES OF THE PEOPLE OF TEXAS,
IN GENERAL CONVENTION,
AT THE TOWN OF WASHINGTON,
ON THE SECOND DAY OF MARCH, 1836.

WHEN A GOVERNMENT has ceased to protect the lives, liberty and property of the people from whom its legitimate powers are derived, and for the advancement of whose happiness it was instituted; and so far from being a guarantee for the enjoyment of those inestimable and inalienable rights, becomes an instrument in the hands of evil rulers for their oppression; when the Federal Republican Constitution of their country, which they have sworn to support, no longer has a substantial existence, and the whole nature of their government has been forcibly changed without their consent, from a restricted federative republic, composed of sovereign states, to a consolidated central military despotism, in which every interest is disregarded but that of the army and the priesthood — both the eternal enemies of civil liberty, and the ever-ready minions of power, and the usual instruments of tyrants; When long after the spirit of the Constitution has departed, moderation is at length, so far lost, by those in power that even the semblance of freedom is removed, and the forms, themselves, of the constitution discontinued; and so far from their petitions and remonstrances being regarded, the agents who bear them are thrown into dungeons; and mercenary armies sent forth to force a new government upon them at the point of the bayonet. When in consequence of such acts of malfeasance and abdication, on the part of the government, anarchy prevails, and civil society is dissolved into its original elements: In such a crisis, the first law of nature, the right of self-preservation — the inherent and inalienable right of the people to appeal to first principles and take their political affairs into their own hands in extreme cases — enjoins it as a right towards themselves and a sacred obligation to their posterity, to abolish such government and create another in its stead, calculated to rescue them from impending dangers, and to secure their future welfare and happiness.

Nations, as well as individuals, are amenable for their acts to the public opinion of mankind. A statement of a part of our grievances is, therefore, submitted to an impartial world, in justification of the hazardous but unavoidable step now taken of severing our political connection with the Mexican people, and assuming an independent attitude among the nations of the earth.

The Mexican government, by its colonization laws, invited and induced the Anglo-American population of Texas to colonize its wilderness under the pledged faith of a written constitution, that they should continue to enjoy that constitutional liberty and republican government to which they had been habituated in the land of their birth, the United States of America. In this expectation they have been cruelly disappointed, inasmuch as the Mexican nation has acquiesced in the late changes made in the government by General Antonio Lopez de Santa Anna, who, having overturned the constitution of his country, now offers us the cruel alternative either to abandon our homes, acquired by so many privations, or submit to the most intolerable of all tyranny, the combined despotism of the sword and the priesthood.

It has sacrificed our welfare to the state of Coahuila, by which our interests have been continually depressed, through a jealous and partial course of legislation carried on at a far distant seat of government, by a hostile majority, in an unknown tongue; and this too, notwithstanding we have petitioned in the humblest terms, for the establishment of a separate state government, and have, in accordance with the provisions of the national constitution, presented the general Congress, a republican constitution which was without just cause contemptuously rejected.

It incarcerated in a dungeon, for a long time, one of our citizens, for no other cause but a zealous endeavor to procure the acceptance of our constitution and the establishment of a state government.

It has failed and refused to secure on a firm basis, the right of trial by jury; that palladium of civil liberty, and only safe guarantee for the life, liberty, and property of the citizen.

It has failed to establish any public system of education, although possessed of almost boundless resources (the public domain) and, although, it is an axiom, in political science, that unless a people are educated and enlightened it is idle to expect the continuance of civil liberty, or the capacity for self-government.

It has suffered the military commandants stationed among us to exercise arbitrary acts of oppression and tyranny; thus trampling upon the most sacred rights of the citizen and rendering the military superior to the civil power.

It has dissolved by force of arms, the state Congress of Coahuila and Texas, and obliged our representatives to fly for their lives from the seat of government; thus depriving us of the fundamental political right of representation.

It has demanded the surrender of a number of our citizens, and ordered military detachments to seize and carry them into the Interior for trial; in contempt of the civil authorities, and in defiance of the laws and constitution.

It has made piratical attacks upon our commerce; by commissioning foreign desperadoes, and authorizing them to seize our vessels, and convey the property of our citizens to far distant ports of confiscation.

It denies us the right of worshipping the Almighty according to the dictates of our own consciences, by the support of a national religion calculated to promote the temporal interests of its human functionaries rather than the glory of the true and living God.

It has demanded us to deliver up our arms; which are essential to our defense, the rightful property of freemen, and formidable only to tyrannical governments.

It has invaded our country, both by sea and by land, with intent to lay waste our territory and drive us from our homes; and has now a large mercenary army advancing to carry on against us a war of extermination.

It has, through its emissaries, incited the merciless savage, with the tomahawk and scalping knife, to massacre the inhabitants of our defenseless frontiers.

It hath been, during the whole time of our connection with it, the contemptible sport and victim of successive military revolutions and hath continually exhibited every characteristic of a weak, corrupt and tyrannical government.

These, and other grievances, were patiently borne by the people of Texas until they reached that point at which forbearance ceases to be a virtue. We then took up arms in defense of the national constitution. We appealed to our Mexican brethren for assistance. Our appeal has been made in vain. Though months have elapsed, no sympathetic response has yet been heard from the Interior. We are, therefore, forced to the melancholy conclusion that the Mexican people have acquiesced in the destruction of their liberty, and the substitution therefor of a military government — that they are unfit to be free and incapable of self-government.

The necessity of self-preservation, therefore, now decrees our eternal political separation.

We, therefore, the delegates, with plenary powers, of the people of Texas, in solemn convention assembled, appealing to a candid world for the necessities of our condition, do hereby resolve and DECLARE that our political connection with the Mexican nation has forever ended; and that the people of Texas do now constitute a FREE, SOVEREIGN and INDEPENDENT REPUBLIC, and are fully invested with all the rights and attributes which properly belong to the independent nations; and, conscious of the rectitude of our intentions, we fearlessly and confidently commit the issue to the decision of the Supreme Arbiter of the destinies of nations.

RICHARD ELLIS, president of the convention and Delegate from Red River.

Charles B Stewart

Tho⁵ Barnett
John S.D. Byrom

Fran^co Ruiz
J. Antonio Navarro
Jesse B. Badgett
Wm D. Lacey
William Menefee
Jno Fisher
Mathew Caldwell
William Mottley
Lorenzo de Zavala
Stephen H. Everitt
Geo W Smyth

Elijah Stapp
Claiborne West

W^m B Scates

M.B. Menard
A.B. Hardin
J.W. Bunton
Tho⁵ J. Gasley
R. M. Coleman
Sterling C. Robertson
Benj Briggs Goodrich
G.W. Barnett
James G. Swisher
Jesse Grimes
S. Rhoads Fisher
John W. Moore
John W. Bower
Saml A Maverick from Bejar
Sam P. Carson
A. Briscoe
J.B. Woods
Jas Collinsworth
Edwin Waller
Asa Brigham
Geo. C. Childress
Bailey Hardeman
Rob. Potter

Thomas Jefferson Rusk
Chas. S. Taylor
John S. Roberts

Robert Hamilton
Collin McKinney
Albert H Latimer
James Power

Sam Houston
David Thomas

Edwd Conrad
Martin Parmer
Edwin O. LeGrand
Stephen W. Blount
Ja^s Gaines
Wm Clark, Jr
Sydney O. Penington
Wm Carrol Crawford
Jno Turner

Test. H.S. Kimble, Secretary

Documents Concerning the Annexation
of Texas to the United States

For an overview of the subject, please see these discussions: The New Handbook of Texas, Texas State Historical Association, Austin, 1996; Vol. 1, pages 192–193. On the web: **https://tshaonline.org/handbook/online/articles/mga02**. Also see, the Texas State Library and Archives website: **www.tsl.state.tx.us/ref/abouttx/annexation/index.html** and the Texas Almanac website: **https://texasalmanac.com/topics/history/timeline/annexation-and-statehood**.

Joint Resolution for Annexing
Texas to the United States

Resolved

by the Senate and House of Representatives of the United States of America in Congress assembled,

That Congress doth consent that the territory properly included within and rightfully belonging to the Republic of Texas, may be erected into a new State to be called the State of Texas, with a republican form of government adopted by the people of said Republic, by deputies in convention assembled, with the consent of the existing Government in order that the same may by admitted as one of the States of this Union.

2. And be it further resolved, That the foregoing consent of Congress is given upon the following conditions, to wit:

First, said state to be formed, subject to the adjustment by this government of all questions of boundary that may arise with other government,

—and the Constitution thereof, with the proper evidence of its adoption by the people of said Republic of Texas, shall be transmitted to the President of the United States, to be laid before Congress for its final action on, or before the first day of January, one thousand eight hundred and forty-six.

Second, said state when admitted into the Union, after ceding to the United States all public edifices, fortifications, barracks, ports and harbors, navy and navy yards, docks, magazines and armaments, and all other means pertaining to the public defense, belonging to the said Republic of Texas, shall retain funds, debts, taxes and dues of every kind which may belong to, or be due and owing to the said Republic;

and shall also retain all the vacant and unappropriated lands lying within its limits, to be applied to the payment of the debts and liabilities of said Republic of Texas, and the residue of said lands, after discharging said debts and liabilities, to be disposed of as said State may direct; but in no event are said debts and liabilities to become a charge upon the Government of the United States.

Third — New States of convenient size not exceeding four in number, in addition to said State of Texas and having sufficient population, may, hereafter by the consent of said State, be formed out of the territory thereof, which shall be entitled to admission under the provisions of the Federal Constitution;

and such states as may be formed out of the territory lying south of thirty-six degrees thirty minutes north latitude, commonly known as the Missouri Compromise Line, shall be admitted into the Union, with or without slavery, as the people of each State, asking admission shall desire;

and in such State or States as shall be formed out of said territory, north of said Missouri Compromise Line, slavery, or involuntary servitude (except for crime) shall be prohibited.

3. And be it further resolved, That if the President of the United States shall in his judgment and discretion deem it most advisable, instead of proceeding to submit the foregoing resolution of the Republic of Texas, as an overture on the part of the United States for admission, to negotiate with the Republic; then,

Be it resolved, That a State, to be formed out of the present Republic of Texas, with suitable extent and boundaries, and with two representatives in Congress, until the next appointment of representation, shall be admitted into the Union, by virtue of this act, on an equal footing with the existing States, as soon as the terms and conditions of such admission, and the cession of the remaining Texian territory to the United States shall be agreed upon by the governments of Texas and the United States:

And that the sum of one hundred thousand dollars be, and the same is hereby, appropriated to defray the expenses of missions and negotiations, to agree upon the terms of said admission and cession, either by treaty to be submitted to the Senate, or by articles to be submitted to the two houses of Congress, as the President may direct.

Approved, March 1, 1845.

Source: Peters, Richard, ed., The Public Statutes at Large of the United States of America, v.5, pp. 797–798, Boston, Chas. C. Little and Jas. Brown, 1850.

Explore the Texas Almanac Archive, 1857–2004
★ 62 Editions ★ Fully Searchable ★ Download pages or entire books ★
https://TexasAlmanac.com/archive

Twenty-Ninth Congress: Session 1 — Resolutions [No. 1.] Joint Resolution for the Admission of the State of Texas into the Union

Whereas

the Congress of the United States, by a joint resolution approved March the first, eighteen hundred and forty-five, did consent that the territory properly included within, and rightfully belonging to, the Republic of Texas, might be erected into a new State, to be called _The State of Texas,_ with a republican form of government, to be adopted by the people of said republic, by deputies in convention assembled, with the consent of the existing government, in order that the same might be admitted as one of the States of the Union;

which consent of Congress was given upon certain conditions specified in the first and second sections of said joint resolution;

and whereas the people of the said Republic of Texas, by deputies in convention assembled, with the consent of the existing government, did adopt a constitution, and erect a new State with a republican form of government, and, in the name of the people of Texas, and by their authority, did ordain and declare that they assented to and accepted the proposals, conditions, and guaranties contained in said first and second sections of said resolution:

and whereas the said constitution, with the proper evidence of its adoption by the people of the Republic of Texas, has been transmitted to the President of the United States and laid before Congress, in conformity to the provisions of said joint resolution:

Therefore—

Resolved by the Senate and House of Representatives of the United States of America in Congress assembled, That the State of Texas shall be one, and is hereby declared to be one, of the United States of America, and admitted into the Union on an equal footing with the original States in all respects whatever.

Sec. 2. And be it further resolved, That until the representatives in Congress shall be apportioned according to an actual enumeration of the inhabitants of the United States, the State of Texas shall be entitled to choose two representatives.

Approved, December 29, 1845.

Source: Minot, Geo., ed., Statutes at Large and Treaties of the United States of America from Dec. 1, 1845, to March 3, 1851, V. IX, p. 108

Constitution of Texas

The complete official text of the Constitution of Texas, including the original document, which was adopted Feb. 15, 1876, plus all amendments approved since then, is available on the State of Texas website:

https://statutes.capitol.texas.gov

An index and search features at that website allow exploration of the 17 Articles and subsequent Sections of the Constitution, along with other Texas Statutes.

For election information, upcoming elections, amendment or other election votes, and voter registration information, go to:

http://www.sos.state.tx.us/elections/index.shtml

According to the **Legislative Reference Library of Texas**, "The Texas Constitution is one of the longest in the nation and is still growing. As of 2017 (the 85th Legislature), the Texas Legislature has proposed a total of 680 amendments. Of these, 498 have been adopted, and 179 have been defeated by Texas voters. Thus, the Texas Constitution has been amended 498 times since its adoption in 1876."

Amending the Texas Constitution requires a two-thirds favorable vote by both the Texas House of Representatives and the Texas Senate, followed by a majority vote of approval by voters in a statewide election.

Prior to 1973, amendments to the constitution could not be submitted by a special session of the Legislature. But the constitution was amended in 1972 to allow submission of amendments if the special session was opened to the subject by the governor.

Constitutional amendments are not subject to a gubernatorial veto. Once submitted, voters have the final decision on whether to change the constitution as proposed.

The table on the next page lists the total number of amendments submitted to voters by the Texas Legislature, how many were adopted, the year in which the Legislature approved them for submission to voters; e.g., the 70th Legislature in 1987 approved 28 bills proposing amendments to be submitted to voters, of which 20 were adopted.

For more information on bills and constitutional amendments, see the Legislative Reference Library of Texas website:

https://lrl.texas.gov

Amendments, 2017

The following seven amendments were submitted to the voters by the 85th Legislature in an election on Nov. 7, 2017:

SJR 1: The constitutional amendment authorizing the legislature to provide for an exemption from ad valorem taxation of all or part of the market value of the residence homestead of the surviving spouse of a first responder who is killed or fatally injured in the line of duty. **Adopted.**

Votes for: 739,452 *Votes against:* 134,167

SJR 6: The constitutional amendment authorizing the legislature to require a court to provide notice to the attorney general of a challenge to the constitutionality of a state statute and authorizing the legislature to prescribe a waiting period before the court may enter a judgment holding the statute unconstitutional. **Adopted.**

Votes for: 554,040 *Votes against:* 300,096

HJR 21: The constitutional amendment authorizing the legislature to provide for an exemption from ad valorem taxation of part of the market value of the residence homestead of a partially disabled veteran or the surviving spouse of a partially disabled veteran if the residence homestead was donated to the disabled veteran by a charitable organization for less than the market value of the residence homestead and harmonizing certain related provisions of the Texas Constitution. **Adopted.**

Votes for: 754,739 *Votes against:* 122,864

SJR 34: The constitutional amendment limiting the service of certain officeholders appointed by the governor and confirmed by the Senate after the expiration of the person's term of office. **Adopted.**

Votes for: 722,753 *Votes against:* 146,390

HJR 37: The constitutional amendment relating to legislative authority to permit credit unions and other financial institutions to award prizes by lot to promote savings. **Adopted.**

Votes for: 511,806 *Votes against:* 345,556

SJR 60: The constitutional amendment to establish a lower amount for expenses that can be charged to a borrower and removing certain financing expense limitations for a home equity loan, establishing certain authorized lenders to make a home equity loan, changing certain options for the refinancing of home equity loans, changing the threshold for an advance of a home equity line of credit, and allowing home equity loans on agricultural homesteads. **Adopted.**

Votes for: 593,052 *Votes against:* 270,780

HJR 100: The constitutional amendment on professional sports team charitable foundations conducting charitable raffles. **Adopted.**

Votes for: 510,363 *Votes against:* 335,582

Amendments, 2019

The following 10 amendments will be submitted to voters by the 86th Legislature in an election on **Nov. 5, 2019**.

HJR 4: Proposing a constitutional amendment providing for the creation of the **flood infrastructure fund** to assist in the financing of drainage, flood mitigation, and flood control projects.

HJR 12: Proposing a constitutional amendment authorizing the legislature to **increase the maximum bond amount** authorized for the **Cancer Prevention and Research Institute of Texas**.

HJR 34: Proposing a constitutional amendment authorizing the legislature to provide for a **temporary exemption from ad valorem taxation** of a portion of the appraised value of **certain property damaged by a disaster**.

HJR 38: Proposing a constitutional amendment **prohibiting the imposition of an individual income tax**.

HJR 72: Proposing a constitutional amendment permitting a person to hold **more than one office as a municipal judge at the same time**.

HJR 95: Proposing a constitutional amendment authorizing the legislature to **exempt from ad valorem taxation precious metal held in a precious metal depository** located in this state.

HJR 151: Proposing a constitutional amendment allowing **increased distributions to the available school fund**.

SJR 24: Proposing a constitutional amendment relating to the appropriation of the net revenue received from the imposition of **state sales and use taxes on sporting goods**.

SJR 32: Proposing a constitutional amendment to allow the **transfer of a law enforcement animal to a qualified caretaker** in certain circumstances.

SJR 79: Proposing a constitutional amendment providing for the issuance of additional **general obligation bonds by the Texas Water Development Board** to provide financial assistance for the development of certain projects in economically distressed areas.

Constitutional Amendments Submitted to Voters by the Texas Legislature
(Proposed/Adopted)

Year	No.	Year	No.	Year	No.
1879	1/1	1931	9/9	1979	12/9
1881	2/0	1933	12/4	1981	10/8
1883	5/5	1935	13/10	1982	3/3
1887	6/0	1937	7/6	1983	19/16
1889	2/2	1939	4/3	1985	17/17
1891	5/5	1941	5/1	1986	1/1
1893	2/2	1943	3/3	1987	28/20
1895	2/1	1945	8/7	1989	21/19
1897	5/1	1947	9/9	1990	1/1
1899	1/0	1949	10/2	1991	15/12
1901	1/1	1951	7/3	1993	19/14
1903	3/3	1953	11/11	1995	14/11
1905	3/2	1955	9/9	1997	15/13
1907	9/1	1957	12/10	1999	17/13
1909	4/4	1959	4/4	2001	20/20
1911	5/4	1961	14/10	2003	22/22
1913	8/0	1963	7/4	2005	9/7
1915	7/0	1965	27/20	2007	17/17
1917	3/3	1967	20/13	2009	11/11
1919	13/3	1969	16/9	2011	10/7
1921	5/1	1971	18/12	2013	10/10
1923	2/1	1973	9/6	2015	7/7
1925	4/4	1975	12/6	2017	7/7
1927	8/4	1977	15/11	2019	10/NA
1929	7/7	1978	1/1		

Source: Legislative Reference Library of Texas.

Texas' Chief Governmental Officials

On this and the following pages are lists of the principal administrative officials who have served the Republic and State of Texas with dates of their tenures of office. In a few instances, there are disputes as to the exact dates of tenures. Dates listed here are those that appear the most authentic.

★ ★ ★ ★ ★ ★ ★

Governors and Presidents

Spanish Royal Governors*

Domingo Terán de los Rios	1691–1692
Gregorio de Salinas Varona	1692–1697
Francisco Cuerbo y Valdés	1698–1702
Mathías de Aguirre	1703–1705
Martín de Alarcón	1705–1708
Simón Padilla y Córdova	1708–1712
Pedro Fermin de Echevers y Subisa	1712–1714
Juan Valdéz	1714–1716
Martín de Alarcón	1716–1719
José de Azlor y Virto de Vera, Marqués de San Miguel de Aguayo	1719–1722
Fernando Pérez de Almazán	1722–1727
Melchor de Mediavilla y Azcona	1727–1731
Juan Antonio Bustillo y Ceballos	1731–1734
Manuel de Sandoval	1734–1736
Carlos Benites Franquis de Lugo	1736–1737
Joseph Fernández de Jáuregui y Urrutia	1737–1737
Prudencio de Orobio y Basterra	1737–1741
Tomás Felipe Winthuisen (or Winthuysen)	1741–1743
Justo Boneo y Morales	1743–1744
Francisco García Larios	1744–1748
Pedro del Barrio Junco y Espriella	1748–1750
Jacinto de Barrios y Jáuregui	1751–1759
Angel de Martos y Navarrete	1759–1767
Hugo Oconór	1767–1770
Juan María Vicencio, Barón de Ripperdá	1770–1778
Domingo Cabello y Robles	1778–1786
Rafael Martínez Pacheco	1787–1790
Manuel Muñoz	1790–1799
Juan Bautista de Elguezábal	1799–1805
Antonio Cordero y Bustamante	1805–1808
Manuel María de Salcedo	1808–1813

(Mexico's War of Independence 1810–1812 created governmental instability.)

Juan Bautista de las Casas *(Revolutionary governor)*	1811–1811
Cristóbal Domínguez, Benito de Armiñan, Mariano Varela, Juan Ignacio Pérez, Manuel Pardo *(ad interim)*	1813–1817
Antonio María Martínez	1817–1821

Some authorities would include Texas under administrations of several earlier Spanish governors. The late Dr. C.E. Castañeda, Latin-American librarian of The University of Texas and authority on the history of Texas and the Southwest, would include the following four: Francisco de Garay, 1523–1526; Pánfilo de Narváez, 1526–28; Nuño de Guzmán, 1528–1530; Hernando de Soto, 1538–1543.

Governors Under Mexican Rule

The first two governors under Mexican rule, Trespalacios and García, were of Texas only as Texas was then constituted. Beginning with Gonzáles, 1824, the governors were for the joint State of Coahuila y Texas.

José Felix Trespalacios	1822–1823
Luciano García	1823–1824
Rafael Gonzáles	1824–1826
Victor Blanco	1826–1827
José María Viesca	1827–1830
Ramón Eca y Músquiz	1830–1831
José María Letona	1831–1832
Ramón Eca y Músquiz	1832–1832
Juan Martín de Veramendi	1832–1833
Juan José de Vidáurri y Villasenor	1833–1834
Juan José Elguezábal	1834–1835
José María Cantú	1835–1835
Agustín M. Viesca	1835–1835
Marciel Borrego	1835–1835
Ramón Eca y Músquiz	1835–1835

Provisional Colonial Governor, Before Independence

Henry Smith (Impeached)	1835–Jan. 1836

(James W. Robinson served as acting governor after Smith was impeached.)

Presidents of the Republic of Texas

David G. Burnet *(provisional)*	Mar. 16, 1836–Oct. 22, 1836
Sam Houston	Oct. 22, 1836–Dec. 10, 1838
Mirabeau B. Lamar	Dec. 10, 1838–Dec. 13, 1841
Sam Houston	Dec. 13, 1841–Dec. 9, 1844
Anson Jones	Dec. 9, 1844–Feb. 19, 1846

Governors Since Annexation

(Abbreviations: (D) Democrat, (R) Republican, (I) Independent. Many of the early Governors ran with no party affiliation.)

J. Pinckney Henderson... Feb. 19, 1846–Dec. 21, 1847
(Albert C. Horton served as acting governor while Henderson was away in the Mexican War.)
George T. Wood .... Dec. 21, 1847–Dec. 21, 1849
Peter Hansbrough Bell ...Dec. 21, 1849–Nov. 23, 1853
(Resigned to enter U.S. House of Representatives.)
J. W. Henderson ....Nov. 23, 1853–Dec. 21, 1853
Elisha M. Pease ....Dec. 21, 1853–Dec. 21, 1857
Hardin R. Runnels (D).....Dec. 21, 1857–Dec. 21, 1859
Sam Houston ....Dec. 21, 1859–Mar. 16, 1861
(Resigned because of state's secession from the Union.)
Edward Clark....................Mar. 16, 1861–Nov. 7, 1861
Francis R. Lubbock .... Nov. 7, 1861–Nov. 5, 1863
(Resigned to enter Confederate Army.)
Pendleton Murrah ....Nov. 5, 1863–June 17, 1865
(Fled to Mexico upon the fall of Confederacy. Lt. Gov. Fletcher S. Stockdale briefly acted as governor after Murrah's departure.)
Andrew J. Hamilton..........June 17, 1865–Aug. 9, 1866
(Hamilton received a commission as "military governor of Texas" from President Abraham Lincoln on Nov. 14, 1862. He appears to have served in that capacity continuously until his "reappointment" as "provisional governor" by President Andrew Johnson on June 17, 1865. Apparently Johnson used the term "reappointment" because Hamilton was already serving as military governor.)
James W. Throckmorton ....Aug. 9, 1866–Aug. 8, 1867
Elisha M. Pease (R) ....Aug. 8, 1867–Sept. 30, 1869
(Appointed under martial law after Throckmorton was removed on July 30, 1867, by Gen. Philip Sheridan. Pease formally took possession of the office on Aug. 8. He resigned and vacated the office Sept. 30, 1869, but no successor was named until Jan. 8, 1870. Some historians extend Pease's term to that date, but in reality Texas was without a head of governemnt for that period.)

Edmund J. Davis (R) .... Jan. 8, 1870–Jan. 15, 1874
(Appointed provisional governor after being elected.)
Richard Coke (D) ....Jan. 15, 1874–Dec. 1, 1876
(Resigned to enter U.S. Senate.)
Richard B. Hubbard (D) .....Dec. 1, 1876–Jan. 21, 1879
Oran M. Roberts (D) ....Jan. 21, 1879–Jan. 16, 1883
John Ireland (D) ....Jan. 16, 1883–Jan. 18, 1887
Lawrence Sullivan Ross (D) .... Jan. 18, 1887–
....Jan. 20, 1891
James Stephen Hogg (D) Jan. 20, 1891–Jan. 15, 1895
Charles A. Culberson (D) Jan. 15, 1895–Jan. 17, 1899
Joseph D. Sayers (D).......Jan. 17, 1899–Jan. 20, 1903
S. W. T. Lanham (D).........Jan. 20, 1903–Jan. 15, 1907
Thos. Mitchell Campbell (D) .... Jan. 15, 1907–
....Jan. 17, 1911
Oscar Branch Colquitt (D) Jan. 17, 1911–Jan. 19, 1915
James E. Ferguson (D)...Jan. 19, 1915–Sept. 25, 1917
*(Impeached in August 1917. Lt. Gov. Hobby served as
acting governor during the impeachment proceedings.
Ferguson was removed from office Sept. 25.)*
William Pettus Hobby (D) Aug. 25, 1917–Jan. 18, 1921
Pat Morris Neff (D) ....Jan. 18, 1921–Jan. 20, 1925
Miriam A. Ferguson (D) ... Jan. 20, 1925–Jan. 17, 1927
Dan Moody (D)..................Jan. 17, 1927–Jan. 20, 1931
Ross S. Sterling (D) .... Jan. 20, 1931–Jan. 17, 1933
Miriam A. Ferguson (D) ... Jan. 17, 1933–Jan. 15, 1935
James V. Allred (D) ....Jan. 15, 1935–Jan. 17, 1939
W. Lee O'Daniel (D) ....Jan. 17, 1939–Aug. 4, 1941
(Resigned to enter U.S. Senate.)
Coke R. Stevenson (D) ......Aug. 4, 1941–Jan. 21, 1947
Beauford H. Jester (D)......Jan. 21, 1947–July 11, 1949
(Died in office. Succeeded by Lt. Gov. Shivers.)
Allan Shivers (D) ....July 11, 1949–Jan. 15, 1957
Price Daniel (D)................Jan. 15, 1957–Jan. 15, 1963
John Connally (D) ....Jan. 15, 1963–Jan. 21, 1969
Preston Smith (D) ....Jan. 21, 1969–Jan. 16, 1973
Dolph Briscoe (D) ....Jan. 16, 1973–Jan. 16, 1979
*(Effective in 1975, the term of office was increased
from 2 to 4 years.)*
William P. Clements (R) ...Jan. 16, 1979–Jan. 18, 1983
Mark White (D) ....Jan. 18, 1983–Jan. 20, 1987
William P. Clements (R) ... Jan. 20, 1987–Jan. 15, 1991
Ann W. Richards (D) ....Jan. 15, 1991–Jan. 17, 1995
George W. Bush (R)........ Jan. 17, 1995–Dec. 21, 2000
(Resigned to become U.S. president.)
Rick Perry (R)..................Dec. 21, 2000–Jan. 20, 2015
Greg Abbott (R)........................ Jan. 20, 2015–present

★ ★ ★ ★ ★ ★ ★

Vice Presidents and Lieutenant Governors

Vice Presidents of the Republic

Lorenzo de Zavala .... Mar. 16, 1836–Oct, 17, 1836
(Provisional.)
Mirabeau B. Lamar .... Oct. 22, 1836–Dec.10, 1838
David G. Burnet .... Dec. 10, 1838–Dec.13, 1841
Edward Burleson ....Dec. 13, 1841–Dec. 9, 1844
Kenneth L. Anderson.......... Dec. 9, 1844–July 3, 1845
(Died in office.)

Lieutenant Governors

Albert C. Horton (D) .... May 2, 1846–Dec. 21, 1847
John A. Greer (D)............ Dec. 21, 1847–Dec. 22, 1851
J. W. Henderson (D) ....Dec. 22, 1851–Nov. 23, 1853
*(Briefly succeeded to governorship when Gov. Bell
resigned to enter U.S. House of Representatives.)*
D. C. Dickson (D) ....Dec. 21, 1853–Dec. 21, 1855
H. R. Runnels (D)............Dec. 21, 1855–Dec. 21, 1857
F. R. Lubbock (D) .... Dec. 21, 1857–Dec. 21, 1859
Edward Clark (I) .... Dec. 21, 1859–Mar. 16, 1861
*(Succeeded Gov. Sam Houston when Houston
refused to take oath to Confederacy.)*
John M. Crockett (D)........... Nov. 7, 1861–Nov. 5, 1863
Fletcher S. Stockdale (D).. Nov. 7, 1863–June 17, 1865
(Fall of Confederacy.)
George W. Jones (D) .... Aug. 9, 1866–July 30, 1867
(Jones was removed by Gen. Philip Sheridan.)
J. W. Flanagan (R) 1869
*(Elected in 1869, Flanagan was appointed U.S. sena-
tor and was never inaugurated as lt. governor.)*
R. B. Hubbard (D) .... Jan. 15, 1873–Dec. 1, 1876
*(Succeeded Gov. Richard Coke when he resigned to
become U.S. senator.)*
J. D. Sayers (D)............... Jan. 21, 1879–Jan. 18, 1881
L. J. Storey (D) .... Jan. 18, 1881–Jan. 16, 1883
Marion Martin (D).............Jan. 16, 1883–Jan. 20, 1885
Barnett Gibbs (D).............Jan. 20, 1885–Jan. 19, 1887
T. B. Wheeler (D) ....Jan. 19, 1887– Jan. 21, 1891
George C. Pendleton (D) ..Jan. 21, 1891–Jan. 17, 1893
M. M. Crane (D) .... Jan. 17, 1893–Jan. 15, 1895
George T. Jester (D) .... Jan. 15, 1895–Jan. 17, 1899
J. N. Browning (D)...........Jan. 17, 1899– Jan. 20, 1903
George D. Neal (D) ....Jan. 20, 1903–Jan. 15, 1907
A. B. Davidson (D) .... Jan. 15, 1907–Jan. 21, 1913
Will H. Mayes (D) .... Jan. 21, 1913–Aug. 14, 1914
(resigned)
William P. Hobby (D) ....Jan. 19, 1915–Aug. 25, 1917

Early Leaders of Texas

The presidents of the Republic of Texas and the state's first Governor, from far left: **David G. Burnet**, provisional president; **Sam Houston**, second and fourth presidents; **Mirabeau B. Lamar**, third president; **Anson Jones**, the Republic's last president; and **J. Pinckney Henderson**, the Lone Star State's first governor.

(Served as acting governor during the impeachment of Gov. Jim Ferguson. Took oath as governor after Ferguson was removed from office Sept. 25.)

W. A. Johnson (D)...........Sept. 29, 1917–Jan. 18, 1921
(Selected as president of the state Senate and acting lt. governor, serving Hobby's unexpired term. He was then elected statewide to the office in 1918.)
Lynch Davidson (D) ....Jan. 18, 1921–Jan. 16, 1923
T. W. Davidson (D)...........Jan. 16, 1923–Jan. 20, 1925
Barry Miller (D).................Jan. 20, 1925–Jan. 20, 1931
Edgar E. Witt (D)..............Jan. 20, 1931–Jan. 15, 1935
Walter Woodul (D)............Jan. 15, 1935–Jan. 17, 1939
Coke R. Stevenson (D)......Jan. 17, 1939–Aug. 4, 1941
(Became governor upon resignation of Gov. W. Lee O'Daniel to become U.S. senator.)
John Lee Smith (D)..........Jan. 19, 1943–Jan. 21, 1947
Allan Shivers (D)...............Jan. 21, 1947–July 11, 1949
(Shivers succeeded to the governorship on death of Gov. Beauford H. Jester.)
Ben Ramsey (D)..............Jan. 16, 1951–Sept. 18, 1961
(Ramsey resigned to become a member of the Texas Railroad Commission.)
Preston Smith (D) ....Jan. 15, 1963–Jan. 21, 1969
Ben Barnes (D) ....Jan. 21, 1969–Jan. 16, 1973
William P. Hobby Jr. (D) ...Jan. 16, 1973–Jan. 15, 1991
Robert D. Bullock (D).......Jan. 15, 1991–Jan. 19, 1999
Rick Perry (R).................Jan. 19, 1999–Dec. 21, 2000
Bill Ratliff (R) .... Dec. 28, 2000–Jan. 14, 2003
(Elected by state Senate when Perry succeeded to governorship.)
David Dewhurst................Jan. 21, 2003–Jan. 20, 2015
Dan Patrick .... Jan. 20, 2015–present

★ ★ ★ ★ ★ ★ ★

Secretaries of State Of the Republic

Raines Yearbook for Texas, 1901, gives the following record of Secretaries of State during the era of the Republic of Texas:

Under David G. Burnet: Samuel P. Carson, James Collingsworth, and W. H. Jack.

Under Sam Houston (first term): Stephen F. Austin, 1836. J. Pinckney Henderson and Dr. Robert A. Irion, 1837–1838.

Under Mirabeau B. Lamar: Bernard Bee appointed Dec. 16, 1838; James Webb appointed Feb. 6, 1839; D. G. Burnet appointed Acting Secretary of State, May 31, 1839; N. Amory appointed Acting Secretary

of State, July 23, 1839; D. G. Burnet appointed Acting Secretary of State, Aug. 5, 1839; Abner S. Lipscomb appointed Secretary of State, Jan. 31, 1840, and resigned Jan. 22, 1841; Joseph Waples appointed Acting Secretary of State, Jan. 23, 1841, and served until Feb. 8, 1841; James S. Mayfield appointed Feb. 8, 1841; Joseph Waples appointed April 30, 1841, and served until May 25, 1841; Samuel A. Roberts appointed May 25, 1841; reappointed Sept. 7, 1841.

Under Sam Houston (second term): E. Lawrence Stickney, Acting Secretary of State until Anson Jones was appointed Dec. 13, 1841. Jones served as Secretary of State throughout this term except during the summer and part of this term of 1842, when Joseph Waples filled the position as Acting Secretary of State.

Under Anson Jones: Ebenezer Allen served from Dec. 10, 1844, until Feb. 5, 1845, when Ashbel Smith became Secretary of State. Allen was again named Acting Secretary of State, March 31, 1845, and later named Secretary of State.

In addition to the above, documents in the Texas State Archives indicate that **Joseph C. Eldredge**, Chief Clerk of the State Department during much of the Republic's existence, signed a number of documents in the absence of the office-holder in the capacity of "Acting Secretary of State."

State Secretaries of State

Charles Mariner .... Feb. 20, 1846–May 4, 1846
David G. Burnet ....May 4, 1846–Jan. 1, 1848
Washington D. Miller...........Jan. 1, 1848–Jan. 2, 1850
James Webb .... Jan. 2, 1850–Nov. 14, 1851
Thomas H. Duval .... Nov. 14, 1851–Dec. 22, 1853
Edward Clark...................... Dec. 22, 1853–Dec. 1857
T. S. Anderson .... Dec. 1857–Dec. 27, 1859
E. W. Cave .... Dec. 27, 1859–Mar. 16, 1861
Bird Holland .... Mar. 16, 1861–Nov. 1861
Charles West............................Nov. 1861–Sept. 1862
Robert J. Townes.................. Sept. 1862–May 2, 1865
Charles R. Pryor .... May 2, 1865–Aug. 1865
James H. Bell ....Aug. 1865–Aug. 1866
John A. Green...........................Aug. 1866–Aug. 1867
D. W. C. Phillips .... Aug. 1867–Jan. 1870
J. P. Newcomb ....Jan. 1, 1870–Jan. 17, 1874
George Clark....................Jan. 17, 1874–Jan. 27, 1874
A. W. DeBerry ....Jan. 27, 1874–Dec. 1, 1876
Isham G. Searcy .... Dec. 1, 1876–Jan. 23, 1879
J. D. Templeton ....Jan. 23, 1879–Jan. 22, 1881
T. H. Bowman...................Jan. 22, 1881–Jan. 18, 1883

J. W. Baines .... Jan. 18, 1883–Jan. 21, 1887
John M. Moore .... Jan. 21, 1887–Jan. 22, 1891
George W. Smith.............. Jan. 22, 1891–Jan. 17, 1895
Allison Mayfield.................. Jan. 17, 1895–Jan. 5, 1897
J. W. Madden .... Jan. 5, 1897–Jan. 18, 1899
D. H. Hardy...................... Jan. 18, 1899–Jan. 19, 1901
John G. Tod......................... Jan. 19, 1901–Jan., 1903
J. R. Curl .... Jan. 1903–April 1905
O. K. Shannon........................... April 1905–Jan. 1907
L. T. Dashiel .... Jan. 1907–Feb. 1908
W. R. Davie .... Feb. 1908–Jan. 1909
W. B. Townsend .... Jan. 1909–Jan. 1911
C. C. McDonald....................... Jan. 1911–Dec. 1912
J. T. Bowman .... Dec. 1912–Jan. 1913
John L. Wortham .... Jan. 1913–June 1913
F. C. Weinert .... June 1913–Nov. 1914
D. A. Gregg .... Nov. 1914–Jan. 1915
John G. McKay .... Jan. 1915–Dec. 1916
C. J. Bartlett .... Dec. 1916–Nov. 1917
George F. Howard...................... Nov. 1917–Nov. 1920
C. D. Mims.............................. Nov. 1920–Jan. 1921
S. L. Staples............................... Jan. 1921–Aug. 1924
J. D. Strickland..................... Sept. 1924–Jan. 1, 1925
Henry Hutchings .... Jan. 1, 1925–Jan. 20, 1925
Mrs. Emma G. Meharg .... Jan. 20, 1925–Jan. 1927
Mrs. Jane Y. McCallum............... Jan. 1927–Jan. 1933
W. W. Heath .... Jan. 1933–Jan. 1935
Gerald C. Mann.................... Jan. 1935–Aug. 31, 1935
R. B. Stanford .... Aug. 31, 1935–Aug. 25, 1936
B. P. Matocha .... Aug. 25, 1936–Jan. 18, 1937
Edward Clark........................ Jan. 18, 1937–Jan. 1939
Tom L. Beauchamp..................... Jan. 1939–Oct. 1939
M. O. Flowers................. Oct. 26, 1939–Feb. 25, 1941
William J. Lawson.............. Feb. 25, 1941–Jan. 1943
Sidney Latham .... Jan. 1943–Feb. 1945
Claude Isbell .... Feb. 1945–Jan. 1947
Paul H. Brown .... Jan. 1947–Jan. 19, 1949
Ben Ramsey...................... Jan. 19, 1949–Feb. 9, 1950
John Ben Shepperd.......... Feb. 9, 1950–April 30, 1952
Jack Ross......................... April 30, 1952–Jan. 9, 1953
Howard A. Carney............. Jan. 9, 1953–Apr. 30, 1954
C. E. Fulgham .... May 1, 1954–Feb. 15, 1955
Al Muldrow .... Feb. 16, 1955–Nov. 1, 1955
Tom Reavley .... Nov. 1, 1955–Jan. 16, 1957
Zollie Steakley................... Jan. 16, 1957–Jan. 2, 1962
P. Frank Lake .... Jan. 2, 1962–Jan. 15, 1963
Crawford C. Martin........... Jan. 15, 1963–Mar. 12, 1966
John L. Hill .... Mar. 12, 1966–Jan. 22, 1968
Roy Barrera...................... Mar. 7, 1968–Jan. 23, 1969
Martin Dies Jr. .... Jan. 23, 1969–Sept. 1, 1971
Robert D. (Bob) Bullock...... Sept. 1, 1971–Jan. 2, 1973
V. Larry Teaver Jr. .... Jan. 2, 1973–Jan. 19, 1973
Mark W. White Jr. .... Jan. 19, 1973–Oct. 27,1977
Steven C. Oaks .... Oct. 27, 1977–Jan. 16, 1979
George W. Strake Jr. .... Jan. 16, 1979–Oct. 6, 1981
David A. Dean .... Oct. 22, 1981–Jan. 18, 1983
John Fainter .... Jan. 18, 1983–July 31, 1984
Myra A. McDaniel .... Sept. 6, 1984–Jan. 26, 1987
Jack Rains...................... Jan. 26, 1987–June 15, 1989
George Bayoud Jr. .... June 19, 1989–Jan. 15, 1991
John Hannah Jr............... Jan. 17, 1991–Mar. 11, 1994
Ronald Kirk .... April 4, 1994–Jan. 10, 1995
Antonio O. "Tony" Garza Jr.Jan. 18, 1995–Dec. 2, 1997
Alberto R. Gonzales .... Dec. 2, 1997–Jan. 10, 1999
Elton Bomer .... Jan. 11, 1999–Dec. 31, 2000
Henry Cuellar .... Jan. 2, 2001–Oct. 5, 2001
Gwyn Shea .... Jan. 2, 2002–Aug. 4, 2003
Geoff Connor .... Sept. 26, 2003–Jan. 1, 2005
J. Roger Williams.................. Jan. 1, 2005–July 1, 2007
Phil Wilson .... July 1, 2007–July 6, 2008
Esperanza (Hope) Andrade
.... July 23, 2008–Nov. 23,2012
John T. Steen Jr. .... Nov. 27, 2012–Jan. 7, 2014

The Capitals of Texas

The Capitals of the six nations that have ruled Texas have been:

SPAIN: Valladolid (before 1551) and Madrid

FRANCE: Paris

MEXICO: Mexico City, D.F.

REPUBLIC OF TEXAS: San Felipe de Austin, Washington-on-the-Brazos, Harrisburg, Galveston Island, Velasco, Columbia, Houston, and Austin

UNITED STATES: Washington, D.C.

CONFEDERATE STATES OF AMERICA: Montgomery, Alabama and Richmond, Virginia

You can learn more about all of the capitals of Texas on the **Texas Almanac website**. Read the full article at:

https://texasalmanac.com/topics/ history/capitals-texas

Nandita Berry...................... Jan. 7, 2014–Jan 21, 2015
Carlos H. Cascos................. Jan 21, 2015–Jan 5, 2017
Rolando B. Pablos.............. Jan 5, 2017–Dec. 17, 2018
David Whitley .... Dec. 17, 2018–May 27, 2019
(Resigned)
Ruth Ruggero Hughs .... Aug. 19, 2019–present

Attorneys General
Of the Republic

David Thomas and Peter W. Grayson
.... Mar. 2–Oct. 22, 1836
J. Pinckney Henderson, Peter W. Grayson,
  John Birdsall, A.S. Thurston..................1836–1838
J.C. Watrous.......................... Dec. 1838–June 1, 1840
Joseph Webb and F.A. Morris 1840–1841
George W. Terrell, Ebenezer Allen............. 1841–1844
Ebenezer Allen..1844–1846

Of the State

Volney E. Howard (D) .... Feb. 21, 1846–May 7, 1846
John W. Harris (D) .... May 7, 1846–Oct. 31, 1849
Henry P. Brewster .... Oct. 31, 1849–Jan. 15, 1850
A. J. Hamilton................... Jan. 15, 1850–Aug. 5, 1850
(The first few attorneys general held office by appointment of the governor. The office was made elective in 1850 by constitutional amendment. Ebenezer Allen was the first elected attorney general.)
Ebenezer Allen................. Aug. 5, 1850–Aug. 2, 1852
Thomas J. Jennings...........Aug. 2, 1852–Aug. 4, 1856
James Willie...................... Aug. 4, 1856–Aug. 2, 1858
Malcolm D. Graham (D)..... Aug. 2, 1858–Aug. 6, 1860
(Confederacy begins)
George M. Flournoy (D).... Aug. 6, 1860–Jan. 15, 1862
N. G. Shelley (D) .... Feb. 3, 1862–Aug. 1, 1864
B. E. Tarver (D) .... Aug. 1, 1864–Dec. 11, 1865
(Reconstruction begins)
Wm. Alexander (Unionist)Dec. 11, 1865–June 25, 1866
W. M. Walton (D)........... June 25, 1866–Aug. 27, 1867
Wm. Alexander (R)........... Aug. 27, 1867–Nov. 5, 1867

Ezekiel B. Turner (I) .... Nov. 5, 1867–July 11, 1870
Wm. Alexander (R)............July 11, 1870–Jan. 27, 1874
(Reconstruction ends)
George Clark (D)...............Jan. 27, 1874–Apr. 25, 1876
H. H. Boone (D)..................Apr. 25, 1876–Nov. 5, 1878
George McCormick.............Nov. 5, 1878–Nov. 2, 1880
J. H. McLeary (D)................Nov. 2, 1880–Nov. 7, 1882
John D. Templeton (D)........ Nov. 7, 1882–Nov. 2, 1886
James S. Hogg (D)..............Nov. 2, 1886–Nov. 4, 1890
C. A. Culberson (D).............Nov. 4, 1890–Nov. 6, 1894
M. M. Crane (D) ....Nov. 6, 1894–Nov. 8, 1898
Thomas S. Smith (D) .... Nov. 8, 1898–Mar. 15,1901
C. K. Bell (D) ....Mar. 20, 1901–Jan. 1904
R. V. Davidson (D) .... Jan. 1904–Dec. 31, 1909
Jewel P. Lightfoot (D).........Jan. 1, 1910–Aug. 31, 1912
James D. Walthall (D) .... Sept. 1, 1912–Jan. 1, 1913
B. F. Looney (D) .... Jan. 1, 1913–Jan., 1919
C. M. Cureton (D) .... Jan. 1919–Dec. 1921
W. A. Keeling (D) .... Dec. 1921–Jan. 1925
Dan Moody (D)...........................Jan. 1925–Jan. 1927
Claude Pollard (D) ....Jan. 1927–Sept. 1929
R. L. Bobbitt (D) .... Sept. 1929–Jan. 1931
(Appointed)
James V. Allred (D) ....Jan. 1931–Jan. 1935
William McCraw (D) ....Jan. 1935–Jan. 1939
Gerald C. Mann (D)......................Jan. 1939–Jan. 1944
(Resigned)
Grover Sellers (D) ....Jan. 1944–Jan. 1947
Price Daniel (D)............................Jan. 1947–Jan. 1953
John Ben Shepperd (D) ....Jan. 1953–Jan. 1, 1957
Will Wilson (D) .... Jan. 1, 1957–Jan. 15, 1963
Waggoner Carr (D).............Jan. 15, 1963–Jan. 1, 1967
Crawford C. Martin (D)......Jan. 1, 1967–Dec. 29, 1972
John Hill (D) .... Jan. 1, 1973–Jan. 16, 1979
Mark White (D) ....Jan. 16, 1979–Jan. 18, 1983
Jim Mattox (D)..................Jan. 18, 1983–Jan. 15, 1991
Dan Morales (D).............. Jan. 15, 1991–Jan. 13, 1999
John Cornyn (R) .... Jan. 13, 1999–Dec. 2, 2002
Greg Abbott (R)................Dec. 2, 2002–Jan. 20, 2015
Ken Paxton (R) .... Jan. 20, 2015–present

★ ★ ★ ★ ★ ★ ★

Treasurers
Of the Republic
Asa Brigham 1838–1840
James W. Simmons.....................................1840–1841
Asa Brigham 1841–1844
Moses Johnson...1844–1846

Of the State
James H. Raymond ....Feb. 24, 1846–Aug. 2, 1858
C.H. Randolph ....Aug. 2, 1858–June 1865
    (Randolph fled to Mexico upon collapse of Confederacy. No exact date is available for his departure from office or for Harris' succession to the post. It is believed Harris took office Oct. 2, 1865.)
Samuel Harris .... Oct. 2, 1865–June 25, 1866
W.M. Royston..................June 25, 1866–Sept. 1, 1867
John Y. Allen .... Sept. 1, 1867–Jan. 1869
George W. Honey ....Jan. 1869–Jan. 1874
    (Honey was removed from office for a short period in 1872 and B. Graham served in his place.)
B. Graham *(short term)* .... beginning May 27, 1872
A. J. Dorn ....Jan. 1874–Jan. 1879
F. R. Lubbock................................Jan. 1879–Jan. 1891
W. B. Wortham...............................Jan. 1891–Jan. 1899
John W. Robbins.........................Jan. 1899–Jan. 1907
Sam Sparks ....Jan. 1907–Jan. 1912
J. M. Edwards .... Jan. 1912–Jan. 1919
John W. Baker ....Jan. 1919–Jan. 1921
G. N. Holton .... July 1921–Nov. 21, 1921

C. V. Terrell...................... Nov. 21, 1921–Aug. 15, 1924
S. L. Staples.................... Aug. 16, 1924–Jan. 15, 1925
W. Gregory Hatcher...........Jan. 16, 1925–Jan. 1, 1931
Charley Lockhart .... Jan. 1, 1931–Oct. 25, 1941
Jesse James .... Oct. 25, 1941–Sept. 29, 1977
Warren G. Harding.............. Oct. 7, 1977–Jan. 3, 1983
Ann Richards ....Jan. 3, 1983–Jan. 2, 1991
Kay Bailey Hutchison...........Jan. 2, 1991–June 1993
Martha Whitehead ....June 1993–Aug. 1996

The office of treasurer was eliminated by constitutional amendment in an election Nov. 7, 1995, effective the last day of August 1996.

★ ★ ★ ★ ★ ★ ★

Railroad Commission of Texas
After the first three names in the following list, each commissioner's name is followed by a surname in parentheses. The name in parentheses is the name of the commissioner whom that commissioner succeeded.

John H. Reagan ....June 10, 1891–Jan. 20, 1903
L. L. Foster..................... June 10, 1891–April 30, 1895
W. P. McLean ....June 10, 1891–Nov. 20, 1894
L. J. Storey (McLean)....... Nov. 21, 1894–Mar. 28,1909
N. A. Stedman (Foster)........ May 1, 1895–Jan. 4, 1897
Allison Mayfield (Stedman)Jan. 5, 1897–Jan. 23, 1923
O. B. Colquitt (Reagan) ....Jan. 21, 1903–Jan. 17, 1911
William D. Williams (Storey)
    .... April 28, 1909–Oct. 1, 1916
John L. Wortham (Colquitt) Jan. 21, 1911–Jan. 1, 1913
Earle B. Mayfield (Wortham)
    ....Jan. 2, 1913–Mar. 1, 1923
Charles Hurdleston (Williams)
    .... Oct. 10, 1916–Dec. 31,1918
Clarence Gilmore (Hurdleston)
    .... Jan. 1, 1919–Jan. 1, 1929
N. A. Nabors (A. Mayfield).Mar. 1, 1923–Jan. 18, 1925
William Splawn (E. Mayfield)
    .... Mar. 1, 1923–Aug. 1, 1924
C. V. Terrell (Splawn) .... Aug. 15, 1924–Jan. 1, 1939
Lon A. Smith (Nabors) ......Jan. 29, 1925–Jan. 1, 1941
Pat M. Neff (Gilmore)...........Jan. 1, 1929–Jan. 1, 1933
Ernest O. Thompson (Neff) .Jan. 1, 1933–Jan. 8, 1965
G. A. (Jerry) Sadler (Terrell)
    .... Jan. 1, 1939–Jan. 1, 1943
Olin Culberson (Smith) ..... Jan. 1, 1941–June 22, 1961
Beauford Jester (Sadler)....Jan. 1, 1943–Jan. 21, 1947
William J. Murray Jr. (Jester)
    ....Jan. 21, 1947–Apr. 10, 1963
Ben Ramsey (Culberson)
    .... Sept. 18, 1961–Dec. 31, 1976
Jim C. Langdon (Murray)
    .... May 28, 1963–Dec. 31, 1977
Byron Tunnell (Thompson)
    ....Jan. 11, 1965–Sept. 15, 1973
Mack Wallace (Tunnell)
    .... Sept. 18, 1973–Sept. 22, 1987
Jon Newton (Ramsey) .... Jan. 10, 1977–Jan. 4, 1979
John H. Poerner (Langdon) .Jan. 2, 1978–Jan. 1, 1981
James E. Nugent (Newton)..Jan. 4, 1979–Jan. 3,1995
Buddy Temple (Poerner)......Jan. 2, 1981–Mar. 2, 1986
Clark Jobe (Temple) .... Mar. 3, 1986–Jan. 5, 1987
John Sharp (Jobe) ....Jan. 6, 1987–Jan. 2, 1991
Kent Hance (Wallace)...... Sept. 23, 1987–Jan. 2, 1991
Robert Krueger (Hance) ....Jan. 3, 1991–Jan. 22, 1993
    (Krueger resigned when Gov. Ann Richards appointed him interim U.S. senator on the resignation of Sen. Lloyd Bentsen.)
Lena Guerrero (Sharp)... Jan. 23, 1991–Sept. 25, 1992
James Wallace (Guerrero)...Oct. 2, 1992–Jan. 4, 1993
Barry Williamson (Wallace) .Jan. 5, 1993–Jan. 4, 1999

Mary Scott Nabers (Krueger)
................................Feb. 9, 1993–Dec. 9, 1994
Carole K. Rylander (Nabers)
................................Dec. 10, 1994–Jan. 4, 1999
Charles Matthews (Nugent)
................................Jan. 3, 1995–Jan. 31, 2005
Antonio Garza (Williamson)
................................Jan. 4, 1999–Nov. 18, 2002
Michael Williams (Rylander)
................................Jan. 4, 1999–Mar. 31, 2011
Victor G. Carrillo (Garza).. Feb. 19, 2003–Jan. 3, 2011
Elizabeth A. Jones (Matthews)
................................Feb. 2, 2005–Feb. 28, 2012
David Porter (Carrillo).......... Jan. 5, 2011–Jan. 2, 2017
Barry T. Smitherman (Williams)
................................July 8, 2011–Jan. 2, 2015
Buddy Garcia (Jones)....... April 16, 2012–Dec. 7, 2012
(Appointed by Gov. Perry.)
Christi Craddick (Garcia)........ Dec. 17, 2012–present
Ryan Sitton (Smitherman).......... Jan 5, 2015–present
Wayne Christian (Porter) ....Jan 9, 2017–present

★ ★ ★ ★ ★ ★ ★

Comptroller of Public Accounts Of the Republic

John H. Money................ Dec. 30, 1835–Jan. 17, 1836
H. C. Hudson.................... Jan. 17, 1836–Oct. 22, 1836
Elisha M. Pease........................ June 1837–Dec. 1837
F. R. Lubbock.............................. Dec. 1837–Jan. 1839
Jas. W. Simmons ....Jan. 15, 1839–Sept. 30, 1840
Jas. B. Shaw .... Sept. 30, 1840–Dec. 24, 1841
F. R. Lubbock....................Dec. 24, 1841–Jan. 1, 1842
Jas. B. Shaw .... Jan. 1, 1842–Jan. 1, 1846

Of the State

Jas. B. Shaw ....Feb. 24, 1846–Aug. 2, 1858
Clement R. Johns ....Aug. 2, 1858–Aug. 1, 1864
Willis L. Robards.............. Aug. 1, 1864–Oct. 12, 1865
Albert H. Latimer..............Oct. 12, 1865–Mar. 27, 1866
Robert H. Taylor............. Mar. 27, 1866–June 25, 1866
Willis L. Robards......... June 25, 1866–Aug. 27, 1867
Morgan C. Hamilton...........Aug. 27, 1867–Jan. 8, 1870
A. Bledsoe..........................Jan. 8, 1870–Jan. 20, 1874
Stephen H. Darden ....Jan. 20, 1874–Nov. 2, 1880
W. M. Brown .... Nov. 2, 1880–Jan. 16, 1883
W. J. Swain ....Jan. 16, 1883–Jan. 18, 1887
John D. McCall.................. Jan. 18, 1887–Jan. 15, 1895
R. W. Finley......................Jan. 15, 1895–Jan. 15, 1901
R. M. Love...........................Jan. 15, 1901–Jan. 1903
J. W. Stephen..............................Jan. 1903–Jan. 1911
W. P. Lane.....................................Jan. 1911–Jan. 1915
H. B. Terrell ....Jan. 1915–Jan. 1920
M. L. Wiginton ....Jan. 1920–Jan. 1921
Lon A. Smith ....Jan. 1921–Jan. 1925
S. H. Terrell ....Jan. 1925–Jan. 1931
Geo. H. Sheppard................ Jan., 1931–Jan. 17, 1949
Robert S. Calvert .... Jan. 17, 1949–Jan., 1975
Robert D. (Bob) Bullock...........Jan. 1975–Jan. 3, 1991
John Sharp........................Jan. 3, 1991–Jan. 2, 1999
Carole Keeton Strayhorn .....Jan. 2, 1999–Jan. 1, 2007
Susan Combs ....Jan. 1, 2007–Jan. 1, 2015
Glenn Hegar .... Jan. 2, 2015–present

★ ★ ★ ★ ★ ★ ★

U.S. Senators from Texas

U.S. Senators were selected by the legislatures of the states until the U.S. Constitution was amended in 1913 to require popular elections. In Texas, the first Senator chosen by the voters in a general election was Charles A. Culberson in 1916. Because of political pressures, however, the rules of the Democratic Party of Texas were changed in 1904 to require that all candidates for office stand before voters in the primary. Consequently, Texas' Senators faced voters in 1906, 1910 and 1912 before the U.S. Constitution was changed.

Following is the succession of Texas representatives in the United States Senate since the annexation of Texas to the Union in 1845:

Houston Succession

Sam Houston (I)................ Feb. 21, 1846–Mar. 4, 1859
John Hemphill (D) .... Mar. 4, 1859–July 11, 1861
(Louis T. Wigfall and W. S. Oldham took their seats in the Confederate Senate, Nov. 16, 1861, and served until the Confederacy collapsed. After that event, the State Legislature on Aug. 21, 1866, elected David G. Burnet and Oran M. Roberts to the U.S. Senate, antici-pating immediate readmission to the Union, but they were not allowed to take their seats.)
Morgan C. Hamilton (R).... Feb. 22, 1870–Mar. 3, 1877
Richard Coke (D) .... Mar. 4, 1877–Mar. 3, 1895
Horace Chilton (D) .... Mar. 3, 1895–Mar. 3, 1901
Joseph W. Bailey (D) ....Mar. 3, 1901–Jan. 8, 1913
(Resigned.)
Rienzi Melville Johnston (D) Jan. 8, 1913–Feb. 3, 1913
(Appointed to fill vacancy.)
Morris Sheppard (D) .... Feb. 13, 1913–Apr. 9, 1941
(Died in office)
Andrew J. Houston (D)........................June 2–26, 1941
(Appointed to fill vacancy; died in office.)
W. Lee O'Daniel (D) .... Aug. 4, 1941–Jan. 3, 1949
Lyndon B. Johnson (D) ......Jan. 3, 1949–Jan. 20, 1961
(Resigned to become U.S. vice president.)
William A. Blakley (D) ..... Jan. 20, 1961–June 15, 1961
(Appointed to fill vacancy.)
John G. Tower (R)........... June 15, 1961–Jan. 21, 1985
Phil Gramm (R) ....Jan. 21, 1985–Dec. 2, 2002
John Cornyn (R) .... Dec. 2, 2002–present

Rusk Succession

Thomas J. Rusk (D) ....Feb 21, 1846–July 29, 1857
(Died in office.)
J. Pinckney Henderson (D) Nov. 9, 1857–June 4, 1858
(Died in office.)
Matthias Ward (D)........... Sept. 29, 1858–Dec. 5, 1859
(Appointed to fill vacancy.)
Louis T. Wigfall (D)............Dec. 5, 1859–Mar. 23, 1861
(Succession was broken by secession. See note above under Houston Succession.)
James W. Flanagan (R).... Feb. 22, 1870–Mar. 3, 1875
Samuel B. Maxey (D).......... Mar. 3, 1875–Mar. 3, 1887
John H. Reagan (D) ....Mar. 3, 1887–June 10, 1891
(Resigned to head Texas Railroad Commission.)
Horace Chilton (D) ....Dec. 7, 1891–Mar. 30,1892
(Appointed to fill vacancy.)
Roger Q. Mills (D) .... Mar. 30, 1892–Mar. 3, 1899
Charles A. Culberson (D) ... Mar. 3, 1899–Mar. 4, 1923
Earle B. Mayfield (D).......... Mar. 4, 1923–Mar. 4, 1929
Tom Connally (D) .... Mar. 4, 1929–Jan. 3, 1953
Price Daniel (D).................Jan. 3, 1953–Jan. 15, 1957
(Resigned to become governor.)
William A. Blakley (D) ....Jan. 15, 1957–Apr. 27, 1957
(Appointed to fill vacancy.)
Ralph W. Yarborough (D).. Apr. 27, 1957–Jan. 12, 1971
Lloyd Bentsen (D) ....Jan. 12, 1971–Jan. 20, 1993
(Resigned to become U.S. Secretary of Treasury.)
Robert Krueger (D) ....Jan. 20, 1993–June 14, 1993
(Appointed to fill vacancy.)
Kay Bailey Hutchison (R)
................................June 14, 1993–Jan. 20, 2013
Ted Cruz (R) .... Jan. 20, 2013–present

★ ★ ★ ★ ★ ★ ★

Commissioners of the General Land Office

Of the Republic

John P. Borden .... Aug. 23, 1837–Dec. 12, 1840
H. W. Raglin .... Dec. 12, 1840–Jan. 4, 1841
Thomas William Ward ...... Jan. 4, 1841–Mar. 20, 1848
(Part of term after annexation.)

Of the State

George W. Smyth .... Mar. 20, 1848–Aug. 4, 1851
Stephen Crosby .... Aug. 4, 1851–Mar. 1, 1858
Francis M. White .... Mar. 1, 1858–Mar. 1, 1862
Stephen Crosby .... Mar. 1, 1862–Sept. 1, 1865
Francis M. White .... Sept. 1, 1865–Aug. 7, 1866
Stephen Crosby .... Aug. 7, 1866–Aug. 27, 1867
Joseph Spence .... Aug. 27, 1867–Jan. 19, 1870
Jacob Kuechler .... Jan. 19, 1870–Jan. 20, 1874
J. J. Groos .... Jan. 20, 1874–June 15, 1878
W. C. Walsh .... July 30, 1878–Jan. 10, 1887
R. M. Hall .... Jan. 10, 1887–Jan. 16, 1891
W. L. McGaughey .... Jan. 16, 1891–Jan. 26, 1895
A. J. Baker .... Jan. 26, 1895–Jan. 16, 1899
George W. Finger .... Jan. 16, 1899–May 4, 1899
Charles Rogan .... May 11, 1899–Jan. 10, 1903
John J. Terrell .... Jan. 10, 1903–Jan. 11, 1909
J. T. Robison .... Jan, 1909–Sept. 11, 1929
J. H. Walker .... Sept. 11, 1929–Jan., 1937
William H. McDonald .... Jan 1937–Jan. 1939
Bascom Giles .... Jan. 1939–Jan. 5, 1955
J. Earl Rudder .... Jan. 5, 1955–Feb. 1, 1958
Bill Allcorn .... Feb. 1, 1958–Jan. 1, 1961
Jerry Sadler .... Jan. 1, 1961–Jan. 1, 1971
Bob Armstrong .... Jan. 1, 1971–Jan. 1, 1983
Garry Mauro .... Jan. 1, 1983–Jan. 7, 1999
David Dewhurst .... Jan. 7, 1999–Jan. 3, 2003
Jerry Patterson .... Jan. 3, 2003–Jan. 2, 2015
George P. Bush .... Jan. 2, 2015–present

★ ★ ★ ★ ★ ★ ★

Speaker of the House

The Speaker of the Texas House of Representatives is the presiding officer of the lower chamber of the Legislature. The official is elected at the beginning of each regular session by a vote of the members of the House.

Of the Republic

Speaker	Term	Congress
Ira Ingram	1836–37	1st
Branch Tanner Archer	1837	2nd
Joseph Rowe	1838	2nd
John M. Hansford	1838–39	3rd
David Spangler Kaufman	1840–41	4th, 5th
Kenneth L. Anderson	1841–42	6th
Nicholas H. Darnell	1842–43	7th
Richardson A. Scurry	1843–44	8th
John M. Lewis	1844–45	9th

Of the State

Speaker, Residence	Term	Leg.
William E. Crump (D), Bellville	1846	1st
John Brown (D), Brownsboro	1846	1st
Edward T. Branch (D), Liberty	1846	1st
William H. Bourland (D), Paris	1846	1st
Stephen W. Perkins (D), Columbia	1846	1st
James W. Henderson (D), Houston	1847–48	2nd
Charles G. Keenan (D), Huntsville	1849–51	3rd
David C. Dickson (D), Anderson	1851–53	4th
Hardin R. Runnels (D), Boston	1853–55	5th
Hamilton P. Bee (D), Laredo	1855–57	6th
William S. Taylor (D), Larissa	1857–58	7th
Matt F. Locke (D), Lafayette	1858–59	7th
Marion DeKalb Taylor (D), Jefferson	1859–61	8th
Constantine W. Buckley (D), Richmond	1861	9th
Nicholas H. Darnell (D), Dallas	1861–62	9th
Constantine W. Buckley (D), Richmond	1863	9th
Marion DeKalb Taylor (D), Jefferson	1863–65	10th
Nathaniel M. Burford (Unionist), Dallas	1866	11th
(Vacant under Congressional Reconstruction and military administration, 1867-1870)		
Ira H. Evans (R), Corpus Christi	1870–71	12th
William H. Sinclair (R), Galveston	1871–73	12th
Marion DeKalb Taylor (D), Jefferson	1873–74	13th
Guy M. Bryan (D), Galveston	1874–76	14th
Thomas R. Bonner (D), Tyler	1876–79	15th
John H. Cochran (D), Dallas	1879–81	16th
George R. Reeves (D), Pottsboro	1881–83	17th
Charles R. Gibson (D), Waxahachie	1883–85	18th
Lafayette L. Foster (D), Groesbeck	1885–87	19th
George C. Pendleton (D), Belton	1887–89	20th
Frank P. Alexander (D), Greenville	1889–91	21st
Robert T. Milner (D), Henderson	1891–93	22nd
John H. Cochran (D), Dallas	1893–95	23rd
Thomas Slater Smith (D), Hillsboro	1895–97	24th
L. Travis Dashiell (D), Jewett	1897–99	25th
J. S. Sherrill (D), Greenville	1899–1901	26th
Robert E. Prince (D), Corsicana	1901–03	27th
Pat M. Neff (D), Waco	1903–05	28th
Francis W. Seabury (D), Rio Grande City	1905–07	29th
Thomas B. Love (D), Lancaster	1907–09	30th
Austin M. Kennedy (D), Waco	1909	31st
(Resigned during 31st session)		
John W. Marshall (D), Whitesboro	1909–11	31st
Sam Rayburn (D), Bonham	1911–13	32nd
Chester H. Terrell (D), San Antonio	1913–15	33rd
John W. Woods (D), Rotan	1915–17	34th
Franklin O. Fuller (D), Coldspring	1917–19	35th
R. Ewing Thomason (D), El Paso	1919–21	36th
Charles G. Thomas (D), Lewisville	1921–23	37th
Richard E. Seagler (D), Palestine	1923–25	38th

R. Lee Satterwhite (D), Amarillo	1925–27	39th
Robert L. Bobbitt (D), Laredo	1927–29	40th
W. S. Barron (D), Bryan	1929–31	41st
Fred H. Minor (D), Denton	1931–33	42nd
Coke R. Stevenson (D), Junction	1933–35	43rd
"	1935–37	44th
Robert W. Calvert (D), Hillsboro	1937–39	45th
R. Emmett Morse (D), Houston	1939–41	46th
Homer L. Leonard (D), McAllen	1941–43	47th
Price Daniel (D), Liberty	1943–45	48th
Claud H. Gilmer (D), Rocksprings	1945–47	49th
William O. Reed (D), Dallas	1947–49	50th
Durwood Manford (D), Smiley	1949–51	51st
Reuben Senterfitt (D), San Saba	1951–53	52nd
"	1953–55	53rd
Jim T. Lindsey (D), Texarkana	1955–57	54th
Waggoner Carr (D), Lubbock	1957–59	55th
"	1959–61	56th
James A. Turman (D), Gober	1961–63	57th
Byron M. Tunnell (D), Tyler	1963–65	58th
Ben Barnes (D), De Leon	1965–67	59th
"	1967–69	60th
Gus F. Mutscher (D), Brenham	1969–71	61st
"	1971–72	62nd
(Resigned during 62nd session)		
Rayford Price (D), Palestine	1972–73	62nd
Price Daniel Jr. (D), Liberty	1973–75	63rd
Bill Clayton (D), Springlake	1975–77	64th
"	1977–79	65th
"	1979–81	66th
"	1981–83	67th
Gib Lewis (D), Fort Worth	1983–85	68th
"	1985–87	69th
"	1987–89	70th
"	1989–91	71st
"	1991–93	72nd
Pete Laney (D), Hale Center	1993–95	73rd
"	1995–97	74th
"	1997–99	75th
"	1999–2001	76th
"	2001–03	77th
Tom Craddick (R), Midland	2003–05	78th
"	2005–07	79th
"	2007–09	80th
Joe Straus (R), San Antonio	2009–11	81st
"	2011–13	82nd
"	2013–15	83rd
"	2015–17	84th
"	2017–19	85th
Dennis Bonnen (R), Angleton	2019–present	86th

★ ★ ★ ★ ★ ★ ★

Chief Justice of the Supreme Court Republic of Texas

James Collinsworth	Dec. 16, 1836–July 23, 1838
John Birdsall	Nov. 19–Dec. 12, 1838
(Senate refused to confirm)	

Thomas J. Rusk	Dec. 12, 1838–Dec. 5, 1840
John Hemphill	Dec. 5, 1840–Dec. 29, 1845

Under Constitutions of 1845 and 1861

John Hemphill	Mar. 2, 1846–Oct. 10, 1858
Royall T. Wheeler	Oct. 11, 1858–April 1864
Oran M. Roberts	Nov. 1, 1864–June 30, 1866

Under Constitution of 1866 (Presidential Reconstruction)

George F. Moore	Aug. 16, 1866–Sept. 10, 1867

(Removed under Congressional Reconstruction by military authorities who appointed members of the next court.)

Under Constitution of 1866 (Congressional Reconstruction)

Amos Morrill	Sept. 10, 1867–July 5, 1870

Under Constitution of 1869

Lemuel D. Evans	July 5, 1870–Aug. 31, 1873
Wesley Ogden	Aug. 31, 1873–Jan. 29, 1874
Oran M. Roberts	Jan. 29, 1874–Apr. 18, 1876

Under Constitution of 1876

Oran M. Roberts	Apr. 18, 1876–Oct. 1, 1878
George F. Moore	Nov. 5, 1878–Nov. 1, 1881
Robert S. Gould	Nov. 1, 1881–Dec. 23, 1882
Asa H. Willie	Dec. 23, 1882–Mar. 3, 1888
John W. Stayton	Mar. 3, 1888–July 5, 1894
Reuben R. Gaines	July 10, 1894–Jan. 5, 1911
Thomas J. Brown	Jan. 7, 1911–May 26, 1915
Nelson Phillips	June 1, 1915–Nov. 16, 1921
C. M. Cureton	Dec. 2, 1921–Apr. 8, 1940
Hortense Sparks Ward	Jan. 8, 1925–May 23, 1925

(Mrs. Ward headed a special Supreme Court to hear one case in 1925.)

W. F. Moore	Apr. 17, 1940–Jan. 1, 1941
James P. Alexander	Jan. 1, 1941–Jan. 1, 1948
J. E. Hickman	Jan. 5, 1948–Jan. 3, 1961
Robert W. Calvert	Jan. 3, 1961–Oct. 4, 1972
Joe R. Greenhill	Oct. 4, 1972–Oct. 25, 1982
Jack Pope	Nov. 29, 1982–Jan. 5, 1985
John L. Hill Jr.	Jan. 5, 1985–Jan. 4, 1988
Thomas R. Phillips	Jan. 4, 1988–Sept. 3 2004
Wallace B. Jefferson	Sept. 14, 2004–Oct. 1, 2013
Nathan L. Hecht	Oct. 1, 2013–present

★ ★ ★ ★ ★ ★ ★

Presiding Judges, Court of Appeals (1876–1891) and Court of Criminal Appeals (1891–present)

Mat D. Ector	May 6, 1876–Oct. 29, 1879
John P. White	Nov. 9, 1879–Apr. 26, 1892
James M. Hurt	May 4, 1892–Dec. 31, 1898
W. L. Davidson	Jan. 2, 1899–June 27, 1913
A. C. Prendergast	June 27, 1913–Dec. 31, 1916
W. L. Davidson	Jan. 1, 1917–Jan. 25, 1921
Wright C. Morrow	Feb. 8, 1921–Oct. 16, 1939
Frank Lee Hawkins	Oct. 16, 1939–Jan. 2, 1951
Harry N. Graves	Jan. 2, 1951–Dec. 31, 1954
W. A. Morrison	Jan. 1, 1955–Jan. 2, 1961
Kenneth K. Woodley	Jan. 3, 1961–Jan. 4, 1965
W. T. McDonald	Jan. 4, 1965–June 25, 1966
W. A. Morrison	June 25, 1966–Jan. 1, 1967
Kenneth K. Woodley	Jan. 1, 1967–Jan. 1, 1971
John F. Onion Jr.	Jan. 1, 1971–Jan. 1, 1989

Michael J. McCormick ....Jan. 1, 1989–Jan. 1, 2001
Sharon Keller ....Jan. 1, 2001–present

★ ★ ★ ★ ★ ★ ★

Administrators of Public Education, Superintendents of Public Instruction

Pryor Lea........................Nov. 10, 1866–Sept. 12, 1867
Edwin M. Wheelock ....Sept. 12, 1867–May 6, 1871
Jacob C. DeGress............. May 6, 1871–Jan. 20, 1874
O. H. Hollingsworth............Jan. 20, 1874–May 6, 1884
B. M. Baker ....May 6, 1884–Jan. 18, 1887
O. H. Cooper..................... Jan 18, 1887–Sept. 1, 1890
H. C. Pritchett.................Sept. 1, 1890–Sept. 15, 1891
J. M. Carlisle .... Sept. 15, 1891–Jan. 10, 1899
J. S. Kendall ....Jan. 10, 1899–July 2, 1901
Arthur Lefevre .... July 2, 1901–Jan. 12, 1905
R. B. Cousins ....Jan. 12, 1905–Jan. 1, 1910
F. M. Bralley ....Jan. 1, 1910–Sept. 1, 1913
W. F. Doughty.....................Sept. 1, 1913–Jan. 1, 1919
Annie Webb Blanton ....Jan. 1, 1919–Jan. 16, 1923
S. M. N. Marrs.................Jan. 16, 1923–April 28, 1932
C. N. Shaver..................... April 28, 1932–Oct. 1, 1932
L. W. Rogers ....Oct. 1, 1932–Jan. 16, 1933
L. A. Woods.............................Jan. 16, 1933–1951

The office of State Superintendent of Public Instruction was abolished by the **Gilmer-Aikin Laws of 1949** and the office of Commissioner of Education was created. The Commissioner is appointed by the State Board of Education, (also created by the Gilmer-Aikin Laws) the members of which are elected by the people.

State Commissioner of Education

J. W. Edgar........................May 31, 1951–June 30, 1974
Marlin L. Brockette.............July 1, 1974–Sept. 1, 1979
Alton O. Bowen .... Sept. 1, 1979–June 1, 1981
Raymon Bynum .... June 1, 1981–Oct. 31, 1984
W. N. Kirby ....April 13, 1985–July 1, 1991
Lionel R. Meno.................... July 1, 1991–Mar. 1, 1995
Michael A. Moses ....Mar. 9, 1995–Aug. 18, 1999
Jim Nelson ....Aug. 18, 1999–Mar. 25, 2002
Felipe Alanis ....Mar. 25, 2002–July 31, 2003
Shirley J. Neeley................Jan. 12, 2004–July 1, 2007
Robert Scott.........................July 1, 2007–July 2, 2012
Michael Williams.............. Sept. 1, 2012–Dec. 31, 2015
Mike Morath ....Jan. 1, 2017–present ☆

Cecilia Abbott.

Photo courtesy of the Office of the First Lady.

First Ladies of Texas

Martha Evans Gindratt Wood 1847–1849
Bell Administration.................................. 1849–1853
(Gov. Peter Hansbrough Bell was not married while in office.)
Lucadia Christiana Niles Pease 1853–57; 1867–69
Runnels Administration 1857–1859
(Gov. Hardin R. Runnels never married.)
Margaret Moffette Lea Houston 1859–1861
Martha Evans Clark 1861
Adele Barron Lubbock............................ 1861–1863
Susie Ellen Taylor Murrah 1863–1865
Mary Jane Bowen Hamilton 1865–1866
Annie Rattan Throckmorton 1866–1867
Ann Elizabeth Britton Davis..................1870–1874
Mary Home Coke...................................1874–1876
Janie Roberts Hubbard 1876–1879
Frances Wickliff Edwards Roberts........ 1879–1883
Anne Maria Penn Ireland...................... 1883–1887
Elizabeth Dorothy Tinsley Ross 1887–1891
Sarah Stinson Hogg............................... 1891–1895
Sally Harrison Culberson....................... 1895–1899
Orlene Walton Sayers............................ 1899–1903
Sarah Beona Meng Lanham.................. 1903–1907
Fannie Brunner Campbell......................1907–1911
Alice Fuller Murrell Colquitt 1911–1915
Miriam A. Wallace Ferguson.................1915–1917
(Miriam A. Wallace Ferguson was Mistress of the Mansion while her husband, James E. Ferguson, was governor, 1915–1917. She served as both Governor and Mistress of the Mansion, 1925–1927 and 1933–1935.)
Willie Cooper Hobby...............................1917–1921
Myrtle Mainer Neff 1921–1925
Mildred Paxton Moody............................1927–1931
Maud Gage Sterling............................... 1931–1933
Jo Betsy Miller Allred 1935–1939
Merle Estella Butcher O'Daniel 1939–1941
Fay Wright Stevenson.............................1941–1942
(Died in the Governor's Mansion on Jan. 3, 1942.)
Edith Will Scott Stevenson 1942–1946
(Mother of Gov. Coke R. Stevenson and Mistress of the Mansion upon the death of the governor's wife.)
Mabel Buchanan Jester........................ 1946–1949
Marialice Shary Shivers........................ 1949–1957
Jean Houston Baldwin Daniel 1957–1963
Idanell Brill Connally............................. 1963–1969
Ima Mae Smith.....................................1969–1973
Betty Jane Slaughter Briscoe............... 1973–1979
Rita Crocker Bass Clements 1979–1983
Linda Gale Thompson White................ 1983–1987
Rita Crocker Bass Clements 1987–1991
Richards Administration 1991–1995
(Gov. Ann Richards was not married while in office.)
Laura Welch Bush.................................1995–2000
Anita Thigpen Perry..............................2000–2015
Cecilia Abbott..........................2015–present

State Government

Texas state government is divided into executive, legislative, and judicial branches under the Texas Constitution adopted in 1876.

The chief executive is the Governor, whose term is for four years. Other elected state officials with executive responsibilities include the Lieutenant Governor, Attorney General, Comptroller of Public Accounts, Commissioner of the General Land Office, and Commissioner of Agriculture. The terms of those officials are also four years.

The Secretary of State and the Commissioner of Education are appointed by the Governor.

Except for making numerous appointments and calling special sessions of the Legislature, the Governor's powers are limited in comparison with those in most states.

The Governor's office welcomes comments and concerns, which are relayed to government officials who may offer assistance. **Send a message through the web-form at:**

https://gov.texas.gov/contact
Or call the **Citizen's Opinion Hotline:**
1 (800) 252-9600

State Government Income and Expenditures

Taxes are the state government's primary source of income. On this and the following pages are summaries of state income and expenditures, percent change from previous year, tax collections, tax revenue by type of tax, a summary of the state budgets for the 2018–2019 and 2020–2021 bienniums, Texas Lottery income and expenditures, and the amount of federal payments to state agencies. **Totals may not sum due to rounding.**

State Revenues by Source and Expenditures by Function
Amounts (in Millions) and Percent Change from Previous Year

Revenues by Source	2018	%	2017	%	2016	%	2015	%	2014	%
Tax Collections	$ 55,585	12.0	$ 49,643	2.4	$ 48,476	(6.2)	$ 51,683	1.4	$ 50,993	672.1
Federal Income	39,618	3.3	38,366	(2.8)	39,474	7.6	36,700	7.1	34,266	5.3
Licenses, Fees, Permits, Fines, and Penalties	6,477	3.5	6,258	2.1	6,128	1.5	6,039	2.1	5,914	0.9
State Health Service Fees and Rebates	7,599	13.4	6,702	201.9	8,071	32.8	6,075	32.6	4,581	15.2
Net Lottery Proceeds	2,229	8.5	2,053	80.2	2,220	17.2	1,894	0.8	1,878	(0.8)
Land Income	2,061	21.6	1,694	48.7	1,140	(26.4)	1,548	(16.9)	1,863	40.6
Interest and Investment Income	1,849	9.3	1,691	24.1	1,362	(2.2)	1,394	(4.8)	1,463	23.7
Settlements of Claims	544	3.2	528	(19.1)	652	20.5	541	(5.9)	575	(5.7)
Escheated Estates	636	(35.0)	979	78.5	548	0.0	548	19.2	460	(47.4)
Sales of Goods and Services	285	(7.5)	308	5.2	293	(36.1)	429	63.4	262	16.1
Other Revenues	3,282	10.4	2,973	1.9	2,918	13.2	2,577	(4.1)	2,687	(3.4)
Total Net Revenues	**$ 120,166**	**8.1**	**$ 111,195**	**(0.1)**	**$ 111,280**	**1.7**	**$ 109,428**	**4.3**	**$ 104,942**	**6.0**
Expenditures by Function	**2018**	**%**	**2017**	**%**	**2016**	**%**	**2015**	**%**	**2014**	**%**
Executive	$ 2,883	3.6	$ 2,783	7.1	$ 2,599	5.5	$ 2,463	3.2	$ 2,386	3.6
Legislative	139	(7.3)	150	8.2	138	(2.5)	142	10.1	129	(4.7)
Judicial	362	4.8	346	3.6	333	5.0	317	0.8	315	16.7
General Government Total	3,384	3.2	3,279	6.8	3,071	5.1	2,923	3.3	2,831	4.5
Education	36,783	3.6	35,505	(1.3)	35,964	3.4	34,790	6.2	32,760	3.9
Employee Benefits	4,760	0.1	4,755	5.6	4,502	11.2	4,050	6.1	3,816	9.7
Health and Human Services	50,421	2.7	49,075	(3.3)	50,734	9.6	46,300	11.0	41,701	7.7
Public Safety and Corrections	5,375	9.1	4,928	2.0	4,829	5.8	4,564	4.7	4,360	1.5
Transportation	9,952	(3.0)	10,261	6.8	9,608	12.9	8,507	(3.8)	8,841	16.3
Natural Resources/ Recreational Services	2,746	34.2	2,046	(28.2)	2,847	9.5	2,601	11.0	2,342	1.7
Regulatory Agencies	312	(10.7)	350	(42.8)	611	26.4	483	(21.2)	614	71.7
Lottery Winnings Paid*	628	12.7	557	(17.2)	672	21.4	554	(8.1)	603	(8.8)
Debt Service – Interest	1,593	26.8	1,256	11.4	1,127	(4.2)	1,178	(8.9)	1,293	(3.1)
Capital Outlay	599	(2.4)	614	2.4	599	44.7	414	(16.3)	495	(11.1)
Total Net Expenditures	**$ 116,554**	**3.5**	**$ 112,625**	**(1.7)**	**$ 114,570**	**7.7**	**$ 106,366**	**6.7**	**$ 99,655**	**6.5**

* Does not include payments made by retailers.
All amounts rounded. Revenue and expenditures exclude trust funds. Fiscal years end August 31.

Source: 2018 State of Texas Annual Cash Report, Revenue and Expenditures of State Funds for the Year Ending August 31, 2018, Comptroller of Public Accounts' Office.

Governor Greg Abbott
P.O. Box 12428
Austin 78711
(512) 463-2000
gov.texas.gov
Salary: $153,750

Lt. Governor Dan Patrick
P.O. Box 12068
Austin 78711
(512) 463-0001
www.ltgov.state.tx.us
Salary: Same as Senator when serving as President of the Senate, same as Governor when serving as Governor.

Attorney General
Ken Paxton
P.O. Box 12548
Austin 78711
(512) 463-2100
www.oag.state.tx.us
Salary: $153,750

Comptroller of Public
Accounts Glenn Hegar
P.O. Box 13528
Austin 78711
(512) 463-4600
www.window.state.tx.us
Salary: $153,750

Texas Land Commissioner
George P. Bush
P.O. Box 12873
Austin 78711
(512) 463-5256
www.glo.texas.gov
Salary: $140,938

Agriculture Commissioner
Sidney C. Miller
P.O. Box 12847
Austin 78711
(512) 463-7476
www.texasagriculture.gov
Salary: $140,938

Secretary of State
Ruth Ruggero Hughs
P.O. Box 12697
Austin 78711
(512) 463-5770
www.sos.state.tx.us
Salary: $132,924

Education Commissioner
Michael H. Morath
1701 N. Congress Ave.
Austin 78701
(512) 463-8985
www.tea.state.tx.us
Salary: $220,375

State Government Budget Summary, 2020–2021 Biennium

Source: Legislative Budget Board; www.lbb.state.tx.us.

The Legislative Budget Board's (LBB) baseline appropriations for state government operations for the 2020–2021 biennium total $250.7 billion from All Funds functions of state government. The funding is a $14.9 billion, or 6.3 percent, increase from the 2018–2019 biennial level of $235.8 billion.

General Revenue Funds, including funds dedicated within the General Revenue Fund, total $118.9 billion for the 2020–2021 biennium, an increase of $10.4 billion, or 9.5 percent, from the adjusted 2018–2019 biennial spending level of $108.5 billion.

The LBB recommended appropriations for the 2020–2021 biennium are within the Comptroller's 2018–2019 Biennial Revenue Estimate.

Article (Governmental Division)		Estimated/ Budgeted 2018–2019*	2020–2021 Budget	Biennial Change	Percentage Change
Art. I:	General Government	$ 7,503.3	$ 7,430.0	$ (73.3)	(1.0)
Art. II:	Health and Human Services	83,584.2	84,368.7	784.5	0.9
Art. III:	Agencies of Education**	81,229.0	94,525.9	13,296.8	16.4
	Public Education**	60,492.7	72,673.1	12,180.3	20.1
	Higher Education	20,736.3	21,852.8	1,116.5	5.4
Art. IV:	The Judiciary	857.1	892.3	35.3	4.1
Art. V:	Public Safety & Criminal Justice	18,378.5	16,040.3	(2,338.3)	(12.7)
Art. VI:	Natural Resources	6.566.0	9,013.0	2,447.1	37.3
Art. VII:	Business & Economic Dev.	36,587.5	37,057.1	469.6	1.3
Art. VIII:	Regulatory	671.7	647.4	(24.3)	(3.6)
Art. IX:	General Provisions**	0.0	285.3	285.3	—
Art. X:	The Legislature	392.8	392.1	(0.8)	(0.2)
	Total, All Articles	**$ 235,770.2**	**$ 250,652.1**	**$ 14,882.0**	**6.3**
	Amount of Tax Relief			(4,980.0)	
	Growth Excluding Property Tax Relief			**$ 9,902.0**	**4.2**

All figures in millions.
Notes: Excludes interagency contracts. Biennial change and percentage change are calculated on
    actual amounts before rounding. Therefore, figure totals may not sum due to rounding.
* Amounts estimated or budgeted for the 2018–19 biennium include supplemental spending adjustments in
    Article II for Medicaid and foster care, but do not include adjustments from Senate Bill 500.
**Contingent funding of $11.5 billion for House Bill 3 has been moved from Article IX to
    Article III, Public Education, for the purposes of this comparison.
    Source: Summary of Conference Committee Report For House Bill 1: Appropriations for the 2020–21 Biennium May 2019.

State Tax Collections 2002–2018

FY	State Tax Collections (in millions)	Resident Tax Population	Per Capita Tax Collections	Taxes as % of Personal Income
2018	$ 55,584.8	28,668,600	$ 1,939	4.0
2017	$ 49,643.4	28,255,300	$ 1,757	3.8
2016	$ 48,476.2	27,845,500	$ 1,741	3.8
2015	$ 51,683.1	27,389,200	$ 1,887	4.0
2014	$ 50,992.6	26,788,600	$ 1,896	4.3
2013	$ 47,781.0	26,399,510	$ 1,810	4.2
2012	$ 44,079.1	26,005,770	$ 1,695	4.0
2011	$ 38,856.2	25,592,790	$ 1,518	3.8
2010	$ 35,368.9	25,191,450	$ 1,404	3.7
2009	$ 37,822.5	24,737,000	$ 1,529	4.1
2008	$ 41,357.9	24,250,000	$ 1,705	4.3
2007	$ 36,955.6	23,778,000	$ 1,554	4.3
2006	$ 33,544.5	23,339,000	$ 1,437	4.1
2005	$ 29,838.3	22,808,000	$ 1,308	4.0
2004	$ 27,913.0	22,409,000	$ 1,246	4.1
2003	$ 26,126.7	22,052,000	$ 1,185	4.1
2002	$ 26,279.1	21,673,000	$ 1,213	4.2

Sources: 2018 State of Texas Annual Cash Report;
historic data collected from older reports.

Tax Revenues, 2017–2018

Type of Tax	FY 2017	%	FY 2018	%
Sales	$ 28,900.0	58.2	$ 31,937.2	57.5
Motor Vehicle Sales and Rentals*	4,532.3	9.1	4,973.4	8.9
Motor Fuels	3,583.7	7.2	3,675.0	6.6
Franchise	3,242.2	6.5	3,685.9	6.6
Insurance	2,376.1	4.8	2,508.4	4.5
Natural Gas Production	982.8	2.0	1,431.1	2.6
Cigarette & Tobacco	1,522.8	3.1	1,320.5	2.4
Alcoholic Beverages	1,217.7	2.5	1,292.0	2.3
Oil Production	2,107.3	4.2	3,391.5	6.1
Utility	439.1	0.9	452.4	0.8
Hotel	530.7	1.1	601.2	1.1
Other Taxes	208.6	0.4	315.9	0.6
Totals	**$ 49,643.4**	**100.0**	**$ 55,584.8**	**100.0**

*Includes tax on manufactured housing sales.
Source: 2018 State of Texas Annual Cash Report.

Federal Revenue by Agency

Source: 2018 State of Texas Annual Cash Report

Texas received $39.6 billion in federal funds during fiscal 2018, a increase of $1.3 billion, or 3.3 percent from fiscal 2017. Federal funds accounted for 33.0 percent of total net revenue, the second-largest source of revenue in fiscal 2018.

	2015	2016	2017	2018
Health and Human Services	$ 23,487.2	$ 25,347.3	$ 24,418.8	$ 25,483.4
Texas Education Agency	4,983.8	5,047.1	5,074.6	5,168.8
Texas Dept. of Transportation	3,113.9	3,961.2	4,250.5	3,875.2
Texas Workforce Commission	936.4	964.7	1,235.2	1,296.9
Texas Department of Public Safety	307.9	312.6	251.0	957.2
Dept. of Agriculture	540.4	582.4	580.6	611.3
Dept. of Family and Protective Services	421.2	417.1	447.5	446.3
Dept. of State Health Services	961.7	987.8	865.8	402.9
General Land Office	633.5	454.8	287.9	341.0
All other Agencies	1,315.0	1,398.7	953.7	1,035.5
Total	$ **36,701.0**	$ **39,473.8**	$ **38,365.6**	$ **39,618.6**

Totals may not sum due to rounding. All figures in millions.

Texas Lottery

Source: Texas Lottery Commission; www.txlottery.org/

The State Lottery Act was passed by the Texas Legislature in July 1991. Texas voters approved a constitutional amendment authorizing a state lottery in an election on Nov. 5, 1991, by a vote of 1,326,154 to 728,994. Since the first ticket was sold on May 29, 1992, the Texas Lottery® has generated more than $95 billion in total sales and more than $28 billion in revenue for the state. More than $61 billion in prizes have been distributed to players through June 2019.

Since 1997, the Texas Lottery has contributed more than $23 billion to the Foundation School Fund, which supports public education. Before September 1997, revenues were only deposited in the General Revenue Fund.

As authorized by the state Legislature, certain Texas Lottery revenues have been earmarked to benefit state programs, including the Fund for Veterans Assistance, which is administered by the Texas Veterans Commission. Sales and unclaimed prizes from the veterans' designated scratch-off games have totaled $117.6 million since 2010.

Other Texas Lottery funds, such as unclaimed prizes, contribute to other causes and programs as authorized by the Texas Legislature.

Distribution of Texas Lottery proceeds for fiscal year 2018:

- 62.5 percent to prizes paid
- 25.4 percent to the Foundation School Fund
- 5.0 percent to retailer commissions
- 3.7 percent for lottery administration
- 0.3 percent to the Texas Veterans Commission. ☆

Texas Lottery Financial Data

Start-up to Aug. 31, 2018. All amounts in millions.

Period	Sales	Value of Prizes Won	Retailer Comm- issions	Revenue to State of Texas*
Start up – FY 1992	$ 591.6	$ 268.9	$ 29.6	$ 250.0
FY 1993	1,856.1	981.7	92.8	656.8
FY 1994	2,760.2	1,528.7	138.0	927.7
FY 1995	3,036.5	1,689.3	151.8	1,015.0
FY 1996	3,432.3	1,951.1	171.7	1,098.3
FY 1997	3,745.5	2,151.7	187.4	1,182.8
FY 1998	3,090.0	1,648.1	154.6	1,097.8
FY 1999	2,571.6	1,329.0	128.8	953.4
FY 2000	2,657.3	1,508.8	133.0	862.8
FY 2001	2,825.3	1,643.2	141.3	864.0
FY 2002	2,966.3	1,715.4	148.4	928.9
FY 2003	3,130.7	1,845.2	156.6	949.1
FY 2004	3,487.9	2,068.6	174.4	1,051.0
FY 2005	3,662.5	2,228.0	183.2	1,070.3
FY 2006	3,774.7	2,310.6	188.8	1,090.3
FY 2007	3,774.2	2,315.3	188.8	1,093.0
FY 2008	3,671.5	2,281.1	183.8	1,034.9
FY 2009	3,720.1	2,299.8	186.1	1,062.2
FY 2010	3,738.4	2,300.2	187.3	1,063.1
FY 2011	3,811.3	2,387.2	190.8	1,023.8
FY 2012	4,190.8	2,632.6	209.8	1,155.5
FY 2013	4,376.3	2,767.4	218.9	1,214.1
FY 2014	4,384.6	2,741.2	219.5	1,220.7
FY 2015	4,529.7	2,858.3	226.7	1,242.7
FY 2016	5,067.5	3,186.4	253.5	1,392.3
FY 2017	5,077.5	3,257.4	253.9	1,334.0
FY 2018	5,626.8	3,666.1	281.5	1,450.5
Totals	$ **95,557.1**	$ **57,561.3**	$ **4,781.0**	$ **28,285.0**

*Revenue to the state presented on an accrual basis.

Help Support the Texas Almanac. Adopt a Town or County at:

GreatTexasLandRush.com

Senators Hinojosa, Flores, Rodríguez, and Nelson discussing legislation. Photo by Senate Media.

Texas Legislature

The Texas Legislature has **181 members: 31 in the Senate** and **150 in the House of Representatives**. Regular sessions convene on the second Tuesday of January in odd-numbered years, but the governor may call special sessions. Article III of the Texas Constitution deals with the legislative branch. On the web: **capitol.texas.gov**

The following lists are of members of the **86th Legislature**, which convened for its Regular Session on Jan. 8, 2019, and adjourned on May 27, 2019. The **87th Legislature** is scheduled to convene on Jan. 12, 2021, and adjourn May 31, 2021.

State Senate

Thirty-one members of the State Senate are elected to four-year, overlapping terms. Salary: The salary of all members of the Legislature, both Senators and Representatives, is $7,200 per year and $124 per diem during legislative sessions; mileage allowance at same rate provided by law for state employees. The per diem payment applies during each regular and special session of the Legislature.

Senatorial Districts include one or more whole counties; some counties have more than one Senator.

The **address of Senators** is Texas Senate, P.O. Box 12068, Austin 78711-2068; phone (512) 463-0200; Fax: (512) 463-0326. On the web: **senate.texas.gov**.

President of the Senate: Lt. Gov. Dan Patrick; **President Pro Tempore**: Kel Seliger; **Secretary of the Senate**: Patsy Spaw; **Sergeant-at-Arms**: Rick DeLeon.

Texas State Senators

District, Member, Party-Hometown, Occupation

1. Bryan Hughes, R-Mineola; attorney.
2. Bob Hall, R-Edgewood; retired military.
3. Robert Nichols, R-Jacksonville; engineer.
4. Brandon Creighton, R-Conroe; attorney.
5. Charles Schwertner, R-Georgetown; surgeon.
6. Carol Alvarado, D-Houston; small-business owner.
7. Paul Bettencourt, R-Houston; tax advisor.
8. Angela Paxton, R-McKinney; consultant, former educator.
9. Kelly G. Hancock, R-North Richland Hills; business owner.
10. Beverly Powell, D-Burleson; education advocate.
11. Larry Taylor, R-Friendswood; insurance agent.
12. Jane Nelson, R-Flower Mound; businesswoman.
13. Borris L. Miles, D-Houston; insurance and real estate developer.
14. Kirk Watson, D-Austin; attorney.
15. John Whitmire, D-Houston; attorney.
16. Nathan Johnson, D-Dallas; attorney.

17. Joan Huffman, R-Houston; attorney.
18. Lois W. Kolkhorst, R-Brenham, business owner.
19. Pete Flores, R-Pleasanton; retired game warden.
20. Juan (Chuy) Hinojosa, D-McAllen; attorney.
21. Judith Zaffirini, D-Laredo; communications specialist, former educator.
22. Brian Birdwell, R-Granbury; retired military.
23. Royce West, D-Dallas; attorney.
24. Dawn Buckingham, R-Lakeway; physician.
25. Donna Campbell, R-New Braunfels; physician.
26. José Menéndez, D-San Antonio; businessman.
27. Eddie Lucio Jr., D-Brownsville; advertising executive.
28. Charles Perry, R-Lubbock; certified public accountant.
29. José R. Rodríguez, D-El Paso; former El Paso County attorney.
30. Pat Fallon, R-Prosper; business owner.
31. Kel Seliger, R-Amarillo; business owner.

House of Representatives

This is a list of the 150 members of the House of Representatives in the 86th Legislature. They were elected for two-year terms from the districts shown below. Representatives and senators receive the same salary.

The **address of all Representatives** is House of Representatives, P.O. Box 2910, Austin, 78768-2910; phone: (512) 463-1000; Fax: (512) 463-5896. On the web: **house. texas.gov**

Speaker, Dennis Bonnen (R-Lake Jackson). **Speaker Pro Tempore**, Joe Moody (R-El Paso). **Chief Clerk**, Robert Haney. **Sergeant-at-Arms**, David Sauceda.

Texas State Representatives

District, Member, Party-Hometown, Occupation

1. Gary VanDeaver, R-New Boston; educator, retired.
2. Dan Flynn, R-Van; rancher, business.
3. Cecil Bell, Jr., R-Magnolia; contractor.
4. Keith Bell, R-Forney; electrical contractor.
5. Cole Hefner, R-Mount Pleasant; insurance agent.
6. Matt Schaefer, R-Tyler; attorney.
7. Jay Dean, R-Longview; self-employed.
8. Cody Harris, R-Palestine; ranch broker.
9. Chris Paddie, R-Marshall; general manager.
10. John Wray, R-Waxahachie; lawyer.
11. Travis Clardy, R-Nacogdoches; attorney.
12. Kyle Kacal, R-College Station; rancher.
13. Ben Leman, R-Anderson; business, rancher.
14. John Raney, R-College Station; bookstore owner.
15. Steve Toth, R-The Woodlands; business owner.
16. Will Metcalf, R-Conroe; banker.
17. John Cyrier, R-Lockhart; general contractor.
18. Ernest Bailes IV, R-Shepherd; self-employed.
19. James White, R-Hillister; educator, rancher.
20. Terry M. Wilson, R-Marble Falls; military, retired.
21. Dade Phelan, R-Beaumont; real estate developer.
22. Joe Deshotel, D-Beaumont; attorney, contractor.
23. Mayes Middleton, R-Wallisville; oil & gas.
24. Greg Bonnen, R-Friendswood; neurosurgeon.
25. Dennis Bonnen, R-Lake Jackson; banking.
26. Rick Miller, R-Sugar Land; leadership consultant.
27. Ron Reynolds, D-Missouri City; attorney.
28. John Zerwas, R-Richmond; anesthesiologist.
29. Ed Thompson, R-Pearland; insurance agent.
30. Geanie W. Morrison, R-Victoria; state representative.
31. Ryan Guillen, D-Rio Grande City; investor.
32. Todd Hunter, R-Corpus Christi; attorney.
33. Justin Holland, R-Heath; real estate broker.
34. Abel Herrero, D-Robstown; attorney.
35. Oscar Longoria, D-Peñitas; attorney.
36. Sergio Muñoz, Jr., D-Palmview; attorney.
37. Alex Dominguez, D-Brownsville; attorney.
38. Eddie Lucio III, D-Brownsville; attorney.
39. Armando Martinez, D-Weslaco; attorney.
40. Terry Canales, D-Edinburg; attorney.
41. R.D. "Bobby" Guerra, D-Mission; attorney.
42. Richard Peña Raymond, D-Laredo; mediator.
43. J. M. Lozano, R-Kingsville; business.
44. John Kuempel, R-Seguin; salesman.
45. Erin Zwiener, R-Driftwood; writer.
46. Sheryl Cole, D-Austin; lawyer, CPA.
47. Vikki Goodwin, D-Austin; real estate broker.
48. Donna Howard, D-Austin; community advocate.
49. Gina Hinojosa, D-Austin; attorney.
50. Celia Israel, D-Austin; realtor.
51. Eddie Rodriguez, D-Austin; business development consultant.
52. James Talarico, D-Round Rock; nonprofit director.
53. Andrew Murr, R-Junction; attorney, rancher.
54. Brad Buckley, R-Salado; veterinarian.
55. Hugh Shine, R-Temple; financial advisor.
56. Charles "Doc" Anderson, R-Waco; veterinarian.
57. Trent Ashby, R-Lufkin; title insurance executive.

58. DeWayne Burns, R-Cleburne; investor, farmer, rancher.
59. J.D. Sheffield, R-Gatesville; physician.
60. Mike Lang, R-Granbury; law enforcement, retired.
61. Phil King, R-Weatherford; attorney.
62. Reggie Smith, R-Van Alstyne; attorney.
63. Tan Parker, R-Flower Mound; business consultant.
64. Lynn Stucky, R-Denton; veterinarian.
65. Michelle Beckley, D-Carrollton; business owner.
66. Matt Shaheen, R-Plano; technology executive.
67. Jeff Leach, R-Plano; attorney.
68. Drew Springer, Jr., R-Muenster; financial services.
69. James B. Frank, R-Wichita Falls; business owner.
70. Scott Sanford, R-McKinney; minister.
71. Stan Lambert, R-Abilene; banker, retired.
72. Drew Darby, R-San Angelo; attorney, business.
73. Kyle Biedermann, R-Fredericksburg; business owner.
74. Poncho Nevárez, D-Eagle Pass; attorney.
75. Mary González, D-Clint; consultant.
76. César Blanco, D-El Paso; consultant.
77. Lina Ortega, D-El Paso; attorney.
78. Joe Moody, D-El Paso; attorney.
79. Art Fierro, D-El Paso.
80. Tracy King, D-Batesville; business.
81. Brooks Landgraf, R-Odessa; attorney, rancher.
82. Tom Craddick, R-Midland; business development manager.
83. Dustin Burrows, R-Lubbock; attorney.
84. John Frullo, R-Lubbock; small-business owner.
85. Phil Stephenson, R-Wharton; CPA.
86. John Smithee, R-Amarillo; attorney.
87. Four Price, R-Amarillo; attorney.
88. Ken King, R-Canadian; oil & gas service executive.
89. Candy Noble, R-Lucas.
90. Ramon Romero, Jr., D-Fort Worth; CEO.
91. Stephanie Klick, R-Fort Worth; registered nurse.
92. Jonathan Stickland, R-Bedford; consultant.
93. Matt Krause, R-Fort Worth; attorney.
94. Tony Tinderholt, R-Arlington; retired.
95. Nicole Collier, D-Fort Worth; attorney.
96. Bill Zedler, R-Arlington; consultant.
97. Craig Goldman, R-Fort Worth; real estate, finance.
98. Giovanni Capriglione, R-Southlake; finance.
99. Charlie Geren, R-River Oaks; restaurant owner and rancher.
100. Eric Johnson, D-Dallas; attorney.
101. Chris Turner, D-Grand Prairie; communications.
102. Ana-Maria Ramos, D-Richardson; attorney, professor.
103. Rafael Anchia, D-Dallas; attorney.
104. Jessica González, D-Dallas; attorney.
105. Terry Meza, D-Irving; attorney.
106. Jared Patterson, R-Frisco; energy management.
107. Victoria Neave, D-Dallas; attorney.
108. Morgan Meyer, R-Dallas; attorney.
109. Carl Sherman, Sr., D-DeSoto; pastor, business.
110. Toni Rose, D-Dallas; mental health liaison.
111. Yvonne Davis, D-Dallas; small-business owner.
112. Angie Chen Button, R-Richardson; marketing.
113. Rhetta Bowers, D-Rowlett; educator.
114. John Turner, D-Dallas; attorney.
115. Julie Johnson, D-Carrollton; attorney.
116. Trey Martinez Fischer, D-San Antonio; contractor.
117. Philip Cortez, D-San Antonio; public relations.
118. Leo Pacheco, D-San Antonio; human resources.
119. Roland Gutierrez, D-San Antonio; attorney.
120. Barbara Gervin-Hawkins, D-San Antonio; education.
121. Steve Allison, R-San Antonio; attorney.
122. Lyle Larson, R-San Antonio; self-employed.
123. Diego Bernal, D-San Antonio; attorney.
124. Ina Minjarez, D-San Antonio; attorney.
125. Ray Lopez, D-San Antonio.
126. Sam Harless, R-Spring; automobile dealer.
127. Dan Huberty, R-Kingwood; finance.
128. Briscoe Cain, R-Baytown; attorney.
129. Dennis Paul, R-Houston; engineer.
130. Tom Oliverson, R-Cypress; anesthesiologist.
131. Alma Allen, D-Houston; educational consultant.
132. Gina Calanni, D-Katy; finance director.
133. Jim Murphy, R-Houston; consultant.
134. Sarah Davis, R-Houston; attorney.
135. Jon Rosenthal, D-Houston; engineer.
136. John Bucy, III, D-Austin; education.
137. Gene Wu, D-Houston; attorney.
138. Dwayne Bohac, R-Houston; small-business owner.
139. Jarvis Johnson, D-Houston; business owner.
140. Armando Walle, D-Houston; legal assistant.
141. Senfronia Thompson, D-Houston; attorney.
142. Harold Dutton, Jr., D-Houston; attorney.
143. Ana Hernandez, D-Houston; attorney.
144. Mary Ann Perez, D-Houston; insurance agent.
145. Christina Morales, D-Houston; funeral director.
146. Shawn Thierry, D-Houston; attorney.
147. Garnet Coleman, D-Houston; business consulting.
148. Jessica Farrar, D-Houston; state representative.
149. Hubert Vo, D-Houston; business.
150. Valoree Swanson, R-Spring; business. ☆

The Supreme Court of Texas: (seated, left to right) Justice Paul W. Green, Chief Justice Nathan L. Hecht, and Justice Eva Guzman; (standing, left to right) Justice Jimmy Blacklock, Justice John Phillip Devine, Justice Debra Lehrmann, Justice Jeffrey S. Boyd, Justice Jeff Brown, and Justice J. Brett Busby. Photo by Ostler McCarthy; Texas Supreme Court.

Texas State Judiciary

The judiciary of the state consists of nine justices of the Supreme Court of Texas; nine judges of the Court of Criminal Appeals; 80 justices of the 14 Courts of Appeals; 459 judges of the State District Courts; 13 judges of the Criminal District Courts; 527 County Court judges; 805 Justice Court judges; and more than 1,200 Municipal Court judges in 944 cities.

Since 1876, judges at all levels are elected by voters in partisan elections. The Judicial Campaign Fairness Act was added to the Texas Election Code in 1995 by the 74th Legislature and limits individual campaign contributions to $5,000 for a statewide judicial office and $1,000–$5,000 for other judicial offices, depending on judicial district population. The exception is law firms, for which a $50 limit is set.

In addition to its system of formal courts, the State of Texas has established 18 **Alternative Dispute Resolution Centers**. The centers are headed by a director and help ease the caseload of Texas courts by using mediation, arbitration, negotiation, and moderated settlement conferences to handle disputes.

Centers are located in Amarillo, Austin, Beaumont, Bryan–College Station, Conroe, Corpus Christi, Dallas, Denton, El Paso, Fort Worth, Houston, Kerrville, Lubbock, Paris, Richmond, San Antonio, San Marcos, and Waco.

(The list of U.S. District Courts in Texas can be found in the Federal Government section, page 515.)

State Higher Courts

The state's higher courts include the Supreme Court, the Court of Criminal Appeals, the Courts of Appeals, and District Courts. Justices of the Supreme Court, Court of Criminal Appeals, and Courts of Appeals are elected to six-year, overlapping terms. District Court judges are elected to four-year terms.

Judicial salaries to be paid by the state for fiscal year 2020 and 2021 are: Supreme Court and Court of Criminal Appeals chief justices, $170,500, justices, $168,000; Court of Appeals chief justices, $156,500; justices, $154,000. Court of Appeals justices also may receive additional compensation paid by counties for extra judicial service, not to exceed $9,000 per year.

District Court judges receive $140,000 from the state. They may receive additional compensation paid by counties, not to exceed $18,000 per year.

The justices listed below are current as of **July 2019**. Notations in parentheses are term of office expiration dates. Elsewhere in this section are lists of District Court judges by district number, district court numbers in each county, and county court judges.

Supreme Court

Chief Justice, Nathan L. Hecht (12/31/20). **Justices**: J. Brett Busby (12/31/20); Jeffrey S. Boyd (12/31/20); Paul W. Green (12/31/22); Eva Guzman (12/31/22); Debra H. Lehrmann (12/31/22); John Phillip Devine (12/31/24); Jeffrey V. Brown (12/31/24); and James D. "Jimmy" Blacklock (12/31/24).

Clerk of Court, Blake A. Hawthorne. Location of court, Austin. Web: **txcourts.gov/supreme.**

Court of Criminal Appeals

Presiding Judge, Sharon Keller (12/31/24). **Judges**: Bert Richardson (12/31/20); Kevin Yeary (12/31/20); David Newell (12/31/20); Michael E. Keasler (12/31/22); Mary Lou Keel (12/31/22), Scott Walker (12/31/22); Barbara Parker Hervey (12/31/24); and Michelle Slaughter (12/31/24). State Prosecuting Attorney, Stacey M. Soule.

Clerk of Court, Deanna Williamson. Location of court, Austin. Web: **http://www.txcourts.gov/cca.**

Courts of Appeals

These courts have jurisdiction within their respective supreme judicial districts. A constitutional amendment approved in 1978 raised the number of associate justices for Courts of Appeals where needed. Judges are elected from the district for six-year terms. An amendment adopted in 1980 changed the name of the old Courts of Civil Appeals to the Courts of Appeals and changed the jurisdiction of the courts.

First District, Houston:* Chief Justice Sherry Radack (12/31/22). **Justices:** Gordon Goodman (12/31/24); Russell Loyd (12/31/20); Evelyn Keyes (12/31/22); Laura Carter Higley (12/31/20); Sarah Beth Landau (12/31/24); Julie Countiss (12/31/24); Richard Hightower (12/31/24); and Peter M. Kelley (12/31/24). **Clerk of Court**, Christopher A. Prine. Counties in the First District: Austin, Brazoria, Chambers, Colorado, Fort Bend, Galveston, Grimes, Harris, Waller, Washington.

Second District, Fort Worth: Chief Justice. Bonnie Sudderth (12/31/24). **Justices:** Dana Womack (12/31/20); Elizabeth Kerr (12/31/22); J. Wade Birdwell (12/31/24); Dabney Bassel (12/31/24); Mark Pittman (12/31/24); and Lee Gabriel (12/31/20). **Clerk of Court**, Debra Spisak. Counties in Second District: Archer, Clay, Cooke, Denton, Hood, Jack, Montague, Parker, Tarrant, Wichita, Wise, Young.

Third District, Austin: Chief Justice Jeff Rose (12/31/20). **Justices:** Edward Smith (12/31/24); Chari L. Kelly (12/31/24); Melissa Goodwin (12/31/22); Thomas Baker (12/31/24); and Gisela Triana (12/31/24). **Clerk of Court**, Jeffrey D. Kyle. Counties in the Third District: Bastrop, Bell, Blanco, Burnet, Caldwell, Coke, Comal, Concho, Fayette, Hays, Irion, Lampasas, Lee, Llano, McCulloch, Milam, Mills, Runnels, San Saba, Schleicher, Sterling, Tom Green, Travis, Williamson.

Fourth District, San Antonio: Chief Justice Sandee Bryan Marion (12/31/20). **Justices:** Beth Watkins (12/31/24); Patricia O'Connel Alvarez (12/31/24); Luz Elena Chapa (12/31/24); Liza Rodriguez (12/31/24); Irene Alarcon Rios (12/31/20); and Rebeca Martinez (12/31/24). **Clerk of Court**, Keith E. Hottle. Counties in the Fourth District: Atascosa, Bandera, Bexar, Brooks, Dimmit, Duval, Edwards, Frio, Gillespie, Guadalupe, Jim Hogg, Jim Wells, Karnes, Kendall, Kerr, Kimble, Kinney, La Salle, Mason, Maverick, McMullen, Medina, Menard, Real, Starr, Sutton, Uvalde, Val Verde, Webb, Wilson, Zapata, Zavala.

Fifth District, Dallas: Chief Justice Robert D. Burns, III (12/31/24). **Justices:** Robbie Partida-Kipness (12/31/24); Ada Brown (12/31/20); Lana Myers (12/31/22); Erin Nowell (12/31/24); David Bridges (12/31/24); David Schenck (11/4/22); Bill Whitehill (12/31/20); Bill Pedersen, III (12/31/24); Amanda Reichek (12/31/24); Cory Carlyle (12/31/24); Ken Molberg (12/31/24); and Leslie Lester Osborne (12/31/24);. **Clerk of Court**, Lisa Matz. Counties in the Fifth District: Collin, Dallas, Grayson, Hunt, Kaufman, Rockwall.

Sixth District, Texarkana: Chief Justice Josh R. Morris, III (12/31/16). **Justices:** Scott Stevens (12/31/24) and Ralph K. Burgess (12/31/20). **Clerk of Court**, Debbie Autrey. Counties in the Sixth District: Bowie, Camp, Cass, Delta, Fannin, Franklin, Gregg, Harrison, Hopkins, Hunt, Lamar, Marion, Morris, Panola, Red River, Rusk, Titus, Upshur, Wood.

Seventh District, Amarillo: Chief Justice Brian P. Quinn (12/31/20). **Justices**: Judy Parker (12/31/24); Patrick A. Pirtle (12/31/24); and James T. Campbell (12/31/22). **Clerk of Court**, Vivian Long. Counties in the Seventh District: Armstrong, Bailey, Briscoe, Carson, Castro, Childress, Cochran, Collingsworth, Cottle, Crosby, Dallam, Deaf Smith, Dickens, Donley, Floyd, Foard, Garza, Gray, Hale, Hall, Hansford, Hardeman, Hartley, Hemphill,

Hockley, Hutchinson, Kent, King, Lamb, Lipscomb, Lubbock, Lynn, Moore, Motley, Ochiltree, Oldham, Parmer, Potter, Randall, Roberts, Sherman, Swisher, Terry, Wheeler, Wilbarger, Yoakum.

Eighth District, El Paso: Chief Justice Ann Crawford McClure (12/31/20). **Justices**: Yvonne Rodriguez (12/31/24) and Gina Palafox (12/31/24). **Clerk of Court**, Elizabeth G. Flores. Counties in the Eighth District: Andrews, Brewster, Crane, Crockett, Culberson, El Paso, Hudspeth, Jeff Davis, Loving, Pecos, Presidio, Reagan, Reeves, Terrell, Upton, Ward, Winkler.

Ninth District, Beaumont: Chief Justice Steve McKeithen (12/31/20). **Justices**: Charles Kreger (12/31/22); Leanne Johnson (12/31/24); and Henry Hollis Horton (12/31/24). **Clerk of Court**, Carol Anne Harley. Counties in the Ninth District: Hardin, Jasper, Jefferson, Liberty, Montgomery, Newton, Orange, Polk, San Jacinto, Tyler.

Tenth District, Waco: Chief Justice Thomas W. Gray (12/31/24). **Justices**: Rex D. Davis (12/31/20) and John Neill. (12/31/22). **Clerk of Court**, Sharri Roessler. Counties in the Tenth District: Bosque, Brazos, Burleson, Coryell, Ellis, Falls, Freestone, Hamilton, Hill, Johnson, Leon, Limestone, Madison, McLennan, Navarro, Robertson, Somervell, Walker.

Eleventh District, Eastland: Chief Justice John Bailey (12/31/24). **Justices**: Mike Wilson (12/31/20) and Keith Stretcher (12/31/24). **Clerk of Court**, Sherry Williamson. Counties in the Eleventh District: Baylor, Borden, Brown, Callahan, Coleman, Comanche, Dawson, Eastland, Ector, Erath, Fisher, Gaines, Glasscock, Haskell, Howard, Jones, Knox, Martin, Midland, Mitchell, Nolan, Palo Pinto, Scurry, Shackelford, Stephens, Stonewall, Taylor, Throckmorton.

Twelfth District, Tyler: Chief Justice James T. Worthen (12/31/20). **Justices**: Brian Hoyle (12/31/22) and Greg Neeley (12/31/24). **Clerk of Court**, Katrina McClenny. Counties in the Twelfth District: Anderson, Angelina, Cherokee, Gregg, Henderson, Houston, Nacogdoches, Rains, Rusk, Sabine, San Augustine, Shelby, Smith, Trinity, Upshur, Van Zandt, Wood.

Thirteenth District, Corpus Christi: Chief Justice Dori Contreras (12/31/24). **Justices**: Nora Longoria (12/31/24); Leticia Hinojosa (12/31/22); Vacant (12/31/24); Gina Benavides (12/31/24); and Gregory Perkes (12/31/20). **Clerk of Court**, Dorian E. Ramirez. Counties in the Thirteenth District: Aransas, Bee, Calhoun, Cameron, DeWitt, Goliad, Gonzales, Hidalgo, Jackson, Kenedy, Kleberg, Lavaca, Live Oak, Matagorda, Nueces, Refugio, San Patricio, Victoria, Wharton, Willacy.

Fourteenth District, Houston†: Chief Justice Kem Frost (12/31/20). **Justices**: Kevin Jewell (12/31/22); Jimmy Zimmerer (12/31/24); Charles A. Spain (12/31/24); Frances Bourliot (12/31/24); Meagan Hassan (12/31/24); Ken Wise (12/31/20); Margaret "Meg" Poissant (12/31/24); and Tracy E. Christopher (12/31/22). **Clerk of Court**, Christopher A. Prine. Counties in the Fourteenth District: Austin, Brazoria, Chambers, Colorado, Fort Bend, Galveston, Grimes, Harris, Waller, Washington.☆

---

*The location of the First Court of Appeals was changed from Galveston to Houston by the 55th Legislature, with the provision that all cases originated in Galveston County be tried in that city and with the further provision that any case may, at the discretion of the court, be tried in either city.

†Because of the heavy workload of the Houston area Court of Appeals, the 60th Legislature in 1967 provided for the establishment of a Fourteenth Appeals Court in Houston.

District Judges in Texas

Sources: Texas Judicial Directory and Texas State Directory.

Below are the names of all district judges in Texas, as of July 2019, listed in district court order. To determine which judges have jurisdiction in specific counties, refer to the **Texas Courts by County** table, on pages 454–455.

Dist.	Judge	Dist.	Judge	Dist.	Judge
1	Craig M. Mixson (R)	65	Yahara Lisa Gutierrez (D)	131	Norma Gonzales (D)
1-A	Delinda Gibbs-Walker (R)	66	A. Lee Harris (R)	132	Ernie B. Armstrong (R)
2	Chris Day (R)	67	Donald J. Cosby (R)	133	Jaclanel McFarland (D)
3	Mark A. Calhoon (R)	68	Martin Hoffman (D)	134	Dale B. Tillery (D)
4	J. Clay Gossett (R)	69	Ron Enns (R)	135	Stephen Williams (R)
5	Bill Miller (R)	70	Denn Whalen (R)	136	Baylor Wortham (D)
6	Wes Tidwell (R)	71	Brad Morin (R)	137	John "Trey" McClendon (R)
7	Kerry L. Russell (R)	72	Ruben G. Reyes (R)	138	Arturo C. Nelson (R)
8	Eddie Northcutt (R)	73	David A. Canales (D)	139	Bobby Flores (D)
9	Phil Grant (R)	74	Gary Coley (R)	140	Jim Bob Darnell (R)
10	Kerry Neves (R)	75	Mark Morefield (R)	141	John P. Chupp (R)
11	Kristen B. Hawkins (D)	76	Angela Saucier (R)	142	George "Jody" Gilles (R)
12	Donald L. Kraemer (R)	77	Patrick Simmons (R)	143	Michael Swanson (R)
13	James Lagomarsino (R)	78	W. Bernard "Barney" Fudge (R)	144	Ray J. Olivarri (R)
14	Eric V. Moye (D)	79	Richard Terrell (R)	145	Campbell Cox II (R)
15	Jim Fallon (R)	80	Larry Weiman (D)	146	Jack Jones (R)
16	Sherry Shipman (R)	81	Lynn Ellison (R)	147	Clifford A. Brown (D)
17	Melody Wilkinson (R)	82	Bryan F. "Rusty" Russ, Jr. (R)	148	Carlos Valdez (D)
18	Sydney B. Hewlett (R)	83	Robert Cadena (R)	149	Terri Tipton Holder (R)
19	Ralph T. Strother (R)	84	Curtis W. Brancheau (R)	150	Monique Diaz (D)
20	John W. Youngblood (R)	85	Kyle Hawthorne (R)	151	Mike Engelhart (D)
21	Carson Campbell (R)	86	Casey Blair (R)	152	Robert Schaffer (D)
22	Bruce Boyer (R)	87	Deborah Oakes Evans (R)	153	Susan McCoy (R)
23	Ben Hardin (R)	88	Earl Stover, III (R)	154	Felix Klein (R)
24	Jack W. Marr (R)	89	Charles M. Barnard (R)	155	Jeff Steinhauser (R)
25	William D. Old, III (R)	90	Stephen Bristow (R)	156	Patrick L. Flanigan (R)
25-A	Jessica R. Crawford (R)	91	Steven R. Herod (R)	157	Tanya Garrison (D)
26	Donna King (R)	92	Luis M. Singleterry (D)	158	Steve Burgess (R)
27	John Gauntt (R)	93	Jaime "Rudy" Tijerina (D)	159	Paul E. White (R)
28	Nanette Hasette (D)	94	Bobby Galvan (R)	160	Aiesha Redmond (D)
29	Michael Moore (R)	95	David W. Evans (R)	161	John W. Smith (R)
30	Jeff McKnight (R)	96	R.H. Wallace, Jr (R)	162	Maricela Moore (D)
31	Steven R. Emmert (R)	97	Jack McGaughey (R)	163	Dennis Powell (R)
32	Glen N. Harrison (R)	98	Rhonda Hurley (D)	164	Alexandra Smoots-Hogan (D)
33	Allan Garrett (R)	99	William C. "Bill" Sowder (R)	165	Ursula A. Hall (D)
34	William E. Moody (D)	100	Stuart Messer (R)	166	Laura Salinas (D)
35	Stephen Ellis (R)	101	Staci Williams (D)	167	David Wahlberg (D)
36	Starr Bauer (R)	102	Jeff M. Addison (R)	168	Marcos Lizarraga (D)
37	Michael E. Mery (D)	103	Janet Leal (D)	169	Gordon G. Adams (R)
38	Camile G. DuBose (R)	104	Lee Hamilton (R)	170	Jim Meyer (R)
39	Shane Hadaway (R)	105	Jack W. Pulcher (R)	171	Bonnie Rangel (D)
40	Bob Carroll (R)	106	Reed Filley (R)	172	Mitch Templeton (R)
41	Anna Perez (D)	107	Benjamin Euresti, Jr. (D)	173	Dan Moore (R)
42	James Eidson (R)	108	Doug Woodburn (R)	174	Hazel B. Jones (D)
43	Craig Towson (R)	109	John L. Pool (R)	175	Catherine Torres-Stahl (D)
44	Bonnie Lee Goldstein (D)	110	William P. Smith (R)	176	Nikita Harmon (D)
45	Mary Lou Alvarez (D)	111	Monica Zapata Notzon (D)	177	Robert Johnson (D)
46	Dan Mike Bird (R)	112	Pete Gomez, Jr. (D)	178	Kelli Johnson (D)
47	Daniel L. Schaap (R)	113	Rabeea Collier (D)	179	Randy Roll (D)
48	David L. Evans (R)	114	Christi Kennedy (R)	180	DaSean Jones (D)
49	Joe Lopez (D)	115	Dean Fowler	181	John B. Board (R)
50	Bobby Burnett (R)	116	Tonya Parker (D)	182	Danilo "Danny" Lacayo (D)
51	Carmen Symes Dusek (R)	117	Sandra Watts (D)	183	Chuck Silverman (D)
52	Trent D. Farrell (R)	118	Timothy Yeats (R)	184	Abigail Anastasio (D)
53	Scott Jenkins (R)	119	Ben Woodward (R)	185	Jason Luong (D)
54	Matt Johnson (R)	120	Maria Salas-Mendoza (D)	186	Jefferson Moore (R)
55	Latosha L. Payne (D)	121	John A. "Trey" Didway (R)	187	Stephanie R. Boyd (D)
56	Lonnie Cox (R)	122	John Ellisor (R)	188	Scott Novy (R)
57	Antonia "Toni" Arteaga (D)	123	LeAnn Kay Rafferty (R)	189	Scot Dollinger (D)
58	Kent Walston (D)	124	F. Alfonso Charles (R)	190	Beau Miller (D)
59	Larry Phillips (R)	125	Kyle Carter (D)	191	Gena Slaughter (D)
60	Justin Sanderson (D)	126	Darlene Byrne (D)	192	Craig Smith (D)
61	Fredericka Phillips (D)	127	R.K. Sandill (D)	193	Bridgett Whitmore (D)
62	Will Biard (R)	128	Courtney Arkeen (D)	194	Ernest B. White III (D)
63	Enrique Fernandez (D)	129	Michael Gomez (D)	195	Hector Garza (D)
64	Danah Zirpoli (R)	130	Craig Estlinbaum (D)	196	Andrew Bench (R)

Dist.	Judge
197	Adolfo Cordova (D)
198	Melvin "Rex" Emerson (R)
199	Angela Tucker (R)
200	Dustin M. Howell (D)
201	Amy Clark Meachum (D)
202	John Tidwell (R)
203	Raquel "Rocky" Jones (D)
204	Tammy Kemp (D)
205	Francisco X. Dominguez (D)
206	Rose Guerra Reyna (D)
207	Jack H. Robison (R)
208	Greg Glass (D)
209	Brian Warren (D)
210	Alyssa G. Perez (D)
211	Brody Shanklin (R)
212	Patricia V. Grady (R)
213	Christopher R. Wolfe (R)
214	Inna Klein (R)
215	Elaine H. Palmer (D)
216	Keith Williams (R)
217	Robert K. Inselmann, Jr. (R)
218	Russell Wilson (R)
219	Jennifer Edgeworth (R)
220	Shaun Carpenter (R)
221	Lisa B. Michalk (R)
222	Roland Saul (R)
223	Phil Vanderpool (R)
224	Cathy Stryker (R)
225	Peter Sakai (D)
226	Velia J. Meza (D)
227	Kevin M. O'Connell (R)
228	Frank Aguilar (D)
229	Baldemar "Balde" Garza (D)
230	Chris Morton (D)
231	Jesus "Jesse" Nevarez Jr. (R)
232	Josh Hill (D)
233	Kenneth E. Newell (R)
234	Lauren Reeder (D)
235	Janelle M. Haverkamp (R)
236	Tom Lowe (R)
237	Les Hatch (R)
238	Elizabeth Leonard (R)
239	Patrick Sebesta (R)
240	Frank J. Fraley (D)
241	Jack M. Skeen, Jr. (R)
242	Lowell "Kregg" Hukill (R)
243	Selena N. Solis (D)
244	James Rush (R)
245	Tristan H. Longino (D)
246	Angela Graves-Harrington (D)
247	Janice Berg (D)
248	Hilary Unger (D)
249	Wayne Bridewell (R)
250	Karin Crump (D)
251	Anna Estevez (R)
252	Raquel West (D)
253	Chap B. Cain III (R)
254	Ashley Wysocki
255	Kim Cooks (D)
256	David Lopez (D)
257	Sandra Peake (D)
258	Travis Kitchens (R)
259	Brooks H. Hagler (D)
260	Steve Parkhurst (R)
261	Lora Livingston (D)
262	Lori C. Gray (D)
263	Amy Martin (D)
264	Paul LePak (R)
265	Jennifer Bennett (D)
266	Jason Cashon (R)
267	Robert E. "Bobby" Bell (R)

Dist.	Judge
268	R. O'Neil Williams (D)
269	Cory Sepolio (D)
270	Dedra Davis (D)
271	Brock Smith (R)
272	Travis B. Bryan III (R)
273	James A. Payne Jr. (R)
274	Gary L. Steel (R)
275	Marla Cuellar (D)
276	Robert Rolston (R)
277	Stacey Mathews (R)
278	Hal R. Ridley (R)
279	Randy Shelton (D)
280	Barbara J. Stalder (D)
281	Sylvia A. Matthews (R)
282	Amber Givens-Davis (D)
283	Lela D. Mays (D)
284	Kristin Bays (R)
285	Aaron Haas (D)
286	Jay M. "Pat" Phelan (R)
287	Gordon H. Green (D)
288	Cynthia Marie Chapa (D)
289	Carlos Quezada (D)
290	Jennifer Peña (D)
291	Stephanie Mitchell (D)
292	Brandon Birmingham (D)
293	Maribel Flores (D)
294	Chris Martin (R)
295	The Honorabble Donna Roth (D)
296	John Roach, Jr. (R)
297	David Hagerman (R)
298	Emily G. Tobolowsky (D)
299	Karen Sage (D)
300	Randall Hufstetler (R)
301	Mary Brown (R)
302	Sandra Jackson (D)
303	Dennise Garcia (D)
304	Andrea Martin (D)
305	Cheryl Lee Shannon (D)
306	Anne Darring (R)
307	Tim Womack (R)
308	Gloria Lopez (D)
309	Linda Marie Dunson (D)
310	Sonya Heath (D)
311	Germaine Tanner (D)
312	Clinton "Chip" Wells (D)
313	Natalia Oakes (D)
314	Michelle Moore (D)
315	Leah Shapiro (D)
316	James Mosley (R)
317	Larry Thorne (D)
318	David W. Lindemood (R)
319	David Stith (R)
320	Pamela C. Sirmon (R)
321	Robert Wilson (R)
322	James B. Munford (R)
323	Alex Kim (R)
324	Jerome S. "Jerry" Hennigan (R)
325	Judith G. Wells (R)
326	Paul Rotenberry (R)
327	Linda Chew (D)
328	Walter Armatys (R)
329	Randy M. Clapp (R)
330	Andrea Plumlee (D)
331	Chantal Melissa Eldridge (D)
332	Mario E. Ramirez, Jr. (D)
333	Daryl Moore (D)
334	Steven E. Kirkland (D)
335	Reva Towslee-Corbett (R)
336	Laurine J. Blake (R)
337	Herb Ritchie (D)
338	Ramona Franklin (D)

Dist.	Judge
339	Maria T. "Terri" Jackson (D)
340	Jay Weatherby (R)
341	Beckie Palomo (D)
342	Kimberly Fitzpatrick (R)
343	Janna Whatley (R)
344	Randy McDonald (R)
345	Jan Soifer (D)
346	Angie J. Barill (D)
347	Missy Medary (R)
348	Mike Wallach (R)
349	Pam Foster Fletcher (R)
350	Thomas Wheeler (R)
351	George Powell (D)
352	Josh Burgess (R)
353	Tim Sulak (D)
354	Kelli Aiken (R)
355	Ryan Sinclair (D)
356	Steven Thomas (R)
357	Juan A. Magallanes (D)
358	W. Stacy Trotter (R)
359	Kathleen A. Hamilton (R)
360	Patricia Baca Bennett (R)
361	Steve Smith (R)
362	Bruce McFarling (R)
363	Tracy Holmes (D)
364	Billy Eichman (R)
365	Amado Abascal (D)
366	Ray Wheless (R)
367	Margaret Barnes (R)
368	Rick J. Kennon (R)
369	C. Michael Davis (R)
370	Noe Gonzalez (D)
371	Mollee Westfall (R)
372	Scott Wisch (R)
377	Eli Garza (R)
378	William D. Wallace (R)
379	Ron Rangel (D)
380	Ben N. Smith (R)
381	Jose L. Garza (D)
382	Brett Hall (R)
383	Mike Herrera (D)
384	Patrick M. Garcia (D)
385	Robin Malone Darr (R)
386	Arcelia Trevino (D)
387	Brenda Mullinix (R)
388	Laura Strathmann (D)
389	Letty Lopez (D)
390	Julie H. Kocurek (D)
391	Brad Goodwin (R)
392	Scott McKee (R)
393	Doug Robison (R)
394	Roy B. Ferguson (D)
395	Ryan D. Larson (R)
396	George Gallagher (R)
397	Brian Keith Gary (R)
398	Keno Vasquez (D)
399	Frank J. Castro (D)
400	Maggie Jaramillo (R)
401	Mark J. Rusch (R)
402	Jeff Fletcher (R)
403	Brenda Kennedy (D)
404	Elia Cornejo Lopez (D)
405	Jared Robinson (R)
406	Oscar "O.J." Hale, Jr. (D)
407	Karen Pozza (D)
408	Angelica Jimenez (D)
409	Sam Medrano, Jr. (D)
410	Jennifer Robin (R)
411	Kaycee Jones (R)
412	Justin R. Gilbert (R)
413	William C. "Bill" Bosworth, Jr. (R)

Dist.	Judge
414	Vicki Menard (R)
415	Graham Quisenberry (R)
416	Andrea Thompson (R)
417	Cynthia Wheless (R)
418	Tracy A. Gilbert (R)
419	Catherine A. Mauzy (D)
420	Edwin Allen "Ed" Klein (R)
421	Chris Schneider (R)
422	B. Michael Chitty (R)
423	Chris Duggan (D)
424	Evan Stubbs (R)
425	Betsy F. Lambeth (R)
426	Fancy H. Jezek (R)
427	Tamara Needles (D)
428	William "Bill" Henry (R)
429	Jill R. Willis (R)
430	Israel Ramon (D)
431	Jonathan Bailey (R)
432	Ruben Gonzalez, Jr. (R)
433	Dibrell "Dib" Waldrip (R)
434	James H. Shoemake (R)
435	Patty Maginnis (R)

Dist.	Judge
436	Lisa K. Jarrett (R)
437	Lori I. Valenzuela (R)
438	Rosie Alvarado (D)
439	David Rakow (R)
440	Grant Kinsey (R)
441	Jeff Robnett (R)
442	Tiffany Haertling (R)
443	Cindy Ermatinger (R)
444	David A. Sanchez (D)
445	Gloria M. Rincones (R)
446	Sara Kate Billingsley (R)
448	Sergio H. Enriquez (D)
449	Renee Rodriguez-Betancourt (D)
450	Brad Urrutia (D)
451	Kirsten Cohoon (R)
452	Robert Hofmann (R)
453	David Junkin (R)
458	Robert L. Rolnick (R)
459	Maya Guerra Gamble (D)
461	Patrick Bulanek (R)
462	Lee Ann Breading (R)
464	Jaime Tijerina (R)

Dist.	Judge
469	Piper McCraw (R)
470	Emily Miskel (R)
471	Andrea Bouressa (R)
505	David Perwin (R)
506	Albert M. McCaig, Jr. (R)
507	Julia Maldonado (D)

Criminal District Courts	
Dallas 1	Tina Yoo Clinton (D)
Dallas 2	Nancy Kennedy (D)
Dallas 3	Gracie Lewis (D)
Dallas 4	Dominique Collins (D)
Dallas 5	Carter Thompson (D)
Dallas 6	Jeanine Howard (D)
Dallas 7	Chika Anyiam (D)
El Paso	Diane Navarette (D)
Jefferson	John B. "Johnny" Stevens (D)
Tarrant 1	Elizabeth Beach (R)
Tarrant 2	Wayne Francis Salvant (R)
Tarrant 3	Robb Catalano (R)
Tarrant 4	Mike Thomas (R)

Administrative Judicial Districts of Texas

There are 11 administrative judicial districts in the state for administrative purposes. Presiding Judges are appointed by the Governor to four-year terms. They must be active or retired district judges or active or retired appellate judges with judicial experience in a district court. They receive extra compensation of $5,000, paid by counties in the administrative district.

The Presiding Judge convenes an annual conference of judges in the administrative district to consult on business in the courts and to adopt rules for administering cases in the district.

The Presiding Judge may assign active or retired district judges residing within the administrative district to any of its district courts. The Presiding Judge of one administrative district may request the Presiding Judge of another administrative district to assign a judge from that district to sit in a district court in the requesting Judge's administrative district.

The Chief Justice of the Supreme Court of Texas convenes an annual conference of the 11 Presiding Judges to determine the need for assignment of judges and to promote the uniform administration of the assignments. The Chief Justice can assign judges of one administrative district for service in another district.

First District: Ray Wheless, McKinney (3/2021): Collin, Dallas, Ellis, Fannin, Grayson, Kaufman, Rockwall.

Second District: Olen Underwood, Conroe (5/2022): Angelina, Bastrop, Brazos, Burleson, Chambers, Grimes, Hardin, Jasper, Jefferson, Lee, Liberty, Madison, Montgomery, Newton, Orange, Polk, San Jacinto, Trinity, Tyler, Walker, Washington.

Third District: Billy Ray Stubblefield, Georgetown (2/2022): Austin, Bell, Blanco, Bosque, Burnet, Caldwell, Colorado, Comal, Comanche, Coryell, Falls, Fayette, Gonzales, Guadalupe, Hamilton, Hays, Hill, Lampasas, Lavaca, Llano, McLennan, Milam, Navarro, Robertson, San Saba, Travis, Williamson.

Fourth District: Sid L. Harle, San Antonio (12/2021): Aransas, Atascosa, Bee, Bexar, Calhoun, De Witt, Dimmit, Frio, Goliad, Jackson, Karnes, La Salle, Live Oak, Maverick, McMullen, Refugio, San Patricio, Victoria, Webb, Wilson, Zapata, Zavala.

Fifth District: Missy Medary, Alice (12/2020): Brooks, Cameron, Duval, Hidalgo, Jim Hogg, Jim Wells, Kenedy, Kleberg, Nueces, Starr, Willacy.

Sixth District: Stephen B. Ables, Kerrville (12/2020): Bandera, Brewster, Crockett, Culberson, Edwards, El Paso, Gillespie, Hudspeth, Jeff Davis, Kendall, Kerr, Kimble, Kinney, Mason, McCulloch, Medina, Menard, Pecos, Presidio, Reagan, Real, Sutton, Terrell, Upton, Uvalde, Val Verde.

Seventh District: Dean Rucker, Midland (4/2023): Andrews, Borden, Brown, Callahan, Coke, Coleman, Concho, Crane, Dawson, Ector, Fisher, Gaines, Garza, Glasscock, Haskell, Howard, Irion, Jones, Kent, Loving, Lynn, Martin, Midland, Mills, Mitchell, Nolan, Reeves, Runnels, Schleicher, Scurry, Shackelford, Sterling, Stonewall, Taylor, Throckmorton, Tom Green, Ward, Winkler.

Eighth District: David L. Evans, Fort Worth (12/2022): Archer, Clay, Cooke, Denton, Eastland, Erath, Hood, Jack, Johnson, Montague, Palo Pinto, Parker, Somervell, Stephens, Tarrant, Wichita, Wise, Young.

Ninth District: Kelly G. Moore, Brownfield (12/2020): Armstrong, Bailey, Baylor, Briscoe, Carson, Castro, Childress, Cochran, Collingsworth, Cottle, Crosby, Dallam, Deaf Smith, Dickens, Donley, Floyd, Foard, Gray, Hale, Hall, Hansford, Hardeman, Hartley, Hemphill, Hockley, Hutchinson, King, Knox, Lamb, Lipscomb, Lubbock, Moore, Motley, Ochiltree, Oldham, Parmer, Potter, Randall, Roberts, Sherman, Swisher, Terry, Wheeler, Wilbarger, Yoakum.

Tenth District: Alfonso Charles, Longview (2/2022): Anderson, Bowie, Camp, Cass. Cherokee, Delta, Franklin, Freestone, Gregg, Harrison, Henderson, Hopkins, Houston, Hunt, Lamar, Leon, Limestone, Marion, Morris, Nacogdoches, Panola, Rains, Red River, Rusk, Sabine, San Augustine, Shelby, Smith, Titus, Upshur, Van Zandt, Wood.

Eleventh District: Susan Brown, Houston (3/2022): Brazoria, Fort Bend, Galveston, Harris, Matagorda, Wharton. ☆

Texas Courts by County

Below are listed the state district court or courts, court of appeals district, administrative judicial district, and U.S. judicial district for each county in Texas as of July 2019. For the names of the district court judges, see table by district number on page 451. Lists of other judges in the Texas court system begin on page 489.

County	State Dist. Court(s)	Ct. of App'ls Dist	Adm. Jud. Dist	U.S. Jud. Dist.
Anderson	3, 87, 349, 369	12	10	E-Tyler
Andrews	109	8	7	W-Midland
Angelina	159, 217	12	2	E-Lufkin
Aransas	36, 156, 343	13	4	S-C.Christi
Archer	97	2	8	N-W. Falls
Armstrong	47	7	9	N-Amarilllo
Atascosa	81, 218	4	4	W-San Ant.
Austin	155	1, 14	3	S-Houston
Bailey	287	7	9	N-Lubbock
Bandera	198	4	6	W-San Ant.
Bastrop	21, 335, 423	3	2	W-Austin
Baylor	50	11	9	N-W. Falls
Bee	36, 156, 343	13	4	S-C.Christi
Bell	27, 146, 169, 264, 426	3	3	W-Waco
Bexar	37, 45, 57, 73, 131, 144, 150, 166, 175, 186, 187, 224, 225, 226, 227, 285, 288, 289, 290, 379, 386, 399, 407, 408, 436, 437, 438	4	4	W-San Ant.
Blanco	33, 424	3	3	W-Austin
Borden	132	11	7	N-Lubbock
Bosque	220	10	3	W-Waco
Bowie	5, 102, 202	6	10	E-Texark.
Brazoria	23, 149, 239, 300, 412	1, 14	11	S-Galves.
Brazos	85, 272, 361	10	2	S-Houston
Brewster	394	8	6	W-Pecos
Briscoe	110	7	9	N-Amarilllo
Brooks	79	4	5	S-C.Christi
Brown	35	11	7	N-S. Angelo
Burleson	21, 335	10	2	W-Austin
Burnet	33, 424	3	3	W-Austin
Caldwell	22, 207, 421	3	3	W-Austin
Calhoun	24, 135, 267	13	4	S-Victoria
Callahan	42	11	7	N-Abilene
Cameron	103, 107, 138, 197, 357, 404, 444, 445	13	5	S-Brownsville
Camp	76, 276	6	10	E-Marshall
Carson	100	7	9	N-Amarilllo
Cass	5	6	10	E-Marshall
Castro	64, 242	7	9	N-Amarilllo
Chambers	253, 344	1, 14	2	S-Galves.
Cherokee	2, 369	12	10	E-Tyler
Childress	100	7	9	N-Amarilllo
Clay	97	2	8	N-W. Falls
Cochran	286	7	9	N-Lubbock
Coke	51	3	7	N-S. Angelo
Coleman	42	11	7	N-S. Angelo
Collin	199, 219, 296, 366, 380, 401, 416, 417, 429, 469, 470	5	1	E-Sherman
Collingsworth	100	7	9	N-Amarilllo
Colorado	25, 25-A	1, 14	3	S-Houston
Comal	22, 207, 274, 433	3	3	W-San Ant.
Comanche	220	11	3	N-Ft. Worth
Concho	119	3	7	N-S. Angelo
Cooke	235	2	8	E-Sherman
Coryell	52, 440	10	3	W-Waco
Cottle	50	7	9	N-W. Falls
Crane	109	8	7	W-Midland
Crockett	112	8	6	N-S. Angelo
Crosby	72	7	9	N-Lubbock
Culberson	205, 394	8	6	W-Pecos
Dallam	69	7	9	N-Amarilllo
Dallas	14, 44, 68, 95, 101, 116, 134, 160, 162, 191, 192, 193, 194,195, 203, 204, 254, 255, 256, 265, 282, 283, 291, 292, 298, 301, 302, 303, 304, 305, 330, 363, Cr. 1, Cr. 2, Cr. 3, Cr. 4, Cr. 5, Cr. 6, Cr. 7	5	1	N-Dallas
Dawson	106	11	7	N-Lubbock

County	State Dist. Court(s)	Ct. of App'ls Dist	Adm. Jud. Dist	U.S. Jud. Dist.
Deaf Smith	222	7	9	N-Amarillo
Delta	8, 62	6	10	E-Sherman
Denton	16, 158, 211, 362, 367, 393, 431, 442, 462	2	8	E-Sherman
DeWitt	24, 135, 267	13	4	S-Victoria
Dickens	110	7	9	N-Lubbock
Dimmit	293, 365	4	4	W-San Ant.
Donley	100	7	9	N-Amarilllo
Duval	229	4	5	S-C.Christi
Eastland	91	11	8	N-Abilene
Ector	70, 161, 244, 358, 446	11	7	W-Midland
Edwards	452	4	6	W-Del Rio
Ellis	40, 378, 443	10	1	N-Dallas
El Paso	34, 41, 65, 120, 168, 171, 205, 210, 243, 327, 346, 383, 384, 388, 409, 448, Cr. 1	8	6	W-El Paso
Erath	266	11	8	N-Ft. Worth
Falls	82	10	3	W-Waco
Fannin	336	6	1	E-Sherman
Fayette	155	3	3	S-Houston
Fisher	32	11	7	N-Abilene
Floyd	110	7	9	N-Lubbock
Foard	46	7	9	N-W. Falls
Fort Bend	240, 268, 328, 387, 400, 434, 458, 505	1, 14	11	S-Houston
Franklin	8, 62	6	10	E-Texark.
Freestone	77, 87	10	10	W-Waco
Frio	81, 218	4	4	W-San Ant.
Gaines	106	11	7	N-Lubbock
Galveston	10, 56, 122, 212, 306, 405	1, 14	11	S-Galves.
Garza	106	7	7	N-Lubbock
Gillespie	216	4	6	W-Austin
Glasscock	118	11	7	N-S. Angelo
Goliad	24, 135, 267	13	4	S-Victoria
Gonzales	25, 25-A	13	3	W-San Ant.
Gray	31, 223	7	9	N-Amarilllo
Grayson	15, 59, 397	5	1	E-Sherman
Gregg	124, 188, 307	6, 12	10	E-Tyler
Grimes	12, 506	1, 14	2	S-Houston
Guadalupe	25, 25-A, 274	4	3	W-San Ant.
Hale	64, 242	7	9	N-Lubbock
Hall	100	7	9	N-Amarilllo
Hamilton	220	10	3	W-Waco
Hansford	84	7	9	N-Amarilllo
Hardeman	46	7	9	N-W. Falls
Hardin	88, 356	9	2	E-B'mont.
Harris	11, 55, 61, 80, 113, 125,127, 129, 133, 151, 152, 157, 164, 165, 174, 176, 177, 178, 179, 180, 182, 183, 184, 185, 189, 190, 208, 209, 215, 228, 230, 232, 234, 245, 246, 247, 248, 257, 262, 263, 269, 270, 280, 281, 295, 308, 309, 310, 311, 312, 313, 314, 315, 333, 334, 337, 338, 339, 351, 507	1, 14	11	S-Houston
Harrison	71	6	10	E-Marshall
Hartley	69	7	9	N-Amarilllo
Haskell	39	11	7	N-Abilene
Hays	22, 207, 274, 428, 453	3	3	W-Austin
Hemphill	31	7	9	N-Amarilllo
Henderson	3, 173, 392	12	10	E-Tyler
Hidalgo	92, 93, 139, 206, 275, 332, 370, 389, 398 , 430, 449, 464	13	5	S-McAllen
Hill	66	10	3	W-Waco
Hockley	286	7	9	N-Lubbock
Hood	355	2	8	N-Ft. Worth
Hopkins	8, 62	6	10	E-Sherman

County	State Dist. Court(s)	Ct. of App'ls Dist	Adm. Jud. Dist	U.S. Jud. Dist.
Houston	3, 349	12	10	E-Lufkin
Howard	118	11	7	N-Abilene
Hudspeth	205, 394	8	6	W-Pecos
Hunt	196, 354	5, 6	10	N-Dallas
Hutchinson	84, 316	7	9	N-Amarillo
Irion	51	3	7	N-S. Angelo
Jack	271	2	8	N-Ft. Worth
Jackson	24, 135, 267	13	4	S-Victoria
Jasper	1, 1-A	9	2	E-B'mont.
Jeff Davis	394	8	6	W-Pecos
Jefferson	58, 60, 136, 172, 252, 279, 317, Cr. 1	9	2	E-B'mont.
Jim Hogg	229	4	5	S-Laredo
Jim Wells	79	4	5	S-C.Christi
Johnson	18, 249, 413	10	8	N-Dallas
Jones	259	11	7	N-Abilene
Karnes	81, 218	4	4	W-San Ant.
Kaufman	86, 422	5	1	N-Dallas
Kendall	451	4	6	W-San Ant.
Kenedy	105	13	5	S-C.Christi
Kent	39	7	7	N-Lubbock
Kerr	198, 216	4	6	W-San Ant.
Kimble	452	4	6	W-Austin
King	50	7	9	N-W. Falls
Kinney	63	4	6	W-Del Rio
Kleberg	105	13	5	S-C.Christi
Knox	50	11	9	N-W. Falls
Lamar	6, 62	6	10	E-Sherman
Lamb	154	7	9	N-Lubbock
Lampasas	27	3	3	W-Austin
La Salle	81, 218	4	4	S-Laredo
Lavaca	25, 25-A	13	3	S-Victoria
Lee	21, 335	3	2	W-Austin
Leon	87, 278, 369	10	10	W-Waco
Liberty	75, 253	9	2	E-B'mont.
Limestone	77, 87	10	10	W-Waco
Lipscomb	31	7	9	N-Amarillo
Live Oak	36, 156, 343	13	4	S-C.Christi
Llano	33, 424	3	3	W-Austin
Loving	143	8	7	W-Pecos
Lubbock	72, 99, 137, 140, 237, 364	7	9	N-Lubbock
Lynn	106	7	7	N-Lubbock
Madison	12, 278	10	2	S-Houston
Marion	115, 276	6	10	E-Marshall
Martin	118	11	7	W-Midland
Mason	452	4	6	W-Austin
Matagorda	23, 130	13	11	S-Galves.
Maverick	293, 365	4	4	W-Del Rio
McCulloch	452	3	6	W-Austin
McLennan	19, 54, 74, 170, 414	10	3	W-Waco
McMullen	36, 156, 343	4	4	S-Laredo
Medina	38	4	6	W-San Ant.
Menard	452	4	6	N-S. Angelo
Midland	142, 238, 318, 385, 441	11	7	W-Midland
Milam	20	3	3	W-Waco
Mills	35	3	7	N-S. Angelo
Mitchell	32	11	7	N-Abilene
Montague	97	2	8	N-W. Falls
Montgomery	9, 221, 284, 359, 410, 418, 435	9	2	S-Houston
Moore	69	7	9	N-Amarillo
Morris	76, 276	6	10	E-Marshall
Motley	110	7	9	N-Lubbock
Nacogdoches	145, 420	12	10	E-Lufkin
Navarro	13	10	3	N-Dallas
Newton	1, 1-A	9	2	E-B'mont.
Nolan	32	11	7	N-Abilene
Nueces	28, 94, 105, 117, 148, 214, 319, 347	13	5	S-C.Christi
Ochiltree	84	7	9	N-Amarillo
Oldham	222	7	9	N-Amarillo
Orange	128, 163, 260	9	2	E-B'mont.
Palo Pinto	29	11	7	N-Ft. Worth
Panola	123	6	10	E-Tyler
Parker	43, 415	2	8	N-Ft. Worth
Parmer	287	7	9	N-Amarillo
Pecos	83, 112	8	6	W-Pecos
Polk	258, 411	9	2	E-Lufkin
Potter	47, 108, 181, 251, 320	7	9	N-Amarillo
Presidio	394	8	6	W-Pecos
Rains	8, 354	12	10	E-Tyler
Randall	47, 181, 251	7	9	N-Amarillo

County	State Dist. Court(s)	Ct. of App'ls Dist	Adm. Jud. Dist	U.S. Jud. Dist.
Reagan	112	8	6	N-S. Angelo
Real	38	4	6	W-San Ant.
Red River	6, 102	6	10	E-Texark.
Reeves	143	8	7	W-Pecos
Refugio	24, 135, 267	13	4	S-Victoria
Roberts	31	7	9	N-Amarillo
Robertson	82	10	3	W-Waco
Rockwall	382, 439	5	1	N-Dallas
Runnels	119	3	7	N-S. Angelo
Rusk	4	6, 12	10	E-Tyler
Sabine	1, 273	12	10	E-Lufkin
San Augustine	1, 273	12	10	E-Lufkin
San Jacinto	258, 411	9	2	S-Houston
San Patricio	36, 156, 343	13	4	S-C.Christi
San Saba	33, 424	3	3	W-Austin
Schleicher	51	3	7	N-S. Angelo
Scurry	132	11	7	N-Lubbock
Shackelford	259	11	7	N-Abilene
Shelby	123, 273	12	10	E-Lufkin
Sherman	69	7	9	N-Amarillo
Smith	7, 114, 241, 321	12	10	E-Tyler
Somervell	18, 249	10	8	W-Waco
Starr	229, 381	4	5	S-McAllen
Stephens	90	11	8	N-Abilene
Sterling	51	3	7	N-S. Angelo
Stonewall	39	11	7	N-Abilene
Sutton	112	4	6	N-S. Angelo
Swisher	64, 242	7	9	N-Amarillo
Tarrant	17, 48, 67, 96, 141, 153, 213, 231, 233, 236, 297, 322, 323, 324, 325, 342, 348, 352, 360, 371, 372, 396, 432, Cr. 1, Cr. 2, Cr. 3, Cr. 4	2	8	N-Ft. Worth
Taylor	42, 104, 326, 350	11	7	N-Abilene
Terrell	63, 83	8	6	W-Del Rio
Terry	121	7	9	N-Lubbock
Throckmorton	39	11	7	N-Abilene
Titus	76, 276	6	10	E-Texark.
Tom Green	51, 119, 340, 391	3	7	N-S. Angelo
Travis	53, 98, 126, 147, 167, 200, 201, 250, 261, 299, 331, 345, 353, 390, 403, 419, 427, 450, 459	3	3	W-Austin
Trinity	258, 411	12	2	E-Lufkin
Tyler	1-A, 88	9	2	E-Lufkin
Upshur	115	6, 12	10	E-Marshall
Upton	112	8	6	W-Midland
Uvalde	38	4	6	W-Del Rio
Val Verde	63, 83	4	6	W-Del Rio
Van Zandt	294	12	10	E-Tyler
Victoria	24, 135, 267, 377	13	4	S-Victoria
Walker	12, 278	10	2	S-Houston
Waller	506	1, 14	2	S-Houston
Ward	143	8	7	W-Pecos
Washington	21, 335	1, 14	2	W-Austin
Webb	49, 111, 341, 406	4	4	S-Laredo
Wharton	23, 329	13	11	S-Houston
Wheeler	31	7	9	N-Amarillo
Wichita	30, 78, 89	2	8	N-W. Falls
Wilbarger	46	7	9	N-W. Falls
Willacy	197	13	5	S-Brownsville
Williamson	26, 277, 368, 395, 425	3	3	W-Austin
Wilson	81, 218	4	4	W-San Ant.
Winkler	109	8	7	W-Pecos
Wise	271	2	8	N-Ft. Worth
Wood	402	6, 12	10	E-Tyler
Yoakum	121	7	9	N-Lubbock
Young	90	2	8	N-W. Falls
Zapata	49	4	4	S-Laredo
Zavala	293, 365	4	4	W-Del Rio

Texas State Agencies

On the following pages is information about several of the many state agencies in Texas. Information was supplied to the Texas Almanac by the agencies, their websites, and from news reports. The web address for more information about state agencies, boards, and commissions is: **www.tsl.texas.gov/apps/lrs/agencies.**

Texas Commission on Environmental Quality

Source: Texas Commission on Environmental Quality; www.tceq.texas.gov

The Texas Commission on Environmental Quality (TCEQ) is the state's leading environmental agency. The TCEQ works to protect Texas' human and natural resources in a manner consistent with sustainable economic development. The agency has about 2,700 employees; of those, about 800 work in the 16 regional offices. The operating budget for the 2019 fiscal year was $370.3 million, of which 84 percent ($309.6 million) was generated by program fees. The remaining revenues came from federal funds ($36.7 million or 10 percent); state general revenue ($16.2 million or 4 percent); and other sources ($7.9 million or 2 percent).

One of the TCEQ's major functions is issuing permits and other authorizations for the control of air pollution, the safe operation of water and wastewater utilities, and the management of hazardous and nonhazardous waste.

The agency promotes voluntary compliance with environmental laws through pollution prevention programs, regulatory workshops, and assistance to businesses and local governments. When environmental laws are violated, the TCEQ has the authority to levy penalties as much as $25,000 a day per violation for administrative cases. In a typical year, the agency conducts more than 105,000 investigations at regulated entities for compliance with state and federal laws and receives about 4,000 complaints.

In fiscal year 2018, the TCEQ issued 1,370 administrative orders, which yielded more than $7.5 million in fines, and directed nearly $3.9 million to supplemental environmental projects benefiting some of the communities in which the environmental violations occurred.

Office of Air

Texas is home to some of the largest U.S. cities, with several metropolitan populations of greater than 1 million people. With these concentrated populations, vehicular traffic and other emissions can create air quality issues among the most challenging in the country.

The state has a fast-growing population, a large industrial base concentrated along the Gulf Coast, and an oil and gas industry expanding throughout much of the state. The TCEQ conducts survey activities along with targeted and/or specialized monitoring activities to evaluate changing air quality conditions across the state.

The TCEQ measures air quality across the state for compliance with federal standards, as well as for localized compounds of concern. Texas' air toxic monitoring network is one of the most comprehensive in the country with more than 80 monitoring sites located across the state.

The TCEQ is responsible for developing a state implementation plan to bring metropolitan areas into compliance with federal air quality standards, such as the ozone standard. The leading areas of concern for ozone issues are the Houston-Galveston-Brazoria and Dallas–Fort Worth areas.

Office of Water

The TCEQ preserves and improves the quality of the state's surface waters by establishing surface water quality standards; monitoring, assessing, and reporting

TCEQ Budget for 2020–2021	
Assessment, Planning and Permitting	$ 389,440,293
Safe Drinking Water	34,907,086
Enforcement and Compliance Support	131,550,963
Pollution Cleanup	84,519,780
River Compact Commissions	5,982,211
Indirect Administration	120,243,484
Total	**$ 766,643,817**

Source: HB1, 2020–2021 State Budget.

conditions; and implementing plans to reduce pollution and improve water quality. It protects surface water users through the water rights permitting process and the watermaster programs.

The TCEQ is also responsible for most state and federal regulatory programs that protect groundwater, administers permits for the discharge of wastewater and stormwater, and conducts Section 401 certifications of federal permits.

The agency enforces the federal Safe Drinking Water Act and oversees the protection of the state's approximately 7,000 public water systems providing drinking water to roughly 27 million customers and has general supervision of water districts.

Office of Waste

Waste management projects at the TCEQ include Superfund projects, pesticide collections, and permits and authorizations for municipal and industrial waste management.

Another major cleanup program focuses on leaking petroleum storage tanks. In 2019, there were 55 Superfund sites in the state, and work continues at another 1,344 sites.

The TCEQ issues permits and other authorizations for municipal and industrial waste management, including landfills and storage, processing, and recycling operations. In addition, the safe recycling of both municipal and industrial waste streams is encouraged.

The TCEQ also regulates the disposal of radioactive material, with the exception of naturally occurring radioactive material (NORM) generated as a result of oil and gas exploration. This includes the regulation of the receipt, processing, storage, and disposal of by-product and low-level radioactive waste, the licensing of uranium and thorium recovery facilities, decommissioning of inactive uranium-recovery facilities, permitting for underground injection control, and legacy radioactive material disposal sites.

Help With Understanding Environmental Rules

The TCEQ offers services to anyone interested in environmental stewardship and navigating TCEQ's programs and regulatory requirements.

Staff members host workshops on recycling and disposal opportunities, and on regulatory and pollution prevention topics.

The TCEQ also offers free compliance assistance to thousands of small businesses and local governments each year. Contact the TCEQ at PO Box 13087, Austin, 78711; (512) 239-1000; www.tceq.texas.gov. ☆

Health and Human Services

Source: Texas Health and Human Services, hhs.texas.gov

Texas Health and Human Services (HHS) is the oversight agency for the state's health and human services system. HHS also administers state and federal programs that provide financial, health, and social services to Texans.

In 2003, the 78th Texas Legislature mandated an unprecedented transformation of the state's health and human services system, blending 12 agencies into five. The system transformed again in 2017, with the goal of removing bureaucratic silos, creating clear lines of accountability, and making it easier for people to find out about services or benefits they might qualify for.

Today's HHS consists of only two agencies: Texas Health and Human Services Commission (HHSC) and the Texas Department of State Health Services (DSHS). The executive commissioner is appointed by the governor and confirmed by the Senate. The Department of Family and Protective Services is an independent agency under the HHSC umbrella.

The state's health and human services agencies spend more than $25 billion per year to administer more than 200 programs, employ more than 55,000 state workers, and operate from more than 1,000 locations.

HHC is located at Brown-Heatly Building, 4900 N. Lamar Blvd., Austin, 78751-2316; Phone: 512-424-6500; TTY: 512-424-6597. The executive commissioner is Dr. Courtney N. Phillips.

Health and Human Services Commission

The HHSC oversees the licensing and credentialing of facilities for long-term care, including nursing homes and assisted living; licenses child care providers; and manages daily operations at state-supported hospitals and living centers.

It also delivers benefits and services such as Medicaid, SNAP food benefits, and TANF cash assistance; services for women and people with special health needs; long-term care for the aging and those with disabilities; and behavioral health services.

Department of State Health Services

DSHS serves as the public health authority for Texas, providing vital statistics and health data to the public, leading the public-health response in times of disaster or outbreaks, and administering chronic and infectious disease prevention and testing. The department also licenses and regulates facilities on topics including youth camps and mobile food establishments. It is led by Commissioner of Public Health Dr. John Hellerstedt.

The client services DSHS previously provided were transferred to HHSC in 2016.

Texas Department of Family and Protective Services

The Texas Department of Family and Protective Services (DFPS) works to protect children and vulnerable adults through prevention programs, investigations, and services and referrals.

Commissioner Hank Whitman resigned in June 2019. His successor has not been named as of press time.

DFPS has five major programs:
- Adult Protective Services
- Child Protective Services
- Investigations
- Prevention and Early Intervention
- Statewide Intake

HHS Budget for 2020–2021	
Dept. of Family and Protective Services	$ 4,428.0
Dept. of State Health Services	1,674.4
Health and Human Services Commission	76,805.3
Total	**$ 82,907.6**

All figures in millions. Total may not sum due to rounding.
Source: HB1, 2020–2021 State Budget.

To report abuse, neglect, or exploitation of children, the elderly or people with disabilities, call 1-800-252-5400 or report online at www.txabusehotline.org. For emergencies call 911.

DFPS headquarters address: 701 W. 51st St., Austin, 78751; Mailing address: PO Box 149030, Austin, 78714-9030; www.dfps.state.tx.us.

Other HHSC Programs

The Family Violence program offers emergency shelter and services to victims and their children.

The Disaster Assistance program processes grant applications for victims of presidentially declared disasters, such as tornados, floods, and hurricanes.

As of 2017, the HHS no longer provides refugee resettlement services. Nonprofit agencies, including U.S. Committee for Refugees and Immigrants (USCRI) have stepped in to provide health services for these groups.☆

Major HHS Programs at a Glance

The **Medicaid** program provides healthcare coverage for one out of every three children in Texas, pays for half of all births, and accounts for 25 percent of the state's total budget. In 2018, an average of 4 million Texans received healthcare coverage through Medicaid.

The Children's Health Insurance Program (CHIP) is designed for families who earn too much money to qualify for Medicaid yet cannot afford private insurance.

The Temporary Assistance for Needy Families (TANF) program provides basic financial assistance for needy children and the parents or caretakers with whom they live. As a condition of eligibility, caretakers must sign and abide by a personal-responsibility agreement. Time limits for benefits have been set by both state and federal welfare-reform legislation.

SNAP food benefits, formerly known as food stamps, is a federally funded program that assists low-income families, the elderly, and single adults obtain a nutritionally adequate diet. Those eligible for food benefits include households receiving TANF or federal Supplemental Security Income benefits, and nonpublic assistance households having incomes below 130 percent of the poverty level. In 2011, more than 3.5 million Texans received SNAP food benefits, and the average monthly benefit amount was about $300.

Both SNAP and TANF benefits are delivered via the electronic benefit transfer (EBT) system, through which clients access benefits at about 12,000 retail locations statewide with the Lone Star card. Information about Medicaid, CHIP, and other health and human services programs can be found at **www.211texas.org**, or by calling **2-1-1**, a toll-free local resource for information on HHS programs.

The General Land Office

Source: General Land Office of Texas, glo.texas.gov

History of the General Land Office

The Texas General Land Office (GLO) is one of the oldest governmental entities in the state, dating back to the Republic of Texas. The first General Land Office was established in 1836 by the Republic's constitution, and the first Texas Congress enacted the provision into law in 1837. The GLO was established to oversee distribution of public lands, register titles, issue patents on land, and maintain records of land granted.

In the early years of statehood, beginning in 1845, Texas established the precedent of using its vast public domain for public benefit. The first use was to sell or trade land to eliminate the huge debt remaining from Texas' War for Independence and the early years of the Republic.

Texas also gave away land to settlers as homesteads; to veterans as compensation for service; for internal improvements, including building railroads, shipbuilding, and improving rivers for navigation; and to build the state Capitol.

The public domain was closed in 1898 when the Texas Supreme Court declared there was no more vacant and unappropriated land in Texas. In 1900, all remaining unappropriated land was set aside by the Legislature to benefit public schools.

Today, 13 million acres of land and minerals, owned by the Permanent School Fund, the Permanent University Fund, various other state agencies, and the Veterans Land Board, are managed by the GLO and the Commissioner of the Texas General Land Office.

This includes over 4 million acres of submerged coastal lands, which consist of bays, inlets, and the area from the Texas shoreline to the three-marine-league line (10.36 miles) in the Gulf of Mexico. It is estimated that more than 1 million acres make up the public domain of the state's riverbeds and another 1.7 million acres are excess lands belonging to the Permanent School Fund.

The GLO is the steward of the Texas Gulf Coast, serving as the premier state agency for protecting and renourishing the coast and fighting coastal erosion. In 1999, the Legislature created the Coastal Erosion Planning and Response Act and put the GLO in charge of facilitating restoration and preservation of eroding beaches, dunes, wetlands, and other bay shorelines along the Texas coast.

The Permanent School Fund owns mineral rights alone in almost 7.4 million acres covered under the Relinquishment Act, the Free Royalty Act, and the various sales acts, and it has outright ownership to about 747,522 upland acres, mostly west of the Pecos River.

Texas Veterans Land Board Programs

The Veterans Land Board (VLB) was formally established by the Legislature to administer benefits for Texas Veterans in 1946 with the first loan made in 1949.

Since then, the programs have evolved to include low-interest land, housing, and home improvement loans. VLB has funded more than 220,000 loans amounting to more than $11 billion for Texas veterans, military members, and their families since its inception.

VLB strives to offer the best benefits program in the nation and works to ensure that Texas veterans are aware of these benefits.

Historic Distribution of the Public Lands of Texas

PURPOSE	ACRES
Settlers	**68,027,108**
Spain and Mexico	24,583,923
Spanish and Mexican Grants south of the Nueces River, recognized by Act of Feb. 10, 1852	3,741,241
Headrights	30,360,002
Republic colonies	4,494,806
Preemption land	4,847,136
Military	**9,874,262**
Bounty	5,354,250
Battle donations	1,162,240
Veterans donations	1,377,920
Confederate	1,979,852
Improvements	**37,155,714**
Road	27,716
Navigation	4,261,760
Irrigation	584,000
Ships	17,000
Manufacturing	111,360
Railroads	32,153,878
Education	**52,329,168**
University, public school, and eleemosynary institutions	52,329,168
Total of distributed lands	**167,386,252**

In a joint effort with the Texas Veterans Commission, the VLB operates the Texas Veterans Call Service Center to connect veterans, military members, and their families with the benefits and services they need. For more information, contact VLB at 1-800-252-VETS (8387) or **www.glo.texas.gov/vlb**.

Texas State Veterans Homes

In 1997, the 75th Legislature approved legislation authorizing the Veterans Land Board to construct and operate Texas State Veterans Homes under a cost-sharing program with the U.S. Department of Veterans Affairs. The homes provide affordable, quality, long-term care for Texas' veterans.

Texas State Veterans Cemeteries

The VLB owns and operates several cemeteries under USDVA guidelines. The USDVA funds the design and construction of the cemeteries, but the land must be donated.

The Alamo

In 2011, the 82nd Legislature granted authority over the Alamo to the GLO. The Alamo hosts millions of visitors from around the world each year. UNESCO designated the Alamo and four other Spanish missions in San Antonio as U.S. World Heritage sites in 2015.

Plans to create a museum and visitors center to house rock legend Phil Collins' donated collection of Alamo and Texana artifacts are under way. ☆

First Methodist Church in Jermyn was built in 1910 and recorded as a Texas Historic Landmark in 1968 by the Texas Historical Commission. Photo by Nicolas Henderson (CC).

Texas Historical Commission

The Texas Historical Commission protects and preserves the state's historic and prehistoric resources. The Texas State Legislature established the Texas State Historical Survey Committee in 1953 to identify important historic sites across the state.

The Texas Legislature changed the agency's name to the Texas Historical Commission in 1973 and increased its mission and its protective powers. Today the agency's concerns include archaeology, architecture, community heritage development, historic sites, history programs, and education. The commission:

- Works with communities and individuals to help identify important historic resources and develop a plan to preserve them.
- Provides leadership and training to county historical commissions, heritage organizations, and museums in Texas' 254 counties.
- Helps protect Texas' diverse architectural heritage, including historic county courthouses.
- Partners with communities to stimulate tourism and economic development.
- Assists Texas cities in the revitalization of their historic downtowns through the Texas Main Street Program.
- Administers the state's historical marker program, which has around 15,000 markers across the state.
- Consults with citizens and groups to nominate properties as Recorded Texas Historic Landmarks, State Archeological Landmarks, and to the National Register of Historic Places.
- Operates 20 state historic sites including house museums, military forts, and archeological sites.
- Works with property owners to save archeological sites on private land and ensures archeological sites are protected as land is developed for highways and other public construction projects.

Mailing address: PO Box 12276, Austin 78711-2276; (512) 463-6100; www.thc.texas.gov.

Railroad Commission of Texas

The Railroad Commission of Texas has primary regulatory jurisdiction over the oil and natural gas industry, pipeline transporters, the natural gas and hazardous liquid pipeline industry, natural gas utilities, the liquefied petroleum gas (LP-gas) industry, rail industry, and coal and uranium surface mining operations. It also promotes the use of LP-gas as an alternative fuel in Texas through research and education.

The commission exercises its statutory responsibilities under provisions of the Texas Constitution, the Texas Natural Resources Code, the Texas Water Code, the Texas Utilities Code, the Coal and Uranium Surface Mining and Reclamation Acts, the Pipeline Safety Acts, and the Railroad Safety Act.

The commission has regulatory and enforcement responsibilities under federal law, including the Federal Railroad Safety Act, the Local Rail Freight Assistance Act, the Surface Coal Mining Control and Reclamation Act, the Pipeline Safety Acts, the Resource Conservation Recovery Act, and the Clean Water Act.

The Railroad Commission was established by the Texas Legislature in 1891 and given jurisdiction over rates and operations of railroads, terminals, wharves, and express companies. In 1917, the legislature declared pipelines to be common carriers and gave the commission regulatory authority over them. It was also given the responsibility to administer conservation laws relating to oil and natural gas production.

The Railroad Commission exists to protect the environment, public safety, and the rights of mineral interest owners; to prevent waste of natural resources; and to assure fair and equitable utility rates in those industries over which it has authority. Mailing address: PO Box 12967, Austin 78711-2967; (512) 463-7288; www.rrc.state.tx.us.

Texas Department of Juvenile Justice

The Texas Department of Juvenile Justice was created on Dec. 1, 2011, by Senate Bill 653, 82nd Legislature. Its creation abolished both the Texas Youth Commission and the Texas Juvenile Probation Commission.

The agency's executive director is Camille Cain, and it has a 13-member commission who are appointed to six-year terms. It is chaired by Wes Ritchey of Bedford.

The **Texas Youth Commission (TYC)** had operated correctional facilities and halfway houses for serious youth offenders. In 2007, widespread sexual and physical abuse was uncovered at many of its facilities. After a number of supervisors were dismissed, the entire TYC board resigned on March 15, 2007, and their powers were transferred to a conservator. The 80th Texas Legislature approved a bill to overhaul the troubled agency.

The **Texas Department of Juvenile Justice** is a unified state juvenile justice agency that works in partnership with local county governments, courts, and communities to promote public safety by providing services to youth from initial contact through end of supervision. Its expressed goals are to:

- Support development of county-based programs and services for youth and families that reduce the need for out-of-home placement;
- Seek alternatives to placing youthful offenders in secure state facilities, while also addressing treatment of youth and protecting the public;
- Locate facilities as geographically close as possible to workforce and other services, and support youths' connection to their families;
- Encourage regional and county collaboration;
- Enhance the continuity of care throughout the juvenile justice system; and
- Use secure facilities of a size that supports effective youth rehabilitation and public safety.

The agency is located at Braker H Complex, 11209 Metric Blvd., Austin 78758. Mailing Address: PO Box 12757, Austin 78711-2757; (512) 490-7130; tjjd.texas.gov.

Texas Workforce Commission

The Texas Workforce Commission (TWC) is the state government agency charged with overseeing and providing workforce development services to employers and job seekers of Texas. Former chair Ruth Ruggero Hughs resigned from the TWC on August 19, 2019 after she was appointed the new Secretary of State by Governor Abbott.

For employers, TWC offers recruiting, retention, training and retraining, outplacement services, and information on labor law and labor market statistics.

For job seekers, TWC offers career development information, job search resources, training programs, and, as appropriate, unemployment benefits. While targeted populations receive intensive assistance to overcome barriers to employment, all Texans can benefit from the services offered by TWC and our network of workforce partners.

The Texas Workforce Commission is part of a local and state network dedicated to developing the workforce of Texas. The network is composed of the statewide efforts of the commission coupled with planning and service provision on a regional level by 28 local workforce boards. This network gives customers access to local workforce solutions and statewide services in a single location — Texas Workforce Centers.

Primary services of the Texas Workforce Commission and our network partners are funded by federal tax revenue and are generally free to all Texans. Mailing address: 101 E. 15th Street, Austin 78778; (512) 463-2222; www.twc.state.tx.us. ☆

Texas State Historical Association
HANDBOOK OF TEXAS

The Handbook of Texas is the largest digital state encyclopedia with:

- More than 27,000 entries by 6,000+ authors
- Topics from the Prehistoric Era to the Modern Age
- 9,000+ images
- 1,000+ video and audio clips
- Entries vetted by our Chief Historian and staff
- 10 million page views annually
- 4.5 million users annually

The Handbook of Texas is accessible for FREE on computers, phones, and tablets.

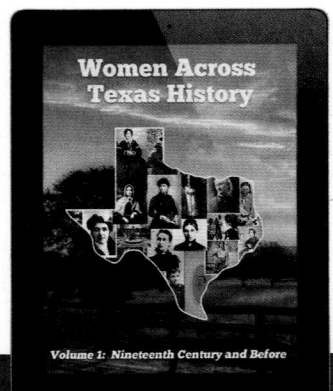

Women Across Texas History

Volume 1: Nineteenth Century and Before

www.tshaonline.org/handbook

Texas State Boards and Commissions

Following is a list of appointees to state boards and commissions, as well as names of other state officials, revised to **August 1, 2019**. Information includes, where available, (1) date of creation; (2) whether the position is elective or appointive; (3) length of term; (4) compensation, if any; (5) number of members; (6) names of appointees, their hometowns, and expiration of terms. In some instances the date of term expiration has passed; in such cases, no new appointment had been made by press time, and the official is continuing to fill the position until a successor is named. Most positions marked "apptv." are appointed by the Governor. Where otherwise, appointing authority is given. Most advisory boards are not listed. Salaries for commissioners and administrators are those that were authorized by the appropriations bill passed by the 85th Legislature for the 2018–2019 biennium. They are "not-to-exceed" salaries: maximum authorized salaries for the positions. Actual salaries may be less than those stated here.

Accountancy, Texas State Board of Public: (1945 with 2-yr. terms; reorganized 1959 as 9-member board with 6-yr. overlapping terms; number of members increased to 12 in 1979; increased to 15 in 1989); per diem and expenses: Chair Timothy L. LaFrey, Austin (1/31/21); Robert M. McAdams, San Antonio (1/31/19); Benjamin Peña, Brownsville (1/31/21); Susan Fletcher, Frisco (1/31/19); Ross T. Johnson, Houston (1/31/21); Lisa A. Friel, San Antonio (1/31/23); Jamie D. Grant, Arlington (1/31/23); Donna J. Hugly, Fredericksburg (1/31/19); James D. Ingram IV, College Station (1/31/23); William Lawrence, Highland Village (1/31/19); Roselyn Morris, San Marcos (1/31/21); Steve D. Peña, Georgetown (1/31/19); Debra S. Sharp, Houston (1/31/23); Kimberly E. Wilkerson, Lubbock (1/31/21). Presiding Officer Manuel Cavazos, 333 Guadalupe, Ste. 3-900, Austin 78701-3900; (512) 305-7800.

Acupuncture Examiners, Texas State Board of: (1993); apptv.; 6-yr.; per diem; 9 members: Chair Raymond J. Graham, El Paso (1/31/17); Donna S. Guthery, Bellaire (1/31/17); Mary E. Hebert, Nacogdoches (1/31/25); Claudine K. Vass, Richmond (1/31/21); Rachelle L. Webb, Austin (1/31/19); Grant E. Weidler, Spring (1/31/23); Jeremy D. Wiseman, Austin (1/31/23); one vacancy. Presiding Officer Allen Cline, 333 Guadalupe, Tower III, #610, Austin 78768; (512) 305-7030.

Ad Valorem Tax Rate, Board to Calculate the: Est. 1907 with 3 ex-officio members: Governor, State Comptroller of Public Accounts, and State Treasurer; consolidated in 1973 with State Tax Board; abolished by 66th Legislature (SB 621, which created the Property Tax Code), effective 1/1/82, and replaced by the Texas State Property Tax Board.

Adjutant General's Dept.: (1836 by Republic of Texas; present office established 1905); apptv.; 2-yr.; 3 members: Adjutant General, Major General Tracy Norris, Austin (1/1/21); ($178,196); Assistant for Army, Brig. Gen. Gregory Chaney, Austin; Assistant for Air, Brig. Gen. Dawn Ferrell, Weatherford. Assistants each serve a term at the pleasure of the Gov.; c/o Camp Mabry, PO Box 5218, Austin 78763-5218; (512) 782-5001.

Administrative Hearings, State Office of: Created in 1991 by 72nd Leg.; apptv.; 2-yr.; 1 member: Chief Admin. Law Judge Kristofer Monson, Driftwood (5/1/21) ($145,278). William P. Clements Building, 300 W. 15th St., Ste. 504, Austin 78701; (512) 475-4993.

Administrative Judicial Districts of Texas, Presiding Judges: Apptv.; term served concurrent with term as District Judge, subject to reappointment if re-elected to bench. No additional compensation. For names of judges, *see* Administrative Judicial Districts in index.

Aging and Disability Services Council, Department of (DADS): Est. 2003 by the 78th Legislature; later abolished by 84th Legislature (Senate Bill 200) effective 9/1/2017 and services merged into Texas Health and Human Services.

Agricultural Finance Authority, Texas: (1987); apptv.; 2-yr.; expenses; 2 ex-officio members: Agriculture Commissioner and Director for Institute for International Agribusiness Studies at Prairie View A&M University; 7 apptd. members: Justin Tucker, Cameron (1/7/20); Kelley Sullivan, Crockett (1/1/20); Lee Norman, Post (2/1/20); John Paul Deneen, Waxahachie (1/1/20); John Crew, Dallas (1/1/20); Ted F. Conover, Tyler (1/1/20); Aaron Wiechman, Lakeway (1/1/20); Barry Smith, Winnsboro (1/1/20); Samuel Brian McCuistion, Aledo (1/1/20). Secretary Prairie View A&M Freddie Richards, PO Box 12847, Austin 78711; (512) 936-0273.

Alcohol and Drug Abuse, Texas Commission on: (1953 as Texas Commission on Alcoholism); abolished by House Bill 2292 and functions merged into Department of State Health Services in January 2004.

Alcoholic Beverage Commission, Texas: (1935 as Liquor Control Board; name changed in 1970); apptv.; 6-yr; per diem and expenses; administrator apptd. by commission; 3 members: Chair Kevin J. Lilly, Houston (11/15/21); Ida Clement Steen, San Antonio (11/15/19); Jason E. Boatright, Dallas (11/15/23). PO Box 13127, Austin 78711-3127; (512) 206-3333.

Alzheimer's Disease & Related Disorders, Texas Council on: (1999); apptv.; 2-yr.; 16 members: Chair Rita Hortenstine, Dallas (8/31/19); Byron Cordes, San Antonio; Laura DeFina, Dallas; Marc Diamond, Dallas; Joe A. Evans, Jr., Beaumont (8/31/21); Vaunette Fay, Houston; Ana Guerrero Gore, Galveston; Char Hu, Georgetown; Eddie Patton, Jr., Sugar Land (3/31/21); Mary Quiceno, Dallas; Sudha Seshadri, San Antonio; Terrance Sommers, Amarillo; Valerie J. Krueger, Austin; Toni Packard, Austin; 2 vacancies. PO Box 149347 Austin, TX 78714-9347;(800) 242-3399.

Angelina and Neches River Authority: (1935 as Sabine-Neches Conservation Dist.; reorganized in 1950 and name changed to Neches River Conservation Dist.; changed to present name in 1977); apptv.; expenses; 6-yr.; 9 members: Chair Jody Anderson, Lufkin (9/5/19); Thomas R. Murphy, Crockett (9/5/19); Skip Ogle, Tyler (9/5/21); David King, Nacogdoches (9/5/19); Dale Morton, Nacogdoches, (9/5/21); Francis G. Spruiell, Center (9/5/21); 3 vacancies. Gen. Mgr. Kelley Holcomb, PO Box 387, Lufkin 75902-0387; (936) 632-7795.

Animal Health Commission, Texas: (1893 as Texas Livestock Sanitary Commission; name changed in 1959; members increased to 9 in 1973; raised to 12 in 1983); apptv.; per diem and expenses; 6-yr.; 13 members: Chair Coleman H. Locke, Hungerford (9/6/21); Joseph G. Osterkamp, Muleshoe (9/6/23); Jim Eggleston, Weatherford (9/6/21); Ken Jordan, San Saba (9/6/19); Wendee C. Langdon, Lubbock (9/6/23); Joe Lynn Leathers, Guthrie (9/6/19); Keith M. Staggs, Gonzales (9/6/23); Thomas Eugene Oates, Huntsville (9/6/19); Leo D. Vermedahl, Dalhart (9/6/23); Michael Louis Vickers, Falfurrias, (9/6/21); Eric Dean White, Mason (9/6/19); Barret J. Klein, Boerne (9/6/19); William Edmiston, Jr., Eldorado (9/9/19). Exec. Dir. Andy

Schwartz ($146,742), PO Box 12966, Austin 78711-2966; (512) 719-0700.

Appraiser Licensing and Certification Board, Texas: (1991); 2-yr.; apptv.; per diem on duty; 9 members; 1 ex officio: Texas General Land Office; 8 app'td.: Chair Jamie Wickliffe, Midlothian (1/31/19); Martha Gayle Reid Lynch, El Paso (1/31/21); Ray Bolton, Bee Cave (1/31/21); James Jeffries, Georgetown (1/31/23); Clayton Black, Stanton (1/31/23); Tony Peña, Lubbock (1/31/21); Alejandro Sostre-Odio, San Antonio (1/31/19); Joyce Yannuzzi, New Braunfels (1/31/19); Earl Renfrow, Austin. Commissioner Douglas E. Oldmixon ($179,375), PO Box 12188, Austin 78711-2188; (512) 936-3001.

Architectural Examiners, Texas Board of: (1937 as 3-member board; raised to 6 members in 1951 and to 9 in 1977); apptv.; 6-yr.; per diem and expenses; 9 members: Chair Debra Marino, San Antonio (8/31/23); Sean Payton, Killeen (8/31/21); Jennifer Walker, Lampasas (8/31/21); Charles H. Anastos, Corpus Christi (8/31/19); Fernando Trevino Jr., San Antonio (8/31/23); Bob Wetmore, Austin (8/31/21); Chase Bearden, Austin (1/31/21); Rosa Salazar, Lubbock (8/31/23); Joyce Smith, San Antonio (8/31/23). Exec. Dir. Julie Hildebrand ($140,005), 333 Guadalupe St., Ste. 2-350, PO Box 12337, Austin 78711-2337; (512) 305-9000.

Arts, Texas Commission on the: (1965 as Texas Fine Arts Commission; name changed to Texas Commission on the Arts and Humanities and members increased to 18 in 1971; name changed to present form in 1979); apptv.; 6-yr.; expenses; members: Chair Dale W. Brock, Fort Worth (8/31/23); S. Shawn Stephens, Houston (8/15/19); Karen Partee, Marshall (8/31/19); Mila B. Gibson, Sweetwater (8/31/21); Marci L. Roberts, Marathon (8/31/21); Adrian Guerra, Roma (8/31/23); Mary Ann Apap Heller, Austin (8/31/19); Deborah Gray Marino, San Antonio (8/31/23); Sean Payton, Killeen (8/31/21). Exec. Dir. Gary Gibbs ($121,041), 920 Colorado St., PO Box 13406, Austin 78711-3406; (512) 463-5535.

Assistive and Rehabilitative Services Council, Department of (DARS): (2004) apptv.; 6-yr.; 9 members: Department was dissolved in September 2016 and programs were transferred to the Texas Workforce Commission.

Athletic Trainers, Advisory Board of: (1971 as Texas Board of Athletic Trainers; name changed in 1975); expenses; 6-yr.; 5 members: Chair David J. Weir, College Station (1/31/25); Darrell Ganus, Kilgore (1/31/21); Britney Webb, Martindale (1/31/21); Michael Fitch, Dallas (1/31/23); David Schmidt, San Antonio (1/31/23). PO Box 149347, MC 1982, Austin 78714-9347; (512) 834-6615.

Attorney, State Prosecuting: (1923) apptd. by Court of Criminal Appeals: Stacey M. Soule ($143,500), 209 W. 14th St., Ste. 203, PO Box 13046, Austin 78711; (512) 463-1660.

Auditor's Office, State: (1929); 2-yr.; apptd. by Legislative Audit Committee, a joint Senate-House committee: State Auditor Lisa R. Collier ($181,128), Robert E. Johnson Bldg., 1501 Congress, P.O. Box 12067, Austin 78711-2067; (512) 936-9500.

Autism and Pervasive Developmental Disorders, Texas Council on: (1987); abolished by the 84th Legislature, S.B. 200. Duties transferred to the Texas Health and Human Services Commission.

Banking, Dept. of: (1923); 2-yr.; apptd. by State Finance Commission; Commissioner Charles G. Cooper ($242,925); 2601 N. Lamar Blvd., Austin 78705-4294; (512) 475-1300. (*See* also Finance Commission of Texas.)

Bar of Texas, State: (1939 as administrative arm of Supreme Court); 30 directors elected by membership; 3-yr. terms; expenses paid from dues collected from membership. Executive director, general counsel, and immediate past chair serve as ex-officio members. Chair of the Board Laura Gibson; Texas Law Center, 1414 Colorado, P.O. Box 12487, Austin 78711; (512) 427-1463.

Barbering Advisory Board, State: (1929 as 3-member Texas Board of Barber Examiners; members increased in 1975; named changed to current in 2005 and functions transferred to Texas Dept. of Licensing and Regulation); 6-yr.; apptd. by dept. commissioners; 5 members: Chair Ron Jemison, Houston (9/29/21); Ronald Weathers, De Soto (9/29/23); Michelle Wasser, Austin (9/29/19); Jenny Hatch, Alpine (9/29/21); James Bowens, Round Rock (9/29/19). c/o Texas Dept. of Licensing and Regulation, 920 Colorado St., PO Box 12884, Austin 78711; (512) 463-6599.

Blind, Texas Commission for the: as of September 2016 the commission was incorporated into the Texas Workforce Commission.

Blind and Visually Impaired Governing Board, Texas School for the: (1979); apptv.; 6-yr.; expenses; 9 members: Joseph Muniz, Harlingen (1/31/21); Mary K. Alexander, Valley View (1/31/21); Ruben Brown, Jr., Pflugerville (1/31/23); Bobby Druesedow, Glen Rose (1/31/19); Michael E. Garrett, Missouri City (1/31/19); Michael P. Hanley, Leander (1/31/23); Brenda W. Lee, Brownwood (1/31/19); Julie Prause, Columbus (1/31/23); B. Lee Sonnenberg, Lubbock (1/31/19). Superintendent William Daugherty ($115,000), 1100 W. 45th St., Austin 78756-3494; (512) 454-8631.

Board of (Note: In most instances, state boards are alphabetized under key word, such as Accountancy, Texas State Board of Public.)

Bond Review Board: (1987); composed of Governor, Lieutenant Governor, House Speaker, and Comptroller of Public Accounts; oversees debt financing for Texas' infrastructure and other public purposes, debt issuance, and debt management functions of state and local entities, and the state's private activity bond allocation; Exec. Dir. Rob Latsha ($117,500); 300 W. 15th St., Ste. 409, PO Box 13292, Austin 78711-3292; (512) 463-1741.

Brazos River Authority: (1929 as Brazos River Conservation and Reclamation District; name changed to present form in 1953); apptv.; 6-yr; expenses; 21 members: Chair Cynthia A. Flores, Round Rock (2/1/21); LeRoy, Tuscola (2/1/19); Salvatore A. Zaccagnino, Caldwell (2/1/19); Richard L. Ball, Mineral Wells (2/1/19); Peter G. Bennis, Fort Worth (2/1/19); Jennifer Henderson, Round Rock (2/1/23); Charles R. Huber III, Granbury (2/1/21); Judy Krohn, Georgetown (2/1/23); Traci LaChance, Danbury (2/1/23); Jim Lattimore, Graford (2/1/19); Royce Lesley, Comanche (2/1/23); Wesley D. Lloyd, Waco (2/1/19); John Henry Luton, Granbury (2/1/21); William J. Rankin, Brenham (2/1/21); Alan Sandersen, Sugar Land (2/1/23); Jarrod Smith, Danbury (2/1/23); Jeffery S. Tallas, Sugar Land (2/1/21); William W. Taylor III, Waco (2/1/21); Wayne Wilson, Bryan (2/1/23); Dave Scott, Richmond (2/1/19). Gen. Mgr./CEO Phillip J. Ford, 4600 Cobbs Drive, PO Box 7555, Waco 76714-7555; (254) 761-3100.

Building and Procurement Commission, Texas: (1919; renamed Texas Facilities Commission in 2007 and some procurement duties transferred to the Comptroller of Public Accounts); *see* Facilities Commission, Texas.

Canadian River Compact Commissioner: (1951); (negotiates with New Mexico and Oklahoma regarding waters of the Canadian): Commissioner Roger S. Cox; Compacts

Coordinator Scott Van Winkle. PO Box 13087, Austin 78711-3087; (512) 239-4730.

Canadian River Municipal Water Authority: (1953); 2-yr; 17 members apptd. by member cities: Pres. Richard Ellis, Levelland; Bill Carder, Borger; Jerry Carlson, Pampa; James O. Collins, Lubbock; Tyke Dipprey, Plainview; Rickey Dunn, Brownfield; William Hallerberg, Amarillo; Jay House, Lubbock; Jay Dee House, Tahoka; Glendon Jett, Borger; Brian Pohlmeir, Plainview; Lenny Sadler, Amarillo; Mac Smith, Pampa; Bruce Vaughn, O'Donnell; Scott Wade, Levelland; Chad Wilson, Slaton; Cris Norris, Lamesa. Gen. Mgr. Kent Satterwhite, PO Box 9, Sanford 79078-0009; (806) 865-3325.

Cancer Prevention & Research Institute of Texas: (1985 as Texas Cancer Council; name changed in 2007); apptv.; 4-yr.; expenses; 11 members; 2 ex officio: Attorney General and Comptroller of Public Accounts; 9 apptd.: Chair Will Montgomery, Dallas (2/1/23); Dee Margo, El Paso (1/31/23); Angelos Angelou, Austin (1/31/19); David A. Cummings, San Angelo (1/31/23), Mahendra C. Patel, San Antonio (1/1/21); William H. Rice, Austin (1/31/19); 3 vacancies. Chief Exec. Dir. Wayne Roberts, ($256,250) 211 E. 7th St., Ste. 300, PO Box 12097, Austin 78711-2097; (512) 463-3190.

Cardiovascular Disease and Stroke, Texas Council on: (1999); apptv.; 6-yr.; 15 members: 4 ex officio: Department of Assistive and Rehabilitative Services, Department of Aging and Disability Services, Texas Education Agency, Texas Department of State Health Services; 11 apptd.: Chair Neal Rutledge, Austin (2/1/23); E'Loria Simon-Campbell, Houston (2/1/19); Janet Hall, Florence (2/1/23); Kyle Sheets, Ovala (2/1/23); Vanessa Hicks-Callaway, Victoria (2/1/19); Sherron Meeks, Midland (2/1/21); Shilpa Shamapant, Austin (2/1/21); Marcie Gonzalez Wilson, Lakeway (2/1/21); Melbert Hillert, Jr., Dallas (2/1/21); Suzanne Hildebrand; Michael M. Hawkins; 4 vacancies. c/o Texas Dept. of State Health Services, PO Box 149347, Austin 78714-9347; (512) 458-7111.

Cemetery Committee, Texas State: (1997); apptv.; 6-yr.; 3 members: Chair Benjamin M. Hanson, Austin (2/1/21); Jim Bayless, Austin (2/1/23); Carolyn Hodges, Houston (2/1/25). 909 Navasota, Austin 78702; (512) 463-6023.

Central Colorado River Authority (*See* Colorado River Authority, Central.)

Chemist, Office of State: (1911); ex officio, indefinite term: State Chemist Timothy J. Herrman, PO Box 3160, College Station 77841-3160; (979) 845-1121.

Childhood Intervention, Interagency Council on Early: Combined 3/1/04 into Department of Assistive and Rehabilitative Services (DARS) of the Health and Human Services Commission.

Chiropractic Examiners, Texas Board of: (1949); apptv.; 6-yr.; expenses; 9 members: Chair Mark R. Bronson, Fort Worth (2/1/21); Nicholas Baucum, Corpus Christi (2/1/21); Karen Campion, Austin (2/1/19); Mindy Neal, Bovina (2/1/23); Debra White, Nacogdoches (2/1/23); Scott Wofford, Abilene (2/1/19); Gus Ramirez, Tyler (2/1/21); John Steinberg, Marion (2/1/19); Ebony Todd, Fort Hood (2/1/23). Exec. Dir. Patrick Fortner ($93,520), 333 Guadalupe, Ste. 3-825, Austin 78701; (512) 305-6700.

Coastal Water Authority: (1967 as Coastal Industrial Water Authority; name changed in 1985); 2-yr.; per diem and expenses; 7 members; 4 apptd. by Houston mayor; 3 apptd. by Gov.: Pres. D. Wayne Klotz, Houston (3/31/19); Thomas Reiser, Houston (4/1/19); Jon M. Sjolander, Dayton (4/1/20); Joseph J. Soliz, Houston (3/31/18); Giti Zarinkelk, Houston (3/31/18); Tony L. Council, Houston (3/31/19); Douglas Walker, Beach City (4/1/19). Exec. Dir.

Donald R. Ripley, ($42,954). 1801 Main, Ste. 800, Houston 77002; (713) 658-9020.

Colorado River Authority, Central: (1935); Abolished December 1, 2017 by S.B. 2262, 85th Legislature. All assets were transferred to Coleman County.

Colorado River Authority, Lower: (1934 as 9-member board; members increased in 1951 and 1975); apptv.; 6-yr.; per diem on duty; 15 members: Chair Timothy Timmerman, Austin (2/1/25); Thomas Michael Martine, Cypress Mill (2/1/25); Stephen F. Cooper, El Campo (2/1/23); Lori A. Berger, Flatonia (2/1/21); Joseph M. Crane, Bay City (2/1/21); Margaret Voelter, Austin, (2/1/25); Laura Figueroa, Brenham (2/1/23); Raymond A. Gill Jr., Horseshoe Bay (2/1/23); Charles B. Johnson, Brownwood (2/1/21); Thomas L. Kelley, Eagle Lake (2/1/23); Robert Lewis, Elgin (2/1/25); George W. Russell, Marble Falls (2/1/21); Michael Allen, Kerrville (2/1/25); Martha Leigh M. Whitten, San Saba (2/1/21); Nancy Yeary, Burnet County (2/1/23). Gen. Man. Phil Wilson, 3700 Lake Austin Blvd., PO Box 220, Austin 78767-0220; (512) 473-3200.

Colorado River Authority, Upper: (1935 as 9-member board; reorganized in 1965); apptv.; 6-yr.; per diem and expenses; 9 members: Chair Eva Horton, San Angelo (2/1/21); Hugh Stone II, San Angelo (2/1/23); Ronny Alexander, Paint Rock (2/1/21); Erica Hall, Abilene (2/1/21); Bill Holland, San Angelo (2/1/19); William Hood, Robert Lee (2/1/19); Martin Lee, Bronte (2/1/19); Wade Mahan, Menard (2/1/23); Kathryn Mews, Menard (2/1/23). Director Chuck Brown, 512 Orient, San Angelo 76903; (325) 655-0565.

Commissioner of (*See* keyword, such as Agriculture, Commissioner of.)

Concho River Water and Soil Conservation Authority, Lower: Established in 1939; abolished by the 81st Texas Legislature on 9/1/09.

Consumer Credit Commissioner: Leslie L. Pettijohn ($196,000), 2601 N. Lamar, Austin 78705-4207; (512) 936-7600. Consumer Help Line: (800) 538-1579.

Cosmetology Advisory Board, Texas: (1935 as 3-member State Board of Hairdressers and Cosmetologists; name changed and members increased in 1971; name changed to current in 2005 and functions transferred to Texas Dept. of Licensing and Regulation); apptv.; per diem and expenses; 6-yr.; 8 members: Chair Ron Robinson, Waco (9/29/19); Anthony Anderson, Spring Branch (9/29/19); Natalie Caballero, Lubbock (9/29/19); Betty Neff, Austin (9/29/23); Aleshia Rivera, Mount Pleasant (9/29/19); Vanessa Robbins, Houston (9/29/21); Mary Paschal-Lindsay, Pearland (9/29/23); Sam Webb, Austin (9/29/21); ex officio, Debbie Wieland, Austin; c/o Texas Dept. of Licensing and Regulation, 920 Colorado, PO Box 12157, Austin 78711; (512) 463-6599.

Counselors, Texas State Board of Examiners of Professional: (1981); apptv.; 6-yr.; expenses; 9 members: Chair Steven D. Christopherson, Pasadena (2/1/19); Loretta Bradley, Lubbock (2/1/21); Brenda Compagnone, San Antonio (2/1/21); Carolyn Stubblefield, Dallas (2/1/23); Christopher Taylor, Dallas (2/1/21); Sarah Abraham, Sugar Land (2/1/19); Steven Hallbauer, Rockwall (2/1/19); Leslie F. Pohl, Austin (2/1/19); Roy Smith, Midland (2/1/23). Exec. Dir. Vacant, c/o Texas Dept. of State Health Services, 1100 W. 49th St., PO Box 149347, Austin 78714-9347; (512) 834-6658.

County and District Retirement System, Texas: (*See* Retirement System, Texas County and District.)

Court Administration, State Office of: (1985); apptd. by State Supreme Court chief justice; 1 member who also serves as executive director of the Texas Judicial Council: Admin. Dir. David Slayton ($196,800); Tom C. Clark State Courts Bldg., 205 W. 14th, 6th Flr., PO Box 12066, Austin 78711; (512) 463-1625.

Court Interpreters Advisory Board, Licensed: Apptv. by Texas Supreme Court; part of Judicial Branch Certification Commission; staggered terms; 6-yr., 5 members: Melissa B. Fischer, San Antonio (2/1/21); Luis Garcia, Keller (N/A); Robert Richter Jr., Houston (2/1/25); Melissa Wallace, San Antonio (2/1/25); Cynthia de Pena, McAllen (2/1/23); 205 W. 14th St., Ste. 101, PO Box 13131, Austin 78711; (512) 463-1630.

Court Reporters Certification Advisory Board: Apptv. by Texas Supreme Court; part of Judicial Branch Certification Commission; staggered terms; 6-yr., 5 members: Chair Hon. William C. Sowder, Lubbock (12/31/21); Board members: Robin Cooksey, Conroe (12/31/21); Janice Eidd-Meadows, Tyler (12/31/21); Deborah K. Hamon, Rockwall (12/31/23); Molly Pela, Houston (12/31/19); Whitney Lehmberg Riley, Boerne (12/31/19); Kim Tindall, San Antonio (12/31/23). Presiding Officer Hon. Lori I. Valenzuela, 205 W. 14th St., Ste. 101, PO Box 13131, Austin 78711; (512) 463-1630.

Credit Union Commission: (1949 as 3-member Credit Union Advisory Commission; name changed and members increased to 6 in 1969; increased to 9 in 1981); apptv.; 6-yr.; expenses; 9 members: Chair Yusuf Farran, El Paso (2/15/21); David Shurtz, Hudson Oaks (2/15/25); Beckie S. Cobb, Deer Park (2/15/21); Steve Gilman, Houston (2/15/25); James L. Minge, Arlington (2/15/23); Kay Swan, Monahans (2/15/25); Ricky Ybarra, Austin (2/15/23); Elizabeth Bayless, Austin (2/15/25); Sherrie Merket, Midland (2/15/23); Karyn Brownlee, Coppell (2/15/23). Commissioner John J. Kolhoff ($185,000), 914 E. Anderson Ln., Austin 78752-1699; (512) 837-9236.

Crime Stoppers Advisory Council: (1981); apptv.; 4-yr.; per diem and expenses; 5 members: Lauren Day, Austin (9/1/20); Perry Gilmore, Amarillo (9/1/20); Carlo Hernandez, Brownsville (9/1/20); 2 vacancies. Texas State University San Marcos, 601 University Dr., San Marcos 78666-4610; (866) 220-4357.

Crime Victims' Institute Advisory Council: (1995 as function of attorney general's office; transferred to Sam Houston State University in 2003); apptv.; 2-yr.; 3 ex-officio: Attorney General, 1 member of House, 1 member of Senate; 14 apptd. members: Shawn Kennington, Pittsburg (1/21/20); Jeff Oldham, Austin (1/21/20); Gene Pack, Houston (1/21/20); JD Robertson, Wimberley (1/21/20); Andrea Sparks, Austin (1/21/20); Hector Villarreal, Alice (1/21/20); Abigail Brookshire, Midlothian (1/21/21); Libby Hamilton, Round Rock (1/21/21); Joan Huffman, Houston (1/21/21); Scott MacNaughton, San Antonio (1/21/21); James White, Hillister (1/21/21); Erleigh Wiley, Forney (1/21/21). Director Leana Bouffard, Crime Victims' Institute, 816 17th St., Sam Houston State University, Huntsville 77340; (936) 294-3100.

Criminal Justice, Texas Board of: (1989: assumed duties of former Board of Corrections, Adult Probation Commission and Board of Pardons and Paroles); apptv; 6-yr.; expenses; 9 members: Chair Dale Wainwright, Austin (2/1/21); R. Terrell McCombs, San Antonio (2/1/19; Eric Gambrell, Dallas (2/1/19); E. F. DeAyala, Houston (2/1/23); Tom Fordyce, Huntsville (2/1/21); Larry Miles, Amarillo (2/1/23); Patrick O'Daniel, Austin (2/1/23); Derrelynn Perryman, Arlington (2/1/21); Thomas Wingate, Mission (2/1/19). Exec. Dir. Dept. of Criminal Justice: Bryan Collier ($266,500), 209 West 14th St., Ste. 500, Price Daniel Bldg., PO Box 13084, Austin 78711-3084; (512) 475-3250.

Deaf, Texas School for the, Governing Board: (1979); apptv.; 6-yr.; expenses; 9 members: Chair Eric Hogue, Wylie (1/31/21); Shawn P. Saladin, Edinburg (1/31/23); Angela O. Wolf, Dripping Springs (1/31/21); Shalia Cowan, Dripping Springs (1/31/23); Ryan D. Hutchison, Austin (1/31/21); Heather Withrow, Austin (N/A); Keith Sibley, Bedford (1/31/25); David Saunders, Waxahachie (1/31/25); Christopher Moreland, New Braunfels (1/31/23). Superintendent Claire Bugen ($148,908), 1102 S. Congress, Austin 78704; (512) 462-5353.

Deaf and Hard of Hearing, Texas Commission for the: Combined into Department of Assistive and Rehabilitative Services (DARS) of the Health and Human Services Commission as of 3/1/04.

Demographer, Office of the State: (2001); created by 77th Legislature: Lloyd Potter, 1700 N. Congress Ave., Ste. 220W, PO Box 13455, Austin 78711; (512) 463-8390.

Dental Examiners, State Board of: (1919 as 6-member board; increased to 9 members in 1971; increased to 12 in 1981; increased to 15 in 1991; sunsetted in 1994; reconstituted with 18 members in 1995; reduced to 15 in 2005); apptv.; 6-yr.; per diem and expenses; 15 members: Chair M. David Tillman, Aledo (2/1/21); Jorge E. Quirch, Missouri City (2/1/21); Kimberly N. Haynes, College Station (2/1/19); Bryan N. Henderson II, Dallas (2/1/23); Robert G. McNeill, Dallas (2/1/21); David H. Yu, Austin (2/1/19); Lorie L. Jones, Magnolia (2/1/23); Margo Y. Melchor, Houston (2/1/21); Lois M. Palermo, League City (2/1/19); Rodney Bustamante, Austin (2/1/21); Kathryn Sisk, Cedar Park (2/1/23); Danielle Franklin, Dallas (2/1/25); Raymond L. Wiggins, Katy (2/1/25); Joanna Allaire, The Woodlands (2/1/25); Jessica Bell, Highland Village (2/1/25). Exec. Dir. Glenn Parker ($116,000), 333 Guadalupe, Tower III, #800, Austin 78701-3942; (512) 463-6400.

Depository Board, State: Abolished in May 1997.

Diabetes Council, Texas: (1983; with 5 ex officio and 6 public members serving 2-yr. terms; changed in 1987 to 3 ex officio and 8 public members; changed to present in 1991; term length changed from 4 to 6 years in 1997); 6-yr.; 14 members: 11 apptv.: Chair Kathy Ann LaCivita, San Antonio (2/1/21); Curtis Triplitt, San Antonio (2/1/19); Jason M. Ryan, Houston (2/1/19); Joan Colgin, Dallas (2/1/21); Felicia Fruia-Edge, Rancho Viejo (2/1/23); Carley Gomez-Meade, Austin (2/1/19); John Griffin, Victoria (2/1/19); Aida Moreno-Brown, El Paso (2/1/21); Feyi Obamehinti, Keller (2/1/23); Ardis Reed, Hideaway (2/1/23); William Sanders, Dallas (2/1/21); 3 ex officio: reps. from Texas Workforce Commission; Health and Human Services Commission; Texas Department of State Health Services. Dir. Ashley Doyle, c/o Texas Dept. of State Health Services, PO Box 149347 Austin 78714-9347; (512) 458-7490.

Dietitians, State Board of Examiners of: All duties transferred to the Texas Department of Licensing and Regulation. Abolished in 2015 by the 84th Legislature, S.B. 202.

Disabilities, Governor's Committee on People with: (1949 as Gov.'s Committee on Employment of the Handicapped; recreated in 1983 as Gov.'s Committee for Disabled Persons; in 1991, given current name and expanded duties); apptv.; 2-yr. and at pleasure of Gov.; 12 members: Chair Aaron W. Bangor, Austin (2/1/18); Ellen M. Bauman, Joshua (2/1/19); Evelyn Cano, Pharr (2/1/20); Andrew Cohen, Round Rock (2/1/19); Elizabeth Dickey, Austin (2/1/19); Archer Hadley, Austin (2/1/19); Richard Martinez, San Antonio (2/1/20); Linda Millstone, Austin (2/1/19); Dylan Rafaty, Plano (2/1/19); Emma F. Rudkin, Boerne (2/1/20); Amy L. Scott, Austin (2/1/20); Marco A. Treviño, Edinburg (2/1/21). Exec. Dir. Angi English, 1100 San Jacinto,

PO Box 12428, Austin 78711-2428; (512) 463-5739; 7-1-1 TDD.

Disabilities, Texas Council for Developmental: (1971); apptv.; 6-yr.; 27 members; 19 apptv.: Chair Richard Browning, Spring (2/1/23); Paul Cardarella, Denton (2/1/25); Maverick Crawford, San Antonio (2/1/25); Randell Resneder, Lubbock (2/1/21); Robert Schier III, Elgin (2/1/23); Eric Shahid, Somerville (2/1/25); Molly Spratt, Austin (2/1/21); Emmett Summers III, San Antonio (2/1/25); Kimberly Torres, Houston (2/1/25); Rebecca Adkins, Lakeway (2/1/21); Kimberly Blackmon, Fort Worth (2/1/21); Gladys Cortez, McAllen (2/1/23); Kristen Cox, El Paso (2/1/21); Andrew Crim, Fort Worth (2/1/21); Mary Durheim, Spring (2/1/23); Scott McAvoy, Cedar Park (2/1/21); Michael Peace, Poteet (2/1/25); Lora Taylor, Katy (2/1/25); John Thomas, Weatherford (2/1/23); 8 ex offico members from various state agencies. Exec. Dir. Beth Stalvey ($123,205), 6201 E. Oltorf, Ste. 600, Austin 78741; (512) 437-5432.

Disabilities, Texas Council on Purchasing from People with: Duties transfered to Texas Workforce Commission in 2015. Abolished by the 84th legislature, S.B. 212.

Disabilities, Texas Office for Prevention of Developmental: Abolished in 2017.

Disaster Recovery and Renewal, Governor's Commission for: (2008); apptv.; terms at pleasure of Gov.; 23 ex-officio members: County judges from the coastal counties of Aransas, Brazoria, Calhoun, Cameron, Chambers, Galveston, Harris, Hidalgo, Jackson, Jefferson, Kenedy, Kleberg, Liberty, Matagorda, Nueces, Orange, Refugio, San Patricio, Starr, Victoria, and Willacy along with the General Land Office Commissioner and the Agriculture Commissioner; 24 apptd. members: Chair Robert Eckels, Houston; Ronnie Acosta, Pearland; William B. Claybar, Orange; Irma Diaz-Gonzalez, Houston; George (Trey) H. Henderson III, Lufkin; Gary L. Hockstra, Lake Jackson; Jo Ann Howard, Austin; Jerry Kane, Corpus Christi; Mary E. Kelly, Austin; William E. King, Houston; H. Thomas Kornegay, Houston; David L. Lakey, Austin; David S. Lopez, Houston; Ross D. Margraves Jr., Houston; Scott McClelland, Houston; Tracye McDaniel, Houston; Allan B. Polunsky, San Antonio; Penny Redington, Austin; Regina Rogers, Beaumont; Rolando Rubiano, Harlingen; Karen A. Sexton, Galveston; Wade E. Upton, Houston; Daniel J. Wolterman, Houston; H. Edwin Young, Houston. c/o Office of the Governor, PO Box 12428, Austin, 78711; (512) 463-2000.

Education Board, Southern Regional: (1969); apptv.; 4-yr.; 5 members: Gov. Greg Abbott ex officio (6/30/23); Pedro Martinez, San Antonio (6/30/19); Mike Morath, Austin (6/30/18); Raymund A. Paredes, Austin (6/30/21); Larry Taylor, Friendswood (6/30/20); 3 apptv.: Rep. Charles Anderson, Waco; Rep. Mike Lang, Eastland; Sen. Donna Campbell, New Braunfels. President Stephen Pruitt, 592 10th St. N.W., Fayetteville, GA 30318-5776; (404) 875-9211.

Education, Commissioner of: (1866 as Superintendent of Public Instruction; 1949 changed to present name by Gilmer-Aiken Act); apptd. by Gov. since 1995; 4-yr.: Mike Morath ($220,375 plus supplement), 1701 N. Congress Ave., Austin 78701-1494; (512) 463-9734.

Education, State Board of: (1866; re-created in 1928 and re-formed in 1949 by Gilmer-Aikin Act to consist of 21 elective members from districts co-extensive with 21 congressional districts at that time; increased to 24 with congressional redistricting in 1971; increased to 27 with congressional redistricting in 1981; reorganized by special legislative session as 15-member apptv. board in 1984;

became elective board again in 1988); expenses; 4-yr.; 15 members: Dist. 1: Georgina C. Pérez (D), El Paso (1/1/21); Dist. 2: Ruben Cortez Jr. (D), Brownsville (1/1/23); Dist. 3: Marisa B. Perez-Diaz (D), Converse (1/1/23); Dist. 4: Lawrence A. Allen Jr. (D), Houston (1/1/23); Dist. 5: Ken Mercer (R), San Antonio (1/1/21); Dist. 6: Donna Bahorich (R), Houston (1/1/21); Dist. 7: Matt Robinson (R), Dickinson (1/1/23); Dist. 8: Barbara Cargill (R), Conroe (1/1/21); Dist. 9: Keven Ellis (R), Lufkin (1/1/21); Dist. 10: Tom Maynard (R), Florence (1/1/21); Dist. 11: Patricia Hardy (R), Fort Worth (1/1/23); Dist. 12: Pam Little (R), Fairview (1/1/23); Dist. 13: Aicha Davis (D), Dallas (1/1/23); Dist. 14: Sue Melton-Malone (R), Robinson (1/1/21); Dist. 15: Marty Rowley (R), Amarillo (1/1/21). c/o Texas Education Agency, 1701 N. Congress Ave., Austin 78701-1494; (512) 463-9007.

Educator Certification, State Board for: (1995); apptv.; 6-yr.; expenses; 14 members; 3 ex officio: rep. of Comm. of Education; rep. of Comm. of Higher Education; 1 dean of a college of education; 11 apptv.: Chair Jill Druesedow, Haskell (2/1/19); Shareefah Nadir-Mason, Dallas (2/1/25); Tommy L. Coleman, Livingston (2/1/25); Sandra D. Bridges, Rockwall (2/1/19); Rohanna Brooks-Sykes, Spring (2/1/21); Edward Hill, Jr., Harker Heights (2/1/23); John P. Kelly, Pearland (2/1/23); Jose M. Rodriguez, Cedar Park (2/1/23); Laurie J. Turner, Corpus Christi (2/1/21); Carlos O. Villagrana, Houston (2/1/21); THECB Rep.: Rex Peebles; TEA Rep.: Martin Winchester; 1701 N. Congress Ave., 5th floor, Austin 78701-1494; (512) 936-8400.

Edwards Aquifer Authority: (1993); 4-yr.; expenses; 17 members (2 apptv. and 15 elected from single-member districts). Elected members: Dist. 1: Carol Patterson, Bexar Co. (12/1/22); Dist. 2: Byron Miller, Bexar Co. (12/1/20); Dist. 3: Abelardo A. Salinas, III, Bexar County (12/1/22); Dist. 4: Benjamin F. Youngblood, Bexar Co. (12/1/20); Dist. 5: Ron Ellis, Bexar Co. (12/1/22); Dist. 6: Deborah Carington, Bexar Co. (12/1/20); Dist. 7: Enrique Valdivia, Bexar Co. (12/1/22); Dist. 8: Kathleen Krueger, Comal Co. (12/1/20); Dist. 9: Ronald J. Walton Sr., Comal & Guadalupe Cos. (12/1/22); Dist. 10: Patrick Stroka, Hays Co. (12/1/20); Dist. 11: Rachel Allyn Sanborn, Hays & Caldwell Cos. (12/1/22); Dist. 12: Scott Yanta, Medina Co. (12/1/20); Dist. 13: Chair Luana Buckner, Medina & Atascosa Cos. (12/1/22); Dist. 14: Don Laffere, Uvalde Co. (12/1/20); Dist. 15: Rader Gilleland, Uvalde Co. (12/1/22). Apptv. members: J. Clark Ward, Medina & Uvalde Cos. (12/1/20); Gary Middleton, South Central Texas Water Advisory Committee (12/1/20). Gen. Mgr. Roland Ruiz, 1615 N. St. Mary's St., San Antonio 78215; (210) 222-2204.

Egg Marketing Advisory Board: Abolished May 1997.

Election Commission, State: (1973); 9 members; 4 ex officio: Chmn. of Democratic State Executive Committee; Chmn. of Republican State Executive Committee; Chief Justice of Supreme Court; Court of Criminal Appeals Presiding Judge; 5 apptv.: 1 justice of the Court of Appeals apptd. by Chief Justice of Supreme Court, 1 District Judge apptd. by presiding judge of Court of Criminal Appeals; 2 county chairmen (1 Democrat, 1 Republican, named by their parties); Secretary of State.

Emergency Communications, Commission on State: (1985 as 17-member Advisory Commission on State Emergency Communications; name changed and members reduced to 12 in 2000); apptv.; 4-yr.; expenses; 12 members: 3 ex officio: reps. of Dept. of State Health Services, Public Utilities Comm., and Dept. of Information Resources; 9 apptd.: Chair William Buchholtz, San Antonio (9/1/21); Kay Alexander, Abilene (9/1/19); James Beauchamp, Midland (9/1/19); Sue Brannon, Midland (9/1/23); Debi Hays, Odessa (9/1/23) Terry Henley, Meadows Place (9/1/19);

Jack D. Miller, Denton (9/1/21); Cathy Skurow, Portland (9/1/23); Von Washington, Sr., El Paso (9/1/21); Clinton Sawyer, Amherst (9/1/19). Exec. Dir. Kelli Merriweather ($123,562), 333 Guadalupe St., Ste. 2-212, Austin 78701-3942; (512) 305-6911.

Emergency Management Council, State: 32 members from state agencies and volunteer organizations. Texas Division of Emergency Management Chief W. Nim Kidd, 5805 N. Lamar Blvd., P.O. Box 4087, Austin 78773; (512) 424-2138.

Emergency Services Retirement System, Texas: (*See* Retirement System, Texas Emergency Services.)

Employment Commission, Texas: (See Workforce Commission, Texas.)

Engineers, Board of Professional: (1937 as 6-member Texas State Board of Registration for Professional Engineers; members increased to 9 in 1981; name changed to present in 1997); apptv.; per diem and expenses; 6-yr.; 9 members: Chair Daniel O. Wong, Houston (9/26/19); Ademola Adejokun, Arlington (9/26/23); Lamberto Balli, San Antonio (9/26/21); Sina K. Nejad, Beaumont (9/26/19); Cathy Norwood, Midland (9/26/21); Rolando Rubiano, Harlingen (9/26/23); Albert Cheng, Houston (9/26/21); Elvira Reyna, Little Elm (9/26/19); Kiran Shah, Richmond (9/26/23). Exec. Dir. Lance Kinney ($158,167), 1917 IH-35 S, Austin 78741; (512) 440-7723.

Environmental Quality, Texas Commission on: (1913 as State Board of Water Engineers; name changed in 1962 to Texas Water Commission; reorganized and name changed in 1965 to Water Rights Commission; reorganized and name changed back to Texas Water Commission in 1977 to perform judicial function for the Texas Dept. of Water Resources; name changed to Texas Natural Resource Conservation Commission in 1993; changed to present form in 2002); apptv.; 6-yr.; 3 members full-time ($189,500): Chair Jon Niermann, Austin (8/31/21); Emily Lindley, Austin (8/31/23); Vacant (8/31/19). Exec. Dir. Toby Baker, PO Box 13087, Austin 78711-3087; (512) 239-3900.

Ethics Commission, Texas: (1991); apptv.; 4-yr.; 8 members: 2 apptd. by House Speaker, 2 apptd. by Lt. Gov, 4 apptd. by Gov.: Chair Chad M. Craycraft, Dallas (11/19/19); Randall H. Erben, Austin (11/19/21); Chris Flood, Houston (11/19/19); Mary K. Kennedy, Houston (11/19/19); Patrick E. Mizell, Houston (11/19/21); Richard S. Schmidt, Corpus Christi (11/19/21); Joseph O. Slovacek, Houston (11/19/21); Steven D. Wolens, Dallas (11/19/19). Interim Exec. Dir. Ian Steusloff ($118,387), 201 E. 14th St., 10th Floor, PO Box 12070, Austin 78711; (512) 463-5800. Disclosure Filing Fax: (512) 463-8808.

Facilities Commission, Texas: (2007; formerly Texas Building and Procurement Commission); apptv.; 6-yr.; 7 members: Chair William Allensworth, Austin (1/31/21); Steven Alvis, Houston (1/31/23); Brian Bailey, Austin (1/31/21); Patti C. Jones, Lubbock (1/31/21); Michael J. Novak, San Antonio (1/31/19); Mike Novak, San Antonio (1/31/19); Rigo Villarreal, Mission (1/31/21); C. Price Wagner, Dallas (1/31/25). Exec. Dir. Mike Novak ($177,982) 1711 San Jacinto, PO Box 13047, Austin 78711; (512) 463-3446.

Family and Protective Services Advisory Council, Department of: (1991 as Dept. of Protective and Regulatory Services; reorganized to present form in 2004); apptv.; 6-yr.; 9 members: Chair Bonnie Hellums, Houston (2/1/23); Omedi Arismendez, Alice (2/1/21); Greg Hamilton, Hutto (2/1/21); Liesa Hackett, Huntsville (2/1/23); Davina Hollin, Corinth (2/1/21); Matt Kouri, Austin (2/1/23); Bonnie Hellums, Houston (2/1/23); Janice Washington, Corpus Christi (2/1/19); Connie Almeida, Richmond (2/1/21). Commissioner Vacant ($220,000), 701 West 51st St., PO Box 149030, Austin 78714; (512) 438-4800. Abuse

Hotline: (800) 252-5400. Ombudsman Hotline: (800) 720-7777.

Finance Commission of Texas: (1923 as Banking Commission; reorganized as Finance Commission in 1943 with 9 members; members increased to 12 in 1983; changed back to 9 members in 1989; increased to 11 in 2009); apptv.; 6-yr.; per diem and traveling expenses; 11 members: Chair Paul Plunket, Dallas (2/1/20); Bob Borochoff, Houston (2/1/22); Molly Curl, Richardson (2/1/22); Lori B. McCool, Boerne (2/1/20); Matt Moore, Amarillo (2/1/22); Vince E. Puente, Sr., Fort Worth (2/1/24); Hector J. Cerna, Eagle Pass (2/1/20); Phillip Holt, Bonham (2/1/22); Stacy G. London, Houston (2/1/22); William Lucas, Center (2/1/24); Cliff McCauley, San Antonio (2/1/24); Robin Armstrong, Friendswood (2/1/22). Banking Commissioner Charles Cooper ($242,925), 2601 N. Lamar Blvd., Austin 78705; (512) 936-6222; appointee of Finance Commission. (*See* also Banking, Dept. of.)

Fire Fighters' Pension Commissioner: (1937); Abolished by the 83 Legislature, S.B. 220. (*See* Retirement System, Texas Emergency Services.)

Fire Protection, Texas Commission on: (1991; formed by consolidation of Fire Dept. Emergency Board and Commission on Fire Protection Personnel Standards and Education); apptv.; 6-yrs.; expenses; 13 members: Chair Robert Moore, Bryan (2/1/21); Joseph Gonzalez, Krugerville (2/1/19); Tommy Anderson, Santa Fe (2/1/21); Carlos Cortez, Jr., Harlingen (2/1/21); Kelly E. Doster, Frisco (2/1/21); Arminda Garza, Harlingen (2/1/19); Mike Jones, Burleson (2/1/23); John T. McMakin, LaRue (2/1/19); Bob Morgan, Fort Worth (2/1/23); Lenny Perez, Brownsville (2/1/19); Mala Sharma, Houston (2/1/23); J.P. Steelman, Longview (2/1/23); Steven C. Tull, Valley Mills (2/1/21). Exec. Dir. Tim Rutland ($107,634), 1701 N. Congress, Ste. 1-105, PO Box 2286, Austin 78768; (512) 936-3838.

Food and Fibers Commission, Texas: Abolished Jan. 1, 2006, and duties transferred to the Texas Dept. of Agriculture Food and Fibers Research Council; PO Box 12847, Austin 78711; (512) 936-2450.

Forensic Science Commission, Texas: (2005); apptv.: 2-yr.; 9 members: 4 apptd. by Gov., 3 apptd. by Lt. Gov., and 2 apptd. by Atty. Gen.: Chair Jeffrey J. Barnard, Dallas (9/1/19); Patrick Buzzini, Spring (9/1/20); Bruce Budowle, North Richland Hills (9/1/20); Mark Daniel, Fort Worth (9/1/19); Nancy Downing, Bryan (9/1/20); Jasmine Drake, Conroe (9/1/20); Dennis Johnson, Austin (9/1/19); Sarah Kerrigan, The Woodlands, (9/1/19); Jarvis Parsons, Bryan (9/1/19). Coor. Leigh M. Tomlin, 1700 N. Congress Ave., Ste. 445, Austin, TX 78701; (888) 296-4232.

Funeral Service Commission, Texas: (1903 as State Board of Embalming; 1935 as State Board of Funeral Directors and Embalmers; name changed to present form in 1987); apptv.; per diem and expenses; 6-yr.; 7 members: Chair Greg Compean, Richmond (2/1/21); Larry Allen, Mesquite (2/1/21); Dianne Hefley, Amarillo (2/1/23); Jonathan Scepanski, McAllen (2/1/25); Kristin Tips, San Antonio (2/1/23); Kevin A. Combest, Lubbock (2/1/25); Melanie Grammar, Whitewright (2/1/25). Exec. Dir. Janice McCoy ($95,318), 333 Guadalupe St., Ste. 2-110, Austin 78701; (512) 936-2474.

General Services Commission: Abolished in February 2002, with most functions taken over by the newly created Texas Building and Procurement Commission, which was renamed Texas Facilities Commission in 2007.

Geoscientists, Texas Board of Professional: (2001); apptv.; expenses; 3-yr.; 9 members (6 professional geoscientists, 3 public members): Chair Charles T. Hallmark, Hearne (2/1/19); W. David Prescott II, Amarillo (2/1/19); Becky L.

The Gulf Coast Authority is charged with protecting our coastal waters, primarily through regional industrial wastewater treatment. Photo by Ed Schipul (CC).

Johnson, Fort Worth (2/1/23); Drusilla Knight-Villarreal, Corpus Christi (2/1/19); Lindsey Lee, Edna (2/1/21); Brandon Stowers, Austin (2/1/23); Bereket Derie, Round Rock (2/1/21); Steven Fleming, Midland (2/1/21); Mark Varhaug, Dallas (2/1/23). Exec. Dir. Rene D. Truan ($96,386), 333 Guadalupe St., Tower 1, Ste. 530; PO Box 13225, Austin 78711; (512) 936-4400.

Guadalupe-Blanco River Authority: (1935); apptv.; per diem and expenses on duty; 6-yr.; 9 members: Chair Dennis L. Patillo, Victoria (2/1/21); Don B. Meador, San Marcos (2/1/19); Kenneth Motl, Port Lavaca (2/1/23); Rusty Brockman, New Braunfels (2/1/23); William R. Carbonara, Cuero (2/1/19); Steve Ehrig, Gonzales (2/1/19); Oscar H. Fogle, Lockhart (2/1/23); Ronald J. Hermes, Seguin (2/1/21); Thomas O. Mathews, Boerne (2/1/21). Gen. Mgr. Kevin Patteson, 933 E. Court St., Seguin 78155; (830) 379-5822.

Guadalupe River Authority Board of Directors, Upper: (1939); apptv.; 6-yr.; 9 members: Pres. Bob Waller, Kerrville (2/1/19); Blake W. Smith, Hunt (2/1/21); James Musgrove, Mountain Home (2/1/21); Diane L. McMahon, Kerrville (2/1/21); Mike L. Allen, Ingram (2/1/19); Aaron C. Bulkley, Hunt (2/1/19); D. Michael Hughes, Ingram (2/1/23); William R. Rector, Kerrville (2/1/23); Margaret B. Snow, Kerrville (2/1/23). Gen. Mgr. Ray Buck Jr., 125 Lehman Dr., Ste. 100, Kerrville 78028-5908; (830) 896-5445.

Guaranteed Student Loan Corporation, Texas: Established 1979 as nonprofit public entity. As of July 21, 2019 the organization is now Trellis Company, a private nonprofit 501(c).

Guardianship Certification Advisory Board: Apptv. by Texas Supreme Court; part of Judicial Branch Certification Commission; staggered terms; 6-yr., 5 members: Jamie MacLean, Austin (2/1/21); Chris Wilmoth, Dallas (2/1/21); Jason S. Armstrong, Lufkin (2/1/25); Gladys Burwell, Friendswood (2/1/25); Toni Rhodes Glover, Ft.

Worth (2/1/23). 205 W. 14th St., Ste. 101, PO Box 13131, Austin 78711; (512) 463-1630.

Gulf Coast Authority: (1969); apptv.; 2-yr.; per diem, expenses on duty; 9 members: 3 apptd. by Gov., 3 by County Commissioners Courts of counties in district, 3 by Mayors Council of cities in district. Franklin D. R. Jones, Jr., Harris Co. (8/31/21); Rita Standridge, Chambers Co. (8/31/20); W. Chris Peden, Galveston Co. (8/31/21); Ron Crowder, Galveston Co. (8/31/21); Robert A. Fry, Harris Co. (8/31/21); Gloria A. Matt, Harris Co. (8/31/21); Lamont E. Meaux, Chambers Co. (8/31/20); Mark Schultz, Chambers Co. (8/31/20); Kevin Scott, Galveston Co. (8/31/20). Gen. Mgr. Lori Traweek, 910 Bay Area Blvd., Houston 77058; (281) 488-4115.

Gulf States Marine Fisheries Commission: (1949 with members from Texas, Alabama, Florida, Louisiana, and Mississippi); apptv.; 3-yr.; 3 Texas members: 2 ex officio: Texas Parks and Wildlife Dept. exec. dir. and 1 member of Legislature; 1 apptd. by Gov.: Troy B. Williamson II, Portland (3/17/20). Exec. Dir. David M. Donaldson, PO Box 726, Ocean Springs, MS 39566-0726; (228) 875-5912.

Health Coordinating Council, Texas Statewide: (1977); apptv.; 6-yr.; 17 members (4 ex officio; 13 apptd. by Gov.): Chair Ayeez A. Lalji, Sugar Land (8/1/19); David Allen, San Antonio (8/1/23); Carol Boswell, Andrews (8/1/21); Salil Deshpande, Houston (8/1/19); Chelsea Elliott, Austin (8/1/23); Elva C. LeBlanc, Fort Worth (8/1/19); Elizabeth Protas, League City (8/1/23); Melinda Rodriguez, San Antonio (8/1/21); Courtney Sherman, Fort Worth (8/1/21); D. Bailey Wynne, Dallas (8/1/23); Nancy Yuill, Sugar Land (8/31/19); Shaukat Zakaria, Houston (8/1/21); Yasser Zeid, Longview (8/1/21). Ex-officio members include 1 each from Texas Dept. of State Health Services, Texas Dept. of Aging and Disability Services, Texas Higher Education Coordinating Board, and Texas Health and Human Services Commission. Coordinator Matt Turner, PO Box 149347, Austin, TX 78714-9347; (512) 776-7261.

Health and Human Services Commission Council: (1991); apptv.; 4-yr.; 9 members: Chair Frank James, Wichita Falls (2/1/21); Gina Hinojosa, Austin (2/1/21); Travis Clardy, Nacogdoches (2/1/21); Joseph Deshotel, Beaumont (2/1/21); Stephanie Klick, Fort Worth (2/1/21); Thresa Meza, Irving (2/1/23); Rick Miller, Sugar Land (2/1/21); Candy Noble, Lucas (2/1/23); Toni Rose, Dallas (2/1/21). Commissioner Courtney Phillips ($275,000; 2/1/21), 4900 North Lamar, PO Box 13247, Austin 78711; (512) 424-6500.

Health and Human Services, Commissioner of: (1879 as State Health Officer; 1955 changed to Commissioner of Health; 1975 changed to Director, Texas Department of Health Resources; 1977 changed to Commissioner, Texas Dept. of Health; changed to present name in 2004); apptv.; 2-yr.: Courtney Phillips ($275,000; 2/1/21), PO Box 13247, Austin 78711-3247; (512) 424-6603.

Health Professions Council: (1993); ex officio; 14 members: 1 from Gov.'s office and 1 each from the following 13 regulating agencies: Texas Board of Chiropractic Examiners, Texas State Board of Dental Examiners, Texas Medical Board, Texas Board of Nursing, Texas Optometry Board, Texas State Board of Pharmacy, Physical Therapy Examiners Board, Texas State Board of Podiatric Medical Examiners, Texas Board of Examiners of Psychologists, Occupational Therapy Examiners Board, Texas Board of Veterinary Medical Examiners, Texas Funeral Service Commission, Texas Department of State Health Services Professional Licensing and Certification Unit. Admin. Officer John Monk, 333 Guadalupe St., Ste. 2-220, Austin 78701; (512) 305-8550.

Health Services Authority, Texas: (2007); apptv.; 2-yr.; expenses; 2 ex officio plus 11 apptd. members: Paula Anthony-McMann, Tyler (6/15/21); Victoria Ai Linh Bryant, Houston (6/15/21); Shannon Calhoun, Goliad (6/15/21); Lourdes Cuellar, Houston (6/15/21); Salil Deshpande, Houston (6/15/21); Emily Hartmann, El Paso (6/15/21); Kenneth James, Volente (6/15/21); Jerome Lisk, Tyler (6/15/21); Leticia Rodriguez, Monahans (6/15/21); Jonathan Sandstrom Hill, Lakeway (6/15/21); Siobhan Shahan, Amarillo (6/15/21); Carlos Vital, Friendswood (6/15/21); Calvin Green, Elgin (6/15/21); Jeffrey Hoogheem, Austin (6/15/21). San Jacinto Building, 221 E. 9th, Ste. 201, Austin 78701; (512) 814-0321.

Health Services Council, Texas Department of State: (1975); Abolished August 31, 2016.

Hearing Instruments, State Committee of Examiners in the Fitting and Dispensing of: (1969); Abolished by the 84th Legislature, S.B 202. As of Oct. 1, 2016, all duties transferred to the Texas Department of Licensing and Regulation.

Higher Education Coordinating Board, Texas: (1953 as temporary board; 1955 as permanent 15-member Texas Commission on Higher Education; 1965 as Texas College and University Systems Coordinating Board; name and membership changed to present form in 1987); apptv.; 6-yr.; expenses; 9 members plus 1 student rep.: Chair Stuart W. Stedman, Houston (8/31/21); Fred Farias III, McAllen (8/31/19); John T. Steen, Jr., San Antonio (8/31/19); Arcilia C. Acosta, Dallas (8/31/19); S. Javaid Anwar, Midland (8/31/21); Michael J. Plank, Houston (8/31/23); Rickey A. Raven, Sugar Land (8/31/21); Donna N. Williams, Arlington (8/31/23); Welcome W. Wilson, Jr., Houston (8/31/23); one vacancy. Commissioner of Higher Education, Raymund A. Paredes, ($212,135 plus supplement) 1200 E. Anderson Lane, PO Box 12788, Austin 78711; (512) 427-6101.

Higher Education Tuition Board, Texas Prepaid: (1995); apptv.; expenses; term at pleasure of Gov.; 6 members, plus 1 ex officio: State Comptroller; 2 apptd. by Gov. and 4 apptd. by Lt. Gov. Gov. appointments: Judy Treviño, San Antonio (2/1/21); Michael Truncale, Beaumont (2/1/21); Javier Villalobos, McAllen (2/1/23); c/o Educational Opportunities & Investments Division, Comptroller of Public Accounts, PO Box 13407, Austin 78711-3407; (800) 445-4723.

Historian, Texas State: (2005); apptv.; 2-yr.; Monte L. Monroe, Lubbock (9/26/20).

Historical Commission, Texas: (1953); apptv.; expenses; 6-yr.; 9 members: Chair John L. Nau III, Houston (2/1/21); Earl P. Broussard Jr., Austin (2/1/23); Monica Burdette, Rockport (2/1/21); Garrett Donnelly, Midland (1/31/23); Lilia Garcia, Raymondville (2/1/21); David Gravelle, Dallas (2/1/21); Laurie Limbacher, Austin (2/1/23); Catherine McKnight, Dallas (1/31/23); Tom Perini, Buffalo Gap (2/1/21); Daisy Sloan White, College Station (2/1/23). Exec. Dir. Mark Wolfe ($150,652), 1511 Colorado St., PO Box 12276, Austin 78711; (512) 463-6100.

Holocaust and Genocide Commission, Texas: (2009); created by 81st Legislature. apptv.; 4-yr.; 18 members: 3 ex officio, 15 apptv.: Chair Lynne Aronoff, Houston (2/1/23); Anne U. Clutterbuck, Houston (2/1/19); Jeffrey Beck, Dallas (2/1/23); Fran Berg, Dallas (2/1/17); Laura Ehrenberg-Chesler, San Antonio (2/1/21); Rabbi Ilan Emanuel, Corpus Christi (2/1/23); Jonathan Gurwitz, San Antonio (2/1/21); Matthew A. Kornhauser, Houston (2/1/19); Sandra B. Lessig, Houston (2/1/19); Elliott Naishtat, Austin (5/10/21); Roger Nober, Fort Worth (2/1/21); David A. Patterson, Dallas (4/13/21); Virginica Prodan, Dallas (2/1/21); Gilbert Tuhabonye, Austin (2/1/21); Edward B. Westerman, San Antonio (2/1/21). Exec. Dir. Matthew Verdugo ($78,000), 1511 Colorado St., PO Box 12276, Austin 78711; (512) 463-8815.

Housing and Community Affairs, Texas Dept. of: (1979 as Texas Housing Agency; merged with Department of Community Affairs and name changed in 1991); apptv.; expenses; 6-yr.; 7 members: Chair J.B. Goodwin, Austin (1/31/21); Paul Braden, Dallas (1/31/23); Leslie Bingham Escareño, Brownsville (1/31/19); Asusena Reséndiz, San Antonio (1/31/19); Sharon Thomason, Wolfforth (1/31/21); Leo Vasquez, Houston (1/31/23); one vacancy. Exec. Dir. David Cervantes ($180,084), 221 East 11th St., PO Box 13941, Austin 78711; (512) 475-3800.

Housing Corp., Texas State Affordable: (1994); 6 yrs.; 5 members: Chair William H. Dietz, Jr., Waco (2/1/21); Valerie Vargas Cardenas, San Juan (2/1/25); Courtney Johnson Rose, Missouri City (2/1/21); Lali Shipley, Austin (2/1/21); Andy Williams, Fort Worth (2/1/23). Pres. David Long, PO Box 12637, Austin 78711-2637; (512) 477-3555.

Human Rights, Texas Commission on: (2004 as part of the Texas Workforce Commission's Civil Rights Division) As of September 1, 2015 the duties and authority of the Texas Commission on Human Rights were transferred to the Texas Workforce Commissioners.

Industrialized Building Code Council, Texas: (1973); apptv.; 2-yr.; 12 members: Presiding Officer Roland L. Brown, Mansfield (2/1/21); Randy Childers, Waco (2/1/20); Stephen Shang, Dallas (2/1/21); Scott A. McDonald, Amarillo (2/1/21); Roland Bown, Midlothian (2/1/21); Douglas O. Robinson, Fort Worth (2/1/19); Edward Martin, Jr., Austin (2/1/21); William F. Smith, III, Dripping Springs (2/1/20); Suzanne R. Arnold, Tyler (2/01/20); Marcela A. Rhoads, Fort Worth (2/1/20); Brian A. Bailey, Dripping Springs (2/1/20); Janet Hoffman, Galveston (2/1/20); c/o Texas Dept. of Licensing and Regulation, PO Box 12157, Austin 78711; (512) 463-6599.

Information Resources, Department of: (1981 as Automated Information and Telecommunications Council; name changed to current in 1990); 6-yr.; expenses; 10 members: 3 ex officio, 7 apptv.: Chair Ben Gatzke, Fort Worth (2/1/23); Christian Alvarado, Austin (2/1/21); Mike Bell, Spring (2/1/23); Stuart Bernstein, Austin (2/1/21); Stacey Napier, Austin (2/1/25); Jeffrey Tayon, Houston (2/1/21); Kara Thompson, Austin (2/1/25); ex-officio members are from Health and Human Services Commission, Texas Dept. of Insurance and Texas Dept. of Transportation. Executive Director Amanda Crawford ($184,792), 300 W. 15th, #1300, PO Box 13564, Austin 78711; (512) 475-4700.

Insurance Commissioner, Texas Dept. of: (1876 as Dept. of Insurance; 1887 as Dept. of Agriculture, Insurance, Statistics and History; 1907 as Dept. of Insurance and Banking; 1923 as Dept. of Insurance); apptv.; 2-yr.; Commissioner Kent Sullivan, Austin (2/1/21), ($202,383), 333 Guadalupe, PO Box 149104, Austin 78714; (512) 463-6169.

Insurance Counsel, Office of Public: (*See* Public Insurance Counsel, Office of.)

Interstate Commission for Adult Offender Supervision: (1937 as Interstate Compact for the Supervision of Parolees and Probationers; 2000 as present name); 50 member states; apptv.: Pam Alexander-Schneider, Lubbock (2/1/21). Compact Admin. for Texas Stuart Jenkins, 8712 Shoal Creek Blvd., Ste. 290, Austin 78757; (512) 406-5990.

Interstate Mining Compact Commission: (1970); 24 member states, plus 2 associate member states; ex officio or apptv., according to Gov's. choice; Texas reps. are appointed from the Texas Railroad Commission. Texas representative: Ryan Sitton. Exec. Dir. Thomas L. Clarke, 445-A Carlisle Dr., Herndon, VA 22170-4802; (703) 709-8654.

Interstate Oil and Gas Compact Commission: (1935); 30 member states, plus 8 associate member states; ex officio or apptv., according to Gov's. choice; per diem and expenses. Official rep. for Texas: Wayne Christian. Exec. Dir. Mike Smith, PO Box 53127, Oklahoma City, OK 73152; (405) 525-3556.

Jail Standards, Texas Commission on: (1975); apptv.; 6-yr.; expenses; 9 members: Chair Bill Stoudt, Longview (1/31/25); Esmaeil Porsa, Parker (1/31/23); Patricia M. Anthony, Garland (1/31/25); Duane Lock, Southlake (1/31/23); Monica McBride, Alpine (1/31/25); Ben Perry, Waco (1/31/23); Kelly Rowe, Lubbock (2/1/21); Melinda Taylor, Austin (1/31/21); Dennis Wilson, Groesbeck (1/31/21). Exec. Dir. Brandon Wood ($108,469), 300 W. 15th St., Ste. 503, PO Box 12985, Austin 78711-2985; (512) 463-5505.

Judicial Compensation Commission: (2007); apptv.; 6-yr.; expenses; 9 members: Chair William Strawn, Austin (2/1/21); Isaac M. Castro, Hamlin (2/1/23); Alejandro Cestero, Houston (2/1/21); Conrith Warren Davis, Sugar Land (2/1/23); Rebeca Aizpuru Huddle, Bellaire (2/1/19); Robert E. Lindsey, III, Goldthwaite (2/1/19); Linda Russel, Houston (2/1/19); Scott J. Salmans, McGregor (2/1/21); Frederick C. Tate, Colleyville (2/1/23); c/o Office of Court Administration, Tom C. Clark Building, 205 W. 14th St., Ste. 600, Austin 78701; (512) 463-1625.

Judicial Conduct, Commission on: (1965 as 9-member Judicial Qualifications Commission; name changed to present in 1977); expenses; 6-yr.; 13 members: 6 apptd. by Supreme Court; 2 apptd. by State Bar; 5 apptd. by Gov.: Chair Catherine N. Wylie, Houston (11/19/21); David C. Hall, Sweetwater (11/19/21); Ronald E. Bunch, Waxahachie (11/19/21); Douglas S. Lang, Dallas (11/19/19); David Patronella, Houston (11/19/21); Ruben G. Reyes, Lubbock (11/19/23). Public Members: Tramer J. Woytek, Hallettsville (11/19/23); Sujeeth B. Draksharam, Sugar Land (11/19/21); Valerie Ertz, Dallas (11/19/23); Darrick L. McGill, Georgetown (11/19/21); David M. Russell, Drip-

ping Springs (11/19/19); Fred Tate, Colleyville (11/19/23);. Attorney Member: Demetrius Bivins, Houston (11/19/19). Exec. Dir. Eric Vinson ($126,660), PO Box 12265, Austin 78711-2265; (512) 463-5533.

Judicial Council, Texas: (1929 as Texas Civil Judicial Council; name changed in 1975); 6-yr.; expenses; 22 members: 16 ex officio and 6 apptd. from general public: Chair Nathan L. Hecht, Dallas (12/31/20); Sharon Keller, Dallas (12/31/24). Legislative Members: Brandon Creighton, Conroe; Jeff Leach, Allen; Andrew Murr, Junction; Judith Zaffirini, Laredo. Judicial Members: Gary Bellair, Ransom Canyon (2/01/19); Bill Boyce, Houston (2/01/21); Jon Gimble, Waco (2/01/25); Scott Jenkins, Austin (2/01/19); Kelly G. Moore, Brownfield (2/01/21); Valencia Nash, Dallas; Sherry Radack, Houston; Polly Spencer, San Antonio; Edward J. Spillane, College Station; Vivian Torres, Hondo. Citizen Members: Kevin Bryant, Dallas (6/30/23); Sonia Clayton, Houston (6/30/19); Allyson Ho, Dallas (6/30/19); Rachel Racz, Fort Worth (6/30/23); Kenneth S. Saks, San Antonio (6/30/21); Evan Young, Austin (6/30/21). Exec. Dir. David Slayton ($196,800), PO Box 12066, Austin 78711; (512) 463-1625.

Judicial Districts Board: (1985); 12 ex-officio members (term in other office); 1 apptv. (4 yrs.); ex officio: Chief Justice of Texas Supreme Court; Presiding Judge, Court of Criminal Appeals; Presiding Judge of each of 9 Administrative Judicial Districts; Gov. apptee.: Thomas R. Phillips, West Lake Hills (12/31/22).

Judicial Districts of Texas, Administrative, Presiding Judges of: (*See* Administrative Judicial Districts, Presiding Judges.)

Juneteenth Cultural and Historical Commission, Texas Emancipation: (1997); abolished by the 82nd Legislature, S.B. 1928.

Juvenile Justice, Texas Department of: (2011); created by Senate Bill 653, 82nd Legislature; combines the Texas Youth Commission and Texas Juvenile Probation Commission; apptv.; 6-yr.; expenses; 13 members: Chair Wesley C. Ritchey, Dalhart (2/1/21); Edeska Barnes, Jr., Jasper (2/1/21); James Castro, Bergheim (2/1/23); Mona Lisa Chambers, Houston (2/1/25); Pama Hencerling, Victoria (2/1/23); Lisa K. Jarrett, San Antonio (2/1/21); Anne Lattimore, Cedar Park (2/1/21); Melissa Martin, Deer Park (2/1/25); David Matthew, Georgetown (2/1/25); Vincent Morales, Jr., Rosenberg (2/1/25); Stephanie Moreno, Beeville (2/1/25); Allison Palmer, San Angelo (2/1/23); James Smith, Midland (2/1/23). Exec. Dir. Camille Cain ($205,879), 11209 Metric Boulevard, P.O. Box 12757, Austin 78711-2757; (512) 424-6130.

Juvenile Probation Commission, Texas: (1981); abolished on Dec. 1, 2011 by the 82nd Legislature, S.B. 653. Its operations and those of the Texas Youth Commission were transferred to the Texas Juvenile Justice Department.

Land Board, School: (1939); 2-yr.; per diem and expenses; 3 members: 1 ex officio: Comm. of General Land Office; 2 apptd.: 1 by Atty. Gen. and 1 by Gov.: Gilbert "Gil" Burciaga, Austin (8/29/19); Scott Rohrman, Dallas (8/31/21); ex officio: George P. Bush; c/o General Land Office, SFA Office Bldg., 1700 N. Congress Ave., Austin 78701-1495; (512) 463-5001.

Land Board, Veterans': (Est. 1949 as 3-member ex-officio board; reorganized 1956); 4-yr.; per diem and expenses; 3 members: 1 ex officio: Comm. of General Land Office; 2 apptd.: Grant Moody, San Antonio (12/29/20); Judson Scott, Bee Cave (12/29/22). Exec. Sec. Vacant, PO Box 12873, Austin 78711-2873; (800) 252-8387.

Land Surveying, Texas Board of Professional: (1979; formed from consolidation of Board of Examiners of

Licensed Land Surveyors, est. 1977, and State Board of Registration for Public Surveyors, est. 1955); apptv.; 6-yr.; 9 members: 1 ex officio: Comm. of General Land Office; 8 apptd.: Chair Jon Hodde, Brenham (1/31/19); Jay Canine, Sugar Land (1/31/23); James H. Cheatham, Aledo (1/31/21); William D. Edwards, Corpus Christi (1/31/21); Coleen Johnson, Leander (1/21/23); Michael McCloskey, Round Rock (1/31/23); William Merten, Houston (1/31/19); Andrew W. Paxton, Lubbock (1/31/21). Interim Exec. Dir. LeAnn Catron ($34,200), 12100 Park 35 Circle, Bldg. A, Ste. 156, MC 230, Austin 78753; (512) 239-5263.

Lands, Board for Lease of University: (1929 as 3-member board; members increased to 4 in 1985); ex officio; term in other office; 4 members: Comm. of General Land Office, 2 members of Board of Regents of The University of Texas, 1 member Board of Regents of Texas A&M University. Sec. Sharon Burks, The University of Texas System; (432) 684-4404.

Lavaca-Navidad River Authority, Board of Directors: (1954 as 7-member Jackson County Flood Control District; reorganized as 9-member board in 1959; name changed to present form in 1969); apptv.; 6-yr.; per diem and expenses; 9 members: President Ronald Kubecka, Deutschburg (5/1/21); Jerry Adelman, Palacios (5/1/23); Terri Parker, Ganado (5/1/23); Michelle Bubela, Edna (5/1/23); Sandy Johs, La Ward (5/1/21); Glenn T. Martin, Edna (5/1/19); Scott Sachtleben, Ganado (5/1/21); Leonard Steffek, Edna (5/1/19); Charlie Taylor, Palacios (5/1/19). Gen. Mgr. Patrick Brzozowski, PO Box 429, Edna 77957; (361) 782-5229.

Law Enforcement Officer Standards & Education, Texas Commission on: (1965); as of 1/1/14 the commission has received a change in name to Texas Commission on Law Enforcement. Name changed by the 83rd Legislature, S.B. 686.

Law Enforcement, Texas Commission on: (2014); created by Senate Bill 686, 83rd Legislature; renamed the Texas Commission on Law Enforcement Officer Standards & Education; apptv.; 6 years; expenses; 9 members: Presiding Officer Joel W. Richardson, Canyon (8/30/19); Jason Hester, Lago Vista (8/30/19); Janna Atkins, Abilene (8/30/23); Patricia Burruss, Olmito (8/30/19); Ron Hood, Dripping Springs (8/30/23); Kim Lemaux, Arlington (8/30/21); Jack Taylor, Austin (8/30/23); Sharon B. Thomas, San Antonio (8/30/21); Tim Whitaker, Richmond (8/30/21). Exec. Dir. Kim Vickers ($127,833), 6330 E. Highway 290, Suite 200, Austin, Texas 78723; (512) 936-7700.

Law Examiners, Texas Board of: (1919); 9 attorneys apptd. by Supreme Court biennially for 2-year terms expiring Sept. 30 of odd-numbered years. Compensation set by Supreme Court not to exceed $20,000 per annum: Chair Harold Odom, Houston; Augustin Rivera, Jr., Corpus Christi; Barbara Ellis, Austin; Teresa Ereon Giltner, Dallas; C. Alfred Mackenzie, Waco; Dwaine M. Massey, Houston; Anna McKim, Lubbock; Cynthia Orr, San Antonio; Carlos Soltero, Austin. Exec. Dir. Susan Henricks, PO Box 13486, Austin 78711-3486; (512) 463-1621.

Law Library Board, Texas State: (1971); ex officio; expenses; 3 members: Atty. Gen., Chief Justice State Supreme Court, Presiding Judge Court of Criminal Appeals. Dir. Dale Propp ($93,534), PO Box 12367, Austin 78711-2367; (512) 463-1722.

Legislative Budget Board: (1949); 10 members; 5 ex-officio: Lt. Gov.; House Speaker; Chmn., Senate Finance Comm.; Chmn., House Appropriations Comm.; Chmn., House Ways and Means Comm.; plus 5 other members of Legislature. Dir. Ursula Parks, PO Box 12666, Austin 78711-2666; (512) 463-1200.

Legislative Council, Texas: (1949); 14 ex-officio members: Lt. Gov.; House Speaker; 6 senators apptd. by Lt. Gov.; 5 representatives apptd. by Speaker; Chmn., House Administration Committee. Exec. Dir. Jeff Archer ($179,826), PO Box 12128, Austin 78711-2128; (512) 463-1155.

Legislative Redistricting Board: (1951); 5 ex-officio members: Lt. Gov., House Speaker, Atty. Gen., Comptroller of Public Accounts and Comm. of General Land Office; PO Box 12128, Austin 78711-2128; (512) 463-1155.

Legislative Reference Library: (*See* Library, Legislative Reference.)

Librarian, State: (Originally est. in 1839; present office est. 1909); apptv., indefinite term: Mark Smith ($143,500), PO Box 12927, Austin 78711-2927; (512) 463-5455.

Library and Archives Commission, Texas State: (1909 as 5-member Library and State Historical Commission; name changed to present form in 1979); apptv.; per diem and expenses on duty; 6-yr.; 7 members: Chair Michael C. Waters, Dallas (9/28/19); David C. Garza, Brownsville (9/28/19); Lynwood Givens, Plano (9/28/21); Larry G. Holt, College Station (9/28/21); Arthur T. Mann, Hillsboro (9/28/23); Darryl Tocker, Austin (9/28/23); Martha Wong, Houston (9/28/21). Dir. and Librarian Mark Smith ($143,500), PO Box 12927, Austin 78711-2927; (512) 463-5455.

Library, Legislative Reference: (1909); 3 ex-officio members: Lt. Gov., House Speaker, Chrm., House Appropriations Committee; 3 Legislative members; indefinite term. Dir. Mary Camp ($131,969), Box 12488, Austin 78711-2488; (512) 463-1252.

Licensing and Regulation, Texas Department on: (1989); apptv.; 6-yr.; expenses; 7 members: Chair Rick Figueroa, Brenham (2/1/21); Thomas F. Butler, Deer Park (2/1/25); Ray Callas, Beaumont (2/1/23); Helen Callier, Kingwood (2/1/21); Nora Castañeda, Harlingen (2/1/25); Joel Garza, Jr., Pearland (2/1/21); Gary Wesson, Bastrop (2/1/23). Exec. Dir. Brian E. Francis ($179,375); PO Box 12157, Austin 78711-2157; (800) 803-9202.

Licensing Standards, Committee on: (2007); abolished by function of law in 2011 as outlined in Chapter 2110 of the Government Code; repealed from HRC Chapter 42 by SB 219 in 2015.

Lottery Commission, Texas: (1993); 6-yr.; apptv.; expenses; 5 members: Chair J. Winston Krause, Austin (2/1/19); Mark Franz, Austin (2/1/25); Robert Rivera, Arlington (2/1/21); Erik Saenz, Houston (2/1/23); one vacancy. Exec. Dir. Gary Grief ($211,191), PO Box 16630, Austin 78761-6630; (512) 344-5000.

Lower Colorado River Authority: (*See* Colorado River Authority, Lower.)

Lower Concho River Water and Soil Conservation Authority: (*See* Concho River Water and Soil Conservation, Lower.)

Lower Neches Valley Authority: (*See* Neches Valley Authority, Lower.)

Manufactured Housing, Governing Board: (1995); apptv.; 6 yrs.; 5 members: Chair Sheila Valles-Pankratz, Mission (1/31/21); Sylvia Acuff, Little Elm (1/31/25); Ronald M. Richards, Clear Lake Shores (1/31/23); Keith C. Thompson, Lubbock (1/31/23), Jason Denny, Austin (1/31/25). Exec. Dir. Joe Garcia, PO Box 12489, Austin 78711-2489; (512) 475-2200.

Marriage & Family Therapists, Texas State Board of Examiners of: (1991); apptv.; 6 yrs.; per diem and transportation expenses; 9 members: Chair Jennifer Smothermon, Abilene (2/1/19); Kenneth Bateman, Garland (2/1/21); Lisa Merchant, Clyde (2/1/23); Keith Rosenbaum, Joshua

(2/1/19); Rich Stoglin, Arlington (2/1/23); George Francis, Georgetown (2/1/23); Michael Miller, Belton (2/1/19); Anthony Scoma, Austin (2/1/21); Evelyn Husband Thompson, Houston (2/1/21). Exec. Dir. Sarah Faszholz ($ 56,382), Texas Dept. of Health Services, PO Box 149347, MC 1982, Austin 78714-9347; (512) 834-6657.

Medical Board, Texas: (1907 as 11-member Texas State Board of Medical Examiners; members increased to 12 in 1931, 15 in 1981, 18 in 1993, and 19 in 2003; changed to present name in 2005 by Senate Bill 419); apptv.; 6-yr.; per diem on duty; 19 members: Chair Sherif Zaafran, Houston (4/13/21); J. Holliday, University Park (4/13/19); George De Loach, Livingston (4/13/23); Kandace Farmer, Highland Village (4/13/21); Jeffrey L. Luna, Livingston (4/13/21); Robert D. Martinez, Mission (4/13/19); Margaret C. McNeese, Houston (4/13/19); Jayaram B. Naidu, Odessa (4/13/21); Manuel M. Quinones, Jr., San Antonio (4/13/23); Karl W. Swann, San Antonio (4/13/19); David Vanderweide, League City (4/13/23); Surendra K. Varma, Lubbock (4/13/19). Public Members: Sharon J. Barnes, Rosharon (4/13/23); Michael E. Cokinos, Houston (4/13/23); Frank S. Denton, Conroe (4/13/19); Robert Gracia, Richmond (4/13/23); Linda G. Molina, San Antonio (4/13/21); LuAnn Morgan, Midland (4/13/21); Timothy Webb, Houston (4/13/19); Exec. Dir. Stephen Brint Carlton ($145,930) plus supplement), PO Box 2018, Austin 78768-2018; (512) 305-7010. Consumer Complaint Hotline: (800) 201-9353.

Medical Physicists, Texas Board of Licensure for Professional: (1991); abolished by the 84th Legislature, S.B. 202. All duties transferred to the Texas Medical Board.

Midwestern State University, Board of Regents: (1959); apptv.; 6-yr.; 9 members: Chair Warren T. Ayres, Wichita Falls (2/25/22); Tiffany D. Burks, Grand Prairie (2/25/22); R. Caven Crosnoe, Wichita Falls (2/25/20); Guy A. Fidelie, Jr., Wichita Falls (2/25/24); Shawn G. Hessing, Fort Worth (2/25/20); Nancy Marks, Wichita Falls (2/25/20); Okechukwu Okeke, Wichita Falls (2/25/24); Karen Liu Pang, Irving (2/25/24); Shelley Sweatt, Wichita Falls (2/25/22). Pres. Dr. Suzanne Shipley, 3410 Taft Blvd., Wichita Falls 76308; (940) 397-4010.

Midwifery Board, Texas: (1999); abolished by the 84th Legislature, S.B. 202. All duties transferred to the Texas Department of Licensing and Regulation.

Military Facilities Commission, Texas: (1935); abolished by the 80th Legislature, S.B. 1724. All duties transferred to the Adjutant General.

Military Preparedness Commission, Texas: (2003); apptv.; some terms at pleasure of Gov.; 2 ex-officio members (1 Senator, 1 House Representative); 13 apptv.: Chair Kevin Pottinger, Fort Worth; Carol Bonds, San Angelo; Garry Bradford, Corpus Christi; Darrell Coleman, Wichita Falls; Tom Duncavage, League City; Woody Gilliland, Abilene; Dennis Lewis, Texarkana; Kenneth Sheets, Mesquite; William Shine, Killeen; Annette Sobel, Lubbock; Shannalea Taylor, Del Rio; A.F. Thomas, El Paso; James Whitmore, New Braunfels; PO Box 12428, Austin, 78711; (512) 463-8800.

Motor Vehicles Board, Texas Dept. of: (2009); 9 members; 6-yr.; Chair Guillermo Treviño, Laredo (2/1/21); Charles Bacarisse, Houston (2/1/25); Stacey Gillman, Houston (2/1/25); Brett Graham, Denison (2/1/23); Tammy McRae, Conroe (2/1/25); Gary Painter, Midland (2/1/21); John M. Prewitt, Cypress (2/1/23); Paul R. Scott, Lubbock (2/1/23); Shelley Washburn, Houston (2/1/21). Exec. Dir. Whitney Brewster ($104,906), 4000 Jackson Ave., Austin, 78731; (888) 368-4689.

Municipal Retirement System, Texas: (*See* Retirement System, Texas Municipal.)

National Guard Armory Board, Texas: (*See* Military Facilities Commission, Texas.)

Natural Resource Conservation Commission, Texas: (*See* Environmental Quality, Texas Commission on.)

Neches River Municipal Water Authority, Upper: (1953 as 9-member board; members decreased to 3 in 1959); apptv.; 6-yr.; 3 members: Jay Steven Herrington, Palestine (2/1/21); Milton Phillip Jenkins, Palestine (2/1/23); Paul Morris, Palestine (2/1/25). Gen. Mgr. Monty D. Shank, PO Box 1965, Palestine 75802; (903) 876-2237.

Neches Valley Authority, Lower: (1933); apptv.; per diem and expenses on duty; 6-yr.; 9 members: Steve Lucas, Beaumont (7/28/19); Juanita Turk, Sour Lake (7/28/21); Lonnie Grissom, Woodville (7/28/21); Kal Kincaid, Beaumont (7/28/23); Steven M. McReynolds, Groves (7/28/19); Clint A. Mitchell, Nederland (4/28/23); Ivy Pate, Beaumont (7/28/21); Charles Spurlock, Woodville (7/28/19); William D. Voigtman, Silsbee (4/28/23). Gen. Mgr. Scott Hall ($126,000), PO Box 5117, Beaumont 77726-5117; (409) 892-4011.

Nueces River Authority: (1953 as Nueces River Conservation and Reclamation District; name changed to present in 1971); apptv.; 6-yr.; per diem and expenses; 22 members: Acting President Dan Leyendecker, Corpus Christi (2/1/19); Tomas Ramirez, III, Devine (2/1/21); Rebecca Bradford, Corpus Christi (2/1/19); W. Alston Beinhorn, Catarina (2/1/23); Allan P. Bloxsom III, Kendalia (2/1/21); Alston Beinhorn, Catarina (2/1/23); Eric L. Burnett, Portland (2/1/21); Chad H. Foster, Jr. Uvalde (2/1/23); Amy Clark, Three Rivers (2/1/21); Marshall Davidson, Ingleside (2/1/23); Chad Foster, Jr., Uvalde (2/1/23); John Galloway, Beeville (2/1/23); Annelise Gonzalez, San Antonio (2/1/23); Debra Young Hatch, Corpus Christi (2/1/23); Karin E. Knolle, Sandia (2/1/21); Joe C. McMillian, Dilley (2/1/19); Travis Pruski, Floresville (2/1/21); David E. Purser, Karnes City (2/1/19); Dina Ramirez, Karnes City (2/1/19); William Schuchman, Jourdanton (2/1/23); Howard Wood, Corpus Christi (2/1/23); Gary W. Moore, Sr., Portland (2/1/21). Exec. Dir. Con Mims, PO Box 349, Uvalde 78802-0349; (830) 278-6810.

Nursing, Texas Board of: (1909 as 5-member Texas Board of Nurse Examiners; members increased to 6 in 1931 and to 9 in 1981; name changed to present and members increased to 13 in 2007); apptv.; per diem and expenses; 6-yr.; 13 members: President Verna Shipp, Lubbock (1/31/23); David Saucedo, II, El Paso (1/31/21); Nina Almasy, Austin (1/31/19); Patricia Clapp, Dallas (1/31/19); Laura Disque, Edinburg (2/1/19); Diana Flores, Helotes (2/1/21); Doris Jackson, Pearland (1/31/23); Mazie Mathews Jamison, Dallas (1/31/23); Kathy Leader-Horn, Granbury (1/31/21); Allison Porter-Edwards, Bellaire (2/1/21); Melissa Schat, Granbury (2/1/19); Francis Stokes, Port Aransas (1/31/19); Kimberly Wright, Big Spring (2/1/23). Exec. Dir. Katherine A. Thomas ($145,864), 333 Guadalupe, Ste. 3-460, Austin 78701; (512) 305-7400.

Nursing Facility Administrators, Texas Board of: Abolished Sept. 1997 and responsibilities transferred to Texas Dept. of Human Services, which itself was abolished in 2004 and responsibilities transferred to Texas Dept. of Aging and Disability Services.

Occupational Therapy Examiners, Texas Board of: (1983 as 6-member board; increased to 9 in 1999); apptv.; 6-yr.; per diem and expenses; 9 members: Chair Stephanie Johnston, Magnolia (2/1/21); Todd Novosad, Bee Cave, (2/1/19); DeLana Honaker, Amarillo (2/1/23); Jennifer Clark, Iola (2/1/19); Karen Gardner, Brenham (2/1/23); Sally Harris King, Houston (2/1/21); Blanca Cardenas, Mission (2/1/23); Amanda Ellis, Austin (2/1/19); Pamela D. Nelon,

Fort Worth (2/1/24). Exec. Dir. John Maline ($70,000), 333 Guadalupe St., Ste. 2-510, Austin 78701-3942; (512) 305-6900.

Offenders with Medical or Mental Impairments, Texas Correctional Office on: Apptv.; 6-yr.; 21 members: 11 ex officio from various state agencies; 10 apptd. by Gov.: Chair Robb Catalano, Fort Worth (2/1/25); Sanjay Adhia, Sugar Land (7/20/21); Allan Cain, Carthage (7/20/23); Robert Chody, Austin (2/1/23); Brian Eby, Wichita Falls (2/1/25); Kathy C. Flanagan, Houston (10/21/19); Trent Marshall, Burleson (2/1/25); Casey O'Neal, Austin (7/20/25); Denise Oncken, Houston (2/1/21); Roger Rodriguez, El Paso (2/1/21); Yolanda Waters, La Marque (9/1/23). Dir. April Zamora ($135,599), 8610 Shoal Creek Blvd., Austin 78757; (512) 406-5406.

Office of Injured Employee Counsel: (2005; represents the interests of workers' compensation claimants); apptv.; 2-yr.; 1 member: Public Counsel Jessica Barta ($143,220), 7551 Metro Center Dr., Ste. 100, Austin 78744-1609; (866) 393-6432.

One-Call Board of Texas: (1997; created by the Underground Facility Damage Prevention and Safety Act and serves as the board for the Texas Underground Facility Notification Corp.); apptv.; 3-yr.; 12 members: Chair Robert DeLeon, Corpus Christi (8/31/19); Joseph Costa, DeSoto (8/31/20); William Geise, Austin (8/31/20); Jeffery Carroll, Austin (8/31/19); Christopher Nowak, Houston (8/31/20); George Spencer, Austin (8/31/20); Richard Tesson, Houston (8/31/21); Barry Calhoun, Grapevine (8/31/19); Sandy Galvan, San Antonio (8/31/19); Marcela Navarrete, El Paso (8/31/21); Manish Seth, Missouri City (8/31/21); Les Stephens, San Marcos (8/31/21). Exec. Dir. Don Ward, PO Box 9764, Austin 78766-9764; (512) 467-9764.

Optometry Board, Texas: (1921 as 6-member State Board of Examiners in Optometry; name changed to present in 1981 and members increased to 9); apptv.; per diem; 6-yr.; 9 members: Chair Mario Gutierrez, San Antonio (1/31/23); Melvin G. Cleveland, Jr., Arlington (1/31/19); Judith Chambers, Austin (1/31/19); Ronald L. Hopping, Houston (1/31/21); Carey A. Patrick, Allen (1/31/21); Ty Sheehan, San Antonio (1/31/23); Virginia Sosa, Uvalde (1/31/19); Bill Thompson, Richardson (1/31/23); Rene D. Peña, El Paso (1/31/21). Exec. Dir. Chris Kloeris ($83,204), 333 Guadalupe St., Ste. 2-420, Austin 78701; (512) 305-8501.

Orthotics and Prosthetics, Texas Board of: abolished by the 83rd Legislature, S.B. 202. All duties transferred to the Texas Department of Licensing and Regulation.

Pardons and Paroles, Texas Board of: (1893 as Board of Pardon Advisers; changed in 1936 to Board of Pardons and Paroles with 3 members; members increased to 6 in 1983; made a division of the Texas Dept. of Criminal Justice in 1990); apptv.; 6-yr.; 7 members (chairman, $176,300; members, $112,750 each): Chair David Gutierrez, Gatesville (2/1/21); D'Wayne Jernigan, Huntsville (2/1/25); Carmella Jones, Angleton (2/1/25); James LaFavers, Amarillo (2/1/23); Brian Long, Palestine (2/1/23); Ed Robertson, Austin (2/1/21); Lionel F. Solis, San Antonio (2/1/21). Parole Commissioners: Lee Ann Eck-Massingill, Gatesville; Ira Evans, Angleton; Mary Farley, Amarillo; Troy Fox, Austin; Roy Garcia, Huntsville; Raymond Gonzalez, Angleton; James Hensarling, Palestine; Elvis Hightower, Austin; Paul Kiel, Palestine; Marsha Moberley, Austin; Anthony Ramirez, San Antonio; Wanda Saliagas, Huntsville; Charles Speier, San Antonio; Roel Tejeda, Gatesville. Gen. Counsel Bettie L. Wells, PO Box 13401, Austin 78711-3401; (512) 406-5852.

Parks and Wildlife Commission, Texas: (1963 as 3-member board; members increased to 6 in 1971 and to 9 in 1983); apptv.; expenses; 6-yr.; 9 members: Jeff Hildebrand, Houston (2/1/25); S. Reed Morian, Houston (2/1/21); Arch Aplin, Lake Jackson (2/1/23); Oliver J. Bell, Houston (2/1/23); Annabel Benavides Galo, Laredo (2/1/19); Jeanne W. Latimer, San Antonio (2/1/21); Bobby Patton, Fort Worth (2/1/25); Richard Scott, Wimberley (2/1/23); James Abell, Tyler (2/1/25); Anna Benavides Galo, Laredo (2/1/21); Reed Morian, Houston (2/1/21). Chairman-Emeritus Lee Marshall Bass, Fort Worth. Exec. Dir. Carter Smith ($200,643), 4200 Smith School Rd., Austin 78744; (512) 389-4800.

Pecos River Compact Commissioner: (1942); apptv.; 6-yr.; salary and expenses; (negotiates with New Mexico regarding waters of the Pecos): Frederic Tate ($33,053), Marfa (1/23/23), PO Box 340, Monahans 79756; (432) 940-1753.

Pension Boards: (For old age, blind and dependent children's assistance, *see* Health and Human Services Commission Council. *See also* listings under Retirement for state and municipal employee and teacher retirement systems.)

Pension Review Board, State: (1979); apptv.; 6-yr.; 9 members (1 senator apptd. by Lt. Gov., 1 representative apptd. by Speaker, 7 apptd. by Gov.): Chair Stephanie Leibe, Austin (1/31/21); Keith Brainard, Georgetown (1/31/25); Andrew Cable, Wimberley (1/31/19); Marcia Dush, Austin (1/31/25); Rossy Fariña-Strauss, Austin (1/31/23); Josh McGee, Houston (1/31/21); Ernest Richards, Irving (1/31/21). Exec. Dir. Anumeha Kumar ($112,750), PO Box 13498, Austin 78711-3498; (512) 463-1736.

Perfusionists, Texas State Board of Examiners of: Abolished September 2005 by the 83rd Legislature, S.B. 202. All duties transferred to the Texas Dept. of Human Services, now part of the Health and Human Services Commission.

Pest Control Board, Texas Structural: Abolished August 2007; responsibilities transferred to the Texas Dept. of Agriculture, Structural Pest Control Service, Pesticide Program.

Pharmacy, Texas State Board of: (1907 as 6-member board; members increased to 9 in 1981); apptv.; 6-yr.; 9 members: Chair Dennis Wiesner, Austin (8/31/19); Bradley A. Miller, Austin (8/31/19); Donald Lewis, Athens (8/31/19); Rick Fernandez, Northlake (8/31/23); Daniel Guerrero, San Marcos (8/31/23); Lori Henke, Amarillo (8/31/23); Suzan Kedron, Dallas (8/31/19); Julie Spier, Katy (8/31/23); Isaac Thornsburg, San Antonio (8/31/21); Rebecca Tijerina, Castle Hills (8/31/21); Jenny Downing Yoakum, Kilgore (8/31/21). Exec. Dir. Allison Vordenbaumen Benz ($132,490), 333 Guadalupe St., Ste. 3-600, Austin 78701-3903; (512) 305-8000. Consumer complaints: (800) 821-3205.

Physical Therapy Examiners, Texas Board of: (1971); apptv.; 6-yr.; expenses; 9 members: Chair Harvey Aikman, Mission (1/31/21); Barbara Sanders, Austin (1/31/23); Liesl Olson, Lubbock (1/31/21); Manuel A. Domenech, Austin (1/31/23); Melissa Skillern, Manvel (1/31/25); Jeffrey Tout, Granbury (1/31/19); Glenda Clausell, Houston (1/31/21); Donivan Hodge, Spicewood (1/31/23); Philip Vickers, Fort Worth (1/31/19). Exec. Dir. John Maline ($104,990), 333 Guadalupe St., Ste. 2-510, Austin 78701-3942; (512) 305-6900.

Physical Therapy and Occupational Therapy Examiners, Executive Council of: (1971); apptv.; 2-yr.; expenses; 5 members: Chair Arthur Roger Matson, Georgetown (2/1/19); Stephanie Johnston, Houston (2/1/21); Barbara Sanders, Austin (2/1/23); Amanda Ellis, Austin (2/1/19); Philip Vickers, Fort Worth (1/31/19). Exec. Dir. John Maline ($104,990), 333 Guadalupe St., Ste. 2-510, Austin 78701-3942; (512) 305-6900.

Physician Assistant Board, Texas: (1993 as Physician Assistant Advisory Council; changed to present name in 1995); apptv.; 6-yr.; 13 members: Chair Karrie Lynn Crosby, Waco (2/1/21); Clay Bulls, Abilene (2/1/21); Jennifer Clarner, Austin (2/1/23); Maribel De Ponce, McAllen (2/1/21); Melinda A. Gottschalk, Round Rock (2/1/19); Victor Ho, Houston (2/1/21); Teralea Davis Jones, Beeville (2/1/19); Janith Mills, Irving (2/1/23); Michael Reis, Woodway (2/1/19); John Scott, Keller (2/1/23); Larry Hughes, Frisco (2/1/25); Jorge Martinez, McAllen (2/1/21); Cameron McElhany, Austin (2/1/23). Exec. Dir. Stephen Brint Carlton ($145,930), 333 Guadalupe, Tower III, #610, Austin 78768; (512) 305-7010. Consumer Complaints: (800) 201-9353.

Plumbing Examiners, State Board of: (1947 as 6-member board; members increased to 9 in 1981); apptv.; expenses; 6-yr.; Chair Julio Cerda, Mission (9/05/19); Ricardo Jose Guerra, Dallas (9/05/21); David Anthony Garza, San Benito (9/05/19); Milton Gutierrez, Fort Worth (9/05/21); Robert F. Jalnos, San Antonio (9/05/19); Edward Thompson, Tyler (9/05/19); 3 vacancies. Exec. Dir. Lisa G. Hill ($114,239), PO Box 4200, Austin 78765-4200; (800) 845-6584.

Podiatric Medical Examiners, Texas State Board of: (1923 as 6-member State Board of Chiropody Examiners; name changed to State Board of Podiatry Examiners in 1967; made 9-member board in 1981; name changed to present in 1996; in 2017 the licensing and regulation of the practice of Podiatry transferred to the Texas Department of Licensing and Regulation); apptv.; 6-yr.; expenses; 9 members: Pres. Travis A. Motley, Colleyville (2/1/23); Leslie Campbell, Plano (2/1/21); Brian B. Carpenter, Paradise (2/1/23); James Michael Lunsford, Spring Branch (2/1/19); Joe E. Martin Jr., College Station (2/1/19); Renee Pietzsch, Georgetown (2/1/21); 3 vacancies. PO Box 12216, Austin 78711-2216; (512) 305-7000. Consumer Complaint Hotline: (800) 821-3205.

Polygraph Examiners Board: (1965); abolished by the 81st Legislature, S.B. 1005. All duties moved from the Texas Department of Public Safety to Texas Department of Licensing and Regulation.

Port Freeport Commission: Apptv.; 6-yr.; 6 members: Paul Kresta, Brazoria (5/31/21); John Hoss, Freeport (5/31/23); Shane Pirtle, Lake Jackson (5/31/23); Bill Terry, Brazoria (5/31/19); Rudy Santos, Angleton (5/31/21); Ravi K. Singhania, Brazosport (5/31/19). Exec. Dir. Phyllis Saathoff, PO Box 615, Freeport 77542-0615; (800) 362-5743.

Preservation Board, State: (1983); 2-yr.; 6 members (3 ex officio: Gov., Lt. Gov., House Speaker); 3 apptv.: 1 apptd. by Gov.: Alethea Swann Bugg, San Antonio (2/1/25); 1 senator apptd. by Lt. Gov.; 1 representative apptd. by Speaker. Exec. Dir. Rod Welsh ($175,990), PO Box 13286, Austin 78711-3286; (512) 463-5495.

Prison Board: (*See* Criminal Justice, Texas Board. of)

Prison Industries Oversight Authority, Private Sector: (1997); abolished by the 81st Legislature, H.B. 1914. All duties transferred to the Texas Department of Criminal Justice.

Private Security Bureau, Texas: (1969 as Board of Private Investigators and Private Security Agencies; reorganized in 1998 as Texas Comm. on Private Security; reestablished in 2004 as a bureau of the Texas Dept. of Public Safety); apptv.; expenses; 6-yr.; 8 members (1 ex officio: Dir., Dept. of Public Safety); 7 apptd. members: Chair Patricia James, Houston (1/31/21); Wade Hayden, San Antonio (1/31/25); Derrick Howard, Universal City (1/31/23); Claude Siems, Houston (1/31/21); Alan Trevino, Austin (1/31/23); Debra Mertz-Ulmer, Houston (1/31/25); Stephen Willeford,

Sutherland Springs (1/31/23). Sr. Mgr. Chris Sims, PO Box 4087, Austin 78773-0001; (512) 424-7710.

Process Server Certification Advisory Board: Apptv. by Texas Supreme Court; part of Judicial Branch Certification Commission; staggered terms; 6-yr., 5 members: Chair Patrick Dyer, Missouri City, (2/1/21); Rhonda Hughey, Kaufman (2/1/19); Eric Johnson, Rosharon (2/1/21); Melissa K. Perez, Waxahachie (2/1/23); Justiss Rasberry, El Paso (2/1/19). PO Box 12248, Austin 78711-2248; (512) 463-2713.

Produce Recovery Fund Board: (1977 as 3-member board; members increased to 5 in 1981); apptv.; expenses; 6-yr.; 5 members: Ralph Diaz, Corpus Christi (1/31/25); Ly H. Nguyen, Lake Jackson (1/31/21); 3 vacancies. Accepting applications for new members. Must meet qualifications in Chapter 101 of the Texas Agricultural Code (https://statutes.capitol.texas.gov/Docs/AG/pdf/AG.101.pdf). Contact Patrick Dudley c/o Texas Dept. of Agriculture, PO Box 12847, Austin 78711-2847; (512) 463-3285.

Psychologists, Texas Board of Examiners of: (1969 as 6-member board; members increased to 9 in 1981); apptv.; 6-yr.; per diem and expenses; 9 members: Chair Tim F. Branaman, Dallas (10/31/19); Lou Ann Todd Mock, Houston (10/31/19); Herman Adler, Houston (10/31/23); Susan Fletcher, Frisco (10/31/21); Ronald Palomares, Dallas (10/31/21); Andoni Zagouris, McAllen (10/31/23); John Bielamowicz, Waxahachie (10/31/21); Ryan Bridges, Houston (10/31/23); Angela A. Downes, Dallas (10/31/19). Exec. Dir. Darrel Spinks ($96,678), 333 Guadalupe St., Ste. 2-450, Austin 78701; (512) 305-7700.

Public Finance Authority, Texas: (1984, assumed duties of Texas Building Authority); apptv.; per diem and expenses; 6-yr.; 7 members: Chair Billy M. Atkinson, Jr., Sugar Land (2/1/23); Ruth C. Schiermeyer, Lubbock (2/1/19); Gerald B. Alley, Arlington (2/1/19); Ramon Manning, Houston (2/1/21); Walker N. Moody, Houston (2/1/19); Rodney K. Moore, Lufkin (2/1/19); Joseph E. Williams, Frisco (2/1/23). Exec. Dir. Lee Deviney ($140,980), PO Box 12906, Austin 78711-2906; (512) 463-5544.

Public Insurance Counsel, Office of: (1995); apptv.; 2-yr.; 1 member: Melissa Hamilton (2/1/21) ($137,734), 333 Guadalupe St., Ste. 3-120; Austin 78701; (512) 322-4143.

Public Safety Commission: (1935 with 3 members; members increased to 5 in 2007); apptv.; expenses; 6-yr.; 5 members: Chair Steven P. Mach, Houston (1/1/21); A. Cynthia Leon, Austin (12/31/20); Jason K. Pulliam, San Antonio (1/1/22). Dir. of Texas Dept. of Public Safety, Steven McCraw ($232,969), PO Box 4087, Austin 78773-0001; (512) 424-2000.

Public Utility Commission: (1975); apptv.; 6-yr., 3 members ($189,500): Chair DeAnn Walker, Austin (9/1/21); Shelly Botkin, Austin (9/1/19); Arthur C. D'Andrea, Austin (9/1/23). Exec. Dir. John Paul Urban ($159,782), PO Box 13326, Austin 78711-3326; (512) 936-7120.

Public Utility Counsel, Office of: (1983); apptv.; 2-yr.; 1 member: Lori Cobos, Austin (2/1/21); ($162,000), PO Box 12397, Austin 78711-2397; (512) 936-7500.

Racing Commission, Texas: (1986); apptv.; 6-yr.; per diem and expenses; 9 members; 2 ex officio: Chmn., Public Safety Commission and Comptroller of Public Accounts; 7 apptv.: Chair John T. Steen III, Houston (2/1/19); Ronald F. Ederer, Corpus Christi (2/01/19); Margaret Martin, Boerne (2/1/21); Connie McNabb, Montgomery (2/1/21); Michael Moore, Fort Worth (2/1/23); Robert C. Pate, Corpus Christi (2/1/23); Arvel Waight Jr., Willow City (2/1/21). Exec. Dir. Chuck Trout ($90,200), PO Box 12080, Austin 78711-2080; (512) 833-6699.

Radiation Advisory Board, Texas: (1961); apptv.; 6-yr.; 18 members: William C. Campbell, Fort Worth (4/16/19); Karen Cuneo Newton, San Antonio (4/16/17); Robert J. Emery, Houston (4/16/17); John Hageman, San Antonio (4/16/17); Gerald T. Powell, Wadsworth (4/16/21); Steve Harris, Dallas (4/16/19); Mark C. Harvey, Houston (4/16/21); John Johnson, San Antonio (4/16/17); Kenneth V. Krieger, Waco (4/16/21); Mitchell Lucas, Granbury (4/16/19); Frank Leavell, Lampasas (4/16/21); Darlene Metter, San Antonio (4/16/19); Simon Trubek, Austin (4/16/21); Judith Raab, Fort Worth (4/16/19); Kevin L. Raabe, Falls City (4/16/17); Darshan J. Sachde, Austin (4/16/19); Mark Silberman, Austin (4/16/17). Control MC 2835, Texas Dept. of State Health Services, PO Box 149347, Austin 78714-9347; (512) 834-6679.

Radioactive Waste Disposal Compact, Texas Low-Level: (1993); apptv.; 6-yr.; expenses; 6 Texas members, plus one member each from Maine and Vermont; Texas apptees.: Chair Brandon T. Hurley, Grapevine (9/1/19); John Matthew Salsman, Driftwood (9/1/23); Richard H. Dolgener, Andrews (9/1/19); Lisa Edwards, Granbury (9/1/23); Linda K. Morris, Waco (9/1/21); Clint Weber, Fort Worth (9/1/19). Radioactive Materials Division MC-233, Texas Commission on Environmental Quality, PO Box 13087, Austin 78711-3087; (512) 239-6466.

Railroad Commission of Texas: (1891); elective; 6-yr.; 3 members, $137,500 each: Wayne Christian (12/31/22); Christi Craddick (12/31/24); Ryan Sitton (12/31/20). Dir. Wei Wang ($180,000), PO Box 12967, Austin 78711-2967; (512) 463-7288.

Real Estate Commission, Texas: (1949 as 6-member board; members increased to 9 in 1979); apptv.; per diem and expenses; 6-yr.; 9 members: Chair R. Scott Kesner, El Paso (1/31/25); Bob Leonard, San Antonio (1/31/21); T.J. Turner, Austin (1/31/21); Jan Fite Miller, Dallas (1/31/23); Barbara Russell, Denton (1/31/25); Rayito Stephens, Pearland (1/31/21); DeLora Wilkinson, Cypress (1/31/23); Jason Hartgraves, Frisco (1/31/25); Micheal Williams, Colleyville (1/31/23). Admin. Douglas E. Oldmixon ($182,700), PO Box 12188, Austin 78711-2188; (512) 459-6544.

Real Estate Research Center Advisory Committee: (1971); apptv.; 6-yr.; 10 members; 1 ex officio: rep. of Texas Real Estate Commission; 9 apptv.: W. Douglas Jennings, Fort Worth (1/31/21); Troy Alley, Jr., DeSoto (1/31/23); Russell Cain, Port Lavaca (1/31/23); Jingjing Clemence, Sugar Land (1/31/23); Alvin Collins, Andrews (1/31/21); Elizabeth Martin, Boerne (1/31/21); Walter F. Nelson, Houston (1/31/19); Stephen D. Roberts, Austin (1/31/19); Christopher Clark Welder, San Antonio (1/31/19). Dir. Gary Maler ($241,448), Texas A&M University Real Estate Center, 2115 TAMU, College Station 77843-2115; (979) 845-0460.

Red River Authority of Texas: (1959); apptv.; 6-yr.; per diem and expenses; 9 members: Pres. Jerry B. Daniel, Truscott (8/11/21); Todd Boykin, Amarillo (8/11/21); Penny C. Carpenter, Silverton (8/11/19); Mike Sandefur, Texarkana (8/11/23); G. Wilson Scaling II, Henrietta (8/11/21); Zackary K. Smith, Canyon (8/11/19); Stephen A. Thornhill, Denison (8/11/19); Joe L. Ward, Telephone (8/11/23); one vacancy. Gen. Mgr. Randy Whiteman, PO Box 240, Wichita Falls 76307-0240; (940) 723-8697.

Red River Compact Commissioner: (1949); apptv.; 4-yr.; salary and expenses; (negotiates with Oklahoma, Arkansas, and Louisiana regarding waters of the Red): Clyde Siebman, Sherman (2/1/23); PO Box 1386, Marshall 75671; (903) 938-4572.

Redistricting Board, Legislative: (*See* Legislative Redistricting Board.)

Rehabilitation Commission, Texas: Combined into Department of Assistive and Rehabilitative Services (DARS) of the Health and Human Services Commission as of 3/1/04.

Residential Construction Commission, Texas: Agency closed 9/1/2010.

Retirement System of Texas, Employees: (1949); apptv.; 6-yr.; 6 members: 1 apptd. by Gov., 1 by Chief Justice of State Supreme Court, 1 by House Speaker; 3 elected by ERS members: Chair I. Craig Hester, Austin (8/31/22); Vice Chair Ilesa Daniels, Houston (8/31/22); Gov.'s apptee: James Kee, San Antonio (8/31/20); Elected members: Doug Danzeiser, Austin (8/31/19); Catherine Melvin, Austin (8/31/23). Exec. Dir. Porter Wilson, 200 East 18th St., PO Box 13207, Austin 78711; (512) 867-7711.

Retirement System of Texas, Teacher: (1937 as 6-member board; members increased to 9 in 1973); 6-yr.; expenses; 9 members; 2 apptd. by State Board of Education, 3 apptd. by Gov., 4 apptd. by Gov. after being nominated by popular ballot of retirement system members: Chair Jarvis V. Hollingsworth, Missouri City (8/31/23); Joe Colonnetta, Dallas (8/31/19); David Corpus, Humble (8/31/19); John Elliott, Austin (8/31/21); Greg Gibson, Schertz (8/31/21); Christopher Moss, Lufkin (8/31/21); James Nance, Hallettsville (8/31/23); Dolores Ramirez, San Benito (8/31/19); Nanette Sissney, Whitesboro (8/31/23). Exec. Dir. Brian Guthrie, 1000 Red River, Austin 78701; (512) 542-6400.

Retirement System, Texas County and District: (1967); apptv.; 6-yr.; 9 members: Chair Robert Eckels, Spring (12/31/19); Bob Willis, Livingston (12/31/19); Chris Davis, Alto (12/31/21); Susan Fletcher, Collin Co. (12/31/23); Deborah Hunt, Georgetown (12/31/21); Bridget McDowell, Baird (12/31/19); Mary Louise Nicholson, Fort Worth (12/31/23); Kara Sands, Nueces Co. (12/31/23); Christopher T. Hill, McKinney (12/31/21). Exec. Dir. Amy Bishop, 901 MoPac Expwy. S., Bldg. IV, Ste. 500, PO Box 2034, Austin 78768-2034; (512) 328-8889.

Retirement System, Texas Emergency Services: (1977; formerly the Fire Fighters' Relief and Retirement Fund); apptv.; expenses; 6-yr.; 9 members: Chair Francisco R. Torres, Raymondville (9/1/19); Edward Keenan, Houston (9/1/23); Rod Ryalls, Burkburnett (9/1/23); Stephanie L. Wagner, Wimberley (9/1/23); Jenny Moore, Lake Jackson (9/1/22); Taylor Allen, Dallas (9/1/19); Dan Key, Friendswood (9/1/20); Courtney G. Bechtol, Rockport (9/1/21); Pilar Rodriguez, Edinburg (9/1/19). Exec. Dir. Kevin Deiters ($99,000), c/o Office of the Fire Fighters' Pension, 920 Colorado, 11th Floor, PO Box 12577, Austin 78711; (512) 936-3372. (*See also* Fire Fighters' Pension Commissioner.)

Retirement System, Texas Municipal: (1947); apptv.; 6-yr.; expenses; 6 members: Jim Parrish, Plano (2/1/23); Bill Philibert, Deer Park (2/1/19); Jesus A. Garza, Kingsville (2/1/23); James P. Jeffers, Nacogdoches (2/1/21); David Landis, Perryton (2/1/21); Julie Oakley, Lakeway (2/1/19). Exec. Dir David R. Gavia, PO Box 149153, Austin 78714-9153; (512) 476-7577.

Rio Grande Compact Commissioner of Texas: (1929); apptv.; 6-yr.; salary and expenses; (negotiates with Colorado and New Mexico regarding waters of the Rio Grande): Patrick R. Gordon ($42,225), El Paso (6/9/25); PO Box 1917, El Paso 79950-1917; (915) 834-7075.

Rio Grande Regional Water Authority: (2003); apptv.; 4-yr.; 18 members: 12 apptd. by Gov.; 6 apptd. by member counties. Gov.'s apptees.: Dario (D.V.) Guerra Jr., Edinburg (2/1/21); Wayne Halbert, Harlingen (2/1/21); Paul Glenn Heller, Mission (2/1/19); Sonny Hinojosa, Edinburg (2/1/21); Sonia Lambert, San Benito (2/1/21); Brian Macmanus, Rio Hondo (2/1/21); Joe Pennington, Raymondville (2/1/21); Roel Rodriguez, McAllen (2/1/19); Bobby Sparks,

Valley Acres (2/1/21); Frank (JoJo) White, Progreso Lakes (2/1/21); Lance Neuhaus, Weslaco (N/A); Troy Allen, Edcouch (N/A). County apptees.: John Bruciak, Cameron Co.; Jim Darling, Hidalgo Co.; Ricardo Gutierrez, Starr Co.; Ike Cabello, Webb Co.; Jimmy Riggan, Willacy Co.; Karran Westerman, Zapata Co.; 322 S. Missouri Ave., Weslaco 78596; (956) 968-3141.

Risk Management, State Office of: apptv.; 2-yr.; 5 members: Chair Lloyd Garland, Lubbock (2/1/19); Rosemary A. Gammon, Plano (2/1/21); Tomas Gonzalez, El Paso (2/1/23); Gerald Ladner, Sr., Austin (2/1/21); John W. Youngblood, Cameron (2/1/19). Exec. Dir. Stephen S. Vollbrecht ($139,582), PO Box 13777, Austin 78711-3777; (512) 475-1440.

Rural Affairs, Texas Department of: (2001 as Office of Rural Community Affairs; name changed to present form in 2009); abolished by the 82nd Legislature, S.B. 1. All duties transferred to the Department of Agriculture.

Sabine River Authority of Texas: (1949); apptv.; per diem and expenses; 6-yr.; 9 members: Cary Abney, Marshall (7/06/21); Thomas Beall, Milam (7/06/23); Jeff Jacobs, Kaufman (7/06/19); David W. Koonce, Center (7/06/19); Andrew Mills, Hemphill (7/6/23); Jeanette Sterner, Holly Lake Ranch (7/6/21); Janie Walenta, Quitman (7/06/23); Earl Williams, Orange (7/06/19); Laurie Woloszyn, Longview (7/06/21). Exec. VP Gen. Mgr. David Montagne, PO Box 579, Orange 77630; (409) 746-2192.

Sabine River Compact Commission: (1953); apptv.; 6-yr.; salary ($8,699) and expenses; (negotiates with Louisiana regarding the waters of the Sabine); 5 members: the chairman, who does not vote, is appointed by the President of United States; Texas and Louisiana each have 2 members. Texas members: Jerry F. Gipson, Longview (7/12/22); Michael H. Lewis, Newton (7/12/25); c/o P.O. Box 13087, Austin 78711; (512) 239-4707.

San Antonio River Authority: (1937); apptv., 6-yr., 12 members: Chair Darrell T. Brownlow, Wilson Co. (11/3/19); Michael W. Lackey, Bexar Co. (11/3/21); Jim Campbell, Bexar Co. (11/7/21); Lourdes Galvan, Bexar Co. (11/5/19); Alicia Lott Cowley, Goliad Co. (11/7/21); John Flieller, Wilson Co. (11/3/21); James Fuller, Goliad Co. (11/13/19); Jerry G. Gonzales, Bexar Co. (11/13/19); Hector Morales, Bexar Co. (11/7/21); Gaylon J. Oehlke, Karnes Co. (11/5/19); Deb Bolner Prost, Bexar Co. (11/13/22); H. B. Ruckman, III, Karnes Co. (11/3/21). Gen. Mgr. Suzanne B. Scott, PO Box 839980, San Antonio 78283-9980; (210) 227-1373.

San Jacinto River Authority, Board of Directors: (1937); apptv.; expenses while on duty; 6-yr.; 6 members: Pres. Lloyd B. Tisdale, Conroe (10/16/19); Ronald Anderson, Mont Belvieu (10/16/21); Mark Micheletti, Kingwood (10/16/23); Jim Alexander, Magnolia (10/16/19); Charles Boulware, Montgomery (10/16/23); Karen Cambio, Kingwood (10/16/19); Brenda Cooper, Montgomery (10/16/21). Gen. Mgr. Jace Houston, PO Box 329, Conroe 77305; (936) 588-1111.

Savings and Mortgage Lending Commissioner: (1961); apptd. by State Finance Commission: Caroline C. Jones ($194,750), 2601 N. Lamar, Ste. 201, Austin 78705; (512) 475-1350. Consumer Complaint Hotline: 877-276-5550.

School Safety Center, Texas: (2001); apptv.; 2-yr.; 6 ex-officio members from the Texas Commissioner of Higher Education, Texas Youth Commission, Texas Education Agency, Dept. of State Health Services, Attorney General's office, and the Texas Juvenile Probation Commission; 10 apptd. members: Chair James R. Pendell, Jill M. Tate, Jenna Heise, Mike D. Cox, Bryan Hedrick, Allison Geddes, Judge Daniel F. Gilliam, Paul A. Robbins, Robert Martinez, Andrew B. Kim, Robert L. Long, III, Dr. Raymund Paredes, Megan Aghazadian, Marie Welsch. Director Kathy Martinez-Prather, 415 N. Guadalupe, Ste. 164, San Marcos 78666; (877) 304-2727.

Securities Board, State: (Est. 1957, the outgrowth of several amendments to the Texas Securities Act, originally passed in 1913); act is administered by the Securities Commissioner, who is appointed by the board members; expenses; 6-yr.; 5 members: Melissa Tyroch, Belton (1/20/25); Robert Belt, Houston (1/20/23); Wally Kinney, Comfort (1/20/25); Kenneth Koncaba, Friendswood (1/20/23); Miguel Romano, Jr., Austin (1/20/21). Commissioner Travis Iles ($147,704), PO Box 13167, Austin 78711-3167; (512) 305-8300.

Seed and Plant Board, State: (1959) Currently inactive.

Sex Offender Treatment, Council on: (1983); apptv.; expenses; 6-yr.; 7 members: Chair Aaron Paul Pierce, Waco (2/1/23); Terri L. Bauer, Sachse (2/1/19); Ezio Leite, Fort Worth (2/1/21); Emily Orozco-Crousen, Abilene (2/1/21); Charissa Dvorak, Heath (2/1/23); Louis Gonzales, III, Round Rock (2/1/19); James Taylor, San Antonio (2/1/21). Exec. Dir. Sarah Faszholz, c/o Texas Dept. of State Health Services, PO Box 149347, Austin 78714-9347; (512) 834-4530

Skill Standards Board, Texas: (1995); abolished and its powers and duties were transferred to the Texas Workforce Investment Council on September 1, 2015.

Social Worker Examiners, Texas State Board of: (1993); apptv.; 6-yr.; per diem and travel expenses; 9 members: Chair Timothy Martel Brown, Dallas (2/1/19); J. Brian Brumley, Sumner (2/1/21); Maria Castro, Weslaco (2/1/19); Beverly Loss, Wolfe City (2/1/21); Martha Mosier, College Station (2/1/23); Audrey Ramsbacher, San Antonio (2/1/23); Megan Graham, Lubbock (2/1/23); Benny Morris, Cleburne (2/1/21); Mark Talbot, McAllen (2/1/19). Exec. Dir. Alice Bradford ($48,000), c/o Texas Dept. of State Health Services, PO Box 149347, Austin 78714-9347; (512) 719-3521.

Soil and Water Conservation Board, Texas State: (1939); 2-yr.; 7 members: 2 apptd. by Gov.; 5 elected by district directors; Chair Barry Mahler, Iowa Park (5/7/21); Marty H. Graham, Rocksprings (5/5/20); José Dodier, Jr., Zapata (5/7/21); David Basinger, Deport (5/1/20); Scott Buckles, Stratford (5/7/21); Gov. Apptee.: Tina Yturria Buford, Harlingen (2/1/20); Carl Ray Polk, Jr., Lufkin (2/1/21). Exec. Dir. Rex Isom ($142,303), 4311 S. 31st St., Ste. 125, PO Box 658, Temple 76503; (254) 773-2250.

Special Education Continuing Advisory Committee, Texas: (1997); apptv.; 4-yr.; 17 members: Agata K. Thibodeaux, Katy (2/1/21); Alicia Giordano, Humble (2/1/21); Amy Litzinger, Austin (2/1/21); Elizabeth A. Donaldson, Stowell (2/1/21); Jana S. Burns, Saginaw (2/1/21); Jana McKelvey, Austin (2/1/23); Jen Stratton, Austin (2/1/23); Jo Ann Garza Wofford, New Braunfels (2/1/21); Kristine H. Mohajer, Leander (2/1/21); Laura Villarreal, Universal City (2/1/23); Laurie Goforth Rodriguez, Dickinson (2/1/21); Rachel A. Dreiling, Dallas (2/1/21); Ray Tijerina, San Antonio (2/1/23); Robin H. Lock, Lubbock (2/1/21); Shemica S. Allen, Allen (2/1/23); Stephanie Martinez, Laredo (2/1/23); Teresa Bronsky, Plano (2/1/23); c/o Texas Education Agency, Division of IDEA Coordination, 1701 N. Congress Ave., Austin 78701-1494; (512) 463-9414; Parent Information Line: 1-800-252-9668.

Speech-Language Pathology and Audiology, State Board of Examiners for: (1983); abolished by the 84th Legislature, S.B. 202. Duties transferred from the Department of State Health Services to the Texas Department of Licensing & Regulation.

Stephen F. Austin State University, Board of Regents: (1969); apptv.; expenses; 6-yr.; 9 members: Chair Brigettee Carnes Henderson, Lufkin (1/31/21); Alton Frailey, Katy (1/31/21); Nelda Luce Blair, Houston (1/31/21); David Alders, Nacogdoches (1/31/25); Scott Coleman, Houston (1/31/21); Karen Gantt, McKinney (1/31/23); Tom Mason, Dallas (1/31/23); Judy Larson Olson, Conroe (1/31/25); Jennifer Winston, Lufkin (1/31/25). Pres. Baker Pattillo, PO Box 13026, SFA Station, Nacogdoches 75962-3026; (936) 468-4048.

Sulphur River Basin Authority: (1985); 7 members; 6-yr.; Region I: Kelly Mitchell, Texarkana (2/1/23); Gary Cheatwood, Bogata (2/1/23); Region 2: Katie Stedman, Mount Pleasant (2/1/21); Chris Spencer, Hughes Spring (2/1/23); Region 3: Bret McCoy, Omaha (2/1/21); Wally Kraft, Paris (2/1/25); Robert Hayter, Paris (6/15/25); 911 N. Bishop St., Ste. C 104, Wake Village 75501; (903) 223-7887.

Sunset Advisory Commission: (1977); 12 members: 5 members of House of Representatives, 5 members of Senate, 1 public member apptd. by Speaker, 1 public member apptd. by Lt. Gov.; 2-yr.; expenses. Public members: Emily Patake, Cedar Park (9/1/19); Ronald G. Steinhart, Dallas (9/1/19). Dir. Jennifer Jones ($165,000), PO Box 13066, Austin 78711-3066; (512) 463-1300.

Teacher Retirement System: (*See* Retirement System of Texas, Teacher.)

Texas A&M University System Board of Regents: (1875); apptv.; 6-yr.; expenses; 9 members: Chair Elaine Mendoza, San Antonio (2/1/23); Tim Leach, Midland (2/1/23); Phil Adams, Bryan/College Station (2/1/21); Robert L. Albritton, Fort Worth (2/1/21); Jay Graham, Houston (2/1/25); Michael Hernandez III, Fort Worth (2/1/25); Bill Mahomes, Dallas (2/1/25); Michael J. Plank, Houston (2/1/25); Cliff Thomas, Victoria (2/1/23). Chancellor John Sharp, PO Box 15812, College Station 77841-5013; (979) 845-9600.

Texas Southern University Board of Regents: (1947); expenses; 6-yr.; 9 members: Chair Hasan K. Mack, Austin (2/1/23); Wesley G. Terrell, Dallas (2/1/21); Marilyn A. Rose, Houston (2/1/21); Ron Price, Mesquite (2/1/23); Marc C. Carter, Houston (2/1/25); Pamela A. Medina, Houston (2/1/25); Derrick M. Mitchell, Houston (2/1/21); Albert H. Myres, Sr., Houston (2/1/25); Jay S. Zeidman, Houston (2/1/25). Pres. Dr. Austin A. Lane. Exec. Admin. Faith Ruiz, 3100 Cleburne St., Hannah Hall, Rm. 104, Houston 77004; (713) 313-7992.

Texas State Technical College Board of Regents: (1960 as Board of the Texas State Technical Institute; changed to present name in 1991); apptv.; expenses; 6-yr.; 9 members: Chair John K. Hatchel, Woodway (2/1/23); Ivan Andarza, Austin (8/31/19); Tony Abad, Waco (8/31/21); Curtis Cleveland, Waco (8/31/21); Keith Honey, Longview (8/31/19); Charles McDonald, Richmond, (8/31/23); Alejandro G. Meade III, Mission (8/31/21); Ellis M. Skinner II, Dallas (8/31/19); Tiffany Tremont, New Braunfels (8/31/23). Chancellor Michael L. Reeser, TSTC System, 3801 Campus Dr., Waco 76705; (254) 867-4891.

Texas State University System, Board of Regents: (1911 as Board of Regents of State Teachers Colleges; name changed in 1965 to Board of Regents of State Senior Colleges; changed to present form in 1975); apptv.; per diem and expenses; 6-yr.; 9 members: Chair William Scott, Nederland (2/1/25); Charlie Amato, San Antonio (2/1/25); Duke Austin, Houston (2/1/23); Garry Crain, The Hills (2/1/23); Veronica M. Edwards, San Antonio (2/1/23); Don Flores, El Paso (2/1/25); Nicki Harle, Baird (2/1/23); David Montagne, Beaumont (2/1/21); Alan L. Tinsley, Madisonville (2/1/21). Chancellor Brian McCall, Thomas

J. Rusk Bldg., 200 E. 10th St., Ste. 600, Austin 78701; (512) 463-1808.

Texas Tech University System, Board of Regents: (1923); apptv.; expenses; 6-yr.; 9 members: Christopher M. Huckabee, Fort Worth (1/31/21); J. Michael Lewis, Dallas (1/31/23); Mark Griffin, Lubbock (1/31/25); Ronnie Hammonds, Houston (1/31/21); Ginger Kerrick, Webster (1/31/25); Mickey L. Long, Midland (1/31/21); John D. Steinmetz, Dallas (1/31/23); John B. Walker, Houston (1/31/23); Dusty Womble, Lubbock (1/31/25); . Chancellor Tedd L. Mitchell, P.O. Box 42011, Lubbock 79409-2011; (806) 742-2161.

Texas Woman's University, Board of Regents: (1901); apptv.; expenses; 6-yr.; 9 members: Chair Jill Jester, Denton (2/1/23); Kathleen Wu, Dallas (2/1/23); Bernadette Coleman, Denton (2/1/23); Teresa Doggett, Austin (2/1/21); Carlos L. Gallardo, Frisco (2/1/21); Robert Hyde, Irving (2/1/25); Stacie McDavid, Fort Worth (2/1/25); Janelle Shepard, Weatherford (2/1/21); Mary Pincoffs Wilson, Austin (2/1/25). Chancellor Dr. Carine M. Feyten, PO Box 425587, TWU Station, Denton 76204-5587; (940) 898-3250.

Transportation Commission, Texas: (1917 as State Highway Commission; merged with Mass Transportation Commission and name changed to State Board of Highways and Public Transportation in 1975; merged with Texas Dept. of Aviation and Texas Motor Vehicle Commission and name changed to present form in 1991) apptv.; 6-yr.; 5 members ($15,914 each): Chair J. Bruce Bugg, Jr. San Antonio (2/1/21); Alvin New, San Angelo (2/1/21); Laura Ryan, Houston (2/1/23); 2 vacancies; Exec. Dir. General James M. Bass ($292,500), 125 E 11th St., Austin 78701-2483; (512) 463-8585.

Transportation, Texas Department of: apptv.; 6-yr.; 5 members ($15,914 each): Chair Tryon D. Lewis, Odessa (2/1/21); Jeff Austin III, Tyler (2/1/19); Bruce Bugg Jr., San Antonio (2/1/21); Jeff Moseley, Houston (2/1/17); Victor Vandergriff, Arlington (2/1/19). Exec. Dir. General Joe Weber ($292,500), 125 E. 11th St., Austin 78701-2483; (512) 463-8585.

Trinity River Authority Board of Directors: (1955); apptv.; per diem and expenses; 6-yr.; 25 members (3 from Tarrant County, 4 from Dallas County, 3 from area-at-large and 1 each from 15 other districts): Chair Kevin Maxwell, Crockett (3/15/21); Cathy Altman, Midlothian (3/15/23); Whitney Beckworth, Chambers Co. (3/15/23); Henry Borbolla III, Fort Worth (3/15/19); Megan Deen, Fort Worth (3/15/23); Tommy G. Fordyce, Huntsville (3/15/19); Jerry House, Leona (3/15/23); John W. Jenkins, Hankamer (3/15/21); Jess A. Laird, Athens (3/15/19); David B. Leonard, Liberty (3/15/19); Victoria Lucas, Terrell (3/15/23); Dennis McCleskey, Apple Springs (3/15/23); Robert F. McFarlane, Palestine (3/15/21); James W. Neale, Dallas (3/15/19); Manny Rachal, Livingston (3/15/21); Steve Roberts, Coldspring (3/15/23); William O. Rodgers, Fort Worth (3/15/23); Amir A. Rupani, Dallas (3/15/19); Ana Laura Saucedo, Dallas (3/15/19); Dudley Skyrme, Palestine (3/15/19); C. Dwayne Somerville, Mexia (3/15/19); Frank H. Steed, Jr., Navarro Co. (3/15/21); Dave Ward, Madisonville (3/15/23); Edward C. Williams III, Dallas Co. (3/15/23). Gen. Mgr. J. Kevin Ward, 5300 S. Collins, PO Box 60, Arlington 76004-0060; (817) 467-4343.

Tuition Board, Prepaid Higher Education: (*See* Higher Education Tuition Board, Texas Prepaid.)

Uniform State Laws, Texas Commission on: (1941) This agency is currently inactive.

University of Houston System Board of Regents: (1963); apptv.; expenses; 6-yr.; 9 members: Chair Tilman J. Fertitta, Houston (8/31/21); Peter K. Taaffe, Austin (8/31/19); Paula M. Mendoza, Houston (8/31/19); Durga D. Agrawal, Houston (8/31/19); Doug H. Brooks, Dallas (8/31/23); Steve I. Chazen, Bellaire (8/31/23); Beth Madison, Houston (8/31/21); Gerald W. McElvy, Southlake (8/31/21); Jack B. Moore, Houston (8/31/23). Chancellor Dr. Renu Khator; Exec. Admin. Gerry Mathisen, 4800 Calhoun, 128 E. Cullen Bldg., Houston 77204-6001; (832) 842-3444.

University of North Texas System Board of Regents: (1949); apptv.; 6-yr.; expenses; 9 members: Chair George Ryan, Dallas (5/22/21); Michael R. Bradford, Dallas (5/22/21); Mary Denny, Aubrey (5/22/23); Milton B. Lee, San Antonio (5/22/23); A.K. Mago, Dallas (5/22/21); Carlos Munguia, University Park (5/22/23); Rusty Reid, Fort Worth (5/22/19); Gwyn Shea, Irving (5/22/19); Glen Whitley, Hurst (5/22/19). Chancellor Lesa B. Roe; Brd. Sec. Rosemary Haggett, 1901 Main St., Dallas 75201; (214) 752-5533.

University of Texas System Board of Regents: (1881); apptv.; expenses; 6-yr.; 9 members: Chair Kevin P. Eltife, Tyler (2/1/23); Janiece Longoria, Houston (2/1/23); James C. Weaver, San Antonio (2/1/23); David J. Beck, Houston (2/1/21); Christina Melton Crain, Dallas (2/1/25); R. Steven Hicks, Austin (2/1/21); Jodi Lee Jiles, Houston (2/1/25); Nolan Perez, Harlingen (2/1/21); Kelcy Warren, Dallas (2/1/25). Chancellor James B. Milliken, 201 W. Seventh St., Ste. 820, Austin 78701-2981; (512) 499-4402.

Utility Commission, Public: (*See* Public Utility Commission.)

Veterans Commission, Texas: (1927 as Veterans State Service Office; reorganized as Veterans Affairs Commission in 1947 with 5 members; name changed to present in 1985); apptv.; 6-yr.; per diem while on duty and expenses; 5 members: Chair Eliseo Cantu Jr., Corpus Christi (12/31/19); Kevin Barber, Houston (12/31/21); Laura Koerner, Fair Oaks Ranch (12/31/23); Daniel P. Moran, Cypress (12/31/19); Kimberlee Shaneyfelt, Argyle (12/31/23). Exec. Dir. Thomas P. Palladino ($145,580), PO Box 12277, Austin 78711-2277; (512) 463-6564.

Veterans' Land Board: (*See* Land Board, Veterans'.)

Veterinary Medical Examiners, Texas State Board of: (1911; revised 1953; made 9-member board in 1981); apptv.; expenses on duty; 6-yr.; 9 members: Chair Jessica Quillivan, Magnolia (8/26/21); Keith Pardue, Austin (8/26/21); Lynn Criner, Needville (8/26/21); Sue Allen, Waco (9/26/19); Samantha Mixon, Boerne (8/26/23); Randall Skaggs, Perryton (8/26/23); Michael White, Conroe (8/26/19). Public Members: George Antuna, Schertz (9/26/19); Carlos Chacon, Houston (8/26/23). Exec. Dir. John Helenberg ($101,787), 333 Guadalupe St., Ste. 3-810, Austin 78701-3942; (512) 305-7555.

Wastewater Treatment Research Council, Texas On-Site: Formed in 1987 as an apptv., 2-yr., 11-member council. Abolished on Sept. 1, 2011, by House Bill 2694.

Water Development Board, Texas: (1957; legislative function for the Texas Dept. of Water Resources, 1977); apptv.; per diem and expenses; 6-yr.; 3 members: Chair Peter M. Lake, Tyler (2/1/21); Kathleen Jackson, Beaumont (12/31/23); Brooke Paup, Austin (12/31/25). Exec. Admin. Jeff Walker ($173,241), 1700 N. Congress Ave., Ste. 690, PO Box 13231, Austin 78711-3231; (512) 463-7847.

Women, Governor's Commission for: (1967); apptv.; 2-yr. term or at pleasure of Gov.; 12 members: Chair Catherine Susser, Corpus Christi (12/31/19); Karen Harris, Lakehills (12/31/19); Tina Yturria Buford, Harlingen (12/31/19); Starr Corbin, Georgetown (12/31/19); Amy Henderson, Amarillo (12/31/19); Karen Manning, Houston (12/31/19); Imelda Navarro, Laredo (12/31/19); Nathali Parker, Round Rock (12/31/19); Rienke Radler, Fort Worth (12/31/19); Jinous Ruhani, Austin (12/31/19); Laura Koenig Young, Tyler (12/31/19). Exec. Dir.: Vacant, 1100 San Jacinto Blvd., Rm. 2.256, PO Box 12428, Austin 78711; (512) 475-2615.

Workers' Compensation Commissioner, Texas: (1991); functions transferred to the Texas Dept. of Insurance Division of Workers' Compensation in 2005; apptv.; 2-yr.; Commissioner Cassie Brown, Austin (2/1/21), PO Box 149104, Austin 78714-9104; (800) 839-5323.

Workforce Commission, Texas: (1936 as Texas Employment Commission; name changed 1995); apptv.; chairman, $189,500; commissioners, $189,500; 6-yr.; 3 members: Chair Vacant, representing the employers; Julian Alvarez III, Harlingen (2/1/23), representing laborers; Bryan Daniel, Georgetown (2/1/25), representing the public. Exec. Dir.: Ed Serna (interim), 101 E. 15th St., Austin 78778-0001; (512) 463-2222.

Workforce Investment Council, Texas: (1993); apptv.; 19 members: 5 ex officio (directors from Economic Development and Tourism, Higher Education Coordinating Board, Texas Education Agency, Texas Health and Human Services Comm., Texas Workforce Comm.); 14 apptd.: Chair Mark Dunn, Lufkin (9/1/19); Vice Chair Sharla Hotchkiss, Midland (9/1/17); Jerry Romero, El Paso (9/1/19); Gina Aguirre Adams, Jones Creek (9/1/21); Mark Barberena, Fort Worth (9/1/19); Lindsey Geeslin, Waco (9/1/23); Carmen Olivas Graham, El Paso (9/1/17); Thomas Halbouty, Southlake (9/1/19); Robert Hawkins, Bellmead (9/1/17); Adam Hutchison, Elm Mott (9/1/23); Paul Jones, Austin (9/1/17); Wayne Oswald, Houston (9/1/23); Paul Puente, Houston (9/1/23); Richard Rhodes, Austin (9/1/19). Dir. Lee Rector ($102,034), 1100 San Jacinto, Ste. 1.100 PO Box 2241, Austin 78768; (512) 936-8100. ☆

TSHA WAS FOUNDED IN 1897, AND OUR MEMBERS' LOVE FOR THE LONE STAR STATE IS AS STRONG AS EVER. AS A MEMBER OF TSHA, YOU ARE PART OF AN ASSOCIATION THAT ENSURES THE STORIED HISTORY OF OUR GREAT STATE IS PASSED ON WELL INTO THE FUTURE.

See all of our membership options on **TSHAonline.org/Membership** and join TSHA today!

A mural in downtown Goliad. Photo by Rosie Hatch.

Local Government

Texas has **254 counties**, a number that has not changed since 1931 when Loving County was organized. Loving has a population of 81, according to the Jan. 1, 2018, Texas Demographic Center estimate, compared with 164 in 1970 and a peak of 285 in 1940. It is the **least-populous county** in Texas. In contrast, Harris County has **the most residents** in Texas, with a 2018 population estimate of **4,660,474**.

Counties range in area from Rockwall's 148.7 square miles to the 6,192.8 square miles in Brewster, which is equal to the combined area of the states of Connecticut and Rhode Island.

The Texas Constitution makes a county a legal subdivision of the state. Each county has a **commissioners court**. It consists of four commissioners, each elected from a commissioner's precinct, and a county judge elected from the entire county. In smaller counties, the county judge retains judicial responsibilities

in probate and insanity cases. **For names of county and district officials, see tables on pages 497–508.**

There are **1,223 incorporated municipalities** in Texas that range in size from 19 residents in Mustang to Houston's 2,307,354, according to the Jan. 1, 2018, Texas Demographic Center estimates. More than 80 percent of the state's population lives in cities and towns, meeting the U.S. Census Bureau definition of urban areas.

Texas had **357 incorporated towns with more than 5,000 population**, according to the 2018 Texas Demographic Center estimates. Under law, these cities may adopt their own charters (called home rule) by a majority vote. Cities of less than 5,000 may be chartered only under the general law.

Some home-rule cities may show fewer than 5,000 residents because population has declined since adopting home-rule charters.

Mayors and City Managers of Texas Cities

This list was compiled from online sources, phone calls, and responses to questionnaires sent out after the municipal elections held May 4, 2019. It includes the name of each city's mayor, as well as the name of the city manager, city administrator, city coordinator,

or other managing executive for municipalities having that form of government. If a town's mail goes to a post office in a different town, the mailing address is included. **Home-rule cities are marked in this list by a single-dagger symbol (†) after the name.**

— A —

Abbott . . . . . Anthony R. Pustejovsky
Abernathy . . . . Lindsey L. Webb
  City Mgr., Mike Cypert
Abilene (†) . . . . . . Anthony Williams
  City Mgr., Robert Hanna
Ackerly . . . . Scott Ragle
Addison (†) . . . . Joe Chow
  City Mgr., Wes Pierson
Adrian . . . . Maggie Gruhlkey

Agua Dulce . . . . John Howard
Alamo (†) . . . . Diana Martinez
  City Mgr., Luciano Ozuna, Jr.
Alamo Heights (†)(6116 Broadway, San Antonio 78209) . . . Bobby Rosenthal
  City Mgr., Buddy Kuhn
Alba . . . . Preston (Sonny) Hass
Albany . . . . Rodney Alexander
  City Mgr., Billy Holson
Aledo . . . . Kit Marshall
  City Admin., Bill Funderburk, Interim

Alice (†) . . . . . . Jolene B. Vanover
  City Mgr., Michael Esparza
Allen (†) . . . . Stephen Terrell
  City Mgr., Eric Ellwanger, Acting
Alma . . . . (vacant)
  City Mgr., Jim Benton
Alpine (†) . . . . Andres (Andy) Ramos
  City Mgr., Jessica Garza
Alto . . . . Jimmy Allen
Alton (†) . . . . Salvador Vela
  City Mgr., Jeff Underwood

— C —

Cactus . . . . Socorro Marquez
City Mgr., Aldo Gallegos
Caddo Mills . . . . . Dwayne Pattison
City Mgr., Matt McMahan
Caldwell . . . . . . Norris L. McManus
City Admin., Camden White
Callisburg . . . . Nathan Caldwell
Calvert . . . . Marcus D. Greaves
City Admin., Kevin O'Carroll
Cameron (†) . . . . . . Connie Anderle
City Mgr., J. Rhett Parker
Campbell. . . . . Carter Ketcham
Camp Wood . . . . Jesse Chavez
Canadian. . . . . Terrill Bartlett
City Mgr., Joe Jarosek
Caney City . . . . Lance Peck
Canton . . . . Lou Ann Everett
City Mgr., Lonny Cluck
Canyon (†) . . . . Gary Hinders
City Mgr., Jon Behrens, Interim
Carbon . . . . Corey Hull
Carl's Corner . . . . . Carl Cornelius
Carmine . . . . Wade Eilers
Carrizo Springs (†) . . . Wayne Seiple
City Mgr., Nora Flores
Carrollton (†) . . . . . Kevin Falconer
City Mgr., Erin Rinehart
Carthage (†) . . . . . Lynn C. Vincent
City Mgr., Stephen K. Williams
Cashion (354 Baker Rd., Wichita Falls
76305) . . . . Debra Carr
Castle Hills (209 Lemonwood Dr., San
Antonio 78213) . . . . . . JR Trevino
City Mgr., Ryan Rapelye
Castroville . . . . . . Phyllis Santleben
City Admin., Lee Elliott, Interim
Cedar Hill (†). . . . . . Stephen Mason
City Mgr., Greg Porter
Cedar Park (†) . . . Corbin Van Arsdale
City Mgr., Brenda Eivens
Celeste . . . . Larry Godwin
Celina (†) . . . . Sean Terry
City Mgr., Jason Laumer
Center (†) . . . . . . David Chadwick
City Mgr., Chad Nehring
Centerville. . . . . . Noal Ray Goolsby
Chandler . . . . Libby Fulgham
City Admin., John Whitsell
Channing . . . . Bob Christian
Charlotte. . . . . Buddy Lee Daughtry
Chester. . . . . Floyd Petri
Chico . . . . Colleen Self
Childress (†). . . . . . . Cary Preston
City Mgr., Kevin Hodges
Chillicothe . . . . Cathy Young
China . . . . . William (Butch) Sanders
China Grove . . . . . Mary Ann Hajek
City Admin., Susan Conaway
Chireno . . . . . Susan Higginbotham
City Admin., Steven Spencer
Christine . . . . Stephen Martinez
Cibolo (†) . . . . Stosh Boyle
City Mgr., Robert T. Herrera
Cisco (†) . . . . Tammy Douglas
City Mgr., Darwin Archer
Clarendon . . . . Sandy Skelton
City Admin., David Dockery
Clarksville . . . . Ann Rushing
City Mgr., Julie Arrington
Clarksville City . (Box 1111, White Oak
75693) . . . . Joe B. Spears
City Mgr., Matt Maines
Claude . . . . Bill Wood
Clear Lake Shores . . . . . Kurt Otten
City Admin., Brent Spier
Cleburne (†) . . . . Scott Cain
City Mgr., Steve Polasek

Cleveland (†) . . . . Otis Cohn
City Mgr., Kelly McDonald
Clifton . . . . Richard Spitzer
City Admin., Pamela K. Harvey
Clint . . . . Dora H. Aguirre
Clute (†) . . . . Calvin Shiflet
City Mgr., CJ Snipes
Clyde . . . . Rodger Brown
City Admin., Mike Murray
Coahoma . . . . Warren Wallace
Cockrell Hill . . . . . . Luis D. Carrera
City Admin., Bret Haney
Coffee City . . . . GeoJan Wright
Coldspring . . . . Pat Eversole
Coleman (†) . . . . . . Tommy Sloan
City Mgr., Diana Lopez
College Station (†) . . . Karl Mooney
City Mgr., Bryan Woods
Colleyville . . . . . . Richard Newton
City Mgr., Jerry Ducay
Collinsville. . . . . Randy Roach
Colmesneil. . . . . Don Baird
Colorado City (†) . . . . . . Tim Boyd
City Mgr., David Hoover
Columbus . . . . Lori An Gobert
City Mgr., Donald Warschak
Comanche . . . . Mary Boyd
City Admin., (vacant)
Combes . . . . Marco Sanchez
Town Admin., Lonnie Bearden
Combine . . . . Tim Ratcliff
Commerce (†) . . . . . Wyman Williams
City Mgr., Darrek Ferrell
Como . . . . Darla Henry
Conroe (†) . . . . Toby Powell
City Admin., Paul Virgadamo, Jr.
Converse (†) . . . . . Alfred (Al) Suarez
City Mgr., Le Ann Piatt
Cool . . (150 FM 113 S., Millsap 76066)
. . . . Dorothy Hall
Coolidge . . . . Jesse Ashmore
Cooper . . . . Darren Braddy
City Admin., Emily Howse
Coppell (†) . . . . Karen Hunt
City Mgr., Mike Land
Copperas Cove (†) . . . . Bradi Diaz
City Mgr., Ryan Haverlah)
Copper Canyon . . . . Ron Robertson
Town Admin., Donna Welsh
Corinth (†) . . . . . . Bill Heidemann
City Mgr., Bob Hart
Corpus Christi (†) . . . Joe McComb
City Mgr., Peter Zanoni
Corrigan . . . . Johnna Gibson
City Mgr., Darrian Hudman
Corsicana (†) . . . . . . Don Denbow
City Mgr., Connie Standridge
Cottonwood . . . . Jeff Gray
Cottonwood Shores . . . . Donald Orr
City Admin., J.C. Hughes
Cotulla . . . . . . Jose Javier Garcia
City Admin., Larry Dovalina
Coupland . . . . Jack Piper
Cove . . . . Leroy Stevens
Covington . . . . . . George Burnett
Coyote Flats . (1800 County Rd. 415,
Cleburne 76031) . . Doug Peterson
Crandall . . . . Danny Kirbie
City Mgr., Jana Shelton
Crane . . . . Mark Pahl
City Admin., Dru Gravens
Cranfills Gap . . . . . . David Witte
Crawford . . . . Franklin Abel
Creedmoor . . . . . . Fran Klestinec
City Admin., Robert Wilhite
Cresson . . . . Bob Cornett
Crockett (†) . . . . . . Ianthia Fisher
City Admin., John Angerstein

Crosbyton . . . . . . Dusty Cornelius
City Admin., Margot Hardin
Cross Plains . . . . Jerry Cassle
City Admin., Debbie Gosnell
Cross Roads. . . . . Bob Gorton
Town Admin., Becky Ross
Cross Timber . . . . Patti Meier
Crowell . . . . Ronnie Allen
Crowley (†). . . . . . . Billy P. Davis
City Mgr., Robert Loftin
Crystal City (†) . . . . Frank Moreno, Jr.
City Mgr., Santos Camarillo
Cuero (†) . . . . . . Sara Post-Meyer
City Mgr., Raymie Zella
Cumby . . . . Kathy Hall-Carter
Cuney . . . . Jessie Johnson
Cushing . . . . Robert Sides
Cut and Shoot . . . . . Nyla Dalhaus

— D —

Daingerfield (†) . . . . Lou Irvin
City Mgr., Rocky Thomasson
Daisetta . . . . Eric Thaxton
Dalhart (†) . . . . Phillip Hass
City Mgr., James Stroud
Dallas (†). . . . . Eric Johnson
City Mgr., T.C. Broadnax
Dalworthington Gardens Laurie Bianco
City Admin., Sherry Roberts
Danbury . . . . Melinda Strong
Darrouzett . . . . Louis Elston
Dawson . . . . Stephen Sanders
Dayton (†) . . . . . Caroline Wadzeck
City Mgr., Theo Melancon
Dayton Lakes . . . . (vacant)
Dean . (6913 State Hwy. 79 N., Wichita
Falls 76035) . . . . Steve L. Sicking
Decatur (†) . . . . . Martin Woodruff
City Mgr., Brett Shannon
DeCordova. . . . . Todd Hall
Deer Park (†). . . . . Jerry Mouton, Jr.
City Mgr., James Stokes
De Kalb. . . . . Dennis Wandrey
City Admin., Abbi Capps
De Leon (†) . . . . Terry Scott
City Admin., David Denman
Dell City . . . . Eddie Chacon
Del Rio (†) . . . . Bruno (Ralphy) Lozano
City Mgr., Matt Wojnowski
Denison (†) . . . . Janet Gott
City Mgr., Jud Rex
Dennis . . . . James Skanowski
Denton (†) . . . . Chris Watts
City Mgr., Todd Hileman
Denver City (†) . . . . . Tommy Hicks
City Mgr., Stan David
Deport . . . . John Mark Francis
DeSoto (†) . . . . . Curtistene McCowan
City Mgr., M. Renee Johnson, Interim
Detroit . . . . Kenneth Snodgrass
Devers . . . . Steven Horelica
Devine . . . . William L. Herring
City Admin., Dora V. Rodriguez, Interim
Diboll (†) . . . . John McClain
City Mgr., Gerry Boren
Dickens . . . . David Warren
City Admin., Lillian Atkinson
Dickinson (†) . . . . . . Julie Masters
City Admin., Chris Heard
Dilley . . . . Mary Ann Obregon
City Admin., David L. Jordan, Interim
Dimmitt (†) . . . . . . Roger Malone
City Mgr., B.J. Potts
Dish . . . . William Sciscoe
Dodd City . . . . Jackie Lackey
Dodson . . . . Steve Kane
Domino . . . . Alfred Campbell

Shops in downtown Baird. Photo by Robert Plocheck.

Donna (†) . . . . .Rick Morales
City Mgr., Carlos Yerena
Dorchester. . . . . David Smith
Double Horn . . . . Cathy Sereno
Double Oak . . . . . . Mike Donnelly
Douglassville . . . . . .DeWitt McCall
Draper . .(14007 Corral City Dr., Argyle
76226) . . . . . . Jamie Sue Harris
Dripping Springs . . . . Todd Purcell
City Admin., Michelle Fischer
Driscoll. . . . . Mark Gonzalez
Dublin . . . . . . David Leatherwood
City Mgr., Nancy Wooldridge
Dumas (†) . . . . . . Bob Brinkmann
City Mgr., Arbie Taylor
Duncanville (†) . . . . Barry L. Gordon
City Mgr., Kevin Hugman

— **E** —

Eagle Lake. . . . . Mary Parr
City Mgr., Gary Broz
Eagle Pass (†) . Ramsey English Cantu
City Mgr., George Antuna
Early . . . . Robert Mangrum
City Admin., Tony Aaron
Earth . . . . Sawnya Bullock
East Bernard . . . . Marvin R. Holub
Eastland (†) . . . . . . .Larry Vernon
City Mgr., Ronald M. Duncan
East Mountain . . (103 Municipal Dr.,
Gilmer 75645) . . . . Marc Covington
Easton . . . . Walter Ward
City Admin., Precious Wafer
East Tawakoni. . . . .Harold Chandler
Ector . . . . Jerry M. Newell
Edcouch . . . . . Virginio Gonzalez, Jr.
City Mgr., Victor Hugo de la Cruz
Eden . . . . .Agapito Torres
Edgecliff Village . . . .Mickey Rigney
City Admin., Veronica Gamboa
Edgewood . . . . . .Steve Steadham
Edinburg (†) . . . . . Richard Molina
City Mgr., Juan G. Guerra
Edmonson . . . . . . .Todd Crawford

Edna (†) . . . . Lance Smiga
City Mgr., Don Doering
Edom. . . . . Barbara Crow
El Campo (†). . . . . . Randy Collins
City Mgr., Courtney Sladek
El Cenizo. . . . . . . Elsa Degollado
City Admin., Jaime Montes
Eldorado . . . . .George Arispe
Electra (†) . . . . Lynda Lynn
City Admin., Steve Bowlin
Elgin (†) . . . . Chris Cannon
City Mgr., Thomas Mattis
Elkhart . . . . Jennifer McCoy
El Lago. . . . . .John Skelton
Elmendorf . . . . .Michael J. Gonzales
City Admin., Cody Dailey
El Paso (†) . . . . .Dee Margo
City Mgr., Tommy Gonzalez
Elsa (†). . . . . Alonzo Perez
City Mgr., JJ Ybarra
Emhouse . . . (3825 Joe Johnson Dr.,
Corsicana 75110). . Johnny Patterson
Emory . . . . .Earl Hill, III
City Admin., Mike Dunn
Enchanted Oaks . (PO Box 5019, Gun
Barrel City 75147) . . . Natalie Onate
Encinal . . . . Sylvano Sanchez
City Mgr., Velma Davila
Ennis (†) . . . . . Angeline Juenemann
City Mgr., Scott Dixon
Escobares . . . . Noel Escobar
Estelline . . . . Jeff Jones
Euless (†) . . . . Linda Martin
City Mgr., Loretta Getchell
Eureka . . . (1305 FM 2859, Corsicana
75109) . . . . . . Tammy Cantrell
Eustace . . . . Dustin Shelton
Evant . . . . Sterling Manning
Everman (†) . . . . . . Ray Richardson
City Mgr., Michael Box

— **F** —

Fairchilds . . . . (8713 Fairchilds Rd.,
Richmond 77469) . . . . Bob Haenel
Fairfield . . . . .Kenneth Hughes
City Admin., Nate Smith
Fair Oaks Ranch (†). . Garry Manitzas
City Mgr., Tobin Maples
Fairview (†) . . . . . .Henry Lessner
Town Mgr., Julie Couch
Falfurrias. . . . . . . David Longoria
City Admin., Lewis David Flores, Jr.
Falls City. . . . . . . Brent Houdmann
Farmers Branch (†) . . . Robert C. Dye
City Mgr., Charles S. Cox
Farmersville . . . . Randy Rice
City Mgr., Benjamin L. White
Farwell . . . . Joe Stanton
Fate (†) . . . . .Joe Burger
City Mgr., Michael Kovacs
Fayetteville . . . . Carl Marino
Ferris . . . . .Jim Swafford
City Mgr., (vacant)
Flatonia . . . . .Bryan Milson
City Mgr., Mark McLaughlin
Florence . . . . Mary Condon
Floresville (†) . . . .
Cecelia (Cissy) Gonzalez-Dippel .City
Mgr., Henrietta Turner
Flower Mound (†) . . . . Steve Dixon
Town Mgr., Jimmy Stathatos
Floydada . . . . Bobby Gilliland
City Mgr., Darrell Gooch
Follett . . . . Lynn Blau
City Mgr., Robert Williamson
Forest Hill (†) . . . . . Gerald Joubert
City Mgr., Sheyi I. Ipaye
Forney (†) . . . . Mary Penn
City Mgr., Tony Carson
Forsan . . . . Steve Park
Fort Stockton . . . . . Chris Alexander
City Mgr., Frank Rodriguez III
Fort Worth (†) . . . . . . Betsy Price
City Mgr., David Cooke
Franklin . . . . Molly Hedrick

Frankston . . . . .Gerald Hall
Fredericksburg (†) . Linda Langerhans
City Mgr., Kent Myers
Freeport (†) . . . . Troy Brimage
City Mgr., Tim Kelty
Freer . . . . Arnold Cantu
City Mgr., Ana A. Garcia
Friendswood (†). . . . . Mike Foreman
City Mgr., Morad Kabiri
Friona . . . . Ricky White
City Mgr., Leander (Lee) Davila
Frisco (†) . . . . Jeff Cheney
City Mgr., George Purefoy
Fritch . . . . .Dwight Kirksey
City Mgr., Drew Brassfield
Frost . . . . Scott Dowdle
Fruitvale . . . . Jennifer Johnston
Fulshear (†) . . . . Aaron Groff
City Mgr., Jack Harper
Fulton . . . . Jimmy Kendrick

— G —

Gainesville (†) . . . .Jim Goldsworthy
City Mgr., Barry Sullivan
Galena Park (†) . . . Esmeralda Moya
Gallatin. . . . . .Juanita Cotton
Galveston (†) . . . . . . Jim Yarbrough
City Mgr., Brian Maxwell
Ganado. . . . . Clinton Tegeler
Garden Ridge . . . . .Larry Thompson
City Admin., Nancy Cain
Garland (†). . . . . Scott LeMay
City Mgr., Bryan Bradford
Garrett . . . . Matt Newsom
Garrison . . . . Russell Wright
Gary . . . . Mark Thornton
Gatesville (†) . . . . . Gary Chumley
City Mgr., William H. (Bill) Parry, III
Georgetown (†) . . . . Dale Ross
City Mgr., David Morgan
George West (†). . . . . Andrew Garza
City Mgr., Georgia Vines
Gholson (155 Wesley Chapel Rd., Waco
76705) . . . . Larry Binnion
Giddings (†) . . . . John Dowell
City Mgr., Ricky Jorgensen
Gilmer (†) . . . . .Tim Marshall
City Mgr., Greg Hutson
Gladewater (†). . . . John (J.D.) Shipp
City Mgr., Ricky Tow
Glenn Heights (†) . . . Harry A. Garrett
City Mgr., David A. Hall
Glen Rose . . . . Pam Miller
City Admin., Michael Leamons
Godley . . . . .David J. Wallis
City Mgr., Stephanie Hodges
Goldsmith . . . . Richard Bradley
Goldthwaite . . . . . . Mike McMahan
City Mgr., Rob Lindsey, III
Goliad . . . . Trudia L. Preston
Golinda. . . . . Joyce Farar
Gonzales (†). . . . . . Connie L. Kacir
City Mgr., Tim Patek
Goodlow . . . . Willie Washington
Goodrich . . . . Kelly Nelson
Gordon . . . . Jack Coleman
Goree. . . . . Greg Fix
Gorman (†). . . . . Robert Ervin
Graford . . . . Carl S. Walston
Graham (†). . . . . . . .Neal Blanton
City Mgr., Brandon Anderson
Granbury (†). . . . . Nin Hulett
City Mgr., Chris Coffman
Grandfalls . . . . . . .Jason Copeland
City Admin., John Kinman

Grand Prairie (†) . . . . Ron Jensen
City Mgr., Tom Hart
Grand Saline. . . . . .Jeremy Gunnels
City Admin., Tully Davidson
Grandview . . . . . . .Zachary Stewart
City Mgr., David D. Henley
Granger . . . . . . Trevor Cheatheam
City Admin., Christy CavnessBradshaw
Granite Shoals (†). . . . .Carl Brugger
City Mgr., Jeffery D. Looney
Granjeno . .(6603 S. FM 494, Mission
78572) . . . . Yvette Cabrera
Grapeland . . . . Balis E. Dailey
Grapevine (†) . . . . . William D. Tate
City Mgr., Bruno Rumbelow
Grays Prairie (Box 116, Scurry 75158)
. . . . .Lorenzo Garza, Jr.
Greenville (†) . . . . . David Dreiling
City Mgr., Summer Spurlock
Gregory . . . . . .Celestino Zambrano
Grey Forest . . . . . . Phillip Howard
Groesbeck. . . . . . Ray O'Docharty
City Admin., Chris Henson
Groom . . . . .Joe Homer
Groves (†) . . . . . . Brad P. Bailey
City Mgr., D.E. Sosa
Groveton . . . . Byron Richards
Gruver . . . . .Buster Davis
City Mgr., Steven McKay
Gun Barrel City (†) . . . .David Skains
City Mgr., Bret Bauer
Gunter . . . . .Mark Millar
City Mgr., Lee Lawrence
Gustine. . . . . Ken Huey

— H —

Hackberry . . . .(119 Maxwell Rd., #B-7,
Frisco 75034). . . . . . Ronald Austin
City Admin., Brenda Lewallen
Hale Center . . . . W.H. Johnson
City Mgr., Dennis Burton
Hallettsville . . . . . . Stephen Hunter
City Admin., Jason T. Cozza
Hallsburg . . . . Mike Glockzin
Hallsville . . . . .Jesse Casey
Haltom City (†) . . . . . An Truong
City Mgr., Keith Lane
Hamilton . . . . Jim McInnis
City Admin., Pete Kampfer
Hamlin . . . . E.C. Ice
City Admin., Bobby Evans
Happy . . . . Sara Tirey
Hardin . . . . .Harry Johnson
Harker Heights (†) . Spencer H. Smith
City Mgr., David Mitchell
Harlingen (†). . . . . . . Chris Boswell
City Mgr., Dan Serna
Hart . . . . Eliazar Castillo
City Admin., Adrian Rosas
Haskell . . . . . . Alberto Alvarez, Jr.
City Admin., Janet Moeller
Haslet . . . . Bob Golden
City Admin., James Quin
Hawk Cove. . . . . . . Brian Prock
City Admin., Rhonda McKeehan
Hawkins . . . . Tom Parker
Hawley . . . . Billy Richardson
Hays . . . . .(Box 1285, Buda 78610)
. . . . Larry Odom
Hearne (†) . . . . . . Ruben Gomez
City Mgr., John Naron
Heath (†) . . . . .Kelson Elam
City Mgr., Aretha L. Adams
Hebron (Box 118916, Carrollton 75011)
. . . . Kelly Clem
Hedley . . . . .Carrie Butler
Hedwig Village . . . . Brian T. Muecke
City Admin., Kelly Johnson

Helotes. . . . . . Thomas A. Schoolcraft
City Admin., Rick A. Schroder
Hemphill . . . . .Robert Hamilton
City Mgr., Laure Morgan
Hempstead (†). . . . Michael Wolfe, Sr.
Henderson (†) . .John W. (Buzz) Fullen
City Mgr., Jay Abercrombie
Henrietta . . . . .Howard Raeke
City Admin., Kelley Bloodworth
Hereford (†) . . . . Tom Simons
City Mgr., Rick L. Hanna
Hewitt (†). . . . . .Charlie Turner
City Mgr., Bo Thomas
Hickory Creek . . . . Lynn Clark
Town Admin., John Smith
Hico . . . . Eddie Needham
City Admin., Adam Niolet
Hidalgo (†) . . . . . . Sergio Coronado
City Mgr., Julian Gonzalez
Hideaway . . . . Ray Hutcheson
Higgins . . . . Michael Callahan
City Mgr., Kim Eggleston
Highland Haven . . . . Olan Kelley
Highland Park (†) . . . Margo Goodwin
Town Admin., Bill Lindley
Highland Village (†). .Charlotte Wilcox
City Mgr., Michael Leavitt
Hill Country Village . . . .
. . . . Gabriel Durand-Hollis
City Admin., Frank Morales
Hillcrest Village (Box 1172, Alvin 77512)
. . . . Tom Wilson
Hillsboro (†) . . . . Edith Turner Omberg
City Mgr., Frank Johnson
Hilshire Village . .(8301 Westview Dr.,
Houston 77055) . . .Russell Herron
City Admin., Susan Blevins
Hitchcock (†) . . . . . Randy Stricklind
City Admin., Marie Gelles
Holiday Lakes . . . Norman Schroeder
Holland. . . . . Stanley Koonsen
Holliday . . . . Allen Moore
Hollywood Park . . . . Chris Murphy
Hondo (†) . . . . . . James W. Danner
City Mgr., Kim Davis
Honey Grove. . . . . . Claude Caffee
Hooks . . . . Jimmy Cochran
Horizon City (†) . . . .Ruben Mendoza
Horseshoe Bay (†) . . . Steve Jordan
City Mgr., Stan R. Farmer
Houston (†) . . . . . . Sylvester Turner
Howardwick . . . . . . Tony Clemishire
Howe . . . . Jeff Stanley
City Admin., Joe Shephard
Hubbard . . . . Mary Alderman
City Mgr., Jason Patrick
Hudson. . . . . Robert Smith
City Admin., James Freeman
Hudson Oaks . . . . . .Marc Povero
City Admin., Patrick Lawler
Hughes Springs. . . . James Samples
City Mgr., George K. Fite
Humble (†) . . . . . . Merle Aaron, Sr.
City Mgr., Jason Stuebe
Hunters Creek Village . . . . (1 Hunters
Creek Pl., Houston 77024)
. . . . Jim Pappas
City Admin., Tom Fullen
Huntington. . . . . . . Frank Harris
City Admin., Bill Stewart
Huntsville (†) . . . . . Andy Brauninger
City Mgr., Aron Kulhavy
Hurst (†) . . . . Henry Wilson
City Mgr., Clay Caruthers
Hutchins . . . . .Mario Vasquez
City Admin., Trudy Lewis
Hutto (†) . . . . Doug Gaul
City Mgr., Odis Jones

Huxley . . (11798 FM 2694, Shelbyville
75973) . . . . Larry Vaughn

— I —

Idalou . . . . David Riley
City Admin., Suzette Williams
Impact . . . . (vacant)
Indian Lake (62 S. Aztec Cove Dr., Los
Fresnos 78566). . . James Chambers
Industry . . . . Mable Meyers
Ingleside (†) . . . . Ronnie Parker
City Mgr., David Huseman
Ingleside on the Bay . . (PO Box 309,
Ingleside 78362) . . . JoAnn Ehmann
Ingram . . . . Brandon Rowan
City Admin., Mark Bosma
Iola . . . . Christina Stover
Iowa Colony . . (12003 County Rd. 65,
Rosharon 77583)
. . . . Michael Byrum-Bratsen
Iowa Park (†). . . . . Ray Schultz
City Mgr., Jerry Flemming
Iraan . . . . Darren Brown
Iredell . . . . Joel Wellborn
Irving (†) . . . . Rick Stopfer
City Mgr., Chris Hillman
Italy . . . . Bryant Cockran
City Admin., Shawn Holden
Itasca . . . . .James Bouldin
City Admin., CinDee Garrett
Ivanhoe (880 Charmaine Dr. E, Ste. A
Woodville 75979). . . . Cathy Bennett

— J —

Jacinto City (†) . . . . Ana Diaz
City Mgr., Lon Squyres
Jacksboro . . . . Alton Morris
City Mgr., Michael Smith
Jacksonville (†) . . . . . Randy Gorham
City Mgr., Greg Smith
Jamaica Beach . . . . . Steve Spicer
City Admin., Sean Hutchison
Jarrell . . . . .Larry Bush
City Mgr., Vanessa Shrauner
Jasper (†) . . . . Gary Gatlin
City Mgr., Denise Kelley
Jayton . . . . .Joe Martinez
Jefferson. . .Charles (Bubba) Haggard
Jersey Village (†) . . .Andrew Mitcham
City Mgr., Austin Bleess
Jewett . . . . John Sitton
Joaquin . . . . William Baker
Johnson City . . . . . .Rhonda Stell
Jolly . . (194 Milton St., Wichita Falls
76310) . . . . . D. LeAnn Skinner
Jones Creek . . . . Gordon Schlemmer
Jonestown . . . . Paul Johnson
City Admin., Ron Wilde
Josephine . . . . Joe Holt
Joshua (†) . . . . Joe Hollarn
City Mgr., Josh Jones
Jourdanton . . . . Robert A. Williams
City Mgr., Lamar Schulz
Junction . . . . . Russell Hammonds
Justin . . . . Alan Woodall
City Mgr., Cori Reaume

— K —

Karnes City . . . . . Leroy T. Skloss
City Mgr., Robert Evans
Katy (†). . . . . Bill Hastings
City Admin., Byron J. Hebert
Kaufman (†) . . . . .Jeff Jordan
City Mgr., Michael T. Slye

Keene (†). . . . . Gary Heinrich
City Mgr., (vacant)
Keller (†) . . . . Pat McGrail
City Mgr., Mark Hafner
Kemah . . . . Terri Gale
City Admin., Wendy Ellis
Kemp . . . . .Laura Peace
City Admin., Regina Kiser
Kempner . . . . Keith L. Harvey
Kendleton . . .Darryl K. Humphrey, Sr.
City Admin., Georgina Ybarra, Acting
Kenedy . . . . James Sutton
City Mgr., Barbara Najvar Shaw
Kenefick . . . . (3564 FM 1008, Dayton
77535) . . . . Martin Wells
Kennard . . . . Jesse Stephens
City Admin., April Wright
Kennedale (†) . . . . . . Brian Johnson
City Mgr., George Campbell
Kerens . . . . Jeffrey Saunders
Kermit (†) . . . . Jerry L. Phillips
City Mgr., Frankie Davis
Kerrville (†) . . . . . . Bill Blackburn
City Mgr., Mark McDaniel
Kilgore (†) . . . . . Ronnie E. Spradlin
City Mgr., Josh Selleck
Killeen (†) . . . . . . Jose L. Segarra
City Mgr., Ronald L. Olson
Kingsbury . . . . Shirley Nolen
Kingsville (†) . . . . .Sam R. Fugate
City Mgr., Deborah Balli, Interim
Kirby (†) . . . . Lisa B. Pierce
City Mgr., Monique Vernon
Kirbyville. . . . . Frank George
Kirvin. . . . . (vacant)
Knollwood . . (100 Collins Dr., Sherman
75090) . . . . . . Richard Roelke
Knox City . . . . Gene Ward
City Admin., Sam Watson
Kosse . . . . .Jarrod Eno
Kountze . . . . Fred Williams
City Admin., Roderick Hutto
Kress . . . . Amparo Becerra
Krugerville. . . . . Jeff Parrent
City Admin., Jeff Parrent
Krum . . . . Ronald G. Harris, Jr.
Kurten . . . . .Philip Mundine
Kyle (†) . . . . Travis Mitchell
City Mgr., Scott Sellers

— L —

La Coste . . . . Andy Keller
City Admin., George Salzman
Lacy Lakeview (†). . . . Sharon Clark
City Mgr., Keith Bond
Ladonia . . . . Jan Cooper
La Feria (†). . . . . Olga H. Maldonado
City Mgr., Jaime S. Sandoval
Lago Vista (†) . . . . . . Ed Tidwell
City Mgr., Joshua Ray
La Grange (†) . . . . . . Janet Moerbe
City Mgr., Shawn Raborn
La Grulla . . . . Pedro A. Flores
City Mgr., Marlen Garza
Laguna Vista (†). . . . .Susie Houston
City Mgr., Rolando Vela
La Joya (†) . . . . Jose A. (Fito) Salinas
City Admin., Mike Alaniz
Lake Bridgeport . . . .Ramon Galvan
Lake City . . . . Dennis Veit
Lake Dallas (†). . . . Michael Barnhart
City Mgr., John Cabrales, Jr.
Lake Jackson (†) . . . . Bob Sipple
City Mgr., William P. Yenne
Lakeport . . (207 Milam Rd., Longview
75603) . . . . . . Johnny Sammons

Lakeside (San Patricio Co.) (Box 787,
Mathis 78368) . . . . . .Jeff Mason
Lakeside (Tarrant Co.) . . . Pat Jacob
Town Admin., Norman Craven
Lakeside City (Box 4287, Wichita Falls
76308) . . . . Cory Glassburn
City Admin., Eric Stevens
Lake Tanglewood . . (100 N. Shore Dr.,
Amarillo 79118). . . . . Don Carver
Lakeview. . . . . Kelly Clark
Lakeway (†) . . . . Sandy Cox
City Mgr., Steve Jones
Lakewood Village . . . . Mark Vargus
Town Admin., Linda Asbell
Lake Worth (†). . . . . Walter Bowen
City Mgr., Stacey Almond
La Marque (†) . . . . . Bobby Hocking
City Mgr., Charles (Tink) Jackson
Lamesa (†). . . . . . . Josh Stevens
City Mgr., Shawna Burkhart
Lampasas (†) . . . . . . Misti Talbert
City Mgr., Finley Degraffenried
Lancaster (†) . . . . Clyde C. Hairston
City Mgr., Opal Mauldin-Jones
La Porte (†) . . . . . . .Louis R. Rigby
City Mgr., Corby Alexander
Laredo (†) . . . . Pete Saenz
City Mgr., (vacant)
Latexo . . . . .Robert Hernandez
La Vernia . . . . . . Robert W. Gregory
La Villa . . . . Alma Moron
City Admin., Arnie Amaro
Lavon . . . . .Vicki Sanson
City Admin., Kim Dobbs
La Ward . . . . Richard Koch
Lawn . . . . .Veronica Burleson
League City (†) . . . . . Pat Hallisey
City Mgr., John Baumgartner
Leakey . . . . Harry Schneemann
Leander (†) . . . . Troy Hill
City Mgr., Gordon Pierce, Interim
Leary . . . (PO Box 1799, Hooks 75561)
. . . . Keith Storey
City Admin., Randy Mansfield
Lefors . . . . Michael Ray
Leona . . . . . . Ernest (Bubba) Oden
Leonard . . . . Steven Bolin
City Admin., Terry McCalpin, Interim
Leon Valley (†) . . . . . . Chris Riley
City Mgr., Kelly Kuenstler
Leroy . . . . Ernest Moravec
Levelland (†). . . . . . Barbra Pinner
City Mgr., Erik Rejino
Lewisville (†) . . . . . Rudy Durham
City Mgr., Donna Barron
Lexington . . . . Allen Retzlaff
Liberty (†) . . . . Carl Pickett
City Mgr., Tom Warner
Liberty Hill . . . . Rick Hall
City Admin., Greg Boatright
Lindale (†) . . . . . . .Jeff Daugherty
City Mgr., Carolyn Caldwell
Linden . . . . Clarence Burns
City Admin., Robert Swisher
Lindsay. . . . . Scott Neu
Lipan . . . . Mike Stowe
Little Elm (†). . . . . . .David Hillock
City Mgr., Matt Mueller
Littlefield . . . . Eric Turpen
City Mgr., Mitch Grant
Little River-Academy . . Drew Lanham
Live Oak (†) . . . . . Mary M. Dennis
City Mgr., Scott Wayman
Liverpool. . . . . Bill Strickland
Livingston . . . . . . Judy B. Cochran
City Mgr., Bill Wiggins
Llano . . . . Gail Lang
City Mgr., Scott Edmonson

Lockhart (†) . . . . Lew White
City Mgr., Steve Lewis
Lockney . . . . Michael DeLeon
City Mgr., Buster Poling, Jr.
Log Cabin . . . . Nancy Ruckstaetter
Lometa . . . . Carlos Garcia
Lone Oak . . . . Doug Williams
Lone Star . . . . Randy Hodges
Longview (†) . . . . Andy Mack
City Mgr., Keith Bonds
Loraine . . . . Dearl Messick
Lorena . . . . Chuck Roper
City Mgr., Joseph R. Pace
Lorenzo . . . . Tim Tiner
City Admin., Christy Forbes
Los Fresnos (†) . . . . . Polo Narvaez
City Mgr., Mark Milum
Los Indios . . . . . . Jaime Gonzalez
City Admin., Jared Hockema
Los Ybanez . . . . . Mary A. Ybanez
City Mgr., John Castillo
Lott . . . . Annita Tindle
Lovelady . . . . William B. Shoemaker
Lowry Crossing (1405 S. Bridgefarmer
Rd., McKinney 75069)
. . . . Derek Stephens
Lubbock (†) . . . . Dan Pope
City Mgr., W. Jarrett Atkinson
Lucas (†) . . . . Jim Olk
City Mgr., Joni Clarke
Lueders . . . . Benny Jarvis
Lufkin (†) . . . . Bob Brown
City Mgr., Keith N. Wright
Luling (†) . . . . . . Mike Hendricks
City Mgr., Mark Mayo
Lumberton (†) . . . . . Don Surratt
City Mgr., Steve Clark
Lyford . . . . . Jose G. (Wally) Solis
Lytle . . . . Mark Bowen
City Admin., Josie Campa

— M —

Mabank . . . . Jeff Norman
City Mgr., Bryant Morris
Madisonville . . . . Bill Parten
City Mgr., Camilla Viator
Magnolia . . . . Todd Kana
City Admin., Paul Mendes
Malakoff . . . . Delois Pagitt
City Admin., Ann Barker
Malone . . . . James Lucko
Manor (†) . . . . Rita G. Jonse
City Mgr., Thomas M. Bolt
Mansfield (†) . . . . . . David L. Cook
City Mgr., Clayton Chandler
Manvel (†) . . . . Debra Marz Davison
City Mgr., Kyle J. Jung
Marble Falls (†) . . . . . John Packer
City Mgr., Mike Hodge
Marfa . . . . Manny Baeza
City Admin., (vacant)
Marietta . . . . Lois Shaddix
Marion . . . . Victor Contreras
City Admin., Micaela Bandel
Marlin (†) . . . . . . Carolyn R. Lofton
City Mgr., Cedric Davis
Marquez . . . . Stynette Clary
City Mgr., Lauren Powers
Marshall (†) . . . . Terri Brown
City Mgr., Mark Rohr
Mart . . . . Len Williams
Martindale . . . . . . Robert Deviney
Mason . . . . Brent Hinckley
City Admin., John Palacio
Matador . . . . Pat Smith
Mathis (†) . . . . Ciri Villarreal
City Mgr., Michael Barrera

Maud . . . . Mickey Williams
City Admin., Pollyanna Moore
Maypearl . . . . Jo Ann Mathers
McAllen (†) . . . . Jim Darling
City Mgr., Roel Roy Rodriguez
McCamey . . . . Patty Jones
McGregor (†) James S. (Jimmy) Hering
City Mgr., Kevin P. Evans
McKinney (†) . . . . . George Fuller
City Mgr., Paul Grimes
McLean . . . . Tanner Hess
McLendon-Chisholm . . . . Keith Short
City Admin., Lisa Palomba
Meadow . . . . Natalie Howard
City Admin., Terri McClanahan
Meadowlakes . . . Mary Ann Raesener
City Mgr., Johnnie Thompson
Meadows Place Charles D. Jessup, IV
Megargel . . . . Paul McQueen
Melissa (†) . . . . Reed Greer
City Mgr., Jason Little
Melvin . . . . Billy Ferris
Memphis . . . . Joe Davis
Menard . . . . Barbara Hooten
City Admin., Don Kerns
Mercedes (†) . . . . . Henry Hinojosa
City Mgr., Sergio Zavala
Meridian . . . . . . Johnnie Hauerland
City Admin., Marie Garland
Merkel . . . . . . Mary Schrampfer
City Mgr., Steve Campbell
Mertens . . . . Barbara Crass
Mertzon . . . . Lisa Hight
Mesquite (†) . . . . Stan Pickett
City Mgr., Cliff Keheley
Mexia (†) . . . . Arthur Busby
City Mgr., Eric Garretty
Miami . . . . Chad Breeding
Midland (†) . . . . Jerry Morales
City Mgr., Courtney Sharp
Midlothian (†) . . . . . . Richard Reno
City Mgr., Chris Dick
Midway . . . . Brenda Ford
Milano . . . . Karl Westbrook
Mildred . . . (5417 FM 637, Corsicana
75109) . . . . Bryan Roach
Miles . . . . . . Sylvester Schwertner
Milford . . . . Bruce Perryman
Miller's Cove . . (PO Box 300 Winfield
75493) . . . . . . Willie B. Garrett
Millsap . . . . Jamie French
City Mgr., Mark Barnes
Mineola . . . . Kevin White
City Admin., Mercy Rushing
Mineral Wells (†) . . . . . Christopher M.
Perricone . . City Mgr., Randy Criswell
Mingus . . . . Milo Moffit
Mission (†) . . . . . Armando O'Caña
City Mgr., Randy Perez
Missouri City (†) . . . . . Yolanda Ford
City Mgr., Anthony J. Snipes
Mobeetie . . . . Bobbie Walker
Mobile City (824 Lilac, Rockwall 75087)
Kenny Phillips
Monahans (†) . . . . David B. Cutbirth
City Mgr., Rex M. Thee
Mont Belvieu (†) . . . . . Nick Dixon
City Mgr., Nathan Watkins
Montgomery . . . . . Sara Countryman
City Admin., Jack Yates
Moody . . . . Jesse Fugit
City Admin., William A. Sterling
Moore Station (4720 County Rd. 4319,
LaRue 75770) . . . Charles Anderson
Moran . . . . Steven W. Taggart
Morgan . . . . Jon Croom, II
Morgan's Point . . . Michel J. Bechtel
City Admin., Brian Schneider

Morgan's Point Resort . Dwayne Gossett
City Mgr., Andrew Bill
Morton . . . . Kim Silhan
City Mgr., Brenda Shaw
Moulton . . . . . . Mark Zimmerman
City Admin., LuAnn D. Rogers
Mountain City (Box 1494, Buda 78610)
. . . . Ralph McClendon
City Admin., Rick Tarr
Mount Calm . . . . Jimmy Tucker
Mount Enterprise . . . . Harvey Graves
City Admin., Khristy Webb, Interim
Mount Pleasant (†) . . Tracy Craig, Sr.
City Mgr., Mike Ahrens
Mount Vernon . . . . . Teresia Wims
City Admin., Tina Rose
Muenster . . . . Tim Felderhoff
City Admin., Stan Endres
Muleshoe (†) . . . . Cliff Black
City Mgr., LeAnn Gallman
Mullin . . . . Jean Smith
Munday . . . . Robert Bowen
City Admin., David Trevino
Murchison . . . . Greg Smith
Murphy (†) . . . . Scott Bradley
City Mgr., Mike Castro
Mustang Ridge . . . . Alisandro Flores

— N —

Nacogdoches (†) . . . Shelley Brophy
City Mgr., Jim Jeffers
Naples . . . . David Betts
Nash . . . . Robert Bunch
City Admin., Doug Bowers
Nassau Bay (†) . . . Mark Denman
City Mgr., Jason Reynolds
Natalia (†) . . . . Tommy Ortiz
City Admin., Lisa S. Hernandez
Navarro . . . (222 S. Harvard Ave.,
Corsicana 75109). . . . Pam Chapman
Navasota (†) . . William A. (Bert) Miller
City Mgr., Brad Stafford
Nazareth . . . . Marlin Durbin
City Mgr., Lacey Farris
Nederland (†) . . . . . Don Albanese
City Mgr., Christopher Duque
Needville . . . . Andrew Bohac
Nevada . . . . Trace Kinnard
Newark . . . . Eric Fleischer
New Berlin . . . . . . Walter Williams
New Boston . . . . Johnny L. Branson
New Braunfels (†) . . Barron Casteel
City Mgr., Robert Camareno
Newcastle . . . . (vacant)
New Chapel Hill (PO Box 132717, Tyler
75713) . . . . Riley Harris
New Deal . . . . Gayla Teeter
New Fairview . . . Joe Max Wilson
New Home . . . . Jim Olsen
New Hope (Box 562, McKinney 75070)
Angel Hamm
New London . . . . . . Dale McNeel
New Summerfield . . . . Jane Barrow
Newton . . . . Mark Bean
City Admin., Donald H. Meek
New Waverly . . . . Nathaniel James
Neylandville . . (2469 County Rd. 4311,
Greenville 75401) . . . Kathy Wilson
Niederwald . . . . . . Reynell Smith
Nixon . . . . Dorothy Riojas
Nocona . . . . Robert Fenoglio
City Mgr., Lynn Henley
Nolanville (†) . . . . . Andy Williams
City Mgr., Kara Escajeda
Nome . . . . Kerry Abney
Noonday . . . . (Box 6425, Tyler 75711)
. . . . J. Mike Turman
Nordheim . . . . . . Katherine Payne

Normangee . . . . Troy Noey
North Cleveland (Box 1266, Cleveland
77327) . . . . Bob Bartlett
Northlake . . . . David Rettig
Town Admin., Drew Corn
North Richland Hills (†) Oscar Trevino
City Mgr., Mark Hindman
Novice . . . . Bobby Green

— O —

Oak Grove . (Box 309, Kaufman 75142)
. . . . .Jeffrey Davis
Oak Leaf . . . . .Jimmie D. Lamb
Oak Point . . . . .Keith Palmer
City Mgr., Stephen Ashley
Oak Ridge (Cooke Co.; 129 Oak Ridge
Dr., Gainesville 76240). Chad Ramsey
Oak Ridge . . . (Kaufman Co. Box 458,
Kaufman 75142) . . . . Al Rudin
Oak Ridge North James M. Kuykendall
City Mgr., Richard Derr
Oak Valley (2211 Oak Valley, Corsicana
75110). . . . . Linda Bennett
Oakwood. . . . . . .Jacquelyn Morrow
O'Brien. . . . . Chris Casillas
Odem. . . . . Billy Huerta
Odessa (†) . . . . . . David R. Turner
City Mgr., Michael Marrero
O'Donnell . . . . Mark Roye
Oglesby . . . . Bruce Pomerenke
Old River-Winfree (PO Box 1169, Mont
Belvieu 77580) . . . . . . .Joe Landry
Olmos Park . . . . Ronald Hornberger
City Mgr., Celia DeLeon
Olney (†) . . . . .Phil Jeske, II
City Admin., Neal Welch
Olton . . . . Mark McFadden
City Admin., Keeley Adams
Omaha. . . . . Ernest Pewitt
Onalaska. . . . B. Milton (Chip) Choate
City Admin., Angela Stutts
Opdyke West . . . (Box 1527, Levelland
79336) . . . . Wayne Riggins
Orange (†) . . . . . . .Larry Spears, Jr.
City Mgr., Kelvin Knauf
Orange Grove . . . . Carl Srp
City Admin., Todd Wright
Orchard . . . . .Rod Pavlock
Ore City . . . . .Gail Weir
Overton . . . . .C.R. Evans
Ovilla . . . . Richard A. Dormier
City Mgr., John R. Dean, Jr.
Oyster Creek . . . . . . .Justin Mills
City Admin., Toby Guenter

— P —

Paducah . . . . Zack Osbourn
Paint Rock . . . . . Ricky Donaldson
Palacios (†) . . . . .Glen Smith
City Mgr., David Kocurek
Palestine (†) . . . . . . Steve Presley
City Mgr., Leslie Cloer, Interim
Palisades (115 Brentwood Rd., Amarillo
79118). . . . . Brad Kiewiet
Palmer . . . . Kenneth Bateman
City Admin., Alicia Baran
Palmhurst . . . . Ramiro J. Rodriguez, Jr.
City Mgr., Lori A. Lopez
Palm Valley . . . (1313 Stuart Place Rd.,
Harlingen 78552). . . . .George Rivera
Palmview (†). . . . . .Ricardo Villareal
City Mgr., Michael Leo
Pampa (†) . . . . Brad Pingel
City Mgr., Shane Stokes
Panhandle . . . . Doyle Robinson
City Mgr., Terry Coffee
Panorama Village . . . . . . Lynn Scott

Pantego . . . . Doug Davis
City Mgr., Matt Fielder
Paradise . . . . Roy Steel
Paris (†) . . . . Steve Clifford
City Mgr., John Godwin
Parker . . . . Lee Pettle
City Admin., Luke Olson
Pasadena (†). . . . . . . Jeff Wagner
Pattison . . . . .Joe Garcia
Patton Village . . . . . . .Leah Tarrant
Payne Springs. . . . Rodney Renberg
Pearland (†) . . . . Tom Reid
City Mgr., Clay Pearson
Pearsall (†). . . . . . . Mary Moore
City Mgr., Josie Carrizales, Interim
Peaster. . . . . .Don Smelley
Pecan Gap . . . . Cole Hoskison
Pecan Hill . . . . . .Stephanie Starrett
City Admin., Shelley Martinez
Pecos (†). . . . . .David Flores
City Mgr., Seth Sorensen
Pelican Bay . . . . Bill Morley
Penelope. . . . . .Ben Neal
Peñitas (†) . . . . Rodrigo (Rigo) Lopez
City Mgr., Omar Romero
Perryton . . . . Kerry Symons
City Mgr., David Landis
Petersburg. . . . . . . Susie Martinez
City Mgr., Ronald Heggemeier
Petrolia. . . . . Buddy Alexander
Petronila . . . . (2475 County Rd. 69,
Robstown 78380) . . . . Todd Wright
Pflugerville (†). . . . . Victor Gonzales
City Mgr., Sereniah Breland
Pharr (†) Ambrosio (Amos) Hernandez
City Mgr., Alex Meade
Pilot Point (†) . . Shea Dane-Patterson
City Mgr., Alan Guard
Pine Forest . . . (305 Nagel Dr., Vidor
77662) . . . . Cathy Nagel
Pinehurst (2497 Martin Luther King Jr.
Dr., Orange 77630) J.L. (Pete) Runnels
City Admin., Robbie Hood
Pine Island . . . (36722 Brumlow Rd.,
Hempstead 77445). . . . Steve Nagy
Pineland . . . . .Randy Burch
Piney Point Village (7676 Woodway Dr.,
#300, Houston 77063) . Mark Kobelan
City Admin., Roger Nelson
Pittsburg (†) . . . . . .David Abernathy
City Mgr., Clint Hardeman
Plains. . . . . Shane McKinzie
City Admin., Steve Vasquez
Plainview (†). . . . . . Wendell Dunlap
City Mgr., Jeffrey Snyder
Plano (†) . . . . Harry LaRosiliere
City Mgr., Mark Israelson
Plantersville. . . . . . . .Karen Hale
Pleak Village . . . .(6621 FM 2218 S.,
Richmond 77469. . . . . Larry Bittner
Pleasanton (†). . . . . . Travis Hall, Jr.
City Mgr., Johnny Huizar
Pleasant Valley (4006 U.S. 287 E, Iowa
Park 76367) . . . . . . Jerry Gholson
Plum Grove . . . (Box 1358, Splendora
77372) . . . . LeeAnn Walker
Point . . . . Johnny Northcutt
Point Blank . . . . . Mark T. Wood
Point Comfort . . . . .Leslie Machicek
City Admin., Ofie Baldera
Point Venture . . . . .Eric Love
Ponder . . . . .Matthew Poole
Port Aransas (†). . . Charles R. Bujan
City Mgr., David Parsons
Port Arthur (†). . Thurman (Bill) Bartie
City Mgr., Rebecca Underhill, Interim
Port Isabel (†) . Juan Jose (JJ) Zamora
City Mgr., Jared Hockema

Portland (†) . . . . Cathy Skurow
City Mgr., Randy L. Wright
Port Lavaca (†) . . . . . Jack Whitlow
City Mgr., William (Bill) DiLibero
Port Neches (†) . . . . Glenn Johnson
City Mgr., André Wimer
Post. . . . . Marvin Self
City Mgr., Deana Smith
Post Oak Bend (1175 County Rd. 278,
Kaufman 75142) . . . . Hank Warden
Poteet . . . . Willie Leal, Jr.
City Admin., Eric A. Jiminez
Poth . . . . .Chrystal Eckel
Pottsboro . . . . Frank Budra
City Mgr., Kevin Farley
Powell . . . . Clay Jackson
Poynor . . . . Dannie Smith
Prairie View (†) . . . . . David Allen
Premont . . . . Priscilla Vargas
Presidio . . . . John Ferguson
City Admin., Jose Portillo
Primera. . . . . . . .R. Dave Kusch
City Admin., Veronica Flores
Princeton . . . . . .John-Mark Caldwell
City Mgr., Derek F. Borg
Progreso. . . . . Gerardo Alanis
City Admin., Alfredo Espinosa
Progreso Lakes . . O.D. (Butch) Emery
Prosper (†). . . . . Ray Smith
Town Mgr., Harlan Jefferson
Providence Village (†) Michael Jordan
Town Mgr., Brian Roberson
Putnam. . . . . . . .Hubert Donaway
Pyote . . . . .Abigail Pritchard

— Q —

Quanah (†). . . . . .Dale Eaton
City Admin., Paula Wilson
Queen City . . . . Harold Martin
Quinlan. . . . . Jacky Goleman
City Admin., John Adel
Quintana . . . . Steve Alongis
City Admin., Tammi Cimiotta
Quitaque . . . . Phil Barefield
City Mgr., Maria Merrell
Quitman . . . . .David Dobbs
City Admin., Rodney Kieke

— R —

Ralls . . . . Don Hamilton
City Admin., Gloria Velasquez
Rancho Viejo . . . . . Cyndie Rathbun
Town Admin., Fred Blanco
Ranger (†) . . . . .Joe Pilgrim
City Mgr., Chad Roberts
Rangerville (31850 Rangerville Rd.,
San Benito 78586) . .Wayne Halbert
Rankin . . . . Brandon Brown
Ransom Canyon . . . . . Jana Trew
City Admin., Maria Elena Quintanilla
Ravenna . . . . Claude L. Lewis
Raymondville (†) . . . Gilbert Gonzales
City Mgr., Eleazar Garcia, Jr.
Red Lick (3193 Old Redlick Rd., Texar-
kana 75503) . . . . .Bob Akin
Red Oak (†) . . . . Mark Stanfill
City Mgr., Todd Fuller
Redwater. . . . . Robert Lorance
Refugio. . . . . Wanda Dukes
Reklaw . . . . Harlan Crawford
Reno (Lamar Co.) . . . . .Bart Jetton
Reno (Parker Co.) . (195 W. Reno Rd.,
Azle 76020). . . . . . . .Eric Hunter
City Admin., Scott Passmore
Retreat . (621 N. Spikes Rd., Corsicana
75110). . . . . . . .Janice Barfknecht

Murals in Sweetwater. Photo by Nicholas Henderson (CC).

Rhome . . Michelle Pittman Di Credico
City Admin., Joe Ashton
Rice. . . . . .Vickie Young
City Admin., Tonya Roberts
Richardson (†) . . . . . . Paul Voelker
City Mgr., Dan ohnson
Richland . . . . Kenneth Guard
Richland Hills (†) . . . . Edward Lopez
City Mgr., Eric Strong
Richland Springs . . . Johnnie Reeves
Richmond (†) . . . . Evalyn W. Moore
City Mgr., Terri Vela
Richwood (†) . . . . . . .Steve Boykin
City Mgr., Michael Coon
Riesel . . . . Kevin Hogg
Rio Bravo (†). . . . . Daisy Lee Valdez
City Admin., Joe Valdez
Rio Grande City (†) . . . Joel Villarreal
City Mgr., Alberto Perez
Rio Hondo . . . Gustavo (Gus) Olivares
City Admin., Ben Medina
Rio Vista . . . William (Keith) Hutchison
Rising Star . . Jimmy Carpenter, Interim
City Admin., Jan Clark
River Oaks (†) . . .Herman D. Earwood
City Admin., Marvin Gregory
Riverside. . . . . John LeMaire
Road Runner . . . . David Ortega, Jr.
Roanoke (†) . . . . . . Scooter Gierisch
City Mgr., Scott Campbell
Roaring Springs. . . . Corky Marshall
Robert Lee . . . . Allyson Crenshaw
Robinson (†). . . . . . .Bert Echterling
City Mgr., Craig Lemin
Robstown (†) Amanda (Mandy) Barrera
Roby . . . . Eli Sepeda
City Mgr., Jack W. Brown
Rochester . . . . Lonnetta Farrar
City Mgr., Gail Nunn
Rockdale (†) . . . . John King
City Mgr., Chris Whittaker
Rockport (†) . . . .Patrick R. (Pat) Rios
City Mgr., Kevin Carruth

Rocksprings. . . . . . . Brian Wood
Rockwall (†) . . . . .Jim Pruitt
City Mgr., Rick Crowley
Rocky Mound . . . . .Noble T. Smith
Rogers . . . . Tammy Cockrum
City Admin., Chris Hill
Rollingwood . . . . . .Michael Dyson
City Admin., Amber Lewis
Roma (†) . . . . . . Roberto A. Salinas
City Mgr., Crisanto Salinas
Roman Forest . . . . Chris Parr
City Admin., Liz Mullane
Ropesville . . . . Brenda Rabel
Roscoe. . . . . .Frank S. (Pete) Porter
City Mgr., Cody Thompson
Rosebud . . . . Roy L. Spivey
City Admin., Keith Whitfield
Rose City . . . . . . Bonnie Stephenson
Rose Hill Acres . . . .(100 Jordan Rd.,
Lumberton 77657) . . . . David Lang
Rosenberg (†) . William T. (Bill) Benton
City Mgr., John Maresh
Ross . . . . Jim Jaska
Rosser . . . . . . Shannon R. Corder
Rotan. . . . . Pete Garcia
City Mgr., Carla Thornton
Round Mountain . . . .Alvin Gutierrez
Round Rock (†) . . . . . Craig Morgan
City Mgr., Laurie Hadley
Round Top . . . . Barry Bone
Rowlett (†) . . . Tammy Dana-Bashian
City Mgr., Brian Funderburk
Roxton . . . . Paul Helms
City Mgr., Janet Wheeler
Royse City (†) . . . . . . Janet Nichol
City Mgr., Carl Alsabrook
Rule. . . . . Jerry Cannon
Runaway Bay . . . . . Herman White
City Admin., Pamela Woods
Runge . . . . .Homer Lott, Jr.
Rusk (†) . . . . Angela Raiborn
City Mgr., Jim Dunaway

— S —

Sabinal . . . . .Charles D. Story
Sachse (†) . . . . Mike Felix
City Mgr., Gina Nash
Sadler . . . . Jackie Moss
City Admin., Jaime Vannoy
Saginaw (†) . . . . Todd Flippo
City Mgr., Gabe Reaume
Saint Hedwig . . . . Dee Grimm
Saint Jo . . . . Lucas Thompson
Salado . . . . Skip Blancett
Village Admin., Don Ferguson
San Angelo (†). . . . . . .Brenda Gunter
City Mgr., Daniel Valenzuela
San Antonio (†) . . . . .Ron Nirenberg
City Mgr., Erik Walsh
San Augustine. . . . . . Leroy Hughes
City Mgr., John Camp
San Benito (†) . Benjamin (Ben) Gomez
City Mgr., Manuel De La Rosa
Sanctuary . . . .(Box 125, Azle 76098)
. . . . Cliff Scallan
San Diego . . . . . Sally Lichtenberger
City Dir., Aleida L. Luera
Sandy Oaks . . . . Micki Ball
City Admin., Ken Roberts, Interim
Sandy Point . . . Charles J. Waller, Jr.
San Elizario . . . . . .Antonio Araujo
City Admin., Maya Sanchez
San Felipe . . . . .Bobby Byars
Sanford . . . . Bernard Pacheco
Sanger (†) . . . . .Thomas Muir
City Mgr., Alina Ciocan
San Juan (†) . . . . Mario Garza
City Mgr., Benjamin Arjona
San Leanna . . . (Box 1107, Manchaca
78652) . . . . Molly Quirk
City Admin., Rebecca Howe
San Marcos (†) . . . . . Jane Hughson
City Mgr., Bert Lumbreras
San Patricio . . .(4615 Main St., Mathis
78368) . . . . Jackie Hale
San Perlita. . . . George M. Guadiana

San Saba. . . . . Ken Jordan
City Mgr., Stan Weik
Sansom Park (5500 Buchanan St., Fort Worth 76114) . . . . Jim Barnett, Jr.
City Admin., Angela Winkle
Santa Anna . . . . .Harold Fahrlender
Santa Clara . (Box 429, Marion 78124)
. . . . .Jeff Hunt
Santa Fe (†) . . . . Jason Tabor
City Mgr., Joe Dickson
Santa Rosa . . . . Bobby de la Fuente
Savoy. . . . . Steve Perkins
Schertz (†). . . . . .Michael Carpenter
City Mgr., Mark Browne
Schulenburg. . . . . . . Elaine Kocian
City Admin., Tami Walker
Scotland . . . . Ron Hoff
Scottsville . . . . Kerry L. Cade
Scurry . . . . Johnny Blazek
Seabrook (†). . . . . . .Thom Kolupski
City Mgr., Gayle Cook
Seadrift . . . . Elmer DeForest
Seagoville (†) . . . Dennis K. Childress
City Mgr., Patrick Stallings
Seagraves . . . . .Charles Evans
Sealy (†) . . . . . . Janice Whitehead
City Mgr., Lloyd Merrell
Seguin (†) . . . . Don Keil
City Mgr., Douglas G. Faseler
Selma . . . . .Tom Daly
City Admin., Johnny Casias
Seminole (†) . . . . John Belcher
City Admin., Tommy Phillips
Seven Oaks (Box 334, Leggett 77350)
. . . . .Centa Evans
Seven Points . . . . Bill Hash
Seymour . . . . Jon Hrncirik
City Admin., Steve Biedermann
Shady Shores . .(Box 362, Lake Dallas 75065) . . . . . Cindy Aughinbaugh
Shallowater . . . . . . .Royking Potter
City Mgr., Russel Moses
Shamrock . . . . Aaron Shannon
City Mgr., Tommey Cole
Shavano Park . . . . Bob Werner
City Mgr., Bill Hill
Shenandoah . . . . . . Ritch Wheeler
City Admin., Kathie Reyer
Shepherd . . . . Charles Minton
Sherman (†) . . . . David Plyler
City Mgr., Robby Hefton
Shiner . . . . Fred Hilscher
Shoreacres . . . . David Jennings
City Mgr., Troy Harison
Silsbee (†) . . . . Mike Tomas
City Mgr., DeeAnn Zimmerman
Silverton . . . . Lane B. Garvin
City Admin., Wade Willson
Simonton . . . . . . Laurie Boudreaux
City Admin., Jennifer Jones Ward
Sinton (†) . . . . Edward Adams
City Mgr., John D. Hobson
Skellytown. . . . . Amanda Dickerson
Slaton (†). . . . . (vacant)
City Admin., Mike Lamberson
Smiley . . . . Michael K. Mills
Smithville . . . . . Scott Saunders, Jr.
City Mgr., Robert Tamble
Smyer . . . . Mary Beth Sims
Snook . . . . John W. See, III
Snyder (†) . . . . Tony Wofford
City Mgr., Merle Taylor
Socorro (†). . . . . .Elia Garcia
City Mgr., Adriana Rodarte
Somerset . . . .
Lydia P. Hernandez. . . . . . . .City Admin., Omar H. Pachecano, Interim
Somerville . . . . . Michael Bradford
City Admin., Danny Segundo

Sonora . . . . Wanda Shurley
City Mgr., Arturo Fuentes
Sour Lake . . . . . . Bruce Robinson
City Mgr., Jack Provost
South Houston . . . . .Joe Soto
Southlake (†) . . . . Laura Hill
City Mgr., Shana Yelverton
Southmayd . . . . .David Turner
South Mountain . . . (107 Barton Ln., Gatesville 76528). . . . Donald Smart
South Padre Island (†) Patrick McNulty
City Mgr., Randy Smith, Interim
Southside Place . . (6309 Edloe Ave., Houston 77005) . . . Pat Patterson
City Mgr., David Moss
Spearman . . . . .Tobe Shields
City Mgr., Suzanne Bellsnyder
Splendora . . . . .Dorothy Welch
Spofford . .(P.O. Box 1541 Bracketville, 78832) . . . . . . .Pablo Resendez
Spring Branch . . . . . James Mayer
Springlake . . . . Gaylon Conner
Springtown . . . . .Greg Hood
City Admin., David Miller
Spring Valley Village (1025 Campbell Rd., Houston 77055) .Tom Ramsey
City Admin., Julie Robinson
Spur . . . . Louise Jones
St. Paul . . . . Opie Walter
Stafford (†). . . . .Leonard Scarcella
Stagecoach . . . . Galen Mansee
Stamford (†) . . . . . . James Decker
City Mgr., Alan Plumlee
Stanton. . . . . Jim Smith
City Admin., Jessie Montez
Staples. . . . . Eddie Daffern
Star Harbor (Box 949, Malakoff 75148)
. . . . Warren Claxton
Stephenville (†) . . . . . Doug Svien
City Mgr., Allen Barnes
Sterling City . . . . . .Lane Horwood
Stinnett . . . . Colin Locke
City Admin., Durk Downs
Stockdale . . . . Ray Wolff
City Mgr., Banks Akin
Stockton Bend . . . . Edward Reiter
Stratford . . . . Ricky Reed
City Admin., Tommy Bogart
Strawn . . . . Tye Jackson
Streetman . . . .Johnny A. Robinson
Sudan . . . . Sam Miller
Sugar Land (†). . . Joe R. Zimmerman
City Mgr., Allen Bogard
Sullivan City (†) . Leonel (Leo) Garcia
City Mgr., Richard Ozuna, Interim
Sulphur Springs (†) . . John A. Sellers
City Mgr., Marc Maxwell
Sundown. . . . .Jonathan Strickland
City Admin., Billy Hernandez
Sunnyvale (†) . . . . . . Saji George
Town Mgr., Susan Guthrie
Sunray . . . . .Bruce Broxson
City Mgr., K.J. Perry
Sunrise Beach Village . Tommy Martin
Sunset Valley . . . . . Rose Cardona
City Admin., (vacant)
Sun Valley (800 Shady Grove Rd., Paris 75462) . . . . Tom Wagnon
Surfside Beach . . . . Larry Davison
Sweeny (†) . . . . Jeff Farley
City Mgr., Cindy King
Sweetwater (†) . . . . . Jim McKenzie
City Mgr., David A. Vela

— T —

Taft . . . . .Pedro Lopez
City Mgr., Denise Hitt

Tahoka . . . . John B. Baker
City Admin., Jerry W. Webster
Talco . . . . Keith Thompson
Talty . . . (9550 Helms Trail, Ste. 500, Forney 75126) . . . Frank Garrison
City Admin., James Stroman
Tatum. . . . . .Phil Cory
Taylor (†). . . . . Brandt Rydell
City Mgr., Brian Laborde
Taylor Lake Village . . . . Jon Keeney
Taylor Landing . . . . . .John Durkay
Teague . . . . James Monks
City Admin., Theresa Prasil
Tehuacana . . . . . . .Roy Cholopisa
Temple (†) . . . . Tim Davis
City Mgr., Brynn Myers
Tenaha . . . . Michael Baker
Terrell (†). . . . . . E. Rick Carmona
City Mgr., Mike Sims, Interim
Terrell Hills (†). . . . .Anne Ballantyne
City Mgr., Greg Whitlock
Texarkana (†) . . . . .Bob Bruggeman
City Mgr., Shirley Jaster
Texas City (†) . . . . Matthew T. Doyle
Texhoma . . . . . . Missy Cartwright
Texline . . . . Jeff Finnegan
City Mgr., Marcia French
The Colony (†). . . . . Joe McCourry
City Mgr., Troy Powell
Thompsons . . . . . Freddie Newsome
Thorndale . . . . . . George Galbreath
City Admin., William Kiesling
Thornton . . . . Kenneth Capps
City Mgr., Victoria Winstead
Thorntonville . . . (Box 740, Monahans 79756) . . . . David Mitchell
Thrall. . . . . Troy Marx
Three Rivers. . . . . . Sam Garcia
City Mgr., Arnold Saenz
Throckmorton. . . . . . . .Will Carroll
Tiki Island . Vernon (Goldie) Teltschick
Timbercreek Canyon . . . . . (101 S. Timbercreek Dr., Amarillo 79118)
. . . . .Bill Young
City Mgr., Kurt Grant
Timpson . . . . Debra Pate Smith
Tioga . . . . Craig Jezek
Tira . . . (801 County Rd. 4612, Sulphur Springs 75482) . . Allen Joslin, Interim
Toco . . . (2103 Chestnut Dr., Brookston 75421) . . . . . J. Jason Waller
Todd Mission (21718 FM 1774, Plantersville 77363) . . . . George C. Coulam
City Mgr., Neal Wendele
Tolar . . . . Terry Johnson
Tomball (†). . . . . . Gretchen Fagan
City Mgr., Robert S. Hauck
Tom Bean . . . . Sherry E. Howard
Tool. . . . . Tawnya Austin
Toyah . . . . Bobby Creamer
Trent . . . . Leanna West
Trenton . . . . . . .Rodney Alexander
Trinidad . . . . Larry Estes
City Admin., Terri Newhouse
Trinity . . . . Wayne Huffman
City Mgr., Steven Jones, Interim
Trophy Club (†) . . . . . Nick Sanders
Town Mgr., Jonathan Phillips, Interim
Troup . . . . .Joe Carlyle
City Mgr., Gene Cottle
Troy. . . . . Michael Morgan
City Admin., Jeff Straub
Tulia (†). . . . . . .Israel Ramirez, Acting
City Mgr., Dion Miller
Turkey . . . . Christy Yates
City Mgr., Larry Plumlee
Tuscola. . . . . Dale Martin
Tye . . . . Roy Votaw
Tyler (†) . . . . Martin Heines
City Mgr., Edward Broussard

— U —

Uhland . . . . Vicki Hunter
City Admin., Karen Gallaher
Uncertain . . . . Greg Jones
Union Grove
(10648 US Hwy. 271 S., Gladewater
75647) . . . . . . Randy Lee Simcox
Union Valley . . . . Craig Waskow
Universal City (†) . . John Williams
City Mgr., Kim Turner
University Park (†) . . Olin B. Lane, Jr.
City Mgr., Robbie Corder
Uvalde (†) . . . . Don McLaughlin
City Mgr., Vince DiPiazza

— V —

Valentine . . . . Jesus Calderon
Valley Mills . . . . Jerry Wittmer
Valley View . . . . . Joshua Brinkley
Van . . . . Don Smith
Van Alstyne . . . . Steven Riley
City Mgr., Lane Jones
Van Horn . . . . Pam Young
City Admin., Francine Malafronte
Vega . . . . Mark Groneman
Venus . . . . James Burgess
City Admin., Michael Boese
Vernon (†) . . . . Doug Jeffrey
City Mgr., Martin Mangum
Victoria (†) . . . . Rawley McCoy
City Mgr., Jesús A. Garza
Vidor (†) . . . . Kimberly Stiebig
City Mgr., Mike Kunst
Village of The Hills . . . . . Eric Ovlen
City Mgr., Wendy Smith May
Vinton . . . . . . Manuel (Manny) Leos
Village Admin., Andrea Carrillo
Volente . . . . David S. Springer
Von Ormy . . . . Sally Martinez

— W —

Waco (†) . . . . Kyle Deaver
City Mgr., Wiley Stem III
Waelder . . . . Roy Tovar
City Mgr., Steven McKay
Wake Village (†) . . . . . Sheryl Collum
City Admin., Jim Roberts
Waller . . . . Danny L. Marburger
Wallis . . . . Steve Bockel
Walnut Springs . . . . . Larry Stafford
Warren City (3004 George Richey Rd.,
Gladewater 75647) . . . Ricky Wallace
Waskom . . . . Jesse Moore
Watauga (†) . . . . . . Arthur L. Miner
City Mgr., Andrea Gardner

Waxahachie (†) . . . . . . David Hill
City Mgr., Michael Scott
Weatherford (†) . . . . . Paul Paschall
City Mgr., Sharon Hayes
Webberville . . . . . Hector Gonzales
Webster (†) . . . . Donna Rogers
City Mgr., Wayne Sabo
Weimar . . . . Milton R. Koller
City Mgr., Mike Barrow
Weinert . . . . Ed Murphy
Weir . . . . Mervin Walker
Wellington . . . . J.D. Hamby
City Mgr., Jon Sessions
Wellman . . . . Todd Ellis
Wells . . . . C.W. Williams
Weslaco (†) . . . . David Suarez
City Mgr., Mike R. Perez
West . . . . Tommy Muska
City Admin., Shelly Nors
Westbrook . . . . Lynn Gaston
West Columbia . . Laurie B. Kincannon
City Mgr., Debbie Sutherland
Westlake . . . . Laura Wheat
Town Mgr., Amanda DeGan
West Lake Hills . . . . . Linda Anthony
City Admin., Robert J. Wood
Weston . . . . Patti Harrington
Weston Lakes (PO Box 1082, Fulshear
77441) . . . . Mary Rose Zdunkewicz
West Orange (†) . . . . . Roy McDonald
Westover Hills (5824 Merrymount, Fort
Worth 76107) . . . . . Kelly Thompson
West Tawakoni . . . Alan Shoemake
City Admin., Susan Roberts
West University Place (†) . Bob Higley
City Mgr., David J. Beach
Westworth Village . . . L. Kelly Jones
City Admin., Sterling Naron
Wharton (†) . . . . Tim Barker
City Mgr., Andres Garza, Jr.
Wheeler . . . . Bob McCain
White Deer . . . . Kent Kelp
Whiteface . . . . Judy Deavours
Whitehouse (†) . . . . Charles Parker
White Oak (†) . . . . Kyle Kutch
City Coord., Charles Smith
Whitesboro . . . . . W.D. (Dee) Welch
City Admin., Michael Marter
White Settlement (†) Ronald A. White
City Mgr., Jeff James
Whitewright . . . . . Jamie Lawrence
Whitney . . . . Trey Jetton
City Admin., Chris Bentley
Wichita Falls (†) . . Stephen Santellana
City Mgr., Darron Leiker
Wickett . . . . Xavier Estrada
Willis (†) . . . . Leonard Reed
City Mgr., Hector Forestier

Willow Park . . . . Doyle Moss
City Admin., Bryan Grimes
Wills Point . . . . Mark Turner
City Admin., Pam Pearson
Wilmer . . Emmanuel Wealthy-Williams
City Admin., John Hubbard, Interim
Wilson . . . . Randy Dunn
Wimberley . . . . Susan Jaggers
City Admin., Shawn Cox
Windcrest (†) . . . . Dan Reese
City Mgr., Rafael Castillo
Windom . . . . Donny Cobb
Windthorst . . . . Greg P. Vieth
Winfield . . . . Debbie Cruitt
Wink . . . . Eric Hawkins
Winnsboro . . . . . Camron Wilcox
City Admin., Craig Lindholm
Winona . . . . Curtis Land
Winters . . . . Lisa Yates
Wixon Valley . (9500 E. State Hwy. 21,
Bryan 77808) . . . James (Jim) Soefje
Wolfe City . . . . Sharion Scott
Wolfforth . . . . . Charles Addington
City Mgr., Darrell G. Newson
Woodbranch Village
(58-A Woodbranch, New Caney
77357) . . . . Vera Craig
Woodcreek . . . . . . William P. Scheel
City Mgr., Brenton B. Lewis
Woodloch . . (Box 1379, Conroe 77305
. . . . Ralph Leino, Jr.
Woodsboro . . . . Kay Roach
Woodson . . . . Bobby Mathiews
Woodville . . . . . Paula M. Jones
City Admin., Mandy K. Risinger
Woodway (†) . . . . Bob Howard
City Mgr., Shawn Oubre
Wortham . . . . Rodney Price
Wylie (†) . . . . Eric Hogue
City Mgr., Chris Holsted

— Y —

Yantis . . . . . John D. (Trey) Norris, III
Yoakum (†) . . . . . Anita R. Rodriguez
City Mgr., Kevin Coleman
Yorktown . . . . Bill Baker
City Admin., John Barth

— Z —

Zavalla . . . . Carlos Guzman
☆

TEXAS READS

★**texas review press**   **to order call 800.826.8911 or visit texasreviewpress.org**

The Fayette County Courthouse in La Grange. Photo by Jerry and Pat Donaho (CC).

County Courts

Each Texas county has one county court created by the Texas Constitution — a constitutional county court — which is presided over by the county judge (see table beginning on **page 497** for a list of county judges). In more populated counties, the Legislature has created statutory county courts, including courts at law, probate courts, juvenile courts, domestic relations courts, and criminal courts at law. Following is a list of statutory county courts and judges, as reported in the Texas Judicial Directory as of July 2019. Other courts with jurisdiction in each county can be found on **pages 454–455**. Other county and district officials can be found on **pages 497–508**.

Anderson: Court at Law, Brendan Jeffrey Doran.

Angelina: Court at Law No. 1, Joe Lee Register; No. 2, Clyde M. Herrington.

Aransas: Court at Law, Richard Bianchi.

Atascosa: Court at Law, Bob Brendel.

Austin: Court at Law, Daniel W. Leedy.

Bastrop: Court at Law, M. Benton Eskew.

Bell: Court at Law No. 1, Jeanne Parker; No. 2, John Michael Mischtian; No. 3, Rebecca DePew.

Bexar: Court at Law No. 1, Helen Petry Stowe; No. 2, Grace M. Uzomba; No. 3, David J. Rodriguez; No. 4, Alfredo Ximenez; No. 5, John Amos Longoria; No. 6, Wayne A. Christian; No. 7, Michael DeLeon; No. 8, Mary D. Roman; No. 9, Gloria Saldana; No. 10, J. Frank Davis; No. 11, Carl (Tommy) T. Stolhandske; No. 12, Yolanda Huff; No. 13, Rosie Gonzalez; No. 14, Carlo R. Key; No. 15, Melissa Vara. **Probate Court** No. 1, Oscar Kazen; No. 2, Veronica Vasquez.

Bosque: Court at Law, Luke A. Giesecke.

Bowie: Court at Law, Craig L. Henry.

Brazoria: Court at Law No. 1 & **Probate Court**, Greg Hill; No. 2 & **Probate Court**, Marc W. Holder; No. 3 & **Probate Court**, Jeremy E. Warren; No. 4 & **Probate Court**, Lori L. Rickert.

Brazos: Court at Law No. 1, Amanda S. Matzke; No. 2, James (Jim) White Locke.

Brown: Court at Law, Sam Clifton Moss.

Burnet: Court at Law, Linda M. Bayless.

Caldwell: Court at Law, Barbara Molina.

Calhoun: Court at Law, Alex R. Hernandez.

Cameron: Court at Law No. 1, Arturo A. McDonald Jr.; No. 2, Laura Betancourt; No. 3, David Gonzales III; No. 4, Sheila Garcia Bence; No. 5, Estela Vasquez Chavez.

Cass: Court at Law, Donald W. Dowd.

Cherokee: Court at Law, Janice C. Stone.

Collin: Court at Law No. 1, Corinne Ann Mason; No. 2, Barnett Walker; No. 3, Lance S. Baxter; No. 4, David D.

Edwards County Courthouse in Rocksprings. Photo by Larry D. Moore (CC).

Rippel; No. 5, Dan K. Wilson; No. 6, Jay A. Bender; No. 7, David Waddill. **Probate Court**, Weldon S. Copeland Jr.

Comal: Court at Law No. 1, Randy C. Gray; No. 2 Charles A. Stephens II.

Cooke: Court at Law, John H. Morris.

Coryell: Court at Law, John R. Lee.

Dallas: Court at Law No. 1, D'Metria Benson; No. 2, Melissa Bellan; No. 3, Sally L. Montgomery; No. 4, Paula Rosales; No. 5, Mark Greenberg. **County Criminal Court** No. 1, Dan Patterson; No. 2, Julia Hayes; No. 3, Audrey Moorhead; No. 4, Nancy Cutler Mulder; No. 5, Lisa Green; No. 6, Angela M. King; No. 7, Remeko Tranisha Edwards; No. 8, Carmen P. White; No. 9, Peggy Hoffman; No. 10, Etta J. Mullin; No. 11, Shequitta Kelly. **Probate Court** No. 1, Brenda Hull-Thompson; No. 2, Ingrid Michelle Warren; No. 3, Margaret R. Jones-Johnson. **County Criminal Court of Appeals** No. 1, Kristin Swanson Wade; No. 2, Pam Luther.

Denton: Court at Law No. 1 & **Juvenile Court**, Kimberly McCary; No. 2, Robert Ramirez. **Probate Court**, Bonnie J. Robison. **Criminal Court at Law** No. 1, Jim E. Crouch; No. 2, Susan Piel; No. 3, Forrest Beadle; No. 4, Chance Oliver; No. 5, Charles (Coby) Waddill.

Ector: Court at Law No. 1, Brooke Hendricks-Green; No. 2, Christopher M. Clark.

Ellis: Court at Law No. 1, Jim Chapman; No. 2, A. Gene Calvert Jr.

El Paso: Court at Law No. 1, Ruth Reyes; No. 2, Julie Gonzalez; No. 3, Javier Alvarez; No. 4, Alejandro Gonzalez; No. 5, Jesus Rodriguez; No. 6, M. Sue Kurita; No. 7, Ruben Morales. **Probate Court** No. 1, Patricia B. Chew; No. 2, Eduardo Gamboa. **Juvenile Court** No. 1, Richard Anise; No. 2, Maria T. Leyva-Ligon. **Criminal**

Court at Law No. 1, Alma R. Trejo; No. 2, Robert S. Anchondo; No. 3, Carlos Carrasco; No. 4, Jesus R. Herrera.

Erath: Court at Law, Blake B. Thompson.

Fannin: Court at Law, Charles Butler.

Fisher: Multicounty Court at Law, David C. Hall (also Mitchell and Nolan counties).

Fort Bend: Court at Law No. 1, Christopher G. Morales; No. 2, Jeffery A. McMeans; No. 3, Juli Mathew; No. 4, toni M. Wallace; No. 5, Teana V. Watson; No. 6, Sherman Hatton, Jr.

Galveston: Court at Law No. 1, John Grady; No. 2, Kerri M. Foley; No. 3, Jack Ewing. **Probate Court**, Kimberly A. Sullivan.

Grayson: Court at Law No. 1, James C. Henderson; No. 2, Carol M. Siebman.

Gregg: Court at Law No. 1, R. Kent Phillips. No. 2, Vincent L. Dulweber.

Grimes: Court at Law, Tuck Moody McLain

Guadalupe: Court at Law No. 1, Bill Squires; No. 2, Frank Follis.

Harris: Civil Court at Law No. 1, George A. Barnstone; No. 2, Jim F. Kovach; No. 3, LaShawn A. Williams; No. 4, Lesley Briones. **County Criminal Court at Law** No. 1, Alex Salgado; No. 2, Ronnisha Bowman; No. 3, Erica Hughes; No. 4, Shannon Baldwin; No. 5, David M. Fleischer; No. 6, Kelley Andrews; No. 7, Andrew A. Wright; No. 8, Franklin Bynam; No. 9, Toria J. Finch; No. 10, Lee Harper Wilson; No. 11, Sedrick T. Walker II; No. 12, Genesis Draper; No. 13, Raul Rodriguez; No. 14, David L. Singer; No. 15, Tonya Jones; No. 16, Darrell William Jordan. **Probate Court** No. 1, Jerry W. Simoneaux; No. 2, Michael B. Newman; No. 3, Jason Cox; No. 4, James Horowitz.

Harrison: Court at Law, Joe M. Black IV.

Hays: Court at Law No. 1, Robert E. Updegrove; No. 2, Chris Johnson; No. 3, Tacie Marie Zelhart.

Henderson: Court at Law No 1, Douglas (Scott) S. Williams; No 2, Nancy Adams Perryman.

Hidalgo: Court at Law No. 1, Rodolfo (Rudy) Gonzalez; No. 2, Jaime (Jay) Palacios; No. 4, Federico (Fred) Garza Jr.; No. 5, Arnoldo Cantu; Jr. No. 6, Albert Garcia; No. 7, Sergio Valdez; No. 8, Omar Maldonado. **Probate Court**, JoAnne Garcia.

Hill: Court at Law, Matthew S. Crain.

Hood: Court at Law, Vincent Messina.

Hopkins: Court at Law, Clay Harrison.

Houston: Court at Law, Sarah Tunnell Clark.

Hunt: Court at Law No. 1, Timothy S. Linden; No. 2, F. Duncan Thomas.

Jefferson: Court at Law No. 1, Gerald W. Eddins; No. 2, Terrence L. Holmes; No. 3, Clint M. Woods.

Jim Wells: Court at Law, Michael Ventura Garcia.

Johnson: Court at Law No. 1, Robert B. Mayfield III; No. 2, F. Steven McClure.

Kaufman: Court at Law No. 1, Tracy Gray; No. 2, Bobby L. Rich, Jr.

Kerr: Court at Law, Susan F. Harris.

Kleberg: Court at Law, Jamie E. Carillo.

Lamar: Court at Law, Bill H. Harris.

Liberty: Court at Law, Thomas A. Chambers.

Lubbock: Court at Law No. 1, Mark J. Hocker; No. 2, Drue A. Farmer; No. 3, Ann-Marie Carruth.

McLennan: Court at Law No. 1, Vikram Deivanayagam; No. 2, T. Bradley Cates.

Medina: Court at Law, Mark Cashion.

Midland: Court at Law No. 1, Kyle Peeler; No. 2, Marvin L. Moore.

Mitchell: Multicounty Court at Law, David C. Hall (also Fisher and Nolan counties).

Montgomery: Court at Law No. 1, Dennis D. Watson; No. 2, Claudia L. Laird; No. 3, Patrice McDonald; No. 4, Mary Ann Turner; No. 5, Keith Mills Stewart.

Moore: Court at Law, Delwin T. McGee.

Nacogdoches: Court at Law, John A. (Jack) Sinz.

Navarro: Court at Law, Amanda D. Putman.

Nolan: Multicounty Court at Law, David C. Hall (also Fisher and Mitchell counties).

Nueces: Court at Law No. 1, Robert J. Vargas; No. 2, Lisa Elisabet Gonzales; No. 3, Deeanne Scoboda Galvan; No. 4, Mark H. Woerner; No. 5, Timothy J. McCoy.

Orange: Court at Law No. 1, Mandy White-Rogers; No 2, Troy Johnson.

Panola: Court at Law, Terry D. Bailey.

Parker: Court at Law No. 1, Jerry D. Buckner; No. 2, Lynn Marie Johnson.

Polk: Court at Law, Tom Brown.

Potter: Court at Law No. 1, Walt Weaver; No. 2, Matt Hand.

Randall: Court at Law No. 1, James W. Anderson; No. 2, Matthew Martindale.

Reeves: Court at Law, Scott W. Johnson.

Rockwall: Court at Law, Brian Williams.

Rusk: Court at Law, Chad W. Dean.

San Patricio: Court at Law, M. Elizabeth Welborn.

Smith: Court at Law No. 1, Jason A. Ellis; No. 2, Taylor Heaton; No. 3, Floyd Thomas Getz.

Starr: Court at Law, Orlando Rodriguez.

Tarrant: Court at Law No. 1, Donald R. Pierson; No. 2, Jennifer Rymell; No. 3, Mike Hrabal. **Criminal Court at Law** No. 1, David Cook; No. 2, Cary F. Walker; No. 3, Bob McCoy; No. 4, Deborah L. Nekhom; No. 5, Jamie Cummings; No. 6, Molly S. Jones; No. 7, Cheril S. Hardy; No. 8, Charles L. Vanover; No. 9, Brent A. Carr; No. 10, Phil A. Sorrels. **Probate Court** No. 1, Christopher W. Ponder; No. 2, Brooke Ulrickson Allen.

Taylor: Court at Law No. 1, Robert Harper; No. 2, Harriett L. Haag.

Tom Green: Court at Law No. 1, Charles (Ben) Nolan; No. 2, Penny Anne Roberts.

Travis: Court at Law No. 1, J. Todd T. Wong; No. 2, Eric M. Shepperd; No. 3, John H. Lipscombe; No. 4, Mike Edward Denton; No. 5, Nancy Hohengarten; No. 6, Brandy Mueller; No. 7, Elisabeth A. Earle; No. 8, Carlos H. Barrera; No. 9, Kim Williams. **Probate Court**, Guy Herman.

Val Verde: Court at Law, Sergio J. Gonzalez.

Van Zandt: Court at Law, Joshua Wintters.

Victoria: Court at Law No. 1, Travis H. Ernst; No. 2, Daniel F. Gilliam.

Walker: Court at Law, Tracy M. Sorensen.

Waller: Court at Law, Carol A. Chaney.

Washington: Court at Law, Eric Thomas Berg.

Webb: Court at Law No. 1, Hugo D. Martinez; No. 2, Victor G. Villarreal.

Wichita: Court at Law No. 1, Gary Wayne Butler; No. 2, Greg King.

Williamson: Court at Law No. 1, Brandy Hallford; No. 2, Laura B. Barker; No. 3, Doug Arnold; No. 4, John B. McMaster.

Wise: Court at Law No. 1, Melton D. Cude; No. 2, Stephen J. Wren. ☆

Regional Councils of Government

Source: Texas Association of Regional Councils; www.txregionalcouncil.org/

The concept of regional planning and cooperation, fostered by enabling legislation in 1965, has spread across Texas since organization of the **North Central Texas Council of Governments** in 1966.

Regional councils are voluntary associations of local governments that deal with problems and planning needs that cross the boundaries of individual local governments or that require regional attention.

These concerns include criminal justice, emergency communications, job-training programs, solid-waste management, transportation, and water-quality management. The councils make recommendations to member governments and may assist in implementing the plans. Financing is provided by local, state, and federal governments.

The **Texas Association of Regional Councils** is at 701 Brazos, Ste. 780, Austin 78701; (512) 478-4715.

Following is a list of the 24 regional councils, member counties, executive director, and contact information:

1. **Panhandle Regional Planning Commission**: Armstrong, Briscoe, Carson, Castro, Childress, Collingsworth, Dallam, Deaf Smith, Donley, Gray, Hall, Hansford, Hartley, Hemphill, Hutchinson, Lipscomb, Moore, Ochiltree, Oldham, Parmer, Potter, Randall, Roberts, Sherman, Swisher, and Wheeler. Kyle Ingham, PO Box 9257, Amarillo 79105-9257; (806) 372-3381; www.prpc.org.

2. **South Plains Association of Governments**: Bailey, Cochran, Crosby, Dickens, Floyd, Garza, Hale, Hockley, King, Lamb, Lubbock, Lynn, Motley, Terry, and Yoakum. Tim Pierce, PO Box 3730, Lubbock 79452-3730; (806) 762-8721; www.spag.org.

3. **Nortex Regional Planning Commission**: Archer, Baylor, Clay, Cottle, Foard, Hardeman, Jack, Montague, Wichita, Wilbarger, and Young. Dennis Wilde, PO Box 5144, Wichita Falls 76307-5144; (940) 322-5281; www.nortexrpc.org.

4. **North Central Texas Council of Governments**: Collin, Dallas, Denton, Ellis, Erath, Hood, Hunt, Johnson, Kaufman, Navarro, Palo Pinto, Parker, Rockwall, Somervell, Tarrant, and Wise. R. Michael Eastland, PO Box 5888, Arlington 76005-5888; (817) 640-3300; www.nctcog.org.

5. **Ark-Tex Council of Governments**: Bowie, Cass, Delta, Franklin, Hopkins, Lamar, Morris, Red River, Titus, and Miller County, Ark. Chris Brown, 4808 Elizabeth St., Texarkana, Texas 75503; (903) 832-8636; www.atcog.org.

6. **East Texas Council of Governments**: Anderson, Camp, Cherokee, Gregg, Harrison, Henderson, Marion, Panola, Rains, Rusk, Smith, Upshur, Van Zandt, and Wood. David Cleveland, 3800 Stone Rd., Kilgore 75662-6297; (903) 984-8641; www.etcog.org.

7. **West Central Texas Council of Governments**: Brown, Callahan, Coleman, Comanche, Eastland, Fisher, Haskell, Jones, Kent, Knox, Mitchell, Nolan, Runnels, Scurry, Shackelford, Stephens, Stonewall, Taylor, and Throckmorton. Tom Smith, 3702 Loop 322, Abilene 79602-7300; (325) 672-8544; www.wctcog.org.

8. **Rio Grande Council of Governments**: Brewster, Culberson, El Paso, Hudspeth, Jeff Davis, Presidio, and Doña Ana County, N.M. Annette Gutierrez, 8037 Lockheed Dr., Ste. 100, El Paso 79925; (915) 533-0998; www.riocog.org.

9. **Permian Basin Regional Planning Commission**: Andrews, Borden, Crane, Dawson, Ector, Gaines, Glasscock, Howard, Loving, Martin, Midland, Pecos, Reeves, Terrell, Upton, Ward, and Winkler. Terri Moore, PO Box 60660, Midland 79711-0660; (432) 563-1061; www.pbrpc.org.

10. **Concho Valley Council of Governments**: Coke, Concho, Crockett, Irion, Kimble, Mason, McCulloch, Menard, Reagan, Schleicher, Sterling, Sutton, and Tom Green. John Austin Stokes, 2801 W. Loop 206, Ste. A, San Angelo 76904; (325) 944-9666; www.cvcog.org.

11. **Heart of Texas Council of Governments**: Bosque, Falls, Freestone, Hill, Limestone, and McLennan. Russell Devorsky, 1514 S. New Road, Waco 76711; (254) 292-1800; www.hotcog.org.

12. **Capital Area Council of Governments**: Bastrop, Blanco, Burnet, Caldwell, Fayette, Hays, Lee, Llano, Travis, and Williamson. Betty Voights, 6800 Burleson Rd., Bldg. 310, Ste. 165, Austin 78744; (512) 916-6000; www.capcog.org.

13. **Brazos Valley Council of Governments**: Brazos, Burleson, Grimes, Leon, Madison, Robertson, and

Washington: Tom Wilkinson Jr., PO Drawer 4128, Bryan 77805-4128; (979) 595-2800; www.bvcog.org.

14. **Deep East Texas Council of Governments**: Angelina, Houston, Jasper, Nacogdoches, Newton, Polk, Sabine, San Augustine, San Jacinto, Shelby, Trinity, and Tyler. Lonnie Hunt, 210 Premier Dr., Jasper 75951; (409) 384-5704; www.detcog.net.

15. **South East Texas Regional Planning Commission**: Hardin, Jefferson, and Orange. Shanna Burke, 2210 Eastex Fwy., Beaumont 77703; (409) 899-8444; www.setrpc.org.

16. **Houston-Galveston Area Council**: Austin, Brazoria, Chambers, Colorado, Fort Bend, Galveston, Harris, Liberty, Matagorda, Montgomery, Walker, Waller, and Wharton. Chuck Wemple, 3555 Timmons Ln., Ste. 120, Houston 77227-2777; (713) 627-3200; www.h-gac.com.

17. **Golden Crescent Regional Planning Commission**: Calhoun, DeWitt, Goliad, Gonzales, Jackson, Lavaca, and Victoria. Joe Brannan, 1908 N. Laurent, Ste. 600, Victoria 77901; (361) 578-1587; www.gcrpc.org.

18. **Alamo Area Council of Governments**: Atascosa, Bandera, Bexar, Comal, Frio, Gillespie, Guadalupe, Karnes, Kendall, Kerr, Medina, and Wilson. Diane Rath, 8700 Tesoro Dr., Ste. 160, San Antonio 78217-6208; (210) 362-5200; www.aacog.com.

19. **South Texas Development Council**: Jim Hogg, Starr, Webb, and Zapata. Robert Mediola, 1002 Dicky Lane, Laredo 78044-2187; (956) 722-3995; www.stdc.cog.tx.us.

20. **Coastal Bend Council of Governments**: Aransas, Bee, Brooks, Duval, Jim Wells, Kenedy, Kleberg, Live Oak, McMullen, Nueces, Refugio, and San Patricio. John P. Buckner, 2910 Leopard St, Corpus Christi 78408; (361) 883-5743; cbcog98.org.

21. **Lower Rio Grande Valley Development Council**: Cameron, Hidalgo, and Willacy. Ron Garza, 301 W. Railroad St., Weslaco 78596; (956) 682-3481; www.lrgvdc.org.

22. **Texoma Council of Governments**: Cooke, Fannin, and Grayson. Eric Bridges, 1117 Gallagher Dr., Ste. 470, Sherman 75090; (903) 813-3514; www.tcog.com.

23. **Central Texas Council of Governments**: Bell, Coryell, Hamilton, Lampasas, Milam, Mills, and San Saba. Jim Reed, PO Box 729, Belton 76513-0729; (254) 770-2210; www.ctcog.org.

24. **Middle Rio Grande Development Council**: Dimmit, Edwards, Kinney, La Salle, Maverick, Real, Uvalde, Val Verde, and Zavala. Nick Gallegos, 307 W. Nopal, Carrizo Springs 78834; (830) 876-3533; www.mrgdc.org. ☆

County Tax Appraisers

The following list of Chief Appraisers for Texas counties was furnished by the State Property Tax Division of the State Comptroller's office. It includes the mailing address for each appraiser and is current to July 2019. (* indicates interim)

Anderson: Carson Wages, PO Box 279, Palestine 75802

Andrews: Susan Brewer, 600 N. Main St., Andrews 79714

Angelina: Tim Chambers, PO Box 2357, Lufkin 75902

Aransas: Mike Soto, 11 Hwy. 35 N., Rockport 78382

Archer: Kimbra York, PO Box 1141, Archer City 76351

Armstrong: Debbie Stribling, P.O. Box 149, Claude 79019

Atascosa: Michelle Cardenas, PO Box 600, Pleasanton 78065

Austin: Greg Cook, 906 E. Amelia St., Bellville 77418

Bailey: Kaye Elliott, 302 Main St., Muleshoe 79347

Bandera: Wendy Grams, PO Box 1119, Bandera 78003

Bastrop: Faun Cullens, PO Box 578, Bastrop 78602

Baylor: Mitzi Welch*, 211 N. Washington, Seymour 76380

Bee: Patricia Davis, 401 N. Washington, Beeville 78102

Bell: Billy White, PO Box 390, Belton 76513

Bexar: Michael Amezquita, PO Box 830248, San Antonio 78283

Blanco: Candice Fry, PO Box 338, Johnson City 78636

Borden: Tracy Cooley, PO Box 298, Gail 79738

Bosque: Marlee Greenwood, PO Box 393, Meridian 76665

Bowie: Mike Brower, PO Box 6527, Texarkana 75505

Brazoria: Cheryl Evans, 500 N. Chenango, Angleton 77515

Brazos: Mark Price, 4051 Pendleton Dr., Bryan 77802

Brewster: Denise Flores, 107 W. Avenue E, #2, Alpine 79830

Briscoe: Pat McWaters, PO Box 728, Silverton 79257

Brooks: Daniel Carcia, PO Drawer A, Falfurrias 78355

Brown: Brett McKibben, 403 Fisk Ave., Brownwood 76801

Burleson: Damon Daughtry*, PO Box 1000, Caldwell 77836

Burnet: Stan Hemphill, PO Box 908, Burnet 78611

Caldwell: Shanna Ramzinski*, PO Box 900, Lockhart 78644

Calhoun: Jesse Hubbell, PO Box 49, Port Lavaca 77979

Callahan: Stephanie McPherson, 132 W. 4th St., Baird 79504

Cameron: Richard Molina, PO Box 1010, San Benito 78586

Camp : Jan Tinsley, 143 Quitman St., Pittsburg 75686

Carson: Beverly Casselberry, PO Box 970, Panhandle 79068

Cass: Anita White, 502 N. Main St., Linden 75563

Castro: Debbie Stribling*, 204 S.E. 3rd (Rear), Dimmitt 79027

Chambers: Mitchell McCullough, PO Box 1520, Anahuac 77514

Cherokee: J.L. Flowers, PO Box 494, Rusk 75785

Childress: Twila Butler, 1710 Ave. F NW, Childress 79201

Clay: Gary Zeitler*, PO Box 108, Henrietta 76365

Cochran: David Greener, 109 S.E. First St., Morton 79346

Coke: Gayle Sisemore, PO Box 2, Robert Lee 76945

Coleman: Bill W. Jones, PO Box 914, Coleman 76834

Collin: Bo Daffin, 250 W. Eldorado, McKinney 75069

Collingsworth: Dwight Bowen, 800 West Ave., Box 9, Wellington, 79095

Colorado: Robert Maes, PO Box 10, Columbus 78934

Comal: Curtis Koehler, PO 900 S. Seguin Ave., New Braunfels 78130

Comanche: JoAnn Hohertz, 8 Huett Cir., Comanche 76442

Concho: Ashley Mayfield, PO Box 68, Paint Rock 76866

Cooke: Doug Smithson, 201 N. Dixon, Gainesville 76240

Coryell: Mitch Fast, 705 E. Main St., Gatesville 76528

Cottle: Nakia Hargrave, PO Box 459, Paducah 79248

Crane: Byron Bitner, 511 W. 8th St., Crane 79731

Crockett: Janet M. Thompson, PO Box 1569, Ozona 76943

Crosby: Kathy Lowrie, PO Box 505, Crosbyton 79322

Culberson: Maricel Gonzalez, PO Box 550, Van Horn 79855

Dallam: Holly McCauley, PO Box 579, Dalhart 79022

Dallas: Ken Nolan, 2949 N. Stemmons Fwy., Dallas 75247

Dawson: Norma J. Brock, PO Box 797, Lamesa 79331

Deaf Smith: Danny Jones, PO Box 2298, Hereford 79045

Delta: Kim Gregory, PO Box 47, Cooper 75432

Denton: Rudy Durham, PO Box 2816, Denton 76202

DeWitt: Beverly Malone, 103 E. Bailey St., Cuero 77954

Dickens: Patti Abbott, PO Box 180, Dickens 79229

Dimmit: Norma Carrillo, 203 W. Houston St., Carrizo Springs 78834

Donley: Paula Lowrie, PO Box 1220, Clarendon 79226

Duval: Raul Garcia, PO Box 809, San Diego 78384

Eastland: Randy Clark, PO Box 914, Eastland 76448

Ector: Anita Campbell, 1301 E. 8th St., Odessa 79761

Edwards: Judy Harris*, PO Box 858, Rocksprings 78880

Ellis: Kathy Rodrigue, PO Box 878, Waxahachie 75168

El Paso: Dinah Kilgore, 5801 Trowbridge Dr., El Paso 79925

Erath: Jerry Lee, 1195 W. South Loop, Stephenville 76401

Falls: Allen McKinley, 403 Craik St., Marlin 76661

Fannin: Michael Jones, 831 W. State Hwy. 56, Bonham 75418

Fayette: Richard Moring, PO Box 836, La Grange 78945

Fisher: Kellen Walker, PO Box 516, Roby 79543

Floyd: Jim Finley, PO Box 249, Floydada 79235

Foard: Jo Ann Vecera, PO Box 419, Crowell 79227

Fort Bend: Glen Whitehead, 2801 B.F. Terry Blvd., Rosenberg 77471

Franklin: Genea Burnaman, PO Box 720, Mount Vernon 75457

Freestone: Bud Black, 218 N. Mount St., Fairfield 75840

Frio: Luciano R. Gonzales, PO Box 1129, Pearsall 78061

Gaines: Gayla Harridge, PO Box 490, Seminole 79360

Galveston: Tommy Watson, 9850 Emmet F Lowry Exp., Ste. A, Texas City 77591

Garza: Diane Josey, PO Drawer F, Post 79356

Gillespie: Scott Fair, 1159 S. Milam, Fredericksburg 78624

Glasscock: Priscilla A. Ginnetti, PO Box 155, Garden City 79739

Goliad: Richard Miller, PO Box 34, Goliad 77963

Gonzales: John Liford, PO Box 867, Gonzales 78629

Gray: Tyson Paronto, PO Box 836, Pampa 79066

Grayson: Shawn Coker, 515 N. Travis, Sherman 75090

Gregg: Libby Neely, 4367 W. Loop 281, Longview 75604

Grimes: Mark Boehnke, PO Box 489, Anderson 77830

Guadalupe: Jamie Osborne, 3000 N. Austin St., Seguin 78155

Hale: Nikki Branscum, PO Box 29, Plainview 79073

Hall: Gina Chavira, 512 W. Main St., Ste. 14, Memphis 79245

Hamilton: Doyle Roberts, 119 E. Henry St., Hamilton 76531

Hansford: Brandi Thompson, 709 W. 7th Ave., Spearman 79081

Hardeman: Richard Petree*, PO Box 388, Quanah 79252

Hardin: Crystal Smith, PO Box 670, Kountze 77625

Harris: Roland Altinger, PO Box 920975, Houston 77292

Harrison: Robert Lisman, PO Box 818, Marshall 75671

Hartley: Debbie Stribling*, PO Box 405, Hartley 79044

Haskell: Wanda Hester, PO Box 467, Haskell 79521

Hays: Laura Raven, 21001 N. IH-35, Kyle 78640

Hemphill: Pam Scates, 223 Main St., Canadian 79014

Henderson: Bill Jackson, PO Box 430, Athens 75751

Hidalgo: Rolando Garza, PO Box 208, Edinburg 78540

Hill: Mike McKibben, PO Box 416, Hillsboro 76645

Hockley: Greg Kelley, PO Box 1090, Levelland 79336

Hood: Greg Stewart, PO Box 819, Granbury 76048

Hopkins: Cathy Singleton, PO Box 753, Sulphur Springs 75483

Houston: Carey Minter, PO Box 112, Crockett 75835

Howard: Lisa Reyna, PO Box 1151, Big Spring 79721

Hudspeth: Adolfo Ramirez, PO Box 429, Sierra Blanca 79851

Hunt: Brent South, PO Box 1339, Greenville 75403

Hutchinson: Joe Raper, PO Box 5065, Borger 79008

Irion: Byron Bitner, PO Box 980, Mertzon 76941

Jack: Kathy R. Conner, PO Box 958, Jacksboro 76458

Jackson: Damon D. Moore, 404 N. Allen St., Edna 77957

Jasper: Lori Barnett*, PO Box 1300, Jasper 75951

Jeff Davis: Everett Quintana, PO Box 373, Fort Davis 79734

Jefferson: Angela Bellard, PO Box 21337, Beaumont 77720

Jim Hogg: Jorge Arellano, PO Box 459, Hebbronville 78361

Jim Wells: J. Sidney Vela, PO Box 607, Alice 78333

Johnson: Jim Hudspeth, 109 N. Main, Cleburne 76033

Jones: Kim McLemore, PO Box 348, Anson 79501

Karnes: Brian Stahl, 915 S. Panna Maria Ave., Karnes City 78118

Kaufman: Sarah Curtis, PO Box 819, Kaufman 75142

Kendall: Shelby W. Presley, 118 Market Ave., Boerne 78006

Kenedy: Thomas G. Denney, PO Box 39, Sarita 78385

Kent: Cindy Watson, PO Box 68, Jayton 79528

Kerr: Sharon Constantinides, PO Box 294387, Kerrville 78029

Kimble: Kenda McPherson, PO Box 307, Junction 76849

King: Kala Briggs, PO Box 117, Guthrie 79236

Kinney: Todd Tate, PO Box 1377, Brackettville 78832

Kleberg: Tina Flores, PO Box 1027, Kingsville 78364

Knox: Mitzi Welch, PO Box 47, Benjamin 79505

Lamar: Jerry Patton, PO Box 400, Paris 75461

Lamb: Lesa Kloiber, PO Box 950, Littlefield 79339

Lampasas: Melissa Gonzales, Box 175, Lampasas 76550

La Salle: Martin Villareal, PO Box 1530, Cotulla 78014

Lavaca: Pamela Lathrop, PO Box 386, Hallettsville 77964

Lee: James Orr, 898 E. Richmond, Ste. 100, Giddings 78942

Leon: Jeff Beshears, PO Box 536, Centerville 75833

Liberty: Lana McCarty, PO Box 10016, Liberty 77575

Limestone: Karen Wietzikoski, PO Drawer 831, Groesbeck 76642

Lipscomb: Angela Peil, PO Box 128, Darrouzett 79024

Live Oak: Debra Morin, PO Box 2370, George West 78022

Llano: Scott Dudley*, 103 E. Sandstone, Llano 78643

Loving: Sherlene Burrows, PO Box 352, Mentone 79754

Lubbock: Tim Radloff, PO Box 10542, Lubbock 79408

Lynn: Marquita Scott, PO Box 789, Tahoka 79373

Madison: Matt Newton, PO Box 1328, Madisonville 77864

Marion: Anna Lummus*, 801 North Tuttle St., Jefferson 75657

Martin: Marsha Graves, PO Box 1349, Stanton 79782

Mason: Liza Trevino, PO Box 1119, Mason 76856

Matagorda: Vince Maloney, 2225 Ave. G, Bay City 77414

Maverick: Maggie Duran, PO Box 2628, Eagle Pass 78853

McCulloch: Zane Brandenberger, 306 W. Lockhart, Brady 76825

McLennan: Andrew J. Hahn Jr., PO Box 2297, Waco 76703

McMullen: Blaine Patterson, PO Box 338, Tilden 78072

Medina: Johnette Dixon, 1410 Ave. K, Hondo 78861

Menard: Kayla Wagner, PO Box 1008, Menard 76859

Midland: Jerry Bundick, PO Box 908002, Midland 79708

Milam: Dyann White, PO Box 769, Cameron 76520

Mills: Codi Ann McCarn, PO Box 565, Goldthwaite 76844

Mitchell: Ryan Eime, 2112 Hickory St., Colorado City 79512

Montague: Kim Haralson, PO Box 121, Montague 76251

Montgomery: Tony Belinoski, PO Box 2233, Conroe 77305

Moore: Alfonso Venegas, PO Box 717, Dumas 79029

Morris: Summer Golden, PO Box 563, Daingerfield 75638

Motley: Jim Finley, PO Box 249, Floydada 79235

Nacogdoches: Gary Woods, 216 W. Hospital St., Nacogdoches 75961

Navarro: Karen Morris, PO Box 3118, Corsicana 75110

Newton: Margie L. Herrin, 109 Court St., Newton 75966

Nolan: Brenda Klepper, PO Box 1256, Sweetwater 79556

Nueces: Ramiro Canales, 201 N. Chaparral, Ste. 206, Corpus Christi 78401

Ochiltree: Burton Jones, 825 S. Main, Ste. 100, Perryton 79070

Oldham: Leann Voyles, PO Box 310, Vega 79092

Orange: Scott Overton, PO Box 457, Orange 77631

Palo Pinto: Donna E. Kozlovsky, PO Box 250, Palo Pinto 76484

Panola: Michael Douglas McPhail, 1736 Ballpark Dr., Carthage 75633

Parker: Larry Hammonds, 1108 Santa Fe Dr., Weatherford 76086

Parmer: Jill Timms, PO Box 56, Bovina 79009

Pecos: Sam Calderon III, PO Box 237, Fort Stockton 79735

Polk: Chad Hill, 114 Matthews St., Livingston 77351

Potter: Jeff Dagley, PO Box 7190, Amarillo 79114

Presidio: Cynthia Ramirez, PO Box 879, Marfa 79843

Rains: Sherri McCall, PO Box 70, Emory 75440

Randall: Jeff Dagley, PO Box 7190, Amarillo 79114

Reagan: Rhonda Shaw, PO Box 8, Big Lake 76932

Real: Juan Saucedo, Box 158, Leakey 78873

Red River: Christie Ussery, PO Box 461, Clarksville 75426

Reeves: John Huddleston, PO Box 1229, Pecos 79772

Refugio: Connie J. Raymond, PO Box 156, Refugio 78377

Roberts: James Morgan, PO Box 458, Miami 79059

Robertson: Nancy Commander, PO Box 998, Franklin 77856

Rockwall: Kevin Passons, 841 Justin Rd., Rockwall 75087

Runnels: PaulScott Randolph, PO Box 524, Ballinger 76821

Rusk: Weldon Cook, PO Box 7, Henderson 75652

Sabine: Cari Papania, PO Box 137, Hemphill 75948

San Augustine: Evelyn Watts, 122 N. Harrison St., San Augustine 75972

San Jacinto: Sherri Schell, PO Box 1170, Coldspring 77331

San Patricio: Robert Cenciw, PO Box 938, Sinton 78387

San Saba: Jan Vanderburg, 423 E. Wallace St., San Saba 76877

Schleicher: Liza Trevino, PO Box 936, Eldorado 76936

Scurry: Jackie Martin, 2612 College Ave., Snyder 79549

Shackelford: Clayton Snyder, PO Box 2247, Albany 76430

Shelby: Robert N. Pigg, 724 Shelbyville St., Center 75935

Sherman: Teresa Edmond, PO Box 239, Stratford 79084

Smith: Michael D. Barnett, 245 South S.E. Loop 323, Tyler 75702

Somervell: Wes Rollen, 112 Allen Dr., Glen Rose 76043

Starr: Rosalva Guerra, 100 N. FM 3167, Ste. 300, Rio Grande City 78582

Stephens: Gary Zeitler, PO Box 351, Breckenridge 76424

Sterling: Ronnie Krejci, PO Box 28, Sterling City 76951

Stonewall: Debra Smith, PO Box 308, Aspermont 79502

Sutton: Mary Bustamante, 300 E. Oak St., Ste. 2, Sonora 76950

Swisher: Debbie Stribling*, PO Box 8, Tulia 79088

Tarrant: Jeff Law, 2500 Handley-Ederville Rd., Fort Worth 76118

Taylor: Gary Earnest, PO Box 1800, Abilene 79604

Terrell: Blain Chriesman, PO Box 747, Sanderson 79848

Terry: Eddie Olivas, PO Box 426, Brownfield 79316

Throckmorton: Dede Smith, Box 788, Throckmorton 76483

Titus: Shirley Dickerson, PO Box 528, Mount Pleasant 75456

Tom Green: Bill Benson, 2302 Pulliam St., San Angelo 76905

Travis: Marya Crigler, PO Box 149012, Austin 78714

Trinity: Greg Gallant, PO Box 950, Groveton 75845

Tyler: David Luther, PO Drawer 9, Woodville 75979

Upshur: Amanda Thibodeaux, 105 Diamond Loch Rd., Gilmer 75644

Upton: Linda Zarate, PO Box 1110, McCamey 79752

Uvalde: Roberto Valdez, 209 N. High St., Uvalde 78801

Val Verde: Cherry Sheedy, 417 W. Cantu Rd., Del Rio 78840

Van Zandt: Scott Hyde, PO Box 926, Canton 75103

Victoria: John Haliburton, 2805 N. Navarro, Ste. 300, Victoria 77901

Walker: Raymond Kiser, PO Box 1798, Huntsville 77342

Waller: Becky Gurrola, PO Box 887, Hempstead 77445

Ward: Norma Valdez, PO Box 905, Monahans 79756

Washington: Willy Dilworth, PO Box 681, Brenham 77834

Webb: Martin Villarreal, 3302 Clark Blvd., Laredo 78043

Wharton: Tylene Gamble, 308 E. Milam, Wharton 77488

Wheeler: Kimberly Morgan, PO Box 1200, Wheeler 79096

Wichita: Lisa Stephens-Musick, PO Box 5172, Wichita Falls 76307

Wilbarger: Sandy Burkett, PO Box 1519, Vernon 76385

Willacy: Agustin Lopez, 688 FM 3168, Raymondville 78580

Williamson: Alvin Lankford, 625 FM 1460, Georgetown 78626

Wilson: Jennifer Coldewey, 1611 Railroad St., Floresville 78114

Winkler: Gary Zeitler*, PO Box 1219, Kermit 79745

Wise: Michael Hand, 400 E. Business 380, Decatur 76234

Wood: Tracy Nichols, PO Box 1706, Quitman 75783

Yoakum: Brooks Barrett, PO Box 748, Plains 79355

Young: Luke Robbins, PO Box 337, Graham 76450

Zapata: Amada Gonzalez, 200 E. 7th Ave., Ste. 240, Zapata 78076

Zavala: Juan Tapia*, 323 W. Zavala, Crystal City 78839 ☆

Wet-Dry Counties

Source: Texas Alcoholic Beverage Commission; www.tabc.state.tx.us

Although the laws regulating the alcoholic beverage industry are consistent statewide, the Alcoholic Beverage Code allows for local-option elections to determine the types of alcoholic beverages that may be sold and how they can be sold.

Elections can be held by counties, cities, or individual justice of the peace precincts. In the time since our last edition went to press, two counties have moved from Dry to Wet or Part Wet:

- Collingsworth County voted to allow alcoholic beverage sales throughout the county.
- Stanton in Martin County voted to allow beer and wine sales (off premises only).

As of August 2019, there were 55 completely wet counties in Texas and 5 completely dry counties.

Over time, Texas has been getting "wetter." In 2003, there were 35 completely wet counties and 51 completely dry. In 1995, there were 53 dry counties, and in 1986, there were 62 dry counties. The list below reflects the wet, part wet, and dry coding on the map.

Counties where all alcoholic beverage sales are legal everywhere (55): Aransas, Austin, Bexar, Brazos, Brewster, Brooks, Burnet, Cameron, Childress, Clay, Collingsworth, Colorado, Comal, Cottle, Crosby, Culberson, Dimmit, Donley, Duval, Ector, El Paso, Fayette, Fisher, Fort Bend, Goliad, Gonzales, Guadalupe, Hidalgo, Hudspeth, Jim Hogg, Kendall, Kenedy, Kinney, Kleberg, La Salle, Midland, Mitchell, Nolan, Nueces, Ochiltree, Presidio, San Saba, Scurry, Sherman, Starr, Sutton, Val Verde, Victoria, Waller, Washington, Webb, Wharton, Wilbarger, Zapata, Zavala.

Kerr, Kimble, King, Knox, Lamar, Lamb, Lampasas, Lavaca, Lee, Leon, Liberty, Limestone, Lipscomb, Live Oak, Llano, Loving, Lubbock, Lynn, Madison, Marion, Martin, Mason, Matagorda, Maverick, McCulloch, McLennan, McMullen, Medina, Menard, Milam, Mills, Montague, Montgomery, Moore, Morris, Motley, Nacogdoches, Navarro, Newton, Oldham, Orange, Palo Pinto, Panola, Parker, Parmer, Pecos, Polk, Potter, Rains, Randall, Reagan, Real, Red River, Reeves, Refugio, Robertson, Rockwall, Runnels, Rusk, Sabine, San Augustine, San Jacinto, San Patricio, Schleicher, Shackelford, Shelby, Smith, Somervell, Stephens, Sterling, Stonewall, Swisher, Tarrant, Taylor, Terrell, Terry, Titus, Tom Green, Travis, Trinity, Tyler, Upshur, Upton, Uvalde, Van Zandt, Walker, Ward, Wheeler, Wichita, Willacy, Williamson, Wilson, Winkler, Wise, Wood, Young, Yoakum.

Counties where no sales of alcoholic beverages are legal anywhere (5): Borden, Hemphill, Kent, Roberts, Throckmorton. ☆

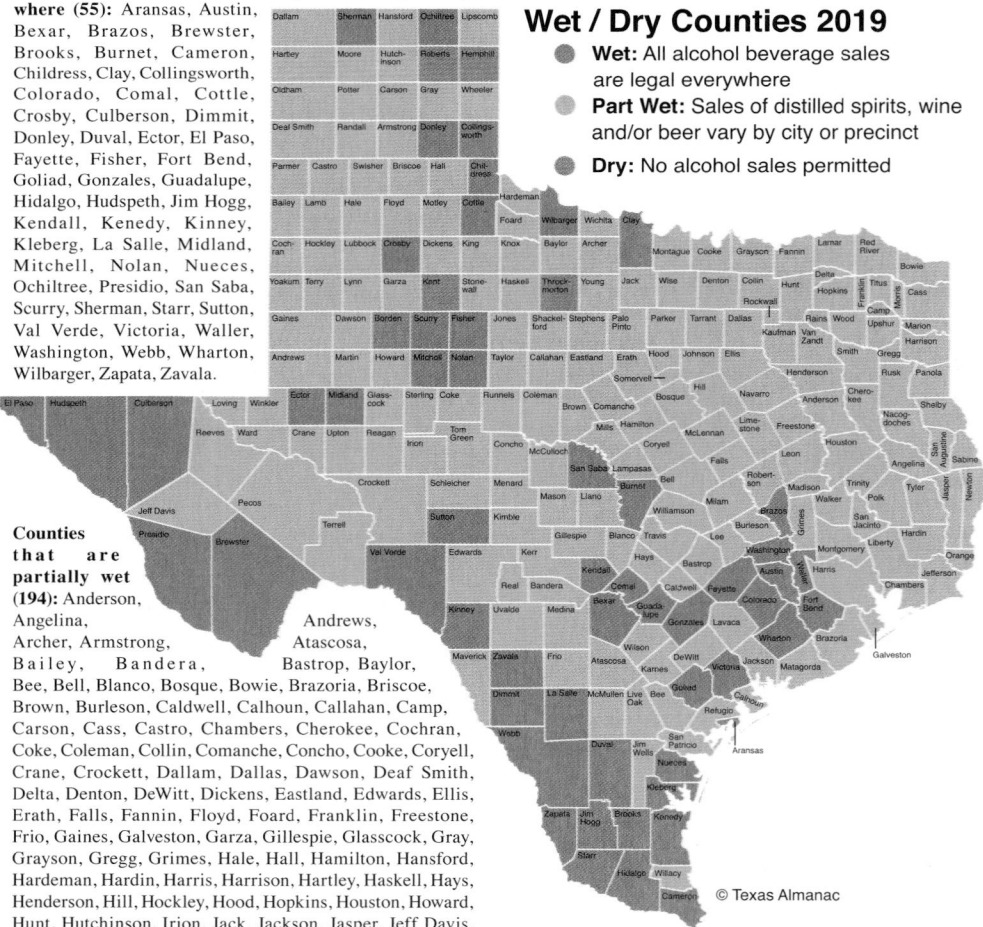

Wet / Dry Counties 2019

- **Wet:** All alcohol beverage sales are legal everywhere
- **Part Wet:** Sales of distilled spirits, wine and/or beer vary by city or precinct
- **Dry:** No alcohol sales permitted

© Texas Almanac

Counties that are partially wet (194): Anderson, Angelina, Archer, Armstrong, Atascosa, Bailey, Bandera, Bastrop, Baylor, Bee, Bell, Blanco, Bosque, Bowie, Brazoria, Briscoe, Brown, Burleson, Caldwell, Calhoun, Callahan, Camp, Carson, Cass, Castro, Chambers, Cherokee, Cochran, Coke, Coleman, Collin, Comanche, Concho, Cooke, Coryell, Crane, Crockett, Dallam, Dallas, Dawson, Deaf Smith, Delta, Denton, DeWitt, Dickens, Eastland, Edwards, Ellis, Erath, Falls, Fannin, Floyd, Foard, Franklin, Freestone, Frio, Gaines, Galveston, Garza, Gillespie, Glasscock, Gray, Grayson, Gregg, Grimes, Hale, Hall, Hamilton, Hansford, Hardeman, Hardin, Harris, Harrison, Hartley, Haskell, Hays, Henderson, Hill, Hockley, Hood, Hopkins, Houston, Howard, Hunt, Hutchinson, Irion, Jack, Jackson, Jasper, Jeff Davis, Jefferson, Jim Wells, Johnson, Jones, Karnes, Kaufman,

Texas County and District Officials — Table No. 1

County Seats, County Judges, County Clerks, County Attorneys, County Treasurers, Tax Assessors-Collectors, and Sheriffs.

See Table No. 2 on **pages 503–508** for District Clerks, District Attorneys, and County Commissioners. Judges in county courts at law, as well as probate courts, juvenile/domestic relations courts, county criminal courts, and county criminal court of appeal, can be on **pages 489–491**. The officials listed here are elected by popular vote. If no county attorney is listed, the district attorney, whose name is listed in Table No. 2, assumes the duties of that office.

County	County Seat	County Judge	County Clerk	County Attorney	County Treasurer	Assessor-Collector	Sheriff
Anderson	Palestine	Robert D. Johnston	Mark Staples	—	Tara Holliday	Teri Garvey Hanks	Greg Taylor
Andrews	Andrews	Charlie Falcon	Vicki Scott	Tim Mason	Office abolished 1/1/1986	Robin Harper	Rusty Stewart
Angelina	Lufkin	Don Lymbery	Amy Fincher	Cary Kirby	Jill Brewer	Billie Page	Greg Sanches
Aransas	Rockport	C.H. (Burt) Mills, Jr.	Valerie Amason	Kristen Barnebey	Alma Cartwright	Jeri Cox	William (Bill) Mills
Archer	Archer City	Randall C. Jackson	Karren Winter	David Levy	Patricia A. Vieth	Dawn Vieth	Staci Williams Beesinger
Armstrong	Claude	Hugh Reed	Tawnee Blodgett	—	Susan Overcast McGrath	Jamie Craig	Fleta Barnett
Atascosa	Jourdanton	Robert Hurley	Diane Gonzales	Lucinda A. Vickers	Laura Pawelek	Loretta Holley	David Soward
Austin	Bellville	Tim Lapham	Carrie Gregor	—	Bryan Haevischer	Kim Rinn	Jack Brandes
Bailey	Muleshoe	Sherri Harrison	Robin Dickerson	Jackie R. Claborn, II	Shonda L. Black	Maria Gonzalez	Richard Wills
Bandera	Bandera	Richard Evans	Tandie Mansfield	Janna Lindig	Beverly Schmidt	Gwenda L. Tschirhart	Dan Butts
Bastrop	Bastrop	Paul Pape	Rose Pietsch	—	Laurie Ingram	Linda Harmon	Maurice Cook
Baylor	Seymour	Rusty A. Stafford	Chris Jakubicek	Cody Robinette	Kevin Hostas	Jeanette Holub	Jason Zeissel
Bee	Beeville	Stephanie Moreno	Nickelle Gonzales	Michael Knight	Office abolished 1/1/1983	Linda G. Bridge	Alden E. Southmayd, III
Bell	Belton	David Blackburn	Shelley Coston	James E. (Jim) Nichols	Gaylon Evans	Shay Luedeke	Eddy Lange
Bexar	San Antonio	Nelson W. Wolff	Lucy Adame-Clark	—	Office abolished 1/1/1985	Albert Uresti	Javier Salazar
Blanco	Johnson City	Brett Bray	Laura Walla	Deborah Earley	Camille Swift	Kristen Spies	Don Jackson
Borden	Gail	Ross D. Sharp	Jana Underwood	Marlo Holbrooks	Shawna Gass	Benny Allison	Benny Allison
Bosque	Meridian	Don Pool	Tab Ferguson	Natalie Koehler	Carla Sigler	Arlene Swiney	Anthony Malott
Bowie	New Boston	James Carlow	Tina Petty	—	Donna Burns	Ramona Dawson-Norman	James Prince
Brazoria	Angleton	L.M. (Matt) Sebesta, Jr.	Joyce Hudman	—	Cathy Campbell	Ro'Vin Garrett	Charles S. Wagner
Brazos	Bryan	Duane Peters	Karen McQueen	Rod Anderson	Laura Taylor Davis	Kristeen Roe	Christopher C. Kirk
Brewster	Alpine	Eleazar R. Cano	Berta Rios-Martinez	J. Steve Houston	Julie K. Morton	Betty Jo Rooney	Ronny Dodson
Briscoe	Silverton	Wayne Nance	Bena Hester	Emily Teegardin	Mary Jo Brannon	Jon Etta Ziegler	Garrett Davis
Brooks	Falfurrias	Eric Ramos	Elvaray B. Silvas	David T. Garcia	Alan Hernandez	Urbino (Benny) Martinez	Urbino (Benny) Martinez
Brown	Brownwood	Paul D. Lilly	Sharon Ferguson	Shane Britton	Ann Krpoun	Christine Pentecost	Vance Hill
Burleson	Caldwell	Keith Schroeder	Anna L. Schielack	Susan Deski	Stephanie Smith	Cheryl Castaneda	Thomas Norsworthy
Burnet	Burnet	James Oakley	Janet Parker	Eddie Arredondo	Karrie Crownover	Sheri Frazier	Calvin Boyd
Caldwell	Lockhart	Hoppy Haden	Teresa Rodriguez	—	Angela Meuth Rawlinson	Darla Law	Daniel C. Law
Calhoun	Port Lavaca	Richard Meyer	Anna Goodman	—	Rhonda Kokena	Gloria Ochoa	Bobbie Vickery
Callahan	Baird	G. Scott Kniffen	Nicole Crocker	Shane Deel	Jan Windham	Tammy Walker	Terry Joy
Cameron	Brownsville	Eddie Treviño, Jr.	Sylvia Garza-Perez	James (Jas) W. Wallace, III	David A. Betancourt	Tony Yzaguirre, Jr.	Omar Lucio
Camp	Pittsburg	A.J. Mason	Elaine Young	—	Kim Pittman	Gale Burns	Alan D. McCandless
Carson	Panhandle	Dan Looten	Celeste Bichsel	Scott Sherwood	Denise Salzbrenner	Jackie Moore	Loren Brand
Cass	Linden	Becky Wilbanks	Amy L. Varnell	—	Donna Early	Angela Young	Larry Rowe
Castro	Dimmitt	Carroll Gerber	JoAnna Blanco	Shalyn Hamlin	Elaine D. Flynt	Pam Rickert	Salvador Rivera
Chambers	Anahuac	Jimmy Sylvia	Heather Hawthorne	Scott R. Peal	Nicole M. Whittington	Denise Hutter	Brian C. Hawthorne

County	County Seat	County Judge	County Clerk	County Attorney	County Treasurer	Assessor-Collector	Sheriff
Cherokee	Rusk	Chris Davis	Laverne Lusk	Dana Young	Erin Curtis	Linda Little	James Campbell
Childress	Childress	Jay Mayden	Barbara Spitzer	Greg Buckley	Brenda Overstreet	Kathy Dobbs	Michael (Mike) Pigg
Clay	Henrietta	Mike Campbell	Sasha Kelton	Seth C. Slagle	Danja Bloodworth	Maribel Longoria	K.R. (Kenny) Lemons, Jr.
Cochran	Morton	Pat Sabala Henry	Shanna Dewbre	Angela Overman	Doris Sealy	Treva Jackson	Jorge De La Cruz
Coke	Robert Lee	Hal Spain	Monica Reyes	Nicholas (Nick) E. Arrott, II	Therese Emert	Josie Dean	Wayne McCutchen
Coleman	Coleman	Billy D. Bledsoe	Stacey Mendoza	Joe Lee Rose	Jerri Ann Chambers	Jamie Trammell	Les Cogdill
Collin	McKinney	Chris Hill	Stacey Kemp	—	Office abolished 1/1/1985	Kenneth Maun	Jim Skinner
Collingsworth	Wellington	John James	Jackie Johnson	Gaylon Davis	Gina Harris	Generah Manuel	Kent Riley
Colorado	Columbus	Ty Prause	Kimberly Menke	Jay E. Johannes	Joyce Guthmann	Mary Jane Poenitzsch	R.H. (Curly) Wied
Comal	New Braunfels	Sherman Krause	Bobbie Koepp	—	Renee Couch	Cathy Talcott	Mark Reynolds
Comanche	Comanche	Stephanie Davis	Ruby Lesley	Craig Willingham	Patsy Phifer	Grace Everhart	Jeff D. Lambert
Concho	Paint Rock	David Dillard	Phyllis F. Lovell	Bryan Clayton	Jenifer Gierisch	Chad Miller	Chad Miller
Cooke	Gainesville	Jason Brinkley	Pam Harrison	Edmund J. Zielinski	Patty Brennan	Brandy Ann Carr	Terry Gilbert
Coryell	Gatesville	Roger A. Miller	Barbara Simpson	Brandon Belt	Randi McFarlin	Justin K. Carothers	Scott Williams
Cottle	Paducah	Karl Holloway	Vickey Wederski	Greg Buckley	Crystal Tucker	Nakia Hargrave	Mark Box
Crane	Crane	Roy Hodges	Judy Crawford	Austin Rawls	Sheila Pahl	Judy Crumrine	Andrew Aguilar
Crockett	Ozona	Fred Deaton	Ninfa Preddy	Jody K. Upham	Laura Conner	Michelle Medley	Robert (Bob) Rodriguez
Crosby	Crosbyton	David Wigley	Tammy Marshall	Michael Sales	Debra Riley	Anna Rodriguez	Ethan Villanueva
Culberson	Van Horn	Carlos G. Urias	Linda McDonald	Stephen Mitchell	Adrian Hinojos	Amalia Hernandez	Oscar Carrillo
Dallam	Dalhart	Wes Ritchey	Terri Banks	Jon King	Kenda McKay	Jami Parr	Shane Stevenson
Dallas	Dallas	Clay Jenkins	John F. Warren	—	Pauline Medrano	John R. Ames	Marian Brown
Dawson	Lamesa	Foy O'Brien	Clare Christy	Steven B. Payson	Terri Stahl	Sylvia Ortiz	Matt Hogg
Deaf Smith	Hereford	D.J. Wagner	Rachel Garman	—	Karen Smith	Teresa Garth	J. Dale Butler
Delta	Cooper	Jason Murray	Jane Jones	Jay Garrett	Debbie Huie	Dawn Stewart	Ricky Smith
Denton	Denton	Andy Eads	Juli Luke	—	Cindy Yeatts Brown	Michelle French	Tracy Murphree
DeWitt	Cuero	Daryl L. Fowler	Natalie Carson	Raymond Reese	Carol Ann Martin	Ashley D. Mraz	Carl Bowen
Dickens	Dickens	Kevin Brendle	Becky Hill	Aaron Clements	Darla Thomason	Rebecca Haney	Terry Braly
Dimmit	Carrizo Springs	Francisco G. Ponce	Mario Z. Garcia	Daniel Gonzalez	Estanislado Martinez	Mary E. Sandoval	Marion Boyd
Donley	Clarendon	John C. Howard	Fay Vargas	Landon Lambert	Wanda Smith	Linda Crump	Charles (Butch) Blackburn
Duval	San Diego	Gilbert N. Saenz	Elodia M. Garza	Baldemar Gutierrez	Sylvia Lazo	Roberto Elizondo	Romeo R. Ramirez
Eastland	Eastland	Rex Fields	Cathy Jentho	—	Christina Dodrill	Andrea May	Wayne Bradford
Ector	Odessa	Debi Hays	Jennifer Martin	Dusty Gallivan	Cleopatra Anderson	Lindy Wright	Mike Griffis
Edwards	Rocksprings	Souli Asa Shanklin	Olga Lydia Reyes	Allen Ray Moody	Lupe Sifuentes-Enriquez	Lorri Garcia Ruiz	Pamela Elliott
Ellis	Waxahachie	Todd Little	Krystal Valdez	Patrick Wilson	Cheryl Chambers	John Bridges	Charles (Chuck) Edge
El Paso	El Paso	Ricardo A. Samaniego	Delia Briones	Jo Anne Bernal	Office abolished 1/1/1986	Ruben P. Gonzalez	Richard D. Wiles
Erath	Stephenville	Alfonso Campos	Gwinda Jones	Lisa Pence	Kimberly Barrier	Jennifer Carey	Matt Coates
Falls	Marlin	Jay Elliott	Linda Watkins	Kathryn (Jody) Gilliam	Sheryl Pringle	Kayci Nehring	Ricky Scaman
Fannin	Bonham	Randy Moore	Tammy Biggar	Richard Glaser	David E. Woodson	Gail Young	Mark Johnson
Fayette	La Grange	Joe Weber	Brenda Fietsam	Peggy Supak	Office abolished 1/2/1988	Rosalinda Adamcik	Keith Korenek
Fisher	Roby	Ken Holt	Pat Thomson	Michael Hall	Jeanna Parks	Jonnye Gibson	Allan Arnwine
Floyd	Floydada	Marty Lucke	Ginger Morgan	Lex Herrington	Lori Morales	Delia Suarez	Paul Raissez
Foard	Crowell	Mark Christopher	Debra Hopkins	Marshall Capps	Darcy Moore	Mike Brown	Mike Brown
Fort Bend	Richmond	KP George	Laura Richard	Roy L. Cordes, Jr.	Bill Rickert	Carrie Surratt	Troy E. Nehls
Franklin	Mount Vernon	Scott Lee	Betty Crane	Gene Stump	Betty Sue Allen	Sue Ann Harper	Ricky Jones

County	County Seat	County Judge	County Clerk	County Attorney	County Treasurer	Assessor-Collector	Sheriff
Freestone	Fairfield	Linda Grant	Linda Jarvis	Brian Evans	Jeannie Keeney	Lisa Foree	Jeremy Shipley
Frio	Pearsall	Arnulfo C. Luna	Angie Tullis	Joseph Sindon	Pete Jasso Martinez	Anna Alaniz	Albert De Leon
Gaines	Seminole	Tom Keyes	Terri Berry	Joe H. Nagy, Jr.	Michael Lord, Jr.	Susan Shaw	Ronny Pipkin
Galveston	Galveston	Mark Henry	Dwight D. Sullivan	—	Kevin C. Walsh	Cheryl E. Johnson	Henry Trochesset
Garza	Post	Lee Norman	Jim Plummer	Ted Weems	LuAnne Terry	Nancy Wallace	Terry Morgan
Gillespie	Fredericksburg	Mark Stroeher	Mary Lynn Rusche	Christopher G. Nevins	Kelly Eckhardt	Vicki J. Schmidt	Buddy Mills
Glasscock	Garden City	Kim Halfmann	Rebecca Batla	Hardy Wilkerson	Alan Dierschke	Tina Flores	Keith Burnett
Goliad	Goliad	Mike Bennett	Mary Ellen Flores	Rob Baiamonte	Bryan Howard	Michelle Garcia	Kirby Brumby
Gonzales	Gonzales	Patrick C. Davis	Lona Ackman	Paul Watkins	Sheryl Barborak	Crystal Cedillo	Matt Atkinson
Gray	Pampa	Chris Porter	Jeanne Horton	Josh Seabourn	Scott Hahn	Gaye Whitehead	Michael Ryan
Grayson	Sherman	Bill Magers	Wilma Bush	—	Gayla Hawkins	Bruce Stidham	Tom Watt
Gregg	Longview	Bill Stoudt	Michelle Gilley	—	Office abolished 1/1/1988	Kirk Shields	Maxey Cerliano
Grimes	Anderson	Joe Fauth, III	Vanessa Burzynski	Jon C. Fultz	Janice Trant	Mary Ann Waters	Donald G. Sowell
Guadalupe	Seguin	Kyle Kutscher	Teresa Kiel	Dave Willborn	Linda Douglass	Daryl John	Arnold S. Zwicke
Hale	Plainview	David Mull	Latrice Kemp	James Tirey	Ida Tyler	Roland Nash	David Cochran
Hall	Memphis	Ray Powell	Raye Bailey	John M. Deaver, II	Janet Bridges	Teresa Altman	Thomas Heck
Hamilton	Hamilton	W. Mark Tynes	Kiesha Baqwell	Mark Henkes	Shawna Dyer	Terry Payne Short	Justin Caraway
Hansford	Spearman	Benny D. Wilson	Janet Torres	Cheryl Nelson	Lynn French	Linda Cummings	Robert Mahaffee
Hardeman	Quanah	Ronald Ingram	Ellen London	Stanley Watson	Traysha Newsom	Jan Evans	Pat Laughery
Hardin	Kountze	Wayne McDaniel	Glenda Alston	Rebecca Walton	Deborah McWilliams	Shirley Cook	Mark Davis
Harris	Houston	Lina Hidalgo	Diane Trautman	Vince Ryan	Dylan Osborne	Ann Harris Bennett	Ed Gonzalez
Harrison	Marshall	Chad Sims	Liz Whipkey	—	Sherry Rushing	Veronica King	Tom McCool
Hartley	Channing	Ronnie Gordon	Melissa Mead	Robert Elliott	Dinkie Parman	Franky Scott	Franky Scott
Haskell	Haskell	Kenny Thompson	Bella Abila	Kris Fouts	Stacia Leach	Connie Benton	Winston Stephens
Hays	San Marcos	Ruben Becerra	Elaine H. Cárdenas	—	Britney Bolton Richey	Jenifer O'Kane	Gary Cutler
Hemphill	Canadian	George Briant	Lisa Johnson	Kyle Miller	Kay Smallwood	Debra L. Ford	Nathan Lewis
Henderson	Athens	Wade McKinney	Mary Margaret Wright	Clint Davis	Michael Bynum	Peggy Goodall	Botie Hillhouse
Hidalgo	Edinburg	Richard F. Cortez	Arturo Guajardo, Jr.	—	Lita Leo	Pablo (Paul) Villarreal, Jr.	J.E. (Eddie) Guerra
Hill	Hillsboro	Justin W. Lewis	Nicole Tanner	David Holmes	Rhonda Burkhart	Krissi Hightower	Rodney B. Watson
Hockley	Levelland	Sharla Baldridge	Jennifer Nicole Palermo	Anna Hord	Denise Bohannon	Debra C. Bramlett	Ray Scifres
Hood	Granbury	Ron Massingill	Katie Lang	Matthew A. Mills	Leigh Ann McCoy	Teresa McCoy	Roger Deeds
Hopkins	Sulphur Springs	Robert Newsom	Tracy Smith	Dusty Rabe	Danny Davis	Debbie Pogue Mitchell	Lewis Tatum
Houston	Crockett	Jim L. Lovell	Terri Meadows	Daphne Lynnette Session	Janis Omelina	Danette Millican	Darrel Bobbitt
Howard	Big Spring	Kathryn Wiseman	Brent Zitterkopf	Joshua Hamby	Sharon Adams	Tiffany Sayles	Stan Parker
Hudspeth	Sierra Blanca	Mike Doyal	Virginia Doyal	C.R. (Kit) Bramblett	Gwen Wilbanks	Patricia Rose	Arvin West
Hunt	Greenville	Bobby W. Stovall	Jennifer Lindenzweig	Joel Littlefield	Brittni Turner	Randy L. Wineinger	Randy Meeks
Hutchinson	Stinnett	Cindy Irwin	Jan Barnes	Mike Milner	Kathy Sargent	Carrie Kimmell	Kirk Coker
Irion	Mertzon	Molly Criner	Shirley Graham Miles	James Ridge	Carolyn Huelster	Joyce Gray	W.A. Estes
Jack	Jacksboro	Brian Keith Umphress	Vanessa James	Michael Brad Dixon	Brad Campsey	Sharon Robinson	Tommy Spurlock
Jackson	Edna	Jill S. Sklar	Katherine R. Brooks	—	Mary Horton	Monica Foster	A.J. (Andy) Louderback
Jasper	Jasper	Mark Allen	Debbie Newman	—	Rene Kelley-Ellis	Bobby Biscamp	Mitchel Newman
Jeff Davis	Fort Davis	Kerith Sproul-Hurley	Jennifer Wright	Teresa L. Todd	Dawn Kitts	William (Bill) Kitts	William (Bill) Kitts
Jefferson	Beaumont	Jeff Branick	Carolyn Guidry	—	Charlie Hallmark	Allison Nathan Getz	Zena Stephens
Jim Hogg	Hebbronville	Juan Carlos Guerra	Zonia G. Morales	Aurora Eliza Garcia	Gloria (Gigi) Benavides	Norma Lisa S. Hinojosa	Erasmo Alarcon, Jr.

County	County Seat	County Judge	County Clerk	County Attorney	County Treasurer	Assessor-Collector	Sheriff
Jim Wells	Alice	Juan Rodriguez, Jr.	J.C. Perez, III	Michael Guerra	Mark Dominguez	Mary Lozano	Danny Bueno
Johnson	Cleburne	Roger Harmon	Becky Ivey	Bill Moore	Kathy Blackwell	Scott Porter	Adam King
Jones	Anson	Dale Spurgin	LeeAnn Jennings	Chad Cowan	Amber Thompson	Gloria Little	Danny Jimenez
Karnes	Karnes City	Wade J. Hedtke	Carol Swize	Jennifer M. Dillingham	Vi Swierc	Brenda Janysek	Dwayne Villanueva
Kaufman	Kaufman	Hal Richards	Laura Hughes	—	Chuck Mohnkern	Brenda Samples	Bryan Beavers
Kendall	Boerne	Darrel L. Lux	Darlene Herrin	—	Sheryl D'Spain	James Hudson	Al Auxier
Kenedy	Sarita	Louis E. (Bud) Turcotte, III	Veronica Vela	Allison Strauss	Cynthia M. Salinas	Sandra G. Burns	Ramon Salinas, III
Kent	Jayton	Jim White	Craig Harrison	Bill Ballard	Christy Long	William Scogin	William Scogin
Kerr	Kerrville	Rob Kelly	Jackie (JD) Dowdy	Heather Stebbins	Tracy Soldan	Bob Reeves	W.R. (Rusty) Hierholzer
Kimble	Junction	Delbert R. Roberts	Haydee Torres	Andrew James Heap	Jolene Williams	Hilario Cantu	Hilario Cantu
King	Guthrie	Duane Lee Daniel	Jammye D. Timmons	—	Denise Beck	Sadie Spitzer	Mike McWhirter
Kinney	Brackettville	Tully Shahan	Rick Alvarado	Todd Durden	Diana Gutierrez	Martha Peña-Padron	Brad Coe
Kleberg	Kingsville	Rudy Madrid	Stephanie G. Garza	Kira Talip	Priscilla Alaniz Cantu	Melissa Trevino-De La Garza	Richard Kirkpatrick
Knox	Benjamin	Stan Wojcik	Lisa Cypert	Lina Reyes Trevino	Rosie Ake	Mitzi Welch	Dean Homstad
Lamar	Paris	Brandon Bell	Ruth Sisson	Gary Young	Nicki Bridgers	Haskell Maroney	Scott Cass
Lamb	Littlefield	James M. DeLoach	Tonya Ritchie	Scott A. Say	Jerry Yarbrough	Brenda Goheen	Gary Maddox
Lampasas	Lampasas	Randall J. Hoyer	Connie Hartman	John K. Greenwood	Melissa Karcher	Linda Crawford	Jesus (Jess) G. Ramos
La Salle	Cotulla	Joel Rodriguez, Jr.	Margarita Esqueda	Elizabeth Martinez	Maria Perez	Dora A. Gonzales	Miguel A. Rodriquez
Lavaca	Hallettsville	Tramer J. Woytek	Elizabeth A. Kouba	John Stuart Fryer	Karen Bludau	Deborah A. Sevcik	Micah Harmon
Lee	Giddings	Paul E. Fischer	Sharon Blasig	Martin Placke	Melinda (Lyndy) Krause	David Matthietz	Rodney W. Meyer
Leon	Centerville	Byron Ryder	Christie Wakefield	James (Caleb) Henson	Brandi S. Hill	Robin Shafer	Kevin Ellis
Liberty	Liberty	Jay H. Knight	Lee Haidusek Chambers	Matthew Posten	Kim Harris	Richard Brown	Robert (Bobby) Rader
Limestone	Groesbeck	Richard Duncan	Kerrie Cobb	William Roy DeFriend	Carol Pickett	Stacy L. Hall	Dennis Wilson
Lipscomb	Lipscomb	Mickey Simpson	Kim Blau	Matthew D. Bartosiewicz	Kimberly L. Long	Gailan Winegarner	Kenneth Eggleston
Live Oak	George West	Jim Huff	Ida Vasquez	Dwayne McWilliams	Nancy Coquat	Mari Gonzales	Larry Busby
Llano	Llano	Ron Cunningham	Marci Hadeler	Rebecca Lange	Teresa Kassell	Kris Fogelberg	Bill Blackburn
Loving	Mentone	Skeet Lee Jones	Mozelle Carr	Stephen Simonsen	Regina Wilkinson	Sherlene Burrows	Chris H. Busse
Lubbock	Lubbock	Curtis Parrish	Kelly Pinion	—	Chris Winn	Ronnie Keister	Kelly S. Rowe
Lynn	Tahoka	Mike Braddock	Susan Tipton	Rebekah Filley	Amy Schuknecht	Donna Willis	Abraham Vega
Madison	Madisonville	A.J. (Tony) Leago	Susanne Morris	—	Judi Delesandri	Karen M. Lane	Travis Neeley
Marion	Jefferson	Leward J. LaFleur	Vickie Smith	Angela Smoak	Terrie S. Neuville	Karen Jones	David McKnight
Martin	Stanton	Bryan Cox	Linda Gonzales	James Napper	Cynthia O'Donnell	Kathy Hull	Brad Ingram
Mason	Mason	Jerry Bearden	Pam Beam	Rebekah Whitworth	Polly McMillan	James (Buster) Nixon	James (Buster) Nixon
Matagorda	Bay City	Nate McDonald	Stephanie Wurtz	Denise M. Fortenberry	Loretta K. Griffin	Cristyn E. Hallmark	Frank D. Osborne
Maverick	Eagle Pass	David Saucedo	Sara Montemayor	Gloria Hernandez	Rito Valdez	Isamari Villarreal	Tom Schmerber
McCulloch	Brady	Bill Spiller	Christine Jones-Patterson	Mark A. Marshall	Steven Estes	Silvia Campos	John Dagen
McLennan	Waco	Scott Felton	Andy Harwell	—	Bill Helton	Randy H. Riggs	Parnell McNamara
McMullen	Tilden	James E. Teal	Mattie S. Sadovsky	Kimberly Kreider-Dusek	Jill Atkinson	Bessilia (Bessie) Guerrero	Emmett Shelton
Medina	Hondo	Chris Schuchart	Gina Champion	Kim Havel	Debbie Southwell	Melissa Lutz	Randy Brown
Menard	Menard	Richard Cordes	Christy Eggleston	Tom Roberson	Ron Wood	Tim Powell	Buck Miller
Midland	Midland	Terry Johnson	Alison Haley	Russell Malm	Mitzi Baker	Karen Hood	Gary Painter
Milam	Cameron	Steve Young	Jodi Morgan	Bill Torrey	Linda Acosta	Sherry Mueck	Chris White
Mills	Goldthwaite	Ed Smith	Carolyn Foster	Gerald Hale	Terrena Busby	Lori King	Clint Hammonds

County	County Seat	County Judge	County Clerk	County Attorney	County Treasurer	Assessor-Collector	Sheriff
Mitchell	Colorado City	Ray Mayo	Debby Carlock	Sterling T. Burleson, II	Jennifer Riveria	Sylvia Clanton	Patrick Toombs
Montague	Montague	Rick Lewis	Glenda Henson	Clay V. Riddle	LaVonda langford	Kathryn Phillips	Marshall Thomas
Montgomery	Conroe	Mark Keough	Mark Turnbull	B.D. Griffin	Melanie K. Bush	Tammy J. McRae	Rand Henderson
Moore	Dumas	Rowdy Rhoades	Brenda McKanna	Scott Higginbotham	Pam Cox	Nikki McDonald	J.E. (Bo) DeArmond
Morris	Daingerfield	Doug Reeder	Scott Sartain	Steve Cowan	Molly Cummings	Kim Thomasson	Jack Martin
Motley	Matador	James B. (Jim) Meador	Lindsey Aldrich	Tom Edwards	Misty Jones	Jana Marshall	Robert Fisk
Nacogdoches	Nacogdoches	Greg Sowell	June Clifton	John Fleming	Denise Baublet	Kim Morton	Jason Bridges
Navarro	Corsicana	H.M. Davenport, Jr.	Sherry Dowd	—	Ryan Douglas	Mike Dowd	Elmer Tanner
Newton	Newton	Kenneth Weeks	Sandra K. Duckworth	—	Ginger Slau	Melissa J. Burks	Billy Rowles
Nolan	Sweetwater	Whitley May	Sharla Keith	Lisa Peterson	Jeanne Wells	Kathy Bowen	David Warren
Nueces	Corpus Christi	Barbara Canales	Kara Sands	Laura Garza Jimenez	*Office abolished 1/1/1988*	Kevin Kieschnick	J.C. Hooper
Ochiltree	Perryton	Charles E. Kelly	Cassi Laxton	Jose N. Meraz	Britney Meraz	Linda Womble	Terry Bouchard
Oldham	Vega	Don R. Allred	Darla Lookingbill	Kent Birdsong	Sherri Johnson	Linda Brown	Brent Warden
Orange	Orange	Carl Thibodeaux	Brandy Robertson	John Kimbrough	Christy Khoury	Karen Fisher	Keith Merritt
Palo Pinto	Palo Pinto	Shane Long	Janette K. Green	Maegan Kostiha	Tanya Fallin	Stacy L. Choate	Brett E. McGuire
Panola	Carthage	LeeAnn Jones	Bobbie Davis	—	Joni Reed	Holly Gibbs	Kevin Lake
Parker	Weatherford	Pat Deen	Lila Deakle	John Forrest	Jenny Barnwell	Jenny Gentry	Larry Fowler
Parmer	Farwell	Trey Ellis	Susie Spring	Jeff W. Actkinson	Sharon May	Awyna Sanchez	Randy Geries
Pecos	Fort Stockton	Joe Shuster	Liz Chapman	Frank Lacy	Sonia Murphy	Santa S. Acosta	Cliff Harris
Polk	Livingston	Sydney Murphy	Schelana Hock	—	Terri Williams	Leslie Jones Burks	Kenneth Hammack
Potter	Amarillo	Nancy Tanner	Julie Smith	Scott Brumley	Leann Jennings	Sherri Aylor	Brian Thomas
Presidio	Marfa	Cinderela Guevara	Virginia Pallarez	Rod Ponton	Frances Garcia	Natalia Williams	Danny Dominquez
Rains	Emory	Wayne Wolfe	Linda Wallace	Robert Vititow	Teresa Northcutt	Sheila Floyd	David Traylor
Randall	Canyon	Ernie Houdashell	Susan Allen	—	Angie Parker	Christina McMurray	Joel W. Richardson
Reagan	Big Lake	Larry Isom	Terri Curry	Chad Elkins	Ginna Hruska	Cynthia Aguilar	Jeff N. Garner
Real	Leakey	Bella A. Rubio	D'Ann Green	Bobby Jack Rushing	Mairi Gray	Donna Brice	Nathan T. Johnson
Red River	Clarksville	L.D. Williamson	Shawn Weemes	Val Varley	Sandra Embrey	Tonya R. Martin	Jimmy Caldwell
Reeves	Pecos	Leo Hung	Dianne O. Florez	Alva Alvarez	Zulema Rodriguez	Rosemary Chabarria	Arturo (Art) Granado
Refugio	Refugio	Robert Blaschke	Ida Ramirez	Deborah A. Bauer	Rita Trojcak	Ida Turner	Raul (Pinky) Gonzales
Roberts	Miami	Rick L. Tennant	Toni Rankin	William P. Weiman	Amy Tennant	Hether Williams	Dana Miller
Robertson	Franklin	Charles L. Ellison	Stephanie Sanders	W. Coty Siegert	Melinda Turner	Michael Brewer	Gerald Yezak
Rockwall	Rockwall	David Sweet	Shelli Miller	—	David Peek	Kim Sweet	Harold Eavenson
Runnels	Ballinger	Barry Hilliard	Julia Miller	Kenneth Slimp	Ann Strube	Robin Burgess	Carl L. Squyres
Rusk	Henderson	Joel Hale	Trudy McGill	Micheal E. Jimerson	Andy Vinson	Lanita Whitehead	Jeff Price
Sabine	Hemphill	Daryl Melton	Janice McDaniel	Robert G. Neal, Jr.	Tricia Jacks	Martha M. Stone	Thomas N. Maddox
San Augustine	San Augustine	Jeff Boyd	Margo Noble	Wesley Hoyt	Pam Smith	Regina Barthol	Robert Cartwright
San Jacinto	Coldspring	Fritz Faulkner	Dawn Wright	—	Dianna (Dee Dee) Adams	Betty Davis	Greg Capers
San Patricio	Sinton	David Krebs	Gracie Alaniz-Gonzales	Tamara Cochran-May	Denise Janak	Dalia Sanchez	Oscar Rivera
San Saba	San Saba	Byron Theodosis	Kim Wells	Randall Robinson	Lois VanBeck	Greg McGregor	Greg McGregor
Schleicher	Eldorado	Charlie Bradley	Mary Ann Gonzalez	Clint T. Griffin	Jennifer L. Henderson	Vanessa Covarrubiaz	David R. Doran
Scurry	Snyder	Dan Hicks	Melody Appleton	Michael Hartman	Nelda Colvin	Jana Young	Trey Wilson
Shackelford	Albany	Robert Skelton	Cheri Hawkins	Colton P. Johnson	Tammy Brown	Edward A. Miller	Edward A. Miller
Shelby	Center	Allison Harbison	Jennifer Fountain	Gary W. Rholes	Ann Blackwell	Debora Riley	Willis Blackwell
Sherman	Stratford	Terri Beth Carter	Laura Rogers	Kim Allen	Doris Parsons	Valerie McAlister	Ted Allen

County	County Seat	County Judge	County Clerk	County Attorney	County Treasurer	Assessor-Collector	Sheriff
Smith	Tyler	Nathaniel Moran	Karen Phillips	—	Kelli R. White	Gary Barber	Larry Smith
Somervell	Glen Rose	Danny L. Chambers	Michelle Reynolds	Andrew Lucas	Susanne Graves	April Campos	Alan West
Starr	Rio Grande City	Eloy Vera	Humberto Gonzalez	Victor Canales, Jr.	Romeo Gonzalez	Ameida Salinas	Rene (Orta) Fuentes
Stephens	Breckenridge	Michael Roach	Jackie Ensey	Gary Trammel	Sharon Trigg	Christie Latham	Will Holt
Sterling	Sterling City	Deborah Horwood	Jerri McCutchen	Lili Hensley	Rhea McGinnis	Julie M. Thomason	Tim A. Sanders
Stonewall	Aspermont	Ronnie Moorhead	Holly McLaury	Riley Branch	Anya Mullen	Jim B. Ward	William (Bill) Mullen
Sutton	Sonora	Steve Smith	Rachel Chavez Duran	David W. Wallace	Janell Schniers	Kathy Sanchez Marshall	Oscar Chavez
Swisher	Tulia	Harold Keeter	C.J. Chasco	J. Michael Criswell	Tricia Speed	Deborah Lemons	Jim McCaslin
Tarrant	Fort Worth	B. Glen Whitley	Mary Louise Nicholson		Office abolished 1/1/1983	Wendy Burgess	Bill E. Waybourn
Taylor	Abilene	Downing A. Bolls, Jr.	Larry Bevill		Lesa Hart Crosswhite	Kay Middleton	Ricky Bishop
Terrell	Sanderson	Santiago Flores	Raeline Thompson	Kenneth D. Bellah	Rebecca Luevano	Keith Hughes	Keith Hughes
Terry	Brownfield	J.D. Wagner	Kim Carter	Kitha Jo'Shae Ferguson-Worley	Karen Grigsby	Rexann W. Furlow	Larry Gilbreath
Throckmorton	Throckmorton	Trey Carrington	Dianna Moore	Jeff Mathiews	Brenda Rankin	Doc Wigington	Doc Wigington
Titus	Mount Pleasant	Brian P. Lee	Joan Newman	John Mark Cobern	Sheryl Preddy	Judy Cook	Tim C. Ingram
Tom Green	San Angelo	Stephen C. Floyd	Elizabeth McGill	Chris Taylor	Dianna Spieker	Becky Robles	David Jones
Travis	Austin	Sarah Eckhardt	Dana DeBeauvoir	David Escamilla	Dolores Ortega Carter	Bruce Elfant	Sally Hernandez
Trinity	Groveton	Doug Page	Shasta Bergman	Joe Warner Bell	B.L. Dockens	Lindy Madden Warren	Woody Wallace
Tyler	Woodville	Jacques L. Blanchette	Donece Gregory		Leann Monk	Lynnette Cruse	Bryan Weatherford
Upshur	Gilmer	Todd Tefteller	Terri Ross		Brandy Vick	Luana Howell	Larry Webb
Upton	Rankin	Dusty Kilgore	LaWanda McMurray	Paige Skehan	Sharon Harper	Monica Zarate	Dan Brown
Uvalde	Uvalde	William R. Mitchell	Valerie Del Toro Romero	John Dodson	Joni Deorsam	Rita C. Verstuyft	Charlie Mendeke
Val Verde	Del Rio	Lewis Owens	Generosa Gracia-Ramon	Ana Markowski Smith	Aaron D. Rodriguez	Beatriz (Bea) I. Muñoz	Joe Frank Martinez
Van Zandt	Canton	Don Kirkpatrick	Susan Strickland		Kenny Edwards	Shirley Chisham	Dale Corbett
Victoria	Victoria	Ben Zeller	Heidi Easley		Sean Kennedy	Rena Scherer	T. Michael O'Connor
Walker	Huntsville	Danny Pierce	Kari French		Amy Klawinsky	Diana L. McRae	Clint McRae
Waller	Hempstead	Carbett (Trey) J. Duhon, III	Debbie Hollan	Elton Mathis	Joan Sargent	Ellen C. Shelburne	Glenn Smith
Ward	Monahans	Greg M. Holly	Denise Valles	Alan Nicholas	Teresa Perry-Stoner	Vicki Heflin	Mikel Strickland
Washington	Brenham	John Durrenberger	Beth A. Rothermel	Renee Ann Mueller	Peggy Kramer	Dot Borchgardt	Otto H. Hanak
Webb	Laredo	Tano E. Tijerina	Margie Ramirez Ibarra	Marco A. Montemayor	Raul Reyes	Rosie Cuellar	Martin Cuellar
Wharton	Wharton	Phillip Spenrath	Barbara Svatek	G.A. (Trey) Maffett	Donna Thornton	Grace Utley	Shannon Srubar
Wheeler	Wheeler	Jerry Hefley	Margaret Dorman	Leslie Standerfer	Renee Warren	Lewis Scott Porter	Wes Crites
Wichita	Wichita Falls	Woodrow W. (Woody) Gossom, Jr.	Lori Bohannon	—	Bob Hampton	Tommy Smyth	David Duke
Wilbarger	Vernon	Greg Tyra	Jana Kennon	Cornell Curtis	Joann Carter	Chris L. Quisenberry	Bill Price
Willacy	Raymondville	Aurelio (Keter) Guerra	Susana R. Garza	Annette C. Hinojosa	Ruben Cavazos	Elizabeth Barnhart	Larry Spence
Williamson	Georgetown	Bill Gravell, Jr.	Nancy E. Rister	Doyle (Dee) Hobbs, Jr.	D. Scott Heselmeyer	Larry Gaddes	Robert Chody
Wilson	Floresville	Richard L. Jackson	Eva S. Martinez	Tom Caldwell	Jan Hartl	Dawn Polasek Barnett	Joe D. Tackitt, Jr.
Winkler	Kermit	Charles M. Wolf	Shethelia Reed	Thomas Duckworth, Jr.	Geneva Baker	Minerva Soltero	Darin Mitchell
Wise	Decatur	J.D. Clark	Sherry Lemon	James Stainton	Katherine Hudson	Monte Shaw	Lane Akin
Wood	Quitman	Lucy Hebron	Kelley Price		Becky S. Burford	Carol Taylor	Thomas Castloo
Yoakum	Plains	Jim Barron	Summer Lovelace		Darla Welch	Jan Parrish	David Bryant
Young	Graham	John C. Bullock	Kay Hardin	Chris Baran	Ann Daily	Nancy Thomas	Travis Babcock
Zapata	Zapata	Joe Rathmell	Mary Jane Villarreal-Bonoan	Said Alfonso Figueroa	Romeo Salinas	Adriana Figueroa	Alonso M. Lopez
Zavala	Crystal City	Joe Luna	Michelle Bonilla	Eduardo Serna	Elizabeth Rodriguez	Cindy Martinez-Rivera	Eusevio Salinas

Texas County and District Officials — Table No. 2

District Clerks, District Attorneys, and County Commissioners

See Table No. 1 on pages 497–502 for County Seats, County Judges, County Clerks, County Attorneys, County Treasurers, Tax Assessors-Collectors, and Sheriffs. Judges in county courts at law, as well as probate courts, juvenile/domestic relations courts, and county criminal courts of appeal, can be on pages 489–491. If more than one district attorney is listed for a county, the district court number is noted in parentheses after each attorney's name. The officials listed here are elected by popular vote. If no district attorney is listed, the county attorney, whose name is listed in Table No. 1, assumes the duties of that office.

County	District Clerk	District Attorney	Comm. Precinct 1	Comm. Precinct 2	Comm. Precinct 3	Comm. Precinct 4
Anderson	Janice Staples	Allyson Mitchell	Greg Chapin	Rashad Q. Mims	Kenneth Dickson	Joey Hill
Andrews	Sherry Dushane	Tim Mason	Barney Fowler	Brad Young	Jeneane Anderegg	Jim Waldrop
Angelina	Reba Squyres	Art Bauereiss	Greg Harrison	Kenneth Timmons	Robert Louis Loggins	Bobby Cheshire
Aransas	Pam Heard	Kristen Barnebey	Jack Chaney	L.E. (Bubba) Casterline Jr.	Charles Smith	Betty Stiles
Archer	Lori Rutledge	Paige Williams	Richard Shelley	Darin Wolf	Pat Martin III	Darryl Lightfoot
Armstrong	Patricia (Trish) Sherrill	Randall C. Sims	John Britten	Parker Stewart	Tom Ferris	Philip Fletcher
Atascosa	Margaret Littleton	Rene M. Peña	Lonnie (Lon) Gillespie	William (Bill) Torans	Freddie Ogden	Bill Carroll
Austin	Sue Murphy	Travis J. Koehn	Reese Turner	Robert Wayne (Bobby) Rinn	Randy Reichardt	Douglas W. King
Bailey	Elaine Parker	Kathryn Gurley	Floyd J. (Butch) Vandiver	Mike Slayden	Joey Kindle	Juan Chavez
Bandera	Tammy Kneuper	Scott Monroe	Robert H. Grimes	Robert A. (Bobby) Harris	Andy Lee Wilkerson Sr.	Jordan (Jody) Rutherford
Bastrop	Sarah Loucks	Bryan Goertz	William M. (Willie) Piña	Clara Beckett	John Klaus	Gary (Bubba) Snowden
Baylor	Chris Jakubicek	David W. Hajek	Rick Gillispie	John Edd Nelson	Don Emsoff	Larry Burnett
Bee	Zenaida Silva	Jose Luis Aliseda Jr.	Carlos Salazar Jr.	Dennis DeWitt	Eloy Rodriguez	Kenneth Haggard
Bell	Joanna Staton	Henry L. Garza	Richard Cortese	Tim Brown	Bill Schumann	John Fisher
Bexar	Donna Kay McKinney	Nicholas (Nico) LaHood	Sergio (Chico) Rodriguez	Paul Elizondo	Kevin A. Wolff	Tommy Calvert
Blanco	Debby Elsbury	Wiley B. (Sonny) McAfee	John F. Wood	James Sultemeier	Chris W. Liesmann	Paul Granberg
Borden	Jana Underwood	Ben R. Smith	Monte Smith	Randy L. Adcock	Ernest Reyes	Joe T. Belew
Bosque	Juanita Miller	B.J. Shepherd	Douglas Day	Durwood Koonsman	Sam Leach	Ronny Liardon
Bowie	Billy Fox	Jerry Rochelle	Sammy Stone	Tom Whitten	Kelly Blackburn	Mike Carter
Brazoria	Rhonda Barchak	Jeri Yenne	Donald W. (Dude) Payne	Ryan Cade	Stacy L. Adams	David Linder
Brazos	Marc Hamlin	Jarvis Parsons	Lloyd Wassermann	Sammy Catalena	G. Kenny Mallard Jr.	Irma Cauley
Brewster	JoAnn Salgado	Rod Ponton	Luc Novovitch	Hugh Garrett	Ruben Ortega	Mike Pallanez
Briscoe	Bena Hester	Becky B. McPherson	Jimmy Burson	Wade Proctor	Dewey Estes	John Burson
Brooks	Noe Guerra	Carlos O. Garcia	Gloria Garza	Vicente Vargas	Carlos Villarreal	Jose A. (Tony) Martinez
Brown	Cheryl Jones	Michael B. Murray	Gary Worley	Joel Kelton	Wayne Shaw	Larry Traweek
Burleson	Dana Fritsche	Julie Renken	Dwayne Beran	Keith Schroeder	David Hildebrand	John B. Landolt Jr.
Burnet	Casie Walker	Wiley B. (Sonny) McAfee	Bill Neve	Russell Graeter	Ronny Hibler	Joe Don Dockery
Caldwell	Tina Morgan Freeman	Fred A. Weber	Alfredo R. Munoz	Edward (Eddie) Moses	Neto Madrigal	Joe Ivan Roland
Calhoun	Pamela Martin Hartgrove	Dan W. Heard	Roger C. Galvan	Vernon Lyssy	Neil E. Fritsch	Kenneth W. Finster
Callahan	Amber Tinsley	Shane Deel	Harold Hicks	Bryan Farmer	Tom F. Windham	Cliff Kirkham
Cameron	Eric Garza	Luis V. Saenz	Sofia C. Benavides	Alex Dominguez	David A. Garza	Dan Sanchez
Camp	Teresa Bockmon	Charles C. Bailey	Bart Townsend	Steven D. Hudnall	L.H. Henderson	Steve Lindley
Carson	Celeste Bichsel	Luke Inman	Mike Britten	James Martin	Mike Jennings	Kevin Howell
Cass	Jamie Albertson	Randal Lee	Brett Fitts	Jon Borseth	Paul Cothren	Darrell Godwin
Castro	JoAnna Blanco	Shalyn Hamlin	Tom McLain	Tim Elliott	Steve Smith	Ralph Brockman
Chambers	Patti L. Henry	Cheryl S. Lieck	Mark Huddleston	Larry G. George	Gary R. Nelson	Rusty Senac

County	District Clerk	District Attorney	Comm. Precinct 1	Comm. Precinct 2	Comm. Precinct 3	Comm. Precinct 4
Cherokee	Janet Gates	Rachel Patton	Kelly Traylor	Steven Norton	Katherine Pinotti	Byron Underwood
Childress	Barbara Spitzer	Luke Inman	Richard Decker	Mark Ross	Lyall Foster	Richard (Rick) Elliott
Clay	Marianne Bowles	Paige Williams	R.L. (Lindy) Choate	Johnny Gee	John McGregor	Richard Keen
Cochran	Shanna Dewbre	Christopher Dennis	Donnie B. Simpson	Bruce Heflin	Stacey Dunn	Reynaldo Morin
Coke	Mary Grim	Allison Palmer	Troy Gene Montgomery	Paul Williams	Gaylon L. Pitcock	Joe Sefcik
Coleman	Margie Mayo	Heath Hemphill	Mark Williams	Rick Beal	Mike Stephenson	Alan Davis
Collin	Lynn Finley	Greg Willis	Susan Fletcher	Cheryl Williams	Chris Hill	Duncan Webb
Collingsworth	Jackie Johnson	Luke Inman	Elmer Keller	Mike Hughs	Eddie Orr	Kirby Campbell
Colorado	Linda Holman	Jay Johannes	Doug Wessels	Darrell Kubesch	Tommy Hahn	Darrell Gertson
Comal	Heather Kellar	Jennifer Anne Tharp	Donna Eccleston	Scott Haag	Kevin Webb	Jen Crownover
Comanche	Brenda Dickey	B.J. Shepard	Gary D. (Corky) Underwood	Russell Gillette	Sherman L. Sides	Jimmy Dale Johnson
Concho	Phyllis F. Lovell	John Best	Trey Bradshaw	Ralph Willberg	Gary Gierisch	Aaron (Sonny) Browning Jr.
Cooke	Susan Hughes	Janice Warder	Gary Hollowell	B.C. Lemons	Alan Smith	Leon Klement
Coryell	Janice M. Gray	Dustin (Dusty) Boyd	Jack Wall	Daren Moore	Don Jones	Wyllis H. Ament
Cottle	Vickey Wederski	David W. Hajek	Jimmy W. Sweeney	Vance D. Thompson	Manuel Cruz Jr.	Marvin G. Powe
Crane	Judy Crawford	Dorothy Holguin	Tom Brown	Dennis Young	Domingo Escobedo	Ruby Martinez
Crockett	Ninfa Preddy	Laurie K. English	Frank Tambunga	Pleas Childress III	Randy Branch	Eligio Martinez
Crosby	Shari Smith	Michael Sales	Gary Jordan	Frank Mullins	Larry Wampler	James Caddell
Culberson	Linda McDonald	Jaime Esparza	Cornelio Garibay	Raul Rodriguez	Gilda Morales	Adrian Norman
Dallam	Terri Banks	David M. Green	Carl McCarty	Corey Crabtree	Don J. Bowers	Floyd French
Dallas	Felicia Pitre	Susan Hawk	Theresa Daniel	Mike Cantrell	John Wiley Price	Elba Garcia
Dawson	Pam Huse	Michael Munk	Ricky Minjarez	Joe Raines	Nicky Goode	Russell Cox
Deaf Smith	Elaine Gerber	Jim English	Pat Smith	Jerry O'Connor	Mike Brumley	Dale Artho
Delta	Jane Jones	Will Ramsay	B.V. (Rip) Templeton	Gary C. Anderson	Loyd Vandygriff	Mark Brantley
Denton	Sherri Adelstein	Paul Johnson	Hugh Coleman	Ron Marchant	Bobbie J. Mitchell	Andrew (Andy) Eads
DeWitt	Tabeth Gardner	Michael A. Sheppard	Curtis G. Afflerbach	James B. Pilchiek Sr.	James Kaiser	Richard Randle
Dickens	Becky Hill	Becky B. McPherson	Dennis Wyatt	Mike Smith	Charlie Morris	Sheldon Parsons
Dimmit	Maricela G. Gonzalez	Roberto Serna	Mike Uriegas	Alonso G. Carmona	Juan R. Carmona	Valerie Rubulcaba
Donley	Fay Vargas	Luke Inman	Mark White	Daniel Ford	Andy Wheatly	Dan Sawyer
Duval	Richard M. Barton	Omar Escobar	Alejo C. Garcia	Rene M. Perez	David Orlando Garza	Gilberto Uribe Jr.
Eastland	Tessa K. Culverhouse	Russell D. Thomason	Andy Maxwell	John (Buzzy) Rutledge	Ronnie Wilson	Robert Rains
Ector	Clarissa Webster	Robert Newton Bland IV	Eddy Shelton	Greg Simmons	Dale Childers	Armando S. Rodriguez
Edwards	Olga Lydia Reyes	Tonya S. Ahlschwede	William Epperson	Lee Sweeten	Matt Fry	Andrew Barnebey
Ellis	Melanie P. Reed	Patrick Wilson	Dennis Robinson	Lane Grayson	Paul Perry	Kyle Butler
El Paso	Norma L. Favela	Jaime E. Esparza	Carlos Leon	David Stout	Vincent Perez	Andrew R. Haggerty
Erath	Wanda Pringle	Alan Nash	Dee Stephens	Herbert Brown	Joe Brown	Scot Jackson
Falls	Christi Wideman	Kathryn Jo (Jody) Gilliam	Milton Albright	F.A. Green	Nelson Coker	Nita Wuebker
Fannin	Nancy Young	Richard Glaser	Gary Whitlock	Stanley Barker	Jerry Magness	Dean Lackey
Fayette	Virginia Wied	Peggy S. Supak	Jason B. McBroom	Gary Weishuhn	Harvey Berckenhoff	Tom Muras
Fisher	Tammy Haley	Ann Reed	Gordon Pippin	Billy Henderson	Preston Martin	Scott Feagan
Floyd	Patty Davenport	Becky B. McPherson	Mike Anderson	Lindan Morris	Nathan Johnson	Amado Morales
Foard	Debra Hopkins	Staley Heatly	Rick Hammonds	Rockne Wisdom	Larry Wright	Anthony Hinsley
Fort Bend	Annie Rebecca Elliott	John Healey Jr.	Richard Morrison	Grady Prestage	W.A. (Andy) Meyers	James Patterson
Franklin	Ellen Jaggers	Will Ramsay	Danny Chitsey	Larkin Jumper	Deryl Carr	Sam Young

County	District Clerk	District Attorney	Comm. Precinct 1	Comm. Precinct 2	Comm. Precinct 3	Comm. Precinct 4
Freestone	Teresa F. Black	Chris Martin	Luke Ward	Craig Oakes	Bodie Emmons	Clyde E. Ridge Jr.
Frio	Ramona B. Rodriguez	Rene M. Peña	Jesus G. (Chuy) Salinas	Richard Graf	Ruben Maldonado	Jose (Pepe) Flores
Gaines	Sharon Taylor	Michael Munk	Danny Yocom	Craig Belt	Blair Tharp	Biz Houston
Galveston	John Kinard	Jack Roady	Ryan Dennard	Joseph Giusti	Stephen W. Holmes	Kenneth F. Clark
Garza	Jim Plummer	Michael Munk	Gary McDaniel	Charles Morris	Ted Brannon	Jerry Benham
Gillespie	Jan Davis	E. Bruce Curry	Curtis Cameron	William A. (Billy) Roeder	Calvin Ransleben	Donnie Schuch
Glasscock	Rebecca Batla	Hardy L. Wilkerson	Jimmy Strube	Mark L. Halfmann	Gary Jones	Michael Hoch
Goliad	Mary Ellen Flores	Michael A. Sheppard	Julian Flores	Alonzo Morales	Ronald W. Bailey	David Bruns
Gonzales	Janice Sutton		Kenneth O. (Dell) Whiddon	Donnie R. Brzozowski	Kevin T. La Fleur	Otis S. (Bud) Wuest
Gray	Jo Mays	Franklin McDonough	Joe Wheeley	Gary Willoughby	Neil Fulton	Jeff Haley
Grayson	Kelly Ashmore	Joseph D. Brown	Jeff Whitmire	David Whitlock	Phyllis James	Bart Lawrence
Gregg	Barbara Duncan	Carl Dorrough	Ronnie McKinney	R. Darryl Primo	Gary W. Boyd	John Mathis
Grimes	Gay Wells	Tuck Moody McLain	Chad Mallett	David E. Dobyanski	Barbara Walker	Gary Husfeld
Guadalupe	Debra Crow	Heather McMinn	Greg Seidenberger	Ralph J. Shanafelt	Jim O. Wolverton	Judy Cope
Hale	Carla Cannon	Wally Hatch	Harold King	Mario Martinez	Kenny Kernell	Benny Cantwell
Hall	Raye Bailey	Luke Inman	Winfred McQueen	Terry Lindsey	Gary Proffitt	James Fuston
Hamilton	Sandy Layhew	B.J. Shepherd	Johnny Wagner	Keith Allen Curry	Lloyd Huggins	Dickie Clary
Hansford	Kim V. Vera	Mark Snider	Ira G. (Butch) Reed	David Thomas	Tim Stedje	Danny Henson
Hardeman	Ellen London	Staley Heatly	Christopher Call	Rodger Tabor	Barry Haynes	Rodney Foster
Hardin	Dana Hogg	David Sheffield	L.W. Cooper Jr.	Chris Kirkendall	Ken Pelt	Alvin Roberts
Harris	Chris Daniel	Kim Ogg	Rodney Ellis	Jack Morman	Steve Radack	R. Jack Cagle
Harrison	Sherry Griffis	Coke Solomon	William Hatfield	Zephaniah Timmins	James Greer	Jay Ebarb
Hartley	Melissa Mead	David M. Green	David Vincent	David Ford	Chad Hicks	Robert (Butch) Owens
Haskell	Penny Anderson	Michael E. Fouts	Billy Wayne Hester	Tiffen Mayfield	Kenny Thompson	Neal Kreger
Hays	Beverly Crumley	Wes Mau	Debbie Gonzales Ingalsbe	Mark Jones	Will Conley	Ray Whisenant
Hemphill	Lisa Johnson	Franklin McDonough	Coleman Bartlett	Tim Alexander	Mark Meek	Nicholas Thomas
Henderson	Betty Herriage	Scott McKee	Scotty Thomas	Wade McKinney	Ronny Lawrence	Ken Geeslin
Hidalgo	Laura L. Hinojosa	Ricardo Rodriguez	A.C. Cuellar Jr.	Eduardo (Eddie) Cantu	Joe M. Flores	Joseph Palacios
Hill	Angelia Orr	Mark Pratt	Danny Bodeker	Larry Crumpton	Larry Wright	Harley F. Davis II
Hockley	Dennis Price	Christopher E. Dennis	Curtis D. Thrash	Larry R. Carter	J.L. (Whitey) Barnett	Thomas R. Clevenger
Hood	Tonna T. Hitt	Robert Christian	James Deaver	Lloyd (Butch) Barton	Jeffrey Tout	Steve Berry
Hopkins	Cheryl Fulcher	Will Ramsay	Beth B. Wisenbaker	Mike Odell	Wade Bartley	Danny Evans
Houston	Carolyn Rains	Donna Gordon Kaspar	Gary Lovell	Willie E. Kitchen	Pat Perry	Kennon Kellum
Howard	Colleen Barton	Hardy L. Wilkerson	Oscar Garcia	Craig Bailey	Jimmie Long	John Cline
Hudspeth	Virginia Doyal	Jaime Esparza	Wayne West	Manuel Galindo Jr.	Jim Ed Miller	Larry Brewton
Hunt	Stacey Landrum	Noble D. Walker Jr.	Eric Evans	Tod McMahan	Phillip Martin	Jim Latham
Hutchinson	Robin Stroud	Mark Snider	Larry Coffman	Jerry D. Hefner	S.T. (Red) Isbell Jr.	Eddie Whittington
Irion	Molly Criner	Allison Palmer	Tia Paxton	Jeff Davidson	John Nanny	Bill (Beaver) McManus
Jack	Tracie J. Pippin	Greg Lowery	Keith Umphress	James L. Brock	James L. Cozart	Terry D. Ward
Jackson	Sharon Mathis	Pam Guenther	Wayne Hunt	Wayne Bubela	Johnny E. Belicek	Dennis Karl
Jasper	Kathy Kent	Steve Hollis	Charles Shofner Jr.	Roy Parker	Willie Stark	Vance Moss
Jeff Davis	Jennifer Wright	Rod Ponton	Larry Francell	Kerith Sproul	Curtis Evans	Albert Miller
Jefferson	Jamie Smith	Bob Wortham	Eddie Arnold	Brent Weaver	Michael (Shane) Sinegal	Everette (Bo) Alfred
Jim Hogg	Zonia G. Morales	Omar Escobar	Linda Jo Soliz	Abelardo (Valo) Alaniz	Sandalio (Sandy) Ruiz	Cynthia Guerra Betancourt

County	District Clerk	District Attorney	Comm. Precinct 1	Comm. Precinct 2	Comm. Precinct 3	Comm. Precinct 4
Jim Wells	R. David Guerrero	Carlos Omar Garcia	Margie H. Gonzalez	Ventura Garcia Jr.	Richard Miller	Emede Garcia
Johnson	David Lloyd	Dale Hanna	Rick Bailey	Kenny Howell	Jerry D. Stringer	Larry Woolley
Jones	Lacey Hansen	Joe Edd Boaz	James Clawson	Steve Lefevre	Ross Davis	Joe Whitehorn
Karnes	Denise Rodriguez	Rene M. Pena	Shelby Dupnik	Pete Jauer	James Rosales	David Reynolds
Kaufman	Rhonda Hughey	Erleigh Norville Wiley	Jimmy Joe Vrzalik	Skeet Phillips	Kenneth Schoen	Jakie Allen
Kendall	Susan Jackson	E. Bruce Curry	Mike Fincke	Richard W. Elkins	Tommy Pfeiffer	Chad Carpenter
Kenedy	Veronica Vela	John T. Hubert	Joe L. Recio	Israel Vela Jr.	Sarita Armstrong Hixon	Gumecinda (Cindy) Gonzales
Kent	Craig Harrison	Michael E. Fouts	Roy W. Chisum	Don Long	Roy H. Parker	Robert Graham
Kerr	Robbin Burlew	Scott Monroe (198th); E. Bruce Curry (216th)	H.A. (Buster) Baldwin	Tom Moser	Jonathan A. Letz	Bob Reeves
Kimble	Haydee Torres	Tonya S. Ahlschwede	Billy Braswell	Charles McGuire	Dennis Dunagan	Chad Gipson
King	Jammye D. Timmons	David W. Hajek	Reggie J. Hatfield	Larry Rush	Bobby J. Tidmore	Jay Hurt
Kinney	Dora Elia Sandoval	Fred Hernandez	Mark Frerich	Joe Montalvo	Dennis Dodson	Pat Melancon
Kleberg	Jennifer Whittington	John T. Hubert	David Rosse	Joe Hinojosa	Roy Cantu	Romeo L. Lomas
Knox	Lisa Cypert	David W. Hajek	Johnny McCowan	Daniel Godsey	Jimmy Urbanczyk	Nathan Urbanczyk
Lamar	Shawntel Golden	Gary Young	Lawrence Malone	Lonnie Layton	Ronnie Bass	Keith Mitchell
Lamb	Stephanie Chester	Scott A. Say	Cory DeBerry	Kent Lewis	Danny Short	Jimmy Young
Lampasas	Cody Reed	John Greenwood	Bobby Carroll	Jim Lindeman	Lowell B. Ivey	Mark Rainwater
La Salle	Margarita A. Esqueda	René M. Peña	Abel B. Gonzalez	Ricardo Garza	Rene Benavidez	Raul Ayala
Lavaca	Sherry T. Henke	Heather McMinn	Edward Pustka	Ronald Berkenhoff	Richard W. Brown	Dennis W. Kocian
Lee	Lisa Teinert	Martin Placke	Maurice Pitts Jr.	Charles Murray	Alan Turner	Steven Knobloch
Leon	Beverly Wilson	Hope L. Knight	Joey Sullivan	David Ferguson	Dean Stanford	David Grimes
Liberty	Donna G. Brown	Logan Pickett	Bruce Karbowski	Greg Arthur	James Reaves	Leon Wilson
Limestone	Carol Sue Jenkins	William Roy DeFriend	John McCarver	W.A. (Sonny) Baker	Jerry Allen	Bobby Forrest
Lipscomb	Kim Blau	Franklin McDonough	Juan Cantu	Merle Miller	Scotty Schilling	Johnie Steele
Live Oak	Melanie Matkin	José Aliseda	Richard Lee	Donna Kopplin Mills	Willie James	Emilio Garza
Llano	Joyce Gillow	Wylie B. McAfee	Peter Jones	Linda Raschke	Ron Wilson	Jerry Don Moss
Loving	Mozelle Carr	Randall W. Reynolds	Harlan Hopper	Ysidro Renteria	Thomas Elgin Jones	William (Bill) Wilkinson
Lubbock	Barbara Sucsy	Matthew D. Powell	Bill McCay	Mark E. Heinrich	Gilbert Flores	Patti Jones
Lynn	Sandra Laws	Michael Munk	Keith Wied	John Hawthorne	Don Blair	Larry Durham
Madison	Joyce Batson	Brian Risinger	Ricky Driskell	Phillip Grisham	Carl Cannon	Sam Cole
Marion	Susan Anderson	Angela Smoak	John Ross (J.R.) Ashley	Joe McKnight	Glenn Dorough	C.W. (Charlie) Treadwell
Martin	Sharon Jones	Hardy L. Wilkerson	Kenny Stewart	Robin Barnes	Bobby Holland	Koy Blocker
Mason	Pam Beam	Tonya Spaeth Ahleschwede	Wayne Hofmann	Will Frey	Stanley Toeppich	Stephen Mutschink
Matagorda	Jamie Bludau	Steven E. Reis	Daniel Pustka	Kent Pollard	James Gibson	Charles R. (Bubba) Frick
Maverick	Leopoldo Vielma	Roberto Serna	Gerardo Morales	Rosy Cantu	Jose Luis Rosales	Roberto Ruiz
McCulloch	Michelle Pitcox	Robert (Bob) Hofmann	Jim Quinn	Gene Edmiston	Jim Ross	Brent C. Deeds
McLennan	Jon Gimble	Abel Reyna	Kelly Snell	Lester Gibson	Will Jones	Ben Perry
McMullen	Mattie Sadovsky	Jose Aliseda	Larry Garcia	Murray Swaim	Scotty McClaugherty	Maximo G. Quintanilla Jr.
Medina	Cindy Fowler	Daniel J. Kindred	Richard C. Saathoff	Larry Sittre	David Lynch	Jerry Beck
Menard	Ann Kothmann	Tonya Ahlschwede	Boyd Murchison	Jay Cunningham	Ed Keith	Larry Burch
Midland	Ross Bush	Teresa Clingman	Jimmy Smith	Robert R. (Robin) Donnelly	Luis D. Sanchez	Randy Prude
Milam	Karen Berry	W.W. (Bill) Torrey	Richard (Opey) Watkins	Donald Shuffield	John Fisher	Jeff Muegge
Mills	Carolyn Foster	Michael B. Murray	Mike Wright	Jed Garren	Robert Hall	Jason Williams

County	District Clerk	District Attorney	Comm. Precinct 1	Comm. Precinct 2	Comm. Precinct 3	Comm. Precinct 4
Mitchell	Belinda Blassingame	Ann Reed	Randy Anderson	Jeremy Strain	Jesse Munoz	Billy H. Preston
Montague	Lesia Darden	Jack McCaughey	Herman Conway	Mike Mayfield	Mark Murphey	Bob Langford
Montgomery	Barbara Gladden Adamick	Brett W. Ligon	Mike Meador	Charlie Riley	James Noack	Jim Clark
Moore	Diane Hoefling	David M. Green	J. Daniel Garcia	Len Sheets	Milton Pax	Lynn Cartrite
Morris	Gwen Oney	J. Stephen Cowan	Dennis Allen	Weldon Lilley	Michael Clair	Todd Freeman
Motley	Jamie Martin	Becky B. McPherson	Guy Campbell	Donnie L. Turner	Franklin Jameson	David Stafford
Nacogdoches	Loretta Cammack	Nicole Lostracco	Jerry Don Williamson	Jerry Stone	Jim Elder	Elton Milstead Jr.
Navarro	Josh Tackett	R. Lowell Thompson	Jason Grant	Dick Martin	David (Butch) Warren	James Olsen
Newton	Bree Allen	Courtney Ponthier	William L. (Bill) Fuller	Thomas Gill	Prentiss L. Hopson	Leonard Powell
Nolan	Jamie Clem	Ann Reed	Terry Willman	Doug Alexander	Tommy White	Tony Lara
Nueces	Patsy Perez	Mark Skurka	Mike Pusley	Joe A. Gonzalez	Oscar O. Ortiz	Joe McComb
Ochiltree	Shawn Bogard	Barrett Dye	Duane Pshigoda	David Peckenpaugh	Richard Burger	Dempsey Malaney
Oldham	Darla Lookingbill	—	Quincy Taylor	Larry Groneman	Roger Morris III	Billy Don Brown
Orange	Vickie Edgerly	John D. Kimbrough	David Dubose	Barry Burton	John Banken	Jody Crump
Palo Pinto	Janie Glover	Michael K. Burns	Curtis Henderson	Louis Ragle	Mike Pierce	Jeff Fryer
Panola	Debra Johnson	Danny Buck Davidson	Ronnie LaGrone	John Gradberg	Hermon E. Reed Jr.	Dale LaGrone
Parker	Sharena Gilliland	Don Schnebly	George Conley	Craig Peacock	Larry Walden	Steve Dugan
Parmer	Sandra Warren	Gordon Green	Kirk Frye	Steve Cockerham	Kenny White	Lloyd Bradshaw
Pecos	Gayle Henderson	Sandy Wilson (83rd); Laurie English (112th)	Tom Chapman	Lupe Dominguez	Mickey Jack Perry	Santiago Cantu Jr.
Polk	Bobbye Richards	William (Lee) Hon	Robert C. (Bob) Willis	Ronnie Vincent	Milton (Milt) Byrd Purvis	C.T. (Tommy) Overstreet
Potter	Caroline Woodburn	Randall C. Sims	H.R. Kelly	Mercy Murguia	Leon Church	Alphonso S. Vaughn
Presidio	Virginia Pallarez	Rod Ponton	Jim White III	Eloy Aranda	Lorenzo Hernandez	Loretto Vasquez
Rains	Deborah Traylor	Robert Vititow	Patsy Marshall	Mike Willis	Michael Godwin	Joe Humphrey
Randall	Jo Carter	James A. Farren	Christy Dyer	Mark Benton	Bob Robinson	Buddy DeFord
Reagan	Terri Curry	Laurie English	Jim O'Bryan	Tim Sellman	Tommy Holt	Thomas Strube
Real	Bella A. Rubio	Daniel J. Kindred	Manuel Rubio	Bryan Shackelford	Gene Buckner	Joe W. Connell Sr.
Red River	Janice Gentry	Val J. Varley	Donnie Gentry	David Hutson	Joe DePriest	Wayne Johnson
Reeves	Patricia Tarin	Randall W. Reynolds	Rojelio (Roy) Alvarado	Louise C. Moore	Paul Hinojos	Tony Trujillo
Refugio	Ruby Garcia	Michael A. Sheppard	Ann Lopez	David Joe Vega	Gary D. Bourland	Rodrigo Bernal
Roberts	Toni Rankin	Franklin McDonough	Cleve Wheeler	Ken R. Gill	Kelly V. Flowers	James F. Duvall Jr.
Robertson	Barbara Axtell	William Coty Siegert	Keith Petitt	Donald Threadgill	Keith Nickelson	Robert Bielamowicz
Rockwall	Kay McDaniel	Kenda Culpepper	Cliff Sevier	Lee Gilbert	Dennis Bailey	David Magness
Runnels	Tammy Burleson	George McCrea	Robert H. (Bobby) Moore	Ronald Presley	Sam Scott	Richard W. (Ricky) Strube
Rusk	Terrie Willard	Micheal E. Jimerson	W.D. (Bill) Hale	Tammy Pepper	Freddy Swann	Harold Howell
Sabine	Tanya Walker	J. Kevin Dutton	Keith C. Clark	Jimmy McDaniel	Doyle Dickerson	Fayne Warner
San Augustine	Jean Steptoe	J. Kevin Dutton	Stanley Jackson	Edward Wilson	Joey Holloway	David McEachern
San Jacinto	Rebecca Capers	Robert H. Trapp	Bay McCoppin	Donnie Marrs	Thomas Bonds	Mark Nettuno
San Patricio	Laura Miller	Michael E. Welborn	Nina G. Treviño	Fred P. Nardini	Alma V. Moreno	Jim Price Jr.
San Saba	Kim Wells	Sonny McAfee	Otis Judkins	Rickey Lusty	Kenley Kroll	Pat S. Pool
Schleicher	Mary Ann Gonzalez	Allison Palmer	Johnny F. Mayo Jr.	Lynn Meador	Kirk Griffin	Matt Brown
Scurry	Candace Jones	Ben Smith	Terry D. Williams	Marianne Randals	David Harrell	Jim Robinson
Shackelford	Cheri Hawkins	Joe Edd Boaz	Steve Riley	Shawn Askew	Lanham Martin	Cody Jordan
Shelby	Lori Oliver	Kenneth Florence	Roscoe McSwain	Jimmy Lout	Travis Rodgers	Bradley Allen

County	District Clerk	District Attorney	Comm. Precinct 1	Comm. Precinct 2	Comm. Precinct 3	Comm. Precinct 4
Sherman	Gina Gray	David M. Green	Dana Buckles	Randy Williams	Jeff Crippen	David Davis
Smith	Lois Rogers	D. Matt Bingham III	Jeff Warr	Cary Nix	Terry Phillips	JoAnn Hampton
Somervell	Michelle Reynolds	Dale Hanna	Larry Hulsey	John Curtis	Kenneth Wood	Don Kranz
Starr	Eloy R. Garcia	Omar Escobar Jr.	Jaime M. Alvarez	Raul (Roy) Peña Jr.	Eloy Garza	Ruben D. Saenz
Stephens	Christie Coapland	Dee Peavy	Ed Russell	D.C. (Button) Sikes	Joe F. High	Rickie Ray Carr
Sterling	Jerri McCutchen	Allison Palmer	John Ross Copeland	Edward J. Michulka Jr.	Deborah H. Horwood	Reed Stewart
Stonewall	Holly McLaury	Michael E. Fouts	David Hoy	Janice Harris	Billy Kirk Meador	Gary Myers
Sutton	Rachel Chavez Duran	Laurie K. English	Miguel (Mike) Villanueva	John Wade	Carl Teaff	Fred Perez
Swisher	C.J. Chasco	J. Michael Criswell	Lloyd Rahlfs	Joe Bob Thompson	Harvey N. Foster	Larry Buske
Tarrant	Thomas A. Wilder	Sharen Wilson	Roy C. Brooks	Andy H. Nguyen	Gary Fickes	J.D. Johnson
Taylor	Tammy Robinson	James M. Eidson	Randall Williams	Kyle Kendrick	Brad Birchum	Charles (Chuck) Statler
Terrell	Martha Allen	Fred Hernandez	Yolanda G. Lopez	Michelle Marquez	Charles Stegall	Jon Tom Lowrance
Terry	Paige Lindsey	Kelly Moore	Mike Swain	Kirby Keesee	Sisillio Castilleja	John R. Franks
Throckmorton	Mary (Susie) Walraven	Michael E. Fouts	Casey Wells	John Jones	Teddy Clark	Wilton Cantrell
Titus	Debra Abston	Charles C. (Chuck) Bailey	Albert Riddle	Mike Fields	Phillip Hinton	Jimmy Parker
Tom Green	Sheri Woodfin	Allison Palmer (51st); George McCrea (119th)	Ralph Hoelscher	Aubrey de Cordova	Steve Floyd	Bill A. Ford
Travis	Velva Price	Margaret Moore	Jeff Travillion	Brigid Shea	Gerald Daugherty	Margaret Gómez
Trinity	Kristen Raiford	Benny Schiro	Grover Worsham	Richard Chamberlin	Neal Smith	Jimmy Brown
Tyler	Chyrl Pounds	Lou Ann Cloy	Martin Nash	James (Rusty) Hughes	Mike Marshall	Jack Walston
Upshur	Karen Bunn	William (Billy) Byrd	Paula Gentry	Don Gross	Frank Berka	Mike Spencer
Upton	Pedro (Pete) Gomez Jr.	Laurie English	Dean Titsworth	Tommy Owens	David Mooney	Leon Patrick
Uvalde	Christina Ovalle	Daniel J. Kindred	Randy Scheide	Mariano Pargas Jr.	Jerry W. Bates	Raul R. Flores
Val Verde	Luz Clara Balderas	Fred Hernandez	Ramiro V. Ramon	Lewis Owens	Robert Beau Nettleton	Gustavo Flores
Van Zandt	Karen Wilson	Chris Martin	Brandon Brown	Virgil Melton Jr.	Bobby Chaney	Ronald G. Carroll
Victoria	Cathy Stuart	Stephen B. Tyler	Danny Garcia Jr.	Kevin M. Janak	Gary E. Burns	Clint C. Ives
Walker	Robyn Flowers	David P. Weeks	B.J. Gaines Jr.	Ronnie White	Bobby Warren	Tim Paulsel
Waller	Liz Pirkle	Elton Mathis	John A. Amsler	Russell Klecka	Jeron Barnett	Justin Beckendorff
Ward	Patricia Oyerbides	Randell W. Reynolds	Julian Florez	Larry Hanna	Dexter Nichols	Eddie Nelms
Washington	Tammy Brauner	Julie Renken	Zeb Heckmann	Luther Hueske	Kirk Hanath	Joy Fuchs
Webb	Esther Degollado	Isidro R. Alaniz	Frank J. Sciaraffa	Rosaura (Wawi) Tijerina	John C. Galo	Jaime A. Canales
Wharton	Kendra Charbula	Ross Kurtz	Leroy Dettling	D.C. (Chris) King	Steven Goetsch	Doug Mathews
Wheeler	Sherri Jones	Franklin McDonough	Daryl G. Snelgrooes	Bob Hink	Richard Kincannon	John Walker
Wichita	Patti Flores	Maureen Shelton	Ray Gonzalez	Lee Harvey	Barry Mahler	Jeff Watts
Wilbarger	Brenda Peterson	Staley Heatly	Richard Jacobs	Phillip Graf	Rodney Johnston	Josh Patterson
Willacy	Gilbert Lozano	Bernard Ammerman	Eliberto Guerra	Oscar De Luna	Alfredo Serrato	Edward (Eddie) Gonzales
Williamson	Lisa David	Shawn Dick	Terry Cook	Cynthia Long	Valerie Covey	Larry Madsen
Wilson	Deborah Bryan	René M. Peña	Albert Gamez Jr.	Paul W. Pfeil	Ricky R. Morales	Larry A. Wiley
Winkler	Sherry Terry	Dorothy Holguin	Billy J. Stevens	James R. (Robbie) Wolf	Randy Neal	Billy Ray Thompson
Wise	Brenda Rowe	Greg Lowery	Danny White	Kevin Burns	Harry Lamance	Gaylord Kennedy
Wood	Jenica Turner	Jim Wheeler	Virgil Holland	Jerry Gaskill	Roger W. Pace	Russell Acker
Yoakum	Sandra Roblez	—	Woody Lindsey	Ray Marion	Ty Powell	Tim Addison
Young	Jamye Rogers	Dee Peavy	Mike Sipes	Matthew Pruitt	Stacey Rogers	Jimmy R. Wiley
Zapata	Dora M. Ramos	Isidro (Chilo) Alaniz	Jose Emilio Vela	Gabriel Villarreal Jr.	Eddie Martinez	Norberto Garza
Zavala	Rachel P. Ramirez	Roberto Serna	Isidro Cantu	Miguel Acosta	Jesse Gonzalez	Fred Enriquez

Texans in Congress

Besides the two members of the U.S. Senate allocated to each state, Texas was allocated 36 members in the U.S. House of Representatives for the 116th Congress. The term of office for members of the House is two years; the terms of all members will expire on Jan. 3, 2021. Senators serve six-year terms. Sen. John Cornyn's term will end in 2021. Sen. Ted Cruz's term will end in 2025.

Addresses and phone numbers of the lawmakers' Washington and district offices are below, as well as the committees on which they serve. Washington zip codes are 20515 for members of the House and 20510 for senators. The telephone area code for Washington is 202. On the Internet, House members can be reached through www.house.gov/writerep.

In 2018, members of Congress received a salary of $174,000. Members in leadership positions received $193,400.

U.S. SENATE

(Total members 100; Republicans 53, Democrats 45, Independents 2.)

CORNYN, John. Republican (Home: Austin); Washington Office: 517 HSOB; (202) 224-2934, Fax 228-2856. www. cornyn.senate.gov.

Texas Offices: 221 W. 6th, Ste. 1530, Austin 78701, (512) 469-6034; 5001 Spring Valley, Ste. 1125 E, Dallas 75244, (972) 239-1310; 222 E. Van Buren, Ste. 404, Harlingen 78550, (956) 423-0162; *John Cornyn.*
5300 Memorial Dr., Ste. 980, Houston 77007, (713) 572-3337; 1500 Broadway, Ste. 1230, Lubbock 79401, (806) 472-7533; 600 Navarro, Ste. 210, San Antonio 78205, (210) 224-7485; 100 E. Ferguson, Ste. 1004, Tyler 75702, (903) 593-0902.

Committees: Finance, Judiciary, Select Committee on Intelligence.

CRUZ, Ted. Republican (Home: Houston); Wash-

ington Office: 404 RSOB; (202) 224-5922. www. cruz.senate.gov.

Texas Offices: 300 E. 8th, Ste. 961, Austin 78701, (512) 916-5834; 3626 N. Hall, Ste. 410, Dallas 75219, (214) 599-8749; 1919 Smith, Ste. 9047, Houston 77002, (713) 718-3057; 200 S. 10th, Ste. 1603, McAllen

Ted Cruz.   78501, (956) 686-7339;
9901 IH-10W, Ste. 950, San Antonio 78230, (210) 340-2885 305; S. Broadway, Ste. 501, Tyler 75702, (903) 593-5130.

Committees: Foreign Relations; Commerce, Science and Transportation; Judiciary; Rules and Administration; Joint Economic Committee.

U.S. HOUSE of REPRESENTATIVES

(Total districts 435; Republicans 197, Democrats 235, 3 vacant. Texas delegation of 36; 23 Republicans, 13 Democrats.)

District 1 — GOHMERT, Louie, R-Tyler; Washington Office: 2267 RHOB; (202) 225-3035, Fax 226-1230; District Offices: 1121 ESE Loop 323, Ste. 206, Tyler 75701, (903) 561-6349; 101 E. Methvin, Ste. 302, Longview 75601, (903) 236-8597; 300 E. Shepherd, Ste. 210, Lufkin 75901, (936) 632-3180; 102 W. Houston, Marshall 75670, (866) 535-6302; 101 W. Main, Ste. 160, Nacogdoches 75961, (936) 715-9514. Committees: Judiciary, Natural Resources.

District 2 — CRENSHAW, Dan, R-Kingwood; Washington Office: 413 CHOB; (202) 225-6565. District Office: 1801 Kingwood Dr., Ste. 240, Kingwood 77339. Committees: Budget, Homeland Security.

District 3 — TAYLOR, Van, R-Plano; Washington Office: 1404 LHOB; (202) 225-4201; District Office: 5600 Tennyson Parkway, Ste. 275, Plano 75204. Committees: Education and Labor; Homeland Security.

District 4 — RATCLIFFE, John, R-Heath; Washington Office, 223 CHOB; (202) 225-6673, Fax 225-3332: District Offices: 6531 Horizon, Ste. A, Rockwall 75032, (972) 771-0100; 100 W. Houston, 1st Floor, Sherman 75090, (903) 813-5270; 2500 N. Robison, Ste. 190, Texarkana 75599, (903) 823-3173. Committees: Intelligence, Judiciary, Homeland Security.

District 5 — GOODEN, Lance, R-Terrell; Washington Office: 425 CHOB; (202) 225-3484. District Office: 18601 LBJ Freeway, Ste. 725, Mesquite 75150. Committee: Financial Services.

District 6 — WRIGHT, Ron, R-Arlington; Washington Office: 428 CHOB; (202) 225-2002; District Offices: 6001 West I-20, Ste. 200, Arlington 76017; 2106 W. Ennis Ave., Ennis 75119. Committees: Education and Labor; Foreign Affairs.

District 7 — FLETCHER, Lizzie Pannill, D-Houston; Washington Office: 1429 LHOB; (202) 225-2571; District Office: 5599 San Felipe Rd., Ste. 950, Houston 77056. Committees: Transportation and Infrastructure; Science, Space, and Technology.

District 8 — BRADY, Kevin, R-The Woodlands; Washington Office: 1011 LHOB; (202) 225-4901, Fax 225-5524. District Offices: 200 River Pointe, Ste. 304, Conroe 77304, (936) 441-5700; 1300 11th St., Ste 400, Huntsville 77340, (936) 439-9532. Committee: Ways and Means.

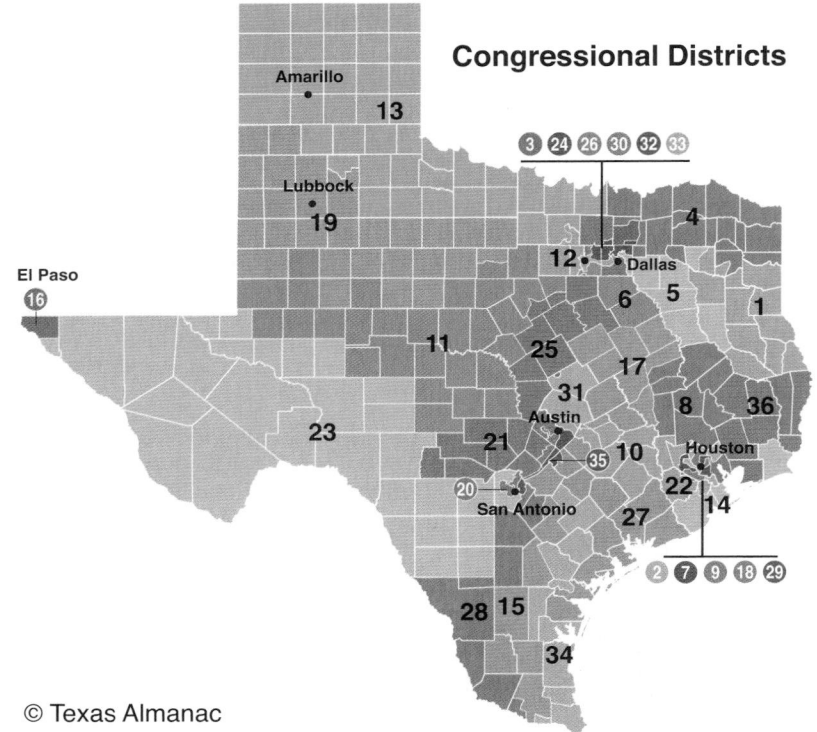

Congressional Districts

© Texas Almanac

District 9 — GREEN, Al, D-Houston; Washington Office: 2347 RHOB; (202) 225-7508; District Office: 3003 South Loop West, Ste. 460, Houston 77054, (713) 383-9234. Committees: Financial Services, Homeland Security.

District 10 — McCAUL, Michael, R-Austin; Washington Office: 2001 RHOB; (202) 225-2401, Fax 225-5955. District Offices: 3301 Northland Dr., Ste. 212, Austin 78731, (512) 473-2357; 2000 S. Market, Ste. 303, Brenham 77833, (979) 830-8497; 1773 Westborough Dr., Ste. 223, Katy 77449, (281) 398-1247; 990 Village Sq., Ste. B, Tomball 77375, (281) 255-8372. Committees: Foreign Affairs, Homeland Security.

District 11— CONAWAY, K. Michael, R-Midland; Washington Office: 2469 RHOB; (202) 225-3605. District Offices: 6 Desta Dr., Ste. 2000, Midland 79705, (432) 687-2390; 501 Center Ave., Brownwood 76801, (325) 646-1950; 132 Houston St., Granbury 76048, (682) 936-2577; 104 W. Sandstone, Llano 78643, (325) 247-2826; 411 W. 8th, Odessa 79761, (866) 882-3811; 33 Twohig, Ste. 307, San Angelo 76903, (325) 659-4010. Committees: Agriculture, Armed Services, Intelligence.

District 12 — GRANGER, Kay, R-Fort Worth; Washington Office: 1026 LHOB; (202) 225-5071, Fax 225-5683; District Office: 1701 River Run Rd., Ste. 407, Fort Worth 76107, (817) 338-0909. Committee: Appropriations.

District 13 — THORNBERRY, William M. (Mac), R-Clarendon; Washington Office: 2208 RHOB; (202) 225-3706, Fax 225-3486; District Offices: 620 S. Taylor, Ste. 200, Amarillo 79101, (806) 371-8844; 2525 Kell Blvd., Ste. 406, Wichita Falls 76308, (940) 692-1700. Committee: Armed Services.

District 14 — WEBER, Randy, R-Friendswood; Washington Office: 107 CHOB; (202) 225-2831. District Offices: 505 Orleans, Ste. 103, Beaumont 77701, (409) 835-0108; 122 West Way, Ste. 301, Lake Jackson 77566, (979) 285-0231; 174 Calder Rd., Ste. 150, League City 77573, (281) 316-0231. Committees: Science, Space and Technology; Transportation and Infrastructure.

District 15 — GONZALEZ, Vicente, D-McAllen; Washington Office: 113 CHOB; (202) 225-2531. District Offices: 131 W. Main St., Benavides 78341, (888) 217-0261; 217 E. Miller, Ste. 200, Falfurrias 78355, (361) 209-3027; 1305 W. Hackberry Ave., McAllen 78501, (956) 682-5545; 404 S. Mier St., San Diego 78384, (888) 217-0261; 1243 Cardinal Ln., Seguin 78155, (830) 358-0497. Committees: Financial Services, Foreign Affairs.

District 16 — ESCOBAR, Veronica, D-El Paso; Washington Office: 1330 LHOB; (202) 225-4831. District Office; 221 N. Kansas, Ste. 1500, El Paso 79901, (915) 541-1400. Committees: Armed Services, Judiciary.

District 17 — FLORES, Bill, R-Bryan; Washington Office: 2440 RHOB; (202) 225-6105; District Offices: 400 Austin Ave., Ste. 302, Waco 76701, (254)

732-0748; 14205 Burnet Rd., Ste. 230, Austin 78728 (512) 373-3378; 3000 Briarcrest Dr., Ste. 406, Bryan 77802, (979) 703-4037. Committees: Budget, Energy and Commerce.

District 18 — JACKSON LEE, Sheila, D-Houston; Washington Office: 2187 RHOB; (202) 225-3816, Fax 225-3317; District Offices: 1919 Smith, Ste. 1180, Houston 77002, (713) 655-0050; 420 W. 19th St., Houston 77008, (713) 861-4070; 6719 W. Montgomery, Ste. 204, Houston 77091, (713) 691-4882; 4300 Lyons Ave., Houston 77020, (713) 227-7740. Committees: Budget, Homeland Security, Judiciary.

District 19 — ARRINGTON, Jodey, R-Lubbock; Washington Office: 1029 LHOB; (202) 225-4005. District Offices: 500 Chestnut St., Abilene 79602, (325) 763-1611; 1312 Texas Ave., Ste. 219, Lubbock 79401, (806) 763-1611. Committee: Ways and Means.

District 20 — CASTRO, Joaquin, D-San Antonio; Washington Office: 2241 RHOB; (202) 225-3236. District Office: 727 E. Cesar E. Chavez Blvd., Ste. B-128, San Antonio 78206, (210) 348-8216. Committees: Education and Labor; Intelligence; Foreign Affairs.

District 21 — ROY, Chip S., R-Austin; Washington Office: 1319 LHOB; (202) 225-4236. District Office: 1100 NE Interstate 410 Loop, #640, San Antonio 78209, (210) 821-5024. Committees: Budget; Oversight and Reform; Veterans' Affairs.

District 22 — OLSON, Pete, R-Sugar Land; Washington Office: 2133 RHOB; (202) 225-5951, Fax 225-5241. District Offices: 1650 Hwy 6, Ste. 150, Sugar Land 77478, (281) 494-2690; 22333 Grand Corner Dr., Ste. 151, Katy 77494, (281) 889-7134. Committees: Energy and Commerce; Science, Space, and Technology.

District 23 — HURD, Will, R-Helotes; Washington Office: 317 CHOB; (202) 225-6625, Fax 225-4511. District Offices; 17721 Rogers Ranch Pkwy., Ste. 120, San Antonio 78258, (210) 921-3130; One University Way, Ste. 202A, San Antonio 78224, (210) 784-5023; 1104 W. 10th St., Del Rio 78840, (830) 422-2040; 100 S. Monroe St., Eagle Pass 78852, (830) 491-7003; 103 W. Callaghan, Fort Stockton 79735, (210) 245-1548; 124 S. Houston, Socorro 79927. Committees: Appropriations, Intelligence.

District 24 — MARCHANT, Kenny, R-Coppell; Washington Office: 2304 RHOB; (202) 225-6605, Fax 225-0074. District Office: 9901 E. Valley Ranch Parkway, Ste. 2060, Irving 75063, (972) 556-0162. Committees: Ethics; Ways and Means.

District 25 — WILLIAMS, Roger, R-Austin; Washington Office: 1708 LHOB; (202) 225-9896. District Offices: 1005 Congress Ave., Ste. 925, Austin 78701, (512) 473-8910; 115 S. Main, Ste. 206, Cleburne 76033, (817) 774-2575. Committee: Financial Services.

District 26 — BURGESS, Michael, R-Lewisville; Washington Office: 2161 RHOB; (202) 225-7772, Fax 225-2919. District Office: 2000 S. Stemmons Fwy., Ste. 200, Lake Dallas 75065, (972) 497-5031. Committees: Energy and Commerce; Rules.

District 27 — CLOUD, Michael, R-Victoria; Washington Office: 1314 LHOB; (202) 225-7742. District Offices: 101 N. Shoreline Blvd., Ste. 300, Corpus Christi 78401, (361) 884-2222; 5606 N. Navarro, Ste. 203, Victoria 77904, (361) 894-6446. Committees: Oversight and Reform; Science, Space, and Technology.

District 28 — CUELLAR, Henry, D-Laredo; Washington Office: 2372 RHOB; (202) 225-1640. District Offices: 602 E. Calton Rd., Laredo 78041, (956) 725-0639; 615 E. Houston, Ste. 451, San Antonio 78205, (210) 271-2851; 117 E. Tom Landry, Mission 78572, (956) 424-3942; 100 N. FM 3167, Rio Grande City 78582, (956) 487-5603. Committee: Appropriations.

District 29 — GARCIA, Sylvia, D-Houston; Washington Office: 1620 LHOB; (202) 225-1688; District Office: 11811 East Fwy., Ste. 430, Houston 77029. Committees: Financial Services, Judiciary.

District 30 — JOHNSON, Eddie Bernice, D-Dallas; Washington Office: 2306 RHOB; (202) 225-8885, Fax 225-1477; District Office: 1825 Market Center Blvd., Dallas 75207, (214) 922-8885. Committees: Science, Space, and Technology; Transportation and Infrastructure.

District 31 — CARTER, John, R-Round Rock; Washington Offices: 2110 RHOB; (202) 225-3864. District Offices: 1717 N. I-35, Ste. 303, Round Rock 78664, (512) 246-1600; 6544B S. General Bruce Dr., Temple 76502, (254) 933-1392. Committee: Appropriations.

District 32 — ALLRED, Colin, D-Dallas; Washington Office: 328 CHOB; (202) 225-2231; District Office: 12750 Merit Dr., Ste. 1434, Dallas 75251, (972) 392-0505. Committees: Foreign Affairs, Transportation and Infrastructure, Veterans' Affairs.

District 33 — VEASEY, Marc, D-Fort Worth; Washington Office: 2348 RHOB; (202) 225-9897. District Offices: 1881 Sylvan Ave., Ste 108, Dallas 75028, (214) 741-1387; 6707 Brentwood Stair Rd., Ste. 200, Fort Worth 76112, (817) 920-9086. Committees: Energy and Commerce; Small Business.

District 34 — VELA, Filemon, D-Brownsville; Washington Office: 437 CHOB; (202) 225-9901. District Offices: 500 E. Main, Alice 78332, (361) 230-9776; 333 Ebony Ave., Brownsville 78520, (956) 544-8352; 1390 W. Expressway 83, San Benito 78586, (956) 276-4497; 301 W. Railroad, Weslaco 78596, (956) 520-8273. Committees: Agriculture, Armed Services.

District 35 — DOGGETT, Lloyd, D-Austin; Washington Office: 2307 RHOB; (202) 225-4865. District Offices: 300 E. 8th, 4th Floor, Austin 78701, (512) 916-5921; 217 W. Travis St., San Antonio 78205, (210) 704-1080. Committees: Budget; Ways and Means.

District 36 — BABIN, Brian, R-Woodville; Washington Office: 2236 RHOB; (202) 225-1555, Fax 226-0396. District Offices: 203 Ivy Ave., Ste 600, Deer Park 77536, (832) 780-0966; 1201 Childers Rd., Orange 77630, (409) 883-8075; 100 W. Bluff Dr., Woodville 75979, (409) 331-8066. Committees: Transportation and Infrastructure; Science, Space and Technology. ☆

U.S. Tax Collections in Texas

Fiscal Year	Individual Income and Employment Taxes	Corporation Income Taxes	Estate Taxes	Gift Taxes	Excise Taxes	TOTAL U.S. Taxes Collected in Texas
	(in thousands) *Information for fiscal years furnished by the Internal Revenue Service.*					
2018	$ 240,169,156	$ 15,756,288	$ 1,395,067	$ 135,733	$ 22,592,120	$ 280,048,364
2017	225,236,761	22,939,596	1,314,828	123,822	21,340,788	270,955,237
2016	218,950,277	19,021,716	1,318,116	140,191	21,698,393	261,138,693
2015	226,945,577	32,083,819	1,167,572	115,516	19,591,942	279,904,425
2014	211,993,178	32,585,544	1,557,068	89,865	19,110,528	265,336,183
2013	195,542,035	33,933,242	890,069	596,861	18,950,003	249,912,209
2012	171,880,127	27,984,282	796,227	180,060	18,619,137	219,459,878
2011	160,086,749	21,880,905	117,936	359,987	15,850,240	198,295,817
2010	147,748,859	24,991,374	1,210,600	287,181	14,904,099	189,142,112
2009	158,798,111	24,235,172	1,780,030	242,918	15,465,279	200,521,512
2008	178,761,539	39,971,658	1,549,767	243,043	15,150,053	235,676,058
2007	160,306,445	41,823,425	1,473,490	218,194	21,569,350	225,390,904
2005	125,816,805	29,186,478	1,196,362	118,231	13,074,838	169,392,715
2000	116,094,820	20,310,672	1,176,278	269,109	14,732,513	152,583,349
1995	69,706,333	10,677,881	869,528	152,683	11,135,857	92,342,282
1990	52,795,489	6,983,762	521,811	196,003	5,694,006	66,191,071
1985	41,497,114	5,637,148	528,106	41,560	6,058,110	53,762,038
1980	25,707,514	7,232,486	453,830	23,722	4,122,538	37,540,089
1970	6,096,961	1,184,342	135,694	20,667	843,724	8,281,389
1960	2,059,075	622,822	70,578	10,583	209,653	2,972,712

Federal Funds Distribution in Texas

	2018		2017
Total all	$ 206.4 billion		$ 193.4 billion
Direct payments	$ 94.9 billion	Direct payments	$ 91.7 billion
Grants	51.9 billion	Grants	51.1 billion
Contracts	46.8 billion	Contracts	44.4 billion
Other financial assistance	12.8 billion	Other financial assistance	5.8 billion
Loans	–21.0 million	Loans	317.2 million
Top 5 by program			
Social Security retirement	$ 47.85 billion	Social Security retirement	$44.71 billion
Medical assistance	21.52 billion	Medical assistance	22.15 billion
Social Security disability	8.98 billion	Social Security disability	3.92 billion
Flood insurance	7.86 billion	Veterans compensation	7.47 billion
Veterans compensation	7.65 billion	Social Security survivors	6.34 billion
Top 5 by agency			
Social Security Administration	$ 67.45 billion	Social Security Administration	$ 64.31 billion
Department of Defense	40.42 billion	Department of Defense	45.37 billion
Department of Health and Human Services	34.44 billion	Department of Health and Human Services	34.96 billion
Department of Veterans Affairs	16.76 billion	Department of Veterans Affairs	15.78 billion
Department of Homeland Security	11.10 billion	Department of Agriculture	10.01 billion
		Information for fiscal years from USAspending.gov.	

Federal Funds Distribution to States, Fiscal 2017

Rank	State	Total	per capita	Rank	State	Total	per capita
1	California	$ 307.7 billion	$ 7,783	12	Tennessee	$ 80.7 billion	$ 12,020
2	Pennsylvania	202.7 billion	15,826	13	South Carolina	80.0 billion	15,916
3	**Texas**	**193.4 billion**	**6,834**	14	Michigan	79.5 billion	7,977
4	Florida	181.9 billion	8,670	15	Arizona	75.8 billion	10,800
5	Indiana	130.0 billion	19.504	16	North Carolina	67.7 billion	6,588
6	Virginia	100.4 billion	11,852	17	Connecticut	67.7 billion	18,857
7	Minnesota	93.9 billion	16,836	18	Maryland	67.6 billion	11,174
8	Kentucky	91.2 billion	20,474	19	Georgia	65.1 billion	6,243
9	Wisconsin	87.3 billion	15,070	20	New Jersey	64.4 billion	7,147
10	Illinois	84.0 billion	6,564				
11	Ohio	83.6 billion	7,170			*Source: USAspending.gov.*	

Major Military Installations

Below are listed the major military installations in Texas in 2018. Data are taken from the U.S. Department of Defense *Base Structure Report 2017* and other sources. "Civilian" refers to Department of Defense and contractor personnel. *In October 2010, Fort Sam Houston, Lackland AFB, and Randolph AFB were merged into Joint Base San Antonio under the jurisdiction of the U.S. Air Force 502nd Air Base Wing.*

U.S. NAVY

Naval Air Station Corpus Christi
Location: Corpus Christi (est. 1941).
Address: NAS Corpus Christi, 11001 D St., Corpus Christi 78418
Main phone number: (361) 961-2811
Personnel: 1,369 active-duty; 395 reserve; 710 civilians.
Major units: Naval Air Training Command Headquarters; Training Air Wing 4; Marine Aviation Training Support Group; Coast Guard Air Group; Corpus Christi Army Depot (est. 1961).

Naval Air Station-Joint Reserve Base Fort Worth
Location: westside Fort Worth (est. 1994) [Carswell, est. in 1942 as Fort Worth Army Air Field, closed in 1993].
Address: NAS-JRB, 1510 Chennault Ave., Fort Worth 76113
Main phone number: (817) 782-3058
Personnel: Active-duty — 2 Army, 232 Navy, 487 Marines, 159 Air Force; Reserve — 605 Army, 2,074 Navy, 1,366 Marines, 975 Air Force, 1,709 Air National Guard; 892 civilians.
Major units: Navy Fleet Logistics Support Squadrons 59; 8th Marine Corps District; Marine Air Group 41; 14th Marine Regiment; Marine Aviation Logistics Squadron 41; Marine Fighter Attach Squadron 112; 136th Airlift Wing, Texas Air National Guard; U.S. Army 90th Aviation Support Battalion; 10th Air Force, 301st Fighter Wing, Air Force Reserve.

Naval Air Station Kingsville
Location: Kingsville (est. 1942).
Address: NAS Kingsville, Texas 78363
Main phone number: (361) 516-6136
Personnel: 363 active-duty; 159 reserve; 243 civilians.
Major units: Training Air Wing Two; Training Squadrons 21 and 22; Naval Auxiliary Landing Field Orange Grove; McMullen Target Range; Escondido Ranch.

U.S. ARMY

Fort Bliss
Location: El Paso (est. 1849).
Address: Fort Bliss, Texas 79916
Main phone number: (915) 568-2121
Personnel: 25,546 active-duty; 260 reserve; 5,660 civilians.
Major units: 1st Armored Division; 32nd Air and Missile Defense Command; 15th Sustainment Brigade; 5th Armored Brigade; Air Defense Artillery School; 11th Air Defense Artillery Brigades; Joint Task Force North; 204th Military Intelligence Battalion; 212th Fires Brigade; 402nd Field Artillery Brigade; Biggs Army Airfield (est. 1916).

Fort Hood
Location: Killeen (est. 1942).
Address: Fort Hood, Texas 76544
Main phone number: (254) 286-5139
Personnel: 36,391 active-duty; 805 reserve; 6,915 civilians.
Major units: III Corps, Headquarters Command; First Army Division West; 1st Cavalry Division; 13th Sustainment Command; 89th Military Police Brigade; 3rd Cavalry Regiment; 41st Fires Brigade; 504th Battlefield Surveillance Brigade; Army Operational Test Command; Darnell Army Medical Center.

Fort Sam Houston*
Location: San Antonio (est. 1878).
Address: Fort Sam Houston, Texas 78234
Main phone number: (210) 221-1211
Personnel: 10,462 active-duty; 692 reserve; 10,506 civilians.
Major units: U.S. Army North; U.S. Army South; Brooke Army Medical Center; Institute of Surgical Research; Army Medical Command; Army Medical Dept. Center and School; 5th Recruiting Brigade; 12th Brigade, Western Region (ROTC); Camp Bullis (est. 1917), training area.

Red River Army Depot
Location: 18 miles west of Texarkana (est. 1941).
Address: Red River Army Depot, Texarkana 75507
Main phone number: (903) 334-2141
Personnel: 19 active-duty; 93 reserve; 3,059 civilians.
Major unit: Defense Distribution Center; U.S. Army Tank-Automotive and Armaments Command.

U.S. AIR FORCE

Dyess Air Force Base
Location: Abilene (est. 1942 as Tye Army Airfield, closed at end of World War II, re-established in 1956).
Address: Dyess Air Force Base, Texas 79607
Main phone number: (325) 696-3113
Personnel: 4,221 active-duty; 425 reserve; 710 civilians.
Major units: 7th Bomb Wing (Air Combat Command); 317th Airlift Group.

Goodfellow Air Force Base
Location: San Angelo (est. 1940).
Address: Goodfellow AFB, San Angelo 76908
Main phone number: (325) 654-3876

Personnel: 3,195 active-duty; 29 reserve; 635 civilians.

Major units: 17th Training Wing; 517th Training Squadron; 17th Medical Group. 17th Mission Support Group.

Lackland Air Force Base*

Location: San Antonio (est. 1942 when separated from Kelly Field).

Address: Lackland Air Force Base, Texas 78236

Main phone number: (210) 671-1110

Personnel: 21,532 active-duty; 4,224 reserve; 9,296 civilians.

Major units: 37th Training Wing; 737th Training Group; 341th, 342nd, 343rd, 344th, and 345th Training Squadrons; Defense Language Institute; Inter-American Air Force Academy; Kelly Field Annex (was Kelly Air Force Base, est. 1916).

Laughlin Air Force Base

Location: Del Rio (est. 1942).

Address: Laughlin Air Force Base, Texas 78843

Main phone number: (830) 298-3511

Personnel: 1,288 active-duty; 82 reserve; 1,108 civilians.

Major unit: 47th Flying Training Wing.

Randolph Air Force Base*

Location: San Antonio (est. 1930).

Address: Randolph Air Force Base, Texas 78150

Main phone number: (210) 652-1110

Personnel: 2,649 active-duty; 538 reserve; 5,177 civilians.

Major units: 12th Flying Training Wing; 359th Medical Group; Air Education and Training Command; 902nd Mission Support Group; Air Force Recruiting Command; Air Force Manpower Agency.

Sheppard Air Force Base

Location: Wichita Falls (est. 1941).

Address: Sheppard Air Force Base, Texas 76311

Main phone number: (940) 676-2511

Personnel: 5,973 active-duty; 131 reserve; 1,603 civilians.

Major units: 82nd Training Wing; 80th Flying Training Wing; NCO Academy.

TEXAS MILITARY FORCES

Camp Mabry

Location: Austin. Just west of MoPac Blvd.

Address: Box 5218, Austin, Texas 78763

Main phone number: (512) 465-5101

Web site: www.tmd.texas.gov

Adjutant General of Texas:

Maj. General Tracy R. Norris

Major units: Joint Force Headquarters, the Standing Joint Interagency Task Force, the 36th Infantry Division, the 147th Reconnaissance Wing, 149th Fighter Wing, and the 136th Airlift Wing. Texas Air National Guard.

Texas Military Forces Museum, open Wednesday–Sunday, 10 a.m. - 4 p.m.

Tracing their history to early frontier days, the Texas Military Forces are organized into the Army and Air National Guard and the Texas State Guard.

The governor is commander-in-chief of the Texas Military Forces. This command function is exercised through the adjutant general appointed by the governor and approved by federal and state legislative authority.

When not in active federal service, Camp Mabry, in west Austin, serves as the administative and storage headquarters. Camp Mabry was established in the early 1890s as a summer encampment of the Texas Volunteer Guard, a forerunner of the Texas National Guard. The name honors Woodford Haywood Mabry, adjutant general from 1891–1898.

The State Guard, an all-volunteer backup force, was created by the Legislature in 1941. It became an active element of the state military forces in 1965 with a mission of reinforcing the National Guard in emergencies, and replacing National Guard units called into federal service. The State Guard had a membership of approximately 2,200 personnel in 2018.

The Army National Guard is available for state and national emergencies and has been used extensively during natural disasters. There were 17,000 Texans serving in the Texas Army National Guard in 2018.

When the military forces were reorganized following World War II, the Texas Air National Guard was added. Its units augment major Air Force commands. Approximately 3,000 men and women currently make up the Air Guard in the state.

Since 2003, some 31,000 National Guard troops from Texas have served in Iraq and Afghanistan.

In 2018, Adjutant General Norris commanded a total of some 22,000 soldiers, airmen, and civilians.

When called into active federal service, National Guard units come within the chain of command of the Army and Air Force units. ☆

Presidential Medal of Freedom

President Donald Trump honored Roger Staubach at the White House with a Presidential Medal of Freedom in 2018. Staubach, who lives in Dallas, was cited for his sports career, his military service, and his work for charitable causes, including United Way, Children's Scholarship Fund, and assistance to armed service members, veterans, and their spouses. White House photo.

Federal Courts in Texas

Source: The following list of U.S. appeals and district court judges and officials was compiled from court websites.

Texas is divided into four federal judicial districts, each of which is comprised of several divisions. Appeal from all Texas federal courts is to the U.S. Fifth Circuit Court of Appeals in New Orleans.

U.S. COURT OF APPEALS, FIFTH CIRCUIT

The Fifth Circuit is composed of Louisiana, Mississippi, and Texas. Sessions are held in each of the states at least once a year and may be scheduled at any location having adequate facilities. U.S. circuit judges are appointed for life and receive a salary of $220,600 in 2018.

Circuit Judges — Chief Judge, Carl E. Stewart, Shreveport.

Judges: Priscilla R. Owen, Austin.

Catharina Haynes, Don R. Willett, and James C. Ho, Dallas.

Edith H. Jones, Greg J. Costa, Jerry E. Smith, and Jennifer Walker Elrod, Houston.

James E. Graves Jr., Leslie H. Southwick, and E. Grady Jolly, Jackson, Miss.

Stuart Kyle Duncan, Lafayette, La.

James L. Dennis, Stephen A. Higginson, and Kurt Damian Engelhardt, New Orleans.

Andrew Stephen Oldham, San Antonio.

Senior Judges: Carolyn Dineen King and Thomas M. Reavley, Houston; Fortunato P. Benavides and Patrick E. Higginbotham, Austin; Rhesa H. Barksdale, Jackson, Miss.; John Malcolm Duhé Jr., Jacques L. Wiener Jr., W. Eugene Davis, and Edith Brown Clement, New Orleans.

Clerk of Court: Lyle W. Cayce, New Orleans.

U.S. DISTRICT COURTS

U.S. district judges are appointed for life and received a salary in 2018 of $208,000.

Northern Texas District
www.txnd.uscourts.gov

District Judges — Chief Judge, Barbara M.G. Lynn, Dallas.

Judges: Sam A. Lindsay, David C. Godbey, Ed Kinkeade, Jane Boyle, Reed O'Connor, and Keren Gren Scholer, Dallas.

Senior Judges: A. Joe Fish and Sidney A. Fitzwater, Dallas; Mary Lou Robinson, Amarillo; Terry R. Means and John H. McBryde, Fort Worth; Sam R. Cummings, Lubbock.

Clerk of District Court: Karen Mitchell, Dallas.

U.S. Attorney: Erin Nealy Cox, Dallas.

Federal Public Defender: Jason Hawkins.

U.S. Marshal: (vacant).

Bankruptcy Judges: Chief Judge, Barbara J. Houser, Dallas. Judges, Stacey G.C. Jernigan and Harlin D. Hale, Dallas; Mark X. Mullin and Russell F. Nelms, Fort Worth; Robert Jones, Lubbock. Court is in continuous session in each division of the Northern Texas District.

Following are the divisions of the Northern District and the counties in each division:

Abilene Division
Callahan, Eastland, Fisher, Haskell, Howard, Jones, Mitchell, Nolan, Shackelford, Stephens, Stonewall, Taylor, and Throckmorton. **Magistrate**: E. Scott Frost, Abilene. **Deputy-in-charge**: Misti Grant.

Amarillo Division
Armstrong, Briscoe, Carson, Castro, Childress, Collingsworth, Dallam, Deaf Smith, Donley, Gray, Hall, Hansford, Hartley, Hemphill, Hutchinson, Lipscomb, Moore, Ochiltree, Oldham, Parmer, Potter, Randall, Roberts, Sherman, Swisher, and Wheeler. **Magistrate**: Lee Ann Reno, Amarillo. **Deputy-in-charge**: Delynda Smith.

Dallas Division
Dallas, Ellis, Hunt, Johnson, Kaufman, Navarro, and Rockwall. **Magistrates**: Irma C. Ramirez, Renee H. Toliver, David L. Horan, and Rebecca Rutherford, Dallas. **Chief Deputy**: Jim Barton.

Fort Worth Division
Comanche, Erath, Hood, Jack, Palo Pinto, Parker, Tarrant, and Wise. **Magistrate**: Jeffrey L. Cureton, Fort Worth. **Division Manager**: Brian Rebecek.

Lubbock Division
Bailey, Borden, Cochran, Crosby, Dawson, Dickens, Floyd, Gaines, Garza, Hale, Hockley, Kent, Lamb, Lubbock, Lynn, Motley, Scurry, Terry, and Yoakum. **Magistrate**: D. Gordon Bryant Jr., Lubbock. **Division Manager**: Erik Paltrow.

San Angelo Division
Brown, Coke, Coleman, Concho, Crockett, Glasscock, Irion, Menard, Mills, Reagan, Runnels, Schleicher, Sterling, Sutton, and Tom Green. **Magistrate**: E. Scott Frost, San Angelo. **Division Manager**: Erik Paltrow.

Wichita Falls Division
Archer, Baylor, Clay, Cottle, Foard, Hardeman, King, Knox, Montague, Wichita, Wilbarger, and Young. **Magistrate**: Hal R. Ray Jr., Wichita Falls. **Deputy-in-Charge**: Teena Timmons.

Western Texas District
www.txwd.uscourts.gov

District Judges — Chief Judge, Orlando Garcia, San Antonio.

Judges: Fred Biery and Xavier Rodriguez, San Antonio.

Kathleen Cardone, Frank J. Montalvo, Philip R. Martinez, and David C. Guaderrama, El Paso.

Robert L. Pitman and Lee Yeakel, Austin.

Alia Moses, Del Rio.

David Counts, Midland-Odessa.

Alan Albright, Waco.

Senior Judges: James R. Nowlin and Sam Sparks, Austin; David Briones, El Paso; Robert A. Junell, Midland and Pecos; David A. Erza, San Antonio.

Clerk of District Court: Jeannette Clack, San Antonio.

U.S. Attorney: John F. Bash.

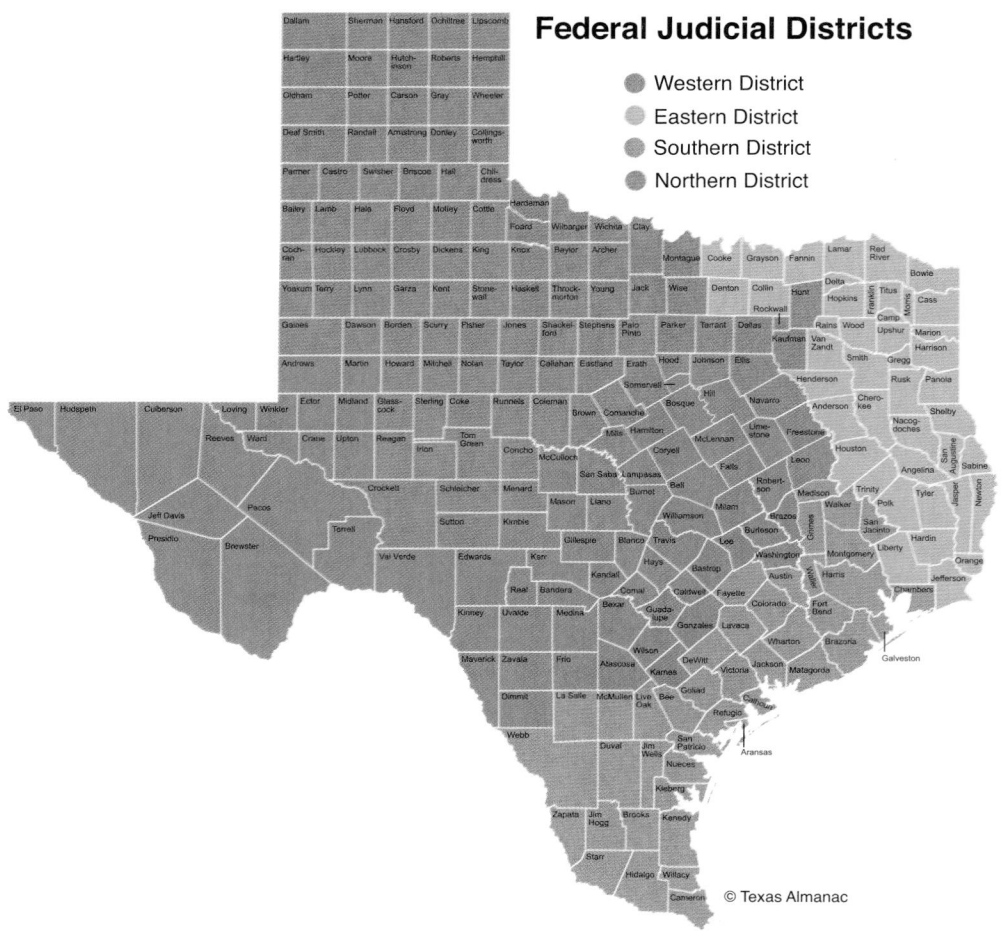

Federal Judicial Districts

- Western District
- Eastern District
- Southern District
- Northern District

© Texas Almanac

Federal Public Defender: Maureen Scott Franco.

U.S. Marshal: Susan L. Pamerleau.

Bankruptcy Judges: Chief Judge, Ronald B. King. Judges, Craig A. Gargotta, H. Christopher Mott and Tony M. Davis, Austin.

Following are the divisions of the Western District, and the counties in each division.

Austin Division

Bastrop, Blanco, Burleson, Burnet, Caldwell, Gillespie, Hays, Kimble, Lampasas, Lee, Llano, Mason, McCulloch, San Saba, Travis, Washington, and Williamson. **Magistrates**: Andrew W. Austin and Mark Lane, Austin. **Divisional Office Manager**: Annette French. **Bankruptcy Court Deputy-in-charge**: Theresa Mills.

Del Rio Division

Edwards, Kinney, Maverick, Terrell, Uvalde, Val Verde, and Zavala. **Magistrates**: Victor Roberto Garcia and Collis White, Del Rio. **Divisional Office Manager**: Trini Barrientez.

El Paso Division

El Paso, Hudspeth. **Magistrates**: Robert F. Castañeda, Anne T. Berton, Miguel A. Torres, and Leon Schydlower, El Paso. **Operations Support Supervisor**: Michael Maiella. **Bankruptcy Court Deputy-in-charge**: Julie Herrera.

Midland-Odessa Division

Andrews, Crane, Ector, Martin, Midland, and Upton. Court for the Midland-Odessa Division is held at Midland, but may, at the discretion of the court, be held in Odessa. **Magistrate**: Ronald C. Griffin, Midland. **Divisional Office Manager**: Jaye Kissler, Midland. **Bankruptcy Court Deputy-in-charge**: Christy L. Carouth.

Pecos Division

Brewster, Culberson, Jeff Davis, Loving, Pecos, Presidio, Reeves, Ward, and Winkler. **Magistrates**: David B. Fannin, Alpine. **Pecos Divisional Office Manager:** Michael Benavides. **Alpine Magistrate Deputy:** Yvette Lujan.

San Antonio Division

Atascosa, Bandera, Bexar, Comal, Dimmit, Frio, Gonzales, Guadalupe, Karnes, Kendall, Kerr, Medina, Real, and Wilson. **Magistrates**: Elizabeth S. Chestney, Richard B. Farrer, and Henry J. Bemporad, San Antonio. **Divisional Office Manager**: Michael F. Oakes. **Clerk of Bankruptcy Court**: Yvette Taylor.

Waco Division

Bell, Bosque, Coryell, Falls, Freestone, Hamilton, Hill, Leon, Limestone, McLennan, Milam, Robertson, and Somervell. **Magistrate**: Jeffrey C. Manske, Waco. **Divisional Office Manager**: Mark G. Borchardt. **Bankruptcy Court Deputy-in-charge**: Bridget Hardage.

Eastern Texas District
www.txed.uscourts.gov

District Judges — Chief Judge, Rodney Gilstrap, Marshall.

Judges: Marcia A. Crone, Rod Clark, and Thad Heartfield, Beaumont.

Michael H. Schneider, Tyler.

Robert W. Schroeder III, Texarkana.

Richard A. Schell, Plano. Amos L. Mazzant III, Sherman.

Clerk of District Court: David O'Toole.

U.S. Attorney: Joseph D. Brown.

Federal Public Defender: G. Patrick Black.

U.S. Marshal: Thomas Smith.

Bankruptcy Judges: Chief Judge, William Parker, Tyler; Brenda Rhoades, Plano.

Following are the divisions of the Eastern District and the counties in each division:

Beaumont Division

Hardin, Jasper, Jefferson, Liberty, Newton, and Orange. **Magistrates**: Zach Hawthorn and Keith F. Giblin. **Deputy-in-charge**: Brandy Fairley.

Lufkin Division

Angelina, Houston, Nacogdoches, Polk, Sabine, San Augustine, Shelby, Trinity, and Tyler. **Deputy-in-charge**: Brandy Fairley.

Marshall Division

Camp, Cass, Harrison, Hopkins, Marion, Morris, and Upshur. **Magistrate**: Roy Payne. **Deputy-in-charge**: Kecia Clendening.

Sherman Division

Collin, Cooke, Delta, Denton, Fannin, Grayson, Hopkins, and Lamar. **Magistrates**: Kimberly C. Priest Johnson and Christine A. Nowak, Plano. **Deputy-in-charge**: Karen Sessions.

Texarkana Division

Bowie, Franklin, Red River, and Titus. **Magistrate**: Caroline M. Craven. **Deputy-in-charge**: Lynn Siebel.

Tyler Division

Anderson, Cherokee, Gregg, Henderson, Panola, Rains, Rusk, Smith, Van Zandt, and Wood. **Magistrates**: K. Nicole Mitchell and John Love, Tyler. **Deputy-in-charge**: Kyla Dean.

Southern Texas District
www.txs.uscourts.gov

District Judges — Chief Judge, Lee H. Rosenthal, Houston.

Judges: Alfred H. Bennett, Keith Ellison, Vanessa Gilmore, Andrew S. Hanen, Lynn N. Hughes, Sim Lake, and Gray H. Miller, Houston.

Nelva Gonzales Ramos, Corpus Christi.

Rolando Olvera and Fernando Rodriguez, Brownsville.

Ricardo H. Hinojosa, Randy Crane, and Micaela Alvarez, McAllen. George C. Hanks Jr., Galveston.

Marina Garcia Marmolejo and Diana Saldaña, Laredo.

Senior Judges: Janis Graham Jack, Corpus Christi; David Hittner, Kenneth M. Hoyt, Nancy F. Atlas, Hilda G. Tagle, and Ewing Werlein Jr., Houston; George P. Kazen, Laredo; Kenneth M. Hoyt and John D. Rainey, Victoria.

Clerk of Court: David J. Bradley, Houston.

U. S. Attorney: Ryan K. Patrick, Houston.

Federal Public Defender: Marjorie A. Meyers.

U.S. Marshal: Gary Blankinship.

Bankruptcy Judges: Chief Judge, David Jones; Judges, Jeff Bohm, Marvin Isgur, Jeffrey P. Norman, and Eduardo V. Rodriguez.

Following are the divisions of the Southern District and the counties in each division:

Brownsville Division

Cameron and Willacy. **Magistrates**: Ronald G. Morgan, Ignacio Torteya III. **Deputy-in-charge**: Rosalina D'Venturi.

Corpus Christi Division

Aransas, Bee, Brooks, Duval, Jim Wells, Kenedy, Kleberg, Live Oak, Nueces, and San Patricio. **Magistrates**: B. Janice Ellington and Jason B. Libby. **Deputy-in-charge**: Marianne Serpa.

Galveston Division

Brazoria, Chambers, Galveston, and Matagorda. **Magistrate**: Andrew M. Edison. **Deputy-in-charge**: Lucia Smith.

Houston Division

Austin, Brazos, Colorado, Fayette, Fort Bend, Grimes, Harris, Madison, Montgomery, San Jacinto, Walker, Waller, and Wharton. **Magistrates**: Dena Hanovice Palermo, Frances H. Stacy, Nancy Johnson, Peter Bray, and Christina Bryan. **Deputy-in-charge**: Darlene Hansen.

Laredo Division

Jim Hogg, La Salle, McMullen, Webb, and Zapata. **Magistrates**: Diana Song Quiroga, John A. Kazen, and Sam S. Sheldon. **Deputy-in-charge**: Kathy Johnson.

McAllen Division

Hidalgo and Starr. **Magistrates**: J. Scott Hacker, Peter Ormsby, and Juan F. Alanis. **Deputy-in-charge**: Velma T. Barrera.

Victoria Division

Calhoun, DeWitt, Goliad, Jackson, Lavaca, Refugio, and Victoria. **Deputy-in-charge**: Lana Tesch. ☆

LAW ENFORCEMENT

Police in Galveston restricting access to damaged structures after Hurricane Ike.
Photo by Robert Kaufmann/FEMA.

TEXAS CRIME HISTORY

CRIME PROFILE OF TEXAS COUNTIES, 2017

TEXAS DEPARTMENT OF CRIMINAL JUSTICE

CORRECTIONAL INSTITUTIONS IN TEXAS

Law Enforcement and Crime Reporting

Source: Texas Department of Public Safety, Austin, www.dps.texas.gov; TDPS report Crime in Texas 2017

The crime statistics in this chapter are all thanks to the **Uniform Crime Reporting (UCR)** programs used by law enforcement agencies in Texas and nationwide. The first of these programs in the United States was the Committee on Uniform Crime Records, developed by the International Association of Chiefs of Police (IACP) in the 1920s. The first IACP crime collection program, in 1930, was voluntary and gathered information from 400 police agencies in 43 states. The FBI was authorized as the national clearinghouse for the information collected by that program.

UCR programs collect data on a summary basis, which provides reliable information about crime but has many limitations. In 1985 a new system was outlined for **Incident Based Reporting (IBR)**, whereby crime data is collected electronically and includes the circumstances of each incident. The national system, called NIBRS, has been slow to grow, but state programs and the FBI have worked in partnership to assist in the transition. In 2015, the Criminal Justice Information Services Division's Advisory Policy Board set a goal to **sunset summary reporting systems and adopt NIBRS by January 1, 2021.**

Texas first adopted the Uniform Crime Report in 1976, and the Department of Public Safety accepted the responsibility of collecting, validating, and tabulating reports from across the state. The Uniform Crime Reporting Section, created specifically for this purpose, is part of the Crime Records Service division of the department.

The state became certified to collect NIBRS data in 1998, and in 2015, House Bill 11 set a goal to transition all of Texas to NIBRS by September 1, 2019. More than 50% of active UCR agencies committed to that goal, and more than 75% have stated commitment to complete the transfer by 2021. The state program will be working to meet the 2021 goal with those agencies that have not yet transitioned.

In Texas, the Department of Public Safety collects data for the national UCR program from police, sheriff's offices, and its own officers. Data are estimated for nonreporting agencies and those that did not have 12 months of data. Agencies that contributed data for the 2017 Crime in Texas report include: 70 college and university police departments, 54 independent school district and zero-population police departments, 250 county sheriff's offices, and 647 city police departments.

Crime Summary, 2017

During 2017, there was a reported total of 842,055 index offenses in Texas. This represents a crime-volume decrease of 5.0 percent when compared to 886,189 reported offenses in 2016.

In 2017, there were 2,975 crimes per 100,000 people, compared with 3,185.2 in 2016, according to data compiled by the Department of Public Safety's UCR program. The crime rate is based on a 2017 population of 28,304,596, compared with a 2016 population of 27,821,692.

Full-Time Law Enforcement Personnel, 2017

Officers	Male	Female	Total
Police Departments	24,256	3,478	27,734
Sheriff Offices	8,510	1,481	9,991
DPS	3,892	295	4,187
Total	**36,658**	**5,254**	**41,912**
Civilians	**Male**	**Female**	**Total**
Police Departments	2,340	5,589	7,929
Sheriff Offices	6,365	6,280	12,645
DPS	1,905	3,560	5,465
Total	**10,610**	**15,429**	**26,039**

Monthly crime variations show that, in general, crime occurrences peaked in the month of May. During 2017, Texas law enforcement officers made 759,550 arrests, a decrease from the 808,634 arrests made in 2016.

Index Crimes

The 2017 violent crime rate increased 0.4 percent from 2016, and the nonviolent, or property, crime rate decreased 7.7 percent from 2016. Of the seven major crime categories, the UCR defines violent crime as murder, rape, robbery, and aggravated assault; property crime is defined as burglary, larceny/theft, and motor vehicle theft.

The value of property stolen during the commission of index crimes in 2017 was more than $1.9 billion, and about 26 percent of that property was recovered.

Texas Crime Rate* per 100,000 people, 2017

Crime	2017	2016	% Change
Murder	5.0	5.3	–5.8%
Rape	50.6	47.9	5.8%
Robbery	113.5	119.5	–5.0%
Aggravated Assault	266.2	261.0	2.0%
Violent Crime Total	**435.3**	**433.7**	**0.4%**
Burglary	470.4	532.2	–11.6%
Larceny/Theft	1,831.6	1,973.1	–7.2%
Motor Vehicle Theft	237.7	246.3	–3.5%
Property Crime Total	**2,539.7**	**2,751.6**	**–7.7%**
Index Crime Total	**2,975.0**	**3,185.2**	**–6.6%**

*Crime rate based on the 2017 Texas population of 28,304,596

Arson

The reported number of arsons committed in Texas in 2017 was 3,294, a decrease of 6.2 percent compared with 3,512 in 2016. In 2017, arson victims suffered losses of $121 million, a 47.2 percent increase when compared with 2016 arson losses of more than $82 million.

Family Violence

Reports of family violence decreased by 0.6 percent in 2017 over 2016. In 2017, there were 185,453 reported incidents of family violence involving 212,307 victims and 207,231 offenders. In 2016, there were 188,992 reported incidents of family violence involving 219,782 victims and 219,785 offenders.

DUI and Drug-Related Crimes

In 2017 there were 69,372 DUI arrests in Texas, an increase of 11.3 percent from 2016. Of those arrests, 6.1 percent were of persons under the age of 21.

Texas reported 147,231 drug abuse arrests in 2017, an increase of 2.2 percent from the previous year. Sales and manufacturing arrests accounted for 19,288 of those arrests (about 13 percent), and the remaining 128,003 arrests (87 percent) were for possession.

In a breakdown by drug type, the arrests for sales and manufacturing were 53.3 percent synthetic narcotics, 21.9 percent opium or cocaine, 11.4 percent marijuana, and 13.4 percent other. By contrast, possession arrests were 50.4 percent marijuana, 19.9 percent opium or cocaine, 10.4 percent synthetic narcotics, and 19.3 percent other.

Hate Crimes

There were 190 hate crimes reported in Texas in 2017, an increase of 6.7 percent from 2016. Incidents involved a total of 229 victims and 209 offenders.

Broken down by bias motivation, 58.6 percent of incidents were motivated by race/ethnicity/ancestry, 21.7 percent by sexual orientation, 14.6 percent by religion, 3 percent by gender identity, 1 percent by disability, and 1 percent by gender. Crimes occurred most frequently in residences, and 47.3 percent of offenders were white, 11.8 percent were black, 11.2 percent were multiracial, and the racial group of 29.6 percent of offenders was unknown.

Law Enforcement Assaults and Deaths

Assaults on law enforcement personnel decreased 4.1 percent in 2017 to 4,553. Injuries resulted from 40.6 percent of incidents. Seven law officers were killed in the line of duty in 2017, and another seven died in duty-related accidents. ☆

Texas Index Crime History, 1993–2017

Year	Murder	Rape*	Robbery	Assault	Violent Crime Total	Change from Prior Year	Burglary	Larceny/ Theft	Motor Vehicle Theft	Property Crime Total	Change from Prior Year
1993	2,149	9,923	40,464	84,892	137,428	N/A	233,944	664,738	124,822	1,023,504	N/A
1994	2,023	9,101	37,639	81,079	129,842	−5.5%	214,698	624,048	110,772	949,518	−7.2%
1995	1,694	8,526	33,666	80,377	124,263	−4.3%	202,637	632,523	104,939	940,099	−1.0%
1996	1,476	8,374	32,796	80,572	123,218	−0.8%	204,335	659,397	104,928	968,660	3.0%
1997	1,328	8,007	30,513	77,239	117,087	−5.0%	200,966	645,174	101,687	947,827	−2.2%
1998	1,343	7,914	28,672	73,648	111,577	−4.7%	194,872	606,805	96,614	898,291	−5.2%
1999	1,218	7,629	29,424	74,165	112,436	0.8%	190,347	614,478	91,992	896,817	−0.2%
2000	1,236	7,821	30,186	73,987	113,230	0.7%	188,205	634,575	92,878	915,658	2.1%
2001	1,331	8,191	35,330	77,221	122,073	7.8%	204,240	669,587	102,838	976,665	6.7%
2002	1,305	8,541	37,599	78,713	126,158	3.3%	212,702	690,028	102,943	1,005,673	3.0%
2003	1,417	7,986	37,000	75,706	122,109	−3.2%	219,733	697,790	98,174	1,015,697	1.0%
2004	1,360	8,401	35,811	75,983	121,555	−0.5%	220,079	696,220	93,844	1,010,143	−0.5%
2005	1,405	8,505	35,781	75,409	121,100	−0.4%	219,733	676,022	93,471	989,226	−2.1%
2006	1,385	8,407	37,271	74,624	121,687	0.5%	215,754	648,083	95,750	959,587	−3.0%
2007	1,415	8,430	38,777	73,570	122,192	0.4%	228,325	662,481	94,026	984,832	2.6%
2008	1,373	8.004	37,757	76,487	115,625	−5.4%	230,263	654,133	85,411	969,807	−1.5%
2009	1,327	8,286	38,041	74,135	121,789	5.3%	240,193	678,340	76,617	995,150	2.6%
2010	1,247	7,626	32,865	71,561	113,299	−7.0%	229,269	654,484	68,220	951,973	−4.3%
2011	1,089	7,445	28,399	68,028	104,961	−7.4%	215,512	613,528	63,379	892,419	−6.3%
2012	1,145	7,692	30,375	67,050	106,262	1.2%	204,976	605,362	64,982	875,320	−1.9%
2013	1,151	7,443	31,852	65,267	105,713	−0.5%	190,567	604,389	65,671	860,627	−1.7%
2014	1,187	11,466	30,857	65,338	108,848	3.0%	166,429	570,385	67,741	804,555	−6.5%
2015	1,314	12,208	31,883	67,358	112,763	3.6%	152,444	555,867	67,081	775,392	−3.6%
2016	1,473	13,320	33,250	72,609	120,652	7.0%	148,073	548,941	68,523	765,537	−1.3%
2017	1,412	14,332	32,120	75,347	123,211	2.1%	133,145	518,414	67,285	718,844	−6.1%

* In 2014, the FBI changed the definition of rape.

Source: Annual crime reports published by TDPS.

Crime Profile of Texas Counties, 2017

County	Reporting Agencies	Commissioned Personnel †	Murder	Rape	Robbery	Assault	Burglary	Larceny/Theft	Auto Theft	Total Index Crimes	Crime Rate per 100,000
Anderson ‡	3	34	2	25	16	141	258	480	57	979	1,700.6
Andrews	2	32	0	8	1	54	57	185	25	330	1,804.8
Angelina ‡	5	59	6	25	38	180	474	1,661	161	2,545	2,897.1
Aransas	4	75	1	19	6	116	353	779	62	1,336	3,956.9
Archer	1	21	0	0	0	10	3	14	2	29	556.9
Armstrong	1	4	0	0	1	4	9	10	5	29	1,550.8
Atascosa ‡	5	50	0	19	16	111	257	694	104	1,201	2,401.7
Austin ‡	5	56	0	11	5	33	97	182	45	373	1,244.9
Bailey ‡	2	9	0	0	1	7	31	53	6	98	1,365.1
Bandera	1	29	0	16	1	14	117	136	26	310	1,411.3
Bastrop ‡	5	77	2	37	39	178	319	951	106	1,632	1,916.6
Baylor	2	9	0	0	1	7	10	14	4	36	975.6
Bee ‡	2	25	1	2	3	69	165	342	26	608	1,850.2
Bell ‡	12	273	30	281	417	831	2,067	5,784	929	10,339	3,008.0
Bexar ‡	27	2,569	143	1,476	2,555	7,741	13,665	63,399	7,774	96,753	4,920.0
Blanco ‡	3	N/A	0	2	1	12	40	52	12	119	1,031.6
Borden	1	2	0	0	0	2	2	14	2	20	3,169.6
Bosque ‡	2	N/A	0	0	0	8	41	72	5	126	818.0
Bowie ‡	7	157	6	67	103	456	547	2,018	202	3,399	3,617.5
Brazoria ‡	22	188	10	105	91	430	945	4,094	366	6,041	1,645.5
Brazos ‡	4	249	6	125	120	399	752	4,011	267	5,680	2,528.9
Brewster ‡	3	12	1	3	0	19	43	49	8	123	1,340.0
Briscoe	1	3	0	1	0	0	4	2	2	9	621.5
Brooks ‡	2	16	0	0	2	15	70	116	0	203	2,816.3
Brown	4	72	1	25	11	87	161	701	34	1,020	2,666.2
Burleson ‡	2	13	0	2	6	28	46	107	9	198	1,207.0
Burnet ‡	5	N/A	0	37	5	73	164	409	47	735	1,559.8
Caldwell ‡	4	35	2	9	13	74	103	415	50	666	1,616.1
Calhoun ‡	3	N/A	1	20	3	86	103	206	33	452	2,282.4
Callahan ‡	3	8	0	4	1	17	48	71	13	154	1,111.4
Cameron ‡	21	131	8	225	191	895	1,788	8,975	350	12,432	2,931.0
Camp ‡	2	7	2	3	4	14	79	152	18	272	2,103.6
Carson ‡	2	4	0	2	0	17	10	24	2	55	911.5
Cass	5	48	0	8	8	55	197	288	34	590	1,970.5
Castro ‡	2	7	0	0	0	5	46	80	13	144	1,897.0
Chambers ‡	3	52	0	25	16	63	148	553	17	822	2,252.7
Cherokee ‡	3	33	1	25	13	168	260	599	72	1,138	2,210.7
Childress	1	5	0	0	0	3	4	8	0	15	1,575.6
Clay	1	14	0	5	2	9	43	75	19	153	1,515.6
Cochran ‡	1	N/A	0	0	0	5	0	1	2	8	281.8
Coke ‡	1	N/A	0	0	0	1	0	1	1	3	92.3
Coleman ‡	2	10	0	0	1	22	24	20	1	68	1,253.5
Collin ‡	18	683	25	249	266	657	1,835	10,486	681	14,199	1,501.3

† The commissioned personnel listed here are fulltime sworn officers employed as of Oct. 31, 2017. Of the 1,022 agencies that provided data for the *2017 Crime in Texas* report, only 478 also provided law enforcement personnel data.

‡ County in which one or more law enforcement agencies did not report data for all of 2017 to the DPS. Data for the county includes estimates for nonreporting agencies to enable the DPS to provide comparable data.

Crime Profile of Texas Counties, 2017

County	Reporting Agencies	Commissioned Personnel †	Murder	Rape	Robbery	Assault	Burglary	Larceny/Theft	Auto Theft	Total Index Crimes	Crime Rate per 100,000
Collingsworth ‡	0	N/A	N/A	N/A	N/A	N/A	N/A	N/A	N/A	N/A	N/A
Colorado ‡	4	16	0	4	1	56	64	110	31	266	1,265.5
Comal ‡	4	29	5	82	36	254	445	1,533	197	2,552	1,688.6
Comanche ‡	3	N/A	0	7	2	28	49	153	4	243	1,814.2
Concho	1	7	0	0	0	7	7	3	4	21	487.7
Cooke ‡	3	40	0	21	13	99	176	465	38	812	2,104.7
Coryell ‡	3	50	2	13	23	231	244	860	50	1,423	1,894.7
Cottle ‡	2	N/A	0	0	0	3	1	1	0	5	361.3
Crane ‡	2	6	0	0	0	3	1	22	3	29	591.1
Crockett	1	9	0	0	0	5	16	16	1	38	1,036.6
Crosby ‡	3	6	0	0	0	1	6	2	0	9	188.0
Culberson ‡	1	N/A	0	0	0	0	0	2	0	0	0
Dallam ‡	2	16	0	11	5	60	113	148	18	355	3,581.9
Dallas ‡	34	5,357	207	1,492	5,975	7,014	16,146	54,544	12,512	97,890	3,390.1
Dawson	2	21	0	5	0	14	35	88	9	151	1,173.9
Deaf Smith	2	40	0	7	5	52	79	300	32	475	2,538.7
Delta	1	11	0	0	0	2	13	10	1	26	499.3
Denton ‡	22	681	10	298	204	582	1,294	6,487	729	9,604	1,535.9
DeWitt ‡	3	15	0	24	1	108	121	202	21	477	2,541.3
Dickens ‡	2	3	0	0	0	7	8	1	0	16	747.0
Dimmit	1	31	0	0	1	16	21	98	6	142	1,300.8
Donley	1	6	0	0	0	2	15	25	2	44	1,313.4
Duval ‡	2	N/A	0	3	2	13	23	21	3	65	914.5
Eastland ‡	6	35	0	11	0	34	55	152	18	270	1,554.4
Ector ‡	4	251	12	86	123	873	868	3,452	470	5,884	3,608.4
Edwards	1	4	0	0	0	0	9	16	1	26	1,372.0
Ellis ‡	9	208	8	52	45	259	440	1,927	197	2,928	1,785.8
El Paso ‡	10	1,058	21	441	432	2,122	1,603	11,758	898	17,275	2,049.5
Erath ‡	4	N/A	1	39	5	50	103	444	27	669	1,582.4
Falls ‡	1	N/A	0	0	0	0	2	6	1	9	95.4
Fannin ‡	2	22	0	22	5	52	149	205	8	441	1,405.2
Fayette ‡	4	N/A	2	11	5	54	65	208	19	364	1,442.9
Fisher	1	4	0	0	0	1	4	2	0	7	182.6
Floyd ‡	2	7	0	4	1	32	36	45	7	125	2,142.6
Foard ‡	2	1	0	0	0	0	0	0	0	0	0
Fort Bend ‡	11	700	13	186	327	874	1,332	6,572	512	9,816	1,346.9
Franklin	1	11	0	6	0	19	45	34	7	111	1,121.9
Freestone ‡	4	N/A	0	5	5	20	69	121	19	239	1,221.1
Frio	3	43	0	0	1	32	132	272	30	467	2,427.5
Gaines	3	32	2	5	2	45	52	147	24	276	1,315.1
Galveston ‡	17	483	15	220	207	497	1,513	6,108	759	9,319	2,669.3
Garza	1	9	0	2	0	11	14	44	3	74	1,150.7
Gillespie ‡	2	28	0	0	3	11	35	177	3	229	855.2

† The commissioned personnel listed here are fulltime sworn officers employed as of Oct. 31, 2017. Of the 1,022 agencies that provided data for the *2017 Crime in Texas* report, only 478 also provided law enforcement personnel data.

‡ County in which one or more law enforcement agencies did not report data for all of 2017 to the DPS. Data for the county includes estimates for nonreporting agencies to enable the DPS to provide comparable data.

Crime Profile of Texas Counties, 2017

County		Reporting Agencies	Commissioned Personnel †	Murder	Rape	Robbery	Assault	Burglary	Larceny/Theft	Auto Theft	Total Index Crimes	Crime Rate per 100,000
Glasscock	‡	1	N/A	0	0	0	4	16	9	2	31	2,334.3
Goliad	‡	1	N/A	1	2	0	13	28	60	4	108	1,428.8
Gonzales		4	52	0	15	3	66	74	169	21	348	1,653.3
Gray	‡	2	14	0	0	6	116	181	576	38	917	4,031.1
Grayson	‡	11	189	6	64	52	250	606	1,663	238	2,879	2,292.7
Gregg	‡	5	167	9	91	116	357	892	2,693	364	4,522	3,425.1
Grimes		2	46	5	7	9	36	107	180	22	366	1,315.5
Guadalupe		4	236	6	98	41	164	456	1,867	147	2,779	1,898.6
Hale	‡	3	38	0	21	11	51	151	484	55	773	2,372.2
Hall ‡		3	3	0	0	0	20	3	7	2	32	1,031.9
Hamilton	‡	2	N/A	0	2	0	18	16	67	5	108	1,563.6
Hansford		2	11	0	0	0	2	6	9	2	19	344.1
Hardeman	‡	2	N/A	0	0	0	0	8	10	1	19	492.0
Hardin	‡	5	35	0	4	8	76	267	424	67	846	1,496.8
Harris	‡	45	8,166	376	2,187	13,288	20,660	27,352	109,057	18,503	191,423	4,070.7
Harrison	‡	4	47	0	36	31	154	504	939	142	1,806	2,794.2
Hartley		1	6	1	0	0	0	4	6	2	13	450.6
Haskell		2	8	0	2	2	5	16	12	4	41	730.7
Hays	‡	5	213	7	104	83	273	568	2,436	319	3,790	1,777.8
Hemphill	‡	1	N/A	0	0	0	0	2	10	1	13	310.7
Henderson	‡	9	35	6	58	20	189	526	789	115	1,703	2,132.4
Hidalgo	‡	22	906	38	411	361	1,696	3,228	17,500	779	24,013	2,807.4
Hill	‡	4	N/A	2	12	6	36	146	452	45	699	2,076.4
Hockley	‡	3	34	1	19	3	109	144	399	38	713	3,057.2
Hood	‡	2	55	1	24	4	90	151	680	51	1,001	1,760.4
Hopkins	‡	3	53	2	10	5	48	51	173	24	313	856.0
Houston	‡	3	20	0	0	5	47	107	207	19	385	1,705.2
Howard	‡	2	37	3	9	23	162	260	816	100	1,373	3,714.6
Hudspeth	‡	1	N/A	0	0	0	1	0	1	1	3	72.0
Hunt	‡	5	111	7	58	40	209	420	960	154	1,848	2,106.7
Hutchinson	‡	2	15	2	32	3	30	181	369	44	661	3,380.7
Irion		1	5	0	0	0	1	11	9	4	25	1,617.1
Jack	‡	2	11	0	3	1	11	14	85	13	127	1,461.3
Jackson	‡	3	15	1	5	4	8	46	116	12	192	1,280.9
Jasper	‡	2	20	1	35	11	90	225	391	45	798	2,384.4
Jeff Davis		1	4	1	0	0	3	5	3	1	13	597.7
Jefferson	‡	7	537	23	133	44	1,275	2,359	5,632	696	10,162	4,143.7
Jim Hogg	‡	1	N/A	0	1	0	6	4	8	3	22	429.9
Jim Wells	‡	4	31	0	29	6	176	461	831	62	1,565	3,888.9
Johnson	‡	8	155	7	81	25	309	579	1,859	248	3,108	1,793.6
Jones	‡	5	20	2	4	3	35	70	97	15	226	1,583.6
Karnes		3	46	0	5	1	33	79	205	17	340	2,221.4
Kaufman	‡	5	138	3	52	48	185	598	1,308	202	2,396	1,986.8

† The commissioned personnel listed here are fulltime sworn officers employed as of Oct. 31, 2017. Of the 1,022 agencies that provided data for the *2017 Crime in Texas* report, only 478 also provided law enforcement personnel data.

‡ County in which one or more law enforcement agencies did not report data for all of 2017 to the DPS. Data for the county includes estimates for nonreporting agencies to enable the DPS to provide comparable data.

Crime Profile of Texas Counties, 2017

County	Reporting Agencies	Commissioned Personnel †	Murder	Rape	Robbery	Assault	Burglary	Larceny/Theft	Auto Theft	Total Index Crimes	Crime Rate per 100,000
Kendall ‡	2	N/A	1	18	1	21	432	393	55	921	2,192.3
Kenedy ‡	1	N/A	0	0	0	3	0	3	0	6	1,492.5
Kent	1	3	0	0	0	0	1	3	0	4	524.9
Kerr	3	104	1	17	7	64	139	651	40	919	1,775.3
Kimble	2	12	0	0	0	5	11	14	4	34	774.3
King	1	1	0	0	0	0	0	0	0	0	0
Kinney	1	6	0	0	1	4	5	0	1	11	575.0
Kleberg ‡	3	70	1	14	24	124	244	774	36	1,217	3,851.6
Knox ‡	3	5	0	2	0	6	17	16	2	43	1,126.8
Lamar ‡	4	86	1	13	32	206	269	777	67	1,365	2,744.5
Lamb ‡	3	10	0	8	1	39	52	101	17	218	1,781.5
Lampasas ‡	2	19	1	2	2	26	79	216	9	335	1,826.2
LaSalle ‡	2	24	0	0	3	9	7	49	1	69	892.5
Lavaca ‡	5	19	0	12	1	28	88	132	8	269	1,217.5
Lee ‡	2	N/A	1	10	2	27	31	165	6	242	1,520.3
Leon ‡	2	N/A	0	1	1	17	45	101	9	174	1,072.1
Liberty ‡	3	39	0	17	22	96	94	530	62	821	3,244.3
Limestone ‡	4	N/A	1	10	12	56	123	386	19	607	2,589.4
Lipscomb ‡	1	N/A	0	0	0	6	4	6	4	20	568.3
Live Oak ‡	3	25	0	2	2	28	78	69	14	193	1,591.0
Llano ‡	2	N/A	0	2	1	6	53	81	7	150	1,059.5
Loving	1	4	0	0	0	0	0	1	0	1	826.4
Lubbock ‡	8	5	13	171	401	2,149	2,649	8,996	1,366	15,745	5,177.9
Lynn ‡	2	N/A	0	0	0	3	28	26	7	64	1,282.6
Madison ‡	3	13	0	2	2	50	87	118	5	264	1,894.4
Marion ‡	2	6	4	6	2	52	73	83	17	237	2,351.4
Martin ‡	2	5	1	1	0	2	4	42	9	59	1,002.5
Mason ‡	1	N/A	0	0	0	6	2	11	2	21	509.3
Matagorda ‡	4	45	3	15	34	123	266	709	27	1,177	3,161.4
Maverick ‡	2	N/A	0	11	9	63	251	661	59	1,054	1,811.8
McCulloch ‡	2	10	0	0	0	7	54	99	7	167	2,048.1
McLennan ‡	15	295	7	199	144	802	1,304	5,323	297	8,076	3,278.6
McMullen ‡	1	N/A	0	0	0	0	0	9	15	0	24	2,926.8
Medina ‡	5	60	2	26	4	71	201	644	81	1,029	2,144.6
Menard	1	6	0	0	0	1	3	2	0	6	285.3
Midland ‡	3	262	2	37	64	328	527	2,391	311	3,660	2,217.6
Milam ‡	4	N/A	2	4	3	49	107	252	15	432	1,736.4
Mills ‡	1	N/A	0	0	0	2	12	8	2	24	490.3
Mitchell ‡	2	8	0	2	0	8	62	117	8	197	2,290.4
Montague ‡	3	15	0	4	3	54	115	210	26	412	2,247.6
Montgomery ‡	13	560	22	149	172	528	1,085	5,014	724	7,694	1,356.5
Moore ‡	3	9	1	8	2	37	73	252	37	410	1,853.7
Morris ‡	5	6	2	3	2	41	63	127	10	248	1,980.7

† The commissioned personnel listed here are fulltime sworn officers employed as of Oct. 31, 2017. Of the 1,022 agencies that provided data for the *2017 Crime in Texas* report, only 478 also provided law enforcement personnel data.

‡ County in which one or more law enforcement agencies did not report data for all of 2017 to the DPS. Data for the county includes estimates for nonreporting agencies to enable the DPS to provide comparable data.

Crime Profile of Texas Counties, 2017

County	Reporting Agencies	Commissioned Personnel †	Murder	Rape	Robbery	Assault	Burglary	Larceny/Theft	Auto Theft	Total Index Crimes	Crime Rate per 100,000
Motley ‡	1	N/A	0	1	0	2	7	5	2	17	1,475.7
Nacogdoches ‡	3	42	2	34	26	99	235	942	44	1,382	2,096.2
Navarro ‡	2	43	2	44	23	143	320	697	58	1,287	2,736.6
Newton ‡	2	22	0	0	0	12	42	43	12	109	783.2
Nolan ‡	3	36	0	3	1	48	178	201	32	463	3,399.2
Nueces ‡	8	464	24	250	491	1,783	2,534	9,591	783	15,456	4,239.4
Ochiltree ‡	2	7	0	0	0	41	39	86	17	183	1,773.4
Oldham ‡	1	N/A	0	0	0	2	7	14	2	25	1,203.1
Orange ‡	6	65	4	14	61	213	396	896	182	1,766	2,081.5
Palo Pinto	2	51	0	1	2	9	76	68	10	166	589.4
Panola	2	37	2	3	5	61	107	383	42	603	2,603.7
Parker ‡	5	90	4	45	12	102	408	1,209	96	1,876	1,450.9
Parmer ‡	4	11	0	4	0	16	33	35	6	94	970.5
Pecos ‡	2	N/A	1	7	3	33	54	164	11	273	1,703.3
Polk ‡	4	13	5	44	5	72	223	544	66	959	1,986.2
Potter ‡	4	97	16	187	238	118	1,720	6,211	1,000	9,490	4,853.4
Presidio ‡	2	N/A	0	1	0	2	6	13	1	23	337.7
Rains	1	12	0	3	0	16	35	46	13	113	994.0
Randall ‡	3	N/A	1	31	4	60	81	285	62	524	1,352.3
Reagan	1	13	0	0	0	6	10	45	3	64	1,753.4
Real ‡	1	N/A	0	0	0	2	13	35	2	52	1,530.8
Red River ‡	3	18	0	4	1	18	67	74	8	172	1,422.7
Reeves ‡	2	19	0	7	5	107	32	219	2	372	2,463.9
Refugio ‡	2	N/A	0	1	0	7	7	18	0	33	451.6
Roberts ‡	1	N/A	0	0	0	1	4	2	0	7	765.9
Robertson ‡	3	16	2	9	2	35	105	165	12	330	2,086.2
Rockwall ‡	5	36	2	29	7	65	128	895	79	1,205	1,347.2
Runnels ‡	3	6	0	2	0	37	34	57	5	135	1,294.6
Rusk ‡	4	29	1	18	8	170	256	674	53	1,180	2,399.7
Sabine ‡	2	4	0	4	2	32	37	82	14	171	1,819.0
San Augustine ‡	2	N/A	1	4	0	26	27	20	16	94	1,142.6
San Jacinto ‡	1	N/A	0	27	3	26	195	198	73	522	1,871.3
San Patricio ‡	9	27	5	20	23	162	315	992	79	1,596	2,637.3
San Saba ‡	2	N/A	0	0	0	6	16	18	5	45	761.6
Schleicher ‡	1	N/A	0	1	0	1	8	22	1	33	1,105.2
Scurry ‡	2	10	0	3	0	33	65	182	6	289	1,662.6
Shackelford	1	7	0	0	0	3	4	8	2	17	514.7
Shelby ‡	2	15	4	9	4	73	92	269	22	473	1,937.0
Sherman ‡	2	3	0	0	0	0	1	2	3	6	195.3
Smith ‡	10	351	9	116	85	892	1,151	4,053	376	6,682	2,804.6
Somervell ‡	1	N/A	0	0	0	7	23	50	1	81	919.1
Starr ‡	5	107	1	27	12	113	191	380	97	821	1,271.7
Stephens ‡	2	18	0	3	0	16	33	86	8	146	1,467.6

† The commissioned personnel listed here are fulltime sworn officers employed as of Oct. 31, 2017. Of the 1,022 agencies that provided data for the *2017 Crime in Texas* report, only 478 also provided law enforcement personnel data.

‡ County in which one or more law enforcement agencies did not report data for all of 2017 to the DPS. Data for the county includes estimates for nonreporting agencies to enable the DPS to provide comparable data.

Crime Profile of Texas Counties, 2017

County	Reporting Agencies	Commissioned Personnel †	Murder	Rape	Robbery	Assault	Burglary	Larceny/Theft	Auto Theft	Total Index Crimes	Crime Rate per 100,000
Sterling	1	4	0	0	0	0	0	0	0	0	0
Stonewall ‡	1	N/A	0	0	0	0	3	5	0	8	565.8
Sutton ‡	2	N/A	0	4	0	1	10	29	2	46	1,199.5
Swisher ‡	4	13	0	2	3	17	22	92	8	144	1,931.6
Tarrant ‡	38	3,928	104	1,068	2,242	4,870	9,265	41,588	5,082	64,219	3,201.5
Taylor ‡	6	299	5	110	139	431	1,173	2,759	272	4,889	3,421.3
Terrell	1	4	0	0	0	2	2	6	3	13	1,662.4
Terry ‡	2	10	0	1	4	23	39	116	17	200	1,561.5
Throckmorton	1	2	0	0	0	2	5	0	1	8	528.1
Titus ‡	2	25	3	35	8	90	158	579	26	899	2,758.4
Tom Green ‡	3	172	4	92	41	165	959	3,580	296	5,137	4,295.2
Travis ‡	15	2,171	39	1,007	1,083	2,831	5,452	29,253	2,409	42,074	3,270.2
Trinity ‡	1	N/A	0	3	1	19	52	108	24	207	1,778.2
Tyler ‡	2	N/A	2	8	2	79	168	118	40	417	1,964.4
Upshur	3	66	3	7	8	135	197	238	37	625	1,707.3
Upton	1	11	0	1	0	7	2	18	0	28	751.1
Uvalde ‡	3	40	1	4	11	31	108	596	14	765	2,792.1
Val Verde	2	100	1	12	11	37	181	594	21	857	1,755.8
Van Zandt ‡	5	46	0	8	2	25	197	303	21	556	1,046.8
Victoria ‡	2	118	5	83	57	178	904	1,945	150	3,322	3,559.1
Walker ‡	2	N/A	4	47	31	151	191	567	119	1,110	1,542.3
Waller ‡	6	60	2	32	16	105	209	401	53	818	1,629.6
Ward ‡	2	11	0	14	3	55	55	127	14	268	2,278.1
Washington	2	64	2	10	4	136	128	275	36	591	1,676.7
Webb ‡	6	470	10	125	156	599	931	5,610	174	7,605	2,771.9
Wharton ‡	3	26	2	16	23	128	209	640	62	1,080	2,586.1
Wheeler ‡	2	10	0	0	0	5	9	26	3	43	772.5
Wichita ‡	6	296	6	98	130	224	878	2,685	288	4,309	3,271.7
Wilbarger ‡	2	18	1	7	4	29	66	270	15	392	3,067.3
Willacy ‡	6	29	1	19	5	114	191	417	15	762	3,508.0
Williamson ‡	12	296	2	188	97	405	925	5,874	333	7,824	1,603.1
Wilson ‡	5	57	2	6	5	37	144	268	52	514	1,040.8
Winkler ‡	3	22	1	2	0	0	10	43	4	60	747.1
Wise ‡	5	66	2	35	4	92	142	432	48	755	1,155.7
Wood ‡	5	51	0	21	3	52	160	298	34	568	1,254.8
Yoakum	2	15	0	4	0	4	16	49	7	80	931.2
Young ‡	3	6	1	6	3	17	54	112	14	207	1,145.6
Zapata ‡	1	N/A	0	0	4	21	113	135	10	283	1,968.0
Zavala ‡	2	10	0	3	1	31	49	67	8	159	1,318.1
TOTAL	**1,021**	**37,541**	**1,412**	**14,332**	**31,726**	**74,638**	**133,149**	**518,400**	**67,272**	**840,929**	**2,975.0**

† The commissioned personnel listed here are fulltime sworn officers employed as of Oct. 31, 2017. Of the 1,022 agencies that provided data for the *2017 Crime in Texas* report, only 478 also provided law enforcement personnel data.

‡ County in which one or more law enforcement agencies did not report data for all of 2017 to the DPS. Data for the county includes estimates for nonreporting agencies to enable the DPS to provide comparable data.

Texas Department of Criminal Justice

Source: Texas Department of Criminal Justice, www.tdcj.texas.gov

The Texas Board of Criminal Justice is composed of nine nonsalaried members who are appointed by the governor for staggered six-year terms. The board employs the Texas Department of Criminal Justice (TDCJ) executive director, sets rules and policies that guide the agency, and considers other agency actions at its meetings.

Board members serve in a separate capacity as the Board of Trustees for the **Windham School District** by hiring a superintendent and providing similar oversight. The Windham School District is a separate entity primarily funded through the Texas Education Agency (TEA).

In addition to hiring the TDCJ executive director, the board appoints an inspector general, a director of internal audits, a director of state counsel for offenders, and a prison rape elimination act ombudsman.

The TDCJ executive director is responsible for the administration and enforcement of statutes relative to the criminal justice system.

The Correctional Institutions Division, Private Facility Contract Monitoring and Oversight Division, Parole Division, and Community Justice Assistance Division are most involved in the everyday confinement and supervision of convicted felons.

The actual supervision of probationers is the responsibility of local community supervision and corrections departments. Victim Services coordinates a central mechanism for crime victims to participate in the criminal justice process.

Divisions of the TDCJ

The **Correctional Institutions Division** (CID) is responsible for the confinement of adult felony and state jail offenders who are sentenced to incarceration in a secure state-operated correctional facility. (More about this division on the next page.)

The **Private Facility Contract Monitoring and Oversight Division** is responsible for oversight and monitoring contracts for privately operated secure facilities, as well as community-based facilities, which include substance abuse treatment services.

The **Parole Division** supervises all offenders released on parole or mandatory supervision, conducts release and transition planning, and verifies compliance with statutory provisions of release.

In addition, this division contracts for electronic monitoring and processing responses to violations, administers programs and services through District Resource Centers and Parole Offices, and coordinates the Interstate Compact for Adult Offender Supervision.

The **Community Justice Assistance Division** (CJAD) administers community supervision, also known as adult probation in Texas. CJAD is responsible for the distribution of formula and grant funds; the development of standards, including best-practice treatment standards; approval of Community Justice Plans and budgets; conducting program and fiscal audits; and providing training and certification of community supervision officers.

Financial Summary 2017

Budget Item	Amount Spent (in millions)	Percent of Total
A: Provide Prison Diversions	$ 315.3	9.18%
B: Special Needs Offenders	25.9	0.76%
C: Incarcerate Felons	2,767.6	80.61%
D: Ensure Adequate Facilities	30.7	0.90%
E: Board of Pardons and Paroles	29.6	0.86%
F: Operate Parole System	192.4	5.60%
G: Indirect Administration	71.8	2.09%
TOTAL	**$ 3,433.5**	**100%**

Source: TDCJ Annual Review 2018.

Inmate Profile
As of Fiscal Year 2018

Sex – Ethnicity – Age	
Male: 91.6%	Hispanic: 33.5%
Black: 32.7%	Other: 0.6%
White: 33.3%	Average age: 39.4

Average Sentences	
Prison: 19.5 years	State jail: 1.1 year

Average Part Of Sentence Served	
Prison: 61.0%	State jail: 99.5%

(Based on offenders released in Fiscal Year 2018.)

Education	
Average IQ	90.7
Percent lacking high school diploma or GED:	81.3%

Source: TDCJ Annual Review 2018.

The remaining divisions support the overall operation of the TDCJ. These include:

- Office of the General Counsel
- Administrative Review and Risk Management
- Business and Finance
- Information Technology
- Manufacturing, Agribusiness and Logistics
- Facilities
- Rehabilitation Programs
- Re-entry and Integration Programs
- Health Services and Human Resources ☆

Correctional Institutions Division

In addition to the incarceration of offenders, the CID has the following support functions: classification and records; counsel substitute; laundry, food, and supply; offender transportation; and correctional training and staff development.

The table below lists all of the correctional institutions in the state alphabetically by county. It includes both those operated by the CID as well as privately-operated facilities, which have been overseen by the **Private Facility Contract Monitoring and Oversight Division** since June 15, 2007.

The town listed is the nearest one to the facility, although the unit may actually be in another county. For instance, the Middleton Transfer Facility is in Jones County, but the nearest city is Abilene, which is in Taylor County. ☆

On-Hand Population	
As of Aug. 31, 2018	
Prisoners	
Prisons	134,152
State Jails	7,433
SAFP (Substance Abuse)	3,434
TOTAL	**145,019**
Parole	
Mandatory Supervision Population	84,495
Probation	
Felony and Misdemeanor*	368,871

*Total adults on direct, indirect, and pretrial supervision, minus transfers

Source: TDCJ Annual Review 2018.

Correctional Institutions in Texas

County	Unit	Nearest Town	Max. Capacity, Gender	Employees	Type* (Operator**)
Anderson	Beto	Tennessee Colony	3,471 Male	633	Prison (CID)
Anderson	Coffield	Tennessee Colony	4,139 Male	879	Prison (CID)
Anderson	Gurney	Tennessee Colony	2,128 Male	437	Transfer (CID)
Anderson	Michael	Tennessee Colony	3,800 Male	816	Prison (CID)
Anderson	Powledge	Palestine	1,137 Male	290	Prison (CID)
Angelina	Diboll	Diboll	518 Male	136	Private Prison (MTC)
Angelina	Duncan	Diboll	606 Male	139	Geriatric (CID)
Bee	Garza East	Beeville	2,458 Male	442	Transfer (CID)
Bee	Garza West	Beeville	2,278 Male	401	Transfer (CID)
Bee	McConnell	Beeville	2,900 Male	542	Prison (CID)
Bexar	Dominguez	San Antonio	2,276 Male	382	State Jail (CID)
Bowie	Telford	New Boston	2,872 Male	706	Prison (CID)
Brazoria	Clemens	Brazoria	1,215 Male	348	Prison (CID)
Brazoria	Darrington	Rosharon	1,931 Male	546	Prison (CID)
Brazoria	Ramsey	Rosharon	1,891 Male	429	Prison (CID)
Brazoria	Scott	Angleton	1,130 Male	307	Prison (CID)
Brazoria	Stringfellow	Rosharon	1,212 Male	313	Prison (CID)
Brazoria	Terrell, C.T.	Rosharon	1,603 Male	466	Prison (CID)
Brazos	Hamilton	Bryan	1,166 Male	256	Pre-Release (CID)
Brown	Havins	Brownwood	596 Male	181	Pre-Release (CID)
Burnet	Halbert	Burnet	612 Female	135	SAFPF (CID)
Caldwell	Lockhart	Lockhart	500 Female, 500 Male	204	Private Prison/Work Program (MTC)
Cherokee	Hodge	Rusk	989 Male	333	DDP (CID)

* **Prison types:** SAFPF (Substance Abuse Felony Punishment Facilities); DDP (Developmentally Disabled Program)
** **Operator abbreviations:** CID (TDCJ Correctional Institutions Division); MTC (Management and Training Corporation); LaSalle (LaSalle Corrections)
1 Employee and capacity data for the Jordan unit in Gray Co. includes those working and held at the nearby Baten facility

Source: TDCJ Unit Directory.

Correctional Institutions in Texas

County	Unit	Nearest Town	Max. Capacity, Gender	Employees	Type* (Operator**)
Cherokee	Skyview	Rusk	562 Female/Male	295	Psychiatric (CID)
Childress	Roach	Childress	1,384 Male	289	Prison (CID)
Coryell	Crain	Gatesville	2,115 Female	711	Prison (CID)
Coryell	Hilltop	Gatesville	553 Female	268	Prison (CID)
Coryell	Hughes	Gatesville	2,984 Male	741	Prison (CID)
Coryell	Mountain View	Gatesville	645 Female	300	Prison (CID)
Coryell	Murray	Gatesville	1,341 Female	341	Prison (CID)
Coryell	Woodman	Gatesville	900 Female	270	State Jail (CID)
Dallas	Hutchins	Dallas	2,276 Male	399	State Jail (CID)
Dawson	Smith	Lamesa	2,234 Male	408	Prison (CID)
DeWitt	Stevenson	Cuero	1,384 Male	272	Prison (CID)
Duval	Glossbrenner	San Diego	612 Male	123	SAFPF (CID)
El Paso	Sanchez	El Paso	1,100 Male	287	State Jail (CID)
Falls	Hobby	Marlin	1,384 Female	299	Prison (CID)
Falls	Marlin	Marlin	606 Female	126	Transfer (CID)
Fannin	Cole	Bonham	900 Male	226	State Jail (CID)
Fannin	Moore, C.	Bonham	1,224 Male	245	Transfer (CID)
Fort Bend	Jester I	Richmond	323 Male	119	SAFPF (CID)
Fort Bend	Jester III	Richmond	1,131 Male	288	Prison (CID)
Fort Bend	Jester IV	Richmond	550 Male	381	Psychiatric (CID)
Fort Bend	Vance	Richmond	378 Male	116	Prison (CID)
Freestone	Boyd	Teague	1,372 Male	298	Prison (CID)
Frio	Briscoe	Dilley	1,384 Male	233	Prison (CID)
Galveston	Hospital Galveston	Galveston	365 Female/Male	496	Medical (CID)
Galveston	Young	Galveston	455 Female	302	Medical (CID)
Gray[1]	Jordan	Pampa	1,008 Male[1]	289[1]	Prison (CID)
Grimes	Luther	Navasota	1,316 Male	323	Prison (CID)
Grimes	Pack	Navasota	1,478 Male	334	Prison (CID)
Hale	Formby	Plainview	1,100 Male	278	State Jail (CID)
Hale	Wheeler	Plainview	576 Male	127	State Jail (CID)
Harris	Kegans	Houston	667 Male	155	State Jail (CID)
Harris	Lychner	Humble	2,276 Male	413	State Jail (CID)
Hartley	Dalhart	Dalhart	1,398 Male	237	Prison (CID)
Hays	Kyle	Kyle	520 Male	117	Private Prison (MTC)
Hidalgo	Lopez	Edinburg	1,100 Male	257	State Jail (CID)
Hidalgo	Segovia	Edinburg	1,224 Male	233	Pre-Release (CID)
Houston	Eastham	Lovelady	2,474 Male	583	Prison (CID)
Jack	Lindsey	Jacksboro	1,031 Male	202	State Jail (MTC)
Jasper	Goodman	Jasper	612 Male	155	Transfer (CID)
Jefferson	Gist	Beaumont	2,276 Male	368	State Jail (CID)
Jefferson	Leblanc	Beaumont	1,224 Male	248	Pre-Release (CID)

* **Prison types:** SAFPF (Substance Abuse Felony Punishment Facilities); DDP (Developmentally Disabled Program)
** **Operator abbreviations:** CID (TDCJ Correctional Institutions Division); MTC (Management and Training Corporation); LaSalle (LaSalle Corrections)
[1] Employee and capacity data for the Jordan unit in Gray Co. includes those working and held at the nearby Baten facility

Source: TDCJ Unit Directory.

Correctional Institutions in Texas

County	Unit	Nearest Town	Max. Capacity, Gender	Employees	Type* (Operator**)
Jefferson	Stiles	Beaumont	2,981 Male	756	Prison (CID)
Johnson	Estes	Venus	1040 Male	191	Private Prison (MTC)
Jones	Middleton	Abilene	2,128 Male	504	Transfer (CID)
Jones	Robertson	Abilene	2,984 Male	683	Prison (CID)
Karnes	Connally	Kenedy	2,148 Male	602	Prison (CID)
La Salle	Cotulla	Cotulla	606 Male	99	Transfer (CID)
Liberty	Cleveland	Cleveland	520 Male	134	Private Prison (MTC)
Liberty	Henley	Dayton	576 Female	124	State Jail (CID)
Liberty	Hightower	Dayton	1,384 Male	335	Prison (CID)
Liberty	Plane	Dayton	2,291 Female	418	State Jail (CID)
Lubbock	Montford	Lubbock	1,044 Male	705	Psychiatric (CID)
Madison	Ferguson	Midway	2,421 Male	578	Prison (CID)
Medina	Ney	Hondo	576 Male	134	State Jail (CID)
Medina	Torres	Hondo	1,384 Male	298	Prison (CID)
Mitchell	Wallace	Colorado City	1,448 Male	255	Prison (CID)
Pecos	Fort Stockton	Fort Stockton	606 Male	114	Transfer (CID)
Pecos	Lynaugh	Fort Stockton	1,416 Male	289	Prison (CID)
Polk	Polunsky	Livingston	2,984 Male	691	Prison (CID)
Potter	Clements	Amarillo	3,798 Male	1,050	Prison (CID)
Potter	Neal	Amarillo	1,732 Male	383	Prison (CID)
Rusk	Bradshaw	Henderson	1,980 Male	266	State Jail (MTC)
Rusk	East Texas	Henderson	224 Female, 2,012 Male	493	Multi-Use (MTC)
Rusk	Moore, B.	Overton	500 Male	109	Private Prison (MTC)
San Saba	San Saba	San Saba	606 Female	135	Transfer (CID)
Scurry	Daniel	Snyder	1,384 Male	224	Prison (CID)
Stephens	Sayle	Breckenridge	632 Male	146	SAFPF (CID)
Swisher	Tulia	Tulia	606 Male	117	Transfer (CID)
Terry	Rudd	Brownfield	612 Male	145	Transfer (CID)
Travis	Travis County	Austin	1,161 Male	264	State Jail (CID)
Tyler	Lewis	Woodville	2,231 Male	570	Prison (CID)
Walker	Byrd	Huntsville	1,365 Male	282	Prison (CID)
Walker	Ellis	Huntsville	2,482 Male	604	Prison (CID)
Walker	Estelle	Huntsville	3,480 Male	980	Prison (CID)
Walker	Goree	Huntsville	1,321 Male	315	Prison (CID)
Walker	Holliday	Huntsville	2,128 Male	435	Transfer (CID)
Walker	Huntsville	Huntsville	1,705 Male	446	Prison (CID)
Walker	Wynne	Huntsville	2,621 Male	697	Prison (CID)
Wichita	Allred	Iowa Park	3,722 Male	939	Prison (CID)
Willacy	Willacy County	Raymondville	1,069 Male	183	State Jail (La Salle)
Wise	Bridgeport	Bridgeport	520 Male	117	Private Prison (MTC)
Wood	Johnston	Winnsboro	612 Male	160	SAFPF (CID)

* **Prison types:** SAFPF (Substance Abuse Felony Punishment Facilities); DDP (Developmentally Disabled Program)
** **Operator abbreviations:** CID (TDCJ Correctional Institutions Division); MTC (Management and Training Corporation); LaSalle (LaSalle Corrections)
[1] Employee and capacity data for the Jordan unit in Gray Co. includes those working and held at the nearby Baten facility

Source: TDCJ Unit Directory.

CULTURE & ARTS

Dinosaur exhibits in the Perot Museum of Nature and Science in Dallas.
Photo by Jonathan Cutrer (jcutrer.com).

ASIAN INDIANS IN TEXAS

MUSEUMS, TEXAS MEDAL OF THE ARTS

TEXAS INSTITUTE OF LETTERS

STATE ARTISTS, POETS, HISTORIANS

FILM AND TELEVISION

HOLIDAYS AND RELIGION

Asian Indians in Texas

By Ayshea Khan

According to U.S. Census estimates, there were 358,002 Asian Indians living in Texas in 2017. The state's thriving job market, educational opportunity, and warm climate have made Texas the fourth-largest concentration of Asian Indians in the United States behind California, New York, and New Jersey.

The Indian Texan community is incredibly diverse, with the Indian continent representing more than 600 languages alongside a myriad of religious and cultural practices. Since the early 1900s, Indian Americans have helped shape the state's economy, public policy, and cultural landscape through their work in education, public health, high technology, medicine, and local business entrepreneurship.

Early Immigration Patterns

Immigration from the Indian subcontinent to the United States prior to 1965 was limited due to a series of racist immigration laws targeted at Asian populations. The Immigration Act of 1917, also known as the Asiatic Barred Zone Act, prohibited immigration from the Asia-Pacific Zone, which included the Indian subcontinent. Asian Indians were targeted specifically in rulings such as the 1923 United States v. Bhagat Singh Thind decision, which decided Asian Indian immigrants such as Bhagat Singh Thind were ineligible for naturalized citizenship.

The 1946 Luce-Celler Act reversed this decision, which allowed 100 Filipinos and 100 Asian Indians into the United States per year. Filipino and Indian Americans were also eligible for naturalization and citizenship under this provision. The Immigration and Nationality Act of 1952 abolished previous racial restrictions outlined in the Immigration Act of 1917, while also providing a quota system for nationalities and regions. Under this new policy, immigration from the "Asiatic barred zone" was capped at 2,000 people annually.

Yet despite these laws, Asian Indians still managed to settle in Texas in the early 1900s. These immigrants were most likely Punjabi Sikhs seeking agricultural work who traveled through Latin America to Texas. By 1930, 49 Indians lived in Texas, many of them attending universities in Dallas, Houston, Lubbock, and College Station. While miscegenation laws that were in place until 1970 prohibited early Asian immigrants from marrying white Texans, many still married Mexican or African American women.

The 1965 Immigration Act led to a swell of Indian immigration to Texas and the rest of the country. The policy removed the quota system based on country of origin. Professionals and others with specialized skills were given priority under this immigration act, resulting in Indians adept in high technology, engineering, energy, manufacturing, and medical fields clustering in major Texas cities. While immigrants prior to 1965 were predominantly male, this policy allowed for an influx of Indian women to the state. Furthermore, the Vietnam War resulted in a severe shortage of nurses in the 1970s. Nurses were recruited from both India and the Philippines to offset this shortage, part of a federal initiative that provided financial and citizenship incentives to relocate to the United States.

> The Asian American population in Texas has increased by 42 percent since 2010, with rapid growth seen in cities such as Austin, Sugar Land, Frisco, Richardson, and Plano. While early immigration stipulations often privileged high-earning Indian professionals, today's Indian Texans are activists, medical providers, artists, software developers, refugees, musicians, small-business owners, service industry workers, and much more.

The 1990 H1-B Visa program permitted Asian immigration for work in the United States for up to six years. Texas companies were able to recruit highly educated workers from overseas when there was a shortage of skilled Americans. This visa program caused the Indian Texan population to double in the 1990s, with skilled Indians flocking to the state for professional and educational opportunity.

The Indian Community of DFW

The Dallas-Fort Worth area is home to one of the oldest Indian American communities in Texas. The city served as a cultural hub for visiting Indian philosophers, lecturers, dancers, and other performers. These visitors came to academic institutions such as Southern Methodist University (SMU) and the University of Texas at Dallas (UT-Dallas). Some of the earliest community members in Dallas included Iqbal "Ike" Singh, who moved to Dallas in 1956 to attend the Graduate School of Business at SMU. Over time he became known as the "patriarch of the Indian community" in Dallas. He welcomed and assisted Indian families new to the area and founded community organizations such as the India Association of North Texas and the Punjabi Cultural Association of North Texas. He was a longtime restaurateur and owned the Safari, La Tunisia, and Commerce Club establishments.

Kumar Pallana was another early Dallas resident. This Indian plate spinner and entertainer was active in the United States vaudeville circuit as "Kumar of India." In the 1960s he settled in Dallas, where he introduced yoga to locals through one of the state's first yoga centers. He and his family also ran the Cosmic Cup Café, which led to Pallana's introduction to filmmaker Wes Anderson. This relationship led to the Indian American appearing in films such as *Bottle Rocket*, *The Royal Tenenbaums*, and *The Terminal*.

Many early Indian entrepreneurs across the state operated motels, often owned by Indians with the surname "Patel," part of the Gujarati Hindu subcaste. By 1984, nearly 14% of all nonchain motels in Texas were owned by families surnamed Patel. Motel ownership in the 1980s helped young Indian families meet requirements for permanent residence status, and these buildings were often operated by leveraging large familial networks. While many families initially began working low-cost independent motels in less desirable areas, many soon branched out to operate much larger commercial chains such as Ramada and Holiday Inn. By 1994, families named Patel owned about 80% of the 90 small motels in Dallas.

From 2000 to 2010 the Asian Indian community of Dallas-Fort Worth more than doubled, with 106,964 Asian Indians residing in Collin, Dallas, Denton, Rockwall, and Tarrant counties. The India Association of North Texas, originally founded in 1962, continues to host a variety of cultural celebrations, social events, and community service projects, which keeps the Indian community base strong and thriving. New immigrants are attracted to the city's job

Photo on previous page: The Sri Meenakshi Devasthanam in Pearland. Photo by I_am_jim (CC).

market, strong school system, and proximity to Indian places of worship, groceries, and other local businesses. In 2012 there were 90 Indian restaurants within a 40-mile radius of Dallas.

The Indian Community of Houston

Houston is home to one of the largest Asian Indian communities in the state. From 1950 to 1965, Houston was the temporary home for a small number of Indians coming to the city to work for a few years before returning to their home country. The oil boom of the 1970s brought thousands of Indians to Houston, with companies such as Humble Oil and Shell Oil attracting Indian engineers and researchers. Texas Medical Center and NASA's Johnson Space Center were also prominent places of employment for Indian immigrants. In these earlier days, the University of Houston's India Student Association served as the center for the Houston Indian community. The association provided support for Indians who had recently relocated due to work, education, or seeking refugee assistance.

Despite the recession of the 1980s and exodus of many Asian Americans from Houston, the Indian American community continued to grow. Today, the influence of the Indian American community can certainly be felt throughout Houston. The community has organized expansive fundraising efforts, such as the campaign supporting the 2001 Gujarat earthquake relief efforts. The city mourned the passing of Kalpana Chawla, the first American of South Asian descent to travel in space and victim in the 2003 *Columbia* shuttle disaster. Chawla earned her Master's degree in aerospace engineering and conducted her astronaut training in Houston in 1994. In 2004, the Asian Advisory Committee was created within the Houston Independent School District to address the growing Asian American student population. The committee has worked to provide translation services for parents, advocate for more diverse curriculum development, and implement Asian cultural celebrations within the classroom.

Other Texan Hubs

Austin

As of 2016, Asian Indians are the fastest-growing Asian ethnic subgroup in the city, comprising roughly 33% of Austin's Asian population. While the city of Austin was home to very few early Indian pioneers, the University of Texas at Austin (UT-Austin) has been a campus known for its active Indian community. Early Indian Americans in Austin included Dr. Shanti Seth and Dr. Jagdishkumar Aggarwal, who both worked at UT-Austin and married each other in the city in 1965. Dr. Shanti Aggarwal came to the United States on an International Peace Scholarship, and her husband became the first non-European professor in the Engineering department. Other early UT-Austin faculty included Sockalingam "Sam" Kannappan, a Tamil graduate student at UT-Austin from 1968-1970, Indian philosopher Raja Rao, and Dr. E.C.G. Sudarshan, who was nominated for the Nobel Prize for his work in particle physics.

Outside of the fields of science, medicine, and technology, UT-Austin's Indian student population engaged in social justice activism and community advocacy. Trikone-Tejas was formed at UT-Austin in 1996 as a progressive coalition of queer students, faculty, and staff of pan-Asian heritage. The organization was committed to ending sexism and homophobia through book and film discussions, workshops, and confidential support groups. Many Indian students were involved with the Asian American Relations Group (ARG!) and the Anti-Racist Organizing Committee in the late 1990s. Through years of protest and student organization, these two organizations fought for the creation of an Asian American Studies program at the university. UT-Austin graduate Raul Mahajan was recognized in Austin for his antiwar activism and won the 2002 Green Party's nomination for Texas governor. Mahajan was the first Asian to ever make the ballot for that office.

Austin was also the birthplace of Saheli, a grassroots community organization that provided assistance to South Asian and other immigrant families dealing with issues related to domestic violence, sexual assault, and trafficking. The organization was started in 1992 and was the first community organization of its kind in the Southwest. A network of South Asian women worked to establish a confidential hotline, host educational discussions and family trainings, provide resources for immigrants, and demonstrate solidarity for broader antiviolence, antiracist work. The nonprofit has evolved from a small grassroots network into a pan-Asian organization now known as Asian Family Support Services of Austin (www.AFSSAustin. org).

Midland-Odessa

The Indian community of Midland-Odessa developed over time due to the fiercely competitive job markets in Dallas and Houston. Midland-Odessa became a center for petrochemical production and distribution, attracting many Indian professionals from medical and related fields. A home was purchased in 1987 to be used as a gathering space for Hindu Indians of Midland-Odessa. By the year 2000, 532 Indian families lived in the area.

Religion

The majority of the Indian Texan community practices the Hindu faith. When there were no temples built in Texas, the Hindu Worship Society of Houston provided Indians the opportunity to practice their faith at services held in family homes. The Society was finally able to establish the first Hindu temple in 1975. Sri Meenakshi Davasthanam was constructed in Pearland in 1982 as the third traditional Hindu temple in the United States. Built for the goddess Meeankshi, the temple now occupies close to 20 acres of land and serves more than 5,000 Indian Houstonians. Houston community member Raj Sayal organized the Hindus of Greater Houston in 1990, which united all local Hindu organizations to participate in celebratory festivals, volunteer projects, and support of Hindu youth. Indian communities in Houston, Dallas, Austin, and elsewhere have held public celebrations for holidays such as Diwali, Holi, and Ratha-Yatra.

Houston is home to the largest Sikh community in Texas. The first gurdwara (Sikh temple) in the American South was constructed in northeast Houston in the early 1970s. Jasbir Sing

Sethi led a group of Sikh Indian Houstonians to advocate for the Sikh Center of the Gulf Coast Area. In 1984 Indian Prime Minister Indira Gandhi was assassinated by her two Sikh bodyguards. The aftermath of the killing included violent anti-Sikh riots and discrimination across India. Sikh Houstonian Hardam Singh Azad helped form the Sikh Association of America in response to the conflict. Azad became a prominent Sikh American and even addressed 2,000 Sikhs in Washington, D.C., in January 1985.

A Malayali Indian community is centered in Houston suburbs including Missouri City, Bellaire, and Stafford. These Malayalam-speaking Christian and Catholic families often have mothers working as nurses while husbands hold nonprofessional jobs. In Dallas, Grace Bible Church hosted Indian worship services until the Malayali groups began organizing the ownership of their own church buildings. There are now approximately 20 Indian Christian congregations in the Dallas-Fort Worth area.

On previous page: Dr. Shanti Seth Aggarwal worked as a research associate at UT-Austin, where she met Dr. Jagdishkumar Aggarwal, who became her husband. Photo courtesy of the Austin History Center.

On this page: Kalpana Chawla immigrated to the U.S. in 1982 and became a citizen in 1991. She was the first American of South Asian decent to travel in space and logged more than 30 hours in space over two missions. Photo courtesy of NASA.

Texas is home to the largest Muslim population in the United States. Today, Dallas is home to the fourth-largest Muslim population in the country and has been described as the "Madinah of America." Mike Ghouse was an Indian Dallas resident and activist who organized the construction of a mosque in Grand Prairie to serve Dallas Indians, Pakistanis, Bangladeshis, Arabs, and Persians. The terrorist attacks on September 11, 2001, spurred a wave of vandalism, violence, and other anti-Muslim and -Sikh discrimination across the United States. Indian children in Texas have shared experiences of bullying, exclusion, and other harassment from their white peers. Solidarity efforts have been spearheaded by Indian and Pakistani Texans in support of the state's mosque communities.

Dallas has also become a hub for South Asian spiritualism connected to Sikh yogis, Tibet's Dalai Lama, the Baha'i faith, Hare Krishna, and transcendental meditation. The Hare Krishna community in Dallas first established a preaching center in 1970, and in 1971 the International Society for Krishna Consciousness purchased a property for a gurukula. Dallas became the site of the first Hare Krishna School in the Western Hemisphere with the opening of TKG Academy in 1972.

other Indian groceries, restaurants, jewelers, clothiers, and other local businesses sprouted up in the area. This included Raja Sweets, operated by the Gahunias family; Himalaya, owned by Kaiser Lashkari; and Shri Balaju Bhavan, offering South Indian vegetarian fare. In 2010 the enclave was officially named the Mahatma Gandhi District. The Dallas suburb of Irving is also known for its exceptional Indian food and street fare, with establishments such as Bombay Sweets & Snacks, Patel Brothers, and Taj Chaat House. Vir Singh owned and operated Indian restaurants in Dallas before opening his Star of India mini-chain of restaurants in Austin, the oldest chain of its kind in the city. Taj Palace is another early Indian Austin establishment, opened in 1990 by Ajay and Kirin Behl. Austin's Indian food has since expanded to include popular restaurants such as Clay Pit and Swad, as well as Indian-Tex-Mex fusion eateries such as The Whip-In and Nasha.

Arts & Culture

Cuisine

As Indian immigration continues to rise in Texas, the country's vibrant food, music, art, and celebrations have left an indelible mark on the state's cultural landscape. While the rich curries and kebabs of Northern India have served as an accessible entry point for many Western palates, Texans from all over now seek the dosas and idlis of South India, the Indochinese influences of Western Bombay, Bengali mutton biriyanis and spiced fish and many more regional dishes.

In 1983 Rupa Vyas opened an Indian American grocery store in the Hillcroft area of southwest Houston. Over subsequent years

Music, Dance & Film

The diaspora of classical Indian music was a product of British colonialization and subsequent Indian immigration to Europe and North America. Renowned Indian musician Ravi Shankar played a major role in popularizing classical Indian music around the world. Dr. Shankar Bhattacharyya came to Texas in the late 1960s to study at Rice University. It was during this time he co-founded the Society for Promotion of Indian Classical Music and Culture Amongst Youth, which has been committed to introducing young Texans to the classical traditions through music concerts, dance performances, and workshops. The Indian Classical Music Circle of Austin (formerly Asian Music

Circle) began in 1975 by Dinkar Rao and Barda Sharma at UT-Austin. The group has brought more than 200 concerts to the Central Texas area. The India Culture Center of Houston has recognized the contributions of David Courtney and his wife Chandrakantha for promoting Indian music in Texas through their involvement with the KPFT radio program *Evening Ragas.*

The Anjali Center for Performing Arts in Sugar Land was founded in 1975 by choreographer Rathna Kumar. This was the first Indian dance school in Texas. The Natyalaya School of Dance, founded by Vinitha Subramanian in 1982, continues to be the largest and oldest Indian classical dance school in the Central Texas area. The school brings the joy of Indian dances such as Bharatanatyam to children of all ages in the Austin area. Classical Indian dancers such as Anuradha Naimpally and Gina Lalli have also made invaluable contributions to the classical Indian dance tradition in Austin.

Indian Americans have also made impressions in the more popular sphere of music. The popularity of Bollywood dance workshops and performances has swept across the state. For example, Bollywood radio programs such as *FunAsiA* of Dallas garner hundreds of thousands of listeners. More contemporary popular artists include Geethali Nora Jones Shankar, daughter of Ravi Shankar and Sue Jones. The artist, known to most as Norah Jones, grew up in Dallas and studied jazz piano at the University of North Texas. Savan Kotecha from Austin is a multiple Grammy and Golden Globe-nominated songwriter known for his collaborations with artists such as Ariana Grande, Usher, Katy Perry, and One Direction.

Texas is the third-largest market for Bollywood films in the country. In addition to its radio program, *FunAsiA* also hosts Bollywood cinema screenings complete with Indian snacks for attendees throughout Dallas and Houston. In addition to Bollywood, nonprofit organizations such as Indie Meme curate South Asian independent film screenings for the Austin and Dallas area. Texans can experience a wide range of Indian cinema at any one of the many film festivals across the state:

- Asian Film Festival of Dallas
- Austin Asian American Film Festival
- DFW South Asian Film Festival
- Houston Asian American & Pacific Islander Film Festival
- Indian Film Festival of Houston
- Indie Meme Film Festival

Yoga

Yoga may be one of the best examples of Indian culture permeating Texas society. An ancient Indian practice, yoga in the United States dates back to the late nineteenth century, with early Indian-born yogis such as Swami Vivekananda and Indra Devi. These yogis would travel from city to city, spreading knowledge of the spiritual practice and philosophy. Texas community members such as Kumar Pallana and other Indian residents spread awareness of the spiritual practices and benefits of yoga in the late 1970s. Yoga studios began to spring up in major Texas  cities, despite some white Texan communities ignorantly referring to the studios as cults or devil worship.

Western sentiments toward the practice have definitely shifted, with nearly 16 million U.S. adults practicing yoga. However, many of these studios have taken a departure from the traditional Indian yoga philosophy and are often run by American non-Asian practitioners.

Festivals

Festivals centered on Indian celebrations and culture attract thousands of attendees each year across the state. The City of Houston's Republic Day Parade, a celebration of national heritage and culture, attracts thousands each January. For the past 25 years, the Greater Dallas Asian American Chamber of Commerce has hosted its annual Asian Festival in celebration of Asian American & Pacific Islander Heritage Month in May. It is known as the largest Asian festival in North Texas and showcases more than 20 Asian countries and cultures. The Islamic Circle of North America Dallas presents an

On previous page: A performance by dancers at the Anjali Performing Arts Center in Houston. Photo courtesy of Anjali Performing Arts.

On this page: An early business card used by Kumar Pallana. Image courtesy of Dipak Pallana and the South Asian American Digital Archive (SAADA).

annual Dallas Muslim Festival, one of the largest annual gatherings of Muslim Texans in the state. The event gives community members the opportunity to connect, share food, and support various Muslim merchants.

Diwali, the traditional Hindu festival of lights, is a fall celebration recognized by major cities across Texas. Each year the Dallas Fort Worth Indian Cultural Society hosts its DFW Diwali Mela, which began as a modest house party of 50 guests hosted by Satish Gupta in 1994. Today, the lavish event is held at the Cotton Bowl and is one of the largest Diwali celebrations in the United States. The event features a re-enactment of the Ramayana, Bollywood singers flown in from India, pop-up restaurants, artisans, and fireworks. Holi is another popular celebration known as the Hindu Festival of Color. The event brings communities together to engage in color play and partake of Indian snacks such as gujiya and malpua. On the eve before Holi, Holika pyres are lit to symbolize Vishnu's triumph over the devil, Holika, and the victory of good over evil. Houston Holi, held at The Crown Festival Park at Sugar Land each year, is the largest Holi Festival in the United States.

Some major Indian festivals held across Texas include:

- AsiaFest in Plano
- Asian Festival, UTSA Institute of Texan Cultures in San Antonio
- Asian Festival in Dallas
- Dallas Muslim Festival
- Diwali Festival celebrated in the fall across Texas
- Festival of Joy held in Dallas
- Festivals of India in Houston
- Holi Festival celebrated in the spring across Texas
- Houston Rath Yatra Festival
- India Republic Day (January 26, 1950), celebrated across Texas
- Indian Independence Day (August 15, 1947) celebrated across Texas
- Pohela Boishakh, or "South Asian New Year Festival," in Austin
- Puranava Indian Culture Fest in Pearland

About the Author

Ayshea Khan currently serves as the Asian American Community Archivist for Austin History Center, the historic division of the Austin Public Library and official archival repository for the City of Austin. Her work is centered on collecting, preserving, and providing access to our diverse local Asian American & Pacific Islander histories. She holds a B.S. in Cinema & Photography from Ithaca College and a MSIS from the University of Texas at Austin School of Information. She is the co-chair of the South Asian American Digital Archive Archivists' Collective and is a core coordinator for the Breaking Library Silos for Social Justice collective.

Further Reading

Benson, Eric. 2016. "Faith And Hope". *Texas Monthly*. https://www.texasmonthly.com/the-culture/faith-and-hope-omar-suleiman/.

Boardman, Amanda. 2012. "Asian Indian Population Booming In Dallas-Fort Worth". *The Dallas Morning News*. https://www.dallasnews.com/news/news/2012/01/11/asian-indian-population-booming-in-dallas-fort-worth.

Brady, M. (2004). *The Asian Texans*. College Station: Texas A & M University Press.

Chen, Angela. 2018. "A Snapshot Of How Asian-Americans Are Changing The South". *Huffpost*. https://www.huffingtonpost.com/entry/asian-american-growth-south_us_5a948133e4b0699553cb5834.

(DADS), Data. 2019. "American Factfinder". United States Census Bureau. https://factfinder.census.gov.

Fox, Margalit. 2013. "Kumar Pallana, Who Went From Yoga To Film, Dies At 94". *The New York Times*. https://www.nytimes.com/2013/10/16/movies/kumar-pallana-94-dies-went-from-yoga-to-film.html.

Handbook of Texas Online, David Marcus, "INDIAN CLASSICAL MUSIC," accessed March 19, 2019, http://www.tshaonline.org/handbook/online/articles/xbi01. Uploaded on April 3, 2015. Modified on September 4, 2015. Published by the Texas State Historical Association.

"Hindus Of Greater Houston". 2019. *Hindus Of Greater Houston*. https://www.hindusofhouston.org/.

"Iqbal Sekhon's Obituary". 2019. *The Dallas Morning News*. https://obits.dallasnews.com/obituaries/dallasmorningnews/obituary.aspx?n=iqbal-sekhon&pid=18129439.

Krishna, Priya. 2019. "If You Missed Diwali In India, Dallas Is The Place To Be". *The New York Times*. https://www.nytimes.com/2017/10/31/dining/diwali-mela-dallas-food.html.

Tang, I. (2008). *Asian Texans*. Austin, Tex.: The it Works.

Varadarajan, Tunku. 1999. "A Patel Motel Cartel?". *The New York Times*. https://www.nytimes.com/1999/07/04/magazine/a-patel-motel-cartel.html.

Yip, Pamela. "Indian grocer achieved success despite her lack of knowledge about the world of business." (Archive) *Houston Chronicle*. March 21, 1993.

Texas Museums of Art, Science, History

Listed below are links to the websites of Texas museums. Where required, some have indication of the area of emphasis of the exhibits.

Abilene
Frontier Texas! (history)
www.frontiertexas.com
Grace Museum (art, history)
www.thegracemuseum.org
National Center for Children's Illustrated Literature
www.nccil.org

Addison
Cavanaugh Flight Museum
www.cavflight.org

Albany
Old Jail Art Center
www.theojac.org

Alpine
Museum of the Big Bend (history)
www.museumofthebigbend.com

Amarillo
Amarillo Museum of Art
www.amarilloart.org
American Quarter Horse Hall of Fame & Museum
www.aqha.com/museum
Don Harrington Discovery Center (science, children's)
www.discoverycenteramarillo.org
Texas Pharmacy Museum
www.ttuhsc.edu/pharmacy/museum/

Angleton
Brazoria County Historical Museum
www.brazoriacountytx.gov/departments/museum

Austin
Blanton Museum of Art
www.blantonmuseum.org
Bob Bullock Texas State History Museum
www.thestoryoftexas.com
Capitol Visitors Center (history)
www.tspb.texas.gov/prop/tcvc/cvc/cvc.html
The Contemporary Austin (art)
www.thecontemporaryaustin.org
Elisabet Ney Museum (art, history)
www.austintexas.gov/elisabetney
French Legation Museum (history)
www.thc.texas.gov/historic-sites/french-legation-state-historic-site
Harry Ransom Humanities Research Center (history, literature)
www.hrc.utexas.edu
Lady Bird Johnson Wildflower Center
www.wildflower.org
Lyndon B. Johnson Presidential Library
www.lbjlibrary.org
Mexic-Arte Museum (Art)
www.mexic-artemuseum.org
O. Henry Museum (history)
www.austintexas.gov/department/o-henry-museum
Pioneer Farms
www.pioneerfarms.org

Texas Memorial Museum (history, natural history)
www.tmm.utexas.edu
Texas Military Forces Museum
www.texasmilitaryforcesmuseum.org
Texas Music Museum
www.texasmusicmuseum.org
Thinkery (children's museum)
thinkeryaustin.org
Umlauf Sculpture Garden & Museum
www.umlaufsculpture.org
Wild Basin Wilderness Preserve
www.parks.traviscountytx.gov/find-a-park/wild-basin
Women and Their Work
www.womenandtheirwork.org

Bay City
Matagorda County Museum and Children's Museum
visitbaycity.org/arts-culture/museum

Beaumont
Art Museum of Southeast Texas
www.amset.org
Edison Museum (science)
www.edisonmuseum.org
Fire Museum of Texas
www.fmotassn.com
Spindletop/Gladys City Boomtown Museum (history)
www.lamar.edu/spindletop-gladys-city/index.html
Texas Energy Museum (history)
www.texasenergymuseum.org

Beeville
Beeville Art Museum
www.bamtexas.org

Belton
Bell County Museum
www.bellcountymuseum.org

Big Spring
Heritage of Big Spring
www.heritagebigspring.com

Bonham
Fannin County Museum of History
www.fannincountymuseum.org
Fort Inglish Village
visitbonham.com/things-to-see/fort-inglish-village
Sam Rayburn Library/Museum
www.cah.utexas.edu/museums/rayburn.php

Borger
Hutchinson County Historical Museum
www.hutchinsoncountymuseum.org

Brownsville
Brownsville Heritage Museum (history)
www.brownsvillehistory.org
Brownsville Museum of Fine Art
bmfa.us
Children's Museum of Brownsville
www.cmofbrownsville.org
Costumes of the Americas Museum
costumesoftheamericasmuseum/net

RGV Commemorative Air Force Museum
www.rgvcaf.org/museum.html
Stillman House Museum (history)
www.brownsvillehistory.org/stillman-house.html

Brownwood
Brown County Museum of History
https://browncountyhistory.org/bcmoh.html
Lehnis Railroad Museum
www.brownwoodtexasgov/228/Lehnis-Railroad-Museum

Bryan-College Station
Brazos Valley African American Museum
www.bvaam.org
Brazos Valley Museum of Natural History
www.brazosvalleymuseum.org
Children's Museum of the Brazos Valley
cmbv.org
George H.W. Bush Presidential Library
https://www.bush41.org
University Art Galleries
uart.tamu.edu

Buffalo Gap
Buffalo Gap Historic Village
https://taylorcountyhistorycenter.com

Burton
Burton Cotton Gin and Museum
www.cottonginmuseum.org

Canadian
The Citadelle Art Foundation
www.thecitadelle.org
River Valley Pioneer Museum
www.rivervalleymuseum.org

Canyon
Panhandle-Plains Historical Museum
www.panhandleplains.org

Carthage
Texas Country Music Hall of Fame & Tex Ritter Museum
www.tcmhof.com

Clarendon
Saints' Roost Museum (history)
www.saintsroostmuseum.com

Clifton
Bosque Museum (history)
www.bosquemuseum.org

Conroe
Heritage Museum of Montgomery County
www.heritagemuseum.us

Corpus Christi
Art Museum of South Texas
artmuseumofsouthtexas.org
Corpus Christi Museum of Science and History
www.ccmuseum.com
Texas State Aquarium
www.texasstateaquarium.org
Texas State Museum of Asian Cultures

Dragonfly sculpture at Austin's Lady Bird Johnson Wildflower Center. Photo by Ron Billings, Texas A&M Forest Service.

www.asianculturesmuseum.org
USS Lexington Museum
   www.usslexington.com

Corsicana
Pearce Western Art/Civil War
   Museum
   http://www.pearcemuseum.com/

Cotulla
Brush Country Historical Museum
   http://www.historicdistrict.com/
   museum

Dalhart
XIT Museum (history)
   www.xitmuseum.com

Dallas
African American Museum
   www.aamdallas.org
Crow Museum of Asian Art
   www.crowcollection.org
Dallas Heritage Village
   www.dallasheritagevillage.org
Dallas Historical Society (Fair Park)
   www.dallashistory.org
Dallas Museum of Art
   www.dma.org
Frontiers of Flight Museum
   www.flightmuseum.com
George W. Bush Presidential Center
   www.georgewbushlibrary.smu.edu
Perot Museum of Nature and Science
   www.perotmuseum.org
Nasher Sculpture Center
   www.nashersculpturecenter.org
Meadows Museum (art)
   meadowsmuseumdallas.org
The Sixth Floor Museum (history)
   www.jfk.org

Denison
Red River Railroad Museum
   www.redriverrailmuseum.org
Denton
Courthouse-on-the-Square Museum
   (history)
   https://dentoncounty.com/Depart-
   ments/History-and-Culture/Of-
   fice-of-History-and-Culture/VISIT.
   aspx
Denton Firefighters Museum
   www.discoverdenton.com/firefight-
   ers-museum/
University of North Texas Art Galleries
   www.gallery.unt.edu
Dublin
Dublin Bottling Works
   www.dublinbottlingworks.com
Dublin Rodeo Heritage Museum
   rodeoheritagemuseum.org
Dumas
Window on the Plains Museum
   www.dumasmuseumandartcenter.
   org
Duncanville
International Museum of Cultures
   www.internationalmuseumofcul-
   tures.org
Edgewood
Edgewood Heritage Park and Historical Village
   edgewoodheritagepark.org
Edinburg
Museum of South Texas History
   www.mosthistory.org

El Campo
El Campo Museum of Natural History
   www.elcampomuseum.org

El Paso
Centennial Museum / Chihuahuan
   Desert Gardens
   www.utep.edu/centennial-muse-
   um
El Paso Museum of Archaeology
   archaeology.elpasotexas.gov
El Paso Museum of Art
   epma.art
El Paso Museum of History
   history.elpasotexas.gov
Fort Davis
Chihuahuan Desert Research
   Institute
   www.cdri.org

Fort Stockton
Annie Riggs Museum (history)
   historicfortstocktontx.com/attrac-
   tions-2/annie-riggs-memorial-mu-
   seum
Fort Worth
Amon Carter Museum (art)
   www.cartermuseum.org
Cattle Raisers Museum
   www.cattleraisersmuseum.org
Fort Worth Museum of Science and
   History
   www.fwmuseum.org
Kimbell Art Museum
   www.kimbellart.org
Log Cabin Village (history)
   www.logcabinvillage.org
Modern Art Museum of Fort Worth
   www.themodern.org
National Cowgirl Museum and Hall
   of Fame
   www.cowgirl.net
Sid Richardson Collection of Western
   Art
   www.sidrichardsonmuseum.org

Texas Civil War Museum
www.texascivilwarmuseum.com

Fredericksburg
Gillespie County Historical Society
www.pioneermuseum.net
National Museum of the Pacific War
www.pacificwarmuseum.org

Frisco
Museum of the American Railroad
museumoftheamericanrailroad.org
National Videogame Museum
www.nvmusa.org

Galveston
The Bryan Museum (art, history)
www.thebryanmuseum.org
Galveston Children's Museum
https://galvestoncm.org
Lone Star Flight Museum
www.lonestarflight.org
Moody Mansion
www.moodymansion.org
Offshore Energy Center / Ocean Star
(science, industry)
www.oceanstaroec.com
Texas Seaport Museum and Tallship
"Elissa"
www.galveston.com/texasseaport-museum/

Gilmer
Flight of Phoenix Aviation Museum
www.flightofthephoenix.org

Greenville
Audie Murphy / American Cotton
Museum
www.cottonmuseum.com

Henderson
The Depot Museum (history)
www.depotmuseum.com

Houston
Blaffer Art Museum, University of
Houston
http://blafferartmuseum.org/
Children's Museum of Houston
www.cmhouston.org
Contemporary Arts Museum
www.camh.org
Czech Center Museum
www.czechcenter.org
The Health Museum
www.thehealthmuseum.org
Houston Center for Contemporary
Craft
www.crafthouston.org
Houston Center for Photography
www.hcponline.org
Houston Fire Museum (history)
www.houstonfiremuseum.org
Houston Museum of Natural Science
www.hmns.org
Lawndale Art Center
www.lawndaleartcenter.org
The Menil Collection (art)
www.menil.org
Museum of Fine Arts
www.mfah.org
Museum of Printing History
www.printingmuseum.org
Rice University Art Gallery
www.ricegallery.org

San Jacinto Museum of History
www.sanjacinto-museum.org
Space Center Houston
www.spacecenter.org

Huntsville
Sam Houston Memorial Museum
www.huntsvilletexas.com/195/
Samuel-Walker-Houston-Muse-um-Cultural-Center
Texas Prison Museum
www.txprisonmuseum.org

Kerrville
Museum of Western Art
www.museumofwesternart.org

Kilgore
East Texas Oil Museum
www.visitkilgore.com/79

Lake Jackson
Lake Jackson Historical Museum
www.lakejacksonmuseum.org

Laredo
Republic of the Rio Grande Museum
www.webbheritage.org/museums/
Texas A&M International University
Planetarium
www.tamiu.edu/coas/planetarium

League City
Butler Longhorn Museum
butlerlonghornmuseum.com
West Bay Common School Children's
Museum (history)
www.oneroomschoolhouse.org

Longview
Longview Museum of Fine Arts
www.lmfa.org

Lubbock
Bayer Museum of Agriculture
www.agriculturehistory.org
Buddy Holly Center (history, music)
https://www.mylubbock.us/depart-mental-websites/departments/
buddy-holly-center/home
Museum of Texas Tech University
(art, humanities, science)
www.depts.ttu.edu/museumttu
National Ranching Heritage Center
www.depts.ttu.edu/nrhc/
Science Spectrum
www.sciencespectrum.org

Lufkin
Naranjo Museum of Natural History
www.naranjomuseum.org
Texas Forestry Museum
www.treetexas.com

Marfa
Chinati Foundation (art)
www.chinati.org

Marshall
Harrison County Historical Museum
http://harrisoncountymuseum.org
Michelson Museum of Art
www.michelsonmuseum.org

McAllen
International Museum of Art &
Science
http://theimasonline.org/welcome/

McKinney
Heard Natural Science Museum
www.heardmuseum.org

Midland
Museum of the Southwest (art,
science, children's)
www.museumsw.org
Petroleum Museum
www.petroleummuseum.org

Mobeetie
Old Mobeetie Texas Association
www.mobeetie.com

Nacogdoches
Millard's Crossing Historic Village
www.mchvnac.com

New Braunfels
McKenna Children's Museum
mckennakids.org
Sophienburg Museum of History and
Culture
www.sophienburg.com

Odessa
Ellen Noel Art Museum
www.noelartmuseum.org
Presidential Archives and Library
http://shepperdinstitute.com/
presidential-archives

Orange
Stark Museum of Art
www.starkculturalvenues.org

Panhandle
Carson County Square House
Museum
www.squarehousemuseum.
weebly.com

Perryton
Museum of the Plains
www.museumoftheplains.com

Plano
Heritage Farmstead Museum
www.heritagefarmstead.org

Port Arthur
Museum of the Gulf Coast (history)
www.museumofthegulfcoast.org

Port Lavaca
Calhoun County Museum (history)
www.calhouncountymuseum.org

Richmond
George Ranch Historical Park
www.georgeranch.org

Rockport
Texas Maritime Museum
www.texasmaritimemuseum.org

Rosenberg
The Black Cowboy Museum
www.blackcowboymuseum.org
Rosenberg Railroad Museum
www.rosenbergrrmuseum.com

Round Top
Henkel Square (history)
www.henkelsquareroundtop.com
Winedale Historical Complex
www.cah.utexas.edu/museums/
winedale.php

San Angelo
Miss Hattie's Bordello Museum
misshatties.com
San Angelo Museum of Fine Arts and
Children's Art Museum
www.samfa.org

San Antonio
The Alamo
www.thealamo.org
Briscoe Western Art Museum
www.briscoemuseum.org
Holocaust Memorial Museum
www.hmmsa.org
Institute of Texan Cultures
www.texancultures.com
Kleberg South Texas Heritage Center
sthc.wittemuseum.org
Magic Lantern Castle Museum
www.magiclanterns.org
The McNay Art Museum
www.mcnayart.org
San Antonio Art League Museum
www.saalm.org
San Antonio Museum of Art
http://www.samuseum.org/
Witte Museum (science, history)
www.wittemuseum.org

San Marcos
LBJ Museum San Marcos
libjuseum.com
Southwestern Writers Collection and
Wittliff Gallery of Southwestern &
Mexican Photography
www.thewittliffcollections.txstate.
edu

Sarita
Kenedy Ranch Museum of South
Texas
https://kenedy.org/museum

Schulenburg
Stanzel Model Aircraft Museum
www.stanzelmuseum.org

Serbin
Texas Wendish Heritage Museum
texaswendish.org

Sherman
Sherman Jazz Museum
shermanjazzmuseum.com

The Sherman Museum (history)
http://theshermanmuseum.org/

Snyder
Scurry County Museum
http://scurrycountymuseum.org

Sulphur Springs
Southwest Dairy Center/Museum
www.southwestdairyfarmers.com

Teague
The B-RI Railroad Museum
www.therailroadmuseum.com

Temple
Czech Heritage Museum
www.czechheritagemuseum.org
Railroad and Heritage Museum
www.templerrhm.org

Texarkana
Museum of Regional History
www.texarkanamuseum.org

The Woodlands
The Woodlands Children's Museum
woodlandschildrensmuseum.org

Thurber
W.K. Gordon Center for Industrial
History of Texas
www.tarleton.edu/gordoncenter/

Tyler
Discovery Science Place
www.discoveryscienceplace.org/
Historic Aviation Memorial Museum
www.tylerhamm.com
Smith County Historical Museum
www.tylertexasonline.com/ty-
ler-texas-museums.htm
Tyler Museum of Art
www.tylermuseum.org

Victoria
Children's Discovery Museum
www.csmgoldencrescent.com
Museum of the Coastal Bend
(history)
www.museumofthecoastalbend.
org
The Nave Museum (art)
www.navemuseum.com

Waco
Dr Pepper Museum (history)
www.drpeppermuseum.com
Martin Museum of Art
www.baylor.edu/martinmuseum/
Mayborn Museum Complex (history,
science)
www.baylor.edu/mayborn
Texas Ranger Hall of Fame /
Museum
www.texasranger.org
Texas Sports Hall of Fame
www.tshof.org

Washington
Star of the Republic Museum
(history)
www.starmuseum.org

Weatherford
Museum of the Americas
www.museumoftheamericas.com
National Vietnam War Museum
www.nationalvnwarmuseum.org

Wharton
20th Century Technology Museum
www.20thcenturytech.com

White Settlement
White Settlement Historical Museum
www.wsmuseum.com

Wichita Falls
Kell House Museum (history)
www.wichita-heritage.org
Museum of Art
http://www.wfmamsu.org/
Museum of North Texas History
www.museumofnorthtexashistory.
org
Professional Wrestling Hall of Fame
& Museum
https://pro-wrestling-hall-of-fame-
museum.business.site

Yoakum
Yoakum Heritage Museum
www.yoakumareachamber.com/
pages/yoakumheritagemuseum.
html ☆

Public Libraries in Texas

Source: Library Development Division of the Texas State Library and Archives in Austin.

Texas public libraries continue to strive to meet the education and information needs of Texans by providing library services of high quality with oftentimes-limited resources.

Each year, services provided by public libraries increase, with more visits to public libraries and higher attendance in library programs.

The challenges facing public libraries in Texas are many and varied. The costs for providing electronic and online sources, in addition to traditional services, are growing faster than budgets.

Urban libraries are trying to serve growing populations, while libraries in rural areas are try-ing to serve remote populations and provide distance learning where possible.

National rankings of public libraries are published by the Institute of Museum and Library Services at **www.imls.gov/research-evaluation/data-collection/public-libraries-survey.**

When comparing Texas statistics to those nationally, Texas continues to rank below most of the other states in most categories, with the exception of public use of internet terminals.

Complete statistical information on public libraries is available on the Texas State Library's website: **www.tsl.texas.gov/landing/statistics.html**. There is also a listing of libraries at: **www.tsl.texas.gov/texshare/libsearch/index.php.** ☆

Texas Institute of Letters Awards

Each year since 1939, the **Texas Institute of Letters** (texasinstituteofletters.org/) has honored outstanding literature and journalism that is either by Texans or about Texas subjects.

Awards have been made for fiction, nonfiction, Southwest history, general information, magazine and newspaper journalism, children's books, translation, poetry, and book design. The awards of recent years are listed below:

Writer/Designer: Title

2019

Ben Fountain: *Beautiful Country Burn Again: Democracy, Rebellion, and Revolution*
Natalia Sylvester: *Everyone Knows You Go Home*
Stephen Markley: *Ohio*
Tarfia Faizullah: *Registers of Illuminated Villages*
Megan Peak: *Girldom*
Brent Nongbri: *God's Library: The Archaeology of the Earliest Christian Manuscripts*
David Bowles: *The Feathered Serpent, Dark Heart of Sky: Myths of Mexico and They Call Me Güero*
Varian Johnson: *The Parker Inheritance*
Chris Barton: *What Can You Do with a Voice Like That?*
Clay Reynolds: "Railroad Man," *New Madrid, and* "Autumn Moon," *New Texas*
Lon Tinkle Award (for career): Naomi Shihab Nye

2018

Jan Reid: *Sins of the Younger Sons*
Chanelle Benz: *The Man Who Shot Out My Eye is Dead*
Roger D. Hodge: *Texas Blood: Seven Generations Among the Outlaws, Ranchers, Indians, Missionaries, Soldiers, and Smugglers of The Borderlands*
Jerry D. Thompson: *Tejano Tiger: José de los Santos Benavides and the Texas-Mexico Borderlands, 1823–1891*
Sasha Pimentel: *For Want of Water: and other poems*
Vanessa Villarreal: *Beast Meridian*
Brett Anthony Johnston: "Miss McElroy," *Ecotone*
Rose Cahalan: "Ride Like a Girl," *Texas Observer*
Michael Merschel: *Revenge of the Star Survivors*
Francisco X. Stork: *Disappeared*
Xelena González and Adriana M. Garcia: *All Around Us*
Philip Boehm: translator of *Chasing the King of Hearts,* by Hanna Krall
Mary Ann Jacob: designer, *The Nueces River, Rio Escondido,* by Margie Crisp and William B. Montgomery
Lon Tinkle Award (for career): Sandra Cisneros

2017

Paulette Jiles: *News of the World*
Amy Gentry: *Good as Gone*
Skip Hollandsworth: *The Midnight Assassin*
Max Krochmal: *Blue Texas: The Making of a Multiracial Democratic Coalition in the Civil Rights Era*
Bruce Bond: *Gold Bee*
Miriam Bird Greenberg: *In the Volcano's Mouth*
Stephen Harrigan: "Off Course," *Texas Monthly*
David Meischen: "Cicada Song," *Salamander*
Kathi Appelt and Alison McGhee: *Maybe a Fox*
Phillippe Diederich: *Playing for the Devil's Fire*
Dianna Hutts Aston: *A Beetle is Shy*
Kristie Lee: *From Tea Cakes to Tamales*
Lon Tinkle Award (for career): Pat Mora

2016

Antonio Ruiz–Camacho: *Barefoot Dogs*
Mary Helen Specht: *Migratory Animals*
Jan Jarboe Russell: *The Train to Crystal City*
Andrew Torget III: *Seeds of Empire*
Laurie Ann Guerrero: *A Crown for Gumecindo*
J. Scott Brownlee: *Requiem for Used Ignition Cap*

W.K. Stratton: "My Brother's Secret," *Texas Monthly*
Brian Van Reet: "The Chaff," *Iowa Review*
Don Tate: *The Remarkable Story of George Moses Horton: Poet*
Brian Yansky: *Utopia, Iowa*
Pat Mora: *The Remembering Day / El dia de los muertos*
Andrea Caillouet: *The Luck Archive: Exploring Belief, Superstition, and Tradition*
Marian Schwartz: translator of *Anna Karenina,* by Leo Tolstoy
Lon Tinkle Award (for career): Sarah Bird

2015

Elizabeth Crook: *Monday, Monday*
Michael Morton: *Getting Life: An Innocent Man's 25-Year Journey from Prison to Peace*
Merritt Tierce: *Love Me Back*
Lawrence T. Jones: *Lens on the Texas Frontier*
Katherine Hoerth: *Goddess Wears Cowboy Boots*
Brian Van Reet: "Eat The Spoil," in *Missouri Review*
Chloe Honum: *The Tulip-Flame*
Pamela Colloff: "The Witness," *Texas Monthly*
Bill Wittliff and Ellen McKie: *The Devil's Backbone,* written by Bill Wittliff, illustrated by Jack Unruh
Nikki Lofton: *Nightingale's Nest*
Glaudia Guadalupe Martinez: *Pig Park*
Pat Mora and Lilbby Martinez: *I Pledge Allegiance*
Lon Tinkle Award (for career): Lawrence Wright

2014

Tom Zigal: *Many Rivers to Cross*
John Taliaferro: *All The Great Prizes: The Life of John Hay from Lincoln to Roosevelt*
Lawrence Wright: *Going Clear: Scientology, Hollywood, and the Prison of Belief*
Nan Cuba: *Body and Bread*
Raúl Coronado: *A World Not to Come: A History of Latino Writing and Print Culture*
Pattiann Rogers: *Holy Heathen Rhapsody*
Bret Anthony Johnston: "To A Good Home," *Virginia Quarterly Review*
Sasha West: *Failure And I Bury The Body*
John MacCormack: "Life On The Shale," *San Antonio Express-News,* series
Lindsay Starr: *Two Prospectors: The Letters of Sam Shepard and Johnny Dark*
Xavier Garza: *Maximilian and the Mystery of the Bingo Rematch*
Kathi Appelt: *The True Blue Scouts of Sugar Man Swamp*
David Bowles: *Flower, Song, Dance: Aztec and Mayan Poetry*
Lon Tinkle Award (for career): Jan Reid

2013

Ben Fountain: *Billy Lynn's Long Halftime Walk*
Margie Crisp: *River of Contrasts*
Kevin Grauke: *Shadows of Men*
Kate Sayen Kirkland: *Captain James A. Baker of Houston: 1857–1941*
Ken Fontenot: *Kingdom of Birds*
James Sanderson: "Bankers," in *Descant*
Kathleen Winter: *Nostalgia for the Criminal Past*
Mellissa Del Bosque: "The Deadliest Place in Mexico," *The Texas Observer,* February, 12, 2012
Kristina Kachele: *In the Country of Empty Crosses,* written by Arturo Madrid
Donna Rubin: *Log Cabin Kitty*
Melodie Cuate: *Journey to Plum Creek*
Lon Tinkle Award (for career): Stephen Harrigan

2012

Stephen Harrigan: *Remember Ben Clayton*
Steven Fenberg: *Unprecedented Power: Jesse Jones, Capitalism, and the Common Good*

Siobhan Fallon: *You Know When the Men Are Gone*
Christopher Long: *The Looshaus*
Jennifer Grotz: *The Needle*
Bret Anthony Johnston: "Paradeability," *American Short Fiction*
Jose Antonio Rodriguez: *The Shallow End of Sleep*
Skip Hollandsworth: "The Lost Boys," *Texas Monthly*, April 2011
Jordan Smith: "The Science of Injustice," *Austin Chronicle*, August 19, 2011
Barbara Werden and Lindsay Starr: *Lone Star Law*, written by Michael Ariens
Dave Oliphant: *After-Dinner Declarations* by Nicanor Parra
Elaine Scott: *Space, Stars and the Beginning of Time*
J.L. Powers: *This Thing Called the Future*
Lon Tinkle Award (for career): Gary Cartwright

2011[1]

Jan Reid: *Comanche Sundown*
Gary Lavergne: *Before Brown: Heman Marion Sweatt, Thurgood Marshall and the Long Road to Justice*
Neil Foley: *Quest for Equality: The Failed Promise of Black-Brown Solidarity*
Bruce Machart: *The Wake of Forgiveness*
Barbara Ras: *The Last Skin*
Elyse Fenton: *Clamor*
Pamela Colloff: "Innocence Lost," *Texas Monthly*, October 2010
C.W. Smith: "Caustic," *Southwest Review*, Summer 2010
Tim Madigan: series on the surgery of a child, *Fort Worth Star-Telegram*
Julie Savasky and DJ Stout: *The Gernsheim Collection*
Diane Gonzales Bertrand: *The Party for Papa Luis/La Fiesta Para Papa Luis*
Dotti Enderle: *Crosswire*
Lon Tinkle Award (for career): C.W. Smith

2009

[1] *Beginning in 2011 the award date reflects the actual date of the presentation. For instance, Larry King's 2009 award was actually presented in 2010.*

Scott Blackwood: *We Agreed to Meet Just Here*
Bryan Burrough: *The Big Rich: The Rise and Fall of the Greatest Texas Oil Fortunes*
John Pipkin: *Woodsburner*
Emilio Zamoro: *Claiming Rights and Righting Wrongs in Texas: Mexican Workers and Job Politics During World War II*
William Virgil Davis: *Landscape and Journey*
John Spong: "Holding Garmsir," *Texas Monthly*, January 2009.
Gwendolyn Zepeda: *Sunflowers/Girasoles*
Marjorie Kempner: "Discovered America," *Southwest Review*, Fall 2009
Lindsay Starr: *"I Do Not Apologize for the Length of This Letter": The Mari Sandoz Letters on Native American Rights, 1940–1965*
Lon Tinkle Award (for career): Larry L. King

2008

Brendan M. Greeley Jr.: *The Two Thousand Yard Stare: Tom Lea's World War II Paintings, Drawings, and Eyewitness Accounts*
Thomas Cobb: *Shavetail*
Ann Weisgarber: *The Personal History of Rachel DuPree*
Rick Bass: "Mary Katherine's First Deer" in *Gray's Sporting Journal*
Todd Benson and Guillermo Contreras: "Texas' Deadliest Export" in the *San Antonio Express-News*
Benjamin Alire Saenz: *The Perfect Season for Dreaming*
Claudia Guadalupe Martinez: *The Smell of Old Lady Perfume*
James Allen Hall: *Now You're the Enemy*
Kerry Neville Bakken: "Indignity" in *Gettysburg Review*
James M. Smallwood: *The Feud that Wasn't: The Taylor Ring, Bill Sutton, John Wesley Hardin, and Violence in Texas*
Barbara Whitehead: *Traces of Forgotten Places*
Reginald Gibbons: translator of Sophocles, *Selected Poems: Odes and Fragments*
Lon Tinkle Award (for career): Carolyn Osborn

SXSW

The four letters above have become internationally recognized for the annual South by Southwest Music, Film, and Interactive Festival held each March in Austin. The festival began in 1987 to promote the Austin music scene. That first event had about 200 musical acts, mostly local, and some 700 registrants.

In 2018, there were more than 2,000 performing acts – music and comedy – from all over the world and a total of 289,000 people attending various events, according to the SXSW report.

The festival has evolved to include film, video, and gaming. Its Interactive portion, which includes all aspects of the Internet, web design, and new technologies, has become the biggest draw in terms of registrants attending: more than 30,000

A musical act at the 2019 SXSW. Photo by Paul Hudson (CC).

in 2017. The film portion attracts celebrities to promote new projects and over the last few years television news and talk shows have relocated to Austin to share some of the spotlight.

The economic impact on the Austin area was reported to be $350.6 million, according to the festival's analysis.

State Cultural Agencies Assist the Arts

Source: Principally, the Texas Commission on the Arts, along with other state cultural agencies.

Culture in Texas, as in any market, is a mixture of activity generated by both the commercial and the nonprofit sectors.

The commercial sector encompasses Texas-based profit-making businesses, including commercial recording artists, nightclubs, record companies, private galleries, assorted boutiques that carry fine art collectibles, and private dance and music halls.

Texas also has extensive cultural resources offered by nonprofit organizations that are engaged in charitable, educational, and humanitarian activities.

The Legislature has authorized five state agencies to administer cultural services and funds for the public good. The agencies are:

Texas Commission on the Arts; Texas Film Commission; Texas Historical Commission; Texas State Library and Archives Commission, and the State Preservation Board.

Although not a state agency, another organization that provides cultural services to the citizens of Texas is Humanities Texas.

The Commission on the Arts was established in 1965 to develop a receptive climate for the arts through the conservation and advancement of Texas' rich and diverse arts and cultural industries.

The Texas Commission on the Arts' goals are:
- Provide grants for the arts and cultural industries in Texas.
- Provide the financial, human, and technical resources necessary to ensure viable arts and cultural communities.
- Promote widespread attendance at arts and cultural performances and exhibitions in Texas.
- Ensure access to arts in Texas through marketing, fund raising, and cultural tourism.

The commission is responsible for several initiatives including:
- Arts Education: programs that serve the curricular and training needs of the state's school districts, private schools, and home schools.
- Marketing and Public Relations: marketing and fund-raising expertise to generate funds for agency operations and increase visibility of the arts in Texas.
- Cultural Tourism: programs that develop and promote tourism destinations featuring the arts.

Information on programs is available on the Texas Commission on the Arts at www.arts.texas.gov. ☆

Master Claudio Muñoz works with dancers at the Houston Ballet Academy. Photo by Houston wikieditor. (CC)

Performing Arts Organizations: Dance, music, theater

The Texas Commission on the Arts provides a listing of performing arts companies and artists in Texas at **www.arts.texas.gov/artroster/roster/show/all#**. There are links arranged by category; dance, theater, music, etc.

There is also **www.arts.texas.gov/resources/ art-in-communities/**, which provides more information about community arts programs, as well as **www. swpap.org**, with performing arts organizations by city.

Texas Medal of the Arts Awards

Source: Texas Commission on the Arts.

The Texas Medals of the Arts were presented to artists and arts patrons with Texas ties in February 2019.

The awards are administered by the Texas Cultural Trust Council. The council was established to raise money and awareness for the Texas Cultural Trust Fund, which was created by the Legislature in 1993 to support cultural arts in Texas (www.txculturaltrust.org).

The medals, awarded every two years, were first presented in 2001. A concurrent proclamation by the state Senate and House of Representatives honors the recipients, and the governor presents the awards in Austin.

2019

Design: Brandon Maxwell, Longview, fashion designer, photographer.

Music: Boz Scaggs, Plano, singer/songwriter.

Visual arts: Trenton Doyle Hancock, Houston and Paris, Tx., artist.

Music Ensemble: Conspirare, Austin, choral ensemble.

Literary: Stephen Harrigan, Austin, Abilene, and Corpus Christi, author, journalist.

Film: Matthew McConaughey, Austin, Uvalde, and Longview, actor.

Multimedia: Mark Seliger, Amarillo and Houston, photographer.

Theater: Jennifer Holliday, Houston, singer, actor.

Arts education: Vidal M. Treviño School of Communications and Fine Arts, Laredo.

Architecture: Elaine Molinar, El Paso, and Craig Dykers, San Antonio.

Matthew McConaughey. Photo by David Torcivia (CC).

2017

Lifetime Achievement Award: Kenny Rogers of Houston.

Multimedia: Kris Kristofferson, Brownsville.

Music: Yolanda Adams, Houston.

Visual arts: Leo Villareal, El Paso, artist.

Dance: Lauren Anderson, Houston.

Literary: John Phillip Santos, San Antonio.

Film: Janine Turner, Euless, actor.

Journalism: Scott Pelley, San Antonio, news broadcaster.

Television: Jaclyn Smith, Houston, actor.

Theater: Renée Elise Goldsberry, Houston.

Arts education: Dallas Black Dance Theatre.

Architecture: Frank Welch, Dallas.

Individual arts patron: Lynn Wyatt, Houston.

Corporate arts patrons: John Paul and Eloise DeJoria, Austin.

Foundation arts patron: Tobin Endowment, San Antonio.

2015

Lifetime Achievement Award: The Gatlin Brothers of Seminole, Abilene, and Odessa.

Multimedia: Emilio Nicolas Sr. of San Antonio, for work as broadcaster.

Music: T Bone Burnett of Fort Worth.

Visual arts: Rick Lowe of Houston, artist.

Jennifer Holliday. Photo by Greg Hernandez (CC).

Dance: Kilgore Rangerettes.

Literary: Lawrence Wright, Austin and Dallas.

Film: Jamie Foxx, Terrell, actor.

Television: Dan Rather, Wharton, news broadcaster.

Television: Chandra Wilson, Houston, actor.

Theater: Robert Schenkkan, Austin.

Arts education: Booker T. Washington High School for the Performing and Visual Arts, Dallas.

Architecture: Charles Renfro, Houston.

Individual arts patron: Margaret McDermott, Dallas.

Corporate arts patron: Dr Pepper Snapple Group, Plano.

Standing Ovation Award: Ruth Altshuler of Dallas.

2013

Multimedia: Eva Longoria of Corpus Christi, for work as actress, author, and philanthropist.

Music: Steve Miller of Dallas.

Visual arts: James Surls, Splendora, artist.

Dance: Houston Ballet.

Television/Film: Ricardo Chavira, San Antonio, actor.

Theater arts: Joe Sears and Jaston Williams, Austin (Greater Tuna fame).

Arts education: Big Thought / Gigi Antoni, Dallas.

Individual arts patron: Gene Jones and Charlotte Jones Anderson, Dallas.

Foundation arts patron: Kimbell Arts Foundation, Fort Worth.

Corporate arts patron: Texas Monthly.

2011

Lifetime Achievement Award: Barbara Smith Conrad from Center Point near Pittsburg, operatic mezzo-soprano and civil rights icon.

Music: ZZ Top of Houston, legendary band that sold over 50 million albums.

Literary: Robert M. Edsel, Dallas, author and founder/president of the Monuments Men Foundation for the Preservation of Art.

Visual arts: James Drake, Lubbock, artist.

Television: Bob Schieffer, Fort Worth, CBS news anchor.

Theater arts: Alley Theatre, Houston.

Multimedia: Ray Benson, Austin, front man for Asleep at the Wheel and co-writer of the play *A Ride with Bob* based on the life of Bob Wills.

Film: Marcia Gay Harden, UT-Austin graduate, Oscar-winning actress.

Film: Bill Paxton, Fort Worth, four-time Golden Globe nominee.

Arts education: Tom Staley, director of the Harry Ransom Center at UT-Austin.

Individual arts patron: Ernest and Sarah Butler of Austin, major donors to Austin arts groups.

Corporate arts patron: H-E-B, grocer with a long history of supporting the arts throughout Texas.

2009

A Standing Ovation Award was presented to former First Lady Laura Bush of Midland and Dallas.

Lifetime Achievement Award: posthumously to artist Robert Rauschenberg, born in Port Arthur.

Music: Clint Black of Katy, country music singer/songwriter.

Literary: T.R. Fehrenbach of San Antonio. Mr. Fehrenbach, born in San Benito, is the author of 18 nonfiction books, including *Lone Star: A History of Texas and Texans*.

Visual arts: Keith Carter of Beaumont, photographer.

Theater arts: Betty Buckley of Fort Worth, Tony Award winner and film actress.

Multimedia: Austin City Limits, the 30-year television series.

Film: Robert Rodriguez of Austin. Mr. Rodriguez, born in San Antonio, is a film director and writer.

Architecture: David Lake of Austin and Ted Flato of Corpus Christi, both now working in San Antonio.

Arts education: Pianist James Dick of Round Top, founder of the International Festival-Institute there.

Individual arts patron: Edith O'Donnell of Dallas.

Corporate arts patron: Anheuser-Busch of St. Louis and Houston.

2007

Lifetime Achievement Award: Broadcast newsman Walter Cronkite of Houston.

Music: Ornette Coleman of Fort Worth, jazz saxophonist.

Dance: Alvin Ailey American Dance Theater. The late Alvin Ailey, born in Rogers, was a creator of African American dance works.

Literary: writer Sandra Brown of Waco.

Visual arts: Jesús Moroles of Corpus Christi/Rockport, sculptor.

Theater arts: actress Judith Ivey of El Paso.

Multimedia: Bill Wittliff of Taft and Austin, publisher, writer, photographer, director, producer.

Arts education: Paul Baker of Hereford/Waelder. Headed drama departments at Baylor and Trinity universities.

Individual arts patron: Diana and Bill Hobby of Houston.

Corporate arts patron: Neiman Marcus, Dallas.

Foundation arts patron: Sid W. Richardson Foundation of Fort Worth.

2005

Lifetime Achievement Award: singer Vikki Carr of El Paso.

Television/theater: actress Phylicia Rashad of Houston.

Music: singer/songwriter Lyle Lovett of Klein.

Dance: Ben Stevenson of Houston and Fort Worth.

Literary arts: Naomi Shihab Nye of San Antonio.

Visual arts: Jose Cisneros of El Paso.

Theater: Robert Wilson of Waco.

Arts education: Ginger Head-Gearheart of Fort Worth, advocate of arts education in public schools.

Individual arts patrons: Joe R. and Teresa Lozano Long of Austin, philanthropists.

Foundation arts patron: Nasher Foundation/Dallas.

2003

Lifetime Achievement: John Graves of Glen Rose, author of *Goodbye to A River*.

Media-film/television acting: Fess Parker of Fort Worth.

Music: country singer Charley Pride of Dallas.

Dance: Tommy Tune of Wichita Falls and Houston.

Theater: Enid Holm of Odessa, actress and former executive director of Texas Nonprofit Theatres.

Literary arts: Sandra Cisneros of San Antonio.

Visual arts: sculptor Glenna Goodacre of Dallas.

Folk arts: Tejano singer Lydia Mendoza of San Antonio.

Architecture: State Capitol Preservation Project of Austin, headed by Dealey Herndon.

Arts education: theater teacher Marca Lee Bircher, Dallas.

Individual arts patron: philanthropist Nancy B. Hamon of Dallas.

Corporate arts patron: Exxon/Mobil based in Irving.

Foundation arts patron: Houston Endowment Inc.

2001

Lifetime Achievement: Van Cliburn of Fort Worth.

Film: actor Tommy Lee Jones of San Saba.

Music: singer-songwriter Willie Nelson of Austin.

Dance: Debbie Allen of Houston, choreographer, director, actress and composer.

Theater: *Texas* musical-drama producer Neil Hess of Amarillo.

Literary arts: playwright Horton Foote of Wharton.

Visual arts: muralist John Biggers of Houston.

Folk arts: musician brothers Santiago Jimenez Jr. and Flaco Jimenez of San Antonio.

Architecture: restoration architect Wayne Bell of Austin.

Arts education: theater arts director Gilberto Zepeda Jr. of Pharr.

Individual arts patron: philanthropist Jack Blanton of Houston.

Corporate arts patron: SBC Communications Inc. of San Antonio.

Foundation arts patron: Meadows Foundation of Dallas. ☆

An artist at Houston's Project Row Houses, co-founded by Rick Lowe, state artist. Carol M. Highsmith photo (CC).

State Artists of Texas

Since 2001, a committee of seven members appointed by the governor, lieutenant governor, and speaker of the House of Representatives selects the poet laureate, state artists, and state musician based on recommendations from the Texas Commission on the Arts. Earlier, the Legislature made the nominations.

The state historian is appointed by the governor and is recommended by both the Texas State Historical Association and the Texas Historical Commission.

Sources: Texas State Library and Archives; Texas Commission on the Arts; The Dallas Morning News.

Years	Artist, Hometown/Residence
1971-72	Joe Ruiz Grandee, Arlington
1972-73	Melvin C. Warren, Clifton
1973-74	Ronald Thomason, Weatherford A.C. Gentry Jr., Tyler, alternate
1974-75	Joe Rader Roberts, Dripping Springs Bette Lou Voorhis, Austin, alternate
1975-76	Jack White, New Braunfels
July 4, 1975 –July 4, 1976	Robert Summers, Glen Rose Bicentennial Artist
1976-77	James Boren, Clifton Kenneth Wyatt, Lubbock, alternate
1977-78	Edward "Buck" Schiwetz, DeWitt County Renne Hughes, Tarrant County, alternate
1978-79	Jack Cowan, Rockport Gary Henry, Palo Pinto County, alternate Joyce Tally, Caldwell County, alternate
1979-80	Dalhart Windberg, Travis County Grant Lathe, Canyon Lake, alternate
1980-81	Harry Ahysen, Huntsville Jim Reno, Simonton, alternate
1981-82	Jerry Newman, Beaumont Raul Guiterrez, San Antonio, alternate
1982-83	Dr. James H. Johnson, Bryan Armando Hinojosa, Laredo, alternate
1983-84	Raul Gutierrez, San Antonio James Eddleman, Lubbock, alternate
1984-85	Covelle Jones, Lubbock Ragan Gennusa, Austin, alternate
1986-87	Chuck DeHaan, Graford
1987-88	Neil Caldwell, Angleton Rey Gaytan, Austin, alternate
1988-89	George Hallmark, Walnut Springs Tony Eubanks, Grapevine, alternate

	Two-dimensional	Three-dimensional
1990-91	Mondel Rogers, Sweetwater	Ron Wells, Cleveland
1991-92	Woodrow Foster, Center	Kent Ullberg, Corpus Christi
	Harold Phenix, Houston, alternate	Mark Clapham, Conroe, alternate
1993-94	Roy Lee Ward, Hunt	James Eddleman, Lubbock
1994-95	Frederick Carter, El Paso	Garland A. Weeks, Wichita Falls
1998-99	Carl Rice Embrey, San Antonio	Edd Hayes, Humble
2000-02	*none designated*	
2003	Ralph White, Austin	Dixie Friend Gay, Houston
2004	Sam Caldwell, Houston	David Hickman, Dallas
2005	Kathy Vargas, San Antonio	Sharon Kopriva, Houston

Year	Two-dimensional	Three-dimensional
2006	George Boutwell, Bosque County	James Surls, Athens
2007	Lee Herring, Rockwall	David Keens, Arlington
2008	Janet Eager Krueger, Encinal	Damian Priour, Austin
2009	René Alvarado, San Angelo	Eliseo Garcia, Farmers Branch
2010	Marc Burckhardt, Austin	John Bennett, Fredericksburg
2011	Melissa Miller, Austin	Jesús Moroles, Rockport
2012	Karl Umlauf, Waco	Bill FitzGibbons, San Antonio
2013	Jim Woodson, Waco, Fort Worth	Joseph Havel, Houston
2014	Julie Speed, Austin, Marfa	Ken Little, Canyon, San Antonio
2015	Vincent Valdez, San Antonio	Margo Sawyer, Houston, Elgin
2016	Dornith Doherty, Houston, Southlake	Dario Robleto, San Antonio, Houston
2017	Kermit Oliver, Refugio, Houston, Waco	Beverly Penn, San Marcos
2018	Sedrick Huckaby, Fort Worth	Beili Liu, Austin
2019	Mary McCleary, Nacogdoches	Rick Lowe, Houston
2020	Earlie Hudnall Jr., Houston	Gabriel Dawe, Dallas

State Historians of Texas

Year	Historian, College
2007-09	Jesús de la Teja, Texas State Univ.
2009-12	Light Cummins, Austin College
2012-16	Bill O'Neal, Panola College
2016-18	vacant
2018-20	Monte Monroe, Texas Tech Univ.

State Musicians of Texas

Year	Artist, Hometown/Residence
2003	James Dick, Round Top
2004	Ray Benson, Austin
2005	Johnny Gimble, Tyler
2006	Billy Joe Shaver, Waco

continued on next page

State Musicians of Texas

Year	Artist, Hometown/Residence
continued from previous page	
2007	Dale Watson, Pasadena/Austin
2008	Shelley King, Austin
2009	Willie Nelson, Abbott/Austin
2010	Sara Hickman, Austin
2011	Lyle Lovett, Klein
2012	Billy Gibbons (ZZ Top), Houston
2013	Craig Hella Johnson, Austin
2014	Flaco Jiménez, San Antonio
2015	Jimmie Vaughn, Dallas/Austin
2016	Joe Ely, Lubbock, Austin
2017	George Strait, Poteet/San Antonio
2018	Marcia Ball, Orange/Austin
2019	Little Joe Hernandez, Temple/San Antonio
2020	Emily Gimble, Austin

State Musician

Little Joe Hernandez has been performing Tejano music since 1955 and as Little Joe y La Familia since 1959. He was named state musician by the Texas Legislature in 2019. File photo.

Poets Laureate of Texas

Years	Poet, Hometown/Residence
1932-34	Judd Mortimer Lewis, Houston
1934-36	Aline T. Michaelis, Austin
1936-39	Grace Noll Crowell, Dallas
1939-41	Lexie Dean Robertson, Rising Star
1941-43	Nancy Richey Ranson, Dallas
1943-45	Dollilee Davis Smith, Cleburne
1945-47	David Riley Russell, Dallas
1947-49	Aline B. Carter, San Antonio
1949-51	Carlos Ashley, Llano
1951-53	Arthur M. Sampley, Denton
1953-55	Mildred Lindsey Raiborn, San Angelo Dee Walker, Texas City, alternate
1955-57	Pierre Bernard Hill, Hunt
1957-59	Margaret Royalty Edwards, Waco
1959-61	J.V. Chandler, Kingsville Edna Coe Majors, Colorado City, alt.
1961	Lorena Simon, Port Arthur
1962	Marvin Davis Winsett, Dallas

Years	Poet, Hometown/Residence
1963	Gwendolyn Bennett Pappas, Houston Vassar Miller, Houston, alternate
1964-65	Jenny Lind Porter, Austin Edith Rayzor Canant, Texas City, alt.
1966	Bessie Maas Rowe, Port Arthur Grace Marie Scott, Abilene, alternate
1967	William E. Bard, Dallas Bessie Maas Rowe, Port Arthur, alt.
1968	Kathryn Henry Harris, Waco Sybil Leonard Armes, El Paso, alt.
1969-70	Anne B. Marely, Austin Rose Davidson Speer, Brady, alt.
1970-71	Mrs. Robby K. Mitchell, McKinney Faye Carr Adams, Dallas, alternate
1971-72	Terry Fontenot, Port Arthur Faye Carr Adams, Dallas, alternate
1972-73	Mrs. Clark Gresham, Burkburnett Marion McDaniel, Sidney, alternate
1973-74	Violette Newton, Beaumont Stella Woodall, San Antonio, alternate
1974-75	Lila Todd O'Neil, Port Arthur C.W. Miller, San Antonio, alternate
1975-76	Ethel Osborn Hill, Port Arthur Gene Shuford, Denton, alternate
1976-77	Florice Stripling Jeffers, Burkburnett Vera L. Eckert, San Angelo, alternate
1977-78	Ruth Carruth, Vernon Joy Gresham Hagstrom, Burkburnett, alternate
1978-79	Patsy Stodghill, Dallas Dorothy B. Elfstroman, Galveston, alt.
1979-80	Dorothy B. Elfstroman, Galveston Ruth Carruth, Vernon, alternate
1980-81	Weems S. Dykes, McCamey Mildred Crabree Speer, Amarillo, alt.
1981-82	*none designated*
1982-83	William D. Barney, Fort Worth Vassar Miller, Houston, alternate
1983-87	*none designated*
1987-88	Ruth E. Reuther, Wichita Falls
1988-89	Vassar Miller, Houston
1989-93	*none designated*
1993-94	Mildred Baass, Victoria
1994-99	*none designated*
2000	James Hoggard, Wichita Falls
2001	Walter McDonald, Lubbock
2002	*none designated*
2003	Jack Myers, Mesquite
2004	Cleatus Rattan, Cisco
2005	Alan Birkelbach, Plano
2006	Red Steagall, Fort Worth
2007	Steven Fromholz, Kopperl, Sugar Land
2008	Larry Thomas, Houston
2009	Paul Ruffin, Huntsville

continued on next page

Poets Laureate of Texas

Years	Poet, Hometown/Residence
continued from previous page	
2010	Karla K. Morton, Denton, Fort Worth
2011	David M. Parsons, Conroe
2012	Jan Seale, McAllen
2013	Rosemary Catacalos, San Antonio

Years	Poet, Hometown/Residence
2014	Dean Young, Austin
2015	Carmen Tafolla, San Antonio
2016	Laurie Ann Guerrero, San Antonio
2017	Jenny Browne, San Antonio
2018	Carol Coffee Reposa, San Antonio
2019	Carrie Fountain, Austin
2020	Emmy Pérez, McAllen

Philosophical Society of Texas Awards of Merit

The Philosophical Society of Texas established the Award of Merit in 2000 and expanded it in 2012 to separate categories, one for fiction and one for nonfiction. In 2015, an award for poetry was introduced. The book must be about Texas or the author must have been born in or have resided within the boundaries claimed by the Republic of Texas in 1836. Award of Merit winners are listed below.

2000		Gregg Cantrell, *Stephen F. Austin, Empresario*, Yale University Press, 1999.
2001		Frank D. Welch, *Philip Johnson & Texas*, University of Texas Press, 2000.
2002		Hal K. Rothman, *LBJ's Texas White House: "Our Heart's Home,"* Texas A&M University Press, 2001.
2003		James L. Haley, *Sam Houston*, University of Oklahoma Press, 2002.
2004		Randolph B. Campbell, *Gone to Texas: A History of the Lone Star State*, Oxford University Press, 2003.
2005		David La Vere, *The Texas Indians*, Texas A&M University Press, 2004.
2006		Mavis P. Kelsey Sr. and Robin Brandt Hutchinon, *Engraved Prints of Texas, 1554–1900*, Texas A&M University Press, 2005
2007		Richard B. McCaslin, *At the Heart of Texas, 100 Years of the Texas State Historical Association, 1897–1997*, Texas State Historical Association Press, 2006.
2008		Stephen Fox, *The Country Houses of John F. Staub*, Texas A&M University Press, 2007.
2009		Pekka Hämäläinen, *The Comanche Empire*, Yale University Press, 2008.
2010		Emilio Zamora, *Claiming Rights and Righting Wrongs in Texas: Mexican Workers and Job Politics During World War II*, Texas A&M University Press, 2009.
2011		Dan K. Utley and Cynthia J. Beeman, *History Ahead: Stories beyond the Texas Roadside Markers*, Texas A&M University Press, 2011.
2012	Fiction	Gerald Duff, *Blue Sabine*, Moon City Press, 2011.
	Non-fiction	Michael Berryhill, *The Trails of Eroy Brown: The Murder Case that Shook the Texas Prison System*, University of Texas Press, 2011.
2013	Fiction	Ben Rehder, *The Chicken Hanger: A Novel*, Texas Christian University Press, 2012.
	Non-fiction	Jan Reid, *Let the People In: The Life and Times of Ann Richards*, UT Press, 2012.
2014	Fiction	Thomas Zigal, *Many Rivers to Cross*, Texas Christian University Press, 2013.
	Non-fiction	Raúl Coronado, *A World Not to Come: A History of Latino Writing and Print Culture*, Harvard University Press, 2013.
2015	Fiction	Sara Bird, *Above the East China Sea*, Knopf, 2014.
	Fiction	James Magnuson, *Famous Writers I have Known: A Novel*, W.W. Norton & Company, 2014.
	Non-fiction	Katie Robinson Edwards, *Midcentury Modern Art in Texas*, University of Texas Press, 2014.
	Poetry	Christian Wiman, *Once in the West*, Farrar, Straus and Giroux, 2014.
2016	Fiction	Sanderia Faye, *Mourner's Bench*, University of Arkansas Press, 2015.
	Non-fiction	Ron J. Jackson Jr. and Lee Spencer White, *Joe: The Slave Who Became an Alamo Legend*, University of Oklahoma Press, 2015.
	Poetry	James Hoggard, *New and Selected Poems*, TCU Press, 2015.
2017	Fiction	Dominic Smith, *The Last Painting of Sara de Vos*, 2016.
	Non-fiction	Kenneth Hafertepe, *The Material Culture of German Texans*, 2016.
	Poetry	Jonathan Fink, *Barbarossa*, 2016.
2018	Fiction	Chanelle Benz, *The Man Who Shot Out My Eye Is Dead*, 2017.
	Non-fiction	Andrew Sansom and William E. Reaves, *Of Texas Rivers and Texas Art*, 2017.
	Poetry	Dan Williams, *Past Purgatory, A Distant Paradise*, 2017.

Holidays, Anniversaries, and Festivals, 2020–2021

Below are listed the principal federal and state government holidays; Christian, Jewish, and Islamic holidays and festivals; and special recognition days for 2020 and 2021. Technically, the United States does not observe national holidays. Each state has jurisdiction over its holidays, which are usually designated by its legislature. This list was compiled partially from the Texas Government Code, the U.S. Office of Personnel Management, and *Astronomical Phenomena 2020* and *Astronomical Phenomena 2021*, which are published jointly by the U.S. Naval Observatory and the United Kingdom Hydrographic Office. See the footnotes for explanations of the symbols.

2020			2021		
New Year's Day	§	Wed., Jan. 1	**New Year's Day**	§	Fri., Jan. 1
Epiphany		Mon., Jan. 6	Epiphany		Wed., Jan. 6
Sam Rayburn Day	‡	Mon., Jan. 6	Sam Rayburn Day	‡	Wed., Jan. 6
Confederate Heroes Day	§	Sun., Jan. 19	**Martin Luther King Jr. Day**	§	Mon., Jan. 18
Martin Luther King Jr. Day	§	Mon., Jan. 20	Confederate Heroes Day	§	Tues., Jan. 19
Valentine's Day		Fri., Feb. 14	Valentine's Day		Sun., Feb. 14
Presidents' Day	§	Mon., Feb. 17	**Presidents' Day**	§	Mon., Feb. 15
Ash Wednesday		Wed., Feb. 26	Ash Wednesday		Wed., Feb. 17
Texas Independence Day	§	Mon., March 2	Texas Independence Day	§	Tues., March 2
Texas Flag Day	‡	Mon., March 2	Texas Flag Day	‡	Tues., March 2
Primary Election Day		Tues., March 3	Palm Sunday		Sun., March 28
César Chávez Day	§	Tues., March 31	Passover (Pesach), first day of		Sun., March 28
Palm Sunday		Sun., April 5	César Chávez Day	§	Wed., March 31
Passover (Pesach), first day of		Thurs., April 9	Good Friday	§	Fri., April 2
Former Prisoners of War Day	‡	Thurs., April 9	Easter Day		Sun., April 4
Good Friday	§	Fri., April 10	Former Prisoners of War Day	‡	Fri., April 9
Easter Day		Sun., April 12	Ramadan, first day of		Tues., April 13
San Jacinto Day	§	Tues., April 21	San Jacinto Day	§	Wed., April 21
Ramadan, first day of		Fri., April 24	Mother's Day		Sun., May 9
Mother's Day		Sun., May 10	Ascension Day		Thurs., May 13
Armed Forces Day		Sat., May 16	Armed Forces Day		Sat., May 15
Ascension Day		Thurs., May 21	Shavuot (Feast of Weeks)		Mon., May 17
Memorial Day	§	Mon., May 25	Whit Sunday — Pentecost		Sun., May 23
Shavuot (Feast of Weeks)		Fri., May 29	Trinity Sunday		Sun., May 30
Whit Sunday — Pentecost		Sun., May 31	**Memorial Day**	§	Mon., May 31
Trinity Sunday		Sun., June 7	Flag Day (U.S.)		Mon., June 14
Flag Day (U.S.)		Sun., June 14	Emancipation Day in Texas (Juneteenth)	§	Sat., June 19
Emancipation Day in Texas (Juneteenth)	§	Fri., June 19	Father's Day		Sun., June 20
Father's Day		Sun., June 21	**Independence Day**	§	Sun., July 4
Independence Day	§	Sat., July 4	Islamic New Year		Tues., Aug. 10
Islamic New Year		Thurs., Aug. 20	Lyndon Baines Johnson Day	§	Fri., Aug. 27
Lyndon Baines Johnson Day	§	Thurs., Aug. 27	**Labor Day**	§	Mon., Sept. 6
Labor Day	§	Mon., Sept. 7	Rosh Hashanah (Jewish New Year)		Tues., Sept. 7
Grandparents Day		Sun., Sept. 13	Grandparents Day		Sun., Sept. 12
Rosh Hashanah (Jewish New Year)		Sat., Sept. 19	Yom Kippur (Day of Atonement)		Thurs., Sept. 16
Yom Kippur (Day of Atonement)		Mon., Sept. 28	Sukkot (Tabernacles), first day of		Tues., Sept. 21
Sukkot (Tabernacles), first day of		Sat., Oct. 3	**Columbus Day**	‡	Mon., Oct. 11
Columbus Day	‡	Mon., Oct.12	Halloween		Sun., Oct. 31
Halloween		Sat., Oct. 31	General Election Day	§	Tues., Nov. 2
General Election Day	§	Tues., Nov. 3	Father of Texas Day	‡	Wed., Nov. 3
Father of Texas Day	‡	Tues., Nov. 3	**Veterans Day**	§	Thurs., Nov. 11
Veterans Day	§	Wed., Nov. 11	**Thanksgiving Day**	§	Thurs., Nov. 25
Thanksgiving Day	§	Thurs., Nov. 26	First Sunday in Advent		Sun., Nov. 28
First Sunday in Advent		Sun., Nov. 29	Hanukkah, first day of		Mon., Nov. 29
Hanukkah, first day of		Fri., Dec. 11	**Christmas Day**	§	Sat., Dec. 25
Christmas Day	§	Fri., Dec. 25			

Federal legal public holidays are shown in bold. If the holiday falls on a Sunday, the following Monday may be treated as a holiday. If the holiday falls on a Saturday, the preceding Friday may be treated as a holiday.

§ **State holiday in Texas**. For state employees, the Friday after Thanksgiving Day, Dec. 24, and Dec. 26 are also holidays. **Option-al holidays** are César Chávez Day, Good Friday, Rosh Hashanah, and Yom Kippur. **Partial-staffing holidays** are Confederate Heroes Day, Texas Independence Day, San Jacinto Day, Emancipation Day in Texas, and Lyndon Baines Johnson Day. State offices will be open on optional holidays and partial-staffing holidays.

‡ **State Recognition Days**, as designated by the Texas Legislature.

Notes on holidays:
• Confederate Heroes Day combines the birthdays of Robert E. Lee (Jan. 19) and Jefferson Davis (June 3).
• Presidents' Day combines the birthdays of George Washington (Feb. 22) and Abraham Lincoln (Feb. 12).
• Jewish and Islamic holidays are tabular, meaning they begin at sunset on the previous evening.
• Between 1939 and 1957, Texas observed Thanksgiving Day on the last Thursday in November. As a result, in a November having five Thursdays, Texas celebrated national Thanksgiving on the fourth Thursday and Texas Thanksgiving on the fifth Thursday. In 1957, Texas changed the state observance to coincide with the national holiday.

Filming on set of the 2012 movie Fort Bliss *outside El Paso. Photo by Sgt. Brandon Bednarek (CC).*

Film and Television Work in Texas

Source: Texas Film Commission at gov.texas.gov/film/

For almost a century, Texas has been one of the nation's top filmmaking states, after California and New York.

More than 1,600 films have been made in Texas since 1910, including **Wings**, the first film to win an Academy Award for Best Picture, which was made in San Antonio in 1927.

Texas' attractions to filmmakers are its diverse locations, abundant sunshine and moderate winter weather, and a variety of support services. The economic benefits of hosting on-location filming over the past decade are estimated at more than $3 billion.

Besides salaries paid to locally hired technicians and actors, as well as fees paid to location owners, the production companies do business with hotels, car rental agencies, lumberyards, restaurants, grocery stores, utilities, security services, and florists.

All types of projects come to Texas besides films, including television features and news organizations, commercials, corporate films, and game videos.

Many projects made in Texas originate in California studios, but Texas is also the home of many independent filmmakers who make films outside the studio system.

Some films and television shows made in Texas have become icons. **Giant**, John Wayne's **The Alamo**, and the long-running TV series **Dallas** all made their mark on the world's perception of Texas.

The Texas Film Commission, a division of the Office of the Governor, markets to Hollywood Texas' locations, support services, and workforce availablity. The legislature funded the Texas Moving Image Incentive Program with $22 million in the 2018–2019 biennium.

The commission's free services include location research, employment referrals for production assistants, red-tape-cutting, and information on weather, travel, and other topics affecting production. ☆

Regional Commissions

Amarillo Film Office
1000 S. Polk, Amarillo 79101
(800) 342-2023
www.visitamarillo.com/film

Austin Film Office
111 Congress Ave., Ste. 700
Austin 78701, (800) 926-2282
www.austinfilmcommission.com

Brownsville Border Film Comm.
1034 E. Levee St.
Brownsville 78520, (956) 548-6156
miriam.suarez@cob.us

Corpus Christi Film Commission
1501 N. Chaparral St.
Corpus Christi 78401

(800) 678-6232
www.corpuschristifilmcommission.com/

Dallas Film Commission
1500 Marilla 2C North
Dallas 75201, (214) 671-9821
www.dallasfilmcommission.com

El Paso Film Commission
One Civic Center Plaza
El Paso 79901, (915) 534-0600
www.filmelpaso.com

Fort Worth Film Commission
111 W. 4th St., Ste. 200
Fort Worth 76102
(800) 433-5747
www.filmfortworth.com

Houston Film Commission

701 Avenida de las Americas
Ste. 200
Houston 77010, (800) 446-8786
www.houstonfilmcommission.com

Northeast Texas Film Commission
P.O. Box 247
Jefferson 75657, (903) 214-1144
www.netexasmovies.com

Rio Grande Valley Film Commission
P.O. Box 2856, Harlingen 78551
(956) 202-1392
www.rgvfilmcommission.com

San Antonio Film Commission
203 S. St. Mary's, Ste. 120
San Antonio 78205,
(210) 207-6730
www.filmsanantonio.com

Recent Movies Made in Texas

Following is a partial list of recent major productions filmed in Texas, in descending order by date. The date is for the year of release of the film, while actual location shots occurred earlier.

Location information is from the Texas Film Commission and other sources.

When only a small portion of the movie is known to have been filmed in Texas, "(part)" is listed next to the movie title.

Some of the major artists who worked on the project are listed in the column at far right.

Sources: Texas Film Commission, and online.

YEAR	MOVIE	LOCATIONS	ARTISTS
2018	The Iron Orchard	Big Spring, Midland, Odessa, Austin	Ty Roberts (director), Austin Nichols
2018	1985	Dallas	Yen Tan (director), Michael Chiklis, Virginia Madsen
2016	Everybody Wants Some	Austin, Bastrop, Elgin, Manor, San Marcos, Taylor, Weimar, Wimberley	Richard Linklater (director), Blake Jenner
2015	My All American	Austin, Dallas, Fort Worth, San Antonio, Elgin, Manor, Smithville	Angelo Pizzo (director), Aaron Eckhart, Finn Wittrock
2013	Boyhood	Alpine, Austin, Houston, San Marcos, Big Bend, Webster, Pedernales State Park	Ethan Hawke, Patricia Arquette, Richard Linklater (director)
2013	Parkland	Dallas, Austin	Billy Bob Thornton, Zac Efron
2011	Bernie	Carthage, Smithville, Georgetown, Bastrop, Lockhart, Austin	Jack Black, Shirley MacLaine, Matthew McConaughey, Richard Linklater (director)
2011	The Tree of Life	Bastrop, Austin, Dallas, Houston, La Grange, Matagorda, San Marcos, Smithville, Waco	Brad Pitt, Sean Penn
2009	Friday the 13th	Austin, Bastrop, La Grange, Marshall, Wimberley	Marcus Nispel (director)
2006	No Country for Old Men (part)	Marfa	Ethan and Joel Coen (directors), Tommy Lee Jones
2006	There Will Be Blood (part)	Marfa, Big Bend National Park	Daniel Day-Lewis
2005	The Three Burials of Melquiades Estrada	Van Horn, Monahans, Santa Elena Canyon, Lajitas, Shafter, Midland/Odessa	Tommy Lee Jones, Julio Cedillo
2004	The Alamo	Dripping Springs, Wimberley, Pedernales Falls State Park, Bastrop, Austin	Dennis Quaid, Jason Patric
2004	Friday Night Lights	Odessa, Notrees, Austin, Houston	Billy Bob Thornton
2003	Texas Chainsaw Massacre	Martindale, Taylor, Austin	
2002	The Rookie	Thorndale, Taylor, Arlington, Big Lake	Dennis Quaid
2000	All the Pretty Horses	Boerne, Helotes, Pipe Creek, Big Bend	Matt Damon, Sam Shepard
2000	Miss Congeniality	Austin, San Antonio	Sandra Bullock, Michael Caine
1999	Where the Heart Is	Austin, Baylor University, Lockhart, Taylor, Kyle, Driftwood, Bastrop, Georgetown	Natalie Portman, Ashley Judd
1999	Boys Don't Cry	Greenville, Dallas area	Hilary Swank
1999	Office Space	Austin, Dallas	Jennifer Aniston, Ron Livingston
1999	Varsity Blues	Elgin, Coupland, Taylor, Georgetown	James Van Der Beek, Jon Voight
1998	Dancer, Texas Pop. 81	Fort Davis, Alpine	Breckin Meyer, Peter Facinelli
1998	Hope Floats	Smithville, Austin	Sandra Bullock, Harry Connick Jr.
1998	The Newton Boys	Bertram, Martindale, Bartlett, Lockhart, Austin, San Antonio	Matthew McConaughey, Ethan Hawke
1996	Bottle Rocket	Hillsboro, Grand Prairie, Dallas	Luke and Owen Wilson, James Caan
1996	Lone Star	Eagle Pass, Del Rio, Laredo	Matthew McConaughey, Kris Kristofferson
1995	Apollo 13	Houston area	Tom Hanks, Kevin Bacon
1993	Dazed and Confused	Austin, Georgetown, Seguin	Richard Linklater (director), Matthew McConaughey

Number of Production Projects in Texas by Year

	2005	2006	2007	2008	2009	2010	2011	2014	2015	2016	2017
Feature Films	31	45	36	27	60	38	16	26	14	24	19
TV Series	13	11	14	12	20	17	15	14	20	15	23
TOTAL	44	56	50	39	80	55	31	40	34	39	42

Sources: Texas Film Commission and the Motion Picture Association of America (2018).

Television series that were recently produced in Texas include **Fixer Upper**, **I Love Dick**, **Day 5**, **Street Stories**, **Real Housewives of Dallas**, **The Little Couple**, **Queen of the South**, **Fast and Loud**, and **Mann & Wife**, and some syndicated programs, in addition to the long-running **Austin City Limits**.

Religious Affiliation Change: 2000 to 2010

Texas remains one of the nation's more "religious" states, even though a smaller portion of Texans is affiliated with a congregation than ten years ago.

At the same time, the estimated number of Muslims in the state increased to 421,972, making it the fifth-largest religious group in the state and making Texas first in the nation in number of Muslims.

Texas ranks in the upper half among the states in percentage of the population belonging to a denomination. According to the *2010 U.S. Religion Census*, at least **56.0 percent** of Texans are adherents to a religion. The national average is 48.8 percent.

The census, sponsored by the Association of Statisticians of American Religious Bodies, is the only U.S. survey to report religious membership down to the county level, as well as at the state level. The census relies on self-reports from congregations for membership numbers.

But in the past, the African-American churches did not participate in the study, and in 2010 less than half of those congregations participated.

Only 345,998 black Protestants were counted in Texas in 2010. According to the U.S. Census of 2010, there were 2,782,876 blacks in Texas, which would mean 87.6 percent of black Texans, who are predominately Protestant, were designated as unaffiliated to any church. This probably leaves out some one million Texas church members.

In 1990, it was estimated that there were 815,000 black Baptists in Texas. An estimate of the membership in black Pentecostal churches was about 300,000. And an estimate for black Methodists in Texas was approximately 200,000.

According to the *2010 U.S. Religion Census*, **Texas ranks**:

— **First** in number of evangelical Protestants, with 6,457,044.

— **First** in number that belong to non-denominational Christian churches, with 1,546,542.

— **First** in number of Muslims, with 421,972 estimated. New York is second with 392,953 estimated.

— **Second**, behind Pennsylvania, in number of Mainline Protestants at 1,641,527.

— **Second**, behind California, in number of Hindus.

— **Third** in number of Buddhists.

— **Third** in number of Catholics.

— **Fifth** in number of Mormons.

Carrying over those estimates into 2010 and adjusting for these additions, the percentage of Texans that are adherents* of a religion would be closer to **59.8 percent** in 2010.

[In addition, the religion census includes denominations that provide numbers of congregations but who have not enumerated the numbers of adherents in each congregation. Even with factoring in an average congregation size of 100 persons for Protestant congregations (a figure used by the census study), the total percentage would vary less than one percent, to **60.7 percent**.]

Although that is higher than the 56.0 percent figure compiled from the reporting churches, still it would be down from **67.1 percent** 20 years ago, indicating a move away from religious affiliation in Texas.

However, with the total state population booming, the churches still reported an **increase of 2.17 million** members, while the total population of Texas increased by 4.29 million from 2000 to 2010.

During the same period, the number of Texans not attached to a religion rose by **2.13 million**.

Thus, according to the Texas Almanac analysis from a variety of sources, there are **10.1 million** persons in the state who are not claimed by a religious group and about 15 million who are congregation members. (The U.S. census counted **25,145,561** persons in Texas in 2010.) — RP.

Largest Religious Bodies	Adherents*	Percent of Texas Population
1. Catholic Church	4,673,500	18.59 %
2. Southern Baptist Convention	3,722,194	14.80 %
3. Non-Denominational Christian	1,546,542	6.15 %
4. United Methodist Church	1,122,736	4.46 %
5. Muslim estimate	421,972	1.68 %
6. Church of Christ	351,129	1.40 %
7. Latter-Day Saints (Mormons)	296,141	1.18 %
8. Assembly of God	275,565	1.10 %
9. Presbyterian Church (U.S.A.)	155,046	0.62 %
10. Episcopal Church	148,439	0.59 %
11. Lutheran (Missouri Synod)	132,508	0.53 %
12. Lutheran (E.L.C.A.)	111,647	0.44 %
Unclaimed by any faith	10,103,455	40.20 %

Adherents include all full members, their children, and others who regularly attend services. All figures used here by the Texas Almanac refer to these adherents.

Religious Adherents

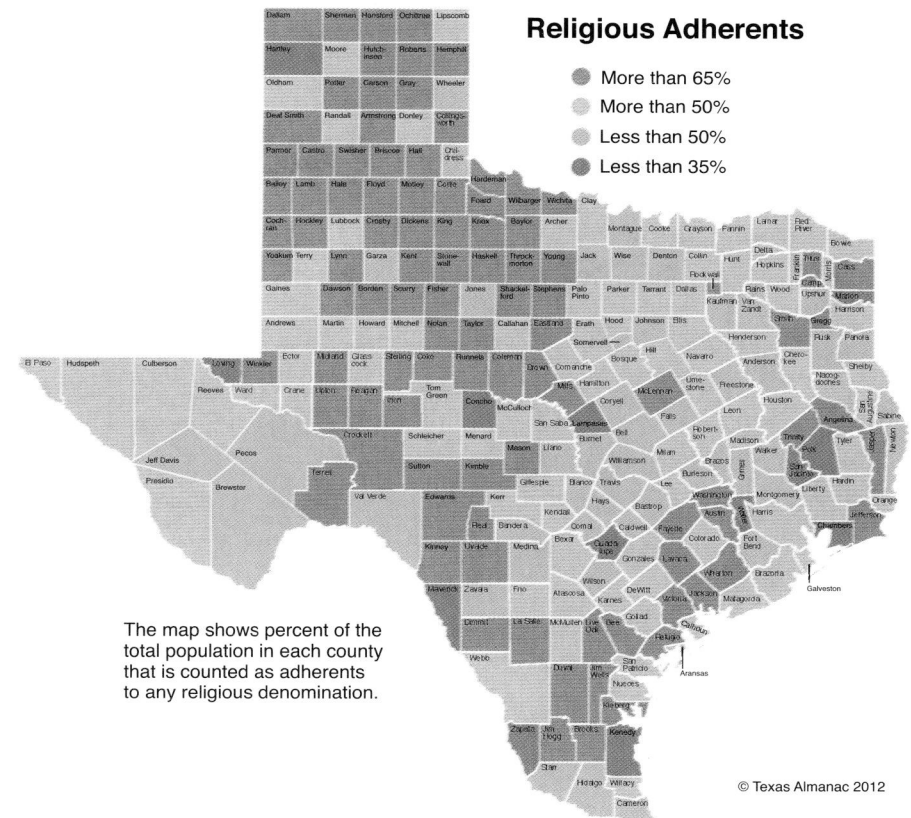

- ● More than 65%
- ◌ More than 50%
- ◌ Less than 50%
- ● Less than 35%

The map shows percent of the
total population in each county
that is counted as adherents
to any religious denomination.

© Texas Almanac 2012

Numbers of Members Statewide by Denomination

Religious Groups in Texas	2000	Change	2010
Adventists	**46,323**	**+ 27,797**	**74,120**
Church of God (Seventh Day) (70 congregations)	—		—
Church of God General Conference	55		65
Seventh-Day Adventists	46,268		74,055
Baha'i	**10,777**	**+ 2,458**	**13,253**
Baptist	**4,537,918**	**+ 52,228**	**4,590,143**
Alliance of Baptists (9 congregations)			—
American Baptist Association	61,272		39,354
American Baptist Churches in the USA	7,057		7,172
Baptist General Conference	340		1,320
Baptist Missionary Association of America	123,198		—
Conservative Baptist Association of America (1 congregation)			—
Free Will Baptist, National Association of, Inc.	2,822		3,111
Independent Baptist Fellowship International (258 cong.)			—
Interstate & Foreign Landmark Missionary Baptists Association	93		—
Landmark Baptist, Indep. Assns. & Unaffil. Churches	964		—
National Primitive Baptist Convention, USA	4,463		—
North American Baptist Conference	1,569		1,157
Primitive Baptists Associations			—
Primitive Baptist Church — Old Line (118 congregations)			—
Progressive Primitive Baptists	197		—
Reformed Baptist Churches of America (27 congregations)			—

Religious Groups in Texas	2000	Change	2010
Regular Baptist Churches, General Assn. of (6 congregations)	684		—
Seventh Day Baptist General Conference			67
Southern Baptist Convention	3,519,459		3,722,194
Southwide Baptist Fellowship (13 congregations)			—
Two-Seed-in-the-Spirit Predestinarian Baptists	29		—
Black Baptists (Estimate)*	(815,771)*		(815,771)*
National Baptist Convention of America, Inc.			89,050
National Baptist Convention, USA, Inc.			59,529
National Missionary Bapist Convention, Inc.			34,039
Progressive National Baptist Convention, Inc.			2,683
Full Gospel Baptist Church Fellowship (52 congregations)			—
Buddhist (95 congregations)	**—**		**66,116**
Mahayana			49,874
Theravada			13,461
Vajrayana			2,781
Catholic Church	**4,368,969**	**+ 304,531**	**4,673,500**
(Christian Scientists) Church of Christ, Scientist (64 cong.)	**—**		**—**
Churches of Christ	**424,907**	**– 30,843**	**394,064**
Church of Christ	377,264		351,129
Independent Christian Churches and Churches of Christ	43,602		40,078
International Churches of Christ	4,041		2,857
(Disciples of Christ) Christian Church	**111,288**	**– 36,471**	**74,817**
Episcopal	**177,910**	**– 29,471**	**148,439**
Episcopal Church, The	177,910		148,439
Reformed Episcopal Church			—
Anglican Church in North America (111 congregations)			—
Hindu (34 congregations in 2000)	**—**		**60,725**
Indian-American Hindu Temple Assn.			36,550
Post-Renaissance			968
Renaissance			98
Traditional Temples			23,109
Holiness	**86,942**	**– 1,738**	**85,204**
Christian & Missionary Alliance, The	3,858		5,465
Church of Christ (Holiness), U.S.A. (4 congregations)			—
Church of God (Anderson, Ind.)	4,669		3,990
Churches of Christ in Christian Union (2 congregations)			—
Free Methodist Church of North America	874		1,864
Missionary Church, The	403		3,119
Nazarene, Church of the	50,528		44,836
Salvation Army	25,070		23,761
Wesleyan Church, The	1,540		2,169
Jain (6 congregations)	**—**		**—**
Jehovah's Witnesses (426 congregations)	**—**		**—**
Judaism, (estimate) *	**(128,000)***	**– 67,355**	**60,645**
Conservative			**17,889**
Orthodox			**8,410**
Reconstructionist			**356**
Reform			**33,990**
Lutheran	**301,518**	**– 29,452**	**272,066**
Church of the Lutheran Brethren of America	—		72
Church of the Lutheran Confession (4 congregations)	—		—
Evangelical Lutheran Church in America	155,019		111,647
Evangelical Lutheran Synod	—		—
Free Lutheran Congregations, The Assoc. of	368		75
Lutheran Church–Missouri Synod, The	140,106		132,508
Lutheran Congregations in Mission for Christ	—		20,936
North American Lutheran Church (26 congregations)	—		—
Wisconsin Evangelical Lutheran Synod	6,025		6,828

Religious Groups in Texas	2000	Change	2010
Mennonite/Amish	**4,930**	**– 1,330**	**3,600**
Amish, Old Order or Conservative Unaffiliated	24		309
Amish, undifferentiated	68		52
Apostolic Christian Church of America, Inc.	27		46
Beachy Amish Mennonite Churches	127		265
Brethren in Christ Church (1 congregation)	—		—
Church of God in Christ (Mennonite)	849		1,068
Church of the Brethren	284		118
Conservative Mennonite Conference	191		106
Evangelical Bible Churches, Fellowship of (was Ev. Menn. Bre.)			—
Eastern Pennsylvania Mennonite Church	65		—
Grace Brethren Churches, Fellowship of (3 congregations)			—
Mennonite Brethren Churches, U.S. Conference of	425		403
Mennonite, other	1,655		—
Mennonite Church USA	1,215		1,233
Messianic Judaism	**—**		**—**
Association of Messianic Congregations (1 congregation)	—		—
Union of Messianic Jewish Congregations (5 congregations)	—		—
Methodist	**1,219,533**	**+ 94,912**	**1,314,445**
Black Methodists (estimate)*	(197,191)*		(150,000)*
African Methodist Episcopal Zion	(2,191)*		1,327
African Methodist Episcopal	(150,000)*		43,839
Christian Methodist Episcopal	(45,000)*		37,986
Congregational Methodist Church	—		2,396
Evangelical Methodist Church (11 congregations)			—
Southern Methodist Church (2 congregations)			—
United Methodist Church, The	1,022,342		1,122,736
(Mormons)	**158,268**	**+ 142,323**	**300,591**
Church of Jesus Christ of Latter-day Saints, The	155,451		296,141
Community of Christ	2,817		4,450
Muslim, estimate	**114,999**	**+ 306,973**	**421,972**
Non-denominational (Evangelical Protestant)	**—**		**1,546,542**
Independent Non-Charismatic Churches	145,249		—
Independent Charismatic Churches	159,449		—
Orthodox (Eastern Christian)	**22,755**	**+ 9,695**	**32,450**
Antiochian Orthodox of North America	4,642		5,348
Armenian Apostolic Church/Cilicia	80		—
Armenian Apostolic Church/Etchmiadzin	1,275		515
Assyrian Apostolic Church			—
Coptic Orthodox Church (8 congregations)	—		3,866
Eritrean Orthodox	—		1,000
Ethiopian Orthodox (4 congregations)			—
Greek Orthodox Archdiocese of America	9,444		12,167
Greek Orthodox Archdiocese of Vasiloupulis	135		—
Malankara Archdiocese/Syrian Orthodox Church in North Amer.	825		1,260
Malankara Orthodox Syrian Church, American Diocese of the	2,675		2,433
Romanian Orthodox Archdiocese in Americas)	413		600
Orthodox Church in America (Territorial Dioceses)	2,096		2,657
Russian Orthodox Church Outside of Russia (4 congregations)	—		1,022
Serbian Orthodox Church in North America	1,110		1,372
Syrian Orthodox Church of Antioch	60		210
Pentecostal/Charismatic	**615,258**	**+ 61,825**	**677,083**
Apostolic Faith Mission of Portland, Ore.	—		135
Assemblies of God	228,098		275,565
Assemblies of God International Fellowship (3 congregations)	—		—
Black Pentecostals (estimate)*	(300,000)*		(300,000)*
Church of God in Christ (estimate)*	(300,000)*		77,545
Church of Our Lord Jesus Christ of Apostolic Faith (22 cong.)	—		—
Calvary Chapel Fellowship Churches (57 congregations)	—		—
Church of God (Cleveland, Tenn.)	38,259		47,709
Church of God of Prophecy	2,906		3,610

Religious Groups in Texas	2000	Change	2010
Church of God of the Apostolic Faith, Inc. (18 congregations)	—		—
Church of Our Lord Jesus Christ of Apostolic Faith (22 cong.)			
Congregational Holiness Church	—		1,280
International Church of the Foursquare Gospel	12,501		11,047
Open Bible Standard Churches, Inc.	—		148
Pentecostal Church of God	11,592		13,486
Pentecostal Holiness Church, International	10,265		15,576
Pentecostal Church International, United (656 congregations)	—		
Vineyard USA	11,637		8,527
Presbyterian	**204,804**	**– 21,514**	**183,290**
Associate Reformed Presbyterian Church	28		223
Cumberland Presbyterian Church	8,422		6,355
Cumberland Presbyterian Church in America (19 cong.)	—		
Evangelical Presbyterian Church	1,449		2,883
Korean Presbyterian Church Abroad (2 congregations)	—		
Korean Presbyterian Church in America (8 congregations)	—		—
Korean-American Presbyterian Church (4 congregations)	—		
Orthodox Presbyterian Church, The	644		824
Presbyterian Church (USA)	180,315		155,046
Presbyterian Church in America	13,946		17,959
Reformed Presbyterian Church General Assembly (1 cong.)	—		—
Reformed Presbyterian Church Hanover Presbytery (1 cong)	—		—
Reformed Presbyterian Church in the United States (1 cong.)	—		—
(Quakers)	**1,074**	**+ 1,700**	**2,774**
Evangelical Friends Church International	—		1,845
Friends General Conference	—		929
Unaffiliated Friends Meetings (2 congregations)	—		—
Reformed/Congregational	**30,308**	**+ 2,599**	**32,907**
Communion of Reformed Evangelical Churches (5 cong.)	—		
Christian Reformed Church in North America	1,936		1,416
Conservative Congregational Christian Conference	25		29
Evangelical Assn. of Reformed, and Congregational (5 cong.)	—		—
Evangelical Free Church of America, The	9,720		13,486
Hungarian Reformed Churches (2 congregations)	—		—
Reformed Church in America	2,040		512
United Church of Christ	16,587		17,464
Sikh (24 congregations)	**—**		**—**
Tao (1 congregation)			
Unitarian Universalist Association	**6,872**	**+ 1,235**	**8,107**
Unity Churches, Association of (43 congregations)	**—**		**—**
Zoroastrian (3 congregations)	**NR**		**1,095**
OTHERS			
Christian Brethren (4 congregations)			—
Evangelical Covenant Church, The	1,022		1,393
Grace Gospel Fellowship (4 congregations)			—
Independent Fundamentalist Churches of America (1 cong.)			—
Metropolitan Community Churches, Universal Fellowship of	5,570		2,765
National Spiritualist Association of Churches (4 congregations)			—
New Apostolic Church of North America (13 congregations)			—
Polish National Catholic Church (3 congregations)			—
Statewide Totals**	**12,875,018**	**+ 2,167,088**	**15,042,106**
Unclaimed (not counted as adherent to religion)	7,976,802	+ 2,126,653	10,103,455

*Texas Almanac estimates. **2000 statewide totals include smaller denominations not reported in 2010 and not listed here.

Compiled from the 2010 survey sponsored by the Association of Statisticians of American Religious Bodies, also other sources, including: Churches and Church Membership in the United States 2000, Glenmary Research Center, Nashville, Tenn., 2002. National Council of Churches of Christ in the USA, New York, Yearbook of American and Canadian Churches, annual. New Handbook of Texas, 1996, various: "Christian Methodist Episcopal Church," by Charles E. Tatum; "African-American Churches," "African Methodist Episcopal Church," and "African Methodist Episcopal Zion Church," by William E. Montgomery; "Religion," by John W. Storey.

HEALTH & SCIENCE

Methodist Dallas Medical Center has served North Texas since 1927.
Photo by Michael Barera (CC).

HONORED SCIENTISTS

RESEARCH FUNDING IN TEXAS

VITAL STATISTICS

HOSPITALS

DRUG TREATMENT

MENTAL HEALTH CARE

Death, Birth Rates Continue Trends in Texas Vital Statistics

Heart disease and cancer remained the major causes of death in 2015, the latest year for which statistical breakdowns were available from the Center for Health Statistics, Texas Department of State Health Services.

Of the 189,166 deaths, heart disease claimed 43,133 lives and cancer claimed 39,018 lives. These two diseases have been the leading causes of death in Texas and the nation since 1950. Chronic respiratory diseases (COPD) ranked third with 10,216 deaths.

These three diseases accounted for nearly half, 49

percent, of all Texas resident deaths in 2015.

The number of babies born to Texas mothers in 2015 was 403,439, an increase from 399,482 in 2014. The state's birth rate in 2015 was 14.7 per 1,000 population, down slightly from 14.8 in 2014. In 1960, the figure was 25.7.

In 2016, the number of induced abortions continued to decline to 54,507 from a high in 2008 of 81,591.

Health Care and Deaths in Texas Counties

County	2018 Physicians	2016 Hospital Beds	Total Deaths 2015	2015 Pregnancy rate*	2016 Abortions	County	2018 Physicians	2016 Hospital Beds	Total Deaths 2015	2015 Pregnancy rate*	2016 Abortions
Statewide Total	**54,233**	**78,578**	**189,166**	**79.9**	**54,507***	Comal	213	348	1,108	84.7	168
Anderson	70	156	655	82.3	30	Comanche	12	25	188	88.6	23
Andrews	11	34	137	97.7	5	Concho	3	16	33	87.9	2
Angelina	188	446	871	75.5	82	Cooke	26	78	413	89.0	43
Aransas	21	0	360	87.8	33	Coryell	35	25	526	62.3	99
Archer	2	0	91	51.7	4	Cottle	0	0	31	48.3	2
Armstrong	0	0	38	71.9	0	Crane	2	25	36	88.6	5
Atascosa	34	67	408	82.1	55	Crockett	1	0	26	94.9	1
Austin	14	32	272	70.6	33	Crosby	1	25	77	81.2	5
Bailey	3	25	50	110.5	2	Culberson	1	14	14	94.8	5
Bandera	6	0	221	63.0	9	Dallam	0	0	38	118.7	5
Bastrop	37	8	660	77.7	107	Dallas	6,862	7,807	15,727	85.5	7,184
Baylor	8	49	61	79.1	1	Dawson	10	23	129	101.5	6
Bee	23	69	271	94.3	44	Deaf Smith	12	42	143	94.8	9
Bell	877	1,005	2,274	97.5	741	Delta	0	0	73	75.3	3
Bexar	4,568	7,287	12,982	82.6	5,093	Denton	1,027	1,297	3,374	63.3	1,251
Blanco	5	0	122	64.8	12	DeWitt	21	49	253	93.2	25
Borden	0	0	10	103.4	1	Dickens	0	0	26	98.5	0
Bosque	10	25	224	72.2	10	Dimmit	9	48	109	102.6	17
Bowie	273	840	1,076	75.5	77	Donley	1	0	51	52.3	5
Brazoria	388	272	2,155	81.7	614	Duval	0	0	149	105.3	18
Brazos	520	586	1,076	57.0	345	Eastland	8	52	265	68.0	11
Brewster	16	25	81	68.9	16	Ector	245	650	1,196	97.2	193
Briscoe	0	0	20	59.6	0	Edwards	1	0	33	83.3	0
Brooks	1	0	90	106.6	9	Ellis	167	164	1,209	70.3	239
Brown	63	188	515	64.4	19	El Paso	1,183	2,419	5,296	82.7	1,317
Burleson	8	25	214	78.2	9	Erath	43	98	323	54.4	65
Burnet	96	71	528	78.0	46	Falls	6	36	178	66.3	13
Caldwell	17	59	320	74.4	64	Fannin	14	25	458	73.5	26
Calhoun	15	25	198	88.3	24	Fayette	31	65	326	78.9	28
Callahan	2	0	179	59.4	10	Fisher	1	14	52	84.0	2
Cameron	499	1,314	2,684	86.9	432	Floyd	6	25	67	74.4	0
Camp	13	25	132	83.4	7	Foard	0	0	16	61.5	0
Carson	1	0	58	54.2	2	Fort Bend	1,003	1,033	2,984	74.5	1,271
Cass	13	43	414	78.6	13	Franklin	3	0	122	73.9	9
Castro	4	17	65	94.4	1	Freestone	5	37	202	73.0	16
Chambers	17	39	290	76.3	57	Frio	15	40	155	98.5	21
Cherokee	62	97	557	96.5	32	Gaines	9	25	128	119.8	4
Childress	11	39	75	68.2	2	Galveston	507	252	2,675	78.4	625
Clay	5	25	131	49.7	2	Garza	0	0	56	82.0	2
Cochran	1	18	31	72.7	2	Gillespie	90	86	318	77.7	20
Coke	0	0	53	90.1	2	Glasscock	0	0	3	80.4	0
Coleman	5	25	131	58.1	5	Goliad	1	0	87	69.6	4
Collin	2,399	2,384	4,005	62.4	1,466	Gonzales	15	33	187	106.5	22
Collingswrth	1	13	39	54.4	1	Gray	20	115	267	92.0	6
Colorado	30	103	256	91.1	19	Grayson	298	600	1,461	77.0	152
						Gregg	382	738	1,274	78.2	113

County	Physicians 2018	Hospital Beds 2016	Total Deaths 2015	Pregnancy rate* 2015	Abortions 2016	County	Physicians 2018	Hospital Beds 2016	Total Deaths 2015	Pregnancy rate* 2015	Abortions 2016
Grimes	13	25	279	87.1	30	Madison	7	25	126	74.3	16
Guadalupe	119	125	1,043	65.0	187	Marion	1	0	167	81.1	1
Hale	33	68	322	76.2	16	Martin	5	18	52	94.9	4
Hall	1	0	57	42.6	1	Mason	1	0	44	101.1	5
Hamilton	14	42	154	79.0	5	Matagorda	31	75	407	91.1	46
Hansford	4	14	53	76.4	1	Maverick	41	101	398	106.4	44
Hardeman	2	45	49	93.8	5	McCulloch	8	25	117	70.9	3
Hardin	16	0	536	69.1	57	McLennan	517	522	2,123	71.4	317
Harris	11,563	14,807	25,342	88.0	13,813	McMullen	0	0	7	96.5	1
Harrison	40	149	677	70.1	55	Medina	24	25	428	76.2	57
Hartley	7	21	51	63.8	1	Menard	1	0	33	57.6	1
Haskell	2	25	62	74.2	1	Midland	263	563	1,098	98.1	168
Hays	272	322	1,007	63.6	492	Milam	17	35	288	87.2	16
Hemphill	5	26	34	105.3	3	Mills	3	0	62	45.1	0
Henderson	78	127	1,084	70.8	58	Mitchell	5	25	109	80.2	5
Hidalgo	981	2,429	4,179	91.9	1,004	Montague	13	87	263	79.3	15
Hill	19	116	455	68.7	29	Montgomery	1,237	1,237	3,623	75.3	687
Hockley	13	48	224	76.7	13	Moore	18	25	164	104.6	8
Hood	81	73	751	87.3	51	Morris	2	0	179	73.6	8
Hopkins	33	96	398	73.0	30	Motley	0	0	17	42.6	0
Houston	7	25	268	78.3	12	Nacgdoches	142	392	605	62.4	97
Howard	32	150	416	85.5	30	Navarro	57	162	568	81.3	64
Hudspeth	1	0	12	76.7	3	Newton	4	0	164	63.6	7
Hunt	97	181	958	68.5	109	Nolan	14	86	178	86.4	6
Hutchinson	14	25	275	78.7	11	Nueces	907	2,035	2,937	78.3	616
Irion	0	0	10	52.4	0	Ochiltree	5	25	83	89.8	3
Jack	6	17	96	79.1	6	Oldham	0	0	17	62.0	1
Jackson	9	25	146	91.5	15	Orange	36	0	947	88.1	95
Jasper	22	59	458	87.8	26	Palo Pinto	26	74	348	77.4	23
Jeff Davis	1	0	16	52.2	2	Panola	15	42	266	70.1	13
Jefferson	547	1,585	2,514	88.6	456	Parker	141	129	1,066	67.4	120
Jim Hogg	0	0	50	106.9	8	Parmer	2	25	75	89.3	2
Jim Wells	33	135	424	94.3	50	Pecos	9	39	114	85.4	12
Johnson	111	137	1,340	73.8	167	Polk	39	66	673	88.7	38
Jones	11	92	214	63.8	3	Potter	445	1,140	1,231	85.4	64
Karnes	7	25	131	97.3	25	Presidio	3	0	36	82.3	3
Kaufman	77	91	897	71.8	164	Rains	1	0	150	62.7	9
Kendall	72	0	377	63.2	34	Randall	69	4	1,050	66.5	70
Kenedy	0	0	3	41.1	0	Reagan	2	21	29	109.4	0
Kent	0	0	9	74.1	0	Real	0	0	38	100.0	3
Kerr	147	124	774	79.0	58	Red River	3	0	180	65.5	7
Kimble	3	15	45	67.4	3	Reeves	10	25	114	98.1	10
King	0	0	0	23.3	0	Refugio	4	20	108	88.6	10
Kinney	0	0	42	102.7	0	Roberts	0	0	6	46.7	0
Kleberg	21	96	243	75.2	48	Robertson	1	0	173	76.6	16
Knox	1	28	61	76.2	2	Rockwall	180	170	545	62.9	114
Lamar	118	393	641	78.0	38	Runnels	14	50	140	69.1	1
Lamb	3	75	147	84.7	5	Rusk	27	96	544	72.9	23
Lampasas	11	25	197	68.8	20	Sabine	3	25	168	81.9	6
La Salle	1	0	61	106.3	14	S. Augustine	2	18	128	66.8	8
Lavaca	18	50	269	81.5	13	San Jacinto	5	0	313	70.9	28
Lee	4	0	183	81.5	21	San Patricio	32	75	642	92.1	75
Leon	5	0	223	87.1	6	San Saba	1	0	54	102.2	7
Liberty	41	29	765	77.0	105	Schleicher	1	14	23	37.7	0
Limestone	21	78	290	86.0	15	Scurry	14	25	179	81.7	4
Lipscomb	0	0	21	76.6	1	Shackelford	2	0	27	84.2	1
Live Oak	1	0	143	81.0	13	Shelby	4	0	300	89.6	17
Llano	10	30	311	86.3	16	Sherman	0	0	34	71.8	4
Loving	0	0	0	—	0	Smith	849	1,204	2,111	76.0	292
Lubbock	736	1,556	2,441	67.3	311	Somervell	12	16	96	53.1	8
Lynn	3	24	51	73.4	3	Starr	22	48	397	100.9	46

County	2018 Physicians	2016 Hospital Beds	Total Deaths 2015	2015 Pregnancy rate*	2016 Abortions
Stephens	8	40	107	87.2	4
Sterling	0	0	9	82.5	0
Stonewall	3	12	29	96.6	0
Sutton	1	12	30	72.4	0
Swisher	4	20	81	95.0	2
Tarrant	4,324	6,284	12,277	76.6	4,258
Taylor	347	829	1,378	77.6	130
Terrell	1	0	17	91.7	0
Terry	4	45	139	97.5	5
Throckmortn	2	0	30	51.9	0
Titus	54	174	311	79.5	28
Tom Green	299	574	973	78.7	116
Travis	3,527	2,881	5,380	70.5	3,321
Trinity	3	45	225	78.5	12
Tyler	7	49	274	76.5	5
Upshur	9	0	471	69.0	20
Upton	1	29	36	101.3	3
Uvalde	37	25	233	88.2	30
Val Verde	44	93	353	101.3	33
Van Zandt	17	52	621	71.7	26
Victoria	217	717	847	84.2	107
Walker	76	123	513	62.0	125
Waller	7	0	305	64.5	65
Ward	4	0	134	100.5	10
Washington	50	60	389	75.7	33
Webb	250	569	1,356	91.6	193

County	2018 Physicians	2016 Hospital Beds	Total Deaths 2015	2015 Pregnancy rate*	2016 Abortions
Wharton	34	208	417	89.6	69
Wheeler	6	41	72	84.2	0
Wichita	305	479	1,304	74.1	154
Wilbarger	16	47	163	85.8	8
Willacy	9	0	151	79.6	28
Williamson	964	833	2,625	66.6	794
Wilson	36	44	410	72.2	52
Winkler	2	19	70	99.1	4
Wise	73	148	554	76.9	43
Wood	33	50	613	72.2	21
Yoakum	6	24	63	99.2	4
Young	21	50	239	73.4	6
Zapata	1	0	85	97.8	18
Zavala	2	0	111	91.5	20

Texas Department of State Health Services: Vital Statistics, 2015, 2016 (by county of residence) and **Center for Health Statistics,** 2019.
Physicians - All M.D.s and D.O.s. in direct patient care. (2018.)
Hospital Beds - Beds (2016) not including military and veteran's hospitals, nor beds in hospitals that were not in compliance with state regulations.
*Pregnancy Rate figured per 1,000 women age 15-44.
*Abortion total statewide includes abortions performed in Texas but county of residence unknown, plus abortions obtained outside the state by Texas residents.

Marriage and Divorce

These charts are for certain years, including 1946, when there was a significant increase in marriages after World War II as well as a significant increase in divorces. Also included are the years 1979-81 when the marriage and divorce rates rearched another peak. *Source: Statistical Abstracts of the United States, National Vital Statistics System.*

	Texas					United States			
Year	Total marriages	Marriage rate*	Total divorces	Divorce rate*	Year	Total marriages	Marriage rate*	Total divorces	Divorce rate*
1940	86,500	13.5	27,500	4.3	1940	1,595,879	12.1	264,000	2.0
1946	143,092	20.5	57,112	8.4	1946	2,291,045	16.4	610,000	4.3
1950	89,155	11.6	37,400	4.9	1950	1,667,231	11.1	385,144	2.6
1955	91,210	10.4	34,921	4.0	1955	1,531,000	9.3	377,000	2.3
1960	91,700	9.6	34,732	3.6	1960	1,523,381	8.5	393,000	2.2
1965	111,500	10.5	41,300	3.9	1965	1,800,200	9.3	479,000	2.5
1970	139,500	12.5	51,500	4.6	1970	2,159,000	10.6	708,000	3.5
1975	153,200	12.5	76,700	6.3	1975	2,152,700	10.1	1,036,000	4.9
1979	172,800	12.9	92,400	6.9	1979	2,331,300	10.6	1,181,000	5.4
1980	181,800	12.8	96,800	6.8	1980	2,390,300	10.6	1,189,000	5.2
1981	194,800	13.2	101,900	6.9	1981	2,422,100	10.6	1,213,000	5.3
1985	213,800	13.1	101,200	6.2	1985	2,425,000	10.2	1,187,000	5.0
1990	182,800	10.5	94,000	5.5	1990	2,443,000	9.8	1,182,000	4.7
1995	188,500	10.1	98,400	5.3	1995	2,336,000	8.9	1,169,000	4.4
2000	196,400	9.6	85,200	4.2	2000	2,329,000	8.2	**944,000	4.0
2005	169,300	7.4	74,000	3.2	2005	2,230,000	7.5	847,000	3.6
2010	174,171	6.9	82,098	3.3	2010	2,096,000	6.8	872,000	3.6
2015	187,415	6.8	71,123	2.6	2015	2,221,579	6.9	800,909	3.1
2016	n/a	7.1	n/a	2.6	2016	2,251,411	7.0	776,288	3.0
2017	n/a	7.1	n/a	2.2	2017	2,236,496	6.9	787,251	2.9

*Rate per 1,000 population.

**Since 2000, the total number of divorces does not include four to six states, including California.

Texans in the National Academy of Sciences

Source: National Academy of Sciences

The National Academy of Sciences is a private organization of researchers dedicated to the furtherance of science and its use for the general welfare. A total of 137 scientists who have had positions with Texas institutions have been named members or associates.

Established by congressional acts of incorporation, which were signed by President Lincoln in 1863, the academy acts as official adviser to the federal government in matters of science and technology.

Election to the academy is one of the highest honors that can be accorded a scientist. As of May 2019, the number of active members was 2,380.

Elected from Texas in 2017 were Guillermina Lozano of the University of Texas MD Anderson Cancer Center, and Marcetta Darensbourg and Ronald DeVore, both of Texas A&M University.

Three foreign associates with ties to Texas institutions have been elected to the academy: in 1970, D.H.R. Barton from Texas A&M; in 1997, Johann Deisenhofer of UTSWMC in Dallas, and, in 2002, Jan-Ake Gustafsson of the University of Houston.

In 1931, Robert Moore (UT-Austin 1920–69) and Hermann Muller (Rice 1915-18, UT-Austin 1920–32) became the first scientists from Texas institutions elected to the academy. ☆

Academy Member	Affiliation*	Elected
Perry L. Adkisson	A&M	1979
Richard W. Aldrich	UT-Austin	2008
James P. Allison	UT-MD Anderson	1997
Abram Amsel †	UT-Austin	1992
Neal R. Amundson †	U of H	1992
Dora E. Angelaki	Baylor Medical	2014
Charles J. Arntzen	A&M	1983
David H. Auston	Rice	1991
Paul F. Barbara †	UT-Austin	2006
Allen J. Bard	UT-Austin	1982
Bonnie Bartel	Rice	2016
Frederic C. Bartter †	UTHSC-SanAntonio	1979
John D. Baxter †	HMRI	2003
Arthur L. Beaudet	Baylor Medical	2011
Brian J.L. Berry	UT-Dallas	1975
Bruce Beutler	UTSWMC	2008
Lewis R. Binford	SMU	2001
R.H. Bing †	UT-Austin	1965
Harold C. Bold †	UT-Austin	1973
Norman E. Borlaug	A&M	1968
Michael S. Brown	UTSWMC	1980
James J. Bull	UT-Austin	2016
Karl W. Butzer †	UT-Austin	1996
Horace R. Byers †	A&M	1952
Luis A. Caffarelli	UT-Austin	1991
C. Thomas Caskey	Baylor Medical	1993
Joseph W. Chamberlain †	Rice	1965
Zhijian (James) Chen	UTSWMC	2014
Wah Chiu	Baylor Medical	2012
C.W. Chu	U of H	1989
Melanie H. Cobb	UTSWMC	2006
Neal G. Copeland	HMRI	2009
F. Albert Cotton †	A&M	1967
Robert F. Curl Jr.	Rice	1997
Marcetta Darensbourg	A&M	2017
Ronald A. DePinho	UT-MD Anderson	2012
Gerard H. de Vaucouleurs †	UT-Austin	1986
Ronald DeVore	A&M	2017
Bryce DeWitt †	UT-Austin	1990
Robert E. Dickinson	UT-Austin	1988
Richard A. Dixon	UNT	2007
Stephen J. Elledge	Baylor Medical	2003
Ronald W. Estabrook †	UTSWMC	1979
Mary K. Estes	Baylor Medical	2007
Karl Folkers †	UT-Austin	1948
Marye Anne Fox	UT-Austin	1994
David L. Garbers †	UTSWMC	1993
Wilson S. Geisler	UT-Austin	2008
Quentin L. Gibson	Rice	1982
Alfred G. Gilman †	UTSWMC	1985
Joseph L. Goldstein	UTSWMC	1980
John B. Goodenough	UT-Austin	2012
William E. Gordon	Rice	1968
Verne E. Grant †	UT-Austin	1968

Academy Member	Affiliation*	Elected
Norman Hackerman †	Welch	1971
Namoi J. Halas	Rice	2013
Carl G. Hartman †	UT-Austin	1937
Dudley Herschbach	A&M	1967
David M. Hillis	UT-Austin	2008
Helen H. Hobbs	UTSWMC	2007
Lora Virginia Hooper	UTSWMC	2015
A. James Hudspeth	UTSWMC	1991
Thomas J.R. Hughes	UT-Austin	2009
Nancy A. Jenkins	MHRI	2008
James L. Kinsey †	Rice	1991
Steven A. Kliewer	UTSWMC	2015
Ernst Knobil †	UTHSC-Houston	1986
Jay K. Kochi †	U of H	1982
P. Kusch †	UT-Dallas	1956
Alan M. Lambowitz	UT-Austin	2004
David M. Lee	A&M	1991
Beth Levine	UTSWMC	2013
Herbert Levine	Rice	2011
Gardner Lindzey †	UT-Austin	1989
Guillermina Lozano	UT-MD Anderson	2017
Alan G. MacDiarmid †	UT-Dallas	2002
David J. Mangelsdorf	UT-Austin	2008
John L. Margrave †	Rice	1974
Martin M. Matzuk	Baylor Medical	2014
S.M. McCann †	UTSWMC	1983
Allan H. MacDonald	UT-Austin	2010
Steven L. McKnight	UTSWMC	1992
David J. Meltzer	SMU	2009
Robert Moore †	UT-Austin	1931
Nancy A. Moran	UT-Austin	2004
Hermann Muller †	Rice, UT-Austin	1931
Hans J. Muller-Eberhard †	UTHSC-Houston	1974
Ferid Murad	UTHSC-Houston	1997
Jack Myers †	UT-Austin	1975
Kyriacos C. Nicolaou	Rice	1996
Robert N. Noyce †	Sematech/Austin	1980
David R. Nygren	UT-Arlington	2000
Eric N. Olson	UTSWMC	2000
Bert W. O'Malley	Baylor Medical	1992
Jose N. Onuchic	Rice	2006
Theophilus Shickel Painter †	UT-Austin	1938
Luis F. Parada	UTSWMC	2011
John Patterson †	UT-Austin	1941
Kenneth L. Pike †	SIL	1985
William H. Press	UT-Austin	1994
Darwin J. Prockop	A&M	1991
Lester J. Reed †	UT-Austin	1973
Peter M. Rentzepis	A&M	1978
Rebecca Richards-Kortum	Rice	2015
Peter J. Rossky	UT-Austin	2011
David W. Russell	UTSWMC	2006
Marlan O. Scully	A&M	2001
Richard E. Smalley †	Rice	1990

Academy Member	Affiliation*	Elected
Esmond E. Snell †	UT-Austin	1955
Richard C. Starr †	UT-Austin	1976
Patrick Stover	A&M	2016
Thomas Südhof	UTSWMC	2002
Max D. Summers	A&M	1989
Harry L. Swinney	UT-Austin	1992
Joseph S. Takahashi	UTSWMC	2003
John T. Tate	UT-Austin	1969
Karen K. Uhlenbeck	UT-Austin	1986
Jonathan W. Uhr	UTSWMC	1984
Roger H. Unger	UTSWMC	1986
H.S. Vandiver †	UT-Austin	1934
Moshe Y. Vardi	Rice	2015
Ellen S. Vitetta	UTSWMC	1994
Salih J. Wakil	Baylor Medical	1990
Xiaodong Wang	UTSWMC	2004
Steven Weinberg	UT-Austin	1972
D. Fred Wendorf	SMU	1987
John Archibald Wheeler †	UT-Austin	1952
Roger J. Williams †	UT-Austin	1946
Jean D. Wilson	UTSWMC	1983

Academy Member	Affiliation*	Elected
Peter G. Wolynes	Rice	1991
James E. Womack	A&M	1999
Masahi Yanagisawa	UTSWMC	2003
Clarence Zener †	A&M	1959
Huda Y. Zoghbi	Baylor Medical	2004

† Deceased
* A&M - Texas A&M University
Baylor Medical - Baylor College of Medicine, Houston
HMRI - Houston Methodist Research Institute
Rice - Rice University
SIL - Summer Institute of Linguistics
SMU - Southern Methodist University
U of H - University of Houston
UNT – University of North Texas
UT-Austin - The University of Texas at Austin
UT-Dallas - The University of Texas at Dallas
UTHSC - Houston - The University of Texas Health
Science Center at Houston
UTHSC - The University of Texas Health Science Center
at San Antonio
UT-MD Anderson Cancer Center - Houston
UTSWMC - The University of Texas Southwestern
Medical Center at Dallas
Welch - Robert A. Welch Foundation

Science Research Funding at Universities

The following chart shows funding for research and development by source at universities in Texas, in order of total R&D funding. The figures are from the National Science Foundation and are for fiscal year 2017.

(Thousands of dollars, $ 000)	All R&D expenditures	Federal gov.	State/local gov.	Business	Nonprofit Org.	Institutional funds
United States	$75,174,941*	$40,237,645	$4,236,505	$4,425,450	$5,116,863	$18,884,298
Texas (all colleges statewide)	**$ 5,495,483**	**$ 2,177,513**	**$ 894,372**	**$ 371,281**	**$ 422,350**	**$ 1,376,041**
1. Texas A&M University	905,474	307,656	207,329	39,928	75,631	264,823
2. U. Texas M.D. Anderson Ctr.	888,029	166,552	255,960	127,759	30,470	173,161
3. University of Texas-Austin	652,187	394,447	27,367	60,282	37,775	124,037
4. Baylor College of Medicine	604,952	292,806	31,849	25,774	76,000	177,568
5. U. Texas Southwestern Med. Dallas	461,797	200,085	77,286	23,391	59,638	60,817
6. U. Texas Health Sci., Houston	246,060	124,461	38,089	12,629	22,007	31,977
7. U. Texas Health Sci., San Antonio	192,557	85,455	18,847	8,637	21,411	57,741
8. Texas Tech University	191,482	31,347	33,007	15,542	13,030	97,944
9. U. Texas Medical Branch Galveston	185,106	104,458	4,923	3,410	18,049	54,266
10. University of Houston	169,431	60,033	43,571	6,474	9,476	49,877
11. Rice University	167,277	84,469	6,191	11,165	16,957	43,505
12. University of Texas-Dallas	113,205	36,097	16,171	5,554	20,859	34,524
13. University of Texas-Arlington	97,197	32,756	19,238	9,012	1,827	34,209
14. University of Texas-El Paso	94,565	44,811	19,327	1,191	4,003	16,476
15. University of Texas-San Antonio	70,163	29,947	10,127	2,664	2,562	23,096
16. Texas State University	60,741	25,132	6,671	910	5,177	22,851
17. U. North Texas, Health Science Ctr.	48,476	26,368	9,313	2,848	1,490	7,973
18. University of North Texas, Denton	43,789	15,668	641	1,447	2,089	23,944
19. Texas Tech U., Health Sci. Ctr.	39,767	9,143	16,806	443	2,136	9,406
20. Southern Methodist University	29,879	14,464	1,019	3,107	1,211	9,865
21. Uni. of Texas-Rio Grande Valley	29,500	14,808	5,725	273	590	8,104
22. Baylor University	29,400	5,265	1,363	1,953	2,048	16,935
23. Texas A&M U.-Corpus Christi	27,993	10,259	5,597	1,340	2,378	4,594
24. Texas A&M University-Kingsville	22,633	7,869	4,940	734	4,628	4,462
25. Texas Tech U. Health Sci., El Paso	16,479	2,410	11,266	617	491	1,688
26. Uni. of Texas Health Science-Tyler	16,292	5,792	2,142	698	2,232	5,428
27. Prairie View A&M University	13,982	8,722	2,876	49	100	2,218
28. Tarleton State University	10,893	4,602	2,914	16	43	3,312
29. St. Edward's University	10,149	7,989	1,095	101	499	455
30. Texas Christian University	7,255	4,035	1,160	1,746	NA	214

Colleges and universities not listed received less. 'NA,' information not available. *Total includes some $2.27 billion from other sources. Source: National Science Foundation.

National Health Expenditures

GDP and Expenditures ($ billion)	1970	1980	1990	2000	2010	2017
Total Health Expenditures	$74.9	$ 255.8	$ 724.3	$ 1,377.2	$ 2,593.6	$ 3,492.1
Percent of GDP	7.2	9.2	12.5	13.8	17.4	17.9
Per capita amount (in dollars)	$ 356	$ 1,110	$2,854	$ 4,878	$ 8,402	$ 10,739
Personal health care expenditure	$ 63.1	$ 217.0	$ 615.3	$ 1,161.5	$ 2,196.1	$ 2,981.0
Cost of private insurance	$ 1.4	$ 7.7	$ 29.1	$ 52.3	$ 108.5	$ 144.1
Hospital care expenditures	$ 27.2	$ 100.5	$ 250.4	$ 415.5	$ 822.3	$ 971.8
Gross Domestic Product (GDP)	$ 1,038	$ 2,788	$ 5,801	$ 9,952	$ 14,527	$ 19,485.4

Source: U.S. Centers for Medicare and Medicaid Services.

Comparison of Vital Statistics

*The most current data available, with selected states: those bordering Texas and other large states. **Lowest and highest with number in bold.***

State/ Country	BIRTH rate*	DEATH rate*	LIFE expec- tancy
Texas	14.7	6.9	78.3
Alaska	15.3	5.8	-
Arkansas	13.1	10.6	-
California	12.6	6.6	-
Florida	11.1	9.5	-
Georgia	12.9	7.8	-
Illinois	12.3	8.3	-
Louisiana	13.9	9.4	-
Michigan	11.4	9.6	-
New Mexico	12.4	8.5	-
New York	12.0	7.8	-
Ohio	12.0	10.2	-
Oklahoma	13.6	10.1	-
Utah	**16.9**	**5.8**	-
New Hampshire	**9.3**	9.0	-
West Virginia	10.7	**12.3**	-
United States	12.4	8.2	80.1
Japan	7.5	9.9	85.5
Brazil	13.9	6.7	74.3
Canada	10.2	8.8	82.0
Afghanistan	37.5	13.2	**52.1**
Germany	8.6	11.8	80.9
Italy	8.5	10.5	82.4
Monaco	**6.5**	10.1	**89.4**
Mexico	18.1	5.4	76.3
Angola	**43.7**	9.0	60.6
Russia	10.7	13.4	71.3
South Sudan	36.9	**19.30**	n/a
Qatar	9.5	**1.6**	79.0
United Kingdom	12.0	9.4	80.9
World	18.2	7.8	69.8

Rates are number during 1 year per 1,000 persons. Sources: National Vital Statistics System 2018; CIA World Factbook, 2018; Texas Vital Statistics Annual Report 2015.

Life Expectancy for Texans by Group

	All	Whites	Blacks	Hispanics
Total population	78.25	78.20	74.75	79.51
Males	75.79	75.74	71.79	77.03
Females	80.65	80.52	77.42	81.83

Source: Texas Department of State Health Services, for 2015.

Texas Births by Race/Ethnicity and Sex

	2015	2000	1990	1980
All Races	403,439	363,325	316,257	273,433
All Male	205,972	185,591	161,522	139,999
All Female	197,467	177,734	154,735	133,434
White Total	136,663	142,553	150,461	151,725
White Male	69,935	72,972	77,134	78,086
White Female	66,728	69,581	73,327	73,639
Black Total	47,515	41,180	43,342	38,544
Black Male	24,140	21,128	21,951	19,501
Black Female	23,375	20,052	21,391	19,043
Hispanic Total	191,080	166,440	115,576	79,324
Hispanic Male	97,469	84,750	58,846	40,475
Hispanic Female	93,611	81,690	56,730	38,849
Other* Total	28,181	13,152	6,687	3,840
Other Male	14,428	6,741	3,591	1,937
Other Female	13,753	6,411	3,287	1,903

*Other includes births of unknown race/ethnicity.
Source: Texas Department of State Health Services.*

Disposition of Bodies in Texas by Percent of Deaths

Year	Burial	Cremation	Donation of body	Removal from state/other
1989	83.7	7.1	0.7	8.5
1995	81.7	11.6	0.8	5.8
2001	75.5	17.3	0.8	6.3
2003	73.1	19.7	0.9	6.2
2011	57.3	34.1	-	-
2013	53.7	37.6	-	-
2014	52.0	39.3	-	-
2015	50.1	41.2	-	-

Sources: Texas DSHS (to 2003) and National Funeral Directors Association.

Nobel Prizes to Texans

Two scientists with Texas connections were awarded the Nobel Prize in 2017 and 2018.

Jim Allison received the Nobel Prize in Medicine in 2018 for his pioneer research that has led to a new type of cancer treatment that frees the immune system to attack tumors.

He is chair of immunology at the MD Anderson Cancer Center in Houston and earned his bachelor's and doctoral degrees at the University of Texas at Austin. He was born in Alice and graduated from high school there.

Michael W. Young received the prize in medicine in 2017 for his work with others on hu-

Young. (CC).

Allison. (CC).

man internal clocks and biorhythms. He graduated from Hurst Bell high school in the Dallas-Fort Worth area.

Young, a professor at Rockefeller University, has also worked at Stanford University and UT-Austin, where he received his bachelor's and doctoral degrees.

Community Hospitals in Texas

Source: The Texas Hospital Association.

– Of the 616 reporting hospitals in Texas in 2017, 528 were considered community hospitals.

(A community hospital is defined as either a non-federal, short-term general hospital or a special hospital whose facilities and services are available to the public. A hospital may include a nursing home-type unit and still be classified as short-term, provided that the majority of its patients are admitted to units where the average length of stay is less than 30 days.)

– The 528 hospitals employed 371,350 full-time equivalent people (FTEs) with a payroll, including benefits, of more than $31.7 billion.

– These hospitals contained some 66,844 beds.

– The average length of stay was 5.3 days in 2017, compared to 6.8 days in 1975. This was less than the U.S. average of 5.5 days.

– The average cost per adjusted admission in Texas was $12,357 or $2,552 per day. This was 5.8 percent less than the U.S. average of $13,126.

– There were 2.7 million admissions in Texas, which accounted for 14.5 million inpatient days.

– There were 45.1 million outpatient visits in 2017, of which 11.9 million were emergency room visits.

– Of the FTEs working in community hospitals within Texas, there were 122,050 registered nurses and 7,700 licensed vocational nurses. ☆

Culberson County Hospital in Van Horn. Photo by Robert Plocheck.

Mental Health and Substance Abuse Admissions

Diagnosis of Adult Clients in Texas / United States: 2016–2017

Diagnosis	Texas clients	% of clients diagnosis		Employed as % of known employment
		Texas	United States	Texas
Schizophrenia	42,023	20.8 %	12.4 %	10.8 %
Bipolar disorder	129,438	64.0 %	40.2 %	23.1 %
Other psychoses	777	0.4 %	2.3 %	18.0 %
All other diagnose	3,393	1.7 %	32.7 %	24.6 %
No diagnosis/deferred	26,628	13.2%	12.5 %	23.7 %
Total	**202,259**	**100.0 %**	**100.0%**	**20.6 %**

Source: U.S. Department of Health and Human Services, Center for Mental Health Services, Uniform Reporting System, 2017.

Readmission Within 180 Days of Mental Health Treatment: 2017

Age	Civil* Texas	Civil U.S.	States / Terr. reporting	Forensic* Texas	Forensic U.S.
		In percent of clients.			
0 to 12	18.2 %	17.3 %	11	–	6.0 %
13 to 17	12.0 %	15.7 %	20	2.7 %	8.5 %
18 to 20	15.2 %	15.5 %	35	2.7 %	10.0 %
21 to 64	19.0 %	20.1 %	51	10.2 %	11.5 %
65 to 74	8.6 %	15.7 %	35	8.6 %	11.3 %
75 and over	13.0 %	10.9 %	24	16.7 %	5.9 %
age not available	–	14.5 %	3		16.7 %
Total	**13.0 %**	**19.2 %**	**52**	**9.5 %**	**11.4 %**

*Forensic services are mental health services provided to persons directed into treatment by the criminal justice system; others are listed as "Civil." *Source: U.S. Department of Health and Human Services, Center for Mental Health Services,* Uniform Reporting System, 2017.

Substance Abuse Treatment in Texas: 2017

Facility operation	No.	%	Clients in treatment on March 31, 2017		
			No.	%	Clients under 18
Private nonprofit	187	43.4	11,403	32.1	905
Private for-profit	190	44.1	17,217	48.5	548
Local / county / community	27	6.3	2,537	7.2	202
State	27	1.6	1,821	5.1	72
Federal	19	4.4	2,476	7.0	–
Tribal	1	0.2	18	0.1	–
Total	**431**	**100.0**	**35,474**	**100.0**	**1,727**

Problem treated					. . . per 100,000 pop.
Alcohol and drug abuse	345	85.4	13,382	37.7	59
Drug abuse only	329	81.4	16,874	74.6	78
Alcohol abuse only	269	66.6	5,218	14.7	24

Source: National Survey of Substance Abuse Treatment Services, 2019.

Estimated Use of Drugs in Texas and Bordering States: 2016–2017

State	Any illicit drug	Marijuana	Other than marijuana[1]	Cigarettes	Binge alcohol[2]	Pain reliever misuse[4]
	*Current users[3] as **percent of population, age 12+ years**. Selected states.*					
U.S. total	10.90	9.23	3.38	18.47	24.37	4.17
Texas	**7.64**	**5.98**	**2.81**	**18.33**	**23.68**	**4.02**
Arkansas	10.51	8.19	3.66	24.65	26.72	5.03
Louisiana	9.29	7.60	3.48	23.92	26.72	4.12
Oklahoma	8.42	6.90	3.22	22.91	22.05	4.38
New Mexico	13.51	11.96	3.68	20.06	24.41	4.15

[1]Marijuana users who have also used another drug are included. [2]Binge use is defined as drinking five or more drinks on the same occasion on at least one day in the past 30 days. [3]Used drugs at least once within month. [4]Within the last year. *Source: U.S. Substance Abuse and Mental Health Services Administration,* National Household Survey on Drug Use and Health, 2018.

State Institutions for Mental Health Services

Source: U.S. Department of Health and Human Servies and the Texas Health and Human Services.

Mental health services were provided to some 379,956 Texans in 2017 in various institutions, including community centers.

In 2004, the Texas Department of State Health Services was created (DSHS), bringing together:
— the Texas Department of Health,
— the Texas Department of Mental Health and Mental Retardation (MHMR),
— Commission on Alcohol and Drug Abuse,
— the Texas Health Care Information Council.

In 2016, Texas Health and Human Services was created by the Legislature with two agencies: the Texas Health and Human Services Commission (HHSC) and DSHS, with many direct client services transferred from DSHS to HHSC, including mental health services.

In 2017, state mental health agency expenditure was $1,070,311,037, with $541 million for community services, according to the federal Uniform Reporting System for the states.

Following is a list of the 10 state hospitals, the year each was founded, and number of beds in 2017, totalling 2,269.

Hospitals for Persons with Mental Illness

Austin State Hospital — Austin; 1857; 263 beds.
Big Spring State Hospital — Big Spring; 1937; 180 beds.
El Paso Psychiatric Center — El Paso; 1974; 71 beds.
Kerrville State Hospital — Kerrville; 1950; 220 beds.
North Texas State Hospital — Wichita Falls (1922), 268 beds and Vernon (1969); 294 beds.
Rio Grande State Center — Harlingen; 1962; 52 beds.
Rusk State Hospital — Rusk; 1919; 288 beds.
San Antonio State Hospital — San Antonio; 1892; 268 beds.
Terrell State Hospital — Terrell; 1885; 291 beds.
Waco Center for Youth — Waco; 1979; 74 beds.

Following is a list of community mental health centers, the year each was founded, and the counties each serves.

Community Mental Health Centers

Abilene — Betty Hardwick Center; 1971; Callahan, Jones, Shackleford, Stephens and Taylor.
Amarillo — Texas Panhandle MHMR; 1968; Armstrong, Carson, Collingsworth, Dallam, Deaf Smith, Donley, Gray, Hall, Hansford, Hartley, Hemphill, Hutchinson, Lipscomb, Moore, Ochiltree, Oldham, Potter, Randall, Roberts, Sherman and Wheeler.
Austin — Austin-Travis County Center; 1967; Travis.
Beaumont — Spindletop MHMR Services; 1967; Chambers, Hardin, Jefferson and Orange.
Big Spring — West Texas Centers; 1997; Andrews, Borden, Crane, Dawson, Fisher, Gaines, Garza, Glasscock, Howard, Kent, Loving, Martin, Mitchell, Nolan, Reeves, Runnels, Scurry, Terrell, Terry, Upton, Ward, Winkler and Yoakum.
Brownwood — Center for Life Resources; 1969; Brown, Coleman, Comanche, Eastland, McCulloch, Mills and San Saba.
Bryan-College Station — MHMR Authority of Brazos Valley; 1972; Brazos, Burleson, Grimes, Leon, Madison, Robertson and Washington.
Cleburne — Johnson-Ellis-Navarro County Center; 1985; Ellis, Johnson, Navarro.

Conroe — Tri-County Services; 1983; Liberty, Montgomery and Walker.
Corpus Christi — Nueces County Community Center; 1970; Nueces.
Dallas — Dallas MetroCare; 1967; Dallas.
Denton — Denton County Center; 1987; Denton.
Edinburg — Tropical Texas Center; 1967; Cameron, Hidalgo and Willacy.
El Paso — Community Center; 1968; El Paso.
Fort Worth — MHMR of Tarrant County; 1969; Tarrant.
Galveston — Gulf Coast Center; 1969; Brazoria and Galveston.
Houston — MHMR Authority/Harris County; 1965; Harris.
Jacksonville — Anderson-Cherokee Community Enrichment Services; 1995; Anderson, Cherokee.
Kerrville — Hill Country Community Center; 1997; Bandera, Blanco, Comal, Edwards, Gillespie, Hays, Kendall, Kerr, Kimble, Kinney, Llano, Mason, Medina, Menard, Real, Schleicher, Sutton, Uvalde and Val Verde.
Laredo — Border Region Community Center; 1969; Jim Hogg, Starr, Webb and Zapata.
Longview — Sabine Valley Center; 1970; Gregg, Harrison, Marion, Panola, Rusk and Upshur.
Lubbock — Lubbock Regional Center; 1969; Cochran, Crosby, Hockley, Lubbock and Lynn.
Lufkin — Burke Center; 1975; Angelina, Houston, Jasper, Nacogdoches, Newton, Polk, Sabine, San Augustine, San Jacinto, Shelby, Trinity and Tyler.
Lytle — Camino Real Community Center; 1996; Atascosa, Dimmit, Frio, La Salle, Karnes, Maverick, McMullen, Wilson and Zavala.
McKinney — LifePath Systems; 1986; Collin.
Midland — Permian Basin Community Centers; 1969; Brewster, Culberson, Ector, Hudspeth, Jeff Davis, Midland, Pecos and Presidio.
Plainview — Central Plains Center; 1969; Bailey, Briscoe, Castro, Floyd, Hale, Lamb, Motley, Parmer and Swisher.
Portland — Coastal Plains Community; 1996; Aransas, Bee, Brooks, Duval, Jim Wells, Kenedy, Kleberg, Live Oak and San Patricio.
Rosenberg — Texana Center; 1996; Austin, Colorado, Fort Bend, Matagorda, Waller and Wharton.
Round Rock — Bluebonnet Trails Community Center; 1997; Bastrop, Burnet, Caldwell, Fayette, Gonzales, Guadalupe, Lee and Williamson.
San Angelo — MHMR Services for the Concho Valley; 1969; Coke, Concho, Crockett, Irion, Reagan, Sterling and Tom Green.
San Antonio — The Center for Health Care Services; 1966; Bexar.
Sherman — MHMR Services of Texoma; 1974; Cooke, Fannin and Grayson.
Stephenville — Pecan Valley Region; 1977; Erath, Hood, Palo Pinto, Parker and Somervell.
Temple — Central Counties Center; 1967; Bell, Coryell, Hamilton, Lampasas and Milam.
Terrell — Lakes Regional Center; 1996; Camp, Delta, Franklin, Hopkins, Hunt, Kaufman, Lamar, Morris, Rockwall and Titus.
Texarkana — Northeast Texas Center; 1974; Bowie, Cass and Red River.
Tyler — Andrews Center; 1970; Henderson, Rains, Smith, Van Zandt and Wood.
Victoria — Gulf Bend Center; 1970; Calhoun, DeWitt, Jackson, Lavaca, Refugio and Victoria.
Waco — Heart of Texas Region Center; 1969; Bosque, Falls, Freestone, Hill, Limestone and McLennan.
Wichita Falls — Helen Farabee Regional Centers; 1969; Archer, Baylor, Childress, Clay, Cottle, Dickens, Foard, Hardeman, Haskell, Jack, King, Knox, Montague, Stonewall, Throckmorton, Wichita, Wilbarger and Young. ☆

EDUCATION

The Lone Star Community College System office in The Woodlands.
Photo courtesy Lone Star Community College.

PUBLIC SCHOOLS

UIL WINNING SCHOOLS

TEXAS HISTORY DAY

UNIVERSITIES AND COLLEGES

Texas Public Schools

Sources: Reports and online directory of the Texas Education Agency, http://tea.texas.gov; Summary of 2020—21 Conference Committee Report for HB1; additional reporting by A.J. Smuskiewicz.

Enrollment in Texas public schools continues to rise. In the 2017-2018 school year, 5,399,682 students were enrolled. That's an increase of 0.8 percent over enrollment in the 2016–2017 school year, and a jump of 15.6 percent above enrollment from 2007-2008, according to the **Texas Education Agency (TEA)**.

In Texas, there are 1,023 independent and common school districts and 177 charter operators. Independent school districts are administered by an elected board of trustees and deal directly with the TEA. Common districts are supervised by elected county school superintendents and county trustees. Charter schools are discussed later in this article.

5 Largest School Districts, by Enrollment (Oct. 2018)		
School District	County	Enrollment
Houston ISD	Harris	209,772
Dallas ISD	Dallas	155,119
Cypress-Fairbanks ISD	Harris	116,512
Northside ISD	Bexar	106,501
Fort Worth ISD	Tarrant	84,510

There were 20 school districts with more than 50,000 students enrolled in their various schools, and 29.8 percent of all students in Texas attend school in those large districts. By contrast, only 1.9 percent of Texas students are enrolled at the 391 smallest districts in Texas, each of which has fewer than 500 students enrolled.

5 Smallest School Districts, by Enrollment (Oct. 2018)		
School District	County	Enrollment
San Vicente ISD	Brewster	13
Doss Consolidated CSD	Gillespie	20
Divide ISD	Kerr	21
Bridgeway Preparatory Academy	Dallas	23
Ramirez CSD	Duval	27

Brief History of Public Education In Texas

Public education was one of the primary goals of the early settlers of Texas, who listed in the Texas Declaration of Independence the failure to provide education as one of their grievances against Mexico.

As early as 1838, President Mirabeau B. Lamar's message to the Republic of Texas Congress advocated setting aside public domain for public schools. His interest caused him to be called the "Father of Education in Texas." In 1839, Congress designated three leagues of land to support public schools for each Texas county and 50 leagues for a state university. In 1840, each county was allocated one more league of land.

The Republic, however, did not establish a public school system or a university. After Texas was admitted into the Union, the 1845 Texas State Constitution advocated public education, instructing the Legislature to designate at least 10 percent of the tax revenue for schools. Further delay occurred until Gov. Elisha M. Pease, on Jan. 31, 1854, signed the bill setting up the Texas public school system.

The public school system was made possible by setting aside $2 million out of $10 million Texas received for relinquishing its claim to land north and west of its present boundaries in the Compromise of 1850.

Early Funding and Administration Changes

During 1854, legislation provided for state apportionment of funds based upon an annual census. Also, railroads receiving grants were required to survey alternate sections to be set aside for public-school financing. The first school census that year showed 65,463 students; state fund apportionment was 62 cents per student.

When adopted in 1876, the present Texas Constitution provided: "All funds, lands, and other property heretofore set apart and appropriated for the support of public schools; all the alternate sections of land reserved by the state of grants heretofore made or that may hereafter be made to railroads, or other corporations, of any nature whatsoever; one half of the public domain of the state, and all sums of money that may come to the state from the sale of any portion of the same shall constitute a perpetual public school fund."

More than 52 million acres of the Texas public domain were allotted for school purposes. (See table, Distribution of the Public Lands of Texas on page 458.)

In 1949, the Gilmer-Aikin Laws reorganized the state system of public schools by making sweeping changes in administration and financing. The Texas Education Agency, headed by the governor-appointed Commissioner of Education, administers the public-school system.

The policy-making body for public education is the 15-member **State Board of Education (SBOE)**, which is elected from separate districts for overlapping four-year terms. Current membership of the board is listed on page 465 in the State Government chapter.

Targeting Student Performance

The 68th Legislature passed one of the most historic education-reform bills of the past 50 years when lawmakers met in special session in the summer of 1984. House Bill 72 came in response to growing concern over deteriorating literacy among Texas' schoolchildren over two decades, reflected in students' scores on standardized tests.

Graduates and Dropouts

School Year	Graduates	*Dropouts
2016–2017	**332,573	33,050
2015–2016	324,311	33,466
2014–2015	313,397	33,437
2013–2014	303,109	35,358
2012–2013	301,418	34,696
2011–2012	292,636	36,276
2010–2011	290,581	34,363
2009–2010	280,520	33,235
2008–2009	264,275	40,923
2007–2008	252,121	45,796
2006–2007	241,193	55,306
2005–2006	240,485	51,841
2004–2005	239,716	18,290

* Grades 7–12.
** Estimate, due to change in reporting at TEA

Texas School Enrollment and Expenditures per Student

School Year	Enrollment	Spending per student
2017–2018	5,399,682	N/A
2016–2017	5,343,893	$12,264
2015–2016	5,284,306	$11,704
2014–2015	5,232,065	$10,971
2013–2014	5,151,925	$9,903
2012–2013	5,058,939	$9,969
2011–2012	4,978,120	$10,335
2010–2011	4,912,385	$11,142
2009–2010	4,824,778	$11,543
2008–2009	4,728,204	$11,567
2007–2008	4,651,516	$10,162
2006–2007	4,576,933	$9,629
2005–2006	4,505,572	$9,269

Provisions of HB 72 raised teachers' salaries, but tied those raises to teacher performance. It also introduced more stringent teacher certification and initiated competency testing for teachers. Lawmakers also created the 22:1 class-size ratio for kindergarten through fourth-grade classes and the no-pass, no-play rule.

Sweeping Reforms

In 1995, the 74th Legislature took on a monumental task and completely rewrote all the state's public education laws.

The Public Schools Reform Act of 1995 increased local control of public schools by limiting the TEA to recommending and reporting on educational goals; overseeing charter schools; managing the permanent, foundation, and available school funds; administering an accountability system; creating and implementing the student testing program; recommending educator appraisal and counselor evaluation instruments; and developing plans for special, bilingual, compensatory, gifted and talented, vocational, and technology education.

It also reduced the authority of the SBOE. The goal was to return as much authority as possible to the local level. However, each subsequent legislature has reinstated some state-level control.

Charter Schools

Charter school legislation in Texas provides for four types of charter schools: the home-rule school district charter, the campus or campus-program charter, the open-enrollment charter, and a university-sponsored charter. A charter contract is typically granted for five years and can be revoked if the school violates its charter.

Since the inception of the charter school movement in Texas, the charter contracts have been granted by the SBOE. However, SB2, which passed during the 2013 legislative session, shifted the authority to grant a charter to the commissioner of education. The SBOE, however, may veto any of his selections.

Public School Personnel and Salaries

Personnel Category	Personnel 2016–2017	Personnel 2017–2018	% Change from Previous	Average Base Salaries 2016–2017	Average Base Salaries 2017–2018	% Change from Previous
Teachers	347,272	342,192	−1.46	$51,891	$50,715	−2.27
Campus Administrators	20,171	19,680	−2.43	$75,654	$74,292	−1.80
Central Administrators	7,340	6,995	−4.70	$99,111	$96,907	−2.22
Professional Support*	67,755	65,119	−3.89	$61,145	$59,791	−2.21
Total Professionals	**442,538**	**433,986**	**−1.93**	—	—	—
Educational Aides	65,702	64,641	−1.61	$20,118	$19,586	−2.64
Auxiliary Staff	179,801	174,514	−2.94	$24,808	$24,237	−2.30
Total Staff	**688,142**	**673,140**	**−2.18**	—	—	—

Note: Totals may not sum because personnel figures are full-time equivalent.
*The Professional Support category includes supervisors, counselors, educational diagnosticians, librarians, nurses/physicians, therapists, and psychologists.

Source: TEA Staff Salary reports for 2016-2017 and 2017-2018

There are currently 171 active charter school districts in Texas. Since 1996, 329 charters have been approved and 154 have closed (including 36 closures due to the charter being revoked). So far, no district has created a home-rule charter, although citizens in Dallas ISD discussed it. There are 56 campus charter schools, which are created by school districts and overseen by each school district's board of trustees.

The most popular form of charter schools is the open-enrollment charter. These are public schools released from some Texas education laws and regulations. Many charter schools have focused efforts on educating young people who are at risk of dropping out of school or who have dropped out and then returned to school. There were 707 open-enrollment schools, representing 296,323 students during the 2017-2018 school year.

The state also approves university-sponsored charters; 29 of such schools are active and in operation, according to a search of TEA's online directory.

During the 2017-2018 school year, about 5.5 percent of the state's public school students attended open-enrollment charter schools.

Today's Public School Challenges

Public education will probably always be a hot-button issue in Texas as parents, teachers, lawmakers, and even the students themselves continue to seek ways to improve our schools. Many residents believe that despite the overall wealth of the state, inadequate attention and finances are directed toward the public education system. Among the problems commonly cited are flaws in the school financing system, relatively low teacher salary, poor test performance by students, debate regarding assessing student and school performance, dropouts from traditional schools in favor of charter schools or other alternatives, gun violence, and mental health issues.

Funding Problems

Funding problems for Texas public schools can be traced to the state's tax system, including a lack of income taxes and a combined state-and-local tax rate that places Texas 46th among the 50 states. Local property taxes and general state revenue together make up the revenue sources for Texas public schools. Between 2008 and 2018, the state revenue stream for schools declined by 12.6 percent while the student population simultaneously increased by 13.7 percent.

In 2019 the 86th Legislature passed HB 3, a sweeping change to school financing. The measure increases per-student funding, funds full-day pre-K for eligible 4-year-olds, and includes money for raises for teachers.

Performance Evaluations

In 2018, the TEA instituted a new "A–F accountability system" for grading the performance of public schools. In this system, 70 percent of a school's grade is based on assessments of student achievement or school progress during the previous year (whichever is greater) and 30 percent is based on closing gaps among students from different subgroups (related to poverty, race, or special education). Student assessment within this system is based largely on their performance on the State of Texas Assessments of Academic Readiness (STAAR) tests for reading, writing, mathematics, science, and social studies, which were first implemented in 2012.

Supporters maintain that this A–F system is more transparent, easier for the public to understand, and more likely to prompt needed policy changes among lawmakers, compared with the previous school assessment system. However, the new system is opposed by many public-school administrators as an overly simplistic way of viewing school conditions and challenges, with too much emphasis on time-consuming standardized testing. The Texas Association of School Administrators has urged the legislature to roll back much of the standardized state assessment system in favor of more control over school assessment by the local districts.

Standardized testing has long been unpopular among Texans. According to a 2017 poll by the University of Texas and *The Texas Tribune*, most Texans believe that reducing the number of standardized tests is the best way to improve public education. The poll respondents believed this option to likely be more effective than increasing funding, raising teacher salaries, grading schools, expanding early childhood (pre-K) education, or using charter schools.

Public School Alternatives

According to TEA statistics available on the "Public School Explorer" website of The Texas Tribune in 2019, more than 50 percent of students are considered to be at risk for dropping out of public school. Reasons for this risk include being economically disadvantaged and having limited proficiency in English. Language is a crucial issue in Texas, where the majority (52.4 percent) of students are Hispanic, many from families in which English is not spoken at home.

Some Texans view charter schools or homeschooling as preferable alternatives to traditional public schools, especially for students at high risk for dropping out. Teacher unions generally oppose charters as being worse than traditional schools for both students and teachers. In February 2019, Louis Malfaro, president of the Texas American Federation of Teachers, argued that the expansion of charters poses a serious threat to the quality of public education, including greater discrimination against certain students, less-qualified teachers, and cuts to traditional funding.

Violence, Mental Health

Other controversial matters in Texas public schools include violence and mental health. The debate over gun violence in schools revolves around tougher gun-control measures and more support for students' mental health. There have been calls for each school to have at least one mental health counselor, who would help students deal with such issues as gun violence, psychological struggles, and suicide risk. Various antigang measures have also been advocated.

State Appropriations

For FY20–21, all funds financing for public education totals $67.5 billion, an increase of $7 billion over the FY18–19 funding level. Most of the funding for public education comes through the Foundation School Program system. The 86th Legislature increased FSP funding by $11.5 billion in General Revenue funding, with the intent to increase salaries for teachers and provide school district property tax relief.

Supplemental appropriation for public education include:

- $100.0 million for school safety enhancements
- $10.9 million to school districts that experienced mass shootings
- $636.0 million for costs attributable to Hurricane Harvey

Permanent School Fund

The Texas public school system was established and the Permanent School Fund (PSF) set up by the Fifth Legislature, Jan. 31, 1854.

The 158-year-old PSF is managed by the SBOE and is the second-largest educational endowment in the United States. It is invested in global markets and broadly diversified.

Every year, a distribution is made from PSF to pay a portion of educational costs in each public school district. The amount distributed is subject to two constraints set in Article VII, Section 5 of the Texas Constitution:

- The SBOE may not approve a distribution rate or transfer to the Available School Fund (ASF) that exceeds 6 percent of the average market value of the fund, excluding real property.
- The total distributions over a 10-year period to the ASF may not exceed the total return on the PSF's investment assets over the same period.

The fund was first established in 1854 with $2.0 million. The amount distributed to schools that year was $40,587. By 1900 the fund had grown to $9.1 million. Funds distributed to schools in 1900 totaled $3.0 million.

The PSF balance, as of Aug. 31, 2018, was $44.1 billion, an increase of $2.6 billion from the prior year.

The PSF also provides a guarantee for bonds issued by local school districts, allowing districts to pay lower interest rates. As of Aug. 31, 2012, PSF assets guaranteed $77.7 billion in school district bonds to 844 public school districts and $1.4 billion in charter district bonds to 14 charter districts. ☆

Permanent School Fund

Year	Fund Value* (in millions)	Funds Distributed to Schools (in millions)
1910	$16.8	$5.9
1920	$25.7	$18.4
1930	$38.7	$27.3
1940	$68.3	$34.6
1950	$161.2	$94.0
1960	$425.8	$164.2
1970	$842.2	$287.2
1980	$2,464.6	$3.0
1990	$7,328.2	$700.3
1991	$10,227.8	$739.2
1992	$10,944.9	$739.5
1993	$11,822.5	$737.7
1994	$11,330.6	$737.0
1995	$12,273.2	$740.0
1996	$12,995.8	$692.7
1997	$15,496.6	$690.8
1998	$16,296.2	$661.9
1999	$19,615.7	$698.5
2000	$22,275.6	N/A
2001	$19,021.8	N/A
2002	$17,047.2	N/A
2003	$18,037.3	N/A
2004	$19,261.8	$825.1
2005	$21,354.3	$880.0
2006	$22,802.7	$841.9
2007	$25,311.8	$843.1
2008	$23,142.4	$716.5
2009	$20,545.3	$716.5
2010	$22,107.8	$60.7
2011	$24,091.6	$1,092.8
2012	$25,503.0	$1,020.9
2013	$27,277.0	$1,020.9
2014	$34,951.2	$838.7
2015	$33,833.5	$838.7
2016	$37,263.9	$1,056.4
2017	$41,418.0	$1,056.4
2018	$44,067.5	$1,235.8

*Prior to 1991, the PSF reported cash, bonds at par, and stock at book value. From 1991 to the present, the PSF has reported cash, bonds and stocks at fair value.

Further Reading

DeMatthews, David, and David S. Knight. "Why Texas public schools are suffering." *Houston Chronicle.* October 11, 2018.

Ramsey, Ross. "Analysis: the challenge of reining in property taxes at no cost to schools." *The Texas Tribune.* February 11, 2019.

Ayala, Eva-Marie. "Are charters better than traditional schools? Texas' A-F grading system suggests maybe not." *Dallas News.* August 24, 2018.

Ayala, Eva-Marie, Corbett Smith, and Nanette Light. "Texas releases new A-F grades for school districts—see how yours rated." *Dallas News.* August 15, 2018.

"The truth about standardized testing in Texas." *Texas Business Leadership Council.* February 2019.

Ramsey, Ross. "Analysis: Texans hate standardized tests, but govern by the results." *The Texas Tribune.* April 13, 2019.

"State of Texas—Public Schools Explorer." *The Texas Tribune.* 2018.

Malfaro, Louis. "A letter from the president on the threat of charter school expansion." *Texas AFT.* February 5, 2019

University Interscholastic League Winning Schools for the 2017–2018 & 2018–2019 School Years

Source: University Interscholastic League, www.uiltexas.org

The **UIL Lone Star Cup** is awarded annually to six high schools, one in each of the six UIL classifications, based on their team performance in district and state championships. The winning schools receive the UIL Lone Star Cup trophy and a $1,000 scholarship.

YEAR	1A	2A	3A	4A	5A	6A
Lone Star Cup Champions						
2018–19	Nazareth	Mason	Brock	Argyle	Highland Park (Dallas)	Southlake Carroll
2017–18	Nazareth	Mason	Brock	Argyle	Prosper	Conroe The Woodlands

State champions in the academic, music, and the arts categories are listed first, then the winners in some sports categories. For other sports results, see page 164. A dash (—) in the box means there was no competition in that conference in that category for that year.

State Champions, Academics

YEAR	1A	2A	3A	4A	5A	6A
Overall State Meet Academic Champions						
2018–19	Borden County	Sabine Pass	Holliday	Argyle	Lovejoy (Lucas)	Cypress Woods
2017–18	Borden County	Sabine Pass	Sabine (Gladewater)	Argyle	Lindale	Clements (Sugar Land)
Accounting						
2018–19	Jayton	Union Grove (Gladewater)	Idalou	Argyle	Hallsville	Cypress Woods
2017–18	Happy	Sabine Pass	Central (Pollok)	Atlanta	Hallsville	Lufkin
Calculator Applications						
2018–19	Santa Anna	Muenster	Ponder	Argyle	Canutillo (El Paso)	North Shore (Houston)
2017–18	Ropes (Ropesville)	Lindsay	Sabine (Gladewater)	Argyle	Prosper	PSJA North (Pharr)
Computer Applications						
2018–19	Springlake-Earth	Vega	Chapel Hill (Mount Pleasant)	Melissa	Waller	Cypress Woods
2017–18	Winters	Sabine Pass	Chapel Hill (Mount Pleasant)	Melissa	Hallsville	North Shore (Houston)
Computer Science						
2018–19	Borden County	Ozona	Ponder	Giddings	Austin LBJ	Cypress Woods
2017–18	Borden County	Ozona	Chapel Hill (Mount Pleasant)	Boerne	Austin LBJ	Richardson
Number Sense						
2018–19	Bellevue	Poolville	Sabine (Gladewater)	Wichita Falls Hirschi	Highland Park (Dallas)	Clements (Sugar Land)
2017–18	Bellevue	Lindsay	City View (Wichita Falls)	Argyle	Highland Park (Dallas)	Clements (Sugar Land)
Mathematics						
2018–19	Fruitvale	Muenster	Sabine (Gladewater)	Salado	Highland Park (Dallas)	Dulles (Sugar Land)
2017–18	Bellevue	Latexo	Sabine (Gladewater)	Salado	Highland Park (Dallas)	Dallas Science-Engr. Magnet
Science						
2018–19	Klondike (Lamesa)	Valley View	Whitney	La Feria	Lubbock	Dulles (Sugar Land)
2017–18	Cross Plains	Lindsay	Whitney	Argyle	Lubbock	Dulles (Sugar Land)
Social Studies						
2018–19	Hartley	Sabine Pass	Tolar	Hereford	Hallsville	Pearland Dawson
2017–18	Hartley	Lindsay	Uplift Summit Intl Prep (Arlington)	Burnet	Hereford	Klein
Current Issues						
2018–19	Borden County	Sabine Pass	Holliday	Argyle	College Station	Humble Atascosita
2017–18	Borden County	Latexo	Holliday	Stephenville	Boerne Champion	Plano West
Literary Criticism						
2018–19	Graford	Sabine Pass	Holliday	Argyle	Sulphur Springs	McKinney
2017–18	Graford	Martin's Mill	Harmony School of Innovation (Fort Worth)	Liberty	Wichita Falls Rider	Katy Seven Lakes

YEAR	1A	2A	3A	4A	5A	6A
Poetry Interpretation						
2018–19	Irion County	Mason	Malakoff	Little Cypress-Mauriceville	Victoria West	Judson (Converse)
2017–18	Trinidad	Stamford	Muleshoe	Princeton	Saginaw	San Angelo Central
Prose Interpretation						
2018–19	Petersburg	West Hardin (Saratoga)	Kemp	Little Cypress-Mauriceville	Tuloso-Midway (Corpus Christi)	Plano
2017–18	McMullen County	Sundown	Muleshoe	Crandall	Denton Ryan	La Joya
Ready Writing						
2018–19	Woodson	Shelbyville	Franklin	Bullard	College Station	Pearland Dawson
2017–18	Zephyr	Port Aransas	Industrial (Vanderbilt)	Needville	Grapevine	Dulles (Sugar Land)
Speech Team						
2018–19	Borden County	Shelbyville	London (Corpus Christi)	North Lamar (Paris)	Lovejoy (Lucas)	Pflugerville Hendrickson
2017–18	Borden County	Cross Roads (Malakoff)	London (Corpus Christi)	Salado	Lindale	Plano West
Informative Speaking						
2018–19	Lometa	Leon (Jewett)	Holliday	North Lamar (Paris)	Mount Pleasant	Plano West
2017–18	Borden County	Three Rivers	Callisburg	North Lamar (Paris)	Lindale	Plano West
Persuasive Speaking						
2018–19	Borden County	Latexo	London (Corpus Christi)	North Lamar (Paris)	Dripping Springs	Plano West
2017–18	Borden County	Lindsay	London (Corpus Christi)	Salado	Magnolia	Austin Anderson
Lincoln-Douglas Debate						
2018–19	Guthrie	Gary	London (Corpus Christi)	Bandera	Lovejoy (Lucas)	Plano West
2017–18	Aspermont	Three Rivers	London (Corpus Christi)	Salado	Frisco Liberty	Klein
Spelling & Vocabulary						
2018–19	Irion County	Brackettville	Holliday	Snyder	Frisco Independence	Midway (Waco)
2017–18	Tioga	Wellington	Holliday	Salado	College Station A&M Consol.	Houston Carnegie Vanguard
Spelling & Vocabulary Team						
2018–19	Kennard	Sabine Pass	Holliday	Burnet	Lubbock	El Paso Coronado
2017–18	Kennard	Sabine Pass	Henrietta	Giddings	Lubbock	Houston Carnegie Vanguard
Journalism Team						
2018–19	Savoy	San Isidro	Gateway (Georgetown)	Wimberley	Leander Rouse	Sterling (Baytown)
2017–18	Grady (Lenorah)	Thrall	Buffalo	Wimberley	Lindale	McKinney
Editorial Writing						
2018–19	Grady (Lenorah)	San Isidro	Coleman	Devine	Lovejoy (Lucas)	Beaumont West Brook
2017–18	Grady (Lenorah)	Archer City	Wall	Wimberley	Randall (Amarillo)	Klein Forest
Feature Writing						
2018–19	Savoy	Mason	Gateway (Georgetown)	Argyle	Lindale	Mansfield
2017–18	Borden County	Claude	Buffalo	Carthage	Lubbock-Cooper	Cypress Creek
Headline Writing						
2018–19	Nazareth	Martin's Mill	Van Alstyne	Bridgeport	PSJA Memorial (Alamo)	Stevens (San Antonio)
2017–18	Happy	West Texas (Stinnett)	Grandview	Argyle	Denton Braswell	Mansfield
News Writing						
2018–19	Savoy	Lindsay	Whitney	Henderson	Gregory-Portland	Sterling (Baytown)
2017–18	Priddy	Stratford	White Oak	Wimberley	Whitehouse	Friendswood

State Champions, Publications

	Yearbooks (Gold Awards)	Print Newspapers (Gold Awards)
2018–19	Vista Ridge (Cedar Park), Texarkana Texas, St. Thomas' Episcopal (Houston), Pleasant Grove (Texarkana), McKinney, Mansfield Legacy, Highland Park (Dallas), Haltom	Texarkana Texas, St. Mark's School of Texas (Dallas), Pleasant Grove (Texarkana), Albany
2017–18	Texarkana Texas, St. Mark's School of Texas (Dallas), Pleasant Grove (Texarkana), McKinney, Mansfield Legacy, Austin Bowie	Texarkana Texas, St. Mark's School of Texas (Dallas), The Hockaday School (Dallas), Pleasant Grove (Texarkana), Lewisville Marcus

State Champions, Music and Theater

YEAR	1A	2A	3A	4A	5A	6A
One-Act Play						
2018–19	Abbott	Sabine Pass	Lago Vista	Salado	Randall (Amarillo)	Keller Central
2017–18	Trinidad	Christoval	Little River Academy	Crandall	Tuloso-Midway (Corpus Christi)	Harlingen South
State Marching Band Contest						
2018–19	—	Valley Mills	—	Canton	—	Vista Ridge (Cedar Park)
2017–18	Whiteface	Clarksville	Mineola	—	Cedar Park	—

State Champions, Athletics

YEAR	1A	2A	3A	4A	5A	6A
Cross Country Team, Boys						
2018–19	Miller Grove (Cumby)	SA Great Hearts Monte Vista	Eustace	Decatur	Eastwood (El Paso)	Conroe The Woodlands
2017–18	Miller Grove (Cumby)	Sundown	Luling	San Elizario	Lovejoy (Lucas)	Conroe The Woodlands
Cross Country Individual, Boys						
2018–19	Hartley	Sundown	Vanderbilt Industrial	Melissa	Aledo	Lewisville Flower Mound
2017–18	Medina	Sundown	Vanderbilt Industrial	San Elizario	Aledo	Lewisville Flower Mound
Cross Country Team, Girls						
2018–19	Happy	San Saba	Tulia	Canyon	Frisco Wakeland	Coppell
2017–18	Nazareth	Sundown	East Bernard	Bandera	Frisco Liberty	Keller
Cross Country Individual, Girls						
2018–19	Claude	Wellington	Academy (Little River)	Llano	McKinney North	Plano
2017–18	Miller Grove (Cumby)	Valley View	Academy (Little River)	Alvarado	McKinney North	Montgomery
Golf Team, Boys						
2018–19	Garden City	Goldthwaite	Columbus	Monahans	Highland Park (Dallas)	Westlake (Austin)
2017–18	Garden City	Grapeland	Pottsboro	Monahans	Highland Park (Dallas	Westlake (Austin)
Golf Individual, Boys						
2018–19	Crowell	Goldthwaite	Pottsboro	Little Cypress-Mauriceville	Sharyland (Mission)	Nelson (Trophy Club)
2017–18	Crowell	Grapeland	Pottsboro	Madisonville	Highland Park (Dallas)	Stratford (Houston)
Golf Team, Girls						
2018–19	Robert Lee	Grapeland	McGregor	Andrews	Grapevine	Westlake (Austin)
2017–18	Blanket	Grapeland	Ingram Moore	Andrews	Grapevine	Westlake (Austin)
Golf Individual, Girls						
2018–19	Phoenix (Greenville)	Martin's Mill	Chapel Hill (Mount Pleasant)	Carrollton Ranchview	Abilene Wylie	Arlington Martin
2017–18	Blanket	Christoval	Rockdale	Carollton Ranchview	Magnolia	Plano East
Tennis, Team						
2018–19	—	—	—	Fredricksburg	Highland Park (Dallas)	Round Rock Westwood
2017–18	—	—	—	Abilene Wylie	Highland Park (Dallas)	Memorial (Houston)

YEAR	1A	2A	3A	4A	5A	6A
Tennis, Boys Singles						
2018–19	Nueces Canyon (Barksdale)	Mason	Brady	Uplift North Hills (Irving)	Nederland	Clear Creek (League City)
2017–18	Grady (Lenorah)	Mason	Brady	Boerne	Amarillo	Katy Tompkins
Tennis, Boys Doubles						
2018–19	Knippa	Mason	Wall	Canyon	College Station A&M Consol.	Clements (Sugar Land)
2017–18	Nazareth	Mason	Wall	Wills Point	Austin LBJ	Westlake (Austin)
Tennis, Girls Singles						
2018–19	Slidell	Thorndale	Jourdanton	Spring Hill (Longview)	Highland Park (Dallas)	Lake Travis (Austin)
2017–18	Eula (Clyde)	Thorndale	London (Corpus Christi)	Boerne	Dripping Springs	Dulles (Sugar Land)
Tennis, Girls Doubles						
2018–19	Nazareth	Mason	Brock	Boerne	Alamo Heights (San Antonio)	Vandegrift (Leander)
2017–18	Nazareth	Mason	Vanderbilt Industrial	Boerne	Alamo Heights (San Antonio)	Plano West
Tennis, Mixed Doubles						
2018–19	Nazareth	Mason	Rockdale	Vernon	Highland Park (Dallas)	Plano West
2017–18	Iredell	Mason	Rockdale	Fredricksburg	Highland Park (Dallas)	Memorial (Houston)
Track & Field, Boys Team						
2018–19	Paducah	Milano	Life Oak Cliff (Dallas)	La Vega (Waco)	Marshall (Missouri City)	Klein Forest
2017–18	Valley (Turkey)	Milano	Yoakum	Dallas Carter	Marshall (Missouri City)	Conroe The Woodlands
Track & Field, Girls Team						
2018–19	Happy	Sunray	Atlanta	Canyon	Lancaster	DeSoto
2017–18	Blum	Refugio	Leonard	Dallas Carter	Mansfield Lake Ridge	DeSoto

Swimming & Diving, Team				
	GIRLS		**BOYS**	
YEAR	5A	6A	5A	6A
2018–19	Montgomery	Carroll (Southlake)	Georgetown	Carroll (Southlake)
2017–18	Dripping Springs	Conroe The Woodlands	Highland Park (Dallas)	Carroll (Southlake)

Wrestling, Boys	
2018–19	**TEAM: 5A** Randall (Amarillo) **6A** Allen **5A Weight Class 106:** Dumas **113:** Lubbock **120:** El Paso Chapin **126:** Frisco **132:** Argyle **138:** Midlothian **145:** Dripping Springs **152:** Pflugerville Weiss **160:** Hereford **170:** Friendswood **182:** Northwest (Justin) **195:** Wylie East **220:** Cedar Park **285:** Highland Park (Dallas) **6A Weight Class 106:** Arlington Martin **113:** Allen **120:** Arlington Martin **126:** Keller **132:** Plano West **138:** Allen **145:** Allen **152:** Allen **160:** Katy **170:** Katy **182:** Arlington Bowie **195:** San Antonio Roosevelt **220:** Killeen Ellison **285:** Allen
2017–18	**TEAM: 5A** Dumas **6A** Allen **5A Weight Class 106:** Frisco **113:** Lubbock **120:** Randall (Amarillo) **126:** Randall (Amarillo) **132:**Corpus Christi Veterans Memorial **138:** Northwest (Justin) **145:** El Paso Bel Air **152:** Hereford **160:** Prosper **170:** Chisholm Trail (Fort Worth) **182:** Bryan **195:** Highland Park (Dallas) **220:** Cedar Park **285:** Foster (Richmond) **6A Weight Class 106:** Allen **113:** Vandegrift (Leander) **120:** Austin Bowie **126:** Allen **132:** El Paso Franklin **138:** Allen **145:** Katy **152:** Carroll (Southlake) **160:** Allen **170:** Allen **182:** Montwood (El Paso) **195:** Allen **220:** Rockwall **285:** Rockwall-Heath
Wrestling, Girls	
2018–19	**TEAM: 5A** Hanks (El Paso) **6A** Keller Timber Creek **5A Weight Class 95:** Azle **102:** Foster (Richmond) **110:** Frisco Liberty **119:** Corpus Christi Veterans Memorial **128:** Hanks (El Paso) **138:** Uvalde **148:** Dallas Kimball **165:** Eastwood (El Paso) **185:** Lovejoy (Lucas) **215:** Corpus Christi Ray **6A Weight Class 95:** Montwood (El Paso) **102:** Arlington Martin **110:** Cypress Creek; **119:** Weatherford **128:** Klein **138:** Nelson (Trophy Club) **148:** Conroe Woodlands College Park **165:** Plano West **185:** Keller Timber Creek **215:** Haltom
2017–18	**TEAM: 5A** Hanks (El Paso) **6A** Cypress Ranch **5A Weight Class 95:** Saginaw **102:** Hanks (El Paso) **110:** Fabens **119:** Hanks (El Paso) **128:** Corpus Christi Veterans Memorial **138:** Eaton (Haslet) **148:** Uvalde **165:** Northwest (Justin) **185:** Humble **215:** Lubbock Monterey **6A Weight Class 95:** Cypress Ranch **102:** Weatherford **110:** Trinity (Euless) **119:** Arlington Martin **128:** Allen **138:** Nelson (Trophy Club) **148:** Katy Cinco Ranch **165:** Cypress Falls **185:** Coppell **215:** Katy Seven Lakes

State and National History Day Contest Winners, 2018 & 2019

Each year thousands of students, encouraged by teachers and parents statewide, participate in the National History Day program in Texas. **Texas History Day**, an affiliate of NHD, is a highly regarded academic program for 6th through 12th grade students. Students that place first or second at the state contest get the chance to compete in the national contest in Washington, D.C. Learn more at **https://tshaonline.org/education/students/texas-history-day/75**

State History Day Winners 2018
Theme: Conflict and Compromise

		Junior	Senior
Documentaries			
Individual		1st: *The Tale of Two Ports*, Baytown Gentry JH	1st: *3/5ths to Thirteenth: The American Compromises of Black Personhood*, Waco HS
		2nd: *The Tie That Binds: The Conflict and Compromise of Adoption Rights and Reform*, Livingston JH	2nd: *Battle of the Old West: The Conflicts and Compromises of Jackson Hole*, Houston Nimitz HS
Group		1st: *The Cuban Missile Crisis: The 13 Days of Conflict That Proved Compromise Is Key*, Livingston JH	1st: *When the Postman Didn't Ring Twice: The 1970 Postal Strike*, Houston Nimitz HS
		2nd: *The Space Race: Conflict and Compromise in New Frontiers*, Baytown Cedar Bayou JH	2nd: *Tapping into the American Civil Rights Movement*, San Antonio Communication Arts HS
Exhibits			
Individual		1st: *Kansas-Nebraska Act: Prelude to Civil War* Edward Gambrell, Sugar Land Macario Garcia Middle School	1st: *"That Damned Fence!" — The Internment of Japanese-Americans during WWII*, Baytown Goose Creek Memorial
		2nd: *Brown v. Board of Education*, Haltom Fossil Hill Middle School	2nd: *Tuskegee Airmen: A War Abroad and at Home*, San Antonio Jay Science and Engineering Academy
Group		1st: *Indian Removal Act: A Compromise Gone Wrong* Mandie Santibanez, Alvaro Perales Jr., Brownsville Lucio Middle School	1st: *The Chamizal Dispute: A Century of Conflict*, Houston Nimitz HS
		2nd: *Emancipation Proclamation: The Turning Point of War*, Bryan Stephen F. Austin Middle School	2nd: *"A Diamond Is Forever"*, Plano East HS
Performances			
Individual		1st: *Hindu, Muslim, Christian, Sikh — Did It Matter? A Compromise That Led to Conflict*, Plano C M Rice Middle School	1st: *The Accidental Activist: How Nadine Gordimer Helped Author a Compromise to End Apartheid*, Waco HS
		2nd: *The Wolves of Yellowstone*, Waco ATLAS Academy	2nd: *A Conflict within the Guatemalan Fields: Rigoberta Menchu*, Houston Nimitz HS
Group		1st: *A Whistle Bought at Just the Right Price*, Baytown Gentry JH	1st: *Mandela and Tambo: The Unseen History of South African Conflict and Compromise*, Plano East HS
		2nd: *It Was All for a Penny: The Newsboys Strike of 1899*, Waco ATLAS Academy	2nd: *An End to Troubles: The Belfast Agreement*, Dallas Highland Park HS
Websites			
Individual		1st: *Radium Girls: Glowing Ghosts Seeking Justice*, Sugar Land Sartartia Middle School	1st: *The End of the Game of Thrones*, Elgin Renaissance Academy
		2nd: *Immigration Reform and Control Act: Trying to Resolve Immigration Conflicts with Compromises*, Fort Worth McLean Middle School	2nd: *Kahlo's Paintbrush: Deconstructing Gender and Constructing Mexicanidad*, Houston MacArthur HS
Group		1st: *N.A.T.O. Freedom & Security*, Houston Grantham Middle School	1st: *The Unionization of General Motors*, Houston Carver HS
		2nd: *Unfairly Interned*, Fort Worth McLean 6th Grade	2nd: *From Subdivision to Superfund: The Toxic Tale of a Texas Neighborhood*, Houston Nimitz HS
Papers			
Individual		1st: *The Cuban Missile Crisis: Compromise Adverts Nuclear Conflict*, Boerne Middle North	1st: *Conflict and Compromise in Negotiating Executive Order 8802*, San Antonio Health Careers HS
		2nd: *Iranian Hostage Crisis and Algiers Accords: The Catalyst of Modern-Day Islamic Terrorism*, El Paso Hornedo Middle School	2nd: *Claiborne: Handling a Maelstrom of Collective Identities*, Houston Eisenhower HS

National History Day 2018

3rd Place, Senior Group Exhibit
The Chamizal Dispute: A Century of Conflict, Humble Nimitz HS

State History Day Winners 2019
Theme: Triumph and Tragedy

	Junior	Senior
Documentaries		
Individual	1st: "It Just Went Like Tinder": The Triumphant Spark That Ignited New Unionism and the Tragedy of the Match Women in History, Livingston JH	1st: Operation Paperclip: A Soaring Triumph, or a Moral Tragedy?, Plano East HS
	2nd: Dr. Takashi Nagai: The Triumphs and Tragedies of the Man Who Loved Others as Himself, San Antonio Rudder Middle School	2nd: 3... Triumphant Missions, 2... Treacherous Deployments, 1... Touching Tragedy, Waco HS
Group	1st: The World Will Not Be the Same: The Triumphs and Tragedies of the Hiroshima and Nagasaki Bombings, Plano C M Rice Middle School	1st: Death in a Promised Land: The Triumph and Tragedy of Black Wall Street, Houston Nimitz HS
	2nd: The Tragedy of the Triangle Shirtwaist Factory Fire, Midland San Jacinto JH	2nd: Project X: How the Tragic Vietnam War Fostered the First Amendment Triumph of the Pentagon Papers, Livingston HS
Exhibits		
Individual	1st: "The March of Misery Led to Victory", San Antonio Rudder Middle School	1st: WWII Women Airforce Service Pilots: The Triumph and Tragedy of Female Flyers, Baytown Goose Creek Memorial
	2nd: Tragedy and Triumph at Tenerife, Brenham JH	2nd: Women's Suffrage: The Necessary Change towards Equality, New Caney HS
Group	1st: Mi Voz, Mi Poder (My Voice, My Power), San Antonio St. Matthew Catholic School	1st: Doolittle Raiders: Ever into Peril, Copperas Cove HS
	2nd: Corrie Ten Boom's Hiding Place, Missouri City Quail Valley Middle School	2nd: Catastrophe in the Canyon: Triumphs from the 1956 Air Tragedy, Houston Nimitz HS
Performances		
Individual	1st: Joni Eareckson Tada: A Tragic Accident That Forged an International Mission, Waco ATLAS Academy	1st: Radium Girls: Triumph in the Face of Tragedy, Plano East HS
	2nd: Sofia Kovaleskaya: Woman in Mathematics, El Paso St. Patrick Cathedral School	2nd: The Death of a Titan, Cypress Lakes HS
Group	1st: We Fight! We Sacrifice! We Triumph!, Waco ATLAS Academy	1st: The Triumphs and Tragedies of Operation Iceberg, Brownsville Veterans Memorial Early College HS
	2nd: The Flight of Pan Am 73, Sugar Land Sartartia Middle School	2nd: Triumphant Paintings of Tragedy: Artemisia Gentileschi, Brownsville Veterans Memorial Early College HS
Websites		
Individual	1st: Finding Family After Slavery, South Belton Middle	1st: The Bracero Program, Arlington Uplift Summit International HS
	2nd: Galveston's 1900 Storm: A City's Triumphant Rise over Waves of Tragedy, Baytown Cedar Bayou JH	2nd: Keep Your Chin Up: How the Tragic Murder of Vincent Chin Triumphantly Ignited the Asian-American Community, Baytown Sterling HS
Group	1st: And Still I Rise: The True Story of Maya Angelou, Irion County HS	1st: Tragedy in a Texas Town: The Texas City Disaster of 1947, Houston Nimitz HS
	2nd: The Muckrakers: Muck, Media, and Reform, Sugar Land Sartartia Middle School	2nd: Deadly Smog Pollution: Profit over People, Houston Carver HS for Applied Tech/Engineering/Arts
Papers		
Individual	1st: The French Occupation of Algeria: The Rise and Fall of a Prince, Austin Renaissance Academy	1st: Still Here: Indigenous Invisibility, Resistance, and Experience through Wounded Knee 1973, Austin Firelight Academy
	2nd: Foreign Relations Pawn: The Triumphant Rise and Tragic Fall of Bobby Fischer, Belmont Home School (Houston)	2nd: New Deal Constitutionalism: The Tragedy of the Great Depression and the Triumph of Judicial Review, Baytown Sterling HS

National History Day 2019

3rd Place, Senior Group Performance	3rd Place, Senior Group Website	Special Award for Latino-American History
The Triumphs and Tragedies of Operation Iceberg, Brownsville Veterans Memorial Early College HS	Tragedy in a Texas Town: The Texas City Disaster of 1947, Houston Nimitz HS	The Bracero Program, Arlington Uplift Summit International HS

Austin Community College graduates awaiting the start of the ceremony. Photo by Austin Community College (CC).

Colleges and Universities

Sources: Texas Higher Education Coordinating Board; www.thecb.state.tx.us/; Legislative Budget Board, "Summary of 2020–21 Conference Committee Report for HB1"

Enrollment in Texas public, independent, career, and private colleges and universities in fall 2018 totaled 1,571,721 students, an increase of 39,221 students, 2.6 percent, above fall 2017 enrollment.

Enrollment in fall 2018 in the 37 public universities was 658,219, a 1.1 percent increase from 2017's enrollment of 651,137. Health-related institutions had enrollment in 2018 of 25,786, a 3.0 percent increase from fall 2017 (25,031) but a decrease of 5.7 percent from fall 2016 (27,353).

The state's public community colleges, Lamar State Colleges, and Texas State Technical College System, which offer two-year degree programs, reported fall 2018 enrollments totaling 758,133 students, an increase over enrollment of 726,699 reported in fall 2017.

Enrollment for fall 2018 at independent and career colleges and universities was 129,583 students, down slightly from the 129,633 students enrolled in fall 2017.

Brief History of Higher Education in Texas

The first permanent institutions of higher education established in Texas were church-supported schools, although there were some earlier efforts:

• Rutersville University was established in 1840 by Methodist minister Martin Ruter in Fayette County and was the predecessor of Southwestern University in Georgetown, which was established in 1843;

• Baylor University, now at Waco, was established in 1845 at Independence, Washington County, by the Texas Union Baptist Association; and

• Austin College, now at Sherman, was founded in 1849 at Huntsville by the Brazos Presbytery of the Old School Presbyterian Church.

Other historic Texas schools of collegiate rank included:

Larissa College, 1848, at Larissa, Cherokee County; McKenzie College, 1841, Clarksville, Red River County; Chappell Hill Male and Female Institute, 1850, Chappell Hill, Washington County; Soule University, 1855, Chappell Hill; Johnson Institute, 1852, Driftwood, Hays County; Nacogdoches University, 1845, Nacogdoches; Salado College, 1859, Salado, Bell County.

Add-Ran College, established in 1873 at Thorp Spring, Hood County, was the predecessor of present-day Texas Christian University, Fort Worth.

Cost of Public Higher Education in Texas 2018		
	2-Year Schools (82)	4-Year Schools (37)
Average Tuition and Fees	$2,506	$9,251
Average Debt	$16,414	$30,825
% of Students with Debt	30.6%	58.5%

Texas A&M University and The University of Texas

The Agricultural and Mechanical College of Texas (now Texas A&M University), authorized by the Legislature in 1871, opened its doors in 1876 to become the first publicly supported institution of higher education in Texas.

In 1881, Texans established The University of Texas in Austin, with a medical branch in Galveston. The Austin institution opened Sept. 15, 1883, and the Galveston school opened in 1891.

First College for Women

In 1901, the 27th Legislature established the Girls Industrial College, which began classes at its campus in Denton in 1903. A campaign to establish a state industrial college for women was led by the State Grange and Patrons of Husbandry.

A bill was signed into law on April 6, 1901, creating the college. It was charged with a dual mission, which continues to guide the university today, to provide a liberal arts education and to prepare young women with a specialized education "for the practical industries of the age."

In 1905, the name of the college was changed to the College of Industrial Arts; in 1934, it was changed to Texas State College for Women.

Since 1957, the institution, which is now the largest university principally for women in the United States, has been the Texas Woman's University.

Historic, Primarily Black Colleges

A number of Texas schools were established primarily for blacks, although collegiate racial integration has long been the status quo. Title III of the Higher Education Act of 1965 established the term Historically Black College/University (HBCU), defined as a school of higher learning that was established and accredited before the 1964 Civil Rights Act and was dedicated to educating African Americans.

Today there are ten HBCUs in Texas: state-supported Prairie View A&M University (originally established as Alta Vista Agricultural College in 1876), Prairie View; and Texas Southern University, Houston; privately supported Huston-Tillotson University, Austin; Jarvis Christian College, Hawkins; Wiley College, Marshall; Paul Quinn College, originally located in Waco, now in Dallas; and Texas College, Tyler.

Predominantly black colleges that are important in the history of higher education in Texas, but which have ceased operations, include Bishop College, established in Marshall in 1881, then moved to Dallas; Mary Allen College, established in Crockett in 1886; and Butler College, originally named the Texas Baptist Academy, in 1905 in Tyler.

Hispanic-Serving Institutions

Title V of the Higher Education Act of 2008 established grant programs for public colleges that qualify as Hispanic-Serving Institutions (HSIs). An HSI is defined as a not-for-profit institution of higher learning

---

Top 5 Undergrad Majors at Public Universities, 2018

1. Business, Management, Marketing, and Related Support Services (20,053 students)
2. Health Professions and Related Programs (11,428 students)
3. Multi/Interdisciplinary Studies (10,855 students)
4. Engineering (8,631 students)
5. Biological and Biomedical Sciences (6,682 students)

Source: Texas Public Higher Education Almanac 2019

---

with a full-time equivalent undergraduate student enrollment that is at least 25 percent Hispanic.

According to the Hispanic Association of Colleges & Universities, Texas has 55 HSIs, including many community colleges, operating today.

State Appropriations

The All Funds appropriation for higher education totals $21.9 billion for FY20–21, an increase of 5.4 percent over the FY18–19 funding level. This amount represents about 8.7 percent of the total state All Funds budget. Within this amount, higher education received $15.9 billion in state General Revenue for FY20–21, an increase of 6.3 percent over the previous biennium.

Rates for all of the higher education formulas were increased over the FY18–19 rates. The core operations piece of the public community and junior colleges formula remained at FY18–19 funding levels.

The General Funds increase includes $485.9 million in new funding and $429.6 million in nonformula support and hold-harmless funding intended for the new mission-specific formulas for the UT Southwestern Medical Center, UT Health Science Center at San Antonio, UT Medical Branch at Galveston, and the UT Health Science Center in Houston.

Funding for tuition revenue bond debt service for FY20–21 decreased by 31.1 million from the FY18–19 funding levels, to $980.9 million.

TEXAS Grant Program funding of $866.4 million increased by $80.0 million from previous levels. This funding is expected to support 70.0 percent of eligible students.

Supplemental appropriations include:

- $16.0 million for deferred maintenance to Texas Southern University
- $29.6 million for abatement and demolition of certain facilities to Texas State Technical College–Waco
- $574 million for wildfire and Hurricane Harvey-related costs to Texas A&M Forest Service
- $58.8 million for expenses related to Hurricane Harvey to "institutions of higher education" ☆

Universities and Colleges

Sources: Texas Higher Education Coordinating Board (www.thecb.state.tx.us/ and http://www.txhighereddata.org) and individual institutions. Dates of establishment may differ from Brief History on page 580 because schools use the date when authorization was given rather than date of first classes.

Name of Institution, Location; (*type or ownership, if private sectarian institution); date of founding; president (unless otherwise noted)	Number of Faculty, 2017	Enrollment Fall Term, 2017	Enrollment Fall Term, 2018	% Change
Abilene Christian University, Abilene; (3–Church of Christ); 1906 (as Childers Classical Institute; as Abilene Christian College, 1914; as university, 1976); Dr. Phil Schubert.	N/A	4,764	4,799	0.7%
ALAMO COLLEGES (9), Dr. Mike Flores, chancellor. 1978 (as San Antonio Community College District; 1982, as Alamo Community College District; current name, 2009). System consists of following colleges and presidents:	2,013	61,415	60,818	-1.0%
Northeast Lakeview College, San Antonio; (7); 2007; Dr. Veronica Garcia.	147	3,860	5,510	42.7%
Northwest Vista College, San Antonio; (7); 1995; Dr. Ric Baser.	556	16,752	16,293	-2.7%
Palo Alto College, San Antonio; (7); 1983; Dr. Robert Garza.	271	9,368	9,852	5.2%
St. Philip's College, San Antonio; (7); 1898; Dr. Adena Williams Loston.	419	12,050	11,590	-3.8%
San Antonio College, San Antonio; (7); 1925; Dr. Robert Vela.	746	19,385	17,573	-9.3%
Alvin Community College, Alvin; (7); 1949; Dr. Christal Albrecht.	322	5,709	5,645	-1.1%
Amarillo College, Amarillo; (7); 1929; Dr. Russell Lowery-Hart.	416	7,525	9,844	30.8%
Amberton University, Garland; (3); 1971 (as Amber University; current name, 2001); Dr. Melinda H. Reagan.	N/A	1,257	1,182	-6.0%
Angelina College, Lufkin; (7); 1968; Dr. Michael J. Simon.	274	5,217	4,819	-7.6%
Angelo State University, San Angelo (See **Texas Tech University**)				
Arlington Baptist University, Arlington; (3–Baptist); 1939 (as Bible Baptist Seminary; 1965 as Arlington Baptist College; name changed to current in 2017); Dr. D. L. Moody.				
Austin College, Sherman; (3–Presbyterian USA); 1849; Dr. Stephen P. O'Day.	N/A	1,237	1,307	5.7%
Austin Community College, Austin; (7); 1972; Dr. Richard M. Rhodes.	1,906	38,462	38,362	-0.3%
Baylor College of Medicine, Houston; (5); 1903 (in Dallas; moved to Houston, 1943; Baptist until 1969; Dr. Paul Klotman, M.D.	N/A	1,575	1,574	-0.1%
Baylor University, Waco; (3–Southern Baptist); 1845 (in Independence; merged with Waco University and moved to Waco, 1887; Dr. Linda A. Livingstone.	N/A	17,059	17,217	0.9%
Blinn College, Brenham; (7); 1883 (as academy; jr. college, 1927); Dr. Mary Hensley Ed. D. chancellor.	624	18,465	19,113	3.5%
Brazosport College, Lake Jackson; (7); 1967; Dr. Millicent M. Valek.	186	4,229	4,304	1.8%
Brookhaven College, Farmers Branch (See **Dallas County Community College District**)				
Cedar Valley College, Lancaster (See **Dallas County Community College District**)				
Central Texas College, Killeen; (7); 1965; Dr. Jim Yeonopolus, chancellor.	580	8,895	9,976	12.2%
Cisco College, Cisco; (7); 1909 (as Cisco Junior College, a private institution; became state school in 1939; name changed to current in 2009); Dr. Thad J. Anglin.	169	3,261	3,358	3.0%
Clarendon College, Clarendon; (7); 1898 (as church school; became state school in 1927); Dr. Robert K. Riza.	74	1,588	1,633	2.8%
Coastal Bend College, Beeville; (7); (1966 as Bee County College, name changed in 1999); Carry DeAtley (interim).	188	4,464	4,633	3.8%
College of the Mainland, Texas City; (7); 1967; Dr. Warren Nichols.	227	4,328	4,673	8.0%
Collin College, McKinney; (7); 1985 (as Collin County Community College); Dr. H. Neil Matkin, district president.	1,356	31,035	32,846	5.8%
Concordia University Texas, Austin; (3–Lutheran Church–Missouri Synod); 1926 (as Concordia Lutheran College; current name, 1995); part of Concordia University System. Dr. Don Christian.	N/A	2,649	2,588	-2.3%
Dallas Baptist University, Dallas; (3–Baptist); 1898 (as Decatur Baptist College; moved to Dallas, name changed to Dallas Baptist College, 1965; became university, 1985); Dr. Adam C. Wright.	N/A	5,066	4,766	-5.9%
Dallas Christian College, Dallas; (3–Christian); 1950; Dr. Brian D. Smith.				
DALLAS COUNTY COMMUNITY COLLEGE DISTRICT (9), Dr. Joe May, chancellor. System consists of following presidents:	2,642	69,089	80,627	16.7%
Brookhaven College, Farmers Branch; (7); 1978; Dr. Thom D. Chesney.	592	9,880	11,065	12.0%
Cedar Valley College, Lancaster; (7); 1977; Dr. Joseph Seabrooks.	273	6,174	6,939	12.4%
Eastfield College, Mesquite; (7); 1970; Dr.Eddie Tealer.	566	10,977	14,502	32.1%
El Centro College, Dallas; (7); 1966; Dr. José Adames.	135	8,885	9,857	10.9%
Mountain View College, Dallas; (7); 1970; Dr. Sharon Davis (interim).	235	8,534	10,913	27.9%
North Lake College, Irving; (7); 1977; Christa Slejko.	279	9,684	10,433	7.7%
Richland College, Dallas; (7); 1972; Dr. Kathryn K. Eggleston.	617	14,955	16,918	13.1%
Del Mar College, Corpus Christi; (7); 1935; Dr. Mark Escamilla.	517	11,476	11,867	3.4%
Eastfield College, Mesquite (See **Dallas County Community College District**)				

*Type: (1) Public University System
(2) Public University
(3) Independent Senior College or University
(4) Public Medical School or Health Science Center
(5) Independent Medical, Dental or Chiropractic School

(6) Public Technical College System
(7) Public Community College
(8) Independent Junior College
(9) Public Community College System
(10) Public Lower-Level Institution

Name of Institution, Location; (*type or ownership, if private sectarian institution); date of founding; president (unless otherwise noted)	Number of Faculty, 2017	Enrollment Fall Term, 2017	Fall Term, 2018	% Change
East Texas Baptist University, Marshall; (3–Baptist); 1913 (as College of Marshall; as East Texas Baptist College, 1944; as university, 1984); Dr. J. Blair Blackburn.	N/A	1,591	1,645	3.4%
El Centro College, Dallas (See **Dallas County Community College District**)				
El Paso Community College, El Paso; (7); 1969; five campuses: Mission del Paso, Northwest, Rio Grande, Transmountain, and Valle Verde; Dr. William Serrata.	1,231	26,896	28,241	5.0%
Frank Phillips College, Borger; (7); 1948; includes campus in Perryton; Dr. Jud Hicks.	85	1,456	1,452	-0.3%
Galveston College, Galveston; (7); 1967; Dr. W. Myles Shelton.	98	2,197	2,423	10.3%
Grayson College, Denison; (7); 1963; Dr. Jeremy McMillen.	203	4,289	4,284	-0.1%
Hardin-Simmons University, Abilene; (3–Southern Baptist); 1891 (as Simmons College; as Simmons University, 1925; current name, 1934); Eric I. Bruntmyer.	N/A	2,252	2,344	4.1%
Hill College, Hillsboro; (7); 1923 (as Hillsboro Junior College; name changed to current, 1962); Dr. Pamela Boehm.	201	4,228	4,421	4.6%
Houston Baptist University, Houston; (3–Baptist); 1960; Dr. Robert B. Sloan Jr.	N/A	3,325	3,432	3.2%
HOUSTON COMMUNITY COLLEGE (9), Cesar Maldonado, chancellor. Houston; 1971. System consists of following colleges and presidents:	2,331	49782	48309	-3.0%
Central College, Houston; (7); Dr. Muddassir Siddiqi.				
Coleman College for Health Sciences, Houston; (7); 2004; Dr. Phil Nicotera.				
Northeast College, Houston; (7); Dr. Destry Dokes (interim).				
Northwest College, Houston; (7); Dr. Zachary R. Hodges.				
Southeast College, Houston; (7); Dr. Melissa Gonzalez.				
Southwest College, Houston; (7); Dr. Madeline Burillo-Hopkins.				
Online College, (7); Dr. Margaret Ford Fisher				
Howard County Junior College District (9), Dr. Cheryl T. Sparks, president. Big Spring, 1945. System consists of the following:	149	4,378	4,629	5.7%
Howard College, Big Spring; (7); 1945; (also has campuses in Lamesa and San Angelo.	133	4,266	4,510	5.7%
Southwest Collegiate Institute for the Deaf, Big Spring; (7)	17	112	119	6.3%
Howard Payne University, Brownwood; (3–Baptist); 1889; Dr. Cory Hines.	N/A	1,043	1,022	-2.0%
Huston-Tillotson University, Austin; (3–United Church of Christ and United Methodist); 1952 (as Huston-Tillotson College, the merger of Tillotson College, 1875, and Samuel Huston College, 1876; current name, 2005); Dr. Colette Pierce Burnette.	N/A	1,103	1,119	1.5%
Jacksonville College, Jacksonville; (8–Missionary Baptist); 1899; Dr. William Michael Smith.				
Jarvis Christian College, Hawkins; (3); 1912; Dr. Lester Newman.	N/A	864	964	11.6%
Kilgore College, Kilgore; (7); 1935; Dr. Brenda Kays.	248	5,396	5,294	-1.9%
Kingwood College, Kingwood (See **Lone Star College System**)				
Lamar University and all branches (See **Texas State University System**)				
Laredo Community College, Laredo; (7); 1946; Dr. Ricardo J. Solis.	274	9,846	10,145	3.0%
Lee College, Baytown; (7); 1934; Dr. Dennis Brown.	405	7,717	7,773	0.7%
LeTourneau University, Longview; (3); 1946 (as LeTourneau Technical Institute; became 4-yr. college, 1961); Dr. Dale A. Lunsford.	N/A	2,860	2,997	4.8%
LONE STAR COLLEGE SYSTEM (9), Dr. Stephen C. Head., chancellor. 1973; formerly North Harris Montgomery Community College District. System consists of following colleges and presidents:	3,403	69,452	78,244	12.7%
Lone Star College–Cy-Fair, Houston; (7); 2003; Dr. Seelpa Keshvala.	873	20,534	20,536	0.0%
Lone Star College–Kingwood, Humble; (7); 1984; Dr. Katherine Persson.	525	**560	11,358	1,928.2%
Lone Star College–Montgomery, Conroe; (7); 1995; Dr. Rebecca L. Riley.	608	13,884	13,088	-5.7%
Lone Star College–North Harris, Houston; (7); 1973; Dr. Gerald F. Napoles.	665	14,577	13,980	-4.1%
Lone Star College–Tomball, Tomball; (7); 1986; Dr. Lee Ann Nutt.	329	7,606	7,639	0.4%
Lone Star College–University Park, Houston; (7); 2012; Shah Ardalan.	506	12,291	11,643	-5.3%
Lubbock Christian University, Lubbock; (3–Church of Christ); 1957; Dr. L. Timothy Perrin.	N/A	1,882	1,810	-3.8%
McLennan Community College, Waco; (7); 1965; Dr. Johnette McKown.	437	8,879	8,954	0.8%
McMurry University, Abilene; (3–Methodist); 1923; Dr. Sandra S. Harper.	N/A	1,108	1,132	2.2%
Midland College, Midland; (7); 1972; Dr. Steve Thomas.	264	5,566	5,259	-5.5%
Midwestern State University, Wichita Falls; (2); 1922; Dr. Suzane Shipley.	377	5,661	5,712	0.9%
Montgomery College, Conroe (See **Lone Star College System**)				
Mountain View College, Dallas (See **Dallas County Community College District**)				
Navarro College, Corsicana; (7); 1946; four campuses: Corsicana, Mexia, Midlothian and Waxahachie; Dr. Kevin G. Fegan.	444	8,830	8,463	-4.2%
North Central Texas College, Gainesville; (7); 1924 (as Gainesville Jr. College; Cooke County College, 1960; present name, 1994); five campuses: Bowie, Corinth, Flower Mound, Gainesville, and Graham. Dr. Brent Wallace, chancellor.	416	10,283	10,171	-1.1%
Northeast Lakeview College, San Antonio (See **Alamo Colleges**)				
Northeast Texas Community College, Mount Pleasant; (7); 1984; Dr. Ron Clinton.	165	3,097	3,090	-0.2%

*Type: (1) Public University System
(2) Public University
(3) Independent Senior College or University
(4) Public Medical School or Health Science Center
(5) Independent Medical, Dental or Chiropractic School
(6) Public Technical College System
(7) Public Community College
(8) Independent Junior College
(9) Public Community College System
(10) Public Lower-Level Institution

** *Lone Star College–Kingwood was forced to cancel in-person classes for Fall 2017 due to Hurricane Harvey.*

Name of Institution, Location; (*type or ownership, if private sectarian institution); date of founding; president (unless otherwise noted)	Number of Faculty, 2017	Enrollment		
		Fall Term, 2017	Fall Term, 2018	% Change
North Harris College, Houston (See **Lone Star College System**)				
North Lake College, Irving (See **Dallas County Community College District**)				
Northwest Vista College, San Antonio (See Alamo Colleges)				
Odessa College, Odessa; (7); 1946; Dr. Gregory Williams.	238	6,240	6,571	5.3%
Our Lady of the Lake University of San Antonio, San Antonio; (3–Roman Catholic); 1895 (as school for girls; as senior college, 1911; as university, 1975); two campuses: San Antonio and Houston; Dr. Diane E. Melby.	N/A	3,212	3,149	-2.0%
Palo Alto College, San Antonio (See **Alamo Colleges**)				
Panola College, Carthage; (7); 1947 (as Panola Junior College; name changed, 1988); Dr. Gregory S. Powell.	142	2,655	2,771	4.4%
Paris Junior College, Paris; (7); 1924; Dr. Pamela Anglin.	184	4,844	4,959	2.4%
Parker University, Dallas; (5); 1982; (as Parker College of Chiropractic; name changed to present in 2011); Dr. William E. Morgan.	N/A	1,205	1,514	25.6%
Paul Quinn College, Dallas; (3–African Methodist Episcopal Church); 1872 (in Waco; moved to Dallas, 1990); Dr. Michael J. Sorrell.	N/A	519	550	6.0%
Prairie View A&M University, Prairie View (See **Texas A&M University System**)				
Ranger College, Ranger; (7); 1926; Dr. William J. Campion.	144	2,411	2,399	-0.5%
Rice University, Houston; (3); chartered, 1891; opened, 1912 (as Rice Institute; as William Marsh Rice University, 1960); Dr. David W. Leebron.	N/A	7,052	7,124	1.0%
Richland College, Dallas (See **Dallas County Community College District**)				
St. Edward's University, Austin; (3–Catholic); 1885; Dr. George E. Martin.	N/A	4,447	4,301	-3.3%
St. Mary's University of San Antonio, San Antonio; (3–Roman Catholic); 1852; Dr. Thomas J. Mengler, J.D.	N/A	3,625	3,617	-0.2%
St. Philip's College, San Antonio (See **Alamo Colleges**)				
Sam Houston State University, Huntsville (See **Texas State University System**)				
San Antonio College, San Antonio (See **Alamo Colleges**)				
SAN JACINTO COLLEGE DISTRICT (9), Dr. Brenda Lang Hellyer, chancellor. System consists of following colleges and provosts	1,253	35455	37895	6.9%
Central, Pasadena; (7); Dr. Van Wigginton.	533	14,438	15,302	6.0%
North, Houston; (7); Dr. William Raffetto.	358	8,995	10,043	11.7%
South, Houston; (7); Dr. Brenda Jones.	418	12,022	12,550	4.4%
Schreiner University, Kerrville; (3–Presbyterian); 1923; Dr. Charlie McCormick.	N/A	1,312	1,418	8.1%
South Plains College, Levelland; (7); 1957; Dr. Robin Satterwhite.	385	9,283	9,279	0.0%
South Texas College, McAllen; (7); 1993; Dr. Shirley A. Reed.	1,096	31,374	31,640	0.8%
South Texas College of Law, Houston; (3); 1923; Michael F. Barry.	N/A	931	950	2.0%
Southern Methodist University, Dallas; (3–Methodist); 1911; Dr. R. Gerald Turner.	N/A	11,789	11,648	-1.2%
Southwest Collegiate Institute for the Deaf, Big Spring (See **Howard County Junior College District**)				
Southwest Texas Junior College, Uvalde; (7); 1946; Dr. Hector Gonzales.	235	6,660	6,894	3.5%
Southwest Texas State University, San Marcos (See **Texas State University System**)				
Southwestern Adventist University, Keene; (3–Seventh-Day Adventist); 1893 (as Keene Industrial Academy; as Southwestern Junior College, 1916; as Southwestern Union College, 1963; as Southwestern Adventist College,1980; as university, 1996); Dr. Ken Shaw.	N/A	819	746	-8.9%
Southwestern Assemblies of God University, Waxahachie; (3–Assemblies of God); 1927 (in Enid, Okla., as Southwestern Bible School; moved to Fort Worth and merged with South Central Bible Institute, 1941; moved to Waxahachie as Southwestern Bible Institute, 1943; as Southwestern Assemblies of God College,1963; as university, 1996); Dr. Kermit S. Bridges.	N/A	2,175	2,121	-2.5%
Southwestern Christian College, Terrell; (3–Church of Christ); 1948 (as Southern Bible Institute in Fort Worth; moved to Terrell and changed name, 1950); Dr. Ervin D. Seamster, Jr.	N/A	122	99	-18.9%
Southwestern University, Georgetown; (3–United Methodist); 1840 (merger of Rutersville College, 1840; McKenzie College, 1841; Wesleyan College, 1846; and Soule University, 1855; first named Texas University; current name, 1875); Dr. Edward B. Burger.	N/A	1,380	1,428	3.5%
Stephen F. Austin State University, Nacogdoches; (2); 1921; Dr. Scott Gordon.	870	12,578	13,058	3.8%
Sul Ross State University, Alpine (See **Texas State University System**)				
Sul Ross State University–Rio Grande College, Uvalde (See **Texas State University System**)				
Tarleton State University, Stephenville (See **Texas A&M University System**)				
TARRANT COUNTY COLLEGE DISTRICT (9), Eugene V. Giovannini, chancellor. Fort Worth; 1965 (as Tarrant County Junior College; name changed, 1999). System consists of following colleges and presidents:	2,156	56,405	56,941	1.0%
Connect Campus, (7); Carlos Morales.	361	6,652	6,762	1.7%
Northeast Campus, Hurst; (7); Dr. Kenya Ayers.	423	9,187	9,012	-1.9%

*Type: (1) Public University System   (6) Public Technical College System
(2) Public University   (7) Public Community College
(3) Independent Senior College or University   (8) Independent Junior College
(4) Public Medical School or Health Science Center   (9) Public Community College System
(5) Independent Medical, Dental or Chiropractic School   (10) Public Lower-Level Institution

Name of Institution, Location; (*type or ownership, if private sectarian institution); date of founding; president (unless otherwise noted)	Number of Faculty, 2017	Enrollment		
		Fall Term, 2017	Fall Term, 2018	% Change
Northwest Campus, Fort Worth; (7); Dr. Zarina Blankenbaker.	520	12,145	12,315	1.4%
South Campus, Fort Worth, (7); Dr. Peter Jordan.	373	8,458	8,997	6.4%
Southeast Campus, Arlington, (7); Dr. William Coppola.	368	7,949	8,018	0.9%
Trinity River Campus, Fort Worth, (7); Dr. S. Sean Madison.	420	12,014	11,837	-1.5%
Temple College, Temple; (7); 1926; Dr. Christy Ponce.	228	4,980	4,910	-1.4%
Texarkana College, Texarkana; (7); 1927; Dr. Jason Smith.	204	4,239	4,234	-0.1%
TEXAS A&M UNIVERSITY SYSTEM (1), Dr. John Sharp, chancellor. System consists of following colleges and presidents:				
Texas A&M University, College Station; (2); 1876 (as Agricultural and Mechanical of Texas; current name,1963); includes College of Veterinary Medicine and College of Medicine at College Station; Dr. Michael K. Young.	5,084	62,802	63,694	1.4%
Texas A&M University at Galveston, Galveston; (2); 1962 (as Texas Maritime Academy; as 4-yr. Moody College of Marine Sciences and Maritime Resources, 1971); Col. Michael E. Fossum USAFR (Ret.), COO.	250	1,998	1,806	-9.6%
Prairie View A&M University, Prairie View; (2); 1876 (as Alta Vista Agricultural College; as Prairie View State Normal Institute, 1879; as Prairie View Normal and Industrial College; as Prairie View A&M College, 1947, as branch of Texas A&M University System; current name, 1973); Dr. Ruth Simmons	510	9,125	9,516	4.3%
Tarleton State University, Stephenville; (2); 1899 (as John Tarleton College; as state-run John Tarleton Agricultural College,1917; as Tarleton State College, 1949; current name, 1973); includes campus in Killeen; Dr. F. Dominic Dottavio.	757	13,019	13,118	0.8%
Texas A&M International University, Laredo; (2); 1970 (as Laredo State University; current name, 1993); Dr. Pablo Arenaz.	383	7,640	7,884	3.2%
Texas A&M University–Corpus Christi, Corpus Christi; (2); 1973 (as upper-level Corpus Christi State University; current name, 1993; 4-year in 1994); Kelly M. Quintanilla.	728	12,236	11,929	-2.5%
Texas A&M University–Kingsville, Kingsville; (2); 1925 (as South Texas Teachers College; as Texas College of Arts and Industries, 1929; as Texas A&I University, 1967; joined University of South Texas System, 1977; joined Texas A&M University System, 1993); Dr. Mark Hussey.	526	8,674	8,541	-1.5%
West Texas A&M University, Canyon; (2); 1910 (as West Texas State Normal College; as West Texas State Teachers College, 1923; as West Texas State College, 1949; as West Texas State Univ., 1963; current name, 1993); Dr.Walter Wendler.	444	10,060	10,030	-0.3%
Texas A&M University–Commerce, Commerce; (2); 1889 (as East Texas State Normal College; as East Texas State Teachers College, 1923; as East Texas State College, 1957; university status conferred and named changed to East Texas State University, 1965; transferred to Texas A&M System, 1995); includes ETSU Metroplex Commuter Facility, Mesquite; Dr. Mark J. Rudin.	734	12,490	12,072	-3.3%
Texas A&M University–Texarkana, Texarkana; (2); 1971 (as East Texas State University at Texarkana; transferred to Texas A&M System and name changed, 1996); Dr. Emily Fourmy Cutrer.	150	2,038	2,067	1.4%
Texas A&M University–Central Texas, Killeen; (2); Dr. Marc A. Nigliazzo.	166	2,575	2,464	-4.3%
Texas A&M University–San Antonio, San Antonio; (2); Dr. Cynthia Teniente-Matson.	327	6,460	6,616	2.4%
Texas A&M University Health Science Center, (4); Includes Baylor College of Dentistry, College of Medicine, Graduate School of Biomedical Sciences, Institute of Biosciences and Technology, School of Rural Public Health, and HSC Statellite locations; Dr. Carrie L. Byington, M.D., Vice Chancellor for Health Services.	841	2,780	2,867	3.1%
Texas Christian University, Fort Worth; (3–Disciples of Christ); 1873 (as AddRan Male and Female College at Thorp Spring; moved to Waco, 1895; as AddRan Christian University, 1889; current name,1902; moved to Fort Worth, 1910); Dr. Victor J. Boschini Jr., chancellor.	N/A	10,469	10,898	4.1%
Texas Chiropractic College, Pasadena; (5); 1908; Dr. Stephen A Foster.	N/A	267	254	-4.9%
Texas College, Tyler; (3–C.M.E.); 1894; Dr. Dwight J. Fennell.	N/A	989	1,059	7.1%
Texas College of Osteopathic Medicine, Fort Worth (See **University of North Texas Health Science Center at Fort Worth**)				
Texas Lutheran University, Seguin; (3–Evangelical Lutheran); 1891 (as Evangelical Lutheran College in Brenham; as Lutheran College of Seguin, 1912; as Texas Lutheran College,1932; as university, 1996); Dr. Debbie Cottrell.	N/A	1,391	1,439	3.5%
Texas Southern University, Houston; (2); 1926 (as Houston Colored Junior College; as 4-yr. Houston College for Negroes, mid-1930s; as Texas State University for Negroes, 1947; present name, 1951); Dr. Austin A. Lane.	659	10,237	9,732	-4.9%
Texas Southmost College, Brownsville; (7); 1926 (as The Junior College of the Lower Rio Grande Valley; 1931 as Brownsville Junior College; current name, 1949); Dr. Jesús Roberto Rodríguez.	222	6,216	7,130	14.7%
TEXAS STATE TECHNICAL COLLEGE SYSTEM (6), Dr. Michael L. Reeser, chancellor. System consists of following colleges and provosts:				
Texas State Technical College–Harlingen, Harlingen; (7) 1967; Cledia Hernandez.	35	412	531	28.9%
Texas State Technical College–Marshall, Marshall; (7) 1991 (as extension center; as independent college, 1999); Barton Day.	194	5,075	4,579	-9.8%

*Type: (1) Public University System	(6) Public Technical College System
(2) Public University	(7) Public Community College
(3) Independent Senior College or University	(8) Independent Junior College
(4) Public Medical School or Health Science Center	(9) Public Community College System
(5) Independent Medical, Dental or Chiropractic School	(10) Public Lower-Level Institution

Name of Institution, Location; (*type or ownership, if private sectarian institution); date of founding; president (unless otherwise noted)	Number of Faculty, 2017	Enrollment		% Change
		Fall Term, 2017	Fall Term, 2018	
Texas State Technical College–Waco, Waco; (7) 1965 (as James Connally Technical Institute; current name, 1969); Dr. Adam Hutchinson.	48	594	586	-1.3%
Texas State Technical College–West Texas, Abilene, Breckenridge, Brownwood and Sweetwater; (7) 1970; Rick Denbow.	22	313	297	-5.1%
Texas State Technical College–North Texas, Red Oak; (7) 2014; Marcus Balch	252	4,236	4,195	-1.0%
Texas State Technical College–Fort Bend, Rosenberg; (7) 2016; Randall Wooten	100	1,596	1,935	21.2%
TEXAS STATE UNIVERSITY SYSTEM (1), Dr. Brian McCall, chancellor. System consists of following colleges and presidents:				
Lamar University, Beaumont; (2); 1923 (as South Park Junior College; as Lamar College, 1932; as Lamar State College of Technology, 1951; present name, 1971; transferred from Lamar University System, 1995); Dr. Kenneth Evans.	625	13,929	14,176	1.8%
Lamar State College–Orange, Orange; (10); 1969 (transferred from Lamar University System, 1995; current name, 2000); Dr. Thomas Johnson.	12	2,293	2,350	2.5%
Lamar State College–Port Arthur, Port Arthur; (10); 1909 (as Port Arthur College; joined Lamar University System, 1975; joined TSU System, 1995; current name, 2000); Dr. Betty J. Reynard.	12	2,293	2,413	5.2%
Lamar Institute of Technology, Beaumont; (10); (joined TSU System, 1995); Dr. Lonnie L. Howard.	16	2,983	3,260	9.3%
Sam Houston State University, Huntsville; (2); 1879; Dr. Dana G. Hoyt.	1,121	20,938	21,025	0.4%
Sul Ross State University, Alpine; (2); 1917 (as Sul Ross State Normal College; as Sul Ross State Teachers College, 1923; as Sul Ross State College, 1949; current name, 1969); Dr. William (Bill) Kibler.	153	1,996	1,885	-5.6%
Sul Ross State University – Rio Grande College, Uvalde, Eagle Pass, Del Rio (2); 1973 (current name, 1995); Dr. William (Bill) Kibler.	47	974	890	-8.6%
Texas State University, San Marcos; (2); 1903 (as Southwest Texas Normal School; as Southwest Texas State Normal College, 1918; as Southwest Texas State Teachers College, 1923; as Southwest Texas State College, 1959; as Southwest Texas State University, 1969; current name, 2003); Dr. Denise M. Trauth.	2,760	38,666	38,644	-0.1%
TEXAS TECH UNIVERSITY SYSTEM (1), Tedd L. Mitchell M.D., chancellor. System consists of following colleges and presidents:				
Angelo State University, San Angelo; (2); 1928 (was part of Texas State University System; joined Texas Tech system, 2007); Dr. Brian J. May.	531	10,189	10,242	0.5%
Texas Tech University, Lubbock; (2); 1923 (as Texas Technological College; current name, 1969); Dr Lawrence Schovanec.	3,395	36,634	37,845	3.3%
Texas Tech University Health Sciences Center, Lubbock; (4); 1972; Dr. Tedd L. Mitchell, M.D.	786	4676	4984	6.6%
Texas Tech University Health Sciences Center, El Paso; (4); 2013; Dr. Richard Lange.	309	662	729	10.1%
Texas Wesleyan University, Fort Worth; (3–United Methodist); 1891 (as college; current name, 1989); Dr. Frederick G. Slabach.	N/A	2,587	2,508	-3.1%
Texas Woman's University, Denton; (2); 1901 (as College of Industrial Arts; as Texas State College for Women, 1934; current name, 1957); Carine M. Feyten, chancellor and president.	1,201	15,321	15,364	0.3%
Tomball College, Tomball (See Lone Star College System)				
Trinity University, San Antonio; (3–Presbyterian U.S.A.); 1869 (at Tehuacana; moved to Waxahachie, 1902; to San Antonio, 1942); Dr. Danny J. Anderson.	N/A	2,595	2,635	1.5%
Trinity Valley Community College, Athens; (7); 1946 (as Henderson County Junior College); includes campus at Terrell; Dr. Jerry King.	257	6,547	6,562	0.2%
Tyler Junior College, Tyler; (7); 1926; Dr. L. Michael Metke, chancellor.	549	9,589	10,019	4.5%
University of Dallas, Irving; (3–Roman Catholic); 1956; Dr. Thomas S. Hibbs.	N/A	2,510	2,542	1.3%
UNIVERSITY OF HOUSTON SYSTEM (1), Dr. Renu Khator, chancellor. System consists of following colleges and presidents:				
University of Houston, Houston; (2); 1927; Dr. Renu Khator.	4,159	45,364	46,324	2.1%
University of Houston–Clear Lake, Houston; (2); 1974; Ira K. Blake.	794	8,542	8,961	4.9%
University of Houston–Downtown, Houston; (2); 1948 (as South Texas College; joined University of Houston System, 1974); Dr. Juan Sánchez Muñoz.	741	13,913	14,261	2.5%
University of Houston–Victoria, Victoria; (2); 1973; Robert K. (Bob) Glenn.	241	4,351	4,381	0.7%
University of the Incarnate Word, San Antonio; (3–Roman Catholic); 1881 (as Incarnate Word College; current name, 1996); Dr. Thomas M. Evans.	N/A	8,192	7,829	-4.4%
University of Mary Hardin-Baylor, Belton; (3–Baptist); 1845; Dr. Randy O'Rear	N/A	3,914	3,888	-0.7%
UNIVERSITY OF NORTH TEXAS SYSTEM (1), Lesa B. Roe, chancellor. System consists of following colleges and presidents:				

*Type: (1) Public University System
(2) Public University
(3) Independent Senior College or University
(4) Public Medical School or Health Science Center
(5) Independent Medical, Dental or Chiropractic School
(6) Public Technical College System
(7) Public Community College
(8) Independent Junior College
(9) Public Community College System
(10) Public Lower-Level Institution

Name of Institution, Location; (*type or ownership, if private sectarian institution); date of founding; president (unless otherwise noted)	Number of Faculty, 2017	Enrollment		% Change
		Fall Term, 2017	Fall Term, 2018	
University of North Texas, Denton; (2); 1890 (as North Texas Normal College; as North Texas State Teachers College, 1923; as North Texas State College, 1949; as university, 1961; current name, 1988); Dr. Neal J. Smatresk.	2,145	38,081	38,087	0.0%
University of North Texas at Dallas, Dallas; (2); (2000); Robert Mong.	250	3,509	3,757	7.1%
University of North Texas Health Science Center at Fort Worth, Fort Worth; (4);1966 (as private college; part of North Texas State University, 1975; current name, 1993); Dr. Michael R. Williams.	418	2270	2258	-0.5%
University of St. Thomas, Houston; (3–Roman Catholic); 1947; Dr. Richard Ludwick.	N/A	3,151	3,213	2.0%
THE UNIVERSITY OF TEXAS SYSTEM (1), James B. Milliken, chancellor. System consists of following colleges and presidents:				
University of Texas at Austin, The, Austin; (2); 1883; Dr. Gregory L. Fenves.	3,739	51,425	51,684	0.5%
University of Texas at Arlington, The, Arlington; (2); 1895 (as Arlington College; as state-run Grubbs Vocational College, 1917; as North Texas Agricultural and Mechanical College, 1923; as Arlington State College, 1949; current name, 1967); Dr. Vistasp M. Karbhari.	1,358	41,712	42,496	1.9%
University of Texas Rio Grande Valley, The, (2); 1973 (as branch of Pan American College; as University of Texas–Pan American at Brownsville, 1989; present name, 2015); Guy Bailey.	2,836	27,708	28,489	2.8%
University of Texas at Dallas, The, Richardson; (2); 1961 (as Graduate Research of the Southwest; as Southwest Center for Advanced Studies, 1967; joined UT System with current name, 1969; full undergraduate program, 1975); Dr. Richard C. Benson.	1,417	27,642	28,755	4.0%
University of Texas at El Paso, The, El Paso; (2); 1913 (as Texas College of Mines and Metallurgy; as Texas Western College of UT, 1949; current name, 1967); Dr. Diana S. Natalicio.	1,346	25,020	25,063	0.2%
University of Texas–Pan American, The, Edinburg. Merged with Brownsville campus in 2015 to form The University of Texas–Rio Grande Valley.				
University of Texas of the Permian Basin, The, Odessa; (2); 1969 (as 2-yr., upper-level institution; expanded to 4-yr., 1991); Dr. Sandra K. Woodley.	291	7,022	5,834	-16.9%
University of Texas at San Antonio, The, San Antonio; (2); 1969; Dr. Taylor Eighmy.	1,735	30,674	32,101	4.7%
University of Texas at Tyler, The, Tyler; (2); 1971 (as Tyler State College; as Texas Eastern University, 1975; joined UT System, 1979); Dr. Michael V. Tidwell.	602	9,934	9,716	-2.2%
University of Texas Health Science Center at Houston, The, Houston; (4); 1972; includes Dental Branch (1905); Graduate School of Biomedical Sciences (1963); Medical School (1970); School of Allied Health Sciences (1973); School of Nursing (1972); School of Public Health (1967); Division of Continuing Education (1958); Dr. Giuseppe N. Colasurdo, M.D.	2,092	5,242	5,335	1.8%
University of Texas Health Science Center at San Antonio, The, San Antonio; (4) 1968; includes Dental School (1970); Graduate School of Biomedical Sciences (1970); Health Science Center (1972); Medical School (1959 as South Texas Medical School of UT; present name, 1966); School of Allied Health Sciences (1976); School of Nursing (1969); Dr. William L. Henrich M.D.	1,623	3270	3280	0.3%
University of Texas Health Science Center at Tyler, The, Tyler; (4); 1949 (as East Texas Tuberculosis Sanatorium; as East Texas Chest Hospital, 1971; joined UT system with current name, 1977); Dr. Kirk A. Calhoun M.D.	133	36	44	22.2%
University of Texas M.D. Anderson Cancer Center, The, Houston; (4); 1941; Dr. Peter W.T. Pisters, M.D.	2,347	357	376	5.3%
University of Texas Medical Branch at Galveston, The, Galveston; (4) 1891; includes Graduate School of Biomedical Sciences (1952); Medical School (1891); School of Allied Health Sciences (1968); School of Nursing (1890); Vacant	1,279	3,302	3,344	1.3%
University of Texas Southwestern Medical Center, The, Dallas; (4); 1943 (as private institution; as Southwestern Medical College of UT, 1948; as UT Southwestern Medical School at Dallas, 1967; joined UT Health Science Center at Dallas, 1972); includes Graduate School of Biomedical Sciences (1947); School of Allied Health Sciences (1968); Southwestern Medical School (1943); Dr. Daniel K. Podolsky M.D.	2,482	2235	2266	1.4%
Vernon College, Vernon; (7); 1970; includes Wichita Falls campus; Dr. Dusty R. Johnston.	162	3,008	3,055	1.6%
Victoria College, Victoria; (7); 1925; Dr. David Hinds.	211	3,945	3,827	-3.0%
Wayland Baptist University, Plainview; (3–Southern Baptist); 1910; Dr. Bobby Hall	N/A	3,441	3,208	-6.8%
Weatherford College, Weatherford; (7); 1869 (as branch of Southwestern University; as denominational junior college, 1922; as municipal junior college, 1949; Dr. Tod Allen Farmer.	304	6,303	6,284	-0.3%
Western Texas College, Snyder; (7); 1969; Dr. Barbara Beebe.	91	2,250	2,179	-3.2%
Wharton County Junior College, Wharton; (7); 1946; Dr. Betty A. McCrohan.	305	7,050	6,768	-4.0%
Wiley College, Marshall; (3–Methodist); 1873; Dr. Herman J. Felton, Jr.	N/A	1,323	1,002	-24.3%

*Type: (1) Public University System
(2) Public University
(3) Independent Senior College or University
(4) Public Medical School or Health Science Center
(5) Independent Medical, Dental or Chiropractic School

(6) Public Technical College System
(7) Public Community College
(8) Independent Junior College
(9) Public Community College System
(10) Public Lower-Level Institution

BUSINESS

Residential construction in Pearland.
Photo by Trong Nguyen/Shutterstock.

ECONOMY AND UNEMPLOYMENT

BANKING, INSURANCE, CONSTRUCTION

COMMERCIAL FISHING AND TOURISM

ELECTRIC GRIDS, OIL, GAS

MINERALS AND MEDIA

Texas Economy: Leading in Job Creation in 2018

Source: Excerpted from the State of Texas Annual Cash Report 2018, Comptroller of Public Accounts.

Texas added more new jobs than any other state in fiscal 2018. From August 2017 to August 2018, the state's economy added 394,500 nonfarm jobs, an increase of 3.2 percent, to reach 12,626,500.

Private-sector employment rose by 3.8 percent. The state's rate of job growth was the highest among the ten most populous states and the fourth highest among all states.

Employment in the goods-producing industries increased by 6.4 percent in 2018, while employment in the service-providing industries grew by 2.7 percent.

Employment growth in the service-providing industries was led by professional and business services (up 92,400) and trade, transportation, and utilities (up 66,200).

The service-providing industries that saw the largest percentage gains in employment were professional and business services (up 5.5 percent) and leisure and hospitality (up 3.7 percent).

The information industry was the only industry to experience an employment decline over the year.

Oil and Gas

Since a decline in 2016, oil and gas industry employment has grown or remained constant in every month, reaching 260,400 in August 2018, an increase of 34,300 (15.2 percent) from August 2017, but still 19 percent below the 2014 peak.

In addition to substantial exploration activities within the state and in the Gulf of Mexico, Texas is headquarters for many of the nation's largest oil and natural gas refining and distribution companies, and has a large number of energy-related jobs in other industries.

As in the mining industry, employment in those industries and sectors has recovered from recent lows.

Consumer Spending

Growth in sales tax collections was up in 2018, by 10.5 percent to reach $31.9 billion.

Sales activity for motor vehicles operating on Texas highways, as measured by state motor vehicle sales tax collections, was also up sharply (by 9.7 percent to reach $5.0 billion).

The Consumer Confidence Index is a monthly measure of consumer optimism, an important factor affecting the sales of housing, automobiles, and other major purchases.

The index for the four-state West South Central Region, which includes Texas, was up by 2.6 percent in fiscal 2018. The index for the nation as a whole was up 1.1 percent.

Service Industries

Texas' service-providing industries, which account for 85 percent of the state's total nonfarm employment, saw job growth of 2.7 percent in 2018. Seven of the eight service-providing industries saw job increases, with the highest growth rate in professional and business services.

The professional and business services added 92,400 jobs (up 5.5 percent). Employment changes varied considerably among industry sectors, with the largest increases in employment services (9.2 percent) and business support services (9.4 percent).

The only sector to experience a decrease was accounting services. The employment services sector, which includes temporary help agencies with many of its jobs in temporary or part-time positions, had the

Gross Domestic Product in Current Dollars

	Millions of dollars			Percent of U.S. total			GDP* 2017	
	2015	2016	2017	2015	2016	2017	China	23,160,000
United States	**18,007,206**	**18,509,998**	**19,263,350**	**100.0**	**100.0**	**100.0**	European Union	20,850,000
1. California	2,510,167	2,619,639	2,746,873	13.9	14.2	14.3	United States	19,390,000
2. Texas	**1,611,958**	**1,601,517**	**1,696,206**	**9.0**	**8.7**	**8.8**	India	9,495,000
3. New York	1,458,253	1,500,152	1,547,116	8.1	8.1	8.0	Japan	5,429,000
4. Florida	890,884	930,375	967,337	4.9	5.0	5.0	Germany	4,171,000
5. Illinois	778,353	796,906	820,362	4.3	4.3	4.3	Russia	4,008,000
6. Pennsylvania	709,722	723,962	752,071	3.9	3.9	3.9	Indonesia	3,243,000
7. Ohio	611,350	624,372	649,127	3.4	3.4	3.4	Brazil	3,240,000
8. New Jersey	563,316	576,228	591,743	3.1	3.1	3.1	United Kingdom	2,914,000
9. Georgia	505,693	532,657	554,269	2.8	2.9	2.9	France	2,836,000
10. North Carolina	502,077	518,378	538,291	2.8	2.8	2.8	Mexico	2,458,000

Source: Bureau of Economic Analysis, U.S. Department of Commerce, 2018.

*Estimated GDP in millions of U.S. dollars, from the World Factbook of the CIA.

largest absolute increase in employment, 26,900. Total professional and business employment was 1,761,700 in August 2018.

The other services industries include a varied mix of business activities, including repair and maintenance services; laundry services; religious, political, and civic organizations; funeral services; parking garages; beauty salons; and a wide range of personal services.

Personal and laundry services employment increased by 4.5 percent, the highest rate among other services sectors. In all, other services industry employment rose by 12,600 to reach 436,700 in August 2018.

Health, Education

The education and health services industry, composed of the educational services and health care and social assistance sectors, added 45,700 jobs in 2018, a growth rate of 2.7 percent. The relatively small educational services sector saw an increase of 14,500 jobs (7.2 percent).

The much larger health care and social assistance sector grew at a 2.1 percent rate (31,200 jobs). In all, Texas education and health services employment reached 1,712,200 in August 2018.

Hospitality

Employment in the leisure and hospitality industry increased by 49,000 (3.7 percent) through 2018. The majority of the industry's job gains occurred in the food services and drinking places sector, which added 33,000 jobs (3.1 percent).

The largest percentage increase was in the amusement, gambling, and recreation industries sector, which grew by 4.2 percent (4,700). Total leisure and hospitality employment in 2018 was 1,372,100, representing about 11 percent of total employment.

Transportation and Utilties

The trade, transportation, and utilities industry, the state's largest employer with 20 percent of total nonfarm jobs in August 2018, added 66,200 jobs (2.7 percent) over the year. Employment in all three industry sector – retail trade; wholesale trade; and transportation, warehousing, and utilities – rose during fiscal 2018.

Wholesale trade employment was up by 5.0 percent (29,800); transportation, warehousing, and utilities employment increased by 19,500 (3.6 percent); and employment in the retail trade sector increased by 16,900 (1.3 percent).

In all, the trade, transportation, and utilities industry provided 2,525,600 jobs in August 2018.

Construction

Construction employment increased by 56,100 (7.9 percent) in 2018 to reach 766,000 in August 2018. Employment in the construction of buildings sector increased at the highest rate of any construction sector, growing by 10.1 percent (16,300).

Total housing construction activity in 2018 was up from 2017. Single-family building permits issued in the year ending in July 2018, at 116,271, were up by 7.3 percent from the same period one year earlier. Building permits for multifamily units rose by 17.6 percent.

According to Multiple Listing Service data from the Texas A&M Real Estate Center, the median sales price for an existing Texas single-family home rose by 5.8 percent, from $226,000 in July 2017 to $239,000 in July 2018. In July 2018, Texas had a 3.5-month inventory of existing homes for sale, down from 3.6 a year before and a substantial improvement from the post-recession high of 8.7 months in mid-2011.

Manufacturing

The manufacturing industry gained 23,400 jobs over the past year, an increase of 2.7 percent. Durable goods employment was up 21,000, led by gains in machinery manufacturing (up 9,900, 11.2 percent). Fabricated metal manufacturing employment also was up substantially over the year (by 5,500, 4.5 percent).

Both sectors are closely associated with oil and natural gas exploration and production, and employment in those sectors has been increasing along with that in the mining industry.

Overall, durable goods employment increased by 3.8 percent. Nondurable-goods manufacturing employment grew by 2,100 (0.7 percent). Total manufacturing employment in August 2018 was 878,500.

Exports

Through July, the value of 2018 exports was 18 percent higher than in the corresponding period of 2017. Texas is the nation's leading exporting state, and has been for more than a decade.

Texas exports comprised 18.0 percent of total U.S. exports through the first 11 months of fiscal 2018.

Finance

In 2018, overall employment in the financial activities industry grew by 2.1 percent (16,000 jobs). The finance and insurance sector grew by 7,200 (1.3 percent), while the real estate and rental and leasing sector grew by 8,800 (4.1 percent).

Financial institutions such as banks are the industry's largest subsector, employing 150,900 as of August 2018.

Total Texas financial activities industry employment reached 775,200 in August 2018.

Information

The information industry is a collection of diverse sectors, representing established sectors of the economy (newspaper publishing, data processing, television broadcasting, and wired telephone services) as well as some newer sectors (cell phone service providers, internet providers, and software).

The information industry was the only one of the 11 major industries to experience a decline in employment over the year. Employment fell 2.8 percent (5,600) to reach 196,000 in August 2018.

Government

Government employment increased by 0.2 percent (4,400) over the year. Federal government employment increased by 1,700, and local government employment increased by 3,500.

State government employment, however, decreased by 800. Total government employment in Texas was 1,942,100 in August 2018. ☆

Texas Gross Domestic Product, 2009–2018, By Industry (in millions)

Industry	2009	2010	2011	2012	2013	2014	2015	2016	2017	2018
Agriculture, Forestry, Fishing/Hunting	$5,523	$9,038	$8,465	$8,218	$10,898	$10,403	$11,888	$8,709	$9,072	$10,898
% change*	(12.3)	63.6	(6.3)	(2.9)	32.6	(4.5)	14.3	(26.7)	4.2	20.1
Natural Resources and Mining	112,575	122,076	146,001	158,861	183,266	199,598	116,107	92,152	115,515	141,191
% change	(36.6)	8.4	19.6	8.8	15.4	8.9	(41.8)	(20.6)	25.4	22.2
Construction	59,866	55,702	56,842	63,588	68,103	75,385	81,424	85,386	87,540	95,486
% change	(7.7)	(7.0)	2.0	11.9	7.1	10.7	8.0	4.9	2.5	9.1
Manufacturing	154,701	176,483	203,495	206,104	224,083	202,685	212,902	197,408	206,063	226,125
% change	(5.1)	14.1	15.3	1.3	8.7	(9.5)	5.0	(7.3)	4.4	9.7
Trade, Transportation, Utilities	212,808	229,191	244,618	266,982	275,782	289,279	306,115	307,889	322,390	345,636
% change	(1.9)	7.7	6.7	9.1	3.3	4.9	5.8	0.6	4.7	7.2
Information	50,353	50,068	50,188	49,328	53,965	53,327	57,767	60,196	62,819	65,308
% change	(6.9)	(0.6)	0.2	(1.7)	9.4	(1.2)	8.3	4.2	4.4	4.0
Financial Activities	159,479	167,358	178,923	192,555	202,323	221,251	234,397	249,593	254,810	265,853
% change	1.4	4.9	6.9	7.6	5.1	9.4	5.9	6.5	2.1	4.3
Professional and Business Services	124,702	131,715	140,676	150,573	157,256	170,065	181,455	184,354	194,950	211,854
% change	(4.2)	5.6	6.8	7.0	4.4	8.1	6.7	1.6	5.7	8.7
Educational and Health Services	80,943	85,445	89,109	92,472	95,613	99,694	107,190	112,839	117,308	121,979
% change	10.5	5.6	4.3	3.8	3.4	4.3	7.5	5.3	4.0	4.0
Leisure and Hospitality Services	37,780	38,945	40,420	43,476	45,459	50,814	56,459	58,500	60,275	62,235
% change	1.3	3.1	3.8	7.6	4.6	11.8	11.1	3.6	3.0	3.3
Other Private Services	24,961	25,294	25,735	27,658	28,889	31,213	32,584	32,924	33,911	35,700
% change	1.5	1.3	1.7	7.5	4.5	8.0	4.4	1.0	3.0	5.5
Government and Schools	139,709	145,880	146,749	151,562	156,612	161,676	170,356	175,750	181,588	185,083
% change	6.1	4.4	0.6	3.3	3.3	3.2	5.4	3.2	3.3	5.5
TOTAL	$1,163,400	$1,237,195	$1,331,221	$1,411,377	$1,502,249	$1,565,390	$1,568,644	$1,565,700	$1,646,211	$1,767,418
% change	(6.0)	6.3	7.6	6.0	6.4	4.2	0.2	(0.2)	5.1	7.4
TOTAL (in 2009 chained** dollars)	$1,271,436	$1,301,727	$1,343,791	$1,411,379	$1,472,104	$1,512,351	$1,590,409	$1,594,408	$1,615,822	$1,672,640
% change	(0.3)	2.4	3.2	5.0	4.3	2.7	5.2	0.3	1.3	3.5

*Percent change from the previous year. ** In 1996, the U.S. Department of Commerce introduced the chained-dollar measure. The new measure is based on the average weights of goods and services in successive pairs of years. It is "chained" because the second year in each pair, with its weights, becomes the first year of the next pair. *Source: 2018 Comprehensive Annual Financial Report for the State of Texas.*

Per Capita Income by County, 2017

Below are listed data for 2017 for total personal income and per capita income by county. Total income is reported in millions of dollars. The middle column indicates the percent of change in total personal income from 2016 to 2017.

In the far right column is the county's rank in the state for per capita income. Kendall County was first with $83,808. The lowest per capita income was in Starr County at $24,981.

Source: Bureau of Economic Analysis, U.S. Department of Commerce, 2018.

Top Ten			Lowest Ten		
County	Major cities	PCI	County	Major cities	PCI
1. Kendall	Boerne	$ 83,808	245. Motley	Matador	$ 28,447
2. Glasscock	Garden City	78,012	246. Cameron	Brownsville	27,741
3. Shackelford	Albany	77,918	247. Zavala	Crystal City	27,695
4. Midland	Midland	75,002	248. Zapata	Zapata	27,325
5. Sherman	Stratford	64,897	249. Walker	Huntsville	27,302
6. Collin	McKinney, Plano, Frisco	64,025	250. Bee	Beeville	27,078
7. Hartley	Dalhart, Channing	62,274	251. Garza	Post	26,482
8. Travis	Austin	62,205	252. Frio	Pearsall	26,421
9. Hansford	Spearman	60,759	253. Hidalgo	McAllen	25,617
10. Cottle	Paducah	60,247	254. Starr	Rio Grande City	24,981

County	Total Income ($ mil)	% change 16 / 17	Per capita income	Rank in State	County	Total Income ($ mil)	% change 16 / 17	Per capita income	Rank in State
United States	$16,820,250	4.4	$51,640	–	Brooks	242	1.8	33,466	217
Metropolitan	15,002,534	4.5	53,617	–	Brown	1,410	3.5	37,041	170
Nonmetro	1,817,716	3.2	39,591	–	Burleson	729	1.2	40,482	113
					Burnet	2,123	2.1	45,350	60
Texas	$1,340,568	2.6	$47,362	–	Caldwell	1,392	3.3	32,889	223
Metropolitan	1,223,760	4.2	48,478	–	Calhoun	796	2.1	36,587	183
Nonmetro	116,809	3.2	38,159	–	Callahan	530	2.5	38,029	153
					Cameron	11,754	1.2	27,741	246
Anderson	1,926	0.5	$33,362	220	Camp	495	2.7	38,491	153
Andrews	764	5.5	43,105	77	Carson	268	4.4	44,364	71
Angelina	3,298	0.2	37,555	160	Cass	1,080	2.8	35,996	190
Aransas	1,146	2.3	44,820	66	Castro	394	7.4	50,209	33
Archer	415	1.7	47,110	53	Chambers	2,148	0.7	51,832	30
Armstrong	85	–1.3	45,262	61	Cherokee	1,790	1.2	34,257	210
Atascosa	1,684	1.2	34,372	208	Childress	212	4.0	29,965	241
Austin	1,467	0.4	49,262	34	Clay	443	1.1	42,522	82
Bailey	316	14.0	44,659	67	Cochran	116	11.0	40,614	109
Bandera	946	1.6	42,330	86	Coke	128	–1.4	38,586	142
Bastrop	2,964	3.6	34,969	197	Coleman	327	3.1	38,788	141
Baylor	142	5.5	39,650	125	Collin	62,078	2.7	64,025	6
Bee	882	2.5	27,078	250	Collingsworth	114	9.9	38,186	151
Bell	14,617	2.5	42,024	91	Colorado	952	3.8	44,836	65
Bexar	85,782	2.5	43,798	74	Comal	7,892	1.0	55,965	18
Blanco	569	1.8	48,978	36	Comanche	541	5.8	39,842	122
Borden	35	–2.3	51,776	31	Concho	88	58.4	32,828	228
Bosque	746	1.5	40,704	108	Cooke	1,889	1.6	47,339	48
Bowie	3,648	2.2	38,807	140	Coryell	2,465	3.0	32,904	222
Brazoria	16,646	0.4	45,925	57	Cottle	84	13.9	60,247	10
Brazos	8,323	3.5	37,352	166	Crane	188	6.6	39,596	127
Brewster	415	1.8	44,418	70	Crockett	131	1.7	36,757	177
Briscoe	52	11.7	34,165	212	Crosby	204	24.1	34,530	206

County	Total Income ($ mil)	% change 16/17	Per capita income	Rank in State	County	Total Income ($ mil)	% change 16/17	Per capita income	Rank in State
Culberson	105	8.8	47,127	52	Hood	2,760	1.2	47,368	47
Dallam	393	6.0	54,562	22	Hopkins	1,382	2.9	37,868	156
Dallas	146,248	2.6	55,859	19	Houston	841	3.0	36,552	185
Dawson	472	16.9	36,857	194	Howard	1,311	5.4	36,367	188
Deaf Smith	784	2.2	41,634	95	Hudspeth	147	-1.9	33,241	221
Delta	184	-3.1	34,737	199	Hunt	3,447	2.3	36,725	180
Denton	45,112	2.5	53,948	24	Hutchinson	899	2.0	42,053	90
DeWitt	1,050	3.5	51,896	29	Irion	84	0.1	55,231	20
Dickens	71	5.9	32,006	231	Jack	345	6.4	39,070	137
Dimmit	334	1.0	32,067	230	Jackson	592	4.0	39,981	120
Donley	146	9.0	44,176	72	Jasper	1,390	1.9	39,105	135
Duval	390	0.9	34,579	205	Jeff Davis	90	-0.7	39,627	126
Eastland	1,036	12.9	56,294	17	Jefferson	10,851	1.8	42,338	85
Ector	6,417	7.7	40,851	106	Jim Hogg	157	-0.1	30,088	235
Edwards	67	1.2	34,266	209	Jim Wells	1,549	0.7	37,906	155
Ellis	7,377	2.6	42,490	83	Johnson	6,682	2.7	39,941	121
El Paso	29,063	2.6	34,582	204	Jones	599	2.9	29,969	240
Erath	1,579	4.7	37,624	159	Karnes	683	5.9	44,986	63
Falls	564	2.2	32,392	226	Kaufman	5,055	2.5	41,140	103
Fannin	1,268	2.6	36,826	174	Kendall	3,690	1.5	83,808	1
Fayette	1,234	3.2	48,833	38	Kenedy	17	-0.1	41,297	100
Fisher	141	-0.7	36,259	189	Kent	37	3.9	48,558	39
Floyd	229	18.7	39,067	138	Kerr	2,446	1.8	47,288	49
Foard	46	2.7	37,809	157	Kimble	181	-5.7	41,007	104
Fort Bend	41,690	0.0	54,510	23	King	11	-26.6	37,689	158
Franklin	413	4.6	38,351	146	Kinney	108	-1.0	28,964	243
Freestone	700	0.8	35,681	193	Kleberg	1,154	3.1	37,123	169
Frio	518	-0.2	26,421	252	Knox	136	0.8	36,564	184
Gaines	758	10.6	36,750	178	Lamar	2,014	4.2	40,610	110
Galveston	16,443	1.1	49,079	35	Lamb	508	11.8	38,465	145
Garza	173	-2.3	26,482	251	Lampasas	1,011	1.5	48,098	41
Gillespie	1,529	1.8	57,382	15	La Salle	263	0.1	34,696	202
Glasscock	105	13.8	78,012	2	Lavaca	961	1.7	47,880	44
Goliad	309	-0.5	40,890	105	Lee	773	4.3	44,991	62
Gonzales	860	6.4	41,154	102	Leon	655	1.9	37,988	154
Gray	936	7.1	41,781	94	Liberty	2,998	0.8	35,840	191
Grayson	5,409	2.1	41,250	101	Limestone	799	2.4	33,945	213
Gregg	5,437	1.0	44,073	73	Lipscomb	185	12.1	54,838	21
Grimes	945	1.8	33,661	216	Live Oak	392	-0.6	32,196	229
Guadalupe	6,868	1.9	43,019	78	Llano	993	1.2	46,826	54
Hale	1,085	5.8	31,778	232	Loving	6	-4.6	45,858	58
Hall	92	11.3	30,033	238	Lubbock	12,646	2.7	41,433	98
Hamilton	479	0.6	56,845	16	Lynn	203	11.5	34,704	201
Hansford	331	11.0	60,759	9	Madison	426	2.3	29,957	242
Hardeman	152	0.8	38,151	152	Marion	367	2.6	36,419	186
Hardin	2,540	2.0	44,456	69	Martin	263	5.0	46,781	55
Harris	247,482	3.9	53,188	25	Mason	178	5.7	42,113	89
Harrison	2,671	1.5	40,068	118	Matagorda	1,504	3.0	40,827	107
Hartley	354	14.3	62,274	7	Maverick	1,667	2.7	28,636	244
Haskell	199	2.3	34,682	203	McCulloch	298	7.0	37,492	164
Hays	8,987	2.6	41,902	92	McLennan	9,985	2.8	39,740	124
Hemphill	212	-8.5	52,632	26	McMullen	46	-14.8	58,513	13
Henderson	3,098	2.1	38,216	148	Medina	1,912	2.5	38,189	150
Hidalgo	22,047	1.1	25,617	253	Menard	75	-4.9	35,475	195
Hill	1,345	2.3	37,502	163	Midland	12,379	-2.1	75,002	4
Hockley	859	-1.1	37,199	167	Milam	920	1.1	36,731	179

County	Total Income ($ mil)	% change 16 / 17	Per capita income	Rank in State	County	Total Income ($ mil)	% change 16 / 17	Per capita income	Rank in State
Mills	181	1.6	36,789	176	Sherman	199	15.5	64,897	5
Mitchell	254	2.1	30,037	237	Smith	10,749	0.9	47,200	51
Montague	764	2.7	39,085	136	Somervell	397	3.8	44,871	64
Montgomery	32,877	2.5	57,585	14	Starr	1,610	0.5	24,981	254
Moore	894	4.4	40,454	115	Stephens	347	–3.1	37,189	168
Morris	527	4.8	42,249	87	Sterling	67	1.2	52,080	27
Motley	35	–2.5	28,447	245	Stonewall	68	3.9	48,863	37
Nacogdoches	2,387	3.4	36,398	187	Sutton	221	7.6	58,599	12
Navarro	1,800	1.9	36,960	172	Swisher	335	12.7	44,632	68
Newton	437	2.6	31,306	234	Tarrant	97,639	1.2	47,525	46
Nolan	595	4.2	40,256	117	Taylor	5,905	1.7	43,329	76
Nueces	15,125	3.0	41,873	93	Terrell	39	–7.0	48,058	43
Ochiltree	506	0.4	50,251	32	Terry	415	12.9	32,649	225
Oldham	102	–4.0	48,409	40	Throckmorton	52	–5.6	33,732	214
Orange	3,692	1.9	43,412	75	Titus	1,099	2.3	33,406	219
Palo Pinto	1,057	1.6	36,987	171	Tom Green	5,038	1.7	42,688	81
Panola	939	4.8	40,411	116	Travis	76,306	4.0	62,205	8
Parker	6,931	2.4	51,930	28	Trinity	504	1.1	34,383	207
Parmer	465	12.5	47,274	50	Tyler	680	0.8	31,551	233
Pecos	523	3.2	33,461	218	Upshur	1,436	1.4	34,783	198
Polk	1,878	0.0	38,210	149	Upton	144	3.6	39,222	132
Potter	4,873	–0.3	40,456	114	Uvalde	998	0.4	36,797	175
Presidio	280	–1.5	39,183	134	Val Verde	1,709	1.0	34,732	200
Rains	381	–1.0	32,379	227	Van Zandt	2,022	2.3	36,649	181
Randall	6,281	1.6	46,718	56	Victoria	3,912	1.0	42,484	84
Reagan	150	4.7	40,496	112	Walker	1,972	1.0	27,302	249
Real	117	2.7	34,198	211	Waller	1,924	0.1	37,508	162
Red River	482	0.4	39,414	129	Ward	477	10.8	41,579	96
Reeves	502	8.6	32,859	224	Washington	1,673	–1.0	47,741	45
Refugio	300	6.9	41,496	97	Webb	8,246	0.9	30,008	239
Roberts	37	2.4	39,397	130	Wharton	1,701	2.2	40,535	111
Robertson	677	1.5	39,350	131	Wheeler	209	4.7	38,978	139
Rockwall	5,683	3.3	58,717	11	Wichita	5,284	–0.1	40,034	119
Runnels	403	2.4	39,215	133	Wilbarger	505	2.0	39,542	128
Rusk	1,876	2.6	35,508	194	Willacy	649	11.5	30,047	236
Sabine	370	3.4	35,371	196	Williamson	26,332	3.2	48,091	42
San Augustine	316	6.1	38,277	147	Wilson	2,082	1.9	42,219	88
San Jacinto	953	1.3	33,712	215	Winkler	325	11.9	42,940	79
San Patricio	2,880	2.8	42,852	80	Wise	2,735	1.5	41,321	99
San Saba	218	–1.0	36,596	182	Wood	1,658	2.4	37,426	165
Schleicher	108	–10.2	35,836	192	Yoakum	341	16.4	39,807	123
Scurry	640	–1.0	37,542	161	Young	816	–1.4	45,405	59
Shackelford	259	–6.0	77,918	3	Zapata	391	6.4	27,325	248
Shelby	983	7.9	38,554	143	Zavala	331	3.6	27,695	247

8 Largest States' Unemployment Rates

Rank	State	April 2019	March 2019	Monthly Change
1.	Florida	3.4 %	3.5 %	– 1.0 %
2.	**Texas**	**3.7 %**	**3.8 %**	**– 1.0 %**
3.	Georgia	3.8 %	3.9 %	– 1.0 %
4.	Pennsylvania	3.8 %	3.9 %	– 1.0 %
5.	New York	3.9 %	3.9 %	0.0 %
6.	North Carolina	4.0 %	4.0 %	0.0 %
7.	Michigan	4.1 %	4.0 %	0.1 %
8.	California	4.3 %	4.3 %	0.0 %

Source: Texas Workforce Commission. April 2019.

Average Work Hours and Earnings

The following table compares the **average weekly earnings**, **hours worked per week**, and **average hourly wage** in Texas for production workers in selected industries in April 2017 and April 2018. Figures are provided by the Texas Workforce Commission.

Industry	Average Weekly Earnings		Average Weekly Hours		Average Hourly Earnings	
	April 2018	April 2017	April 2018	April 2017	April 2018	April 2017
Mining and Logging	$ 1,277.46	$ 1,188.14	45.3	44.6	$ 28.20	$ 26.64
Mining (including Oil & Gas)	1,283.68	1,185.91	45.2	44.6	28.40	26.59
Manufacturing	1,017.12	986.62	43.3	42.6	23.49	23.16
Durable Goods	1,145.88	1,063.42	44.5	42.3	25.75	25.14
Fabricated Metal Product Mfg.	1,026.48	869.46	47.0	43.3	21.84	20.08
Nondurable Goods	788.16	852.52	41.2	43.1	19.13	19.78
Trade, Transportation, Utilities						
Wholesale Trade	1,023.00	944.15	42.2	40.4	24.83	23.37
Machinery, Equipment, Supplies	1,048.71	1,067.24	41.5	42.1	25.27	25.35
Retail Trade						
Auto Dealers/Parts	648.49	621.33	36.7	36.7	17.67	16.93
Building Material/Garden Equip.	462.35	499.46	32.4	34.0	14.27	14.69
Food/Beverage Stores	413.62	384.62	33.6	33.1	12.31	11.62
Gasoline Stations	377.48	376.88	32.5	34.2	11.63	11.02
Clothing/Accessories Stores	278.41	256.46	21.4	20.8	13.01	12.33

Employment in Texas by Industry

Employment in Texas reached 12,727,600 in April 2019, up 294,200 jobs since April 2018. The following table shows Texas Workforce Commission estimates of the nonagricultural labor force by industry for April 2019 and the percent change during the year in the number employed. *Source: Texas Workforce Commission. Additional information available at the website twc. texas.gov*

Industry	April 2019	Monthly Change	Annual Change	Annual % Change
Total Nonagricultural	12,727,600	28,900	294,200	2.4
Private	10,768,900	28,700	283,000	2.7
Goods-Producing	1,928,500	8,800	80,500	4.4
Mining & Logging (oil, gas)	257,500	2,700	16,400	6.8
Construction	766,500	5,800	32,500	4.4
Manufacturing	904,500	300	31,600	3.6
Service-Providing	10,799,100	20,100	213,700	2.0
Trade, Transportation, Utilities	2,510,800	800	35,000	1.4
Information	202,000	− 100	− 1,400	− 0.7
Financial Activities	793,400	3,400	20,900	2.7
Professional & Business Services	1,766,900	8,400	45,900	2.7
Education & Health Services	1,729,900	4,300	42,300	3.4
Leisure & Hospitality	1,391,700	3,200	45,500	3.4
Other Services	445,700	− 100	14,300	3.3
Government	1,958,700	200	11,200	0.6

Help Wanted: Top Online Postings of Job Vacancies

Occupation	April 2019	March 2019	Employer	April 2019	March 2019
Registered Nurses	20,668	19,131	HCA - Healthcare Company	4,576	4,411
Software Developers	19,202	17,518	University of Texas System	3,952	3,697
Supervisors, Retail	14,609	12,805	Family Dollar	3,641	1,206
Retail Sales	13,890	12,991	Christus Health	3,321	3,096
Customer Service	11,191	9,538	Robert Half International	3,204	3,350
Truck Drivers	10,509	10,067	Baylor Scott & White Health	2,821	2,682
Maintenance/Repair	7,726	7,218	Pizza Hut	2,526	2,528

Source: Texas Workforce Commission from Conference Board Help Wanted Online Data Series.

Largest Banks Operating in Texas by Asset Size

Source: Texas Department of Banking, December 31, 2018
Abbreviations: NA, not available; N.A. National Association.

	Name	City	Class	Assets	Loans
				(thousands of dollars)	
1	JP Morgan Chase Bank	New York NY	National	$ 180,252,645	NA
2	Bank of America	Charlotte NC	National	121,074,038	NA
3	USAA Federal Savings Bank	San Antonio	State	81,620,818	$ 46,135,612
4	Wells Fargo Bank	San Francisco CA	National	72,632,829	NA
5	Comerica Bank	Dallas	State	70,737,276	50,162,764
6	Compass Bank	Birmingham AL	State	38,706,859	NA
7	Frost Bank	San Antonio	State	32,355,408	14,099,733
8	Texas Capital Bank N.A.	Dallas	National	28,246,367	22,560,574
9	Prosperity Bank	El Campo	State	22,689,286	10,340,946
10	ZB (formerly Zion First National)	Salt Lake City UT	National	10,969,210	NA
11	PlainsCapital Bank	Dallas	State	10,105,549	6,352,095
12	Independent Bank	McKinney	State	9,842,314	7,881,957
13	Capital One	New Orleans LA	National	9,129,641	NA
14	LegacyTexas Bank	Plano	State	9,058,559	7,761,524
15	International Bank of Commerce	Laredo	National	8,469,038	4,862,164
16	NexBank SSB	Dallas	National	8,305,036	4,714,229
17	First Financial Bank N.A.	Abilene	National	7,703,083	3,953,635
18	Wells Fargo Bank South Central N.A.	Houston	National	7,137,879	751,533
19	Branch Banking & Trust	Winston-Salem NC	State	6,285,058	NA
20	Southside Bank	Tyler	State	6,117,745	3,312,799
21	BOKF	Tulsa OK	National	6,024,038	NA
22	Woodforest National Bank	The Woodlands	National	5,923,725	4,621,673
23	Allegiance Bank	Houston	State	4,653,896	3,708,306
24	TBK Bank SSB	Dallas	State	4,524,838	3,597,849
25	Amarillo National Bank	Amarillo	National	4,367,991	3,393,578
26	Cadence Bank N.A.	Birmingham AL	National	4,190,000	NA
27	Citibank	Sioux Falls SD	National	4,183,000	NA
28	Broadway National Bank	San Antonio	National	3,653,723	2,074,953
29	Regions Bank	Birmingham AL	State	3,648,905	NA
30	Happy State Bank	Happy	State	3,444,514	2,385,061
31	CommunityBank of Texas N.A.	Beaumont	National	3,280,197	2,446,823
32	Veritex Community Bank	Dallas	State	3,207,962	2,555,494
33	American National Bank of Texas	Terrell	National	3,156,040	1,930,480
34	Inwood National Bank	Dallas	National	2,817,297	1,786,134
35	First United Bank & Trust	Durant OK	State	2,772,332	NA
36	City Bank	Lubbock	State	2,710,801	1,957,197
37	Texas Bank and Trust Company	Longview	State	2,528,019	2,112,727
38	TIB The Independent BankersBank	Farmers Branch	State	2,513,109	1,062,314
39	VeraBank N.A.	Henderson	National	2,308,542	1,369,932
40	Guaranty Bank & Trust N.A.	Mount Pleasant	National	2,266,909	1,660,095
41	Iberia Bank	Lafayette LA	State	2,265,341	NA
42	Bancorp South Bank	Tupelo MS	State	2,212,340	NA
43	Lone Star National Bank	Pharr	National	2,209,580	1,166,786
44	Beal Bank SSB	Plano	State	2,123,922	1,155,091
45	Bank of the Ozarks	Little Rock AR	State	2,123,922	NA
46	Vantage Bank Texas	San Antonio	State	1,916,572	1,470,284
47	BTH Bank N.A.	Quitman	National	1,915,036	1,302,216
48	Jefferson Bank	San Antonio	State	1,905,588	1,312,131
49	First National Bank Texas	Killeen	National	1,874,272	958,060
50	WestStar Bank	El Paso	State	1,823,484	1,251,155

Deposits/Assets of Commercial Banks by County

Source: Federal Reserve Bank of Dallas as of Dec. 31, 2018.
(thousands of dollars)

County	Banks	Deposits	Assets	County	Banks	Deposits	Assets
Andrews	2	$ 786,813	$ 891,775	El Paso	2	1,762,700	2,069,095
Angelina	1	209,518	253,557	Erath	1	80,827	90,526
Atascosa	2	156,141	179,741	Fannin	1	86,664	99,674
Austin	5	2,247,370	2,640,246	Fayette	4	1,234,697	1,386,252
Bailey	1	82,066	95,914	Fisher	1	72,316	79,543
Bandera	2	200,559	222,443	Floyd	1	98,753	110,149
Bastrop	2	732,743	832,163	Foard	1	35,591	39,756
Baylor	1	144,154	164,051	Franklin	1	137,570	191,004
Bee	1	394,903	434,881	Frio	2	651,437	747,255
Bell	4	3,272,585	3,878,149	Galveston	4	2,443,359	2,818,052
Bexar	8	35,295,268	41,739,510	Gillespie	1	856,602	1,027,574
Blanco	1	103,668	118,188	Gonzales	1	358,672	405,478
Bosque	2	212,576	235,388	Gray	1	46,957	55,419
Bowie	2	403,265	457,687	Grayson	3	531,304	603,838
Brazoria	7	1,064,722	1,202,395	Gregg	3	2,738,363	3,154,115
Brazos	2	1,376,265	1,702,781	Grimes	2	286,326	329,785
Briscoe	1	48,994	58,522	Guadalupe	3	740,993	840,515
Brooks	1	70,721	78,668	Hale	1	28,433	41,842
Brown	2	597,258	692,419	Hall	1	52,154	60,348
Burleson	1	518,430	585,429	Hansford	3	383,962	442,146
Burnet	1	216,982	246,255	Hardeman	1	54,058	59,433
Caldwell	2	299,387	337,880	Harris	17	19,229,546	22,831,273
Calhoun	1	288,038	317,838	Harrison	1	196,806	219,573
Callahan	1	361,301	417,210	Haskell	1	61,248	69,714
Cameron	4	2,035,806	2,399,293	Henderson	2	511,511	574,094
Camp	1	456,470	574,188	Hidalgo	5	2,837,932	3,245,212
Carson	1	31,919	35,898	Hill	1	147,021	174,653
Cass	2	418,016	485,983	Hockley	2	169,732	189,546
Castro	1	1,108,104	1,315,753	Hood	2	552,532	621,225
Chambers	1	107,951	121,100	Hopkins	2	1,287,599	1,468,635
Cherokee	2	1,939,996	2,323,662	Houston	3	149,554	171,239
Childress	1	100,825	109,158	Howard	1	355,314	392,240
Coke	1	35,596	41,227	Hunt	1	45,217	49,406
Coleman	2	146,726	164,425	Irion	1	413,042	443,331
Collin	4	15,351,268	19,740,097	Jack	1	214,449	240,334
Collingsworth	1	346,069	397,725	Jackson	1	52,037	55,733
Colorado	4	429,944	509,599	Jasper	1	224,576	257,831
Comanche	1	84,215	92,919	Jeff Davis	1	77,685	85,847
Concho	2	180,945	205,992	Jefferson	1	2,811,864	3,280,197
Cooke	2	1,105,043	1,257,696	Jim Hogg	1	77,858	93,485
Coryell	2	628,133	702,303	Johnson	1	183,874	202,974
Cottle	1	45,174	49,436	Jones	1	57,552	62,995
Crockett	1	226,569	255,317	Karnes	2	742,308	820,886
Crosby	2	744,025	854,498	Kaufman	2	2,934,672	3,243,517
Dallas	24	98,710,887	124,594,733	Kendall	1	131,506	147,556
Dawson	1	317,970	350,327	Kerr	1	144,894	159,550
Deaf Smith	1	148,705	169,091	Kimble	2	104,219	114,513
Delta	2	70,832	82,931	Kleberg	1	439,043	528,374
Denton	4	1,014,778	1,154,602	Lamar	3	503,771	598,254
DeWitt	2	373,066	426,164	Lamb	1	1,232,126	1,401,066
Dickens	1	40,782	45,300	Lampasas	1	120,111	137,448
Dimmit	1	65,660	75,849	La Salle	1	87,693	98,237
Donley	1	35,155	42,941	Lavaca	2	901,613	1,014,153
Duval	2	95,912	108,840	Lee	1	188,031	209,953
Ector	2	741,013	835,144	Leon	2	904,919	1,029,838
Edwards	1	69,285	79,024	Liberty	1	265,398	307,164
Ellis	4	1,329,849	1,514,241	Limestone	2	263,888	305,100

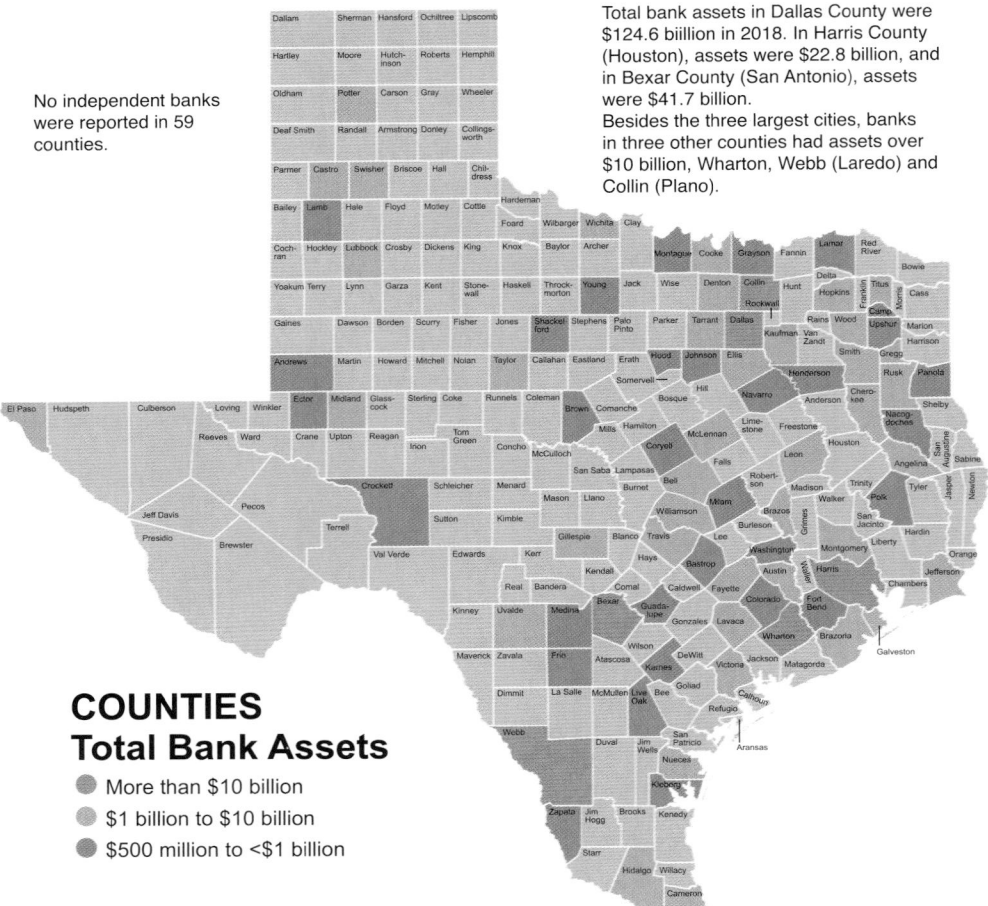

Total bank assets in Dallas County were $124.6 biillion in 2018. In Harris County (Houston), assets were $22.8 billion, and in Bexar County (San Antonio), assets were $41.7 billion.
Besides the three largest cities, banks in three other counties had assets over $10 billion, Wharton, Webb (Laredo) and Collin (Plano).

No independent banks were reported in 59 counties.

COUNTIES
Total Bank Assets
- ⬤ More than $10 billion
- ◯ $1 billion to $10 billion
- ⬤ $500 million to <$1 billion

County	Banks	Deposits	Assets
Live Oak	2	473,387	541,096
Llano	2	324,676	364,865
Lubbock	9	7,202,629	8,437,114
Lynn	1	48,239	53,804
Martin	1	204,361	223,418
Mason	2	139,674	170,695
McCulloch	2	246,566	275,947
McLennan	12	3,601,061	4,121,667
Medina	3	544,978	615,950
Menard	1	31,988	36,668
Midland	5	4,546,544	5,152,536
Milam	3	753,409	865,275
Mills	1	284,812	315,242
Mitchell	1	113,904	125,272
Montague	1	600,346	694,569
Montgomery	1	5,338,201	5,923,725
Morris	2	174,566	229,772
Nacogdoches	1	649,877	727,918
Navarro	4	865,304	999,160
Nolan	2	266,816	296,100
Nueces	5	2,322,016	2,636,085
Ochiltree	1	150,362	172,423
Orange	1	190,459	208,340

County	Banks	Deposits	Assets
Palo Pinto	1	90,435	105,391
Panola	2	473,116	603,570
Parker	2	533,691	592,673
Parmer	1	140,134	158,719
Pecos	2	352,805	388,375
Polk	3	719,847	843,224
Potter	3	4,930,457	5,774,064
Presidio	1	111,062	129,531
Randall	1	140,739	159,818
Rockwall	1	56,079	62,457
Runnels	3	354,889	393,200
Rusk	2	2,463,609	2,805,100
Sabine	1	53,507	61,500
San Jacinto	2	147,118	162,736
San Patricio	1	126,919	142,889
San Saba	1	52,416	60,969
Schleicher	1	50,905	60,537
Scurry	2	217,249	246,149
Shackelford	1	516,595	592,295
Shelby	2	395,923	455,099
Sherman	1	211,463	244,798
Smith	4	5,420,176	7,478,325
Starr	1	71,385	84,166

County	Banks	Deposits	Assets
Sterling	1	173,449	183,532
Stonewall	1	57,348	67,891
Sutton	1	340,941	423,400
Swisher	2	2,902,560	3,488,531
Tarrant	9	3,270,178	3,860,943
Taylor	3	6,407,214	7,846,262
Titus	2	1,963,071	2,367,052
Tom Green	1	235,462	270,620
Travis	3	242,106	315,275
Trinity	1	52,297	57,825
Tyler	1	129,181	144,198
Upshur	2	510,368	587,879
Uvalde	1	1,589,321	1,734,034
Val Verde	1	23,455	28,288
Van Zandt	1	125,454	145,753

County	Banks	Deposits	Assets
Walker	1	412,049	469,922
Ward	1	157,971	176,873
Washington	4	763,614	860,573
Webb	4	8,811,325	11,650,632
Wharton	3	18,334,982	23,884,829
Wheeler	1	66,550	75,402
Wichita	4	1,796,545	2,130,172
Wilbarger	1	248,340	294,284
Williamson	4	1,249,028	1,396,930
Wilson	1	41,929	51,535
Wise	2	240,164	279,433
Wood	2	1,551,311	2,052,193
Young	3	650,882	767,275
Zapata	2	378,887	513,078
Zavala	1	56,042	64,839

Texas Total Bank Resources and Deposits: 1905–2018

On Dec. 31, 2018, Texas had 409 national and state banks, the lowest number since our records began in 1905. In 1986, the number of independent banks in the state peaked at 1,972. In 2018, total assets were the highest ever at nearly $400 billion. Deposits peaked in 2018 at $328.9 billion. *Source: Federal Reserve Bank of Dallas.*

Date	National Banks			State Banks			Combined Total		
	No. Banks	Assets (add 000)	Deposits (add 000)	No. Banks	Assets (add 000)	Deposits (add 000)	No. Banks	Assets (add 000)	Deposits (add 000)
Sept. 30, 1905	440	$ 189,484	$ 101,285	29	$ 4,341	$ 2,213	469	$ 193,825	$ 103,498
Nov. 10, 1910	516	293,245	145,249	621	88,103	59,766	1,137	381,348	205,015
Dec. 29, 1920	556	780,246	564,135	1,031	391,127	280,429	1,587	1,171,373	844,564
Dec. 31, 1930	560	1,028,420	826,723	655	299,012	231,909	1,215	1,327,432	1,058,632
Dec. 31, 1940	446	1,695,662	1,534,702	393	227,866	179,027	839	1,923,528	1,713,729
Dec. 31, 1950	442	6,467,275	6,076,006	449	1,427,680	1,338,540	891	7,894,955	7,414,546
Dec. 31, 1960	468	10,520,690	9,560,668	532	2,997,609	2,735,726	1,000	13,518,299	12,296,394
Dec. 31, 1970	530	22,087,890	18,384,922	653	8,907,039	7,958,133	1,183	30,994,929	26,343,055
Dec. 31, 1980	641	75,540,334	58,378,669	825	35,186,113	31,055,648	1,466	110,726,447	89,434,317
Dec. 31, 1985	1,058	144,674,908	111,903,178	878	64,349,869	56,392,634	1,936	209,024,777	168,295,812
Dec. 31, 1986	1,077	141,397,037	106,973,189	895	65,989,944	57,739,091	1,972	207,386,981	164,712,280
Dec. 31, 1987	953	135,690,678	103,930,262	812	54,361,514	47,283,855	1,765	190,052,192	151,214,117
Dec. 31, 1988	802	130,310,243	106,740,461	690	40,791,310	36,655,253	1,492	171,101,553	143,395,714
Dec. 31, 1989	687	133,163,016	104,091,836	626	40,893,848	36,652,675	1,313	174,056,864	140,744,511
Dec. 31, 1990	605	125,808,263	103,573,445	578	45,021,304	40,116,662	1,183	170,829,567	143,690,107
Dec. 31, 1993	502	139,409,250	111,993,205	510	44,566,815	39,190,373	1,012	183,976,065	151,183,578
Dec. 31, 1994	481	140,374,540	111,881,041	502	47,769,694	41,522,943	983	188,144,234	153,403,984
Dec. 31, 1995	456	152,750,093	112,557,468	479	49,967,946	42,728,454	935	202,718,039	155,285,922
Dec. 31, 1996	432	152,299,695	122,242,990	445	52,868,263	45,970,674	877	205,167,958	168,213,664
Dec. 31, 1997	417	180,252,942	145,588,677	421	54,845,186	46,202,808	838	235,098,128	191,791,485
Dec. 31, 1998	402	128,609,813	106,704,893	395	50,966,996	42,277,367	797	179,576,809	148,982,260
Dec. 31, 1999	380	128,878,607	99,383,776	373	52,266,148	42,579,986	753	181,144,755	141,963,762
Dec. 31, 2000	358	112,793,856	88,591,657	351	53,561,550	43,835,525	709	166,355,406	132,427,182
Dec. 31, 2001	342	85,625,768	72,812,548	344	59,047,520	47,843,799	686	144,673,288	120,656,347
Dec. 31, 2002	332	95,308,420	79,183,418	337	62,093,220	49,715,186	669	157,401,640	128,898,604
Dec. 31, 2003	316	75,003,613	62,567,943	337	61,448,617	49,790,333	653	136,452,230	112,358,276
Dec. 31, 2004	311	82,333,800	67,977,669	328	69,127,411	54,950,601	639	151,461,211	122,928,270
Dec. 31, 2005	302	96,505,262	77,688,463	324	76,697,256	61,257,128	626	173,202,518	138,945,591
Dec. 31, 2006	286	97,936,270	79,389,737	322	83,910,356	66,132,394	608	181,846,626	145,522,131
Dec. 31, 2007	282	107,260,539	83,637,302	330	154,283,181	114,537,280	612	261,543,720	198,174,582
Dec. 31, 2008	267	108,816,852	84,802,191	327	164,658,101	115,186,285	594	273,474,953	199,988,476
Dec. 31, 2009	263	153,639,579	109,552,071	318	162,958,865	120,962,911	581	316,598,444	230,514,982
Dec. 31, 2010	253	149,498,073	120,827,780	314	162,772,458	127,925,865	567	312,270,531	248,753,645
Dec. 31, 2011	250	159,621,331	129,799,399	302	169,525,070	137,180,187	552	329,146,401	266,979,586
Dec. 31, 2012	227	156,392,247	139,945,006	293	205,788,318	169,156,089	520	362,180,565	302,101,095
Dec. 31, 2013	211	138,785,446	118,373,970	283	216,540,710	181,010,324	494	355,326,156	299,384,294
Dec. 31, 2014	203	128,134,221	108,506,074	267	235,388,932	197,078,456	470	363,523,153	305,584,530
Dec. 31, 2015	195	117,391,368	99,420,411	252	246,932,641	204,350,121	477	364,324,009	303,770,532
Dec. 31, 2016	186	122,431,838	104,027,309	244	254,560,238	208,323,981	430	376,992,076	312,351,290
Dec. 31, 2017	183	133,291,358	111,896,128	240	259,417,028	212,732,825	423	392,708,386	324,628,953
Dec. 31, 2018	176	$137,477,382	$114,245,832	233	$262,400,881	$214,562,067	409	$399,878,263	$328,907,699

Texas State Banks

Consolidated Statement, Foreign and Domestic
Offices, as of Dec. 31, 2018
Source: Federal Reserve Bank of Dallas

Number of Banks	233
(thousands of dollars)	

Assets

Cash and balances due from banks:
Non-interest-bearing balances
and currency and coin .... $ 4,962,045
Interest-bearing balances 13,098,333
Held-to-maturity securities 13,547,370
Available-for-sale securities 47,367,624
Equity securities not held for trading 54,182
Federal funds sold in domestic offices 1,365,496
Securities purchases under agreements to resell 11,642
Loans and lease financing receivables:
Loans and leases held for sale 1,665,108
Loans and leases held for investment...........163,989,470
Less: allowance for loan and lease losses....... 1,811,630
Loans and leases, net 162,177,840
Trading Assets 141,420
Premises and fixed assets............................. 3,902,016
Other real estate owned 178,289
Investments in unconsolidated subsidiaries
and associated companies. 49,909
Direct/indirect investments in real estate ventures... 12,944
Intangible assets..6,070,415
Other assets 7,796,248

Total Assets .... **$ 262,400,881**

Liabilities

Deposits:
In domestic offices .... $ 214,164,380
Non-interest-bearing.................................... 79,784,426
Interest-bearing 134,379,960
In foreign offices, edge & agreement subsidiaries
and IBFs... 497,687
Non-interest-bearing.......................................264,633
Interest-bearing balances.............................. 233,054
Federal funds purchased and securities sold under
agreements to repurchase:
funds in domestic offices......................................451,840
securities sold under agreement to repurchase .2,280,725
Trading liabilities 299,103
Other borrowed money (mortgages/leases)......... 9,615,243
Subordinated notes and debentures 580,055
Other liabilities.. 2,000,675

Total Liabilities .... **$ 229,889,708**

Equity Capital

Perpetual preferred stock .... $ 4,906
Common stock.. 482,034
Surplus (exclude surplus related to
preferred stock) 16,457,220
Retained earnings 16,645,362
Accumulated other comprehensive income........ −1,077,974
Other equity capital components..............................−7,519
Total bank equity capital 32,504,029
Minority interest in cons. subsidiaries.............. 7,144

Total Equity Capital .... **$ 32,511,173**

Total liabilities, minority interest and
equity capital .... **$ 262,400,881**

Texas National Banks

Consolidated Statement, Foreign and Domestic
Offices, as of Dec. 31, 2018
Source: Federal Reserve Bank of Dallas

Number of Banks	176
(thousands of dollars)	

Assets

Cash and balances due from banks:
Non-interest-bearing balances
and currency and coin .... $ 2,708,378
Interest-bearing balances.............................. 9,238,424
Held-to-maturity securities 2,771,738
Available-for-sale securities 21,161,149
Equity securities not held for trading 37,944
Federal funds sold in domestic offices 3,375,562
Securities purchases under agreements to resell 125,000
Loans and lease financing receivables:
Loans and leases held for sale 5,646,116
Loans and leases held for investment............. 87,674,263
Less: allowance for loan and lease losses........ 1,005,273
Loans and leases, net of allowance 86,668,990
Trading Assets 27,594
Premises and fixed assets................................... 1,595,444
Other real estate owned 74,985
Investments in unconsolidated subsidiaries
and associated companies..................................29,807
Direct/indirect investments in real estate ventures...... 2,099
Intangible assets..847,772
Other assets 3,166,380

Total Assets .... **$ 137,477,382**

Liabilities

Deposits:
In domestic offices .... $ 114,245,638
Non-interest-bearing.................................... 30,220,646
Interest-bearing 84,024,992
In foreign offices, edge & agreement subsidiaries
and IBFs... 0
Non-interest-bearing.......................................0
Interest-bearing balances..............................0
Federal funds purchased and securities sold under
agreements to repurchase:
funds in domestic offices......................................792,297
securities sold under agreement to repurchase 883,402
Trading liabilities 21,011
Other borrowed money (mortgages/leases)..........5,861,778
Subordinated notes and debentures 223,153
Other liabilities.. 975,172

Total Liabilities .... **$ 123,002,451**

Equity Capital

Perpetual preferred stock .... $ 160,750
Common stock.. 357,986
Surplus (exclude surplus related to
preferred stock) 4,607,653
Retained earnings 9,621,463
Accumulated other comprehensive income.......... − 278,689
Other equity capital components............................. − 7,973
Total bank equity capital 14,461,190
Minority interest in consolidated subsidiaries 13,741

Total Equity Capital .... **$ 14,474,937**

Total liabilities, minority interest and
equity capital .... **$ 137,477,382**

Savings and Loan Associations in Texas

This table includes all thrifts that are not also classified as banks under federal law: that is, it includes federal savings and loan associations and federal savings banks. *Source: Texas Department of Savings and Mortgage Lending.*

Year ending	Number of Inst.	Total Assets	Mortgage Loans	Cash/ Securities	Deposits	FHLB/ Borrowed Money	†Net Worth
				(in thousands of dollars)			
Dec. 31, 2018	5	$ 83,782,803	$ 6,020,272	$ 43,883,996	$ 73,570,292	$ 153,368	$ 8,284,160
Dec. 31, 2017	5	82,642,161	7,155,350	41,128,877	73,813,038	62,068	7,559,159
Dec. 31, 2016	6	80,671,509	48,621,797	29,471,795	73,504,651	349,316	7,166,859
Dec. 31, 2015	6	73,722,445	47,512,693	24,727,034	65,397,606	213,039	6,703,177
Dec. 31, 2014	8	71,253,195	45,943,853	29,164,768	62,899,043	379,957	6,470,089
Dec. 31, 2013	8	66,605,862	41,812,008	34,083,458	59,101,594	196,784	5,941,114
Dec. 31, 2012	12	64,448,340	41,967,892	20,925,955	57,004,423	579,846	5,645,916
Dec. 31, 2011	12	57,857,491	40,757,220	15,671,590	50,819,345	657,598	5,079,133
Dec. 31, 2010	19	53,980,441	17,005,657	14,230,550	46,935,007	987,211	4,840,466
Dec. 31, 2009	19	46,524,327	17,810,587	9,702,023	40,272,742	973,610	4,254,794
Dec. 31, 2008	22	87,572,855	49,816,471	31,763,898	52,606,655	27,137,730	6,582,759
Dec. 31, 2005	19	55,755,096	42,027,293	9,140,789	30,565,411	11,299,136	4,228,103
Dec. 31, 2000	25	55,709,391	43,515,610	1,512,444	28,914,234	17,093,369	4,449,097
Dec. 31, 1995	45	52,292,519	27,509,933	5,971,364	28,635,799	15,837,632	3,827,249
Dec. 31, 1994	50	50,014,102	24,148,760	6,790,416	29,394,433	15,973,056	3,447,110
Dec. 31, 1990 §	131	72,041,456	27,475,664	20,569,770	56,994,387	17,738,041	–4,566,656
Conservatorship	51	14,952,402	6,397,466	2,188,820	16,581,525	4,304,033	–6,637,882
Privately Owned	80	57,089,054	21,078,198	18,380,950	40,412,862	13,434,008	2,071,226
Dec. 31, 1989 §	196	90,606,100	37,793,043	21,218,130	70,823,464	27,158,238	–9,356,209
Conservatorship	81	22,159,752	11,793,445	2,605,080	25,381,494	7,103,657	–10,866,213
Privately Owned	115	68,446,348	25,999,598	18,613,050	45,441,970	20,054,581	1,510,004
Dec. 31, 1988	204	110,499,276	50,920,006	26,181,917	83,950,314	28,381,573	–4,088,355
Dec. 31, 1985	273	91,798,890	60,866,666	10,426,464	72,806,067	13,194,147	3,903,611
Dec. 31, 1980	318	$ 34,954,129	$ 27,717,383	$ 3,066,791	$ 28,439,210	$ 3,187,638	$ 1,711,201

Texas Savings Banks

The savings bank charter was approved by the Legislature in 1993, and the first savings bank was chartered in 1994. Savings banks operate similarly to savings and loans associations in that they are housing-oriented lenders. Under federal law a savings bank is categorized as a commercial bank and not a thrift. Therefore savings-bank information is also reported with state and national bank information. *Source: Texas Department of Savings and Mortgage Lending.*

Year ending	Number of Inst.	Total Assets	Mortgage Loans	Cash/ Securities	Deposits	FHLB/ Borrowed Money	†Net Worth
				in thousands of dollars (000)			
Dec. 31, 2018	24	$ 24,434,061	$ 11,003,911	$ 9,104,353	$ 17,635,204	$ 3,653,055	$ 2,877,779
Dec. 31, 2017	24	22,355,393	10,721,196	7,199,404	16,479,408	3,194,283	2,462,036
Dec. 31, 2016	28	18,715,828	13,394,235	2,937,083	14,032,907	1,813,466	2,679,435
Dec. 31, 2015	28	13,790,890	10,291,788	2,597,416	10,218,604	1,199,403	2,202,693
Dec. 31, 2014	29	11,031,064	8,211,320	2,947,322	8,257,801	659,216	1,977,443
Dec. 31, 2013	30	10,194,983	7,148,798	3,389,771	7,739,381	499,261	1,812,736
Dec. 31, 2012	30	10,142,623	6,816,212	2,630,941	7,610,074	699,816	1,674,039
Dec. 31, 2011	30	9,530,011	6,132,972	2,650,324	7,247,147	568,547	1,543,269
Dec. 31, 2010	29	8,559,443	4,568,866	4,164,611	6,720,417	332,684	1,329,943
Dec. 31, 2009	29	8,372,892	4,283,372	1,237,215	6,330,896	307,494	1,201,409
Dec. 31, 2008	28	3,988,377	1,980,651	538,162	3,119,082	411,119	434,893
Dec. 31, 2007	26	9,967,678	6,471,833	1,027,709	6,162,709	2,328,467	1,372,231
Dec. 31, 2006	22	9,393,482	6,444,178	836,821	5,721,314	2,453,757	1,138,780
Dec. 31, 2005	19	8,720,497	5,605,678	985,535	5,308,639	1,967,673	1,352,882
Dec. 31, 2004	22	12,981,650	6,035,081	1,654,978	8,377,409	3,000,318	1,482,078
Dec. 31, 2003	23	17,780,413	8,396,606	3,380,565	11,901,441	3,315,544	2,422,317
Dec. 31, 2000	25	11,315,961	9,613,164	514,818	8,644,826	1,455,497	1,059,638
Dec. 31, 1995	13	7,348,647	5,644,591	1,106,557	4,603,026	2,225,793	519,827
Dec. 31, 1994	8	$ 6,347,505	$ 2,825,012	$ 3,139,573	$ 3,227,886	$ 2,628,847	$ 352,363

† Net worth includes permanent stock and paid-in surplus general reserves, surplus and undivided profits. § In 1989 and 1990, the Office of Thrift Supervision, U.S. Department of the Treasury, separated data on savings and loans (thrifts) into two categories: those under the supervision of the Office of Thrift Supervision (Conservatorship Thrifts) and those still under private management (Privately Owned).

Credit Unions: End of 2018

	# Credit Unions	Members	Surplus Funds	Savings	Loans	Assets
Texas	454	9.0 million	$ 21.6 billion	$ 88.8 billion	$ 78.1 billion	$ 104.4 billion
U.S.	5,572	117.5 million	$ 350.6 billion	$ 1,234.8 billion	$ 1,058.9 billion	$ 1,470.8 billion

Sources: Texas Credit Union Department and Credit Union National Association.

	U.S. Credit Union History				**Texas Credit Union History**			
Year	# Credit Unions	Members (million)	Savings ($ billion)	Loans ($ billion)	# Credit Unions	Members (million)	Savings ($ billion)	Loans ($ billion)
2017	5,800	113.6	1,181.0	978.4	NA	8.8	86.1	73.3
2016	6,022	109.2	1,114.4	889.5	NA	8.5	81.7	68.1
2015	6,259	105.0	1.029.1	804.9	478	8.3	77.6	63.2
2014	6,513	101.5	971.2	728.9	490	8.2	73.2	NA
2013	6,795	98.4	930.0	659.4	503	8.1	70.1	55.0
2010	7,605	92.6	804.3	580.3	550	7.5	58.9	43.3
2005	9,198	87.0	591.4	474.2	625	6.8	40.2	32.7
2000	10,860	79.8	380.9	309.3	714	6.5	28.4	22.6
1995	12,230	69.3	278.8	198.4	819	5.4	20.3	14.7
1990	14,549	61.6	201.1	141.3	954	4.4	13.9	8.9
1980	21,465	43.9	61.7	48.7	1,379	3.2	4.8	3.7
1970	23,687	22.8	15.4	14.1	1,435	1.5	1.0	1.0
1960	20,094	12.0	4.8	4.4	1,159	0.7	0.3	0.3
1950	10,586	4.6	0.9	0.7	484	0.2	0.04	0.04

Source: Credit Union National Association.

Credit Unions in Texas

Source: Texas Credit Union Department, National Credit Union Administration, and Credit Union National Association.

Credit unions are chartered at federal and state levels. The National Credit Union Administration (NCUA) is the regulatory agency for the federal-chartered credit unions in Texas.

The Texas Credit Union Department is the regulatory agency for the state-chartered credit unions. It was established in 1969 as a separate agency by the 61st Legislature. In 2018, it supervised 182 active credit unions. These state-chartered credit unions served 3.9 million Texans and had approximately $41.9 billion in assets in 2018.

The department is supervised by the nine-member Texas Credit Union Commission, which is appointed by the governor to staggered terms of six years, with the terms of one-third of the members expiring Feb. 15 of each odd-numbered year.

The Texas Credit Union League was the state association for federal and state credit unions beginning in 1934. It is now called Cornerstone Credit Union League and includes Oklahoma and Arkansas. The league's address is 6801 Parkwood Blvd., Ste. 300, Plano 75024.

The address for the Texas Credit Union Department is 914 East Anderson Lane, Austin 78752. Their website is cud.texas.gov. ☆

Comparison of Texas credit unions
as of Dec. 31, 2018

	State	Federal
No. of instituions	182	272
Total assets	$41.9 billion	$62.2 billion
Asset growth	3.4%	2.0%
Avg. asset size	$230.2 million	$229.8 million
No. with <$5 mil. asset	28	40
Net Income	$363.8 million	$508.6 million

Source: Texas Credit Union Department.

Credit Outstanding by Lenders 2018

	U.S. Outstanding ($ billion)	Market share
Banks / Savings Insti.	$ 1,682.0	42.0%
Finance Companies	534.0	13.3%
Credit Unions	469.2	**11.7%**
Federal Government*	1,236.6	30.8%
Educational Insitutions*	30.4	0.8%
Nonfinancial business	38.6	1.0%
Pools of Securitized Assets	18.3	0.5%
Total	$ 4,009.2	

* Includes student loans. Source: Federal Reserve Board.

Insurance in Texas

Source: 2018 Annual Report, Texas Dept. of Insurance.

The Texas Department of Insurance reported that on Aug. 31, 2018, there were 2,819 entities licensed to handle insurance business in Texas and 641,371 agents and adjusters.

Under reforms in 1993-94, a three-member State Board of Insurance was replaced by the department, with a Commissioner of Insurance appointed by the governor for a two-year term in each odd-numbered year and confirmed by the Texas Senate.

On Sept. 1, 2005, legislation passed by the 79th Legislature took effect, transferring functions of the Texas Workers' Compensation Commission to the department and creating within it the Division of Worker's Compensation.

Also established was the office of Commissioner of Workers' Compensation, appointed by the governor, to enforce and implement the Texas Workers' Compensation Act.

Property/Casualty filings in Texas

A single-form filing submission may contain multiple policy forms and endorsements.

Type form	2015	2016	2017	2018
Personal liability	57	61	55	43
Bond/miscellaneous	327	470	363	304
Certificate of insurance	-	-	12	8
Commercial automobile	498	487	487	286
Commercial property	450	495	437	316
General liability	1,711	1,222	1,348	824
Homeowners	409	311	414	319
Inland marine	415	295	173	169
Identity theft	1	11	13	1
Commercial multi-peril	1,279	1,145	1,082	798
Personal automobile	373	461	431	256
Professional liability	546	584	512	375
Workers' compensation	115	96	103	98
Cyber risk	-	-	15	27
Total filing submissions	**6,386**	**5,786**	**5,588**	**3,930**
Actual forms received	**31,184**	**26,022**	**28,744**	**28,042**

Inspection Operations in Texas

The inspections office of the Texas Department of Insurance oversees amusement rides for building code standards as well as commercial and residential buildings for windstorm compliance.

Windstorm operations	2015	2016	2017	2018
Applications processed	24,773	44,320	33,983	50,341
Inspections completed	8,804	9,276	5,517	6,828
Certificates of compliance	31,734	41,604	32,020	47,784
Amusement ride safety	**2015**	**2016**	**2017**	**2018**
Inspection certif. approved	9,558	9,334	10,521	9,597
Injuries reported	121	110	89	77
Non-compliant operators	169	326	334	301

Agent/adjuster licensing

Licenses, certificates, and registrations.

Agents / Adjusters	2015	2016	2017	2018
Life, accident, health	206,868	226,348	236,521	240,844
Property, casualty	123,103	133,203	139,221	142,146
Adjusters	109,067	119,848	130,855	145,328
Life only	31,427	37,534	42,359	44,477
Total, including other types	**529,509**	**581,834**	**616,957**	**641,371**

Premium Rates Compared

Auto Insurance: Average for Coverage by State, 2019

The U.S. average is $1,355. Maine has the least expensive at 925. Most expensive states listed below:

1. Michigan............................ $ 2,484
2. Louisiana............................ 2,190
3. Florida................................ 1,823
4. Connecticut......................... 1,771
5. New York............................ 1,759
6. Kentucky 1,752
7. Nevada............................... 1,746
8. DC...................................... 1,723
9. Rhode Island...................... 1,688
10. Delaware............................1,646
11. Oklahoma........................... 1,643
12. Pennsylvania.................... 1,522
26. **Texas 1,300**

In dollars, twelve-month rates. Information not available from some states. Source: carinsurance.com.

Homeowners Insurance: Average Premiums by State, 2018

The national average rate was $1,228. Most expensive states listed below:

1. Florida ....$ 3,575
2. Louisiana 2,979
3. Oklahoma 2,651
4. Alabama 2,314
5. Mississippi 2,290
6. Arkansas...............................2,063
7. **Texas....................................1,945**
8. Kansas 1,939
9. Missouri 1,722
10. Nebraska 1,583

In dollars, twelve-month rates. $200,000 dwelling with $1,000 deductible and $100,000 liability. Source: homeinsur.com.

Texas Insurance Premiums, Payments				Capital/Surplus of Texas Companies
Year	Total Premiums	Claim Payments	Ratio	
2017	$ 160.5 billion	$ 134.4 billion	83.7	$ 1.3 trillion
2016	$ 152.3 billion	$ 119.3 billion	78.3	$ 1.2 trillion
2015	$ 128.8 billion	$ 91.7 billion	72.1	$ 1.1 trillion
2014	$ 139.2 billion	$ 97.9 billion	70.3	$ 1.1 trillion

Texas Top 5 Auto Insurers / 2018		
Group	Premiums	% of market
1. State Farm IL	$ 3,563,120,430	16.83
2. Berkshire Hathaway	$ 2,637,489,162	12.46
3. Allstate Ins.	$ 2,362,583,959	11.16
4. Progressive	$ 2,041,345,038	9.64
5. Farmers Ins.	$ 1,842,735,338	8.70

Texas Top 5 Homeowners Insurers / 2018		
1. State Farm	$ 1,837,352,539	21.01
2. Allstate	$ 1,124,648,161	12.86
3. Farmers Ins.	$ 952,430,570	10.89
4. USAA	$ 850,439,148	9.72
5. Liberty Mutual	$ 709,880,064	8.12

Texas Top 5 Health Insurers / 2018		
1. UnitedHealth	$ 14,614,229,813	19.85
2. Health Care Service Corp.	$ 12,759,816,533	17.33
3. Centene Corp.	$ 6,529,067,988	8.87
4. Humana	$ 6,084,977,858	8.26
5. Anthem Inc.	$ 4,812,609,465	6.54

Texas Top 5 Life Insurers / 2018		
1. Metropolitan	$ 834,490,639	6.87
2. New York Life	$ 741,516,556	6.11
3. Northwestern Mutual	$ 631,216,174	5.20
4. Lincoln National	$ 569,322,386	4.69
5. Prudential of Am.	$ 505,842,958	4.17

Personal Auto	
Companies in state	288
Groups in state	65
Policies (liability)	18,693,457
Total Premiums	$21,170,412,785

Homeowners Insurance	
Companies in state	148
Groups in state	61
Homeowners	4,675,125
Dwelling	784,347
Tenants	1,460,336
Total Premiums	$8,747,056,947

Health Insurance	
Companies in state	468
Groups in state	194
Insured Texans	23,019,956
Texans without insurance	4,816,968
Texas estimated pop.	27,836,924
Total Premiums	$73,640,197,125

Life Insurance	
Companies in state	441
Groups in state	163
Total Premiums	$12,144,660,095

Ten-year history, number of insurance companies operating in Texas

	2008	2009	2010	2011	2012	2013	2014	2015	2016	2017
Life/Health										
Texas	170	161	161	157	153	149	146	145	145	140
Non-Texas	520	514	504	499	485	483	479	477	475	474
Non-U.S.	0	0	0	0	7	6	6	6	6	6
subtotal	690	675	665	656	645	638	638	628	626	620
Property/Casualty										
Texas	250	250	243	238	236	225	224	235	245	221
Non-Texas	942	948	948	947	935	948	946	952	940	941
Non-U.S.	0	0	0	0	18	17	16	15	16	17
subtotal	1,192	1,198	1,191	1,185	1,189	1,190	1,186	1,202	1,201	1,179
Other*										
Texas	348	353	350	332	324	301	303	295	298	295
Non-Texas	486	504	515	512	487	464	467	462	480	494
Non-U.S.	0	0	0	0	7	6	6	6	6	7
subtotal	834	857	865	844	818	771	776	763	784	796
Grand Total	**2,716**	**2,730**	**2,721**	**2,685**	**2,652**	**2,599**	**2,600**	**2,593**	**2,611**	**2,595**

Other includes: Nonprofit legal services corporations, third-party administrators, continuing care retirement communities, and health maintenance organizations.

Source: 2017 Annual Report, Texas Department of Insurance.

Construction: Texas Non-Residential Contract Awards

The chart below shows the total value of non-residential construction contract awards in Texas by month **in billions of dollars**. The **change over the period from January 2018 to January 2019** was an increase of **21.9 percent**.

Month	Total Awards	Month	Total Awards	Month	Total Awards
September 2015	$ 2.572	November 2016	1.803	January 2018	2.212
October 2015	3.261	December 2016	2.312	February 2018	1.938
November 2015	2.140	January 2017	2.952	March 2018	2.194
December 2015	1.697	February 2017	2.007	April 2018	1.689
January 2016	2.410	March 2017	2.447	May 2018	2.907
February 2016	1.469	April 2017	2.938	June 2018	4.517
March 2016	2.540	May 2017	3.561	July 2018	4.595
April 2016	1.840	June 2017	2.904	August 2018	2.192
May 2016	2.147	July 2017	3.415	September 2018	1.774
June 2016	2.455	August 2017	2.469	October 2018	1.834
July 2016	2.009	September 2017	2.345	November 2018	1.998
August 2016	2.373	October 2017	4.794	December 2018	2.567
September 2016	3.090	November 2017	2.152	January 2019	$ 2.697
October 2016	2.517	December 2017	1.822		

Source: State Comptroller, 2019.

State Expenditures for Highways

The chart below shows net expenditures (excluding trusts) for state highway construction and maintenance by fiscal year and percent change from the previous year.

Year	Net Expenditures	Percent change
2007	$ 5,359,397,359	4.4
2008	$ 5,208,591,565	– 2.8
2009	$ 4,252,879,534	– 18.3
2010	$ 3,353,467,064	– 21.1
2011	$ 3,774,008,186	12.5
2012	$ 4,186,493,637	10.9
2013	$ 4,491,601,827	7.3
2014	$ 5,305,157,884	18.1
2015	$ 5,192,484,124	– 2.1
2016	$ 6,159,245,504	18.6
2017	$ 6,748,220,204	9.6
2018	$ 6,381,670,144	– 5.4

Source: Texas Annual Cash Reports.

Federal Funds for Highways

The chart below shows fiscal 2019 dispersement of Federal Highway Administration funds for construction and maintenance in **thousands of dollars**. The column at right shows dollars per capita.

State	Highway Funds Total	Highway Funds Lane-miles
U.S. Total	$ 42,355,403	8,804,092
1. California	3,963,775	394,383
2. Texas	**3,790,154**	**679,917**
3. Florida	2,046,153	274,149
4. New York	1,812,763	239,763
5. Pennsylvania	1,771,931	251,271
6. Illinois	1,535,424	306,614
7. Ohio	1,447,596	262,377
8. Georgia	1,394,444	272,017
9. Michigan	1,137,059	256,207
10. North Carolina	1,126,340	227,544
11. Virginia	1,098,983	163,648

Source: Federal Highway Administration, 2019.

Texas Single-Family Building Permits

Year	No. of Dwelling Units Units	No. of Dwelling Units % change	Avg. Value per Unit ($) Value	Avg. Value per Unit ($) % change
1980	67,870	–	$ 51.900	–
1981	66,161	– 2.5	55,700	7.3
1982	78,714	19.0	53,800	– 3.4
1983	103,252	31.2	63,400	17.8
1984	84,565	– 18.1	68,000	7.3
1985	67,964	– 19.6	71,000	4.4
1986	59,143	– 13.0	72,200	1.7
1987	43,975	– 25.6	77,700	7.6
1988	35,908	– 18.3	83,900	8.0
1989	36,658	2.1	90,400	7.7
1990	38,233	4.3	95,500	5.6
1991	46,209	20.9	92,800	– 2.8
1992	59,543	28.9	95,400	2.8
1993	69,964	17.5	96,400	1.0
1994	70,452	0.7	99,500	3.2
1995	70,421	0.0	100,300	0.8
1996	83,132	18.1	102,100	1.8
1997	82,228	– 1.1	108,900	6.7
1998	99,912	21.5	112,800	3.6
1999	101,928	2.0	118,800	5.3
2000	108,782	6.7	127,100	7.0
2001	111,915	2.9	124,700	– 1.9
2002	122,913	9.8	126,400	1.4
2003	137,493	11.9	128,800	1.9
2004	151,384	10.1	137,600	6.8
2005	166,203	9.8	144,300	4.9
2006	163,032	– 1.9	155,100	7.5
2007	120,366	– 26.2	169,000	9.0
2008	81,107	– 32.6	174,100	3.0
2009	68,230	– 15.9	167,900	– 3.6
2010	68,170	– 0.1	179,200	6.7
2011	67,254	– 1.3	191,100	6.6
2012	81,926	21.8	192,300	0.6
2013	93,478	14.1	197,500	2.7
2014	103,045	10.2	208,900	5.8
2015	105,448	2.3	217,100	3.9
2016	106,511	1.0	220,300	1.5
2017	116,766	9.6	$ 226,100	2.6

Real Estate Center at Texas A&M University, 2019.

Commercial Fishing in Texas

Total Texas coastwide landings in 2017 were more than 93.3 million pounds, valued at more than $236.9 million. Shrimp accounted for most of the weight and value of all seafood landed (see chart at bottom).

The Coastal Fisheries Division of the Texas Parks and Wildlife Department manages the marine fishery resources of Texas' four million acres of saltwater, including the bays and estuaries and out to nine nautical miles in the Gulf of Mexico.

The division works toward sustaining fishery populations at levels that are necessary to ensure replenishable stocks of commercially and recreationally important species.

It also focuses on habitat conservation and restoration and leads the agency research on all water-related issues, including assuring adequate in-stream flows for rivers and sufficient freshwater inflows for bays and estuaries. ☆

Top Fishing Ports for Texas in 2017

Rank	Port	Pounds (000)	Dollars (000)
1	Brownsville–Port Isabel	23,000	$ 62,800
2	Palacios	20,200	54,500
3	Galveston	18,800	48,700
4	Port Arthur	17,100	37,100

Source: National Ocean Economics Program, 2019.

Landings by State 2017

Rank	States	Pounds (000)	Dollars (000)
	Total, U.S.	9,923,678	$ 5,428,140
1	Alaska	6,004,882	1,764,462
2	Massachusetts	242,137	605,250
3	Maine	208,677	511,315
4	Louisiana	898,425	370,222
5	Washington	215,976	277,740
6	Florida	87,818	238,855
7	**Texas**	**93,361**	**236,993**
8	Virginia	343,964	183,203

Source: National Marine Fisheries Service, 2019.

Leading U.S. Ports in 2017

Rank	Port	Value in Dollars (in millions)
1	New Bedford, MA	$ 389.5
2	Dutch Harbor, AK	173.0
3	Naknek-King Salmon, AK	154.0
4	Kodiak, AK	152.0
5	Alaska Peninsula, AK	111.5
14	**Brownsville–Port Isabel, TX**	**62.2**

Source: National Ocean Economics Program, 2019.

Oyster fishermen returning to Fulton. Photo by Robert Plocheck.

Texas Commercial Fishery Landings by Species

Species	2017		2015		2012	
	Pounds	Value	Pounds	Value	Pounds	Value
Shrimp, Brown	49,857,425	$ 115,006,107	52,552,655	$ 96,897,374	43,707,869	$ 92,254,541
Shrimp, White	28,914,208	74,195,669	16,644,175	45,591,742	24,100,143	62,970,321
Oyster, Eastern	3,503,518	20,403,679	1,582,685	8,232,088	5,817,191	21,302,111
Snapper, Red	2,212,786	9,881,455	2,151,587	9,387,187	1,122,665	4,447,884
Shrimp, marine, other	101,960	62,835	25,844	9,794	1,023,748	4,021,505
Crab, Blue	4,126,389	5,415,937	3,914,228	5,109,692	2,849,739	2,875,694
Drum, Black	1,926,052	2,457,801	1,812,617	2,003,383	1,612,023	1,485,663
Snapper, Vermilion	149.071	442.915	306,820	919,931	511,224	1,433,985
Croaker, Atlantic	87,768	766,557	90,084	745,8567	88,918	740,110
Total, including others	**93,361,097**	**$236,992,832**	**80,356,029**	**$173,418,614**	**90,557,774**	**$213,313,076**

Source: National Ocean Economics Program and National Marine Fisheries Service, 2019.

Tourism, Travel Impact Estimates by County, 2017

This analysis covers most travel in Texas including business, pleasure, shopping, to attend meetings and other destinations. **Spending** is all spending on goods and services by visitors at a destination. **Earnings** are wages and salaries of employees and income of proprietors of businesses that receive travel expenditures. Employment associated with these businesses are listed under **jobs**. **Local tax** receipts are from hotel taxes, local sales taxes, auto rental taxes, etc., as separate from state tax receipts, as well as spending by travel employees and property taxes attributable to travel businesses and employees. *Source: Office of the Governor, Economic Development and Tourism.*

County	Spending ($000)	Earnings ($000)	Jobs	Local tax ($000)	County	Spending ($000)	Earnings ($000)	Jobs	Local tax ($000)
Anderson	$ 54,813	$ 14,056	681	$ 1,575	Coryell	44,308	13,006	497	1,298
Andrews	29,194	6,705	433	752	Cottle	1,677	181	10	12
Angelina	130,608	31,166	1,530	3,140	Crane	3,322	626	36	85
Aransas	102,093	33,087	1,288	3,397	Crockett	27,688	3,068	185	303
Archer	1,864	172	9	17	Crosby	1,609	442	25	30
Armstrong	1,226	95	8	6	Culberson	37,033	5,482	184	809
Atascosa*	64,047	21,762	740	2,178	Dallam	14,121	6,144	283	618
Austin	42,686	10,011	420	847	Dallas	9,045,095	4,363,486	97,079	427,939
Bailey	4,441	1,298	73	132	Dawson	17,710	3,443	210	373
Bandera	29,633	21,615	734	2,178	Deaf Smith	16,175	3,605	178	461
Bastrop	155,312	69,207	1,973	6,997	Delta	1,515	311	14	21
Baylor	6,299	772	28	72	Denton	713,091	245,921	6,806	27,936
Bee*	40,094	9,350	393	1,009	DeWitt*	58,669	15,336	607	1,514
Bell	445,138	137,258	5,352	14,207	Dickens	483	137	7	11
Bexar	7,106,223	2,398,606	69,220	314,164	Dimmit*	31,312	5,483	245	887
Blanco	15,969	4,366	194	522	Donley	6,418	1,905	94	225
Borden	108	12	1	0	Duval	10,187	1,060	59	114
Bosque	16,614	8,002	200	692	Eastland	16,171	4,416	245	555
Bowie	189,350	36,794	1,874	4,247	Ector	425,258	86,756	2,522	14,726
Brazoria	372,276	111,490	4,843	11,817	Edwards	873	178	7	10
Brazos	479,396	151,433	6,162	17,196	Ellis	167,432	47,721	1,256	5,452
Brewster	74,300	39,438	1,583	3,489	El Paso	1,465,780	440,993	13,850	50,597
Briscoe	1,271	166	8	10	Erath	44,969	13,134	493	1,334
Brooks	12,926	1,903	77	235	Falls	10,267	2,303	99	255
Brown	50,158	16,441	642	1,827	Fannin	14,966	2,640	119	310
Burleson	14,514	4,256	161	342	Fayette	48,373	10,680	484	1,233
Burnet	82,449	32,877	1,130	3,425	Fisher	992	167	7	13
Caldwell	33,108	8,582	213	788	Floyd	4,916	685	32	46
Calhoun	42,702	10,801	393	1,504	Foard	370	94	4	8
Callahan	3,839	1,065	54	74	Fort Bend	518,759	173,847	4,998	18,545
Cameron	801,598	212,848	9,571	27,058	Franklin	9,456	1,770	112	200
Camp	15,975	1,693	86	127	Freestone	46,148	5,662	380	666
Carson	5,837	414	22	27	Frio*	34,848	8,474	375	1,004
Cass	20,510	5,267	270	463	Gaines	16,778	3,689	166	439
Castro	2,502	447	21	32	Galveston	989,973	289,894	10,840	40,726
Chambers	39,120	8,064	248	1,630	Garza	9,724	2,923	102	225
Cherokee	34,960	8,793	449	784	Gillespie	102,974	30,436	1,001	4,688
Childress	14,453	3,241	188	619	Glasscock	258	44	3	2
Clay	20,575	778	44	56	Goliad	10,214	1,883	62	217
Cochran	870	200	13	13	Gonzales*	28,781	5,255	217	680
Coke	3,472	709	45	44	Gray	42,017	13,062	537	1,246
Coleman	6,742	1,518	80	154	Grayson	208,497	39,849	1,632	4,404
Collin	1,500,619	645,351	15,658	66,202	Gregg	219,822	60,375	2,586	6,303
Collingswrth	1,889	246	15	19	Grimes	19,130	5,604	229	500
Colorado	55,988	13,652	507	1,195	Guadalupe	165,633	70,231	2,002	6,524
Comal	405,262	148,845	4,690	15,611	Hale	48,242	12,610	703	1,382
Comanche	13,744	2,665	130	256	Hall	2,283	311	13	34
Concho	1,200	407	10	27	Hamilton	6,171	1,365	56	160
Cooke	60,728	16,502	577	1,792	Hansford	2,026	338	21	45

*Oil and gas production in recent years may affect travel impact estimates.

Travel Impacts by Origin of Visitor, 2017

Origin	Spending ($Billions)	Earnings ($Billions)	Jobs (Thousand)	Tax Receipts ($Millions)		
				Local	State	**Federal
Other U.S.	$ 28.1	$ 10.3	283.8	$ 783	$ 1,459	$ 1,754
International	$ 6.8	$ 1.9	62.6	$ 150	$ 344	$ 280
Texas	$ 29.7	$ 9.0	284.6	$ 595	$ 1,536	$ 1,414
All visitors	**$ 64.6**	**$ 21.2**	**631.0**	**$ 1,528**	**$ 3,338**	**$ 3,448**
Other Travel*	$ 10.2	$ 4.5	46.6	0	0	$ 1,106
Total Travel	**$ 74.7**	**$ 25.7**	**677.6**	**$ 1,528**	**$ 3,338**	**$ 4,554**

*Other Travel includes resident air travel, travel arrangement, and convention / trade shows. ** Federal includes motor vehicle fuel and airline ticket taxes, as well as income taxes attributable to travel industry income.
Source: Survey for the Office of Governor.

County	Spending ($000)	Earnings ($000)	Jobs	Local tax ($000)	County	Spending ($000)	Earnings ($000)	Jobs	Local tax ($000)
Hardeman	5,701	885	62	104	Lamar	70,867	21,008	867	2,099
Hardin	43,916	10,275	493	1,138	Lamb	12,804	1,905	101	175
Harris	12,165,938	5,247,543	109,463	594,078	Lampasas	15,165	3,361	164	402
Harrison	88,366	15,150	688	1,189	Lavaca	16,967	4,178	143	450
Hartley	1,053	205	12	15	Lee	24,239	6,297	207	513
Haskell	5,829	1,416	97	216	Leon	32,534	5,156	247	630
Hays	348,914	120,122	3,820	12,830	Liberty	53,195	18,276	438	1,633
Hemphill	8,637	1,517	65	344	Limestone	18,430	2,810	132	405
Henderson	110,527	21,561	496	1,980	Lipscomb	2,232	200	8	12
Hidalgo	1,268,691	389,497	16,863	38,656	Live Oak*	35,765	5,181	261	710
Hill	58,226	10,199	502	946	Llano	106,885	47,838	2,202	4,136
Hockley	24,281	6,627	347	548	Loving	44	7	1	0
Hood	63,134	17,087	532	1,951	Lubbock	757,603	279,900	8,672	25,832
Hopkins	66,320	13,099	532	1,230	Lynn	1,096	252	15	17
Houston	32,484	5,913	237	433	Madison	10,890	2,260	104	308
Howard	114,305	19,329	862	3,079	Marion	8,540	2,062	129	213
Hudspeth	5,138	414	16	20	Martin	17,482	1,737	93	101
Hunt	108,037	30,989	826	2,747	Mason	3,045	738	52	85
Hutchinson	38,076	9,210	397	1,013	Matagorda	66,052	23,286	1,045	2,808
Irion	10,120	416	16	21	Maverick*	59,383	14,697	657	1,830
Jack	4,347	747	39	66	McCulloch	18,494	2,546	156	471
Jackson	11,836	2,443	102	252	McLennan	556,876	149,083	5,772	16,348
Jasper	38,870	11,408	520	1,198	McMullen*	1,960	468	13	19
Jeff Davis	8,699	4,360	115	188	Medina	43,673	8,968	379	768
Jefferson	548,993	128,520	6,088	16,527	Menard	2,612	305	14	25
Jim Hogg	5,015	1,251	55	99	Midland	544,447	104,044	3,687	16,187
Jim Wells	66,125	16,358	736	1,251	Milam	28,447	6,931	314	627
Johnson	150,770	34,509	1,155	3,954	Mills	2,784	492	21	56
Jones	8,247	2,585	123	175	Mitchell	9,703	1,863	62	242
Karnes*	54,288	13,195	446	1,434	Montague	18,370	5,146	287	493
Kaufman	137,285	26,809	825	2,798	Montgomery	632,996	311,864	7,133	31,168
Kendall	87,004	32,197	1,276	2,814	Moore	42,936	7,343	389	1,287
Kenedy	829	320	13	13	Morris	5,510	995	43	79
Kent	714	142	7	7	Motley	736	101	5	7
Kerr	98,360	40,388	1,543	3,936	Nacgdoches	78,953	21,569	1,120	2,620
Kimble	16,466	2,580	138	388	Navarro	50,688	12,329	599	1,426
King	43	7	0	0	Newton	4,796	716	32	57
Kinney	5,691	2,081	108	115	Nolan	25,312	9,195	399	1,235
Kleberg	57,610	14,091	524	1,539	Nueces	1,140,074	385,275	14,895	49,230
Knox	2,760	375	18	29	Ochiltree	18,856	3,658	196	527
La Salle*	37,187	14,650	595	1,745	Oldham	8,595	934	53	87

*Oil and gas production in recent years may affect travel impact estimates.

County	Spending ($000)	Earnings ($000)	Jobs	Local tax ($000)
Orange	120,943	27,933	1,099	2,940
Palo Pinto	71,755	13,719	555	1,178
Panola	17,446	3,559	194	567
Parker	110,602	25,987	855	2,631
Parmer	4,856	731	39	64
Pecos	62,303	9,803	586	2,496
Polk	56,603	18,565	795	1,490
Potter	755,558	207,026	8,312	26,748
Presidio	15,432	2,947	79	655
Rains	8535	2,888	92	204
Randall	113,680	23,831	1,260	2,411
Reagan	11,551	3,030	172	160
Real	7,497	2,420	94	181
Red River	4,298	1,002	33	70
Reeves	120,899	25,076	1,342	5,471
Refugio	21,609	2,531	108	257
Roberts	1,004	43	2	2
Robertson	22,106	4,572	246	700
Rockwall	97,352	27,912	891	3,534
Runnels	6,898	1,441	82	126
Rusk	36,560	7,641	346	786
Sabine	12,601	2,428	117	139
S.Augustne	7,437	1,918	109	131
SanJacinto	11,857	2,774	151	158
SanPatricio	140,681	37,759	1,326	4,704
San Saba	4,489	1,025	74	101
Schleicher	457	130	7	9
Scurry	37,976	12,099	572	1,176
Shackelford	2,288	1,533	84	112
Shelby	34,918	8,878	527	893
Sherman	5,086	453	29	31
Smith	354,399	104,858	3,924	10,487
Somervell	17,600	4,252	156	608
Starr	27,636	5,628	245	632
Stephens	7,147	1,766	82	192
Sterling	2,356	226	16	16
Stonewall	1,057	280	20	17

County	Spending ($000)	Earnings ($000)	Jobs	Local tax ($000)
Sutton	7,937	2,059	138	326
Swisher	3,536	860	44	68
Tarrant	5,613,557	4,283,738	76,486	345,928
Taylor	422,356	100,711	3,789	12,755
Terrell	1,098	199	14	8
Terry	11,335	3,480	201	411
Throckmrton	3,336	202	11	13
Titus	55,034	11,298	518	1,326
Tom Green	218,875	77,976	3,354	6,920
Travis	5,666,532	2,009,187	56,325	267,471
Trinity	10,993	5,977	225	390
Tyler	10,935	2,415	140	235
Upshur	22,334	3,725	180	344
Upton	3,252	801	54	94
Uvalde	82,685	20,689	834	2,964
Val Verde	55,972	16,178	662	1,854
Van Zandt	51,397	10,934	485	1,004
Victoria	215,854	41,638	1,524	5,326
Walker	106,675	24,187	1,132	2,568
Waller	50,695	8,400	229	1,223
Ward	53,952	15,760	856	2,459
Washington	91,919	17,082	672	1,904
Webb*	568,444	154,510	6,103	16,024
Wharton	41,084	9,963	484	1,292
Wheeler	19,477	3,033	155	409
Wichita	219,588	56,433	3,371	6,643
Wilbarger	22,532	5,211	255	705
Willacy	25,687	4,199	162	386
Williamson	627,148	176,440	5,620	21,953
Wilson*	34,179	10,101	395	850
Winkler	11,658	1,667	93	294
Wise	58,350	17,172	898	1,668
Wood	26,630	8,406	366	566
Yoakum	6,360	1,435	73	199
Young	23,258	7,276	313	666
Zapata	15,747	2,947	181	218
Zavala	7,351	902	45	80

Tourists at Barton Warnock Environmental Center in Lajitas. Photo by Earl Nottingham, Texas Parks & Wildlife.

Telecommunications Trends to High-Speed, Wireless

The chart below shows the move to wireless communications, and the decline in the number of telephone land lines in Texas and nationwide. The chart also shows the growth of high-speed Internet use in the state and in the United States. *Sources: Federal Communications Commission and Public Utility Commission of Texas.*

	2000	2005	2009	2011	2013	2016
Mobile Wireless Telephone Subscribers						
Texas	6,705,000	14,424,000	21,008,000	23,482,000	24,890,000	28,840,000
U.S.	90,643,000	192,053,000	261,284,000	290,304,000	310,691,000	395,900,000
Local Telephone Wirelines/Landlines						
Texas	13,657,444	12,310,000	10,500,000	9,590,000	8,840,000	8,110,000
U.S.	188,499,586	157,041,487	152,945,000	143,319,000	133,233,000	121,331,000
Internet Connections						
Texas	253,000	2,943,000	7,484,000	17,487,000	23,612,000	30,171,000
U.S.	4,107,000	42,518,000	102,043,000	206,124,000	275,608,000	369,416,000

U.S. Internet Lines by Technology (in thousands)

	aDSL	Cable Modem	Fiber	Satellite	Fixed Wireless	Mobile Wireless	Total
2013	30,657	52,760	7,250	1,623	810	190,706	284,692
2017	25,506	64,059	12,906	1,826	1,245	302,562	408,816

Cell phones. Photo by Daniel Wilson (CC).

The chart below shows the percent of the population that in 2016 had access to advanced, high-quality voice, data, graphics, and video offerings. The chart shows that almost 28 percent of the rural population in Texas is without that access. *Source: Federal Communications Commission 2018 Broadband Progress Report.*

Percent with access to advanced telecommunications, 2016 (25 Mbps/3 Mbps)

	Population with access		Urban with access		Rural with access	
	Total	Percent	Population	Percent	Population	Percent
Texas	27,763,538	93.4 %	23,251,241	97.6 %	4,512,297	72.3 %
U.S.	313,389,000	81.2 %	226,701,000	89.7 %	27,694,000	45.7 %

Texas Electric Grids: Demand and Capacity

- The Electric Reliability Council of Texas (**ERCOT**) operates the electric grid for 75 percent of the state.
- The Panhandle, South Plains, and a corner of Northeast Texas are under the Southwest Power Pool (**SPP**).
- El Paso and the far western corner of the Trans Pecos are under the Western Electric Coordinating Council (**WECC**).
- The southeast corner of Texas is under the **SERC** Reliability Corporation.

The councils were first formed in 1968 to ensure adequate bulk power supply.

	Actual (in megawatts)						Estimate		Projected
	2011	2012	2013	2014	2015	2016	2017	2018	2019
ERCOT demand	68,416	66,548	67,245	66,454	69,877	71,110	69,512	73,473	74,853
capacity	69,595	73,219	74,396	73,950	76,798	78,466	78,251	77,558	78,085
% margin*	1.7	9.1	9.6	10.1	9.0	9.4	11.1	9.3	7.4
SPP demand	54,991	53,177	47,647	46,076	48,894	51,883	51,577	51,687	52,422
capacity	62,044	72,802	71.897	65,302	63,426	63,350	67,780	68,714	67,618
% margin	11.4	27.0	33.8	29,4	22.9	18.1	31.4	32.9	29.0
WECC demand	117,755	130,465	132,875	127,092	131,072	139,431	136,903	136,679	136,244
capacity	147,147	147,527	167,171	162,119	164,417	165,881	160,337	164,960	163,492
% margin	20.0	11.6	20.5	21.6	20.3	15.9	14.6	17.1	16.1
SERC demand	161,995	158,041	121,810	123,866	127,742	128,985	127,575	128,851	129,811
capacity	201,103	198,140	165,171	159,822	159,279	160,896	160,253	161,117	162,434
% margin	19.4	20.2	26.3	22.5	19.8	19.8	20.4	20.3	20.1
U.S. demand	759,642	768,943	759,310	723,411	741,056	768,510	752,080	755,578	760,642
capacity	892,426	927,060	944,515	917,167	916,439	923,873	931,379	963,135	996,104
% margin	14.9	17.1	19.6	21.1	19.1	16.8	19.3	21.6	23.6

*Capacity Margin is the amount of unused available capability of an electric power system at **summer peak** load as a percentage of capacity resources. Source: Federal Energy Information Administration, March 2019. 2017–2019 data from ERCOT.

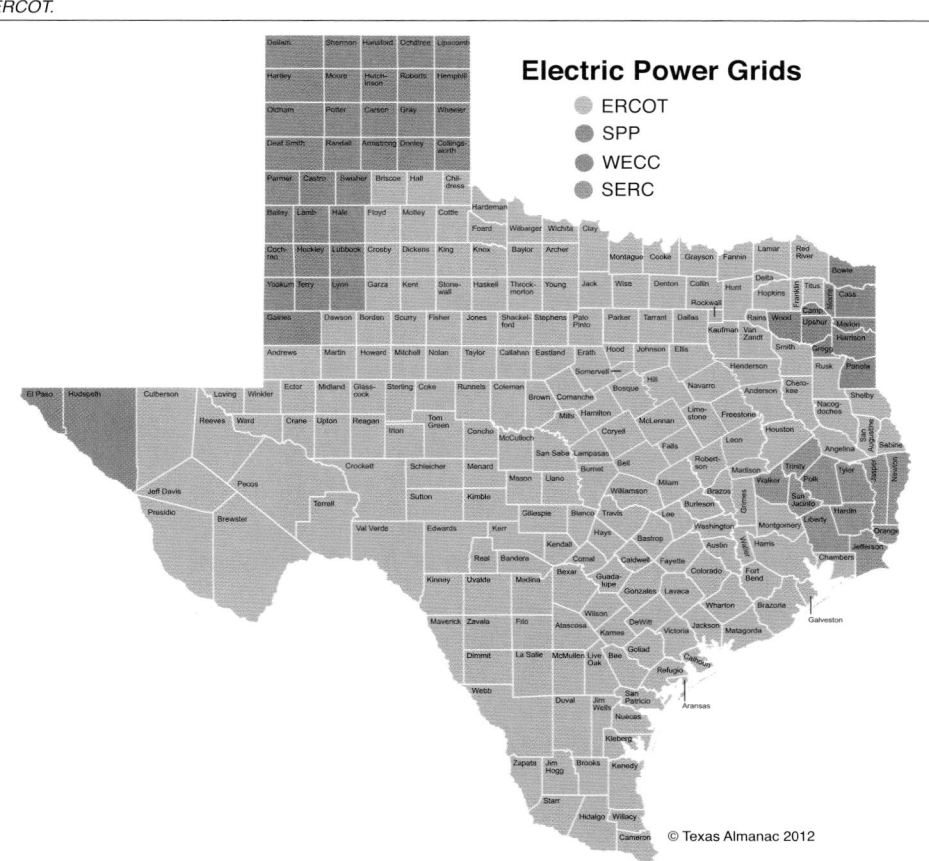

Electric Power Grids

- ERCOT
- SPP
- WECC
- SERC

© Texas Almanac 2012

Wind turbines in San Patricio County off FM 3284. Photo by Rosie Hatch.

Wind Energy Continues Expansion in State

Sources: U.S. Energy Information Administration and the American Wind Energy Association, 2019.

Texas continues to lead the nation in installed wind capacity and generation. In the first quarter of 2019, Texas had 25 percent of the nation's installed wind capacity, reaching almost 25,000 megawatts. Iowa was second in installed wind capacity, at 8,957 megawatts.

With Texas' significant growth in turbine development, wind generation was responsible for about 16 percent of total electricity generation in the state in 2018, more than double what it was in 2011 at 6.9 percent.

The Texas plains continue to see rapid growth in wind farms, while more recently expansion has begun offshore on the Gulf Coast.

In all, Texas has five of the ten largest wind generation projects in the country. Roscoe Wind Farm, which stretches across Nolan, Mitchell, Scurry, and Fisher counties, is the largest in the state, with a capacity of 782 MW.

It is third in the nation to Alta farm in California at 1,548 MW and Shepherds Flat in Oregon at 845 MW. ☆

Installed Wind Capacity in megawatts (MW)		
YEAR	Texas	U.S.
2019 (Q1)	24,895	97,227
2018	24,899	96,487
2017	22,637	89,078
2016	20,321	82,183
2015	14,208	66,008
2014	14,098	65,879
2013	12,354	61,110
2012	10,648	49,802
2011	10,394	46,919
2010	10,089	40,267
2009	9,403	34,863
2008	7,427	24,651
2007	4,296	16,596
2005	1,995	9,149
2000	181	2,566

2018 Renewable Energy as Portion of Net Generation of Electricity
[in thousand megawatthours.]

State	Total Electric	Total Renewable	% Renewable	Hydroelectric	Wind
1. Washington	116,763	90,734	77.7 %	81,576	7,356
2. California	197,227	84,302	42.7 %	25,898	13,650
3. Texas	474,777	82,104	17.3 %	1,433	75,753
4. Oregon	84,836	45,679	53.8 %	36,729	7,137
5. New York	134,356	38,000	28.3 %	30,911	4,383
6. Iowa	64,187	22,922	35.7 %	999	21,685
United States	4,178,000	713,000	17.1 %	292,000	275,000
Source: Energy Information Administration, 2019.					

Texas Oil Production History

The table shows the year of oil or gas discovery in each county, oil production in 2017 and 2018, and total oil production from date of discovery to Jan. 1, 2019. **The 15 counties omitted have not produced oil.**

The table has been compiled by the *Texas Almanac* from information provided in past years by the Texas Mid-Continent Oil & Gas Assoc., which used data from the U.S. Bureau of Mines and the Texas state comptroller. Since 1970, production figures have been compiled from records of the Railroad Commission of Texas. The figures in the final column are cumulative of all previously published figures. The change in sources, due to different techniques, may create some discrepancies in year-to-year comparisons among counties.

County	Year of Discovery	Production in Barrels* 2017	Production in Barrels* 2018	Total Production to Jan. 1, 2019	County	Year of Discovery	Production in Barrels* 2017	Production in Barrels* 2018	Total Production to Jan. 1, 2019
Anderson	1928	583,789	653,788	309,438,663	Crockett	1925	8,905,249	7,893,047	460,214,077
Andrews	1929	37,704,866	41,711,797	3,212,512,677	Crosby	1955	1,165,290	1,003,845	37,029,740
Angelina	1936	5,653	4,886	1,002,699	Culberson	1953	16,818,361	24,197,908	100,054,095
Aransas	1936	242,485	167,667	89,372,098	Dallam	2015	0	0	116
Archer	1911	932,211	895,921	509,121,007	Dallas	1986	0	0	232
Atascosa	1917	20,811,279	21,499,395	289,278,259	Dawson	1934	3,518,338	3,629,269	434,485,755
Austin	1915	387,383	414,936	121,550,435	Delta	1984	0	0	65,089
Bandera	1995	1,780	1,532	44,365	Denton	1937	208,744	177,710	11,918,979
Bastrop	1913	76,846	110,590	18,774,091	DeWitt	1930	61,579,364	64,301,925	514,415,184
Baylor	1924	100,491	85,875	59,510,478	Dickens	1953	491,175	485,737	29,649,071
Bee	1929	370,096	321,156	114,838,422	Dimmit	1943	52,728,024	55,789,071	468,806,748
Bell	1980	0	0	446	Donley	1967	276	103	3,143
Bexar	1889	83,240	78,318	37,365,364	Duval	1905	962,824	1,013,113	602,212,841
Borden	1949	2,987,187	4,536,573	455,349,043	Eastland	1917	191,964	171,308	160,259,245
Bosque	2006	0	0	309	Ector	1926	20,972,753	19,738,203	3,400,515,417
Bowie	1944	34,074	29,639	7,196,887	Edwards	1946	3,853	1,920	613,731
Brazoria	1902	3,330,376	3,986,713	1,311,126,131	Ellis	1953	157	9	844,828
Brazos	1942	4,723,019	4,637,399	185,516,389	Erath	1917	6,138	5,083	2,296,827
Brewster	1969	0	0	56	Falls	1937	2,087	1,007	894,141
Briscoe	1982	0	0	4,065	Fannin	1980	0	0	13,354
Brooks	1935	676,172	617,927	183,043,400	Fayette	1943	2,016,915	1,884,530	178,798,788
Brown	1917	105,012	88,829	54,908,588	Fisher	1928	841,432	984,932	259,717,501
Burleson	1938	6,800,091	12,154,039	244,881,389	Floyd	1952	0	0	268,610
Caldwell	1922	1,240,047	1,206,047	297,425,995	Foard	1929	68,347	90,339	25,386,546
Calhoun	1935	132,094	170,059	108,525,382	Fort Bend	1919	1,014,996	968,404	713,956,205
Callahan	1923	126,339	108,879	88,436,257	Franklin	1936	481,564	428,939	183,327,247
Cameron	1944	632	755	480,603	Freestone	1916	79,803	76,984	47,258,550
Camp	1940	98,463	88,222	31,310,122	Frio	1934	7,276,270	7,962,150	192,409,474
Carson	1921	123,601	120,526	183,984,141	Gaines	1935	23,787,060	24,031,983	2,521,582,943
Cass	1936	366,222	381,776	118,509,294	Galveston	1922	277,567	247,158	464,787,666
Chambers	1916	3,272,116	2,886,167	938,864,889	Garza	1926	2,356,412	2,295,846	377,907,799
Cherokee	1926	716,952	558,467	76,568,128	Glasscock	1925	29,869,563	42,138,864	474,424,490
Childress	1961	7,480	7,656	1,807,450	Goliad	1930	237,943	287,038	89,279,420
Clay	1917	439,788	438,615	211,898,782	Gonzales	1902	31,445,218	34,380,919	305,314,634
Cochran	1936	2,740,803	2,773,018	550,784,921	Gray	1925	925,299	924,354	687,067,472
Coke	1942	399,360	367,240	231,296,485	Grayson	1930	1,138,018	1,085,001	274,270,246
Coleman	1902	270,287	233,061	98,525,284	Gregg	1931	1,634,070	1,641,592	3,318,949,930
Collin	1963	0	0	53,000	Grimes	1952	625,809	490,201	26,355,571
Collngswrth	1936	724	3,666	1,295,351	Guadalupe	1922	718,433	708,396	217,599,114
Colorado	1932	534,863	589,462	48,205,576	Hale	1946	1,298,414	1,240,040	204,474,922
Comanche	1918	97,182	74,767	6,534,714	Hamilton	1938	819	119	164,677
Concho	1940	274,057	286,153	30,715,765	Hansford	1937	247,960	406,959	42,311,173
Cooke	1924	1,304,593	1,178,116	418,688,248	Hardeman	1944	687,993	733,117	95,869,159
Coryell	1964	0	0	1,100	Hardin	1893	1,226,255	1,193,294	462,699,154
Cottle	1955	192,143	147,836	6,511,486	Harris	1905	1,014,173	958,154	1,395,210,707
Crane	1926	7,247,571	6,972,207	1,869,291,048	*Total includes condensate production.				

County	Year of Discovery	Production in Barrels* 2017	Production in Barrels* 2018	Total Production to Jan. 1, 2019
Harrison	1928	757,758	793,111	104,001,737
Hartley	1937	170,935	199,584	11,100,474
Haskell	1929	576,953	642,575	122,793,780
Hays	1956	0	0	296
Hemphill	1955	3,445,757	2,892,151	74,620,271
Henderson	1934	939,083	595,246	183,649,738
Hidalgo	1934	760,293	759,747	136,159,258
Hill	1929	0	1	80,670
Hockley	1937	12,654,484	12,367,200	1,854,064,818
Hood	1958	81,740	82,596	2,860,142
Hopkins	1936	252,774	163,985	92,868,464
Houston	1934	818,812	772,626	78,483,013
Howard	1925	38,376,051	61,954,939	1,024,865,204
Hudspeth	2008	0	0	59
Hunt	1942	880	610	2,027,018
Hutchinson	1923	551,044	635,087	540,617,621
Irion	1928	9,775,060	10,575,007	191,854,413
Jack	1923	838,827	785,072	218,642,669
Jackson	1934	1,660,668	2,268,350	696,632,390
Jasper	1928	913,446	1,010,019	45,841,640
Jeff Davis	1980	0	0	20,866
Jefferson	1901	1,379,104	1,022,776	577,712,951
Jim Hogg	1921	87,726	82,446	114,373,618
Jim Wells	1931	105,702	88,204	464,524,919
Johnson	1962	13,586	12,660	556,906
Jones	1926	498,487	417,429	229,751,997
Karnes	1930	108,747,629	116,825,823	791,767,631
Kaufman	1948	59,037	51,523	25,663,542
Kenedy	1947	295,737	310,180	43,126,726
Kent	1946	3,278,086	3,451,715	625,367,479
Kerr	1982	0	0	79,044
Kimble	1939	237	310	102,070
King	1943	1,991,815	1,872,910	201,074,099
Kinney	1960	0	0	402
Kleberg	1919	262,157	250,045	342,454,958
Knox	1946	149,146	169,855	64,769,357
Lamb	1945	262,699	60,818,722	428,001,771
Lampasas	1985	0	226,907	43,890,960
La Salle	1940	55,071,001	0	111
Lavaca	1941	4,731,058	6,564,227	74,072,301
Lee	1939	1,142,734	2,089,783	152,724,586
Leon	1936	965,959	796,516	78,827,823
Liberty	1904	1,213,902	1,045,763	561,544,441
Limestone	1920	96,409	90,909	121,303,462
Lipscomb	1956	3,144,368	2,749,900	97,883,343
Live Oak	1930	12,317,711	12,303,210	198,564,193
Llano	1978	0	0	647
Loving	1921	57,541,224	97,210,789	360,427,143
Lubbock	1941	1,037,099	988,758	87,241,073
Lynn	1950	359,690	319,721	24,139,213
Madison	1946	3,015,524	2,334,275	64,933,743
Marion	1910	561,109	570,946	59,134,526
Martin	1945	58,240,211	83,237,044	687,120,540
Matagorda	1901	395,293	407,932	291,669,254
Maverick	1929	854,305	899,836	67,751,013
McCulloch	1938	43,594	41,567	2,617,751
McLennan	1902	702	587	349,990
McMullen	1922	31,175,488	32,328,179	354,893,731
Medina	1901	116,580	104,989	12,340,501
Menard	1946	104,589	95,092	9,294,394
Midland	1945	108,326,105	144,358,136	1,158,254,263
Milam	1921	488,940	912,370	27,828,511
Mills	1982	0	0	28,122
Mitchell	1920	2,891,205	2,640,515	273,330,024
Montague	1919	1,824,134	1,508,168	354,955,747
Montgmry	1931	873,735	854,974	789,205,497
Moore	1926	342,037	267,483	34,002,201
Morris	2004	21,263	31,475	74,045
Motley	1957	34,572	36,455	11,415,510
Nacgdches	1866	103,464	85,199	7,347,864
Navarro	1894	176,799	155,681	222,575,215
Newton	1937	681,945	659,271	73,757,922
Nolan	1939	1,424,154	1,159,108	217,976,991
Nueces	1930	410,560	401,276	574,701,635
Ochiltree	1951	5,005,991	5,108,431	216,982,678
Oldham	1957	403,706	339,331	20,109,486
Orange	1913	712,900	749,647	171,602,317
Palo Pinto	1902	175,228	160,596	28,568,407
Panola	1917	1,673,088	1,589,064	121,729,904
Parker	1942	82,176	88,041	5,633,745
Parmer	1963	0	0	144,000
Pecos	1926	15,410,157	22,255,314	1,924,256,783
Polk	1930	1,299,953	1,170,050	144,362,515
Potter	1925	679,612	768,949	14,144,180
Presidio	1980	0	0	4,641
Rains	1955	0	0	148,911
Reagan	1923	39,185,396	46,601,612	747,946,043
Real	2003	86	65	29,435
Red River	1951	85,773	78,007	9,329,479
Reeves	1939	85,024,477	137,453,599	445,484,644
Refugio	1920	2,304,275	2,280,572	1,367,197,524
Roberts	1945	2,037,776	1,930,607	75,349,990
Robertson	1944	1,162,950	1,199,852	44,374,832
Runnels	1927	369,945	353,417	154,066,263
Rusk	1930	2,041,378	1,991,194	1,865,397,650
Sabine	1981	13,679	2,383	4,992,685
S.Augustine	1947	55,260	43,154	3,476,166
S. Jacinto	1940	152,816	171,954	30,024,937
S. Patricio	1930	504,256	618,328	497,827,294
San Saba	1982	0	0	499,480
Schleicher	1934	399,429	344,390	94,303,319
Scurry	1923	14,677,072	14,963,393	2,246,960,566
Shackelford	1910	434,009	404,852	190,642,702
Shelby	1917	70,920	65,756	6,074,574
Sherman	1938	61,878	61,866	10,313,604
Smith	1931	1,165,160	1,304,825	283,989,711
Somervell	1978	4,107	4,334	95,568
Starr	1929	853,157	902,764	317,435,578
Stephens	1916	1,953,906	1,860,560	369,774,494
Sterling	1947	848,935	750,640	103,286,965
Stonewall	1938	2,170,606	2,036,793	283,965,745
Sutton	1948	83,582	65,271	9,204,951
Swisher	1981	0	0	6

*Total includes condensate production.

County	Year of Discovery	Production in Barrels*		Total Production to Jan. 1, 2019	County	Year of Discovery	Production in Barrels*		Total Production to Jan. 1, 2019
		2017	2018				2017	2018	
Tarrant	1969	13,245	12,362	368,843	Washngtn	1915	489,133	1,538,326	39,011,695
Taylor	1929	420,959	402,846	150,299,854	Webb	1921	15,228,136	13,645,772	283,832,235
Terrell	1952	91,433	94,943	10,791,981	Wharton	1925	1,010,655	923,931	365,389,908
Terry	1940	3,652,601	3,395,723	495,259,112	Wheeler	1910	3,919,583	4,008,552	177,561,715
Thrckmrton	1925	760,012	871,397	231,948,402	Wichita	1910	1,721,751	1,608,255	856,009,697
Titus	1936	478,880	426,677	218,056,998	Wilbarger	1915	737,040	702,919	274,031,059
Tm Green	1940	411,533	505,959	99,266,425	Willacy	1936	236,712	199,531	121,787,619
Travis	1934	4,592	3,930	794,472	Williamson	1915	8,485	7,932	9,677,618
Trinity	1946	24,206	27,766	1,667,069	Wilson	1941	1,897,095	1,295,401	68,238,818
Tyler	1937	1,494,387	1,275,116	74,685,808	Winkler	1926	9,280,334	14,440,366	1,146,879,635
Upshur	1931	271,268	271,902	293,812,746	Wise	1942	615,740	619,319	116,255,026
Upton	1925	53,222,275	62,226,181	1,213,844,817	Wood	1940	3,443,646	3,395,954	1,249,796,544
Uvalde	1950	0	0	1,814	Yoakum	1936	23,831,920	26,808,701	2,386,906,401
Val Verde	1935	695	2,233	159,521	Young	1917	951,749	945,858	326,025,049
Van Zandt	1929	489,008	485,998	559,359,262	Zapata	1919	121,190	122,249	50,860,580
Victoria	1931	799,574	1,871,472	264,184,173	Zavala	1937	6,531,203	5,998,124	96,000,562
Walker	1934	122,743	79,240	1,145,926	Source: Railroad Commission, 2017–18 production reports.				
Waller	1934	286,696	219,008	35,455,945	*Total includes condensate production.				
Ward	1928	25,297,184	35,677,151	974,489,969					

Rig Counts and Wells Drilled by Year

Year	Rotary rigs active*		Permits†	Texas wells completed		Wells drilled**
	Texas	U.S.	Texas	Oil	Gas	Texas
1982	994	3,117	41,224	16,296	6,273	27,648
1985	680	1,980	30,878	16,543	4,605	27,124
1990	348	1,009	14,033	5,593	2,894	11,231
1995	251	723	11,244	4,334	3,778	9,785
1996	283	779	12,669	4,061	4,060	9,747
1997	358	945	13,933	4,482	4,594	10,778
1998	303	827	9,385	4,509	4,907	11,057
1999	226	622	8,430	2,049	3,566	6,658
2000	343	918	12,021	3,111	4,580	8,854
2001	462	1,156	12,227	3,082	5,787	10,005
2002	338	830	9,716	3,268	5,474	9,877
2003	449	1,032	12,664	3,111	6,336	10,420
2004	506	1,192	14,700	3,446	7,118	11,587
2005	614	1,381	16,914	3,454	7,197	11,154
2006	746	1,649	18,952	4,761	8,534	12,764
2007	834	1,769	19,994	5,084	8,643	13,778
2008	898	1,880	24,073	6,208	10,361	16,615
2009	432	1,086	12,212	5,860	8,706	14,585
2010	659	1,541	18,029	5,392	4,071	9,477
2011	838	1,875	22,480	5,380	3,008	8,391
2012	899	1,919	22,479	10,936	3,580	14,535
2013	835	1,761	21,471	19,249	4,917	24,166
2014	882	1,862	25,792	24,999	3,585	29,554
2015	430	977	10,549	15,578	2,787	19,503
2016	236	510	8,113	7,813	2,129	10,468
2017	430	876	12,600	5,394	1,022	6,914
2018	513	1,032	13,307	8,588	1,813	10,986

Texas Railroad Commission. *Source for rig count: Baker Hughes Inc. This is an annual average from monthly reports.
†Totals after 1988 are number of drilling permits issued; data for previous years were total drilling applications received.
Wells drilled are oil and gas well **completions and dry holes drilled/plugged.

Top Oil-Producing Counties since Discovery

There are 38 counties that have produced more than 500 million barrels of oil since discovery. The counties are ranked below. The column at right lists the number of regular producing oil wells in the county in February 2019.

Rank	County	Barrels	Oil Wells	Rank	County	Barrels	Oil Wells
1.	Ector	3,400,515,417	7,145	21.	Wichita	856,009,697	4,769
2.	Gregg	3,318,949,930	2,451	22.	Karnes	791,767,631	2,714
3.	Andrews	3,212,512,677	10,514	23.	Montgomery	789,205,497	122
4.	Gaines	2,521,582,943	3,917	24.	Reagan	747,946,043	4,992
5.	Yoakum	2,386,906,401	3,870	25.	Fort Bend	713,956,205	292
6.	Scurry	2,246,960,566	2,448	26.	Jackson	696,632,390	257
7.	Pecos	1,924,256,784	3,156	27.	Martin	687,120,540	5,897
8.	Crane	1,869,291,048	4,006	28.	Gray	687,067,472	2,451
9.	Rusk	1,865,397,650	1,744	29.	Kent	625,367,479	538
10.	Hockley	1,854,064,818	3,843	30.	Duval	602,212,841	545
11.	Harris	1,395,210,707	240	31.	Jefferson	577,712,951	200
12.	Refugio	1,367,197,524	564	32.	Nueces	574,701,635	127
13.	Brazoria	1,311,126,131	264	33.	Liberty	561,544,441	491
14.	Wood	1,249,796,544	625	34.	Van Zandt	559,359,262	240
15.	Upton	1,213,844,817	5,623	35.	Cochran	550,784,921	1,632
16.	Midland	1,158,254,263	6,701	36.	Hutchinson	540,617,621	2,154
17.	Winkler	1,146,879,635	1,669	37.	DeWitt	514,415,184	1,154
18.	Howard	1,024,865,204	4,915	38.	Archer	509,121,007	2,818
19.	Ward	974,489,969	3,502	*Source: Texas Railroad Commission.*			
20.	Chambers	938,864,899	188				

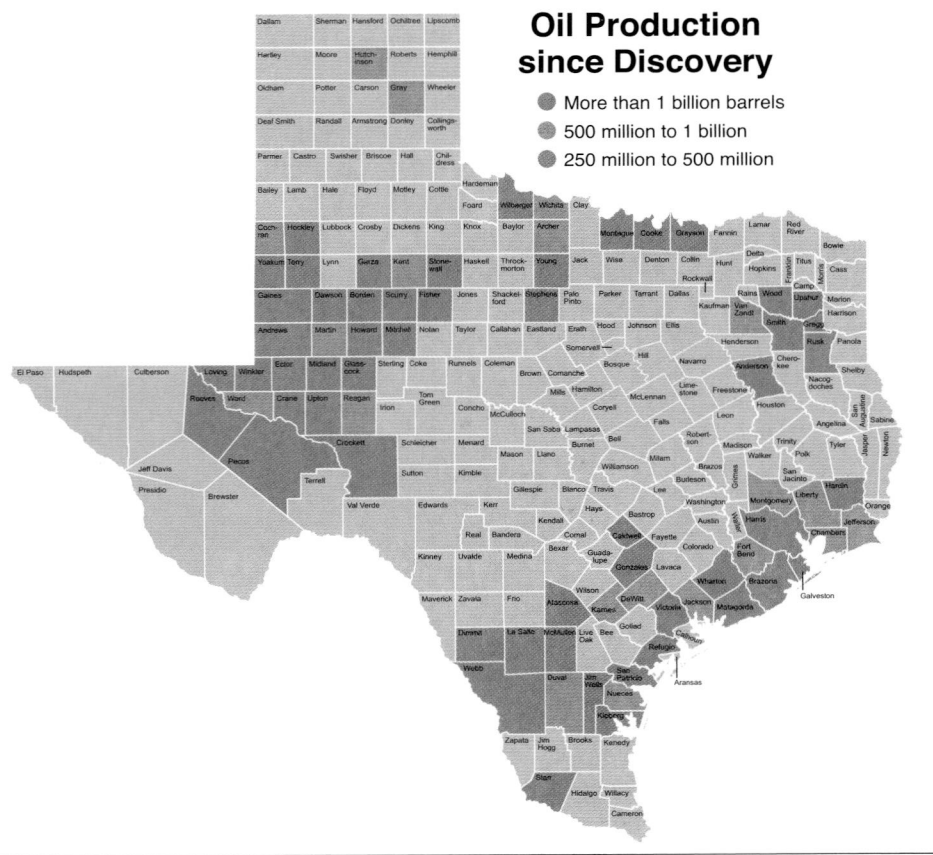

Oil Production since Discovery

- More than 1 billion barrels
- 500 million to 1 billion
- 250 million to 500 million

Oil and Gas Production by County, 2018

In 2018 in Texas, the total natural gas production from gas wells was 5,742,977,699 thousand cubic feet (MCF) and total crude oil production from oil wells was 1,334,186,860 barrels (BBL). Total condensate was 191,151,636 barrels. Total casinghead production was 3,106,361,360 MCF. **Counties not listed in the chart below had no production in 2018.** *Source: Texas Railroad Commission.*

County	Oil (BBL)	Casinghead (MCF)	GW Gas (MCF)	Conden-sate (BBL)	County	Oil (BBL)	Casinghead (MCF)	GW Gas (MCF)	Conden-sate (BBL)
Anderson	619,327	724,733	2,385,960	34,461	Edwards	1,375	0	5,365,211	545
Andrews	41,516,979	67,222,631	3,462,831	194,818	Ellis	9	12	2,798,479	0
Angelina	0	0	49,416,911	4,886	Erath	1,992	327	2,376,359	3,091
Aransas	32,275	199,590	4,766,288	135,392	Falls	1,007	0	0	0
Archer	895,800	290,973	15,700	121	Fayette	1,619,731	5,113,444	9,277,696	264,799
Atascosa	21,476,804	23,423,428	2,184,625	22,591	Fisher	984,570	966,636	23,139	362
Austin	397,606	365,222	2,249,969	17,330	Foard	90,339	26,431	42,396	0
Bandera	1,532	0	6,198	0	Fort Bend	808,345	535,070	6,403,675	160,059
Bastrop	106,920	72,876	36,245	3,670	Franklin	407,705	155,874	1,270,355	21,234
Baylor	85,875	8,732	0	0	Freestone	29,706	43,459	94,708,464	47,278
Bee	235,866	264,582	10,795,826	85,290	Frio	7,949,734	10,353,852	957,770	12,416
Bexar	78,318	12	0	0	Gaines	24,023,705	20,324,710	3,314,178	8,278
Borden	4,536,573	3,786,039	0	0	Galveston	208,508	98,572	1,359,015	38,650
Bowie	25,276	3,253	18,786	4,363	Garza	2,295,846	520,256	0	0
Brazoria	3,300,168	878,390	13,878,487	686,545	Glasscock	42,125,127	137,543,995	629,457	13,737
Brazos	4,528,975	6,569,846	2,109,920	108,424	Goliad	209,254	203,525	7,891,676	77,784
Brooks	196,520	209,695	16,911,899	421,407	Gonzales	34,378,110	53,233,447	242,991	2,809
Brown	86,932	229,847	559,178	1,897	Gray	921,973	1,676,131	6,239,156	2,381
Burleson	12,102,422	12,158,608	1,411,497	51,617	Grayson	1,074,655	3,954,783	1,044,829	10,346
Caldwell	1,206,047	33,931	0	0	Gregg	1,458,160	1,966,748	33,909,134	183,432
Calhoun	122,010	142,206	1,750,323	48,049	Grimes	471,047	2,675,229	5,509,825	19,154
Callahan	107,142	193,098	340,192	1,737	Guadalpe	708,396	10	0	0
Cameron	0	0	83,904	755	Hale	1,240,040	2,220,353	0	0
Camp	88,222	0	291,687	0	Hamilton	35	0	92,106	84
Carson	98,300	606,427	6,786,416	22,226	Hansford	345,263	1,471,759	9,382,430	61,696
Cass	378,232	388,462	361,239	3,544	Hardeman	733,117	295,384	0	0
Chambers	2,750,438	940,306	4,906,869	135,729	Hardin	935,819	982,167	4,474,393	257,475
Cherokee	197,886	495,488	25,688,642	360,581	Harris	822,467	606,007	9,133,297	135,687
Childress	7,656	0	0	0	Harrison	364,675	1,222,385	104,948,945	428,436
Clay	433,531	1,239,300	254,871	5,084	Hartley	199,584	133,967	771,472	0
Cochran	2,772,918	1,829,138	62,255	100	Haskell	642,575	433,332	0	0
Coke	361,624	2,211,946	313,415	5,616	Hemphill	487,424	4,634,958	108,580,307	2,404,727
Coleman	230,225	471,806	313,178	2,836	Hendrson	575,662	4,742,756	7,165,215	19,584
Collingswth	3,666	54,763	849,966	0	Hidalgo	56,504	18,874	53,191,551	703,243
Colorado	140,378	297,261	14,322,526	449,084	Hill	1	0	10,073,659	0
Comnche	70,781	115,662	407,264	3,986	Hockley	12,365,711	7,648,807	32,814	1,489
Concho	285,652	87,025	157,940	501	Hood	0	684	35,266,391	82,596
Cooke	1,028,755	2,272,495	12,316,807	149,361	Hopkins	159,229	83,180	59,039	4,756
Cottle	116,981	17,142	2,888,957	30,855	Houston	578,527	835,508	3,519,052	194,099
Crane	6,915,241	33,058,879	8,226,100	56,966	Howard	61,952,932	88,509,963	255,351	2,007
Crockett	7,725,356	62,256,584	44,783,945	167,691	Hunt	610	0	0	0
Crosby	1,003,845	69,897	0	0	Hutchinson	496,407	2,340,050	4,990,120	138,680
Culberson	1,181,586	5,189,785	245,466,217	23,016,322	Irion	10,562,025	113,516,208	1,275,776	12,982
Dallas	0	0	9,242,190	0	Jack	704,461	8,633,690	7,452,047	80,611
Dawson	3,629,269	1,561,223	0	0	Jackson	2,219,097	662,479	2,942,297	49,253
Denton	18,192	677,045	170,182,806	159,518	Jasper	477,598	1,077,721	9,503,338	532,421
DeWitt	47,988,735	133,515,692	131,399,308	16,313,190	Jefferson	619,208	482,798	6,788,333	403,568
Dickens	485,737	18,261	0	0	Jim Hogg	14,949	2,602	6,924,782	67,497
Dimmit	36,938,322	105,773,024	173,472,771	18,850,749	Jim Wells	69,946	193,755	2,951,681	18,258
Donley	0	0	8,406	103	Johnson	0	0	188,548,765	12,660
Duval	970,774	180,557	8,170,079	42,339	Jones	417,429	188,602	7,480	0
Eastland	157,099	457,205	1,616,582	14,209	Karnes	100,328,631	200,799,593	133,939,973	16,497,192
Ector	19,729,607	49,777,612	3,645,027	8,596	Kaufman	51,523	16,110	0	0

County	Oil (BBL)	Casinghead (MCF)	GW Gas (MCF)	Condensate (BBL)	County	Oil (BBL)	Casinghead (MCF)	GW Gas (MCF)	Condensate (BBL)
Kenedy	114,212	211,666	16,237,097	195,968	Rusk	1,426,150	1,937,536	111,475,148	565,044
Kent	3,451,715	6,846,603	0	0	Sabine	2,383	11,406	794,709	0
Kimble	310	0	15,948	0	S.Augustine	17,328	313,871	161,217,613	25,826
King	1,872,614	252,099	156,830	296	SanJacinto	40,846	153,627	3,401,650	131,108
Kleberg	70,752	383,536	7,241,742	179,293	SanPatricio	425,755	685,540	5,254,454	192,573
Knox	169,855	87,639	0	0	Schleicher	304,642	2,411,890	5,307,593	39,748
La Salle	56,930,040	105,170,600	140,523,049	3,888,682	Scurry	14,963,393	39,708,406	0	0
Lamb	226,907	256,856	0	0	Shackelford	390,955	593,013	998,895	13,897
Lavaca	6,064,351	9,381,656	22,671,906	499,876	Shelby	28,228	398,256	48,290,501	37,528
Lee	2,078,303	3,964,256	604,232	11,480	Sherman	60,149	35,526	12,114,290	1,717
Leon	754,663	1,655,257	29,927,503	41,853	Smith	1,144,743	1,251,788	16,761,643	160,082
Liberty	824,942	475,236	7,233,279	220,821	Somervell	0	0	4,117,117	4,334
Limestone	65,647	12	34,914,262	25,262	Starr	485,638	1,074,846	35,190,173	417,126
Lipscomb	1,175,191	12,339,174	39,177,304	1,574,709	Stephens	1,823,941	2,518,257	7,066,589	36,619
Live Oak	8,453,356	25,881,804	48,694,375	3,849,854	Sterling	725,063	5,727,901	2,621,702	25,577
Loving	76,870,328	185,462,577	130,899,360	20,340,461	Stonewall	2,036,793	3,407,451	0	0
Lubbock	988,758	97,653	0	0	Sutton	20,278	51,505	23,860,027	44,993
Lynn	319,721	113,604	0	0	Tarrant	0	0	428,822,907	12,362
Madison	2,080,324	7,458,374	2,784,168	253,951	Taylor	402,846	207,899	16,447	0
Marion	548,261	127,793	1,489,891	22,685	Terrell	33,152	332,153	19,740,903	61,791
Martin	83,236,933	132,967,264	9,131	111	Terry	3,395,723	1,643,932	0	0
Matagrda	241,253	280,252	9,152,818	166,679	Throckmrtn	869,427	2,527,996	109,826	1,970
Maverick	857,419	2,110,511	1,704,672	42,417	Titus	426,677	1,406	0	0
McCulloch	41,567	0	0	0	TomGreen	502,002	2,168,482	474,950	3,957
McLennan	587	0	0	0	Travis	3,930	0	0	0
McMullen	31,318,777	46,483,125	39,553,336	1,009,402	Trinity	23,339	0	382,402	4,427
Medina	104,989	7,591	2,580	0	Tyler	456,362	568,628	7,077,635	818,754
Menard	95,092	7,418	19,921	0	Upshur	89,084	30,786	19,269,313	182,818
Midland	144,243,169	309,616,672	5,163,189	114,967	Upton	62,058,096	177,680,261	10,979,460	168,085
Milam	912,138	450,962	19,418	232	Val Verde	2,030	0	4,657,287	203
Mills	0	0	4,142	0	Van Zandt	482,001	180,222	1,100,165	3,997
Mitchell	2,640,515	684,568	0	0	Victoria	1,817,952	1,261,676	2,775,170	53,520
Montague	1,026,721	11,394,231	51,455,375	481,447	Walker	44,019	1,112,054	898,679	35,221
Montgomry	832,878	1,277,415	2,519,087	22,096	Waller	207,024	433	1,554,833	11,984
Moore	259,598	1,357,393	15,933,401	7,885	Ward	35,023,511	72,051,734	16,196,030	653,640
Morris	31,475	20,502	0	0	Washngton	1,053,417	4,709,872	25,118,054	484,909
Motley	36,455	4,621	0	0	Webb	305,124	1,676,740	802,646,228	13,340,648
Nacgdches	11,811	47,261	73,012,363	73,388	Wharton	767,742	774,916	9,793,106	156,189
Navarro	144,213	151,697	370,841	11,468	Wheeler	1,279,596	9,656,534	110,418,680	2,728,956
Newton	502,552	948,722	2,372,982	156,719	Wichita	1,608,255	427,587	0	0
Nolan	1,158,330	1,828,519	261,433	778	Wilbarger	702,919	93,001	0	0
Nueces	176,919	361,145	9,158,915	224,357	Willacy	159,903	96,955	3,865,441	39,628
Ochiltree	4,810,731	22,190,299	13,383,979	297,700	Willimson	7,932	0	0	0
Oldham	339,298	965,329	22,038	33	Wilson	1,295,365	678,253	1,159	36
Orange	418,493	1,060,988	5,237,158	331,154	Winkler	13,549,876	23,267,098	13,432,511	890,490
Palo Pinto	114,961	2,200,883	7,774,113	45,635	Wise	157,355	3,442,396	181,026,416	461,964
Panola	284,322	1,876,102	316,481,298	1,304,742	Wood	3,321,295	54,511,219	1,738,125	74,659
Parker	1,412	145,497	59,100,489	86,629	Yoakum	26,808,701	38,841,458	175,556	0
Pecos	22,199,337	52,715,731	47,148,689	55,977	Young	933,739	1,424,077	970,527	12,119
Polk	401,760	325,879	35,466,091	768,290	Zapata	64,398	179,234	73,181,329	57,851
Potter	730,664	2,180,838	4,328,563	38,285	Zavala	5,998,008	6,211,611	275,133	116
Reagan	30,228,335	135,067,870	1,418,392	28,340	Source: Texas Railroad Commission.				
Real	65	0	65,848	0					
Red River	78,007	0	0	0					
Reeves	89,736,060	246,631,838	408,851,747	47,717,539					
Refugio	2,265,215	7,987,289	1,602,347	15,357					
Roberts	1,446,499	11,686,809	29,739,098	484,108					
Robertson	1,193,756	650,712	69,847,931	6,096					
Runnels	350,907	777,568	113,248	2,510					

Top Gas-Producing Counties, 1993–2019

The top 37 natural gas-producing counties are listed in the chart below. The fourth column at the right lists the number of producing gas wells in the county in February 2019. Sixty-one counties have produced more than 500 billion cubic feet of natural gas since 1993 (see map). (**MCF** is thousand cubic feet.)

Rank	County	Gas (MCF)	Gas Wells	Rank	County	Gas (MCF)	Gas Wells
1.	Webb	10,499,360,593	6,023	20.	Limestone	1,562,766,679	1,116
2.	Tarrant	7,461,247,725	4,007	21.	Sutton	1,561,344,481	5,610
3.	Panola	7,256,665,029	4,949	22.	Lavaca	1,505,174,330	418
4.	Zapata	6,369,311,386	2,838	23.	Reeves	1,478,956,204	804
5.	Hidalgo	5,152,105,674	1,281	24.	Loving	1,424,691,042	470
6.	Johnson	4,801,942,701	2,925	25.	Terrell	1,419,294,969	647
7.	Freestone	4,391,998,895	2,949	26.	Dimmit	1,357,828,396	1,691
8.	Wise	4,141,818,464	4,213	27.	Parker	1,307,373,065	1,522
9.	Pecos	4,101,227,884	1,283	28.	Brooks	1,302,032,716	386
10.	Denton	3,424,697,743	2,875	29.	Duval	1,289,029,271	367
11.	Starr	2,971,824,615	1,071	30.	Leon	1,274,466,025	568
12.	Hemphill	2,960,230,802	2,401	31.	Gregg	1,265,008,192	859
13.	Wheeler	2,781,928,534	1,872	32.	Lipscomb	1,220,691,655	1,382
14.	Crockett	2,577,714,355	5,649	33.	Wharton	1,195,569,679	308
15.	Robertson	2,560,786,795	894	34.	Shelby	1,181,859,897	637
16.	Rusk	2,550,157,906	2,309	35.	Upshur	1,160,638,006	704
17.	Harrison	2,532,856,448	2,294	36.	La Salle	1,140,478,091	982
18.	Nacogdoches	1,791,188,959	1,361	37.	Moore	1,136,233,811	1,376
19.	DeWitt	1,581,517,485	790				

Source: Texas Railroad Commission.

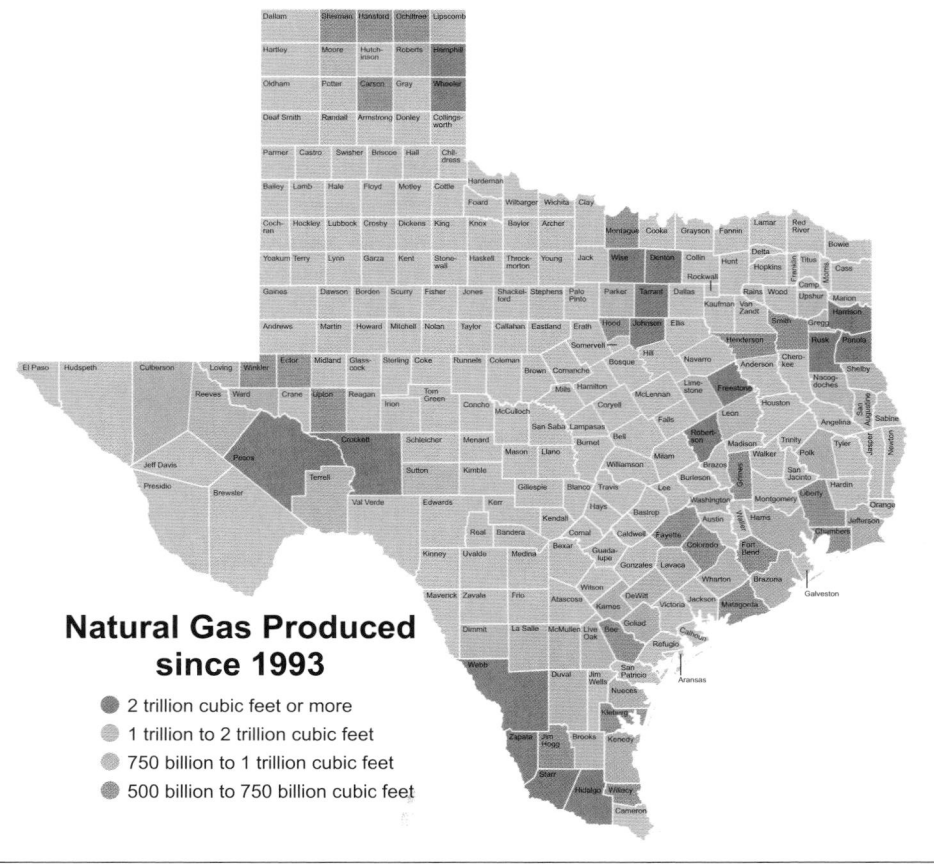

Natural Gas Produced since 1993

- 2 trillion cubic feet or more
- 1 trillion to 2 trillion cubic feet
- 750 billion to 1 trillion cubic feet
- 500 billion to 750 billion cubic feet

Petroleum Production and Income in Texas

Year	Crude Oil Production (thousand barrels)	Crude Oil Value (add 000)	Crude Oil Average Price per barrel (nominal)	Crude Oil *Average price per barrel (2005 $)	Natural Gas Production (million cubic feet)	Natural Gas Value (add 000)	Natural Gas Wellhead Price (cents per **Mcf)
1915	24,943	$ 13,027	$ 0 .52	NA	13,324	$ 2,594	19.5
1925	144,648	262,270	1.81	NA	134,872	7,040	5.2
1935	392,666	367,820	0.94	NA	642,366	13,233	2.1
1945	754,710	914,410	1.21	NA	1,711,401	44,839	2.6
1955	1,053,297	2,989,330	2.84	NA	4,730,798	378,464	8.0
1965	1,000,749	2,962,119	2.96	NA	6,636,555	858,396	12.9
1970	1,249,697	4,104,005	3.28	NA	8,357,716	1,203,511	14.4
1975	1,221,929	9,336,570	7.64	NA	7,485,764	3,885,112	51.9
1980	977,436	21,259,233	21.84	47.74	7,115,889	10,673,834	150.0
1981	945,132	32,692,116	35.06	67.14	7,050,207	12,598,712	178.7
1982	923,868	29,074,126	31.77	57.33	6,497,678	13,567,151	208.8
1983	876,205	22,947,814	29.35	50.95	5,643,183	14,672,275	225.0
1984	874,079	25,138,520	28.87	48.31	5,864,224	13,487,715	230.0
1985	860,300	23,159,286	26.80	43.52	5,805,098	12,665,114	218.0
1986	813,620	11,976,488	14.73	23.40	5,663,491	8,778,410	155.0
1987	754,213	13,221,345	17.55	27.10	5,516,224	7,612,389	138.0
1988	727,928	10,729,660	14.71	21.96	5,702,643	7,983,700	141.0
1989	679,575	12,123,624	17.81	25.62	5,595,190	8,113,026	145.0
1990	672,081	15,047,902	22.37	30.98	5,533,771	8,281,372	149.7
1991	672,810	12,836,080	19.04	25.47	5,509,990	7,713,986	143.0
1992	642,059	11,820,306	18.32	23.94	5,436,408	8,643,888	174.0
1993	572,600	9,288,800	16.19	20.70	5,606,498	7,365,800	204.0
1994	533,900	7,977,500	14.98	18.76	5,675,748	6,220,300	185.0
1995	503,200	8,177,700	16.38	20.09	5,672,105	5,305,200	155.0
1996	478,100	9,560,800	20.31	24.44	5,770,255	6,945,000	217.0
1997	464,900	8,516,800	18.66	22.07	5,814,745	8,134,200	232.0
1998	440,600	5,472,400	12.28	14.36	5,772,080	6,362,900	196.0
1999	337,100	5,855,800	17.29	19.93	5,538,929	6,789,700	219.0
2000	348,900	10,037,300	28.60	32.26	5,645,972	12,837,600	368.0
2001	325,500	7,770,500	23.41	25.82	5,668,602	13,708,700	400.0
2002	335,600	8,150,400	23.77	25.80	5,611,958	9,840,800	295.0
2003	333,300	9,708,600	29.13	30.96	5,671,689	14,797,800	488.0
2004	327,910	12,762,650	38.79	40.08	5,817,227	17,077,700	546.0
2005	327,600	12,744,600	52.61	52.61	5,700,613	16,399,400	733.0
2006	314,600	19,353,500	61.31	59.38	6,077,786	23,500,800	639.0
2007	311,830	21,341,100	68.30	64.30	6,421,375	22,968,420	625.0
2008	315,896	30,409,170	96.85	89.28	7,271,815	34,415,890	797.0
2009	349,391	18,455,530	57.40	52.31	7,573,033	12,167,800	367.0
2010	369,953	26,054,900	76.23	68.88	7,246,042	11,796,700	448.0
2011	448,903	39,420,500	91.99	81.15	7,051,594	13,646,300	395.0
2012	724,422	55,145,600	92.50	NA	7,128,775	12,959,100	266.0
2013	749,876	73,666,700	95.80	NA	7,725,119	15,358,900	373.0
2014	927,417	85,962,300	87.02	NA	8,171,230	18,034,000	428.0
2015	1,004,774	48,132,920	48.79	NA	7,871,200	8,827,180	263.0
2016	974,612	32,854,310	42.40	NA	6,996,000	20,566,930	255.0
2017	1,026,765	49,869,976	48.57	NA	6,300,292	20,664,957	328.0
2018	1,274,569	$76,359,429	$ 59.91	NA	5,742,978	$ 19,468,695	339.0

Revised May 2019. *In chained (2005) dollars, from the U.S. Energy Information Administration (EIA). (NA, not available.) **Mcf (thousand cubic feet).
Sources: Previously from the Texas Railroad Commission, Texas Mid-Continent Oil & Gas Association and, beginning in 1979, data are from Department of Energy. Data since 1993 are from the state comptroller and EIA and the railroad commission. Federal figures do not include gas that is vented or flared or used for pressure maintenance and repressuring, but do include non-hydrocarbon gases.

Offshore Production History – Oil and Gas

The cumulative offshore natural gas production as of Jan. 1, 2019, was **4,207,288,591** thousand cubic feet (Mcf). The cumulative offshore oil production was **42,538,000** barrels.

Production in Recent Years

YEAR	Crude Oil BBL	Casing-head Mcf	Gas Well Gas Mcf	Conden-sate BBL
2000	548,046	335,415	44,086,237	220,309
2005	450,378	389,301	28,589,312	452,049
2006	310,625	262,049	26,870,964	295,034
2007	232,602	124,942	30,051,725	410,375
2008	210,897	120,986	42,029,079	393,594
2009	480,514	1,673,140	37,235,149	918,357
2010	477,080	1,159,787	27,577,237	843,630
2011	522,307	925,166	23,573,021	566,413
2012	605,389	902,900	16,811,048	435,049
2013	500,209	460,876	15,083,228	369,599
2014	424,102	547,256	12,454,823	354,670
2015	291,428	233,094	9,982,738	281,510
2016	154,005	48,816	8,337,712	231,975
2017	118,474	35,054	6,049,351	183,464

2018 Production by Area

Offshore Area	Crude Oil BBL	Casing-head Mcf	Gas Well Gas Mcf	Conden-sate BBL
Brazos-LB	0	0	24,695	72
Brazos-SB	0	0	0	0
Galveston-LB	69,706	27,153	272,999	136,656
Galveston-SB	0	0	0	0
High Island-LB	0	0	1,849,487	13,091
High Island-SB	0	0	0	0
Matagrda Is.-LB	57,532	31,048	0	0
Matagrda Is.-SB	0	0	0	0
Mustang Is.-LB	0	0	590,791	9,586
Mustang Is.-SB	2,247	2,928	1,252,230	44,535
N. Padre Is.-LB	0	0	0	0
Sabine Pass	0	0	0	0
Total	**129,485**	**61,129**	**3,990,202**	**203,940**

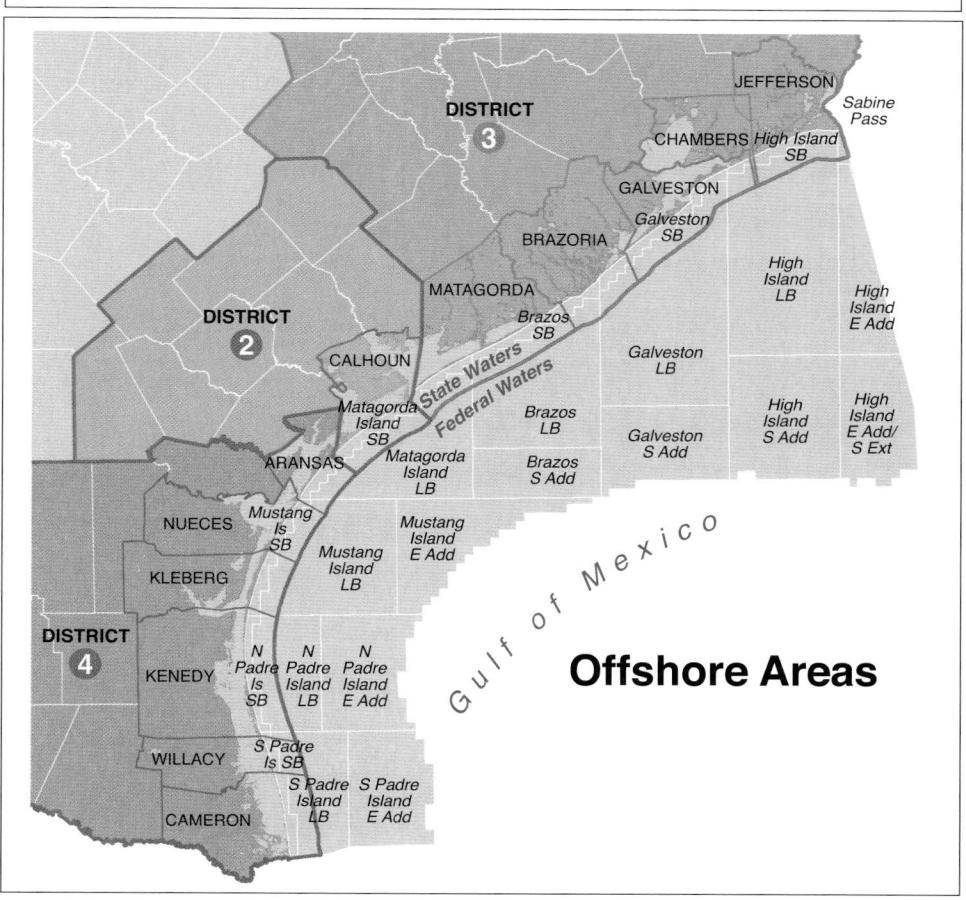

Offshore Areas

Receipts by Texas from Tidelands

The Republic of Texas had proclaimed its Gulf boundaries as three marine leagues, recognized by international law as traditional national boundaries. These boundaries were never seriously questioned when Texas joined the Union in 1845. But, in 1930 a congressional resolution authorized the U.S. Attorney General to file suit to establish offshore lands as properties of the federal government. Congress returned the disputed lands to Texas in 1953, and the U.S. Supreme Court confirmed Texas' ownership in 1960. In 1978, the federal government also granted states a "fair and equitable" share of the revenues from offshore leases within three miles of the states' outermost boundary. States did not receive any such revenue until 1986.

The table shows annual receipts from tidelands in the Gulf of Mexico by the Texas General Land Office from 1963 to Aug. 31, 2018. It does not include revenue from bays and other submerged area owned by Texas. Totals include previous years not shown in this chart. Source: General Land Office.

From	To	Total	Bonus	Rental	Royalty	Lease
9-01-1963	8-31-1964	$ 3,656,236.75	$ 2,435,244.36	$ 525,315.00	$ 695,677.39	...
9-01-1964	8-31-1965	54,654,576.96	53,114,943.63	755,050.12	784,583.21	...
9-01-1965	8-31-1966	22,148,825.44	18,223,357.84	3,163,475.00	761,992.60	...
9-01-1966	8-31-1967	8,469,680.86	3,641,414.96	3,711,092.65	1,117,173.25	...
9-01-1967	8-31-1968	6,305,851.00	1,251,852.50	2,683,732.50	2,370,266.00	...
9-01-1968	8-31-1969	6,372,268.28	1,838,118.33	1,491,592.50	3,042,557.45	...
9-01-1969	8-31-1970	10,311,030.48	5,994,666.32	618,362.50	3,698,001.66	...
9-01-1970	8-31-1971	9,969,629.17	4,326,120.11	726,294.15	4,917,214.91	...
9-01-1971	8-31-1972	7,558,327.21	1,360,212.64	963,367.60	5,234,746.97	...
9-01-1972	8-31-1973	9,267,975.68	3,701,737.30	920,121.60	4,646,116.78	...
9-01-1973	8-31-1974	41,717,670.04	32,981,619.28	1,065,516.60	7,670,534.16	...
9-01-1974	8-31-1975	27,321,536.62	5,319,762.85	2,935,295.60	19,066,478.17	...
9-01-1975	8-31-1976	38,747,074.09	6,197,853.00	3,222,535.84	29,326,685.25	...
9-01-1976	8-31-1977	84,196,228.27	41,343,114.81	2,404,988.80	40,448,124.66	...
9-01-1977	8-31-1978	118,266,812.05	49,807,750.45	4,775,509.92	63,683,551.68	...
9-01-1978	8-31-1979	100,410,268.68	34,578,340.94	7,318,748.40	58,513,179.34	...
9-01-1979	8-31-1980	200,263,803.03	34,733,270.02	10,293,153.80	155,237,379.21	...
9-01-1980	8-31-1981	219,126,876.54	37,467,196.97	13,100,484.25	168,559,195.32	...
9-01-1981	8-31-1982	250,824,581.69	27,529,516.33	14,214,478.97	209,080,586.39	...
9-01-1982	8-31-1983	165,197,734.83	10,180,696.40	12,007,476.70	143,009,561.73	...
9-01-1983	8-31-1984	152,755,934.29	32,864,122.19	8,573,996.87	111,317,815.23	...
9-01-1984	8-31-1985	140,561,690.79	32,650,127.75	6,837,603.70	101,073,959.34	...
9-01-1985	8-31-1986	516,503,771.08	6,365,426.23	4,241,892.75	78,289,592.27	$ 427,606,859.83
9-01-1986	8-31-1987	60,066,571.05	4,186,561.63	1,933,752.50	44,691,907.22	9,254,349.70
9-01-1987	8-31-1988	56,875,069.22	14,195,274.28	1,817,058.90	28,068,202.53	12,794,533.51
9-01-1988	8-31-1989	61,793,380.04	12,995,892.74	1,290,984.37	35,160,568.40	12,345,934.53
9-01-1989	8-31-1990	68,701,751.51	7,708,449.54	1,289,849.87	40,331,537.06	19,371,915.04
9-01-1990	8-31-1991	90,885,856.99	3,791,832.77	1,345,711.07	70,023,601.01	15,724,712.14
9-01-1991	8-31-1992	51,154,511.34	4,450,850.00	1,123,585.54	26,776,191.35	18,803,884.45
9-01-1992	8-31-1993	60,287,712.60	3,394,230.00	904,359.58	34,853,679.68	21,135,443.34
9-01-1993	8-31-1994	57,825,043.59	3,570,657.60	694,029.30	32,244,987.95	21,315,368.74
9-01-1994	8-31-1995	62,143,227.78	8,824,722.93	674,479.79	34,691,023.35	17,951,001.71
9-01-1995	8-31-1996	68,166,645.51	13,919,246.80	1,102,591.39	32,681,315.73	20,463,491.59
9-01-1996	8-31-1997	90,614,935.93	22,007,378.46	1,319,614.78	41,605,792.50	25,682,150.19
9-01-1997	8-31-1998	104,016,006.75	36,946,312.49	2,070,802.90	38,760,320.91	26,238,570.45
9-01-1998	8-31-1999	53,565,810.30	5,402,171.00	2,471,128.47	23,346,515.93	22,345,994.90
9-01-1999	8-31-2000	55,465,763.99	3,487,564.80	2,171,636.35	24,314,241.99	25,492,320.85
9-01-2000	8-31-2001	68,226,347.58	9,963,608.68	1,830,378.11	23,244,034.74	33,188,326.05
9-01-2001	8-31-2002	30,910,283.91	9,286,015.20	1,545,583.01	13,369,771.56	6,708,914.14
9-01-2002	8-31-2003	50,881,515.90	15,152,092.40	1,071,377.60	19,648,641.39	15,009,404.51
9-01-2003	8-31-2004	54,379,791.20	14,448,555.70	1,094,201.41	25,199,635.21	13,637,398.88
9-01-2004	8-31-2005	53,594,809.87	9,148,220.20	1,624,666.50	32,406,328.78	10,415,594.39
9-01-2005	8-31-2006	60,829,271.63	22,565,845.14	1,605,090.30	23,287,994.53	13,370,341.66
9-01-2006	8-31-2007	52,513,621.85	15,879,784.44	2,022,859.80	18,785,626.55	15,825,351.06
9-01-2007	8-31-2008	86,705,980.28	4,632,175.50	1,485,080.97	68,408,943.01	12,179,780.80
9-01-2008	8-31-2009	65,835,625.76	3,896,795.20	1,020,204.33	53,166,364.50	7,752,261.73
9-01-2009	8-31-2010	49,647,832.14	3,352,431.20	603,406.00	41,901,754.81	3,790,240.13
9-01-2010	8-31-2011	50,360,843.36	4,088,819.06	546,404.80	43,602,027.62	2,123,591.88
9-01-2011	8-31-2012	37,561,595.54	2,436,420.00	217,356.00	33,327,417.09	1,580,402.45
9-01-2012	8-31-2013	32,676,026.13	1,079,400.00	339,941.00	30,353,820.49	902,864.64
9-01-2013	8-31-2014	28,103,953.40	217,000.00	193,125.00	26,665,893.97	1,027.934.53
9-01-2014	8-31-2015	17,922,043.53	969,600.00	71,894.00	16,302,558.59	577,990.94
9-01-2015	8-31-2016	7,053,383.42	0.00	112,350.00	6,819,050.31	121,983.11
9-01-2016	8-31-2017	7,422,396.66	100,800.00	48,712.00	7,172,244.48	100,640.18
9-01-2017	8-31-2018	10,237,935.90	0.00	48,000.00	5,759,255.41	4,430,680.49
Totals		$ 3,974,612.907.55	$ 774,513,049,71	$ 147,166,154.10	$ 2,213,663,471.20	$ 839,270.232.54
Inside three-mile line		$ 533,256,002.78	$ 180,838,499.91	$ 39,193,553.27	$ 313,223,949.60	0.00
Between three-mile and three marine-league line		$ 2,599,261,306.65	$ 591,022,465.41	$ 107,734,519.64	$1,900,439,521.60	0.00
Outside three marine-league line		$ 842,095,598,12	$ 2,652,084.39	$ 173,281.19	0.00	$ 839,270,232,54

Nonpetroleum Minerals

Sources: U.S. Geological Survey's mineral industry surveys, www.usgs.gov/centers/nmic/mineral-industry-surveys; Bureau of Economic Geology, The University of Texas at Austin, www.beg.utexas.edu

There are many nonpetroleum, or nonfuel, minerals found in Texas. Although they are overshadowed by production of petroleum, natural gas, and natural gas liquids, many are important to the economy.

In 2018, Texas nonfuel mineral production was valued at **$6.0 billion**, a 15 percent increase from the $5.2 billion in total value for 2017, and accounted for 7.3 percent of the total U.S. nonfuel mineral production value of $82.2 billion. Among all 50 states, **Texas ranked third in nonfuel mineral production** for the fourth year in a row (since 2015), behind Arizona ($6.7 billion in 2018) and Nevada ($7.9 billion).

The nonfuel mineral commodities produced in Texas in 2018 include: barite, cement, gold, gypsum, helium, lime, ammonia, salt, sand and gravel (both construction and industrial), selenium, stone (both crushed and dimension), sulfur, talc, tellurium, vanadium, and zeolites (clinoptilolite).

Texas was the leader in crushed stone production, and second to California in sand and gravel (construction).

Texas was **the only state that produced tellurium** in 2018, though the amount and value has been withheld to avoid disclosing proprietary data for the company involved.

ALUMINUM: No aluminum ores are mined in Texas, but three Texas plants process aluminum materials in one or more ways. Plants in San Patricio and Calhoun counties produce aluminum oxide (alumina) from imported raw ore (bauxite), and a plant in Milam County reduces the oxide to aluminum.

ASBESTOS: Small occurrences of amphibole-type asbestos have been found in the state. In West Texas, richterite, a white, long-fibered amphibole, is associated with some of the talc deposits northwest of Allamoore in Hudspeth County. Another type, tremolite, has been found in the Llano Uplift of Central Texas where it is associated with serpentinite in eastern Gillespie and western Blanco counties. No asbestos is mined in Texas.

ASPHALT (NATIVE): Asphalt-bearing Cretaceous limestones crop out in Burnet, Kinney, Pecos, Reeves, Uvalde, and other counties. The most significant deposit is in southwestern Uvalde County, where asphalt occurs naturally in pore spaces of the Anacacho Limestone. The material is quarried and used extensively as road-paving material. Asphalt-bearing sandstones occur in Anderson, Angelina, Cooke, Jasper, Maverick, Montague, Nacogdoches, Uvalde, Zavala, and other counties.

BARITE: Deposits of a heavy, nonmetallic mineral, barite (barium sulphate), have been found in many localities, including Baylor, Brown, Brewster, Culberson, Gillespie, Howard, Hudspeth, Jeff Davis, Kinney, Live Oak, Llano, Taylor, Val Verde, and Webb counties. During the 1960s, there was small, intermittent production in the Seven Heart Gap area of the Apache Mountains in Culberson County, where barite was mined from open pits. Most of the deposits are known to be relatively small, but the Webb County deposit has not been evaluated. Grinding plants, which prepare barite mined outside of Texas for use chiefly as a weighting agent in well-drilling muds and as a filler, are located in Brownsville, Corpus Christi, El Paso, Galena Park, Galveston, and Houston.

BASALT (TRAP ROCK): Masses of basalt, a hard, dark-colored, fine-grained igneous rock, crop out in Kinney, Travis, Uvalde, and several other counties along the Balcones Fault Zone, and also in the Trans-Pecos area of West Texas. Basalt is quarried near Knippa in Uvalde County for use as road-building material, railroad ballast, and other aggregate.

BENTONITE (see CLAYS).

BERYLLIUM: Occurrences of beryllium minerals at several Trans-Pecos localities have been recognized for several years.

BRINE (see also SALT, SODIUM SULPHATE): Many wells in Texas produce brine by solution mining of subsurface salt deposits, mostly in West Texas counties such as Andrews, Crane, Ector, Loving, Midland, Pecos, Reeves, Ward, and others. These wells in the Permian Basin dissolve salt from the Salado Formation, an enormous salt deposit that extends in the subsurface from north of the Big Bend northward to Kansas, has an east-west width of 150 to 200 miles, and may have several hundred feet of net salt thickness. The majority of the brine is used in the petroleum industry, but it also is used in water softening, the chemical industry, and other uses. Three Gulf Coast counties, Fort Bend, Duval, and Jefferson, have brine stations that produce from salt domes.

BUILDING STONE (DIMENSION STONE): Granite and limestone currently are quarried for use as dimension stone. The granite quarries are located in Burnet, Gillespie, Llano, and Mason counties; the limestone quarries are in Shackelford and Williamson counties. Past production of limestone for use as dimension stone has been reported in Burnet, Gillespie, Jones, Tarrant, Travis, and several other counties. There also has been production of sandstone in various counties for use as dimension stone.

CEMENT MATERIALS: Cement is currently manufactured in Bexar, Comal, Dallas, Ector, Ellis, Hays, McLennan, Nolan, and Potter counties. Many of these utilize Cretaceous limestones and shales or clays as raw materials for the cement. On the Texas High Plains, a cement plant near Amarillo uses impure caliche as the chief raw material. Iron oxide, also a constituent of cement, is available from the iron ore deposits of East Texas and from smelter slag. Gypsum, added to the cement as a retarder, is found chiefly in the North-Central, Central, and Trans-Pecos areas.

A new greenfields white cement production plant has been proposed near Brady, but it has been delayed due to local opposition. It would be the third of its kind in the U.S.

Cement Production in Texas
(metric tons)

Type	2018	2017
Portland and Blended	11,757,243	11,465,785
Masonry	291,718	304,320
Clinker	10,573,886	10,128,636
	Source: Industry surveys at USGS	

CHROMIUM: Chromite-bearing rock has been found in several small deposits around the margin of the Coal Creek serpentinite mass in northeastern Gillespie County and northwestern Blanco County. Exploration has not revealed significant deposits.

CLAYS: Texas has an abundance and variety of ceramic and nonceramic clays and is one of the country's leading producers of clay products.

Almost any kind of clay, ranging from common clay used to make brick and tile to clays suitable for manufacture of specialty whitewares, can be used for ceramic purposes. Fire clay suitable for use as refractories occurs chiefly in East and North-Central Texas; ball clay, a high-quality plastic ceramic clay, is found in East Texas.

Ceramic clay suitable for quality structural clay products, such as structural building brick, paving brick, and drain tile, is especially abundant in East and North-Central Texas.

Common clay suitable for use in the manufacture of cement and ordinary brick is found in most counties of the state. Many of the Texas clays will expand or bloat upon rapid firing and are suitable for the manufacture of lightweight aggregate, which is used mainly in concrete blocks and highway surfacing.

Nonceramic clays are utilized without firing. They are used primarily as bleaching and absorbent clays, fillers, coaters, additives, bonding clays, drilling muds, catalysts, and potentially as sources of alumina. Most of the nonceramic clays in Texas are bentonites and fuller's earth. These occur extensively in the Coastal Plain and locally in the High Plains and Big Bend areas. Kaolin clays in parts of East Texas are potential sources of such nonceramic products as paper coaters and fillers, rubber fillers, and drilling agents. Relatively high in alumina, these clays also are a potential source of metallic aluminum.

COAL (see also LIGNITE): Bituminous coal, which occurs in North-Central, South, and West Texas, was a significant energy source in Texas prior to the large-scale development of oil and gas. During the period from 1895–1943, Texas mines produced more than 25 million tons of coal. The mines were inactive for many years, but the renewed interest in coal as a major energy source prompted a revaluation of Texas' coal deposits. In the late 1970s, bituminous coal production resumed in the state on a limited scale when mines were opened in Coleman, Erath, and Webb counties.

Much of the state's bituminous coal occurs in North-Central Texas. Deposits are found there in Pennsylvanian rocks within a large area that includes Coleman, Eastland, Erath, Jack, McCulloch, Montague, Palo Pinto, Parker, Throckmorton, Wise, Young, and other counties. Before the general availability of oil and gas, underground coal mines near Thurber, Bridgeport, Newcastle, Strawn, and other points annually produced significant coal tonnages. Preliminary evaluations indicate substantial amounts of coal may remain in the North-Central Texas area. The coal seams there are generally no more than 30 inches thick and are commonly covered by well-consolidated overburden. Ash and sulphur content are high. Beginning in 1979, two bituminous coal mine operations in North-Central Texas, one in southern Coleman County and one in northwestern Erath County, produced coal to be used as fuel by the cement industry. Neither mine is currently operating.

In South Texas, bituminous coal occurs in the **Eagle Pass district of Maverick County**, and bituminous cannel coal is present in the Santo Tomas district of Webb County. The Eagle Pass area was a leading coal-producing district in Texas during the late 1800s and early 1900s. The bituminous coal in that area, which occurs in the Upper Cretaceous Olmos Formation, has a high ash content and a moderate moisture and sulfur content. According to reports, Maverick County coal beds range from four to seven feet thick.

The cannel coals of western Webb County occur near the Rio Grande in middle Eocene strata. They were mined for more than 50 years and used primarily as a boiler fuel. Mining ceased from 1939 until 1978, when a surface mine was opened 30 miles northwest of Laredo to produce cannel coal for use as fuel in the cement industry and for export. An additional mine has since been opened in that county. Tests show that the coals of the Webb County Santo Tomas district have a high hydrogen content and yield significant amounts of gas and oil when distilled. They also have a high sulfur content. A potential use might be as a source of various petrochemical products.

Coal deposits in the Trans-Pecos country of West Texas include those in the Cretaceous rocks of the Terlingua area of Brewster County, the Eagle Spring area of Hudspeth County, and the San Carlos area of Presidio County. The coal deposits in these areas are believed to have relatively little potential for development as a fuel. They have been sold in the past as a soil amendment (see **LEONARDITE**).

COPPER: Copper minerals have been found in the Trans-Pecos area of West Texas, in the Llano Uplift area of Central Texas, and in redbed deposits of North Texas. No copper has been mined in Texas during recent years, and the total copper produced in the state has been relatively small. Past attempts to mine the North Texas and Llano Uplift copper deposits resulted in small shipments.

Practically all the copper production in the state has been from the Van Horn–Allamoore district of Culberson and Hudspeth counties in the Trans-Pecos area. Chief output was from the Hazel copper-silver mine of Culberson County that yielded over 1 million pounds of copper during 1891–1947. Copper ores and concentrates from outside of Texas are processed at smelters in El Paso and Amarillo.

CRUSHED STONE: Texas is among the leading states in the production of crushed stone. Most production consists of limestone; other kinds of crushed stone produced in the state include basalt (trap rock), dolomite, granite, marble, rhyolite, sandstone, and serpentinite. Large tonnages of crushed stone are used as aggregate in concrete, as road material, and in the manufacture of cement and lime. Some is used as riprap, terrazzo, roofing chips, filter material, and fillers, as well as other purposes. In 2018, Texas led the country in the production of crushed stone, followed by Pennsylvania, Florida, and North Carolina.

Crushed Stone Production

Year	Quantity (thous. met. tons)	Value (millions)
2018	172,000	$1,900
2017	164,000	$1,750
2016	163,000	$1,690
2015	163,000	$1,630
	Source: Industry surveys at USGS	

DIATOMITE (DIATOMACEOUS EARTH): Diatomite is a very lightweight siliceous material consisting of the remains of microscopic aquatic plants (diatoms). It is used chiefly as a filter and filler; other uses are for thermal insulation, as an abrasive, as an insecticide carrier, as a lightweight aggregate, and for other purposes. The diatomite was deposited in shallow, fresh-water lakes that were present in the High Plains during portions of the Pliocene and Pleistocene epochs. Deposits have been found in Armstrong, Crosby, Dickens, Ector, Hartley, and Lamb counties. No diatomite is mined in Texas.

DOLOMITE ROCK: Dolomite rock, which consists largely of the mineral dolomite (calcium-magnesium carbonate), commonly is associated with limestone in Texas. Areas in which dolomite rock occurs include Central Texas, the Callahan Divide, and parts of the Edwards Plateau, High Plains, and West Texas. Some of the principal deposits of dolomite rock are found in Bell, Brown, Burnet, Comanche, Edwards, El Paso, Gillespie, Lampasas, Mills, Nolan, Taylor, and Williamson counties. Dolomite rock can be used as crushed stone (although much of Texas dolomite is soft and not a good aggregate material), in the manufacture of lime, and as a source of magnesium.

FELDSPAR: Large crystals and crystal fragments of feldspar minerals occur in the Precambrian pegmatite rocks that crop out in the Llano Uplift area of Central Texas, including Blanco, Burnet, Gillespie, Llano, and Mason counties, and in the Van Horn area of Culberson and Hudspeth counties in West Texas. Feldspar has been mined in Llano County for use as roofing granules and as a ceramic material. Feldspar is currently mined in Burnet County for use as an aggregate.

FLUORSPAR: The mineral fluorite (calcium fluoride), which is known commercially as fluorspar, occurs in both Central

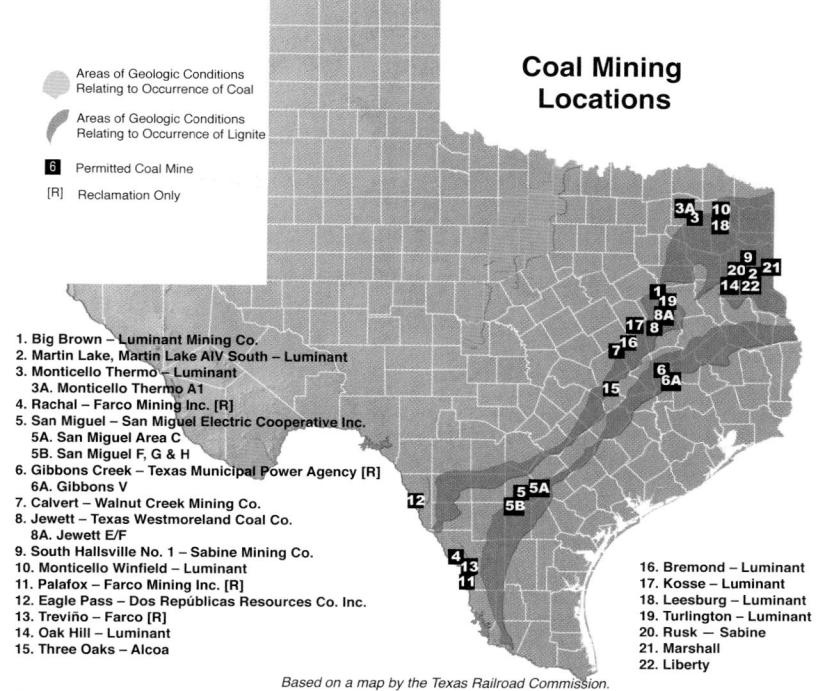

Coal Mining Locations

Areas of Geologic Conditions Relating to Occurrence of Coal

Areas of Geologic Conditions Relating to Occurrence of Lignite

6   Permitted Coal Mine

[R]   Reclamation Only

1. Big Brown – Luminant Mining Co.
2. Martin Lake, Martin Lake AIV South – Luminant
3. Monticello Thermo – Luminant
   3A. Monticello Thermo A1
4. Rachal – Farco Mining Inc. [R]
5. San Miguel – San Miguel Electric Cooperative Inc.
   5A. San Miguel Area C
   5B. San Miguel F, G & H
6. Gibbons Creek – Texas Municipal Power Agency [R]
   6A. Gibbons V
7. Calvert – Walnut Creek Mining Co.
8. Jewett – Texas Westmoreland Coal Co.
   8A. Jewett E/F
9. South Hallsville No. 1 – Sabine Mining Co.
10. Monticello Winfield – Luminant
11. Palafox – Farco Mining Inc. [R]
12. Eagle Pass – Dos Repúblicas Resources Co. Inc.
13. Treviño – Farco [R]
14. Oak Hill – Luminant
15. Three Oaks – Alcoa

16. Bremond – Luminant
17. Kosse – Luminant
18. Leesburg – Luminant
19. Turlington – Luminant
20. Rusk — Sabine
21. Marshall
22. Liberty

Based on a map by the Texas Railroad Commission.

Coal and Lignite Mine Production
(in short tons)

Mine	Acres Bonded	2016	2017	2018	Cumulative Total
1. Big Brown	4,363.1	0	0	0	171,155,954
2. Martin Lake	17,167.7	2,864,517	2,344,708	2,471,147	315,025,965
Martin Lake AIV South	2,308.0	0	0	0	6,771,850
3. Monticello-Thermo	1,876.1	0	0	0	42,849,720
Monticello-Thermo A-1	278.9	59,120	0	0	792,213
4. Rachal	615.9	0	0	0	963,827
5. San Miguel	10,424.1	530,939	584,779	1,981,967	89,557,389
San Miguel Area C	3,668.2	2,245,919	2,463,764	195,081	22,747,139
San Miguel F, G, & H	1,996.0	-	-	787,644	787,644
6. Gibbons Creek	4,976.6	0	0	0	30,431,174
Gibbons Creek V	1,796.1	0	0	0	12,547,611
7. Calvert	6,072.0	2,123,225	1,992,150	2,030,297	53,440,419
8. Jewett	9,593.2	3,643,619	0	0	173,220,612
Jewett E/F	3,917.0	21,372	0	0	35,937,586
9. South Hallsville No. 1	16,299.9	2,177,192	1,312,181	1,221,253	112,544,241
10. Monticello-Winfield	13,269.0	0	0	0	277,049,944
11. Palafox	2,575.2			0	5,355,519
12. Eagle Pass	5,848.0	1,788,007	2,437,496	2,146,219	7,026,808
13. Treviño	531.9			0	890,453
14. Oak Hill	18,064.9	1,186,697	0	0	129,763,914
15. Three Oaks	11,654.9	6,983,347	7,149,478	93,632	75,274,543
16. Bremond	3,370.6	0	0	0	236
17. Kosse	11,440.6	9,299,300	10,076,011	8,683,043	79,680,543
18. Leesburg	4,293.0	0	0	0	0
19. Turlington	3,614.3	1,415,346	1,239,905	0	16,504,979
20. Rusk	8,825.0	2,020,588	2,526,625	2,313,432	11,739,784
21. Marshall	1,101.0	213,647	240,240	185,097	851,509
22. Liberty	3,424.8	2,567,044	3,048,198	2,734,143	10,550,417
Statewide Total	**173,446.8**	**39,139,879**	**35,415,535**	**24,842,955**	***1,843,692,437**

* Statewide cumulative total includes the cumulative amount mined from the following "no longer permitted" mines: Little Bull Creek (428,932), Powell Bend (1,569,875), Thurber (465,984), Darco (6,798,881), and Sandow (150,966,982).

Source: Coal Production through 2018 report, Railroad Commission of Texas

and West Texas. In Central Texas, the deposits that have been found in Burnet, Gillespie, and Mason counties are not considered adequate to sustain mining operations. In West Texas, deposits have been found in Brewster, El Paso, Hudspeth, Jeff Davis, and Presidio counties. Fluorspar has been mined in the Christmas Mountains of Brewster County and processed in Marathon. Former West Texas mining activity in the Eagle Mountains district of Hudspeth County resulted in the production of approximately 15,000 short tons of fluorspar during the peak years of 1942–1950. No production has been reported in Hudspeth County since that period. Imported fluorspar is processed in Brownsville, Eagle Pass, El Paso, and Houston. Fluorspar is used in the steel, chemical, aluminum, magnesium, ceramics, and glass industries, and for various other purposes.

FULLER'S EARTH (see CLAYS).

GOLD: No major deposits of gold are known in Texas. Small amounts have been found in the Llano Uplift region of Central Texas and in West Texas; minor occurrences have been reported on the Edwards Plateau and the Gulf Coastal Plain of Texas. Nearly all of the gold produced in the state came as a by-product of silver and lead mining at Presidio mine, near Shafter in Presidio County. Additional small quantities were produced as a by-product of copper mining in Culberson County and from residual soils developed from gold-bearing quartz stringers in metamorphic rocks in Llano County. No gold mining has been reported in Texas since 1952. Total gold production in the state from 1889–1952 amounted to more than 8,419 troy ounces, according to U.S. Bureau of Mines figures. Most of the production, at least 73 percent and probably more, came from the Presidio mine.

GRANITE: Granites in shades of red and gray and related intrusive igneous rocks occur in the Llano Uplift of Central Texas and in the Trans-Pecos country of West Texas. Deposits are found in Blanco, Brewster, Burnet, El Paso, Gillespie, Hudspeth, Llano, McCulloch, Mason, Presidio, and other counties. Quarries in Burnet, Gillespie, Llano, and Mason counties produce Precambrian granite for a variety of uses, such as dimension stone and crushed stone.

GRAPHITE: Graphite, a soft, dark-gray mineral, is a form of very high-grade carbon. It occurs in Precambrian schist rocks of the Llano Uplift of Central Texas, notably in Burnet and Llano counties. Crystalline-flake graphite ore formerly was mined from open pits in the Clear Creek area of western Burnet County and processed at a plant near the mine. The mill now occasionally grinds imported material. Uses of natural crystalline graphite are refractories, steel production, pencil leads, lubricants, foundry facings, and crucibles, as well as other purposes.

GRINDING PEBBLES (ABRASIVE STONES): Flint pebbles, suitable for use in tube-mill grinding, are found in the Gulf Coastal Plain, where they occur in gravel deposits along rivers and in upland areas. Grinding pebbles are produced from Frio River terrace deposits near the McMullen–Live Oak county line, but the area is now part of the Choke Canyon Reservoir area.

GYPSUM: Gypsum is widely distributed in Texas. Chief deposits are bedded gypsum in the area east of the High Plains, in the Trans-Pecos country, and in Central Texas. It also occurs in salt-dome caprocks of the Gulf Coast. The massive, granular variety, which is known as rock gypsum, is the kind most commonly used by industry. Other varieties include alabaster, satin spar, and selenite.

Gypsum is one of the important industrial minerals in Texas. Bedded gypsum is produced from surface mines in Culberson, Fisher, Gillespie, Hardeman, Hudspeth, Kimble, Nolan, and Stonewall counties. Gypsum was formerly mined at Gyp Hill salt dome in Brooks County and at Hockley salt dome in Harris County. Most of the gypsum is calcined and used in the manufacture of gypsum wallboard, plaster, joint compounds, and other construction products. Crude gypsum is used chiefly as a retarder in portland cement and as a soil conditioner.

HELIUM: Helium is a very light, nonflammable, chemically inert gas. The U.S. Interior Department has ended its helium operation near Masterson in the Panhandle. The storage facility at Cliffside gas field near Amarillo and the 425-mile pipeline system will remain in operation until the government sells its remaining unrefined, crude helium. Helium is used in cryogenics, welding, pressurizing and purging, leak detection, synthetic breathing mixtures, and for other purposes. **In 2018, there were four helium extraction plants in Texas.**

IRON: Iron oxide (limonite, goethite, and hematite) and iron carbonate (siderite) deposits occur widely in East Texas, notably in Cass, Cherokee, Marion, and Morris counties, and also in Anderson, Camp, Harrison, Henderson, Nacogdoches, Smith, Upshur, and other counties. Magnetite (magnetic, black iron oxide) occurs in Central Texas, including a deposit at Iron Mountain in Llano County. Hematite occurs in the Trans-Pecos area and in the Llano Uplift of Central Texas. The extensive deposits of glauconite (a complex silicate containing iron) that occur in East Texas and the hematitic and goethitic Cambrian sandstone that crops out in the northwestern Llano Uplift region are potential sources of low-grade iron ore.

Limonite and other East Texas iron ores are mined from open pits in Cherokee and Henderson counties for use in the preparation of portland cement, as a weighting agent in well-drilling fluids, as an animal feed supplement, and for other purposes. East Texas iron ores also were mined in the past for use in the iron-steel industry.

KAOLIN (see CLAYS).

LEAD AND ZINC: The lead mineral galena (lead sulfide) commonly is associated with zinc and silver. It formerly was produced as a by-product of West Texas silver mining, chiefly from the Presidio mine at Shafter in Presidio County, although lesser amounts were obtained at several other mines and prospects. Deposits of galena also are known to occur in Blanco, Brewster, Burnet, Gillespie, and Hudspeth counties.

Zinc, primarily from the mineral sphalerite (zinc sulphide), was produced chiefly from the Bonanza and Alice Ray mines in the Quitman Mountains of Hudspeth County. In addition, small production was reported from several other areas, including the Chinati and Montezuma mines of Presidio County and the Buck Prospect in the Apache Mountains of Culberson County. Zinc mineralization also occurs in association with the lead deposits in Cambrian rocks of Central Texas.

LEONARDITE: Deposits of weathered (oxidized) low-Btu value bituminous coals, generally referred to as "leonardite," occur in Brewster County. The name leonardite is used for a mixture of chemical compounds that is high in humic acids. In the past, material from these deposits was sold as soil conditioner. Other uses of leonardite include modification of viscosity of drill fluids and as sorbants in water-treatment.

LIGHTWEIGHT AGGREGATE (see CLAYS, DIATOMITE, PERLITE, VERMICULITE).

LIGNITE: Almost all current coal production in Texas is located in the Tertiary-aged lignite belts that extend across the Texas Gulf Coastal Plain from the Rio Grande in South Texas to the Arkansas and Louisiana borders in East Texas. The Railroad Commission of Texas (RRC) reported that in 2018, Texas produced 24.8 million short tons of lignite from 12 mines. Cumulative production in 2018 was 1.8 billion short tons of lignite and coal. See the map and table opposite for more detail on coal and lignite mining.

The near-surface lignite resources, occurring at depths of less than 200 feet in seams of three feet or thicker, are estimated at 23 billion short tons. Recoverable reserves of strippable lignite, those that can be economically mined under current conditions of price and technology, are estimated by the EIA to be 722 million short tons.

Additional lignite resources of the Texas Gulf Coastal Plain occur as deep-basin deposits. Deep-basin resources, those that occur at depths of 200 to 2,000 feet in seams of five feet or thicker, are comparable in magnitude to near-surface resources. The deep-basin lignites are a potential energy resource that conceivably could be utilized by in situ (in place) recovery methods such as underground gasification.

As with bituminous coal, lignite production was significant prior to the general availability of oil and gas. Remnants of old underground mines are common throughout the area of lignite occurrence. Large reserves of strippable lignite have again attracted the attention of energy suppliers, and Texas is now the nation's sixth leading producer of coal, 99 percent of it lignite. Twelve large strip mines are now producing lignite that is burned for mine-mouth electric-power generation, and additional mines are planned. Mines are located in Atascosa, Franklin, Freestone, Harrison, Hopkins, Leon, Limestone, McMullen, Milam, Panola, Robertson, Rusk, and Titus counties.

Texas Coal and Lignite Production
(short tons)

Year	Total
2018	24,842,955
2017	35,415,535
2016	39,139,879
2015	36,277,112
2014	43,633,881
2013	42,449,594
2012	43,536,176
2011	45,587,404
2010	41,419,857
2009	37,099,067
2008	40,152,112
2007	38,403,681
2006	46,128,231
2005	47,168,916
2004	45,680,097
2003	48,179,875
2002	44,683,793
pre-2002	1,143,894,272

Source: Railroad Commission of Texas

LIME MATERIAL: Limestones, which are abundant in some areas of Texas, are heated to produce lime (calcium oxide) at a number of plants in the state. High-magnesium limestone and dolomite are used to prepare lime at a plant in Burnet County. Other lime plants are located in Bexar, Bosque, Comal, Hill, Johnson, and Travis counties. Lime production captive to the kiln's operator occurs in several Texas counties. Lime is used in soil stabilization, water purification, paper and pulp manufacture, metallurgy, sugar refining, agriculture, construction, removal of sulfur from stack gases, and for many other purposes.

LIMESTONE (see also BUILDING STONE): Texas is one of the nation's leading producers of limestone, which is quarried in more than 60 counties. Limestone occurs in nearly all areas of the state with the exception of most of the Gulf Coastal Plain and High Plains. Although some of the limestone is quarried for use as dimension stone, most of the output is crushed for uses such as bulk building materials (crushed stone, road base, concrete aggregate), chemical raw materials, fillers or extenders, lime and portland cement raw materials, agricultural limestone, and removal of sulfur from stack gases.

MAGNESITE: Small deposits of magnesite (natural magnesium carbonate) have been found in Precambrian rocks in Llano and Mason counties of Central Texas. At one time, there was small-scale mining of magnesite in the area; some of the material was used as agricultural stone and as terrazzo chips. Magnesite also can be calcined to form magnesia, which is used in metallurgical furnace refractories and other products.

MAGNESIUM: On the Texas Gulf Coast in Brazoria County, magnesium chloride is extracted from sea water at a plant in Freeport and used to produce magnesium compounds and magnesium metal. During World War II, high-magnesium Ellenburger dolomite rock from Burnet County was used as magnesium ore at a plant near Austin.

MANGANESE: Deposits of manganese minerals, such as braunite, hollandite, and pyrolusite, have been found in several areas, including Jeff Davis, Llano, Mason, Presidio, and Val Verde counties. Known deposits are not large. Small shipments have been made from Jeff Davis, Mason, and Val Verde counties, but no manganese mining has been reported in Texas since 1954.

MARBLE: Metamorphic and sedimentary marbles suitable for monument and building stone are found in the Llano Uplift and nearby areas of Central Texas and the Trans-Pecos area of West Texas. Gray, white, black, greenish black, light green, brown, and cream-colored marbles occur in Central Texas in Burnet, Gillespie, Llano, and Mason counties. West Texas metamorphic marbles include the bluish-white and the black marbles found southwest of Alpine in Brewster County and the white marble from Marble Canyon north of Van Horn in Culberson County. Marble can be used as dimension stone, terrazzo, and roofing aggregate, and for other purposes.

MERCURY (QUICKSILVER): Mercury minerals, chiefly cinnabar, occur in the Terlingua district and nearby districts of southern Brewster and southeastern Presidio counties. Mining began there about 1894, and from 1905–1935, Texas was one of the nation's leading producers of quicksilver. Following World War II, a sharp drop in demand and price, along with depletion of developed ore reserves, caused abandonment of all the Texas mercury mines.

With a rise in the price, sporadic mining took place from 1951–1960. In 1965, when the price of mercury moved to a record high, renewed interest in the Texas mercury districts resulted in the reopening of several mines and the discovery of new ore reserves. By April 1972, however, the price had declined, and the mines have reported no production since 1973.

MICA: Large crystals of flexible, transparent mica minerals in igneous pegmatite rocks and mica flakes in metamorphic schist rocks are found in the Llano Uplift area of Central Texas and the Van Horn area of West Texas. Most Texas deposits do not meet specifications for sheet mica, and although several attempts have been made to produce West Texas sheet mica in Culberson and Hudspeth counties, sustained production has not been achieved. A mica quarry operated for a short time in the early 1980s in the Van Horn Mountains of Culberson and Hudspeth counties to mine mica schist for use as an additive in rotary drilling fluids.

MOLYBDENUM: Small occurrences of molybdenite have been found in Burnet and Llano counties, and wulfenite, another molybdenum mineral, has been noted in rocks in the Quitman Mountains of Hudspeth County. Molybdenum minerals also occur at Cave Peak north of Van Horn in Culberson County, in the Altuda Mountain area of northwestern Brewster County, and in association with uranium ores of the Gulf Coastal Plain.

PEAT: This spongy organic substance forms in bogs from plant remains. It has been found in the Gulf Coastal Plain in several localities including Gonzales, Guadalupe, Lee, Milam, Polk, and San Jacinto counties. There has been intermittent, small-scale production of some of the peat for use as a soil conditioner.

PERLITE: Perlite, a glassy igneous rock, expands to a lightweight, porous mass when heated. It can be used as a lightweight aggregate, filter aid, horticultural aggregate, and for other purposes. Perlite occurs in Presidio County, where it has been mined in the Pinto Canyon area north of the Chinati Mountains. No perlite is currently mined in Texas, but perlite mined outside of Texas is expanded at plants in Bexar, Dallas, El Paso, Guadalupe, Harris, and Nolan counties.

PHOSPHATE: Rock phosphate is present in Paleozoic rocks in several areas of Brewster and Presidio counties in West Texas and in Central Texas, but the known deposits are not large. In Northeast Texas, sedimentary rock phosphate occurs in thin conglomeratic lenses in Upper Cretaceous and Tertiary rock units; possibly some of these low-grade phosphorites could be processed on a small scale for local use as a fertilizer. Imported phosphate rock is processed at a plant in Brownsville.

POTASH: The potassium mineral polyhalite is widely distributed in the subsurface Permian Basin of West Texas and has been found in many wells in that area. During 1927–1931, the federal government drilled a series of potash-test wells in Crane, Crockett, Ector, Glasscock, Loving, Reagan, Upton, and Winkler counties. In addition to polyhalite, which was found in all of the counties, these wells revealed the presence of the potassium minerals carnallite and sylvite in Loving County and carnallite in Winkler County. The known Texas potash deposits are not as rich as those in the New Mexico portion of the Permian Basin and have not been developed.

PUMICITE (VOLCANIC ASH): Deposits of volcanic ash occur in Brazos, Fayette, Gonzales, Karnes, Polk, Starr, and other counties of the Texas Coastal Plain. Deposits also have been found in the Trans-Pecos area, High Plains, and in several counties east of the High Plains. Volcanic ash is used to prepare pozzolan cement, cleansing and scouring compounds, and soaps and sweeping compounds, as well as a carrier for insecticides and for other purposes. It has been mined in Dickens, Lynn, Scurry, Starr, and other counties.

QUICKSILVER (see MERCURY).

RARE-EARTH ELEMENTS AND METALS: The term "rare-earth elements" is commonly applied to elements of the lanthanide group (atomic numbers 57 through 71) plus yttrium. Yttrium, atomic number 39 and not a member of the lanthanide group, is included as a rare-earth element because it has similar properties to members of that group and usually occurs in nature with them. The metals thorium and scandium are sometimes termed "rare metals" because their occurence is often associated with the rare-earth elements.

The majority of rare-earth elements are consumed as catalysts in petroleum cracking and other chemical industries. Rare earths are widely used in the glass industry for tableware, specialty glasses, optics, and fiber optics. Cerium oxide has growing use as a polishing compound for glass, gem stones, cathode-ray tube faceplates, and other polishing. Rare earths are alloyed with various metals to produce materials used in the aeronautic, space, and electronics industries. The addition of rare-earth elements may improve resistance to metal fatigue at high temperatures, reduce potential for corrosion, and selectively increase conductivity and magnetism of the metal.

Various members of this group, including thorium, have anomalous concentrations in the rhyolitic and related igneous rocks of the Quitman Mountains and the Sierra Blanca area of Trans-Pecos, Texas.

SALT (SODIUM CHLORIDE) (see also BRINES): Salt resources of Texas are virtually inexhaustible. Enormous deposits occur in the subsurface Permian Basin of West Texas and in the salt domes of the Gulf Coastal Plain. Salt also is found in the alkali playa lakes of the High Plains, the alkali flats or salt lakes in the Salt Basin of Culberson and Hudspeth counties, and along some of the bays and lagoons of the South Texas Gulf Coast.

Texas is one of the leading salt-producing states. Rock salt is obtained from underground mines in salt domes at Grand Saline in Van Zandt County and Hockley Dome in Harris County. Salt is produced from rock salt and by solution mining as brines from wells drilled into the underground salt deposits.

SAND, INDUSTRIAL: Sands used for special purposes, due to high silica content or to unique physical properties,

command higher prices than common sand. Industrial sands in Texas occur mainly in the Central Gulf Coastal Plain and in North-Central Texas. They include abrasive, blast, chemical, engine, filtration, foundry, glass, hydraulic-fracturing (proppant), molding, and pottery sands. Recent production of industrial sands has been from Atascosa, Colorado, Hardin, Harris, Liberty, Limestone, McCulloch, Newton, Smith, Somervell, and Upshur counties.

SAND AND GRAVEL (CONSTRUCTION): Sand and gravel are among the most extensively utilized resources in Texas. Principal occurrence is along the major streams and in stream terraces. Sand and gravel are important bulk construction materials, used as railroad ballast, base materials, and for other purposes. In 2018, Texas was second only to California in production of sand and gravel (construction). Arizona and Washington were the next two largest producers.

Construction Sand and Gravel Production		
Year	Quantity (thous. met. tons)	Value (millions)
2018	99,100	$ 1,000
2017	84,300	$ 828
2016	81,700	$ 817
	Source: Industry surveys at USGS	

SANDSTONE: Sandstones of a variety of colors and textures are widely distributed in a number of geologic formations in Texas. Some of the sandstones have been quarried for use as dimension stone in El Paso, Parker, Terrell, Ward, and other counties. Crushed sandstone is produced in Freestone, Gaines, Jasper, McMullen, Motley, and other counties for use as road-building material, terrazzo stone, and aggregate.

SERPENTINITE: Several masses of serpentinite, which formed from the alteration of basic igneous rocks, are associated with other Precambrian metamorphic rocks of the Llano Uplift. The largest deposit is the Coal Creek serpentinite mass in northern Blanco and Gillespie counties from which terrazzo chips have been produced. Other deposits are present in Gillespie and Llano counties. (The features that are associated with surface and subsurface Cretaceous rocks in several counties in or near the Balcones Fault Zone and that are commonly known as "serpentine plugs" are not serpentine at all, but are altered igneous volcanic necks and pipes, and mounds of altered volcanic ash, palagonite, that accumulated around the former submarine volcanic pipes.)

SHELL: Oyster shells and other shells in shallow coastal waters and in deposits along the Texas Gulf Coast have been produced in the past chiefly by dredging. They were used to a limited extent as raw material in the manufacture of cement, as concrete aggregate and road base, and for other purposes. No shell has been produced in Texas since 1981.

SILVER: During the period 1885–1952, the production of silver in Texas, as reported by the U.S. Bureau of Mines, totaled about 33 million troy ounces. For about 70 years, silver was the most consistently produced metal in Texas, although always in moderate quantities. All of the production came from the Trans-Pecos country of West Texas, where the silver was mined in Brewster County (Altuda Mountain), Culberson and Hudspeth counties (Van Horn Mountains and Van Horn–Allamoore district), Hudspeth County (Quitman Mountains and Eagle Mountains), and Presidio County (Chinati Mountains area, Loma Plata mine, and Shafter district).

Chief producer was the Presidio mine in the Shafter district, which began operations in the late 1800s, and, through September 1942, produced more than 30 million ounces of silver, more than 92 percent of Texas' total silver production. Water in the lower mine levels, lean ores, and low price of silver resulted in the closing of the mine in 1942. Another important silver producer was the Hazel copper-silver mine in the Van Horn–Allamoore district in Culberson County, which accounted for more than 2 million ounces.

An increase in the price of silver in the late 1970s stimulated prospecting for new reserves, and exploration began near the old Presidio mine, near the old Plata Verde mine in the Van Horn Mountains district, at the Bonanza mine in the Quitman Mountains district, and at the old Hazel mine. A decline in the price of silver in the early 1980s, however, resulted in reduction of exploration and mine development in the region. The recent rise in the value of silver has sparked new interest in the Shafter mining district of West Texas.

SOAPSTONE (see TALC AND SOAPSTONE).

SODIUM SULFATE (SALT CAKE): Sodium sulfate minerals occur in salt beds and brines of the alkali playa lakes of the High Plains in West Texas. In some lakes, the sodium sulfate minerals are present in deposits a few feet beneath the lakebeds. Sodium sulfate is found in underground brines in the Permian Basin. Current production is from brines and dry salt beds at alkali lakes in Gaines and Terry counties. Past production was reported in Lynn and Ward counties. Sodium sulfate is used chiefly by the detergent and paper and pulp industries. Other uses are in the preparation of glass and other products.

STONE (see BUILDING STONE and CRUSHED STONE).

STRONTIUM: Deposits of the mineral celestite (strontium sulfate) have been found in a number of places, including localities in Brown, Coke, Comanche, Fisher, Lampasas, Mills, Nolan, Real, Taylor, Travis, and Williamson counties. Most of the occurrences are very minor, and no strontium is currently produced in the state.

SULFUR: Texas is one of the world's principal sulfur-producing areas. The sulfur is mined from deposits of native sulfur, and it is extracted from sour (sulfur-bearing) natural gas and petroleum. Recovered sulfur accounted for more than 90 percent of all 2018 sulfur production in the United States. Native sulfur is found in large deposits in the caprock of some of the salt domes along the Texas Gulf Coast and in some of the surface and subsurface Permian strata of West Texas, notably in Culberson and Pecos counties.

Native sulfur obtained from the underground deposits is known as Frasch sulfur, so called because of Herman Frasch, the chemist who devised the method of drilling wells into the deposits, melting the sulfur with superheated water, and forcing the molten sulfur to the surface. Most of the production now goes to the users in molten form.

Frasch sulfur is produced from only one Gulf Coast salt dome in Wharton County and from West Texas underground Permian strata in Culberson County. Operations at several Gulf Coast domes have been closed in recent years. During the 1940s, acidic sulfur earth was produced in the Rustler Springs district in Culberson County for use as a fertilizer and soil conditioner. Sulfur is recovered from sour natural gas and petroleum at plants in numerous Texas counties.

Sulfur is used in the preparation of fertilizers and organic and inorganic chemicals, in petroleum refining, and for many other purposes.

TALC AND SOAPSTONE: Deposits of talc are found in the Precambrian metamorphic rocks of the Allamoore area of eastern Hudspeth and western Culberson counties. Soapstone, containing talc, occurs in the Precambrian metamorphic rocks of the Llano Uplift area, notably in Blanco, Gillespie, and Llano counties. Current production is from surface mines in the Allamoore area. Talc is used in ceramic, roofing, paint, paper, plastic, synthetic rubber, and other products.

TIN: Tin minerals have been found in El Paso and Mason counties. Small quantities were produced during the early 1900s in the Franklin Mountains north of El Paso. Cassiterite (tin dioxide) occurrences in Mason County are believed to be very minor. The only tin smelter in the United States, built at Texas City by the federal government during World War II and later sold to a private company, processes tin concentrates from ores mined outside of Texas, tin residues, and secondary tin-bearing materials.

TITANIUM: The titanium mineral rutile has been found in small amounts at the Mueller prospect in Jeff Davis County. Another titanium mineral, ilmenite, occurs in sandstones in Burleson, Fayette, Lee, Starr, and several other counties. Deposits that would be considered commercial under present conditions have not been found.

TRAP ROCK (see BASALT).

TUNGSTEN: The tungsten mineral scheelite has been found in small deposits in Gillespie and Llano counties and in the Quitman Mountains in Hudspeth County. Small deposits of other tungsten minerals have been prospected in the Cave Peak area north of Van Horn in Culberson County.

URANIUM: Uranium deposits were discovered in the Texas Coastal Plain in 1954 when abnormal radioactivity was detected in the Karnes County area. A number of uranium deposits have since been discovered within a belt of strata extending more than 250 miles from the middle Coastal Plain southwestward to the Rio Grande.

Various uranium minerals also have been found in other areas of Texas, including the Trans-Pecos, the Llano Uplift, and the High Plains. With the exception of small shipments from the High Plains during the 1950s, all the uranium production in Texas has been from the Coastal Plain. Uranium has been obtained from surface mines extending from northern Live Oak County, southeastern Atascosa County, across northern Karnes County, and into southern Gonzales County. Uranium is produced by in-situ leaching, brought to the surface through wells, and stripped from the solution at recovery operations.

In 1999, uranium mining shut down because of decreased value and demand. Production resumed in Texas in late 2004, when inventories were depleted and market prices rose to economic levels that allowed resumption of production. A total of 1.4 million pounds (606.5 tons) of eU$_3$O$_8$ was produced in South Texas in 2007.

There are no active uranium recovery operations in Texas, though as of 2017 there are 10 permits for uranium exploration in seven counties: Bee, Brooks, Duval, Goliad, Jim Hogg, Kleberg, and Live Oak.

VERMICULITE: Vermiculite, a mica-like mineral that expands when heated, occurs in Burnet, Gillespie, Llano, Mason, and other counties in the Llano Uplift region. It has been produced at a surface mine in Llano County. Vermiculite, mined outside of Texas, is exfoliated (expanded) at plants in Dallas, Houston, and San Antonio. Exfoliated vermiculite is used for lightweight concrete aggregate, horticulture, insulation, and other purposes.

VOLCANIC ASH (see PUMICITE).

ZEOLITES: The zeolite minerals clinoptilolite and analcime occur in Tertiary lavas and tuffs in Brewster, Jeff Davis, and Presidio counties in West Texas. Clinoptilolite also is found associated with Tertiary tuffs in the southern Texas Coastal Plain, including deposits in Karnes, McMullen, and Webb counties, and currently is produced in McMullen County. Zeolites, sometimes called "molecular sieves," can be used in ion-exchange processes to reduce pollution, as a catalyst in oil cracking, in obtaining high-purity oxygen and nitrogen from air, in water purification, and for many other purposes.

ZINC (see LEAD AND ZINC). ☆

Texas Newspapers, Radio, and Television Stations

Sources: 2019 Texas Newspaper Directory; FCC, https://www.fcc.gov/media/filing-systems-and-databases

Texas is rich with newspapers and broadcast media, many of which have long histories. In the following list, only printed, subscription newspapers appear, and their frequency of publication is indicated by the following codes: (D) daily or at least four days a week, (TW) triweekly, (S) semiweekly, (SM) semimonthly, (M) monthly; all others are weeklies. Radio and TV stations are those with valid operating licenses as of May 2019. Not included are those with construction permits or pending applications.

—A—

Abernathy: Newspaper: *Abernathy Advocate.*

Abilene: Newspaper: *Abilene Reporter-News* (D). Radio-AM: KSLI, 1280 kHz; KWKC, 1340; KYYW, 1470; KZQQ, 1560. Radio-FM: KGNZ, 88.1 MHz; KACU, 89.5; KAGT, 90.5; KAQD, 91.3; KMWX, 92.5; KULL, 100.7; KEAN, 105.1; KKHR, 106.3; KEYJ, 107.9. TV Stations: KXVA-Ch. 15; KTAB-Ch. 24; KRBC-Ch. 29.

Agua Dulce: Radio-FM: KOUL, 107.7 MHz.

Alamo: Radio-FM: KJAV, 104.9 MHz.

Alamo Heights: Radio-AM: KDRY, 1100 kHz.

Albany: Newspaper: *Albany News.*

Aledo: Newspaper: *The Community News.*

Alice: Newspaper: *Alice Echo-News Journal* (S). Radio-AM: KOPY, 1070 kHz. Radio-FM: KAWV, 88.3 MHz; KOPY, 92.1; KNDA, 102.9.

Allen: Radio-FM: KESN, 103.3 MHz.

Alpine: Newspaper: *Alpine Avalanche.* Radio-AM: KVLF, 1240 kHz. Radio-FM: KBAL, 90.3 MHz; KALP, 92.7.

Alvin: Newspaper: *Alvin Sun.* Radio-AM: KTEK, 1110 kHz. Radio-FM: KACC, 89.7 MHz. TV Station: KFTH-Ch. 36.

Amarillo: Newspaper: *Amarillo Globe-News* (D). Radio-AM: KGNC, 710 kHz; KIXZ, 940; KTNZ, 1010; KZIP, 1310; KDJW, 1360; KPUR, 1440. Radio-FM: KJRT, 88.3 MHz; KXLV, 89.1; KACV, 89.9; KAVW, 90.7; KXRI, 91.9; KQIZ, 93.1; KMXJ, 94.1; KXSS, 96.9; KGNC, 97.9; KPRF, 98.7; KBZD, 99.7; KXGL, 100.9; KATP, 101.9; KEYU, 102.9; KJJP, 105.7. TV Stations: KVII-Ch. 7; KFDA-Ch. 10; KCIT-Ch. 15; KAMR-Ch. 19.

Anahuac: Newspaper: *The Progress.*

Andrews: Newspaper: *Andrews County News* (S). Radio-AM: KACT, 1360 kHz. Radio-FM: KACT, 105.5 MHz.

Anson: Newspaper: *Western Observer.* Radio-FM: KTLT, 98.1 MHz.

Aransas Pass: Newspaper: *Aransas Pass Progress.* Radio-FM: KKWV, 88.1 MHz.

Archer City: Newspaper: *Archer County News.* Radio-FM: KPMA, 91.9 MHz.

Arlington: Radio-FM: KLTY, 94.9 MHz. TV Station: KPXD-Ch. 42.

Arroyo: Radio-FM: KVJS, 88.1 MHz.

Athens: Newspaper: *Athens Daily Review* (D). Radio-AM: KLVQ, 1410 kHz.

Atlanta: Newspaper: *Atlanta Citizens Journal.* Radio-AM: KPYN, 900 kHz. Radio-FM: KNRB, 100.1 MHz.

Austin: Newspapers: *Austin American-Statesman* (D); *Austin Business Journal; The Daily Texan* (D); *West Austin News* (SM); *Westlake Picayune.* Radio-AM: KLBJ, 590 kHz; KVET, 1300; KTSN, 1490. Radio-FM: KAZI, 88.7 MHz; KMFA, 89.5; KUT, 90.5; KVRX, 91.7; KLBJ, 93.7; KKMJ, 95.5; KVET, 98.1; KASE, 100.7; KPEZ, 102.3. TV Stations: KTBC-Ch. 7; KXAN-Ch. 21; KLRU-Ch. 22; KVUE-CH. 33; KEYE-Ch. 43; KNVA-Ch. 49.

Austwell: Radio-FM: KIBQ, 105.9 MHz.

Azle: Newspaper: *Azle News.* Radio-FM: KYDA,101.7 MHz.

—B—

Baird: Newspaper: *Baird Banner.* Radio-FM: KABW, 95.1 MHz.

Balch Springs: Radio-AM: KSKY, 660 kHz.

Ballinger: Newspaper: *Runnels County Register.* Radio-AM: KRUN, 1400 kHz. Radio-FM: KKCN, 103.1 MHz.

Bandera: Newspaper: *Bandera Bulletin.* Radio-FM: KEEP, 103.1 MHz.

Bangs: Radio-FM: KBNX, 97.9 MHz.

Bartlett : Newspaper: *Tribune-Progress.*

Bastrop: Newspaper: *Bastrop Advertiser* (S). Radio-FM: KHIB, 88.5 MHz; KLZT, 107.1.

Batesville: Radio-FM: KRZU, 90.7 MHz; KQSA, 97.9

Bay City: Newspaper: *The Bay City Tribune* (S). Radio-FM: KQUE, 88.1 MHz; KZBJ, 89.5; KNTE, 101.7; KMKS, 102.5.

Baytown: Newspaper: *Baytown Sun* (D). Radio-AM: KWWJ, 1360. TV Station: KUBE-Ch. 41.

Beaumont: Newspaper: *The Beaumont Enterprise* (D). Radio-AM: KLVI, 560 kHz; KZZB, 990; KIKR, 1450. Radio-FM: KLBT, 88.1 MHz; KGHY, 88.5; KTXB, 89.7; KVLU, 91.3; KQXY, 94.1; KYKR, 95.1; KTCX, 102.5; KQQK, 107.9. TV Stations: KBMT-Ch. 12; KFDM-Ch. 25; KITU-Ch. 33.

Bee Cave: Radio-FM: KTXX, 104.9 MHz.

Beeville: Newspaper: *Beeville Bee-Picayune* (S). Radio-AM: KIBL, 1490 kHz. Radio-FM: KVFM, 91.3 MHz; KTKO, 105.7; KRXB, 107.1.

Bellaire: Radio-AM: KGOW, 1560 kHz.

Bellmead: Radio-FM: KBHT, 104.9 MHz.

Bells: Radio-FM: KMKT, 93.1 MHz.

Bellville: Newspaper: *The Bellville Times.* Radio-AM: KULF, 1090 kHz.

Belton: Newspaper: *The Belton Journal.* Radio-FM: KOOC, 106.3 MHz. TV Station: KNCT-Ch. 46.

Benavides: Radio-FM: KXTM, 94.3 MHz.

Benbrook: Radio-AM: KFLC, 1270 kHz. Radio-FM: KESS, 107.1 MHz.

Big Lake: Newspaper: *Big Lake Wildcat.*

Big Sandy: Newspaper: *The Big Sandy–Hawkins Journal.* Radio-FM: KTAA, 90.7 MHz.

Big Spring: Newspaper: *Big Spring Herald* (D). Radio-AM: KBYG, 1400 kHz; KBST, 1490. Radio-FM: KBCX, 91.5 MHz; KBTS, 94.3; KBST, 95.7; KBUG, 100.9. TV Station: KCWO-Ch. 33.

Big Wells: Radio-FM: KHBE, 102.1 MHz.

Bishop: Radio-FM: KMZZ, 106.9 MHz.

Blanco: Newspaper: *Blanco County News.* TV Station: KNIC-Ch. 18.

Blanket: Radio-FM: KQMJ, 104.7 MHz

Bloomington: Radio-FM: KHVT, 91.5 MHz; KLUB, 106.9.

Blossom: Radio-FM: KISY, 92.7 MHz

Boerne: Newspaper: *Boerne Star* (S). Radio-AM: KBRN, 1500 kHz.

Bogata: Newspaper: *Bogata News–Talco Times.*

Bonham: Radio-AM: KFYN, 1420 kHz.

Booker: Newspaper: *Booker News.*

Borger: Newspaper: *Borger News-Herald* (D). **Radio-AM:** KQTY, 1490 kHz. **Radio-FM:** KWAS, 88.7 MHz; KQFX, 104.3; KQTY, 106.7. **TV Station:** KEYU-Ch. 31.

Bovina: Radio-FM: KKNM, 96.5 MHz.

Bowie: Newspaper: *The Bowie News* (S). **Radio-AM:** KNTX, 1410 kHz.

Brackettville: Radio-FM: KUDR 94.7 MHz.

Brady: Newspaper: *Brady Standard-Herald.* **Radio-AM:** KNEL, 1490 kHz. **Radio-FM:** KNEL, 95.3 MHz.

Breckenridge: Newspaper: *Breckenridge American.* **Radio-AM:** KROO, 1430 kHz. **Radio-FM:** KQXB, 89.9 MHz; KLXK, 93.5.

Brenham: Newspaper: *Brenham Banner-Press* (D). **Radio-AM:** KWHI, 1280 kHz. **Radio-FM:** KUBJ, 89.7 MHz; KLTR, 94.1; KTTX, 106.1.

Bridgeport: Newspaper: *Bridgeport Index.* **Radio-FM:** KBOC, 98.3 MHz.

Brookshire: Newspaper: *The Times Tribune.* **Radio-AM:** KCHN, 1050 kHz.

Brownfield: Newspaper: *Brownfield News* (S). **Radio-AM:** KKUB, 1300 kHz. **Radio-FM:** KLTB, 89.7 MHz; KEJS, 104.3.

Brownsville: Newspaper: *The Brownsville Herald* (D). **Radio-AM:** KVNS, 1700 kHz. **Radio-FM:** KBNR, 88.3 MHz; KKPS, 99.5. **TV:** KVEO-Ch. 24.

Brownwood: Newspaper: *Brownwood Bulletin* (TW). **Radio-AM:** KXYL, 1240 kHz; KBWD, 1380. **Radio-FM:** KBUB, 90.3 MHz; KHBW, 91.7; KQBZ, 96.9; KPSM, 99.3; KOXE, 101.3.

Bryan: Newspaper: *The Eagle* (D). **Radio-AM:** KTAM, 1240 kHz; KAGC, 1510. **Radio-FM:** KORA, 98.3 MHz; KNFX, 99.5; KKYS, 104.7. **TV Stations:** KYLE-Ch. 29; KBTX-Ch. 50.

Buda: Radio-FM: KROX, 101.5 MHz.

Buffalo: Newspapers: *Buffalo Express*; *The Buffalo Press.* **Radio-FM:** WTAW, 103.5 MHz.

Buffalo Gap: Radio-FM: KBGT, 93.3 MHz.

Bullard: Radio-FM: KZXM, 94.3 MHz.

Buna: Newspaper: *The Buna Beacon.*

Burkburnett: Newspaper: *Burkburnett Informer Star.* **Radio-FM:** KYYI, 104.7 MHz.

Burke: Radio-FM: KAGZ, 97.7 MHz.

Burleson: Newspaper: *Burleson Star.* **Radio-AM:** KCLE, 1460 kHz.

Burnet: Newspapers: *Burnet Bulletin*; *Citizens Gazette.* **Radio-FM:** KMPN 95.9 MHz; KBEY, 103.9.

Bushland: Radio-FM: KTXP, 91.5 MHz.

—C—

Caldwell: Newspaper: *Burleson County Tribune.* **Radio-FM:** KALD, 91.9 MHz; KAPN, 107.3.

Callisburg: Radio-FM: KPFC, 91.9 MHz.

Cameron: Newspaper: *The Cameron Herald.* **Radio-AM:** KTON, 1330 kHz. **Radio-FM:** KMIL, 105.1 MHz.

Campbell: Radio-FM: KRVA, 107.1 MHz.

Canadian: Newspaper: *The Canadian Record.* **Radio-FM:** KHHC, 91.3 MHz.

Canton: Newspaper: *Canton Herald.* **Radio-AM:** KWJB, 1510 kHz.

Canyon: Newspaper: *The Canyon News* (S). **Radio-AM:** KNSH, 1550 kHz. **Radio-FM:** KWTS, 91.1 MHz; KARX, 107.1; KZRK, 107.9.

Carrizo Springs: Newspaper: *Carrizo Springs Javelin.* **Radio-AM:** KBEN, 1450 kHz. **Radio-FM:** KCZO, 92.1 MHz.

Carrollton: Radio-AM: KJON, 850 kHz.

Carthage: Newspaper: *The Panola Watchman* (S). **Radio-AM:** KGAS, 1590 kHz. **Radio-FM:** KRTG, 88.3 MHz; KTUX, 98.9; KGAS, 104.3.

Castroville: Newspaper: *Castroville News Bulletin.*

Cedar Lake: Radio-FM: KQVI, 89.9 MHz.

Cedar Park: Newspaper: *Hill Country News Weekender.* **Radio-FM:** KGSR, 93.3 MHz.

Celina: Newspaper: *Celina Record.*

Center: Newspaper: *The Light and Champion* (S). **Radio-AM:** KDET, 930 kHz. **Radio-FM:** KQBB, 100.5 MHz.

Centerville: Newspaper: *Centerville News.* **Radio-FM:** KKEE, 101.3 MHz; KUZN, 105.9.

Chandler: Newspaper: *Chandler & Brownsboro Statesman.*

Channing: Radio-FM: KAMT, 105.1 MHz.

Charlotte: Radio-FM: KSAQ, 102.3 MHz.

Chico: Newspaper: *Chico Texan.*

Childress: Newspaper: *The Red River Sun.* **Radio-AM:** KCTX, 1510 kHz. **Radio-FM:** KCTX, 96.1 MHz; KCHT 99.7.

Christine: Radio-FM: KWYU, 96.9 MHz.

Christoval: Radio-FM: KQTC, 99.5 MHz.

Clarendon: Newspaper: *Clarendon Enterprise.* **Radio-FM:** KYCL, 88.9 MHz; KEFH, 99.3.

Clarksville: Newspaper: *Clarksville Times.* **Radio-AM:** KHDY, 1350 kHz. **Radio-FM:** KXQJ, 90.1 MHz; KHDY, 98.5.

Claude: Newspaper: *The Claude News.* **Radio-FM:** KPUR, 95.7 MHz.

Cleburne: Newspaper: *Cleburne Times-Review* (D). **Radio-AM:** KHFX, 1140 kHz.

Cleveland: Newspaper: *The News Advocate.* **Radio-FM:** KTHT, 97.1 MHz.

Clifton: Newspaper: *The Clifton Record.* **Radio-FM:** KWOW, 104.1 MHz.

Clute: Newspaper: *The Facts* (D).

Clyde: Newspaper: *Clyde Journal.*

Coahoma: Radio-FM: KXCS, 105.5 MHz.

Cockrell Hill: Radio-AM: KRVA, 1600 kHz.

Coleman: Newspaper: *Chronicle & Democrat-Voice.* **Radio-AM:** KSTA, 1000 kHz. **Radio-FM:** KXYL, 102.3 MHz.

College Station: Newspaper: *The Battalion* (D). **Radio-AM:** KZNE, 1150 kHz; KWBC, 1550; WTAW, 1620. **Radio-FM:** KEOS, 89.1 MHz; KLGS, 89.9; KAMU, 90.9; KNDE, 95.1. **TV Station:** KAMU-Ch. 12.

Colorado City: Newspaper: *Colorado City Record.* **Radio-AM:** KVMC, 1320 kHz. **Radio-FM:** KEHM, 99.3 MHz; KAUM, 107.1

Columbus: Newspapers: *The Banner Press Newspaper*; *Colorado County Citizen.* **Radio-FM:** KULM, 98.3 MHz.

Comanche: Newspaper: *The Comanche Chief.* **Radio-AM:** KCOM, 1550 kHz. **Radio-FM:** KYOX, 94.3 MHz; KCXX 103.9.

Comfort: Newspaper: *The Comfort News.* **Radio-FM:** KMYO, 95.1 MHz.

Commerce: Newspaper: *Commerce Journal.* **Radio-FM:** KETR, 88.9 MHz; KYJC, 91.3.

Comstock: Radio-FM: KDER, 99.3 MHz.

Concan: Radio-FM: KHCU, 93.1 MHz.

Conroe: Newspaper: *The Courier* (D). **Radio-AM:** KJOZ, 880 kHz; KYOK, 1140. **Radio-FM:** KHPT, 106.9 MHz. **TV Stations:** KPXB-Ch. 32; KTBU-Ch. 42.

Converse: Radio-AM: KTMR, 1130 kHz.

Cooper: Newspaper: *Cooper Review.* **Radio-FM:** KPCO, 89.9 MHz; KIKT, 93.5.

Coppell: Newspaper: *Citizens' Advocate.*

Copperas Cove: Newspaper: *Copperas Cove Leader-Press* (S). **Radio-FM:** KSSM, 103.1 MHz.

Corpus Christi: Newspapers: *Corpus Christi Caller-Times* (D); *Coastal Bend Legal & Business News* (D). **Radio-AM:** KCTA, 1030 kHz; KCCT, 1150; KSIX, 1230; KKTX, 1360; KUNO, 1400; KEYS, 1440. **Radio-FM:** KPLV, 88.7 MHz; KEDT, 90.3; KBNJ, 91.7; KMXR, 93.9; KBSO, 94.7; KZFM, 95.5; KLTG, 96.5; KRYS, 99.1. **TV Stations:** KIII-Ch. 8; KZTV-Ch. 10; KRIS-Ch. 13; KEDT-Ch. 23; KORO-Ch. 27; KSCC-Ch. 38.

Corrigan: Radio-FM: KYTM, 99.3 MHz.

Corsicana: Newspaper: *Corsicana Daily Sun* (D). **Radio-AM:** KAND, 1340 kHz.

Cotulla: Radio-FM: KCOT, 96.3 MHz; KWMJ, 100.7.

Crane: Newspaper: *Crane News.* **Radio-AM:** KXOI, 810 kHz. **Radio-FM:** KMMZ, 101.3 MHz.

Creedmoor: Radio-AM: KZNX, 1530 kHz.

Crockett: Newspaper: *Houston County Courier.* **Radio-AM:** KIVY, 1290 kHz. **Radio-FM:** KCKT, 88.5 MHz; KIVY, 92.7; KBPC, 93.5.

Cross Plains: Newspaper: *Cross Plains Review.*

Crowell: Newspaper: *Foard County News.* **Radio-FM:** KKKQ, 98.9 MHz.

Crystal City: Newspaper: *Zavala County Sentinel.* **Radio-FM:** KHER, 94.3 MHz.

Cuero: Newspaper: *Cuero Record.* **Radio-FM:** KTLZ, 89.9 MHz.

Cuney: Radio-FM: KOEE, 99.7 MHz.

Cypress: Radio-AM: KYND, 1520 kHz.

—D—

Daingerfield: Newspaper: *The Steel Country Bee.* **Radio-AM:** KNDF, 1560 kHz.

Dalhart: Newspaper: *Dalhart Texan* (S). **Radio-AM:** KXIT, 1240 kHz. **Radio-FM:** KTDH, 89.3 MHz; KTDA, 91.7; KBEX 96.1.

Dallas: Newspapers: *The Dallas Morning News* (D); *Dallas Business Journal*; *Daily Commercial Record* (D); *Park Cities News*; *Texas Jewish Post.* **Radio-AM:** KLIF, 570 kHz; KGGR, 1040; KRLD, 1080; KFXR, 1190; KTCK, 1310; KBXD, 1480. **Radio-FM:** KNON, 89.3 MHz; KERA, 90.1; KCBI, 90.9; KKXT, 91.7; KZPS, 92.5; KBFB, 97.9; KLUV, 98.7; KJKK, 100.3; WRR, 101.1; KDMX, 102.9; KKDA, 104.5; KRLD, 105.3. **TV Stations:** WFAA-Ch. 9; KERA-Ch. 14; KDAF-Ch. 32; KDFW-Ch. 35; KDFI-Ch. 36; KXTX-Ch. 40; KDTX-Ch. 45.

Decatur: Newspaper: Wise County Messenger (S). **Radio-FM:** KDKR, 91.3 MHz; KRNB, 105.7. **TV Station:** KMPX-Ch. 30.

Deer Park: Radio-FM: KAMA, 104.9 MHz.

De Leon: Newspaper: *De Leon Free Press.*

Dell City: Newspaper: *Hudspeth County Herald.*

Del Mar Hills: Radio-AM: KVOZ, 890 kHz.

Del Rio: Newspaper: *Del Rio News-Herald* (D). **Radio-AM:** KDRN, 1230 kHz; KWMC, 1490. **Radio-FM:** KVFE, 88.5 MHz; KTPD, 89.3; KDLI, 89.9; KDLK, 94.1; KTDR, 96.3. **TV Station:** KYVV-Ch. 28.

Del Valle: Radio-AM: KIXL, 970 kHz.

Denison: Radio-FM: KYFB, 91.5 MHz.

Denton: Newspaper: *Denton Record-Chronicle* (D). **Radio-FM:** KNTU, 88.1 MHz; KFZO, 99.1; KHKS, 106.1. **TV Station:** KDTN-Ch. 43.

Denver City: Newspaper: *Denver City Press.*

Deport: Newspaper: *Deport Times-Blossom Times.*

DeSoto: Newspaper: *Focus Daily News* (D).

Detroit: Newspaper: *Detroit Weekly.* **Radio-FM:** KFYN, 104.3 MHz.

Devine: Newspaper: *The Devine News.* **Radio-FM:** KRPT, 92.5 MHz.

Diboll: Radio-AM: KSML, 1260 kHz. **Radio-FM:** KAFX, 95.5 MHz.

Dilley: Radio-FM: KKDL, 93.7 MHz; KVWG, 95.3; KLMO, 98.9.

Dimmitt: Newspaper: *The Castro County News.* **Radio-AM:** KDHN, 1470 kHz. **Radio-FM:** KNNK, 100.5 MHz.

Doss: Radio-FM: KGKV, 88.1 MHz.

Dripping Springs: Newspapers: *Dripping Springs Century News*; *News-Dispatch.* **Radio-FM:** KLLR, 91.9 MHz.

Dublin: Newspaper: *The Dublin Citizen.* **Radio-FM:** KSTV, 93.1 MHz.

Dumas: Newspaper: *Moore County News-Press* (S). **Radio-AM:** KDDD, 800 kHz. **Radio-FM:** KDDD, 95.3 MHz.

—E—

Eagle Lake: Newspaper: *Eagle Lake Headlight.* **Radio-FM:** KJJB, 95.3 MHz.

Eagle Pass: Radio-AM: KEPS, 1270 kHz. **Radio-FM:** KEPI, 88.7 MHz; KEPX, 89.5; KINL, 92.7. **TV Station:** KVAW-Ch. 18.

Early: Radio-FM: KJKB, 106.7 MHz.

East Bernard: Newspaper: *East Bernard Express.*

Eastland: Newspaper: *Eastland County Today.* **Radio-FM:** KQXE, 91.1 MHz; KATX, 97.7.

Eden: Newspaper: *Eden Echo.* **Radio-FM:** KPDE, 91.5 MHz.

Edinburg: Radio-AM: KURV, 710 kHz. **Radio-FM:** KOIR, 88.5 MHz; KBFM, 104.1; KVLY, 107.9.

Edna: Newspaper: *Jackson County Herald-Tribune.* **Radio-FM:** KIOX, 96.1 MHz.

El Campo: Newspaper: *El Campo Leader-News* (S). **Radio-AM:** KULP, 1390 kHz. **Radio-FM:** KXBJ, 96.9 MHz.

Eldorado: Newspaper: *Eldorado Success.* **Radio-FM:** KOPE, 88.9 MHz; KLDE, 104.9; KPEP, 106.5.

Electra: Newspaper: *Electra Star-News.* **Radio-FM:** KOLI, 94.9 MHz.

Elgin: Newspaper: *Elgin Courier.* **Radio-AM:** KTAE, 1260 kHz.

Elkhart: Radio-FM: KATG, 88.1 MHz.

Ellinger: Radio-FM: KTIM, 89.1 MHz.

El Paso: Newspaper: *El Paso Times* (D). **Radio-AM:** KROD, 600 kHz; KTSM, 690; KAMA, 750; KQBU, 920; KXPL, 1060; KHRO, 1150; KVIV, 1340; KHEY, 1380; KELP, 1590; KSVE, 1650. **Radio-FM:** KTEP, 88.5 MHz; KKLY; 89.5; KVER, 91.1; KOFX, 92.3; KSII, 93.1; KINT, 93.9; KYSE, 94.7; KLAQ, 95.5; KHEY, 96.3; KBNA, 97.5; KTSM, 99.9; KPRR, 102.1. **TV Stations:** KCOS-Ch. 13; KFOX-Ch. 15; KTSM-Ch. 16; KVIA-Ch. 17; KDBC-Ch. 18; KTFN-Ch. 20; KINT-Ch. 25; KSCE-Ch. 39.

Emory: Newspaper: *Rains County Leader.*

Encinal: Radio-FM: KQBI, 91.7 MHz; KELT, 102.5; KZPL, 105.1.

Encino: Radio-FM: KZTX, 91.1 MHz.

Ennis: Newspaper: *The Ennis Daily News* (S).

Escobares: Radio-FM: KERG, 104.7 MHz.

Estelline: Radio-FM: KZES, 91.3 MHz.

—F—

Fabens: Radio-FM: KPAS, 103.1 MHz.

Fairfield: Newspapers: *Freestone County Times*; *The Fairfield Recorder.* **Radio-FM:** KNES, 99.1 MHz.

Falfurrias: Newspaper: *Falfurrias Facts.* **Radio-AM:** KLDS, 1260 kHz. **Radio-FM:** KRVP, 91.5 MHz; KDFM, 103.3; KPSO, 106.3.

Fannett: Radio-FM: KZFT, 90.5 MHz.

Farmersville: Newspaper: *Farmersville Times.* **Radio-AM:** KFCD, 990 kHz. **Radio-FM:** KXEZ, 92.1

MHz.

Farwell: Newspaper: *State Line Tribune.* **Radio-AM:** KIJN, 1060 kHz. **Radio-FM:** KIJN, 92.3 MHz; KICA, 98.3. **TV Station:** KPTF-Ch. 18.

Ferris: Newspaper: *The Ellis County Press.* **Radio-AM:** KDFT, 540 kHz.

Flatonia: Newspaper: *The Flatonia Argus.*

Floresville: Newspaper: *Wilson County News.* **Radio-FM:** KJMA, 89.7 MHz; KTFM, 94.1.

Flower Mound: Radio-FM: KTCK, 96.7 MHz.

Floydada: Newspaper: *Floyd County Hesperian-Beacon.* **Radio-AM:** KFLP, 900 kHz. **Radio-FM:** KFLP, 106.1 MHz.

Forney: Newspaper: *Forney Messenger.*

Fort Davis: Newspaper: *Jeff Davis County Mt. Dispatch.*

Fort Stockton: Newspaper: *Fort Stockton Pioneer.* **Radio-AM:** KFST, 860 kHz. **Radio-FM:** KRAF, 88.3 MHz; KFST, 94.3.

Fort Worth: Newspapers: *Fort Worth Star-Telegram* (D); *Commercial Recorder* (D); *Tarrant County Commercial Record* (S); *Fort Worth Business Press.* **Radio-AM:** WBAP, 820 kHz; KFJZ, 870; KHVN, 970; KKGM, 1630. **Radio-FM:** KTCU, 88.7 MHz; KLNO, 94.1; KSCS, 96.3; KEGL, 97.1; KPLX, 99.5; KDGE, 102.1; KMVK, 107.5. **TV Stations:** KFWD-Ch. 9; KTVT-Ch. 19; KTXA-Ch. 29; KXAS-Ch. 41.

Franklin: Newspapers: *Franklin News Weekly; Franklin Advocate.* **Radio-FM:** KVLX, 103.9 MHz.

Frankston: Newspaper: *The Frankston Citizen.* **Radio-FM:** KOYE, 96.7 MHz.

Fredericksburg: Newspaper: *Fredericksburg Standard-Radio Post.* **Radio-AM:** KNAF, 910 kHz. **Radio-FM:** KIVM, 91.1 MHz; KBLC, 91.5; KNAF, 105.7. **TV Station:** KCWX-Ch. 5.

Freeport: Radio-FM: KJOJ, 103.3 MHz.

Freer: Radio-FM: KBTD, 89.1 MHz; KQCI, 91.5; KBRA, 95.9.

Friendswood: Newspapers: *Friendswood Journal; Friendswood Reporter News.*

Friona: Newspaper: *Friona Star.* **Radio-FM:** KGRW, 94.7 MHz.

Frisco: Radio-AM: KATH, 910 kHz.

Fritch: Newspaper: *The Eagle Press.*

—**G**—

Gail: Newspaper: *Borden Star.*

Gainesville: Newspaper: *Gainesville Daily Register* (D). **Radio-AM:** KGAF, 1580 kHz. **Radio-FM:** KZMJ, 94.5 MHz.

Galveston: Newspaper: *The Galveston County Daily News* (D). **Radio-AM:** KGBC, 1540 kHz. **Radio-FM:** KOVE, 106.5 MHz. **TV Stations:** KLTJ-Ch. 23; KTMD-Ch. 48.

Ganado: Radio-FM: KHTZ, 94.9 MHz.

Gardendale: Radio-FM: KFZX, 102.1 MHz.

Garland: Radio-AM: KAAM, 770 kHz. **TV Station:** KUVN-Ch. 23.

Gatesville: Newspaper: *Gatesville Messenger and Star Forum* (S). **Radio-FM:** KVLW, 88.1 MHz.

Georgetown: Newspapers: *Williamson County Sun; Sunday Sun.* **Radio-FM:** KHFI, 96.7 MHz; KLJA, 107.7.

George West: Radio-FM: KGWT, 93.5 MHz; KXAF 97.9.

Giddings: Newspaper: *Giddings Times & News.* **Radio-FM:** KANJ, 91.1 MHz; KGID 96.3.

Gilmer: Newspaper: *Gilmer Mirror.* **Radio-FM:** KFRO, 95.3 MHz.

Ginger: Radio-FM: KYFA, 91.5 MHz.

Gladewater: Newspaper: *Gladewater Mirror.* **Radio-AM:** KEES, 1430 kHz.

Glen Rose: Newspaper: *Glen Rose Reporter.*

Radio-FM: KTFW, 92.1 MHz.

Goldsmith: Radio-FM: KTXO, 94.7 MHz.

Goldthwaite: Newspaper: *Goldthwaite Eagle.* **Radio-FM:** 107.3 MHz.

Goliad: Newspaper: *Advance-Guard Press.* **Radio-FM:** KHMC, 95.9 MHz; KPQG 104.3.

Gonzales: Newspaper: *Gonzales Inquirer.* **Radio-AM:** KCTI, 1450 kHz. **Radio-FM:** KCTI, 88.1 MHz; KMLR, 106.3.

Graham: Newspaper: *The Graham Leader* (S). **Radio-AM:** KSWA, 1330 kHz. **Radio-FM:** KWKQ, 94.7 MHz.

Granbury: Newspaper: *Hood County News* (S). **Radio-AM:** KPIR, 1420 kHz.

Grand Prairie: Radio-AM: KKDA, 730 kHz.

Grand Saline: Newspaper: *Grand Saline Sun.*

Grape Creek: Radio-FM: KPTJ 104.5 MHz.

Grapeland: Newspaper: *The Messenger* (S).

Greenville: Newspaper: *Herald-Banner* (D). **Radio-AM:** KGVL, 1400 kHz. **Radio-FM:** KTXG, 90.5 MHz. **TV Station:** KTXD-Ch. 46.

Greenwood: Radio-FM: KAGP 89.1 MHz.

Gregory: Radio-FM: KPUS, 104.5 MHz.

Groesbeck: Newspaper: *Groesbeck Journal.*

Groom: Newspaper: *Groom-McLean-Lefors News.*

Groves: Radio-FM: KCOL, 92.5 MHz.

Groveton: Radio-FM: KFON, 93.9 MHz.

Guthrie: Radio-FM: KJAG, 107.7 MHz

—**H**—

Hallettsville: Newspaper: *Hallettsville Tribune-Herald.* **Radio-FM:** KTXM, 99.9 MHz.

Haltom City: Radio-FM: KLIF, 93.3 MHz.

Hamilton: Newspaper: *Hamilton Herald-News.* **Radio-AM:** KCLW, 900 kHz.

Hamlin: Newspaper: *The Hamlin Herald.* **Radio-FM:** KCDD, 103.7 MHz.

Hardin: Radio-FM: KGBV, 90.7 MHz.

Harker Heights: Radio-FM: KUSJ, 105.5 MHz.

Harlingen: Newspaper: *Valley Morning Star* (D). **Radio-AM:** KGBT, 1530 kHz. **Radio-FM:** KJJF, 88.9 MHz; KFRQ, 94.5; KBTQ, 96.1. **TV Stations:** KGBT-Ch. 31; KLUJ-Ch. 34; KMBH-Ch. 38.

Harper: Radio-FM: KZAH, 99.1 MHz.

Haskell: Radio-FM: KVRP, 97.1 MHz.

Hawley: Radio-FM: KTJK, 101.7 MHz.

Hearne: Newspaper: *Robertson County News.* **Radio-FM:** KEDC, 88.5 MHz; KVJM, 103.1.

Hebbronville: Newspapers: *Hebbronville View; Jim Hogg County Enterprise.* **Radio-FM:** KOTX 98.7 MHz; KEKO, 101.7; KUFA, 104.3.

Helotes: Radio-FM: KONO, 101.1 MHz.

Hemphill: Newspaper: *The Sabine County Reporter.* **Radio-FM:** KTHP, 103.9 MHz.

Hempstead: Radio-FM: KTWL, 105.3 MHz.

Henderson: Newspaper: *The Henderson News* (S). **Radio-AM:** KWRD, 1470 kHz.

Henrietta: Newspaper: *Clay County Leader.*

Hereford: Newspaper: *Hereford Brand* (S). **Radio-AM:** KPAN, 860 kHz. **Radio-FM:** KRLH, 90.9 MHz; KJNZ, 103.5; KPAN, 106.3.

Hewitt: Radio-FM: KIXT, 106.7 MHz.

Hico: Newspaper: *Hico News Review.* **Radio-FM:** KITT, 106.5 MHz; KCBN, 107.7.

Highland Park: Radio-AM: KBDT, 1160 kHz. **Radio-FM:** KVIL, 103.7 MHz.

Highlands: Newspaper: *Highlands Star/Crosby Courier.*

Highland Village: Radio-FM: KWRD, 100.7 MHz.

Hillsboro: Newspaper: *Hillsboro Reporter* (S). **Radio-AM:** KHBR, 1560 kHz. **Radio-FM:** KBRQ, 102.5 MHz.

Holliday: Radio-FM: KGVB, 90.9 MHz; KWFB, 100.9.

Hondo: Newspaper: *Hondo Anvil Herald.* **Radio-AM:** KCWM, 1460 kHz. **Radio-FM:** KZIC, 89.9 MHz; KAHL, 105.9.

Hooks: Radio-FM: KTRG, 94.1 MHz; KPWW, 95.9.

Hornsby: Radio-FM: KOOP, 91.7 MHz.

Houston: Newspapers: *Houston Chronicle* (D); *Houston Business Journal; Daily Court Review* (D); *Jewish Herald-Voice.* **Radio-AM:** KILT, 610 kHz; KTRH, 740; KBME, 790; KEYH, 850; KPRC, 950; KLAT, 1010; KNTH, 1070; KCOH, 1230; KXYZ, 1320; KSHJ, 1430; KMIC, 1590. **Radio-FM:** KUHF, 88.7 MHz; KPFT, 90.1; KTSU, 90.9; KXNG, 91.7; KQBT, 93.7; KTBZ, 94.5; KKHH, 95.7; KHMX, 96.5; KBXX, 97.9; KODA, 99.1; KILT, 100.3; KLOL, 101.1; KMJQ, 102.1; KLTN, 102.9; KRBE, 104.1; KHCB, 105.7. **TV Stations:** KUHT-Ch. 8; KHOU-Ch. 11; KTRK-Ch. 13; KTXH-Ch. 19; KZJL-Ch. 21; KETH-Ch. 24; KRIV-Ch. 26; KPRC-Ch. 35; KIAH-Ch. 38.

Howe: Radio-FM: KHYI, 95.3 MHz.

Hudson: Radio-FM: KZXL, 96.3 MHz.

Humble: Radio-AM: KGOL, 1180 kHz. **Radio-FM:** KSBJ, 89.3 MHz.

Hunt: Radio-FM: KYRT, 97.9 MHz; KLKV, 99.9.

Huntington: Radio-FM: KSML, 101.9 MHz.

Huntsville: Newspaper: *The Huntsville Item* (D). **Radio-AM:** KM2XVL, 1220 kHz; KHCH, 1410; KHVL, 1490. **Radio-FM:** KSHU, 90.5 MHz; KVST, 99.7; KSAM, 101.7.

Hurst: Radio-AM: KMNY, 1360 kHz.

Hutto: Radio-FM: KYLR, 92.1 MHz.

—I—

Idalou: Newspaper: *Idalou Beacon.* **Radio-FM:** KRBL, 105.7 MHz; KLZK, 107.7.

Ingleside: Newspaper: *Ingleside Index.* **Radio-FM:** KAJE, 107.3 MHz.

Ingram: Newspaper: *West Kerr Current.* **Radio-FM:** KTXI, 90.1 MHz; KFXE, 96.5.

Iowa Park: Newspaper: *Iowa Park Leader.* **Radio-FM:** KXXN, 97.5 MHz.

Irving: Newspaper: *The Irving Rambler.* **TV Station:** KSTR-Ch. 48.

—J—

Jacksboro: Newspaper: *Jacksboro Herald-Gazette.* **Radio-FM:** KFWR, 95.9 MHz.

Jacksonville: Newspaper: *Jacksonville Progress* (TW). **Radio-AM:** KEBE, 1400 kHz. **Radio-FM:** KBJS, 90.3 MHz; KEBE, 95.1; KLJT, 102.3; KOOI, 106.5. **TV Station:** KETK-Ch. 22.

Jasper: Newspaper: *The Jasper Newsboy.* **Radio-AM:** KCOX, 1350 kHz. **Radio-FM:** KTXJ, 102.7 MHz; KJAS, 107.3.

Jefferson: Newspaper: *Jefferson Jimplecute.* **Radio-FM:** KHCJ, 91.9 MHz; KJTX, 104.5.

Jewett: Newspaper: *Jewett Messenger.*

Johnson City: Newspaper: *Johnson City Record-Courier.* **Radio-FM:** KFAN, 107.9 MHz.

Jourdanton: Radio-FM: KLEY, 95.7 MHz.

Junction: Newspaper: *Junction Eagle.* **Radio-AM:** KMBL, 1450 kHz. **Radio-FM:** KYKK, 93.5 MHz.

—K—

Karnes City: Newspaper: *The Karnes Countywide.* **Radio-FM:** KHHL, 103.1 MHz.

Katy: Newspaper: *Katy Times.* **TV Station:** KYAZ-Ch. 25.

Kaufman: Newspaper: *The Kaufman Herald.*

Keene: Radio-FM: KJRN, 88.3 MHz.

Kempner: Radio-FM: KOOV, 106.9 MHz.

Kenedy: Radio-AM: KAML, 990 kHz. **Radio-FM:** KCAF, 92.1 MHz.

Kerens: Newspaper: *The Kerens Tribune.* **Radio-FM:** KRVF, 106.9 MHz.

Kermit: Newspaper: *The Winkler County News.* **Radio-FM:** KDCJ, 91.5 MHz; KWXW, 93.7; KERB, 106.3.

Kerrville: Newspapers: *Kerrville Daily Times* (D); *Hill Country Community Journal.* **Radio-AM:** KERV, 1230 kHz. **Radio-FM:** KKER, 88.7 MHz; KHKV, 91.1; KRNH, 92.3; KRVL, 94.3; KKVR, 106.1. **TV Station:** KMYS-Ch. 32.

Kilgore: Newspaper: *Kilgore News Herald* (S). **Radio-AM:** KDOK, 1240 kHz. **Radio-FM:** KZLO, 88.7 MHz; KKTX, 96.1.

Killeen: Newspaper: *Killeen Daily Herald* (D). **Radio-AM:** KRMY, 1050 kHz. **Radio-FM:** KNCT, 91.3 MHz; KIIZ, 92.3. **TV Station:** KAKW-Ch. 13.

Kingsland: Radio-FM: KHSB, 104.7 MHz.

Kingsville: Newspaper: *Kingsville Record & Bishop News* (S). **Radio-AM:** KINE, 1330 kHz. **Radio-FM:** KTAI, 91.1 MHz; KKBA, 92.7; KFTX, 97.5.

Kirbyville: Newspaper: *Kirbyville Banner.*

Krum: Radio-FM: KNOR, 93.7 MHz.

Kurten: Radio-FM: KPWJ, 107.7 MHz.

Kyle: Newspaper: *Hays Free Press.*

—L—

La Feria: Newspaper: *La Feria News.*

La Grange: Newspaper: *The Fayette County Record* (S). **Radio-AM:** KVLG, 1570 kHz. **Radio-FM:** KBUK, 104.9 MHz.

Lake Dallas: TV Station: KAZD-Ch. 39.

Lake Jackson: Radio-FM: KYBJ, 91.1 MHz; KGLK, 107.5.

Lakeway: Newspaper: *Lake Travis View.*

Lamesa: Newspaper: *Lamesa Press Reporter* (S). **Radio-AM:** KPET, 690 kHz. **Radio-FM:** KBKN, 91.3 MHz; KTXC, 104.7.

Lampasas: Newspaper: *Lampasas Dispatch Record* (S). **Radio-AM:** KCYL, 1450 kHz.

La Porte: Newspaper: *Bay Area Observer.* **Radio-FM:** KHJK, 103.7 MHz.

Laredo: Newspaper: *Laredo Morning Times* (D). **Radio-AM:** KLAR, 1300 kHz; KLNT, 1490. **Radio-FM:** KHOY, 88.1 MHz; KBNL, 89.9; KJBZ, 92.7; KQUR, 94.9; KRRG, 98.1; KNEX, 106.1. **TV Stations:** KGNS-Ch. 8; KLDO-Ch. 19.

Laughlin AFB: Radio-FM: KDRX, 106.9 MHz.

La Vernia: Newspaper: *La Vernia News.*

League City: Radio-AM: KHCB, 1400 kHz.

Leander: Radio-FM: KUTX, 98.9 MHz.

Lefors: Radio-FM: KBDW, 91.7 MHz.

Leonard: Newspaper: *The Leonard Graphic.*

Levelland: Newspaper: *Levelland & Hockley County News-Press* (S). **Radio-AM:** KLVT, 1230 kHz. **Radio-FM:** KJDL, 105.3 MHz.

Lewisville: Radio-FM: KDXX, 107.9 MHz.

Lexington: Newspaper: *Lexington Leader.*

Liberty: Newspaper: *The Vindicator.* **Radio-FM:** KSHN, 99.9 MHz.

Liberty Hill: Newspaper: *The Liberty Hill Independent.*

Lindale: Newspaper: *Lindale News & Times.*

Linden: Newspaper: *The Cass County Sun.*

Lindsay: Newspaper: *Lindsay Letter.*

Littlefield: Newspaper: *Lamb County Leader-News* (S). **Radio-AM:** KZZN, 1490 kHz.

Livingston: Newspaper: *Polk County Enterprise* (S). **Radio-AM:** KETX, 1440 kHz. **Radio-FM:** KETX, 92.3 MHz.

Llano: Newspaper: *The Llano News.* **Radio-FM:** KVHL, 91.7 MHz; KITY, 102.9. **TV Station:** KBVO-Ch. 27.

Lockhart: Newspaper: *Lockhart Post-Register.* **Radio-AM:** KFIT, 1060 kHz.

Lometa: Radio-FM: KACQ, 101.9 MHz.

Longview: Newspaper: *Longview News-Journal* (D). **Radio-AM:** KFRO, 1370 kHz. **Radio-FM:** KYKX, 105.7 MHz. **TV Stations:** KCEB-Ch. 26; KFXK-Ch. 31.

Lorena: Radio-FM: KYAR, 98.3 MHz.

Lorenzo: Radio-FM: KKCL, 98.1 MHz.

Los Ybañez: Radio-FM: KJJT, 98.5 MHz.

Louise: Radio-FM: KABA, 90.3 MHz.

Lovelady: Radio-FM: KHMR, 104.3 MHz.

Lubbock: Newspaper: *Lubbock Avalanche-Journal* (D). **Radio-AM:** KRFE, 580 kHz; KFYO, 790; KJTV, 950; KKAM, 1340; KWBF, 1420; KBZO, 1460; KDAV, 1590. **Radio-FM:** KTXT, 88.1 MHz; KTTZ, 89.1; KAMY, 90.1; KKLU, 90.9; KLBB, 93.7; KFMX, 94.5; KLLL, 96.3; KQBR, 99.5; KONE, 101.1; KZII, 102.5; KXTQ, 106.5. **TV Stations:** KCBD-Ch. 11; KPTB-Ch. 16; KTTZ-Ch. 25; KAMC-Ch. 27; KJTV-Ch 35; KLBK-Ch. 40.

Lufkin: Newspaper: *Lufkin Daily News* (D). **Radio-AM:** KRBA, 1340 kHz. **Radio-FM:** KLDN, 88.9 MHz; KSWP, 90.9; KAVX, 91.9; KYBI, 100.1; KYKS, 105.1. **TV Station:** KTRE-Ch. 9.

Luling: Newspaper: *Luling Newsboy and Signal.* **Radio-FM:** KAMX, 94.7 MHz.

Lumberton: Radio-AM: KLLS, 1300 kHz. **Radio-FM:** KKHT, 100.7 MHz.

Lytle: Newspapers: *Leader News*; *Medina Valley Times.* **Radio-FM:** KZLV, 91.3 MHz.

—M—

Mabank: Newspaper: *The Monitor* (S). **Radio-AM:** KTXV, 890 kHz.

Madisonville: Newspaper: *Madisonville Meteor.* **Radio-AM:** KMVL, 1220 kHz. **Radio-FM:** KHML, 91.5 MHz; KAGG, 96.1; KMVL, 100.5.

Malakoff: Newspaper: *The News.* **Radio-FM:** KCKL, 95.9 MHz.

Manor: Radio-AM: KTXW, 1120 kHz; KELG, 1440.

Marble Falls: Newspaper: *The Highlander* (S). **Radio-FM:** KBMD, 88.5 MHz.

Marathon: Radio-FM: KDKY, 91.5 MHz.

Marfa: Newspaper: *The Big Bend Sentinel.* **Radio-FM:** KRTS, 93.5 MHz.

Marion: Radio-AM: KBIB, 1000 kHz.

Markham: Radio-FM: KKHA, 92.5 MHz; KBYC, 104.5.

Marlin: Newspaper: *The Marlin Democrat.* **Radio-FM:** KRMX, 92.9 MHz.

Marshall: Newspaper: *Marshall News Messenger* (D). **Radio-AM:** KZEY, 1410 kHz; KMHT, 1450. **Radio-FM:** KBWC, 91.1 MHz; KCUL, 92.3; KMHT, 103.9.

Mart: Newspaper: *Mart Messenger.* **Radio-FM:** KWAA, 88.9 MHz.

Mason: Newspaper: *Mason County News.* **Radio-FM:** KZZM, 101.7 MHz; KHLB, 102.5.

McAllen: Newspaper: *The Monitor* (D). **Radio-AM:** KRIO, 910 kHz. **Radio-FM:** KHID, 88.1 MHz; KVMV, 96.9; KGBT, 98.5. **TV Station:** KNVO-Ch. 49.

McCook: Radio-FM: KCAS, 91.5 MHz.

McCoy: Radio-FM: KMPI, 90.5 MHz.

McGregor: Newspaper: *McGregor Mirror & Crawford Sun.*

McKinney: Newspaper: *Collin County Commercial*

Record (S). **Radio-FM:** KNTU, 88.1 MHz.

McQueeney: Radio-FM: KZAR, 97.7 MHz.

Memphis: Radio-FM: KHNZ, 101.5 MHz; KLSR, 105.3.

Menard: Newspaper: *Menard News and Messenger.* **Radio-FM:** KTCY, 105.3 MHz.

Mercedes: Newspaper: *The Mercedes Enterprise.* **Radio-FM:** KTEX, 100.3 MHz.

Meridian: Newspaper: *Meridian Tribune.* **Radio-FM:** KOME, 95.3 MHz.

Merkel: Newspaper: *The Merkel Mail.* **Radio-AM:** KMXO, 1500 kHz. **Radio-FM:** KHXS, 102.7 MHz.

Mertzon: Radio-FM: KMEO, 91.9 MHz; KBTP, 101.1; KBJX, 103.5.

Mesquite: Radio-FM: KEOM, 88.5 MHz.

Mexia: Newspaper: *The Mexia News* (S). **Radio-AM:** KLRK, 1590 kHz.

Meyersville: Radio-FM: 100.1 MHz.

Miami: Newspaper: *Miami Chief.*

Midland: Newspaper: *Midland Reporter-Telegram* (D). **Radio-AM:** KCRS, 550 kHz; KWEL, 1070; KLPF, 1180; KMND, 1510. **Radio-FM:** KVDG, 90.9 MHz; KNFM, 92.3; KZBT, 93.3; KQRX, 95.1; KCRS, 103.3; KCHX, 106.7. **TV Stations:** KUPB-Ch. 18; KMID-Ch. 26.

Midlothian: Newspaper: *Midlothian Mirror.*

Miles: Newspaper: *Miles Messenger.* **Radio-FM:** KMLS, 95.5 MHz.

Mineola: Newspaper: *Wood County Monitor.* **Radio-FM:** KMOO, 99.9 MHz.

Mineral Wells: Newspaper: *Mineral Wells Index* (S). **Radio-AM:** KVTT, 1110 kHz. **Radio-FM:** KYQX, 89.3 MHz.

Mirando City: Radio-FM: KBDR, 100.5 MHz.

Mission: Newspaper: *Progress Times.* **Radio-AM:** KIRT, 1580 kHz. **Radio-FM:** KQXX, 105.5 MHz.

Missouri City: Radio-AM: KBRZ, 1460 kHz.

Monahans: Newspaper: *The Monahans News.* **Radio-AM:** KCKM, 1330 kHz. **Radio-FM:** KMRA, 91.1 MHz; KBAT, 99.9.

Mont Belvieu: Radio-FM: KFNC, 97.5 MHz.

Moody: Radio-FM: 99.1 MHz.

Moran: FM-Radio: 104.1 MHz.

Morton: Radio-FM: KQOA, 91.1 MHz; KPGA, 91.9.

Moulton: Newspaper: *Moulton Eagle.*

Mountain Home: Radio-FM: KAXA, 103.7 MHz.

Mount Pleasant: Newspaper: *Mount Pleasant Tribune* (S). **Radio-AM:** KIMP, 960 kHz. **Radio-FM:** KYZQ, 88.3 MHz.

Mount Vernon: Newspaper: *Mount Vernon Optic-Herald.*

Muenster: Newspaper: *Muenster Enterprise.* **Radio-FM:** KTMU, 88.7 MHz; KZZA, 106.7.

Muleshoe: Newspaper: *Muleshoe Journal.*

Munday: Newspaper: *The Knox County News-Courier.*

Murphy: Newspaper: *Murphy Monitor.*

—N—

Nacogdoches: Newspaper: *Nacogdoches Daily Sentinel* (D). **Radio-AM:** KSFA, 860 kHz. **Radio-FM:** KSAU, 90.1 MHz; KJCS, 103.3; KTBQ, 107.7. **TV Station:** KYTX-Ch. 18.

Naples: Newspaper: *The Monitor.*

Natalia: Radio-FM: KYRQ, 90.3 MHz.

Navasota: Newspaper: *The Navasota Examiner.* **Radio-FM:** KWUP, 92.5 MHz.

Nederland: Radio-AM: KBED, 1510 kHz.

Needville: Newspaper: *Hometown Journal.*

New Boston: Newspaper: *Bowie County Citizens Tribune.* **Radio-AM:** KLBW, 1530 kHz. **Radio-FM:** KEWL, 95.1 MHz; KZRB, 103.5; KTTY, 105.1.

New Braunfels: Newspaper: *New Braunfels Herald-Zeitung* (D). **Radio-AM:** KGNB, 1420 kHz. **Radio-FM:** KNBT, 92.1 MHz.

Newcastle: Radio-FM: KBLY, 100.5 MHz.

New Deal: Radio-FM: KTTU, 97.3 MHz.

Newton: Newspaper: *Newton County News.*

New Ulm: Newspaper: *New Ulm Enterprise.* **Radio-FM:** KNRG, 92.3 MHz.

New Waverly: Radio-FM: KNLY, 91.1 MHz.

Nocona: Newspaper: *Nocona News.*

Nolanville: Radio-FM: KLFX, 107.3 MHz.

Normangee: Newspaper: *The Normangee Star.*

—O—

Oakwood: Radio-FM: 94.5 MHz.

O'Brien: Radio-FM: KZOB, 105.5 MHz.

Odem: Radio-FM: KMJR, 98.3 MHz.

Odessa: Newspaper: *Odessa American* (D). **Radio-AM:** KFLB, 920 kHz; KOZA, 1230. **Radio-FM:** KBMM, 89.5 MHz; KLVW, 90.5; KXWT, 91.3; KMRK, 96.1; KMCM, 96.9; KODM, 97.9; KHKX, 99.1; KQLM, 107.9. **TV Stations:** KOSA-Ch. 7; KWES-Ch. 9; KMLM-Ch. 15; KPEJ-Ch. 23; KWWT-Ch. 30; KPBT-Ch. 38.

O'Donnell: Newspaper: *O'Donnell Index-Press.* **Radio-FM:** 97.7 MHz.

Olney: Newspaper: *Olney Enterprise.*

Olton: Newspaper: *Olton Enterprise.*

Orange: Newspaper: *The Orange Leader* (S). **Radio-AM:** KOGT, 1600 kHz. **Radio-FM:** KKMY, 104.5 MHz; KIOC, 106.1.

Ore City: Radio-FM: KAZE, 106.9 MHz.

Overton: Radio-FM: KTYK, 100.7 MHz.

Ozona: Newspaper: *Ozona Stockman.* **Radio-FM:** KYXX, 94.3 MHz; KCMZ, 105.5.

—P—

Paducah: Newspaper: *Paducah Post.* **Radio-FM:** KPZX, 94.7 MHz.

Paint Rock: Newspaper: *The Concho Herald.*

Palacios: Newspaper: *Palacios Beacon.* **Radio-FM:** KPAL, 91.3 MHz.

Palestine: Newspaper: *Palestine Herald-Press* (D). **Radio-AM:** KNET, 1450 kHz. **Radio-FM:** KYFP, 89.1 MHz; KYYK, 98.3.

Pampa: Newspaper: *The Pampa News* (TW). **Radio-AM:** KGRO, 1230 kHz. **Radio-FM:** KAVO, 90.9 MHz; KOMX, 100.3; KDRL, 103.3.

Panhandle: Newspaper: *Panhandle Herald, White Deer News.* **Radio-FM:** KPQP, 106.1 MHz.

Paris: Newspaper: *The Paris News* (D). **Radio-AM:** KZHN, 1250 kHz; KPLT, 1490. **Radio-FM:** KHCP, 89.3 MHz; KQPA, 91.9; KOYN, 93.9; KBUS, 101.9; KPLT, 107.7.

Pasadena: Newspaper: *The Pasadena Citizen* (S). **Radio-AM:** KIKK, 650 kHz; KLVL, 1480. **Radio-FM:** KFTG, 88.1 MHz; KKBQ, 92.9.

Pearland: Newspapers: *Pearland Journal*; *Pearland Reporter News.*

Pearsall: Newspaper: *Frio-Nueces Current.* **Radio-AM:** KMFR, 1280 kHz. **Radio-FM:** KSAG, 103.3 MHz; KSAH, 104.1.

Pecan Grove: Radio-AM: KREH, 900 kHz.

Pecos: Newspaper: *Pecos Enterprise.* **Radio-AM:** KIUN, 1400 kHz. **Radio-FM:** KPKO, 91.3 MHz; KDNZ, 97.3; KPTX, 98.3.

Perryton: Newspaper: *Perryton Herald* (S). **Radio-AM:** KEYE, 1400 kHz. **Radio-FM:** KEYE, 93.7 MHz.

Pflugerville: Radio-AM: KOKE, 1600 kHz.

Pharr: Newspaper: *The Advance News Journal.* **Radio-AM:** KVJY, 840 kHz.

Pilot Point: Newspaper: *Pilot Point Post-Signal.* **Radio-FM:** KZMP, 104.9 MHz.

Pineland: Radio-FM: KFAH, 99.1 MHz.

Pittsburg: Newspaper: *The Pittsburg Gazette.* **Radio-FM:** KGWP, 91.1 MHz; KPIT, 91.7; KSCN, 96.9; KMPA, 103.1.

Plains: Radio-FM: KPHS, 90.3 MHz.

Plainview: Newspaper: *Plainview Herald* (D). **Radio-AM:** KVOP, 1090 kHz; KREW, 1400. **Radio-FM:** KPMB, 88.5 MHz; KBAH, 90.5; KWLD, 91.5; KRIA, 103.9; KKYN, 106.9.

Plano: Radio-AM: KEXB, 620 kHz.

Pleasanton: Newspaper: *Pleasanton Express.* **Radio-AM:** KWMF, 1380 kHz.

Pleasant Valley: Radio-FM: KZAM, 98.7 MHz.

Point Comfort: Radio-FM: KJAZ, 94.1 MHz.

Port Aransas: Newspaper: *Port Aransas South Jetty.*

Port Arthur: Newspaper: *The Port Arthur News* (D). **Radio-AM:** KDEI, 1250 kHz; KOLE, 1340. **Radio-FM:** KQBU, 93.3 MHz; KTJM, 98.5. **TV Station:** KBTV-Ch. 27.

Port Isabel: Newspaper: *Port Isabel/South Padre Press.* **Radio-FM:** KNVO, 101.1 MHz; KLME, 105.5.

Portland: Radio-FM: KSGR, 91.1 MHz; KLHB, 105.5.

Port Lavaca: Newspaper: *Port Lavaca Wave.* **Radio-FM:** KNAL, 93.3 MHz.

Port Neches: Radio-AM: KBPO, 1150 kHz.

Port O'Connor: Radio-FM: KHPO, 91.9 MHz.

Post: Newspaper: *The Post Dispatch.* **Radio-FM:** KSSL, 107.3 MHz.

Pottsboro: Newspaper: *Pottsboro Sun.*

Prairie View: Radio-FM: KPVU, 91.3 MHz.

Premont: Radio-FM: KLBD, 88.1 MHz.

Presidio: Newspaper: *The Presidio International.*

Princeton: Newspaper: *Princeton Herald.*

—Q—

Quanah: Newspaper: *Quanah Tribune-Chief.* **Radio-AM:** KOLJ, 1150 kHz. **Radio-FM:** KQTX, 98.1 MHz.

Quemado: Radio-FM: KQMD, 88.1 MHz.

Quinlan: Newspaper: *The Quinlan-Tawakoni News.*

Quitaque: Newspaper: *Valley Tribune.*

—R—

Ralls: Newspaper: *Crosby County News.*

Ranchitos Las Lomas: Radio-FM: KLIT, 93.3 MHz.

Ranger: Radio-FM: KWBY, 98.5 MHz.

Rankin: Radio-FM: KXFS, 93.7 MHz.

Raymondville: Newspaper: *Chronicle/Willacy County News.* **Radio-AM:** KSOX, 1240 kHz. **Radio-FM:** KVHI, 88.7 MHz; KBUC, 102.1; KBIC, 105.7.

Refugio: Radio-FM: KRIK, 100.5 MHz; KXAI, 103.7; KXHM, 106.1.

Reno: Radio-FM: KLOW, 98.9 MHz.

Richardson: Radio-AM: KKLF, 1700 kHz.

Riesel: Newspaper: *Riesel Rustler.*

Rio Grande City: Radio-FM: KXJT, 88.3 MHz; KRGX, 95.1; KQBO, 107.5. **TV Station:** KTLM-Ch. 40.

Robert Lee: Newspaper: *Observer/Enterprise.* **Radio-FM:** KJVI, 105.7 MHz.

Robinson: Radio-FM: KWPW, 107.9 MHz.

Robstown: Newspaper: *Nueces County Record-Star.* **Radio-AM:** KROB, 1510 kHz. **Radio-FM:** KLUX, 89.5 MHz; KSAB, 99.9; KMIQ, 104.9.

Rockdale: Newspaper: *Rockdale Reporter.* **Radio-FM:** KRXT, 98.5 MHz.

Rockport: Newspaper: *The Rockport Pilot* (S)

Radio-FM: KKPN, 102.3 MHz.

Rocksprings: Newspaper: *Texas Mohair Weekly/Rocksprings Record.*

Rollingwood: Radio-AM: KJCE, 1370 kHz.

Roma: Radio-FM: KRIO, 97.7 MHz.

Rosebud: Newspaper: *Rosebud News.*

Rosenberg: Newspaper: *Fort Bend Herald* (D). **Radio-AM:** KQUE, 980 kHz. **TV Station:** KXLN-Ch. 45.

Rotan: Newspaper: *Double Mountain Chronicle.*

Round Rock: Newspaper: *Round Rock Leader* (S). **Radio-FM:** KNLE, 88.1 MHz; KFMK, 105.9.

Rowena: Newspaper: *The Rowena Press.*

Roxton: Newspaper: *Roxton Progress* (SM).

Royse City: Newspaper: *Royse City Herald Banner.*

Rudolph: Radio-FM: KTER, 90.7 MHz.

Rusk: Newspaper: *Cherokeean Herald.* **Radio-AM:** KTLU, 1580 kHz.

—S—

Sabinal: Radio-FM: KHAV, 107.1 MHz.

Sachse: Newspaper: *Sachse News.*

Saint Jo: Newspaper: *Saint Jo Tribune.*

Salado: Newspaper: *Salado Village Voice.*

San Angelo: Newspaper: *San Angelo Standard-Times* (D). **Radio-AM:** KGKL, 960 kHz; KKSA, 1260; KCRN, 1340. **Radio-FM:** KLRW, 88.5 MHz; KNAR, 89.3; KNCH, 90.1; KLTP, 90.9; KDCD, 92.9; KSAO, 93.9; KIXY, 94.7; KGKL, 97.5; KELI, 98.7; KCLL, 100.1; KWFR, 101.9; KMDX, 106.1; KSJT, 107.5. **TV Stations:** KLST-Ch. 11; KSAN-Ch. 16; KIDY-Ch. 19.

San Antonio: Newspapers: *San Antonio Express-News* (D); *San Antonio Business Journal*; *Hart Beat* (TW). **Radio-AM:** KTSA, 550 kHz; KSLR, 630; KKYX, 680; KTKR, 760; KONO, 860; KRDY, 1160; WOAI, 1200; KZDC, 1250; KAHL, 1310; KXTN, 1350; KCHL, 1480; KEDA, 1540. **Radio-FM:** KPAC, 88.3 MHz; KSTX, 89.1; KSYM, 90.1; KYFS, 90.9; KRTU, 91.7; KROM, 92.9; KXXM, 96.1; KAJA, 97.3; KISS, 99.5; KCYY, 100.3; KQXT, 101.9; KJXK, 102.7; KZEP, 104.5; KVBH, 107.5. **TV Stations:** KLRN-Ch. 9; KSAT-Ch. 12; KHCE-Ch. 16; KABB-Ch. 30; KVDA-Ch. 38; KENS-Ch. 39; KWEX-Ch. 41; WOAI-Ch. 48.

San Augustine: Newspaper: *San Augustine Tribune.* **Radio-FM:** KXXE, 92.5 MHz.

San Benito: Newspaper: *San Benito News.* **Radio-FM:** KHKZ, 106.3 MHz.

Sanderson: Radio-FM: KEVG, 102.7 MHz.

San Diego: Radio-FM: KXAM, 102.5 MHz; KUKA, 105.9.

Sanger: Radio-FM: KAWA, 89.7 MHz.

San Juan: Radio-AM: KUBR, 1210 kHz.

San Marcos: Newspaper: *San Marcos Daily Record* (D). **Radio-FM:** KTSW, 89.9 MHz; KBPA, 103.5.

San Saba: Newspaper: *San Saba News & Star.* **Radio-AM:** KROY, 1410 kHz. **Radio-FM:** KNUZ, 106.1 MHz.

Santa Anna: Radio-FM: KXXU, 104.3 MHz; KSZX, 105.5.

Santa Fe: Radio-FM: KJIC, 90.5 MHz.

Savoy: Radio-FM: KQDR, 107.3 MHz.

Schertz: Radio-FM: KBBT, 98.5 MHz.

Schulenburg: Newspaper: *Schulenburg Sticker.*

Scotland: Radio-FM: KXPN, 95.5 MHz.

Seabrook: Radio-FM: KROI, 92.1 MHz.

Seadrift: Radio-FM: KMAT, 105.1 MHz.

Sealy: Newspaper: *The Sealy News.* **Radio-FM:** KQLC, 90.7 MHz.

Seguin: Newspaper: *Seguin Gazette* (D). **Radio-AM:** KWED, 1580 kHz. **Radio-FM:** KSMG, 105.3 MHz.

Seminole: Newspaper: *Seminole Sentinel* (S). **Radio-AM:** KIKZ, 1250 kHz. **Radio-FM:** KSEM, 106.3 MHz.

Seymour: Newspaper: *Baylor County Banner.* **Radio-AM:** KSEY, 1230 kHz. **Radio-FM:** KSEY, 94.3 MHz.

Shamrock: Newspaper: *County Star-News.* **Radio-FM:** KSNZ, 92.9 MHz.

Shepherd: Newspaper: *San Jacinto News-Times.*

Shenandoah: Radio-AM: KRCM, 1380 kHz.

Sherman: Newspaper: *Herald Democrat* (D). **Radio-AM:** KJIM, 1500 kHz. **TV Station:** KXII-Ch. 12.

Shiner: Newspaper: *The Shiner Gazette.*

Silsbee: Newspaper: *Silsbee Bee.* **Radio-FM:** KAYD, 101.7 MHz.

Sinton: Newspaper: *The News of San Patricio.* **Radio-AM:** KDAE, 1590 kHz. **Radio-FM:** KNCN, 101.3 MHz.

Slaton: Newspaper: *The Slatonite.* **Radio-FM:** KVCE, 92.7 MHz.

Smiley: Radio-FM: KSXT, 90.3 MHz; KBQQ, 103.9.

Smithville: Newspaper: *Smithville Times.*

Snyder: Newspaper: *Snyder Daily News* (D). **Radio-AM:** KSNY, 1450 kHz. **Radio-FM:** KTPR, 89.9 MHz; KGWB, 91.1; KHMZ 94.9; KLYD, 98.9; KSNY, 101.5. **TV Station:** KPCB-Ch. 17.

Somerset: Radio-AM: KYTY, 810 kHz.

Somerville: Radio-FM: KXBT, 88.1 MHz.

Sonora: Newspaper: *Devil's River News.* **Radio-FM:** KHOS, 92.1 MHz.

South Padre Island: Radio-FM: KESO, 92.7 MHz; KZSP, 95.3.

Spearman: Newspaper: *Reporter-Statesman.* **Radio-FM:** KTOT, 89.5 MHz; KXDJ, 98.3.

Springtown: Newspaper: *Springtown Epigraph.* **Radio-FM:** KSQX, 89.1 MHz.

Spur: Newspaper: *Texas Spur.*

Stamford: Newspapers: *Stamford American*; *The Stamford & Haskell Star.* **Radio-AM:** KVRP, 1400 kHz. **Radio-FM:** KLGD, 106.9 MHz.

Stanton: Newspaper: *Martin County Messenger.* **Radio-FM:** KFLB, 88.1 MHz; KXQT, 105.9.

Stephenville: Newspaper: *Stephenville Empire Tribune* (S). **Radio-AM:** KSTV, 1510 kHz. **Radio-FM:** KQXS, 89.1 MHz; KEQX, 89.7; KTRL, 90.5.

Sterling City: Radio-FM: KNRX, 96.5 MHz.

Stockdale: Radio-AM: KQQB, 1520 kHz.

Stratford: Newspaper: *Stratford Star.* **Radio-FM:** KOGW, 91.5 MHz.

Sulphur Bluff: Radio-FM: KETE, 99.7 MHz.

Sulphur Springs: Newspaper: *News-Telegram* (TW). **Radio-AM:** KSST, 1230 kHz. **Radio-FM:** KGPF, 91.1 MHz; KZRF, 91.9; KSCH, 95.9.

Sunset Valley: Radio-FM: KVLR, 92.5 MHz.

Sweetwater: Newspaper: *Sweetwater Reporter* (D). **Radio-AM:** KXOX, 1240 kHz. **Radio-FM:** KXOX, 96.7. **TV Station:** KTXS-Ch. 20.

—T—

Taft: Radio-FM: KYRK, 106.5 MHz.

Tahoka: Newspaper: *Lynn County News.* **Radio-FM:** KMMX, 100.3 MHz; KAMZ, 103.5.

Tatum: Radio-FM: KZQX, 100.3 MHz.

Taylor: Newspaper: *Taylor Press* (S). **Radio-FM:** KLQB, 104.3 MHz.

Teague: Newspaper: *Teague Chronicle.*

Temple: Newspaper: *Temple Daily Telegram* (D). **Radio-AM:** KTEM, 1400 kHz. **Radio-FM:** KVLT, 88.5 MHz; KBDE, 89.9; KLTD, 101.7. **TV Station:**

KCEN-Ch. 9.

Terrell: Newspaper: *The Terrell Tribune.* **Radio-AM:** KPYK, 1570 kHz.

Terrell Hills: Radio-AM: KLUP, 930 kHz. **Radio-FM:** KTKX, 106.7 MHz.

Texarkana: Newspaper: *Texarkana Gazette* (D). **Radio-AM:** KCMC, 740 kHz; KTFS, 940; KKTK, 1400. **Radio-FM:** KTXK, 91.5 MHz; KTAL, 98.1; KKYR, 102.5. **TV Station:** KTAL-Ch. 15.

Texas City: Newspaper: *The Post Newspaper* (S). **Radio-AM:** KYST, 920 kHz.

Thorndale: Newspaper: *Thorndale Champion.* **Radio-FM:** KOKE, 99.3 MHz.

Three Rivers: Newspaper: *The Progress.* **Radio-FM:** KEMA, 94.5 MHz.

Throckmorton: Newspaper: *Throckmorton Tribune.*

Timpson: Newspaper: *East Texas Press.*

Tomball: Radio-AM: KSEV, 700 kHz.

Tom Bean: Radio-FM: KLAK, 97.5 MHz.

Trent: Radio-FM: KGDL, 92.1 MHz.

Trenton: Newspaper: *Trenton Tribune.*

Trinity: Newspaper: *Trinity County News-Standard.* **Radio-FM:** KTYR, 89.7 MHz.

Troup: Radio-FM: KTBB, 97.5 MHz.

Tulia: Newspaper: *Swisher County News.* **Radio-FM:** KBTE, 104.9 MHz.

Turkey: Newpaper: *Caprock Courier.*

Tye: Radio-FM: KBCY, 99.7 MHz.

Tyler: Newspaper: *Tyler Morning Telegraph* (D). **Radio-AM:** KTBB, 600 kHz; KGLD, 1330; KYZS, 1490. **Radio-FM:** KVNE, 89.5 MHz; KGLY, 91.3; KRWR, 92.1; KTYL, 93.1; KNUE, 101.5; KKUS, 104.1. **TV Station:** KLTV-Ch. 7.

—U—

Umbarger: Radio-FM: KRBG, 88.7 MHz.

Universal City: Radio-AM: KSAH, 720 kHz.

University Park: Radio-AM: KTNO, 1440 kHz; KZMP, 1540.

Uvalde: Newspaper: *Uvalde Leader-News* (S). **Radio-AM:** KGWU, 1400 kHz. **Radio-FM:** KHPS, 88.9 MHz; KBNU, 93.9; KUVA, 102.3; KVOU, 104.9. **TV Station:** KPXL-Ch. 26.

Uvalde Estates: Radio-FM: KEWP, 103.5 MHz.

—V—

Valley Mills: Newspaper: *Valley Mills Progress.*

Valley View: Radio-FM: KQFZ, 89.1 MHz.

Van Alstyne: Newspaper: *Van Alstyne Leader.*

Van Horn: Newspaper: *The Van Horn Advocate.* **Radio-FM:** KVHR, 91.5 MHz.

Vega: Newspaper: *Vega Enterprise.*

Vernon: Newspaper: *Vernon Record* (S). **Radio-AM:** KVWC, 1490 kHz. **Radio-FM:** KVED, 88.5 MHz; KVWC, 103.1.

Victoria: Newspaper: *Victoria Advocate* (D). **Radio-AM:** KVNN, 1340 kHz; KITE, 1410. **Radio-FM:** KAYK, 88.5 MHz; KBRZ, 89.3; KVRT, 90.7; KQVT, 92.3; KTXN, 98.7; KBAR, 100.9; KVIC, 104.7; KIXS, 107.9. **TV Stations:** KVCT-Ch. 11; KAVU-Ch. 15.

Vidor: Newspaper: *Vidor Vidorian.*

—W—

Waco: Newspaper: *Waco Tribune-Herald* (D). **Radio-AM:** KBBW, 1010 kHz; KWTX, 1230; KRZI, 1660. **Radio-FM:** KWBT, 94.5; KBGO, 95.7; KWTX, 97.5; WACO, 99.9; KWBU, 103.3. **TV Stations:** KWTX-Ch. 10; KXXV-Ch. 26; KWKT-Ch. 44.

Wake Village: Radio-FM: KHTA, 92.5 MHz.

Wallis: Newspaper: *Wallis News-Review.*

Waskom: Radio-FM: KQHN, 97.3 MHz.

Waxahachie: Newspaper: *Waxahachie Daily Light* (TW). **Radio-AM:** KBEC, 1390 kHz.

Weatherford: Newspaper: *Weatherford Democrat* (D). **Radio-AM:** KZEE, 1220 kHz. **Radio-FM:** KMQX, 88.5 MHz.

Webster: Newspaper: *Bay Area Citizen.*

Weimar: Newspaper: *Weimar Mercury.*

Wellington: Radio-FM: KSIF 91.7 MHz.

Wells: Radio-FM: KVLL, 94.7 MHz.

Weslaco: Radio-AM: KRGE, 1290 kHz. **TV Station:** KRGV-Ch. 13.

West: Newspaper: *The West News.*

West Lake Hills: Radio-AM: KTXZ, 1560 kHz.

West Odessa: Radio-FM: KFRI, 88.7 MHz.

Wharton: Newspaper: *Wharton Journal-Spectator* (S). **Radio-AM:** KANI, 1500 kHz.

Wheeler: Newspaper: *The Wheeler Times.* **Radio-FM:** KPDR, 90.3 MHz; 98.9.

Wheelock: Radio-FM: KVMK 100.9 MHz.

Whitehouse: Radio-FM: KISX, 107.3 MHz.

White Oak: Newspaper: *White Oak Independent.* **Radio-FM:** KAPW, 99.3 MHz.

Whitesboro: Newspaper: *Whitesboro News-Record.* **Radio-FM:** KMAD, 102.5 MHz.

Whitewright: Newspaper: *Whitewright Sun.*

Wichita Falls: Newspaper: *Times Record News* (D). **Radio-AM:** KWFS, 1290. **Radio-FM:** KMCU, 88.7 MHz; KMOC, 89.5; KZKL, 90.5; KNIN, 92.9; KLUR, 99.9; KWFS, 102.3; KQXC, 103.9; KBZS, 106.3. **TV Stations:** KJTL-Ch. 18; KAUZ-Ch. 22; KFDX-Ch. 28.

Willis: Radio-FM: KAFR, 88.3 MHz.

Wills Point: Newspapers: *Van Zandt News*; *Wills Point Chronicle.*

Wimberley: Newspaper: *Wimberley View.*

Winfield: Radio-FM: KALK, 97.7 MHz.

Winnie: Newspapers: *The Hometown Press*; *Seabreeze Beacon.* **Radio-FM:** KKHT, 100.7 MHz; KXXF 105.3.

Winnsboro: Newspaper: *Winnsboro News.* **Radio-FM:** KWNS, 104.7 MHz.

Winona: Radio-FM: KBLZ, 102.7 MHz.

Winters: Radio-FM: KORQ, 96.1 MHz.

Wixon Valley: Radio-FM: KBXT, 101.9 MHz.

Wolfforth: Radio-FM: KAIQ, 95.5 MHz. **TV Station:** KLCW-Ch. 43.

Woodville: Newspaper: *Tyler County Booster.*

Wylie: Newspaper: *The Wylie News.* **Radio-AM:** KHSE, 700 kHz.

—Y—

Yoakum: Newspaper: *Yoakum Herald-Times.* **Radio-FM:** KYKM, 94.3 MHz.

Yorktown: Newspaper: *Yorktown News-View.* **Radio-FM:** KGGB, 96.3 MHz.

—Z—

Zapata: Newspaper: *Zapata County News.* **Radio-FM:** KHEM, 89.3 MHz; KQHM 102.7; KJJS, 103.9. ☆

TRANSPORTATION

A loaded container ship leaving the Port of Houston.
Photo by Mark Taylor Cunningham/Shutterstock.

RAILROADS

HIGHWAYS AND MOTOR VEHICLES

FREIGHT GATEWAYS

CONSULATES AND FOREIGN TRADE ZONES

PORTS AND AVIATION

Freight Railroads in Texas

In Texas in 2017, there were three Class I railroad companies operating. The local or switching lines in operation made up about 20 percent of the state's total track mileage. In 2017, railroads in the state carried some 330 million tons of freight. The leading commodities handled are listed below. A complete list of the 52 railroads in the state is in the Counties section on page 193. *Source: Association of American Railroads.*

Railroads in State	Miles Operated
Class I (3, *see list at right*)	12,220
Regional	0
Local (29)	1,274
Switching & Terminal (20)	1,012
Total	**14,506**
Total excluding trackage rights*	**10,506**

Railroads in State	Miles Operated
Class I	
Union Pacific Railroad Co.	6,307
BNSF Railway Co.	4,984
Kansas City Southern Railway Co.	929

Trackage rights — track provided by another railroad. Numbers in parentheses represent the number of railroad companies in each category.

Freight Traffic in Texas by Kind – 2017

Carloads originated		Tons	Carloads terminated		Tons
Chemicals	442,600	40.4 million	Nonmetallic minerals	536,400	58.3 million
Nonmetallic minerals	309,200	32.7 million	Coal	382,900	45.9 million
Intermodal	1,025,800	12.9 million	Chemicals	337,200	31.3 million
Petroleum	123,100	11.3 million	Farm products	174,600	18.6 million
Glass and stone	36,600	3.8 million	Intermodal	1,145,600	14.7 million
All Other	257,900	11.6 million	All Other	710,300	48.8 million
Total	**2,195,200**	**112.6 million**	**Total**	**3,287,000**	**217.5 million**

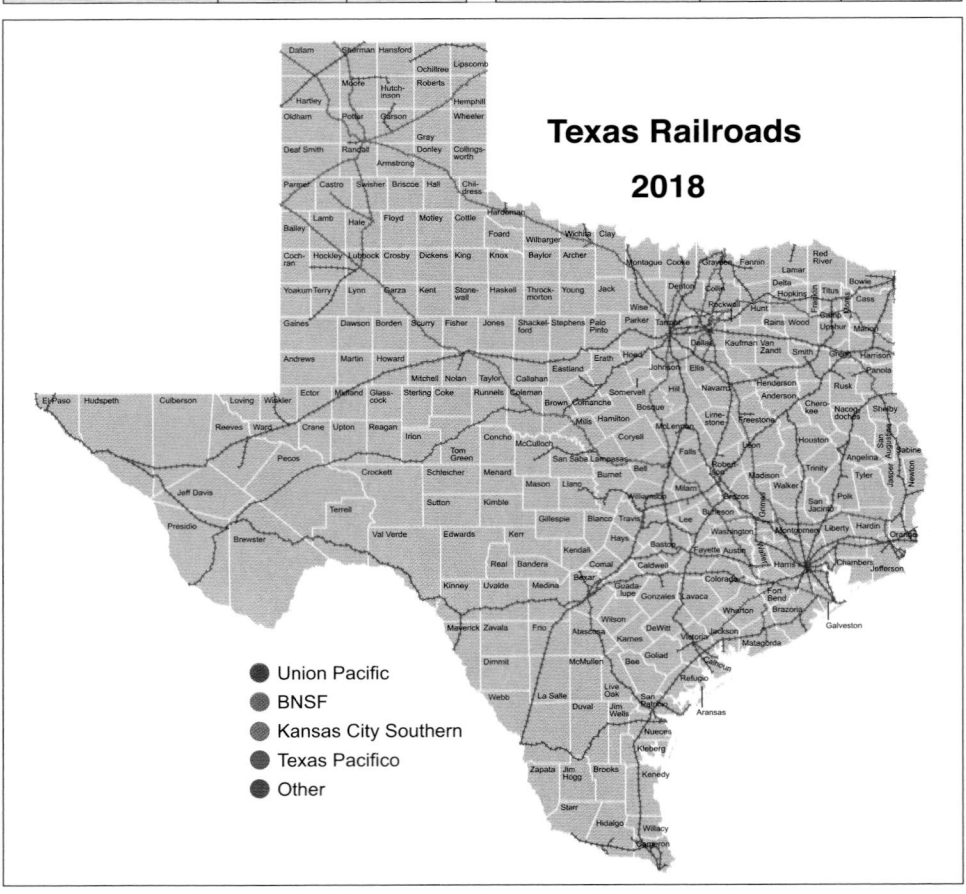

Texas Railroads 2018

- Union Pacific
- BNSF
- Kansas City Southern
- Texas Pacifico
- Other

Interstate 69 through Houston. Photo by Carol M. Highsmith, Library of Congress (CC).

Highway Miles, Construction, Maintenance, Vehicles: 2018

Texans drove more than 24 million motor vehicles in 2018 over 300,000 miles of roadways, including city- and county-maintained roads. That driving is calculated to have included more than 540 million miles driven daily on the 196,307 miles of state-maintained highways alone.

The Texas Department of Transportation (TxDOT) is responsible for state highway construction and maintenance, planning for future road expansion, administering Texas tollways and toll tags, and operating the state's 12 official Texas Travel Information Centers and 100 safety rest areas.

Mileage, maintenance, and construction figures (listed by county) refer only to roads that are maintained by the state: Interstates, U.S. highways, state highways, farm-to-market roads, and some loops around urban areas. Not included are city- or county-maintained streets and roads. A lane mile is one lane for one mile; i.e., one mile of four-lane highway equals four lane miles. Sources: Texas Department of Transportation and Department of Motor Vehicles.

County	Vehicles Registered	Lane Miles of Highway	Vehicle Miles Driven Daily	State Construction Expenditures	Combined Construction Maintenance Expenditures	Total Vehicle Registration Fees	State Net Receipts	County Net Receipts
Anderson	50,786	989	1,225,145	$ 12,795,233	$25,646,420	$ 3,563,732	$ 2,635,684	$ 925,825
Andrews	21,719	554	748,298	6,254,102	10,781,995	2,241,982	1,741,527	498,745
Angelina	84,124	941	1,992,167	19,707,733	35,776,284	6,539,465	5,144,803	1,391,588
Aransas	26,285	203	545,634	73,435	7,084,272	1,615,934	1,086,091	526,069
Archer	11,811	572	382,718	2,665,979	6,135,782	784,464	331,963	451,460
Armstrong	2,849	379	319,032	154,698	2,008,848	176,599	9,279	167,277
Atascosa	50,769	1,011	1,924,036	5,383,346	33,215,009	3,611,115	2,716,556	891,449
Austin	41,746	630	1,453,404	18,811,489	37,128,243	2,936,182	2,120,324	813,021
Bailey	6,774	491	215,583	14,010	2,079,942	520,609	117,087	403,344
Bandera	28,255	414	424,038	980,479	4,172,551	1,719,453	1,083,081	633,113
Bastrop	93,673	805	2,357,868	9,509,504	24,210,462	6,846,782	5,340,274	1,497,895
Baylor	4,445	531	205,987	346,751	2,976,181	284,180	38,752	244,793
Bee	24,027	673	605,081	825,260	6,936,799	1,737,708	1,126,566	610,047
Bell	307,744	1,553	7,467,154	72,350,253	157,215,753	21,385,144	17,086,187	4,278,279
Bexar	1,612,495	3,392	32,120,226	281,970,861	441,851,580	142,209,413	103,875,725	38,227,608
Blanco	18,144	462	630,644	43,982	2,516,715	1,266,925	806,293	458,389
Borden	1,070	344	62,136	12,803	2,061,174	48,029	3,161	44,802
Bosque	23,692	696	502,919	1,227,700	6,515,905	1,372,748	780,650	590,705
Bowie	88,560	1,207	3,013,402	11,968,005	41,200,080	6,196,542	4,796,997	1,393,703
Brazoria	332,413	1,372	6,289,252	28,955,251	44,963,929	23,142,780	18,982,151	4,136,247
Brazos	158,654	982	3,731,565	18,469,812	35,667,930	12,076,488	9,595,937	2,451,862

County	Vehicles Registered	Lane Miles of Highway	Vehicle Miles Driven Daily	State Construction Expenditures	Combined Construction Maintenance Expenditures	Total Vehicle Registration Fees	State Net Receipts	County Net Receipts
Brewster	10,766	607	229,893	$ 1,761,918	$ 8,663,280	$ 649,089	$ 297,433	$ 347,475
Briscoe	2,070	326	43,011	122,554	1,706,958	114,275	7,409	106,770
Brooks	6,594	340	662,718	5,780,326	10,293,350	400,500	126,124	274,200
Brown	43,786	766	800,341	3,485,597	10,868,234	3,208,622	2,299,682	906,478
Burleson	24,059	535	800,953	2,675,987	12,016,287	1,652,100	1,024,074	626,285
Burnet	57,861	805	1,475,843	3,353,359	14,846,703	4,079,505	2,978,880	1,093,434
Caldwell	42,957	716	1,325,861	2,984,416	9,119,093	2,987,579	2,118,295	867,254
Calhoun	23,597	406	547,893	1,488,560	12,346,233	1,887,121	1,297,601	588,073
Callahan	16,655	744	977,385	1,138,016	18,219,255	1,337,446	768,338	567,985
Cameron	317,364	1,826	6,391,519	30,249,578	55,297,729	27,119,500	19,167,966	7,939,385
Camp	17,771	265	267,268	1,798,543	3,537,114	1,560,898	1,078,636	481,231
Carson	7,591	780	801,178	363,787	15,012,305	537,310	125,178	411,860
Cass	33,886	975	842,484	2,618,924	10,559,716	2,082,381	1,375,889	705,375
Castro	8,142	533	277,332	260,817	2,160,785	769,845	314,859	454,518
Chambers	48,112	809	2,621,281	19,425,446	29,173,290	3,407,493	2,578,390	825,163
Cherokee	49,792	1,144	1,182,932	6,760,369	18,103,086	3,292,889	2,384,746	905,907
Childress	6,372	479	387,101	327,206	9,435,072	381,175	64,956	315,843
Clay	13,742	777	764,889	1,253,671	14,281,015	1,008,896	478,314	529,590
Cochran	3,048	467	97,594	46,910	2,277,822	212,849	10,162	202,529
Coke	4,614	369	190,158	45,747	2,026,210	261,875	40,290	221,321
Coleman	11,370	753	401,173	575,757	4,506,471	667,707	198,577	468,887
Collin	799,926	1,463	9,306,643	143,122,968	171,214,736	62,262,739	50,617,571	11,555,069
Collingsworth	3,395	454	67,438	349,890	4,727,899	218,510	12,425	205,886
Colorado	29,896	767	1,959,491	7,759,763	18,769,237	2,174,022	1,488,059	683,921
Comal	168,163	716	4,431,111	41,970,821	57,492,015	14,406,980	11,751,224	2,633,058
Comanche	17,106	744	457,662	1,377,651	5,629,410	1,275,335	718,760	555,778
Concho	3,468	477	295,055	1,216,508	8,281,270	193,059	11,330	181,530
Cooke	57,910	850	1,865,249	4,008,048	13,354,029	4,907,576	3,900,501	1,003,291
Coryell	60,215	736	1,123,020	4,453,659	21,989,925	3,351,870	2,409,993	938,356
Cottle	1,707	390	71,057	78,363	1,574,233	96,307	5,670	90,524
Crane	5,075	319	289,810	2,625,510	4,459,718	361,307	138,721	222,564
Crockett	5,271	783	675,150	2,100,774	9,529,791	349,260	71,053	277,972
Crosby	5,996	566	177,680	3,355,026	6,560,365	356,137	41,444	314,339
Culberson	2,249	750	831,124	1,871,463	7,889,694	139,833	8,396	131,295
Dallam	8,141	687	369,158	3,321,064	7,583,178	710,255	262,111	448,063
Dallas	2,155,995	3,377	39,374,100	551,810,638	627,648,168	170,789,799	143,736,397	26,916,955
Dawson	11,877	710	463,310	9,297,999	11,558,720	1,020,369	503,411	514,842
Deaf Smith	20,986	603	423,317	1,691,857	5,910,874	1,889,179	1,267,733	620,374
Delta	6,747	353	162,983	6,522,974	12,737,150	372,289	94,175	277,940
Denton	680,143	1,634	10,314,719	149,404,143	173,518,210	48,693,843	39,699,365	8,921,118
Dewitt	25,915	660	646,406	11,575,748	21,876,139	1,775,929	1,144,512	629,961
Dickens	2,752	468	95,598	716,029	4,613,666	145,073	8,432	136,553
Dimmit	12,091	505	556,152	8,348,368	25,766,910	935,852	559,492	375,921
Donley	3,438	469	455,036	214,260	3,671,498	216,914	13,231	203,421
Duval	11,948	636	405,093	532,981	2,703,262	800,931	356,221	444,365
Eastland	24,621	1,025	1,295,152	31,968,953	38,653,371	2,126,396	1,486,105	639,288
Ector	182,479	971	2,998,995	5,819,661	13,908,599	18,290,396	15,706,241	2,579,014
Edwards	2,976	499	77,128	12,595	8,736,280	173,189	9,669	163,455
Ellis	181,071	1,527	5,683,974	107,173,331	116,821,875	12,103,729	9,780,517	2,311,676
El Paso	676,142	1,725	11,695,340	193,830,046	243,255,251	56,771,308	41,956,777	14,793,624
Erath	42,479	841	1,069,070	11,365,019	42,569,173	2,939,938	2,127,053	809,494
Falls	18,268	746	758,355	4,091,307	22,483,267	1,310,291	727,633	582,013
Fannin	38,906	982	758,016	6,611,234	24,710,908	2,650,505	1,849,817	798,211
Fayette	35,792	1,032	1,827,381	1,406,036	21,790,077	2,363,559	1,627,124	733,294
Fisher	4,839	558	159,761	291,195	7,580,223	277,269	15,413	261,622
Floyd	7,077	702	174,153	223,350	3,084,680	555,522	132,982	422,148
Foard	1,701	298	46,581	36,379	7,942,198	97,777	5,123	92,654
Fort Bend	622,718	1,247	8,002,186	136,613,633	144,387,887	47,216,342	38,666,914	8,491,396
Franklin	12,782	339	551,899	1,049,412	26,463,206	807,497	398,608	408,284

County	Vehicles Registered	Lane Miles of Highway	Vehicle Miles Driven Daily	State Construction Expenditures	Combined Construction Maintenance Expenditures	Total Vehicle Registration Fees	State Net Receipts	County Net Receipts
Freestone	23,887	823	1,575,846	$ 784,513	$ 12,534,264	$ 1,602,525	$ 994,101	$ 607,797
Frio	15,556	759	1,287,738	3,489,072	12,653,605	1,096,002	603,268	492,248
Gaines	22,034	661	708,465	973,523	3,844,170	1,597,423	1,184,471	412,466
Galveston	299,733	1,067	5,328,064	129,312,692	142,812,294	20,166,217	16,464,311	3,672,695
Garza	4,971	458	488,658	2,130,083	10,660,862	320,010	69,949	249,587
Gillespie	36,842	690	818,097	417,303	4,561,570	2,346,462	1,552,678	788,430
Glasscock	2,566	357	421,230	448,595	3,659,354	164,692	8,627	155,932
Goliad	9,527	535	323,701	1,133,849	4,198,931	509,112	141,060	367,420
Gonzales	25,455	885	1,506,732	6,482,675	10,503,639	1,824,372	1,195,569	627,904
Gray	23,553	760	621,147	481,872	20,316,655	1,734,212	1,094,323	638,216
Grayson	135,410	1,265	3,462,221	19,266,486	32,302,937	9,862,493	7,836,330	2,013,835
Gregg	130,036	816	2,747,267	22,169,663	42,583,249	11,670,818	9,793,281	1,870,166
Grimes	35,143	615	1,100,857	14,735,523	32,816,116	2,317,753	1,588,271	726,991
Guadalupe	153,546	1,014	3,716,362	16,418,466	37,672,486	10,533,792	8,291,756	2,229,149
Hale	29,713	1,056	908,996	438,726	10,194,199	2,268,151	1,553,022	713,693
Hall	3,185	457	195,441	439,379	3,536,324	194,920	10,997	183,689
Hamilton	11,612	581	349,475	1,228,717	8,485,947	715,628	241,864	472,999
Hansford	6,840	526	123,761	160,272	3,286,947	524,161	125,747	398,214
Hardeman	3,862	465	355,924	2,386,232	9,583,592	248,400	13,618	234,672
Hardin	59,862	580	1,363,904	7,685,845	14,719,074	4,402,149	3,308,202	1,090,502
Harris	3,595,373	5,152	62,024,466	537,913,406	595,697,034	299,063,451	248,051,245	50,736,193
Harrison	70,967	1,185	2,577,939	3,631,663	189,594,590	4,969,462	3,712,453	1,252,293
Hartley	6,923	540	392,516	3,157,110	32,732,172	677,207	327,029	349,612
Haskell	6,055	668	229,645	43,693	3,902,468	429,774	76,078	353,161
Hays	187,219	716	5,146,756	25,286,605	31,587,248	13,873,068	11,289,871	2,559,839
Hemphill	5,777	392	175,530	2,296,898	13,315,199	361,694	81,915	279,271
Henderson	92,494	1,035	1,781,405	22,204,256	33,393,129	5,915,980	4,546,213	1,364,802
Hidalgo	621,505	2,453	11,226,433	78,966,054	99,094,555	54,924,886	40,843,624	14,061,195
Hill	44,544	1,097	2,571,215	14,785,238	46,894,344	3,270,670	2,442,657	825,750
Hockley	27,011	751	696,269	493,587	13,341,837	1,931,077	1,291,654	636,517
Hood	70,735	402	1,018,060	5,811,010	10,251,625	5,189,158	3,995,694	1,186,356
Hopkins	43,222	961	1,739,746	2,994,461	21,685,945	3,061,090	2,208,928	849,305
Houston	23,793	868	634,897	2,130,281	28,682,383	1,418,023	826,594	590,176
Howard	30,968	887	1,328,675	37,198,882	53,211,801	2,268,499	1,558,284	708,627
Hudspeth	3,696	827	1,470,618	1,096,421	21,360,677	218,136	12,238	205,740
Hunt	98,556	1,349	2,816,140	20,809,822	32,656,769	7,034,122	5,407,933	1,619,814
Hutchinson	25,016	487	330,856	111,018	10,991,311	1,767,173	1,172,653	593,192
Irion	3,594	246	315,600	2,218,167	9,725,104	298,317	88,185	209,954
Jack	11,486	576	324,192	1,349,364	6,117,262	829,927	383,903	445,716
Jackson	18,110	637	938,816	340,025	5,591,497	1,127,414	592,434	534,188
Jasper	41,928	774	1,041,308	658,479	10,993,955	2,727,441	1,908,138	817,963
Jeff Davis	2,831	468	198,287	409,153	12,081,215	166,596	34,646	131,362
Jefferson	219,441	1,121	5,231,963	23,680,306	34,755,877	15,985,271	13,053,644	2,917,525
Jim Hogg	4,710	288	168,214	833,832	41,060,887	338,773	101,798	236,702
Jim Wells	43,389	715	1,182,962	5,138,819	8,305,401	3,358,310	2,501,910	854,777
Johnson	178,013	995	3,225,988	8,468,788	24,386,349	14,513,594	11,738,062	2,764,027
Jones	17,196	1,006	469,366	5,542,032	21,792,090	1,388,974	818,689	568,792
Karnes	20,045	692	799,860	5,261,116	22,353,155	1,313,129	767,628	545,048
Kaufman	124,760	1,215	4,165,598	33,602,556	63,119,853	8,357,030	6,486,947	1,864,568
Kendall	62,857	453	1,197,250	13,460,038	46,931,276	5,836,788	4,480,633	1,344,290
Kenedy	723	193	455,459	429,871	11,174,566	30,431	2,767	27,479
Kent	1,184	323	43,835	10,379	2,037,792	55,619	4,748	50,827
Kerr	60,266	711	1,228,974	584,146	8,519,255	4,196,976	3,145,338	1,038,974
Kimble	6,470	685	659,642	422,750	8,093,643	368,016	77,690	290,043
King	509	206	76,474	37,049	800,760	19,787	1,351	18,392
Kinney	3,658	408	217,894	1,426,039	9,101,314	230,384	61,534	168,652
Kleberg	26,271	374	774,162	3,368,275	8,400,728	2,011,878	1,430,376	579,525
Knox	4,396	466	121,014	224,177	2,427,007	306,038	42,056	263,785
Lamar	53,166	1,004	1,178,026	7,395,122	21,999,010	3,878,331	2,894,240	981,755

County	Vehicles Registered	Lane Miles of Highway	Vehicle Miles Driven Daily	State Construction Expenditures	Combined Construction Maintenance Expenditures	Total Vehicle Registration Fees	State Net Receipts	County Net Receipts
Lamb	13,710	799	460,254	$ 210,834	$ 4,156,607	$ 945,560	$ 434,300	$ 510,288
Lampasas	26,070	518	689,393	45,786	2,407,593	1,895,882	1,206,210	687,567
La Salle	8,184	648	1,229,392	3,568,089	13,147,376	678,579	339,439	339,006
Lavaca	29,663	671	592,000	992,807	12,052,420	1,659,674	1,022,748	635,251
Lee	25,213	529	704,816	1,275,291	6,218,264	1,779,257	1,174,985	602,760
Leon	24,402	839	1,582,499	4,788,670	27,645,229	1,592,223	1,005,602	585,476
Liberty	84,616	843	2,056,439	5,449,122	16,212,060	6,146,330	4,836,543	1,306,537
Limestone	24,850	770	649,289	6,107,897	16,941,781	1,537,695	920,392	616,194
Lipscomb	4,327	412	119,564	303,812	8,766,066	324,125	44,792	279,160
Live Oak	15,092	1,008	1,492,788	4,343,846	26,029,063	1,012,158	497,641	513,857
Llano	28,387	499	495,061	592,319	3,901,711	1,733,726	1,050,162	679,344
Loving	224	68	193,701	598,940	1,283,126	10,598	704	9,895
Lubbock	247,697	1,726	4,060,813	72,878,849	99,114,305	20,288,054	16,766,058	3,481,341
Lynn	6,480	713	415,188	684,931	3,314,340	383,227	53,921	328,203
Madison	14,349	617	1,069,261	2,203,492	7,882,768	1,478,061	987,756	489,560
Marion	10,635	330	270,449	161,594	2,596,642	692,311	265,992	426,120
Martin	7,100	578	850,492	688,420	8,276,333	644,731	208,561	435,725
Mason	6,604	422	184,987	472,029	4,991,918	375,750	85,993	289,467
Matagorda	37,912	691	988,435	2,929,794	11,188,910	2,406,859	1,644,651	760,210
Maverick	48,434	499	964,788	8,612,775	15,327,616	3,729,832	2,845,298	882,655
McCulloch	10,133	608	378,058	1,567,937	6,661,481	730,767	280,636	449,107
McLennan	224,356	1,687	6,762,304	65,541,195	114,623,449	17,422,114	13,997,874	3,408,140
McMullen	2,448	320	265,816	2,985,334	13,443,789	132,271	7,593	124,568
Medina	56,542	766	1,383,166	1,239,037	10,963,645	4,124,339	3,091,974	1,028,687
Menard	2,935	348	145,469	2,184,471	6,363,069	162,666	17,559	144,766
Midland	215,431	1,079	4,159,490	22,234,858	47,224,486	21,340,241	18,469,904	2,854,002
Milam	30,431	707	860,996	785,444	7,647,416	1,875,383	1,200,599	673,438
Mills	7,270	450	302,072	338,429	4,054,656	452,510	94,036	357,993
Mitchell	7,557	662	695,380	1,663,799	6,275,324	435,863	84,839	350,803
Montague	26,657	850	698,494	1,788,944	14,097,514	1,746,661	1,102,201	642,716
Montgomery	544,940	1,312	10,628,294	202,352,643	219,265,381	38,889,007	32,234,176	6,600,975
Moore	23,937	479	519,054	7,180,429	11,492,504	1,818,964	1,249,080	568,995
Morris	14,031	359	490,282	173,885	3,150,356	892,842	469,585	422,906
Motley	1,802	331	54,347	295,501	2,313,357	93,498	5,668	87,742
Nacogdoches	58,915	980	1,717,468	13,891,831	29,555,181	4,247,568	3,151,906	1,091,425
Navarro	52,355	1,192	2,178,862	79,334,778	94,046,337	3,739,338	2,776,609	960,663
Newton	13,920	554	349,652	875,898	7,928,896	846,466	347,448	498,564
Nolan	14,974	690	1,146,814	3,424,641	21,931,068	1,052,570	534,271	516,940
Nueces	287,512	1,530	6,817,759	205,783,277	250,815,427	22,586,216	18,698,966	3,866,741
Ochiltree	12,308	429	260,500	2,205,720	5,151,027	1,011,213	511,195	499,545
Oldham	3,021	467	844,302	71,154	2,181,778	212,115	36,973	175,053
Orange	84,481	626	2,826,820	13,414,746	40,293,637	5,246,656	4,016,086	1,226,300
Palo Pinto	33,952	823	1,048,023	3,371,576	14,403,760	2,344,709	1,646,477	695,766
Panola	27,750	773	954,019	8,929,867	19,859,242	1,728,251	1,268,086	458,837
Parker	155,377	887	3,469,196	24,544,342	48,191,204	12,851,529	10,422,090	2,414,197
Parmer	10,381	614	422,640	325,724	3,648,090	779,366	305,641	473,459
Pecos	16,304	1,687	1,349,906	4,106,628	21,113,399	1,347,628	799,496	547,260
Polk	56,826	865	1,621,513	4,806,170	18,252,707	4,526,549	3,443,141	1,080,378
Potter	105,106	906	2,571,948	35,575,785	79,016,375	8,596,911	7,024,672	1,562,953
Presidio	8,045	547	163,591	4,705,394	9,523,290	544,270	204,046	339,906
Rains	15,232	268	337,720	224,632	9,586,435	936,381	487,199	448,351
Randall	136,758	888	1,513,355	60,543,825	64,932,498	10,957,006	8,746,232	2,193,321
Reagan	5,524	319	474,120	3,726,247	5,247,532	476,724	158,895	317,696
Real	4,705	295	103,510	123,402	3,705,825	300,193	75,024	224,811
Red River	14,921	752	397,982	1,533,438	10,779,662	862,252	358,747	503,103
Reeves	13,227	1,178	1,743,468	14,618,143	32,101,281	1,289,778	783,224	506,117
Refugio	8,784	464	704,748	1,020,231	4,995,572	599,707	261,409	337,663
Roberts	1,322	242	81,777	211,602	1,826,007	62,598	4,652	57,924
Robertson	20,270	661	977,025	1,325,626	6,553,177	1,381,070	791,129	589,043

County	Vehicles Registered	Lane Miles of Highway	Vehicle Miles Driven Daily	State Construction Expenditures	Combined Construction Maintenance Expenditures	Total Vehicle Registration Fees	State Net Receipts	County Net Receipts
Rockwall	91,492	346	2,018,706	$ 31,598,976	$53,770,530	$ 7,647,601	$ 6,162,054	$ 1,473,821
Runnels	13,127	734	363,772	1,162,335	6,217,495	884,142	394,577	488,627
Rusk	53,337	1,181	1,242,739	1,720,109	17,114,146	3,622,623	2,646,001	974,214
Sabine	13,354	483	279,417	197,115	5,164,406	806,467	347,783	458,088
San Augustine	9,503	540	291,026	3,145,957	12,773,804	665,068	257,526	407,106
San Jacinto	29,163	529	738,791	3,296,631	9,784,035	1,906,997	1,210,992	694,374
San Patricio	68,332	989	2,259,281	5,394,762	24,104,001	4,839,977	3,610,598	1,223,787
San Saba	8,132	435	176,112	612,699	2,255,097	487,004	102,409	384,261
Schleicher	4,348	362	134,741	26,639	2,172,003	256,162	47,145	208,727
Scurry	22,605	686	648,709	1,880,815	7,689,018	2,045,864	1,441,584	603,464
Shackelford	4,899	355	148,101	365,951	2,658,457	381,317	101,359	279,696
Shelby	28,721	880	743,511	3,000,529	18,218,671	2,065,399	1,363,998	700,259
Sherman	3,156	431	254,274	632,085	1,972,333	228,213	11,738	216,421
Smith	220,345	1,611	5,403,806	15,522,144	54,882,499	17,146,779	13,665,176	3,464,798
Somervell	12,057	197	248,377	426,652	3,006,752	679,435	323,012	355,468
Starr	55,348	531	1,073,231	6,959,697	11,317,271	3,787,588	2,834,627	951,419
Stephens	10,655	559	215,356	3,966,295	13,050,077	706,387	292,686	413,040
Sterling	2,549	309	259,512	216,211	1,719,283	131,848	28,188	103,572
Stonewall	2,092	327	79,865	345,548	2,342,807	119,397	5,097	114,212
Sutton	5,781	590	625,873	1,535,001	5,521,227	371,834	107,189	264,258
Swisher	7,150	804	430,970	224,459	3,602,488	442,134	79,269	362,397
Tarrant	1,718,938	3,305	31,844,601	428,471,708	541,950,754	141,523,004	119,240,226	22,073,188
Taylor	131,320	1,211	2,554,538	7,838,159	31,477,366	10,534,877	8,556,326	1,967,935
Terrell	1,329	373	78,254	9,656	2,577,482	60,530	4,310	56,198
Terry	11,424	628	507,238	261,755	2,372,926	820,277	327,147	492,500
Throckmorton	2,045	343	72,641	673,201	4,616,569	132,398	6,308	125,978
Titus	31,813	584	1,216,987	17,526,453	34,374,659	2,615,754	1,850,245	764,277
Tom Green	117,074	1,041	1,837,796	12,160,351	30,216,135	9,156,535	7,172,876	1,972,718
Travis	993,424	2,154	20,589,706	224,443,453	317,273,663	76,065,112	62,432,106	13,485,712
Trinity	15,950	443	368,118	851,506	9,161,652	964,527	469,365	494,452
Tyler	22,415	519	503,970	436,959	9,371,844	1,363,341	761,235	601,211
Upshur	43,815	790	994,467	633,379	12,287,321	2,643,780	1,834,007	808,241
Upton	4,368	391	297,912	4,387,439	8,269,970	320,104	100,676	219,339
Uvalde	27,459	760	724,010	771,788	7,059,093	2,024,171	1,413,483	609,236
Val Verde	47,272	735	528,336	4,577,866	15,665,577	3,391,148	2,524,584	863,442
Van Zandt	64,183	1,161	2,365,291	9,780,969	34,029,930	4,151,845	3,027,328	1,122,199
Victoria	92,184	911	2,173,413	28,652,262	40,653,775	6,898,121	5,420,542	1,468,699
Walker	55,718	812	2,493,181	62,248,183	83,004,387	3,809,166	2,787,414	1,016,644
Waller	53,819	591	2,083,617	29,370,803	35,306,644	3,949,142	2,997,439	949,146
Ward	15,067	670	1,205,307	2,791,256	15,080,669	1,349,316	1,046,031	302,677
Washington	42,639	656	1,191,865	3,086,241	15,724,374	3,102,746	2,263,619	835,445
Webb	206,404	1,243	3,494,692	42,480,734	59,574,724	20,107,427	15,292,896	4,808,120
Wharton	48,830	883	1,724,826	16,845,678	34,516,406	3,724,182	2,817,289	904,692
Wheeler	7,603	674	562,207	123,453	5,084,818	479,694	106,566	372,632
Wichita	113,509	1,138	2,127,316	2,741,111	18,980,795	8,226,415	6,576,954	1,641,889
Wilbarger	12,763	717	636,062	2,793,539	12,765,446	1,006,717	477,639	527,969
Willacy	15,913	516	486,438	4,953,800	12,079,638	1,051,713	533,506	517,785
Williamson	458,794	1,671	8,462,468	60,170,925	92,563,740	35,996,886	29,165,540	6,767,916
Wilson	57,366	742	1,148,517	9,553,275	37,240,419	3,635,794	2,678,439	954,453
Winkler	9,943	292	588,572	412,152	2,621,197	819,930	502,279	317,249
Wise	88,614	909	2,309,258	5,808,948	13,583,625	6,832,052	5,422,668	1,403,551
Wood	52,903	909	934,569	685,794	10,357,970	3,542,362	2,582,690	955,369
Yoakum	11,486	430	298,486	182,742	2,684,871	1,023,823	542,225	481,047
Young	23,080	705	369,015	3,539,757	11,107,101	1,630,759	1,020,485	608,596
Zapata	12,294	274	290,951	1,549,019	4,803,048	833,252	445,042	388,143
Zavala	9,053	541	377,749	377,397	5,814,310	624,457	269,999	354,332
				$	$	$	$	$
Total	24,862,981	196,307	540,367,474	5,130,989,400	8,583,389,516	2,094,922,232	1,640,921,713	422,152,298

Texas Major Toll Roads

Facilities	Authority	2010	2014	2015	2016
Roads	(Tolls Collected in thousands of dollars, 000)				
Camino Colombia Toll Road	TxDOT	$ 3,352	NA	$ 4,079	$ 6,997
Central Texas Toll Facilities[1]	Central Texas Turnpike System and Regional Authority	90,006	$ 165,131	202,582	239,165
Fort Bend Toll Roads	Fort Bend Toll Road Authority	15,675	23,510	26,860	29,481
Harris County Toll Facilities[2]	Harris County Toll Road Authority	464,269	622,209	745,373	759,276
North Texas Toll Facilities	North Texas Tollway Authority	399,054	580,045	615,488	671,961
East Texas Toll Facilities	North East Texas Regional Authority	–	6,651	8,340	8,731
Total, roads		$ 972,356	$ 1,397,546	$ 1,602,722	$ 1,715,611

[1]Including U.S. 183A and Manor Expressway. [2]Including Jesse Jones Memorial Toll Bridge. NA, not available.
Source: Highway Statistics annual, Federal Highway Administration; and local toll authorities.

Toll Bridges

Facilities	Authority	2010	2013	2014	2015
Bridge	(Tolls Collected in thousands of dollars, 000)				
Cameron County International	Cameron County	$ 22,102	$ 14,850	$ 15,172	$ 21,273
Del Rio International	City of Del Rio	4,144	4,972	5,216	6,558
Eagle Pass International	City of Eagle Pass	8,106	8,043	9,701	10,737
Laredo International	City of Laredo	41,449	44,735	54,402	69,215
McAllen International	City of McAllen	11,036	13,232	13,548	19,799
Pharr International	City of Pharr	10,639	11,665	12,362	13,196
Roma International	Starr County	2,081	1,816	1,871	2,988
San Luis Pass–Vacek	Galveston County	1,265	512	507	3,128
Zaragosa	City of El Paso	16,094	17,581	19,625	21,499
TOTAL tolls collected, roads & bridges		$ 1,089,272	$ 1,364,894	$ 1,529,950	$ 1,771,115

Source: Highway Statistics annual, Federal Highway Administration.

Driver Licenses

The following list shows the number of licensed drivers by year for Texas and for all the states. Sources are the Texas Department of Public Safety (for state figures) and the Federal Highway Administration.

Year	Texas licensed drivers	Total U.S. licensed drivers	Year	Texas licensed drivers	Total U.S. licensed drivers
2018	18,000,274	N/A	2003	15,091,776	196,165,666
2017	17,675,389	225,346,257	2002	14,639,132	194,295,633
2016	17,326,113	221,711,918	2001	14,303,799	191,275,719
2015	16,970,365	218,084,465	2000	14,024,305	190,625,023
2014	16,579,591	214,092,472	1995	12,369,243	176,628,482
2013	16,230,209	212,159,728	1990	11,136,694	167,015,250
2012	15,950,297	211,814,830	1985	10,809,078	156,868,277
2011	16,880,877	211,874,649	1980	9,287,286	145,295,036
2010	16,808,359	210,114,939	1975	7,509,497	129,790,666
2009	16,602,416	209,618,386	1970	6,380,057	111,542,787
2008	16,551,156	208,320,601	1965	5,413,887	98,502,152
2007	16,330,825	205,741,845	1960	4,352,168	87,252,563
2006	16,096,985	202,810,438	1955	3,874,834	74,685,949
2005	15,831,852	200,548,972	1950	2,687,349	59,322,278
2004	15,562,484	198,888,912			

Motor Vehicles Crashes, Losses in Texas

Year	Number killed	†Number injured	Crashes by Kind				Vehicle Miles Traveled		Economic loss (in millions)
			Fatal	†Injury	†Non-injury	†Total	Number (in millions)	Deaths per 100 mill miles	
1960	2,254	127,980	1,842	71,100	239,300	312,242	46,353	4.9	$ 350
1965	3,028	186,062	2,460	103,368	365,160	470,988	* 52,163	5.8	498
1966	3,406	208,310	2,784	115,728	406,460	524,972	55,261	6.2	557
1970	3,560	223,000	2,965	124,000	886,000	1,012,965	* 68,031	5.2	1,042
1975	3,429	138,962	2,945	92,510	373,141	468,596	84,575	4.1	1,440
1980	‡ 4,424	185,964	‡ 3,863	123,577	§ 305,500	432,940	103,255	4.3	3,010
1982	4,271	204,666	3,752	135,859	312,159	451,770	* 124,910	3.4	3,375
1983	‡ 3,823	208,157	‡ 3,328	137,695	302,876	443,899	129,309	3.0	3,440
1984	3,913	220,720	3,466	145,543	293,285	442,294	137,280	2.9	¶ 3,795
1985	3,682	231,009	3,270	151,657	300,531	452,188	143,500	2.6	3,755
1986	3,568	234,120	3,121	154,514	298,079	452,593	150,474	2.4	3,782
1987	3,261	226,895	2,881	146,913	246,175	395,969	151,221	2.2	3,913
1988	3,395	238,845	3,004	152,004	237,703	392,711	152,819	2.2	4,515
1989	3,361	243,030	2,926	153,356	233,967	390,249	159,679	2.1	4,873
1990	3,243	262,576	2,882	162,424	216,140	381,446	163,103	2.0	4,994
1991	3,079	263,430	2,690	161,470	207,288	371,448	162,780	1.9	5,604
1992	3,057	282,025	2,690	170,513	209,152	382,355	162,769	1.9	6,725
1993	3,037	298,891	2,690	178,194	209,533	390,417	167,988	1.8	¶ 11,784
1994	3,142	326,837	2,710	192,014	219,890	414,614	172,976	1.8	12,505
1995	3,172	334,259	2,790	196,093	152,190	351,073	183,103	1.7	13,005
1996	3,738	350,397	3,247	204,635	§ 90,261	298,143	187,064	2.0	¶ 7,766
1997	3,508	347,881	3,079	205,595	97,315	305,989	194,665	1.8	7,662
1998	3,576	338,661	3,160	202,223	102,732	308,115	201,989	1.8	8,780
1999	3,519	339,448	3,106	203,220	105,375	311,701	213,847	1.6	8,729
2000	3,775	341,097	3,247	205,569	110,174	318,990	210,340	1.8	9,163
2001	3,739	340,554	3,319	207,043	113,596	323,958	216,276	1.73	9,348
2002	3,826	315,061	3,544	196,211	113,089	** 324,651	215,873	1.77	¶ 21,100
2003	3,823	308,543	3,372	190,926	§ 245,607	†† 460,025	218,209	1.75	20,700
2004	3,725	288,715	3,286	180,556	245,000	447,691	229,345	1.62	19,400
2005	3,559	293,583	3,157	184,093	257,532	464,541	234,232	1.52	19,200
2006	3,523	272,779	3,120	173,861	243,970	439,027	236,852	1.49	20,400
2007	3,463	267,305	3,098	173,052	264,098	459,689	241,746	1.43	20,600
2008	3,477	243,547	3,116	159,760	257,154	438,996	234,593	1.48	22,900
2009	3,108	234,704	2,807	154,685	251,850	428,273	232,055	1.34	20,300
2010	3,050	‡‡ 217,381	2,772	141,554	233,573	391,101	234,261	1.30	22,200
2011	3,015	211,006	2,751	138,624	226,949	381,463	235,602	1.28	21,900
2012	3,417	230,957	3,037	152,301	247,679	417,707	237,831	1.44	26,000
2013	3,407	232,599	3,065	154,458	272,601	445,829	244,536	1.39	27,800
2014	3,538	237,941	3,189	158,833	297,934	476,875	242,989	1.46	38,000
2015	3,582	247,652	3,186	165,199	332,891	521,389	258,122	1.39	36,600
2016	3,794	265,077	3,404	176,381	351,153	551,971	271,263	1.40	38,800
2017	3,721	253,852	3,432	160,926	343,680	537,970	274,580	1.36	38,401

(Note: The highest death rate was in 1966 at 6.2.)

*Method of calculating vehicle miles traveled revised. Last changed in 1982 by TxDOT.

†In August 1967, amended estimating formula received from National Safety Council (NCS). Starting 1972, actual reported injuries are listed rather than estimates.

‡Change in counting fatalities. In 1978, counted when injury results in death within 90 days of accident. In 1983, counted when injury results in death within 30 days.

§Change in counting Non-injury acci-dents. For 1996–2002, only crashes having at least **one vehicle towed** were tabulated.

¶Economic loss formula changed. Last changed in 2002, when figures are calculated using NCS Average Calculable Cost on a per death basis figure for the year identified. Figures are rounded to the nearest hundred million. For 1996–2001, only prop-erty damage in crashes having at least one vehicle towed was tabulated.

**Beginning with 2002 data, the "Total" crash figure includes "Unknown Severity Crashes" which are not included on this chart. Prior to 2002 these crashes were counted in the Non-injury or Injury category.

††Beginning with 2003 crashes, only those resulting in injury or death or damage to property to the apparent extent of $1,000 are tabulated.

‡‡Beginning in 2010, number injured includes incapacitating, non-incapac-itating, and possible injuries.

Source: Texas Department of Transportation (TxDOT) since 2001. Earlier statistics are from the Texas Department of Public Safety (DPS).

Foreign Consulates in Texas

In the list below, these abbreviations appear after the name of the city: (CG) Consulate General; (C) Consulate; (VC) Vice Consulate. The letter "H" before the designation indicates honorary status. Compiled from "Foreign Consular Offices in the United States," U.S. Dept. of State, April 2016; also Texas Secretary of State.

Angola: Houston (CG); 3040 Post Oak Blvd., Ste. 780, 77056. (713) 212-3840. en.angolaconsulate-tx.org.

Argentina: Houston (CG); 2200 West Loop S, 77027. (713) 871-8935. www.chous.mrecic.gov.ar.

Australia: Houston (CG); 3009 Post Oak Blvd., Ste. 1310, 77056. usa.embassy.gov.au/houston.

Austria: Houston (HC); 11000 Brittmoore Park Dr., 77041. (713) 723-9979. austrianconsulatehouston.org

Barbados: Houston (HC); 3027 Sleepy Hollow Dr., Sugar Land 77479. (832) 725-5566.

Belarus: Houston (HC); 25227 Grogans Mill, Ste. 201, The Woodlands, 77380. (832) 868-6392.

Belgium: Houston (HC); 12222 Ashford Way, Kingwood 77339. (281) 650-9621.
Dallas (HC): 1308 Danbury Dr., Mansfield, 76063. (817) 229-4259
San Antonio (HC); 106 S. St. Mary's, Ste. 200, 78205. (210) 271-0630.

Belize: Houston (CG); 7101 Breen Dr., 77086. (281) 999-4484.
Dallas (HC); 8035 East R.L. Thorton Fwy., Ste. 221, 75228.
San Antonio (HC); 3510 Pinto Pony La., 78247. (210) 859-8234.

Bolivia: Houston (HC); 2401 Fountain View Dr., Ste. 110, 77057. (832) 916-4200. www.boliviatx.org.

Botswana: Houston (HC); 3330 Chevy Chase Dr., 77019. (713) 256-1717.

Brazil: Houston (CG); 1233 West Loop South, Ste. 1150, 77027. houston.itamaraty.ogv.br.

Cameroon: Houston (HC); 1319 Gamma, Crosby 77532. (713) 499-3502.

Canada: Dallas (CG); 500 N. Akard St., Ste. 2900, 75201. (214) 922-9806.
Houston (C); 5847 San Felipe St., Ste. 1700, 77057. (713) 821-1440.

Chile: Houston (CG):1300 Post Oak Blvd., Ste. 1130, 77056; (832) 668-5853. chile.og.cl/houston/en/
Dallas (HC); 5200 Keller Springs Rd., Ste. 633, 75248.

China: Houston (CG); 3417 Montrose, Ste. 700, 77006. (713) 520-1462. houston.china-consulate.org.

Colombia: Houston (CG); 2400 Augusta Dr., Ste. 400, 77057; (713) 979-0844. houston.consulado.gov.co.

Costa Rica: Houston (CG); 3100 Wilcrest, Ste. 260, 77042. (713) 266-0484.

Cote d'Ivoire: Houston (HC); 1302 Waugh Dr., Ste. 482, 77019. (713) 410-0472.

Croatia: Houston (HC); 1415 Congress St., Ste. 300. 77002. (713) 444-1442.

Czech Republic: Houston (HC); Czech Center Museum, 4920 San Jacinto, 77004.

Denmark: Dallas (HC); 3819 Maple Ave., 75219. (214) 661-7036.
Houston (HC); 320 Westcott St., Ste. 106, 77007. (713) 622-9018.

Ecuador: Houston (CG); 2603 Augusta Dr., No. 810, 77057. (713) 572-8731. houston.consulado.gob.ec.
Dallas (HC); 6574 Gerrard St., Frisco, 75034. (972) 712-9107.

Egypt: Houston (CG); 5718 Westheimer, Ste. 1350, 77057. (713) 961-4915.
consulateofegypthouston.com.

El Salvador: Dallas (CG); 1250 W. Mockingbird Lane, Ste. 240, 75247. (214) 637-1500.
consuladodallas.rree.gob.sv.
Houston (CG); 8300 Bissonet, Ste. 400, 77074.

(346) 571-5198.,consuladohouston.rree.gob.sv.

Equatorial Guinea: Houston (CG); 6401 Southwest Fwy., 77074. (713) 776-9900.

Estonia: Houston (HC); 23010 Holly Creek Tr., Tomball 77377. (713) 351-7610.

Ethiopia: Houston (HC); 9301 Southwest Freeway, Ste. 250, 77074. (713) 271-7567.

Finland: Dallas (HC); 1601 Elm, Ste. 3000, 75201. (214) 999-4472.

France: Houston (CG); 777 Post Oak Blvd., Ste. 600, 77056. (713) 572-2799. houston.consulfrance.org.
Austin (HC); 3900 Petes Path, 78731.
Dallas (HC); 12720 Hillcrest, Ste. 730, 75230. (972) 789-9305.
El Paso (HC); 1357 Rancho Grande, 79936.
San Antonio (HC); 311 Basin Dr., 78216.

Germany: Houston (CG); 1330 Post Oak Blvd., Ste. 1850, 77056. (713) 627-7770.
Dallas (HC); 17130 Dallas Pkwy., Ste 240, 75248. (469) 687-2502.

Ghana: Houston (HC); 3535 Westheimer Rd., Ste. 235, 77027. (713) 960-1950. ghanaconsulatehouston.com.

Greece: Houston (CG); 2401 Fountain View Dr., Ste. 850, 77057. (713) 840-7522.
www.mfa.gr/usa/en/consulate-in-houston/

Guatemala: Houston (CG); 3013 Fountain View Dr., Ste. 210, 77057. (713) 953-9531.
conshouston.minex.gob.gt
Del Rio (CG); 106 Foster Dr., 78840. (830) 422-2230.
McAllen (CG); 709 Broadway St., 78501. (956) 429-3413.

Haiti: Houston (HC); 6310 Auden St., 77005.

Honduras: Houston (CG); 3731 Briarpark Dr., Ste. 155, 77042. (346) 201-6711.
Irving (C); 2520 W. Irving Blvd., Ste. 400, 75061. (214) 347-4441.

Hungary: Houston (HCG); 11850 Hempstead, Ste. 230, 77092. (713) 476-0497.
hungary.honoraryconsulate.network

Iceland: Dallas (HC); 6827 Northwood Rd., 75225, (214) 415-2311.

India: Houston (CG); 4300 Scotland St., 77007. (713) 626-2148. cgihouston.gov.in

Indonesia: Houston (CG); 10900 Richmond Ave., 77042. (713) 785-1691. kemlu.go.id

Ireland: Austin (CG); 515 Congress Ave., Ste. 1720, 78701. (512) 792-5500.
www.dfa.ie/irish-consulate/austin

Israel: Houston (CG); 24 Greenway Plz., Ste. 1500, 77046. (832) 301-3500.
embassies.gov.il/houston/Pages/Home.aspx

Italy: Houston (CG); 1300 Post Oak Blvd., Ste. 660, 77056. (713) 850-7520. conshouston.esteri.it

Jamaica: Houston (HC); 6001 Savoy Dr., Ste 509, 77036. (713) 782-8494.

Japan: Houston (CG); 909 Fannin, Ste. 3000, 77010. (713) 652-2977. houston.us.emb-japan.go.jp
Dallas (HC); 5819 Edinburgh St., 75252. (972) 713-8683.

Korea: Houston (CG); 1990 Post Oak Blvd., Ste. 1250, 77056. (713) 961-0186.
overseas.mofa.go.kr/us-houston-en/index.do
Dallas (C); 14001 N. Dallas Parkway, Ste. 450, 75240. (972) 701-0180.
overseas.mofa.go.kr/us-dallas-en/index.do

Latvia: Houston (HC); 2120 Troon Rd., 77019. (832) 263-1635.

Lebanon: Houston (HC); 2400 Augusta Dr., Ste. 308, 77057. (713) 268-1640.

Lesotho: Austin (HC); 7400 Valburn Dr., 78731.

Lithuania: Houston (HC); 4030 Case, 77005. (713) 665-4218.

Luxembourg: Austin (HC); 2700 Via Fortuna Dr., Ste. 500. (512) 634-3782.

Mali: Austin (HC); 2000 Lipanese Trail, 78733.

Malta: Dallas (CG); 500 N. Akard, Ste. 4170. (214) 855-9897.
Houston (HC); 2602 Commonwealth St., 77006. (713) 654-7900.

Mexico: Austin (CG); 5202 E. Ben White, Ste. 150, 78741. (512) 478-2866. consulmex.sre.gob.mx/austin/
Brownsville (C); 301 Mexico Blvd., Ste. F2, 78520. (956) 542-4431.
Dallas (CG); 1210 River Bend Dr., 75247. (214) 932-8670. consulmex.sre.gob.mx/dallas/
Del Rio (C); 2207 N. Bedell Ave., 78840. (830) 775-2352.
Eagle Pass (C); 2252 E. Garrison, 78852. (830) 773-9255.
El Paso (CG); 910 E. San Antonio Ave., 79901. (915) 533-3644.
Houston (CG); 4506 Caroline St., 77004. (713) 271-6800. consulmex.sre.gob.mx/houston/
Laredo (CG); 1612 Farragut St., 78040. (956) 723-6369. consulmex.sre.gob.mx/laredo/
McAllen (C); 600 S. Broadway, 78501. (956) 686-0243.
Presidio (C); 319 W. De Marzo St., 79845. (915) 229-2788.
San Antonio (CG); 127 Navarro St., 78205. (210) 227-9145.
San Antonio (Office of Mexican Attorney General); 613 NW Loop 410, Ste. 610, 78216. (210) 344-1131.

Monaco: Dallas (HC); 11020 Tibbs St., 75230. (214) 991-2916.

Mongolia: San Antonio (HC); P.O. Box 399, Comfort, 78013. (830) 995-5014.

Morocco: Dallas (HC); 325 N. St. Paul St., Ste. 4200, 75201. (214) 965-8402.

Namibia: San Antonio (HC); 106 S. St. Mary's St., Ste. 200, 78205. (210) 271-0630.

Netherlands: Houston (HC); 10777 Westheimer Rd., Ste. 1055, 77042. (713) 785-2200.

Nicaragua: Houston (CG); 8989 Westheimer, Ste. 103, 77063. (713) 789-2762.

Norway: Houston (CG); 3410 W. Dallas St., Ste. 100, 77019. (713) 620-4200.
Dallas (HC); 8623 Royalbrook Ct. 75243. (214) 707-2213.

Pakistan: Houston (CG); 11850 Jones Rd. 77070. (281) 890-2223. www.pakistanconsulatehouston.org

Panama: Houston (CG); 24 Greenway Plaza, Ste. 1307, 77046. (713) 622-4451. conpahouston.com
Austin (HC) 101 Knarr St., 78734. (512) 386-1461.

Papua New Guinea: Houston (HCG); 4900 Woodway Dr., Ste. 1200, 77056. (713) 966-2500.

Paraguay: Houston (HC); 4707 Welford Dr., Bellaire, 77401. (713) 444-9887.

Peru: Houston (C); 5177 Richmond Ave., Ste. 695, 77056. (713) 355-9438.
www.consulado.pe.en/Houston/
Dallas (CG); 13601 Preston Rd., Ste. E650, 75240. www.consulado.pe/es/Dallas/

Philippines: Houston (CG) 9990 Richmond Ave., Ste. 100N, 77042. (832) 668 -5139.
Dallas (HC); 8315 Navisota Dr., Lantana, 76226. (940) 728-2222.

Poland: Houston (HC); 3040 Post Oak Blvd., Ste. 825, 77056. (713) 993-9685. houston.msz.gov.pl/pl/

Portugal: Houston (HC); 721 Buckingham Dr., 77024. (713) 515-5272.

Qatar: Houston (CG); 1990 Post Oak Blvd, Ste. 900, 77056. (713) 355-8221.

Romania: Dallas (HC); 1412 Main St., Ste. 1800, 75202. (214) 522-3799.
Houston (HC); 4265 San Felipe, Ste. 220, 77027. (713) 629-1551.

Russia: Houston (CG); 1333 West Loop South, Ste. 1300, 77027. (713) 337-3300. rusconhouston.mid.ru/

Rwanda: Houston (HCG); 70 Terra Bella Dr., Manvel, 77578.

Saudi Arabia: Houston (CG); 5718 Westheimer, Ste. 1500, 77057. (713) 785-5577.

Sierra Leone: Dallas (HC); 2301 Forest Lane., Ste. 400, Garland, 75042. (214) 552-5613.

Slovakia: Dallas (HC); 10830 N. Central Expwy., Ste. 400, 75231. (214) 251-8020.

Slovenia: Houston (HC); 11300 Kingsworthy Lane, 77024. (713) 278-1366.

South Africa: Dallas (HC); 1510 N. Hampton St., Ste. 340, DeSoto 75115. (512) 463-5887.

Spain: Houston (CG); 1800 Bering Dr., Ste. 660, 77057. (713) 783-6200.
www.exteriores.gob.es/Consulados/HOUSTON/
Austin (HC); 2201 Woodmont Ave., 78703.
Corpus Christi (HC); 7314 Kolda Dr., 78414. (361) 994-7517.
Dallas (HC); 5454 La Sierra Dr., Ste. 200, 75231.
El Paso (HC); 14 Cumberland Ci. 79903. (915) 307-7689.
San Antonio (HC); 200 E. Grayson, Ste. 203, 78215.

Sweden: Houston (HC); 3730 Kirby Dr., 77098. (713) 953-1417.
Dallas: (HC); 3808 Miramar Ave., 75205. (214) 521-2312.

Switzerland: Houston (HC); 2000 Edwards St., 77007. (713) 467-9887.
Dallas (HC); 2651 N. Harwood, Floor 14, 75201. (214) 965-1025.

Thailand: Houston (HC); 3 Greenway Plaza, Ste. 800, 77046. (713) 335-3995.
www.thaiconsulatehouston.com
Dallas (HC); 5301 Spring Valley Rd., Ste. 200, 75254. (972) 450-7342.

Trinidad/Tobago: Houston (HC); 9 Parkside Rd, 77063. (713) 816-6477.

Tunisia: Dallas (HC); 4227 N. Capistrano Dr., 75287. (972) 267-4191.

Turkey: Houston (CG); 1990 Post Oak Blvd., Ste.1300, 77056. (713) 622-5849. houston.cg.mfa.gov.tr/Mission

Ukraine: Houston (HC); 123 N. Post Oak, Ste 410. (281) 242-6654.

United Arab Emirates: Houston (CG); 7505 South Main St., Ste. 510, 77030. (832) 956-6666.

United Kingdom: Houston (CG); 1301 Fannin St., Floor 24, 77002. (713) 210-4000.
Dallas (HC); 1900 N. Akard St., 75201. (214) 978-8989.
San Antonio (HC); 254 Spencer Lane, 78201. (210) 735-9393.

Uruguay: Houston (HC); 1220 S. Ripple Creek Dr., 77057. (713) 781-3993.

Venezuela: Houston (CG); 2401 Fountain View Dr., Ste. 220, 77057. (7130 974-0028.
venezuela-us.org/houston/index.php/es/

Vietnam: Houston (CG); 5251 Westheimer Rd., Ste. 1100, 77056. (713) 850-1233. ☆

Foreign Trade Zones in Texas

Source: U.S. Department of Commerce.

Foreign-trade-zone status endows a domestic site with certain customs privileges, causing it to be considered outside customs territory and therefore available for activities that might otherwise be carried on overseas.

Operated as public utilities for qualified corporations, the zones are established under grants of authority from the Foreign-Trade Zones board, which is chaired by the U.S. Secretary of Commerce. Zone facilities are available for operations involving storage, repacking, inspection, exhibition, assembly, manufacturing, and other processing.

A foreign-trade zone is especially suitable for export processing or manufacturing operations when foreign components or materials with a high U.S. duty are needed to make the end product competitive in markets abroad.

Source: U.S. Department of Commerce.

In 2018 there were 32 Foreign-Trade Zones in Texas.

Amarillo, FTZ 252
City of Amarillo
801 S. Fillmore, Ste. 205, Amarillo 79101

Athens, FTZ 269
Athens Economic Development Corp.
201 W. Corsicana, Ste. 3, Athens 75751

Austin, FTZ 183
FTZ of Central Texas Inc.
535 E. 5th St., Austin 78701

Beaumont, FTZ 115
Port Arthur, FTZ 116
Orange, FTZ 117
FTZ of Southeast Texas Inc.
P.O. Drawer 2297, Beaumont 77704

Bowie County, FTZ 258
TexAmericas Center
107 Chapel Lane, New Boston 75570

Brownsville, FTZ 62
Brownsville Navigation District
1000 Foust Road, Brownsville 78521

Calhoun/Victoria Counties FTZ 155
Calhoun-Victoria FTZ Inc.
P.O. Drawer 397, Point Comfort 77978

Conroe, FTZ 265
City of Conroe
PO Box 3066, Conroe 77305

Corpus Christi, FTZ 122
Port of Corpus Christi Authority
222 Power St.
Corpus Christi 78401

Dallas/Ft.Worth, FTZ 39
D/FW International Airport Board
Drawer 619428,
D/FW Airport 75261

Dallas/Fort Worth, FTZ 168
Metroplex International Trade Development Corp.
P.O. Box 613307, Dallas 75361

Eagle Pass, FTZ 96
City of Eagle Pass
P.O. Box 3693, Eagle Pass 78853

Ellis County, FTZ 113
Ellis County Trade Zone Corp.
P.O. Box 788
Midlothian 76065

El Paso, FTZ 68
City of El Paso
501 George Perry, Ste. I,
El Paso 79925

El Paso, FTZ 150
Westport Economic Dev. Corp.
1865 Northwestern Dr., El Paso 79912

Fort Worth, FTZ 196
Alliance Corridor Inc.
13600 Heritage Pkwy., Ste. 200
Fort Worth 76177

Freeport, FTZ 149
Port Freeport
1100 Cherry St., Freeport 77541

Galveston, FTZ 36
Board of Trustees of the Galveston Wharves
P.O. Box 328, Galveston 77553

Gregg County, FTZ 234
Gregg County
269 Terminal Circle, Longview 75603

Harris County, FTZ 84
Port of Houston Authority
111 East Loop North, Houston 77029

Laredo, FTZ 94
City of Laredo
5210 Bob Bullock Loop, Laredo 78041

Liberty County, FTZ 171
Liberty Co. Economic Dev. Corp.
P.O. Box 857, Liberty 77575

Lubbock, FTZ 260
City of Lubbock
1500 Broadway, 6th Floor,
Lubbock 79401

McAllen, FTZ 12
McAllen Economic Dev. Corp.
6401 South 33rd St., McAllen 78503

Midland, FTZ 165
City of Midland
P.O. Box 60305, Midland 79711

San Antonio, FTZ 80
City of San Antonio Economic Development Department
100 W. Houston, Ste. 1900,
San Antonio 78205

Starr County, FTZ 95
Starr County Industrial Foundation
P.O. Box 502, Rio Grande City 78582

Texas City, FTZ 199
Texas City FTZ Corp.
P.O. Box 2608, Texas City 77592

Waco, FTZ 246
City of Waco
P.O. Box 1220, Waco 76703

Weslaco, FTZ 156
City of Weslaco
255 S. Kansas Ave., Weslaco 78596

A tanker being towed from Ingleside to the Gulf of Mexico. Photo by Rosie Hatch.

Annual Tonnage Handled by Major/Minor Texas Ports

Table below gives consolidated tonnage (x1,000) handled by Texas ports. All figures are in short tons (2,000 lbs.). Note that " - " indicates no commerce was reported, "0" means tonnage reported was less than 500 tons. *Source: U.S. Corps of Engineers.*

Port	2017	2010	2005	2000	1995	1990	1985
Beaumont	89,437	76,959	78,887	76,894	20,937	26,729	26,842
Brownsville	7,763	4,616	5,105	3,268	2,656	1,372	1,443
Corpus Christi	87,323	73,663	77,637	81,164	70,218	60,165	41,057
Freeport	24,484	26,676	33,602	28,966	19,662	14,526	12,918
Galveston	7,836	13,949	8,008	10,402	10,465	9,620	7,792
Houston	260,071	227,133	211,666	186,567	135,231	126,178	90,669
Matagorda Channel (Port Lavaca)	4,279	8,879	11,607	10,552	9,237	6,097	4,366
Port Arthur	39,203	30,232	26,385	20,524	49,800	30,681	15,755
Sabine Pass	13,885	2,494	641	910	231	631	547
Texas City	37,751	56,591	57,839	58,109	50,403	48,052	33,441
Victoria Channel	4,337	2,792	3,224	5,104	4,624	3,740	3,414
Anahuac	-	-	-	-	-	0	53
Aransas Pass	280	173	128	6	181	169	10
Arroyo Colorado	-	411	791	837	994	765	692
Cedar Bayou	1,785	931	1,172	1,002	473	219	219
Chocolate Bayou	1,108	1,005	3,537	3,488	3,480	3,463	4,077
Clear Creek	-	-	-	-	-	0	0
Colorado River	541	671	501	445	576	476	480
Dickinson	545	93	688	904	657	556	195
Double Bayou	-	-	257	0	-	0	21
Greens Bayou	6,416	5,523	3,768	0	0	0	0
Harbor Island (Port Aransas)	27	1	10	151	209	na	na
Liberty Channel	-	5	-	-	-	0	0
Orange	659	684	627	681	693	710	648
Palacios	-	-	-	-	-	0	10
Port Isabel	8	0	-	5	130	269	280
Port Mansfield	-	-	-	-	20	102	204
Rockport	-	-	-	-	-	644	0
San Bernard River	117	371	773	633	653	534	519
Other Ports	0	0	0	0	0	0	307
TOTAL*	524,583	486,658	487,100	452,991	371,021	335,312	245,959

Excludes duplication.

Foreign/Domestic Commerce: Breakdown for 2017

Data below represent inbound and outbound tonnage for major ports. Note that "-" means no tonnage was reported. *Does not include Canadian. Source: U.S. Corps of Engineers* (All figures in short tons x1000)

Port	Foreign*		Domestic		
	Imports	Exports	Receipts	Shipments	Local
Beaumont	27,534	26,159	8,720	25,070	1,954
Brownsville	3,425	894	3,205	238	1
Corpus Christi	22,225	38,023	5,338	17,752	3,984
Freeport	9,171	10,184	2,460	2,669	0
Galveston	1,551	2,257	2,353	1,657	18
Houston	72,386	100,825	35,745	30,068	21,057
Matagorda Chl. (Port Lavaca)	506	1,220	536	2,017	0
Port Arthur	10,084	19,265	4,703	5,001	152
Sabine Pass	1	13,751	0	134	-
Texas City	10,301	11,190	4,531	10,910	139
Victoria	-	-	1,167	3,170	-

Gulf Intracoastal Waterway by Commodity (Texas portion)

(All figures in short tons x1000) *Source: U.S. Army Corps of Engineers*

Commodity	2017	2010	2005	2000	1995
Coal	342	93	335	121	162
Petroleum products	55,711	49,219	39,538	34,816	40,496
Chemicals	16,891	17,553	20,668	21,382	26,818
Raw materials	3,363	3,123	4,898	5,822	6,544
Manufactured goods	2,331	1,646	2,449	2,301	2,056
Food, farm products	455	574	473	960	1,216
Total	79,444	72,917	69,549	66,440	78,386

U.S. ports ranked by tonnage, 2017
(millions)

1. S. Louisiana............ 275.1
2. Houston................. 260.1
3. New York 135.9
4. New Orleans.............. 96.3
5. Beaumont................. 89.4
6. Corpus Christi.......... 87.3
7. Long Beach 86.0
8. Baton Rouge.............. 77.0
9. Virginia...................... 67.3
10. Los Angeles............. 65.9

States ranked by tonnage, 2017
(x1,000)

1. Louisiana............. 572,065
2. Texas.................. 524,583
3. California 244,063
4. New Jersey.......... 144,184
5. Washington...........119,422
6. Florida................. 103,590
7. Illinois.................... 90,563
8. Kentucky............... 89,944
9. Ohio 82.982
10. Pennsylvania 72,569

U.S. Freight Gateways, 2017

[**In billions of dollars** ($214.8 represents $214,800,000,000)]. Top gateways ranked by value of ship-ments, with Texas gateways highlighted. *Source: U.S. Bureau of Transportation Statistics, National Transportation Statistics, annual.*

Rank	Port	Mode	Exports	Imports	Total trade	Exports as a percent of total
1	Los Angeles, CA	Water	$ 36.0	$ 178.7	$ 214.8	16.8 %
2	Laredo, TX	Land	93.8	114.2	208.0	45.1 %
3	Port of New York/New Jersey, NY/NJ	Water	43.0	150.0	193.0	22.3 %
4	John F. Kennedy, NY	Air	86.3	96.5	182.8	47.2 %
5	Long Beach, CA	Water	33.3	136.0	169.3	19.6 %
6	Chicago, IL	Air	47.0	112.9	159.9	29.4 %
7	Detroit, MI	Land	73.9	59.6	133.5	55.3 %
8	Houston, TX	Water	71.3	59.3	130.7	54.6 %
9	Los Angeles International Airport, CA	Air	55,7	55,2	113.0	50.3 %
10	Savannah, GA	Water	25.6	64.3	89.9	28.5 %
11	Port Huron, MI	Land	40.2	44.8	85.0	47.3 %
12	Norfolk, VA	Water	31.5	46.2	77.7	40.5 %
13	New Orleans, LA	Air	31.6	43.4	75.0	42.1 %
14	Buffalo-Niagara Falls, NY	Land	38.8	34.7	73.6	52.8 %
15	Charleston, SC	Water	24.9	45.1	70.0	35.6 %
16	El Paso, TX	Land	28.8	36.5	65.3	44.1 %
17	San Francisco International Airport, CA	Air	29.1	34.5	63.6	45.8 %
18	Miami International Airport, FL	Air	34.1	24.9	59.0	57.8 %
19	Cleveland, OH	Air	32.1	23.9	56.1	57.3 %
20	Anchorage, AK	Air	13.9	40.9	54.8	25.4 %
21	Dallas-Fort Worth Airport, TX	Air	22.9	31.3	54.2	42.2 %
22	Baltimore, MD	Water	15.8	38.1	53.8	29.3 %
23	Tacoma, WA	Water	9.2	41.4	50.5	18.2 %
24	Oakland, CA	Water	19.3	28.2	47.4	40.6 %
25	Atlanta, GA	Air	15.8	29.7	45.4	34.7 %
28	Hidalgo, TX	Land	11.6	20.8	32.3	36.8 %
29	Eagle Pass, TX	Land	8.1	22.5	30.7	26.6 %
35	Corpus Christi, TX	Water	15.9	6.8	22.7	70.1 %
45	Beaumont, TX	Water	10.7	8.0	18.7	57.4 %

Border Crossings at U.S. Ports of Entry, 2010 and 2018

Below are statistics for selected states as to incoming border traffic at ports of entry into the United States. *Data are from the U.S. Bureau of Transportation Statistics.* (**Total in thousands**. Percent of U.S. total.)

Entering at border (thousands 000)	U.S. total	%	Texas	California	New York	Arizona	Michigan
2010							
Vehicle passengers	182,538	53 %	53,356	45,611	18,189	14,726	12,251
Personal vehicles	92,929	27 %	31,349	25,260	8,573	6,651	6,566
Pedestrians	40,306	12 %	17,156	14,740	262	7,648	17
Trucks	10,187	3 %	3,194	1,089	1,452	373	2,165
Containers (truck)	7,346	2 %	2,149	678	1,145	291	1,805
2018							
Vehicle passengers	196,421	52 %	68,523	56,654	16,558	17,781	11,066
Personal vehicles	103,821	27 %	34,702	31,999	7,905	9,335	6,288
Pedestrians	46,660	12 %	18,479	20,160	363	7,110	14
Trucks	12,142	3 %	4,384	1,400	1,533	396	2,454
Containers (truck)	8,864	2 %	3,144	981	1,254	328	1,732

Aviation: Passenger Traffic Continues Upward Trend

Air transportation is a vital and vigorous part of the Texas economy, and Texans are major users of air transportation. The airport system ranks as one of the busiest and largest in the nation.

The state's 54,446 active pilots represent 8.6 percent of the nation's pilots. The number of active general aviation aircraft in the state totals 20,143, almost 10 percent of the nation's total.

Twenty-six airports continue to provide commercial service to Texas communities, including the Texarkana Regional Airport, which is physically located in Arkansas.

Scheduled passenger traffic (air carrier and commuters) increased from 2015 to 2017, continuing an upward trend that began in 2010. Enplanements increased by approximately 2 million, or 2.5 percent, over the two-year period.

Ten airports saw their enplanements increase, while sixteen airports experienced a decrease. Of the seven largest airports in the state, all but George Bush Houston Intercontinental experienced increases in passenger enplanements. Austin-Bergstrom International and Dallas Love Field led with increases of 16.6 percent and 16.0 percent respectively.

The two large hub airports, Dallas-Fort Worth International and Houston Bush, saw their enplanements increase slightly 0.3% and decrease 3.9%, respectively. The four medium hub airports, Austin (16.6%),

Dallas Love (16.0%), Houston Hobby (10.9%), and San Antonio (6.0%) led the state in passenger growth.

In 2017, Texas airports enplaned 80,258,207 passengers. D/FW, Dallas Love, Houston Bush, and Houston Hobby together accounted for 81 percent of the passengers, or 64,919,423 enplanements.

More than 90 percent of the state's population lived within 50 miles of an airport with scheduled passenger service.

Smaller airports

Among the smaller airports, only two saw their enplanements increase, Longview and Harlingen. Fourteen of the 16 saw their enplanements decrease over the two-year period.

Of those airports losing enplanements, eight airports experienced double-digit losses, including College Station (-18.3%), Brownsville (-18.9%), Beaumont (-30.0%), and Tyler (-36.7%). United Airlines discontinued service to and from Tyler in early 2016.

Texas has also seen increases in service provided by the ultra-low-cost carriers that now provide service to several Texas airports both year-round and seasonally. Air service continues to be an area of concern for some communities as the airlines removed excess capacity from the system in an effort to return to, and maintain, profitability.

While the economy has continued to improve, some

Public Administration

Source: Texas Transportation Institute

In 1945, the Texas Aeronautics Commission (TAC) was created and directed by the legislature to encourage, foster, and assist in the development of aeronautics within the state, and to encourage the establishment of airports and air navigational facilities.

The Commission's first annual report of Dec. 31, 1946, stated that Texas had 592 designated airports and 7,756 civilian aircraft.

The TAC's to providing air transportation was strengthened in 1989 when the TAC became the Texas Department of Aviation (TDA). And on Sept. 1, 1991, when the Texas Department of Transportation (TxDOT) was created, the TDA became the Aviation Division within the department.

The primary responsibilities of the Aviation Division include providing engineering and technical services for planning, constructing, and maintaining aeronautical facilities in the state. It is also responsible for long-range aviation facility development planning (statewide system of airports) and applying for, receiving, and disbursing federal funds.

In the Texas Airport System Plan, TxDOT has identified 289 airports and three heliports. Of the airports, **26 are commercial airports, 24 are reliever airports, and 239 are general aviation airports.**

Additionally, TxDOT's Aviation Division has requested Federal Aviation Administration Reliever status for five airports. These include the privately owned Austin Executive and Houston Executive airports, as well as the publicly owned New Braunfels Municipal, Mid-Way Regional, and Cleburne municipal airports.

Commercial-service airports provide scheduled passenger service. Reliever airports are a special class of general aviation airports designated by the Federal Aviation Administration (FAA). They provide alternative landing facilities in the metropolitan areas separate from the commercial service airports and, together with the business/corporate airports, provide access for business and executive turbine-powered aircraft.

The community-service and basic-service airports provide access for single- and multi-engine, piston-powered aircraft to smaller communities throughout the state. Some community-service airports are also capable of accommodating light jets.

TxDOT is charged by the legislature with planning, programming, and implementing improvement projects at the general aviation airports. In carrying out these responsibilities, TxDOT channels the Airport Improvement Program (AIP) funds provided by the FAA for all general aviation airports in Texas.

Since 1993, TxDOT has participated in the FAA's state block grant demonstration program. Under this program, TxDOT assumes most of the FAA's responsibility for the administration of the AIP funds for airports.

The Aviation Facilities Development Program (AFDP) oversees planning and research, assists with engineering and technical services, and provides financial assistance through state grants to public bodies operating airports for the purpose of establishing, constructing, reconstructing, enlarging, or repairing airports, airstrips, or navigational facilities.

The 85th Legislature appropriated funds to TxDOT, which subsequently allocated a portion of those funds to the Aviation Division. TxDOT allocated approximately $15 million annually for the 2018-2019 biennium to the Aviation Division to help implement and administer the AFDP. These funds are in addition to the block grant funds received through the FAA's AIP.

Drones

The past few years have seen the advent and proliferation of unmanned aircraft systems (UASs), commonly called drones.

They have woven their way into our everyday lives as hobbyists and various professionals use them for a variety of functions that include aerial photography, real estate, construction/industrial, agriculture, emergency management/law enforcement, and insurance.

Nationwide, more than 900,000 hobbyists registered UASs as of Dec. 31, 2018, and the FAA estimates there are some 1.25 million units that can be identified as distinctly hobbyist.

Commercial UAS operator registrations number more than 277,000 since online registration began in April 2016. The commercial UAS industry is still at a very early stage and growth is expected to accelerate in the years to come. The FAA says the fleet today exceeds 835,000.

Related to UASs are the remote pilots that fly

A military drone being prepared for flight at Corpus Christi Naval Air Station. U.S. Navy photo (CC).

them. The FAA issues Remote Pilot Certificates under the Small UAS Rule (14 CFR Part 107), which took effect on Aug. 29, 2016. This rule also provided the regulatory structure for the operation of small UASs for commercial purposes.

As of December 2018, the FAA had issued more than 116,000 Remote Pilot Certificates.

---

small communities remain vulnerable to decreases in air service. In 2013, Del Rio lost its commercial service. Victoria has also seen its service cut. Many of the smaller airports in the state have struggled to maintain their enplanements.

Aviation Trends

Despite solid economic growth in 2018, the U.S. airline industry saw profits fall because of increased energy and labor costs. No major consolidation or restructuring in the airline industry has taken place since 2015, when American and US Airways combined their networks and reservation systems.

Nationwide, enplanements increased 4.7 percent in 2018. Load factors in 2018 also continued to increase, matching the record high of 84.7 percent first hit in 2016. Airlines continued their efforts to generate additional revenue through fees that typically have been included in the airfare, such as meals and baggage, as well as those services that have not typically been provided, such as premium boarding.

The airlines posted profits in 2018, the tenth year in a row, as they continued their shift towards returns on invested capital and away from gaining market share. Expansion in activity by the ultra-low-cost carriers (i.e., Spirit and Allegiant) contributed to keeping prices down. General aviation continues to be an important part of both the aviation industry and the national economy as the demand for general aviation aircraft is closely related to economic growth.

Moderate fuel prices has led to two consecutive years of increasing aircraft shipments and a turnaround in aircraft billings, which increased in 2018 for the first time since they began to slide in 2015.

Total aircraft shipments, which peaked in 2007, and billings, which peaked in 2008, both increased in 2018.

Worldwide Trends

Billings for general aviation aircraft worldwide increased in 2018 but at a slower pace than shipments.

Total billings increased from $20.2 billion in 2017 to $20.6 billion in 2018 after dropping from an all-time high of $24.8 billion in 2008.

In both worldwide and U.S. manufacturing, piston aircraft showed an increase in shipments in 2018 from 2016.

Turbine shipments also increased for both worldwide manufactured aircraft and U.S. manufactured aircraft over the same period.

Business Aviation

Business aviation has long been a leader in the industry, and that is not expected to change. While light jets and air taxi companies once dominated the talk of the industry, this is no longer the case. These have given way to improving the operating efficiencies of a range of business jets.

Some new concepts have dominated the aviation conversation in the last year. Chief among them is that of Urban Air Mobility popularized by Uber Elevate.

This concept involves utilizing electric vertical takeoff and landing aircraft to move people and goods across large urban areas using both existing facilities and newly developed vertiports.

Finally, the economic impact of civil aviation in Texas includes total employment of 643,800 workers, a total payroll of $29.5 billion, and total economic output of $110 billion.

Sources: Federal Aviation Administration, General Aviation and Part 135 Activity Survey - CY2017; U.S. Civil Airmen Statistics 2018; General Aviation Manufacturer's Association General Aviation Statistical Databook and Industry Outlook: 2018 Annual Report; FAA Terminal Area Forecasts 2018; Texas Department of Transportation, Aviation Division; FAA Aerospace Forecasts 2019-2039; The Economic Impact of Civil Aviation on the U.S. Economy, Federal Aviation Administration, September 2017.

Passenger Enplanement by Airport

Airport	2007	2009	2011	2013	2015	Percent change	2017
Abilene	90,507	81,451	80,030	78,847	88,959	−2.89%	86,386
Amarillo	455,539	404,903	399,997	373,946	347,304	−3.80%	334,102
Austin	4,112,023	4,019,088	4,409,094	4,809,854	5,643,251	16.60%	6,580,031
Beaumont	35,352	22,310	14,323	26,070	35,557	−30.03%	24,880
Brownsville	91,262	77,438	84,465	88,292	147,831	−18.89%	119,912
Brownwood*	-	-	-	-	-	-	-
College Station	89,830	73,462	70,869	84,379	91,243	−18.29%	74,552
Corpus Christi	418,674	353,868	327,534	309,480	339,105	−5.98%	318,810
D/FW	28,395,711	26,548,401	27,464,158	28,946,438	31,356,173	0.25%	31,433,095
Dallas/Love	3,912,856	3,704,594	3,841,785	3,971,077	6,495,869	16.03%	7,537,325
Del Rio**	17,386	13,851	9,331	6,846	-	-	-
El Paso	1,676,738	1,489,619	1,469,168	1,377,876	1,370,243	5.28%	1,442,605
Harlingen	442,117	374,232	361,494	354,717	263,423	2.91%	271,086
Houston/Bush	20,717,170	19,168,962	19,491,854	18,821,429	20,346,164	−3.88%	19,556,778
Houston/Hobby	4,219,867	4,032,037	4,646,710	5,213,512	5,765,544	10.89%	6,392,225
Houston/Ellington*	-	-	-	-	-	-	-
Killeen-Ft. Hood	193,722	202,226	189,330	175,992	153,698	−14.22%	131,836
Laredo	110,971	100,308	105,631	106,524	113,176	−16.09%	94,970
Longview	26,076	24,201	21,360	20,207	19,871	4.08%	20,682
Lubbock	575,774	533,635	505,381	454,661	446,081	1.70%	453,680
McAllen	411,431	360,608	335,008	332,769	390,358	−13.12%	339,132
Midland	489,845	435,979	472,177	502,303	533,049	−6.53%	498,248
San Angelo	69,738	60,315	55,304	60,127	64,901	−7.46%	60,061
San Antonio	3,907,118	3,809,114	3,967,764	3,998,343	4,057,345	5.99%	4,300,499
Texarkana	35,280	27,530	28,626	31,214	35,469	−2.52%	34,574
Tyler	77,117	73,177	73,334	81,277	77,543	−36.71%	49,075
Victoria	8,829	6,113	5,115	4,204	3,129	4.15%	3,259
Waco	75,496	66,116	60,479	59,809	63,256	−3.03%	61,340
Wichita Falls	46,297	43,376	38,941	43,994	45,426	−14.01%	39,064
Total	70,702,726	66,106,914	68,529,262	70,334,187	78,293,968	2.51%	80,258,207

Percent change 2015 to 2017. *Not currently a commercial airport. ** Del Rio lost commercial service in 2013. Calendar year data.
Source: FAA Terminal Area Forecast 2018.

Texas Air History

Passengers enplaned in Texas by scheduled carriers. (Texarkana not included.) Fiscal year data. *Source: Federal Aviation Administration.*

Year	Passengers
1950	1,169,051
1960	3,113,582
1965	5,757,689
1970	10,256,691
1975	13,182,957
1980	26,216,873
1985	40,659,223
1990	49,317,029
1995	57,166,515
2000	65,090,784
2005	65,718,669
2008	69,906,579
2009	66,155,323
2010	66,850,320
2011	68,505,347
2012	69,059,805
2013	70,305,633
2014	73,714,180
2015	78,261,315
2016	80,187,617
2017	80,223,633

Top U.S. Air Routes, City-to-City, 2018

Rank	Routes	Passengers
1.	Los Angeles – New York	6,495
2.	Chicago – New York	6,269
3.	New York – Orlando	5,651
4.	Fort Lauderdale – New York	5,182
5.	New York – San Francisco/Oakland	5,157
6.	Los Angeles – San Francisco/Oakland	4,987
7.	Atlanta – New York	4,304
8.	Miami – New York	3,631
9.	**Dallas/Fort Worth – New York**	**3,148**
10.	Chicago – Los Angeles	3,113

(Average daily passengers each way. Includes all airports in the city.)
Source: U.S. Department of Transportation.

Leading U.S. Airlines, 2018

Rank	Airline	Passengers
1.	**Southwest Airlines**	**163,605,692**
2.	Delta Air Lines	152,028,678
3.	**American Airlines**	**148,180,840**
4.	United Airlines	113,197,102
5.	JetBlue Airways	42,235,977
6	SkyWest Airlines	38,955,705
7.	Alaska Airlines	33,502,928
8.	Spirit Airlines	28,683,265

Texas-based airlines in bold. Source: U.S. Department of Transportation.

AGRICULTURE

Squash growing at Tree Grace Farms near Lubbock.
Photo by USDA NRCS Texas.

PRINCIPAL CROPS

VEGETABLE CROPS

FRUITS AND NUTS

LIVESTOCK AND THEIR PRODUCTS

Agriculture in Texas

Information was provided by Texas A&M AgriLife Extension specialists, Texas Agricultural Statistics Service, U.S. Department of Agriculture, and U.S. Department of Commerce. Caroline Gleaton, Administrative Associate V; John Robinson, Professor and Extension Specialist-Cotton Marketing; and Mark Welch, Extension Economist-Grain Marketing, Texas A&M AgriLife Extension Service coordinated the information. All references are to Texas unless otherwise specified. For information on the lumber industry, see page 75 in the Environment chapter.

Agribusiness, the combined phases of food and fiber production, processing, transporting, and marketing, is a leading Texas industry. Most of the following discussion is devoted to the initial phase of **production on farms and ranches**.

Texas agriculture is an important industry. Cash receipts from agricultural producers in 2017 were estimated at $22.8 billion, compared with $20.7 billion in 2016. Agricultural production is associated with considerable upstream and downstream economic activity. Many businesses, financial institutions, and individuals are involved in providing supplies, credit, and services to farmers and ranchers, and in processing and marketing agricultural commodities.

The potential for further growth is favorable. With the increasing demand for food and fiber throughout the world, and because of the importance of agricultural exports to the nation's trade balance, agriculture in Texas is destined to play an important role in the future.

Major efforts of research and educational programs by the Texas A&M University System are directed toward developing the state's agricultural industry to its fullest potential. The goal is to capitalize on natural advantages that agriculture has in Texas because of the relatively warm climate, productive soils, and availability of excellent export and transportation facilities.

Texas Farms

The number and nature of farms have changed over time. The number of farms in Texas has decreased from 420,000 in 1940 to 247,500 in 2018, with an average size of 514 acres. The number of small farms is increasing, but many are operated by part-time farmers and ranchers.

Mechanization of farming continues as new and larger machines replace manpower and smaller equipment. Even though machinery price tags are higher than in the past, machines are technologically advanced and efficient. Tractors, mechanical harvesters, and numerous cropping machines have virtually eliminated menial tasks that for many years were traditional to farming.

Revolutionary agricultural chemicals and genetically engineered traits have appeared along with improved plants and animals. Many of the natural hazards of farming and ranching have been reduced by better use of weather information, machinery, and other improvements, but rising costs, labor availability, and high-energy costs have added to concerns of farmers and ranchers.

Changes in Texas agriculture in the last 50 years include:

1. More detailed record keeping that assists in management and marketing decisions
2. More restrictions on choice or inputs/practices

3. Precision agriculture will take on new dimensions through the use of satellites, computers, Global Positioning Systems (GPS), and other high-tech tools to help producers manage inputs such as seed, fertilizers, pesticides, and water.

Farms have become fewer, larger, specialized, and much more expensive to own and operate, but are also far more productive. Meanwhile, the number of small farms operated by part-time farmers is increasing. Land ownership is becoming more of a lifestyle used mostly for recreational purposes. Off-farm landowners are increasing.

Irrigation continues to be an important factor in crop production. Crops and livestock have made major changes in production areas, as in the concentration of cotton on the High Plains and livestock increases in Central and East Texas. Pest and disease control methods have greatly improved. Herbicides are relied upon for weed control.

Feedlot finishing, commercial broiler production, artificial insemination, improved pastures and brush control, reduced feed requirements, and other changes have greatly increased livestock and poultry efficiency. Biotechnology and genetic engineering promise new breakthroughs in reaching even higher levels of productivity. Horticultural plant and nursery businesses have expanded. Improved wildlife management has increased deer, turkey, and other wildlife populations. The use of land for recreation and ecotourism is growing.

Farmers and ranchers are better educated and informed, and more science- and business-oriented. Today, agriculture operates in a global, high-tech, consumer-driven environment.

Cooperation among farmers in marketing, promotion, and other fields has increased. Also, agricultural producers have become increasingly dependent on off-the-farm services to supply production inputs such as feeds, chemicals, credit, and other essentials.

Agribusiness

Texas farmers and ranchers have developed considerable dependence upon agribusiness. With many producers specializing in the production of certain crops and livestock, they look beyond the farm and ranch for supplies and services. On the input side, they rely on suppliers of production needs and services and, on the output side, they need assemblers, processors, and distributors.

Since 1940, the proportion of Texans whose livelihood is linked to agriculture has changed greatly. In 1940, about 23 percent of Texans were producers on farms and ranches, and about 17 percent were suppliers or were engaged in assembly, processing, and distribution of agricultural products. The agribusiness alignment in 2008 reflected less than 2 percent on farms and ranches, with about 15 percent of the labor force providing production or marketing supplies and services and retailing food and fiber products.

Cash Receipts

Farm and ranch cash receipts in 2017 totaled $22.8 billion, with estimates of $936.6 million for federal farm program, conservation, and indemnity payments. Realized gross farm income totaled $27.2 billion, with farm production expenses of $22.8 billion and net farm income totaling $4.4 billion.

Percent of Income from Products

Livestock and livestock products accounted for 63 percent of the $22.8 billion cash receipts from farm marketings in 2017, with the remaining 37 percent from crops. Receipts from livestock have trended up largely because of increased feeding operations and reduced crop acreage associated with farm programs and low prices. However, these relationships change continuously because of variations in commodity prices and volume of marketings.

Cattle and calves accounted for 38.8 percent of total cash receipts (excluding government payments) received by Texas farmers and ranchers in 2017. Milk made up 9.7 percent of receipts, poultry and eggs 11.8 percent, hogs 0.9 percent, and miscellaneous livestock 1.9 percent.

Cotton accounted for 16 percent of total receipts, while feed crops was 7.7 percent, food grains 1.5 percent, vegetables and melons 1.9 percent, oil crops

1.0 percent, fruits and nuts 0.9 percent, and other crops 8.1 percent.

Texas' Rank among States

Measured by cash receipts from crops and livestock, Texas ranked third in 2017; California ranked first; Iowa, second; and Nebraska, fourth.

Texas normally leads all other states in numbers of: farms and ranches; farm and ranch land; cattle slaughtered; cattle on feed; calf births; sheep and lambs; goats; cash receipts from livestock marketings; cattle and calves; beef cows; sheep and lambs; wool production; mohair production; and exports of fats, oils, and greases. The state also usually leads in production of cotton.

Texas Agricultural Exports

The value of Texas' share of agricultural exports in fiscal year 2017 was $7.2 billion. Cotton accounted for $2.6 billion of the exports; corn and processed grain products, $384.9 million; feed and other feedgrains, $294.7 million; wheat, $198.3 million; vegetable oils, $16.0 million; rice, $104.2 million; hides and skins, $192.7 million; beef and veal and pork, $1.0 billion; broiler meat and other poultry products, $301.9 million; fresh fruits, $43.3 million; processed fruits and tree nuts, $117.6 million; soybeans and soybean meal, $33.3 million; fresh and processed vegetables, $128.6 million; dairy products, $314.0 million; and miscellaneous and other products, $1.4 billion.

Cash Receipts by Commodities, 2013–2017

COMMODITIES	2013	2014	2015	2016	2017	Percent of 2017
	(All values in thousands of dollars)					
All Commodities	$ 22,308,658	$ 24,583,483	$ 23,492,427	$ 20,660,480	$ 22,769,150	100.0%
Animals and products	15,377,060	16,950,166	16,674,279	13,152,605	14,337,401	63.0%
Meat animals	10,334,495	11,183,779	11,680,410	8,657,563	9,025,154	39.6%
Cattle and calves	10,097,183	10,938,332	11,459,962	8,467,800	8,827,816	38.8%
Hogs	237,312	245,447	220,448	189,763	197,338	0.9%
Dairy products, milk	1,955,544	2,529,372	1,818,675	1,848,140	2,213,152	9.7%
Poultry and eggs	2,716,006	2,851,685	2,828,041	2,266,336	2,677,569	11.8%
Broilers	2,184,957	2,261,860	2,030,358	1,835,520	2,231,814	9.8%
Misc. livestock †	371,015	385,330	347,153	380,566	421,526	1.9%
Crops	6,931,597	7,633,317	6,818,148	7,507,875	8,431,749	37.0%
Food grains	611,497	595,699	591,711	424,269	350,375	1.5%
Rice	160,759	155,703	127,907	122,768	146,418	0.6%
Wheat	448,427	436,840	460,006	297,599	198,603	0.9%
Feed crops	2,072,211	2,374,706	2,026,948	2,121,556	1,743,402	7.7%
Corn	1,170,787	1,308,204	1,067,346	1,170,850	1,011,237	4.4%
Cotton	1,615,716	2,076,186	1,710,731	2,366,886	3,638,010	16.0%
Oil crops	228,650	188,997	198,264	160,312	227,345	1.0%
Vegetables and melons	445,129	399,779	364,459	387,286	430,167	1.9%
Fruits and nuts	145,698	201,124	155,646	204,673	204,024	0.9%
All other crops ‡	1,812,696	1,796,827	1,770,388	1,842,893	1,838,425	8.1%

† Includes catfish, honey, mohair, wool, chicken eggs, farm chickens, turkeys, and other animals and products.
‡ Includes miscellaneous vegetables and other field crops.
Values are rounded to the nearest thousand. Sub-categories may not sum to total because not all sub-categories are reported.

Source: USDA/ERS Farm Income and Wealth Statistics.

In 2016, Texas' exports of $6.1 billion of farm and ranch products compares with $6.0 billion in 2015 and $6.3 billion in 2014.

Hunting

The management of wildlife as an economic enterprise through leasing for hunting makes a significant contribution to the economy of many counties. Leasing the right of ingress on a farm or ranch for the purpose of hunting is the service marketed. After the leasing, the consumer — the hunter — goes onto the land to seek the harvest of the wildlife commodity. Hunting lease income to farmers and ranchers in 2018 was estimated at $697 million.

The demand for hunting opportunities is growing while the land capable of producing huntable wildlife is decreasing. As a result, farmers and ranchers are placing more emphasis on wildlife management practices to help meet requests for hunting leases.

Irrigation

Agricultural irrigation in Texas peaked in 1974 at 8.6 million acres. Over the next 20 years, irrigation declined due to many factors, including poor farm economics, falling water tables in certain regions, energy costs for irrigation pumping, and the movement of much of the vegetable production from South Texas to Mexico. For the past 15 years, total irrigated area has stabilized and fluctuates from year to year between 6 and 6.4 million acres. This puts Texas third in the nation, behind California and Nebraska in agricultural irrigation.

Although some irrigation is practiced in nearly every county of the state, about 60 percent of the total irrigated acreage is on the High Plains of Texas. Other concentrated areas of irrigation are the Upper Gulf Coast rice-producing area, the Lower Rio Grande Valley, the Winter Garden area of South Texas, and the Trans-Pecos area of West Texas.

Sprinkler irrigation is used on about 75 percent of the total irrigated acreage, with surface irrigation methods, primarily furrow and surge methods, on much of the remaining irrigated area. Texas growers are continuing the switch to center pivot irrigation machines. Texas farmers lead the nation in the adoption of efficient irrigation technologies, particularly LEPA (low energy precision application) and LESA (low elevation spray application) center pivot systems, both of which were developed by Texas A&M AgriLife Research and the Texas A&M AgriLife Extension Service.

The use of drip irrigation continues to increase and accounts for about 10 percent of the total irrigated acreage. Drip irrigation is routinely used for vegetables, vineyards, and tree crops such as citrus, pecans, and peaches. Some drip irrigation of cotton, forages, and peanuts is being practiced in West Texas. Farmers continue to experiment with drip irrigation, but the relatively high costs and management requirements are limiting more widespread use.

Agricultural irrigation uses about 60 percent of all fresh water in the state, and landscape irrigation accounts for about 40 percent of total municipal water use.

Texas is one of only a handful of states that require a state irrigator's license for the design and installation of landscape and residential irrigation systems. Cities of 20,000 persons or larger are required to have irrigation inspectors to ensure that landscape irrigation systems meet state design and installation requirements. However, no license or certification is

Export Shares of Commodities

Commodity*	2014	2015	2016	2017	2017 % of U.S. Total
	(All values in millions of dollars)				
Beef and veal	$ 958.3	$ 925.7	$ 845.8	$ 952.0	13.1%
Pork	61.5	59.5	59.2	60.7	0.9%
Hides and skins	302.9	288.0	201.0	192.7	10.2%
Other livestock products [1]	159.3	129.2	140.6	183.9	6.0%
Dairy products	363.7	266.7	251.5	314.0	5.8%
Broiler meat	280.4	212.1	201.8	232.2	7.4%
Other poultry products [2]	90.4	78.7	60.7	69.7	3.6%
Total animal products	2,216.5	1,959.8	1,760.5	2,005.3	6.9%
Vegetables, fresh	45.4	37.4	41.9	44.7	1.8%
Vegetables, processed	86.5	71.5	81.1	83.9	1.8%
Fruits, fresh	36.4	31.4	38.7	43.3	0.9%
Fruits, processed	32.8	30.8	36.6	37.8	0.9%
Tree nuts	72.8	73.5	85.4	79.8	0.9%
Rice	88.9	91.8	93.4	104.2	6.1%
Wheat	268.2	274.6	180.0	198.3	3.3%
Corn	254.1	187.8	248.0	226.0	2.5%
Feeds/feed grains [3]	369.5	377.9	339.9	294.7	3.5%
Grain products, processed	172.5	174.2	170.4	158.9	3.6%
Soybeans	24.2	18.2	20.6	28.2	0.1%
Soybean meal	5.6	4.6	3.7	5.1	0.1%
Vegetable oils	14.3	17.5	11.0	16.0	0.5%
Other oilseeds and products [4]	191.8	143.7	128.0	147.2	7.1%
Cotton	1,287.8	1,403.4	1,708.2	2,610.5	44.7%
Other plant products [5]	1,101.7	1,055.3	1,109.3	1,110.8	6.4%
Total plant products	4,052.6	3,993.5	4,296.2	5,189.4	4.8%
Total agricultural exports	$ 6,269.2	$5,953.3	$6,056.7	$7,194.6	5.2%

*Totals may not add due to rounding.
[1] Includes other nonpoultry meats, animal fat, live farm animals, and other animal parts.
[2] Includes turkey meat, eggs, and other fowl products.
[3] Includes processed feeds, fodder, barley, oats, rye, and sorghum.
[4] Includes peanuts (oilstock), other oil crops, corn meal, other oilcake and meal, protein substances, bran, and residues.
[5] Includes sweeteners and products, other horticulture products, planting seeds, cocoa, coffee, and other processed foods.

Source: USDA Economic Research Service; USDA Foreign Agricultural Service (Global Agricultural Trade System).

required for the design or installation of agricultural irrigation systems.

To meet future water demand for our rapidly growing cities and industries, several regions of the state are looking at water transfers from agriculture. The largest water transfer project currently under construction is the **San Antonio Water System Vista Ridge Pipeline**, which will transfer 16 billion gallons per year from the Carrizo and Simsboro aquifers in Burleson County to San Antonio. The long-term effects on water availability in Burleson County are uncertain.

Texas water planning documents estimate that as much as 30 percent of future water demand could be met through agricultural irrigation conservation. However, state funding for such programs continues to decline. In about 20 percent of the irrigated area, water is delivered to farms through canals and pipelines by irrigation and other types of water districts and by river authorities. Many of these delivery networks are aging, in poor condition, and have high seepage losses. Estimates are that over 30 percent of all water diverted by irrigation districts is lost in the conveyance systems.

Approximately 80 percent of the state's irrigated acreage is supplied with water pumped from wells. Surface water sources supply the remaining area. The severe droughts of the early to mid-2010's greatly impacted water availability from surface sources, such as rivers and reservoirs. As a result, the number of groundwater wells increased rapidly throughout South and West Texas, which could impact future water availability.

Declining groundwater levels in several major aquifers is a serious problem, particularly in the Ogallala Aquifer in the Texas High Plains, and the southern portion of the Carrizo-Wilcox formation. *See "Major Aquifers of Texas" on page 44.*

Texas common law grants the landowner with broad rights to exploit the underlying groundwater. Laws and regulations governing groundwater use enacted in Texas over the last 50 years attempt to recognize the landowner's right to beneficially use the water, while giving water districts certain powers to manage and restrict water use. Legal battles are ongoing between these two interests.

However, an increasing number of groundwater conservation districts are establishing water use limits for agricultural irrigation. The Edwards Aquifer Authority has a voluntary irrigation "op-out" program, the first of its kind in Texas, where farmers receive payments in exchange for not irrigating during drought years.

Irrigation is an important factor in the productivity of Texas agriculture. The value of crop production from irrigated acreage is 50 to 60 percent of the total value of all crop production, although only about 30 percent of the state's total harvested cropland acreage is irrigated.

Cotton

Cotton has been a major crop in Texas for more than a century. Since 1880, Texas has led all states in cotton production in most years, and today the annual Texas cotton harvest amounts to around 37.5 percent of total production in the United States. The annual Texas cotton crop has averaged 5.8 million 480-lb. bales since 1996.

A center pivot sprinkler irrigating young cotton plants, which are growing in wheat residue as a cover crop. Photo by USDA NRCS Texas.

Principal Crops

In most recent years, the value of crop production in Texas is less than 37 percent of the total value of the state's agricultural output. Cash receipts from farm sales of crops are reduced somewhat because some grain and roughage is fed to livestock on farms where produced. Drought has reduced receipts in recent years.

Receipts from all Texas crops totaled $8.4 billion in 2017, $7.5 billion in 2016, and $6.8 billion in 2015.

Cotton, corn, grain sorghum, and wheat account for a large part of the total crop receipts. In 2017, cotton contributed about 43.2 percent of the crop total; corn, 12.0 percent; and wheat, 2.4 percent. Hay, cottonseed, vegetables, peanuts, rice, soybeans, and grain sorghum are other important cash crops.

Value of upland cotton produced in Texas in 2018 was $2.4 billion. Cottonseed value in 2018 was $341.0 million, making the value of the Texas crop around $2.7 billion.

Upland cotton was harvested from 4.4 million acres in 2018 and American-Pima from 17,500 acres. Yield for upland cotton in 2018 was 756 pounds per harvested acre, with American-Pima yielding 933 pounds per acre. Upland cotton acreage harvested in 2017 totaled 5.5 million, and American-Pima harvested 13,000 acres for total cotton acreage of 5.51 million. The yield for upland cotton was 809 pounds per acre and 960 pounds per acre for American-Pima. Total cotton production amounted to 6.9 million bales in 2018 and 9.3 million in 2017.

Cotton is the raw material for processing operations at gins, oil mills, compresses, and a small number of textile mills in Texas. Cotton in Texas is machine harvested. Field storage of harvested seed cotton has become common practice as gins decline in number.

Most of the Texas cotton crop is exported. China, Turkey, Mexico, and various Pacific Rim countries are major buyers. With the continuing development of fiber-spinning technology and the improved quality of Texas cotton, the export demand for Texas cotton has grown. Spinning techniques can efficiently produce high-quality yarn from relatively strong, short or longer staple upland cotton with fine mature fiber.

Grain Sorghum

The value of Texas grain sorghum in 2018 was second highest in the nation, behind Kansas. Much of the grain is exported or used in livestock and poultry feed throughout the state. Recently, Texas sorghum has also seen demand in ethanol production.

Total production of grain sorghum in 2018 was 62.1 million bushels, with 46 bushels per acre yield from 1.4 million acres harvested. With an average price of $6.85 per cwt., the total value reached $238.2 million.

In 2017, 1.5 million acres of grain sorghum were harvested, yielding an average of 63 bushels per acre for a total production of 94.5 million bushels. It was valued at $6.30 per cwt., for a total value of $333.4 million.

In 2016, 1.8 million acres were harvested with an average of 66 bushels per acre, or 115.5 million bushels. The season's average price was $5.94 per cwt. for a total value of $384.2 million.

Although grown to some extent in all counties where crops are important, the largest concentrations are in the High Plains, Coastal Bend, and Lower Rio

Value of Cotton & Cottonseed 1900–2018				
	Upland Cotton		Cottonseed	
Crop Year	Production (Bales)	Value	Production (Tons)	Value
	(All figures in thousands)			
1900	3,438	$157,306	1,531	$20,898
1910	3,047	$210,260	1,356	$31,050
1920	4,345	$376,080	1,934	$41,350
1930	4,037	$194,080	1,798	$40,820
1940	3,234	$162,140	1,318	$31,852
1950	2,946	$574,689	1,232	$111,989
1960	4,346	$612,224	1,821	$75,207
1970	3,191	$314,913	1,242	$68,310
1980*	3,320	$1,091,616	1,361	$161,959
1981	5,645	$1,259,964	2,438	$207,230
1982	2,700	$664,848	1,122	$90,882
1983	2,380	$677,443	1,002	$162,324
1984	3,680	$927,360	1,563	$157,863
1985	3,910	$968,429	1,635	$102,156
1986	2,535	$560,945	1,053	$82,118
1987	4,635	$1,325,981	1,915	$157,971
1988	5,215	$1,291,651	2,131	$238,672
1989	2,870	$812,784	1,189	$141,491
1990	4,965	$1,506,182	1,943	$225,388
1991	4,710	$1,211,789	1,903	$134,162
1992	3,265	$769,495	1,346	$145,368
1993	5,095	$1,308,396	2,147	$255,493
1994	4,915	$1,642,003	2,111	$215,322
1995	4,460	$1,597,037	1,828	$201,080
1996	4,345	$1,368,154	1,784	$230,136
1997	5,140	$1,482,787	1,983	$226,062
1998	3,600	$969,408	1,558	$204,098
1999	5,050	$993,840	1,987	$160,947
2000	3,940	$868,061	1,589	$162,078
2001	4,260	$580,723	1,724	$159,470
2002	5,040	$967,680	1,855	$191,065
2003	4,330	$1,199,237	1,616	$202,000
2004	7,740	$1,493,510	2,895	$301,080
2005	8,440	$1,879,757	2,869	$289,739
2006	5,800	$1,288,992	2,066	$243,776
2007	8,250	$2,391,840	2,861	$443,409
2008	4,450	$935,568	1,547	$351,192
2009	4,620	$1,328,342	1,634	$254,904
2010	7,840	$3,006,797	2,685	$413,490
2011	3,500	$1,375,920	1,228	$354,892
2012	5,000	$1,675,200	1,669	$442,285
2013	4,170	$1,493,194	1,368	$347,472
2014	6,175	$1,753,814	1,959	$363,629
2015	5,720	$1,564,992	1,844	$413,056
2016	8,100	$2,593,296	2,528	$490,432
2017	9,270	$2,950,085	2,852	$393,576
2018	6,850	$2,384,640	2,088	$341,004

* Beginning in 1971, the basis for cotton prices was changed to 480 pound net weight bale from 500 pound gross weight; to compute comparable prices for previous years, multiply price times 1.04167.

Sources: Texas Agricultural Facts@, USDA/NASS Crop Production Annual Summary, January; and Crop Values Annual Summary, February. USDA/NASS Quick Stats data system.

Realized Gross Income* and Net Income from Farming 1980–2017

Year	**Realized Gross Farm Income	Farm Production Expenses	Net Change In Farm Inventories	***Total Net Farm Income	***Total Net Income Per Farm
	(Values in millions of dollars)				(dollars)
1980	$ 9,611.4	$ 9,081.1	$ –542.5	$ 456.9	$ 2,331.0
1981	11,545.7	9,643.1	699.9	1,902.6	9,756.8
1982	11,404.5	10,008.2	–127.8	1,396.3	7,197.6
1983	11,318.1	9,778.9	–590.7	1,539.2	7,933.8
1984	11,692.6	10,257.3	186.1	1,435.3	7,398.3
1985	11,375.3	9,842.8	–9.0	1,532.5	7,981.9
1986	10,450.1	9,272.8	–349.0	1,177.3	6,196.6
1987	12,296.6	10,038.7	563.2	2,257.9	12,010.1
1988	12,842.3	10,331.7	–128.4	2,510.6	13,076.2
1989	12,843.1	10,328.4	–798.6	2,514.7	12,962.1
1990	14,421.5	11,012.9	343.9	3,408.6	17,391.0
1991	14,376.4	11,270.3	150.0	3,106.1	15,767.0
1992	14,482.5	10,617.6	464.1	3,864.9	19,519.8
1993	15,817.0	11,294.6	197.0	4,522.5	20,745.4
1994	15,394.5	11,134.7	107.7	4,259.9	19,363.0
1995	15,678.9	12,537.3	243.7	3,141.6	14,151.3
1996	15,025.0	12,006.6	–290.1	3,018.4	13,475.1
1997	16,430.7	12,718.5	709.2	3,712.3	16,498.9
1998	15,506.0	12,047.4	–817.1	3,458.6	15,269.7
1999	17,469.5	12,441.9	196.0	5,027.6	22,099.3
2000	16,810.1	12,707.8	–50.2	4,102.3	17,968.9
2001	18,089.1	13,106.6	113.4	4,982.5	21,795.7
2002	16,567.7	11,372.8	436.8	5,195.1	22,686.0
2003	20,105.7	13,687.6	–137.7	6,418.1	28,026.6
2004	21,826.4	14,343.8	539.0	7,482.5	32,674.7
2005	21,928.5	15,371.6	306.7	6,556.8	28,507.8
2006	20,329.6	16,010.9	–753.8	4,318.7	18,777.0
2007	24,738.0	19,800.2	948.6	4,937.7	19,950.3
2008	22,523.4	19,674.0	–1,174.8	2,849.4	14,282.1
2009	20,648.8	18,562.9	–980.9	2,085.9	9,133.8
2010	23,474.2	18,807.4	46.6	4,666.8	22,404.4
2011	26,004.5	21,429.7	–2,494.0	4,574.9	21,811.9
2012	27,430.8	23,839.1	–1,075.4	3,591.8	NA
2013	29,673.0	24,177.7	–170.9	5,495.3	NA
2014	30,689.3	26,465.5	401.8	4,223.7	NA
2015	29,511.6	22,999.9	–454.1	6,511.8	NA
2016	25,036.4	22,127.9	–77.7	2,908.5	NA
2017	27,192.6	22,784.6	–574.5	4,408.0	NA

* Details for items may not add to totals because of rounding.
** Cash receipts from farm marketings, government payments, value of home consumption, and gross rental value of farm dwellings.
*** Farm income of farm operators.
NA= Not available
NOTE: A positive value of inventory change represents current-year production not sold by Dec. 31. A negative value is an offset to production from prior years included in current-year sales.

Sources: "Economic Indicators of the Farm Sector, State Financial Summary, 1985, 1987, 1989, 1993," USDA/ERS; "Farm Business Economics Report," August 1996; "Texas Agricultural Statistics Service, October 2010"; USDA/ERS.

Grande Valley areas. Research to develop high-yielding hybrids resistant to diseases and insect damage continues.

Rice

Rice, which is grown in about 20 counties on the Coastal Prairie of Texas, ranked third in value among Texas crops for a number of years. However, in 2018, cotton, hay, corn, wheat, and grain sorghum outranked rice.

Rice farms are highly mechanized, producing rice through irrigation and using airplanes for much of the planting, fertilizing, and application of insecticides and herbicides.

Texas farmers grow long- and medium-grain rice only. The Texas rice industry, which grew from 110 acres in 1850 to a high of 642,000 planted acres in 1954, has been marked by significant yield increases and improved varieties. Record production was in 1981, with 27.2 million cwt. harvested. The highest yield was 8,370 pounds per acre in 2012.

Several different types of rice milling procedures are in use today. The simplest and oldest method produces a product known as **regular milled white rice**, the most prevalent on the market currently.

During this process, rice grains are subjected to additional cleaning to remove chaff, dust, foreign seed, etc., and then husks are removed from the grains. This results in a product that is the whole unpolished grain of rice with only the outer hull and a small amount of bran removed. This product is called **brown rice** and is sometimes sold without further treatment other than grading. It has a delightful nutlike flavor and a slightly chewy texture.

When additional layers of the bran are removed, the rice becomes white in color and begins to appear as it is normally recognized at retail level. The removal of the bran layer from the grain is performed in a number of steps using two or three types of machines. After the bran is removed, the product is ready for classification as to size. Rice is more valuable if the grains are not broken. In many cases, additional vitamins are added to the grains to produce what is called "**enriched rice.**"

Another process may be used in rice milling to produce a product called **parboiled rice**. In this process, the rice is subjected to a combination of steam and pressure prior to the time it is milled in the manner described above. This process gelatinizes the starch in the grain, the treatment aiding in the retention of much of the natural vitamin and mineral content. After cooking, parboiled rice tends to be fluffy, more separate, and plump.

Still another type of rice is **precooked rice**, which is actually milled rice that, after milling, has been cooked. Then the moisture is removed through a dehydration process. Precooked rice requires a minimum of preparation time since it needs merely to have the moisture restored to it.

The U.S. produces only a small part of the world's total rice, but it is **one of the leading exporters**. American rice is popular abroad and is exported to more than 100 foreign countries.

Mature wheat planted on ridges in a cotton field near Lubbock. Photo by USDA NRCS Texas.

Texas rice production in 2018 totaled 15.1 million cwt. from 189,000 harvested acres, with a yield of 7,970 pounds per acre. The crop value totaled $188.3 million.

Rice production was 11.47 million cwt. in 2017 on 158,000 harvested acres, yielding 7,260 pounds per acre. Total value in 2017 was $136.5 million.

Rice production was 13.77 million cwt. in 2016 on 187,000 harvested acres. Production in 2016 was valued at $143.2 million, with a yield of 7,360 pounds per acre.

Wheat

Wheat for grain is one of the state's most valuable cash crops. In 2018, wheat was exceeded in value by cotton, hay, and corn. Wheat pastures also provide considerable winter forage for cattle that is reflected in value of livestock produced.

Texas wheat production totaled 56.0 million bushels in 2018 as yield averaged 32.0 bushels per acre. Planted acreage totaled 4.5 million acres and 1.8 million acres were harvested. With an average price of $5.15 per bushel, the 2018 wheat value totaled $288.4 million.

In 2017, Texas wheat growers planted 4.7 million acres and harvested 2.4 million acres. The yield was 29.0 bushels per acre for 2017, with total production of 68.2 bushels at $3.89 per bushel valued at $265.1 million.

Texas wheat growers planted 5.0 million acres in 2016 and harvested grain from 2.8 million acres. The yield was 32.0 bushels per acre for a total production of 89.6 million bushels valued at $317.2 million or $3.54 per bushel.

Wheat was first grown commercially in Texas near Sherman about 1833. The acreage expanded greatly in North Central Texas after 1850 because of rapid settlement of the state and introduction of the well-adapted Mediterranean strain of wheat. A major family flour industry was developed in the Fort Worth/Dallas/Sherman area between 1875 and 1900. Now, around half of the state acreage is planted on the High Plains and about a third of it is irrigated.

Most of the Texas wheat acreage is of the hard red winter class. Because of the development of varieties with improved disease resistance and the use of wheat for winter pasture, there has been a sizable expansion of acreage in Central and South Texas.

Most all wheat harvested for grain is used in some phase of the milling industry. The better-quality hard red winter wheat is used in the production of commercial bakery flour. Lower grades and varieties of soft red winter wheat are used in family flours. By-products of milled wheat are used for feed.

Corn

Interest in corn production throughout the state has increased since the 1970s as yields improved with new varieties. Once the principal grain crop, corn acreage declined as plantings of grain sorghum increased. Only 500,000 acres were harvested annually until the mid-1970s, when new hybrids were developed.

Harvested acreage was 1.8 million in 2018; 2.2 million in 2017; and 2.6 million in 2016. Yields for the corresponding years were 108, 140, and 127 bushels per acre, respectively.

Most of the acreage and yield increase has occurred in Central and South Texas. In 2018, corn ranked third in value among the state's crops. It was valued at $774.9 million in 2018; $1.2 billion in 2017; and $1.2 billion in 2016. The grain is largely used for livestock feed, but other important uses are in ethanol and food products.

Texas Crop Production, 2018

Crop	Harvested Acres (thousands)	Yield Per Acre	Unit	Total Production (thousands)	Cash Value (thousands)
Corn, grain	1,750.0	108.0	bushel	189,000.0	$774,900
Corn, silage	270.0	16.0	ton	4,320.0	—
Cotton, American-Pima	17.5	933.0	lb:bale	(D)	—
Cotton, Upland	4,350.0	756.0	lb:bale	6,850.0	$2,384,640
Cottonseed	—	—	ton	2,088.0	$341,004
Grapefruit *	15.7	306	box	4,800.0	$65,080
Hay, Alfalfa	140.0	5.6	ton	784.0	$159,936
Hay, Other	4,600.0	1.65	ton	7,590.0	$903,210
Hay, All	**4,740.0**	**1.77**	**ton**	**8,374.0**	**$1,063,146**
Oats	50.0	50.0	bushel	2,500.0	$12,375
Dry Onions	11.0	300.0	cwt.	3,300.0	$61,380
Oranges *	8.7	216.0	box	1,880.0	$35,538
Peaches *	—	—	ton	2.4	—
Peanuts	145.0	3,300.0	lb.	478,500.0	$119,625
Potatoes	14.0	425.0	cwt.	5,950.0	$75,565
Rice	189.0	7,970.0	lb:cwt.	15,060.0	$188,250
Sorghum, Grain	1,350.0	46.0	bushel	62,100.0	$238,216
Sorghum, Silage	80.0	13.0	ton	1,040.0	—
Soybeans	135.0	32.0	bushel	4,320.0	$33,048
Sugarcane for sugar & seed	38.9	36.6	ton	1,425.0	—
Sunflowers	23.5	1,174.0	lb.	27,580.0	$5,342
Vegetables, Principal	62.0	—	cwt.	16,181.7	$305,255
Wheat, Winter	1,750.0	32.0	bushel	56,000.0	$288,400
Total of Listed Crops	**15,000.3**	**—**	**—**	**—**	**$5,991,764**

* Reflects 2017/2018 crop year. Grapefruit, Texas 80-lb./box. Oranges, Texas 85-lb./box
†Sugarcane value will be published in *Crop Values* released February 2020. Sugarcane for sugar and seed value of production in 2017 was $31,040,000.
(D) Withheld to avoid disclosing data for individual operations
Source: USDA/NASS, annual crop production, January, annual crop values, February.

The sugarcane grinding mill operated at Santa Rosa in Cameron County is considered one of the most modern mills in the United States. Texas sugarcane-producing counties include Cameron, Hidalgo, and Willacy.

At a yield of 36.6 tons per acre, sugarcane and seed production in 2018 totaled 1.4 million tons from 38,900 harvested acres. *(The value of the 2018 crop will not be released until February 2020.)*

In 2017, 40,500 acres were harvested for total production of 1.5 million tons valued at $29.8 million. The yield was 36.8 tons per acre.

In 2016, 37,700 acres were harvested, from which 1.4 million tons of sugarcane were milled. The yield averaged 37.0 tons per acre for a total value of $28.6 million.

Oats

Oats are grown extensively in Texas for winter pasture, hay, silage, and greenchop feeding, and some acreage is harvested for grain.

Of the 450,000 acres planted to oats in 2018, 50,000 acres were harvested. The average yield was 50.0 bushels per acre. Production totaled 2.5 million bushels with a value of $12.4 million, or $4.95 per bushel.

In 2017, 455,000 acres were planted. From the plantings, 60,000 acres were harvested, with an average yield of 45.0 bushels per acre for a total production of 2.7 million bushels. Average price per bushel was $4.28, and total production value was $11.6 million.

Texas farmers planted 470,000 acres of oats in 2016. They harvested 60,000 acres that averaged 50.0 bushels per acre for a total production of 3.0 million bushels at an average price of $4.03 per bushel with an estimated value of $12.1 million. Most of the acreage was used for grazing.

Almost all oat grain produced in Texas is utilized as **feed for livestock** within the state. A small acreage is grown exclusively for planting seed.

Sugarcane

Sugarcane is grown from seed cane planted in late summer or fall. It is harvested 12 months later and milled to produce **raw sugar and molasses**. Raw sugar requires additional refining before it is in final form and can be offered to consumers.

Hay, Silage, and Other Forage Crops

A large proportion of Texas' agricultural land is devoted to forage crop production. This acreage produces forage needs and provides essentially the total feed requirements for most of the state's large domestic livestock population as well as game animals.

Approximately 87.9 million acres of pasture and rangeland, which are primarily in the western half of Texas, provide grazing for beef cattle, sheep, goats, horses, and game animals. An additional 8.3 million acres are devoted to cropland used only for pasture or grazing. The average annual acreage of forage land used for hay, silage, and other forms of machine-harvested forage is around 5 million acres.

All hay accounts for a large amount of this production with some corn and sorghum silage being produced. The most important hay crops are annual and perennial grasses and alfalfa. Production in 2018 totaled 8.4 million tons of hay from 4.7 million harvested acres at a yield of 1.8 tons per acre. Value of hay was $1.1 billion, or $137 per ton.

In 2017, 9.5 million tons of hay were produced from 4.5 million harvested acres at a yield of 2.1 tons per acre. The value in 2017 was $1.0 billion or $116 per ton. In 2016, the production of hay was 11.7 million tons from 4.6 million harvested acres with a value of $1.2 billion or $112 per ton, at a yield of 2.5 tons per acre.

Alfalfa hay production in 2018 totaled 784,000 tons with 140,000 acres harvested with a yield of 5.6 tons per acre. At a value of $204 per ton, total value was $159.9 million. In 2017, 528,000 tons of alfalfa hay were harvested from 120,000 acres at a yield of 4.4 tons per acre. Value was $95.6 million, or $181 per ton. Alfalfa hay was harvested from 130,000 acres in 2016, producing an average of 5.3 tons per acre for total production of 689,000 tons valued at $121.3 million, or $176 per ton.

An additional sizable acreage of annual forage crops is grazed, as well as much of the small grain acreage. Alfalfa, sweet corn, vetch, arrowleaf clover, grasses, and other forage plants also provide income as seed crops.

Peanuts

Well over three-fourths of the annual peanut production is from irrigated acreage. In 2018, Texas ranked fourth nationally in production of peanuts. Among Texas crops, peanuts rank ninth in value.

Until 1973, essentially all of the Texas acreage was planted to the Spanish type, which was favored because of its earlier maturity and better drought tolerance than other types. The Spanish variety is also preferred for some uses due to its distinctive flavor. The Florunner variety, a runner market type, is now planted on a sizable proportion of the acreage where soil moisture is favorable. This variety matures later but provides better yields than Spanish varieties under good growing conditions. Florunner peanuts have acceptable quality to compete with the Spanish variety in most products.

In 2018, peanut production totaled 478.5 million pounds from 155,000 acres planted and 145,000 harvested, yielding 3,300 pounds per acre. At 25.0 cents per pound, value of the crop was estimated at $119.6 million. In 2017, peanut production amounted to 697.2 million pounds from 275,000 acres planted and 210,000 harvested. With an average yield of 3,320 pounds per acre and average price of 28.6 cents per pound, the 2017 value of production was $199.4 million.

Production in 2016 amounted to 559.7 million pounds of peanuts from 305,000 acres planted and 205,000 acres harvested, or an average of 2,730 pounds per harvested acre valued at 23.2 cents per pound for a $129.8 million value.

Soybeans

Soybean production is located in the areas of the Upper Coast, irrigated High Plains, and Red River Valley of Northeast Texas. Soybeans are adapted to the same general soil climate conditions as corn, cotton, or grain sorghum, provided moisture, disease, and insects are not limiting factors.

In low-rainfall areas, yields have been too low or inconsistent for profitable production under dryland conditions. Soybeans' need for moisture in late summer minimizes economic crop possibilities in the Blacklands and Rolling Plains. In the Blacklands, cotton root rot seriously hinders soybean production. Limited moisture at critical growth stages may occasionally prevent economical yields, even in

Fields of red grain sorghum near Edmonson. Photo by USDA NRCS Texas.

high-rainfall areas of Northeast Texas and the Coastal Prairie.

Because of day length sensitivity, soybeans should be planted in Texas during the long days of May and June to obtain sufficient vegetative growth for optimum yields. Varieties planted during this period usually cease vegetative development and initiate reproductive processes during the hot, dry months of July and August.

When moisture is insufficient during the blooming and fruiting period, yields are drastically reduced. In most areas of the state, July and August rainfall is insufficient to permit economical dryland production. The risk of dryland soybean production in the Coastal Prairie and Northeast Texas is considerably less when compared to other dryland areas because moisture is available more often during the critical fruiting period.

The 2018 soybean crop totaled 4.3 million bushels and was valued at $33.0 million, or $7.65 per bushel. Of the 175,000 acres planted, 135,000 were harvested with an average yield of 32.0 bushels per acre. In 2017, the Texas soybean crop averaged 37.0 bushels per acre from 185,000 acres harvested. Total production of 6.8 million bushels was valued at $60.9 million, or $8.90 per bushel. In 2016, the Texas soybean crop averaged 31.0 bushels per acre from 145,000 acres harvested. Total production of 4.5 million bushels was valued at $41.2 million, or $9.16 per bushel.

Sunflowers

Sunflowers constitute one of the most important annual oilseed crops in the world. The cultivated types, which are thought to be descendants of the common wild sunflower native to Texas, have been successfully grown in several countries, including Russia, Argentina, Romania, Bulgaria, Uruguay, Western Canada, and portions of the northern United States.

Extensive trial plantings conducted in the Cotton Belt states since 1968 showed sunflowers have considerable potential as an oilseed crop in much of this area, including Texas. This crop exhibits good cold and drought tolerance, is adapted to a wide range of soil and climate conditions, and tolerates higher levels of hail, wind, and sand abrasion than other crops normally grown in the state.

In 2018, sunflower production totaled 27.6 million pounds and was harvested from 23,500 acres at a yield of 1,174 pounds per acre. With an average price of $19.40 per cwt., the crop was valued at $5.3 million. In 2017, 43,000 of the 46,000 acres planted to sunflowers were harvested with an average yield of 1,423 pounds per acre. Total production of 61.2 million pounds was valued at $11.7 million, or $19.20 per cwt.

In 2016, of 45,500 acres planted to sunflowers, 38,500 acres were harvested, yielding 1,309 pounds per acre for a total yield of 50.4 million pounds valued at $9.4 million, or $18.70 per cwt.

Reasons for growing sunflowers include the need for an additional cash crop with low water and plant nutrient requirements, the development of sunflower

Vegetable Production, 2018

Crop	Harvested Acres	Yield Per Acre, Cwt.	Production, Cwt.	Value (thousands of dollars)
Cabbage	5,000	270	1,350,000	$27,405
Cantaloupes	2,000	110	220,000	$5,060
Carrots	1,600	250	400,000	$3,785
Chile Peppers ‡	2,500	55	138,000	$8,873
Cucumbers	4,900	97	475,000	$8,746
Dry Onions	11,000	300	3,300,000	$61,380
Potatoes	14,000	425	5,950,000	$75,565
Spinach	2,800	250	700,000	$13,346
Squash	1,500	59	89,000	$3,481
Watermelons	23,000	340	7,820,000	$143,387
Total for Fresh Market *	**68,300**	**—**	**20,442,000**	**$351,028**

* Includes some quantities processed.

‡ Chile peppers are defined as all peppers, excluding bell peppers. Estimates include both fresh and dry product combined.

Sources: USDA/NASS, Annual Vegetable Summary, February 2019; "2018 State Agriculture Overview, Texas"

hybrids, and interest by food processors in Texas sunflower oil which has high oleic acid content. Commercial users have found many advantages in this high oleic oil, including excellent cooking stability, particularly for use as a deep-frying medium for potato chips, corn chips, and similar products.

Sunflower meal is a high-quality protein source free of nutritional toxins that can be included in rations for swine, poultry, and ruminants. The hulls constitute a source of roughage, which can also be included in livestock rations.

Nursery Crops

The trend to increase production of nursery crops continues to rise as transportation costs on long-distance hauling increases. This has resulted in a marked increase in the production of container-grown plants within the state. This increase is noted especially in the production of bedding plants, foliage plants, sod, and woody landscape plants.

Plant rental services have become a multi-million-dollar business. This relatively new service provides the plants and maintains them in office buildings, shopping malls, public buildings, and even in some homes for a fee. The response has been good, as evidenced by the growth of companies providing these services.

The interest in plants for interior landscapes is confined to no specific age group as both retail nurseries and florist shops report that people of all ages are buying their plants.

Texas A&M AgriLife Extension specialists estimated cash receipts from nursery crops in Texas to be around $1.9 billion in 2018. Texans are creating colorful and green surroundings by improving their landscape plantings.

A winter cabbage field in Texas. Photo by IrinaK/Shutterstock.

Vegetable Crops

Some market vegetables are produced in almost all Texas counties. In 2017, Hidalgo County was the leading Texas county in vegetable acres harvested, followed by Hartley and Frio counties. Other leading producing counties are: Terry, Guadalupe, Medina, Uvalde, Yoakum, and Waller.

Texas is one of the seven leading states in the production of fresh market vegetables. Nationally, in 2018, Texas ranked seventh in production, exceeded by California, Washington, Florida, Georgia, Minnesota, and Michigan, and fifth in value of fresh market vegetables.

In 2018, fresh market vegetable production of 20.4 million cwt. was valued at $351.0 million from 68,300 acres harvested. In 2017, Texas growers harvested total fresh market vegetable crops valued at $283.2 million from 67,600 acres with a production of 14.7 million cwt. Texas growers harvested 16.5 million cwt. of fresh market vegetable crops from 64,600 acres, valued at $240.3 million in 2016.

Dry Onions

Dry onion production in 2018 totaled 3.3 million cwt. from 11,000 harvested acres and was valued at $61.4 million, at a yield of 300 cwt. per acre. In 2017, 3.0 million cwt. of dry onions were harvested from 11,500 acres and valued at $73.9 million, at a yield of 260 cwt. per acre. A total of 2.7 million cwt. of dry onions were produced from 9,200 harvested acres and valued at $64.3 million in 2016, yielding 295 cwt. per acre.

Carrots

Carrot production in 2018 totaled 400,000 cwt. from 1,600 harvested acres at a yield of 250 cwt. per acre. Production was valued at $3.8 million. In 2017, carrots were harvested from 1,900 acres with a value of $4.8 million. At a yield of 240 cwt. per acre, 2017 production was 456,000 cwt. Carrot production in 2016 totaled 590,000 cwt. from 2,000 harvested acres. At a yield of 295 cwt. per acre, production value was $6.6 million.

The winter carrot production from South Texas accounts for about three-fourths of total production during the winter season.

All Potatoes

In 2018, all potatoes were harvested from 14,000 acres with production of 6.0 million cwt. valued at $75.6 million at a yield of 425 cwt. per acre. All potatoes were harvested from 22,800 acres with production of 8.9 million cwt. valued at $135.2 million in 2017, yielding 390 cwt. per acre. This compares with 21,000 acres harvested valued at $141.8 million in 2016 with production of 8.3 million cwt. and a yield of 395 cwt. per acre.

Cantaloupes

Cantaloupe production in 2018 totaled 220,000 cwt. from 2,000 harvested acres and was valued at $5.1 million at a yield of 110 cwt. per acre. In 2017, cantaloupes were harvested from 2,000 acres for total production of 220,000 cwt. valued at $5.3 million, yielding 110 cwt. per acre. Of the 1,900 harvested acres in 2016, 237,500 cwt. cantaloupes were produced at a yield of 125 cwt. per acre and were valued at $5.2 million.

Five pound and fifty pound bags of pecans, grown near Crystal City. Photo by USDA.

Watermelons

Watermelon production in 2018 was 7.8 million cwt. from 23,000 acres with a value of $143.4 million, yielding 340 cwt. per acre. In 2017, at a yield of 290 cwt. per acre, 6.4 million cwt. watermelons were harvested from 22,000 acres and valued at $91.7 million. Watermelon production was 7.3 million cwt. from 25,000 acres in 2016, with a value of $74.0 million at a yield of 290 cwt. per acre.

Cabbage

In 2018, 5,000 acres were harvested and yielded total production of 1.4 million cwt. that was valued at $27.4 million. Yield was 270 cwt. per acre. In 2017, 6,000 acres of cabbage were harvested yielding total production of 1.8 million cwt., or 300 cwt. per acre, valued at $32.0 million. The 5,700 acres of cabbage harvested in Texas in 2016 brought a value of $35.9 million. At a yield of 350 cwt. per acre, total production was 2.0 million cwt.

Spinach

Spinach production is primarily concentrated in the Winter Garden area of South Texas.

The 2018 production value of spinach was estimated at $13.3 million. Production of 700,000 cwt. was harvested from 2,800 acres with a yield of 250 cwt. per acre. In 2017, 2,800 acres were harvested with a value of $19.4 million. At a yield of 240 cwt. per acre, production was 672,000 cwt. The 4,000 acres harvested in 2016 produced 980,000 cwt. at a yield of 245 cwt. per acre and valued at $10.2 million.

Cucumbers

In 2018, 4,900 acres of cucumbers were harvested. Production totaled 475,300 cwt. and was valued at $8.8 million. The yield was 97 cwt. per acre. In 2017, 6,100 acres of cucumbers were harvested with a value of $11.6 million. Production was 610,000 cwt. with a yield of 100 cwt. per acre. At a yield of 105 cwt. per acre, the 672,000 cwt. cucumber crop in Texas during 2016 was harvested from 6,400 acres and valued at $12.1 million.

Fruits and Nuts

Texas is noted for producing a wide variety of fruits. The pecan is the only commercial nut crop in the state. The pecan is native to most of the state's river valleys and is the Texas state tree. Citrus is produced commercially in the three southernmost counties in the Lower Rio Grande Valley. Peaches represent the next most important Texas fruit crop, and there is considerable interest in growing apples.

Citrus

Texas ranks with Florida and California as leading states in the production of citrus. Most of the Texas production is in Cameron, Hidalgo, and Willacy counties of the Lower Rio Grande Valley. In 2017/18, grapefruit production was estimated at 4.8 million boxes at $13.56 per box or $65.1 million. Grapefruit production in 2016/17 was 4.8 million boxes for a total value of $62.3 million. Production in 2015/16 was 4.8 million boxes with a value of $50.4 million.

Production of oranges in 2017/18 was 1.9 million boxes for a total value of $35.5 million. In 2016/17, production was 1.4 million boxes for a total value of $24.3 million. Production was 1.7 million boxes in 2015/16 for a value of $30.3 million.

Peaches

Primary production areas are East Texas, the Hill Country, and the West Cross Timbers. Production varies substantially due to adverse weather conditions. Low-chilling varieties for early marketings are being grown in Atascosa, Frio, Webb, Karnes, and Duval counties.

The Texas peach crop's production totaled 2,420 tons in 2018. In 2017, production was 2,500 tons. Value of production was $6.3 million. In 2016, production was 4,200 tons that was valued at $9.2 million.

Pecans

The pecan, the state tree, is one of the most widely distributed trees in Texas. It is native to over 150 counties and is grown commercially in some 30 additional counties. The pecan is also widely used as a dual-purpose yard tree. The commercial plantings of pecans have accelerated in Central and West Texas, with many of the new orchards being irrigated. Many new pecan plantings are being established under trickle-irrigation systems.

In 2018, pecan orchards yielded 300 pounds per acre from 112,000 harvested acres. The utilized production was 33.6 million pounds with a value of $56.1 million or $1.67 per pound. In 2017, a yield of 426 pounds per acre was harvested from 115,000 acres. The utilized production was 49 million pounds with a value of $110.0 million or $2.25 per pound. The 2015 crop totaled 39 million pounds from 100,000 harvested acres at a yield of 390 pounds per acre. The value was $94.0 million or $2.41 per pound.

Nationally, Texas ranked third behind New Mexico and Georgia in utilized pecan production in 2018.

Livestock and Animal Products

Livestock and animal products accounted for about 63 percent of the agricultural cash receipts in Texas in 2017. The state ranks first nationally in all cattle, beef cattle, cattle on feed, sheep and lambs, wool, goats, and mohair.

Cattle and calves account for around 61.6 percent of cash receipts from marketings of livestock and animal products. Sales of livestock and animal products in 2017 totaled $14.3 billion, up from $13.2 billion in 2016. The January 1, 2019, inventory of all cattle and calves in Texas totaled 13 million head, valued at $13.0 billion, compared to 12.5 million as of January 1, 2018, valued at $13.5 billion, and 12.3 million as of January 1, 2016, valued at $12.7 billion.

On January 1, 2019, the sheep and lamb inventory stood at 750,000 head, valued at $135.8 million, compared with 750,000 head as of January 1, 2018, valued at $138.8 million. January 1, 2017 showed an inventory of 710,000 valued at $109.2 million. Sheep and lambs numbered 3.2 million on January 1, 1973, down from a high of 10.8 million in 1943.

Wool production decreased from 26.4 million pounds valued at $23.2 million in 1973 to 1.8 million pounds valued at $3.2 million in 2018. Production was 1.8 million pounds in 2017 valued at $2.9 million. The price of wool per pound was 88 cents in 1973, compared to $1.80 in 2018, $1.63 in 2017, and $1.75 in 2016.

Mohair production in Texas has dropped from a 1965 high of 31.6 million pounds to 465,000 pounds in 2018. Production was valued at $3.3 million or $7.20 per pound. In 2017, production was 470,000 pounds valued at $3.1 million or $6.60 per pound. Mohair production in 2016 was 510,000 pounds valued at $3.1 million or $6.00 per pound.

Beef Cattle

Raising beef cattle is the most extensive agricultural operation in Texas. In 2017, cattle and calves were 38.8 percent of total cash receipts — $8.8 million of $22.8 million, compared with $8.5 million of $20.7 million in 2016 (41.0%) and $11.5 million of $23.5 million in 2015 (48.8%). The next leading commodity is poultry and eggs.

Nearly all of the 254 counties in Texas derive more revenue from cattle than from any other agricultural commodity, and those that don't usually rank cattle second in importance.

Within the boundaries of Texas are 13.7 percent of all the cattle in the U.S., as are 14.7 percent of the beef breeding cows, and 14.1 percent of the calf crop as of January 1, 2019, inventory.

The number of all cattle in Texas on January 1, 2019 totaled 13 million, compared with 12.5 million on January 1, 2018, and 12.3 million on January 1, 2017.

Calves born on Texas farms and ranches in January 1, 2018, totaled 4.8 million, compared with 4.4 million in 2017, and 4.3 million in 2016.

Dairy Product Manufacturing

The major dairy products manufactured in Texas include condensed, evaporated and dry milk; creamer; butter; and cheese. However, specifics of production and value are not available because of the small number of manufacturing plants producing these products.

Dairying

All cow's milk sold by Texas dairy farmers is marketed under the terms of Federal Marketing Orders. Most Texas dairymen are members of one of four marketing cooperatives. Associate Milk Producers, Inc. is the largest, representing the majority of the state's producers.

Texas dairy farmers received an average price for milk of $16.90 per hundred pounds in 2018, $18.40 in 2017, and $17.20 in 2016. A total of 12.9 billion pounds of milk was sold to plants and dealers in 2018, bringing in cash receipts from milk to dairy farmers of $2.2 billion. This compared with 12.1 billion pounds sold in 2017 that brought in $2.2 billion in cash receipts. In 2016, Texas dairymen sold 10.8 billion pounds of milk, which brought in cash receipts of $1.8 billion.

Cattle on the Birdwell Clark Ranch in Henrietta. Photo by USDA NRCS Texas.

The annual average number of milk cows in Texas was 545,000 head as of January 1, 2019, inventory. This compared with 530,000 head as of January 1, 2018, and 500,000 as of January 1, 2017. Average milk production per cow in the state has increased steadily over the past several decades. The average milk production per cow in 2018 was 23,933 pounds. Milk per cow in 2017 was 23,406 pounds. In 2016, milk per cow was 22,585 pounds. Total milk production in Texas was 12.9 billion pounds in 2018, 12.1 billion pounds in 2017, and 10.8 billion pounds in 2016.

There were 467 farms reporting milk cows in Texas in 2017. In 2012, 985 farms reported milk cows, and in 2007, 1,293 farms reported milk cows in Texas.

Swine

Texas had 1.1 million head of swine on hand, December 1, 2018 — only 1.5 percent of the U.S. swine herd.

Although the number of farms producing hogs has steadily decreased, the size of production units has increased substantially. There is favorable potential for increased production.

In 2018, 2.7 million head of hogs were marketed in Texas, producing 445.3 million pounds of pork valued at $225.4 million. In 2017, 2.1 million head of hogs were marketed, producing 366.1 million pounds of pork valued at $194.0 million. Comparable figures for 2016 were 2.1 million head marketed, and 366.0 million pounds of pork produced with a value of $181.8 million.

Goats and Mohair

All goats in Texas numbered 842,000 on January 1, 2019. This compares with 869,000 on January 1, 2018, and 892,000 on January 1, 2017.

Though data for the all-goat inventory are limited, the goatherd consists of Angora goats for mohair production. Angora goats totaled 75,000 as of January 1, 2019; 75,000 as of 2018; and 80,000 as of January 1, 2017.

Mohair production during 2018 totaled 465,000 pounds. This compares with 470,000 in 2017 and 510,000 pounds in 2016. Average price per pound in 2018 was $7.20 from 75,000 goats clipped for a total value of $3.3 million. In 2017, producers received $6.60 per pound from 77,000 goats clipped for a total value of $3.1 million. In 2016, producers received $6.00 per pound from 80,000 goats clipped for a total value of $3.1 million.

Over half of the world's mohair and over 55 percent of the U.S. clip are produced in Texas.

Sheep and Wool

Sheep and lambs in Texas numbered 750,000 head on January 1, 2019, compared to 750,000 as of January 1, 2018, and 710,000 as of January 1, 2017. All sheep were valued at $135,750,000 on January 1, 2019, compared with $138,750,000 as of January 1, 2018, and $129,220,000 as of January 1, 2017.

Breeding ewes one year old and over numbered 455,000 as of January 1, 2019; 465,000 as of January 1, 2018; and 440,000 as of January 1, 2017. Replacement lambs less than one year old totaled 100,000 head as

Hog Production 1960–2018

Year	Production (lbs.)	Avg. Price Per Cwt.	Gross Income
1960	288,844,000	$14.70	$44,634,000
1970	385,502,000	$22.50	$75,288,000
1980	315,827,000	$35.90	$111,700,000
1981	264,693,000	$41.70	$121,054,000
1982	205,656,000	$49.60	$112,726,000
1983	209,621,000	$45.20	$95,343,000
1984	189,620,000	$45.50	$95,657,000
1985	168,950,000	$43.40	$72,512,000
1986	176,660,000	$47.30	$82,885,000
1987	216,834,000	$50.60	$103,983,000
1988	236,658,000	$41.30	$100,029,000
1989	224,229,000	$39.90	$93,178,000
1990	196,225,000	$48.20	$92,222,000
1991	207,023,000	$45.10	$97,398,000
1992	217,554,000	$36.40	$79,436,000
1993	221,130,000	$39.90	$90,561,000
1994	224,397,000	$35.10	$78,394,000
1995	221,323,000	$35.50	$81,509,000
1996	204,476,000	$45.90	$94,962,000
1997	224,131,000	$47.40	$103,050,000
1998	271,444,000	$30.70	$86,349,000
1999	274,572,000	$27.50	$71,604,000
2000	328,732,000	$36.60	$115,105,000
2001	260,875,000	$39.10	$105,217,000
2002	223,441,000	$28.70	$67,255,000
2003	197,876,000	$33.60	$67,998,000
2004	202,199,000	$44.90	$90,349,000
2005	223,375,000	$45.40	$105,989,000
2006	257,644,000	$40.80	$108,844,000
2007	273,213,000	$39.70	$95,581,000
2008	328,356,000	$40.50	$143,249,000
2009	286,069,000	$37.60	$135,077,000
2010	149,934,000	$50.20	$96,676,000
2011	168,718,000	NA	$153,517,000
2012	414,904,000	NA	$288,652,000
2013	285,822,000	NA	$240,322,000
2014	305,146,000	NA	$248,928,000
2015	373,991,000	NA	$222,851,000
2016	369,354,000	NA	$193,529,000
2017	369,146,000	NA	$199,298,000
2018	445,348,000	NA	$232,243,000

NA = not available

Sources:"1985 Texas Livestock, Dairy and Poultry Statistics", USDA, Bulletin 235, June 1986, pp. 32, 46; 1991 "Texas Livestock Statistics", USDA,; "1993 Texas Livestock Statistics", Bulletin 252, Texas Agricultural Statistics Service, August 1994; "Texas Agricultural Facts, 2009", October, 2010; "Texas Ag Facts", various years. "Meat Animals - Prod., Disp., & Income", April 2018 and April 2019; (December 1 previous year); USDA/NASS Quick Stats. Numbers from previous years revised.

Sheep and Wool Production 1850–2019

Year	Sheep Number	Sheep Value	Wool Production (lbs)	Wool Value
1850	100,530	NA	131,917	NA
1860	753,363	NA	1,493,363	NA
1870	1,223,000	$2,079,000	NA	NA
1880	6,024,000	$12,048,000	NA	NA
1890	4,752,000	$7,128,000	NA	NA
1900	2,416,000	$4,590,000	9,630,000	NA
1910	1,909,000	$5,536,000	8,943,000	$1,699,170
1920	3,360,000	$33,600,000	22,813,000	$5,019,000
1930	6,304,000	$44,758,000	48,262,000	$10,135,000
1940	10,069,000	$49,413,000	79,900,000	$23,171,000
1950	6,756,000	$103,877,000	51,480,000	$32,947,000
1960	5,938,000	$85,801,000	51,980,000	$21,832,000
1970	3,708,000	$73,602,000	30,784,000	$11,082,000
1980	2,400,000	$138,000,000	18,300,000	$17,751,000
1981	2,360,000	$116,820,000	20,500,000	$24,600,000
1982	2,400,000	$100,800,000	19,300,000	$16,212,000
1983	2,225,000	$86,775,000	18,600,000	$15,438,000
1984	1,970,000	$76,830,000	17,500,000	$16,100,000
1985	1,930,000	$110,975,000	16,200,000	$13,284,000
1986	1,850,000	$107,300,000	16,400,000	$13,284,000
1987	2,050,000	$133,250,000	16,400,000	$19,844,000
1988	2,040,000	$155,040,000	18,200,000	$35,854,000
1989	1,870,000	$133,445,000	18,000,000	$27,180,000
1990	2,090,000	$133,760,000	17,400,000	$19,662,000
1991	2,000,000	$108,000,000	16,700,000	$13,861,000
1992	2,140,000	$111,280,000	17,600,000	$16,896,000
1993	2,040,000	$118,320,000	17,000,000	$11,050,000
1994	1,895,000	$106,120,000	14,840,000	$15,582,000
1995	1,700,000	$100,300,000	13,468,000	$15,488,000
1996	1,650,000	$108,900,000	9,900,000	$8,316,000
1997	1,400,000	$100,800,000	10,950,000	$11,607,000
1998	1,530,000	$122,400,000	9,230,000	$5,815,000
1999	1,350,000	$95,850,000	7,956,000	$3,898,000
2000	1,200,000	$94,800,000	7,506,000	$3,678,000
2001	1,150,000	$92,000,000	6,003,000	$3,122,000
2002	1,130,000	$88,140,000	5,950,000	$4,046,000
2003	1,040,000	$82,160,000	5,600,000	$5,040,000
2004	1,100,000	$105,600,000	5,600,000	$5,712,000
2005	1,070,000	$112,350,000	5,550,000	$5,328,000
2006	1,090,000	$124,260,000	4,900,000	$4,459,000
2007	1,050,000	$111,300,000	4,500,000	$5,445,000
2008	960,000	$97,920,000	4,200,000	$4,872,000
2009	870,000	$87,870,000	3,500,000	$3,640,000
2010	830,000	$83,000,000	3,450,000	$5,451,000
2011	850,000	$109,650,000	2,600,000	$5,746,000
2012	670,000	$102,510,000	2,100,000	$3,507,000
2013	700,000	$99,400,000	2,300,000	$4,048,000
2014	730,000	$118,990,000	2,100,000	$3,297,000
2015	720,000	$126,000,000	1,950,000	$3,198,000
2016	725,000	$131,950,000	1,700,000	$2,975,000
2017	700,000	$127,400,000	1,800,000	$2,934,000
2018	750,000	$138,750,000	1,760,000	$3,168,000
2019	750,000	$135,750,000	NA	NA

NA = not available

Sources: "1985 Texas Livestock, Dairy and Poultry Statistics", USDA Bulletin 235, June 1986. "Texas Agricultural Facts" Annual Summary, Crop and Livestock Reporting Service, various years, "1993 Texas Livestock Statistics", Texas Agricultural Statistics Service, Bulletin 252, August 1994; "Texas Agricultural Statistics, 2009", October 2010, "Texas Ag Fact", February and March 2011; Texas Sheep and Wool report, February 28, 2019, Agricultural Prices, February 28, 2017, NASS/TASS Quick Stats.

of January 1, 2019; 100,000 as of January 1, 2018; and 95,000 as of January 1, 2017. Sheep and lamb farms in Texas were estimated to be 14,672 as of January 1, 2017; compared to 10,674 in 2012.

Texas wool production in 2018 was 1.8 million pounds from 210,000 sheep. Value totaled $3.2 million or $1.80 per pound. This compared with 1.8 million pounds of wool from 240,000 sheep valued at $2.9 million or $1.63 per pound in 2017; and 1.8 million pounds from 260,000 sheep valued at $3.2 million or $1.75 per pound in 2016.

Most sheep and lambs in Texas are concentrated in the Edwards Plateau area of West Central Texas and nearby counties.

San Angelo has long been the largest sheep and wool market in the nation and the center for wool and mohair warehouses, scouring plants and slaughterhouses.

Poultry and Eggs

Poultry and eggs contribute about 11.8 percent of the total cash receipts of Texas farmers in 2017. On January 1, 2018, Texas ranked sixth among the states in broilers produced and fifth in eggs produced.

In 2017, cash receipts to Texas producers from the production of poultry and eggs totaled $2.7 billion. This compares with $2.3 billion in 2016 and $2.8 in 2015.

Broiler production in 2018 totaled 653.5 million birds, compared with 651.2 million in 2017 and 629.5 million in 2015.

Horses

Nationally, Texas ranks as one of the leading states in horse numbers and is the headquarters for many national horse organizations. The largest single breed registry in America, the American Quarter Horse Association, has its headquarters in Amarillo. The National Cutting Horse Association and the American Paint Horse Association are both located in Fort Worth. In addition to these national associations, Texas also has active state associations that include Palominos, Arabians, Thoroughbreds, Appaloosa, and ponies.

Horses are still used to support the state's giant beef cattle and sheep industries. However, the largest horse numbers within the state are near urban and suburban areas, where they are mostly used for recreation activities. Horses are most abundant in the heavily populated areas of the state. State participation activities consist of horse shows, trail rides, play days, rodeos, polo and horse racing. Residential subdivisions have been developed within the state to provide facilities for urban and suburban horse owners. ☆

Goats and Mohair 1900–2019

Year	Goats		Mohair	
	Number	Farm Value	Production (lbs)	Value
1900	627,000	$924,000	961,000	$268,000
1910	1,135,000	$2,514,000	1,998,000	$468,000
1920	1,753,000	$9,967,000	6,786,000	$1,816,000
1930	2,965,000	$14,528,000	14,800,000	$4,995,000
1940	3,300,000	$10,560,000	18,250,000	$9,308,000
1950	2,295,000	$13,082,000	12,643,000	$9,735,000
1960	3,339,000	$29,383,000	23,750,000	$21,375,000
1970	2,572,000	$19,033,000	17,985,000	$7,032,000
1980	1,400,000	$64,400,000	8,800,000	$30,800,000
1981	1,380,000	$53,130,000	10,100,000	$35,350,000
1982	1,410,000	$57,810,000	10,000,000	$25,500,000
1983	1,420,000	$53,250,000	10,600,000	$42,930,000
1984	1,450,000	$82,215,000	10,600,000	$48,160,000
1985	1,590,000	$76,797,000	13,300,000	$45,885,000
1986	1,770,000	$70,977,000	16,000,000	$40,160,000
1987	1,780,000	$82,592,000	16,200,000	$42,606,000
1988	1,800,000	$108,180,000	15,400,000	$29,876,000
1989	1,850,000	$100,270,000	15,400,000	$24,794,000
1990	1,900,000	$93,100,000	14,500,000	$13,775,000
1991	1,830,000	$73,200,000	14,800,000	$19,388,000
1992	2,000,000	$84,000,000	14,200,000	$12,354,000
1993	1,960,000	$84,280,000	13,490,000	$11,197,000
1994	1,960,000	$74,480,000	11,680,000	$30,602,000
1995	1,850,000	$81,400,000	11,319,000	$20,940,000
1996	1,900,000	$89,300,000	7,490,000	$14,606,000
1997	1,650,000	$70,950,000	6,384,000	$14,556,000
1998	1,400,000	$71,400,000	4,650,000	$12,044,000
1999	1,350,000	$71,550,000	2,550,000	$9,384,000
2000	1,300,000	$74,100,000	2,346,000	$10,088,000
2001	1,400,000	$105,000,000	1,716,000	$3,775,000
2002	1,250,000	$106,250,000	1,944,000	$3,110,400
2003	1,200,000	$110,400,000	1,680,000	$2,856,000
2004	1,200,000	$115,200,000	1,620,000	$3,402,000
2005	1,250,000	$138,430,000	1,250,000	$3,750,000
2006	1,284,000	$140,170,000	1,100,000	$4,400,000
2007	1,272,000	$150,800,000	960,000	$3,840,000
2008	1,185,000	$120,871,000	820,000	$3,116,000
2009	1,120,000	$129,920,000	700,000	$2,170,000
2010	1,110,000	$108,290,000	730,000	$3,066,000
2011	980,000	NA	530,000	$2,703,000
2012	905,000	NA	470,000	$2,256,000
2013	872,000	NA	490,000	$2,695,000
2014	906,000	NA	580,000	$3,654,000
2015	908,000	NA	480,000	$3,408,000
2016	865,000	NA	510,000	$3,060,000
2017	892,000	NA	470,000	$3,102,000
2018	869,000	NA	465,000	$3,348,000
2019	842,000	NA	NA	NA

NA = Not Available

Sources: ""1985 Texas Livestock, Dairy and Poultry Statistics", USDA Bulletin 235, June 1986. "Texas Agricultural Facts", Crop and Livestock Reporting Service, various years; "1993 Texas Livestock Statistics", Texas Agricultural Statistics Service, Bulletin 252, August 1994; "Texas Agricultural Statistics, 2009", October 2010; "Texas Ag Facts", February and March 2011. USDA/TASS Texas Goat Inventory, February 28, 2019.

Located in the state's southernmost region, the **Texas Tropical Trail Region** covers **20 counties**, **23,000 square miles**, and is home to **1.7 million residents**. For over **200 miles** in both directions, the Tropical Trail borders the nation of Mexico and the Gulf of Mexico. The region boasts a variety of experiences including diverse cuisine, music, nature, history, culture, and architecture. Historic sites include battlegrounds, architecture, museums, lighthouses and landmarks. For the adventurous, the region offers beachcombing, hiking, hunting, camping, golfing, boating, fishing, and a wide variety of water sports. Nature lovers can take in birding, wildlife preserves, ranches, sanctuaries, and wetlands. And the mild weather is perfect year-round for multicultural and historic events and festivals.

TEXAS TROPICAL TRAIL

TEXAS HISTORICAL COMMISSION
TEXAS HERITAGE TRAILS PROGRAM

VISIT: https://texastropicaltrail.com/ & GO!

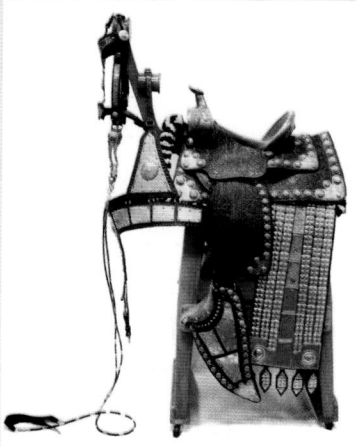

Western Treasures

★ Fine Western Art
★ Antique Western photos
★ Antique Bits & Spurs
★ Saddles
★ Antique American Indian Beadwork & Artifacts

"All things West of the Pecos"

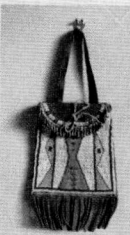

www.western-treasures.com   info@western-treasures.com

TEXAS ALMANAC ONLINE

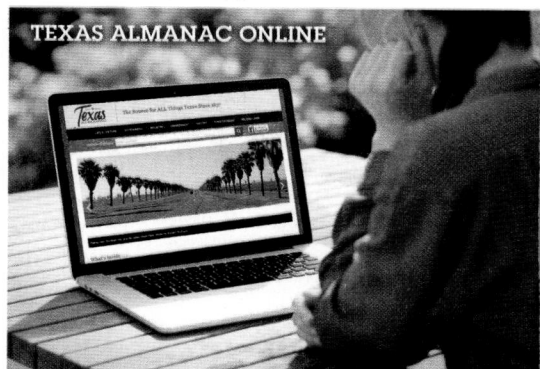

On the Texas Almanac website you'll find a searchable town database, featured articles searchable archive of Texas Almanacs dating back to the very first edition, published in 1857., more pictures, and a FREE electronic version of the Texas Almanac 2020-2021.

You can even adopt your favorite town or county! The Great Texas Land Rush gives you a place to show your appreciation for Texas by leaving a special message on our site.

EST 1857

Texas ALMANAC

VISIT US AT TEXASALMANAC.COM

APPENDIX

Bluebonnets along the road to Enchanted Rock.
Photo by TimothyJ (CC).

Obituaries: July 2017 – July 2019

Allred, Sammy, 84; nationally known as one of the Geezinslaw Brothers (with Dewayne Smith) from gigs starting on Arthur Godfrey's radio program to later appearances on late-night television talk shows; Austin humorist, country singer, and a deejay for more than 30 years; Austin native; in Austin, May 10, 2018.

Artis, Orsten, 74; the 6-foot-1 co-captain of the Texas Western (now the University of Texas at El Paso) basketball team; in 1966 they were the first team of African-American starters to win the NCAA national championship, defeating the University of Kentucky; the story was portrayed in the 2006 film *Glory Road;* born in Gary, Ind., where he had a long career as a police detective; in Merrillville, Ind., Dec. 26, 2017.

Avery, James, 96; creator of the jewelry empire that began as a one-man operation in Kerrville in 1954; at his death the company had 80 stores across the South; Wisconsin native's service at Lackland Air Force Base in San Antonio during World War II brought him to settle in the Hill Country a few years later; in Boerne, April 30, 2018.

Bean, Alan, 86; in November 1969 became fourth person to walk on the moon; returned to space in July 1973 as commander of the flight to the orbiting space research station Skylab; native of Wheeler in the Panhandle, grew up in Fort Worth, University of Texas 1955; he left NASA in 1981 to became a full-time artist; in Houston, May 26, 2018

Bode, Elroy, 86; the author of ten books about El Paso and the Hill Country was born in Kerrville; after serving as an officer in the Air Force he moved in 1958 to El Paso, a city he came to love and where he taught high school creative writing and English for 30 years; his work also appeared in the *Southwest Review*, the *Texas Observer*, and other publications; at hims home in El Paso, Sept. 10, 2017.

Brazelton, T. Berry, 99; Waco native was nationally known pediatrician and best-selling author of books on childhood development; awarded the Presidential Citizens Medal in 2013; maintained a farm and historical home in Marlin that he inherited from his family; on Cape Cod, Mass., March 13, 2018.

Bush, Barbara, 92; born Barbara Pierce in New York, she became only the second woman (after Abigail Adams) to be both the wife and the mother of U.S. presidents; she and husband George H.W. (with little George W.) moved to Odessa in 1949, then Midland, and to Houston in 1959; in Houston, April 17, 2018.

Bush, George H.W., 94; son of U.S. Sen. Prescott Bush of Connecticut, became 41st president of the United States in 1989 after serving in numerous government positions including vice president; in 1949 moved his young family to West Texas to work in the oil business; Republican elected to Congress from Houston in 1966; in Houston, Nov. 30, 2018, just months after the death of his wife.

Caldwell, Neil, 88; state legislator from Brazoria County (1960-1977) was one of the "Dirty Thirty", the bipartisan group that exposed corruption in the state government in the 1970s; a progressive described as an intellectual and humorist; former state artist; served as district judge; received law degree from the University of Texas in 1957; at his home near Angleton, Feb. 6, 2018.

Cavazos, Richard, 88; the first Hispanic four-star general in the U.S. Army; completed the ROTC program at Texas Tech University in 1951; awarded the Distinguished Service Cross in both Korea and Vietnam; born in Kingsville the son of a King Ranch cowhand; in San Antonio, Oct. 29, 2017.

Cavender, James, 87; founder of the western wear store; opened his first clothing store in Pittsburg in East Texas in 1965; the Tyler-based company grew to 80 stores in 12 states; in Tyler, May 29, 2018.

Clements, Rita, 86; former Texas First Lady, wife of Gov. Bill Clements (1979-1983 and 1987-1991); active in Republican politics beginning in 1952 volunteering in the presidential campaign of Dwight Eisenhower; Kansas native, her family moved to Brady when she was 10; graduate of Hockaday School in Dallas 1949; University of Texas 1953; on the UT board of regents from 1996-2007; in Dallas, Jan. 6, 2018.

Frost, Tom, 90; headed for 35 years Frost Bank founded by his great-grandfather in San Antonio in 1868; civic leader worked to develop the city's medical center, HemisFair '68, and bring the NBA Spurs to town; in San Antonio, Aug. 10, 2018.

Garcia, Gus, 84; longtime Austin political leader who became the city's first elected Hispanic mayor in 2001; also served on the city council, and the first Hispanic elected to the Austin school board in 1972, where he later served as president; born in Zapata, raised in Laredo; Army veteran, graduate of the University of Texas 1959; in Austin, Dec. 17, 2018.

Garrido, Augie, 79; baseball coach at the University of Texas at Austin for 20 years where he led the Longhorns to national championships in 2002 and 2005; with stints as coach at California State-Fullerton and other schools he retired as the coach with the most wins in college baseball history, 1,975; in Newport Beach, Calif., March 15, 2018.

Gerron, Peggy Sue, 78; the inspiration for the 1957 Buddy Holly hit "Peggy Sue" when she was dating a fellow Crickets musician; she became a dental assistant in California; returned to Lubbock in 1995 to care for her mother; in Lubbock, Oct. 1, 2018.

Graham, Don, 79; University of Texas professor considered the leading scholar on Texas literature and culture; author of a biography of World War II hero Audie Murphy and books on how Hollywood sees Texas, including the 2018 book *Giant* about the making of the 1956 film in Marfa; native of Lucas, raised in McKinney and Carrollton; graduate of the University of North Texas; PhD 1971 from UT; in Austin, June 22, 2019.

Dr. T. Berry Brazelton, left.. Photo by John Mathew Smith (CC).

President George H.W. Bush and Barbara Bush, right, in the late 1980s. Photo by Jane Boursaw (CC).

John Hillerman, far left. CBS Television photo (CC).

Katherine Helmond, left. Photo by Alan Light (CC).

Dorothy Malone, right. ABC Television photo (CC).

Hale, DeWitt, 100; served in the legislature for 28 years from the 1950s to the 1970s, spearheading passage of bills allowing mixed bar drinks and women serving on juries; first elected in 1938 at age 21 while still a student at the University of Texas; Caddo Mills native grew up in Farmersville and moved to Corpus Christi after serving in World War II; in Austin, Feb. 20, 2018.

Hall, Ralph, 95; elected to Congress 17 times, first as a Democrat and later as a Republican, becoming the oldest ever to serve in the U.S. House of Representatives, until 2014; born in Fate, served as a Navy pilot in World War II, earned a law degree at Southern Methodist Univerisity in 1951; at his home in Rockwall, March 7, 2019.

Hardin, Ty, 87; TV western star in the series *Bronco*, which ran in the late 1950s and early 1960s; Manhattan native was brought at age 2 to Houston; he graduated from Houston's Lamar High School, attended Blinn College on a football scholarship, served in the Army before ending up playing tight end for Bear Bryant at Texas A&M University; in Huntington Beach, Calif., Aug. 3, 2017.

Helmond, Katherine, 89; actress best known for her roles on the television series *Soap* (1977-1981) and *Who's the Boss?* (1984-1992); received seven Emmy nominations and won two Golden Globes; worked in movies and on Broadway; born in Galveston where her father was a firefighter; after attending Ball High School she worked in theater in Houston and Dallas before moving to New York; at her home in Los Angeles, Feb. 23, 2019.

Hillerman, John, 84; *Magnum, P.I.'s* uptight butler Higgins, the role the Denison native played with a British accent, and which brought him an Emmy and a Golden Globe; other TV roles included *Ellery Queen*, *The Betty White Show*, and *One Day at a Time*; in Houston, Nov. 9, 2017.

Hooper, Tobe, 74; director of the 1974 cult horror film *The Texas Chain Saw Massacre*; native of Austin also directed the 1987 sequel with Dennis Hopper, *Poltergeist*, in 1982 with Steve Spielberg, and worked on other films, and various television programs; in Los Angeles, Aug. 26, 2017.

Jenkins, Dan, 90; sportswriter for nearly 25 years for *Sports Illustrated* and author of *Semi-Tough*, the 1972 novel about pro football culture, also wrote *Baja Oklahoma* and others; avid golfer; first wrote on sports with fellow student Bud Shrake at Fort Worth Paschal High School; graduate of Texas Christian University; started in professional journalism at the *Fort Worth Press* in the 1950s; in Fort Worth, March 7, 2019.

Jones, Delwin, 94; cotton farmer who represented the Lubbock area in the state House of Representatives from 1964-1972 as a Democrat and from 1989-2011 as a Republican; played key role in bringing a medical school and law school to Texas Tech University where he also served on the board of regents; in Lubbock, July 25, 2018.

Kelleher, Herb, 87; Southwest Airlines co-founder (with Rollin King) in 1967; years of legal battles from competing airlines delayed operations of the low-fare carrier

until 1971 when it began with flights between Dallas, Houston, and San Antonio; company grew to be a major national carrier with more than 120 million passengers a year; New Jersey native moved his law practice to San Antonio in 1961; in Dallas, Jan. 3, 2019.

Kinchlow, Ben, 82; co-host with Pat Robertson of the *700 Club* on the Christian Broadcasting Network from 1975-1988 and 1992-1996; born in Uvalde where he went to Southwest Texas Junior College; served in the Air Force for 13 years; ordained in the African Methodist Episcopal Church in 1971; conducted a youth ministry in Killeen before joining the television program; in Virginia, July 18, 2019.

Kraft, Christopher, 95; the face and voice of NASA's mission control during the early space flights, including the first moon landing in 1969; as the ground commander in Houston he explained what was happening on the flights at news conferences seen around the world; in Houston, July 22, 2019, two days after the 50th anniversary of Apollo 11.

Liberto, Frank, 84; his family's concession-supply company came up with the cheese sauce that allowed for the nation's first "concession nachos" to be introduced in 1976 at a Texas Ranger baseball game; native of San Antonio, Central Catholic High School, St. Mary's University 1955; in San Antonio, Nov. 5, 2017.

Lindsey, Roland, 78; barbecue icon founded Bodacious Bar-B-Q in Longview in 1968; the company eventually expanded to 22 locations statewide; grew up in Dallas where he learned to barbecue at his father's cafe; in Longview, Sept. 20, 2018.

Love, Dan, 88; Austin television and radio broadcaster in the 1950s and 1960s on KTBC and KHFI; served on the Austin city council in the 1970s; born Marvin Love in Dallas; Sunset High School 1947, University of Texas 1952; in Elgin, Oct. 13, 2017.

Malone, Dorothy, 93; actress discovered by a Hollywood talent agent in a 1943 production at Southern Methodist University; won an Academy Award for the 1956 film *Written on the Wind*; best known as a star in the 1960s television series *Peyton Place*; in Dallas where she had lived since 1971, Jan. 19, 2018.

Mann, Carol, 77; star of the Ladies Professional Golf Association in the 1960s and 1970s; served as the LPGA president; retired from golf in 1981 to become a television commentator; elected to the Texas Golf Hall of Fame in 2010; at her home in The Woodlands, May 20, 2018.

McCurdy, Dan, 76; broadcaster and advertising director who was co-creator of the slogan "Oh Thank Heaven for 7-Eleven" in 1967; also helped introduce the Slurpee frozen drink; began in radio in high school in Stamford; retired to Sherman; in Dallas, Feb. 5, 2018.

McFaddin, Jean, 75; Lufkin native credited with making the Macy's Thanksgiving Day parade a supreme New York and national event; was events planner for Macy's for 24 years; graduate of Lufkin High School 1960, University of Texas in 1964, and master's in theater production in 1966; in New York, April 17, 2018.

McNair, Bob, 81; the energy mogul who brought the NFL back to Houston in 1999 when he was awarded the franchise that would become the Texans; raised in North Carolina, moved to Houston in 1960 where his philanthropic contributions included $100 million to Baylor College of Medicine and $1 million each for relief after hurricanes Katrina and Harvey; in Houston, Nov. 23, 2018.

Mendelsohn, John, 82; led MD Anderson Cancer Center to national prominence as president from 1996 to 2011; under his tenure the center expanded facilities, doubled in staff and patients, and annual revenues quadrupled to $3.1 billion as it became recognized as the nation's top cancer hospital; at his Houston home, Jan. 7, 2019.

Merryman, Jerry, 86; co-inventor of the pocket calculator; at Texas Instruments starting in 1965, he along with Jack Kilby and James Van Tassel created the prototype now in the Smithsonian Institution; the team also pioneered rechargeable batteries and thermal printing; native of Hearne, learned electronics as a boy reading a book called *Radio Engineering*, attended Texas A&M University; in Dallas, Feb. 27, 2019.

Moon, Wally, 87; baseball and basketball star at Texas A&M University 1949-1950; Arkansas native was National League rookie of the year for the St. Louis Cardinals in 1954, helped lead the Los Angeles Dodgers to World Series titles in 1959, 1963, and 1965; retired to Bryan where he died Feb. 9, 2018.

Nobis, Tommy, 74; University of Texas football great on the Longhorns' 1963 national championship team, played linebacker for the Atlanta Falcons in the NFL; native of San Antonio where he attended Thomas Jefferson High School; in suburban Atlanta, Ga., Dec. 13, 2017.

Overton, Richard, 112; the nation's oldest World War II veteran and believed to be the oldest living man in the United States; born in Bastrop County in 1906; enlisted in the Army in September 1940 and served in the South Pacific with the all-black 1887th Engineer Aviation Battalion; in Austin, Dec. 27, 2018.

Perot, Ross, 89; Texarkana native and computer services billionaire who ran for president as an independent in 1992, receiving almost 19 percent of the vote – he ran less successfully in 1996 – advocating a balanced budget; after graduating from the U.S. Naval Academy in 1953, he started as a salesman for IBM; founded Electronic Data Systems in 1962; philanthropist for education and financier of missions to aid Americans held in Vietnam and Iran; in Dallas, July 9, 2019.

Powers, Bill, 72; president of the University of Texas for almost ten years, until 2015; raised $3.1 billion, overhauled the undergraduate curriculum, launched the Longhorn (TV) Network, and helped establish the Dell Medical School at UT; came to teach at the UT law school in 1977, later served as dean; in Austin, March 10, 2019.

Priest, Micael, 66; artist of the era of Armadillo World Headquarters when he created the widely recognized posters for Austin's music events of the time; raised partly in Bedford, first moved to Austin in 1969; attended UT-Austin and UT-Arlington; in Austin, Sept. 11, 2018.

Primas, Emma, 112; one of the oldest Texans, born in Maynard, San Jacinto County, in 1905; owned a neighborhood grocery in northeast Houston for many years; spent her last years in Fort Bend County; in Houston, Jan. 30, 2018.

Roberts, Hisako Tsuchiyama, 104; co-founder with her husband of the renowned Salt Lick in Driftwood; met Thurman Roberts in her native Hawaii during World War II and together they opened the barbecue restaurant in 1967; she held a master's degree in psychology from the University of California, Los Angeles; in Austin, Jan. 18, 2018.

Robinson, Frank, 83; Beaumont native became the first African-American manager in major league baseball in 1975 with the Cleveland Indians; raised in California, he was known as a slugger when he played for 21 seasons mostly for the Cincinnati Reds and Baltimore Orioles; the only player to win the MVP title in both leagues; at his Los Angeles home, Feb. 7, 2019.

Salling, Mark, 35; actor who played Puck on the television series *Glee* from 2008 to 2013; native of Dallas; 2001 graduate of Lake Highlands High School where he was a member of the wrestling team; in Los Angeles, Jan. 30, 2018, an apparent suicide.

Schmidt, Harvey, 88; co-creator of *The Fantasticks*, the romance that opened Off-Broadway in 1960 and became the world's longest-running musical; he and collaborator Tom Jones were students at the University of Texas at Austin when Jones wrote the book and lyrics and Schmidt wrote the music, including "Try to Remember"; born in Dallas; in Tomball, Feb. 28, 2018.

Schmidt, Rick, 73; owner of the well-known Kreuz Market in Lockhart where he served barbecue without forks or sauce; in 2011 he sold the business to his son; Rick moved the market from downtown in 1999 to a new building down the road after a well-publicized dispute with his sister, the feud ended years later with a joint barbecue venture in Bee Cave; Feb. 11, 2019.

Schwartz, A.R. "Babe", 92; Democratic state senator from Galveston from 1960 until 1981, where he was leader of liberal causes; championed environmental protections and public access to Texas beaches; graduate of Galveston Ball High School, Texas A&M University, and UT law school; at his home in Houston, Aug. 10, 2018.

Seldin, Donald W., 97; Brooklyn native came to Dallas in 1951 to head the University of Texas Southwestern Medical Center department of internal medicine; served 36 years guiding Southwestern into a national leader in biomedicine; faculty would include six Nobel laureates; in Dallas, April 25, 2018.

Shearer, William, 81; doctor to Houston's famed "Bubble Boy" David Vetter who because of an immune disorder

Ross Perot. U.S. Department of Veterans Affairs photo..

Hisako Tsuchiyama Roberts, above, co-founder of the Salt Lick in Driftwood. Roberts Family photo.

Mark Salling. Photo by Kristin Dos Santos (CC).

Gov. Mark White, far left. Photo by Bill Malone for Texas State Archives (CC).

Frank Robinson, left, Beaumont native. Sporting News archives (CC).

Rip Torn, right. Photo by Alan LIght (CC).

was isolated to a plastic bubble from 1978 to 1984 when he died; Shearer was one of the nation's leading immunologists at Baylor College of Medicine and Texas Children's Hospital for 40 years; in Houston, Oct. 9, 2018.

Shivers, R.A. "Bud", 72; investor and son of Gov. Allan Shivers was an influential backer of George W. Bush in Texas politics and a philanthropist, assisting Austin's Seton hospital by setting up a fund for financial support; served on the boards of St. Edward's University in Austin and the University of St. Thomas in Houston; in Austin, Jan. 8, 2019.

Smith, Liz, 94; Fort Worth native whose gossip columns ran in various New York newspapers for 33 years; attended Hardin-Simmons University in Abilene before completing a degree in journalism at the University of Texas in Austin in 1949; besides her newspaper columns she also served as a commentator for the local Fox TV channel in New York and E! Entertainment Television; in New York, Nov. 12, 2017.

Tatro, Amber, 42; center of the 1984 Supreme Court case that gave rights to disabled students; the unanimous decision said the Irving school district should provide certain health care measures that did not required a doctor; in Dallas, Aug. 8, 2018, from complications of infections resulting from her congenital spinal defect.

Taylor, Lonn, 79; Smithsonian Institution historian beginning in 1984, retiring in 2002 to Fort Davis; author of a book on the Star-Spangled Banner; director (1970-1977) of the Winedale Historical Complex near Round Top; also worked on the 1968 HemisFair and with the Dallas Historical Society and Museum of New Mexico; attended high school in Fort Worth; graduate of Texas Christian University; in Fort Davis, June 26, 2019.

Tittle, Y.A., 90; famed New York Giants quarterback was born Yelberton Abraham Tittle Jr. in Marshall where he attended high school before playing football at Louisiana State University 1944-1947; he began pro football with the old Baltimore Colts of the All-America Football Conference and then played for the San Francisco 49ers, who traded him to New York in 1961; in Stanford, Calif., Oct. 8, 2017.

Torn, Rip, 88; actor born in Temple; Taylor (Tx.) High School Class of 1948; studied agriculture at Texas A&M University, then switched to drama at the University of Texas; after service in the U.S. Army he moved to Hollywood; nominated for an Oscar in 1984; received an Emmy in 1996 as supporting actor in the HBO series *The Larry Sanders Show*; also appeared on Broadway; at his home in Lakeville, Conn., July 9, 2019.

Turman, Jimmy, 91; one-term speaker of the state House of Representatives during the establishment of the state sales tax in 1961-1962; Fannin County native; teacher with degrees from what is now Texas A&M University-Commerce and a Ph.D. from the University of Texas in Austin in 1957; in Austin, Feb. 13, 2019.

Uher, Tom, 81; Democratic legislator served for 35 years representing Brazoria, Matagorda, and Wharton coun-

ties; focused on education issues, also authored bill to allow direct access to MD Anderson cancer center without doctor referral; law degree from the University of Texas in 1962; in his native Bay City, March 9, 2019.

Watson, Murray Jr., 86; prominent Democratic legislator from 1957 to 1973 serving from his native McLennan County; champion of higher education who as state senator was the proponent for establishing the Texas State Technical College, which now has 10 campuses around the state; graduate of Baylor University; in Waco, July 24, 2018.

Watson, W. Marvin, 93; headed the White House staff of Lyndon B. Johnson from 1965 until 1968, when he was appointed U.S. postmaster general, then a Cabinet-level position; a Johnson ally since 1948 when he saw LBJ campaigning in Waco, where Watson was attending Baylor University; native of Oakhurst, San Jacinto County; in The Woodlands, Nov. 26, 2017.

Wedgeworth, Ann, 83; actress in film and on Broadway, won a Tony Award for her role in Neil Simon's *Chapter Two*; was the flirty divorcee on the TV series *Three's Company*; born in Abilene where her father was an educator; graduate of Southern Methodist University; in New Jersey, Nov. 16, 2017.

White, Mark, 77; Democratic governor of Texas, 1983-1987, when he championed education reform including the "no pass, no play" rule for high school athletes and limiting class size in elementary schools; Henderson native received his bachelor's and law degrees from Baylor University, he also served as Texas secretary of state and attorney general; in Houston, Aug. 5, 2017.

Whittier, Julius, 68; first black football letterman at the University of Texas; the UT board of regents had dropped its ban on black players in 1963, but not until 1970 did Whittier become the first to make varsity; San Antonio Highlands High School graduate 1969; earned a law degree at UT and was a longtime prosecutor in Dallas; in Dallas, Sept. 25, 2018.

Williams, Don, 78; country singer whose 1980 hit "I Believe in You" topped the country charts and crossed over to the pop Top 40; born in Floydada the son of a mechanic who moved frequently; eventually the singer graduated from Gregory-Portland High School in 1958; his popularity was international, in Latin America, Africa, and especially England where *County Music People* magazine named him artist of the decade in 1980; in Mobile, Ala., Sept. 8, 2017.

Wittliff, Bill, 79; writer, filmmaker, and photographer who adapted *Lonesome Dove* into the hit 1989 mini-series; wrote and directed the 1986 film *Red Headed Stranger*, and wrote the screenplay for the 1981 film *Raggedy Man*; he and his wife published Texas authors at their Encino Press and founded the Southwestern Writers Collection at Texas State University in San Marcos; native of Taft, grew up in Edna and Gregory; graduated from the University of Texas in 1963; at his home in Austin, June 9, 2019. ☆

Texas Almanac Pronunciation Guide

Texas' rich cultural diversity is reflected nowhere better than in the names of places. Standard pronunciation is used in many cases, but purely colloquial pronunciation often is used, too.

In the late 1940s, George Mitchel Stokes, a graduate student at Baylor University, developed a list of pronunciations of 2,300 place names across the state. Stokes earned his doctorate and eventually was the director of the speech division in the communications studies department at Baylor University. He retired in 1983.

In the following list based on Stokes longer list, pronunciation is by respelling and diacritical marking. Respelling is employed as follows: "ah" as in the exclamation, ah, or the "o" in tot; "ee" as in meet; "oo" as in moot; "yoo" as in use; "ow" as in cow; "oi" as in oil; "uh" as in mud.

Note that ah, uh and the apostrophe(') are used for varying degrees of neutral vowel sounds, the apostrophe being used where the vowel is barely sounded. Diacritical markings are used as follows: bāle, băd, lĕt, rīse, rĭll, ōak, brōōd, fŏŏt.

The stressed syllable is capitalized. Secondary stress is indicated by an underline as in Atascosa — ăt uhs KŌ suh.

A

Abbott — Ă buht
Abernathy — Ă ber nă thĭ
Abilene — ĂB uh leen
Acala — uh KĂ luh
Ackerly — ĂK er lĭ
Acme — ĂK mĭ
Acton — ĂK t'n
Acuff — Ă kuhf
Adamsville — Ă d'mz vĭl
Addicks — Ă dĭks
Addielou — ă dĭ LŌŌ
Addison — A di s'n
Adkins — ĂT kĭnz
Adrian — Ā drĭ uhn
Afton — ĀF t'n
Agua Dulce — ah wuh DŌŌL sĭ
Agua Nueva — ah wuh nyōō Ā vuh
Aiken — Ā kĭn
Alamo — ĂL uh mō
Alamo Heights — ăl uh mō HĪTS
Alanreed — ĂL uhn reed
Alba — ĂL buh
Albany — AWL buh nĭ
Albert — ĂL bert
Aledo — uh LEE dō
Alexander — ĕl ĭg ZĂN der
Alfred — ĂL frĕd
Algoa — ăl GŌ uh
Alice — Ă lĭs
Alief — Ā leef
Allen — Ă lĭn
Allenfarm — ălĭn FAHRM
Alleyton — Ă lĭ t'n
Allison — ĂL uh s'n
Alma — AHL muh
Alpine — ĂL pīn
Altair — awl TĂR
Alto — ĂL tō
Altoga — ăl TŌ guh
Alvarado — ăl vuh RĂ dō
Alvin — ĂL vĭn
Alvord — ĂL vord
Amarillo — ăm uh RĬL ō
Amherst — AM herst
Ammannsville — ĂM 'nz vĭl

Anahuac — ĂN uh wăk
Anderson — ĂN der s'n
Andice — ĂN dĭs
Andrews — ĂN drōōz
Angelina — ăn juh LEE nuh
Angleton — ĂNG g'l t'n
Anna — ĂN uh
Annona — ă NŌ nuh
Anson — ĂN s'n
Antelope — ĂNT uh lōp
Anton — ĂNT n
Appleby — Ă p'l bĭ
Apple Springs — ă p'l SPRĬNGZ
Aquilla — uh KWĬL uh
Aransas — uh RĂN zuhs
Aransas Pass — uh răn zuhs PĂS
Arbala — ahr BĂ luh
Arcadia — ahr KĂ dĭ uh
Archer — AHR cher
Archer City — ahr cher SĬT ĭ
Arcola — ahr KŌ luh
Argo — AHR gō
Argyle — ahr GĪL
Arlington — AHR lĭng t'n
Arneckeville — AHR nĭ kĭ vĭl
Arnett — AHR nĭt
Arp — ahrp
Artesia Wells — ahr tee zh' WĔLZ
Arthur City — ahr ther SĬT ĭ
Asherton — ĂSH er t'n
Aspermont — ĂS per mahnt
Atascosa — ăt uhs KŌ suh
Athens — Ă thĕnz
Atlanta — ăt LĂN tuh
Atlas — ĂT l's
Attoyac — AT uh yăk
Aubrey — AW brĭ
Augusta — aw GUHS tuh
Austin — AWS t'n
Austonio — aws TŌ nĭ ō
Austwell — AWS wĕl
Avalon — ĂV uhl n
Avery — Ā vuh rĭ
Avinger — Ă vĭn jer
Avoca — uh VŌ kuh
Axtell — ĂKS t'l
Azle — Ā z'l

B

Bagwell — BĂG w'l
Bailey — BĀ lĭ
Baileyboro — BĀ lĭ ber ruh
Baileyville — BĀ lĭ vĭl
Baird — bärd
Bakersfield — BĀ kers feeld
Balch Springs — bawlch or bawlk SPRĬNGZ
Ballinger — BĂL ĭn jer
Balmorhea — băl muh RĀ
Bandera — băn DĔR uh
Bangs — băngz
Banquete — băn KĔ tĭ
Barclay — BAHRK lĭ
Bardwell — BAHRD w'l
Barker — BAHR ker
Barksdale — BAHRKS dāl
Barnhart — BAHRN hahrt
Barnum — BAHR n'm
Barry — BĂ rĭ
Barstow — BAHRS tō
Bartlett — BAHRT lĭt
Bassett — BĂ sĭt
Bastrop — BĂS trahp
Batesville — BĀTS v'l
Batson — BĂT s'n
Baxter — BĂKS ter
Bay City — ba SĬT ĭ
Baylor — BĀ ler
Bayside — BĀ sīd
Baytown — BĀ town
Beasley — BEEZ lĭ
Beaukiss — bō KĬS
Beaumont — BŌ mahnt
Bebe — bee bee
Beckville — BĔK v'l
Becton — BĔK t'n
Bedias — BEE dīs
Bee — bee
Beehouse — BEE hows
Beeville — BEE vĭl
Belcherville — BĔL cher vĭl
Bell — bĕl
Bellaire — bĕl ĂR
Bellevue — BĔL vyōō

Bellmead — bĕl MEED
Bells — bĕlz
Bellville — BĔL vĭl
Belmont — BĔL mahnt
Belton — BĔL t'n
Ben Arnold — bĕn AHR n'ld
Benavides — <u>bĕn</u> uh VEE d's
Ben Bolt — bĕn BŌLT
Benbrook — BĬN brŏŏk
Benchley — BĔNCH lĭ
Bend — bĕnd
Ben Franklin — bĕn FRĂNGk lĭn
Ben Hur — bĕn HER
Benjamin — BĔN juh m'n
Bennett — BĔN ĭt
Bentonville — BĔNT n vĭl
Ben Wheeler — bĭn HWEE ler
Berclair — ber KLĂR
Bertram — BERT r'm
Bessmay — bĕs MĂ
Best — bĕst
Bettie — BĔT ĭ
Bexar — BA är or băr
Beyersville — BĬRZ vĭl
Biardstown — BĂRDZ t'n
Bigfoot — BĬG fŏŏt
Big Lake — bĭg LĂK
Big Sandy — bĭg SĂN dĭ
Big Spring — bĭg SPRĬNG
Big Wells — bĭg WĔLZ
Birdville — BERD vĭl
Birome — bĭ RŌM
Birthright — BERTH rĭt
Bishop — BĬ sh'p
Bivins — BĬ vĭnz
Black — blăk
Blackfoot — BLĂK fŏŏt
Blackwell — BLĂK w'l
Blair — blăr
Blanchard — BLĂN cherd
Blanco — BLĂNG kō
Blanket — BLĂNG kĭt
Bleakwood — BLEEK wŏŏd
Bledsoe — BLĔD sō
Blessing — BLĔ sĭng
Blewett — BLŌŌ ĭt
Blooming Grove — <u>blŏŏ</u> mĭng
    GRŌV
Bloomington — BLŌŌM ĭng t'n
Blossom — BLAH s'm
Blue Grove — blŏŏ GRŌV
Blue Ridge — blŏŏ RĬJ
Bluff Dale — BLUHF dāl
Bluffton — BLUHF t'n
Blum — bluhm
Boerne — BER nĭ
Bogata — buh GŌ duh
Boling — BŌL ĭng
Bolivar — BAH lĭ ver
Bomarton — BŌ mer t'n
Bonham — BAH n'm
Bonita — bō NEE tuh
Bonney — BAH nĭ
Bonus — BŌ n's
Bon Wier — bahn WEER

Booker — BŎŎ ker
Boonsville — BŎŎNZ vĭl
Booth — bŏŏth
Borden — BAWRD n
Borger — BŎR ger
Bosque — BAHS kĭ
Boston — BAWS t'n
Bovina — bō VEE nuh
Bowie — BŎŎ Ĭ
Boxelder — bahks ĔL der
Boyce — bawĭs
Boyd — boĭd
Brachfield — BRĂCH feeld
Bracken — BRĂ kĭn
Brackettville — BRĂ kĭt vĭl
Bradford — BRĂD ferd
Bradshaw — BRĂD shaw
Brady — BRĂ dĭ
Brandon — BRĂN d'n
Brashear — bruh SHĬR
Brazoria — bruh ZŌ rĭ uh
Brazos — BRĂZ uhs
Breckenridge — BRĔK uhn rĭj
Bremond — <u>bree</u> MAHND
Brenham — BRĔ n'm
Brewster — BRŎŎ ster
Brice — brĭs
Bridgeport — BRĬJ pŏrt
Briggs — brĭgz
Briscoe — BRĬS kō
Britton — BRĬT n
Broaddus — BRAW d's
Brock — brahk
Bronson — BRAHN s'n
Bronte — brahnt
Brookeland — BRŎŎK l'nd
Brookesmith — BRŎŎK smith
Brooks — brŏŏks
Brookshire — BRŎŎK sher
Brookston — BRŎŎKS t'n
Brown — brown
Browndel — brown DĔL
Brownfield — BROWN feeld
Brownsboro — BROWNZ <u>buh</u> ruh
Brownsville — BROWNZ vĭl
Brownwood — BROWN wŏŏd
Bruceville — BRŎŎS v'l
Brundage — BRUHN dĭj
Bruni — BRŎŎ nĭ
Brushy Creek — bruh shĭ KREEK
Bryan — BRĬ uhn
Bryans Mill — brī 'nz MĬL
Bryarly — BRĬ er lĭ
Bryson — BRĬ s'n
Buchanan Dam — buhk <u>hăn</u> uhn
    DĂM
Buckholts — BUHK hōlts
Buckhorn — BUHK hawrn
Buda — BYŎŎ duh
Buena Vista — <u>bwā</u> nuh VEES tuh
Buffalo — BUHF uh lō
Buffalo Gap — <u>buhf</u> uh lō GĂP
Buffalo Springs — <u>buhf</u> uh lō
    SPRĬNGZ
Bula — BYŎŎ luh

Bullard — BŎŎL erd
Bulverde — bŏŏl VER dĭ
Buna — BYŎŎ nuh
Burkburnett — <u>berk</u> ber NET
Burkett — BER kĭt
Burkeville — BERK vĭl
Burleson — BER luh s'n
Burlington — BER lĭng t'n
Burnet — BER nĕt
Burton — BERT n
Bushland — BŎŎSH l'nd
Bustamante — <u>buhs</u> tuh MAHN tĭ
Butler — BUHT ler
Byers — BĬ erz
Bynum — BĬ n'm
Byrd — berd

C

Cactus — KĂK t's
Caddo Mills — <u>kă</u> dō MĬLZ
Calallen — kăl ĂL ĭn
Calaveras — kăl uh VĔR's
Caldwell — KAHL wĕl
Calhoun — kăl HŎŎN
Call — kawl
Calliham — KĂL uh hăm
Callisburg — KĂ lĭs berg
Call Junction — kawl JUHNGK sh'n
Calvert — KĂL vert
Camden — KĂM dĭn
Cameron — KĂM uh r'n
Camilla — kuh MEEL yuh
Camp — kămp
Campbell — KĂM uhl
Campbellton — KĂM uhl t'n
Camp Wood — kămp WŎŎD
Canadian — <u>kuh</u> NĂ dĭ uhn
Candelaria — kăn duh LĔ rĭ uh
Canton — KĂNT n
Canyon — KĂN y'n
Caplen — KĂP lĭn
Caps — kăps
Caradan — KĂR uh dăn
Carbon — KAHR b'n
Carey — KĂ rĭ
Carlisle — KAHR lĭl
Carlsbad — KAHR uhlz băd
Carlton — KAHR uhl t'n
Carmine — kahr MEEN
Carmona — <u>kahr</u> MŌ nuh
Caro — KAH rō
Carrizo Springs — kuh <u>ree</u> zuh
    SPRĬNGZ
Carrollton — KĂR 'l t'n
Carson — KAHR s'n
Carthage — KAHR thĭj
Cash — kăsh
Cason — KĂ s'n
Cass — kăs
Castell — kăs TĔL
Castro — KĂS trō
Castroville — KĂS tro vĭl
Catarina — kăt uh REE nuh
Cat Spring — kăt SPRĬNG
Caviness — KĂ vĭ nĕs

Downtown Brownsville, Cameron County. Photo by Robert Plocheck.

Cayuga — kā YŌŌ guh
Cedar Bayou — <u>see</u> der BĪ ō
Cedar Creek — <u>see</u> der KREEK
Cedar Hill — <u>see</u> der HĬL
Cedar Lake — <u>see</u> der LĀK
Cedar Lane — <u>see</u> der LĀN
Cedar Park — <u>see</u> der PAHRK
Cedar Valley — <u>see</u> der VA lǐ
Cee Vee — <u>see</u> VEE
Celeste — suh LĔST
Celina — suh LĪ nuh
Center — SENT er
Center City — sĕn ter SĬT ĭ
Center Point — sĕn ter POINT
Centerville — sĕn ter vĭl
Centralia — sĕn TRĀL yuh
Chalk — chawlk
Chalk Mountain - chawlk MOWNT n
Chambers — CHĂM berz
Chandler — CHĂND ler
Channelview — <u>chăn</u> uhl VYŌŌ
Channing — CHĂN ĭng
Chapman Ranch — chăp m'n
  RĀNCH
Chappell Hill — chă p'l HĬL
Charco — CHAHR kō
Charleston — CHAHR uhls t'n
Charlie — CHAHR lǐ
Charlotte — SHAHR l't
Chatfield — CHĂT feeld
Cheapside — CHEEP sīd
Cheek — cheek
Cherokee — CHĔR uh <u>kee</u>
Chester — CHĔS ter
Chico — CHEE kō
Chicota — chǐ KŌ tuh

Childress — CHĬL drĕs
Chillicothe — <u>chǐl</u> ǐ KAH thǐ
Chilton — CHĬL t'n
China — CHĪ nuh
China Spring — chī nuh SPRĬNG
Chireno — sh' REE nō
Chisholm — CHĬZ uhm
Chita — CHEE tuh
Chocolate Bayou — <u>chah</u> kuh lǐt
  BĪ ō
Choice — chois
Chriesman — KRĬS m'n
Christine — krǐs TEEN
Christoval — krǐs TŌ v'l
Cibolo — SEE bō lō
Circle Back — SER k'l băk
Circleville — SER k'l vǐl
Cisco — SĬS kō
Cistern — SĬS tern
Clairemont — KLĂR mahnt
Clairette — klăr ǐ ĔT
Clarendon — KLĂR ǐn d'n
Clareville — KLĂR vǐl
Clarksville — KLAHRKS vǐl
Clarkwood — KLAHRK wōōd
Claude — klawd
Clawson — KLAW s'n
Clay — klā
Clayton — KLĀT n
Clear Lake — KLĬR lăk
Clear Spring — klǐr SPRĬNG
Cleburne — KLEE bern
Clemville — KLĔM vǐl
Cleveland — KLEEV l'nd
Clifton — KLĬF t'n
Cline — klīn

Clint — klǐnt
Clodine — klaw DEEN
Clute — klōōt
Clyde — klīd
Coahoma — kuh HŌ muh
Cockrell Hill — kahk ruhl HĬL
Coke — kōk
Coldspring — KŌLD sprǐng
Coleman — KŌL m'n
Colfax — KAHL făks
Collegeport — kah lǐj PŌRT
College Station — <u>kah</u> lǐj STĀ sh'n
Collin — KAH lǐn
Collingsworth — KAH lǐnz werth
Collinsville — KAH lǐnz vǐl
Colmesneil — KŌL m's neel
Colorado — <u>kahl</u> uh RAH dō
Colorado City — kah luh <u>rā</u> duh or
  kah luh <u>rah</u> duh SĬT ǐ
Columbus — kuh LUHM b's
Comal — KŌ măl
Comanche — kuh MĂN chǐ
Combes — kōmz
Comfort — KUHM fert
Commerce — KAH mers
Como — KŌ mō
Comstock — KAHM stahk
Concan — KAHN kăn
Concepcion — kuhn sep sǐ ŌN
Concho — KAHN chō
Concord — KAHN kawrd
Concrete — kahn KREET
Cone — kōn
Conlen — KAHN lǐn
Conroe — KAHN rō
Converse — KAHN vers

Diacritical markings are used as follows: bāle, băd, lĕt, rīse, rĭll, ōak, brōōd, fŏŏt. The stressed syllable is capitalized. Secondary stress is indicated by an underline as in Atascosa — ăt uhs KŌ suh. TEXAS ALMANAC ©.

Conway — KAHN wā
Cooke — kŏŏk
Cookville — KŎŎK vĭl
Coolidge — KŎŎ lĭj
Cooper — KŎŎ per
Copeville — KŎP v'l
Coppell — kahp pĕl or kuhp PĔL
Copperas Cove — kahp ruhs KŌV
Corbett — KAWR bĭt
Cordele — kawr DĔL
Corinth — KAH rĭnth
Corley — KAWR lĭ
Corpus Christi — <u>kawr</u> p's KRĬS tĭ
Corrigan — KAWR uh g'n
Corsicana — <u>kawr</u> sĭ KĂN uh
Coryell — kō rĭ ĔL
Cost — kawst
Cottle — KAH t'l
Cotton Center — <u>kaht</u> n SĔNT er
Cotton Gin — KAHT n jĭn
Cottonwood — KAHT n wŏŏd
Cotulla — kuh TŎŎ luh
Coupland — KŌP l'n
Courtney — KŌRT nĭ
Covington — KUHV ĭng t'n
Coy City — koi SĬT ĭ
Craft — krăft
Crafton — KRĂF t'n
Crandall — KRĂN d'l
Crane — krăn
Cranfills Gap — krăn f'lz GĂP
Crawford — KRAW ferd
Creedmoor — KREED mōr
Cresson — KRĔ s'n
Crisp — krĭsp
Crockett — KRAH kĭt
Crosby — KRAWZ bĭ
Crosbyton — KRAWZ bĭ t'n
Cross — kraws
Cross Cut — KRAWS kuht
Cross Plains — kraws PLĂNZ
Cross Roads — KRAWS rōdz
Crow — krō
Crowell — KRŌ uhl
Crowley — KROW li
Crystal City — krĭs t'l SĬT ĭ
Crystal Falls — krĭs t'l FAWLZ
Cuero — KWĔR o
Culberson — KUHL ber s'n
Cumby — KUHM bĭ
Cuney — KYŎŎ nĭ
Cunningham — KUHN ĭng hăm
Currie — KER rĭ
Cushing — KŎŎ shĭng
Cuthand — KUHT hănd
Cyclone — SĪ klōn
Cypress — SĪ prĕs

D

Dabney — DĂB nĭ
Dacosta — duh KAHS tuh
Dacus — DĂ k's
Daingerfield — DĀN jer feeld
Daisetta — dā ZĔT uh
Dalby Springs — dĂl bĭ SPRĬNGZ

Dale — dāl
Dalhart — DĂL hahrt
Dallam — DĂL uhm
Dallas — DĂ luhs
Damon — DĂ m'n
Danbury — DĂN bĕrĭ
Danciger — DĂN sĭ ger
Danevang — DĂN uh văng
Darrouzett — dăr uh ZĔT
Davilla — duh VĬL uh
Dawn — dawn
Dawson — DAW s'n
Dayton — DĀT n
Deadwood — DĔD wŏŏd
Deaf Smith — dĕf SMĬTH
Deanville — DEEN vĭl
DeBerry — duh BĔ rĭ
Decatur — <u>dee</u> KĀT er
Deer Park — dĭr PAHRK
De Kalb — dĭ KĂB
De Leon — da lee AHN
Del Rio — dĕl REE ō
Delta — DĔL tuh
Del Valle — dĕl VĂ lĭ
Delwin — DĔL wĭn
Denhawken — DĬN haw kĭn
Denison — DĔN uh s'n
Denning — DĔN ĭng
Dennis — DĔ nĭs
Denton — DĔNT n
Denver City — <u>dĕn</u> ver SĬT ĭ
Deport — DEE pōrt or dĭ PŌRT
Derby — DER bĭ
Desdemona — <u>dĕz</u> dĭ MŌ nuh
DeSoto — dĭ SŌ tuh
Detroit — dee TROIT
Devers — DĔ vers
Devine — duh VĬN
Dew — dyŏŏ
Deweyville — DYŎŎ ĭ vĭl
DeWitt — dĭ WĬT
Dewville — DYŎŎ vĭl
Dexter — DĔKS ter
D'Hanis — duh HĂ nĭs
Dialville — DĪ uhl vil
Diboll — DĪ bawl
Dickens — DĬK ĭnz
Dickinson — DĬK ĭn s'n
Dike — dĭk
Dilley — DĬL i
Dilworth — DĬL <u>werth</u>
Dimebox — dĭm BAHKS
Dimmit — DĬM ĭt
Dinero — dĭ NĔ rō
Direct — duh RĔKT
Dixon — DĬK s'n
Dobbin — DAH bĭn
Dobrowolski — <u>dah</u> bruh WAHL skĭ
Dodd City — dahd SĬT ĭ
Dodge — DAH j
Dodson — DAHD s'n
Donie — DŌ nĭ
Donley — DAHN lĭ
Donna — dah nuh
Doole — DOO lĭ
Dorchester — dawr CHĔS ter

Doss — daws
Doucette — DŎŎ sĕt
Dougherty — DAHR tĭ
Douglass — DUHG l's
Douglassville — DUHG lĭs vĭl
Downing — DOWN ĭng
Downsville — DOWNZ vĭl
Dozier — DŌ zher
Draw — draw
Driftwood — DRĬFT wŏŏd
Dripping Springs — drĭp ĭng SPRĬNGZ
Driscoll — DRĬS k'l
Dryden — DRĪD n
Dublin — DUHB lĭn
Duffau — DUHF ō
Dumas — DŎŎ m's
Dumont — DYŎŎ mahnt
Dundee — DUHN dĭ
Dunlap — DUHN lăp
Dunlay — DUHN lĭ
Dunn — duhn
Durango — duh RĂNG gō
Duval — DŎŎ vawl

E

Eagle — EE g'l
Eagle Lake — <u>ee</u> g'l LĀK
Eagle Pass — <u>ee</u> g'l PĂS
Earth — erth
East Bernard — <u>eest</u> ber NAHRD
Easterly — EES ter lĭ
Eastland — EEST l'nd
Easton — EES t'n
Ector — ĔK ter
Edcouch — ĕd KOWCH
Eddy — E di
Eden — EED n
Edge — ĕj
Edgewood — ĔJ wŏŏd
Edinburg — ĔD n <u>berg</u>
Edmonson — ĔD m'n s'n
Edna — ED nuh
Edom — EE d'm
Edroy — ĔD roi
Edwards — ĔD werdz
Egan — EE g'n
Egypt — EE juhpt
Elbert — ĔL bert
El Campo — ĕl KĂM pō
Eldorado — <u>ĕl</u> duh RĂ duh
Electra — ĭ LĔK truh
Elgin — ĔL gĭn
Eliasville — <u>ee</u> LĪ uhs vĭl
El Indio — ĕl ĬN dĭ ō
Elkhart — ĔLK hahrt
Ellinger — ĔL ĭn jer
Elliott — ĔL ĭ 't
Ellis — ĔL uhs
Elmendorf — ĔLM 'n dawrf
Elm Mott — ĕl MAHT
Elmo — ĔL mō
Eloise — ĔL o <u>eez</u>
El Paso — ĕl PĂS ō
Elsa — ĔL suh

Elysian Fields — uh lee zh'n
   FEELDZ
Emhouse — ĔM hows
Emory — ĔM uh rĭ
Encinal — ĕn suh NAHL
Encino — ĕn SEE nō
Energy — ĔN er jĭ
Engle — ĔN g'l
English — ĬNG glĭsh
Enloe — ĔN lō
Ennis — ĔN ĭs
Enochs — EE nuhks
Eola — ee Ō luh
Era — EE ruh
Erath — EE räth
Esperanza — ĕs per RĂN zuh
Estelline — ĔS tuh leen
Etoile — ĭ TOIL
Etter — ĔT er
Eula — YŌŌ luh
Euless — YŌŌ lĭs
Eureka — yōō REE kuh
Eustace — YŌŌS t's
Evadale — EE vuh dāl
Evant — EE vänt
Evergreen — Ĕ ver green
Everman — Ĕ ver m'n

F

Fabens — FĀ b'nz
Fairbanks — FĂR bangks
Fairfield — FĂR feeld
Fairlie — FĂR lee
Fair Play — fär PLĀ
Fairview — FĂR vyōō
Fairy — FĂ rĭ
Falfurrias — făl FYŌŌ rĭ uhs
Falls — fawlz
Falls City — fawlz SĬT ĭ
Fannett — fä NĔT
Fannin — FĂN ĭn
Fargo — FAHR gō
Farmers Branch — fahr merz
   BRĂNCH
Farmersville — FAHRM erz vĭl
Farnsworth — FAHRNZ werth
Farrar — FĂR uh
Farrsville — FAHRZ vĭl
Farwell — FAHR w'l
Fashing — FĂ shĭng
Fate — fāt
Fayette — fä ĔT
Fayetteville — FĀ uht vĭl
Fentress — FĔN trĭs
Ferris — FĔR ĭs
Field Creek — feeld KREEK
Fieldton — FEEL t'n
Fife — fīf
Fischer — FĪ sher
Fisher — FĪSH er
Fisk — fĭsk
Flagg — flăg
Flat — flăt
Flatonia — flä TŌN yuh
Flint — flĭnt

Flomot — FLŌ maht
Florence — FLAH ruhns
Floresville — FLŌRZ vil
Florey — FLŌ ri
Floyd — floid
Floydada — floi DĀ duh
Fluvanna — flōō VĂN uh
Flynn — flĭn
Foard — fōrd
Foard City — fōrd SĬT ĭ
Fodice — FŌ dĭs
Follett — fah LĔT
Fordtran — fōrd TRĂN
Forest — FAW rĕst
Forestburg — FAW rĕst berg
Forney — FAWR nĭ
Forreston — FAW rĕs t'n
Forsan — FŌR săn
Fort Bend — fōrt BĔND
Fort Chadbourne — fōrt CHĂD bern
Fort Davis — fōrt DĀ vĭs
Fort Griffin — fōrt GRĬF ĭn
Fort Hancock — fōrt HĂN kahk
Fort McKavett — fōrt muh KĂ vĕt
Fort Stockton — fōrt STAHK t'n
Fort Worth — fōrt WERTH
Fowlerton — FOW ler t'n
Francitas — frän SEE t's
Franklin — FRĂNGK lĭn
Frankston — FRĂNGS t'n
Fred — frĕd
Fredericksburg — FRĔD er rĭks
   berg
Fredonia — free DŌN yuh
Freeport — FREE pört
Freer — FREE er
Freestone — FREE stōn
Frelsburg — FRĔLZ berg
Fresno — FRĔZ nō
Friday — FRĪ dĭ
Friendswood — FRĔNZ wōōd
Frio — FREE ō
Friona — free Ō nuh
Frisco — FRĬS kō
Fritch — frĭch
Frost — frawst
Fruitland — FRŌŌT länd
Fruitvale — FRŌŌT väl
Frydek — FRĪ dĕk
Fulbright — FŌŌL brĭt
Fulshear — FUHL sher
Fulton — FŌŌL t'n

G

Gail — gāl
Gaines — gānz
Gainesville — GĂNZ vuhl
Galena Park — guh lee nuh PAHRK
Gallatin — GĂL uh t'n
Galveston — GĂL vĕs t'n
Ganado — guh NĂ dō
Garceno — gahr SĂ nō
Garciasville — gahr SEE uhs vĭl
Garden City — GAHRD n sĭt ĭ
Gardendale — GAHRD n dāl

Garden Valley — gahrd n VĂ lĭ
Garland — GAHR l'nd
Garner — GAHR ner
Garrett — GĂR ĭt
Garrison — GĂ rĭ s'n
Garwood — GAHR wōōd
Gary — GĔ rĭ
Garza — GAHR zuh
Gatesville — GĂTS vil
Gause — gawz
Gay Hill — gä HĬL
Geneva — juh NEE vuh
Georgetown — JAWRJ town
George West — jawrj WĔST
Geronimo — juh RAH nĭ mō
Giddings — GĬD ĭngz
Gillespie — guh LĔS pĭ
Gillett — juh LĔT
Gilliland — GĬL ĭ l'nd
Gilmer — GĬL mer
Ginger — JĬN jer
Girard — juh RAHRD
Girvin — GER vĭn
Gladewater — GLĂD wah ter
Glasscock — GLĂS kahk
Glazier — GLĀ zher
Glen Cove — glĕn KŌV
Glendale — GLĔN däl
Glenfawn — glĕn FAWN
Glen Flora — glĕn FLŌ ruh
Glenn — glĕn
Glen Rose — GLĔN rōz
Glidden — GLĬD n
Gober — GŌ ber
Godley — GAHD lĭ
Golden — GŌL d'n
Goldfinch — GŌLD fĭnch
Goldsboro — GŌLZ buh ruh
Goldsmith — GŌL smith
Goldthwaite — GŌLTH wät
Goliad — GŌ lĭ ăd
Golinda — gō LĬN duh
Gonzales — guhn ZAH l's
Goodland — GŌŌD l'n
Goodlett — GŌŌD lĕt
Goodnight — GŌŌD nīt
Goodrich — GŌŌD rĭch
Gordon — GAWRD n
Gordonville — GAWRD n vĭl
Goree — GŌ ree
Gorman — GAWR m'n
Gouldbusk — GŌŌLD buhsk
Graford — GRĀ ferd
Graham — GRĀ 'm
Granbury — GRĂN bĕ rĭ
Grandfalls — gränd FAWLZ
Grand Saline — grän suh LEEN
Grandview — GRĂN vyōō
Granger — GRĂN jer
Grapeland — GRĀP l'nd
Grapevine — GRĂP vĭn
Grassland — GRĂS l'nd
Grassyville — GRĂ sĭ vĭl
Gray — grā
Grayburg — GRĀ berg
Grayson — GRA s'n

The refinery in Goldsmith, Ector County. Photo by Robert Plocheck.

Green — green
Greenville — GREEN v'l
Greenwood — GREEN wŏŏd
Gregg — grĕg
Gregory — GRĔG uh rĭ
Grimes — grīmz
Groesbeck — GRŌZ bĕk
Groom — grōŏm
Groveton — GRŌV t'n
Grow — grō
Gruene — green
Grulla — GRŌŌL yuh
Gruver — GRŌŌ ver
Guadalupe — gwah duh LŌŌ pĭ or gwah duh LŌŌ pā
Guerra — GWĔ ruh
Gunter — GUHN ter
Gustine — GUHS teen
Guthrie — GUHTH rĭ
Guy — gī

H

Hackberry — HĂK bĕ rĭ
Hagansport — HĂ gĭnz pŏrt
Hainesville — HĀNZ v'l
Hale — hāl
Hale Center — hāl SĔNT er
Hall — hawl
Hallettsville — HĂL ĕts vĭl
Hallsville — HAWLZ vĭl
Hamilton — HĂM uhl t'n
Hamlin — HĂM lĭn
Hammond — HĂM 'nd
Hamon — HĂ m'n

Hamshire — HĂM sher
Handley — HĂND lĭ
Hankamer — HĂN kăm er
Hansford — HĂNZ ferd
Happy — HĂ pĭ
Hardeman — HAHR duh m'n
Hardin — HAHRD n
Hare — hăr
Hargill — HAHR gĭl
Harleton — HAHR uhl t'n
Harlingen — HAHR lĭn juhn
Harper — HAHR per
Harris — HĂ rĭs
Harrison — HĂ rĭ s'n
Harrold — HĂR 'ld
Hart — hahrt
Hartburg — HAHRT berg
Hartley — HAHRT lĭ
Harwood — HAHR wŏŏd
Haskell — HĂS k'l
Haslam — HĂZ l'm
Haslet — HĂS lĕt
Hasse — HĂ sĭ
Hatchell — HĂ ch'l
Hawkins — HAW kĭnz
Hawley — HAW lĭ
Hays — hāz
Hearne — hern
Heath — heeth
Hebbronville — HĔB r'n vĭl
Hebron — HEE br'n
Hedley — HĔD lĭ
Heidenheimer — HĪD n hīmer
Helena — HĔL uh nuh
Helotes — hĕl Ō tĭs

Hemphill — HĔMP hĭl
Hempstead — HĔM stĕd
Henderson — HĔN der s'n
Henly — HĔN lĭ
Henrietta — hĕn rĭ Ĕ tuh
Hereford — HER ferd
Hermleigh — HER muh lee
Hewitt — HYŌŌ ĭt
Hicks — hĭks
Hico — HĪ kō
Hidalgo — hĭ DĂL gō
Higgins — HĬ gĭnz
High — hī
Highbank — HĪ băngk
High Island — hī Ī l'nd
Highlands — HĪ l'ndz
Hightower — HĪ tow er
Hill — hĭl
Hillister — HĬL ĭs ter
Hillsboro — HĬLZ buh ruh
Hindes — hĭndz
Hiram — HĪ r'm
Hitchcock — HĬCH kahk
Hitchland — HĬCH l'nd
Hobson — HAHB s'n
Hochheim — HŌ hĭm
Hockley — HAHK lĭ
Holland — HAHL 'nd
Holliday — HAH luh dā
Hondo — HAHN dō
Honey Grove — HUHN ĭ grōv
Honey Island — huhn ĭ Ī l'nd
Honey Springs — huhn ĭ SPRĬNGZ
Hood — hŏŏd
Hooks — hŏŏks

Hopkins — HAHP kǐnz
Houston — HYŌŌS t'n or YŌŌS t'n
Howard — HOW erd
Howe — how
Howland — HOW l'nd
Hubbard — HUH berd
Huckabay — HUHK uh bǐ
Hudspeth — HUHD sp'th
Huffman — HUHF m'n
Hufsmith — HUHF smǐth
Hughes Springs — hyōōz SPRǏNGZ
Hull — huhl
Humble — UHM b'l
Hungerford — HUHNG ger ferd
Hunt — huhnt
Hunter — HUHNT er
Huntington — HUHNT ǐng t'n
Huntsville — HUHNTS v'l
Hurlwood — HERL wōōd
Hutchins — HUH chǐnz
Hutchinson — HUH chǐn s'n
Hutto — HUH tō
Hye — hī
Hylton — HǏL t'n

I

Iago — ī Ā gō
Idalou — Ǐ duh lōō
Imperial — ǐm PǏR ǐ uhl
Inadale — Ǐ nuh dāl
Independence — ǐn duh PĚN d'ns
Indian Creek — ǐn dǐ uhn KREEK
Indian Gap — ǐn dǐ uhn GĂP
Industry — ǏN duhs trǐ
Inez — ī NĚZ
Ingleside — ǏNG g'l sīd
Ingram — ǏNG gr'm
Iola — ī Ō luh
Iowa Park — ī uh wuh PAHRK
Ira — Ǐ ruh
Iraan — ī ruh ĂN
Iredell — Ǐ ruh děl
Ireland — Ǐ rǐ l'nd
Irene — ī REEN
Irion — ǏR i uhn
Ironton — ǏRN t'n
Irving — ER vǐng
Italy — ǏT uh lǐ
Itasca — ī TĂS kuh
Ivan — Ǐ v'n
Ivanhoe — Ǐ v'n hō

J

Jack — jǎk
Jacksboro — JĂKS buh ruh
Jackson — JĂK s'n
Jacksonville — JĂK s'n vǐl
Jamestown — JĂMZ town
Jardin — JAHRD n
Jarrell — JĂR uhl
Jasper — JĂS per
Jayton — JĀT n
Jean — jeen
Jeddo — JĚ dō

Jeff Davis — jěf DA vǐs
Jefferson — JĚF er s'n
Jericho — JĚ rǐ kō
Jermyn — JER m'n
Jewett — JŌŌ ǐt
Jiba — HEE buh
Jim Hogg — jǐm HAWG
Jim Wells — jǐm WĚLZ
Joaquin — waw KEEN
Johnson — JAHN s'n
Johnson City — jahn s'n SǏT ǐ
Johntown — JAHN town
Johnsville — JAHNZ vǐl
Joinerville — JOI ner vǐl
Jolly — JAH lǐ
Jollyville — JAH lǐ vǐl
Jonah — JŌ nuh
Jones — jōnz
Jonesboro — JŌNZ buh ruh
Jonesville — JŌNZ vǐl
Josephine — JŌ suh feen
Joshua — JAH sh' wa
Jourdanton — JERD n t'n
Joy — joi
Joyce — jawǐs
Juliff — JŌŌ lǐf
Junction — JUHNGK sh'n
Juno — JŌŌ nō
Justiceburg — JUHS tǐs berg
Justin — JUHS tǐn

K

Kalgary — KĂL gě rǐ
Kamay — KĀ ǐm ā
Kanawha — KAHN uh wah
Karnack — KAHR näk
Karnes — kahrnz
Karnes City — kahrnz SǏT ǐ
Katemcy — kuh TĚM sǐ
Katy — KĀ tǐ
Kaufman — KAWF m'n
Keechi — KEE chǐ
Keene — keen
Kellerville — KĚL er vǐl
Kemah — KEE muh
Kemp — kěmp or kǐrmp
Kemp City — kěmp SǏT ǐ
Kempner — KĚMP ner
Kendalia — kĚn DĀL yuh
Kenedy — KĚN uh dǐ
Kennard — kuh NAHRD
Kennedale — KĚN uh dāl
Kent — kěnt
Kerens — KER 'nz
Kermit — KER mǐt
Kerr — ker
Kerrville — KER vǐl
Kildare — KǏL dǎr
Kilgore — KǏL gōr
Killeen — kuh LEEN
Kimble — KǏM b'l
King — kǐng
Kingsbury — KǏNGZ bě rǐ
Kingsland — KǏNGZ l'nd

Kingsmill — kǐngz MǏL
Kingston — KǏNGZ t'n
Kingsville — KǏNGZ vǐl
Kinney — KǏN ǐ
Kirby — KER bǐ
Kirbyville — KER bǐ vǐl
Kirkland — KERK l'nd
Kirvin — KER vǐn
Kleberg — KLĀ berg
Klondike — KLAHN dǐk
Knickerbocker — NǏK uh bah ker
Knippa — kuh NǏP uh
Knott — naht
Knox — nahks
Knox City — nahks SǏT ǐ
Kosciusko — kuh SHŌŌS kō
Kosse — KAH sǐ
Kountze — kōōntz
Kress — kres
Krum — kruhm
Kurten — KER t'n
Kyle — kīl

L

La Blanca — lah BLAHN kuh
La Coste — luh KAWST
Ladonia — luh DŌN yuh
LaFayette — lah fǐ ĚT
Laferia — luh FĚ rǐ uh
Lagarto — luh GAHR tō
La Gloria — lah GLŌ rǐ uh
La Grange — luh GRĀNJ
Laguna — luh GŌŌ nuh
Laird Hill — lǎrd HǏL
La Joya — luh HŌ yuh
Lake Creek — lǎk KREEK
Lake Dallas — lǎk DĂL uhs
Lake Jackson — lǎk JĂK s'n
Laketon — LĂK t'n
Lake Victor — lǎk VǏK ter
Lakeview — LĂK vyōō
Lamar — luh MAHR
La Marque — luh MAHRK
Lamasco — luh MĂS kō
Lamb — lǎm
Lamesa — luh MEE suh
Lamkin — LĂM kǐn
Lampasas — lǎm PĂ s's
Lancaster — LĂNG k's ter
Laneville — LĀN vǐl
Langtry — LĂNG trǐ
Lanier — luh NǏR
La Paloma — lah puh LŌ muh
La Porte — luh PŌRT
La Pryor — luh PRǏ er
Laredo — luh RĀ dō
Lariat — LĂ ri uht
Larue — luh RŌŌ
La Salle — luh SĂL
Lasara — luh SĚ ruh
Lassater — LĂ sǐ ter
Latch — lǎch
Latexo — luh TĚKS ō
Lavaca — luh VĂ kuh

La Vernia — luh VER nĭ uh
La Villa — lah VĬL uh
Lavon — luh VAHN
La Ward — luh WAWRD
Lawn — lawn
Lawrence — LAH r'ns
Lazbuddie — LĂZ buh dĭ
League City — <u>leeg</u> SĬT ĭ
Leakey — LĀ kĭ
Leander — lee ĂN der
Leary — LĬ er ĭ
Ledbetter — LĔD bĕt er
Lee — lee
Leesburg — LEEZ berg
Leesville — LEEZ vĭl
Lefors — lĭ FŌRZ
Leggett — LĔ gĭt
Leigh — lee
Lela — LEE luh
Lelia Lake — <u>leel</u> yuh LĀK
Leming — LĔ mĭng
Lenorah — lĕ NŌ ruh
Leo — LEE ō
Leon — lee AHN
Leona — <u>lee</u> Ō nuh
Leonard — LĔN erd
Leon Springs — lee ahn SPRĬNGZ
Leroy — LEE roi
Levelland — LĔ v'l lănd
Levita — luh VĬ tuh
Lewisville — LŌŌ ĭs vĭl
Lexington — LĔKS ĭng t'n
Liberty — LĬB er tĭ
Liberty Hill — Ĭ ber tĭ HĬL
Lillian — LĬL yuhn
Limestone — LĬM stōn
Lincoln — LĬNG k'n
Lindale — LĬN dāl
Linden — LĬN d'n
Lindenau — lĭn duh NOW
Lindsay — LĬN zĭ
Lingleville — LĬNG g'l vĭl
Linn — lĭn
Lipan — lĭ PĂN
Lipscomb — LĬPS k'm
Lissie — LĬ sĭ
Little Elm — lĭt l ĔLM
Littlefield — LĬT uhl feeld
Little River — lĭt uhl RĬV er
Live Oak — LĬV ōk
Liverpool — LĬ ver pōōl
Livingston — LĬV ĭngz t'n
Llano — LĂ nō
Locker — LAH ker
Lockett — LAH kĭt
Lockhart — LAHK hahrt
Lockney — LAHK nĭ
Lodi — LŌ dĭ
Lohn — lahn
Lolita — lō LEE tuh
Loma Alto — lō muh ĂL tō
Lometa — lō MEE tuh
London — LUHN d'n
Lone Grove — lōn GRŌV
Lone Oak — LŌN ōk
Long Branch — lawng BRĂNCH

Long Mott — lawng MAHT
Longview — LAWNG vyōō
Longworth — LAWNG werth
Loop — lōōp
Lopeno — lō PEE nō
Loraine — lō RĀN
Lorena — lō REE nuh
Los Angeles — laws AN juh l's
Los Ebanos — lōs ĔB uh nōs
Los Fresnos — lōs FRĔZ nōs
Los Indios — lōs ĬN dĭ ōs
Losoya — luh SAW yuh
Lott — laht
Louise — LŌŌ eez
Lovelady — LUHV lā dĭ
Loving — LUH vĭng
Lowake — lō WĀ kĭ
Lubbock — LUH buhk   or   LUH b'k
Lueders — LŌŌ derz
Luella — lōō ĔL uh
Lufkin — LUHF kĭn
Luling — LŌŌ lĭng
Lund — luhnd
Lutie — LŌŌ tĭ
Lyford — LĬ ferd
Lynn — lĭn
Lyons — LĬ 'nz
Lytton Springs — lĭt n SPRĬNGZ

M

Mabank — MĀ băngk
Macune — muh KŌŌN
Madison — MĂ dĭ s'n
Madisonville — MĂ duh s'n vĭl
Magnolia — măg NŌL yuh
Magnolia Springs — măg nol yuh
   SPRINGZ
Malakoff — MĂL uh kawf
Malone — muh LŌN
Malta — MAWL tuh
Manchaca — MĂN shăk
Manchester — MĂN chĕs ter
Manheim — MĂN hĭm
Mankins — MĂN kĭnz
Manor — MĂ ner
Mansfield — MĂNZ feeld
Manvel — MĂN v'l
Maple — MĂ puhl
Marathon — MĂR uh th'n
Marble Falls — mahr b'l FAWLZ
Marfa — MAHR fuh
Margaret — MAHR guh rĭt
Marietta — mĕ rĭ Ĕ tuh
Marion — MĔ rĭ uhn
Markham — MAHR k'm
Marlin — MAHR lĭn
Marquez — mahr KĀ
Marshall — MAHR sh'l
Mart — mahrt
Martin — MAHRT n
Martindale — MAHRT n dāl
Martinsville — MAHRT nz vĭl
Maryneal — mā rĭ NEEL
Marysville — MĂ rĭz vĭl
Mason — MĂ s'n

Matador — MĂT uh dör
Matagorda — măt uh GAWR duh
Mathis — MĂ thĭs
Maud — mawd
Mauriceville — maw REES vĭl
Maverick — MĂV rĭk
Maxey — MĂKS ĭ
Maxwell — MĂKS w'l
May — mā
Maydell — MĂ dĕl
Maypearl — <u>mā</u> PERL
Maysfield — MĂZ feeld
McAdoo — MĂK uh dōō
McAllen — măk ĂL ĭn
McCamey — muh KĂ mĭ
McCaulley — muh KAW lĭ
McCoy — muh KOI
McCulloch — muh KUH luhk
McFaddin — măk FĂD n
McGregor — muh GRĔ ger
McKinney — muh KĬN ĭ
McLean — muh KLĀN
McLennan — muhk LĔN uhn
McLeod — măk LOWD
McMahan — măk MĂN
McMullen — măk MUHL ĭn
McNary — măk NĀ rĭ
McNeil — măk NEEL
McQueeney — muh KWEE nĭ
Meadow — MĔ dō
Medicine Mound — <u>mĕd</u> uhs n
   MOWND
Medill — mĕ DĬL
Medina — muh DEE nuh
Megargel — muh GAHR g'l
Melissa — muh LĬS uh
Melrose — MĔL röz
Melvin — MĔL vĭn
Memphis — MĔM fĭs
Menard — muh NAHRD
Mendoza — mĕn DŌ zuh
Mentone — mĕn TŌN
Mercedes — <u>mer</u> SĂ deez
Mercury — MER kyuh ri
Mereta — muh RĔT uh
Meridian — muh RĬ dĭ uhn
Merit — MĔR ĭt
Merkel — MER k'l
Mertens — <u>mer</u> TĔNZ
Mertzon — MERTS n
Mesquite — muhs KEET
Mexia — muh HĂ uh
Meyersville — MĬRZ vĭl
Miami — mĭ ĂM uh or mĭ ĂM ĭ
Mico — MEE kō
Middleton — MĬD uhl t'n
Midfields — MĬD feeldz
Midland — MĬD l'nd
Midlothian — <u>mĭd</u> LŌ thĭ n
Midway — MĬD wā
Milam — MĬ l'm
Milano — mĭ LĂ nō
Mildred — MĬL drĕd
Miles — mīlz
Milford — MĬL ferd
Miller Grove — mĭl er GRŌV

Millersview — MĬL erz vyōō
Millett — MĬL ĭt
Millheim — MĬL hīm
Millican — MĬL uh kuhn
Mills — mĭlz
Millsap — MĬL săp
Minden — MĬN d'n
Mineola — mĭn ĭ Ō luh
Mineral — MĬN er uhl
Mineral Wells — mĭn er uhl WĔLZ
Minerva — mĭ NER vuh
Mingus — MĬNG guhs
Minter — MĬNT er
Mirando City — mĭ răn duh SĬT ĭ
Mission — MĬSH uhn
Mission Valley — mĭsh uhn VĂ lĭ
Missouri City — muh zōōr uh SĬT ĭ
Mitchell — MĬ ch'l
Mobeetie — mō BEE tĭ
Moline — mō LEEN
Monahans — MAH nuh hănz
Monaville — MŌ nuh vĭl
Monkstown — MUHNGKS town
Monroe — MAHN rō
Monroe City — mahn rō SĬT ĭ
Montague — mahn TĀG
Montalba — mahnt ĂL buh
Mont Belvieu — mahnt BĔL vyōō
Montell — mahn TĔL
Montgomery — mahnt GUHM er ĭ
Monthalia — mahn THĂL yuh
Moody — MŌŌ dĭ
Moore — mōr
Morales — muh RAH lĕs
Moran — mō RĂN
Morgan — MAWR g'n
Morgan Mill — mawr g'n MĬL
Morse — mawrs
Morton — MAWRT n
Moscow — MAHS kow
Mosheim — MŌ shĭm
Moss Bluff — maws BLUHF
Motley — MAHT lĭ
Moulton — MŌL t'n
Mound — mownd
Mountain Home — mownt n HŌM
Mount Calm — mownt KAHM
Mount Enterprise — mownt ĔN
   ter prīz
Mount Pleasant — mownt PLĔ z'nt
Mount Selman — mownt SĔL m'n
Mount Sylvan — mownt SĬL v'n
Mount Vernon — mownt VER n'n
Muenster — MYŌŌNS ter
Muldoon — muhl DŌŌN
Muleshoe — MYŌŌL shōō
Mullin — MUHL ĭn
Mumford — MUHM ferd
Munday — MUHN dĭ
Murchison — MER kuh s'n
Murphy — MER fĭ
Mykawa—mĭ KAH wuh
Myra — MĪ ruh
Myrtle Springs — mert l SPRĬNGZ

N

Nacogdoches — năk uh DŌ chĭs
Nada — NĀ duh
Naples — NĀ p'lz
Nash — năsh
Natalia — nuh TĂL yuh
Navarro — nuh VĂ rō
Navasota — năv uh SŌ tuh
Nazareth — NĂZ uh r'th
Neches — NĀ chĭs
Nederland — NEE der l'nd
Needville — NEED vĭl
Nelsonville — NĔL s'n vĭl
Neuville — NYŌŌ v'l
Nevada — nuh VĂ duh
Newark — NŌŌ erk
New Baden — nyōō BĀD n
New Berlin — nyōō BER lin
New Boston — nyōō BAWS t'n
New Braunfels — nyōō BRAHN f'ls
   or BROWN fĕlz
Newby — NYŌŌ bĭ
New Caney — nyōō KĀ nĭ
Newcastle — NYŌŌ kăs uhl
New Gulf — nyōō GUHLF
New Home — NYŌŌ hōm
New Hope — nyōō HŌP
Newlin — NYŌŌ lĭn
New London — nyōō LUHN d'n
Newman — NYŌŌ m'n
Newport — NYŌŌ pōrt
New Salem — nyōō SĀ l'm
Newsome — NYŌŌ s'm
New Summerfield — nyōō SUHM
   er feeld
Newton — NYŌŌT n
New Ulm — nyōō UHLM
New Waverly — nyōō WĀ ver lĭ
New Willard — nyōō WĬL erd
Nimrod — NĬM rahd
Nineveh — NĬN uh vuh
Nixon — NĬKS uhn
Nocona — nō KŌ nuh
Nolan — NŌ l'n
Nolanville — NŌ l'n vĭl
Nome — nōm
Noonday — NŌŌN dā
Nopal — NŌ păl
Nordheim — NAWRD hīm
Normandy — NAWR m'n dĭ
Normangee — NAWR m'n jee
Normanna — nawr MĂN uh
Northrup — NAWR thr'p
North Zulch — nawrth ZŌŌLCH
Norton — NAWRT n
Novice — NAH vĭs
Nueces — nyōō Ā sĭs
Nugent — NYŌŌ j'nt
Nursery — NER suh rĭ

O

Oakalla — ō KĂL uh
Oak Grove — ōk GRŌV
Oak Hill — ōk HĬL

Oakhurst — ŌK herst
Oakland — ŌK l'nd
Oakville — ŌK vĭl
Oakwood — ŌK wōōd
O'Brien — ō BRĪ uhn
Ochiltree — AH k'l tree
Odell — Ō dĕl or ō DĔL
Odem — Ō d'm
Odessa — ō DĔS uh
O'Donnell — ō DAH n'l
Oenaville — ō EEN uh v'l
Oglesby — Ō g'lz bĭ
Oilton — OIL t'n
Oklaunion — ōk luh YŌŌN y'n
Olden — ŌL d'n
Oldenburg — ŌL dĭn berg
Oldham — ŌL d'm
Old Glory — ōld GLŌ rĭ
Olivia — ō LĬV ĭ uh
Olmito — awl MEE tuh
Olmos Park — ahl m's PAHRK
Olney — AHL nĭ
Olton — ŌL t'n
Omaha — Ō muh haw
Omen — Ō mĭn
Onalaska — uhn uh LĂS kuh
Oplin — AHP lĭn
Orange — AHR ĭnj
Orangefield — AHR ĭnj feeld
Orange Grove — AHR ĭnj GRŌV
Orchard — AWR cherd
Ore City — ōr SĬT ĭ
Osceola — ō sĭ Ō luh
Otey — Ō tĭ
Otis Chalk — ō tĭs CHAWLK
Ottine — ah TEEN
Otto — AH tō
Ovalo — ō VĂL uh
Overton — Ō ver t'n
Owens — Ō ĭnz
Ozona — ō ZŌ nuh

P

Paducah — puh DYŌŌ kuh
Paige — pāj
Paint Rock — pānt RAHK
Palacios — puh LĂ sh's
Palestine — PAL uhs teen
Palito Blanco — p' lee to BLAHNG
   kō
Palmer — PAH mer
Palo Pinto — pă lō PĬN tō
Paluxy — puh LUHK sĭ
Pampa — PĂM puh
Pandora — păn DŌR uh
Panhandle — PĂN hăn d'l
Panna Maria — păn uh muh REE
   uh
Papalote — pah puh LŌ tĭ
Paradise — PĂR uh dīs
Paris — PĂ rĭs
Parker — PAHR ker
Parmer — PAH mer
Parnell — pahr NĔL
Parsley Hill — pahrs lĭ HĬL

Diacritical markings are used as follows: bāle, băd, lĕt, rīse, rĭll, ōak, brōōd, fōōt. The stressed syllable is capitalized. Secondary stress is indicated by an underline as in Atascosa — ăt uhs KŌ suh. TEXAS ALMANAC ©.

Pasadena — păs uh DEE nuh
Patricia — puh TRĬ shuh
Patroon — puh TROŌN
Pattison — PĂT uh s'n
Pattonville — PĂT n vĭl
Pawnee — paw NEE
Paxton — PĂKS t'n
Peacock — PEE kahk
Pearl — perl
Pearland — PĂR länd
Pearsall — PEER sawl
Peaster — PEES ter
Pecan Gap — pĭ kahn GĂP
Pecos — PĀ k's
Penelope — puh NĔL uh pĭ
Penitas — puh NEE t's
Pennington — PĔN ĭng t'n
Penwell — PĬN wĕl
Peoria — pee Ō rĭ uh
Percilla — per SĬL uh
Perrin — PĔR ĭn
Perry — PĔ rĭ
Perryton — PĔ rĭ t'n
Peters — PEET erz
Petersburg — PEET erz berg
Petrolia — puh TRŌL yuh
Petteway — PĔT uh wā
Pettit — PĔT ĭt
Pettus — PĔT uhs
Petty — PĔT ĭ
Pflugerville — FLOŌ ger vĭl
Pharr — fahr
Phelps — fĕlps
Phillips — FĬL uhps
Pickton — PĬK t'n
Pidcoke — PĬD kŏk
Piedmont — PEED mahnt
Pierce — PĬ ers
Pilot Point — pī l't POINT
Pine Forest — pīn FAW rĕst
Pine Hill — pĭn HĬL
Pinehurst — PĬN herst
Pineland — PĬN land
Pine Mills — pĭn MĬLZ
Pine Springs — pĭn SPRĬNGZ
Pioneer — pī uh NĬR
Pipecreek — pĭp KREEK
Pittsburg — PĬTS berg
Placedo — PLĂS ĭ dō
Placid — PLĂ sĭd
Plains — plānz
Plainview — PLĀN vyoō
Plano — PLĂ nō
Plantersville — PLĂN terz vĭl
Plaska — PLĂS kuh
Plateau — plă TŌ
Pleasant Grove—plĕ z'nt GRŌV
Pleasanton — PLĒZ uhn t'n
Pledger — PLĔ jer
Plum — pluhm
Point — point
Pointblank — pint BLĂNGK
Polk — pōlk
Pollock — PAHL uhk
Ponder — PAHN der

Ponta — pahn TĀ
Pontotoc — PAHNT uh tahk
Poolville — POŌL vĭl
Port Aransas — pōrt uh RĂN zuhs
Port Arthur — pōrt AHR ther
Port Bolivar — pōrt BAH lĭ ver
Porter Springs — pōr ter SPRĬNGZ
Port Isabel — pōrt ĬZ uh bĕl
Portland — PŌRT l'nd
Port Lavaca — pōrt luh VĂ kuh
Port Neches — pōrt NĀ chĬs
Port O'Connor — pōrt ō KAH ner
Posey — PŌ zĭ
Post — pōst
Postoak — PŌST ōk
Poteet — pō TEET
Poth — pōth
Potosi — puh TŌ sĭ
Potter — PAHT er
Pottsboro — PAHTS buh ruh
Pottsville — PAHTS vĭl
Powderly — POW der lĭ
Powell — POW w'l
Poynor — POI ner
Prairie Dell — prĕr ĭ DĔL
Prairie Hill — prĕr ĭ HĬL
Prairie Lea — prĕr ĭ LEE
Prairie View — prĕr ĭ VYOŌ
Prairieville — PRĔR ĭ vĭl
Premont — PREE mahnt
Presidio — pruh SĬ dĭ ō
Priddy — PRĬ dĭ
Primera — pree MĔ ruh
Princeton — PRĬNS t'n
Pritchett — PRĬ chĭt
Proctor — PRAHK ter
Progreso — prō GRĔ sō
Prosper — PRAHS per
Purdon — PERD n
Purley — PER lĭ
Purmela — per MEE luh
Putnam — PUHT n'm
Pyote — PĬ ōt

Q

Quail — kwāl
Quanah — KWAH nuh
Queen City — kween SĬT ĭ
Quemado — kuh MAH dō
Quihi — KWEE hee
Quinlan — KWĬN l'n
Quintana — kwĭn TAH nuh
Quitaque — KĬT uh kwa
Quitman — KWĬT m'n

R

Rainbow — RĂN bō
Rains — ränz
Ralls — rahlz
Randall — RĂN d'l
Randolph — RĂN dahlf
Ranger — RĂN jer
Rangerville — RĂN jer vĭl
Rankin — RĂNG kĭn

Ratcliff — RĂT klĭf
Ravenna — rĭ VĔN uh
Rayburn — RĀ bern
Raymondville — RĀ m'nd vĭl
Raywood — RĀ woŏd
Reagan — RĀ g'n
Real — REE awl
Realitos — ree uh LEE t's
Redford — RĔD ferd
Red Oak — RĔD ōk
Red River — rĕd RĬ ver
Red Rock — rĕd RAHK
Red Springs — rĕd SPRĬNGZ
Red Water — RĔD wah ter
Reeves — reevz
Refugio — rĕ FYOŌ rĭ ō
Reilly Springs — rĭ lĭ SPRĬNGZ
Reklaw — RĔK law
Reno — REE nō
Rhineland — RĪN l'nd
Rhome — rōm
Rhonesboro — RŌNZ buh ruh
Ricardo — rĭ KAHR dō
Rice — rīs
Richards — RĬCH erdz
Richardson — RĬCH erd s'n
Richland — RĬCH l'nd
Richland Springs — rĭch l'nd
    SPRĬNGZ
Richmond — RĬCH m'nd
Ridge — rĭj
Ridgeway — RĬJ wā
Riesel — REE s'l
Ringgold — RĬNG gōld
Rio Frio — ree ō FREE ō
Rio Grande City — ree ō grahn dĭ
    or ree ō grän SĬT ĭ
Rio Hondo — ree ō HAHN dō
Riomedina — ree ō muh DEE nuh
Rios — REE ōs
Rio Vista — ree ō VĬS tuh
Rising Star — rĭ zĭng STAHR
River Oaks — rĭ ver ŌKS
Riverside — RĬ ver sĭd
Riviera — ruh VĬR uh
Roane — rōn
Roanoke — RŌN ōk or RŌ uh
    nōk
Roans Prairie — rōnz PRĔR Ĭ
Roaring Springs — rōr ĭng
    SPRĬNGZ
Robert Lee — rah bert LEE
Roberts — RAH berts
Robertson — RAH bert s'n
Robinson — RAH bĭn s'n
Robstown — RAHBZ town
Roby — RŌ bĭ
Rochelle — rō SHĔL
Rochester — RAH chĕs ter
Rockdale — RAHK däl
Rock Island — rahk Ī l'nd
Rockland — RAHK l'nd
Rockport — rahk PŌRT
Rocksprings — rahk SPRĬNGZ
Rockwall — rahk WAWL

Diacritical markings are used as follows: bāle, băd, lĕt, rīse, rĭll, ōak, broōd, foōt. The stressed syllable is capitalized. Secondary stress is indicated by an underline as in Atascosa — ăt uhs KŌ suh. TEXAS ALMANAC ©.

Texas 83 outside Seagraves, Gaines County. Photo by Robert Plocheck.

Rockwood — RAHK wōōd
Roganville — RŌ g'n vĭl
Rogers — RAH jerz
Roma — RŌ muh
Romayor — rō MÃ er
Roosevelt — RŌ suh v'lt or RŌŌ suh v'lt
Ropesville — RŌPS vĭl
Rosanky — rō ZĂNG kĭ
Roscoe — RAHS kō
Rosebud — RŌZ b'd
Rose Hill — rōz HĬL
Rosenberg — RŌZ n berg
Rosenthal — RŌZ uhn thawl
Rosewood — RŌZ wōōd
Rosharon — rō SHĚ r'n
Rosita — rō SEE tuh
Ross — raws
Rosser — RAW ser
Rosston — RAWS t'n
Rossville — RAWS vĭl
Roswell — RAHZ w'l
Rotan — rō TĂN
Round Rock — ROWND rahk
Round Top — ROWN tahp
Rowena — rō EE nuh
Rowlett — ROW lĭt
Roxton — RAHKS t'n
Royalty — ROI uhl tĭ
Royse City — roi SĬT ĭ
Royston — ROIS t'n
Rugby — RUHG bĭ
Ruidosa — ree uh DŌ suh
Rule — rōōl
Runge — RUHNG ĭ
Runnels — RUHN 'lz
Rural Shade — rōōr uhl SHĀD
Rusk — ruhsk
Rutersville — RŌŌ ter vĭl
Rye — rī

S

Sabinal — SĂB uh năl
Sabine — suh BEEN
Sabine Pass — suh been PĂS
Sabinetown — suh been TOWN
Sachse — SĂK sĭ
Sacul — SĂ k'l
Sadler — SĂD ler
Sagerton — SĂ ger t'n
Saginaw — SĂ guh naw
Saint Jo — sănt JŌ
Saint Paul — sănt PAWL
Salado — suh LĀ dō
Salesville — SĂLZ vĭl
Salineno — suh LEEN yō
Salmon — SĂL m'n
Salt Gap — sawlt GĂP
Saltillo — săl TĬL ō
Samfordyce — săm FOR dis
Sample — SĂM p'l
Samnorwood — săm NAWR wōōd
San Angelo — săn ĂN juh lō
San Antonio — săn ăn TŌ nĭ ō
San Augustine — săn AW g's teen
San Benito — săn buh NEE tuh
Sanderson — SĂN der s'n
Sandia — săn DEE uh
San Diego — săn dĭ Ā gō
Sandy Point — săn dĭ POINT
San Elizario — săn ĕl ĭ ZAH rĭ ō
San Felipe — săn fuh LEEP
Sanford — SĂN ferd
San Gabriel — săn GĀ brĭ uhl
Sanger — SĂNG er
San Jacinto — săn juh SĬN tuh or juh SĬN tō
San Juan — săn WAHN
San Marcos — săn MAHR k's
San Patricio — săn puh TRĬSH ĭ ō
San Perlita — săn per LEE tuh
San Saba — săn SĂ buh

Santa Anna — săn tuh ĂN uh
Santa Elena — săn tuh LEE nuh
Santa Maria — săn tuh muh REE uh
Santa Rosa — săn tuh RŌ suh
Santo — SĂN tō
San Ygnacio — săn ĭg NAH sĭ ō
Saragosa — sĕ ruh GŌ suh
Saratoga — sĕ ruh TŌ guh
Sargent — SAHR juhnt
Sarita — suh REE tuh
Saspamco — suh SPĂM kō
Satin — SĂT n
Savoy — suh VOI
Schattel — SHĂT uhl
Schertz — sherts
Schleicher — SHLĪ ker
Schroeder — SHRĀ der
Schulenburg — SHŌŌ lĭn berg
Schwertner — SWERT ner
Scotland — SKAHT l'nd
Scottsville — SKAHTS vĭl
Scranton — SKRĂNT n
Scurry — SKUH rĭ
Scyene — sī EEN
Seabrook — SEE brōōk
Seadrift — SEE drĭft
Seagoville — SEE gō vĭl
Seagraves — SEE grāvz
Seale — seel
Sealy — SEE lĭ
Sebastopol — suh BĂS tuh pōōl
Sebastian — suh BĂS tĭ 'n
Security — sĭ KYŌŌR ĭ tĭ
Segno — SĔG nō
Segovia — sĭ GŌ vĭ uh
Seguin — sĭ GEEN
Selfs — sĕlfs
Selma — SĔL muh
Seminole — SĔM uh nōl
Seymour — SEE mōr
Shackelford — SHĂK uhl ferd

Diacritical markings are used as follows: bāle, băd, lĕt, rīse, rĭll, ōak, brōōd, fŏŏt. The stressed syllable is capitalized. Secondary stress is indicated by an underline as in Atascosa — ăt uhs KŌ suh. TEXAS ALMANAC ©.

Shady Grove — shā dǐ GRŌV
Shafter — SHĂF ter
Shallowater — SHĂL uh wah ter
Shamrock — SHĂM rahk
Shannon — SHĂN uhn
Sharp — shahrp
Sheffield — SHĔ feeld
Shelby — SHĔL bǐ
Shelbyville — SHĔL bǐ vǐl
Sheldon — SHĔL d'n
Shepherd — SHĔ perd
Sheridan — SHĔ rǐ dn
Sherman — SHER m'n
Sherwood — SHER wood
Shiner — SHĪ ner
Shiro — SHĪ rō
Shive — shīv
Sidney — SĬD nǐ
Sierra Blanca — sǐer ruh BLĂNG kuh
Siloam — suh LŌM
Silsbee — SĬLZ bǐ
Silver Lake — sǐl ver LĀK
Silverton — SĬL ver t'n
Silver Valley — sǐl ver VĂ lǐ
Simms — sǐmz
Simonton — SĪ m'n t'n
Singleton — SĬNG g'l t'n
Sinton — SĬNT n
Sipe Springs — SEEP sprǐngz
Sisterdale — SĬS ter dāl
Sivells Bend — sǐ v'lz BĔND
Skellytown — SKĔ lǐ town
Skidmore — SKĬD mōr
Slaton — SLĀT n
Slayden — SLĀD n
Slidell — slī DĔL
Slocum — SLŌ k'm
Smiley — SMĪ lǐ
Smith — smǐth
Smithfield — SMĬTH feeld
Smithland — SMĬTH l'nd
Smithson Valley — smǐth s'n VĂ lǐ
Smithville — SMĬTH vǐl
Smyer — SMĪ er
Snook — snook
Snyder — SNĪ der
Somerset — SUH mer sĕt
Somervell — SUH mer vĕl
Somerville — SUH mer vǐl
Sonora — suh NŌ ruh
Sour Lake — sowr LĀK
South Bend — sowth BĔND
South Bosque — sowth BAHS kǐ
South Houston — sowth HYOOS t'n
Southland — SOWTH l'nd
Southmayd — sowth MĀD
South Plains — sowth PLĀNZ
Spade — spād
Spanish Fort — spă nǐsh FŌRT
Sparenberg — SPĂR ǐn berg
Speaks — speeks
Spearman — SPĬR m'n
Spicewood — SPĪS wood
Splendora — splĕn DŌ ruh
Spofford — SPAH ferd

Spring — sprǐng
Springdale — SPRǏNG dāl
Springlake — sprǐng LĀK
Springtown — SPRǏNG town
Spur — sper
Spurger — SPER ger
Stacy — STĀ sǐ
Stafford — STĂ ferd
Stamford — STĂM ferd
Stanton — STĂNT n
Staples — STĀ p'lz
Starr — stahr
Stephens — STEE vĕnz
Stephenville — STEEV n vǐl
Sterley — STER lǐ
Sterling — STER lǐng
Sterling City — ster lǐng SĬT ǐ
Stiles — stīlz
Stinnett — stǐ NĔT
Stockdale — STAHK dāl
Stoneburg — STŌN berg
Stoneham — STŌN uhm
Stone Point — stōn POINT
Stonewall — STŌN wawl
Stout — stowt
Stowell — STŌ w'l
Stranger — STRĂN jer
Stratford — STRĂT ferd
Strawn — strawn
Streeter — STREET er
Streetman — STREET m'n
Study Butte — styoo dǐ BYOOT
Sublime — s'b LĪM
Sudan — SOO dăn
Sugar Land — SHOO ger lănd
Sullivan City — suh luh v'n SĬT ǐ
Sulphur Bluff — suhl fer BLUHF
Sulphur Springs — suhl fer SPRǏNGZ
Summerfield — SUHM er feeld
Sumner — SUHM ner
Sundown — SUHN down
Suniland — SUH nǐ lănd
Sunny Side — SUH nǐ sīd
Sunray — SUHN rā
Sunset — SUHN sĕt
Sutherland Springs — suh ther l'nd SPRǏNGZ
Sutton — SUHT n
Swan — swahn
Sweeny — SWEE nǐ
Sweet Home — sweet HŌM
Sweetwater — SWEET wah ter
Swenson — SWĔN s'n
Swift — swǐft
Swisher — SWĬ sher
Sylvester — sil VES ter

T

Taft — tăft
Tahoka — tuh HŌ kuh
Talco — TĂL kō
Talpa — TĂL puh
Tanglewood — TĂNG g'l wood
Tankersley — TĂNG kers lǐ

Tarrant — TAR uhnt
Tarzan — TAHR z'n
Tascosa — tăs KŌ suh
Tatum — TĀ t'm
Tavener — TĂV uh ner
Taylor — TĀ ler
Teague — teeg
Tehuacana — tuh WAW kuh nuh
Telephone — TĔL uh fōn
Telferner — TĔLF ner
Tell — tĕl
Temple — TĔM p'l
Tenaha — TĔN uh haw
Tennyson — TĔN uh s'n
Terlingua — TER lǐng guh
Terrell — TĔR uhl
Terrell Hills — ter uhl HILZ
Terry — TĔR ǐ
Texarkana — tĕks ahr KĂN uh
Texas City — tĕks ĕz SĬT ǐ
Texhoma — tĕks Ō muh
Texline — TĔKS līn
Texon — tĕks AHN
Thalia — THĂL yuh
The Grove — th' GRŌV
Thicket — THĬ kǐt
Thomaston — TAHM uhs t'n
Thompsons — TAHMP s'nz
Thorndale — THAWRN dāl
Thornton — THAWRN t'n
Thorp Spring — thawrp SPRING
Thrall — thrawl
Three Rivers — three RǏ verz
Throckmorton — THRAHK mawrt n
Thurber — THER ber
Tilden — TĬL d'n
Timpson — TĬM s'n
Tioga — tǐ Ō guh
Titus — TĪT uhs
Tivoli — tǐ VŌ luh
Tokio — TŌ kǐ ō
Tolar — TŌ ler
Tolbert — TAHL bert
Tolosa — tuh LŌ suh
Tomball — TAHM bawl
Tom Bean — tahm BEEN
Tom Green — tahm GREEN
Tool — tool
Topsey — TAHP sǐ
Tornillo — tawr NEE yō
Tow — tow
Toyah — TOI yuh
Toyahvale — TOI yuh vāl
Trawick — TRĂ wǐk
Travis — TRĂ vǐs
Trent — trĕnt
Trenton — TRĔNT n
Trickham — TRĬK uhm
Trinidad — TRĬN uh dăd
Trinity — TRĬN ǐ tǐ
Troup — troop
Troy — TRAW ǐ
Truby — TROO bǐ
Trumbull — TRUHM b'l
Truscott — TRUHS k't
Tucker — TUHK er

Tuleta — tōō LEE tuh
Tulia — TŌŌL yuh
Tulsita — tuhl SEE tuh
Tundra — TUHN druh
Tunis — TŌŌ nĭs
Turkey — TER kĭ
Turlington — TER lĭng t'n
Turnersville — TER nerz vĭl
Turnertown — TER ner town
Turney — TER nĭ
Tuscola — tuhs KŌ luh
Tuxedo — TUHKS ĭ dō
Twin Sisters — twĭn SĬS terz
Twitty — TWĬ tĭ
Tye — tī
Tyler — TĪ ler
Tynan — TĪ nuhn

U

Uhland — YŌŌ l'nd
Umbarger — UHM bahr ger
Union — YŌŌN y'n
Upshur — UHP sher
Upton — UHP t'n
Urbana — er BĀ nuh
Utley — YŌŌT lĭ
Utopia — yōō TŌ pĭ uh
Uvalde — yōō VĂL dĭ

V

Valdasta — văl DĂS tuh
Valentine — VĂL uhn tīn
Valera — vuh LĬ ruh
Valley Mills — vă lĭ MĬLZ
Valley Spring — vă lĭ SPRĬNG
Valley View — vă lĭ VYŌŌ
Van — văn
Van Alstyne — văn AWLZ teen
Vancourt — VĂN kört
Vanderbilt — VĂN der bĭlt
Vanderpool — VĂN der pōōl
Van Horn — văn hawrn
Van Vleck — văn VLĔK
Van Zandt — văn ZĂNT
Vashti — VĂSH tĭ
Vaughan — vawn
Vega — VĀ guh
Velasco — vuh LĂS kō
Venus — VEE n's
Vera — VĬ ruh
Veribest — VĔR ĭ bĕst
Verhalen — ver HĂ lĭn
Vernon — VER n'n
Vickery — VĬK er ĭ
Victoria — vĭk TŌ rĭ uh
Vidor — VĪ der
Vienna — vee ĔN uh
View — vyōō
Village Mills — vĭl ĭj MĬLZ
Vincent — VĬN s'nt
Vinegarone — vĭn er guh RŌN
Vineyard — VĬN yerd
Violet — VĪ ō lĕt
Voca — VŌ kuh
Von Ormy — vahn AHR mĭ

Voss — vaws
Votaw — VŌ taw

W

Waco — WĀ kō
Wadsworth — WAHDZ werth
Waelder — WĔL der
Waka — WAH kuh
Walberg — WAWL berg
Waldeck — WAWL dĕk
Walker — WAWL ker
Wall — wawl
Waller — WAW ler
Wallis — WAH lĭs
Wallisville — WAH lĭs vĭl
Walnut Springs — wawl n't
  SPRĬNGZ
Walton — WAWL t'n
Warda — WAWR duh
Ward — wawrd
Waring — WĀR ĭng
Warren — WAW rĭn
Warrenton — WAW rĭn t'n
Washburn — WAHSH bern
Washington — WAHSH ĭng t'n
Waskom — WAHS k'm
Wastella — wahs TĔL uh
Watauga — wuh TAW guh
Water Valley — wah ter VĂ lĭ
Waxahachie — wawks uh HĀ chĭ
Wayland — WĀ l'nd
Weatherford — WĔ ther ferd
Weaver — WEE ver
Webb — wĕb
Webberville — WĔ ber vĭl
Webster — WĔBS ter
Weches — WEE chĭz
Weesatche — WEE săch
Weimar — WĬ mer
Weinert — WĬ nert
Weir — weer
Welch — wĕlch
Welcome — WĔL k'm
Weldon — WĔL d'n
Wellborn — WĔL bern
Wellington — WĔL ĭng t'n
Wellman — WĔL m'n
Wells — wĕlz
Weser — WEE zer
Weslaco — WĔS luh kō
West — wĕst
Westbrook — WĔST brŏŏk
Westfield — WĔST feeld
Westhoff — WĔS tawf
Westminster — wĕst MĬN ster
Weston — WĔS t'n
Westover — WĔS tō ver
Westphalia — wĕst FĀL yuh
West Point — wĕst POINT
Wharton — HWAWRT n
Wheeler — HWEE ler
Wheelock — HWEE lahk
White Deer — HWĬT Deer
Whiteface — HWĬT făs
Whiteflat — hwĭt FLĂT
Whitehouse — HWĬT hows

Whitesboro — HWĬTS buh ruh
Whitewright — HWĬT rīt
Whitharral — HWĬT hăr uhl
Whitney — HWĬT nĭ
Whitsett — HWĬT sĭt
Whitson — HWĬT s'n
Whitt — hwĭt
Whon — hwahn
Wichita — WĬCH ĭ taw
Wichita Falls — wĭch ĭ taw FAWLZ
Wickett — WĬ kĭt
Wiergate — WEER găt
Wilbarger — WĬL bahr ger
Wildorado — wĭl duh RĀ dō
Willacy — WĬL uh sĭ
Williamson — WĬL yuhm s'n
Willis — WĬ lĭs
Wills Point — wĭlz POINT
Wilmer — WĬL mer
Wilson — WĬL s'n
Wimberley — WĬM ber lĭ
Winchester — WĬN ches ter
Windom — WĬN d'm
Windthorst — WĬN thr'st
Winfield — WĬN feeld
Wingate — WĬN găt
Winkler — WĬNGK ler
Winnie — WĬ nĭ
Winnsboro — WĬNZ buh ruh
Winona — wĭ NŌ nuh
Winterhaven — WĬN ter hā v'n
Winters — WĬN terz
Wise — wīz
Wizard Wells — wĭ zerd WĔLZ
Woden — WŌD n
Wolfe City — wŏŏlf SĬT ĭ
Wolfforth — WŌŌL forth
Wood — wŏŏd
Woodbine — WŌŌD bīn
Woodlake — wŏŏd LĀK
Woodland — WŌŌD l'nd
Woodlawn — wŏŏd LAWN
Woodrow — WŌŌD rō
Woodsboro — WŌŌDZ buh ruh
Woodson — WŌŌD s'n
Woodville — WŌŌD v'l
Wortham — WERTH uhm
Wright City — rĭt SĬT ĭ
Wrightsboro — RĪTS buh ruh
Wylie — WĪ lĭ

Y

Yancey — YĂN sĭ
Yantis — YĂN tĭs
Yoakum — YŌ k'm
Yorktown — YAWRK town
Young — yuhng
Youngsport — YUHNGZ pört
Ysleta — ĭs LĔT uh

Z

Zapata — zuh PAH tuh
Zavalla — zuh VĂL uh
Zephyr — ZĔF er
Zuehl — ZEE uhl

Diacritical markings are used as follows: bāle, băd, lĕt, rīse, rĭll, ōak, brōōd, fŏŏt. The stressed syllable is capitalized. Secondary stress is indicated by an underline as in Atascosa — ăt uhs KŌ suh. TEXAS ALMANAC ©.

ADVERTISER INDEX

GENERAL INDEX

For cities and towns not listed in the index, see lists on pages 380–407 and pages 478–488. For full information about cities, see "Cities and towns" entry in this index. For full information about counties, also look under the cities and towns in the county, as well as the "Counties" index entry. Page numbers in italics refer to photographs and artwork and their captions.

A panoramic view of Big Ben National Park. Photo by Jonathan Cutrer (jcutrer.com).

For CITIES and TOWNS not listed in the Index, see complete list on pages 380–407.

A grey day on Galveston Island. Photo by Yinan Chen.

Bluebonnets in Muleshoe recreation area. Photo by Kan Khampanya (Shutterstock).

A sunset over Lake Ray Hubbard during the 2015 drought. Photo by Nelo Hotsuma (CC).

For CITIES and TOWNS not listed in the Index, see complete list on pages 380–407.

Texas Lakes

Bodies of water with a normal capacity of 5,000 acre-feet or larger. *Italicized* reservoirs are usually dry.

● PANHANDLE PLAINS
1. Palo Duro Reservoir
2. Lake Rita Blanca
3. Lake Meredith
4. Bivins Lake
5. *Buffalo Lake*
6. Mackenzie Reservoir
7. Greenbelt Lake
8. Baylor Lake
9. White River Lake
10. Lake Alan Henry
11. Lake J.B. Thomas
12. Sulphur Springs Draw Reservoir
13. *Natural Dam Lake*
14. Red Draw Reservoir
15. Lake Colorado City
16. Champion Creek Reservoir
17. Mitchell County Reservoir
18. Lake Sweetwater
19. E.V. Spence Reservoir
20. Oak Creek Reservoir
21. O.C. Fisher Lake
22. Twin Buttes Reservoir
23. Lake Nasworthy
24. Ballinger Lake
25. O.H. Ivie Reservoir
26. Hords Creek Lake
27. Lake Winters
28. Lake Abilene
29. Lake Coleman
30. Lake Brownwood
31. Lake Clyde
32. Lake Kirby
33. Lake Fort Phantom Hill
34. Lake Stamford
35. Lake Davis
36. Truscott Brine Lake
37. Santa Rosa Lake
38. Lake Electra
39. Lake Kemp
40. Lake Diversion
41. Lake Kickapoo
42. North Fork Buffalo Creek Reservoir
43. Lake Wichita
44. Lake Arrowhead
45. Millers Creek Reservoir
46. Lake Cooper/Olney
47. Lake Graham
48. Lost Creek Reservoir
49. Possum Kingdom Lake
50. Hubbard Creek Reservoir
51. Lake Daniel
52. Lake Cisco

53. Lake Palo Pinto
54. Lake Leon
55. Proctor Lake

● BIG BEND
56. Red Bluff Reservoir
57. Balmorhea Lake
58. Imperial Reservoir
59. Amistad International Reservoir

● HILL COUNTRY
60. Brady Creek Reservoir
61. Lake Buchanan
62. Inks Lake
63. Lake Lyndon B. Johnson
64. Lake Marble Falls
65. Lake Travis
66. Lake Austin
67. Lady Bird Lake
68. Lake Walter E. Long
69. Lake Georgetown
70. Granger Lake
71. Canyon Lake
72. Medina Lake

● PRAIRIES AND LAKES
73. Lake Nocona
74. Hubert H. Moss Lake
75. Lake Texoma
76. Randell Lake
77. Valley Lake
78. Lake Bonham
79. Coffee Mill Lake
80. Pat Mayse Lake
81. Lake Crook
82. River Crest Lake
83. Cooper Lake
84. Lake Sulphur Springs
85. Lake Cypress Springs
86. Greenville City Lakes
87. Lake Tawakoni
88. Terrell City Lake
89. Lake Lavon
90. Lake Ray Hubbard
91. Lake Kiowa
92. Lake Ray Roberts
93. Lewisville Lake
94. Grapevine Lake
95. North Lake
96. White Rock Lake
97. Mountain Creek Lake
98. Joe Pool Lake
99. Lake Arlington
100. Lake Worth
101. Eagle Mountain Lake
102. Lake Weatherford
103. Lake Amon G. Carter

104. Lake Bridgeport
105. Lake Mineral Wells
106. Benbrook Lake
107. Lake Granbury
108. Squaw Creek Reservoir
109. Lake Pat Cleburne
110. Lake Waxahachie
111. Bardwell Lake
112. Cedar Creek Reservoir
113. Forest Grove Reservoir
114. Lake Athens
115. Trinidad Lake
116. Lake Halbert
117. Richland-Chambers Reservoir
118. Fairfield Lake
119. Navarro Mills Lake
120. Aquilla Lake
121. Lake Whitney
122. Lake Waco
123. Tradinghouse Creek Reservoir
124. Lake Creek Lake

125. Belton Lake
126. Stillhouse Hollow Lake
127. Alcoa Lake
128. Lake Limestone
129. Twin Oaks Reservoir
130. Camp Creek Lake
131. Lake Bryan
132. Gibbons Creek Reservoir
133. Somerville Lake
134. Lake Bastrop
135. Fayette County Reservoir
136. Lake Dunlap
137. Lake Gonzales
138. Eagle Lake

● PINEYWOODS
139. Wright Patman Lake
140. Monticello Reservoir
141. Lake Winnsboro
142. Lake Bob Sandlin
143. Welsh Reservoir

144. Ellison Creek Reservoir
145. Lake O' the Pines
146. Johnson Creek Reservoir
147. Caddo Lake
148. Lake Fork Reservoir
149. Lake Quitman
150. Lake Holbrook
151. Lake Hawkins
152. Gilmer Reservoir
153. Lake Gladewater
154. Eastman Lakes
155. Brandy Branch Reservoir
156. Lake Cherokee
157. Martin Creek Lake
158. Murvaul Lake